AN

ARABIC-ENGLISH LEXICON

AN

ARABIC-ENGLISH LEXICON

BY

EDWARD WILLIAM LANE

IN EIGHT PARTS

PART 1 ا - ث

مَدُّ ٱلْقَامُوسِ

AN

ARABIC-ENGLISH LEXICON,

DERIVED FROM THE BEST AND THE MOST COPIOUS EASTERN SOURCES;

COMPRISING A VERY LARGE COLLECTION
OF WORDS AND SIGNIFICATIONS OMITTED IN THE ḲÁMOOS,
WITH SUPPLEMENTS TO ITS ABRIDGED AND DEFECTIVE EXPLANATIONS,
AMPLE GRAMMATICAL AND CRITICAL COMMENTS,
AND EXAMPLES IN PROSE AND VERSE:

COMPOSED BY MEANS OF THE MUNIFICENCE OF THE MOST NOBLE
ALGERNON,
DUKE OF NORTHUMBERLAND, K.G.,
ETC. ETC. ETC.,
AND THE BOUNTY OF
THE BRITISH GOVERNMENT:

BY EDWARD WILLIAM LANE.

IN TWO BOOKS:

THE FIRST CONTAINING ALL THE CLASSICAL WORDS AND SIGNIFICATIONS COMMONLY KNOWN
TO THE LEARNED AMONG THE ARABS:
THE SECOND, THOSE THAT ARE OF RARE OCCURRENCE AND NOT COMMONLY KNOWN.

BOOK I.—PART 1.

ا — ث

KALPAZ

ISBN: 978-93-5128-814-5(Set)
ISBN: 978-93-5128-823-7(PB)

First Published in 1863
Indian Reprint in 2017

Published by

Kalpaz Publications
C-30, Satyawati Nagar,
Delhi – 110052
E-mail: kalpaz@hotmail.com
Website: kalpazpublications.com
Ph.: +91-9212142040

Cataloging in Publication Data—DK

Courtesy: D.K. Agencies (P) Ltd. <docinfo@dkagencies.com>

Lane, Edward William, 1801-1876, **author.**

Madd al-qa˜mu˜s = An Arabic-English lexicon : derived from the best and the most copious eastern sources, comprising a very large collection of words and significations omitted in the Kamoos, with supplements to its abridged and defective explanations, ample grammatical and critical comments, and examples in prose and verse : composed by means of the munificence of the most noble algernon, Duke of Northumberland, K. G., etc. etc. etc., and the bounty of the British Government / by Edward William Lane.

volumes cm

English and Arabic.

Parts 6-8 edited with a memoir by Stanley Lane Poole.

"First published in 1863"—Title page verso.

"In two books: the first containing all the words and significations commonly known to the learned among the Arabs : the second, those that are of rare occurrence and not communly known."
ISBN 9789351288145 (set :

1. Arabic language—Dictionaries—English. 2. English language—Dictionaries—Arabic. I. Lane-Poole, Stanley, 1854-1931, editor. II. Title. III. Title: Arabic-English lexicon.

PJ6640.L36 2017 DDC 492.7321 23

PREFACE.

In the year 1842, a most generous offer made to me by the present Duke of Northumberland (then Lord Prudhoe) enabled me to undertake the composition of this work; and to His Grace's princely aid I have ever since been mainly indebted for the means of accomplishing the project thus originated.

The object proposed was not to do in English little more than what Golius and others had already done in Latin, by translating and composing from a few Arabic lexicons of the class of epitomes or abstracts or manuals; but to draw chiefly from the most copious Eastern sources; one of which, comprising in about one seventh part of its contents the whole of the celebrated Ḳámoos, I knew to exist in Cairo. There, also, I had reason to believe that I might find other sources unknown in Europe, and obtain more aid in the prosecution of my design than I could elsewhere; and thither, therefore, I betook myself for this purpose.

On my arrival at Cairo, I first had recourse, for help in making my preparations, to an accomplished Arabic Scholar, the late M. Fulgence Fresnel, with whom, during a former residence in Egypt, I had contracted an intimate friendship. Previously informed by me of my project, he had tested the qualifications of several learned natives for the task of assisting me in collecting, transcribing, and collating, the materials from which my lexicon was to be composed; and he recommended to me, as the person whom he esteemed the most fit, the sheykh Ibráheem (surnamed 'Abd-el-Ghaffár) Ed-Dasooḳee. To have engaged as my coadjutor a sheykh respected for his character and learning, and to have been disappointed in him, and obliged to dismiss him, might have made him my enemy, and enabled and induced him to baffle my scheme; but my experience led me to believe that a person better qualified for the services that I required of him, than the sheykh Ibráheem Ed-Dasooḳee, could not have been found by me in Cairo; and I had no occasion to employ any other assistant, except, occasionally, transcribers, under his supervision.

The assistance that I received from my friend M. Fresnel was not limited to the favour mentioned above. With a generosity rarely equalled, he insisted upon transferring to me the most valuable of his Arabic manuscripts, to remain with me during the whole period of the composition of my lexicon, and in case of his death during that period to become my absolute property. Most deeply do I deplore his not having lived to see how greatly those precious manuscripts have contributed to the accuracy and value of my work, and to have them restored to him. They consist of two copies of the Ṣiḥáḥ and a copy of the Ḳámoos. One of the copies of the former lexicon is a manuscript of extraordinary excellence: it was finished in the year of the Flight 676 (A.D. 1277); and forms a large quarto-volume. The other copy of the same lexicon is in three volumes: the second volume surpasses in accuracy every other copy of the same work that I have seen, and is enriched with numerous important extracts, in its margins, from the celebrated Annotations of Ibn-Barree and El-Busṭee: the first volume is similarly enriched, and little inferior to the second in accuracy: the third is of the ordinary quality. The copy of the Ḳámoos, which is written in a very small and compact hand, and forms a single octavo-volume, I believe to be unique: it contains, in its margins, (with other annotations and with various readings,) copious extracts from the great work which is the main source of my own lexicon; and its text, of which the transcription was finished in the year of the Flight 1120 (A.D. 1708-9), has been carefully collated. These valuable acquisitions I made almost immediately after my arrival at Cairo.

It was indispensable, I believe, to the success of my undertaking, that I should most carefully avoid whatever might draw down disrespect from the 'Ulamà of Cairo, or others of the Muslim inhabitants, either upon myself or upon the sheykh who was to assist me in procuring the chief materials for the composition of my work. For it was only by his means that I could reasonably hope to obtain the use of manuscripts in the libraries of mosques; that is, by his borrowing those manuscripts as though for his own use: and one of the librarians showed himself to be desirous of urging any pretext in order to refuse the loan of the work that I most needed. I therefore made my place of residence to be as far as I could from the quarters frequented by Franks, and conformed with such of the general usages of the Muslims as did not involve a profession of their religion. But my precautions did not suffice to secure me from every difficulty. Even the Viceroy, Moḥammad 'Alee Páshá, though almost an absolute prince, could not enable me to overcome them. Hearing of my project, I know not how, he spontaneously informed me, by his Prime Minister, that he was desirous of showing his respect for my Patron by rendering me any assistance within his power. I replied that his Highness would very greatly aid me by granting me authority to demand the loan of certain manuscripts in the libraries of mosques. But it was feared that the wardens of the mosques would in this case urge the necessity of an order from the Sulṭán, or abstract considerable portions from those manuscripts and so defeat my plan. I could therefore only endeavour to obtain, according to the usual custom, through the sheykh my assistant, a small portion at a time of each of the required manuscripts: and even this I was unable to do until after the lapse of some weeks. In the mean time, however, I had the good fortune to acquire a large folio-volume, consisting of nearly the whole of the first tenth portion, of a copy of the great work to which I have alluded before as comprising in about one seventh part of its contents the whole of the celebrated Ḳámoos. This work, entitled "Táj el-'Aroos" (تاج العَرُوس), a compilation from the best and most copious Arabic lexicons, in the form of a running commentary on the Ḳámoos, with necessary critical and other illustrations, original, and selected from various authors of high repute, fully justified my expectation. I found, from the portion before me, that it would of itself alone suffice to supply the means of composing an Arabic lexicon far more accurate and perspicuous, and incomparably more copious, than any hitherto published in Europe. But I should not have been satisfied with making use of it for such a purpose without being able to refer to several of the most important of the works from which it was compiled.

Of these works, and others particularly deserving of notice, as well as of the Táj el-'Aroos itself, and of the principles of Arabic lexicology, I must now endeavour to give a brief account. In doing this, I shall frequently have occasion to cite the "Muzhir" of Es-Suyooṭee, a compilation of the utmost value to students in general, and more especially to lexicographers, of the Arabic language. Its author died in the year of the Flight 911, a date to be borne in mind in perusing my extracts from it. I possess a most excellent copy of it, (written by a learned man, the sheykh Naṣr El-Hooreenee, with the exception of a portion which, while he was suffering from an attack of ophthalmia, was written for him by one of his disciples,) transcribed from the best that is known to exist in Cairo, (namely, that of Es-Sejá'ee, in the library of the great mosque El-Azhar,) and enriched with copious marginal notes.

What is called the classical language of Arabia, often termed by the Arabs "the language of Ma'add," and "the language of Muḍar," is a compound of many sister-dialects, very little differing among themselves, which were spoken throughout nearly the whole of the Peninsula before the religion of Moḥammad incited the nation to spread its conquering armies over foreign countries. Before that period, feuds among the tribes, throughout the whole extent of their territory, had prevented the blending of their dialects into one uniform language; but this effect of disunion was counteracted in a great measure by the institution of the sacred months, in which all acts of hostility were most strictly interdicted, and by the annual pilgrimage, which had obtained from time immemorial, and the yearly fair held at 'Okáḍh, at which the poets of various tribes, during a period of about a century before the birth of Moḥammad, or perhaps during a somewhat longer period, contended for the meed of general admiration.*

---

* Respecting this fair, see some extracts from the first of M. Fresnel's "Lettres sur l'Histoire des Arabes avant l'Islamisme" in Note 18 to the first chapter of my Translation of the Thousand and One Nights.

"Ḳatádeh says that the tribe of Ḳureysh used to cull what was most excellent in the dialects of the Arabs, so that their dialect became the most excellent of all." (Táj el-'Aroos, in article عرب: and the like is said in the 9th Section of the Muzhir.) This assertion, however, is not altogether correct: for many of the children of the tribe of Ḳureysh, in the time of Moḥammad, were sent into the desert to be there nursed in order to their acquiring the utmost chasteness of speech. Moḥammad himself was sent to be nursed among the tribe of Saad Ibn-Bekr Ibn-Hawázin, descendants of Muḍar, but not in the line of Ḳureysh: and he is said to have urged the facts of his being of Ḳureysh and having grown up among the tribe of Saad as the grounds of his claim to be the most chaste in speech of the Arabs. It is evident, therefore, that Ḳureysh, in his time, were less chaste in speech than some other tribes; though the truth of this asserted saying of his rests, I believe, only on the authority of a Saadee, who may have forged it in order to raise the reputation of his own tribe for purity of speech. From distant tribes, Ḳureysh probably borrowed little. The dialect of Ḥimyer, confined mainly to El-Yemen, and allied much more to the Ethiopic and the Hebrew than to the language of Ma'add, contributed to this last language little more than a small proportion of words. For our knowledge of it, which is very scanty, we are chiefly indebted to the researches of M. Fresnel, who discovered a surviving idiom of it, spoken chiefly in the district of Mahreh, between Ḥaḍramowt and 'Omán: hence it has been termed "Mahree;" and from the name of the tribe who speak it, M. Fresnel gave it the appellation of "Ehhkili," or "Ehkili." The author of the "Miṣbáḥ" (El-Feiyoomee) says, in article مهر, "The language of the people of Mahreh, which is a district of 'Omán, is quick, and scarcely, or not at all, intelligible [to other Arabs], and is of the ancient Ḥimyeree."

The language of Ma'add was characterized by its highest degree of perfection, copiousness, and uniformity, in the time of Moḥammad; but it soon after declined, and at length lost almost all that constituted its superiority over the other branches of the Semitic stock in the states in which these are known to us. It is evident that all the Semitic languages diverged from one form of speech: and the known history of the Arabic is sufficient, I think, to show that the mixture of the several branches of the Shemites, in different degrees, with different foreign races, was the main cause, if not of the divergence, at least of the decay, of their languages, as exemplified by the Biblical Hebrew and Chaldee, and the Christian Syriac. That their divergence also was thus mainly caused, we cannot prove; but that this was the case I do not doubt, judging from the differences in their vocabularies, more especially from the differences of this kind in the Hebrew and Phœnician from the other Semitic languages. The existence of at least one language widely differing from the Semitic very long before the age of Moses is proved by the remains of the ancient Egyptian, from the time of the Pyramids; a language predominantly Semitic in its grammar, but predominantly Non-Semitic in its vocabulary; and evidently a compound of two heterogeneous forms of speech. The opinion, common among the learned of the Arabs, that the Arabic is the offspring of the Syriac, apparently suggested by a comparison of their vocabularies and by false notions of development, is simply absurd, unless by "the Syriac" we understand a lost language very different from that which is known to us by this appellation.* Every language without a written literature tends to decay more than to development by reason of foreign influences; and the history of the Arabic exhibits an instance of decay remarkably rapid, and extraordinary in degree. An immediate consequence of the foreign conquests achieved by the Arabs under Moḥammad's first four successors was an extensive corruption of their language: for the nations that they subdued were naturally obliged to adopt in a great measure the speech of the conquerors, a speech which few persons have ever acquired in such a degree as to be secure from the commission of frequent errors in grammar without learning it from infancy. These nations, therefore, and the Arabs dwelling among them, concurred in forming a simplified dialect, chiefly by neglecting to observe those inflections and grammatical rules which constitute the greatest difficulty of the classical Arabic: in the latter half of the first century of the Flight, this simplified dialect became generally spoken in the foreign towns and villages inhabited by the Arabs; and it gradually became the general language throughout the deserts, as well as the towns and villages, of Arabia itself. That such a change took place, in the language of the Arabs inhabiting foreign towns and villages, at this period, is shown by several anecdotes interspersed in Arabic works, and amply confirmed in

---

* Many among the Jews, the Syrians, and the Fathers of the Christian Church, held that the Aramaic or the Syriac was the language of Adam.

the older Arabic lexicons and other lexicological works by instances of the necessity of appeals to contemporary Arabs of the desert, respecting points of grammar, by learned men whose parents lived in the first century of the Flight. The celebrated lexicologist El-Aṣma'ee, who was born in the year of the Flight 123, and lived to the age of 92 or 93, was not a sound grammarian. (See De Sacy's "Anthol. Gr. Ar." p. 49 of the Arabic text.) And even Seebaweyh, who was contemporary, during the whole of his comparatively short life, with El-Aṣma'ee, appears to have erred in grammar. (See p. 133 of the present work.) Ibn-Seedeh says, in the "Moḥkam," in art. سرط, (voce سِرَاطٌ,) that El-Aṣma'ee was not a grammarian: and in art. شرب, (voce شُرُوبٌ, as pl. of شَارِبٌ,) he remarks that Ibn-El-Aạrábee (who calls شروب pl. of شَرْبٌ) was ignorant of grammar. In short, not a single instance is known of any one's having acquired a perfect knowledge of the grammar of the classical Arabic otherwise than by being brought up among Arabs who retained that language uncorrupted. The Khaleefeh El-Weleed (who reigned near the close of the first century of the Flight), the son of 'Abd-El-Melik, spoke so corrupt a dialect that he often could not make himself understood by the Arabs of the desert. A ridiculous instance of the mistakes occasioned by his use of the simplified language which is now current is related by Abu-l-Fidà. The rapid progress of the corruption of the language among the learned is the more remarkable when it is considered that many of these, in the first and second centuries of the Flight, were very long-lived: for in a list of the most celebrated Arabic lexicologists and grammarians, in the 48th Section of the Muzhir, the first five whose lengths of life are defined attained the following ages: 92, 74, 93, 96 or 97 or 98 or 99, and 92 or 93: the first of these (Yoonus) was born in the year 90 of the Flight; and the last, in the year 123; this being El-Aṣma'ee. This series of five is broken only by one, whose length of life is not known. In some few spots, the language of Ma'add long lingered; and it may perhaps even survive to the present day; as appears from the following curious statement in the Ḳámoos (article عكد): "'Akád is a certain mountain, near Zebeed, [a well-known city in the western seaboard of El-Yemen,] the inhabitants of which retain the chaste language:" to which is added in the Táj el-'Aroos, that they retain this language "to the present time [the middle of the eighteenth century]: and the stranger remains not with them more than three nights, [the period prescribed by the law for the entertainment of a stranger,] by reason of [their] fear for [the corruption of] their language." But instances of the corruption of the classical Arabic are related (in the 44th Section of the Muzhir) as having occurred even in the life-time of Moḥammad.

Such being the case, it became a matter of the highest importance to the Arabs to preserve the knowledge of that speech which had thus become obsolescent, and to draw a distinct line between the classical and post-classical languages. For the former language was that of the Ḳur-án and of the Traditions of Moḥammad, the sources of their religious, moral, civil, criminal, and political code: and they possessed, in that language, preserved by oral tradition,—for the art of writing, in Arabia, had been almost exclusively confined to Christians and Jews,—a large collection of poetry, consisting of odes and shorter pieces, which they esteemed almost as much for its intrinsic merits as for its value in illustrating their law. Hence the vast collection of lexicons and lexicological works composed by Arabs, and by Muslims naturalized among the Arabs; which compositions, but for the rapid corruption of the language, would never have been undertaken. In the aggregate of these works, with all the strictness that is observed in legal proceedings, as will presently be shown, the utmost care and research have been employed to embody everything that could be preserved or recovered of the classical language; the result being a collection of such authority, such exactness, and such copiousness, as we do not find to have been approached in the case of any other language after its corruption or decay.

The classical language they called, by reason of its incomparable excellence, "el-loghah," or "the language:" and the line between this and the post-classical was easily drawn, on account of the almost sudden commencement, and rapid progress, of the corruption. It was decided by common consent, that no poet, nor any other person, should be taken as an absolute and unquestionable authority with respect to the words or their significations, the grammar, or the prosody, of the classical language, unless he were one who had died before the promulgation of El-Islám, or who had lived partly before and partly after that event; or, as they term it, unless he were a "Jáhilee" or a "Mukhadram," or (as some pronounce it) "Mukhadrim," or "Muḥaḍram," or "Muḥaḍrim." A poet of the class next after the Mukhaḍrams is termed an "Islámee:" and as the corruption of the language had become considerable in his time, even among those who aimed at chasteness of speech, he is not cited as an authority absolutely and unquestionably like the two preceding classes. A poet of the next class, which is the last, is termed a "Muwelled:" he is absolutely post-classical; and is cited as an unquestionable authority with respect only to the rhetorical sciences. The commencement of the period of the Muwelleds is not distinctly stated: but it must have preceded the middle of the second century of the Flight; for the classical age may be correctly defined as having nearly ended with the first century, when very few persons born before the establishment of El-Islám through Arabia were living. Thus the best of the Islámee poets may be regarded, and are generally regarded, as holding classical rank, though not as being absolute authorities with respect to the words and the significations, the grammar, and the prosody, of the classical language. The highest of all authorities, however, on such points, prosody of course excepted, is held by the Arabs to be the Ḳur-án. The Traditions of Moḥammad are also generally held to be absolute authorities with respect to everything relating to the prose of the classical language; but they are excluded by some from the class of absolute authorities, because traditions may be corrupted in language, and interpolated, and even forged. Women are often cited as authorities of equal rank with men: and in like manner, slaves reared among the Arabs of classical times are cited as authorities equally with such Arabs. (See the word شَاعِرٌ in the present work; and see also جَاهِلِيٌّ and مُخَضْرَمٌ and إِسْلَامِيٌّ and مُوَلَّدٌ.)

The poetry of the Jáhilees and Mukhaḍrams consists, first, of *odes* (termed قَصَائِدُ, plural of قَصِيدَةٌ), which were regarded as complete poems, and which were all designed to be chanted or sung: secondly, of shorter compositions, termed *pieces* (قِطَعٌ, plural of قِطْعَةٌ); many of which were also designed to be chanted or sung: and thirdly, of *couplets*, or *single verses*. In the first of these classes are usually included all poems of more than fifteen verses: but few odes consist of much less than fifty verses or much more than a hundred. Of such poems, none has been transmitted, and none is believed to have existed, of an age more than a few generations (probably not more than three or four or five) anterior to that of Moḥammad. It is said in the 49th Section of the Muzhir, on the authority of Moḥammad Ibn-Selám El-Jumaḥee, that "the pristine Arabs had no poetry except the few verses which a man would utter in his need: and odes (ḳaṣeedehs) were composed, and poetry made long, only [for the first time] in the age of 'Abd-El-Muṭṭalib [Moḥammad's grandfather], or Ḥáshim Ibn-'Abd-Menáf [his great-grandfather]." And shortly after, in the same Section of that work, it is said, on the same authority, that "the first who composed poems of this kind was El-Muhelhil Ibn-Rabee'ah Et-Teghlibee, on the subject of the slaughter of his brother Kuleyb:" "he was maternal uncle of Imra-el-Ḳeys* Ibn-Ḥojr El-Kindee." "Or, according to 'Omar Ibn-Shebbeh, each tribe claimed priority for its own poet; and not merely as the author of two or three verses, for such they called not a poem: the Yemánees claimed for Imra-el-Ḳeys; and Benoo-Asad, for 'Abeed Ibn-El-Abraṣ; and Teghlib, for [El-] Muhelhil; and Bekr, for 'Amr Ibn-Ḳamee-ah and El-Murakḳish El-Akbar; and Iyád, for Aboo-Du-ád: and some assert that El-Afwah El-Azdee was older than these, and was the first who composed ḳaṣeedehs: but these for whom priority in poetry was claimed were nearly contemporary; the oldest of them probably not preceding the Flight by a hundred years, or thereabout. Thaalab says, in his 'Amálee,' El-Aṣma'ee says that the first of the poets of whom is related a poem extending to thirty verses is [El-] Muhelhil: then, Dhu-eyb Ibn-Kaab Ibn-'Amr Ibn-Temeem Ibn-Ḍamreh, a man of Benoo-Kináneh; and El-Aḍbaṭ Ibn-Ḳureyạ: and he says, Between these and El-Islám was four hundred years: and Imra-el-Ḳeys was long after these." But this is inconsistent with the assertion of Ibn-Selám mentioned above, made also by En-Näwawee in his "Tahdheeb el-Asmà," p. 163, that El-Muhelhil was maternal uncle of Imra-el-Ḳeys: and as the majority refer El-Muhelhil to a period of about a century before the Flight, we have a double reason for holding this period (not that of four hundred years) to be the more probably

* This name is generally pronounced thus, or "Imr-el-Ḳeys," by the learned among the Arabs in the present day; for most of them regard it as pedantic to pronounce proper names in the classical manner. The classical pronunciation is "Imraü-l-Ḳeys" and "Imruü-l-Ḳeys" and Imru-l-Ḳeys;" in the last instance without hemzeh, because (as is said in the Tahdheeb and the Táj el-'Aroos on the authority of El-Kisá-ee and El-Farrà) this letter is often dropped.

correct. According to Ibn-Ḳuteybeh, the time of Imra-el-Ḳeys was forty years before that of Moḥammad; as is stated in the Calcutta edition of the Mo'allaḳát. M. Fresnel contends that the honour commonly ascribed to El-Muhelhil is due to Zuheyr Ibn-Jenáb El-Kelbee, of whose poetry at least seventy-nine verses have been preserved, fragments of different poems, including a piece of fifteen verses, of which the first hemistich of the first verse rhymes with the second hemistich, according to rule. But this Zuheyr, during a portion of his life, is related to have been contemporary with El-Muhelhil. In a fragment ascribed to him, he represents himself (if the fragment be genuine) to have lived two hundred years: and one tradition assigns to him a life of two hundred and fifty years; another, four hundred years; and another, four hundred and fifty years!*—Upon the whole, then, it seems that we may with probability refer the first ḳaṣeedeh to a period within a century and a half, at the utmost, before the Flight.

Moḥammad said, on being asked, "Who is the best of the poets?" "Imra-el-Ḳeys will be the leader of the poets to Hell." And in the general estimation of the Arabs, he is the most excellent of all their poets. His Mo'allaḳah is most especially admired by them. Of the pagan and unbelieving poets who flourished before and during the time of Moḥammad, El-Beyḍáwee sarcastically remarks (on chap. xxvi. verses 224 and 225 of the Ḳur-án, in which, and in the verse that next follows, they are censured as seducers, bewildered by amorous desire, and vain boasters,) "Most of their themes are unreal fancies, and their words chiefly relate to the description of the charms of women under covert, and amorous dalliance, and false arrogations or professions, and the rending of reputations, and the impugning of the legitimacy of parentages, and false threatening, and vain boasting, and the praise of such as do not deserve it, with extravagance therein." The like is also said in the Keshsháf, (on the same passage of the Ḳur-án,) and in too large a degree we must admit it to be just; but it is very far from being unexceptionable. The classical poetry is predominantly objective, sensuous, and passionate; with little imagination, or fancy, except in relation to phantoms, or spectres, and to jinn, or genii, and other fabulous beings; and much less artificial than most of the later poetry, many of the authors of which, lacking the rude spirit of the Bedawees, aimed chiefly at mere elegancies of diction, and plays upon words. Generally speaking, in the classical poetry, the descriptions of nature, of the life of the desert, of night-journeyings and day-journeyings, with their various incidents, of hunting, and stalking, and lurking for game, of the tending of camels, of the gathering of wild honey, and similar occupations, are most admirable. And very curious and interesting, as will be shown by many citations in the present work, are its frequent notices (mostly by early Muslim poets) of the superstitions that characterized, in the pagan times, the religion most generally prevailing throughout Arabia; in which, with the belief in a Supreme Deity, with strange notions of a future state, and with angelolatry, astrolatry, and idolatry, was combined the lowest kind of fetishism, chiefly the worship of rocks and stones and trees, probably learned from Negroes, of whom the Arabs have always had great numbers as slaves, and with whom they have largely intermixed. Sententious language consisting of parallel clauses, like that of the so-called "poetical books" of the Bible, was probably often employed by the Arabs of every age. It seems to be almost natural to their race when excited to eloquence. But the addition of rhyme in this style of language appears to have become common in the later times. Moḥammad Ibn-Eṭ-Ṭeiyib El-Fásee says (in article خطب of his Annotations on the Ḳámoos) that the oration termed خُطْبَة, in the Pagan and the early Muslim ages, was, in most instances, not in rhyming prose. The remains of classical prose are often used as authorities; but being more liable to corruption, they are regarded as less worthy of reliance than the poetry.†

---

* See the first and second and third of M. Fresnel's "Lettres sur l'Histoire des Arabes avant l'Islamisme:" the second and third in the "Journal Asiatique," 3rd Series, vols. 3 and 5.

† Those who desire to pursue the study of the history of the classical Arabic beyond the limits to which I have here confined my remarks, together with that of its sister-languages, will find much learned and valuable information in M. Renan's "Histoire Générale et Système Comparé des Langues Sémitiques;" though his scepticism in relation to questions merely philological (as well as to sacred matters) is often, in my opinion, ill-grounded and unreasonable. I must particularly remark upon his erroneous assertion that the poems of the age anterior to El-Islám make no allusion to the ancient religions of Arabia, and hence appear to have been expurgated by Muslims, so as to efface all traces of paganism. Many of such allusions, by pagan poets, might be adduced from lexicons, grammars, and scholia; and some examples of them will be found in the present work, in articles دور and عز and مور &c.; the

[first

Such are the principal original sources from which the Arabic lexicons and lexicological works have been derived. Another source consisted of phrases and single words transmitted from the Arabs of classical times, or from those later Arabs of the desert who were believed (though they were not regarded as unquestionable authorities) to have retained the pure language of their ancestors. The earlier of these are often called, by the lexicologists, العرب العاربة; as in the 1st Section of the Muzhir, where it is said that the transmission (النقل) should be "from such as العرب العاربة, like [the descendants of] Ḳaḥṭán and Ma'add and 'Adnán; not from those after them; after the corruption of their language, and the varying of the Muwelleds." El-Jowharee, as will presently be seen, applies the appellation العرب العاربة even to desert-Arabs of his own time; but in doing so, he deviates from the general usage of the lexicologists. As is said in the 6th Section of the Muzhir, the transmitter must be a trustworthy person; but may be a woman, and may be a slave, as we have before stated. The degrees of credit to which the phrases and words thus transmitted are entitled are distinguished by ranging them in the following classes: 1st, (as is stated in the 3rd Section of the Muzhir,) the term متواتر is applied to that which has been transmitted by such a number of persons as cannot be supposed to have agreed to a falsehood: 2ndly, آحاد (plural of أحد), to what have been transmitted by some of the lexicologists, but are wanting in that which is required to justify the application, thereto, of the former term; and what is thus transmitted is also termed مظنون: 3rdly, (as is said in the 5th Section,) أفراد (plural of فرد), to what have been transmitted by only one of the lexicologists; and what is thus transmitted, if the transmitter is a person of exactness, as Aboo-Zeyd and El-Khaleel and others, is admitted: 4thly, (as is said in the 15th Section,) مفاريد (plural of مفرود), to words known to be spoken only by one Arab. It was only when all other sources failed to supply what was wanted, that recourse was had, by the writers of lexicons and lexicological works, to contemporary Arabs of the desert; and I do not find that much reliance was often placed upon these after the end of the third century of the Flight. El-Jowharee, who died near the close of the next century, states, in the short preface to his "Ṣiḥáḥ," that what he had collected in El-'Irák for his lexicon he "rehearsed by lip to [those whom he terms] العرب العاربة in their abodes in the desert (البادية):" but this he seems to have done rather to satisfy any doubts that he may have had, and to obtain illustrations, than with the view of taking such persons as authorities for words or phrases or significations. It is related of Aboo-Zeyd, in the 7th Section of the Muzhir, that he said, "I do not say 'the Arabs say' unless I have heard it from these: Bekr Ibn-Hawázin and Benoo-Kiláb and Benoo-Hilál; or from [the people of] the higher portion of the lower region, or [of] the lower of the higher:"* and that Yoonus used the expression "the Trustworthy (الثقة) told me from the Arabs;" that being asked, "Who is the Trustworthy?" he answered, "Aboo-Zeyd;" and being asked, "And wherefore dost thou not name him?" he answered, "He is a tribe, so I do not name him."†

Most of the contents of the best Arabic lexicons was committed to writing, or to the memories of students, in the latter half of the second century of the Flight, or in the former half of the next century. Among the most celebrated lexicological

---

first of these from the Mo'allaḳah of Imra-el-Ḳeys. It would have been strange, indeed, if this had not been the case: for, except the Ḳur-án, nothing was so highly prized by the lexicologists as the pagan poetry: every fragment of it was most valuable in their estimation, and most carefully sought after and preserved; and the intentional corruption of it they regarded as almost a crime.

* "Aboo-'Amr said, 'The most chaste in speech, of men, are the higher [in respect of territory] of [the tribe of] Temeem, and the lower of [the tribe of] Ḳeys:' and Aboo-Zeyd said, 'The most chaste in speech, of men, are [the people of] the lower portion of the higher region, and the higher of the lower,' meaning the rear of [the tribe of] Hawázin; the people of the higher region being the people of El-Medeeneh, and those around it, and those next it, and those near it, whose dialect he held to be not the same as that [of Hawázin]." (Muzhir, 49th Section.) According to the Ḳámoos, the higher region (العالية) is "what is above Nejd, to the land of Tihámeh, to the part behind Mekkeh; and certain towns, or villages, outside El-Medeeneh."

† The exclusion of post-classical words and significations in the best Arabic lexicons, or their specification as such when they occur therein, is of very great importance to us in the use that we are often obliged to make of those lexicons in interpreting the Hebrew Scriptures. Thus the triumph of El-Islám, by occasioning the corruption of the Arabic language and the composition of such lexicons, has rendered us a most signal service. I have seldom noticed correspondences between the Arabic on the one side and the Hebrew and other Semitic languages on the other, because, though these are often illustrated by means of the incomparable copiousness of the Arabic, the Arabic is rarely illustrated by them, and because we have no such authorities for the interpretation of those languages as we have for the interpretation of the Arabic.

works, general and special, of this period, are the "'Eyn," commonly ascribed to El-Khaleel, who died in the year of the Flight 160 or 170 or 175 (aged 74); the "Nawádir" of El-Kisá-ee, who died in 182 or 183 or 189 or 192; the "Jeem" and the "Nawádir" and the work entitled "El-Ghareeb el-Muṣannaf" of Aboo-'Amr Esh-Sheybánee, who died in 205 or 206 or 213 (aged 110 or 111 or 118); the "Nawádir" and the "Loghát" of El-Farrà, who died in 207 (aged 67); the "Loghát" of Aboo-'Obeydeh, who died in 208 or 209 or 210 or 211 (aged 96 or 97 or 98 or 99); the "Nawádir" and the "Loghát" of Aboo-Zeyd, who died in 214 or 215 or 216 (aged 93); the "Ajnás" of El-Aṣma'ee, who died in 215 or 216 (aged 92 or 93); the work entitled "El-Ghareeb el-Muṣannaf" of Aboo-'Obeyd, who died in 223 or 224 or 230 (aged 67); and the "Nawádir" of Ibn-El-Aaṛábee, who died in 231 or 233 (aged 81 or 83): all mentioned near the close of the 1st Section of the Muzhir. From these and similar works, either immediately or through the medium of others in which they are cited, and from oral tradition, and, as long as it could be done with confidence, by collecting information from Arabs of the desert, were composed all the best lexicons, and commentaries on the classical poets &c. The most authoritative of such works are the lexicons; and the most authoritative of these are, of course, generally speaking, the later, because every succeeding lexicographer profited by the critical research of his predecessors, and thus avoided or corrected errors committed by earlier authors. The commentaries on the poets and on the Traditions have contributed largely to the lexicons. They often present explanations that have been disallowed or questioned by eminent lexicographers; and therefore their statements, when unconfirmed by other authorities, must be received with caution: but in many cases their explanations are unquestionably accurate, and they afford valuable aid by giving examples of words and phrases of doubtful meanings. The danger of relying upon a single early authority, however high that authority may be, in any matter of Arabic lexicology, will be shown by innumerable instances in the present work. I here speak of errors of judgment. In addition to these, we have mistranscriptions. A word once mistranscribed is repeated in copy after copy; and at length, from its having been found in several copies, is confidently regarded as correct.* The value of the larger and later and more esteemed lexicons cannot, therefore, be too highly rated.

The first of the general lexicons is that which is commonly ascribed to El-Khaleel, entitled the "'Eyn" (كِتَاب العَيْن); and this has served in a great measure as the basis of many others. In it the words are mentioned according to their radical letters, as in all the best lexicons; but the letters are arranged, with the exception of ا and ى, which are classed with و for obvious reasons, nearly in the order of their places of utterance, as follows; commencing with ع (whence the title):

ع ح ه خ غ ق ك ج ش ض ص س ز ط د ت ظ ذ ث ر ل ن ف ب م و ا ى

Under each of these letters, in the foregoing order, except the last three which are necessarily classed together, are mentioned all the words of which the roots contain that letter without any letter of those preceding it in this arrangement: first, the biliteral-radical words: then, the triliteral-radical; of which are placed first the sound; secondly the unsound in one letter; and thirdly the unsound in two letters: next, the quadriliteral-radical: and lastly, the quinqueliteral-radical. Thus, under the letter ع are mentioned all the words of which the roots contain that letter: under ح, all the words of which the roots contain that letter without ع: under ه, all of which the roots contain that letter without ع or ح: and so on. For instance, in the section of the letter ل, we find, in the first division, first, لن; then, لف and فل; and so on: and in the second division, first, نعل

* For instance, M. Fresnel quoted (in the second of his "Lettres sur l'Histoire des Arabes avant l'Islamisme," in the "Journal Asiatique," 3rd Series, vol. iii. pp. 330 et seq.,) an extract from the "Kitáb el-Aghánee," as containing, in the phrases ما حملت واحدا منهم تصعا ولا ولدته تينا, two words supposed by him, and by his and my learned friend the sheykh Moḥammad 'Eiyád Eṭ-Ṭanṭáwee, (see pp. 324 et seq. of that letter,) to be wanting in all the Arabic dictionaries. One of these words is written تصعا, as above, in one of M. Fresnel's copies of the "Kitáb el-Aghánee," three in number; in another copy, تضعا; and in the third copy, قضعا: the other is in all the copies تينا, as above: and they are explained in that work, on the authority of Abu-l-Yaḳdhán El-Joạfee, as meaning فى دُبُرِ الطُّهْرِ وَقُبُلِ الحَيْضِ and ان تخرج رجلاه قبل راسه. The former word is correctly تُضْعًا or تَضْعًا, both infinitive nouns of وَضَعَتْ. The other word is a mistranscription for يَتْنًا. My lamented friend M. Fresnel was always glad to receive and admit a correction of any of his own *rare* mistakes; and in his "Fourth Letter" he announced that the sheykh Moḥammad had afterwards rectified these two errors.

* كَفَى المَرْءَ نُبْلًا أَنْ تُعَدَّ مَعَايِبُهْ *

and فلن ; then, بن and نبل ; and so on : all the combinations of the same radical letters being arranged consecutively; and the same order of letters being observed in all cases. Respecting the question of its authorship, which is involved in much uncertainty, I have gathered from the 1st Section of the Muzhir what here follows. Es-Seeráfee says that El-Khaleel composed the first part of the 'Eyn. But most men deny [absolutely] its being his composition. Some say that it is by Leyth [or El-Leyth] Ibn-Naṣr Ibn-Seiyár El-Khurásánee. El-Azheree says that El-Leyth composed it, and ascribed it to El-Khaleel in order that it might become in much request. Some say that El-Khaleel composed the portion from the beginning to the end of the letter ع, and El-Leyth completed it; and therefore it is that the first part does not resemble the rest. Ibn-El-Moạtezz relates, on the authority of the "Moạjam el-Udabà" of Yáḳoot El-Ḥamawee, that El-Khaleel made himself solely and peculiarly an associate of El-Leyth; and when he composed the 'Eyn, assigned it to him: that El-Leyth held it in very great estimation, and gave him a hundred thousand [dirhems]; and committed the half of it to memory:* but it happened that he purchased a highly-prized female slave, who, becoming jealous of the daughter of his paternal uncle [i. e. of his wife], and desiring to enrage him, which she could not do with respect to money as he would not care for her doing this, burned that book: and as no one else possessed a copy of it, and El-Khaleel had then died, El-Leyth dictated the half that he retained in his memory, and employed persons to complete it uniformly with that half: and they made this composition which is in the hands of men. To account for the mistakes occurring in the 'Eyn, Thaạlab says, "El-Khaleel sketched it out, but did not fill it up; and had he filled it up, he had spared nothing in it; for El-Khaleel was a man of whom the like has not been seen: certain learned men filled it up, on whose authority nothing has been related." It is also said that El-Khaleel composed, of this book, only the section of the letter ع, and his companion El-Leyth composed the rest, and named himself "El-Khaleel" [i. e. "the friend"]; and that when he says, in the book, "El-Khaleel Ibn-Aḥmad says," it is El-Khaleel; and when he says, absolutely, "El-Khaleel says," he speaks of himself: and that every flaw in the book is from him; not from El-Khaleel. En-Nawawee says that [according to some of the learned] the 'Eyn ascribed to El-Khaleel is only what El-Leyth collected from El-Khaleel.† The mistakes in the 'Eyn are numerous; and there are many interpolations in copies thereof. Several authors have applied themselves to point out and correct these faults: some, in works specially devoted to this object: some, in abridgments of the 'Eyn or in other lexicons. But in general the mistakes are confined to matters of inflection and derivation; not extending to the insertion of false or unknown words: and such mistakes are of light account.‡

The following notices of other celebrated lexicons, composed after the 'Eyn, so far as to include the Ḳámoos, I borrow chiefly from the same section of the Muzhir; distinguishing my own additions by enclosing them within square brackets.

Among the celebrated lexicons composed after the model of the 'Eyn, is the "Jemharah" of Ibn-Dureyd, [who is said to have died in the year of the Flight 321, and to have lived 93 years.] Some say that it is one of the best of lexicons; and it has been taken as an authority by Aboo-'Alee El-Fárisee and Aboo-'Alee El-Ḳálee and Es-Seeráfee and other eminent authors. Ibn-Jinnee disparages it for faults similar to those of the 'Eyn: and Nifṭaweyh, whom Ibn-Dureyd had satirized, pronounced it to be untrustworthy; but without justice.

---

* Many of the Arabs have been remarkable for a tenacity of memory almost miraculous. Several of them are related to have composed and dictated from memory large works, including even lexicons. At school, they generally learn the whole of the Ḳur-án by heart, aided to do so by its being composed in rhyming prose: and many students, among them, when unable to purchase works necessary to them, borrow such works, a portion at a time, from the libraries of the mosques, and commit their entire contents to memory. Hence, in numerous instances, the variations in copies of the same Arabic work; copies being often written from the dictation of persons who have learned a work by heart.

† En-Nawawee also says, (see the printed edition of his Biographical Dictionary, page 231,) that, according to some of the learned, "much of what El-Azheree has transcribed in the Tahdheeb el-Loghah from the 'Eyn is of the mistakes of Leyth:" but this is inconsistent with the estimation in which the Tahdheeb is held by lexicographers of the highest repute. El-Azheree often points out what he terms mistakes of El-Leyth, and corrects them.

‡ In the present work, whatever is given as on the authority of El-Leyth is from the 'Eyn; I believe, through the medium of the Tahdheeb of El-Azheree, except, perhaps, in a very few instances: and from the 'Eyn also is generally derived (probably in almost every instance) what is given as on the authority of El-Khaleel.

The "Tahdheeb" of El-Azheree, [who was born in the year of the Flight 282, and died in the year 370 or 371. This is a very excellent lexicon, and one from which I have largely drawn, immediately and through the medium of the Lisán el-'Arab and of the Táj-el-'Aroos. Its arrangement is the same as that of the 'Eyn, which it calls "the book of El-Leyth," and from which its contents are in a great measure derived. I possess a large portion of this work in a volume of the "Tahdheeb et-Tahdheeb;" and a small portion, consisting of 193 pages, of a copy in large 8vo., corresponding to a part of the former.]

The "Moḥeeṭ" of the Ṣáḥib Ibn-'Abbád. [Ibn-Khillikán* states that he was born in the year of the Flight 326, and died in 385: and describes this work as "in seven volumes; arranged in the order of the letters of the alphabet; copious in words, but having few confirmatory examples:" thus resembling the Ḳámoos. Much has been drawn from it in my own lexicon.]

The "Mujmal" of Ibn-Fáris, [who died in the year of the Flight 390 or 395.] He restricted himself, in his lexicon, to the mention of genuine words; excluding the unfamiliar and ignored; on the authority of oral tradition, and from books of good repute; aiming, as he says, at abridgment and conciseness. [His work is highly esteemed. The arrangement is that of the usual order of the letters of the alphabet.]

The "Ṣiḥáḥ," or, as some call it, "Ṣaḥáḥ," of El-Jowharee, [commonly, now, pronounced "El-Jóharee," who died, according to Abu-l-Fidà, in the year of the Flight 398, and "was from Fáráb, a city of the country of the Turks, beyond the river," that is, beyond the Seyhoon: or, according to Ibn-Esh-Shiḥneh, he died in the year 397, as I find in two copies of his history in my possession: or, according to Ḥájjee Khaleefeh, in 393.] Et-Tebreezee says that it is commonly known by the title of the صِحَاح, which is pl. of صَحِيح; but that some call it the صَحَاح, which is synonymous with صَحِيح. As its title imports, the author restricted himself to the mention of genuine words, like Ibn-Fáris, his contemporary. [But his lexicon is far more comprehensive, and more excellent in every respect, than that of Ibn-Fáris.] As he says in his preface, he composed it in an order which none had before pursued, [mentioning each word according to the place of the last letter of the root, and then the first and second, in the usual order of the alphabet,] after collecting the contents in El-'Irák, and rehearsing them by lip [as I have before mentioned] to [those whom he terms] العَرَب العَارِبَة in their abodes in the desert (البَادِيَة). Eth-Tha'álibee says that he was one of the wonders of the age. His lexicon, however, is not free from instances of inadvertence or mistakes, like all great books; and such as cannot be attributed to the copyists. Yáḳoot says, in the "Moạjam el-Udabà," that the cause of the mistranscriptions in it was this: when he had composed it, it was read to him as far as [the section of] the letter ض, and an evil suggestion occurred to his mind, in consequence of which he cast himself from a housetop, and died: so the rest of the book remained a rough draught, not pruned, or trimmed, nor fairly copied out; and his disciple Ibráheem Ibn-Ṣáliḥ El-Warráḳ made a fair copy of it, and committed mistakes in some places in it. Ibn-Barree wrote a commentary, or series of annotations, (حَوَاشٍ, plural of حَاشِيَة,) on the Ṣiḥáḥ, [an extremely valuable work] in which he reached the middle [of the section] of the letter س; and the sheykh 'Abd-Allah Ibn-Moḥammad El-Busṭee completed it. [But I have invariably found passages from every part of it cited as the sayings of Ibn-Barree.] And Eṣ-Saghánee, or, as he is called by some, Eṣ-Ṣághánee, wrote a Tekmileh (تَكْمِلَة, i. e. Supplement) to the Ṣiḥáḥ; exceeding it in bulk. [Some further remarks on the Ṣiḥáḥ (my own copies of which have been already described) will be found in my account of the Ḳámoos. The abridgment entitled "Mukhtár eṣ-Ṣiḥáḥ" is well known: it is too scanty to be of much use except to those who desire to commit to memory the most usual words and significations. A very superior abridgment is the "Jámi'" of the seyyid Moḥammad Ibn-es-seyyid-Ḥasan, which was finished, according to Ḥájjee Khaleefeh, in the year of the Flight 854. It is copious, well digested, and enriched with additions from the Mughrib of El-Muṭarrizee, the Fáïḳ of Ez-Zamakhsheree, the Niháyeh of Ibn-El-Atheer, &c. Of this work I possess a very good copy.]

---

* I have the express authority of the Táj el-'Aroos (in art. خلك) for thus writing the name of this author.

The "Jámi'" of El-Ḳazzáz, [who died in the year of the Flight 412. Ḥájjee Khaleefeh mentions it as "an esteemed book, but rare." It is not unfrequently cited in the Táj el-'Aroos.]

The "Moo'ab" (thus, with fet-ḥ to the ع,) of Aboo-Ghálib Ibn-Temám, [or, according to Ibn-Khillikán, Aboo-Ghálib Temám,] known by the appellation of Ibn-Et-Teiyánee, [who died in the year of the Flight 436;] a work of very great utility, consisting of what is correct of the contents of the 'Eyn, not omitting anything of the confirmatory examples from the Ḳur-án and the Traditions and the genuine poems of the Arabs, but rejecting what it contains of examples respecting which there is disagreement, and of mistranscribed words, and faulty formations; and adding what Ibn-Dureyd has added in the Jemharah. It is rarely found; for people have not persevered in transcribing it, but have rather inclined to the Jemharah of Ibn-Dureyd and the Moḥkam of Ibn-Seedeh and the Jámi' of El-Ḳazzáz and the Ṣiḥáḥ &c.

The "Moḥkam" of Ibn-Seedeh the Andalusian, who was blind, [as was also his father; and who died in the year of the Flight 458, aged about 60 years.] This is the greatest of the lexicological books [i. e. of the lexicons] composed since the age of the Ṣiḥáḥ [to the time of the author of the Muzhir, of those known to him. It follows the arrangement of the 'Eyn; and it is held in very high estimation for its copiousness, its accuracy, its critical remarks, and its numerous examples from classical poets. In copiousness and in some other respects, it is superior, and in others hardly (if at all) inferior, to the Ṣiḥáḥ. It is one of the two chief sources of the Ḳámoos; the other being the 'Obáb of Eṣ-Ṣagháneе: and I have drawn from it very largely, both immediately and through the medium of the Lisán el-'Arab and of the Táj el-'Aroos, for my own lexicon. I possess the last fifth part of it in a volume of the "Tahdheeb et-Tahdheeb;" and another large portion, and a smaller portion, of a most admirable copy which has been dispersed, written in the year of the Flight 675, for the library of a Sulṭán, apparently the celebrated Beybars.]

[The "Asás" of Ez-Zamakhsheree, who was born in the year of the Flight 467, and died in 538. This lexicon is a very excellent repertory of choice and chaste words and phrases; and especially and peculiarly valuable as comprising a very large collection of tropical significations, distinguished as such, which has greatly contributed, by indirectly illustrating proper significations as well as otherwise, to the value of my own lexicon, as my numerous citations of it will show, although I have generally been obliged to draw from it through the medium of the Táj el-'Aroos, which often does not name it in quoting it. Its order is the same as that of the Mujmal, apparently in most copies: but some, which are said to be abridged, follow the order of the Ṣiḥáḥ.]

[The "Mughrib" of El-Muṭarrizee, who was born in Khuwárezm, in the year of the Flight 536, and died in 610. This is a lexicon of select words and phrases, and particularly of such as occur in books of Traditions, and other works relating to the law. It forms a very valuable companion and supplement to the other lexicons; and I have constantly consulted it and drawn from it in composing the present work. Its arrangement of the roots is that of the usual order of the alphabet, with respect to the first, second, and third letters of each. I possess a very excellent copy of it, written in the year of the Flight 977, presented to me by the Rev. J. R. T. Lieder, late of the English Church-Mission in Cairo.]

The "'Obáb" of Eṣ-Ṣagháneе, or Eṣ-Ṣágháneе, [who was born in the year of the Flight 577, and died in 660, according to the Muzhir (48th Section), or, as is said in the Táj el-'Aroos (art. صغن), in 655, on the authority of one who attended his funeral.] This, after the Moḥkam, is the greatest of the lexicological works composed since the age of the Ṣiḥáḥ [to the time of the author of the Muzhir, of those known to him. It was left unfinished. If, as I believe is the case, it follow the order of the Ṣiḥáḥ, the portion completed was somewhat more than three fourths; for] the author reached, in it, to the section of بكم: which occasioned the saying,

• إِنَّ ٱلصَّغَانِىَّ ٱلَّذِى • حَازَ ٱلْعُلُومَ وَٱلْحِكَمْ • كَانَ قُصَارَى أَمْرِهِ • أَنِ ٱنْتَهَى إِلَى بَكَمْ •

[" Verily Eṣ-Ṣaghánee, who mastered the sciences and the doctrines of philosophy, the utmost of his case was that he reached to بَكَّر," which signifies "dumbness," &c.—Though a man of extensive learning, he was opiniative, and addicted to unjust criticism of his superiors. A copy of the 'Obáb, and a copy of the same author's Supplement to the Ṣiḥáḥ, before mentioned, used by the author of the Táj el-'Aroos, belonged to the library of the mosque of the Emeer Ṣarghatmish, in Cairo; but on my causing an inquiry to be made for them, the librarian declared that they were no longer found there. They have probably been stolen; or had not been returned by the author of the Táj el-'Aroos when he died; on which occasion, it is said, his house was plundered of the books &c. that he left.]

[The "Lisán el-'Arab" of Ibn-Mukarram, who was born in the year of the Flight 630, and died in 711. In the copy of his lexicon in the library of the collegiate mosque called the "Ashrafeeyeh," in Cairo, consisting of twenty-eight quarto-volumes, he is styled "Jemál-ed-Deen Moḥammad Ibn-esh-sheykh-el-imám-el-marḥoom-Jelál-ed-Deen-Abi-l-'Izz-Mukarram Ibn-esh-sheykh-Nejeeb-ed-Deen-Abi-l-Ḥasan-El-Anṣáree:" but in the Táj el-'Aroos, he is almost always called Ibn-Mandhoor (ابن منظور). I shall give an account of this great work in describing the Táj el-'Aroos.]

[The "Tahdheeb et-Tahdheeb" of Maḥmood Et-Tanookhee, who died in the year of the Flight 723. It is a combination of the contents of the Moḥkam and Tahdheeb (the former occupying the first place in each article) with a few additions from other sources. Thus it forms one of the best and most comprehensive of the Arabic lexicons, without any exceptions known to me but the Lisán el-'Arab and the Táj el-'Aroos. Of the original autograph copy of this work, in five full-paged, large quarto-volumes, I possess the last volume, consisting of 501 pages. I made a diligent search for the other volumes, but without success.]

[The "Miṣbáḥ" of El-Feiyoomee (Aḥmad Ibn-Moḥammad Ibn-'Alee El-Muḳri). Its full title is "El-Miṣbáḥ el-Muneer fee Ghareeb esh-Sharḥ el-Kebeer." This is a lexicon similar to the Mughrib, above mentioned; but much more comprehensive; forming a most valuable companion and supplement to the larger lexicons. Notwithstanding its title, it comprises a very large collection of classical words and phrases and significations of frequent occurrence; in many instances with more clear and full explanations than I have found elsewhere. I have therefore constantly drawn from it in composing my own lexicon; possessing a very accurate copy of it, a full-paged quarto-volume of 742 pages. Its author states in it that he finished its composition in the year of the Flight 734.]

[The "Mughnee," as it is commonly called, or "Mughni-l-Lebeeb," of the celebrated grammarian Ibn-Hishám, who was born in the year of the Flight 708, and died in 761 or the following year. A large work, whereof a little more than one half consists of an elaborate lexicon of the particles and similar words, for which it is my chief authority, as it was, also, that of the author of the Ḳámoos, whose explanations of the particles are, however, very meagre and unsatisfactory. I am fortunate in possessing a most excellent copy of it, a quarto-volume of 609 pages.]

The "Ḳámoos" of El-Feyroozábádee, [or, as some pronounce it, El-Feeroozábádee, (from the city of Férózábád, or Feerózábád, pronounced by the Arabs Feyroozábád, or Feeroozábád,) who was born in the year of the Flight 729, and died in 816.*] This, after the Moḥkam and the 'Obáb, is the greatest of the lexicological works composed since the age of the Ṣiḥáḥ [to the time of the author of the Muzhir, of those known to him]: but none of these three [he adds] has attained to be as much used as the Ṣiḥáḥ; nor has the rank of the Ṣiḥáḥ, nor its celebrity, been diminished by the existence of these; because it is restricted to what is genuine, so that it is, among the books of lexicology, like the Ṣaḥeeḥ of El-Bukháree among the books

* It is stated at the end of article وجد in the Táj el-'Aroos that the author of the Ḳámoos wrote at the end of the first volume of the second copy of that work made by his own hand, which volume ended with the article above mentioned, that he finished the transcription of that volume in Dhu-l-Ḥijjeh 768.

of traditions; for the point upon which turns the title to reliance is not the copiousness of the collection, but the condition of genuineness, or correctness. [The judgment thus expressed, as to the rank and celebrity of the Ṣiḥáḥ, in comparison with the Ḳámoos, I have found to agree with the opinion of the most learned men among the Arabs with whom I have been acquainted. But to insinuate that the words and significations added in the latter of these lexicons to those of the former are generally less genuine, or less correct, is not just: they may be truly said to be generally less chaste, inasmuch as they are less usual: but their collector has undoubtedly rendered a great service to the students of Arabic by these additions, which have of late years caused the copies of his lexicon to become much more numerous than those of the Ṣiḥáḥ. The value of the Ṣiḥáḥ consists in its presenting a very judicious collection of the most chaste words, with critical illustrations from the best of the lexicologists, and examples from the best of the classical poets. The Ḳámoos is little more than what may be termed an enormous vocabulary; a collection of words and significations from preceding lexicons and similar works, (for otherwise, according to the principles of Arabic lexicology as universally taught, they would be of no authority,) mainly from the Moḥkam and the 'Obáb; with very few critical observations, many of which are false,* and scarcely any examples from the poets. Thus it resembles the Moheeṭ of Ibn-'Abbád, before mentioned. In order to make room for his numerous additions, desiring that the bulk of his book should be nearly the same as that of the Ṣiḥáḥ, the author has often abridged his explanations in such a manner as to render them unintelligible to the most learned of the Arabs, and has omitted much of what is most valuable of the contents of the latter work. But he has frequently deviated from this his usual practice for the purpose of inserting criticisms of others, without acknowledgment, and apparently some few of his own, upon points in the Ṣiḥáḥ in which its author is asserted to have erred; and this he has often done so as to lead to the belief that the author of the Ṣiḥáḥ has affirmed what he has merely quoted from another. Many of these criticisms I have found to have been borrowed from the Annotations on the Ṣiḥáḥ by Ibn-Barree and El-Busteo, or from the Supplement to the Ṣiḥáḥ by Eṣ-Ṣagháneo: generally when they are false, (which is often the case,) though sometimes when they are correct, from the latter of these works. I have felt it to be my duty to make these remarks in defence of El-Jowharee, and for the sake of truth. Abundant proofs of their correctness will be found in my own lexicon. They may surprise many, who have not known the fact that the Ḳámoos is very little more than an abridged compilation from other works: and another fact, to be mentioned in the next paragraph, which will be in a measure supplementary to this brief account of the Ḳámoos, will probably surprise them more.—This is the latest of the lexicons noticed in the Muzhir: therefore I have no further occasion for the use of the square brackets to distinguish my own statements or opinions from those of the author of that work, which has thus far afforded me so much aid in my account of the principles of Arabic lexicology, and of the most celebrated Arabic lexicons, as well as in my remarks on the history of the language. My own, most valuable, manuscript-copy of the Ḳámoos, which I have already described, has been of very great use to me, though its text is generally most correctly given in the Táj el-'Aroos. I have also constantly had before me the edition printed at Calcutta. This is certainly more accurate than most of the manuscript-copies; but it contains countless false readings, which show that, in many instances, the editor, notwithstanding his unquestionable learning and his possession of eleven copies, did not understand what he edited. It seems that he must often have given the worst of the readings of his originals, from neglecting to study the passages in which they occur. I have not thought it necessary to mention *all* of the false readings in his edition; but I have mentioned *many* of them.]

The "Lámi'" of El-Feyroozábádee. Its full title is "El-Lámi' el-Moạlam el-'Oját el-Jámi' beyn el-Moḥkam wa-l-'Obáb." From some words in the preface to the Ḳámoos, it has been inferred that the author of that work had composed a lexicon in sixty volumes, bearing the foregoing title, from which, chiefly, he composed, or abridged, the Ḳámoos, in two volumes. But in a very learned work, of Annotations on the Ḳámoos, by Moḥammad Ibn-Eṭ-Ṭeiyib El-Fásee, it is clearly

* The judgment and memory of its author are often in fault: for instance, in article بيض he disallows the expression الأَيَّامُ البِيضُ, and in art. وضح he uses it; and in article ضح he disallows ضِيحٌ as syn. with ضَحٌّ, and in article ضيح he authorizes it: and many similar instances might be mentioned.

shown that the words from which this inference has been drawn really signify that the author of the Lámi' *commenced* (*not* that he *completed*) this work, and made it, as far as it extended, to surpass every other work of a similar kind; but that he imagined it would be, in sixty volumes, too large for students to acquire or read; and, being requested to compose *before it* a concise lexicon, he applied himself to the composition of the Ḳámoos, and abridged the matter of which the Lámi' was to have consisted, so as to comprise the essence of each thirty of the intended volumes in one volume. Thus the words in question are so far from being a proof of the completion of the Lámi', that their literal meaning indicates the very contrary of this. They are not, however, the only evidence that we have on this point: for the same eminent scholar to whose Annotations on the Ḳámoos I have referred above quotes, from the biographical memoir of the author of the Lámi' in the "Ṭabaḳát en-Noḥáh" of Es-Suyooṭee, the direct assertion that this work was never completed. He also states, as does likewise the author of the Táj el-'Aroos, that more than one writer has transmitted, on the authority of the handwriting of its author, a proof of its non-completion: for they relate the fact of his having written upon the back of the Lámi' that, if he had been able to complete it, it would have composed a hundred volumes, [of what size he does not give the least notion,] and that he completed five volumes of it. This, it should be observed, is not inconsistent with what has been said before: it appears that the work would have consisted of a hundred volumes, each of the size of one of the five volumes that were completed; or would have composed sixty *larger* volumes. But I rather incline to think that its author roughly calculated, at one time, that the whole would consist of a hundred volumes; and at another time, that it would consist of sixty; and that both estimates are greatly beyond the truth. The non-completion of the Lámi' is therefore certain; but this is not so much to be regretted as some persons might imagine from its author's statement respecting it in his preface to the Ḳámoos; for the work appears, from its title, to have been, as far as it extended, with respect to the words and significations, mainly a compilation uniting the contents of the Moḥkam and the 'Obáb, and neither of these lexicons has been lost to the world. From a reference to it in article نكه of the Ḳámoos, (in which the author asserts his having disproved an opinion respecting the signification of نَكِهَةٌ without stating that El-Azheree had done so more than five centuries before,) it seems that the Lámi' (seeing how small a portion of it was completed) followed the order of the 'Eyn and the Moḥkam; for article نكه is in the third of the main divisions of these two works, but in the last but two of those of the Ḳámoos. Considering this fact, and that the main divisions of the 'Eyn and the Moḥkam necessarily decrease in length from first to last, I suppose that the author of the five volumes of the Lami' wrote them, agreeably with a common practice, with large margins for additions, and calculated that, with these additions, each of the five volumes would form at least three.

The "Táj el-'Aroos," the enormous extent of which I have mentioned in the second paragraph of this preface, is said to have been commenced, in Cairo, soon after the middle of the last century of our era, by the seyyid Murtaḍà Ez-Zebeedee. At the end of a copy of it in his own handwriting, he states that it occupied him fourteen years and some days. According to the modern historian of Egypt, El-Jabartee, he was born A.D. 1732 or 1733: came to Cairo A.D. 1753: finished the Táj el-'Aroos A.D. 1767 or 1768: and died A.D. 1791 (in the year of the Flight 1205). And the same historian says that Moḥammad Bey Abu-dh-Dhahab, for the copy of that work which is in the library of his mosque, gave him a hundred thousand dirhems (or drachms) of silver. It is a compilation from the best and most copious of the preceding Arabic lexicons and other lexicological works, in the form of an interwoven commentary on the Ḳámoos; exhibiting fully and clearly, from the original sources, innumerable explanations which are so abridged in the latter work as to be unintelligible to the most learned men of the East; with copious illustrations of the meanings &c., corrections of mistakes in the Ḳámoos and other lexicons, and examples in prose and verse; and a very large collection of additional words and significations, mentioned under the roots to which they belong. Of the works from which it is compiled, though I believe that it was mainly derived in the first instance from the Lisán el-'Arab, more than a hundred are enumerated by the seyyid Murtaḍà in his preface. Among these are—1. The "Ṣiḥáḥ," a copy in eight volumes, in the handwriting of Yáḳoot Er-Roomee, with useful marginal notes determining the correct readings &c. by Ibn-Barree [and El-Busṭee] and Aboo-Zekereeyà Et-Tebreezee; in the library [of the collegiate mosque] of the Emeer Ezbek.—2. The "Tahdheeb" of El-Azheree, a copy in sixteen volumes.—3. The "Moḥkam" of Ibn-Seedeh, a copy in eight volumes.—4. The "Tahdheeb el-Abniyeh wa-l-Af'ál," by Ibn-El-Ḳaṭṭáa, in two volumes.—5. The "Lisán el-'Arab," by the Imám Jemál-ed-Deen Moḥammad Ibn-'Alee El-Ifreeḳee, [whose appellations I have more fully given before, commonly called (in the Táj el-'Aroos) "Ibn-Manḍhoor,"] in twenty-eight volumes, the copy transcribed from the original draught of the author, during his life-time: [of this copy I have often made use in composing my own lexicon; and I have found it very helpful, especially in enabling me to supply syllabical signs, which are too often omitted in the copies of the Táj el-'Aroos:] its author followed closely, in its composition, the Ṣiḥáḥ, the Tahdheeb, the Moḥkam, the Niháyeh, the Annotations of Ibn-Barree [and El-Busṭee on the Ṣiḥáḥ], and the Jemharah of Ibn-Dureyd: [he also drew from innumerable other sources, to which he refers in his work.]—6. The "Tahdheeb et-Tahdheeb" of Abu-th-Thenà Maḥmood Ibn-Abee-Bekr Ibn-Ḥámid Et-Tanookhee, a copy in five volumes, [of which, as I have already mentioned, I possess the last,] the original draught of the author, who closely followed, in its composition, the Ṣiḥáḥ, the Tahdheeb, and the Moḥkam, with the utmost accuracy: he died in the year of the Flight 723.—7. The "Kitáb el-Ghareebeyn" of Aboo-'Obeyd El-Harawee.—8. The "Niháyeh fee Ghareeb el-Ḥadeeth," by Ibn-El-Atheer [Mejd-ed-Deen] El-Jezeree.—9. The "Kifáyet el-Mutaḥaffiḍh," by Ibn-El-Ajdábee, with Expositions thereof.—10. The "Faṣeeḥ" of Thaalab, with three Expositions thereof.—11 and 12. The "Fiḳh el-Loghah" and the work entitled "El-Muḍáf wa-l-Mensoob," each by Aboo-Manṣoor Eth-Tha'álibee.—13 and 14. The "'Obáb" and the "Tekmileh fi-ṣ-Ṣiḥáḥ," each by Er-Raḍee Eṣ-Ṣaghánee, in the library [of the mosque] of the Emeer Ṣarghatmish.—15. The "Miṣbáh" [of El-Feiyoomee].—16. The "Taḳreeb" of Ibn-Khaṭeeb.—17. The "Mukhtár eṣ-Ṣiḥáḥ," by Er-Rázee.—18, 19, and 20. The "Asás" and the "Fáïḳ" and the "Mustaḳṣee fi-l-Amthál," all three by Ez-Zamakhsheree.—21. The "Jemharah" of Ibn-Dureyd, in four volumes, in the library [of the mosque] of El-Mu-eiyad.—22. The "Iṣláḥ el-Manṭiḳ" of Ibn-Es-Sikkeet.—23 and 24. The "Khaṣáïṣ" of Ibn-Jinnee, and the "Sirr eṣ-Ṣiná'ah" of the same author.—25. The "Mujmal" of Ibn-Fáris.—Many other works of great value are included in the same list. And the Annotations on the Ḳámoos by his preceptor, Moḥammad Ibn-Eṭ-Ṭeiyib El-Fásee, (before mentioned, in my account of the Lámi',) must be especially noticed as a very comprehensive and most learned work, from which the seyyid Murtaḍà derived much valuable matter to incorporate in the Táj el-'Aroos. From these Annotations of Moḥammad El-Fásee, which have often served to explain to me obscure passages in the Táj el-'Aroos, and from several others of the most celebrated of the works used by the seyyid Murtaḍà, I have drawn much matter which he omitted as not necessary to Eastern scholars, but which will be found to be highly important to the Arabic students of Europe. He made very little use of a commentary on the Ḳámoos entitled the "Námoos," by Mullà 'Alee el-Ḳári, as it is not a work held in high estimation, and he was most careful to include among his authorities none but works of high repute. It must also be mentioned that he has bestowed great pains upon the important task of settling the true text of the Ḳámoos, according to the authorities of several celebrated copies; and that he has inserted the various readings that he regarded as being worthy of notice. And here I may state that most of the illustrations of the text of the Ḳámoos that are incorporated in the Turkish translation of that work, whenever I have examined them, which has often been the case, I have found to be taken from the Táj el-'Aroos, of which the Translator ('Áṣim Efendee) is said to have had a copy in the author's handwriting: but generally speaking, what is most precious of the contents of the latter work has been omitted in that translation.

As the Táj el-'Aroos is the medium through which I have drawn most of the contents of my lexicon, I must more fully state the grounds upon which I determined to make so great a use of it. Not long after I had become acquainted with this enormous work, I found it to be asserted by some persons in Cairo that the seyyid Murtaḍà was not its author: that it was compiled by a certain learned man (whose name I could not ascertain) who, coming to Cairo with this work, on his way from Western Africa to Mekkeh as a pilgrim, and fearing to lose it in the desert-journey, committed it to the seyyid Murtaḍà to be safely kept until his return: that he died during his onward-journey, or during his return towards Cairo: and that the seyyid Murtaḍà published it as his own composition. This grave accusation brought against the reputed author of the Táj el-'Aroos, unsupported by the knowledge of the name of the person whom he is thus asserted to have wronged, I did not find to be credited by any of the learned, nor do I myself believe it: but it imposed upon me the necessity of proving or disproving, not the *genuineness* of the book (a matter of no importance except as affecting the reputation of the seyyid Murtaḍà*), but, its *authenticity.* I was therefore obliged to make a most laborious collation of passages quoted in it with the same passages in the works quoted: and in every instance I found that they had been faithfully transcribed. Thus the authenticity of the Táj el-'Aroos was most satisfactorily established. But in comparing large portions of it with the corresponding portions of the Lisán el-'Arab, I made the unexpected discovery that, in most of the articles in the former, from three-fourths to about nine-tenths of the additions to the text of the Ḳámoos, and in many articles the whole of those additions, existed verbatim in the Lisán el-'Arab. I cannot, therefore, acquit the seyyid Murtaḍà of a want of candour, and of failing to render due honour to one of the most laborious of compilers, by not stating either that the Táj el-'Aroos was mainly derived in the first instance from the Lisán el-'Arab (which I believe to have been the case) or that the contents of the former are mainly found in the latter. This circumstance has induced me very often to compose articles of my lexicon principally from the Lisán el-'Arab in preference to the Táj el-'Aroos, comparing the contents afterwards with the latter; and when they agreed, giving the latter as my authority in most instances (though not always†) because I could only undertake to have the latter transcribed. The only copy of the Lisán el-'Arab known to me is that which I have already mentioned. It was lent to me, in successive portions, from the library of the collegiate mosque called "the Ashrafeeyeh," in Cairo. It is written in several different hands, nearly resembling one another, of a peculiar cursive kind, which none can correctly read without studying sufficiently to understand thoroughly; for which reason, if I had been able to obtain any copy made from it (for it bears statements of its having been several times partially or wholly transcribed some centuries ago) I could not have placed much reliance upon it. Since the time of the seyyid Murtaḍà, it has suffered much injury, chiefly from the rotting of the paper; in many places, the whole of the written portion of a page having fallen out, the margin only remaining.

Having fully satisfied myself of the authenticity of the Táj el-'Aroos, as well as of its intrinsic value, my next object was to cause a careful transcription of it to be commenced without delay, although, while I remained in Cairo, I made use of copies belonging to the libraries of mosques. The following are all the copies of that work, or of portions thereof, respecting which I have been able to procure any information.—1. The copy made use of by 'Áṣim Efendee in writing his Turkish Translation of the Ḳámoos. This belonged, according to his own statement, made to me, to Yaḥyà Efendee the Ḥakeem, who for many years composed the annual Egyptian Almanac published by order of the Government. He said that it was in the handwriting of the author, in two very large volumes; which, though hardly credible, is not absolutely impossible; for the handwriting of the seyyid Murtaḍà was small and compact: that the Grand Vezeer who was in Egypt during the contest between our own forces in that country and the French borrowed it of him, and sent it to Constantinople without his permission: and that he had caused many inquiries to be made for it there, but never learned any tidings of it.—2. A copy believed to have been in fourteen folio-volumes, in the handwriting of the author. Of this, the last volume and the last but two are in the library of the Riwáḳ of the Syrians in the great mosque El-Azhar. The rest of it seems to have been lost. It may be a portion of a copy which the author retained for himself. When he died, his family kept his death secret for two days; after which, the officers of the Government Treasury plundered his house of much property, among which, perhaps, was this copy; and if so, it may have fallen into different hands; one person taking a portion; and another person, another portion.—3. A copy sent by the author as a present to the King of Ṣan'à. So I was informed on the authority of a person living in Cairo, who asserted that he conveyed it for the author, and who must have attained to manhood some years before the author's death. He may perhaps be mistaken as to the work that he conveyed; but this is not probable.—4. The copy in the library of the mosque of Moḥammad Bey Abu-dh-Dhahab, before mentioned; said to be in eight thick, full-paged folio-volumes;‡ not in the author's handwriting,

* By various other works, he earned a high reputation for learning; and I believe that his ability to compose such a work as the Táj el-'Aroos was never called in question.

† In the articles of which the last radical letter is و, and in those of which the last is ى, I have generally deviated from my usual plan by indicating the authority of the Lisán el-'Arab rather than that of the Táj el-'Aroos in order to convey some notion of the value of the former work.

‡ I was informed that the number of its volumes is eight; but I was never allowed to see the whole copy, and, in the course of transcription, I neglected to note where each volume ended.

but transcribed under his superintendence, and in part, and perhaps entirely, revised by him. This copy wants a portion from the commencement of the first main division of the lexicon; i. e., of باب الهمزة: it also wants some other, smaller, portions. I shall have to say more respecting it in the next paragraph.—5. A portion in the handwriting of the author, in my possession; from the commencement of باب الهمزة to the words لغة فى رثى الميّت, in article رثأ: supplying more than the main portion that is wanting in the copy of Moḥammad Bey. It is of a small quarto-size, and ends in the middle of a page.—6. A copy in the library of the late Ibráheem Páshá, transcribed from that of Moḥammad Bey, and said to be incorrectly written.—7. A large folio-volume, in my possession, before mentioned, consisting of nearly the whole of the first tenth portion; evidently transcribed from the copy of Moḥammad Bey, for it wants what is deficient in باب الهمزة in the latter copy.

The copy transcribed for me, which is in twenty-four thick quarto-volumes, is partly from the portion, in the handwriting of the author, in the great mosque El-Azhar; but mainly from the copy of Moḥammad Bey; what is wanting in this last, in باب الهمزة, being copied from the MS. No. 5 in the foregoing list; and very nearly the whole of the other (smaller) portions that are wanting therein being supplied from the principal source, namely, the Lisán el-'Arab. It is therefore far superior to the other known copies, in respect of completeness, except the first and third of the copies mentioned in the next preceding paragraph if these exist and be still entire. But it will not always serve as a perfect test of the correctness of my own lexicon, although it has been carefully collated with its originals, as I made use of the copy of Moḥammad Bey as long as I remained in Egypt, and have used the Lisán el-'Arab and other lexicons for the supplying of syllabical signs &c. wanting in that copy and in my own. In my copy, diacritical points have often been omitted when not thought by the transcriber to be absolutely necessary; as is the case in almost all copies of lexicons: also syllabical signs that are in the originals are not unfrequently omitted: and my copy is more irregular than its originals in the manner of writing the letter hemzeh. The copy of Moḥammad Bey will probably, in a few years, be in many places illegible; for the ink with which it is written is of a corrosive nature, and has already, in those parts, eaten through the paper, though hitherto not to such an extent as to present any difficulty to the reader: or rather I should say that such was the case just before my own copy was made; for while I was translating from portions of it already transcribed for me, small pieces often dropped out from its leaves, in spite of my utmost care. I believe that if I had not undertaken the composition of the present work, the means of composing such a work would not much longer have existed. For not only was the sole copy of the Táj el-'Aroos that was nearly complete, and that was worthy of reliance, of those known to exist, rapidly decaying; but many of the most precious of the manuscripts from which it was compiled have been mutilated; many are scattered, no one knows whither; and several, of which no other copies are known to be in existence, and for which one would have to search from city to city, exploring the libraries of mosques, are said to have perished. The transcription of my own copy, and its collation, extended over a period of more than thirteen years. It might have been accomplished in much less time, had less care been bestowed upon it: but for several years I could find no competent and willing transcriber except the sheykh Ibráheem Ed-Dasooḳee, who was unable to devote the whole of his time to this object. Upon him the task of transcription mainly devolved; and the collation was performed wholly by him in conjunction with myself or with another sheykh.

As soon as a few pages of my copy of the Táj el-'Aroos had been transcribed, I commenced the work of translation and composition from its originals. I did not hesitate to write my lexicon in English rather than in Latin, because the latter language is not sufficiently perspicuous nor sufficiently copious. For several years I continued to collect all that I required for a lexicon as complete as it was possible for me to make it. But I then considered that about one third of what I had compiled consisted of the explanations of words rarely occurring; many of them, words that no one student was likely ever to meet with; and not a few, such as are termed آحاد or أفراد or مفاريد (before explained, in page xi. of this preface); these last being words known only as having been *spoken*, each by a single Arab, or as only once occurring in any *writing*. I considered also that the undertaking which I had thus long been prosecuting was one which would require many more years for its completion; and that it was incumbent on me to take into account the uncertain duration of my appointed term of life, and to occupy myself first with what was most important. I therefore finally determined to divide my lexicon into two Books: the first to contain all the classical words and significations commonly known to the learned among the Arabs: the other, those that are of rare occurrence and not commonly known. And I have made such subdivisions as will enable the purchaser of a copy to bind it in the manner that he may deem most convenient: in two volumes, or in four, or in eight; each to consist of a portion of Book I. with the corresponding portion of Book II.; or so that all the words in Book I. of which the roots commence with one letter may be immediately followed by the words in Book II. of which the roots commence with the same letter. The Second Book will be small in comparison with the First, of which the Part to be first published (ا to ث inclusive) will form about one eighth. In order that it may be possible to bind the whole work in two volumes, I have chosen for it a thin paper.

Nearly twenty years have now elapsed since I commenced this work. Had I foreseen that the whole labour of the composition must fall upon me or the project be abandoned, and had I also foreseen the length of time that it would require of me, unaided, I should certainly not have had the courage to undertake it. I had hoped that I should have at least one coadjutor: and I continued to hope for some years that such might be the case; but by no one have I been aided in the least degree, except, occasionally, in discussions of difficult points, by the sheykh Ibráheem Ed-Dasookee; who has written the results of some of these discussions on the margins of pages of my copy of the Táj el-'Aroos, generally in his own words, but often in words dictated by me. For seven years, in Cairo, I prosecuted my task on each of the work-days of the week, after an early breakfast, until within an hour of midnight, with few and short intervals of rest, (often with no interruption but that of a few minutes at a time for a meal, and half an hour for exercise,) except on rare occasions when I was stopped by illness, and once when I devoted three days to a last visit to the Pyramids: I seldom allowed myself to receive a visiter except on Friday, the Sabbath and leisure-day of the Muslims: and more than once I passed a quarter of a year without going out of my house. But I must not be supposed to claim much credit for the exercise of self-denial with respect to the pleasures of society; for during those seven years passed in Cairo, I had my wife and sister and the latter's two sons residing with me. Nor would I here make mention of the severe labour which this work has cost me but for the purpose of guarding against the imputation of my having been wanting in energy or industry. To convey a due idea of the difficulties of my task would be impossible. While mainly composing from the Táj el-'Aroos, I have often had before me, or by my side, eight or ten other lexicons, (presenting three different arrangements of the roots, and all of them differing in the order, or rather disorder, of the words explained,) requiring to be consulted at the same time. And frequently more than a day's study has been necessary to enable me thoroughly to understand a single passage: for the strict rules of Arabic lexicology demand that every explanation be given as nearly as possible in the words in which some person of authority has transmitted it; and many explanations perfectly intelligible when they were first given became less and less so in succeeding ages, and at length quite unintelligible to the most learned of living Arabs. Even Ibn-Seedeh often confesses, in the Moḥkam, his inability to understand an explanation or some other statement that he has transmitted. Many explanations, moreover, present instances of what is termed تَسَامُح; and instances of a worse kind of license, termed تَسَاهُل, are not of unfrequent occurrence: by the former term is meant a deficiency in what an author writes relying upon the understanding of the reader; and by the latter term, a deficiency in what he writes *without* relying upon the reader's knowledge. Often, two synonymous words are used to explain each other. Numerous cases of this kind occur in the Ḳámoos: such, for instance, are حُجَّةٌ and بُرْهَانٌ, سَاوَرَهُ and وَاثَبَهُ, اِعْتَقَدَ and اِعْتَقَدَ, and تَلَزَّجَ and تَلَجَّنَ: and in these cases I have not always found the information that I required by referring to other lexicons. More frequently, in lieu of an explanation, we find merely the word مَعْرُوفٌ, meaning "well known:" and in a very large proportion of such cases, what was once "well known" has long ceased to be so. Still more frequently, significations are only indicated by the context: in many instances, as clearly as they could be expressed by any words of explanation: but in many other instances, very obscurely. Many words are rendered by others which are not elsewhere explained in the same lexicon; many, by words meant to be understood in senses not elsewhere explained in that lexicon; many, by words meant to be understood in tropical senses; and many, by words meant to be understood in post-classical senses. In these last cases, I have often found in my knowledge of modern Arabic a solution of a difficulty: but without great caution, such knowledge would frequently have misled me, in consequence of the changes which have taken place in the applications of many words since the classical age. Great caution is likewise requisite in the attempt to elicit the significations of words by means of analogy; as I could easily show by giving all the principal words of one article with their significations, and then requiring any student to divine the significations of the other words of the same article by such means, and comparing his explanations with those that have been authoritatively transmitted. Perfect reliance is not to be placed upon vowel-signs and the like when they are merely written, without their being either described in words or shown by the statement that the word of which the pronunciation is to be fixed is similar to some other word well known. Even when they are described, one has to consider what rule the author follows; and in some lexicons the rules followed by the authors are not explained. For instance, when a noun of three letters is said to be with fet-ḥ, if in the Ḳámoos, tne meaning is that it is of the measure فَعْل: but in some other lexicons it means that it is of the measure فَعَل. If we find such a noun in the Ḳámoos written as of the measure فَعَل and said to be with fet-ḥ, we must infer that فَعْل (not فَعَل) is the correct measure: and if in the same lexicon we find such a noun that is to be explained written otherwise than as of the measure فَعْل, without its being followed by any indication of its measure, we must infer that فَعْل is probably its true measure, unless it be a word commonly known. But these and other technical difficulties are comparatively small, or become so after a little time spent in the study of different lexicons with a previous knowledge of the principles of Arabic lexicology and lexicography. Among the graver difficulties are those which are often presented by verses cited as confirmatory examples, or as illustrations, without either context or explanation; many of which I have inserted in my lexicon as being either absolutely necessary or such as I could not omit with entire satisfaction. Various other obstacles that I have had to encounter I refrain from mentioning, hoping that I shall be deemed to have said enough to excuse myself for the length of time that has elapsed since the commencement of my work. I have, however, been unusually favoured by circumstances; and especially by my having acquired, in familiar intercourse with Arabs, an acquaintance with their manners and customs, and their mental idiosyncrasies, indispensably requisite to success in my undertaking. Encouraged by these circumstances, I applied myself to the working of the rich mine that I had discovered, with the resolution expressed in the saying of a poet,*

• لَأَسْتَسْهِلَنَّ الصَّعْبَ أَوْ أُدْرِكَ المُنَى • فَمَا انْقَادَتِ الآمَالُ إِلَّا لِصَابِرِ •

When I had prosecuted my task in Cairo during a period of nearly six years, I understood it to be the desire of my Patron that the British Government might be induced to recognise the importance of my work by contributing to the expense of its composition. I therefore submitted to the Head of Her Majesty's Government a request that my undertaking might be thus honoured and promoted: and I did so in a time peculiarly auspicious; the Premier being Lord John Russell, now Earl Russell. His Lordship graciously and promptly replied to my appeal by granting me an annual allowance from the Fund for Special Service; and through his recommendation, this was continued to me by one of his successors in office, another Nobleman who added eminence in letters to elevation of birth and station, the late Earl of Aberdeen. And here I must especially and gratefully acknowledge my obligations to the learned Canon Cureton, for his friendly offices on these and other occasions. I must also add that Professor Lepsius and Dr. Abeken, and the late Baron Bunsen, kindly exerted themselves to obtain permission for my lexicon to be printed at Berlin, at the joint expense of the Prussian Government and the Academy of Sciences; and several of the learned Orientalists of Germany seconded their endeavours; but conditions were proposed to me to which I could not willingly accede.

After a stay of somewhat more than seven years in Cairo, a considerable portion of which period was spent by me in collecting and collating the principal materials from which my lexicon is composed, I returned to England; leaving to the sheykh Ibráheem Ed-Dasooḳee the task of completing the transcription of those materials, a task for which he had become fully qualified.

---

* Cited in page 123 of this work.

I must now add some explanations necessary to facilitate the use of my lexicon.

The arrangement that I have adopted is, in its main features, the same as that of Golius: the words being placed according to their radical letters; and the roots being arranged according to the order of their letters (commencing with the first of those letters) in the usual alphabet.

Words of three different classes, in which the radical letters are the same, but different in number, I place in the same article. The first of these classes consists of words of two radical letters; as بَلْ: the second class, of reduplicative triliteral-radical words, in which the first and second radical letters are the same as those of the first class, and the third the same as the second of that class; as بَلَّ and بُلَّ and بَلَل &c.: and the third class, of reduplicative quadriliteral-radical words, in which the first and third radical letters are the same as the first of the first class, and the second and fourth the same as the second of that class; as بَلْبَلَ and بَلْبَلَة and بِلْبَال &c. These three classes are included in the same article in all the best Arabic lexicons; and two reasons may be given for my following the same plan. One reason is similarity of signification. Words of the first and second corresponding classes very seldom exhibit an alliance in signification; but instances of such alliance in words of the first and third classes are less rare; and instances of alliance in signification in words of the second and third classes are very numerous. The other reason is, that such words are generally held to be derived from the same root. Some of the Arabian lexicologists hold that a word of the class of بَلَّ is a biliteral-radical word; so that the letters of its root are represented by فع: but most of them regard it as, absolutely, a triliteral-radical word; so that the letters of its root are represented by فعل. With respect to a word such as بَلْبَلَ, the opinion held by El-Farrà and others, and ascribed to El-Khaleel, is, that it is to be represented by فَعْفَع; so that the letters of its root are represented by فع: another opinion, ascribed to El-Khaleel and his followers among the Basrees and Koofees, is, that it is to be represented by فَعْفَل; so that the letters of its root are represented by فعل: another, ascribed to Seebaweyh and his companions, is, that it is originally a word to be represented by فَعَّل, and that the third radical letter is changed, and made the same as the first; so that the letters of its root are represented by the same letters as if the word itself were to be represented by فَعْفَل: the opinion commonly obtaining among the Basrees is, that it is to be represented by فَعْلَل; so that the letters of its root are represented, in this case also, by فعل; and as the last of these modes of representing the word is the one most usual, I generally adopt this mode in my lexicon, except in quoting from an author who uses another mode. The triliteral root, in both of these classes of words, is that which is preferred in the Muzhir, where, in the 40th Section, not far from the commencement, these different opinions are stated.

Agreeably with the same principle, quasi-quadriliteral-radical words (the conjugations and varieties of which will be found in a table inserted in this preface) I class with the triliteral-radical words from which they are derived by the Arabian lexicologists and grammarians.

What is commonly called "the Verb of Wonder" I mention among the verbs. The Koofees say that it is a noun, meaning an epithet. (See مَا أُمَيْلِحَ زَيْدًا, in article ملح.)

Dialectic variants, synonyms, and words nearly synonymous, from the same root, are mentioned and explained in one paragraph: but every word thus explained in a paragraph headed by another word is also mentioned by itself, or accompanied by a word or words nearly resembling it in form, with a reference to that paragraph. (In order to facilitate the reference, an arrow-head (▼) is inserted to render conspicuous a word explained in a paragraph headed by another word.) Several obvious advantages result from this arrangement; not the least of which is a considerable saving of room. In these cases, when I have found it possible to do so, I have placed the most common word first, or otherwise distinguished it from the rest: sometimes I have shown which words are more or less common by the authorities that I have indicated for them.

When a noun is not found at the head of a paragraph, or by itself, or with another nearly resembling it in form, it is to be looked for among the infinitive nouns, which are mentioned with their respective verbs. And plurals are to be found under their singulars.

Words that are regularly formed, *ad libitum*, (such as active and passive participial nouns, and nouns denoting the comparative and superlative degrees, &c.,) are not mentioned, unless for special reasons.

In respect of the places which I have assigned to arabicized words, I have generally followed the usual practice of the Arabian lexicographers; that is, I have generally placed them as though they were derived from Arabic roots; because most students look for them under the headings beneath which I have mentioned them, and because many of them have derivatives formed from them in the regular Arabic manner. But, properly speaking, every letter in an arabicized word is regarded by most of the Arabian lexicologists as radical.

When several significations are assigned to one word &c., connected by "or," it is often the case that one is right in one instance, and another in another; and not unfrequently, that all are correct in different instances.

Whenever I have found it possible to do so, I have distinguished (by the mark ‡) what is affirmed to be tropical from what is proper; generally on the authority of the Asás. I have also generally distinguished (by the mark †) what I regard as evidently, or probably, tropical, when I have found no express authority for asserting such to be the case. Thus I have often been enabled to draw clearly what may be termed the "genealogies" of significations. Always, in the arrangement of significations, I have, to the utmost of my ability, paid attention to their relations, one to another. The mark — is used to denote a break in the relations of significations &c.; and ═ denotes an extraordinary, or a complete, dissociation.

Numerous words in the Ṣiḥáḥ and Ḳámoos and most other Arabic lexicons are merely said to be the names of certain plants or animals. Of these I have generally found and given explanations which have either enabled me to determine the particular species to which they apply or may enable others to do so, and which will show that the applications of many of these words have been changed in post-classical times. For the names and descriptions of plants, my chief authority is Aboo-Ḥaneefeh Ed-Deenawaree, who is generally held to have adhered to the original nomenclature more accurately than any other writer on the Arabian flora, enabled to do so in many cases by his own careful investigations, and by consulting Arabs of the desert, at a sufficiently early period, in the third century of the Flight. I have been induced to mention the properties commonly attributed by the Arabs to plants and drugs &c., though they are generally fanciful, because they sometimes help to point out what is meant by an explanation otherwise vague, and sometimes elucidate far-fetched comparisons or allusions.

The explanations of the particles are extremely defective in almost all the Arabic lexicons; but of this very important class of words, generally more difficult to explain than any other class, I have found, in the Mughnee, illustrations even more ample than I required. Though I have generally omitted the statement of opinions evidently erroneous, and refuted in the Mughnee, I have in some degree imitated the author of that work by endeavouring to treat such words rather too largely than too scantily.

Of the learning of Golius, and the industry of Freytag, I wish to speak with sincere respect, and with gratitude for much benefit derived by me from their works before circumstances gave me advantages which they did not enjoy. But lest I should be charged with omitting important matters in some of the originals from which my work is composed, it is necessary for me to state that, in countless instances, both of those lexicographers have given explanations, more or less full, as from the Ṣiḥáḥ or Ḳámoos or both, when not one word thereof, nor even an indication, is found in either of those originals:* and that much of what Freytag has given as from the Ḳámoos is from the Turkish Translation of that lexicon, of which I have before spoken, a work of considerable learning, but of no authority when no voucher is mentioned in it.† I have myself occasionally cited the Turkish Translation of the Ḳámoos, but only when I have not found what I wanted in any other work, and, in a case of this kind, only when I have felt confidence in its correctness, or when I have desired a confirmation of my own opinion. In very few instances have I adopted its explanations; having often found them to be glaringly incorrect; in some cases, from its author's having partially misunderstood what he had to translate; but in more cases, from his having altogether failed to understand, and therefore having given literal renderings which are far from conveying the meanings intended.

Proper names of persons and of places, and post-classical words and significations, I have, with very few exceptions, excluded from my lexicon. A dictionary of words of the former class, such as would satisfy the wants of students, would of itself alone form a large volume; for the sources from which it might be drawn are abundant, and not difficult of access. A dictionary of post-classical Arabic, worthy of being so called, could not be composed otherwise than by a considerable number of students in different cities of Europe where good libraries of Arabic manuscripts are found, and by as many students in different countries of Asia and Africa; partly from books, and partly from information to be acquired only by intercourse with Arabs; and several of those who should contribute to its composition would require to be well versed in the sciences of the Muslims. In excluding almost all post-classical words and significations, I have followed the example of every one of the most esteemed Arabian lexicographers; and the limits that I have assigned to my labours have certainly been rather too wide than too narrow, as will be sufficiently shown by the fact that the quantity of the matter comprised in the first eighth part of my First Book (ا to ث inclusive) is treble the quantity of the corresponding portion of Freytag's Lexicon, although I leave rare words &c. for my Second Book.

I have inserted nothing in my lexicon without indicating at least one authority for it, except interwoven additions of my own which I have invariably distinguished by enclosing them between square brackets. Throughout Part I of the First Book, I have generally made the indications of the authorities as numerous as I conveniently could; but I have not thought it desirable to do so throughout, as these indications occupy much space, and what is most important is to note the oldest authority mentioned in any of my originals, with one or more of good repute to confirm it. A table of the authorities inserted in this preface will show which of them I have cited through the medium of the Táj el-'Aroos or the Lisán el-'Arab. Such authorities I have often indicated without any addition.‡ When two or more indications of authorities are given, it is to be understood that they agree essentially, or mainly; but not always that they agree in words. When any authority is, in an important degree, less full, or less clear, than another or others by which it is accompanied, I distinguish it by an asterisk placed after the initial

* By this remark, I may perhaps provoke the retort that, in composing an Arabic-English lexicon wholly from Arabic sources, I am myself doing what may be resolved into something like reasoning in a circle. But such is not the case; for the words employed in explanations in the Arabic lexicons are generally still used in the senses in which they are there employed; and the intended meanings of words that are not still used in such senses are, with few exceptions, easily determined by examples in which they occur, or by the general consent of the learned among the Arabs in the present day. Of the exceptional difficulties of interpretation, I have already said enough; and for my own sake, as well as for the sake of truth, I by no means wish to underrate them.

† In Freytag's first volume, the authorities are seldom indicated.—Sometimes explanations given by Golius as from the Ṣiḥáḥ or Ḳámoos or both, and not found in either of those works, are copied by Freytag without his stating such to be the case, and without his indicating the authorities or authority assigned by Golius: for example, three such instances occur in the short article دبح.

‡ In a few instances, in the Táj el-'Aroos, where its author has drawn from the Tahdheeb or the Moḥkam through the medium of the Lisán el-'Arab, I have found the Tahdheeb erroneously named as his authority instead of the Moḥkam, or the Moḥkam instead of the Tahdheeb.—Sometimes an authority is mentioned by a surname borne by two or more, so that the person meant is doubtful.

or initials &c. by which it is indicated. Frequently it happens that an explanation is essentially the same in the Lisán el-'Arab and the Táj el-'Aroos, but more full, or more clear, in the former: in cases of this kind I have generally indicated only the latter as my authority.

Sometimes I have been obliged to employ English terms which have not, to my knowledge, been used by any other writer; but I have been careful to invent only such as will, I believe, be easily understood. For example, I have applied the epithet "auroral" to certain risings and settings of stars or asterisms, to denote the restriction of those risings and settings to the whole period of the morning-twilight: the epithet "heliacal," applied to such risings, would restrict them overmuch. Lexicological and grammatical terms employed in my lexicon will be found in one of the tables inserted in this preface.

I have supposed the student who will make use of this work to be acquainted with the *general* rules of grammar. These he must bear in mind when he meets with *particular* rules mentioned by me. For instance, from his finding it stated, in page 77 of this lexicon, that, when إِلَّا is used in the sense of غَيْرُ, the noun which follows it is put in the same case as that which precedes it, he must not imagine that exceptions to this rule are presented by such phrases as لَا إِلٰهَ إِلَّا ٱللّٰهُ (*There is no deity other than,* i. e. *but, God*) and مَا هٰذَا شَيْئًا إِلَّا كِتَابٌ (*This is not anything but a writing*) and مَا جَآءَ مِنْ أَحَدٍ إِلَّا زَيْدٌ (*No one came but Zeyd*) and لَيْسَ هٰذَا بِشَىْءٍ إِلَّا كِتَابًا (which means the same as the second of these phrases): for in each of these examples the noun preceding إِلَّا is regarded as being virtually in the same case as the noun following it. (See a note in De Sacy's Arabic Grammar, 2nd ed., vol. ii. p. 404.)

Considering the size of this work, the quantity of Arabic type that it comprises, the minuteness of many of the characters employed in it, and the excessive care required in the placing of those small characters, no student can reasonably hope to find it entirely free from typographical faults, whether they be such as have originated from the compositors and have escaped the scrutiny of the author, or such as are almost inevitable in the process of printing. I shall use my utmost endeavours to detect such faults, and to note them for correction.

The following tables will, I believe, supply all further explanations that will be needed.

I.—*Table of the Conjugations of Arabic Verbs.*

1. (1st variety) فَعَلَ, يَفْعُلُ : (2nd) فَعَلَ, يَفْعِلُ : (3rd) فَعَلَ, يَفْعَلُ : (4th) فَعِلَ, يَفْعَلُ : (5th) فَعُلَ, يَفْعُلُ : (6th) فَعِلَ, يَفْعِلُ.

2. فَعَّلَ : variations قَصَّى (for قَصَّصَ) and the like.

3. فَاعَلَ.

4. أَفْعَلَ.

5. تَفَعَّلَ : variations اِفَّعَّلَ, in the cases of verbs of which the ف is ت, ث, ج, د, ذ, ز, س, ش, ص, ض, ط, or ظ : also تَظَنَّى (for تَظَنَّنَ) and the like : تَفَعَّلُ &c. (for تَتَفَعَّلُ &c.)

6. تَفَاعَلَ : variations اِفَّاعَلَ, in cases like those in which تَفَعَّلَ sometimes becomes اِفَّعَّلَ : also تَفَاعَلُ &c. (for تَتَفَاعَلُ &c.)

7. اِنْفَعَلَ : variations اِنَّصَرَ (for اِنْنَصَرَ) and the like; and اِمَّلَسَ (for اِنْمَلَسَ) and the like.

8. اِفْتَعَلَ : variations فَعَّلَ, فِعَّلَ, فِتَعَّلَ, or فَعَّلَ, in the cases of verbs of which the ع is ت, ث, ج, د, ذ, ز, س, ش, ص, ض, ط, or ظ : also such as اِتَّبَعَ (for اِتْتَبَعَ), اِتَّغَرَ and اِثَّغَرَ and اِدَّغَرَ (for اِثْتَغَرَ), اِجْدَمَعَ (for اِجْتَمَعَ), اِدَّرَكَ (for اِدْتَرَكَ), اِدَّكَرَ and اِذَّكَرَ and اِذْدَكَرَ (for اِذْتَكَرَ), اِزْدَادَ (for اِزْتَادَ), اِصْطَبَرَ and اِصَّبَرَ (for اِصْتَبَرَ), اِضْطَرَبَ and اِضَّرَبَ (for اِضْتَرَبَ), اِضْطَرَدَ (for اِطْتَرَدَ), اِطَّبَعَ (for اِطْتَبَعَ), اِطَّلَمَ and اِظْطَلَمَ and اِظَّلَمَ (for اِظْتَلَمَ), اِتَّقَى (for اِوْتَقَى), اِتَّسَرَ (for اِيْتَسَرَ) : اِعَّذَرَ and اِعِذَّرَ (for اِعْتَذَرَ).

9. اِفْعَلَّ : variations اِفْعَلَلَ, in the case of a verb of which the ل is unsound; as اِرْعَوَى : and اِفْعَأَلَّ; as اِبْيَضَّ.

10. اِسْتَفْعَلَ : variations اِسْطَاعَ and اِسْتَاعَ (for اِسْتَطَاعَ).

11. اِفْعَالَّ : variation اِفْعَالَلَ, in the case of a verb of which the ل is unsound; as اِحْوَاوَى.

12. اِفْعَوْعَلَ.

13. اِفْعَوَّلَ.

Q. 1. فَعْلَلَ. Q. 2. تَفَعْلَلَ. Q. 3. اِفْعَنْلَلَ. Q. 4. اِفْعَلَلَّ.

R. Q. 1. Verbs of the classes of بَلْبَلَ (in which the first and third radical letters are the same, and the second and fourth,) and جَلْبَبَ (in which the third and fourth radical letters are the same).

R. Q. 2. Verbs of the classes of تَبَلْبَلَ and تَجَلْبَبَ.

R. Q. 3. Verbs of the class of اِقْعَنْسَسَ.

R. Q. 4. Verbs of the class of اِبْيَضَضَّ, mentioned above, (see 9,) as variations of اِفْعَلَّ, may be classed under this head.

Q. Q. 1. فَعْلَسَ; فَعْلَمَ; فَعْلَنَ (as عَلْوَنَ according to some, and عَشْرَنَ); فَعْلَى : فَعَّالَ; فَعْمَلَ; فَعْنَلَ; فَعْهَلَ; فَعْوَلَ; فَعْيَلَ : فَأْعَلَ; فَتْعَلَ; فَنْعَلَ; فَهْعَلَ; فَوْعَلَ; فَيْعَلَ : تَفْعَلَ; سَفْعَلَ; مَفْعَلَ; نَفْعَلَ; هَفْعَلَ; يَفْعَلَ.

Q. Q. 2. تَفَعْلَتَ; تَفَعْلَى : تَفَعْنَلَ; تَفَعْوَلَ; تَفَعْيَلَ : تَفَوْعَلَ; تَفَيْعَلَ : تَمَفْعَلَ.

Q. Q. 3. اِفْعَنْلَأَ; اِفْعَنْلَى; اِفْعَأْلَلَ; اِفْعَلَّلَ; اِفْعَوْلَلَ; اِفْعَيَّلَ : اِفْتَعْأَلَ : اِفْوَنْعَلَ.

Q. Q. 4. اِفْعَالَّ; اِفْعَهَلَّ : اِفْلَعَلَّ; اِفْمَعَلَّ; اِفْوَعَلَّ : اِنْفَعَلَّ.

Beside these, there are some other forms of Q. Q. verbs, not to be classed with any of the foregoing. And probably there are some other varieties of Q. Q. 2; each quasi-passive of Q. Q. 1.

II.—*Table of Lexicological and Grammatical Terms &c. used in the following work.*

Accord., *for* according.

Accus. case, *for* accusative case, نَصْبٌ.

Act., *for* active, مَبْنِيٌّ لِلْفَاعِلِ or لِلْمَعْلُومِ.

Act. part. n., *for* active participial noun, اِسْمُ فَاعِلٍ.

Adv. n., *for* adverbial noun, ظَرْفٌ, and sometimes صِفَةٌ; of place, ظَرْفُ مَكَانٍ; and of time, ظَرْفُ زَمَانٍ.

Agent, فَاعِلٌ.

Analogous, or regular, قِيَاسِيٌّ and مَقِيسٌ.

Analogy, قِيَاسٌ.

Anomalous, or irregular, غَيْرُ قِيَاسِيٍّ and غَيْرُ مَقِيسٍ or شَاذٌّ (see "Dev.") or نَادِرٌ (see "Extr.").

Aor., *for* aorist, مُضَارِعٌ.

Aplastic, applied to a noun and to a verb, جَامِدٌ.

App., *for* apparently.

Appositive, تَابِعٌ.

Attribute, or predicate, مُسْنَدٌ and خَبَرٌ.

Broken pl., *for* broken plural, جَمْعٌ مُكَسَّرٌ.

Coll. gen. n., *for* collective generic noun, اِسْمُ جِنْسٍ جَمْعِيٌّ; also called a lexicological plural, جَمْعٌ لُغَوِيٌّ.

Complement of a prefixed noun, مُضَافٌ إِلَيْهِ.

Complete, *i. e.* attributive, verb, فِعْلٌ تَامٌّ.

Conj., *for* conjugation, بَابٌ.

Conjunct, مَوْصُولٌ: conjunct noun, مَوْصُولٌ اِسْمِيٌّ: conjunct particle, مَوْصُولٌ حَرْفِيٌّ.

Conjunction, حَرْفُ عَطْفٍ and حَرْفٌ عَاطِفٌ.

Contr., *for* contrary.

Conventional term, اِصْطِلَاحٌ. — Conventional language, عُرْفٌ.

Corroborative, تَأْكِيدٌ and تَوْكِيدٌ.

Decl., *for* declinable, مُعْرَبٌ: perfectly decl., مُنْصَرِفٌ and مَصْرُوفٌ: imperfectly decl., غَيْرُ مُنْصَرِفٍ and غَيْرُ مَصْرُوفٍ.

Defective verb, *i. e.* having و or ى for the last radical letter, فِعْلٌ نَاقِصٌ.

Dev., *for* deviating; as in the phrase, Deviating from the constant course of speech (with respect to analogy, or rule, or with respect to usage); شَاذٌّ. This term and نَادِرٌ (see "Extr.") are often used in the lexicons indiscriminately.

Dial., *for* dialect, لُغَةٌ.

Dial. var. of, *for* dialectic variant of, لُغَةٌ فِى.

Dim., *for* diminutive, مُصَغَّرٌ.

Enunciative, خَبَرٌ.

Epithet, and epithetic phrase, نَعْتٌ and وَصْفٌ and صِفَةٌ.

Ex., *for* example.

Expl., *for* explained.

Expos., *for* exposition, شَرْحٌ and تَفْسِيرٌ: the latter particularly applied to an exposition of the Ḳur-án.

Extr., *for* extraordinary (with respect to analogy, or rule, or with respect to usage), نَادِرٌ. (See "Dev.")

Fem., *for* feminine, مُؤَنَّثٌ.

Fut., *for* future, مُسْتَقْبَلٌ.

Gen. case, *for* genitive case, خَفْضٌ and جَرٌّ.

Gen. n., *for* generic noun, اِسْمُ جِنْسٍ.

Hollow verb, فِعْلٌ أَجْوَفُ.

Homonym, مُشْتَرَكٌ, for مُشْتَرَكٌ فِيهِ.

I. q., *for* idem quod.

Ideal (as opposed to real) subst., اِسْمُ مَعْنًى, or simply مَعْنًى.

Imitative sequent, إِتْبَاعٌ.

Imperative, أَمْرٌ.

Inchoative, مُبْتَدَأٌ.

Incomplete, *i. e.* non-attributive, verb, فِعْلٌ نَاقِصٌ, or فِعْلٌ غَيْرُ تَامٍّ.

Indecl., *for* indeclinable, مَبْنِيٌّ.

Inf. n., *for* infinitive noun, مَصْدَرٌ. Inf. n. of unity, مَصْدَرٌ لِلْمَرَّةِ. Inf. n. of modality, مَصْدَرٌ لِلنَّوْعِ.

Instrumental noun, اِسْمُ آلَةٍ.

Intrans., *for* intransitive, غَيْرُ مُتَعَدٍّ and لَازِمٌ.

Irreg., *for* irregular: see "Anomalous."

Lit., *for* literally.

Mahmooz verb, فِعْلٌ مَهْمُوزٌ.

Manṣoob aor., *for* manṣoob aorist, مُضَارِعٌ مَنْصُوبٌ.

Masc., *for* masculine, مُذَكَّرٌ.

Measure, وَزْنٌ.

Mejzoom aor., *for* mejzoom aorist, مُضَارِعٌ مَجْزُومٌ.

Metaphor, اِسْتِعَارَةٌ.

Metaphorical, اِسْتِعَارِيٌّ.

Metonymy, كِنَايَةٌ.

N., *for* noun, اِسْمٌ.

N. un., *for* noun of unity, وَاحِدَةٌ and وَاحِدٌ.

Nom. case, *for* nominative case, رَفْعٌ.

Objective complement of a verb, مَفْعُولٌ or مَفْعُولٌ بِهِ.

Part. n.: see "act. part. n." and "pass. part. n."

Particle, حَرْفٌ.

Pass., *for* passive, مَبْنِيٌّ لِلْمَفْعُولِ or لِلْمَجْهُولِ.

Pass. part. n., *for* passive participial noun, اِسْمُ مَفْعُولٍ.

Perfect pl., *for* perfect plural, جَمْعٌ سَالِمٌ; also called a sound pl., جَمْعٌ صَحِيحٌ.

Perfect verb, *i. e.* one which has not two radical letters alike, nor has ء nor و nor ى for one of its radical letters, فِعْلٌ سَالِمٌ. (See also "Sound verb.")

Pers., *for* person (of a verb).

Pl., *for* plural, جَمْعٌ. Pl. of pauc., *for* plural of paucity, جَمْعُ قِلَّةٍ. Pl. of mult., *for* plural of multitude, جَمْعُ كَثْرَةٍ. Pl. pl., *for* plural of a plural, جَمْعُ جَمْعٍ.

Possessive noun or epithet (such as تَامِرٌ and لَابِنٌ &c.), اِسْمٌ عَلَى النَّسَبِ (a kind of relative noun).

Post-classical, مُوَلَّدٌ and مُحْدَثٌ.

Predicate: see "Attribute."

Prefixed noun, مُضَافٌ.

Prep., *for* preposition, حَرْفُ جَرٍّ, and sometimes صِفَةٌ.

Pret., *for* preterite, مَاضٍ.

Prov., *for* proverb, مَثَلٌ.

Q., *for* quadriliteral-radical verb, فِعْلٌ رُبَاعِيٌّ.

Q. Q., *for* quasi-quadriliteral-radical verb, فِعْلٌ مُلْحَقٌ بِالرُّبَاعِيِّ.

Q. v., *for* quod vide.

Quasi-coordinate, مُلْحَقٌ: see art. لحق.

Quasi-inf. n., *for* quasi-infinitive noun, اِسْمُ مَصْدَرٍ and اِسْمٌ لِلْمَصْدَرِ.

Quasi-pass., *for* quasi-passive, مُطَاوِعٌ.

Quasi-pl. n., *for* quasi-plural noun, اِسْمُ جَمْعٍ.

Quasi-sound verb, i. e. one having و or ى for its first radical letter, فِعْلٌ مِثَالٌ.

R. Q., *for* reduplicative quadriliteral-radical verb, فِعْلٌ رُبَاعِيٌّ مُضَاعَفٌ.

Real (as opposed to ideal) subst., اِسْمُ عَيْنٍ, or simply عَيْنٌ, and اِسْمُ ذَاتٍ or simply ذَاتٌ.

Receptacular noun, اِسْمُ وِعَاءٍ.

Reg., *for* regular: see "Analogous."

Rel. n., *for* relative noun, اِسْمٌ مَنْسُوبٌ, or نِسْبَةٌ.

Simple subst. (as opposed to inf. n.), اِسْمٌ.

Sing., *for* singular, مُفْرَدٌ and وَاحِدٌ.

Sound pl., *for* sound plural: see "Perfect pl."

Sound verb, *i. e.* one which is not of the class termed "perfect," but which has not و nor ى for one of its radical letters: or, as used in the 'Eyn and several other lexicons, one that has not و nor ى nor ء for one of its radical letters: فِعْلٌ صَحِيحٌ. (See "Perfect verb.")

Specificative, or discriminative, تَمْيِيزٌ.

State, denotative of, حَالٌ.

Subject (as correlative of attribute or predicate), مُسْنَدٌ إِلَيْهِ.

Subst., *for* substantive, اِسْمٌ.

Substitute, بَدَلٌ.

Syll. signs, *for* syllabical signs, شَكْلٌ.

Syn., *for* synonym and synonymous, مُرَادِفٌ and مُتَرَادِفٌ. Syn. with, *for* synonymous with, لُغَةٌ فِى.

Trad., *for* tradition, حَدِيثٌ.

Trans., *for* transitive, مُتَعَدٍّ and وَاقِعٌ.

Transposition, قَلْبٌ. Formed by transposition, مَقْلُوبٌ.

Tropical, مَجَازٌ and مَجَازِيٌّ.

Unsound verb, *i. e.* one having و or ى for one of its radical letters: or, as used in the 'Eyn and several other lexicons, one having و or ى or ء for one of its radical letters: فِعْلٌ مُعْتَلٌّ.

V., *for* verb, فِعْلٌ.

Verbal noun, اِسْمُ فِعْلٍ.

---

‡ means asserted to be tropical.
‡‡ „ asserted to be doubly tropical.
† „ supposed by me to be tropical.

III.—*Chronological list of the more celebrated of the Lexicologists and Grammarians cited in the following work, extracted from the 48th Section of the Muzhir: with some additions, which are marked with an asterisk.*

*Ibn-'Abbás: died in the year of the Flight	68
*Mujáhid: said to have lived 83 years; and to have died in	100 or 101 or 102 or 103
*Ḳatádeh: born in 60: died in	117 or 118
Aboo-'Amr Ibn-El-'Alà: (*born at Mekkeh, in the year of the Flight 70 or 68 or 65:) died in	151 (*or 154) or 159
El-Khaleel: lived to the age of 74	160 or 170 or 175
*El-Leyth Ibn-Naṣr Ibn-Seiyár El-Khurásánee: contemporary with, and companion of, El-Khaleel.	
Yoonus: born in the year 90	182 *or 183
*Abu-d-Duḳeysh: contemporary with Yoonus.	
El-Kisá-ee	182 or 183 or 189 or 192
Seebaweyh: lived 32 years, or 40 and odd years: died in	161 (*or 177) or 180 or 188 or 194
Aboo-Moḥammad El-Yezeedee: lived 74 years: died in	202
En-Naḍr Ibn-Shumeyl: died in	203 or 204
Ḳuṭrub	206
El-Farrà: lived 67 years	207
Aboo-'Obeydeh (*Maạmar Ibn-El-Muthennà Et-Teymee): born in 112: died in	208 or 209 or 210 or 211
Aboo-'Amr Esh-Sheybánee: lived 110 (*or 111) or 118 years: died in	205 or 206 or 213
Aboo-Zeyd (*El-Anṣáree:) lived 93 years: died in	214 or 215 or 216
El-Aṣma'ee: born in 123 (*or 122): died in	(*214 or) 215 or 216 *or 217
*El-Liḥyánee: contemporary with El-Kisá-ee and Aboo-'Obeydeh and Aboo-Zeyd and El-Aṣma'ee.	
Abu-l-Ḥasan El-Akhfash	210 or 215 or 221
*Abu-l-Heythem: a preceptor of Aboo-'Obeyd.	
*Ibn-Buzurj: contemporary with Abu-l-Heythem.	
Aboo-'Obeyd: lived 67 years: died in	223 or 224 or 230
Ibn-El-Aạrábee: born in 150: died in	231 or 233
*Shemir: contemporary with Ibn-El-Aạrábee.	
Ibn-Es-Sikkeet (*Yaạḳoob)	244
Aboo-Ḥátim Es-Sijistánee: lived nearly 90 years: died in	248 or 250 or 254 or 255
*Es-Sukkaree (author of an "Exposition of the Deewán El-Hudhaleeyeen"): born in 212: died in	270 or 275
Ibn-Ḳuteybeh: [also called El-Ḳutabee, and by some, (among whom is the author of the Táj-el-'Aroos,) less properly, El-Ḳuteybee: (see the Biogr. Dictionary of En-Nawawee, p. 771:)] born in 213: died in	267 *or 270 or 271 or 276
*Aboo-Ḥaneefeh Ed-Deenawaree (author of the "Book of Plants")	282
El-Mubarrad: born in 210: died in	282 or 285 *or 286
Thaạlab (*Abu-l-'Abbás Aḥmad Ibn-Yaḥyà, author of the "Faṣeeḥ"): born in 200: died in	291
Kuráạ	cir. 310
Ez-Zejjáj (*Aboo-Is-ḥáḳ)	311
*Ibn-Dureyd (author of the "Jemharah"): born in 223, or [about five years later, for] it is said that he lived 93 years, not more, and died in	321
*Ibraheem Ibn-Moḥammad Ibn-'Arafeh (Nifṭaweyh): born in 244 or 250: died in	323
Aboo-Bekr Ibn-El-Ambáree: born in 271: died in	(*327 or) 328
Ez-Zejjájee	(*337 or) 339 or 340
*El-Fárábee	343
Ibn-Durustaweyh: born in 258: died in	347
Ibn-El-Ḳooṭeeyeh	367
Es-Seeráfee: born before the year 270: died in	368
Ibn-Khálaweyh	370
El-Azheree (author of the "Tahdheeb"): *born in 282: died in	*370 or 371
Aboo-'Alee El-Fárisee: (*lived more than 90 years:) died in	(*376 or) 377
Aboo-Bekr Ez-Zubeydee (author of an abridgment of the "'Eyn"	379
*Ibn-'Abbád (the Ṣáḥib, author of the "Moḥeeṭ"): born in 326: died in	385
*El-Khaṭṭábee	388
Ibn-Jinnee (*Abu-l-Fet-ḥ 'Othmán): born before the year 330: died in	392
Ibn-Fáris	(*390 or) 395
El-Jowharee (author of the "Ṣiḥáḥ")	*393 or 397 or 398
El-Harawee (author of the "Ghareebeyn")	401
*Moḥammad Ibn-Jaạfar El-Ḳazzáz	412
El-Jawáleeḳee	425
*Ibn-Et-Teiyánee (author of the "Moo'ab")	436
Ibn-Seedeh (*author of the "Moḥkam"): lived about 60 years: died in	458
El-Khaṭeeb Et-Tebreezee: born in 421: died in	502
*Er-Rághib El-Iṣfahánee: died in the early part of century five.	
Ibn-El-Ḳaṭṭáạ: born in 433: died in	515
*El-Meydánee: died in	518
Ibn-Es-Seed El-Baṭalyowsee: born in 444: died in	521
Ez-Zamakhsheree (*author of the "'Asás" and "Keshsháf," &c.): born in 467: died in	538
*Es-Suheylee (author of the "Rowḍ")	581
Ibn-Barree (*author of "Annotations on the Ṣiḥáḥ")	582
*Ibn-El-Atheer El-Jezeree, (Mejd-ed-Deen, author of the "Niháyeh")	606
*El-Fakhr Er-Rázee	606
*El-Muṭarrizee (author of the "Mughrib"): born in 536: died in	610
Eṣ-Ṣaghánee (*or Eṣ-Ṣághánee, author of the "'Obáb" and of the "Tekmileh fi-ṣ-Ṣiḥáḥ"): born in 577: died in	660
Er-Raḍee Esh-Sháṭibee: born in 601: died in	684
*El-Beyḍáwee	685 or 690 or 691
El-Jemál Ibn-Málik: born in 600: died in	692
*Ibn-Mukarram (author of the "Lisán el-'Arab"): born in 630: died in	711
*El-Feiyoomee (author of the "Miṣbáh," which he finished in 734).	
Aboo-Ḥeiyán: born in 654: died in	745
*Ibn-Hishám (author of the "Mughnee"): born in 708: died in	761 or 762
El-Feyroozábádee (author of the "Ḳámoos" *and the "Baṣáïr"): born in 729: died in	816
*The seyyid Murtaḍà Ez-Zebeedee (author of the "Táj el-Aroos"): died in	1205

IV.—*Indications of Authorities.*

From all these authorities I have drawn through the medium of the Táj el-'Aroos or the Lisán el-'Arab, except those distinguished by the mark ‡, which denotes those whence I have always drawn immediately: from many of them I have also drawn through the medium of some other lexicon than the two above named: and from those distinguished by the mark † I have often, or generally, drawn immediately. What is meant by an asterisk placed after any indication of an authority in my lexicon has been explained in page xxvi.

†A, The “Asás” of Ez-Zamakhsheree.

AA, Aboo-'Amr Ibn-El-'Alà, and Aboo-'Amr Esh-Sheybánee: each being cited simply by the name of “Aboo-'Amr.”

AAF, Aboo-'Alee El-Fárisee.

ADḳ, Abu-d-Duḳeysh.

AḤát, Aboo-Ḥátim Es-Sijistánee.

AḤei, Aboo-Ḥeiyán.

AHeyth, Abu-l-Heythem.

AḤn, Aboo-Ḥaneefeh Ed-Deenawaree, author of the “Book of Plants.”

†AM, Aboo-Manṣoor (same as Az).

AO, Aboo-'Obeydeh.

A'Obeyd, Aboo-'Obeyd.

AZ, Aboo-Zeyd.

Aṣl, El-Aṣlam.

Akh, El-Akhfash.

Aṣ, El-Aṣma'ee.

†Az, El-Azheree (same as AM), author of the “Tahdheeb.”

B, The “Baṣáïr,” by the author of the “Ḳámoos.”

†Bḍ, El-Beyḍáwee's “Exposition of the Ḳur-án.”

Bkh, El-Bukhárec.

Bṭl, El-Baṭalyowsee.

‡CḲ, The Calcutta edition of the “Ḳámoos.”

Dmr, Ed-Demeeree.

‡EM, The “Exposition of the Mo'allaḳát,” printed at Calcutta.

†F, El-Feyroozábádee, author of the “Ḳámoos.”

†Fei, El-Feiyoomee, author of the “Miṣbáḥ.”

Fr, El-Farrà.

Fṣ, The “Faṣeeḥ” of Thaalab.

†Ḥam, The “Exposition of the Ḥamáseh,” (“Hamasæ Carmina,”) by Et-Tebreezee.

‡Ḥar, El-Ḥareeree's “Maḳámát,” the Commentary on; 2nd edit. of Paris.

Hr, El-Harawee.

IAạr, Ibn-El-Aạrábee.

I'Ab, Ibn-'Abbás.

‡I'Aḳ, Ibn-'Aḳeel's “Exposition of the Alfeeyeh of Ibn-Málik,” edited by Dr. Dieterici.

IAmb, Ibn-El-Ambáree.

IAth, Ibn-El-Atheer El-Jezeree, (Mejd-ed-Deen,) author of the “Niháyeh.”

IB, Ibn-Barree, author of the “Annotations on the Ṣiḥáḥ,” with El-Bustee.

†IDrd, Ibn-Dureyd, author of the “Jemharah” &c.

IDrst, Ibn-Durustaweyh.

IF, Ibn-Fáris, author of the “Mujmal.”

†IHsh, Ibn-Hishám, author of the “Mughnee.”

IJ, Ibn-Jinnee.

IKh, Ibn-Khálaweyh.

IḲooṭ, Ibn-El-Ḳooṭeeyeh.

IḲt, Ibn-Ḳuteybeh.

IḲṭṭ, Ibn-El-Ḳaṭṭáṭ.

†IM, Ibn-Mukarram, (commonly called in the Táj el-'Aroos “Ibn-Manḍhoor,”) author of the “Lisán el-'Arab.”

IO, Ibn-'Odeys.

†ISd, Ibn-Seedeh, author of the “Moḥkam.”

ISh, Ibn-Shumeyl (En-Naḍr).

ISk, Ibn-Es-Sikkeet (Yaạḳoob).

‡IbrD, Ibráheem Ed-Dasooḳee.

†J, El-Jowharee, author of the “Ṣiḥáḥ.”

‡JK, A MS. supposed to be the “Jámi'” of El-Karmánee: a lexicon founded upon the “'Eyn,” with additions from the “Tekmilet el-'Eyn” of El-Khárzenjee.

‡JM, The “Jámi'” of the seyyid Moḥammad.

‡Jel, The “Exposition of the Ḳur-án” by the Jeláleyn.

Jm, The “Jemharah” of Ibn-Dureyd.

†Ḳ, The “Ḳámoos.”

ḲI, The ḳáḍee 'Iyáḍ.

‡KL, The “Kenz el-Loghah,” of Ibn-Maạroof; an Arabic-Persian Dictionary.

‡KT, The “Kitáb et-Taạreefát.”

Kf, The “Kifáyet el-Mutaḥaffiḍh.”

Kh, El-Khaleel, commonly supposed to be the author of the “'Eyn.”

†Kr, Kuráạ, author of the “Munjid.”

Ks, El-Kisá-ee.

†Ksh, The “Keshsháf” of Ez-Zamakhsheree.

Ḳt, El-Ḳuteybee.

Ḳṭr, Ḳuṭrub.

‡Kull, The “Kulleeyát” of Abu-l-Baḳà.

†Ḳur, The “Ḳur-án.”

Ḳz, El-Ḳazzáz.

†Ḳzw, El-Ḳazweenee.

†L, The “Lisán el-'Arab.”

Lb, El-Leblee.

Lḥ, El-Liḥyánee.

Lth, El-Leyth Ibn-Naṣr Ibn-Seiyár, held by El-Azheree to be the author of the “'Eyn,” which he calls “Kitáb Leyth.”

†M, The “Moḥkam.”

‡MA, The “Muḳaddamet el-Adab” of Ez-Zamakhsheree

†MF, Moḥammad Ibn-Eṭ-Ṭeiyib El-Fásee, author of “Annotations on the Ḳámoos.”

†MṢ, The “Mukhtár eṣ-Ṣiḥáḥ.”

Mbr, El-Mubarrad.

†Meyd, El-Meydánee's “Proverbs.”

†Mgh, The “Mughrib” of El-Muṭarrizee.

Mj, The “Mujmal” of Ibn-Fáris.

†Mṣb, The “Miṣbáḥ” of El-Feiyoomee.

†Mṭr, El-Muṭarrizee, author of the “Mughrib.”

†Mughnee, The “Mughni-l-Lebeeb” of Ibn-Hishám.

†Mz, The “Muzhir” of Es-Suyooṭee.

Nh, The “Niháyeh” of Ibn-El-Atheer El-Jezeree (Mejd ed-Deen).

Ns, En-Nesa-ee.

O, The “'Obáb” of Eṣ-Ṣaghánee.

‡PṢ, The “Persian Translation of the Ṣiḥáḥ.”

R, The “Rowḍ” (“Er-Rowḍ el-Unuf”) of Es-Suheylee.

†Ṣ, The “Ṣiḥáḥ.”

‡SM, The seyyid Murtaḍà, author of the “Táj el-'Aroos.”

Sb, Seebaweyh.

Seer, Es-Seeráfee.

Ṣgh, Eṣ-Ṣaghánee, author of the “'Obáb” and of the “Tekmileh fi-ṣ-Ṣiḥáḥ.”

Sh, Shemir.

†Skr, Es-Sukkaree, author of an “Exposition of the Deewán El-Hudhaleeyeen.”

Suh, Es-Suheylee, author of the “Rowḍ.”

†T, The “Tahdheeb” of El-Azheree.

‡TA, The “Táj el-'Aroos.”

‡TK, The “Turkish Translation of the Ḳámoos.”

TṢ, The “Tekmileh fi-ṣ-Ṣiḥáḥ” of Eṣ-Ṣaghánee.

†TT, The “Tahdheeb et-Tahdheeb.”

Th, Thaalab, author of the “Faṣeeḥ.”

†W, El-Wáḥidee's “Exposition of the Deewán of El-Mutanebbee,” edited by Dr. Dieterici.

Yoo, Yoonus.

Yz, El-Yezeedee.

†Z, Ez-Zamakhsheree.

Zbd, Ez-Zubeydee, author of an “Abridgment of the 'Eyn.”

†Zj, Ez-Zejjáj.

I have now, to the best of my ability, supplied all the necessary apparatus for the use of my lexicon, except, only, such information as I suppose the student to have acquired from other sources.

The Arabic title مَدُّ القَامُوس (which the Arabs in general, in the present day, the learned as well as the unlearned, would pronounce "Medd el-Ḳámoos," as they deem it pedantic to pronounce the titles of books in the classical manner,) I have adopted in imitation of that given to his lexicon by El-Feyroozábádee. It has two meanings: "The Flow of the Sea" and "The Extension of the Ḳámoos."

Not only the main expenses incurred in the composition of this work, but also the cost of the printing, and that of the Arabic type, have been defrayed by the munificence of His Grace the Duke of Northumberland. The Arabic characters have often been considerably altered by the Arabs themselves and by other Easterns; and still more by Europeans, to adapt them to the purpose of printing. For this purpose, I have myself innovated a modification of one medial form and one final form, and ح. My Nephew, Mr. Edward Stanley Poole, who possesses unusual skill in Arabic caligraphy, designed, under my superintendence, the whole of the Arabic type employed for this work; and has also assisted me occasionally in the collation of the proofs, previously to my own examination and correction of them; and often in other affairs connected with the printing of my lexicon.

E. W. L.

December, 1862.

A CALAMITY that has recently befallen me, in common with multitudes of other persons,—the decease of the ILLUSTRIOUS DUKE by whom this work was originated, and whose munificence has constantly supplied the chief means of its support,—requires me to announce that the event so widely and deeply deplored will not cause any interruption of the publication.

His princely patronage, granted spontaneously, and with a kindness and delicacy not to be surpassed, has been continued during nearly a quarter of a century. The carrying-out of his intentions, with respect to my Lexicon, now devolves upon HIS WIDOW, HER GRACE THE DUCHESS OF NORTHUMBERLAND, by her own particular desire.

The intense interest that has ever been felt by HER GRACE in all the great deeds whereby the departed DUKE has established countless claims upon the gratitude of his country is well known; and it is, to me, a source of the utmost thankfulness and pride that my own undertaking is included among the objects that have been honoured by the patronage, and stamped with the approval, of them both.

E. W. L.

March, 1865.

POSTSCRIPT TO THE PREFACE.

Since the publication of the foregoing Preface, two occurrences have induced me to append to it this Postscript, without waiting for the completion of my work.

The first of these occurrences was my receiving the unexpected information that the copy of the 'Obáb which I had sought, without success, to discover in Cairo had been found and purchased, had been brought to London, and was offered to me for sale. A most exorbitant price was demanded of me for it, and refused by me: but my late lamented Patron, by means of a person employed to treat for it by my Nephew Mr. Reginald Stuart Poole, bought it, for a sum which, though large, was not greater than that which I would myself willingly have paid for it if I had been a man of wealth; and most kindly entrusted it to me, for my use during the progress of the printing of my Lexicon.

The 'Obáb is, as I supposed it to be, and as I have since found to be stated by Ḥájjee Khaleefeh, composed in the order of the Ṣiḥáḥ, ending in article بكم; so that its author completed a little more than three fourths of his intended work. To what he has borrowed from the Ṣiḥáḥ, which he has freely and literally copied throughout the 'Obáb, but usually without acknowledgment, he has made large additions, with due acknowledgments, chiefly from the Jemharah of Ibn-Dureyd and the Moḥeeṭ of Ibn-'Abbád. Whether his less numerous additions be from the original sources or from citations in other lexicons, I have not been able to determine. Of all the lexicons of earlier authors, his work most resembles the Moḥkam; which, though it is in my opinion decidedly superior to the 'Obáb in critical accuracy and in other respects, he seems to have strangely neglected; thereby suggesting to the author of the Ḳámoos the project of composing the Lámi', and subsequently the composition of the Ḳámoos itself.* In a notice of its author and of his other works, in article صغن in the Táj el-'Aroos, the 'Obáb is said to be "in twenty volumes;" and the same is said by Ḥájjee Khaleefeh: but the copy of it mentioned above is in ten large quarto volumes, written in a very large hand, and generally with all the vowel-signs and the like that are absolutely requisite. Several portions of it, not, however, amounting to much in proportion to the rest, had been lost when it was brought to England: but as the work was never completed, this is less to be regretted than it would be otherwise. In many parts it has been injured by worms; and in some parts, by larger vermin. In other respects, it is in good preservation. I have often found it very useful in the cases of doubtful passages in the Táj el-Aroos; and not unfrequently in its affording me valuable additions to the contents of the latter work, though notes in its margins in the handwriting of the Seyyid Murtaḍà show that he consulted it with much careful and critical consideration.

The second reason for my appending here this Postscript to my Preface is to correct the dates of the birth and death of El-Azheree. The paragraph relating to his Lexicon, the "Tahdheeb," I had inserted in its right relative place; but I was afterwards led to transpose it, while the Preface was in type, by observing that the place was inconsistent with the dates of his birth and death which I had there given on the authority of two most excellent copies of the Muzhir and had repeated in another page; and I did not discover that these dates were incorrect until it was too late to rectify the mistakes otherwise than by reprinting two leaves, after the Preface had been published. El-Azheree, as is stated by Ibn-Khillikán, was born in the year of the Flight 282; and died in the latter part of 370,

---

* Throughout Part V. of my Lexicon, I have generally endeavoured to show (by the indications of my authorities) the degrees in which the 'Obáb has borrowed from the contents of the Ṣiḥáḥ and contributed to the contents of the Ḳámoos.

or, as some say, 371; so that he lived 88 or 89 years (lunar reckoning). In the year 311, being then about 20 years old, he became a prisoner among the Ḳarmaṭees, falling to the lot of a party of Arabs of the Desert. Among these people he appears to have remained several years; for he is related to have mentioned his having passed two winters with them in Eṣ-Ṣammán, but usually to have wintered with them in the Dahnà. And while wandering and sojourning with them in these and other parts of Central and Northern Arabia, he collected many words and phrases, which he has mentioned in his Lexicon; but expressly distinguishing them as having been heard by him from the Arabs or from Arabs of the Desert (in both cases meaning the same) or as having been heard by him in the Desert, lest he should be supposed to claim for them less questionable authority. His opinion of these additions to the "Tahdheeb" is shown by his insertion of them, and also by a citation from a statement in his own handwriting, that in the speech of the people among whom he was in captivity, themselves Arabs of the Desert, a gross inaccuracy or mistake was seldom or never found. Thus we learn a very important fact respecting the gradual corruption of the dialects of Arabic: the utmost that can be said of the dialect spoken by the wandering tribes more than nine centuries ago in the North-Central region, where the vernacular language has continued to the present day to be least exposed to foreign influences and therefore least affected thereby, is, that it was free from gross inaccuracies. That the language of the settled inhabitants throughout Arabia had long before become too much corrupted for their words or phrases to be cited in lexicons, unless for the purpose of discriminating them as post-classical, is admitted and affirmed by all the lexicologists who have had occasion to mention the subject: but the language now spoken in the towns of the North-Central region (which language is well known by reason of that region's being still traversed by one of the great pilgrim-routes and often visited by learned men from Egypt and from Syria) is said to be less corrupt than are the dialects of the Bedawees of the same and of other parts.

More than seventeen hundred printed pages of my Lexicon are now before me; and when it is considered that this portion comprises about thrice as much matter as the corresponding portion (one half) of Freytag's unabridged Lexicon, I hope that the time which the printing has occupied will not be thought unreasonably long. Notwithstanding the time and pains that I have devoted to the scrutiny necessary for the detection and correction of typographical and other errors, the errata that I have since casually observed and noted down are not so few as I hoped and expected them to be: but I have generally found them to be such as any one qualified to make a profitable use of my work may easily discover and rectify without my aid.

E. W. L.

December, 1869.

The first letter of the alphabet [according to the order in which the letters are now commonly disposed; and also according to the original order, which see in art. ابجد]: called أَلِفٌ. [This name, like most of the other names of Arabic letters, is traceable to the Phœnician language, in which it signifies "an ox;" the ancient Phœnician form of the letter thus called being a rude representation of an ox's head.] It is, of all the letters, that which is most frequent in speech: and some say that, in الٓمٓ, in the Ḳur [ch. ii. &c.], it is a name of God. (TA.) Its name is properly fem., as is also that of every other letter; [and hence its pl. is أَلِفَاتٌ;] but it may be made masc.: so says Ks: Sb says that all the letters of the alphabet are masc. and fem., like as اللِّسَانُ is masc. and fem. (M.) As a letter of the alphabet, it is abbreviated, [or short, and is written ا, as it also is generally when occurring in a word, except at the end, when, in certain cases, it is written ى,] and is pronounced with a pause after it: and it is also prolonged: (Ṣ, Ḳ,* TA:) [in the latter case, it is written آءٌ; and] this is the case when it is made a subst.: and when it is not called a letter, [i.e. when one does not prefix to it the word حَرْفٌ,] it is [properly] fem. (Ṣ.) Its dim. is أُيَيَّةٌ, meaning *an* ا *written small*, or *obscure*, (Ṣ, IB,) according to those who make it fem. and who say, زَيَّيْتُ زَايًا and ذَيَّلْتُ ذَالًا; but أُوَيَّةٌ according to those who say, زَوَّيْتُ زَايًا. (IB.)——أَلِفٌ [properly so called] is *one of the letters of prolongation* and *of softness* and *of augmentation;* the letters of augmentation being ten, which are comprised in the saying, أَلْيَوْمَ تَنْسَاهُ ["to-day thou wilt forget it"]. (Ṣ.) There are two species of الف; namely, لَيِّنَةٌ [or *soft*], and مُتَحَرِّكَةٌ [or *movent*]; the former of which is [properly] called أَلِفٌ; and the latter, هَمْزَةٌ; (Ṣ, TA;) which is a faucial letter, pronounced in the furthest part of the fauces [by a sudden emission of the voice after a total suppression, so that it resembles in sound a feebly-uttered ع, whence the form of the character (ء) whereby it is represented]: but this latter is sometimes tropically called الف; and both [as shown above] are of the letters of augmentation. (Ṣ in art. او, and TA.) There are also two other species of الف; namely, أَلِفُ وَصْلٍ [*the alif of conjunction* or *connexion*, or *the conjunctive* or *connexive alif*]; and أَلِفُ قَطْعٍ [*the alif of disjunction*, or *the disjunctive alif*]; every one that is permanent in the connexion of words being of the latter species; and that which is not permanent, [i. e. which is not pronounced, unless it is an alif of prolongation,] of the former species; and this is without exception augmentative; [but it is sometimes a substitute for a suppressed radical letter, as in اِبْنٌ, originally بَنَىٌ or بَنَوٌ;] whereas the alif of disjunction is sometimes augmentative, as in the case of the interrogative alif [to be mentioned below, and in other cases]; and sometimes radical, as in أَخَذَ and أَمَرَ: (Ṣ, TA:) or, according to Aḥmad Ibn-Yaḥyà and Moḥammad Ibn-Yezeed, (T, TA,) the primary أَلِفَات are three; the rest being subordinate to these: namely, أَلِفٌ أَصْلِيَّةٌ [*radical alif*], (T, Ḳ, TA,) as in إِلْفٌ and أَكَلَ (T) and أَخَذَ; (Ḳ;) and أَلِفٌ قَطْعِيَّةٌ [*disjunctive alif*], as in أَحْمَدُ (T, Ḳ) and أَحْمَرُ (T) and أَحْسَنَ; (T, Ḳ;) and أَلِفٌ وَصْلِيَّةٌ [*conjunctive* or *connexive alif*], (T, Ḳ,) as in اِسْتِخْرَاجٌ (T) and اِسْتَخْرَجَ. (T, Ḳ.)——The أَلِف which is one of the letters of prolongation and of softness is called الأَلِفُ السَّاكِنَةُ [*the quiescent alif*, and الأَلِفُ الهَادِئَةُ, which signifies the same]: (MF, TA:) it is an aerial letter, (Mughnee, MF, TA,) merely a sound of prolongation after a fet-ḥah; (T, TA;) and cannot have a vowel, (IB, Mughnee, MF,) wherefore it cannot commence a word: (Mughnee:) when they desire to make it movent, if it is converted from و or ى, they restore it to its original, as in عَصَوَانِ and رَحَيَانِ; and if it is not converted from و or ى, they substitute for it hemzeh, as in رَسَائِلُ, in which the hemzeh is a substitute for the ا in [the sing.] رِسَالَةٌ. (IB.) IJ holds that the name of this letter is لَا, [pronounced *lá* or *lé*, without, or with, imáleh, like the similar names of other letters, as بَا and تَا and ثَا &c.,] and that it is the letter which is mentioned [next] before ى in reckoning the letters; the ل being prefixed to it because it cannot be pronounced at the beginning of its name, as other letters can, as, for instance, ص and ج; and he adds that the teachers [in schools] err in pronouncing its name لَامْ أَلِفْ. (Mughnee.)——The grammarians have other particular appellations for alifs, which will be here mentioned. (T, TA.)——الأَلِفُ المَجْهُولَةُ [*The unknown alif*] is such as that in فَاعِلٌ [or فَاعَلَ] and فَاعُولٌ; i. e., every ا, (T, Ḳ,) of those having no original [from which they are converted, not being originally أ nor و nor ى, but being merely a formative letter, and hence, app., termed "unknown"], (T,) inserted for the purpose of giving fulness of sound to the fet-ḥah in a verb and in a noun; (T, Ḳ;) and this, when it becomes movent, becomes و, as in the case of خَاتَمٌ and خَوَاتِمُ, becoming و in this case because it is movent, and followed by a quiescent ا, which ا is the ا of the pl., and is also مجهولة. (T.)——أَلِفَاتُ المَدَّاتِ [*The alifs of prolongations*] are such as those [which are inserted for the same purpose of giving fulness of sound to the fet-ḥah] in كَلْكَالٌ, for كَلْكَلٌ, and خَاتَامٌ, for خَاتَمٌ, and دَانَاقٌ, for دَانَقٌ. (T, Ḳ.) In like manner, و is inserted after a ḍammeh, as in أَنْظُورُ; and ى after a kesreh, as in شِيمَالٌ. (TA.) An alif of this species is also called أَلِفُ الإِشْبَاعِ [*The alif added to give fulness of sound* to a fet-ḥah preceding it]: and so is the alif in مَنَا used in imitation [of a noun in the accus. case; as when one says, رَأَيْتُ رَجُلًا (pronounced رَجُلَا) "I saw a man," and the person to whom these words are addressed says, مَنَا *Whom?*]. (Mughnee.)——أَلِفُ الصِّلَةِ [*The alif of annexation*, or *the annexed alif*,] is that which is an annex to the fet-ḥah of a rhyme, (T, Ḳ,) and to that of the fem. pronoun هَا: in the former case as in

بَانَتْ سُعَادُ وَأَمْسَى حَبْلُهَا آنْقَطَعَا

in which ا is made an annex to the fet-ḥah of the ع [of the rhyme]; and in the saying in the Ḳur [xxxiii. 10], وَتَظُنُّونَ بِاللّٰهِ الظُّنُونَا, in which the ا after the last ن is an annex to the fet-ḥah of that ن; and in other instances in the final words of verses of the Ḳur-án, as قَوَارِيرَا and سَلْسَبِيلَا [in lxxvi. 15 and 18]: in the other case as in ضَرَبْتُهَا and مَرَرْتُ بِهَا. (T.) The difference between it and أَلِفُ الوَصْلِ is, that the latter is in the beginnings of nouns and verbs, and the former is in the endings of nouns [and verbs]. (T, Ḳ.) It is also called أَلِفُ الإِطْلَاقِ [*The alif of unbinding*, because the vowel ending a rhyme prevents its being مُقَيَّد, i. e. "bound" by the preceding consonant]; (Mughnee;) and أَلِفُ الفَاصِلَةِ [*the alif of the final word of a verse of poetry* or *of a verse of the Ḳur-án* or *of a clause of rhyming prose*]. (TA.) [This last appellation must not be confounded with that which here next follows.]——الأَلِفُ الفَاصِلَةُ [*The separating alif*] is the ا which is written after the و of the pl. to make a separation between that و and what follows it, as in شَكَرُوا (T, Ḳ) and كَفَرُوا, and in the like of يَغْزُوا and يَدْعُوا [and يَرْضَوْا]; but when a pronoun is affixed to the verb, this ا, being needless, does not remain: (T:) also the ا which makes a separation between the ن which is a sign of the fem. gender and the heavy [or doubled] ن [in the corroborated form of the aor. and imperative], (T, Ḳ,) because a triple combination of ن is disliked, (T,) as in [يَفْعَلْنَانِّ and تَفْعَلْنَانِّ and] اِفْعَلْنَانِّ (T, Ḳ) and لَا تَفْعَلْنَانِّ. (T.)——أَلِفُ النُّونِ الخَفِيفَةِ [*The alif of the light*, or *single, noon* in the contracted corroborated form of the aor. and imperative], as in the phrase in the Ḳur [xcvi. 15], لَنَسْفَعًا بِالنَّاصِيَةِ [explained in art. سفع], (T, Ḳ,) and the phrase [in xii. 32], وَلَيَكُونًا مِنَ الصَّاغِرِينَ [*And he shall assuredly be of those in a state of vileness*, or *ignominy*], in both of which instances the pause is made with ا [only, without tenween, so that one says لَنَسْفَعَا and لَيَكُونَا, and this seems to be indicated in Expositions of the Ḳur-án as the proper pronunciation of these two words in the phrases here cited, the former of which, and the first word of the latter,

I find thus written in an excellent copy of the Mughnee, with a fet-ḥah only instead of tenween, though I find them written in copies of the Ḳur-án and of the Ḳ with tenween, and for this reason only I have written them therewith in the first places above], this ا being a substitute for the light ن, which is originally the heavy نّ: and among examples of the same is the saying of El-Aạshà,

وَلَا تَحْمَدِ المُثْرِينَ وَٱللّٰهَ فَٱحْمَدَا

[*And praise not thou the opulent, but God do thou praise*], the poet meaning فَاحْمَدَنْ, but pausing with an ا: (T:) and accord. to 'Ikrimeh Ed-Ḍabbee, in the saying of Imra-el-Ḳeys,

قِفَا نَبْكِ مِنْ ذِكْرَى حَبِيبٍ وَمَنْزِلِ

[what is meant is, *Do thou pause that we may weep by reason of the remembrance of an object of love, and of a place of abode,* for] the poet means قِفَنْ, but substitutes ا for the light ن; (TA;) or, accord. to some, قفا is in this case [a dual] addressed to the poet's two companions. (EM p. 4.) —— أَلِفُ العِوَضِ [*The alif of exchange*] is that which is substituted for the tenween (T, Ḳ) of the accus. case when one pauses upon it, (T,) as in رَأَيْتُ زَيْدَا (T, Ḳ [and so in the copy of the Mughnee mentioned above, but in the copies of the T I find زَيْدًا,]) and فَعَلْتُ خَيْرَا and the like. (T.) —— أَلِفُ التَّعَايِى [*The alif of inability to express what one desires to say*], (T,) or أَلِفُ التَّغَابِى [*the alif of feigning negligence* or *heedlessness*], (Ḳ,) [but the former is evidently, in my opinion, the right appellation,] is that which is added when one says إِنَّ عُمَرَ, and then, being unable to finish his saying, pauses, saying إِنَّ عُمَرَا, [in the CḲ عُمَرًا,] prolonging it, desiring to be helped to the speech that should reveal itself to him, (T, Ḳ,) and at length saying مُنْطَلِقٌ, meaning to say, if he were not unable to express it, إِنَّ عُمَرَ مُنْطَلِقٌ [*Verily 'Omar is going away*]. (T.) The ا in a case of this kind is [also] said to be لِلتَّذَكُّرِ [*for the purpose of endeavouring to remember*]; and in like manner, و, when one desires to say, يَقُومُ زَيْدٌ, and, forgetting زيد, prolongs the sound in endeavouring to remember, and says يَقُومُو. (Mughnee in the sections on ا and و.) It is also added to a curtailed proper name of a person called to, or hailed, as in يَا عُمَا for يَا عُمَرُ [which is an ex. contrary to rule, as عُمَر is masc. and consists of only three letters]. (T.) —— أَلِفُ النُّدْبَةِ [*The alif of lamentation*], as in وَا زَيْدَاهْ [*Alas, Zeyd!*], (T, Ḳ,) i. e. the ا after the د; (T;) and one may say وَا زَيْدَا, without the ه of pausation. (Alfeeyeh of Ibn-Málik, and I 'Aḳ p. 272.) —— أَلِفُ الاِسْتِنْكَارِ [*The alif of disapproval*], (T,) or الأَلِفُ لِلْإِنْكَارِ [which means the same], (Mughnee,) is similar to that next preceding, as in أَأَبُو عُمَرَاهْ [*What! Aboo-'Omar?*] in reply to one who says, "Aboo-'Omar came;" the ه being added in this case after the letter of prolongation like as it is in وَا فُلَانَاهْ said in lamentation. (T.) [The ex. given in the Mughnee is آ عُمَرَاهْ, as said in reply to one who says, "I met 'Amr;" and thus I find it written, with آ; but this is a mistranscription of the interrogative أ, which see below.] In this case it is only added to give fulness of sound to the vowel; for you say, أَلرَّجُلُوهْ [*What! the man?* for أَأَلرَّجُلُوهْ,] after one has said "The man stood;" and أَلرَّجُلَاهْ in the accus. case; and أَلرَّجُلِيهْ in the gen. case. (Mughnee in the section on و. [But in my copy of that work, in these instances, the incipient ا, which is an ا of interrogation, is written آ.]) —— الأَلِفُ المُنْقَلِبَةُ عَنْ يَآءِ الإِضَافَةِ [*The alif that is converted from the affixed pronoun* ى], as in يَا غُلَامَا أَقْبِلْ [*O my boy, advance thou*,] for يَا غُلَامِى; (TA in art. حرز;) [and (I 'Aḳ p. 271) يَا عَجَبَا لِزَيْدٍ *O my wonder at Zeyd!* for يا عجبى لزيد;] and in يَا وَيْلَتَا for يَا وَيْلَتِى, and يَا أَبَتَا for يَا أَبَتِى, and يَا بِأَبَا and يَا بِأَبَاهْ for يَا بِأَبِى. (T and TA in art. بأ.) [This is sometimes written ى, but preceded by a fet-ḥah.] —— الأَلِفُ المُحَوَّلَةُ [*The transmuted alif*, in some copies of the Ḳ أَلِفُ المُحَوَّلَةِ, which, as MF observes, is put for the former,] is every ا that is originally و or ى (T, Ḳ) movent, (T,) as in قَالَ [originally قَوَلَ], and بَاعَ [originally بَيَعَ], (T, Ḳ,) and غَزَا [originally غَزَوَ], and قَضَى [originally قَضَيَ], and the like of these. (T.) —— أَلِفُ التَّثْنِيَةِ [*The alif of the dual*, or rather, *of dualization*], (T, Ḳ,) in verbs, (TA,) as in يَجْلِسَانِ and يَذْهَبَانِ, (T, Ḳ,) and in nouns, (T,) as in الزَّيْدَانِ (T, Ḳ) and العَمْرَانِ; (T;) [i. e.] the ا which in verbs is a dual pronoun, as in فَعَلَا and يَفْعَلَانِ, and in nouns a sign of the dual and an indication of the nom. case, as in رَجُلَانِ. (Ṣ.) —— It is also indicative of the accus. case, as in رَأَيْتُ فَاهُ [*I saw his mouth*]. (Ṣ.) —— أَلِفُ الجَمْعِ [*The alif of the plural*, or *of pluralization*], as in مَسَاجِد and جِبَال (T, Ḳ) and فُرْسَان and فَوَاعِل. (T.) —— أَلِفُ التَّأْنِيثِ [*The alif denoting the fem. gender*], as in حُبْلَى (Mughnee, Ḳ) and سَكْرَى [in which it is termed مَقْصُورَة *shortened*], and the meddeh in حَمْرَآء (Ḳ) and بَيْضَآء and نُفَسَآء [in which it is termed مَمْدُودَة *lengthened*]. (TA.) —— أَلِفُ الإِلْحَاقِ [*The alif of adjunction*, or *quasi-coordination*; *that which renders a word an adjunct to a particular class*, i. e. *quasi-coordinate to another word, of which the radical letters are more in number than those of the former word*, (see the sentence next following,)], (Mughnee, TA,) as in أَرْطًا (Mughnee) [or أَرْطَى; and the meddeh in عِلْبَآء &c.]. —— أَلِفُ التَّكْثِيرِ [*The alif of multiplication*, i. e. *that merely augments the number of the letters of a word without making it either fem. or quasi-coordinate to another, unaugmented, word*], as in قَبَعْثَرَى (Mughnee, TA) [correctly قَبَعْثَرًى], in which the ا [here written ى] is not to denote the fem. gender, (Ṣ and Ḳ in art. قبعثر,) because its fem. is قَبَعْثَرَاةٌ, as Mbr. says; (Ṣ and TA in that art.;) nor to render it quasi-coordinate to another word, (Ḳ and TA in that art.,) as is said in the Lubáb, because there is no noun of six radical letters to which it can be made to be so; but accord. to Ibn-Málik, a word is sometimes made quasi-coordinate to one comprising augmentative letters, as اِقْعَنْسَسَ is to اِحْرَنْجَمَ. (TA in that art.) ═ أَلِفَاتُ الوَصْلِ [*The alifs of conjunction* or *connexion*, or *the conjunctive* or *connexive alifs*], (T, Ḳ,) which are in the beginnings of nouns, (T,) [as well as in certain well-known cases in verbs,] occur in ٱبْنٌ (T, Ḳ) and ٱبْنُمٌ (Ḳ) and ٱمْرَأَةٌ and ٱمْرُؤٌ and ٱثْنَتَانِ and ٱثْنَانِ and ٱبْنَةٌ and ٱسْمٌ and ٱسْتٌ, (T, Ḳ,) which have a kesreh to the ا when they commence a sentence, [or occur alone, i. e., when immediately preceded by a quiescence,] but it is elided when they are connected with a preceding word, (T,) [by which term "word" is included a particle consisting of a single letter with its vowel,] and ٱيْمُنُ and ٱيْمُ [and variations thereof, which have either a fet-ḥah or a kesreh to the ا when they commence a sentence, or occur alone], (Ḳ,) and in the article ٱلْ, the ا of which has a fet-ḥah when it commences a sentence. (T.) ═ أَلِفُ القَطْعِ [*The alif of disjunction*, or *the disjunctive alif*,] is in the beginnings of sing. nouns and of pl. nouns: it may be known by its permanence in the dim., and by its not being a radical letter: thus it occurs in أَحْسَنُ, of which the dim. is أُحَيْسِنُ: (I Amb, T:) in pls. it occurs in أَزْوَاجٌ and أَلْوَانٌ (I Amb, T, Ḳ) and أَلْسِنَةٌ [&c.]: (I Amb, T:) [it also occurs in verbs of the measure أَفْعَلَ, as أَكْرَمَ; in which cases it is sometimes لِلسَّلْبِ, i. e. *privative*, (like the Greek alpha,) as in أَقْسَطَ "he did away with injustice," which is termed قُسُوطٌ and قَسْطٌ, inf. ns. of قَسَطَ:] it is distinguished from the radical ا, as shown above: (I Amb, T:) or it is sometimes augmentative, as the interrogative أ [to be mentioned below]; and sometimes radical, as in أَخَذَ and أَمَرَ; and is thus distinguished from the conjunctive ا, which is never other than augmentative. (Ṣ.) —— أَلِفُ التَّفْضِيلِ وَالتَّقْصِيرِ [*The alif denoting excess and deficiency*, i. e., *denoting the comparative and superlative degrees*], as in فُلَانٌ أَكْرَمُ مِنْكَ [*Such a one is more generous*, or *noble, than thou*], (T, Ḳ,*) and أَلْأَمُ مِنْكَ [*more ungenerous*, or *ignoble, than thou*], (T,) and أَجْهَلُ النَّاسِ [*the most ignorant of men*]. (T, Ḳ.*) —— أَلِفُ العِبَارَةِ [*The alif of signification*], (T, Ḳ,) as though, (T,) or because, (TA,) significant of the speaker, (T, TA,) also called العَامِلَةُ [*the operative*], as in أَنَا أَسْتَغْفِرُ ٱللّٰهَ [*I beg forgiveness of God*], (T, Ḳ,) and أَنَا أَفْعَلُ كَذَا [*I do thus*]. (T.) —— أَلِفُ الاِسْتِفْهَامِ [*The alif of interrogation*, or *the interrogative alif*], (T, Ṣ, Mṣb in art. همز, Mughnee,) as in أَزَيْدٌ قَائِمٌ [*Is Zeyd standing?*], (Mughnee,) and أَزَيْدٌ عِنْدَكَ أَمْ عَمْرٌو [*Is Zeyd with thee, or at thine abode, or 'Amr?*], (Ṣ,) and أَقَامَ زَيْدٌ [*Did Zeyd stand?*], said when the asker is in ignorance, and to which the answer is نَعَمْ or لَا; (Mṣb;) and in a negative phrase, as أَلَمْ نَشْرَحْ [*Did we not dilate*, or *enlarge?* in the Ḳur xciv. 1]. (Mughnee.)

When this is followed by another hemzeh, an ا is interposed between the two hemzehs, [so that you say أَاأَنْتَ, also written آأَنْتَ,] as in the saying of Dhu-r-Rummeh,

• أَيَا ظَبْيَةَ الوَعْسَآءِ بَيْنَ جُلَاجِلٍ •
• وَبَيْنَ النَّقَا أَاأَنْتِ أَمْ أُمُّ سَالِمِ •

[*O thou doe-gazelle of El-Waasà between Jeléjil and the oblong gibbous hill of sand, is it thou, or Umm-Sálim?*]; (T, Ṣ;) but some do not this. (T.) [It is often conjoined with إِنَّ, as in the Ḳur xii. 90, أَئِنَّكَ لَأَنْتَ يُوسُفُ *Art thou indeed Joseph?*] It is sometimes used to make a person acknowledge, or confess, a thing, (T, Mṣb in art. همز, Mughnee,) and to establish it, (Mṣb,) as in the phrase in the Ḳur [v. 116], أَأَنْتَ قُلْتَ لِلنَّاسِ [*Didst thou say to men?*], (T,) and أَلَمْ نَشْرَحْ or أَأَنْتَ [explained above], (Mṣb in art. همز,) and in أَأَنْتَ ضَرَبْتَ or أَضَرَبْتَ زَيْدًا [*Didst thou beat Zeyd?*], and أَزَيْدًا ضَرَبْتَ [*Zeyd didst thou beat?*]. (Mughnee.) And for reproving, (T, Mughnee,) as in the phrase in the Ḳur [xxxvii. 153], أَصْطَفَى ٱلْبَنَاتِ عَلَى ٱلْبَنِينَ [*Hath He chosen daughters in preference to sons?*], (T,) [but see the next sentence,] and [in the same ch., verse 93,] أَتَعْبُدُونَ مَا تَنْحِتُونَ [*Do ye worship what ye hew out?*]. (Mughnee.) And to express a nullifying denial, as in [the words of the Ḳur xvii. 42,] أَفَأَصْفَاكُمْ رَبُّكُمْ بِٱلْبَنِينَ وَٱتَّخَذَ مِنَ ٱلْمَلَائِكَةِ إِنَاثًا [*Hath then your Lord preferred to give unto you sons, and gotten for himself, of the angels, daughters?*]. (Mughnee.) And to denote irony, as in [the Ḳur xi. 89,] أَصَلَوَاتُكَ تَأْمُرُكَ أَنْ نَتْرُكَ مَا يَعْبُدُ آبَاؤُنَا [*Do thy prayers enjoin thee that we should leave what our fathers worshipped?*]. (Mughnee.) And to denote wonder, as in [the Ḳur xxv. 47,] أَلَمْ تَرَ إِلَى رَبِّكَ كَيْفَ مَدَّ ٱلظِّلَّ [*Hast thou not considered the work of thy Lord, how He hath extended the shade?*]. (Mughnee.) And to denote the deeming a thing slow, or tardy, as in [the Ḳur lvii., 15,] أَلَمْ يَأْنِ لِلَّذِينَ آمَنُوا [*Hath not the time yet come for those who have believed?*]. (Mughnee.) And to denote a command, as in [the Ḳur iii. 19,] أَأَسْلَمْتُمْ, meaning أَسْلِمُوا [*Enter ye into the religion of El-Islám*]. (Mughnee, and so Jel.) And to denote equality, occurring after سَوَآءٌ and مَا أُبَالِى and مَا أَدْرِى and لَيْتَ شِعْرِى, and the like, as in [the Ḳur lxiii. 6,] سَوَآءٌ عَلَيْهِمْ أَسْتَغْفَرْتَ لَهُمْ أَمْ لَمْ تَسْتَغْفِرْ لَهُمْ [It will be *equal to them whether thou beg forgiveness for them or do not beg forgiveness for them*], and in مَا أُبَالِى أَقُمْتَ أَمْ قَعَدْتَ [*I care not whether thou stand or sit*]: and the general rule is this, that it is the hemzeh advening to a phrase, or proposition, of which the place may be supplied by the inf. n. of its verb; for one may say, سَوَآءٌ عَلَيْهِمُ ٱلْاِسْتِغْفَارُ وَعَدَمُهُ [*Equal to them will be the begging of forgiveness and the not doing so*], and مَا أُبَالِى بِقِيَامِكَ وَعَدَمِهِ [*I care not for thy standing and thy not doing so*]. (Mughnee.) —— أَلِفُ النِّدَآءِ [*The alif of calling, or vocative alif*], (T, Ṣ,* Mughnee,* Ḳ,) as in أَزَيْدُ, meaning يَا زَيْدُ [*O Zeyd*], (T, Ḳ,) and in أَزَيْدُ أَقْبِلْ [*O Zeyd, advance*], (Ṣ,) used in calling him who is near, (Ṣ, Mughnee,) to the exclusion of him who is distant, because it is abbreviated. (Ṣ.) آ, with medd, is a particle used in calling to him who is distant, (Mughnee, Ḳ,) as in آزَيْدُ أَقْبِلْ [*Ho there*, or *soho*, or *holla, Zeyd, advance*]. (TA.) Az says, You say to a man, in calling him, آفُلَانُ and أَفُلَانُ and آيَا فُلَانُ (TA) or أَيَا. (Ṣ and Ḳ in art. ايا.) —— إِى وَٱللّٰهِ, for إِى: see إِى. —— In a dial. of some of the Arabs, hemzeh is used in a case of pausing at the end of a verb, as in their saying to a woman, قُولِئْ [*Say thou*], and to two men, قُولَأْ [*Say ye two*], and to a pl. number, قُولُؤْ [*Say ye*]; but not when the verb is connected with a word following it: and they say also لَأْ, with a hemzeh, [for لَا,] in a case of pausation. (T.) But Aḥmad Ibn-Yaḥyà says, All men say that when a hemzeh occurs at the end of a word, [i. e. in a case of pausation,] and has a quiescent letter before it, it is elided in the nom. and gen. cases, though retained in the accus. case [because followed by a quiescent ا], except Ks alone, who retains it in all cases: when it occurs in the middle of a word, all agree that it should not be dropped. (T.) AZ [however] says that the people of El-Ḥijáz, and Hudheyl, and the people of Mekkeh and El-Medeeneh, do not pronounce hemzeh [at all]: and 'Eesà Ibn-'Omar says, Temeem pronounce hemzeh, and the people of El-Ḥijáz, in cases of necessity, [in poetry,] do so. (T.) —— Ks cites, [as exhibiting two instances of a rare usage of ا, or آ, in a case of pausing, in the place of a suppressed word,]

• دَعَا فُلَانٌ رَبَّهُ فَأَسْمَعَا • اَلْخَيْرُ خَيْرَانِ وَإِنْ شَرٌّ فَآ •
• وَلَا أُرِيدُ الشَّرَّ إِلَّا أَنْ تَآ •

[written without the syll. signs in the MS. from which I transcribe this citation, but the reading seems to be plain, and the meaning, *Such a one supplicated his Lord, and made* his words *to be heard*, saying, *Good is double good; and if evil* be my lot, *then evil; but I desire not evil unless Thou wilt* that it should befall me]: and he says, he means, إِلَّا أَنْ تَشَآءَ; this being of the dial. of Benoo-Saad, except that it is [with them] تَا, with a soft ا [only]: also, in replying to a person who says, "Wilt thou not come?" one says, فَا, meaning فَٱذْهَبْ بِنَا [*Then go thou with us*]: and in like manner, by فَآ, in the saying above, is meant فَشَرٌّ. (TA.) ═ Hemzeh also sometimes occurs as a verb; إِهْ, i. e. إِ with the ه of pausation added, being the imperative of وَأَى as syn. with وَعَدَ. (Mughnee.) ═ [As a numeral, ا denotes *One*.]

اب

1. أَبَّ, (T, Ṣ, M, &c.,) aor. ـِ, (M, Ḳ,) agreeably with analogy in the case of an intrans. verb of this class, (TA,) and ـُ, (AZ, T, Ṣ, M, Ḳ,) contr. to analogy, (TA,) inf. n. أَبٌّ (T, Ṣ, M, Ḳ) and أَبِيبٌ (M, Ḳ) and أَبَابٌ and أَبَابَةٌ (Ṣ, M, Ḳ) and إِبَابَةٌ; (M;) and ائْتَبَّ [written with the disjunctive alif اِيتَبَّ]; (T, Ḳ;) *He prepared himself*, (AZ, Ṣ, M, A, Ḳ,) and *equipped himself*, (AZ, Ṣ, A,) for (لِ) departing, or going away, (AZ, Ṣ,) or for journeying: (M, A, Ḳ:) or *he determined upon journeying, and prepared himself*. (T.) El-Aashà says,

• صَرَمْتُ وَلَمْ أَصْرِمْكُمُ وَكَصَارِمٍ •
• أَخٌ قَدْ طَوَى كَشْحًا وَأَبَّ لِيَذْهَبَا •

(T, Ṣ, M, TA,) i. e. *I cut* [in effect, *while I did not* really *cut*] *you: for like one who cuts is a brother who has determined and prepared to go away*. (TA.) [Hence,] لَا عَبَابَ وَلَا أَبَابَ, [or لا عَبَابِ ولا أَبَابِ,] a prov. [which see explained in art. عب]. (TA.) [And hence the saying,] هُوَ فِى أَبَابِهِ, (Ṣ, M, Ḳ,) and أَبَابَتِهِ, and إِبَابَتِهِ, (M,) *He is in his* [*state of*, or *he is engaged in his*,] *preparation* or *equipment* [for departing or journeying]. (Ṣ, M, Ḳ.) The hemzeh in أَبَّ is sometimes changed into و; and thus وَبَّ, inf. n. وَبٌّ, signifies *He prepared himself to assault*, or *charge, in battle*. (T, TA.) —— أَبَّتْ أَبَابَتُهُ, and إِبَابَتُهُ, *His way*, or *course, of acting*, or *conduct*, or *the like, was*, or *became, rightly directed*, or *ordered*. (M, Ḳ.) —— أَبَّ أَبَّهُ ✝ i. q. قَصَدَ قَصْدَهُ, (Ḳ,) which signifies *He tended, repaired, betook himself*, or *directed his course, towards him*, or *it*: (Ṣ and Mṣb in art. قصد:) and also, *he pursued his* (another's) *course, doing as he* (the latter) *did*. (L in art. وكد.) —— أَبَّ إِلَى وَطَنِهِ, (M, Ḳ,) aor. ـِ, (IDrd, M, Ḳ) and ـُ, (Ḳ,) inf. n. أَبٌّ (AA, Ṣ, M, Ḳ) and إِبَابَةٌ and أَبَابَةٌ (M, Ḳ) and أَبَابٌ, (TA,) *He yearned for, longed for*, or *longed to see, his home*. (AA, Ṣ, M, Ḳ.)

8: see 1, first signification.

10. اِسْتَأَبَّهُ *He adopted him as a father*; an extr. form; (IAar, M;) from أَبٌّ, a dial. var. of أَبٌ: (TA:) regularly, اِسْتَأْبَاهُ. (M.) And اِسْتَأَبَّ أَبًّا and اِسْتَأْبَبَ أَبًّا *He adopted a father*. (TA in art. ابو.)

أَبٌّ: see art. ابو.

أَبٌّ *Herbage*, (M, Ḳ,) *whether fresh or dry*: (M,* Ḳ,* TA:) or *pasture*, or *herbage which beasts feed upon*, (Fr, AḤn, Zj, T, Ṣ, M, A, Mṣb, Ḳ,) *of whatever kind*, (AḤn, Zj,) [or] *not sown by men*: (Mṣb:) it is, *to cattle and other beasts, what fruit is to men*: (Mujáhid, T, Mṣb:) or *whatever grows upon the face of the earth*; ('Aṭà, Th, T, M;) *whatever vegetable the earth produces*: (Ḳ,* TA:) and also, *green herbage*, or *plants*: (Ḳ,* TA:) and, as some say, *straw*, (Jel in lxxx. 31, and TA,) because cattle eat it: (TA:) or *herbage prepared for pasture and for cutting*: (TA:) accord. to IF, (Mṣb,) *dried fruits*; because prepared for winter (Bḍ in lxxx. 31, and Mṣb) and for journeying: (Mṣb:) pl. [of pauc.] أُبُوبٌ, originally أَأْبُبٌ. (I'Aḳ p. 367.) You say, فُلَانٌ رَاعَ لَهُ الحَبُّ وَطَاعَ لَهُ الأَبُّ, meaning *Such a one's seed-produce* [or grain] *increased, and his pasture became ample.* (A.) — Also a dial. var. of أَبٌ, *A father.* (T, and MF from the Tes-heel of Ibn-Málik.) — أُبٌ أُبَّهُ : see 1.

أَبَابَةٌ and إِبَابَةٌ *A way,* or *course, of acting,* or *conduct,* or *the like.* (M, Ḳ.) [See 1.]

إِبَّانٌ The *time,* or *season,* of a thing: (Mṣb:) or the *time of the preparing,* or *making ready,* of a thing: (Mgh:) as, for instance, of fruit: (Mgh, Mṣb:) it is of the measure فِعْلَانٌ, (Mgh, Mṣb,) from أَبٌّ in the first of the senses assigned to it above, (Mgh,) the ن being augmentative; (Mṣb;) or of the measure فِعَّالٌ, (Mgh, Mṣb,) from أَبَنَ "he watched" or "observed" a thing, (Mgh,) the ن being radical: (Mṣb:) but the former derivation is the more correct. (Mgh.) [See also art. ابن.]

ابجد

أَبْجَدُ *The first of a series of eight words comprising the letters of the Arabic alphabet* [*in the order in which they were originally disposed,* agreeing with that of the Hebrew and Aramaic, but with six additional letters: they are variously written and pronounced; generally as follows: أَبْجَدْ هَوَّزْ حُطِّى كَلَمَنْ سَعْفَصْ قَرَشَتْ ثَخَذْ ضَظَغْ: but the Arabs of Western Africa write the latter four thus: صعفض قرست ثخذ ظغش]: (Ḳ and TA in art. بجد: [in both of which are related several fables concerning the origin of these words:]) accord. to the general opinion, the word ابجد is of foreign origin, [like each of the words following it,] and therefore its first letter [as well as each of the others] is a radical. (TA.) [Hence, الأَبْجَدُ signifies *The alphabet.* You say حُرُوفُ الأَبْجَدِ *The letters of the alphabet.* — It is probable (as De Sacy has observed in his Ar. Gram., 2nd ed., i. 8,) that the Arabic alphabet originally consisted of only twenty-two letters: for some of the ancient Arabs called Saturday ابجد, Sunday هوّز, and so on to قرشت inclusive; calling Friday عَرُوبَة. — In the lexicon entitled "El-'Eyn," the letters of the alphabet are arranged nearly according to their places of utterance; as follows: ع، ح، ه، خ، غ، ق، ك، ج، ش، ض، ص، س، ز، ط، د، ت، ظ، ذ، ث، ر، ل، ن، ف، ب، م، و، ا، ى: and this order has been followed in the Tahdheeb and Moḥkam and some other lexicons.]

ابد

1. أَبَدَ, aor. ـِ, inf. n. أُبُودٌ, *He remained, stayed, abode,* or *dwelt,* (T, Ṣ, M, Ḳ,) *constantly, continually,* or *permanently, without quitting,* (T, L,) بِمَكَانٍ *in a place;* (T, Ṣ, M, Ḳ;) and so أَبَدَ having for its aor. ـُ. (TA.) — أَبَدَ, (Ṣ, M, A, &c.,) aor. ـِ and ـُ, (T, Ṣ, M, L, Mṣb, Ḳ,) inf. n. أُبُودٌ; (M, L, Mṣb;) and ▼ تَأَبَّدَ; (T, M, A, Mgh, L;) *He* (a beast) *became wild,* or *shy;* syn. تَوَحَّشَ: (Ṣ, M, A, Mgh, L, Mṣb, Ḳ:) [because wild animals live long, unless killed by accident; accord. to what is said by Aṣ and others in explanation of أَوَابِدُ (sing. آبِدَةٌ) applied to animals, as meaning wild:] *took fright, and fled,* or *ran away at random:* (Mgh:) *took fright at, and shunned, mankind.* (T, Mṣb.) أُبُودٌ also signifies The *shrinking* from a thing, or *shunning* it; syn. نُفُورٌ. (Kull pp. 30 and 31.) And أَبِدَ, (Ṣ, Ḳ,) aor. ـَ; (Ḳ;) and ▼ تَأَبَّدَ; (A, Ḳ;) *He* (a man, Ṣ, A) *became unsocial, unsociable, unfamiliar,* or *shy; like a wild animal;* syn. تَوَحَّشَ. (Ṣ, A, Ḳ.) — [Hence,] أَبَدَ, (Ḳ,) aor. ـِ, inf. n. أُبُودٌ, (TA,) ‡ *He* (a poet) *made use, in his verses, of words,* or *phrases, strange, unusual, unfamiliar,* or *far from being intelligible,* (Ḳ,* TA,) *such as were not understood* (Ḳ) *at first sight,* or *on first consideration.* (TA.) — [And perhaps from أَبَدَ in the sense explained above, but more probably, I think, by the substitution of أ for و,] أَبِدَ, aor. ـَ, (T, Ṣ, &c.,) inf. n. أَبَدٌ, (L,) *He* (a man, Ṣ) *was angry;* (T, Ṣ, M, L, Ḳ;) as also أَمِدَ and وَبِدَ and وَمِدَ and عَبِدَ. (T, L.) You say, أَبِدَ عَلَيْهِ *He was angry with him.* (L.)

2. أَبَّدَ, inf. n. تَأْبِيدٌ, *He made,* or *rendered, perpetual.* (Ṣ, Ḳ.) [See also the pass. part. n. below.] لَمْ أَفْعَلْ تَأْبِيدًا is a phrase used as though meaning ▼ لَمْ آتِ بِآبِدَةٍ [*I did not a deed ever to be remembered,* or *mentioned*]. (Ḥam p. 191.) — *He,* or *it, made* [a beast] *to take fright; to become wild,* or *shy.* (KL.)

5. تَأَبَّدَ: see 1, in two places. — *He* (a man) *was long distant from his home;* expl. by طَالَتْ غُرْبَتُهُ; (Ḳ;) or *was long in a state of celibacy;* طالت عُزْبَتُهُ, as in one copy of the Ḳ; (TA;) *and became little in need,* or *little desirous, of women.* (Ḳ.) — *It* (a place of abode or sojourning) *became deserted* [*by mankind*]: (T, M, Ḳ:) and *became inhabited by wild animals.* (T, M, A.)

أَبِدٌ: see إِبِدٌ.

أَبَدٌ *Time,* syn. دَهْرٌ, (Ṣ, M, Mṣb, Ḳ,) *in an absolute sense:* (TA:) or *a long time,* syn. دَهْرٌ طَوِيلٌ: (A, and Mgh: [and this may be meant in the Ṣ &c. by the syn. دَهْرٌ alone, q. v.:]) or, properly, *a long time* (دهر طويل) *that is unlimited:* (Mṣb, TA:) or *an extended space of time that is indivisible;* for you say زَمَانُ كَذَا "the time of such a thing," but not أَبَدُ كَذَا: (Er-Rághib:) [and generally, *time,* or *duration,* or *continuance,* or *existence, without end; endless time,* &c.; *prospective eternity;* opposed to أَزَلٌ, which signifies "time, or duration, &c., without beginning:" (see the latter word for further explanations, &c.:) each of these significations may be meant by the explanation in the Ṣ and M and Ḳ, which is also given in the Mṣb: each correctly applies in particular instances:] pl. [of pauc.] آبَادٌ (Ṣ, M, Mṣb, Ḳ) and [of mult.] أُبُودٌ (Ṣ, M, Ḳ) [and أَبَدُونَ, of which an ex. will be found below]: but the use of these pls. is restricted to particular cases, to signify portions of time, or to serve as corroboratives to the sing.: (MF:) as signifying an extended indivisible space of time, [or the like,] أَبَدٌ should have neither dual nor pl.; but آبَادٌ is sometimes said, when the sing. is restricted to denote a particular part, or portion, of the whole of that to which it applies, in like manner as a generic noun is restricted to a special and partial signification: some, however, have mentioned آبَادٌ as being post-classical; not of the language of the Arabs called العَرَبُ العَرْبَاءُ. (Er-Rághib.) طَالَ الأَبَدُ عَلَى لُبَدٍ [*The time became long to Lubad,* the last, and the longest of life, of Luḳmán's seven vultures, to the term of the life of which his own term of life was decreed to extend,] is a proverb applied to any thing that has been of long duration. (M.) And you say, رَزَقَكَ ٱللّٰهُ عُمْرًا طَوِيلَ الآبَادِ بَعِيدَ الآمَادِ [*May God grant thee a life long in duration* (lit. *durations,* the pl. form being used not in its proper sense, but to give intensiveness of signification), *and remote in limit* (lit. *limits*)]. (A.) And كَانَ هٰذَا فِى آبَادِ الدَّهْرِ *This was a long time ago.* (Mgh.) And أَبَدٌ ▼ أَبِدٌ (TA) and أَبَدٌ ▼ أَبِيدٌ, (Ṣ, M, TA,) meaning دَائِمٌ [in an intensive sense]; (TA;) [*A long,* or *an endless, period of time;*] like as you say, دَهْرٌ دَاهِرٌ (Ṣ) or دَهْرٌ دَهِيرٌ. (M.) [In each of these phrases, the latter word is added as a corroborative, or to give intensiveness to the signification.] لِلْأَبَدِ and لِأَبَدٍ and [in an intensive sense, as will be seen below,] لِأَبَدِ الأَبَدِ and لِأَبَدٍ أَبَدٍ, accord. to different recitals of a trad., signify *To the end of time; for ever;* and *for ever and ever.* (TA.) أَبَدًا is an adv. n., of which the signification includes all future time; [meaning *Ever;* like قَطُّ in relation to past time;] (El-Khafájee, El-Bedr Ed-Demámeenee, MF;) and عَلَى الأَبَدِ signifies the same. (TA.) [So, too, does الأَبَدَ, unless used in a limited sense known to the hearer.] When you say, لَا أُكَلِّمُهُ أَبَدًا, you mean, [*I will not speak to him as long as I live,* or *henceforth,* or *ever;* or *I will never speak to him;* i. e.,] from the time of your speaking to the end of your life. (Mṣb.) [In this case, أَبَدًا may also be considered as a mere corroborative. It is used in both these ways (لِلتَّوْكِيدِ and لِلتَّأْبِيسِ) in affirmative as well as negative sentences. For exs. of its use in affirmative sentences, see the Ḳur xviii. 2 and iv. 60, &c.] One also says, لَا آتِيهِ أَبَدَ الآبَادِ, (T, Ḳ,) and لَا أَفْعَلُهُ أَبَدَ الآبَادِ, (Ṣ, M, A,) and (T, M, A, Ḳ,) which, though of classical authority, is said to be no evidence of the use of آباد as a pl. of أَبَدٌ in a general way by the Arabs of the classical ages, as it is here added merely as a corroborative, as آزال is in the phrase أَزَلَ الآزَالِ; (MF;) and أَبَدَ الأَبَدِينَ, (M, A, Ḳ,) in which the latter word is not a rel. n., for if so it would be الأَبَدِيِّينَ, but app. a pl., (M,) like أَرَضُونَ; (M, Ḳ;) and ▼ أَبَدَ الآبِدِينَ, (Ṣ, Ḳ,) like as you say, دَهْرَ الدَّاهِرِينَ; (Ṣ;) and ▼ أَبَدَ الأَبَدِيَّةِ; (M, Ḳ;) and ▼ أَبَدَ الأَبِيدِ; (T, Ṣ, M, A, Ḳ;) and أَبِيدَ أَبَدَ الأَبَدِ; (Ḳ;) and أَبَدَ ▼ الأَبِيدِ; (M, Ḳ;) and

الدَّهْرِ ; (M, Ḳ; [in the T يَدَ الدَّهْرِ ;]) all of which phrases are the same in meaning; (Ḳ;) [i. e. *I will not do it*, and *I will not come to him*, (or لا آتيه may here mean the same as لا افعله,) *during the endless space of all future times, or time;* or *the like;* or *for ever and ever; εἰς αἰῶνα τῶν αἰώνων; in seculum seculorum; in omne ævum;*] the last word in every case being a corroborative. (MF.) —— Also, [for ذُو أَبَدٍ, and (applied to a fem. n.) ذَاتُ أَبَدٍ,] *Lasting:* or *everlasting.* (Ṣ, A, Ḳ.) So in the saying, الدُّنْيَا أَمَدٌ وَالآخِرَةُ أَبَدٌ [*The present state of existence is limited in duration, but the final state of existence is everlasting*]. ('Obeyd Ibn-'Omeyr and L.) And الأَبَدُ signifies [*The Everlasting;* i. e. God; because He alone is ▼ البَاقِى الأَبَدِىُّ *The Enduring without end* or *cessation;* for the Muslims hold that all living creatures (even the angels) must die, and be raised again to life: or] *The Ancient without beginning.* (Ḳ.) ═══ Also *Offspring that is a year old.* (Ḳ.)

أَبِدٌ *Unsocial, unsociable, unfamiliar,* or *shy; like a wild animal;* applied to a man, and to a young camel: (Ṣ, L:) and ▼ إِبِدٌ, applied to a female slave, and to a she-ass, signifies *shunning mankind, shy,* or *wild.* (Ḳ.) [See also آبِدٌ.] ═══ See also إِبِدٌ, in four places.

إِبِدٌ: see أَبِدٌ. ═══ This word, (Lth, ISh, Ṣ, Ḳ,) said by Lth and ISh to be the only word of its measure heard from the Arabs except إِبِلٌ and بِلِزٌ and نِكِحٌ, but Az says that he had not heard the last two from any person worthy of reliance, and that they are pronounced نِكْحٌ and بِلِزٌ, (L,) [see إِبِلٌ,] and ▼ أَبِدٌ and ▼ أَبَدٌ, (Ḳ,) which are thought by Az to be dial. vars. of the first, (L,) applied to a female slave, and to a she-ass, signify *Prolific; that breeds,* or *brings forth, plentifully;* (Ṣ, Ḳ;) and ▼ أَبِدٌ and ▼ أَبِدَةٌ (Aboo-Málik, TA) and ▼ إِبِدَةٌ, (Aboo-Málik, Ḳ,) applied to a she-camel, signify the same: (Aboo-Málik, Ḳ, TA:) and إِبِدٌ (Lth, ISh, L) and ▼ أَبِدٌ, (M, L,) applied to a female slave, (M, L,) and to a she-ass, (Lth, ISh, M, L,) and to a mare, (M, L,) *that brings forth every year;* (Lth, ISh, L;) or applied as a pl. to the female slave and the mare and the she-ass, *that breed,* or *bring forth:* (M, L:) and الإِبِدَانِ *the female slave and the mare.* (Ḳ, TA.) In the following saying,

لَنْ يُقْلِعَ الجَدُّ النَّكِدْ • إِلَّا بِجَدِّ ذِى الإِبِدْ •

فِى كُلِّ مَا عَامٍ تَلِدْ •

[*Hard fortune will not depart save with the fortune* which is the necessary attendant *of the possessor of the female slave,* as long as he possesses her, (or, if we take ذى in the sense of هٰذِه, *save with the fortune of this female slave,*) *who every year* (ما being redundant) *brings forth,*] الابد means the female slave because her being prolific is an obstacle to prosperity, and is not good fortune; i. e., she only increases evil [and brings reproach upon her master by bearing him children; for the Arab in ancient times was considered as dishonoured by his having a child by a slave]. (Ṣ.) The Arabs also said, لَنْ يَبْلُغَ الجَدَّ النَّكِدْ إِلَّا ▼ الأَبِدْ, meaning *Nothing will attain to the object of removing hard fortune save female slaves and beasts or cattle which breed,* or *bring forth.* (M, L: [in the latter of which is added, فِى كُلِّ عَامٍ تَلِدْ *in every year bringing forth.*])

أَبِدَةٌ : } see أَبِدٌ.
إِبِدَةٌ : }

أَبَدِىٌّ: see أَبَدٌ, last sentence but one.

أَبَدِيَّةٌ [The *quality,* or *attribute, of unlimited, indivisible,* or *endless, duration; everlastingness*]. (M, Ḳ.) See أَبَدٌ. —— أَبَدِيَّاتٌ a term applied to *Sayings of which the following is an ex.:* لَا آتِيكَ مَا بَلَّ بَحْرٌ صُوفَةً. (M in art. صوف [q. v.]; &c.)

أَبُودٌ: see آبِدٌ.

أَبِيدٌ: see أَبَدٌ, in three places.

آبِدٌ *Remaining, staying, abiding,* or *dwelling, constantly, continually,* or *permanently,* in a place; applied to a man [and to a bird]. (L.) And أَوَابِدُ [pl. of آبِدَةٌ] Birds *that remain in a country constantly, winter and summer;* (T, L;) *contr. of* قَوَاطِعُ. (A, L.) —— For the phrases أَبَدٌ آبِدٌ and أَبَدَ الآبِدِينَ, see أَبَدٌ. —— A *wild* animal; (M, L, Mṣb;) *that shuns, and takes fright at, mankind, &c.:* (L, Mṣb:) fem. with ة: pl. [properly fem.] أَوَابِدُ, (M, Mgh, L,) and [masc. and fem.] أُبَّدٌ: (M, L:) and ▼ أَبُودٌ is syn. with آبِدٌ; (M;) as also ▼ مُتَأَبِّدٌ. (A.) Wild animals are called أَوَابِدُ (Ṣ, M, L, Ḳ) and أُبَّدٌ (M, L, Ḳ) because they endure for a long, or [naturally] unlimited, time; (M, L;) because they do not die a natural death, (Aṣ, M, L, Ḳ,) but from some evil accident; and the same is asserted of the serpent. (Aṣ, M, L.) [See also أَبِدٌ.] [Hence,] قَيْدُ الأَوَابِدِ † *The light,* or *active, horse, which overtakes the wild animals, and which they can hardly,* or *never, escape:* so called because he prevents their escaping the pursuer like a shackle. (Mṣb.) [See also art. قيد.] [Hence also the saying,] النِّعَمُ أَوَابِدُ فَقَيِّدُوهَا بِالشُّكْرِ ‡ [*Benefits are fugitive,* or *fleeting; therefore detain ye them by gratitude*]. (A trad.)

آبِدَةٌ fem. of آبِدٌ, q. v. —— Also, [as a subst.,] † *A deed,* (Ḥar p. 364,) or *a calamity,* (Ṣ, M, Ḳ,) *ever to be remembered,* or *mentioned,* (Ṣ, M, Ḳ, Ḥar,) *by reason of its extraordinary nature, and its grievousness:* (Ḥar:) or *a great,* or *formidable, event, at which people take fright,* or *are alarmed:* (TA:) or *a strange, abominable,* or *evil, thing:* (Ḥam p. 627:) pl. أَوَابِدُ. (Ḳ.) You say, جَآءَ فُلَانٌ بِآبِدَةٍ *Such a one did,* or *brought to pass,* [*a deed* or] *calamity ever to be remembered,* or *mentioned.* (Ṣ.) See also 2. —— ‡ *A strange, an unusual,* or *an unfamiliar, word* or *saying; one far from being intelligible;* (M;) pl. أَوَابِدُ, signifying *expressions of subtile meanings;* so called because *remote from perspicuity.* (Mṣb.) —— The pl. also signifies ‡ *Strange, unusual, unfamiliar,* or *extraordinary, rhymes,* or *verses,* or *poems;* syn. شَوَارِدُ مِنَ القَوَافِى, (Ṣ,) or قَوَافٍ شُرَّدٌ. (Ḳ.) El-Farezdak says,

• لَنْ تُدْرِكُوا كَرَمِى بِلُؤْمِ أَبِيكُمُ •

• وَأَوَابِدِى بِتَنَحُّلِ الأَشْعَارِ •

[*Ye will not attain to my nobility with the ignobleness of your father, nor to my extraordinary verses by arrogating to yourselves the verses of other men*]. (Ṣ.) [See أَبَدٌ.]

مُؤَبَّدٌ [*Made,* or *rendered, perpetual*]. You say, وَقَفَ أَرْضَهُ وَقْفًا مُؤَبَّدًا *He made his land an unalienable bequest for pious uses in perpetuity, not to be sold nor to be inherited.* (T.) —— Also, with ة, A she-camel that is *wild, and intractable,* or *unmanageable;* syn. وَحْشِيَّةٌ مُعْتَاصَةٌ. (Ḳ.)

مُتَأَبِّدٌ: see آبِدٌ.

ابر

1. أَبَرَ الكَلْبَ, (Ṣ, Ḳ,) aor. ـِ and ـُ, (Ḳ,) inf. n. أَبْرٌ, (TA,) *He gave the dog, to eat, a needle in bread:* (Ṣ, Ḳ:) and [app., in like manner, أَبَرَ الشَّاةَ *he gave the sheep,* or *goat, to eat, a needle in its fodder:* for you say,] أُبِرَتِ الشَّاةُ *the sheep,* or *goat, ate a needle in the fodder.* (A.) —— أَبَرَتْهُ العَقْرَبُ ‡ *The scorpion stung him with the extremity of its tail.* (Ṣ, M, A, Ḳ.) —— أَبَرَهُ ‡ *He spoke evil of him behind his back,* or *in his absence,* or *otherwise, with truth,* or *though it might be with truth;* or *defamed him;* (IAạr, T, A, Ḳ;) and *annoyed him,* or *hurt him.* (IAạr, T, A.) ═══ أَبَرَ, (T, Ṣ, A, Mṣb, Ḳ,) aor. ـُ and ـِ, inf. n. أَبْرٌ (M, Mṣb, Ḳ) and إِبَارٌ and إِبَارَةٌ, (M, Ḳ,) *He fecundated* a palm-tree [by means of the spadix of the male tree, which is bruised, or brayed, and sprinkled upon the spadix of the female; or by inserting a stalk of a raceme of the male tree into the spathe of the female, after shaking off the pollen of the former upon the spadix of the female (see أَلْقَحَ)]; (T, Ṣ, A, Mṣb;) as also ▼ أَبَّرَ, (Ṣ, A,) inf. n. تَأْبِيرٌ: (Ṣ:) or the latter has an intensive and frequentative signification [meaning the doing so much, or frequently, or to many palm-trees]: (Mṣb:) and the former (Ṣ, M, A, Ḳ) and ▼ latter, (M, A, Ḳ,) *he dressed,* or *put into a good* or *right* or *proper state,* a palm-tree, (Ṣ, M, A, Ḳ,) and seed-produce, (M, Ḳ,) or any thing, as, for instance, a snare for catching game. (A Ḥn, M.) You say also, أُبِرَتِ النَّخْلَةُ, and ▼ أُبِّرَتْ, and وُبِرَتْ, *The palm-tree was fecundated.* (Aboo-'Amr Ibn-El-'Alà, L.) ═══ أَبِرَ, aor. ـَ, *He,* (a man, TA,) or *it, was,* or *became, in a good* or *right* or *proper state.* (T, Ḳ.)

2: see 1, in three places.

5. تَأَبَّرَ *It* (a palm-tree, A and Mṣb, or a young palm-tree, Ṣ) *admitted,* or *received, fecundation:* (Ṣ, A, Mṣb:) *it became fecundated of itself.* (Ṣ.)

8. اِئْتَبَرَهُ [written with the disjunctive alif إِيتَبَرَهُ] *He asked him to fecundate,* or *to dress,* or *put into a good* or *right* or *proper state, his palm-trees,* or *his seed-produce.* (T, Ṣ, M, * Ḳ.) ═══ See also بَأَرَ.

إِبْرَةٌ *A needle;* (T, Mṣb;) *an iron* مِسَلَّةٌ: (M,

Ḳ:) pl. إِبَرٌ (T, Ṣ, M, Mṣb, Ḳ) and إِبَارٌ. (M, Ḳ.) — ‡ The *sting*, or *extremity of the tail*, of a scorpion; (Ṣ,* M, A, Ḳ;) as also ▼ مِئْبَرٌ; of which latter the pl. is مَآبِرُ: (A:) and of a bee. (A.) — ‡ The *extremity* of a horn. (A.) — ‡ The [*privy*] *member* of a man. (TA.) — إِبْرَةُ الذِّرَاعِ ‡ *The extremity of the elbow*; (Zj in his Khalḳ el-Insán; and A;) *the extremity of the* ذِرَاع [here meaning the *ulna*] *of the arm*, (Ḳ,) *from which the measurer by the cubit measures*; (TA;) [this being always done from the extremity of the elbow;] *the extremity of the bone from which the measurer by the cubit measures*: the extremity of the os humeri which is next to the elbow is called the قَبِيح; and the زُجّ of the elbow is between the قبيح and the ابرة الذراع: (T:) or *a small bone, the head of which is large, and the rest slender, compactly joined to the* قبيح: (TA voce قبيح:) or *the slender part of the* ذراع: (Ṣ, M: or *a bone*, (as in some copies of the Ḳ,) or *small bone*, (as in other copies of the Ḳ and in the M,) which latter is the right reading, (TA,) *even with the extremity of the* زَنْد [which is applied to the *ulna* and to the *radius*] *of*, or *from*, (مِن,) *the* ذراع [or *fore arm*] *to the extremity of the finger*. (M, Ḳ.) — الإِبْرَةُ also signifies ‡ *The bone of what is termed* وَتَرَةُ العُرْقُوبِ [i. e. *of the heel-tendon* of a man, or *of the hock* of a beast], (M, Ḳ,) *which is a small bone adhering to the* كَعْب [i. e. to the *ankle* or to the *hock*]: (M, TA:) and [app. more correctly "or"] *the slender part of the* عرقوب [or *hock*] *of the horse*: (M,* Ḳ,* TA:) in the عرقوبان [or two hocks] are [what are termed] إِبْرَتَانِ, which are *the external extremity of each hock*. (Ṣ.) — See also مِئْبَرَةٌ.

أَبَّارٌ: see إِبَرِيٌّ.

إِبَارٌ a subst. [signifying The *fecundation* of a palm-tree]: (Ṣ:) or it is an inf. n.: [see 1:] or it signifies *a palm-tree whereof the spadix is used for the purpose of fecundation*. (Mṣb.)

أَبُورٌ: see مِئْبَرٌ.

أَبَّارٌ *A maker of needles*: (T, M, Ḳ:) and *a seller thereof*: or the latter is called ▼ إِبَرِيٌّ, of which إِبَرِيٌّ is a corruption. (Ḳ.) — † The *flea*. (Ḳ.) — See also بَأَّارٌ, in art. بأر.

آبِرٌ One *who fecundates* a palm-tree, or palm-trees: *who dresses*, or *puts into a good* or *right* or *proper state*, a palm-tree, or palm-trees, or seed-produce; (T, TA;) or any work of art; and hence applied to the fecundater of the palm-tree. (Aboo-'Abd-Er-Raḥmán, TA.) — مَا بِهَا آبِرٌ † *There is not in it* [namely the house (الدار)] *any one*. (TA from the Expositions of the Fṣ.)

مَأْبَرٌ: see مِئْبَرٌ.

مِئْبَرٌ The *place* [or *case*] *of the needle*. (Ḳ.) — † The *tongue*. (L.) — See also إِبْرَةٌ: — and مِئْبَرَةٌ. — Also, (T, L, Ḳ,) and ▼ مَأْبَرٌ, (T, L,) and ▼ أَبُورٌ, (Mṣb,) *That*, (Mṣb, Ḳ,) [namely] *what is called* جُشْر, (T, TT,) or جُشّ, (so in a copy of the T,) [in the L and TA it is said to be "like (what is termed) الحشّ," thus written with the unpointed ح, and without any syll. signs, perhaps a mistranscription for حُشْر, and doubtless meaning the *anthers*, or the *pollen*,] *with which palm-trees are fecundated*. (T, L, Mṣb, Ḳ.)

مِئْبَرَةٌ (Lḥ, Ṣ, M, Ḳ) and ▼ مِئْبَرٌ and ▼ إِبْرَةٌ (M, Ḳ) ‡ *Malicious and mischievous misrepresentation*; *calumny*; or *slander*; (Lḥ, Ṣ, M, Ḳ;) and the † *marring*, or *disturbance*, *of the state of union* or *concord* or *friendship* or love *between a people* or *between two parties*: (Lḥ, Ṣ, Ḳ, TA:) pl. مَآبِرُ. (Ṣ, M.) You say, خَبُثَتْ مِنْهُمُ الْمَخَابِرُ فَمَشَتْ بَيْنَهُمْ بِالمَآبِرِ ‡ [*Their internal states*, or *qualities*, *became bad*, or *evil*, or *corrupt*, *and in consequence calumnies became current among them*]. (A.)

مُؤَبَّرٌ: see what follows.

مَأْبُورٌ A dog *that has had a needle given him, to eat, in bread*: (Ṣ:) and, with ة, applied to a sheep or goat (شَاة) *that has eaten a needle in its fodder, and in whose inside it has stuck fast*; in consequence of which the animal eats nothing, or, if it eat, the eating does it no good. (TA.) It is said in a trad., المُؤْمِنُ كَالْكَلْبِ المَأْبُورِ *The believer is like the dog that has had a needle given to him, to eat, in bread*. (Ṣ.) [Accord. to Ibr D, the meaning is, that he is generous and incautious, so that he is easily deceived.] — Also, (T, Ṣ, A,) and ▼ مُؤَبَّرٌ, (Ṣ,) A palm-tree *fecundated*: (T, Ṣ, A:) and the same, and seed-produce, *dressed*, or *put into a good* or *right* or *proper state*. (T, TA.) The former is the meaning in the phrase سِكَّةٌ مَأْبُورَةٌ, (T, Ṣ,) occurring in a trad., [q. v. voce مَأْمُورٌ,] i. e. *A row of palm-trees* [or perhaps *a tall palm-tree*] *fecundated*: or, as some say, this phrase means *a ploughshare properly prepared for ploughing*. (TA.)

ابض

1. أَبَضَهُ, aor. ـِ (Ṣ, A, Ḳ) and ـُ, (L,) inf. n. أَبْضٌ (Ṣ) and أُبُوضٌ, (L,) *He tied*, or *bound*, *the pastern of his* (a camel's) *fore leg to his* (the camel's) عَضُد [or *arm*], *so that his fore leg became raised from the ground*; (Ṣ, A, Ḳ;) as also ▼ تَأَبَّضَهُ: (Ṣ, Ḳ:) and accord. to IAạr, أَبْضٌ signifies [simply] the act of *tying*, or *binding*. (TA.) — [Also, inf. n. أَبْضٌ, *He loosed him*, or *it*: for] أَبْضٌ also signifies the act of *loosing*; syn. تَخْلِيَةٌ; i. e. *contr. of* شَدٌّ: (IAạr, Ḳ:) thus bearing two contr. significations. (TA.) — Also, (Ḳ,) inf. n. أَبْضٌ, (TA,) *He hit*, or *hurt*, *his vein called the* إِبَاض. (Ḳ, TA.) — أَبِضَ, (Ṣ, L, Ḳ,) inf. n. أَبَضٌ; (TA;) and أَبَضَ; (Ṣ, L, Ḳ;) *It* (the vein called النَّسَا) *became contracted*, (Ṣ, L, Ḳ,) *and strengthened the hind legs*; (L;) as also ▼ تَأَبَّضَ: (Ṣ, L:) and ▼ تَأَبُّضٌ in the hind legs signifies their *being contracted* (A, TA) *and tense*: (TA:) تَأَبُّضٌ of the hind legs of a horse, and تَشَنُّج [or contraction] of the vein above mentioned, are qualities approved; and the latter is known by means of the former. (AO, TA.) — أَبْضٌ also signifies The *being in a state of rest*, or *motionless*. (IAạr, Ḳ.) — And The *being in a state of motion*: (IAạr, Ḳ:) thus, again, having two contr. significations. (TA.)

5. تَأَبَّضَ *He* (a camel) *had his pastern of his fore leg tied*, or *bound*, *to his arm*, *so that his fore leg became raised from the ground*. (Ṣ, Ḳ.) You say, تَقَبَّضَ كَأَنَّمَا تَأَبَّضَ [*He contracted himself as though he had his leg thus bound*]. (A, TA.) — تَأَبَّضَتْ *She* (a woman) *sat in the posture of the* ▼ مُتَأَبِّض [app. meaning *having her shanks pressed back against her thighs*]. (TA.) — See also أَبِضَ, in two places. — تَأَبَّضَهُ: see أَبَضَهُ.

أُبْضٌ, or إِبْضٌ, or أَبْضٌ, or أُبُضٌ: see مَأْبِضٌ. — Also, the first, *i. q.* دَهْرٌ [*Time*; or *a long period of time*; or *a period of time whether long or short*; &c.]: pl. آبَاضٌ. (Ṣ, Ḳ.)

إِبَاضٌ The *cord*, or *rope*, *with which the pastern of a camel's fore leg is tied*, or *bound*, *to his arm*, *so that his fore leg is raised from the ground*: (Aṣ, Ṣ, A, Ḳ:) pl. أُبُضٌ. (Ḳ.) The dim. is ▼ أُبَيْضٌ. (Ṣ.) — *A certain vein* (عِرْق) *in the hind leg* (AO, Ḳ) *of a horse*. (AO.)

أَبُوضٌ, (Ḳ,) or أَبُوضُ النَّسَا, (ISh,) A *very swift* horse: (ISh, Ḳ:) as though he bound up his hind legs by the quickness with which he raised them when he put them down. (ISh.)

أُبَيْضٌ: see إِبَاضٌ.

مَأْبِضٌ The *inner side of the knee* (Ṣ, A, Ḳ) of any thing: (Ṣ:) or the inner sides of the two knees are called مَأْبِضَا السَّاقَيْنِ: (T, TA:) or *any part upon which a man bends*, or *folds*, *his thigh*: or *what is beneath each thigh*, *in the prominent places of the lower parts thereof*: or the *inner side of each thigh*, *as far as the belly*: and also the *wrist*; the *joint of the hand in the fore arm*: (TA:) and in the camel, (Ḳ,) [i. e.] in each of the fore legs of the camel, (T, TA,) the *inner side of the elbow*: (T, Ḳ, TA:) as also ▼ أُبْضٌ; (IDrd, Ḳ;) or, as in [some of] the copies of the Ṣ in art. بيض, ▼ أَبْضٌ; [in one copy of the Ṣ ▼ أُبُضٌ; and in another, imperfectly written;] but some write it ▼ إِبْضٌ: and one says, أَخَذَ بِإِبْضِهِ, meaning *He put his hands*, or *arms*, *beneath his knees*, *from behind*, *and then carried him*. (TA.) The pl. of مَأْبِضٌ is مَآبِضُ. (Ṣ.)

مَأْبُوضٌ A camel *having the pastern of his fore leg tied*, or *bound*, *to his arm*, *so that his fore leg is raised from the ground*; (A,* TA;) as also ▼ مُتَأَبِّضٌ: (Ṣ:) or the latter, *having his fore shank bound to his arm with the* إِبَاض. (Ḳ.) — *Hit*, or *hurt*, *in the vein called the* إِبَاض. (TA.)

مُؤْتَبِضُ النَّسَا *The crow*: because it hops as though it were مَأْبُوض. (Ḳ.)

مُتَأَبِّضٌ: see مَأْبُوضٌ: and see 5. — Also *Having the vein called* إِبَاض *in a tense state*. (TA.)

ابط

1. أَبَطَهُ *i. q.* هَبَطَهُ, q. v.: (IAạr, Az, Ṣgh, Ḳ:) said of God. (Ḳ.)

5. تَأَبَّطَهُ *He put it* (a thing, Ṣ, Mgh, Mṣb) *beneath his* إِبْط [or *arm-pit*]; (Ṣ, Mṣb, Ḳ;) or *in*

his إِبْط. (Mgh.) — Hence, (K,) تَأَبَّطَ شَرًّا, the surname of Thábit the son of Jábir (Ṣ, Ḳ) El-Fahmee: (Ṣ:) because they assert that the sword never quitted him: (Ṣ:) or because he put beneath his arm-pit a quiver of arrows, and took a bow, or put beneath his arm-pit a knife, and came to an assembly of Arabs, and smote some of them. (Ḳ.) It is invariable: but if you desire to express the dual or pl., you say, ذَوَا تَأَبَّطَ شَرًّا and ذَوُو تَأَبَّطَ شَرًّا, or you say كِلَاهُمَا and كُلُّهُمْ. (Ṣ.) It does not admit of the formation of a dim., nor is it abridged: (Ṣ, Ḳ:) but some of the Arabs used to say تَأَبَّطُ [so written with refa], using a single word, accord. to Sb, as is said in the L. (TA.) Its rel. n. is ▼ تَأَبَّطِىٌّ. (Ṣ, Ḳ.) — [Hence also] تأبّط فُلَانٌ فُلَانًا † *Such a one placed such a one under his protection.* (TA.) — تأبّط also signifies *He put his* رِدَآء, (Ṣ,) or *garment*, (Mgh, Ḳ,) *under his right arm, and then threw* [*a portion of*] *it over his left shoulder*, (Ṣ, Mgh, Ḳ,) in prayer, or in إِحْرَام; (Mgh;) as also اِضْطَبَعَ. (Ṣ.) [See also تَوَشَّحَ.]

إِبْطٌ [The *armpit*;] the *inner side of the shoulder-joint*: (ISd, Ḳ:) or the *part beneath the* جَنَاح [which signifies the *arm*, *upper arm*, *armpit*, and *wing*, &c.]: (Ṣ, Mṣb:) also written ▼ إِبِطٌ; (Mṣb, Ḳ;) which is said to be a dial. var. by some of the moderns; but this is strange, on account of what is said respecting إِبِلٌ; (Mṣb;) for Sb says that there are only two substs. of the measure فِعِلٌ, which are إِبِلٌ and حِبِرٌ; and one epithet, namely بِلِزٌ: other instances have been mentioned, but their transmission from Sb is not established: (Mṣb, in art. ابل:) it is also said that there is no other word like إِبِلٌ; but this means, in its original form, and does not deny that there are words like it by the insertion of a second vowel like the first, such as this and many other words: (TA:) [see also إِبِلٌ:] it is fem.; (Mgh;) or masc. and fem.; (Ṣ, Mṣb;) sometimes the latter; (Lḥ, Ḳ;) but the making it masc. is more approved: (TA:) Fr cites, from certain of the Arabs, the phrase, فَرَفَعَ السَّوْطَ حَتَّى بَرَقَتْ إِبْطُهُ (Ṣ,) [*And he raised the whip so that his armpit shone*]: (Ṣ, Mṣb:) the pl. is آبَاطٌ. (Ṣ, Mṣb, Ḳ.) — [Hence,] ضَرَبَ آبَاطَ الأُمُورِ وَمَغَابِنَهَا ‡ [*He hit the secret and occult particulars of the affairs*]. (A, TA [followed by the words وَأَشْتَقَّ ضَمَائِرَهَا وَبَوَاطِنَهَا, a pleonastic addition, merely explaining what goes before.]) — And ضَرَبَ آبَاطَ المَفَازَةِ ‡ [*He traversed the recesses of the desert*]. (TA.) — And إِبْطُ جَبَلٍ † *The foot*, or *bottom*, or *lowest part*, (سَفْح,) *of a mountain*. (TA.) — And إِبْطُ رَمْلٍ † *The place where the main body of sand ends*: (Ṣ:) or *what is thin, of sand*: (Ḳ:) or *the lowest part of an oblong tract of sand collected together and elevated, where the main body thereof ends, and it becomes thin*. (TA.) — And إِبْطُ الشِّمَالِ † *Evil fortune; ill luck*. (TA.)

إِبِطٌ: see إِبْطٌ.

إِبْطِىٌّ [*Of*, or *relating to, the armpit*]. — الإِبْطِىُّ *The axillary vein.* (Golius, on the authority of Meyd.)

السَّيْفُ إِبَاطُ لِى *The sword is beneath my* إِبْط [or *armpit*]: and السَّيْفُ عِطَافِى وَإِبَاطِى *I put*, or *place, the sword upon my side, and beneath my* إِبْط. (TA.) And جَعَلْتُهُ إِبَاطِى *I put it* (namely the sword, TA) *next my* إِبْط. (Ḳ, TA.) The Hudhalee, (Ṣ, TA,) El-Mutanakhkhil, describing water to which he came to drink, (TA,) says, (Ṣ, TA,) accord. to the Deewán, but some ascribe the words to Taäbbata-Sharrà, (TA,)

* شَرِبْتُ بِجَمِّهِ وَصَدَرْتُ عَنْهُ *
* وَأَبْيَضُ صَارِمٌ ذَكَرٌ إِبَاطِى *

meaning [*I drank of the main body thereof, and returned from it, and a sharp steel-edged sword was*] *beneath my* إِبْط: (Ṣ, TA:) or, accord. to one relation, the poet said, بِأَبْيَضَ صَارِمٍ ذَكَرٍ: and accord. to another, وَعَضْبٌ صَارِمٌ: Skr says that the last word of the verse is a contraction of آبَاطِى: and Ibn-Es-Seeráfee, that it is originally ▼ إِبَاطِىٌّ; and if so, it is an epithet. (TA.)

إِبَاطِىٌّ: see what next precedes.

تَأَبَّطِىٌّ: see 5.

ابق

1. أَبَقَ, aor. ـِ, (Ṣ, Mgh, Mṣb, Ḳ, &c.,) which is the most common form, (Mṣb,) and ـُ, (Ṣ, TṢ, Mgh, Mṣb,) and ـَ, (Ḳ,) so in the copies of the Ḳ in the place of ـُ; (TA;) and أَبِقَ, aor. ـَ; (IDrd, Mṣb, Ḳ;) inf. n. إِبَاقٌ (Ṣ, Mgh, Mṣb) and أَبْقٌ and أَبَقٌ, (Ḳ,) or the first of these is a simple subst., and the second and third are the inf. ns.; (Mṣb;) *He* (a slave) *ran away*, or *fled*, (T, Ṣ, Mgh, Mṣb,) or *went away*, (Ḳ,) *from his master*, (T, Mṣb,) *without* [*being induced to do so by*] *fear, or severity of work*: (Mṣb, Ḳ:) thus the signification is restricted in the 'Eyn: (Mṣb:) and in this case, the law ordains that the slave shall be restored; but if the act arise from severity of work or from fear, he is not to be restored: (Lth, TA:) in the Ḳur xxxvii. 140, it is said of Jonas, (T, Bḍ,) because he fled from his people without the permission of his Lord: (Bḍ:) and it is also, tropically, said of a fish: (Mgh:) or *he* (a slave) *hid himself, and then went away*: (M, Ḳ:) as also ▼ تَأَبَّقَ: (M:) or this signifies, simply, *he hid*, or *concealed, himself*: or *he confined, restricted, limited, restrained*, or *withheld, himself*: (Ṣ, Ḳ:) or it has both of the last two significations: (Ṣgh:) and *he abstained* from a thing, *as from a sin*, or *crime*. (IAạr, Ḳ*.) A poet says, (Ṣ,) namely, 'Ámir Ibn-Kaạb, (AZ,) or 'Ámán Ibn-Kaạb, or, as some say, Ghámán, (AA,)

* أَلَا قَالَتْ بَهَانِ وَلَمْ تَأَبَّقْ ▼ *
* كَبِرْتَ وَلَا يَلِيقُ بِكَ النَّعِيمُ *

[*Now surely Baháni said, and she did not hide herself*, or *did not restrain herself, Thou hast grown old, and enjoyment doth not befit thee*]: (Ṣ:) or *she did not hide herself* [or *her mind*], *but said openly*: (TA:) or *she did not go far* [*from the person whom she addressed, or from the truth*]; so says AZ, taking it from إِبَاق as relating to a slave: (TA:) or *she did not abstain* from her speech, *as from a sin*, or *crime*: (IAạr:) or *she did not disdain*, or *scorn*. (TA.) AḤát says that he asked Aṣ respecting ▼ تَأَبَّق, and he answered that he knew it not. (TA.)

5: see 1, in three places. — تَأَبَّقَتْ *She* (a camel) *withheld her milk*. (TA.) — تَأَبَّقَ الشَّىْءَ [or مِنَ الشَّىْءِ] *He denied*, or *disacknowledged, the thing*. (Ḳ.) One says to a man, "Verily in thee is such a quality;" and he replies, مَا أَتَأَبَّقُ *I do not deny*, or *disacknowledge*: and one says, "O son of such a woman;" and the man replies, مَا أَتَأَبَّقُ مِنْهَا *I do not deny*, or *disacknowledge, her*. (IF.)

أَبُوقٌ: } see آبِقٌ.
أَبَّاقٌ: }

آبِقٌ A slave *running away*, or *fleeing*, &c.; a *runaway*, or *fugitive*, slave; part. n. of أَبَقَ; (Mgh, Mṣb, Ḳ;) as also ▼ أَبُوقٌ [but in an intensive, or frequentative, sense, i. e. *who runs away*, or *flees, &c., much*, or *often*; and so ▼ أَبَّاقٌ, occurring in the Ḳ, in art. ملخ]: (IF, Ḳ:) pl. أُبَّاقٌ (Mgh, Mṣb, Ḳ) and أَبَقٌ. (Ḳ.)

ابل

1. أَبِلَ, aor. ـَ; (Ṣ, M, Ḳ;) and أَبَلَ, aor. ـُ; (Ḳ;) inf. n. أَبَالَةٌ, (Ṣ, M, Ḳ,) of the former verb, (Ṣ, M, TA,) or, accord. to Sb, إِبَالَةٌ, because it denotes an office, and, if so, of the latter verb, (TA,) and أَبَلٌ, (M, Ḳ,) which is of the former verb, (M, TA,) and أَبَلَةٌ [like غَلَبَةٌ]; (T;) *He* (a man, Ṣ) *was*, or *became, skilled in the good management of camels* (Ṣ, M, Ḳ) and *of sheep* or *goats*. (M, Ḳ.) إِبَالَةٌ, like كِتَابَةٌ [in measure], signifies The *management*, or *tending*, (A, Ḳ, TA,) *of* مَال [meaning *camels* or *other beasts*]. (A, TA.) You say, هُوَ حَسَنُ الإِبَالَةِ *He is good in the management*, or *tending, of his* مال [or *camels*, &c.]. (A, TA.) — أَبَلَ, aor. ـُ: see 2, second signification. — أَبَلَتِ الإِبِلُ *The camels were gotten*, or *acquired, as permanent property*. (Ṣ, TA.) — أَبِلَتِ الإِبِلُ, aor. ـَ; and أَبَلَتْ, aor. ـُ; (Ḳ;) inf. n. [of the former] أَبَلٌ and [of the latter] أُبُولٌ; (TA;) *The camels became many*, or *numerous*. (Ḳ.) — Also أَبَلَتِ الإِبِلُ, (Ṣ, M, Ḳ,) and the like is said of wild animals, (Ṣ, M,) or others, (Ḳ,) aor. ـُ and ـِ, inf. n. أُبُولٌ (Ṣ, M, Ḳ) and أَبِلَ; (M, Ḳ;) and أَبِلَتْ; and ▼ تَأَبَّلَتْ; (M, Ḳ;) *The camels were content*, or *satisfied, with green pasture, so as to be in no need of water*: (Ṣ, M, Ḳ:) the last verb is mentioned by Z, and he says that it is tropical, and hence أَبِيلٌ applied to "a monk." (TA.) — [Hence,] أَبَلَ الرَّجُلُ عَنِ امْرَأَتِهِ, and ▼ تَأَبَّلَ, (Ṣ, M, Ḳ,); *The man was content to abstain from conjugal intercourse with his wife*; syn. اِجْتَزَأَ عَنْهَا; (M;) *the man abstained from conjugal*, or *carnal, intercourse with his wife*. (Ṣ, Ḳ, TA.) — [Hence also] أَبَلَ, (Ḳ,)

inf. n. أَبْلٌ, (TA,) ‡ *He devoted himself to religious exercises; or became a devotee;* (K, TA;) as also أَبُلَ, like فَقُهَ, inf. n. أَبَالَةٌ: or this signifies *he became a monk.* (TA.) — And أَبَلَ, aor. (Kr, M, K,) inf. n. أَبْلٌ, (Kr, M,) † *He overcame, and resisted,* or *withstood;* (Kr, M, K;) as also ▼ أَبَّلَ, (K,) inf. n. تَأْبِيلٌ; (TA;) but the word commonly known is أَبَلَ. (M, TA.) — Also (K, TA, but in the CK "or") أَبَلَتِ الإِبِلُ signifies *The camels were left to pasture at liberty, and went away, having with them no pastor:* (K:) or *they became wild,* or *shy.* (K,* TA.) — And *The camels sought by degrees,* or *step by step,* or *bit by bit, after the* أُبُل [q. v.], i. e. *the* خِلْفَة *of the herbage* or *pasture.* (TA.) — And, inf. n. أُبُولٌ, *The camels remained,* or *abode,* in the place: (M, K:) or *remained,* or *abode, long* in the pasturage, and in the place. (El-Moheet, TA.) — أَبَلَ العُشْبُ, inf. n. أُبُولٌ, *The herbage became tall, so that the camels were able to feed upon it.* (K.) — أَبَلَ الشَّجَرُ, inf. n. أُبُولٌ, *The trees had green* [*such, app., as is termed* أُبُل] *growing in its dried parts, mixing therewith, upon which camels,* or *the like, fatten.* (Ibn-'Abbád.) = أَبَلَهُ, inf. n. أَبْلٌ, *He assigned to him,* or *gave him,* (جَعَلَ لَهُ,) *pasturing camels,* or *camels pasturing by themselves.* (K.)

2. أَبَّلَ, (S, K,) inf. n. تَأْبِيلٌ, (K,) *He took for himself, got, gained,* or *acquired, camels; he acquired them as permanent property.* (S, K.) [See also 5.] — *He was one whose camels had become numerous;* (T, M, K;) as also ▼ أَبِلَ, (M, K,) inf. n. إِبَالٌ; (TA;) and ▼ أَبَلَ, aor. (K,) inf. n. أَبْلٌ. (TK.) — تَأْبِيلُ الإِبِلِ *The managing,* or *taking good care, of camels;* (M;) and *the fattening of them:* (M, K:) mentioned by AHn, on the authority of Aboo-Ziyád El-Kilábee. (M.) = See also 1.

4: see 2.

5: see 1, in two places: — and see 8. = تَأَبَّلَ إِبِلًا *He took for himself, got, gained,* or *acquired, camels;* (AZ, T, M, K;) like تغنّم غنمًا. (AZ, T.) [See also 2.]

8. لَا يَأْتَبِلُ, (S, M, K,) in the O ▼ لَا يَتَأَبَّلُ, (TA,) *He does not,* or *will not, keep firmly,* or *steadily, to the pasturing of camels, nor tend them well;* (M, K;) *he does not,* or *will not, manage them,* or *take care of them, in such manner as to put them in good condition:* (As, A'Obeyd, T, S:) or it signifies, (M, K,) or signifies also, (S,) *he does not,* or *will not, keep firmly,* or *steadily, upon them when riding them;* (T, S, M, K, TA;) used in this sense by a man excusing himself for not putting on a camel his aged father who was walking. (T.)

أَبْلٌ: see إِبِلٌ: — and أَبِلٌ.

أُبُلٌ: see أُبْلَةٌ.

أَبِلٌ *Skilled in the good management of camels* (S, M, K) and *of sheep or goats;* (M, K;) as also ▼ آبِلٌ: (S, M, K:) and أَبِلٌ بِالإِبِلِ, and in poetry ▼ إِبِلٌ, *skilled in the management,* or *care, of camels.* (T.) — A man *possessing camels;* (Fr, M, K;) as also ▼ آبِلٌ, (M, K,) similar to تَامِرٌ and لَابِنٌ, (Ham p. 714,) but this is disapproved by Fr; (TA;) and ▼ إِبَلِىٌّ, (S, M, O,) with fet-h to the ب, (S, O,) because several kesrehs together are deemed uncouth; (O;) in the K, erroneously, ▼ أَبَلِىٌّ, with two fet-hahs; (TA;) and ▼ إِبِلِىٌّ also, (M, K,) with two kesrehs. (K.) — بَعِيرٌ أَبِلٌ *A fleshy he-camel.* (Ibn-'Abbád, K.) — نَاقَةٌ أَبِلَةٌ *A she-camel blessed, prospered,* or *made to have increase, in respect of offspring.* (Ibn-'Abbád, K.) In one place in the K, مِنَ الوَلَدِ is put for فِى الوَلَدِ. (TA.)

أُبُلٌ [mentioned in two places in the latter part of the first paragraph,] The خِلْفَة *of herbage,* (K,) i. e., *of dry herbage;* [app. meaning *what grows in the season called* الصَّيْف, or *summer, among herbage that has dried up;*] *growing after a year; upon which camels,* or *the like, fatten.* (TA.)

إِبِلٌ, (T, S, M, Msb, K, &c.,) said by Sb to be the only subst. of this form except حِبِرٌ, and to have none like it among epithets except بِلِزٌ; for though other instances are mentioned, they are not of established authority; (Msb;) but IJ mentions, with these, حِبِكٌ and إِطِلٌ [which may be of established authority]; (TA;) [and to these may be added إِبِطٌ and إِبِدٌ, and perhaps نِكِحٌ and خِطِبٌ; respecting which see إِبِدٌ;] and for إِبِلٌ one says also ▼ إِبْلٌ, (S, Msb, K, &c.,) sometimes, by way of contraction; (S, Msb;) or this may be a dial. var. of the former; (Kr, MF;) [*Camels:* and *a herd of camels:* or] *at the least,* applied to a صِرْمَة; i. e. *a number* [*of camels*] *more than a* ذَوْد [*which is at least nine,*] *up to thirty;* after which is the هَجْمَة, i. e. forty and upwards; and then, هُنَيْدَةٌ, which is a hundred of إِبِل: (T:) or, accord. to Ibn-'Abbád, *a hundred of* إِبِل: (TA:) it is a quasi-pl. n.; (Az, S, ISd, Z, O, Msb, &c.;) a word having no proper sing.; (S, M, O, Msb;) and is of the fem. gender, because the quasi-pl. n. that has no proper sing. is necessarily fem. (S, O, Msb) when not applied to human beings, (S, O,) or when applied to irrational beings, (Msb,) and has ة added in the dim.; (S, Msb;) the dim. of إِبِل being ▼ أُبَيْلَةٌ: (S, Msb, K:) it is said in the K that it is a sing. applied to a pl. number, and is not a pl., nor a quasi-pl. n.; but in this assertion together with the saying that the dim. is as above is a kind of contradiction; for if it be a sing., and not a quasi-pl. n., what is the reason of its being fem.? (TA:) the pl. is آبَالٌ (S, M, Msb, K) and أَبِيلٌ [like عَبِيدٌ pl. of عَبْدٌ, q. v.]; (Msb, TA;) the pl. meaning *herds* [*of camels*]; and in like manner أَغْنَامٌ and أَبْقَارٌ mean flocks of sheep or goats and herds of bulls or cows: (Msb, TA:) and the dual, إِبِلَانِ, means *two herds* [*of camels*], (Sb, T, S, M, Msb,) each with its pastor; (T;) like as غَنَمَانِ means two flocks of sheep or goats: (S:) or, accord. to Ibn-'Abbád, the dual means *two hundreds of* إِبِل. (TA.) — الإِبِلُ الصُّغْرَى [*The smaller camels*] is an appellation applied to *sheep;* because they eat more than goats. (IAar in TA art. ضبط.) — It is said in the Kur [lxxxviii. 17], أَفَلَا يَنْظُرُونَ إِلَى ٱلْإِبِلِ كَيْفَ خُلِقَتْ, meaning, accord. to 'Aboo-Amr Ibn-El-'Alà, (T, TA,) ‡ [*Will they not then consider*] *the clouds that bear the water for rain,* [*how they are created?*] (T, K, TA:) but accord. to him who reads الإِبِل, the meaning is, *the camels.* (T, TA.)

أَبَلَةٌ *A blight, blast, taint,* or *the like:* (T, K:) thus written by IAth, agreeably with the authority of Aboo-Moosà; (TA;) occurring in a trad., in which it is said that one should not sell dates until he is secure from الأَبَلَة; (T, TA;) but accord. to a commentary on the Nh, it is correctly written ▼ أُبْلَةٌ [q. v.] (TA.)

إِبْلَةٌ *Enmity; hostility.* (Kr, M, K.)

أُبْلَةٌ *Unwholesomeness and heaviness* of food; (S, M, K;) originally وُبْلَةٌ, like as أَحَدٌ is originally وَحَدٌ; (S;) as also ▼ أُبُلٌ. (K.) It is said in a trad. that this departs from every property for which the poor-rate has been paid. (S, M.) — See also أَبَلَةٌ. — *An evil quality* of herbage or pasture. (AHn, TA in art. نشر.) — *A cause of harm* or *injury; evil; mischief.* (TA.) — *A consequence* of an action, or *a claim which one seeks to obtain for an injury;* and *a cause of blame* or *dispraise:* having these meanings in the saying, إِنْ فَعَلْتَ ذَاكَ فَقَدْ خَرَجْتَ مِنْ أُبْلَتِهِ [*If thou do that, thou wilt escape from its consequence,* &c.]. (T.) — *A fault, vice,* or *the like.* (Aboo-Málik, T.) So in the saying, مَا عَلَيْكَ فِى هٰذَا الأَمْرِ أُبْلَةٌ [*There is not to be charged against thee, in this affair, any fault,* &c.]. (T.) — *A crime; a sin; an unlawful action.* (K.) — *Rancour, malevolence, malice,* or *spite.* (IB.)

أَبَلِىٌّ: see أَبِلٌ.

إِبِلِىٌّ: see أَبِلٌ.

إِبَلِىٌّ, with fet-h to the ب, because several kesrehs together are deemed uncouth, *Of,* or *relating to, camels.* (S.) — See also أَبِلٌ.

إِبِلِىٌّ: see أَبِلٌ.

أَبِيلٌ † *A Christian monk;* (S, M, Msb, K;) so called because of his abstaining (تَأَبُّلِهِ) from women: (TA:) or the *chief monk:* (T:) or *a devotee:* (TA:) or *an old man,* or *elder:* (M:) or the *chief,* or *head-man, of the Christians:* (M, K:) or the *man who calls them to prayer by means of the* نَاقُوس; (A Heyth, M,* K;) the *beater of the* ناقوس: (IDrd:) as also ▼ أَيْبُلِىٌّ, (M and K, but according to the M as meaning "a monk,") which is either a foreign word, or changed by the relative ى, or of the same class as إِنْقَحْلٌ [in which the first letter as well as th second is augmentative], for Sb says that there is not in the language an instance of the measure فَيْعَلٌ; (M;) and ▼ أَيْبَلِىٌّ, and هَيْبَلِىٌّ, and ▼ أَبِيلِىٌّ, and ▼ أَيْبُلٌ, (K,) which last is disallowed by Sb for the reason stated above; (TA;) and ▼ أَيْبِلٌ, like أَيْنُقٌ; and ▼ أَيْبِلِىٌّ; (K;) the last with fet-h to the hemzeh, and kesr to the ب, and with the [first] ى quiescent; or أَيْبِلِىٌّ [app. a mistranscription for أَيْبِلِىٌّ] is used by poetic licence for ▼ أَيْبِلِىٌّ, like أَيْنُقٌ for أَنْوُقٌ: (TA:) pl. آبَالٌ (M, K) and أَبْلٌ, or أُبْلٌ, [accord. to different copies of the K,] with damm [which indicates that the former is meant, though it is irregular]. (K.) By أَبِيلُ الأَبِيلِينَ is meant 'Eesá [or Jesus], (S, K,) the Messiah. (S.) — In the Syriac language it signifies *Mourning*, or *sorrowing*. (K.) ═ Also *A staff*, or *stick*. (M, K.) — See also إِبَالَةٌ.

أُبَالَةٌ: see the next paragraph.

إِبَّالَةٌ: see إِبَّوْلٌ. ═ Also *A bundle of firewood*; (T, S, Msb;) and so ▼ إِبَالَةٌ: (T, S:) or *a great bundle of firewood*; and so ▼ أُبَالَةٌ and بُلَّةٌ (K) and ▼ إِبَالَةٌ: (Bd in cv. 3; but there explained only as signifying *a great bundle*:) or *a bundle of dry herbage*; (M, TA;) and so ▼ إِبَالَةٌ (K) and ▼ أَبِيلٌ and ▼ أَبِيلَةٌ (M, K) and ▼ إِيبَالَةٌ, (K, [in the CK أَيْبالَةٌ,]) with one of the two ب changed into ى, and mentioned by Az, but it is said in the S and O that this is not allowable, because this change may not be made in a word of the measure فِعَّالَةٌ, with ة, but only in one without ة, as in the cases of قِيرَاطٌ and دِينَارٌ; (TA;) and وَبِيلَةٌ signifies the same, (K,) belonging to art. وبل. (TA.) Hence the prov., (S, TA,) ضِغْثٌ عَلَى إِبَّالَةٍ and ▼ إِبَالَةٍ, (S, K, &c.,) but the former is the more common, and ▼ إِيبَالَةٍ, which is allowed by Az but disallowed by J; (TA;) [lit. *A handful of herbage, or the like, upon a bundle*, or *great bundle, of firewood*, or *a bundle of dry herbage*;] meaning † *a trial*, or *trying event, upon another* (S, O, K) *that had happened before*: (S, O:) or *plenty* (خِصْبٌ) *upon plenty*; as though bearing two contr. significations. (K.)

أَبِيلَةٌ: see إِبَّالَةٌ.

أُبَيْلَةٌ dim of إِبِلٌ, q. v. (S, Msb, K.)

أَيْبِلِىٌّ: see أَبِيلٌ.

أَبَابِيلُ: see إِبَّوْلٌ.

آبِلٌ *A pastor of camels*, (M, K, TA,) *who manages them*, or *takes care of them, well*. (TA.)

إِبَّالٌ: see the next paragraph.

إِبَّوْلٌ, (T, S, M, Msb, K,) like عِجَّوْلٌ, (S, Msb, K, [in the CK, erroneously, عُجُول,]) *A separate*, or *distinct, portion* of a number of birds, and of horses, and of camels, (M, K,) and of such following one another; (K;) as also ▼ إِبِّيلٌ, and ▼ إِبَّالَةٌ, (M, K,) and ▼ إِبَالَةٌ, and ▼ إِيبَالٌ: (K:) or it signifies *a bird separating itself from the row of other birds*; (T, TA;) accord. to IAar. (TA.) It is said to be the sing. of ▼ أَبَابِيلُ: (T, S, M, and Jel in cv. 3:) Ks says, I used to hear the grammarians say that this latter has for its sing. إِبَّوْلٌ, like عِجَّوْلٌ, of which the pl. is عَجَاجِيلُ: (Msb:) or its sing. is ▼ إِبِّيلٌ; (S, Msb;) but he who says this adds, I have not found the Arabs to know a sing. to it: (S:) or each of these is its sing.; (M, Jel;) and so is ▼ إِبَّالٌ: (Jel:) or its sing. is ▼ إِبَّالَةٌ, (Bd in cv. 3, and Msb,) originally signifying "a great bundle:" (Bd:) it is said that this seems to be its sing.; and so ▼ أُبَالَةٌ: or the sing. may be ▼ إِيبَالَةٌ, like as دِينَارٌ is sing of دَنَانِيرُ: (T:) or it has no sing., (T, S, M, Bd, Msb, K,) accord. to Fr (T, Msb) and Akh (S) and AO, (T, M,) like شَمَاطِيطُ (Fr, T, Bd) and عَبَادِيدُ. (AO, M, Bd.) أَبَابِيلُ signifies, accord. to some, *A company in a state of dispersion*: (M:) or *dispersed companies, one following another*: (Msb:) or *distinct*, or *separate, companies*, (Akh, S, Msb, K,) *like leaning camels*: (Msb:) or *companies in a state of dispersion*. (AO, Msb.) One says, جَآءَتْ إِبِلُكَ أَبَابِيلَ *Thy camels came in distinct*, or *separate, companies*. (Akh, S.) And طَيْرٌ أَبَابِيلُ [in the Kur cv. 3 means *Birds in distinct*, or *separate, flocks* or *bevies*]: (Akh, S:) [or] *birds in companies from this and that quarter*: or *following one another, flock after flock*: (Zj, T:) or † *birds in companies*; (Bd, Jel;) likened to great bundles, in respect of their compactness. (Bd.) [Respecting these birds, Fei, in the Msb, quotes many fanciful descriptions, which I omit, as absurd.]

إِبِّيلٌ: see إِبَّوْلٌ, in two places.

إِبَّالَةٌ: see إِبَّوْلٌ.

إِيبَالَةٌ: see إِبَّالَةٌ, in three places: — and إِبَّوْلٌ, in two places.

آبَلُ *More, and most, skilled in the good management of camels*. (S, M, K, TA.) Hence the prov., آبَلُ مِنْ حُنَيْفِ الحَنَاتِمِ [*More skilled* &c. *than Honeyf-el-Hanátim*]. (TA.) And the phrase, هُوَ مِنْ آبَلِ النَّاسِ [*He is of the most skilled* &c. *of men*]. (S, M, K.) Mentioned by Sb, who says that there is no verb corresponding to it. (M.) [But see 1, first signification.]

آبِلٌ: see أَبِلٌ, in two places. — إِبِلٌ أَوَابِلُ, (S, M, K,) and أُبَّلٌ, and آبَالٌ, (M,) [all pls. of آبِلٌ or آبِلَةٌ,] and ▼ مُؤَبَّلَةٌ, (M,) *Many*, or *numerous, camels*: (S, M, K:) or this, [app. meaning the last,] as some say, *put in distinct herds*; (M;) and so آبَالٌ: (TA:) or *gotten, gained*, or *acquired, for permanent possession*: (M:) this last is the meaning of the last of the epithets above. (S, K.) — آبِلٌ, applied to a camel, also signifies *Content*, or *satisfied, with green pasture, so as to be in no need of water*: pl. أُبَّالٌ: (S, K:) and so أَوَابِلُ, applied to she-camels, (T,* TA,) and to wild animals. (S in art. جزأ.) — And إِبِلٌ آبِلَةٌ *Camels seeking by degrees*, or *step by step*, or *bit by bit, after the* أُبُلْ [q. v.], i. e. *the* خُلَّة *of the herbage or pasture*. (TA.) — And إِبِلٌ أُبَّلٌ *Camels left to themselves*, (S, M, K, TA,) *without a pastor*. (TA.)

أُبُلٌ and أَيْبُلٌ: see أَبِيلٌ.

أَيْبَلِىٌّ and أَيْبِلِىٌّ and أَيْبُلِىٌّ: see أَبِيلٌ.

إِيبَالٌ: see إِبَّوْلٌ.

إِيبَالَةٌ: see إِبَالَةٌ, in two places: — and see إِبَّوْلٌ.

أَرْضٌ مَأْبَلَةٌ *A land having camels*. (S, K.)

إِبِلٌ مُؤَبَّلَةٌ: see آبِلٌ.

ابن

1. أَبَنَهُ, aor. ـُ and ـِ, inf. n. أَبْنٌ, *He made him an object of imputation*, or *suspected him*: and *he found fault with him*, or *blamed him*: (M:) or *he cast a foul*, or *an evil, imputation upon him*. (IAar, T.) You say, أَبَنَهُ بِشَىْءٍ, (S, K,) or بِشَرٍّ, (as in one copy of the S,) or بِخَيْرٍ وَشَرٍّ, (Lh, M,) aor. as above, (Lh, S, M, K,) and so the inf. n., (Lh, M,) *He made him an object of imputation*, or *suspected him*, (Lh, S, M, K,) *of a thing*, (S, K,) or *of evil*, (S, accord. to one copy,) or *of good, and evil*: (Lh, M:) and ▼ أَبَّنَهُ signifies the same. (M.) And فُلَانٌ يُؤْبَنُ ▼ بِخَيْرٍ, or بِشَرٍّ, *Such a one is made an object of imputation*, or *suspected, of good*, or *of evil*: (AA,* Lh, T [as in the TT; but perhaps يُؤْبَنُ is a mistranscription for يُؤَبَّنُ; for it is immediately added, فَهُوَ مَأْبُونٌ:]) when, however, you say يُؤْبَنُ [i. e. يُؤْبَنُ or ▼ يُؤَبَّنُ] alone, it relates to evil only. (AA, T. [But see 2.]) And فُلَانٌ يُؤْبَنُ بِكَذَا, or ▼ يُؤَبَّنُ, *Such a one is evil spoken of by the imputation of such a thing*. (S, accord. to different copies.) And it is said respecting the assembly of the Prophet, لَا تُؤْبَنُ ▼ فِيهِ الحُرَمُ, (T, and so in a copy of the S,) or لا تُؤَبَّنُ, (so in some copies of the S,) i. e. *Women* (T) *shall not be mentioned in an evil manner therein*: (T, S:) or *shall not have evil imputations cast upon them, nor be found fault with, nor shall that which is foul be said of them, nor that which ought not, of things whereof one should be ashamed*. (IAar, T.) — Also, and ▼ أَبَّنَهُ, (M, K,) inf. n. تَأْبِينٌ, (K,) *He found fault with him*, or *blamed him, to his face*; (M, K;) and *he upbraided him*, or *reproached him*. (M.)

2. أَبَّنَ الشَّىْءَ, (AZ, S,) inf. n. تَأْبِينٌ, (K,) *He watched*, or *observed, the thing*; or *he expected it*, or *waited for it*. (AZ, S, K.) — أَبَّنَ الأَثَرَ, (M,) inf. n. as above, (As, T, S, K,) *He followed the traces*, or *footprints*, or *footsteps*, (As, T, S, M, K,) *of a thing*; (As, S, K;) as also ▼ تَأَبَّنَ. (K.) And hence the next signification. (As, T.) ═ أَبَّنَ الرَّجُلَ, (S, M,) inf. n. as above, (Sh, T, S, K,) *He praised the man*, or *spoke well of him*, (Sh, Th, T, S, M, K,) *after his death*, (Th, S, M, K,) or *in death and in life*, (Sh, T,) used in poetry to signify praise of the living; (M;) and *wept for him*: (S:) *he praised him; and enumerated*, or *recounted, his good qualities* or *actions*: you say, لَمْ يَزَلْ يُقَرِّظُ أَحْيَاءَكُمْ وَيُؤَبِّنُ مَوْتَاكُمْ [*He ceased not to eulogize your living and to praise your dead*]: (Z, TA:) for he who praises the dead traces his [good] deeds. (As, T.) — See also 1, in six places.

5: see 2.

اِبْنٌ: see art. بنى.

أُبْنَةٌ *A knot in wood*, or *in a branch*; (S, M, K;) or *in a staff*, or *stick*; (T;) and *in a bow*, (TA,) [i. e.] the *place of the shooting forth of a branch in a bow*, (M,) which is a fault therein; (TA;) and *in a rope*, or *cord*: (M in art. اتل:)

pl. أُبَنٌ. (T, Ṣ.) — Hence, (M,) ‡ *A fault, defect,* or *blemish,* (T, M, Ḳ, TA,) in one's grounds of pretension to respect, (T, TA,) and in speech, or language. (M, TA.) — † Particularly The *enormity that is committed with one who is termed* مَأْبُون. (TA.) — And ‡ *Rancour, malevolence, malice,* or *spite:* (Ḳ, TA:) and *enmity:* pl. as above. (TA.) You say, بَيْنَهُمْ أُبَنٌ ‡ (Ṣ, TA) *Between them are enmities.* (Ṣ.) — Also The [*part called*] غَلْصَمَة [meaning the *epiglottis*] of a camel. (M, Ḳ.)

إِبْنَةٌ: see art. بنى.

إِبَّانٌ The *time* of a thing; (T, Ṣ, M, Ḳ, and Mṣb in art. اب;) the *season* of a thing; (Mṣb in that art.;) the *time of the preparing,* or *making ready,* of a thing; (Mgh in that art.;) as, for instance, of fruit, (Ṣ, Mgh, Mṣb,) of the fresh ripe dates, and of the gathering of fruits, and of heat or cold: (T.:) or the *first* of a thing. (M, Ḳ.) You say, أَخَذَ الشَّىْءَ بِإِبَّانِهِ *He took the thing in its time:* or *in,* or *with, the first thereof.* (M.) The ن is radical, so that it is of the measure فِعَّالٌ; or, as some say, augmentative, so that it is of the measure فِعْلَانٌ. (TA.) [See art. اب.]

مُؤَبَّنٌ occurs as meaning *Dead,* or *dying;* i. e., [properly,] *wept for.* (Ṣ.) [See 2.]

مُؤَبِّنٌ *A praiser of the dead;* because he traces his [good] deeds. (Aṣ, T.)

مَأْبُونٌ *Made an object of imputation,* or *suspected, of evil:* thus when used alone: otherwise you add بِخَيْرٍ [of good], and بِشَرٍّ [of evil]. (M, Ḳ.) — Hence, [*A catamite;*] *one with whom enormous wickedness is committed;* (TA;) *i. q.* مُخَنَّثٌ. (Idem, voce دُعْبُوثٌ.) — Also One who is *imprisoned;* because suspected of a foul fault, or crime. (T.)

ابنس, accord. to the Mṣb; or بنس, accord. to the TA.

آبَنُوسٌ, with medd to the ا and kesr to the ب, (TA,) or with ḍamm to the ب, [i. e. آبُنُوسٌ, and by some written آبَنُوسٌ,] or with the ب quiescent, [i. e. آبْنُوسٌ,] and without و, [app. آبْنُسٌ,] (Mṣb,) [*Ebony;*] *a thing well known, which is brought from India:* an arabicized word: (Mṣb [in which is added the proper Arabic appellation; but the word in my copy of that work is imperfectly written; app. جعفر; which, however, does not seem to be the word intended:]) some say that it is the *same as* سَاسَمٌ: others, that it is *different therefrom:* and respecting the measure of the word, authors differ. (TA.)

ابه

1. أَبَهَ لَهُ, (JK, Ḳ,) and بِهِ; (Ḳ;) and أَبِهَ; aor. [of both] يَأْبَهُ; inf. n. أَبْهٌ, (JK, Ḳ,) of the former, (TA,) and أُبُوهٌ, [also of the former,] (JK,) and أَبَهٌ, (JK, Ḳ,) which is of the latter; (TA;) *He knew it;* or *understood it;* or *knew it,* or *understood it, instinctively:* or *he recognised it readily; knew it,* or *understood it, readily, after he had forgotten it.* (Ḳ.) You say, مَا أَبَهْتُ لَهُ, (AZ, JK, Ṣ, Mgh,) aor. أَبَهَ, inf. n. أَبْهٌ; (AZ, Ṣ;) and مَا أَبِهْتُ لَهُ, (JK, Ṣ,) aor. as above, inf. n. أَبَهٌ; (Ṣ;) *I did not know it,* or *understand it;* or *did not know of it; was not cognizant of it:* (JK, Mgh:) or *I did not have my attention roused to it after I had forgotten it:* (AZ, Ṣ:) the former is like وَبَهْتُ; (Mgh;) and the latter, like [وَبِهْتُ and] نَبِهْتُ. (Ṣ.) — لَا يُؤْبَهُ لَهُ (Mgh, Ḳ, TA) *He will not be cared for, minded,* or *regarded,* because of his lowness of condition, or abjectness. (Mgh, TA.) — أَبَهْتُهُ بِكَذَا *I imputed to him,* or *suspected him of, such a thing.* (JK, Ḳ, TA.)

2. أَبَّهْتُهُ, inf. n. تَأْبِيهٌ, *I roused his attention:* and *I made him to know,* or *understand.* (Kr, Ḳ.) The two meanings are nearly alike. (TA.) And ▼ آبَهْتُهُ *I made him to know; informed, apprized, advertised,* or *advised, him; gave him information, intelligence, notice,* or *advice.* (IB.)

4: see 2.

5. تَأَبَّهَ *He magnified himself; behaved proudly,* or *haughtily.* (JK, Ṣ, Ḳ.) You say, تَأَبَّهَ الرَّجُلُ عَلَى فُلَانٍ *The man magnified himself against such a one, and held himself above him.* (JK,* TA.) And تَأَبَّهَ عَنْ كَذَا *He shunned, avoided,* or *kept himself far from, such a thing;* (JK, Z, Ḳ;) *he was disdainful of it, he disdained it,* or *held himself above it.* (Z, Ḳ.)

أُبَّهَةٌ *Greatness,* or *majesty;* (JK, Ṣ, Ḳ;) *a quality inspiring reverence or veneration;* (TA;) *goodliness and splendour;* (Ḳ;) and *goodliness of aspect:* (TA:) and *pride, self-magnification,* or *haughtiness.* (JK,* Ṣ,* Ḳ.)

ابو

1. أَبَوْتُ, [third pers. أَبَا,] (T, Ṣ, M, Ḳ,) and أَبِيتُ, [third pers. أَبِىَ,] (T, M, Ḳ,) the latter accord. to Yz, (T,) aor. يَأْبُو, (TḲ,) inf. n. أُبُوَّةٌ, (Yz, T, Ṣ, Mṣb,) or this is a simple subst., (M,) *I became a father.* (T,* Ṣ,* M, Ḳ.) — أَبَوْتُهُ, (ISk, T, M, Ḳ,) aor. آبُوهُ, (IAạr, ISk, T,) inf. n. إِبَاوَةٌ, (M, Ḳ,) *I was,* (IAạr, ISk, T,) or *became,* (M, Ḳ,) *a father to him.* (IAạr, ISk, T, M, Ḳ.) — [Hence, *I fed him,* or *nourished him;* and *reared him,* or *brought him up.*] You say, فُلَانٌ يَأْبُو هٰذَا اليَتِيمَ, inf. n. إِبَاوَةٌ, *Such a one feeds,* or *nourishes, this orphan, like as the father does his children.* (Lth, T.) And مَا لَهُ أَبٌ يَأْبُوهُ (ISk, T, Ṣ) *He has not a father to feed him,* or *nourish him,* and *to rear him,* or *bring him up.* (Ṣ.)

2. أَبَّيْتُهُ, inf. n. تَأْبِيَةٌ, *I said to him* بِأَبِى [meaning فُدِيتَ بِأَبِى *Mayest thou be ransomed with my father!* or the like: see أَبٌ, below]. (Ḳ, TA. [In the CḲ, erroneously, يا أبى.])

5. تَأَبَّاهُ *He adopted him as a father;* (M, Ḳ, TA;) as also ▼ اِسْتَأْبَاهُ; (M in art. اب;) and so تَأَبَّاهُ أَبًا, accord. to A'Obeyd: (TA:) [or,] accord. to A'Obeyd, you say, تَأَبَّيْتُ أَبًا *I adopted a father:* (T:) and you say also, اِسْتَأْبَبَ أَبًا and اِسْتَأْبَ أَبًا, *he adopted a father.* (TA.)

10: see 5.

أَبٌ is originally أَبَوٌ, (Ṣ, Mṣb, Ḳ,) as is shown by the first of its dual forms and of its pl. forms mentioned below; (Ṣ, Mṣb;) and signifies *A father* [in the ordinary sense: and also as meaning † *an ancestor*]: (M:) as also ▼ أَبًا, a dial. var., (M, Ḳ,) the same in the nom. and accus. and gen. cases, like قَفًا: (M:) and أَبٌّ is a dial. var. of the same, [the second letter being doubled to compensate for the و suppressed, as is the case in أَخٌّ, (TA voce أَخٌ,)] but is rare. (Mṣb.) Accord. to the dial. commonly obtaining, when you use it as a prefixed noun, you decline it with the letters و and ا and ى, saying, هٰذَا أَبُوهُ [*This is his father*], (Mṣb,) and أَبُوكَ [*thy father*]; (M;) and رَأَيْتُ أَبَاهُ [*I saw his father*]; and مَرَرْتُ بِأَبِيهِ [*I passed by his father*]: (Mṣb:) but accord. to one dial., you say, هٰذَا أَبَاهُ, (Mṣb,) and أَبَاكَ; (M;) and رَأَيْتُ أَبَاهُ; and مَرَرْتُ بِأَبَاهُ: (Mṣb:) and accord. to one dial., which is the rarest of all, it is defective in every case, like يَدٌ and دَمٌ; (Mṣb;) and [thus] you say, هٰذَا أَبُكَ [&c.]. (M.) The dual is أَبَوَانِ, (Ṣ, M, Mṣb,) meaning [*two fathers,* and] *father and mother;* and some say أَبَانِ: (Ṣ, M:) you say, هُمَا أَبَوَاهُ, meaning *They two are his father and mother;* and in poetry you may say, هُمَا أَبَاهُ; and in like manner, رَأَيْتُ أَبَيْهِ [*I saw his father and mother*], (T,) and أَبَيْكَ [*thy father and mother*]; (Ṣ;) but the usual, or chaste, form is رَأَيْتُ أَبَوَيْهِ. (T.) The pl. is آبَآءٌ, (T, Ṣ, M, Mṣb, Ḳ,) the best form, (T,) and أَبُونَ, (T, Ṣ, M, Ḳ,) and أُبُوٌّ, (M, Ḳ, [in the CḲ الاَبُو is erroneously put for الأُبُوُّ,]) and أُبُوَّةٌ, (Lḥ, T, Ṣ, M, Ḳ,*) like عُمُومَةٌ and خُؤُولَةٌ: (T, Ṣ:) you say, هٰؤُلَآءِ أَبُوكُمْ, meaning آبَاؤُكُمْ [*These are your fathers*]; (T;) and hence, in the Ḳur [ii. 127], accord. to one reading, وَإِلٰهَ أَبِيكَ إِبْرٰهِيمَ وَإِسْمٰعِيلَ وَإِسْحٰقَ [*And the God of thy fathers, Abraham and Ishmael and Isaac*], meaning the pl. of أَبٌ, i. e. أَبِينَكَ, of which the ن is suppressed because the noun is prefixed [to the pronoun]; (Ṣ;) and some of the Arabs say, أَبُوَّتُنَا أَكْرَمُ الآبَآءِ [*Our fathers are the most generous of fathers*]. (T.) The dim. is ▼ أُبَىٌّ; originally أُبَيْوٌ, with the final radical letter restored. (Mṣb.) — مَا يَدْرِى لَهُ مِنْ أَبٍ, and مَا أَبٌ, meaning *He knows not who is his father,* and *what is his father,* are sayings mentioned by Lḥ on the authority of Ks. (M.) — لَا أَبَا لَكَ, (T, Ṣ, M, Ḳ, &c.,) [accord. to the dial. of him who says أَبًا instead of أَبٌ,] as also لَا أَبَ لَكَ, and لَا أَبَاكَ, (Ṣ, Ḳ,) [the last, accord. to J, because the ل (meaning the ل in لك in the preceding phrases) is as though it were redundant, but he seems not to have known the dial. var. أَبًا, and I rather think that لَا أَبَاكَ is for لَا أَبْقَى ٱللّٰهُ أَبَاكَ, or the like,] and لَا أَبَكَ, (Mbr, Ṣgh, Ḳ,) and لَابَ لَكَ, (Ḳ,) which is for لَا أَبَ لَكَ, (M,) means Thou art, in my estimation, one deserving of its being said to him, *Mayest thou have no father!* it is used in the manner of a proverb, is of frequent occurrence in poetry, (M,) is said to him who has a father and to him who has not a father, and is an imprecation as to the meaning, of necessity, though enunciative as to the letter; (M, Ḳ;) and hence the saying of Jereer,

* يَا تَيْمَ تَيْمَ عَدِىٍّ لَا أَبَا لَكُمُ *

[*O Teym, Teym of 'Adee, may ye have no*

father!]; which is the strongest evidence of its being a proverb, and not having a literal meaning; for all of [the tribe of] Teym could not have one father, but all of them were fit objects of imprecation and rough speech: (M:) it is an expression of praise: (Ṣ:) [i. e.] it is an imprecation against him to whom it is addressed, not, however, said with the desire of its having effect, but on an occasion of intense love, like لَا أُمَّ لَكَ, &c.: (Ḥar p. 165:) and sometimes in dispraise, like لَا أُمَّ لَكَ: and in wonder, like لِلّٰهِ دَرُّكَ: (TA:) or, as A Heyth says, on the authority of Aboo-Sa'eed Eḍ-Ḍareer, it expresses the utmost degree of reviling; [meaning *Thou hast no* known *father;*] and لَا أُمَّ لَكَ expresses reviling also, but means Thou hast no free, or ingenuous, mother: (Meyd in Ḥar p. 165: [see أُمٌّ:]) sometimes it means *Strive, or exert thyself, in thine affair;* for he who has a father relies upon him in some circumstances of his case: (TA:) accord. to Kh, it means *Thou hast none to stand thee in stead of thyself:* (ISh, TA:) Fr says that it is a phrase used by the Arabs [parenthetically, i. e.,] to divide their speech: (TA:) [thus, for instance,] Zufar Ibn-El-Ḥárith says,

* أَرِينِى سِلَاحِى لَا أَبَا لَكَ إِنَّنِى *
* أَرَى الحَرْبَ لَا تَزْدَادُ إِلَّا تَمَادِيَا *

[*Show thou me my weapons: (mayest thou have no father! or thou hast no father: &c.:) verily I see the war, or battle, increases not save in perseverance*]. (TA.) [Aboo-'Alee, as cited in the M, observes that the ا (meaning the final ا) in أَبَا, in the phrase لَا أَبَا لَكَ, indicates that it is a prefixed noun, and determinate; whereas the ل in لك together with the government exercised upon the noun by لا indicates that it is, on the contrary, indeterminate, and separate from what follows it: but it seems that he was unacquainted with the dial. var. أَبًا; for لَا أَبَا لَكَ in the dial. of him who uses the form أَبًا instead of أَبٌ is the same grammatically as لَا أَبَ لَكَ in the dial. of him who uses the form أَبٌ.] Suleymán Ibn-'Abd-El-Melik heard an Arab of the desert, in a year of drought, say, أَنْزِلْ عَلَيْنَا الغَيْثَ لَا أَبَا لَكَ, and Suleymán put the best construction upon it, [as though it meant, *Send down upon us rain: Thou hast no father*], and said, I testify that He hath no father nor female companion nor offspring. (TA.) They say also, in paying honour [to a person], لَا أَبَ لِشَانِئِكَ, and لَا أَبَا لِشَانِئِكَ, (TA,) i. e. *May thy hater have no father!* or, accord. to ISk, each is a metonymical expression for لَا أَبَا لَكَ. (Ṣ in art. شنأ, q. v.) — One also says, on the occasion of an occurrence that is approved and commended, by way of expressing wonder and praise, لِلّٰهِ أَبُوكَ, meaning *To God, purely, is attributable* [*the excellence of*] *thy father, seeing that he begat thee a generous son, and produced the like of thee!* (TA;) [or *to God be attributed (the excellence of) thy father!*] it means that to God [alone] belongs the power to create the like of this man [to whom it relates], from whom has proceeded this wonderful action. (Ḥar p. 44.) — And هِىَ بِنْتُ أَبِيهَا, meaning *She resembles her father in strength of mind,* or *spirit, and sharpness of disposition, and in hastening,* or *striving to be first, to do things:* said of Ḥafṣah, by 'Áïsheh. (TA.) — بِأَبِى, (TA,) or بِأَبِى أَنْتَ, (T in art. بأ,) [said to a person,] means [فُدِيتَ بِأَبِى *Mayest thou be ransomed with my father!* (see the next sentence but one;) or] أَفْدِيكَ بِأَبِى [*I will ransom thee with my father*]; (T ubi suprà;) or أَنْتَ مَفْدِىٌّ بِأَبِى *Thou art,* or *shalt be, ransomed with my father*]; or فَدَيْتُكَ بِأَبِى [*I have* in my heart *ransomed thee,* or *I would ransom thee, with my father*]; the ب being dependent upon a word suppressed, which, accord. to some, is a [pass. participial] noun, and accord. to others, a verb; and this word is suppressed because of the frequent usage of the phrase. (TA.) You say also, بِأَبِى أَنْتَ وَأُمِّى [*With my father mayest thou be ransomed, and* with *my mother!*]. (TA.) And بِأَبِى مَنْ وَدِدْتُهُ, i. e. فُدِىَ بِأَبِى مَنْ وَدِدْتُهُ [*May he whom I love be ransomed with my father!*], meaning *may he* [*my father*] *be made a ransom for him* [*whom I love*]! (El-Wáḥidee on the Deewán of El-Mutanebbee, in De Sacy's Chrest. Arabe, sec. ed. vol. iii. p. 35 of the Arabic text.) Sometimes they change the ى into ا: a poet says,

* وَقَدْ زَعَمُوا أَنِّى جَزِعْتُ عَلَيْهِمَا *
* وَهَلْ جَزَعٌ أَنْ قُلْتُ وَا بِأَبَا هُمَا *

[*And they have asserted that I have become impatient on account of them two: but is it* an evidence of *impatience that I said, Alas, with my father may they two be ransomed?*]; meaning وَا بِأَبِى هُمَا. (Ṣ.) And some of the Arabs used to say, وَا بِأَبَا أَنْتَ [*Alas, with my father mayest thou be ransomed!*]: this, says AM, being like يَا وَيْلَتَا for يَا وَيْلَتِى; as also يَا بِيَبَا, with the hemzeh changed into ى, originally يَا بِأَبَا, meaning يَا بِأَبِى: and hence what is related, in a trad., of Umm-'Aṭeeyeh; that she used not to mention the Prophet without saying, بِيَبَا [for بِأَبِى هُوَ]. (TA in art. بأ.) A woman said,

* يَا بِأَبِى أَنْتَ وَيَا فَوْقَ البِيَبْ *

[O thou to whom I would say, *With my father mayest thou be ransomed! and O* thou who art *above* him to whom I would address *the saying, With my father mayest thou be ransomed!*]; respecting which Fr observes that the two words [ب and أَب] are made as one [by prefixing the article] because of their frequent occurrence; (Ṣ;) and Aboo-'Alee says that the ى in بِيَب is substituted for ء, not necessarily; but ISk quotes the words as commencing with يَا بِيَبَا, which is the right reading, in order that this expression may agree with البِيَب, which is derived from it: Et-Tebreezee, however, relates Abu-l-'Alà's reciting the words as ending with البِئَبْ; saying that this is compounded from the phrase بِأَبِى, and that therefore the ء is preserved. (TA.) [See also the first paragraph in art. بأ.] — You say also, يَا أَبَتِ [meaning *O my father*], (Ṣ, M, Ḳ,) as in يَا أَبَتِ افْعَلْ [*O my father, do thou* such a thing]; (Ṣ;) and يَا أَبَتَ; (Ṣ, M, Ḳ;) and يَا أَبَتُ; (Z in the Ksh xii. 4;) and يَا أَبَهْ (Ṣ, M, Ḳ) when you pause after it. (Ṣ, M.) The ة, [here written ت,] (Kh, M,) the sign of the fem. gender, (Ṣ, Z,) is substituted for the [pronominal] affix ى, (Kh, Ṣ, M, Z,) as in يَا أُمَّتِ; (Ṣ;) and is like the ة in عَمَّة and خَالَة, as is shown by your saying, in pausing, يَا أَبَهْ, like as you say, يَا خَالَهْ: (Kh, M:) the annexing of the fem. ت to a masc. noun in this case is allowable, like as it is in حَمَامَةٌ ذَكَرٌ and شَاةٌ ذَكَرٌ and رَجُلٌ رَبْعَةٌ and غُلَامٌ يَفَعَةٌ: its being made a substitute for the affix ى is allowable because each of these is an augmentative added at the end of a noun: and the kesreh is the same that is in the phrase يَا أَبِى: (Z ubi suprà:) the ت does not fall from اب in the phrase يَا أَبَتِ when there is no pause after it, though it [sometimes] does from أُمّ in the like phrase in that case, because the former word, being of [only] two letters, is as though it were defective. (Ṣ.) يَا أَبَتَ is for يَا أَبَتَاهُ, (Aboo-'Othmán El-Mázinee, Ṣ,* M, [the latter expression mentioned also in the Ḳ, but not as being the original of the former,]) the ا [and ه] being suppressed; (the same Aboo-'Othmán and M;) or for يَا أَبَتَا, the ا being suppressed, like as the ى is in يَا غُلَامِ; or it may be after the manner of يَا أَبِى. (Z ubi suprà.) يَا أَبَتُ is thus pronounced after the usual manner of a noun ending with the fem. ة, without regard to the fact that the ت is in the former a substitute for the suffix ى. (Z ubi suprà.) يَا أَبَهْ is said in a case of pause, except in the Ḳur-án, in which, in this case, you say, يَا أَبَتْ, following the written text; and some of the Arabs pronounce the fem. ة, in a case of pause, ت [in other instances], thus saying, يَا طَلْحَتْ. (Ṣ.) يَا أَبَاهْ is also said; (M, Ḳ;) though scarcely ever. (M.) A poet uses the expression يَا أَبَاتَ, for يَا أَبَتَاهُ: (Ṣ, M:) IB says that this is used only by poetic license, in a case of necessity in verse. (TA.) — أَبٌ is tropically applied to signify ‡ *A grandfather,* or *any ancestor.* (Mṣb.) — It is also applied to signify † *A paternal uncle;* as in the Ḳur ii. 127, quoted before. (M.) — [It is also (like أُمّ and اِبْن and بِنْت) prefixed to nouns of various significations. Most of the compounds thus formed will be found explained in the arts. to which belong the nouns that occupy the second place. The following are among the more common, and are therefore here mentioned, as exs. of different kinds.] — أَبُو المَرْأَةِ † *The woman's husband:* (Ibn-Ḥabeeb, M:) it is said in the TṢ that الأَبُ, in certain of the dials., signifies *the husband:* MF deems this meaning strange. (TA.) أَبُو المَثْوَى † *The master of the dwelling,* or *of the place of abode:* (TA:) and † *the guest.* (Ḳ in art. ثوى.) أَبُو الأَضْيَافِ † *The very hospitable man.* (TA.) — أَبُو الحَارِثِ † *The lion.* (TA.) أَبُو جَعْدَةَ † *The wolf.* (TA.) أَبُو الحُصَيْنِ † *The fox.* (TA.) — أَبُو جَابِرٍ † *Bread.* (Ṣ and Ḳ in art. جبر.) — أَبُو مَالِكٍ † *Extreme old age:* (TA:) and † *hunger.* (MF in art. جبر.)

أَبًا: see أَبٌ.

إِبْوَآءٌ or أُبْوَآءٌ: see أُبُوَّةٌ.

أُبُوِّىٌّ *Of, or relating or belonging to, a father; paternal.* (Ṣ, TA.)

أُبَىٌّ dim. of أَبٌ, q. v. (Mṣb.)

أُبُوَّةٌ [in copies of the Ḳ ♦ إِبْوَاءٌ, and in the CḲ ♦ أَبْوَاءٌ, both app. mistranscriptions for أُبُوَّةٌ, which is well known,] *Fathership; paternity;* the *relation of a father.* (Ṣ,* M.) You say, بَيْنِى وَبَيْنَ فُلَانٍ أُبُوَّةٌ [*Between me and such a one is a tie of fathership*]. (Ṣ.)

ابى

1. أَبَى, aor. يَأْبَى, (Ṣ, M, Mṣb, Ḳ,) which is anomalous, (Ṣ, M, Mṣb,) because it has no faucial letter (Ṣ, Mṣb) for its second or third radical, (Mṣb,) and يَأْبِى, (M, Mṣb, Ḳ,) mentioned by IJ as sometimes said, (M,) agreeably with analogy, (TA,) and يِئْبَى, which is doubly anomalous, first because the pret. is of the measure فَعَلَ, and this pronunciation of the ى of the aor. is [regularly allowable only] in the case of a verb of the measure فَعِلَ, aor. يَفْعَلُ, and secondly because it is only in an aor. like يِيجَلُ, (Sb, M,) i. e., of a verb of which the first radical letter is و or ى, (TA in art. وجل,) and يِئْبِى, (IB, [who cites as an ex. a verse ending with the phrase حَتَّى تِئْبِيَهْ,]) inf. n. إِبَآءٌ (Ṣ, M, Mgh, Mṣb, Ḳ) and إِبَآءَةٌ, (Ḳ,) or إِبَاةٌ, (so in a copy of the M,) or إِبَايَةٌ, (so in the Mṣb,) *He refused;* or *refrained, forbore, abstained,* or *held back;* syn. اِمْتَنَعَ; (Ṣ, Mṣb, MF, Bḍ in ii. 32, Kull p. 8,) *voluntarily,* or *of his own free will* or *choice:* (Bḍ ubi suprà, Kull:) [thus when used intransitively: and it is also used transitively:] you say, أَبَى الأَمْرَ *he refused assent,* or *consent, to the thing,* or *affair; disagreed to it;* and *did not desire* [*to do*] *it:* (Mṭr in Ḥar p. 483:) *he did not assent to, consent to, approve,* or *choose, it; he disallowed it; rejected it:* (Mgh:) and أَبَى الشَّىْءَ *he disliked, was displeased with, disapproved of,* or *hated, the thing.* (M, Ḳ.) Fr says that there is no verb with fet-ḥ to its medial radical letter in the pret. and fut. [or aor.] unless its second or third radical is a faucial letter, except أَبَى: that AA adds رَكَنَ: but that one says رَكَنَ with يَرْكُنُ for its fut., and رَكِنَ with يَرْكَنُ for its fut.: (T:) so that the instance mentioned by AA is one of an intermixture of two dial. vars.: (TA:) Th adds قَلَى and غَسَا and شَجَا; and Mbr adds جَبَا: but most of the Arabs say يَقْلِى and يَشْجُو and يَغْسُو and يَجْبِى. (T.) [Some other instances are mentioned by other authors; but these are verbs of which the aors. are rarely with fet-ḥ, or are instances of the intermixture of two dial. vars.] أَبَيْتَ اللَّعْنَ is a greeting which was addressed to kings in the time of ignorance; meaning *Mayest thou refuse,* or *dislike,* (ISk,* Ṣ,* M,* Ḥar p. 491,) to do a thing that would occasion thy *being cursed!* (ISk, Ṣ, M;) or, to do that for which thou wouldst deserve *the being cursed!* for it implies the meaning of a prayer; i. e., may God make thee to be of those who dislike the being cursed! and hence it occurs parenthetically. (Ḥar ubi suprà.) You say also, أَبَى أَنْ يُضَامَ [*He refused,* or *did not submit, to be harmed,* or *injured*]. (T.) [And sometimes لَا is inserted after أَنْ, and is either redundant, or corroborative of the meaning of the verb, as in the case of أَنْ لَا or أَلَّا after مَنَعَ.] It is said in the Ḳur ix. 32, وَيَأْبَى اللّٰهُ إِلَّا أَنْ يُتِمَّ نُورَهُ, meaning *But God will not consent* or *choose* [*save to complete,* or *perfect, his light*]. (Bḍ.) And in the same xvii. 91, فَأَبَى أَكْثَرُ النَّاسِ إِلَّا كُفُورًا, i. e. [*But the greater number of men have not consented to,* or *chosen,* aught] *save denying* [its truth, or *disbelieving* it]; this phrase with إِلَّا being allowable because it is rendered by means of a negative. (Bḍ.) You also say, كَانَ يَأْبَى اللَّحْمَ [*He used to refuse,* or *dislike, flesh-meat*], (Ḳ,) or أَكْلَ اللَّحْمِ [*the eating of flesh-meat*]. (Mgh.) And أَبَى فُلَانٌ المَآءَ [*Such a one refused,* or *disliked, water,* or *the water*]: (Ṣ:) or أَبَى مِنْ شُرْبِ المَآءِ [*he refused,* or *voluntarily refrained from, the drinking of water,* or *the water*]. (AAF, M.) And أَبَى عَلَيْهِ الأَمْرَ, (Mgh, and Mṭr [author of the Mgh] in Ḥar p. 483,) and ♦ تَأَبَّاهُ عَلَيْهِ, both signify *He refused him his assent,* or *consent, to the thing,* or *affair.* (Mṭr ubi suprà, in Ḥar.) Hence, (Mṭr ubi suprà,) أَبَى عَلَيْهِ, (Mgh, and Mṭr ubi suprà,) and ♦ تَأَبَّى عَلَيْهِ, (T, Ṣ, and Mṭr ubi suprà,) *He was incompliant,* or *unyielding, to him; he resisted him, withstood him,* or *repugned him;* syn. اِمْتَنَعَ (T, Ṣ, Mgh, and Mṭr ubi suprà) عَلَيْهِ: (T:) thus explained because the objective complement (الأَمْرَ) is suppressed. (Mṭr ubi suprà.) —— أَبِيتُ الطَّعَامَ, (Ḳ,) or مِنَ الطَّعَامِ, and اللَّبَنَ, (M, TA, [in a copy of the former of which the verb is written أَبَيْتُ, but this I suppose to be a mistranscription, on account of what here follows,]) like رَضِيتُ, (Ḳ,) inf. n. أَبًى, (M, and so in some copies of the Ḳ,) or إِبًى, (so in some copies of the Ḳ,) with kesr, and with the short final alif, (TA, [i. e. like رِضًى, but perhaps this may have been supposed to be the right reading only because the verb is likened to رَضِيتُ, of which رِضًى is the most common inf. n.,]) *I left,* or *relinquished, the food,* (M, Ḳ,) and *the milk,* (M, TA,) *without being satiated,* or *satisfied.* (M, Ḳ.) —— أَبِىَ الفَصِيلُ, and أُبِىَ, inf. n. أَبًى, *The young camel,* or *young weaned camel, suffered indigestion from the milk, and became affected with a dislike of food.* (M, Ḳ.) —— أَبَيْتُ as syn. with أَبَوْتُ: see the latter.

4. آبَيْتُهُ إِيَّاهُ [in the CḲ, erroneously, أَبَيْتُهُ] *I made him to refuse it; or to refrain, forbear, abstain,* or *hold back, from it, voluntarily,* or *of his own free will* or *choice:* (Ṣ: [this meaning being there implied, though not expressed:]) or *I made him to dislike it, to be displeased with it, to disapprove of it,* or *to hate it:* (M, Ḳ:) namely, water [&c.]. (Ṣ, M.) One says, فُلَانٌ بَحْرٌ لَا يُؤْبَى, (ISk, Ṣ, Ḳ,* [in the CḲ, erroneously, لا يُوبى,]) i. e., لَا يَجْعَلُكَ تَأْبَاهُ [*Such a one is like a sea,* or *great river, that will not make thee to refuse it,* or *dislike it,* &c.]; (Ḳ;) i. e., *that will not fail,* or *come to an end,* (ISk, Ṣ, Ḳ,) *by reason of its abundance.* (ISk, Ṣ.) In like manner one says, of any water, مَآءٌ لَا يُؤْبَى [*Water that will not fail,* or *come to an end*]. (TA.) And عِنْدَنَا مَآءٌ مَا يُؤْبَى *With us,* or *at our abode, is water that does not become scanty,* or *little in quantity.* (Lḥ, T, M.) And آبَى المَآءُ *The water decreased,* or *became deficient.* (AA, from El-Mufaḍḍal.) And قَلِيبٌ لَا يُؤْبَى *A well that will not become exhausted:* (IAạr, M:) one should not say, يُوبَى. (M, TA.) In like manner, also, one says, كَلَأٌ لَا يُؤْبَى *Herbage,* or *pasture, that will not fail,* or *come to an end.* (Ṣ.) And عِنْدَهُ دَرَاهِمُ لَا تُؤْبَى *He has dirhems,* or *money, that will not fail,* or *come to an end.* (TA.) And آبَى المَآءُ signifies also *The water* [in a well] *was,* or *became, difficult of access* (اِمْتَنَعَ), *so that no one was able to descend to it but by exposing himself to peril* or *destruction:* (M:) if a drawer of water descend into the well, (T, TA,) and the water be altered for the worse in odour, (TA,) he exposes himself to peril, or destruction. (T, TA.)

5. تَأَبَّى عَلَيْهِ الأَمْرَ: and تَأَبَّى عَلَيْهِ alone: see 1, latter half of the paragraph.

إِبْيَةٌ *A paucity,* or *deficiency, and revulsion, of the milk in the breast:* (Fr, TṢ:) or *a revulsion of the milk in the udder;* (Ḳ;) but the saying "in the udder" requires consideration. (TA:) You say to a woman, when she has a fever on the occasion of childbirth, إِنَّمَا هٰذِهِ الحُمَّى إِبْيَةُ ثَدْيِكِ [*This fever is only* occasioned by *the paucity,* or *deficiency, and revulsion, of the milk in thy breast.*] (TA.)

أَبْيَانٌ and أُبْيَانٌ and أُبَيَانٌ: see آبٍ, in four places.

أُبَآءٌ, (T, Ṣ, M,) or أُبَآءٌ مِنَ الطَّعَامِ, (Ḳ,) *A dislike,* or *loathing, of food:* (T, Ṣ, M, Ḳ:) of the measure فُعَالٌ, (Ṣ, M,) with ḍamm, (Ṣ, Ḳ,) because it is like a disease, and nouns significant of diseases are generally of that measure. (M.) You say, أَخَذَهُ أُبَآءٌ (T, Ṣ, M, Ḳ) مِنَ الطَّعَامِ (Ḳ) *He was,* or *became, taken,* or *affected, with a dislike,* or *loathing, of food.* (T, Ṣ, M, Ḳ.)

إِبَآءٌ inf. n. of أَبَى, q. v. (Ṣ, M, &c.) —— See also أُبِيَّةٌ.

أَبِىٌّ and أَبِيَّةٌ: see آبٍ, in three places. —— Also, the former (أَبِىٌّ), She [app. a camel, or any beast,] *that refuses,* or *refrains from, fodder, by reason of her suffering from indigestion:* and she *that refuses,* or *refrains from, the stallion, by reason of her having little appetency.* (AA.) [See also أَوَابٍ, voce آبٍ.]

أَبَّآءٌ A man *who refuses,* or *does not submit,* to *be harmed,* or *injured.* (T.)

أُبِيَّةٌ, with ḍamm, (Ḳ,) and kesr to the ب, and with teshdeed of this letter and of the ى, (TA,) [in the CḲ أَبِيَّةٌ,] *Pride; self-magnification,* or *greatness,* or *majesty:* (Ḳ:) and ♦ إِبَآءٌ [also] signifies *pride, self-magnification,* or *haughtiness.* (Ḥam p. 118.)

آبٍ, and ♦ أَبِىٌّ, (Ṣ, M, Mṣb, Ḳ, TA,) and ♦ أَبْيَانٌ,

(Ṣ, TA,) part. ns. of أَبَى, signifying *Refusing*; or *refraining, forbearing, abstaining,* or *holding back* [*voluntarily*, or *of his own free will* or *choice*]: (Ṣ, Mṣb, TA:*) [*refusing assent* or *consent*; &c.:] *disliking, being displeased* with a thing, *disapproving* of it, or *hating* it: (M,* Ḳ,* TA:) or the first and second, a man *disliking*, or *loathing, food*: (M, Ḳ, TA:) and the third, (Ḳ,) and ↓ أَبْيَانٌ, (so in a copy of the M,) or أَبَيَانٌ, (Ḳ,) a man *who refuses*, or *refrains from*, or *dislikes*, or *hates*, (يَأْبَى,) *food*; or, *things that are base* or *mean*, (M, Ḳ, TA,) *and causes of dispraise* or *blame*: (TA:) or the second (أَبِىٌّ), a man *who refuses*, or *refrains*, &c., *vehemently*, or *much*; *incompliant, unyielding, resisting, withstanding*, or *repugning*: (T:) and ↓ أَبْيَانٌ and أَبَيَانٌ, a man *having vehement* اباء [app. أُبَآء, i. e. *dislike*, or *loathing, of food*; agreeably with a common quality of words of the measure فَعَلَان]: (T, TA: [but in copy of the T, accord. to the TT, اباء in this last explanation is written إِبَآء: in the TA it is without any vowel-sign:]) the pl. of آبٍ is آبُونَ and أُبَاةٌ (M, Ḳ) and أُبِىٌّ, (Ḳ,) with ḍamm, then kesr, and then teshdeed, (TA, [in the CḲ أَبِىّ, and in a copy of the M أُبِين,]) and أُبَّآءٌ, (M, TA,) or إِبَآءٌ, (Ḳ, TA,) like رِجَالٌ: (TA: [in the CḲ أَبَاء:]) the pl. of ↓ أَبِىٌّ is أَبِيُّونَ; (M, Ḳ;) of which an instance occurs wherein the pl. ن is likened to a radical ن; the gen. case being written, at the end of a verse, أَبِيِّينِ: (M:) the pl. of ↓ أَبْيَانٌ, (M,) or أَبَيَانٌ, (Ḳ,) is إِبْيَانٌ. (Kr, M, Ḳ.) — [Hence,] الآبِى *The lion*. (Ḳ.) — And آبِيَةٌ, (M,) so in some copies of the Ḳ, but in others ↓ أَبِيَّةٌ, (TA,) She [app. a camel] *that dislikes*, or *loathes, and will not drink, water*: and she *that desires not the evening-food*: and she (a camel) *that is covered and does not conceive*, or *become pregnant*: (M, Ḳ:) and أَوَابٍ, [its pl.,] she-camels *that refuse*, or *refrain from, the stallion*. (TA. [See also أَبِىٌّ.]) It is said in a prov., العَاشِيَةُ تَهِيجُ الآبِيَةَ [*She that is eating her evening-food*, or *pasturing in the evening, excites her that has no desire for that food*]; i. e., when the camels that desire not the evening-food see the camels eating that food, they follow them, and pasture with them. (M, and so in the Ṣ in art. عشو.)

مُؤْبٍ [act. part. n. of 4, q. v.] Water *failing*, or *coming to an end*: (TA:) or water that is *scanty*, or *little in quantity*.] (Lḥ, M, TA.)

مَآءٌ مَأْبَاةٌ, (M,) or مَآءَةٌ مَأْبَاةٌ, (Ḳ,) *Water which the camels refuse*, or *dislike*. (M, Ḳ.)

اتب

2. أَتَّبَهَا إِتْبًا, (M, Ḳ, [but in the latter the pronoun is masc.,]) and بِإِتْبٍ, (M,) or simply أَتَّبها, (Ṣ,) inf. n. تَأْتِيبٌ, (Ṣ, Ḳ,) *He put on her*, or *clad her with, an* إِتْب: (Ṣ, M, Ḳ:) or أَتَّبها signifies *he put on her*, or *clad her with, a shift*. (AZ, T.) — أُتِّبَ, (M, Ḳ,) inf. n. as above, (Ḳ,) *It* (a garment, or piece of cloth,) *was made into an* إِتْب. (M, Ḳ.)

5. تَأَتَّبَ بِإِتْبٍ, (M, Ḳ,) and ↓ ائتتب, [written with the disjunctive alif إِيتَتَبَ], (M,) or ↓ ائتب, (Ḳ, [but this I think a mistranscription,]) *He put on himself*, or *clad himself with, an* إِتْب: (M, Ḳ:) or ↓ ائتتبت, alone, *she put on herself*, or *clad herself with, an* إِتْب. (AZ, T, Ṣ, M.) — تَأَتَّبَ الدِّرْعَ وَالسِّلَاحَ † *He put on* (i. e. on himself) *the coat of mail, and the arms*, or *weapons*. (A.) And تَأَتَّبَ القَوْسَ † *He put forth his shoulder-joints from the belt of the bow*, [*the belt being across his breast*,] *so that the bow was on his shoulder-blades*: (A:) accord. to AḤn, (M,) تَأَتُّبٌ signifies † a man's *putting the suspensory of the bow across the breast, and putting forth the shoulder-joints from it*, (M, Ḳ,) *so that the bow is on the shoulder-joints*: (M:) and you say also, تَأَتَّبَ قَوْسَهُ عَلَى ظَهْرِهِ † [*he put his bow in the manner above described upon his back*]. (Ṣ.) — [And hence,] تأتّب signifies also † *He prepared himself*, or *made himself ready*, (Ḳ,) لِلْأَمْرِ [*for the affair*]. (TḲ.) — And † *He acted*, or *behaved, with forced hardness, firmness, strength, hardiness, courage*, or *vehemence*. (Ḳ.)

8: see 5, in two places.

9: see 5.

إِتْبٌ (T, Ṣ, M, A, Ḳ) and ↓ مِئْتَبَةٌ (M, Ḳ) *A* بَقِير (Ṣ,) or بَقِيرَة, (M, Ḳ,) i. e., (Ṣ, M, [but in the Ḳ what here follows is given as a meaning distinct from that of بقيرة,]) *a* بُرْد [q. v.], (Ṣ, M, Ḳ,) or *piece of cloth*, (Ṣ, A,) *which is slit* (Ṣ, M, A, Ḳ) *in the middle*, (Ṣ,) *and worn by a woman*, (A, Ḳ,) *who throws it upon her neck*, (Ṣ, M,) [*putting her head through the slit*;] *having neither an opening at the bosom* (a جَيْب), *nor sleeves*: (Ṣ, M, A, Ḳ:) and *a woman's shift*: (T, M, Ḳ:) and, (Ḳ,) or accord. to some, (M,) *a garment that is short, reaching half-way down the shank*: (M, Ḳ:) or [*a garment like*] *drawers*, or *trousers, without legs*; (M, Ḳ;) *i. q.* نُقْبَةٌ: (M:) or *a shirt without sleeves*, (Ṣ voce بَقِير, M, Ḳ,) *worn by women*: (Ṣ ubi suprà:) the first explanation alone is given in most lexicons: (TA:) some say that *it is different from the* إِزَار; that it *has no band like that of drawers* or *trousers, and is not sewed together after the manner of drawers* or *trousers, but is a shirt of which the two sides are not sewed together*: (M:) or *i. q.* عِلْقَةٌ and صِدَارٌ and شَوْذَرٌ; all signifying one and the same thing: (T:) pl. [of pauc.] آتُبٌ (M, Ḳ [in the CḲ and a MS. copy of the Ḳ written أَتَابٌ]) [originally أَأْتُبٌ which is mentioned as one of the pls. by MF] and آتُبٌ [originally أَأْتُبٌ which is also mentioned as one of the pls. by MF] and by transposition أَتْؤُبٌ, (MF,) and [of mult.] أُتُوبٌ, (Ṣ,) or إِتَابٌ, (M,) or both. (Ḳ.) — [Hence,] إِتْبٌ also signifies † The *husk* of barley. (M, Ḳ.)

مِئْتَبٌ *A* [*wrapper*, or *wrapping garment, such as is called*] مِشْمَل. (T.)

مِئْتَبَةٌ: see إِتْبٌ.

مُؤَتَّبُ الظُّفُرِ † A man *whose nail is crooked*. (Ḳ.)

اتم

1. أَتْمٌ, (M, Ḳ,) in, or in relation to, a سِقَآء [or skin for water or milk], (TA,) signifies The *having two punctures of a seam* (خُرْزَتَانِ) *rent so as to become one*. (M, Ḳ.) You say, أَتَمَتِ القِرْبَةُ, aor. ِ, inf. n. أَتْمٌ, *The water-skin had its two punctures* (خرزتاها) [or rather *two of its punctures*, agreeably with the explanation of the inf. n. in the M and Ḳ, as given above,]) *rent so that they became one*. (TḲ.) — [And hence,] The *meeting together of the* مَسْلَكَانِ [or *vagina and rectum*]: whence أَتُومٌ [q. v.] as an epithet applied to a woman. (Ḥam p. 373.) — [It seems to be indicated in the T, that one says, أَتَمَ النِّسَآءُ, aor. ِ, and أَتَمَ, aor. ُ; as meaning, or perhaps the former only, *The women assembled*, or *came together*: for I there find, immediately after مَأْتَمٌ as signifying "a place in which women assemble," "one says, أَتَمَ, aor. ِ, and أَتَمَ, aor. ُ:" but it is then added that, accord. to Khálid Ibn-Yezeed, مأتم is from أَتَمَ, aor. ِ.] — *I. q.* فَتْقٌ [The act of *rending, rending asunder, ripping*, or *the like*; or *undoing the sewing* of a thing]. (TA.) — The act of *cutting*. (Ṣgh, Ḳ.) You say, أَتَمَهُ *He cut it*. (TḲ.) — أَتَمَ, aor. ِ, also signifies *He brought together*, or *united*, two things. (T.) [See أَتُومٌ, and مَأْتَمٌ.] — أَتَمَ بِالمَكَانِ, (Ṣgh, Mṣb,) with two forms of aor., [app. ِ and ُ,] (Mṣb,) inf. n. أُتُومٌ, (Ṣgh, Ḳ,) or أُتُومٌ; (Mṣb;) and أَتِمَ, aor. َ; (Mṣb;) *He stayed, remained, dwelt*, or *abode, in the place*. (Ṣgh, Mṣb, Ḳ.)

2: see 4.

4. آتَمَهَا, inf. n. إِيتَامٌ; and ↓ أَتَّمَهَا, inf. n. تَأْتِيمٌ; *He rendered her such as is termed* أَتُوم, q. v. (O, Ḳ.)

أَتُومٌ is primarily used in relation to the سِقَآء [or skin for water or milk; as meaning] *Having two punctures of a seam* (خُرْزَتَانِ) *rent so that they become one*. (Ṣ.) — And hence, (Ṣ,) or from أَتَمَ as meaning "he brought together, or united," two things, (T,) A woman *whose* مَسْلَكَانِ [or *vagina and rectum*] *meet together in one*, [*by the rupture of the part between them*,] (T, M,) *becoming conjoined, so that the* فَرْج *is enlarged thereby*, (TA,) *on the occasion of devirgination*; (M;) *i. q.* مُفْضَاةٌ, (T, Ṣ, M,) as some say; (T;) or مُفَاضَةٌ; (Ḳ; [said in the TA to be a mistake: but مُفْضَاةٌ and مُفَاضَةٌ are said in the M, in art. فيض, to have the same signification;]) a woman *whose* مَسْلَكَانِ *have become one*: (Ḥam p. 271:) or, as some say, *small in the* فَرْج [or *vagina*]: (M:) or it has these two contr. significations. (Ḳ.)

مَأْتَمٌ is a quasi-inf. n. of أَتَمَ in the last of the senses explained above. (Mṣb.) [Thus it signifies *A staying, remaining, dwelling*, or *abiding*, in a place. But it more commonly signifies] The *assembling* of women [and of men also] *in a case of rejoicing* and *of mourning*. (Ḥar p. 234.) —

It is also a noun of time from the same. (Msb.) [Thus it signifies *A time of staying* or *remaining*, &c.] — And it is also a noun of place from the same. (Msb.) [And thus it signifies *A place of staying* or *remaining*, &c. But it more commonly signifies] *A place of assembling* of women [and of men also] *in a case of rejoicing* and *of mourning*: from أَتَمَ, aor. ـِ , accord. to Khálid Ibn-Yezeed. (T.) — And hence, tropically, (Msb,) ‡ *Women assembling together* (T, Ṣ, M, Mgh, Msb, Ḳ) *in a case of rejoicing* and *of mourning*, (T, M, Mgh, Ḳ,) or *in a case of good* and *of evil*: (Ṣ, Msb:) or *any assembly*, (M, Ḳ,) *of men* and *of women*, (M,) *in a case of mourning* or *of rejoicing*: (M, Ḳ:) or particularly *of young women*; (M, Ḳ,) accord. to some; but it is not so: and some assert that the word is derived from أَتْمٌ, in the first of the senses explained in this art.; and from أَتُومٌ, as an epithet applied to a woman; because it signifies *women coming together, and meeting face to face, in a case of good* and *of evil*: (M:) the pl. is مَآتِمُ. (Ṣ, Mgh.) Abu-l-'Aṭà Es-Sindee says,

* عَشِيَّةَ قَامَ النَّائِحَاتُ وَشُقِّقَتْ *
* جُيُوبٌ بِأَيْدِى مَأْتَمٍ وَخُدُودُ *

[*In the evening when arose the wailing women* to wail, *and openings at the necks and bosoms* of garments *were rent with the hands of assembled* mourning *women, and cheeks* also were lacerated]: (Ṣ, M, Mgh:) i. e., بِأَيْدِى نِسَآءٍ. (Ṣ.) And another says,

* حَتَّى تَرَاهُنَّ لَدَيْهِ قُيَّمَا *
* كَمَا تَرَى حَوْلَ الأَمِيرِ المَأْتَمَا *

[*So that thou seest them* (referring to women) *standing in his presence*, or *at*, or *by, it, like as thou seest the assembly of men around the prince*, or *commander*]: المأتم here necessarily denoting men. (M.) — IKt says, (Msb,) it is used by the vulgar to denote *An affliction*, or *evil accident*; (Ṣ, Mgh, Msb;) [and Mtr adds,] and *a wailing*: (Mgh:) they say, كُنَّا فِى مَأْتَمِ فُلَانٍ [meaning *We were present at the affliction of such a one*]: (Ṣ, Msb:) or كُنَّا فِى مَأْتَمِ بَنِى فُلَانٍ [meaning *We were present at the affliction*, and *wailing, of the sons of such a one*]: (Mgh:) but the correct word in this case, (Ṣ, Mgh,) or the better, (Msb,) is مَنَاحَةٌ: (Ṣ, Mgh, Msb:) so says IAmb. (Mgh.) But accord. to IB, nothing forbids that it may occur in the sense of *A place of wailing*; and in the sense of *mourning*, and *wailing*, and *weeping*; for therefore do women assemble: and thus it may be in the saying of Et-Teymee, respecting Manṣoor Ibn-Ziyád,

* وَالنَّاسُ مَأْتَمُهُمْ عَلَيْهِ وَاحِدٌ *
* فِى كُلِّ دَارٍ رَنَّةٌ وَزَفِيرُ *

[*The people's mourning*, &c., *for him was one: in every house was a moaning, and a sighing*]: and in the saying of another,

* أَضْحَى بَنَاتُ النَّبِىِّ إِذْ قُتِلُوا *
* فِى مَأْتَمٍ وَالسِّبَاعُ فِى عُرُسٍ *

i. e. [*The daughters of the captives, when they were slain, became, in the early part of the day*,] *in a state of mourning; and the beasts of prey, in a state of rejoicing*. (TA.)

اتن

1. أَتَنَ بِالمَكَانِ, (Ṣ, M, Msb, Ḳ,*) aor. ـِ , (Msb,) or ـُ , (Ḳ,) inf. n. أُتُونٌ (M, Msb, Ḳ) and أَتْنٌ, (Ḳ,) *He remained, continued, stayed*, or *abode, in the place*; (Ṣ, M, Msb, Ḳ;*) or *became fixed*, or *settled, therein*. (M.)

10. استأتن [lit.] *He* (an ass) *became a she-ass*. (M.) The saying, كَانَ حِمَارًا فَٱسْتَأْتَنَ, said of a man, [lit.] signifies [*He was a he ass*,] *and he became a she ass*; meaning † *he was mighty*, or *of high condition*, [like the wild he-ass,] *and he became base, abject*, or *vile*. (Ṣ, TA.) — Also, (Ṣ, TA,) or استأتن أَتَانًا, (M,) *He* (a man) *purchased a she-ass*; (Ṣ;) *he took for himself a she-ass*. (Ṣ, M.)

أَتَانٌ (T, Ṣ, M, Msb, Ḳ) and ↓ إِتَانٌ, (Ḳ,) but one should not say أَتَانَةٌ, (ISk, Ṣ, Msb,) or this is of rare occurrence, (Ḳ,) occurring in certain of the trads., (IAth,) *A she-ass* [*domestic* or *wild*]: (Ṣ, M, Msb, Ḳ:) pl. (of pauc., T, Ṣ, Msb) آتُنٌ and (of mult., T, Ṣ, Msb) أُتُنٌ (T, Ṣ, M, Msb, Ḳ) and أُتْنٌ and (quasi-pl. n., M) ↓ مَأْتُونَآءُ. (Ṣ, M, Ḳ.) — Hence, أَتَانٌ signifies ‡ *A foolish and soft* or *weak woman*; as being likened to a she-ass. (TA.) — Also The *station of the drawer of water at the mouth of the well*; (Ṣ, M, Ḳ;) and so ↓ إِتَانٌ. (M, Ḳ.) And *A rock*, or *great mass of stone*, (AA, T, Ṣ, M,) *in water*; (AA, T, M;) or, as some say, *at the bottom of the casing of a well, so that it is next the water*. (AA, T.) And *A large, round mass of rock, which, when it is in shallow water, is called* أَتَانُ الضَّحْلِ; and a she camel is likened thereto, in respect of her hardness: (Ṣ:) or أَتَانُ الضَّحْلِ signifies *a large mass of rock projecting from the water*. (T:) or *a mass of rock*, (M, Ḳ, TA,) *large and round, in the water*, (TA,) *at the mouth of the well, overspread with* [*the green substance called*] طُحْلُب, *so that it is smooth*, (M, Ḳ, TA,) *more smooth than other parts*: (M, TA:) or *a mass of rock, part of which is immerged* (غَامِرٌ, M, Ḳ) *in the water*, (Ḳ,) *and part apparent*. (M, Ḳ.) And أَتَانُ الثَّمِيلِ signifies *A large mass of rock in the interior of the water-course, which nothing raises or moves, of the measure of the stature of a man in length and likewise in breadth*. (ISh.) — Also The [*piece of wood called*] قَاعِدَة [*which is one of four forming the support*] *of the* هَوْدَج [more commonly called هَوْدَج, q. v.]: pl. أُتُنٌ, (Ḳ, TA,) with medd. (TA: [but in the CḲ أُتُنٌ.])

إِتَانٌ: see أَتَانٌ, in two places.

أَتُونٌ (T, M, Mgh, Msb, Ḳ) and أَتُّونٌ, (Ḳ,) or, accord. to J, (Msb,) it is thus, with teshdeed, but pronounced without teshdeed by the vulgar, (Ṣ, Msb,) *A certain place in which fire is kindled*, (Ṣ, Mgh,) *called in Persian* كُلْخَن [or كُلْخَنْ], *pertaining to a bath*: and metaphorically applied to: *that in which bricks are baked, and called in Persian* دَاشُوزَنْ *and* تُونَكْ [or simply تُونْ and دَاشْ]: (Mgh:) accord. to Az, (Msb,) it is *that of the bath, and of the place in which gypsum is made*: (T, Msb:) or the *trench, hollow*, or *pit, of the* جَيَّار [or *lime-burner*, (in the CḲ, erroneously, the خَبَّاز,)] and *of the preparer of gypsum*; (M, Ḳ, TA;) and *the like*: (Ḳ:) the pl. [said in the TA to be of the latter, but it is implied in the T and M and Mgh that it is of the former,] is أَتَاتِينُ, (T, Ṣ, M, Mgh, Msb, Ḳ, [in the CḲ, erroneously, أَتَانِينُ,]) by common consent of the Arabs, (Mgh,) with two ت's, (T,) accord. to Fr, who says that they sometimes double a letter in the pl. when they do not double it in the sing., (T,) and accord. to IJ, who says that it seems as though they changed أَتُونٌ to أَتُّونٌ; (M;) and [of أَتُونٌ, as is said in the TA and implied in the M,] أُتُنٌ. (M, Ḳ.) [J says that] it is said to be post-classical; (Ṣ;) [and ISd says,] I do not think it to be Arabic. (M.)

مَأْتُونَآءُ: see أَتَانٌ.

اتو

1. أَتَا, aor. يَأْتُو; (Msb;) and أَتَوْتُهُ, (T, Ṣ, M, Ḳ,) aor. آتُوهُ; (Ṣ;) inf. n. أَتْوٌ, (M, Msb,) or أَتْوَةٌ, (Ṣ,) or the latter is an inf. n. of un.; (T, TA;) *He came*; (Msb;) and *I came to him*, or *it*; (Ṣ;) the former a dial. var. of أَتَى, aor. يَأْتِى; (Msb;) and the latter, of أَتَيْتُهُ. (T, Ṣ, M, Ḳ.) [See art. اتى, to which, as well as to the present art., belong several words mentioned in this.] = أَتَا, aor. as above, (TḲ,) inf. n. أَتْوٌ, (M, Ḳ, TḲ,) also signifies *He pursued a right, direct, straight*, or *even, course*, in going, or pace. (M, Ḳ, TḲ.) — And *He* (a man, TḲ) *hastened, made haste*, or *sped*; or *he was quick, hasty, speedy, rapid, swift*, or *fleet*. (M, Ḳ, TḲ.) — And أَتَتِ النَّاقَةُ, inf. n. as above, *The she-camel returned her fore legs*, [*drawing the feet back towards the body, and lifting them high*,] *in her going*. (M.) You say, مَا أَحْسَنَ أَتْوَ يَدَىْ هٰذِهِ النَّاقَةِ, and أَتَى يَدَيْهَا, *How good*, or *beautiful, is this she-camel's returning of her fore legs in her going!* i. e. رَجْعَ يَدَيْهَا فِى سَيْرِهَا. (T,* Ṣ, M.) — And أَتْوٌ signifies also The act of *impelling*, or *propelling*; particularly, of an arrow from a bow. (TA.) See also this word below. = أَتَوْتُهُ, (Ṣ, M, Msb, Ḳ,) aor. آتُوهُ, (Ṣ, Msb,) inf. n. إِتَاوَةٌ, (Ṣ, M, Msb, Ḳ,) so accord. to A'Obeyd, (M,) and mentioned by Ṣgh on the authority of AZ, (TA,) and أَتْوٌ, (Ṣ, TA,) [*I gave him what is termed* إِتَاوَة, as meaning *the tax called* خَرَاج: this is the signification which seems to be indicated in the Ṣ: or] *I bribed him; gave him a bribe*. (M, Msb, Ḳ.) [See also إِتَاوَةٌ below.] = أَتَتِ النَّخْلَةُ, (T, Ṣ, M, Ḳ,) and الشَّجَرَةُ, (M, Ḳ,) aor. تَأْتُو, (Ṣ,) inf. n. إِتَآءٌ, with kesr, (Kr, M, Ḳ,) [in a copy of the T, and in two copies of the Ṣ, أَتَآءٌ, but this is said in the M to be a subst.,] and أَتْوٌ; (M, Ḳ;) and ↓ أَتَّتِ النخلة, inf. n. إِيتَآءٌ; (T;) *The palm-tree* [and *the tree*]

bore: (Ṣ:) or *put forth its fruit:* or *showed its being in a good state:* (M, Ḳ:) or *bore much:* (T, M, Ḳ:) and اتآء signifies also the *increasing,* or *thriving,* of seed-produce. (T.) — And أَتَتِ المَاشِيَةُ, inf. n. إِتَآءٌ, [in a copy of the M أَتَآءٌ,] *The cattle, or camels &c., increased,* or *yielded increase.* (M, Ḳ. [In the CḲ, immediately before this phrase, وَالثِّمَارِ is erroneously put for وَالنَّمَآءُ.]) ═ تَأَتَّى for تَأَتْوَى: see 1 in art. اوى.

4: see 1, near the end of the paragraph.

أَتْوٌ an inf. n. of 1, q. v. ═ *A way, course, mode,* or *manner.* (M, Ḳ.) You say, of speech, or language, (M,) and of a speaker, or reciter of a خُطْبَة, (IAạr, M,) مَا زَالَ عَلَى أَتْوٍ وَاحِدٍ *It,* and *he, ceased not to follow one* [*uniform*] *way,* &c. (M.) ═ *An impulsion; a propulsion;* particularly *an act of shooting* an arrow from a bow: so in a trad., where it is said, كُنَّا نَرْمِى الأَتْوَ وَالأَتْوَيْنِ *We used to shoot one shooting and two shootings;* meaning, of arrows from bows, after the prayer of sunset. (TA.) ═ *Death:* or [so in the T, but in the Ḳ "and,"] *a trial;* or *an affliction.* (T, Ḳ.) You say, أَتَى عَلَى فُلَانٍ أَتْوٌ *Death came upon such a one:* or *a trial;* or *an affliction.* (ISh, T.) And إِنْ أَتَى عَلَىَّ أَتْوٌ فَغُلَامِى حُرٌّ *If I die,* [or *if death befall me,*] *my slave shall be free.* (T.) — *A vehement sickness* or *disease:* (T, Ḳ:) or the *fracture of an arm,* or *of a leg.* (T.) ═ *A gift.* (Ṣ, Ḳ.) — *Butter;* (Ṣ;) as also ↓أَتَآءٌ, (A,) or ↓إِتَآءٌ. (TA: [in which it is said to be like كِتَابٌ; but this I think a mistake: see أَتَآءٌ below.]) You say, when a skin of milk is agitated, and its butter comes, قَدْ جَآءَ أَتْوُهُ [*Its butter has come*]. (Ṣ, TA.) And you say, لَبَنٌ ذُو اتآءٍ ↓ *Milk having butter.* (A, TA.) ═ *A great body* or *corporeal form* or *person* (شَخْصٌ عَظِيمٌ). (AZ, Ṣgh, Ḳ.)

أَتْوَةٌ *A single coming;* as also أَتْيَةٌ. (T.)

أَتْوَانٌ a corroborative [or imitative sequent] of أَسْوَانٌ, which signifies *grieving, mourning,* or *sorrowful:* (TA:) or *i. q.* حَرِيصٌ [*vehemently desirous; eager;* &c.]. (Mirḳát el-Loghah, cited by Golius.)

أَتَآءٌ, (T, Ṣ, M,) or إِتَآءٌ, like كِتَابٌ, (Ḳ, [but it is said in the M that the former is a subst. and the latter an inf. n.,] *Increase;* syn. نَمَآءٌ, (Ṣ, M, Ḳ, [in the CḲ وَالثِّمَارِ is erroneously put for وَالنَّمَآءُ,]) and بَرَكَةٌ: (Ṣ:) *increase, and produce,* or *net produce,* of land; as though from الإِتَاوَةُ signifying الخَرَاجُ: (TA:) *gain,* or *revenue, arising from the increase of land,* or *from the rent thereof,* or *the like:* (TA, and so in a copy of the Ṣ:) the *produce of land,* and *fruits, &c.:* (Aṣ, T:) *what is produced of the fruits* (آكَالٌ [in the CḲ أُكَالٌ]) *of trees:* (M, Ḳ:) the *fruit of palm-trees.* (Ṣ.) — See also أَتْوٌ, in three places.

أَتِىٌّ (Ṣ, M, Ṣgh, Ḳ) and ↓أُتِىٌّ [respecting which see what follows] and ↓إِتِىٌّ, (Ṣgh, Ḳ,) of all which, the first is said by A'Obeyd to be the form used by the Arabs, (TA,) [and all belong to art. اتى, as well as to the present art.,] and ↓أَتَاوِىٌّ (M, Ṣgh, Ḳ) and ↓إِتَاوِىٌّ and ↓أُتَاوِىٌّ, (Ṣgh, Ḳ,) all these, and the three preceding them, mentioned by Ṣgh on the authority of AA, but the last of all said by him to be strange, (TA,) *A rivulet for which a man makes a way* or *channel,* or *an easy course* or *passage, to his land:* (Ṣ, M, Ḳ:) or a *torrent,* or *flow of water, from another region* or *quarter:* (M, Ḳ: [both these meanings mentioned in the M in art. اتو, and the former in art. اتى also, of that work:]) or أَتِىٌّ signifies *a conduit of water;* and *any channel in which water is made to have an easy course;* as also ↓أُتِىٌّ, mentioned by Sb; or, as some say, this is a pl.: (M:) or *any rivulet:* (Aṣ, T:) or *a rivulet less than the* [*trench called*] نُؤْى: (IB:) and سَيْلٌ أَتِىٌّ (Lḥ, T, Ṣ, M) and ↓أَتَاوِىٌّ, (Lḥ, Ṣ, M,) *a torrent,* or *flow of water, that comes one knows not whence:* (M:) or *that comes when the rain that has produced it has not fallen upon the people to whom it comes:* (Lḥ, Ṣ, M:) or *that comes from a land upon which rain has fallen to a land upon which rain has not fallen.* (T, Mṣb.) — Hence, (T, M,) or the reverse is the case, (T, M, Mṣb,) all the words above, (AA, T, Ḳ,) or أَتِىٌّ and ↓أَتَاوِىٌّ, (Ṣ, M, Mgh, Mṣb, [the last said in the T to be the most approved,]) *A stranger;* or a man *not of one's own people,* or *not of one's own kindred:* (AA, T, Ṣ, M, Mgh:) or a man *who asserts his relation to a people of whom he is not:* (Mṣb:) or أَتِىٌّ signifies *one who is among a people of whom he is not:* (Aṣ, T:) and أَتَاوِىٌّ, *a stranger, who is not in his own country;* or, accord. to Ks, *a stranger, who is not in his own home:* (T:) the pl. of this last is أَتَاوِيُّونَ: (Ṣ:) [the fem. sing. is أَتَاوِيَّةٌ:] and the pl. fem. أَتَاوِيَّاتٌ. (T, Ṣ, M.)

إِتَاوَةٌ *i. q.* خَرَاجٌ [i. e. *A tax, a tribute,* or *an impost*], (T, Ṣ, M, Ḳ,) *such, for instance, as is levied on land,* (TA in the present art.,) and *such as is imposed on a slave;* (TA in art. ضرب;) and *any tax or other exaction that is taken by compulsion,* or *against the will,* or *that is apportioned to a people:* (M: [in the TA "to a place" instead of "to a people:"]) and also, *a bribe:* or, (accord. to some, M,) particularly, *a bribe for water:* (M, Ḳ:) the pl. is أَتَاوَى, (T, M, Ḳ, TA, [but in some copies of the Ḳ أَتَاوِى, and accord. to copies of the Ṣ it is أَتَاوٍ, being written, with the article, الأَتَاوِى; both of which appear to be wrong; for it is said to be] like عَلَاوَى and هَرَاوَى, pls. of عِلَاوَةٌ and هِرَاوَةٌ, (M, TA,) and like سَكَارَى; (TA;) changed, [in the accus. case, with the article prefixed,] at the end of a verse, into الأَتَاوِيَا, for the sake of the rhyme: (M, TA:) this occurs in a verse of El-Jaadee: (Ṣ:) it has also for a pl. إِتَاوَاتٌ, (T,) and أُتًى, [in the CḲ, erroneously, أَتِى,] which is extr., (M, Ḳ,) as though its sing. were أَتْوَةٌ, being like رُشًى, pl. of رُشْوَةٌ, (M,) and like عُرًى, pl. of عُرْوَةٌ. (TA.) You say, أَدَّى إِتَاوَةَ أَرْضِهِ [*He payed the tax of his land*]; i. e. خَرَاجَهَا: and ضُرِبَتْ عَلَيْهِمُ الإِتَاوَةُ [*The tax,* or *tribute,* or *impost, was imposed upon them*]; i. e. الجِبَايَةُ: and some assert it to be tropical. (TA.) You say also, شَكَمَ فَاهُ بِالإِتَاوَةِ [*He stopped* (lit. *bitted*) *his mouth with the bribe*]; i. e. بِالرِّشْوَةِ. (TA.)

أَتَاوِىٌّ and its vars.: see أَتِىٌّ, above.

اتى

1. أَتَى, aor. يَأْتِى, (Mṣb,) and, in the dial. of Hudheyl, يَأْتِ, without ى; (Ṣ;) and أَتَيْتُهُ, (T, Ṣ, M, Mṣb, Ḳ,) [aor. آتِيهِ;] and in the imperative, some of the Arabs say, تِ, suppressing the ا, like as is done in خُذْ and كُلْ and مُرْ; (IJ, M;) inf. n. إِتْيَانٌ, (T, Ṣ,* M, Mgh, Mṣb, Ḳ,) or this is a simple subst., (Mṣb,) and إِتْيَانَةٌ, (M, Ḳ,) which should not be used as an inf. n. of un., unless by a bad poetic licence, (Lth, T,) and أَتْىٌ (T, Ṣ, M, Mṣb, Ḳ) and أُتِىٌّ and إِتِىٌّ and مَأْتَاةٌ; (M, Ḳ;) *He* [or *it*] *came;* (Mṣb;) and *I came to him,* or *it;* (Ṣ, M, Mgh,* Mṣb, Ḳ;) or *was,* or *became, present at it,* namely, a place: (Mgh:) as also أَتَا, aor. يَأْتُو; (Mṣb;) and أَتَوْتُهُ, (T, Ṣ, M, Ḳ), aor. آتُوهُ: (Ṣ:) for which reason, we assign the generality of the words mentioned in art. اتو to the present art. also. (M.) [Accord. to the authorities here indicated for the signification of أَتَى, this verb and جَآءَ are syn.: some attempt to distinguish them; but contradict one another in so doing: the slight distinctions that exist between them will be best seen by a comparison of the exs. in this art. with those in art. جيأ:] accord. to Er-Rághib, the proper [or primary] signification of الإِتْيَانُ is *The coming with ease.* (TA.) — أَتَاهَا, (Mgh, Mṣb,) inf. n. إِتْيَانٌ, (Mṣb,) [lit. *He came to her,*] means † *he lay with her;* syn. جَامَعَهَا; (Mgh, Mṣb;) namely, a woman, (Mgh,) or his wife. (Mṣb.) Hence an expression in the Ḳur xxvi. 165. (TA.) — أَتَى القَوْمَ [*He came to the people:* and hence,] *he asserted his relationship to the people, not being of them.* (Mṣb.) [See أَتِىٌّ in art. اتو.] — أَتَى بِهِ [*He came with,* or *brought, him,* and *it;* or] *he made him* (a man), and *it* (a thing, such, for instance, as property), *to come.* (Kull.) [See also 4: and see, in what follows, other significations of أَتَى trans. by means of بِ. Hence, أَتَى بِوَلَدٍ *He begot a child,* or *children.* And أَتَتْ بِهِ *She brought him forth; gave birth to him.*] Accord. to Aboo-Is-ḥáḳ, the meaning of the words in the Ḳur [ii. 143] أَيْنَمَا تَكُونُوا يَأْتِ بِكُمُ اللّٰهُ جَمِيعًا is, *Wherever ye be, God will bring you all back unto Himself.* (M.) [You say also, أَتَى بِبَيِّنَةٍ *He adduced a proof.*] See also 3. — أَتَى الأَمْرَ [*He entered into, engaged in,* or *occupied himself with, the thing,* or *affair:* and, as also أَتَى بِهِ,] *he did, executed,* or *performed, the thing,* or *affair;* (M, Ḳ;) and in like manner, الذَّنْبَ, [and بِالذَّنْبِ,] *the crime, sin,* or *offence.* (M.) It is said in the Ḳur [ix. 54], وَلَا يَأْتُونَ الصَّلَاةَ إِلَّا وَهُمْ كُسَالَى, meaning *And they do not enter into,* or *engage in, prayer, unless when they are heavy,* or *sluggish.* (TA.) And you say, أَتَى الفَاحِشَةَ, [and بِالفَاحِشَةِ,

(see Ḳur iv. 23 and lxv. 1,)] *He entered into, engaged in, or occupied himself with*, [or *he did, or committed*,] *that which was excessively foul or evil.* (TA.) And أَتَى بِالجَيِّدِ مِنْ قَوْلٍ أَوْ فِعْلٍ [*He said, gave utterance to, uttered, or expressed, or he brought to pass, did, or effected, what was good, or excellent; he said, or did, well, or excellently*]. (Mṣb in art. جود.) And أَتَى بِجَرْيٍ بَعْدَ جَرْيٍ [*He* (a horse) *performed, or fetched, run after run*]. (Ṣ in art. تأم, &c.) — وَلَا يُفْلِحُ السَّاحِرُ حَيْثُ كَانَ أَتَى [in the Ḳur xx. 72] means [*And the enchanter shall not prosper where he is, or wherever he may be*]; (M, Bḍ, Ḳ;) and *where he cometh*: (Bḍ:) or حَيْثُ أَتَى بِسِحْرِهِ [*where he cometh with his enchantment; or where he performeth his enchantment*]: (Jel:) and it is said to mean that where the enchanter is, he must be slain: such is the doctrine of the lawyers. (M.) — Z mentions that أَتَى occurs in the sense of صَارَ [*He, or it, became*; like as we sometimes say, *he, or it, came, or came to be*]; like جَآءَ in the saying, جَآءَ البِنَآءُ مُحْكَمًا. (Kull.) [So you say, أَتَى البِنَآءُ مُحْكَمًا *The building became, or came to be, firm, strong, or compact.*] — The saying, in the Ḳur [xvi. 1], أَتَى أَمْرُ اللّٰهِ فَلَا تَسْتَعْجِلُوهُ, means [*The threatened punishment ordained of God hath approached: therefore desire not ye to hasten it*:] *its coming hath approached.* (TA.) [And in like manner,] أُتِىَ فُلَانٌ, like عُنِىَ, means *Such a one was approached by the enemy come in sight of him.* (Ḳ.) أُتِيتَ يَا فُلَانُ [*Thou art approached &c., O such a one,*] is said when one is warned of an enemy that has come in sight of him. (Ṣgh, TA.) And أَتَى عَلَيْهِمُ العَدُوُّ means *The enemy came to them,* [or *came down upon them*, for, as MF observes, أَتَى when trans. by means of عَلَى seems to imply the meaning of نَزَلَ,] *overcoming*, or *overpowering, them.* (Bḍ in xviii. 40.) — Hence, أَتَى عَلَيْهِ [and أَتَاهُ, as will be seen by what follows,] † *He destroyed him,* or *it.* (Bḍ ubi suprà.) And hence, from إِتْيَانُ العَدُوِّ, (Mgh,) أَتَى عَلَيْهِ الدَّهْرُ ‡ *Time, or fortune, destroyed him.* (M, Mgh, Mṣb, Ḳ.) Destruction is meant in the Ḳur [lix. 2], where it is said, فَأَتَاهُمُ اللّٰهُ مِنْ حَيْثُ لَمْ يَحْتَسِبُوا † [*But God brought destruction upon them whence they did not reckon, or expect*]. (Es-Semeen, TA.) And it is said in the Ḳur [xvi. 28], فَأَتَى اللّٰهُ بُنْيَانَهُمْ مِنَ القَوَاعِدِ, i. e. † *But God removed their building from the foundations, and demolished it* upon them, so that He destroyed them. (TA.) أَتَى عَلَيْهِ also signifies † *He caused it to come to an end; made an end of it; consumed it;* [*devoured it;*] *exhausted it; came to, or reached, the end of it;* namely, a thing; (Kull;) as, for instance, what was in a bowl; (Ḳ in art. جردم;) and what was in a vessel; (Ḳ in art. جرجب;) like فَرَغَ مِنْهُ: (ISd cited in the TA in art. نكش:) or i. q. مَرَّ بِهِ [which may be rendered *he went away with it*; but this, as an explanation of أَتَى عَلَيْهِ, has another meaning, which see in what follows]. (Kull.) And one says, أُتِىَ فُلَانٌ مِنْ مَأْمَنِهِ † *Destruction came to such a one from the quarter whence he felt secure.* (TA.) And أُتِىَ عَلَى يَدِ فُلَانٍ † *Property belonging to such a one perished.* (T.) And يُؤْتَى دُونَهُ † *He is taken away, or carried off, and overcome.* (TA.) A poet says,

أَتَى دُونَ حُلْوِ العَيْشِ حَتَّى أَمَرَّهُ • نُكُوبٌ عَلَى آثَارِهِنَّ نُكُوبُ •

meaning † [*Misfortunes, in the footsteps of which were misfortunes,*] *took away* [*what was sweet, of life, and rendered it bitter*]. (TA.) One says also, مِنْ هٰهُنَا أُتِيتَ, [so I find it written, but I think that the last word should be أُتِيتَ, agreeably with a preceding phrase from the T,] † *Hence the trial, or affliction, came in upon thee.* (Mgh.) And أُتِىَ مِنْ جِهَةِ كَذَا, with the verb in the passive form, † *He missed* [*his object in respect of such a thing*] *by laying hold upon it when it was not fit to be laid hold upon.* (Mṣb.) And أُتِىَ الرَّجُلُ, [also] like عُنِىَ, † *The man was deceived, or deluded, and his faculty of sense became altered to him, so that he imagined that to be true which was not true.* (TA.) — أَتَى عَلَيْهِ is also *syn.* with مَرَّ بِهِ [meaning *He*, or *it*, (as, for instance, a period of time,) *passed by him*, or *over him*]. (Mṣb.) You say, أَتَى عَلَيْهِ حَوْلٌ [*A year passed over him; or he became a year old*]. (Ṣ, Ḳ, Mṣb, in art. حول; &c.) — أَتَتِ النَّاقَةُ, and مَا أَحْسَنَ أَتْيَ يَدَىْ هٰذِهِ النَّاقَةِ: see art. اتو.

2. أَتَّى لِلْمَآءِ, (T, Ṣ, M,) or المَآءَ, (Ḳ,) or both, (TA,) inf. n. تَأْتِيَةٌ and تَأَتٍّ, *He smoothed, made easy, or prepared,* (سَهَّلَ, Ṣ, Ḳ, or هَيَّأَ, T,) *the way, course, passage, or channel, of the water,* (T, Ṣ, Ḳ,) *in order that it might pass forth to a place;* (Ṣ;) *he directed a channel for it* (M, TA) *so that it ran to the places wherein it rested or remained.* (TA.) And أَتَّى لِأَرْضِهِ أَتِيًّا *He made a rivulet, or a channel for water, to run to his land.* (M.) — أَتَّى اللّٰهُ لِفُلَانٍ أَمْرَهُ, inf. n. تَأْتِيَةٌ, (T, M,* TA,) *God prepared, disposed, arranged, or put into a good or right state,* [and thus *rendered feasible or practicable or easy,*] *for such a one, his affair.* (M,* TA.)

3. آتَاهُ, [inf. n. as below,] *He requited, compensated, or recompensed, him.* (M, Ḳ.) The saying, in the Ḳur [xxi. 48], وَإِنْ كَانَ مِثْقَالَ حَبَّةٍ مِنْ خَرْدَلٍ أَتَيْنَا بِهَا, some read thus, (M,* TA,) meaning [*Though it be the weight of a grain of mustard,*] *we will bring it* [forward for requital]: others read آتَيْنَا بِهَا, meaning *we will give* [a recompense] *for it;* in which case the verb is of the measure أَفْعَلَ: or *we will requite for it;* in which case the verb is of the measure فَاعَلَ. (M, TA.) — آتَيْتُهُ عَلَى الأَمْرِ, (T, Ṣ, M, Mṣb,) inf. n. مُؤَاتَاةٌ, (T, Ṣ,) *I agreed with him, or was of one mind or opinion with him, upon, or respecting, the thing, or affair; I complied with him respecting it;* (T, Ṣ, M, Mṣb;) *in a good manner:* (T:) the vulgar say, وَاتَيْتُهُ: (Ṣ:) this is of the dial. of the people of El-Yemen, inf. n. مُوَاتَاةٌ; and is the form commonly current: (Mṣb:) but it should not be used, except in the dial. of the people of El-Yemen. (T.) — [Hence, app., آتَى as meaning *He aided*; a signification mentioned by Golius, on the authority of Z and Ibn-Maaroof.]

4. آتَاهُ, (Ṣ, M, &c.,) inf. n. إِيتَآءٌ, (TA,) i. q. أَتَى بِهِ [*He came with, or brought, him, or it*]; (Ṣ;) *he made it* (a thing) *to come,* إِلَيْهِ *to him;* (TA;) *he made, or caused, him, or it, to be present;* (Ksh, TA;) *he made, or caused, it* (a thing) *to go, pass,* or *be conveyed* or *transmitted,* (syn. سَاقَهُ,) إِلَيْهِ *to him.* (M, Ḳ.) It is said in the Ḳur [xviii. 61], آتِنَا غَدَآءَنَا, i. e. إِيتِنَا بِهِ [*Come thou to us with,* or *bring thou to us, our morning-meal*]. (Ṣ.) — Hence, (Ksh, TA,) inf. n. as above, (T, Ṣ,) *He gave him* (T, Ṣ, M, Mṣb, Ḳ) a thing, (M, Ḳ,) or property: (Mṣb:) and you say, آتِ in the sense of the [imperative] هَاتِ [*give thou*]. (T.) We read in the Ḳur. [v. 60, &c.] وَيُؤْتُونَ الزَّكَاةَ [*And they give the portion of property which is the due of the poor*]. (TA.) And in [xxvii. 23 of] the same, وَأُوتِيَتْ مِنْ كُلِّ شَيْءٍ, meaning *And she hath been given somewhat of everything.* (M, TA.) [You say also, أُوتِىَ كَذَا, as meaning *He was gifted,* or *endowed, with such a thing;* as, for instance, a faculty.] See also 3. — آتَيْتُ المُكَاتَبَ *I made a gift to the slave between whom and me was a contract that he should become free on payment of a certain sum: or I abated, or took off, somewhat of his appointed part-payments, or instalments.* (Mṣb.) — مَا آتَاكُمُ الرَّسُولُ, in the Ḳur lix. 7, means *What the Apostle giveth you,* of the [spoil termed] فَىْء, (Bḍ, Jel,) &c.: (Jel:) or *what command he giveth you:* (Bḍ:) or *what he commandeth you* [*to receive*]. (Kull.) — أُوتِىَ فِى شَىْءٍ *A dispute, or an altercation, was held before him, respecting the meaning of a thing:* [perhaps more properly signifying *he was given authority to decide respecting a thing:*] occurring in a trad. (Mgh.)

5. تَأَتَّى لَهُ *It* (an affair, T, Mgh, Mṣb, Ḳ, or a thing, Ṣ, M) *was, or became, prepared, disposed, arranged, or put into a good or right state, for him;* (T,* Ṣ, M, Mgh, Mṣb, Ḳ;) and hence, *it* (a thing) *was, or became, feasible or practicable, and easy, to him;* (Mgh;) *it* (an affair) *was, or became, facilitated, or easy, to him;* (Mṣb;) *the way thereof* (i. e. of an affair) *was, or became, facilitated, or easy, to him.* (TA.) The following is an ex.:

• تَأَتَّى لَهُ الدَّهْرُ حَتَّى انْجَبَرْ •

[*Fortune became well, or rightly, disposed for him, so that he became restored to wealth, or competence*]: (T:) or تَأَتَّى لَهُ الخَيْرُ الخ [*good fortune, or prosperity, became prepared, &c., for him, &c.*]. (So in the TA.) And hence the saying, هٰذَا مِمَّا يَتَأَتَّى لِىَ المَضْغُ *This is of the things which it is feasible or practicable, and easy, to me to chew.* (Mgh). — *He applied himself to it with gentleness,* (Aṣ, Ṣ, Ḳ,) and so تَأَتَّى لَهَا, meaning لِحَاجَتِهِ, *to his needful affair or business,* (T,) *and entered into it, engaged in it, occupied himself with it, did it, executed it, or performed it, by the way, or manner, proper, or suitable, to it.* (Aṣ, T, Ṣ, Ḳ. [In the CḲ, for أَتَاهُ مِنْ وَجْهِهِ, we find أتاهُ عن وَجْهِهِ.]) And تَأَتَّى فِى أَمْرِهِ *He used gentleness, or acted gently, in his affair.* (Mṣb.) — تَأَتَّى لَهُ بِسَهْمٍ حَتَّى أَصَابَهُ *He sought him leisurely or repeatedly* [*with an arrow,* app. *taking aim in one direction and then in another, until he hit him*]. (Z, TA.) — جَآءَ فُلَانٌ يَتَأَتَّى is explained by Fr as meaning يَتَعَرَّضُ لِمَعْرُوفِكَ [*Such a one came, or has come, addressing, or applying, or directing, himself, or his regard, or attention, or mind, to obtain thy favour, or bounty*]. (Ṣ.) And you say, تَأَتَّى لَهُ, meaning تَعَرَّضَ لِمَعْرُوفِهِ [*He addressed, applied, or directed, himself, &c., to obtain his favour, or bounty*]. (TA.) — Some say that تَأَتَّى signifies *He prepared himself to rise, or stand.* (TA.)

10. اِسْتَأْتَى فُلَانًا *He asked such a one to come, deeming him slow, or tardy.* (Ḳ.) — اِسْتَأْتَتِ النَّاقَةُ *The she-camel desired to be covered;* (A, TA;) *desired the stallion;* (Ṣ, M, Ḳ;) *being excited by lust.* (Ṣ, A.)

إِتْى : see أُتِىٌّ.

أَتْيَةٌ *A single coming;* as also أَتْوَةٌ; but not ▾إِتْيَانَةٌ, unless by a bad poetic licence. (T.) — See also أُتِيَّةُ الجُرْحِ.

إِتْيَانٌ is either an inf. n. of أَتَى, or a simple subst. [signifying *A coming*]. (Mṣb.)

إِتْيَانَةٌ an inf. n. of 1 [q. v.]: (M, Ḳ:) see also أَتْيَةٌ.

أَتَآءٌ or إِتَآءٌ : see أُتِىٌّ.

أُتِىٌّ as syn. with أَتَاوِىٌّ : see art. اتو. — Also, (M, and so in some copies of the Ḳ, where it is said to be like رُضِىٌّ,) or ▾إِتِىٌّ, like رِضِىٌّ, (so in other copies of the Ḳ,) and ▾أَتَآءٌ, (M, Ḳ,) written by some إِتَآءٌ, (TA,) *What falls, of wood or leaves, into a river:* (M, Ḳ:) from الإِتْيَانُ: (M:) pl. أَتَآءٌ [in the CḲ إِتاء] and أُتِىٌّ. (M, Ḳ.) — رَجُلٌ أَتِىٌّ *A man who is sharp, energetic, vigorous, and effective, in affairs; who applies himself to them with gentleness, and enters into them, or performs them, by the way, or manner, proper, or suitable, to them.* (M.) — فَرَسٌ أَتِىٌّ : see مُسْتَأْتٍ.

أُتِيَّةُ الجُرْحِ, (so in a copy of the M,) or ▾أَتِيَّتُهُ, (so in some copies of the Ḳ, and accord. to the TA,) or ▾أُتِيَّتُهُ, (so in other copies of the Ḳ,) and ▾أَتِيْتُهُ, (so in the M, and in some copies of the Ḳ,) or ▾إِتِيْتُهُ, (so in some copies of the Ḳ, and accord. to the TA,) or أُتَيْتُهُ, (so in a copy of the Ḳ,) *The matter which comes from the wound:* (M, Ḳ:) from Aboo-'Alee. (TA.)

أَتَّى *i. q.* حَتَّى; (Ḳ;) a dial. var. of the latter. (TA.)

أُتِيَّةُ الجُرْحِ and أُتِيَّتُهُ : see إِتْيَةُ الجُرْحِ.

آتٍ [*Coming;* (see also مَأْتِىٌّ;) applied to a man, &c.; and to time, meaning *future:* also *a comer:* — and hence,] *An angel.* (Mgh, Mṣb.)

آتِيَةُ الجُرْحِ : see أُتِيَّةُ الجُرْحِ.

مَأْتًى *A place of coming.* (Mṣb.) [And ▾مَأْتَاةٌ signifies the same: or *A road,* or *way, by which one comes; a way of access; an approach;* as also مَأْتِىٌّ: or, more properly, *a means of coming.*] — مَأْتَى المَرْأَةِ [*The place of access of the woman;* i. e. *the meatus of her vagina;* or *her vagina* itself;] *the* مَحِيض, or *place of menstruation, of the woman.* (Zj in the TA in art. حيض.) — مَأْتَى الأَمْرِ and ▾مَأْتَاتُهُ *The way,* or *manner,* (وَجْه, Ṣ, or جِهَة, M, Ḳ,) *of the affair,* (Ṣ, M, Ḳ,) *by which it is, or is to be, entered into, engaged in, done, executed, or performed;* like as you say مَعْنَى الكَلَامِ and مَعْنَاتُهُ, meaning the same by both. (Ṣ.) You say, أَتَيْتُ الأَمْرَ مِنْ مَأْتَاهُ and ▾مَأْتَاتِهِ, (Ṣ, M,) i. e., مِنْ وَجْهِهِ الَّذِى يُؤْتَى مِنْهُ [*I entered into, engaged in, did, executed, or performed, the affair by the way, or manner, whereby it should be entered into, &c.*], (Ṣ,) or مِنْ جِهَتِهِ [which means the same]. (M.)

مُؤْتًى : see مُسْتَأْتٍ.

مَأْتَاةٌ : see مَأْتًى, in three places.

مَأْتِىٌّ [pass. part. n. of 1; *Come: come to:*] is of the measure مَفْعُولٌ; the و being changed into ى and incorporated into the ى which is the final radical letter. (Ṣ.) In the saying, in the Ḳur [xix. 62], إِنَّهُ كَانَ وَعْدُهُ مَأْتِيًّا, the meaning is ▾آتِيًا [*Verily that which He hath promised,* or *the fulfilment of his promise, is coming*]; like as, in the phrase حِجَابًا مَسْتُورًا, in the Ḳur [xvii. 47], سَاتِرًا is meant: or it may be a pass. part. n. [in signification as well as form]; for what cometh to thee, of that which God commandeth, thou comest thereto. (Ṣ.) It is said in a prov., مَأْتِىٌّ أَنْتَ أَيُّهَا السَّوَادُ [lit. *Thou art come to, O thou person*], meaning *there is no escape for thee from this event.* (TA.) — Applied to a man, it also signifies أُتِىَ فِيهِ [in a sense indicated in the Ḳur xxvi. 165]. (TA.)

طَرِيقٌ مِيتَآءٌ *A road to which people come* (Th, M, Mgh, Mṣb) *much, or often;* (Mgh, Mṣb;) the latter word being of the measure مِفْعَالٌ, (Th, M, Mgh, Mṣb,) originally مِئْتَاىٌ or مِئْتَاوٌ; (Mṣb;) from أَتَيْتُ, (Th, M,) or الإِتْيَانُ; [or from أَتَوْتُ;] like دَارٌ مِحْلَالٌ, i. e. a house where people alight or abide much, or often: (Mgh, Mṣb:) *a road that is frequented* (Ṣ, M, Ḳ) *and conspicuous:* (M, Ḳ:) in [some of] the copies of the Ḳ, incorrectly, مِيتَآءَةٌ: (TA:) A'Obeyd has inadvertently written it without [the radical] ء, and in the category of فِعْلَاء. (M.) Death is thus termed in a trad., as being a way which every one travels: (TA:) and as that trad. is related, it is without [the radical] ء. (M.) — مِيتَآءُ الطَّرِيقِ *The main part, or middle, of the road;* or *the part of the road along which one travels:* (Sh, TA:) or *the space within which the road is comprised;* (Ṣ, Mṣb, Ḳ;) as also مِيدَآءُ الطريق: (TA:) or this last, as also مِيتَآءُ الطريق, signifies *the measure of the two sides, and the distance, of the road.* (L in art. ميت.) — مِيتَآءٌ also signifies *The extreme limit of the distance to which horses run;* (Ṣ, Mṣb;) and so مِيدَآءٌ. (Ṣ, TA.) — And *i. q.* تِلْقَآءٌ. (Ḳ.) You say, دَارِى بِمِيتَآءِ دَارِ فُلَانٍ *My house is opposite to the house of such a one; facing it,* or *fronting it;* and so بِمِيدَآءِ دَارِهِ; (Ṣ;) and بِمِيتَآءِ دَارِهِ. (L in art. ميت.) — And بَنَى القَوْمُ بُيُوتَهُمْ عَلَى مِيتَآءٍ وَاحِدٍ (Ṣ) and مِيدَآءٍ وَاحِدٍ (Ṣ, and L in art. ميد,) *The people built their houses, or constructed their tents, after one mode, manner, fashion, or form.* (L in art. ميد.) — رَجُلٌ مِيتَآءٌ *A man who requites, compensates, or recompenses; who gives much, or largely.* (M, Ḳ.)

فَرَسٌ مُسْتَأْتٍ, and ▾مُؤْتًى, and ▾أَتِىٌّ, and مستوتى, [so I find it written, perhaps for مُسْتَوْتٍ, which may be a dial. var. of مُسْتَأْتٍ, like as وَاتَيْتُهُ is of آتَيْتُهُ,] *A mare desiring the stallion.* (TA.)

اث

1. أَثَّ, aor. ـِ (T, Ṣ, M, L, Ḳ) and ـُ and ـَ, (M, L, Ḳ,) inf. n. أَثَاثَةٌ (T, Ṣ, M, L, Ḳ) and أَثَاثٌ (M, L, Ḳ) and أُثُوثَةٌ, (M,) or أُثُوثٌ, (L, Ḳ,) *It* (anything) *was, or became, much in quantity, abundant, or numerous:* and *great,* or *large:* (M, L:) *it* (herbage, or a herb,) *was, or became, abundant, or plenteous, and tangled, or luxuriant;* (T, Ṣ, Ḳ;) or *abundant and tall:* (M:) *it* (hair) *was, or became, abundant and long.* (M, TA.) — أَثُثَتْ, (M, Ḳ,) aor. ـُ, inf. n. أَثٌّ, (M,) said of a woman, *She was, or became, large in the hinder parts.* (M, Ḳ.)

2. أَثَّثَهُ *He made it plain, level, smooth, soft, or easy to lie or ride or walk upon.* (M, Ḳ.)

5. تَأَثَّثَ *He obtained, or acquired, goods, household-goods, or furniture and utensils and the like; or abundance of the goods, conveniences, or comforts, of life;* (Ṣ;) or *property;* (Ṣ, M;) or *wealth;* or *what was good.* (M.)

أَثٌّ, fem. with ة : see أَثِيثٌ, in two places.

أَثَاثٌ *Goods;* or *utensils and furniture of a house or tent; household-goods;* syn. مَتَاعٌ; (T, M;) or مَتَاعُ بَيْتٍ; (Ṣ, Mṣb, Ḳ;) *of whatever kind; consisting of clothes, and stuffing for mattresses or the like, or outer garments* [*&c.*]: (M, TA:) or (so accord. to the M and Ḳ, but in the T "also,") *all property,* (AZ, T, Ṣ, M, Ḳ,) [*consisting of*] *camels, and sheep or goats, and slaves, and utensils and furniture or household-goods:* (AZ, T, Ṣ:) or *abundant property:* or *abundance of property:* (M, TA:) [in which last sense it is an inf. n. used as simple subst.:] or *what is made, or taken, for use,* and *i. q.* مَتَاعٌ; *not what is for merchandise:* or *what is new, of the utensils and furniture of a house or tent; not what is old and worn out:* (TA:) [it is a coll.

gen. n., and] the n. un. is with ة: (AZ, T, Ṣ, M, Mṣb, Ḳ:) or it has no n. un.: (Fr, T, Ṣ, Mṣb, Ḳ:) if you form a pl. from اثاث, you say, ثَلَاثَةُ آثَّةٍ, [originally أَأْثِثَةٍ, like أَطْعِمَة, pl. of طَعَام,] and أُثُثٌ كَثِيرَةٌ. (Fr, T.)

أَثِيثٌ *Much in quantity, abundant,* or *numerous:* and *great,* or *large:* as also ▼ أَثٌّ; (M, Ḳ;) which is, in my opinion, [says ISd, originally أَثِثٌ,] of the measure فَعِلٌ: (M:) the fem. is أَثِيثَةٌ: and the pl. is إِثَاثٌ and أَثَائِثُ; (M, Ḳ;*) both being pls. of the masc. and of the fem.; (Ḳ;) or the latter is pl. of the fem. only; (M,* MF;) but the former is [pl. of the masc.,] like كِرَامٌ as pl. of كَرِيمٌ, (TA,) and is pl. of the fem. also. (M.) You say, نَبَاتٌ أَثِيثٌ *Herbage,* or *a herb, that is abundant,* or *plenteous, and tangled,* or *luxuriant:* (T, Ṣ:) or *abundant and tall.* (M.) And شَعَرٌ أَثِيثٌ *Hair that is abundant, and tangled,* or *luxuriant:* (Ṣ:) or *abundant* (T, M) *and long.* (M.) And لِحْيَةٌ أَثِيثَةٌ, and ▼ أَثَّةٌ, *A thick beard.* (M, TA.) And اِمْرَأَةٌ أَثِيثَةٌ *A fleshy woman:* (M, TA:) pl. أَثَائِثُ, (M,) signifying *fleshy* women; (Ṣ, M, Ḳ;) as also إِثَاثٌ: (M:) or the former of these pls. signifies *tall, full-grown,* women. (Ḳ.)

أُثَاثِىُّ *i. q.* أُثَافِىُّ, (Ḳ,) i. e. The [*three*] *stones which are set up and upon which the cooking-pot is placed:* the [second] ث is said to be a substitute for ف, and some hold the hemzeh to be augmentative. (TA.)

اثر

1. أَثَرَ خُفَّ البَعِيرِ, aor. ـِ, inf. n. أَثْرٌ, *He made an incision in the foot of the camel* [*in order to know and trace the footprints*]; as also ▼ أَثَّرَهُ. (M.) And أَثَرَ البَعِيرَ *He made a mark upon the bottom of the camel's foot with the iron instrument called* مِئْثَرَة *in order that the footprints upon the ground might be known:* (T, TT:) or *he scraped the inner* [i. e. *under*] *part of the camel's foot with that instrument in order that the footprints might be traced.* (Ṣ.) — أَثَرَ الحَدِيثَ, (T, Ṣ, M, A, &c.,) عَنِ القَوْمِ, (M,) aor. ـُ (Ṣ, M, Mṣb, Ḳ) and ـِ, (M, Ḳ,) inf. n. أَثْرٌ (T, Ṣ, M, Mṣb, Ḳ) and أَثَارَةٌ and أُثْرَةٌ, (M, Ḳ,) the last from Lḥ, but in my opinion, [says ISd,] it is correctly speaking a subst., and syn. with مَأْثَرَةٌ and مَأْثُرَةٌ, (M,) *He related,* or *recited, the tradition, narrative,* or *story, as received,* or *heard, from the people; transmitted the narrative,* or *story, by tradition, from the people:* (T, Ṣ,* M, A, L, Mṣb,* Ḳ:*) or *he related that wherein they had preceded* [*as narrators:* so I render أَنْبَأَهُمْ بِمَا سَبَقُوا فِيهِ, believing هم to have been inserted by a mistake of a copyist in the M, and hence in the L also:] from الأَثَرُ. (M, L.) [See أَثَرٌ.] You say also, أَثَرَ عَنْهُ الكَذِبَ, meaning *He related, as heard from him, what was false.* (L, from a trad.) — أَثَرَ, aor. ـُ, (M,) inf. n. أَثْرٌ, (M, Ḳ,) also signifies *Multum inivit* camelus camelam. (M, Ḳ.) — أَثِرَ لِلْأَمْرِ, aor. ـَ, *He applied,* or *gave, his whole attention to the thing,* or *affair, having his mind unoccupied by other things.* (Ḳ.) — أَثِرَ عَلَى الأَمْرِ *He determined, resolved,* or *decided, upon the thing,* or *affair.* (T, Ḳ.) — لَقَدْ أَثِرْتُ أَنْ أَفْعَلَ كَذَا وَكَذَا, (Lth, T, L,) inf. n. أَثَرٌ and أَثْرٌ, (L,) *I have assuredly purposed to do such and such things.* (Lth, T, L.) — See also 4. — And see 10.

2. أَثَّرَ فِيهِ, inf. n. تَأْثِيرٌ, *He,* or *it, made,* (Mṣb,) or *left,* (M, Ḳ,) or *caused to remain,* (Ṣ,) *an impression,* or *a mark,* or *trace, upon him,* or *it.* (Ṣ,* M, Mṣb, Ḳ.*) It is said of a sword, [meaning *It made,* or *left, a mark,* or *scar, upon him,* or *it,*] and in like manner of a blow. (T, TA.) [Whence,] أَثَّرَ فِى عِرْضِهِ † [*He scarred his honour*]. (Ḳ in art. وحش.) You say also, أَثَّرَ بِوَجْهِهِ وَبِجَبِينِهِ السُّجُودُ [*Prostration in prayer made,* or *left, a mark,* or *marks, upon his face and upon his forehead*]. (T,* TA.) See also 1, first sentence. — *He,* or *it, made an impression,* or *produced an effect, upon him,* or *it; impressed, affected,* or *influenced, him,* or *it.* (The Lexicons passim.) — أَثَّرَ كَذَا بِكَذَا, (T, TT,) or ▼ آثَرَ, (Ḳ,) *He,* or *it, made such a thing to be followed by such a thing.* (T, TT, Ḳ.*)

4: see 2, last sentence. — [Hence, app.,] آثَرَهُ, (Aṣ, T, M, Mṣb,) inf. n. إِيثَارٌ, (Aṣ, T,) *He preferred him,* or *it.* (Aṣ, T, M, Mṣb, TA.) You say, آثَرَهُ عَلَيْهِ *He preferred him before him:* so in the Ḳur xii. 91. (Aṣ, M.) And آثَرْتُ فُلَانًا عَلَى نَفْسِى [*I preferred such a one before myself*], from الإِيثَار. (Ṣ.) And قَدْ آثَرْتُكَ بِهِ *I have preferred for thee it; I have preferred to give thee it, rather than any other thing.* (T.) And آثَرَ أَنْ يَفْعَلَ كَذَا *He preferred doing such a thing;* as also ▼ أَثِرَ, inf. n. أَثَرٌ; and أَثَّرَ. (M.) — آثَرَ also signifies *He chose,* or *elected,* or *selected.* (Ḳ.) — And آثَرَهُ *He honoured him; paid him honour.* (M, Ḳ.)

5. تَأَثَّرَ *It received an impression,* or *a mark,* or *trace; became impressed,* or *marked.* (Mṣb.) — *He,* or *it, had an impression made,* or *an effect produced, upon him,* or *it; became impressed, affected,* or *influenced.* (The Lexicons passim.) = See also 8.

8. اِئْتَثَرَهُ, [written with the disjunctive alif اِيتَثَرَهُ,] and ▼ تَأَثَّرَهُ, *He followed his footsteps:* (M, Ḳ:) or *did so diligently,* or *perseveringly.* (TA.)

10. اِسْتَأْثَرَ عَلَى أَصْحَابِهِ; (ISk, Ṣ, Ḳ;) and ▼ أَثِرَ عَلَيْهِمْ, aor. ـَ; (Ḳ;) *He chose for himself* [*in preference to his companions*] (ISk, Ṣ, Ḳ) *good things,* (Ḳ,) *in partition,* (TA,) or *good actions, and qualities of the mind.* (ISk, Ṣ.) And استأثر بِالشَّىْءِ, (Ṣ, Ḳ,) or الشَّىْءَ, (Mṣb,) *He had the thing to himself, with none to share with him in it:* (Ṣ, Mṣb, Ḳ:) and the former signifies *he appropriated the thing to himself exclusively,* (M, Ḳ,) عَلَى غَيْرِهِ *in preference to another* or *others.* (M.) It is said in a trad., إِذَا اسْتَأْثَرَ اللّٰهُ بِشَىْءٍ فَالْهَ عَنْهُ *When God appropriateth a thing to Himself exclusively, then be thou diverted from it so as to forget it.* (M.) And one says, اِسْتَأْثَرَ اللّٰهُ بِفُلَانٍ (and فُلَانًا, TA,) [*God took such a one to Himself,*] when a person has died and it is hoped that he is forgiven. (Ṣ, M, A, Ḳ.)

أَثْرٌ, (AZ, T, Ṣ, A, L, Ḳ, &c.,) said by Yaḳḳoob to be the only form known to Aṣ, (Ṣ,) and ▼ أُثُرٌ, which is a form used by poetic licence, (M, L,) and ▼ إِثْرٌ, (M, L, Ḳ,) and ▼ أَثَرٌ, (M,) and ▼ أُثْرٌ, which is in like manner a sing., not a pl., (T, L,) and ▼ أُثْرَةٌ, (El-Leblee,) and ▼ أَثِيرٌ, (Ḳ,) *The diversified wavy marks, streaks,* or *grain,* of a sword; syn. فِرِنْدٌ; (Aṣ, T, Ṣ, M, A, L, Ḳ;) and دِيبَاجَةٌ; and تَسَلْسُلٌ; (AZ, T;) and its *lustre,* or *glitter:* (M, L:) pl. [of the first] أُثُورٌ: (T, M, L, Ḳ:) the pl. of أُثْرَةٌ is أُثَرٌ. (El-Leblee.) Khufáf Ibn-Nudbeh Es-Sulamee says, [describing swords,]

> جَلَاهَا الصَّيْقَلُونَ فَأَخْلَصُوهَا
> خِفَافًا كُلُّهَا يَتْقِى بِأَثْرِ

[*The furbishers polished them, and freed them from impurities, making them light: each of them preserving itself from the evil eye by means of its lustre*]: i. e., each of them opposes to thee its فِرِنْد: (Ṣ, L:) يَتْقِى is a contraction of يَتَّقِى; and the meaning is, when a person looks at them, their bright rays meet his eye, so that he cannot continue to look at them. (L.)

أَثْرٌ The *scar of a wound, remaining when the latter has healed;* (Aṣ, Sh, T, Ṣ, M, Ḳ;) as also ▼ أُثْرٌ (Ṣ, Ḳ) and ▼ أُثُرٌ: (Sh, T:) pl. آثَارٌ, though properly إِثَارٌ, with kesr to the ا; [but why this is said, I do not see; for آثَارٌ is a regular pl. of all the three forms of the sing.;] and أُثُورٌ may be correctly used as a pl. (Sh, T, L.) — *A mark made with a hot iron upon the inner* [i. e. *under*] *part of a camel's foot, by which to trace his footprints:* (M, Ḳ:) pl. أُثُورٌ. (M.) [See also أُثْرَةٌ.] — *Lustre,* or *brightness,* of the face: as also ▼ أُثْرٌ. (M, Ḳ.) — See أَثَرٌ. = See also إِثْرٌ.

أُثْرٌ: see أَثْرٌ, in three places: — and أُثُرٌ: — and see أَثَرٌ, in two places. = Also, (Ṣ, M, Ḳ,) and ▼ إِثْرٌ, (M, Ḳ,) but the latter is disallowed by more than one authority, (TA,) *What is termed the* خُلَاصَة [q. v.] *of clarified butter:* (Ṣ, M, Ḳ:) or, as some say, the *milk when the clarified butter has become separated from it.* (M.) [See also قِشْدَة.]

أَثَرٌ *A remain,* or *relic,* of a thing; (M, Mṣb, Ḳ;) as of a house; as also ▼ أَثَارَةٌ: (Mṣb:) *a trace remaining* of a thing; and of the stroke, or blow, of a sword: (Ṣ:) see also أُثْرٌ: *a sign, mark,* or *trace;* opposed to the عَيْن, or thing itself: (TA:) *a footstep, vestige,* or *track; a footprint;* the *impression,* or *mark, made by the foot of a man* [*&c.*] *upon the ground;* as also ▼ إِثْرٌ: and *an impress,* or *impression,* of anything: (El-Wá'ee:) pl. آثَارٌ (M, Mṣb, Ḳ) and أُثُورٌ. (M, Ḳ.) [The sing. is also frequently used in a pl. sense: and the former of these pls. is often used to signify *Remains,* or *monuments,* or *memorials,* of *anti-*

quity, or of any past time.] It is said in a prov., لَا أَطْلُبُ أَثَرًا بَعْدَ عَيْنٍ *I will not seek a trace*, or *vestige*, [or, as we rather say in English, *a shadow*,] *after* suffering *a reality*, or *substance*, to escape me: or, as some relate it, لَا تَطْلُبْ *seek not thou.* (Ḥar pp. 120 and 174.) And one says, قَطَعَ ٱللّٰهُ أَثَرَهُ [*May God cut short his footsteps*]: meaning may *God render him crippled*: for when one is crippled, his footsteps cease. (TA.) And فُلَانٌ لَا يَصْدُقُ أَثَرُهُ, and أَثَرَهُ, *Such a one*, if asked, *will not tell thee truly whence he comes*: (M in art. صدق:) a prov. said of a liar. (TA.) And خَرَجْتُ, (Ṣ, M,* Ḳ,) and جِئْتُ, (El-Wá'ee, Mṣb,) فِى أَثَرِهِ, and ▼ فِى إِثْرِهِ, (T, Ṣ, M, Mṣb, Ḳ,) the former of which is said by more than one to be the more chaste, (TA,) [but the latter seems to be the more common,] and عَلَى أَثَرِهِ, and ▼ على إِثْرِهِ, (El-Wá'ee, Mṣb,) *I went out*, (Ṣ, &c.,) and *I came*, (El-Wá'ee, Mṣb,) *after him*: (M, A, Ḳ:) or *at his heel*: (Expos. of the Fṣ:) or *following near upon him*, or *hard upon him*, or *near after him*, or *following him nearly*: (Mṣb:) *as though treading in his footsteps.* (El-Wá'ee.) And أَثَرَ ذِى أَثِيرَيْنِ: see آثِرَ. (Ḳ.) — *An impress* or *impression, a mark, stamp, character*, or *trace, in a fig. sense; an effect.* (The Lexicons passim.) You say, عَلَى مَاشِيَتِهِ أَثَرٌ حَسَنٌ *Upon his camels*, or *sheep*, or *goats, is an impress of a good state*, or *condition; of fatness, and of good tending*; like إِصْبَعٌ. (TA in art. صبع.) And إِنَّهُ لَحَسَنُ الأَثَرِ فِى مَالِهِ *Verily he has the impress of a good state*, or *condition, in his camels*, or *sheep*, or *goats*; like حَسَنُ الإِصْبَعِ, and البِسِّ. (TA ubi suprà.) And عَلَيْهِ أَثَرُ كَذَا *He*, or *it, bears the mark, stamp, character*, or *trace, of such a thing.* (The Lexicons passim.) — [The pl.] آثَارٌ also signifies *Signs*, or *marks, set up to show the way.* (Ḳ.) — Also the sing., *i. q.* أُثْرٌ, q. v. (M, L.) — Also i. q. خَبَرٌ [both of which words are generally held to be syn., as meaning *A tradition*, or *narration relating or describing a saying or an action &c., of Mohammad*]: (M, Ḳ:) or, accord. to some, the former signifies *what is related as received from* [one or more of] *the Companions of Mohammad*; (TA;) but it may also be applied to *a saying of the Prophet*; (Kull p. 152;) and the latter, what is from Mohammad himself; (TA;) or from another; or from him or another: (Kull p. 152:) or the former signifies *i. q.* سُنَّةٌ [*a practice or saying*, or *the practices and sayings collectively, of Mohammad, or any other person who is an authority in matters of religion, namely, any prophet, or a Companion of Mohammad, as handed down by tradition*]: (Ṣ, A:) pl. آثَارٌ. (Ṣ, M.) You say, وَجَدْتُهُ فِى الأَثَرِ [*I found it in the traditions of the practices and sayings of the Prophet*; &c.]: and فُلَانٌ مِنْ حَمَلَةِ الآثَارِ [*Such a one is of those who bear in their memories, knowing by heart, the traditions of the practices and sayings of the Prophet*; &c.]. (A.) — A man's *origin*; as in the sayings, مَا يُدْرَى لَهُ أَيْنَ أَثَرٌ *It is not known where was his origin*; and مَا يُدْرَى لَهُ مَا أَثَرٌ *It is not known what is his origin.* (Ks, Lḥ, M.) — *The term*, or *period, of life*: so called because it follows life: (Mṣb, TA:) or from the same word as signifying the print of one's foot upon the ground; because when one dies, his footprints cease to be seen. (TA.) — [For the former of these two reasons,] آثَارَهُمْ in the Ḳur xxxvi. 11 means *The rewards and punishments of their good and evil lives.* (M, L.) ═ آثَارٌ is also a pl. of ثَأْرٌ, q. v.; formed by transposition from أَثْآرٌ. (Yaạḳoob, and M in art. ثأر.)

أَثُرٌ A man *who chooses for himself* [in preference to his companions] (ISk, Ṣ, M, Ḳ) *good things*, (Ḳ,) *in partition*, (M, TA,) or *good actions, and qualities of the mind*; (ISk, Ṣ;) as also ▼ أَثِرٌ. (M, Ḳ.)

أَثِرٌ: see أَثُرٌ.

أُثْرٌ: see أَثْرٌ, in two places: — and see أُثُرٌ.

أَثْرَةٌ: see أَثَارَةٌ.

أُثْرَةٌ: see أَثَارَةٌ. — *A mark which is made by the Arabs of the desert upon the inner* [i. e. *under*] *part of a camel's foot*; as also ▼ تَأْثُورٌ, and, accord. to some, ▼ تُؤْثُورٌ; whence one says, رَأَيْتُ أُثْرَتَهُ, and ▼ تُؤْثُورَهُ, *I saw the place of his footsteps upon the ground*: (M:) or the *abrasion of the inner* [i. e. *under*] *part of a camel's foot with the instrument of iron called* مِئْثَرَة *and* تُؤْثُور, *in order that his footprints may be traced.* (Ṣ.) [See also أَثْرٌ.] — See also أَثَرٌ. — And see مَأْثُرَةٌ. — *Preference.* (A.) You say, لَهُ عِنْدِى أُثْرَةٌ *He has a preference in my estimation.* (A.) And هُوَ ذُو أُثْرَةٍ عِنْدَ الأَمِيرِ *He has a preference in the estimation of the prince*, or *commander.* (A.) And فُلَانٌ ذُو أُثْرَةٍ عِنْدَ فُلَانٍ, (TA,) or ▼ أَثَرَةٍ, (T,) *Such a one is a favourite with such a one.* (T, TA.) See also أَثَرَةٌ, in two places. — أُثْرَةَ ذِى أَثِيرٍ: see آثِرَ. ═ *Dearth, scarcity, drought*, or *sterility*, (جَدْبٌ [in the CḲ جَذْب],) *and an unpleasant state* or *condition.* (M, Ḳ.)

إِثْرَةٌ: see أَثَرَةٌ. — إِثْرَةَ مَا: see آثِرَ.

أَثَرَةٌ: see أَثَارَةٌ. — A subst. [signifying The *appropriation of a thing or things to oneself exclusively*: the *having a thing to oneself, with none to share with him in it*:] from اِسْتَأْثَرَ بِالشَّىْءِ. (Ṣ, M.) And, as also ▼ أُثْرَةٌ and ▼ إِثْرَةٌ and ▼ أُثْرَى, The *choice for oneself* [in preference to his companions] *of good things*, (M,* Ḳ,* TA,) *in partition*; (M, TA;) the *choice and preference of the best of things, and taking it*, or *them, for oneself*: (TA:) the pl. of the second is أُثَرٌ. (TA.) You say, أَخَذَهُ بِلَا أَثَرَةٍ, and ▼ بلا أُثْرَةٍ, [&c.,] *He took it without a choice and preference of the best of the things, and the taking the best for himself.* (T, TA.) And a poet says,

فَقُلْتُ لَهُ يَا ذِئْبُ هَلْ لَكَ فِى أَخٍ
يُوَاسِى بِلَا أُثْرَى ▼ عَلَيْكَ وَلَا بُخْلِ

[*And I said to him, O wolf, hast thou a desire for a brother who will share without choice of the best things for himself in preference to thee, and without niggardness?*]. (M, TA.) See also أُثْرَةٌ.

أُثْرَى: see أَثَرَةٌ, in two places.

أَثِيرٌ: see أَثُرٌ. — [*That makes a large footprint*, or *the like.*] You say, دَابَّةٌ أَثِيرَةٌ *A beast that makes a large footprint upon the ground with its hoof*, (AZ, Ṣ, M, Ḳ,) or *with its soft foot, such as that of the camel.* (AZ, Ṣ.) — A man *possessing power and authority; honoured*: pl. أُثَرَآءُ: fem. أَثِيرَةٌ. (M.) — فُلَانٌ أَثِيرِى *Such a one is my particular friend*: (Ṣ, Ḳ:) or *is the person whom I prefer.* (A.) فُلَانٌ أَثِيرٌ عِنْدَ فُلَانٍ *Such a one is a favourite with such a one.* (T.) — أَوَّلَ ذِى أَثِيرٍ, and آثِرَ ذِى أَثِيرٍ, &c.: see آثِرَ. — شَىْءٌ كَثِيرٌ أَثِيرٌ [*A thing very abundant, copious*, or *numerous*]: أثير is here an imitative sequent, (Ṣ, Ḳ,*) like بَثِيرٌ. (Ṣ.) ═ الأَثِيرُ [ὁ αἰθήρ, *The ether*;] *the ninth, which is the greatest, sphere, which rules over* [*all*] *the other spheres*: [said to be] so called because it affects the others (يُؤَثِّرُ فِى غَيْرِهِ). (MF.) [It is also called فَلَكُ الأَطْلَسِ, and فَلَكُ العَرْشِ; and is said to be next above that called فَلَكُ الكُرْسِىِّ.]

أَثَارَةٌ: see أَثَرٌ. You say, سَمِنَتِ الإِبِلُ عَلَى أَثَارَةٍ, (Ṣ, M,*) or عَلَى أَثَارَةٍ مِنْ شَحْمٍ, (A,) *The camels acquired fat, upon*, or *after, remains of fat.* (Ṣ, M,* A.) And غَضِبَ عَلَى أَثَارَةٍ قَبْلَ ذَاكَ *He became angry the more, having been angry before that.* (Lḥ, M.) And أَغْضَبَنِى فُلَانٌ عَلَى أَثَارَةِ غَضَبٍ *Such a one angered me when anger yet remained in me.* (A.) And أَثَارَةٌ مِنْ عِلْمٍ, and ▼ أَثَرَةٌ, (T, Ṣ, M, Ḳ,) and ▼ أُثْرَةٌ, (M, Ḳ,) or ▼ أَثْرَةٌ, (T,) the first of which is the most approved, (M,) and is [originally] an inf. n., [see أَثَرَ الحَدِيثَ,] (T,) signify *A remain*, or *relic, of knowledge*, (Zj, T, Ṣ, M, Ḳ, and Jel in xlvi. 3 of the Ḳur,) *transmitted*, or *handed down*, (Ḳ, Jel,) *from the former generations*: (Jel:) or *what is transmitted*, or *handed down, of knowledge*: (Zj, M:) or *somewhat transmitted from the writings of the former generations*: (TA:) by the knowledge spoken of [in the Ḳur ubi suprà] is meant that of writing, which was given to certain of the prophets. (I 'Ab.)

آثِرٌ One *who relates*, or *recites, a tradition, narrative*, or *story*, or *traditions, &c., as received*, or *heard, from another*, or *others*; *a narrator thereof.* (T, Ṣ,* L.) The saying of 'Omar, on his being forbidden by Mohammad to swear by his father, مَا حَلَفْتُ بِهِ ذَاكِرًا وَلَا آثِرًا, means *I did not swear by him uttering (the oath) as proceeding in the first instance from myself, nor repeating (it) as heard from another particular person.* (A'Obeyd, T, Ṣ, TA.) — اِفْعَلْ هٰذَا آثِرًا مَّا, (IAạr, T, Ṣ, Ḳ,) and آثِرًا without ما, (IAạr, T,) and ▼ آثِرَ ذِى أَثِيرٍ, (Ṣ, Ḳ,) mean *I will do this the first of every thing.* (Ṣ, Ḳ.*) And in like manner, after لَقِيتُهُ [*I met him, or it*], one says, آثِرًا مَّا, [and ▼ آثِرَ ذِى أَثِيرٍ,] and ▼ أَوَّلَ ذِى أَثِيرٍ, (M, Ḳ,) and

آثِرَ ذَاتِ يَدَيْنِ, (M,) or ذَاتِ يَدَيْنِ, (Ḳ,) and ▼ أَثِيرَةَ ذِي أَثِيرٍ, (IAạr, M, Ḳ,) and ذِي يَدَيْنِ, آثِرَ ذِي أَثِيرَيْنِ, (Ḳ,) and ▼ أُثْرَةَ ▼ ذِي أَثِيرٍ, (M, as from Lḥ,) or ▼ أَثَرَ ▼ ذِي أُثَيرَيْنِ, (Ḳ,) and ▼ إِثْرَةً ▼ مَّا, and ▼ إِثْرَ ▼ ذِي أَثِيرَيْنِ: (Lḥ, M, Ḳ:) or, as some say, ▼ الأَثِيرُ signifies *the daybreak*, or *dawn*; and ▼ ذُو أَثِيرٍ, *the time thereof.* (M, TA.) Fr says that ابْدَأْ بِهٰذَا آثِرًا مَّا, and ▼ آثِرَ ذِي أَثِيرٍ, and ▼ أَثِيرَ ذِي أَثِيرٍ, signify *Begin thou with this first of every thing.* (TA.) One says also, افْعَلْهُ آثِرًا مَّا, (T, M, TA,) and ▼ إِثْرًا مَّا, (M, TA,) meaning *Do thou it* [*at least*], *if thou do nothing else:* (T, M, TA:) or, as some say, *do thou it in preference to another thing*, or *to other things:* ما being redundant, but [in this case] not to be omitted, because [it is a corroborative, and] the meaning of the phrase is, do thou it by choice, or preference, and with care. (M, TA.) Mbr says that the phrase خُذْ هٰذَا آثِرًا مَّا means *Take thou this in preference;* i. e., I give it thee in preference; as though one desired to take, of another, one thing, and had another thing offered to him for sale: and ما is here redundant. (T, TA.)

أُثْرَة: see تَأْثُورٌ.

تُؤْثُورٌ: see أُثْرَةٌ, in two places: and see مِئْثَرَةٌ, in two places.

مَأْثُرَةٌ (T, Ṣ, M, Ḳ, &c.) and مَأْثَرَةٌ (Ṣ, M, Ḳ) and ▼ أُثْرَةٌ (M, Ḳ) *A generous quality or action;* (AZ, Ṣ;) so called because related, or handed down, by generation from generation: (Ṣ:) or *a generous quality that is inherited by generation from generation:* (M, Ḳ:) *a generous quality*, or *action, related*, or *handed down by tradition from one's ancestors:* (A:) *a cause of glorying:* (AZ:) and *precedence in* حَسَب [or *grounds of pretension to respect*, &c.]: pl. of the first and second, مَآثِرُ. (AZ, T.)

مِئْثَرَةٌ and ▼ تُؤْثُورٌ *An iron instrument* (Ṣ, M, Ḳ) *with which the bottom of a camel's foot is marked, in order that his footprints upon the ground may be known:* (M:) or, *with which the inner* [i. e. *under*] *part of a camel's foot is scraped, in order that his footprints may be traced:* (Ṣ, Ḳ:) or ▼ تؤثور has a different meaning, explained above, voce أُثْرَةٌ. (M.) The مِيثَرَة of a horse's saddle is without hems. (Ṣ.)

مَأْثُورٌ A camel *having a mark made upon the bottom of his foot with the iron instrument called* مِئْثَرَةٌ, *in order that his footprints upon the ground may be known:* (T:) or *having the inner* [i. e. *under*] *part of his foot scraped with that instrument, in order that his footprints may be traced.* (Ṣ.) — A sword *having in its* مَتْن [or *broad side;* or *the middle of the broad side, of the blade,*] *diversified wavy marks, streaks,* or *grain,* or *lustre* or *glitter:* (M, Ḳ: [in some copies of the latter of which, instead of أَثْرٌ, I find أُثُرٌ:]) or *having its* متن *of female,* or *soft, iron, and its edge of male iron,* or *steel:* (Ḳ:) or *that is said to be of the fabric of the jinn,* or *genii;* (Ṣ, M, Ḳ;*) and not from الأَثْرُ, as signifying الفِرِنْد: (Ṣ, M:) so says Aṣ: (Ṣ:) [ISd says,] مأثور is in my opinion a pass. part. n. that has no verb: (M:) or it signifies an *ancient* sword, *which has passed by inheritance from great man to great man.* (A.) — A tradition, narrative, or story, *handed down from one to another, from generation to generation.* (T, Ṣ, A.)

اثف

1. أَثَفَ القِدْرَ: see 2. — أَثَفَهُ, aor. ـِ, (T, Ṣ, M, Ḳ,) inf. n. أَثْفٌ, (T, M,) *He followed him.* (Ks, T, Ṣ, M, Ḳ.) — *He drove away,* or *drove away and pursued closely,* or *hunted, him;* syn. طَرَدَهُ. (Ibn-'Abbád, Ḳ.) — *He sought,* or *sought after,* or *pursued after, him,* or *it:* in which sense the aor. is ـُ, (AA, Ḳ,) and ـِ also. (So in some copies of the Ḳ.)

2. اثّف القِدْرَ, (T, Ṣ, M, Ḳ,) inf. n. تَأْثِيفٌ, (Ṣ, Ḳ,) *He put the cooking-pot upon the* أَثَافِى [pl. of أُثْفِيَّةٌ, q. v.]; (T,* Ṣ, M,* Ḳ;) as also ▼ أَثَفَهَا, (M, TA,) inf. n. أَثْفٌ; (TA;) or ▼ آثَفَهَا, (so in some copies of the Ḳ in art. ثفى,) inf. n. إِيثَافٌ; (TA in that art.;) the first of which is a dial. var. of ثَفَّاهَا, inf. n. تَثْفِيَةٌ; (Ṣ;) and ▼ أَثْفَاهَا, whence قِدْرٌ مُؤَثْفَاةٌ. (M.)

4: see 2.

5. تَأَثَّفَتِ القِدْرُ *The cooking-pot was put upon the* أَثَافِى. (TA.) — تَأَثَّفُوهُ *They surrounded him,* or *it:* (Ṣ, Ḳ:*) *they became around him,* or *it, like the* أُثْفِيَّة [or rather *like the* أَثَافِى]: (M:) *they collected themselves together around him,* or *it.* (A, TA.) — تأثّف المَكَانَ, (T, Ṣ, Ḳ,) or بِالمَكَانِ, (M,) *He* (a man, Ṣ) *kept to the place;* (T, Ḳ;) *remained in it;* (M;) *did not quit it.* (AZ, T, Ṣ, M.) — تَأَثَّفَهُ also signifies *He followed after him, and pressed* or *importuned him, and ceased not to incite him.* (T, Ḳ.) In my opinion, [says Az,] this is not in any way derived from الأُثْفِيَّةُ; but from أَثَفْتُ الرَّجُلَ, meaning "I followed the man." (T.) — And تَأَثَّفُوا عَلَى الأَمْرِ *They aided,* or *assisted, one another to do,* or *accomplish, the thing,* or *affair.* (M, L.)

Q. Q. 1. أَثْفَى القِدْرَ: see 2. [But accord. to Az, in the T, يُؤَثْفِى, as aor. of أَثْفَى, is يُثْفِى reduced to its original form; and the like is said in the Ṣ and M in art. ثفى. If this be the case, مُؤَثْفَاةٌ, q. v., may be مُثْفَاةٌ reduced in the same manner, i. e., to its original form.]

أَثْفٌ [probably a mistake for ▼ آثِفٌ] *Continuing, permanent, constant, firm,* or *established:* (Ḳ, TA:) so in the Moheeṭ. (TA.) — Also, (Ḳ, and so in a copy of the Ṣ,) or ▼ آثِفٌ, [agreeably with analogy, and therefore more probably the correct form,] (so in other copies of the Ṣ and in the T,) *Following.* (Ks, T, Ṣ, Ḳ.)

أُثْفِيَّةٌ and إِثْفِيَّةٌ [the former of which is the more common, and this only I find in copies of the T,] The *stone* [*which is one of the three*] *whereon the cooking-pot is placed:* (A'Obeyd, M, Ḳ:) it is, with the Arabs, *a stone like the head of a man:* (T:) the pl. is أَثَافِىُّ and أَثَافٍ; (T, Ṣ, [in which latter it is written differently in different copies, with the article prefixed, الأَثَافِىُّ and الأَثَافِى, but in both manners in art. ثفى,] M, Ḳ;) the latter being allowable; (T;) or, accord. to Akh, the latter only is used by the Arabs; (M;) applied to the *three stones mentioned above:* (TA in art. سفع; &c.:) upon these the cooking-pot is set up; but what is of iron, having three legs, is not called اثفيّة, but مِنْصَبٌ; (T;) [and this is what is meant by أُثْفِيَّةٌ مِنْ حَدِيدٍ in art. سفع in the Ḳ;] i. e. an iron trivet upon which a cooking-pot is set up. (TA in art. نصب.) أُثْفِيَّةٌ may be of the measure فُعْلُويَةٌ [from اثف], and it may be of the measure أُفْعُولَةٌ [from ثفى; in either case originally أُثْفُوِيَةٌ]. (A, L.) ثَالِثَةُ الأَثَافِى signifies *The part, not detached, of a mountain; by the side of which, two pieces are put* [*for the cooking-pot to be set thereon*]. (A'Obeyd, T, Ḳ.) And hence the saying, (A'Obeyd, T,) رَمَاهُ ٱللّٰهُ بِثَالِثَةِ الأَثَافِى (A'Obeyd, T, Ḳ) *May God smite him with the mountain;* meaning, ‡ *with a calamity;* (Th, TA, Ḳ in art. ثفى;) *with a calamity like the mountain* [*in greatness*]; (Th, M;) for when they do not find the third of the اثافى, they rest the cooking-pot [partly] upon the mountain: (M, Ḳ, in art. ثفى:) or, *with difficulties,* or *troubles,* or *calamities:* (Aṣ, T:) or, *with all evil;* evils being likened to one اثفيّة after another, and the third being the last: (T, Ḳ:) so says Aboo-Sa'eed: (T:) or, *with the last of evil;* and *the last of everything hateful:* (AO in Ḥar p. 84:) or, *with a great calamity.* (Ḥar ib.) One says also, فُلَانٌ ثَالِثَةُ الأَثَافِى, meaning ‡ *Such a one is the heaviest, most burdensome,* or *most troublesome, of the people.* (Ḥar ubi suprà.) — [Hence also,] الأَثَافِى is a name applied to † *certain stars* [accord. to Ideler, as mentioned by Freytag in his Lex., *the stars* σ *and* τ *and* υ *Draconis*] *over against the head of the* قِدْر; which is the name of certain stars disposed in a round form. (AḤát, Ḳ.) [Also] a name given by the vulgar to † [*The three chief stars in the constellation called*] الشَّلْيَاقُ [i. e. *Lyra*]. (Ḳzw.) — The sing., (Ḳ,) i. e. each of the two forms thereof, but written in the copies of the Ṣ with ḍamm [only], (TA in art. ثفى,) or [only] the latter, with kesr, (M, and so in the Ḳ in art. ثفى,) also signifies † *A number,* (M,) or *a great number,* (Ḳ, and so in the Ṣ in art. ثفى,) and *a company,* or *congregated body, of men:* (M, Ḳ:) pl. as above. (M.) You say, هُمْ عَلَيْهِ أُثْفِيَّةٌ وَاحِدَةٌ † [*They are against him one band*]. (TA.) And بَقِيَتْ مِنْ بَنِى فُلَانٍ أُثْفِيَّةٌ خَشْنَاءُ *There remained of the sons of such a one a great number.* (Ṣ in art. ثفى.)

آثِفٌ: see أَثْفٌ, in two places.

مُؤَثَّفٌ † *Short, broad, plump, and fleshy.* (Ḳ.) — And, with ة, ‡ A woman *whose husband has two wives beside her; she being the third of them:* they being likened to the أَثَافِى of the cooking-pot. (M.) [See also مُثْفَاةٌ, in art. ثفى.]

قِدْرٌ مُؤَثْفَاةٌ *A cooking-pot put upon the* أَثَافِى

[pl. of أُثْفِيَّةٌ, q. v.]. (M, and Ḳ in art. ثفى: in some copies of the latter, مُؤَثْفَاةٌ.) [See Q. Q. 1.]

اثكل

إِثْكَالٌ and أُثْكُولٌ i. q. شِمْرَاخٌ [A fruit-stalk of the raceme of a palm-tree, upon which are the dates]; like عِثْكَالٌ and عُثْكُولٌ: the hemzeh in each is a substitute for ع; but by J [and others] it is held to be augmentative, and the words are mentioned in art. ثكل, q. v. (TA.)

اثل

1. أَثَلَ, aor. ـِ, inf. n. أُثُولٌ, It (anything, M) had, or came to have, root, or a foundation; or it was, or became, firm, or established, and firmly rooted or founded; as also ↓ تأثّل. (M, Ḳ.) — Also, inf. n. as above, It (dominion) was, or became, great; (TA;) and so ↓ the latter verb. (M, Ḳ.*) — And أَثُلَ, inf. n. أَثَالَةٌ, said of high rank, or nobility, It was, or became, old, of ancient origin, or of long standing. (TA.) — See also 5.

2. أثّلهُ, (M, Ḳ,) inf. n. تَأْثِيلٌ, (Ṣ, Ḳ,) He made it (his wealth, or property, M, Ḳ, and so applied it is tropical, TA) to have root, or a foundation; or to become firm, or established, and firmly rooted or founded; syn. أَصَّلَهُ. (Ṣ,* M, Ḳ.) — He (God, T, M,* TA) made it (a man's dominion, T, M, Ḳ) to be, or become, firm, firmly established, stable, or permanent: (T:) or great: (M, Ḳ:) and he (a man) made it (a thing) lasting, or permanent. (TA.) IAạr cites the following verse,

* تُؤَثِّلُ كَعْبٌ عَلَىَّ القَضَا *
* فَرَبِّى يُغَيِّرُ أَعْمَالَهَا *

[app. meaning Kaab would oblige me to make payment, or the like, (as though establishing against me the duty of doing so,) but my Lord changes their actions,] explaining it by saying, i. e. تُلْزِمُنِى; but (ISd says,) I know not how this is. (M.) — He (God, M) made it (a man's wealth, or property,) to increase; or put it into a good, or right, state, or condition; syn. زَكَّاهُ. (M, Ḳ.) — أَثَّلْتُهُ بِرِجَالٍ I multiplied him [meaning his party] by men. (TA.) — أَثَّلْتُ عَلَيْهِ الدُّيُونَ I collected against him the debts. (TA.) — أَثَّلَ أَهْلَهُ He clad his family with the most excellent of clothing: (M:) or he clad them (M, Ḳ) with the most excellent of clothing, (Ḳ,) and did good to them, or acted well towards them. (M, Ḳ.) — أَثَّلَ, [used intransitively,] (M, Ḳ,) inf. n. as above, (TA,) He (a man, Ḳ) became abundant in his wealth, or property. (M, Ḳ.)

5. تأثّل: see 1, in two places. — Also It (a thing) became collected together. (Ḳ.) — He took for himself, got, or acquired, what is termed أَثَلَةٌ, i. e. مِيرَةٌ [meaning victuals, or provision]; (M, Ḳ;) بَعْدَ حَاجَةٍ [after want]. (M.) — He took for himself, got, or acquired, a source, stock, or fund, (أَصْلٌ,) of wealth, or property. (Ṣ, TA.) — And تأثّل مَالًا He collected, or gained, or acquired, wealth, or property, (M, Ḳ,) and took it for himself: (M:) [said in the TA to be tropical:] or he collected wealth, or property, and took it for himself, or got it, or acquired it, as a source, stock, or fund: (Mgh:) and أَثَّلَ ↓ مَالًا, inf. n. أُثُولٌ, signifies the same as تأثّلهُ. (TA.) — هُمْ يَتَأَثَّلُونَ النَّاسَ They take أُثَال, i. e. wealth, or property, from men. (TA.) — تأثّل بِئْرًا He dug a well (T, Ṣ, M, Ḳ) for himself. (T, TA.)

أَثْلٌ A kind of trees; (Ṣ, Ḳ;) a species of the طَرْفَآء [or tamarisk; so applied in the present day; termed by Forskål (Flora Aeg. Arab. p. lxiv.) tamarix orientalis]; (Ṣ, TA;) or a kind of trees, (T, M,) or a certain tree, (Mgh,) resembling the طرفآء, (T, M, Mgh,) except that it is of a better kind, (T,) or except that it is larger, and better in its wood, (M,) of which are made yellow and excellent [vessels of the kind called] أَقْدَاح, and of which was made the Prophet's pulpit; it has thick stems, of which are made doors and other things; and its leaves are of the kind called عَبَل, like those of the طرفآء: (TA:) AḤn says, on the authority of Aboo-Ziyád, that it is of the kind termed عِضَاه, tall, and long in its wood, which is excellent, and is carried to the towns and villages, and the clay houses of these are built upon it; [app. meaning that its wood is used in forming the foundations of the walls;] its leaves are of the kind called هَدَب, [syn. with عَبَل,] long and slender, and it has no thorns; of it are made [bowls of the kinds called] قِصَاع and جِفَان; and it has a red fruit, like a knot of a rope: (M:) or a kind of large trees, having no fruit: (Mṣb:) or i. q. طرفآء, having no fruit: (Bḍ in xxxiv. 15:) n. un. with ة; (Ṣ, M, Mṣb, Ḳ;) explained in the A as the سَمُرَة [or gum-acacia tree]: or a tall, straight [tree such as is termed] عِضَاهَة, of which are made the like of أَقْدَاح: (TA:) the pl. [of أَثْل] is أُثُولٌ (M, Ḳ) and [of أَثْلَةٌ] أَثَلَاتٌ. (Ṣ, Ḳ, TA (in the CḲ [أَثْلاتٌ]).) — [See also أَثْلَةٌ, below.] — فُلَانٌ أَثْلُ مَالٍ Such a one is a collector of wealth, or property. (Ibn-'Abbád.)

أَثْلَةٌ n. un. of أَثْلٌ, q. v. (Ṣ, M, &c.) Because of the tallness of the tree thus called, and its erectness, and beauty of proportion, the poets liken thereto a woman of perfect stature and erect form. (M.) — Metaphorically, (Mṣb,) ‡ Honour, or reputation; or grounds of pretension to respect on account of the honourable deeds or qualities of one's ancestors, &c.; syn. عِرْضٌ; (Mṣb, TA;) or حَسَبٌ. (Ṣ, O, Ḳ, TA.) So in the saying, فُلَانٌ يَنْحِتُ أَثْلَتَنَا, or يَنْحَتُ, (Ṣ accord. to different copies, and so in the O, but in the copies of the Ḳ, incorrectly, يَنْحَتُ فِى أَثْلَتِنَا, TA,) ‡ Such a one speaks evil of, (Ṣ, O,) or impugns, or speaks against, (Ḳ,) our honour, or reputation, &c. (Ṣ, O, Ḳ.) And نَحَتَ أَثْلَتَهُ ‡ He detracted from his reputation; spoke against him; impugned his character; censured him; blamed him. (A, Mṣb.) And فُلَانٌ تُنْحَتُ أَثْلَاتُهُ ‡ [Such a one's grounds of pretension to respect, &c., are impugned]. (TA.) And هُوَ لَا تُنْحَتُ أَثْلَتُهُ ‡ He has not any vice, or fault, nor any imperfection, or defect. (Mṣb.) — The root, foundation, origin, source, stock, or the like, syn. أَصْلٌ; (T, Ṣ, M, Mgh, Ḳ;) of a thing, and of a man; (T;) of anything; (M;) [a source, stock, or fund,] of wealth, or property: (Mgh, TA:) pl. إِثَالٌ. (Ḳ.) So in the saying, لَهُ أَثْلَةُ مَالٍ [He has a source, or stock, or fund, of wealth, or property]. (TA.) — Victuals, or provision; syn. مِيرَةٌ. (M, Ḳ.) — The goods, furniture, and utensils, of a house or tent; as also ↓ أَثَلَةٌ. (M, Ḳ.*) — Apparatus, accoutrements, implements, or the like. (Ibn-'Abbád, Ḳ.) So in the saying, أَخَذْتُ أَثْلَةَ الشِّتَآءِ [I took the apparatus, &c., of, i. e. for, the winter]. (Ibn-'Abbád.)

أَثَلَةٌ: see أَثْلَةٌ, near the end.

أَثَالٌ, (T, Ṣ, M,) with fet-ḥ, (Ṣ,) or أُثَالٌ, with ḍamm, (Mgh,) or both, (Ḳ,) ‡ Glory, honour, dignity, nobility, or high rank. (AA, T, Ṣ, M, Mgh, Ḳ.) You say, لَهُ أَثَالٌ كَأَنَّهُ أُثَالٌ ‡ He has glory, or honour, &c., as though it were the mountain called Othál. (TA.) [But the next signification seems to be here more appropriate.] — † Wealth, or property. (Mgh.)

أَثِيلٌ A place of growth of trees of the kind called أَرَاك [perhaps a mistranscription for أَثْل]: mentioned by Th, from IAạr. (T.) — Abundant, and luxuriant, or long, hair. (TA.) — See also مُؤَثَّلٌ, in two places.

آثِلٌ: see مُؤَثَّلٌ.

مُؤَثَّلٌ Having root, or a foundation; or firm, or established, and firmly rooted or founded: (Ṣ:) or having a permanent source, or firm foundation: (Munjid of Kr:) or of old foundation or origin: or collected together so as to [become stable or permanent, or] have root or a foundation: (T:) or old; of ancient origin; or of long standing: (M, TA:) or permanent: (IAạr:) ‡ applied to glory, honour, dignity, nobility, or high rank; (T, Kr, Ṣ, M, TA;) and so ↓ أَثِيلٌ: (Ṣ, TA:) and to wealth, or property: (Kr, Ṣ:) and to anything; (T, M;) and so ↓ أَثِيلٌ, and ↓ مُتَأَثِّلٌ: (M:) and ↓ آثِلٌ, also, has the first of these significations, applied to dominion. (T.) — Prepared, disposed, arranged, or put into a right or good state. (AA.)

مُتَأَثِّلٌ: see مُؤَثَّلٌ. — Also Taking for oneself, getting, or acquiring, a source, stock, or fund, (أَصْل,) of wealth, or property: (Ṣ, TA:) or collecting wealth, or property, (T, Mgh,) and taking it for oneself, or getting it, or acquiring it, as a source, stock, or fund. (Mgh.) So in a trad. on the subject of a charge respecting the orphan, يَأْكُلُ مِنْ مَالِهِ غَيْرَ مُتَأَثِّلٍ مَالًا [He may eat of his wealth, or property, not taking for himself a source, stock, or fund, of wealth, or property: or, not collecting &c.]: (T, Ṣ, Mgh:*) or, accord. to Bkh, not acquiring abundance of wealth: but the former explanation is more correct lexically. (Mgh.)

اثم

1. أَثِمَ, (Lth, Ṣ, M, &c.,) aor. ـَ, (Lth, M, Mṣb, Ḳ,) inf. n. إِثْمٌ, (Ṣ, Ḳ,) or أَثَمٌ, the former being a simple subst., (Mṣb,) and مَأْثَمٌ, (Ṣ, Ḳ,) He fell

into what is termed إِثْمٌ [i. e. *a sin*, or *crime*, &c.]; (Lth, T, Ṣ, M, Mṣb,* Ḳ*;) [*he sinned; committed a sin*, or *crime*;] *he did what was unlawful:* (M,* Ḳ:) and ▼ تَأْثِيمٌ signifies the same as إِثْمٌ: (Ḳ:) it may be either an inf. n. of ▼ أَثَّمَ, which [says ISd] I have not heard, or, as Sb holds it to be, a simple subst. like تَنْبِيتٌ: (M:) and is said to be used in the sense of إِثْمٌ in the Ḳur lii. 23 [and lvi. 24]. (TA.) [It should be added also, that ▼ تَأْثَامٌ, like تَكْذَابٌ, is syn. with تَأْثِيمٌ and إِثْمٌ; and, like تَأْثِيمٌ, may be an inf. n. of ▼ أَثَّمَ, or a simple subst.: see an ex. voce بَرُوقٌ.] In the dial. of some of the Arabs, the first letter of the aor. is with kesr, as in تِعْلَمُ and نِعْلَمُ; and as the hemzeh in إِثْمٌ is with kesr, the radical hemzeh [in the aor.] is changed into ى; so that they say إِيثَمُ and تِيثَمُ [for آثَمُ and تَأْثَمُ]. (TA.) In the saying,

• لَوْ قُلْتَ مَا فِي قَوْمِهَا لَمْ تِيثَمِ •
• يَفْضُلُهَا فِي حَسَبٍ وَمِيسَمِ •

the meaning is, [*Shouldst thou say, thou wouldst not sin*, or *do wrong*, in so saying,] *There is not, among her people*, any one *who excels her* [*in grounds of pretension to respect, and in impress*, or *character, of beauty*]. (M.) — أَثَمَهُ ٱللّٰهُ فِي كَذَا, aor. ـُ (Ṣ, Ḳ) and ـِ, (Ṣ,) or ـَ, (Ḳ,) but there is no other authority than the Ḳ for this last, nor is there any reason for it, as the medial radical letter is not faucial, nor is the final, and in the Iḳtiṭáf el-Azáhir the aor. is said to be ـِ and ـُ, (MF, TA,) [*God reckoned him to have sinned*, or *committed a crime* or *the like, in such a thing*; or] *God reckoned such a thing against him as an* إِثْم: (Ṣ, Ḳ:) or أَثَمَهُ, aor. ـِ (Fr, T, M, Mṣb) and ـُ, (Mṣb,) inf. n. أَثْمٌ (Fr, T, Mṣb) and أَثَامٌ (Fr, T, TA) and إِثَامٌ, (Fr, TA,) *He* (God) *requited him*, (Fr, T,) or *punished him*, (M,) *for what is termed* إِثْم [i. e. *sin*, or *crime*, &c.]: (Fr, T, M:) [see also أَثَامٌ below:] or *he* (a man) *pronounced him to be* آثِم [i. e. *a sinner*, or *the like*]: (Mṣb:) [or] ▼ آثَمَهُ, aor. يُؤْثِمُهُ, has this last signification, said of God; and also signifies *He found him to be so.* (T.) — You say also, أَثِمَتِ ٱلنَّاقَةُ ٱلْمَشْىَ, aor. ـِ, inf. n. أَثْمٌ, *The she-camel was slow.* (M.)

2. أَثَّمَهُ, (Ṣ, Mṣb, Ḳ,) inf. n. تَأْثِيمٌ, (Mṣb, Ḳ,) *He said to him* أَثِمْتَ [*Thou hast fallen into a sin*, or *crime*, &c.; *hast sinned*, &c.]. (Ṣ, Mṣb, Ḳ.) — See also 1, first and second sentences.

4. آثَمَهُ *He made him*, or *caused him, to fall into what is termed* إِثْم [i. e. *a sin*, or *crime*, &c.], (Zj, Ṣ, M, Ḳ,) or *what is termed* ذَنْب. (Mṣb.) — See also 1, last sentence but one.

5. تَأَثَّمَ *He abstained from what is termed* إِثْم [i. e. *sin*, or *crime*, &c.]; (T, Ṣ, M, Mṣb, Ḳ;) like تَحَرَّجَ meaning "he preserved himself from what is termed حَرَج:" (Mṣb:) or *he did a work*, or *deed, whereby he escaped from what is termed* إِثْم: (TA:) and *he repented of what is so termed*, (M, Ḳ,) *and begged forgiveness of it*; as though he removed the إِثْم itself by repentance and by begging forgiveness; or sought to do so by those two means. (M.) You say also, تَأَثَّمَ مِنْ كَذَا *He abstained from such a thing as a sin*, or *crime*; syn. تَحَنَّثَ, q. v. (Ṣ, Ḳ, in art. حنث.)

إِثْمٌ [accord. to some, an inf. n.; see أَثِمَ: accord. to others, only a simple subst., signifying] *A sin, a crime, a fault, an offence*, or *an act of disobedience*, syn. ذَنْبٌ, (Ṣ, M, Mṣb, Ḳ,) *for which one deserves punishment*; differing from ذَنْب inasmuch as this signifies both what is intentional and what is unintentional: (Kull:) or [so accord. to the M, but in the Ḳ "and,"] *an unlawful deed:* (M, Ḳ:) or *a deed which retards from recompense:* or, accord. to Fr, *what is exclusive of the* [*punishment termed*] حَدّ: accord. to Er-Rághib, it is a term of more general import than عُدْوَانٌ: (TA:) ▼ مَأْثَمٌ [which is originally an inf. n. of أَثِمَ] is syn. with إِثْمٌ; (T,* Mgh;) and so, too, is ▼ أَثَامٌ, (Mṣb,) or ▼ إِثَامٌ, signifying *a deed retarding recompense:* (TA:) the pl. of إِثْمٌ is آثَامٌ: (M:) and the pl. of ▼ مَأْثَمٌ is مَآثِمُ. (T.) — [Sometimes it is prefixed to a noun or pronoun denoting its object: — and sometimes it means † *The punishment of a sin* &c.: see explanations of a passage in the Ḳur v. 32, voce بَآءَ.] — ‡ *Wine:* (Aboo-Bekr El-Iyádee, T, Ṣ, M, Ḳ:) sometimes used in this sense; (Ṣ;) but tropically; not properly: (IAmb:) I think, [says ISd,] because the drinking thereof is what is thus termed. (M.) — [And for a like reason,] † *Contention for stakes*, or *wagers, in a game of hazard*; syn. قِمَارٌ; (M, Ḳ;) which is a man's destruction of his property. (M.) It is said in the Ḳur [ii. 216, respecting wine and the game called ٱلْمَيْسِر,] قُلْ فِيهِمَا إِثْمٌ كَبِيرٌ وَمَنَافِعُ لِلنَّاسِ [*Say thou, In them both are great sin and means of profit to men*]: and Th says, when they contended in a game of this kind, and won, they gave food and alms, and these were means of profit. (M.)

أَثَامٌ: see إِثْمٌ. — Also *The requital*, or *recompense, of* إِثْم [i. e. *sin*, or *crime*, &c.]: (T, Ṣ, M, Mṣb:) so says Zj, (T, M,) and in like manner say Kh and Sb: (T:) or *punishment* (Yoo, Lth, T, M, Ḳ) *thereof:* (Lth, T, M:) and ▼ إِثَامٌ and ▼ مَأْثَمٌ signify the same; (M, Ḳ;) the latter like مَقْعَدٌ. (TA. [In the CḲ this is written مَأْثِمٌ.]) So in the Ḳur [xxv. 68], يَلْقَ أَثَامًا [*He shall find a requital*, or *recompense*, or *a punishment, of sin*]: (T, Ṣ, M:) in my opinion, [says ISd,] the correct meaning is, *he shall find the punishment of* آثَام [or *sins*]: but some say, the meaning is that which here follows. (M.) — *A valley in Hell.* (M, Ḳ.)

إِثَامٌ: see إِثْمٌ: — and أَثَامٌ.

أَثُومٌ: see أَثِيمٌ; and أَثِمٌ.

أَثِيمٌ: see آثِمٌ. — Also *A great*, or *habitual, liar*; or one *who lies much*; and so ▼ أَثُومٌ. (Ḳ.) So in the Ḳur ii. 277: or it there signifies *Burdened with* إِثْم [or *sin*, &c.]. (TA.) In the Ḳur xliv. 44, it means, accord. to Fr, *The unrighteous*, or *sinning*; like ▼ آثِمٌ: (T:) or *the unbeliever:* (TA:) or, accord. to Zj, in this instance, (M,) by the اثيم is meant *Aboo-Jahl.* (M, Ḳ.) — Also *The commission of* إِثْم [*sin*, or *crime*, &c.,] *much*, or *frequently*; and so ▼ أَثِيمَةٌ. (M, Ḳ.)

أَثِيمَةٌ: see أَثِيمٌ.

أَثَّامٌ: see آثِمٌ.

آثِمٌ *Falling into what is termed* إِثْم [i. e. *a sin*, or *crime*, &c.]; (Ṣ, Mṣb,* Ḳ;*) [*sinning; committing a sin*, or *crime*;] *doing what is unlawful:* (Ḳ:) and in like manner, (Ṣ, Mṣb, Ḳ,) but having an intensive signification, (Mṣb,) ▼ أَثِيمٌ, and ▼ أَثُومٌ, (Ṣ, M, Mṣb, Ḳ,) and ▼ أَثَّامٌ: (M, Mṣb, Ḳ: [in the CḲ, erroneously, without teshdeed:]) the pl. of the first of these three is أُثَمَآءُ; that of the second, أُثُمٌ; and that of the third, أَثَّامُونَ. (M.) See also أَثِيمٌ. — آثِمَةٌ, (Ṣ,) and آثِمَاتٌ, (Ṣ, M, Ḳ, [in the CḲ, erroneously, أَثِمَاتٌ.]) A she-camel, (Ṣ,) and she-camels, *slow*, or *tardy*; (Ṣ, M, Ḳ;) *weary, fatigued*, or *jaded*. (Ḳ. [In the CḲ, we find مُعْيِبَاتٌ erroneously put for مُعْيِيَاتٌ.]) Some pronounce it with ت. (Ṣgh.) [In like manner,] ▼ مُؤَاثِمٌ signifies That is *slack*, or *slow, in pace*, or *going*; ٱلَّذِى يُكَذِّبُ فِى ٱلسَّيْرِ. (Ṣgh, Ḳ. [In Golius's Lex., as from the Ḳ, ٱلَّذِى يَكْذِبُ ٱلسَّيْرَ. Both are correct, signifying the same.])

تَأْثَامٌ : } see 1.
تَأْثِيمٌ : }

مَأْثَمٌ: see إِثْمٌ, in two places: — and see أَثَامٌ.

مَأْثُومٌ [*Reckoned to have sinned*, or *the like*;] *having a thing reckoned against him as an* إِثْم: (Ṣ:) or *requited for what is termed* إِثْم. (Fr, T.)

مُؤَاثِمٌ: see آثِمٌ.

اثن

إِثْنَانِ and إِثْنَتَانِ: see art. ثنى.

اج

1. أَجَّتِ ٱلنَّارُ, (Ṣ, A, Mṣb,) aor. ـُ (Ṣ, Mṣb) and ـِ, (M, TA,) [the former contr. to analogy, and the latter agreeable therewith, in the case of an intrans. verb of this class,] inf. n. أَجِيجٌ, (Ṣ, A, Mṣb, Ḳ,) *The fire burned, burned up, burned brightly*, or *fiercely*, (Mṣb,) *blazed*, or *flamed*, or *blazed* or *flamed fiercely*; (Ṣ, A, Mṣb, Ḳ;) as also ▼ تَأَجَّجَت (Ṣ, A, Ḳ) and ▼ ٱئْتَجَّت [written with the disjunctive alif إِيتَجَّت]: (Ṣ, Ḳ:) or *made a sound by its blazing* or *flaming*. (ISd, TA.) — أَجَّ, aor. ـُ, (Ṣ, Ḳ, &c.,) contr. to analogy, (TA,) and ـِ, (Jm, TṢ, L, Ḳ,) but this is rejected by AA, (MF,) inf. n. أَجٌّ (Ṣ) and أَجِيجٌ, (TA,) ‡ *He* (an ostrich) *ran, making a* [*rustling*] *sound*, or *noise, such as is termed* حَفِيف. (Ṣ, L, Ḳ, &c.) And, aor. ـُ, (T, A,) inf. n. أَجٌّ, (T, TA,) † *He hastened*, or *was quick, in his pace*; *walked quickly*; or *went a pace between a walk and a run*; (T, Nh;) said of a man; (Nh, from a trad.;) and of a camel: (IB:) or ‡ *he made a sound*, or *noise*, in his pace or going, *like that of the blazing*, or *flaming, of fire*. (A.) You say, أَجَّ أَجَّةَ ٱلظَّلِيمِ

‡ [*He made a rustling sound* in going along, *like that of the ostrich*]. (A.) And أَجَّ, aor. ـُ, [so in the TA,] inf. n. أَجِيجٌ, † *It* (a camel's saddle) *made a sound* or *noise* [produced by his running]. (AZ, TA.) And أَجِيجٌ signifies also † The *sounding* of water *in pouring forth*. (TA.) — أَجَّ, (Ṣ, Ḳ,) aor. ـُ, (Ṣ, L,) inf. n. أُجُوجٌ, (Ṣ, Ḳ,) *It* (water) *was*, or *became*, *such as is termed* أُجَاجٌ. (Ṣ, L, Ḳ.) = أَجَّهُ *He rendered it* (namely water) *such as is termed* أُجَاجٌ. (Ḳ.)

2. أَجَّجَ النَّارَ, (Ṣ, A, Ḳ,) inf. n. تَأْجِيجٌ, (Ḳ,) *He made the fire to* [*burn, burn up, burn brightly* or *fiercely*, (see 1,)] *blaze*, or *flame*, or *blaze* or *flame fiercely*. (Ṣ, A, Ḳ.) — [Hence,] أَجَّجَ بَيْنَهُمْ شَرًّا † *He kindled evil*, or *mischief*, *among them*. (TA.)

5: see 1. — Hence تَأَجَّجَ also signifies *It gave light*; *shone*; or *shone brightly*. (TA, from a trad.) — See also 8, where a contracted form of this verb is mentioned.

8: see 1. — [Hence,] ائْتَجَّ النَّهَارُ [written with the disjunctive alif ايْتَجَّ] *The day was*, or *became*, *intensely hot*, or *fiercely burning*; (Ṣ, Ḳ;) as also ▼ تَأَجَّ and تَأَجَّجَ. (Ḳ.)

أَجَّةٌ *Intenseness of heat*, and *its fierce burning*; (Ṣ, Ḳ;) as also ▼ أَجِيجٌ [inf. n. of 1], and ▼ أَجَاجٌ, and ▼ ائْتِجَاجٌ [inf. n. of 8]: pl. إِجَاجٌ. (Ṣ.) You say, جَآءَتْ أَجَّةُ الصَّيْفِ *The intense heat*, or *fierce burning*, *of summer came*. (TA.) — The *sound* of fire; as also ▼ أَجِيجٌ. (ISd, TA.) — ‡ The *sound*, or *noise*, *and commotion*, of an ostrich running, and of people walking or passing along. (A.) You say, أَجَّ أَجَّةَ الظَّلِيمِ [explained above: see 1]. (A.) — † *Confusion*: (Ṣ, Ḳ:) or, as also ▼ أَجِيجٌ, the *confusion arising from the talking* of a people, and the *sound*, or *noise*, *of* their *walking* or *passing along*. (L.) You say, القَوْمُ فِى أَجَّةٍ *The people are in a state of confusion* [&c.]. (Ṣ.)

أَجَاجٌ: see أَجَّةٌ.

أُجَاجٌ Anything *burning to the mouth, whether salt or bitter or hot*. (MF.) [Hence,] مَآءٌ أُجَاجٌ, (Ṣ, A, Ḳ, &c.,) and ▼ إِجَاجٌ, (Mṣb,) *Water that burns by its saltness*: (A:) or *salt water*: or *bitter water*: (TA:) or *salt, bitter water*: (Ṣ, Ḳ:) or *very salt water*: (I'Ab:) or *bitter and very salt water*: (Mṣb:) or *very salt water, that burns by reason of its saltness*: or *very bitter water*: or *water very salt and bitter, like the water of the sea*: (TA:) or *water of which no use is made for drinking, or for watering seed-produce, or for other purposes*: (El-Ḥasan:) or *very hot water*: (TA:) the pl. is the same [as the sing.; or أُجَاجٌ is also used as a quasi-pl. n.]. (TA.)

إِجَاجٌ: see أُجَاجٌ.

أَجُوجٌ *Giving light; shining*; or *shining brightly*. (AA, Ṣ, Ḳ.)

أَجِيجٌ inf. n. of 1, which see: and see also أَجَّةٌ, in three places.

هَجِيرٌ أَجَّاجٌ [*A vehemently hot*, or *fiercely-burning, summer-midday*]. (A.)

آجٌّ; fem. with ة: see الأَوَاجِجُ, below.

آجُوجٌ: see يَأْجُوجُ, below.

السَّمَائِمُ الأَوَاجِجُ [*The fiercely-burning hot winds*; the latter word being pl. of ▼ آجَّةٌ, fem. of ▼ آجٌّ, which is the act. part. n. of أَجَّ;] is used by poetic licence for الأَوَاجُّ. (TA.)

ائْتِجَاجٌ inf. n. of 8, which see: and see also أَجَّةٌ.

مَأْجُوجُ: see what follows.

يَأْجُوجُ One *who walks quickly*, and *runs*, *in this and that manner*. (Ḳ,* TA.) — يَأْجُوجُ and ▼ مَأْجُوجُ, (Ṣ, Mṣb, Ḳ,) imperfectly decl., (Ṣ,) [*Gog and Magog*;] *two tribes of God's creatures*; (TA;) or *two great nations*; (Mṣb;) or *two tribes of the children of Japheth the son of Noah*: or, as some say, *the former, of the Turks*; and *the latter, of the Jeel* [meaning *Jeel-Jeelán*, said in the TA in art. جيل, on the authority of ISd, to be *a people beyond the Deylem*; and on the authority of Az, to be *believers in a plurality of gods*; (*the Geli* and *Gelæ* of Ptolemy and Strabo, as observed by Sale, in a note on ch. xviii. v. 93 of the Ḳur, on the authority of Golius in Alfrag. p. 207;)]: (Bḍ in xviii. 93:) [said by the Arabs to be *Scythians of the furthest East*; *particularly those on the north of the Chinese*: (Golius:) or, as some say, *the descendants of Japheth, and all the nations inhabiting the north of Asia and of Europe*: (Freytag:)] *said* in a rad., (TA,) on the authority of I'Ab, (Mṣb,) *to compose nine tenths of mankind*: (Mṣb, TA:) or يأجوج is the name of *the males*, and مأجوج is that of *the females*: (Mṣb:) he who pronounces them thus, and makes the ا a radical letter, says that the former is of the measure يَفْعُولُ, and the latter of the measure مَفْعُولُ; as though from أَجِيجُ النَّارِ; (Akh, Ṣ, Mṣb;*) or from مَآءٌ أُجَاجٌ; (TA;) or from أَجَّ said of an ostrich; and imperfectly decl. as being determinate and fem.: (Bḍ ubi suprà:) he who pronounces them without ء, making the ا in each an augmentative letter, says that the former is from يَجَجْتُ, and the latter from مَجَجْتُ: (Akh, Ṣ, Ḳ:) this is the case if they be Arabic: (TA:) but some say that they are foreign names; (Mṣb, TA;) their being imperfectly decl. is said to indicate this; (Bḍ ubi suprà;) and if so, the ا in them is similar to that in هَارُوت and مَارُوت and دَاوُود and the like; and the ء, anomalous, as that in عَأْلَمٌ and the like; and their measure is فَاعُولُ. (Mṣb.) Ru-beh used to read ▼ آجُوجُ and مَاجُوجُ [in the CḲ مَأْجُوجُ]; and Aboo-Mo'ádh, يَمْجُوجُ. (Ḳ.)

اجر

1. أَجَرَهُ, aor. ـِ and ـُ, (Ṣ, Mgh, Mṣb, Ḳ,) which latter form of the aor., though known to most of the lexicologists, is disacknowledged by a few of them, (TA,) inf. n. أَجْرٌ; (Ṣ, Mṣb;) and ▼ آجَرَهُ, (Ṣ, Mgh, Mṣb, Ḳ,) a form disacknowledged by Aṣ, but said by some to be the more chaste of the two, of the form أَفْعَلَ, not فَاعَلَ, as IḲṭṭ by evident inadvertence makes it to be by saying that its aor. is يُؤَاجِرُ, (TA,) inf. n. إِيجَارٌ; (Ṣ;) *He* (God, Ṣ, A, Mgh, Mṣb, and a man, Mgh) *recompensed, compensated*, or *rewarded, him*, (Ṣ, A, Mgh, Mṣb, Ḳ,) عَلَى مَا فَعَلَ *for what he had done*. (A.) [See أَجْرٌ, below.] أُجِرَ فُلَانٌ خَمْسَةً مِنْ وَلَدِهِ [*Such a one became entitled to a reward for five of his children*, by their death, (for it is believed that the Muslim will be rewarded in Paradise for a child that has died in infancy)], (Ṣ,) and أُجِرَ وَلَدَهُ, (A,) and أُجِرَ فِى أَوْلَادِهِ, (Ḳ,) mean that his children died, and became [causes of] his reward. (Ṣ, A, Ḳ.) — أَجَرَهُ, (Ḳ,) aor. ـِ, (Ṣ,) [*He served him for hire, pay*, or *wages*;] *he became his hired man*, or *hireling*. (Ṣ, Ḳ.) So in the Ḳur xxviii. 27. (TA.) — أَجَرَهُ, aor. ـِ, (L, Mṣb, Ḳ,) and ـُ, (Mṣb, Ḳ,) inf. n. أَجْرٌ, (L, Ḳ,) *He let him* (namely his slave) *on hire*, or *for pay*, or *wages*; (L,* Mṣb,* Ḳ;) as also ▼ آجَرَهُ, inf. n. إِيجَارٌ; ('Eyn, Mgh, Mṣb, Ḳ;) and ▼ آجَرَهُ, inf. n. مُؤَاجَرَةٌ: (Ḳ:) all these are good forms of speech, used by the Arabs: (L:) or ▼ آجره having for its inf. n. مؤاجرة signifies *he appointed him* (namely another man) *hire, pay*, or *wages, for his work*; (Mj, Mgh;) or *he engaged with him to give him hire, pay*, or *wages*; (A, Mgh, Mṣb;) and can have only one objective complement: whereas, ▼ when it is of the measure أَفْعَلَ it is doubly trans.; (Mgh, Mṣb;) so that one says, آجَرَنِى ▼ مَمْلُوكَهُ *He let me his slave on hire*. (Mgh.) One also says, أَجَرَ الدَّارَ, aor. ـِ and ـُ, inf. n. أَجْرٌ, *He let the house on hire*; and so آجَرَ ▼ الدَّارَ, [inf. n. إِيجَارٌ:] (Mṣb, TA:) and آجَرَهُ ▼ الدَّارَ, [inf. n. إِيجَارٌ,] *He let to him the house on hire*: (Ṣ, A, Mgh, Mṣb:) the latter verb being of the measure أَفْعَلَ, not of the measure فَاعَلَ: (A, Mgh, Mṣb:) and the vulgar say, وَاجَرَ: (Ṣ:) some, however, say, آجَرْتُ ▼ الدَّارَ, inf. n. مُؤَاجَرَةٌ, making the verb of the measure فاعل: (Mṣb, TA:) some also say, آجَرْتُ ▼ الدَّارَ زَيْدًا [*I let the house to Zeyd*], inverting the order of the words: (Mṣb, TA:) and the lawyers say, آجَرْتُ ▼ الدَّارَ مِنْ زَيْدٍ [in the same sense, like as بِعْتُ زَيْدًا الدَّارَ means the same as بِعْتُ مِنْ زَيْدٍ الدَّارَ]. (Mṣb: [but in the Mgh, the like of this is said to be vulgar.])

3. آجر, inf. n. مُؤَاجَرَةٌ: see 1, latter half, in three places: and see 10. One says also, of a woman, (Ḳ,) or a whorish female slave, (TA,) آجَرَتْ, [of the measure فَاعَلَتْ, not أَفْعَلَتْ, (see مُؤْجِرٌ, below,)] meaning *She prostituted herself for hire*. (Ḳ.)

4. آجر, inf. n. إِيجَارٌ: see 1, first sentence: — and see the latter half of the same paragraph, in seven places.

8. ائتجر [written with the disjunctive alif ايتجر] *He gave alms, seeking thereby to obtain a reward*

[*from God*]: (L, Ḳ*:) and ائتجر بِهِ *He gave it as alms, seeking thereby a reward.* (L.) اتَّجَرَ for ائتجر is not allowable, because ء cannot be incorporated into ت: [or, accord. to some, this is allowable, as in اتَّزَرَ for ائتزر, and اتَّمَنَ for ائتمن &c.:] Hr allows it; and cites an ex. in a trad.; but IAth says that the proper reading in this instance is يَأْتَجِرُ, not يَتَّجِرُ; or, if the latter be allowed, it is from التِّجَارَةُ, not from الأَجْرُ. (L.) —— أُوتُجِرَ عَلَيْهِ بِكَذَا [in which the radical ء is changed into و because the alif preceding it is made disjunctive and with ḍamm, (in one copy of the Ṣ, and in the L and TA, erroneously written اِيتُجِرَ,)] *He was hired to do it for such a sum* or *thing*, (see مُؤْتَجَرٌ, below,)] is from الأُجْرَةُ. (Ṣ, L.)

10. اِسْتَأْجَرَهُ, (Ṣ, Ḳ,) and ▼ آجَرَهُ, (Ḳ,) [the latter of the measure فَاعَلَ, as has been clearly shown above, from the A and Mgh and Mṣb,] *He hired him; took him as a hired man,* or *hireling.* (Ṣ, Ḳ, TA.) You say also, اِسْتَأْجَرَ الدَّارَ [*He hired the house; took it on hire*]. (A, Mgh.)

أَجْرٌ *A recompense, compensation,* or *reward,* (Ṣ, Ḳ, &c.,) *for what one has done;* (Ḳ;) i. q. ثَوَابٌ; (Ṣ;) as also ▼ إِجَارَةٌ and ▼ أُجَارَةٌ and ▼ أَجَارَةٌ, (Ḳ,) of which three forms the first is the most generally known and the most chaste, (TA,) and ▼ أُجْرَةٌ: (TA:) or, as some say, there is a distinction between أَجْرٌ and ثَوَابٌ: El-'Eynee says, in the Expos. of El-Bukhâree, that what is obtained by the fundamental practices of the law, and by obligatory religious services, is termed ثواب; and what is obtained by supererogatory acts of religion, اجر; for ثواب is properly a substitute for a thing itself; and اجر, for the profit arising from a thing; though each is sometimes used in the sense of the other: (TA:) it is well known that اجر signifies *a recompense,* or *reward, from God to a man, for righteous conduct;* (MF;) and ▼ إِجَارَةٌ, *recompense, compensation, hire, pay,* or *wages, from one man to another, for work;* (Mgh, MF;) and hence الأَجِيرُ; (MF;) and ▼ أُجْرَةٌ also has this latter signification, (Mgh, TA,) and is syn. with كِرَآءٌ; (Ṣ, Mgh, Ḳ;) [signifying likewise *rent* for a house, and *the like;*] but أَجْرٌ is used [sometimes] in the sense of إِجَارَةٌ and in that of أُجْرَةٌ: (Mṣb:) the pl. of أَجْرٌ is أُجُورٌ (Mṣb, Ḳ) and آجَارٌ; (Ḳ;) but the latter form was unknown to MF: (TA:) the pl. of ▼ أُجْرَةٌ is أُجَرٌ and أُجُرَاتٌ and أُجْرَاتٌ. (Mṣb.) [One says, أَجْرُكَ عَلَى ٱللّٰهِ *Thy recompense is due from God.* And, to console a person for the death of a relation or friend, عَظَّمَ ٱللّٰهُ أَجْرَكَ فِيهِ *May God largely compensate thee for him!* i. e., for the loss of him.] By the expression أَجْرٌ كَرِيمٌ in the Ḳur xxxvi. 10 is said to be meant *Paradise.* (TA.) —— ‡ *A dowry,* or *nuptial gift; a gift that is given to,* or *for, a bride:* (Ḳ:) pl. أُجُورٌ: so in the Ḳur xxxiii. 49 [&c.]. (TA.) —— † *Praise; good fame.* (Ḳ.) So, as some say, in the Ḳur xxix. 26. (TA.)

أُجْرٌ and أُجُرٌ: see آجُرٌ.

أُجْرَةٌ: see أَجْرٌ, in three places.

إِجْرِيَّآءٌ and إِجْرِيًّا: see إِجِّيرَى.

أَجُورٌ: see آجُرٌ.

أَجِيرٌ (Ṣ, Ḳ, &c.) *A hired man; a hireling:* (L:) or of the measure فَعِيلٌ in the sense of the measure مُفَاعَلٌ, i. e. *a man with whom one has engaged to give him hire, pay,* or *wages:* (Mgh, Mṣb:*) pl. أُجَرَآءُ. (L, Mṣb.)

إِجَارَةٌ and أُجَارَةٌ and أَجَارَةٌ: see أَجْرٌ, in four places. —— إِجَارَةٌ also signifies The *giving of usufructs for a compensation.* (Mgh.) —— And *Land which its owners have let to him who will build upon it:* so explained by the lawyers. (Mgh.)

إِجَّارٌ (Ṣ, M, IAth, Mgh, Ḳ) and ▼ إِجَّارَةٌ (M) and ▼ إِنْجَارٌ (Mgh, Ḳ) The *flat top,* or *roof, of a house,* (Ṣ, M, IAth, Mgh, Ḳ,) *that has not around it anything to prevent a person's falling from it:* (M,* IAth:) of the dial. of the people of Syria and of El-Ḥijáz: (Ṣ:) pl. [of the first and second] أَجَاجِيرُ and أَجَاجِرَةٌ; (A'Obeyd, Ṣ, Ḳ;) and [of the third] أَنَاجِيرُ. (Mgh, Ḳ.)

إِجَّارَةٌ: see إِجَّارٌ.

إِجِّيرَى (ISk, Ḳ) and ▼ إِجْرِيًّا and ▼ إِجْرِيَّآءٌ (Ṣ in art. هجر) *A custom; a habit.* (ISk, Ḳ, and Ṣ ubi suprà.) The hemzeh is said to be a substitute for ه [in هِجِّيرَى &c.] (TA.) You say, مَا زَالَ ذٰلِكَ إِجْرِيَّآءَهُ *That ceased not to be his custom,* or *habit.* (ISk.)

آجَرٌ and آجُرٌ and آجِرٌ, and the pls. آجُرُونَ and آجِرُونَ: see what next follows.

آجُرٌ (Ṣ, Mgh, Mṣb, Ḳ) and ▼ آجِرٌ (AA, Ks, Ḳ) and ▼ آجُورٌ (Ṣ, Ḳ) and ▼ أَجُورٌ and ▼ يَأْجُورٌ (Ḳ) and ▼ أُجُرٌ (as in some copies of the Ḳ) and ▼ آجَرٌ, (as in some copies of the Ḳ and in the TA,) or ▼ أُجْرٌ, (as in other copies of the Ḳ,) and ▼ آجِرٌ [to which is erroneously added in the CK آجِرَةٌ] and [the pls.] ▼ آجُرُونَ and ▼ آجِرُونَ (Ḳ) are syn., (Ṣ, Ḳ,) of Persian origin, (Ṣ,) [from آكُورْ or آكُرْ,] arabicized, (Ṣ, Mgh, Ḳ,) signifying *Baked bricks;* (Mṣb;) *baked clay,* (Mgh, L,) *with which one builds:* (Ṣ, L:) آجُرٌ and آجُورٌ and آجَرٌ [&c.] are pls., [or rather coll. gen. ns., except the two forms ending with و and ن,] and their sings. [or rather ns. un.] are with ة, i. e. آجُرَّةٌ &c. (L.)

آجُورٌ: see آجُرٌ.

إِنْجَارٌ: see إِجَّارٌ.

مُؤْجَرٌ [A slave, or] a house, *let on hire;* (Akh, T, Mṣb;) as also ▼ مَأْجُورٌ; (L;) and some say, ▼ مُؤَاجَرٌ. (Akh, Mṣb.)

مُؤْجِرٌ One *who lets on hire* [a slave, or] a house: one should not say ▼ مُؤَاجِرٌ; for this is wrong with respect to the classical language, and abominable with respect to the conventional acceptation and common usage; a foul reproach being meant thereby [as is shown by the explanation of آجَرَتْ, given above: or, accord. to some, it is allowable when it relates to a house: (see أُجْرَةٌ:) it seems to be disallowed only when used absolutely]. (A, Mgh.)

مَأْجُورٌ } see مُؤْجَرٌ.
مُؤَاجَرٌ }

مُؤَاجِرٌ: see مُؤْجِرٌ.

مُؤْتَجَرٌ [part. n. of أُوتُجِرَ]. Moḥammad Ibn-Bishr El-Khárijee, not [as is said in the Ṣ] Aboo-Dahbal, says, (L,)

• يَا لَيْتَ أَنِّى بِأَثْوَابِى وَرَاحِلَتِى •
• عَبْدٌ لِأَهْلِكِ هٰذَا الشَّهْرَ مُؤْتَجَرُ •

[*O would that I were, with my clothes and my riding-camel, a hired slave to thy family, this month*]: (Ṣ, L.) i. e., مَعَ أَثْوَابِى. (Ṣ.)

يَأْجُورٌ: see آجُرٌ.

اجص

إِجَّاصٌ [The *plum;*] *a certain fruit,* (Ḳ, TA,) *of the description termed* فَاكِهَة, (TA,) *well known;* (Mṣb, Ḳ;) *cold and moist;* or, *as some say, of moderate temperature;* (TA;) *which facilitates the flow of the yellow bile;* (Ḳ;) i. e., *its juice,* or *water, does so, when drunk with sugar-candy* (طَبَرْزَد) *and manna* (تَرَنْجَبِين) *added to it;* (TA;) *and allays thirst, and heat of the heart;* (Ḳ;) *but it relaxes the stomach, and does not agree with it; and it generates a watery mixture; and its injurious effect is repelled by the drinking of sugary* سَكَنْجَبِين [or *oxymel*]: *it is of several kinds:* (TA:) [*the most common is the Damasc,* or *Damascene, plum:*] *the best is* (Ḳ, TA) *the Armenian,* (TA,) *that which is sweet and large:* (Ḳ, TA:) *the sour,* or *acid, is less laxative, and more cold:* (TA:) the n. un. is with ة: (Ṣ, Mṣb, Ḳ:) you should not say إِنْجَاصٌ; (Yaạḳoob, Ṣ, Ḳ;) or this is a word of weak authority, (Ḳ, TA,) and you say إِجَّاصٌ and إِنْجَاصٌ like as one says إِجَّارٌ and إِنْجَارٌ: (TA:) in the dial. of the Syrians, the إِجَّاص [or إِنْجَاص or إِنْجَاس accord. to common modern usage among them] is the [*pear* which they formerly called] مِشْمِش and [which others call] كُمَّثْرَى: (Ḳ:) *it is of the growth of the country of the Arabs:* (AḤn:) اجّاص is an adventitious word, (Ṣ, Ḳ,) or arabicized, (Mṣb,) because ج and ص do not both occur in any Arabic word: (Ṣ, Mṣb, Ḳ:) or, accord. to Az, they do so occur; as, for instance, in جَصَّصَ, and in صَجَّ. (TA.)

اجل

1. أَجِلَ, aor. ـَ, (Mṣb, Ḳ,) inf. n. أَجَلٌ, (Mṣb,) *It* (a thing, Mṣb, [as, for instance, a thing purchased, and the price thereof, and a thing promised or threatened or foretold, and also payment for a thing purchased, and the fulfilment of a promise or threat or prediction, and any event,]) *was,* or *became, delayed, postponed, kept back;* [and therefore, *future;*] syn. تَأَخَّرَ; (Ḳ;) and أَجَلَ, aor. ـُ, inf. n. أُجُولٌ, signifies the same. (Mṣb.) [See أَجَلٌ and آجِلٌ. The primary signification seems to be, *It had a term,* or *period, appointed for it, at which it should fall due,* or

come to pass.] — أَجَلَهُ, aor. ـُ, (Ḳ,) inf. n. أَجْلٌ; (TA;) and ▼ أَجَّلَهُ, (Ḳ,) inf. n. تَأْجِيلٌ; (TA;) and ▼ آجَلَهُ, (Ḳ,) inf. n. مُؤَاجَلَةٌ; (TḲ;) *He confined, restricted, restrained, withheld, debarred, hindered,* or *prevented, him.* (Ḳ, TA.) Hence the phrase, أَجَلُوا مَالَهُمْ *They confined, restricted, &c., their cattle from the pasturage.* (TA.) — أَجَلَ عَلَيْهِمْ شَرًّا, (Ṣ, Mṣb,) or الشَّرَّ, (Ḳ,) aor. ـِ (Ṣ, Mṣb, Ḳ) and ـُ, (Ṣ, Ḳ,) inf. n. أَجْلٌ, (Ṣ, Mṣb,) *He committed against them evil,* (Ṣ, Mṣb, Ḳ,) and *drew it,* or *procured it, to them:* (Mṣb:) and (Ṣ, in the Ḳ "or") *he excited it, stirred it up,* or *provoked it, against them:* (Ṣ, Ḳ:) or, accord. to AZ, أَجَلْتُ عَلَيْهِمْ, inf. n. as above, signifies *I committed a crime against them:* and AA says that جَلَبْتُ عَلَيْهِمْ and جَرَرْتُ and أَجَلْتُ have one and the same signification. (TA.) — And أَجَلَ لِأَهْلِهِ, (Lḥ, Ḳ,) inf. n. as above, (TA,) *He gained, acquired,* or *earned,* and *collected,* and *brought,* or *purveyed,* and *exercised skill in the management of affairs, for his family.* (Lḥ, Ḳ.)

2. أَجَّلَ الأَجَلَ, (TA,) inf. n. تَأْجِيلٌ, (Ḳ, TA,) *He defined the term,* or *period;* (Ḳ,* TA;) *assigned, appointed,* or *specified, it.* (TA.) It is said in the Ḳur [vi. 128], وَبَلَغْنَا أَجَلَنَا ٱلَّذِى أَجَّلْتَ لَنَا [*And we have reached our term which Thou hast assigned,* or *appointed, for us;*] meaning, the day of resurrection; (Bḍ,* Jel;) or the term of death; or, as some say, the term of extreme old age. (TA.) And أَجَّلْتُهُ, inf. n. as above, signifies *I assigned,* or *appointed, for him,* or *it, a term,* or *period.* (Mṣb.) — أَجَّلَنِى *He granted me a delay,* or *postponement.* (TA.) You say, ▼ اِسْتَأْجَلْتُهُ فَأَجَّلَنِى إِلَى مُدَّةٍ (Ṣ, Ḳ, TA) *I desired, asked, demanded,* or *requested, of him a term,* or *period,* [*of delay,* or *postponement,*] *and he granted me a delay,* or *postponement, to a certain term,* or *period.* (TA.) — See also 1.

3. آجَلَهُ, inf. n. مُؤَاجَلَةٌ: see 1.

5. تَأَجَّلَ i. q. ▼ اِسْتَأْجَلَ; (Ḳ, TA;) i. e. *He asked,* or *requested, that a term,* or *period, should be assigned, appointed,* or *specified, for him.* (TA.) It is said in a trad. of Mek-ḥool, كُنَّا مُرَابِطِينَ بِالسَّاحِلِ فَتَأَجَّلَ مُتَأَجِّلٌ [*We were keeping post on the frontier of the enemy, in the tract on the sea-coast, and*] *a person asked,* or *requested, that a term,* or *period, should be assigned,* or *appointed,* or *specified, for him,* and that permission should be granted him to return to his family. (TA.)

10: see 2 and 5.

أَجْلٌ is originally the inf. n. of أَجَلَ شَرًّا "he committed evil;" and is used to indicate the causation of crimes; and afterwards, by extension of its application, to indicate any causation: (Bḍ in v. 35:) one says, فَعَلْتُهُ مِنْ أَجْلِكَ, and ▼ مِنْ إِجْلِكَ, (Ṣ, Ḳ,) and فَعَلْتُهُ أَجْلَكَ, and ▼ إِجْلَكَ, (so in some copies of the Ḳ,) and مِنْ إِجْلَاكَ, and مِنْ أَجْلَاكَ, (Ḳ, [belonging to art. جلو, in which also they are mentioned,]) and مِنْ إِجْلَالِكَ, and مِنْ أَجْلَالِكَ, (so in some copies of the Ḳ and in the TA, [belonging to art. جل,]) i. e. [*I did it*] مِنْ جَرَّاكَ, (Ṣ,) which means [originally] *in consequence of thy committing it:* (Bḍ ubi suprà:) [and then, by extension of its application, as shown above, *because of thee,* or *of thine act* &c.; *on thine account; for thy sake;* as also لِأَجْلِكَ, which is more common in the present day:] or مِنْ جَلَلِكَ: (Ḳ:) and مِنْ أَجْلِهِ كَانَ كَذَا, i. e. بِسَبَبِهِ [*Because of him,* or *it, it was thus,* or *such a thing was*]. (Mṣb.) An instance of its occurrence without مِنْ [or لِ] is presented by the saying of 'Adee Ibn-Zeyd,

أَجْلَ أَنَّ ٱللّٰهَ قَدْ فَضَّلَكُمْ

[*Because that God hath made you to have excellence,* or *hath preferred you*]. (TA.)

إِجْلٌ, whence فَعَلْتُهُ إِجْلَكَ, and فَعَلْتُهُ مِنْ إِجْلِكَ: see أَجْلٌ, in two places.

أَجَلْ, (Ṣ, Mughnee, Ḳ,) with the ل quiescent, (Mughnee,) is written with kesr and with fet-ḥ [to the medial letter, i. e. ▼ أَجِلْ as well as أَجَلْ] like نعم [which is written نَعِمْ as well as نَعَمْ]: (TA:) it is a particle (Mughnee) denoting a reply; like نَعَمْ; (Ṣ, Mughnee, Ḳ;) importing acknowledgment of the truth of the speaker, to him who gives information; and the making a thing known, to him who asks information; and a promise, to him who seeks, or demands; (Mughnee;) i. e. *It is as thou sayest* [in the first case; and *yes,* or *yea,* in the same, and in the other cases]; (Ḳ voce بَجَلْ;) therefore it occurs after such sayings as "Zeyd stood" and "did Zeyd stand?" and "beat thou Zeyd:" but El-Málakee restricts the information to that which is affirmative, and the saying expressive of seeking or demanding to that which is without prohibition: and it is said by some that it does not occur after an interrogation: (Mughnee:) Er-Radee says, in the Expos. of the Káfiyeh, after Z and others, that it is to denote acknowledgment of the truth of information, and does not occur after a saying in which is the meaning of seeking, or demanding: (TA:) or, accord. to Z and Ibn-Málik and others, it relates particularly to information: and accord. to Ibn-Kharoof, it occurs mostly after information: (Mughnee:) in the Expos. of the Tes-heel, it is said to be for denoting acknowledgment of the truth of information, past or other, affirmative or negative, and not to occur after an interrogation: (TA:) Akh says that it is better than نَعَمْ (Ṣ, Mughnee, Ḳ*) after information, (Mughnee,) in acknowledging the truth of what is said; (Ṣ, Mughnee, Ḳ;) and نعم is better than it after an interrogation: (Ṣ, Mughnee, Ḳ:) so that when one says, سَوْفَ تَذْهَبُ [Thou wilt, or shalt, go away], thou sayest أَجَلْ [*Yes*]; and it is better than نعم: but when one says, أَتَذْهَبُ [Wilt thou go away?], thou sayest نعم; and it is better than اجل. (Ṣ.)

أَجَلٌ The *term,* or *period,* of a thing: (Ṣ, Ḳ:) its *assigned, appointed,* or *specified, term* or *period:* this is the primary signification: (TA:) or the *term,* or *period,* and *time of falling due,* of a thing: (Mṣb:) pl. آجَالٌ. (Mṣb, Ḳ.) — Hence, The *period of* women's *waiting, before they may marry again, after divorce:* as in the Ḳur ii. 231 and 232. (TA.) — The *period,* or *extremity of time, in which falls due a debt* (Ḳ, TA) and *the like.* (TA.) You say, بَاعَهُ إِيَّاهُ إِلَى أَجَلٍ [*He sold it to him for payment at an appointed period*]: and سَلَّمَ الدَّرَاهِمَ فِى طَعَامٍ إِلَى أَجَلٍ [*He delivered the money for wheat,* or *the like, to be given at an appointed period*]. (Mṣb in art. كلأ.) — The *term,* or *period, of death;* (Ḳ;) the *time in which God has eternally decreed the end of life by slaughter or otherwise:* or, as some say, the *whole duration of life:* and its *end:* a man's *life* being thus termed: and his *death, by which it terminates:* (Kull p. 17:) the *assigned,* or *appointed, duration of the life* of a man. (TA.) One says, دَنَا أَجَلُهُ, meaning *His death drew near;* originally, ٱسْتِيفَآءُ الأَجَلِ *the completion of the duration of life.* (TA.) In the Ḳur vi. 128, (see 2, above,) the meaning is, The *term of death:* or, as some say, the *term of extreme old age:* (TA:) or the *day of resurrection.* (Bḍ,* Jel.) The words of the Ḳur [vi. 2] ثُمَّ قَضَى أَجَلًا وَأَجَلٌ مُسَمًّى عِنْدَهُ mean [*Then He decreed a term,*] *the term of death,* and [*there is a term named with Him,*] *the term of the resurrection:* or *the period between the creation and death,* and *the period between death and the resurrection;* for اجل is applied to the *end of a space of time* and to the *whole thereof:* (Bḍ:) or the meaning is, *the period of sleep,* and *the period of death:* (Bḍ, TA:) or *the period of those who have passed away,* and *the period of those who remain and those who are to come:* (Bḍ:) or *the period of remaining in this world,* and *the period of remaining in the world to come:* or in both instances *death* is meant; [*accidental,* and *natural;*] for the اجل of some is by accidental means, as the sword, and drowning, and burning, and eating what disagrees, and other means of destruction; while some have their full periods granted to them and are preserved in health until they die a natural death: or the اجل of some is that of him who dies in a state of happiness and enjoyment; and of others, that of him who reaches a limit beyond which God has not appointed, in the natural course of this world, any one to remain therein; and to both of these, reference is made in the Ḳur [xvi. 72 and] xxii. 5. (TA.) — Sometimes, also, it means *Destruction:* and thus it has been explained as occurring in the Ḳur [vii. 184], where it is said, وَأَنْ عَسَى أَنْ يَكُونَ قَدِ ٱقْتَرَبَ أَجَلُهُمْ [*And that, may be, their destruction shall have drawn near*]. (TA.)

أَجِلْ: see أَجَلْ.

أَجِلٌ: see آجِلٌ.

أَجِيلٌ *Having a delay,* or *postponement, granted to him, to a certain time;* i. q. ▼ مُؤَجَّلٌ إِلَى وَقْتٍ. (Lth.) — See also آجِلٌ.

آجِلٌ *Delayed; postponed; kept back;* syn. مُتَأَخِّرٌ; [but in some copies of the Ḳ, for آجِلٌ, we find ▼ أَجِلٌ;] as also ▼ أَجِيلٌ, of which the pl. is أُجْلٌ: (Ḳ:) and therefore, (TA,) *not present; future; to come; contr. of* عَاجِلٌ: (Ṣ, Mṣb, TA:)

and ▼ مُتَأَجِّلٌ, also, signifies *delayed, deferred,* or *postponed, to the time of the end of a period;* originally, *contr. of* مُتَعَجِّلٌ. (Mgh.) [See also أَجِيلٌ.] — [Hence,] الآجِلَةُ *The [future,] latter, ultimate,* or *last, dwelling,* or *abode,* or *life; the world to come;* syn. الآخِرَةُ; (Ḳ, TA;) *contr. of* العَاجِلَةُ. (Ṣ, TA.) = *Committing* a crime; or a *committer* of a crime. (Ṣ, TA.)

مُؤَجَّلٌ *Determined, defined,* or *limited, as to time;* applied to a writing: so in the Ḳur iii. 139: (Bḍ, Jel, TA:) and to a debt; *contr. of* حَالٌّ, q. v. (Mgh in art. حل.) — See also أَجِيلٌ.

مُتَأَجِّلٌ: see آجِلٌ.

اجم

1. أَجِمَهُ, with kesr, [aor. َ,] (AZ, Ṣ, O,) inf. n. أَجَمٌ; (KL, PṢ;) or أَجَمَهُ, aor. ُ, (so in the Ḳ,) inf. n. أَجْمٌ; (TḲ;) [but أَجِمَ is the form commonly known; and if it were incorrect, the author of the Ḳ would probably, accord. to his usual custom, have charged J with error respecting it;] *He loathed it; disliked it; was,* or *became, disgusted with it;* namely, food; (AZ, Ṣ, O, Ḳ;) &c.; (Ḳ;) *from constantly keeping to it;* (AZ, Ṣ, O;) or *because of its not agreeing with him:* (TA:) *he reckoned it bad:* (KL:) and ▼ تَأَجَّمَهُ also signifies *he disliked, disapproved,* or *hated, it;* or *he expressed,* or *showed, dislike, disapprobation,* or *hatred, of it;* syn. تَكَرَّهَهُ. (TA.) = أَجَمَ فُلَانًا, aor. ُ, (Ḳ,) inf. n. أَجْمٌ, (TḲ,) *He incited,* or *urged, such a one to do that which he disliked, disapproved,* or *hated.* (Ḳ.)

2: see 4.

4. يُؤْجِمُ النَّاسَ, or ▼ يُؤَجِّمُ النَّاسَ, [accord. to different copies of the Ḳ, the former being the reading in the TA,] *He makes men's own selves to be objects of dislike, disapprobation,* or *hatred, to them.* (Ḳ voce أُجُومٌ.) [Accord. to the TḲ, you say, أَجَمَهُ مِنْهُ, inf. n. إِيجَامٌ, meaning *He made him to be an object of dislike, disapprobation,* or *hatred, to him.*]

5. تَأَجَّمَ *He* (a lion) *entered his* أَجَمَة [or *thicket*]. (Ḳ.) = تَأَجَّمَهُ: see 1.

أُجُمٌ *Any square, roofed, house:* (Ḳ:) mentioned by ISd as on the authority of Yaạḳoob: but see أُجُمٌ as explained by J [in the Ṣ] on the same authority. (TA.)

أُجْمٌ: see أُجُمٌ. = It is also a pl. of أَجَمَةٌ. (M, Ḳ.)

أُجُمٌ: see أَجَمَةٌ.

أُجُمٌ *A fortress;* (Mgh, Mṣb, Ḳ;) like أُطُمٌ: (Mgh:) pl. آجَامٌ. (Mgh, Mṣb, Ḳ.) الأُجُمُ [is the name of] *A fortress* (Ṣ, Ḳ) *in El-Medeeneh,* (Ḳ,) *built of stones by the people of that city:* and Yaạḳoob says that أُجُمٌ signifies *any square, roofed, house.* (Ṣ, Ṣgh.) Imra-el-Ḳeys says, [describing a vehement rain,]

• وَتَيْمَاءَ لَمْ يَتْرُكْ بِهَا جِذْعَ نَخْلَةٍ •
• وَلَا أُجُمًا إِلَّا مَشِيدًا بِجَنْدَلِ •

[*And Teymá,* (a town so called,) *it left not therein a trunk of a palm-tree, nor a square, roofed, house, unless raised high with stones:* but in the Calc. ed. of the Mo'allaḳát, (p. 54,) for أُجُمًا, we find أُطُمًا, which has the same meaning]. (Ṣ, Ṣgh.) See also أُجُمٌ. (TA.) Accord. to Aṣ, it is also pronounced ▼ أُجْمٌ. (Ṣ.)

أَجَمَةٌ *A thicket, wood,* or *forest; a collection,* (Mgh, Mṣb,) or *an abundant collection,* (Ḳ,) *of tangled, confused,* or *dense, trees,* or *shrubs:* (Mgh, Mṣb, Ḳ:) or it is *of reeds,* or *canes:* (Ṣ:) or a [*place such as is termed*] مَغِيض *of water collected together, in which, in consequence thereof, trees grow:* (Ṣ in art. غيض:) [or] it signifies also *a bed,* or *place of growth, of canes* or *reeds:* (Mgh:) the pl. is أَجَمَاتٌ and أُجُمٌ (Ṣ, M, Ḳ) and أُجْمٌ (M, Ḳ) and ▼ أَجَمٌ, (Ṣ, M, Mgh, Mṣb, Ḳ,) [or rather this last is a coll. gen. n., of which أَجَمَةٌ is the n. un.,] and إِجَامٌ (Ṣ, M, Ḳ) and [pl. of pauc.] آجَامٌ, (Ṣ, M, Mgh, Ḳ,) or the last but one is pl. of أَجَمٌ, (M,) and so is the last. (Lḥ, M, Mṣb.) And hence, The *haunt of a lion.* (TA in art. حرب.) — آجَامٌ [in the CḲ أَجام] also signifies *Frogs.* (Ṣgh, Ḳ.) [App. because frogs are generally found in beds of canes or reeds.]

أُجُومٌ signifies يُؤْجِمُ النَّاسَ, or مَنْ يُؤَجِّمُ النَّاسَ; [accord. to different copies of the Ḳ; see 4;] i. e. One *who makes men's own selves to be objects of dislike, disapprobation,* or *hatred, to them.* (Ḳ.)

آجِمٌ *Loathing, disliking,* or *regarding with disgust.* (Ṣ, TA.) = مَآءٌ آجِمٌ *i. q.* ▼ مَأْجُومٌ [*Water that is loathed, disliked,* or *regarded with disgust*]. (TA.)

مَأْجُومٌ: see آجِمٌ.

اجن

1. أَجَنَ, (Ṣ, Mgh, Mṣb, Ḳ,) aor. ِ and ُ; (Ṣ, Mṣb, Ḳ;) and أَجِنَ, (Ṣ, Mgh, &c.,) aor. َ, (Ṣ, Mṣb,) mentioned by Yz; (Ṣ;) inf. n. of the former أُجُونٌ (Ṣ, Mgh, Mṣb, Ḳ*) and أَجْنٌ; (Ṣ, Mṣb, Ḳ;*) and of the latter أَجَنٌ; (Ṣ, Mgh, Mṣb, Ḳ;) *It* (water) *became altered for the worse* (Ṣ, Mgh, Mṣb, Ḳ) *in taste and colour,* (Ṣ, Mgh, Ḳ,) *from some such cause as long standing,* (TA,) *but was drinkable:* (Mgh, Mṣb:) or *became altered for the worse in its odour by oldness:* or *became covered with* [*the green substance called*] طُحْلُب *and with leaves:* (Mgh:) أُجِنَ, also, said of water, signifies *it became altered for the worse:* (Th:) and in the Iḳtiṭáf occurs أَجَنَ, aor. َ, which is unknown, but may be a mixture of two dial. vars. [namely of أَجَنَ having for its aor. ِ and ُ, and يَأْجَنُ having for its pret. أَجِنَ]. (MF) = أَجَنَ *He* (a قَصَّار, or whitener of cloth) *beat* a piece of cloth or a garment [in washing it]. (Ṣ, Ḳ.)

أَجْنٌ: } see آجِنٌ.
أَجِنٌ: }

أُجْنَةٌ (Ṣ, Ḳ) and أُجُنَةٌ and إِجْنَةٌ (Ḳ) *i. q.* وَجْنَةٌ [*The ball,* or *elevated part, of the cheek*]. (Ṣ, Ḳ.)

أَجِينٌ: see آجِنٌ.

إِجَّانَةٌ (Ṣ, Mgh, Mṣb, Ḳ) and ▼ إِنْجَانَةٌ, (Lḥ, Ḳ,) the latter of the dial. of Ṭeiyi, (Lḥ, TA,) or this is a vulgar form, (Mgh,) not allowable, (Ṣ,) and ▼ إِيجَانَةٌ, (Ḳ,) with ى, (TA,) *A thing well known;* (Ḳ;) *a vessel in which clothes are washed;* (Mṣb;) a [*vessel also called*] مِرْكَن, *resembling a* لَقَن [which is a *kind of basin*], *in which clothes are washed:* (Mgh:) or *what is called in Persian* پنگان [i. e. پِنْگَان *a small cup*]: (PṢ:) [it probably received this last meaning, and some others, in post-classical times: Golius explains it as meaning "*lagena, phiala, crater:*" adding, "hinc vulgo Fingiána [i. e. فِنْجَانَة] *calix* vocatur: item *Urceus: hydria:* [referring to John ii. 6:] *Vas dimidiæ seriæ simile, in quo aqua et similia ponuntur:*" on the authority of Ibn-Maạroof: and, on the same authority, "*Labrum* seu *vas lapideum instar pelvis, in quo lavantur vestes:*"] pl. أَجَاجِينُ: (Ṣ, Mgh, Mṣb, Ḳ:) meaning [also] *what resemble troughs, surrounding trees.* (Mṣb.)

آجِنٌ (Ṣ, Mgh, Mṣb, Ḳ) and ▼ أَجِنٌ (Ṣ, Mṣb, Ḳ) and ▼ أَجْنٌ (ISd, TA) and ▼ أَجِينٌ (TA) Water *altered for the worse* (Ṣ, Mgh, Mṣb, Ḳ) *in taste and colour,* (Ṣ, Mgh, Ḳ,) *from some such cause as long standing,* (TA,) *but still drinkable:* (Mgh, Mṣb:) or *altered for the worse in its odour by oldness:* or *covered with* [*the green substance called*] طُحْلُب *and with leaves:* (Mgh:) pl. أُجُونٌ; thought by ISd to be pl. of أَجْنٌ and آجِنٌ. (TA.)

إِنْجَانَةٌ: } see إِجَّانَةٌ.
إِيجَانَةٌ: }

مِئْجَنَةٌ [in Golius's Lex. مِئْجَن] The *instrument for beating used by the* قَصَّار [or *whitener of cloth, in washing*]: but better without ء, [written مِيجَنَةٌ,] because the pl. is مَوَاجِنُ; or, accord. to IB, the pl. is مَآجِنُ. (TA.)

احد

2. أَحَّدَهُ, [inf. n. تَأْحِيدٌ,] *He made it one;* or *called it one:* as also وَحَّدَهُ. (TA in art. وحد.) You say, أَحِّدِ الاِثْنَيْنِ *Make thou the two to become one.* (Ḳ.) It is related in a trad., that Mohammad said to a man who was making a sign with his two fore fingers in repeating the testimony of the faith, [There is no deity but God, &c.,] أَحِّدْ أَحِّدْ [meaning that he should make the sign with one finger only]. (Ṣ.) And أَحَّدَ ٱللّٰهَ means *He declared God to be one; he declared,* or *professed, the unity of God;* as also وَحَّدَهُ. (T and L in art. وحد.) — أَحِّدِ العَشَرَةَ, (Ṣ, Ḳ,) inf. n. تَأْحِيدٌ, (Ḳ,) *Make thou the ten to become eleven,* (Ṣ, Ḳ,) is a phrase mentioned by Fr on the authority of an Arab of the desert. (Ṣ.)

8. اِتَّحَدَ: see art. وحد: and see what here next follows.

10. اِسْتَأْحَدَ *He* (a man, Ṣ) *was,* or *became, alone, by himself, apart from others,* or *solitary;*

syn. اِنْفَرَدَ; (Ṣ, Ḳ;) as also ▼ اِتَّحَدَ [written with the disjunctive alif اِتَّحَدَ, originally اِوْتَحَدَ or اِوْتَحَدَ], (Ḳ, TA,) or تَوَحَّدَ. (CḲ.) —— مَا اَسْتَأْحَدَ بِهِ *He did not know it; did not know,* or *had not knowledge, of it; did not understand it; did not know the minute circumstances of it;* or *did not perceive it by any of the senses;* syn. لَمْ يَشْعُرْ بِهِ; (L, Ḳ;) i. e., a thing, or an affair: of the dial. of El-Yemen. (L.)

أَحَدٌ, originally وَحَدٌ, the و being changed into أ, (Mṣb,) *One; the first of the numbers;* (Ṣ;) syn. [in many cases] with وَاحِدٌ; (Ṣ, Mṣb, Ḳ;) with which it is interchangeable in two cases, to be explained below: (Mṣb:) pl. آحَادٌ and أُحْدَانٌ (Ḳ) and أَحَدُونَ, which last occurs in a phrase hereafter to be mentioned; (TA;) or it has no pl. in this sense; (Mṣb, Ḳ,* TA;) and as to آحَادٌ, it may be pl. of وَاحِدٌ, [and originally أَوْحَادٌ,] like أَشْهَادٌ as pl. of شَاهِدٌ, (Th, Mṣb,) a pl. of pauc. (Mṣb.) The fem. is ▼ إِحْدَى only; and this is only used in particular cases, to be shown below: (Mṣb:) most agree that the ى in this word is the characteristic of the fem. gender: but some say that it is to render it quasi-coordinate to the quadriliteral-radical class: [this, however, is inconsistent with its pronunciation, which is invariably إِحْدَى, not إِحْدًى:] (TA:) its pl. is إِحَدٌ, as though the sing. were إِحْدَةٌ, like as is said of ذِكَرٌ as pl. of ذِكْرَى: one of the expositors of the Tes-heel writes it أُحَدٌ, with ḍamm and then fet-ḥ; but a pl. of this measure is not applicable to a sing. of the measure فِعْلَى, with kesr. (MF.) The dim. of أَحَدٌ is ▼ أُحَيْدٌ; and that of إِحْدَى is ▼ أُحَيْدَى. (L in art. وحد.) —— It is interchangeable with وَاحِدٌ in two cases: first, when it is used as an epithet applied to God: (Mṣb:) for الأَحَدُ, as an epithet, is applied to God alone, (Mṣb, Ḳ,) and signifies *The One; the Sole; He who has ever been one and alone:* or *the Indivisible:* or *He who has no second* [*to share*] *in his lordship, nor in his essence, nor in his attributes:* (TA:) you say, هُوَ الوَاحِدُ and هُوَ الأَحَدُ: and in like manner, أَحَدٌ, without the article, is used as an epithet specially in relation to God, and is interchangeable in this case [but not in other cases] with وَاحِدٌ: therefore you do not say رَجُلٌ أَحَدٌ nor دِرْهَمٌ أَحَدٌ and the like [but رَجُلٌ وَاحِدٌ and دِرْهَمٌ وَاحِدٌ &c.] (Mṣb.) [See also وَاحِدٌ, in art. وحد.] In the phrase in the Ḳur [cxii. 1], قُلْ هُوَ اللّٰهُ أَحَدٌ [*Say, He is God, One* God], أَحَدٌ is a substitute for اللّٰه; for an indeterminate noun is sometimes a substitute for a determinate noun, as in another passage in the Ḳur, xcvi. 15 and 16. (Ṣ.) Secondly, it is interchangeable with وَاحِدٌ in certain nouns of number: (Mṣb:) you say أَحَدَ عَشَرَ [masc.] and إِحْدَى عَشْرَةَ [fem.] (Ṣ) [meaning *Eleven:* and in these two cases you may not substitute وَاحِدٌ and وَاحِدَةٌ for أَحَدٌ and إِحْدَى: but] in أَحَدٌ وَعِشْرُونَ [*One and twenty,* and the like,] أَحَدٌ is interchangeable with وَاحِدٌ. (Mṣb.) Ks says, When you prefix the article ال to a number, prefix it to every number; therefore you should say, مَا فَعَلَتِ الأَحَدَ العَشَرَ الأَلْفُ الدِّرْهَمِ [*What did the eleven thousand dirhems?*]: but the Baṣrees prefix it to the first only, and say, ما فعلت الأَحَدَ عَشَرَ أَلْفَ دِرْهَمٍ. (Ṣ.) —— In [most] cases differing from these two, there is a difference in usage between أَحَدٌ and وَاحِدٌ: the former is used in affirmative phrases as a prefixed noun only, governing the noun which follows it in the gen. case; [as in exs. which will be found below;] and is used absolutely in negative phrases; [as will also be seen in exs. below;] whereas وَاحِدٌ is used in affirmative phrases as a prefixed noun and otherwise: the fem. إِحْدَى, also, is only used as a prefixed noun, except in numbers (Mṣb) [and in one other instance, which see below]. Using أَحَدٌ and its fem. in affirmative phrases as prefixed nouns, you say, قَامَ أَحَدُ الثَّلَاثَةِ [*One of the three stood*]; and قَالَتْ إِحْدَاهُمَا [*One of them two* (females) *said*]; and خُذْ إِحْدَى الثَّلَاثَةِ [*Take thou one of the three*]. (TA.) The phrase إِحْدَى بَنَاتِ طَبَقٍ means *A calamity:* (Ḳ:) or, as some say, (TA, but in the Ḳ "and,") *a serpent;* (Ḳ, TA;) so called because it twists itself round so as to become like a طَبَق. (TA.) And the phrase إِحْدَى الإِحَدِ, (L, Ḳ, TA,) in which the latter word has kesr to the إ and fet-ḥ to the ح, and is pl. of the former, also written الأُحَدِ, but this form is disapproved by MF, as has been shown above, (TA, [in several copies of the Ḳ incorrectly written الأَحَدِ,]) [lit. means *One of the ones;* and] is applied to *a great,* or *mighty, event;* (L, Ḳ, TA;) *one that is difficult, distressing, grievous,* or *terrible.* (L, TA.) You say, أَتَى بِإِحْدَى الإِحَدِ [the last of which words is here again written in several copies of the Ḳ الأَحَدِ] *He brought to pass a grievous, and great,* or *mighty, event,* (Ḳ, TA,) when you desire to express the greatness and terribleness of an event. (TA.) You also say, فُلَانٌ أَحَدُ الأَحَدِينَ, and وَاحِدُ الأَحَدِينَ, (Ḳ, TA,) the latter in one copy of the Ḳ written وَاحِدُ الوَاحِدِينَ, in which the latter word is pl. of the former, (TA,) and وَاحِدُ الآحَادِ, and إِحْدَى الإِحَدِ, (Ḳ, TA,) like a phrase before mentioned, only the former is applied to a calamity, and this to an intelligent being, and written in the two manners before mentioned, the difference being only in application, (TA, [in several copies of the Ḳ here again written إِحْدَى الأَحَدِ, and in the CḲ أَحَدِيُّ الأَحَدِ,]) and إِحْدَى الأَحَدِينَ, (Et-Tes-heel,) and إِحْدَى الآحَادِ, (TA,) which are expressions of the utmost praise, (IAar, AHeyth, Ḳ,) [lit. *Such a man is one of the ones;* meaning] *such a one is unique among the uniques;* (TA;) *one who has no equal; unequalled; incomparable.* (IAar, Tes-heel.) It seems that the form of pl. used in the phrase أَحَدُ الأَحَدِينَ is used only as applied to rational beings; but it is said in the Expositions of the Tes-heel that this phrase signifies *One of the calamities;* the form of the rational pl. being given to nouns significant of things deemed great, mighty, or grievous. (AHeyth.) In the phrase إِحْدَى الإِحَدِ, the fem. forms are said to be used for the purpose of giving intensiveness to the signification, as though the meaning were دَاهِيَةُ الدَّوَاهِي, the word داهية being [an intensive epithet] from دَهَآءٌ as signifying intelligence, or intelligence mixed with craft or cunning and forecast; or by داهية being meant a calamity. (Expositions of the Fṣ, TA.) AHei thought أَحَدُ الأَحَدِينَ to be an epithet applied to a male, and إِحْدَى الإِحَدِ to be applied to a female: but his opinion has been refuted by Ed-Demámeenee in the Expos. of the Tes-heel: and this latter author there remarks, that in expressions meant to denote praise [of a man], أَحَدٌ and إِحْدَى are prefixed to their own proper pls., as أَحَدٌ and أَحَدُونَ; or to an epithet, as in the case of أَحَدُ العُلَمَآءِ [*One of the learned*]; but that they have not been heard prefixed to generic nouns. (TA.) You say likewise, هُوَ ابْنُ إِحْدَاهَا *He is born of noble,* or *generous, ancestors, both on the father's and the mother's side;* speaking of a man and of a camel. (L and Ḳ in art. وحد.) And لَا يَقُومُ بِهٰذَا الأَمْرِ إِلَّا ابْنُ إِحْدَاهَا *None will manage this thing,* or *affair, but a noble,* or *generous, man.* (AZ, L in art. وحد.) And ▼ لَا يَسْتَطِيعُهَا إِلَّا ابْنُ إِحْدَاتِهَا [*None will be able to perform it but a noble,* or *generous, man*]. (L in art. وحد.) —— One instance is mentioned, of the occurrence, in a trad., of إِحْدَى not used as a part of a number [i. e. not as a part of the compound إِحْدَى عَشْرَةَ] nor as a prefixed noun; viz., إِحْدَى مِنْ سَبْعٍ [*One of seven*]; in which سبع is said to mean the nights of 'Ád [during which that tribe was destroyed], or the years of Joseph [during which Egypt was afflicted with dearth]. (MF, from the Fáïḳ &c.) —— Used in a negative phrase, أَحَدٌ signifies *Any one with whom one may talk or speak:* and in this manner it is used without variation as sing. and pl. and fem. (Ṣ) as well as masc. (Mṣb.) You say, لَا أَحَدَ فِي الدَّارِ [*There is not any one in the house*]: but you do not say, فِيهَا أَحَدٌ [as meaning the contrary]. (Ṣ.) We read in the Ḳur [lxix. 47, this ex. of its use as a masc. pl.], فَمَا مِنْكُمْ مِنْ أَحَدٍ عَنْهُ حَاجِزِينَ [*And not any persons of you should have withheld me from* punishing *him*]. (Ṣ.) And in the same [xxxiii. 32, we find this ex. of its use as a fem. pl.], لَسْتُنَّ كَأَحَدٍ مِنَ النِّسَآءِ [*Ye are not like any* others *of women*]. (Ṣ.) —— It is also used in interrogative phrases; as in the saying, هَلْ أَحَدٌ رَأَى مِثْلَ هٰذَا [*Has any one seen the like of this?*]; (A'Obeyd, L;) and in the saying, يَا أَحَدُ رَآهَا [for يَا أَحَدُ, *O, has any one seen her,* or *it?*]. (L, from a trad.) —— It is [said to be] also used in the sense of شَيْءٌ [meaning *Anything*], applied to an irrational being; as in the saying, مَا بِالدَّارِ مِنْ أَحَدٍ إِلَّا حِمَارًا *There is not in the house anything,* rational or irrational, *except an ass:* so that the thing excepted is united in kind to that from which the exception is made [accord. to this rendering; but this instance is generally regarded as one in which the thing excepted is disunited in kind from that from which the exception is made].

(Mṣb.) So too in the Ḳur lx. 11, accord. to the reading of Ibn-Mes'ood: (Mṣb:) but others there read شَىْءٌ, which may mean any one or any thing. (Bḍ, Jel.) — الأَحَدُ, (Ḳ,) as also يَوْمُ الأَحَدِ, (Ṣ, Mṣb,) as a proper name, (Mṣb,) is applied to *A certain day;* (Ḳ;) [*Sunday;*] *the first day of the week;* or, as some say, [i. e. as some term it,] *the second of the week;* (TA;) for the Arabs are said, by IAạr, to have reckoned the Sabbath, or Saturday, as the first, though they called Sunday the first of the days: (Mṣb in art. جمع:) it is sing., and masc.: (Lḥ:) pl. [as above, i. e.] آحَادٌ (Ṣ, Mṣb, Ḳ) and أُحْدَانٌ: (Ḳ:) or it has no pl. (Ḳ: [but in the TA this last observation is very properly restricted, as relating only to أَحَدٌ as syn. with وَاحِدٌ, and as applied to any unknown person.]) In this sense, it has no dim. (Sb, in Ṣ, art. امس.) — الآحَادُ in lexicology signifies *What have been transmitted by some of the lexicologists, but not by such a number of them as cannot be supposed to have agreed to a falsehood:* what has been transmitted by this larger number is termed مُتَوَاتِرٌ. (Mz 3rd نوع.)

إِحْدَى: } fems. of أَحَدٌ, q. v.
إِحْدَاةٌ: }

أَحَدِيَّةٌ *The unity* of God; (Mṣb;) as also وَحْدَانِيَّةٌ. (L and Ḳ in art. وحد.)

أُحَادَ [accus. of أُحَادُ] is imperfectly decl., because of its deviation from its original, (Ṣ, Ḳ,) both in form and in meaning; (Ṣ;) [being changed in form from وَاحِدًا, and in meaning from وَاحِدًا وَاحِدًا to: (see ثُلَاثُ:)] you say, جَاؤُوا أُحَادَ أُحَادَ, [احاد being repeated for the purpose of corroboration,] meaning, *They came one [and] one, one [and] one;* or *one [by] one, one [by] one.* (Ṣ, Ḳ.) The dim. of أُحَادُ is ▼ أُحَيِّدُ, perfectly decl., like ثُلَيْثٌ [q. v.] &c. (Ṣ, in art. ثلث.)

أُحَيْدٌ dim. of أَحَدٌ, q. v.

أُحَيِّدُ : see أُحَادُ.

أُحَيْدَى dim. of إِحْدَى fem. of أَحَدٌ, q. v.

احن

1. أَحِنَ (Ṣ, Mṣb, Ḳ) عَلَيْهِ, (Ṣ, TA,) aor. ـَ, (Mṣb, Ḳ,) inf. n. أَحَنٌ, (Mṣb,) or أَحْنٌ, and إِحْنَةٌ, (TA,) or this last is a simple subst.; (Mṣb;) and أَحَنَ عَلَيْهِ, aor. ـِ, inf. n. أَحْنٌ; (Kr, TA;) *He retained enmity against him in his bosom, watching for an opportunity to indulge it, or exercise it;* or *hid enmity against him in his bosom;* or *bore rancour, malevolence, malice, or spite, against him:* (Ṣ, Mṣb, Ḳ:*) and *he was affected with anger* (Ḳ, TA) *against him, such as came upon him suddenly from the retention or hiding of enmity in the bosom, or from rancour, malevolence, malice, or spite.* (TA.)

3. آحَنَهُ, (TA,) inf. n. مُؤَاحَنَةٌ, (Ṣ, Ḳ,) *He treated him, or regarded him, with enmity,* or *hostility.* (Ṣ,* Ḳ,* TA.)

إِحْنَةٌ *Retention of enmity in the bosom, with watchfulness for an opportunity to indulge it, or exercise it;* or *concealment of enmity in the bosom;* or *rancour, malevolence, malice,* or *spite:* (Ṣ, Mṣb, Ḳ:) and *anger* (Ḳ, TA) *coming upon one suddenly therefrom:* (TA:) pl. إِحَنٌ. (Ṣ, Mṣb, Ḳ.) It is said in the Ṣ that one should not say حِنَةٌ; and this is disallowed by Aṣ and Fr and Ibn-El-Faraj: in the T it is said that it is not of the language of the Arabs; and Aṣ is related to have disapproved of Eṭ-Ṭirimmáḥ for using its pl. in poetry: but it is said in a trad., مَا بَيْنِى وَبَيْنَ العَرَبِ حِنَةٌ [*There is not between me and the Arabs retention of enmity in the bosom,* &c.]; and it occurs in another trad., in a similar phrase; and the pl., in a third trad.; therefore we say that it is a dial. var. of rare occurrence. (TA.)

اخ

أَخٌ: see art. اخو.

اخت

أُخْتٌ fem. of أَخٌ, q. v. in art. اخو.

اخذ

1. أَخَذَ, (Ṣ, A, L, &c.,) in the first pers. of which, أَخَذْتُ, [and the like,] the ذ is generally changed into ت, and incorporated into the [augmentative] ت, [but in pronunciation only, for one writes أَخَذْتُ and the like,] aor. ـُ, imperative خُذْ, originally أُوْخُذْ, (Ṣ, L,) which latter form sometimes occurs, [but with و in the place of ؤْ when the ا is pronounced with ḍamm,] (TA,) inf. n. أَخْذٌ (Ṣ, L, Mṣb, Ḳ, &c.) and تَأْخَاذٌ, (Ṣ, L, Ḳ,) the latter having an intensive signification; (MF;) and وَخَذَ is a dial. var., as mentioned by Ibn-Umm-Ḳásim and others on the authority of AḤei; (MF in art. تخذ;) *He took; he took with his hand; he took hold of;* (Ṣ, A, L, Mṣb, Ḳ;) a thing. (Ṣ, L.) You say, خُذِ الخِطَامَ, and خُذْ بِالخِطَامِ *Take thou,* or *take thou with thy hand,* or *take thou hold of, the nose-rein* of the camel: (Ṣ, L, Mṣb:) the ب in the latter phrase being redundant. (Mṣb.) [And أَخَذَ بِيَدِهِ, lit. *He took his hand, or arm;* meaning † *he aided, or assisted, him:* a phrase of frequent occurrence.] And أَخَذَ عَلَى يَدِ فُلَانٍ † *He prevented, restrained, or withheld, such a one from doing that which he desired; as though he laid hold upon his hand, or arm:* (L:) and أَخَذَ عَلَى يَدِهِ دُونَ مَا يُرِيدُهُ [signifies the same]. (Ḳ in art. لغد.) — Also, inf. n. أَخْذٌ, *He took,* or *received; contr. of* أَعْطَى. (L.) [Hence,] أَخَذَ عَنْهُ, † *He received from him traditions,* and the like. (TA passim.) — † [*He took,* or *derived,* or *deduced,* a word, a phrase, and a meaning.] — ‡ *He took, received, or admitted, willingly,* or *with approbation; he accepted.* (B, MF.) So in the Ḳur [vii. 198], خُذِ العَفْوَ ‡ [*Take thou willingly,* or *accept thou, superfluous property,* or *such as is easily spared* by others]. (MF.) So too in the same [iii. 75], وَأَخَذْتُمْ عَلَى ذٰلِكُمْ إِصْرِى ‡ [*And do ye accept my covenant to that effect?*]. (B.) [And in the phrases, أَخَذْنَا مِيثَاقَكُمْ بِالعَمَلِ بِمَا فِى التَّوْرَاةِ, (Jel ii. 60,) and عَلَى العَمَلِ بِمَا فِى التوراة, (Idem ii. 87,) † *We accepted your covenant to do according to what is in the Book of the Law revealed to Moses.*] خُذْ عَنْكَ [is elliptical, and] means خُذْ مَا أَقُولُ وَدَعْ عَنْكَ الشَّكَّ وَالمِرَآءَ † [*Accept thou what I say, and dismiss from thee doubt and obstinate disputation*]. (Ṣ, L.) — *He took* a thing *to,* or *for, himself; took possession of* it; *got,* or *acquired,* it; syn. حَازَ; (Z, Er-Rághib, B;) which, accord. to Z and Er-Rághib and others, is the primary signification; (MF;) and حَصَّلَ. (B.) [See also 8.] — [*He took and kept;*] *he retained; he detained:* as in the Ḳur [xii. 78], فَخُذْ أَحَدَنَا مَكَانَهُ [*Therefore retain thou one of us in his stead*]. (B.) — [*He took,* as meaning *he took away.* Hence,] أَخَذَ مِنْهُ السَّيْرُ *Journeying, or travel, took from him strength;* (القُوَّةَ being understood;) *weakened him.* (Ḥar p. 520.) And أَخَذَ مِنَ الشَّارِبِ, (Mgh,) and مِنَ الشَّعَرِ, (Mṣb,) *He clipped,* or *cut off from,* (Mgh, Mṣb,) *the mustache,* (Mgh,) and *the hair.* (Mṣb.) — *He,* or *it, took by force;* or *seized:* (B:) † *he,* or *it, overcame, overpowered,* or *subdued:* said by some to be the primary signification. (MF.) [See also أَخَذَهُ عَلْوًا, &c., in art. علو: and أَخَذَهُ مِنْ فَوْقُ, &c., in art. فوق.] It is said in the Ḳur [ii. 256], لَا تَأْخُذُهُ سِنَةٌ وَلَا نَوْمٌ † *Neither drowsiness nor sleep shall seize* [or *overcome*] *Him.* (B.) [And] you say, أَخَذَتْهُ رِعْدَةٌ † *A tremour seized, took, affected,* or *influenced, him.* And أَخَذَهُ بَطْنُهُ † *His belly affected him with a desire to evacuate it.*] You say also, أَخَذَ فِيهِ الشَّرَابُ † *The wine affected him, or influenced him, so that he became intoxicated.* (TA in art. ثمل.) And أَخَذَ الرَّأْسَ (Mṣb in art. سور, &c.) and أَخَذَ بِالرَّأْسِ (Ḳ in art. حمى, &c.) † [*It had an overpowering influence upon the head*]; meaning wine. (Mṣb, Ḳ.) And أَخَذَ بِالحَلْقِ [*It* (food, &c.) *choked*]. (IAạr in art. نشب in the TA, and Ṣ in art. بشع, &c.) And لَا يَأْخُذُ فِيهِ قَوْلُ قَائِلٍ † [*Nothing that any one may say will have any power, or effect, or influence, upon him*]; meaning that he obeyeth no one. (L in art. ليت.) — *He took captive.* (L, Mṣb, B.) So in the Ḳur [ix. 5], فَاقْتُلُوا المُشْرِكِينَ حَيْثُ وَجَدْتُّمُوهُمْ وَخُذُوهُمْ [*Then slay ye the believers in a plurality of gods wherever, or whenever, ye find them, and take them captives*]. (Bḍ, L, B.) — See also 2, in three places. — *He gained the mastery over* a person, *and killed,* or *slew,* him; (Zj, L;) as also ▼ آخَذَ: (L:) or simply, † *he killed,* or *slew.* (B.) It is said in the Ḳur [xl. 5], وَهَمَّتْ كُلُّ أُمَّةٍ بِرَسُولِهِمْ لِيَأْخُذُوهُ, meaning [*And every nation hath purposed against their apostle*] *that they might gain the mastery over him, and slay him;* (Zj, L;) or † *that they might slay him.* (B.) — † *He* (God, Mṣb) *destroyed* a person: (Mṣb, MF:) and † *extirpated,* or *exterminated.* (MF.) فَأَخَذَهُمُ اللّٰهُ بِذُنُوبِهِمْ [in the Ḳur iii. 9 and xl. 22] means *But God destroyed them for their sins.* (Jel.) — ‡ *He punished,* or *chastised;* (L, Mṣb, B, Ḳ, MF;) as also ▼ آخَذَ: (L, Mṣb, MF:) as in the phrases, أَخَذَهُ بِذَنْبِهِ

(Mṣb, Ḳ*) and ▼ آخَذَهُ بِهِ, inf. n. of the latter مُؤَاخَذَةٌ, (Ṣ, L, Mṣb, Ḳ,) ‡ *he punished,* or *chastised, him for his sin,* or *offence:* (Mṣb:) and أُخِذَ بِذَنْبِهِ means † *he was restrained and requited and punished for his sin,* or *offence:* (L:) or, accord. to some, أَخَذَ signifies *he extirpated,* or *exterminated;* and ▼ آخذ *he punished,* or *chastised, without extirpating,* or *exterminating.* (MF.) [For ▼ آخذ,] some say وَاخَذَ, (Ṣ, L,) which is not allowable, (Ḳ,) accord. to some; but accord. to others, it is a chaste form; (MF;) of the dial. of El-Yemen, and used by certain of the seven readers [of the Ḳur-án] in the instance of لَا يُوَاخِذُكُمُ ٱللّٰهُ [ii. 225 and v. 91]; and the inf. n. in that dial. is مُوَاخَذَةٌ, and the imperative is وَاخِذْ. (Mṣb.) — ‡ *He made a violent assault upon* a person, *and wounded* him *much.* (Ḳ, TA.) [You say also, أَخَذَهُ بِلِسَانِهِ, meaning † *He assailed him with his tongue; vituperated him; spoke against him.*] — [*He took, took to,* or *adopted.*] You say, أَخَذَ أَخْذَهُمْ and إِخْذَهُمْ &c.: see أَخْذٌ, below. And أَخَذَ فِى طَرِيقِ كَذَا [*He took such a road*]: and أَخَذَ عَنْ يَمِينِهِ أَوْ يَسَارِهِ [*he took the way by,* or *on, the right of him,* or *it, or the left of him,* or *it*]. (Ṣ in art. نظر.) [And أَخَذَ بِالحَزْمِ, and فِى الحَزْمِ, (the former the more common, the latter occurring in art. حوط in the Ḳ,) † *He took the course prescribed by prudence, discretion, precaution,* or *good judgment; he used precaution:* and, like أَخَذَ بِالثِّقَةِ, † *he took the sure course* in his affair.] And أَخَذَ حِذْرَهُ † *He took care; became cautious,* or *vigilant.* (Bḍ in iv. 73 and 103.) [And أَخَذَ بِمَا قَالَ فُلَانٌ † *He took to,* or *adopted and followed,* or *adhered to, what such a one said:* see Ḥar p. 367; where it is said that اخذ when thus used is made trans. by means of ب because it implies the meaning of تَشَبَّثَ.] — *He took to, set about, began,* or *commenced;* as in the saying, أَخَذَ يَفْعَلُ كَذَا *He took to, set about, began,* or *commenced, doing such a thing;* in which case, accord. to Sb, اخذ is one of those verbs which do not admit of one's putting the act. part. n. in the place of the verb which is its enunciative: [i. e., one may not say فَاعِلًا in the place of يفعل in the phrase above:] and as in أَخَذَ فِى كَذَا *He began, commenced,* or *entered upon, such a thing.* (L.) — [It is used in a variety of other phrases, in which the primary meaning is more or less apparent; and several of these will be found explained with other words occurring therein. The following instances may be here added.] — طَرِيقٌ يَأْخُذُ فِى رَمْلَةٍ [*A road leading into,* or *through, a tract of sand*]. (Ḳ in art. فزر.) And أَخَذَ بِهِمُ الطَّرِيقُ فِى غَيْرِ المَحَجَّةِ [*The road lead them otherwise than in the beaten track*]. (T* and A in art. بهرج.) — مَا أَخَذْتُكَ عَيْنِى مُنْذُ حِينٍ † *My eye hath not seen thee for some time;* like مَا ظَفِرَتْكَ. (T in art. ظفر.) And مَا فِى الحَىِّ أَحَدٌ تَأْخُذُهُ عَيْنِى [explained to me by Ibr D as meaning † *There is not in the tribe any one whom my eye regards as worthy of notice* or *respect* by reason of his greatness therein]. (TA in art. جهر.) — أَخَذْتُ عِنْدَهُ يَدًا, and مَعْرُوفًا: see

8. — أَخِذَ, aor. ـَ, inf. n. أَخَذٌ, (Ṣ, L, Ḳ,) *He* (a young camel) *suffered heaviness of the stomach, and indigestion, from the milk:* (Ṣ:) or *became disordered in his belly, and affected with heaviness of the stomach, and indigestion, from taking much milk.* (L.) — *He* (a camel, L, Ḳ, or a sheep or goat, L) *became affected by madness,* or *demoniacal possession;* (Ḳ;) or *by what resembled that.* (L.) — أَخِذَتْ عَيْنُهُ, aor. ـَ, inf. n. أَخَذٌ, *His eye became affected by inflammation, pain, and swelling,* or *ophthalmia.* (Ibn-Es-Seed, L, Ḳ.*) — أَخُذَ, aor. ـُ, inf. n. أُخُوذَةٌ, *It* (milk) *was,* or *became, sour.* (Ḳ.) [See آخِذٌ.]

2. أَخَّذَتْهُ, (Ṣ, L, K,*) inf. n. تَأْخِيذٌ, (Ṣ, L,) *She captivated,* or *fascinated, him,* (namely, her husband,) *and restrained him, by a kind of enchantment,* or *charm,* and especially *so as to withhold him from carnal conversation with other women;* (Ṣ,* L, Ḳ,* TA;) as also ▼ أَخَذَتْهُ; and ▼ آخَذَتْهُ [of which the inf. n. is app. إِيخَاذٌ]. (L, TA.) A woman says, أُؤَخِّذُ جَمَلِى *I captivate,* or *fascinate, my husband, by a kind of enchantment,* or *charm, and withhold him from other women.* (L, from a trad.) And one says, of a man, يُؤَخِّذُ عَنِ ٱمْرَأَتِهِ *He withholds others* [*by a kind of enchantment,* or *charm,*] *from carnal conversation with his wife.* (Mṣb.) The sister of Ṣubḥ El-'Ádee said, in bewailing him, when he had been killed by a man pushed towards him upon a couch-frame, or raised couch, ▼ أَخَذْتُ عَنْكَ الرَّاكِبَ وَالسَّاعِىَ وَالمَاشِىَ وَالقَاعِدَ وَالقَائِمَ وَلَمْ أُأَخِّذْ عَنْكَ النَّائِمَ [*I withheld from thee by enchantment the rider and the runner and the walker and the sitter and the stander, and did not so withhold from thee the prostrate*]. (L.) And one says of a beautiful garment, ▼ أَخَذَ القُلُوبَ مَأْخَذَهُ [*It captivated hearts in a manner peculiar to it*]: (Ḳ in art. حصر: [in the CḲ, incorrectly, اَخَذَتْ and القُلُوبُ:]) and اخذ بِقَلْبِهِ [*He,* or *it, captivated his heart;* or] *he* [or *it*] *pleased him,* or *excited his admiration.* (TA in art. اله.) — أَخَّذَ اللَّبَنَ, inf. n. as above, *He made the milk sour.* (Ḳ.) [See آخِذٌ.]

3. آخذ, inf. n. مُؤَاخَذَةٌ: see 1, in the middle portion of the paragraph, in five places.

4. آخذ, inf. n., app., إِيخَاذٌ: see 2.

8. اتّخذ [written with the disjunctive alif إِيتَخَذَ] occurs in its original form; and is changed into ٱتَّخَذَ [with the disjunctive alif إِتَّخَذَ]; this being of the measure افتعل from أَخَذَ, the [radical] ء being softened, and changed into ت, and incorporated [into the augmentative ت]: hence, when it had come to be much used in the form of افتعل [thus changed], they imagined the [former] ت to be a radical letter [unchanged], and formed from it a verb of the measure فَعِلَ, aor. يَفْعَلُ; saying, تَخِذَ, aor. يَتْخَذُ, (Ṣ, L, Mṣb,*) inf. n. تَخْذٌ and تَخَذٌ: (Mṣb:) and ▼ ٱسْتَخَذَ [written with the disjunctive alif إِسْتَخَذَ], of which exs. will be found below, is also used for ٱتَّخَذَ; one of the two ت being changed into س, like as س is changed into ت in سِتٌّ [for سِدْسٌ]: or استخذ may be of the

measure استفعل from تَخِذَ; one of the two ت being suppressed; after the manner of those who say ظَلْتُ for ظَلِلْتُ: (Ṣ, L:) and IAth says that ٱتَّخذ, in like manner, is of the measure افتعل from تَخِذَ; not from أَخَذَ: (L and Ḳ in art. تخذ:) but IAth is not one who should contradict J, whose opinion on this point is corroborated by the fact that they say ٱتَّزَرَ from إِزَارٌ, and ٱتَّمَنَ from أَمْنٌ, and ٱتَّهَلَ from أَهْلٌ; and there are other instances of the same kind: or, accord. to some, ٱتّخذ is from وَخَذَ, a dial. var. of أَخَذَ, and is originally اِوْتَخَذَ. (MF.) [The various significations of اتّخذ and تَخِذَ and استخذ will be here given under one head.] — You say, إِتَّخَذُوا فِى القِتَالِ, فِى الحَرْبِ, (Ṣ, L, Ḳ,*) and (Mṣb,) with two hemzehs, (Ṣ, L, Ḳ,) or, correctly, إِيتَخَذُوا, with one hemzeh, [or إِاتَّخَذُوا,] as two hemzehs cannot occur together in one word, (marginal note in a copy of the Ṣ,) [but in a case of waṣl, the first hemzeh being suppressed, the second remains unchanged,] *They took,* or *seized,* (أَخَذُوا,) *one another* (Ṣ, L, Mṣb, Ḳ) *in fight,* (Ṣ, L,) and *in war;* (Mṣb;) and so ٱتَّخَذُوا. (Mṣb.) And إِيتَخَذَ القَوْمُ *The people,* or *company of men, wrestled together, each taking hold in some manner upon him who wrestled with him, to throw him down.* (L, TA.) — [اتّخذ, as also ▼ استخذ, and] تَخِذَ, aor. ـَ, (Ḳ in art. تخذ,) inf. n. تَخْذٌ and تَخَذٌ, (TA in art. تخذ,) likewise signifies *i. q.* أَخَذَ, (Ḳ in art. تخذ, and B and TA in the present art.,) as meaning *He took* a thing *to,* or *for, himself; took possession of* it; *got,* or *acquired,* it; syn. حَازَ and حَصَّلَ. (B, TA.) Some read, [in the Ḳur, xviii. 76,] لَتَخِذْتَ عَلَيْهِ أَجْرًا [*Thou mightest assuredly have taken for thyself a recompense for it*]: (Ṣ, L, Ḳ in art. تخذ, and TA in the present art.:) this is the reading of Mujáhid, (Fr, TA,) and is authorized by I'Ab, and is that of Aboo-'Amr Ibn-El-'Alà and AZ, and so it is written in the model-copy of the Ḳur, and so the readers [in general] read: (AM, L, TA:) so read Ibn-Ketheer and the Baṣrees; he and Yaạḳoob and Ḥafṣ pronouncing the ذ; the others incorporating it [into the ت]: (Bḍ:) some read لَاتَّخَذْتَ; (L and Ḳ in art. تخذ;) but these read at variance with the scripture. (AM, L, TA.) ▼ استخذ أَرْضًا is a phrase mentioned by Mbr as used by some of the Arabs, (Ṣ, L,) and signifies *i. q.* ٱتَّخَذَهَا [*He took for himself a piece of land*]. (Ṣ, L, Ḳ.) And ٱتّخذ وَلَدًا [in the Ḳur, ii. 110, &c.,] signifies *He got a son,* or *offspring.* (Bḍ &c. See also below.) And تَخِذَ, aor. ـَ, inf. n. تَخْذٌ and تَخَذٌ, also signifies *He gained, acquired,* or *earned,* wealth, (L, and Mṣb in arts. اخذ and تخذ,) or a thing. (Mṣb.) — ▼ استخذ عَلَيْهِمْ يَدًا and عِنْدَهُمْ signify alike, *i. q.* ٱتّخذ [*He did to them a benefit,* or *favour;* as though he earned one for himself in prospect, making it to be incumbent on them as a debt to him]: (ISh:) and ٱتَّخَذْتُ عِنْدَهُ مَعْرُوفًا means [in like manner, ٱتَّخَذَ as also ▼ أَخَذْتُ عنده معروفا, and يَدًا, (and فِيهِ حُسْنًا has a similar meaning; see Ḳur xviii.

85;)] *I did to him a benefit*, or *favour*; syn. أَسْدَيْتُهُ إِلَيْهِ. (Mṣb in art. سدى.) — اتّخذ also signifies *He made* a thing; syn. عَمِلَ; like تَخِذَ, [aor. ـَ,] inf. n. تَخْذٌ and تَخَذٌ: (L:) *he made*, or *manufactured*, a bow, a water-skin, &c., مِنْ كَذَا *of such a thing*: *he made*, or *prepared*, a dish of food, a medicine, &c.: either absolutely or *for himself*. (The Lexicons passim.) — Also *He made*, or *constituted*, or *appointed*; syn. جَعَلَ; doubly trans.; (B, Mṣb;) and so تَخِذَ. (Mṣb in art. تخذ.) You say, اتَّخَذَهُ صَدِيقًا *He made him* [or *took him as*] *a friend*; (Mṣb in the present art.;) and so تَخِذَهُ. (Idem in art. تخذ.) And اتَّخَذَهُ هُزُؤًا [in the Ḳur ii. 63 and 231, &c.,] means *He made him*, or *it, a subject of derision*. (Bḍ, Jel.) And اتَّخَذَهُ وَلَدًا [in the same, xii. 21 and xxviii. 8,] *He made him*, or *took* or *adopted him as, a son*. (Bḍ. See also above.)

10. اِسْتَأْخَذَ, written with the disjunctive alif اِسْتَأْخَذَ: see 8, in four places. [Other meanings may be inferred from explanations of مُسْتَأْخِذٌ, q. v. infrà.]

أَخْذٌ inf. n. of أَخَذَ, q. v. — † *A way*, or *manner, of life*; as also ▼ إِخْذٌ. (Ṣ, L, Ḳ.) You say, ذَهَبَ بَنُو فُلَانٍ وَمَنْ أَخَذَ أَخْذَهُمْ, (Ṣ, L, Ḳ,*) and ▼ إِخْذَهُمْ, (L, Ḳ,) the former of the dial. of Temeem, and the latter of the dial. of El-Ḥijáz, (TA,) meaning † *The sons of such a one went away*, or *passed away, and those who took to their way of life*, (Ṣ, L, Ḳ,) *and adopted their manners*, or *dispositions*: (Ḳ:) and مَنْ أَخَذَ أَخْذُهُمْ and ▼ مَنْ أَخَذَهُ إِخْذُهُمْ, and [in the CḲ أَخْذُهُمْ] and ▼ إِخْذُهُمْ, signify [virtually] the same: (Ḳ:) or مَنْ أَخَذَ أَخْذَهُمْ and ▼ إِخْذَهُمْ signify [properly] مَنْ أَخَذَهُ أَخْذُهُمْ وَسِيرَتُهُمْ [*those whom their way of life took*, or *influenced*]. (ISk, Ṣ, L.) One says also, اُسْتُعْمِلَ فُلَانٌ عَلَى الشَّامِ وَمَا أَخَذَ إِخْذَهُ ▼, with kesr, meaning † [*Such a one was appointed prefect over Syria*,] *and he did not take to that good way of life which it was incumbent on him to adopt*: you should not say أَخْذَهُ: (AA, Ṣ, L:) or it means *and what was adjacent to it*: (Fr, L:) or, accord. to the Wá'ee, one says, in this case, ▼ وَمَا أَخَذَ إِخْذُهُ and أَخْذُهُ and ▼ أُخْذُهُ, with kesr and fet-ḥ and ḍamm [to the hemzeh, and with the ذ marfooah, as in instances before]. (Et-Tedmuree, MF.) One also says, ▼ لَوْ كُنْتَ مِنَّا لَأَخَذْتَ بِإِخْذِنَا, (Ṣ, L,) with kesr to the ا, (L,) [in a copy of the Ṣ بِأَخْذِنَا, which seems to be also allowable, accord. to the dial. of Temeem,] meaning *Wert thou of us, then thou hadst taken to*, or *wouldst take to, our manners*, or *dispositions, and fashion*, (Ṣ, L,) *and garb, and way of life*. (L.) The words of the poet,

فَلَوْ كُنْتُمْ مِنَّا أَخَذْنَا بِإِخْذِكُمْ ▼

IAạr explains as meaning *And were ye of us, we had caught and restored to you your camels*: but no other says so. (L.) — نُجُومُ الأَخْذِ *The Mansions of the Moon*; (Ṣ, L, Ḳ;) also called نُجُومُ الأَنْوَاءِ; (L; [see art. نوء;]) called by the former appellation because the moon every night enters (يَأْخُذُ فِي) one of those mansions: (Ṣ, L:) or *the stars which are cast at those* [*devils*] *who listen by stealth* [*to the conversations of the angels*]: (L, Ḳ:) but the former explanation is the more correct. (L.) — See also إِخَاذٌ.

أُخُذٌ, whence مَا أَخَذَ أُخُذَهُ: see أَخْذٌ. — It is also a pl. of إِخَاذٌ; (Ṣ, L;) and of إِخْذٌ or إِخْذَةٌ, explained below with إِخَاذٌ. (L.)

إِخْذٌ [The *act of taking, taking with the hand*, &c.], a subst. from أَخَذَ. (Ṣ, L, Mṣb.) — See also أَخْذٌ, in nine places. — And see إِخَاذٌ. — Also *A mark made with a hot iron upon a camel's side when a disease therein is feared*. (Ḳ.)

أَخَذٌ *Heaviness of the stomach, and indigestion*, of a young camel, *from the milk*. (Ḳ.) [See أَخِذٌ.] — See also أُخُذٌ.

أَخِذٌ A young camel *disordered in his belly, and affected with heaviness of the stomach, and indigestion, from taking much milk*. (AZ, Fr, L.) [See also صُبْحَانٌ.] — A camel, or a young camel, or a sheep or goat, *affected by what resembles madness*, or *demoniacal possession*. (L.) — A man *affected with inflammation of the eye; with pain and swelling of the eye; with ophthalmia*; (Ṣ, L;) as also ▼ مُسْتَأْخِذٌ. (L.) See also this latter. — See also آخِذٌ.

أُخُذٌ (Ṣ, L, Ḳ) and ▼ أَخَذٌ, (Ibn-Es-Seed, L, Ḳ,) which latter is the regular form, (L,) *Inflammation of the eye; pain and swelling of the eye; ophthalmia*. (Ṣ, L, Ḳ.)

أَخْذَةٌ [inf. n. un. of أَخَذَ, *An act of taking*, &c.: *an act of punishment*, or *chastisement*, or *the like*; as in the Ḳur lxix. 10: pl. أَخَذَاتٌ]. — أَخَذُوا أَخَذَاتِهِمْ *They took their places of abode*. (IAth and L, from a trad.)

أُخْذَةٌ *A manner of taking*, or *seizing*, of a man with whom one is wrestling: pl. أُخَذٌ. (L.) — *A kind of enchantment*, or *fascination, like* سِحْر, (Ṣ, L, Mṣb,* Ḳ,) *which captivates the eye and the like*, (L,) *and by which enchantresses withhold their husbands from other women*; called by the vulgar رِبَاطٌ and عَقْدٌ; and practised by the women in the time of ignorance: (TA:) or *a kind of bead* (خَرَزَةٌ, Ṣ, L, Ḳ) *with which one captivates*, or *fascinates*, or *restrains*; (Ḳ;) *with which women captivate*, or *fascinate*, or *restrain, men*, (Ṣ, L,) *and withhold them from other women*: (L:) or *i. q.* رُقْيَةٌ. (A.) — *A pitfall dug for catching a lion*. (A, TA.) — بَادِرْ بِزَنْدِكَ أُخْذَةَ النَّارِ [*Strive thou to be before the time called* (that of) اخذة النار *with thy wooden instrument for producing fire*; i. e. *haste thou to use it before that time*;] means *the time a little after the prayer of sunset*; asserted to be the worst time in which to strike fire. (Ḳ.)

إِخْذَةٌ: see إِخَاذٌ.

إِخَاذٌ and ▼ إِخَاذَةٌ *A pool of water left by a torrent*: pl. أُخُذٌ: (AO, Ḳ:) both signify the same: (L:) or ▼ إِخَاذَةٌ signifies *a thing like a pool of water left by a torrent*; and إِخَاذٌ is its pl. [or a coll. gen. n.]; and the pl. of this latter is أُخُذٌ, like as كُتُبٌ is pl. of كِتَابٌ, and sometimes it is contracted into أُخْذٌ: (Ṣ, L:) the like of this is said by Aboo-'Adnán: (L:) and إِخَاذَاتٌ is also a pl. of إِخَاذَةٌ, occurring in a trad., and signifying *pools which receive the rain-water, and retain it for drinkers*: (IAth, L:) or the correct word is إِخَاذٌ, without ة, and it signifies *a place where beasts assemble at a pool of water left by a torrent*; and its pl. is أُخُذٌ (AA, A'Obeyd, L) and آخَاذٌ, which latter is extr.: (L:) but as to ▼ إِخَاذَةٌ, it has a different signification, which will be found below; i. e. land of which a man takes possession for himself, &c.: (AA, L:) or إِخَاذٌ is a coll. gen. n., and ▼ إِخَاذَةٌ is its n. un., and signifies *a receptacle made for water to collect therein*: and ▼ أَخْذٌ signifies *a thing that one digs for himself, in the form of a watering-trough, which retains water for some days*; and its pl. is أُخْذَانٌ: (L:) and ▼ إِخْذٌ and ▼ إِخْذَةٌ also signify *a thing that one digs in the form of a watering-trough*; and the pl. is أُخُذٌ and إِخَاذٌ. (L.) In a trad. of Mesrooḳ Ibn-El-Ajda', إِخَاذ are likened to the Companions of Moḥammad; and it is added, that one ▼ إِخَاذَة suffices for a rider; and one, for two riders; and one, for a company of men: (Ṣ, L:) meaning that among them were the young and the old, and the possessor of knowledge and the possessor of more knowledge. (L.) — See also إِخَاذَةٌ.

أَخِيذٌ *i. q.* ▼ مَأْخُوذٌ [*Taken; taken with the hand*; &c.]. (Mṣb.) — *A captive*: (Ṣ, L, Mṣb, Ḳ:) fem. with ة. (Ṣ, L.) Hence the saying, أَكْذَبُ مِنْ أَخِيذِ الجَيْشِ *More lying than the captive of the army*: meaning him whom his enemies have taken captive, and whom they desire to conduct them to his people, and who lies to them to his utmost. (Fr, L.) [See another ex. voce صُبْحَانٌ.] — *A strange*, or *foreign, old man*. (Ḳ.)

إِخَاذَةٌ *Land which a man*, (Ṣ, L, Ḳ,) *or a Sulṭán*, (Ṣ, L,) *takes for himself*; as also ▼ إِخَاذٌ: (Ṣ, L, Ḳ:) or *land which a man takes for himself, and brings into a state of cultivation after its having been waste*: (AA, Mgh, L:) or *waste land which the owner gives to him who shall cultivate it*: (Mgh:) and *land which the Imám gives to one, not being property*, (Ḳ,) or *not being the property of another*. (TA, as from the Ḳ.) — See also إِخَاذٌ, in five places. — Also The *handle* of a [shield of the kind called] حَجَفَة; (Ḳ; [in the L written جحفة, with the ج before the ح;]) also called its ثِقَاف. (L.)

أَخِيذَةٌ *A thing that is taken by force*. (L.) [See also أَخِيذٌ.]

أَخَّاذٌ One *who takes eagerly*, or *greedily*: whence the saying, مَا أَنْتَ إِلَّا أَخَّاذٌ نَبَّاذٌ *Thou art none other than one who taketh a thing eagerly, or greedily, and then throweth it away quickly*. (A.)

آخِذٌ, (as in some copies of the Ḳ, in both of

the senses here explained,) or ▼ أُخُذٌ, (as in other copies of the Ḳ, and in the L and TA, [but the former is the more agreeable with the form of the pl.,]) A camel *beginning to become fat*; (L, Ḳ;) or *to become aged*: (Ḳ:) pl. أَوَاخِذُ. (L.) ═ Milk *that bites the tongue*; syn. قَارِصٌ. (Ḳ.) [See أُخُذٌ.]

مَأْخَذٌ [*A place where, or whence, a thing is taken*: pl. مَآخِذُ.] [Hence,] مَآخِذُ الطَّيْرِ *The places whence birds are taken*. (Ḳ, TA.) — [*The source of derivation* of a word or phrase or meaning.] — *A way* [*which one takes*]; as in the phrase, سَلَكَ المَأْخَذَ الأَقْرَبَ *He went the nearest way*. (Mṣb. in art. حصر.) — [See also 2, last sentence but one.]

مَأْخُوذٌ: see أَخِيذٌ.

رَجُلٌ مُؤَخَّذٌ عَنِ النِّسَآءِ *A man withheld* [*by a kind of enchantment* or *charm* (see 2)] *from women*. (L.)

مُؤْتَخِذٌ: see what follows.

مُسْتَأْخِذٌ [*Requiring to be clipped*; i. e.] *long*; applied to hair. (Ḳ.) ═ *Lowering his head*, or *stooping*, (Aṣ, Ṣ, L, Ḳ,) *by reason of inflammation of the eyes*, or *ophthalmia*, (Aṣ, Ṣ, L,) or *by reason of pain*, (Aṣ, Ṣ, L, Ḳ,) or *from some other cause*; (L;) as also ▼ أَخِذٌ, q. v. (TA.) *Lowly*, or *submissive*, (AA, L, Ḳ,) by reason of disease; as also ▼ مُؤْتَخِذٌ. (AA, L.)

اخر

2. أَخَّرَ, (Ṣ, Ḳ, &c.,) inf. n. تَأْخِيرٌ, (Ḳ,) is trans. (Ṣ, Ḳ, &c.) and intrans.: (Ḳ:) as a trans. verb it signifies *He made to go back* or *backwards, to recede, retreat, retire*, or *retrograde*: *he put*, or *drove, back*: *he put*, or *placed, behind*, or *after*; *back*, or *backward*: *he made to be behind*, or *posterior*, or *last*: *he made to remain behind, hold back, hang back*, or *lag behind*: *he kept*, or *held, back*: *he postponed, put off, procrastinated, deferred, delayed*, or *retarded*: *he made backward*, or *late*: contr. of قَدَّمَ. (Mṣb, TA.) — أَخَّرَنِى إِلَى مُدَّةٍ *He granted me a delay*, or *postponement, to a certain term*, or *period*. (TA in art. اجل.) ═ For its significations as an intrans. verb, see 5, in two places.

5. تأخّر is quasi-pass. of the trans. verb أَخَّرَ; (Ṣ, A, Mṣb;) i. e. *He*, or *it, went back* or *backwards, drew back, receded, retreated, retired*, or *retrograded*: *became put*, or *driven, back*: *became put*, or *placed, behind*, or *after*: *became behind, posterior*, or *last*: *he remained behind*, or *in the rear*; *held back, hung back, lagged behind*, or *delayed*; *was*, or *became, backward*, or *late*: *it was*, or *became, kept back, postponed, put off, procrastinated, deferred, delayed*, or *retarded*: contr. of تَقَدَّمَ: (TA:) and ▼ استأخر is syn. therewith; (Ṣ, Ḳ;) and ▼ أَخَّرَ, inf. n. تَأْخِيرٌ, signifies the same, being intrans. as well as trans. (Ḳ.) An ex. of the latter occurs in a saying of Moḥammad to 'Omar: أَخِّرْ عَنِّى *Retire thou from me*: or the meaning is, أَخِّرْ عَنِّى رَأْيَكَ [*hold thou back from me thine opinion*; or *reserve thou thine opinion until after mine shall have been given*]. (TA.) You say, تَأَخَّرَ عَنْهُ تَأْخُرَةً وَاحِدَةً [*He went back, &c., from him*, or *it, once*]. (Lḥ.) And تَأَخَّرَ عَنِ الشَّىْءِ, or الأَمْرِ, *He went back, &c., from the thing*, or *the affair*: *he was*, or *became, behind, behindhand*, or *backward, with respect to it*: *he held back, hung back, refrained*, or *abstained, from it*; and ▼ استأخر عَنْهُ signifies the same. (The Lexicons in many places.) فَإِذَا جَآءَ أَجَلُهُمْ لَا يَسْتَأْخِرُونَ ▼ سَاعَةً, in the Ḳur vii. 32 and other places, means *And when their time is come*, for punishment, *they will not remain behind*, or *be respited*, [*any while*, or] *the shortest time*: or *they shall not seek to remain behind*, by reason of intense terror. (Bḍ.)

10: see 5, in three places.

أَخِرٌ [an epithet variously explained]. One says, in reviling, (Ṣ, TA,) but not when the object is a female, (TA,) أَبْعَدَ ٱللّٰهُ الأَخِرَ, (Th, Ṣ, A, &c.,) and ▼ الآخِرَ, (M, &c.,) or this latter is wrong, (Meshárik of 'Iyáḍ, Mgh, Mṣb,) as is also ▼ الأَخَرَ, (Meshárik of 'Iyáḍ,) meaning ‡ *May God alienate*, or *estrange, from good*, or *prosperity*, or *may God curse, him who is absent from us*, (A, Mṣb, TA,) *distant*, or *remote*: (A, Mṣb:) or *the outcast*; *the alienated*: (Mṣb:) or *him who is put back*, and *cast away*: so says Sh: or, accord. to ISh, *him who is put back, and remote from good*: and he adds, I think that ▼ الأَخِير is meant: (L:) or *the base fellow*: or *the most ignoble*: or *the miserable wretch*: (Et-Tedmuree and others:) or *the last speaker*: (Nawádir of Th:) or الاخر is here a metonymy for *the devil*: (Lb:) it is a word used [for the reason explained voce أَبْعَدَ] in relating what has been said by one of two persons cursing each other, to the other; (Expositions of the Fṣ;) and the phrase above mentioned is meant to imply a prayer for those who are present [by its contrasting them with the person to whom it directly applies]. (A.) One also says, لَا مَرْحَبًا بِالأَخِرِ, [alluding to a particular person,] meaning [*May the place*, or *land, not be ample*, or *spacious*, or *roomy*,] *to the remote from good*. (TA.) It is said in a trad. of Mázin, إِنَّ الأَخِرَ قَدْ زَنَى *Verily the outcast*, (Mgh, Mṣb,) or *he who is remote, and held back, from good*, (Mgh,* TA,) *hath committed adultery*, or *fornication*: the speaker meaning himself; (Mgh, Mṣb;) as though he were an outcast. (Mṣb.) And in another trad. it is said, المَسْأَلَةُ أَخِرُ كَسْبِ المَرْءِ *Begging is the most ignoble* [mode of] *gain of man*: but El-Khaṭṭábee relates it with medd, [i. e. ▼ آخِرُ,] explaining it as meaning *begging is the last thing whereby man seeks sustenance* when unable to gain [by other means]. (TA.)

أُخُرٌ The *back, hinder*, or *latter, part*: the *hindermost*, or *last, part*: contr. of قُدُمٌ. (Ḳ.) [See also مُؤْخِرٌ; from which it appears to be distinguished by its being used only adverbially, or with a preposition: and see آخِرٌ.] You say, شُقَّ ثَوْبُهُ أُخُرًا, and مِنْ أُخُرٍ, (Ṣ, Ḳ,*) *His garment was rent*, or *slit, in its back*, or *hinder, part*, (Ṣ,) or *behind*. (Ḳ.) And تَأَخَّرَ أُخُرًا [*He retired backwards*]. (A.) And جَآءَ أُخُرًا: see آخِرٌ, in two places.

أُخْرَةٌ and بِأُخْرَةٍ: see آخِرٌ.

أُخَرَةٌ and بِأَخَرَةٍ: see آخِرٌ, in five places.

بِعْتُهُ بِأَخِرَةٍ *I sold it* (namely the article of merchandise, TA) *with postponement of the payment*; *upon credit*; *for payment to be made at a future period*; syn. بِنَظِرَةٍ; (Ṣ, A, Ḳ;) i. e. بِنَسِيْئَةٍ. (Ṣ.)

أُخُرَةٌ and بِأُخُرَةٍ: see آخِرٌ.

أُخْرَى: see آخَرُ, of which it is the fem.: and see also آخِرٌ.

أُخْرَاةٌ another fem. of آخَرُ. (Ḳ.)

أُخْرِيًّا and إِخْرِيًّا and إِخِرِيًّا: see آخِرٌ.

[أُخْرَوِىٌّ and أُخْرَاوِىٌّ *Relating to the other state of existence*, or *the world to come*.]

أَخِيرٌ and أَخِيرًا: see آخِرٌ, in five places. See also أَخِرٌ.

أُخَيْرَى dim. of أُخْرَى, fem. of آخَرُ, q. v. (Ṣ.)

آخَرُ a subst., of the measure أَفْعَلُ, but implying the meaning of an epithet, (Ṣ,) from أَخَّرَ in the sense of تَأَخَّرَ, (TA,) *Another*; the *other*; *a thing* [or *person*] *other than the former* or *first*; (L;) i. q. غَيْرٌ; (Ḳ;) as in the phrases, رَجُلٌ آخَرُ *another man*, and ثَوْبٌ آخَرُ *another garment* or *piece of cloth*: (TA:) or *one of two things* [or *persons*]; (Ṣ, Ṣgh, Mṣb;) as when you say, جَآءَ القَوْمُ فَوَاحِدٌ يَفْعَلُ كَذَا وَآخَرُ كَذَا *The people came, and one was doing thus, and one* [i. e. *another*] *thus*: (Ṣgh, Mṣb:) originally meaning *more backward*: (TA:) fem. ▼ أُخْرَى (Ṣ, Mṣb, Ḳ) and ▼ أُخْرَاةٌ; (Ḳ;) which latter is not well known: (MF:) pl. masc. آخَرُونَ and أُخَرُ; (Ṣ, Ḳ;) [the latter irreg. as such;] and, applied to irrational things, أَوَاخِرُ, like as أَفَاضِلُ is pl. of أَفْضَلُ: (Mṣb:) and pl. fem. أُخْرَيَاتٌ and أُخَرُ; (Ṣ, Mṣb, Ḳ;) which latter is imperfectly decl.; for an epithet of the measure أَفْعَلُ which is accompanied by مِنْ has no [dual nor] pl. nor fem. as long as it is indeterminate; but when it has the article ال prefixed to it, or is itself prefixed to another noun which it governs in the gen. case, it has a dual and a pl. and a fem.; but it is not so with آخَرُ; for it has a fem. [and dual] and pl. without مِنْ and without the article ال and without its being prefixed to another noun: you say, مَرَرْتُ بِرَجُلٍ آخَرَ, and بِرِجَالٍ أُخَرَ and آخَرِينَ, and بِٱمْرَأَةٍ أُخْرَى, and بِنِسْوَةٍ أُخَرَ, [*I passed by another man*, and *by other men*, and *by another woman*, and *by other women*;] therefore, as it [namely أُخَرُ] is thus made to deviate from its original form, [i. e. آخَرُ, (I'Aḳ p. 287,) which is of a class of words used, when indeterminate, alike as sing. and dual and pl.,] and is [essentially and originally] an epithet, it is imperfectly decl., though a pl.: but when you name thereby a man, it is perfectly decl., when indeterminate, accord. to Akh, or imperfectly decl. accord. to Sb. (Ṣ, L.) The dim. of آخَرُ is ▼ أُوَيْخِرُ; the ا with the ء suppressed following the same rule as the ا in ضَارِبٌ: (TA:) and the dim. of أُخْرَى is ▼ أُخَيْرَى. (Ṣ.) See also أُخْرَى voce آخِرٌ. —— لَا أَفْعَلُهُ أُخْرَى اللَّيَالِى, (Ṣ, Ḳ,) or أُخْرَى المَنُونِ, (Ḳ,) means *I will not do it ever:* (Ṣ, Ḳ:) or the latter, *I will not do it to the end of time.* (Ṣ.) And أُخْرَى القَوْمِ, *The last of the people.* (Ṣ, Ḳ.) One says, جَآءَ فِى أُخْرَى القَوْمِ *He came among the last of the people.* (TA.) And جَآءَ فِى أُخْرَيَاتِ النَّاسِ *He came among those who were the last of the people.* (Ṣ, A, Ḳ.) [See also آخِرٌ.] —— In أَبْعَدَ اللّٰهُ الآخَرَ, the last word is a mistake for الأَخِرَ, q. v. (Meshárik of 'Iyáḍ.)

آخِرٌ, (Ṣ, Mṣb, Ḳ,) an epithet, of the measure فَاعِلٌ, (Ṣ,) and ▼ أَخِيرٌ, (Ṣ, Mṣb,) *The last; aftermost; hindmost:* and *the latter; after; hinder:* and [as a subst.] *the end: contr. of* أَوَّلُ: [or *of* أَوَّلٌ when used as a subst.:] (A, Mṣb, Ḳ:) or *of* مُتَقَدِّمٌ: (Lth, Mṣb:) or *what is after the first* or *former:* (Ṣ:) fem. of the former آخِرَةٌ: (Ṣ, Mṣb, Ḳ:) pl. [masc.] آخِرُونَ (Ḳur xxvi. 64, &c.,) and (masc. and fem., Mṣb) أَوَاخِرُ (Ṣ, Mṣb) and fem. آخِرَاتٌ also: (Th:) and ▼ مَآخِيرُ is syn. with أَوَاخِرُ; as in مَآخِيرُ اللَّيْلِ [occurring in the Ṣ and Ḳ in art. جهر, meaning *The last,* or *latter, parts,* or *portions, of the night*]. (TḲ in art. جهر.) You say, جَآءَ آخِرًا and ▼ أَخِيرًا and ▼ أُخُرًا and ▼ بِأَخَرَةٍ, all meaning the same [*He came lastly,* or *latterly*]: and in like manner, مَا عَرَفْتُهُ إِلَّا أَخِيرًا ▼ and ▼ إِلَّا بِأَخَرَةٍ [*I did not know it save at the last,* or *lastly,* or *latterly*]: (Ṣ:) or ▼ جَآءَ أَخِيرًا and ▼ أُخُرًا and ▼ أَخَرَةً and ▼ بِأَخَرَةٍ and ▼ أُخْرَةً and ▼ بِأُخْرَةٍ, (Ḳ,) or ▼ أُخْرَةً and ▼ بِأُخْرَةٍ, (Lḥ, L,) and ▼ إِخْرِيًّا and ▼ أُخْرِيًّا and ▼ إِخِرِيًّا (TA) and بِآخِرَةٍ and ▼ آخِرِيًّا (Ḳ) mean *he came lastly of everything.* (Ḳ.) It is said in a trad., respecting Mohammad, كَانَ يَقُولُ بِأَخَرَةٍ ▼ إِذَا أَرَادَ أَنْ يَقُومَ مِنَ المَجْلِسِ كَذَا وَكَذَا *He used to say, at the end of his sitting, when he desired to rise from the place of assembly, thus and thus:* or, accord. to IAth, it may mean, *in the last,* or *latter, part of his life.* (TA.) And you say, أَتَيْتُكَ آخِرَ مَرَّتَيْنِ and آخِرَةَ مَرَّتَيْنِ (IAạr, M, Ḳ) app. meaning (M) [*I came to thee the latter of two times;*] *the second of two times.* (M, Ḳ.*) And لَا أُكَلِّمُهُ آخِرَ الدَّهْرِ *I will not speak to him* [*to the end of time,* or] *ever.* (A.) [See a similar phrase above, voce آخَرُ.] And جَاؤُوا عَنْ آخِرِهِمْ [*They came with the last of them;* عن being here syn. with ب; meaning *they came all, without exception*]. (A.) [And كَانَ ذٰلِكَ فِى آخِرِ الشَّهْرِ, and السَّنَةِ; and فى أَوَاخِرِهِمَا, *That was in the end of the month,* and *of the year;* and *in the last days thereof.*] And النَّهَارُ يَجُرُّ عَنْ آخِرٍ فَآخِرٍ [*The day lengthens*] *hour by hour.* (A.) See also أَخَرُ, last sentence. —— الآخِرُ is a name of God, signifying [*The last;* or] *He who remaineth after all his creatures, both vocal and mute, have perished.* (Nh.) —— الآخِرَانِ *The two hinder dugs* of the she-camel; opposed to the قَادِمَانِ; (TA;) *the two dugs that are next the thighs.* (Ḳ.) —— الآخِرَةُ, (Ḳ,) for الدَّارُ الآخِرَةُ, (Bḍ in ii. 3,) [and الحَيَاةُ الآخِرَةُ,] and ▼ الأُخْرَى, (Ḳ,) [*The latter, ultimate,* or *last,* and *the other, dwelling,* or *abode,* and *life;* i. e. *the latter, ultimate,* or *last,* and *the other, world; the world,* or *life, to come;* and *the ultimate state of existence, in the world to come;*] *the dwelling,* or *abode,* [*and life,*] *of everlasting duration:* (Ḳ:) [each] an epithet in which the quality of a subst. predominates. (Z, and Bḍ ubi suprà.) [Opposed to الدُّنْيَا.] And آخِرَةٌ also signifies The *enjoyments, blessings,* or *good, of the ultimate state; of the other world;* or *of the world,* or *life, to come:* in which sense likewise it is opposed to دُنْيَا: (see an ex. of both voce بَاعَ, in art. بيع: so too ▼ أُخْرَى.)] —— آخِرَةُ الرَّحْلِ, (Ṣ, Mṣb, Ḳ,) and السَّرْجِ, (Mṣb,) and آخِرُهُ, (Ṣ in art. قدم, and Ḳ,) and مُؤْخِرَتُهُ, (Ṣ, Mgh, Mṣb, Ḳ,) which is a rare form, or, accord. to Yaạkoob, not allowable, (Ṣ,) and ▼ مُؤْخِرُهُ, and ▼ مُؤَخِّرَتُهُ, and ▼ مُؤَخَّرُهُ, (Ṣ in art. قدم, and Ḳ,) and ▼ مُؤَخَّرَتُهُ, (Mṣb, Ḳ,) or this is a mistake, (Mgh, Mṣb,) and ▼ مُؤَخِّرُهُ, (Ḳ,) but the first of all is the most chaste, (Mṣb,) *The thing,* (Ṣ,) or *piece of wood,* (Mṣb,) *of the camel's saddle,* (Ṣ, Mṣb,) and *of the horse's,* (Mṣb,) *against which the rider leans* [*his back*]; (Ṣ, Mṣb;) *the contr. of its* قَادِمَة [by which term قادمة is meant the واسط]: (Ḳ:) the واسط of the camel's saddle is the tall fore part which is next to the breast of the rider; and its آخرة is *its hinder part;* (Az, L;) i. e. *its broad piece of wood,* (Mgh,) or *its tall and broad piece of wood,* (Az, L,) *which is against,* or *opposite to,* (تُحَاذِى,) *the head* [*and back*] *of the rider:* (Az, Mgh, L:) [for] the آخرة and the واسط are the شَرْخَانِ, between which the rider sits: this is the description given by En-Naḍr [ISh]; and all of it is correct: there is no doubt respecting it: (Az, L:) the pl. of آخرة is أَوَاخِرُ. (Mṣb.) —— آخِرَةُ العَيْنِ: see مُؤْخِرُ العَيْنِ. —— آخِرٌ and ▼ أَخِيرٌ [accord. to some] also signify *Absent.* (Ḳ.) But see أَخِرٌ, second sentence.

آخِرِيًّا: see آخِرٌ.

أُوَيْخِرٌ dim. of آخَرُ, q. v. (TA.)

مُؤْخِرُ العَيْنِ, (T, Ṣ, A, Mgh, Mṣb, Ḳ, [in the CḲ مُؤَخَّرُها,]) said by AO, (Mṣb,) or A'Obeyd, (TA,) to be better without teshdeed, from which observation it is to be understood that teshdeed in this case is allowable, though rare, but Az disallows it, (Mṣb, TA,) and مُؤْخِرَتُهَا, and ▼ آخِرَتُهَا, (Ḳ,) [*The outer angle of the eye;*] *the part of the eye next the temple;* (Ṣ, A, Mgh, Mṣb;) *the part next the* لِحَاظ: (Ḳ:) opposed to its مُقْدِم, which is the extremity thereof next the nose: (Ṣ, Mgh, Mṣb:) pl. مَآخِرُ. (Mgh.) You say, نَظَرَ إِلَىَّ بِمُؤْخِرِ عَيْنِهِ [*He looked at,* or *towards, me from* (lit. *with*) *the outer angle of his eye*]. (Ṣ.) —— مُؤْخِرُ الرَّحْلِ, and مُؤْخِرَتُهُ: see آخِرٌ.

مُؤَخَّرٌ The *back, hinder,* or *latter, part* of anything: its *hindermost,* or *last, part: contr. of* مُقَدَّمٌ: as in the phrase, ضَرَبَ مُؤَخَّرَ رَأْسِهِ [*He struck the back,* or *hinder part, of his head*]. (Ṣ, Mṣb.) [See also أُخُرٌ and آخِرٌ.] —— مُؤَخَّرُ الرَّحْلِ, and مُؤَخَّرَتُهُ: see آخِرٌ.

المُؤَخِّرُ a name of God, [*The Postponer,* or *Delayer;*] *He who postpones,* or *delays, things, and puts them in their places:* [or *He who puts,* or *keeps, back,* or *backward:* or *He who degrades:*] *contr. of* المُقَدِّمُ. (TA.) —— مُؤَخِّرُ الرَّحْلِ, and مُؤَخِّرَتُهُ: see آخِرٌ.

نَخْلَةٌ مِئْخَارٌ *A palm-tree of which the fruit remains until the end of winter:* (AḤn, Ḳ:) and *until the end of the time of cutting off the fruit of palm-trees:* (Ṣ, M, Ḳ:) *contr. of* مِبْكَارٌ *and* بَكُورٌ: pl. مَآخِيرُ. (A.)

مَآخِيرُ [reg. pl. of مِئْخَارٌ]: see آخِرٌ, first sentence.

مُتَأَخِّرٌ: see its verb. —— [An author, or other person, *of the later,* or *more modern, times.*]

المُسْتَأْخِرِينَ in the Ḳur xv. 24 is said by Th to mean *Those who come to the mosque after others,* or *late:* (TA:) or it means *those who are later in birth and death:* or *those who have not yet come forth from the loins of men:* or *those who are late,* or *backward, in adopting the Muslim religion and in fighting against unbelievers and in obedience.* (Bḍ.)

اخو

1. أَخُوتَ, [third pers. أَخَا,] (Ṣ, Ḳ,) aor. تَأْخُو, (Ṣ,) inf. n. أُخُوَّةٌ; (Ṣ, Ḳ, &c.;) and ▼ آخَيْتَ, (Ḳ, TA,) [in the CḲ أَخَيْتَ, which is wrong in respect of the pers., and otherwise, for it is correctly] with medd, (TA,) inf. n. إِخَآءٌ and مُؤَاخَاةٌ; (Lth;) and ▼ تَأَخَّيْتَ; (Ḳ;) *Thou becamest a brother* [in the proper sense of this word, and also as meaning *a friend,* or *companion,* or *the like*]. (Ṣ,* Ḳ,* TA.) ▼ أُخُوَّةٌ is also [used as] a simple subst., (TA,) signifying *Brotherhood; fraternity;* the *relation of brother;* as also ▼ إِخَآءٌ and مُؤَاخَاةٌ; and ▼ تَآخٍ: (Lth, TA:) and the *relation of sister.* (Ṣ.) You say, بَيْنِى وَبَيْنَهُ أُخُوَّةٌ and ▼ إِخَآءٌ [&c., meaning] *Between me and him is brotherhood.* (JK, TA.) And ▼ بَيْنَ السَّمَاحَةِ وَالحَمَاسَةِ تَآخٍ † [*Between liberality and courage is a relation like that of brothers*]. (TA.) And خُوَّةٌ is a dial. var. of أُخُوَّةٌ, occurring in a trad. (IAth, TA.) ═ [It is also trans.] You say, أَخُوتُ عَشَرَةً *I was,* or *became, a brother to ten.* (TA.)

2. أَخَّيْتُ لِلدَّابَّةِ, (Ṣ, Ḳ,) or الدَّابَّةَ, (Mṣb, [so accord. to a copy of that work, but probably this is a mistranscription,]) inf. n. تَأْخِيَةٌ, (Ṣ, Mṣb, Ḳ,) *I made an* آخِيَة [q. v.] *for the beast,* (Mṣb, Ḳ,) *and tied the beast therewith;* (Mṣb;) [and

so, app., ▼ آخَيْتُ (which, if correct, is probably of the measure أَفْعَلْتُ); for it is related that] an Arab of the desert said to another, آخِ ▼ لِي آخِيَّةً أَرْبِطْ إِلَيْهَا مُهْرِي [*Make thou for me an* آخِيَّة *to which I shall tie my colt*]. (TA.) And you say, آخَى ▼ فُلَانٌ فِي فُلَانٍ آخِيَّةً فَكَفَرَهَا † *Such a one did a benefit to such a one, and he was ungrateful for it.* (TA.) [But perhaps آخِ and آخَى in these two exs. are mistranscriptions for أَخِ and أَخَى.]

3. آخَاهُ, (Ṣ, Ḳ,) vulgarly وَاخَاهُ, (Ṣ,) or the latter is a dial. var. of weak authority, (Ḳ,* TA,) said by some to be of the dial. of Ṭeiyi, (TA,) inf. n. مُؤَاخَاةٌ and إِخَآءٌ (Ṣ, Ḳ) and وِخَآءٌ (Ḳ) and [quasi-inf. n.] ▼ إِخَاوَةٌ (Fr, Ḳ) and وِخَاوَةٌ, (CḲ,) *He fraternized with him; acted with him in a brotherly manner:* (Ṣ,* Ḳ,* PṢ, TḲ:) A'Obeyd mentions, on the authority of Yz, آخَيْتُ and وَاخَيْتُ, and آسَيْتُ and وَاسَيْتُ, and آكَلْتُ and وَاكَلْتُ: the pret. is said to be thus assimilated to [a form of] the fut.; for they used [sometimes] to say, يُوَاخِي, changing the hemzeh into و. (IB, TA.) —— It is said in a trad., آخَى بَيْنَ المُهَاجِرِينَ وَالأَنْصَارِ, meaning *He united the emigrants* [to El-Medeeneh] *with the assistants* [previously dwelling there] *by the brotherhood of El-Islám and of the faith.* (TA.) You say also, آخَيْتُ بَيْنَ الشَّيْئَيْنِ [*I united the two things as fellows,* or *pairs*]; and sometimes one says, وَاخَيْتُ, like as one says, وَاسَيْتُ, for آسَيْتُ; mentioned by ISk. (Mṣb.) —— See also 1, in three places.

4: see 2, in three places.

5. تَأَخَّيْتُ, and the inf. n. تَأَخٍّ: see 1, in three places. —— تَأَخَّيْتُ أَخًا *I adopted a brother:* (Ṣ, Ḳ:) or [تَأَخَّيْتُهُ signifies] *I called him brother.* (Ḳ.) —— تَأَخَّيْتُ الشَّىْءَ, (Ṣ, Ḳ, TA,) or بِالشَّىْءِ, (Mṣb,) *I sought, endeavoured after, pursued,* or *endeavoured to reach* or *attain* or *obtain, the thing;* (Ṣ, Mṣb, Ḳ, TA;) *as the brother does the brother;* and in the same manner the verb is used with a man for its object: but تَوَخَّيْتُ, in the same sense, is more common. (TA.) You say, تَأَخَّيْتُ مَحَبَّتَكَ *I sought,* &c., *thy love,* or *affection.* (TA in art. وخى.)

6. تَآخَيَا *They became brothers,* or *friends* or *companions* or *the like, to each other.* (Ṣ,* TA.)

أَخٌ, (Ṣ, Mṣb, Ḳ,) originally أَخَوٌ, (Kh, Ṣ, Mṣb,) as is shown by the first of its dual forms mentioned below, and by its having a pl. like آبَآءٌ, (Ṣ,) and أَخٌّ, (Ḳ,) with the second letter doubled to compensate for the و suppressed, as is the case in أَبٌّ, (TA,) and ▼ أَخًا, [like أَبًا,] and ▼ أَخُو, (IAạr, Ḳ, TA, [the last, with the article prefixed to it, erroneously written in the CḲ الأَخُو,]) and ▼ أَخْوٌ, like دَلْوٌ, (Kr, Ḳ,) a well-known term of relationship, (Ḳ, TA,) i. e. *A brother;* the *son of one's father and mother,* or *of either of them:* and also applied to *a foster-brother:* (TA:) and † *a friend;* and *a companion, an associate,* or *a fellow:* (Ḳ:) derived from آخِيَّةٌ [q. v.]; as though one أَخ were tied and attached to another like as the horse is tied to the آخِيَّة: (Ḥar p. 42:) or, accord. to some of the grammarians, it is from وَخَى meaning قَصَدَ; because the أَخ has the same aim, endeavour, or desire, as his أَخ: (TA:) when أَخ is prefixed to another noun, its final vowel is prolonged: (Kh:) you say, هٰذَا أَخُوكَ [*This is thy brother,* &c.], and مَرَرْتُ بِأَخِيكَ [*I passed by thy brother,* &c.], and رَأَيْتُ أَخَاكَ [*I saw thy brother,* &c.]: (Ṣ: [in which it is also asserted that one does not say أَخُو without prefixing it to another noun; but this is inconsistent with the assertion of IAạr and F, that الأَخُو is a syn. of الأَخُ:]) the dual is أَخَوَانِ, (Ṣ, Mṣb, Ḳur xlix. 10, Ḥam p. 434,) or أَخْوَانِ, with the خ quiescent, (TA, [but this I have found nowhere else,]) and some of the Arabs say أَخَانِ, (Ṣ, Mṣb,) and Kr mentions أُخُوَانِ, with ḍamm to the خ, said by IB to occur in poetry, and held by ISd to be dual of أُخُو, with ḍamm to the خ: (TA:) the pl. is إِخْوَةٌ and إِخْوَانٌ, (Ṣ, Mṣb, Ḳ, &c.,) the former generally applied to *brothers,* and the latter to *friends* [or *the like*], (T, Ṣ,*) but not always, as in the Ḳur xlix. 10, where the former does not denote relationship, and in xxiv. 60 of the same, where the latter does denote relationship, (T, TA,) and sometimes the former is applied to a [single] man, as in the Ḳur iv. 12, (Ṣ,) and أُخْوَةٌ, (Fr, Ṣ, Mṣb, Ḳ, [in the CḲ أَخْوَةٌ,]) or this is a quasi-pl. n., (Sb, TA,) and أُخْوَانٌ, (Kr, Mṣb, Ḳ,) and آخَآءٌ, (Ṣ, Ḳ,) like آبَآءٌ, (Ṣ,) and أُخُوٌّ, and أُخُوَّةٌ, (ISd, Ḳ,) the last mentioned by Lḥ, and thought by ISd to be formed from the next preceding by the addition of ة characterizing the pl. as fem., (TA,) and أُخُونَ, (Ṣ, Mṣb, Ḳ,) and اخاوون. (Mṣb: [there written without any syll. signs, and I have not found it elsewhere.]) The fem. of أَخ is ▼ أُخْتٌ [meaning *A sister:* and † *a female friend,* &c.]: (Ṣ, Mṣb, Ḳ, &c.:) written with ḍamm to show that the letter which has gone from it is و; (Ṣ;) the ت being a substitute for the و; (TA;) not to denote the fem. gender, (Ḳ, TA,) because the letter next before it is quiescent: this is the opinion of Sb, and [accord. to SM] it is the correct opinion: for Sb says that if you were to use it as a proper name of a man, you would make it perfectly decl.; and if the ت were to denote the fem. gender, the name would not be perfectly decl.; though in one place he incidentally says that it *is* the sign of the fem. gender, through inadvertence: Kh, however, says that its ت is [originally] ه [meaning ة]: and Lth, that أُخْتٌ is originally أَخَةٌ: and some say that it is originally أَخْوَةٌ: (TA:) the dual. is أُخْتَانِ: (Kh:) and the pl. is أَخَوَاتٌ. (Kh, Ṣ, Mṣb, Ḳ.) The saying لَا أَخَا لَكَ بِفُلَانٍ [*Thou hast no brother,* or † *friend, in such a one*] means لَيْسَ لَكَ بِأَخٍ [*such a one is not a brother,* or *friend, to thee*]. (Ṣ, Ḳ.) It is said in a prov., مَنْ لَكَ بِأَخِيكَ كُلِّهِ [*Who will be responsible to thee for thy brother,* or † *thy friend, altogether?* i. e., for his always acting to thee as a brother, or friend]. (JK.) And in another, رُبَّ أَخٍ لَكَ لَمْ تَلِدْهُ أُمُّكَ [† *There is many a brother to thee whom thy mother has not brought forth*]. (TA.) And in another, أَخُوكَ أَمِ الذِّئْبُ [*Is it thy brother,* or *the wolf?*]; said in suspecting a thing: as also أَخُوكَ أَمِ اللَّيْلُ [*Is it thy brother, or is it the night* that deceives thee?]. (Ḥar p. 554.) And another saying is, الرُّمْحُ أَخُوكَ وَرُبَّمَا خَانَكَ [† *The spear is thy brother, but sometimes,* or *often, it is unfaithful to thee*]. (TA.) —— Ibn-'Arafeh says that when أُخُوَّةٌ does not relate to birth, it means conformity, or similarity; and combination, agreement, or unison, in action: hence the saying, هٰذَا الثَّوْبُ أَخُو هٰذَا [† *This garment,* or *piece of cloth, is the like,* or *fellow, of this*]: and hence the saying in the Ḳur [xvii. 29], كَانُوا إِخْوَانَ الشَّيَاطِينِ † *They are the likes,* or *fellows, of the devils:* and in the same [xliii. 47], إِلَّا هِيَ أَكْبَرُ مِنْ أُخْتِهَا ▼ † *But it was greater than its like,* or *fellow;* i. e., than what was like to it in truth &c. (TA.) It is said in a trad., النَّوْمُ أَخُو المَوْتِ [*Sleep is the like of death*]. (El-Jámi' eṣ-Ṣagheer.) One says also, لَقِىَ فُلَانٌ أَخَا المَوْتِ, † *Such a one met with the like of death.* (Mṣb, TA.) And they said, رَمَاهُ ٱللّٰهُ بِلَيْلَةٍ لَا أُخْتَ ▼ لَهَا [† *God afflicted him with a night having none like to it*], i. e., a night in which he should die. (TA.) And لَا أُكَلِّمُهُ إِلَّا أَخَا السِّرَارِ † *I will not speak to him save the like of secret discourse.* (Aṣ, TA.) [And hence,] أُخْتَا ▼ سُهَيْلٍ [† *The two sisters of Canopus;*] *the two stars called* الشِّعْرَى العَبُورُ *and* الشِّعْرَى الغُمَيْصَآءُ. (Ṣ and Ḳ in art. شعر, q. v.) —— يَا أَخَا بَكْرٍ, or تَمِيمٍ, means † *O thou of* [the tribe of] *Bekr,* or *Temeem.* (Ḥam p. 284.) —— Lḥ mentions, on the authority of Abu-d-Deenár and Ibn-Ziyád, the saying, القَوْمُ بِأَخِى الشَّرِّ, as meaning † *The people,* or *company of men, are in an evil state* or *condition.* (TA.) [But accord. to others,] one says, تَرَكْتُهُ بِأَخِى الخَيْرِ, meaning ‡ *I left him in an evil state* or *condition:* (JḲ,* Mṣb, Ḳ, TA:) and بِأَخِى الشَّرِّ ‡ *in a good state* or *condition.* (TA.) —— You say also, هُوَ أَخُو الصِّدْقِ † *He is one who cleaves,* or *keeps, to veracity.* (Mṣb.) —— أَخُو, as a prefixed noun, is also used in the sense of أَهْلٌ, meaning † *Worthy,* or *deserving,* of a thing: and *meet, fit,* or *fitted,* for it. So in the phrase أَخُو ثِقَةٍ † *Worthy,* or *deserving, of trust,* or *confidence;* expl. by W (p. 91) as meaning *a person in whom one trusts,* or *confides.* And so in the prov., لَيْسَ أَخُو الكِظَاظِ مَنْ يَسْأَمُهُ † *He who is fit,* or *fitted, for vehement striving for the mastery is not he who turns away from it with disgust:* see art. كظ.] —— It is also used in the sense of ذُو: as in the phrase, هُوَ أَخُو الغِنَى [† *He is possessed,* or *a possessor, of wealth,* or *competence,* or *sufficiency*]. (Mṣb.) [So too in the phrase, أَخُو الخَيْرِ † *Possessed,* or *a possessor, of good,* or *of what is good.* And in like manner,] أَخُو الخَنَعِ means الذَّلِيلُ, i. e. ذُو الذِّلَّةِ, i. e.] ذُو الخَنَعِ [† *The low, base,* or *abject*]. (Ḥam p. 44.) [So too] سَيْرُنَا أَخُو الجَهْدِ means سَيْرُنَا ذُو الجَهْدِ, i. e.] سَيْرُنَا جَاهِدٌ

[† *Our journeying is laborious*: see an ex. in the first paragraph of art. غدر]. (TA.) — حُمَّى الأَخَوَيْنِ † *A fever that affects the patient two days, and quits him two days; or that attacks on Saturday, and quits for three days, and comes* [*again*] *on Thursday; and so on.* (Mṣb.) — دَمُ الأَخَوَيْنِ : see دَمٌ, in art. دمى.

أَخًا : } see أَخٌ.
أَخُو :
أَخُو :

أُخْتٌ : see أَخٌ, in four places.

[أُخَىٌّ and أُخَيَّةٌ dims. of أَخٌ and أُخْتٌ.]

أَخَوِىٌّ *Brotherly; fraternal; of,* or *relating to, a brother,* and *a friend* or *companion:* and also, *sisterly; of,* or *relating to, a sister;* because you say أَخَوَاتٌ [meaning "sisters"]; but Yoo -used to say ▼ أُخْتِىٌّ, which is not agreeable with analogy. (Ṣ, TA.)

أُخْتِىٌّ : see أَخَوِىٌّ.

إِخْوَانٌ, besides being a pl. of أَخٌ, q. v., is a dial. var. of خِوَانٌ. (TA. [See art. خون.])

إِخَاوَةٌ : see 3.

أُخُوَّةٌ an inf. n. of 1: and also [used as] a simple subst. (TA.) See 1. — When it does not relate to birth, it means † *Conformity,* or *similarity;* and *combination, agreement,* or *unison, in action.* (Ibn-'Arafeh, TA.)

آخِيَّةٌ, (Lth, Ṣ, Mṣb, Ḳ, &c.,) originally of the measure فَاعُولَةٌ, [i. e. آخُوِيَةٌ,] (Mṣb,) and آخِيَةٌ, (Lth, Mṣb, Ḳ,) and أَخِيَّةٌ, (JK, Ḳ, TA, [but in the Ḳ the orthography of these three words is differently expressed in different copies, and somewhat obscurely in all that I have seen,]) *A piece of rope of which the two ends are buried in the ground,* (ISk, JK, Ṣ,) *with a small staff* or *stick,* or *a small stone, attached thereto,* (ISk, Ṣ,) *a portion thereof, resembling a loop, being apparent,* or *exposed, to which the beast is tied;* (ISk, JK, Ṣ;) it is made in soft ground, as being more commodious to horses than pegs, or stakes, protruding from the ground, and more firm in soft ground than the peg, or stake: (TA:) or *a loop tied to a peg,* or *stake, driven* [*into the ground*], *to which the beast is attached:* (Mṣb:) or *a stick,* or *piece of wood,* (Ḳ, TA,) *placed crosswise* (TA) *in a wall,* or *in a rope of which the two ends are buried in the ground, the* [*other*] *end* [or *portion*] *protruding, like a ring, to which the beast is tied:* (Ḳ, TA:) or *a peg,* or *stake, to which horses are tied:* (Ḥar p. 42:) [see also آرِىٌّ:] the pl. of the first is أَوَاخِىُّ; (JK, Ṣ, Mṣb, Ḳ;*) and of the second, أَوَاخٍ; (Mṣb;) and of the third, أَخَايَا, (JK, Ḳ,*) like as خَطَايَا is pl. of خَطِيَّةٌ. (TA.) In a trad., the believer and belief are likened to a horse attached to his آخِيَّة; because the horse wheels about, and then returns to his آخِيَّة; and the believer is heedless, and then returns to believe. (TA.) And in another, men are forbidden to make their backs like the أَخَايَا of beasts; i. e., in prayer; meaning that they should not arch them therein, so as to make them like the loops thus called. (TA.) — Also *i. q.* طُنُبٌ; (Ḳ;) i. e. The *kind of tent-rope thus called.* (TA in art. طنب, q. v.) — And † *A sacred,* or *an inviolable, right* or *the like;* syn. حُرْمَةٌ and ذِمَّةٌ. (Ṣ, Ḳ.) You say, لِفُلَانٍ أَوَاخِىُّ وَأَسْبَابٌ تُرْعَى [† *To such a one belong sacred,* or *inviolable, rights, and ties of relationship and love, to be regarded*]. (Ṣ.) And لَهُ عِنْدِى آخِيَّةٌ † *He has, with me,* or *in my estimation, a strong, sacred,* or *inviolable, right;* and *a near tie* or *connexion,* or *means of access* or *intimacy* or *ingratiation.* (TA.) — In a trad. of 'Omar, in which it is related that he said to El-'Abbás, أَنْتَ آخِيَّةُ آبَاءِ رَسُولِ ٱللّٰهِ, it is used in the sense of بَقِيَّة; [and the words may therefore be rendered *Thou art the most excellent of the ancestors of the Apostle of God;*] as though he meant, thou art he upon whom one stays himself, and to whom one clings, of the stock of the Apostle of God. (TA.)

اد

1. أَدَّتْهُ دَاهِيَةٌ, aor ـُ (T, Ṣ, M, Ḳ) and ـِ, (M, Ḳ,) but this latter is strange, [anomalous,] and unknown, (TA,) and ـَ, (M, Ḳ,) mentioned by Lḥ, whence it seems that he made the pret. to be of the measure فَعِلَ, or that it is co-ordinate to أَبَى, aor يَأْبَى, (M,) inf. n. أَدٌّ, (T, Ṣ, M,) *A calamity befell him.* (M, Ḳ.) And in like manner, أَدَّهُ أَمْرٌ, aor. and inf. n. as above, *An event befell him:* (M:) or *oppressed him, distressed him,* or *afflicted him.* (Bḍ in xix. 91.) — See also 5.

5. تَأَدَّدَ; (T, Ḳ;) and ▼ أَدَّ, inf. n. أَدٌّ; (TA;) *i. q.* تَشَدَّدَ [*He acted,* or *behaved, with forced hardness, firmness, strength, vigour,* &c.]. (T, Ḳ.)

أَدٌّ (Ṣ, M, Ḳ) and ▼ إِدٌّ (T, Ḳ) and ▼ أَدٌّ (Ḳ) *Strength; power; force:* (Ṣ, M, Ḳ:) *superior power* or *force* or *influence; mastery; conquest; predominance.* (M, Ḳ, TA.) — See also إِدٌّ, in two places. — Also, the first, The *sound of treading.* (T.)

إِدٌّ : see أَدٌّ. — Also, and ▼ إِدَّةٌ, *A wonder,* or *wonderful thing:* (M, L, Ḳ:) *a very evil, abominable, severe, thing,* or *affair:* (Ṣ, M, A, L, Ḳ:) *a calamity;* (Ṣ, A, L, Ḳ;) or thus the former word signifies; (M;) as also ▼ أَدٌّ, (as in the copies of the Ḳ,) or ▼ آدٌّ, [originally آدِدٌ,] of the measure فَاعِلٌ: (so in the Ṣ and L:) pl. (of إِدٌّ, M, TA) إِدَادٌ, (Ḳ, TA,) or أَدَادٌ, (T, CḲ, [but this, if correct, is a quasi-pl. n.,]) or أَدَادٌ, (M,) and (of إِدَّةٌ, Ṣ, M) إِدَدٌ. (T, Ṣ, M, Ḳ.) You say also أَمْرٌ إِدٌّ [meaning as above], using إِدٌّ as an epithet, accord. to Lḥ. (M.) And ▼ دَاهِيَةٌ إِدَّةٌ [*A very evil, abominable,* or *severe, calamity*]. (A.) Hence the saying in the Ḳur [xix. 91], لَقَدْ جِئْتُمْ شَيْئًا إِدًّا *Verily ye have done a very evil,* or *abominable, thing:* (Ṣ, M:*) or, accord. to one reading, ▼ أَدًّا; both meaning *great,* or *grievous:* and some of the Arabs say, ▼ بِشَىْءٍ آدٍّ, which means the same. (T, TA.)

إِدَّةٌ : see إِدٌّ, in two places.

آدٌّ : see أَدٌّ : — and see إِدٌّ, in two places.

ادب

1. أَدَبَ, aor. ـِ, inf. n. أَدْبٌ, *He invited* (people, Ṣ, or a man, Ḳ) *to his repast,* or *banquet;* (Ṣ, Ḳ;) as also ▼ آدَبَ, (Ḳ,) or آدَبَ إِلَى طَعَامِهِ, aor يُودِبُ [or يُؤْدِبُ], (AZ, Ṣ,) inf. n. إِيدَابٌ [originally إِئْدَابٌ]. (AZ, Ṣ, Ḳ.) You say, أَدَبَ القَوْمَ, (Ṣ,) or أَدَبَ عَلَى القَوْمِ, aor. as above, (T,) *He invited the people to his repast.* (T, Ṣ.) And أَدَبَهُمْ عَلَى الأَمْرِ *He collected them together for the affair.* (A.) And ▼ أُودِبُ جِيرَانَكَ لِتُشَاوِرَهُمْ [*I will collect thy neighbours in order that thou mayest consult with them*]. (A.) The primary signification of أَدْبٌ is The act of *inviting.* (T.) — [Hence,] أَدَبَ, aor. ـِ; (Mṣb, Ḳ;) or أَدُبَ, aor. ـُ; (so in a copy of the M;) inf. n. أَدْبٌ, (M, Mgh, Mṣb,) or أَدَبٌ; (Ḳ;) *He made a repast,* or *banquet,* (M, Mṣb, Ḳ,) *and invited people to it;* (Mṣb;) as also ▼ آدَبَ, (M,) aor. and inf. n. as above: (TA:) or *he collected and invited people to his repast.* (Mgh.) — [Hence also, as will be seen below, voce أَدَبٌ,] أَدَبَهُ, aor. ـِ, inf. n. أَدْبٌ, *He taught him the discipline of the mind, and the acquisition of good qualities and attributes of the mind* or *soul;* (Mṣb;) and ▼ أَدَّبَهُ, [inf. n. تَأْدِيبٌ, signifies *the same;*] *he taught him what is termed* أَدَبٌ [or *good discipline of the mind and manners,* &c.; i. e. *he disciplined him,* or *educated him, well; rendered him well-bred, well-mannered, polite; instructed him in polite accomplishments;* &c.]: (Ṣ, M, A, Mgh, Ḳ:) or the latter verb, inf. n. تَأْدِيبٌ, signifies *he taught him well,* or *much, the discipline of the mind, and the acquisition of good qualities and attributes of the mind* or *soul:* and hence, this latter also signifies *he disciplined him, chastised him, corrected him,* or *punished him, for his evil conduct;* because discipline, or chastisement, is a means of inviting a person to what is properly termed الأَدَبُ. (Mṣb.) — أَدُبَ, aor. ـُ, (AZ, T, Ṣ, M, Ḳ,) inf. n. أَدَبٌ, (M, Ḳ,) *He was* or *became, characterized by what is termed* أَدَبٌ [or *good discipline of the mind and manners,* &c.; i. e., *well disciplined, well-educated, well-bred,* or *well-mannered, polite, instructed in polite accomplishments,* &c.]. (AZ, T, Ṣ, M, Ḳ.)

2 : see 1.

4 : see 1, in three places. — آدَبَ البِلَادَ, aor. and inf. n. as above, † *He filled the provinces,* or *country, with justice,* or *equity.* (Ḳ,* TA.)

5. تَأَدَّبَ *He learned,* or *was taught, what is termed* أَدَبٌ [or *good discipline of the mind and manners,* &c.; i. e. *he became,* or *was rendered, well-disciplined, well-educated, well-bred, well-mannered, polite, instructed in polite accomplishments,* &c.]; as also ▼ اِسْتَأْدَبَ. (Ṣ, Mgh, Ḳ.)

10 : see 5.

أُدْبٌ, (Ṣ, M, Ḳ,) or, accord. to some, ▼ إِدْبٌ, (TA,) *Wonderful*; or *a wonderful thing*; syn. عَجَبٌ; (Ṣ, M, Ḳ;) as also ▼ أُدْبَةٌ [used in the latter sense]. (Ḳ.) You say, ▼ جَآءَ فُلَانٌ بِأَمْرٍ إِدْبٍ *Such a one did a wonderful thing.* (Aṣ, T.*) ═ See also أَدَبٌ, last sentence.

إِدْبٌ: see أُدْبٌ, in two places.

أَدَبٌ, so termed because it invites men to the acquisition of praiseworthy qualities and dispositions, and forbids them from acquiring such as are evil, (T, Mgh,) signifies *Discipline of the mind*; and *good qualities and attributes of the mind* or *soul*: (Mṣb:) or *every praiseworthy discipline by which a man is trained in any excellence*: (AZ, Mgh, Mṣb:) [*good discipline of the mind and manners; good education; good breeding; good manners; politeness; polite accomplishments*:] *i. q.* ظَرْفٌ [as meaning *excellence*, or *elegance, of mind, manners, address, and speech*]: and *a good manner of taking* or *receiving* [what is given or offered or imparted, or what is to be acquired]: (M, A, Ḳ:) or *good qualities and attributes of the mind* or *soul*, and the *doing of generous* or *honourable actions*: (El-Jawáleekee:) or the *practice of what is praiseworthy both in words and actions*: or the *holding*, or *keeping, to those things which are approved*, or *deemed good*: or the *honouring of those who are above one, and being gentle, courteous*, or *civil, to those who are below one*: (Towsheeḥ:) or *a faculty which preserves him in whom it exists from what would disgrace him*: (MF:) it is of two kinds, أَدَبُ النَّفْسِ [which embraces all the significations explained above], and أَدَبُ الدَّرْسِ [which signifies *the discipline to be observed in the prosecution of study, by the disciple with respect to the preceptor, and by the preceptor with respect to the disciple*: see "Haji Khalfæ Lexicon," Vol. I. p. 212]: (Ṣ, Bṣl, Mgh:) [also *deportment*, or *a mode of conduct* or *behaviour*, absolutely; for one speaks of good أَدَب and bad أَدَب:] the pl. is آدَابٌ [which is often employed, and so is the sing. also, as signifying the *rules of discipline to be observed in the exercise of a function*, such as that of a judge, and of a governor; and *in the exercise of an art*, such as that of the disputer, and the orator, and the poet, and the scribe; &c.]. (Mṣb.) — عِلْمُ الأَدَبِ signifies [*The science of philology*; or] *the science by which one guards against error in the language of the Arabs, with respect to words and with respect to writing*; ("Haji Khalfæ Lexicon," Vol. I. p. 215;) [and so, simply, الأَدَبُ: which is also used to signify *polite literature*: but in this sense, and likewise] as applied to *the sciences relating to the Arabic language*, [or *the philological sciences*, which are also termed ▼ العُلُومُ الأَدَبِيَّاتُ,] الأَدَبُ is a post-classical term, innovated in the time of El-Islám. (El-Jawáleekee.) ═ أَدَبُ البَحْرِ, (A, Ḳ,) or ▼ أُدْبُ البَحْرِ, (T, L,) ‡ *The abundance of the water of the sea.* (T, A, L, Ḳ.)

أُدْبَةٌ: see مَأْدُبَةٌ: ═ and see also أُدْبٌ.

أَدَبِىٌّ [*Of*, or *relating to, what is termed* أَدَب, or الأَدَب. Hence, العُلُومُ الأَدَبِيَّاتُ: see أَدَبٌ, last sentence but one.]

أَدِيبٌ *Characterized by what is termed* أَدَب [or *good discipline of the mind and manners*, &c.; i. e. *well-disciplined, well-educated, well-bred*, or *well-mannered*; *polite*; *instructed in polite accomplishments*, or *an elegant scholar*; &c.]: (T, Ṣ, M, Mgh, Ḳ:) pl. أُدَبَآءُ. (M, Ḳ.) — See also مُؤَدَّبٌ.

آدَبُ [originally أَأْدَبُ, *More*, or *most, characterized by what is termed* أَدَب; i. e. *better*, or *best, disciplined, educated, bred*, or *mannered*; *more*, or *most, polite*; &c.]. You say, هُوَ مِنْ آدَبِ النَّاسِ [*He is of the best disciplined*, &c., *of men*]. (A.)

آدِبٌ One *who invites people to a repast*, or *banquet*: (T, Ṣ, Mṣb:) pl. أَدَبَةٌ. (TA.)

مَأْدَبَةٌ: see what next follows, in two places.

مَأْدُبَةٌ *A repast*, or *banquet, to which guests are invited*; (A'Obeyd, T, Ṣ, M, Mgh, Mṣb, Ḳ;) or *made on account of a wedding*: (M, Ḳ:) as also ▼ مَأْدَبَةٌ, (Ṣ, M, Mṣb, Ḳ,) or, accord. to A'Obeyd, this latter has a different signification, as will be seen below, (TA,) and ▼ مَأْدِبَةٌ, (IJ,) and ▼ أُدْبَةٌ: (M, Ḳ:) pl. مَآدِبُ. (Ṣ.) In a trad., the Ḳur-án is called مَأْدُبَةُ اللّٰهِ فِى الأَرْضِ, or ▼ مَأْدَبَةٌ; and A'Obeyd says that, if we read مَأْدُبَة, the meaning is, *God's repast which He has made in the earth, and to which He has invited mankind*; but if we read مَأْدَبَة, this word is of the measure مَفْعَلَةٌ from الأَدَبُ, [and the meaning is, *a means which God has prepared in the earth for men's learning good discipline of the mind*, &c.; it being a noun similar to مَثْرَاةٌ and مَكْثَرَةٌ &c.:] El-Aḥmar, however, makes both words synonymous. (T, M,* TA.)

مَأْدِبَةٌ: see what next precedes.

مُؤَدَّبٌ ▼ أَدِيبٌ A camel *well-trained and broken.* (T, L.)

مَأْدُوبَةٌ, occurring in a verse of 'Adee, [which I do not anywhere find quoted,] She [app. a bride] *for whom a repast*, or *banquet, has been made.* (TA.)

ادر

1. أَدِرَ, aor. ـَ, (T, M, Mṣb, Ḳ,) inf. n. أَدَرٌ (Lth, T, Ṣ, Mgh) and أُدْرَةٌ, (Lth, TA,) or أَدَرَةٌ, (as in the TT,) or أُدْرَةٌ is a simple subst., (M, Ḳ,) and so is أَدَرَةٌ, (Ḳ,) *He* (a man, Ṣ) *had the disorder termed* أُدْرَة. (T, Ṣ, M, &c.)

أُدْرَةٌ a subst. from أَدِرَ; [see آدَرُ, below;] (Ḳ;) as also ▼ أَدَرَةٌ: (M, Ḳ:) the former signifies [*A scrotal hernia*;] *an inflation in the* خُصْيَة [or the *testicle*, or the *scrotum*]: (T,* Ṣ:) or *an inflation of the* خُصْيَة: (Mṣb:) or *a disorder consisting in an inflation*, or *a swelling, of the* خُصْيَتَانِ, *and their becoming greatly enlarged with matter* or *wind therein*: (Esh-Shiháb, on the Soorat el-Aḥzáb:) or *a largeness of the* خُصَى: (Mgh:) and ▼ أَدَرَةٌ also signifies what is vulgarly termed قِيلَةٌ [meaning in the present day *a scrotal hernia*]: or, accord. to some, *i. q.* خُصْيَةٌ. (TA.) [See also 1.]

أَدَرَةٌ: see أُدْرَةٌ, in two places. [See also 1.]

آدَرُ (T, Ṣ, M, Mgh, Mṣb, Ḳ) and ▼ مَأْدُورٌ (M, Ḳ) A man (Ṣ) [*having a scrotal hernia*; or] *having an inflation in the* خُصْيَة [or the *testicle*, or the *scrotum*]: (T,* Ṣ:) or *having an inflation of the* خُصْيَة: (Mṣb:) or *having his* صِفَاق [or *inner skin*] *ruptured, so that* [*some of*] *his intestines fall into his scrotum*; *the rupture being in every instance only in the left side*: or *afflicted by a rupture in one of his* خُصْيَانِ [or *in either half of the scrotum*]: (M, Ḳ:) or *having a largeness of the* خُصَى (Mgh:) pl. of the former, أُدْرٌ; (Mṣb, Ḳ;) and of the latter, مَآدِيرُ. (Ḳ.) Accord. to some, (M,) خُصْيَةٌ أَدْرَآءُ signifies [*A testicle*, or *scrotum*,] *large, without rupture.* (M, Ḳ.)

مَأْدُورٌ: see آدَرُ.

ادم

1. أَدَمَ الخُبْزَ, aor. ـِ, (M, Mṣb, Ḳ,) inf. n. أَدْمٌ; (M, Mṣb;) and ▼ آدَمَهُ, (Mṣb, Ḳ,) inf. n. إِيدَامٌ; (TḲ;) *He mixed the bread with* أُدْم [or *seasoning*; i. e. *he seasoned it*]; (M, Ḳ;) *he made the swallowing of the bread to be good*, or *agreeable, by means of* إِدَام [or *seasoning*]. (Mṣb.) You say also, أَدَمَ الخُبْزَ بِاللَّحْمِ, aor. ـِ, [*He seasoned the bread*, or *rendered it savoury, with flesh-meat*,] from أُدْم and إِدَام, signifying مَا يُؤْتَدَمُ بِهِ. (Ṣ.) — أَدَمَ القَوْمَ, aor. ـِ, (Ḳ,) inf. n. أَدْمٌ; (TA;) or ▼ آدَمَهُمْ; (M;) or both; (TA;) *He seasoned for the people*, or *company of men*, (أَدَمَ لَهُمْ, [in the CḲ, erroneously, أَدامَ لهم,]) *their bread*; (M, Ḳ, TA;) i. e., *mixed it* [*for them*] *with* إِدَام. (TA.) — [From أَدْم in the first of the senses explained above, is app. derived the phrase,] أَدَمَهُ بِأَهْلِهِ *He mixed him, associated him*, or *united him in company, with his family.* (M.) [And in like manner,] أَدَمَ بَيْنَهُمَا, (T, Ṣ,) or بَيْنَهُمْ, (M, Mṣb,* Ḳ,) aor. ـِ, (T, M, Mṣb, Ḳ,) inf. n. أَدْمٌ; (T, M, Mṣb;) and ▼ آدَمَ, (T, Ṣ, M, Mṣb, Ḳ,) inf. n. إِيدَامٌ; (T, TA;) *He* (God, T, Ṣ, M, or a man, Mṣb) *effected a reconciliation between them*; *brought them together*; (Ṣ, M, Mṣb, Ḳ; [expl. in the M and Ḳ by لَأَمَ, for which we find in the CḲ لَأَمَ;]) *made them sociable*, or *familiar, one with another*; (Ṣ, Mṣb, TA;) *and made them to agree*: (TA:) or *induced love and agreement between them*: held by A'Obeyd to be from أُدْم, because thereby food is made good and pleasant. (T.) It is said in a trad., فَإِنَّهُ أَحْرَى أَنْ يُؤْدَمَ بَيْنَكُمَا, meaning *For it is most fit*, or *meet, that there should be, between you two, love and agreement*: (T, Ṣ:) or, *that peace*, or *reconciliation, and friendship, should continue between you two.* (Mṣb.) And a poet says,

* وَالبِيضُ لَا يُؤْدِمْنَ ▼ إِلَّا مُؤْدَمَا ▼ *

i. e. [*And the pure*, or *free from faults*, among

women,] *do not love any save one who is made an object of love* [by his good qualities], (T, Ṣ,) *a proper object of love.* (T.) —— أَدَمَهُمْ, (T, M, Ḳ,) aor. ـِ, (T,) or ـُ, (M, Ḳ,) inf. n. أَدْمٌ, (M,) ‡ *He was, or became, to them, what is termed* أُدْمَة; (T, M, Ḳ;) i. e., *one who made people to know them;* (T;) or *a pattern, an exemplar, an example,* or *one who was imitated,* or *to be imitated; and one by means of whom they were known:* (M, Ḳ:) so says IAạr. (M.) —— أَدَمَ الأَدِيمَ *He pared,* or *removed the superficial part of, the hide:* (T,* TA:) and ✝ آدَمَ الأَدِيمَ, with medd, *he pared off the* أَدَمَة [q. v.] *of the hide:* (TA:) or the latter signifies *he exposed to view the* أَدَمَة [in the CḲ, erroneously, the أُدْمَة] *of the hide.* (M, Ḳ.) —— أَدِمَ, aor. ـَ, (M, Ḳ,) inf. n. أَدَمٌ; (TḲ;) and أَدُمَ, aor. ـُ, (M, Ḳ,) inf. n. أُدُومَةٌ (T, Ḳ) [or, more probably, أُدْمَةٌ, like سُمْرَةٌ &c.]; *He* (a camel, and a gazelle, and a man,) *was,* or *became, of the colour termed* أُدْمَة, q. v. infrà. (M, Ḳ.)

2. أَدَّمَهُ, inf. n. تَأْدِيمٌ, *He put much* إِدَام [or *seasoning*] *into it.* (TA.)

4: see 1, in five places.

8. ائتدم به [written with the disjunctive alif ايتدم] *He made use of it* [*to render his bread pleasant,* or *savoury*]; namely أُدْم, (M,* TA,) or إِدَام. (M.) [إِدَام is explained in the T and Ṣ &c. by the words مَا يُؤْتَدَمُ بِهِ, meaning *That which is used for seasoning* bread.] —— ائتدم العُودُ ‡ *The wood,* or *branch, had the sap* (المَآء) *flowing in it.* (Z, Ḳ.)

10. استأدمهُ *He sought,* or *demanded, of him* إِدَام [or *seasoning*]. (Z, TA.)

أَدْمٌ: see أَدَمَةٌ. —— هُوَ أَدْمُ أَهْلِهِ: see أُدْمَةٌ.

أُدْمٌ: see إِدَامٌ. —— هُوَ أُدْمُ أَهْلِهِ and أُدْمُ بَنِى أَبِيهِ: see أُدْمَةٌ.

أَدَمٌ: see أَدِيمٌ, in two places: —— and أَدَمَةٌ. —— أُدُمٌ: see أَدَمٌ.

أَدَمَةٌ: هُوَ أَدَمَةُ أَهْلِهِ: see أُدْمَةٌ.

أُدْمَةٌ *A state of mixing, or mingling, together* [*in familiar, or social, intercourse*]. (Lth, T, M, Ḳ.) You say, بَيْنَهُمَا أُدْمَةٌ *Between them two is a mixing,* &c. (Lth, T.) —— Also, (M, Ḳ,) or ✝ أَدْمٌ, (Ṣ,) *Agreement:* (Ṣ, M, Ḳ, TA:) and *familiarity, sociableness, companionship,* or *friendship.* (Ṣ, TA. [The meanings in this sentence are assigned in the Ṣ only to the latter word: in the TA, only to the former.]) —— And the former, *Relationship.* (M, Ḳ.) —— And *A means of access* (وَسِيلَةٌ, Fr, T, Ṣ, M, Ḳ) to a thing, (Fr, T, Ṣ,) and to a person; (Fr, T;) as also ✝ أَدَمَةٌ. (Ḳ.) You say, فُلَانٌ أُدْمَتِى إِلَيْكَ *Such a one is my means of access to thee.* (Fr, T.) —— And [hence,] *A present which one takes with him in visiting a friend or a great man;* in Persian دَسْت آوِيز. (Ḳ, L.) —— هُوَ أُدْمَةُ أَهْلِهِ: and هُوَ أُدْمَةٌ لِفُلَانٍ: see أُدْمَةٌ. —— In camels, *A colour intermixed,* or *tinged, with blackness,* or *with whiteness;* or *clear whiteness;* (M, Ḳ;) or, as some say, (TA,) *intense whiteness;* (Ṣ, TA;) or *whiteness, with blackness of the eyeballs:* (Nh, TA:) and in gazelles, *a colour intermixed,* or *tinged, with whiteness:* (M, Ḳ:) or in gazelles and in camels, *whiteness:* (T:) and in human beings, (M, Ḳ,) *a tawny colour;* or *darkness of complexion;* syn. سُمْرَةٌ [q. v.]; (Ṣ, M, Ḳ;) or *an intermixture,* or *a tinge, of blackness;* (Lth, T;) or *intense* سُمْرَة [or *tawniness*]; and it is said to be from أُدْمَةُ الأَرْضِ, meaning *the colour of the earth:* (Nh, TA:) or [in men,] *i. q.* حُمْرَةٌ [which, in this case, signifies *whiteness* of complexion]: (TA:) accord. to AḤn, it signifies *whiteness;* syn. بَيَاضٌ. (M.) [See also آدَمُ.]

أَدَمَةٌ: see أُدْمَةٌ. —— هُوَ أَدَمَةُ أَهْلِهِ, (M, Ḳ,) and ✝ أُدْمَتُهُمْ, (M,) or ✝ أَدَمَتُهُمْ, (Ḳ,) and ✝ أَدْمُهُمْ, (M,) or ✝ أُدْمُهُمْ, and ✝ إِدَامُهُمْ, (Ḳ,) ‡ *He is the pattern, exemplar, example,* or *object of imitation, of his people,* or *family, by means of whom they are known:* (M, Ḳ:) so says IAạr. (M.) And جَعَلْتُ فُلَانًا أَدَمَةَ أَهْلِى ‡ *I made such a one to be the pattern, exemplar, example,* or *object of imitation, of my people,* or *family.* (T, Ṣ.) And هُوَ أَدَمَةٌ لِفُلَانٍ, and ✝ أُدْمَةٌ, ‡ *He is a pattern,* &c., *to such a one.* (Fr, TA.) And فُلَانٌ أَدَمَةُ بَنِى فُلَانٍ ‡ *Such a one is he who makes people to know the sons of such a one.* (T.) And هُوَ أَدَمَةُ قَوْمِهِ ‡ *He is the chief,* and *provost, of his people.* (A, TA.) And فُلَانٌ إِدَامُ قَوْمِهِ, and أُدْمُ بَنِى أَبِيهِ, ‡ *Such a one is the aider, and manager of the affairs,* and *the support,* and *right orderer of the affairs, of his people,* and *of the sons of his father.* (A, TA.) —— [The *inner skin;* the *cutis,* or *derma;*] the *interior of the skin, which is next to the flesh;* (Ṣ, M, Ḳ;) the exterior thereof being called the بَشَرَة: (Ṣ:) or (as some say, M) the *exterior thereof, upon which is the hair;* the interior thereof being called the بَشَرَة: (M, Ḳ:) and ✝ أَدَمٌ may be its pl.; [or rather, a coll. gen. n.;] or, accord. to Sb, it is a quasi-pl. n. (M.) —— Accord. to some, (M,) *What appears of the skin of the head.* (M, Ḳ. [See بَشَرَة.]) —— And † The *interior* of the earth or ground; (M, Ḳ;) the surface thereof being called its أَدِيم: (M, TA:) or, as some say, its *surface.* (TA.)

أَدَمِىٌّ *A seller of* [أَدَم, or] *skins,* or *hides:* (TA:) and ✝ أَدَّامٌ signifies the same; and particularly *a seller of goats' skins.* (Golius, from the larger work entitled Mirḳát el-Loghah.)

أُدْمَانٌ and أُدْمَانَةٌ: see آدَمُ.

إِدَامٌ (T, Ṣ, M, Mgh, Mṣb, Ḳ) and ✝ أُدْمٌ (the same except the Ḳ) [*Seasoning,* or *condiment,* for bread; and *any savoury food;*] *what is used for seasoning* (مَا يُؤْتَدَمُ بِهِ, T, Ṣ, M,* Mgh, Mṣb, Ḳ) *with bread;* (T, TA;) *that which renders bread pleasant and good and savoury;* (IAmb, Mgh;) *whether fluid or not fluid;* (Mgh, Mṣb;) صِبْغٌ and صِبَاغٌ being peculiarly applied to that which is fluid: (Mgh:) or أُدْمٌ is *anything that is eaten with bread:* (TA:) the pl. [of mult.] of إِدَامٌ is أُدُمٌ, (Mgh, Mṣb,) and, by contraction, أُدْمٌ, which is also used as the sing., (Mṣb,) and [pl. of pauc.] آدِمَةٌ (M, Ḳ) and آدَامٌ; (Ḳ;) or this last is pl. of أُدْمٌ. (M, Mgh, Mṣb, TA.) It is said in a trad., نِعْمَ الإِدَامُ الخَلُّ [*Excellent,* or *most excellent, is the seasoning, vinegar!*]. (T, TA.) And in another, سَيِّدُ آدَامِ الدُّنْيَا وَالآخِرَةِ اللَّحْمُ [*The prince of the seasonings of the present world and of the world to come is flesh-meat*]. (TA.) —— هُوَ إِدَامُ أَهْلِهِ, and إِدَامُ قَوْمِهِ: see أَدَمَةٌ. —— Anything *conforming,* or *conformable; agreeing,* or *agreeable; suiting,* or *suitable.* (M, Ḳ.) [Used also as a pl.: thus,] 'Ádiyeh Ed-Dubeyreeyeh says,

* كَانُوا لِمَنْ خَالَطَهُمْ إِدَامَا *

[*They were, to those who mixed with them in social intercourse, conformable,* or *agreeable.*] (M.)

طَعَامٌ أَدِيمٌ *i. q.* ✝ مَأْدُومٌ [*Seasoned*]: (T:) or ✝ مَأْدُومٌ [*seasoned food*]; (M, Ḳ;) *food in which is* إِدَام. (TA.) Hence the prov., سَمْنُكُمْ هُرِيقَ فِى أَدِيمِكُمْ [*Your clarified butter is poured into your seasoned food*]; (T, TA;) applied to a niggardly man; (Ḥar p. 462;) meaning, your good, or wealth, returns unto you: (TA:) or, as some say, the meaning is, *into your* سِقَآء [or *skin*]: (T, Ḥar* ubi suprà:) and the vulgar say, فِى دَقِيقِكُمْ [*into your flour*]. (TA.) And the saying, سَمْنُهُمْ فِى أَدِيمِهِمْ [*Their clarified butter is in their seasoned food*]; meaning, their good, or wealth, returns unto them. (M.) And the saying of Khadeejeh to the Prophet, إِنَّكَ لَتَكْسِبُ المَعْدُومَ ✝ وَتُطْعِمُ المَأْدُومَ (M, TA) *Verily thou gainest what is denied to others,* or *makest others to gain what they have not, of the things they want,* or *makest the poor to gain,* (TA in art. عدم,) *and givest to eat food in which is* إِدَام. (TA in the present art.) [Hence also,] أَطْعَمْتُكَ ✝ مَأْدُومِى (M, Ḳ) meaning أَتَيْتُكَ بِعُذْرِى [*I gave thee my excuse;* or, perhaps, *my virginity;* see عُذْرَةٌ]: (Ḳ:) [or,] as some say, the meaning is, *my good manners:* said by the wife of Dureyd Ibn-Eṣ-Ṣimmeh, on the occasion of his divorcing her. (M, TA.) —— And hence, (Ḥam p. 205, Mgh,) *Tanned skin* or *hide; leather:* (M, Ḥam, Mgh, Mṣb:) or *skin,* or *hide,* (M, Ḳ,) *in whatever state it be:* (M:) or *red skin or hide:* (M, Ḳ:) or *skin,* or *hide, in the state after that in which it is termed* أَفِيق; *that is, when it is complete* [*in its tanning*] *and has become red:* (M:) or the *exterior of the skin* of anything: (T:) pl. [of pauc.] آدِمَةٌ (Ṣ, M, Ḳ) and آدَامٌ and [of mult.] أُدُمٌ, (M, Ḳ,) the last from Lḥ, and [says ISd] I hold that he who says أُدْمٌ says رُسْلٌ, (M,) and ✝ أَدَمٌ, (T, Ṣ, Mṣb, Ḳ,) or this is a quasi-pl. n., (Sb, M, Mgh,) [often used as a gen. n.,] of which آدَامٌ may be pl. (M.) —— ابْنُ أَدِيمٍ and ابْنُ أَدِيمَيْنِ and ابْنُ ثَلَاثَةِ آدِمَةٍ: see ابْنٌ, in art. بنى. One says, إِنَّمَا يُعَاتَبُ الأَدِيمُ ذُو البَشَرَةِ [lit.] *Only the hide that has the exterior part, upon which the hair grows, is put again into the tan:* (T:) a prov.; (TA;) meaning, only he is disciplined, or reproved, who is an object of hope, and in whom is full intelligence, and strength; (T, TA, and AHn in TA, art. بشر [where, however, in the TA, دون is erroneously put for ذو];) and only he is disputed with in whom is place for dispute. (TA.) — أَدِيمُ الحَرْبِ is used metaphorically for أَهْلُ الحَرْبِ ‡ [*The skin of the warriors*, or *of the people engaged in war* or *fight*]. (M.) — فُلَانٌ صَحِيحُ الأَدِيمِ [lit. *Such a one is sound of skin*] means ‡ *such a one is sound in respect of origin,* and *of honour*, or *reputation.* (Ḥar p. 135.) You say also, فُلَانٌ بَرِىْءُ الأَدِيمِ مِمَّا لُطِخَ بِهِ [meaning ‡ *Such a one is clear in honour*, or *reputation, of that with which he has been aspersed*]. (M,* TA.) And ▼ مَزَّقَ أَدَمِى ‡ *He rent my honour*, or *reputation.* (Ḥar ubi suprà.) — أَدِيمٌ also signifies ‡ The *surface* of the earth or ground: (Ṣ, M:) [see also أَدَمَةٌ, last sentence:] or *what appears* thereof, (Ḳ,) and of the sky. (M, Ḳ.) — And ‡ The *first part* of the period called الضُّحَى. (M, Ḳ, TA.) You say, جِئْتُكَ أَدِيمَ الضُّحَى ‡ *I came to thee in the first part of the* ضحى; (Lḥ, M;) app. meaning, عِنْدَ ٱرْتِفَاعِ الضُّحَى [*when the morning was becoming advanced; when the sun was becoming high*]. (M.) — And ‡ The *whiteness* of day: (IAar, M, Ḳ, TA:) and ‡ the *darkness* of night: (IAar, M, TA:) or ‡ the *whole* of the day, (M, A, Ḳ, TA,) and of the night. (A, TA.) You say, ظَلَّ أَدِيمَ النَّهَارِ صَائِمًا وَأَدِيمَ اللَّيْلِ قَائِمًا ‡ *He continued the whole of the day fasting, and the whole of the night standing* [in prayer, &c.]. (A, TA.)

أَدَامٌ: see أَدَمِىٌّ.

آدَمُ *Of the colour termed* أُدْمَةٌ: pl. أُدْمٌ and ▼ أُدْمَانٌ; (Ṣ, M, Ḳ;) the latter like حُمْرَانٌ as a pl. of أَحْمَرُ: (M:) the fem. sing. is أَدْمَآءُ and ▼ أَدْمَانَةٌ; (Ṣ, M, Ḳ;) the latter anomalous; (Ḳ;) occurring in poetry, but disapproved (Ṣ, M) by Aṣ; (Ṣ;) said by Aboo-'Alee to be like خُمْصَانَةٌ; (M;) and the fem. pl. is أُدْمٌ: (Ṣ, M, Ḳ:) applied to a camel, *of a colour intermixed*, or *tinged, with blackness*, or *with whiteness*; or *of a clear white*; (M, Ḳ;) or, as some say, *intensely white*; (TA;) or *white, and black in the eyeballs*; (Ṣ;) or *white*; (Aṣ, T;) and so applied to a gazelle: (T:) or, applied to a gazelle, *of a colour intermixed*, or *tinged, with whiteness*; (M, Ḳ;) Lth, however, says that أَدْمَآءُ is applied to a female gazelle, but he had not heard آدَمُ applied to the male gazelle; (TA;) and Aṣ says, (Ṣ,) أُدْمٌ applied to gazelles signifies *white, having upon them streaks in which is a dust-colour*, (Ṣ, M,) *inhabiting the mountains*, and *of the colour of the mountains*; (Ṣ;) if of a pure white colour, they are termed آرَامٌ: (T, TA:) or, accord. to ISk, *white in the bellies, tawny in the backs, and having the colour of the bellies and of the backs divided by two streaks of the colour of musk*; and in like manner explained by IAar: (T:) applied to a human being, آدَمُ signifies *tawny*; or *dark-complexioned*; syn. أَسْمَرُ; (Ṣ, M, Ḳ;) or, thus applied, it signifies أَحْمَرُ اللَّوْنِ [which, in this case, means *white of complexion*]; (TA;) and the pl. is أُدْمَانٌ. (Ṣ.) The Arabs say, قُرَيْشُ الإِبِلِ أُدْمُهَا وَصُهْبُهَا, meaning *The best of camels are those of them which are* أُدْم *and those of them which are* صُهْب; [see أَصْهَبُ;] like as Ḳureysh are the best of men. (M.) — Also [*Adam*,] *the father of mankind*; (Ṣ, M, Ḳ;) and likewise ▼ أُدْمُ; but this is extr.: (Ḳ:) there are various opinions respecting its derivation; but [these it is unnecessary to mention, for] the truth is that it is a foreign word, [i. e. Hebrew,] of the measure فَاعَلُ, like آزَرُ: (MF:) and [therefore] its pl. is أَوَادِمُ. (Ṣ, M, Ḳ.)

آدَمِىٌّ [*Of*, or *relating to, Adam*: and hence, *human*: and *a human being*:] a rel. n. from آدَمُ. (TA.)

إِيدَامَةٌ † *Level, hard, but not rugged, ground*: (Aṣ:) or *hard ground without stones*; (Ḳ;) from أَدِيمٌ signifying the "surface" of the earth or ground: (TA:) or *ground somewhat elevated; not much so; only found in plains, and producing vegetation, which, however, is disapproved, because its situation is rugged, and little water remains in it*: (ISh:) pl. أَيَادِيمُ, (Aṣ, Esh-Sheybánee, IB, Ḳ,) which J erroneously says has no sing.: (Ḳ:) for he says, [in the Ṣ,] أَيَادِيمُ signifies *hard and elevated tracts* (مُتُون) *of ground*; and has no sing. (TA.)

مُؤْدَمٌ, as in an ex. cited above, (see 1,) *Made an object of love*; (T, Ṣ;) *a proper object of love.* (T.) — رَجُلٌ مُؤْدَمٌ مُبْشَرٌ ‡ *A man who is skilful, and experienced in affairs*, (M, Ḳ,) *who combines* [*qualities like*] *softness of the interior skin and roughness of the exterior skin*: (T, Ṣ, M, Ḳ:) or *who combines softness and hardness*, or *gentleness and force, with knowledge of affairs*: (T:) or *who combines such qualities that he is suited to hardship and to easiness of circumstances*: (Aṣ, T:) or, accord. to IAar, *having a thick and good skin*: (M:) or *beloved*: (TA:) the fem. is with ة: (M, Ḳ:) you say, اِمْرَأَةٌ مُؤْدَمَةٌ مُبْشَرَةٌ, meaning ‡ *a woman goodly in her aspect and faultless in her intrinsic qualities*: and sometimes the former epithet, with and without ة, as applied to a woman and to a man respectively, is put after the latter. (M.) See also art. بشر.

مَأْدُومٌ: see أَدِيمٌ, in four places.

ادو

4. آدَى *He took his* أَدَاة [q. v.]; (M;) *he prepared himself*; (M, Ḳ; [mentioned in the latter in art. ادى;]) or *equipped*, or *accoutred, himself*; or *furnished*, or *provided, himself with proper*, or *necessary, apparatus, equipments*, or *the like*; (M;) or *he was*, or *became, in a state of preparation*; (Yaạḳoob, T, Ṣ;) لِلسَّفَرِ *for journeying*, or *the journey*: (Yaạḳoob, T, Ṣ, M, Ḳ:) part. n. مُؤْدٍ. (Yaạḳoob, T, Ṣ.) And ▼ تَآدَى *He took his* أَدَاة, [or *prepared himself*, &c.,] لِلْأَمْرِ *for the affair*: (M:) or ▼ تَآدَى *he prepared, furnished, equipped*, or *accoutred, himself* for the affair; (Ibn-Buzurj, Az, TA;) from الأَدَاةُ: (Az, TA:) or ▼ the former of these two verbs, (so in some copies of the Ṣ and Ḳ,) or ▼ the latter of them, (so in other copies of the Ṣ and Ḳ, and in the TA,) *he took his* أَدَاة [or *equipments*, &c., i. e. *he prepared himself*,] *for* [*the vicissitudes of*] *fortune*: (Ṣ, Ḳ:) and ▼ تَآدَوْا, inf. n. تَآدٍ, *they took the apparatus, equipments*, or *the like, that should strengthen*, or *fortify, them against* [*the vicissitudes of*] *fortune* &c.: (T:) [accord. to some,] التَّآدِى is [irregularly derived] from الأَدُّ, meaning "strength." (TA.) — *He was*, or *became, completely armed*; (T, TA;) part. n. as above; (T, Ṣ, M, Mṣb;) from الأَدَاةُ: (T, TA:) or *he was*, or *became, strong by means of weapons and the like*; part. n. as above: (Mṣb:) or *he was*, or *became, strong* [in an absolute sense]; (Ṣ, Ḳ; [mentioned in the latter in art. ادى;]) said of a man; from الأَدَاةُ; (Ṣ;) part. n. as above. (Ḳ.) — آدَاهُ is originally أَعْدَاهُ; the second ا [in آ, for أَا,] being hemzeh substituted for ع in the original; meaning *He aided*, or *assisted, him*: [or *he avenged him*:] or it may be from الأَدَاةُ; meaning *he made him to have*, or *gave him*, or *assigned to him, weapons*, or *arms*. (Ḥam p. 387.) [In either case, it should be mentioned in the present art.; as اعدى belongs to art. عدو, and الاداة has for its pl. الأَدَوَاتُ.] You say, آدَاهُ عَلَى كَذَا, aor. يُؤْدِيهِ, inf. n. إِيدَآءٌ, *He strengthened him*, and *aided him*, or *assisted him, against such a thing*, or *to do such a thing*. (Ṣ.) And آدَاهُ عَلَى فُلَانٍ, meaning أَعْدَاهُ and أَعَانَهُ [*He avenged him of such a one*; or *he aided*, or *assisted, him against such a one*]. (M and Ḳ in art. عدى.) And مَنْ يُؤْدِينِى عَلَى فُلَانٍ *Who will aid me*, or *assist me, against such a one?* (Ṣ.) The people of El-Ḥijáz say, ▼ اِسْتَأْدَيْتُهُ عَلَى فُلَانٍ, meaning اِسْتَعْدَيْتُهُ فَأَعْدَانِى (T, Ṣ) and فَآدَانِى عَلَيْهِ أَعَانَنِى (T) [*I asked of him* (namely the Sultán, T, or the Emeer, Ṣ) *vengeance of such a one*, or *aid against such a one, and he avenged me of him*, or *aided me against him*].

5: see 4, in two places.

6: see 4, in three places.

10. اِسْتَأْدَاهُ عَلَيْهِ i. q. اِسْتَعْدَاهُ [*He asked of him aid*, or *assistance, against him*; or *vengeance of him*]: (T, Ṣ, M, Ḳ:*) or *he complained to him of his* (another's) *deed to him, in order that he might exact his* (the complainant's) *right*, or *due, from him*. (TA.) See also 4, last sentence.

أَدَاةٌ *An instrument*; *a tool*; *an implement*; *a utensil*: and *instruments*; *tools*; *implements*; *utensils*; *apparatus*; *equipments*; *equipage*; *accoutrements*; *furniture*; *gear*; *tackling*: syn. آلَةٌ: (T, Ṣ, M, Mṣb, Ḳ:) of any tradesman or craftsman; with which he performs the work of his trade or craft: and of war; أَدَاةُ الحَرْبِ signifying *weapons*, or *arms*: (Lth, T:) and for an affair [of any kind]: (M:) [applied also to the *apparatus* of a camel, or of a camel's saddle, &c.: (see حِدْجٌ:)] and ▼ أَدَاوَةٌ signifies the same; (M, TA;) and ▼ إِدَاوَةٌ: (TA:) and ▼ أَدِىٌّ, (Ṣ, TA,) like غَنِىٌّ, (TA,) [in some copies of the Ṣ آدِىٌّ,] signifies *apparatus*, *equipments, equipage, accoutrements, furniture, gear, tackling, implements, tools, or the like;* syn. أُهْبَةٌ: (Ṣ, TA:) the pl. of أَدَاةٌ is أَدَوَاتٌ. (T, Ṣ, Mṣb, Ḳ.) You say, أَخَذَ أَدَاتَهُ [*He took his apparatus,* &c.; or *prepared, furnished, equipped,* or *accoutred, himself*]; (Ṣ, M, Ḳ;) لِلْأَمْرِ [*for the affair*], and لِلسَّفَرِ [*for journeying,* or *the journey*], (M,) and لِلدَّهْرِ [*for* the vicissitudes of *fortune*]: (T, Ṣ, Ḳ:) and it is related on the authority of Ks, that they said أَخَذَ هَدَاتَهُ; substituting ه for أ. (Lḥ, M). And أَخَذْتُ لِذٰلِكَ الأَمْرِ أَدِيَّهُ ♦ i. e. أُهْبَتَهُ [*I took for that affair its apparatus,* &c.]. (Ṣ, TA.) And نَحْنُ عَلَى أَدِيٍّ ♦ لِلصَّلَاةِ *We are in a state of preparation for prayer.* (Ṣ, TA.) — [Hence, in grammar, *A particle;* as being a kind of auxiliary; including the article ال, the preposition, the conjunction, and the interjection; but not the adverbial noun.]

أَدِيٌّ: see أَدَاةٌ, in three places. — Also *A journey;* or *a journeying:* from آدَى لِلسَّفَرِ. (M.)

أَدَاوَةٌ: see أَدَاةٌ.

إِدَاوَةٌ *i. q.* مِطْهَرَةٌ; (Ṣ, M, Mgh, Mṣb, Ḳ;) i. e. *A small vessel* [or *bag*] *of skin, made for water, like the* سَطِيحَة: (TA:) or, as some say, only *of two skins put face to face:* (M, TA:) pl. أَدَاوَى; (Ṣ, Mgh, Mṣb, Ḳ;) originally, by rule, أَدَائِى; which is changed, as in the cases of خَطَايَا and مَطَايَا, from the measure فَعَائِلُ to the measure فَعَالَى, so that the و in أَدَاوَى is a substitute for the augmentative ا in the sing., and the final alif [written ى] in أَدَاوَى is a substitute for the و in the sing. (Ṣ.) — See also أَدَاةٌ.

آدَى [a noun denoting the comparative and superlative degrees, irregularly formed from the verb آدَى; like as the noun آدَى in art. ادى is irregularly formed from the verb أَدَّى in that art.]. You say, هُوَ آدَى شَىْءٍ, meaning أَقْوَاهُ and أَعْدَاهُ [*It is the strongest kind of thing,* and, app., *the most effectual to aid* or *assist,* or *to avenge*]. (TA.) — See also art. ادى.

مُؤْدٍ part. n. of the intrans. verb آدَى [q. v.]. (T, Ṣ, M, &c.) — [And act. part. n. of آدَاهُ.] — مُودٍ, without ء, is from أَوْدَى signifying "he perished" [&c.]. (Ṣ.)

ادى

2. أَدَّاهُ, (T, Ṣ, M, &c.,) inf. n. تَأْدِيَةٌ (T, Ṣ, Ḳ) and أَدَآءٌ, (T,) or the latter is a simple subst., (Ṣ, M, Mṣb, Ḳ,) [and so, accord. to the Mṣb, is the former also, but this is a mistake,] *He made it,* or *caused it, to reach, arrive,* or *come* [to the appointed person or place &c.]; *he brought, conveyed,* or *delivered, it;* syn. أَوْصَلَهُ; (M, Mṣb, Ḳ;) namely, a thing; (M;) as, for instance, الأَمَانَةَ إِلَى أَهْلِهَا [*the thing committed to his trust and care, to its owner*]: (Mṣb:) *he delivered it, gave it up,* or *surrendered it:* (T:) *he payed it,* or *discharged it;* (Ṣ, Ḳ;) namely, his debt, (Ṣ,) a bloodwit, a responsibility, and the like; (Mṣb in art. غرم;) [and hence,] أَدَّى مَا عَلَيْهِ [*he acquitted himself of that which was incumbent on him;* or *payed,* or *discharged, what he owed*]: (T:) *he performed, fulfilled,* or *accomplished, it;* namely, [for instance,] الحَجَّ [*the pilgrimage*]; (Mṣb in art. قضى;) and in like manner, المَنَاسِكَ [*the religious rites and ceremonies of the pilgrimage*]. (Jel in ii. 196, and Mṣb ubi suprà.) It is said in the Ḳur [xliv. 17], أَنْ أَدُّوا إِلَىَّ عِبَادَ ٱللّٰهِ, meaning *Deliver ye to me* [*the servants of God,*] the children of Israel: or, as some say, the meaning is, أَدُّوا إِلَىَّ مَا أَمَرَكُمُ ٱللّٰهُ بِهِ يَا عِبَادَ ٱللّٰهِ [*perform ye to me that which God hath commanded you* to do, *O servants of God*]: or it may mean *listen ye,* or *give ye ear, to me;* as though the speaker said, أَدُّوا إِلَىَّ سَمْعَكُمْ; the verb being used in this sense by the Arabs. (T.) And one says, تَأَدَّيْتُ ♦ لَهُ, (Ḳ, TA,) and إِلَيْهِ, in the place of لَهُ, مِنْ حَقِّهِ, meaning أَدَّيْتُهُ; (TA;) i. e. *I payed him his due,* or *right.* (Ḳ, TA.) And a man says, مَا أَدْرِى كَيْفَ أَتَأَدَّى ♦ [*I know not how to pay*]. (TA.) One says also, أَدَّى عَنْهُ [meaning *He payed,* or *made satisfaction, for him*]: and أَدَّى عَنْهُ الخَرَاجَ [*He payed for him,* or *in his stead, the land-tax*]. (Mgh in art. جزأ.) [Hence,] El-Akhnas says,

فَأَدَّيْتُ عَنِّى مَا ٱسْتَعَرْتُ مِنَ الصِّبَا
وَلِلْمَالِ عِنْدِى اليَوْمَ رَاعٍ وَكَاسِبُ

i. e. *But I have put away from me* [*what I had borrowed,* or *assumed, of the foolishness of youth, and amorous dalliance,*] *and now I am* [or *there is at my abode*] *a keeper and collector to the camels,* or *cattle,* or *property.* (Ḥam p. 346.) — [أَدَّى إِلَى كَذَا is a phrase often used as meaning *It brought, conducted, led,* or *conduced, to such a thing* or *state;* as, for instance, crime to punishment or to ignominy.]

4. آدَى, intrans. and trans.: see art. ادو.

5. تَأَدَّى إِلَيْهِ الخَبَرُ *The information,* or *news, reached him.* (Ṣ.) — See also 2, in two places.

10. اِسْتَأْدَاهُ مَالًا *He desired,* or *sought, to obtain from him property,* or *sued,* or *prosecuted, him for it,* or *demanded it of him,* (Ṣ, Ḳ,) *and extracted it,* (Ṣ,) or *took it,* or *received it,* (Ḳ,) *from him.* (Ṣ, Ḳ.) — See also art. ادو.

أَدَآءٌ a subst. from 2 [signifying The *act of making,* or *causing, to reach, arrive,* or *come* to the appointed person or place &c.; *of bringing, conveying,* or *delivering;* *of giving up,* or *surrendering;* *payment,* or *discharge,* of a debt &c.; the *act of acquitting oneself* of that which is incumbent on him; *performance, fulfilment,* or *accomplishment*]. (Ṣ, M, Mṣb, Ḳ.) — [Hence,] هُوَ حَسَنُ الأَدَآءِ *He has a good manner of pronouncing,* or *uttering, the letters.* (TA.) — أَدَآءٌ as a term of the law signifies The *performance* of an act of religious service [such as prayer &c.] *at the appointed time:* opposed to قَضَآءٌ, performance at a time other than that which is appointed. (Mṣb and TA in art. قضى.)

أَدِىٌّ: see art. ادو.

آدَى [a noun denoting the comparative and superlative degrees, irregularly formed from the verb أَدَّى; like as the noun آدَى mentioned in art. ادو is irregularly formed from the verb آدَى]. You say, هُوَ آدَى لِلْأَمَانَةِ [*He is more,* or *better, disposed to deliver, give up,* or *surrender, the thing committed to his trust and care*] (T, Ṣ, M, Ḳ) مِنْكَ [*than thou*], (Ṣ,) or مِنْ غَيْرِهِ [*than another than he*]. (M,* Ḳ.) [Az says,] the vulgar say, أَدَّى لِلْأَمَانَةِ; but this is incorrect, and not allowable; and I have not known any one of the grammarians allow آدَى, because أَفْعَل denoting wonder [and the comparative and superlative degrees] is not formed but from the triliteral [verb], and one does not say, أَدَى in the sense of أَدَّى: the proper phrase is أَحْسَنُ أَدَآءً. (T.) — See also art. ادو.

مُؤَدٍّ: see art. ادو.

اذ

إِذْ a word denoting past time: (Lth, T, Ṣ, M, L, Mughnee, Ḳ:) it is a noun, (Ṣ, L, Mughnee, Ḳ,) indecl., with its last letter quiescent; and properly is prefixed to a proposition; (Ṣ, L, Ḳ;) as in جِئْتُكَ إِذْ قَامَ زَيْدٌ [*I came to thee when Zeyd stood*], and إِذْ زَيْدٌ قَائِمٌ and إِذْ زَيْدٌ يَقُومُ [*When Zeyd was standing*]. (Ṣ, L.) The proposition to which it is prefixed is either nominal, as in [the words of the Ḳur viii. 26,] وَٱذْكُرُوا إِذْ أَنْتُمْ قَلِيلٌ [*And remember ye when ye were few*]; or verbal, having the verb in the pret. as to the letter and as to the meaning, as in [the Ḳur ii. 28, &c.,] وَإِذْ قَالَ رَبُّكَ لِلْمَلَائِكَةِ [*And when thy Lord said unto the angels*]; or verbal with the verb in the pret. as to the meaning but not as to the letter, as in [the Ḳur ii. 121,] وَإِذْ يَرْفَعُ إِبْرٰهِيمُ القَوَاعِدَ [*And when Abraham was rearing the foundations*]; all three of which kinds are comprised in the Ḳur where it is said, [ix. 40,] إِلَّا تَنْصُرُوهُ فَقَدْ نَصَرَهُ ٱللّٰهُ إِذْ أَخْرَجَهُ ٱلَّذِينَ كَفَرُوا ثَانِىَ ٱثْنَيْنِ إِذْ هُمَا فِى الغَارِ إِذْ يَقُولُ لِصَاحِبِهِ لَا تَحْزَنْ إِنَّ ٱللّٰهَ مَعَنَا [*If ye will not aid him, verily God aided him, when those who disbelieved expelled him, being the second of two, when they two were in the cave, when he was saying to his companion, Grieve not thou, for God is with us*]. (Mughnee.) But sometimes one half of the proposition is suppressed, as in إِذْ ذَاكَ, [also written إِذَّاكَ,] meaning إِذْ ذَاكَ كَذٰلِكَ [*When that was so*], or إِذْ ذَاكَ كَائِنٌ [*When that was, i. e. then, at that time*]. (Mughnee.) And sometimes the whole of the proposition is suppressed, (M, Mughnee,) as being known, (Mughnee,) and tenween is substituted for it; the ذ receiving kesreh because of the occurrence of two quiescent letters together, (M, Mughnee,) namely the ذ and the tenween, (M,) and thus one says, يَوْمَئِذٍ; the kesreh of the ذ not being, as Akh holds it to be, the kesreh of declension, although اذ here occupies the place of a noun governed in the gen. case by another prefixed to it, (M, Mughnee,) for it still requires a proposition to be understood after it, (Mughnee,) and is held to be indecl. (M, Mughnee) by general consent, like كَمْ and مَنْ, (M,) as being composed of two letters. (Mughnee.) [J says,] when إِذْ is not prefixed to a proposition, it has tenween: (Ṣ:) and hence Aboo-Dhu-eyb says, (Ṣ, M,)

* نَهَيْتُكَ عَنْ طِلَابِكَ أُمَّ عَمْرٍو *
* بِعَافِيَةٍ وَأَنْتَ إِذٍ صَحِيحُ *

[*I forbade thy suing Umm-'Amr in health, thou being then sound*]; (Ṣ, M, L, Mughnee, TA; [but in two copies of the Ṣ, for بِعَافِيَةٍ, I find بِعَاقِبَةٍ; and in the L it is without any point;]) in which [J says] the poet means حِينَئِذٍ, like as one says يَوْمَئِذٍ and لَيْلَتَئِذٍ: (Ṣ:) and Fr says that some of the Arabs say, كَانَ كَذَا وَكَذَا وَهُوَ إِذٍ صَبِىٌّ, meaning هُوَ إِذْ ذَاكَ صَبِىٌّ [*Such and such things were, he being then a boy*]. (T.) إِذِى also occurs for اذ [app. إِذْ, but whether this or إِذَ is not clear in the MS. from which I take this]. (M.) When إِذْ is adjoined to nouns signifying times, the Arabs join it therewith in writing, in certain instances: namely حِينَئِذٍ [*At that time*, or *then*], and يَوْمَئِذٍ [*In*, or *on*, or *at, that day*], and لَيْلَتَئِذٍ [*In*, or *on*, or *at, that night*], and غَدَاتَئِذٍ [*In*, or *on, that morning*], and عَشِيَّتَئِذٍ [*In*, or *on, that evening*], and سَاعَتَئِذٍ [*In that hour*: or *at that time; then*], and عَامَئِذٍ [*In that year*], [and وَقْتَئِذٍ *At that time; then*]; but they did not say الآنَئِذٍ, because الآنَ denotes the nearest present time, except in the dial. of Hudheyl, in which it has been found to occur. (T.) When it is followed by a verb, or by a noun not having the article ال prefixed to it, or [rather] by any movent letter, the ذ of إِذْ is quiescent; but when it is followed by a noun with ال, [or by any ٱ,] the ذ is mejroorah, as in the saying,

* إِذِ القَوْمُ كَانُوا نَازِلِينَ بِكَاظِمَةْ *

[*When the people*, or *company of men, were alighting*, or *taking up their abode, at Kádhimeh*]. (T.) —— In general, (Mughnee, Ḳ,) it is an adverbial noun denoting past time, (M, Mughnee, Ḳ,) when it is a noun denoting such time, (Mughnee, Ḳ,) as in وَإِذْ قَالَ رَبُّكَ لِلْمَلَائِكَةِ [explained above], (M,) and in فَقَدْ نَصَرَهُ ٱللّٰهُ إِذْ أَخْرَجَهُ ٱلَّذِينَ كَفَرُوا [also explained above, and in other instances already mentioned]: (Mughnee, Ḳ:) in the former of which instances, AO says that it is redundant; (M, Mughnee;) but Aboo-Is-ḥáḳ says that this is a bold assertion of his; (M;) [and IHsh says,] this assertion is of no account, and so is that of him who says that it here denotes certainty, like قَدْ: (Mughnee:) [J holds the opinion of AO on this point; for he says,] إِذْ is sometimes redundant, like إِذَا, as in the saying in the Ḳur [ii. 48], وَإِذْ وَاعَدْنَا مُوسَى, meaning وَوَاعَدْنَا مُوسَى [*And We appointed a time with Moses*; but instances of this kind are most probably elliptical: see the next sentence]. (Ṣ.) As a noun denoting past time, it is [said to be] also an objective complement of a verb, as in [the Ḳur vii. 84,] وَٱذْكُرُوا إِذْ كُنْتُمْ قَلِيلًا [*And remember ye when ye were few*]: (Mughnee, Ḳ:) and generally in the commencements of narratives in the Ḳur, it may be an objective complement of أُذْكُرْ understood, as in وَإِذْ قَالَ رَبُّكَ لِلْمَلَائِكَةِ [before cited], and the like. (Mughnee: but see the third of the sentences here following.) As such, it is [said to be] also a substitute for the objective complement of a verb, as in [the Ḳur xix. 16,] وَٱذْكُرْ فِى ٱلْكِتَابِ مَرْيَمَ إِذِ ٱنْتَبَذَتْ [*And mention thou*, or *remember thou, in the Scripture, Mary, the time when she withdrew aside*], where اذ is a substitute of implication for مريم. (Mughnee, Ḳ: but see the second of the sentences here following.) As such, it also has prefixed to it a noun of time, of such a kind that it is without need thereof, as in يَوْمَئِذٍ, or not of such a kind that it is without need thereof, as in [the Ḳur iii. 6,] بَعْدَ إِذْ هَدَيْتَنَا [*After the time when Thou hast directed us aright*]. (Mughnee, Ḳ.) And it is generally asserted, that it never occurs otherwise than as an adverbial noun, or as having a noun prefixed to it; that in the like of وَٱذْكُرُوا إِذْ كُنْتُمْ قَلِيلًا, it is an adverbial noun relating to an objective complement suppressed, i. e. وَٱذْكُرُوا نِعْمَةَ ٱللّٰهِ عَلَيْكُمْ إِذْ كُنْتُمْ قَلِيلًا [*And remember ye the grace of God towards you when ye were few*]; and in the like of إِذِ ٱنْتَبَذَتْ, that it is an adverbial noun relating to a suppressed prefixed noun to [that which becomes by the suppression] the objective complement of a verb, i. e. [in this instance] وَٱذْكُرْ قِصَّةَ مَرْيَمَ [*And mention thou*, or *remember thou, the case of Mary*]: and this assertion is strengthened by the express mention of the [proper] objective complement in [the Ḳur iii. 98,] وَٱذْكُرُوا نِعْمَةَ ٱللّٰهِ عَلَيْكُمْ إِذْ كُنْتُمْ أَعْدَآءً [*And remember ye the grace of God towards you when ye were enemies*]. (Mughnee.) —— Also, (Mughnee, Ḳ,) accord. to some, (T, Mughnee,) it is used (T, Mughnee, Ḳ) as a noun (Mughnee, Ḳ) to indicate future time, (T, Mughnee, Ḳ,) and إِذَا is said to denote past time, (T,) [i. e.] each of these occurs in the place of the other; (TA;) the former being used to indicate future time in the Ḳur [xxxiv. 50], where it is said, وَلَوْ تَرَى إِذْ فَزِعُوا [*And couldst thou see the time when they shall be terrified*], meaning the day of resurrection; this usage being allowable, says Fr, only because the proposition is like one expressing a positive fact, since there is no doubt of the coming of that day; (T;) and in [the Ḳur xcix. 4,] يَوْمَئِذٍ تُحَدِّثُ أَخْبَارَهَا [*On that day, she* (the earth) *shall tell her tidings*]; (Mughnee, Ḳ;) this being generally regarded as similar to the expression of a future event which must necessarily happen as though it had already happened; but it may be urged in favour of those who hold a different opinion that it is said in the Ḳur [xl. 72 and 73], فَسَوْفَ يَعْلَمُونَ إِذِ الأَغْلَالُ فِى أَعْنَاقِهِمْ [*They shall hereafter know, when the collars* shall be *on their necks*]; for يعلمون is a future as to the letter and the meaning because of its having سوف conjoined with it, and it governs اذ, which is therefore in the place of إِذَا. (Mughnee.) —— It also indicates a cause, as in [the Ḳur xliii. 38,] لَنْ يَنْفَعَكُمُ ٱلْيَوْمَ إِذْ ظَلَمْتُمْ [*It will not profit you this day, since*, or *because, ye have acted wrongfully*], (Mughnee, Ḳ,) i. e. because of your having acted wrongfully in the sublunary state of existence; (Bḍ, Mughnee;) but it is disputed whether it be in this instance a particle in the place of the causative لِ, or an adverbial noun: (Mughnee:) Aboo-'Alee seems to hold that اذ ظلمتم [as meaning *when ye have acted wrongfully*] is a substitute for, or a kind of repetition of, اليوم; an event happening in the present world being spoken of as though it happened in the world to come because the latter immediately follows the former. (IJ, M, L, Mughnee.) You say also, الحَمْدُ لِلّٰهِ إِذْ جِئْتَ [*Praise be to God because*, or *that, thou camest*, or *hast come*]. (Ṣ in art. جيأ.) —— It is also used to denote one's experiencing the occurrence of a thing when he is in a particular state; (Ṣ, L;) or to denote a thing's happening suddenly, or unexpectedly; (Ṣ, Mughnee, Ḳ;) like إِذَا; (Ṣ;) and in this case is only followed by a verb expressing an event as a positive fact, (Ṣ, L,) and occurs after بَيْنَا and بَيْنَمَا; (Mughnee, Ḳ;) as [in exs. voce بَيْنَ; and] in بَيْنَمَا أَنَا كَذَا إِذْ جَآءَ زَيْدٌ [*While I was thus*, or *in this state, lo*, or *behold*, or *there*, or *then, at that time*, (accord. to different authorities, as will be seen below,) *Zeyd came*]; (Ṣ, L;) and as in the saying of a poet,

* اِسْتَقْدِرِ ٱللّٰهَ خَيْرًا وَٱرْضَيَنَّ بِهِ *
* فَبَيْنَمَا ٱلْعُسْرُ إِذْ دَارَتْ مَيَاسِيرُ *

[*Beg thou God to appoint for thee good, and do thou be content therewith; for while* there has been *difficulty, lo, easy circumstances have come about*]: (Mughnee, Ḳ:*) but it is disputed whether it be [in this case] an adverbial noun of place, (Mughnee, Ḳ,) as Zj and AHei hold; (TA;) or of time, (Mughnee, Ḳ,) as Mbr holds; (TA;) or a particle denoting the sudden, or unexpected, occurrence of a thing, (Mughnee, Ḳ,) as IB and Ibn-Málik hold; (TA;) or a corroborative, i. e. [grammatically] redundant, particle, (Mughnee, Ḳ,) an opinion which Ibn-Ya'eesh holds, and to which Er-Raḍee inclines. (TA.) —— It is also a conditional particle, but only used as such coupled with ما, (Ṣ, L, Mughnee,*) and causes two aorists to assume the mejzoom form, (Mughnee,) as when you say, إِذْمَا تَأْتِنِى آتِكَ [*When*, or *whenever, thou shalt come to me, I will come to thee*], like as you say, إِنْ تَأْتِنِى وَقْتًا آتِكَ [If thou come to me at some, or any, time, I will come to thee]; and you say also إِذْمَا أَتَيْتَ [like as you say, إِنْ أَتَيْتَ, using the pret. in the sense of the future]: (Ṣ, L:) it is a particle accord. to Sb, used in the manner of the conditional إِنْ; but it is an adverbial noun accord. to Mbr and Ibn-Es-Sarráj and El-Fárisee. (Mughnee.) —— [What I have translated from the Ṣ, L, Ḳ, and TA, in this art., is mostly from فصل الهمزة of باب الذال: the rest, from باب الالف اللينة.]

اذا

إِذَا denotes a thing's happening suddenly, or unexpectedly; (Mughnee, Ḳ;) or one's experiencing the occurrence of a thing when he is in a particular state; (Ṣ;) like إِذْ: (Ṣ voce إِذْ:) it pertains only to nominal phrases; does not require to be followed by a reply, or the complement of a condition; does not occur at the commencement of a sentence; and signifies the present time, (Mughnee, Ḳ,) not the future; (Mughnee;) as in خَرَجْتُ فَإِذَا الأَسَدُ بِالبَابِ [*I went forth, and lo,* or *behold,* or *there,* or *then, at that present time,* (accord. to different authorities, as will be seen below,) *the lion was at the door*]; and (in the saying in the Ḳur [xx. 21], TA,) فَإِذَا هِىَ حَيَّةٌ تَسْعَى [*And lo,* or *behold,* &c., *it was a serpent running*]; (Mughnee, Ḳ;) and in the saying, خَرَجْتُ فَإِذَا زَيْدٌ قَائِمٌ, which means *I went forth, and Zeyd presented himself to me suddenly,* or *unexpectedly, at the time, by standing.* (Ṣ, TA.) Accord. to Akh, it is a particle, (Mughnee, Ḳ,) and his opinion is rendered preferable by their saying, خَرَجْتُ فَإِذَا إِنَّ زَيْدًا بِالبَابِ [*I went forth, and lo,* or *behold, verily Zeyd was at the door*]; for [اذا cannot here be a noun governed in the accus. case, as] what follows إِنَّ, which is with kesr, does not govern what precedes it: (Mughnee:) accord. to Mbr, it is an adverbial noun of place: accord. to Zj, an adverbial noun of time. (Mughnee, Ḳ.) Ibn-Málik adopts the first of these opinions; Ibn-'Osfoor, the second; (Mughnee;) and so El-Fenjedeehee; (TA;) and Z, the third; and he asserts that its governing word is a verb understood, derived from المُفَاجَأَةُ; [agreeably with the explanation cited above from the Ṣ;] but others hold that the word which governs it in the accus. case is the enunciative, which is either expressed, as in خَرَجْتُ فَإِذَا زَيْدٌ جَالِسٌ [*I went forth, and there, in that place,* or *then, at that time, Zeyd was sitting*], or meant to be understood, as in فَإِذَا الأَسَدُ, i. e. حَاضِرٌ [*And there,* or *then, the lion was present*]; or if it be supposed to be [itself] the enunciative, its governing word is مُسْتَقِرٌّ or اسْتَقَرَّ [understood]: and in the last of the phrases here mentioned, it may be an enunciative accord. to the opinion of Mbr, the meaning being فَبِالحَاضِرَةِ الأَسَدُ [*And among the things present was the lion*]; but not accord. to the opinion of Zj, because a noun signifying time cannot be the enunciative of one signifying a corporeal thing; nor accord. to the opinion of Akh, because a particle cannot be used to denote the enunciative of such a thing; or, as signifying time, it may be the enunciative of such a thing if we suppose a prefixed noun to be suppressed, the meaning of فَإِذَا الأَسَدُ being فَإِذَا حُضُورُ الأَسَدِ [*And then was the presence of the lion*]. (Mughnee.) You may say either خَرَجْتُ فَإِذَا زَيْدٌ جَالِسٌ or جَالِسًا [*I went forth, and lo,* or *behold,* &c., *Zeyd was sitting* or *Zeyd* was there *sitting*], with the nom. as an enunciative and with the accus. as a denotative of state. (Mughnee.) The Arabs said, قَدْ كُنْتُ أَظُنُّ أَنَّ العَقْرَبَ أَشَدُّ لَسْعَةً مِنَ الزُّنْبُورِ فَإِذَا هُوَ هِىَ [*I used to think that the scorpion was more vehement in stinging than the hornet, and lo, he is* (as vehement as) *she*], and also, فَإِذَا هُوَ إِيَّاهَا, which Sb disallowed, in contending with Ks, who allowed it, and appealed for confirmation thereof to certain Arabs, whose judgment was pronounced in his favour; but it is said that they were bribed to give this judgment, or that they knew the place which Ks held in the estimation of Er-Rasheed; and if the latter expression be of established authority, it is irregular and unchaste. (Mughnee.) — It also denotes the complement of a condition, like فَ, (Ṣ, Mṣb,) with which it is in this case syn., (Mṣb,) as in the words of the Ḳur [xxx. 35], وَإِنْ تُصِبْهُمْ سَيِّئَةٌ بِمَا قَدَّمَتْ أَيْدِيهِمْ إِذَا هُمْ يَقْنَطُونَ [*And if an evil befall them for that which their hands have sent before,* (i. e. for sins which they have committed,) *then they despair*]. (Ṣ, Mṣb.) — It is also an adverbial noun denoting future time, (Ṣ, Mṣb, Mughnee, Ḳ,*) and implying the meaning of a condition, (Mṣb, Mughnee,) and this is generally the case when it is not used in the manner first explained above. (Mughnee.) In this case it is not used otherwise than as prefixed to a proposition, (Ṣ, Mughnee,) which is always verbal, as in the words of the Ḳur [xxx. 24], ثُمَّ إِذَا دَعَاكُمْ دَعْوَةً مِنَ الأَرْضِ إِذَا أَنْتُمْ تَخْرُجُونَ [*Then, when He shall call you,* or *when He calleth you,* (for, as in Arabic, so in English, a verb which is properly present is often tropically future,) *with a single call from out the earth, lo,* or *behold,* or *then, ye shall come forth*], in which occur both the usages of اذا here mentioned; (Mughnee;) and in the phrase, إِذَا جِئْتَ أَكْرَمْتُكَ [*When thou shalt come, I will treat thee with honour*]; (Mṣb;) and in the phrase, أَجِيئُكَ إِذَا احْمَرَّ البُسْرُ [*I will come to thee when the full-grown unripe dates shall become red*], and إِذَا قَدِمَ فُلَانٌ [*when such a one shall arrive*], which shows it to be a noun because this is equivalent to يَوْمَ يَقْدَمُ فُلَانٌ [on the day when such a one shall arrive]: (Ṣ:) or in the phrase قُمْ إِذَا احْمَرَّ البُسْرُ [and in many other cases] it denotes time divested of any accessory idea, the meaning being [*Arise thou*] *at the time of the full-grown unripe dates' becoming red:* and so in the saying of Esh-Sháfi'ee, If a man were to say, أَنْتِ طَالِقٌ إِذَا لَمْ أُطَلِّقْكِ, or مَتَى لم اطلّقك, [*Thou art divorced when I do not divorce thee,*] and then be silent for a time sufficient for the divorce to be pronounced therein, she would be divorced; but should he make it dependent upon a thing in the future, the divorce would be delayed to that time, as if he said, اذا احمرّ البسر [using it in the sense first assigned to this phrase above]. (Mṣb.) The verb after it is in most cases a pret.: in other cases, an aor.: both occur in the saying of Aboo-Dhu-eyb,

* وَالنَّفْسُ رَاغِبَةٌ إِذَا رَغَّبْتَهَا *
* وَإِذَا تُرَدُّ إِلَى قَلِيلٍ تَقْنَعُ *

[*And the soul is desirous when thou makest it desirous; and when thou reducest it,* or *restrictest it, to little, it is content*]. (Mughnee.) When it is immediately followed by a noun, as in [the phrase in the Ḳur lxxxiv. 1,] إِذَا السَّمَآءُ انْشَقَّتْ, the noun is an agent with a verb suppressed, explained by what follows it; contr. to the opinion of Akh; (Mughnee;) the complete phrase being إِذَا انْشَقَّتِ السَّمَآءُ انْشَقَّتْ [*When the heaven shall be cleft,* (when) *it shall be cleft*]; and in like manner, إِنْ, as in the saying, in the Ḳur [ix. 6], وَإِنْ أَحَدٌ مِنَ المُشْرِكِينَ اسْتَجَارَكَ. (I 'Aḳ p. 123.) And in the saying of the poet,

* إِذَا بَاهِلِىٌّ تَحْتَهُ حَنْظَلِيَّةٌ *
* لَهُ وَلَدٌ مِنْهَا فَذَاكَ المُدَرَّعُ *

كَانَ is meant to be understood after اذا [so that the meaning is, *When a Báhilee* (a man of the tribe of Báhileh) *has,* or *shall have, as his wife a Ḥandhaleeyeh* (a woman of the tribe of Ḥandhaleh, who were renowned for generosity), *he having offspring from her, that* (offspring) *is,* or *will be, the mail-clad*]. (Mughnee.) — Sometimes it denotes past time, (Mughnee, Ḳ,) like as إِذْ sometimes denotes future time, (Mughnee,) as in [the saying in the Ḳur lxii. 11,] وَإِذَا رَأَوْا تِجَارَةً أَوْ لَهْوًا انْفَضُّوا إِلَيْهَا [*And when they saw merchandise or sport, they dispersed themselves to it*]. (Mughnee, Ḳ.) [Thus] it occurs in the place of إِذْ, like as إِذْ occurs in the place of إِذَا. (TA.) — And sometimes it denotes the present time; and this is after an oath, as in [the phrase in the Ḳur xcii. 1,] وَاللَّيْلِ إِذَا يَغْشَى [*By the night when it covereth* with its darkness]. (Mughnee, Ḳ.) — It also occurs in the sense of the conditional إِنْ, as in the saying, أُكْرِمُكَ إِذَا أَكْرَمْتَنِى, meaning إِنْ أَكْرَمْتَنِى [*I will treat thee with honour if thou treat me with honour*]: (T:) [for] what is possible is made dependent upon it as well as what is known to be certain, as in the phrases, إِذَا جَآءَ زَيْدٌ [*If Zeyd come*] and إِذَا جَآءَ رَأْسُ الشَّهْرِ [*When the beginning of the month shall come*]; or, accord. to Th, there is a difference between إِذَا and إِنْ; (Mṣb;) the latter being held by him to denote what is possible, and the former to denote what is ascertained; so that one says, إِنْ جَآءَ زَيْدٌ and إِذَا جَآءَ رَأْسُ الشَّهْرِ. (Mṣb in art. ان.) — When a verb in the first person sing. of the pret. is explained by another verb after it immediately preceded by إِذَا, [تَقُولُ is understood before the former verb, and therefore] the latter verb must be in the second pers. sing., as in لُجْتُهُ إِذَا أَدَرْتَهُ فِى فِيكَ [meaning Thou sayest (of a thing) لُجْتُهُ *when,* or *if, thou hast turned it about in thy mouth*]. (MF in art. لوج. See also أَىْ; last sentence but one.) — It is sometimes redundant, like as إِذْ is sometimes [accord. to some], as in the saying of 'Abd-Menáf Ibn-Ribạ El-Hudhalee,

* حَتَّى إِذَا أَسْلَكُوهُمْ فِى قُتَائِدَةٍ *
* شَلًّا كَمَا تَطْرُدُ الجَمَّالَةُ الشُّرُدَا *

[*Until they made them to pass along Ḳutáïdeh,* (here meaning a certain mountain-road so named, Ṣ in art. قتد,) *urging on, like as the owners,* or *attendants, of camels drive those that take fright and run away*]; for it is the end of the poem; or he may have abstained from mentioning the enunciative because of its being known to the hearer. (Ṣ.) When إِذَا is preceded by حَتَّى, [as in this instance,] it is generally held that اذا is not governed by حَتَّى in the gen. case, but is still an adverbial noun, حَتَّى being an inceptive particle without government. (Mughnee.) — As to what it is that governs إِذَا in the accus. case, there are two opinions; that it is its conditional proposition; or a verb, or the like, in the complement thereof: (Mughnee, Ḳ:) the former is the opinion of the critical judges; so that it is in the predicament of مَتَى and حَيْثُمَا and أَيَّانَ. (Mughnee.) — Sometimes it is used so as not to denote a condition, as in the words of the Ḳur [xlii. 35], وَإِذَا مَا غَضِبُوا هُمْ يَغْفِرُونَ [*And when*, or *whenever*, *they are angry, they forgive*], in which it is an adverbial noun relating to the enunciative of the inchoative after it; for if it denoted a condition, and the nominal proposition were a complement, it would be connected by فَ: and the same is the case when it is used after an oath, as in an ex. given above. (Mughnee.) — See also what follows.

إِذًا, (Mṣb, TA, the latter as on the authority of Lth,) with tenween, (TA,) or إِذَنْ, (T, Ṣ, M, Mṣb, Mughnee, Ḳ, the first as on the authority of Lth,) written in the former manner, (TA,) or in the latter, (T,) when connected with a following proposition, (T, TA,) and in a case of pause written ✝ إِذَا, (T, Ṣ, M, Mṣb, Mughnee, Ḳ, TA,) and therefore the Basrees hold that in other cases it should be written إِذًا, (Mṣb,) though El-Mázinee and Mbr hold that it should be in this case also with ن, while Fr holds that it should be written with ا when it governs, and otherwise with ن, in order to distinguish between it and [the adverbial noun] إِذَا: (Mughnee:) a particle, (Ṣ, Mṣb, Mughnee, TA,) accord. to the general opinion; and accord. to this opinion, it is a simple word, not compounded of إِذْ and أَنْ; and as being simple, it is that which renders an aor. manṣoob, not أَنْ suppressed and meant to be understood after it: some say that it is a noun: (Mughnee:) [but a knowledge of its meaning is necessary to the understanding of the reason given for asserting it to be a noun.] It denotes a response, or reply, corroborating a condition; (Lth, T, TA;) or compensation, or the complement of a condition; (Mṣb;) or a response, or reply, (Sb, Ṣ, Mughnee, Ḳ,) in every instance; (TA;) and compensation, or the complement of a condition, (Sb, Ṣ, M, Mughnee, Ḳ,) though not always: (Mughnee, TA:) and its virtual meaning is [*Then*; i. e., *in that case*; or] *if the case*, or *affair*, *be as thou hast mentioned*, (M, Ḳ, TA,) or *as has happened*: (M, TA:) [and hence,] accord. to those who say that it is a noun, the original form of the phrase إِذَنْ أُكْرِمَكَ [*Then*, or *in that case*, or *if the case be so*, *I will treat thee with honour*, said in reply to one who says "I will come to thee,"] is إِذَا جِئْتَنِى أُكْرِمُكَ [*When thou shalt come to me, I will treat thee with honour*]; then the proposition [جِئْتَنِى] is thrown out, and tenween [or ن] is substituted for it, (Mughnee,) for which reason, and to distinguish between it and [the adverbial] إِذَا, the Koofees hold that it should be written with ن, (Mṣb,) and أَنْ [preceded by يَجِبُ عَلَىَّ or the like] is suppressed and meant to be understood [as that which renders the aor. manṣoob; so that when one says إِذَنْ أُكْرِمَكَ, it is as though he said إِذَا جِئْتَنِى يَجِبُ عَلَىَّ أَنْ أُكْرِمَكَ *When thou shalt come to me, it will be incumbent*, or *obligatory*, *on me to treat thee with honour*]. (Mughnee.) It renders an aor. following it manṣoob on certain conditions: (Mughnee, TA:) to have this effect, the aor. must have a future signification, (T, Ṣ, Mughnee, TA,) not present: (TA:) اذا must commence the phrase in which the aor. occurs; (Mughnee, TA;) [or, in other words,] the aor. must not be syntactically dependent upon what precedes اذا: (TA:) and there must be nothing intervening between اذا and the aor., (T, Mughnee, TA,) unless it is a particle, (T,) or an oath, (T, Mughnee,) or the negative لَا: (Mughnee:) therefore, to a person who says, "To-night I will visit thee," (Ṣ,) or who says, "I will come to thee," (Mughnee,) you say, إِذَنْ أُكْرِمَكَ [*Then*, or *in that case*, &c., *I will treat thee with honour*]; (T, Ṣ, Mughnee;) and to one who says, "I will treat thee with honour," you say, إِذًا أَجِيْئَكَ [*Then*, or *if the case be so*, *I will come to thee*]. (TA.) When the verb after اذن has the present signification, it does not govern: (Ṣ, Mughnee, TA:) therefore, to a person who says, "I love thee," you say, إِذَنْ أَظُنُّكَ صَادِقًا [*Then*, or *if the case be so*, *I think thee veracious*]; for this is a mere reply: (Mughnee:) and to one talking to thee, إِذًا أَظُنُّكَ كَاذِبًا [*Then I think thee to be lying*]. (TA.) When it is put in a middle place, (Ṣ,) not commencing the phrase, (Mughnee,) the verb after it not being syntactically dependent upon what is before it, (Ṣ, TA,) it does not govern: (Ṣ, Mughnee, TA:) therefore, to one who says, "I will come to thee," (Mughnee, TA,) you say, أَنَا إِذَنْ أُكْرِمُكَ [*I, in that case, will treat thee with honour*]: (Ṣ, Mughnee, TA:) for اذن among the words which govern verbs is likened to الظَّنُّ among those which govern nouns: (Ṣ:) and when it is put at the end, it does not govern; as when you say, أُكْرِمُكَ إِذًا [*I will treat thee with honour in that case*]. (Ṣ.) The saying [of the poet, or rájiz],

لَا تَتْرُكَنِّى فِيهِمُ شَطِيرَا
إِنِّى إِذًا أَهْلِكَ أَوْ أَطِيرَا

is explained by regarding it as an instance of the suppression of the enunciative of إِنَّ, so that the meaning is, إِنِّى لَا أَقْدِرُ عَلَى ذٰلِكَ, and then a new phrase commences [wherefore the verse means *Do not thou leave me among them remote, or a stranger: verily* I cannot endure that: *in that case I should perish, or I should flee*]. (Mughnee.) When it is immediately preceded by a conjunction such as وَ or فَ, the aor. may be either marfooạ or manṣoob. (Ṣ, Mughnee.) When a noun is introduced between it and the aor., the latter is marfooạ, (T, Mughnee,) as in the saying, إِذَنْ أَخُوكَ يُكْرِمُكَ [*Then*, or *in that case, thy brother will treat thee with honour*], (T,) or إِذًا يَا عَبْدَ ٱللّٰهِ أُكْرِمَكَ [*Then*, or *in that case, O 'Abd-Allah, I will treat thee with honour*]; but Ibn-'Oṣfoor allows the intervention of an adverbial noun [without annulling the government]; and Ibn-Bábshádh, that of the vocative, and of a prayer; and Ks and Hishám, that of a word governed by the verb; but Ks in this case prefers naṣb; and Hishám, rafạ. (Mughnee.) When you put an oath in the place of the noun, you make the aor. manṣoob, as in the saying, إِذًا وَٱللّٰهِ تَنَامَ [*Then*, or *if the case be so, by God, thou wilt sleep*]: but if you prefix لَ to the verb with the oath, you make the aor. marfooạ, saying, إِذَنْ وَٱللّٰهِ لَتَنْدَمُ [*Then*, or *if the case be so, by God, assuredly thou wilt regret*, or *repent*]. (T.) When you introduce a particle between it and the aor., you make the latter either marfooạ or manṣoob, saying, إِذَنْ لَا أُكْرِمَكَ and لَا أُكْرِمُكَ [*Then*, or *in that case, I will not treat thee with honour*]. (T.) — Sometimes the أ is rejected, and they say, ذَنْ لَا أَفْعَلُ [*Then*, (a word exactly agreeing with ذَنْ in sound as well as in meaning,) or *in that case, I will not do* such a thing]. (M, Ḳ,* TA.) — IJ relates, on the authority of Khálid, that إِذًا is used in the dial. of Hudheyl for إِذْ. (M.) — [إِذَنْ or إِذًا is mentioned and explained in the Ṣ and Ḳ and TA in art. اذن, and in the TA in باب الألف اللَّيِّنة also.]

اذر

آذَارُ *The sixth of the Greek* [or *Syrian*] *months* [*corresponding to March O. S.*]. (Ḳ.) [This is not to be confounded with آذَرُ or أَذَرُ, which is the ninth month of the Persian calendar.]

اذن

1. أَذِنَ لَهُ (T, Ṣ, M, Mṣb, Ḳ) and إِلَيْهِ, (M, Ḳ,) aor. ـَ, (T, Mṣb, Ḳ,) inf. n. أَذَنٌ, (T, Ṣ, Mṣb, Ḳ,) *He* [*gave ear* or] *listened to it*, (T, Ṣ, M, Mṣb, Ḳ,) or *him*: (T, Ṣ, M, Ḳ:*) or it signifies, (Ḳ,) or signifies also, (M,) *he listened to it*, or *him*, *pleased*, or *being pleased*. (M, Ḳ.) It is said in a trad., (T,) مَا أَذِنَ ٱللّٰهُ لِشَىْءٍ كَأَذَنِهِ لِنَبِىٍّ يَتَغَنَّى بِالقُرْآنِ (T, Ṣ) *God hath not listened to anything* [in a manner] *like his listening* [*to a prophet chanting the Ḳur-án*]. (T.) And in the Ḳur [lxxxiv. 2 and 5], وَأَذِنَتْ لِرَبِّهَا *And shall listen to its Lord*, (M, Bḍ, Jel,) *and obey*; (Jel;) i. e., shall submit to the influence of his power as one listens to the commander and submits to him. (Bḍ.) And you say, أَذِنَ لِلَّهْوِ *He listened and inclined to sport*, or *play*. (M.) — [Hence, perhaps,] أَذِنَ لِرَائِحَةِ الطَّعَامِ † *He desired eagerly*, or *longed for*, *the food*, [*perceiving its odour*,] (ISh, Ḳ,) and *inclined to it*. (ISh, TA.) — [Hence also, app.,] أَذِنَ لَهُ فِى الشَّىْءِ, (Ṣ, M, Ḳ,) or فِى كَذَا, (T,) or فِى أَمْرِ كَذَا, (Mṣb,) aor. ـَ, (T, Ḳ,) inf. n. إِذْنٌ, (T, Ṣ, M, Ḳ,) or this is a simple subst., (Mṣb,) and أَذِينٌ, (Ḳ,) [as though originally signifying *He gave ear to him in respect of such a thing*; and then] *he permitted him, allowed him*, or *gave him permission* or *leave*, *to do the thing*, or *such a thing*. (M, Mṣb, Ḳ.) [See also إِذْنٌ, below.] You say, أَذِنْتُ لِلْعَبْدِ فِى التِّجَارَةِ [*I gave permission*, or *leave*, *to the slave to traffic*]. (Mṣb.) — أَذِنَ

لَهُ عَلَيْهِ *He took*, or *got*, *permission*, or *leave*, *for him from him*. (M.) You say, إِيذَنْ لِى عَلَى الأَمِيرِ (Ṣ, TA) *Take thou*, or *get thou*, *permission for me from the commander*, or *governor*, or *prince*. (TA.) El-Aʼazz Ibn-ʻAbd-Allah says,

• وَإِنِّى إِذَا ضَنَّ الأَمِيرُ بِإِذْنِهِ •
• عَلَى الإِذْنِ مِنْ نَفْسِى إِذَا شِئْتُ قَادِرُ •

[*And verily I, when the prince is niggardly of his permission, am able to take permission of myself when I will*]. (TA.) And a poet says,

• قُلْتُ لِبَوَّابٍ لَدَيْهِ دَارُهَا •
• تِيذَنْ فَإِنِّى حَمْؤُهَا وَجَارُهَا •

[*I said to a door-keeper, near by whom was her house, take thou*, or *get thou*, *permission* for me to enter, *for I am her husband's father, and her neighbour*]: meaning, says Aboo-Jaafar, لِتَأْذَنْ; for the suppression of the ل is allowable in poetry, and the pronunciation with kesr to the ت is accord. to the dial. of him who says أَنْتَ تِعْلَمُ. (Ṣ.) —— أَذِنَ بِالشَّىْءِ, (Ṣ,* M, Mṣb, Ḳ,) aor. ـَ, (Ṣ, M, Ḳ,) inf. n. إِذْنٌ and أَذَنٌ and أَذَانٌ and أَذَانَةٌ, (M, Ḳ,) *He knew the thing; knew of it; had knowledge of it; became informed*, or *apprized*, *of it*. (Ṣ, M, Mṣb, Ḳ.) It is said in the Ḳur [ii. 279], فَأْذَنُوا بِحَرْبٍ مِنَ ٱللّٰهِ وَرَسُولِهِ (Ṣ, M, Ḳ) *Then be ye informed*, or *apprized*, *of war* [that shall come upon you] *from God and his apostle*: (M, Ḳ:) or *then be ye sure*, or *assured*, &c. (T.) [See also إِذْنٌ, below.] ═ أَذَنَهُ, (T, Ṣ, M, Ḳ,) inf. n. أَذْنٌ, (T,) *He hit*, or *hurt*, *his ear*; (T, Ṣ, M, Ḳ;) or *struck his ear*; (so in some copies of the Ṣ;) and ▼ آذَنَهُ signifies the same, (M, Ḳ,) inf. n. إِيذَانٌ. (TA.) [See also 2.] —— أُذِنَ [as though originally signifying *He had his ear hit or hurt*;] *he complained*, or *had a complaint*, *of his ear*; (Ḳ;) said of a man. (TA.)

2. أَذَّنَهُ, (Ṣ, M, Ḳ,) inf. n. تَأْذِينٌ, (Ḳ,) *He wrung*, or *twisted*, (عَرَكَ,) *his* (a boy's, Ṣ) *ear*: (Ṣ, Ḳ:) or *he struck*, (ضَرَبَ, TA,) or *struck with his finger*, or *fillipped*, (نَقَرَ, M, TA,) *his ear*. (M, TA.) [See also أَذَنَهُ.] They say, (in a prov., TA in art. جوز,) لِكُلِّ جَابِهٍ جَوْزَةٌ ثُمَّ يُؤَذَّنُ, (M, TA,) i. e. *For every one that comes to water is a single watering* for his family and his cattle; *then his ear is struck*, to apprize him that he has nothing more to receive from them: (TA in the present art., and the like is said in the same in art. جوز:) or, † *then he is repelled from the water*: (TA in art. جوز:) [for أَذَّنَهُ signifies also] —— † *He repelled him*, (IAạr, T, M, Ḳ,) namely, a man, (IAạr, T, M,) *from drinking*, (Ḳ,) *and did not give him to drink*. (M, Ḳ.) You say also, أَذِّنُوا عَنِّى أَوْلَهَا, [in which the pronoun appears, from the context, to relate to camels,] † *Send ye away from me the first ones of them*. (En-Naḍr, T.) ═ أَذَّنَ النَّعْلَ, (inf. n. as above, Ṣ,) *He put to the sandal what is termed* أُذُن, q. v. infrà: (Ṣ, M, Ḳ:) and in like manner one says with respect to other things. (Ṣ, Ḳ.) ═ أَذَّنَ, (M, Ḳ,) inf. n. as above, (Ḳ,) also signifies *He made known*, or *notified*, a thing (بِشَىْءٍ) *much*; (M, Ḳ;*) *he proclaimed*, or *made proclamation*; syn. نَادَى: (Jel in vii. 42, and Bḍ and Jel in xii. 70 and xxii. 28:) Sb says that some of the Arabs make أَذَّنَ and ▼ آذَنَ to be syn.: but some say that the former signifies *he called out publickly*; and the latter, i. q. أَعْلَمَ [*he made to know*, &c.: see 4]. (M, TA.) It is said in the Ḳur [xxii. 28], وَأَذِّنْ فِى النَّاسِ بِالْحَجِّ (M) *And proclaim thou, among the people, the pilgrimage*. (Bḍ, Jel.) —— Also, (Ṣ, Ḳ,) or أَذَّنَ بِالصَّلَاةِ, (Mṣb,) inf. n. as above, (M, Ḳ,) or أَذَانٌ, (Ṣ,) or both, (TA,) or the latter is [properly speaking] a simple subst. [used as an inf. n.], as in the instances of وَدَّعَ وَدَاعًا and سَلَّمَ سَلَامًا and كَلَّمَ كَلَامًا &c., (Mṣb,) *He called to prayer*; (M, Ḳ;) *he notified*, or *made known*, or *proclaimed*, [i. e., *chanted*, from the مِئْذَنَة,] *the time of prayer*; (Ṣ,* Mṣb,* TA;) and ▼ آذَنَ signifies the same, (Ḳ,) inf. n. إِيذَانٌ. (TA.) IB says, the phrase أَذَّنَ العَصْرُ, with the verb in the act. form, [a phrase commonly obtaining in the present day,] is wrong; the correct expression being أُذِّنَ بِالعَصْرِ [*The time of the prayer of afternoon was proclaimed*, i. e., *chanted*], with the verb in the pass. form, and with the preposition to connect it with its subject. (Mṣb.) —— You say also, أَذَّنَ بِإِرْسَالِ إِبِلِهِ *He spoke of sending away his camels*. (En-Naḍr, T.)

4. آذَنَهُ: see 1, last sentence but one. —— [Hence, app.,] inf. n. إِيذَانٌ, † *He prevented him*, or *forbade him*; (Ḳ;) and *repelled him*. (TA.) [See also 2.] —— And † *It* (a thing, M) *pleased*, or *rejoiced*, *him*, (M, Ḳ,) *and he therefore listened to it*. (M.) ═ آذَنْتُهُ, inf. n. إِيذَانٌ, (T, Mṣb,) in the place of which the subst. أَذَانٌ is also used, (T,) signifies أَعْلَمْتُهُ [*I made him to know*, or *have knowledge; informed, apprized, advertised*, or *advised, him; gave him information, intelligence, notice*, or *advice*: and *I made it known, notified it*, or *announced it*]: (T, Mṣb:) and ▼ تَأَذَّنْتُ, also, signifies أَعْلَمْتُ [as meaning *I made to know*, &c.: and *I made known*, &c.]. (Mṣb.) You say, آذَنَهُ بِالأَمْرِ, (T, Ḳ, [in the CḲ, erroneously, أَذَنَهُ,]) or بِالشَّىْءِ, (Ṣ,) and آذَنَهُ الأَمْرَ, (M, Ḳ,) inf. n. إِيذَانٌ, (T,) meaning أَعْلَمَهُ [*He made him to know*, or *have knowledge of, the thing; informed, apprized, advertised*, or *advised, him of it; gave him information, intelligence, notice*, or *advice, of it; made it known, notified it*, or *announced it, to him*]; (T, Ṣ, M, Ḳ;) as also ▼ تَأَذَّنَهُ الأَمْرَ. (M.) So, accord. to one reading, in the Ḳur [ii. 279], فَآذِنُوا بِحَرْبٍ مِنَ ٱللّٰهِ *Then make ye known*, or *notify ye*, or *announce ye, war from God*. (M. [For the more common reading, see 1, latter part.]) And so in the Ḳur [vii. 166], وَإِذْ ▼ تَأَذَّنَ رَبُّكَ *And when thy Lord made known*, or *notified*, or *announced*: (Zj, Ṣ, M, Ḳ:*) or the meaning here is, *swore*: (M, Ḳ:*) [for] you say, ▼ تَأَذَّنَ لَيَفْعَلَنَّ, meaning *he swore that he would assuredly do* [such a thing]: (M:) Lth says that ▼ تَأَذَّنْتُ لَأَفْعَلَنَّ كَذَا وَكَذَا signifies the making the action obligatory. (T.) You say also, ▼ تَأَذَّنَ الأَمِيرُ فِى النَّاسِ *The commander*, or *governor*, or *prince, proclaimed* (نَادَى) *among the people, with threatening* (Ṣ, Ḳ) *and prohibition*; i. e. تَقَدَّمَ and أَعْلَمَ. (Ṣ.) And you say of a building that has cracked in its sides, آذَنَ بِالٱنْهِدَامِ وَالسُّقُوطِ † [*It gave notice of becoming a ruin and of falling down*]. (Mṣb in art. دعو.) [See also a similar ex. in a verse cited voce أَلْ. And hence,] آذَنَ العُشْبُ [in the CḲ (erroneously) أَذَنَ] ‡ *The herbage began to dry up; part of it being still succulent, and part already dried up*. (M, Ḳ, TA.) And آذَنَ الحَبُّ † *The grain put forth its* أُذُنَة, or *leaves*. (TA.) See also 2, latter half, in two places. ═ آذَنَ and ▼ تَأَذَّنَ are [also] used in one and the same sense [as meaning *He knew; had knowledge*; or *became informed, apprized, advertised*, or *advised*, of a thing]; like as one says تَيَقَّنَ and أَيْقَنَ. (Ṣ, TA.) You say, ▼ تَأَذَّنْ, meaning إِعْلَمْ [*Know thou*]; like as you say تَعَلَّمْ, meaning إِعْلَمْ. (M.)

5: see 4, in eight places.

10. اِسْتَأْذَنَهُ *He asked*, or *demanded, of him permission*, or *leave*, (M, Mṣb, Ḳ,) فِى كَذَا *to do such a thing*. (Mṣb.) [You say, اِسْتَأْذَنَ meaning *He asked*, or *demanded, permission*, or *leave, to enter*, or *to come into the presence of another*; and *to go*. And اِسْتَأْذَنَ فِى الدُّخُولِ عَلَيْهِ, and, elliptically, اِسْتَأْذَنَ عليه, *He asked*, or *demanded, permission*, or *leave, to go in to him*.]

أُذْنٌ: see أُذُنٌ.

إِذْنٌ [is held by some to be an inf. n., like ▼ أَذِينٌ: (see 1:) by others, to be] a simple subst.; (Mṣb;) signifying *Permission; leave*; or *concession of liberty*, to do a thing: and sometimes *command*: and likewise *will*; (Mṣb, TA;) as in the phrase بِإِذْنِ ٱللّٰهِ *by the will of God*: (Mṣb:) or, accord. to El-Ḥarállee, the *withdrawal*, or *removal, of prevention* or *prohibition*, and the *giving of power* or *ability, in respect of being and creation*: or, accord. to Ibn-El-Kemál, the *rescission of prohibition, and concession of freedom of action, to him who has been prohibited by law*: or, accord. to Er-Rághib, the *notification of the allowance* or *permission of a thing, and of indulgence in respect of it*; as in إِلَّا لِيُطَاعَ بِإِذْنِ ٱللّٰهِ, [in the Ḳur iv. 67,] meaning [*but that he may be obeyed*] *by the will of God*, and [also] *by his command*: (TA:) or, as explained in the Ksh, *facilitation*; an explanation founded upon the opinion that the actions of men are by their own effective power, but facilitated by God; and in this sense, Esh-Shiháb regards it as a metaphor, or a non-metaphorical trope: (MF:) and *accommodation*; syn. تَوْفِيقٌ; (Hr in explanation of a clause of iii. 139 of the Ḳur [which see below];) but Es-Semeen says that this requires consideration. (TA.) —— Also *Knowledge*; syn. عِلْمٌ; (T, M, Ḳ;) and so ▼ أَذِينٌ; (M, Ḳ;) as in the saying فَعَلَهُ بِإِذْنِى (T,* M, Ḳ) and ▼ بِأَذِينِى (M, Ḳ) [*He did it with my knowledge*]: or إِذْنٌ has a more particular signification than عِلْمٌ, being scarcely ever, or never, used save of that [*knowledge*] *wherein is will, conjoined with command* or *not conjoined therewith;* for in the saying [in the Ḳur iii. 139, referred to above,] وَمَا كَانَ لِنَفْسٍ أَنْ تَمُوتَ إِلَّا بِإِذْنِ ٱللّٰهِ [*And it is not for a soul to die save with the knowledge of God*], it is known that there are will and command; and in the saying [in the Ḳur ii. 96], وَمَا هُمْ بِضَارِّينَ بِهِ مِنْ أَحَدٍ إِلَّا بِإِذْنِ ٱللّٰهِ [*But they do not injure thereby any one save with the knowledge of God*], there is will in one respect, for there is no difference of opinion as to the fact that God hath made to exist in man a faculty wherein is the power of injuring another: (Er-Rághib:) but Es-Semeen says that this plea is adduced by Er-Rághib because of his inclining to the persuasion of the Moạtezileh. (TA.) You say also, فَعَلْتُ كَذَا بِإِذْنِهِ meaning *I did thus by his command.* (T.)

أَذْنٌ: see أُذْنَةٌ.

أُذُنٌ and ▼ أُذْنٌ, (Ṣ, M, Mṣb, Ḳ,) the latter a contraction of the former, [which is the more common,] (Mṣb,) [The *ear;*] *one of the organs of sense;* (M, TA;) *well known:* (M:) of the fem. gender: (Ṣ, M, Mṣb, Ḳ:) as also ▼ أَذِينٌ: (Ḳ:) pl. آذَانٌ, (Ṣ, M, Mṣb, Ḳ,) its only pl. form: (M:) dim. ▼ أُذَيْنَةٌ; but when used as a proper name of a man, أُذَيْنٌ, though أُذَيْنَةٌ has been heard. (Ṣ.) You say, جَآءَ نَاشِرًا أُذُنَيْهِ [*He came spreading,* or, as we say, *pricking up, his ears:* meaning] ‡ *he came in a state of covetousness,* or *eagerness.* (T, Ḳ, TA. [See also نَشَرَ.]) And وَجَدْتُ فُلَانًا لَابِسًا أُذُنَيْهِ ‡ *I found such a one feigning himself inattentive,* or *heedless.* (T, TA.) And لَبِسْتُ أُذُنَىَّ لَهُ ‡ *I turned away from him, avoided him,* or *shunned him:* or *I feigned myself inattentive,* or *heedless, to him.* (Ḳ, TA. [See also لَبِسَ.]) — ‡ A man *who listens to what is said to him:* (M, Ḳ, TA:) or a man *who hears the speech of every one:* (Ṣ:) or *who relies upon what is said to him;* as also وَابِصَةُ ٱلسَّمْعِ: (M in art. وبص:) applied as an epithet to one and to a pl. number, (Ṣ, M, Ḳ,) alike, (Ṣ, M,) and to two, and to a woman; not being pluralized nor dualized [nor having the fem. form given to it]: (IB:) you say رَجُلٌ أُذُنٌ (AZ, Ṣ, M) and أُذْنٌ, and رِجَالٌ أُذُنٌ and أُذْنٌ [&c.]: (AZ, M:) and sometimes it is applied to a man as a name of evil import. (M.) It is said in the Ḳur [ix. 61], وَيَقُولُونَ هُوَ أُذُنٌ قُلْ أُذُنُ خَيْرٍ لَكُمْ (T, M) *And they say, "He is one who hears and believes everything that is said to him:"* as though, by reason of the excess of his listening, he were altogether the organ of hearing; like as a spy is termed عَيْنٌ; or أُذُن is here from أَذِنَ "he listened," and is like أُنُفٌ and شُلُلٌ in its derivation: (Bḍ:) for among the hypocrites was he who found fault with the Prophet, saying, "If anything be told him from me, I swear to him, and he receives it from me, because he is an أُذُن:" (M:) therefore he is commanded to answer, Say, "*A hearer of good for you.*" (T, M, Bḍ.) — † *A sincere,* or *faithful, adviser* of a people, *who counsels to obedience:* (Mṣb:) a man's *intimate, and special,* or *particular, friend.* (TA.) — ‡ *A certain appertenance* of the heart; (M;) [i. e. either *auricle* thereof;] أُذُنَا ٱلْقَلْبِ signifying *two appendages* (زَنَمَتَانِ) *in the upper part of the heart:* (K:) and ‡ of a نَصْل [or arrow-head or the like; i. e. either *wing* thereof]: and ‡ of an arrow; آذَانُ ٱلسَّهْمِ signifying *the feathers of the arrow,* as AḤn says, when they are attached thereon; and ذُو ثَلَاثِ آذَانٍ [*a thing having three such feathers*] meaning *an arrow:* all so called by way of comparison: (M:) and † of a sandal; (Ṣ, M, Ḳ;) i. e. the *part* thereof *that surrounds the* قِبَال [q. v.]: (M:) or أُذُنَا ٱلنَّعْلِ signifies *the two parts,* [or *loops,*] *of the sandal, to which are tied the* عَضُدَانِ *of the* شِرَاك, [or *two branches of the thong that is attached to another thong between two of the toes, which two branches, however, sometimes pass through the* أُذُنَانِ, *encompassing the heel,*] *behind the narrow part* (خَصْر) *of the sole.* (AO in an anonymous MS in my possession. See also خَصْرٌ.) — ‡ *A handle,* (M,) or [*a loop-shaped,* or *an ear-shaped, handle, such as is termed*] عُرْوَةٌ, (T, Ḳ,) of anything; (M, Ḳ;) as, for instance, (M,) of a كُوز [or mug]; (T, M;) and of a دَلْو [or bucket]: so called by way of comparison: and in all cases fem.: (M:) pl. as above. (T.) — ‡ *What becomes sharp,* or *pointed, and then falls off,* or *out,* of the plants called عَرْفَج and ثُمَام when they put forth their خُوص [q. v.], or when their خوص become perfect; because it has the shape of an ear. (AḤn, M.)

إِذَنْ, also written إِذًا: see art. اذا.

أَذَنَةٌ The *leaves of trees,* (En-Naḍr, T,) or *of grain.* (Ḳ.) — [The *kind of leaf called* خُوصَة *of the* ثُمَام.] — ‡ The *young ones of camels* and *of sheep* or *goats;* (En-Naḍr, T, Ḳ;) as being likened to the خُوصَة of the ثُمَام. (TA.) — *A piece of straw:* pl. [or rather coll. gen. n.] ▼ أَذَنٌ [in the CḲ أُذُنٌ]. (IAạr, T, Ḳ.) — *Appetite, appetency, longing, yearning,* or *strong desire.* (En-Naḍr, T.) You say, هٰذِهِ بَقْلَةٌ تَجِدُ بِهَا ٱلْإِبِلُ أَذَنَةً شَدِيدَةً *This is a herb for which the camels feel a strong appetite* &c. (En-Naḍr, T.) And هٰذَا طَعَامٌ لَا أَذَنَةَ لَهُ *This is food for the odour of which there is no appetite.* (Ḳ,* TA.)

أَذَانٌ *A making known; a notification; an announcement.* (T, Ṣ, Mgh.) [See 4.] So in the Ḳur [ix. 3], وَأَذَانٌ مِنَ ٱللّٰهِ وَرَسُولِهِ إِلَى ٱلنَّاسِ [*And a notification,* or *an announcement, from God and his apostle to men,* or *the people*]. (T, Mgh.) — Also, and ▼ أَذِينٌ, (T, Ṣ, M, Ḳ,) and تَأْذِينٌ, [the last an inf. n. of 2, and the second a quasi-inf. n. of the same, which see,] (M, Ḳ,) The *notification,* or *announcement, of prayer,* and *of the time thereof;* (T, Ṣ;) the *call to prayer.* (M, Ḳ.) [The words of this call (which is usually chanted from the مِئْذَنَة, or turret of the mosque,) are ٱللّٰهُ أَكْبَرُ (four times) أَشْهَدُ أَنْ لَا إِلٰهَ إِلَّا ٱللّٰهُ (twice) أَشْهَدُ أَنَّ مُحَمَّدًا رَسُولُ ٱللّٰهِ (twice) حَيَّ عَلَى ٱلصَّلَاةِ (twice) حَيَّ عَلَى ٱلْفَلَاحِ (twice) ٱللّٰهُ أَكْبَرُ (twice) لَا إِلٰهَ إِلَّا ٱللّٰهُ.] — ٱلْأَذَانُ also signifies *The* [*notification,* or *announcement, called*] إِقَامَة; (M, Ḳ;) because it is a notification to be present at the performance of the divinely-ordained prayers. (TA.) [This (which is chanted in the mosque) consists of the words of the former أَذَان with the addition of قَدْ قَامَتِ ٱلصَّلَاةُ pronounced twice after حَيَّ عَلَى ٱلْفَلَاحِ.] — ٱلْأَذَانَانِ signifies *The* أَذَان [*more commonly so called*] *and the* إِقَامَة. (TA.)

أَذُونٌ [An animal *having an ear;* as distinguished from صَمُوخ, which means "having merely an ear-hole"]. (Mṣb in art. بيض.)

أَذِينٌ: see أُذُنٌ. — See also إِذْنٌ, in three places. — And see أَذَانٌ. — *I. q.* ▼ مُؤْذِنٌ [*Making to know* or *have knowledge,* بِأَمْرٍ *of a thing; informing, apprizing, advertising,* or *advising; giving information, intelligence, notice,* or *advice; making known, notifying,* or *announcing*]: like أَلِيمٌ and وَجِيعٌ as meaning مُؤْلِمٌ and مُوجِعٌ. (M.) — See also مُؤَذِّنٌ. — One who is *responsible, answerable, amenable,* or *a surety;* [بِأَمْرٍ *for a thing;* and perhaps also بِغَيْرِهِ *for another person;*] syn. كَفِيلٌ (Ṣ, M, Ḳ) and زَعِيمٌ [which signifies the same as كَفِيلٌ, and is plainly shown in the M to be here used as a syn. of this latter; but SM assigns to it here another meaning, namely رَئِيسٌ, in which sense I find no instance of the use of أَذِينٌ]; (AO, M;) and ▼ آذِنٌ also is syn. with أَذِينٌ in the sense of كَفِيلٌ. (Ḳ.) — Also *A place to which the* أَذَان [or *call to prayer*] *comes* [or *reaches*] *from* [or *on*] *every side.* (Ṣ, Ḳ.)

أُذَيْنَةٌ dim. of أُذُنٌ, q. v. (Ṣ.)

أُذَانِىٌّ (Ṣ, M, Mgh, Ḳ) and ▼ آذَنُ (M, Ḳ) *Large-eared;* (Ṣ, M, Mgh, Ḳ;) *long-eared;* (M;) applied to a man, (Ṣ, M, Ḳ,) and to a camel, and to a sheep or goat: (M:) [or] the latter epithet is applied to a ram; and its fem. أَذْنَآءُ to a ewe. (T, Ṣ, M.)

أُذُنِىٌّ One *who hears everything that is said:* but this is a vulgar word. (TA.) [See أُذُنٌ.]

آذَنُ: see أُذَانِىٌّ.

آذِنٌ [act. part. n. of 1. As such, *Permitting,* or *allowing;* one *who permits,* or *allows.* And hence,] *A doorkeeper,* or *chamberlain.* (Ṣ, Ḳ.) — See also أَذِينٌ.

مَأْذُونٌ: see مُؤْذَنٌ.

مُؤْذِنٌ: see أَذِينٌ. You say, سِيمَاهُ بِٱلْخَيْرِ مُؤْذِنَةٌ *His impress notifies* [or *is indicative of*] *goodness.* (TA.) — مُؤْذِنَاتٌ, signifying The *women who notify,* or *announce, the times of festivity and rejoicing,* [*particularly on the occasions of weddings,*] is a vulgar word. (TA.) — Herbage *beginning to dry up; part of it being still succulent, and part already dried up:* and a branch, or wood, *that has dried, but has in it some succulency.* (TA.)

مَأْذَنَةٌ : } see what next follows.
مُؤْذَنَةٌ :

مِئْذَنَةٌ (which may also be pronounced مِيذَنَةٌ, Mṣb) The *place* [generally *a turret of a mosque*] *upon which the time of prayer is notified, made known,* or *proclaimed*; (T, M,* Ḳ;*) *i. q.* مَنَارَةٌ [which has this meaning and others also]; (AZ, T, Ṣ, Mṣb;) as also ▼ مُؤْذَنَةٌ: (AZ, T:) or it signifies, (as in some copies of the Ḳ,) or signifies also, (as in other copies of the same,) *i. q.* مَنَارَةٌ: and صَوْمَعَةٌ: [see these two words:] (Ḳ:) or *i. q.* مَنَارَةٌ, meaning صَوْمَعَةٌ; (Lḥ, M, TA;) by way of comparison [to the turret first mentioned]: but as to ▼ مَأْذَنَةٌ, it is a vulgar word: (TA:) the pl. is مَآذِنُ, agreeably with the original form of the sing. (Mṣb.)

مُؤَذِّنٌ *One who notifies, makes known,* or *proclaims,* [by a chant,] *the time of prayer*; (M,* Mṣb, Ḳ;*) [i. e., *who chants the call to prayer*;] as also ▼ أَذِينٌ. (M, Ḳ.)

مَأْذُونٌ, as meaning A slave *permitted,* or *having leave given him, by his master, to traffic,* is used for مَأْذُونٌ لَهُ, (Mṣb, TA,) by the lawyers. (Mṣb.) —— Also *Having his ear hit,* or *hurt*; and so ▼ مُؤْذَنٌ. (TA.)

اذى

1. أَذِىَ, aor. ـَ, inf. n. أَذًى, (T, M, Mṣb, Ḳ,) in [some of] the copies of the Ḳ written أَذًا, and so by IB, (TA,) and أَذَاةٌ, (CḲ, [but not found by me in any MS. copy of the Ḳ nor in any other lexicon,]) and, accord. to IB, أَذَاةٌ and أَذِيَّةٌ, (TA,) or these two are simple substs.; (M, Ḳ;) and ▼ تَأَذَّى; (T, Ṣ, M, Mṣb, Ḳ;) [*He was,* or *became, annoyed, molested, harmed,* or *hurt*;] *he experienced,* or *suffered, slight evil,* [i. e., *annoyance, molestation, harm,* or *hurt,*] *less than what is termed* ضَرَر; (El-Khaṭṭábee;) or *he experienced,* or *suffered, what was disagreeable,* or *hateful,* or *evil,* (Mṣb, Ḳ,) *in a small degree*; (Ḳ;) بِهِ [*by him,* or *it*]; (T, Ṣ, M, Ḳ;) [and مِنْهُ *from him,* or *it*:] ▼ التَّأَذِّى signifies *the being affected by what is termed* الأَذَى [i. e. *what annoys, molests, harms,* or *hurts, one*]: and also *the showing the effect thereof*; which is forbidden by the saying of 'Omar, إِيَّاكَ وَالتَّأَذِّىَ ▼ بِالنَّاسِ [*Avoid thou,* or *beware thou of, showing the being annoyed, molested, harmed,* or *hurt, by men*]; for this is what is within one's power. (Mgh.) —— Also, aor. and inf. n. as above, *It* (a thing) *was unclean, dirty,* or *filthy.* (Mṣb.)

4. آذى signifies فَعَلَ الأَذَى [*He did what annoyed, molested, harmed,* or *hurt*]. (M, Ḳ.) —— And آذَاهُ, (T, Ṣ, M, Mṣb, Ḳ,) aor. يُؤْذِيهِ, (Ṣ,) inf. n. إِيذَآءٌ (T, IB, Mṣb) and [quasi-inf. n.] أَذِيَّةٌ, (T,) or أَذًى and أَذَاةٌ and أَذِيَّةٌ, (Ṣ, Ḳ,) but IB refuses his assent to this, saying that these three are inf. ns. of أَذِىَ, and MF says of إِيذَآءٌ, which is expressly disallowed by the author of the Ḳ, though he himself uses it, that others assert it to have been heard and transmitted, and to be required by rule, but he adds that he had searched for examples of it in the language of the Arabs, and investigated their prose and their poetry, without finding this word; (TA;) [*He,* or *it, annoyed him, molested him, harmed him,* or *hurt him*; or] *he did what was disagreeable,* or *hateful,* or *evil, to him.* (Bḍ in xxxiii. 53, Mṣb.) It is said in the Ḳur [xxxiii. 47], وَدَعْ أَذَاهُمْ, meaning *And leave thou the requiting of them* until thou receive a command respecting them; (M, Bḍ, Jel;) namely, the hypocrites: (M:) or *leave thou unregarded their doing to thee what is* [*annoying, molesting, harmful, hurtful,* or] *disagreeable,* &c., *to thee.* (Bḍ.)

5: see 1, in three places.

أَذًى inf. n. of 1. (T, M, Mṣb, Ḳ.) [As a simple subst., *A state of annoyance* or *molestation.*] —— And [*Annoyance, molestation, harm,* or *hurt*: quasi-] inf. n. of آذَاهُ. (Ṣ, Ḳ.) —— It signifies also, [like ▼ أَذِيَّةٌ and ▼ أَذَاةٌ,] كُلُّ مَا تَأَذَّيْتَ بِهِ [*Anything by which thou art annoyed, molested, harmed,* or *hurt*]; (T;) or مَا يُؤْذِيكَ [*a thing that annoys, molests, harms,* or *hurts thee*]: (Mgh:) or *a slight evil*; *less than what is termed* ضَرَر. (El-Khaṭṭábee.) You say, أَمَاطَ الأَذَى عَنِ الطَّرِيقِ *He removed,* or *put away,* or *put at a distance, what was hurtful from the road,* or *way.* (Mgh and TA in art. ميط.) —— Also *A thing held to be unclean, dirty,* or *filthy*: so in the Ḳur ii. 222. (Mgh, Mṣb.) [*Filth*; *impurity*: often used in this sense in books on practical law.]

أَذٍ *Experiencing,* or *suffering,* [*annoyance, molestation, harm, hurt,* or] *what is disagreeable,* or *hateful,* or *evil,* (M,* Ḳ,* Mṣb,) *in a great,* or *vehement, degree*; (M, Ḳ;) applied to a man; (M, Mṣb;) as also ▼ أَذِىٌّ: (M, Ḳ:) and both signify *the contr.*; i. e. *doing what is disagreeable,* or *hateful,* or *evil, in a great,* or *vehement, degree.* (Ḳ.) —— Also, applied to a camel, *That will not remain still in one place, by reason of a natural disposition, not from pain,* (El-Umawee, A'Obeyd, Ṣ, M, Ḳ,) *nor disease*; (Ḳ;) as also ▼ أَذِىٌّ: (M:) fem. of the former أَذِيَةٌ; (El-Umawee &c.;) and of the latter ▼ أَذِيَّةٌ. (TA.)

أَذًا: and إِذًا: see art. اذا.

أَذَاةٌ an inf. n. of 1. (IB.) —— And [quasi-] inf. n. of آذَاهُ. (Ṣ, Ḳ.) —— See also أَذًى and أَذِيَّةٌ.

أَذِىٌّ, and أَذِيَّةٌ as its fem.: see أَذٍ, in three places.

أَذِيَّةٌ an inf. n. of 1. (IB.) —— And [quasi-] inf. n. of آذَاهُ. (Ṣ, Ḳ.) —— And a subst. from آذَاهُ; (Mṣb;) or, as also ▼ أَذَاةٌ, a subst. from أَذِىَ and تَأَذَّى; (M, Ḳ;) signifying *A thing that is disagreeable,* or *hateful,* or *evil, in a small degree.* (Ḳ.) See also أَذًى.

آذِىٌّ, (Ṣ, M, Ḳ, &c.,) with medd and teshdeed, (TA, [in the CḲ, erroneously, أَذِىٌّ,]) *Waves* (Ṣ, M, Ḳ) *of the sea*: (Ṣ:) or *vehement waves*: (TA:) or the أَطْبَاق [app. meaning *rollers,* because they fall over like folds,] *which the wind raises from the surface of the water, less than* (دُونَ [but this sometimes signifies *above*]) *what are termed* مَوْج: (ISh, TA:) pl. أَوَاذِىُّ. (Ṣ.)

ار

1. أَرَّهَا, aor. يَؤُرُّ, (Ṣ,) inf. n. أَرٌّ, (Ṣ, Ḳ,) *Inivit eam*; *he compressed her.* (Ṣ, Ḳ.)

إِرْ إِرْ, (M, TT, L, [and so in the present day,]) or أَرْ أَرْ, (Ḳ,) *A cry by which sheep or goats are called.* (M, L, Ḳ.)

مِئَرٌّ A man (Ṣ,) *much addicted to venery*: (Ṣ, Ḳ:) so accord. to A'Obeyd, as related by Sh and El-Iyádee, but thought by Az to be مِئْيَرٌ, of the same measure as مِعْيَرٌ, i. e., مِفْعَلٌ, [originally مِأْيَرٌ,] from آرَهَا. (T.)

ارب

1. أَرُبَ, aor. ـُ, (T, Ṣ, M, Ḳ,) inf. n. أَرَابَةٌ (AZ, T, Ṣ, M, Ḳ) and إِرْبٌ, like صِغَرٌ, (Ṣ, Ḳ,) *He was,* or *became, cunning, characterized by intelligence with craft and forecast,* or simply *intelligent, excellent in judgment, sagacious,* (T, [in which it is said that Aṣ is related to have assigned this signification to أَرِبَ, aor. ـَ, inf. n. أَرَبٌ,] Ṣ, M, Ḳ,) *and knowing in affairs.* (M.) [The TA assigns the former inf. n. to it when it signifies simply intelligence, and the latter when it has the more comprehensive signification of cunning.] —— أَرِبَ بِالشَّىْءِ, [aor. ـَ,] *He became expert,* or *skilful, in the thing*: (M:) or *he became accustomed to,* or *practised* or *exercised in, the thing,* (Ṣ, Ḳ,*) *and became knowing,* or *skilful* [*therein*]. (Ṣ.) —— أَرِبَ, inf. n. أَرَبٌ, is also *syn. with* أَنِسَ [app. as meaning *He became familiar* with a person or thing]. (M.) —— And أَرِبَ بِالشَّىْءِ also signifies *He devoted,* or *addicted, himself,* or *clave,* or *kept, to the thing*: (T, Ḳ:) and *he was,* or *became, niggardly, avaricious,* or *tenacious, of the thing.* (T, M, TA.) —— And أَرِبَ فِى الأَمْرِ, and ▼ تَأَرَّبَ فِيهِ, *He exerted,* or *employed, his power and ability in the affair, and understood it*: (ISh, T:) or تَأَرَّبَ signifies *he exerted his strength, force,* or *energy*; or *strained himself*; (Aṣ, Ṣ, M;) فِى الشَّىْءِ [*in the thing*]; (Aṣ, Ṣ;) and فِى حَاجَتِهِ [*in his needful affair,* or *in the accomplishment of his want*]. (Aṣ, Ṣ, M.) —— أَرِبَ عَلَيْهِ *He had,* or *obtained, power over him,* or *it.* (M.) ═══ أَرِبَ, aor. ـَ, (T, Ṣ, Ḳ,) inf. n. أَرَبٌ, (T, Ṣ,) *He was,* or *became, in want,* or *need.* (T, Ṣ, Ḳ.) [See أَرِبْتَ عَنْ ذِى يَدَيْكَ, and two other phrases following it, in a later part of this paragraph.] —— أَرِبَ إِلَيْهِ, (M, Mṣb,) or بِهِ, (T,) aor. and inf. n. as above, *He wanted it*; *was,* or *became, in want,* or *need, of it*; (T, M, Mṣb;) and *sought it,* or *desired it*; (T;) namely, a thing. (T, Mṣb.) —— أَرِبَ الدَّهْرُ *Fortune was,* or *became, hard,* or *adverse*: (T, Ṣ, Ḳ:) as though it wanted something of us, for which it pressed hard. (M, TA.) And أَرِبَ عَلَيْهِ *He was,* or *became, hard upon him* in his demand. (TA, from a trad.) ═══ أَرَبَهُ, [from إِرْبٌ,] *He struck upon a member,* or *limb, belonging to him.* (Ḳ,*

TA.) —— أُرِبَ, (T, Ṣ, Ḳ, TA,) *His member,* or *limb,* (generally meaning the *arm,* or *hand,* M,) *was cut off:* (M, Ḳ:) or *dropped off:* (T:) and *his members,* or *limbs,* (generally relating to [the *members,* or *fingers, of*] *the arm,* or *hand,* TA,) *dropped off, one after another,* (Ṣ, Ḳ, TA,) *in consequence of his being affected by the disease termed* جُذَام: (TA:) and *it* (said of a member, or limb,) *dropped off.* (TA.) The phrase, أَرِبْتَ مِنْ ذِى يديك, (T, TA,) or عَنْ ذِى يَدَيْكَ, (Ṣ, TA, [and said in the latter to be likewise found in the T, but I have consulted two copies of the T and found only عن,]) or فِى ذى يديك, (IAạr, as related by Sh,) or مِنْ يَدَيْكَ, (Ḳ,) but MF says that من in this phrase is a mistranscription, (TA,) means, *May the members* [or *fingers*] *of thy hands,* or *arms, drop off:* (Ṣ, Ḳ, TA:) or it means, *may what is in thy hands depart from thee, so that thou shalt be in want:* occurring in a trad. (IAạr, T, TA.) And أَرِبَ مَا لَهُ, said by Moḥammad on the occasion of a man's coming to him and asking him to acquaint him with some work that should introduce him into Paradise, means, accord. to Ḳt, *May his members,* or *limbs, drop off,* or *be cut off: what aileth him?* (TA:) or, accord. to IAạr, *may he become in want: what aileth him?* (T, TA:) but IAth says that this has been related in three different ways: first, أَرِبَ, signifying an imprecation, [as rendered above,] and used as expressive of wonder: secondly, أَرَبٌ ▼ مَا لَهُ; i. e. حَاجَةٌ لَهُ; مَا being [syntactically] redundant, denoting littleness; the meaning being, *he has some little want:* or, as some say, *a want hath brought him: what aileth him?* thirdly, ▼ أَرِبٌ; i. e. هُوَ أَرِبٌ; meaning *he is intelligent,* or *sagacious,* or *skilful,* [as is said in the T,] *and perfect: what aileth him?* or *what is his affair?* the inchoative being suppressed. (TA.) مَا لَهُ أَرِبَتْ يَدُهُ, (M, Ḳ,*) another form of imprecation, (M,) means *What aileth him? may his arm,* or *hand, be cut off:* or, *may he become poor, and want what is in the hands of others.* (M, Ḳ.*) —— [Hence, perhaps,] أَرِبَتْ مَعِدَتُهُ *His stomach became vitiated, disordered,* or *in an unsound state.* (Ḳ.) —— أَرِبَ also signifies *He prostrated himself firmly,* or *fixedly, upon his* [*seven*] *members* [*mentioned in the explanations of the word* إِرْبٌ]. (T.)

2. أرّب, inf. n. تَأْرِيبٌ, *He,* or *it,* [*made,* or *rendered, cunning,* or *intelligent, excellent in judgment, sagacious, and knowing in affairs;* (see أَرُبَ;)] *made to have knowledge,* or *skill;* or *made to understand.* (M, TA.) ═ *He was,* or *became, avaricious;* [*in a state of vehement want* of a thing;] *eagerly desirous.* (A'Obeyd, TA.) [See also 1.] ═ *He cut up,* or *cut into pieces,* (T, A, Mgh,) a sheep, or goat, (A, Mgh,) *limb by limb.* (T, A, Mgh.) —— *He cut off* a member, or limb, *entire.* (M, TA.) —— *He made entire,* or *complete,* (T, Ṣ, M, Ḳ,) a thing, (Ṣ,) a lot, or portion, (T, TA,) or anything. (M.)

3. آرَبَهُ, (Ṣ, A,) inf. n. مُؤَارَبَةٌ, (M, A,) *He strove,* or *endeavoured, to outwit, deceive, beguile,* or *circumvent, him;* syn. دَاهَاهُ. (Ṣ, M,* A.*) It is said in a trad., (TA,) مُؤَارَبَةُ الأَرِيبِ جَهْلٌ وَعَنَآءٌ [*The striving to outwit the cunning,* or *intelligent,* or *sagacious, is ignorance, and labour* without profit]: (A, TA:) i. e., the intelligent is not to be outwitted. (TA.) And آرب به signifies *He practised an artifice, a stratagem,* or *a fraud, upon him.* (TA, from a trad.)

4. آرب عَلَيْهِمْ, (T, Ṣ, M, Ḳ,) of the measure أَفْعَلَ, (T,) inf. n. إِيرَابٌ [originally إِئْرَابٌ], (Ḳ,) *He was successful against them, and overcame them.* (T, Ṣ, M, Ḳ.)

5. تأرّب *He affected,* or *endeavoured to acquire,* (تَكَلَّفَ,) *cunning,* or *intelligence, and excellence of judgment,* (Ḳ, TA,) *and deceit, guile,* or *artifice, and wickedness, mischievousness,* or *malignity.* (TA.) [See إِرْبٌ.] —— تَأَرَّبَ فِى الأَمْرِ: see 1.

أَرْبٌ: see what next follows, in two places.

إِرْبٌ *Cunning, intelligence with craft and forecast,* or simply *intelligence, excellence of judgment, sagacity,* (T, Ṣ, M, L, Ḳ,) *and knowledge in affairs;* (M, L;) as also ▼ إِرْبَةٌ and ▼ أُرْبَةٌ (M, Ḳ) and ▼ أَرَبٌ, (M, A,) or ▼ أَرْبٌ. (L.) You say, هُوَ ذُو إِرْبٍ [*He is a possessor of cunning,* or *intelligence,* &c.]. (Ṣ.) —— *Intelligence and religion.* (Th, M, Ḳ.) —— *Deceit, guile, artifice,* or *fraud;* syn. مَكْرٌ: so in the L and other lexicons: in the Ḳ, نُكْرٌ [i. e. "cunning," &c., as above]: (TA:) and so ▼ إِرْبَةٌ; syn. حِيلَةٌ. (Ḳ.) —— *Wickedness, mischievousness,* or *malignity; hidden rancour, malevolence,* or *malice.* (Ḳ, TA.) [In a trad. it occurs in this sense written, in the TA, ▼ أَرَب.] ═ See also أَرَبٌ, in four places. ═ Also *A member; a distinct and complete part of an animal body; a limb;* (T, Ṣ, M, Mgh, Mṣb, Ḳ;) or *such as is made complete,* or *entire, not wanting anything:* (M:) pl. آرَابٌ (Ṣ, M, Mgh, Mṣb) and أَرْآبٌ; (Ṣ, Mgh;) the latter formed by transposition. (Mgh.) You say, قَطَّعْتُهُ إِرْبًا إِرْبًا *I cut him up, member by member,* or *limb by limb.* (TA.) And السُّجُودُ عَلَى سَبْعَةِ آرَابٍ or أَرْآبٍ *Prostration* [in prayer] *is* [performed] *on seven members;* (Ṣ, Mgh;) namely, the forehead, the hands, the knees, and the feet. (TA.) —— Also The *membrum genitale;* the *pudendum;* syn. فَرْجٌ: (M, Ḳ:) but some say that this signification is not known: [see أَرَبٌ:] in some copies of the Ḳ, the explanation is written فَرْخ, with the unpointed ح. (TA.) —— آرَابٌ [the pl.] also signifies *Pieces of flesh,* or *of flesh-meat.* (M.)

أَرَبٌ: see إِرْبٌ. ═ *Want,* or *need;* (T, Ṣ, M, Mgh, Mṣb, Ḳ;) as also ▼ إِرْبٌ and ▼ إِرْبَةٌ (the same, and A) and ▼ أُرْبَةٌ (Ḳ) and ▼ مَأْرَبَةٌ and ▼ مَأْرُبَةٌ (T, Ṣ, M, A, Mṣb, Ḳ) and ▼ مَأْرِبَةٌ (Ḳ) and ▼ مَأْرَبٌ: (M, A:) the pl. [of أَرَبٌ or إِرْبٌ] is آرَابٌ, and [of إِرْبَةٌ, and perhaps of the other sings. commencing with ا,] إِرَبٌ; (M;) and the pl. of مأربة is مَآرِبُ. (T, Mṣb.) It is said in a trad., respecting Moḥammad, كَانَ أَمْلَكَكُمْ لارِبه *He had the most power, of you, over his want, and desire:* (M,* Mgh,* Mṣb,* TA:) IAth says that the most common reading is لِأَرَبِهِ, meaning لِحَاجَتِهِ: but some read ▼ لِإِرْبِهِ, [as in the M and Mgh,] i. e., either the same as above, [and so in the Mgh,] or لِعُضْوِهِ, by which is specially meant the membrum genitale: (TA:) but this is not known. (M.) Respecting the phrase أَرَبٌ مَّا لَهُ, see 1. You say also, مَا إِرْبُكَ ▼ إِلَى هٰذَا *What is* [the reason of] *thy want of this?* (A.) And مَا لِى فِيهِ إِرْبٌ ▼ *I have no want of it.* (A.) By غَيْرِ أُولِى الإِرْبَةِ ▼, in the Ḳur [xxiv. 31], are meant *Idiots;* or *persons deficient in intellect:* [from إِرْبَةٌ as meaning "intelligence:"] (Sa'eed Ibn-Jubeyr, Ṣ:) or *not such as have need of women.* (Jel.) مَأْرُبَةٌ ▼ لَا حَفَاوَةٌ, (Ṣ, A,) or مَأْرَبٌ ▼ لَا حَفَاوَةٌ, (M,) is a proverb, (Ṣ, A,) meaning He only honours thee *for the sake of something which he wants* of thee; *not for love* of thee: (A, Meyd:) or only thy *want* brought thee; *not* the object of *paying extraordinary honour* to me. (M.) [See also Freytag's Arab. Prov., ii. 690.] You say also, الْحَقْ بِمَأْرَبِكَ ▼ مِنَ الأَرْضِ, meaning, *Go thou whither thou wilt* [*so as to attain thy want*]. (A.)

أَرِبٌ: see أَرِيبٌ. —— Also [*Expert; skilful:* (see أَرُبَ, of which it is the part. n.:) or] *accustomed to,* or *practised* or *exercised in, a thing, and knowing,* or *skilful.* (Ṣ, TA.) See also 1, in the latter part of the paragraph. ═ أَرِبٌ بِشَىْءٍ [or إِلَى شَىْءٍ; (see أَرِبَ,)] or ▼ آرِبٌ, of the measure فَاعِلٌ, (Mṣb,) *Wanting, needing,* or *desiring, a thing.* (Mṣb,* TA in art. مهر, &c.)

أُرْبَةٌ: see إِرْبٌ: ═ and أَرَبٌ.

إِرْبَةٌ: see إِرْبٌ, in two places: ═ and أَرَبٌ, in two places.

أُرَبَى *Calamity; misfortune:* (T, Ṣ, M, A, Ḳ:) [said to be] the only word of this measure except شُعَبَى and أُرَمَى [names of two places]. (TA.)

أُرْبَانٌ (M, Ḳ):
أُرْبُونٌ (TA):
أَرَبُونٌ (TA):
dial. vars. of عُرْبَانٌ and عُرْبُونٌ and عَرَبُونٌ. (M,* Ḳ,* TA.)

أَرِيبٌ *Cunning, characterized by intelligence with craft and forecast,* or simply *intelligent* [as in the Ṣ], *excellent in judgment, sagacious,* (T, Ṣ,* M, Ḳ,) *and knowing in affairs;* (M;) as also ▼ أَرِبٌ: (Ḳ:) pl. of the former أُرَبَآءُ. (T, M.) ═ قِدْرٌ أَرِيبَةٌ *A wide, an ample,* or *a capacious, cooking-pot.* (Ḳ.)

آرَبُ *More,* or *most, cunning,* or *intelligent, excellent in judgment,* or *sagacious.* (A.) [See أَرِيبٌ.]

أَرِبٌ: see آرِبٌ.

مَأْرَبٌ: see أَرَبٌ, in three places.

مَأْرَبَةٌ and مَأْرُبَةٌ and مَأْرِبَةٌ: see أَرَبٌ, in four places.

مُؤَرَّبٌ A member, or limb, *cut off entire:* (T:)

or an *entire, unbroken*, member, or limb: (Ṣ:) and anything *made entire, complete,* or *perfect.* (Ṣ, Ḳ.) You say, كَتِفٌ مُؤَرَّبَةٌ *A shoulder cut off entire,* (Mgh, TA,) *having none of its flesh taken from it,* (Mgh,) *without any deficiency.* (TA.)

ارث

1. أَرَثَ: see 2.

2. أَرَّثَ, (M, A,) inf. n. تَأْرِيثٌ, (T, Ṣ, Ḳ,) *He kindled,* or *lighted,* a fire; or *made it to burn, burn up, burn brightly* or *fiercely, blaze,* or *flame;* (T, Ṣ, M, A, Ḳ;) as also ▼ أَرَثَ, aor. ِ, (T, Ḳ,) inf. n. أَرْثٌ; (Ḳ; in a copy of the A إِرْثٌ;) but this [says SM] no leading lexicographer has mentioned, nor have I found any example of it. (TA.) [See also وَرَثَ.] — [Hence,] تَأْرِيثٌ also signifies ‡ *The exciting discord, dissension, disorder, strife, quarrelling,* or *animosity, between a people.* (Ṣ, Ḳ.) You say, أَرَّثَ بَيْنَ القَوْمِ, (M, A,) and أَرَّثَ بَيْنَهُمُ الشَّرَّ وَالحَرْبَ, (T, TA,) ‡ *He excited discord, dissension, disorder, strife, quarrelling,* or *animosity, between,* or *among, the people,* or *company of men;* (T, M, A;) *kindled the fire of discord, dissension, &c.,* [or *evil,* and *war,*] *between them,* or *among them.* (T,* TA.)

5. تَأَرَّثَتِ النَّارُ *The fire became kindled,* or *lighted;* or *it burned, burned up, burned brightly* or *fiercely, blazed,* or *flamed.* (Ṣ, M, Ḳ.)

إِرْثٌ, originally وِرْثٌ, (T, Ṣ,) *Inheritance;* or a person's *obtaining possession of property left* to him *by one who has died.* (MF.) — *An inheritance,* or *a heritage; what is inherited.* (Ṣ, A, Ḳ.) — *An old condition, case,* or *state of things, which the last has inherited from the first.* (Ṣ, A, Ḳ.) So in the phrase, هُوَ عَلَى إِرْثٍ مِنْ كَذَا [*He is conforming, in respect of such a thing, with an old state of things,* or *an old usage, which he has inherited from his ancestors*]. (Ṣ.) And in the following ex., from a trad., إِنَّكُمْ عَلَى إِرْثٍ مِنْ إِرْثِ أَبِيكُمْ إِبْرَاهِيمَ [*Verily ye are conforming with an old state of things,* or *an old usage, which ye have inherited from your father Abraham*], the meaning is, that his religion was their heritage. (T,* TA.) [See also وِرْثٌ.] — *A remainder,* or *what remains,* (M, L, Ḳ,) of a thing, (Ḳ,) or *of the original* of a thing: (M, L:) pl. إِرَاثٌ. (L.) — And [hence, app.,] *Ashes.* (M, Ḳ.) — Also *Origin, race,* or *stock.* (Ṣ, M, A, Ḳ.) You say, هُوَ فِي إِرْثِ صِدْقٍ *He is of an excellent origin, race,* or *stock.* (Ṣ.) And إِنَّهُ لَفِي إِرْثِ مَجْدٍ [*Verily he is of a glorious origin, race,* or *stock*]; as also إِرْفِ مَجْدٍ, by a change of letters. (Yaạkoob, M.) Accord. to IAạr, إِرْثٌ relates to حَسَبٌ [or grounds of pretension to respect or honour, on account of one's ancestors' or one's own deeds or qualities, &c.]; and وِرْثٌ, to property, or wealth. (M.) [See art. ورث.]

أُرْثَةٌ: see إِرَاثٌ, in three places.

إِرَاثٌ *Fire;* (T, M, L, Ḳ;) as also ▼ إِرَاثَةٌ and ▼ أَرِيثٌ: (TA:) or (so accord. to the M and L, but in the Ḳ "and") *tinder,* and *the like, prepared for fire;* (M, L, Ḳ;) [as also ▼ إِرَاثَةٌ and ▼ أُرْثَةٌ; or these two words signify *a means of kindling* or *inflaming;* as will be seen from what follows:] or *a lump of the dung of a horse or the like,* or *a similar thing, with which one kindles a fire;* as also ▼ أُرْثَةٌ: (A:) or this last signifies *dung of camels or horses or the like,* (Ṣ, Ḳ,) or *wood,* or *a stick,* (T,) *that is prepared,* or *put in readiness, by the ashes,* (Ṣ, Ḳ,) or *buried in them,* (T,) *for the time when it may be wanted* (T, Ṣ, Ḳ) *for fuel.* (T.) It is said in a prov., mentioned in the collection of Meyd, النَّمِيمَةُ ▼ إِرَاثَةُ العَدَاوَةِ [*Calumny,* or *slander, is a means of kindling,* or *inflaming, enmity*]. (TA: but in Freytag's Arab. Prov., ii. 773, in the place of اراثة, we find ▼ أُرْثَة.)

أَرِيثٌ: see the paragraph next preceding.

إِرَاثَةٌ: see إِرَاثٌ, in three places.

ارج

1. أَرِجَ, aor. َ, inf. n. أَرَجٌ (Ṣ, A, Mṣb, Ḳ) and أَرِيجٌ (Ṣ, A, Ḳ) and أَرِيجَةٌ, (Ḳ, [in which it is only mentioned as syn. with the first and second of these ns., so that it may be a simple subst.,]) *It* (perfume) *diffused,* or *exhaled, its odour;* (Ṣ, A;) as also ▼ تَأَرَّجَ: (A:) *it had a hot,* or *strong, odour;* syn. تَوَهَّجَ رِيحُهُ. (Ṣ, A, Ḳ.) — *It* (a place) *was,* or *became, strongly fragrant.* (Mṣb.) — أَرَجَ: see 2, in three places.

2. أَرَّجَ, [and app. ▼ أَرَجَ also,] *He perfumed* a thing; *made it fragrant.* (Ḥam p. 135.) — [Both also app. signify *He made* perfume *to diffuse,* or *exhale, its odour:* or *made it to have a hot,* or *strong, odour.* — And hence,] أَرَّجَ, inf. n. تَأْرِيجٌ; (Ṣ, Ḳ;) and ▼ أَرَجَ, (TA,) aor. ُ, (TḲ,) inf. n. أَرْجٌ; (Ḳ, TA;) † *He excited discord, dissension, disorder, strife, quarrelling,* or *animosity,* (Ṣ, Ḳ, TA,) بَيْنَ القَوْمِ *between,* or *among, the people,* or *company of men,* like أَرَّشَ, (Ṣ, TA,) and فِى الحَرْبِ *in war.* (TA.) And أَرَّجَ الحَرْبَ, (Ṣ, Ḳ, TA, and Ḥam ubi suprà,) and ▼ أَرَجَهَا, (TA,) † *He kindled war,* or *the war;* (Ṣ, TA, and Ḥam ubi suprà;) and in like manner, النَّارَ *the fire.* (IAạr, Ḥam.)

5: see 1.

أَرَجٌ (L) and ▼ أَرِيجٌ and ▼ أَرِيجَةٌ (ISd, TA) *A sweet odour:* (ISd, L, TA:) pl. of the last, أَرَائِجُ. (ISd, TA.) [See also 1.]

أَرِجٌ Perfume *diffusing,* or *exhaling, its odour: having a hot,* or *strong, odour.* (TA.) — Applied also to a place: you say, مَكَانٌ أَرِجٌ *A strongly fragrant place:* (Mṣb:) and بَيْتٌ أَرِجٌ بِالطِّيبِ [*a house,* or *chamber, fragrant,* or *strongly fragrant, with perfume*]. (A.)

أَرِيجٌ : } see أَرَجٌ.
أَرِيجَةٌ : }

أَرَّاجٌ (Ḳ) and ▼ مِئْرَجٌ (TA) † *A liar:* and one *who excites discord, dissension, disorder, strife, quarrelling,* or *animosity, among people.* (Ḳ,* TA.)

مِئْرَجٌ: see what next precedes.

المُؤَرِّجُ † *The lion.* (Ḳ.)

ارخ

1. أَرَخَ الكِتَابَ: see 2.

2. أَرَّخَ الكِتَابَ, (Ṣ, Mgh, Mṣb, Ḳ,) inf. n. تَأْرِيخٌ; (Ṣ, Mgh;) and ▼ أَرَخَهُ, (IḲṭṭ, Mṣb, Ḳ,) inf. n. أَرْخٌ; (TA;) but the former is the more common, (Mṣb,) and the latter is by some rejected, though correct accord. to IḲṭṭ and others; (MF;) and ▼ آرَخَهُ, (Ḳ,) inf. n. مُؤَارَخَةٌ; (TA;) as also وَرَّخَهُ, inf. n. تَوْرِيخٌ; (Ṣ, Mgh,* Mṣb;) in which the و is a substitute for the ء; (Yaạkoob, Mṣb;) a form seldom used; (Mṣb;) *He dated the writing,* or *letter; inscribed it with a date,* or *note of the time when it was written.* (Ṣ, Mgh, Mṣb, Ḳ.) You say also, أَرَّخَ الكِتَابَ بِيَوْمِ كَذَا *He inscribed the writing,* or *letter, with the date of such a day.* (Ṣ, L.) And أَرَّخَ البَيِّنَةَ *He dated,* or *mentioned the date of, the evidence, proof,* or *voucher:* in the contr. case saying, أَطْلَقَ. (Mṣb.) Some say that تَأْرِيخٌ is an arabicized word, (L, Mṣb,) borrowed by the Muslims from the people of the Bible: [i. e., from the Jews or Christians; app. from the Hebr. יָרֵחַ the "moon," or יֶרַח "a month;" or from the Chald. יְרַח "a month;" as observed by Golius:] (L:) others say that it is [pure] Arabic: (Mṣb, TA:) some, that it is formed by transposition from تَأْخِيرٌ. (TA.)

3: see 2.

أَرْخَةٌ: see what next follows.

تَأْرِيخٌ inf. n. of 2. — Also, [as a subst., generally pronounced without ء,] *A date; an era; an epoch;* (Mṣb;) and ▼ أَرْخَةٌ is a subst. [signifying the same,] from أَرَخَ. (Ḳ.) تَأْرِيخُ الهِجْرَةِ is *The era,* or *epoch, of the Emigration* [or *Flight* (for such it really was)] of Mohammad [from Mekkeh to El-Medeeneh], (L, Mṣb,) which his companions, in the time of 'Omar, agreed to make their era, commencing the year from the first appearance of the new moon of [the month] El-Moharram, [two months before the Flight itself,] and making the day to commence from sunset: (Mṣb:) it is also called تَأْرِيخُ المُسْلِمِينَ *the era,* or *epoch, of the Muslims.* (L.) — Also The *utmost limit, term,* or *time,* of anything: whence the saying, فُلَانٌ تَأْرِيخُ قَوْمِهِ *Such a one is the person from whom date the nobility,* or *eminence, and dominion,* or *authority, of his people.* (Eṣ-Ṣoolee, Mgh, TA.) — [Also, *A chronicle; a book of annals; a history:* pl. تَوَارِيخُ, from تَوْرِيخٌ.]

[مُؤَرِّخٌ *A chronicler; a writer of annals; a historian.*]

ارز

أَرْزٌ and ▾أُرُزٌ The *pine-tree*; syn. شَجَرُ الصَّنَوْبَرِ: (Ḳ:) or this is called ▾أَرْزَةٌ, and أَرْزٌ is the pl.: (A'Obeyd, Ṣ:) [or rather أَرْزٌ is a coll. gen. n., and أَرْزَةٌ is the n. un.:] or the *male of that kind of tree*; (AḤn, Ḳ;) as also ▾أَرْزَةٌ; (Ḳ;) and the author of the Minháj adds, it is *that which does not produce fruit; but pitch* (زِفْت) *is extracted from its trunks and roots, and its wood is employed as a means of light, like as candles are employed; and it grows not in the land of the Arabs:* A'Obeyd says, ▾أَرْزَةٌ is the *name of a tree well known in Syria, called with us* صَنَوْبَر, *because of its fruit:* he says also, I have seen this kind of tree, called أَرْزَة, and it is called in El-'Irák صَنَوْبَر, but this last is the name of the fruit of the أَرْز: (TA:) or *i. q.* عَرْعَر [a name given to the *cypress* and to the *juniper-tree*]. (Ḳ.) It is said in a trad., مَثَلُ الكَافِرِ مَثَلُ الأَرْزَةِ ▾ المُجْذِيَةِ عَلَى الأَرْضِ حَتَّى يَكُونَ انْجِعَافُهَا بِمَرَّةٍ وَاحِدَةٍ [*The similitude of the unbeliever is the similitude of the pine-tree standing firmly upon the ground until it is pulled up at once*]: respecting which AA and AO say that it is ▾الأَرَزَة, with fet-ḥ to the ر; meaning the tree called الأَرْزَن: but A'Obeyd thinks this to be a mistake, and that it is ▾الأَرْزَة, with the ر quiescent. (L.)

أُرُزٌ: see أَرْزٌ: ═ and see also أُرْزٌ.

أَرُزٌ: } see أُرُزٌ.
أُرْزٌ: }

أَرْزَةٌ: see أَرْزٌ, in five places.

أَرَزَةٌ The *tree called* أَرْزَن [which is *a hard kind, from which staves are made*]: (AA, Ṣ, Ḳ:) some say that it is ▾آرِزَةٌ, of the measure فَاعِلَةٌ; but A'Obeyd disapproves of this. (TA.) See also أَرْزٌ.

أَرُزٌّ and ▾أُرُزٌّ and ▾أُرُزٌ and ▾أُرْزٌ (Ṣ, Mṣb, Ḳ) and ▾آرُزٌ and ▾أَرُزٌ (Kr, Ḳ) and رُزٌّ (Ṣ, Mṣb, Ḳ) and رُنْزٌ, (Ṣ, Ḳ,) the first of which is the form commonly obtaining among persons of distinction; the last but one, that commonly obtaining among the vulgar; (TA;) and the last, of the dial. of 'Abd-El-Ḳeys; (Ṣ, TA;) [*Rice;*] *a certain grain*, (Ṣ, Ḳ,) *well known:* (Ḳ:) [said in the TA to be a species of بُرّ; but this is an improper explanation:] *there are several kinds; Egyptian and Persian and Indian; and the best kind is the* جوهرى [perhaps a mistake for مِصْرِىّ, or Egyptian]: *it is cold and dry in the second degree*; or, as some say, *moderate*; or, as some say, *hot in the first degree; and its husk is poisonous.* (El-Minháj, TA.)

آرُزٌ: } see أُرُزٌ.
أَرُزٌّ: }

آرِزَةٌ: see أَرَزَةٌ.

ارش

1. أَرَشَهُ, (TA,) aor. ِ, (TḲ,) inf. n. أَرْشٌ, (Ḳ, TA,) *He scratched with the nails*, or *lacerated, him*, [a man,] or *it*, [the skin, or (as in the TḲ) the face,] *little* or *much, so as to bring blood* or *not*; syn. خَدَشَهُ. (Ḳ,* TA.) [This signification is probably derived from أَرْش as syn. with تَأْرِيش, in which sense it seems to be the inf. n. of an obsolete verb.] ═ أَرَشَهُ, (TA,) inf. n. as above, (Ḳ, TA,) *He gave him* (Ḳ,* TA) *the fine*, or *mulct, for a wound.* (TA.) — أَرَشُوهُ, inf. n. as above, *They sold the milk of their camels for the water of his well.* (Ṣgh.) ═ أُرِشَ, like عُنِىَ, (Ṣgh,) inf. n. as above, (Ṣgh, Ḳ,) *He sought to obtain*, or *demanded, the fine*, or *mulct, for a wound.* Ṣgh, Ḳ.*)

2. أَرَّشَ بَيْنَ القَوْمِ, (Ṣ, L, Mṣb,) and بَيْنَ الرَّجُلَيْنِ, (TA,) inf. n. تَأْرِيشٌ, (Ṣ, Mṣb,) *He made mischief; or excited disorder, disturbance, disagreement, discord, dissension, strife,* or *quarrelling;* (Ṣ, L, Mṣb, TA;) *between*, or *among, the people*, or *company of men*, (Ṣ, L, Mṣb,) and *between the two men:* (TA:) accord. to some, its original is حَرَّشَ. (Mṣb.) — And أَرَّشَ النَّارَ, inf. n. as above, *He kindled the fire;* or *made it to burn:* (Ṣ, Ḳ:) and in like manner, الحَرْبَ † *war*, or *the war.* (Ṣ.)

8. ٱئْتَرِشْ مِنْهُ خُمَاشَتَكَ [written with the disjunctive alif إِيتَرِشْ] *Take thou from him the fine*, or *mulct, for thy* خُمَاشَة, q. v. (Ḳ.) — ٱئْتَرَشَ لِلْخُمَاشَةِ [*He surrendered himself to pay the fine*, or *mulct, for the injury termed* خُمَاشَة,] is like ٱسْتَسْلَمَ لِلْقِصَاصِ. (Ḳ.)

أَرْشٌ *The making mischief; or exciting disorder, disturbance, disagreement, discord, dissension, strife,* or *quarrelling;* [like تَأْرِيش; see 2, and see also 1;] syn. فَسَادٌ [in the sense of إِفْسَادٌ]; (Mṣb;) and إِغْرَآءٌ. (Ḳ.) — *Disagreement, discord,* or *dissension; and contention,* or *altercation:* you say, بَيْنَهُمَا أَرْشٌ *Between them two is disagreement*, &c. (Ḳ.) ═ *A fine*, or *mulct, for a wound:* (Ṣ, Mgh, Mṣb, Ḳ:) from the first of the significations in this paragraph; (Mṣb;) or from its being one of the causes of contention, or altercation; or, accord. to AM, from the same word as inf. n. of أَرَشَ in the first of the senses explained in this art.; accord. to IF, originally هَرْشٌ: (TA:) pl. أُرُوشٌ. (Mgh, Mṣb.) Hence the saying mentioned by IAạr, انْتَظِرْنِى حَتَّى تَعْقِلَ فَلَيْسَ لَكَ عِنْدَنَا أَرْشٌ إِلَّا الأَسِنَّةُ [*Wait thou for me until thou accept a fine for a wound in lieu of retaliation; for thou hast no compensation for a wound to receive from us except the spear-heads*]: meaning, thou shalt not slay a man for whom we will ever give bloodwit. (L, TA.) — *What is diminished* [*of the price*] *by reason of a defect in a garment or piece of cloth:* as being a cause of contention, or altercation. (Ḳ,* TA.) — *What is payed* [*by way of adjustment of the difference*] *between freedom from defect and defect in an article of merchandise:* (Ḳt, Ḳ:) for when the purchaser of a garment or piece of cloth as being free from defect discovers in it a hole or other defect, contention ensues between him and the seller. (TA.) — *A bribe.* (Aboo-Nahshal, Sh, Ḳ.)

مَأْرُوشٌ *Scratched with the nails*, or *lacerated, little* or *much, so as to bleed* or *not.* Ru-beh says,

* فَقُلْ لِذَاكَ المُزْعِجِ المَحْنُوشِ *
* أَصْبِحْ فَمَا مِنْ بَشَرٍ مَأْرُوشِ *

Then say thou to that man who is *disquieted* by envy, and as though he were *stung, Act thou gently*, for [*there is no scarf-skin scratched*; meaning,] my honour is uninjured, having in it no defect nor scratch. (L,* TA.)

ارض

1. أَرُضَتِ الأَرْضُ, (Ṣ, Ḳ, [in two copies of the Ṣ أَرِضَت, but this is evidently a mistake,]) with ḍamm, (Ṣ,) like كَرُمَتْ, (Ḳ,) inf. n. أَرَاضَةٌ, (Ṣ, M, Ḳ,) *The land became thriving*, or *productive;* (Ṣ, Ḳ;) as also ▾اسْتَأْرَضَت; (TA;) *it became pleasing to the eye, and disposed by nature to yield good produce;* (Ḳ, TA;) *it became fruitful, and in good condition;* (M;) *it collected moisture, and became luxuriant with herbage; it became soft to tread upon, pleasant to sit upon, productive, and good in its herbage* or *vegetation:* (AḤn:) and أَرِضَتِ الأَرْضُ, (Ḳ,) aor. ِ, (TA,) *the land became abundant in herbage*, or *pasture.* (Ḳ.) — أَرُضَ, inf. n. أَرَاضَةٌ, is also said of a man, meaning † *He was*, or *became, lowly*, or *submissive, and naturally disposed to good*, or *to do good.* (L, TA,) ═ أَرَضَ الأَرْضَ *He found the land to be abundant in herbage*, or *pasture.* (Ḳ.) ═ أُرِضَتِ الخَشَبَةُ, (Ṣ, A, Mṣb, TA,) in the pass. form, (Mṣb,) like عُنِىَ, (TA,) aor. تُؤْرَضُ, (Ṣ, TA,) inf. n. أَرْضٌ, (Ṣ, A, TA,) with sukoon [to the ر]; (Ṣ, TA;) and some add أَرِضَت, aor. تَأْرَضُ, inf. n. as above; (TA; [and so in a copy of the Ṣ in the place of what here precedes;]) *The piece of wood was*, or *became, eaten by the* أَرَضَة, q. v. (Ṣ, A, Mṣb, TA.) ═ أَرِضَتِ القُرْحَةُ, (Ṣ, M, Ḳ,) aor. ِ, (Ṣ, Ḳ,) inf. n. أَرَضٌ, (Ṣ, M,) *The ulcer*, or *sore, became blistered*, (Ṣ, M, Ḳ,) *and wide*, (M,) *and corrupt* (Ṣ, M, Ḳ) *by reason of thick purulent matter*, (Ṣ,) *and dissundered;* (M;) so says Aṣ; (TA;) as also ▾اسْتَأْرَضَت. (Ṣgh, Ḳ.) ═ أُرِضَ, like عُنِىَ, (Ḳ,) inf. n. أَرْضٌ; (TA;) or أَرِضَ, like سَمِعَ, aor. ِ, inf. n. أَرَضٌ; (L;) *He was*, or *became, affected with* زُكَام [or *rheum*]. (L, Ḳ.)

2. أَرَّضَ, (TḲ,) inf. n. تَأْرِيضٌ, (Ḳ,) *He depastured the herbage of the earth*, or *land:* and *he sought after it:* (Ḳ:) or, accord. to some, تَأْرِيض denotes this latter signification with respect to a place of alighting, or abiding: (TA:) and you say [also], تَأَرَّضَ ▾ المَنْزِلَ *he sought after, and chose, the place for alighting*, or *abiding:* (M, TA:) and تَرَكْتُ الحَىَّ يَتَأَرَّضُونَ ▾ لِلْمَنْزِلِ *I left the tribe seeking after a tract of country in which to alight*, or *abide.* (TA.) ═ *He*, or *it, rendered heavy;* [app. meaning *slow*, or *sluggish*; see 5;] syn. ثَقَّلَ. (Ibn-'Abbád, Ḳ.) — *He made to tarry; to tarry and wait,* or *expect;* or *to be patient, and tarry, and wait,* or *expect.* (Ibn-'Abbád, Ḳ.)

4. آرض, inf. n. إِيرَاضٌ: see 5. ═ مَا آرَضَ هٰذَا المَكَانَ *How abundant is the herbage* (عُشْب) *of this place!* or, as some say, مَا آرَضَ هٰذِهِ الأَرْضَ *How level, or soft, and productive, and good, is this land!* (Lh, AHn.) ═ آرَضَهُ, (Ṣ, Ḳ, [in the CḲ, incorrectly, أَرَضَهُ,]) inf. n. as above, (Ṣ,) *He* (God) *caused him to be affected with* زُكَام [or *rheum*]. (Ṣ, Ḳ.)

5. تَأَرَّضَ *It* (herbage) *became in such a state that it might be cut.* (Ṣ, Ḳ.) ═ *He clave,* or *kept, to the ground, not quitting it:* (A:) and ▼ آرض, inf. n. إِيرَاضٌ, *he remained upon the ground:* and تأرّض بِالمَكَانِ *he remained fixed in the place, not quitting it:* or *he waited,* or *expected, and stood upon the ground:* and, as also ▼ استأرض بالمكان, *he remained, and tarried,* or *tarried in expectation, in the place:* or *he remained fixed therein:* (TA:) and تأرّض alone, *he tarried, loitered, stayed, waited,* or *paused in expectation:* (Ṣ, TA:) and *he was,* or *became, heavy, slow,* or *sluggish, inclining,* or *propending, to the ground;* (Ṣ, Ḳ;) [as also ▼ استأرض, accord. to IB's explanation of its act. part. n.] You say, فُلَانٌ إِنْ رَأَى مَطْعَمًا تَأَرَّضَ وَإِنْ أَصَابَ مَطْعَمًا أَعْرَضَ [*Such a one, if he see food, cleaves,* or *keeps, to the ground, not quitting it; and if he obtain food, turns away:* or تأرّض may here be rendered agreeably with the explanation next following]. (A, TA.) — جَآءَ فُلَانٌ يَتَأَرَّضُ لِى (Ṣ, Ḳ,* TA) *Such a one came asking,* or *petitioning, for a thing that he wanted, to me;* syn. يَتَصَدَّى, and يَتَعَرَّضُ; (Ṣ, Ḳ, TA;) and تَضَرَّعَ is also a syn. of تأرّض, used in this manner. (TA.) ═ See also 2, in two places.

10: see 5, in two places. — استأرض السَّحَابُ *The clouds expanded,* or *spread:* or, as some say, *became fixed,* or *stationary.* (M, TA.) ═ See also 1, first signification: ═ and see 1 again, last signification but one.

الأَرْضُ [*The earth;*] *that whereon are mankind:* (TA:) [and *earth, as opposed to heaven:* and *the ground,* as meaning *the surface of the earth, on which we tread and sit and lie;* and *the floor:* without ال signifying *a land,* or *country:* and *a piece of land* or *ground:* and *land,* or *soil,* or *ground, considered in relation to its quality:*] it is fem.: (Ṣ, A, Mṣb, Ḳ:) and is a coll. gen. n.; (Ṣ, A, Ḳ;) of which the n. un. should be أَرْضَةٌ, but this they did not say: (Ṣ:) or a pl. having no sing.; (A, Ḳ;) for أَرْضَةٌ has not been heard: (Ḳ:) its pl. is أَرَضَاتٌ, (Ṣ, Ḳ,) in [some of] the copies of the Ḳ أَرْضَاتٌ, (TA,) for they sometimes form the pl. of a word which has not the fem. ة with ا and ت, as in the instance of عُرُسَاتٌ; (Ṣ;) and أَرَضُونَ, [which is more common,] (AZ, AHn, Ṣ, Mgh, Mṣb, Ḳ,) with fet-ḥ to the ر, (AZ, AHn, Mgh, Mṣb,) and with و and ن, though a fem. has not its pl. formed [regularly] with و and ن unless it is of the defective kind, like ثُبَةٌ and ظُبَةٌ, but they have made the و and ن [in this instance] a substitute for the ا and ت which they have elided [from أَرَضَاتٌ], and have left the fet-ḥah of the ر as it was; (Ṣ;) but they also said أَرْضُونَ, (AZ, AHn, Ṣ,) sometimes, making the ر quiescent; (Ṣ;) and أُرُوضٌ (AZ, AHn, Mṣb, Ḳ) is sometimes used as a pl., as in the saying مَا أَكْثَرَ أُرُوضَ بَنِى فُلَانٍ [*How many are the lands of the sons of such a one!*]; (TA;) and another [and very common] pl. is [أَرَاضٍ, with the article written] الأَرَاضِى, contr. to rule, (Ṣ, Mṣb, Ḳ,) as though they had formed a pl. from آرْض; (Ṣ;) thus written in all the copies of the Ṣ; [accord. to SM; but in one copy of the Ṣ, I find كَأَنَّهُمْ جَمَعُوا اراضا; and in another, ارضا;] and in one copy [is added], "thus it is found in his [J's] handwriting;" but IB says that correctly he should have said أَرْضَى, like أَرْطَى; for as to آرْض, its regular pl. would be أَوَارِض; and [SM says] I have found it observed in a marginal note to the Ṣ that the pl. of أَرْض would be أَآرِض, like as أَكَالِبُ is pl. of أَكْلُب; and wherefore did he not say that الاراضى is a pl. of an unused sing., like لَيَالٍ and أَهَالٍ, so that it is as though it were pl. of أَرْضَاةٌ, like as لَيَالٍ is pl. of لَيْلَاةٌ? yet if any one should propose the plea that it may be formed by transposition from أَأْرُض, he would not say what is improbable; its measure being in this case أَعَالِفُ; the word being أَرَاضِئُ, and the ء being changed into ى: (TA:) accord. to Abu-l-Khaṭṭáb, (Ṣ,) آرَاض is also a pl. of أَرْض, (Ṣ, Ḳ,) like as آهَال is a pl. of أَهْل; (Ṣ;) but IB says that, in the opinion of the critics, the truth with respect to what is related on the authority of Abu-l-Khaṭṭáb is, that from أَرْض and أَهْل are formed أَرَاض and أَهَال, as though they were pls. of أَرْضَاةٌ and أَهْلَاةٌ; like as they said لَيْلَةٌ and لَيَالٍ, as though this were pl. of لَيْلَاةٌ. (TA.) It is said in proverbs, أَجْمَعُ مِنَ الأَرْضِ [*More comprehensive than the earth*]: (TA:) and آمَنُ مِنَ الأَرْضِ [*More trustworthy than the earth,* in which treasures are securely buried]: and أَشَدُّ مِنَ الأَرْضِ [*Harder than the earth,* or *ground*]: (A, TA:) and أَذَلُّ مِنَ الأَرْضِ [*More vile,* or *more submissive, than the earth,* or *ground*]. (TA.) And you say, مَنْ أَطَاعَنِى كُنْتُ لَهُ أَرْضًا ‡ [*Whoso obeyeth me, I will be to him as ground* whereon one treads]; denoting submissiveness. (A, TA.) And فُلَانٌ إِنْ ضُرِبَ فَأَرْضٌ ‡ [*Such one, if he be beaten, is like ground*]; i. e. he cares not for beating. (A, TA.) One says also, لَا أَرْضَ لَكَ [*Mayest thou have no land,* or *country!* or *thou hast no land,* or *country*]; like as one says, لَا أُمَّ لَكَ. (Ṣ, Ḳ.) — [And hence,] هُوَ ٱبْنُ أَرْضٍ *He is a stranger,* (A, Ḳ, TA,) *of whom neither father nor mother is known.* (TA.) — اِبْنُ الأَرْضِ [with the art. ال prefixed to the latter word] is *A certain plant,* (AHn, Ḳ,) *which comes forth upon the summits of the* [*hills called*] آكَام, *having a stem* (أَصْل), *but not growing tall,* (AHn,) *which resembles hair, and is eaten,* (AHn, Ḳ,) *and quickly dries up;* (AHn;) *a species of* بَقْل, as also بِنْتُ الأَرْضِ: (Ṣ in art. بنى:) and بَنَاتُ الأَرْضِ *plants:* (M in art. بسر:) and *the places which are concealed from the pastor.* (Ṣ in that art.) Also *The pool that is left by a torrent:* (T in art. بنى:) and بَنَاتُ الأَرْضِ *pools in which are remains of water:* (IAạr in TA art. بسر:) and *rivulets.* (T in art. بنى.) — أَرْضٌ is also used to signify † *A carpet;* or *anything that is spread:* and in this sense, in poetry, it is sometimes made masc. (Mṣb.) — And † *Anything that is low.* (Ṣ, Ḳ.) And ‡ The *lower,* or *lowest, part of the legs* of a horse or the like: (Ṣ, Ḳ:) or the *legs* of a camel or of a horse or the like: and the *part that is next to the ground thereof.* (TA.) You say بَعِيرٌ شَدِيدُ الأَرْضِ ‡ *A camel strong in the legs.* (TA.) And فَرَسٌ بَعِيدُ مَا بَيْنَ أَرْضِهِ وَسَمَائِهِ ‡ *A horse that is large and tall.* (A, TA.) — Also, of a man, ‡ The *knees and what is beneath,* or *below,* (lit. *after,*) *them.* (TA.) — And of a sandal, † [The *lower surface of the sole;*] the *part that touches the ground.* (TA.) ═ *A febrile shivering; a tremor:* (Ṣ, Ḳ:) or *vertigo:* or it signifies also *vertigo arising from a relaxed state, and occasioning a defluxion from the nose and eyes.* (TA.) I'Ab is related to have said, on the occasion of an earthquake, أَزُلْزِلَتِ الأَرْضُ أَمْ بِى أَرْضٌ, (Ṣ,) i. e. [*Hath the earth been made to quake, or is there in me*] *a tremor?* or *a vertigo?* (TA.) [أَهْلُ الأَرْضِ signifies *A certain class of the jinn,* or *genii;* by whom human beings are believed to be possessed, and affected by an involuntary tremor; whence it seems that this appellation may perhaps be from أَرْض as signifying "a tremor." See مَأْرُوض: and see خَبَل, as explained in the Ṣ.] — Also *Rheum;* syn. زُكَام: (Ṣ, Ḳ:) in this sense masc.; or, accord. to Kr, fem., on the authority of Ibn-Ahmar. (TA.) ═ See also مَأْرُوض.

أَرِضٌ: see أَرِضَةٌ.

أَرْضَةٌ: see what next follows.

أِرْضَةٌ of herbage, *What suffices the camels,* or *other pasturing animals, for a year:* (IAạr, AHn, M:) or *abundant herbage* or *pasture;* as also ▼ أَرْضَةٌ and ▼ إِرَضَةٌ. (Ḳ.)

أَرَضَةٌ [The *wood-fretter;*] *a certain insect that eats wood,* (Ṣ, A, Mṣb, Ḳ,) *well known;* (A, Ḳ;) it is *a white worm, resembling the ant, appearing in the days of the* [*season called*] رَبِيع: (TA:) there are two kinds: *one kind is small, like the large of the* ذَرّ [or *grubs of ants*]; *and this is the bane of wood in particular:* (AHn, TA:) or *this kind is the bane of wood and of other things, and is a white worm with a black head, not having wings, and it penetrates into the earth, and builds for itself a habitation of clay,* or *soil; and this is said to be that which ate the staff of Solomon* [as is related in the Ḳur xxxiv. 13, where it is called دَابَّةُ الأَرْضِ, as is said in the A]: (TA:) the other kind [*is the termite,* or *white ant; termes fatale* of Linn.; called by Forskål (in his Descr. Animalium &c., p. 96,) *termes arda, destructor;* and *this*] *is like a large common ant, having wings; it is the bane of everything that is of wood, and of plants; except that it does not attack what is moist,* or *succulent; and it has legs:* (AHn, TA:)

the pl. is ▼ أَرْضٌ (AḤn, Mṣb, TA) and أَرَضَاتٌ; (Mṣb;) or, as some [more properly] say, أَرَضٌ is a quasi-pl. [or coll. gen.] n. (AḤn, TA.) It is said in a prov., آكَلُ مِنَ الأَرَضَةِ [*More consuming than the wood-fretter, or the termite*]. (TA.) And in another, أَفْسَدُ مِنَ الأَرَضَةِ [*More marring, or injuring, or destructive, than the wood-fretter, or the termite.*] (A, TA.)

أَرِضَةٌ: see أَرِيضٌ.

إِرَضَةٌ: see أُرْضَةٌ.

أُرُوضٌ: see أَرِيضٌ.

أَرِيضٌ part. n. of أَرُضَ. — You say أَرْضٌ أَرِيضَةٌ (Ṣ, A, Ḳ) and ▼ أَرِضَةٌ (TA) *Land that is thriving, or productive;* (Ṣ, A, Ḳ;) *pleasing to the eye;* (AA, Ṣ, A, Ḳ;) *and disposed by nature to yield good produce:* (A, Ḳ, TA:) or *fruitful; increasing in plants or herbage:* (IAạr:) or *level, or soft:* (ISh:) or *that collects moisture, and becomes luxuriant with herbage; that is soft to tread upon, pleasant to sit upon, productive, and good in its herbage* or *vegetation:* (AḤn:) it also signifies *a wide land;* syn. عَرِيضَةٌ: (TA:) and إِرَاضٌ [as pl. of أَرِيضٌ] is syn. with عِرَاضٌ and وِسَاعٌ; (AA, Ḳ, TA;) as though the ء were a substitute for the ع. (TA.) — أَرِيضٌ is also an imitative sequent to عَرِيضٌ; (Ṣ, Ḳ;) as in the phrase شَىْءٌ عَرِيضٌ أَرِيضٌ [*A very wide thing*]: (Ṣ:) or it signifies *fat*, as an epithet: (Ḳ:) some use it in this sense without عريض, applied to a kid. (Ṣ.) And you say, اِمْرَأَةٌ عَرِيضَةٌ أَرِيضَةٌ [*A very wide, or wide and fat, woman;* or, as seems to be indicated in the TA in art. عرض, *prolific and perfect*]; and in like manner, ▼ مُؤْرَضَةٌ. (TA.) You say also رَجُلٌ أَرِيضٌ, (Ṣ,) and ▼ أَرُوضٌ لِلْخَيْرِ, (A,) *A man lowly, or submissive;* (Ṣ;) *naturally disposed to good, or to do good.* (Ṣ, A.) And نَفْسٌ وَاسِعٌ أَرِيضٌ: see رَابِطٌ.

هُوَ آرَضُهُمْ بِهِ *He is the most adapted, meet, suited, fitted,* or *fit, of them, for it;* or *most worthy of them of it.* (Ḳ.) And هُوَ آرَضُهُمْ أَنْ يَفْعَلَ ذٰلِكَ *He is the most adapted,* &c., or *most worthy, of them to do that.* (Aṣ, Ṣ.)

مُؤْرَضَةٌ: see أَرِيضٌ.

مَأْرُوضٌ Wood *eaten by the* أَرَضَة [or *wood-fretter*, or *termite*, but generally meaning the former]; (Ṣ, A, Mṣb, Ḳ;) as also ▼ أَرِضٌ. (TA.) — A person *affected with* خَبَل [q. v.] *from the jinn, or genii, and* [*what are called*] أَهْلُ الأَرْضِ, (Ṣ, Ḳ,) i. e. (so accord. to the Ṣ and TA, but in the Ḳ "and") *he who moves about his head and body involuntarily.* (Ṣ, Ḳ.) — A person *affected with* زُكَام [*or rheum*]: (Ṣ, Ḳ:) accord. to Ṣgh, [who seems, like J, not to have known أُرِضَ,] from آرَضَهُ; (Ṣgh, TA;) whereas by rule, [if from آرَضَهُ,] it should be مُؤْرَضٌ. (TA.)

فَسِيلٌ مُسْتَأْرِضٌ, and وَدِيَّةٌ مُسْتَأْرِضَةٌ, *A young palm-tree,* and *a small young palm-tree, having a root in the ground:* such as grows forth from the trunk of the mother-tree is called رَاكِبٌ. (Ṣ, Ḳ.) — مُسْتَأْرِضٌ also signifies *Heavy, slow,* or *sluggish, inclining,* or *propending, to the ground.* (IB.)

ارط

1. [The unaugmented verb from this root seems to be unknown, if it were ever in use, for it is not mentioned, though the pass. part. n., مَأْرُوطٌ, is mentioned as having three significations, which see below.]

2: see 4.

4. آرَطَتِ الأَرْضُ, (AHeyth, Ḳ,) of the measure أَفْعَلَتْ, [originally] with two alifs, (TA,) [aor. يُؤْرِطُ, inf. n. إِيرَاطٌ,] *The land produced the kind of trees called* أَرْطًى [or أَرْطَى]; (AHeyth, Ḳ;) as also أَرْطَتْ, inf. n. إِرْطَآءٌ; or this is a corruption, attributable to J: so says the author of the Ḳ, following AHeyth: but it is no corruption, for it is mentioned by the authors on verbs and by ISd and others; (MF, TA;) for instance, by AḤn, in his book on plants, and by IF, in the Mj: (TA:) [and J mentions it in its proper place, in art. رطو, as well as in the present art.:] ▼ أَرَّطَتْ, with the ر musheddedeh, has also been found in the handwriting of certain of the men of letters; but this is a corruption. (Ḳ.)

أُرْطٌ *A colour like that of the* أَرْطَى [or أَرْطًى]. (Ṣgh, Ḳ.)

أَرْطًى, (Mbr, Ṣ, Ḳ,) of the measure فَعْلَى, because you say أَدِيمٌ مَأْرُوطٌ, [explained below,] (Mbr, Ṣ,) the alif (Mbr, Ṣ, Ḳ) ending it (Mbr) [written ى] being a letter of quasi-coordination, (Ṣ, Ḳ,) not to denote the fem. gender, (Mbr, Ṣ,) its n. un. being أَرْطَاةٌ, (Mbr, Ṣ, Ḳ,) wherefore it is with tenween when indeterminate, but not when determinate: (Ṣ, Ḳ:) or it is of the measure أَفْعَلُ, (Mbr,* Ṣ,) the last letter being radical, (Mbr,) because you say أَدِيمٌ مَرْطِىٌّ, (Mbr, Ṣ,) and in this case it should be mentioned among words with an infirm letter [for the last radical], and is with tenween both when determinate and when indeterminate; (Ṣ;) [but this is a mistake, for when it is determinate, it can be with tenween only if used as a proper name; therefore,] IB observes, that if you make its last letter radical, its measure is أَفْعَلُ, and a word of this measure, if a subst., is imperfectly decl. when determinate, but perfectly decl. when indeterminate: (TA:) [the author of the Ḳ copies the error of the Ṣ, saying, "or its alif is radical," (meaning its last letter,) "and in this case it is always with tenween;" and he adds, "or," (for which he should have said "and,") its measure is أَفْعَلُ: to all which it is necessary to add, that some of the grammarians hold it to be also of the measure فَعْلَى, ending with a fem. alif, and therefore assign to it no n. un.:] *A kind of tree,* (Ṣ, Ḳ,) *of those growing in sands,* (Ṣ, TA,) *resembling the kind called* عِضَاه, *growing as a branch* [in the TA عَصًا, for which I read غُصْنًا,] *from a single stem, to the height of the stature of a man, the leaves whereof are what are termed* هَدَب [q. v., and are included among those termed خُوص], (AḤn, TA,) *and its flower is like that of the* خِلَاف [or *salix ægyptia*], (AḤn, Ḳ,) *save in being smaller, the colour being one; and the odour thereof is pleasant: it grows in sands, and therefore the poets make frequent mention of the wild bulls' and cows' taking refuge among this and other trees of the sands, burrowing at their roots to hide themselves there, and to protect themselves from the heat and cold and rain, but not among the trees in hard ground, for burrowing in the sand is easy:* (AḤn, TA:) *its fruit is like the* عُنَّاب [or *jujube*], *bitter, and is eaten by camels in its fresh moist state, and its roots are red,* (AḤn, Ḳ,) *intensely red:* (AḤn, TA:) AḤn adds, a man of the Benoo-Asad informed me, that *the leaves* (هَدَب) *of the* ارطى *are red like the red pomegranate: its fruit also is red:* (TA:) the dual is أَرْطَيَانِ: (AḤn, TA:) and the pl. أَرْطَيَاتٌ and أَرَاطَى and أَرَاطٍ, (AḤn, Ḳ,) in the accus. case أَرَاطِىَ. (TA.)

أَرْطَوِىٌّ: } see what next follows.
أَرْطَاوِىٌّ: }

مَأْرُوطٌ A hide *tanned with* أَرْطًى; (Ṣ, Ḳ;) i. e. *with the leaves thereof;* (Ṣ in art. رطو;) as also ▼ مُؤَرْطًى; (TA;) and so مَرْطِىٌّ. (Ṣ.) — A camel *having a complaint from eating* أَرْطًى: (L, Ḳ:*) and a camel *that eats* أَرْطًى, (AZ, Ṣ, Ḳ,) *and keeps to it;* (Ḳ;) as also ▼ أَرْطَوِىٌّ (AZ, Ṣ, Ḳ) and ▼ أَرْطَاوِىٌّ. (Ibn-'Abbád, Ṣgh, L, Ḳ.)

مُؤَرْطًى: see what next precedes.

ارف

2. أَرَّفَهَا, (T, M, Mgh,) namely الدَّارَ, and الأَرْضَ, (T, M,) inf. n. تَأْرِيفٌ, (T,) *He set,* or *put, limits,* or *boundaries,* [أُرَف,] *to it;* (M, Mgh;) *and marked it out:* (Mgh:) or *he divided it; and set,* or *put, limits,* or *boundaries, to it:* (T:) namely *the house,* and *the land.* (T, M.) And أُرِّفَ عَلَى المَالِ, (Ṣ, Mgh, Mṣb,) or على الأَرْضِ, inf. n. as above, (Ḳ,) *The property,* (Ṣ, Mgh, Mṣb,) or *the land,* (Ḳ,) *had limits,* or *boundaries, set,* or *put, to it,* (Ṣ, Mṣb, Ḳ,) or *around it;* (Mgh;) and *was divided.* (Ḳ.) When this is done, it is said that there is no شُفْعَة [or right of preemption] with respect to the property. (Ṣ, Mgh, Mṣb.) — تَأْرِيفٌ also signifies The *tying* a rope, or cord, *so as to form a knot* or *knots.* (Ḳ.)

إِرْفٌ *i. q.* إِرْثٌ مَجْدٍ: إِنَّهُ لَفِى إِرْفِ مَجْدٍ [*Verily he is of a glorious origin, race,* or *stock*]: mentioned by Yaạḳoob as an instance of a change of letters. (M.)

أُرْفَةٌ *A limit,* or *boundary,* (Aṣ, T, Ṣ, M, Mgh, Mṣb, Ḳ,) *making a separation* (Mgh) *between two pieces of land;* (Mṣb, Ḳ;) *a sign,* or *mark,* (Aṣ, T, Ṣ, Mgh,) *of the limits,* or *boundaries, between two pieces of land:* (Ṣ:) and *a separation between houses and estates:* (M:) and *a dam between two pieces of land sown or for sowing:* (Th, M:) Yaạḳoob asserts that its ف is a substitute for the ث of أُرْثَةٌ [which is, however, less common]: (M:) the pl. is أُرَفٌ, (T, Ṣ, M, &c.,) signifying, accord. to Lḥ, like أُرَثٌ, *limits*, or *boundaries, between two pieces of land* [&c.]; (T;) and it is said in a trad., that these cut off الشُّفْعَة [i. e. the right of preemption]; (T, Ṣ, Mgh;) meaning, in the language of the people of El-Ḥijáz, *signs*, or *marks*, and *limits*, or *boundaries*. (T.) Th relates that an Arab woman said, جَعَلَ عَلَىَّ زَوْجِى أُرْفَةً لَا أَجُوزُهَا, i. e. *My husband set me a sign*, or *mark*, [or *limit*,] *beyond which I should not pass*. (M.) And أُرْفَةُ أَجَلٍ signifies *An extreme limit of a period of existence*. (TA, from a trad.) —— Also *A knot*. (Sgh, Ḳ.)

أُرْفِىٌّ *A measurer of land*, (Ḳ,* TA,) *who marks it with limits*, or *boundaries*. (TA.)

هُوَ مُؤَارِفِى *He has his limit*, or *boundary, next to mine, in dwelling*, and *in place*: (Ḳ:) a phrase like هُوَ مُتَاخِمِى. (TA.)

ارق

1. أَرِقَ, aor. َ, inf. n. أَرَقٌ, (T, Ṣ, Ḳ, &c.,) *He was sleepless*, or *wakeful*, or *sleep departed from him*, (JK, T,) *by night*; (T;) *i. q.* سَهِرَ (Ṣ, Mgh, Sgh, Ḳ) بِاللَّيْلِ; (Sgh, Ḳ;) or *i. q.* سَهِدَ: (Ṣ, and L and Ḳ in art. سهد:) or *sleep departed from him by reason of a malady, or a distracting accident* or *event*: (M:) or *he was sleepless* or *wakeful* (سَهِرَ) *in a case that was disliked*, or *evil*; سَهِرَ having a general sense: (M, F:) or *he shut his eyes one while and opened them another*, [*being unable to continue sleeping*,] whereas سَهِرَ signifies he did not sleep at all: (Deewán of the Hudhalees, cited by Freytag in his Lex.:) or أَرَقٌ signifies *sleeplessness*, or *wakefulness, engendered by anxiety and grief*: (Ḥar p. 162:) and ↓ ائترق [with the disjunctive alif written اِيتَرَقَ] signifies the same as أَرِقَ. (Ṣ, Ḳ.) ═ أُرِقَتِ النَّخْلَةُ [and أُرِقَ الزَّرْعُ] *The palm-tree* [and *the seed-produce*] *was affected*, or *smitten, by what is termed* أَرَقَان. (JK.)

2. أَرَّقَنِى كَذَا, (JK, Ṣ, Ḳ,*) inf. n. تَأْرِيقٌ, (Ṣ, Mgh,) *Such a thing rendered me*, or *caused me to be, sleepless* or *wakeful*; (JK, Ṣ, Mgh,* Ḳ;*) as also ↓ آرَقَنِى, (Ḳ,) inf. n. إِيرَاقٌ. (TA.)

4: see 2.

8: see 1.

أَرْقٌ: see أَرَقَانٌ.

أَرُقٌ: see what next follows.

أَرِقٌ *Sleepless* or *wakeful* (Ṣ, Ḳ) *by night* (Ḳ) [*by reason of a malady, or a distracting accident* or *event*, &c. (see 1)]; as also ↓ آرِقٌ (IF, Ḳ) and ↓ أَرُقٌ and ↓ أُرُقٌ; or the last signifies *habitually so*. (TA.)

أُرُقٌ: see what next precedes.

أَرَقَانٌ (JK, Ṣ, Ḳ) and أُرْقَانٌ and أَرْقَانٌ and إِرْقَانٌ and ↓ أُرَاقٌ and ↓ أَرْقٌ and إِرَقَانٌ (Ḳ) *i. q.* يَرَقَانٌ; (JK, Ṣ, Ḳ;) أَرَقَانٌ being a dial. var. of this last; (Ṣ;) or the hemzeh is a substitute for the ى; (L;) and يرقان is the word most commonly known; (Ḳ;) *A blight*, or *disease, which affects*, or *smites, seed-produce*: (JK, Ṣ, Ḳ:) and *a disease* [namely *jaundice*] *which affects*, or *smites, man*, (Ṣ, Ḳ,) *causing the person to become yellow* [or *blackish*]; (TA;) it is *a disease which changes the colour of the person excessively to yellowness or blackness, by the flowing of the yellow or black humour to the skin and the part next thereto, without putridity*. (Ibn-Seenà [Avicenna], Ḳ.)

أُرَاقٌ: see أَرَقَانٌ.

آرِقٌ: see أَرِقٌ.

زَرْعٌ مَأْرُوقٌ *Seed-produce affected*, or *smitten, with a blight*, or *disease*, (JK, Ṣ, Ḳ,) *such as is termed* أَرَقَان; (JK, Ṣ;) as also مَيْرُوقٌ [from يَرَقَان]: (Ṣ, Ḳ:) and نَخْلَةٌ مَأْرُوقَةٌ *a palm-tree affected*, or *smitten, therewith*. (JK, TA.)

ارك

1. أَرَكَتِ الإِبِلُ, aor. ُ and ِ, inf. n. أُرُوكٌ, *The camels fed upon the kind of tree called* أَرَاك: (Ṣ, Mṣb, Ḳ:) or *remained*, or *continued, among trees of that kind*, (ISk, Ṣ, Ḳ,) i. e., *what are termed* حَمْض, (ISk, Ṣ,) *eating them*: (Ḳ:) or *found*, or *lighted on, any trees whatever, and remained*, or *continued, among them*: (Ḳ:) or, accord. to Aṣ, *kept* in a place (بِمَكَانٍ), *not removing* therefrom: (ISk, Ṣ:) or *remained*, or *continued*, in a place *for the purpose of feeding upon the* اراك: and hence the signification next following, which is tropical. (Er-Rághib.) —— أَرَكَ بِالْمَكَانِ, (Ṣ, Mṣb, Ḳ,) aor. and inf. n. as above, (Mṣb, TA,) ‡ *He* (a man, Ṣ) *remained, continued*, or *abode, in the place*, (Ṣ, Mṣb, Ḳ,) *not quitting it*; (TA;) as also أَرِكَ, aor. َ, (Ḳ,) inf. n. أَرَكٌ. (TA.) —— And أَرَكَ, (Ḳ,) inf. n. أَرْكٌ and أُرُوكٌ, (TA,) † *He persisted*, or *persevered*, syn. لَجَّ, (Ḳ,) i. e. أَصَرَّ, (T, Ḳ,) in an affair. (T, Ḳ.) —— And, (Ḳ,) inf. n. أُرُوكٌ, (TA,) † *He held back*, or *drew back*, (تَأَخَّرَ,) in an affair. (Ḳ.) ═ أَرَكَ الإِبِلَ, (Ḳ,) aor. ُ, (TA,) inf. n. أَرْكٌ, (Ḳ,) *He fed the camels*, or *made them to feed, upon the kind of tree called* أَرَاك: or *made them to remain, or continue, among trees of that kind*: or *brought them to any trees whatever, and made them to remain, or continue, among them*. (Ḳ.) —— أَرَكَ الأَمْرَ فِى عُنُقِهِ, (L, Ḳ,) inf. n. أُرُوكٌ, so in the L, (TA,) † *He compelled him*, or *constrained him, to do the thing*, or *affair*; or *made him to keep*, or *cleave, to it*. (L, Ḳ.) ═ أَرِكَتِ الإِبِلُ, aor. َ, (Ṣ, Ḳ,) inf. n. أَرَكٌ; (Ṣ;) and أَرُكَتْ, aor. ُ; and أُرِكَتْ; (Ḳ;) *The camels had a complaint*, or *suffered pain*, (Ṣ, Ḳ,) *of*, or *in, their bellies*, (Ṣ,) *from eating the* أَرَاك. (Ṣ, Ḳ.)

2. أَرَّكَهَا, inf. n. تَأْرِيكٌ, *He concealed her* (namely a woman, TA) *by means of an* أَرِيكَة, q. v. (K.)

8. ائترك [written with the disjunctive alif اِيتَرَكَ] *It* (the kind of tree called أَرَاك) *became firm, strong*, or *compact, and big*: (O, Ḳ:) or *attained to maturity*: (Ḳ:) or *became tangled*, or *luxuriant, and abundant*. (TA.)

إِرَكٌ: see أَرَاكٌ. —— عُشْبٌ لَهُ إِرْكٌ *Herbage in which the camels remain*, or *continue*. (Ibn-'Abbád, Ḳ.)

أَرَاكٌ أَرِكٌ *Abundant, and tangled*, or *luxuriant, trees of the kind called* اراك; (Ḳ, TA; [in the CḲ أَرْكٌ, but said in the TA to be like كَتِفٌ;]) as also ↓ مُؤْتَرِكٌ. (Ḳ.) —— أَرْضٌ أَرِكَةٌ *Land abounding with the kind of trees called* اراك. (Ḳ.) —— إِبِلٌ أَرِكَةٌ and أَرَاكَى, [the latter being the pl.,] *Camels having a complaint*, or *suffering pain*, (Ṣ, Ḳ,) *of*, or *in, their bellies*, (Ṣ,) *from eating the* اراك. (Ṣ, Ḳ.)

أَرَاكٌ The [*kind of trees termed*] حَمْض; (AḤn, Ḳ;) as also ↓ إِرَكٌ: (Ibn-'Abbád, Ḳ:) and (Ḳ) *certain trees of the kind termed* حَمْض, (T, Ṣ, Mṣb, Ḳ,) *well known, bearing what resemble bunches of grapes*, (T, TA,) *and of which sticks for cleaning the teeth are made*, (AḤn, Aboo-Ziyád, Mṣb, Ḳ,) *that is, of its branches*, (AḤn, Aboo-Ziyád, Mṣb,) *and of its roots, which latter are more esteemed for this purpose*: (Aboo-Ziyád:) *it is the best of the trees of which the branches are used for this purpose, and the best of those upon which beasts feed with respect to the odour of the milk* [*yielded by those beasts*]: (AḤn:) or *one of the large thorny trees, upon which camels feed: the milk of* [*the camels that feed upon*] *it is the best of milk: and it is not allowable to prohibit the public from feeding their beasts upon it*: (Mgh:) or *a kind of tall, smooth*, or *soft, tree, abounding with leaves and branches, the wood of which is weak, and which has a fruit in bunches*, or *racemes, called* بَرِير, *one* [*bunch*] *of which will fill the hand*: (Mṣb:) n. un. with ة: (Ṣ, Mṣb:) pl. (of the n. un., T) أُرُكٌ (T, Ḳ) and أَرَائِكُ, (IB, Ḳ,) which is a form sometimes used, and is also pl. of the n. un. (IB.) —— *A piece of land* (Ḳ, TA) *in which are trees of the kind thus called*. (TA.)

أَرِيكٌ: see the end of the next paragraph.

أَرِيكَةٌ *A raised couch* (سَرِير) *in a* حَجَلَة, (Ḳ, and Jel in xviii. 30,) *which is a tent*, or *pavilion*, or *chamber*, (بَيْت,) *adorned with cloths and curtains*, [or *a kind of curtained canopy* or *alcove* or *the like*,] *for a bride*; (Jel ubi suprà;) *a raised couch* (سرير) *in a* حَجَلَة, *and having before it a curtain*; when alone, not thus called: (TA:) or *a bed*, or *thing spread upon the ground to sit or lie upon, in a* حَجَلَة: (Zj, TA:) or *a raised couch* (سرير), *absolutely, whether in a* حجلة or *not*: (TA:) or [in the CḲ "and"] *anything upon which one reclines such as is termed* سَرِير or فِرَاش or مِنَصَّة: (Ḳ, TA:) or [in some copies of the Ḳ "and"] *a raised couch* (سرير) *ornamentally furnished and decorated, in a* [*tent*, or *pavilion*, or *the like, such as is termed*] قُبَّة, or *in a chamber*, or *an apartment*, (بَيْت, [or by this may be meant here *a tent of any kind*, though I think that in this instance it more probably denotes *an inner apartment*, or *an alcove*,]) *which, when there is not in it a* سرير, *is termed* حَجَلَة: (Ṣ, Sgh, Ḳ:) accord. to Er-Rághib, so named because originally made of [the wood of] the أَرَاك; or because it is a place of abode; from أَرَكَ بِالمَكَانِ "he abode in the place:" (TA:) pl. أَرَائِكُ (Ṣ, Ḳ) and [coll. gen. n.] ▼ أَرِيكٌ. (Ḳ.)

إِبِلٌ أَرَاكِيَّةٌ: see what next follows.

إِبِلٌ أَرِكَةٌ *Camels feeding upon the kind of tree called* أَرَاك; (Ṣ, Mṣb;) as also ▼ أَرَاكِيَّةٌ: (Ḳ:) or *remaining*, or *continuing, among trees of that kind*, i. e., *what are termed* حَمْض: or *keeping* in a place, *not removing* therefrom: (Ṣ:) pl. أَوَارِكُ. (Ṣ, Mṣb.) Their milk is said to be the best of milk. (TA.)

قَوْمٌ مُؤْرِكُونَ *A people*, or *company of men, alighting and abiding by trees of the kind called* أَرَاك, (Ḳ,) *feeding their camels upon those trees.* (AḤn, Ḳ.*)

أَرَاكٌ مُؤْتَرِكٌ: see أَرِكَ.

ارم

1. أَرَمَهُ, (Ṣ, Ḥar p. 99,) aor. ـِ, inf. n. أَرْمٌ, (Ṣ,) *He took away*, or *removed, its* أَرُومَة, or أَصْل: (Ḥar ubi suprà:) [*he extirpated it; eradicated it:*] *he ate it.* (Ṣ.) You say, أَرَمَتِ السَّائِمَةُ المَرْعَى, aor. as above, *The pasturing beasts consumed*, or *made an end of, the pasturage, not leaving of it anything.* (AḤn, M.) And أَرَمَ مَا عَلَى الخِوَانِ, (T,) or المَائِدَةِ, (Th, M, Ḳ,) aor. as above, (M,) *He ate what was on the table,* (Th, T, M, Ḳ,) *not leaving anything.* (Ḳ.) And أَرَمَتْهُمُ السَّنَةُ, (AHeyth, T, M, Ḳ,) aor. ـُ, (so in the T, as on the authority of AHeyth,) inf. n. as above, (M,) *The year of dearth*, or *drought*, or *sterility, extirpated them;* (T;) or *devoured them;* (AHeyth, T;) or *cut them off.* (M, Ḳ.) And أَرَمَتِ السَّنَةُ بِأَمْوَالِنَا *The year of dearth*, or *drought*, or *sterility, devoured everything* [*of our property* or *cattle*]. (Ṣ.) And أَرَمَتِ الأَرْضُ المَيِّتَ *The earth consumed the dead body.* (T.) — أَرِمَ المَالُ, aor. ـَ, *The property*, or *cattle, perished*, or *came to nought.* (TA.)

أَرْمٌ: see إِرَمٌ.

أَرِمٌ [part. n. of أَرِمَ]. You say أَرْضٌ أَرِمَةٌ, meaning *Land upon which rain has not fallen for a long time:* (T:) or *land which does not give growth to anything.* (TA.) [Not to be confounded with آرِمَةٌ, q. v.] — See also what next follows.

إِرَمٌ (T, Ṣ, M, Ḳ) and ▼ أَرِمٌ, (M, Ḳ,) like كَتِفٌ, (Ḳ,) or ▼ إِرْمٌ, (so in a copy of the M,) and ▼ إِرَمِيٌّ and ▼ أَرَمِيٌّ, (M, Ḳ,) from Lḥ, (TA,) or ▼ أَرْمِيٌّ, from Lḥ, (so in a copy of the M,) and ▼ إِرْمِيٌّ, from Lḥ, (TA,) and يَرَمِيٌّ, (M, Ḳ,) from Lḥ, (TA,) and أَيْرَمِيٌّ, (T, Ḳ,) *A sign*, or *mark, set up to show the way;* (M, Ḳ;) *stones set up as a sign*, or *mark, to show the way in the desert:* (Ṣ:) or particularly *one belonging to* [*the tribe of*] *'Ád:* (M, Ḳ:) accord. to ISh, the إِرَم is [*a thing*] *like a man in a standing posture upon the head of a hill, whereby one is directed to the right way, and whereby the land is marked, composed of stones set one upon another, and is only the work of the Muslims, and such is made by people in the present day, upon the road:* (T:) or *such as was made by the people in the time of ignorance, who were accustomed, when they found a thing in their way and could not take it with them, to leave upon it some stones, whereby to know it, until, when they returned, they took it:* (TA:) the pl. [of pauc.] is آرَامٌ and [of mult.] أُرُومٌ: (ISh, T, Ṣ, M, Ḳ:) or أُرُومٌ signifies the *graves*, or *sepulchres, of* [*the tribe of*] *'Ád.* (M, Ḳ.) — [إِرَمُ in the phrase إِرَمَ ذَاتِ العِمَادِ (see art. عمد) is a proper name; but whether of a place, or a tribe, or an individual, is disputed: it is commonly believed to be the name of *The terrestrial paradise of Sheddád the son of 'Ád:* see Bḍ lxxxix. 6.]

أَرْضٌ أَرْمَآءُ *Land in which there is not a root, or stock, of a tree; as though it were* ▼ مَأْرُومَة [or *extirpated*]: (O:) or *land in which neither root nor branch is left;* as also ▼ مَأْرُومَةٌ. (M, Ḳ.)

أَرْمِيٌّ and إِرْمِيٌّ and أَرَمِيٌّ and إِرَمِيٌّ: see إِرَمٌ.

أُرُومٌ: see what next follows.

أَرُومَةٌ (T, M, Ḳ) and أُرُومَةٌ, (M, Ḳ,) the latter of the dial. of Temeem, (TA,) or this is not allowable, (T,) or ▼ أُرُومٌ, (Ṣ,) or this is the pl., (M, Ḳ,) [or a coll. gen. n.,] The *root*, or *base*, or *lowest part*, syn. أَصْل, (T, Ṣ, M, Ḳ,) of a tree (T, Ṣ) of any kind; (T;) and of a horn: (Ṣ:) or, of a tree, [or plant, the *root-stock*, or *rhizoma*, or] the *part from which branch off the* عُرُوق [or *roots properly so called*]. (Ḳ in art. عرق. [See an instance of its use voce جَنْبَةٌ; another, voce جِنْثٌ; and another, voce جَزْرٌ.]) — And [hence,] † The *origin*, or *stock*, of a man: (TA:) ‡ The *origin* of حَسَب [or grounds of pretension to respect or honour, &c.]. (Ḥar p. 99.)

سَنَةٌ آرِمَةٌ (Ṣ, Ḳ, TA [in the CḲ, erroneously, أَرِمَةٌ]) *An extirpating year of dearth* or *drought* or *sterility:* (Ṣ:) or *a year of dearth &c. cutting off people.* (Ḳ.)

أَرْضٌ مَأْرُومَةٌ: see أَرْمَآءُ, in two places.

اري

1. أَرَتِ الدَّابَّةُ مَرْبِطَهَا, (M, Ḳ,) and مَعْلَفَهَا, [aor. تَأْرِي,] inf. n. أَرْيٌ, (M,) *The beast kept to its place where it was tied,* (M, Ḳ,) and *to its manger.* (M.) — أَرَتِ الدَّابَّةُ إِلَى الدَّابَّةِ, (Ḳ,) aor. as above, (Ṣ,) and so the inf. n., (TA,) *The beast joined itself*, or *became joined, to the beast, and kept with it to one manger.* (Ṣ, Ḳ.)

2. أَرَّيْتُ لِلدَّابَّةِ, (Ṣ, M, Ḳ,) and الدَّابَّةَ, (M, Ḳ,) inf. n. تَأْرِيَةٌ, (Ṣ, M, Ḳ,) *I made for the beast an* آرِيّ [q. v.], (Ṣ,* M,) or *an* آرِيَة. (Ḳ: [in the CḲ أَرِيَّة; but this and آرِيَّة are probably mistakes of copyists.]) — أَرَّى الشَّىْءَ, inf. n. as above, *He rendered the thing permanent*, or *steadfast; confirmed it; established it.* (M, Ḳ.) Hence, in a trad., اَللّٰهُمَّ أَرِّ مَا بَيْنَهُمْ, i. e. *O God, make permanent*, or *confirm*, or *establish, what is between them, of love*, or *affection;* said in praying for a man and his wife. (M, TA.) Mohammad is also related to have said, with this intention, اَللّٰهُمَّ أَرِّ بَيْنَهُمَا, meaning *O God, render permanent*, or *confirm, the union*, or *concord*, or *love, of them two;* (A'Obeyd, TA;) or *cause union to subsist, and render permanent*, or *confirm, love*, or *affection, between them two:* (IAth, TA:) or اَللّٰهُمَّ أَرِّ كُلَّ وَاحِدٍ مِنْهُمَا صَاحِبَهُ, meaning *O God, confine each of them two to the other, so that the heart of neither may become turned away to any but that other:* the correct form of speech, however, is عَلَى صَاحِبِهِ, unless it be like تَعَلَّقْتُ فُلَانًا for تَعَلَّقْتُ بِفُلَانٍ. (IAmb, TA.)

4. آرَيْتُ الدَّابَّةَ *I joined the beast to another beast, and made it to keep with the other to one manger:* (Ṣ, in the present art.; and Ḳ:) or آرَيْتُ الدَّابَّتَيْنِ *I joined the two beasts together, and made them both keep to one manger.* (So accord. to the Ṣ in art. وار.)

5. تَأَرَّى بِالمَكَانِ *He remained, stayed*, or *abode, in the place:* (Ṣ, Mgh, Mṣb:) or *he became confined*, or *he confined himself, therein;* (T, M, Ḳ;) as also ▼ ائترى [written with the disjunctive alif ايتَرَى]. (M, Ḳ.) — تَأَرَّى عَنْهُ *He remained behind him, not going with him; held back*, or *hung back, from him.* (M, Ḳ.)

8: see 5.

أَرِيٌّ: }
أَرِيَّةٌ: } see what next follows.
آرٍ: }

آرِيٌّ, (T, Ṣ, M, Mgh, Mṣb, Ḳ,) with medd and teshdeed, (TA,) [originally آرُويٌ,] of the measure فَاعُول, (T, Ṣ, Mgh, Mṣb,) from تَأَرَّى بِالمَكَانِ as explained above, (Mgh,) or hence this verb, (Mṣb,) and ▼ أَرِيٌّ, (M, Ḳ,* [but accord. to the latter, the second form may be either thus (as it is written in the M) or ▼ آرٍ, (agreeably with the latter of the two pls. mentioned below,) for the two forms are there expressed by الآرِيُّ وَيُخَفَّفُ, (in the CḲ, erroneously, الأَرِيُّ وَيُخَفَّفُ,) and in another place in the Ḳ we find it written ▼ آرِيَّةٌ, or, as in the CḲ, ▼ أَرِيَّةٌ,]) The *place of confinement of a beast:* (ISk, T, Ṣ:) or *i. q.* آخِيَّةٌ; (M, Mgh, Mṣb, Ḳ;) used in this sense by the Arabs; (Mgh, Mṣb;) or sometimes having this application; meaning *a rope to which a beast is tied in its place of confinement;* (Ṣ;) or *a loop of a rope to which a beast is tied in that place:* (Mgh:) so called because it withholds beasts from escaping: (TA:) sometimes, (Mṣb,) improperly, (ISk, T, Ṣ,) by the vulgar, and by the lawyers, (Mgh,) applied to *a manger:* (ISk, T, Ṣ, Mgh, Mṣb:) pl. أَوَارِيُّ (T, Ṣ, Mgh, Mṣb) and أَوَارٍ. (Ṣ.) — Hence, أَوَارِيُّ is metaphorically applied to ‡ The *places* (أَحْيَاز) *that are made, in shops, for grain and other things:* and to ‡ the *water-tanks*, or *troughs*, *in a bath.* (Mgh.) — El-'Ajjáj says, describing a [wild] bull, and his covert,

وَٱعْتَادَ أَرْبَاضًا لَهَا آرِىُّ

meaning [*And he frequented lodging-places*] *having a firm foundation for the quiet of the wild animals therein* [as having been from the first occupied by such animals and unfrequented by men]. (Ṣ.) — آرِىٌّ is also said to signify *Land of a kind between even and rugged.* (M.)

آرِيَةٌ: see آرِىٌّ.

از

1. أَزَّتِ القِدْرُ, (Ṣ, Ḳ,) or البُرْمَةُ, (A,) aor. ـِ (Ṣ, Ḳ) and ـُ, (Ḳ,) inf. n. أَزِيزٌ (Ṣ, A, Ḳ) and أَزٌّ and أَزَازٌ, (Ḳ,) *The cooking-pot made a sound in boiling:* (Ṣ, accord. to an explanation there given of the inf. n.; and A:) or *boiled:* (Ṣ:) or *boiled vehemently;* (Ḳ;) as also ↓ ائتزّت [written with the disjunctive alif ايتزّت], (Ṣ, Ḳ,) inf. n. ٱئْتِزَازٌ; (Ṣ;) and ↓ تأزّت, (Ḳ,) inf. n. تَأَزُّزٌ: (TA:) or all signify *it boiled not vehemently.* (Ḳ.) It is said in a trad., كَانَ يُصَلِّى وَلِجَوْفِهِ أَزِيزٌ كَأَزِيزِ ٱلْمِرْجَلِ مِنَ ٱلْبُكَاءِ ‡ [*He used to pray, his inside making a sound like the sound of the boiling of the cooking-pot, by reason of weeping*]: (Ṣ, A, Mgh:) this is said of Moḥammad: ازيز meaning *boiling,* or the *sound thereof.* (Mgh.) — أَزَّتِ السَّحَابَةُ *The cloud made a sound from afar.* (Ḳ.) [In this instance, the TA assigns only one form to the aor., namely ـِ, and gives only أَزٌّ and أَزِيزٌ as inf. ns.] أَزِيزٌ signifies The *sounding* of thunder; (Ṣ, A;*) and of a mill-stone. (A.) You say, هَالَنِى أَزِيزُ الرَّعْدِ [*The sounding of the thunder terrified me*]: and صَدَّعَنِى أَزِيزُ الرَّحَى [*The sounding of the mill-stone made my head to ache*]. (A, TA.) — Also, inf. n. أَزِيزٌ, *It flamed,* or *blazed, like fire in firewood, and was in motion, or in a state of commotion.* (AO.) — أَزَّ بِالقِدْرِ, [aor. ـُ,] inf. n. أَزٌّ, *He kindled a fire,* or *made it to burn* or *to burn fiercely, beneath the cooking-pot, in order that it might boil:* or you say, أَزَّ القِدْرَ, inf. n. as above, meaning *he collected firewood beneath the cooking-pot so that the fire flamed,* or *blazed:* and *he made the fire to flame,* or *blaze, beneath the cooking-pot.* (TA.) And أَزَّ النَّارَ, (Ḳ,) aor. ـُ, inf. n. أَزٌّ, (TA,) *He kindled the fire,* or *made it to burn* or *to burn fiercely.* (Ḳ, TA.) — أَزَّ الشَّىْءَ, (Ḳ,) aor. ـُ, inf. n. أَزٌّ and أَزِيزٌ, (TA,) *He put the thing into a state of violent motion* or *commotion:* (ISd, Ḳ:) so accord. to IDrd: (ISd:) but Ibráheem El-Ḥarbee explains أَزٌّ only as signifying the act of *moving.* (TA.) — أَزَّهُ, (A, TA,) aor. ـُ, (TA,) inf. n. أَزٌّ, (Ṣ, TA,) *He put him in motion; disquieted him;* (A,* TA;) *stirred up, roused,* or *provoked, him;* and *incited, urged,* or *instigated, him;* (Ṣ,* A,* TA;) عَلَى كَذَا *to do such a thing.* (A, TA.*) It is said in the Ḳur [xix. 86], أَلَمْ تَرَ أَنَّا أَرْسَلْنَا ٱلشَّيَاطِينَ عَلَى ٱلْكَافِرِينَ تَؤُزُّهُمْ أَزًّا *Seest thou not that we have sent the devils against the unbelievers inciting them strongly* to acts of disobedience? (Ṣ, TA.) Or أَزٌّ signifies The *inciting* a man to do a thing *by artifice,* or *cunning,* and *gentleness.* (El-Ḥarbee.)

5. تأزّت القِدْرُ: see 1.

8. ائتزّت القِدْرُ: see 1. — هُوَ يَأْتَزُّ مِنْ كَذَا *He becomes angry, and distressed, and disquieted* or *disturbed, by reason of such a thing.* (A, TA.)

أَزَّةٌ *A sound, or noise.* (TA.)

أَزِيزٌ inf. n. of 1. — *Sharpness;* syn. حِدَّةٌ. (TA.)

ازب

1. أَزَبَ, aor. ـِ, (A, Ḳ,) inf. n. أَزْبٌ, (TḲ,) *It* (water) *flowed* or *ran;* (A, Ḳ;) like وَزَبَ. (TA.)

مِئْزَابٌ, (Ṣ, A, Mgh, Mṣb, Ḳ,) and مِيزَابٌ, (Ṣ, Mṣb,) *A water-spout; a pipe,* or *channel, that spouts forth water:* (Mgh, TA:) or *that by which water pours down from a high place:* (Towsheeḥ:) or *a water-spout of wood,* or *the like, to convey away the water from the roof of a house:* (MF in art. زوب:) the former is from the verb above mentioned: (A, Ḳ:) or it is arabicized, (A, Mgh, Ḳ,) from the Persian, (Mgh, Ḳ,) signifying "make water:" (Ḳ:) its pl. is مَآزِيبُ: (ISk, Ṣ, Mgh, Mṣb:) and the pl. of ميزاب is مَيَازِيبُ and مَوَازِيبُ, from وَزَبَ, said of water, meaning "it flowed," (Mgh, Mṣb,) accord. to IAạr; (Mgh;) or this is arabicized; or post-classical: (Mṣb:) but ميزاب, without ء, is altogether disallowed by Yaạḳoob [i. e. ISk]: (Mgh:) it is also called مِرْزَابٌ, (T, Ṣ, Mṣb,) accord. to IAạr; (T, Mṣb;) but this is disallowed by ISk, Fr, and AḤát, (Mṣb,) and by Az [the author of the T]; (Mgh;) and مِزْرَابٌ also, accord. to IAạr and Lth and others, as is mentioned in the T. (Mṣb.)

ازج

2. أزّج, inf. n. تَأْزِيجٌ, (Mṣb, Ḳ,) *He built a structure of the kind called* أَزَجٌ, *and made it long:* (Ḳ:) or *he built* a house, or chamber, *in the form of what is so called.* (Mṣb.)

أَزَجٌ *A certain kind of structure;* (Ṣ, Ḳ;) or *a house, or chamber, built in a long,* or *an oblong, form;* (Mgh, L, Mṣb;) *called in Persian* أُوسْتَانْ, (Mgh, L,) *and also, in the same language,* سَغْ, *and* كَمَرْ: (Mgh:) [i. e. *an oblong, arched,* or *vaulted, structure* or *edifice;* (*such as a bridge;* see قَنْطَرَةٌ;) *a portico, gallery,* or *piazza;* accord. to Golius and Freytag, *ædificii genus oblongum et fornicatum, porticus instar;* to which Freytag adds, *portæ arcus superior:*] or, accord. to some, *a roof:* (Mṣb:) pl. [of pauc.] آزَاجٌ (Ṣ, Mṣb, Ḳ) and آزُجٌ (Ṣ, Ḳ) and [of mult.] إِزَجَةٌ. (Ḳ.)

ازر

1. أَزَرَهُ, aor. ـُ, (TḲ,) inf. n. أَزْرٌ, (IAạr, Ḳ,) *It surrounded,* or *encompassed, it,* (IAạr,* Ḳ,* TA,) namely, a thing. (TḲ.) — See also 2, in two places: and see 3.

2. أزّرهُ, inf. n. تَأْزِيرٌ, *He put on him,* or *clad him with, an* إِزَار; (Ṣ;) as also ↓ أَزَرَهُ. (TA.) — *It covered it:* (Ḳ,* TA:) as in the phrase, أزّر النَّبْتُ الأَرْضَ *The herbage covered the ground,* or *land.* (TA.) — ‡ *He repaired the lower part of it,* (namely, a wall,) *and thus made that part like an* إِزَار: (Mgh, Mṣb:*) *he cased* [*the lower part of*] *it,* (namely, a wall,) *and thus strengthened it.* (A.) — ‡ *He strengthened him,* or *it;* (Ḳ, TA;) as also ↓ أَزَرَهُ, (Fr,) inf. n. أَزْرٌ. (Fr, Ḳ.) [See also 3.]

3. آزَرَهُ, (Fr, Ṣ, A, Mṣb,) for which the vulgar say وَازَرَهُ, (Fr, Ṣ,) the latter an extr. form, (Ḳ,) inf. n. مُؤَازَرَةٌ; (Mṣb, Ḳ;) and ↓ أَزَرَهُ; (TA;) *He aided, assisted,* or *helped, him;* (Fr, Ṣ, A, Mṣb, Ḳ;*) *and strengthened him.* (Mṣb.) [See also 2.] You say, آزَرْتُ الرَّجُلَ عَلَى فُلَانٍ *I aided, assisted,* or *helped, and strengthened, the man against such a one.* (Zj.) And أَرَدْتُ كَذَا فَآزَرَنِى عَلَيْهِ فُلَانٌ *I desired to do such a thing, and such a one aided, assisted,* or *helped, me to do it.* (A, TA.) — آزَرَ الزَّرْعُ بَعْضُهُ بَعْضًا, (A,) inf. n. as above, (Ḳ,) ‡ *The seed-produce became tangled,* or *luxuriant,* (A, Ḳ,) *one part reaching to another,* (A,) *and one part strengthening another;* (Ḳ;) as also ↓ تآزر الزَّرْعُ: (TA:) or تآزر النَّبْتُ signifies *the herbage became tangled,* or *luxuriant, and strong.* (Ṣ.) — آزَرَ الشَّىْءُ الشَّىْءَ, (TA,) inf. n. as above, (Ḳ,) *The thing equalled,* or *was equal to, the thing: the thing matched,* or *corresponded to, the thing.* (Ḳ,* TA.) In some copies of the Ḳ, in the place of المُسَاوَاةُ, is found المُوَاسَاةُ: the former is the correct reading. (TA.)

5: see 8, in two places: — and see also 3, in two places.

8. ايتزر, (Ṣ, Mgh, Mṣb,) originally ٱئْتَزَرَ, (Mgh, Mṣb,) and ↓ تآزر, (Ṣ,) or ايتزر بالإِزَار, and ↓ تآزر بِهِ, (Ḳ,) *He put on,* or *wore, the* إِزَار: (Ṣ, Mgh, Mṣb, Ḳ:) اِتَّزَرَ is wrong, (Nh,) or vulgar, (Mgh,) and should not be said: it occurs in certain of the trads., but is probably a corruption of the relaters: (Ḳ:) or it is a correct form, [like اِتَّخَذَ &c., (see art. اخذ,)] (Mṣb, MF,) accord. to El-Karmánee and Ṣgh and others. (MF.)

أَزْرٌ *Strength.* (IAạr, Ṣ, A, Ḳ.) — And (or as some say, TA) *Weakness:* thus bearing two contr. significations. (IAạr, Ḳ.) — And The *back.* (IAạr, Ṣ, Ḳ.) أُشْدُدْ بِهِ أَزْرِى, in the Ḳur [xx. 32], means *Strengthen Thou by him my back:* (IAạr, Ṣ:) or *confirm Thou by him my strength:* or *strengthen Thou by him my weakness.* (IAạr.) — *Aid, assistance,* or *help.* (Mṣb.) — Also, (Ṣ,) or ↓ أُزْرٌ, (Ḳ,) The *place,* (Ḳ,) or *part of* [*each of*] *the two flanks,* (Ṣ,) *where the* إِزَار *is tied in a knot.* (Ṣ, Ḳ.)

أُزْرٌ: see أَزْرٌ.

إِزْرٌ: see إِزَارٌ.

إِزْرَةٌ *Any particular mode, or manner, of putting on, or wearing, the* إِزَار. (Ṣ, Ḳ.) You say, إِنَّهُ لَحَسَنُ الإِزْرَةِ [*Verily he has a good manner of putting on,* or *wearing, the* ازار]. (A.) And ايتزر إِزْرَةً حَسَنَةً *He put on,* or *wore, the* ازار *in* a good manner. (Ṣ.) And it is said in a trad., إِزْرَةُ المُؤْمِنِ إِلَى نِصْفِ السَّاقِ وَلَا جُنَاحَ عَلَيْهِ فِيمَا بَيْنَهُ وَبَيْنَ الكَعْبَيْنِ [*The believer's mode of wearing the* ازار *is to have it reaching to the middle of the shank; and there shall be no sin chargeable to him with respect to what is between that and the two ankles*]. (TA.)

إِزَارٌ, masc. and fem., and ↓إِزَارَةٌ, and ↓مِئْزَرٌ, (Ṣ, Mṣb, Ḳ,) and ↓مِئْزَرَةٌ, (Lḥ,) and ↓إِزْرٌ, (Ḳ,) *A thing well known;* (Ṣ, Mṣb;) [*a waist-wrapper;*] *a wrapper for covering,* or *which covers, the lower part of the body,* [*from the waist downwards, concealing the thighs, and generally the upper half, or more, of the shanks,* (see أُزْرٌ, or أُزُرٌ, and إِزْرَةٌ,)] *not sewed:* or *such as is beneath the shoulders,* or *on the lower half of the body:* the رِدَآء is that which covers the upper half of the body; or that which is upon the shoulders and back; and this also is not sewed: each of these explanations is correct: (MF:) or *i. q.* مِلْحَفَةٌ: (Ḳ:) [in the present day, إِزَار, vulgarly pronounced إِيزَار, is also applied to *a woman's outer covering,* or *wrapper, of white calico;* described in my "Modern Egyptians:" and ↓مِئْزَر, to *a pair of drawers:* and app., in post-classical writings, to *anything resembling a waist-wrapper, worn on any part of the person, and in any manner; sometimes as a turban:*] and إِزَارٌ also signifies *anything with which one is veiled, concealed,* or *covered:* (Th, Ḳ:) its pl. is آزِرَةٌ, (Ṣ, Mṣb, Ḳ,) a pl. of pauc., (Ṣ, Mṣb,) and (of mult., S, Mṣb) أُزُرٌ (Ṣ, Mṣb, Ḳ) and أُزْرٌ, (Ḳ,) which is of the dial. of Temeem, or, accord. to MF, a contraction of أُزُرٌ: (TA:) and the pl. of مِئْزَرٌ is مَآزِرُ. (Mṣb.) You say, شَدَّ لِلْأَمْرِ ↓مِئْزَرَهُ ‡ *He prepared himself for the thing, affair,* or *business.* (A.) And شَدَّ ↓المِئْزَرَ ‡ *He abstained from sexual intercourse:* or *he prepared himself for religious service.* (TA, from a trad.) And اِخْضَرَّ إِزَارِى ‡ (*The place of*) *my* ازار *became black:* or, rather, *became of a* [*blackish*] *hue inclining to green:* because the hair when it first grows is of that hue. (Ḥar p. 404.) And دَارِى إِزَارِى [*My house is my covering*]: said by Es-Sarawee to IAar, on the latter's expressing his surprise at the former's walking in his house naked. (TA.) — ‡ *Continence; chastity.* (Ḳ, TA.) You say, فُلَانٌ عَفِيفُ الإِزَارِ, and ↓المِئْزَرِ ‡ *Such a one is continent, abstaining from women with whom it is unlawful to him to have commerce:* (A 'Obeyd:) and in like manner, فُلَانٌ طَيِّبُ الإِزَارِ. (TA in art. حجز.) — ‡ One's *wife:* (Ṣ, M, Ḳ:) or one's *self:* (IḲt, Suh:) or one's *wife and family:* or one's *family and self.* (TA.) One says, فِدًى لَكَ إِزَارِى ‡ *May my wife be a ransom for thee:* (Aboo-'Omar El-Jarmee, Ṣ:) or *myself.* (IḲt, Suh.) And it is said in a trad. respecting the vow of allegiance made at the 'Aḳabeh, لَنَمْنَعَنَّكَ مِمَّا نَمْنَعُ مِنْهُ أُزُرَنَا ‡ *We will assuredly defend thee from that from which we defend our wives and our families:* or *ourselves.* (TA.) — ‡ *A ewe.* (Ḳ, TA.) [But see شَاةٌ مُؤَزَّرَةٌ.] And إِزَارْ إِزَارْ is *A cry by which a ewe is called to be milked.* (Ḳ.)

إِزَارَةٌ: see إِزَارٌ.

فَرَسٌ آزَرُ, and آزَرَآءُ, [which is the fem.,] ‡ *A horse, and a mare, white in the hinder part,* (A, TA,) which is the place of the إِزَار of a man; (TA;) [i. e., it corresponds to the lower part of the body of a man:] when the whiteness descends to the thighs, the epithet مُسَرْوَلٌ is employed: (A:) or the former signifies *a horse white in the thighs, and having his fore parts black,* or *of any colour:* (AO, Ḳ:) pl. أُزْرٌ. (A.)

مِئْزَرٌ: see إِزَارٌ, in five places.

مِئْزَرَةٌ: see إِزَارٌ.

شَاةٌ مُؤَزَّرَةٌ ‡ *A ewe,* or *she-goat, that is* [*black in the hinder part*] *as though attired with a black* إِزَار. (A; [in which is added, وَيُقَالُ لَهَا إِزَارٌ, which may mean, "and one says, She has an ازار;" or "and one calls her ازار;" but more probably the former is meant thereby;] and Ḳ; [in which نَعْجَةٌ, "a ewe," is put in the place of شَاةٌ.]) — نَصْرٌ مُؤَزَّرٌ ‡ *Aid* [*made*] *effective and powerful:* (Ḳ, TA:) occurring in a trad. (TA.)

مَأْزُورَاتٌ for مَوْزُورَاتٌ: see art. وزر.

ازف

1. أَزِفَ, aor. َ, inf. n. أَزَفٌ (Ṣ, Mṣb, Ḳ) and أُزُوفٌ, (Mṣb, Ḳ,) *It* (departure) *was,* or *became,* or *drew, near:* (Ṣ, Mṣb, Ḳ:) and in like manner, a time. (TA.) Hence, in the Ḳur [liii. 58], أَزِفَتِ الآزِفَةُ *The resurrection draweth near.* (Ṣ, Mṣb.) — *He* (a man) *hastened,* or *was quick:* (Ṣ, Ḳ:) or *he drew near, and hastened,* or *was quick.* (A, TA.)

4. آزَفَنِى *He* (a man, TA) *incited me,* or *urged me, to hasten,* or *be quick:* (Ḳ, TA:) it is of the measure أَفْعَلَنِى. (TA.)

5. تَأَزُّفٌ The *stepping with contracted steps.* (Ḳ.) But see خَطْوٌ مُتَآزِفٌ, below. (TA.)

6. تَآزَفُوا *They drew near together, one to another.* (IF, Ḳ.)

آزِفٌ, applied to a man, *Hastening,* or *quick:* (Ṣ, TA:) and *endeavouring to hasten,* or *be quick.* (TA.)

الآزِفَةُ *The resurrection:* so in the Ḳur liii. 58, (Ṣ, Mṣb,) and xl. 18: (Bḍ:) or in the latter place it means *the near event,* or *case, of being on the brink of the fire* [*of Hell*]: or, as some say, *death.* (Bḍ.)

مُتَآزِفٌ, of the measure مُتَفَاعِلٌ, applied to a man, (TA,) *Short;* (Ṣ, A, Ḳ;) as being contracted in make; (A, TA;) *having his several parts near together.* (Ṣ, Ḳ.) [In the CḲ it is written مُتَأَزِّف, in this sense and others, following.] — *A strait,* or *narrow, place.* (O, L, Ḳ.) — *A contracted* stepping: you say, خَطْوٌ مُتَآزِفٌ: so in the O and L. (TA.) — ‡ A man (Ṣgh, TA) *evil in disposition; narrow-minded:* (Ṣgh, Ḳ, TA:) *weak; cowardly.* (TA.)

ازق

1. أَزَقَ, aor. ُ; (Ḳ;) and أَزِقَ, aor. َ; (IDrd, Ḳ;) inf. n. (of the former, TA) أَزْقٌ, (Ṣ, O, Ḳ,) and (of the latter, TA) أَزَقٌ, (IDrd, Ḳ,) or the latter is used by poetic licence for the former; (Aṣ, Ṣgh;) *He,* or *it,* (said of a man, MF, or of a man's bosom or mind, Ḳ,) *became strait,* or *straitened;* (IDrd, Ṣ,* O,* Ḳ, MF;) أَزْقٌ being thus *syn. with* أَزْلٌ: (Ṣ, O:) or *it* (a man's bosom or mind) *became straitened in war* or *fight;* (Ḳ;) or *he* (a man) *became straitened in his bosom* or *mind, in war* or *fight:* (TA:) as also ↓تَأَزَّقَ, with respect to both these significations; (Ḳ;) or this signifies *it* (a man's bosom or mind) *became strait,* or *straitened;* like تَأَزَّلَ; (Fr, Ṣ;) and ↓تَآزَقَ signifies the same as تَأَزَّقَ. (Z, in Golius.) [See also 10.] — أَزَقَهُ, inf. n. أَزْقٌ, *He straitened him:* the verb being trans. and intrans. (MF.)

5 and 6: see 1.

10. اُسْتُؤْزِقَ عَلَى فُلَانٍ *The place became strait to such a one,* (Ḳ, TA,) *so that he was unable to go forth* [*into it, to war or fight*]. (TA.)

مَأْزِقٌ *A place of straitness,* or *a strait place,* (Ṣ, Ḳ, TA,) *in which people fight.* (TA.) And hence, *A place of war* or *fight.* (Ṣ.) And مَأْزِقُ العَيْشِ *The place of straitness of life,* or *living.* (Lḥ.) Pl. مَآزِقُ. (TA.)

ازل

1. أَزَلَ, (Ṣ, Ḳ,) aor. ِ, inf. n. أَزْلٌ, (Ṣ,) *He* (a man) *became in a state of straitness,* or *narrowness, and suffering from dearth* or *drought* or *sterility.* (Ṣ, Ḳ.) [See also the pass. form of the verb here following; and see 5.] — أَزَلَهُ, aor. as above, (Ḳ,) and so the inf. n., (TA,) *He confined, restricted, restrained, withheld, debarred, hindered,* or *prevented, him;* (Ḳ,* TA;) and *straitened him; in consequence of distress,* or *adversity,* and *fear.* (TA.) — *He shortened his* (a horse's) *rope,* [or *tether,*] *and then left him to pasture at pleasure* (Lth, Ḳ, [in the CḲ, شَيْئَهُ is put for سَيْبَهُ,]) *in the place of pasturage.* (Lth.) — أَزَلُوا مَالَهُمْ, (Ṣ,) or أَمْوَالَهُمْ, (Ḳ,) aor. as above, (Ṣ,) *They confined, restricted,* or *debarred, their cattle from the place of pasturage,* (Ṣ,) or *did not take,* or *send, them forth thereto,* (Ḳ,) *in consequence of fear,* (Ṣ, Ḳ,) or *dearth* or *drought* or *sterility.* (Ḳ.) — It is said in a trad. respecting Ed-Dejjál, and his besieging the Muslims in Beyt-el-Maḳdis, [or Jerusalem,] فَيُؤْزَلُونَ أَزْلًا شَدِيدًا *And they will be straitened with a vehement straitening.* (TA.) And أُزِلَ النَّاسُ signifies *The people suffered,* or *were afflicted with, drought,* or *want of rain.* (TA.)

4. آزَلَتِ السَّنَةُ *The year became severe, distressful, calamitous,* or *adverse.* (TA.) — آزَلَهُمُ اللّٰهُ *God afflicted them with drought,* or *want of rain.* (TA.)

5. تَأَزَّلَ *It* (a man's bosom or mind) *became*

strait, or *straitened*; (Fr, Ṣ, Ḳ;) as also تَآزَقَ. (Fr, Ṣ.)

أَزْلٌ *Straitness; distress; difficulty;* (Ṣ,* Ḳ;) and *drought*, or *want of rain*. (TA.) — *Vehemence of might*, or *of strength, in war*, or *fight; of courage, valour*, or *prowess:* or *of war*, or *fight:* or *of fear:* or *of punishment:* syn. شِدَّةُ بَأْسٍ. (TA.) ═ It is also used as an epithet, meaning *Strait; narrow; confined.* (Ḥam p. 339.)

إِزْلٌ *A calamity;* (Ḳ;) because of its distressing character. (TA.) — *Lying*, or *falsehood*. (Yaạḳoob, Ṣ, Ḳ.)

أَزَلٌ *i. q.* قِدَمٌ [i. e. *Eternity, with respect to past time*, or *considered retrospectively; existence from eternity;* or *ancientness*] (Ṣ, Ḳ, TA) *that is without beginning;* (TA;) or the *continuance of existence in decreed times interminable in respect of the past;* like as أَبَدٌ is the continuance of existence in decreed times interminable in respect of the future; (KT;) or *that* [*existence*, or *time*,] *which has no extremity in its beginning;* like قِدَمٌ; and أَبَدٌ is that which has no extremity in its latter part; like بَقَآءٌ: the former is *existence without any beginning:* (Kull p. 31:) said to be from the phrase لَمْ يَزَلْ ["he, or it, has not ceased" to be &c.; i. e. "has ever" been &c. (see أَزَلِىٌّ)]: or, accord. to some, from أَزْلٌ signifying "narrowness;" because the intellect is prevented by its narrowness from perceiving its beginning: (MF:) ازل is a name for *that of which the mind is prevented by its narrowness from determining the limit of the beginning;* from أَزْلٌ meaning "narrowness;" and ابد is a name for that of which the mind shrinks from, or shuns, the determining the limit of the end; from أُبُودٌ meaning the act of "shrinking" from a thing, or "shunning" it. (Kull pp. 30 and 31.) Hence the saying, كَانَ فِى الأَزَلِ قَادِرًا عَالِمًا [*He was*, or *has been, ever, powerful, knowing*]. (A, TA.) The phrase أَزَلَ الآزَالِ [*During the space, without beginning, of all past times;* or *ever, in all past times;*] is like the phrase أَبَدَ الآبَادِ; said to be no evidence of the use of آزَالٌ as a pl. of أَزَلٌ in a general way by the Arabs of the classical ages, as it is here added merely as a corroborative. (MF in art. ابد.) [See also أَزَلِىٌّ.]

أَزِلٌ: see آزِلٌ.

أَزَلِىٌّ [*Eternal, with respect to past time; existing from eternity;* or *ancient without beginning;* as is implied in the Ṣ and Ḳ &c.;] a thing, or being, *which has not been preceded by non-existence:* it is applied to God: and to [his] knowledge: that which exists must be one of three kinds only: أَزَلِىٌّ أَبَدِىٌّ [*existing from eternity*, and consequently *existing to eternity*]; and this is God [who is also called القَدِيمُ الأَزَلِىُّ *the Ancient without beginning*]: and لَا أَزَلِىٌّ وَلَا أَبَدِىٌّ [*not existing from eternity nor existing to eternity*]; and such is the present world: and أَبَدِىٌّ غَيْرُ أَزَلِىٍّ [*existing to eternity without existing from eternity*]; and such is the world to come; the reverse of which [last] is impossible: (TA:) it is a rel. n. from أَزَلٌ: or, accord. to some, it is not [genuine] Arabic: (TA:) or it is originally يَزَلِىٌّ, a rel. n. from لَمْ يَزَلْ, (Ṣ, Ḳ,) a phrase applied to that which is قَدِيمٌ; and is formed by contraction; (Ṣ;) then, the ى is changed into ا, as being easier of pronunciation; as in أَزَنِىٌّ, applied to a spear, in relation to ذُو يَزَنٍ; (Ṣ, Ḳ,* Ṣgh, TA;) and as in أَثْرِبِىٌّ, applied to a blade, (Ṣ, Ṣgh, TA,) in relation to يَثْرِبُ: (TA:) so say some of the learned. (Ṣ.)

أَزَلِيَّةٌ The *quality*, or *attribute, of* أَزَلٌ [*eternity, with respect to past time*, &c.]: but it is a forged term, not of the [genuine] language of the Arabs. (A, TA.)

سَنَةٌ أَزُولٌ *A severe, distressful, calamitous*, or *adverse, year:* pl. أُزُلٌ. (Ḳ.)

آزِلٌ A man *in a state of straitness, distress, adversity*, or *difficulty*. (TA.) — A man *in a state of straitness in consequence of fever:* or *who is unable to go forth in consequence of pain:* or *confined, restricted, withheld*, or *prevented* [*from going forth*]. (TA.) — لَبُونٌ آزِلَةٌ [*A milch camel*] *confined*, or *restricted, not pasturing at pleasure, having her shank tied up to her arm, on account of her owner's fear of a hostile incursion:* occurring in a poem of El-Aạshà. (TA.) — أَزْلٌ آزِلٌ, in the Ḳ, erroneously, ↓ أَزِلٌ, *Severe*, or *vehement, straitness, distress*, or *difficulty*. (Ḳ,* TA.)

مَأْزِلٌ *A place of straitness*, or *a strait place;* (Ṣ, Ḳ;) like مَأْزِقٌ: (Ṣ:) or *a place of war* or *fight, when strait*. (Lḥ.) And مَآزِلُ العَيْشِ *The place where the means of subsistence are strait*, or *narrow*. (Lḥ.)

سُنَيَّةٌ حَمْرَآءُ مُؤْزِلَةٌ [*A severe year of dearth*, or *sterility*,] *afflicting with drought*. (TA, from a trad.)

مَأْزُولٌ A horse *having his rope* [or *tether*] *shortened, and then left to feed at pleasure in the place of pasturage*. (Lth.)

ازم

1. أَزَمَ, aor. ـِ, inf. n. أَزْمٌ and أُزُومٌ, *He bit with the whole mouth, vehemently:* (Ḳ:) or *with the canine teeth:* or you say, أَزَمَهُ, and أَزَمَ عَلَيْهِ, meaning *he bit it, and then repeated* [*the action*] *upon it, not letting it go:* or *he seized upon it with his mouth:* (TA:) or أَزَمَهُ signifies [simply] *he bit it:* (Ṣ:) and أَزَمَ عَلَيْهِ, aor. ـِ, inf. n. أَزْمٌ; and أَزِمَ, aor. ـَ, inf. n. أَزَمٌ; *the same;* or *he seized*, or *took hold, upon it with his teeth:* (Mṣb:) and أَزَمْتُ يَدَ الرَّجُلِ *I bit the arm*, or *hand, of the man most vehemently*. (TA.) أَزَمَ بِهَا occurs in a trad. as meaning *He bit it*, (referring to a ring of a coat of mail,) *and held it between two of his central teeth*. (AO.) And in another trad., أَزَمَ فِى يَدِهِ, meaning *He bit his arm*, or *hand*. (TA.) And you say, أَزَمَ الفَرَسُ عَلَى فَأْسِ اللِّجَامِ *The horse seized* [*with his teeth*, or *champed*,] *upon the* فَأْس [q. v.] *of the bit*. (Ḳ.) And أَزْمٌ signifies also The *cutting with the canine tooth*, and *with a knife*, (Ḳ,) and *with other things*. (TA.) — [And hence,] أَزَمَ عَلَيْنَا, (Ṣ, Mṣb,* Ḳ,*) aor. ـِ, inf. n. أَزْمٌ (Ṣ) and أُزُومٌ, (TA,) said of a time, (Ṣ, Mṣb,) or a year, (Ḳ,) *It was*, or *became, distressful*, or *afflictive, to us*, [*as though it bit us*,] *by drought, dearth*, or *scarcity;* (Ṣ, Mṣb, Ḳ;) *and scant in its good things;* (Ṣ;) as also أَزِمَ, aor. ـَ, inf. n. أَزَمٌ. (Mṣb.) And أَصَابَتْهُمْ سَنَةٌ أَزَمَتْهُمْ, (Ṣ, Ḳ,*) inf. n. أَزْمٌ, (Ṣ,) *A year*, or *year of dearth* or *drought* or *sterility, befell them, which extirpated them:* (Ṣ, Ḳ:*) or, accord. to Sh, the verb in this sense is only with ر. (TA. [See art. ارم.]) — [Hence also,] أَزَمَ بِهِ, (AZ, Ṣ, Ḳ,) inf. n. أَزْمٌ, (TA,) *He clave to him*, namely, his companion; (AZ, Ṣ, Ḳ;) and *to it*, namely, a place. (Ḳ.) And أَزَمَ عَلَيْهِ, (Ḳ,) aor. ـِ, inf. n. أَزْمٌ, (TA,) *He kept, attended*, or *applied himself, constantly, perseveringly*, or *assiduously, to it;* (Ḳ;) *he clave to it*. (TA.) And أَزَمَ بِضَيْعَتِهِ, or لَهَا, (accord. to different copies of the Ḳ, the former being the reading in the TA,) and عَلَيْهَا, (TA,) inf. n. أُزُومٌ, (AZ, TA,) *He kept, attended*, or *applied himself, constantly, perseveringly*, or *assiduously, to his* ضيعة [or *land*, &c.]. (AZ, Ḳ, TA.) — أَزَمَ, (Nh, Ḳ,) inf. n. أَزْمٌ, (Nh, TA,) also signifies *He held his teeth together, one upon another:* (Nh:) [and *he compressed*, or *put together, his lips:* (see آزِمٌ:)] and *he closed*, or *locked*, a door. (Ḳ, TA.) It is said in a trad., السِّوَاكُ تَسْتَعْمِلُهُ عِنْدَ تَغَيُّرِ الفَمِ مِنَ الأَزْمِ *The stick for cleaning the teeth, thou shalt use it on the occasion of the mouth's becoming altered in odour from the holding of the teeth together*. (Nh.) — [And hence,] أَزَمَ, (Ṣ, Nh, Mṣb,) inf. n. أَزْمٌ, (Mṣb, Ḳ,) *He held, refrained*, or *abstained*, (Ṣ, Ḳ,*) عَنِ الشَّىْءِ *from the thing:* (Ṣ, TA:) and *he held, refrained*, or *abstained, from desiring much:* (TA:) and *from food* (Mṣb, Ḳ*) *and drink;* (Mṣb;) as also أَزِمَ, aor. ـَ, inf. n. أَزَمٌ: (Mṣb:) and *from speech;* (Nh, Ḳ;*) *like as does the faster from food:* and hence, (Nh,) or from the next preceding signification, (Mṣb,) حِمْيَةٌ [meaning as explained in what follows] is termed أَزْمٌ: (Nh, Mṣb:) but accord. to the relation commonly known, of a trad. in which أَزْمٌ is said to occur in the last of the senses explained above, the word is أَرْمٌ, with ر, and with teshdeed in the case of the م. (Nh.) It is related in a trad., that 'Omar having asked El-Ḥárith Ibn-Keledeh, the طَبِيب of the Arabs, "What is the [best] remedy?" (Ṣ,) or having asked him respecting [the best] medical, or curative, treatment, (Mṣb,) the latter said, الأَزْمُ, meaning الحِمْيَةُ; (Ṣ, Mṣb;) both these words here meaning *The practising abstinence;* (PṢ;) or *the abstaining*, or *desisting, from eating:* (TA:) or, in this instance, (TA,) الأَزْمُ signifies *the not putting in food upon food:* and (some say, TA) *the being silent:* (Ḳ, TA:) and it signifies also *strength*. (TA.) — أَزَمَ الشَّىْءُ *The thing became contracted; became drawn together*, or *compressed;* as also أَزِمَ, aor. ـَ. (Ḳ.)

5. تَأَزَّمَ القَوْمُ, (TA,) or تَأَزَّمَ القَوْمُ دَارَهُمْ, (Ṣ,) *The people, or company of men, stayed, remained, or dwelt, long in their abode.* (Ṣ, TA.)

أَزْمٌ: see أَزْمَةٌ.

أَزِمٌ [part. n. of أَزِمَ; fem. with ة]: see أَزْمَةٌ.

أَزْمَةٌ [inf. n. of un. of 1: and hence,] *A single act of eating;* (Ḳ, TA;) i. e. *an eating but once in the course of the day;* like وَجْبَةٌ [q. v.]. (TA.) — Also, (Fr, Ṣ, Mṣb, Ḳ,) and ▼أَزْمَةٌ and ▼أَزَمَةٌ, (Fr, Ḳ, [the last in the CḲ like the first,]) *Straitness, hardness, or distress;* (Ṣ, Mṣb, Ḳ;) *drought, dearth, or sterility:* (Ṣ, Mṣb:) pl. (of the first, TA) ▼أَزْمٌ, (Ḳ,) [or rather this is a coll. gen. n.,] like as تَمْرٌ is of تَمْرَةٌ, (TA,) [but originally an inf. n. of أَزَمَ, q. v.,] and إِزَمٌ, (Ḳ,) like as بِدَرٌ is of بَدْرَةٌ. (TA.) Hence the trad., اشْتَدِّى أَزْمَةُ تَنْفَرِجِى, meaning *Become severe, O year of drought, or dearth, or sterility: then thou wilt pass away:* though it has been strangely asserted that ازمة is here the proper name of a woman, to whom, on an occasion of her being taken with the pains of labour, these words were said by the Prophet. (TA.) You also say سَنَةٌ أَزْمَةٌ and ▼أَزِمَةٌ, (Ḳ,) so in the copies of the Ḳ, there said to be like فَرِحَةٌ, but correctly ▼آزِمَةٌ, as in the M &c., (TA,) [or both are correct, being part. ns., respectively, of أَزِمَ and أَزَمَ,] and ▼أَزُومَةٌ, meaning *A distressful, or an afflictive, year;* (Ḳ;) *a year of vehement drought or dearth or sterility.* (TA.) And أَوَازِمُ [pl. of ▼آزِمَةٌ, used as a subst.,] signifies *Distressful, or afflictive, years.* (TA.) ▼أَزَامِ, also, (Ḳ,) or, accord. to Aboo-'Alee, ▼أَزُومُ, (IB,) [each a proper name, as denoting a kind of personification,] signifies *The year of drought or dearth or sterility.* (Ḳ.) And you say, نَزَلَتْ بِهِمْ أَزَامِ ▼ and ▼أَزُومُ *Severe straitness, or distress, befell them.* (Ṣ, TA.*)

أَزِمَةٌ : } see أَزْمَةٌ.
أَزَمَةٌ : }

أَزَامِ: see أَزْمَةٌ, in two places.

أَزَامٌ: see what next follows.

أَزُومٌ: see آزِمٌ, in three places. — أَزُومُ: see أَزْمَةٌ, in two places. — Also, the former, *Cleaving to a thing;* (Ḳ;) and so ▼أَزَامٌ. (Ṣgh, Ḳ.)

أَزُومَةٌ: see أَزْمَةٌ.

آزِمٌ act. part. n. of أَزَمَ; *Biting with the whole mouth, vehemently:* [&c.:] as also ▼أَزُومٌ: (Ḳ: [in the CḲ the former is erroneously written آزَمْ:]) or the latter signifies *that has a habit of biting;* or *that bites much;* syn. عَضُوضٌ: (Ḥam p. 532:) pl. of the former أُزُومٌ: (Ḥam p. 360:) and of the latter أُزُمٌ. (Ḥam p. 600.) [Hence,] ▼الأَزُومُ *The biting lion;* or *the lion that bites much, or vehemently;* الأَسَدُ العَضُوضُ. (TA.) — [Hence also,] The *canine tooth;* syn. نَابٌ; and so ▼آزِمَةٌ; and ▼أَزُومٌ: pl. of the first أُزَّمٌ; and of the second أَوَازِمُ; and of the third أُزُمٌ. (M, Ḳ.) — Also *Having his lips compressed, or put together.* (AZ, Ṣ.)

آزِمَةٌ: see آزِمٌ: — and see also أَزْمَةٌ, in three places.

مَأْزِمٌ *A narrow, or strait, place; a place of narrowness or straitness;* (Ṣ, Ḳ;) like مَأْزِلٌ; (Ṣ;) of a land, and of the pudendum muliebre, and of life, (Ḳ,) or of the means of subsistence; (Lḥ, Ḳ;) or *of any kind:* (TA:) *any narrow road between two mountains:* (Ṣ, Mṣb:) *a narrow place in mountains, such that one part meets another, and the place beyond widens:* (TA:) pl. مَآزِمُ. (Ṣ, Ḳ.) — And hence, (Mṣb,) *A place of war or fight;* (Ṣ, Mṣb;) because of the straitness of the state thereof, and the difficulty of escape from it. (Mṣb.)

مُتَأَزِّمٌ *Smitten, or afflicted, by* أَزْمَة [or *straitness,* &c.]: (Ḳ:) or *expressing pain or grief,* or *lamenting,* or *complaining, on account of the straitness,* or *distressfulness,* or *afflictiveness,* (شِدَّة and أَزْمَة,) *of time,* or *fortune.* (TA.)

ازى

2. أَزَّى الحَوْضَ, inf. n. تَأْزِيَةٌ (Ṣ, Ḳ) and تَأْزِىءٌ, or تَوْزِىءٌ, (accord. to different copies of the Ṣ, [the latter irregular,]) or both, (accord. to the TA,) *He put, or made, an* إِزَآء [q. v.], *to the watering-trough or tank;* (Ṣ, Ḳ;) i. e. *he put upon its mouth a stone,* or *a* جُلَّة [explained below, voce إِزَآء], or *the like;* (TA;) as also ▼آزَاهُ, inf. n. إِيزَآءٌ; (Ṣ, TA;) or ▼تَأْزَاهُ. (Ḳ.)

3. آزَاهُ, (Ṣ, Ḳ,) inf. n. مُؤَازَاةٌ, (Mṣb in art. حذو, and TA in art. وزى, &c., [though it would seem from the Ḳ to be إِيزَآءٌ,]) *He* (a man, Ṣ) *was,* or *became, over against it,* or *opposite to it; he faced,* or *fronted, him,* or *it.* (Ṣ,* Ḳ,* TA in art. وزى.) Accord. to the Ṣ, one should not say, وَازَاهُ: but it is said in a trad. respecting the prayer of fear, فَوَازَيْنَا العَدُوَّ, i. e. *And we faced,* or *fronted, the enemy:* (TA:) and the inf. n. is مُوَازَاةٌ. (TA in art. وزى.) [Its syn. حَاذَاهُ is more common.] — [Hence مُؤَازَاةٌ signifying *A conformity, a mutual resemblance, or a correspondence, with regard to sound, of two words occurring near together;* like اِزْدِوَاجٌ &c.: see art. زوج.] — [Hence, likewise,] آزاه also signifies *He contended with him,* syn. جَارَاهُ; (Ḳ, TA;) and *opposed,* or *withstood, him,* syn. قَاوَمَهُ. (TA.) Whence the saying in a trad., وَفِرْقَةٌ آزَتِ المُلُوكَ فَقَاتَلَتْهُمْ عَلَى دِينِ ٱللّٰهِ [*And a party contended with, and opposed, or withstood, the kings, and fought with them for the religion of God*]. (TA.)

4. آزى الحَوْضَ i. q. أَزَّاهُ, q. v. (Ṣ, TA.) — And *He repaired,* or *put into a right* or *proper state, the* إِزَآء [q. v.] *of the watering-trough* or *tank.* (IAạr, TA.) — And *He poured forth the water from its* إِزَآء. (TA.) — And آزى فِيهِ *He poured forth upon its* إِزَآء. (TA.)

5: see 2.

نَاقَةٌ أَزِيَةٌ, (accord. to some copies of the Ṣ,) or ▼آزِيَةٌ, (accord. to other copies of the Ṣ,) or both, (IAạr, TA,) each after the manner of a relative noun, [having no verb,] (TA,) *A she-camel that drinks from the* إِزَآء [q. v.]: (TA:) or *that will not drink save from the* إِزَآء *of the trough* or *tank;* and عَقِرَةٌ signifies one "that will not drink save from the عُقْر [thereof]:" (Ṣ, TA, and IAạr in art. عقر in the TA:) or, accord. to IAạr, *that will not come to the watering-trough* or *tank, to drink, until they leave it unoccupied for her;* as also قَذُورٌ. (TA in the present art.)

الإِزَآءُ i. q. الحِذَآءُ [*The front,* as meaning the *part, place,* or *location, that is over against, opposite, facing, fronting,* or *in front*]. (Mṣb, and Ḳ &c. in art. حذو.) You say, هُوَ بِإِزَائِهِ *He is over against, opposite to, facing, fronting,* or *in front of, him;* syn. بِحِذَائِهِ, (Ṣ,) or مُحَاذِيهِ. (Mṣb.) — [Hence, بِإِزَائِهِ signifies also *Corresponding to it;* as when one says,] الأَبْجَلُ عِرْقٌ مِنَ الفَرَسِ وَالبَعِيرِ بِإِزَآءِ الأَكْحَلِ مِنَ الإِنْسَانِ [*The* ابجل *is a vein of the horse and the camel, corresponding to the* اكحل *of man*]. (TA in art. بجل.) [You say also, وَضَعَ لَفْظًا بِإِزَآءِ مَعْنًى *He applied a word,* or *phrase, as correspondent to an idea,* or *a meaning.*] — إِزَآءٌ is also applied to a man, and to a woman, and to a number of persons, in senses here following. (TA.) You say, هُوَ إِزَآءُ الأَمْرِ *He is the manager, conductor, orderer, regulator,* or *superintendent, of the affair.* (Ṣ, Mṣb, TA.) And in the same sense the word is used by Ḥomeyd, in the phrase إِزَآءُ مَعَاشٍ [*The manager,* or *orderer, of the means of subsistence*], applied to a woman. (TA.) And in an instance in which a poet likens the إِزَآء of a watering-trough or tank to the [stinking animal called] ظَرِبَان: (Ṣ, TA:) in this case it means The *water-drawer* [of the trough or tank]. (Aṣ, IB, TA.) [But in relation to a watering-trough or tank, it generally has another meaning, which see below.] You say also, فُلَانٌ إِزَآءُ مَالٍ (Ṣ) [*Such a one is*] *a manager, tender,* or *superintendent, of cattle,* or *camels* &c.; (Ḳ,* TA;) *a good pastor thereof.* (TA.) And إِزَآءُ الحَرْبِ *The vigorous wager,* or *prosecutor, of war.* (Ḳ.) And فُلَانٌ إِزَآءُ فُلَانٍ *Such a one is the fellow and assistant of such a one.* (TA.) And هُمْ إِزَاؤُهُمْ *They are their fellows,* (Ḳ, TA,) *who assist them, and order,* or *set in order, their affairs:* (TA:) or *they are those who order,* or *set in order, their affairs.* (Mṣb.) And إِنَّهُ لَإِزَآءُ خَيْرٍ, and شَرٍّ, *Verily he is a possessor of goodness,* and *of evilness.* (TA.) — Also, الإِزَآءُ, (Ḳ,) or إِزَآءُ العَيْشِ, (TḲ,) *The means of sustenance:* or *what has been caused,* or *occasioned, of plentifulness and easiness, and of superabundance, of sustenance.* (Ḳ.) — Also The *place where the water is poured into the watering-trough* or *tank;* (Aṣ, Ṣ, Ḳ;) i. e. *its fore part;* [the *part next to the well or other source whence it is filled;*] the hinder part, where the camels stand when they come to water, being called the عُقْر: (Ṣ in art. عقر:) or, accord. to AZ, *a mass of stone, and what is put for protection* [*of the brink of the trough* or *tank* (as it is generally constructed of stones cemented and plastered with mud)] *upon the place where the water is poured when the bucket is emptied:* (Ṣ in the present art.:) or the *whole* (جميع [said in the TA to be a mistake for جمع, but this I think extremely improbable,]) *of what is between the watering-trough* or *tank and the cavity of the well,* [namely,] *of the* [*casing of stones,* or *bricks, called*] طَىّ: (Ḳ:) or *a stone,* or *skin,* or جُلَّة [i. e. *a thing made of palm-leaves woven together,* generally used as a receptacle for dates], *put* [*for protection*] *upon the mouth* [or *part of the border where the water is poured in*] *of the watering-trough* or *tank:* (Ḳ,* TA:) in the Ḳ, يوضع عَلَيْهَا is erroneously put for يوضع عَلَى فَمِ الحَوْضِ. (TA.)

نَاقَةٌ آزِيَةٌ: see أَزِيَةٌ.

اس

1: see 2, in two places.

2. أَسَّسَهُ, (Ṣ, M, Mṣb,) inf. n. تَأْسِيسٌ, (Ṣ, Mṣb, Ḳ,) *He founded it;* or *made,* or *laid, a foundation,* or *basis, for it;* (Ṣ,* Mṣb;) namely, a building, (Ṣ,) or a wall: (Mṣb:) *he marked out the limits of it,* (namely, of a house,) *and raised its foundations: he built its foundation,* or *basis:* (Ḳ:) *he commenced it;* namely, a building; as also ▼ أَسَّهُ, aor. يَؤُسُّهُ, inf. n. أَسٌّ: (M:) *he built it;* namely, a house; (TA;) as also ▼ أَسَّهُ. (Ḳ.) You say, هٰذَا تَأْسِيسٌ حَسَنٌ [*This is a good founding,* or *foundation*]. (TA.) And مَنْ لَمْ يُؤَسِّسْ مِلْكَهُ بِالعَدْلِ هَدَمَهُ ‡ [*He who does not lay the foundation of his property with equity,* or *justice, destroys it*]. (A, TA.) — أَسِّسْ زَادًا: see زَادٌ, in art. زود.

أُسٌّ: see what next follows, in six places.

أُسٌّ *The foundation, basis,* or *lowest part,* (Ṣ, A, Mgh, Mṣb, Ḳ,) of a building, (Ṣ, A, Ḳ,) or of a wall; (Mgh, Mṣb;) as also ▼ أُسٌّ and ▼ إِسٌّ (A, Ḳ) and ▼ أَسَاسٌ (Ṣ, A, Mgh, Mṣb, Ḳ) and ▼ أَسَسٌ, (Ṣ, Ḳ,) which is a contraction of أَسَاسٌ: (Ṣ:) or the *commencement* of a building: and *any commencement* of a thing; as also ▼ أُسٌّ and ▼ أَسَاسٌ and ▼ أَسَسٌ: (M:) and the *origin, source, stock,* or *root,* (أَصْلٌ,) of a man; as also ▼ أُسٌّ: or of anything; (M, Ḳ;) as also ▼ أُسٌّ (M, Ḳ) and ▼ إِسٌّ and ▼ أَسِيسٌ: (Ḳ:) and the *heart* of a man; because [the Arabs believe that] it is the first thing that comes into existence in the womb: (M, Ḳ:) pl. آسَاسٌ (Ṣ, M, Mgh, Mṣb, Ḳ) and إِسَاسٌ (M, Mṣb, Ḳ) and أُسُسٌ; (M, Mgh, Mṣb, Ḳ;) the first of which is pl. of أُسٌّ, (Mgh, Mṣb,) like as أَقْفَالٌ is of قُفْلٌ; (Mṣb;) or of أَسَسٌ, like as أَسْبَابٌ is of سَبَبٌ; (Ṣ;) or, as some say, of أُسُسٌ, [like as أَعْنَاقٌ is of عُنُقٌ,] so that it is a pl. pl.; (TA;) and the second, of أُسٌّ, like as عِسَاسٌ is of عُسٌّ; (Mṣb;) and the third, of أَسَاسٌ, (Mgh, Mṣb,) like as عُنُقٌ is of عَنَاقٌ. (Mṣb.) You say, بَنَى بَيْتَهُ عَلَى أَسَاسِهِ الأَوَّلِ [*He built his house upon its first foundation.*] (A.) And قَلَعَهُ مِنْ أُسِّهِ [*He uprooted it from its foundation*]. (A.) And فُلَانٌ أَسَاسُ ▼ أَمْرِهِ الكَذِبُ ‡ [*Such a one, the foundation of his affair,* or *case, is falsehood*]. (A, TA.) And كَانَ ذٰلِكَ عَلَى أُسِّ الدَّهْرِ, (Ṣ, M, A, Ḳ,) and ▼ أَسِّهِ, and ▼ إِسِّهِ, (Ṣ, M, Ḳ,) ‡ *That was in old,* or *ancient, time;* (Ṣ, M, Ḳ;) *at the beginning of time;* (Ṣ, A,* Ḳ;) and in like manner, عَلَى آسْتِ الدَّهْرِ. (A.) — Also *A remain, relic, trace, vestige, sign, mark,* or *track,* of anything. (Ḳ.) You say, خُذْ أُسَّ الطَّرِيقِ, or أَسَّ ▼ الطَّرِيقِ, [accord. to different copies of the Ḳ, meaning, *Take thou to the track of the way,*] when one guides himself by any mark or track, or by camels' dung: but when the way is manifest, you say, خُذْ شَرَكَ الطَّرِيقِ. (Ḳ.) أُسٌّ also signifies The *remains of ashes* (M, Ḳ) *between the* أَثَافِى, q. v.: (M:) occurring in a verse of En-Nábighah Edh-Dhubyánee; but accord. to most relaters of this verse, it is آسٌ. (TA.)

أِسٌّ:
أَسَسٌ:
أَسَاسٌ:
أَسِيسٌ:
} see أُسٌّ, in several places.

اسب

4. آسَبَتِ الأَرْضُ *The land produced* [*herbage such as is termed*] عُشْب; syn. أَعْشَبَتْ. (Ḳ.)

إِسْبٌ The *hair of the pubes:* (M, Ḳ:) or *of the pudendum:* (Th, M, Ḳ:) or *of the podex:* (Ṣ, Ḳ:) it may be, (Ṣ,) or is said to be, (M,) from وِسْبٌ, (Ṣ, M,) which signifies "herbage," or "plants," (Ṣ,) or "abundance of herbage:" (M:) the و being changed into ء, as in the case of إِرْثٌ and وِرْثٌ: (Ṣ:) pl. أُسُوبٌ, and, accord. to IJ, آسَابٌ. (M.)

مُؤَسَّبٌ A ram *having much wool.* (M, Ḳ.)

است

اِسْتٌ, signifying The *podex,* or the *anus,* (Ḳ,) or signifying the former, and sometimes used as meaning the latter, (Ṣ in art. سته,) is with a conjunctive hemzeh, [written آسْتٌ, when not immediately preceded by a quiescence,] and its final radical letter is elided; for the original form is سَتَهٌ; (Mṣb;) and it is mentioned in art. سته. (Ḳ.) [It is of the fem. gender.] It is said in a prov., applied to him who fails of attaining the object that he seeks, أَخْطَأَتِ آسْتُهُ الحُفْرَةَ [*His anus missed the hole in the ground*]. (Meyd.) — [Hence,] اِسْتُ الدَّهْرِ ‡ *The first,* or *beginning, of time;* (A;) *old,* or *ancient, time.* (IB, A,* Ḳ.*) One says, مَا زَالَ عَلَى آسْتِ الدَّهْرِ مَجْنُونًا ‡ [*He ceased not,* or *has not ceased, from the beginning of time,* or *from old time, to be insane,* or *mad;* or] *he always was,* or *always has been, known as being insane,* or *mad:* like as one says, عَلَى إِسِّ الدَّهْرِ. (AZ, Ṣ.) And Aboo-Nukheyleh says,

• مَا زَالَ مُذْ كَانَ عَلَى آسْتِ الدَّهْرِ •
• ذَا حُمُقٍ يَنْمِى وَعَقْلٍ يَحْرِى •

‡ [*He ceased not,* or *has not ceased, to be, since he was in the beginning of time,* or *in old time,* i. e., *from the first of his existence, a person of increasing foolishness, and of decreasing intellect*]. (AZ, Ṣ.) IB says, J has erred in mentioning است in this section [of the Ṣ]; its proper place being in art. سته, where he has also mentioned it; for its hemzeh is conjunctive, by common consent; and if conjunctive, it is augmentative: also, his saying that they have changed the [final] س in إِسٌّ into ت, like as they have changed the [final] س of طَسٌّ into ت, making this word طَسْتٌ, is a mistake; for, were it so, the hemzeh of است would be disjunctive [in every case; whereas it is always conjunctive except after a pause, when it is pronounced with kesr]: moreover, he has attributed this assertion to AZ, who never made it, but only mentioned است الدهر with اسّ الدهر because of their agreement in meaning. (TA.) — [Hence also,] اِسْتُ الكَلْبَةِ † *Calamity,* or *misfortune:* (Ḳ:) *adversity; difficulty; distress; affliction:* (TA:) *what is hated, disliked, disapproved, foul, abominable,* or *evil.* (Ḳ.) — And اِسْتُ المَتْنِ † *The desert:* (Ḳ:) or *the wide desert.* (TA.) — See also art. سته.

أُسْدِىٌّ The *warp* of cloth; (Ḳ;) as also أُسْتِىٌّ and أُزْدِىٌّ: (TA:) but it is improperly mentioned in this art.; for it is [originally أُسْتُوِىٌّ,] of the measure أُفْعُولٌ. (Ḳ.)

إِسْتِىٌّ *Of,* or *relating to, the* اِسْت. (TA in art. سته.)

استاذ

أُسْتَاذٌ a foreign word, pronounced to be such because س and ذ do not occur in any one Arabic word, (Mṣb,) not found in the poetry of the pagan times, (Ibn-Dihyeh in TA art. ستذ,) nor in the language of those times, (Shifá el-Ghaleel, ibid.,) [arabicized from the Persian أُسْتَاذْ,] *A master:* (MF:) *a skilful man, who is held in high estimation:* (Mṣb:) *a preceptor; a tutor; a teacher: a craftsmaster:* (Ibn-Dihyeh; and Golius on the authority of Meyd:) [and so in the present day; as also أُسْطَا and أُسْتَا:] also applied by the vulgar to *a eunuch;* because he generally tutors children: (Shifá el-Ghaleel, and Ibn-Dihyeh:) pl. أُسْتَاذُونَ: (Ḥar p. 377) [and أَسَاتِذَةٌ and أَسَاتِيذُ; and vulgarly, in the present day, أُسْتَوَاتٌ and أُسْطَوَاتٌ].

استبرق

إِسْتَبْرَقٌ: see art. برق, in which, and in art. سرق, it is mentioned: but this is its proper place, if it be an arabicized word: in the T it is mentioned in art. ستبرق.

اسد

1. أَسِدَ, (Ṣ, M, A, Ḳ,) aor. ـَ, (Ḳ,) inf. n. أَسَدٌ, (TA,) ‡ *He* (a man, M) *was,* or *became, like a lion,* (Ṣ, M, A, Ḳ,) *in his boldness,* (A,) *and his*

other dispositions; (Ṣ, A, TA;) as also ▼ استأسد; (M, A, Ḳ;) [and ▼ تأسّد; (see أَسِدَ;)] عَلَيْهِ *towards him*, or *against him*. (A.) You say أَسَدٌ بَيِّنُ الأَسَدِ [*A lion bearing evidence of being like a lion in boldness*]: an extr. phrase, like حِقَّةٌ بَيِّنَةُ الحِقَّةِ; (TA;) which is [said to be] the only other instance of the kind. (TA in art. حق.) [Hence the saying,] إِذَا دَخَلَ فَهِدَ وَإِذَا خَرَجَ أَسِدَ ‡[*When he comes in, he is like a lynx; and when he goes out, he is like a lion*: see فَهِدَ]. (Ṣ, from a trad.) You say also, أَسِدَ عَلَيْهِ meaning † *He became emboldened against him*; (TA;) as also ▼ استأسد. (Ṣ, Mṣb, Ḳ.) And † *He was*, or *became, angry with him*: (M, L, Ḳ:*) or (so accord. to the M and L, but in the Ḳ "and,") *behaved in a light and hasty manner*, or *foolishly*, or *ignorantly, towards him*. (M, L, Ḳ.*) — أَسِدَ, (Ṣ, Ḳ,) aor. as above, (Ḳ,) and so the inf. n., (TA,) also signifies † *He* (a man, Ṣ) *became stupified* (Ṣ, Ḳ) *by fear* (Ṣ) *at seeing a lion*. (Ṣ, Ḳ.) Thus it has two contr. meanings. (Ḳ.) ═ أَسَدَ, aor. ـِ, *i. q.* سَبَعَ [† *He bit another with his teeth, like as does the beast of prey*: or *he reviled, vilified*, or *vituperated*, another; *charged him with a vice or fault or the like*; or *assailed him with foul language, such as displeased* him]. (Ḳ.) — See also 4.

2: see 4.

4. آسَدَهُ, (Ṣ, M, Mṣb, Ḳ,) or آسَدَهُ بِالصَّيْدِ, (A,) inf. n. إِيسَادٌ; (TA;) and اوسدهُ, (Ṣ, Ḳ,) in which the أ [i. e. the second أ, for آسدهُ is originally أَأْسَدَهُ,] is changed into و; (Ṣ;) and ▼ أَسَّدَهُ; (Ḳ;) ‡ *He incited him* (namely a dog) *to the chase*. (Ṣ, M, A, Mṣb, Ḳ.*) — آسد بَيْنَ الكِلَابِ ‡ *He incited the dogs to attack one another*. (A.) And آسد بَيْنَ القَوْمِ, (Ṣ, M, A, L, Mṣb,) inf. n. إِيسَادٌ; (Mṣb;) or ▼ أَسَدَ, aor. ـِ; (Ḳ;) ‡ *He excited discord, dissension, disorder, strife, quarrelling*, or *animosity, between*, or *among, the people*, or *company of men*. (Ṣ, M, A, L, Mṣb, Ḳ.) ═ آسد السَّيْرَ *He journeyed with energy*; syn. أَسْأَدَهُ; (IJ, M;) from which it is probably formed by transposition. (M.)

5: see 1.

10. استأسد *He called a lion*. (M.) ═ See 1, in two places. — † *He became accustomed*, or *habituated*, [to a thing, as a dog to the chase,] *and emboldened*; syn. ضَرِىَ. (Mṣb.) — ‡ *It* (a plant, or herbage,) *became strong, and tangled*, or *luxuriant*: (Ṣ:) or *became tall and large*: or *grew to its utmost height*: (M:) or *attained its full growth, and became tangled*, or *luxuriant*, (M,) *and strong*: (TA:) or *became tall, and dry* (جَفَّ [perhaps a mistake for الْتَفَّ, as in the Ṣ and M,]) *and large*, (A, TA,) *and spread every way*: (A:) or *became tall, and attained its full growth*. (Ḳ.) ═ أَسْتَوْسَدَ (Ḳ, TA, [or أُسْتُوسِدَ,] in the CḲ اَسْتُوسَدَ) † *He* (a man, TA) *was*, or *became, excited, roused, provoked*, (هُيِّجَ, Ḳ, TA, in the CḲ هَيَّجَ,) or *incited*. (TA.)

أَسَدٌ [The *lion*;] *a certain beast of prey*, (M, TA,) *well known*: (M, A, Mṣb, Ḳ:) IKh and others have mentioned more than five hundred names for it; and it is said to have a thousand names [in the Arabic language; but these, with few exceptions, are epithets used as substs.]: (TA:) pl. [of pauc.] آسُدٌ (Ṣ, Ḳ [in the TA with two hemzehs, أَأْسُدٌ, which is the original form, but deviating from the regular pronunciation,]) and آسَادٌ (Ṣ, M, Ḳ) and [of mult.] أُسُودٌ (Ṣ, M, Mṣb, Ḳ) and أُسُدٌ (Ṣ) and أُسْدٌ, (Ṣ, M, Mṣb, Ḳ,) the last two of which are contractions of the form next preceding them, (Ṣ,) and أُسْدَانٌ (Ḳ) and ▼ مَأْسَدَةٌ, (Mṣb, Ḳ,) the last called by some a pl., but [rightly] said by others to be a quasi-pl. n.: (TA:) the female is called أَسَدَةٌ; (AZ, Ks, Ṣ; M, A, Mṣb, Ḳ;) or أَسَدٌ is applied to the male and the female, and sometimes the female is called أَسَدَةٌ. (Mṣb.) — لَقِيتُ مِنْهُ أَسَدًا is a phrase [meaning *I found him to be a man of exceeding boldness*; being] expressive of an intensive degree of boldness. (Mughnee in art. ب.) — الأَسَدُ † *The constellation Leo*. (Ḳzw, &c.) [See الذِّرَاعُ.] — And † *The star Cor Leonis*, or *Regulus*. (Ḳzw, &c.) [See الجَبْهَةُ.]

أَسِدٌ ‡ [*Like a lion*;] *bold; daring*; as also ▼ أَسِيدٌ and ▼ مُتَأَسِّدٌ [and ▼ مُسْتَأْسِدٌ (see 10)]. (Mṣb.) You say أَسَدٌ أَسِدٌ [*A bold*, or *fierce, lion*], adding the latter word to give intensiveness of signification. (IAạr, M.) — [Its fem.] أَسِدَةٌ [app. applied to a bitch] signifies † *Accustomed*, or *habituated*, [to the chase,] *and emboldened*; syn. ضَارِيَةٌ. (Ḳ, TA, in the CḲ صارِيَة.) [See also 10.]

أَسَدَةٌ *A* [*kind of enclosure for the protection of camels, sheep, or goats, such as is called*] حَظِيرَة. (Ḳ.) [Like أَصِيدَةٌ.] ═ [See also أَسَدٌ, of which it is the fem.]

أُسْدِىٌّ, with ḍamm, (IB, Ḳ,) thus correctly written, (IB,) in the L [and Ṣ] أُسْدِىٌّ, (TA,) *A kind of garments* or *cloths* (ثِيَاب, Ṣ, for which is put, in the Ḳ, erroneously, نَبَات, TA): occurring in a poem of El-Ḥoṭeiah, (Ṣ,) who likens thereto an extensive, even, waterless desert. (L.) IB says that he is in error who mentions it in the present art.: Aboo-'Alee says that أُسْدِىٌّ and أُسْتِىٌّ are quasi-pls. of سَدًى and سَتًى as signifying ثَوْبٌ مُسْدًى, and originally أُسْدُوىٌ and أُسْتُوىٌ; like as أُمْعُوزٌ is a quasi-pl. of مَعْزٌ. (L.) [But see art. سدو and سدى.]

أَسِيدٌ: see أَسِدٌ.

إِسَادَةٌ (Ṣ, Ḳ) and أَسَادَةٌ (Ḳ) *i. q.* وِسَادَةٌ [*A pillow*, &c.]: (Ṣ, Ḳ:) like إِشَاحٌ for وِشَاحٌ. (TA.)

مُؤْسِدٌ ‡ One *who trains a dog*, or *dogs, to the chase*. (L, Mṣb.)

مَأْسَدَةٌ *A place in which are lions*: (Mṣb, Ḳ:) or أَرْضٌ مَأْسَدَةٌ *a land having lions in it*: (Ṣ, A:) or *a land abounding with lions*: (M, R:) pl. مَآسِدُ. (A.) — See also أَسَدٌ.

مُتَأَسِّدٌ: } see أَسِدٌ.
مُسْتَأْسِدٌ: }

اسر

1. أَسَرَهُ, (Ṣ, M, A,) aor. ـِ, inf. n. أَسْرٌ (Ṣ, M, Ḳ) and إِسَارٌ, (M, TA,) *He bound, braced*, or *tied, him*, [namely, his captive,] or *it*, (Ṣ, M, A, Ḳ,) namely, his قَتَب [or camel's saddle], (Ṣ, A,) or his horse's saddle, (A,) *with an* إِسَار, i. e. *a thong of untanned hide*, (Ṣ, A,) *by tying the two extremities of the* عَرْقُوَتَانِ *of the camel's saddle*, or *of the curved pieces of wood of the horse's saddle*. (A.) — Also, aor. as above, and so the inf. n., i. e. أَسْرٌ (Ṣ, Mṣb) and إِسَارٌ, (Lth, Ṣ,) *He made him a captive; captived him*; or *took him a prisoner; whether he bound him with an* إِسَار *or did not*; (Ṣ;) as also ▼ آسَرَهُ, of the same form as أَكْرَمَ; (Mṣb;) and ▼ استأسرهُ, accord. to a trad., in which it occurs thus used, transitively: (Mgh:) and *he imprisoned him*. (TA, from a trad.) — Also, (Ṣ, Mṣb,) inf. n. أَسْرٌ, (Mṣb,) † *He* (God) *created him*, or *formed him*, (Ṣ, Mṣb,) *in a goodly manner*. (Mṣb.) You say, أَسَرَهُ اللّٰهُ أَحْسَنَ الأَسْرِ *God created him*, or *formed him, in the best manner*. (Fr, TA.) — أُسِرَ, (Ṣ, A,) aor. يُؤْسَرُ; (Ṣ;) or أَسِرَ, aor. يَأْسَرُ; (IḲṭṭ;) or أُسِرَ بَوْلُهُ; (M;) inf. n. أُسْرٌ, (M, and so in a copy of the Ṣ,) or the latter is a simple subst.; (M, IḲṭṭ;) *He* (a man, Ṣ, A) *suffered suppression of his urine*. (Ṣ, M, IḲṭṭ, A.) [See أُسْرٌ, below.]

[2. أسّر *He bound*, or *tied, tight, fast*, or *firmly*. (So accord. to Golius; but for this he names no authority.)]

4: see 1.

5. تَأَسَّرَ عَلَيْهِ فُلَانٌ † *Such a one excused himself to him, and was slow*, or *tardy*: (AZ, T, Ḳ:*) thus as related by Ibn-Hánee from AZ: as A'Obeyd relates it from him, تَأَسَّنَ; but this is a mistake: it is correctly with ر. (T.)

8. يَأْتَسِرُ, inf. n. اِئْتِسَارٌ [written with the disjunctive alif إِيتِسَارٌ]; for يَتَّسِرُ, inf. n. اِتِّسَارٌ: see art. يسر.

10. استأسر لِلْعَدُوِّ *He submitted himself as a captive to the enemy*. (Mgh.) You say, اِسْتَأْسِرْ, meaning *Be thou a captive to me*. (Ṣ.) ═ See also 1.

أَسْرٌ *i. q.* إِسَارٌ, q. v. (Ṣ.) Hence the saying, هٰذَا الشَّىْءُ لَكَ بِأَسْرِهِ *This thing is for thee*, or *is thine*, [lit.] *with its thong of untanned hide* [wherewith it is bound]; meaning, *altogether*; like as one says, بِرُمَّتِهِ. (Ṣ.) And خُذْهُ بِأَسْرِهِ *Take thou it all*, or *altogether*. (Mṣb.) And جَآءَ القَوْمُ بِأَسْرِهِمْ *The people came altogether*. (Aboo-Bekr.) — *Strength of make*, or *form*. (M, Ḳ.) [Accord. to the copies of the Ḳ in my hands, it also signifies *Strength of natural disposition*; but instead of وَالخُلُقِ, in those copies, we should read وَالخَلْقَ, agreeably with other lexicons, as is implied in the TA: see 1.] You say, فُلَانٌ شَدِيدُ أَسْرِ الخَلْقِ ‡ *Such a one is of strong, firm, or compact, make, or form.* (TA.) —— شَدَدْنَا أَسْرَهُمْ, in the Ḳur [lxxvi. 28], means ‡ *We have strengthened their make, or form:* (Ṣ, A, Mṣb:) or, *their joints:* or, *their two sphincters which serve as repressers of the urine and fæces* (مَصَرَّتَي البَوْلِ وَالغَائِطِ), which contract when the excrement has passed forth; or the meaning is, that these two things do not become relaxed before one desires. (IAạr, Ḳ.)

أُسْرٌ, (Ṣ, M, IḲṭṭ, A,) a subst., (M, IḲṭṭ,) as also ▾ أُسُرٌ, (M, Lb,) meaning *Suppression of the urine:* (Ṣ, M, &c.:) suppression of the fæces is termed حُصْرٌ: (Ṣ:) or *a dribbling of the urine, with a cutting pain in the bladder, and pangs like those of a female in the time of parturition.* (IAạr.) You say, أَخَذَهُ الأُسْرُ [*Suppression of urine, &c., took him,* or *affected him*]. (A.) And أَنَالَهُ ٱللّٰهُ أُسْرًا [*May God give him a suppression of urine, &c.*]: a form of imprecation. (A.) —— Hence, (M,) عُودُ أُسْرٍ (IAạr, Ṣ, M, A, Ḳ) and عُودُ الأُسْرِ and عُودُ أُسُرٍ (Expositions of the Fṣ) and عُودُ يُسْرٍ, (IAạr, Ḳ,) or this is a corruption, (Ḳ,) or a vulgar mistake, (A,) and should not be said, (Fr, Ṣ, A,) unless meant to be used as ominous of good, (A,) *A stick,* or *piece of wood, which is put upon the belly of a man affected by a suppression of his urine,* (Ṣ, A, Ḳ, &c.,) *and which cures him.* (A.)

أُسُرٌ: see أُسْرٌ.

أُسْرَةٌ † A man's *kinsmen that are more,* or *most, nearly related to him;* his *near kinsmen:* (Ṣ,* M, A,* Mṣb,* Ḳ:) or a man's *nearer,* or *nearest, relations on his father's side:* (Aboo-Jaạfar En-Naḥḥás:) so called because he is strengthened by them. (Ṣ, A.)

إِسَارٌ *A thing with which one binds;* (M, Ḳ;) *a thong of untanned hide,* (Ṣ, A, Mṣb,) *with which one binds a camel's saddle,* (Aṣ, Ṣ,) [as also إِصَارٌ,] *and a captive;* and so أَسْرٌ, q. v.: (Ṣ:) and *a rope,* or *cord, with which a captive is bound:* and *a pair of shackles:* (TA:) pl. أُسُرٌ. (M, Ḳ.) [See also 1.] You say, حَلَّ إِسَارَهُ فَأَطْلَقَهُ *He untied his thong of untanned hide wherewith he was bound, and released him.* (A.) —— See also أَسِيرٌ.

أَسِيرٌ i. q. ▾ مَأْسُورٌ; (Ṣ, TA;) *Bound with an* إِسَار: (M, TA:) *shackled:* (Ḳ:) *imprisoned:* (Mujáhid, M, Ḳ:) *captived,* or *a captive;* (Ṣ, M, Ḳ;) *absolutely,* (TA,) *although not bound with an* اسار: (Ṣ:) and ▾ إِسَارٌ is sometimes used in the same sense. (Mṣb.) اسير is also applied as an epithet to a woman, (Mgh, Mṣb,) when the woman is mentioned; but otherwise أَسِيرَةٌ is used as the fem.: you say, قَتَلْتُ الأَسِيرَةَ [*I slew the female captive*], like as you say, رَأَيْتُ القَتِيلَةَ. (Mṣb.) The pl. is أَسْرَى (Ṣ, M, Mṣb, Ḳ) and أُسَرَاءُ (M, Ḳ) and (accord. to several authors, pls. of أَسْرَى, TA) أُسَارَى (Ṣ, M, Mṣb, Ḳ) and أَسَارَى: (M, Ḳ:) the first of these forms of pl. is proper to epithets applied to those who are hurt or afflicted in their bodies or their intellects: (Aboo-Is-ḥáḳ:) it is used in this instance because a captive is like one wounded or stung. (Th, M.)

تَآسِيرُ السَّرْجِ [in the CḲ, erroneously, تَأْسِير] *The thongs of the horse's saddle, whereby it is bound:* (Ḳ:) accord. to the more correct opinion, a pl. without a sing. (MF.)

مَأْسُورٌ: see أَسِيرٌ. A camel's saddle *bound with an* إِسَار: pl. مَآسِيرُ. (TA.) —— † A man, and a beast, *having strongly-knit joints.* (M.) —— A man *suffering suppression of his urine.* (Ṣ.)

اسطرلاب

أَسْطُرْلَابٌ or أُسْطُرْلَابٌ, [accord. to different copies of the Ḳ,] and with ص in the place of س, [from the Greek ἀστρολαβόν, *An astrolabe:* a word of which F gives the following fanciful derivation:] لاب was a man who traced some lines, and founded upon them calculations; whence أَسْطُرُ لَابٍ [the lines of Láb], from which was formed the compound word اسطرلاب, and اصطرلاب, the س being changed into ص because of the ط following. (Ḳ in art. لوب.) It is either an arabicized or a post-classical word: accord. to the Niháyet el-Adab, the names of all the instruments by which time is known, whether by means of calculation or water or sand, are foreign to the Arabic language. (MF.)

اسف

1. أَسِفَ, aor. ـَ, inf. n. أَسَفٌ, (M, Mṣb, Ḳ,) *He grieved, lamented,* or *regretted:* and *he was angry:* (Mṣb:) or *he grieved exceedingly:* and *he was exceedingly angry:* (M:) or *he grieved most intensely:* (Ḳ:) some say that أَسَفٌ signifies the *grieving* for a thing that has escaped; not in an absolute sense: (MF:) or it properly signifies the *rising,* or *swelling,* or *mantling, of the blood of the heart,* from desire of vengeance; and when this is against an inferior, it is *anger;* but when against a superior, it is *grief.* (Er-Rághib.) Moḥammad, being asked respecting sudden death, answered, saying, رَاحَةٌ لِلْمُؤْمِنِ وَأَخْذَةُ أَسَفٍ لِلْكَافِرِ, or accord. to one recital, ▾ أَسِفٍ, i. e. [*Rest,* or *ease, to the believer, and an act of punishment*] *of anger* [*to the unbeliever*], or *of one who is angry.* (Ḳ.) You say, أَسِفَ عَلَى مَا فَاتَهُ, inf. n. as above; (Ṣ;) and ▾ تَأَسَّفَ; (Ṣ, M,* Ḳ;*) *He grieved,* or *lamented, for,* or *at,* or *regretted, most intensely, what had escaped him:* (Ṣ, M,* Ḳ:) and أَسِفَ عَلَيْهِ, (Ṣ, Ḳ,) inf. n. as above, (Ṣ,) *he was angry with him,* or *at it:* (Ṣ, Ḳ:) or أَسِفَ فُلَانٌ عَلَى كَذَا وَكَذَا, and ▾ تَأَسَّفَ, signify, accord. to some, *such a one grieved,* or *lamented, for,* or *at, such and such things* which had escaped him: or, accord. to others, *grieved,* or *lamented, most intensely.* (IAmb.) أَسَفًا in the Ḳur xviii. 5 means, accord. to Ed-Ḍaḥḥák, جَزَعًا [i. e. *In grief,* or *in most violent grief,* &c.]: or, accord. to Ḳatádeh, *in anger.* (TA.) And يَا أَسَفَا عَلَى يُوسُفَ, in the Ḳur [xii. 84], means يَا جَزَعَاهُ [*O my grief for Joseph:* or *O my most violent grief*]. (TA.)

4. آسَفَهُ (in [some of] the copies of the Ḳ, erroneously, أَسَفَهُ, TA) *He angered him; made him angry:* (Ṣ, M,* O, L, Mṣb, Ḳ:) and *he grieved him; made him to grieve,* or *lament.* (M,* TA.)

5: see 1, in two places. —— تَأَسَّفَتْ يَدُهُ ‡ i. q. تَشَعَّثَتْ [app. meaning *His hand became bruised,* or *mangled;* or *became cracked,* or *chapped*]. (M, TA.)

أَسَفٌ inf. n. of 1, which see throughout. [Used as a subst., i. q. أَسَافَةٌ.]

أَسِفٌ (M, Mgh, Mṣb) and ▾ آسِفٌ and ▾ أَسْفَانُ and ▾ أَسِيفٌ (M, TA) and ▾ أَسُوفٌ (M) *Angry:* (Mgh, Mṣb, TA:) or *exceedingly angry.* (M.) For an ex. of the first, see 1. See also أَسِيفٌ, in two places.

أَسْفَانُ: see أَسِفٌ: and أَسِيفٌ.

إِسَافٌ (Ṣ, M, Ṣgh, &c.) and أَسَافٌ (IAth, Ḳ) *A certain idol,* (Ṣ, M, Ḳ,) *belonging to Ḳureysh,* (Ṣ, M,) *as was also* نَائِلَةُ; (Ṣ;) *the former of which was placed, by 'Amr Ibn-Lohei, upon Eṣ-Ṣafà, and the latter upon El-Marweh; and he used to sacrifice to them, in front of the Kaabeh:* (Ṣ, Ḳ:) or, (Ṣ, M, Ḳ,) as some assert, (Ṣ,) *these two were two persons of Jurhum,* (Ṣ, Ḳ,) *a man and a woman,* (M,) اساف *the son of 'Amr, and* نائلة *the daughter of Sahl,* (Ṣ, Ḳ,) *who committed fornication in the Kaabeh, and were therefore changed into two stones,* (Ṣ, M, Ḳ,) *which Ḳureysh afterwards worshipped.* (Ṣ, Ḳ.) [Other accounts of them are also given, slightly differing from the latter above.]

أَسُوفٌ: see أَسِيفٌ, in two places: and see أَسِفٌ.

أَسِيفٌ *Grieving, lamenting,* or *regretting,* (Ḳ,* TA,) *most intensely, on account of a thing that has escaped:* (M, TA:) and *quickly affected with grief,* (Ṣ, Mgh, Ḳ,) *and tender-hearted;* as also ▾ أَسُوفٌ: (Ṣ, Ḳ:) or, as also ▾ أَسُوفٌ (M) and ▾ أَسْفَانُ and ▾ آسِفٌ (M, TA) and ▾ أَسِفٌ, (M,) *grieving exceedingly:* (M:) or *grieved:* (TA:) and sometimes the first signifies *angry, and at the same time grieving,* or *lamenting:* (Ṣ:) pl. أُسَفَاءُ. (M.) See also أَسِفٌ. —— *A slave:* (ISk, Ṣ, M, Ḳ:) and *a hired man:* (ISk, M, Ḳ:) because of their state of abasement and subjection: fem. with ة: (M:) and pl. as above. (Ṣ, M.) —— *A captive.* (TA.) —— *A very old man:* (Ḳ:) pl. as above: so in a trad., in which the slaying of such is forbidden. (TA.) —— One *who scarcely,* or *never, becomes fat.* (Ḳ.) —— † *A region,* or *country, that does not give growth to anything,* or *produce any vegetation;* as also أَسِيفَةٌ and ▾ أَسَافَةٌ and ▾ أَسَافَةٌ: (M:) and ▾ أَسَافَةٌ also signifies † *thin,* or *shallow, earth:* (AḤn, M:) and أَرْضٌ أَسِيفَةٌ, ‡ *thin,* or *shallow, earth, which scarcely,* or *never, gives growth to anything,* or *produces any vegetation:* (Ṣ:) or *which is not commended for its vegetation:* (A, TA:) or, as also ▾ أَسَافَةٌ and ▾ أَسَافَةٌ, † *thin,* or *shallow, earth:* or *such as does* not produce vegetation: and ▼ أَرْضٌ أَسِفَةٌ † *land which scarcely, or never, produces vegetation.* (Ḳ.)

أَسَافَةٌ [*Grief, lamentation,* or *regret:* and *anger:* (see 1:) or] *excessive grief:* and *excessive anger:* (M:) or *most intense grief:* (Ḳ:) a subst. from أَسِفَ. (M, Ḳ.) —— The *state,* or *condition, of a slave:* (M, Ḳ:) and, *of a hired man.* (M.) —— ‡ The *state,* or *condition, of land which scarcely,* or *never, produces vegetation.* (Ḳ, TA.) ═ See أَسِيفٌ, in three places.

أُسَافَةٌ: see أَسِيفٌ, in two places.

آسِفٌ: see أَسِيفٌ: and أَسِفٌ.

اسفيداج

إِسْفِيدَاجٌ [*Ceruse; or white lead;*] *ashes of lead* (رَمَادُ الرَّصَاصِ وَالآنُكِ, Ḳ, which last word is as though it were added to explain that immediately preceding, TA): when subjected to a fierce heat, it becomes what is termed إِسْرَنْجٌ: [so in the CḲ: more probably إِسْرِنْجٌ:] it has clearing and mitigating properties, (Ḳ,) and other useful qualities: (TA:) an arabicized word [from the Persian اسفيداج isfédáj]. (Ḳ.)

اسك

1. أَسَكَهَا, aor. ـِ, inf. n. أَسْكٌ, *He hit, hurt,* or *wounded, her* (a woman's) إِسْكَتَانِ. (TA.) And أُسِكَتْ *She* (a woman) *was hurt,* or *wounded, in a place not that of circumcision,* [i. e., *in her* إِسْكَتَانِ,] *by the circumcising woman's missing the proper place.* (Mṣb.) [See بَظْرٌ.]

أَسْكٌ: see الإِسْكَتَانِ.

إِسْكٌ: see الإِسْكَتَانِ. —— Also The *side of the* اسْت [i. e., of the *podex,* or of the *anus*]. (Sh, TA.) [Hence,] one says of a man, إِنَّمَا هُوَ إِسْكُ أَمَةٍ, meaning *He is but a stinking fellow.* (TA.)

الإِسْكَتَانِ (T, Ṣ, M, Mgh, Ṣgh, Mṣb, Ḳ) and الأَسْكَتَانِ, (M, Ḳ,) The *two sides* [or *labia majora*] *of the vulva,* or *external portion of the female organs of generation,* (T, Ṣ, Mgh, Mṣb,) i. e., *of a woman, above* [or rather *within*] *the* شُفْرَانِ; (Mgh; the شُفْرَانِ being the two borders thereof; T, Mṣb;) i. e. the قُذَّتَانِ *thereof;* (Ṣ and M and L in art. قذ;) the *two sides, on the right and left, of the vulva,* or *external portion of the organs of generation, of a woman, between which is the* مَشَقّ: (Zj in his "Khalḳ el-Insán":) or [accord. to some, but incorrectly,] the شُفْرَانِ [in the CḲ the شَفْر] *of the* رَحِم [here meaning, as in many other instances, the *vulva,* i. e. فَرْج], (M, Ḳ,) or *of the* حَيَآء [which also means the vulva, but seldom that of a woman]: (El-Khárzenjee:) or [agreeably with general usage, and with the explanations given before this last,] *its two sides, next to its* شُفْرَانِ: (M, Ḳ:) or, [what is the same,] *its* قُذَّتَانِ: (Ḳ:) pl. إِسَكٌ (El-Khárzenjee, Ḳ) and [quasi-pl. ns.] ▼ إِسْكٌ and ▼ أَسْكٌ. (M, Ḳ.)

مَأْسُوكَةٌ A woman *hit, hurt,* or *wounded, in her* إِسْكَتَانِ: (TA:) a woman (Mṣb) *hurt,* or *wounded, in a place not that of circumcision, by the circumcising woman's missing the proper place;* (Ṣ, Mṣb, Ḳ;) [i. e.,] *hurt,* or *wounded, by that cause, in her* إِسْكَتَانِ. (T, TA.)

اسل

أَسُلَ, aor. ـُ, (Ṣ, M, Ḳ,) inf. n. أَسَالَةٌ, (Ṣ, M, IAth,) *It was smooth and even:* (M:) *it* (anything) *was lank:* (Ṣ:) *it* (a cheek, M, IAth, Ḳ) *was smooth and long:* (M:) or *long,* or *oblong, and not high in its ball:* (IAth:) or *long,* (Ḳ, TA,) *soft in make,* (TA,) *and lank.* (Ḳ, TA.) أَسَالَةٌ in the cheek of a horse is approved, and is an indication of generous quality: you say, تُنْبِئُ أَسَالَةُ خَدِّهِ عَنْ أَصَالَةِ جَدِّهِ [*The smoothness and longness, &c., of his cheek tells of the generous origin of his ancestor*]. (AO, Z.) ═ See also 2.

2. أَسَّلَهُ *He made it* (an iron thing) *thin.* (TA.) [*He made it* (anything) *sharp,* or *pointed.* (See the pass. part. n., below.)] —— أَسَّلَ المَطَرُ, inf. n. تَأْسِيلٌ, *The rain moistened to the measure of the* أَسَلَة [or *thin part*] *of the arm.* (Ḳ.) When it has moistened to the measure of the عَظَمَة [or thick part] of the arm, you say of it, عَظَّمَ, inf. n. تَعْظِيمٌ: one says, كَيْفَ كَانَتْ مَطَرَتُكُمْ أَسَّلَتْ أَمْ عَظَّمَتْ [*How was your rain? Did it moisten to the measure of the thin part of the arm, or did it moisten to the measure of the thick part thereof?*]. (TA.) And أَسَّلَ الثَّرَى, (TA,) or ▼ أَسَلَ, (M, [so in a copy of that work, but probably a mistranscription,]) *The moisture reached to the measure of the* أَسَلَة. (M, TA.)

5. تَأَسَّلَ أَبَاهُ, (M, Ḳ,) as also تَأَسَّنَهُ, (M, TA,) *He resembled his father,* (M, Ḳ, TA,) *and assumed his natural dispositions;* and so تَقَيَّلَهُ. (TA.) [See آسَالٌ, below.]

أَسَلٌ [*Rush,* or *rushes:* so called in the present day:] *a kind of trees:* (Ṣ:) or [rather] *a kind of plant,* (M, Mgh, TA,) *having shoots* (M, Mgh) *which are slender,* (Mgh,) *without leaves;* (M, Mgh;) or *of which the shoot is slender, and of which sieves are made;* as is said in the A; and Ṣgh adds, [*growing*] *in El-'Irák:* (TA:) AḤn says, (TA,) accord. to Aboo-Ziyád, *it is of the kind called* أَغْلَاث, *and comes forth in slender shoots, not having branches growing out from them, nor wood,* (M, TA,) *and sometimes men beat them, and make of them well-ropes and other cords,* (TA,) *and it seldom or never grows but in a place wherein is water, or near to water:* (M, TA:) AḤn says [also], it signifies *shoots,* or *twigs, growing* (M, Ḳ) *long and slender and straight,* (M,) *without leaves; of which mats are made:* (M, Ḳ:) or أَسَلَةٌ, (Ḳ,) which is the n. un. of أَسَلٌ applied to the plant mentioned above, (M, Ḳ,) signifies *any shoot,* or *twig, in which is no crookedness.* (Ḳ.) —— Hence, (M,) ‡ *Spears;* (Ṣ, M, Ḳ;) as being likened to the plant mentioned above, in respect of its evenness and length and straightness and the slenderness of its extremities: n. un. as above: (M:) and † *arrows,* or *Arabian arrows;* syn. نَبْلٌ; (M, Ḳ:) applied to both of these in a trad. of 'Omar, which refutes an assertion that it is peculiarly applied to spears, or long spears, and not to نبل: (A 'Obeyd, TA:) Sh says that it is applied to spears because of the points of the heads fixed upon them. (TA.) —— † *Any thin thing of iron, such as a spear-head,* and *a sword,* and *a knife.* (TA.) —— ‡ The *prickles of palm-trees:* (M, Ḳ:) n. un. as above: (M:) by way of comparison [to the plant mentioned above]: (TA:) or *any long thorns,* or *prickles, of a tree.* (Ṣ.) —— [See also what next follows.]

أَسَلَةٌ n. un. of أَسَلٌ, q. v. (M, Ḳ.) —— Hence, by way of comparison, the significations here following from the Ḳ. (TA.) —— ‡ *Anything in which is no crookedness.* (M.) —— ‡ The *thin part* of a blade of iron, such as that of an arrow &c.: (M, Ḳ:) and of the fore arm; (Ṣ, M, Ḳ;) i. e. the *half* thereof *next the hand;* the half next the elbow being called the عَظَمَة. (Ḳ in art. عظم.) —— ‡ The *thin part,* (Ṣ,) or *extremity,* or *tip,* (M, Ḳ,) of the tongue; (Ṣ, M, Ḳ;) the thick part thereof being called the عَظَمَة. (Ḳ in art. عظم.) One says, أَسَلَاتُ أَلْسِنَتِهِمْ أَمْضَى مِنْ أَسِنَّةِ أَسَلِهِمْ ‡ [*The tips of their tongues are sharper than the heads of their spears*]. (A, TA.) —— ‡ The *nerves,* (Ḳ,) or the *extremity thereof,* (M,) of a camel. (M, Ḳ.) —— ‡ The *head,* [or what we term the *toe,* or *foremost extremity,* also called ذُؤَابَة and أَنْف,] of a sandal; (M, Ḳ;) *which is tapering.* (M.)

أَسَلِيَّةٌ an epithet applied to the letters ز and س and ص because *Pronounced with the tip of the tongue.* (TA.)

أَسِيلٌ *Smooth and even:* (M, Ḳ:) anything *lank;* (Ṣ, A;) syn. سَبْطٌ, (A,) [i. e.] مُسْتَرْسِلٌ: (Ṣ, A:) applied to a cheek, (AZ, Ḳ, TA,) [*smooth and long:* or *long,* or *oblong, and not high in its ball:* (see 1:) or] *soft, tender, thin, and even:* (AZ:) or *long,* (Ḳ, TA,) *soft in make,* (TA,) *and lank.* (Ḳ, TA.) You say رَجُلٌ أَسِيلُ الخَدِّ *A man having the cheek soft and long:* (Ṣ:) and in like manner, فَرَسٌ *a horse.* (TA.) And كَفٌّ أَسِيلَةُ الأَصَابِعِ *A hand small and slender, and lank, or long, in the fingers.* (TA.)

آسَالٌ a pl. having no sing.: (Ḳ:) mentioned by ISk as a word of which he had not heard any sing. (Ṣ.) You say, هُوَ عَلَى آسَالٍ مِنْ أَبِيهِ [in the CḲ, erroneously, أَسَالٍ,] *He is of a semblance and of characteristics and natural dispositions which are those of his father;* (Ṣ, Ḳ;) like آسَانٍ. (Ṣ.)

مُؤَسَّلٌ Anything *sharpened,* or *pointed.* (M, Ḳ.) You say أُذُنٌ مُؤَسَّلَةٌ *An ear* [of a horse or the like] *slender, pointed, and erect.* (M.)

اسم

1. أَسَمَهُ a dial. var. of وَسَمَهُ, q. v. (TA.)

إِسْمٌ: see art. سمو.

أُسَامَةُ, determinate, (Ṣ, M, Ḳ,) and imperfectly decl., (M, Mṣb,) as a proper name, (Mṣb, Ḳ,)

The lion; (Ṣ, M, Mṣb, Ḳ;) as also الأُسَامَةُ. (Ṣgh, Ḳ.)

اسن

1. أَسَنَ, aor. ـِ (Ṣ, M, Mgh, Mṣb, Ḳ) and ـُ, (Ṣ, M, Ḳ,) inf. n. أُسُونٌ (Ṣ, M, Mṣb) and أَسْنٌ; (M;) and أَسِنَ, aor. ـَ, (Ṣ, M, &c.,) inf. n. أَسَنٌ; (Ṣ, M, Mṣb;) said of water, *i. q.* أَجَنَ *and* أَجِنَ; (Ṣ, Ḳ;) [i. e.] *It became altered for the worse* (M, Mgh, Mṣb) *in odour,* (M,) [or *in taste and colour, from some such cause as long standing,* (see أَجَنَ,)] *but was drinkable;* (M;) or *so as not to be drunk,* (Mṣb, TA,) thus differing from أَجَنَ and أَجِنَ. (TA.) [See also أَصِلَ.]

أَسْنٌ: see what follows.

آسِنٌ (Ṣ, Mgh, Mṣb, Ḳ) and ↓ أَسِنٌ, (Ṣ, Mgh, Mṣb,) applied to water, (Ṣ, Mgh, &c.,) *i. q.* آجِنٌ [and أَجِنٌ]; (Ṣ, Ḳ;) [i. e.] *Altered for the worse* (Mgh, Mṣb) *in odour,* (Mgh,) [or *in taste and colour, from some such cause as long standing, but drinkable;* (see above, and see آجِنٌ;)] or *so as not to be drunk,* (Mṣb, TA,) thus differing from آجِنٌ and أَجِنٌ: (TA:) pl. [of the former] أُسَّانٌ [like as أَطْهَارٌ is pl. of طَاهِرٌ, or perhaps it may have for its sing. أَسْنٌ, like أَجْنٌ]. (M, TA.) مِنْ مَآءٍ غَيْرِ آسِنٍ, in the Ḳur [xlvii. 16], is explained by Fr as meaning *Of water not altered for the worse; not* آجِن. (TA.)

اسو

1. أَسَا الجُرْحَ, (aor. يَأْسُو, Ṣ,) inf. n. أَسْوٌ and أَسًا, [but in the Ṣ, the latter seems to be mentioned as a simple subst.,] *He dressed the wound; treated it curatively,* or *surgically.* (Ṣ, M, Ḳ.) —— [Hence,] † هٰذَا أَمْرٌ لَا يُؤْسَى كَلْمُهُ [*This is an affair of which the evil* (lit. *the wound*) *will not be remedied*]. (Ṣ.) —— [Hence also,] أَسَا بَيْنَهُمْ (first pers. أَسَوْتُ, Ṣ, Mṣb, inf. n. أَسْوٌ, Ṣ, M,) ‡ *He made peace, effected a reconciliation,* or *adjusted a difference, between them;* (Ṣ, M, Mṣb, Ḳ;) as also ↓ أَسَّى بينهم. (El-Muärrij, TA.) ═ أَسِىَ, aor. يَأْسَى, inf. n. أَسًا or أَسًى, *He grieved,* or *mourned,* (Ṣ, M, Mṣb, Ḳ,) عَلَيْهِ [*for him,* or *it*], (M, Ḳ,) and عَلَى مُصِيبَةٍ [*for an affliction*], and لِفُلَانٍ [*for such a one*]. (Ṣ.) [This belongs to the present art. and to art. اسى; but is distinguished in the M and Ḳ by being mentioned only in the latter art.; though the inf. n. is mentioned in the Ḳ in both arts.] Hence the saying, الإِسَآءُ يَدْفَعُ الأَسَا [*Medicine dispels grief,* or *mourning*]. (TA.)

2. أَسَّى بَيْنَهُمْ: see 1. ═ أَسَّاهُ, (Ṣ, M, Ḳ,) inf. n. تَأْسِيَةٌ, (Ṣ, Ḳ,) *i. q.* عَزَّاهُ [*He exhorted him,* or *enjoined him, to be patient; to take patience;* or *to take example by,* or *console himself by the example of, him who had suffered the like affliction*]; (Ṣ, M, Ḳ, TA;) *saying to him, Wherefore dost thou grieve,* or *mourn, when such a one is thine example* (إِسْوَتُكَ)? i. e. *what has befallen thee befell him, and he was patient; therefore take thou example by him and so be consoled* (تَأَسَّ بِهِ). (TA.) You say, أَسَّاهُ بِمُصِيبَةٍ i. e. عَزَّاهُ [*He exhorted him,* or *enjoined him, to be patient,* &c., *by* mentioning *an affliction* that had befallen another; unless بمصيبة be a mistranscription for لِمُصِيبَةٍ *on account of an affliction*]; as also ↓ آسَاهُ, with medd. (TA.)

3. آسَيْتُهُ بِمَالِى, (Ṣ, Mgh,) inf. n. مُؤَاسَاةٌ, (Ṣ, M, Ḳ,) *I made him my object of imitation* (إِسْوَتِى), [meaning *I made myself like him,*] *in respect of my property:* (Ṣ:) or *I made him an object of imitation* [*with,* or *in respect of, my property*], *I imitating his example, and he imitating my example:* (Mgh:) and وَاسَيْتُهُ is a dial. var., but of weak authority: (Ṣ, Mgh:) and آسَانِى [alone] *he made me an object of imitation to him by giving me of his property* [*and thus reducing himself to my condition in some degree while in the same degree raising me to his*]; (Ḥam p. 696;) and أُوَاسِيهِ [thus without a second ء] *I make him the object of my own imitation and so share with him my property:* (Id p. 198:) or آسَاهُ بِمَالِهِ signifies *he gave him of his property, and made him an object of imitation in respect of it:* or only, *of food sufficient for his want;* not of what is superabundant: (M, Ḳ:) whence the saying, رَحِمَ اللّٰهُ رَجُلًا أَعْطَى مِنْ فَضْلٍ وَوَاسَى مِنْ كَفَافٍ [*May God have mercy on a man who has given of superabundance, and imparted of food only sufficient for his want so as to make himself equal with him to whom he imparts of such food*]: (TA:) [and آسَاهُ signifies *he shared with him:* and *he was,* or *became, equal with him:* for] المُوَاسَاةُ occurs often in trads., signifying the *sharing with another,* or *making another to share with one, in the means of subsistence* [*&c.*]; and is originally [المُؤَاسَاةُ,] with ء: also, the *being,* or *becoming, equal with another:* (TA:) and you say, آسَيْتُهُ بِنَفْسِى, meaning *I made him equal with myself;* in the dial. of El-Yemen وَاسَيْتُهُ. (Mṣb.) آسِ بَيْنَ النَّاسِ فِى وَجْهِكَ, in a letter of 'Omar, means *Make thou the people to share* [*alike*], *one with another, in thy consideration and regard:* or, as some say, *make thou them equal* [*in respect thereof*]. (Mgh.) The saying مَا يُؤَاسِى فُلَانٌ فُلَانًا is explained in three different ways: accord. to El-Mufaddal Ibn-Mohammad, it means *Such a one does not make such a one to share with him:* accord. to El-Muärraj, *does not good to such a one;* from the saying of the Arabs, آسِ فُلَانًا بِخَيْرٍ *Do thou good to such a one:* or, as some say, *does not give such a one any compensation for his love,* or *affection, nor for his relationship;* from الأَوْسُ, meaning العَوَضُ; being originally يُؤَاوِسُهُ, then يُؤَاسِوُهُ, and then يُؤَاسِيهِ: or it may be from أَسَوْتُ الجُرْحَ. (IDrd, TA.) [See also an ex. voce أَثَرَةٌ.]

4. آسَاهُ: see 2.

5. تَأَسَّى: see 8. —— *I. q.* تَعَزَّى [*He took patience;* or *constrained himself to be patient;* or *he took example by,* or *became consoled by the example of, another who had suffered in like manner and had been patient*]. (Ṣ, M, Ḳ.) You say, تَأَسَّى بِهِ, i. e. تَعَزَّى بِهِ [*He took patience,* or *constrained himself to be patient, by reflecting upon him, or it;* or *he took example by him,* or *became consoled by his example,* meaning the example of a person who had suffered in like manner and had been patient]. (Ṣ.) [See 2.]

6. تَآسَوْا signifies آسَى بَعْضُهُمْ بَعْضًا [*They imitated one another with their property, one giving of his property to another, so that they thus equalised themselves; they imitated one another and so shared together their property; they shared, one with another, in the means of subsistence, &c.; they were,* or *became, equal, one with another:* see 3]. (Ṣ, Ḳ.) A poet says,

* وَإِنَّ الأُولَى بِالطَّفِّ مِنْ آلِ هَاشِمٍ *
* تَآسَوْا فَسَنُّوا لِلْكِرَامِ التَّآسِيَا *

(Ṣ,) in which تآسوا is from المُؤَاسَاةُ; not from التَّأَسِّى, as it is stated to be by Mbr, who says that تآسوا means تَوَاسَوْا and تَعَزَّوْا. (IB, TA.) [This verse is cited and translated in art. الى, voce أُلَى, q. v.]

8. ائتسى به [written with the disjunctive alif إِيتَسَى] *He imitated him; followed his example; did as he did, following his example,* or *taking him as an example, an exemplar, a pattern,* or *an object of imitation; he took example by him;* (Ṣ, Mgh, Mṣb, TA;) as also ↓ تَأَسَّى بِهِ: (Mṣb, TA:) *he made him an object of imitation* (إِسْوَة) [*to himself*]. (M, Ḳ.) One says, لَا تَأْتَسِ بِمَنْ لَيْسَ لَكَ بِإِسْوَةٍ *Do not thou imitate him who is not for thee a* [*fit*] *object of imitation.* (Ṣ, M.*)

Q. Q. 1. أَسْوَيْتُهُ بِهِ [*I made him to imitate him, to follow his example,* or *to take example by him;*] *I made him an example, an exemplar, a pattern,* or *an object of imitation, to him:* (M, Ḳ:) from IAạr: and if from الإِسْوَةُ, as he asserts it be, the measure of this verb is فَعْلَيْتُ, like دَرْبَيْتُ and جَعْبَيْتُ. (M.)

أَسًا or أَسْىٌ *Curative,* or *surgical, treatment.* (Ṣ.) [See the verb أَسَا.] ═ *Grief,* or *mourning.* (Ṣ, Ḳ.) [See the verb أَسِىَ.]

أَسْوَانُ: see أَسِىٌّ.

أُسًى *Patience.* (Ṣ.) ═ Also pl. of أُسْوَةٌ, like as إِسًى is pl. of إِسْوَةٌ. (Ṣ,* Ḳ,* TA.)

أَسْوَةٌ : } see what next follows.
أُسْوَةٌ : }

إِسْوَةٌ and ↓ أُسْوَةٌ (Ṣ, M, Mgh, Mṣb, Ḳ) and ↓ أَسْوَةٌ, mentioned by Er-Rághib in one of his works, (MF,) *An example; an exemplar; a pattern; an object of imitation; a person by whom one takes example;* syn. قِدْوَةٌ or قُدْوَةٌ; (Ṣ, M, Mṣb, Ḳ;) each a subst. from إِيتَسَى بِهِ; (Mgh;) i. e. مَا يُؤْتَسَى بِهِ: (TA:) explained by Er-Rághib as meaning the *condition in which is a man in respect of another's imitating* [*him*], *whether good or bad, pleasing or hurtful:* (TA:) also *a thing* [or *person*] *by which one who is in grief*, or *mourning*, *takes example*, (Ṣ, Ḳ,) *for the being consoled* (لِلتَّعَزِّى) *thereby*: (Ṣ:) pl. إِسًى and أُسًى; (Ṣ, Ḳ;) the former of the first sing., and the latter of the second. (TA.) The first of these meanings is intended in the saying, لِى فِى فُلَانٍ إِسْوَةٌ and أُسْوَةٌ [*I have in such a one an example*, &c.]. (Ṣ.) The saying, مَا سِوَى التُّرَابِ مِنَ الأَرْضِ إِسْوَةُ التُّرَابِ is tropical, meaning ‡ *There is nothing but the dust of the earth*, or *ground*, *that follows the dust*. (Mgh.) — Also an inf. n., [or rather a quasi-inf. n.,] syn. with ٱئْتِسَآءٌ [inf. n. of 8]. (TA.)

أَسْوَانُ *Grieving*, *mourning*, or *sorrowful*; (M, Ḳ;) as also أَسْيَانُ and ▼ أَسٍ, (M in art. اسى,) or ▼ آسٍ, (Ḳ in art. اسى, [to which alone the first of these three belongs, but the second and third may be regarded as belonging either to that art. or to the present,]) or ▼ أَسِىٌّ. (Mṣb.) [See art. اسى.] It is [sometimes] followed by أَتْوَانُ [as an imitative sequent corroborating its meaning]. (M.)

إِسَآءٌ and ▼ أَسْوٌ *A medicine*, or *remedy*; (Ṣ, M, Ḳ;) the latter, (Ṣ,) or each, (TA,) particularly *a vulnerary*: (Ṣ, TA:) pl. [of each, as is indicated in the TA,] آسِيَةٌ. (M, Ḳ.) — The former is also a pl. of آسٍ. (Ṣ, M, Ḳ.)

أَسْوٌ: see what next precedes.

أَسِىٌّ *i. q.* ▼ مَأْسُوٌّ; (Ṣ, M, Ḳ;) i. e., *Dressed*; or *treated curatively*, or *surgically*; applied to a wound. (Ṣ, M.*) — See also أَسْوَانُ.

أَسَاوَةٌ *Medical*, *curative*, *therapeutical*, [or *surgical*,] *treatment*. (Ibn-El-Kelbee, Ṣgh, Ḳ.) By rule it should be [إِسَاوَةٌ,] with kesr. (Ṣgh, TA.)

آسٍ *A physician*; *one skilled in medical*, *curative*, *therapeutical*, [or *surgical*,] *treatment* [*particularly of wounds*]: pl. أُسَاةٌ and إِسَآءٌ; (Ṣ, M, Ḳ;) said by IJ to be the only instance of فُعَلَةٌ and فِعَالٌ interchangeable except رُعَاةٌ and رِعَآءٌ, pls. of رَاعٍ: (M:) and آسُونَ occurs [as its pl.] in a verse of Ḥoteiäh. (Ṣ, TA.) — With the people of the desert, (Ṣ,) [its fem.] آسِيَةٌ signifies ‡ *A female circumciser* [*of girls*]. (Ṣ, Ḳ: [mentioned in the latter in art. اسى.]) — See also أَسْوَانُ.

مَأْسُوٌّ: see أَسِىٌّ.

اسى

1. أَسِىَ, aor. يَأْسَى, inf. n. أَسًى or أَسًا, *He grieved*, or *mourned*, (Ṣ, M, Mṣb, Ḳ,) عَلَيْهِ [*for him or it*]. (M, Ḳ.) See art. اسو.

أَسٍ, [agreeably with analogy, as part. n. of أَسِىَ,] (M,) or ▼ آسٍ, (Ḳ,) or ▼ أَسِىٌّ, (Mṣb,) and ▼ أَسْيَانُ, (M, Ḳ,) a dial. var. of أَسْوَانُ, (TA, [see art. اسو,]) *Grieving*, *mourning*, or *sorrowful*: (M, Mṣb, Ḳ:) fem. [of the first, or second,] أَسِيَةٌ, (M,) or آسِيَةٌ, (Ḳ,) and [of اسيان] أَسْيَانَةٌ (M, Ḳ) and أَسْيَى: (TA:) pl. [of اسيان] أَسْيَانُونَ (M, Ḳ) and أَسَايُونَ [which is extr. and somewhat doubtful] (Ḳ) and [of اسيانة] أَسْيَانَاتٌ and [of اسيى or of أَسِيَةٌ] أَسَايَا (M, Ḳ) and [of اسيى] أَسْيَيَاتٌ. (Ḳ.)

أَسْيَانُ:
أَسِىٌّ:
آسٍ:
} see above.

آسِيَةٌ, mentioned in this art. in the Ḳ: see آسٍ in art. اسو.

اشب

1. أَشَبَهُ, aor. ـِ, (M, Ḳ,) inf. n. أَشْبٌ, (M, TA,) *He mixed it*. (M, Ḳ.) And أَشَبْتُ القَوْمَ; (Ṣ;) or ▼ أَشَّبْتُهُمْ, inf. n. تَأْشِيبٌ; (TA;) *I mixed the people together*. (Ṣ, TA.) — Also, aor. as above, (Ṣ, Ḳ,) and ـُ, (Ḳ,) inf. n. as above, (Ṣ,) † *He charged him with a vice*, *fault*, or *the like*; *blamed*, *censured*, or *reprehended*, *him*: (Ṣ, Ḳ:) or *he aspersed*, *reviled*, or *reproached*, *him*, *and mixed up falsehood in his aspersion of him*. (TA.) You say also, أَشَبَهُ بِشَرٍّ [i. e. بِشَرٍّ or بِشَرٍّ] † *He cast upon him a stigma*, or *mark of dishonour*, *by which he became known*: (Lḥ, TA:) or *he cast a censure*, or *reproach*, *upon him*, *and involved him in it*. (TA.) — أَشِبَ الشَّجَرُ, aor. ـَ, (A, Ḳ,) inf. n. أَشَبٌ; (TA;) and ▼ تَأَشَّبَ; (Ḳ;) or أَشِبَتِ الغَيْضَةُ; (Ṣ;) *The collection of trees*, or *the thicket*, *was*, or *became*, *dense*, *tangled*, *confused*, *intertwined*, or *complicated*: (Ṣ, Ḳ:) or *very dense*, or *much tangled* or *confused*, *so as to be impassable*. (AḤn, A.) — [Hence,] أَشِبَ الكَلَامُ بَيْنَهُمْ † *Their speech*, *one with another*, *became confused*, or *intricate*. (TA.) — And أَشِبَ الشَّرُّ لِلَّئِيمِ *Evil clave to the ignoble*. (A.)

2. أَشَّبَهُ, inf. n. تَأْشِيبٌ, *He rendered it* (a collection of trees) *dense*, *tangled*, *confused*, *intertwined*, or *complicated*. (Ḳ.) — أَشَّبْتُ القَوْمَ: see 1. — أَشَّبَ الكَلَامَ بَيْنَهُمْ † *He made their speech*, *one with another*, *confused*, or *intricate*. (TA.) — أَشَّبَ الشَّرَّ بَيْنَهُمْ † *He occasioned confusion*, *discord*, or *mischief*, *between them*. (Lth.) And hence, (TA,) تَأْشِيبٌ signifies also The *exciting discord*, *dissension*, *disorder*, *strife*, *quarrelling*, or *animosity*, (Ṣ, Ḳ, TA,) بَيْنَ قَوْمٍ *between*, or *among*, a people. (Ṣ, TA.)

5. تَأَشَّبَ: see 1. — تَأَشَّبُوا † *They were*, or *became*, *mixed*, or *confounded together*; as also ▼ ٱئْتَشَبُوا [written with the disjunctive alif إِيتَشَبُوا]. (Ṣ, Ḳ.) — ‡ *They assembled*, or *congregated*, *themselves* (A, Ḳ) *from different parts*; (TA;) as also ▼ ٱئْتَشَبُوا. (Ḳ.) And تَأَشَّبُوا إِلَيْهِ † *They drew themselves together to him*, (Ḳ, TA,) *and crowded densely upon him*; *or collected themselves together to him*, *and surrounded him*. (TA.)

8: see 5, in two places.

أَشَبٌ inf. n. of أَشِبَ. (TA.) — [Hence,] *Confusedness*; *dubiousness*: so in the saying, ضَرَبْتُ فِيهِ فُلَانَةُ بِعِرْقٍ ذِى أَشَبٍ; i. e. ذِى ٱلْتِبَاسٍ. (Ṣ.) See art. ضرب. — Also *An abundance of trees*. (TA.) In a trad. of Ibn-Umm-Mektoom, إِنِّى رَجُلٌ ضَرِيرٌ بَيْنِى وَبَيْنَكَ أَشَبٌ فَرَخِّصْ لِى فِى العِشَآءِ وَالفَجْرِ means *Verily I am a blind man*, [and] *between me and thee are palm-trees confusedly disposed*; *therefore grant thou me indulgence with respect to* [coming to thee to perform the prayers of] *the nightfall and the daybreak*. (Ḳ,* MF, TA.)

أَشِبٌ *Dense*, *tangled*, *confused*, *intertwined*, or *complicated*; applied to a collection of trees: (Ṣ, TA:) or *so dense*, or *so much tangled* or *confused*, *as to be impassable*; applied to a thicket: (A:) and a place *abounding with trees*: (TA:) applied also to ‡ a collection of clouds, meaning *commingled*: (A:) and to † a number, meaning *intricate*, or *confused*. (Ṣ, TA.) It is said in a prov., عِيصُكَ مِنْكَ وَإِنْ كَانَ أَشِبًا, (A,) meaning ‡ [*Thy stock is an appertenance of thine*] *although it be thorny and intricate* or *confused*. (TA. [See art. عيص.])

أُشَابَةٌ ‡ *A medley*, or *mixed* or *promiscuous multitude* or *assemblage*, of men, or people; (Ṣ, A, L, Ḳ;) *congregated from every quarter*: (L:) pl. أَشَائِبُ. (Ṣ, Ḳ.*) You say, هٰؤُلَآءِ أُشَابَةٌ ‡ *These are a collection* [of people] *from different places*. (TA.) — Also ‡ *Mixtures of unlawful and lawful kinds* of property: (A:) or *what is mixed with that which has been unlawfully acquired*; (Ḳ, TA;) *that in which is no good*; (TA;) of gains: pl. as above. (Ḳ, TA.)

مَأْشُوبُ الحَسَبِ † *Not pure in his grounds of pretension to respect*. (ISd, TA.) [See also what follows.]

مُؤْتَشِبٌ and جَمْعٌ مُؤْتَشِبٌ ‡ [*A mixed collection of people*]. (A.) — فُلَانٌ مُؤْتَشِبٌ, (Ṣ, Ḳ,*) with fet-ḥ [to the ش], (Ḳ,) in one copy of the Ḳ, مُؤْتَشَبٌ, (TA,) † *Such a one is of mixed*, *not of pure*, *race*, or *lineage*. (Ṣ, Ḳ.)

اشر

1. أَشَرَ, (Ṣ, Mṣb, Ḳ,) aor. ـِ, (ISk, MṢ,) or ـُ, (Mṣb,) inf. n. أَشْرٌ, (Mṣb,) *He divided* [or *sawed*] a piece of wood (ISk, Mṣb, Ḳ) with the مِئْشَار; (Ṣ, Mṣb, Ḳ;) as also وَشَرَ and نَشَرَ. (Mṣb, TA.) — أَشَرَتْ أَسْنَانَهَا, aor. ـِ, [or, accord. to the Mṣb, it seems to be ـُ,] inf. n. أَشْرٌ; (Ḳ;) and ▼ أَشَّرَتْهَا, (Ḳ,) inf. n. تَأْشِيرٌ; (Ṣ;) *She* (a woman, TA) *made her teeth serrated*, (Ṣ, Ḳ,) *and sharpened their extremities*, (Ṣ,) to render them like those of a young person: but a curse is denounced in a trad. against her who does this. (TA.) [See also art. وشر.] — أَشِرَ, aor. ـَ, (Ṣ, Mṣb, Ḳ,) inf. n. أَشَرٌ, (Ṣ, A, Mṣb,) *He exulted*, or *exulted greatly*, or *excessively*; *and behaved insolently and unthankfully*, or *ungratefully*: (Ṣ,* A,* Mṣb, Ḳ,* TA:) or *he exulted by reason of wealth*, *and behaved with pride*, *and self-conceitedness*, *and boastfulness*, *and want of thankfulness*: or *he behaved with the utmost exultation*, &c.: or *he rejoiced*, *and rested his mind upon things agreeable with natural desire*. (TA.) [See بَطِرَ.]

2: see 1.

[8. ٱئْتَشَرَتْ, written with the disjunctive alif إِيتَشَرَتْ, *She invited another to make her teeth serrated and to sharpen their extremities;* as also ▼ استأشرت. See the act. part. ns. below: and see also استوشرت.]

10: see 8.

أُشُرٌ :
أُشْرٌ : } see أَشِرٌ.
أُشُرٌ :

أَشِرٌ (Ṣ, A, Mṣb, Ḳ) and ▼ أَشُرٌ and ▼ أُشْرٌ and ▼ أُشُرٌ (Ḳ) and ▼ أَشْرَانُ (Ṣ, Ḳ) *Exulting,* or *exulting greatly,* or *excessively; and behaving insolently and unthankfully,* or *ungratefully:* (Ṣ,* A,* Mṣb, Ḳ,* TA:) or *exulting by reason of wealth, and behaving with pride, and self-conceitedness, and boastfulness, and want of thankfulness:* or *behaving with the utmost exultation,* &c.: or *rejoicing, and resting the mind upon things agreeable with natural desire:* (TA:) pl. [of the first] أَشِرُونَ and [of the second] أَشُرُونَ (L, Ḳ) and [of the first four] أُشُرٌ (Ḳ [accord. to the TA, but not in the copies of the Ḳ in my hands,]) and (of أَشْرَانُ, TA) أَشْرَى (Ḳ) and أَشَارَى (Ṣ, Ḳ) and أُشَارَى. (Ḳ.) One says, أَشِرٌ أَفِرٌ, and ▼ أَشْرَانُ أَفْرَانُ, using the latter word in each instance as an imitative sequent. (TA.) — بَرْقٌ أَشِرٌ ‡ *Lightning flashing repeatedly to and fro.* (A.) — نَبْتٌ أَشِرٌ ‡ *A plant,* or *herbage, extending beyond its proper bounds.* (A.)

أُشْرٌ: see what next follows.

بِأَسْنَانِهِ أُشُرٌ and ▼ أُشْرٌ and ▼ أُشُورٌ, (Ṣ, Ḳ,) which last is a pl., (Ḳ,) *In his teeth is a serration,* (Ṣ, Ḳ,) *and a sharpness of the extremities* [such as is seen in the teeth of young persons]; (Ṣ;) which is sometimes natural and sometimes artificial; (Ḳ;) and [naturally] only in the teeth of young persons. (TA.) Hence the prov., أَعْيَيْتِنِى أُشُرٌ فَكَيْفَ بِدُرْدُرٍ. (Ṣ.) [See art. در.] — أُشُرُ المِنْجَلِ ‡ *The teeth of the reaping-hook,* or *sickle.* (Ḳ.)

أُشَرَةٌ, and its dual: see آشِرٌ.

أُمْنِيَّةٌ أَشِرَةٌ *A very exulting wish:* occurring in the Mo'allakah of El-Ḥárith Ibn-Ḥillizeh. (EM p. 272.)

أَشْرَانُ: see أَشِرٌ, in two places.

أُشُورٌ: see أُشُرٌ.

آشِرٌ *Dividing* [or *sawing*], or one *who divides* [or *saws*], wood, with the مِئْشَار. (Mṣb.) — [Hence,] The *prickles* [or *serrated parts*] *of the shanks of the locust;* (Ḳ;) as also ▼ تَأْشِيرٌ. (TA.) — Also, and ▼ أُشَرَةٌ and ▼ مِئْشَارٌ, *A joint* (عُقْدَةٌ) *at the extremity of the tail of the locust, like two claws;* (Ḳ;) which two things are also called ▼ أُشَرَتَانِ and ▼ مِئْشَارَانِ. (TA.) — آشِرَةٌ A woman *who sharpens the extremities of her teeth* [and *makes them serrated:* see 1]. (Mṣb.) — يَدٌ آشِرَةٌ *An arm,* or *a hand, sawn off; i. q.* ▼ مَأْشُورَةٌ: (ISk, Ṣ, Mṣb, Ḳ:*) like عِيشَةٌ رَاضِيَةٌ in the sense of مَرْضِيَّةٌ. (Ṣ.)

تَأْشِيرٌ, or تَأْشِيرَةٌ, as in different Lexicons, (TA,) [the former in the Ḳ,] The *thing with which the locust bites:* pl. تَآشِيرُ. (Ḳ.) — See also the pl. voce آشِرٌ.

مُؤَشَّرٌ Anything (TA) *made thin* [and *serrated*]. (Ḳ.) [Hence,] ثَغْرٌ مُؤَشَّرٌ *A front tooth serrated and sharpened at the extremity.* (TA.) And hence, (TA,) مُؤَشَّرُ العَضُدَيْنِ is applied to the beetle [as meaning *Having the fore shanks formed thin, and serrated*]. (Ṣ, TA.)

مِئْشَارٌ (Ṣ, Mṣb, Ḳ, &c.) [*A saw;*] *an instrument with which wood is divided;* (Mṣb, Ḳ;) as also مِيشَارٌ, from وَشَرَ; (Mṣb, TA;) and مِنْشَارٌ: (TA:) pl. مَآشِيرُ. (ISk, Mṣb, TA.) — See also this word and its dual voce آشِرٌ.

مَأْشُورٌ Wood *divided* [or *sawn*] with the مِئْشَار. (Mṣb.) See also آشِرٌ. — مَأْشُورَةٌ A woman *who has the extremities of her teeth sharpened* [and *serrated artificially:* see 1]. (Mṣb.)

مِئْشِيرٌ, applied alike to the male and the female, (Ṣ,) to a she-camel and a courser, (Ṣ, Ḳ,) and a man and a woman, (TA,) *Brisk; lively; sprightly.* (Ṣ,* Ḳ.)

مُؤْتَشِرَةٌ and ▼ مُسْتَأْشِرَةٌ A woman *who invites* [*another*] *to make her teeth serrated* [*and to sharpen their extremities:* see 1]. (Ḳ.)

مُسْتَأْشِرَةٌ: see what next precedes.

اشف

إِشْفَى, of the measure فِعْلَى, [and therefore fem., and imperfectly decl.,] (Ṣ, Mṣb,) accord. to some; but accord. to others, of the measure إِفْعَلُ, like إِصْبَعُ, as Kh is related to have said, (Mṣb,) which latter is said by IB to be the correct measure, the [incipient] ا being augmentative, and the word [masc.,] with tenween, [i. e. إِشْفًى,] perfectly decl.: (TA:) The *instrument belonging to the* إِسْكَاف [or *sewer of skins,* or *leather*]; (Ṣ,* Mṣb, TA;) i. e., *with which he sews;* and the *instrument with which he bores,* or *perforates:* (TA:) the *instrument for boring,* or *perforating,* (Ḳ in art. شفى,) *belonging to the* أَسَاكِفَة; said by ISk to be that *which is used for water-skins,* or *milk-skins, and leather water-bags, and the like;* that used for sandals, or shoes, being called مِخْصَفٌ: (Ṣ and TA in art. شفى:) and the [*instrument called*] مِخْرَزٌ *with which skin,* or *leather, is sewed:* (Ḳ in art. شفى:) *i. q.* مِخْرَزٌ: (Mgh in art. شفى:) pl. أَشَافٍ. (Ṣ, Mgh, Mṣb, Ḳ: [in the CḲ, erroneously, أَشَافِى.]) In the Ḳ, in the present art., الإِسْكَافُ is put, by a mistake of the copyists, for لِلْإِسْكَافِ. (TA.) See also art. شفى.

اشك

1. أَشُكَ ذَا خُرُوجًا *i. q.* وَشُكَ, q. v. (TA.)

اشن

5. تَأَشَّنَ *He washed his hands with* أُشْنَان [q. v. infrà]. (Mṣb, Ḳ.)

أُشْنَةٌ [applied in the present day to *Moss:* and particularly, *tree-moss:* in Persian أُشْنَهْ: but] Lth says, (TA,) it is *a thing that winds itself upon the trees called* بَلُّوط *and* صَنَوْبَر [*oak and pine*] *as though it were pared off from a root* (كَأَنَّهُ مَقْشُورٌ مِنْ عِرْقٍ); and it is *sweet in odour, and white:* (Ḳ, TA:) Az says, I do not think it to be [genuine] Arabic. (TA.)

أُشْنَانٌ and إِشْنَانٌ, (Mṣb, Ḳ,) but the former is of higher authority than the latter, (TA,) *i. q.* حُرُضٌ [*Kali,* or *glasswort*]: (Mṣb in the present art.; and Ṣ, A, Mgh, Mṣb, Ḳ, in art. حرض:) [and also *potash,* which is thence prepared;] *a thing,* or *substance, well known,* (Ḳ, TA,) *with which clothes and the hands are washed;* (TA; [see قِلْى;]) *good,* or *profitable,* [*as a remedy*] *for the mange,* or *scab, and the itch; clearing to the complexion, cleansing, emmenagogue, and abortive.* (Ḳ.)

أُشْنَانَةٌ *A vessel for* حُرُض [or *for* أُشْنَان as meaning *potash*]; syn. مِحْرَضَةٌ. (A in art. حرض.)

أُشْنَانِىٌّ *A seller of* أُشْنَان. (TA.)

اصد

2. أَصَّدَهُ, inf. n. تَأْصِيدٌ, is from أُصْدَةٌ: (Ṣ, Ḳ:) [app. meaning *He made it an* أُصْدَة: or *he wore it as an* أُصْدَة: and hence مُؤَصَّدٌ or مُؤَصَّدَةٌ as explained below: or] *he clad him with an* أُصْدَة. (TḲ.)

4. آصد [in some copies of the Ḳ أَصَدَ, which is a mistake, (see the pass. part. n. مُؤْصَدٌ, below,)] *He closed* (أَغْلَقَ, Ṣ, A, Ḳ, and so in the M in art. وصد, or أَطْبَقَ, as in the M in the present art.) a door, or an entrance; as also اوصد; (Ṣ, M, A, Ḳ;) of which it is a dial. var. (Ṣ.) And *He covered,* or *covered over,* a cooking-pot. (M.)

أُصْدَةٌ (Ṣ, M, Ḳ, and Ḥam p. 223) and ▼ أَصِيدَةٌ (M, Ḳ) and ▼ مُؤَصَّدٌ, (Ṣ,* M,) or ▼ مُؤَصَّدَةٌ, (Ḳ,) *A garment of the kind called* صِدَار *worn by a young girl:* when a girl attains to the age of puberty, she is clad with a دِرْع: (M:) or *a small shirt for a little girl:* or *worn beneath the* ثَوْب; (Ḳ:) or the أُصْدَة is *a garment without sleeves, worn by a bride and by a little girl:* (M:) or *a small shirt* or *shift, worn beneath the* ثوب; and *also worn by little girls:* (Ṣ:) or *a garment of which the sewing is not complete:* or *i. q.* بَقِيرَةٌ: or *i. q.* صُدْرَةٌ. (Ḥam ubi suprà.) Kutheiyir says,

* وَقَدْ دَرَّعُوهَا وَهْىَ ذَاتُ مُؤَصَّدٍ ▼ *
* مَجُوبٍ وَلَمَّا يَلْبَسِ الدِّرْعَ رِيدُهَا *

[*They clad her with a* دِرْع *when she wore a* مُؤَصَّد *with an opening cut out at the neck and bosom, when her equal in age had not yet worn the* درع]. (Ṣ, M.)

أَصِيدٌ *A court;* or *an open* or *a wide space in front of a house,* or *extending from its sides;* (Ṣ, M, Ḳ;) a dial. var. of وَصِيدٌ, (Ṣ,) which is the more common form: (M:) or the *extreme and exterior part of a house:* (Mirkát el-Loghah, and Meyd, as rendered by Golius:) or *an intermediate place between the threshold or door and the house; a place which looks neither upon the public nor upon the interior parts, whether it be an area or a vestibule.* (Ibn-Maạroof, as rendered by Golius.)

أُصِيدَةٌ : see أُصُدَةٌ. — *A* [*kind of enclosure for the protection of camels, sheep, or goats, such as is called*] حَظِيرَةٌ : (M, Ḳ:) or *like a* حظيرة, (Ṣ, and Ḥam p. 223,) [*but made*] *of rocks,* or *great masses of stone:* (Ḥam:) a dial. var. of وَصِيدَةٌ [q. v.]: (Ṣ:) pl. إِصَادٌ. (Ḥam.)

مُؤْصَدٌ *Closed; closed over,* or *covered:* occurring in the Ḳur [xc. 20 and] civ. 8; (L;) in which AA reads مُؤْصَدَةٌ [with hemz; others reading this word without hemz]. (Ṣ, L.) You say بَابٌ مُؤْصَدٌ [*A closed door*]. (A.) And قِدْرٌ مُؤْصَدَةٌ *A covered cooking-pot.* (A.) And بَابُ العَفْوِ عَنْهُ مُؤْصَدٌ † [*The door of forgiveness is closed from him;* i. e., *against him*]. (A.)

مُؤْصَدٌ, or مُؤْصَدَةٌ : see أُصُدَةٌ, in three places.

اصر

1. أَصَرَهُ, aor. ـِ , inf. n. أَصْرٌ, *He,* or *it,* (a thing, Ks,) *confined, restricted, limited, kept close, kept within certain bounds or limits, shut up, imprisoned, held in custody, detained, retained, restrained, withheld, debarred, hindered, impeded,* or *prevented, him,* or *it:* (Ks, Ṣ, M, A,* Ḳ:) *it straitened him.* (TA.) You say, أَصَرْتُ الرَّجُلَ عَلَى ذٰلِكَ الأَمْرِ *I confined,* or *restricted, the man to that thing,* or *affair.* (Ks.) And أَصَرْتُهُ عَنْ حَاجَتِهِ, and عَمَّا أَرَادَهُ, *I withheld, restrained,* or *debarred, him from the thing that he wanted,* and *from the thing that he desired.* (IAạr.) — أَصَرَ البَيْتَ, aor. and inf. n. as above, *He made,* or *put, to the tent an* إِصَار. (Ḳ,* TḲ.) — Also, aor. and inf. n. as above, *He broke it.* (El-Umawee, Ṣ, M, Ḳ.*) — *He inclined,* or *bent, it.* (M, Ḳ,* TA.) — *It inclined him,* (Aṣ, Ṣ, Ḳ,) عَلَى فُلَانٍ *to such a one.* (Aṣ, Ṣ.) See an ex. voce آصِرَةٌ.

[3. آصَرَهُ, inf. n. مُؤَاصَرَةٌ, *He was his neighbour, having the* إِصَار *of his tent by the side of the* إِصَار *of the tent of the other.* See the act. part. n. below.]

[6. تَآصَرُوا *They were neighbours; they dwelt,* or *abode, near together.* See the act. part. n. below.]

أُصْرٌ : } see إِصْرٌ; each in three places.
أَصْرٌ :

إِصْرٌ *A covenant, compact,* or *contract;* (Ṣ, Ḳ;) as also ▼ أُصْرٌ and ▼ أَصْرٌ: (Ḳ:) [see also وِصْرٌ:] *any bond arising from relationship,* or *from a covenant* or *compact* or *contract,* (Aboo-Is-ḥáḳ,) and *from an oath:* (ISh:) *a covenant, compact,* or *contract, which one does not fulfil, and for the neglecting and breaking of which one is punished:* so in the Ḳur ii. 286: (I 'Ab:) [see also what follows, in two places:] or *a heavy,* or *burdensome, covenant, compact,* or *contract:* so in the Ḳur iii. 75: (ISh, M:) so, too, in the same vii. 156: (T, M:) pl. آصَارٌ, a pl. of pauc.: (M:) or *a heavy,* or *burdensome, command;* such as was given to the Children of Israel to slay one another: so in the Ḳur ii. 286, accord. to Zj. (TA.) — *A weight,* or *burden;* (Ṣ, M, Ḳ;) as also ▼ أُصْرٌ and ▼ أَصْرٌ: (Ḳ:) so called because it restrains one from motion: (TA:) pl. as above. (M.) — *A sin; a crime; an offence;* (Ṣ, M, Ḳ;) as also ▼ أُصْرٌ and ▼ أَصْرٌ: (Ḳ:) so called because of its weight, or burdensomeness: (TA:) or the *sin of breaking a compact,* or *covenant:* (Fr, Sh:) or *a grievous punishment of a sin:* so accord. to AM in the Ḳur ii. 286. (TA.) — *A thing that inclines one to a thing.* (M, Ḳ.) [See also آصِرَةٌ. It is said in the Ḥam (p. 321) that أَوَاصِرُ is pl. of the former word: but it is evidently pl. of the latter.] — *A swearing by an oath which obliges one to divorce* or *emancipate* or *to pay a vow.* (Ḳ, TA.) So in a trad., in which it is said, مَنْ حَلَفَ عَلَى يَمِينٍ فِيهَا إِصْرٌ فَلَا كَفَّارَةَ لَهَا [*Whoso sweareth an oath in which is an obligation to divorce* or *emancipate* or *to pay a vow, for it there is no expiation*]: for such is the heaviest of oaths, and that from which the way of escape, or evasion, is most strait: the original meaning of اصر being *a burden,* and *a binding.* (TA.) — The *ear-hole:* pl. آصَارٌ (IAạr, Ḳ) and إِصْرَانٌ. (Ḳ.)

إِصَارٌ and ▼ أَيْصَرٌ (Ṣ, M, Ḳ) and ▼ إِصَارَةٌ and ▼ آصِرَةٌ (M, Ḳ) *A short rope,* (Ṣ,) or *small rope,* (Ḳ,) *by which the lower part of the* [*kind of tent called*] خِبَآء *is tied,* or *bound,* (Ṣ, Ḳ,) *to the peg:* (Ṣ:) or *a short peg, for the* [*ropes called*] أَطْنَاب, *with which the lower part of the* [*kind of tent called*] خباء *is fastened:* (M:) [or] إِصَار signifies also *the peg,* (Ḳ,) or *short peg,* (TA,) *of the* [*kind of tent-rope called*] طُنُب: (Ḳ:) or *a peg of the* خباء: (Ibn-Es-Seed, TA:) pl. of the first أُصُرٌ (Ṣ, M) and آصِرَةٌ; (M;) and of the second أَيَاصِرُ. (Ṣ.) ISd thinks that ▼ آصِرَات is the pl. of ▼ آصِرَةٌ used in the first of the senses explained above in in the following verse:

• لَعَمْرُكَ لَا أَدْنُو لِوَصْلِ دَنِيَّةٍ •
• وَلَا أَتَصَبَّى آصِرَاتِ خَلِيلِى •

the poet meaning [*By thy life, I will not approach to hold loving communion,* or *intercourse, with an ignoble,* or *a low, female;*] *nor will I direct my regard to the short ropes which bind* [*to the pegs*] *the lower part of the tent of my friend,* coveting his wife, and the like: or he may mean *nor will I direct my regard to the female relations of my friend,* such as his paternal aunt, and his maternal aunt, and the like. (TA.) [See آصِرَةٌ, below.] — Also, the first, *A thing by which things are tied firmly,* or *made firm* or *fast.* (TA.) — *A thong of untanned hide which binds together the* عَضُدَانِ *of a camel's saddle:* and إِسَار is a dial. var. thereof. (M.) — Also, (M, Ḳ,) and ▼ أَيْصَرٌ, (AZ, Aṣ, Ḳ,) *A* [*garment of the kind called*] كِسَآء *in which dry herbage,* or *fodder, is collected:* (M, Ḳ:) or *a* كساء *filled with herbage, and tied:* (AZ:) or *a* كساء *in which is dry herbage,* or *fodder:* otherwise it is not thus called: (Aṣ:) pl. [of the former] أُصُرٌ and آصِرَةٌ; (Ḳ;) and of the latter أَيَاصِرُ. (AZ.) — And both words, (the former accord. to the Ṣ and M and Ḳ, and the latter accord. to Aṣ and the Ṣ and M and Ḳ,) *Dry herbage,* or *fodder:* (Ṣ, Ḳ:) or *dry herbage,* or *fodder, collected together:* (TA:) or *dry herbage,* or *fodder, in a* [*garment of the kind called*] كِسَآء: otherwise it is not thus called: (Aṣ:) or *dry herbage,* or *fodder, contained in a* مِحَشّ. (M.) [The following saying is cited as an ex. of the first of these significations:] لِفُلَانٍ مَحَشٌّ لَا يُجَزُّ ▼ أَيْصَرُهُ [*To such a one belongs a place,* or *land, abounding with dry herbage,*] *the dry herbage whereof will not be cut;* (Ṣ;) meaning, because of its abundance. (TA.) — Also, the former, *A basket* (زَبِيل or زِنْبِيل, as in different copies of the Ḳ) *in which goods,* or *commodities,* (مَتَاع,) *are carried:* so called as being likened to the thing in which dry herbage is put. (TA.)

إِصَارَةٌ : see إِصَارٌ.

كَلَأٌ آصِرٌ *Pasturage that detains those that are on it* [*by reason of its abundance*]: (M, TA:) or, *to which one goes because of its abundance.* (TA.)

آصِرَةٌ, and its pl. آصِرَاتٌ : see إِصَارٌ, in three places: of which last word, the first is also a pl. — *The thing termed* آخِيَّة and آرِىّ [*to which a beast is tied*]. (TA.) — *A tie of kindred,* or *relationship,* (Ṣ, M, Ḳ,) or *of affinity,* (Ṣ,) or *a favour,* or *benefit,* (Ṣ, Ḳ,) *that inclines one to a man;* (Ṣ;) or because it inclines one: (M:) pl. أَوَاصِرُ. (Ḳ.) One says, مَا تَأْصِرُنِى ▼ عَلَى فُلَانٍ آصِرَةٌ *No tie of relationship, nor any favour,* or *benefit, inclines me to such a one.* (Ṣ.) And عَطَفَ عَلَىَّ بِغَيْرِ آصِرَةٍ وَنَظَرَ فِى أَمْرِى بِغَيْرِ بَاصِرَةٍ [*He inclined to me without any tie of relationship, &c., and examined my case without eye*]. (A.) [See also إِصْرٌ.]

أَيْصَرٌ : see إِصَارٌ, in three places.

مَأْصَرٌ and مَأْصِرٌ *A place in which a person or thing is confined, shut up,* or *imprisoned:* pl. مَآصِرُ; for which the vulgar say, مَعَاصِرُ. (Ṣ, Ḳ.) — Also, the former, (M, A,) or مَاصِرٌ; (TA;) either of the measure مَفْعَلٌ from الأَصْرُ, or of the measure فَاعِلٌ from المَصْرُ; *A thing intervening between two other things and preventing the passage from one to the other; a barrier:* (A:) *a rope across a road or river, preventing the passage of travellers and ships or boats,* (M, L,) *for the taking of the tithes from them.* (L.)

مُؤَاصِرٌ *A neighbour:* (Ḳ:) [or *a close,* or *near, neighbour:* as in the saying,] هُوَ جَارِى مُؤَاصِرِى *He is my neighbour, having the* إِصَار *of his tent by the side of the* إِصَار *of my tent.* (El-Aḥmar, Ṣ.)

حَىٌّ مُتَآصِرُونَ *A tribe dwelling,* or *abiding, near together.* (Ṣ, Ḳ.*)

اصطبل

إِصْطَبْلٌ *A stable* (Ḳ) *for* دَوَابّ [i. e. *horses* or *mules* or *asses*]: (Ṣ [in some copies of which it is omitted] and Ḳ:) the ا is radical, because an augmentative does not occur at the beginning of a word of four or five letters unless derived from a verb: (Ṣ:) [probably from the barbarous Greek σταβλίον:] AA says that it is not of the [genuine] language of the Arabs: (Ṣ:) IB says that it is a foreign word, used by the Arabs: (TA:) accord. to some, (TA,) it is of the dial. of Syria: (Ḳ, TA:) the pl. is أَصَاطِبُ: and the dim. أُصَيْطِبٌ. (TA.)

اصطرلاب

أُصْطُرْلَابٌ or أَصْطُرْلَابٌ: see اسطرلاب.

اصل

1. أَصُلَ, (Ḳ,) inf. n. أَصَالَةٌ; (TA;) or أَصِلَ; (M;) *It* (a thing, M) *had*, or *came to have, root*, or *a foundation*; (M, Ḳ;) as also ↓ تأصّل: (M:) or *it was*, or *became, firm*, or *established*, and *firmly rooted* or *founded*; as also ↓ تأصّل: (Ḳ:) and [in like manner] ↓ استأصل *it* (a thing) *was*, or *became, firm in its root* or *foundation, and strong*. (Mṣb.) You say, ↓ اِسْتَأْصَلَتِ الشَّجَرَةُ *The tree* [*took root*; or] *grew, and became firm in its root*. (TA.) — [Hence,] أَصُلَ, (Ṣ, M, Ḳ,) inf. n. as above, (Ṣ, M,) *He* (a man, Ṣ,* M) *was*, or *became, firm*, (Ṣ, M, Ḳ,) or *sound*, (Ṣ,) *of judgment*; (Ṣ, M, Ḳ;) *intelligent*. (M: [and so, probably, in correct copies of the Ḳ; but in a MS. copy of the Ḳ and in the CḲ and TA, instead of عَاقِل, the reading in the M, I find عَاقِب.]) — Also, (Ṣ,* Ḳ,) inf. n. as above, (Ṣ, TA,) *It* (judgment, or opinion,) *was*, or *became, firm*, or *sound*, (Ṣ,* TA,) or *good*. (Ḳ.) — And, inf. n. as above, *It* (a thing) *was*, or *became, eminent, noble*, or *honourable*. (Mṣb.) = أَصَلَهُ, [aor. and inf. n. as in what follows next after this sentence,] *He hit*, or *struck, its root*, or *foundation; that by being which it was what it was*, or *in being which it consisted*; or *its ultimate constituent*. (A, TA.) — And hence, (A, TA,) أَصَلَهُ عِلْمًا, (A, Ḳ, TA,) aor. ـِ, inf. n. أَصْلٌ; (TA;) or ↓ آصَلَهُ [with medd, (which I think to be a mistake, unless this be a dial. var.,) and without علما]; (so in a copy of the M;) † *He knew it completely*, or *thoroughly*, or *superlatively well*, syn. قَتَلَهُ, (Ḳ,) [i. e.] قَتَلَهُ عِلْمًا, *so that he was acquainted with its* أَصْل [or *root*, or *foundation*, or its *ultimate constituent*, as is indicated in the A and TA]: (M:) or this is from أَصَلَةٌ, as meaning "a certain very deadly serpent;" (A, TA;) [whence the phrase,] أَصَلَتْهُ الأَصَلَةُ, (Ḳ,) inf. n. أَصْلٌ, (TA,) *The* [*serpent called*] اصلة *sprang upon him* (Ḳ, TA) *and slew him*. (TA.) = أَصِلَ, aor. ـَ, (M, Ḳ,) inf. n. أَصَلٌ, (M,) said of water, *i. q.* أَسِنَ; (M, Ḳ;) i. e. *It became altered for the worse* (M, TA) *in its taste and odour*, (TA,) *from fetid black mud* (Ḳ, TA) *therein*: so says Ibn-'Abbád: (TA:) and said of flesh-meat, *it became altered* (Ḳ, TA) *in like manner*. (TA.) = أَصَلَ فُلَانٌ يَفْعَلُ كَذَا وَكَذَا *Such a one set about*, or *commenced, doing thus and thus*, or *such and such things*. (TA.)

2. أصّلهُ, inf. n. تَأْصِيلٌ, *He made it to have a firm*, or *fixed, root*, or *foundation, whereon to build*, (Mṣb, TA,) i. e., *whereon another thing might be built*. (El-Munáwee, TA.) [Hence,] أصّل مَالَهُ i. q. أَثَّلَهُ [*He made his wealth*, or *property, to have root*, or *a foundation*; or *to become firm*, or *established*, and *firmly rooted* or *founded*: see, below, أَصْلُ مَالٍ, and مَالٌ لَهُ أَصْلٌ]. (M and Ḳ in art. اثل.) — أَصَّلَ الأُصُولَ [*He disposed, arranged, distributed, classified*, or *set in order, the fundamentals, fundamental articles, principles, elements*, or *rudiments*, of a science, &c.,] is a phrase similar to بَوَّبَ الأَبْوَابَ and رَتَّبَ الرُّتَبَ. (TA.)

4. آصل, (inf. n. إِيصَالٌ, TA,) *He entered upon the time called* أَصِيل, q. v. (Ṣ, M, Ḳ.) = See also أَصَلَهُ عِلْمًا.

5. تأصّل: see 1, first sentence, in two places.

10. استأصل: see 1, in two places, first and second sentences. = استأصلهُ *He uprooted it; unrooted it; eradicated it; extirpated it; pulled it up*, or *out*, or *off, from its root*, or *foundation*, or *lowest part*, (Ṣ, TA,) or *with its roots*, or *foundations*, or *lowest parts*; (TA;) *he cut it off* (M, Mṣb) *from its root*, or *lowest part*, (M,) or *with its roots*, or *lowest parts*. (Mṣb.) You say, اِسْتَأْصَلَ اللّٰهُ شَأْفَتَهُمْ, a precative phrase, meaning *May God* [*extirpate* or] *remove* (*from them*) *their* شأفة; which is an ulcer, or a purulent pustule, that comes forth in the foot, and is cauterized, and in consequence goes away: (M:) or استأصل شأفتهم [in general usage] means *he extirpated them*, or *may he extirpate them*; or *he cut off*, or *may he cut off, the last remaining of them*. (TA. [See also art. شأف.]) And استأصل القَوْمَ, i. e. قَطَعَ أَصْلَهُمْ [*He cut off the root, race*, or *stock, of the people*; i. e. *he extirpated them*]. (M.) And استأصل اللّٰهُ الكُفَّارَ *God destroyed altogether* or *entirely*, or *may God destroy altogether* or *entirely, the unbelievers*. (Mṣb.) And استأصل الخِتَانَ *He performed the circumcision so as to remove the prepuce utterly*. (TA in art. سحت.)

أَصْلٌ The *lower*, or *lowest, part* of a thing; [i. e. its *root, bottom*, or *foot*;] (M, Mṣb, Ḳ;) as also ↓ يَأْصُولٌ: (M, Ḳ:) so of a mountain: and of a wall; (TA;) i. e. its *foundation*, or *base*: (Mṣb:) and of a tree [or plant]; (TA;) i. e. [its *stem*, or *trunk*, or *stock*, or] the *part from which the branches are broken off*: (TA in art. كسر:) [and also its *root*, or *foot*; for] the سَاق of a tree is said to be the part between its أَصْل and the place where its branches shoot out: (TA in art. سوق:) [and *a stump* of a tree: and hence, *a block* of wood: (see exs. voce نَقِير:)] pl. أُصُولٌ (Ṣ, M, Mṣb, Ḳ) and [pl. of pauc.] آصُلٌ: (AḤn, Ḳ:) [ISd says that] the former is its only pl.: (M:) [but] the latter pl. occurs in a verse of Lebeed, (which see below,) as cited by AḤn. (TA.) You say, قَعَدَ فِى أَصْلِ الجَبَلِ *He sat upon*, or *at, the lowest part* [&c.] *of the mountain*; and فِى أَصْلِ الحَائِطِ *at the lowest part* [&c.] *of the wall*. (TA.) And قَلَعَهُ مِنْ أَصْلِهِ [*He pulled it up*, or *out*, or *off, from its root*, or *foundation*, or *lowest part*]; and بِأُصُولِهِ [*with its roots*, or *foundations*, or *lowest parts*; both meaning, *utterly, entirely*, or *altogether*]. (TA in explanation of استأصلهُ, q. v.) And قَلَعَ أَصْلَ الشَّجَرَةِ *He pulled up*, or *out, the lowest part*, [or *stem* or *stock* or *root* or *foot* or *stump*,] *of the tree*. (TA.) Lebeed says, [of a wild cow,]

• تَجْتَافُ آصُلَ قَالِصٍ مُتَنَبِّذٍ •
• بِعُجُوبِ أَنْقَآءٍ يَمِيلُ هَيَامُهَا •

[*She enters into the midst of the stems of trees with high branches, apart from others*, i. e. from other trees, *in the hinder parts of sand-hills, the fine loose sand thereof inclining* upon her]: (AḤn, TA:) but as some relate it, أَصْلًا قَالِصًا. (TA. [See EM, p. 161.]) — *A thing upon which another thing is built* or *founded* [either properly or tropically]: (KT, Kull p. 50, TA:) the *foundation*, or *basis*, of a thing, [either properly or tropically,] *which being imagined to be taken away*, or *abstracted, by its being taken away*, or *abstracted, the rest thereof becomes also taken away*, or *abstracted*: (Er-Rághib, TA:) *that upon which the existence* of anything *rests* [or *depends*]; so the father is اصل to the offspring, and the river is اصل to the streamlet that branches off from it: (Mṣb:) or *a thing upon which another thing depends as a branch*; as the father in relation to the son: (Kull:) [i. e. the *origin, source, beginning*, or *commencement*, of a thing: the *origin, original, root, race*, or *stock*, from which a man springs. Hence شَىْءٌ لَهُ أَصْلٌ *A thing having root*, or *a foundation*; and consequently, *having rootedness, fixedness, immobility, stability*, or *permanence*; *rooted, fixed, immoveable, stable*, or *permanent*. Whence,] مِلْكٌ ثَابِتٌ لَهُ أَصْلٌ, (Mgh voce عَقَار,) and مَالٌ لَهُ أَصْلٌ, (Mṣb in explanation of that word,) and مَا لَهُ أَصْلٌ, (KT in explanation of the same,) [*Real*, or *immoveable, property*;] *property such as consists in a house or land yielding a revenue*; (Mgh;) or *such as a house and palm-trees*; (Mṣb;) or *such as land and a house*. (KT.) [Hence, also, أَصْلُ مَالٍ signifying *A source of wealth* or *profit*; *a stock, fund, capital*, or *principal*. You say,] اِتَّخَذْتُهُ لِنَفْسِى أَصْلَ مَالٍ لِلنَّسْلِ لَا لِلتِّجَارَةِ [*I took it for myself as a source of wealth or profit, for breeding, not for traffic*]. (Mgh in art. قنو.) You say also, بَاعَ أَصْلَ أَرْضِهِ [meaning *He sold the fundamental property*, i. e. *the property itself, of his land*]. (Ṣ voce عُكْر.) [See also an ex. in conjugation 4 in art. بقى: and another in the first paragraph of art. حبس.] And أَخَذَهُ بِأَصْلِهِ [*He took it as it were with its root*, or *the like*; meaning, *entirely*]. (Ḳ. [See أَصِيلَةٌ.]) And قَطَعَ أَصْلَهُمْ [*He cut off their root, race*, or *stock*; i. e. *he extirpated them*]. (M.) And فُلَانٌ فِى أَصْلِ صِدْقٍ, (Ṣ and L in art. ضنأ,) and

فِى أَصْلِ سُوْءٍ, (L ibid.,) *Such a one is of an excellent origin*, or *race*, or *stock*, (Ṣ, L,) and *of a bad origin*, or *race*, or *stock*; (L;) اصل being here syn. with ضِنْءٌ (Ṣ, L) and مَعْدِن. (Ṣ.) And فُلَانٌ فِى أَصْلِ الكَرَمِ *Such a one is of* [a race] *the source of generosity*, or *nobleness*; اصل being here syn. with بُؤْبُؤٌ. (Ṣ in art. بأ.) And لَا أَصْلَ لَهُ وَلَا فَصْلَ *He has no* حَسَب [i. e. *grounds of pretension to respect or honour*; or *rank*, or *nobility*, or *the like*]; *nor tongue* [i. e. *eloquence*]: (Ks, Ṣ, O, Mṣb:) or *he has no intellect*, (IAạr, Mṣb, El-Munáwee,) *nor eloquence*: (El-Munáwee, TA:) or *he has no lineage, nor tongue*: (L:) or *he has no father, nor child*: (Kull p. 53:) [or *he has no known stock nor branch*; for] فَصْل is the contr. of أَصْل, and in relationship signifies *a branch*. (Mṣb in art. فصل.) You say also, مَا فَعَلْتُهُ أَصْلًا, meaning *I have not done it ever*; and *I will not do it ever*; the last word being in the accus. case as an adverbial noun; i. e. *I have not done it at any time*; and *I will not do it at any time*. (Mṣb, El-Munáwee, TA.) — [It also signifies The *original*, or *elemental, matter, material, substance*, or *part*, of a thing; syn. with عُنْصُرٌ;] *that from which a thing is taken* [or *made*]. (KT voce دَاخِل.) — [The *fundamental*, or *essential, part* of a thing. Hence, sing. of أُصُولٌ as signifying The *fundamentals, fundamental articles* or *dogmas, principles, elements*, or *rudiments*, of a science &c. Whence,] عِلْمُ الأُصُولِ, (TA,) [meaning] عِلْمُ أُصُولِ الدِّينِ [*The science of the fundamentals, fundamental articles* or *dogmas*, or *principles, of religion*; *the science of theology*, or *divinity*; *according to the system of the Muslims, as distinguished from that of the philosophers*;] *the science of the articles*, or *tenets, of belief*; also called الفِقْهُ الأَكْبَرُ; (Kull. voce فقه;) and [more commonly] عِلْمُ الكَلَامِ. (Ḥájjee Khaleefeh.) [See also 2.] — *A radical* (as opposed to an augmentative) *letter*; as being an essential element of a word. (The Lexicons passim.) — The *original form* of a word. (The same passim.) — The *original*, or *primary, signification* of a word. (The same passim.) — *An original copy* of a book: and *a copy* of a book *from which one quotes*, or *transcribes, any portion*. (TA, &c., passim.) — [The *original*, or *primary, state*, or *condition*: or] the *old state*, or *condition*. (Kull p. 50.) You say, الأَصْلُ فِى الأَشْيَآءِ الإِبَاحَةُ وَالطَّهَارَةُ *The old state, or condition, of things is that of being allowable, or lawful, and that of being pure, or clean.* (Kull ubi suprà.) And رَجَعَتْ إِلَى أَصْلِهَا *She returned*, or *reverted*, [*to her original*, or *old, state*, or *condition*; or *to her natural disposition*;] *to a natural disposition which she had relinquished*. (Ṣ voce عِتْر.) — [The *utmost point*, or *degree*, *to which a person*, or *thing, can go*, or *be brought* or *reduced*: and, app., the *utmost that one can do*. Hence the saying,] لَأَضْطَرَّنَّكَ إِلَى أَصْلِكَ [*I will assuredly impel thee, or drive thee, against thy will, to the utmost point to which thou canst go, or be brought or reduced*: or, *constrain thee to do thine utmost*]. (IAạr in L, art. قح [where it is given in explanation of the phrases لَأَضْطَرَّنَّكَ إِلَى قُرِّكَ and قُحَاحِكَ; and so in the T in art. قر in explanation of the former of these two phrases; which is said in the M, in art. قر, to mean *I will assuredly make thee to have recourse to thine utmost effort*, or *endeavour*; and in the L in art. قح this is given as another explanation of the latter of the same two phrases. See also the saying, لَأُلْجِئَنَّكَ إِلَى قُرِّ قَرَارِكَ, explained voce قَرَارٌ.]) — [*That by being which a thing is what it is*, or *in being which it consists*; or its *ultimate constituent*; syn. حَقِيقَةٌ; a meaning well known; and indicated, in the A and TA, by the coupling of حَقِيقَة with أَصْل, evidently as an explicative adjunct.] — [The *prime* of a thing; the *principal, purest, best*, or *choicest, part* thereof; *what is*, or *constitutes, the most essential part* thereof; its *very essence*. Hence;] أَصْلُ دَارٍ [*The principal part of a country*]; (Aṣ, Ṣ, Mṣb, Ḳ, voce عُقْر;) [which is] *the place where the people dwell*, or *abide*. (Aṣ and Ṣ ibid. [See عُقْر.]) And أَصْلُ قَوْمٍ [*The principal place of abode of a people*]. (Ṣ and Ḳ voce بَيْضَةٌ. [See this word.]) And هُوَ فِى أَصْلِ قَوْمِهِ *He is of the prime*, or *of the purest in race*, *the best*, or *the choicest, of his people*; i. q. صُيَّابَتِهِمْ, and صُيَّابِهِمْ. (TA in art. صيب.) — *What is most fit*, or *proper*: as when one says, الأَصْلُ فِى الإِنْسَانِ العِلْمُ [*What is most fit, or proper, in man, is knowledge*]; i. e., knowledge is more fit, or proper, than ignorance: and الأَصْلُ فِى المُبْتَدَإِ التَّقْدِيمُ *What is* [*most*] *fit*, or *proper, in the case of the inchoative, is the putting* [it] *before* [the enunciative], whenever there is no obstacle. (Kull p. 50.) — *What is preponderant in relation to what is preponderated*: as, in language, the word used in its proper sense [in relation to that used in a tropical sense]. (Kull ibid.) — *What is* [*essential*, or] *requisite*, or *needful*: as when one says الأَصْلُ فِى الحَيَوَانِ الغِذَآءُ [*What is essential, or requisite, or needful, in the case of the animal, is food*]. (Kull ibid.) — *A* [*primary*, or] *universal*, or *general, rule*, or *canon*. (Kull ibid.) — *An indication, an evidence*, or *a proof, in relation to that which is indicated*, or *evidenced*, or *proved*. (Kull ibid.)

أَصَلٌ: see its n. un., أَصَلَةٌ.

أَصِلٌ, (Ḳ,) or ▼ أَصِيلٌ, (M,) i. q. ▼ مُسْتَأْصِلٌ. (M, Ḳ.) You say قَلْعٌ أَصِلٌ *Eradicating*, or *extirpating, evulsion*: (TA:) or ▼ قَطْعٌ أَصِيلٌ *extirpating excision*. (M.)

أُصُلٌ, said by some to be a pl., and by others to be a dial. var., of أَصِيلٌ: see the latter word, in two places.

أَصَلَةٌ: see أَصِيلَةٌ. — Also *A kind of serpent, the most malignant*, or *noxious, of serpents*: (Ṣ:) or *a serpent*, (M, Ḳ,) *short*, (M, [where, in the only copy to which I have access, I find added, كَالرِّئَةِ, app. a mistranscription, for كَالرُّمَّةِ, *like the fragment of a rope*,]) or *small*, (Ḳ,) *red, but not intensely red*, (M,) *very deadly, of the most malignant*, or *noxious, kind*, (TA,) *having one leg, upon which it stands*, (M, TA,) *then turns round, then springs*, (TA,) *that springs upon a man, and blows, killing everything upon which it blows*: (M:) or, as some say, *a great serpent*, (M, Ḳ,) *that kills by its blowing*: (Ḳ:) or *one of the very crafty kinds of serpents, short and broad, said to be like the shaft of an arrow, and it springs upon the horseman*: (Mṣb:) pl. ▼ أَصَلٌ, (Ṣ, M. Mṣb, Ḳ,) [or rather this is a coll. gen. n.,] and [pl. of pauc.] آصَالٌ. (Mṣb.) — [Hence, app.,] † *Short and broad*: applied to a man and to a woman. (TA.)

أَصْلِىٌّ [*Radical*; *fundamental*; *primitive*; *original*; *underived*: an epithet of extensive application; and particularly applied to a letter of a word, as opposed to augmentative; and to a signification]. (The Lexicons &c. passim.)

أَصْلِيَّةٌ [The *quality denoted by the epithet* أَصْلِىٌّ; *radicalness*, &c.:] a term used by IJ [and others] in the place of تَأَصُّلٌ: see 5. (M.)

أَصِيلٌ [*Having root*, or *a foundation*; and consequently, *having rootedness, fixedness, immobility, stability*, or *permanence*; *rooted, fixed, immoveable, stable*, or *permanent*]. You say, إِنَّ النَّخْلَ فِى أَرْضِنَا لَأَصِيلٌ *Verily the palm-trees in our land remain permanently, not perishing*. (A, TA.) — A man *having* أَصْل, (Ḳ, TA,) i. e., *lineage*, or *pedigree*: (TA:) or *established in his* أَصْل: (Abu-l-Baḳà, TA:) or *noble*, or *generous*. (Mṣb.) — A man *firm of judgment, and intelligent*. (M, Ḳ.* [Accord. to the copies of the latter, the signification is عَاقِبٌ ثَابِتُ الرَّأْىِ: but I think that the right reading of the first word is عَاقِلٌ, as in the M, in which this word occupies the last place in the explanation.]) And أَصِيلُ الرَّأْىِ *A man firm*, or *sound, of judgment*. (Ṣ.) And رَأْىٌ أَصِيلٌ *Judgment having* أَصْل [i. e. *firmness*]. (M.) And مَجْدٌ أَصِيلٌ *Glory, honour, dignity*, or *nobility, having a firm root* or *foundation*. (Ṣ.) And شَرٌّ أَصِيلٌ *Vehement evil* or *mischief*. (Ibn-'Abbád.) — See also أَصِلٌ, in two places. — [Hence, app.,] الأَصِيلُ *Destruction*: and *death*: as also, in both senses, ▼ الأَصِيلَةُ. (Ḳ.) — [The *evening*; or] i. q. عَشِىٌّ; (M, Ḳ, Mṣb, TA;) i. e. (Mṣb, TA) the *time from the* عَصْر, (Ṣ, TA,) *from the prayer of the* عصر, (Mṣb,) *to sunset*; (Ṣ, Mṣb, TA;) as also ▼ أَصِيلَةٌ: (R, TA:) the pl. is أُصُلٌ, (Ṣ, M, R, Mṣb, Ḳ,) or ▼ this is a sing., (TA,) or it may be a sing., (M,) for it is used as such, (M, TA,) and أُصْلَانٌ, (Ṣ, M, Ḳ,) and آصَالٌ, (Ṣ, M, Ṣgh, Ḳ,) [a pl. of pauc.,] or, accord. to Eṣ-Ṣaláḥ Eṣ-Ṣafadee, this is a pl. of أُصُلٌ, the sing., not the pl., (TA,) or it is pl. of أُصُلٌ, (Zj, M,) which may be a pl. or a sing., (M,) and أَصَائِلُ, (Ṣ, M, Ḳ,) as though pl. of أَصِيلَةٌ, (Ṣ,) or it is pl. of this last word. (R, TA.) You say, لَقِيتُهُ أَصِيلًا and ▼ أُصُلًا, i. e. [*I met him in the evening*,] عَشِيًّا. (A, TA.) From the pl. أُصْلَانٌ is formed the dim. ▼ أُصَيْلَانٌ, (Ṣ, M, Ḳ,) which is extr., (M, Ḳ,) because the dim. of a pl. is [regularly] formed only from a pl. of pauc., which اصلان is not; or, if اصلان be a sing., like رُمَّانٌ and قُرْبَانٌ, this dim. is regular: (M:) sometimes, (Ḳ,) one says also ▼ أُصَيْلَال, (Ṣ, M, Ḳ,) substituting ل for the [final] ن. (Ṣ, M.*) You say, ▼ لَقِيتُهُ أُصَيْلَانًا and ▼ أُصَيْلَالًا, meaning, as above, عَشِيًّا: (A, TA:) and Lḥ mentions ▼ لقيته أُصَيْلًا. (So in two copies of the Ṣ.)

أَصِيلَةٌ A man's *whole property*: (M, Ḳ:) or his *palm-trees*: (Ḳ, TA: in the CḲ his *palm-tree*:) thus in the dial. of El-Ḥijáz. (O, TA.) — أَخَذَهُ بِأَصِيلَتِهِ, (Ṣ, M, Ḳ,) and ▼ بِأَصَلَتِهِ, (IAạr, M, Ḳ,) *He took it altogether*, (Ṣ, M, Ḳ,) [as it were] *with its root*, (Ṣ, M,) *not leaving aught of it*. (TA.) And جَاؤُوا بِأَصِيلَتِهِمْ *They came altogether; the whole of them*. (Ṣ, Z.) — لِفُلَانٍ أَرْضٌ أَصِيلَةٌ *To such a one belongs land long possessed*, or *inherited from his parents, by means of which he has his living*: a phrase of the people of Eṭ-Ṭáïf. (TA.) — See also أَصِيلٌ, in two places.

أُصُولِيٌّ One *skilled in the science termed* عِلْمُ الأُصُولِ: see أَصْلٌ. (TA.)

لَقِيتُهُ أُصَيْلًا: see أَصِيلٌ, last sentence.

أُصَيْلَانٌ and أُصَيْلَالٌ: see أَصِيلٌ, in four places, last two sentences.

لَقِيتُهُ مُؤْصِلًا *I met him entering upon the time called the* أَصِيل. (TA.) And أَتَيْنَا مُؤْصِلِينَ *We came entering upon the time so called*. (Ṣ.)

أَصْلٌ مُؤَصَّلٌ [*A root*, or *foundation*, or *the like, made firm*, or *fixed*, or *established*]. (Ṣ.) [See also أَصِيلٌ.]

شَاةٌ مُسْتَأْصَلَةٌ *A sheep, or goat, whose horn has been taken from its root*. (TA.)

مُسْتَأْصِلٌ: see أَصِيلٌ.

بَأْصُول: see أَصْلٌ, first sentence.

اط

1. أَطَّ, (Ṣ, Ḳ,) aor. ـِ, (Ḳ,) inf. n. أَطِيطٌ (Ṣ, Ḳ) and أَطٌّ, (TA,) *It produced, made, gave, emitted*, or *uttered, a sound, noise, voice, or cry*; (Ṣ, Ḳ;) [and particularly, *it creaked*; and *it moaned*;] said of a camel's saddle, (Ṣ,* Ḳ, [in the CḲ, الرَّجُل is put by mistake for الرَّحْل,]) [and particularly of a new camel's saddle,] and the like, (Ḳ,) such as a [plaited or woven girth called] نِسْع, and of everything of which the sound resembles that of a new camel's saddle, (TA,) and of a palm-trunk, and of a tree of the kind called سِدْر, (Ṣ, TA,) or of the kind called سَرْح, (TA,) and of a cane or reed on the occasion of its being straightened, [in which instance it is said to be tropical, but if so it is tropical in several other instances,] and of a bow, (TA,) and of the belly by reason of emptiness, (Ṣ,* TA,) and, in a trad. of Aboo-Dharr, ‡ of heaven, or the sky, notwithstanding there being [really] no أَطِيط in this instance, for it is meant to denote [the presence of] multitude, and confirmation of the majesty of God. (TA.) [It is also said of other things, as will be shown by phrases here following, and by explanations of أَطِيط below.] You also say, أَطَّتِ الإِبِلُ, (Ḳ,) aor. as above, inf. n. أَطِيطٌ, (TA,) *The camels moaned by reason of fatigue*, or *uttering their yearning cry to their young*, (Ḳ, TA,) and sometimes *by reason of fulness of their udders with milk*. (TA.) And لَا آتِيكَ مَا أَطَّتِ الإِبِلُ *I will not come to thee as long as camels utter cries* [or *moan*] *by reason of the heaviness of their loads*. (Ṣ.) And لَا أَفْعَلُ ذٰلِكَ مَا أَطَّتِ الإِبِلُ, meaning *I will not do that ever*. (TA.) And مَا لَنَا بَعِيرٌ يَئِطُّ *We have not a camel that moans*, or *cries*; meaning *we have not any camel*; for the camel cannot but do so. (TA, from a trad.) [See also أَطِيط, below.] And أَطَّتْ لَهُ رَحِمِي ‡ [*My feeling of relationship*, or *sympathy of blood*,] *became affected with tenderness*, or *compassion*, and *became moved*, [or rather *pleaded*,] *for him* [or *in his favour*]: (Ḳ, TA:) and hence ▼ التَّأَطُّط [inf. n. of the verb in the syn. phrase تَأَطَّطَتْ لَهُ رَحِمِي]. (Sgh, TA.) And أَطَّتْ بِكَ الرَّحِمُ [*The feeling of relationship*, or *sympathy of blood, pleaded*, or *hath pleaded, in thee*;] i. e., *inclined thee to favour*. (Ḥam p. 765.) [See another ex. voce نَحَاسَةٌ.]

5: see 1, near the end.

أَطٌّ: see أَطِيط, below.

نُسُوعٌ أُطُطٌ [pl. of أَطٌّ, part. n. of 1,] *Creaking* [*plaited*, or *woven, thongs*]. (Ḳ.)

أَطِيطٌ [as explained in what here follows seems to be properly an inf. n., though, like all inf. ns., it may be used as a subst.:] The *sounding*, or *the like*, or the *sound*, or *the like*, [and particularly the *creaking*, or *creaking sound*, and the *moaning*, or *moaning sound*,] of a camel's saddle (Ṣ, Ḳ, TA) when new; (TA;) and so ▼ أَطٌّ, of the litters and saddles of camels when the riders are heavy thereon; and the former, also, of a door; said, in a trad., of the gate of paradise, by reason of its being crowded; (TA;) and of a plaited or woven thong when stretching; (Ez-Zejjájee, TA;) and of the back [when strained]; (Ḳ;) and of the bowels, (TA,) and of the belly, or inside, by reason of hunger, (Ḳ,) or by reason of vehement hunger; (TA;) and of camels, (Ṣ, Ḳ,) by reason of their burdens, (Ḳ,) or by reason of the heaviness of their burdens; (Ṣ;) and the *prolonging of the cries* of camels: (TA:) but 'Alee Ibn-Ḥamzeh says that the cry of camels is termed رُغَاءٌ, and that أَطِيط signifies the *sounding*, or *sound*, of their bellies, or insides, *by reason of repletion from drinking*. (IB, TA.) أَهْلُ صَهِيلٍ وَأَطِيطٍ, occurring in a trad., means † *Possessors of horses and of camels*. (TA.) — Also † *Hunger*, (Ḳ, TA,) itself, as well as the sound of the bowels or belly by reason thereof: from Ez-Zejjájee. (TA.)

أَطَّاطٌ *Sounding much; noisy*; (Ḳ, TA;) *having a sound*: applied [to any of the things mentioned above in the explanations of أَطّ and أَطِيط; and] to a hide; and to a camel repleted with drink; and to a road: fem. with ة: which, applied to a woman, signifies one *whose* فَرْج *has a sound* إِذَا جُومِعَتْ. (TA.)

اطر

1. أَطَرَهُ, aor. ـِ (Ṣ, Mṣb, Ḳ) and ـُ, (Ḳ,) inf. n. أَطْرٌ; (Ṣ, Mṣb, Ḳ;) and ▼ أَطَّرَهُ, inf. n. تَأْطِيرٌ; (Ḳ;) *He bent it, or curved it*; (Ṣ, Mṣb, Ḳ, &c.;) namely, a bow, (Ṣ, A,) and a twig, or the like: (A:) *he laid hold upon one of its two extremities, and curved it*: *he bent it, or curved it*; namely, anything; عَلَى شَىْءٍ *upon a thing*: and the latter verb, [or both,] *he bent it into the form of a hoop, bringing its two extremities together*. (TA.) — It is said of Adam, كَانَ طُوَالًا فَأَطَّرَهُ ▼ اللّٰهُ *He was tall, and God bent him, and diminished his height*. (TA.) — And one says, أَخَذَ عَلَى يَدَيِ الظَّالِمِ وَأَطَرَهُ عَلَى الحَقِّ ‡ [*He laid hold upon the two hands*, or *arms, of the wrongdoer*, or *prevented, restrained*, or *withheld, him from doing that which he desired*,] *and bent him to* [*conformity with*] *what was right*. (AA, from a trad.) And أَطَرْتَ فُلَانًا عَلَى مَوَدَّتِكَ ‡ [*Thou hast bent such a one to love thee*]. (A.) — أَطَرَ السَّهْمَ, (Ṣ, Ḳ,) aor. ـِ and ـُ, (Ḳ,) inf. n. as above, (Ṣ, Ḳ,) *He wound an* أُطْرَة *upon the arrow*. (Ṣ, Ḳ.) — أَطَرَ البَيْتَ, (TḲ,) inf. n. as above, (Ḳ,) *He made an* إِطَار, which is *a thing resembling a zone or belt, to the tent or house*. (Ḳ, TḲ.)

2: see 1, in two places. — أَطَّرَتْ, inf. n. تَأْطِير, *She* (a girl, IAạr) *remained in the house*, or *tent, of her father, some time*, or *long*, (IAạr, Ḳ,) *without marrying*. (IAạr.) [See also 5.]

5. تَأَطَّرَ *It* (a spear) *bent*: (Ṣ, Ḳ:) *it* (a thing) *became crooked, curved*, or *bent*; as also ▼ انأطر: (Ḳ, TA:) *it became bent into the form of a hoop, its two extremities being brought together*. (TA.) — تَأَطَّرَتْ *She affected a bending of her person, body*, or *limbs, in her gait*. (A.) — *He confined himself* (Ḳ, TA) in a place. (TA.) — تَأَطَّرَتْ *She* (a woman) *remained*, or *stayed, in her house*, or *tent*; (Ṣ, Ḳ;) *she kept to it*. (TA.) [See also 2.]

7: see 5.

أَطْرٌ The *place of curvature* (مُنْحَنًى) of a bow, and of a cloud: (Ḳ, TA:) an inf. n. used as a subst., and, being so used, admitting the dual form: or the *bent*, or *curved, part of the extremity* of a bow; to which Ṭarafeh likens the curving of the ribs of a she-camel: (TA:) and *what resembles a curvature, seen in the clouds*: an inf. n. in the sense of a pass. part. n. (Skr, TA.)

أُطْرَةٌ The *sinew that is wound immediately above the notch of an arrow*; (Ṣ, Ḳ;) as also ▼ إِطَارٌ. (Ḳ.) — The *edge of the glans* of the penis; (Ḳ,* TA;) as also ▼ the latter word. (Ḳ, TA.) — The *flesh surrounding the nail*: (Ḳ:) pl. أُطَرٌ and إِطَارٌ. (TA.) — *A mixture of ashes and blood with which a fracture in a cooking-pot is smeared* (Ṣ, Ḳ) *and repaired*. (TA.)

إِطَارٌ *Anything that surrounds another thing*: (Ṣ, A, Mṣb, Ḳ:) as the *hoop* of a tambourine, (A, Mgh, TA,) and of a sieve. (Ṣ, A, Mgh, Ḳ.) — *A ring of hair surrounding the head, the middle of it being bald.* (TA.) —— *The branches of a vine, bent, or wreathed, so as to form a covering over-head.* (Ḳ.) —— See also أُطْرَةٌ, in two places. —— إِطَارُ الحَافِرِ *The part of the hoof of a horse or the like which surrounds, or extends around, the* أَشْعَر [q. v.]. (Ṣ.) —— إِطَارُ الشَّفَةِ (Ṣ, Ḳ, &c.) ‡ *The part,* (A,) or *flesh,* (Mṣb,) *surrounding the lip:* (A, Mṣb:) or *the part that separates between the lip and the hairs of the mustache:* (Ḳ:) or *the edge of the upper lip, between the lip itself and the parts where the hair grows:* (IAth:) or *the rising edge,* or *ridge, between the part where the mustache is clipped and the lip, intermixing with the mouth.* (A'Obeyd.) The Muslim should clip his mustache so that this part shall appear. (Mṣb, TA.) —— إِطَارُ بَيْتٍ *A thing resembling a zone,* or *belt, of a tent* or *house.* (Ḳ.) —— إِطَارٌ مِنَ النَّاسِ ‡ *A ring,* or *circle, of men.* (Ḳ.) One says, هُمْ إِطَارٌ لِبَنِى فُلَانٍ ‡ *They have alighted and taken up their abode* [*so that they form a ring*] *around the sons of such a one.* (A, Mṣb.)

أَطِيرٌ *A sin; a crime; an offence.* (Ṣ, Ḳ.) One says, أَخَذَنِى بِأَطِيرِ غَيْرِى *He punished me for the sin, crime,* or *offence, of another than myself.* (Ṣ.)

مَأْطُورَةٌ *A bow.* (A.) —— *A milking-vessel of skin* (عُلْبَة) *for the head of which a twig is bent into the form of a hoop, and put round, after which its lip is covered;* (Ḳ, TA;) or, *sometimes, the edges of the skin of the* علبة *are folded upon the hoop-formed twig, and dry upon it.* (TA.)

اطم

أُطْمٌ and أُطُمٌ, (Ṣ, Ḳ,) like أُجْمٌ and أُجُمٌ, (Ṣ, and Mgh in art. اجم,) *A fortress:* or, as some say, *any lofty building:* (Mgh:) or *a* [*building such as is termed*] قَصْر [q. v.]: (IAạr, Ḳ:) and *any fortress built of stones:* and *any square, roofed, house:* (Ḳ:) pl. (of pauc., TA) آطَامٌ (Ṣ, Mgh, Ḳ) and (of mult., TA) أُطُومٌ: (Ḳ:) آطَامٌ signifies *fortresses of the people of El-Medeeneh:* and one of these is termed ▼ أُطُمَةٌ: (Ṣ:) or this signifies [simply] *a fortress;* and its pl. is آطَامٌ. (TA.)

أُطُمَةٌ: see above.

آطَامٌ مُؤَطَّمَةٌ *Lofty* [*fortresses, &c.*]: (A, TA:) [or it may signify *fortresses, &c., disposed in order,* or *grouped together;* for it is said to be] a phrase like أَبْوَابٌ مُبَوَّبَةٌ, (O, TA,) or like أَجْنَادٌ مُجَنَّدَةٌ. (Ḳ.)

اف

1. أَفَّ, aor. يَؤُفُّ (IDrd, M, Mgh, Ḳ) and يَئِفُّ, (IDrd, M, Ḳ,) the latter agreeable with analogy, (TA,) [but the former, though irregular, is the more common,] inf. n. أَفٌّ; (M, Mgh;) and ▼ أَفَّفَ, inf. n. تَأْفِيفٌ; (Ṣ, Mgh, Ḳ;) and ▼ تَأَفَّفَ; (M, Ḳ;) *He said* أُفٍّ [q. v.], (IDrd, Ṣ, M, Mgh, Ḳ,) by reason of anxiety, or disquietude of mind, or by reason of vexation, distress of mind, or disgust: (IDrd, M, Ḳ:) held by Sb to be of the same class as سَبَّحَ and هَلَّلَ meaning "he said سُبْحَانَ ٱللّٰهِ" and "he said لَا إِلٰهَ إِلَّا ٱللّٰهُ." (M.) You say also, ▼ تَأَفَّفَ بِهِ, and ▼ أَفَّفَ بِهِ, and ▼ أَفَّفَهُ, meaning *He said to him* أُفٍّ. (M.) And جَعَلَ فُلَانٌ يَتَأَفَّفُ ▼ مِنْ رِيحٍ وَجَدَهَا *Such a one began to say* أُفٍّ أُفٍّ *by reason of a smell which he perceived.* (T.) And إِنَّهُ يَتَأَفَّفُ ▼ عَلَيْهِ *Verily he is angry with him, or enraged against him.* (TA.)

2: see 1, in three places.

5: see 1, in four places.

أُفْ and أُفِّ and أُفِّ, or أُفِ: see أُفٌّ.

إِفْ and its vars. (differing only in having the ف movent): see the next paragraph.

أُفٌّ *Dirt,* or *filth;* as also ▼ أُفَّةٌ: (Ṣ:) you say, أُفًّا لَهُ, and ▼ أُفَّةً, *Dirt,* or *filth, to him;* in which the tenween is for the purpose of rendering them indeterminate; (Ṣ;) and أُفٌّ لَهُ وَتُفٌّ; (T;) and أُفًّا وَتُفًّا; and أُفَّةً ▼ وَتُفَّةً; (T, Ṣ;) the latter of which is an imitative sequent: (Ṣ:) or أُفٌّ signifies the *dirt of the ear;* and تُفٌّ, the *dirt of the nails;* (Aṣ, T, M, Ḳ; but in the last, *of the nail;*) the phrases mentioned above being used on the occasion of deeming a thing dirty or filthy, and afterwards on the occasion of experiencing annoyance or disgust at anything; (Aṣ, T, M,* TA;) and ▼ أَفَفٌ, also, has the former of these two meanings: (TA:) or أُفٌّ signifies the *dirt around the nail;* (M;) or the *dirt of the nail;* (Ḳ;) and تُفٌّ, the *dirt in the nail:* (M:) or the former, *a paring of the nail:* and *a piece of stick,* or *a reed, which one takes up from the ground:* (Ḳ:) in these various senses they are explained as used in the saying, أُفًّا لَهُ وَتُفًّا: (TA:) or the former signifies *stink:* (Zj, TA:) or *paucity;* (T, M, Ḳ;) as also ▼ أَفَفٌ; (M;) or from ▼ أَفَفٌ signifying *a thing little in quantity;* (T; and the same meaning is assigned to this word in the Ḳ;) and تُفٌّ is an imitative sequent, (T, M, Ḳ,) of the same meaning. (M.) —— أُفِّ, also, is a word expressive of vexation, distress of mind, or disgust; (M, Mgh;) or of dislike, displeasure, or hatred; (Ḳ;) and has six forms; (T, Ṣ;) mentioned by Akh; (Ṣ;) or ten; (M;) or forty; (Ḳ;) or more; (TA;) as follow: أُفِّ and أُفَّ and أُفُّ and أَفِّ and أُفًّا and أُفٌّ (T, Ṣ, M, Ḳ) and أُفِ and أُفُ and أُفِ and أُفًّا and أُفٌّ (Ḳ) and أُفْ (M, Ḳ) and أُفٍّ and ▼ أُفَّى, pronounced with imáleh, (M, Ḳ,) i. e. with pure imáleh, and ▼ أُفَّى with intermediate imáleh, and ▼ أُفَّى without imáleh, the alif [written ى] in these three denoting the fem. gender, and ▼ أُفِّى, with kesr to the ف, (Ḳ,) i. e., as a prefixed noun with its complement, [the latter being the pronoun of the first pers.,] (TA,) and ▼ أُفُّوهْ, (Ḳ,) with ḍamm to the أ and ف, which latter is with teshdeed, and with the و and ه quiescent, (TA,) and ▼ أُفَّهْ [in a copy of the M ▼ أُفَّةٌ] and أُفَّهُ and ▼ أُفَّهْ (Ḳ) and ▼ أُفِّ and ▼ إِفِّ and ▼ إِفٌّ and ▼ إِفِ and ▼ إِفًّا and ▼ إِفٍّ and ▼ إِفِّ and ▼ إِفًّا and ▼ إِفٌّ and ▼ إِفُّ, with ḍamm to the ف, which is with teshdeed, [in a copy of the M ▼ إِفٌّ,] and ▼ إِفًّا, like إِنَّا, and ▼ إِفَّى, pronounced with imáleh, and ▼ إِفِّى, with kesr, (Ḳ,) i. e., prefixed to the pronoun of the first person, (IAmb,) and ▼ أَفْ and ▼ أَفِّ (Ḳ) and ▼ أَفِّ, or ▼ أُفْ, and ▼ آفْ, or ▼ آفِّ, and ▼ آفْ, or ▼ آفِّ, (accord. to different copies of the Ḳ,) [all these forms, making the number (forty) mentioned by the author of the Ḳ, I have drawn from a comparison of three copies of that work, and I believe them to be correct: some other forms are mentioned by SM as perhaps indicated in the Ḳ; but I see no good reason for this: he then adds,] and ▼ أُفَّهْ and ▼ أُفُوهْ and ▼ أَفَّهْ, the last mentioned by IB on the authority of IḲṭṭ. (TA.) أُفِّ, [with its variants,] in its primary sense, denotes one's blowing at a thing that falls upon him, such as dust or ashes; or at the place, to remove therefrom what is annoying; therefore people say, at anything that they deem troublesome, or displeasing, or hateful, أُفٍّ لَهُ [as though meaning *A puff,* or *blast of breath, to it*]: (Ḳt, T:) or [rather] it is a word imitative of a sound; [like *ugh* in English, both in sound and meaning; and in meaning like our interjections *foh* and *faugh;*] (Bḍ on the ex. in the Ḳur which will be found below, and TA;) denoting vexation, or distress of mind, or disgust; (Bḍ ubi suprà;) or denoting contempt: (TA:) or it is a verbal noun, meaning *I am vexed,* or *distressed in mind,* or *disgusted:* (Bḍ ubi suprà:) or it is an imperative verbal noun [denoting disgust or abhorrence, like *out,* and *away*]: (IJ, M:) or he who says أُفًّا لَكَ uses it in the manner of an imprecation, like as one says وَيْلًا لِلْكَافِرِينَ; and he who says أُفٌّ لَكَ puts it in the nom. case because of the ل, like as one says وَيْلٌ لِلْكَافِرِينَ; and he who says أُفِّ لَكَ puts it in the gen. case likening it to words imitative of sounds. (IAmb.) It is said in the Ḳur [xvii. 24], وَلَا تَقُلْ لَهُمَا أُفٍّ, (T, Ṣ, TA,) or أُفِّ, (TA, [in which other readings also are mentioned,]) [*And say not thou to them* (i. e. to thy father and mother) *Ugh, &c.,*] meaning, do not thou deem anything of their affairs burdensome, nor be contracted in bosom thereby, nor be rough, or harsh, or coarse, to them: (Ḳt, T:) or do not thou say to them anything expressive of the least disgust, when they have become old, but take upon thyself their service; أُفِّ signifying *stink.* (Zj, T.)

إِفٌّ and its vars. (differing only in having the ف movent): see أُفٌّ. —— For إِفٌّ, see also إِفَّانٌ, in three places.

أُفَّةٌ: see إِفَّانٌ, in two places.

أُفَّةٌ: see أُفٌّ, in four places. —— Also *A dirty, a filthy, an unclean, man:* (Ḳ:) from أُفٌّ signifying the "dirt of the nail." (TA.) —— *One in want; poor; possessing little:* (Ḳ:) from أَفَفٌ signifying "a thing little in quantity." (TA.) ——

A coward: (K:) as though originally ذُو أُفَّةٍ, i. e. *holding back, by reason of disgust,* (مُتَأَفِّفٌ,) *from fight:* (TA:) or *experiencing vexation* or *disgust,* and *languid* or *sluggish, in war:* (IAar:) also *heavy,* or *sluggish.* (IAth.)

إِفَّةٌ : see إِفَّانٌ, in three places.

أَفَفٌ *Vexation, distress of mind,* or *disgust.* (T, IAth, K.) — See also أُفٌّ, in three places. — And see إِفَّانٌ, in three places.

أُفَّهْ and أُفَّهٍ and أُفَّهٌ and أُفَّهُ and أُفَّهَ : see أُفٌّ.

أُفِّي, pronounced in three different ways; and أُفَّى : see أُفٌّ.

أُفًّا and أُفِّى and إِفِّى : see أُفٌّ.

أُفُوهْ : see أُفٌّ.

أُفُوفَةٌ : see what next follows.

أُفَّافٌ A man *who says* أُفٍّ *much* or *often;* (M, TA;) as also ▼ أُفُوفَةٌ, accord. to the copies of the O and TS and K; but in other lexicons ▼ أُفُوفَةٌ: in the O, one *who ceases not to say to another* أُفٍّ لَكَ: in the Jm, the last of these three words is explained as meaning one *who ceases not to say this at some of his affairs.* (TA.)

إِفَّانٌ (T, S, M, K) and أَفَّانٌ (T, TS, L, K) and ▼ إِفَّةٌ (S, M, K) and ▼ أَفَفٌ (T, L, K) and ▼ إِفٌّ (L, M) and ▼ أَفَّةٌ (M) and ▼ تَئِفَّةٌ, (T, M, S, K, &c.,) of the measure تَفْعِلَةٌ, [being originally تَأْفِفَةٌ,] accord. to J, who appears to be right in saying so, (IB,) and so accord. to Aboo-'Alee, who states, on authority of Aboo-Bekr, that it is thus in some of the copies of the Book of Sb, (L,) though in other copies of that book said to be of the measure فَعِلَّةٌ, (IB, L,) *A time;* (T, S, M, K;) as in the sayings, كَانَ ذٰلِكَ عَلَى إِفِّ ▼ ذٰلِكَ and إِفَّانِهِ (S, TA) and ▼ أَفَفِهِ, and ▼ إِفَّتِهِ, and ▼ تَئِفَّتِهِ, (TA,) *That was at the time of that;* (S, TA;) and أَتَانِي فِي إِفَّانِ ذٰلِكَ, (IAar, L,) and عَلَى إِفَّانِ ذلك, (IAar, T, M, L,) and أَفَّانِهِ, (T, L,) and ▼ إِفِّهِ, (M, L,) and ▼ أَفَفِهِ, (IAar, T, L,) and ▼ إِفَّتِهِ, (M, L,) and ▼ أَفَّتِهِ, (M,) and ▼ تَئِفَّتِهِ, (IAar, T, S, M, L,) preceded by على, (IAar, T, S, &c.,) and by فى, (L,) *He came to me at the time of that.* (IAar, T, &c.)

أُفُوهْ : see أُفٌّ.

آفِ and آفٍ and آفٌ : see أُفٌّ.

أُفَّافٌ : see أُفُوفَةٌ.

تَئِفَّةٌ : see إِفَّانٌ, in three places.

مُتَأَفِّفٌ عَنِ القِتَالِ [app. *Holding back, by reason of disgust, from fight;* as though saying أُفٍّ at the mention thereof: see أُفَّةٌ]. (TA.)

افخ

1. أَفَخَهُ, (A'Obeyd, S, L, &c.,) aor. ـَ, inf. n. أَفْخٌ, (L,) *He,* [or *it*] *struck him,* or *hit him,* [or *hurt him,*] *on the part of his head called the* يَأْفُوخ. (A'Obeyd, S, L, Msb, K.) He who pronounces يافوخ without ء says يَفَخَهُ. (Msb.)

مَأْفُوخٌ A man *having his head broken in the part called the* يَأْفُوخ. (L.)

يَأْفُوخٌ, (Lth, Az, S, Msb, K,) as also يَافُوخٌ, without ء, but the former is the more correct and the better, (Lth, Az, Msb,) and is of the measure يَفْعُولٌ, (Lth, Az, S, Msb,) whereas the latter is of the measure فَاعُولٌ, (Lth, Az, Msb,) [*The top, vertex,* or *crown, of the head;* or the *part of the top of the head which is crossed by the coronal suture, and comprises a portion of the sagittal suture;*] the *part where the anterior and posterior bones of the head meet;* (K;) the *place that is in a state of commotion in the head of an infant;* (S;) the *place which, in the head of a child, does not close up until after some years;* or *does not become knit together in its several parts;* and this is *where the bone of the anterior part of the head and that of its posterior part meet;* (Zj in his "Khalk el-Insán;") the *place that is soft, in a child's head, before the two bones called the* نَمَّاغَة *and* رَمَّاعَة *meet, between the* هَامَة [or *middle of the head*] *and the forehead:* (L:) or the *middle of the head when it has become hard and strong;* before which it is not thus called: (Msb:) pl. يَآفِيخُ; (S;) so in the old lexicons [in general]; but in the T and K يَوَافِيخُ [which is pl. of يافوخ without ء; or, as pl. of يافوخ, is like تَوَارِيخُ as pl. of تَأْرِيخٌ]; and because of this form of the pl., F says that J is in error in mentioning the word in the present art.: it has been shown, however, that J is not in error in this case. (TA.) — [Hence the saying,] أَنْتُمْ يَآفِيخُ الشَّرَفِ † *Ye are the centres and summits of the heads of nobility.* (L, from a trad.) And يَآفِيخُ اللَّيْلِ † *The main* [or *middle*] *part of the night.* (S, K.) — [See also art. يفخ.]

افق

1. أَفَقَ, (JK, S, K,) aor. ـِ, (JK, K,) inf. n. أَفْقٌ, (TK,) *He went his own way, at random,* or *heedlessly,* (رَكِبَ رَأْسَهُ,) *and went away in the* آفَاق [or *regions, &c., of the land*]: (Lth, JK, K:) or *he went away in,* or *into, the land,* or *country:* (S:) and *he took his way into the* آفاق [or *regions,* &c.,] *of the land.* (JK.) — [Hence, app.,] أَفَقَ, aor. as above; thus, says IB, accord. to Kz, and thus it is given on the authority of Kr; (TA;) [see أَفِقَ;] or أَفِقَ, aor. ـَ, (S, O, K,) inf. n. أَفَقٌ; (S;) *He attained the utmost degree,* [as though he reached the أُفُق (or horizon, or furthest point of view,)] *in generosity;* (S, O, K;) or *in knowledge,* or *science;* or *in chasteness of speech,* or *eloquence, and in the combination of excellent qualities.* (K.) — Also, أَفَقَ, aor. ـِ, (Kr, Ibn-'Abbád, JK, K,) inf. n. أَفْقٌ, (JK, TA,) *He overcame,* or *surpassed.* (Kr, Ibn-'Abbád, JK, K.) — And, inf. n. أُفُوقٌ, *He was goodly,* or *beautiful; he possessed the quality of exciting admiration and approval by his beauty and the pleasingness of his aspect:* said of a camel, and of a horse. (JK.) — أَفَقَ عَلَيْهِ (JK, TA) *He* (a man) *excelled him;* namely, another man: (JK:) or *he preceded him in excellence;* or *outwent him therein;* as also أَفَقَهُ, aor. ـِ. (TA.) [It is like فَاقَهُ.] — أَفَقَ فِي العَطَآءِ, aor. ـِ, (S, K,) inf. n. أَفْقٌ, (TA,) *He gave to some more than to others.* (S, K.) So in the saying of El-Aashà,

وَلَا المَلِكُ النُّعْمَانُ يَوْمَ لَقِيتُهُ
بِغِبْطَتِهِ يُعْطِى القُطُوطَ وَيَأْفِقُ

[*Nor the King En-Noamán, on the day that I met him, in his goodly,* or *happy, condition, giving gifts,* or *stipends,* or *written obligations conferring gifts, and giving to some more than to others*]: (S:) or the meaning is, *writing* [*writs of*] *gifts,* and *sealing* them: or, as some say, *taking his way into the* آفاق [or *regions,* &c.,] *of the land.* (JK.) — أَفَقَهُ, aor. ـِ, (S, Msb, K,) inf. n. أَفْقٌ, (S, Msb,) *He tanned it* (namely a hide) *until it became what is termed* أَفِيقٌ. (S, Msb,* K.)

5. تَأَفَّقَ بِنَا *He* (a man, As, TA) *came to us* مِنْ أُفُقٍ [*from a region,* &c., *of the land*]: (As, K:) or *came to us, and alighted at our abode as a guest:* and in the Nawádir el-Aaráb, تأفّق به is said to signify *he reached him,* or *overtook him;* as also تلفّق به. (TA.)

أُفْقٌ : see أُفُقٌ.

أَفَقٌ The *main and middle part* (سَنَن) of a road; (K;) the *face,* or *surface,* thereof: (IAar, K:) pl. آفَاقٌ. (K.) Hence the saying, قَعَدَ فُلَانٌ عَلَى أَفَقِ الطَّرِيقِ [*Such a one sat upon the main and middle part,* or *face,* or *surface, of the road*]. (TA.) — The *flanks,* or *ilia:* or, as some say, *skins;* or *skin;* as in the saying, شَرِبْتُ حَتَّى مَلَأْتُ أَفَقِى *I drank until I filled my skin:* (JK:) pl. [or rather coll. gen. n.] of ▼ أَفَقَةٌ; (IAar;) which signifies the *flank;* (IAar, K;) as does also ▼ أَفَقَةٌ. (Th, K.) — Also pl., (S, K,) or [rather] quasi-pl. n., (M, K,) of أَفِيقٌ, q. v. (S, M, K.)

أَفِقٌ : see أَفِيقٌ, in two places.

أُفُقٌ (JK, S, Mgh, Msb, K, &c.) and ▼ أُفْقٌ (S, K) *A side;* meaning *a lateral,* or *an outward* or *adjacent, part* or *portion;* or *a part, region, quarter,* or *tract, considered with respect to its collocation* or *juxtaposition* or *direction,* or *considered as belonging to a whole;* or *a remote side;* syn. نَاحِيَةٌ; (JK, S, Mgh, Msb, K;) and *a border,* or *an extremity;* (JK;) of a land, or of the earth; and of the sky, or heavens: (JK, Mgh, Msb:) [or the *horizon,* or *part next to the horizon, of the sky* and *of the earth;*] or *what appears of the sides* (النَّوَاحِى) *of the celestial sphere,* (K, TA,) and *of the borders,* or *extremities, of the earth:* (TA:) or the *place whence blows the south wind,* and *the north wind,* and *the west wind,* and *the east wind:* (K,* TA:) pl. آفَاقٌ: (JK, S, Mgh, Msb, K:) and the sing. also is used as a pl.; like فُلْكٌ, as is said in the Nh: (MF:) thus in the verse of El-'Abbás, in praise of the Prophet:

• أَنْتَ لَمَّا وُلِدْتَ أَشْرَقَتِ الأَرْ •
• ضُ وَضَآءَتْ بِنُورِكَ الأُفُقُ •

[*When thou wast born, the earth became bright, and the tracts of the horizon*, or *the regions, shone with thy light*]: or, as some say, الافق is made fem. by him as meaning النَّاحِيَةُ. (TA.) The phrase حِينَ يَغِيبُ الأُفُقُ means *When the redness*, or *whiteness, in the* أُفُق [or horizon] *disappears*. (Mgh.) —— Also, in like manner, The *side*, or *lateral part*, of a tent: (JK:) or the *part between the* [*two*] *anterior* [*pieces of wood called the*] زِرَان, *in the* [*fore part called the*] رِوَاق, of a tent: (K:) and the *sides*, or *lateral parts*, of a tent of the kind belonging to the Arabs of the desert. (TA.) ═ أُفُق is also said to be a pl. of أَفِيق; but this is disallowed by Lh. (TA.) ═ See also أَفَق.

أَفِقَةٌ: see أَفَقٌ. ═ Also *A burying of a skin, or hide, in the earth, so that its hair may be removed, and it may become ready for tanning.* (Lth, K,* TA.) [See أَفِيق.]

أُفُقِىٌّ, (ISk, JK, T, Ṣ, Mgh, Mṣb, K,) contr. to rule, (T, Mṣb,) and ▾ أَفَقِىٌّ, (Aṣ, ISk, Ṣ, Mgh, Mṣb, K,) agreeably with rule, (Ṣ,) being a rel. n. from أُفُق, (Mṣb,) and some (namely the lawyers, in relation to pilgrimage and the like, MF) say ▾ آفَاقِىٌّ, (Mgh, MF,) which is incorrect, (Mgh, Mṣb,) or whether it be correct, after the manner of أَنْصَارِىٌّ and the like, requires consideration, (MF,) an epithet applied to a man, (ISk, Ṣ, Mṣb,) meaning One *who is from the* آفَاق [or *lateral parts*, or *regions*,] *of the land*; (ISk,* Ṣ, Mṣb;*) mentioned by Aboo-Naṣr: (Ṣ, referring to the first form of the word:) or one *who goes about in the* آفَاق: (JK:) or one *who goes through the* آفَاق *of the land in search of sustenance*: (K,* TA:) as also ▾ أَفَاقٌ. (K, TA.) أُفُقِىٌّ مَكَّةَ or أَفَقِىٌّ مَكَّةَ means *He who is without the places where the pilgrims coming to Mekkeh enter upon the state of* إِحْرَام. (Mgh.)

أَفَقِىٌّ: see أُفُقِىٌّ.

أَفِيقٌ: see آفَقٌ. —— Applied also to a bucket (دَلْو), meaning *Excelling other buckets*. (AA, K.) ═ Also, (Aṣ, Th, JK, Ṣ, Mgh, Mṣb, K,) and ▾ أَفِيقَةٌ, (K,) or the latter is a more particular term than the former, like as جِلْدَةٌ is more so than جِلْدٌ, (Mgh,) and ▾ أَفَقٌ, (K, [but see what follows,]) The *skin, or hide, that is not completely tanned*, (Ṣ, Mgh, Mṣb, K,) *so that it is unsubstantial, not firm*, or *strong*, or *tough*: (Mgh:) when its tanning is complete, and it becomes red, it is termed أَدِيم: therefore أَفِيق is of the measure فَعِيلٌ in the sense of the measure مَفْعُولٌ: (Mṣb:) or *in the second stage of its tanning*; for in the first stage it is termed مَنِيئَةٌ; then, افيق; and then, اديم: (TA:) or *that is tanned, but before it is sewed*: (Aṣ, Ṣ, K:) or *before it is cut*, or *slit*: (K:) or *when it comes forth from the tan, its tanning being finished*, (JK, TA,) *its* [*original*] *odour being* [*still*] *in it*: (TA:) or *after it is tanned*: (Mṣb:) or *not tanned*: (Th, TA:) or *that is tanned without* قَرَظ or أَرْطَى or *any of the tans of the people of Nejd*: (TA:) ISd says, I think that Th has mentioned ▾ أَفَقٌ as syn. with أَفِيقٌ, and explained it as signifying the *skin*, or *hide, that is not tanned*; but I am not sure of it: (TA:) the pl. is أَفَقٌ, (Lh, JK, Ṣ, Mṣb, K,) like as أَدَمٌ is pl. of أَدِيمٌ, (Ṣ,) or this is a quasi-pl. n., (M, K,) and أُفُقٌ (JK, K) is allowable, (JK,) or, accord. to Lh, it is not allowable, (TA,) and [pl. of pauc.] آفِقَةٌ, (Aṣ, Ṣ, K,) like as آدِمَةٌ and أَرْغِفَةٌ are pls. of أَدِيمٌ and رَغِيفٌ. (Aṣ, Ṣ.) ▾ أَفِيقَةٌ signifies also *A* سِقَآء [or *skin for water or milk* &c.] *made of a hide of the kind termed* أَفِيق. (Mgh.) And أَفِيقٌ also signifies The *skin* of a man, and of any beast. (TA.)

أَفِيقَةٌ: see أَفِيقٌ, in two places.

أُفَاقٌ: see أُفُقِىٌّ.

آفِقٌ, (Ṣ, K, &c.,) of the measure فَاعِلٌ, (Ṣ, Kz, TA, [in the CK آفَق, and in like manner in a copy of the JK,]) from أَفَقَ, (Ṣ, K,) or, as IB says, accord. to Kz, from أَفِقَ, aor. ـَ, and so accord. to Kr, and shown to be of the measure فَاعِلٌ by several verses in which it occurs, (TA,) One *who has attained the utmost degree in generosity*; (Ṣ, K;) or *in knowledge*, or *science*; or *in chasteness of speech*, or *eloquence, and in the combination of excellent qualities*; (K;) as also ▾ أَفِيقٌ: (K:) fem. with ة. (IF, K.) Also applied to a horse, *Generous with respect to both parents*: fem. with ة. (Ṣ.) And applied to a camel, *That excites admiration and approval by his generousness, excellence, high blood, or the like*; (JK;) and so ▾ أُفُقٌ, (JK, Ṣ, K,) applied to a horse, (Ṣ, K,) and a mare, (JK, Ṣ, K,) and a she-camel. (JK.)

آفِقَةٌ: see أَفَقٌ.

آفَاقِىٌّ: see أُفُقِىٌّ.

افك

1. أَفَكَهُ, aor. ـِ, inf. n. أَفْكٌ, (with fet-ḥ, Ṣ, TA, its only form, TA, [in the CK إِفْك,]) *He changed his*, or *its, manner of being*, or *state*; (Ṣ, K;) and *he turned him*, or *it*, (i. e., anything, Mṣb,) *away*, or *back*; (Ṣ, Mṣb, K;) عَنِ الشَّىْءِ [*from the thing*]; (Ṣ;) or عَنْ وَجْهِهِ [*from his*, or *its, mode*, or *manner, of being*, &c.]: (Mṣb:) so in the Kur xlvi. 21, أَجِئْتَنَا لِتَأْفِكَنَا عَنْ آلِهَتِنَا *Hast thou come to us to turn us away*, or *back, from our gods?* (Bd:) or *he turned him away*, or *back, by lying*: (TA:) or *he changed*, or *perverted, his judgment*, or *opinion*: (K:) or *he deceived him*, or *beguiled him, and so turned him away*, or *back*: and simply *he deceived him*, or *beguiled him*: and أُفِكَ signifies *he was turned from his judgment*, or *opinion, by deceit*, or *guile*. (TA.) It is said in the Kur [li. 9], يُؤْفَكُ عَنْهُ مَنْ أُفِكَ, i. e., *He will be turned away from it* (namely, the truth,) *who is turned away* in the foreknowledge of God: (TA:) or, accord. to Mujáhid, يُؤْفَنُ عَنْهُ مَنْ أُفِنَ [*he will be weak in intellect and judgment so as to be thereby turned away from it who is weak in intellect and judgment*]. (Ṣ, TA.) You say also, أُفِكَ الرَّجُلُ عَنِ الخَيْرِ *The man was turned away*, or *back, from good*, or *prosperity*. (Sh.) And أَفَكَهُ, (K, TA,) inf. n. as above, (TA,) *He forbade him what he wished*, (K, TA,) *and turned him away*, or *back, from it*. (TA.) —— أَفَكَ, aor. ـِ; (Mṣb, K;) and أَفِكَ, aor. ـَ; (IAạr, K;) inf. n. إِفْكٌ (Mṣb, K) and أَفْكٌ and أُفُكٌ and أُفُوكٌ; (K;) *He lied; uttered a falsehood; said what was untrue*; (Mṣb, K;) as also ▾ أَفَّكَ, (K,) inf. n. تَأْفِيكٌ: (TA:) because a lie is a saying that is turned from its proper way, or mode. (Bd in xxiv. 11.) —— أَفَكَ النَّاسَ, aor. ـِ, inf. n. أَفْكٌ, *He told the people what was false*; أَفَكَ and أَفَكْتُهُ being like كَذَبَ and كَذَبْتُهُ. (Az, TA.) —— أَفَكَ فُلَانًا, (K,) inf. n. أَفْكٌ; (TA;) or the verb is ▾ آفَكَ; (so in the printed edition of Bd, xlvi. 27;) *He*, or *it, made such a one to lie, or say what was untrue*. (K.) —— أُفِكَ *He was weak* [*as though perverted*] *in his intellect and judgment* or *opinion*. (K,* TA.) But أَفَكَهُ اللّٰهُ as meaning *God rendered weak his intellect* is not used. (L, TA.) —— ‡ *It* (a place) *was not rained upon, and had no vegetation*, or *herbage*. (K, TA.)

2: see 1.

4: see 1.

8. اِئْتَفَكَتِ البَلْدَةُ [written with the disjunctive alif اِيتَفَكَتْ], (Ṣ, K,) بِأَهْلِهَا, (Ṣ,) *The land*, or *district*, or *the town*, or *the like, was*, or *became, overturned*, or *subverted*, (Ṣ, K,) *with its inhabitants*: (Ṣ:) as were the towns of the people of Lot. (TA.) —— Hence it is said of El-Baṣrah, قَدِ ٱئْتَفَكَتْ بِأَهْلِهَا مَرَّتَيْنِ, meaning ‡ *It has been submerged with its inhabitants twice*; as though subverted. (Sh.) —— You say also, اِيتَفَكَتْ تِلْكَ الأَرْضُ ‡ *That land has been burnt up by drought*. (IAạr.)

إِفْكٌ [an inf. n. used as a subst.;] *A lie*; *a falsehood*; (Ṣ, TA;) as also ▾ أَفِيكَةٌ: pl. (of the latter, K) أَفَائِكُ. (Ṣ, K.) You say, ▾ يَا لَلْأَفِيكَةِ, and ▾ يَا لِلْأَفِيكَةِ; [and ▾ يَا لَلْأُفَيْكَةِ, using the dim. form for the purpose of enhancement; i. e. *O the lie!* and *O the great lie!*] the ل with fet-ḥ denoting calling to aid; and with kesr denoting wonder, as though the meaning were, O man, wonder thou at this great lie. (TA.)

افكة [so in the TA, without any syll. signs; app. either أَفْكَةٌ, an inf. n. of un., or ▾ آفِكَةٌ, like دَاهِيَةٌ;] *A punishment sent by God, whereby the dwellings of a people are overturned*: occurring in a trad. relating to the story of the people of Lot. (TA.)

سَنَةٌ أَفِكَةٌ ‡ *A year of drought* or *sterility*: (K,

TA:) pl. أَوَافِكُ [contr. to rule, as though the sing. were ▾ آفِكَةٌ]. (Z, TA.)

أُفُوكٌ: see أَفَّاكٌ.

أَفِيكٌ One who is *turned from his judgment*, or *opinion, by deceit*, or *guile*; as also ▾ مَأْفُوكٌ. (Ḳ.) —— *Lacking strength* or *power* or *ability, and having little prudence and artifice.* (Lth, Ḳ.) —— See also أَفَّاكٌ.

أَفِيكَةٌ: see إِفْكٌ, in three places. —— Also *A severe*, or *distressing, calamity.* (Ibn-Abbád.)

أُفَيْكَةٌ: see إِفْكٌ.

أَفَّاكٌ *A great*, or *habitual, liar*; (Ṣ, Mṣb, Ḳ;) as also ▾ أَفُوكٌ, (Mṣb, Ḳ,) and ▾ أَفِيكٌ: (Ḳ:) fem. of the first [and last] with ة: but the second is both masc. and fem.: (Mṣb:) the pl. of the second is افك with ḍamm [i. e. أُفُكٌ, accord. to the rule of the Ḳ, but the TA seems to indicate that it is أُفُكٌ, by likening it to the pl. of صَبُورٌ]. (Ḳ.)

آفِكَةٌ: see افكة: —— and see سَنَةٌ أَفِكَةٌ.

مَأْفُوكٌ [*Changed in his*, or *its, manner of being*, or *state: turned away*, or *back, from a thing*: &c.]: see أَفِيكٌ. —— *Weak* [*as though perverted*] *in his intellect* (AZ, Ṣ, Ḳ) *and judgment* or *opinion*; as also مَأْفُونٌ: (AZ, Ṣ:) accord. to A'Obeyd, (or AA, as in one copy of the Ṣ,) a *man who does not attain*, or *obtain, good*, or *prosperity.* (Ṣ.) —— Also, (Ḳ,) fem. with ة, (Ṣ, Ḳ,) † *A place*, (Ḳ,) or land, (أَرْضٌ, Ṣ, Z,) *not rained upon, and having no vegetation*, or *herbage.* (Ṣ, Z, Ḳ.)

المُؤْتَفِكَاتُ (Ṣ, Ḳ) and المُؤْتَفِكَةُ, (TA,) both occurring in the Ḳur, [the former in ix. 71 and lxix. 9, and the latter in liii. 54,] *The cities overthrown*, or *subverted, by God, upon the people of Lot.* (Ṣ, Ḳ.) —— The former also signifies *The winds that turn over* [*the surface of*] *the earth*, or *ground*: (Ḳ:) or *the winds that blow from different quarters*: it is said (by the Arabs, Ṣ) that when these winds blow much, the earth (i. e. its seed-produce, TA) thrives, or yields increase. (Ṣ, Ḳ, TA.)

افل

1. أَفَلَ, (T, Ṣ, Mṣb, Ḳ,) said of a thing, (Mṣb,) or of the moon, (T,) and أَفَلَتْ, said of the sun, (T, Ṣ, M,) and of the stars, (M,) aor. ـِ and ـُ, inf. n. أُفُولٌ (T, Ṣ, M, Mṣb, Ḳ) and أَفْلٌ, (M, Mṣb,) *It was*, or *became, absent*, or *hidden*, or *concealed*; (T, Ṣ, Mṣb, Ḳ;) *it set*; (T, Ṣ, M, &c.;) and so أَفِلَ, aor. ـَ. (Ḳ.) —— Hence, أَفَلَ فُلَانٌ عَنِ البَلَدِ *Such a one became absent*, or *went away, from the country*, or *town.* (Mṣb.)

أَفِيلٌ *A young camel such as is termed* اِبْنُ مَخَاضٍ [i. e. *that has entered its second year*]; (Aṣ, El-Fárábee, Ṣ, M, Mṣb, Ḳ;) and *the like*; (Ṣ;) or, and also *such as is above this* [*in age*]; (El-Fárábee, M, Mṣb, Ḳ;) or, and also *such as is termed* اِبْنُ لَبُونٍ [i. e. *that has entered the third year*]; beyond which it is not so called: (Aṣ, TA:) or *that is seven months old*, or *eight*: (Aṣ, Mṣb:) or *a youthful camel*: (AZ, Mṣb:) and also (M, Ḳ) *a young weaned camel*; syn. فَصِيلٌ: (T, M, Mṣb, Ḳ:) fem. with ة: (Aṣ, Ṣ:) pl. إِفَالٌ (T, Ṣ, M, Ḳ) and أَفَائِلُ, (Sb, Ṣ, M, Ḳ,) which latter they liken to ذَنَائِبُ as pl. of ذَنُوبٌ. (M.) [In my copy of the Mṣb, the pl. is said to be إفالة: and it is also there said, on the authority of IF, that افالة signifies the *young ones of sheep*.] It is said in a prov., إِنَّمَا القَرْمُ مِنَ الأَفِيلِ [*The stallion-camel is only* that which has increased in growth *from the young one in its second year*, &c.]; i. e. what is great has begun small. (TA.)

آفِلٌ part. n. of 1, (T, TA,) applied to the moon, and to any star: (TA:) fem. with ة: (T, TA:) pl. آفِلُونَ (Ḳur vi. 76 [the rational form of the pl. being there used because it is applied to stars as being likened to gods]) and أُفَّلٌ and أُفُولٌ. (TA.)

افه

أَفُوهٌ and أُفَّهْ and أُفَّهٌ and أُفَّهَ and أُفَّهُ and أَفُّوهُ and أُفُّوهٌ: see أُفٌّ.

افيون

أَفْيُونٌ, [like صَعْفُوقٌ, but this is of a very extr. measure; or, as some write it, أُفْيُونٌ, like عُصْفُورٌ &c.;] or إِفْيُونٌ, [like بِرْذَوْنٌ;] (accord. to different copies of the Ḳ, art. فين;) [an arabicized word, from the Greek ὄπιον, either immediately or through the Persian أَبْيُونْ; meaning *Opium*:] the *milk* [or *juice*] *of the black Egyptian* خَشْخَاش [or *poppy*, or *papaver somniferum*]; (Ḳ;) or the *milk of the* خشخاش, *the best of which is the black Egyptian*; (TA;) or the *expressed juice of the black Egyptian* خشخاش, *dried in the sun*: *cold and dry in the fourth degree*: (Ibn-Seenà, or Avicenna, i. 133:) *beneficial for hot tumours, especially in the eye*; *torporific* (*to the intellect*, TA): *in a small quantity, beneficial, and soporific*: *in a large quantity, a poison*: (Ḳ:) [the lexicographers regard the word as Arabic:] some, among whom is the author of the Ḳ, hold that it belongs to art. فين: others, that it belongs to art. افن. (TA.)

اقحوان

أُقْحُوَانٌ: see art. قحو.

اقط

1. أَقَطَهُ, aor. ـِ, (Ṣ, Ḳ,) inf. n. أَقْطٌ, (Ṣ,) *He made it* (namely food) *with* أَقِط, q. v. infrà. (Ṣ, Ḳ.) —— Also, (aor. and inf. n. as above, TA,) *He fed him with* أقط: (A'Obeyd, Ḳ:) like لَبَنَهُ from لَبَنٌ, and لَبَأَهُ from لِبَأٌ: Lḥ mentions the verb in this sense as used without its being made transitive. (TA.) —— [أَقَطَ in the CḲ is a mistake for أَقَطَ, q. v.]

4. أَقَطَ, (Lḥ, Ḳ, [in the CḲ, incorrectly, أَقِطَ,]) of the measure أَفْعَلَ, agreeably with a common rule, applying to anything, (Lḥ, TA,) *He had much* أقط; *his* أقط *became much*, or *abundant.* (Lḥ, Ḳ.)

8. ائتقط [written with the disjunctive alif اِيتَقَطَ] *He made*, or *prepared*, أقط: (Ṣ:) strangely omitted in the O and in the Ḳ. (TA.)

أَقِطٌ (Fr, Az, Ṣ, Mṣb, Ḳ) and إِقْطٌ (Fr, O, Ḳ) and أَقْطٌ (Fr, Ḳ) and إِقِطٌ, (Ṣ, O, Mṣb, Ḳ,) the last sometimes occurring in poetry, and formed from the first, by transferring the vowel of the ق to the preceding letter, (Ṣ,) or a contraction of the second, accord. to a common usage of [the tribe of] Temeem in the cases of words of this measure, (O,) and أُقْطٌ (Ḳ) and أُقُطٌ, (Aṣ, Ḳ,) of all which the first is the most chaste, and the last is strange, (TA,) [*A preparation of dried curd*;] *a preparation of*, or *thing made from, milk* (Az, Mṣb, Ḳ) *of sheep or goats*, (Ḳ,) *which has been churned, and of which the butter has been taken*, (Az, Mṣb, Ḳ,) *cooked, and then left until it becomes concrete*: (Az, Mṣb:) or *made from the milk of camels*, in particular: (IAạr:) or *milk which is dried, and has become hard, like stone*; *with which one cooks*; repeatedly mentioned in trads.: (TA:) or *a thing made from milk*; *being a kind of cheese*: (Ḥar p. 587:) pl. أُقْطَانٌ. (Ḳ.)

أَقَّاطٌ *A maker of* أقط. (TA.)

مَأْقُوطٌ Food *made with* أقط. (Ṣ.)

اكد

1. أَكَدَ *He trod* wheat. (IAạr, Ḳ.)

2. أَكَّدَ, inf. n. تَأْكِيدٌ, *i. q.* وَكَّدَ, (Ṣ, Mṣb, Ḳ,) of which it is a dial. var.; (Ṣ;) but it is not so chaste as the latter, and by some is disallowed. (TA.)

4. آكد *i. q.* أَوْكَدَ. (Ṣ in art. وكد.)

5. تأكّد *i. q.* تَوَكَّدَ. (Ṣ and Ḳ in art. وكد.)

إِكَادٌ sing. of أَكَائِدُ and تَآكِيدُ, (Ḳ,) both of which are irreg. in relation to their sing., (TA,) signifying (i. e. the pls.) *Thongs*, or *straps, by which the* قَرَبُوس *is bound to the two side-boards of a horse's saddle.* (Ḳ.) [See also وِكَادٌ.]

أَكِيدٌ *Firm*; (Ḳ, TA;) applied to a covenant, or compact. (TA.)

اكر

1. أَكَرَ, aor. ـُ, inf. n. أَكْرٌ, *He tilled* the ground; *ploughed* it *up for sowing.* (Mṣb.) —— *He dug* the ground. (TA.) —— *He cut*, or *dug, a river*, or *canal*, or *rivulet.* (Mṣb.) —— And أَكَرَ, aor. ـِ, (TA,) inf. n. as above; (Ḳ;) and ▾ تَأَكَّرَ; (Ḳ;) *He dug a hollow*, or *cavity, in the ground, for water to collect therein and to be baled out therefrom clear*: (Ḳ, TA:) or ▾ تأكّر أُكَرًا signifies *he dug hollows*, or *cavities, in the ground.* (Ṣ.)

3. آكَرَهُ, (TḲ,) inf. n. مُؤَاكَرَةٌ, (Ṣ, Ḳ,) *He made a contract*, or *bargain, with him to till and sow and cultivate land for a share of its produce*; syn. of the inf. n. مُخَابَرَةٌ. (Ṣ, Ḳ, TA.) The doing of this is forbidden. (TA.)

5: see 1, in two places.

أُكْرَةٌ *A hollow*, or *cavity, dug in the ground*, (Ṣ, Mṣb, Ḳ,) *in which water collects, and from which it is baled out clear*: (Ḳ:) pl. أُكَرٌ. (Ṣ, Mṣb.) — Also a dial. var. of كُرَةٌ, (Ḳ,) [*A ball*] *with which one plays*: (TA:) [and *a sphere*, or *globe*:] but it is of weak authority. (Ḳ.)

إِكَارَةٌ, as used in practical law, *Land which is given by its owners to men who sow and cultivate it* [app. *for a certain share of its produce*: see 3]. (Mgh.)

أَكَّارٌ *A tiller*, or *cultivator*, *of land*: (Mṣb, Ḳ:) pl. أَكَرَةٌ; as though it were pl. of آكِرٌ, (Ṣ, Mṣb, Ḳ,) like as كَفَرَةٌ is pl. of كَافِرٌ. (Mṣb.)

اكف

2. أَكَّفَ الإِكَافَ, inf. n. تَأْكِيفٌ, *He made the* اكاف; (Ḳ;) as also وَكَّفَهُ, inf. n. تَوْكِيفٌ; which latter, accord. to IF, is the original form. (TA.) — See also 4.

4. آكَفَ الحِمَارَ, (Ṣ, Mgh, Mṣb, Ḳ,) inf. n. إِيكَافٌ, (Ḳ,) *He bound*, (Ṣ, Ḳ, TA,) or *put*, (Mṣb, TA,) *the* إِكَاف *upon the ass*; (Ṣ, Mṣb, Ḳ;) as also ▾ أَكَّفَهُ; (Ṣgh, Ḳ;) and اوكفه; (Ṣ, Mgh, Ḳ;) which is of the dial. of the people of El-Ḥijáz; the first being of the dial. of Benoo-Temeem: and in like manner, البَغْلَ *the mule*. (Lḥ.)

إِكَافٌ (Ṣ, Mgh, Mṣb, Ḳ) and أُكَافٌ, (Ḳ,) as also وِكَافٌ (Ṣ, Mgh, Mṣb, Ḳ) and وُكَافٌ, (Ḳ in art. وكف,) The بَرْذَعَة, [i. e. *pad*, or *stuffed saddle, generally stuffed with straw*,] (Ḳ,) of the ass, (Ṣ, Mgh, Mṣb, Ḳ,) and also used for the mule, and for the camel; (TA in art. وكف;) a saddle like the رَحْل and قَتَب: (TA:) and *a saddle* of a horse *made in the form of the ass's* اكاف, *having at its fore part* [or *pommel*] *a thing resembling a pomegranate*: (Mgh:) [see also قَتَبٌ:] pl. [of pauc.] آكِفَةٌ (TA) and [of mult.] أُكُفٌ. (Ṣ, Mgh, Mṣb, TA.) Yaḳoob asserts that the ا in إِكَاف is a substitute for the و in وِكَاف. (TA.) A rájiz says,

إِنَّ لَنَا أَحْمِرَةً عِجَافَا •
يَأْكُلْنَ كُلَّ لَيْلَةٍ إِكَافَا •

meaning [*Verily we have some lean asses*] *which eat every night* the price of an اكاف. (TA.)

أَكَّافٌ The *maker of the kind of saddle called* إِكَاف. (Ḳ.)

اكل

1. أَكَلَهُ, [aor. ـُ,] inf. n. أَكْلٌ and مَأْكَلٌ, [*He ate it*,] (Ṣ, Ḳ,) namely, food. (Ṣ.) Er-Rummánee says that أَكْلٌ properly signifies The *swallowing* food *after chewing* it; so that the swallowing of pebbles is not properly thus termed: (Mṣb:) or, accord. to Ibn-El-Kemál, the *conveying*, or *transmitting*, *to the belly* what may be chewed, *whether* [*the thing be*] *chewed or not*; so that it does not apply to milk, nor to سَوِيق: and as to the saying of the poet,

مِنَ الآكِلِينَ المَآءَ ظُلْمًا فَمَا أَرَى •
يَنَالُونَ خَيْرًا بَعْدَ أَكْلِهِمُ المَآءَ •

† [*Of the eaters of* what they purchase with the price of *water*, *wrongfully*, *I do not see* any *attain good after their eating of* what they have purchased with the price of *the water*,] he means a people who used to sell water and purchase with the price thereof what they would eat: (TA:) [for you say, أَكَلَ كَذَا as meaning † *He ate the price of such a thing*: see another ex. voce إِكَافٌ; and another voce ثَدْىٌ.] — The saying, in the Ḳur [v. 70], لَأَكَلُوا مِنْ فَوْقِهِمْ وَمِنْ تَحْتِ أَرْجُلِهِمْ [*They should eat* things *above them and* things *beneath their feet*] means, their means of subsistence should be made ample; (Bḍ, TA;) by the pouring of the blessings of the heaven and the earth upon them; or by the abundance of the fruit of the trees, and the produce of the grains sown; or by their being blessed with gardens of ripe fruits, so that they should gather them from the upper part of each tree, and pick up what should have fallen upon the ground. (Bḍ.) — إِنْقَطَعَ أُكُلُهُ [lit. *His eating became cut off*, or *stopped*,] means ‡ *he died*; [see also أُكُلٌ;] and so إِسْتَوْفَى أُكُلَهُ [lit. *he completed his eating*]. (TA.) — أَكَلَ رَوْقَهُ [lit. *He ate his life*,] means ‡ *he became extremely aged, and his teeth fell out, one after another*. (TA.) — هُوَ يَأْكُلُ النَّاسَ, and يَأْكُلُ لُحُومَ النَّاسِ [*He eats men*, and *eats the flesh of men*,] means ‡ *he defames men*; or *does so in their absence*: (TA:) and the action thus signified may be [*with words*, or *by making signs*] *with the side of the mouth*, and *with the eye*, and *with the head*. (TA in art. همز.) It is said in the Ḳur [xlix. 12], أَيُحِبُّ أَحَدُكُمْ أَنْ يَأْكُلَ لَحْمَ أَخِيهِ مَيْتًا [lit. *Would any one of you like to eat the flesh of his brother when dead?*]; defamation, or defamation of the absent, being meant thereby. (Ṣ,* Ibn-'Arafeh, Bḍ, Jel.) — أَكَلَ غَنَمِى وَشَرِبَهَا ‡ [*He ate* the flesh of *my sheep, and drank* the milk of *them*, means, like أَكَلَ مَالِى, *he ate, fed upon, devoured*, or *consumed*, *my wealth*, or *property*: see 2]. (TA.) — أَكَلَتِ النَّارُ الحَطَبَ ‡ *The fire devoured*, or *consumed*, *the firewood*. (Ṣ, Mgh.) — أَكَلَتْ أَظْفَارَهُ الحِجَارَةُ ‡ [*The stones wore away his nails*]. (TA.) — مَرْنِىّ الوَاوُ فِى مَرْنِىّ أَكَلَتْهَا اليَآءُ † [*The* و *in* مرنى, *the* ى *has swallowed it up*]; because it is originally مَرْنُوِى: a phrase occurring in the 'Eyn. (TA.) — أَكَلَ عُمْرَهُ ‡ *He consumed his life*. (Mgh.) — It is said in a trad., (TA,) أُمِرْتُ بِقَرْيَةٍ تَأْكُلُ القُرَى ‡ [*I have been commanded to have given unto me a town which shall devour the* other *towns*]; (Ḳ, TA;) said to be Yethrib [afterwards called El-Medeeneh]; (TA;) i. e., the people of which shall conquer the [other] towns and make spoil of their possessions: or it denotes the superior excellence of that town; and is like the saying, هٰذَا حَدِيثٌ يَأْكُلُ الأَحَادِيثَ [*This is a tradition which does away with*, or *overrules*, the other *traditions*]. (Ṣgh, Ḳ, TA.) — أَكَلَ السِّكِّينُ اللَّحْمَ means ‡ *The knife's cutting the flesh*. (TA.) — أَكَلَنِى رَأْسِى, inf. n. إِكْلَةٌ and أُكَالٌ and أَكَالٌ, ‡ *My head itched*. (Ḳ, TA.) An Arab was heard to say, [as is often said in the present day,] جِلْدِى يَأْكُلُنِى ‡ *My skin itches*. (TA.) — أَكِلَ, aor. ـَ, (Ḳ,) inf. n. أَكَلٌ, (TA,) ‡ *It* (a limb, or member, [and a sore,] and a piece of stick, or wood,) *became corroded* or *cankered*, or *decayed*, *by the mutual eating away of its several parts*; as also ▾ ائتكل [written with the disjunctive alif إِيتَكَلَ], and ▾ تَأَكَّلَ. (Ḳ, TA.) — أَكِلَتِ الأَسْنَانُ, (Ṣ, Mṣb, Ḳ,) aor. and inf. n. as in the next preceding sentence, (Mṣb,) ‡ *The teeth rubbed together and wasted away*; by reason of age; (Ṣ;) or *fell out, one after another*: (Mṣb:) or *broke in pieces*, or *became much broken*: (Ḳ:) and ▾ تَأَكَّلَتْ signifies the same; (Ṣ, Mṣb;) and so ▾ ائتكلت. (Ṣ.) — أَكِلَتِ النَّاقَةُ, aor. ـَ, inf. n. أَكَالٌ, † *The she-camel experienced an itching and annoyance in her belly*, (Ṣ, O, Ḳ,) *from the growth of the hair*, (Ṣ, O,) or *from the growth of the fur*, (Ḳ,) *of her fœtus*. (Ṣ, O, Ḳ.)

2. أَكَّلَهُ, [inf. n. تَأْكِيلٌ, *He made him to eat* a thing.] — أَكَّلَ مَالِى وَشَرَّبَهُ, (Ṣ, Ḳ,) inf. n. as above, (Ḳ,) [lit. *He made* people *to eat my property, and made* them *to drink it*,] means ‡ *he fed men*, or *the people*, *with my property*, or *cattle*. (Ṣ, Ḳ, TA.) — ظَلَّ مَالِى يُؤَكَّلُ وَيُشَرَّبُ, (so in some copies of the Ḳ and in the TA,) or يُؤَكِّلُ وَيُشَرِّبُ, (so in two copies of the Ṣ and in a copy of the Ḳ,) [of which the former is app. the right reading, as the lit. meaning seems to be *My cattle passed the day made to eat and made to drink*,] i. e., ‡ *pasturing as they pleased*. (Ṣ, Ḳ, TA.) — أَكَّلَهُ الشَّىْءَ, inf. n. as above, ‡ *He charged against him*, or *accused him of doing, the thing*; as also ▾ آكَلَهُ, (Ḳ, TA,) inf. n. إِيكَالٌ. (TA.) In [some of] the copies of the Ḳ, for إِدَّعَاهُ, we here find, erroneously, دَعَاهُ. (TA.) You say, أَكَّلْتَنِى مَا لَمْ آكُلْ [lit. *Thou hast made me to eat what I have not eaten*,] meaning ‡ *thou hast charged against me*, or *accused me of doing, what I have not done*; as also ▾ آكَلْتَنِى. (Ṣ, TA.) So too, أَشْرَبْتَنِى مَا لَمْ أَشْرَبْ. (Ṣ and Ḳ in art. شرب.)

3. آكَلَهُ, inf. n. مُؤَاكَلَةٌ (Ṣ, Ḳ) and إِكَالٌ, (Ḳ,) *He ate with him*; (Ṣ, Ḳ;) as also وَاكَلَهُ, though of weak authority; (Ḳ;) or this latter is not allowable. (Ṣ, Ṣgh.) — مُؤَاكَلَةٌ which is forbidden in a trad. is † *A debtor's giving a thing to his creditor in order that he may abstain from taking the debt*. (TA.)

4. آكَلَ, [inf. n. إِيكَالٌ,] said of the palm-tree, and of seed-produce, (Ṣ, Ḳ,) and of anything, (Ṣ,) *It had ripe fruit*; *it supplied food*. (Ṣ, Ḳ.) — آكَلَهُ الشَّىْءَ, (Ṣ, Ḳ,) inf. n. as above, (Ṣ,) *He gave him to eat the thing*; *he fed him with the thing*. (Ṣ,* Ḳ.) — See also 2, in two places. — آكل النَّارَ † *He fed*, or *supplied*, *the fire with fuel*. (Ṣ.) — آكل بَيْنَ النَّاسِ, (A, Ḳ,) inf. n. as above, (Ṣ, O,) ‡ *He busied himself among the people with propagating calumnies*: (Ṣ, O, TA:) or *he created*, or *excited*, *disagreement*, *dissension*, or

strife, among them; or *made,* or *did, mischief among them:* (A, TA:) or *he incited them, one against another.* (Ḳ.) — آكَلْتُكَ فُلَانًا, (Ṣ,) or آكَلَ فُلَانًا فُلَانًا, (Ḳ, [in the CḲ, erroneously, فُلَانٌ فُلَانًا,]) ‡ *I made thee,* (Ṣ,) or *he made such a one,* (Ḳ,) *to have dominion,* or *authority,* or *power, over such a one.* (Ṣ, Ḳ.)

5. تَأَكَّلَ: see 1, latter part, in two places: — and see also 8. — Also, said of a sword, (Ṣ, Ḳ,) and of silver (Ḳ, TA) molten, (TA,) and of lightning, and of collyrium, and of aloes, (Ḳ,) and of anything shiny, (TA,) ‡ *It shone, gleamed,* or *glistened,* (Ṣ, Ḳ, TA,) *much,* or *intensely;* (Ḳ;) when said of a sword, *by reason of its sharpness.* (Ṣ, TA.)

8. ائتكل [with the disjunctive alif اِيتَكَلَ]: see 1, latter part, in two places. — أَمَا تَنْفَكُّ تَأْتَكِلُ *Dost thou not cease to eat our flesh,* [i. e., *to wound our reputations,* (see 1,)] *and to defame us?* (Aboo-Naṣr, TA.) But see below. — ائتكلت النَّارُ ‡ *The fire flamed,* or *blazed, vehemently;* as though *one part thereof devoured another.* (TA.) — ائتكل غَضَبًا, (Ḳ,) or مِنَ الغَضَبِ, (Ṣ,) ‡ *He burned,* or *burned fiercely, with,* or *by reason of, anger.* (Ṣ, Ḳ.) The phrase mentioned above, اما تنفك تأتكل, is also cited as an ex. of this meaning. (Ṣ, TA.) You say likewise, ائتكل مِنْهُ ‡ *He was,* or *became, angry with him, and excited,* or *provoked, against him,* (Ḳ, TA,) *and vehement,* or *severe;* (TA;) as also منه ▼ تأكّل. (Ḳ.)

10. استأكله الشَّىْءَ ‡ *He asked,* or *begged, of him to assign to him the thing,* or *to make it be to him, as a means of subsistence,* or *a thing to be eaten.* (Ḳ, TA.) — يَسْتَأْكِلُ الضُّعَفَآءَ ‡ *He takes* (Ṣ, Ḳ, TA) *and devours* (TA) *the possessions of the weak ones.* (Ṣ, Ḳ, TA.)

أُكْلٌ: see أُكُلٌ.

أَكَلٌ inf. n. of أَكِلَ [q. v.]. — فِى أَسْنَانِهِ أَكَلٌ ‡ *In his teeth is a rubbing together and wasting away;* by reason of age. (Ṣ, TA.) See also أُكَالٌ.

أَكِلٌ [part. n. of أَكِلَ]. — نَاقَةٌ أَكِلَةٌ † *A she-camel experiencing an itching and annoyance in her belly,* (Ṣ, Ḳ,) *from the growth of the hair,* (Ṣ,) or *from the growth of the fur,* (Ḳ,) *of her fœtus.* (Ṣ, Ḳ.) — [الأَكَلُ is erroneously put, in the CḲ, for الآكِلُ, in a sense explained below.]

أُكُلٌ and ▼ أُكْلٌ; (Ṣ, Mṣb, Ḳ, &c.;) the latter a contraction of the former; (Mṣb;) *What is eaten;* (Ṣ, Mṣb, TA;) as also ▼ أُكْلَةٌ and ▼ أَكِلَةٌ (Lḥ, TA) and ▼ مَأْكَلَةٌ and ▼ مَأْكُلَةٌ (Mṣb, Ḳ) and ▼ مَأْكُولٌ; (Lḥ, Mṣb;) *any eatable;* i. e. *anything that is eaten;* (Ṣ;) and ▼ أَكَالٌ signifies [*the same, an eatable,* or] *food.* (Ṣ, TA.) You say of one who is dead, اِنْقَطَعَ أُكُلُهُ [*His food has become cut off,* or *stopped:* in the TA, أَكْلُهُ: see 1]. (Ṣ.) And مَا ذُقْتُ أَكَالًا ▼ *I have not tasted food.* (Ṣ, TA.) — *Fruit* (Ṣ, Ḳ [in the latter of which, in some copies, الثَّمَرُ is put for الثُّمُرُ, erroneously, as is said in the TA]) of palm-trees and other trees [&c.]. (Ṣ.) So in the Ḳur [xiii. 35], أُكُلُهَا دَائِمٌ [*Its fruit* shall be *perpetual*]: (Ṣ, TA:) meaning that the fruits thereof shall be not as those of the present world, which come to one at one time and not at another. (TA.) [Pl. آكَالٌ; occurring in the M and Ḳ in art. اتو.] — ‡ *Means of subsistence:* (Ḳ:) *worldly good fortune,* (Ṣ, Ḳ,) *and ample means of subsistence.* (Ṣ.) You say, فُلَانٌ ذُو أُكُلٍ ‡ *Such a one is possessed of worldly good fortune, and ample means of subsistence:* (Ṣ:) and عَظِيمُ الأُكُلِ ‡ *possessed of* [*great*] *good fortune;* or *of a* [*great and*] *good share of the means of subsistence.* (TA.) — ‡ *Thickness, substantialness,* or *closeness* or *compactness of texture,* of a garment, or piece of cloth; (Ṣ, Ḳ, TA;) and *strength* thereof. (Ḳ.) You say ثَوْبٌ ذُو أُكُلٍ ‡ *A garment,* or *piece of cloth, having thickness,* &c.: and قِرْطَاسٌ ذُو أُكُلٍ ‡ *paper having thickness,* &c. (Ṣ, TA.) — ‡ *Intelligence; judgment;* (Aboo-Naṣr, Ṣ, Ḳ;) *firmness of intellect.* (Ḳ, TA.) You say رَجُلٌ ذُو أُكُلٍ ‡ *A man possessing intelligence and judgment.* (Aboo-Naṣr, Ṣ, TA.)

أَكْلَةٌ *A single act of eating* (Ṣ, Mgh, Mṣb, Ḳ) *until one is satisfied.* (Ṣ.) Hence the saying, المُعْتَادُ أَكْلَتَانِ الغَدَآءُ وَالعَشَآءُ, meaning *That to which people are accustomed is two acts of eating,* the eating of *the morning-meal* and that of *the evening-meal.* (Mgh.) — See also أُكْلَةٌ, in two places. — And see أُكُلٌ, first sentence.

أُكْلَةٌ *A morsel,* or *small mouthful,* of food. (Ṣ, Mgh, Mṣb, Ḳ.) [For the pl., see below.] You say, أَكَلْتُ أُكْلَةً وَاحِدَةً *I ate one morsel.* (Ṣ.) And أَكَلَ بِأَخِيهِ أُكْلَةً † [*He ate a morsel by means of defaming his brother*] is said, in a trad., of a man who is on terms of brotherhood with another, and then goes to his enemy, and speaks of him in a manner not good, in order that he may give him a present for doing so. (TA.) — *A small round cake of bread;* syn. قُرْصَةٌ; (Ṣ, Ḳ;) *a single* قُرْص: (Mgh:) pl. أُكَلٌ, as below. (TA.) — See also أُكُلٌ. — Also † *i. q.* طُعْمَةٌ; (Ṣ, Ḳ;) which is also syn. with ▼ مَأْكَلَةٌ; (Ṣ, Mṣb, Ḳ, in art. طعم;) i. e. *An assigned,* or *appointed, means of subsistence; such as a grant of a tract of land; and a tax, or portion of a tax or taxes; and the like;* (Mgh in explanation of طُعْمَةٌ, and TA in explanation of the same and of مَأْكَلَةٌ in art. طعم;) and [it is also said that] ▼ مَأْكَلَةٌ signifies *a thing that is assigned,* or *appointed,* or *granted, to a man, so that he is not to be reckoned with,* or *called to account, for it:* (TA in the present art.:) [thus it applies to *any absolute grant, either of land,* (*as an allodium, an appanage, &c.,*) *or of revenue:*] pl. أُكَلٌ (Ḳ) [and app. also آكَالٌ, which see below]. You say, هٰذَا الشَّىْءُ أُكْلَةٌ لَكَ *This thing is a* طُعْمَة *to thee,* or *for thee.* (Ṣ.) — See also أَكِيلَةٌ. — Also, and ▼ إِكْلَةٌ (Ṣ, Z, Ṣgh, Ḳ) and ▼ أَكَلَةٌ, (Kr, Ḳ,) ‡ *Defamation;* or *defamation of the absent.* (Ṣ, Z, Ṣgh, Ḳ.) You say, إِنَّهُ لَذُو أُكْلَةٍ and ▼ إِكْلَةٍ (Ṣ, TA) and ▼ أَكَلَةٍ (TA) ‡ *Verily he is one who defames men;* or, *who does so in their absence.* (Ṣ, TA.)

إِكْلَةٌ *A mode,* or *manner,* (Ḳ,) or *state,* or *condition,* (Ṣ, Ḳ,) *in which one eats:* (Ṣ, Ḳ:*) like جِلْسَةٌ and رِكْبَةٌ: (Ṣ, TA:) and the *posture of the eater, reclining or sitting.* (TA.) You say, إِنَّهُ لَحَسَنُ الإِكْلَةِ [*Verily he has a good mode,* &c., *of eating*]. (Ṣ.) — See also أُكْلَةٌ, last two sentences. — ‡ The *itch:* or *an itching:* (Ṣ, Ḳ:) as also ▼ أُكَالٌ, (Aṣ, Ṣ, Ḳ,) [see أَكَلَنِى رَأْسِى, of which both are said to be inf. ns.,] and ▼ أَكِلَةٌ: (Ḳ:) so the last is written accord. to the correct copies of the Ḳ: accord. to Esh-Shiháb, in the Shifá el-Ghaleel, it would seem to be أُكْلَةٌ; but this is at variance with the authority of the leading lexicologists: the same word, أَكِلَةٌ, is also explained in the Ḳ as signifying *a disease in a limb,* or *member, in consequence of which one part is* [*as it were*] *eaten by another;* [a meaning which I believe to be correct, (see أُكَالٌ,) although SM says,] but this is identical with the *itch,* or *an itching:* and ▼ أُكْلَانٌ is a vulgar term for the same; and so is ▼ آكِلَةٌ, with medd, given as correct by Eth-Thaʼálibee, in [his book entitled] the Mudáf and Mensoob, but disallowed by El-Khafájee. (TA.) One says, إِنِّى لَأَجِدُ فِى جَسَدِى إِكْلَةً ‡ [*Verily I experience in my body an itching.*] (Ṣ.)

أَكِلَةٌ: see إِكْلَةٌ.

أَكُولَةٌ: see أَكُولٌ.

أُكْلَانٌ: see إِكْلَةٌ.

أَكَالٌ: see أُكُلٌ, first and second sentences.

أُكَالٌ ‡ *A corrosion,* or *cankering,* or *decaying,* of a limb, or member, [and of a sore,] *from the mutual eating away of its several parts;* as also ▼ إِكَالٌ. (Ḳ, TA.) [See also أَكِلَةٌ, voce إِكْلَةٌ, where a similar meaning is assigned to the former of these two words; and the same seems to be indicated in the Mṣb.] — See also another signification voce إِكْلَةٌ. — بِهَا أُكَالٌ, said of a she-camel, † *She has an itching and annoyance in her belly,* (Ṣ, Ḳ,) *from the growth of the hair,* (Ṣ,) or *of the fur,* (Ḳ,) *of her fœtus.* (Ṣ, Ḳ.)

إِكَالٌ: see أُكَالٌ.

أَكُولٌ and ▼ أَكُولَةٌ and ▼ أَكِيلٌ all signify the same; (Ḳ;) i. e. *A man who eats much;* [*who is a great eater; edacious; voracious;*] as also ▼ أَكَّالٌ. (TA.)

أَكِيلٌ *One who eats with another.* (Ṣ, TA.) — See also أَكُولٌ: — and see آكِلٌ. — *I. q.* ▼ مَأْكُولٌ [as signifying *Eaten*]. (TA.) — See also أَكِيلَةٌ.

أَكُولَةٌ *A sheep,* or *goat, which is set apart* (Ṣ, Mṣb, Ḳ) *to be eaten,* (Ṣ, Mgh, Ḳ,) [i. e.] *to be slaughtered,* (Mṣb,) *and which is fattened,* (Ṣ, Mgh,) *and the taking of which by the collector of the poor-rate is disapproved;* (Ṣ;) *not left to pasture by itself, being of the best of the beasts:* (Mṣb:) and ▼ أَكِيلَةٌ occurs in the same sense, applied to a sheep, or goat, fattened to be eaten. (Mgh.) Hence the prov., مَرْعًى وَلَا أَكُولَةٌ [lit. *Pasturage, and no* اكولة]; meaning † *wealth collected together, and none expended.* (TA.) — Also *Barren;* applied to a sheep or goat [app. because such is generally eaten]. (Ḳ.)

أَكُولَةٌ: see what next follows.

أَكِيلَةٌ and ▾ أَكِيلٌ and ▾ أُكُولَةٌ, with two dammehs, (Ḳ,) so in the copies of the Ḳ, but perhaps a mistake for ▾ أُكْلَةٌ, (TA,) a word of a bad dial., (Ḳ,* TA,) and ▾ مَأْكُولٌ and ▾ مُؤَاكِلٌ, (Ḳ, TA, [in some copies of the former of which, instead of وَهِىَ قَبِيحَةٌ وَالْمَأْكُولِ وَالْمُؤَاكِلِ, meaning, as is said in the TA, وَهِىَ لُغَةٌ قَبِيحَةٌ &c., we find وَهِىَ قَبِيحَةُ الْمَأْكُولِ وَالْمُؤَاكِلِ,]) *A sheep,* or *goat, which is set* (Ḳ, TA) *in the lurking-place of a hunter* (TA) *for the purpose of catching thereby the wolf and the like.* (Ḳ, TA.) — And the first two words, (Ḳ,) or أَكِيلَةُ سَبُعٍ, (Ṣ, Mgh, Mṣb,) *A beast which has been eaten,* (Ṣ,* Ḳ,) or *partly eaten,* (Mgh, Mṣb,) *by a beast or bird of prey,* (Ṣ, Mgh, Mṣb, Ḳ,) *and then rescued from it:* (Mgh, TA:) the ة in اكيلة being added because the quality of a subst. is predominant in it. (Ṣ.) — See also أُكُولَةٌ.

أَكَّالٌ: see أَكُولٌ.

آكِلٌ *Eating;* or *an eater;* as also ▾ أَكِيلٌ: pl. أَكَلَةٌ. (Ṣ, Ḳ.) You say, هُمْ أَكَلَةُ رَأْسٍ [lit. *They are eaters of a head*]; meaning † *they are few; one head satisfying their stomachs.* (Ṣ.) — آكِلَةُ اللَّحْمِ ‡ *Pasturing beasts.* (Ḳ, TA.) — ‡ *The knife;* (Ḳ, TA;) because it cuts the flesh: (TA:) and *the pointed staff* or *stick;* (Ḳ, TA;) as being likened thereto: (TA:) and *fire:* (Ḳ:) and *whips;* (Sh, Ḳ;) because they burn the skin. (TA.) — الآكِلُ, [in the CḲ, erroneously, الأَكِلُ,] ‡ *The king.* (Ḳ, TA.) [Opposed to المَأْكُولُ, q. v.] — آكِلُ الرِّبَا ‡ [*The receiver of usury*]: occurring in a trad., in which it is said, لُعِنَ آكِلُ الرِّبَا وَمُؤْكِلُهُ ▾ ‡ [*The receiver of usury is cursed, and the giver thereof*]. (TA.)

آكِلَةٌ fem. of آكِلٌ, q. v. — See also إِكْلَةٌ.

آكَالٌ [app. a pl. of pauc. of أُكْلٌ, q. v., and of أُكُلٌ, agreeably with analogy,] ‡ The [*grants termed*] مَآكِل of kings; (Ḳ;) their طُعَم [pl. of طُعْمَةٌ, explained above, voce أُكْلَةٌ]. (TA.) — † The *stipends* of soldiers. (Ḳ.) — ذَوُو الآكَالِ, for which J has erroneously put الآكال, [in the Ṣ,] (TṢ, Ḳ,) without ذوو, (TA,) ‡ *The lords,* or *chiefs, of the tribes, who take the* مِرْبَاع [or *fourth part of the spoil,* which was the chief's portion in the time of ignorance] (Ṣ, TṢ, Ḳ, TA) *&c.* (TA.)

مَأْكَلٌ, (Ṣ,) [in measure] like مَقْعَدٌ, (TA,) [an inf. n. of أَكَلَ, q. v.: — and also signifying] *Gain.* (Ṣ, TA.) — [Also *A place,* and *a time, of eating:* pl. مَآكِلُ.]

مُؤْكَلٌ † *Fortunate; possessed of good fortune; prosperous.* (Aboo-Sa'eed, Ḳ.)

مُؤْكِلُ الرِّبَا ‡ [*The giver of usury:* see آكِلٌ, last sentence]. (TA.)

مَأْكَلَةٌ and ▾ مَأْكُلَةٌ: see أُكْلٌ: — and for the former, see also أُكْلَةٌ, in two places. — Also, both words, *i. q.* مِيرَةٌ [i. e. *Corn,* or *any provision, which a man brings,* or *purveys, for himself* or *his family,* or *for sale*]. (Ḳ.) — Also used in the sense explained above, voce أُكْلٌ, [as a subst.,] and likewise as an epithet, so that one says شَاةٌ مَأْكَلَةٌ [as meaning *A sheep,* or *goat, that is eaten*]. (Ḳ.) — Both words signify [also] *A place whence one eats.* (Ṣ, O.) — [And hence] one says, اتَّخَذْتُ فُلَانًا مَأْكَلَةً and مَأْكُلَةً † [*I took for myself such a one as a person from whom to obtain what to eat*]. (Ṣ, O.) — [The pl. is مَآكِلُ: of which see an ex. voce آكَالٌ.]

مَأْكُلَةٌ: see the paragraph next preceding, throughout.

مِئْكَلَةٌ *Anything in* [i. e. *out of*] *which one eats:* (Lḥ, Ḳ:) or [*bowls of the kind called*] صِحَاف, (Ṣ,) or a [*bowl of the kind called*] صَحْفَةٌ, (TA,) *in which the tribe find it easy to cook,* (so in a copy of the Ṣ and in the TA,) or *to put,* (so in another copy of the Ṣ,) *flesh-meat and* [*the kind of porridge called*] عَصِيدَة: (Ṣ, TA:) or *a bowl not so large as a* صَحْفَة, *but next to it in size, that satisfies the stomachs of two men,* or *three:* (Ṣ voce صَحْفَةٌ:) [or] *a small* [*bowl of the kind called*] قَصْعَة, *that satisfies the stomachs of three:* and *a small* [*cooking-pot such as is called*] بُرْمَة. (Ḳ.)

مَأْكُولٌ: see أَكِيلٌ: — and أُكْلٌ: — and أَكِيلَةٌ. — ‡ The *subjects* of a king. (Z, Ḳ, TA.) Hence the trad., مَأْكُولُ حِمْيَرَ خَيْرٌ مِنْ آكِلِهَا ‡ *The subjects of Ḥimyer are better than their king,* or *ruler.* (Z, TA.)

مِئْكَالٌ *A spoon:* (Ḳ:) because one eats with it. (TA.)

مُؤَاكِلٌ: see أَكِيلَةٌ. — Also, [like ▾ مُسْتَأْكِلٌ,] ‡ One *who takes and devours the possessions of men.* (TA.)

مُسْتَأْكِلٌ: see what next precedes.

اكم

2. تَأْكِيمٌ The *being big in the* كَفَل [i. e. the *hinder parts,* or *posteriors,* also termed مَأْكَمَة]. (O, Ḳ.) You say, أُكِّمَتِ المَرْأَةُ *The woman was large in the* كَفَل. (TḲ.)

10. استأكم *It* (a place) *became what are termed* أَكَمٌ, q. v. (Ḳ.) — استأكم مَجْلِسَهُ *He* (a man, TA) *found his sitting-place to be plain, smooth, soft,* or *easy to sit upon.* (Ḳ.)

أُكُمٌ: see what next follows.

أَكَمَةٌ *A hill,* or *mound,* syn. تَلٌّ, (Mṣb, Ḳ,) [in an absolute sense, or] *of what is termed* قُفّ [q. v.], (Ḳ,) or, as in the M, (TA,) *of a single collection of stones:* or it is *inferior to mountains:* or *a place that is more elevated than what is around it, and is rugged, not to the degree of being stone:* (Ḳ:) or *an isolated mountain:* (Ḳ voce جَبَلٌ:) or *an eminence like what is termed* رَابِيَة: *a collection of stones in one place, sometimes rugged and sometimes not rugged:* (Mṣb:) or *i. q.* قُفّ, *except that the* اكمة *is higher and greater:* (ISh, TA:) or *what is higher than the* قُفّ, *compact and round, rising into the sky, abounding with stones:* (TA:) pl. أَكَمَاتٌ (Ṣ, Mṣb) and ▾ أَكَمٌ, [or this is rather a coll. gen. n. of which أَكَمَةٌ is the n. un.,] (Ṣ, Mṣb, Ḳ,) and إِكَامٌ, (Ḳ, TA,) or this is pl. of أَكَمٌ, (Ṣ, Mṣb, TA,) and أُكُمٌ, (Ḳ, TA,) or this is pl. of إِكَامٌ, (Ṣ, Mṣb, TA,) and آكَامٌ [a pl. of pauc.], (Ḳ,) or this is pl. of أُكُمٌ, (Ṣ, Mṣb, TA,) and آكُمٌ [which is also a pl. of pauc.], (IJ, Ḳ,) or this is a pl. of أَكَمٌ: (TA:) IHsh says that أَكَمٌ is the only word like ثَمَرٌ in its series of pls.; for its sing. [or n. un.] is أَكَمَةٌ, and the pl. of this [or the coll. gen. n.] is أَكَمٌ, and the pl. of this is إِكَامٌ, and the pl. of this is أُكُمٌ, and the pl. of this is آكَامٌ, and the pl. of this is أَكَامِيمُ [or أَوَاكِيمُ?]. (MF in art. ثمر.) It is said in a prov., used in ridiculing any one who has told of his committing some fault, not desiring to reveal it, حَسِّنُونِى وَوَرَاءَ الأَكَمَةِ مَا وَرَاءَهَا [in which I think the first word to be a mistranscription, for جِئْتُمُونِى, and the literal meaning to be, *Ye have come to me; but behind the hill is what is behind it*]: related on the authority of Zeyd Ibn-Kethweh. (TA.) And one says, لَا تَبُلْ عَلَى أَكَمَةٍ, meaning ‡ *Publish not what is secret of thine affair.* (TA.)

مَأْكِمٌ and مَأْكَمٌ: see what next follows.

مَأْكَمَةٌ, (El-Fárábee,) or مَأْكِمَةٌ, (Ṣ,) or both, and ▾ مَأْكَمٌ and ▾ مَأْكِمٌ, (IAth, Ḳ,) The *hinder part, posteriors, buttocks,* or *rump,* of a woman; syn. عَجِيزَةٌ: (Ṣ:) or *a portion of flesh on the head of the* وَرِك [or *haunch*]; *one of two such portions:* (Zj in his "Khalḳ el-Insán," and Ḳ:) or these are *two protuberances of flesh on the heads of the upper parts of the* وَرِكَانِ [or *haunches*]; *on the right and left:* (TA:) or they are *two portions of flesh conjoining the* عَجُز [or *buttocks*] *and the* مَتْنَانِ [or *two portions of flesh and sinew next the back-bone, on each side*]; (Ḳ, TA;) or, as in the Nh, *conjoining the* عَجْب [or *rump-bone*] *and the* مَتْنَان: or *two portions of flesh at the root of the* وَرِكَانِ: (TA:) pl. مَآكِمُ. (Ṣ, Ḳ.) Lḥ mentions the saying, إِنَّهُ لَعَظِيمُ المَآكِمِ [*Verily he is big in the hinder parts*]; as though they called every portion thereof مأكم. (TA.) And one says in reviling a person, يَا ٱبْنَ أَحْمَرِ المَأْكَمَةِ, meaning *O son of him who is red in the* سَفِلَة. (TA.)

مُؤَكَّمَةٌ: see what follows.

مُؤْكَمَةٌ [in the CḲ, erroneously, مُؤَاكَمَةٌ] and ▾ مُؤَكَّمَةٌ She *who is large in the* مَأْكَمَتَانِ. (Ḳ.)

ال

أَلْ is a particle of determination: (Mughnee &c.:) or, accord. to some, it is a conjunct noun, and this is the correct opinion; but some say it is a conjunct particle; and some, a particle of determination: (I 'Aḳ p. 40:) [it is equivalent to our article *The*;] as in الرَّجُلُ [*The man*]: (Ṣ and Ḳ in art. لوم, and I 'Aḳ p. 48:) accord. to Kh, [what is termed] the determinative is أَلْ [altogether, and therefore it is called by some "the determinative alif and lám"]; but accord. to Sb, it is the ل alone; [wherefore it is called by some, as in the Ṣ &c., "the lám of determination;"] so that accord. to Kh, the hemzeh is a hemzeh of disjunction; but accord. to Sb, it is a hemzeh of conjunction: (I 'Aḳ ubi suprà:) [J says,] the ل being quiescent, the conjunctive ا is prefixed to it in order that it may commence therewith; but when it is conjoined with what precedes it, the ا is dropped, as in لِلرَّجُلِ. (Ṣ in art. لوم.) Sometimes the Arabs suppress hemzeh after it; and sometimes they also suppress the ا of the article itself: thus, for الأَحْمَرُ, they say الَحْمَرُ, and لَحْمَرُ. (Zj, cited in TA in art. ايك.) In the dial. of some of the people of El-Yemen, (TA in art. ام, q. v.,) or in the dial. of Ḥimyer, (TA in art. طيب,) اَمْ is used in the sense of ال. (TA.) — It is used to distinguish a noun as known [to the hearer or reader in a particular and definite sense]: (Mughnee, I 'Aḳ ubi suprà:) first, by its being mentioned [before]; (Mughnee;) as in [the words of the Ḳur lxxiii. 15 and 16,] كَمَا أَرْسَلْنَا إِلَى فِرْعَوْنَ رَسُولًا فَعَصَى فِرْعَوْنُ الرَّسُولَ [*Like as we sent unto Pharaoh an apostle, and Pharaoh disobeyed the apostle*]; (Mughnee, I 'Aḳ;) in which case, the pronoun may supply the place which it and the noun that it accompanies occupies: secondly, by its being conceived in the mind; as in [the Ḳur ix. 40,] إِذْ هُمَا فِى الغَارِ [*When they two were in the cave*]: and thirdly, by its being applied to a thing present; and accord. to Ibn-'Oṣfoor, this does not occur except after nouns of indication, as in جَآءَنِى هٰذَا الرَّجُلُ [*This man* (lit. *this, the man,*) *came to me*]; or after أَىّ in calling, as in يَا أَيُّهَا الرَّجُلُ [*O man*]; or after إِذَا denoting a thing's happening suddenly, or unexpectedly, as in خَرَجْتُ فَإِذَا الأَسَدُ [*I went forth, and lo, there was the lion*]; or after the noun denoting the present time, as ٱلْآنَ [*Now*]: but this requires consideration; for you say to the reviler of a man in your presence, لَا تَشْتِمِ الرَّجُلَ [*Revile not thou the man*]; and because that which is after إِذَا does not render determinate anything present at the time of speaking; and because that in الآن is really redundant, being inseparable, which the determinative is never known to be: the good example in this case is the saying in the Ḳur [v. 5,] اَلْيَوْمَ أَكْمَلْتُ لَكُمْ دِينَكُمْ [*This day I have completed for you your religion*]. (Mughnee.) — It is also used to denote the species: first, to denote the totality of the individuals of the species; and this may have its place supplied by كُلّ used in its proper sense; (Mughnee, I 'Aḳ* ubi suprà;) as in [the Ḳur iv. 32,] وَخُلِقَ ٱلْإِنْسَانُ ضَعِيفًا [*For man was created weak*]: secondly, to denote the totality of the properties of the individuals, or the combination of all those properties in one thing; and this may have its place supplied by كُلّ used in a tropical sense; as in زَيْدٌ الرَّجُلُ عِلْمًا [*Zeyd is the man in respect of knowledge*; as though he combined in himself the knowledge of all the individuals of his species]; i. e., he is the complete, or perfect, [or we would rather say, preeminent,] in knowledge; and hence, [in the Ḳur ii. 1,] ذٰلِكَ الكِتَابُ [*That is the book*, or *scripture*; as though combining in itself the excellences of all other books or scriptures; or meaning that is preeminently the book, or scripture]: and thirdly, to denote the quiddity, or essence; and this may not have its place supplied by كُلّ used either properly or tropically; as in the saying, [in the Ḳur xxi. 31,] وَجَعَلْنَا مِنَ ٱلْمَآءِ كُلَّ شَىْءٍ حَىٍّ [*And we have made of water* (meaning, accord. to common opinion, sperma genitale,) *everything living*]; or, accord. to some, it is used in this case to distinguish a thing as known [in a particular sense] by its being conceived in the mind. (Mughnee.) — It is also used to denote predominance of application; as in المَدِينَةُ [*The city*], meaning the city of the Apostle; and الكِتَابُ [*The book*], meaning the book of Seebaweyh: and in this case, it may not be suppressed, except when the noun is used vocatively, or when it is prefixed to another noun which it governs in the gen. case; and in some anomalous instances, as in هٰذَا عَيُّوقٌ طَالِعًا [*This is the star Capella, rising*], originally العَيُّوقُ. (I 'Aḳ p. 51.) [In a case of this kind, it is said in the Mughnee to be redundant; but I think it is clearly not so in any of the instances here mentioned, except the last; and this I would rather assign to a category yet to be noticed, in which ال is certainly redundant, and, by rule, inseparable.] — It is also prefixed to a noun transferred from its original application to that of a proper name; it being so prefixed to convey an allusion to the original signification; and such noun being generally an epithet, as حَارِثٌ; but sometimes an inf. n., as فَضْلٌ; and sometimes a generic noun, as نُعْمَانٌ; so that in any of these cases you may prefix ال, saying الحَارِثُ and الفَضْلُ and النُّعْمَانُ, with a view to the original signification; and you may suppress it, with a view to the actual state [which is that of a proper name]: for when you mean that a name of this kind is given as one ominous of good, you prefix the ال in order to indicate this; as when you say الحَارِثُ with a view to a person's being thus named to prognosticate that he will live and be a tiller, or cultivator; but when you only consider it as a proper name, you do not prefix the ال: thus the prefix ال conveys a meaning not obtained without it; and therefore it is not redundant, as some assert it to be. (I 'Aḳ p. 50.) [The author of the Mughnee is one of those who consider ال redundant in this case.] — It is in some cases redundant: and in some of these, it is inseparable; as in [a proper name which cannot be used with a view to an original application from which it has been transferred to that of a proper name though it may have been so transferred, such as] اللَّاتُ, which is the name of a certain idol that was at Mekkeh [so called because a man used to moisten سَوِيق with clarified butter, for the pilgrims, at the place thereof]; and, accord. to some, [as before mentioned,] in الآنَ; and in the conjunct nouns الَّذِى and its variations, accord. to those who hold that a noun of this kind is rendered determinate by its complement: in other cases, where it is redundant, it is separable; and this is when it is prefixed to a proper name by poetic licence, as in بَنَاتُ الأَوْبَرِ for بَنَاتُ أَوْبَرَ, a species of truffle; or, accord. to Mbr, this is not a proper name, and the ال is not redundant; and when it is prefixed to a specificative, as in طِبْتَ النَّفْسَ for طِبْتَ نَفْسًا, accord. to the Baṣrees, who hold, in opposition to the Koofees, that the specificative may only be indeterminate; (I 'Aḳ p. 49;) [and, in like manner, as redundant and separable,] it is irregularly prefixed [by poetic licence] in الأَمْسِ [q. v.], when it is left in its original form with kesr. (T.) — Accord. to the Koofees, and some of the Baṣrees, and many of the later authors, it may also supply the place of the affixed pronoun; and such they hold to be the case in the saying in the Ḳur [lxxix. 41], فَإِنَّ ٱلْجَنَّةَ هِىَ ٱلْمَأْوَى [*Verily Paradise, it shall be his place of abode*]; and in مَرَرْتُ بِرَجُلٍ حَسَنٍ الوَجْهُ [*I passed by a man beautiful in his face*]; and ضُرِبَ زَيْدٌ الظَّهْرُ وَالبَطْنُ [*Zeyd was beaten, his back and his belly*]; when الوجه and الظهر and البطن are thus in the nom. case: but those who deny its being used in this manner hold that لَهُ is to be understood in the verse of the Ḳur, and مِنْهُ in the other examples: and Ibn-Málik restricts the licence to cases not including the صِلَة [or complement of ال used in the manner which is here next to be explained]. (Mughnee.) — It is also a conjunct noun in the sense of الَّذِى and its variations; and as such is prefixed to an act. part. n., and to a pass. part. n., and, as some say, to a simple epithet; (Mughnee, and I 'Aḳ p. 43;) as الضَّارِبُ [which is equivalent to الَّذِى يَضْرِبُ], and المَضْرُوبُ [which is equivalent to الَّذِى ضُرِبَ], and الحَسَنُ الوَجْهِ: (I 'Aḳ:) but this last is not to be regarded, as it cannot be rendered by means of a verb. (Mughnee.) As such, also, it is sometimes prefixed to an adverbial noun, (Mughnee and I 'Aḳ,) extraordinarily; (I 'Aḳ;) as in the saying,

• مَنْ لَا يَزَالُ شَاكِرًا عَلَى ٱلْمَعَهْ •
• فَهْوَ حَرٍ بِعِيشَةٍ ذَاتِ سَعَهْ •

[*Whoso ceases not to be grateful*, or *thankful, for what is with him*, or *what he has, he is worthy of a state of life such as is attended with plenty.*] (Mughnee and I 'Aḳ.) As such it is also sometimes prefixed to a nominal proposition; as in the saying,

• مِنَ القَوْمِ الرَّسُولُ ٱللهِ مِنْهُمْ •
• لَهُمْ دَانَتْ رِقَابُ بَنِى مَعَدِّ •

[*Of the people of whom is the apostle of God*, of those *to whom the necks of the sons of Ma'add have become abased*]. (Mughnee and I 'Aḳ.) And as such it is also sometimes prefixed to a verbal proposition, of which the verb is an aor.; which shows that it is not [in this case] a particle of determination; (Mughnee;) as in the phrase, صَوْتُ الحِمَارِ اليُجَدَّعُ [*The voice of the ass that has his ear*, or *ears, cut off*]. (T and Mughnee.) But all these three cases are peculiar to poetry; contrary to the opinion of Akh, and, with respect to the last case, to that of Ibn-Málik. (Mughnee.) [Respecting the last instance, see also art. جدع.] Another instance of its usage prefixed in this sense to an aor. is the saying,

• مَا أَنْتَ بِالْحَكَمِ التُّرْضَى حُكُومَتُهُ •

[*Thou art not the judge whose judgment is approved*]; (IAmb, T, I 'Aḳ;) a saying of El-Farezdaḳ: (IAmb, T:) it is an extraordinary case; (I 'Aḳ;) and is [said to be] an instance of a bad poetic license, the like of which in prose would be an error by common consent. (Expos. of the Shudhoor edh-Dhahab.) In like manner, one says, accord. to AZ, هٰذَا اليَضْرِبُكَ, meaning *This is he who beats thee;* and رَأَيْتُ اليَضْرِبُكَ *I saw him who beats thee;* and هٰذَا الوَضْعُ لِلشِّعْرِ *This is what is appropriated to poetry.* (T: [in which this last ex. is perhaps intended to intimate that the prefixing of ال in this manner to a verb is allowable only in poetry.]) — The Arabs also say, هُوَ الحَصِينُ أَنْ يُرَامَ وَهُوَ العَزِيزُ أَنْ يُضَامَ, meaning أَحْصَنُ مِنْ أَنْ يُرَامَ وَأَعَزُّ مِنْ أَنْ يُضَامَ [*He is more strongly fortified,* or *protected against attack, than that he will be sought,* or *desired, and he is more mighty than that he will be injured;* i. e., *too strongly fortified,* or *protected against attack, to be sought,* or *desired, and too mighty to be injured:* see مِن.]. (TA in art. لوم. [But الحِصْنُ is there erroneously put for الحَصِينُ.]) ═ Among strange usages, is that of أَلْ as an interrogative, mentioned by Ḳṭr; as in أَلْ فَعَلْتَ in the sense of هَلْ فَعَلْتَ [*Didst thou do? or hast thou done?*]. (Mughnee.)

إِلٌّ *Anything which has a quality requiring it to be regarded as sacred,* or *inviolable; which has some right pertaining to it:* and thus used in particular senses here following. (R, TA.) — *Relationship;* or *nearness with respect to kindred;* (Fr, T, Ṣ, M, R, Ḳ;) as also ↓إِلَّةٌ, (Fr, T, Ḳ,) of which the pl. is إِلَلٌ. (Ḳ.) So in the Ḳur [ix. 8], لَا يَرْقُبُوا فِيكُمْ إِلًّا (Fr, T) *They will not regard, with respect to you, relationship;* (Bḍ, Jel;) accord. to some. (Bḍ.) And so in a trad. of 'Alee, يَخُونُ العَهْدَ وَيَقْطَعُ الإِلَّ [*He is unfaithful to the covenant, and cuts the tie of relationship*]. (TA.) Ḥassán Ibn-Thábit says,

• لَعَمْرُكَ إِنَّ إِلَّكَ مِنْ قُرَيْشٍ •
• كَإِلِّ السَّقْبِ مِنْ رَأْلِ النَّعَامِ •

[*By thy life, thy relationship to Kureysh is like the relationship of the young camel to the young of the ostrich*]. (Ṣ.) — *Good origin.* (Ḳ.) So, accord. to some, in a saying of Aboo-Bekr, which see below. (TA.) — *I. q.* مَعْدِنٌ, (Ḳ,) or مَعْدِنٌ صَحِيحٌ [as meaning *A place,* or *person, whence a thing,* or *person, originates, free from imperfection,* or *from everything that would induce doubt or suspicion or evil opinion*]. (El-Muärrij, TA: [in which the verse of Ḥassán cited above is given as an ex. of this signification.]) — *A compact,* or *covenant;* or *one by which a person becomes responsible for the safety, or safe-keeping, of a person or thing;* syn. عَهْدٌ: (AO, Aboo-Is-ḥáḳ, T, Ṣ, M, R, Ḳ:) *a confederacy,* or *league;* syn. حِلْفٌ; (Aboo-Is-ḥáḳ, T, M, Ḳ;) and so, accord. to some, in the Ḳur ubi suprà: (Bḍ:) *a covenant between two parties by which either is bound to protect the other;* syn. جُوَارٌ: (Aboo-Is-ḥáḳ, T, R:) *a promise,* or *an assurance, of security* or *safety;* or *indemnity;* syn. أَمَانٌ; (Ḳ;) a meaning which it has, accord. to some, in the verse of the Ḳur cited above. (TA.) Hence, وَفِىُّ الإِلِّ *A fulfiller, performer,* or *keeper, of the compact,* or *covenant.* (TA, from a trad.) — *Lordship;* syn. رُبُوبِيَّةٌ. (M, Ḳ.) So in the Ḳur ubi suprà, accord. to some. (Bḍ.) And so in the saying of Aboo-Bekr, above referred to, when he heard the rhyming prose of Museylimeh, هٰذَا كَلَامٌ لَمْ يَخْرُجْ مِنْ إِلٍّ [*This is language which did not proceed from lordship*]: so explained by A'Obeyd: (Suh, TA:) or it has here another signification, mentioned before; the meaning being, which did not come from the origin whence came the Ḳur-án: or, accord. to some, it has here the signification next following. (TA.) — *Revelation,* or *inspiration.* (Ḳ, TA.) — الإِلُّ also signifies *God:* [like the word אֵל, or rather הָאֵל, as used in Hebrew:] (T, Ṣ, M, Ḳ:) so say Mujáhid and Esh-Shaabee: (T:) and so it is said to signify in the verse of the Ḳur cited above: (T, TA:) [and so it seems to signify in the saying of Aboo-Bekr, also cited above, accord. to the M:] but Aboo-Is-ḥáḳ disallows this; and so does Suh, in the R. (TA.) Ibn-El-Kelbee says, (M,) when إِلٌّ ends any name, it has this meaning, and is the complement of a prefixed noun; and so إِيلُ; (M, Ḳ;) as in جَبْرَئِلُ [and جَبْرَئِيلُ &c.]; and so say most of the learned: (TA:) but this is not a valid assertion; for were it so, جَبْرَئِلُ and the like would be perfectly decl.: (M:) some say that these names are constructed inversely, after the manner of the language of the 'Ajam; ال and ايل meaning *servant,* and the first part of the name being a name of God. (Suh, TA.) ═ *I. q.* شَخْصٌ [used in a pl. sense]. (Mughnee in art. أَلَا. [See what is said to be an ex. of this meaning in a verse of Dhu-r-Rummeh cited in art. الا in the present work.]) — [It is said that] إِلٌّ is also syn. with جَارٌ [*A neighbour;* &c.]. (Ḳ: [and so, accord. to the TA, in the M; but I have consulted the M without finding this explanation, and think it to be probably a mistranscription for جُوَارٌ, (see above,) as in the T and R.])

إِلَّةٌ: see إِلٌّ.

أَمْرٌ إِلِّىٌّ *A thing,* or *an affair, relating,* or *attributable, to* الإِلّ, meaning either *God,* or *revelation* or *inspiration.* (TA.)

الا

أَلَا [in its primitive acceptation, being composed of the interrogative hemzeh and the negative لَا,] denotes an interrogation respecting a negative, as in the saying [of the poet],

• أَلَا ٱصْطِبَارَ لِسَلْمَى أَمْ لَهَا جَلَدٌ •
• إِذَا أُلَاقِى ٱلَّذِى لَاقَاهُ أَمْثَالِى •

[*Is there not any patience belonging to Selmà, or has she hardiness, when I experience what persons like me have experienced?*]: (Mughnee, Ḳ:) and when used in this manner, it is put before a nominal proposition only, and governs like the negative لا [when used without the interrogative hemzeh]. (Mughnee.) — It also denotes a wish; as in the saying [of the poet],

• أَلَا عُمْرَ وَلَّى مُسْتَطَاعٌ رُجُوعُهُ •
• فَيَرْأَبَ مَا أَثْأَتْ يَدُ الغَفَلَاتِ •

[*May there not be a life which has declined whereof the returning is possible, so that it may repair what the hand of negligences hath marred?*]; for which reason يرأب is manṣoob, because it is the complement of a wish, coupled with فَ: and used in this manner, also, it is put before a nominal proposition only, [وَلَّى in the verse above being a qualificative, like an epithet,] and it governs like the negative لا [without the interrogative hemzeh], and has no enunciative either expressed or understood. (Mughnee.) — It also denotes reproof, or reproach, (T, Mughnee, Ḳ,) and disapproval; as in the saying [of the poet],

• أَلَا ٱرْعِوَآءَ لِمَنْ وَلَّتْ شَبِيبَتُهُ •
• وَآذَنَتْ بِمَشِيبٍ بَعْدَهُ هَرَمُ •

[*Is there no self-restraint to him whose youth hath declined, and announced hoariness, after which is to follow decrepitude?*]: (Mughnee, Ḳ:) and used in this manner, also, it is put before a nominal proposition only, and governs as in the cases mentioned above, (Mughnee,) or before a verb [also], which is always marfooa; as in the phrases أَلَا تَنْدَمُ عَلَى فِعَالِكَ [*Dost not thou repent of thine actions?*] and أَلَا تَسْتَحْيِى مِنْ جِيرَانِكَ [*Art not thou ashamed for thyself,* or *of thyself, with respect to thy neighbours?*] and أَلَا تَخَافُ رَبَّكَ [*Dost not thou fear thy Lord?*]. (T.) — It also denotes عَرْضٌ, (T,) or العَرْضُ, and التَّحْضِيضُ, both of which signify the asking, or requiring, a thing; (Mughnee, Ḳ;*) but the former means the doing so with gentleness; (Mughnee, Ḳ;) and the latter, the doing so with urgency: (Mughnee:) and when used in this manner, [also,] it is said to be composed of لا with the interrogative hemzeh; (TA;) and is put before a verbal proposition only; (Mughnee;) as in the saying [in the Ḳur xxiv. 22], أَلَا تُحِبُّونَ أَنْ يَغْفِرَ ٱللّٰهُ لَكُمْ [*Do not ye,* or *wherefore do not ye,* (see أَمَا,) *like that God should forgive you?*] (Mughnee, Ḳ,) and [in the same, ix. 13,] أَلَا تُقَاتِلُونَ قَوْمًا نَكَثُوا أَيْمَانَهُمْ [*Will not ye,* or *wherefore will not ye, fight a people who have broken their oaths?*]; (Mughnee;) or before a mejzoom or marfooạ aor., both of these forms being mentioned on the authority of the Arabs, as in أَلَا تَنْزِلُ تَأْكُلُ and أَلَا تَنْزِلْ تَأْكُلْ [*Wilt not thou, or wherefore wilt not thou, alight and eat?*]. (Ks, T.) —— It is also an inceptive particle, (Ṣ, Mughnee, Ḳ,) of which those who parse show the place but neglect the meaning, (Mughnee,) used to give notice of something about to be said, [like as *Now*, and *why*, (by the former of which I think it is generally best rendered when thus used,) are often employed in our language, and like as ἀλλὰ (which is remarkable for its near agreement with it in sound) is often used in Greek,] (Ṣ, Mughnee, Ḳ,) and importing averment, because it is composed of the interrogative hemzeh and the negative لَا, which, when thus composed, have this import, (Mughnee, Ḳ,) like أَلَمْ, and أَلَيْسَ, because the interrogative particle resembles the particle of negation, and the negation of a negation is an affirmation, (Ḥam p. 589,) and like أَمَا before an oath: (Z, Mughnee:) [it may therefore be further rendered by our word *surely*; for this word (as Dr. Johnson says in his Dictionary) "is often used rather to intend and strengthen the meaning of the sentence, than with any distinct and explicable meaning:"] or it signifies حَقًّا [*verily*, or *truly*]: (M voce أَمَا:) it is put before both the [kinds of] propositions, [the nominal and the verbal;] (Mughnee;) as in the saying [in the Ḳur ii. 12], أَلَا إِنَّهُمْ هُمُ ٱلسُّفَهَآءُ [meaning *Now surely it is they who are the lightwitted*], (Mughnee, Ḳ,) and [in the same, xi. 11,] أَلَا يَوْمَ يَأْتِيهِمْ لَيْسَ مَصْرُوفًا عَنْهُمْ [meaning *Now surely, on the day of its coming to them, it shall not be averted from them*], (Mughnee,) in which يَوْمَ يَأْتِيهِمْ appears to be the object of government of مَصْرُوفًا, which is the enunciative of لَيْسَ; whence it has been argued that, as the object of government of the enunciative of ليس precedes that verb, the enunciative itself may precede it: (I 'Aḳ pp. 74 and 75:) [J says,] you say, أَلَا إِنَّ زَيْدًا خَارِجٌ [*Now surely Zeyd is going forth*], like as you say, اِعْلَمْ أَنَّ زَيْدًا خَارِجٌ [*Know thou that Zeyd is going forth*]: (Ṣ:) Ks says, أَلَا is used to give notice of what is about to be said, and is followed by a command and a prohibition and an enunciation, as in أَلَا قُمْ [*Now stand thou*], and أَلَا لَا تَقُمْ [*Now stand not thou*], and أَلَا إِنَّ زَيْدًا قَدْ قَامَ [*Now surely Zeyd has stood*, or *has just now stood*]. (T.) When it is put before the particle [يَا] used to give notice of what is about to be said, it is merely an inceptive, as in the saying [of the poet],

• أَلَا يَا ٱسْلَمِى يَا دَارَ مَىَّ عَلَى البِلَى •

[*Now be thou free from evil, O abode of Meiyá, during wear and tear*]. (AAF, M.) —— Lth says, sometimes أَلَا is immediately followed by another لَا; and he cites the following ex.:

• فَقَامَ يَذُودُ النَّاسَ عَنَّا بِسَيْفِهِ •
• يَقُولُ أَلَا لَا مِنْ سَبِيلٍ إِلَى هِنْدِ •

[*Then he began to drive away the people from us, saying, Now is there no way to Hind?*]: and one says to a man, "Did such and such things happen?" and he answers, أَلَا لَا [*Why no*]: he holds الا to be used to give notice of what is about to be said, and لا to be a negative. (T.)

أُلَا and أُلَآءِ, and أُولَآءِ &c.: see art. الى.

أَلَّا is a particle denoting تَحْضِيض; (Mṣb in art. حض, Mughnee, Ḳ;) i.e., when followed by a future, exciting to an action, and seeking or desiring or demanding the performance of it; and when followed by a preterite, reproof for not doing a thing; (Mṣb ubi suprà;) syn. with هَلَّا: (T, TA;) and peculiar to enunciative verbal propositions, (Mughnee, Ḳ,) like the other particles used for the same purpose. (Mughnee.) You say, أَلَّا تَفْعَلُ كَذَا [*Wherefore wilt not thou do such a thing?* and] أَلَّا فَعَلْتَ كَذَا [*Wherefore didst not thou such a thing?*] (T, TA,) meaning, (TA,) or as though meaning, (T,) لِمَ لَمْ تَفْعَلْ كَذَا (T, TA.) —— It also means أَنْ لَا; the ن being incorporated into the ل, which is written with teshdeed: (T, TA:) in which case, it is not to be confounded with the foregoing particle. (Mughnee.) You say, أَمَرْتُهُ أَلَّا يَفْعَلَ ذَاكَ [*I commanded him that he should not do that*]; and you may say, أَمَرْتُهُ أَنْ لَا يَفْعَلَ ذَاكَ: it occurs in the old copies of the Ḳur written in the former manner in some places, and in the latter manner in other places. (T, TA.) In the saying in the Ḳur [xxvii. 31], أَلَّا تَعْلُوا عَلَىَّ, [which may mean *That ye exalt not yourselves against me*, or *exalt ye not yourselves against me*,] it may be a compound of أَنْ governing a manṣoob aor. and the negative لَا, or of the explicative أَنْ and the prohibitive لَا. (Mughnee.) [It often has لِ prefixed to it, forming the compound لِئَلَّا, which signifies *That*, or *in order that, . . . not*; and may frequently be rendered by *lest*; as in the Ḳur ii. 145, لِئَلَّا يَكُونَ لِلنَّاسِ عَلَيْكُمْ حُجَّةٌ *That*, or *in order that, there may not be*, or *lest there should be, to men, against you, any allegation*.]

إِلَّا, [regarded as a simple word,] not to be confounded with the compound of the conditional إِنْ and the negative لَا, (Mughnee at the end of the article on this word,) is used in four manners. (The same in the beginning of the art.) First, (Mughnee,) it is used (as a particle, Ṣ, Mṣb,) to denote exception; [meaning *Except, save*, or *saving*; and sometimes *but*; and sometimes *but not*; as will be seen below;] (T, Ṣ, Mṣb, Mughnee, Ḳ; [in which last it is mentioned in art. ال, and again, as in the Ṣ, in the last division of the work;]) and to denote exception, it is used in five manners; after an affirmation, and a negation, and a portion of a sentence devoid of the mention of that from which the exception is made, and when the thing excepted precedes that from which the exception is made, and when these two are disunited in kind, in which last case it has the meaning of لٰكِنَّ [*but* when the sentence is negative, and *but not* when the sentence is affirmative]. (Ṣ, TA.) You say, قَامَ القَوْمُ إِلَّا زَيْدًا [*The people*, or *company of men, stood, except Zeyd*]; i.e., Zeyd was not included in the predicament of the people, or company of men: (Mṣb:) and it is said in the Ḳur [ii. 250], (T,) فَشَرِبُوا مِنْهُ إِلَّا قَلِيلًا مِنْهُمْ [*And they drank of it, except a few of them*]: (T, Mughnee, Ḳ:) here قليلا is governed in the accus. case by إِلَّا, (Mughnee, Ḳ,) accord. to the most correct opinion: (Mughnee:) accord. to Th, it is so because there is no negation in the beginning of the sentence. (T.) And it is also said in the Ḳur [iv. 69], (T,) مَا فَعَلُوهُ إِلَّا قَلِيلٌ مِنْهُمْ [*They had not done it*, or *they would not do it, except a few of them*]: (T, Mughnee, Ḳ:) here قليل is in the nom. case as being a partial substitute, (Mughnee, Ḳ,) accord. to the Baṣrees, (Mughnee,) i.e., as being a [partial] substitute for the [pronoun] و [in فعلوه], for it may here be so without perversion of the meaning, whereas it cannot be so without such perversion when the sentence is affirmative: (TA:) accord. to the Koofees, إِلَّا is a conjunction, like the conjunctive لَا: (Mughnee:) accord. to Th, قليل is here in the nom. case because the sentence commences with a negative: (T:) or in a sentence [like this,] which is not affirmative, in which the thing excepted is united in kind to that from which the exception is made, accord. to the opinion which is generally preferred and which commonly obtains, the noun signifying the thing excepted is a substitute for the noun signifying that from which the exception is made; but it is allowable to put it in the accus. case according to the general rule respecting exception; so that one says, مَا قَامَ أَحَدٌ إِلَّا زَيْدٌ and إِلَّا زَيْدًا [*There stood not any one, except Zeyd*]: and the same is the case in a prohibitive sentence; as in لَا يَقُمْ أَحَدٌ إِلَّا زَيْدٌ and إِلَّا زَيْدًا [*Let not any one stand, except Zeyd*]; and in an interrogative sentence; as in هَلْ قَامَ أَحَدٌ إِلَّا زَيْدٌ and إِلَّا زَيْدًا [*Did any one stand, except Zeyd?*]; when, in such sentences, the thing excepted is united in kind to that from which the exception is made. (I 'Aḳ p. 162.) You say also, مَا جَآءَنِى إِلَّا زَيْدٌ [*There came not to me any, save Zeyd*], without mentioning that from which the exception is made; (TA;) and مَا ضَرَبْتُ إِلَّا زَيْدًا [*I beat not any, save Zeyd*]; and مَا مَرَرْتُ إِلَّا بِزَيْدٍ [*I passed not by any, save by Zeyd*]; (I 'Aḳ p. 164;) the case of the noun signifying the thing excepted being the same as if الا were not mentioned: (I 'Aḳ ubi suprà, and TA:*) but you may not say, affirmatively, ضَرَبْتُ إِلَّا زَيْدًا, or the like. (I 'Aḳ ubi suprà.) When the thing excepted precedes that from which the exception is made, if the sentence is affirmative, the noun signifying the former must be in the accus. case; as in قَامَ إِلَّا زَيْدًا القَوْمُ [*Except Zeyd, the people*, or *company of men, stood*]: and so, accord. to the usage generally preferred, when the sentence is not affirmative; as in مَا قَامَ إِلَّا زَيْدًا القَوْمُ [*Except Zeyd, the people*, or *company of men, stood not*]; but recorded instances allow one's saying also, مَا قَامَ إِلَّا زَيْدٌ القَوْمُ. (I 'Aḳ p. 163.) When the thing excepted is disunited in kind from that from which the exception is made, if the sentence is affirmative, the noun signifying the former must likewise be in the accus. case; as in قَامَ القَوْمُ إِلَّا حِمَارًا [*The people*, or *company of men, stood, but* *not an ass*], and ضَرَبْتُ القَوْمَ إِلَّا حِمَارًا [*I beat the people, but not an ass*], &c.: (I 'Aḳ p. 162:) and so, accord. to the generality of the Arabs, when the sentence is negative; as in مَا قَامَ القَوْمُ إِلَّا حِمَارًا [*The people stood not, but an ass*]; (I 'Aḳ p. 163;) and مَا رَأَيْتُ القَوْمَ إِلَّا حِمَارًا [*I saw not the people, but an ass*]; إِلَّا being here syn. with لٰكِنَّ; as also in the Ḳur [xlii. 22], where it is said, لَا أَسْأَلُكُمْ عَلَيْهِ أَجْرًا إِلَّا ٱلْمَوَدَّةَ فِى ٱلْقُرْبَى [*I ask not of you a recompense for it, but affection in respect of relationship*]; (Mṣb;) and in the same xx. 1 and 2, مَا أَنْزَلْنَا عَلَيْكَ ٱلْقُرْآنَ لِتَشْقَى إِلَّا تَذْكِرَةً [*We have not sent down unto thee the Ḳur-án that thou shouldest suffer fatigue, but as an admonition*]; (Bḍ, Jel;) or it is here syn. with بَلْ [which in this case means the same as لٰكِنَّ]: (Ṣ:) so, too, when the sentence resembles a negative, being prohibitive or interrogative; (I 'Aḳ p. 163, explained in p. 162;) [thus, لَا تَضْرِبِ القَوْمَ إِلَّا حِمَارًا means *Beat not thou the people, but an ass*; and] فَلَوْلَا كَانَتْ قَرْيَةٌ آمَنَتْ فَنَفَعَهَا إِيمَانُهَا إِلَّا قَوْمَ يُونُسَ [in the Ḳur x. 98] means *And wherefore did not any* inhabitants of a *town believe*, before the punishment befell them, *and their belief profit them, but the people of Jonas?* for these were different from the former. (T.) When إِلَّا is repeated for the purpose of corroboration, it has no effect upon what follows it, except that of corroborating the first exception; as in مَا مَرَرْتُ بِأَحَدٍ إِلَّا زَيْدٍ إِلَّا أَخِيكَ [*I passed not by any one, except Zeyd, except thy brother*], in which اخيك is a substitute for زيد, for it is as though you said, مَا مَرَرْتُ بِأَحَدٍ إِلَّا زَيْدٍ أَخِيكَ; and as in قَامَ القَوْمُ إِلَّا زَيْدًا وَإِلَّا عَمْرًا [*The people stood, except Zeyd, and except 'Amr*], originally إِلَّا زَيْدًا وَعَمْرًا. When the repetition is not for that purpose, if the sentence is devoid of the mention of that from which the exception is made, you make the governing word [which is the verb] to affect one, whichever you please, of the nouns signifying the things excepted, and put the others in the accus. case, so that you say, مَا قَامَ إِلَّا زَيْدٌ إِلَّا عَمْرًا إِلَّا بَكْرًا [*There stood not any, save Zeyd, save 'Amr, save Bekr*]; but if the sentence is not devoid of the mention of that from which the exception is made, different rules are observed accord. as the things excepted are mentioned before that from which the exception is made or after it: in the former case, all must be put in the accus., whether the sentence be affirmative or not affirmative; as in قَامَ إِلَّا زَيْدًا إِلَّا عَمْرًا إِلَّا بَكْرًا القَوْمُ [*Except Zeyd, except 'Amr, except Bekr, the people stood*], and مَا قَامَ إِلَّا زَيْدًا إِلَّا عَمْرًا إِلَّا بَكْرًا القَوْمُ [*Except Zeyd, except 'Amr, except Bekr, the people stood not*]: in the latter case, when the sentence is affirmative, all must likewise be put in the accus., so that you say, قَامَ القَوْمُ إِلَّا زَيْدًا إِلَّا عَمْرًا إِلَّا بَكْرًا [*The people stood, except Zeyd, except 'Amr, except Bekr*]; but when the sentence is not affirmative, the same rule is observed with respect to one of them as when the exception is not repeated, accord. to the usage generally preferred, or it may be put in the accus., which is rarely done, and the rest must be put in the accus., so that you say, مَا قَامَ أَحَدٌ إِلَّا زَيْدٌ إِلَّا عَمْرًا إِلَّا بَكْرًا [*There stood not any one, except Zeyd, except 'Amr, except Bekr*, accord. to the more approved usage], زيد being a substitute for احد, or you may make the other nouns which remain to be substitutes. (I 'Aḳ pp. 164—166.) — Secondly, (Mughnee,) it is used as a qualificative, (Ṣ, Mṣb, Mughnee, Ḳ,) in the manner of غَيْرٌ, (Mughnee, Ḳ,) [i. e.] in the place of غَيْرٌ, (Ṣ,) [i. e.] as *syn. with* غَيْرٌ, (T, Mṣb,) *and* سِوَى; (T;) [both meaning the same, i. e. *Other than*; or *not*, as used before a subst. or an adjective;] but its primary application is to denote exception, and its use as a qualificative is adventitious; whereas the primary application of غَيْرٌ is as a qualificative, and its use to denote exception is adventitious. (Ṣ.) It [generally] follows an indeterminate, unrestricted pl.; (Mṣb;) or an indeterminate pl., or the like thereof, is qualified by it and by that which follows it; (Mughnee, Ḳ;) the noun which follows it being put in the same case as that which precedes it. (Ṣ.) The following is an ex. of the indeterminate pl.: (Mughnee, Ḳ:) لَوْ كَانَ فِيهِمَا آلِهَةٌ إِلَّا ٱللّٰهُ لَفَسَدَتَا [*If there had been in them* (namely the heavens and the earth) *deities other than God*, or *not God, assuredly they would have become in a state of disorder*, or *ruin*; occurring in the Ḳur xxi. 22]; (Fr, T, Ṣ, Mṣb, Mughnee, Ḳ;) الّا here meaning سِوَى, (Fr, T,) or غَيْرٌ, (Mṣb, TA,) and الّا الله being a qualificative of آلِهَةٌ. (TA.) And the following is an ex. of the like of an indeterminate pl.:

أُنِيخَتْ فَأَلْقَتْ بَلْدَةً فَوْقَ بَلْدَةٍ
قَلِيلٍ بِهَا الأَصْوَاتُ إِلَّا بُغَامُهَا

[*She* (the camel) *was made to lie down, and threw her breast upon a tract of ground in which were few sounds other than her broken yearning cry for her young one*]; for the determination of الاصوات [by the article ال] is generical: (Mughnee, Ḳ:) this verse is by Dhu-r-Rummeh. (Ṣ in art. بلد.) The following is an ex. of the like of a pl.: (Mughnee:) it is by Lebeed: (T:)

لَوْ كَانَ غَيْرِى سُلَيْمَى اليَوْمَ غَيَّرَهُ
وَقْعُ الحَوَادِثِ إِلَّا الصَّارِمُ الذَّكَرُ

[*If it had been other than I,* (O) *Suleymá, today, the befalling of misfortunes would have altered him; other than the sharp sword diversified with wavy marks* or *streaks* or *grain*, or *of which the edge is of steel and the middle of the broad side of soft iron*]. (T, Mughnee. [But in the latter, in the place of اليَوْمَ, I find الدَّهْرَ, i. e. *ever*.]) What Sb says necessarily implies its not being a condition that the word qualified must be a pl. or the like thereof; for he gives as an ex., لَوْ كَانَ مَعَنَا رَجُلٌ إِلَّا زَيْدٌ لَغُلِبْنَا [*If there had been with us a man other than Zeyd, we should have been overcome*]. (Mughnee.) Another ex. of the same usage of إِلَّا is the following: جَآءَنِى القَوْمُ إِلَّا زَيْدٌ [*The people came to me, others than Zeyd*, or *not Zeyd*]. (Ṣ.) [And مَا أَنْتُمْ إِلَّا بَشَرٌ مِثْلُنَا *Ye are no other than human beings like us*. (Ḳur xxxvi. 14.)] And the saying [in the Ḳur xliv. 56], لَا يَذُوقُونَ فِيهَا ٱلْمَوْتَ إِلَّا ٱلْمَوْتَةَ ٱلْأُولَى [*They shall not taste therein death, other than the first death*]; الّا here meaning سِوَى: (T:) or, accord. to some, it here means بَعْدَ [*after*]. (Jel.) And the saying of 'Amr Ibn-Maạdee-kerib,

وَكُلُّ أَخٍ مُفَارِقُهُ أَخُوهُ
لَعَمْرُ أَبِيكَ إِلَّا الفَرْقَدَانِ

[*And every brother, his brother forsakes him*, or *separates himself from him, by the life of thy father, other than the Farḳadán*; which is the name of the two stars β and γ of Ursa Minor]; as though he said غَيْرُ الفَرْقَدَيْنِ: (Ṣ:) but Ibn-El-Ḥájib regards this instance as a deviation from a general rule; for he makes it a condition of the use of الّا as a qualificative that it must be impossible to use it for the purpose of denoting exception: (Mughnee:) Fr says that this verse has the meaning of a negation, and therefore الّا here governs the nom. case; as though the poet said, There is not any one but his brother forsakes him, except the Farḳadán. (T.) When it is used as a qualificative, it differs from غَيْرٌ inasmuch as that the noun qualified by it may not be suppressed; so that one may not say, جَآءَنِى إِلَّا زَيْدٌ [meaning *There came to me not Zeyd*]; whereas one says, جَآءَنِى غَيْرُ زَيْدٍ: and, accord. to some, in this also; that it may not be used as such unless it may be used to denote exception; so that one may say, عِنْدِى دِرْهَمٌ إِلَّا دَانِقٌ [*I have a dirhem, not a dánik*], because one may say إِلَّا دَانِقًا [*except a dánik*]; but not إِلَّا جَيِّدٌ [*not a good one*], because one may not say إِلَّا جَيِّدًا [*except a good one*]; but it may be said that this is at variance with what they assert respecting the phrase لَوْ كَانَ فِيهِمَا آلِهَةٌ, and with the ex. given by Sb, and with the saying of Ibn-El-Ḥájib mentioned above. (Mughnee.) — Thirdly, (Mughnee,) sometimes, (Ṣ, Mṣb,) it is used as a conjunction, (Mughnee, Ḳ,) in the manner of وَ, (Ṣ, Mughnee, Ḳ,) consociating both literally and as to the meaning, as mentioned by Akh and Fr and AO, (Mughnee,) [i. e.] as *syn. with* وَ [*And*]. (Mṣb.) Thus in the saying, لِئَلَّا يَكُونَ لِلنَّاسِ عَلَيْكُمْ حُجَّةٌ إِلَّا ٱلَّذِينَ ظَلَمُوا [*That there may not be to men, against you, any allegation, and* (meaning *nor*) *to those who have acted wrongfully*]; (Mṣb, Mughnee, Ḳ;) occurring in the Ḳur [ii. 145]; (Mṣb;) so accord. to Akh and Fr and AO; (Mughnee;) i. e., and those who have acted wrongfully also, to them there shall not be, against you, any allegation: (Mṣb:) Fr explains it as meaning that the wrongdoer has no allegation of which account should be taken; and this is correct, and is the opinion held by Zj. (T.) Thus, too, in the saying [in the Ḳur xxvii. 10 and 11], لَا يَخَافُ لَدَىَّ ٱلْمُرْسَلُونَ إِلَّا مَنْ ظَلَمَ ثُمَّ بَدَّلَ حُسْنًا بَعْدَ سُوْءٍ [*The apostles shall not fear in my presence, and* neither shall *he who hath acted wrongfully, then hath done good instead, after evil*; as some explain it; but others say that الّا here denotes exception]. (Mughnee, in which it is explained as meaning وَلَا مَنْ ظَلَمَ; and Ḳ.) And thus in the saying of the poet, [namely, El-Mukhabbal Es-Saạdee, (Ṣ in art. خلد,)]

وَأَرَى لَهَا دَارًا بِأَغْدِرَةِ السِّـ • سِيدَانِ لَمْ يَدْرُسْ لَهَا رَسْمُ •
إِلَّا رَمَادًا هَامِدًا دَفَعَتْ • عَنْهُ الرِّيَاحَ خَوَالِدٌ سُحْمُ •

[*And I see a dwelling* formerly *belonging to her, at the pools of Es-Seedán*, (a hill so called,) *the remains of which have not become effaced, and ashes wasted and compacted together, from which three black pieces of stone whereon the cooking-pot was wont to be placed turned back the winds*]: he means, أَرَى لَهَا دَارًا وَرَمَادًا. (Ṣ.) — Fourthly, (Mughnee,) it is redundant, as in the following verse, (Ṣ in art. فلذ, Mughnee, Ḳ,) of Dhu-r-Rummeh, (Ṣ ubi suprà, Mughnee,) accord. to Aṣ and IJ: (Mughnee:)

حَرَاجِيجُ مَا تَنْفَكُّ إِلَّا مُنَاخَةً • عَلَى الْخَسْفِ أَوْ نَرْمِى بِهَا بَلَدًا قَفْرَا •

[She-camels *long-bodied*, or *lean*, (but other meanings are assigned to the word which I thus render,) *that cease not to be made to lie down in a state of hunger, or with which we direct our course to a desert region*]; (Ṣ ubi suprà, Mughnee; [but in one copy of the former, in the place of نَرْمِى, I find يُرْمَى; and in my copy of the latter, تَرْمِى;]) meaning, ما تنفكّ مناخةً: (Ṣ ubi suprà:) but it is said that this is a mistake of the poet: (Mughnee:) so says Aboo-'Amr Ibn-El-'Alà; for, he says, إِلَّا is not to be introduced after تَنْفَكُّ and تَزَالُ: (TA:) and some say that the right reading is إِلًّا, with tenween, [perhaps a mistranscription, for آلًا,] meaning شَخْصًا [in a pl. sense]: and some, that تنفكّ is a complete [or an attributive] verb, and مناخة is a denotative of state; [consequently, that إِلَّا is a compound of إِنْ and لَا, as in some other instances hereafter to be mentioned;] the meaning being, *that are not disengaged*, or *not free, from fatigue* [*unless when made to lie down*]. (Mughnee.) The following is also given as an ex. of the same kind:

أَرَى الدَّهْرَ إِلَّا مَنْجَنُونًا بِأَهْلِهِ •

[*I see fortune*, or *time*, to be like *a water-wheel, with its people*]: but the reading which is remembered to have been heard is وَمَا الدَّهْرُ: and if the former be correct, it may be explained on the supposition that ارى is the complement of an oath meant to be understood, and that لا is suppressed, as in [the saying in the Ḳur xii. 85,] تَاللّٰهِ تَفْتَأُ تَذْكُرُ يُوسُفَ; [so that the meaning is, *I see not fortune*, or *time*, to be aught *save a water-wheel, with its people*;] the form of the exceptive sentence which is devoid of the mention of that from which the exception is made indicating such an explanation. (Mughnee.) — [Fifthly,] it occurs as *syn. with* لَمَّا [as a particle denoting exception, equivalent to our *But*; meaning both *except* and (after an oath or the like) *only*, or *nothing more than*]; as in the saying in the Ḳur [xxxviii. 13], إِنْ كُلٌّ إِلَّا كَذَّبَ الرُّسُلَ [*There was not any one but* such as *accused the apostles of lying*], in which 'Abd-Allah reads, in its place, لَمَّا; and for كُلٌّ he reads كُلُّهُمْ; and as in the saying, أَسْأَلُكَ بِاللّٰهِ إِلَّا أَعْطَيْتَنِى [*I ask*, or *beg*, or *beseech, thee by God but that thou give me*; i. e., I do not ask of thee anything save thy giving me; the preterite here, as in many instances in which it is preceded by لَمَّا (q. v.), not being a preterite in meaning]; for which one says also لَمَّا اعطيتنى. (T.) ═ It is also a particle [or rather a compound of two words] denoting the complement of a condition; originally إِنْ لَا, which form a compound that does not admit of [the pronunciation termed] imáleh, because إِنْ and لَا are particles. (T.) [It signifies, lit., *If not.*] It is followed by a fut., which it renders mejzoom; [and in this case it may be rendered as above, or by *unless*;] as in the saying in the Ḳur [viii. 74], إِلَّا تَفْعَلُوهُ تَكُنْ فِتْنَةٌ فِى الْأَرْضِ [*If ye do it not*, or *unless ye do it, there will be a weakness of faith and an appearing of unbelief in the earth*]. (T.) [In like manner,] in a saying such as the following, [in the Ḳur ix. 40,] إِلَّا تَنْصُرُوهُ فَقَدْ نَصَرَهُ اللّٰهُ [*If ye do not*, or *will not, aid him, certainly God aided him*], it is only a compound of two words, the conditional إِنْ and the negative لَا, and is distinct from إِلَّا of which the usages have been mentioned before, though Ibn-Málik has included it therewith. (Mughnee.) [Often in post-classical works, and perhaps in classical also, but seldom except when it is preceded by a condition with its complement, the verb or verbal proposition which should immediately follow it is suppressed; as in the like of the saying, إِنْ فَعَلْتَ كَذَا عَفَوْتُ عَنْكَ وَإِلَّا قَتَلْتُكَ *If thou do such a thing, I forgive thee*, or *cancel thine offence; but if* thou wilt *not* do it (i. e., إِلَّا تَفْعَلْهُ,) *I kill thee*: sometimes also it ends a sentence, by an aposiopesis; the whole of what should follow it being suppressed: and sometimes the complement of the condition which precedes, as well as the verb or verbal proposition which should immediately follow it, is suppressed; so that you say, إِنْ فَعَلْتَ كَذَا وَإِلَّا قَتَلْتُكَ *If thou do such a thing*, excellent will it be, or the like, (فَنِعِمَّا هُوَ, or the like, being understood,) *but if not, I kill thee*. Hence,] it sometimes has the meaning of إِمَّا, [signifying *Or*, denoting an alternative, corresponding to a preceding إِمَّا, which signifies "either,"] as in the saying, إِمَّا أَنْ تُكَلِّمَنِى وَإِلَّا فَاسْكُتْ [*Either do thou speak to me or else* (meaning وَإِلَّا تُكَلِّمْنِى *or if thou wilt not speak to me*) *be silent*], i. e., وَإِمَّا أَنْ تَسْكُتَ. (Ṣ.) [It is also followed by أَنْ, as in إِلَّا أَنْ يَشَآءَ اللّٰهُ *Unless God should please*; in the Ḳur vi. 111, &c. And by و as a denotative of state, as in لَا تَمُوتُنَّ إِلَّا وَأَنْتُمْ مُسْلِمُونَ *Do not ye die unless ye be Muslims*; in the Ḳur ii. 126 and iii. 97. And sometimes it is preceded by أَللّٰهُمَّ; for the effect of which, in this case, see art. اله.]

الب

1. أَلَبَ, (Th, M, Ḳ,) aor. ـِ and ـُ, inf. n. أَلْبٌ, (M,) *It* (a thing, Th, M) *was*, or *became, collected*; or *compact*; syn. اِجْتَمَعَ; (Th, Ḳ;) or تَجَمَّعَ. (M.) — أَلَبَ إِلَيْهِ الْقَوْمُ *The people came to him from every direction*: (M, Ḳ:) or أَلَبَ الْقَوْمُ [signifies *the people multiplied themselves, and hastened*; for it] denotes الإِكْثَار and الإِسْرَاع: (T in art. ضبب:) and أَلَبَ, (T, Ḳ,) aor. as above, (T,) signifies *he hastened*, or *went quickly*. (T, Ḳ.) — أَلَبَتِ الإِبِلُ *The camels obeyed the driver, and collected themselves together*. (M, Ḳ.) [See also 5.] — أَلَبَ إِلَيْهِ *He returned to him*, or *it*. (Ḳ,* TA.) — أَلَبَتِ السَّمَآءُ, (M, Ḳ,) aor. ـِ, (M,) *The sky rained with long continuance*. (M, Ḳ.) ═ أَلَبَ, (Ṣ, Mṣb, Ḳ,) aor. ـِ, inf. n. أَلْبٌ, (Mṣb,) *He collected* (Ṣ, Mṣb, Ḳ) an army, (Ṣ,) or a people; (Mṣb;) as also ↓ أَلَّبَ, (M,) inf. n. تَأْلِيبٌ: (TA:) and camels also: (TA:) or أَلَبَ الإِبِلَ aor. ـِ (T,* Ṣ, M, Ḳ) and ـُ, (Ṣ, M, Ḳ,) inf. n. أَلْبٌ, (T, Ṣ,) signifies *he collected the camels, and drove them* (Ṣ, TA) *vehemently*: (TA:) or *he drove them*: (T,* Ḳ:) or *he drove them vehemently*. (M.) — أَلَبَ, (TA,) inf. n. as above, (Ḳ, TA,) also signifies *He drove, pursued, chased*, or *hunted, with vehemence*: (Ḳ, TA:) and *he drove away* a people. (Mṣb.) You say, أَلَبَ الْحِمَارُ طَرِيدَتَهُ *The* [wild] *ass chased*, or *pursued, the object of his chase* [i. e. his female, as is shown by MF,] *with vehemence*; (M, Ḳ;) as also ↓ أَلَّبَهَا. (Ḳ.)

2: see 1, in two places. — تَأْلِيبٌ also signifies The act of *exciting, instigating*, or *rousing to ardour*: (Ṣ, Ḳ:) and the *exciting of discord*, or *strife*, or the *making of mischief*. (Ḳ.) You say, أَلَّبَ بَيْنَهُمْ *He excited discord* or *strife*, or *made mischief, between them*. (M.)

5. تَأَلَّبُوا *They collected themselves together*. (Ṣ, A, Mṣb.) [See also 1.] You say also, تَأَلَّبُوا عَلَيْهِ *They leagued together*, or *collected themselves together, and aided one another, against him*. (T.)

أَلْبٌ (T, Ṣ, Mṣb) and ↓ إِلْبٌ (Ṣ, Mṣb) *Persons*, or *people, collected together*; (Ṣ;) *an assembly*; *a collected body*: (Mṣb:) or *a collection of many people*: (T:) and ↓ أَلْبٌ أَلُوبٌ *a great assembly* or *congregation*. (M.) — Also *A people*, or *company of men, combining in hostility* against a man. (TA, from a trad.) You say, هُمْ عَلَيْهِ أَلْبٌ وَاحِدٌ, and ↓ إِلْبٌ, (but the former is the better known, M,) *They are* [*one body of men*] *assembled against him with injustice and enmity* or *hostility*: (Lth, T, M, Ḳ:) like وَعْلٌ وَاحِدٌ and صَدْعٌ وَاحِدٌ and ضِلَعٌ وَاحِدٌ. (T, TA.)

إِلْبٌ: see أَلْبٌ, in two places.

أَلَبٌ a dial. var. of يَلَبٌ; (M;) *Helmets of camels' skins*: or, as some say, it signifies *steel*: (T:) أَلَبَةٌ is [its n. un., being] a dial. var. of يَلَبَةٌ. (Ḳ,* TA.) [See also يَلَبٌ.]

أَلُوبٌ: see أَلْبٌ. — Also One *who hastens*, or *is quick*; (T;) and ↓ مِئْلَبٌ likewise signifies [the same; or] *quick*, or *swift*: (Ibn-Buzurj, T, Ḳ:) or the former signifies *quick in drawing forth the bucket*: (IAạr, M, Ḳ:) or *brisk, lively, sprightly, active, agile*, or *prompt, and quick*; (Ḳ, TA;)

applied to a man. (TA.) —— رِيحٌ أَلُوبٌ *A cold wind,* (M,) *that raises and scatters the dust.* (M, Ḳ.) —— سَمَآءٌ أَلُوبٌ *A sky raining with long continuance.* (M.)

أَلُوبٌ : see مِئْلَبٌ.

حَسُودٌ مُؤَلِّبٌ [An *envious* man,] *who excites discord* or *strife,* or *makes mischief.* (Ṣ,* TA.)

الت

1. أَلَتَ, aor. ـِ , inf. n. أَلْتٌ, *It* (a thing) *decreased; diminished; lessened; became defective, deficient, incomplete,* or *imperfect.* (Mṣb.) ═ أَلَتَهُ حَقَّهُ, (Ṣ, M, A, Ḳ,) aor. ـِ , (Ṣ, M, Ḳ,) inf. n. أَلْتٌ (Ṣ, M) and إِلَاتَةٌ; (M;) and أَلِتَهُ, aor. ـَ; (Fr;) and ▼ آلَتَهُ, (M, Ḳ,) inf. n. إِيلَاتٌ; (Ḳ;) as also أَلاَتَهُ, inf. n. إِلَاتٌ, (so in a MS. copy of the Ḳ,) or إِلَاتَةٌ; (so in the L: [agreeably with analogy, and therefore probably the correct reading: see art. ليت, to which it belongs: in SM's copy of the Ḳ, and in the CḲ, the verb is written أَلاَتَهُ, and the inf. n. إِلَاتٌ: by MF, the verb is written ▼ آلَتَهُ, of the measure فَاعَلَ, and the inf. n. إِلَاتٌ, like قِتَالٌ:]) [and لَاتَهُ, aor. يَلِيتُ; and وَلَتَهُ; and أَوْلَتَهُ;] *He diminished to him his right,* or *due; abridged him,* or *defrauded him, of a portion of it:* (Fr, Ṣ, M, A, Ḳ:) and in like manner, أَلَتَهُ مَالَهُ, and ▼ آلَتَهُ, &c., *he diminished to him his property;* or *abridged him,* or *defrauded him, of a portion of it:* (M, TA:) and أَلَتَ الشَّىْءَ *he diminished the thing.* (Mṣb.) [Hence,] مَا أَلَتْنَاهُمْ مِنْ عَمَلِهِمْ مِنْ شَىْءٍ [in the Ḳur lii. 21, *We will not diminish to them aught of* the reward *of their work*]: (T, A:) or, accord. to one reading, (that of Ibn-Ketheer, TA,) مَا أَلِتْنَاهُمْ. (T, TA.) [See also art. ليت.] ═ أَلَتَهُ, (T, Ṣ, Ḳ,) or أَلَتَهُ عَنْ وَجْهِهِ, (TA,) aor. ـِ; (T;) as also لَاتَهُ; these being two dial. vars., one of the other, mentioned by Yz, on the authority of AA; (Ṣ;) [and أَلاَتَهُ; (see art. ليت;)] *He withheld him,* or *restrained him,* (Ṣ, Ḳ,) and *turned him,* or *averted him,* (T, Ṣ, Ḳ,) *from his course, purpose,* or *object.* (Ṣ, TA.) ═ أَلَتَهُ, (M, Ḳ,) or أَلَتَهُ يَمِينًا, (Aṣ, T, Ṣ,) aor. ـِ , inf. n. أَلْتٌ, *He made him to swear,* or *take an oath:* (Aṣ, T, Ṣ, Ḳ:) or *he desired of him that he should swear,* or *give his testimony, for him.* (M, Ḳ.) And أَلَتَهُ بِيَمِينٍ, inf. n. as above, *He pressed him,* or *pressed hard upon him, with an oath.* (M.) It is related that a man said to 'Omar, "Fear God, O prince of the faithful:" and another, hearing him, said, أَتَأْلِتُ عَلَى أَمِيرِ الْمُؤْمِنِينَ, meaning *Dost thou lower the dignity of the prince of the faithful?* or *dost thou diminish to him* [*the respect that is due to him*]? accord. to IAạr.: or rather, *dost thou conjure the prince of the faithful?* his saying "Fear God" being as though he conjured him by God: for the Arabs say, أَلَتُّكَ بِاللّٰهِ لَمَّا فَعَلْتَ كَذَا, meaning *I conjure thee by God but that thou do thus,* or *such a thing.* (T.)

3: see 1.

4: see 1, in two places.

أَلْتٌ *Deficiency:* as in the saying مَا فِى مَزَاوِدِهِمْ أَلْتٌ [*There is not, in their provision-bags, any deficiency*]. (A.) ═ *A swearing;* syn. حَلِفٌ. (M, TA.) [Perhaps an inf. n. in this sense.] —— *An oath:* as in the saying, when one has not given thee thy right, or due, قَيِّدْهُ بِالأَلْتِ [*Bind thou him by oath*]. (T.) ═ *Calumny, slander,* or *false accusation.* (Kr, M, Ḳ.) [Perhaps an inf. n. in this sense also.]

أَلْتَةٌ *A small gift.* (AA, T, Ḳ.) ═ *An oath such as is termed* غَمُوسٌ, q. v. (AA, T, Ḳ.)

الد

إِلَادَةٌ &c. for وِلَادَةٌ &c.: see art. ولد.

الف

1. أَلِفَهُ, (T, Ṣ, M, Mṣb, Ḳ,) aor. ـَ , (Ṣ, Mṣb, Ḳ,) inf. n. إِلْفٌ (Ṣ, M, Mṣb, Ḳ) and أَلْفٌ (Ḳ) and إِلَافٌ and وِلَافٌ, which is anomalous, and أَلَفَانٌ, (M, TA,) *He kept,* or *clave, to it;* (A'Obeyd, T, M, Mṣb,* TA;) namely, a thing, (A'Obeyd, T, M, TA,) or a place; (Ṣ, Mṣb, TA;) as also أَلَفَهُ, aor. ـِ; (TA;) and ▼ آلَفَهُ, (A'Obeyd, T, Ṣ, M, Mṣb,) aor. يُؤْلِفُ, (Ṣ, TA,) inf. n. إِيلَافٌ; (Ṣ, Mṣb, TA;) and ▼ آلَفَهُ, aor. يُؤَالِفُ, inf. n. مُؤَالَفَةٌ and إِلَافٌ: (Ṣ, Mṣb, TA:) [*he frequented it,* or *resorted to it habitually;* namely, a place:] *he became familiar with it;* or *accustomed,* or *habituated, to it;* namely, a thing: (AZ, T:) *he became familiar, sociable, companionable, friendly,* or *amicable, with him:* (AZ, T, Mṣb:) *he loved,* or *affected, him; liked, approved,* or *took pleasure in, him.* (Mṣb.) You say, أَلِفَتِ الطَّيْرُ الحَرَمَ [*The birds kept to the sacred territory*], and البُيُوتَ [*the houses*]: and آلَفَتِ ▼ الظِّبَآءُ الرَّمْلَ *The gazelles kept to the sands.* (T.) —— There are three manners of reading the passage in the Ḳur [cvi. 1 and 2], لِإِيلَافِ قُرَيْشٍ ▼ إِيلَافِهِمْ رِحْلَةَ الشِّتَآءِ وَالصَّيْفِ; the second and third being لِإِلَافِ and لِإِلْفِ; the first and second of which have been adopted; (Aboo-Is-ḥáḳ, T, TA;) and the third also; this being the reading of the Prophet [himself]: (TA:) [accord. to all these readings, the passage may be rendered, *For the keeping of Ḳureysh, for their keeping to the journey of the winter and of the summer,* or *spring;* the chapter going on to say, for this reason "let them worship the Lord of this House," &c.: or] the second and third readings are from أَلِفَ, aor. يَأْلَفُ; [and accord. to these readings, the passage may be rendered as above;] but accord. to the first reading, the meaning is, *for the preparing and fitting out* [&c.; i. e., *preparing and fitting out* men and beasts *in the journey of the winter* &c.]: so says IAmb; and Fr explains in the same manner the third reading: but IAạr says that, accord. to this reading, the meaning is, *the protecting* [&c.]: he says that the persons who protected were four brothers, Háshim and 'Abd-Shems and El-Muttalib and Nowfal, the sons of 'Abd-Menáf: these gave protection to Ḳureysh in their procuring of corn: (T:) Háshim obtained a grant of security from the king of the Greeks, and Nowfal from Kisrà, and 'Abd-Shems from the Nejáshee, and El-Muttalib from the kings of Ḥimyer; and the merchants of Ḳureysh used to go to and from the great towns of these kings with the grants of security of these brothers, and none opposed them: Háshim used to give protection (يُؤْلِفُ [in the copies of the Ḳ يُؤَلِّفُ]) [to those journeying] to Syria, and 'Abd-Shems to Abyssinia, and El-Muttalib to El-Yemen, and Nowfal to Persia: (T, Ḳ:*) or ▼ إِيلَافٌ in the Ḳur signifies *a covenant,* or *an obligation;* and *what resembles permission,* (إِجَازَةٌ, as in some copies of the Ḳ and in the TA,) or *protection,* (إِجَارَةٌ, as in the CḲ,) *with an obligation involving responsibility for safety;* first obtained by Háshim, from the kings of Syria; (Ḳ,* TA;) and the explanation is, that Ḳureysh were dwelling in the sacred territory, (Ḳ,) having neither seed-produce nor udders [to yield them milk], (TA,) secure in the procuring of their provisions from other parts, and in their changes of place, in winter and summer, or spring; the people around them having their property seized; whereas, when any cause of mischief occurred to them, they said, "We are people of the sacred territory," and then no one opposed them: (Ḳ:) so in the O: (TA:) or the ل is to denote wonder; and the meaning is, *wonder ye at the* ايلاف *of Ḳureysh* [&c.]: (Ḳ:) some say that the meaning is connected with what follows; i. e., let them worship the Lord of this House for the ايلاف [&c., agreeably with the first explanation which we have given]: others, that it is connected with what precedes; as J says; (TA;) the meaning being, I have destroyed the masters of the elephant *to make Ḳureysh remain* at Mekkeh, and *for their uniting the journey of the winter and of the summer,* or *spring;* that when they finished one, they should commence the other; (T, Ṣ;) and this is like the saying, ضَرَبْتُهُ لِكَذَا لِكَذَا, with suppression of the [conjunctive] وَ: (Ṣ:) but Ibn-'Arafeh disapproves of this, for two reasons: first, because the phrase "In the name of God" &c. occurs between the two chapters: [Bd, however, mentions that in Ubei's copy, the two compose one chapter:] secondly, because ايلاف signifies the *covenants,* or *obligations, which they obtained when they went forth on mercantile expeditions, and whereby they became secure.* (TA.) ▼ إِلَافٌ [in like manner] signifies *A writing of security, written by the king for people, that they may be secure in his territory:* and is used by Musáwir Ibn-Hind in the sense of إِيلَافٌ, [as is also إِلْفٌ,] when he says, in satirizing Benoo-Asad,

• زَعَمْتُمْ أَنَّ إِخْوَتَكُمْ قُرَيْشٌ •
• لَهُمْ إِلْفٌ وَلَيْسَ لَكُمْ إِلَافُ •

meaning *Ye asserted* [*that your brothers are Ḳureysh;* i. e.,] *that ye are like Ḳureysh:* but how should ye be like them? for *they have* [*an alliance whereby they are protected in*] the *trade* of El-Yemen and Syria; *and ye have not* that [*alliance*]. (Ḥam p. 636.) [Hence,] إِلَافُ اللّٰهِ, [a phrase used in the manner of an oath,] accord. to some, signifies *The safeguard,* or *protection, of God:* or, accord. to others, *an honourable station from God.* (TA.) ═ أَلَفَهُ, aor. ـُ , *He gave him a thousand*; (Ṣ, Ḳ;) of articles of property, and of camels. (TA.)

2. أَلَّفَ بَيْنَهُمْ, inf. n. تَأْلِيفٌ, (T, Mṣb, Ḳ,) *He united them, or brought them together,* (T, Mṣb, TA,) *after separation;* (T, TA;) *and made them to love one another;* (Mṣb;) *he caused union,* or *companionship,* (أُلْفَة,) *to take place between them.* (Ḳ.) And أَلَّفْتُ بَيْنَ الشَّيْئَيْنِ, inf. n. as above, [*I united, or put together, the two things.*] (Ṣ.) And أَلَّفَ الشَّىْءَ *He united, or connected,* (T,) or *gathered* or *collected* or *brought together,* (M,) *the several parts of the thing.* (T, M.) — Hence, تَأْلِيفُ الكُتُبِ [*The composition of books*]. (T, TA.) — تَأْلِيفٌ is The *putting many things into such a state that one name becomes applicable to them, whether there be to some of the parts a relation to others by precedence and sequence, or not:* so that it is a more general term than تَرْتِيبٌ: (KT:) or the *collecting together*, or *putting together, suitable things;* from الالفة [i. e. الأُلْفَة]; and is a more particular term than تَرْكِيبٌ, which is the putting together things, whether suitable or not, or placed in order or not. (Kull p. 118.) — أَلَّفُوا إِلَى كَذَا: see 5. — أَلَّفَ أَلِفًا *He wrote an alif;* (Ḳ;) like as one says جَمَّمَ جِيمًا. (TA.) — See also 4, in three places.

3. آلَفَهُ: see 1, first sentence. — آلَفَ, (M, TA,) inf. n. مُؤَالَفَةٌ, (TA,) [app., *He made a covenant with another to be protected during a journey for the purpose of trade,* or *traffic:* (see 1:) and hence,] *he* (a man) *traded,* or *trafficked.* (M, TA.) — شَارَطَهُ مُؤَالَفَةً *He made a condition with him for a thousand:* (IAạr, M:) like as one says, شَارَطْتُهُ مُمَاآةً, meaning, for a hundred. (IAạr, M, Ḳ, in art. مأى.)

4. آلَفَهُ, inf. n. إِيلَافٌ: see 1, in three places. — آلَفَهُ الشَّىْءَ, (T, M,) or المَوْضِعَ, (Ṣ,) or مَكَانَ كَذَا, (Ḳ,) inf. n. as above, (T,) *He made him to keep, or cleave, to the thing, or to the place, or to such a place.* (T, Ṣ,* M, Ḳ.*) — آلَفْتُ الشَّىْءَ *I joined, conjoined, or united, the thing.* (T.) — آلَفْتُ القَوْمَ, (T,* Ṣ, Ḳ,*) inf. n. as above, (Ṣ,) *I made the people, or company of men, to be a thousand complete* [*by adding to them myself*]; (T, Ṣ, Ḳ, TA;) they being before nine hundred and ninety-nine. (T, TA.) And آلف العَدَدَ *He made the number to be a thousand;* as also ▼ أَلَّفَهُ: (M:) or آلف ▼ الأَلْفَ *he completed the thousand.* (Ḳ.) And in like manner, (Ṣ,) آلَفْتُ الدَّرَاهِمَ *I made the dirhems to be a thousand* (Ṣ, Ḳ) *complete.* (Ṣ.) And ▼ أَلَّفُوا تُمِرَ الأَعْمَارِ *They said to them, May you live a thousand years.* (A in art. عمر.) — آلَفُوا *They became a thousand* (T, Ṣ, M) *complete.* (Ṣ.) And آلَفَتِ الدَّرَاهِمُ *The dirhems became a thousand* (Ṣ, Ḳ) *complete.* (Ṣ.)

5. تَأَلَّفَ القَوْمُ, (Mṣb, Ḳ,) and ▼ اِئْتَلَفُوا [written with the disjunctive alif اِيتَلَفُوا], (T, Ḳ,) *The people, or party, became united, or came together,* (Mṣb, Ḳ,) [*after separation,* (see 2, of which each is said in the TA to be quasi-pass.,)] *and loved one another:* (Mṣb:) or the meaning of ▼ اِئْتِلَافٌ [and تَأَلُّفٌ also] is the *being in a state of union, alliance, agreement, congruity,* or *congregation:* (Mṣb:) and the *being familiar, sociable, companionable, friendly,* or *amicable, one with another.* (TA.) And تَأَلَّفَا is said of two things; [meaning *They became united,* or *put together;* (see 2;)] as also ▼ ائتلفا. (Ṣ.) And ▼ ائتلف الشَّىْءُ signifies *The several parts of the thing kept,* or *clave, together.* (M.) And تألّف *It became put together in order.* (M.) — تَأَلَّفُوا *They sought, desired,* or *asked,* [*a covenant to ensure them*] *protection,* (IAạr, T, M,) إِلَى كَذَا [meaning in a journey for the purpose of trade, or traffic, *to such a place,* as is shown in the T by an explanation of the words of IAạr, كَانَ هَاشِمٌ يُؤَلِّفُ إِلَى الشَّامِ, in a passage in which the foregoing signification is assigned to تَأَلَّفُوا]; (M;) as also أَلَّفُوا الى كذا. (M.) — تَأَلَّفَهُ *He treated him with gentleness* or *blandishment, coaxed him,* or *wheedled him;* (Ḳ;) *behaved in a sociable, friendly,* or *familiar, manner with him;* (TA;) *attracted him,* or *allured him; and gave him a gift,* or *gifts;* (T, Ḳ;*) *in order to incline him to him:* (Ḳ:) or *he affected sociableness, friendliness,* or *familiarity, with him.* (Mgh.) You say, تَأَلَّفْتُهُ عَلَى الإِسْلَامِ [*I attracted him,* or *allured him; and gave him a gift,* or *gifts, in order to incline him; to embrace El-Islám*]. (Ṣ.)

8: see 5, in four places.

أَلْفٌ, meaning *A certain number,* (Ṣ, M, Ḳ,) *well known,* (M,) i. e. *a certain round number,* (Mṣb,) [namely *a thousand,*] is of the masc. gender: (T, Ṣ, Mṣb, Ḳ:) you say ثَلَاثَةُ آلَافٍ [*Three thousand*], not ثَلَاثُ آلَافٍ; (TA;) and هٰذَا أَلْفٌ وَاحِدٌ [*This is one thousand*], not وَاحِدَةٌ; (Ṣ;) and أَلْفٌ أَقْرَعُ, [*A complete thousand*], (T, Ṣ,) not قَرْعَاءُ: (Ṣ:) it is not allowable to make it fem.: so say IAmb and others: (Mṣb:) or it is allowable to make it fem. as being a pl.: (T:) or, accord. to ISk, it is allowable to say, هٰذِهِ أَلْفٌ as meaning هٰذِهِ الدَّرَاهِمُ أَلْفٌ [*These dirhems are a thousand*]; (Ṣ, Ḳ;*) and Fr and Zj say the like: (Mṣb:) the pl. is آلُفٌ, applied to three, (M,) and آلَافٌ, (T, Ṣ, M, Mṣb, Ḳ,) applied to a number from three to ten, inclusively, (TA,) and أُلُوفٌ, (T, Ṣ, M, Mṣb, Ḳ,) used to denote more than ten; (T;) and الآلُفُ [in the TA الأَلُف] is used by poetic licence for الآلَافُ, by suppression of the [radical] ل. (M.)

إِلْفٌ [originally an inf. n. of أَلِفَهُ, q. v.,] He *with whom one is familiar, sociable, companionable, friendly,* or *amicable;* he *to whom one keeps* or *cleaves;* [*a constant companion* or *associate; a mate; a fellow; a yoke-fellow; one who is familiar, &c., with another* or *others;* (see مُؤَالِفٌ;)] (M;) *i. q.* ▼ أَلِيفٌ; (T, Ṣ, M, Ḳ;) which is an act. part. n. of أَلِفَهُ; (Mṣb;) as is also ▼ آلِفٌ: (Mṣb, Ḳ;) and ▼ أَلْفٌ also is syn. with أَلِيفٌ: (Ḳ:) the female is termed إِلْفَةٌ and إِلْفٌ; (M;) both of these signifying *a woman with whom thou art familiar, &c., and who is familiar, &c., with thee:* (Ḳ:) and the fem. of ▼ آلِفٌ is آلِفَةٌ: (Ḳ:) the pl. of إِلْفٌ is آلَافٌ; (T, M;) which is also pl. of ▼ أَلْفٌ: (TA:) and that of ▼ أَلِيفٌ is الأَلَائِفُ (Ṣ, Ḳ, TA) and أُلَفَاءُ: (M, TA:) and that of ▼ آلِفٌ is أُلَّافٌ (T, Ṣ, Mṣb, Ḳ) and آلَافٌ, like as أَنْصَارٌ is pl. of نَاصِرٌ, (TA,) and so, (M, TA,) in my opinion, [says ISd,] (M,) is أُلُوفٌ, like as شُهُودٌ is pl. of شَاهِدٌ, (M, TA,) though some say that it is pl. of إِلْفٌ: (M:) and the pl. of ▼ آلِفَةٌ is أَوَالِفُ and آلِفَاتٌ. (Ḳ.) You say, فُلَانٌ إِلْفِى and ▼ أَلِيفِى [*Such a one is my constant companion* or *associate, &c.*] (T.) And حَنَّتِ الإِلْفُ إِلَى الإِلْفِ [*The female mate yearned towards the mate*]. (Ṣ.) And نَزَعَ البَعِيرُ إِلَى آلَافِهِ [*The camel yearned towards his mates*]. (T.) أُلَّافٌ, (T,) or آلَافٌ, (TA,) is said by IAạr to mean *Persons who keep to the large towns,* or *cities.* (T, TA.) أُلُوفٌ in the Ḳur ii. 244 is said by some to be pl. of إِلْفٌ or of ▼ آلِفٌ: but by others, to signify "thousands." (Bḍ, L, TA.) ▼ أَوَالِفُ الطَّيْرِ signifies *The birds that keep to Mekkeh and the sacred territory:* and ▼ أَوَالِفُ الحَمَامِ, *Domestic pigeons.* (T.)

أَلِفٌ: see إِلْفٌ, in two places. — As some say, (O,) it also signifies *A man having no wife.* (O, Ḳ.) — *One of the letters of the alphabet;* (M;) the *first thereof;* (Ḳ;) as also ▼ أَلِيفٌ: (M:) Ks says that, accord. to the usage of the Arabs, it is fem., and so are all the other letters of the alphabet; [and hence its pl. is أَلِفَاتٌ;] but it is allowable to make it masc.: Sb says that every one of them is masc. and fem., like as is لِسَانٌ. (M.) See art. ا. — ‡ *A certain vein lying in the interior of the upper arm,* [*extending*] *to the fore arm:* (Ḳ, TA:) so called as being likened to an ا: (TA:) the two are called الأَلِفَانِ. (Ḳ.) — ‡ *One of any kind of things:* (Ḳ, TA:) as being likened to the ا; for it denotes the *number one.* (TA.)

أُلْفَةٌ *A state of keeping* or *cleaving* [to a person or thing]: (M:) *a state of union, alliance, agreement, congruity,* or *congregation;* (Mṣb;) a subst. from الاِئْتِلَافُ: (Mṣb, Ḳ, TA:) and, as such, (TA,) signifying also *familiarity, sociableness, socialness, companionableness, friendliness, fellowship, companionship, friendship,* and *amity.* (Mṣb, TA.*)

أَلْفِىٌّ *Of,* or *relating to,* or *belonging to, the number termed* أَلْفٌ [*a thousand*]. (TA.)

[قَامَةٌ أَلِفِيَّةٌ *A stature resembling the letter alif.* Often occurring in late works.]

إِلَافٌ an inf. n. of أَلِفَهُ: and used as a subst.: see 1. — بَرْقٌ إِلَافٌ *Lightning of which the flashes are consecutive* or *continuous.* (TA.)

أَلُوفٌ *Having much* أُلْفَة [meaning *familiarity, sociableness, &c.*]: pl. أُلُفٌ. (Ḳ.)

أَلِيفٌ: see إِلْفٌ, in three places: — and see أَلِفٌ.

آلِفٌ and آلِفَةٌ; and أَوَالِفُ, the pl. of the latter: see إِلْفٌ, in seven places.

إِيلَافٌ an inf. n.: and used as a subst.: see 1.

مَأْلَفٌ [*An accustomed place;*] *a place to which a man keeps* or *cleaves;* [*which he frequents,* or *to which he habitually resorts;*] *with which he is familiar,* or *to which he is accustomed;* (Mṣb;) *a place with which men* or *camels* [or *birds* and *the like*] *are familiar,* &c. (Ḳ,* TA.) — And hence, *Leafy trees to which animals of the chase draw near.* (AZ, Ḳ.)

مُؤْلِفُونَ, with fet-ḥ, [i. e. مُؤْلَفُونَ or ▼ مُؤَلَّفُونَ,] *Possessors of thousands;* or *men whose camels have become, to each, a thousand.* (TA.)

مُؤَلَّفٌ and ▼ مَأْلُوفٌ *Kept to,* or *clove to;* applied to a thing [and to a person; and meaning when applied to the latter, *with whom one is familiar, sociable,* &c.]. (T.) It is said in a trad., الْمُؤْمِنُ إِلْفٌ ▼ مَأْلُوفٌ [*The believer is one who is familiar,* or *sociable,* &c., *with others,* and *with whom others are familiar,* &c.]. (TA.) — الْمُؤَلَّفَةُ قُلُوبُهُمْ *Those whose hearts are made to incline,* or *are conciliated, by beneficence and love* or *affection:* (Ṣ,* Mṣb:) as used in the Ḳur [ix. 60], it is applied to *certain chief persons of the Arabs, whom the Prophet was commanded to attract,* or *allure, and to present with gifts,* (T, Ḳ,) *from the poor-rates,* (TA,) *in order that they might make those after them desirous of becoming Muslims,* (T, Ḳ,) *and lest care for things which they deemed sacred,* or *inviolable, together with the weakness of their intentions, should induce them to combine in hostility with the unbelievers against the Muslims; for which purpose, he gave them, on the day of Ḥoneyn, eighty* [in the TA *two hundred*] *camels:* (T:) they were *certain men of eminence, of the Arabs, to whom the Prophet used to give gifts from the poor-rates; to some of them, to prevent their acting injuriously; and to some, from a desire of their becoming Muslims,* (Mgh, Mṣb,) *and their followers also;* (Mṣb;) *and to some, in order that they might remain stedfast as Muslims, because of their having recently become such;* but when Aboo-Bekr became appointed to the government, he forbade this practice. (Mgh, Mṣb.) — أَلْفٌ مُؤَلَّفَةٌ [These are *a thousand*] *made complete.* (Ṣ.) — See also مؤلفون.

[مُؤَلِّفٌ *A composer of a book* or *books; an author.*]

مَأْلُوفٌ: see مُؤَلَّفٌ, in two places.

الق

1. أَلَقَ, (JK, Ḳ, TA,) aor. ـِ; (Ḳ, TA;) or أَلِقَ, aor. ـَ; (CḲ; [in which it would seem, from what follows in this paragraph and the next, that the pret. is wrong, but that the aor. is right;]) inf. n. أَلْقٌ and إِلَاقٌ; (JK, Ḳ;) *It* (lightning) *lied;* (AHeyth, Ḳ;) [i. e.] *it was without rain.* (JK.) — See also 5. — Also, أَلَقَ, aor. ـِ, inf. n. أَلْقٌ, *He lied; spoke falsely:* whence the reading of Aboo-Jaafar and Zeyd Ibn-Aslam, [in the Ḳur xxiv. 14,] إِذْ تَأْلِقُونَهُ بِأَلْسِنَتِكُمْ [*When ye spoke it falsely with your tongues*]. (TA.)

5. تألّق *It* (lightning) *shone, gleamed,* or *glistened;* as also ▼ ائتلق [written with the disjunctive alif إِيتَلَقَ]; (JK, Ṣ, IJ, Ḳ;) and so ▼ أَلَقَ, aor. ـِ. (TA.) Ibn-Aḥmar has made the second trans., using the phrase تَأَلَّقُ ▼ الْعُيُونَ, either by suppressing a prep., [meaning *She shines to the eyes,*] or meaning thereby *she ravishes the eyes.* (TA.) — And تَأَلَّقَتْ, said of a woman, *She adorned herself:* (Ṣgh, Ḳ:) or *she became active and quick to engage in contention* or *altercation, and prepared herself for evil* or *mischief, and raised her head:* (IF, Ḳ:) or *she became like the* إِلْقَة [fem. of إِلْقٌ, q. v.]. (IAar.)

8: see 5, in two places.

إِلْقٌ *A he-wolf:* fem. with ة: (IAar, Ṣ, Ḳ:) and the fem. is also applied to *a she-ape* or *monkey;* the male of which is not called إِلْقٌ, but قِرْدٌ, (Ṣ, Ḳ,) and رُبَّاحٌ. (S.) — † *Evil in disposition,* applied to a man; and so with ة applied to a woman: and the latter, *a* [*demon of the kind called*] سِعْلَاة; because of its evil, or malignant, nature: (TA:) and a *bold* woman; (Lth, Ḳ;) for the same reason. (TA.)

إِلَاقٌ [an inf. n. (see 1) used as an epithet;] *Lying,* or *fallacious,* lightning; (Ḳ;) *that has no rain;* (JK, Ḳ;) as also ▼ أَلَّاقٌ: (Ḳ,* TA:) ▼ أَلَقٌ, likewise, is an epithet applied to lightning [in the same sense; or as signifying *shining, gleaming,* or *glistening:* see 1 and 5]: and so is ▼ أَلَّقٌ, as *syn. with* خُلَّبٌ [*that excites hope of rain, but deceives the expectation*]. (TA.) — Also, applied to a man, *Lying:* (JK:) or *lying much,* or *often,* or *habitually:* (TA:) and *very deceitful, and variable in disposition.* (TA.)

أَلِيقٌ [app. an inf. n. of أَلَقَ; (see 5;)] The *shining, gleaming,* or *glistening,* of lightning. (TA.)

أَلَّقٌ: see إِلَاقٌ.

إِلَّقٌ, like إِمَّعٌ, [in a copy of the JK incorrectly written أَلْقٌ,] *i. q.* مُتَأَلِّقٌ [*Shining, gleaming,* or *glistening*]; (Ṣ, Ḳ;) applied to lightning. (JK.) — Also † An *inconstant* man; from التَّأَلُّقُ as relating to lightning. (JK: there, in this instance, written إِلْقٌ.)

أَلَّاقٌ: } see إِلَاقٌ.
آلِقٌ: }

الك

1. أَلَكَ اللِّجَامَ, (ISd, Ḳ,) [aor. ـُ or ـِ,] inf. n. أَلْكٌ, (ISd, TA,) *He* (a horse) *chewed,* or *champed, the bit;* syn. عَلَكَهُ. (ISd, Ḳ.) One says, of a horse, يَأْلُكُ اللُّجُمَ *He chews,* or *champs, the bits:* but the verb commonly known is يَلُوكُ, or يَعْلُكُ. (Lth.) — [Hence, accord. to some, (see أَلُوكٌ,)] أَلَكَ بَيْنَ الْقَوْمِ, (Mṣb, TA,) aor. ـِ, inf. n. أَلْكٌ and أَلُوكٌ, (Mṣb,) *He acted as a messenger* (تَرَسَّلَ) *between the people.* (Mṣb, TA.) — And أَلَكَهُ, aor. ـِ, inf. n. أَلْكٌ, *He conveyed,* or *communicated, to him a message.* (Kr.) — And أَلَكَ *He sent.* (IB in art. لوك.)

4. أَلِكْنِى is from أَلَكَ signifying "he sent;" and is originally أَأْلِكْنِى; the [second] hemzeh being transposed and placed after the ل, it becomes أَلْئِكْنِى; then the hemzeh has its vowel transferred to the ل, and is thrown out; as is done in the case of مَلَكٌ, which is originally مَأْلَكٌ, then مَلْأَكٌ, and then مَلَكٌ: (IB in art. لوك:) it means *Be thou my messenger;* and *bear thou my message;* and is often used by the poets. (Ṣ in art. لوك.) Accord. to IAmb, one says, أَلِكْنِى إِلَى فُلَانٍ, meaning *send thou me to such a one:* [but I do not know any instance in which this meaning is applicable:] and the original form is أَلْئِكْنِى; or, if from الأَلُوكُ, the original form is أَأْلِكْنِى: and he also says that it means *be thou my messenger to such a one.* (TA.) One says also, أَلِكْنِى إِلَيْهَا بِرِسَالَةٍ, which should properly mean *Send thou me to her with a message:* but it is an inverted phrase; since the meaning is, *be thou my messenger to her with this message* [or rather *with a message*]: and أَلِكْنِى إِلَيْهَا بِالسَّلَامِ i. e. *convey thou,* or *communicate thou, to her my salutation;* or *be thou my messenger to her* [*with salutation*]: and sometimes this [prep.] ب is suppressed, so that one says, أَلِكْنِى إِلَيْهَا السَّلَامَ: sometimes, also, the person sent is he to whom the message is sent; as in the saying, أَلِكْنِى إِلَيْكَ السَّلَامَ [virtually meaning *receive thou my salutation;* but literally] *be thou my messenger to thyself with salutation.* (TA.) Lḥ mentions the phrase أَلَكْتُهُ إِلَيْهِ, with respect to a message, aor. أُلِيكُهُ, inf. n. إِلَاكَةٌ; in which case, the hemzeh [in the aor. and inf. n.] is converted into a letter of prolongation. (TA in art. لاك.)

5: see أَلُوكٌ.

10. استألك مَأْلُكَتَهُ *He bore,* or *conveyed, his message;* (Ḳ;) as also استلأك. (TA.)

أَلُوكٌ *A thing that is eaten* [or rather *chewed,* as will be seen below]: so in the phrases, عَلُوكُ صِدْقٍ and عَلُوجُ صِدْقٍ like هٰذَا أَلُوكُ صِدْقٍ [*This is an excellent thing that is chewed*], and مَا تَأَلَّكْتُ ▼ بِأَلُوكٍ [or مَا تَلَوَّكْتُ بِأَلُوكٍ] (Ḳ in art. علج) like مَا تَعَلَّجْتُ بِعَلُوجٍ [app. meaning *I have not occupied myself in chewing with anything that is chewed*]. (TA.) — [And hence, accord. to some,] *A message,* or *communication sent from one person or party to another;* (Lth, Ṣ, M, Ḳ, &c.; [in the CḲ, after الرِّسَالَةُ, by which الأَلُوكُ is explained in the Ḳ &c., we find قِبَلَ المَلِكِ مُشْتَقٌّ مِنْهُ, in which the first two words should be قِيلَ المَلْأَكُ, as in other copies of the Ḳ and in the TA; and الأُلُوكُ is erroneously put, in the CḲ, for الأَلُوكُ;]) said by Lth and ISd to be so called because it is [as it were] chewed in the mouth; (TA;) as also ▼ أَلُوكَةٌ (ISd, Ṣgh, Ḳ) and ▼ مَأْلَكَةٌ (Lth, Ṣ, Mṣb, Ḳ, &c.) and ▼ مَأْلُكَةٌ (Mṣb, Ḳ) and ▼ مَأْلُكٌ: (Ṣ, M, Mṣb, Ḳ, &c.:) accord. to Kr, (TA,) this last is the only word of the measure مَفْعُلٌ: (Ḳ, TA:) but accord. to Sb and Akh, there is no word of this measure: (TA:) [i. e. there is none originally of this measure:] other instances have been mentioned; namely, مَكْرُمٌ and مَعُونٌ [originally مَعْوُنٌ] and مَقْبُرٌ and مَهْلُكٌ and مَيْسُرٌ, which last occurs in the Ḳur [ii. 280], accord. to one reading, in the words فَنَظِرَةٌ إِلَى مَيْسُرِهِ; but it is said that each of these, and مَأْلُكٌ also, may be regarded as originally with ة; or, accord. to AḤei, each is [virtually, though not in the language of the grammarians,] a pl. of the same with ة; (MF, TA;) and Akh says the same with respect to مَكْرُمٌ and مَعُونٌ: (TA:) Seer says that each is curtailed of ة by poetic licence; but this assertion will not apply to مَيْسُرٌ, as it occurs in the Ḳur. (MF, TA.) — أَلُوكٌ also signifies *A messenger.* (Ibn-'Abbád, Ḳ. [In the CḲ here follows, وَالمَأْلُوكُ وَالمَأْلُوقُ: but the right reading is وَالمَأْلُوكُ المَأْلُوقُ, as in other copies and in the TA.])

أَلُوكَةٌ: see أَلُوكٌ.

مَأْلَكٌ is said to be the original form of مَلَكٌ [*An angel;* so called because he conveys, or communicates, the message from God; (Ḳ,* TA, in art. لأك;)] derived from أَلُوكٌ; (Mṣb, Ḳ, TA; [but in the CḲ is a mistake here, pointed out above, voce أَلُوكٌ;]) so that the measure of مَلَكٌ is مَعَلٌ: (Mṣb:) مَلَكٌ is both sing. and pl.: Ks says that it is originally مَأْلَكٌ, from أَلُوكٌ signifying "a message;" then, by transposition, مَلْأَكٌ, a form also in use; and then, in consequence of frequency of usage, the hemzeh is suppressed, so that it becomes مَلَكٌ; but in forming the pl., they restore it to مَلْأَكٌ, saying مَلَائِكَةٌ, and مَلَائِكُ also: (Ṣ in art. ملك:) or, accord. to some, it is from لَأَكَ "he sent;" so that the measure of مَلَكٌ is مَفَلٌ: and there are other opinions respecting it: (Mṣb:) some say that its م is a radical: see art. ملك. (TA in art. لأك.)

مَأْلُكٌ: } see أَلُوكٌ.
مَأْلَكَةٌ: }
مَأْلُكَةٌ: }

الم

1. أَلِمَ, aor. ـَ, inf. n. أَلَمٌ, *It,* (as, for instance, the belly, T, Ṣ, or the head, Mṣb,) or *he,* (a man, T, Ṣ, Mṣb,) *was in pain; had,* or *suffered, pain; ached.* (T, Ṣ, M, Mṣb, Ḳ.) أَلِمَ بَطْنَهُ [*He was in pain,* or *had pain, in his belly*] (M) and أَلِمْتَ بَطْنَكَ [*thou wast in pain,* or *hadst pain, in thy belly*] (T, Ṣ) or رَأْسَكَ [*in thy head*] (Mṣb) are like سَفِهَ رَأْيَهُ (M) and رَشِدْتَ أَمْرَكَ (Ṣ, T) and وَجِعْتَ رَأْسَكَ; (Mṣb;) the noun being in the accus. case accord. to Ks as an explicative, though explicatives are [by rule] indeterminate, as in ضِقْتُ بِهِ ذَرْعًا and قَرِرْتُ بِهِ عَيْنًا; (T;) the regular form being [أَلِمَ بَطْنُهُ and] أَلِمَ بَطْنُكَ, (T, Ṣ,) as the verb is intrans. (T.)

4. آلَمْتُهُ, (Ṣ, M, Mṣb, Ḳ,) inf. n. إِيلَامٌ, (Ṣ, Mṣb,) *I caused him pain* or *aching.* (Ṣ,* M, Mṣb, Ḳ.)

5. تَأَلَّمَ *He was,* or *became, pained:* (M,* Mṣb, Ḳ:*) or *he expressed pain, grief,* or *sorrow; lamented; complained; made lamentation* or *complaint; moaned;* syn. تَوَجَّعَ, (T, Ṣ,) and شَكَى. (T.) You say, تَأَلَّمَ فُلَانٌ مِنْ فُلَانٍ [*Such a one expressed pain,* &c., *on account of* the conduct or the like of *such a one; complained of such a one*]: (T:) and لِأَزْمَةِ الزَّمَانِ [*on account of the hardness of the time*]. (TA in art. ازم.)

أَلَمٌ: see أَلِمٌ.

أَلَمٌ *Pain; ache;* (T, Ṣ, M, Ḳ;) as also ↑ أَيْلَمَةٌ: (T, M, Ḳ:) pl. (of the former, T, M) آلَامٌ. (T, M, Ḳ.) You say, مَا أَجِدُ أَيْلَمَةً وَلَا أَلَمًا *I do not find pain nor ache;* i. e. وَجَعًا: so says AZ: and IAạr says, ↑ أَيْلَمَةً وَلَا أَلَمَةً as meaning the same. (T.) And the Arabs say, لَأُبِيتَنَّكَ عَلَى ↑ أَيْلَمَةٍ, meaning *I will assuredly bring upon thee* [lit. *make thee to pass the night in*] *distress,* or *difficulty.* (Sh.)

أَلِمٌ *Being in pain; having,* or *suffering, pain; aching.* (M, Ḳ.)

أَلَمَةٌ: see أَلَمٌ.

إِلَامَ a contraction of إِلَى مَا: see إِلَى, last sentence.

أَلِيمٌ *Causing pain* or *aching; painful;* (Ṣ, Ḳ;) *i. q.* ↑ مُؤْلِمٌ; (T, M, Mṣb;) like سَمِيعٌ as syn. with مُسْمِعٌ: (Ṣ:) so when applied to punishment [or torment or torture]: (T, Mṣb:) or, thus applied, *painful,* or *causing pain* or *aching, in the utmost degree.* (M, Ḳ.)

أُلُومَةٌ *Lowness, ignobleness, baseness, vileness,* or *meanness.* (O, Ḳ.)

أَيْلَمَةٌ: see أَلَمٌ, in three places. — Accord. to IAạr, (T,) *A sound,* or *voice.* (T, Ḳ.) You say, مَا سَمِعْتُ لَهُ أَيْلَمَةً *I heard not any sound,* or *voice, of,* or *belonging to, him,* or *it.* (IAạr, T.) — Accord. to AA, (T,) *Motion.* (T, Ḳ.)

مُؤْلِمٌ: see أَلِيمٌ.

المس

أَلْمَاسُ, or أَلْمَاسُ: see art. موس.

اله

1. أَلَهَ, (Ṣ, and so in some copies of the Ḳ,) with fet-ḥ, (Ṣ,) or أَلِهَ, (Mgh, Mṣb, and so in some copies of the Ḳ,) like تَعِبَ, aor. ـَ, (Mṣb,) inf. n. إِلَاهَةٌ (Ṣ, Mṣb, Ḳ) and أُلُوهَةٌ and أُلُوهِيَّةٌ, (Ḳ,) *He served, worshipped,* or *adored;* syn. عَبَدَ. (Ṣ, Mṣb, Ḳ.) Hence the reading of I 'Ab, [in the Ḳur vii. 124,] وَيَذَرَكَ وَإِلَاهَتَكَ [*And leave thee, and the service,* or *worship,* or *adoration, of thee;* instead of وَآلِهَتَكَ *and thy gods,* which is the common reading]; for he used to say that Pharaoh was worshipped, and did not worship: (Ṣ:) so, too, says Th: and IB says that the opinion of I 'Ab is strengthened by the sayings of Pharaoh [mentioned in the Ḳur lxxix. 24 and xxviii. 38], "I am your lord the most high," and "I did not know any god of yours beside me." (TA.) = أَلِهَ, aor. ـَ, (Ṣ, Ḳ,) inf. n. أَلَهٌ, (Ṣ,) *He was,* or *became, confounded,* or *perplexed, and unable to see his right course;* (Ṣ, Ḳ;) originally وَلِهَ. (Ṣ.) — أَلِهَ عَلَى فُلَانٍ *He was,* or *became, vehemently impatient,* or *affected with vehement grief,* or *he manifested vehement grief and agitation, on account of such a one;* (Ṣ, Ḳ;) like وَلِهَ. (Ṣ.) — أَلِهَ إِلَيْهِ *He betook himself to him by reason of fright* or *fear, seeking protection;* or *sought,* or *asked, aid,* or *succour, of him: he had recourse,* or *betook himself, to him for refuge, protection,* or *preservation.* (Ḳ.) — أَلِهَ بِالمَكَانِ *He remained, stayed, abode,* or *dwelt, in the place.* (MF.) = أَلَهَهُ, (Ḳ,) like مَنَعَهُ, (TA,) [in the CḲ أَلَّهَهُ,] *He protected him; granted him refuge; preserved, saved, rescued,* or *liberated, him; aided,* or *succoured, him;* or *delivered him from evil: he rendered him secure,* or *safe.* (Ḳ.)

2. تَأْلِيهٌ [inf. n. of أَلَّهَهُ *He made him,* or *took him as, a slave; he enslaved him;*] *i. q.* تَعْبِيدٌ. (Ṣ, Ḳ.) — [The primary signification of أَلَّهَهُ seems to be, *He made him to serve, worship,* or *adore.* — Accord. to Freytag, besides having the former of the two meanings explained above, it signifies *He reckoned him among gods; held him to be a god; made him a god:* but he does not mention his authority.]

5. تَأَلَّهَ *He devoted himself to religious services* or *exercises; applied himself to acts of devotion.* (JK, Ṣ, Mṣb, Ḳ.)

أُلَاهِيَّةٌ: see إِلَاهَةٌ.

إِلَٰهٌ, or إِلَاهٌ, [the former of which is the more common mode of writing the word,] is of the measure فِعَالٌ (Ṣ, Mṣb, Ḳ) in the sense of the measure مَفْعُولٌ, (Ṣ, Mṣb,) like كِتَابٌ in the sense of مَكْتُوبٌ, and بِسَاطٌ in the sense of مَبْسُوطٌ, (Mṣb,) meaning ↑ مَأْلُوهٌ [*An object of worship* or *adoration;* i. e. *a god, a deity*]; (Ṣ, Mṣb, Ḳ;) *anything that is taken as an object of worship* or *adoration, accord. to him who takes it as such:* (Ḳ:) with the article ال, properly, *i. q.* اَللّٰهُ; [see this word below;] but applied by the believers in a plurality of gods to *what is worshipped* by them *to the exclusion of* الله: (Mṣb:) pl. آلِهَةٌ: (Mṣb, TA:) which signifies *idols:* (JK, Ṣ, TA:) in the Ḳ, this meaning is erroneously assigned to إِلَاهَةٌ: (TA:) [not so in the CḲ; but there, الآلِهَةُ is put in a place where we should read الإِلَاهَةُ, or إِلَاهَةٌ without the article:] ↑ الإِلَاهَةُ [is the fem. of الإِلَاهُ, and] signifies [the *goddess:* and particularly] *the serpent:* [(a meaning erroneously assigned in the CḲ to الآلِهَةُ; as also other meanings here following:) because it was a special object of the worship of some of the ancient Arabs:] (Ḳ:) or *the great serpent:* (Th:) and *the* [*new moon;* or *the moon when it is termed*] هِلَال: (Th, Ḳ:) and, (Ṣ, Ḳ,) as also ↑ إِلَاهَةُ, without ال, the former perfectly decl., and the latter imperfectly decl., (Ṣ,) and ↑ الأُلَاهَةُ, (IAạr, Ḳ,) and ↑ الأُلَهَةُ, (IAạr, TA,) and ↑ الأُلُوهَةُ, (Ḳ,) [and app. ▼ أَلَاهَةٌ,] and ▼ الأُلَيْهَةُ, (Ḳ,) *the sun;* (Ṣ, Ḳ;) app. so called because of the honour and worship which they paid to it: (Ṣ:) or *the hot sun.* (Th, TA.) [إِلٰهٌ is the same as the Hebrew אֱלוֹהַּ and the Chaldee אֱלָהּ; and is of uncertain derivation: accord. to some,] it is originally وِلَاهٌ, like as إِشَاحٌ is originally وِشَاحٌ; meaning that mankind yearn towards him who is thus called, [seeking protection or aid,] in their wants, and humble themselves to him in their afflictions, like as every infant yearns towards its mother. (TA.) [See also the opinions, cited below, on the derivation of اَللّٰهُ.]

أَلَاهَةٌ and الأَلَاهَةُ: see إِلٰهٌ.

أُلَاهَةٌ and الأُلَاهَةُ: see إِلٰهٌ. ═ أُلَاهَةٌ: see إِلَاهَةٌ.

إِلَاهَةٌ inf. n. of 1, q. v. (Ṣ, Mṣb, Ḳ.) ═ *Godship; divinity;* (Ḳ;) as also ▼ أُلُوهَةٌ (CḲ [not found by me in any MS. copy of the Ḳ) and ▼ أُلُوهِيَّةٌ. (Ḳ.) ═ إِلَاهَةٌ and الإِلَاهَةُ: see إِلٰهٌ.

الأُلَيْهَةُ: see إِلٰهٌ.

[إِلٰهِىٌّ, or إِلَاهِىٌّ, *Of, or relating to, God or a god; divine: theological:* Hence, العِلْمُ الإِلٰهِىُّ or الإِلَاهِىُّ: see what next follows.]

[الإِلٰهِيَّةُ, or الإِلَاهِيَّةُ, *Theology; the science of the being and attributes of God, and of the articles of religious belief;* also termed عِلْمُ الإِلٰهِيَّاتِ or الإِلَاهِيَّاتِ, and ▼ العِلْمُ الإِلٰهِىُّ or الإِلَاهِىُّ.]

اَللّٰهُ, [written with the disjunctive alif أَللّٰهُ, meaning *God, i. e. the only true god,*] accord. to the most correct of the opinions respecting it, which are twenty in number, (Ḳ,) or more than thirty, (MF,) is a proper name, (Mṣb, Ḳ,) applied to *the Being who exists necessarily, by Himself, comprising all the attributes of perfection;* (TA;) a proper name denoting *the true god,* comprising all the excellent divine names; a unity comprising all the essences of existing things; (Ibn-El-'Arabee, TA;) the ال being inseparable from it: (Mṣb:) not derived: (Lth, Mṣb, Ḳ:) or it is originally إِلٰهٌ, or إِلَاهٌ, (Sb, AHeyth, Ṣ, Mṣb, Ḳ,) of the measure فِعَالٌ in the sense of the measure مَفْعُولٌ, meaning مَأْلُوهٌ, (Ṣ, Ḳ,*) with [the article] ال prefixed to it, (Sb, AHeyth, Ṣ, Mṣb,) so that it becomes الإِلَاهُ, (Sb, AHeyth, Mṣb,) then the vowel of the hemzeh is transferred to the ل [before it], (Mṣb,) and the hemzeh is suppressed, (Sb, AHeyth, Ṣ, Mṣb,) so that there remains اَلِلٰهُ, or اَلِلَاهُ, after which the former ل is made quiescent, and incorporated into the other: (Sb, AHeyth, Mṣb:) the suppression of the hemzeh is for the purpose of rendering the word easy of utterance, on account of the frequency of its occurrence: and the ال is not a substitute for the hemzeh; for were it so, it would not occur therewith in الإِلَاهُ: (Ṣ:) so says J; but IB says that this is not a necessary inference, because الإِلَاهُ applies to God (اللّٰه) and also to the idol that is worshipped; whereas اللّٰه applies only to God; and therefore, in using the vocative form of address, one may say, يَا أَللّٰهُ [*O God*], with the article ال and with the disjunctive hemzeh; but one may not say, يَا الإِلَاهُ either with the disjunctive or with the conjunctive hemzeh: (TA:) Sb allows that it may be originally لَاهٌ: see art. ليه: (Ṣ:) some say that it is from أَلِهَ, either because minds are confounded, or perplexed, by the greatness, or majesty, of God, or because He is the object of recourse for protection, or aid, in every case: or from أَلَهَهُ, meaning "he protected him," &c., as explained above: see 1, last sentence. (TA.) The ال is pronounced with the disjunctive hemzeh in using the vocative form of address [يَا أَللّٰهُ] because it is inseparably prefixed as an honourable distinction of this name; (Ṣ;) or because a pause upon the vocative particle is intended in honour of the name; (Ṣ in art. ليه;) and AAF says that it is also thus pronounced in a form of swearing; as in أَفَأَللّٰهِ لَتَفْعَلَنَّ [an elliptical phrase, as will be shown below, meaning *Then, by God, wilt thou indeed do* such a thing?]; though he denies its being thus pronounced because it is inseparable; regarding it as a substitute for the suppressed hemzeh of الإِلَاهُ: (Ṣ in the present art.:) Sb mentions this pronunciation in يَا أَللّٰهُ; and Th mentions the pronunciation of يَا اللّٰهُ also, with the conjunctive hemzeh: Ks, moreover, mentions, as used by the Arabs, the phrase يَلَهْ اغْفِرْ لِى [*O God, forgive me*], for يَا أَللّٰهُ; but this is disapproved. (ISd, TA.) The word is pronounced in the manner termed تَفْخِيمٌ, [i. e., with the broad sound of the lengthened fet-ḥ, and with a full sound of the letter ل,] for the purpose of showing honour to it; but when it is preceded by a kesreh, [as in بِاللّٰهِ *By God,* and بِسْمِ اللّٰهِ *In the name of God,*] it is pronounced in the [contr.] manner termed تَرْقِيقٌ: AḤát says that some of the vulgar say, لَا وَاللّٰهْ [*No, by God*], suppressing the alif, which should necessarily be uttered, as in الرَّحْمٰنُ, which is in like manner written without alif; and he adds that some person has composed a verse in which the alif [in this word] is suppressed, erroneously. (Mṣb.) You say, اَللّٰهَ اَللّٰهَ فِى كَذَا, [a verb being understood,] meaning *Fear ye God, fear ye God, with respect to such a thing.* (Marginal note in a copy of the Jámi' eṣ-Ṣagheer. [See another ex. voce كَرَّةٌ.]) And اَللّٰهِ لَأَفْعَلَنَّ and لِلّٰهِ لَأَفْعَلَنَّ [*By God, I will assuredly do* such a thing]: in the former is understood a verb significant of swearing; and in the latter, [or in both, for a noun is often put in the accus. case because of a particle understood,] a particle [such as بِ or وَ] denoting an oath. (Bḍ in ii. 1.) And وَاللّٰهِ مَا فَعَلْتُ and لِلّٰهِ مَا فَعَلْتُ, meaning [*By God, I did not,* or *have not done,* such a thing]. (JK.) And لِلّٰهِ دَرُّكَ ‡ *To God be attributed thy deed!* (A in art. در:) or *the good that hath proceeded from thee!* or *thy good deed!* or *thy gift!* and *what is received from thee!* [and *thy flow of eloquence!* and *the like*]: a phrase expressive of admiration of anything: (TA in art. در:) [when said to an eloquent speaker or poet, it may be rendered *divinely art thou gifted!*]. And لِلّٰهِ دَرُّهُ ‡ *To God be attributed his deed!* [&c.]. (Ṣ and Ḳ in art. در.) And لِلّٰهِ القَائِلُ [meaning *To God be attributed (the eloquence of) the sayer!* or] *how good,* or *beautiful, is the saying of the sayer,* or *of him who says* [such and such words]! or it is like the phrase لِلّٰهِ دَرُّهُ, meaning ‡ *To God be attributed his goodness!* and *his pure action!* (Ḥar p. 11.) And لِلّٰهِ فُلَانٌ [*To God be attributed (the excellence,* or *goodness,* or *deed, &c., of) such a one!*] explained by Az as meaning *wonder ye at such a one: how perfect is he!* (Ḥar ibid.) [And لِلّٰهِ أَبُوكَ: see art. ابو.] And لَاهِ أَنْتَ, meaning لِلّٰهِ أَنْتَ [lit. *To God be thou attributed!* i. e. *to God be attributed thine excellence!* or *thy goodness!* or *thy deed!* &c.]. (JK.) [Similar to لِلّٰهِ, thus used, is the Hebrew expression לֵאלֹהִים after an epithet signifying "great" or the like.] إِنَّا لِلّٰهِ وَإِنَّا إِلَيْهِ رَاجِعُونَ, in the Ḳur [ii. 151], said on the occasion of an affliction, means *Verily to God we belong,* as property and servants, He doing with us what He willeth, *and verily unto Him we return* in the ultimate state of existence, and He will recompense us. (Jel.) AZ mentions the phrase الحَمْدُ لَاهِ [meaning الحَمْدُ لِلّٰهِ *Praise be to God*]: but this is not allowable in the Ḳur-án: it is only related as heard from the Arabs of the desert, and those not knowing the usage of the Ḳur-án. (Az, TA.) — ▼ اَللّٰهُمَّ is an expression used in prayer; as also لَاهُمَّ; (JK, Mṣb;) meaning يَا أَللّٰهُ [*O God*]; the م being a substitute for [the suppressed vocative particle] يا; (Ṣ in art. ليه, and Bḍ in iii. 25;) but one says also, يَا أَللّٰهُمَّ, (JK, and Ṣ ibid,) by poetic licence: (Ṣ ibid:) or the meaning, accord. to some, is يَا أَللّٰهُ أُمَّنَا بِخَيْرٍ [*O God, bring us good*]; (JḲ, and Bḍ ubi suprà;) and hence the origin of the expression. (Bḍ.) You say also اَللّٰهُمَّ إِلَّا [which may be rendered, inversely, *Unless, indeed;* or *unless, possibly*]: the former word being thus used to denote that the exception is something very rare. (Mṭr in the commencement of his Expos. of the Maḳámát of El-Ḥareeree, and Ḥar pp. 52 and 53.) And اَللّٰهُمَّ نَعَمْ [which may be rendered, inversely, *Yes, indeed;* or *yea, verily*]: the former word being used in this case as corroborative of the answer to an interrogation, negative and affirmative. (Ḥar p. 563.)

اَللّٰهُمَّ: see what next precedes.

مَأْلُوهٌ: see إِلٰهٌ.

الو

1. أَلَا, (Ṣ, M, Mgh, Ḳ,) aor. يَأْلُو, (Ṣ, Mgh,) inf. n. أَلْوٌ (T, M, Mgh, Ḳ) and أُلُوٌّ (Ḳ, TA [in a copy of the M أَلُوٌّ]) and أُلِىٌّ; (Ḳ, TA; [in a copy of the M أَلِىٌّ, and in a copy of the Mgh written with fet-ḥ and ḍamm to the أ;]) and ▼ أَلَّى, (Ṣ, M, Ḳ,) aor. يُؤَلِّى, inf. n. تَأْلِيَةٌ; (Ṣ;) and ▼ ائتلى [written with the disjunctive alif إِيتَلَى]; (Ṣ, M, Ḳ;) [and ▼ تَأَلَّى, as appears from an ex. in a verse cited in art. نشب, q. v.;] *He fell short;* or *he fell short of doing what was requisite,* or *what he ought to have done;* or *he*

flagged, or *was remiss*; syn. قَصَّرَ: (S, M, K; and Fr, IAar, T, Mgh, in explanation of the first of these verbs:) and *he was slow*, or *tardy*: (M, K; and AA, T, S, in explanation of the second verb:) or *he flagged*, or *was remiss*, or *languid, and weak.* (AHeyth and T in explanation of all of the above-mentioned verbs except the last.) You say, أَلَا فِى الأَمْرِ, (Mgh,) and ▼ ائتلى فيه, (S,) *He fell short*, &c., (قَصَّرَ,) *in the affair.* (S, Mgh.) In the saying, لَمْ يَأْلُ أَنْ يَعْدِلَ فِى ذٰلِكَ, i. e. *He did not fall short*, &c., (لَمْ يُقَصِّرْ,) *in acting equitably and equally in that*, فى is suppressed before ان: but in the phrase, لَمْ يَأْلُ مِنَ العَدْلِ, as some relate it, [the meaning intended seems to be, *They did not hold back*, or the like, *from acting equitably*; for here] the verb is made to imply the meaning of another verb: and such is the case in the saying, لَا آلُوكَ نُصْحًا, meaning *I will not refuse to thee, nor partially or wholly deprive thee of, sincere, honest*, or *faithful, advice*: (Mgh:) or this last signifies *I will not flag*, or *be remiss, nor fall short, to thee in giving sincere, honest*, or *faithful, advice.* (T, S.*) It is said in the Kur [iii. 114], لَا يَأْلُونَكُمْ خَبَالًا, meaning *They will not fall short*, or *flag*, or *be remiss, in corrupting you.* (IAar, T.) And the same meaning is assigned to the verb in the saying وَلَا يَأْتَلِ ▼ أُولُو ٱلْفَضْلِ مِنْكُمْ, in the Kur [xxiv. 22], by A 'Obeyd: but the preferable rendering in this case is that of AHeyth, which will be found below: see 4. (T.) Ks mentions the phrase, أَقْبَلَ بِضَرْبَةٍ لَا يَأْلُ [*He came with a blow, not falling short*, &c.], for لا يَأْلُو like لَا أَدْرِ [for لا أَدْرِى]. (S, M: [but in the copies of the former in my hands, for بِضَرْبَةٍ, I find بِضَرْبِهِ.]) ▼ أَلَّى [with teshdeed] is also said of a dog, and of a hawk, meaning *He fell short of attaining the game that he pursued.* (TA.) And of a cake of bread, meaning *It was slow in becoming thoroughly baked.* (IAar, IB.) [See also the phrase لَا دَرَيْتَ وَلَا ٱئْتَلَيْتَ in a later part of this paragraph.] —— You say also, مَا أَلَوْتُ الشَّىْءَ, (K,) or مَا أَلَوْتُ أَنْ أَفْعَلَهُ, (M,) inf. n أَلْوٌ (M, K) and أُلُوٌّ, (K, TA, [in a copy of the M أُلُوٌّ,]) meaning *I did not leave, quit, cease from, omit*, or *neglect*, (M, K,) *the thing*, (K,) or *doing it.* (M.) And فُلَانٌ لَا يَأْلُو خَيْرًا *Such a one does not leave, quit*, or *cease from, doing good.* (M.) And مَا أَلَوْتُ جُهْدًا *I did not leave, omit*, or *neglect, labour, exertion, effort*, or *endeavour*: and the vulgar say, مَا آلُوكَ جُهْدًا; but this is wrong: so says As. (T. [See, however, similar phrases mentioned above.]) —— أَلَا, aor. as above, (TA,) inf. n. أُلُوٌّ, (IAar, T, TA,) also signifies *He strove*, or *laboured*; *he exerted himself*, or *his power* or *ability*; (IAar, T, TA;) as also ▼ تَأَلَّى: (T, TA:) the contr. of a signification before mentioned; i. e. "he flagged," or "was remiss, or languid, and weak." (TA.) You say, أَتَانِى فِى حَاجَةٍ فَأَلَوْتُ فِيهَا *He came to me respecting a want, and I strove*, or *laboured*, &c., *to accomplish it.* (T.) —— And أَلَا, aor. as above, (T, S,) inf. n. أَلْوٌ, (IAar, T, S,) *He was*, or *became, able to do it*: (IAar, T, S:) and ▼ أَلَّى, inf. n. تَأْلِيَةٌ, also signifies *he was*, or *became, able*; (TA;) and so ▼ ائتلى. (ISk, S, TA.) You say, هُوَ يَأْلُو هٰذَا الأَمْرَ *He is able to perform*, or *accomplish, this affair.* (T.) And مَا أَلَوْتُهُ *I was not able to do it.* (T, M, K.) And أَتَانِى فُلَانٌ فِى حَاجَةٍ فَمَا أَلَوْتُ رَدَّهُ *Such a one came to me respecting a want, and I was not able to rebuff him.* (T.) It is said in a trad., مَنْ صَامَ الدَّهْرَ فَلَا صَامَ وَلَا أَلَّى ▼ [*He who fasts ever*, or *always, may he neither fast*] *nor be able* to fast: as though it were an imprecation: or it may be enunciative: another reading is وَلَا آلَ, explained as meaning وَلَا رَجَعَ: [see art. اول:] but El-Khattábee says that it is correctly أَلَّى and أَلَا. (TA.) And the Arabs used to say, (S, M,) [and] accord. to a trad. it will be said to the hypocrite [in his grave], on his being asked respecting Mohammad and what he brought, and answering "I know not," (T in art. تلو,) لَا دَرَيْتَ وَلَا ٱئْتَلَيْتَ ▼, (T, S, M, K,) meaning, accord. to As, (T,) or ISk, (S,) *Mayest thou not know, nor be able* to know: (T, S:*) or, accord. to Fr, *nor fall short*, or *flag*, in seeking to know; that the case may be the more miserable to thee: (T:) or وَلَا أَلَيْتَ, as an imitative sequent [for ولا أَلَوْتَ, to which the same explanations are applicable]: (MK:) or لَا دَرَيْتَ وَلَا تَلَيْتَ, the latter verb being assimilated to the former, (ISk, T in art. تلو, S,) said to mean وَلَا تَلَوْتَ, i. e. *nor mayest thou read nor study*: (T in art. تلو:) or لَا دَرَيْتَ وَلَا أَتْلَيْتَ, i. e. [*mayest thou not know*,] *nor mayest thou have camels followed by young ones.* (Yoo, ISk, T, S, M, K.) —— Also, (IAar, T,) inf. n. أَلْوٌ, (IAar, T, K,) *He gave him a thing*: (IAar, T, K:*) [doubly trans.:] the contr. of a signification before mentioned, (also given by IAar, T and TA,) which is that of "refusing" [a person anything: see, above, لَا آلُوكَ نُصْحًا]. (TA.)

2: see 1, in four places.

4. آلَى, (T, S, M, &c.,) aor. يُؤْلِى, inf. n. إِيلَآءٌ, (T, S, Mgh,) [and in poetry إِلَآءٌ, (see a reading of a verse cited voce أَلِيَّةٌ,)] *He swore*; (T, S, M, Mgh, K;) as also ▼ تَأَلَّى, and ▼ ائتلى. (T, S, M, K.) You say, آلَيْتُ عَلَى الشَّىْءِ and آلَيْتُهُ [*I swore to do the thing*]. (M.) [And آلَيْتُ لَا أَفْعَلُ كَذَا *I swore that I would not do such a thing*; and, emphatically, *I swear that I will not do such a thing.* And آلَى يَمِينًا *He swore an oath.*] It is said in the Kur [xxiv. 22], وَلَا يَأْتَلِ ▼ أُولُو ٱلْفَضْلِ مِنْكُمْ, meaning, accord. to AHeyth and Fr, *And let not those of you who possess superabundance swear* [that they will not give to relations &c.]; for Aboo-Bekr [is particularly alluded to thereby, because he] had sworn that he would not expend upon Mistah and his relations who had made mention of [the scandal respecting] 'Áisheh: and some of the people of El-Medeeneh read وَلَا يَتَأَلَّ ▼, but this disagrees with the written text: A 'Obeyd explains it differently: see 1: but the preferable meaning is that here given. (T.) And it is said in a trad., آلَى مِنْ نِسَائِهِ شَهْرًا *He swore that he would not go in to his wives for a month*: the verb being here made trans. by means of من because it implies the meaning of اِمْتِنَاع, which is thus trans. (TA.) [See also an ex. of the verb thus used in the Kur ii. 226.] التَّأَلِّى ▼ عَلَى ٱللّٰهِ is said to mean One's *saying, By God, such a one will assuredly enter the fire* [*of Hell*], *and God will assuredly make to have a good issue the work of such a one*: but see the act. part. n. below. (TA.) —— آلَتْ, inf. n. as above, *She* (a woman) *took for herself*, or *made*, or *prepared, a* مِئْلَاة, q. v. (TA.)

5: see 1, in two places: —— and see 4, in three places.

8: see 1, in five places: —— and see 4, in two places.

أَلُو, or إِلُو: see إِلَى in art. الى.

أُلُو, (so in some copies of the S, and so in the K in the last division of that work, and in the CK in art. ال, [and thus it is always pronounced,] but in some copies of the K in art. ال it is written أُلُونَ, [as though to show the original form of its termination,]) or أُولُو, (so in the M, and in some copies of the S, [and thus it is generally written,]) *i. q.* ذَوُو [*Possessors of*; *possessed of*; *possessing*; *having*]; a pl. which has no sing. (S, M, K) of its own proper letters, (S, K,) its sing. being ذُو: (S:) or, as some say, a quasi-pl. n., of which the sing. is ذُو: (K:) the fem. is أُلَاتُ, (so in some copies of the S and K, [and thus it is always pronounced,]) or أُولَاتُ, (so in other copies of the S and K, [and thus it is generally written,]) of which the sing. is ذَاتُ: (S, K:) it is as though its sing. were أَلٌ, (M, K, [in the CK أُلٌ,]) the [final] و [in the masc.] being the sign of the pl., (M,) for it has و [for its termination] in the nom. case, and ى in the accus. and gen. (M, K.) It is never used but as a prefixed noun. (M, K.) The following are exs. of the nom. case: نَحْنُ أُولُو قُوَّةٍ وَأُولُو بَأْسٍ شَدِيدٍ [*We are possessors of strength, and possessors of vehement courage*], in the Kur [xxvii. 23]; and أُولُو ٱلْأَرْحَامِ بَعْضُهُمْ أَوْلَى بِبَعْضٍ [*The possessors of relationships, these have the best title* to inheritance, *one with respect to another*], in the same [viii. last verse and xxxiii. 6]; (TA;) and جَآءَنِى أُولُو ٱلْأَلْبَابِ [*The persons of understandings came to me*]; and أُولَاتُ ٱلْأَحْمَالِ [*Those who are with child*; occurring in the Kur lxv. 4]: (S:) and the following are exs. of the accus. and gen. cases: وَذَرْنِى وَٱلْمُكَذِّبِينَ أُولِى ٱلنَّعْمَةِ [*And leave thou me*, or *let me alone, with the beliers*, or *discrediters*, (i. e., commit their case to me,) *the possessors of ease and plenty*], in the Kur [lxxiii. 11]; and لَتَنُوٓءُ بِٱلْعُصْبَةِ أُولِى ٱلْقُوَّةِ [*Would weigh down the company of men possessing strength*], in the same [xxviii. 76]. (TA.) وَأُولِى ٱلْأَمْرِ مِنْكُمْ, in the Kur [iv. 62], [*And those, of you, who are possessors of command*], (M, K,*) accord. to Aboo-Is-hák, (M,) means *the companions of the Prophet, and the men of knowledge their followers,* (M, Ḳ,) *and the possessors of command, who are their followers, when also possessors of knowledge and religion:* (Ḳ:) or, as some say, [simply] *the possessors of command;* for when these are possessors of knowledge and religion, and take, or adopt and maintain, and follow, what the men of knowledge say, to obey them is of divine obligation: and in general those who are termed أُولُو الأَمْرِ, of the Muslims, are *those who superintend the affairs* of such *with respect to religion, and everything conducing to the right disposal of* their *affairs.* (M.)

إِلَى, accord. to Sb, is originally with و in the place of the [ى, i.e. the final] alif; and so is عَلَى; for the alifs [in these two particles] are not susceptible of imáleh; [i. e., they may not be pronounced ilè and 'alè;] and if either be used as the proper name of a man, the dual [of the former] is إِلَوَانِ and [that of the latter] عَلَوَانِ; but when a pronoun is affixed to it, the alif is changed into yé, so that you say إِلَيْكَ and عَلَيْكَ; though some of the Arabs leave it as it was, saying إِلَاكَ and عَلَاكَ. (Ṣ.) It is a prep., or particle governing a noun in the gen. case, (Ṣ, Mughnee, Ḳ,) and denotes the end, as opposed to [مِنْ, which denotes] the beginning, of an extent, or of the space between two points or limits; (Ṣ, M;) or the end of an extent (T, Mughnee, Ḳ) of place; [signifying *To,* or *as far as;*] as in the phrase [in the Ḳur xvii. 1], مِنَ المَسْجِدِ الحَرَامِ إِلَى المَسْجِدِ الأَقْصَى [*From the Sacred Mosque to,* or *as far as, the Furthest Mosque;* meaning from the mosque of Mekkeh to that of Jerusalem]; (Mughnee, Ḳ;) or in the saying, خَرَجْتُ مِنَ الكُوفَةِ إِلَى مَكَّةَ [*I went forth from El-Koofeh to Mekkeh*], which may mean that you entered it, [namely, the latter place,] or that you reached it without entering it, for the end includes the beginning of the limit and the furthest part thereof, but does not extend beyond it. (Ṣ.) [In some respects it agrees with حَتَّى, q. v. And sometimes it signifies *Towards;* as in نَظَرَ إِلَيَّ *He looked towards me;* and مَالَ إِلَيْهِ *He,* or *it, inclined towards him,* or *it.*] — It also denotes the end of a space of time; [signifying *To, till,* or *until;*] as in the saying [in the Ḳur ii. 183], ثُمَّ أَتِمُّوا الصِّيَامَ إِلَى اللَّيْلِ [*Then complete ye the fasting to,* or *till,* or *until, the night*]. (Mughnee, Ḳ.) [Hence, إِلَى أَنْ (followed by a manṣoob aor.) *Till,* or *until:* and إِلَى مَتَى *Till,* or *until, what time,* or *when?* i. e. *how long?* and also *to, till,* or *until, the time when.* See also the last sentence in this paragraph.] — [In like manner it is used in the phrases إِلَى آخِرِهِ, and إِلَى غَيْرِ ذٰلِكَ, meaning, (*And so on,*) *to other things,* and *to the end thereof;* equivalent to *et cætera.*] — Sometimes, (Ṣ,) it occurs in the sense of مَعَ, (T, Ṣ, M, Mughnee, Ḳ,) when a thing is joined to another thing; (Mughnee, Ḳ;) as in the phrase [in the Ḳur iii. 45 and lxi. 14], مَنْ أَنْصَارِى إِلَى ٱللّٰهِ [*Who will be my aiders with,* or *in addition to, God?*], (Ṣ, Mughnee, Ḳ,) accord. to the Koofees and some of the Baṣrees; (Mughnee;) i. e. *who will be joined to God in aiding me?* (M, TA;) and as in the saying [in the Ḳur iv. 2], وَلَا تَأْكُلُوا أَمْوَالَهُمْ إِلَى أَمْوَالِكُمْ [*And devour not ye their possessions with,* or *in addition to, your possessions*]; (T, Ṣ;) and [in the same, ii. 13,] وَإِذَا خَلَوْا إِلَى شَيَاطِينِهِمْ [*And when they are alone with their devils*]; (Ṣ;) and in the saying, الذَّوْدُ إِلَى الذَّوْدِ إِبِلٌ [*A few she-camels with,* or *added to, a few she-camels are a herd of camels*], (Ṣ, Mughnee, Ḳ,) a prov., meaning † *a little with a little makes much;* (Ṣ and A in art. ذود, q. v.;) though one may not say, إِلَى زَيْدٍ مَالٌ meaning مَعَ زَيْدٍ مَالٌ: (Mughnee:) so too in the saying, فُلَانٌ حَلِيمٌ إِلَى أَدَبٍ وَفِقْهٍ [*Such a one is clement,* or *forbearing, with good education,* or *polite accomplishments, and intelligence,* or *knowledge of the law*]; (M, TA;) and so, accord. to Kh, in the phrase, أَحْمَدُ ٱللّٰهَ إِلَيْكَ [*I praise God with thee:* but see another rendering of this phrase below]. (ISh.) In the saying in the Ḳur [v. 8], فَٱغْسِلُوا وُجُوهَكُمْ وَأَيْدِيَكُمْ إِلَى المَرَافِقِ, it is disputed whether [the meaning be *Then wash ye your faces, and your arms with the elbows,* or, *and your arms as far as the elbows;* i. e., whether] the elbows be meant to be included among the parts to be washed, or excluded therefrom. (T.) A context sometimes shows that what follows it is included in what precedes it; as in قَرَأْتُ القُرْآنَ مِنْ أَوَّلِهِ إِلَى آخِرِهِ [*I read,* or *recited, the Ḳurán, from the beginning thereof to the end thereof*]: or that it is excluded; as in ثُمَّ أَتِمُّوا الصِّيَامَ إِلَى اللَّيْلِ [explained above]: when this is not the case, some say that it is included if it be of the same kind [as that which precedes]; some, that it is included absolutely; and some, that it is excluded absolutely; and this is the right assertion; for with the context it is in most instances excluded. (Mughnee.) — It is also used to show the grammatical agency of the noun governed by it, after a verb of wonder; or after a noun of excess importing love or hatred; [as in مَا أَحَبَّهُ إِلَيَّ *How lovely,* or *pleasing, is he to me!* (TA in art. حب,) and مَا أَبْغَضَهُ إِلَيَّ *How hateful,* or *odious, is he to me!* (Ṣ in art. بغض;) and] as in the saying [in the Ḳur xii. 33], رَبِّ السِّجْنُ أَحَبُّ إِلَيَّ [*O my Lord, the prison is more pleasing to me*]. (Mughnee, Ḳ.) [This usage is similar to that explained in the next sentence.] — It is *syn. with* عِنْدَ; (Ṣ, M, Mughnee, Mṣb, Ḳ;) as in the phrase, هُوَ أَشْهَى إِلَيَّ مِنْ كَذَا [*It is more desirable,* or *pleasant, in my estimation than such a thing*]; (Mṣb;) and in the saying of the poet,

* أَمْ لَا سَبِيلَ إِلَى الشَّبَابِ وَذِكْرُهُ *
* أَشْهَى إِلَيَّ مِنَ الرَّحِيقِ السَّلْسَلِ *

[*Is there no way of return to youth, seeing that the remembrance thereof is more pleasant to me,* or *in my estimation, than mellow wine?*] (Mughnee, Ḳ:) and accord. to this usage of إِلَى in the sense of عِنْدَ may be explained the saying, أَنْتِ طَالِقٌ إِلَى سَنَةٍ, meaning *Thou art divorced at the* commencement of *a year.* (Mṣb.) — It is also *syn.* with لِ; as in the phrase, وَالأَمْرُ إِلَيْكَ [*And command,* or *to command, belongeth unto Thee,* meaning God, as in the Ḳur xiii. 30, and xxx. 3], (Mughnee, Ḳ,) in a trad. respecting supplication: (TA:) or, as some say, it is here used in the manner first explained above, meaning, *is ultimately referrible to Thee:* and they say, أَحْمَدُ ٱللّٰهَ إِلَيْكَ, meaning, *I tell the praise of God unto thee:* (Mughnee:) [but see another rendering of this last phrase above:] you say also, ذٰلِكَ إِلَيْكَ *That is committed to thee,* or *to thy arbitration.* (Ḥar p. 329.) — It also occurs as *syn. with* عَلَى; as in the saying in the Ḳur [xvii. 4], وَقَضَيْنَا إِلَى بَنِى إِسْرَائِيلَ [*And we decreed against the children of Israel*]: (Mṣb:) or this means *and we revealed to the children of Israel* (Bḍ, Jel) *decisively.* (Bḍ.) — It is also syn. with فِى; (M, Mughnee, Ḳ;) as in the saying [in the Ḳur iv. 89 and vi. 12], لَيَجْمَعَنَّكُمْ إِلَى يَوْمِ القِيَامَةِ [*He will assuredly collect you together on the day of resurrection*]: (Ḳ:) thus it may be used in this instance accord. to Ibn-Málik: (Mughnee:) and it is said to be so used in the saying [of En-Nábighah, (M, TA,)]

* فَلَا تَتْرُكَنِّى بِالوَعِيدِ كَأَنَّنِى *
* إِلَى النَّاسِ مَطْلِىٌّ بِهِ القَارُ أَجْرَبُ *

[*Then do not thou leave me with threatening, as though I were, among men, smeared with tar,* being like a *mangy* camel]; (M, Mughnee;) or, accord. to some, there is an ellipsis and inversion in this verse; الى being here in dependence upon a word suppressed, and the meaning being, *smeared with pitch,* [like a camel,] *yet being united to men:* or, accord. to Ibn-'Oṣfoor, مطلىّ is here considered as made to import the meaning of *rendered hateful,* or *odious;* for he says that if الى were correctly used in the sense of فى, it would be allowable to say, زَيْدٌ إِلَى الكُوفَةِ: (Mughnee:) [or the meaning may be, *as though I were, compared to men, a mangy* camel, *smeared with pitch:* for] I 'Ab said, after mentioning 'Alee, عِلْمِى إِلَى عِلْمِهِ كَالقَرَارَةِ فِى المُثْعَنْجَرِ, meaning *My knowledge compared to his knowledge is like the* قرارة [*or small pool of water left by a torrent*] *placed by the side of the middle of the sea* [or *the main deep*]. (Ḳ in art. ثعجر.) It is also [said to be] used in the sense of فى in the saying in the Ḳur [lxxix. 18], هَلْ لَكَ إِلَى أَنْ تَزَكَّى [*Wilt thou purify thyself* from infidelity?] because it imports the meaning of invitation. (TA.) — It is also used [in a manner contr. to its primitive application, i. e.,] to denote beginning, [or origination,] being *syn. with* مِنْ; as in the saying [of a poet],

* تَقُولُ وَقَدْ عَالَيْتُ بِالكُورِ فَوْقَهَا *
* أَيُسْقَى فَلَا يَرْوَى إِلَىَّ ٱبْنُ أَحْمَرَا *

[*She says,* (namely my camel,) *when I have raised the saddle upon her, Will Ibn-Aḥmar be supplied with drink and not satisfy his thirst from me?* i. e., will he never be satisfied with drawing forth my sweat?]. (Mughnee, Ḳ.) — It is also used as a corroborative, and is thus [syntactically] redundant; as in the saying in the Ḳur [xiv. 40], فَٱجْعَلْ أَفْئِدَةً مِنَ النَّاسِ تَهْوِى إِلَيْهِمْ, with fet-ḥ to the و [in تهوى], (Mughnee, Ḳ,) accord.

to one reading, (Mughnee,) meaning تَهْوَاهُمْ [i. e. *And make Thou hearts of men to love them*]: (Ḳ:) so says Fr: but some explain it by saying that تهوى imports the meaning of تَمِيلُ; or that it is originally تَهْوِى, with kesr, the kesreh being changed to a fet-ḥah, and the yé to an alif, as when one says رَضَا for رَضِىَ, and نَاصَاةٌ for نَاصِيَةٌ: so says Ibn-Málik; but this requires consideration; for it is a condition in such cases that the ى in the original form must be movent. (Mughnee.) [See art. هوى.] — اَللّٰهُمَّ إِلَيْكَ, occurring in a trad., [is elliptical, and] means *O God, I complain unto Thee*: or *take Thou me unto Thee*. (TA.) — And أَنَا مِنْكَ وَإِلَيْكَ means *I am of thee, and related to thee*. (TA.) — You say also, اِذْهَبْ إِلَيْكَ, meaning *Betake*, or *apply, thyself to*, or *occupy thyself with, thine own affairs*. (T, Ḳ.*) And similar to this is the phrase used by El-Aạshà, فَاذْهَبِى مَا إِلَيْكِ. (TA.) And إِلَيْكُمْ [alone is used in a similar manner, elliptically, or as an imperative verbal noun, and] means *Betake*, or *apply, yourselves to*, or *occupy yourselves with, your own affairs*, (اِذْهَبُوا إِلَيْكُمْ,) *and retire ye*, or *withdraw ye, to a distance*, or *far away, from us*. (ISk.) And إِلَيْكَ عَنِّى means *Hold*, or *refrain, thou from me*: (T, Ḳ:) or *remove, withdraw*, or *retire, thou to a distance from me*: اليك used in this sense is an imperative verbal noun. (Ḥar p. 508.) Sb says, (M,) or Akh, (Ḥar ubi suprà,) I heard an Arab of the desert, on its being said to him إِلَيْكَ, reply, إِلَىَّ; as though it were said to him *Remove, withdraw*, or *retire, thou to a distance*, and he replied, *I will remove*, &c. (M.) Aboo-Fir'own says, satirizing a Nabathæan woman of whom he asked for water to drink,

إِذَا طَلَبْتَ المَآءَ قَالَتْ لَيْكَا

[*When thou shalt demand water, she will say, Retire thou to a distance*]; meaning, [by ليكا, i. e. لَيْكَ with an adjunct alif for the sake of the rhyme,] إِلَيْكَ, in the sense last explained above. (M.) — One also says, إِلَيْكَ كَذَا, meaning, *Take thou such a thing*. (T, Ḳ.) — When إِلَى is immediately followed by the interrogative مَا, both together are written إِلَامَ [meaning, *To what? whither?* and *till*, or *until, what time*, or *when?* i. e. *how long?*]; and in like manner one writes عَلَامَ for عَلَى مَا, (Ṣ* and Ḳ voce ما,) and حَتَّامَ for حَتَّى مَا. (Ṣ voce حَتَّى.)

أَلْوَةٌ and أُلْوَةٌ and إِلْوَةٌ: see أَلِيَّةٌ.

أَلُوٌّ One *who swears much*; *who utters many oaths*: (IAạr, T, Ḳ:) mentioned in the Ḳ in art. الى; but the present is its proper art. (TA.)

أَلِيَّةٌ [*A falling short*; or *a falling short of what is requisite*, or *what one ought to do*; or *a flagging*, or *remissness*; and *slowness*, or *tardiness*:] a subst. from أَلَا as signifying قَصَّرَ and أَبْطَأَ. (M.) Hence the prov., (M,) إِلَّا حَظِيَّةٌ فَلَا أَلِيَّةٌ, i. e. *If I be not in favour, and high estimation, I will not cease seeking, and labouring, and wearying myself, to become so*: (M, Ḳ:*) or *if thou fail of good fortune in that which thou seekest, fall not short*, or *flag not*, or *be not remiss, in showing love, or affection, to men*; may-be thou wilt attain somewhat of that which thou wishest: originally relating to a woman who becomes displeasing to her husband: (Ṣ in art. حظو:) it is one of the proverbs of women: one says, *if I be not in favour, and high estimation, with my husband, I will not fall short*, or *flag*, or *be remiss, in that which may render me so, by betaking myself to that which he loveth*: (T and TA in art. حظو:) Meyd says that the two nouns are in the accus. case because the implied meaning is إِلَّا أَكُنْ حَظِيَّةً فَلَا أَكُنْ أَلِيَّةً; the latter noun being [accord. to him] for ▼ آلِيَةً, for which it may be put for the sake of conformity [with the former]; and the former having the signification of the pass. part. n. of أَحْظَى, or that of the part. n. of حَظِىَ [or حَظِيتُ]. (Ḥar p. 78.) — *An oath*; (T, Ṣ, M, Mgh, Ḳ;) as also ▼ أَلْوَةٌ (M, Ḳ) and ▼ أَلْوَةٌ (T, Ṣ, M, Ḳ) and ▼ أُلْوَةٌ and ▼ إِلْوَةٌ: (Ṣ, M, Ḳ: [in the CḲ, والأَلْوَةُ مُثَلَّثَةٌ is erroneously put for والأَلْوَةُ مثلثةٌ:]) it is [originally أَلِيوَةٌ,] of the measure فَعِيلَةٌ: (Ṣ:) pl. أَلَايَا. (Ṣ, Mgh.) A poet says, (namely, Kutheiyir, TA,)

قَلِيلُ الأَلَايَا حَافِظٌ لِيَمِينِهِ
وَإِنْ سَبَقَتْ مِنْهُ الأَلِيَّةُ بَرَّتِ

[*A person of few oaths, who keeps his oath from being uttered on ordinary* or *mean occasions*; *but if the oath has proceeded from him at any former time*, or *hastily, it proves true*]: (Ṣ, TA:) or, as IKh relates it, قَلِيلُ الإِلَآءِ; meaning, he says, قَلِيلُ الإِيلَآءِ; the ى being suppressed: see 4. (TA.)

أَلِيًّا: see the latter part of the paragraph next preceding.

آلٍ *Falling short*; or *falling short of what is requisite*, or *what one ought to do*; or *flagging*, or *remiss*: [and *slow*, or *tardy*: &c.: see 1:] fem. with ة: and pl. of this latter أَوَالٍ. (Ṣ, TA.) See أَلِيَّةٌ, used, accord. to Meyd, for آلِيَةٌ. — *Niggardly, penurious*, or *avaricious*; *impotent to fulfil duties* or *obligations*, or *to pay debts*. (Ḥar p. 78.)

مِئْلَاةٌ *The piece of rag which a woman holds in wailing*, (Ṣ, TA,) *and with which she makes signs*: (TA:) [it is generally dyed blue, the colour of mourning; and the woman sometimes holds it over her shoulders, and sometimes twirls it with both hands over her head, or before her face:] pl. مَآلٍ: (Ṣ, TA:) which also signifies *rags used for the menses*. (TA in art. غبر.)

مُتَأَلٍّ [part. n. of 5]. It is said in a trad., وَيْلٌ لِلْمُتَأَلِّينَ مِنْ أُمَّتِى, explained as meaning *Woe to those of my people who pronounce sentence against God, saying, Such a one is in Paradise, and such a one is in the fire* [*of Hell*]: but see the verb. (TA.)

الى

1. أَلِىَ, (Ṣ, Ḳ,) aor. يَأْلَى, inf. n. أَلًى, (Ṣ,) *He* (a man, Ṣ) *was*, or *became, large in the* أَلْيَة, q. v. (Ṣ, Ḳ.*) — لَا دَرَيْتَ وَلَا أَلَيْتَ: see 1 in art. الو.

أَلَى : } see إِلَى : — and see also أَلْيَانُ.
أَلًى : }

إِلًى : see إِلَى.

أُلَى, (so in some copies of the Ṣ and in the M,) accord. to Sb, or أُلَا, (so likewise in the M, in which it is mentioned in art. الى, [and thus it is always pronounced,]) or أُولَى; (so in several copies of the Ṣ and in the Ḳ, in the last division of each of those works, [and thus it is generally written;]) and with the lengthened ا, [and this is the more common form of the word, i. e. ▼ أُلَآءِ, as it is always pronounced, or أُولَآءِ, as it is generally written, both of which modes of writing it I find in the M.,] (Ṣ, M, Ḳ,) of the same measure as غُرَابٍ, (M,) indecl., with a kesreh for its termination; (Ṣ;) [*These* and *those*,] a pl. having no proper sing., (Ṣ, Ḳ,) or a noun denoting a pl., (M,) or its sing. is ذَا for the masc. and ذِهْ for the fem., (Ṣ, Ḳ,) for it is both masc. and fem., (Ṣ,) and is applied to rational beings and to irrational things. (M.) [Thus,] هُمْ أُولَآءِ عَلَى أَثَرِى, in the Ḳur xx. 86, means [*They are these, following near after me*; or] *they are near me, coming near after me*. (Jel, and Bḍ says the like.) And in the same, iii. 115, هَا أَنْتُمْ أُولَآءِ تُحِبُّونَهُمْ وَلَا يُحِبُّونَكُمْ *Now ye*, O ye *these* believers, *love them, and they love not you*. (Jel.) — The particle (M) هَا (Ṣ, Ḳ) used as an inceptive to give notice of what is about to be said is prefixed to it, [i. e., to the form with the lengthened ا,] (Ṣ, M, Ḳ,) so that you say, ▼ هٰؤُلَآءِ [meaning *These*, like as هٰذَا means "this"]. (Ṣ, Ḳ.) And AZ says that some of the Arabs say, هٰؤُلَآءٍ قَوْمُكَ [*These are thy people*], (Ṣ, M,*) and ▼ رَأَيْتُ هٰؤُلَآءٍ [*I saw these*], (M,) with tenween and kesr (Ṣ, M) to the hemzeh; (Ṣ;) and this, says IJ, is of the dial. of Benoo-'Okeyl. (M.) — And the ك of allocution is added to it, so that you say, أُولٰئِكَ, [or أُولَآئِكَ, which is the same, and أُولٰئِكُمْ, or أُولَآئِكُمْ, &c.,] and أُولَاكَ, (Ṣ, Ḳ,) and أُولَالِكَ, (so in some copies of the Ṣ and in the Ḳ,) or أُلَالِكَ, (so in some copies of the Ṣ and in the M,) in which the [second] ل is augmentative, (M,) and ▼ أُلَّاكَ, with teshdeed, (Ḳ,) [all meaning *Those*, like as ذَاكَ and ذٰلِكَ mean "that;" and hence] Ks says that when one says أُولٰئِكَ, the sing. is ذٰلِكَ; and when one says أُولَاكَ, the sing. is ذَاكَ; (Ṣ;) or أُلَالِكَ [or أُولَالِكَ, each with an augmentative ل, like ذٰلِكَ, (and this, I doubt not, is the correct statement,)] is as though it were pl. of ذٰلِكَ: (M:) but one does not say هٰؤُلَالِكَ, or هٰأُولَالِكَ, (M,) [nor هٰؤُلَآئِكَ, or the like.] [Thus it is said in the Ḳur ii. 4, أُولٰئِكَ عَلَى هُدًى مِنْ رَبِّهِمْ وَأُولٰئِكَ هُمُ الْمُفْلِحُونَ *Those follow a right direction from their Lord, and those are they who shall prosper*.] And sometimes أُولٰئِكَ is applied to irrational things, as in the phrase بَعْدَ أُولَآئِكَ الأَيَّامِ [*After those days*]; and in the Kur [xvii. 38], where it is said, إِنَّ ٱلسَّمْعَ وَٱلْبَصَرَ وَٱلْفُؤَادَ كُلُّ أُولَآئِكَ كَانَ عَنْهُ مَسْؤُولًا [*Verily the ears and the eyes and the heart, all of those shall be inquired of*]. (Ṣ.) —— The dims. are ♦ أُلَيَّا and ♦ أُلَيَّآءِ, (Ṣ, M) and ♦ هٰؤُلَيَّآءِ: (M:) for the formation of the dim. of a noun of vague application does not alter its commencement, but leaves it in its original state, with fet-ḥ or ḍamm, [as the case may be,] and the ى which is the characteristic of the dim. is inserted in the second place if the word is one of two letters, [as in the instance of ذَيَّا, dim. of ذَا,] and in the third place if it is a word of three letters. (Ṣ.) ═ الأُلَى, (as in some copies of the Ṣ and T,) of the same measure as العُلَى; (Ṣ; [wherefore the author of the TA prefers this mode of writing it, which expresses the manner in which it is always pronounced;]) or الأُلَا; (ISd, TA;) or الأُولَى; (so in some copies of the Ṣ and T;) is likewise a pl. having no proper sing., [meaning *They who, those which,* and simply *who,* and *which,*] its sing. being الَّذِى; (Ṣ;) or is changed from being a noun of indication so as to have the meaning of الَّذِينَ; as also ♦ الأُلَآءِ; wherefore they have the lengthened as well as the shortened alif, and that with the lengthened alif is made indecl. by terminating with a kesreh. (ISd.) A poet says,

- وَإِنَّ الأُولَى بِالطَّفِّ مِنْ آلِ هَاشِمٍ
- تَآسَوْا فَسَنُّوا لِلْكِرَامِ التَّآسِيَا

[*And they who are in Et-Ṭaff, of the family of Háshim, shared their property, one with another, and so set the example, to the generous, of the sharing of property*]. (T, and Ṣ in art. اسو, where, in one copy, I find الأُلَى in the place of الأُولَى.) And another poet says,

- وَإِنَّ الأُلَآءِ يَعْلَمُونَكَ مِنْهُمُ

[*And verily they who know thee, of them*]: which shows what has been said above, respecting the change of meaning. (ISd.) Ziyád El-Aajam uses the former of the two words without ال, saying,

- فَأَنْتُمْ أُولَى جِئْتُمْ مَعَ البَقْلِ وَالدَّبَى
- فَطَارَ وَهٰذَا شَخْصُكُمْ غَيْرُ طَائِرِ

[*For ye are they who came with the herbs,* or *leguminous plants, and the young locusts, and they have gone away, while these, yourselves, are not going away*]: (T:) he means that their nobility is recent. (Ḥam p. 678; where, instead of فانتم and اولى, we find وَأَنْتُمْ and أُلَا.) —— In the phrase العَرَبُ الأُولَى, (as in the L, and in some copies of the Ṣ and Ḳ,) or الأُلَى, (as also in the L, and in other copies of the Ṣ and Ḳ, [and thus it is always pronounced,]) الاولى or الالى may also signify الَّذِينَ, the verb سَلَفُوا being suppressed after it, because understood; [so that the meaning is, *The Arabs who have preceded,* or *passed away;*] so says Ibn-Esh-Shejeree: (L:) or it is formed by transposition from الأُوَلُ, being pl. of أُولَى [fem. of أَوَّلُ], like أُخَرُ as is pl. of آخَرُ: and it is thus in the phrase, ذَهَبَتِ العَرَبُ الأُولَى or الأُلَى [*The first Arabs have passed away*]. (Ṣ, Ḳ.) 'Obeyd Ibn-El-Abraṣ uses the phrase, نَحْنُ الأُلَى [as meaning *We are the first*]. (TA.)

إِلَى : see إِلَى.

إِلَى : see إِلًى : ═ and see also art. الو.

إِلًى (T, Ṣ, M, Ḳ) and ♦ أَلًى, (Ṣ, M, Ḳ,) the latter said by Zekereeyà to be the most common, and the same is implied in the Ṣ, but MF says that this is not known, (TA,) and ♦ إِلْوٌ, (T,) or ♦ أَلْوٌ, (Es-Semeen, Ḳ,) like دَلْوٌ, (Es-Semeen, TA,) [belonging to art. الو,] and ♦ إِلْىٌ (T, M, Ḳ) and ♦ أَلْىٌ (M, Ḳ) and ♦ أُلْىٌ (Es-Sakháwee, Zekereeyà, TA) and ♦ إِلًى, (the same,) or إِلًا, occurring at the end of a verse, but it may be a contraction of إِلًّا, meaning عَهْدًا, (M,) *A benefit, benefaction, favour, boon,* or *blessing:* pl. آلَآءٌ. (T, Ṣ, M, Ḳ, &c.) IAmb says that أَلًى and إِلًى are originally وَلًا and وِلًا. (TA.)

أَلْيَةٌ The *buttock,* or *buttocks, rump,* or *posteriors,* syn. عُجَيْزَةٌ, (Ḳ,) or [more properly] عَجُزٌ, (M,) of a man &c., (M,) or of a sheep or goat, (Lth, T, Ṣ,) and of a man, (Lth, T,) or of a ewe: (ISk, T:) or the *flesh and fat thereon:* (M, Ḳ:) you should not say ♦ إِلْيَةٌ, (T, Ṣ, Ḳ,) a form mentioned by the expositors of the Fṣ, but said to be vulgar and low; (TA;) nor لِيَّةٌ, (T, Ṣ, Ḳ,) with kesr to the ل, and with teshdeed to the ى, as in the Ṣ, [but in a copy of the Ṣ, and in one of the T, written without teshdeed,] a form asserted to be correct by some, but it is rarer and lower than إِلْيَةٌ, though it is the form commonly obtaining with the vulgar: (TA:) the dual. is ♦ أَلْيَانِ, (AZ, T, Ṣ,) without ت; (Ṣ;) but أَلْيَتَانِ sometimes occurs: (IB:) أَلَصُّ الأَلْيَتَيْنِ is an epithet applied to the Zenjee, (Ḳ in art. لص,) meaning *having the buttocks cleaving together:* (TA in that art.:) the pl. is أَلَيَاتٌ (T, M, Ḳ) and أَلَايَا; (M, Ḳ;) the latter anomalous. (M.) Lḥ mentions the phrase, إِنَّهُ لَذُو أَلَيَاتٍ [*Verily he has large buttocks*]; as though the term أَلْيَةٌ applied to every part of what is thus called. (M.) —— *Fat,* as a subst.: (M:) and *a piece of fat.* (M, Ḳ.) —— The *tail,* or *fat of the tail,* (Pers. دُنْبَهْ,) of a sheep. (KL.) [Both of these significations (the "tail," and "fat of the tail," of a sheep) are now commonly given to لِيَّة, a corruption of أَلْيَةٌ mentioned above: and in the Ḳ, voce طُنْبُورٌ, it is said that the Pers. دُنْبَهْ بَرَهْ signifies أَلْيَةُ الحَمَلِ.] —— أَلْيَةُ السَّاقِ *The muscle of the shank;* syn. حَمَاةُ السَّاقِ [which see, in art. حمو]. (AAF, M, Ḳ.) —— أَلْيَةُ الإِبْهَامِ *The portion of flesh that is at the root of the thumb;* (Ṣ, M;) *and which is also called its* ضَرَّة; (M;) or *the part to which corresponds the* ضَرَّة; (Ṣ;) *and which is also called* أَلْيَةُ الكَفِّ; the ضَرَّة being the portion of flesh in (فِى [app. a mistranscription for مِنْ *from*]) the little finger to the prominent extremity of the ulna next that finger, at the wrist: (TA:) or *the portion of flesh in the* ضَرَّة *of the thumb.* (Ḳ.) —— أَلْيَةُ الخِنْصِرِ *The portion of flesh that is beneath the little finger;* [app. *what is described above, as called the* ضَرَّة, *extending from that finger to the prominent extremity of the ulna, at the wrist;*] *also called* أَلْيَةُ اليَدِ. (Lth, T.) —— أَلْيَتَا الكَفِّ *The* أَلْيَة *of the thumb* [*described above as also called by itself* أَلْيَةُ الكَفِّ] *and the* ضَرَّة *of the little finger* [respecting which see the next preceding sentence]. (TA, from a trad.) —— أَلْيَةُ القَدَمِ *The part of the human foot upon which one treads, which is the portion of flesh beneath* [or next to] *the little toe.* (M.) —— أَلْيَةُ الحَافِرِ *The hinder part of the solid hoof.* (Ṣ, M.)

إِلْيَةٌ : see أَلْيَةٌ.

أَلْيَانُ : see أَلْيَانٌ.

أَلْيَانِ an irreg. dual of أَلْيَةٌ, q. v.

أَلْيَانٌ (T, Ṣ, M, Ḳ) and ♦ أَلْيَانٌ (M, Ḳ) and ♦ آلَى, (T, Ṣ, Ḳ,) of the measure أَفْعَلُ, (Ṣ,) and ♦ آلٍ, (M,) or ♦ أَلِى, (so in some copies of the Ḳ, and so accord. to the TA,) or ♦ أَلْىٌ, (so in a copy of the Ḳ,) or ♦ أَلِىٌّ, (accord. to the CḲ,) and ♦ آلٍ, (M, Ḳ,) applied to a ram, *Large in the* أَلْيَة, q. v.: (T,* Ṣ, M,* Ḳ,* TA:) and so, applied to a ewe, أَلْيَانَةٌ, (T, M, Ḳ, [in the CḲ أَلْيَانَة,]) fem. of أَلْيَانُ; (T;) and ♦ أَلْيَآءُ, (T, Ṣ, M, Ḳ,) fem. of آلَى: (T, Ṣ:) and in like manner these epithets [masc. and fem. respectively, آلَى, however, being omitted in the M,] are applied to a man and to a woman; (M, Ḳ;) or, accord. to Aboo-Is-ḥáḳ, (M,) آلَى is applied to a man, and عَجْزَآءُ to a woman, but not أَلْيَآءُ, (Ṣ, M,) though [it is asserted that] some say this, (Ṣ,) Yz saying so, accord. to A 'Obeyd, (IB,) but A 'Obeyd has erred in this matter: (M:) the pl. is أُلْىٌ, (T, Ṣ, M, Ḳ, [in the CḲ erroneously written with fet-ḥ to the أ,]) pl. of آلَى, (T, Ṣ, M,) or of آلٍ; of the former because an epithet of this kind is generally of the measure أَفْعَلُ, or of the latter after the manner of بُزْلٌ as pl. of بَازِلٌ, and عُوذٌ as pl. of عَائِذٌ; (M;) applied to rams (T, Ṣ, M) and to ewes, (T, Ṣ,) and to men and to women; (M, Ḳ;) and أَلْيَانَاتٌ, (Ṣ, M, Ḳ, [in the CḲ أَلْيَانَات,]) pl. of أَلْيَانَةٌ, (TA,) [but] applied to rams (Ṣ) [as well as ewes], or to women, (M, Ḳ,) and, also applied to women, إِلَآءٌ, (M, and so in a copy of the Ḳ, [in the CḲ أَلَآء,]) or آلَآءٌ, (so in some copies of the Ḳ, and in the TA,) with medd, pl. of أَلْيَآءُ, (TA,) and أَلَايَا, (Ḳ,) pl. of أَلْيَانُ. (TA.)

الأُلَآءِ and هٰؤُلَآءِ and أُلَآءِ : see أُلَى.

أَلِىٌّ, mentioned in this art. in the Ḳ: see art. الو: ═ and see also أَلْيَانُ.

أُلَيَّا and أُلَيَّآءِ and هٰؤُلَيَّآءِ : see أُلَى.

أَلَّآءٌ A man *who sells fat, which is termed* أَلْيَةٌ. (M.)

أَلِىٌّ‎ : see أَلْآنَ.

آلٍ : } see أَلْيَانُ.
آلٍ :

آلَى, and its fem. أَلْيَآءُ : see أَلْيَانُ, in two places.

امر

1. أَمَّهُ, (T, Ṣ, M, &c.,) aor. ـُ, (T, M, Mṣb,) inf. n. أَمٌّ, (T, Ṣ, M, Mṣb,) *He tended, repaired, betook himself,* or *directed his course, to,* or *towards, him,* or *it; aimed at, sought, endeavoured after, pursued,* or *endeavoured to reach* or *attain* or *obtain, him,* or *it; intended it,* or *purposed it;* syn. قَصَدَهُ, (Lth, T, Ṣ, M, Mgh, Mṣb, Ḳ,) and تَوَجَّهَ إِلَيْهِ, تَوَخَّاهُ, (T,) and تَعَمَّدَهُ, (Mgh,) and (TA;) as also ↓ أَمَّمَهُ, and ↓ تَأَمَّمَهُ, (T, Ṣ, M, Mgh, Mṣb, Ḳ,) and ↓ ائْتَمَّهُ, (M, Ḳ,) and ↓ يَمَّمَهُ, (T, M, Ḳ,) and ↓ تَيَمَّمَهُ; (T, M, Mgh, Ḳ;) the last two being formed by substitution [of ى for أ]. (M.) Hence, يَا أَللّٰهُ أُمَّنَا بِخَيْرٍ [*O God, bring us good*]. (JK in art. اله, and Bḍ in iii. 25.) And لَأَمَّ مَا هُوَ, occurring in a trad., meaning *He has indeed betaken himself to,* or *pursued, the right way:* or it is used in a pass. sense, as meaning *he is in the way which ought to be pursued.* (TA.) And انْطَلَقْتُ أَتَأَمَّمُ ↓ رَسُولَ ٱللّٰهِ, in another trad., *I went away, betaking myself to the Apostle of God.* (TA.) Hence, also, تَيَمَّمَ ↓ الصَّعِيدَ لِلصَّلَاةِ [*He betook himself to dust,* or *pure dust,* to wipe his face and his hands and arms therewith, *for prayer*]: (T,* M,* Mgh, TA:) as in the Ḳur iv. 46 and v. 9: (ISk, M, TA:) whence التَّيَمُّمُ as meaning *the wiping the face and the hands and arms with dust;* (ISk, T,* M,* Mgh, TA;) i. e. *the performing the act termed* تَوَضُّؤ *with dust:* formed by substitution [of ى for أ]: (M, Ḳ:) originally التَّأَمُّمُ. (Ḳ.) — See also 8. — أَمَّهُ, (Ṣ, M, Mgh, &c.,) aor. ـُ, (M, Mgh,) inf. n. أَمٌّ, (M, Mgh, Ḳ,) *He broke his head, so as to cleave the skin,* (Ṣ, Mṣb,) *inflicting a wound such as is termed* آمَّة [q. v.]; (Ṣ;) [i. e.] *he struck,* (M, Mgh, Ḳ,) or *wounded,* (M, Ḳ,) the أُمّ [q. v.] *of his head,* (M, Mgh, Ḳ,) with a staff, or stick. (Mgh.) — أَمَّهُمْ, (Ṣ, M, Ḳ) and أَمَّ بِهِمْ, (M, Ḳ,) [aor. ـُ,] inf. n. إِمَامَةٌ, (Ṣ, [but in the M and Ḳ it seems to be indicated that this is a simple subst.,]) *He preceded them; went before them; took precedence of them;* or *led them, so as to serve as an example,* or *object of imitation;* syn. تَقَدَّمَهُمْ; (M, Ḳ;) [and particularly] فِى الصَّلَاةِ [*in prayer*]. (Ṣ.) And أَمَّهُ and أَمَّ بِهِ *He prayed as* إِمَام [q. v.] *with him.* (Mṣb.) And أَمَّ الصُّفُوفَ *He became* [or *acted as*] إِمَام *to the people composing the ranks* [in a mosque &c.]. (Ḥar p. 680.) You say also, لَا يَؤُمُّ الرَّجُلَ الرَّجُلُ فِى سُلْطَانِهِ [*A man shall not take precedence of a man in his authority*]; meaning, in his house, and where he has predominance, or superior power, or authority; nor shall he sit upon his cushion; for in doing so he would show him contempt. (Mgh in art. سلط.) — أَمَّتْ, (Ṣ, M, Ḳ,) [first pers. أَمُمْتُ,] aor. ـُ, (M,) inf. n. أُمُومَةٌ, (M, Ḳ,) *She* (a woman, Ṣ) *became a mother;* (Ṣ, M, Ḳ;) [as also أَمِمْتُ having for its first pers. أَمِمْتُ, aor. ـَ; for] you say, مَا كُنْتِ أُمًّا وَلَقَدْ أَمِمْتِ [*Thou wast not a mother, and thou hast become a mother*], (Ṣ, M, Ḳ, [in the last فَأَمِمْتِ,]) with kesr, (Ḳ,) inf. n. أُمُومَةٌ. (Ṣ, M, Ḳ.) — أَمَمْتُهُ *I was to him a mother.* (A in art. ربض.) IAạr, speaking of a woman, said, كَانَتْ لَنَا عَمَّةٌ تَؤُمُّهَا, meaning [*She had,* lit. *there was to her, a paternal aunt*] *who was to her like the mother.* (M.)

2. أَمَّمَهُ and يَمَّمَهُ : see 1, first sentence, in two places.

3. آمَّهُ *It agreed with it, neither exceeding nor falling short.* (M.) — [See also the part. n. مُؤَامّ, voce أَمَرَ; whence it seems that there are other senses in which آمَّ may be used, intransitively.]

5. تَأَمَّمَ and تَيَمَّمَ : see 1, former part, in four places. — تَأَمَّمَ بِهِ : see 8. — تَأَمَّمْتُ *I took for myself,* or *adopted, a mother.* (Ṣ.) And تَأَمَّمَهَا *He took her for himself,* or *adopted her, as a mother;* (Ṣ,* M, Ḳ;) as also ↓ اسْتَأَمَّهَا, (M, Ḳ,) and تَأَمَّهَا. (M.)

8. ائْتَمَّهُ [written with the disjunctive alif إِيتَمَّهُ]: see 1, first sentence. — ائْتَمَّ بِهِ *He followed his example; he imitated him; he did as he did, following his example;* or *taking him as an example, an exemplar, a pattern,* or *an object of imitation;* (Ṣ, Mgh, Mṣb;) as also ↓ أَمَّهُ: (Bḍ in xvi. 121:) the object of the verb is termed إِمَام; (Ṣ, M, Mgh, Mṣb, Ḳ;) applied to a learned man, (Mṣb,) or a head, chief, or leader, or some other person. (M, Ḳ.) *He made it an* أُمَّة or إِمَّة [i. e. *a way, course,* or *rule, of life* or *conduct;* as explained immediately before in the work whence this is taken]; as also ↓ تَأَمَّمَ بِهِ. (M.) You say, ائْتَمَّ بِالشَّىْءِ and ائْتَمَى بِهِ, by substitution [of ى for م], (M, Ḳ,) disapproving of the doubling [of the م]. (M.)

10: see 5.

أَمْ is a conjunction, (Ṣ, M, Ḳ,) connected with what precedes it (Mṣb, Mughnee) so that neither what precedes it nor what follows it is independent, the one of the other. (Mughnee.) It denotes interrogation; (M, Ḳ;) or is used in a case of interrogation, (Ṣ, Mṣb,) corresponding to the interrogative أ, and meaning أَىّ, (Ṣ,) or, as Z says, أَىُّ ٱلْأَمْرَيْنِ كَائِنٌ; [for an explanation of which, see what follows;] (Mughnee;) or, [in other words,] corresponding to the interrogative أ, whereby, and by أَمْ, one seeks, or desires, particularization: (Mughnee:) it is as though it were an interrogative after an interrogative. (Lth, T.) Thus you say, أَزَيْدٌ فِى ٱلدَّارِ أَمْ عَمْرٌو [*Is Zeyd in the house, or 'Amr?*]; (Ṣ, Mughnee;) i. e. which of them two (أَيُّهُمَا) is in the house? (Ṣ;) therefore what follows ام and what precedes it compose one sentence; and it is not used in commanding nor in forbidding; and what follows it must correspond to what precedes it in the quality of noun and of verb; so that you say, أَزَيْدٌ قَائِمٌ أَمْ قَاعِدٌ [*Is Zeyd standing, or sitting?*] and أَقَامَ زَيْدٌ أَمْ قَعَدَ [*Did Zeyd stand, or sit?*]. (Mṣb.) It is not to be coupled with أ after it: you may not say, أَعِنْدَكَ زَيْدٌ أَمْ أَعِنْدَكَ عَمْرٌو. (Ṣ.) — As connected in like manner with what goes before, it is preceded by أ denoting equality [by occurring after سَوَآءٌ &c.], and corresponds thereto, as in [the Ḳur lxiii. 6,] سَوَآءٌ عَلَيْهِمْ أَسْتَغْفَرْتَ لَهُمْ أَمْ لَمْ تَسْتَغْفِرْ لَهُمْ [It will be *equal to them whether thou beg forgiveness for them or do not beg forgiveness for them*]. (Mughnee.) — It is also unconnected with what precedes it, (Ṣ, Mṣb, Mughnee,) implying always digression, (Mughnee,) preceded by an enunciative, or an interrogative, (Ṣ, Mṣb, Mughnee,) other than أ, (Mughnee,) or by أ not meant [really] as an interrogative but to denote disapproval, (Mughnee,) and signifies بَلْ, (Lth, Zj, T, Ṣ, M, Mughnee, Ḳ,) or بَلْ and أ together, (Mṣb,) and this is its meaning always accord. to all the Baṣrees, but the Koofees deny this. (Mughnee.) Thus, using it after an enunciative, you say, إِنَّهَا لَإِبِلٌ أَمْ شَآءٌ [*Verily they are camels: nay,* or *nay but, they are sheep,* or *goats:* or *nay, are they sheep,* or *goats?*]: (Ṣ, Mṣb, Mughnee:) this being said when one looks at a bodily form, and imagines it to be a number of camels, and says what first occurs to him; then the opinion that it is a number of sheep or goats suggests itself to him, and he turns from the first idea, and says, أَمْ شَآءٌ, meaning بَلْ, because it is a digression from what precedes it; though what follows بل is [properly] a thing known certainly, and what follows ام is opined. (Ṣ, TA.) And using it after an interrogative in this case, you say, هَلْ زَيْدٌ مُنْطَلِقٌ أَمْ عَمْرٌو [*Is Zeyd going away? Nay rather,* or, *or rather, is 'Amr?*]: you digress from the question respecting Zeyd's going away, and make the question to relate to 'Amr; so that ام implies indecisive opinion, and interrogation, and digression. (Ṣ.) And thus using it, you say, هَلْ زَيْدٌ قَامَ أَمْ عَمْرٌو [*Did Zeyd stand? Nay rather,* or *or rather, did 'Amr?*]. (Mṣb.) And an ex. of the same is the saying [in the Ḳur xiii. 17], هَلْ يَسْتَوِى ٱلْأَعْمَى وَٱلْبَصِيرُ أَمْ هَلْ تَسْتَوِى ٱلظُّلُمَاتُ وَٱلنُّورُ [*Are the blind and the seeing equal? Or rather are darkness and light equal?*]. (Mughnee.) And an ex. of it preceded by أ used to denote disapproval is the saying [in the Ḳur vii. 194], أَلَهُمْ أَرْجُلٌ يَمْشُونَ بِهَا أَمْ لَهُمْ أَيْدٍ يَبْطِشُونَ بِهَا [*Have they feet, to walk therewith? Or have they hands to assault therewith?*]: for أ is here equivalent to a negation. (Mughnee.) [It has been shown above that] أَمْ is sometimes introduced immediately before هَلْ: (Ṣ, Ḳ:) but IB says that this is when هل occurs in a phrase next before it; [as in the ex. from the Ḳur xiii. 17, cited above;] and in this case, the interrogative meaning of ام is annulled; it being introduced only to denote a digression. (TA.) — It is also used as a simple interrogative; accord. to the assertion of AO; in the sense of هَلْ; (Mughnee;) or in the sense of the interrogative أَ; (Lth, T, Ḳ;) as in the saying, أَمْ عِنْدَكَ غَدَآءٌ حَاضِرٌ, meaning *Hast thou a morning-meal ready?* a good form of speech used by the Arabs; (Lth, T;) and allowable when preceded by another phrase. (T.) — And sometimes it is redundant; (AZ, T, Ṣ, Mughnee, Ḳ;) in the dial. of the people of El-Yemen; (T;) as in the saying,

• يَا دَهْنَ أَمْ مَا كَانَ مَشْيِى رَقَصَا •

• بَلْ قَدْ تَكُونُ مِشْيَتِى تَوَقُّصَا •

(T, Ṣ,* [in the latter, يا هِنْدُ, and only the former hemistich is given,]) meaning *O Dahnà,* (the curtailed form دَهْنَ being used for دَهْنَآءُ,) *my walking was not,* as now in my age, [a feeble movement like] *dancing: but* in my youth, *my manner of walking used to be a bounding:* (T:) this is accord. to the opinion of AZ: but accord. to another opinion, ام is here [virtually] conjoined with a preceding clause which is suppressed; as though the speaker had said, يَا دَهْنَ أَكَانَ مَشْيِى رَقَصًا أَمْ مَا كَانَ كَذٰلِكَ. (A'Hát, TA.) = It is also used (T, Mughnee) in the dial. of the people of El-Yemen, (T,) or of Ṭeiyi and Ḥimyer, (Mughnee,) in the sense of ال, (T,) to render a noun determinate. (Mughnee.) So in the trad., لَيْسَ مِنَ آمْبِرِّ آمْصِيَامُ فِى آمْسَفَرِ, (T, Mughnee,) i. e. لَيْسَ مِنَ البِرِّ الصِّيَامُ فِى السَّفَرِ [*Fasting in journeying is not* an act *of obedience* to God]. (T, and M in art. بر.) So too in the trad., اَلْآنَ طَابَ آمْضَرْبُ *Now fighting has become lawful;* as related accord. to the dial. of Ḥimyer, for الضَّرْبُ. (TA in art. طيب.) It has been said that this form ام is only used in those cases in which the ل of the article does not become incorporated into the first letter of the noun to which it is prefixed; as in the phrase, خُذِ الرُّمْحَ وَآرْكَبِ آمْفَرَسَ [*Take thou the spear, and mount the mare,* or *horse*], related as heard in El-Yemen; but this usage may be peculiar to some of the people of that country; not common to all of them; as appears from what we have cited above. (Mughnee.) = أَمْ for أَمَا, before an oath: see art. اما. = And أَمُ ٱللّٰهِ and أَمِ ٱللّٰهِ &c.: see أَيْمُنُ ٱللّٰهِ, in art. يمن.

أُمٌّ *A mother* (T, Ṣ, M, Mṣb, Ḳ, &c.) [of a human being and] of any animal; (IAạr, T;) as also ♦ إِمٌّ, (Sb, M, Mṣb, Ḳ,) and ♦ أُمَّةٌ, (T, M, Mṣb, Ḳ,) and ♦ أُمَّهَةٌ, (Ṣ, M, Mṣb, Ḳ,) which last is the original form (Ṣ, Mṣb) accord. to some, (Mṣb,) or the ه in this is augmentative (M, Mṣb) accord. to others: (Mṣb:) the pl. is أُمَّهَاتٌ (Lth, T, Ṣ, M, Mṣb, Ḳ) and أُمَّاتٌ; (Ṣ, M, Mṣb, Ḳ;) or the former is applied to human beings, and the latter to beasts; (T, Ṣ;) or the former to rational beings, and the latter to irrational; (M, Ḳ;) or the former is much applied to human beings, and the latter to others, for the sake of distinction; (Mṣb;) but the reverse is sometimes the case: (IB:) IDrst and others hold the latter to be of weak authority: (TA:) the dim. of أُمٌّ is ♦ أُمَيْمَةٌ (T, Ṣ, Ḳ) accord. to some of the Arabs; but correctly, [accord. to those who hold the original form of أُمٌّ to be أُمَّهَةٌ,] it is ♦ أُمَيْهَةٌ. (Lth, T, TA. [In a copy of the T, I find this latter form of the dim. written اميهة.]) — لَا أُمَّ لَكَ denotes dispraise; (Ṣ;) being used by the Arabs as meaning *Thou hast no* free, or ingenuous, *mother;* because the sons of female slaves are objects of dispraise with the Arabs; and is only said in anger and reviling: (AHeyth, T:) or, as some say, it means *thou art one* who has been picked up as a foundling, *having no* known *mother:* (TA:) [or] it is also sometimes used in praise; (A 'Obeyd, T, Ṣ, Ḳ;) and is used as an imprecation without the desire of its being fulfilled upon the person addressed, being said in vehemence of love, [lit. meaning *mayest thou have no mother!*], like ثَكِلَتْكَ أُمُّكَ, and لَا أَبَا لَكَ, [and قَاتَلَكَ ٱللّٰهُ,] &c. (Ḥar p. 165.) — Some elide the ا of أُمّ; as in the saying of 'Adee Ibn-Zeyd,

• أَيُّهَا العَائِبُ عِنْدِمُّ زَيْدٍ •

[*O thou who art blaming in my presence the mother of Zeyd*]; meaning, عِنْدِى أُمَّ زَيْدٍ; the ى of عندى being also elided on account of the occurrence of two quiescent letters [after the elision of the ا of أُمّ]: (Lth, T, Ṣ:) and as in the phrase وَيْلُمِّهِ, (Ṣ,) which means وَيْلٌ لِأُمِّهِ. (Ṣ, and Ḳ in art. ويل, q. v.) — هُمَا أُمَّاكَ means *They two are thy two parents:* or *thy mother and thy maternal aunt.* (Ḳ.) [But] فَدَاهُ بِأُمَّيْهِ is said to mean [*He expressed a wish that he* (another) *might be ransomed with*] *his mother and his grandmother.* (TA.) — One says also, يَا أُمَّتِ ♦ لَا تَفْعَلِى [*O my mother, do not thou* such a thing], and [in like manner] يَا أَبَتِ ٱفْعَلْ; making the sign of the fem. gender a substitute for the [pronominal] affix ى; and in a case of pause, you say يَا أُمَّهْ. (Ṣ.) — And one says, مَا أُمِّى وَأُمُّهُ, and مَا شَكْلِى وَشَكْلُهُ, meaning [*What relationship have I to him, or it?* or *what concern have I with him, or it?* or] *what is my case and* [what is] *his* or *its, case?* because of his, or its, remoteness from me: whence, (T,)

• وَمَا أُمِّى وَأُمُّ الوَحْشِ لَمَّا •

• تَفَرَّعَ فِى مَفَارِقِى الْمَشِيبُ •

[*And what concern have I with the wild animals when hoariness hath spread in the places where my hair parts?*]; (T, Ṣ;) i. e. مَا أَنَا وَطَلَبُ الوَحْشِ بَعْدَ مَا كَبِرْتُ [i. e. مَا أَمْرِى وَطَلَبُ الوَحْشِ: in one copy of the Ṣ, وَطَلَبَ, i. e. with وَ as a prep. denoting concomitance, and therefore governing the accus. case: both readings virtually meaning *what concern have I with the pursuing of the wild animals after I have grown old?*]: he means, the girls: and the mention of أُمّ in the verse is superfluous. (Ṣ.) — أُمٌّ also relates to inanimate things that have growth; as in أُمُّ الشَّجَرَةِ [*The mother of the tree*]; and أُمُّ النَّخْلَةِ [*the mother of the palm-tree*]; and أُمُّ المَوْزَةِ [*the mother of the banana-tree;* of which see an ex. in art. موز]; and the like. (M, TA.) — And it signifies also The *source, origin, foundation,* or *basis,* (Ṣ, M, Mṣb, Ḳ,) of a thing, (Ṣ, Mṣb, [in the former of which, this is the first of the meanings assigned to the word,]) or of anything; (M, Ḳ;) its *stay, support,* or *efficient cause of subsistence.* (M, Ḳ.) — *Anything to which other things are collected together,* or *adjoined:* (IDrd, M, Ḳ:) *anything to which the other things that are next thereto are collected together,* or *adjoined:* (Lth, T:) the *main,* or *chief, part* of a thing; the *main body* thereof: and that which is *a compriser, or comprehender,* of [other] things: (Ḥam p. 44:) the *place of collection, comprisal,* or *comprehension,* of a thing; the *place of combination* thereof. (En-Naḍr, T.) — And hence, (IDrd, M,) The *head,* or *chief,* of a people, or company of men; (IDrd, Ṣ, M, Ḳ;) because others collect themselves together to him: (IDrd, TA:) so in the phrase أُمُّ عِيَالٍ [lit. *the mother of a household*], in a poem of Esh-Shenfarà: (IDrd, M:) or in this instance, it has the signification next following, accord. to Esh-Sháfi'ee. (T.) — *A man who has the charge of the food and service* of a people, or company of men; accord. to Esh-Sháfi'ee: (T:) or their *servant.* (Ḳ.) — A man's *aged wife.* (IAạr, T, Ḳ.) — *A place of habitation or abode.* (Ḳ.) So in the Ḳur [ci. 6], فَأُمُّهُ هَاوِيَةٌ *His place of habitation* or *abode* [shall be] *the fire* [of Hell]: (Bḍ, Jel, TA:) or, as some say, the meaning is أُمُّ رَأْسِهِ هَاوِيَةٌ فِيهَا [*his brain shall fall into it,* namely, the fire of Hell]. (TA.) — The *ensign,* or *standard, which an army follows.* (Ṣ.) [See أُمُّ الرُّمْحِ, below.] — It is said in a trad., respecting the prophets, أُمَّهَاتُهُمْ شَتَّى, meaning that, though their religion is one, *their laws,* or *ordinances,* or *statutes, are various,* or *different:* or the meaning is, *their times are various,* or *different.* (TA in art. شت.) — See also أُمَّةٌ, in two places. — أُمٌّ is also prefixed to nouns significant of many things. (M.) [Most of the compounds thus formed will be found explained in the arts. to which belong the nouns that occupy the second place. The following are among the more common, and are therefore here mentioned, with the meanings assigned to them in lexicons in the present art., and arranged in distinct classes.] — أُمُّ الرَّجُلِ *The man's wife;* and *the person who manages the affairs of his house* or *tent.* (TA.) And أُمُّ مَثْوَى الرَّجُلِ *The man's wife, to whom he betakes himself for lodging,* or *abode:* (T:) *the mistress of the man's place of abode.* (Ṣ, M.) — أُمُّ عَامِرٍ *The hyena,* or *female hyena;* as also أُمُّ عَمْرٍو; (TA;) and أُمُّ الطَّرِيقِ. (Ṣ, TA. [See also other significations of the first and last below.]) أُمُّ حِلْسٍ [or أُمُّ الحِلْسِ (as in the Ṣ and Ḳ in art. حلس)] *The she-ass.* (TA.) أُمُّ البَيْضِ *The female ostrich.* (Ṣ, Ḳ.) — أُمُّ الرَّأْسِ *The brain:* (T, M, Ḳ:) or *the thin skin that is upon it:* (IDrd, M, Ḳ:) or *the bag in which is the brain:* (T:) or *the skin that comprises the brain;* [*the meninx,* or *dura mater and pia mater;*] (Ṣ, Mgh;) which is called

أُمُّ الدِّمَاغِ (Ṣ, Mṣb) likewise. (Ṣ.) — أُمُّ النُّجُومِ *The Milky way*; (Ṣ, M, Ḳ;) because it is the place where the stars are collected together [in great multitude]: (M:) or, as some say, *the sun*; which is the greatest of the stars. (Ḥam pp. 43 and 44.) Because of the multitude of the stars in the Milky way, one says, مَا أَشْبَهَ مَجْلِسَكَ بِأُمِّ النُّجُومِ ‡ [*How like is thine assembly to the Milky way!*]. (TA.) — أُمُّ القُرَى [*The mother of the towns; the metropolis*: particularly] *Mekkeh*; (T, Ṣ, M, Ḳ;) because asserted to be in the middle of the earth; (M, Ḳ;) or because it is the Kibleh of all men, and thither they repair; (M, Ḳ;*) or because it is the greatest of towns in dignity: (M, Ḳ:) and every city is the أُمّ of the towns around it. (T.) أُمُّ التَّنَائِفِ *The most difficult of deserts* or *of waterless deserts*: (T:) or *a desert*, or *waterless desert*, (Ṣ, Ḳ,) *far extending*. (Ṣ.) أُمُّ الطَّرِيقِ (T, Ṣ, M) and ↓ أُمَّةُ الطَّرِيقِ (M, Ḳ) *The main part* [or *track*] *of the road*: (T, Ṣ, M, Ḳ:) *when it is a great road* or *track, with small roads* or *tracks around it* [or *on either side*], *the greatest is so called*. (T. [The former has also another signification, mentioned above.]) أُمُّ عَامِرٍ *The cemetery*, or *place of graves*. (T. [This, also, has another signification, mentioned before.]) أُمُّ الرُّمْحِ *The ensign*, or *standard*; (M, Ḳ;) also called أُمُّ الحَرْبِ; (TA;) [and simply الأُمُّ, as shown above;] and *the piece of cloth which is wound upon the spear*. (T, M.*) أُمُّ جَابِرٍ *Bread*: and also *the ear of corn*. (T.) أُمُّ الخَبَائِثِ [*The mother of evil qualities* or *dispositions*; i. e.] *wine*. (T.) أُمُّ الكِتَابِ [in the Ḳur iii. 5 and xiii. 39] (Ṣ, M, &c.) *The original of the book or scripture* [i. e. *of the Ḳur-án*]: (Zj, M, Ḳ:) or *the Preserved Tablet*, اللَّوْحُ المَحْفُوظُ: (M, Mṣb, Ḳ:) or it signifies, (M, Ḳ,) or signifies also, (Mṣb,) *the opening chapter of the Ḳur-án*; *the* فَاتِحَة; (M, Mṣb, Ḳ;) because every prayer begins therewith; (M;) as also أُمُّ القُرْآنِ: (Mṣb, Ḳ:) or the former, *the whole of the Ḳur-án*, (I 'Ab, Ḳ,) *from its beginning to its end*: (TA:) and the latter, *every plain, or explicit, verse of the Ḳur-án, of those which relate to laws and statutes and obligatory ordinances*. (T, Ḳ.) أُمُّ الشَّرِّ *Every evil upon the face of the earth*: and أُمُّ الخَيْرِ *every good upon the face of the earth*. (T.)

إِمٌّ: see أُمٌّ, first sentence.

أَمَّةٌ: see أُمَّةٌ.

أُمَّةٌ *A way, course, mode, or manner, of acting, or conduct, or the like*; (AZ, Ṣ;) as also ↓ إِمَّةٌ: (AZ, Ṣ, Ḳ:) Fr assigns this meaning to the latter, and that next following to the former: (T:) *a way, course, or rule, of life, or conduct*; (Fr, T, M, Ḳ;) as also ↓ إِمَّةٌ. (M, Ḳ.) — *Religion*; as also ↓ إِمَّةٌ: (AZ, Ṣ, M, Ḳ: [one of the words by which this meaning is expressed in the M and Ḳ is شِرْعَة; for which Golius found in the Ḳ سُرْعَة:]) *one course, which people follow, in religion*. (T.) You say, فُلَانٌ لَا أُمَّةَ لَهُ *Such a one has no religion; no religious persuasion*. (Ṣ.) And a poet says,

وَهَلْ يَسْتَوِى ذُو أُمَّةٍ وَكَفُورُ

[*And are one who has religion and one who is an infidel equal?*]. (Ṣ.) — *Obedience* [app. *to God*]. (T, M, Ḳ.) — The *people of a* [*particular*] *religion*: (Akh, Ṣ:) *a people to whom an apostle is sent*, (M, Ḳ,) *unbelievers and believers*; such being called his أُمَّة: (M:) *any people called after a prophet* are said to be his أُمَّة: (Lth, T:) the *followers of the prophet*: pl. أُمَمٌ. (T, Mṣb.) It is said in the Ḳur [ii. 209], كَانَ النَّاسُ أُمَّةً وَاحِدَةً, meaning *Mankind was* [*a people*] *of one religion*. (Zj, T, TA.) — *A nation; a people; a race; a tribe, distinct body*, or *family*; (Lth, T, M, Ḳ;) of mankind; (Lth, T;) or of any living beings; as also ↓ أُمٌّ: (M, Ḳ:) *a collective body* [of men or other living beings]; (T, Ṣ;) a sing. word with a pl. meaning: (Akh, Ṣ:) *a kind, genus*, or *generical class*, (T, Ṣ, M, Ḳ,) *by itself*, (T,) of any animals, or living beings, (T, Ṣ, M, TA,) others than the sons of Adam, (T,) as of dogs, (T, Ṣ, M,) and of other beasts, and of birds; (T, M,* TA;) as also ↓ أُمٌّ; (M, Ḳ;) pl. of the former أُمَمٌ; (Ṣ, M;) which occurs in a trad. as relating to dogs; (Ṣ;) and in the Ḳur vi. 38, as relating to beasts and birds. (T, M,* TA.) — A man's *people, community, tribe, kinsfolk*, or *party*; (M, Ḳ, TA;) his *company*. (TA.) — *A generation of men*; or *people of one time*: pl. أُمَمٌ: as in the saying, قَدْ مَضَتْ أُمَمٌ *Generations of men have passed away*. (T.) — The *creatures of God*. (M, Ḳ.) You say, مَا رَأَيْتُ مِنْ أُمَّةِ ٱللّٰهِ أَحْسَنَ مِنْهُ [*I have not seen, of the creatures of God, one more beautiful than he*]. (M.) — *I. q.* إِمَامٌ; (T, M, Ḳ;) accord. to A 'Obeyd, applied in this sense to Abraham, in the Ḳur xvi. 121. (T.) — *A righteous man who is an object of imitation*. (T.) — *One who follows the true religion, holding, or doing, what is different from, or contrary to, all other religions*: (M, Ḳ:) [said to be] thus applied to Abraham, ubi suprà. (M.) — *One who is known for goodness*: (Fr, T:) and so explained by Ibn-Mes'ood as applied to Abraham: (TA:) or, so applied, it has the signification next following: (TA:) *a man combining all kinds of good qualities*: (T, M, Ḳ:) or, as some say, *repaired to*: or *imitated*. (Bḍ.) — *A learned man*: (T, M, Ḳ:) *one who has no equal*: (T:) the *learned man of his age, or time, who is singular in his learning*: (Mṣb:) and *one who is alone in respect of religion*. (T.) — See also أُمٌّ, first sentence. Hence, يَا أُمَّتِ, which see in the same paragraph. — The *stature of a man; tallness, and beauty of stature*; or *justness of stature*; syn. قَامَةٌ; (T, Ṣ, M, Mṣb, Ḳ;) and شَطَاطٌ: (M, TA: [in the Ḳ, the signification of نَشَاطٌ is assigned to it; but this is evidently a mistake for شَطَاطٌ; for the next three significations before the former of these words in the Ḳ are the same as the next three before the latter of them in the M; and the next five after the former word in the Ḳ are the same as the next five after the latter in the M, with only this difference, that one of these five is the first of them in the M and the third of them in the Ḳ:]) pl. أُمَمٌ. (T, Ṣ, M.*) You say, إِنَّهُ لَحَسَنُ الأُمَّةِ, i. e. الشَّطَاطِ [*Verily he is beautiful in justness of stature*]. (M.) And El-Aạshà says,

حِسَانُ الوُجُوهِ طِوَالُ الأُمَمْ

[*Beautiful in respect of the faces*,] *tall in respect of the statures*. (T, Ṣ, M.* [In the last, بِيضُ الوُجُوهِ.]) — The *face*. (T, M, Ḳ.) — أُمَّةُ الوَجْهِ *The form of the face*: (AZ, T:) or *the principal part thereof*; (M, Ḳ;) *the part thereof in which beauty is usually known to lie*. (M.) You say, إِنَّهُ لَحَسَنُ أُمَّةِ الوَجْهِ *Verily he is beautiful in the form of the face*: and إِنَّهُ لَقَبِيحُ أُمَّةِ الوَجْهِ *verily he is ugly in the form of the face*. (AZ, T.) — أُمَّةُ الطَّرِيقِ: see أُمٌّ. — *A time; a period of time; a while*. (T, Ṣ, M, Ḳ.) So in the Ḳur [xii. 45], وَٱدَّكَرَ بَعْدَ أُمَّةٍ [*And he remembered, or became reminded, after a time*]: (Ṣ, M:) or, *after a long period of time*: but some read ↓ إِمَّةٍ, i. e., after *favour* had been shown him, in his escape: and some read أَمَهٍ, i. e., forgetting. (Bḍ.) And so in the same [xi. 11], وَلَئِنْ أَخَّرْنَا عَنْهُمُ العَذَابَ إِلَى أُمَّةٍ مَعْدُودَةٍ [*And verily, if we kept back from them the punishment*] *until a short period of time*. (Ṣ,* Bḍ.)

إِمَّةٌ: see أُمَّةٌ, in three places; first and second sentences. — *I. q.* ↓ إِمَامَةٌ (Ḳ) [i. e. The *office of* إِمَام, q. v.: or] the *acting as*, or *performing the office of*, إِمَام: (T in explanation of إِمَّة, and M and Mṣb in explanation of إِمَامَة:) and the *mode*, or *manner, of performing that office*. (T.) — *I. q.* هَيْئَةٌ (Lḥ, M, Ḳ) and شَأْنٌ (M, Ḳ) and حَالٌ (M) and حَالَةٌ (M, Ḳ) [all as meaning *State, condition*, or *case*: or by the first may be here meant *external state* or *condition*; *form*, or *appearance*; or *state with respect to apparel and the like*]. — *An easy and ample state of life*; (T;) *easiness*, or *pleasantness of life*; *ampleness of the conveniences of life, or of the means of subsistence*; *ease and enjoyment*; *plenty*; *prosperity*; *welfare*. (IAạr, M, Ḳ.*) You say of an old man when he has strength remaining, فُلَانٌ بِإِمَّةٍ, meaning *Such a one is returning to a state of well-being and ease and enjoyment*. (TA.) — *Dominion; mastership; authority*. (Fr, T, IḲṭṭ.) — *A blessing*, or *what God bestows upon one*; *a benefit, benefaction, favour*, or *boon*; *a cause of happiness*; (T, Ṣ, M, Mṣb, Ḳ;) as being that which men aim at, pursue, or endeavour to obtain. (T.) See أُمَّةٌ, last sentence but one. — Accord. to IḲṭṭ, it signifies also *i. q.* أُمَمٌ [but in what sense is not said]. (TA.)

أَمَمٌ *Nearness*. (Ṣ, M, Ḳ.) — [*Near; nigh*.] You say, أَخَذْتُ ذٰلِكَ مِنْ أَمَمٍ *I took that from near; from nigh*. (Ṣ, TA.) And دَارُكُمْ أَمَمٌ *Your house is near*, or *nigh*. (M, TA.) And هُوَ أَمَمٌ مِنْكَ *He, or it, is near to thee*: and in like manner you say of two: (M, TA:) and of a pl. number. (Ṣ, M, TA.) And دَارِى أَمَمَ دَارِهِ *My house is opposite to, facing,* or *in front of, his house.* (Ṣ.) —— *Easy:* (Ṣ, M, Ḳ:) *near at hand; near to be reached,* or *laid hold of.* (T, TA.) —— *Between near and distant.* (ISk, T, Ṣ.) —— *Conforming,* or *conformable, to the just mean:* (M, Ḳ:*) and ▼ مُؤَامٌّ, (AA, T, Ṣ, M, Ḳ,) [in form] like مُضَارٌّ, (Ṣ,) originally مُؤَامِمٌ, (TA,) *the same;* (T;) *of a middle,* or *middling, kind* or *sort; neither exceeding, nor falling short of, what is right;* (AA, T, Ṣ, M;) applied to an affair, or a case, (T, Ṣ,) and a thing [of any kind]; (Ṣ;) as also ▼ مُؤَمٌّ; (TA;) and *convenient,* or *suitable:* (M, Ḳ:) and أَمَمٌ and ▼ مُؤَامٌّ both signify an affair, or a case, that is *manifest, clear,* or *plain,* (M, Ḳ,) *not exceeding the due bounds* or *limits.* (M.)

أَمَامٌ *The location that is before;* (M, Mṣb,* Ḳ;) *contr. of* وَرَآءٌ. (M, Ḳ.) It is used [absolutely] as a noun, and adverbially, (M, Mṣb,* Ḳ,) necessarily prefixed to another noun: (Mgh:) and is fem., (Ks, M,) and sometimes masc.: (M, Ḳ:) or it is masc., and sometimes fem. as meaning the جِهَة: or, as Zj says, they differ as to making it masc. and making it fem. (Mṣb.) You say, كُنْتُ أَمَامَهُ *I was before him, in respect of place.* (Ṣ.) In the saying of Moḥammad, to Usámeh, الصَّلَاةُ أَمَامَكَ, the meaning is *The time of prayer* [*is before thee*], or *the place thereof;* and by the prayer is meant the prayer of sunset. (Mgh.) You also say, أَمَامَكَ [i. e. Look *before thee;* meaning *beware thou;* or *take thou note;*] when you caution another, (M, Ḳ,) or notify him, of a thing. (M.)

إِمَامٌ *A person,* (Ṣ, Mgh,) or *learned man,* (Mṣb,) *whose example is followed,* or *who is imitated;* (Ṣ, Mgh, Mṣb;) *any exemplar,* or *object of imitation,* (T, M, Ḳ,) *to a people,* or *company of men,* (T,) *such as a head, chief,* or *leader,* or *some other person,* (M, Ḳ,) *whether they be following the right way or be erring therefrom:* (T:) applied alike to a male and to a female: (Mgh, Mṣb:) applied to a female, it occurs in a phrase in which it is written by some with ة: (Mgh:) but this is said to be a mistake: (Mṣb:) it is correctly without ة, because it is a subst., not an epithet: (Mgh, Mṣb:) or it is allowable with ة, because it implies the meaning of an epithet: (Mṣb:) and ▼ أُمَّةٌ signifies the same: (T, M, Ḳ:) the pl. of the former is أَيِمَّةٌ, (T, Ṣ, M, Ḳ, [but omitted in the CḲ,]) originally أَأْمِمَةٌ, (T, Ṣ,) of the measure أَفْعِلَةٌ, like أَمْثِلَةٌ, pl. of مِثَالٌ, (T,) but as two meems come together, the former is incorporated into the latter, and its vowel is transferred to the hemzeh before it, which hemzeh, being thus pronounced with kesr, is changed into ى; (T, Ṣ;*) or it is thus changed because difficult to pronounce; (M;) or, as Akh says, because it is with kesr and is preceded by another hemzeh with fet-ḥ: (Ṣ:) but some pronounce it أَئِمَّةٌ, (Akh, T, Ṣ, M, Ḳ,) namely, those who hold that two hemzehs may occur together; (Akh, Ṣ;) the Koofees reading it thus in the Ḳur ix. 12; (M;) but this is anomalous: (M, Ḳ:) it is mentioned as on the authority of Aboo-Is-ḥáḳ, and [Az says,] I do not say that it is not allowable, but the former is the preferable: (T:) or the pl. is أَئِمَّةٌ, originally أَأْمِمَةٌ, like أَمْثِلَةٌ; one of the two meems being incorporated into the other after the transfer of its vowel to the hemzeh [next before it]; some of the readers of the Ḳur pronouncing the [said] hemzeh with its true sound; some softening it, agreeably with analogy, in the manner termed بَيْنَ بَيْنَ; and some of the grammarians changing it into ى; but some of them reckon this incorrect, saying that there is no analogical reason for it: (Mṣb:) and accord. to some, (M,) its pl. is also إِمَامٌ, (M, Ḳ,) like the sing., (Ḳ,) occurring in the Ḳur xxv. 74; (M;) not of the same category as عَدْلٌ (M, Ḳ) and رِضًى, (M,) because they sometimes said إِمَامَانِ, but a broken pl.: (M, Ḳ:*) or, accord. to A 'Obeyd, it is in this instance a sing. denoting a pl.: (M, Ṣ:*) or it is pl. of آمٌّ, [which is originally آمِمٌ,] like as صِحَابٌ is pl. of صَاحِبٌ: (M:) the dim. of أَيِمَّةٌ is ▼ أُوَيْمَّةٌ; or, as El-Mázinee says, ▼ أُيَيْمَّةٌ. (Ṣ.) —— الإِمَامُ also signifies *The Prophet:* (Ḳ:) he is called إِمَامُ أُمَّتِهِ [*the exemplar, object of imitation, leader,* or *head, of his nation,* or *people*]; (T;) or إِمَامُ الأُمَّةِ [*the exemplar,* &c., *of the nation,* or *people*]; (M;) it being incumbent on all to imitate his rule of life or conduct. (T.) —— *The Khaleefeh:* (Mṣb, Ḳ:) he is called إِمَامُ الرَّعِيَّةِ [*the exemplar,* &c., *of the people,* or *subjects*]. (M.) The title of الإِمَامُ is still applied to the Kings of El-Yemen: Aboo-Bekr says, you say, فُلَانٌ إِمَامُ القَوْمِ, meaning *such a one is the first in authority over the people,* or *company of men:* and إِمَامُ المُسْلِمِينَ means *the head, chief,* or *leader, of the Muslims.* (TA.) —— *The person whose example is followed,* or *who is imitated,* [i. e. *the leader,*] *in prayer.* (Mṣb.) —— [*The leading authority,* or *head, of a persuasion,* or *sect.* The four أَيِمَّة or أَئِمَّة are the heads of the four principal persuasions, or sects, of the Sunnees; namely, the Ḥanafees, Sháfi'ees, Málikees, and Ḥambelees. And the Ḥanafees call the two chief doctors of their persuasion, after Aboo-Ḥaneefeh, namely, Aboo-Yoosuf and Moḥammad, الإِمَامَانِ *The two Imáms.*] —— *The leader* of an army. (M, Ḳ.) —— *The guide:* (Ḳ:) he is called إِمَامُ السَّفْرِ [*the leader of the travellers*]. (M.) —— *The conductor,* or *driver, of camels* (M, Ḳ) is called إِمَامُ الإِبِلِ, though he be behind them, because he guides them. (M.) —— *The manager,* or *conductor,* and *right disposer, orderer,* or *rectifier,* of anything. (M, Ḳ.*) —— *The Ḳur-án* (M, Ḳ) is called إِمَامُ المُسْلِمِينَ [*the guide of the Muslims*]; (M;) because it is an exemplar. (TA.) [*The model-copy,* or *standard-copy, of the Ḳur-án,* namely the copy of the Khaleefeh 'Othmán, is particularly called الإِمَامُ.] —— [*The scripture* of any people: and, without the article, *a book,* or *written record.*] It is said in the Ḳur [xvii. 73], يَوْمَ نَدْعُو كُلَّ أُنَاسٍ بِإِمَامِهِمْ *The day when we shall call every one of mankind with their scripture:* or, as some say, *with their prophet and their law:* or, as some say, *with their book in which their deeds are recorded.* (T.) It is also said in the Ḳur [xxxvi. 11], وَكُلَّ شَيْءٍ أَحْصَيْنَاهُ فِى إِمَامٍ مُبِينٍ, meaning, says El-Ḥasan, [*And everything have we recorded*] *in a perspicuous book,* or *writing;* (Ṣ, Jel;) i. e., *on the Preserved Tablet.* (Bḍ, Jel.) —— *The lesson* of a boy, *that is learned each day* (T, M, Ḳ) *in the school:* (T:) also called السَّبَقُ. (TA.) —— *The model,* or *pattern,* of a semblance, or shape. (M, Ḳ.) —— *The builder's wooden instrument* [or *rule*] *whereby he makes the building even.* (Ṣ, Ḳ.*) —— *The cord which the builder extends to make even, thereby, the row of stones or bricks of the building;* also called التُّرُّ and المِطْمَرُ; (T;) *the string which is extended upon,* or *against, a building, and according to which one builds.* (M, Ḳ.*) —— إِمَامٌ signifies also *A road,* or *way:* (Ṣ, [but omitted in some copies,] M, Ḳ:) or *a manifest road,* or *way.* (TA.) It is said in the Ḳur [xv. 79], وَإِنَّهُمَا لَبِإِمَامٍ مُبِينٍ (Ṣ, M) *And they were both, indeed, in a way pursued and manifest:* (M:) or *in a way which they travelled in their journeys.* (Fr.) —— The *direction* (تِلْقَآء) of the Ḳibleh. (M, Ḳ.*) —— *A tract, quarter,* or *region, of land,* or *of the earth.* (Ṣ.) —— *A string* [of a bow or lute &c.]; syn. وَتَرٌ. (Ṣgh, Ḳ.)

أَمِيمٌ *Beautiful in stature;* (Ḳ;) applied to a man. (TA.) ═ *I. q.* ▼ مَأْمُومٌ; (Ṣ, M, Mṣb, Ḳ;) i. e. one *who raves,* or *is delirious,* (يَهْذِى, [in two copies of the Ṣ يُهْذِى, but the former appears, from a remark made voce أَمَّةٌ, to be the right reading,]) *from* [*a wound in*] *what is termed* أُمُّ رَأْسِهِ [see أُمٌّ]: (Ṣ:) or *wounded in what is so termed;* (M, Ḳ;) *having a wound such as is termed* آمَّةٌ, q. v. (Mṣb.) It is also used, metaphorically, in relation to other parts than that named above; as in the saying,

* وَحَشَاىَ مِنْ حَرِّ الفِرَاقِ أَمِيمُ *

‡ [*And my bowels are wounded by reason of the burning pain of separation*]. (M.) ═ *A stone with which the head is broken:* (Ṣ, O:) but in the M and Ḳ ▼ أُمَيْمَةٌ, [in a copy of the M, however, I find it without any syll. signs, so that it would seem to be ▼ أَمِيمَةٌ,] explained as signifying *stones with which heads are broken:* (TA:) pl. أَمَائِمُ. (Ṣ, TA.)

أُمَامَةُ *Three hundred camels:* (M, Ḳ:) so explained by Abu-l-'Alà. (M.)

إِمَامَةٌ: see إِمَّةٌ.

أَمِيمَةٌ: see أَمِيمٌ. —— Also, (Ṣgh,) or ▼ أُمَيْمَةٌ, (Ḳ,) *A blacksmith's hammer.* (Ṣgh, Ḳ.)

أُمَيْمَةٌ dim. of أُمٌّ, q. v. (T, Ṣ, Ḳ.) ═ See also أَمِيمٌ: —— and أَمِيمَةٌ.

الإِمَامِيَّةُ *One of the exorbitant sects of the Shee'ah,* (TA,) *who asserted that 'Alee was expressly appointed by Moḥammad to be his successor.* (Esh-Shahrastánee p. 122, and KT.)

أُمَيْمِيَّةٌ [dim. of أُمِّيَّةٌ]: see أُمٌّ, first sentence.

أُمِّىٌّ (T, M, Mgh, Mṣb, Ḳ) and ↑ أُمَّانٌ (Ḳ) [the former a rel. n. from أُمَّةٌ, and thus properly meaning *Gentile:* whence, in a secondary, or tropical, sense, † *a heathen;*] † one *not having a revealed scripture;* (Bḍ in iii. 19 and 69;) so applied by those having a revealed scripture: (Bḍ in iii. 69:) [and particularly] an *Arab:* (Jel in iii. 69, and Bḍ and Jel in lxii. 2:) [or] in the proper language [of the Arabs], *of,* or *belonging to,* or *relating to, the nation* (أُمَّة) *of the Arabs,* who did not write nor read: and therefore metaphorically applied to ‡ any one *not knowing the art of writing nor that of reading:* (Mgh:) or † one *who does not write;* (T, M, Ḳ;) because the art of writing is acquired; as though he were thus called in relation to the condition in which his mother (أُمّ) brought him forth: (T:) or † one *who is in the natural condition of the nation* (الأُمَّة) *to which he belongs,* (Zj,* T, M,* Ḳ,*) *in respect of not writing,* (T,) or *not having learned writing; thus remaining in his natural state:* (M, Ḳ:) or † one *who does not write well;* said to be a rel. n. from أُمّ; because the art of writing is acquired, and such a person is as his mother brought him forth, in respect of ignorance of that art; or, as some say, from أُمَّةُ العَرَبِ; because most of the Arabs were of this description: (Mṣb:) the art of writing was known among the Arabs [in the time of Moḥammad] by the people of Eṭ-Ṭáïf, who learned it from a man of the people of El-Ḥeereh, and these had it from the people of El-Ambár. (T.) أُمِّيُّونَ لَا يَعْلَمُونَ الكِتَابَ, in the Ḳur ii. 73, means *Vulgar persons,* [or *heathen,*] *who know not the Book of the Law revealed to Moses:* (Jel:) or *ignorant persons, who know not writing,* so that they may read that book; or, *who know not the Book of the Law revealed to Moses.* (Bḍ.) Moḥammad was termed أُمِّىّ [meaning *A Gentile,* as distinguished from an Israelite: or, accord. to most of his followers, meaning *illiterate;*] because the nation (أُمَّة) of the Arabs did not write, nor read writing; and [they say that] God sent him as an apostle when he did not write, nor read from a book; and this natural condition of his was one of his miraculous signs, to which reference is made in the Ḳur [xxix. 47], where it is said, "thou didst not read, before it, from a book, nor didst thou write it with thy right hand:" (T, TA:) but accord. to the more correct opinion, he was not well acquainted with written characters nor with poetry, but he discriminated between good and bad poetry: or, as some assert, he became acquainted with writing after he had been unacquainted therewith, on account of the expression "before it" in the verse of the Ḳur mentioned above: or, as some say, this may mean that he wrote though ignorant of the art of writing, like as some of the kings, being أُمِّيُّون, write their signs, or marks: (TA:) or, accord. to Jaafar Eṣ-Ṣádiḳ, he used to read from the book, or scripture, if he did not write. (Kull p. 73.) [Some judicious observations on this word are comprised in Dr. Sprenger's Life of Moḥammad (pp. 101—2); a work which, in the portion already published (Part I.), contains much very valuable information.] — Also, (Ḳ,) or [only] أُمِّىٌّ, (AZ, T, M,) applied to a man, (AZ, T,) *Impotent in speech,* (عَيِىّ, in the Ḳ incorrectly written غَبِىّ, TA,) *of few words, and rude, churlish, uncivil,* or *surly.* (AZ, T, M, Ḳ.)

أُمِّيَّةٌ The *quality denoted by the epithet* أُمِّىّ: (TA:) [*gentilism:* † *heathenism:* &c.:] † the *quality of being* [*in the natural condition of the nation to which one belongs,* or] *as brought forth by one's mother, in respect of not having learned the art of writing nor the reading thereof.* (Kull p. 73.)

أُمَّانٌ: see أُمِّىّ: and see also art. امن.

أُمَيْمَةٌ: see أُمّ.

آمٌّ [act. part. n. of 1;] *i. q.* قَاصِدٌ: [see 1, first sentence:] (TA:) pl. إِمَامٌ, like as صِحَابٌ is pl. of صَاحِبٌ, (M, Ḳ,) accord. to some, but others say that this is pl. of إِمَامٌ [q. v.; the sing. and pl. being alike]; (M;) and آمُّونَ. (TA.) Hence, in the Ḳur [v. 2], وَلَا آمِّينَ ٱلْبَيْتَ ٱلْحَرَامَ [*Nor those repairing to the Sacred House*]. (TA.)

آمَّةٌ (Ṣ, Mṣb) and ↑ مَأْمُومَةٌ, as some of the Arabs say, (IB, Mṣb,) because it implies the meaning of a pass. part. n., originally; (Mṣb;) but 'Alee Ibn-Ḥamzeh says that this is a mistake; for the latter word is an epithet applied to the part called أُمّ الدِّمَاغ when it is broken; (IB;) or شَجَّةٌ آمَّةٌ and ↑ مَأْمُومَةٌ; (M, Mgh, Ḳ;) *A wound by which the head is broken,* (Ṣ, M, Mṣb, Ḳ,) *reaching to the part called* أُمّ الدِّمَاغ, (Ṣ, Mṣb,) or, [which means the same,] أُمّ الرَّأْس, (M, Ḳ,) *so that there remains between it and the brain* [*only*] *a thin skin:* (Ṣ:) it is the most severe of شِجَاج [except that which reaches the brain (see شَجَّة)]: ISk says that the person suffering from it roars, or bellows, (يَصْعَقُ,) like thunder, and like the braying of camels, and is unable to go forth into the sun: (Mṣb:) the mulct for it is one third of the whole price of blood: (TA:) IAạr assigns the meaning of [this kind of] شَجَّة to ↑ أَمِيمَة; which seems, therefore, to be either a dial. var. or a contraction of آمَّة: (Mṣb:) the pl. of آمَّة is أَوَامُّ (Mgh, Mṣb) and ↑ مَآمِيمُ; or this latter has no proper sing.: (M, TA:) the pl. of ↑ مَأْمُومَة is مَأْمُومَاتٌ. (Mgh, Mṣb.)

أَوَمُّ and أَيَمُّ *Better in the performance of the office termed* إِمَامَة; followed by مِنْ: (Zj, T, M, Ḳ:) originally أَأَمُّ: the second hemzeh being changed by some into و and by some into ى. (Zj, T, M.)

أُوَيْمَةٌ, or أُيَيْمَةٌ, dim. of أَيِمَّةٌ, pl. of إِمَامٌ, q. v. (Ṣ.)

مُؤَمٌّ: see أَمِيرٌ.

مِئَمٌّ A camel *that leads and guides:* (M:) or *a guide that shows the right way:* and a camel *that goes before the other camels:* (Ḳ:) fem. with ة; (M, Ḳ;) applied to a she-camel (M, TA) *that goes before the other she-camels, and is followed by them.* (TA.)

مَأْمُومٌ: see أَمِيمٌ. — Also A camel *having his hump bruised internally by his being much ridden,* or *having his hump swollen in consequence of the galling of the saddle and the cloth beneath it, and bruised, and having his hump corroded:* (Ṣ:) or *whose fur has gone from his back in consequence of beating,* or *of galls,* or *sores, produced by the saddle or the like.* (M, Ḳ.) — مَأْمُومَةٌ: see آمَّةٌ, in three places.

مُؤَامٌّ: see أَمِيمٌ, in two places.

مُؤْتَمٌّ act. part. n. of ٱئْتَمَّ بِهِ; *Following as an example; imitating; taking as an example, an exemplar, a pattern,* or *an object of imitation.* (Mṣb.) — مُؤْتَمٌّ بِهِ pass. part. n. of the same; *Followed as an example; imitated;* &c.: thus distinguished from the former by the preposition with the object of its government. (Mṣb.)

مَآمِيمُ: see آمَّةٌ.

اما

أَمَا, used to denote an interrogation, is a compound of the interrogative hemzeh and the negative مَا: (M:) it is a mere interrogative [respecting a negative, like أَلَا]; as in the saying, أَمَا تَسْتَحْيِى مِنَ ٱللّٰهِ [*Art not thou ashamed for thyself,* or *of thyself, with respect to God?*]. (Lth, T.) — [IHsh says, after explaining two other usages of أَمَا which we have yet to mention,] El-Málaḳee adds a third meaning of أَمَا, saying that it is a particle denoting عَرْض [or the asking, or requiring, a thing in a gentle manner], like [أَلَا (q. v.) and] لَوْلَا; and is connected peculiarly with a verb; as in أَمَا تَقُومُ [*Wherefore wilt not thou stand?*], and أَمَا تَفْعَلُ [*Wherefore wilt not thou do such a thing?*]; which may be explained by saying that the hemzeh is used as an interrogative to make one confess, or acknowledge, a thing, as it is in أَلَمْ and أَلَا, and that مَا is a negative. (Mughnee.) — It is also an inceptive word, used in the manner of أَلَا: (M:) followed by إِنَّهُ, it is *syn. with* أَلَا: (Ṣ:) [meaning *Now:* or *now surely:* or] both of these meaning *verily,* or *truly;* i. e. حَقًّا: and for this reason Sb allows one's saying, أَمَا إِنَّهُ مُنْطَلِقٌ and أَمَا أَنَّهُ مُنْطَلِقٌ [*Verily,* or *truly, he is going away*]; with kesr after the manner of أَلَا إِنَّهُ, and with fet-ḥ after the manner of حَقًّا أَنَّهُ: and هَمَا وَٱللّٰهِ لَقَدْ كَانَ كَذَا is mentioned as meaning أَمَا وَٱللّٰهِ [&c., i. e. *Verily,* or *truly, by God, such a thing did indeed happen*]; the ه being a substitute for the hemzeh: (M:) so too حَمَا وَٱللّٰهِ [or حَمَا وَٱللّٰهِ]: (Ṣgh and Ḳ in art. حمى:) it denotes the truth of the words which follow it; as when you say, أَمَا إِنَّ زَيْدًا عَاقِلٌ, meaning *Truly,* or *properly speaking,* not tropically, *Zeyd is intelligent;* and أَمَا وَٱللّٰهِ قَدْ ضَرَبَ زَيْدٌ عَمْرًا [*Truly,* &c., *by God, Zeyd beat,* or *struck, 'Amr*]: (Ṣ in art. امو:) [in other words,] it corroborates an oath and a sentence; as in

أَمَا وَٱللّٰهِ لَئِنْ سَهِرْتُ لَكَ لَيْلَةً لَأَدَعَنَّكَ نَادِمًا [*Verily, or now surely, by God, if I remain awake for thee a night, then will I indeed leave thee repenting*]; and أَمَا لَوْ عَلِمْتُ مَكَانَكَ لَأَزْعَجْتُكَ مِنْهُ [*Verily, or now surely, if I had known thy place of being, then had I unsettled thee, or removed thee, from it*]; and أَمَا إِنَّهُ لَرَجُلٌ كَرِيمٌ [*Verily, or now surely, he is* (emphatically) *a generous man*]: (T:) or it is an inceptive particle, used in the manner of أَلَا; [meaning *now:* or *now surely:*] (Mughnee:) or a particle used to give notice of what is about to be said: only put before a proposition [as in exs. mentioned above]: (TA:) and often occurring before an oath [as in exs. mentioned above]: and sometimes its hemzeh is changed into ه or ع, before the oath; each with the ا remaining; [written هَمَا or عَمَا;] and with the ا elided; [written هَمَ or عَمَ;] or with the ا elided, but without the substitution; [written أَمَ;] and when ان occurs after أَمَا, it is with kesr, as it is after أَلَا: and it also means حَقًّا [*verily*, or *truly*]: or أَحَقًّا [*verily?* or *truly?*]: accord. to different opinions: and in this case, ان after it is with fet-h, as it is after حَقًّا: accord. to Ibn-Kharoof, this is a particle: but some say that it is a noun in the sense of حَقًّا: and others, that it consists of two words, namely, the interrogative hemzeh and مَا as a noun in the sense of شَىْءٌ; i. e. أَذٰلِكَ ٱلشَّىْءُ حَقٌّ [*is that thing true?*]; so that the meaning is أَحَقًّا: [if so, أَمَا أَنَّهُ مُنْطَلِقٌ means *Verily*, or *truly, is he going away?*] and this, which is what Sb says, is the correct opinion: مَا is virtually in the accus. case, as an adverbial noun, like as حَقًّا is literally: and أَنَّ with its complement is an inchoative, of which the adverbial noun is the enunciative: but Mbr says that حَقًّا is the inf. n. of يَحِقُّ, which is suppressed, and that أَنَّ with its complement is an agent. (Mughnee.)

أَمَّا is a conditional and partitive and corroborative particle; and is sometimes written أَيْمَا, by the change of the first م into ى. (Mughnee, Ḳ.) — It is used as a conditional particle in the words of the Ḳur [ii. 24], فَأَمَّا ٱلَّذِينَ آمَنُوا فَيَعْلَمُونَ أَنَّهُ ٱلْحَقُّ مِنْ رَبِّهِمْ وَأَمَّا ٱلَّذِينَ كَفَرُوا فَيَقُولُونَ مَاذَا أَرَادَ ٱللّٰهُ بِهٰذَا مَثَلًا [*For as for those who have believed, they know that it is the truth from their Lord; but as for those who have disbelieved, they say, What is it that God meaneth by this as a parable?*]. (Mughnee,* Ḳ,* TA.) That it denotes a condition is shown by the necessary occurrence of ف after it; for if this ف were a conjunction, it would not be prefixed to the enunciative; and if it were redundant, it might be dispensed with; but it may not be dispensed with except in a case of necessity in poetry or in a case of an ellipsis. — In most cases, (Mughnee, Ḳ,) it is used as a partitive, (Ṣ, Mughnee, Ḳ,) implying the meaning of a condition; (Ṣ; [in which it is mentioned with أَمَا;]) and thus it is used in the passage of the Ḳur cited above; (Mughnee;) and in the following exs. [in the Ḳur xviii. 78 and 79 and 81], أَمَّا ٱلسَّفِينَةُ فَكَانَتْ لِمَسَاكِينَ يَعْمَلُونَ فِى ٱلْبَحْرِ and وَأَمَّا ٱلْغُلَامُ فَكَانَ أَبَوَاهُ مُؤْمِنَيْنِ and وَأَمَّا ٱلْجِدَارُ فَكَانَ لِغُلَامَيْنِ يَتِيمَيْنِ [*As for the ship, it belonged to poor men who worked on the sea . . . and as for the boy, his two parents were believers . . . and as for the wall, it belonged to two orphan boys*]. (Mughnee,* Ḳ,* TA.) [It is a partitive also in the phrase أَمَّا بَعْدُ, which see in art. بعد.] — Few have mentioned its use as a corroborative: (Mughnee:) it is thus used in the phrase أَمَّا زَيْدٌ فَذَاهِبٌ [*Whatever be the case*, or *happen what will* or *what may*, or *at all events, Zeyd is going away*], when you mean that Zeyd is inevitably going away, and determined, or decided, upon doing so: (Z cited in the Mughnee, and Ḳ:) therefore Sb explains it as meaning, in this case, مَهْمَا يَكُنْ مِنْ شَىْءٍ [*whatever be the case*, &c., as above, or, in some instances, *happen what would* or *what might*]; thereby showing it to be a corroborative, and to have a conditional meaning: (Z cited in the Mughnee: [and the same explanation of it is given, with a similar ex., in the Ṣ, in art. امو:]) the ف, in this case, is transferred from its proper place before the inchoative, and put before the enunciative. (I 'Aḳ p. 306.) Ks says that أَمَّا is used in commanding and forbidding and announcing: you say, أَمَّا ٱللّٰهَ فَٱعْبُدْ [*Whatever be the case*, or *happen what will*, &c., *God worship thou*]: and أَمَّا ٱلْخَمْرَ فَلَا تَشْرَبْهَا [i. e. أَمَّا ٱلْخَمْرَ فَلَا تَشْرَبْ لَا تَشْرَبْهَا (as is shown in the case of a similar ex. in the Mughnee, though you may say أَمَّا ٱلْخَمْرَ فَلَا تَشْرَبْهَا, without an ellipsis, like as you say أَمَّا ثَمُودُ فَهَدَيْنَاهُمْ as well as أَمَّا ثَمُودَ, in the Ḳur xli. 16, accord. to different readers,) *Whatever be the case*, &c., *wine (drink not), drink not thou it*]: and أَمَّا زَيْدٌ فَخَرَجَ [*Whatever be the case*, &c., *with respect to other things, Zeyd has gone forth*; or *whatever be the case with respect to others, as for Zeyd, he has gone forth*]: whereas إِمَّا [which see in the next paragraph] is used in expressing a condition and in expressing doubt and in giving option and in taking option. (T.) — [IHsh says that in his opinion,] in the phrase أَمَّا ٱلْعَبِيدَ فَذُو عَبِيدٍ, thus heard, with العبيد in the accus. case, the meaning is, مَهْمَا ذَكَرْتَ [&c., i. e. *Whenever thou mentionest the slaves, he is a possessor of slaves*: but I would rather say that the meaning is, أَمَّا ذِكْرُكَ ٱلْعَبِيدَ, &c., i. e. *as for thy mentioning the slaves*, &c.]: and so in similar phrases which have been heard. (Mughnee.) ═ Distinct from the foregoing is أَمَّا in the saying in the Ḳur [xxvii. 86], أَمَّا ذَا كُنْتُمْ تَعْمَلُونَ [*Or rather, what is it that ye were doing?*]: for here it is a compound of the unconnected أَمْ and the interrogative مَا. (Mughnee.) ═ So too in the saying of the poet,

أَبَا خُرَاشَةَ أَمَّا أَنْتَ ذَا نَفَرٍ *
فَإِنَّ قَوْمِىَ لَمْ تَأْكُلْهُمُ ٱلضَّبُعُ *

[*O Aboo-Khurásheh, because thou wast possessor of a number of men* dost thou boast? *Verily, my people, the year of dearth*, or *of sterility, hath not consumed them*]: for here it is a compound of the أَنْ termed مَصْدَرِيَّةٌ [which combines with a verb following it to form an equivalent to an inf. n.] and the redundant مَا: أَمَّا أَنْتَ is for لِأَنْ كُنْتَ; the preposition and the verb are suppressed for the sake of abridgment, so that the pronoun [تَ in كُنْتَ] becomes separate; and مَا is substituted for the verb [thus deprived of its affixed pronoun], and the ن [of ان] is incorporated into the م [of ما]. (Mughnee.) [See another reading of this verse voce إِمَّا; and there also, immediately after, another ex. (accord. to the Mughnee) of أَمَّا used in the manner explained above. See also أَنْ as a conditional particle, like إِنْ.] ═ Also i. q. إِمَّا, q. v. (Mughnee, Ḳ.)

إِمَّا is sometimes written أَمَّا, and sometimes its first م is changed into ى, [forming أَيْمَا or إِيمَا or both, as will be shown below,] (Mughnee, [in my copy of which it is written أَيْمَا, and so in some copies of the Ḳ,] and Ḳ, [in some copies of which it is written إِيمَا,]) and it is held by Sb to be a compound of إِنْ and مَا, (Mughnee,) or as denoting the complement of a condition it is a compound of إِنْ and مَا. (M, Ḳ.) — It denotes doubt; (Ks, T, Mughnee, Ḳ;) as in مَا أَدْرِى مَنْ قَامَ إِمَّا زَيْدٌ وَإِمَّا عَمْرٌو [*I know not who stood: either Zeyd or 'Amr*]: (Ks, T:) and جَآءَنِى إِمَّا زَيْدٌ وَإِمَّا عَمْرٌو [*There came to me either Zeyd or 'Amr*], said when one knows not which of them came. (Mughnee, Ḳ.) — It also denotes vagueness of meaning; as in [the Ḳur ix. 107,] إِمَّا يُعَذِّبُهُمْ وَإِمَّا يَتُوبُ عَلَيْهِمْ [*Either He will punish them or He will turn unto them with forgiveness*]. (Mughnee, Ḳ.) — It also denotes giving option; as in [the Ḳur xviii. 85,] إِمَّا أَنْ تُعَذِّبَ وَإِمَّا أَنْ تَتَّخِذَ فِيهِمْ حُسْنًا [*Either do thou punish, or do thou what is good to them*]. (Mughnee, Ḳ.) — It also denotes the making a thing allowable; as in تَعَلَّمْ إِمَّا فِقْهًا وَإِمَّا نَحْوًا [*Learn thou either law or syntax*; (an ex. given in the T, on the authority of Ks, as an instance of the usage of إِمَّا to denote giving option;)] but its use with this intent is disputed by some, (Mughnee, Ḳ,) while they assert it of أَوْ. (Mughnee.) — It is also used as a partitive; as in [the Ḳur lxxvi. 3,] إِمَّا شَاكِرًا وَإِمَّا كَفُورًا [*Either*, or *whether, being thankful or being unthankful*]; (Mughnee, Ḳ;) the two epithets being here in the accus. case as denotatives of state: or, accord. to the Koofees, إِمَّا may be here [a compound of] the conditional إِنْ and the redundant مَا; كَانَ, accord. to Ibn-Esh-Shejeree, being understood after it: (Mughnee:) and Fr says that the meaning is, إِنْ شَكَرَ وَإِنْ كَفَرَ [*if he be thankful and if he be unthankful*]. (T.) — It also denotes taking option; as in the saying, لِى دَارٌ بِالْكُوفَةِ فَأَنَا خَارِجٌ إِلَيْهَا فَإِمَّا أَنْ أَسْكُنَهَا وَإِمَّا أَنْ أَبِيعَهَا [*I have a house in El-Koofeh, and I am going forth to it, and either I will inhabit it or I will sell it*: but this is similar to the usage first mentioned above]. (Ks, T.) — It is a conjunction, (Ṣ in art. امو, and Mughnee,) accord. to most authorities, i. e., the second إِمَّا in the like of the saying, جَآءَنِى إِمَّا زَيْدٌ وَإِمَّا عَمْرٌو [mentioned above]; (Mughnee;) used in the manner of أَوْ in all its cases except this one, that in the use of او you begin with assurance, and then doubt comes upon you; whereas you begin with إِمَّا in doubt, and must repeat it; as in the saying last mentioned: (Ṣ: [and the like is said in the Mughnee, after the explanations of the meanings:]) but some assert that it is like the first إِمَّا, not a conjunction; because it is generally preceded by the conjunction و: and some assert that و conjoins the noun with the noun, and the إِمَّا conjoins إِمَّا with إِمَّا; but the conjoining of a particle with a particle is strange. (Mughnee.) — Sometimes the و is suppressed; as in the following verse, (Mughnee,) of El-Aḥwaṣ; (Ṣ;)

يَا لَيْتَمَا أُمُّنَا شَالَتْ نَعَامَتُهَا
أَيْمَا إِلَى جَنَّةٍ أَيْمَا إِلَى نَارِ

[*O, would that our mother took her departure, either to Paradise or Hell-fire!*]; (Ṣ,* Mughnee, Ḳ;) cited by Kṣ, with ايما for إِمَّا: (T:) and sometimes it is with kesr [i. e. إِيمَا]: (Ṣ:) IB says that it is correctly إِيمَا, with kesr; asserting the original to be إِمَّا, with kesr, only. (TA.) — And sometimes the former إِمَّا is dispensed with; as in the following verse, (Mughnee,) which shows also that مَا is sometimes suppressed;

سَقَتْهُ الرَّوَاعِدُ مِنْ صَيِّفٍ
وَإِنْ مِنْ خَرِيفٍ فَلَنْ يَعْدَمَا

[*The thundering clouds of summer-rain watered him, or of autumn-rain; so he will not want* sufficient drink]: i. e. إِمَّا مِنْ صَيِّفٍ وَإِمَّا مِنْ خَرِيفٍ. (Mughnee, Ḳ.) Mbr and Aṣ say that إِنْ is here conditional, and that the ف is its complement: but this assertion is of no weight; for the object is the description of a mountain-goat as having sufficient drink in every case: AO says that إِنْ in this verse is redundant. (Mughnee.) — Sometimes, also, one does not require to mention the second إِمَّا, by mentioning what supplies its place; as in the saying, إِمَّا أَنْ تَتَكَلَّمَ بِخَيْرٍ وَإِلَّا فَاسْكُتْ [*Either do thou speak what is good or else be silent*]. (Mughnee.) [See art. الا, near its end.] — Distinct from the foregoing is إِمَّا in the saying in the Ḳur [xix. 26], فَإِمَّا تَرَيِنَّ مِنَ ٱلْبَشَرِ أَحَدًا [*And if thou see, of mankind, any one*]: for this is [a compound of] the conditional إِنْ and the redundant مَا. (Ṣ* in art. امو, and Mughnee.) [In like manner,] you say, in expressing a condition, إِمَّا تَشْتِمَنَّ زَيْدًا فَإِنَّهُ يَحْلُمُ عَنْكَ [*If thou revile Zeyd, he will treat thee with forbearance*]. (Ks, T.) And إِمَّا تَأْتِنِى أُكْرِمْكَ [*If thou come to me, I will treat thee with honour*]. (Ṣ.) — In the following saying, إِمَّا أَنْتَ مُنْطَلِقًا ٱنْطَلَقْتُ [*If thou be going away, I go away*], the مَا is not that which restrains the particle to which it is subjoined from governing, but is a substitute for a verb; (Ḳ and TA in art. مَا;) as though the speaker said, إِنْ صِرْتَ [or rather إِذَا صِرْتَ] مُنْطَلِقًا. (TA in that art.) And hence the saying of the poet, [of which a reading different from that here following has been given voce أَمَّا,]

أَبَا خُرَاشَةَ إِمَّا أَنْتَ ذَا نَفَرٍ
فَإِنَّ قَوْمِى لَمْ تَأْكُلْهُمُ ٱلضَّبُعُ

[*O Aboo-Khurásheh, if thou be possessor of a number of men, verily, my people, the year of dearth,* or *of sterility, hath not consumed them*]; as though he said, إِنْ كُنْتَ ذَا نَفَرٍ. (TA in that art.) [But IHsh states the case differently; saying,] An instance of مَا not used to restrain from governing, but as a substitute for a verb, occurs in the saying, أَمَّا أَنْتَ مُنْطَلِقًا ٱنْطَلَقْتُ [*Because thou wast going away, I went away*]; originally, ٱنْطَلَقْتُ لِأَنْ كُنْتَ مُنْطَلِقًا: [for an explanation of which, see what is said of أَمَّا أَنْتَ in a reading of the verse commencing with أَبَا خُرَاشَةَ voce أَمَّا:] but accord. to El-Fárisee and IJ, the government belongs to مَا; not to كَانَ [or كُنْتَ]. (Mughnee in art. مَا.) — So too in the saying, اِفْعَلْ هٰذَا إِمَّا لَا, meaning إِنْ كُنْتَ لَا تَفْعَلُ غَيْرَهُ [i. e. *Do thou this if thou wilt not do another thing;* or *do thou this at least*]; (Mughnee and Ḳ, each in art. مَا;) indicating a person's refusal to do [fully] that which he is ordered to do: (TA in that art.:) or إِمَّا لَا فَٱفْعَلْ كَذَا, meaning *if thou wilt not do that, then do thou this;* the three particles [إِنْ and مَا and لَا] being made as one word: so says Lth: (T:) [J says,] إِمَّا لَا فَٱفْعَلْ كَذَا is pronounced with imáleh, [i. e. "immá-lè,"] and is originally إِنْ لَا with مَا as a connective; and the meaning is, *if that thing will not be, then do thou thus:* (Ṣ in art. لَا:) [but] AḤát [disallows this pronunciation, and] says, sometimes the vulgar, in the place of اِفْعَلْ ذٰلِكَ إِمَّا لَا, say, اِفْعَلْ ذٰلِكَ بَارِى [*Do thou that at least*]; but this is Persian, and is rejected as wrong: and they say also, أُمَّالِى, with damm to the ا [and with imáleh in the case of the final vowel, and thus it is vulgarly pronounced in the present day]; but this too is wrong; for it is correctly إِمَّا لَا, [with kesr, and] not pronounced with imáleh, for particles [in general] are not thus pronounced: (T:) and the vulgar also convert the hemzeh into ه with damm [saying هُمَّالِى]. (TA in art. مَا.) [Fei says,] لَا is a substitute for the verb in the saying, إِمَّا لَا فَٱفْعَلْ هٰذَا, the meaning being *If thou do not that, then* [*at least*] *do thou this:* the origin thereof is this; that certain things are incumbent on a man to do, and he is required to do them, but refuses; and then one is content with his doing some, or a part, of them, and says to him thus: i. e., *if thou wilt not do all, then do thou this:* then the verb is suppressed, on account of the frequency of the usage of the phrase, and مَا is added to give force to the meaning: and some say that it is for this reason that لَا is here pronounced with imáleh; because it serves for the verb; like as بَلَى is, and the vocative يَا: but it is said that it is correctly pronounced without imáleh; because particles [in general] are not pronounced therewith; as Az says. (Mṣb in art. لَا.) [El-Ḥareeree says that] إِمَّا لَا is properly [a compound of] three particles, which are إِنْ and مَا and لَا, made as one word, and the ا at the end thereof is like the ا of حُبَارَى [in which it is written ى, agreeably with rule]; wherefore it is pronounced with imáleh, like as is the ا of this latter word. (Durrat el-Ghowwáṣ, in De Sacy's Anthol. Gr. Ar. p. 57 of the Arabic text.) In the Lubáb it is said that لَا is used as a negative of the future, as in لَا تَفْعَلْ; and the verb [in إِمَّا لَا] is suppressed; so it [لا] serves as a substitute in the saying, اِفْعَلْ هٰذَا إِمَّا لَا; therefore they pronounce its ا with imáleh: and IAth says that the Arabs sometimes pronounced لَا with a slight imáleh; and the vulgar make the imáleh thereof full, so that its ا becomes ى; but this is wrong. (TA.) You say also, خُذْ هٰذَا إِمَّا لَا, meaning *Take thou this if thou take not that.* (T.) It is related that the Prophet saw a runaway camel, and said, "To whom belongeth this camel?" when, lo, some young men of the Anṣár said, "We have drawn water upon him during twenty years, and yet he has in him fat; so we desired to slaughter him; but he escaped from us." He said, "Will ye sell him?" They answered, "No: but he is thine." And he said, إِمَّا لَا فَأَحْسِنُوا إِلَيْهِ حَتَّى يَأْتِيَهُ أَجَلُهُ, meaning *If ye will not sell him, act well to him until his term of life come to him.* (T.)

امت

1. أَمَتَهُ, (T, Ṣ, M, Ḳ,) aor. ـِ, (T, M, Ḳ,) inf. n. أَمْتٌ, (T, Ṣ, M,) *He measured it; determined its measure, quantity,* or *the like; computed,* or *conjectured, its measure, quantity, &c.;* (T, Ṣ,* M, Ḳ;) as also ↓ أَمَّتَهُ, (M, Ḳ,) inf. n. تَأْمِيتٌ. (TA.) You say, أَمِتْ يَا فُلَانُ هٰذَا لِى كَمْ هُوَ *Compute thou, O such a one, this, for me, how many it is.* (T.) And أَمَتَ ٱلْقَوْمَ *He computed,* or *conjectured, the number of the people,* or *company of men.* (T.) And أَمَتَ ٱلْمَآءَ *He measured,* or *computed, the distance between him and the water.* (T.) — Also, (Ṣ, Ḳ,) aor. as above, (Ḳ,) and so the inf. n., (Ṣ,) i. q. قَصَدَهُ [*He tended, repaired, betook himself,* or *directed his course, to it,* or *towards it; aimed at it; sought after it;* or *intended,* or *purposed, it*]; (Ṣ, Ḳ;) namely, a thing. (Ṣ.)

2. أَمَّتَهُ: see 1. — أُمِّتَ بِٱلشَّرِّ *He was suspected of evil.* (M, TA.)

أَمْتٌ *A measure of distance* [&c.]; as in the saying, كَمْ أَمْتُ مَا بَيْنَكَ وَبَيْنَ ٱلْكُوفَةِ *What is the measure of the distance between thee and El-Koofeh?* (T, TA.) — *Doubt:* (Th, T, M:) said to be so termed because this word signifies the "computing, or conjecturing, measure, quantity, and the like," in which there is doubt. (T, TA.) [See 1.] So in the following ex.: ٱلْخَمْرُ حُرِّمَتْ لَا أَمْتَ فِيهَا *Wine is unlawful: there is no doubt respecting* the unlawfulness of *it:* (Sh, Th, T, Ḳ:) or the meaning is, *there is no indulgence,* or *lenity, with respect to it;* from أَمْتٌ as signifying "feebleness, or weakness," in a journey, or pace. (T, TA.) And in the saying, لَيْسَ فِى ٱلْخَمْرِ أَمْتٌ

There is no doubt respecting wine, that it is unlawful. (Th, M.) [Or in the like of these two instances it signifies] *Disagreement,* or *diversity of opinion,* (اِخْتِلَاف,) respecting a thing (فِى شَىْءٍ). (M, Ḳ.) ═ *Curvity, crookedness, distortion,* or *unevenness:* (M, Ḳ:) *ruggedness in one place and smoothness in another;* (Ḳ;) [*inequality of surface;*] *one part being higher,* or *more prominent, than another:* (TA:) *an elevated place:* (T, Ṣ, Ḳ:) *small mounds:* (Fr, Th, T, Ṣ, M, Ḳ:) or *what is elevated, of ground:* or, as some say, *water-courses of valleys, such as are low,* or *depressed:* (Fr, T, TA:) *small hills; hillocks:* (M, TA:) *a hollow,* or *depressed place, between any two elevated portions of ground &c.:* (IAạr, T, M:) *depression and elevation,* or *lowness and highness,* (Ṣ, M, A, Ḳ,) in the ground; (A;) used in this sense in the Ḳur xx. 106; (Ṣ;) and the same in a water-skin not completely filled: (Ṣ, A:*) or *laxity in a water-skin when it is not well filled so as to overflow:* (T,* TA:) or *a* [*consequence of*] *pouring* [*water*] *into a skin until it doubles,* or *creases, and not filling it; so that one part of it is higher,* or *more prominent, than another:* (M, TA:) pl. إِمَاتٌ (M, Ḳ, TA, but in some copies of the Ḳ آمَاتٌ, and in the CḲ أَمَاتٌ,) and أُمُوتٌ. (M, Ḳ.) You say, اِسْتَوَتِ الأَرْضُ فَمَا بِهَا أَمْتٌ *The earth,* or *ground, was even, so that there was not in it any depression and elevation.* (A, TA.) And اِمْتَلَأَ السِّقَآءُ فَمَا بِهِ أَمْتٌ *The skin became full, so that there was not in it any depression* [*of one part of its surface*] *and elevation* [*of another part*]. (Ṣ, A.*) Az says, (TA,) I have heard the Arabs say, قَدْ مَلَأَ القِرْبَةَ مَلْأً لَا أَمْتَ فِيهِ *He had filled the water-skin so full that there was no laxity in it.* (T, TA.) — *A fault, a defect, an imperfection, a blemish,* or *the like,* (T, M, Ḳ,) in the mouth, and in a garment, or piece of cloth, and in a stone. (M, Ḳ.) [Hence the saying,] أَمْتٌ فِى الحَجَرِ لَا فِيكَ i. e. [*May there be a defect,* or *the like,*] *in stones; not in thee:* meaning, may God preserve thee when the stones shall have perished: (Sb, M:) امت is here put in the nom. case, though the phrase is significant of a prayer, because it is not a verbal word: the phrase is like التُّرَابُ لَهُ: and the commencing the sentence with an indeterminate noun is approvable because it is virtually a prayer. (M.) This prov. is mentioned by the expositors of the Tes-heel: not by Meyd. (TA.) — *Weakness; feebleness;* (T, Ḳ;) *langour; remissness.* (TA.) You say, سِرْنَا سَيْرًا لَا أَمْتَ فِيهِ *We performed a journey,* or *went a pace, in which was no weakness,* or *feebleness* [&c.]. (T, TA.) ═ *A good way, course, mode,* or *manner, of acting,* or *conduct,* or *the like.* (T, Ḳ.)

مُؤَمَّتٌ *Suspected* of evil and the like. (Ḳ.) [See 2.] ═ [A water-skin] *filled* [*so as to be equally distended:* see أَمْتٌ]. (Ḳ.)

مَآءٌ مَأْمُوتٌ *A water of which the distance is computed,* or *conjectured.* (TA.) — هُوَ إِلَى أَجَلٍ مَأْمُوتٍ *It is until a determined, defined,* or *definite, period.* (Ṣ, Ḳ.*) — شَىْءٌ مَأْمُوتٌ *A thing that is known.* (M, TA.) [And so مَوْمُوتٌ.]

امد

1. أَمِدَ عَلَيْهِ, aor. ـَ, inf. n. أَمَدٌ, *He was angry with him:* (Ṣ, M, Mṣb,* Ḳ:) like أَبِدَ (Ṣ) and وَمِدَ and وَبِدَ and عَبِدَ. (T in art. ابد.)

2. أَمَّدَ, inf. n. تَأْمِيدٌ, *He declared the time, considered with regard to its end;* or *the utmost,* or *extreme, extent, term, limit, point,* or *reach;* expl. by بَيَّنَ الأَمَدَ. (Ḳ.)

أَمَدٌ *Time, considered with regard to its end:* زَمَانٌ being time considered with regard to its end and its beginning: (Er-Rághib:) [but sometimes it is interchangeable with زَمَانٌ, as will be seen in what follows:] or *the utmost,* or *extreme, extent, term, limit, point,* or *reach.* (Ṣ, M, A, Mṣb, Ḳ.) You say, بَلَغَ أَمَدَهُ *He,* or *it, reached,* or *attained, his,* or *its, utmost,* or *extreme, extent, term,* &c. (Mṣb.) And ضَرَبَ لَهُ أَمَدًا [*He assigned,* or *appointed, for him,* or *it, a term,* or *limit*]. (A.) And هُوَ بَعِيدُ الآمَادِ [*He is one whose limits are remote:* آمَادٌ being the pl.]. (A.) — *The period of life which one has reached;* as in the saying, مَا أَمَدُكَ *What is thy period of life which thou hast reached?* (Ṣ.) — *Each of the two terms of the life* of a man; i. e. the *time of* his *birth,* and the *time of* his *death.* (Sh, T.) El-Ḥasan [El-Baṣree], being asked by El-Ḥajjáj, مَا أَمَدُكَ, meaning *What was the time of thy birth?* answered by saying that it was two years before the expiration of 'Omar's reign as Khaleefeh. (T, L, from a trad.) — *The starting-place,* and *the goal,* of horses in a race. (Sh, T, L.) — ‡ *Any space of time:* (Er-Rághib:) *a space of time of unknown limit.* (Kull pp. 9 and 10.) — Sometimes, † *A particular time;* as in the phrase أَمَدُ كَذَا *The time of such a thing;* like زَمَانُ كَذَا. (Kull p. 10.) — [It is also used for ذُو أَمَدٍ, and (applied to a fem. n.) ذَاتُ أَمَدٍ, *Having a term,* or *limit; limited in duration;* as in the saying,] الدُّنْيَا أَمَدٌ وَالآخِرَةُ أَبَدٌ [*The present state of existence is limited in duration, but the final state of existence is everlasting*]. ('Obeyd Ibn-'Omeyr, L in art. ابد.)

أُمْدَةٌ *A remainder,* or *what remains,* (Ḳ,) of anything. (TA.)

سِقَآءٌ مُؤَمَّدٌ *A skin* [*exhausted;*] *in which there remains not a gulp,* or *as much as is swallowed at once, of water.* (Ḳ.)

أَمَدٌ مَأْمُودٌ *An extreme term, limit,* or *point, reached,* or *attained.* (Ḳ.)

امر

1. أَمَرَهُ, (T, Ṣ, M, &c.,) aor. ـُ, (M, &c.,) inf. n. أَمْرٌ (T, Ṣ, M, Mṣb, Ḳ) and إِمَارٌ, (M, L, Ḳ,) which latter, however, is disapproved by MF, (TA,) and إِيمَارٌ is syn. therewith, (Ḳ,) but this also is disapproved by MF, and deemed by him strange, [being by rule the inf. n. of ▼آمَرَهُ, respecting which see what follows,] (TA,) and آمِرَةٌ, (M, Ḳ,) which is one of the inf. ns. [or quasi-inf. ns.] of the measure فَاعِلَةٌ, like عَافِيَةٌ and عَاقِبَةٌ, (M,) *He commanded him; ordered him; bade him; enjoined him;* the inf. n. signifying the contr. of نَهْىٌ; (T, M, Ḳ;) as also ▼آمَرَهُ, (Kr, M, Ḳ,) mentioned by A'Obeyd also as a dial. var. of أَمَرَهُ: (Mṣb:) but A'Obeyd says that آمَرْتُهُ and أَمَرْتُهُ are syn. [in a sense different from that explained above, i. e.] as meaning كَثَّرْتُهُ. (TA.) You say, أَمَرَهُ بِهِ, (Ṣ, M, Ḳ,) and أَمَرَهُ إِيَّاهُ, suppressing the prep., (M,) *He commanded, ordered, bade,* or *enjoined, him to do it.* (M, Ḳ.) And أَمَرْتُكَ أَنْ تَفْعَلَ, and لِتَفْعَلَ, and بِأَنْ تَفْعَلَ, *I commanded, ordered, bade,* or *enjoined, thee to do* [such a thing]. (M.) [And أَمَرَهُ بِكَذَا as meaning *He commanded him,* or *ordered him, to make use of such a thing;* or *the like:* whence, in a trad.,] أُمِرْتُ بِالسِّوَاكِ [*I have been commanded to make use of the tooth-stick*]. (El-Jámi' eṣ-Ṣagheer.) [And *He enjoined him such a thing;* as, for instance, patience.] The imperative of أَمَرَ is مُرْ; originally أُؤْمُرْ; which also occurs [with و in the place of ؤ when the ا is pronounced with ḍamm]: (M:) but [generally] when it is not preceded by a conjunction, (Mṣb,) i. e., by وَ or فَ, (T,) you suppress the ء, [i. e. the radical ء, and with it the conjunctive ا preceding it,] contr. to rule, and say, مُرْهُ بِكَذَا [*Command,* or *order,* or *bid,* or *enjoin, thou him to do such a thing*]; like as you say, كُلْ and خُذْ: when, however, it is preceded by a conjunction, the practice commonly obtaining is, to restore the ء, agreeably with analogy, and thus to say, وَأْمُرْ بِكَذَا. (Mṣb.) — [You say also, أَمَرَ بِهِ فَقُتِلَ *He gave an order respecting him, and accordingly he was slain.* And أَمَرَ لَهُ بِكَذَا *He ordered that such a thing should be done,* or *given, to him.*] — In the Ḳur [xvii. 17], أَمَرْنَا مُتْرَفِيهَا فَفَسَقُوا فِيهَا, so accord. to most of the readers, (T, &c.,) means *We commanded* [*its luxurious inhabitants*] to obey, *but they transgressed therein,* or *departed from the right way,* or *disobeyed:* (Fr, T, Ṣ, &c.:) so says Aboo-Is-ḥáḳ; adding that, although one says, أَمَرْتُ زَيْدًا فَضَرَبَ عَمْرًا, meaning *I commanded Zeyd to beat 'Amr, and he beat him,* yet one also says, أَمَرْتُكَ فَعَصَيْتَنِى [*I commanded thee, but thou disobeyedst me*]: or, accord. to some, the meaning is, *We multiplied its luxurious inhabitants;* (T;) and this is agreeable with another reading, namely, ▼آمَرْنَا; (TA;) and a reading of El-Ḥasan, namely, أَمِرْنَا, like عَلِمْنَا, may be a dial. var., of the same signification: (M:) see 4, in two places: or it may be from الإِمَارَةُ; (Ṣ, TA;) [in which case it seems that we should read ▼أَمَّرْنَا; or, perhaps, أَمُرْنَا: see 2:] Abu-l-'Áliyeh reads ▼أَمَّرْنَا, and this is agreeable with the explanation of I'Ab, who says that the meaning is, *We made its chiefs to have authority, power,* or *dominion.* (TA.) — أَمَرَهُ, aor. ـُ, also signifies *He commanded, ordered, bade,* or *enjoined, him to do that which it behooved him to do.* (A.) [*He counselled,* or *advised, him.*] One says, مُرْنِى, meaning *Counsel thou me; advise thou me.* (A.) — أَمَرَ بِٱقْتِبَاسٍ, said

of a wild animal, means *He rendered* the beholder *desirous of capturing* him. (M.) — أَمُرَ, (Aṣ, Fr, Th, T, Ṣ, M, Mṣb, Ḳ,) aor. ـُ; (Mṣb, TA;) and أَمَرَ, aor. ـُ; (Ṣ, M, IKṭṭ, Ḳ;) and أَمِرَ, aor. ـَ; (M, Ḳ, and several other authorities; but by some this is disallowed; TA;) inf. n. أَمْرٌ (Ḳ) and إِمْرَةٌ (Ṣ) and إِمَارَةٌ; (Aṣ, T, Ṣ;) or the second is a simple subst.; (Ḳ;) or perhaps it is meant in the Ṣ that this and the third are quasi-inf. ns.; (MF;) *He had,* or *held, command; he presided as a commander, governor, lord, prince,* or *king;* (M, Mṣb, Ḳ;) *he became an* أَمِير; (Aṣ, T, Ṣ;) عَلَى القَوْمِ *over the people.* (M,* Mṣb, Ḳ.) [See also 5.] أُمِرَ فُلَانٌ وَأَمِرَ عَلَيْهِ, or وَأُمِّرَ ▾ عليه, (as in different copies of the Ṣ,) [*Such a one has held command and been commanded,*] is said of one who has been a commander, or governor, after having been a subject of a commander, or governor; meaning *such a one is a person of experience;* or *one who has been tried,* or *proved and strengthened, by experience.* (Ṣ.) — أَمَرَهُ as syn. with آمَرَهُ: see 4. — أَمِرَ, (Ṣ, M, Mṣb, Ḳ,) aor. ـَ, (Mṣb, Ḳ,) inf. n. أَمَرٌ and أَمَرَةٌ; (M, Ḳ, TA; the latter written in the CḲ أَمْرَةٌ;) and أَمُرَ, aor. ـُ; (IKṭṭ;) † *It* (a thing, M, Mṣb, or a man's property, or camels or the like, Abu-l-Ḥasan and Ṣ, and a people, T, Ṣ) *multiplied;* or *became many,* or *much,* or *abundant;* (T, Ṣ, M, Mṣb, Ḳ;) and *became complete.* (M, Ḳ.) — And the former, † *His beasts multiplied;* or *became many;* (M, Ḳ;) [as also ▾ آمر; for you say,] آمر ▾ بَنُو فُلَانٍ, inf. n. إِيمَارٌ, † *The property,* or *camels* or *the like, of the sons of such a one multiplied;* or *became many,* or *abundant.* (M.) — أَمِرَ الأَمْرُ, (Akh, Ṣ, Ḳ,) aor. ـَ, inf. n. أَمَرٌ, (Akh, Ṣ,) † *The affair,* or *case,* (i. e., a man's affair, or case, Akh, Ṣ,) *became severe, distressful, grievous,* or *afflictive.* (Akh, Ṣ, Ḳ.)

2. أَمَّرَهُ, inf. n. تَأْمِيرٌ, *He made him,* or *appointed him, commander, governor, lord, prince,* or *king.* (Ṣ,* Mgh, Mṣb.) [And it seems to be indicated in the Ṣ that ▾ أَمَرَهُ, without teshdeed, signifies the same.] See 1, in three places. You say also, أُمِّرَ عَلَيْنَا (A, TA) *He was made,* or *appointed, commander,* &c., *over us.* (TA.) — Also *He appointed him judge,* or *umpire.* (Mgh.) — أَمَّرَ القَنَاةَ † *He affixed a spear-head to the cane or spear.* (T, M.) [See also the pass. part. n., below.] — أَمَّرَ أَمَارَةً *He made* [a thing] *a sign,* or *mark, to show the way.* (T.)

3. آمَرَهُ فِى أَمْرِهِ, (T,* Ṣ, M, Mṣb,) inf. n. مُؤَامَرَةٌ, (Ṣ, Ḳ,) *He consulted him respecting his affair,* or *case;* (T,* Ṣ, M, Mṣb, Ḳ,* TA;) as also وَامَرَهُ; (TA;) or this is not a chaste form; (IAth, TA;) or it is vulgar; (Ṣ, TA;) and ▾ استأمره, (M,) inf. n. اِسْتِئْمَارٌ; (Ṣ, Ḳ;) and ▾ ائتمره, (T,) inf. n. اِئْتِمَارٌ. (Ṣ, Ḳ.) It is said in a trad., آمِرُوا النِّسَآءَ فِى أَنْفُسِهِنَّ *Consult ye women respecting themselves,* as to marrying them. (TA.) And in another trad., آمَرَتْ نَفْسَهَا, meaning *She consulted herself,* or *her mind;* as also ▾ استأمرت نفسها. (TA.) [See another ex. voce نَفْسٌ. And see also 8.]

4. آمر, inf. n. إِيمَارٌ: see 1, last sentence but one, in two places. — آمَرَهُ; (Ṣ, M, Mṣb, Ḳ;) and ▾ أَمَرَهُ, (Ṣ, M, Mṣb, Ḳ,) accord. to some, (M,) aor. ـُ, (Mṣb, Ḳ,) inf. n. أَمْرٌ; (Mṣb;) both signifying the same accord. to AO, (Ṣ,) or A 'Obeyd, (TA,) but the latter is of weak authority, (Ḳ,) or is not allowable; (M;) and, accord. to El-Ḥasan's reading of xvii. 17 of the Ḳur, (see 1,) ▾ أَمِرَهُ also; (M;) † *He* (a man) *multiplied it;* or *made it many,* or *much,* or *abundant:* (Ṣ, Mṣb:) *He* (God) *multiplied,* or *made many* or *much* or *abundant, his progeny,* and *his beasts:* (M, Ḳ:) and آمر مَالَهُ † *He* (God) *multiplied,* &c., *his property,* or *camels* or *the like.* (Ṣ.) — See also 1, first sentence, in two places.

5. تأمّر *He became made,* or *appointed, commander, governor, lord, prince,* or *king;* (Mṣb;) *he received authority, power,* or *dominion;* عَلَيْهِمْ *over them.* (Ṣ, Ḳ.) [See also أَمُرَ.] — See also 8.

6: see 8, in three places.

8. ائتمر [written with the disjunctive alif اِيتَمَرَ] *He obeyed,* or *conformed to, a command;* (Ṣ,* M, Mgh, Ḳ;*) *he heard and obeyed.* (Mṣb.) You say, ائتمر بِخَيْرٍ, meaning *He was as though his mind commanded him to do good and he obeyed the command.* (M.) And [you use it transitively, saying,] ائتمر الأَمْرَ *He obeyed,* or *conformed to, the command.* (Ṣ.) And لَا يَأْتَمِرُ رُشْدًا *He will not do right of his own accord.* (A.) Imra el-Ḳeys says, (Ṣ,) or En-Nemir Ibn-Towlab, (T,)

• وَيَعْدُو عَلَى المَرْءِ مَا يَأْتَمِرْ •

[*And that which man obeys wrongs him,* or *injures him*]; meaning, that which his own soul commands him to do, and which he judges to be right, but in which often is found his destruction: (Ṣ:) or, accord. to Ḳt, *that evil which man purposes to do:* (T:) or *that which man does without consideration, and without looking to its result.* (A 'Obeyd, T.) [See what follows.] — *He undertook a thing without consulting;* (Ḳt, T;) as though his soul, or mind, ordered him to do it and he obeyed it: (TA:) *he followed his own opinion only.* (Mgh.) One says, أَمَرْتُهُ فَأْتَمَرَ وَأَبَى أَنْ يَأْتَمِرَ, (A, Mgh,) meaning *I commanded him, but he followed his own opinion only, and refused to obey.* (Mgh.) — *He formed an opinion, and consulted his own mind, and determined upon it.* (Sh, T.) And ائتمر رَأْيَهُ *He consulted his own mind,* or *judgment,* respecting what was right for him to do. (Sh, T.) — ائتمروا, (A, Mṣb,) inf. n. اِئْتِمَارٌ; (Ṣ, Ḳ;) and ▾ تآمروا, (A,) inf. n. تَآمُرٌ, of the measure تَفَاعُلٌ; (Ṣ;) and ▾ تأمّروا, (TA,) inf. n. تَأَمُّرٌ; (Ḳ;) *They consulted together:* (Ṣ,* A, Mṣb, Ḳ:*) or ائتمروا and ▾ تآمروا signify *they commanded, ordered, bade,* or *enjoined, one another;* like as one says, اقتتلوا and تقاتلوا, and اختصموا and تخاصموا: (T:) or ائتمروا عَلَى الأَمْرِ and ▾ تآمروا عَلَيْهِ, *they determined,* or *settled, their opinions respecting the affair,* or *case:* (M:) and ائتمروا بِهِ, (Ṣ, Mṣb,) inf. n. as above, (Ḳ,) signifies *they purposed it,* (Ṣ, Mṣb, Ḳ,*) namely, a thing, (Mṣb, Ḳ,) *and consulted one another respecting it.* (Ṣ.) It is said in the Ḳur [lxv. 6], وَأْتَمِرُوا بَيْنَكُمْ بِمَعْرُوفٍ *And command ye,* or *enjoin ye, one another to do good:* [such is app. the meaning,] but God best knoweth: (T:) or, accord. to Ḳt, *purpose ye among yourselves to do good.* (TA.) And in the same [xxviii. 19], إِنَّ الْمَلَأَ يَأْتَمِرُونَ بِكَ لِيَقْتُلُوكَ, meaning *Verily the chiefs command one another respecting thee, to slay thee:* (Zj, T:) or *consult together against thee, to slay thee:* (AO, T:) or *purpose against thee, to slay thee:* (Ḳt, T:) but the last but one of these explanations is better than the last. (T.) — See also 3. — Accord. to El-Bushtee, ائتمره also signifies *He gave him permission:* but this has not been heard from an Arab. (Az, TA.)

10: see 3, in two places.

أَمْرٌ *A command; an order; a bidding; an injunction; a decree; an ordinance; a prescript:* (Ṣ,* Mṣb,* TA, &c.:) pl. أَوَامِرُ: (Ṣ, Mṣb, &c.:) so accord. to common usage; and some writers of authority justify and explain it by saying that أَمْرٌ is [originally] مَأْمُورٌ بِهِ; that it is then changed to the measure فَاعِلٌ; [i. e., to آمِرٌ;] like أَمْرٌ عَارِفٌ, which is originally مَعْرُوفٌ; and عِيشَةٌ رَاضِيَةٌ, originally مَرْضِيَّةٌ; &c.; [and then, to أَمْرٌ;] and that فَاعِلٌ becomes in the pl. فَوَاعِلُ; so that أَوَامِرُ is the pl. of مَأْمُورٌ: others say that it has this form of pl. to distinguish it from أَمْرٌ in the sense of حَالٌ [&c.], in which sense it has for its pl. أُمُورٌ. (Mṣb, TA.) [But I think that أَوَامِرُ may be properly and originally pl. of آمِرَةٌ, for آيَةٌ آمِرَةٌ, or the like. MF says that, accord. to the T and M, the pl. of أَمْرٌ in the sense explained in the beginning of this paragraph is أُمُورٌ: but he seems to have founded his assertion upon corrupted copies of those works; for in the M, I find nothing on this point; and in the T, not, as he says, الأَمْرُ ضِدُّ النَّهْيِ وَاحِدُ الأُمُورِ, but قَالَ اللَّيْثُ الأَمْرُ مَعْرُوفٌ نَقِيضُ النَّهْيِ وَالأَمْرُ وَاحِدُ الأُمُورِ, evidently meaning that أَمْرٌ signifies the contr. of نَهْىٌ, and is also, in another sense, the sing. of أُمُورٌ.] [Hence,] أُولُو الأَمْرِ *Those who hold command or rule, and the learned men.* (M, Ḳ. [See Ḳur iv. 62.]) And أَمْرُ اللّٰهِ *The threatened punishment of God:* so in the Ḳur x. 25, and xi. 42, and xvi. 1; in which last place occur the words, أَتَى أَمْرُ اللّٰهِ فَلَا تَسْتَعْجِلُوهُ, meaning *The threatened punishment ordained of God hath, as it were, come:* so near is it, that it is as though it had already come: *therefore desire not ye to hasten it.* (Zj, M, TA.) And *The purpose of God.* (Bḍ and Jel in lxv. 3; &c.) And الأَمْرُ قَرِيبٌ *The resurrection,* or *the time thereof, is near.* (Mgh, from a trad.) And مَا فَعَلْتُهُ عَنْ أَمْرِى, in the Ḳur xviii. 81, *I did it not of my own judgment:* (Bḍ:) or, *of my own choice.* (Jel.) [Hence also الأَمْرُ, in grammar, signifies *The imperative form of a verb.*] — Also *A thing; an affair; a business; a matter; a concern: a state, of a person or thing,* or *of persons or things* or *affairs* or *circumstances*; *a condition*; *a case*: *an accident*; *an event*: *an action*: syn. شَأْنٌ: (M, F, TA:) and حَالٌ, (Mṣb, TA,) and حَالَةٌ: (Mṣb:) and حَادِثَةٌ: (Ḳ:) and فِعْلٌ: (MF, TA:) and *a thing that is said*; *a saying*: (TA voce أُولُو, at the end of art. ال:) pl. أُمُورٌ; (Ṣ, M, Ḳ, &c.;) its only pl. in the senses here explained. (TA.) You say, أَمْرُ فُلَانٍ مُسْتَقِيمٌ [*The affair, or the like, of such a one is in a right state*]: and أُمُورُهُ مُسْتَقِيمَةٌ [*His affairs are in a right state*]. (Ṣ, A.) And شَتَّتَ أَمْرَهُ *He dissipated, disorganized, disordered, unsettled,* or *broke up, his state of things,* or *affairs.* (Aṣ, TA in art. شعب.) [امر seems to be here used, as in many other instances, rather in the sense of the pl. than in that of the sing.] — أَمْرٌ كُلِّىٌّ [*A universal,* or *general, prescript, rule,* or *canon*]. (Mṣb voce قَاعِدَةٌ, KT voce قَانُونٌ, &c.)

إِمْرٌ a subst. from أَمِرَ الأَمْرُ in the sense of اِشْتَدَّ; (Ṣ;) or a subst. from أَمِرَ as signifying كَثُرَ and تَمَّ; (M;) † [*A severe, a distressful, a grievous,* or *an afflictive, thing*: or] *a terrible, and foul,* or *very foul, thing*: or *a wonderful thing.* (TA.) Hence, [used as an epithet, like أَمِرٌ, q. v.,] in the Ḳur [xviii. 70], لَقَدْ جِئْتَ شَيْئًا إِمْرًا † *Verily thou hast done a severe, a distressful, a grievous,* or *an afflictive, thing*: (Ṣ:) or *a terrible, and foul,* or *very foul, thing*: (TA:) or *a wonderful thing*: (Ṣ:) or *an abominable, a foul,* or *an evil, and a wonderful, thing*: (Ks, M, Ḳ:*) or *a terrible and an abominable thing*; signifying more than نُكْرًا, [which occurs after, in verse 73,] inasmuch as the [presumed] drowning of the persons in the ship was more abominable than the slaying of one person: (Zj, T:) or *a crafty, and an abominable,* or *a foul,* or *an evil, and a wonderful, thing*; and derived from أَمِرَ القَوْمُ as meaning كَثُرُوا. (Ks.)

أَمَرٌ a coll. gen. n. of which أَمَرَةٌ (q. v.) is the n. un. ═ See also تَأْمُورٌ.

أَمِرٌ: see إِمْرٌ. ═ † *Multiplied*; or *become many,* or *much,* or *abundant.* (M, Ḳ.) [See أَمِرَ.] You say زَرْعٌ أَمِرٌ † *Abundant seed-produce.* (Lḥ, M.) — † A man *whose beasts have multiplied,* or *become many* or *abundant.* (M.) † A man *blessed,* or *prospered,* (Ibn-Buzurj, M, Ḳ,*) *in his property*: (M:) fem. with ة. (Ibn-Buzurj.) And with ة, † A woman *blessed to her husband* [*by her being prolific*]: from the signification of كَثْرَة. (M.) ═ † *Severe*; *distressful*; *afflictive.* (TA.) [See also إِمْرٌ.]

أَمْرَةٌ *A single command, order, bidding,* or *injunction*: as in the saying, لَكَ عَلَىَّ أَمْرَةٌ مُطَاعَةٌ *Thou hast authority to give me one command, order, bidding,* or *injunction,* which shall be *obeyed* by me. (Ṣ, M,* A, Mṣb, Ḳ.) You should not say, [in this sense,] إِمْرَةٌ, with kesr. (T, Ṣ.) ═ See also إِمْرَةٌ.

إِمْرَةٌ a subst. from أَمَرَ [q. v.]; *Possession of command*; the *office,* and *authority, of a commander, governor, lord, prince,* or *king*; (M,* Mṣb, Ḳ;) as also ▼ إِمَارَةٌ (Mgh, Mṣb, Ḳ) and ▼ أَمَارَةٌ; (L, Ḳ;) but this last is by some disallowed, and is said in the Fṣ and its Expositions to be unknown. (MF.) It is said in a trad., لَعَلَّكَ سَآءَتْكَ إِمْرَةُ ٱبْنِ عَمِّكَ *Perhaps thy paternal uncle's son's possession of command hath displeased thee.* (TA.) — [And hence, † *Increase,* or *abundance,* or *the like*; as also other forms mentioned in what follows.] You say, فِى وَجْهِ مَالِكَ تَعْرِفُ إِمْرَتَهُ † *In the face of thy property,* [meaning such as consists in camels or the like, and also money,] *thou knowest its increase and abundance,* and *its expense*: (Ṣ:) or ▼ إِمَّرَتَهُ, and ▼ إِمِّرَتَهُ, which latter is a dial. var. of weak authority, and ▼ أَمَرَتَهُ, i. e., *its increase and abundance*: (M:) or ▼ إِمَّرَتَهُ as meaning *its prosperous state*; as also ▼ أَمَارَتَهُ, and ▼ أَمْرَتَهُ: (Ibn-Buzurj:) accord. to AHeyth, who reads ▼ تُعْرَفُ إِمَّرَتُهُ, the meaning is, *its decrease*; but the correct meaning is, *its increase,* as Fr explains it. (T, TA.) It is said respecting anything of which one knows what is good in it at first sight: (Lḥ, M:) and means, on a thing's presenting itself, thou knowest its goodness. (T.) One says also, مَا أَحْسَنَ ▼ أَمَارَتَهُمْ † *How good is their multiplying, and the multiplying of their offspring and of their number!* (M.) And لَا جَعَلَ ٱللّٰهُ فِيهِ ▼ إِمَّرَةً † *May God not make an increase to be therein.* (T.)

أَمَرَةٌ *Stones*: (Ḳ:) [or *a heap of stones*:] or it is the n. un. of أَمَرٌ, which signifies *stones*: (M:) or the latter signifies *stones set up in order that one may be directed thereby to the right way*: (Ḥam p. 409:) and the former also signifies *a hill*; (M, Ḳ;) and أَمَرٌ is [used as] its pl.: (M:) and *a sign,* or *mark, by which anything is known*; (M, Ḳ;) as also ▼ أَمَارٌ and ▼ أَمَارَةٌ; (Aṣ, Ṣ;) and أَمَرٌ is [used as] its pl. in this sense also: (M:) or *a sign,* or *mark, set up to show the way*; (AA, Fr;) as also ▼ أَمَارٌ and ▼ أَمَارَةٌ: (Ḳ:) or *a small sign,* or *mark, of stones, to show the way, in a waterless desert*; (Ṣ;) as also ▼ أَمَارٌ [and ▼ أَمَارَةٌ]; and *any sign,* or *mark, that is prepared*: (TA:) or *a structure like a* مَنَارَة [here app. meaning *a tower of a mosque*], *upon a mountain, wide like a house or tent, and larger, of the height of forty times the stature of a man, made in the time of 'Ád and Irem; in some instances its foundation being like a house, though it consists only of stones piled up, one upon another, cemented together with mud, appearing as though it were of natural formation*: (IṢh, T:) the pl. (in all the senses above, Ḳ) [or rather the coll. gen. n.,] is أَمَرٌ. (Ṣ, Ḳ.) ═ See also إِمَّرَةٌ.

أَمَارٌ and ▼ أَمَارَةٌ *A sign, mark,* or *token.* (Aṣ, Ṣ, Mgh.) See also each voce أَمَرَةٌ, in three places. You say, هِىَ أَمَارَةُ مَا بَيْنِى وَبَيْنَكَ *It is a sign,* or *token, of what is between me and thee.* (T,* TA.) And a poet says,

إِذَا طَلَعَتْ شَمْسُ ٱلنَّهَارِ فَإِنَّهَا
أَمَارَةُ تَسْلِيمِى عَلَيْكِ فَسَلِّمِى

[*When the sun of day rises, it is a sign of my saluting thee, therefore do thou salute*]. (TA.) — Also *A time*: (Aṣ, Ṣ, Ḳ:) so IAạr explains the latter word, not particularizing the time as definite or otherwise: (M:) or *a definite time*: (TA:) or *a time,* or *place, of promise* or *appointment*; *an appointed time* or *place*; syn. مَوْعِدٌ: (M, Mgh, Ḳ:) or, accord. to some, the former word is pl. [or rather coll. gen. n.] of the latter. (TA.) El-'Ajjáj says,

إِذْ رَدَّهَا بِكَيْدِهِ فَٱرْتَدَّتِ
إِلَى أَمَارٍ وَأَمَارِ مُدَّتِى

When He (meaning God) *brings it,* (namely my soul,) *by his skilful ordering,* and his power, [*and it is thus brought,* or *it thus comes, to a set time,* and] *to the time of the end of my appointed period*: امار مدّتى being as above; the former word being prefixed to the latter, governing it in the gen. case. (IB. [In the Ṣ we find وَأَمَارُ مُدَّتِى.])

أَمُورٌ [an intensive epithet from أَمَرَهُ]. You say, إِنَّهُ لَأَمُورٌ بِٱلْمَعْرُوفِ وَنَهُوٌّ عَنِ ٱلْمُنْكَرِ *Verily he is one who strongly commands,* or *enjoins, good conduct, and who strongly forbids evil conduct.* (Ṣ in art. نهى, and A.*)

أَمِيرٌ *One having, holding,* or *possessing, command*; (Ṣ;) *a commander*; *a governor*; *a lord*; (M,* Mṣb;) *a prince,* or *king*: (M, Ḳ:) fem. with ة: (Ṣ, Ḳ:) pl. أُمَرَآءُ. (M, Mṣb, Ḳ.) — *A leader of the blind.* (M, Ḳ.) So in the saying of El-Aạshà:

إِذَا كَانَ هَادِى ٱلْفَتَى فِى ٱلْبِلَا
دِ صَدْرَ ٱلْقَنَاةِ أَطَاعَ ٱلْأَمِيرَا

[*When the young man's guide in the countries,* or *lands,* or *the like, is the top of the cane, he obeys the leader of the blind*]. (M.) — A woman's *husband.* (A.) — *A neighbour.* (Ḳ.) — *A person with whom one consults*: (A, Ḳ:) *any one of whom one begs counsel,* or *advice, in a case of fear.* (TA.) You say, هُوَ أَمِيرِى *He is the person with whom I consult.* (A.)

أَمَارَةٌ: see إِمْرَةٌ, in three places: — and see also أَمَرَةٌ, in three places; and أَمَارٌ.

إِمَارَةٌ: see إِمْرَةٌ. — الإِمَارَةُ is also used for صَاحِبُ الإِمَارَةِ, i. e. الأَمِيرُ. (Mgh.)

أَمَّرٌ: see the next paragraph, in two places.

إِمَّرٌ A man *who consults every one respecting his case*; as also ▼ أَمَّرٌ and ▼ إِمَّرَةٌ: (M:) or a man *resembling* [*in stupidity*] *a kid*: [see the latter part of this paragraph:] (Th, M:) or, as also ▼ إِمَّرَةٌ (Ṣ, M, Ḳ, &c.) and أَمَّرٌ and ▼ أَمَّرَةٌ, (Ḳ,) a man *having weak judgment,* (Ṣ, Ḳ,) *stupid,* (T, M,) or *weak, without judgment,* (M, L,) or *without intellect,* or *intelligence,* (T,) *who obeys the command of every one,* (T, Ṣ,) *who complies with what every one desires to do in all his affairs*; (Ḳ;) *a stupid man, of weak judgment, who says to another, Command me to execute thine affair.* (IAth.) It is said in a trad., مَنْ يُطِعْ ▼ إِمَّرَةً لَا يَأْكُلْ ثَمَرَةً [*He who obeys a stupid man, &c., shall not eat fruit*: or the meaning is] *he who obeys a stupid woman shall be debarred from good.* (IAth.) ▼ إِمَّرَةٌ is applied to a woman and to a man: when it is applied to a man, the ة is added to give intensiveness to the signification. (ISh.) The following saying, إِذَا طَلَعَتِ الشِّعْرَى سَفَرًا فَلَا تُرْسِلْ فِيهَا إِمَّرَةً ▼ وَلَا إِمَّرًا, in rhyming prose, means [*When Sirius rises in the clear twilight,*] *send not thou among them* (meaning the camels) *a man without intelligence* [*in a great degree, nor one who is so in a less degree; or a woman without intelligence, nor a man without intelligence;*] to manage them. (Sh.) — Also, (M, Ḳ,) and ▼ إِمَّرَةٌ and ▼ أَمَّرٌ and ▼ أَمَّرَةٌ, (Ḳ,) *A young lamb:* (M, Ḳ:) or the first (إِمَّرٌ) and the second, *a young kid:* (M, TA:) or the former of these two, *a male lamb:* (M, TA:) or *a young male lamb:* (Ṣ:) and the latter of them, *a female lamb:* (M, TA:) or *a young female lamb.* (Ṣ, M.) One says, مَا لَهُ إِمَّرٌ وَلَا إِمَّرَةٌ ▼, meaning *He has not a male lamb nor a female lamb:* (M, TA:) or *he has not anything.* (T, Ṣ, M.)

أُمَّرَةٌ : see إِمَّرٌ, in two places.

إِمَّرَةٌ : see إِمَّرٌ, in six places: — and see إِمَّرَةٌ, in four places.

إِمَّرَةٌ : see إِمَّرَةٌ.

أَمَّارٌ [*Wont to command*]. [Hence,] النَّفْسُ الأَمَّارَةُ [*The soul that is wont to command*]; (A;) *the soul that inclines to the nature of the body, that commands to the indulgence of pleasures and sensual appetites, drawing the heart downwards, so that it is the abode of evils, and the source of culpable dispositions.* (KT.) [See نَفْسٌ.]

أَمَّارَةٌ fem. of أَمَّارٌ [q. v.]. — See also إِمَّرٌ.

آمِرٌ [act. part. n. of أَمَرَهُ]. — آمِرٌ and ▼ مُؤْتَمِرٌ *Two days,* (Ṣ,) *the last,* (Ḳ,) *the former being the sixth, and the latter the seventh,* (M,) *of the days called* أَيَّامُ العَجُوزِ: (Ṣ, M, Ḳ: [but see عَجُوزٌ:]) as though the former commanded men to be cautious, and the latter consulted them as to whether they should set forth on a journey or stay at home: (Ṣ:) accord. to Az, the latter is applied as an epithet to the day as meaning يُؤْتَمَرُ فِيهِ. (TA.)

تَأْمُرِىٌّ : see تَأْمُورٌ, in two places.

تُؤْمُرِىٌّ, and without ء : see تَأْمُورٌ, in six places.

تَأْمُورٌ and ▼ تَأْمُورَةٌ are properly mentioned in this art.; the measure of the former being تَفْعُولٌ; (Ḳ;) and that of the latter, تَفْعُولَةٌ: (TA:) not as J has imagined; [who writes them without ء, and mentions them in art. تمر;] (Ḳ;) their measures accord. to him being فَاعُولٌ and فَاعُولَةٌ. (TA.) [But in all the senses here explained, they appear to be with and without ء.] — The former signifies The *soul:* (Ṣ in art. تمر, where it is written without ء; and M, A, Ḳ:) because it is that which is wont to command. (A.) One says, قَدْ عَلِمَ تَأْمُورُكَ ذٰلِكَ *Thy soul,* or *self, hath known that.* (AZ, and T in art. تمر.) — The *intellect:* (M:) as in the saying, عَرَفْتُهُ بِتَأْمُورِى *I knew it by my intellect.* (M in art. تمر, without ء; and TA.) You say also, هُوَ ابْنُ تَأْمُورِهَا, meaning *He is the knowing with respect to it.* (TA in art. بنى.) — The *heart,* (T in art. تمر without ء, and M, A, Ḳ,) *itself.* (M, TA.) Hence the saying, حَرْفٌ فِى تَأْمُورِى خَيْرٌ مِنْ عَشْرَةٍ فِى وِعَائِكَ [*One word in my heart is better than ten in thy receptacle*]. (T in art. تمر, and TA.) — The *pericardium.* (M in art. تمر, without ء.) — The *core,* or *black* or *inner part,* or *clot of blood,* (حَبَّة, M, Ḳ, or عَلَقَة, TA,) and *life,* and *blood, of the heart:* (M, Ḳ:) or *blood,* (Aṣ, Ṣ, M, in art. تمر, and K,) absolutely: (TA:) and تَأْمُورُ النَّفْسِ signifies *the life-blood:* (Aṣ, Ṣ:) or *the blood of the body:* (Ṣ in art. نفس:) and *the life of the soul.* (M, Ḳ.) — Also, as being likened to blood, (TA,) ‡ *Wine;* and so ▼ تَأْمُورَةٌ: (M, Ḳ:) and — ‡ *A dye:* (M, TA:) and — ‡ *Saffron.* (Aṣ, Ḳ.) — [Hence also,] ‡ *Water.* (M, Ḳ.) You say, مَا فِى الرَّكِيَّةِ تَأْمُورٌ, (T, Ṣ in art. تمر, and M,) or تَأْمُورٌ, (A,) ‡ *There is not in the well any water.* (T, Ṣ, M, A.) — The *wezeer* (وَزِير) *of a king:* (M, Ḳ:) because his command is effectual. (TA.) — *Any one:* as in the saying, مَا بِهَا تَأْمُورٌ, (T in art. تمر, A, Ḳ,) as also ▼ تُؤْمُورٌ, (T in art. تمر, and Ḳ,) each with an augmentative ت, and without ء as well as with it, accord. to Er-Radee and others, (TA,) and ▼ تَأْمُرِىٌّ, and ▼ تَأْمُورِىٌّ, (M,) and ▼ تُؤْمُرِىٌّ, (T in art. تمر, M, TA,) or without ء, (Ṣ, M, Ḳ, in art. تمر,) and ▼ أَمَّرٌ, (M, Ḳ,) *There is not in it* (i. e. in the house, الدار, M, A, TA) *any one.* (M, A, Ḳ, and T and Ṣ in art. تمر.) You say also, بِلَادٌ خَلَآءٌ لَيْسَ فِيهَا تُومُرِىٌّ ▼ *Vacant regions wherein is not any one.* (Ṣ in art. تمر.) ▼ تُؤْمُرِىٌّ (M, Ḳ) and تَأْمُرِىٌّ ▼ (Ṣ in art. تمر) and ▼ تَأْمُورِىٌّ and تُومُرِىٌّ (M, Ḳ) also signify *A man,* or *human being.* (Ṣ,* M, Ḳ.) You say, speaking of a beautiful woman, مَا رَأَيْتُ تُومُرِيًّا ▼ أَحْسَنَ مِنْهَا *I have not seen a human being,* or *creature, more beautiful than she:* (Ṣ and M in art. تمر:) and مَا رَأَيْتُ تُومُرِيًّا ▼ أَحْسَنَ مِنْهُ [*I have not seen a man more beautiful than he*]. (T and Ṣ in art. تمر.) Accord. to some, they are used only in negative phrases; but accord. to others, they are also used in such as are affirmative. (MF.) — Also *Anything:* as in the saying أَكَلَ الذِّئْبُ الشَّاةَ فَمَا تَرَكَ مِنْهَا تَأْمُورًا [*The wolf ate the sheep, or goat, and left not of it anything*]. (T and Ṣ in art. تمر.) — *A child, young one,* or *fœtus;* syn. وَلَدٌ. (M, Ḳ.) — The *receptacle* (وِعَآء) *of the child, young one,* or *fœtus.* (M in art. تمر, without ء; and Ḳ.) — *A* وِعَآء [*in the ordinary sense;* i. e. *a bag,* or *receptacle, for travelling-provisions and for goods or utensils &c.*]. (M, Ḳ.) Hence the saying, أَنْتَ أَعْلَمُ بِتَأْمُورِكَ *Thou art best acquainted with what thou hast with thee; and with thine own mind.* (M.) — Also, (Ḳ,) and ▼ تَأْمُورَةٌ, (M, [in which the former is not given in the following senses,] and Ḳ,) or ▼ تَأْمُورَةٌ, (Ṣ in art. تمر,) *A ewer,* syn. إِبْرِيقٌ, (Ṣ, M, Ḳ,) *for wine:* (Ṣ:) and, (M, Ḳ,) or, as some say, (TA,) *a* حُقَّة (M, Ḳ, TA) *in which wine is put.* (TA.) — Also the first, (M, Ḳ,) or ▼ third, (T and Ṣ in art. تمر,) The *chamber,* or *cell,* (صَوْمَعَة, T and M in art. تمر, without ء, and Ṣ and Ḳ, and نَامُوس, M, Ḳ,) *of a monk.* (M, Ḳ.) — And hence, (TA,) the first, (Ḳ,) and ▼ second, (M, Ḳ,) or ▼ third, of these three words, (T and Ṣ in art. تمر,) ‡ The *covert,* or *retreat, of a lion.* (T, Ṣ, M, Ḳ.) Whence, فُلَانٌ أَسَدٌ فِى تَأْمُورَتِهِ ▼ ‡ *Such a one is a lion in his covert:* (T and Ṣ in art. تمر:) a saying borrowed from 'Amr Ibn-Maadee-Kerib: (T and Ṣ ibid:) or, accord. to some, it means, *a lion in the greatness of his courage,* and *in his heart.* (TA.) — Also (i. e. the first only) *Play,* or *sport, of girls* or *of boys.* (Th, M in art. تمر without ء, and Ḳ.) — See also يَأْمُورٌ.

تُؤْمُورٌ *A sign,* or *mark, set up to show the way in a waterless desert;* (Ḳ, TA;) *consisting of stones piled up, one upon another:* (TA:) pl. تَآمِيرُ. (Ḳ.) [See أَمَرَةٌ.] — See also تَأْمُورٌ.

تَأْمُورَةٌ, and without ء : see تَأْمُورٌ, in eight places. — Also The *pericardium;* the *integument* (غِلَاف) *of the heart.* (Ṣ in art. تمر: there written without ء.)

تَأْمُورِىٌّ : see تَأْمُورٌ, in two places.

مِئْمَرٌ *Counsel; advice:* as in the saying, فُلَانٌ بَعِيدٌ مِنَ المِئْمَرِ قَرِيبٌ مِنَ المِئْبَرِ *Such a one is far from counsel,* or *advice: near to calumny,* or *slander.* (A.)

مُؤَمَّرٌ *Made,* or *appointed, commander, governor, lord, prince,* or *king:* (Ṣ, M, Ḳ:*) *made to have authority, power,* or *dominion:* (Ṭ, M, Ḳ:) in which latter sense it is explained by Khálid, as applied by Ibn-Mukbil to a spear. (T.) — † A cane, or spear-shaft, *having a spear-head affixed to it.* (Ḳ.) — † A spear-head (T, TA) *sharpened;* syn. مُحَدَّدٌ. (T, M, Ḳ, TA.) — *Distinguished,* or *defined,* (مُحَدَّدٌ,) *by signs,* or *marks:* (TA:) or, as some say, (TA,) *marked with a hot iron;* syn. مَوْسُومٌ. (Ḳ, TA.)

مَأْمُورٌ [pass. part. n. of أَمَرَهُ, q. v.]. — It is said in a trad., (Ṣ, &c.,) خَيْرُ المَالِ مُهْرَةٌ مَأْمُورَةٌ وَسِكَّةٌ مَأْبُورَةٌ ‡ *The best of property are a prolific filly* [*and a row of palm-trees,* or perhaps *a tall palm-tree, fecundated*]; (AZ, A 'Obeyd, T, Ṣ, A, Ḳ;) as though the filly were commanded [by God] to be so: (A, in which the epithet مأمورة thus used is said to be tropical:) [or] مأمورة is thus for the sake of conformity to مأبورة, and is originally مُؤْمَرَةٌ, (Ṣ, M,* Ḳ,) from آمَرَهَا اللّٰهُ: (TA:) or it is a dial. var. of weak authority; (Ḳ;) though, accord. to AZ, it signifies *made to have abundant offspring,* from أَمَرَ اللّٰهُ المُهْرَةَ, meaning "God made the filly to have abundant offspring," a dial. var. of آمَرَهَا, as A 'Obeyd also asserts it to be. (TA.)

مَأْمَرٌ and مَأْمِيرٌ : see what next follows.

مُؤْتَمِرٌ [*Obeying, or conforming to, a command;* &c.: see 8. —] One *who acts according to his own opinion;* (T;) *who follows his own opinion only:* or *who hastes to speak.* (M.) ═ See also امر. — Also, and ♦المُؤْتَمِرُ, [*The month which is now commonly called*] المُحَرَّمُ: (M, Ḳ:) the former appellation (مؤتمر) is that by which the tribe of 'Ád called it: (Ibn-El-Kelbee:) pl. ♦مَآمِرُ and مَآمِيرُ [both anomalous]. (M, Ḳ.) [See شَهْرٌ.]

يَأْمُورٌ; (M, Ḳ;) so in all the copies of the Ḳ; but in the L and other lexicons, ♦تَأْمُورٌ; (TA;) *A certain beast of the sea:* or, as some say, *a small beast:* (M:) and *a kind of mountain-goat:* (M, Ḳ:) or *a certain wild beast,* (Ḳ, TA,) or *a beast resembling the mountain-goat,* (M,) *having a single branching horn in the middle of his head.* (M, TA.) [See يَحْمُورٌ, the *oryx.*]

امس

أَمْسِ, meaning *Yesterday,* or *the day before the present day* (Mṣb, Ḳ) *by one night,* (Ḳ,) and tropically applied to ‡ *what is before that,* (Mṣb,) or *a short time before,* (Bḍ in x. 25,) [used as a subst. and as an adv.,] is indecl., with any of the three vowels for its termination: (Ḳ:) [written أَمْسُ and أَمْسَ and أَمْسِ:] or it is an adv. n., indecl., with kesr for its termination, unless made indeterminate, or made determinate [by the article ال]; and sometimes indecl. with fet-ḥ: (Ez-Zejjájee, M, TA:) or, accord. to IHsh, the termination with fet-ḥ is a rejected form; and that with ḍamm is not mentioned by any of the grammarians: (TA:) but مُذْ أَمْسَ [*Since yesterday*] occurs, used by poetic licence: (Sb, Ṣ:) أَمْسِ is a noun of which the last letter is made movent to avoid the concurrence of two quiescent letters: and the Arabs differ respecting it: (Ṣ:) most of them make it indecl., with kesr for its termination, when it is determinate [without the article ال]: but some of them make it [imperfectly] decl. when it is determinate [in the same manner]: (Ṣ, Ḳ:*) [accord. to the most approved usage,] you say, [رَأَيْتُهُ أَمْسِ, and بِالأَمْسِ, which is more common, and الأَمْسَ, *I saw him yesterday;* and] مَا رَأَيْتُهُ مُذْ أَمْسِ [*I have not seen him since yesterday*]; and if you have not seen him [since the day next] before that, you say, مَا رَأَيْتُهُ مُذْ أَوَّلَ مِنْ أَمْسِ [*I have not seen him since the day before yesterday*]; and if you have not seen him [since] two days before that, you say, مَا رَأَيْتُهُ مُذْ أَوَّلَ مِنْ أَوَّلَ مِنْ أَمْسِ [*I have not seen him since the day before the day before yesterday*]. (ISk, TA.) The phrase رَأَيْتُهُ أَمْسٍ [*I saw him yesterday*] has also been heard, but it is extr. (Ḳ.) The people of El-Ḥijáz make أَمْسِ indecl., with kesr for its termination; and the Benoo-Temeem do the same when it is in the accus. or gen. case; but these latter make it [imperfectly] decl. when it is in the nom. case, saying, ذَهَبَ أَمْسُ بِمَا فِيهِ [*Yesterday has gone with what* happened *during it*]; whereas the people of El-Ḥijáz say, ذَهَبَ أَمْسِ بِمَا فِيهِ, because it is [held by them to be] indecl. on account of its implying that it has the determinative article ال [understood as prefixed to it], the kesreh being added to avoid the concurrence of two quiescent letters; while the Benoo-Temeem hold it to be, in the nom. case, a deviation from الأَمْسُ, and therefore imperfectly decl., because of its being determinate, [and so resembling a proper name,] and its deviation from the original form, like سَحَرُ in the like case: (IB, TA:) all of the Arabs, however, make it decl. when the article ال is prefixed to it, (Ṣ, Ḳ,*) and when it is made indeterminate, or is prefixed to another noun: (Ṣ:) they say, using it indeterminately, كُلُّ غَدٍ صَائِرٌ أَمْسًا [*Every morrow becomes a yesterday*]; (Ṣ,* IB;) and making it determinate by the article ال, they say, كَانَ الأَمْسُ طَيِّبًا [*The yesterday was good*], (IB,) and مَضَى الأَمْسُ المُبَارَكُ [*The blessed yesterday has past*]; (Ṣ;) and prefixing it to another noun, كُلُّ أَمْسِنَا كَانَ طَيِّبًا [*All of our yesterday was good*], (IB,) and مَضَى أَمْسُنَا [*Our yesterday has past*]: (Ṣ:) [therefore,] in the following verse,

وَإِنِّى وَقَفْتُ اليَوْمَ وَالأَمْسِ قَبْلَهُ
بِبَابِكَ حَتَّى كَادَتِ الشَّمْسُ تَغْرُبُ

[*And verily I stood to-day, and yesterday before it, at thy door until the sun was almost setting*], (thus related by IAạr in two different ways, الأَمْسِ and الأَمْسَ,) if we read الأَمْسِ, the ال is redundant, because it is implied in the word أَمْسِ; but if we read الأَمْسَ, the ال is not implied in أَمْسَ, and therefore is prefixed to make it determinate. (IJ, M.) The pl. is آمُسٌ and آمَاسٌ, (Zj, Ḳ,) both pls. of pauc., (Zj, TA,) and أُمُوسٌ, (Zj, Ḳ, TA, [in the CḲ, incorrectly, أَمُوسٌ,]) which is a pl. of mult. (Zj, TA.) There is no dim. form of أَمْسِ; like as there is none of غَدٌ and أَىٌّ and مَتَى and أَيْنَ and كَيْفَ and البَارِحَةُ and عِنْدَ and مَا and the names of the months and those of the days of the week, except الجُمُعَةُ. (Sb, Ṣ.)

إِمْسِىٌّ, contr. to analogy, (M, TA,) and أَمْسِىٌّ [which is agreeable with analogy] is allowable, as related by Ṣgh on the authority of Fr, but the former is the more chaste, (TA,) *Of,* or *relating to,* or *belonging to, yesterday.* (M, TA.)

امل

1. أَمَلَهُ, (T, Ṣ, M, &c.,) aor. ـُ, (T, Ṣ, M, Mṣb,) and ـِ, (so in the M accord. to the TT,) inf. n. أَمْلٌ, (T, Ṣ, M, &c.,) this being the inf. n. accord. to IJ, [as distinguished from أَمَلٌ and إِمْلٌ,] (M,) *He hoped it;* or *hoped for it;* syn. رَجَاهُ; (Ṣ,* M,* [see أَمَلٌ below,] Ḳ;) meaning, what was good for him; (Ṣ;) as also ♦أَمَّلَهُ, (T,* M, Ḳ,) inf. n. تَأْمِيلٌ: (Ṣ, T:) or *he expected it;* [or *had a distant,* or *remote, expectation of it;* for] it is mostly used in relation to that of which the occurrence, or coming to pass, is deemed remote; as in the saying of Zuheyr,

أَرْجُو وَآمُلُ أَنْ تَدْنُو مَوَدَّتُهَا

[*I hope, and have a distant expectation, that her love may approach*]: he who has determined upon a journey to a distant town or country says, أَمَلْتُ الوُصُولَ [*I have formed an expectation,* or *a distant expectation, of arriving*]; but he does not say, طَمِعْتُ, until he has become near thereto; for طَمَعٌ relates only to that of which the occurrence, or coming to pass, is [deemed] near: and الرَّجَآءُ is between الأَمَلُ and الطَّمَعُ; for it is sometimes attended with fear that the thing expected may not come to pass, wherefore it is used in the sense of fear; and when the fear is strong, [lest the thing expected should not come to pass, it denotes distant expectation, and thus] it is used in the sense of الأَمَلُ; whence the usage in the verse of Zuheyr; but otherwise it is used in the sense of الطَّمَعُ: (Mṣb:) or الرجاء signifies the expectation of benefit, or advantage, from some preceding cause or means: so says El-Ḥarállee: or it is properly syn. with الأَمَلُ; and in common conventional language, means the clinging of the heart to the coming to pass of a future desired event: so says Ibn-El-Kemál: or, accord. to Er-Rághib, an opinion requiring the coming to pass of an event in which will be a cause of happiness: (TA:) and ♦أَمَّلَهُ, inf. n. تَأْمِيلٌ, signifies *he expected it much;* and is more commonly used than the form without teshdeed. (Mṣb.)

2: see 1, in two places. ═ تَأْمِيلٌ also signifies The *inducing* [one] *to hope* or *expect.* (KL.)

5. تَأَمَّلَ الشَّىْءَ [*He considered the thing,* or *studied it,* or *contemplated it, carefully,* or *attentively, with investigation;*] *he looked at the thing endeavouring to obtain a clear knowledge of it:* (Ṣ:) or *i. q.* تَدَبَّرَهُ; (Mṣb, TA;) i. e., (Mṣb,) *he looked into the thing, considered it, examined it,* or *studied it, repeatedly,* (Mṣb, TA,) *in order to know it,* or *until he knew it,* (Mṣb,) or *in order to ascertain its real case:* (TA:) or *he looked intently,* or *hardly, at,* or *towards, the thing:* (TA:) or تَأَمَّلَ signifies *he acted,* or *proceeded, deliberately, not hastily,* syn. تَثَبَّتَ, (T, M,) or *he paused,* or *waited,* syn. تَلَبَّثَ, (Ḳ,) *in an affair,* and *in consideration;* (M, Ḳ, TA;) *he paused, and acted with deliberation.* (TA.) فِيهِ تَأَمُّلٌ [meaning *It requires careful,* or *attentive, consideration,* or simply *it requires consideration,*] is a phrase [of frequent occurrence in the larger lexicons &c., used to imply doubt, and also to insinuate politely that the words to which it relates are false, or wrong,] like فِيهِ نَظَرٌ [q. v.]. (MF in art. صفح.)

أَمْلٌ: } see أَمَلٌ.
إِمْلٌ: }

أَمَلٌ (T, Ṣ, M, Mṣb, Ḳ) and ♦إِمْلٌ (IJ, M, Ḳ) and ♦أَمْلٌ, (Ḳ,) the first of which is an inf. n., accord. to IJ, (M,) and is the form commonly known, (TA,) *Hope;* syn. رَجَآءٌ: (Ṣ, M, Ḳ:) or *expectation;* [or *distant,* or *remote, expectation;* being] mostly used in relation to that of which the occurrence, or coming to pass, is deemed remote: applied also to *an affection of the heart from some good to be attained:* (Mṣb, TA: [in both of which are further explanations, for which see 1:]) ♦إِمْلَةٌ, also, signifies the same as أَمَلٌ,

(Ṣ, M, Ḳ,) or تَأْمِيلٌ; (Lḥ, M, Ḳ;) [or *a manner of hoping* or *expecting*; for J adds,] and it is like جِلْسَةٌ and رِكْبَةٌ: (Ṣ:) and ▼ مُؤَمَّلٌ, likewise, signifies the same as أَمَلٌ: (TA:) the pl. of أَمَلٌ and إِمْلٌ and أَمْلٌ is آمَالٌ. (M,* Ḳ, TA.) You say, خَابَ سَعْيُهُ وَأَمَلُهُ [*His labour, and his hope,* or *expectation, were disappointed, frustrated,* or *balked*]. (A and TA in art. خيب.) And مَا أَطْوَلَ إِمْلَتَهُ ▼ *How far-reaching is his hope,* or *expectation!* (T,* Ṣ, M, Ḳ:) [or *his manner of hoping* or *expecting!*] from الأَمَلُ. (T.) —— Also, the first, *An object of hope.* (Jel in xviii. 44.)

إِمْلَةٌ: see أَمَلٌ, in two places.

آمِلٌ act. part. n. of 1; [*Hoping:* or] *expecting.* (Mṣb.) [See 1.]

مُؤَمَّلٌ One *whose beneficence may be hoped for.* (Ḥar p. 183.) —— المُؤَمَّلُ *The eighth of the horses that are started together in a race;* (Ḳ;) these being ten: (TA:) or *the ninth thereof:* (TA in explanation of السُّكَيْتُ:) or *the seventh thereof.* (Ḥam p. 46.) ═ See also أَمَلٌ.

مَأْمُولٌ pass. part. n. of 1; [*Hoped:* or] *expected.* (Mṣb.)

امن

1. أَمِنَ, (T, Ṣ, M, &c.,) aor. ـَ, (T, Mṣb, Ḳ,) inf. n. أَمْنٌ (T, Ṣ, M, Mṣb, Ḳ) and إِمْنٌ (Zj, M, Ḳ) and أَمَنٌ (M, Ḳ) and أَمَنَةٌ (T, Ṣ, M, Ḳ) and إِمْنَةٌ (T) and أَمَانٌ (M, Ḳ) [and app. أَمَانَةٌ, for it is said in the Ṣ that this is syn. with أَمَانٌ,] and آمِنٌ, an instance of an inf. n. of the measure فَاعِلٌ, which is strange, (MF,) or this is a subst. like فَالِجٌ, (M,) *He was,* or *became,* or *felt, secure, safe,* or *in a state of security* or *safety;* originally, *he was,* or *became, quiet,* or *tranquil, in heart,* or *mind;* (Mṣb;) *he was,* or *became, secure,* or *free from fear;* أَمْنٌ signifying the *contr. of* خَوْفٌ, (Ṣ, M, Ḳ,) and so أَمَنَةٌ (Ṣ) and آمِنٌ [&c.]: (M, Ḳ:) *he was,* or *became,* or *felt, free from expectation of evil,* or *of an object of dislike* or *hatred, in the coming time;* originally, *he was,* or *became, easy in mind, and free from fear.* (El-Munáwee, TA.) [See أَمْنٌ, below.] You say also, يَأْمَنُ عَلَى نَفْسِهِ [*He is secure,* or *safe,* or *free from fear, for himself*]. (M.) And أَمِنَ البَلَدُ, meaning *The inhabitants of the country,* or *district,* or *town, were in a state of security,* or *confidence, therein.* (Mṣb.) The verb is trans. by itself, and by means of the particle مِنْ; as in أَمِنَ زَيْدٌ الأَسَدَ and أَمِنَ مِنَ الأَسَدِ, meaning *Zeyd was,* or *became,* or *felt, secure from, safe from,* [or *free from fear of,*] *the lion.* (Mṣb.) You say also, أَمِنَ كَذِبَ مَنْ أَخْبَرَهُ [*He was secure from,* or *free from fear of, the lying of him who informed him*]. (M.) And لَا آمَنُ أَنْ يَكُونَ كَذٰلِكَ [*I am not free from fear of its being so; I am not sure but that it may be so*]. (Mgh in art. نبل; and other lexicons passim.) And, of a strong-made she camel, أَمِنَتْ أَنْ تَكُونَ ضَعِيفَةً [*She was secure from,* or *free from fear of, being weak*]: (M: [in a copy of the Ṣ أَمِنَتْ:]) and أَمِنَتِ العِثَارَ وَالإِعْيَآءَ [*She was secure from,* or *free from fear of, stumbling, and becoming jaded*]: (M:) and أُمِنَ عِثَارُهَا [*Her stumbling was not feared*]. (So in a copy of the Ṣ.) And, of a highly-prized camel, أُمِنَ أَنْ يُنْحَرَ [*It was not feared that he would be slaughtered; or his being slaughtered was not feared*]. (M.) [أَمِنَهُ sometimes means *He was,* or *became, free from fear, though having cause for fear, of him,* or *it;* i. e. *he thought himself secure,* or *safe, from him,* or *it.* (See Ḳur vii. 97.)] —— أَمِنَهُ (inf. n. أَمْنٌ TḲ) [and accord. to some copies of the Ḳ ▼ آمَنَهُ] and ▼ أَمَّنَهُ (inf. n. تَأْمِينٌ Ḳ) and ▼ ائْتَمَنَهُ ([written with the disjunctive alif إِيتَمَنَهُ, and] also written اتَّمَنَهُ, on the authority of Th, which is extr., like اتَّهَلَ [&c.], M) and ▼ استأمنهُ all signify the same (M, Ḳ, TA) [*He trusted,* or *confided, in him;* (as also آمن به, q. v.;) *he intrusted him with,* or *confided to him, power, authority, control,* or *a charge; he gave him charge* over a thing or person: these meanings are vaguely indicated in the M and Ḳ and TA.]. You say, يَأْمَنُهُ النَّاسُ وَلَا يَخَافُونَ غَائِلَتَهُ [*Men,* or *people, trust,* or *confide, in him, and do not fear his malevolence,* or *mischievousness*]. (T, M.) And أَمِنَهُ عَلَى كَذَا and ▼ ائتمنهُ (Ṣ, Mgh,* Mṣb*) and عَلَيْهِ, (Ṣ, Mṣb, Ḳ,) [*He trusted,* or *confided, in him with respect to such a thing; he intrusted him with,* or *confided to him, power, authority, control,* or *a charge, over it; he gave him charge over it;*] *he made him,* or *took him as,* أَمِين *over such a thing.* (Mgh.) Hence, in a trad., the مُؤَذِّن is said to be مُؤْتَمَن; i. e. يَأْتَمِنُهُ ▼ النَّاسُ عَلَى الأَوْقَاتِ الَّتِى يُؤَذِّنُ فِيهَا [*Men trust,* or *confide, in him with respect to the times in which he calls to prayer*], and know, by his calling to prayer, what they are commanded to do, as to praying and fasting and breaking fast. (Mgh.) It is said in the Ḳur [xii. 11], مَا لَكَ لَا تَأْمَنُنَا عَلَى يُوسُفَ and [تَأْمَنَّا] with idghám [i. e. *What aileth thee that thou dost not trust,* or *confide, in us with respect to Joseph?* or, *that thou dost not give us charge over Joseph?*]; (Ṣ;) meaning, why dost thou fear us for him? (Bḍ;) some pronouncing the verb in a manner between those of the former and the latter modes of writing it; but Akh says that the latter is better: (Ṣ:) some read تِيمَنَّا. (Bḍ.) You say also, ▼ أُوتُمِنَ فُلَانٌ [*Such a one was trusted,* or *confided, in;* &c.;] when it begins a sentence, changing the second ء into و; in like manner as you change it into ى when the first is with kesr, as in إِيتَمَنَهُ; and into ا when the first is with fet-ḥ, as in آمَنَ. (Ṣ.) The phrase ▼ أُوتُمِنَ أَمَانَةً, in a saying of Mohammad, if it be not correctly عَلَى أَمَانَةٍ, may be explained as implying the meaning of اُسْتُحْفِظَ أَمَانَةً [*He was asked to take care of a deposite; or he was intrusted with it*]. (Mgh.) [You also say, أَمِنَهُ بِكَذَا, meaning *He intrusted him with such a thing;* as, for instance, money or other property: see two exs. in the Ḳur iii. 68.] ═ أَمُنَ, (M, Mgh, Ḳ,) or أَمِنَ, (Mṣb,) inf. n. أَمَانَةٌ, (M, Mgh, Mṣb,) *He was,* or *became, trusted in,* or *confided in:* (M, Ḳ:) or *he was,* or *became, trusty, trustworthy, trustful, confidential,* or *faithful:* said of a man. (Mgh.)

2. أَمَّنَهُ, inf. n. تَأْمِينٌ: see 4: —— and see also أَمِنَهُ. ═ أَمَّنَ, inf. n. as above, also signifies *He said* آمِينَ or أَمِينَ, (T, Ṣ, Mṣb,) after finishing the Fátiḥah, (T,) or عَلَى الدُّعَآءِ *on the occasion of the prayer,* or *supplication.* (Mṣb.)

4. آمَنَ is originally أَأْمَنَ; the second ء being softened. (Ṣ.) You say, آمَنَهُ, [inf. n. إِيمَانٌ;] (Ṣ, M, Mṣb;) and ▼ أَمَّنَهُ, [inf. n. تَأْمِينٌ;] (M, TA;) meaning *He rendered him secure,* or *safe;* (Mṣb;) *he rendered him secure,* or *free from fear;* (Ṣ, M, TA;) *contr. of* أَخَافَهُ: (TA:) so in آمَنْتُهُ مِنْهُ *I rendered him secure,* or *safe, from him,* or *it.* (Mṣb.) And of God you say, آمَنَ عِبَادَهُ مِنْ أَنْ يَظْلِمَهُمْ [*He hath rendered his servants secure from his wronging them*]. (Ṣ.) And يُؤْمِنُ عِبَادَهُ مِنْ عَذَابِهِ [*He rendereth his servants secure from his punishment*]. (M.) You say also, آمَنْتُ الأَسِيرَ, meaning *I gave,* or *granted,* الأَمَان [i. e. *security* or *safety,* or *protection* or *safeguard,* or *the promise* or *assurance of security* or *safety,* or *indemnity,* or *quarter,*] *to the captive.* (Mṣb.) And آمَنَ فُلَانٌ العَدُوَّ [*Such a one granted security,* &c., *to the enemy*], inf. n. as above. (T.) It is said in the Ḳur ch. ix. [verse 12], accord. to one reading, لَا إِيمَانَ لَهُمْ *They have not the attribute of granting protection;* meaning that when they grant protection, they do not fulfil their engagement to protect. (T.) ═ إِيمَانٌ also signifies The *believing* [a thing, or in a thing, and particularly in God]; syn. تَصْدِيقٌ; (T, Ṣ, &c.;) by common consent of the lexicologists and other men of science: (T:) its primary meaning is the *becoming true to the trust with respect to which God has confided in one, by a firm believing with the heart; not by profession of belief with the tongue only, without the assent of the heart;* for he who does not firmly believe with his heart is either a hypocrite or an ignorant person. (T, TA.) Its verb is intrans. and trans. (TA, from a Commentary on the Mutowwal.) You say, آمَنَ, meaning *He believed.* (T.) And it is said to be trans. by itself, like صَدَّقَ; and by means of بِ, considered as meaning إِعْتِرَافٌ [or *acknowledgment*]; and by means of لِ, considered as meaning إِذْعَانٌ [or *submission*]. (TA.) [Thus] you say, [آمَنَهُ and] آمَنَ بِهِ, (inf. n. إِيمَانٌ, T, Ḳ,) meaning *He believed it* or *in it,* (T, M, Ḳ,) namely, a thing. (T, M.) And آمَنَ بِٱللّٰهِ *He believed in God.* (T.) It seems to be meant by what is said in the Ksh [in ii. 2], that آمن به [or آمَنَهُ] properly signifies آمَنَهُ التَّكْذِيبَ [*He rendered him secure from being charged with lying,* or *falsehood*]; and that the meaning *he believed him,* or *in him,* is tropical; but this is at variance with what its author says in the A; and Es-Saad says that this latter meaning is proper. (TA.)

The phrase in the Ḳur [ix. 61], وَيُؤْمِنُ لِلْمُؤْمِنِينَ, accord. to Th, means *And he believeth the believers; giveth credit to them.* (M.) —— Sometimes it is employed to signify The *acknowledging with the tongue* only; and hence, in the Ḳur [lxiii. 3], ذٰلِكَ بِأَنَّهُمْ آمَنُوا ثُمَّ كَفَرُوا *That is because they acknowledged with the tongue, then disacknowledged with the heart.* (TA.) —— Also † The *trusting*, or *confiding*, or *having trust* or *confidence.* (M, Ḳ.) [You say, آمَنَ بِهِ, meaning *He trusted*, or *confided*, *in him*, or *it*: for] the verb of ايمان in this sense is trans. by means of بِ, without implication; as Bḍ says. (TA.) [And it is also trans. by itself: for] you say, مَا آمَنَ أَنْ يَجِدَ صَحَابَةً, meaning ‡ *He trusted not that he would find companions*; (M,* Ḳ,* TA;) said of one who has formed the intention of journeying: or the meaning is مَا كَادَ [i. e. *he hardly*, or *scarcely*, *found* &c.; or *he was not near to finding* &c.]. (M, Ḳ.) See also أَمَنَةٌ. —— Also The *manifesting humility* or *submission, and the accepting the Law*, (Zj, T,* Ḳ,) *and that which the Prophet has said or done, and the firm believing thereof with the heart*; (Zj, T, M;) without which firm belief, the manifesting of humility or submission, and the accepting that which the Prophet has said or done, is termed إِسْلَام, for which one's blood is to be spared. (T.) [In this sense, it is trans. by means of لِ, accord. to some, as shown above; or by means of بِ, for, accord. to Fei,] you say, آمَنْتُ بِاللّٰهِ, inf. n. as above, meaning *I submitted*, or *resigned, myself to God.* (Mṣb.) [There are numerous other explanations which it is needless to give, differing according to different persuasions. —— See also إِيمَانٌ below.]

8: see 1, in five places.

10. اِسْتَأْمَنَهُ *He asked*, or *demanded*, *of him* الأَمَان [i. e. *security* or *safety*, or *protection* or *safeguard*, or *the promise* or *assurance of security* or *safety*, or *indemnity*, or *quarter*]. (T,* Mṣb, TA.) —— See also أَمِنَهُ. —— اِسْتَأْمَنَ إِلَيْهِ *He entered within the pale of his* أَمَان [or *protection*, or *safeguard*]. (Ṣ, Mṣb.)

أَمْنٌ [an inf. n. of أَمِنَ: as a simple subst. it signifies *Security*, or *safety*: (see أَمِنَ:) or] *security* as meaning *freedom from fear*; contr. of خَوْف; (Ṣ, M, Ḳ;) as also ▼ إِمْنٌ (Zj, M, Ḳ) and ▼ أَمَنٌ (M, Ḳ) and ▼ أَمَنَةٌ (Ṣ, M, Ḳ) [and ▼ إِمْنَةٌ (see أَمِنَ)] and ▼ أَمَانٌ and ▼ آمِنٌ, (M, Ḳ,) which last is an inf. n. of أَمِنَ [like the rest], (MF,) or a subst. like فَالِجٌ; (M;) and ▼ أَمَانَةٌ is syn. with أَمَانٌ, (Ṣ,) both of these signifying *security*, or *safety*, and *freedom from fear*: (PṢ:) or أَمْنٌ signifies *freedom from expectation of evil*, or *of an object of dislike* or *hatred, in the coming time*; originally, *ease of mind, and freedom from fear.* (El-Munáwee, TA.) You say, أَنْتَ فِى أَمْنٍ [*Thou art in a state of security*], (T, M,) ▼ مِنْ ذٰلِكَ [*from that*]; and فِى أَمَانٍ signifies the same; (T;) and so ▼ فِى آمِنٍ. (M.) And ▼ أَمَنَةً نُعَاسًا, in the Ḳur [iii. 148], means *Security* (أَمْنًا) [and *slumber*]. (Ṣ.) ▼ أَمَانٌ also signifies *Protection*, or *safeguard*: and [very frequently] *a promise*, or *an assurance, of security* or *safety*; *indemnity*; or *quarter*: in Pers. پناه and زِنْهَار: (KL:) syn. إِلٌّ. (Ḳ in art. ال.) You say, ▼ دَخَلَ فِى أَمَانِهِ [*He entered within the pale of his protection*, or *safeguard*]. (Ṣ, Mṣb.) [And كُنْ فِى أَمَانِ ▼ اللّٰهِ *Be thou in the protection*, or *safeguard, of God.*] And ▼ أَعْطَيْتُهُ الأَمَانَ [*I gave*, or *granted, to him security* or *safety*, or *protection* or *safeguard*, or *the promise* or *assurance of security* or *safety*, or *indemnity*, or *quarter*]; namely, a captive. (Mṣb.) And طَلَبَ ▼ مِنْهُ الأَمَانَ [*He asked*, or *demanded*, *of him security* or *safety*, or *protection* or *safeguard*, &c., as in the next preceding ex.]. (Mṣb, TA.) —— أَمْنًا in the Ḳur ii. 119 means ذَا أَمْنٍ [*Possessed of security* or *safety*]: (Aboo-Is-ḥáḳ, M:) or مَوْضِعَ أَمْنٍ [*a place of security* or *safety*; like مَأْمَنًا]. (Bḍ.) —— See also آمِنٌ. —— You say also, مَا أَحْسَنَ أَمْنَكَ, and ▼ أَمَنَكَ, meaning *How good is thy religion! and thy natural disposition!* (M, Ḳ.)

إِمْنٌ: see أَمْنٌ.

أَمَنٌ: see أَمْنٌ, first and last sentences.

أَمِنٌ: see آمِنٌ. —— Also, (Ḳ, [there said to be like كَتِفٌ,]) or ▼ آمِنٌ, (M, [so written in a copy of that work,]) *Asking*, or *demanding*, or *seeking, protection, in order to be secure*, or *safe*, or *free from fear, for himself*: (M, Ḳ:) so says IAạr. (M.)

إِمْنَةٌ: see أَمْنٌ.

أَمَنَةٌ: see أَمْنٌ, in two places: —— and see also أَمَانَةٌ. ═ Also A man *who trusts*, or *confides, in every one*; (T, Ṣ, M;) and so ▼ أُمْنَةٌ: (Ṣ:) and *who believes in everything that he hears*; *who disbelieves in nothing*: (Lḥ, T:) or *in whom men*, or *people, trust*, or *confide, and whose malevolence*, or *mischievousness, they do not fear*: (T, M:) and ▼ أُمَنَةٌ signifies *trusted in*, or *confided in*; [like أَمِينٌ;] and by rule should be أُمْنَةٌ, because it has the meaning of a pass. part. n. [like لُعْنَةٌ and ضُحْكَةٌ and لُقْطَةٌ &c. (see لَقَطَ)]: (M:) or both signify one *in whom every one trusts*, or *confides*, *in*, or *with respect to, everything.* (Ḳ.) —— See also أَمِينٌ.

أُمَنَةٌ: see أَمَنَةٌ, in two places.

امان: see أَمْنٌ, in seven places.

أَمُونٌ, applied to a she camel, of the measure فَعُولٌ in the sense of the measure مَفْعُولَةٌ, like عَصُوبٌ and حَلُوبٌ, ‡ *Trusted*, or *confided, in*; (T;) *firmly, compactly*, or *strongly, made*; (T, Ṣ, M, Ḳ;) *secure from*, or *free from fear of, being weak*: (Ṣ, M:) also, that is *secure from*, or *free from fear of, stumbling, and becoming jaded*: (M:) or *strong, so that her becoming languid is not feared*: (A, TA:) pl. أُمُنٌ. (M, Ḳ.) [See also what next follows.]

أَمِينٌ *Trusted; trusted in; confided in*; (T,* Ṣ,* M, Mṣb,* Ḳ;) as also ▼ أَمَّانٌ; (Ṣ, M, Ḳ;) *i. q.* ▼ مَأْمُونٌ (Ṣ, M, Ḳ) and ▼ مُؤْتَمَنٌ: (ISk, T, Ḳ:) [*a person in whom one trusts* or *confides*; *a confidant*; *a person intrusted with*, or *to whom is confided, power, authority, control*, or *a charge*, عَلَى شَىْءٍ *over a thing*; *a person intrusted with an affair*, or *with affairs*, i. e., *with the management*, or *disposal, thereof*; *a confidential agent*, or *superintendent*; *a commissioner*; *a commissary*; *a trustee*; *a depositary*;] *a guardian*: (TA:) *trusty*; *trustworthy*; *trustful*; *confidential*; *faithful*: (Mgh, Mṣb:*) pl. أُمَنَاءُ, and, accord. to some, ▼ أَمَنَةٌ, as in a trad. in which it is said, أَصْحَابِى أَمَنَةٌ لِأُمَّتِى, meaning *My companions are guardians to my people*: or, accord. to others, this is pl. of ▼ آمِنٌ [app. in a sense mentioned below in this paragraph, so that the meaning in this trad. is *my companions are persons who accord trust, or confidence, to my people*]. (TA.) Hence,

> أَلَمْ تَعْلَمِى يَا أَسْمَ وَيْحَكِ أَنَّنِى
> حَلَفْتُ يَمِينًا لَا أَخُونُ أَمِينِى

[*Knowest thou not, O Asmá* (أَسْمَآءُ, curtailed for the sake of the metre), *mercy on thee!* or *woe to thee! that I have sworn an oath that I will not act treacherously to him in whom I trust?*] i. e. ▼ مَأْمُونِى: (Ṣ:) or the meaning here is, *him who trusts*, or *confides, in me*; (ISk, T;) [i. e.] it is here *syn. with* ▼ آمِنِى. (M.) [Hence also,] أَمِينٌ, الأَمِينُ فِى القِمَارِ, (Ḳ voce مُجْمِدٌ, &c.,) or أَمِينُ القِمَارِ, [*The person who is intrusted, as deputy, with the disposal of the arrows in the game called* المَيْسِر; or] *he who shuffles the arrows*; الَّذِى يَضْرِبُ بِالقِدَاحِ. (EM p. 105.) [Hence also,] الرُّوحُ الأَمِينُ [*The Trusted*, or *Trusty, Spirit*]; (Ḳur xxvi. 193;) applied to Gabriel, because he is intrusted with the revelation of God. (Bḍ.) ▼ أَمَّانٌ, mentioned above, and occurring in a verse of El-Aạshà, applied to a merchant, is said by some to mean *Possessed of religion and excellence.* (M.) ▼ مُؤْتَمَنٌ is applied, in a trad., to the مُؤَذِّن, as meaning that men trust, or confide, in him with respect to the times in which he calls to prayer, and know by his call what they are commanded to do as to praying and fasting and breaking fast. (Mgh.) هُوَ ▼ مَأْمُونُ المُعَامَلَةِ means *He is* [*trusty*, or *trustworthy, in dealing with others*; or] *free from exorbitance and deceit* or *artifice* or *craft to be feared.* (Mṣb.) —— *An aid*, or *assistant*; syn. عَوْنٌ [here app. meaning, as it often does, *an armed attendant*, or *a guard*]; because one trusts in his strength, and is without fear of his being weak. (M.) —— † The *strong*; syn. قَوِىٌّ. (Ḳ, TA: [in the latter of which is given the same reason for this signification as is given in the M for that of عون; for which قوى may be a mistranscription; but see أَمُونٌ.]) —— One *who trusts*, or *confides, in* another; (ISk, T, Ḳ;) [as also ▼ آمِنٌ, of which see an ex. voce حَفِرَ;] so accord. to ISk in the verse cited above in this paragraph: (T:) thus it bears two contr. significations. (Ḳ.) —— See also آمِنٌ, in five places. ═ And see آمِينَ.

أَمَانَةٌ : see أَمْنٌ, first sentence. — *Trustiness; trustworthiness; trustfulness; faithfulness; fidelity;* (M, Mgh, Ḳ;) as also ↓ أَمَنَةٌ. (M, Ḳ.) أَمَانَةُ ٱللّٰهِ [for مَا أُقْسِمُ بِهِ or أَمَانَةُ ٱللّٰهِ قَسَمِى *The faithfulness of God is my oath* or *that by which I swear*] is composed of an inf. n. prefixed to the agent, and the former is in the nom. case as an inchoative; the phrase being like لَعَمْرُ ٱللّٰهِ, as meaning an oath; and the enunciative being suppressed, and meant to be understood: accord. to some, you say, أَمَانَةَ ٱللّٰهِ [app. for نَشُدُكَ أَمَانَةَ ٱللّٰهِ *I adjure thee*, or *conjure thee, by the faithfulness of God*, or *the like*], making it to be governed in the accus. case by the verb which is to be understood: and some correctly say, وَأَمَانَةِ ٱللّٰهِ [*By the faithfulness of God*], with the و which denotes an oath: (Mgh:) or this last is an oath accord. to Aboo-Ḥaneefeh; but Esh-Sháfi'ee does not reckon it as such: and it is forbidden in a trad. to swear by ٱلْأَمَانَة; app. because it is not one of the names of God. (TA.) [Or these phrases may have been used, in the manner of an oath, agreeably with explanations here following.] ═ *A thing committed to the trust and care of a person; a trust; a deposite;* (Mgh, Mṣb;) and *the like:* (Mṣb:) *property committed to trust and care:* (TA:) pl. أَمَانَاتٌ. (Mgh, Mṣb.) It is said in the Ḳur [viii. 27], وَتَخُونُوا أَمَانَاتِكُمْ [*Nor be ye unfaithful to the trusts committed to you*]. (Mgh.) And in the same [xxxiii. 72], إِنَّا عَرَضْنَا الْأَمَانَةَ عَلَى السَّمٰوَاتِ وَالْأَرْضِ وَالْجِبَالِ فَأَبَيْنَ أَنْ يَحْمِلْنَهَا وَأَشْفَقْنَ مِنْهَا وَحَمَلَهَا الْإِنْسَانُ [*Verily we proposed*, or *offered, the trust* which we have committed to man *to the heavens and the earth and the mountains, and* (accord. to explanations of Bḍ and others) *they refused to take it upon themselves*, or *to accept it, and they feared it, but man took it upon himself*, or *accepted it:* or, (accord. to another explanation of Bḍ, also given in the T, and in the Ḳ in art. حمل, &c.,) *they refused to be unfaithful to it, and they feared it, but man was unfaithful to it:* but in explaining what this trust was, authors greatly differ: accord. to some,] الامانة here means *obedience;* so called because the rendering thereof is incumbent: or *the obedience which includes that which is natural and that which depends upon the will:* [for] it is said that when God created these [celestial and terrestrial] bodies, He created in them understanding: or it may here [and in some other instances] mean *reason*, or *intellect:* [and *the faculty of volition:* and app. *conscience:* these being trusts committed to us by God, to be faithfully employed: (see an ex. voce جَذْرٌ:)] and *the imposition of a task* or *duty* or *of tasks* or *duties* [app. *combined with reason* or *intellect, which is necessary for the performance thereof*]: (Bḍ:) or it here means *prayers and other duties for the performance of which there is recompense and for the neglect of which there is punishment:* (Jel:) or, accord. to I 'Ab and Sa'eed Ibn-Jubeyr, (T,) *the obligatory statutes which God has imposed upon his servants:* (T, Ḳ:*) or, (T, Ḳ,) accord. to Ibn-'Omar, [*the choice between*] *obedience and disobedience* was offered to Adam, and he was informed of the recompense of obedience and the punishment of disobedience: but, in my opinion, he says, (T,) it here means *the intention which one holds in the heart*, (T, Ḳ,) *with respect to the belief which he professes with the tongue, and with respect to all the obligatory statutes which he externally fulfils;* (Ḳ;) because God has confided to him power over it, and not manifested it to any [other] of his creatures, so that he who conceives in his mind, with respect to the acknowledgment of the unity of God, (T, Ḳ,) and with respect to belief [in general], (T,) the like of that which he professes, he fulfils the امانة [or trust], (T, Ḳ,) and he who conceives in his mind disbelief while he professes belief with the tongue is unfaithful thereto, and every one who is unfaithful to that which is confided to him is [termed] حَامِلٌ, (T,) or حَامِلُ الأَمَانَةِ, and مُحْتَمِلُهَا: (Bḍ:) and by الإِنْسَانُ is here meant the doubting disbeliever. (T.) — Also, [as being a trust committed to him by God, A man's] *family*, or *household;* syn. أَهْلٌ. (TA.)

أُمَّانٌ : see أَمِينٌ, in two places. ═ Also One *who does not write;* as though he were (كَأَنَّهُ [in the CḲ لِأَنَّهُ because he is]) an أُمِّىّ. (Ḳ, TA.) [But this belongs to art. امّ; being of the measure فُعْلَانٌ, like عُرْيَانٌ.] — And *A sower*, or *cultivator of land;* [perhaps meaning *a clown*, or *boor;*] syn. زَرَّاعٌ: (CḲ:) or *sowers*, or *cultivators of land;* syn. زُرَّاعٌ: (Ḳ, TA:) in one copy of the Ḳ زِرَاعٌ. (TA.)

آمِنٌ *Secure, safe*, or *free from fear;* as also ↓ أَمِينٌ (Lḥ, T,* Ṣ,* M, Mṣb, Ḳ) and ↓ أَمِنٌ. (M, Ḳ.) Hence, in the Ḳur [xcv. 3], وَهٰذَا ٱلْبَلَدِ ٱلْأَمِينِ ↓ [*And this secure town*]; (Akh, Lḥ, T, Ṣ, M;) meaning Mekkeh. (M.) بَلَدٌ آمِنٌ and ↓ أَمِينٌ means *A town*, or *country*, or *district, of which the inhabitants are in a state of security*, or *confidence, therein.* (Mṣb.) It is also said in the Ḳur [xliv. 51], إِنَّ ٱلْمُتَّقِينَ فِى مَقَامٍ أَمِينٍ ↓, meaning [*Verily the pious shall be in an abode*] *wherein they shall be secure from the accidents*, or *casualties, of fortune.* (M.) [And hence,] ٱلْأَمِينُ ↓ is one of the epithets applied to God, (Mgh, Ḳ,) on the authority of El-Ḥasan; (Mgh;) an assertion requiring consideration: it may mean *He who is secure with respect to the accidents*, or *casualties, of fortune:* but see المُؤْمِنُ, which is [well known as] an epithet applied to God. (TA.) آمِنُ المَالِ means *What is secure from being slaughtered, of the camels, because of its being highly prized;* by المال being meant الإِبِل: or, as some say, ‡ *what is highly esteemed, of property of any kind;* as though, if it had intellect, it would feel secure from being exchanged. (M.) You say, أَعْطَيْتُهُ مِنْ آمِنِ مَالِى, (Ḳ, TA, [in the CḲ آمَنِ,]) meaning ‡ *I gave him of the choice*, or *best, of my property; of what was highly esteemed thereof;* (Ḳ, TA;) and مِنْ أَمِنِ ↓ مَالِى, which Az explains as meaning *of the choice*, or *best, of my property.* (TA: [in which is given a verse cited by ISk showing that أَمِن, thus used, is not a mistranscription for آمن.]) And آمِنُ الحِلْمِ means *Steadfast in forbearance* or *clemency;* of *whose becoming disordered in temper, and free from self-restraint, there is no fear.* (M.) — See also أَمِينٌ, in three places: — and see أَمِنٌ. ═ See also أَمْنٌ, in two places.

آمِينَ [in the CḲ, erroneously, آمِينُ] and ↓ أَمِينَ; (Th, T, Ṣ, M, Mgh, Mṣb, Ḳ;) both chaste and well known, (TA,) the latter of the dial. of El-Ḥijáz, (Mṣb, TA,) as some say, (TA,) [and this, though the less common, is the original form, for] the medd in the former is only to give fulness of sound to the fet-ḥah of the أ, (Th, M, Mṣb, TA,) as is shown by the fact that there is no word in the Arabic language of the measure فَاعِيلٌ; (Mṣb, TA;) and some pronounce the former آمِّينَ, (Ḳ,) which is said by some of the learned to be a dial. var., (Mṣb,) but this is a mistake, (Ṣ, Mṣb,) accord. to authorities of good repute, and is one of old date, originating from an assertion of Aḥmad Ibn-Yaḥyà, [i. e. Th,] that آمِينَ is like عَاصِينَ, by which he was falsely supposed to mean its having the form of a pl., [and being consequently آمِّينَ,] (Mṣb, [and part of this is said in the M,]) whereas he thereby only meant that the م is without teshdeed, like the ص in عَاصِينَ; (M;) beside that the sense of قَاصِدِينَ [which is that of آمِّينَ, from أَمَّ,] would be inconsistent after the last phrase of the first chapter of the Ḳur [where آمِينَ is usually added]; (Mṣb;) and sometimes it is pronounced with imáleh, [i. e. "émeena,"] as is said by El-Wáḥidee in the Beseeṭ; (Ḳ;) but this is unknown in works on lexicology, and is said to be a mispronunciation of some of the Arabs of the desert of El-Yemen: (MF:) each form is indecl., (Ṣ,) with fet-ḥ for its termination, like أَيْنَ and كَيْفَ, to prevent the occurrence of two quiescent letters together: (T, Ṣ, TA:) it is a word used immediately after a prayer, or supplication: (Ṣ,* M:) [it is best expressed, when occurring in a translation, by the familiar Hebrew equivalent *Amen:*] El-Fárisee says that it is a compound of a verb and a noun; (M;) meaning *answer Thou me;* [i. e. *answer Thou my prayer;*] (M, Mgh;*) or *O God, answer Thou:* (Zj, T, Mṣb, Ḳ:) or *so be it:* (AḤát, Ṣ, Mṣb, Ḳ:) or *so do Thou*, (Ḳ, TA,) *O Lord:* (TA:) it is strangely asserted by some of the learned, that, after the Fátiḥah, [or Opening Chapter of the Ḳur-án,] it is a prayer which implies all that is prayed for in detail in the Fátiḥah: so in the Towsheeḥ: (MF:) or it is *one of the names of God:* (M, Mṣb, Ḳ:) so says El-Ḥasan (M, Mṣb) El-Baṣree: (Mṣb:) but the assertion that it is for يَا أَللّٰهُ [*O God*], and that ٱسْتَجِبْ [*answer Thou*] is meant to be understood, is not correct accord. to the lexicologists; for, were it so, it would be with refa, not naṣb. (T.)

إِيمَانٌ [inf. n. of 4, q. v. — Used as a simple subst., *Belief;* particularly *in God, and in his word and apostles &c.: faith: trust*, or *confidence:* &c.] — Sometimes it means *Prayer;* syn. صَلَاةٌ: as in the Ḳur [ii. 138], where it is said, وَمَا كَانَ ٱللّٰهُ لِيُضِيعَ إِيمَانَكُمْ, (Bḍ, Jel, TA,) i. e. [*God will not make to be lost*] *your prayer* towards Jerusalem, (Bḍ,* Jel,) as some explain it. (Bḍ.) — Sometimes, also, it is used as meaning *The law brought by the Prophet.* (Er-Rághib, TA.)

مَأْمَنٌ *A place of security* or *safety* or *freedom from fear;* or *where one feels secure.* (M, TA.)

مُؤْمَنٌ pass. part. n. of آمَنَهُ. (T.) It is said in the Ḳur [iv. 96], accord. to one reading, (T, M,) that of Aboo-Jaạfar El-Medenee, (T,) لَسْتَ مُؤْمَنًا [*Thou art not granted security,* or *safety,* &c.; or] *we will not grant thee security,* &c. (T, M.)

مُؤْمِنٌ [act. part. n. of 4; *Rendering secure,* &c.]. المُؤْمِنُ is an epithet applied to God; meaning *He who rendereth mankind secure from his wronging them:* (T, Ṣ:) or *He who rendereth his servants secure from his punishment:* (M, IAth:) i. q. المُهَيْمِنُ, (M,) which is originally المُؤَامِنُ; [for the form مُفَيْعِلٌ is originally مُؤَفْعِلٌ;] the second ء being softened, and changed into ى, and the first being changed into ه: (Ṣ:) or *the Believer of his servants* (Th, M, TA) *the Muslims, on the day of resurrection, when the nations shall be interrogated respecting the messages of their apostles:* (TA:) or *He who will faithfully perform to his servants what He hath promised them:* (T, TA:) or *He who hath declared in his word the truth of his unity.* (T.) — [Also *Believing,* or *a believer;* particularly *in God, and in his word and apostles &c.: faithful: trusting,* or *confiding:* &c.: see 4.]

مَأْمُونٌ: see أَمِينٌ, in three places. — مَأْمُونَةٌ A woman *whose like is sought after and eagerly retained because of her valuable qualities.* (M.)

مَأْمُونِيَّةٌ *A certain kind of food; so called in relation to El-Ma-moon.* (TA.)

مُؤْتَمَنٌ: see أَمِينٌ, in two places.

امه

1. أَمِهَ, aor. ـَ, inf. n. أَمَهٌ, *He forgot.* (Ṣ, Ḳ.) Hence the reading of I'Ab, [in the Ḳur xii. 45,] وَادَّكَرَ بَعْدَ أَمَهٍ [*And he remembered,* or *became reminded, after forgetting*]. (Ṣ.) AHeyth is said to have read بَعْدَ أَمْهٍ; and accord. to AO, أَمَهٌ signifies نِسْيَانٌ [like أَمَهٌ]; but this is not correct. (Az, TA.) — *He confessed,* or *acknowledged:* (Ṣ, Ḳ:) occurring in this sense in a trad. of Ez-Zuhree; but not well known. (Ṣ.) The reading of I'Ab, mentioned above, بَعْدَ أَمَهٍ, is explained by A'Obeyd as meaning *after confessing,* or *acknowledging.* (TA.)

5. تَأَمَّهَ أُمًّا *He adopted a mother;* (M, Ḳ;) as also ▼تَأَمَّمَهَا. (M in art. أم.)

أُمَّهَةٌ i. q. أُمٌّ [*A mother* of a human being and of any animal]: (M, Ḳ:) the former is [said by some to be] the original of the latter: (Ṣ:) Aboo-Bekr says that the ه in the former is a radical letter: (TA:) or the former applies to a rational creature; and the latter, to [a rational and] an irrational: (Ḳ:) or, accord. to Az, the pl. of the former applies to the rational; and that of the latter, to the irrational: (TA:) the former sing. sometimes applies to an irrational creature: (IJ, TA:) [for some further remarks on both of these words and their pls., see the latter of them:] the pl. [of the former] is أُمَّهَاتٌ and [that of the latter is] أُمَّاتٌ: (T, Ṣ:) Az says that the ه is added in the former for the purpose of distinguishing between the daughters of Adam [to whom it is generally applied] and other animate beings. (TA.)

امو

1. أَمَتْ, (Ṣ,* M, Ḳ, [in the CḲ, erroneously, آمَتْ,]) second pers. أَمَوْتِ; (Ṣ;) and أَمِيَتْ, (M, Ḳ,) like سَمِعَتْ; (Ḳ;) and أَمُوَتْ, (Lḥ, M, Ḳ,) like كَرُمَتْ; (Ḳ;) inf. n. أُمُوَّةٌ; (Ṣ, M, Ḳ;) *She* (a woman) *became a slave;* (Ṣ,* M, Ḳ;) as also ▼تَأَمَّتْ. (Mṣb.) — أَمَتِ السِّنَّوْرُ, aor. تَأْمُو, inf. n. أُمَاءٌ, *The cat* [*mewed,* or] *uttered a cry;* (Ṣ, Ḳ;) like مَاءَتْ, aor. تَمُوءُ, inf. n. مُوَاءٌ. (Ṣ.)

2. أَمَّاهَا, (M, Ḳ,) inf. n. تَأْمِيَةٌ, (Ḳ,) *He made her a slave.* (M, Ḳ.)

5. تَأَمَّتْ: see 1. — تَأَمَّى أَمَةً *He took for himself a female slave;* (Ṣ, M, Mṣb, Ḳ;) as also ▼اِسْتَأْمَاهَا. (Ṣ, Ḳ.)

8. هُوَ يَأْتَمِى بِهِ *He follows his* (another person's) *example; imitates him;* i. q. يَأْتَمُّ بِهِ. (TA in the present art.) And اِئْتَمَى بِالشَّىْءِ [written with the disjunctive alif اِيتَمَى] is used for اِئْتَمَّ بِهِ [*He made the thing to be a rule of life* or *conduct*], by substitution [of ى for م], (M and Ḳ in art. أم,) the doubling [of the م] being disapproved. (M in that art.)

10: see 5.

أَمَةٌ, originally أَمَوَةٌ, (Mṣb,) [but whether أَمْوَةٌ or أَمَوَةٌ is disputed, as will be seen in what follows,] *A female slave;* (M, Ḳ;) *a woman whose condition is that of slavery;* (T;) contr. of حُرَّةٌ: (Ṣ:) [in relation to God, best rendered *a handmaid:*] dual أَمَتَانِ: (Mṣb:) pl. آمٍ, (Lth, T, Ṣ, M, Mṣb, Ḳ, &c.,) like قَاضٍ, (Mṣb,) a pl. of pauc. [respecting which see what follows after the other pls.], (Lth, T,) and إِمَآءٌ [the most common form] (T, Ṣ, M, Mgh, Mṣb, Ḳ) and إِمْوَانٌ (T, Ṣ, M, Mṣb, Ḳ) and أُمْوَانٌ (Ḳ, and so in some copies of the M) and أَمْوَانٌ (Ḳ, and so in some copies of the M) [the last, or last but one, accord. to different copies of the M, on the authority of Lḥ,] and أَمَوَاتٌ, (M, Mṣb, Ḳ,) for which one may say أَمَاتٌ. (Ibn-Keysán, TA.) Accord. to Sb (M) and Mbr (TA) it is originally أَمَوَةٌ, (Ṣ, M, Ḳ,) because it has for a pl. آمٍ, (Ṣ, M,) which is [originally أَأْمُوٌ,] of the measure أَفْعُلٌ, (Lth, T, Ṣ,) like آكُمٌ, pl. of أَكَمَةٌ, (Sb, M,) and like أَيْنُقٌ, [pl. of نَاقَةٌ, which is originally نَوَقَةٌ,] for a sing. of the measure فَعْلَةٌ has not a pl. of this form; (Ṣ;) and Mbr says that there is no noun of two letters but a letter has been dropped from it, which it indicates by its pl. or dual, or by a verb if it is derived therefrom: (TA:) or it is originally فَعْلَةٌ: (AHeyth, T, Ḳ:) AHeyth says that they suppressed its final radical letter, and, forming a pl. from it after the manner of نَخْلَةٌ and نَخْلٌ, instead of saying أَمْرٌ, which they disliked as being of only two letters, they transposed the suppressed و, changing it into ا, and placing it between the ا and م. (T: [in which this opinion, though it does not account for the termination of the pl. آمٍ, is said to be preferable.]) One says, جَآءَتْنِى أَمَةُ ٱللّٰهِ [*The handmaid of God came to me*]: and in the dual, جَآءَتْنِى أَمَتَا ٱللّٰهِ: and in the pl., جَآءَنِى إِمَآءُ ٱللّٰهِ and إِمْوَانُ ٱللّٰهِ and أَمَوَاتُ ٱللّٰهِ; and one may also say, أَمَاتُ ٱللّٰهِ. (Ibn-Keysán, TA.) [ISd says,] رَمَاهُ ٱللّٰهُ مِنْ كُلِّ أَمَةٍ بِحَجَرٍ is mentioned by IAạr as said in imprecating evil on a man; but I think it is مِنْ كُلِّ أَمْتٍ [*May God cast a stone at him from every elevated place,* or the like]. (M.)

أَمَوِىٌّ *Of,* or *relating* or *belonging to, a female slave.* (Ṣ.)

أُمَيَّةٌ dim. of أَمَةٌ; (Ṣ, Mṣb;) originally أُمَيْوَةٌ. (Mṣb.)

ان

1. أَنَّ, aor. يَئِنُّ, inf. n. أَنِينٌ and أُنَانٌ (Ṣ, M, Mṣb, Ḳ) and تَأْنَانٌ (Ṣ, Ḳ) and أَنٌّ, (M, Ḳ,) *He moaned;* or *uttered a moan,* or *moaning,* or *prolonged voice of complaint;* or *said, Ah!* syn. تَأَوَّهَ; (M, Ḳ;) by reason of pain: (Ṣ, TA:) *he complained* by reason of disease or pain: (TA:) *he uttered a cry* or *cries:* (Mṣb:) said of a man. (Ṣ, Mṣb.) — أَنَّتِ القَوْسُ, aor. تَئِنُّ, inf. n. أَنِينٌ, *The bow made a gentle and prolonged sound.* (AḤn, M.) — لَا أَفْعَلُهُ مَا أَنَّ فِى السَّمَآءِ نَجْمٌ means *I will not do it as long as there is a star in the heaven:* (Ṣ, M, Ḳ:) أَنَّ being here a dial. var. of عَنَّ. (Ṣ.) You say also, مَا أَنَّ فِى الفُرَاتِ قَطْرَةٌ *As long as there is a drop in the Euphrates.* (T, Ṣ.) And لَا أَفْعَلُهُ مَا أَنَّ فِى السَّمَآءِ سَمَآءٌ [*I will not do it as long as there is rain in the heaven*]. (Ṣ.) [It is said in the M that Lḥ mentions the last two sayings; but it is there indicated that he read قَطْرَةً and سَمَآءً: and] ISk mentions the saying, لَا أَفْعَلُهُ مَا أَنَّ فِى السَّمَآءِ نَجْمًا, (T, M,) and مَا عَنَّ فِى السَّمَآءِ نَجْمٌ; (T;) [in the former of which, أَنَّ must be a particle (which see below); but it seems that it should rather be إِنَّ, in this case, as ISd thinks; for he says,] I know not for what reason أَنَّ is here with fet-ḥ, unless a verb be understood before it, as ثَبَتَ or وُجِدَ: [and he adds,] Lḥ mentions مَا أَنَّ ذٰلِكَ الجَبَلَ مَكَانَهُ [*as long as that mountain is in its place*]: and مَا أَنَّ حِرَآءً مَكَانَهُ [*as long as Mount Ḥirá is in its place*]: but he does not explain these sayings. (M.)

أَنْ is a pronoun, denoting the speaker, [*I,* masc. and fem.,] in the language of some of the Arabs: they say, أَنْ فَعَلْتُ [*I did*], with the ن quiescent: but most of them pronounce it [▼أَنَ] with fet-ḥ when conjoined with a following word; (Mughnee, Ḳ;) saying, أَنَ فَعَلْتُ: (TA:) and [▼أَنَا] with ا in a case of pause: (Mughnee, Ḳ:) and some pronounce it with ا also when it is conjoined with a following word; saying, أَنَا فَعَلْتُ; [as we generally find it written in books;] but this is of a bad dialect: (TA:) [this last assertion, however, requires consideration; for the dial. here said to be bad is that of Temeem, accord. to what here follows:] the Basrees hold that the pronoun consists of the ء and the ن, and that the [final] ا is redundant, because it is suppressed in a case of conjunction with a following word; but the Koofees hold that the pronoun is composed of all the three letters, because the ا is preserved in a case of conjunction with a following word in the dial. of Temeem. (Marginal note in a copy of the Mughnee.) [Accord. to Az,] it is best to say ♦ أَنَا in a case of pause; and ♦ أَنَ in a case of conjunction with a following word, as in أَنَ فَعَلْتُ ذَاكَ [I did that]; but some of the Arabs say, أَنَا ♦ فَعَلْتُ ذَاكَ; and some make the ن quiescent in a case of this kind, though this is rare, saying, أَنْ قُلْتُ ذَاكَ [I said that]; and Kudá'ah prolong the former ا, saying, آنَ ♦ قُلْتُهُ. (T.) [Accord. to J,] ♦ أَنَا is a pronoun denoting the speaker alone, and is made to end invariably with fet-h to distinguish it from the particle أَنْ which renders the aor. mansoob; the final ا being for the purpose of showing what is the vowel in a case of pause; but when it occurs in the middle [or beginning] of a sentence, it is dropped, except in a bad dialect. (S.) [Accord. to ISd,] ♦ أَنَ is a noun denoting the speaker; and in a case of pause, you add ا at the end, [saying ♦ أَنَا,] to denote quiescence; (M;) [or] it is better to do this, though it is not always done: (TA:) but it is said, on the authority of Ktr, that there are five dial. vars. of this word; namely, أَنَ فَعَلْتُ, and ♦ آنَ, and ♦ أَنَا, and ♦ أَنْ, and ♦ أَنَهْ, all mentioned by IJ; but there is some weakness in this: IJ says that the ه in ♦ أَنَهْ may be a substitute for the ا in أَنَا, because the latter is the more usual, and the former is rare; or it may be added to show what is the vowel, like the ا, and be like the ه in كِتَابِيَهْ and حِسَابِيَهْ. (M.) For the dual, as well as the pl., only نَحْنُ is used. (Az, TA.) — It is also a pronoun denoting the person addressed, or spoken to, by assuming the form ♦ أَنْتَ [Thou, masc.]; ت being added to it as the sign of the person addressed, (S, M, Mughnee, K,) and أَنْ being the pronoun, (M, Mughnee, K,) accord. to the general opinion; (Mughnee, K;) the two becoming as one; not that one is prefixed to the other as governing it in the gen. case: (S:) and so ♦ أَنْتِ, (S, M, Mughnee, K,) addressed to the female: (S, M:) and ♦ أَنْتُمَا, (M, Mughnee, K,) addressed to two; not a regular dual, for were it so it would be أَنْتَانِ; but like كُمَا in ضَرَبْتُكُمَا: (M:) and ♦ أَنْتُمْ and ♦ أَنْتُنَّ, (S, Mughnee, K,) which are [respectively] the masc. and fem. pls. (TA.) — To each of these the ك of comparison is sometimes prefixed; so that you say, ♦ أَنْتَ كَأَنَا [Thou art like me, or as I], and ♦ أَنَا كَأَنْتَ [or أَنَ كَأَنْتَ I am like thee, or as thou]; as is related on the authority of the Arabs; for though the ك of comparison is not prefixed to the [affixed] pronoun, and you say, أَنْتَ كَزَيْدٍ, but not أَنْتَ كِي, yet the separate pronoun is regarded by them as being in the same predicament as the noun; and therefore the prefixing it to the latter kind of pronoun is approved. (S.) It is said in the Book of لَيْسَ, by IKh, that there is no such phrase, in the language of the Arabs, as أَنْتَ كِي, nor as أَنَا كَكَ, except in two forged verses; wherefore Sb says that the Arabs, by saying أَنْتَ مِثْلِي and أَنَا مِثْلُكَ, have no need of saying أَنْتَ كِي and أَنَا كَكَ: and the two verses are these:

• فَلَوْلَا الحَيَآءُ لَكُنَّا كَهُمْ • وَلَوْلَا البَلَآءُ لَكَانُوا كَنَا •

[And but for the sense of shame, we had been like them, or as they: and but for trial, or affliction, they had been like us, or as we]: and

• إِنْ تَكُنْ كِي فَإِنَّنِي كَكَ فِيهَا •
• إِنَّنَا فِي المَلَامِ مُصْطَحِبَانِ •

[If thou art like me, or as I, verily I am like thee, or as thou, in respect of her, or it, or them: verily we, in respect of blame, are companions]. (TA.) Az mentions his having heard some of the Benoo-Suleym say, كَمَا أَنْتَنِي, [the latter word being a compound of the pronoun أَنْتَ, regularly written separately, and the affixed pronoun نِى,] meaning Wait thou for me in thy place. (TA.) ═ It is also a particle: and as such, it is—First, a particle of the kind called مَصْدَرِيٌّ, rendering the aor. mansoob: (Mughnee, K:) i. e., (TA,) it combines with a verb [in this case] in the future [or aor.] tense, following it, to form an equivalent to an inf. n., and renders it mansoob: (S, TA:) you say, أُرِيدُ أَنْ تَقُومَ [I desire that thou stand, or that thou wouldst stand, or that thou mayest stand]; meaning أُرِيدُ قِيَامَكَ [I desire thy standing]. (S.) It occurs in two places: first, in that of the inchoative, or in the beginning of a phrase, so that it is in the place of a nom. case; as in the saying [in the Kur ii. 180], وَأَنْ تَصُومُوا خَيْرٌ لَكُمْ [And that ye fast is better for you]; (Mughnee, K;) i. e. صِيَامُكُمْ [your fasting]. (TA.) And, secondly, after a word denoting a meaning which is not that of certainty: and thus it is in the place of a nom. case; as in the saying [in the Kur lvii. 15], أَلَمْ يَأْنِ لِلَّذِينَ آمَنُوا أَنْ تَخْشَعَ قُلُوبُهُمْ [Hath not the time that their hearts should become submissive, i. e. the time of their hearts' becoming submissive, yet come unto those who have believed?]: and in the place of an accus. case; as in the saying [in the Kur x. 38], وَمَا كَانَ هٰذَا القُرْآنُ أَنْ يُفْتَرَى [And this Kur-án is not such that it might be forged; i. e., افْتِرَآءً; so in Bd and Jel; and so in a marginal note to a copy of the Mughnee, where is added, meaning مُفْتَرًى forged]: and in the place of a gen. case; as in the saying [in the Kur lxiii. 10], مِنْ قَبْلِ أَنْ يَأْتِىَ أَحَدَكُمُ المَوْتُ [Before that death come unto any one of you; i. e. before death's coming unto any one of you]. (Mughnee, K.) Sometimes it makes the aor. to be of the mejzoom form, (Mughnee, K,) as some of the Koofees and AO have mentioned, and as Lh has stated on the authority of certain of the Benoo-Sabbáh of Dabbeh; (Mughnee;) as in this verse:

• إِذَا مَا غَدَوْنَا قَالَ وِلْدَانُ أَهْلِنَا •
• تَعَالَوْا إِلَى أَنْ يَأْتِنَا الصَّيْدُ نَحْطِبِ •

[When we went away in the morning, the youths of our family, or people, said, Come ye, until that the chase come to us, (i. e. until the coming of the chase to us,) let us collect firewood]. (Mughnee, K.) And sometimes it is followed by an aor. of the marfooa form; as in the saying [in the Kur ii. 233], accord. to the reading of Ibn-Moheysin, لِمَنْ أَرَادَ أَنْ يُتِمُّ الرَّضَاعَةَ [For him who desireth that he may complete the time of sucking; i. e. the completing thereof]; (Mughnee, K;) but this is anomalous, (I 'Ak p. 101, and TA,) or أَنْ is here a contraction of أَنَّ [for أَنَّهُ]: (I 'Ak:) and in the saying of the poet,

• أَنْ تَقْرَآنِ عَلَى أَسْمَآءَ وَيْحَكُمَا •
• مِنِّى السَّلَامَ وَأَنْ لَا تُشْعِرَا أَحَدَا •

[That ye two convey, or communicate, to Asmá, (mercy on you! or woe to you!) from me, salutation, and that ye inform not any one]; but the Koofees assert that أَنْ is here [in the beginning of the verse] a contraction of أَنَّ, and anomalously conjoined with the verb; whereas the Basrees correctly say that it is أَنْ which renders the aor. mansoob, but is deprived of government by its being made to accord with its co-ordinate مَا, termed مَصْدَرِيَّة; (Mughnee;) or, as IJ says, on the authority of Aboo-'Alee, أَنْ is here used by poetic licence for أَنَّكُمَا; and the opinion of the Baghdádees [and Basrees], that it is likened to مَا, and therefore without government, is improbable, because أَنْ is not conjoined with a verb in the present tense, but only with the preterite and the future. (M.) When it is suppressed, the aor. may be either mansoob or marfooa; but the latter is the better; as in the saying in the Kur [xxxix. 64], أَفَغَيْرَ ٱللّٰهِ تَأْمُرُونِّى أَعْبُدُ [Other than God do ye bid me worship?]. (S.) If it occurs immediately before a preterite, it combines with it to form an equivalent to an inf. n. relating to past time; being in this case without government: you say, أَعْجَبَنِى أَنْ قُمْتَ [It pleased me that thou stoodest]; meaning thy standing that is past pleased me: (S:) and thus it is used in the saying [in the Kur xxviii. 82], لَوْلَا أَنْ مَنَّ ٱللّٰهُ عَلَيْنَا [Were it not for that God conferred favour upon us; i. e., for God's having conferred favour upon us]. (Mughnee.) It is also conjoined with an imperative; as in the phrase mentioned by Sb, كَتَبْتُ إِلَيْهِ بِأَنْ قُمْ [I wrote to him, Stand; i. e. I wrote to him the command to stand]; which shows that AHei is wrong in asserting that whenever it is conjoined with an imperative it is an explicative [in the sense of أَىْ], and that in this particular instance the ب may be redundant, which it cannot here be, because, whether redundant or not, it is not put immediately before anything but a noun or what may be rendered by a noun. (Mughnee.) — Secondly, it is a contraction of أَنَّ; (Mughnee, Ḳ;) and occurs after a verb denoting certainty, or one used in a manner similar to that of such a verb: (Mughnee:) so in the saying [in the Ḳur lxxiii. 20], عَلِمَ أَنْ سَيَكُونُ مِنْكُمْ مَرْضَى [*He knoweth that* (*the case will be this:*) *there will be among you some diseased*; the affixed pronoun ه, meaning الشَّأْنُ, being understood after أَنْ, which therefore stands for أَنَّهُ, i. e. أَنَّ الشَّأْنَ]: (Mughnee, Ḳ:*) and in the phrase, بَلَغَنِى أَنْ قَدْ كَانَ كَذَا وَكَذَا [*It has come to my knowledge*, or *been related to me*, or *been told to me*, or *it came to my knowledge*, &c., *that* (*the case is this:*) *such and such things have been*]; a phrase of this kind, in which أَنْ occurs with a verb, not being approved without قَدْ, unless you say, بَلَغَنِى أَنَّهُ كَانَ كَذَا وَكَذَا: (Lth, T:) [for] when the contracted أَنْ has for its predicate a verbal proposition, of which the verb is neither imperfectly inflected, like لَيْسَ and عَسَى, nor expressive of a prayer or an imprecation, it is separated from the verb, according to the more approved usage, by قَدْ, or the prefix سَ, or سَوْفَ, or a negative, as لَا &c., or لَوْ: (I 'Aḳ pp. 100 and 101:) but when its predicate is a nominal proposition, it requires not a separation; so that you say, عَلِمْتُ أَنْ زَيْدٌ قَائِمٌ [*I knew that* (*the case was this:*) *Zeyd was standing*]; (I 'Aḳ p. 100;) and بَلَغَنِى أَنْ زَيْدٌ خَارِجٌ [*It has come to my knowledge*, or *been related to me*, or *been told to me*, &c., *that* (*the case is this:*) *Zeyd is going*, or *coming, out*, or *forth*]; (TA;) except in the case of a negation, as in the saying in the Ḳur [xi. 17], وَأَنْ لَا إِلٰهَ إِلَّا هُوَ [*And that* (*the case is this:*) *there is no deity but He*]. (I 'Aḳ p. 100.) Thus used, it is originally triliteral, and is also what is termed مَصْدَرِيَّةٌ; [عَلِمَ أَنْ, in the first of the exs. above, for instance, meaning عَلِمَ أَنَّهُ, i. e. عَلِمَ أَنَّ الشَّأْنَ, which is equivalent to عَلِمَ كَوْنَ الشَّأْنِ;] and governs the subject in the accus. case, and the predicate in the nom. case: and its subject must be a pronoun, suppressed, [as in the exs. given above, where it means الشَّأْن, and in a verse cited before, commencing أَنْ تَقْرَآنِ, accord. to Aboo-'Alee,] or expressed; the latter, accord. to the more correct opinion, being allowable only by poetic license: and its predicate must be a proposition, unless the subject is expressed, in which case it may be either a single word or a proposition; both of which kinds occur in the following saying [of a poet]:

* بِأَنْكَ رَبِيعٌ وَغَيْثٌ مَرِيعٌ *
* وَأَنْكَ هُنَاكَ تَكُونُ الثِّمَالَا *

[he is speaking of persons coming as guests to him whom he addresses, when their provisions are exhausted, and the horizon is dust-coloured, and the north wind is blowing, (as is shown by the citation of the verse immediately preceding, in the T,) and he says, They know *that thou art like rain that produces spring-herbage, and* like *plenteous rain, and that thou, there, art the aider and the manager of the affairs of people*]. (Mughnee. [In the T, for رَبِيعٌ, I find الرَّبِيعُ; and for وَأَنْكَ, I there find وَقِدْمًا: but the reading in the Mughnee is that which is the more known.]) [J says,] أَنْ is sometimes a contraction of أَنَّ, and does not govern [anything]: you say, بَلَغَنِى أَنْ زَيْدٌ خَارِجٌ [explained above]; and it is said in the Ḳur [vii. 41], وَنُودُوا أَنْ تِلْكُمُ ٱلْجَنَّةُ [*And it shall be proclaimed to them that* (*the case is this:*) *that is Paradise*]: (Ṣ:) [here, however, أَنْ is regarded by some as an explicative, as will be seen below:] but in saying this, J means that it does not govern as to the letter; for virtually it does govern; its subject being meant to be understood; the virtual meaning being أَنَّهُ تِلْكُمُ ٱلْجَنَّةُ. (IB.) [In another place, J says,] You may make the contracted أَنْ to govern or not, as you please. (Ṣ.) Aboo-Ṭálib the Grammarian mentions an assertion that the Arabs make it to govern; as in the saying [of a poet, describing a beautiful bosom],

* كَأَنْ ثَدْيَيْهِ حُقَّانِ *

[*As though its two breasts were two small round boxes*]: but [the reading commonly known is

* كَأَنْ ثَدْيَاهُ حُقَّانِ *

(this latter reading is given in De Sacy's Anthol. Gram. Ar. p. 104 of the Ar. text; and both are given in the Ṣ;) كَأَنْ here meaning كَأَنَّهُ; and] Fr says, We have not heard the Arabs use the contracted form and make it to govern except with a pronoun, in which case the desinential syntax is not apparent. (T.) The author of the Ḳ says in the B that you say, عَلِمْتُ أَنْ زَيْدًا لَمُنْطَلِقٌ [*I knew that Zeyd was indeed going away*], with ل when it is made to govern; and عَلِمْتُ أَنْ زَيْدٌ مُنْطَلِقٌ [*I knew that* (*the case was this:*) *Zeyd was going away*], without ل when it is made to have no government. (TA. [But in the latter ex. it governs the subject, which is understood, as in other exs. before given.]) [See an ex. in a verse ending with the phrase وَكَأَنْ قَدِ cited voce قَدْ, where كَأَنْ is for كَأَنَّهُ, meaning كَأَنَّ الشَّأْنَ, and a verb is understood after قد. And see also أَنَّ, below.] — Thirdly, it is an explicative, (Mughnee, Ḳ,) meaning أَىْ, (Ṣ, M, and so in some copies of the Ḳ,) or [rather] used in the manner of أَىْ; (Mughnee, and so in some copies of the Ḳ;) [meaning قَائِلِينَ, or قَائِلًا; or يَقُولُ, or يَقُولُونَ; or some other form of the verb قَالَ; i. e. *Saying*; &c.;] as in the saying [in the Ḳur xxiii. 27], فَأَوْحَيْنَا إِلَيْهِ أَنِ ٱصْنَعِ ٱلْفُلْكَ [*And we revealed*, or *spake by revelation, unto him, saying, Make thou the ark*]; (Mughnee, Ḳ;) and [in the Ḳur vii. 41,] وَنُودُوا أَنْ تِلْكُمُ ٱلْجَنَّةُ [*And it shall be proclaimed to them, being said, That is Paradise*]; or in these two instances it may be regarded as what is termed مَصْدَرِيَّةٌ, by supposing the preposition [ب] understood before it, so that in the former instance it is the biliteral, because it is put before the imperative, and in the second it is the contraction of أَنَّ, because it is put before a nominal proposition; (Mughnee;) and [in the Ḳur xxxviii. 5,] وَٱنْطَلَقَ ٱلْمَلَأُ مِنْهُمْ أَنِ ٱمْشُوا (Ṣ, M, Mughnee) i. e. [*And the chief persons of them*] *broke forth*, or *launched forth, with their tongues*, or *in speech*, [*saying*,] *Go ye on*, or *continue ye, in your course of action* &c. (Mughnee.) For this usage of أَنْ, certain conditions are requisite: first, that it be preceded by a proposition: secondly, that it be followed by a proposition; so that you may not say, ذَكَرْتُ عَسْجَدًا أَنْ ذَهَبًا, but you must say أَىْ in this case, or must omit the explicative: thirdly, that the preceding proposition convey the meaning of القَوْلُ, as in the exs. above; in the last of which, انطلق has the meaning assigned to it above; not that of walking or going away: fourthly, that there be not in the preceding proposition the letters of القَوْلُ; so that one may not say, قُلْتُ لَهُ أَنِ ٱفْعَلْ; or, if there be in it those letters, that the word which they compose shall be interpreted by another word; as in the saying, in the Ḳur [v. 117], مَا قُلْتُ لَهُمْ إِلَّا مَا أَمَرْتَنِى بِهِ أَنِ ٱعْبُدُوا ٱللّٰهَ, which may mean, as Z says, *I have not commanded them* [aught *save that which Thou commandedst me, saying, Worship ye God*]; (Mughnee;) in which instance Fr says that it is an explicative: (T:) fifthly, that there be not a preposition immediately before it; for if you say, كَتَبْتُ إِلَيْهِ بِأَنِ ٱفْعَلْ كَذَا, it is what is termed مَصْدَرِيَّةٌ [as we have before shown]. (Mughnee.) When it may be regarded as an explicative and is followed by an aor. with لا, as in أَشَرْتُ إِلَيْهِ أَنْ لَا تَفْعَلْ كَذَا, it may be marfooạ, [namely, the aor.,] on the supposition that لا is a negative; or mejzoom, on the supposition that it is a prohibitive; and in both cases ان is an explicative; [so that the meaning is, *I made a sign to him*, as though *saying, Thou wilt not do such a thing*, in the former case; or, in the latter, *Do not thou such a thing*;] or manṣoob, on the supposition that لا is a negative and that ان is what is termed مَصْدَرِيَّةٌ: but if لا is wanting, it may not be mejzoom, but may be marfooạ [if we use ان as an explicative] or manṣoob [if ان be what is termed مَصْدَرِيَّةٌ]. (Mughnee.) — Fourthly, it is redundant, as a corroborative, (Mughnee, Ḳ,) like whatever else is redundant: and thus it is in four cases: one of these, which is the most common, being when it occurs after لَمَّا denoting time; [and this is mentioned in the M;] as in the saying [in the Ḳur xxix. 32], وَلَمَّا أَنْ جَآءَتْ رُسُلُنَا لُوطًا [*And when our apostles came to Lot*]: (Mughnee:) [or,] accord. to J, (TA,) it is sometimes a connective to لَمَّا; as in the saying in the Ḳur [xii. 96], فَلَمَّا أَنْ جَآءَ ٱلْبَشِيرُ [*And when that* (like as we say, "now that,") *the announcer of good tidings came*]: and sometimes it is redundant; as in the saying in the Ḳur [viii. 34], وَمَا لَهُمْ أَنْ لَا يُعَذِّبَهُمُ ٱللّٰهُ [as though it might be rendered ***But what reason have they, God should not punish them?***]: (Ṣ, TA:) but IB says that the connective is redundant; and [that ان is not redundant in the latter instance, for] if it were redundant in this verse of the Ḳur it would not render the [aor.] verb manṣoob. (TA. [The author of the Mughnee, like IB, disallows that ان is redundant in a case of this kind, which Kh asserts it to be; and says that فِى is understood before it.]) The second case is when it occurs between لَوْ and a verb signifying swearing, the latter being expressed; as in this verse:

فَأُقْسِمُ أَنْ لَوِ ٱلْتَقَيْنَا وَأَنْتُمُ
لَكَانَ لَنَا يَوْمٌ مِنَ ٱلشَّرِّ مُظْلِمُ

[*And I swear, had we and you met, there had been to us a dark day of evil*]: and when that verb is omitted; as in the following ex.:

أَمَا وَٱللّٰهِ أَنْ لَوْ كُنْتَ حُرًّا
وَمَا بِٱلْحُرِّ أَنْتَ وَلَا ٱلْعَتِيقِ

[*Verily*, or *now surely, by God, if thou wert freeborn; but thou art not the freeborn nor the emancipated*]: so say Sb and others: Ibn-'Oṣfoor holds it to be a particle employed to connect the complement of the oath with the oath; but this is rendered improbable by the fact that it is in most cases omitted, and such particles are not. (Mughnee.) The third case, which is extr., is when it occurs between the كَ [of comparison] and the noun governed by it in the genitive case; as in the saying,

وَيَوْمًا تُوَافِينَا بِوَجْهٍ مُقَسَّمٍ
كَأَنْ ظَبْيَةٍ تَعْطُو إِلَى وَارِقِ ٱلسَّلَمْ

[*And on a day thou comest to us with a beautiful face, like a doe-gazelle raising her head towards the goodly green-leaved tree of the selem kind*], accord. to the reading of him who makes ظبية to be governed in the genitive case [instead of the accus. or the nom.; for if we read it in the accus. or the nom., أَنْ is a contraction of أَنَّ; in the former case, ظبية being its subject, and its predicate being suppressed; and in the latter case, the meaning being كَأَنَّهَا ظَبْيَةٌ, so that the subject of ان is suppressed]. (Mughnee.) The fourth case is when it occurs after إِذَا; as in the following ex.:

فَأُمْهِلُهُ حَتَّى إِذَا أَنْ كَأَنَّهُ
مُعَاطِى يَدٍ فِى لُجَّةِ ٱلْمَآءِ غَامِرُ

[*And I leave him alone until when he is as though he were a giver of a hand to be laid hold upon, in the fathomless deep of the water immerged*]. (Mughnee.) — [Fifthly,] among other meanings which have been assigned to it, (Mughnee,) it has a conditional meaning, like إِنْ: (Mughnee, Ḳ:) so the Koofees hold; and it seems to be most probably correct, for several reasons: first, because both these forms occur, accord. to different readings, in several instances, in one passage of the Ḳur; as in [ii. 282,] أَنْ تَضِلَّ إِحْدَاهُمَا [*If one of them twain* (namely, women,) *err*]; &c.: secondly, because [the prefix] فَ often occurs after it; as in a verse commencing with أَمَّا خُرَاشَةَ [as cited voce أَمَّا, accord. to some who hold that أَمَّا in that verse is a compound of the conditional أَنْ and the redundant مَا; and as in the Ḳur ii. 282, where the words quoted above are immediately followed by فَتُذَكِّرَ إِحْدَاهُمَا ٱلْأُخْرَى]: thirdly, because it is conjoined with إِنْ [which forms a part of the compound إِمَّا] in this ex.:

إِمَّا أَقَمْتَ وَأَمَّا أَنْتَ مُرْتَحِلًا
فَٱللّٰهُ يَكْلَأُ مَا تَأْتِى وَمَا تَذَرُ

[*If thou remain, and if thou be going away* (أَمَّا meaning أَنْ كُنْتَ, as syn. with إِنْ كُنْتَ), *may God guard* thee (يَكْلَأُ being marfooạ because of the ف) *as long as thou doest and as long as thou leavest undone*]: thus related, with kesr to the former ان [in إِمَّا] and with fet-ḥ to the latter [in أَمَّا]. (Mughnee.) — [Sixthly,] it is a negative, like إِنْ: (Mughnee, Ḳ:) so, as some say, in [the Ḳur iii. 66,] أَنْ يُؤْتَى أَحَدٌ مِثْلَ مَا أُوتِيتُمْ [meaning accord. to them *Not any one is given the like of that* scripture *which ye have been given*]: but it is said [by others] that the meaning is, [taken with what precedes it,] And believe not ye *that* (بِأَنْ) *any one is given the like of that* scripture *which ye have been given*, except it be given to him who followeth your religion; and that the phrase "say thou, Verily the direction is the direction of God," is parenthetic. (Mughnee.) — [Seventhly,] it is syn. with إِذْ, (AZ, T, Mughnee, Ḳ, [in Freytag's Lex., from the Ḳ, إِذْ قِيلَ, but قيل in the Ḳ relates to what there follows,]) as some say, in [the Ḳur l. 2,] بَلْ عَجِبُوا أَنْ جَآءَهُمْ مُنْذِرٌ مِنْهُمْ [*Verily they wonder because a warner from among themselves hath come unto them*]; (Mughnee, Ḳ;) and in other instances; but correctly, in all these instances, ان is what is termed مَصْدَرِيَّة, and لِ denoting cause is understood before it. (Mughnee.) [See also أَمَّا and إِمَّا.] — [Eighthly,] it is *syn. with* لِئَلَّا, accord. to some, in [the Ḳur iv. last verse,] يُبَيِّنُ ٱللّٰهُ لَكُمْ أَنْ تَضِلُّوا [*God explaineth to you* (the ordinances of your religion, Jel), *lest ye should err*, or *in order that ye may not err*]; (Mughnee, Ḳ;) and in the saying,

نَزَلْتُمْ مَنْزِلَ ٱلْأَضْيَافِ مِنَّا
فَعَجَّلْنَا ٱلْقِرَى أَنْ تَشْتُمُونَا

[*Ye became*, or *have become, in the condition of our guests; so we hastened*, or *have hastened, the entertainment, lest ye should revile us*, or *in order that ye should not revile us*]: (Mughnee:) but correctly, in such a case [likewise], ان is what is termed مَصْدَرِيَّة, and the original wording is كَرَاهَةَ أَنْ تَضِلُّوا [*from a motive of dislike that ye should err*], (Mughnee, Ḳ,) and مَخَافَةَ أَنْ تَشْتُمُونَا [*from a motive of fear that ye should revile us*]: so say the Baṣrees: some say, extravagantly, that لِ is meant to be understood before it, and لَا after it. (Mughnee.) — [Ninthly,] it occurs in the sense of ٱلَّذِى; as in the saying, زَيْدٌ أَعْقَلُ مِنْ أَنْ يَكْذِبَ [*Zeyd is more reasonable than he who lies;* which is equivalent to saying, *Zeyd is too reasonable to lie:* but respecting its usage in a phrase of this kind, and respecting the form of the aor. after it in such a case, see مِنْ]. (Kull p. 78.) — By a peculiarity of pronunciation termed عَنْعَنَةٌ, the tribe of Temeem say عَنْ instead of أَنْ. (M.)

إِنْ is used in various ways: first, as a conditional particle, (Ṣ, M, Mṣb, Mughnee, Ḳ,) denoting the happening of the second of two events in consequence of the happening of the first, (Ṣ, Mṣb,*) whether the second be immediate or deferred, and whether the condition be affirmative or negative; (Mṣb;) [and as such it is followed by a mejzoom aor., or by a pret. having the signification of an aor.;] as in the saying, إِنْ تَفْعَلْ أَفْعَلْ [*If thou do* such a thing, *I will do* it; and] إِنْ تَأْتِنِى آتِكَ [*If thou come to me, I will come to thee*]; and إِنْ جِئْتَنِى أَكْرَمْتُكَ [*If thou come to me, I will treat thee with honour*]; (Ṣ;) and إِنْ فَعَلْتَ فَعَلْتُ [*If thou do, I will do*] for which the tribe of Ṭeiyi say, as IJ relates on the authority of Ḳṭr, هِنْ فَعَلْتَ فَعَلْتُ; (M;) and إِنْ قُمْتَ قُمْتُ [*If thou stand, I will stand*]; and إِنْ دَخَلْتِ ٱلدَّارَ أَوْ لَمْ تَدْخُلِى ٱلدَّارَ فَأَنْتِ طَالِقٌ [*If thou enter the house, or if thou enter not the house, thou shalt be divorced*]; (Mṣb;) and [in the Ḳur viii. 39,] إِنْ يَنْتَهُوا يُغْفَرْ لَهُمْ مَا قَدْ سَلَفَ [*If they desist, what hath already past shall be forgiven them*]; and [in verse 19 of the same ch.,] وَإِنْ تَعُودُوا نَعُدْ [*But if ye return* to attacking the Apostle, *we will return* to assisting him]. (Mughnee, Ḳ.) [On the difference between it and إِذَا, see the latter.] When either it or إِذَا is immediately followed by a noun in the nom. case, the said noun is governed in that case by a verb necessarily suppressed, of which it is the agent; as in the saying, in the Ḳur [ix. 6], وَإِنْ أَحَدٌ مِنَ ٱلْمُشْرِكِينَ ٱسْتَجَارَكَ; the complete phrase being وَإِنِ ٱسْتَجَارَكَ أَحَدٌ مِنَ ٱلْمُشْرِكِينَ ٱسْتَجَارَكَ [*And if any one of the believers in a plurality of gods demand protection of thee,* (if) *he demand protection of thee*]: so accord. to the generality of the grammarians. (I 'Aḳ p. 123.) Sometimes it is conjoined with the negative لَا, and the ignorant may imagine it to be the exceptive إِلَّا; as in [the saying in the Ḳur ix. 40,] إِلَّا تَنْصُرُوهُ فَقَدْ نَصَرَهُ ٱللّٰهُ [*If ye will not aid him, certainly God did aid him*]; and [in the next preceding verse,] إِلَّا تَنْفِرُوا يُعَذِّبْكُمْ [*If ye will not go forth to war, He will punish you*]. (Mughnee, Ḳ.*) It is sometimes used to denote one's feigning himself ignorant; as when you say to one who asks, "Is thy child in the house?" and thou hast knowledge thereof, إِنْ كَانَ فِى ٱلدَّارِ أَعْلَمْتُكَ بِهِ [*If he be in the house, I will inform thee thereof*]. (Mṣb.) And to denote one's putting the knowing in the predicament of the ignorant, in order to incite to the doing or continuing an action; as when you say, إِنْ كُنْتَ ٱبْنِى فَأَطِعْنِى [*If thou be my son, obey me*]; as though you said, "Thou knowest that thou art my son, and it is incumbent on the son to obey the father, and thou art not obedient; therefore do what thou art commanded to do." (Mṣb.) And sometimes it is divested of the conditional meaning, and becomes *syn. with* لَوْ; as in the saying, صَلِّ وَإِنْ عَجَزْتَ عَنِ ٱلْقِيَامِ [*Pray thou though thou be unable to stand;*] i. e. pray *thou whether thou be able to stand or unable to do so*; and in the saying, أَكْرِمْ زَيْدًا وَإِنْ قَعَدَ i. e. [*Treat thou Zeyd with honour*] *though he be sitting*; or, *whether he sit or not*. (Mṣb.) [إِمَّا as a compound of the conditional إِنْ and the redundant مَا, see in an art. of which اما is the heading.] — [Secondly,] it is a negative, (Ṣ, Mughnee, Ḳ,) *syn. with* مَا; (Ṣ;) and is put before a nominal proposition; (Mughnee, Ḳ;) as in the saying [in the Ḳur lxvii. 20], إِنِ ٱلْكَافِرُونَ إِلَّا فِى غُرُورٍ [*The unbelievers are not* in aught *save in a deception*]; (Ṣ, Mughnee, Ḳ;) and before a verbal proposition; as in [the Ḳur ix. 108,] إِنْ أَرَدْنَا إِلَّا ٱلْحُسْنَى [*We desired not*, or *meant not*, aught *save that which is best*]. (Mughnee, Ḳ.) The assertion of some, that the negative إِنْ does not occur except where it is followed by إِلَّا, as in the instances cited above, or by لَمَّا, with teshdeed, which is syn. therewith, as, accord. to a reading of some of the Seven [Readers], in the saying [in the Ḳur lxxxvi. 4], إِنْ كُلُّ نَفْسٍ لَمَّا عَلَيْهَا حَافِظٌ, i. e., مَا كُلُّ نَفْسٍ إِلَّا عَلَيْهَا حَافِظٌ [*There is not any soul but over it is a guardian*], is refuted by the sayings in the Ḳur [x. 69 and lxxii. 26], إِنْ عِنْدَكُمْ مِنْ سُلْطَانٍ بِهٰذَا [meaning, accord. to the Jel., *Ye have no proof of this* that ye say], and إِنْ أَدْرِى أَقَرِيبٌ مَا تُوعَدُونَ [*I know not whether that with which ye are threatened be nigh*]. (Mughnee, Ḳ.*) The conditional and the negative both occur in the saying in the Ḳur [xxxv. 39], وَلَئِنْ زَالَتَا إِنْ أَمْسَكَهُمَا مِنْ أَحَدٍ مِنْ بَعْدِهِ [*And I swear that, if they should quit their place, not any one should withhold them after Him*]: the former is conditional; and the latter is negative, and is [part of] the complement of the oath which is denoted by the ل prefixed to the former; the complement of the condition being necessarily suppressed. (Mughnee.) When it is put before a nominal proposition, it has no government, accord. to Sb and Fr; but Ks and Mbr allow its governing in the manner of لَيْسَ; and Sa'eed Ibn-Jubeyr reads, [in the Ḳur vii. 193,] إِنِ ٱلَّذِينَ تَدْعُونَ مِنْ دُونِ ٱللّٰهِ عِبَادًا أَمْثَالَكُمْ [*Those whom ye invoke beside God*, or *others than God, are not men like you*]: also, the people of El-'Áliyeh have been heard to say, إِنْ أَحَدٌ خَيْرًا مِنْ أَحَدٍ إِلَّا بِالعَافِيَةِ [*Any one is not better than any* other *one, except by means of health*, or *soundness*]; and إِنْ ذٰلِكَ نَافِعَكَ وَلَا ضَارَّكَ [*That is not profitable to thee nor injurious to thee*]: as an ex. of its occurrence without government, which is mostly the case, the saying of some, إِنَّ قَائِمٌ, may be explained as originally إِنْ أَنَا قَائِمٌ [*I am not standing*]; the أ of أَنَا being elided for no reason in itself, and the ن of إِنْ being incorporated into the ن of أَنَا, and the ا of this latter being elided in its conjunction with the following word; but إِنَّ قَائِمًا has also been heard. (Mughnee.) Sometimes it occurs [as a negative] in the complement of an oath: you say, وَٱللّٰهِ إِنْ فَعَلْتُ, meaning مَا فَعَلْتُ [*By God, I did not*]. (Ṣ.) — [Thirdly,] it is a contraction of إِنَّ, and is put before a nominal and before a verbal proposition. (Mughnee, Ḳ.) In the former case, it is made to govern and is made to have no government: (Ṣ,* Ḳ:) [i. e.] in this case, it is allowable to make it govern; contr. to the opinion of the Koofees: (Mughnee:) Lth says that he who uses the contracted form of إِنَّ uses the nom. case with it, except that some of the people of El-Ḥijáz use the accus. case with it: (T:) thus it is said, accord. to one reading, [in the Ḳur xi. 113,] إِنْ كُلًّا لَمَّا لَيُوَفِّيَنَّهُمْ رَبُّكَ أَعْمَالَهُمْ [*Verily all* of them, *thy Lord will indeed fully render them* the recompense of *their works*]: (T, Mughnee:) Fr says, We have not heard the Arabs use the contracted form and make it to govern, unless with a pronoun, in which case the desinential syntax is not apparent; and he adds that in the instance cited above, they make كُلًّا to be governed in the accus. case by لَيُوَفِّيَنَّهُمْ; as though the phrase were لَيُوَفِّيَنَّهُمْ كُلًّا; and that كُلٌّ would be proper; for you say, إِنْ زَيْدٌ لَقَائِمٌ [*Verily Zeyd is standing*]: (T:) the ex. given by Sb is, إِنْ عَمْرًا لَمُنْطَلِقٌ [*Verily 'Amr is going away*]. (Mughnee.) But it is [most] frequently made to have no government; as in the saying [in the Ḳur xliii. 34 accord. to one reading], وَإِنْ كُلُّ ذٰلِكَ لَمَا مَتَاعُ ٱلْحَيَاةِ ٱلدُّنْيَا [*And verily all that is the furniture of the present life*]; and, accord. to the reading of Ḥafṣ, [and of 'Áṣim and Kh, in the Ḳur xx. 66, respecting which see إِنَّ,] إِنْ هٰذَانِ لَسَاحِرَانِ [*Verily these two are enchanters*]; &c. (Mughnee.) When it is put before a verbal proposition, it is necessarily made to have no government: (Mughnee, Ḳ:) and in most cases the verb is a preterite and of the kind called نَاسِخ [which effects a change of the grammatical form or of the meaning in a nominal proposition before which it is placed]; as in the saying [in the Ḳur ii. 138], وَإِنْ كَانَتْ لَكَبِيرَةً [*And verily it was a great matter*]; and [in the Ḳur xvii. 75,] وَإِنْ كَادُوا لَيَفْتِنُونَكَ [*And verily they were near to seducing thee*]; (Mughnee;) in which last ex. AZ says, it means لَقَدْ, i. e. *without doubt*; and so in the same ch. vv. 78 and 108: (T:) less frequently it is an aor. of a verb of this kind; as in the saying [in the Ḳur xxvi. 186], وَإِنْ نَظُنُّكَ لَمِنَ ٱلْكَاذِبِينَ [*And verily we think thee to be* of the number *of the liars*]: and both these kinds of expression may be taken as exs. to be imitated: less frequently than this it is a preterite of a verb not of the kind termed نَاسِخ; as in the saying [of a poet],

• شَلَّتْ يَمِينُكَ إِنْ قَتَلْتَ لَمُسْلِمًا •

[*May thy right arm*, or *hand, dry up*, or *become unsound! verily thou hast slain a Muslim*]; but this may not be taken as an ex. to be imitated; contr. to the opinion of Akh; for he allows the phrase, إِنْ قَامَ لَأَنَا [*Verily I stood*], and إِنْ قَعَدَ لَأَنْتَ [*Verily thou sattest*]: and less frequently than this it is an aor. of a verb not of the kind termed نَاسِخ; as in the saying, إِنْ يَزِينُكَ لَنَفْسُكَ وَإِنْ يَشِينُكَ لَهِيَهْ [*Verily thy soul* is that which *beautifies thee, and it* is that which *deforms thee*]; and this, by common consent, may not be taken as an ex. to be imitated. (Mughnee.) Wherever you find إِنْ with لَ after it, decide that it is originally إِنَّ; (Mughnee, Ḳ;) as in the exs. above: but respecting this ل there is a difference of opinion: see this letter. (Mughnee.) J says, (TA,) إِنْ is sometimes a contraction of إِنَّ, and this must have ل put before its predicate, to compensate for what is elided, of the doubled letter; as in the saying in the Ḳur [lxxxvi. 4, accord. to him who reads لَمَا instead of لَمَّا], إِنْ كُلُّ نَفْسٍ لَمَا عَلَيْهَا حَافِظٌ [*Verily every soul hath over it a guardian*]; and in the saying, إِنْ زَيْدٌ لَأَخُوكَ [*Verily Zeyd is thy brother*]; in order that it may not be confounded with إِنْ which is syn. with the negative مَا: (Ṣ, TA:) but IB says, ل is here introduced to distinguish between negation and affirmation, and this إِنْ has neither subject nor predicate; so J's saying that the ل is put before its predicate is without meaning: and this ل is sometimes introduced with the objective complement of a verb; as in إِنْ ضَرَبْتُ لَزَيْدًا [*Verily I struck*, or *beat, Zeyd*]; and with the agent; as in إِنْ قَامَ لَزَيْدٌ [*Verily Zeyd stood*]. (TA.) When the contracted إِنْ governs, this ل is not necessary; so you may say, إِنْ زَيْدًا قَائِمٌ [*Verily Zeyd is standing*]; because in this case it cannot be confounded with the negative; for the negative does not render the subject manṣoob and the predicate marfooạ: and when it does not govern, if the meaning is apparent, the ل is not needed; as in

• وَنَحْنُ أُبَاةُ ٱلضَّيْمِ مِنْ آلِ مَالِكٍ •
• وَإِنْ مَالِكٌ كَانَتْ كِرَامَ ٱلمَعَادِنِ •

[*And we are persons who refuse to submit to injury, of the family of Málik: and verily* the family of *Málik are generous in respect of* their *origins*]; كَانَتْ being here for لَكَانَتْ. (I 'Aḳ p. 99.) — [Fourthly,] it is redundant, (Ṣ, Mughnee, Ḳ,) occurring with مَا; as in the saying, مَا إِنْ يَقُومُ زَيْدٌ [*Zeyd does not stand*]; (Ṣ;) and in the saying [of a poet],

• مَا إِنْ أَتَيْتَ بِشَىْءٍ أَنْتَ تَكْرَهُهُ •

[*Thou didst not a thing which thou dislikest*]. (Mughnee, Ḳ: in the CḲ أَتَيْتُ.) It is mostly thus used after the negative ما, when put before a verbal proposition; as above; or before a nominal proposition; as in the saying,

• وَمَا إِنْ طِبُّنَا جُبْنٌ وَلٰكِنْ • مَنَايَانَا وَدَوْلَةُ آخَرِينَا •

[*And our habit is not cowardice; but our destinies and the good fortune of others* caused our being defeated]: and in this case it prevents the government of ما, as in this verse: but in the saying,

• بَنِى غُدَانَةَ مَا إِنْ أَنْتُمْ ذَهَبًا •
• وَلَا صَرِيفًا وَلٰكِنْ أَنْتُمُ ٱلخَزَفُ •

[*Sons of Ghudáneh, ye are not indeed gold, nor silver*, or *pure silver, but ye are pottery*], accord. to him who relates it thus, saying ذهبا and صريفا, in the accus. case, it is explained as a negative, corroborative of ما: (Mughnee:) and accord. to J,

(TA,) the negatives مَا and إِنْ are sometimes thus combined for corroboration; as in the saying of the rájiz, (El-Aghlab El-'Ijlee, TA,)

• مَا إِنْ رَأَيْنَا مَلِكًا أَغَارَا • أَكْثَرَ مِنْهُ قِرَةً وَقَارَا •

[*We have not indeed seen a king who has made a hostile incursion possessing more numerous sheep, or goats, and camels, than he*]; (Ṣ, TA;) but IB says that ان is here redundant, not a negative. (TA.) Sometimes it is redundant after the conjunct noun مَا; as in the saying,

• يُرَجِّى الْمَرْءُ مَا إِنْ لَا يَرَاهُ •

• وَتَعْرِضُ دُونَ أَدْنَاهُ الْخُطُوبُ •

[*Man hopes for that which he will not see; for calamities intervene as obstacles in the way to what is nearest thereof*]. (Mughnee.) And after the termed مَصْدَرِيَّة مَا, (Mughnee,) [i. e.,] after the adverbial مَا [which is of the kind termed مصدريّة]; (TA;) as in the saying (of Maslooṭ El-Ḳurey'ee, cited by Sb, TA),

• وَرَجِّ الْفَتَى لِلْخَيْرِ مَا إِنْ رَأَيْتَهُ •

• عَلَى السِّنِّ خَيْرًا لَا يَزَالُ يَزِيدُ •

[*And hope thou that the youth is* destined *for good as long as thou hast seen him not ceasing to increase in good with age*]. (Mughnee.) And after the inceptive أَلَا; as in the saying,

• أَلَا إِنْ سَرَى لَيْلِى فَبِتُّ كَئِيبًا •

• أُحَاذِرُ أَنْ تَنْأَى النَّوَى بِغَضُوبَا •

[*Now he journeyed on*, or *during*, that *my night, and I passed the night in an evil state, broken in spirit by grief, being fearful that the distance* to which he was going *with Ghaḍoob* (a woman so named) *would become far*]. (Mughnee.) And before the meddeh denoting disapproval: [for] Sb heard a man, on its being said to him, "Wilt thou go forth if the desert become plentiful in herbage?" reply, أَأَنَا إِنِيهْ [*What, I, indeed?*] disapproving that he should think otherwise than that. (Mughnee. [See also art. انى.]) — [Fifthly,] it is *syn. with* قَدْ: so it is said to be in the saying [in the Ḳur lxxxvii. 9], إِنْ نَفَعَتِ ٱلذِّكْرَى [*Admonition hath profited*], (T, Mughnee, Ḳ,) by IAạr (T) and by Ḳṭr: (Mughnee:) and Abu-l-'Abbás relates that the Arabs say, إِنْ قَامَ زَيْدٌ meaning قَدْ قَامَ زَيْدٌ [*Zeyd has stood*]; and he adds, that Ks states his having heard them say so, and having thought that it expressed a condition, but that he asked them, and they answered that they meant قَدْ قَامَ زَيْدٌ, and not مَا قَامَ زَيْدٌ. (T.) [So too, accord. to the Ḳ, in all the exs. cited in the next sentence as from the Mughnee; but this is evidently a mistake, occasioned by an accidental omission.] — [Sixthly,] it is asserted also by the Koofees, that it is *syn. with* إِذْ, in the following exs.: in the Ḳur [v. 62], وَٱتَّقُوا ٱللّٰهَ إِنْ كُنْتُمْ مُؤْمِنِينَ [*And fear ye God, because ye are believers*: and so, accord. to AZ, as is said in the T, in a similar instance in the Ḳur ii. 278: and in the same, iv. 62]: and [in the Ḳur xlviii. 27,] لَتَدْخُلُنَّ ٱلْمَسْجِدَ ٱلْحَرَامَ إِنْ شَآءَ ٱللّٰهُ آمِنِينَ [*Ye shall assuredly enter the sacred mosque, because God hath willed, in security*]: and in like instances, when the verb therein expresses what is held sure to happen or to have happened: and in the saying,

• أَتَغْضَبُ إِنْ أُذْنَا قُتَيْبَةَ حُزَّتَا •

• جِهَارًا وَلَمْ تَغْضَبْ لِقَتْلِ ٱبْنِ خَازِمِ •

[*Art thou angry because the ears of Ḳuteybeh have been cut, openly,* or *publicly, and wast not angry for the slaughter of Ibn-Ḥázim?*]: (Mughnee:) but in all these instances [it is sufficiently obvious that] ان may be otherwise explained. (Mughnee, Ḳ.) — [Seventhly,] it is sometimes *syn. with* إِذَا; as in the Ḳur [ix. 23], لَا تَتَّخِذُوا آبَآءَكُمْ وَإِخْوَانَكُمْ أَوْلِيَآءَ إِنِ ٱسْتَحَبُّوا ٱلْكُفْرَ عَلَى ٱلْإِيمَانِ [*Take not ye your fathers and your brethren as friends when they love unbelief above belief*]; and in the same [xxxiii. 49], وَٱمْرَأَةً مُؤْمِنَةً إِنْ وَهَبَتْ نَفْسَهَا لِلنَّبِيِّ [*And a believing woman when she giveth herself to the Prophet*]: so says AZ. (T.) — [Eighthly,] it is used for إِمَّا, (Mughnee and Ḳ, voce إِمَّا,) distinct from إِمَّا which is a compound of the conditional إِنْ and the redundant مَا. (Mughnee ibid.) [See an ex. in a verse cited voce إِمَّا in the present work, commencing with the words سَقَتْهُ ٱلرَّوَاعِدُ.]

أَنَ: see أَنْ, in four places.

أَنَّ is one of the particles which annul the quality of the inchoative; and is originally إِنَّ; therefore Sb has not mentioned it among those particles [as distinct from إِنَّ, from which, however, it is distinguished in meaning]: (I 'Aḳ p. 90:) it is a corroborative particle; (I 'Aḳ, Mughnee;) a particle governing the subject in the accus. case and the predicate in the nom. case, (Ṣ, I 'Aḳ, Mughnee, Ḳ,) combining with what follows it to form an equivalent to an inf. n., (Ṣ,) [for,] accord. to the most correct opinion, it is a conjunct particle, which, together with its two objects of government, is explained by means of an inf. n. (Mughnee.) If the predicate is derived, the inf. n. by means of which it is explained is of the same radical letters; so that the implied meaning of بَلَغَنِى أَنَّكَ تَنْطَلِقُ [*It has come to my knowledge*, or *been related to me*, or *been told to me*, or *it came to my knowledge*, &c., *that thou goest away*], or أَنَّكَ مُنْطَلِقٌ [*that thou art going away*], is بَلَغَنِى الِانْطِلَاقُ [or rather ٱنْطِلَاقُكَ *thy going away has come to my knowledge*, &c.]; and hence, the implied meaning of بَلَغَنِى أَنَّكَ فِى الدَّارِ [*It has come to my knowledge, &c., that thou art in the house*] is بَلَغَنِى ٱسْتِقْرَارُكَ فِى الدَّارِ [*thy remaining in the house has come to my knowledge*, &c.], because the predicate is properly a word suppressed from مُسْتَقِرٌّ or ٱسْتَقَرَّ: and if the predicate is underived, the implied meaning is explained by the word كَوْنٌ; so that the implied meaning of بَلَغَنِى أَنَّ هٰذَا زَيْدٌ [*It has come to my knowledge, &c., that this is Zeyd*] is بَلَغَنِى كَوْنُهُ زَيْدًا [*his being Zeyd has come to my knowledge*, &c.]; for the relation of every predicate expressed by an underived word to its subject may be denoted by a word signifying "being;" so that you say, هٰذَا زَيْدٌ and, if you will, هٰذَا كَائِنٌ زَيْدًا; both signifying the same. (Mughnee.) There are cases in which either أَنَّ or إِنَّ may be used: [see the latter, in twelve places:] other cases in which only the former may be used: and others in which only the latter. (I 'Aḳ p. 91.) The former only may be used when the implied meaning is to be explained by an inf. n. (I 'Aḳ, Ḳ.) Such is the case when it occurs in the place of a noun governed by a verb in the nom. case; as in يُعْجِبُنِى أَنَّكَ قَائِمٌ [*It pleases me that thou art standing*], i. e. قِيَامُكَ [*thy standing* pleases me]: or in the place of a noun governed by a verb in the accus. case; as in عَرَفْتُ أَنَّكَ قَائِمٌ [*I knew that thou wast standing*], i. e. قِيَامَكَ [*thy standing*]: or in the place of a noun governed in the gen. case by a particle; as in عَجِبْتُ مِنْ أَنَّكَ قَائِمٌ [*I wondered that thou wast standing*], i. e. مِنْ قِيَامِكَ [*at*, or *by reason of, thy standing*]: (I 'Aḳ p. 91:) [and sometimes a preposition is understood; as in لَا شَكَّ أَنَّهُ كَذَا, for لَا شَكَّ فِى أَنَّهُ كَذَا *There is no doubt that it is thus*, i. e. لَا شَكَّ فِى كَوْنِهِ كَذَا *There is no doubt of its being thus*:] and أَنَّ must be used after لَوْ; as in لَوْ أَنَّكَ قَائِمٌ لَقُمْتُ [*If that thou wert standing, I had stood*, or *would have stood*, i. e. لَوْ قِيَامُكَ ثَابِتٌ, or لَوْ ثَبَتَ قِيَامُكَ, accord. to different opinions, both meaning *if thy standing were a fact*: see I 'Aḳ pp. 305 and 306]. (Ḳ.) Sometimes its أ is changed into ع; so that you say, عَلِمْتُ عَنَّكَ مُنْطَلِقٌ [meaning *I knew that thou wast going away*]. (M.) — With كَ prefixed to it, it is a particle of comparison, (Ṣ,* M, TA,) [still] governing the subject in the accus. case and the predicate in the nom. case: (TA:) you say, كَأَنَّ زَيْدًا عَمْرٌو [*It is as though Zeyd were 'Amr*], meaning that Zeyd is like 'Amr; as though you said, إِنَّ زَيْدًا كَائِنٌ كَعَمْرٍو [*verily, Zeyd is like 'Amr*]: [it is to be accounted for by an ellipsis: or] the كَ is taken away from the middle of this proposition, and put at its commencement, and then the kesreh of إِنَّ necessarily becomes changed to a fet-ḥah, because إِنَّ cannot be preceded by a preposition, for it never occurs but at the commencement [of a proposition]. (IJ, M.) Sometimes, كَأَنَّ denotes denial; as in the saying, كَأَنَّكَ أَمِيرُنَا فَتَأْمُرَنَا [*As though thou wert our commander so that thou shouldst command us*], meaning *thou art not our commander* [*that thou shouldst command us*]. (TA.) It also denotes wishing; as in the saying, كَأَنَّكَ بِى قَدْ قُلْتُ الشِّعْرَ فَأُجِيدَهُ, meaning *Would that I had poetized*, or *versified, so that I might do it well*: (TA:) [an elliptical form of speech, of which the implied meaning seems to be, *would that I were as though thou sawest me that I had poetized*, &c.; or the like: for] you say [also], كَأَنِّى بِكَ meaning كَأَنِّى أَبْصُرُ بِكَ [*It is as though I saw thee*]; i. e. I know from what I witness of thy condition to-day how thy condition will be to-morrow; so that it is as though I saw thee in that condition: (Ḥar p. 126: [see also بِ; near the end of the paragraph:]) [thus,] كَأَنَّ also denotes knowing; and also thinking; [the former as in the saying immediately preceding, and] as when you say, كَأَنَّ ٱللّٰهَ يَفْعَلُ مَا يَشَآءُ [*I know,* or rather *it appears, as though seen, that God does what He wills*]; and [the latter as when you say,] كَأَنَّكَ خَارِجٌ [*I think,* or rather *it seems, that thou art going forth*]. (TA.) — [When it has the affixed pronoun of the first person, sing. or pl., you say, أَنِّى and أَنَّنِى, and أَنَّا and أَنَّنَا: and when it has also the ك of comparison prefixed to it,] you say, كَأَنِّى and كَأَنَّنِى, [and كَأَنَّا and كَأَنَّنَا,] like as you say, لَكِنِّى and لَكِنَّنِى [&c.]. (Ṣ.) — As أَنَّ is a derivative from إِنَّ, it is correctly asserted by Z that أَنَّمَا imports restriction, like ↓ إِنَّمَا; both of which occur in the saying in the Ḳur [xxi. 108], قُلْ إِنَّمَا ↓ يُوحَى إِلَىَّ أَنَّمَا إِلٰهُكُمْ إِلٰهٌ وَاحِدٌ [*Say thou, It is only revealed to me that your God is only one God*]: the former is for the restricting of the quality to the qualified; and the latter, for the reverse: (Mughnee, Ḳ:) i. e. the former is for the restricting of the revelation to the declaration of the unity; and the latter, for the restricting of "your God" to unity: (Marginal note in a copy of the Mughnee:) but these words of the Ḳur do not imply that nothing save the unity was revealed to the Prophet; for the restriction is limited to the case of the discourse with the believers in a plurality of gods; so that the meaning is, there has not been revealed to me [aught], respecting the godhead, except the unity; not the attribution of any associate to God. (Mughnee.) [أَنَّمَا, however, does not always import restriction; nor does always even ↓ إِنَّمَا: in each of these, مَا is what is termed كَافَّةٌ; i. e., it restricts the particle to which it is affixed from exercising any government; and sometimes has no effect upon the signification of that particle: (see art. مَا; and see إِنَّمَا, below, voce إِنَّ:) thus, for instance, in the Ḳur viii. 28, وَٱعْلَمُوا أَنَّمَا أَمْوَالُكُمْ وَأَوْلَادُكُمْ فِتْنَةٌ means *And know ye that your possessions and your children are a trial;* not that they are *only a trial.* When it has the ك of comparison prefixed to it, it is sometimes contracted; as in the following ex.:] a poet says,

* كَأَمَّا يَخْتَطِينَ عَلَى قَتَادِ *
* وَيَسْتَضْحِكْنَ عَنْ حَبِّ ٱلْغَمَامِ *

[*As though,* by reason of their mincing gait, *they were walking upon tragacanthas; and they were laughing so as to discover* teeth like *hailstones*]: كَأَمَّا being for كَأَنَّمَا. (IAạr.) — أَنَّ is sometimes contracted into أَنْ; (Ṣ, Mughnee;) and in this case, it governs in the manner already explained, voce أَنْ. (Mughnee.) — It is also *syn. with* لَعَلَّ; (Sb, Ṣ, M, Mughnee, Ḳ;) as in the saying, ٱيتِ ٱلسُّوقَ أَنَّكَ تَشْتَرِى لَنَا شَيْئًا [*Come thou to the market; may-be thou wilt buy for us something;* ٱيتِ being originally ٱئْتِ]; i. e. لَعَلَّكَ: (Sb, M, Mughnee, Ḳ:*) and, accord. to some, (M, Mughnee, Ḳ,) so in the Ḳur [vi. 109], where it is said, وَمَا يُشْعِرُكُمْ أَنَّهَا إِذَا جَآءَتْ لَا يُؤْمِنُونَ [*And what maketh you to know?* (meaning, maketh you to know that they will believe when it cometh? i. e. ye do not know that: Jel:) *May-be, when it cometh, they will not believe*]: (Ṣ, M, Mughnee, Ḳ:) thus accord. to this reading: (Mughnee, Ḳ:) and Ubei here reads لَعَلَّهَا. (Ṣ.) أَنَّ and لَأَنَّ and لَوْ أَنَّ are all *syn. with* عَلَّ and لَعَلَّ; and أَنِّى and أَنَّنِى, and لَأَنِّى and لَأَنَّنِى, and لَوْ أَنِّى and لَوْ أَنَّنِى, with عَلِّى and لَعَلِّى. (Ḳ voce لَعَلَّ.) — It is also syn. with أَجَلْ [*Yes,* or *yea;* or *it is as thou sayest*]. (M, TA.) [See also إِنَّ, as exemplified by a verse commencing with وَيَقُلْنَ and by a saying of Ibn-Ez-Zubeyr.]

إِنَّ is one of the particles which annul the quality of the inchoative, like أَنَّ, of which it is the original: (I 'Aḳ p. 90:) it is a corroborative particle, (I 'Aḳ, Mughnee,) corroborating the predicate; (Ṣ, Ḳ;) governing the subject in the accus. case and the predicate in the nom. case; (Ṣ, I 'Aḳ, Mughnee, Ḳ;) [and may generally be rendered by *Verily,* or *certainly,* or the like; exactly agreeing with the Greek ὅτι, as used in Luke vii. 16 and in many other passages in the New Testament; though it often seems to be nothing more than a sign of inception, which can hardly be rendered at all in English; unless in pronunciation, by laying a stress upon the predicate, or upon the copula;] as in the saying, إِنَّ زَيْدًا قَائِمٌ [*Verily,* or *certainly, Zeyd is standing;* or simply, *Zeyd is standing,* if we lay a stress upon *standing,* or upon *is*]. (I 'Aḳ p. 90.) But sometimes it governs both the subject and the predicate in the accus. case; as in the saying,

* إِذَا ٱشْتَدَّ جُنْحُ ٱللَّيْلِ فَلْتَأْتِ وَلْتَكُنْ *
* خُطَاكَ خِفَافًا إِنَّ حُرَّاسَنَا أُسْدَا *

[*When the darkness of night becomes,* or *shall become, intense, then do thou come, and let thy steps be light: verily our guardians are lions*]; (Mughnee, Ḳ; [but in the latter, for ٱشْتَدَّ, we find ٱسْوَدَّ, so that the meaning is, *when the first portion of the night becomes,* or *shall become, black,* &c.;]) and as in a trad. in which it is said, إِنَّ قَعْرَ جَهَنَّمَ سَبْعِينَ خَرِيفًا [*Verily the bottom of Hell is* a distance of *seventy years* of journeying]: (Mughnee, Ḳ:) the verse, however, is explained by the supposition that it presents a denotative of state [in the last word, which is equivalent to شُجْعَانًا or the like], and that the predicate is suppressed, the meaning being, تَلْقَاهُمْ أُسْدًا [*thou wilt find them lions*]; and the trad. by the supposition that قَعْرَ is an inf. n., and سَبْعِينَ is an adverbial noun, so that the meaning is, *the reaching the bottom of hell is* [to be accomplished in no less time than] *in seventy years.* (Mughnee.) And sometimes the inchoative [of a proposition] after it is in the nom. case, and its subject is what is termed ضَمِيرُ شَأْنٍ, suppressed; as in the saying of Mohammad, إِنَّ مِنْ أَشَدِّ ٱلنَّاسِ عَذَابًا يَوْمَ ٱلْقِيٰمَةِ ٱلْمُصَوِّرُونَ [*Verily,* (*the case is this:*) *of the men most severely to be punished, on the day of resurrection, are the makers of images*], originally إِنَّهُ, i. e. إِنَّ ٱلشَّأْنَ; (Mughnee, Ḳ;*) and as in the saying in the Ḳur [xx. 66], إِنَّ هٰذَانِ لَسَاحِرَانِ, [accord. to some,] as will be seen in what follows. (TA.) — Of the two particles إِنَّ and ↓ أَنَّ, in certain cases only the former may be used; and in certain other cases either of them may be used. (I 'Aḳ p. 91.) The former must be used when it occurs inceptively, (Kh, T, I 'Aḳ p. 92, Mughnee, Ḳ,) having nothing before it upon which it is syntactically dependent, (Kh, T,) with respect to the wording or the meaning; (Ḳ;) as in إِنَّ زَيْدًا قَائِمٌ [*Verily Zeyd is standing*]. (I 'Aḳ, Ḳ.) It is used after أَلَا, (I 'Aḳ, Ḳ,) the inceptive particle, (I 'Aḳ,) or the particle which is employed to give notice [of something about to be said]; (Ḳ;) as in أَلَا إِنَّ زَيْدًا قَائِمٌ [*Now surely Zeyd is standing*]. (I 'Aḳ, Ḳ.) And when it occurs at the commencement of the complement of a conjunct noun; (I 'Aḳ, Ḳ;*) as in جَآءَ ٱلَّذِى إِنَّهُ قَائِمٌ [*He who is standing came*]; (I 'Aḳ;) and in the Ḳur [xxviii. 76], وَآتَيْنَاهُ مِنَ ٱلْكُنُوزِ مَا إِنَّ مَفَاتِحَهُ لَتَنُوْءُ بِٱلْعُصْبَةِ أُولِى ٱلْقُوَّةِ [*And we gave him, of treasures, that whereof the keys would weigh down the company of men possessed of strength*]. (I 'Aḳ,* Ḳ,* TA.) And in the complement of an oath, (I 'Aḳ, Ḳ,) when its predicate has لَ, (I 'Aḳ,) or whether its subject or its predicate has لَ or has it not; (Ḳ;) as in وَٱللّٰهِ إِنَّ زَيْدًا لَقَائِمٌ [*By Allah, verily Zeyd is standing*], (I 'Aḳ,) and إِنَّهُ قَائِمٌ: or, as some say, when you do not employ the لَ, the particle is with fet-ḥ; as in وَٱللّٰهِ أَنَّكَ ↓ قَائِمٌ [*I swear by Allah that thou art standing*]; mentioned by Ks as thus heard by him from the Arabs: (TA:) but respecting this case we shall have to speak hereafter. (I 'Aḳ.) And when it occurs after the word قَوْلٌ or a derivative thereof, in repeating the saying to which that word relates; (Fr, T, I 'Aḳ,* Ḳ;*) as in the saying [in the Ḳur iv. 156], وَقَوْلِهِمْ إِنَّا قَتَلْنَا ٱلْمَسِيحَ [*And their saying, Verily we have slain the Messiah*]; (Fr, T;) and قُلْتُ إِنَّ زَيْدًا قَائِمٌ [*I said, Verily Zeyd is standing*]; (I 'Aḳ;) and [in the Ḳur v. 115,] قَالَ ٱللّٰهُ إِنِّى مُنَزِّلُهَا عَلَيْكُمْ [*God said, Verily I will cause it to descend unto you*]; accord. to the dial. of him who does not pronounce it with fet-ḥ: (Ḳ:) but when it occurs in explaining what is said, you use ↓ أَنَّ; as in the saying, قَدْ قُلْتُ لَكَ كَلَامًا حَسَنًا أَنَّ أَبَاكَ شَرِيفٌ وَأَنَّكَ عَاقِلٌ [*I have said to thee a good saying; that thy father is noble and that thou art intelligent*]; (Fr, T;) or when the word signifying "saying" is used as meaning "thinking;" as in أَتَقُولُ أَنَّ زَيْدًا قَائِمٌ [*Dost thou say that Zeyd is standing?*], meaning أَتَظُنُّ [*Dost thou think?*]. (I 'Aḳ.) Also, when it occurs in a phrase denotative of state; (I 'Aḳ;) [i. e.,] after the و denotative of state; (Ḳ;) as in زُرْتُهُ وَإِنِّى ذُو أَمَلٍ [*I visited him, I verily having hope,* or *expectation*]; (I 'Aḳ;) and in جَآءَ زَيْدٌ وَإِنَّ يَدَهُ عَلَى رَأْسِهِ [*Zeyd came, he verily having his hand upon his head*]. (Ḳ.) And when it occurs in a phrase which is the predicate of a proper (as opposed to an ideal) substantive; (I 'Aḳ, Ḳ;*) as in زَيْدٌ إِنَّهُ قَائِمٌ [*Zeyd, verily he is standing*], (I 'Aḳ,) or ذَاهِبٌ [*going away*]; contr. to the assertion of Fr. (Ḳ.) And when it occurs before the ل which suspends the grammatical government of a verb of the mind, preceding it, with respect to its objective complements; (I 'Aḳ, Ḳ;*) as in عَلِمْتُ إِنَّ زَيْدًا لَقَائِمٌ [*I knew Zeyd verily was standing*]; (I 'Aḳ;) and in [the Ḳur lxiii. 1,] وَٱللّٰهُ يَعْلَمُ إِنَّكَ لَرَسُولُهُ [*And God knoweth thou verily art his apostle*]: (Ḳ:) but if the ل is not in its predicate, you say, ↓ أَنَّ; as in عَلِمْتُ أَنَّ زَيْدًا قَائِمٌ [*I knew that Zeyd was standing*]. (I 'Aḳ.) And in the like of the saying in the Ḳur [ii. 171], وَإِنَّ ٱلَّذِينَ ٱخْتَلَفُوا فِى ٱلْكِتَابِ لَفِى شِقَاقٍ بَعِيدٍ [*And verily they who differ among themselves respecting the book are in an opposition remote from the truth*]; because of the ل [of inception] which occurs after it, in لَفِى: (Ks, A 'Obeyd:) the ل of inception which occurs before the predicate of إِنَّ should properly commence the sentence; so that إِنَّ زَيْدًا لَقَائِمٌ [*Verily Zeyd is standing*] should properly be لَإِنَّ زَيْدًا قَائِمٌ; but as the ل is a corroborative and إِنَّ is a corroborative, they dislike putting two particles of the same meaning together, and therefore they put the ل later, transferring it to the predicate: Mbr allows its being put before the predicate of ↓ أَنَّ; and thus it occurs in an unusual reading of the saying [in the Ḳur xxv. 22], إِلَّا أَنَّهُمْ لَيَأْكُلُونَ ٱلطَّعَامَ [*But they ate food*]; but this is explained by the supposition that the ل is here redundant: (I 'Aḳ p. 95:) this is the reading of Sa'eed Ibn-Jubeyr: others read, إِلَّا إِنَّهُمْ لَيَأْكُلُونَ ٱلطَّعَامَ [*but verily they ate food*]: and إِنَّ [as well as ↓ أَنَّ] is used after the exceptive إِلَّا when it is not followed by the ل [of inception]. (TA.) Also, when it occurs after حَيْثُ; as in اِجْلِسْ حَيْثُ إِنَّ زَيْدًا جَالِسٌ [*Sit thou where Zeyd is sitting*]. (I 'Aḳ p. 92, and Ḳ.) And after حَتَّى; as in مَرِضَ زَيْدٌ حَتَّى إِنَّهُمْ لَا يَرْجُونَهُ [*Zeyd has fallen sick, so that verily they have no hope for him*]: whereas after a particle governing the gen. case, [i. e. a preposition,] you say, ↓ أَنَّ. (IHsh in De Sacy's Anthol. Gr. Ar. p. 76.) — Either of these two forms may be used after إِذَا denoting a thing's happening suddenly, or unexpectedly; as in خَرَجْتُ فَإِذَا إِنَّ زَيْدًا قَائِمٌ [*I went forth, and lo, verily Zeyd was standing*], and فَإِذَا أَنَّ ↓ زَيْدًا قَائِمٌ [*and lo,* or *at that present time, Zeyd's standing*]; in which latter case, أَنَّ with its complement is [properly] an inchoative, and its enunciative is إِذَا; the implied meaning being, *and at that present time was the standing of Zeyd*: or it may be that the enunciative is suppressed, and that the implied meaning is, [*and lo,* or *at that present time,*] *the standing of Zeyd* was an event come to pass. (I 'Aḳ p. 93.) Also, when occurring in the complement of an oath, if its enunciative is without ل: (I 'Aḳ:) [see exs. given above:] or, as some say, only ↓ أَنَّ is used in this case. (TA.) Also, when occurring after فَ denoting the complement of a condition; as in مَنْ يَأْتِنِى فَإِنَّهُ مُكْرَمٌ [*He who cometh to me, verily he shall be treated with honour*], and أَنَّهُ ↓ مُكْرَمٌ; in which latter case, أَنَّ with its complement is an inchoative, and the enunciative is suppressed; the implied meaning being, *honourable treatment of him* shall be an event come to pass: or it may be an enunciative to an inchoative suppressed; the implied meaning being, his recompense shall be *honourable treatment*. (I 'Aḳ p. 94.) Also, when occurring after an inchoative having the meaning of a saying, its enunciative being a saying, and the sayer being one; as in خَيْرُ ٱلْقَوْلِ إِنِّى أَحْمَدُ [*The best saying is, Verily I praise* God], and أَنِّى ↓ أَحْمَدُ; in which latter case, أَنَّ with its complement is an enunciative of خَيْرُ; the implied meaning being, *the best saying is the praising* of God [or *my praising* of God]. (I 'Aḳ ubi suprà.) You also say, لَبَّيْكَ إِنَّ ٱلْحَمْدَ لَكَ [*At thy service! Verily praise belongeth to Thee!* O God]; commencing [with إِنَّ] a new proposition: and sometimes one says, ↓ أَنَّ; meaning بِأَنَّ ٱلْحَمْدَ لَكَ [*because praise belongeth to Thee*]. (Mṣb.) — The cases in which إِن may not be used in the place of أَنَّ have been mentioned above, voce أَنَّ. — [When it has the affixed pronoun of the first person, sing. or pl.,] you say, إِنِّى and إِنَّنِى, (Ṣ,) and إِنَّا and إِنَّنَا, (TA,) like as you say لَكِنِّى and لَكِنَّنِى [&c.]. (Ṣ.) إِنَّ as a contraction of إِنْ أَنَا has been mentioned above, as occurring in the phrase إِنَّ قَائِمٌ, voce إِنْ, q. v. — Accord. to the grammarians, (T,) إِنَّمَا is a compound of إِنَّ and مَا, (T, Ṣ,) which latter prevents the former's having any government: (T:) it imports restriction; like أَنَّمَا, which see above, voce أَنَّ, in three places: (Mughnee, Ḳ:) [i. e.] it imports the restriction of that which it precedes to that which follows it; as in إِنَّمَا زَيْدٌ مُنْطَلِقٌ [*Zeyd is only going away*], and إِنَّمَا يَنْطَلِقُ زَيْدٌ [*Only Zeyd goes away*]: (Bḍ in ii. 10:) [in other words,] it is used to particularize, or specify, or distinguish a thing from other things: (Ṣ:) it affirms a thing in relation to that which is mentioned after it, and denies it in relation to other things; (T, Ṣ;) as in the saying in the Ḳur [ix. 60], إِنَّمَا ٱلصَّدَقَاتُ لِلْفُقَرَآءِ [*The contributions levied for pious uses are only,* or *but, for the poor*]: (Ṣ:) but El-Ámidee and AḤei say that it does not import restriction, but only corroboration of an affirmation, because it is a compound of the corroborative إِنَّ and the redundant مَا which restrains the former from exercising government, and that it has no application to denote negation implied in restriction, as is shown by the trad., إِنَّمَا ٱلرِّبَا فِى ٱلنَّسِيْئَةِ [which must mean, *Verily usury is in the delay of payment*], for usury is in other things beside that here mentioned, as رِبَا ٱلْفَضْلِ [or profit obtained by the superior value of a thing received over that of a thing given], by common consent: (Kull p. 76:) some say that it necessarily imports restriction: J says what has been cited above from the Ṣ: some say that it has an overt signification in denoting restriction, and is susceptible of the meaning of corroboration: some say the reverse of this: El-Ámidee says that if it were [properly] restrictive, its occurrence in another sense would be at variance with the original import; but to this it may be replied, that if it were [properly] corroborative, its occurrence in another sense would be at variance with the original import: it [therefore] seems that it is susceptible of both these meanings, bearing one or the other according as this or that suits the place. (Mṣb.) إِنَّمَا is to be distinguished from إِنَّ with the conjunct [noun] مَا, which does not restrain it from governing [though its government with this is not apparent, and which is written separately]; as in إِنَّ مَا عِنْدَكَ حَسَنٌ meaning *Verily what is with thee is good*, and in إِنَّ مَا فَعَلْتَ حَسَنٌ meaning *Verily thy deed is good*. (I 'Aḳ pp. 97 and 98.) — إِنَّ is sometimes contracted into إِنْ; (Ṣ, Mughnee, Ḳ;) and in this case, it is made to govern and is made to have no government: (Ṣ:) it is seldom made to govern in this case; often made to have no government: the Koofees say that it is not contracted; (Mughnee, Ḳ;) and that when one says, إِنْ زَيْدٌ لَمُنْطَلِقٌ [the meaning is virtually *Verily Zeyd is going away*, but] إِنْ is a negative and the ل is syn. with إِلَّا; but this assertion is refuted by the fact that some make it to govern when contracted, as in exs. cited above, voce إِنْ, q. v. (Mughnee.) — It is also *syn. with* نَعَمْ [*Even so; yes; yea*]; (Mughnee, Ḳ;) contr. to the opinion of AO. (Mughnee.) [See also أَنَّ, last sentence.] Those who affirm it to have this meaning cite as an ex. the following verse (Mughnee, Ḳ*) of 'Obeyd-Allah Ibn-Ḳeys-er-Ruḳeiyát: (Ṣ,* TA:)

* وَيَقُلْنَ شَيْبٌ قَدْ عَلَا * كَ وَقَدْ كَبِرْتَ فَقُلْتُ إِنَّهْ *

[*And they say,* (namely, the women,) *Hoariness hath come upon thee, and thou hast become old: and I say, Even so,* or *yes,* or *yea*]: (Mughnee, Ḳ:) but this has been rebutted by the saying, We do not concede that the ه is here added to denote the pause, but assert that it is a pronoun, governed by إِنَّ in the accus. case, and the predicate is suppressed; the meaning being, إِنَّهُ كَذٰلِكَ [*Verily it,* i. e. *the case, is thus*]. (Mughnee.) [J says,] The meaning is, إِنَّهُ قَدْ كَانَ كَمَا تَقُلْنَ [*Verily it,* i. e. *the case, hath been as ye say*]: A 'Obeyd says, This is a curtailment of the speech of the Arabs; the pronoun being deemed sufficient because the meaning is known: and as to the saying of Akh, that it signifies نَعَمْ, he only means thereby that it may be so rendered, not that it is originally applied to that signification: he says that the ه is here added to denote the pause. (Ṣ.) There is, however, a good ex. of إِنَّ in the sense of نَعَمْ in the saying of Ibn-Ez-Zubeyr, to him who said to him, "May God curse a she camel which carried me to thee," إِنَّ وَرَاكِبَهَا, i. e. *Even so,* or *yes,* or *yea; and* may God curse *her rider*: for the suppression of both the subject and the predicate is not allowable. (Mughnee.) And hence, accord. to Mbr, the saying in the Ḳur [xx. 66], as thus read, إِنَّ هٰذَانِ لَسَاحِرَانِ [meaning, if so, *Yes, these two are enchanters*]. (Mughnee.) [But this phrase has given rise to much discussion, related in the Mughnee and other works. The following is a brief abstract of what has been said respecting it by several of the leading authorities.] Aboo-Is-ḥáḳ says that the people of El-Medeeneh and El-Koofeh read as above, except 'Áṣim, who is reported to have read, إِنْ هٰذَانِ, without teshdeed, and so is Kh; [so too is Ḥafṣ, as is said above, voce إِنْ;] and that AA read إِنَّ هٰذَيْنِ, the former word with teshdeed, and the latter in the accus. case: that the argument for إِنَّ هٰذَانِ, with teshdeed and the nom. case, [or rather what is identical in form with the nom. case,] is, that it is of the dial. of Kinánch, in which the dual is formed by the termination ان in the nom. and accus. and gen. cases alike, as also in the dial. of Benu-l-Ḥárith Ibn-Kaab: but that the old grammarians say that ه is here suppressed; the meaning being, إِنَّهُ هٰذَانِ: (T:) this last assertion, however, is weak; for what is applied to the purpose of corroboration should not be suppressed, and the instances of its suppression which have been heard are deviations from general usage, except in the case of أَنَّ, with fet-ḥ, contracted into أَنْ: (Mughnee:) Aboo-Is-ḥáḳ then adds, that some say, إِنَّ is here syn. with نَعَمْ: this last opinion he holds to be the best; the meaning being, نَعَمْ هٰذَانِ لَهُمَا سَاحِرَانِ [*Yes, these two, verily they are two enchanters*: for this is not a case in which the ل (which is the ل of inception) can be regarded as transferred from its proper place, at the commencement of the sentence or proposition, as it is in some instances mentioned in the former half of this paragraph: but it is said in the Mughnee that this explanation is invalidated by the fact that the combining of the corroborative ل and the suppression of the inchoative is like the combining of two things inconsistent, or incompatible; as is also the opinion that the ل is redundant, because the redundant ل prefixed to the enunciative is peculiar to poetry]: next in point of goodness, in the opinion of Aboo-Is-ḥáḳ, is, that it is of the dial. of Kinánch and Benu-l-Ḥárith Ibn-Kaab: the reading of AA he does not allow, because it is at variance with the written text: but he approves the reading of 'Áṣim and Kh. (T.) — إِنَّ also occurs as a verb: it is the third person pl. fem. of the pret. from الأَيْنُ, syn. with التَّعَبُ; or from آنَ syn. with قَرُبَ: or the third person sing. masc. of the pret. passive from الأَنِينُ, in the dial. of those who, for رُدَّ and حُبَّ, say رِدَّ and حِبَّ, likening these verbs to قِيلَ and بِيعَ: or the sing. masc. of the imperative from the same: or the pl. fem. of the imperative from الأَيْنُ; or from آنَ syn. with قَرُبَ: or the sing. fem. of the corroborated form of the imperative from وَأَى, syn. with وَعَدَ. (Mughnee.)

أَنَا, signifying *I*: see أَنْ, in seven places.

أَنَهْ, signifying *I*: see أَنْ, in two places.

أَنَّةٌ *i. q.* أَنِينٌ [inf. n. of أَنَّ, but app. a simple subst., signifying *A moan, moaning*, or *prolonged voice of complaint*; or *a saying Ah*: or *a complaint*: or *a cry*]. (TA.)

أَنْتَ, signifying *Thou*: fem. أَنْتِ; dual أَنْتُمَا; pl. masc. أَنْتُمْ, and pl. fem. أَنْتُنَّ: see أَنْ, in six places.

أُنَنَةٌ, أُنَانٌ } see أَنَّانٌ

أَنَّانٌ One *who moans*; *who utters a moaning*, or *prolonged voice of complaint*; or *who says Ah*; *much*, or *frequently*; as also ▼أُنَانٌ and ▼أُنَنَةٌ: (M, Ḳ:) or this last signifies one *who publishes complaint*, or *makes it public, much*, or *frequently*: (M:) or one *who talks and grieves and complains much*, or *frequently*; and it has no verb derived from it: (T:) and you say, رَجُلٌ أُنَنَةٌ قُنَنَةٌ, [in which the latter epithet is app. an imitative sequent to the former,] meaning *an eloquent man*. (TA.) The fem. of أَنَّانٌ is with ة: (M, Ḳ:) and is said to be applied to a woman *who moans*, or *says Ah, and is affected with compassion, for a dead husband, on seeing another whom she has married after the former*. (MF.) [See also حَنَّانَةٌ, voce حَنَّانٌ.]

آنَ, signifying *I*: see أَنْ, in two places.

آنٌّ part. n. of أَنَّ, [*Moaning*; or *uttering a moan* or *moaning* or *a prolonged voice of complaint*; or *saying Ah*; by reason of pain: *complaining* by reason of disease or pain: or] *uttering a cry* or *cries*: fem. with ة. (Mṣb.) [Hence,] you say, مَا لَهُ حَانَّةٌ وَلَا آنَّةٌ *He has not a she camel nor a sheep*, or *goat*: (Ṣ, M, A, Ḳ:) or *he has not a she camel nor a female slave* (M, Ḳ) *that moans by reason of fatigue*. (M.)

مَئِنَّةٌ, occurring in a trad., (Ṣ, Mgh, Ḳ, &c., in the first and last in art. مأن, and in the second in the present art.,) where it is said, إِنَّ طُولَ الصَّلَاةِ وَقِصَرَ الخُطْبَةِ مَئِنَّةٌ مِنْ فِقْهِ الرَّجُلِ, (Ṣ, Mgh, TA, &c.,) is of the measure مَفْعِلَةٌ, [originally مَأْنِنَةٌ,] from إِنَّ, (Ṣ, Z in the Fáïḳ, IAth, Mgh, Ḳ,) the corroborative particle; (Z, IAth, Mgh;) like مَعْسَاةٌ from عَسَى; (Ṣ, Ḳ;) but not regularly derived from إِنَّ, because a word may not be so derived from a particle; or it may be said that this is so derived after the particle has been made a noun; (Z, IAth;) or neither of these modes of derivation is regular: (MF:) the meaning is, [*Verily the longness of the prayer and the shortness of the oration from the pulpit are* (together)] *a proper ground for one's saying, Verily the man is a person of knowledge* or *intelligence*: (Z,* Mgh, Ḳ in art. مأن:) this is the proper signification: accord. to AO, the meaning is, *a thing whereby one learns the knowledge*, or *intelligence, of the man*: (Mgh:) or it means *a thing suitable to*, (Ṣ, Mgh,) *and whereby one knows*, (Ṣ,) *the knowledge*, or *intelligence, of the man*: (Ṣ, Mgh:) or *a sign* (Aṣ, Ṣ, Ḳ) *of the knowledge*, or *intelligence, of the man*; and *suitable thereto*: (Aṣ, Ṣ:) or *an evidence thereof*: (M:) or *an indication*, or *a symptom, thereof*; everything that indicates a thing being said to be مَئِنَّةٌ لَهُ: [so that مَئِنَّةٌ لِكَذَا may be well rendered *a thing that occasions one's knowing*, or *inferring*, or *suspecting, such a thing*; and in like manner, *a person that occasions one's doing so*: or, more properly, *a thing*, &c., *in which such a thing is usually known to take place*, or *have place*, or *be*, or *exist*, like مَظِنَّةٌ:] one of the strangest of the things said of it is, that the ء is a substitute for the ظ of مَظِنَّةٌ: (IAth:) this seems to have been the opinion of Lḥ: (Az, L:) accord. to AA, it is *syn. with* آيَةٌ [*a sign*, &c.]. (TA.) Aṣ says (Ṣ,* Ḳ, TA, all in art. مأن) that the word is thus, with teshdeed to the ن, in the trad. and in a verse of poetry, as these are related; (Ṣ, TA;) but correctly, in his opinion, it should be مَئِينَةٌ, of the measure فَعِيلَةٌ, (Ṣ, Ḳ,* TA,) unless it be from إِنَّ, as first stated above: (Ṣ, TA:) AZ used to say that it is مَئِتَّةٌ, with ت, (Ṣ, Ḳ,* TA,) meaning *a thing* (lit. *a place*) *meet, fit*, or *proper*, or *worthy* or *deserving*, and *the like*; of the measure مَفْعِلَةٌ, [originally مَأْتِتَةٌ,] from أَتَّهُ meaning "he overcame him with an argument or the like:" (Ṣ, Ḳ, TA:) but some say that it is of the measure فَعِلَّةٌ, from مَأَنَ meaning اِحْتَمَلَ: see art. مأن. (Ḳ in that art.) You say also, هُوَ مَئِنَّةٌ لِلْخَيْرِ, from إِنَّ, *He is a person fit*, or *proper, for one's saying of him, Verily he is good*; and in like manner, مَعْسَاةٌ, from عَسَى, as meaning "a person fit, or proper, for one's saying of him, May-be he will do good." (A, TA.) And إِنَّهُ لَمَئِنَّةٌ أَنْ يَكُونَ كَذَا *Verily it is meet, fit*, or *proper, for one's saying of it, Verily it is thus*; or *is worthy*, or *deserving, of one's saying* &c.: or *verily it is a thing meet, fit*, or *proper, for one's saying* &c.; or *is a thing worthy*, or *deserving, of one's saying* &c.: of the measure مَفْعِلَةٌ, from إِنَّ. (Ḳ in the present art.) And إِنَّهُ لَمَئِنَّةٌ أَنْ يَفْعَلَ ذٰلِكَ *Verily he is meet, fit*, or *proper, for doing that*; or *is worthy*, or *deserving, of doing that*: or *verily he is a person meet, fit*, or *proper, for doing that*; or *is a person worthy*, or *deserving, of doing that*: and in like manner you say of two, and of more, and of a female: but مَئِنَّةٌ may be of the measure فَعِلَّةٌ [from مأن], i. e. a triliteral-radical word. (M.) — You also say, أَتَاهُ عَلَى مَئِنَّةِ ذٰلِكَ, meaning *He came to him at the time*, or *season*, [or *fit* or *proper time*,] *of that*; and *at the first thereof*. (M.)

انا

أَنَا (pronoun of the first person sing.): see art. ان.

انب

2. أَنَّبَهُ, inf. n. تَأْنِيبٌ, *He blamed, reproved, reprehended, chid*, or *reproached, him*: (Ṣ, M, A, Ḳ:) or *he did so severely*, or *angrily*: (ISk, T, Ṣ, M, A, Ḳ:) or, *with the utmost severity* or *harshness*: (T, M, TA:) or *he repulsed him*, meaning a person who asked something of him, *in the most abominable manner*. (M,* Ḳ,* TA.)

أُنْبُوبٌ *An internodal portion*, or the *portion between any two joints*, or *knots*, of a cane, or reed, and of a spear-shaft: (T:) [and] *a spear*, or *lance*: pl. أَنَابِيبُ: mentioned in this art. [in the T, and] by Ibn-El-Mukarram [in the L]. (TA.) [See also art. نب.]

انت

أَنْتَ, أَنْتِ, أَنْتُمَا, أَنْتُمْ, and أَنْتُنَّ: see أَنْ, in art. ان.

انث

1. [أَنُثَ, aor. ـُ, inf. n. أَنَاثَةٌ and أُنُوثَةٌ, (see the former of these two ns. below,) *It was*, or *became, female, feminine*, or *of the feminine gender*. — And hence, أَنُثَتْ, said of land (أَرْض), ‡ *It was*, or *became, such as is termed* أَنِيثَةٌ. — Hence also,] أَنُثَ, said of iron, ‡ *It was*, or *became, soft*. (Golius, from the larger of two editions of the lexicon entitled مرقاة اللغة.) Accord. to IAạr, softness is the primary signification. (M.) [But accord. to the A, the second and third of the meanings given above are tropical: (see أَنِيثٌ:) and the verb in the first of the senses here assigned to it, if not proper, is certainly what is termed حَقِيقَةٌ عُرْفِيَّةٌ, i. e., conventionally regarded as proper.]

2. أَنَّثَهُ, inf. n. تَأْنِيثٌ, *He made it* (namely, a noun [&c.], Ṣ and Mṣb) *feminine*; (Ṣ, M, L, Mṣb;) *he attached to it*, or *to that which was syntactically dependent upon it, the sign of the feminine gender*. (Mṣb.) — †*He*, or *it, rendered him effeminate*. (KL.) [See the pass. part. n., below.] — أَنَّثَ لَهُ, inf. n. as above, ‡ *He acted gently*, [or *effeminately*] *towards him*; as also ▼ تَأَنَّثَ لَهُ. (Ḳ, TA.) And أَنَّثَ فِى أَمْرِهِ, inf. n. as above, (T, A,) ‡ *He acted gently in his affair*: (A:) or *he applied himself gently to his affair*: (T:) and some say, ▼ تأنّث فى امره, meaning *he acted effeminately in his affair*. (T, TA.)

4. آنَثَتْ, (Ṣ, M, A, Ḳ,) inf. n. إِينَاثٌ, (Ḳ,) *She* (a woman) *brought forth a female*, (Ṣ, A, Ḳ,) or *females*. (M.) — [And hence,] †*It* (land, أَرْض,) *was*, or *became, such as is termed* مِئْنَاثٌ. (A.)

5. تأنّث *It* (a noun [&c.]) *was*, or *became*, or *was made, feminine*. (Ṣ, L.) — See also 2, in two places.

أُنْثَى *Female*; *feminine*; *of the female*, or *feminine, sex*, or *gender*; contr. of ذَكَرٌ: (T, Ṣ, M:) an epithet applied to anything of that sex or gender: (T:) IAạr asserts, that a woman is termed انثى from the phrase بَلَدٌ أَنِيثٌ, q. v., because of her softness; she being more soft than a man: (M, L:) [but see the observation at the end of the first paragraph of this art.:] the pl. is إِنَاثٌ; (T, Ṣ, M, A, Mṣb, Ḳ;) and sometimes one says أُنُثٌ, as though it were pl. of إِنَاثٌ; (Ṣ;) or it is [truly] pl. of إِنَاثٌ, like as نُمُرٌ is of نِمَارٌ; (T;) and أَنَاثَى, (T, A, Mṣb, Ḳ,) which last occurs in poetry. (T.) You say, هٰذَا طَائِرٌ وَأُنْثَاهُ [*This is a (male) bird and his female*]: not أُنْثَاتُهُ. (ISk, T.) In the Ḳur iv. 117, I'Ab reads أُنُثًا [in the place of أُنُثًا or إِنَاثًا]; and Fr says that it is pl. of وَثَنٌ, the و in وُثُنٌ being changed into أ as in أُقِّتَتْ [for وُقِّتَتْ]. (T, L.) — اِمْرَأَةٌ أُنْثَى ‡ [*A feminine woman*,] means *a perfect woman*; (T, A, Ḳ;) a woman being thus termed in praise; like as a man is termed رَجُلٌ ذَكَرٌ. (T, A.) — [The pl.] إِنَاثٌ also signifies † *Inanimate things*; (Lḥ, T, M, Ḳ;) as trees and stones (T, Ḳ) and wood. (T.) In the passage of the Ḳur mentioned above, إِنَاثًا is said to have this meaning: (T, M:) [or it there means *females*; for] Fr says that El-Lát and El-'Ozzà and the like were said by the Arabs to be feminine divinities. (T, TA.) — Also † *Small stars*. (Ḳ.) — And [the dual] الأُنْثَيَانِ ‡ *The two testicles*; syn. الخُصْيَانِ: (Ṣ, Ḳ;) or الخُصْيَتَانِ [which is said by some to mean *the scrotum*; but the former is generally, though app. not always, meant by الانثيان]. (M, Mgh, Mṣb.) — And ‡ *The two ears*: (Aṣ, T, Ṣ, M, A, Mgh, Ḳ:) because they are of the fem. gender. (TA.) — And † *The two tribes of Bejeeleh and Ḳuḍá'ah*. (Ḳ) — And أُنْثَيَا الفَرَسِ † *The inner parts* (الرَّبَلَتَانِ) *of the thighs of the horse*. (M, L.) — And الأُنْثَى is also used to signify † *The* [*engine of war called*] مَنْجَنِيق; because the latter word is [generally] of the feminine gender. (M.)

أَنِيثٌ: see مُؤَنَّثٌ. — أَرْضٌ أَنِيثَةٌ, (AA,* IAạr, T, Ṣ, M, Ḳ,) and ▼ مِئْنَاثٌ, (ISh, T, M, Ḳ,) ‡ *Plain, even*, or *soft, land*, or *ground*, (ISh, IAạr, T, M, Ḳ,) *that produces many plants*, or *much herbage*; (AA, T, M, Ḳ;) or *that produces herbs*, or *leguminous plants, and is plain, even*, or *soft*; (El-Kilábee, Ṣ;) or *fitted for producing plants*, or *herbage*; *not rugged*. (ISh, T, L.) And مَكَانٌ أَنِيثٌ *A place in which the herbage grows quickly, and becomes abundant*. (T, L.) And بَلَدٌ أَنِيثٌ † *A country*, or *district, of which the soil is soft, and plain*, or *even*. (IAạr, M, L.) — حَدِيدٌ أَنِيثٌ ‡ *Female iron*; *that which is not what is termed* ذَكَر: (Ṣ, M, L, Ḳ:) *soft iron*. (T and Ḳ in art. انف.) And سَيْفٌ أَنِيثٌ ‡ *A sword of female iron*: (M, L:) or *a sword that is not sharp*, or *cutting*; *a blunt sword*: (T, M,* L:) and ▼ سَيْفٌ مِئْنَاثٌ, and ▼ مِئْنَاثَةٌ, (T, M, L, Ḳ,) mentioned by Lḥ, (T, L,) *a blunt sword*; (Ḳ;) as also ▼ مُؤَنَّثٌ: (TA:) or *a sword of soft iron*. (T, L.)

أَنَاثَةٌ [inf. n. of أَنُثَ, q. v.:] The *female*, or *feminine, nature*, or *quality*, or *gender*; (M;) as also ▼ أُنُوثَةٌ. (A.) — ‡ The *quality of land which is termed* أَنِيثَةٌ. (A.) — [‡ *Softness* of iron: see أَنِيثٌ.]

أُنُوثَةٌ: see the paragraph next preceding.

مُؤْنِثٌ A woman *bringing forth*, or *who brings forth, a female*, (Ṣ, Ḳ,) or *females*. (M.)

مِئْنَاثٌ A woman *who usually brings forth females*: (Ṣ, M, Ḳ:) and a man *who usually begets female children*; for the measure مِفْعَالٌ applies equally to both sexes: (Ṣ:) the contr. epithet is مِذْكَارٌ. (TA.) — See also مُؤَنَّثٌ, in two places. — أَرْضٌ مِئْنَاثٌ: see أَنِيثٌ. — سَيْفٌ مِئْنَاثٌ, and مِئْنَاثَةٌ: see أَنِيثٌ.

مُؤَنَّثٌ [A *feminine* word; a word *made feminine*. — Also,] (T, A, Ḳ,) and ▼ أَنِيثٌ, (AA, T,) and ▼ مِئْنَاثٌ, (Ḳ,) and ▼ مِئْنَاثَةٌ, (TA,) ‡ i. q. مُخَنَّثٌ, (AA, T, A, Ḳ,) i. e. An *effeminate* man; one *who resembles a woman* (AA, T, TA) *in gentleness, and in softness of speech, and in an affectation of languor of the limbs*: (TA:) or a man *in the form*, or *make, of a female*. (T.) — سَيْفٌ مُؤَنَّثٌ: see أَنِيثٌ. — طِيبٌ مُؤَنَّثٌ † *Perfume that is used by women*; *such as* خَلُوق *and* زَعْفَرَان, (Sh, T, L,) *and what colours the clothes*: (L:) ذُكُورَةُ الطِّيبِ being such perfumes as have no colour; such as غَالِيَة and كَافُور and مِسْك and عُود and عَنْبَر and the like, which leave no mark. (T, L.)

انح

1. أَنَحَ, aor. ـِ, inf. n. أَنْحٌ and أَنِيحٌ and أُنُوحٌ, *He* (a man, Ṣ) *breathed hard*, or *violently, in consequence of heaviness*, or *oppression, experienced by him as an effect of disease*, or *of being out of breath*, (Ṣ, Ḳ, TA,) *as though he made a reiterated hemming in his throat*, (كَأَنَّهُ يَتَنَحْنَحُ,) *and did not speak clearly*, or *plainly*: (Ṣ, TA:) or *he made a reiterated hemming in his throat* (تَنَحْنَحَ), when asked for a thing, *by reason of niggardliness*: (L:) or *he uttered a long*, or *vehement, sigh*, or *a kind of groaning sound*, (زَفَرَ,) when asked for a thing. (A.) You say, يَأْنِحُ عَلَى مَالِهِ *He utters a long*, or *vehement, sigh*, or *a kind of groaning sound, over his property* [from unwillingness to part with it]. (A.) — It is said in a trad. of Ibn-'Omar, رَأَى رَجُلًا يَأْنِحُ بِبَطْنِهِ, meaning, [it is asserted, though this seems doubtful, *He saw a man*] *raising*, or *lifting, his belly with an effort, oppressed by its weight*: from أُنُوح in the last of the senses assigned to it below. (TA.)

أُنَّحٌ: see آنِحٌ, with which it is syn., and of which it is also pl.

أَنُوحٌ: see آنِحٌ, in two places.

أُنُوحٌ: [see 1:] it is also explained as signifying *A sound like that which is termed* زَفِير, *arising from grief*, or *anger*, or *repletion of the belly*, or *jealousy*: (L:) *a sound accompanied by a reiterated hemming in the throat* (صَوْتٌ مَعَ تَنَحْنُحٍ): (Aṣ:) and *a sound that is heard from a man's inside, with breathing, and a shortness of breath*, or *panting for breath, which affects fat men*; as also ▼ أَنِيحٌ. (L.)

أَنِيحٌ: see أُنُوحٌ. [See also 1.]

أَنِحٌ: see آنِحٌ.

آنِحٌ act. part. n. of 1; A man *breathing hard*, or *violently*, &c.: and a man *who, when he is asked for a thing, makes a reiterated hemming in his throat* (يَتَنَحْنَحُ), *by reason of niggardliness*; as also ↓ أُنُوحٌ, and ↓ أُنَّحٌ, (Ṣ, Ḳ,) and ↓ أَنَّاحٌ: (Lḥ:) or ↓ أُنُوحٌ signifies a man *who hangs back from*, or *falls short of, doing generous deeds*; as also أُزُوحٌ: (El-Ghanawee and Ṣ in art. ازح, and TA in the present art.:) and is also applied to a horse, meaning *that runs, and makes a kind of groaning noise*; إِذَا جَرَى قَرْقَرَ: this is the right reading in the Ḳ: in some copies اذا جرى قرقر [*that makes a rumbling sound in his belly when he runs*]: (TA:) the pl. of آنِحٌ is أُنَّحٌ. (Ṣ, Ḳ.) — آنِحَةٌ, applied to a female, signifies *Short*. (Ḳ.)

انس

1. أَنِسَ بِهِ, (AZ, Ṣ, M, A, Mṣb, Ḳ,) and إِلَيْهِ, (A,) aor. ـَ; (Mṣb, TA;) and أَنَسَ, (Ṣ, M, A, Mṣb, Ḳ,) aor. ـِ (M, Mṣb, TA) and ـُ; (M;) and أَنُسَ, aor. ـُ; (M, Ṣgh, Ḳ;) inf. n. أُنْسٌ and أُنْسَةٌ, (Ṣ, Ḳ,) both of أَنِسَ, (Ṣ,) or إِنْسٌ, (AZ, AHát, T, M, Mṣb,) also of أَنِسَ, (AZ, AHát, Mṣb, TA,) but this is rare, (T, TA,) and أُنْسٌ, (T, Ṣ, M, A, Ḳ,) which is the more common, (T, TA,) and is of أَنِسَ, (Ṣ,) or أُنْسٌ has a different signification from إِنْسٌ the inf. n. of أَنِسَ, [see أُنْسٌ below,] (AZ, AHát,) or it is a subst. from أَنِسَ بِهِ, (Mṣb,) and أُنْسَةٌ; (M;) [but this also is probably a subst.;] one says أُنْسٌ and أُنْسَةٌ, like as one says بُعْدٌ and بُعْدَةٌ; (Ḥam p. 768;) *He was*, or *became, sociable, companionable, conversable, inclined to company or converse, friendly, amicable*, or *familiar, with him*, or *by means of him*, and *to him*: and [انس به] *he was*, or *became, cheered*, or *gladdened, by his company* or *converse*, or *by his*, or *its, presence*; or *cheerful, gay*, or *gladsome*: the inf. n. signifying the *contr. of* وَحْشَةٌ: (T, Ṣ, A, Ḳ:) or *he was*, or *became, at ease*, or *tranquil, with him*: (M:) or *his heart was*, or *became, at ease*, or *tranquil, with him*; *without shrinking*, or *aversion*: (Mṣb:) and ↓ اِسْتَأْنَسَ بِهِ, (Ṣ, M, A, Mṣb,) and إِلَيْهِ, (A,) and ↓ تَأَنَّسَ بِهِ, signify the same, (Ṣ, M, Mṣb,) i. e., the same as أَنِسَ (M, A, Mṣb, TA) and أَنَسَ (M, Mṣb) and أَنُسَ: (M:) أَنِسَ بِفُلَانٍ is likewise explained as signifying *he delighted*, or *rejoiced, in such a one*; *he was happy*, or *pleased, with him*: (IAạr, TA:) [and ↓ آنَسَهُ, a form of frequent occurrence, inf. n. مُؤَانَسَةٌ, which occurs in this art. in the TA, also signifies *he was*, or *became, sociable*, &c., *with him*; like أَنِسَ بِهِ &c.: it is also said in the TA that ↓ آنَسَ بِهِ and أَنِسَ بِهِ are syn., meaning, app., like استأنس به and تأنّس به, and that آنس in this case is therefore of the measure فَاعَلَ; but this admits of some doubt, as it is said immediately after آنسهُ as meaning the contr. of أَوْحَشَهُ:] and ↓ اِسْتَأْنَسَ, (Ḳ, TA,) said of a wild animal, (TA,) signifies [*he became familiar*, or *tame*, or *domesticated*; or] *his wildness* (تَوَحُّشُهُ) *departed*: (Ḳ, TA:) you say إِذَا جَآءَ ٱللَّيْلُ ٱسْتَأْنَسَ كُلُّ وَحْشِيٍّ وَٱسْتَوْحَشَ كُلُّ إِنْسِيٍّ [*When the night comes, every wild animal becomes familiar with his kind, and every human being becomes shy of his kind*, i. e., of such thereof as he does not know, when meeting them in the dark]. (A, TA, Mṣb in art. وحش.)

2: أَنَّسَهُ, inf. n. تَأْنِيسٌ, *He rendered him familiar*; or *tame*. (KL.) — See also 4, in three places.

3: see 1, in two places.

4. آنَسَهُ, (M, Ḳ,) inf. n. إِينَاسٌ, (Ṣ,) *He behaved in a sociable, friendly*, or *familiar, manner with him*; [see 1, in two places;] *he*, or *it, cheered him*, or *gladdened him, by his company or converse*, or *by his*, or *its, presence*; *he*, or *it, solaced*, or *consoled, him*; *contr. of* أَوْحَشَهُ; (Ṣ,* Ḳ;) as also ↓ أَنَّسَهُ, (Ḳ,) inf. n. تَأْنِيسٌ: (Ṣ, Ḳ:) or *he*, or *it, rendered him easy, at ease*, or *tranquil*; as also ↓ the latter verb, occurring in the following ex.: سَمَّاهَا بِالْمُؤْنِسَاتِ لِأَنَّهُنَّ يُؤَنِّسْنَهُ بِأَقْرَانِهِ فَيُؤَمِّنَّهُ أَوْ يُحَسِّنَّ ظَنَّهُ [*He has called them* (referring to weapons) المؤنسات *because they render him at ease with his adversaries, and secure, or cause him to have a good opinion* of his safety, and thus, cheer him, or solace him, by their presence]. (M: [and the like is said in the A.]) — *He perceived it*; syn. of the inf. n. إِدْرَاكٌ. (TA.) — *He saw him*, or *it*, (Ṣ, M, A,* Mṣb, Ḳ,) and *looked at him*, or *it*; (M, TA;) as also ↓ أَنَّسَهُ, inf. n. تَأْنِيسٌ; (Ḳ;) and ↓ اِسْتَأْنَسَهُ: (M:) or *he saw it so that there was no doubt or uncertainty in it*: or *he saw it*, meaning a thing by the sight or presence of which he was cheered, gladdened, solaced, or consoled; إِينَاسٌ signifying إِبْصَارُ مَا يُؤْنَسُ بِهِ: (Bḍ in xx. 9:) or *he saw it, not having before known it*, or *been acquainted with it*. (TA.) — *He heard it*; namely, a sound or voice. (Ṣ, Ḳ.) — *He felt it*; *was sensible of it*; (M, Ḳ, TA;) *experienced it in himself*; (TA;) namely, [for instance,] fright, or fear. (A, TA.) — *He knew it*: (Ṣ, M, Mṣb, Ḳ:) *he was acquainted with it*: (TA:) *he had certain knowledge of it*; *was certain of it*. (M, TA.) You say, آنَسْتُ مِنْهُ رُشْدًا (Ṣ, A, TA) *I knew him to be characterized by* رُشْد, (Ṣ, TA,) i. e., *maturity of intellect, and rectitude of actions, and good management of affairs*. (TA.) [See Ḳur iv. 5.] And it is said in a prov., بَعْدَ ٱطِّلَاعٍ إِينَاسٌ, i. e. *After appearance* [*is knowledge*, or *certain knowledge*]. (Fr, TA.)

5. تأنّس به: see 1. — تَأَنَّسَ ٱلْبَازِى *The falcon looked, raising his head* (M, A, Ḳ) *and his eyes*. (A.) — تأنّس لهُ: see 10.

10. اِسْتَأْنَسَ, and استأنس به and إِلَيْهِ: see 1. — استأنس signifies also *He* (a wild animal) *became sensible of the presence or nearness of a human being*. (Ṣ, Ḳ.) — *He looked*; as in the phrase اِذْهَبْ فَٱسْتَأْنِسْ هَلْ تَرَى أَحَدًا [*Go thou and look if thou see any one*]: (Fr, TA:) *he considered*, or *examined, endeavouring to obtain a clear knowledge of a thing*; (Ḳ, TA;) *and looked aside*, or *about, to ascertain if he could see any one*: (TA:) *he sought*, or *asked for, knowledge*, or *information*; *he inquired*: (M, TA:) and hence, (Bḍ in xxiv. 27,) *he asked permission*. (Fr, Zj, Ḳ, TA, and Bḍ ubi suprà.) It is said in the Ḳur [xxiv. 27], لَا تَدْخُلُوا بُيُوتًا غَيْرَ بُيُوتِكُمْ حَتَّى تَسْتَأْنِسُوا وَتُسَلِّمُوا [*Enter ye not houses other than your own houses*] *until ye inquire* whether its inhabitants desire that ye should enter or not; [*and salute*:] (M:) or (which is essentially the same, M) *until ye ask permission*: (Fr, Zj, M, TA:) but Fr says that the sentence presents an inversion, and that the meaning is, *until ye salute, and ask if ye shall enter or not*: (TA:) I 'Ab says that تستأنسوا is a mistranscription; and he and Ubei and Ibn-Mes'ood read تَسْتَأْذِنُوا, which signifies the same: (Az, TA:) [it is said that] استأنس also signifies *he made a reiterated hemming, like a slight coughing*; [as a man does to notify his nearness;] syn. تَنَحْنَحَ: and so some explain it in the text of the Ḳur quoted above. (TA.) — استأنس لَهُ *He listened to*, or *endeavoured* or *sought to hear, him*, or *it*; as also ↓ تأنّس. (A.) [See the Ḳur xxxiii. 53.] — اِسْتَأْنَسَهُ: see 4.

أُنْسٌ *Sociableness*; *companionableness*; *conversableness*; *inclination to company* or *converse*; *friendliness*; *amicableness*; *socialness*; *familiarity*: *cheerfulness*; *gayness*; *gladsomeness*: *contr. of* وَحْشَةٌ: (T, Ṣ, A, Ḳ:) *joy*; *gladness*; *happiness*: (Ḥar p. 652:) or *ease*, or *tranquillity*: (M:) or *ease*, or *tranquillity, of heart, and freedom from shrinking*, or *from aversion*: (Mṣb:) an inf. n. of 1, (Ṣ, M,) as are also ↓ أَنَسٌ and ↓ أُنْسَةٌ (Ṣ, Ḳ) and ↓ إِنْسٌ, (M,) but this is rare as signifying the contr. of وَحْشَةٌ: (T, TA:) or ↓ إِنْسٌ is the inf. n. of أَنِسَ بِهِ; but أُنْسٌ is not: (AZ, AHát, Mṣb, TA:) this latter is a subst. from that verb [signifying as explained above]: (Mṣb:) or only signifying *converse, and companionship*, or *familiarity, with women*; (AZ, AHát, TA;) or *amatory conversation and conduct*; or the *talk of young men and young women*: (Fr, TA:) [but of all the forms above, أُنْسٌ is that which is most commonly used, at least in post-classical works, as signifying the contr. of وَحْشَةٌ.] — [Also † *Delight*, as meaning *a cause of delight*, or *thing that gives delight*.] A poet says,

* يَا سَاكِنِي مَكَّةَ لَا زِلْتُمْ *
* أُنْسًا لَنَا إِنِّى لَمْ أَنْسَكُمْ *
* مَا فِيكُمْ عَيْبٌ سِوَى قَوْلِكُمْ *
* عِنْدَ ٱللِّقَا أَوْحَشْتَنَا أُنْسُكُمْ *

[*O inhabitants of Mekkeh, may ye not cease to be a delight to us*: *verily I have not forgotten you*: *there is in you no fault beside your saying, at meeting, Your sociableness*, or *companiableness*, &c., *has made us feel lonely and sad*; meaning, in your absence]. (TA in art. وحش.) [See أَوْحَشَ. But this signification, though allowable as tropical, is perhaps post-classical.] — اِبْنُ أُنْسٍ: كَيْفَ ٱبْنُ أُنْسِكَ and فُلَانٌ ٱبْنُ أُنْسِ فُلَانٍ: and كَيْفَ تَرَى ٱبْنَ أُنْسِكَ: see إِنْسٌ.

إِنْسٌ: see أُنْسٌ, in two places. — ‡ *A chosen, select, particular*, or *special, friend* or *companion*; (Ṣ, Ḳ;) as also ↓ اِبْنُ إِنْسٍ, (Ṣ, Ḳ,) or ↓ اِبْنُ أُنْسٍ. (So in a copy of the A.) You say, هٰذَا إِنْسِى; (Ṣ;) and إِنْسُكَ, and اِبْنُ إِنْسِكَ; (Ḳ;) ‡ *This is my chosen*, or *particular, friend*; (Ṣ;) and *thy chosen*, or *particular, friend*. (Ḳ.) And فُلَانٌ اِبْنُ إِنْسِ فُلَانٍ, (Ṣ,) or ↓ فلان ابن أُنْسٍ, (A,)

‡ *Such a one is the chosen*, or *particular, friend of such a one.* (Ṣ, A.) One also says, كَيْفَ تَرَى ٱبْنَ إِنْسِكَ and ▼ أُنْسِكَ, (Ṣ, M,) or كَيْفَ تَرَى ٱبْنَ إِنْسِكَ (AZ, Fr, A) and ▼ أُنْسِكَ, (A,) meaning himself, (AZ, Fr, Ṣ, TA,) i. e., ‡ *How dost thou regard me in my companionship with thee?* (Ṣ:) or the meaning is, ‡ *how dost thou find thyself?* (A:) or *how is thyself?* (M, TA.) ═ *Mankind*; (Ṣ, M, A, Ḳ;) the *opposite of* جِنٌّ; (Mṣb;) as also ▼ أُنْسٌ, (Akh, Ṣ, TA,) and ▼ إِنْسَانٌ; (A, Ḳ;) the last being a gen. n., (Mṣb,) but applied to the male (Ṣ,* Mṣb) and female, (Ṣ, Mṣb, Ḳ,) and sing. and pl.: (Mṣb:) one is [also] termed ▼ إِنْسِىٌّ and ▼ أُنْسِىٌّ; (Ṣ, Ḳ;) the former of which is a rel. n. from إِنْسٌ; (M;) [and the latter, from أُنْسٌ: the fem. of each is with ة:] the vulgar apply to a woman, instead of ▼ إِنْسَانٌ, [which is the more approved,] ▼ إِنْسَانَةٌ: (Ṣ, Ḳ:) this latter [accord. to some] should not be used: (Ṣ:) but it is correct, though rare: it is said in the Ḳ to occur in poetry, but supposed to be post-classical: it occurs, however, in classical poetry, and has been transmitted by several authors: (MF:) the pl. (of إِنْسٌ, M, TA) is آنَاسٌ; (M, Ḳ, TA;) and (of the same, Ḳ in art. نوس, or of ▼ إِنْسَانٌ, M) أُنَاسٌ, (M, Ḳ ubi suprà,) with which نَاسٌ is syn., (Ṣ, M, Mṣb, Ḳ,) being a contraction thereof; (Sb, Ṣ, M, Mṣb;) and (of ▼ أُنْسِىٌّ, Ṣ, M, or ▼ إِنْسِىٌّ, Ṣ, or of ▼ إِنْسَانٌ, Lḥ, Ṣ, M, Mṣb) أَنَاسِىُّ, (Lḥ, Ṣ, M, Mṣb, Ḳ,) like as كَرَاسِىُّ is pl. of كُرْسِىٌّ, or like as سَرَاحِينُ is pl. of سِرْحَانٌ, but ى being substituted for ن, (M, TA,) after the same manner as they say أَرَانٍ for أَرَانِبُ; (Fr, TA;) and أَنَاسٍ, (Lḥ, M,) in the accus. case أَنَاسِىَ, as the word is read in the Ḳur xxv. 51, by Ks, (TA,) and by Yaḥyà Ibn-El-Ḥárith, (Ḳ, TA,) dropping the ى between the second and last radical letters, [for, with some others, it seems, they held the word to be derived from the root نسى,] (TA,) and أَنَاسِيَةٌ, (Ṣ, M, Ḳ,) in which the ة is a substitute for one of the two yás in أَنَاسِىُّ, a pl. of إِنْسِىٌّ; or, accord. to Mbr, أَنَاسِيَةٌ is pl. of إِنْسَانٌ, [in the TA, of إِنْسِيَّةٌ, which I regard as a mistranscription,] and is like زَنَادِقَةٌ for زَنَادِيقُ, and فَرَازِنَةٌ for فَرَازِينُ; (M, TA;) and you say also إِنْسُونَ. (TA.) نَاسٌ is masc., as in the Ḳur ii. 10, &c.; and sometimes fem., as meaning *A tribe*, or *a body of men*, قَبِيلَةٌ, or طَائِفَةٌ; as in the phrase, mentioned by Th, جَآءَتْكَ النَّاسُ, meaning, *The tribe*, or *portion of people* (قِطْعَةٌ), *came to thee.* (M, TA.) ▼ بَنُو الإِنْسَانِ means *The sons of Adam.* (M.) And النَّاسُ النَّاسُ, an expression mentioned by Sb, means, *Men in every place and in every state are men*: a poet says,

بِلَادٌ بِهَا كُنَّا وَكُنَّا نُحِبُّهَا

إِذِ ٱلنَّاسُ نَاسٌ وَٱلْبِلَادُ بِلَادُ

meaning [*A country in which we were, and which we used to love,*] *since the men were ingenuous men, and the country was a fruitful country.* (M.) The following trad., لَوْ أَطَاعَ ٱللّٰهُ ٱلنَّاسَ فِى ٱلنَّاسِ لَمْ يَكُنْ نَاسٌ *If God complied with the prayer of men with respect to men there would be no men*, is said to mean, that men love to have male children born to them, and not females, and if there were no females, or if the females were not, men would cease to be. (TA.) It is related that a party of the jinn, or genii, came to a company of men, and asked permission to go in to them, whereupon the latter said to them, Who are ye? and they answered, نَاسٌ مِنَ الجِنِّ [*A people of the jinn*], making their answer to accord. with common usage; for it is customary for men, when it is said to them, Who are ye? to answer, نَاسٌ مِنْ بَنِى فُلَانٍ [*Men of the sons of such a one*]. (IJ, M, L: but in the L, for ناس, in both instances, we find أُنَاسٌ.) [See also نَاسٌ in art. نوس.] Respecting the derivation of ▼ إِنْسَانٌ, authors differ, though they agree that the final ن is augmentative: the Baṣrees say that it is from الإِنْسُ; (Mṣb;) and its measure is فِعْلَانٌ; (Ṣ, Mṣb;) but an addition, of ى, is made in its dim., [which is أُنَيْسِيَانٌ,] like as an addition is made in رُوَيْجِلٌ, the dim. of رَجُلٌ: (Ṣ:) [but it should be observed that رُوَيْجِلٌ is more probably the dim. of رَاجِلٌ:] some say that it is from إِينَاسٌ, signifying "perception," or "sight," and "knowledge," and "sensation;" because man uses these faculties: (TA:) and Moḥammad Ibn-'Arafeh El-Wásiṭee says that men are called إِنْسِيُّونَ because they are seen (يُؤْنَسُونَ, i. e. يُرَوْنَ), and that the jinn are called جِنٌّ because they are [ordinarily] concealed (مُجْتَنُّونَ, i. e. مُتَوَارُونَ,) from the sight of men: (TA:) [it is said in the B, as cited in the TA, that the form أُنْسَان is also used for إِنْسَانٌ; as though it were a dual, meaning "a double associate," i. e., an associate with the jinn and with his own kind; for it is added, أُنْسٌ بِٱلْجِنِّ وَأُنْسٌ بِٱلْخَلْقِ:] some derive the word from النَّوْسُ, signifying "motion:" (TA:) some (namely, the Koofees, Mṣb) say that it is originally إِنْسِيَانٌ, (Ṣ, Mṣb, TA,) of the measure إِفْعِلَانٌ, (Ṣ, Mṣb,) from النِّسْيَانُ ["forgetfulness"], (Mṣb,) and contracted to make it more easy of pronunciation, because of its being so often used; (Ṣ;) but it is restored to its original in forming the dim., (Ṣ, Mṣb,) which is أُنَيْسِيَانٌ: (Mṣb, TA:) this form of the dim., they say, shows the original form of the word which is its source; (TA;) and they adduce as an indication of its derivation the saying of I 'Ab, إِنَّمَا سُمِّىَ إِنْسَانًا لِأَنَّهُ عُهِدَ إِلَيْهِ فَنَسِىَ [*He* (meaning the first man) *was only named* انسان *because he was commanded and he forgot*]: (Ṣ, TA:) [in like manner,] it is said that النَّاسُ is originally النَّاسِى; the former of these, accord. to one reading, and the latter accord. to another, occurs in the Ḳur ii. 195; the latter referring to Adam, and to the words of the Ḳur in xx. 114: (TA:) but Az holds that إِنْسِيَانٌ is of the measure فِعْلِيَانٌ, from الإِنْسُ, and similar to خِرْصِيَانٌ. (L, TA.*)

أُنْسٌ i. q. أُنْسٌ, q. v. (Ṣ, Ḳ.) ═ Also i. q. إِنْسٌ, q. v. (Akh, Ṣ, TA.) — Also *A numerous company of men*; (Ḳ,* TA;) *many men.* (TA.) — *A tribe* (حَىٌّ) *staying, residing, dwelling*, or *abiding*: (Ṣ, Ḳ:) the *people of a place of alighting or abode*: (M, TA: [but in the latter, in one place, said to be إِنْسٌ, with kesr; though a verse cited in both, as an ex., shows it to be أَنَسٌ:]) the *inhabitants of a house*: (AA, TA:) pl. (of the word in the first sense, of these three, TA, and in the second, M, TA) آنَاسٌ. (M, TA.) — *One with whom a person is sociable.* (Ḥam p. 136.) You say also, هُمْ أَنَسُ فُلَانٍ *They are they with whom such a one is sociable* (ٱلَّذِينَ يَسْتَأْنِسُ إِلَيْهِمْ). (Lḥ, M.) And هُوَ أَنَسُ خِدْمَتِهِ *He is much accustomed to the serving of him.* (Ḥar p. 472.)

أَنَسَةٌ i. q. أُنْسٌ, q. v. (Ṣ, Ḳ.)

إِنْسِىٌّ *Of*, or *belonging to, mankind*; *human*; [as also ▼ أُنْسِىٌّ, and ▼ إِنْسَانِىٌّ;] a rel. n. from إِنْسٌ. (M.) — *A human being*; *a man*; as also ▼ أُنْسِىٌّ, (Ṣ, Ḳ,) and ▼ إِنْسَانٌ. (Ṣ, A, Mṣb, Ḳ.) See إِنْسٌ, in two places. — [*Domestic, as opposed to wild.* Ex.] حُمُرٌ إِنْسِيَّةٌ *Domestic asses*; *asses that are accustomed to the houses*: commonly known as written with kesr to the ء: but in the book of Aboo-Moosà is an indication of its being with damm to the ء [أُنْسِيَّةٌ]: and as some relate a trad. in which it occurs, أَنَسِيَّةٌ, which is said to be of no account. (TA.) — The *left side* (AZ, Ṣ, M, Mṣb, Ḳ) of an animal, (Mṣb,) or of a beast and of a man, (M,) or of anything: (AZ, Ṣ, Ḳ:) or the *right side*: (Aṣ, Ṣ:) [but the latter seems to be a mistake:] Az says that Lth has well explained this term and its contrary وَحْشِىٌّ, saying that the latter is the right side of every beast; and the former, the *left* side; agreeably with those of the first authority in sound learning; and [that] it is related of El-Mufaḍḍal and Aṣ and AO, that all of them asserted the latter to be, of every animal except man, [the "far" side, or "off" side,] the side on which it is not milked nor mounted; and the former, [the *near* side,] the side *on which the rider mounts and the milker milks*: (TA in art. وحش:) [and the like is said, as a citation from Az, in the Mṣb in art. وحش: but after this, in my copy of the Mṣb, there seems to be an omission; for it is immediately added, "But Az says, This is not correct in my opinion:"] it is said that everything that is frightened declines to its right side; for the beast is approached to be mounted and milked on the left side, and, fearing thereat, runs away from the place of fear, which is the left side, to the place of safety, which is the right side: (Ṣ,* IAmb in Mṣb; both in art. وحش:) [accordingly,] Er-Rá'ee describes a beast as declining to the side termed الوحشى because frightened on the left side: (Ṣ and Mṣb in art. وحش:) and 'Antarah alludes to one's shrinking with the side so termed from the whip, [which he likens to a cat,] because the whip of the rider is in his right hand: (Ṣ in art. وحش:) but Abu-l-'Abbás says that people differ respecting these two terms when relating to a man: that, accord. to some, they mean the same in this case as in the cases of horses and other beasts of carriage, and of camels: but some say, that in the case of a man, the latter term means the part next the shoulder-blade; and the former, the *part next the arm-pit.* (TA in art. وحش.) Of every double member of a man, as the upper half of each arm, and the two fore arms, and the two feet, it means *That* [side] *which is towards the man;* and وَحْشِىٌّ, that which turns away from him: (Aṣ, Ṣ:) or, of the foot, the former means *that* [side] *which is towards the other foot;* [i. e., the *inner* side;] and the latter, the contrary of the former. (TA in art. وحش.) Of a bow, (Ṣ, M, Ḳ,) or of a Persian bow, (TA in art. وحش,) *That* [side] *which is towards thee;* (Ṣ, Ḳ;) and وَحْشِىٌّ, the back: (Ṣ and Ḳ in art. وحش:) or the former, *that* [side] *which is next to the archer;* and the latter, that which is next to the animal shot at: (M, TA:) or of a bow, whether Persian or not is not said, [the former means the side *against which the arrow lies;* and] the latter, the side against which the arrow does not lie. (TA in art. وحش.)

أُنَسِىٌّ: see إِنْسٌ and إِنْسِىٌّ, each in two places.

إِنْسَانٌ and إِنْسَانَةٌ: see إِنْسٌ, passim; and إِنْسِىٌّ. — إِنْسَانُ العَيْنِ ‡ *The image that is seen* [*reflected*] *in the black of the eye;* (Ṣ, Ḳ;) *what is seen in the eye, like as is seen in a mirror, when a thing faces it:* (Zj in his "Khalḳ el-Insán:") or *the pupil,* or *apple,* (نَاظِر,) *of the eye:* (M:) or *the black* (حَدَقَة) *of the eye:* (Mṣb:) pl. أَنَاسِىُّ, (Ṣ, Mṣb, Ḳ,) but not أَنَاسٌ. (Ṣ.)

إِنْسَانِىٌّ: see إِنْسِىٌّ, first signification.

[إِنْسَانِيَّةٌ *Human nature; humanity;* as also نَاسُوتٌ, which is probably post-classical, opposed to لَاهُوتٌ, q. v., in art. لِيه.]

أَنُوسٌ A *tame,* or *gentle, dog; contr. of* عَقُورٌ: pl. أُنُسٌ. (M, A, Ḳ.) — See also آنِسَةٌ.

أَنِيسٌ *i. q.* ▼ مُؤَانِسٌ [generally used as an epithet in which the quality of a subst. is predominant, meaning, *A sociable, companionable, conversable, friendly,* or *familiar, person; a cheerful companion*]: (Ṣ, Ḳ:) *one with whom one is sociable, companionable, conversable, friendly, familiar,* or *cheerful:* (Ḳ:) *a person,* (A,) or *anything,* (Ṣ,) *by whose company,* or *converse,* or *presence, one is cheered, gladdened, solaced,* or *consoled.* (Ṣ, A.) You say, مَا بِالدَّارِ أَنِيسٌ (or, as in some copies of the Ḳ, مِنْ أَنِيسٍ,) *There is not in the house any one by whose company,* or *converse,* or *presence, one is cheered, gladdened, solaced,* or *consoled:* (A:) or *there is not in the house any one.* (Ṣ, M, Ḳ.) [See also آنِسَةٌ.] — الأَنِيسُ † *The domestic cock;* (AA, Ḳ;) also called الشُّقَرُ. (TA.) — الأَنِيسَةُ ‡ *The fire;* (IAạr, A, Ḳ;) as also ▼ مَأْنُوسَةُ, [imperfectly decl., being a proper name and of the fem. gender,] (M,) and ▼ المَأْنُوسَةُ, (M, Ḳ,) of which [says ISd] I know no verb: (M:) because, when a man sees it in the night, he becomes cheerful and tranquil thereat, even if it be in a desert land. (TA.) You say, بَاتَتِ الأَنِيسَةُ أَنِيسَتَهُ ‡ *The fire was during night his cheerful companion,* or *his cheerer by its presence*]. (A, TA.)

آنَسُ [*More,* and *most, sociable,* &c.]. Hence, آنَسُ مِنَ الحُمَّى † [*A closer companion than fever*]: a saying of the Arabs, meaning, that fever scarcely ever quits the patient; as though it were sociable with him. (M, TA.)

جَارِيَةٌ آنِسَةٌ *A girl of cheerful mind,* (Lth, A, Ḳ, TA,) *whose nearness,* and *conversation,* or *discourse, thou lovest,* (Lth, TA,) or *whose conversation,* or *discourse,* and *nearness, are loved:* (A:) or *a girl of pleasant conversation* or *discourse;* as also ▼ أَنُوسٌ: (M:) and آنِسَةُ الحَدِيثِ *who becomes sociable, companionable, conversable, friendly, familiar,* or *cheerful, by means of thy conversation* or *discourse:* it does not mean who cheers thee [by conversation or discourse]: (Ṣ:) pl. أَوَانِسُ (Lth, A, TA) and آنِسَاتٌ: (Lth, TA:) and the pl. of أَنُوسٌ is أُنُسٌ. (M, TA.) [See also أَنِيسٌ.]

مَأْنَسٌ [app. *i. q.* مَكَانٌ مَأْنُوسٌ, q. v.] (A.)

مُؤْنِسٌ † A name which the Arabs, (Ṣ, M,) and the ancients, (M,) used to give to *Thursday;* (Ṣ, M;) because on that day they used to incline to places of pleasure; and 'Alee is related to have said that God created *Paradise* on Thursday, and named it thus. (M, TA.) — المُؤْنِسَاتُ ‡ *Weapons:* (M, A:) or *all weapons:* (Ḳ:) or *the spear and the* مِغْفَر *and the* تِجْفَاف *and the* تَسْبِغَة *and the* تُرْس (Fr, Ḳ) *and the sword and the helmet:* (IḲṭṭ, TA:) so called because they render their possessor at ease with his adversaries, and secure, or cause him to have a good opinion [of his safety, and thus, cheer him, or solace him, by their presence: see 4]. (M, A.*) — See also بَابُونَج.

مَكَانٌ مَأْنُوسٌ, (M,) and مَحَلٌّ مَأْنُوسٌ, (A,) [*A place,* and] *a place of alighting* or *abode, in which is* أُنْس [i. e. *sociableness,* &c.]: (A:) مأنوس is a kind of possessive noun, because they did not say أَنَسْتُهُ, nor أَنَسْتُ المَكَانَ. (M, L.) — مَأْنُوسَةُ and المَأْنُوسَةُ: see أَنِيسٌ.

مُؤَانِسٌ: see أَنِيسٌ.

المُسْتَأْنِسُ † *The lion;* (TṢ, Ḳ;) as also ▼ المُتَأَنِّسُ: (TṢ, TA:) or *he that is sensible of the prey from afar,* (Ḳ, TA,) *and examines and looks about for it.* (TA.)

المُسْتَأْنِسُ: see what next precedes.

انف

1. أَنَفَهُ, (T, Ṣ, M, Ḳ,) aor. ـُ (M, Ḳ) and ـِ, (Ḳ,) inf. n. أَنْفٌ, (M,) *He struck,* (T, Ṣ, Ḳ,) or *hit,* or *hurt,* (M,) *his nose;* (T, Ṣ, M, Ḳ;) namely, a man's. (Ṣ.) — *It* (the water) *reached his nose,* (T, Ṣ, Ḳ,) on the occasion of his descending into a river; (Ṣ;) as also ▼ آنَفَهُ, (Ḳ, [but in some copies written again أَنَفَهُ,]) inf. n. إِينَافٌ. (TḲ.) = أَنَفَتِ الإِبِلُ, (inf. n. as above, TA,) *The camels trod herbage,* or *pasture, such as is termed* أُنُفٌ, (ISk, Ṣ, Ḳ,) i. e., *which had not been pastured upon.* (Ṣ.) [But in the TT, as from the M, I find ▼ ائتنف, (which should rather be written ائْتَنَفَ, or, accord. to the more usual mode, آتَنَفَ,) *He trod such herbage,* or *pasture.*] = أَنِفَ, aor. ـَ, (Ṣ, M, Ḳ,) inf. n. أَنَفٌ, (M,) *He* (a camel) *had a complaint of,* or *suffered pain in, his nose, from the* بُرَة [or *nose-ring*]: (Ṣ, M, Ḳ:) from ISk. (Ṣ.) — أَنِفَتِ الإِبِلُ, accord. to certain of the Kilábees, means *The flies alighted upon the noses of the camels, and they sought places which they did not seek before.* (T.) — أَنِفَ مِنْهُ, aor. ـَ, inf. n. أَنَفٌ (Ṣ, M, Mṣb, Ḳ) and أَنَفَةٌ, (Ṣ, M, Ḳ,) or the latter is a simple subst., (Mṣb,) [*He turned up his nose at it;*] *he disdained it; scorned it; abstained from it,* or *refused to do it, by reason of disdain and pride;* (Ṣ, M, Mṣb, Ḳ;) *he disliked it,* or *hated it, and his soul was above it;* (L;) namely, a thing: (Ṣ, M, L, Mṣb:) and *he shunned it, avoided it,* or *kept himself far from it:* (Mṣb:) and *he disliked it,* or *hated it;* namely, a saying. (AZ, T, Mṣb.) You say, مَا رَأَيْتُ أَحْمَى أَنْفًا مِنْ فُلَانٍ [*I have not seen any one more vehemently disdainful,* or *scornful, than such a one*]. (Ṣ.) And حَمَلَ مِنْ ذٰلِكَ أَنَفًا *He conceived, in consequence of that, disdain,* or *scorn, arising from indignation and anger.* (TA, from a trad.) [The verb is also trans. without مِنْ: you say,] يَأْنَفُ أَنْ يُضَامَ [*He disdains,* or *scorns,* or *refuses to bear,* or *to submit to, being injured*]. (Ḳ.) [When immediately trans.,] أَنِفَ also signifies *He loathed, disliked,* or *regarded with disgust.* (IAạr, T.) You say, أَنِفَ البَعِيرُ الكَلَأَ *The camel loathed, disliked,* or *regarded with disgust, the herbage,* or *pasture.* (T.) And أَنِفَ الطَّعَامَ وَغَيْرَهُ *He disliked the food &c.* (M.) And أَنِفَتْ فَرَسِى هٰذِهِ هٰذَا البَلَدَ *This my mare disliked this region.* (T, as heard from an Arab of the desert.) And تَأْنَفُ فَحْلَهَا *She* (a woman, and a mare, and a camel, being pregnant,) *dislikes her male,* or *stallion.* (T.) And أَنِفَتْ, said of a woman, signifies *She, being pregnant, had no appetite for anything.* (Ibn-'Abbád, Ḳ.)

2: see 4. = تَأْنِيفٌ also signifies † The *sharpening,* or *making pointed, the extremity* of a thing. (Ṣ.) You say of a spear-head, or an arrow-head, or a blade, أُنِّفَ, inf. n. تَأْنِيفٌ, (Ḳ,) † *It was sharpened* or *pointed* [*at its extremity*]. (TA.) — [Used as a subst.,] †*Sharpness of the extremity* of the hock; which, in a horse, is approved. (TA.) — أُنِّفَ تَأْنِيفَ السَّيْرِ, said by an Arab of the desert in describing a horse, means †*He was made even, like as is made even the cut thong* or *strap.* (M.) = † The *seeking after herbage,* or *pasture,* (Ḳ, TA,) *such as is termed* أُنُفٌ. (TA.) — أَنَّفَ مَالَهُ, (T,) or الإِبِلَ, (Ḳ,) inf. n. as above; and ▼ آنَفَهَا, (T, Ṣ, Ḳ,) inf. n. إِينَافٌ; (T;) † *He pastured his beasts upon the first of the herbage:* (T:) or *he pursued, with the camels, repeatedly,* or *gradually,* or *step by step,* (Ṣ, Ḳ, TA,) *after the first of the herbage,* (Ṣ,) or *after the herbage* *which had not been pastured upon*: (Ḳ,* TA:) or *he went with them thereto.* (L.)

4. آنفهُ, (Ṣ, M, Ḳ,) inf. n. إِينَافٌ, (Ṣ,) *He,* (Ṣ,) or *it,* (M,) *made him to have a complaint of,* or *to suffer pain in, his nose.* (Ṣ, M, Ḳ.) — See also أَنَّفَهُ. — *He,* or *it, induced him to feel disdain, scorn, indignation, and anger;* (IF, M, Ḳ, TA;) as also ▾ انّفهُ, inf. n. تَأْنِيفٌ: (Ḳ:) or *caused him to dislike,* or *hate,* or *to loath,* or *feel disgust.* (T.) — † *He hastened it;* namely, his affair. (Ibn-'Abbád, Ḳ.) — See also 2. — آنف as an intrans. verb: see 1.

5. تَتَأَنَّفُ الشَّهَوَاتِ † *She desires of her husband, with eagerness, one thing after another, by reason of intense longing in pregnancy.* (T, the Moḥeeṭ, L, Ḳ.*) — يَتَأَنَّفُ الإِخْوَانَ ‡ *He seeks the brethren, they disdaining,* or *scorning,* or *disliking; not holding social intercourse with any one.* (TA.)

8: see 10.

10. استأنفهُ and ▾ ائتنفهُ [written with the disjunctive alif إِيتَنَفَهُ] † *He took* [*its* أَنْف, i. e.,] *the first of it:* (M:) *he began it,* or *commenced it:* (Ṣ,* M, Mṣb, Ḳ:*) or *i. q.* اِسْتَقْبَلَهُ [which has also the latter of the two significations mentioned above, (Mgh in art. قبل,) and moreover signifies *he anticipated it;* and from what follows here, it seems to be probable that this last signification, as well as the other, may be meant by it in this instance]: (T, M:) namely, a thing, (M, Mṣb,) or an affair. (T.) You say, استأنفهُ بِوَعْدٍ †*He made him a promise in anticipation; without his asking it of him.* (M.) And, of a woman, أُسْتُؤْنِفَتْ بِالنِّكَاحِ أَوَّلًا † [*She was just married,* or *bedded, for the first time*]. (M.) See also أُنُفٌ, last sentence. — [Hence, حَرْفُ ٱسْتِئْنَافٍ, in grammar, *An inceptive particle, placed at the commencement of a new proposition grammatically independent of that which precedes it.*]

أَنْفٌ a word of well-known meaning; (Lth, T, Ḳ;) The *nose;* syn. مَعْطِسٌ; (Mṣb;) the *aggregate composed of the two nostrils and the septum and the* [*bone called*] قَصَبَة, which is the hard part of the انف; (MF;) *i. q.* مَنْخِرٌ [which is evidently an explanation by a synecdoche, as this word properly signifies *nostril*]: (M:) it pertains to man and to others: (Ṣ:) ▾ أُنْفٌ is a dial. var. of the same; (MF, TA;) and so is ▾ إِنْفٌ, which is a form used by the vulgar peculiarly: (TA:) the pl. [of pauc.] is آنُفٌ and آنَافٌ (Ṣ, M, Mṣb, Ḳ) and [of mult.] أُنُوفٌ. (T, Ṣ, M, Mṣb, Ḳ.) The dual is applied to The *two nostrils;* as in the saying of Muzáḥim El-'Oḳeylee, يَسُوفُ بِأَنْفَيْهِ النِّقَاعَ [*He scents with his two nostrils the dust*]. (TA.) You say also, هُوَ يَتَتَبَّعُ أَنْفَهُ ‡ *He scents, or sniffs, the odour, and follows it.* (T, [in which, however, I find يَتْبَعُ in the place of يتتبّع,] O, L, Ḳ, TA.) And, of a she-camel, تَرْأَمُ بِأَنْفِهَا † [*She makes a show of affection with her nose, by smelling her young one;* not having true love]. (Ṣ, M, Ḳ, voce مُذَائِرٌ; &c.: see also مُعَارِضٌ.) And مَاتَ حَتْفَ أَنْفِهِ, (Ṣ, Ḳ, &c., in art. حتف,) and حَتْفَ أَنْفَيْهِ, (Ḳ ibid.,) † *He died* [*a natural death,*] *on his bed,* (Ḳ,) *without being slain or beaten* (Ṣ, Ḳ) *or drowned or burned.* (Ḳ. [See art. حتف.]) And حَمِىَ أَنْفُهُ ‡ *He became vehemently angry,* or *enraged;* as also وَرِمَ أَنْفُهُ. (IAth. [See also art. حمى.]) And رَجُلٌ حَمِىُّ الأَنْفِ ‡ *A disdainful,* or *scornful, man; who disdains,* or *scorns, being injured.* (T, Ḳ, TA. [See, again, art. حمى.]) And سَمِىُّ الأَنْفِ † [lit. *High-nosed,* signifies the same;] *i. q.* أَنِفَانُ. (T, Ḳ.) And أَنْفٌ فِى السَّمَآءِ وَٱسْتٌ فِى المَآءِ † [*A nose in the sky and a rump in the water*]; a prov., applied to him who magnifies himself in words and is little in actions. (Ḥar p. 641.) And جَعَلَ أَنْفَهُ فِى قَفَاهُ ‡ [lit. *He put his nose in the back of his neck*]; meaning *he turned away from the truth,* or *what was right, and betook himself to what was false,* or *vain:* (Ḳ, TA:) expressing the utmost degree of turning away, or turning the head, from a thing. (TA.) And أَضَاعَ مَطْلَبَ أَنْفِهِ, (M, Ḳ,) and مَوْضِعَ أَنْفِهِ, (M,) † [*He neglected,* or *left unprotected,*] *the womb from which he had come forth:* (Th, M:) or *the* فَرْج *of his mother.* (Ibn-'Abbád, Ḳ.) And هُوَ الفَحْلُ لَا يُقْرَعُ أَنْفُهُ, and لَا يُقْدَعُ, † *He is the speaker,* or *orator, who is not to be rebutted.* (TA.) أَنْفُ الأَسَدِ † [*The nose of the lion*] is *the asterism called* النَّثْرَةُ, q. v. (Ḳzw in his Description of the Mansions of the Moon.) — † [*A prominent part* of anything, as being likened to a nose;] the *extremity* of anything. (M.) [Thus,] أَنْفُ جَبَلٍ ‡ *A prominence,* or *projecting part, of a mountain.* (T, Ṣ, M, Mṣb, TA.) أَنْفُ النَّابِ, (Ṣ, M, Ḳ, TA,) in [some of] the copies of the Ḳ, erroneously, البَابِ, (TA,) ‡ *The extremity,* (Ṣ, M, Ḳ, TA,) or *edge,* (M, TA,) *of the canine tooth,* or *tush, when it comes forth.* (Ṣ, M, Ḳ, TA.) أَنْفُ خُفِّ البَعِيرِ † *The extremity of the* مَنْسِم [i. e. *toe,* or *each of the two nails of the foot,*] *of the camel.* (T, Ḳ.) أَنْفُ اللِّحْيَةِ ‡ *The fore part,* (M, TA,) or *side,* (Ḳ,) *of the beard.* (M, Ḳ, TA.) أَنْفُ النَّعْلِ † *The toe,* or *foremost extremity, of the sandal* [also called its أَسَلَة and its ذُنَابَة]. (M.) أَنْفَا القَوْسِ † *The two extremities which are in the inner sides of the two curved ends of the bow.* (M.) — † The *first,* or *first part,* of anything; (Ṣ, M, Ḳ;) relating also to times; (M;) as also ▾ مُسْتَأْنَفٌ. (M, TA.) Thus, أَنْفُ المَرْعَى † *The first of the herbage,* or *pasture.* (Ṣ,* M.) أَنْفُ المَطَرِ † *The first vegetation produced by the rain.* (T, Ḳ.) جَآءَ فِى أَنْفِ الخَيْلِ ‡ [*He came among the first of the horses,* or *horsemen*]. (TA.) سَارَ فِى أَنْفِ النَّهَارِ ‡ [*He journeyed in the first part of the day*]. (TA.) هٰذَا أَنْفُ عَمَلِ فُلَانٍ ‡ *This is the first of the things which such a one has begun to do.* (T, TA.) أَنْفُ الشَّدِّ, (T, Ṣ, M,) and العَدْوِ, (M,) † *The first of the run,* or *running:* (T:) *the most vehement thereof.* (T, Ṣ, M, Ḳ.*) أَنْفُ البَرْدِ † *The first of the cold:* (T:) *the most vehement thereof;* (T, Ṣ, M;) so says Yaạḳoob. (Ṣ.) — ‡ *A lord,* or *chief.* (IAar, T, Ḳ.) You say, هُوَ أَنْفُ قَوْمِهِ ‡ *He is the lord,* or *chief, of his people.* (TA.) — ‡ *A piece broken off of a cake of bread.* (Ḳ, TA.) — † *A part of ground, or land, that is hard, and lying open, exposed to the sun.* (IF, Ḳ.)

أُنْفٌ: see أَنْفٌ, first sentence: and see أُنُفٌ.

إِنْفٌ: see أَنْفٌ, first sentence.

أَنِفٌ A camel *having a complaint of,* or *suffering pain in, his nose, from the* بُرَة [or *nose-ring*]: (ISk, Ṣ, M, Ḳ:) or *wounded by the nose-rein, whether it be with a* خِشَاش *or* بُرَة (A 'Obeyd, T, M) *or* خِزَامَة [all of which are different kinds of nose-rings]. (A' Obeyd, T.) And consequently, *Submissive, and tractable:* (Ṣ, TA:) or *submissive and obedient, that dislikes chiding and beating, and goes as he is able to do spontaneously and easily:* (Aboo-Sa'eed, TA:) and ▾ آنِفٌ signifies the same; (A 'Obeyd, M, Ḳ;) but the former is the more correct and the more chaste: (Ṣgh, Ḳ:) by rule, it should be مَأْنُوفٌ, like مَصْدُورٌ, (T, Ṣ, M,) and مَبْطُونٌ. (T, Ṣ.) To such a camel, the believer is likened in a trad.; (T, Ṣ, M;) because he ceases not to complain, or suffer pain; (M;) or because he does not require to be chidden nor to be punished, but endures and performs what is incumbent on him. (Aboo-Sa'eed, TA.) — *Disdaining,* or *disdainful; scorning,* or *scornful; i. q.* حَمِىُّ الأَنْفِ: and ▾ أَنِفَانٌ [signifies the same;] *i. q.* سَمِىُّ الأَنْفِ. (T, Ḳ.) — See also آنِفٌ.

رَوْضَةٌ أُنُفٌ ‡ *A meadow of new herbage,* (Mṣb,) *not pastured upon* (Ṣ, Mṣb, Ḳ) *by any one;* (Ṣ;) as also ▾ مُؤْنِفٌ: (Ibn-'Abbád, Ḳ:) or *untrodden:* contracted, by poetic licence, into ▾ أُنْفٌ, in a verse of Abu-n-Nejm. (M.) And كَلَأٌ أُنُفٌ † *Herbage not pastured upon* (Ṣ, M) *by any one.* (M.) — كَأْسٌ أُنُفٌ † *A cup of wine not drunk:* (Ḳ:) or *from which one has not drunk before;* as though the drinking thereof were [but just] begun; like رَوْضَةٌ أُنُفٌ: (Ṣ:) or † *full:* and in like manner, مَنْهَلٌ أُنُفٌ † [*a full watering-place*]; (M;) or ‡ *not before drunk from.* (TA.) And خَمْرٌ أُنُفٌ ‡ *Wine of which none has before been taken from its jar.* (M, TA.*) — أَرْضٌ أُنُفٌ *i. q.* أَنِيفَةٌ, q. v. (M, TA.) — نَقِيذَةٌ أُنُفٌ † *A long* [as though *new and undiminished*] *coat of mail.* (L in art. نقذ, from El-Mufaḍḍal.) — أَمْرٌ أُنُفٌ † *An event brought to pass at the first, not being before decreed:* (Ḳ, TA:) accord. to those who assert that there is no decreeing [by God]. (TA.) — مِشْيَةٌ أُنُفٌ † *A goodly* [as though *novel*] *gait,* or *manner of walking.* (Ibn-'Abbád, Ḳ.) — آتِيكَ مِنْ ذِى أُنُفٍ is like the phrase مِنْ ذِى قُبُلٍ; i. e., فِيمَا يُسْتَقْبَلُ [*I will come to thee in what is* (now) *to be begun* (of time)]; meaning, *immediately;* nearly the same as آنِفًا, but relating to the nearest future time, whereas this latter relates to the nearest past time]. (Ṣ, Ḳ.) And افْعَلْ ذَاكَ مِنْ ذِى أُنُفٍ,

i. e., ▼ فِيمَا يُسْتَأْنَفُ [*I will do that in what is* (*now*) *to be begun* &c.]; like مِنْ ذِى عَوْضٍ. (Ḳ in art. عوض.)

أُنُفَةُ الصَّلَاةِ † *The beginning*, or *commencement*, *of prayer*; (Ḳ;) i. e. *the first saying of* ٱللّٰهُ أَكْبَرُ: (TA:) accord. to a relation of a trad., in which it occurs, with ḍamm, [أُنُفَةٌ,] (IAth, Ḳ,) but correctly with fet-ḥ. (Hr, IAth, Ḳ.) The ة seems to be here added to أُنُف as it is in ذَنَبَةٌ for ذَنَبٌ. (Ṣgh.)

أَنَفَةٌ *Disdain*; *scorn*; *disdainful and proud incompliance* or *refusal*; (Mṣb;) *indignation*; and *anger*: (TA:) a subst. [or, accord. to the Ṣ and M and Ḳ, an inf. n.] from أَنِفَ مِنْهُ. (Mṣb.)

أَنْفَانُ: see أَنِفَ.

أَنْفِيَّةٌ *Snuff, for the nose*: but this is post-classical. (TA.)

أَنُوفٌ A man *very disdainful, scornful*, or *indignant*; *very disdainfully and proudly incompliant* or *refusing*; (M;) *who disdains*, or *scorns*, *exceedingly, to do ignoble deeds*: (Ḥur p. 312:) pl. أُنُفٌ. (M.) —— A woman *whose nose has a pleasant odour*: (Ṣ, M, Ḳ:) or *whom one likes to smell*: (IAạr, M:) or *who disdains, scorns, abstains from, shuns*, or *dislikes, that in which is no good*. (Ibn-'Abbád, Ṣgh, Ḳ.)

أَنِيفٌ † A mountain *which produces vegetation before other regions*. (Ibn-'Abbád, Ḳ.) And أَرْضٌ أَنِيفَةٌ, (T, M,) or أَنِيفَةُ النَّبْتِ, (Ṣ, Ḳ,) † *Land that produces its vegetation early*: (T:) or *that produces vegetation quickly*: (Eṭ-Ṭáëe, ISk, Ṣ, Ḳ:) or *that produces vegetation*; as also ▼ أَنُفٌ. (M.) ═ Applied to iron, *i. q.* أَنِيثٌ; i. e. *Soft*. (Aboo-Turáb, T, Ḳ.)

أُنَافِىٌّ (with ḍamm, Ḳ) *Having a large nose*; (Yaạḳoob, Ṣ, M, Ḳ;) applied to a man: (M, Ḳ:) similar to عُضَادِىٌّ and أُذَانِىٌّ. (TA.)

آنَفُ [*More*, and *most, disdainful*, &c.]. You say, مَا رَأَيْتُ آنَفَ مِنْ فُلَانٍ *I have not seen any one more disdainful*, or *scornful*, or *indignant, than such a one*. (Ṣ, TA.) ═ هٰذِهِ آنَفُ بِلَادِ ٱللّٰهِ *This is the speediest, in producing vegetation, of the countries of God*. (T, Ṣ,* M,* Ḳ.*)

آنِفٌ: see أَنِفَ. ═ آنِفًا means † *In the beginning*, or *first part, of this present time in which we are*; from أَنْفٌ as meaning the "first," or "first part," of a thing: and hence what here immediately follows. (Ḥam p. 348.) مَا ذَا قَالَ آنِفًا, (T, Ṣ,* M, Ḳ,* &c.,) and ▼ أُنُفًا, (IAạr, Bḍ, Ḳ, Jel,) in the Ḳur [xlvii. 18], (M, &c.,) means ‡ *What was this that he said just now?* (Zj, T, M, Bḍ, Jel:) or, *a little while ago?* (IAạr, T, Ḳ:) i. e., *in the first time near to us?* (Zj, T, M:) from ٱسْتَأْنَفْتُ ٱلشَّىْءَ "I began the thing." (Zj, T, M.) You say also, أَتَيْتُ فُلَانًا آنِفًا ‡ [*I came to such a one a little while ago*]; like as you say, مِنْ ذِى قِبَلٍ. (Lth, T.) And جَآءَ آنِفًا ‡ *He came a little while ago*; syn. قُبَيْلُ. (M.) And ▼ فَعَلَهُ بِآنِفَةٍ, mentioned by IAạr, but not explained by him; in my opinion, [says ISd,] like فَعَلَهُ آنِفًا ‡ [*He did it a little while ago*: or *just now*]. (M.) And it is said in a trad., أُنْزِلَتْ عَلَىَّ سُورَةٌ آنِفًا *A chapter of the Ḳur-án has been sent down to me now*. (TA.)

آنِفَةٌ ‡ The *first part of life* (مَيْعَة and أَوَّلِيَّة) of a boy. (Ks, Ḳ, TA.) —— See also آنِفٌ.

مُؤَنَّفٌ: its fem., with ة, see voce مُؤْنَفٌ.

مُؤْنَفٌ: see أَنْفٌ.

مُؤَنَّفٌ †*Sharpened at its extremity*; or *pointed*; (M, Ḳ;) applied to a spear-head, or an arrow-head, or a blade, (Ḳ,) or anything. (M.) —— †*Made even*: a thong, or strap, *made of a certain measure, and evenly*. (M.) ═ إِبِلٌ مُؤَنَّفَةٌ † *Camels with which one pursues repeatedly*, or *gradually*, or *step by step, after the first of the herbage*; and so ▼ مُؤْتَنَفَةٌ: (M:) and the former epithet is applied to sheep or goats. (Ḳ.) —— The former of these two epithets, applied to a woman, signifies † *Just married* or *bedded*, (ٱلَّتِى ٱسْتُؤْنِفَتْ بِالنِّكَاحِ,) *for the first time*. (M.)

مَأْنُوفٌ A camel *that is urged on by* [*means of the rein attached to*] *his nose*. (M.)

مُؤْتَنِفٌ † A man *who begins to make use of the places of pasturing and alighting*; (M;) *who pastures his beasts upon the first of the herbage*. (Aṣ, T, Ḳ.* [In the CḲ, أُنُفَ الكَلَأِ is put for أَنْفَ الكَلَأِ.]) —— † A man (TA) *journeying in the beginning*, or *first part, of the night*: (Ḳ:) so in all the copies of the Ḳ; but correctly, as in the Moḥeeṭ and the O, *in the beginning*, or *first part, of the day*. (TA.)

مُؤْتَنَفٌ † [A place] *from which nothing has been eaten*; as also ▼ مُتَأَنَّفٌ; (Ḳ;) which latter is explained by Ibn-'Abbád as signifying a place *not eaten* [*from*] *before*. (TA.) —— جَارِيَةٌ مُؤْتَنَفَةُ ٱلشَّبَابِ † A girl [*in the prime of youth*;] *in whom no trace of agedness appears*. (Ṣgh, Ḳ.)

مُتَأَنَّفٌ: see مُؤْتَنَفٌ.

مُسْتَأْنَفٌ: see أَنْفٌ, in the latter part of the paragraph.

انق

1. أَنِقَ, aor. ـَ, inf. n. أَنَقٌ, *It excited admiration and approval by its beauty* or *goodliness*; *it pleased*, or *rejoiced*. (Mṣb.) —— Also, aor. and inf. n. as above, *He rejoiced*; *was joyful, happy*, or *pleased*. (Ṣ, Ḳ.) You say, أَنِقْتُ بِهِ, (Lth, JK, Mṣb, Ḳ,) aor. and inf. n. as above, (Lth, JK,) *I was pleased with it*, or *by it*; or *was rejoiced by it*. (Lth, JK, Mṣb, Ḳ. [In the CḲ أُعْجِبَ is erroneously put for أَعْجَبَ.]) It is said in a trad., مَا مِنْ عَاشِيَةٍ أَشَدُّ أَنَقًا وَلَا أَبْعَدُ شِبَعًا مِنْ طَالِبِ عِلْمٍ *There is not any eater by night* [i. e. any man] *who hath more pleasure and approval and desire and love* [in his pursuit, *nor any who is further from satiation* therein, *than the student*, or *pursuer, of science*]; meaning that the man of learning is excessively greedy and insatiable, persevering in vehement desire. (L.) —— And أَنِقَ ٱلشَّىْءَ, (AZ, Ḳ,) inf. n. as above, (AZ,) *He loved the thing*. (AZ, Ḳ.)

2. أَنَّقَ, inf. n. تَأْنِيقٌ, *He made*, or *caused, to wonder*. (Ḳ, TA.)

4. آنَقَنِى, (Ṣ, Mṣb, Ḳ,) inf. n. إِينَاقٌ and نِيقٌ, (Ḳ,) [but the latter is properly a quasi-inf. n.,] *It excited my admiration and approval*; *pleased me*; or *rejoiced me*. (Ṣ, Mṣb, Ḳ.) —— مَا آنَقَهُ فِى كَذَا *How vehemently does he seek*, or *pursue*, or *desire, such a thing!* or *how vehement is he in seeking, pursuit*, or *desire, with respect to such a thing!* (JK, Ḳ.)

5. تَأَنَّقَ *He sought, pursued*, or *desired, the most pleasing of things*; (TA;) [*he affected nicety*, or *refinement*; *he was dainty, nice, exquisite, refined*, or *scrupulously nice and exact*; or *chose what was excellent*, or *best*; and *he exceeded the usual bounds*; as also تَنَوَّقَ and تَنَيَّقَ, in all these senses;] فِى ٱلْمَطْعَمِ, *in respect of food, never eating anything but what was clean* [*and choice*]; and فِى ٱلْمَلْبَسِ, *in respect of apparel, never dressing otherwise than well*; and فِى ٱلْكَلَامِ, *in respect of speech, never speaking otherwise than chastely*; and فِى جَمِيعِ ٱلْأُمُورِ, *in respect of all affairs*. (TA in art. نطس.) تَأَنَّقَ فِيهِ is like تَنَوَّقَ; (JK, Ṣ, Ḳ;) i. e. *He did it*, or *performed it* (namely, a thing, or an affair,) *with* نِيقَة [i. e. *daintiness, nicety, exquisiteness, refinement, neatness*, or *scrupulous nicety and exactness*; or *in a manner exceeding what is usual*]: (Ṣ:) or *he chose what was excellent*, or *best, to be done in it, and did it admirably*: (TA:) or *he did it* (namely, his work, Mṣb) *firmly, solidly, soundly*, or *thoroughly*, (Mṣb, Ḳ,) *and skilfully*. (Ḳ: [but in this last sense, 'Alee Ibn-Ḥamzeh allows only the latter of these two verbs. TA in art. نوق.]) You say also, تَأَنَّقَ فُلَانٌ فِى ٱلرَّوْضَةِ *Such a one found himself in the meadow*, or *garden*, (وَقَعَ فِيهَا,) *pleased*, or *rejoiced, therewith*: (Ṣ:) or *he found it pleasant* or *delightful, delighted in it*, or *took pleasure* or *delight in it, and enjoyed its beauties*: and *he sought after its beauties, step by step, and was pleased*, or *rejoiced, therewith, and enjoyed it*. (TA.) And تَأَنَّقَ ٱلْمَكَانَ *He was pleased*, or *rejoiced, with the place, and attached to it, not quitting it*: (L:) *he loved the place*. (Fr, Ḳ.) It is said in a trad. of Ibn-Mes'ood, إِذَا وَقَعْتُ فِى آلِ حٰمٓ وَقَعْتُ فِى رَوْضَاتٍ أَتَأَنَّقُهُنَّ, or, as in the T, أَتَأَنَّقُ فِيهِنَّ, meaning [*When I find myself in the chapters of the Ḳur-án commencing with Ḥá Meem*,] *I find myself in meadows*, or *gardens, the beauties of which I seek after step by step, and with which I am pleased*, or *rejoiced, and which I enjoy*: i. e., I find pleasure, or delight, in reading them, or reciting them, and enjoy their beauties. (TA.)

أَنَقٌ inf. n. of 1 [q. v.]. (Lth, JK, &c.) —— [Hence, *A pleasing*, or *rejoicing, state*, or *condition*.] You say, هُوَ فِى أَنَقٍ مِنْ عَيْشِهِ وَخِصْبٍ [*He is in a pleasing*, or *rejoicing, state*, or *condition, in respect of his life, and in a state of plenty*]. (JK.) —— *Goodliness*, or *beauty, and pleasingness, of aspect,* or *outward appearance:* or, as some say, *a uniform and uninterrupted state of verdure before the eye;* because it pleases, or rejoices, its beholder. (TA.) —— *Herbage,* or *pasturage,* (Ḳ, TA,) *that is goodly,* or *beautiful, and pleasing,* or *rejoicing:* an inf. n. used as a subst. (TA.)

أَنِقٌ : see أَنِيقٌ.

مَا لَهُ فِى الشَّىْءِ أَنَقَةٌ *He has no pleasure,* or *pride, in the thing.* (JḲ.)

أَنُوقٌ *A certain bird;* (Ṣ;) i. e. the رَخَمَة [or *female of the vultur percnopterus*]; (IAạr, Ṣ;) called by Kumeyt ذَاتُ ٱسْمَيْنِ [*possessor of two names*] because having these two appellations: (Ṣ:) or the *eagle:* and also the *former bird:* (Ḳ:) ISk cites 'Omárah as saying that it is in his opinion the eagle; but that people say it is the رخمة; and he adds, [alluding to a prov., which see below,] that the eggs of the رخمة are found in ruins, and in plain country: (TA:) or the *male of the* رَخَم: (JK, TA:) or *a certain black bird, having what resembles the* عُرْف [or *comb of the cock*], (AA, Ḳ,) *that deposits its eggs in remote places:* (AA:) or *a certain black bird,* (AA, Ḳ,) *like a great hen,* (AA,) *bald in the fore part of the head,* (AA, Ḳ,) *having a yellow bill,* (Ḳ,) or *having a long bill:* (AA:) she guards her eggs, and defends her young one, and keeps with her offspring, and submits not herself to any but her mate, and migrates among the first of the migrating birds, and returns among the first of the returning birds, and will not fly while moulting, and will not be deceived by her small feathers but waits until they become quills and then flies, and will not remain constantly in the nests, and will not alight upon the quiver (Ḳ) knowing it to contain arrows: (TA:) the word is sing. and pl.: (TA:) or its pl. is أُنُقٌ. (JK.) Hence the prov., (JK, Ṣ,) أَعَزُّ مِنْ بَيْضِ ٱلْأَنُوقِ [*More rare than the eggs of the anook*]: (JK, Ṣ, Ḳ:) because this bird guards its eggs, so that they are hardly ever, or never, found; for its nests are on the tops of mountains, and in difficult and distant places; (Ṣ, Ḳ;) notwithstanding which, it is said to be stupid: (Ṣ:) ISd says that the female bird called رخمة may be meant thereby; or the male, because the eggs of the male exist not; or the eggs of the latter may be meant because he often guards them, like as does the male ostrich. (TA.)

أَنِيقٌ *Goodly,* or *beautiful;* (Ṣ, Ḳ;) *pleasing,* or *rejoicing;* (JK, Ṣ, Mṣb, Ḳ;) as also ▼ أَنِقٌ: (JK, TA:) and *loved.* (TA.) You say, رَوْضَةٌ أَنِيقٌ *A meadow,* or *garden, that is loved:* and رَوْضَةٌ أَنِيقَةٌ *a meadow,* or *garden, that is pleasing,* or *rejoicing.* (TA.)

لَهُ إِنَاقَةٌ and أَنَاقَةٌ (Ḳ, and so in some copies of the Ṣ,) *He has goodliness,* or *beauty,* and *pleasingness:* but in the L, [and in some copies of the Ṣ,] لَهُ إِنَاقَةٌ وَلَبَاقَةٌ; and what precedes it indicates that the meaning is *he has a faculty of doing well* or *excellently* [*and of nice* or *refined skilfulness*]. (TA.)

آنَقُ [originally أَأْنَقُ] *More,* or *most, pleasing* or *rejoicing.* (TA.)

مُتَأَنِّقٌ [part. n. of 5; *Seeking, pursuing,* or *desiring, the most pleasing of things; affecting nicety,* or *refinement; dainty, nice, exquisite, refined,* &c.; in respect of food, apparel, speech, &c.:] one *who is in a pleasing condition* (فِى أَنَقٍ) *in respect of his life, and in a state of plenty.* (JK.) It is said in a prov., لَيْسَ ٱلْمُتَعَلِّقُ كَٱلْمُتَأَنِّقِ, (JK, TA,) i. e. *He who is content with what is little,* (Ṣ, Ḳ, in art. علق,) or *what is barely sufficient, of sustenance,* (TA in the present art.,) *is not like him who seeks, pursues, or desires, the most pleasing of things,* or *who is dainty,* &c., (مَنْ يَتَأَنَّقُ,) *and eats what he pleases,* (Ṣ, Ḳ, in art. علق,) or *him who is not content save with the most pleasing of things.* (TA in the present art.)

انك

آنُكٌ *Pure* رَصَاص [or *lead*]: or *black* رصاص: (Mṣb:) *i. q.* أُسْرُبٌ; (Ṣ, Ḳ;) i. e. رَصَاصٌ قَلْعِىٌّ; so says Ḳt; and Az says, I think it is an arabicized word: (TA:) or *white* اسرب: or *black* اسرب: or *pure* اسرب: (Ḳ:) or *i. q.* قَزْدِيرٌ [which is applied in the present day to *tin,* and *pewter*]: (Kr:) El-Ḳásim Ibn-Maan says, I heard an Arab of the desert say, هٰذَا رَصَاصٌ آنُكٌ, i. e. [*this is*] *pure* [*lead*]: (TA:) it is of the measure أَفْعُلٌ, [originally أَأْنُكٌ,] (Ṣ, Ḳ,) which is one of the forms of pls., (Ṣ,) like أَفْلُسٌ; (Mṣb;) and there is no other word of this measure, (Az, Ṣ, Ḳ,) among sing. nouns, (Az, Ṣ,) except أَشُدٌّ [originally أَشْدُدٌ], (Ṣ, Ṣgh, Ḳ,) and آجُرٌ in the dial. of those who pronounce it without teshdeed: (Ṣgh:) it is disputed, however, whether أَشُدٌّ be a sing. or a pl.: (Az, TA:) [and as to آجُرٌ, see what follows:] or, accord. to some, (Mṣb,) آنُكٌ is of the measure فَاعُلٌ, (Kr, Mṣb,) and is the only word of that measure in Arabic: (Kr:) or it is a foreign word; and so are آجُرٌ and [the proper names] آمُلُ and كَابُلُ. (Mṣb.) It is said, in a trad., that he who listens to a singing female slave, آنُكٌ shall be poured into his ears (Ṣ, TA) on the day of resurrection. (TA.)

انم

ٱلْأَنَامُ (T, M, Mṣb, Ḳ) and ▼ ٱلْآنَامُ (Ḳ) and ▼ ٱلْأَنِيمُ, (M, Ḳ,) the last allowable in poetry, (M,) *i. q.* ٱلْخَلْقُ; (M, Ḳ, and Bḍ and Jel in lv. 9;) i. e. [*Mankind;* for such is the general meaning of ٱلْخَلْقُ, or] *mankind and the jinn* (or *genii*) *and others:* (Jel ubi suprà:) or *the jinn and mankind:* (T, Mṣb, Ḳ:) or *what are on the face of the earth of all that are termed* ٱلْخَلْقُ [or *created beings*]: (Lth, T, Mṣb:) or *all that is on the face of the earth:* (Ḳ:) or *everything having a* رُوح [i. e. *soul,* or *spirit*]: (Bḍ ubi suprà:) or *every one who is subject to sleep.* (TA [as though it were derived from ٱلنَّوْمُ.]) الانام is not mentioned by J, though occurring in the Ḳur-án. (TA.)

ٱلْأَنِيمُ : } see above.
ٱلْآنَامُ : }

انما

إِنَّمَا : see إِنَّ, in art. ان.

انو

إِنْوٌ : see إِنًى, in two places.

انى

1\. أَنَى, (Ṣ, M, Ḳ,) aor. يَأْنِى, (Ṣ,) inf. n. إِنًى (Ṣ, M, Ḳ) and أَنْىٌ and أَنَآءٌ, (M, Ḳ,) or, accord. to [some of the copies of] the M, أَنًى, (TA, [in which this is said to be the right form,]) or أَنًا, (as written in the CḲ,) said of a thing, *Its time came;* or *it was,* or *became,* or *drew, near;* syn. أَنَى وَقْتُهُ, and جَآءَ أَنَاهُ; (Bḍ lvii. 15 [in explanation of a passage cited voce أَنْ];) or حَانَ: (Ṣ, M, Ḳ:) or أَنَى, aor. يَأْنِى, inf. n. أَنْىٌ, signifies *it was,* or *became,* or *drew, near;* and *it was,* or *became, present.* (Mṣb.) You say, أَنَى لَكَ أَنْ تَفْعَلَ, aor. يَأْنِى; and آنَ لك, aor. يَئِينُ; and أَنَالَ لك, aor. يَنِيلُ; and نَالَ لك; all meaning حَانَ لَكَ [*The time has come,* or *has drawn near, for thee that thou shouldst do* such a thing: or *the time of thy doing* such a thing *has come to thee:* or *thy doing* such a thing *has drawn near*]: so says Zj; and Fr says the like: but the best of these is أَنَى لَكَ. (T.) And أَنَى ٱلرَّحِيلُ *The time of departure came,* or *drew near;* syn. حَانَ وَقْتُهُ. (TA, from a trad.) —— *It came,* or *attained, to its time; to its full,* or *final, time* or *state; to maturity,* or *ripeness; it became mature,* or *ripe;* (T, Ṣ, M, IAmb,* Mṣb,* Ḳ;) or, accord. to some, only when said of a plant; (M, Ḳ;) [or it signifies also] *it became thoroughly cooked.* (T, Mṣb.*) Hence, in the Ḳur [xxxiii. 53], غَيْرَ نَاظِرِينَ إِنَاهُ *Not waiting,* or *watching, for its becoming thoroughly cooked;* or *for its cooking becoming finished.* (T, Ṣ,* M.) [See also إِنًى, below.] You say also, أَنَى ٱلْحَمِيمُ, (inf. n. أَنْىٌ, TA,) *The hot water became heated to the utmost degree.* (Ṣ, Ḳ.) And أَنَى ٱلْمَآءُ *The water became hot to the utmost degree.* (M.) == أَنِىَ, aor. يَأْنَى, inf. n. أَنْىٌ, *It* (a thing) *was,* or *became, behind,* or *after, its time:* (Lth, T:) or أَنَى, inf. n. أُنِىٌّ, *it,* or *he,* (a man, TA,) *was,* or *became, behind, backward,* or *late; it,* or *he, delayed,* or *held back;* (M, Ḳ;) as also أَنِىَ, aor. يَأْنَى, inf. n. إِنًى; and ▼ تَأَنَّى, inf. n. تَأَنِّيَةٌ. (Ḳ.) —— See also 5, in two places.

2: see 4, in two places: == and see 1. —— You say also, أَنَّيْتُ فِى ٱلشَّىْءِ *I fell short,* or *fell short of what was requisite* or *what I ought to have done,* or *flagged,* or *was remiss, in,* or *in respect of, the thing.* (TA. [The verb is there written without any syll. signs; but the context seems to indicate that it is as above.])

4\. آنى and ▼ أَنَّى signify the same. (IAạr, T, M.) You say, آنَاهُ, (T, Ṣ, M, Mṣb, Ḳ,) with medd, (Mṣb,) aor. يُؤْنِيهِ, (Ṣ,) inf. n. إِينَآءٌ, (Ṣ, Ḳ,) [in the CḲ, آنَيْتُهُ إِنًا is erroneously put for آنَيْتُهُ إِينَآءً,] *He postponed it, put it off, deferred it, delayed it, retarded it;* (T, Ṣ, M, Mṣb, Ḳ;) *restrained* *it, withheld it, impeded it;* (Ṣ, TA;) whatever the thing be. (T.) And أَنَّيْتُ ↓ الطَّعَامَ فِى النَّارِ *I kept the food long upon the fire.* (TA.) And لَا تُؤَنِّ فُرْصَتَكَ *Postpone not thou, or defer not, thine opportunity, or the time when thou art able to do a thing.* (T.) And it is said in a trad., respecting the prayer of Friday, رَأَيْتُكَ آنَيْتَ وَآذَيْتَ (M,* Mgh,* TA) *I see thee to have delayed* coming, *and to have done what is annoying* to others by stepping over the necks [of those already in their places in the mosque]: (Aṣ, Mgh,* TA:) a saying of 'Omar. (Mgh.) ═ آنَاهُ also signifies *He made him, or it, to be distant, remote,* or *far off; removed far away, alienated,* or *estranged, him, or it;* like أَنْآهُ [from which it is formed by transposition]. (TA.) [Hence,] يُؤْنِيكَ occurs in a verse of Es-Sulameeyeh; (M, TA;) meaning يُنْئِيكَ; the ء being put before the ن. (M.)

5. تَأَنَّى *He acted deliberately,* or *leisurely, not hastily;* as also ↓ اِسْتَأْنَى; and ↓ أَنِىَ, (M, Ḳ,) aor. يَأْنَى, (Ḳ,) inf. n. أَنْىٌ: (TA:) *he acted with moderation, gently, deliberately,* or *leisurely; without haste;* and *with gravity, staidness, sedateness,* or *calmness;* فِى الأَمْرِ *in the affair;* as also ↓ اِسْتَأْنَى: (Mgh:) or *he acted gently;* (IAạr, T, TA;) as also ↓ أَنِىَ, aor. and inf. n. as above: (TA:) or *he acted gently, and waited;* فِى الأَمْرِ *in the affair:* (Ṣ:) or *he waited,* or *was patient,* or *waited with patience,* (T, Mṣb,) *and did not hasten,* in an affair. (Mṣb.) التَّأَتِّى and التَّأَنِّى are nearly syn.: you say, تَأَنَّى لَهُ *He acted gently with him,* [or *to him,*] *and did not hasten in his affair.* (Mgh.) You say also, اِسْتَأْنَى ↓ بِهِ *He waited patiently with him;* or *waited, and had patience, with him;* (Ṣ, TA;) *he did not hasten him;* (Lth, T;) as also ↓ اِسْتَأْنَاهُ. ('Eyn, Ḥar p. 67.) And أُسْتُؤْنِىَ ↓ بِهِ حَوْلًا [*He was waited patiently with for a year*]. (Ṣ.) And اِسْتَأْنِ ↓ فِى أَمْرِكَ *Hasten not in thine affair.* (Lth, T.) And اِسْتَأْنَيْتُ ↓ فِى الطَّعَامِ *I waited for the food to become perfectly prepared* or *cooked.* (Ḥar p. 67.) And تَأَنَّيْتُ الرَّجُلَ (and عَلَيْهِ, M and Ḳ in art. نظر, [see اِنْتَظَرَهُ,]) *I waited for the man;* as also ↓ اِسْتَأْنَيْتُ بِهِ: whence, يُسْتَأْنَى ↓ بِالْجِرَاحَاتِ *One should wait for the issues,* or *consequences,* or *results, of wounds.* (Mgh.) And تَأَنَّيْتُكَ حَتَّى لَا أَنَاةَ بِى [*I have waited patiently for thee until there is no disposition to wait patiently in me*]. (Ṣ.)

10: see 5, passim.

أَنْىٌ: see what next follows.

إِنْىٌ (AO, T, Ṣ, M, Mṣb, Ḳ) and ↓ إِنًى, (Akh, T, Ṣ, Mṣb,) the latter in [some of] the copies of the Ḳ erroneously written أَنَآءٌ, (TA,) [and in other copies of the same omitted,] and ↓ إِنْوٌ, (Akh, Th, T, Ṣ, M, Ḳ,) with و substituted for ى, (AAF, M,) and ↓ أَنْىٌ (Ḳ) and ↓ أَنًى, (M, IAmb,) *An hour,* or *a short portion,* or *a time,* or *an indefinite time,* (سَاعَةٌ,) *of the night:* (Zj, T, Ṣ, M, Ḳ:) or *a time* or *season* (وَقْتٌ) of the night: (M in art. انو:) or i. q. وَهْنٌ [*the period about midnight;* or *the time after an hour,* or *a short period, of the night;* or *when the night is departing*]: (M, Ḳ:) or *any* سَاعَة [i. e. *hour,* or *short portion,* or *time,*] (M, Ḳ) of the night: (M:) [and *any period of time;* as will be seen below:] or, accord. to some, (M,) ↓ إِنًى signifies *the whole day;* (M, Ḳ;) as also ↓ أُنِىٌّ: (Ḳ:) the pl. is آنَآءٌ (T, Ṣ, M, Mṣb, Ḳ) and أُنِىٌّ and إِنِىٌّ. (M, Ḳ.) You say, مَضَى إِنْىٌ مِنَ اللَّيْلِ and ↓ إِنْوٌ [&c.] *A time,* or *season,* [&c.,] (وَقْتٌ, [&c.,]) *of the night passed:* (M in art. انو:) dual إِنْوَانِ and إِنْيَانِ. (Ṣ.) And a poet says,

أَتَمَّتْ حَمْلَهَا فِى بَعْضِ شَهْرٍ
وَحَمْلُ الحَامِلَاتِ إِنًى طَوِيلُ

[*She completed her gestation in a portion of a month; but the gestation of the pregnant* in general *is a long period of time*]. (IAạr, T.) Another uses the phrase ضَحَّاكُ الأَنْىِ, occurring at the end of a verse, [for ضَحَّاكُ الأَنِىِّ,] meaning *Found to be laughing whenever one comes to him.* (M.)

أَنًى: see إِنْىٌ, in two places. — The *utmost point, reach,* or *degree,* (M, Ḳ,) of a thing; (M;) as also ↓ إِنًى: so in the phrase, بَلَغَ أَنَاهُ and إِنَاهُ *It* (a thing, M) *attained its utmost point, reach,* or *degree:* (M, Ḳ:) or this means, [or, accord. to the CḲ, "and" it means,] *its state of being thoroughly cooked; its state of maturity;* or *its full,* or *final, time* or *state.* (Ḳ.) [See 1, where an ex. from the Ḳur xxxiii. 53 is cited. Both words are said to be inf. ns.] ═ See also أَنَاةٌ.

إِنًى: see إِنْىٌ, in two places: — and see أَنًى.

أَنَآءٌ [*Postponement; a putting off; a deferring; a delaying; a retarding: restraint; a withholding; an impeding:*] a subst. from آنَاهُ, aor. يُؤْنِيهِ, inf. n. إِينَآءٌ, meaning "he postponed it," &c.: (Ṣ, Mṣb,* TA:) the context of the Ḳ erroneously requires it to be understood as a subst. from أَنِىَ, aor. يَأْنَى. (TA.)

إِنَآءٌ *A certain thing of which one makes use,* (M,) *well known;* (Ṣ, Ḳ;) namely, *a vessel,* or *receptacle,* (Mgh, Mṣb,) *for water* [&c.]: (Mgh:) pl. آنِيَةٌ, (T, Ṣ, M, Mgh, Mṣb, K,) originally أَأْنِيَةٌ; (M;) and أَوَانٍ; (T, Ṣ, M, Mgh, Ḳ;) the former a pl. of pauc.; and the latter a pl. of mult., (Mgh,) pl. of آنِيَةٌ. (T, Ṣ, M.)

أَنَاةٌ *Moderation; gentleness; deliberateness; a leisurely manner of proceeding,* or *of deportment,* &c.; *patience,* as meaning *contr. of hastiness:* and *gravity; staidness; sedateness; calmness:* a subst. from تَأَنَّى; (Ṣ, Mṣb;) syn. تُؤَدَةٌ; (T;) and رِفْقٌ; (Ḥam p. 317;) and حِلْمٌ and وَقَارٌ; (M, Mgh, Ḳ;) as also ↓ أَنًى. (M, Ḳ, TA. [In the CḲ, كَالأَنِّى is erroneously put for كَالأَنَى.]) — Also *Hope:* [in this sense, accord. to the TA, written with kesr; but this is doubtless a mistake, probably occasioned by a mistranscription:] so in the charge of 'Orweh to his sons; يَا بَنِىَّ إِذَا رَأَيْتُمْ خَلَّةً رَائِعَةً مِنْ رَجُلٍ فَلَا تَقْطَعُوا أَنَاتَكُمْ مِنْهُ وَإِنْ كَانَ عِنْدَ النَّاسِ رَجُلَ سَوْءٍ [*O my sons, when ye see a quality exciting admiration and approval, in a man, cut not ye off your hope of him, though he be in the estimation of the people a bad man*]. (M.) ═ A woman *in whom is a languor on the occasion of rising,* or *standing up;* (T, Ṣ, Ḳ;) *and a gentle,* or *grave, deportment:* (Ṣ:) or *in whom is a languor impeding from rising,* or *standing up:* (Aṣ:) and وَهْنَانَةٌ signifies the like: (T:) Sb says that it is originally وَنَاةٌ, like as أَحَدٌ is originally وَحَدٌ; from الوَنَى: (Ṣ:) the people of El-Koofeh say that it is only وَنَاةٌ: so says Lth: and he says that أَنَاةٌ signifies, as applied to a woman, *blessed, prospered,* or *abounding in good,* as it is explained also by ADḳ, and *forbearing, gentle, grave, staid, sedate,* or *calm,* and *compliant,* or *agreeing with another in mind* or *opinion:* and the pl. is أَنَوَاتٌ: or, as some say, it signifies a *grave, staid, sedate,* or *calm,* woman, *who does not clamour, nor utter foul language.* (T.)

آنٍ, as part. n. of 1, A thing *of which the time has come,* or *drawn near:* and *which has come,* or *attained, to its time; to its full,* or *final, time* or *state; to maturity,* or *ripeness:* but accord. to some, only applied to a plant. (M, Ḳ.) [Compare آنٌ.] ═ *Behind,* or *after, the time; backward,* or *late; delayed,* or *held back;* (Ḳ, TA; [but wanting in a MS. copy of the former in my possession, and in the CḲ;]) as also ↓ آنٍ. (TA.)

إِنِيهْ a word expressive of disapproval, and of deeming a thing remote or improbable: Sb relates that it was said to an Arab of the desert, who had taken up his abode in a town, or place, "Wilt thou go forth when the desert shall have become plentiful in herbage?" and he said, أَأَنَا إِنِيهْ [*What, I, indeed?*], meaning "Do ye say this to me when I am known to do thus?" as though he disapproved of their questioning him: but there is much diversity of opinion respecting this word: (TA:) [accord. to some,] it is composed of the redundant إِنْ and the meddeh denoting disapproval [followed by the ه of silence]. (Mughnee voce إِنْ.) [See what is said of the redundant اِنْ in the present work.]

أَنَّى signifies *Whence?* syn. مِنْ أَيْنَ; (T, Ṣ, M;) being an interrogative respecting the direction, or quarter, from which a thing is: (Mṣb:) and *whence* [used to denote a condition]: (TA:) and *where?* and *where* [used to denote a condition]; syn. أَيْنَ: (T, Ḳ: [in which latter the first signification is not mentioned:]) and as one of the adverbial nouns used to denote a condition, *whencesoever; from whatever direction* or *quarter:* (Ṣ:) and *wherever; wheresoever:* (Lth, T:) and *when?* and *when* [used to denote a condition]; syn. مَتَى: (T, Ḳ: [but in the latter of these, in art. ان, in the place of مَتَى we find حَيْثُ, which I regard as a mistake:]) and *how?* syn. كَيْفَ: (Lth, T, Ṣ, M, Ḳ:) and *however.* (Lth, TA.) [I mention all these significations together because one of them is assigned by some authorities and another by others to أَنَّى in one and the same instance.] You say, أَنَّى يَكُونُ هٰذَا *Whence, from what direction* or *quarter, from what way, will,* or *should, be this?* (Mṣb.) And أَنَّى لَكَ هٰذَا *Whence* [came, or cometh,] *to thee this?* (Ṣ.) It is said in the Ķur [iii. 32], يَا مَرْيَمُ أَنَّى لَكِ هٰذَا *O Mary, whence* [came] *to thee this?* (T.) And in the same [xxxiv. 51], وَأَنَّى لَهُمُ ٱلتَّنَاوُشُ مِنْ مَكَانٍ بَعِيدٍ, meaning [*But*] *whence* [*shall the attaining* of belief *be* possible *to them from a distant place,* i. e., (as explained in the Ṣ in art. نوش,) in the world to come, when they have disbelieved in the present world? or *but how* &c.?]. (T.) And in the same [lxxx. 25], accord. to one reading, أَنَّى صَبَبْنَا ٱلْمَآءَ صَبًّا, meaning *Where have we poured forth the water, pouring?* but in this is an allusion to the direction [whence the rain comes]; and it may be rendered *whence?* &c.; and accord. to this reading, the pause upon طَعَامِهِ [immediately preceding] is complete. (IAmb, T.) And you say, أَنَّى تَأْتِنِى آتِكَ, (Ṣ, Ķ,) meaning *Whencesoever,* or *from whatever direction* or *quarter, thou shalt come to me, I will come to thee.* (Ṣ.) In the saying of 'Alkameh,

• وَمُطْعَمُ ٱلْغُنْمِ يَوْمَ ٱلْغُنْمِ مُطْعَمُهُ •
• أَنَّى تَوَجَّهَ وَٱلْمَحْرُومُ مَحْرُومُ •

the meaning is, [*And he who is given spoil to enjoy,* (lit., who is fed therewith,) *on the day of spoil, is given it to enjoy*] *wherever he repairs,* or *however he repairs,* [*and the prohibited is prohibited.*] (Lth, T, TA.) The saying in the Ķur [iii. 159], قُلْتُمْ أَنَّى هٰذَا means *Ye say, When is this?* or *How is this?* (T,) or *Whence is this?* (T, Bḍ, Jel.) And أَنَّى شِئْتُمْ, in the same, [ii. 223,] may mean *Whence,* or *when,* or *how, ye will.* (TA.) You say also, أَنَّى لَكَ أَنْ تَفْتَحَ ٱلْحِصْنَ, meaning *How* [*is it,* or *will it be, possible for thee to open, or conquer, the fortress*]? (Ṣ.)

آنٍ *Hot,* or *heated, to the utmost degree:* applied to hot water, (Ṣ, M, Ķ,) in the Ķur lv. 44: (Ṣ, M:) fem. آنِيَةٌ; occurring in the Ķur lxxxviii. 5. (M.) — See also أَنِىٌّ. — Also A man *much characterized by moderation, gentleness,* or *deliberateness; by a leisurely manner of proceeding,* or *of deportment, &c.; by patience,* as meaning *contr. of hastiness; by gravity, staidness, sedateness,* or *calmness.* (Ṣ, Ķ.*)

أَتَيْتُهُ آنِيَةً بَعْدَ آنِيَةٍ is a phrase mentioned by AAF, meaning *I came to him time after time:* in which, [says ISd,] I am of opinion that آنِيَة is of the measure فَاعِلَة from ٱلْإِنَى: but the word commonly known is آوِنَة [pl. of أَوَان; or آيِنَة, which is syn. with آوِنَة: see أَوَان]. (M.)

انيه

إِنْيَهْ: see art. انى.

اه

1. أَهَّ, (Ṣ in art. اوه, and Ķ,) inf. n. أَهٌّ (Ķ) and أَهَّةٌ (Ṣ,* Ķ) and the same without teshdeed; (Ķ,* TA;) [app. meaning أَهَةٌ, which, however, belongs to art. اوه, q. v.;]) or إِهَّةٌ; (so in the CĶ; [but in some copies of the Ķ, and ▼ أَهَّهَ, as in the TĶ, where it is said that the inf. n. of this form of the verb is تَأْهِيهٌ;]) and ▼ تَأَهَّهَ; (Ķ;) [*i. q.* أَوَّهَ *and* آهَ *and* تَأَوَّهَ; or] *He expressed pain* or *grief* or *sorrow,* or *he lamented* or *complained* or *moaned,* (Ṣ, Ķ,) *as one in an evil state, and broken in spirit by grief* or *mourning, and said* آه, or هَاهْ. (Ķ.) [See a verse cited in art. اوه, voce آهَةٌ.]

2 and 5: see above.

إِهْ, i. e. إِ with the ه of pausation; imperative of وَأَى, q. v. (Mughnee in art. الف.)

آهِ and أَهْ and آهًا &c.: see art. اوه.

اهب

2. أَهَّبَهُ لِلْأَمْرِ, [inf. n. تَأْهِيبٌ,] *He furnished, prepared, equipped,* or *accoutred, him, for the thing,* or *affair; he furnished him,* or *provided him, with the apparatus, gear, tackling, implements, instruments, tools,* or *the like, proper,* or *necessary, for it.* (MF.) — أَهَّبَ ٱلْأَمْرَ *He prepared the thing,* or *affair.* (MF.) — See also 5.

5. تَأَهَّبَ *He furnished, prepared, equipped,* or *accoutred, himself; furnished,* or *provided, himself with proper,* or *necessary, apparatus, gear, tackling, implements, instruments, tools,* or *the like;* (Ṣ, A, Mṣb, Ķ;) لِلسَّفَرِ *for journeying;* (Mṣb;) or لِلْأَمْرِ *for the thing,* or *affair;* as also ▼ أَهَّبَ. (Ķ.)

أَهَبٌ: see إِهَابٌ.

أُهْبَةٌ *Apparatus, equipments, equipage, accoutrements, furniture, gear, tackling, implements, instruments, tools,* or *the like;* (Ṣ, A, Mṣb, Ķ;) as in أُهْبَةُ ٱلْحَرْبِ [*the apparatus, arms, weapons, equipage,* or *accoutrements, of war*]; (Ṣ;) as also هُبَةٌ: (Ķ:) pl. of the former, أُهَبٌ. (Ṣ, Mṣb.) You say, أَخَذَ لِذٰلِكَ ٱلْأَمْرِ أُهْبَتَهُ [*He took his apparatus,* &c., *for that thing,* or *affair;* also meaning, *he made his preparation,* or *he prepared himself, for it*]. (TA.)

إِهَابٌ *A skin,* or *hide,* (A, Mṣb, Ķ,) in an absolute sense, (A,) of a bull or cow, sheep or goat, or wild animal: (TA:) or *a skin,* or *hide, not yet tanned:* (Ṣ, A, Mgh, Mṣb, Ķ:) and sometimes applied to the ‡ *skin* of a man: (Mṣb:) pl. (of pauc., TA) آهِبَةٌ (IAạr, Ķ) and (of mult., TA) أُهُبٌ, (Ṣ, A, Mgh, Mṣb, Ķ,) with two dammehs, (Mgh, Mṣb,) and ▼ أَهَبٌ, (Ṣ, Mṣb, Ķ,) contr. to rule, (Ṣ, Mṣb,) or, accord. to Sb, (L,) this last is a quasi-pl. n.: (Mgh, L:) in one copy of the Ķ, it is written أُهْبٌ. (TA.) You say, جَاعُوا حَتَّى أَكَلُوا ٱلْأُهُبَ [*They hungered so that they ate the skins,* or *hides*]. (A.) And كَادَ يَخْرُجُ مِنْ إِهَابِهِ فِى عَدْوِهِ † [*He almost issued from his skin in his running*]. (A.) And حَقَنَ ٱلدِّمَآءَ فِى أُهُبِهَا † [*He spared the people's blood in their bodies*]. (TA, from a trad.)

اهل

1. أَهَلَ, aor. ـُ, inf. n. أُهُولٌ; (Mṣb;) or أُهِلَ, like عُنِىَ; (Ķ, TA;) *It* (a place, Mṣb, TA) *was,* or *became, peopled,* or *inhabited.* (Mṣb, Ķ, TA.) — أَهَلَ, aor. ـُ and ـِ, inf. n. as above, *He married,* or *took a wife;* (Yoo, Ṣ, Mṣb, Ķ;) as also ▼ تَأَهَّلَ; (Ṣ, Mgh, Mṣb, Ķ;) and ▼ ٱتَّهَلَ, [written with the disjunctive alif إِتَّهَلَ, like ٱتَّخَذَ and ٱتَّزَرَ and ٱتَّمَنَ &c.,] (Ķ,) of the measure افتعل. (TA.) — أَهَلَ; (Ks, Ṣ, Mṣb;) or أَهِلَ, aor. ـَ; (Ķ;) or both; (JK;) بِهِ, (JK,) i. e. بِٱلرَّجُلِ, (Ks, Ṣ,) or بِٱلشَّىْءِ; (Mṣb;) *i. q.* أَنِسَ [*He was,* or *became, sociable, companionable, friendly, amicable,* or *familiar, with him,* i. e. *the man;* or *he was,* or *became, cheered,* or *gladdened, by his company* or *converse,* or *by his,* or *its* (*the thing's*) *presence*]. (JK, Ṣ, Mṣb, Ķ.)

2. أَهَّلَ بِهِ, (Ķ,) or أَهَّلَهُ, (Ḥam p. 184,) inf. n. تَأْهِيلٌ, (Ḥam, Ķ,) *He said to him* أَهْلًا: (Ḥam:) or *he said to him* مَرْحَبًا وَأَهْلًا: (Ķ:) like رَحَّبَ بِهِ: (TA:) [see أَهْلٌ:] IB says that [the first pers. of] the aor. of this verb is with fet-ḥ to the ء [contr. to rule: a strange assertion]. (TA.) — أَهَّلَهُ لِذٰلِكَ, inf. n. as above; and ▼ آهَلَهُ; *He saw him, judged him, thought him,* or *held him, to be worthy,* or *deserving, of that; to merit it; to have a right,* or *just title* or *claim, to it:* (Ķ,* TA:) or *he made him to be worthy,* or *deserving, of that;* &c. (TA.) You say, أَهَّلَكَ ٱللّٰهُ لِلْخَيْرِ [*May God make thee worthy,* or *deserving, of good, good fortune, prosperity,* or *the like*]. (Ṣ.)

4. آهَلَكَ ٱللّٰهُ فِى ٱلْجَنَّةِ, inf. n. إِيهَالٌ, *May God make thee to enter with thy wife into Paradise:* (AZ, Ṣ, TA:) or *may God make thee to have a family in Paradise, and unite thee with them* [*therein*]. (TA.) — See also 2.

5: see 1.

8: see 1.

10. اِسْتَأْهَلَهُ as signifying *He was,* or *became, worthy,* or *deserving, of it,* or *he merited it,* or *he had a right,* or *just title* or *claim, to it,* is not allowable: (Mṣb,* MF:) not only does J disallow it, but the generality of those before him do so; saying that it is not chaste: in the Fṣ it is said to be of weak authority; and the expositors thereof confirm this assertion, saying that it occurs, but is inferior to other words in chasteness; and El-Ḥareeree asserts it to be erroneous: (MF:) or it is good in this sense; and J's disallowance of it is of no account: (Ķ:) Az and Z and Ṣgh and others assert it to be good: and Az says, in the T, some have asserted the saying فُلَانٌ يَسْتَأْهِلُ أَنْ يُكْرَمَ أَوْ يُهَانَ, as meaning [*Such a one*] *is worthy,* or *deserving,* [*of being treated with honour, or of being held in light estimation,*] to be erroneous; and ٱلِٱسْتِئْهَالُ to be only from ٱلْإِهَالَةُ; but I do not disallow it, nor charge with error him who says thus; for I have heard the verb thus used by a chaste Arab of the desert, of the Benoo-Asad, and there was present a number of Arabs of the desert who did not disapprove his saying: and this is confirmed by the saying in the Ķur

[lxxiv. 55], هُوَ أَهْلُ التَّقْوَى وَأَهْلُ المَغْفِرَةِ [explained below: see أَهْلٌ]. (T.) —— استأهل, (JK, Ḳ,) or استأهل الإِهَالَةَ, (Mṣb,) *He took the* إِهَالَة: (JK, Ḳ:) or *he ate the* اهالة: see this word below. (Mṣb, TA.)

أَهْلٌ [The *people* of a house or dwelling, and of a town or village, and of a country: and the *family* of a man:] a man's *cohabitants of one dwelling* or *place of abode*, (Er-Rághib, Kull p. 84,) and *of one town* or *country*: (Er-Rághib:) afterwards applied to a man's *fellow-members of one family* or *race*, and *of one religion*, and *of one craft* or *art* or *the like*: (Er-Rághib, Kull:) or, as some say, *relations, whether they have followers* or *dependents, or not*; whereas آل signifies relations with their followers or dependents: (Kull:) or it originally signifies *relations*: and sometimes is applied to *followers* or *dependents*: and signifies also the أَهْل [i. e. *people*, or *inhabitants*, or *family*,] *of a house* or *tent*: (Mṣb:) or a man's *nearer*, or *nearest*, *relations by descent from the same father or ancestor*; or his *kinsfolk*; his *relations*: (Ḳ:) or, accord. to [the Imám] Moḥammad, a man's *wife* [or *wives*] *and his children and household who are the objects of his expenditure*; and thus, *any brother and sister*, or *paternal uncle and son of a paternal uncle*, or *strange* or *distantly-related child*, *whom a man feeds or sustains in his abode*: the *most particular*, or *most special*, *dependents*, or *the like*, of a man: on the authority of El-Ghooree: (Mgh:) [J indicates some of these meanings merely by saying that it signifies] the أَهْل of a man, and the أَهْل of a house; as also ↓ أَهْلَةٌ: (Ṣ:) [see also آل; in the explanations of which, certain distinctions between it and أَهْل will be found mentioned:] the pl. is أَهْلُونَ, [like أَرْضُونَ, a form sometimes used for أَرَضُونَ,] (Mgh, Mṣb, Ḳ,) and أَهَالٍ, (Ṣ, Mgh, Mṣb, Ḳ,) with an additional ى, [implied by the tenween, and expressed in the accus. case, and when the word is determinate, as in الأَهَالِى,] (Ṣ,) contr. to rule, (Ṣ, Mgh,) like لَيَالٍ, pl. of لَيْلٌ, (Ṣ,) [and like أَرَاضٍ, respecting which and أَهَالٍ and لَيَالٍ, see أَرْضٌ,] and آهَالٌ, (Ṣ, Ḳ,) a pl. [of pauc.] sometimes occurring in poetry, (Ṣ,) [like آرَاضٌ,] and أَهَلَاتٌ and أَهْلَاتٌ [as though pls. of أَهْلَةٌ]. (Ṣ, Ḳ.) —— أَهْلُ البَيْتِ The [*people* or] *inhabitants* [or *family*] *of the house* or *tent*. (Mgh, Ḳ.) But أَوْصَى لِأَهْلِ بَيْتِهِ means the same as اوصى لِجِنْسِهِ, i. e. *He left by will*, of his property, *to the children of his father*, [or *his kindred by the father's side*,] *exclusively of all relations of the mother*. (Mgh in art. جنس.) [See also أَهْلُ الرَّجُلِ, below.] —— أَهْلُ القُرَى *The* [*people* or] *inhabitants of the towns* or *villages*. (TA.) And أَهْلُ البَلَدِ *The settled*, or *constant*, *inhabitants of the country* or *town*. (Mṣb.) And أَهْلُ الحَضَرِ *The people of the region*, or *regions*, *of cities, towns*, or *villages, and of cultivated land*. (A in art. حضر.) And أَهْلُ المَدَرِ وَالوَبَرِ (Ṣ in art. مدر, &c.) [*The people of the towns* or *villages*, or] *the inhabitants of the buildings, and of the tents*, (Kull,) or *deserts*. (TA in art. وبر.) —— [أَهْلُ القُبُورِ, and المَقَابِرِ, *The people of the graves, and of the places of graves*; i. e., *those buried therein*.] —— [أَهْلُ الجَنَّةِ *The people of Paradise*.] —— [أَهْلُ النَّارِ *The people of the fire*, i. e., *of Hell*.] —— See also أَهْلَةٌ. —— The following is an ex. of اهل as explained above in the first sentence on the authority of the Ḳ: الأَهْلُ إِلَى الأَهْلِ أَسْرَعُ مِنَ السَّيْلِ إِلَى السَّهْلِ a prov. [meaning *Kinsfolk are quicker of tendency to kinsfolk than the torrent to the plain*]. (TA.) So, too, a saying of a poet cited voce خفض. (TA.) [And] أَهْلَكَ وَاللَّيْلَ a prov. meaning بَادِرْ أَهْلَكَ وَٱحْذَرِ اللَّيْلَ وَظُلْمَتَهُ [*Betake thyself early to thy family, and beware of the night and its darkness*]. (Ḥar p. 175.) [And] مَرْحَبًا وَأَهْلًا (Ṣ, Ḳ) a saying meaning *Thou hast come to an ample*, or *a spacious*, or *roomy*, *place, and to* [people like thine own] *kinsfolk*; therefore be cheerful, or sociable, not sad, or shy: (Ṣ:) or *thou hast found*, or *met with*, [*an ample*, or *a spacious*, or *roomy*, *place, and*] *kinsfolk, not strangers*. (Ḳ.) [And] أَهْلًا وَسَهْلًا وَمَرْحَبًا *Thou hast come to a people who are* [like] *kinsfolk, and to a place that is plain, even, not rugged, and that is ample, spacious*, or *roomy*; therefore rejoice thyself, and be not sad, or shy. (Mṣb.) —— أَهْلُ النَّبِىِّ *The* [*family* or] *wives and daughters of the Prophet, and his son-in-law 'Alee*: or *his women*; *and* (as some say, TA) *the men who are his* آل; (Ḳ, TA;) *comprising the grandchildren* (أَحْفَاد) *and* [*other*] *progeny*: and so أَهْلُ البَيْتِ as used in the Ḳur xxxiii. 33, occurring also [in a like sense] in xi. 76: (TA:) and الأَهْلُ is conventionally applied to *the nearer*, or *nearest*, *kinsfolk of the Prophet*. (Er-Rághib.) —— أَهْلُ كُلِّ نَبِىٍّ also means *The people to whom any prophet is sent*; (Ḳ, TA;) and *those who are of his religion*. (TA.) —— In the phrase آلُ ٱللّٰهِ وَرَسُولِهِ, meaning *The friends*, or *the like*, (أَوْلِيَآء, Ḳ, TA,) and *the assistants*, (TA,) *of God and of his apostle*, the first word is originally أَهْل. (Ḳ, TA.) —— أَهْلُ ٱللّٰهِ is also an appellation which used to be applied to *The readers* or *reciters* [*of the Ḳur-án*]. (TA.) —— أَهْلُ الرَّجُلِ also signifies ‡ *The man's wife*; (Mgh,* Mṣb,* Ḳ;) as well as *his wife and children*; (TA;) [so, too, in the present day, أَهْلُ بَيْتِ الرَّجُلِ;] and so, too, ↓ أَهْلَتُهُ. (Ḳ.) Hence the phrase بَنَى عَلَى أَهْلِهِ [see art. بنى]: (Kull:) and دَخَلَ بِأَهْلِهِ and دَخَلَ عَلَى أَهْلِهِ [see art. دخل]. (Ḥar p. 502; &c.) —— أَهْلُ مَذْهَبٍ [*The people of*, or] *those who follow*, (Ḳ, TA,) *and believe*, (TA,) *a certain persuasion*, or *body of tenets*. (Ḳ, TA.) [Hence,] أَهْلُ السُّنَّةِ [*Those who conform to the institutes of Moḥammad*]. (TA.) [And] أَهْلُ الأَهْوَآءِ [*The people of erroneous opinions*;] *those whose belief is not that of the class termed* أَهْلُ السُّنَّةِ, *but who have the same* قِبْلَة. (TA.) [And] أَهْلُ الإِسْلَامِ *Those who follow the religion of El-Islám*. (Mgh.) [And] أَهْلُ القُرْآنِ *Those who read*, or *recite, the Ḳur-án, and perform the duties enjoined thereby*. (Mgh.) [And] أَهْلُ الكِتَابِ [*The people of the Scripture*, or *Bible*: and] *the readers*, or *reciters*, *of the Mosaic Law, and of the Gospel*. (TA.) —— أَهْلُ العِلْمِ [*The people of knowledge*, or *science*;] *those who are characterized by knowledge*, or *science*. (Mṣb.) —— أَهْلُ الأَمْرِ [*The possessors of command*: or] *those who superintend the affairs* [*of others*]; (Ḳ, TA;) like أُولُو الأَمْرِ, q. v. (TA.) —— أَهْلُ المَرَاتِبِ [*The people of exalted stations, posts of honour*, or *dignities*]. (TA in art. رتب.) —— أَهْلُ الذِّمَّةِ (Mgh in art. ذم) and أَهْلُ العَهْدِ (TA in art. عهد) *Those persons*, (Mgh, TA,) *of the unbelievers*, (Mgh,) [namely, *Christians, Jews*, and *Sabians*, but no others,] *who have a compact*, or *covenant*, *with the Muslims*, (Mgh, TA,) *paying a poll-tax, whereby they are secure of their property and blood*, (Mgh,) or *whereby the Muslims are responsible for their security* [*and freedom and toleration*] *as long as they act agreeably to the compact*. (TA.) —— أَهْلٌ also signifies The *possessors*, or *owners*, of property: as in the Ḳur iv. 61. (TA.) —— أَهْلٌ لِكَذَا A person, (Ṣ, Ḳ,) and persons, for it is used as a sing. and as a pl., (Ḳ,) *having a right*, or *just title, to such a thing*; *entitled thereto*; *worthy*, or *deserving*, *thereof*; *meet*, or *fit*, *for it*: (Ṣ, Ḳ:) the vulgar say ↓ مُسْتَأْهِلٌ, which is not allowable: (Ṣ:) or this assertion of J's is of no account. (Ḳ: see 10.) You say, هُوَ أَهْلٌ لِلْإِكْرَامِ *He is entitled to be*, or *worthy of being*, *treated with honour*. (Mṣb.) And هُوَ أَهْلَةٌ ↓ لِكُلِّ خَيْرٍ [*He is entitled to*, or *worthy of*, *all that is good*]. (Ibn-'Abbád.) And ↓ أَهْلَةُ وُدٍّ *He who is*, or *they who are*, *entitled to*, or *worthy of*, *love*, or *affection*. (Ṣ, Ṣgh.) And hence, in the Ḳur [lxxiv. last verse], هُوَ أَهْلُ التَّقْوَى وَأَهْلُ المَغْفِرَةِ (TA) *He is the Being entitled to be regarded with pious fear, and the Being entitled to forgive* those who so regard Him. (Jel.) In the phrase أَهْلَ الثَّنَآءِ وَالمَجْدِ [*O Thou who art the Being entitled to praise and glory*], occurring in a form of prayer, the first word is manṣoob as a vocative: and it may be marfooʼ, as the enunciative of an inchoative suppressed; i. e. أَنْتَ أَهْلُ [*Thou art the Being entitled* &c.]. (Mṣb.) —— [Frequently, also, أَهْلٌ signifies The *author*, or, more commonly, *authors*, of a thing; like صَاحِبٌ and أَصْحَابٌ; as in أَهْلُ البِدَعِ *The author*, or *authors*, *of innovations*; and أَهْلُ الظُّلْمِ *The author*, or *authors*, *of wrong*.]

أَهْلِىٌّ: see أَهِلٌ.

أَهْلَةٌ: see أَهْلٌ, in four places: —— and see أَهِلَةٌ.

أَهِلَةٌ *i. q.* مَالٌ [*Property*; or *cattle*]: so in the saying إِنَّهُمْ لَأَهْلُ أَهِلَةٍ (JK, Ḳ) [app. meaning *Verily they are sojourners*, or *settlers*, *possessed of property*, or *cattle*]: ↓ أَهْلٌ here signifying حُلُولٌ [pl. of حَالٌّ]. (JK, TA.) [But] Yoo says that هُمْ أَهْلُ ↓ أَهْلَةٍ and أَهِلَة means *They are people of the distinguished sort*. (TA.)

أَهِلٌ ↓ أَهْلِىٌّ *A domestic* beast [or bird]; a beast [or bird] *that keeps to the dwelling* [*of its owner*];

(JK, Mṣb, Ḳ, TA;) *contr. of* وَحْشِىٌّ; (TA;) as also ↓ أَهِلٌ. (Ḳ.) You say حُمُرٌ أَهْلِيَّةٌ [*Domestic asses*]: (JK, TA:) occurring in a trad., in which their flesh is forbidden to be eaten. (TA.)

أَهْلِيَّةٌ The *quality of having a right*, or *just title*, to a thing; *worthiness*, or *desert; meetness*, or *fitness*; in Pers. سَزَاوَارِى: (Golius, app. from a gloss. in a copy of the KL:) the *state*, or *quality, of meetness*, or *fitness*, [of a person,] *for the bindingness of the rights which the law imposes for one* or *upon him*. (TA.)

إِهَالَةٌ *Grease*: (Ṣ:) or *melted grease*: (Mṣb:) or *fat*: or *melted fat*: or *olive-oil*: and *anything that is used as a seasoning* or *condiment*: (Ḳ:) *such as fresh butter*, and *fat*, and *oil of sesame*: (TA:) or *melted fat of a sheep's tail* and *the like*. (JK.) Hence, سَرْعَانَ ذَا إِهَالَةً, a prov., mentioned in art. سرع; (Ḳ,* TA;) or, as some say, وَشْكَانَ. (TA.)

آهِلٌ, (JK, Ṣ, Mṣb, Ḳ,) [said by those unacquainted with the verb أَهَلَ in the first of the senses explained in this art. to be] a kind of rel. n., (TA,) and ↓ مَأْهُولٌ, (JK, Ḳ,) *A place peopled*, or *inhabited*: (Mṣb:) or a place *having people*: (JK:) or the former has this signification; and the latter signifies *having its people in it*: (ISk, Ḳ:) or the former has this last signification: (Yoo, Ṣ:) pl. of the latter مَآهِلُ, occurring in a poem of Ru-beh [app. by poetic licence for مَآهِيلُ]. (TA.) You say قَرْيَةٌ آهِلَةٌ *A peopled*, or *inhabited, town* or *village*. (Mṣb.) And أَمْسَتْ نِيرَانُهُمْ آهِلَةً *Their fires became in the evening attended by many people*. (TA.)

مَأْهُولٌ: see آهِلٌ. — ثَرِيدَةٌ مَأْهُولَةٌ [*A mess of crumbled bread*] *having much* إِهَالَة, q. v. (A, TA.)

مُتَأَهِّلٌ *Having a wife*. (Ḥar p. 571.)

مُسْتَأْهِلٌ: see أَهْلٌ; latter part of the paragraph. — Also *Taking*, or *eating*, إِهَالَة, q. v. (Ṣ.)

او

أَوْ a conjunction, (M, Mughnee, Ḳ,) to which the later authors have ascribed meanings amounting to twelve: (Mughnee:) a particle which, when occurring in an enunciative phrase, [generally] denotes doubt, and vagueness of meaning; and when occurring in an imperative or a prohibitive phrase, [generally] denotes the giving of option, or choice, and the allowing a thing, or making it allowable. (Ṣ.) — First, (Mughnee,) it denotes doubt. (T, Ṣ, M, Mṣb, Mughnee, Ḳ.) So in the saying, رَأَيْتُ زَيْدًا أَوْ عَمْرًا [*I saw Zeyd or 'Amr*]. (T,* Ṣ, Mṣb.) And جَآءَنِى رَجُلٌ أَوِ امْرَأَةٌ [*A man or a woman came to me*]. (Mbr, T.) And لَبِثْنَا يَوْمًا أَوْ بَعْضَ يَوْمٍ [in the Ḳur xviii. 18 and xxiii. 115, *We have remained a day or part of a day*]. (Mughnee.) — Secondly, (Mughnee,) it denotes vagueness of meaning. (Ṣ, Mṣb, Mughnee, Ḳ.) So [it may be used] in the first of the exs. given above. (Mṣb.) And so in the saying, وَإِنَّا أَوْ إِيَّاكُمْ لَعَلَى هُدًى أَوْ فِى ضَلَالٍ مُبِينٍ [*And verily we or ye are following a right direction or in manifest error*], (Ṣ, Mughnee,) in the Ḳur [xxxiv. 23]; (Ṣ;) the ex. being in the former او. (Mughnee.) — Thirdly, (Mughnee,) it denotes the giving of option, or choice. (T, Ṣ, M, Mughnee, Ḳ.) So in the saying, كُلِ السَّمَكَ أَوِ اشْرَبِ اللَّبَنَ [*Eat thou the fish, or drink thou the milk*]; i. e. do not thou both of these actions; (Mbr, T, Ṣ;) but choose which of them thou wilt. (Mbr, T.) And تَزَوَّجْ هِنْدًا أَوْ أُخْتَهَا [*Take thou as wife Hind or her sister*]. (Mughnee.) And [in like manner] it denotes the making choice. (T.) [So when you say, سَأَتَزَوَّجُ هِنْدًا أَوْ أُخْتَهَا, meaning *I will take as wife Hind or her sister*; whichever of them I choose.] — Fourthly, (Mughnee,) it denotes the allowing a thing, or making it allowable. (T, Ṣ, Mṣb, Mughnee, Ḳ.) So in the saying, جَالِسِ الحَسَنَ أَوِ ابْنَ سِيرِينَ [*Sit thou with El-Hasan or Ibn-Seereen*]. (Mbr, T, Ṣ.) And قُمْ أَوِ اقْعُدْ [*Stand thou or sit*]: and the person to whom this is said may do [one or] both of these actions. (Mṣb.) [And similar exs. are given in the Mughnee.]) But وَلَا تُطِعْ مِنْهُمْ آثِمًا أَوْ كَفُورًا [in the Ḳur lxxvi. 24, *And obey not thou, of them, a sinner or a person very ungrateful to God*,] means that thou shalt not obey either of such persons: (Mbr, T, Mughnee:) in which case او is more forcible than وَ; for when you say to a person, لَا تُطِعْ زَيْدًا وَعَمْرًا [*Obey not thou Zeyd and 'Amr*], he may obey one of them, since the command is that he shall not obey the two. (Zj, T.) — Fifthly, (Mughnee,) it denotes unrestricted conjunction. (Mughnee, Ḳ.) So in the saying, in the Ḳur [iv. 46 and v. 9], أَوْ جَآءَ أَحَدٌ مِنْكُمْ مِنَ الغَائِطِ [*And if any one of you cometh from the privy*]; (TA;) [where, however, it may also be rendered *or*, though] meaning وَجَآءَ; (T, TA;) the و in this explanation being what is termed a denotative of state. (T.) So, too, accord. to AZ, in the expression أَوْ يَزِيدُونَ [*And they exceeded* that number], in the Ḳur [xxxvii. 147]: but see below. (TA.) And so in the words, أَوْ أَنْ نَفْعَلَ فِى أَمْوَالِنَا مَا نَشَآءُ [*And our doing, in respect of our possessions, what we will*], in the Ḳur [xi. 89]. (T, TA.) — Sixthly, it denotes transition, (Mughnee,) used in the sense of [the adversative particle] بَلْ, (T, Ṣ, M, Mughnee, Ḳ,) in a case of amplification of speech; (Ṣ;) accord. to Sb, on two conditions; that it shall be preceded by a negation or a prohibition, and that the agent shall be mentioned a second time; as in مَا قَامَ زَيْدٌ أَوْ مَا قَامَ عَمْرٌو [*Zeyd did not stand: nay, rather 'Amr did not stand*]; and لَا يَقُمْ زَيْدٌ أَوْ لَا يَقُمْ عَمْرٌو [*Let not Zeyd stand: nay, rather let not 'Amr stand*]. (Mughnee.) Accord. to Fr, (Th, M, Mughnee,) it has this meaning in أَوْ يَزِيدُونَ [*Nay, rather they exceeded* that number], (Th, Ṣ, M, Mughnee,) in the Ḳur [xxxvii. 147, cited above]: (Ṣ:) or the meaning is, *or they would exceed* [that number] in your estimation: or these words with those preceding them in the same verse mean, we sent him to a multitude of whom, if ye saw them, ye would say, They are a hundred thousand, *or they exceed* [that number]; (M, Mughnee;*) so that it denotes doubt on the part of men, not of God, for He is not subject to doubt: (M:) or we sent him to a hundred thousand in the estimation of men, *or they exceeded* [that number] in the estimation of men; for God does not doubt: (Ṣ:) or او is here used to denote vagueness of meaning: (IB, Mughnee:) or, it is said, to denote that a person might choose between saying, "they are a hundred thousand," and saying, "they are more;" but this may not be when one of the two things is the fact: or, accord. to some of the Koofees, it has the meaning of وَ: and each of these meanings, except the last, has been assigned to او as occurring in the Ḳur ii. 69 and xvi. 79. (Mughnee.) — Seventhly, it denotes division; (Mughnee, Ḳ;*) as in the saying, الكَلِمَةُ اسْمٌ أَوْ فِعْلٌ أَوْ حَرْفٌ [*The word is a noun or a verb or a particle*]: so said Ibn-Málik: or, as he afterwards said, in preference, it denotes separation (التَّفْرِيق) divested of the attribute of denoting doubt and vagueness of meaning and the giving of option or choice; adducing as one of his exs. of this meaning the saying, وَقَالُوا كُونُوا هُودًا أَوْ نَصَارَى [in the Ḳur ii. 129, *And they said, "Be ye Jews" or "Christians"*]; because the use of و in division is better; as when you say, الكَلِمَةُ اسْمٌ وَفِعْلٌ وَحَرْفٌ: or it denotes, accord. to some, distinction (التَّفْصِيل); and the meaning of the ex. last cited, say they, is, *and the Jews said, "Be ye Jews," and the Christians said, "Be ye Christians."* (Mughnee.) It is [said to be] used in this last sense (that of التفصيل) in the saying, كُنْتُ آكُلُ اللَّحْمَ أَوِ العَسَلَ [*I used to eat flesh-meat or honey*]; i. e. *I used to eat flesh-meat one time and honey another time*: and so in the Ḳur vii. 3 and x. 13. — Eighthly, (Mughnee,) it is used in the sense of the exceptive إِلَّا, (Mughnee, Ḳ,) or إِلَّا أَنْ; (M;) and in this case the aor. after it is manṣoob, because of أَنْ suppressed. (Mughnee, Ḳ.) So in the saying, لَأَقْتُلَنَّهُ أَوْ يُسْلِمَ [*I will assuredly slay him or he shall become a Muslim*; i. e., *unless he become a Muslim*]. (Mughnee. [And a similar ex. is given in the M.]) So, too, in the saying,

• وَكُنْتُ إِذَا غَمَزْتُ قَنَاةَ قَوْمٍ •
• كَسَرْتُ كُعُوبَهَا أَوْ تَسْتَقِيمَا •

[*And I used, when I pinched and pressed the spear of a people, to break its knots*, or *joints*, or *its internodal portions*, (the shaft being a cane,) *or*, i. e. *unless, it became straight*]: (Mughnee, Ḳ:*) a prov., of which the author is Ziyád El-Aajam; meaning, when a people behaved with hardness to me, I endeavoured to soften them: (TA in art. غمز:) thus related by Sb, the verb ending it being rendered manṣoob by او; and thus he heard it from some one or more of the Arabs; but in the original verses, which are but three, it is تَسْتَقِيمُ, with refa. (IB and TA in art. غمز.) [And similar to these above are the sayings,] إِنَّهُ لَفُلَانٍ أَوْ مَا بِنَجْدٍ قَرَظَةٌ [*Verily it belongs to such a one or there is not*, i. e. *unless there be not, in Nejd, a* قَرَظَة (see art. قرظ)]: and لَآتِيَنَّكَ أَوْ مَا بِنَجْدٍ قَرَظَةٌ [*I will assuredly come to thee or there* is not, i. e. *unless there be not, in Nejd, a* قَرَظَة]; meaning *I will assuredly come to thee, in truth.* (T.) — Ninthly, (Mughnee,) it is used in the sense of إِلَى, (Mughnee, Ḳ,) or إِلَى أَنْ; (Ṣ;) in which case also the aor. after it is manṣoob, because of أَنْ suppressed: (Mughnee:) and in the sense of حَتَّى [which is also syn. with إِلَى]. (Fr, T, M, Ḳ.) So in the saying, لَأَضْرِبَنَّهُ أَوْ يَتُوبَ [*I will assuredly beat him until he repent*]. (Ṣ. [And similar exs. of او as explained by حَتَّى are given in the T (from Fr) and in the M and in the Mughnee.]) And so in the saying of the poet,

لَأَسْتَسْهِلَنَّ الصَّعْبَ أَوْ أُدْرِكَ المُنَى •
فَمَا آنْقَادَتِ الآمَالُ إِلَّا لِصَابِرِ •

[*I will assuredly deem easy what is difficult until I attain the objects of wish; for hopes become not easy of accomplishment save to one who is patient*]. (Mughnee.) — Tenthly, some say, (Mughnee,) it denotes nearness [of one event or thing to another]; as in the saying, مَا أَدْرِى أَسَلَّمَ أَوْ وَدَّعَ [*I know not whether he saluted or bade farewell*]: (Mughnee, Ḳ: [but in the CḲ this ex. is misplaced:]) this, however, is manifestly wrong; او being here used to denote doubt, and the denoting of nearness being only inferred from the fact of the saluting being confounded in the mind with the bidding farewell, since this is impossible or improbable when the two times are far apart. (Mughnee.) — Eleventhly, (Mughnee,) it occurs as a conditional, (T, Mughnee, Ḳ,) accord. to Ks alone; (T;) or rather as a conjunctive and conditional; وَإِنْ being meant to be understood in its place; though in truth the verb that precedes it indicates that the conditional particle [إِنْ] is meant to be understood [before that verb], and او retains its proper character, but forms part of that which has a conditional meaning because conjoined with a preceding conditional phrase. (Mughnee.) So in the saying, لَأَضْرِبَنَّهُ عَاشَ أَوْ مَاتَ, (Mughnee, Ḳ,) i. e., إِنْ عَاشَ بَعْدَ الضَّرْبِ وَإِنْ مَاتَ [*I will assuredly beat him if he live* (after the beating) *or if he die*]: so says Ibn-Esh-Shejeree. (Mughnee.) — Twelfthly, accord. to Ibn-Esh-Shejeree, on the authority of some one or more of the Koofees, (Mughnee,) it denotes division into parts, or portions; as in the saying [in the Ḳur ii. 129, before cited,] وَقَالُوا كُونُوا هُودًا أَوْ نَصَارَى, (Mughnee, Ḳ,) i. e. *And they said, "Be ye, some of you, Jews, and, some of you, Christians:"* (TA:) but [IHsh says,] it appears to me that the meaning here is that of التَّفْصِيل mentioned before. (Mughnee.) — [In the Ḳ it is said to occur also in the sense of أَنْ: but this is evidently a mistake, app. originating in one of the two principal sources of the Ḳ, namely, the M, in which the same is said, but is exemplified by a phrase in which it is explained by إِلَّا أَنْ, the eighth of the meanings of أَوْ mentioned above.] — See also أَوٌّ, below.

أَوَ in أَوَلَمْ يَرَوْا &c. is [the conjunction] وَ with the interrogative ا prefixed to it. (Fr, T.)

أَوْ مِنْ كَذَا (T, M) and أَوِ (M) [*Alas, on account of,* or *for, such a thing!*] an expression denoting complaint of distress, or of anxiety, or of grief or sorrow; (T;) or an expression of grief or sorrow; (M;) like ▼ آوِ and ▼ آوِ and ▼ أَوْتَاهُ, (Ḳ and TA in art. اوه,) or ▼ أَوَّتَاهُ, (CḲ in that art.,) or ▼ أَوْتَاهْ, or ▼ آوَّتَاهْ, (Ṣ in that art., [the ه in one copy of which is marked as quiescent,]) and like آهِ and أَوْهِ and &c. (Ṣ and Mṣb and Ḳ in art. اوه: see آهِ in that art.) AZ says, one says, أَوْهِ عَلَى زَيْدٍ [meaning *Alas, for Zeyd!*] with kesr to the ه, and ▼ أَوَّتَا عَلَيْكَ [thus without ه, meaning *Alas, for thee!*] with ت; an expression of regret for a thing, whether of great or mean account. (T.)

أَوٌّ The *word* ▼ أَوْ *when made a noun.* (T, Ḳ.) So say the grammarians. (T.) You say, هٰذِهِ أَوٌّ حَسَنَةٌ [*This is a good* أَوْ]. (T.) And to one who uses the phrase أَفْعَلُ كَذَا أَوْ كَذَا, (T,) you say, دَعِ الأَوَّ جَانِبًا [*Let thou,* or *leave thou, the word* أَوْ *alone*]. (T, Ḳ.)

أَوَّةٌ [*A moaning* (see its syn. آهَةٌ in art. اوه)] is said by some to be of the measure فَعْلَةٌ, in which the ة is the sign of the fem. gender; for they say, سَمِعْتُ أَوَّتَكَ [*I heard thy moaning*], making it ت: and so says Lth; أَوَّةٌ is after the manner of فَعْلَةٌ: (T:) you say, أَوَّةً لَكَ [May God cause *moaning to thee!*], (Lth, T, and Ṣ in art. اوه,) and آهَةً لَكَ: [but accord. to J, the former of these is cognate with the latter; for he says that] the former is with the ه suppressed, and with teshdeed to the و. (Ṣ in art. اوه, where see آهَةٌ.) — أَوَّتَا عَلَيْكَ; and أَوَّتَاه, or آوَّتَاه, or أَوْتَاه, or أَوْتَاهُ: see أَوِ مِنْ كَذَا.

أَوَّةٌ i. q. دَاهِيَةٌ [*A calamity, a misfortune,* &c.: or, perhaps, *very cunning,* applied to a man]: pl. أَوُوٌ; (AA, T, Ḳ, TA; [but in copies of the Ḳ, written أُوُوٌ;]) which is one of the strangest of the things transmitted from the Arabs; the regular form being أُوًى, like قُوًى, pl. of قُوَّةٌ; but the word occurring as above in the saying of the Arabs, مَا هُوَ إِلَّا أَوَّةٌ مِنَ الأَوُوِ [*It is no other thing than a calamity of the calamities*: or, perhaps, *he is no other than a very cunning man of the very cunning*]. (AA, T, TA.)

آوِ and آوِ: see أَوِ: and see آهِ in art. اوه.

أَوِيٌّ and أُوَوِيٌّ: see آيَةٌ, in art. اى.

آوَّتَاه: see أَوِ.

اوب

1. آبَ, aor. يَؤُوبُ, (T, Ṣ, &c.,) inf. n. أَوْبٌ (Ṣ, M, Mṣb, Ḳ) and إِيَابٌ and أَوْبَةٌ (T, Ṣ, M, Ḳ) and أَيْبَةٌ, (M, Ḳ,) ى taking the place of و, (M,) and إِيبَةٌ (Lḥ, M, Ḳ) and مَآبٌ [like مَآلٌ], (Mṣb, TA,) *He* (an absent person, T) *returned* (T, Ṣ, M, A, Mgh, Mṣb, Ḳ) to his place, (Sh,) or to a thing, (M,) or from his journey; (Mṣb;) as also ▼ أَوَّبَ, (M,) inf. n. تَأْوِيبٌ and تَأْيِيبٌ; (Ḳ;) and ▼ تَأَوَّبَ; (M, Ḳ;) and ▼ ائتاب [written with the disjunctive alif إِيتَابَ]; (Ṣ;) and ▼ أَيَّبَ, [a quasi-quadriliteral-radical verb, originally أَيْوَبَ,] of the measure فَيْعَلَ, (M,) inf. n. إِيَابٌ, (M, Ḳ,) originally إِيوَابٌ, of the measure فِيعَالٌ, (M, TA,) or, accord. to Fr, إِيَابٌ is incorrect, and the right word is إِيَّابٌ: (TA:) [and if so, أَيَّبَ is perhaps changed from أَوَّبَ, like as أَيْبَةٌ is from أَوْبَةٌ; and تَأْيِيبٌ is perhaps its inf. n., changed from تَأْوِيبٌ:] or, as some say, إِيَابٌ signifies only the *returning* to one's family *at night*: (M, TA:) and ▼ تَأَوَّبَ أَهْلَهُ and ▼ ائتاب اهله [as well as آبَ إِلَى أَهْلِهِ] signify *he returned to his family at,* or *in, the night*: (T, TA:) or آبَ إِلَيْهِمْ, (Ṣ,) [or آبَهُمْ, accord. to a copy of the A, where we find أُبْتُ بَنِى فُلَانٍ,] aor. as above; (TA;) and ▼ تَأَوَّبَهُمْ (Ṣ, A, Ḳ) and ▼ تَأَيَّبَهُمْ, (Ḳ,) ى taking the place of و, (TA,) inf. n. مُتَأَوَّبٌ and مُتَأَيَّبٌ, (M,* [in which the two forms of the verb are also given, but with the sing. pronoun of the third pers. instead of the pl.,] and Ḳ,) each in the form of a pass. part. n.; (TA;) *he came to them at night*: (Ṣ, M,* A, Ḳ:) and آبَ المَآءَ, (M,) inf. n. أَوْبٌ, (Ḳ,) signifies *he came to the water, to drink, at night*; as also ▼ ائتابهُ; (M, Ḳ;) and ▼ تَأَوَّبَهُ: (M:) or, accord. to AZ, تَأَوَّبْتُ signifies *I came in the beginning of the night.* (Ṣ.) You say also, آبَتِ الشَّمْسُ, (T, Ṣ, &c.,) aor. تَؤُوبُ, (M,) inf. n. مَآبٌ, (T,) or إِيَابٌ [in the CḲ أَيابٌ] and أُيُوبٌ, (M, Ḳ,) *The sun returned from its place of rising, and set*: (Mṣb:) or *the sun set*; (T, Ṣ, M, A, Ḳ;) as though it returned to the place whence it commenced its course; (M;) [or] it is a dial. var. of غَابَتْ. (Ṣ.) And آبَ إِلَيْهِ نَاسٌ *People came to him from every direction,* or *quarter.* (TA, from a trad.) The poet Sá'ideh Ibn-El-'Ajlán uses the expression, لَآبَكَ مُرْهَفٌ, meaning *A thin sword would have come to thee*; in which the verb may be trans. by itself, or the prep. إِلَى may be understood. (M, TA.) — *He returned from disobedience to obedience; he repented.* (TA.) And آبَ إِلَى ٱللّٰهِ *He returned unto God from his sin,* or *offence, and repented.* (Mṣb.) — آبَ بِهِ إِلَيْهِ *He made him to return to him,* or *it*; as also ▼ أَوَّبَهُ إِلَيْهِ. (M.) And آبَ يَدَهُ إِلَى سَيْفِهِ, (as in a copy of the T,) or بِيَدِهِ, (as in a copy of the A, [which is probably here the more correct],) *He put back his hand to his sword* to draw it: (Lth, T, A:) and الى قوسه [*to his bow*] to draw it: and الى سهمه [*to his arrow*] to shoot it. (A.) — See also 2.

2. أَوَّبَ: see 1, first sentence: — and the same again, near the end. — *He repeated,* or *echoed, the praises of God*: thus in the saying [in the Ḳur xxxiv. 10], يَا جِبَالُ أَوِّبِى مَعَهُ *O mountains, repeat ye,* or *echo ye, the praises of God with him*; [i. e., with David;] (Ṣ,* M, TA;) but some read ▼ أُوبِى معه, meaning *return ye with him in praising as often as he returneth therein*: (M, TA:) or, accord. to the former reading, the meaning is, *O mountains, labour ye with him in praising God all the day, until the night*: (T:)

for آوَبَ, (T, A,) inf. n. تَأْوِيبٌ, (T, A, K,) also signifies *It* (a company of men) *journeyed by day:* (Aboo-Málik, T:) or *all the day,* (T, A, K,) *to the night,* (T,) *without alighting to rest:* (TA:) تأويب being the same kind of day-journeying as إِسْآد is of night-journeying: (T, M:) or *he journeyed all the day, and alighted at night:* (T, Ṣ:) or *he journeyed by night:* (Mṣb:) or تأويب (M, L, K) and ▼ مُؤَاوَبَة (Lth, T, L, K) signify the *vying, one with another,* of travelling-camels, *in pace,* or *going.* (Lth, T, M, L, K.) A poet says,

وَإِنْ تُؤَاوِبْهُ ▼ تَجِدْهُ مِثْوَبَا ▼

[*And if thou,* or *they,* (meaning camels,) *vie with him in pace,* or *going, thou wilt,* or *they will, find him to be one that overcomes therein*]: so as related by Lth: but as related by others, تُؤَوِّبْهُ. (T.)

3. آوب, inf. n. مُؤَاوَبَةٌ: see 2, in two places.

5. تأوّب and تأيّب: see 1, in five places.

8. ائتاب: see 1, in three places.

Q. Q. 1. أَيَّبَ, originally أَيْوَبَ: see 1, first sentence.

آبُ *The name of a* [*Syrian*] *month* [*corresponding to August, O. S.*]: an arabicized word. (IAạr, M, K.)

أَوْبٌ an inf. n. of 1. (Ṣ, M, Mṣb, K.) — Also *The returning of the fore and hind legs* of a beast *in going along:* (T, M, A,* K:) or *quickness in the changing,* or *shifting, of the fore and hind legs in going along:* (Ṣ:) and simply *quickness,* or *swiftness.* (M, K.) One says, مَا أَعْجَبَ أَوْبَ يَدَيْهَا *How wonderful is the returning* [or *quick shifting*] *of her fore legs!* (A.) And to one going at a quick pace, one says, الأَوْبَ الأَوْبَ [meaning *Keep to the quick changing,* or *shifting, of the legs;* a verb being understood: or *Trot on! Trot on!*]. (A.) — *A right,* or *direct, way, course,* or *tendency;* syn. قَصْدٌ and اِسْتِقَامَةٌ. (M [in which these two syns. are mentioned together] and K [in which another explanation intervenes between them, namely عَادَة, as though they were meant to be understood in different senses, which I do not think to be the case].) — *A direction:* as in the saying, رَمَى أَوْبًا أَوْ أَوْبَيْنِ [*He shot,* or *cast, in one direction, or in two directions*]. (M, A.) — *A course, way, mode,* or *manner, of acting,* or *conduct,* or *the like:* (A:) *custom.* (Lḥ, M, A, K.) You say, كُنْتُ عَلَى صَوْبِ فُلَانٍ وَأَوْبِهِ *I was* [proceeding] *in the course, way, mode,* or *manner, of acting,* &c., *of such a one.* (A.) And مَا زَالَ هٰذَا أَوْبَهُ *This ceased not to be his course, way, mode,* or *manner,* &c.: (A:) or *his custom.* (Lḥ, M, A.) — *A way,* or *road:* (M, Mṣb, K:) *a quarter:* ('Eyn, M, A, K:) *a tract,* or *side:* ('Eyn, Ṣ:) *a place:* (Ṣ:) *a place to which one returns* [like مَآب]. (A, Mṣb.) You say, جَاؤُوا مِنْ كُلِّ أَوْبٍ *They came from every way,* or *road,* (M, Mṣb,) or *quarter,* ('Eyn, M, A,) or *tract,* or *side,* ('Eyn, Ṣ,) *and place,* (Ṣ,) or *place to which one returns.* (A, Mṣb.) And أَوْبَا الوَادِي signifies *The two sides of the valley.* (A.) ═ *Bees:* (M, K:) a quasi-pl. n.: as though the sing. were آئِبٌ: AḤn says that they are so called because of their returning to the مَبَاءَة, i. e. the place where they hive for the night. (M, TA.) See آئِبٌ. — *The clouds.* (K.) — *The wind.* (K.)

أَوْبَةٌ and ▼ أَيْبَةٌ *Return;* (T, A, K;) as also ▼ إِيَابَةٌ, a subst. from آبَ. (Mṣb.) You say, لِيَهْنِئْكَ أَوْبَةُ الغَائِبِ [*May the return of the absent give thee joy*]. (TA.) And فُلَانٌ سَرِيعُ الأَوْبَةِ and ▼ الأَيْبَةِ *Such a one is quick in return.* (A'Obeyd, T, Ṣ.*) — *Return from disobedience to obedience; repentance.* (TA in art. ايب.) — كَلَامٌ لَا أَوْبَةَ لَهُ *Speech,* or *language, without profit.* (A.) ═ أَوْبَةٌ is also the sing. of أَوْبَاتٌ, which signifies *The legs of a beast.* (K, TA.)

أَيْبَةٌ: see أَوْبَةٌ, in two places. ═ Also, (as in some copies of the K,) or ▼ إِيبَةٌ, (accord. to the CK,) or ▼ آئِبَةٌ, (accord. to the TK,) *A noon-day draught* or *drink.* (K.)

إِيبَةٌ: see what next precedes.

أَؤُوبٌ A she-camel *quick in the changing,* or *shifting, of her fore and hind legs in going along.* (Ṣ.)

إِيَابَةٌ: see أَوْبَةٌ.

أَوَّابٌ *Frequent in returning.* (T.) — *Frequent in returning unto God, from one's sins;* (M, TA;) *wont to repent,* or *frequent in repenting:* (Zj, T, A, Mgh, Mṣb:) or *turning from disobedience to obedience:* (Ṣ, L:) or *a praiser of God;* (Sa'eed Ibn-Jubeyr, TA;) by which is here meant, in the prayer of the period of the forenoon called الضُّحَى, when the sun is high, and the heat violent; hence termed صَلَاةُ الأَوَّابِينَ; which is performed when the young camels feel the heat of the sun from the parched ground: (TA:) or *obedient:* (Katádeh, TA:) or one *who reflects upon his sins in solitude, and prays God to forgive them:* (TA:) or one *who keeps,* or *is mindful of, the ordinances prescribed by God,* (حَفِيظٌ, [which is thus explained by Bḍ and Jel as occurring in the Kur l. 31,]) *and does not rise from his sitting-place until he begs forgiveness of God:* ('Obeyd Ibn-'Omeyr, T, TA:* [but this is evidently meant as an explanation of أَوَّابٌ together with حَفِيظٌ: see the Kur ubi suprà:]) or one *who sins, and then returns to obedience, and then sins, and then returns to obedience.* (TA.)

آئِبٌ act. part. n. of آبَ; *Returning:* [&c.:] (M, Mṣb:) pl. أُوَّابٌ and أُيَّابٌ and ▼ أَوْبٌ [q. v.]: (M, K:) or, accord. to some, the last is a quasi-pl. n. (M, TA.)

آئِبَةٌ The *coming* of camels *to water, to drink, every night:* whence the saying,

لَا تَرِدَنَّ المَاءَ إِلَّا آئِبَهْ

[*Do not thou come to the water, to drink, unless coming to it every night*]. (IAạr, M.) — See also أَيْبَةٌ.

مَآبٌ *A place to which one returns:* (T, Ṣ, K:) *a settled,* or *fixed, abode,* or *dwelling-place:* (TA:) the *place to which one is translated,* or *removed, by death:* (K, TA:) *the goal to which the course of life ultimately leads one;* or *place to which one returns in the ultimate state,* or *world to come.* (T, TA.) — The *place where the sun sets.* (TA.) — [*A day-journey:* pl. مَآوِبُ; as in the saying,] بَيْنَهُمَا ثَلَاثُ مَآوِبَ *Between them two are three day-journeys.* (K.)

مِثْوَبٌ [A camel *that overcomes in vying with another,* or *others, in pace,* or *going*]: see an ex. voce أَوَّبَ. (T.)

مَآبَةُ البِئْرِ [*The place where the water flows again into the well to supply the deficiency occasioned by drawing;*] *the* مَبَاءَة *of the well;* i. e., *the place where the water collects in the well.* (TA.)

رِيحٌ مُؤَوِّبَةٌ, (IB, CK,) or مُؤَوَّبَةٌ, (as in a copy of the M, and in some copies of the K,) *A wind blowing throughout the whole day:* (M, K:) or *a wind that comes at night.* (IB.)

مُؤْتَابٌ: see مُتَأَوِّبٌ, in two places.

مُتَأَوَّبٌ an inf. n. of 5, q. v.; as also ▼ مُتَأَيَّبٌ. (M,* K.)

مُتَأَوِّبٌ *Returning to one's family at,* or *in, the night;* as also ▼ مُؤْتَابٌ: (TA:) or, as also ▼ مُتَأَيِّبٌ, *coming at night:* or *coming in the beginning of the night:* (Ṣ:) [and so ▼ مُؤْتَابٌ, as in the following ex.:]

وَمَنْ يَتَّقِ فَإِنَّ اللّٰهَ مَعْهُ ✱ وَرِزْقُ اللّٰهِ مُؤْتَابٌ وَغَادِ

[*And whoso feareth God, verily God is with him; and the supply of God cometh* to him *at night,* or *in the beginning of the night, and cometh early in the morning:* يَتَّقِ being here put for يَتَّقِى, by a necessary poetical licence: see art. وقى]. (Ṣ.)

مُتَأَيَّبٌ: see مُتَأَوَّبٌ.

مُتَأَيِّبٌ: see مُتَأَوِّبٌ.

اود

1. أَوِدَ, aor. يَأْوَدُ, inf. n. أَوَدٌ, *It* (a thing, T, Ṣ, M, or an arrow, AḤn, M) *was,* or *became, of itself, crooked, curved,* or *bent.* (T, Ṣ, M, A,* K.) [See also 5.] ═ آدَ, aor. يَؤُودُ, inf. n. أَوْدٌ, *It* (the day) *receded,* in the evening. (T, L.) — *It* (the evening, T, Ṣ) *declined.* (T, Ṣ, K.) — *It* (a thing, L) *returned.* (M, L, K.) — آدَتِ الظِّلَالُ *The shadows returned, and inclined towards the east.* (L.) — آدَ عَلَيْهِ *He inclined towards him;* or *pitied him.* (M.) ═ آدَهُ, (T, Ṣ, Mṣb,) first pers. أَدْتُهُ, (M,) or أُدْتُهُ, (K, TA, [in the CK, erroneously, إِدْتُهُ,]) aor. يَؤُودُ, inf. n. أَوْدٌ, (Aṣ, T, M, Mṣb,) *He crooked, curved,* or *bent, it;* (Aṣ, T, Ṣ, L, Mṣb, K;) i. e., a stick, (Aṣ, T, L,) or other thing; (L;) as also ▼ أَوَّدَهُ. (L, K.) — آدَهُ, aor. يَؤُودُ, (T, Ṣ, M, &c.,) inf. n. أَوْدٌ (Ṣ, M, K) and أُؤُودٌ, (M, K,) *It* (a load) *oppressed him by its weight; pressed heavily upon him; burdened him.* (AZ, T, Ṣ, A, Mṣb.) And *It* (a thing, or an affair,) *oppressed, distressed,* or *afflicted, him:* (M, L, K:) and [in like manner] ▼ تَأَوَّدَهُ, (L, K,)

or ♦ تَآوَدَهُ, (T,) as also تَآدَاهُ, (L, Ḳ,) the last formed by transposition (T, L) from the second, (T,) or first, (L,) said of an affair, *it pressed heavily upon him; oppressed him.* (T, L, Ḳ.) You say, ♦ مَا آدَكَ فَهُوَ لِى آئِدٌ *What hath burdened* [or *distressed*] *thee, it* (that thing) *is burdening* [or *distressing*] *to me.* (Ṣ.)

2: see 1.

5. تَأَوَّدَ *It* (a stick, T, L, or some other thing, L) *became, by an extraneous operation, crooked, curved,* or *bent;* (T, Ṣ, M, A, L, Ḳ;) as also ♦ اِنْآدَ. (T, Ṣ, M, L, Ḳ: [in the CḲ فَآتَادَ is erroneously put for فَانْآدَ.]) El-'Ajjáj says,

لَمْ يَكُ يَنْآدُ ♦ فَأَمْسَى انْآدَا

[*He used not to become bent, and he has become bent*], making the pret. to be a denotative of state because قَدْ is meant to be understood, as in the saying in the Ḳur [iv. 92], أَوْ جَاؤُوكُمْ حَصِرَتْ صُدُورُهُمْ. (Ṣ.) You say also, تَأَوَّدَتْ فِى قِيَامِهَا *She* (a woman) *bent in her rising, by reason of her heaviness.* (T and L in art. وأد.) — تَأَوَّدَهُ: see آدَهُ.

6. تَآوَدَهُ: see آدَهُ.

7. اِنْآدَ: see 5, in two places. — Also *He became oppressed,* or *burdened* [by a load]. (Mṣb.)

أَوَدٌ; (T, M;) or ♦ آوَدُ, fem. أَوْدَآءُ; (Ḳ;) *Crooked, curved,* or *bent.* (T, M, Ḳ.)

آوَدُ; fem. أَوْدَآءُ: see what next precedes.

آئِدٌ *Burdening* [or *distressing*]. (Ṣ.) See 1, last sentence.

مَؤُودٌ *Oppressed, pressed heavily upon,* or *burdened,* by a load. (Ṣ.)

مَآوِدُ *Calamities:* (IAạr, M, L, Ḳ:) as also مَوَائِدُ, which is app. formed by transposition. (M, L.) Some say that مآود is pl. of مُؤْيِدٌ, and derive this word [which see in art. ايد] from آدَهُ, aor. يَؤُودُ, meaning "it oppressed him by its weight:" (T, L:) or it has no sing. (IAạr, M.)

اوز

إِوَزٌّ (Ṣ, Mṣb, Ḳ) and إِوَزَّةٌ, (Ṣ,) or the latter is the n. un. of the former, [which is a coll. gen. n.,] (Mṣb,) *i. q.* بَطٌّ [The *goose,* or *geese;* and the *duck,* or *ducks;* but اوز is generally applied to the former of these birds; and بط, to the latter; agreeably with a statement in the Jm, that بَطٌّ is applied by the Arabs to the *small,* and إِوَزٌّ to the *large*]; (Ṣ, Ḳ;) as also وَزٌّ, of which the n. un. is وَزَّةٌ: (Mṣb:) إِوَزٌّ is of the measure فِعَلٌّ: (Mṣb:) [but see what follows:] the pl. is إِوَزُّونَ, (Ṣ, Mṣb, Ḳ,) a form which is sometimes used, (Ṣ, Mṣb,) and which is anomalous. (Mṣb.) [See also كُرْكِىٌّ.] — [Hence,] إِوَزٌّ also signifies † *Short and thick:* (Ḳ:) *fleshy without being tall:* (Lth, TA:) fem. with ة. (TA.) El-'Okbaree asserts that the ا is augmentative, because it is followed by three radical letters: (MF, TA:) but ISd says that it is of the measure فِعَلٌّ, and may not be of the measure إِفْعَلٌ, [i. e., originally إِوْزَزٌ,] because this does not occur as the measure of an epithet. (TA.) [It seems, however, that اوز is in this case a subst. used tropically as an epithet, after the manner of many nicknames.] — Also, applied to a man, and to a horse, and to a camel, *Firm in make:* (AḤei in the Expos. of the Tes-heel, and TA:) or, applied to a horse, *compact and strong in make.* (TA.)

إِوَزَّى *A manner of walking in which is a moving up and down: or leaning on one side;* (Ḳ;) [the latter omitted in the CḲ;] *at one time on the right and at another on the left* [*like a goose or duck*]: (TA:) and the *walk of a sprightly horse.* (TA.) Az says that it may be of the measure إِفْعَلَّى, [i. e., originally إِوْزَزَّى,] or فِعَلَّى; but Abu-l-Ḥasan holds the latter to be the more correct, because it is the measure of many words relating to walking; as جِيَضَّى, and دِفَقَّى. (TA.)

أَرْضٌ مَأْوَزَةٌ *A land abounding with the birds called* إِوَزّ. (Ṣgh, Ḳ.)

اوس

آسٌ [*The myrtle;*] *a certain kind of tree,* (Ṣ, Mṣb, Ḳ,) *well known,* (Ṣ, Ḳ,) *fragrant,* (IDrd, M, Mṣb,) *and evergreen, abundant in the land of the Arabs, growing in the plains and mountains, and increasing so as to become a great tree:* (AḤn, M, TA:) n. un. with ة: (AḤn, M, Mṣb, Ḳ:) IDrd says, I think it an adventitious word, although used by the Arabs, and occurring in chaste poetry. (M, TA.)

اوف

1. آفَتِ البِلَادُ, aor. تَؤُوفُ, inf. n. أَوْفٌ and آفَةٌ (M, TA) and أُوُوفٌ, (M,) or أُؤُوفٌ, (TA,) *The country,* or *countries, had therein what is termed* آفَة [i. e. *a blight* or *blast* or *the like,* or *a pest* or *plague* or *the like*]. (M, TA.) And إِيفَ الطَّعَامُ, (Ibn Buzurj, T,) or الزَّرْعُ, (Ḳ,) or الشَّىْءُ, with the verb in the pass. form, (Mṣb,) like قِيلَ, (Ḳ,) *The wheat,* or *seed-produce,* or *thing, became affected,* or *smitten, with what is termed* آفَة [i. e. *a blight, blast, taint, canker,* or *the like*]. (T, Ḳ, Mṣb.) And آفَ القَوْمُ, (M, TA,) and أُوفُوا, (Ḳ,) thus in a correct copy of the 'Eyn, (TA,) and إِيفُوا, (Lth, T, Ḳ,) and أُفُوا, (Ḳ, TA,) [in the CḲ أُفِّفُوا,] and إِفُوا, (Lth, T, Ḳ, [in the CḲ أُفُوا,]) the last, namely, إِفُوا, with the ا termed مُمَالَة, having a quiescent letter [i. e. ى] rendered apparent by utterance but not by writing, between it and the ف, (T, Ḳ,* [in which is a strange omission, of the words سَاكِنٌ بَيْنَهُ اللَّفْظُ لَا الخَطُّ as in the T, or سَاكِنَةٌ بَيْنَهَا الخ as in the TA,] TA,) *The people became affected,* or *smitten, with what is termed* آفَة [i. e. *a pest* or *plague* or *the like*]. (Lth, T, M, Ḳ.) Lth says, in this case one says إِفُوا, and in one dial. إِيفُوا: (T:) in several copies of his book, in one dial. أُفِّفُوا, with two distinct ف s, of which the former is with teshdeed: but in some copies as mentioned just before. (Ṣgh, TA.)

آفَةٌ [*A blight, blast, taint, canker, disease, bane, pest, plague,* or *the like; any evil affection; an evil; a cause of mischief or harm or injury; anything that is noxious or destructive; a calamity;*] *i. q.* عَاهَةٌ; (Ṣ, Mṣb, Ḳ;) i. e. (Mṣb, [in the Ḳ "or,"]) *an accident that mars,* or *corrupts, that which it affects,* or *befalls,* or *smites:* (T, M, O, Mṣb, Ḳ:) pl. آفَاتٌ. (Mṣb, Ḳ.) [See 1.] One says, آفَةُ الظَّرْفِ الصَّلَفُ وَآفَةُ العِلْمِ النِّسْيَانُ [*The bane of elegance in manners, or the like, is the overpassing the due limits therein, and arrogating to oneself superiority therein, through pride; and the bane of science is forgetfulness*]. (T.) And it is said in a trad., آفَةُ الحَدِيثِ الكَذِبُ وَآفَةُ العِلْمِ النِّسْيَانُ [*The bane of discourse is lying; and the bane of science is forgetfulness*]. (TA.) And hence the saying, لِكُلِّ شَىْءٍ آفَةٌ وَلِلْعِلْمِ آفَاتٌ [*To everything there is a bane; and to science there are banes*]. (TA.)

مَؤُوفٌ, (Ks, T, Ṣ, M, Mṣb, Ḳ,) originally مَأْوُوفٌ, (Mṣb,) and ♦ مَئِيفٌ, (Ibn-Buzurj, T, Ḳ,) *Affected,* or *smitten, with what is termed* آفَة; (T, Ṣ, M, &c.;) applied to wheat, (Ks, Ibn-Buzurj, T, M,) or seed-produce, (Ṣ, Ḳ,) &c. (Mṣb.)

مَئِيفٌ: see مَؤُوفٌ.

اوق

أُوقِيَّةٌ: see art. وقى.

اول

1. آلَ, aor. يَؤُولُ, (T, Ṣ, M, &c.,) inf. n. أَوْلٌ (T, M, Mgh, Mṣb, Ḳ) and مَآلٌ (M, Ḳ) and إِيَالٌ, which last is used as a subst. in relation to objects of the mind, (Mṣb,) and أَيْلُولَةٌ [like دَيْمُومَةٌ], (TA,) *He,* or *it, returned;* syn. رَجَعَ; (T, Ṣ, M, Mgh, Mṣb, Ḳ;) and عَادَ; (T;) [and *he resorted;* (see an instance voce إِيَّلٌ;)] إِلَيْهِ *to it;* (M, Ḳ;) namely a thing [of any kind; the thing, or place, whence he, or it, originated, or came; his, or its, origin, or source; his, or its, original state, condition, quantity, weight, &c.; any place; and a former action, or saying, or the like: see رَجَعَ, by which, as the explanation of آلَ, may be meant to be implied some other significations, here following, which these two verbs have in common]: (M:) and آلَ عَنْهُ *he* (a man, M) *returned,* or *reverted, from it.* (M, Ḳ.) — From آلَ as syn. with رَجَعَ is the phrase, فُلَانٌ يَؤُولُ إِلَى كَرَمٍ [meaning either *Such a one returns to generosity,* or, as كَرَمٌ is used in the sense of كِرَامٌ, *is referable to generous,* or *noble, ancestors*]. (TA.) [And hence the phrase,] آلَ إِلَيْهِ بِنَسَبٍ [*He bore a relation to him, as a member to a head, by kindred*], and بِدِينٍ [*by religion*]. (Ibn-'Arafeh.) And the saying, in a trad., مَنْ صَامَ الدَّهْرَ فَلَا صَامَ وَلَا آلَ, i. e. ‡ [*He who fasts ever,* or *always, may he neither fast*] *nor return to what is good.* (TA. [In the Mgh, art. دهر, for آلَ I find أَفْطَرَ; and it is there said that this is an imprecation uttered by the Prophet, lest a man should believe

this kind of fasting to be ordained by God; or, through impotence, should become insincere; or because, by fasting all the days of the year, he would do so on the days on which fasting is forbidden. See other readings voce أَلَا in art. الو.]) — Hence also the saying, آلَتِ الضَّرْبَةُ إِلَى النَّفْسِ, meaning † *The blow, or stroke, resulted in destroying life; in slaying, or killing.* (Mgh.) — Hence also, آلَ الأَمْرُ إِلَى كَذَا [*The affair, or case, became ultimately reduced to such a state, or condition; came to such a result; came to be thus*]. (Mṣb.) — Hence also, طَبَخْتُ الشَّرَابَ فَآلَ إِلَى قَدْرِ كَذَا *I cooked the wine, or beverage, and it became reduced* (رَجَعَ) *to such a quantity.* (Ṣ.) And طَبَخَهُ حَتَّى آلَ إِلَى الثُّلُثِ أَوِ الرُّبُعِ *He cooked it* (namely نَبِيذ [i. e. must, or mead, or wort,]) *until it became reduced* (رَجَعَ) *to the third, or to the fourth:* (T:) or, said of the same, (Mgh,) or of medicine, (TA,) حَتَّى آلَ المَنَّانِ مَنًّا وَاحِدًا, (Mgh,) or إِلَى مَنٍّ وَاحِدٍ, (TA,) *until twice the quantity, or weight, of a* مَنّ *became* [*reduced to*] (صَارَ) *one* مَنّ. (Mgh.) — [Hence also, مَجَازُ الأَوْلِ *The proleptic, or anticipative, trope;* as فَصِيل applied to "a young camel" before it is weaned, because it is to be weaned.] — [And hence also, app.,] آلَ الشَّىْءُ, inf. n. مَآلٌ, *The thing* [*became reduced in quantity or size;*] *decreased; diminished; or became defective, or deficient.* (M, Ḳ.) And آلَ لَحْمُ النَّاقَةِ *The flesh of the she-camel went away, so that she became lean, or slender and lean, or lean and lank in the belly.* (T, Ḳ.) — آلَ, (T, Ṣ, M, Ḳ,) inf. n. أَوْلٌ (T, M, Ḳ) and إِيَالٌ, (M, Ḳ,) is also said of tar, (T, Ṣ, M,) and of honey, (Ṣ,) and of milk, (M,) and of wine, or beverage, (TA,) and of urine, (M,) or of the urine of camels that have been contented with green pasture instead of water, at the end of their being in that state, (T,) and of oil, (M, Ḳ,) and other things, (Ḳ,) as meaning *It became thick:* (T, Ṣ, M, Ḳ:) said of milk, *it thickened and coagulated:* (M:) said of wine, or beverage, *it thickened, and became intoxicating in its utmost degree:* (Az, TA:) and said of oil, *it attained its full perfume, or sweetness of odour, by being well prepared or compounded.* (T.) — مَا لَكَ تَؤُولُ إِلَى كَتِفَيْكَ [written in the TA without any vowel-signs, app. meaning ‡ *What aileth thee that thou shruggest thy shoulders? lit., drawest thyself together to thy two shoulder-blades?*] is said [to a man] إِذَا انْضَمَّ إِلَيْهِمَا وَاجْتَمَعَ [when he draws himself together to them, and contracts himself]; and is a tropical phrase: so says Z. (TA.) — آلَ مِنْ فُلَانٍ *He escaped, or became safe or secure, from such a one:* a dial. var. of وَأَلَ: (T, Ḳ:) of the dial. of the Anṣár. (TA.) — You say also, آلَ, aor. يَؤُولُ; (T, Mṣb;) or أَوِلَ, aor. يَأْوَلُ; (Ḳ;) meaning *He, or it, preceded; went before; was, or became, before, beforehand, first, or foremost;* (T, Mṣb, Ḳ;) *and came:* (Mṣb:) with this, also, وَأَلَ is syn.; and from it [says Az] is most probably derived أَوَّلُ, so that its original form is أَأْوَلُ: [or, as Fei says,] hence is derived the phrase, used by the vulgar, العَشْرُ الأَوَّلُ with fet-ḥ to the hemzeh [as meaning "the first, or preceding, ten (nights of the month)," for الأُوَلُ, pl. of الأُولَى, fem. of الأَوَّلُ; but this is generally regarded as being originally الأَوَّالُ, from وَأَلَ]. (Mṣb.) = آلَهُ: see 2. — Accord. to Lth, (TA,) أُلْتُهُ, (M, Ḳ,) aor. أَؤُولُهُ, inf. n. أَوْلٌ, (TA,) signifies *I made it* (namely, milk, M, or oil &c., Ḳ) *to thicken,* (M, Ḳ,) *and to coagulate;* (M;) the verb being both intrans. and trans.: (Ḳ:) but Az says that it is not known as trans., in this sense, in the language of the Arabs [of the classical ages]. (TA.) = آلَ رَعِيَّتَهُ, (Ṣ, M, Mṣb, Ḳ,) aor. يَؤُولُ, inf. n. أَوْلٌ (Ṣ) and إِيَالٌ, (Ṣ, M, Ḳ,) of which the simple subst. is إِيَالَةٌ, (Ṣ,* Mṣb,) *He* (a prince or commander, Ṣ, or a king, M, Ḳ) *ruled, or governed, his subjects; presided over their affairs, as commander or governor;* (Ṣ, M, Mṣb, Ḳ;) *and did so well:* (Ṣ:) and آلَ عَلَيْهِمْ, inf. n. أَوْلٌ and إِيَالٌ and إِيَالَةٌ, [or this last, as said above, is a simple subst.,] *he presided over them; held command, or authority, over them;* (M, Ḳ;) namely, a people, or company of men; (Ḳ;) or, *over their affairs.* (TA.) It is said in a prov., (M,) قَدْ أُلْنَا وَإِيلَ عَلَيْنَا (T, Ṣ, M) *We have ruled and been ruled;* (T;) *we have presided and been presided over.* (M.) — آلَ مَالَهُ, (T, Ṣ, M,* Mṣb, Ḳ,) inf. n. إِيَالَةٌ, (T, Mṣb,) *He put into a good, or right, state, or condition, and managed, or tended, his* مال [meaning *cattle*]; (T, Ṣ, M,* Ḳ;) as also ↓ ائْتَالَهُ [written with the disjunctive alif إِيْتَالَهُ], (Ḳ,) inf. n. إِيتِيَالٌ: (Ṣ:) or *he managed his camels, and his sheep or goats, in such a manner that they throve, or became in a good state or condition, by his management.* (Mṣb.) Lebeed describes a female singer

• بِمُوَتَّرٍ تَأْتَالُهُ ↓ إِبْهَامُهَا •

(T, Ṣ,) meaning *with a stringed lute,* (EM p. 169,) *which her thumb adjusts;* (Ṣ, EM;) from أُلْتُ, (T, Ṣ,) signifying *I put into a good, right, or proper, state, or condition.* (T. [But see another reading in the first paragraph of art. اوى.]) You say also, أُلْتُ الشَّىْءَ meaning *I composed, or collected together, the thing, and put it into a good, right, or proper, state, or condition:* and some of the Arabs say, أَوَلَ ↓ آللّٰهُ عَلَيْكَ أَمْرَكَ, i. e. *May God compose for thee thine affair:* and, by way of imprecation, لَا أَوَلَ ↓ آللّٰهُ عَلَيْهِ شَمْلَهُ [*May God not compose for him his discomposed, disorganized, deranged, or unsettled, affair, or affairs*]. (T.) — أُلْتُ الإِبِلَ, inf. n. أَوْلٌ and إِيَالٌ, also signifies *I drove the camels:* (M:) or, accord. to the T, *I bound the camels' udders with the* أَصِرَّة (صِرَارُهَا) *until the time of milking, when I loosed them.* (TA.)

2. أَوَّلَهُ إِلَيْهِ, (M, Ḳ,) inf. n. تَأْوِيلٌ, (TA,) *He returned it* (namely, a thing, M) *to him, or it; he made it, or caused it, to return to him, or it;* syn. رَجَعَهُ: (M, Ḳ: in the CḲ رَجَّعَهُ:) and ↓ آلَهُ also signifies the same; syn. رَدَّهُ. (TA.) You say, أَوَّلَ آللّٰهُ عَلَيْكَ ضَالَّتَكَ *May God restore to thee thy stray;* (T,* TA;) *cause it to return to thee;* (TA;) *bring together thee and it.* (T.) And أَوَّلْتُهُ إِلَى كَذَا *I caused him, or it, to come to such a state or condition; brought, or reduced, him, or it, thereto;* syn. صَيَّرْتُهُ إِلَيْهِ. (T.) — See also 1, near the end of the paragraph, in two places. — تَأْوِيلٌ also signifies The *discovering, detecting, revealing, developing, or disclosing,* or the *explaining, expounding, or interpreting, that to which a thing is, or may be, reduced, or that which it comes, or may come, to be:* (Ṣ, O, TA:) you say, أَوَّلْتُهُ, inf. n. تَأْوِيلٌ; and ↓ تَأَوَّلْتُهُ, inf. n. تَأَوُّلٌ; in one and the same sense: and hence the saying of El-Aạshà:

• عَلَى أَنَّهَا كَانَتْ تَأَوُّلُ ↓ حُبِّهَا •

• تَأَوُّلُ ↓ رِبْعِيِّ السِّقَابِ فَأَصْحَبَا •

(Ṣ:) or تَأَوَّلُ ↓ حُبَّهَا: (so in a copy of the T: [the former word being, accord. to this reading, a contraction of تَتَأَوَّلُ; but this does not altogether agree with what here follows:]) AO says, تَأَوُّلُ حُبِّهَا means تَفْسِيرُهُ وَمَرْجِعُهُ: [i. e., the explanation of her love, or of the (poet's) love of her, and the state, or condition, to which it eventually came, is this:] (Ṣ:) it was small in his heart, and ceased not to grow until it became great; like as the little young camel [born in the season called ربيع, or in the beginning of the breeding-time,] ceases not to grow until he becomes great like his mother, (T,* Ṣ,) and has a son accompanying him: (Ṣ:) [or] أَوَّلَهُ and ↓ تَأَوَّلَهُ, (M, Ḳ,) inf. n. of the former as above, (Ḳ,) when said of language, signify دَبَّرَهُ وَقَدَّرَهُ وَفَسَّرَهُ [*he considered its end, or what it might be to which it led or pointed, and compared one part of it with another, and then explained, or expounded, or interpreted, it*]: (M, Ḳ:) hence, [if the explanation in the M and Ḳ be meant to denote three distinct meanings, which I do not think to be the case,] it would seem as though تَأْوِيلٌ and تَفْسِيرٌ were syn.; but accord. to other authorities, they differ: (TA:) [Az says,] accord. to Aḥmad Ibn-Yaḥyà, these two words and مَعْنًى are all one: but تأويل seems to me to signify the *collecting the meanings of dubious expressions by such expression as is clear, or plain, without dubiousness:* or, accord. to Lth, it is the *interpreting of language that has different meanings; and this cannot be rightly done but by an explanation which changes the expression;* as also ↓ تَأَوُّلٌ: (T:) or the *turning a verse of the Ḳur-án from its apparent meaning to a meaning which it bears, or admits, when the latter is agreeable with the Scripture and the Sunneh:* for instance, in the words of the Ḳur [vi. 95, &c.], يُخْرِجُ ٱلْحَىَّ مِنَ ٱلْمَيِّتِ, if the meaning be [thus explained] "He produceth the bird from the egg," this is تفسير: and if [it be explained as meaning] "He produceth the believer from the unbeliever," or "the knowing from the ignorant," this is تأويل: so says Ibn-El-Kemál: (TA:) [hence, although it may often be rendered by *interpretation,* like تفسير, it more properly signifies the *rendering in a manner not according to the letter, or overt sense; explaining the covert, or virtual,* *meaning; interpreting in a manner not according to the obvious meaning:*] or the *reducing a thing to its ultimate intent, whether it be a saying or an action:* (Er-Rághib, TA:) or تفسير signifies the "discovering, detecting, revealing, or disclosing, what is meant by a dubious expression;" and تأويل, the *reducing one of two senses,* or *interpretations, which an expression bears,* or *admits, to that which suits the apparent meaning:* (L and Ḳ in art. فسر, and TA in that and in the present art.:) or the former signifies the "expounding, explaining, or interpreting, the narratives which occur collected without discrimination in the Ḳur-án, and making known the significations of the strange words or expressions, and explaining the occasions on which the verses were revealed;" and the latter, the *explaining the meaning of that which is* مُتَشَابِه, [or *what is equivocal,* or *ambiguous,*] i. e., *what is not understood without repeated consideration.* (TA: [in which are some further explanations; but these add nothing of importance.])—[Hence, أَوَّلَ لَفْظًا, in grammar, *He rendered a word,* or *an expression,* or *a phrase, in grammatical analysis, by another word,* or *expression,* or *phrase.*]— And [hence likewise,] تَأْوِيلٌ signifies also The *interpretation,* or *explanation,* of a dream; the *telling the final sequel,* or *result,* thereof: (M, Ḳ:) as in the Ḳur xii. 101. (M.)— It is also used [as a simple subst.] to signify The *end, issue, result,* or *final sequel,* of a thing; syn. عَاقِبَةٌ; (Bḍ in iv. 62 and xvii. 37;) or ▼مَآلٌ; (Jel in the same places;) or مَرْجِعٌ, and مَصِيرٌ; as in the Ḳur [iii. 5], وَمَا يَعْلَمُ تَأْوِيلَهُ إِلَّا ٱللّٰهُ [*But none knoweth the end,* &c., *thereof, except God*]: (A'Obeyd, T:) or this phrase means, *but none knoweth when will be the resurrection, and to what the case will eventually come,* (T, M,) *when the hour shall arrive,* (TA,) *except God:* (T, M:) so says Aboo-Is-ḥáḳ: (T:) and in like manner, [in the Ḳur vii. 51,] هَلْ يَنْظُرُونَ إِلَّا تَأْوِيلَهُ means *Do they wait for aught save the result to which their case will come by the resurrection?* (Aboo-Is-ḥáḳ, T, M:) or, *the result to which it will come* (Bḍ, Jel) *in the manifestation of its truth by the appearance of the promises and threats of which it has told?* (Bḍ:) in like manner, also, the saying, تَقْوَى ٱللّٰهِ أَحْسَنُ تَأْوِيلًا means *The fear of God is best in respect of result;* syn. عَاقِبَةً. (TA.)

5: see 2, in the former half of the paragraph, in six places.—تأوّل فيه الخير *He discovered in him the existence of good,* or *goodness, from its outward signs:* and *he sought,* or *looked for, good,* or *goodness, in him.* (TA.) You say also, تَأَوَّلْتُ فِي فُلَانٍ ٱلْأَجْرَ *I sought,* or *looked for, recompense in* (or *of* or *from*) *such a one.* (T.)

8: see 1, near the end of the paragraph, in two places.

10. استأل الرُّؤْيَا *He sought the interpretation of the dream, by consideration.* (TA in art. سوأ.)

آلٌ A man's أَهْلٌ [or *family*]; (T, Ṣ, M, Mṣb, Ḳ;) i. e. his *relations:* (Mṣb:) his عَشِيرَة [or *kinsfolk;* or *nearer,* or *nearest, relations by descent from the same father or ancestor;* &c.]; from أَوْلٌ as signifying رُجُوعٌ, because recourse is had to them in all affairs: (Ḥar p. 578:) and his *household;* (Ṣ, TA;) the *people of* his *house:* (Mṣb:) and his *followers;* (Ṣ, Mṣb, Ḳ;) including *soldiers:* (Ṣ, TA:) and his أَوْلِيَآء [i. e. *friends,* and *the like*]: (Ḳ:) *those who bear a relation* to him, *as members to a head,* (مَنْ آلَ إِلَيْهِ,) *by religion* or *persuasion* or *kindred;* as in the Ḳur iii. 9 and viii. 54 and 56 &c.: (Ibn-'Arafeh:) [or in these and many other instances, it may be rendered *people:*] but in general it is not used save in relation to that in which is eminence, or nobility; so that one does not say, آلُ ٱلْإِسْكَافِ, like as one says أَهْلُهُ: (Ḳ:) and it is peculiarly used as a prefix to the proper names of rational beings; not to indeterminate nouns, nor to nouns of places or of times; so that one says, آلُ فُلَانٍ; but not آلُ رَجُلٍ, nor آلُ زَمَانِ كَذَا, nor آلُ مَوْضِعِ كَذَا, like as one says, [أَهْلُ رَجُلٍ, and أَهْلُ زَمَانٍ, and] أَهْلُ بَلَدِ كَذَا and مَوْضِعِ كَذَا: (TA:) Ks disallows its being prefixed to a pronoun; so that one should not say, آلُهُ, but أَهْلُهُ; but his opinion in this matter is not correct: it is originally أَوْلٌ; the و being changed into ا, (M,* Mṣb,) as in قَالَ [which is originally قَوَلَ]: so say some: (Mṣb:) or it is originally أَهْلٌ, (T, M, Mṣb, Ḳ,) then أَأْلٌ, and then آلٌ: (Ḳ:) so say some, arguing thus from its having أُهَيْلٌ for its dim.: (T, Mṣb:) but accord. to Ks, it assumes the form ▼أُوَيْلٌ as a dim.: (T:) or each of these is its dim. (M, Ḳ.) By the آل of the Prophet are meant, accord. to some persons, *His followers, whether relations or others:* and *his relations, whether followers or not:* (Aḥmad Ibn-Yaḥyà, T:) or, as some say, *his family* (أَهْلُهُ [q. v.]) *and his wives:* [but it seems to be indicated that what I have rendered "and his wives" is meant as an explicative adjunct to اهله:] or, as some say, *the people of his religion:* (Esh-Sháfi'ee, T:) being himself asked who were his آل, he answered *all pious persons:* (Anas, TA:) but in a trad. in which it is said that the poor-rates are prohibited to him and to his آل, by this is meant those to whom was appropriated the fifth [of the spoils] instead of the poor-rates; and these were the genuine descendants of Háshim and El-Muṭṭalib. (Esh-Sháfi'ee, T.)— يَا لَزَيْدٍ and يَالَ زَيْدٍ, accord. to the Koofees, are contractions of يَا آلَ زَيْدٍ [*O family of Zeyd*]. (Mughnee, on the letter ل; and El-Ashmoonee on the Alfeeyeh of Ibn-Málik, section الاستغاثة. [See the letter ل.])—[See also إِيَالَةٌ.]═‡ *I. q.* شَخْصٌ [meaning The *body,* or *corporeal form* or *figure* or *substance,* (of anything, as is said in the T,) *which one sees from a distance;* or, in this case, often, though not always, the *person,* or *self*]; (AA, T, Ṣ, M, Ḳ;) of a man: a metaphorical application, from آل as signifying أَهْلٌ and عَشِيرَةٌ; because comprising the members and the senses. (Ḥar p. 578.)— Sometimes, it is redundant, or pleonastic; [being only used for the sake of metre in verse, or to give more force to an expression;] as in the following instance:

• أَلَاقِي مِنْ تَذَكُّرِ آلِ لَيْلَى •
• كَمَا يَلْقَى ٱلسَّلِيمُ مِنَ ٱلْعِدَادِ •

[*I experience, from remembrance of Leylà,* or *of Leylà's person* or *self, the like of what the person bitten* or *stung* by a venomous reptile *experiences from the paroxysm of pain occasioned by the bite* or *sting*]. (TA.) [See also another ex., voce جَابٌ; and another, voce مِزْمَارٌ.]—[Like شَخْصٌ, it seems to be sometimes applied to *Any material thing that is somewhat high, and conspicuous:* and hence, perhaps, the signification next following.]— مَا أَشْرَفَ مِنَ ٱلْبَعِيرِ [app. meaning The *overtopping,* or *higher, part,* or *parts, of the camel*]. (M, Ḳ.)— *A* [*tent of the kind called*] خَيْمَة. (M.)— The *poles of the* خَيْمَة; (M, Ḳ;) as also ▼آلَةٌ; of which the pl. is آلَاتٌ: (Ḳ:) or ▼آلَةٌ is the sing. of آلٌ and آلَاتٌ, [or n. un. of the former and pl. of the latter,] which signify the *pieces of wood* (خَشَبَات) *upon which the* خيمة *is raised,* or *constructed:* and hence Kutheiyir likens the legs of his she-camel to four آلَات of the [wood of the tree called] طَلْح. (Ṣ.)— The *pieces of wood* (خَشَب, T, M, Ḳ) of خِيَم [or tents], (M,) *stripped* [*of the tent-cloths*]. (T, TA.)— Also, [app. because rising from the general surface of the ground,] The *extremities and sides* of a mountain. (M, Ḳ.*)═The سَرَاب [or *mirage*]: (Aṣ, T, M, Ḳ:) or peculiarly applied to *that which is in the first part of the day,* (Ḳ,) *as though raising figures seen from a distance* (شُخُوص), *and making them to quiver:* (TA:) or *that which one sees in the first part of the day, and in the last part thereof, as though raising figures seen from a distance* (شخوص); *not the same as the* سراب: (Ṣ:) or *what resembles the* سراب: (Mṣb:) or, as some say, *that which is in the* ضُحَى [or *early part of the day when the sun is yet low*], *like water between the sky and the earth,* [*in appearance*] *raising figures seen from a distance* (شخوص), *and making them to quiver;* whereas the سراب is that which is at mid-day, [apparently] cleaving to the ground, as though it were running water: Th says, *the* آل *is in the first part of the day:* (M:) Aṣ says that *the* آل *and the* سراب *are one:* but others say that *the former is from the* ضُحَى [see above] *to the declining of the sun from the meridian;* whereas the سراب is after the declining of the sun from the meridian to the prayer of the عَصْر; and in favour of their assertion they urge, that *the former* [*in appearance*] *raises everything so that it becomes what is termed* آل, *i. e.* شخص; for the آل of everything is its شخص; and that the سراب [in appearance] lowers every شخص in it so that it becomes [as though it were] cleaving to the ground, having no شخص: Yoo says, the Arabs say that *the* آل *is from the* غُدْوَة [or *period between the prayer of daybreak and sunrise*] *to the time when the sun is very high,* or *near the meridian;* then it is called سراب for the rest of the day: ISk says, *the* آل *is that which* [*in appearance*] *raises figures seen from a distance* (شخوص),

and is in the ضُحًى [explained above]; and the سراب is that which is upon the surface of the ground, as though it were water, and is at mid-day: and this, I [namely Az] say, is what I have found the Arabs in the desert to say: (T:) El-Ḥareeree speaks of the glistening of the آل; app. using this word in the sense of سراب; for it is the latter that glistens; not the former: (Ḥar p. 363:) the word is masc. and fem. (Mṣb, Ḳ.) The phrase يَرْفَعُ ٱلْآلَ, ending a verse (Ṣ, M) of En-Nábighah, (M, TA,) i. e. Edh-Dhubyánee, (TA,) or El-Jaadee, (Ṣ,) [variously cited in the Ṣ and M and TA,] is an instance of inversion; the meaning being يَرْفَعُهُ ٱلْآلُ [*The* آل *raising it*]: (Ṣ, TA:) or the meaning is, *making the* آل *conspicuous* more than it would otherwise be; the agent of the verb being a prominent portion of a mountain, which, being itself raised [in appearance] by the آل, has the effect of doing this. (M.) = See also the next paragraph. = And see أَلْيَانٌ, in art. الى.

آلَةٌ *i. q.* أَدَاةٌ [i. e. *An instrument; a tool; an implement; a utensil:* and *instruments; tools; implements; utensils; apparatus; equipments; equipage; accoutrements; furniture; gear; tackling;*] (Ṣ, M, Ḳ) *with which one works, for himself* or *for another:* it is both sing. and pl.: (M, Ḳ:) or, (Ḳ,) as some say, (M,) it is a pl. having no sing. (M, Ḳ) as to the letter: (M:) [but it is very often used as a sing.:] and the pl. is آلَاتٌ. (Ṣ, Ḳ.) In the saying of 'Alee, يَسْتَعْمِلُ آلَةَ ٱلدِّينِ فِى طَلَبِ ٱلدُّنْيَا [lit. *He makes use of the instrument of religion in seeking the goods of the present world*], † *science*, or *knowledge*, is meant; because thereby only is religion. (M.) — [*A musical instrument;*] *a lute; a musical reed,* or *pipe;* the [*kind of mandoline called*] طُنْبُور. (TA.) — The *male organ of generation.* (TA.) — The *bier of a corpse.* (Abu-l-'Omeythil, Ṣ, M, Ḳ.) Thus, accord. to some, in the following verse, (Ṣ,* M,) of Kaab Ibn-Zuheyr:

• كُلُّ ٱبْنِ أُنْثَى وَإِنْ طَالَتْ سَلَامَتُهُ •
• يَوْمًا عَلَى آلَةٍ حَدْبَآءَ مَحْمُولُ •

[*Every son of a female, though his health,* or *safety, long continue, is one day borne upon a gibbous bier:* for the bier of the Arabs of the desert was generally composed of two poles connected by a net-work of cords upon which the corpse lay depressed]: (Ṣ, M:) or, as some say, [*in a distressing state,* or *condition;* for, they say,] آلة here signifies حَالَة. (TA.) — See also آل, in two places, near the middle of the paragraph. = *A state,* or *condition; i. q.* حَالَةٌ [as mentioned above]: (T, Ṣ, M, Ḳ:) pl. [or rather coll. gen. n.] ✝آلٌ. (T, S.) You say, هُوَ بِآلَةِ سَوْءٍ [*He is in an evil state* or *condition*]. (Ṣ.) — *I. q.* شِدَّةٌ [*Straitness; difficulty; distress;* &c.]. (M, Ḳ.)

إِيلَةٌ sometimes signifies The *relations to whom one goes* [or *is traced*] *back in genealogy.* (Ibn-'Abbád.) [See also آلٌ.] — You say also, رَدَدْتُهُ إِلَى إِيلَتِهِ *I made him to go back,* or *revert, to his natural disposition:* or, *to his* [*original*] *state* or *condition.* (Ibn-'Abbád.)

أُولُو, in the gen. and accus. أُولِى: see أُلُو, in art. الو.

أُولَى fem. of أَوَّلُ: see the latter in art. وأل. = أُولَى as a pl., and its var. أُولَآءِ; and أُولٰئِكَ, or أُولَالِكَ; &c.: see أُلَى, in art. الى.

أُوَالُ *A certain idol of* [*the tribes of*] *Bekr and Teghlib,* (Ḳ, TA,) *the two sons of Wáïl.* (TA.)

أُوَيْلٌ dim. of آلٌ, q. v. (Ks, T, M, Ḳ.)

إِيَالٌ The *vessel,* or *receptacle, of thickening,* or *thick, milk:* (M:) [or, accord. to the Ḳ, this seems to be termed ✝أُيَّلٌ: see آئِلٌ:] or, *in which wine* (شَرَاب), or *expressed juice,* or *what is pressed,* or *squeezed, so that its juice is forced out,* or *the like thereof, is made to thicken.* (TA.) = [Also an inf. n. of 1, which see throughout.]

إِيَالَةٌ *Rule,* or *government:* (Ṣ, Mṣb:) [accord. to some, an inf. n. of آلَ as a trans. verb: accord. to others,] a simple subst. (Mṣb.)

أَوَّلٌ and its variations &c., see art. وأل: some, on account of difference of opinion from others respecting its radical letters, have mentioned this word in the present art. (TA.)

أَيْلٌ: see إِيَّلٌ: = and see also آئِلٌ, last sentence.

أُيَّلٌ: see إِيَّلٌ: = and see also آئِلٌ, in four places; and إِيَالٌ.

إِيَّلٌ and ✝أُيَّلٌ (T, Ṣ, Mgh, Mṣb, Ḳ, the first and third and fourth in art. ايل) and ✝أَيِّلٌ, (T, Ḳ,) the last on the authority of IAar, (TA,) but A 'Obeyd says that it is إِيَّلٌ, with kesr, (T,) and this is the approved form, (TA,) The [*animal called*] وَعِلٌ: (Ḳ:) or the *male* وَعِل; (ISh, T, Ṣ, Mgh, Mṣb;) i. e. the *mountain-goat:* (Mṣb:) accord. to some, (Ṣ,) what is called in Persian كَوَزْن; (Ṣ, Mgh;) by which word Sh explains the word إِيَّلٌ: ISh says, it is the *animal that is very wide between the horns, and bulky, like the domestic bull:* (T:) [see بَقَرُ الوَحْشِ in art. بقر:] and Lth says, it is called thus because it resorts (يَؤُولُ) to the mountains: sometimes the ى is changed into ج: the fem. is of the same three forms with ة: (TA:) and the pl. is أَيَائِلُ [like سَيَائِدُ pl. of سَيِّدٌ]. (Lth, T, Mgh, Mṣb.) — See also آئِلٌ, in two places.

آئِلٌ [act. part. n. of 1 in all its senses: and thus, particularly,] *Thickening,* or *thick;* (T, Ṣ, M, TA;) applied to the urine of camels that have been contented with green pasture instead of water, at the end of their being in that state; (T;) or to milk, (Ṣ, M, TA,) and to oil, and other things, such as tar, and honey, and wine, or beverage: (TA:) pl. ✝أُيَّلٌ: (Ṣ, M:) which last word [in one copy of the M written إِيَّلٌ, but this I think a mistranscription,] signifies also the *remains of thickening,* or *thick, milk;* or, as some say, the [*seminal*] *water in the womb:* (M:) or this same word (أُيَّلٌ) has the last of these significations; and also, [as a sing. epithet,] the first of the meanings explained in this paragraph; as also آئِلٌ, applied to milk; (Ḳ;) or to milk *thickening,* or *thick, and mixed; not excessively thick, but in a somewhat good degree, and changed in its flavour:* (AHát, TA:) or it [app. أُيَّلٌ, as in the TḲ,] signifies the *vessel,* or *receptacle, thereof;* (Ḳ;) [a meaning assigned in the M to إِيَالٌ;] *in which milk thickens:* (TA:) Sh says that ✝إِيَّلٌ signifies the *milk of the* أَيَائِل [pl. of إِيَّلٌ]; and so says AA: but AHeyth says that this is absurd; and that the right word is ✝أُيَّلٌ, having the signification first explained in this paragraph, i. e. *thickening,* or *thick,* milk: En-Nadr says that ✝إِيَّلٌ signifies *thick urine of she-goats of the mountain;* which, when drunk by a woman, excites her venereal faculty: (T:) or this last word is used to signify *milk of an* إِيَّل, which is said to strengthen in the venereal faculty, and to fatten, as Ibn-Ḥabeeb asserts; and ✝أُيَّلٌ, which he affirms to be wrong, is a dial. var. thereof; and it may also be a quasi-pl. n. thereof: (M:) as a pl. [of آئِلٌ], applied to milk, ✝أُيَّلٌ is extr. in two respects; as a pl., of this form, of an epithet not applied to an animal; and as being regularly أُوَّلٌ. (IJ, M.) = إِنَّهُ لَآئِلُ مَالٍ and ✝أُيَّلُ مَالٍ *Verily he is a good manager,* or *tender, of cattle,* or *camels,* or *the like.* (M, TA.)

تَأْوِيلٌ used as a simple subst. in the sense of عَاقِبَةٌ &c.: see 2, last sentence.

مَآلٌ inf. n. of آلَ, in two senses pointed out above. (M, Ḳ, TA.) — [Hence, مَآلُهُ إِلَى كَذَا *His,* or *its, return,* or *course,* or *transition, is to such a state* or *condition.*] = Also, [as a noun of place &c.,] *i. q.* مَرْجِعٌ [as signifying *A place,* and *a state,* or *condition, to which a person,* or *thing, returns;* and, *to which he,* or *it, ultimately,* or *eventually, comes*]. (TA, [where this is given as a signification not mentioned in the Ḳ; so that مرجع is not here used as an inf. n.: it is, moreover, a signification well known.]) See also 2, last sentence. — *A refuge:* applied in this sense to God. (Ḥar p. 361.)

هُوَ مُؤْتَالٌ لِقَوْمِهِ مُقْتَالٌ عَلَيْهِمْ *He is ruler,* or *governor, of his people; a possessor of dictatorship over them,* or *of authority over them to judge* or *give judgment* or *pass sentence* or *decide judicially.* (A, TA.)

هٰذَا مُتَأَوَّلٌ حَسَنٌ [app. *This is a good discovery made from outward signs*]. (TA, where it immediately follows تَأَوَّلَ فِيهِ ٱلْخَيْرَ with its explanations given above.)

مُتَأَوِّلٌ: see its verb. — [Sometimes it signifies] *Veracious:* opposed to مُتَقَوِّلٌ. (Ḥar p. 256.)

اولو

أُولُو, in the gen. and accus. أُولِى: see أُلُو in art. الو.

اولى

أُولَى fem. of أَوَّلُ: see the latter in art. وأل. =

أُولَى as a pl., and its var. أُولَآءِ; and أُولٰئِكَ, or أُولَالِكَ; &c.: see أُلَى, in art. الى.

اوم

أُوْمٌ for أُمٌّ: see art. ام.

اون

1. آنَ, aor. يَؤُونُ, inf. n. أَوْنٌ, *He was, or became, at rest, or at ease; he rested* in a journey. (IAạr, T.) —— أُنْتُ, aor. and inf. n. as above, *I enjoyed a life of ease and plenty; a state of freedom from trouble* or *inconvenience, and toil* or *fatigue; a state of ease, repose,* or *tranquillity.* (AZ, T, Ṣ, M, Ḳ.) —— *I was,* or *became, grave, staid, steady, sedate,* or *calm.* (Ṣ, Ḳ.) —— *I was,* or *became, gentle;* or *I acted gently:* (T, Ṣ, M, Mṣb, Ḳ:) and *I acted,* or *proceeded, with moderation, without haste* or *hurry,* in pace or journeying: (M:) *I went gently, softly,* or *in a leisurely manner:* (Ṣ, Ḳ:) أَوْنٌ [the inf. n.] is formed by substitution [of ا for ه] from هَوْنٌ. (Ṣ.) You say, أُنْتُ بِالشَّىْءِ, and عَلَى الشَّىْءِ, *I was gentle,* or *I acted gently, with the thing;* (M;) and فِى الأَمْرِ *in the affair.* (Mṣb.) And أُنْ عَلَى نَفْسِكَ *Act thou gently with thyself,* or *be thou gentle, in pace* or *journeying:* and *proceed thou with moderation, without haste* or *hurry:* (T, Ṣ:) said in the latter sense to one who has become unsteady, or irresolute. (T.) [In like manner,] you say, أَوِّنْ ▾ عَلَى قَدْرِكَ, meaning اِتَّئِدْ عَلَى نَحْوِكَ [app. *Act thou with moderation, gentleness, deliberation,* or *in a leisurely manner, according to thine ability,* or *to the measure of thine ability;* for قَدْرٌ and نَحْوٌ are both syn. with مِقْدَارٌ]. (T, Ḳ.) And أَوِّنُوا ▾ فِى سَيْرِكُمْ *Proceed ye with moderation in your course* or *pace* or *journeying.* (ISk, T.) And تَأَوَّنَ ▾ فِى الأَمْرِ *He paused,* or *was patient, in the affair.* (M.) —— أَوْنٌ also signifies The *being weary,* or *fatigued;* like أَيْنٌ. (M.) [Whether, in this sense, it have a verb, is doubtful: see its syn. here mentioned.] —— Also The *putting oneself to trouble,* or *inconvenience, for the sake of what one may expend upon himself and his family.* (M.) And hence, accord. to one [whose name is imperfectly written in the TA], the word ▾ مَؤُونَةٌ, [as being originally مَأُونَةٌ,] of the measure مَفْعُلَةٌ: but others say that it is of the measure فَعُولَةٌ, from مَأَنْتُ. (TA.) —— آنَ أَوْنُكَ ▾ and أَوَانُكَ [and أَيْنُكَ] signify the same. (M.) [See art. اين.]

2: see 1, in two places.

5: see 1.

الآنَ and its vars.: see art. اين. [Accord. to some, it belongs to the present art., in which it is mentioned in the Mṣb.]

أَوْنٌ: see 1 [of which it is the inf. n.]: and see also what next follows.

أَوَانٌ (T, Ṣ, M, Mṣb, Ḳ) and ▾ إِوَانٌ, (T, M, Mṣb, Ḳ,) the latter mentioned by Ks on the authority of Aboo-Jámi', but the former is the usual mode of pronouncing it, (T,) and ▾ أَوْنٌ, (M,) *A time; a season:* pl. آوِنَةٌ; (T, Ṣ, M, Mṣb, Ḳ;) but Sb says آوِنَاتٌ; (M; [so in a copy of that work; app. آوِنَاتٌ, as though pl. of آوِنَةٌ;]) and آيِنَةٌ is syn. with آوِنَةٌ. (AA, T, Ḳ.) You say, جَآءَ أَوَانُ البَرْدِ [*The time,* or *season, of cold came*]. (T.) And فُلَانٌ يَصْنَعُ ذٰلِكَ الأَمْرَ آوِنَةً, (Ṣ, Ḳ,*) and آيِنَةً, (Ḳ, [in the CḲ آئِنَةً,]) *Such a one does that thing sometimes, leaving it undone sometimes.* (Ṣ, Ḳ.*) And أَتَيْتُهُ آيِنَةً بَعْدَ آيِنَةٍ *I came to him times after times.* (AA, T.) And آوِنَةٌ signifies *Time after time.* (TA, from a trad.) In the saying (of Aboo-Zubeyd, L),

طَلَبُوا صُلْحَنَا وَلَاتَ أَوَانٍ

(M,) or إِوَانٍ, (L,) [*They sought our reconciliation* with them, *but it was not the time* that reconciliation should be sought], accord. to Abu-l-'Abbás, the tenween of the last word is not a sign of the genitive case, but is, as in the instance of إِذٍ, because of the suppression of a proposition to which the word should be prefixed, as when you say, جِئْتُ أَوَانَ قَامَ زَيْدٌ *I came at the time that Zeyd stood.* (M, L.) —— [Hence, أَوَانَئِذٍ *At that time* or *season; then;* like حِينَئِذٍ.]

إِوَانٌ: see أَوَانٌ: —— and see also إِيوَانٌ.

آئِنٌ [part. n. of 1:] A man *enjoying a life of ease and plenty; a state of freedom from trouble* or *inconvenience, and toil* or *fatigue; a state of ease, repose,* or *tranquillity.* (AZ, T, Ṣ, Ḳ.) —— [Hence the saying,] رِبْعٌ آئِنٌ خَيْرٌ مِنْ غِبٍّ خَضْخَاضٍ [*An easy,* or *a gentle, journey in which the camels are watered only on the first and fourth days is better than a laborious,* or *quick, journey in which they are watered only on the first and third days*]. (TA.) [The fem. is آئِنَةٌ: the pl. of which is أَوَائِنُ and آئِنَاتٌ.] You say, بَيْنَنَا وَبَيْنَ مَكَّةَ ثَلَاثُ لَيَالٍ أَوَائِنُ *Between us and Mekkeh are three nights of easy,* or *gentle, journeying:* (Ṣ, Ḳ:*) and عَشْرُ لَيَالٍ آئِنَاتٌ *ten nights of easy journeying.* (Ṣ, M, Ḳ.)

إِيوَانٌ and ▾ إِوَانٌ (T, Ṣ, M, Mṣb, Ḳ) [each] a foreign word, [i. e. Persian,] (M,) *A chamber,* or *an apartment,* (T, Mṣb,) or *a large* صُفَّة [i. e. *porch,* or *roofed vestibule,* or *the like*], (Ṣ, Ḳ,) *similar to an* أَزَج [or *oblong arched* or *vaulted structure,* or *a portico*], (T, Ṣ, M, Ḳ,) or *built in the form of an* أَزَج, (Mṣb,) *not closed in the front,* or *face:* (T, M, Mṣb:*) [and *a palace;* often used in this sense in Arabic as well as in Persian: and in the present day, the former, and more commonly لِيوَان, which is Persian, is also applied to *an estrade; a slightly-raised portion of the floor, generally extending nearly from the door to the end,* or *to each end, of a room:*] pl. of the former, أَوَاوِينُ, (T, Ṣ, Ḳ,) because the sing. is originally إِوَّوَانٌ, (Ṣ,) and إِيوَانَاتٌ; and pl. of the latter, أُوُنٌ. (T, Ṣ, Ḳ.) Hence, إِيوَانُ كِسْرَى [*The great porch,* or *the palace, of Kisrà,* or *Chosroes,* who is called صَاحِبُ الإِيوَانِ]. (T, Ṣ, Mṣb.) —— Also the latter, [and app., accord. to the Mṣb, the former also,] *Any prop,* or *support,* of a thing: (T, Mṣb:) particularly, *a pole of a* [*tent of the kind called*] خِبَآء. (T.) —— The إِيوَان of the لِجَام [is The *headstall of the bridle;* and] has for its pl. إِيوَانَاتٌ. (T, Ḳ.)

مَؤُونَةٌ: see 1, and see art. مأن.

اوه

1 and 2: see 5.

5. تَأَوَّهَ; (Ṣ, Mgh, Mṣb, Ḳ;) and ▾ أَوَّهَ, (Ṣ, Mgh, Ḳ,) inf. n. تَأْوِيهٌ; (Ṣ, Ḳ;) and ▾ آهَ, inf. n. أَوْهٌ; (Ḳ;) *He said* آهِ or أَوْهِ &c. [i. e. *Ah!* or *alas!*]; (Ṣ, Mgh, Ḳ;) *he moaned;* or *uttered a moan,* or *moaning,* or *prolonged voice of complaint;* (Ṣ, TA;) i. q. تَوَجَّعَ. (Mṣb.)

آهِ, (Az, Ṣ, Mṣb, Ḳ, &c.,) as also آهٍ, (IAmb, Ḳ,) and آهًا, and آهَةَ ▾, (TA,) and ▾ أَوْهِ, (Ṣ, Mṣb, Ḳ,) and ▾ أَوْهٍ, (ISd, Ḳ,) and ▾ أَوْهُ, (Ḳ,) and ▾ أَوَّهْ, (Ṣ,) or ▾ أَوِّهِ, (Ḳ,) and ▾ أَوَّهُ, (Hr, Mgh, Mṣb, Ḳ,) so in some copies of the Ṣ, but in a copy in the author's handwriting ▾ آوَّهْ, there said to be with medd, and with teshdeed and fet-ḥ to the و, and with the ه quiescent, (TA,) [or,] accord. to Aboo-Ṭálib, آوَّهْ, with medd, thus pronounced by the vulgar, is wrong, (T in art. او,) and ▾ أَوَّاه, and ▾ أَوُّوه, [in both of which, and in some other forms which follow, it is doubtful whether the ه be quiescent or movent, and if movent, with what vowel,] (TA,) and ▾ آوُوهُ, (Ḳ, TA,) or ▾ أَوُوهُ, but said by ISd to be with medd, and mentioned by AHát as heard from the Arabs, (TA,) and ▾ أَوْتَاهُ, (Ḳ, TA,) or أَوْتَاهُ, (CḲ,) or ▾ أَوْتَاه, and ▾ آوْتَاه, (Ṣ, [in one copy of which the ه is marked as quiescent,]) and ▾ آوِيَاه, (Ḳ, TA,) with medd, (TA,) or ▾ أَوِيَاهُ, (CḲ,) and أَوِ, (Ṣ, Mṣb, Ḳ,) and آوِ, and آوِ, (Ḳ, TA,) and وَاهًا, and هَاهُ or هَاهْ, (TA,) [*Ah!* or *alas!*] a word imitative of the voice, cry, or exclamation, of the مُتَأَلِّه; (Az and TA in explanation of آهِ;) [i. e.] a word expressive of pain, grief, sorrow, lamentation, complaint, or moaning; (Ṣ, Mgh, Mṣb, Ḳ, TA;) denoting the prolongation of the voice with complaint: (Ṣ, TA, after أَوَّهْ or آوَّهْ:) sometimes, also, a man says آهِ from a motive of affection, or pity, or compassion, and of impatience: (Az, TA:) [and it is also said that] آهًا is a word expressive of grief or lamentation, or of most intense grief or lamentation or regret; [that] it is put in the accus. case as being used in the manner of inf. ns.; and [that] the hemzeh is originally و: but IAth says, آهًا is a word expressive of pain, grief, sorrow, lamentation, complaint, or moaning, used in relation to evil, like as وَاهًا is used in relation to good: (TA in art. اه:) and أَوَّهْ and آوَّهْ and أَوِ are cries uttered to horses, to make them return. (ISh and TA in art. اوى. See 2 in that art. in the present work.) You say, آهِ مِنْ كَذَا [*Ah,* or *alas, on account of,* or *for, such a thing!*]; (Ṣ, Mṣb;) and in like manner, أَوْهِ [&c.], followed by مِنْ, and by لِ, (Ṣ, TA,) and by عَلَى. (TA.) [See also أَوِ in art. او.]

آهَةٌ a subst. from تَأَوَّهَ; occurring in the saying of El-Muthakkib El-'Abdee,

* إِذَا مَا قُمْتُ أَرْحَلُهَا بِلَيْلٍ *

* تَأَوَّهُ آهَةَ الرَّجُلِ الحَزِينِ *

[*When I arise to saddle her, by night, she moans with the moaning of the sorrowful man*]: (Ṣ, ISd:) ISd says that, in his opinion, the subst. is here put in the place of the inf. n., i. e. تَأَوُّه: (TA:) but some recite the verse differently, saying, أَهَّةَ, from أَهَّ meaning تَوَجَّعَ: (Ṣ:) and some say, تَهَوُّهُ هَاهَةَ. (TA.) And hence the saying, in imprecating evil on a man, آهَةً لَكَ [*May God cause moaning to thee!*], and أَوَّةً لَكَ, with the ه suppressed, and with teshdeed to the و. (Ṣ.) [See also أَوَّةً in art. او.] And see آهِ above. ═ [Also] *Measles*: thus in the phrase, used in imprecating evil on a man, آهَةً وَمَاهَةً [May God cause] *measles and small-pox* [to befall thee]! (Ḳ,* TA,) mentioned by Lḥ on the authority of Aboo-Khálid. (TA.)

آهٍ and أَوْهِ and أَوَّهْ and أَوْهُ &c.: see آهِ.

أَوَّاهٌ A man *often saying Ah! or alas!* or *often moaning*: (Mgh:) or one *who says Ah!* or *alas! from a motive of affection*, or *pity*, or *compassion*, and *fear*: or *mourning*, or *sorrowing*, *much*, or *often*: (TA:) or *compassionate*; *tender-hearted*: or *often praying*, or *frequent in prayer*: (Ḳ,* TA:) or one *who celebrates the praises of God*, or *praises Him greatly*, or *glorifies Him*: or *who praises much*, or *often*: or *who abases himself*, or *addresses himself with earnest supplication*, [*to God*], *confident of his prayer's being answered*: (TA:) or one *having certain knowledge* (Ḳ, TA) *of his prayer's being answered*: (TA:) or *inviting much*, or *often*, *to what is good*: (TA:) or *skilled in the law*: or *a believer*; so in the Abyssinian language: (Ḳ:) occurring in the Ḳur [ix. 115 and xi. 77]. (TA.) ═ See also آهِ.

أَوُّوهُ, or أَوُوهْ, and أَوُّوهْ:
آوَتَاه, or أَوَّتَاهُ, or أَوَّتَاهْ, and أَوَّتَاه:
آوِيَاه, or أَوِيَاهْ:
} see آهِ.

مُتَأَوِّهٌ [*Saying Ah!* &c.: (see the verb:) and] *abasing himself*; or *addressing himself with earnest supplication* [*to God*]. (TA.) [See also أَوَّاهٌ.]

اوى

1. أَوَى إِلَيْهِ, (T, Ṣ, M, Mgh, Mṣb, Ḳ,) and أَوَّاهُ, (M, Mṣb, Ḳ,) aor. يَأْوِى, (T, Ṣ, Mṣb,) imperative ايو, (T,) inf. n. أُوِىٌّ, (T, Ṣ, M, Mgh, Mṣb, Ḳ,) with ḍamm, (Ḳ,) of the measure فُعُولٌ, [originally أُوُوىٌ,] (Ṣ,) and إِوِىٌّ, (Fr, M, Ḳ,) with kesr, (Ḳ,) and إِوَآءٌ; (Ṣ;) and ▼ أَوَّى اليه, (M, Ḳ,) inf. n. تَأْوِيَةٌ; (Ḳ;) and ▼ تَأَوَّى; (M, Ḳ;) and ▼ ائْتَوَى, (thus [more commonly اِئْتَوَى] accord. to a copy of the M,) or ▼ اِتَّوَى, (Ḳ,) like اِتَّخَذَ, (TḲ,) and ▼ اِيتَوَى, (M, Ḳ,) both of the measure افتعل; (TA;) and ▼ آوَى is used by some in the same sense, but rejected, in this sense, by several; (Mṣb;) the pronoun relating to a place of abode; (T, Ṣ, M, Mṣb, Ḳ;) *He betook himself to it*, or *repaired to it, for lodging, covert, or refuge*; (Mgh;) and [simply] *he got him* or *got himself, betook himself, repaired*, or *resorted, to it*; (T, Mgh;) *he returned to it*; (M;) *he took up his abode in it*; *he lodged*, or *abode*, or *dwelt, in it*. (Mṣb, Ḳ.) Hence, in the Ḳur [xi. 45], سَآوِى إِلَى جَبَلٍ يَعْصِمُنِى مِنَ المَآءِ [*I will betake myself for refuge to a mountain that shall preserve me from the water*]. (Ṣ.) الأُوِىُّ properly relates to living beings; but is used otherwise, metaphorically. (M.) In the saying of Lebeed,

* بِصَبُوحِ صَافِيَةٍ وَجَذْبِ كَرِينَةٍ *

* بِمُوَتَّرٍ تَأْتَى ▼ لَهُ إِبْهَامُهَا *

[*With a morning-potation of clear wine* (خَمْر being understood), *and a female singer's straining of her chords, with a stringed instrument to which her thumb returns* after the straining], he means تَأْتَوِى لَهُ, of the measure تَفْتَعِلُ, from أَوَيْتُ إِلَيْهِ signifying عُدْتُ; the و being changed into ا [written ى], and the ى, which is the final radical, being elided. (M. [But see another reading near the end of the first paragraph of art. اول.]) أَوَى, aor. as above, inf. n. أُوِىٌّ, also signifies *He turned away*: and hence, [it is said,] إِذْ أَوَى الفِتْيَةُ إِلَى الكَهْفِ [*When the young men turned away to the cave*: though the verb may be here well rendered *betook themselves for refuge*]. (Ḥar p. 246.) You say also, أَوَيْتُ إِلَى فُلَانٍ, (A 'Obeyd, T,) or لَهُ, (as afterwards written in a copy of the T,) [*I betook myself to such a one*, or *repaired to him, for lodging, covert, or refuge*; or] *I joined myself, got myself, betook myself, repaired*, or *resorted, to such a one*: and accord. to AHeyth, أَوَيْتُ فُلَانًا signifies the same; but he did not know أَوَيْتُ to be syn. with آوَيْتُ as explained below. (T.) And أَوَى إِلَى اللّٰهِ *He returned unto God*. (TA, from a trad.) — أَوَى said of a wound: see 5. ═ See also 4, in seven places. ═ أَوَى لَهُ, (T, Ṣ, M, Mgh, Ḳ,) like رَوَى, (Ḳ, TA,) but it would have been more explicit if the author of the Ḳ had said like رَمَى, (TA,) [as is shown by the false reading in the CḲ, أَوِىَ لَهُ كَرَوِىَ,] aor. يَأْوِى, (T, Ṣ, Mgh,) inf. n. أَوْيَةٌ (Ṣ, Ḳ) and إِيَّةٌ, (Ṣ, Mgh, Ḳ,) with kesr, (TA,) [originally إِوْيَةٌ,] the و being changed into ى because of the kesreh before it, (Ṣ,) or because combined with ى and preceded by sukoon [a mistake for "kesreh"], (IB as cited in the TA,) [in a copy of the T written ايّة, and in a copy of the M and in the CḲ آيَة,] and مَأْوِيَةٌ, (Ṣ, M, Ḳ,) without teshdeed, (Ṣ, TA,) [in my copy of the Mgh written with teshdeed,] and مَأْوَاةٌ, (Ṣ, M, Ḳ,) *He compassionated him*; *felt compassion*, or *pity, for him*; (T, Ṣ, M, Mgh, Ḳ;) as also ▼ ائتوى, (T, Ḳ,) of the measure افتعل. (TA.) In using the imperative form, you say, اِوِ لَهُ, [unless this be a mistranscription for اِيوِ لَهُ,] meaning *Be thou compassionate to him*. (T, TA.)

2: see 1, first sentence: ═ and see 4. ═ أَوَّيْتُ بِالخَيْلِ (ISh, T) [*I drew together the horses*: this meaning seems to be indicated in the T, by the context: or] *I called out to the horses* أَوْهْ, *in order that they should return at hearing my voice*: (ISh:) and in like manner one says to them ▼ آوِ or آوْ; (ISh, T, TA;) a well-known call of the Arabs to horses; and sometimes آىْ, with a long meddeh, is said to them from afar. (T, TA.) [See also 5.]

4. آوَاهُ, (T, Ṣ, M, Mgh, Mṣb, Ḳ,) inf. n. إِيوَآءٌ; (T, Ṣ, Mgh;) and ▼ أَوَّاهُ; (Ḳ;) and ▼ أَوَاهُ; (T, Ṣ, M, Mgh, Mṣb, Ḳ;) the first of which is the [most] approved; (T;) the last used by some; (T, Mṣb;) both given on the authority of AZ, (Ṣ,) and of A 'Obeyd, accord. to whom you say, أَوَيْتُهُ, with the short ا only; (T, M;) *He*, or *it, gave him*, or *afforded him, lodging, covert*, or *refuge*; *harboured him*; *sheltered him*; *protected him*; (Mgh;) *he lodged him*, or *lodged him with himself*; *made him his guest*; or *gave him refuge* or *asylum*, absolutely, or *with himself*; syn. أَنْزَلَهُ; (Ḳ;) or أَنْزَلَهُ بِهِ. (T, Ṣ, TA.) You say also, آوَيْتُهُ and ▼ أَوَيْتُ الرَّجُلَ إِلَىَّ [*I took the man to me to lodge, to be my guest*, or *to give him refuge* or *asylum*]. (M.) And آوَاهُ سَقْفٌ [*A roof sheltered him*]. (Mgh.) And آوَيْتُهَا and ▼ أَوَيْتُ الإِبِلَ [*I lodged the camels in their nightly resting-place*]; both meaning the same. (T.) And it is said in a trad., الحَمْدُ لِلّٰهِ الَّذِى كَفَانَا وَآوَانَا i. e. [*Praise be to God who hath sufficed us and*] *hath brought us to a place of abode for us*, and not made us to be scattered like the beasts. (TA.) AHeyth disallowed ▼ أَوَيْتُ as syn. with آوَيْتُ; but it is correct. (T.) It is said in a form of divorce, لَا يَأْوِينِى ▼ وَإِيَّاكِ بَيْتٌ [*A house, or tent, shall not lodge*, or *comprise, me with thee*]. (Mgh.) And among other instances, is the saying of the Prophet, (T,) لَا يَأْوِى ▼ الضَّالَّةَ إِلَّا ضَالٌّ [*No one will harbour the stray beast but a person straying from the right course of conduct*]. (T, Mgh.) And his saying, لَا قَطْعَ فِى ثَمَرٍ حَتَّى يَأْوِيَهُ ▼ الجَرِينُ i. e. [*There shall be no cutting off* of the hand *in the case of* stealing *fruit*] *unless the place where the fruit is dried contain it* [at the time of the stealing thereof]. (TA.) — Hence, إِيوَآءُ خَشَبِ الفَحْمِ *The throwing of dust, or earth, upon the wood of which charcoal is made, and covering it therewith*. (Mgh.) ═ See also 1, first sentence.

5: see 1, first sentence. — تَأَوَّتِ الطَّيْرُ *The birds collected*, or *flocked, together*; (Lth, T, Ṣ, M, Ḳ;) as also ▼ تَآوَتْ: (Ḳ:) the latter is allowable. (T.) And in like manner one says of other things. (M.) [Thus,] one says, تَأَوَّتِ الخَيْلُ *The horses drew*, or *gathered, themselves together*: and تَأَوَّى النَّاسُ *The men did so*. (T.) You say also, of a wound, ▼ تَأَوَّى, and ▼ أَوَى, meaning *It drew together, for healing*; and so تَآزَى, and أَزَى: so in the Nawádir el-Aaráb. (T.) ═ One may also say, يَتَأَوَّى, without saying it with ه, [i. e. يَتَأَوَّهُ,] meaning *He says* أَوْه. (Fr and T in art. او.) [See also 2; and see art. اوه.]

6: see 5, in two places.

8. اِئْتَوَى, or اِتَّوَى, or اِئتوى, and اِيتَوَى, and تَأَتَّى for تَأَتَّوِى: see 1, first part of the paragraph, in four places. — See also the last sentence but one of the same paragraph.

10. اِسْتَأْوَيْتُهُ *I asked him*, or *desired him, to compassionate me*, or *have mercy on me*; syn. اِسْتَرْحَمْتُهُ. (T.) A poet (namely, Dhu-r-Rummeh, TA) says,

وَلَوْ أَنِّى ٱسْتَأْوَيْتُهُ مَا أَوَى لِيَا

[*And if I had asked him, or desired him, to compassionate me, he would not have compassionated me*]. (T, Ṣ.)

أُوَيَّةٌ dim. of آيَةٌ: see the letter ا.

آوٍ or آوٍ: see 2. — آوٍ [the part. n. of 1] has for its pl. أُوِىٌّ [like one of the inf. ns. of 1]. (T, Ṣ.) The latter is applied to birds, signifying *Collecting, or flocking, together*; (T, Ṣ, M,* Ḳ;*) syn. ▼مُتَأَوِّيَةٌ (Lth, T) and مُتَأَوِّيَاتٌ. (Lth, T, Ṣ, M, Ḳ.)

ابْنُ آوَى, a determinate noun, (Ṣ, M,) [*The jackal*; vulgarly called in the present day وَاوِى;] *a certain small beast*, (M, Ḳ,) *called in Persian* شَغَال, (Ṣ,) or *in that language* [or *in Turkish*] چَقَال: (TA:) it has been said to be *the offspring of the wolf*; but is well known to be not of the wolf-kind: (Mṣb:) آوَى is inseparable from ابن: (M:) it is imperfectly decl., (T, Ṣ, Mṣb,) being of the measure أَفْعَلُ, (Ṣ,) or regarded as such; (Lth, T;) or because it has the quality of a proper name and the measure of a verb: (Mṣb:) the pl. is بَنَاتُ آوَى, (T, Ṣ, Mṣb, Ḳ,) though applying to males [as well as females], like بَنَاتُ أَعْوَجَ and بَنَاتُ لَبُونٍ. (AHeyth, T.)

أَوَوِىٌّ and أَوِىٌّ, said to be rel. ns. of آيَةٌ; which see, in art. اى.

آيَةٌ, said by some to be originally أَوَيَةٌ: see art. اى.

مَأْوًى (Ṣ, M, Mṣb, Ḳ) and ▼مَأْوٍ and ▼مَأْوَاةٌ (M, Ḳ [but respecting these two forms see what follows]) nouns of place from the first of the verbs in this art.; (M, Ḳ;) [*A place to which one betakes himself, or repairs, for lodging, covert, or refuge; a refuge; an asylum; a place of resort*; (see 1;)] *any place to which a thing betakes itself*, &c., (يَأْوِى إِلَيْهِ,) *by night or by day*; (Ṣ;) the *lodging-place*, or *abode*, of any animal; the *nightly resting-place* of sheep or goats; (Mṣb;) and of camels: (Idem in art. روح:) ▼مَأْوٍ is used peculiarly in relation to camels: (Ṣ:) مَأْوِى الإِبِلِ being a dial. var. of مَأْوَى الإِبِلِ, but anomalous, (Fr, T, Ṣ, Mṣb,) and the only instance of the kind except مَأْقِى العَيْنِ: (Fr, T, M: [but see art. مأق:]) مُوْق and مَأْوًى and مَأْقٌ are the forms preferred: (Fr, T:) [Az also says,] I have heard the chaste in speech of the Benoo-Kiláb use, for مَأْوَى الإِبِلِ, the word ▼مَأْوَاةٌ. (T.) جَنَّةُ المَأْوَى, in the Ḳur [liii. 15], is said to mean *The paradise to which repair the souls of the martyrs*, (M, Bḍ, Jel, TA,) or *the pious*, (Bḍ, Jel,) or *the angels*: (Jel:) or *that in which the night is passed*. (TA.)

مَأْوٍ: } see مَأْوًى, in four places.
مَأْوَاةٌ:

مَاوِيَّةٌ: see art. موه.

مُتَأَوِّيَةٌ: see آوٍ.

اى

2. أَيَّا آيَةً, [inf. n., by rule, as below,] *He put, or set, a sign, token, or mark, by which a person or thing might be known*. (M.) — أَيَّا بِالإِبِلِ, (inf. n. تَأْيِيَةٌ, Lth, T,) *He chid the camels, saying to them* أَيَايَا, (Lth, T, M, and Ḳ in art. أيا,) or أَيَايَهْ, (M,) or يَايَا, (Ḳ,) or يَايَهْ. (M, Ḳ.)

5. تَأَيَّا, as a trans. verb: see 6. — *He paused, stopped, stayed, remained*, or *tarried*, (T, Ṣ, M, Ḳ,*) بِالْمَكَانِ *in the place*; (M, Ḳ;* [in the latter explained by تَلَبَّثَ عَلَيْهِ; but this seems to be a mistake, arising from the omission of part of a passage in the M, (one of the chief sources of the Ḳ,) running thus; تَأَيَّا بِالْمَكَانِ تَلَبَّثَ وَتَمَكَّثَ وَتَأَيَّا عَلَيْهِ ٱنْصَرَفَ فِى تُؤَدَةٍ;]) and *confined, restricted, limited, restrained*, or *withheld, himself*. (T.) In the sense of its inf. n., [by rule, تَأَيٍّ, originally تَأَيُّىٌ,] they said ▼تَأْيِيَةٌ, or تَئِيَّةٌ or تَئِيَّةٌ; [thus differently written in different places in copies of the T and Ṣ;] as in the ex. لَيْسَ مَنْزِلُكُمْ بِدَارِ تَائِيَّةٍ or تَئِيَّةٍ, (IAạr, T,) or لَيْسَ مَنْزِلُكُمْ هٰذَا بِمَنْزِلِ تَأْيِيَةٍ or تَئِيَّةٍ, (Ṣ,) i. e. *Your abode*, or *this your abode, is not an abode of tarriance and confinement*. (IAạr, T, Ṣ.) — *He expected*, or *waited for, a thing*: (Lth, T:) and *he acted with moderation, gently, deliberately*, or *leisurely*; *without haste*; or *with gravity, staidness, sedateness*, or *calmness*; (Lth, T, Ḳ;) فِى الأَمْرِ *in the affair*; inf. n. تَأَيٍّ. (Lth, T.) تَأَيَّيْتُ عَلَيْهِ, in a verse of Lebeed, means *I acted with moderation*, &c., as above, *and paused, stopped, stayed, remained*, or *tarried, upon him*, i. e., upon my horse: (T:) or *I remained firm upon him*: (TA, as on the authority of Az:) but it is explained by Lth as meaning *I turned away*, or *back, deliberately*, or *leisurely, upon him*. (T: and the like is said in the M.)

6. تَآيَيْتُهُ, (T, Ṣ, M,* Ḳ,) and ▼تَأَيَّيْتُهُ, (Ṣ, Ḳ,) *I directed my course*, or *aim, to*, or *towards*, (T, Ṣ, M,* Ḳ,) *his* آيَة, (Ṣ, M,) i. e., (M,) *his* شَخْص [or *body*, or *corporeal form* or *figure* or *substance, seen from a distance*; or *person*]. (T, M, Ḳ.) The following is an ex., as some relate it, of the former verb; and as others relate it, of the latter:

ٱلْحُصْنُ أَوْلَى لَوْ تَآيَيْتِهِ
مِنْ حَثْيِكِ التُّرْبَ عَلَى الرَّاكِبِ

[*Modest behaviour were more proper, if thou directedst thy course towards his person, than thy throwing dust upon the rider*]: (Ṣ, TA: [in two copies of the former of which, for أَوْلَى, I find أَدْنَى:]) said by a woman to her daughter, on the latter's relating, in a couplet, that a rider, passing along, had seen her, and she had thrown dust in his face, purposely. (IB.)

أَىْ a vocative particle, (Ṣ, M, Mughnee, Ḳ,) addressed to the near, (Ṣ, Ḳ,) not to the distant: (Ṣ:) or to the near, or the distant, or the intermediate; accord. to different authorities. (Mughnee.) You say, أَىْ زَيْدُ أَقْبِلْ [*O Zeyd, advance*: or, if it may be used in addressing one who is distant, *ho there, soho*, or *holla*: and if used in addressing one who is between near and distant, *ho*, or *what ho*]: (Ṣ:) and أَىْ رَبِّ [*O my Lord*]; occurring in a trad.: and sometimes it is pronounced ▼آىْ. (Mughnee.) — Also an explicative particle. (Ṣ, M, Mughnee, Ḳ.) You say, أَىْ كَذَا in the sense of يُرِيدُ كَذَا [*He means such a thing*, or يَعْنِى كَذَا, which has the same signification; or أُرِيدُ, or أَعْنِى, *I mean*; or the like; for all of which, we may say, *meaning*; or *that is*]; (Ṣ;) as in عِنْدِى عَسْجَدٌ أَىْ ذَهَبٌ [*I have* عَسْجَد, *that is*, (I have) ذَهَب, or *gold*]. (Mughnee.) What follows it is an adjunct explicative of what precedes it, or a substitute. (Mughnee.) AA says that he asked Mbr respecting what follows it, and he answered that it may be a substitute for what precedes, and may be a word independent of what precedes it, and may be a noun in the accus. case: and that he asked Th, and he answered that it may be an explicative, or a word independent of what precedes it, or a noun governed in the accus. case by a verb suppressed: you say, جَآءَنِى أَخُوكَ أَىْ زَيْدٌ [*Thy brother came to me*; *that is, Zeyd*]; and you may say, أَىْ زَيْدًا [*I mean Zeyd*]: and رَأَيْتُ أَخَاكَ أَىْ زَيْدًا [*I saw thy brother*; *I mean*, or *that is, Zeyd*]; and you may say, أَىْ زَيْدٌ [*that is, Zeyd*]: and مَرَرْتُ بِأَخِيكَ أَىْ زَيْدٍ [*I passed by thy brother*; *that is, by Zeyd*]; and you may say, أَىْ زَيْدًا [*I mean, Zeyd*]; and أَىْ زَيْدٌ [*that is, Zeyd*]. (T, TA.) When it occurs after تَقُولُ, in a case like the following, [i. e., when a verb following it explains a verb preceding it,] one says, تَقُولُ ٱسْتَكْتَمْتُهُ الحَدِيثَ أَىْ سَأَلْتُهُ كِتْمَانَهُ [*Thou sayest*, استكتمته الحديث, *meaning* سألته كتمانه *I asked of him the concealment of it*, namely, the discourse, or story; and so when تَقُولُ is understood, as is often, or generally, the case in lexicons]; with ḍamm to the ت: but if you put إِذَا in the place of أَىْ, you say, إِذَا سَأَلْتَهُ, with fet-ḥ, because اذا is an adverbial noun relating to تَقُولُ. (Mughnee.) — See also أَىٌّ, near the beginning of the paragraph, in three places.

إِىْ is a particle denoting a reply, meaning نَعَمْ [*Yes*, or *yea*]; importing acknowledgment of the truth of an enunciation; and the making a thing known, to him who asks information; and a promise, to him who seeks or demands; therefore it occurs after such sayings as "Zeyd stood" and "Did Zeyd stand?" and "Beat thou Zeyd," and the like; as does نَعَمْ: Ibn-El-Ḥájib asserts that it occurs only after an interrogation; as in the saying [in the Ḳur x. 54], وَيَسْتَنْبِئُونَكَ أَحَقٌّ هُوَ قُلْ إِى وَرَبِّى [*And they will ask thee to inform them, saying, Is it true? Say, Yea, by my Lord!*]: but accord. to all, it does not occur otherwise than before an oath: and when one says, إِى وَٱللّٰهِ [*Yea, by God!*], and then drops the و, the ى may be quiescent, and with fet-ḥ, and elided; [so that you say, إِىْ ٱللّٰهِ, and إِىَ ٱللّٰهِ, and إِ ٱللّٰهِ;] in the first of which cases, two quiescent letters occur together, irregularly. (Mughnee.) Lth says, إِى is an oath, as in إِى وَرَبِّى, meaning, says Zj, نَعَمْ وَرَبِّى: IAạr is also related to have said the like; and this is the correct explanation. (T.) [J says,] It is a word preceding an oath, meaning بَلَى [q. v.]; as in إِى وَرَبِّى and إِى وَٱللّٰهِ. (Ṣ.) [ISd and F say,] It is syn. with نَعَمْ, and is conjoined with an oath: and one says also هِى. (M, Ḳ.)

أَىٌّ is a noun, used in five different manners. (Mughnee.) One of its meanings is that of an interrogative, (T, Ṣ, M, Mughnee, Ḳ,) relating to intellectual beings and to non-intellectual things; [meaning *Who? which?* and *what?*] (Ṣ, M, Ḳ;) and as such, it is a decl. noun: (Ṣ:) it is said in the Ḳ to be a particle; (MF;) and so in the M; (TA;) but this is wrong: (MF:) and it is added in the Ḳ that it is indecl.; (MF;) and it is said to be so in the M, accord. to Sb, in an instance to be explained below; (TA;) but this is only when it is a conjunct noun [like ٱلَّذِى], or denotes the object of a vocative: (MF:) or, accord. to some, it is decl. as a conjunct noun also. (Mughnee.) You say, أَيُّهُمْ أَخُوكَ [*Who,* or *which, of them, is thy brother?*]. (Ṣ.) Another ex. is the saying [in the Ḳur vii. 184, and last verse of lxxvii.], فَبِأَىِّ حَدِيثٍ بَعْدَهُ يُؤْمِنُونَ [*And in what announcement, after it, will they believe?*]. (Mughnee.) Sometimes it is without teshdeed; as in the saying (of El-Farezdaḳ, M),

• تَنَظَّرْتُ نَصْرًا وَٱلسِّمَاكَيْنِ أَيْهُمَا ♦ •
• عَلَىَّ مِنَ ٱلْغَيْثِ ٱسْتَهَلَّتْ مَوَاطِرُهْ •

[*I looked for rain,* or *aid from the clouds, and the two Simáks* (stars so called). *Of which of them two did the rains pour vehemently upon me from the clouds?*]: (M, Mughnee, Ḳ:* [in the last of which, only the former hemistich is given, with نَسْرًا (meaning the star or asterism so called) instead of نَصْرًا:]) so by poetic licence: (M:) IJ says that for this reason the poet has elided the second ى, but should have restored the first ى to و, because it is originally و. (TA. [But this assertion, respecting the first ى, I regard as improbable.]) أَيْمِ ♦, also, is a contraction of أَىُّ مَا, meaning أَىُّ شَىْءٍ: so in the saying, أَيْمِ هُوَ يَا فُلَانُ [*What thing is it, O such a one?*]: and أَيْمِ تَقُولُ [*What thing sayest thou?*]. (TA in art. ايم.) In like manner, also, ♦ أَيْشٍ is used as a contraction of أَىُّ شَىْءٍ. (Ks, TA in art. جوم.) A poet speaks of his companions as being بِأَىِّ وَأَيْنَمَا; making أَىّ the name of the quarter (جِهَة); so that, being determinate and of the feminine gender, it is imperfectly declinable. (M. [See أَيْنَ; under which head two other readings are given; and where it is said that the verse in which this occurs is by Ḥomeyd Ibn-Thowr.]) أَىّ is never without a noun or pronoun to which it is prefixed, except in a vocative expression and when it is made to conform with a word to which it refers, as in cases to be exemplified hereafter. (Mughnee.) Being so prefixed, it is determinate; but sometimes, [as in the latter of the cases just mentioned,] it is not so prefixed, yet has the meaning of a prefixed noun. (Ṣ.) When used as an interrogative, it is not governed, as to the letter, though it is as to the meaning, by the verb that precedes it, but by what follows it; as in the saying in the Ḳur [xviii. 11], لِنَعْلَمَ أَىُّ ٱلْحِزْبَيْنِ أَحْصَى [*That we might know which of the two parties was able to compute*]; and in the same [xxvi. last verse], وَسَيَعْلَمُ ٱلَّذِينَ ظَلَمُوا أَىَّ مُنْقَلَبٍ يَنْقَلِبُونَ [*And they who have acted wrongly shall know with what a translating they shall be translated*]: (Fr,* Th, Mbr, T, Ṣ:*) when it is governed by the verb before it, it has not the interrogative meaning, as will be shown hereafter. (Fr, T.) In the saying of the poet,

• تَصِيحُ بِنَا حَنِيفَةُ إِذْ رَأَتْنَا •
• وَأَىَّ ٱلْأَرْضِ تَذْهَبُ لِلصِّيَاحِ •

[*Ḥaneefeh* (the tribe so named) *shout to us when they see us. And to what* place *of the earth,* or *land, will they go for the shouting?*], أَىّ is in the accus. case because the prep. إِلَى is suppressed before it. (Ṣ.) When they separate it [from what follows it, not prefixing it to another noun], the Arabs say أَىٌّ, and in the dual أَيَّانِ, and in the pl. أَيُّونَ; and they make it fem., saying أَيَّةٌ, and [in the dual] أَيَّتَانِ, and [in the pl.] أَيَّاتٌ: but when they prefix it to a noun, properly so called, not a pronoun, they make it sing. and masc., saying أَىُّ ٱلرَّجُلَيْنِ [*Who,* or *which, of the two men?*], and أَىُّ ٱلْمَرْأَتَيْنِ [*Who,* or *which, of the two women?*], and أَىُّ ٱلرِّجَالِ [*Who,* or *which, of the men?*], and أَىُّ ٱلنِّسَآءِ [*Who,* or *which, of the women?*]: and when they prefix it to a fem. pronoun, they make it masc. [as when they prefix it to a masc. pronoun] and fem., saying أَيُّهُمَا and أَيَّتُهُمَا [*Who,* or *which, of them two?*], meaning women; (Fr, T;) [the latter of which seems to be the more common; for ISd says,] sometimes they said أَيُّهُنَّ [*Who,* or *which, of them?* referring to women], meaning أَيَّتُهُنَّ. (M.) It is said in the Ḳur [xxxi. last verse], وَمَا تَدْرِى نَفْسٌ بِأَىِّ أَرْضٍ تَمُوتُ [*And a person knoweth not in what land he will die*]: (Ṣ:) but some read بِأَيَّةِ أَرْضٍ; and Sb compares this fem. form to كُلَّتُهُنَّ. (Bḍ.) When it is used as an interrogative relating to an indeterminate noun in a preceding phrase, أَىّ is made to conform with that indeterminate noun in case-ending and in gender and in number; and this is done [alike, accord. to some,] in the case of its connexion with a following word and in the case of a pause; so that, [in the case of a pause,] to him who says, جَآءَنِى رَجُلٌ [A man came to me], you say, [accord. to the authorities alluded to above,] أَىٌّ [*Who?*]; and to him who says, رَأَيْتُ رَجُلًا [I saw a man], أَيًّا [*Whom?*]; and to him who says, مَرَرْتُ بِرَجُلٍ [I passed by a man], أَىٍّ [*Whom?*]: and in like manner, [accord. to all authorities,] in the case of its connexion with a following word; as أَىٌّ يَا فَتَى [*Who, O young man?*], and أَيًّا يَا فَتَى [*Whom, O young man?*], and أَىٍّ يَا فَتَى [*Whom, O young man?*]: and in the case of the fem. you say, أَيَّةٌ and أَيَّةً and أَيَّةٍ [in the nom. and accus. and gen. respectively]; and in the dual, أَيَّانِ and أَيَّتَانِ in the nom. case [masc. and fem. respectively], and أَيَّيْنِ and أَيَّتَيْنِ in the accus. and gen. cases [masc. and fem. respectively]; and in the pl., [with the like distinction of genders,] أَيُّونَ and أَيَّاتٌ in the nom. case, and أَيِّينَ and أَيَّاتٍ in the accus. and gen. cases. (I 'Aḳ p. 319.) [Exs. in cases of pause, agreeing with the foregoing rules, are given in the T; and exs. in cases of connexion with following words, agreeing with the foregoing, are given in the Mughnee: but J gives rules differing from the foregoing in some respects; and IB gives rules differing in some points both from the foregoing and from those of J.] It is said in the Ṣ, أَىّ is made to conform with indeterminate nouns significant of intellectual beings and of non-intellectual things, and is used as an interrogative; and when it is thus used in reference to an indeterminate noun, you make it to have a case-ending like that of the noun respecting which it demands positive information; so that when it is said to you, مَرَّ بِى رَجُلٌ [A man passed by me], you say, أَىٌّ يَا فَتَى [*Who, O young man?*], thus giving it a case-ending [like that of رَجُلٌ] when it is in connexion with a following word; and you indicate the case-ending [by the pronunciation termed ٱلرَّوْمُ, saying أَىُّ, with a somewhat obscure utterance of the final vowel,] in pausing; and if one says, رَأَيْتُ رَجُلًا [I saw a man], you say, أَيًّا يَا فَتَى [*Whom, O young man?*], giving it a case-ending [like that of رَجُلًا], with tenween, when it is [thus] in connexion with a following word; and you pause upon the ا, saying أَيَّا; and when one says, مَرَرْتُ بِرَجُلٍ [I passed by a man], you say, أَىٍّ يَا فَتَى [*Whom, O young man?* in a case of connexion with a following word; and أَىِّ in a case of pausing]: you conform with what the other has said, in the nom. and accus. and gen. cases, in the case of connexion with a following word and in that of pausing: but IB says that this is correct only in the case of connexion with a following word; for in the case of a pause, you say only أَىّْ, in the nom. and gen., with sukoon; and you imitate in both of these cases only when you use the dual form or the pl.: it is added in the Ṣ, you say in the cases of the dual and pl. and fem. like as we have said respecting مَنْ: when one says, جَآءَنِى رِجَالٌ [Men came to me], you say, أَيُّونْ [*Who?*], with the ن quiescent; and أَيِّينْ in the accus. and gen.: but IB says, the correct mode is to say, أَيُّونَ and أَيِّينَ, with fet-ḥ to the ن in both; [meaning that this is the only allowable mode in the case of connexion with a following word, and app. that it is the preferable mode in the case of a pause;] the quiescent ن being allowable only in the case of a pause, and with respect to مَنْ, for you say مَنُونْ and مَنِينْ with the quiescent ن only: it is then added in the Ṣ, you say, also, أَيَّهْ [*Who?* and *whom?*] in using the fem. [in a case of pause]; but in a case of connexion with a following word, [when referring to a noun in the accus.,] you say, أَيَّةً يَا هٰذَا [*Whom, O thou?* in the sing.], and أَيَّاتٍ [in the pl.; and in like manner, أَيَّةٌ in the nom. sing., and أَيَّةٍ in the gen. sing.; and أَيَّاتٌ in the nom. pl., and أَيَّاتٍ in the gen. pl.]: but when the interrogation refers to a determinate noun, أَيٌّ is in the nom. case (with refʿ) only. (TA.) [See also أَيَّانَ, below.] — [In other cases, now to be mentioned, it is used alike as sing., dual, and pl.] — It also denotes a condition; (T, Ṣ, M, Mughnee;) in which case, also, it is a decl. noun, applied to an intellectual being and to a non-intellectual thing. (Ṣ.) So in the saying, أَيُّهُمْ يُكْرِمْنِى أُكْرِمْهُ [*Whichever of them treats me with honour, I will treat him with honour*]. (Ṣ.) So, too, in the saying [in the Ḳur xvii. 110], أَيًّا مَا تَدْعُوا فَلَهُ الْأَسْمَآءُ الْحُسْنَى [*Whichever ye call Him, He hath the best names*]. (T,* Mughnee.) And in the saying [in the same, xxviii. 28], أَيَّمَا الْأَجَلَيْنِ قَضَيْتُ فَلَا عُدْوَانَ عَلَىَّ [*Whichever of the two terms I fulfil, there shall be no wrongdoing to me*]. (Mughnee.) One says also, صَحِبَهُ ٱللّٰهُ أَيًّا مَا تَوَجَّهَ, meaning أَيْنَمَا تَوَجَّهَ [*May God accompany him wherever he goeth*]. (AZ, T.) And Zuheyr uses the expression أَيَّةَ وِجْهَةٍ سَلَكُوا for أَيَّةً سَلَكُوا [*Whatever tract they travelled,* or *travel*]. (T.) The saying, أَيِّى وَأَيُّكَ كَانَ شَرًّا فَأَخْزَاهُ ٱللّٰهُ [*Whichever of me and thee be evil, may God abase him!*] was explained by Kh to Sb as meaning أَيُّنَا كَانَ شَرًّا [*whichever of us* two *be evil*]; and as being like the saying, أَخْزَى ٱللّٰهُ الْكَاذِبَ مِنِّى وَمِنْكَ, meaning مِنَّا. (M. [And in a similar manner, the former clause of that saying, occurring in a verse, with مَا after أَيِّى, is said in the T to have been explained by Kh to Sb.]) — It is also a conjunct noun; (Mughnee;) [i. e.] it is sometimes used in the manner of الَّذِى, and therefore requires a complement; as in the saying, أَيُّهُمْ فِى الدَّارِ أَخُوكَ [*He, of them, who is in the house is thy brother*]: (Ṣ:) [i. e.] it is syn. with الَّذِى. (M, Mughnee.) So in the saying [in the Ḳur xix. 70], ثُمَّ لَنَنْزِعَنَّ مِنْ كُلِّ شِيعَةٍ أَيُّهُمْ أَشَدُّ عَلَى الرَّحْمٰنِ عِتِيًّا [*Then we will assuredly draw forth, from every sect, him, of them, who is most exorbitantly rebellious against the Compassionate*]: so says Sb: but the Koofees and a number of the Baṣrees disagree with him, holding that the conjunct noun أَيٌّ is always decl., like the conditional and the interrogative: Zj says, "It has not appeared to me that Sb has erred except in two instances, whereof this is one; for he has conceded that it is decl. when separate, and how can he say that it is indecl. when it is a prefixed noun?" and El-Jarmee says, "I have gone forth from El-Baṣrah, and have not heard, from my leaving the Khandaḳ to Mekkeh, any one say, لَأَضْرِبَنَّ أَيُّهُمْ قَائِمٌ [as meaning *I will assuredly beat him, of them, who is standing*], with ḍamm:" these assert, that it is, in the verse above, an interrogative, and that it is an inchoative, and اشدّ is an enunciative: but they differ as to the objective complement of the verb: Kh says that this is suppressed, and that the implied meaning is, *we will assuredly draw forth those of whom it will be said, Which of them is most* &c.? and Yoo says that it is the proposition [ايّهم &c.], and that the verb is suspended from governing, as in the instance in the Ḳur xviii. 11, cited above: and Ks and Akh say that it is كُلّ شيعة, that من is redundant, and that the interrogative proposition is independent of what precedes it; this being grounded on their saying that the redundance of مِنْ is allowable in an affirmative proposition: but these [following] facts refute their sayings; viz. that the suspension of government is peculiar to verbs significant of operations of the mind; and that it is not allowable to say, لَأَضْرِبَنَّ الْفَاسِقُ, with refʿ, as meaning by implication "I will assuredly beat him of whom it is said, He is the transgressor;" and that the redundance of مِنْ in an affirmative proposition is not correct. (Mughnee. [Some further remarks on the same subject, in that work, mentioning other opinions as erroneous, I omit. Another reading of the passage in the Ḳur cited above (xix. 70) will be found in what here follows.]) [ISd states that] they said, لَأَضْرِبَنَّ أَيُّهُمْ أَفْضَلُ [*I will assuredly beat him, of them, who is most excellent*], and أَيٌّ أَفْضَلُ [*him who is most excellent*]; أَيّ being indecl., accord. to Sb, and therefore the verb does not govern it [save as to the meaning]. (M.) And [that] you say, اِضْرِبْ أَيُّهُمْ أَفْضَلُ [*Beat thou him, of them, who is most excellent*], and أَيُّهُمْ أَفْضَلُ [meaning the same, or *whichever of them,* &c.]; suppressing the relative هُوَ after ايّهم. (M in a later part of the same art.) Fr says that when أَيّ is governed by the verb before it, it has not the interrogative meaning; and you may say, لَأَضْرِبَنَّ أَيُّهُمْ يَقُولُ ذٰلِكَ [*I will assuredly beat him, of them,* or *whichever of them, says that*]: and he says that he who reads أَيَّهُمْ, in the accus. case, in the passage of the Ḳur cited above (xix. 70) makes it to be governed by لَنَنْزِعَنَّ. (T.) Ks says, you say, لَأَضْرِبَنَّ أَيُّهُمْ فِى الدَّارِ [*I will assuredly beat him, of them,* or *whichever of them, is in the house*]; but you may not say, ضَرَبْتُ أَيُّهُمْ فِى الدَّارِ: thus he distinguishes between the actual occurrence and that which is expected. (Ṣ.) Akh says, also, that it may be indeterminate and qualified by an epithet; as when one says, مَرَرْتُ بِأَيٍّ مُعْجِبٍ لَكَ, like as one says, بِمَنْ مُعْجِبٍ لَكَ [*I passed by one pleasing to thee*]: but this has not been heard [from the Arabs]. (Mughnee.) — It also denotes perfection, or consummateness: and in this case it is an epithet applying to an indeterminate noun; as in زَيْدٌ رَجُلٌ أَىُّ رَجُلٍ ‡ [*Zeyd is a man; what a man!*], meaning that he is complete, or consummate, in the qualities of men: and it is a denotative of state relating to a determinate noun; as in مَرَرْتُ بِعَبْدِ ٱللّٰهِ أَىَّ رَجُلٍ ‡ [*I passed by 'Abd-Allah; what a man was he!*]: (Mughnee:) and used in this sense, it is tropical. (Ḥar p. 534.) [J says,] it is sometimes an epithet applying to an indeterminate noun: you say, مَرَرْتُ بِرَجُلٍ أَيِّ رَجُلٍ and أَيِّمَا رَجُلٍ † [*I passed by a man; what a man!*]; and مَرَرْتُ بِٱمْرَأَةٍ أَيَّةِ ٱمْرَأَةٍ † [*I passed by a woman; what a woman!*], and بِٱمْرَأَتَيْنِ أَيَّتِمَا ٱمْرَأَتَيْنِ [*by two women; what two women!*]; and هٰذِهِ ٱمْرَأَةٌ أَيَّةُ ٱمْرَأَةٍ † [*This is a woman; what a woman!*]: and أَيَّتُمَا ٱمْرَأَتَيْنِ † [*What two women!*]; ما being redundant: and in the case of a determinate noun, you say, هٰذَا زَيْدٌ أَيَّمَا رَجُلٍ † [*This is Zeyd; what a man is he!*]; putting it in the accus. case as a denotative of state; and هٰذِهِ أَمَةُ ٱللّٰهِ أَيَّتَمَا جَارِيَةٍ † [*This is the handmaid of God; what a girl,* or *young woman, is she!*]: you say, also, [in using an indeterminate noun,] أَىُّ ٱمْرَأَةٍ جَآءَتْكَ and أَيَّةُ ٱمْرَأَةٍ جَآءَتْكَ † [*What a woman came to thee!*]; and مَرَرْتُ بِجَارِيَةٍ أَيِّ جَارِيَةٍ † [*I passed by a girl,* or *young woman; what a girl,* or *young woman!*]; and جِئْتُكَ بِمُلَآءَةٍ أَيِّ مُلَآءَةٍ and أَيَّةِ مُلَآءَةٍ † [*I brought thee a body-wrapper; what a body-wrapper!*]: all are allowable. (Ṣ.) [In all these it evidently denotes admiration, or wonder, at some good or extraordinary quality in the person or thing to which it relates; notwithstanding that J says afterwards,] and sometimes it is used to denote wonder; as in the saying of Jemeel,

• بُثَيْنَ ٱلْزَمِى لَا إِنَّ لَا إِنْ لَزِمْتِهِ •
• عَلَى كَثْرَةِ ٱلْوَاشِينَ أَىُّ مَعُونِ •

† [*O Butheyneh,* (بُثَيْنَ being a curtailed form of بُثَيْنَة, a woman's name,) *adhere thou to "No:" verily "No," if thou adhere to it, notwithstanding the numbers of the slanderers, what a help* will it be!]: (Ṣ:) i. e., an excellent help will be thy saying "No" in repelling, or rebutting, the slanderers, though they be many. (TA in art. عون.) Fr gives as exs. of its use to denote wonder the sayings, أَىُّ رَجُلٍ زَيْدٌ [*What a man is Zeyd!*], and أَىُّ جَارِيَةٍ زَيْنَبُ [*What a girl,* or *young woman, is Zeyneb!*]. (T.) It denotes wonder at the sufficiency, and great degree of competence, of the person [or thing] to whom [or to which] it relates. (M.) El-Ḳattál El-Kilábee says,

• وَلَمَّا رَأَيْتُ أَنَّنِى قَدْ قَتَلْتُهُ •
• نَدِمْتُ عَلَيْهِ أَىَّ سَاعَةِ مَنْدَمِ •

[*And when I saw that I had slain him, I repented of it; in what an hour,* or *time, of repentance!*]: i. e., when I slew him, I repented of it, in a time when repentance did not profit: أَىَّ being here in the accus. case as an adv. n.; for, as it denotes the part of a whole, its predicament is made to be the same as that of the affixed noun, of whatever kind this may be. (Ham p. 95.) —— It also has ك prefixed to it; and thus it becomes changed in signification so as to denote numerousness, being *syn. with the enunciative* كَمْ [*How many!*]; (S, K;) or *syn. with* رُبَّ [as meaning *many*]: (Sb, M:) [and sometimes it is syn. with the interrogative كَمْ, meaning *how many?* or *how much?* as will be shown below:] thus it is written كَأَيٍّ, (M,) or كَأَيِّنْ, (S, M, K,) its tenween being written ن; (S, K;) and كَآءٍ, (M,) or [more commonly] كَائِنْ, (S, M, K, [in some copies of the S and K كَأْيِنْ,]) like كَاعِنْ, (S,) said by IJ, on the authority of Aboo-'Alee, to be formed from كَأَيِّنْ, by putting the double ى before the ء, after the manner of the transposition in قِسِىّ and a number of other words, so that it becomes كَيَّأٍ [or كَيَّئِنْ], then suppressing the second ى, as is done in مَيْتٌ and هَيْنٌ and لَيْنٌ, so that it becomes كَيْءٍ [or كَيْئِنْ], and then changing the [remaining] ى into ا, as in [طَيْئِىٌّ, which becomes] طَائِىٌّ, and in [حِيرِىٌّ, which becomes] حَارِىٌّ, so that it becomes كَآءٍ [or كَائِنْ]; (M;) and it has other dial. vars.; namely كَيْئِنْ [one of the intermediate forms between كَأَيِّنْ and كَائِنْ mentioned above]; (K; [in one copy of the K written كَيِّئِنْ, and so accord. to the TK;]) and كَأْيٍ, (M, K,) of the measure of رَمْىٍ, and most probably formed by transposition from كَيْءٍ, mentioned above; (M;) and كَإٍ, of the measure of عَمٍ, (M, TA,) incorrectly written in the copies of the K كَاءٍ, i. e. like كَاعٍ, (TA,) formed by the suppression of ى in كَيْءٍ; a change not greater than that from أَيْمُنُ ٱللّٰهِ to مُ ٱللّٰهِ and مِ ٱللّٰهِ. (M.) You say, كَأَيِّنْ رَجُلًا لَقِيتُ [*How many a man have I met!* or *many a man* &c.], (S, K,*) putting the noun following كَأَيِّنْ in the accus. case as a specificative; (S;) and كَأَيِّنْ مِنْ رَجُلٍ لَقِيتُ; (S, K;*) and the introduction of مِنْ after كَأَيِّنْ is more common, and better. (S. [And Sb, as cited in the M, says the like.]) You say also, كَأَيِّنْ قَدْ أَتَانِى رَجُلًا [*How many a man has come to me!* or *many a man* &c.]. (Sb, M.) And بِكَأَيِّنْ, i. e. بِكَمْ تبيع, تَبِيعُ هٰذَا ٱلثَّوْبَ [*For how much wilt thou sell this garment*, or *piece of cloth?*]. (S.) Kh says that if any one of the Arabs made it to govern the gen. case, perhaps he did so by making مِنْ to be implied, as is allowable with كَمْ: (M:) [so that you may say, بِكَأَيِّنْ دِرْهَمٍ ٱشْتَرَيْتَ هٰذَا *For how many a dirhem didst thou buy this?* for] it is allowable to make the noun that follows كَمْ to be governed in the gen. case by مِنْ implied, when كم immediately follows a preposition; as in بِكَمْ دِرْهَمٍ ٱشْتَرَيْتَ هٰذَا; but when it is not thus preceded by a preposition, the noun after it must be in the accus. case. (I 'Ak p. 317.) It always holds the first place in a proposition, like كَمْ. (Idem, next p.) —— It is also a connective of the vocative يَا with the noun signifying the person or persons or thing called, when this noun has the article ال prefixed to it; (S, M, Mughnee, K;) and with a noun of indication, as ذَا; and with a conjunct noun having ال prefixed to it, as ٱلَّذِى: (I 'Ak p. 268:) it is a noun formed for serving as such a connective; (M, K;) and has هَا affixed to it. (S, M, &c.) You say, يَا أَيُّهَا ٱلرَّجُلُ [which seems to be best rendered *O thou man*; more agreeably with the original, *O thou, the man*; or, accord. to Akh, *O thou who art the man*; lit., *O he who is the man*; often written يَأَيُّهَا]; (T, S, M, Mughnee, K;) and يَا أَيُّهَا ٱلرَّجُلَانِ [*O ye two men*]; and يَا أَيُّهَا ٱلرِّجَالُ [*O ye men*]; (M;) and يَا أَيَّتُهَا ٱلْمَرْأَةُ [*O thou woman*]; (S, M;) and يَا أَيَّتُهَا ٱلْمَرْأَتَانِ [*O ye two women*]; and يَا أَيَّتُهَا ٱلنِّسْوَةُ [*O ye women*]; and يَا أَيُّهَا ٱلْمَرْأَةُ, and ٱلْمَرْأَتَانِ, and ٱلنِّسْوَةُ; (M;) and يَا أَيُّهَا ذَا [*O thou, this* person or thing]; and يَا أَيُّهَا ٱلَّذِى فَعَلَ كَذَا [*O thou who didst*, or *hast done, thus*]. (I 'Ak p. 267.) In the first of the exs. here given, أَىّ is a noun of vague signification, (Zj, T, S,) denoting the person called, (Zj, T,) of the sing. number, (Zj, T, S,) rendered determinate by the vocative [يا], (S,) indecl., with damm for its termination; (Zj, T, S;) and هَا is a particle employed to rouse attention, or to give notice, a substitute for the noun to which أَىّ is in other cases prefixed; and ٱلرَّجُلُ is a qualificative to أَىّ, (Zj, T, S,) wherefore it is in the nom. case. (S.) Akh asserts, [as we have indicated above,] that أَىّ is here the conjunct noun, and that the first member of its complement, namely the relative هُوَ, is suppressed; the meaning being, يَا مَنْ هُوَ ٱلرَّجُلُ: but this assertion is refuted by the fact that there is no relative pronoun that must be suppressed, nor any conjunct noun that necessarily requires that its complement should be a nominal proposition: though he might reply to these two objections by arguing that ما in the saying لَا سِيَّمَا زَيْدٌ is in like manner [virtually] in the nom. case [as a conjunct noun syn. with ٱلَّذِى, and that the first member of its complement, namely هُوَ, an inchoative of which زَيْدٌ is the enunciative, is suppressed]. (Mughnee.) The putting of the qualificative of أَىّ in the accus. case, as in the saying يَا أَيُّهَا ٱلرَّجُلَ أَقْبِلْ [*O thou man, advance*], is allowed (M, K) by El-Mázinee; but it is not known [as heard from the Arabs]. (M.) أَيُّهَا and أَيَّتُهَا are also used for the purpose of particularizing; [in which case they are not preceded by يا;] as when one says, أَمَّا أَنَا فَأَفْعَلُ كَذَا أَيُّهَا ٱلرَّجُلُ [*As for me, I will do thus*, or *such a thing, thou man*], meaning himself; and as in the saying of Kaab Ibn-Málik, related in a trad., فَتَخَلَّفْنَا أَيَّتُهَا ٱلثَّلَاثَةُ [*And we remained behind*, or *held back, ye three*], meaning, by the three, those particularized as remaining behind [with him], or holding back. (TA.)

أَيَا : see art. ايا. —— أَيَا : see the next paragraph.

إِيَا ٱلشَّمْسِ, [the former word, when alone and indeterminate, perhaps (as when determinate) without tenween, for it is explained (with its dial. vars.) in the S and K in باب الالف اللينة, though it is also explained in some copies of the S in the present art.,] and ↓ إِيَاةُ ٱلشَّمْسِ, (T, S, M, Mgh, K,) and ↓ أَيَاةُ ٱلشَّمْسِ, (S, M, K,) and ↓ أَيَآءُ ٱلشَّمْسِ, (T, M, Mgh, K, and in a copy of the S,) with fet-h and medd, (T, Mgh, K, and so in a copy of the S,) *The light of the sun*, (S, M, Mgh, K,) and *its beauty*: (M, K:) or *its rays*, and *its light*: (T:) or, as some say, ↓ اياة الشمس signifies *the halo of the sun; that, with respect to the sun, which is like the* هَالَة *with respect to the moon*; i. e. *the* دَارَة *around the sun*: (S:) the pl. [of ↓ إِيَاةٌ] is ↓ أَيًا and إِيَآءٌ; [or rather the former is a coll. gen. n.;] like أَكَمٌ and إِكَامٌ in relation to أَكَمَةٌ. (M.) Tarafeh says, (T, S, Mgh,) describing the fore teeth (ثَغْر) of his beloved, (EM p. 62,)

سَقَتْهُ إِيَاةُ ↓ ٱلشَّمْسِ إِلَّا لِثَاتِهِ *

[*The light of the sun has shed its lustre upon them, except their gums*]. (T, S, Mgh.) —— And hence, by way of comparison, (M,) إِيَا ٱلنَّبَاتِ, and ↓ أَيَاتُهُ, (M, K,) and ↓ إِيَاتُهُ, and ↓ أَيَاؤُهُ, (K,) ‡ *The beauty of herbage*, (M, K,) and *its blossoms*, (M,) and *brightness*, (K, TA,) *in its verdure and growth*. (TA.) —— أَيَا إِيَاهُ أَقْبِلْ : see أَيَا, in art. ايا.

أَيَآءٌ :
أَيَاةٌ :
إِيَاةٌ : } see the next preceding paragraph, throughout.

أُيَيَّةٌ dim. of آءَةٌ: see the letter ا.

أُيَيَّةٌ dim. of آيَةٌ, q. v. (T.)

أَيَّا : see إِيَّا, in art. ايا.

إِيَّا : see art. ايا. [Az says,] I have not heard any derivation of إِيَّا; but I think, without being certain, that it is from تَآيَيْتُهُ as explained above; as though it were a noun from that verb, of the measure فِعْلَى, like ذِكْرَى from ذَكَرْتُ; so that the meaning of إِيَّاكَ is *I direct myself*, or *my aim, to*, or *towards, thee*, and *thy person*. (T.)

أَيِّىٌّ [a rel. n. of أَىّ]. When you ask a man respecting his كُورَة [i. e. district, or city, or town], you say, ٱلْأَيِّىُّ [*The person of what district*, &c., *art thou?*]; like as you say, in asking him respecting his قَبِيلَة [or tribe], ٱلْمَنِّىُّ [from مَنْ]: and you say also, أَيِّىٌّ أَنْتَ [*A person of what district, &c., art thou?*]; and مَنِّىٌّ أَنْتَ. (T.) [See also مَنِّىٌّ, in art. من.]

أَيَّانَ : see art. اين. Lth says that it is used in the manner of مَتَى; [signifying *When?*]; and that some say its ن is radical; others, that it is augmentative: (T:) IJ says, it must be from أَىّ, not from أَيْنَ, for two reasons: first, because أَيْنَ denotes place; and أَيَّانَ, time: and secondly, because nouns of the measure فَعَّالٌ are few; and those of the measure فَعْلَانٌ, many: so that if you name a man أَيَّانُ, it is imperfectly decl.: and he adds, that أَىٌّ means a part of a whole; so that it applies as properly to times as it does to other things: (TA:) Fr says that it is originally أَىَّ أَوَانٍ [*at what time?*]. (T.) One says, of a stupid, or foolish, person, لَا يَعْرِفُ أَيَّانَ [*He knows not when*]. (IB.)

أَىٌ : see أَىٌّ :— and see also 2 in art. اوى.

— آىٌ : see what next follows, in two places.

آيَةٌ *A sign, token,* or *mark, by which a person or thing is known;* syn. عَلَامَةٌ (IAar, T, Ṣ, M, Mṣb, Ḳ) and أَمَارَةٌ: (M, Ḳ:) it properly signifies *any apparent thing inseparable from a thing not equally apparent, so that when one perceives the former, he knows that he perceives the other, which he cannot perceive by itself, when the two things are of one predicament; and this is apparent in the object of sense and in that of the intellect:* (Er-Rághib, TA:) it is of the measure فَعَلَةٌ, (M, Ḳ,) originally أَيَيَةٌ; the [former] ى being changed to ا because the letter before it is with fet-ḥ, though this is an extraordinary change: (M:) this is related as on the authority of Sb: (TA:) or it is of the measure فَعْلَةٌ, (M, Ḳ,) accord. to Kh; (M;) originally أَوْيَةٌ; (Ṣ;) [for, accord. to J and Fei,] Sb said that its medial radical letter is و, and that the final is ى, because words of this class are more common than those of which the medial and final radical letters are both ى; (Ṣ, Mṣb;) and the rel. n. is أَوَوِىٌّ: (Ṣ:) but IB says, Sb did not state that the medial radical letter of آيَةٌ is و, as J states; but he said that it is originally أَيَّةٌ, and that the quiescent ى is changed into ا; and he relates of Kh, that he allowed the rel. n. of آيَةٌ to be آئِىٌّ ↓ and آيِىٌّ ↓ and آوِىٌّ; but as to أَوَوِىٌّ, he says, I know not any one who has said it except J: (TA:) or it is of the measure فَاعِلَةٌ, (Ṣ, Mṣb, Ḳ,) originally آيِيَةٌ, contracted by the suppression of its final radical letter [with the preceding kesreh]: so accord. to Fr: [but see what follows (after the pls.), where this is said to be the opinion of Ks, and disallowed by Fr:] (Ṣ, Mṣb:) the pl. is آيَاتٌ and آىٌ ↓, (Ṣ, M, Mṣb, Ḳ,) [or the latter is rather a coll. gen. n.,] and pl. pl. آيَآءٌ: (M, Ḳ:) J says that one of its pls. is آيَاىٌ; [and we find the same also in some copies of the Ḳ;] but this is a mistake for آيَآءٌ, which is pl. of آىٌ, not of آيَةٌ: (IB, TA:) and this pl., being of the measure أَفْعَالٌ, has been adduced as evidence that the medial radical letter is ى, not و: (TA:) the dim. is إِيَيَّةٌ ↓, [of the measure فُعَيْلَةٌ changed to فِعَيْلَةٌ because of the medial radical ى,] which, accord. to Fr, shows the opinion of Ks, that آيَةٌ is of the measure فَاعِلَةٌ rendered defective by the suppression of its final radical letter, to be incorrect, because [Fr holds, in opposition to some others, that] a noun of this measure has not its dim. formed on the measure فُعَيْلَةٌ unless it is a proper name. (T.) They said, اِفْعَلْهُ بِآيَةِ كَذَا [*Do thou it at the sign of such a thing*]; like as you say, بِعَلَامَةِ كَذَا and بِأَمَارَةِ كَذَا. (M.) And [in this sense, as is indicated by the context in the M,] it is one of the nouns that are prefixed to verbs [as virtually governing the gen. case], (M, Ḳ,*) because of the nearness of its meaning to the meaning of *time:* (Ḳ:) as in the saying [of a poet],

* بِآيَةِ تُقْدِمُونَ الخَيْلَ شُعْثًا *

[*At the sign of your urging forward the horses, unsmoothed in their coats,* or *not curried;* which means nearly the same as "at the time of your urging" &c.]. (M.) — *A sign* as meaning *an indication, an evidence,* or *a proof.* (TA.) — *A sign* as meaning *a miracle;* [and *a wonder;* for] آيَاتُ اللّٰهِ means *the wonders of God.* (TA.) — *An example,* or *a warning;* (Fr, T, M, Mṣb, Ḳ;) as, for instance, the case of Joseph and his brethren, related in the Ḳur: (Fr, T:) pl. آىٌ ↓ (M, Ḳ) and آيَاتٌ. (Fr, T.) — *A message,* or *communication sent from one person or party to another;* syn. رِسَالَةٌ. (TA.) — The *body,* or *corporeal form* or *figure* or *substance,* (Ṣ, M, Ḳ,) of a man, (Ṣ,) *which one sees from a distance;* [as being a kind of sign;] or *a person,* or *an individual;* syn. شَخْصٌ. (Ṣ, M, Ḳ.) — *A whole company* of people: as in the saying, خَرَجَ القَوْمُ بِآيَتِهِمْ *The people,* or *party, went forth with their whole company, not leaving behind them anything.* (AA, Ṣ, M.) — [Hence, accord. to some, *A verse* of the Ḳur-án; as being] *a collection of words* of the Book of God: (Ṣ:) or *a connected form of words* of the Ḳur-án *continued to its breaking off;* (Ḳ, TA;) accord. to Aboo-Bekr, so called because it is a sign of the breaking off: (TA:) or *a portion* of the Ḳur-án *after which a suspension of speech is approvable:* (Mṣb:) or *a portion* of the Ḳur-án *denoting any statute,* or *ordinance, of God, whether it be* [*what is generally termed*] *an* آيَة, [i. e. *a verse,*] *or a chapter* (سُورَة), *or an aggregate* [*and distinct*] *portion of the latter.* (Er-Rághib, Kull, TA.*) [الآيَةَ, written after a quotation of a part of a verse of the Ḳur-án, means اِقْرَإِ الآيَةَ *Read thou the verse.*]

آيَا : see أَيَا, in art. ايا.

آئِىٌّ and آيِىٌّ, accord. to Kh, rel. ns. of آيَةٌ, q. v. (IB.)

تَآيَةٌ, or تَأْيِيَةٌ or تَئِيَّةٌ: see 5.

ايا

أَيَا a vocative particle, (Ṣ, M, Ḳ,) used in calling him who is near and him who is distant: [in the former case, like *O:* in the latter, like *ho there,* or *soho,* or *holla:*] you say, أَيَا زَيْدُ أَقْبِلْ [*O Zeyd, advance:* or *ho there,* or *soho,* or *holla,* &c.]: (Ṣ:) or J is in error in saying this: it is used in calling to him who is distant: (Mughnee, Ḳ:) so say Ibn-El-Ḥájib, in the Káfiyeh, and El-Fakhr El-Járabardee; and the latter adds, or to him who is in a predicament like that of him who is distant, being sleeping or inadvertent; the person who calls thereby being eager for the person called to advance to him: (TA:) or not used in calling to him who is near: (Ḳ:) and ه is substituted for its hemzeh; (M, Ḳ;) so that one says, هَيَا. (M.) AZ says, I have heard them say, أَيَا إِيَاهُ أَقْبِلْ. (T in بَابُ الأَلْقَابِ.) [Accord. to the TA, (art. ا,) one says also آيَا.]

إِيَا الشَّمْسِ, and النَّبَاتِ; and إِيَاةٌ, and أَيَاةٌ, and آيَا: see art. اى.

إِيَّا (Ṣ, M, Ḳ, &c.) and أَيَّا, (M, Ḳ,) the latter form used by some, as related on the authority of Ḳṭr; (M;) accord. to some, (M,) a noun of vague signification, (Ṣ, M, Ḳ,) used metonymically for a noun in the accus. case, (M,) with which are connected all the affixed pronouns that denote the accus. case: you say إِيَّاكَ [*Thee*] and إِيَّاهُ [*him*] and إِيَّاىَ [*me*] (Ṣ, Ḳ) and إِيَّانَا [*us,* &c.]: (Ṣ:) and the hemzeh is changed into ه, so that you say هِيَّاكَ (Ṣ, M, Ḳ*) and هَيَّاكَ; (Ḳṭr, IJ, M, Ḳ;*) and sometimes into و, so that you say وِيَّاكَ [and app. وَيَّاكَ also; both of which are used by some of the Arabs in the present day, very commonly in Egypt, for وَإِيَّاكَ as meaning مَعَكَ]; like as one says وَزَيْدًا, meaning [مَعَ زَيْدٍ]: (Ḳ:) the ك and ه and ى [&c.] are put to show the object meant, in order that the person addressed may be known from the absent [&c.]; and have no place in the analysis of a sentence, like the ك in ذٰلِكَ and أَرَأَيْتَكَ: (Ṣ, M: in the former of which is added, and like the ا and ن in أَنْتَ:) and this is identical with the opinion of Akh: (M, TA:) thus إِيَّا is the noun, and what follows it is to denote allocution, [&c.,] and the two become as one thing; for nouns of vague signification are not prefixed to other nouns to govern them in the gen. case, nor are any of the pronouns, being themselves determinate. (Ṣ.) Ibn-Keysán says, (Ṣ, M,) some of the grammarians say that إِيَّاكَ, altogether, is a noun; and he adds, but some say (M) that the ك and ه &c. are the nouns, and that إِيَّا is a support thereto, because they cannot stand by themselves, (Ṣ, M,) like the ك &c. which occupy the latter place in يَضْرِبُكَ &c.; so when the ك &c. are put first, [as in إِيَّاكَ ضَرَبْتُ *Thee I beat,* or *struck,*] they are supported by ايا, and the whole becomes as one thing: (Ṣ:) and you may also say, ضَرَبْتُ إِيَّاىَ [*I beat,* or *struck, me*]; because it is not allowable to say, ضَرَبْتُنِى: (Ṣ as corrected by IB:) but you may not say, ضَرَبْتُ إِيَّاكَ [*I beat,* or *struck, thee*]; because you only require إِيَّاكَ when you cannot use the ك [alone]; though you may say, ضَرَبْتُكَ إِيَّاكَ [*I beat,* or *struck, thee, thee*]; because the ك is made to be syntactically dependent upon the verb, so when you repeat it you require إِيَّا. (Ṣ.) In the saying of the poet, (Ṣ,) Dhu-l-Iṣba' El-'Adwánee, (TA,)

* كَأَنَّا يَوْمَ قُرَّى إِنَّمَا نَقْتُلُ إِيَّانَا *

[*As though we, on the day of Ḳurrá, only killed ourselves*], he has separated it from the verb only because the Arabs do not make the action of the agent to fall upon the agent itself by the adjunction of the pronoun: they do not say, قَتَلْتُنِى, but only قَتَلْتُ نَفْسِى: so the poet has used إِيَّانَا in the same manner as أَنْفُسَنَا. (Ṣ, TA.) Some of the grammarians say that إِيَّا is prefixed to what follows it, governing it in the gen. case; and adduce as an evidence thereof a saying which see below, commencing with إِذَا بَلَغَ الرَّجُلُ. (Ṣ.)

Zj says that it is an explicit noun, [not a pronoun,] which is prefixed to all the pronouns, governing them in the gen. case; but only to pronouns; so that if one said, إِيَّا زَيْدٍ حَدَّثْتُ, it would be bad. (M.) Kh holds that it is a pronoun prefixed to the ك [&c.], governing it in the gen. case; (M, Ḳ;) and the like is related to have been the opinion of El-Mázinee: and Sb relates of Kh that he said, if any one were to say إِيَّاكَ نَفْسَكَ [*Thee, thyself*], I would not severely blame him, for this ك is [virtually] governed in the gen. case. (M.) But accord. to Akh, it is a simple, or uncompounded, pronoun, the ending of which becomes altered, as the endings of pronouns are wont to become, because of the varying of the numbers of the persons using them; (M, Ḳ; [in both of which the last of the words thus rendered is المضمرين; accord. to a copy of the M, المضمرين, i. e. المُضْمِرِينَ; in a copy of the Ḳ, without any syll. signs; and in the CḲ, المُضْمَرِيْنِ; of which readings, I have followed that found in the M; supposing the meaning to be, that ايّا has different endings according as it is used by one speaking to another, or by one speaking of another, or by one speaking of himself, or to, or of, two or more, and the like;]) and the ك of ايّاك is like the ك of ذٰلِكَ, inasmuch as it is an indication of allocution only, divested of the idea of its being a sign of the pronoun. (M.) Of all these varying opinions, IJ says that he has found none to be correct when investigated, except that of Akh; with whose opinion, that stated in the begining of this art. is identical [except as to the affix, which is there said to be a pronoun, not merely a particle of allocution]. (M, TA.) Zj, being asked to explain the meaning of the phrase إِيَّاكَ نَعْبُدُ, [in the Ḳur i. 4,] answered, حَقِيقَتَكَ نَعْبُدُ [*Thine essence we worship*]; and said that it is derived from آيَةٌ, meaning "a sign by which a thing is known:" but IJ does not approve of this. (M.) [Respecting the phrase, فَإِذَا هُوَ إِيَّاهَا, in which ايّاها is used in the place of a noun in the nom. case, and which is therefore disallowed by Sb, see إِذَا.] — It is also used for the purpose of cautioning, or putting one on his guard. (T, Ṣ.) You say, إِيَّاكَ وَالأَسَدَ [*Beware thou of*, or *avoid thou*, or *remove thyself far from, the lion*]: it is a substitute for a verb; as thou you said, بَاعِدْ: and you say also, هِيَّاكَ; like as you say أَرَاقَ and هَرَاقَ: (Ṣ:) [or ايّاك in this case is governed by a verb understood: for] Ibn-Keysán says, when you say, إِيَّاكَ وَزَيْدًا [*Beware thou of*, or *avoid thou*, or *remove thyself far from, Zeyd*], you caution him whom you address against Zeyd, and the verb governing the accus. case is not apparent: the meaning is, أُحَذِّرُكَ زَيْدًا [*I caution thee against Zeyd*]; as though you said, أُحَذِّرُكَ إِيَّاكَ وَزَيْدًا [*I caution thee, thee with Zeyd*]; or as though you said, بَاعِدْ نَفْسَكَ عَنْ زَيْدٍ وَبَاعِدْ زَيْدًا عَنْكَ [*Remove thyself far from Zeyd, and remove Zeyd far from thee*]; so that the verb governs the word signifying the person cautioned and that signifying him against whom that person is cautioned: (TA:) [and Az says,] when you say, إِيَّاكَ وَرُكُوبَ الفَاحِشَةِ, the verb is suppressed: it is as though you said, أُحَذِّرُكَ رُكُوبَ الفَاحِشَةِ [*I caution thee against the committing of that which exceeds the bounds of rectitude*]. (T.) Kh is related to have heard an Arab of the desert say, (T,* M, the latter on the authority of Sb.,) إِذَا بَلَغَ الرَّجُلُ السِّتِّينَ فَإِيَّاهُ وَإِيَّا الشَّوَابِّ [*When the man attains to sixty years, I caution him against*, or *let him avoid, the young women*]; (T, Ṣ, M;) prefixing ايّا to الشوابّ, and putting the latter in the gen. case: (Ṣ:) but accord. to Akh, it is not allowable to say [thus, or] إِيَّاكَ وَإِيَّا زَيْدٍ. (M.) Sometimes the و is suppressed, as in the saying of the poet,

* فَإِيَّاكَ إِيَّاكَ المِرَآءَ فَإِنَّهُ *
* إِلَى الشَّرِّ دَعَّآءٌ وَلِلشَّرِّ جَالِبُ *

[*Then avoid thou, avoid thou obstinate disputation, for it is wont to invite to evil, and an attracter of evil*]; meaning, إِيَّاكَ وَالمِرَآءَ; i. e., إِيَّاكَ وَأَنْ تُمَارِىَ. (TA.) You say [properly], إِيَّاكَ وَأَنْ تَفْعَلَ كَذَا [*Beware thou of*, or *avoid thou, doing such a thing*]: but [in strict propriety] you should not say, إِيَّاكَ أَنْ تَفْعَلَ كَذَا, without و. (Ṣ.) See also art. اى.

أَيَايَا (Lth, T, Ṣ, M, Ḳ) and أَيَايَهْ, (M,) or يَايَا, (Ḳ,) and يَايَهْ, (M, Ḳ,) *A cry by which camels are chidden.* (Lth, T, Ṣ, M, Ḳ.) [See 2 in art. اى.]

ايب

For words which might be supposed to be properly mentioned under this head, see art. اوب.

ايد

1. آدَ, aor. يَئِيدُ, inf. n. أَيْدٌ, *He*, (a man, AZ, T, &c.,) or *it*, (a thing, L,) *was*, or *became, strong:* (AZ, T, Ṣ, M, Ḳ, &c.:) and ▼ ايّد, inf. n. إِيَادٌ, *he became possessed of strength.* (AHeyth, T, L.) — آدَتْ ضِيَافَتُهُ ‡ *His coming as a guest was*, or *became, frequent.* (A.) [See أَيِّدٌ.]

2. أَيَّدَ, inf. n. تَأْيِيدٌ; (T, Ṣ, M, &c.;) and ▼ آيد, (T, Ṣ, Ḳ,) of the measure فَاعَلَ, (Ṣ,) inf. n. مُؤَايَدَةٌ; (Ḳ;) *He strengthened:* (Ṣ, M, L, Mṣb, Ḳ:) *he aided*, or *rendered victorious.* (L.) You say, أَيَّدَهُ عَلَى الأَمْرِ *He strengthened him to accomplish the affair.* (M, L.)

3: see 2.

4: see 1.

5. تَأَيَّدَ *He*, or *it*, (a thing, Ṣ,) *became strengthened.* (T, Ṣ, Ḳ.)

أَيْدٌ and آدٌ *Strength*; syn. صُلْبٌ, (M, L, Ḳ,) and قُوَّةٌ [which is one of the significations of صُلْبٌ, and that which is here meant]; as also ▼ أَيْدٌ [which is an inf. n.: see 1]. (Ṣ, M, Ḳ.)

آدٌ: see أَيْدٌ.

أَيِّدٌ *Strong:* (Ṣ, A, Mgh, Mṣb, Ḳ:) an epithet applied [to God, and] to a man. (Ṣ.) A poet says,

* إِذَا القَوْسُ وَتَّرَهَا أَيِّدٌ * رَمَى فَأَصَابَ الكُلَى وَالذُّرَى *

[lit. *When a strong one strings the bow, he shoots, and hits the kidneys, and the tops of the humps of the camels*]; meaning, when God strings [or stretches] the bow that is in the clouds, He casts fat into the kidneys and humps of the camels, by means of the herbage that is produced by the rain. (Ṣ.) — إِنَّهُ لَأَيِّدُ الغَدَآءِ وَالعَشَآءِ means ‡ *Verily he is often present at the morning and evening meals.* (A.)

إِيَادٌ *Anything by which a person or thing is strengthened*, (M, L, Ḳ,) or *guarded, defended*, or *protected:* (T, L:) *a thing by which one is protected*, or *veiled*, or *concealed:* the *side; shade*, or *shadow*; or *protection*: *a place of refuge:* (M, L, Ḳ:) *either side* of anything, *that strengthens* it: (Lth, T:) *anything that is in the vicinity* of a thing: (T:) *each wing* of an army: (Ṣ, M, L, Ḳ:) *earth that is put round a watering-trough* or *tank*, or *round a tent*, (Ṣ, M, L, Ḳ,) *to strengthen it*, or *to keep away from it the rain-water:* (Ṣ, L:) *any fortification*: *a fortified mountain:* (M, L, Ḳ:) *a mountain that is inaccessible*, or *difficult of access.* (IAạr, T.) [In the place of one signification, Golius gives "cortex;" having found لحاء in the place of لَجَأ.] — *An elevated tract*, or *a heap, of sand.* (M, Ḳ.) — *Abundance of camels* [because they strengthen their owner]. (Ḳ.) — The *air*; syn. هَوَآءٌ. (Ḳ.)

مُؤْيِدٌ: see مُؤْيَدٌ: = and see what next follows.

مُؤْيِدٌ, of the same measure as مُؤْمِنٌ, *A great, mighty*, or *severe, thing*; (Ṣ, L, Ḳ;) *a calamity:* (T, Ṣ, M, L, Ḳ:) or, accord. to Aṣ, it is ▼ مُؤْيَدٌ, with fet-ḥ to the ى, and signifies *anything rendered strong*, or *hard*, or *severe.* (L.) [See مَأْوِدٌ, in art. اود.]

مُؤَيَّدٌ and ▼ مُؤْيَدٌ (the latter irreg., by rule being مُؤَايَدٌ, TḲ,) *Strengthened:* (Ṣ, L, Ḳ:) *aided*; or *rendered victorious:* (L:) and the former, *strong*, applied to a building. (M.)

مُؤَيِّدٌ *Strengthening:* (Ṣ, L:) *aiding*; or *rendering victorious.* (L.) The dim. also has this form. (Ṣ.)

اير

1. آرَهَا, aor. يَئِيرُ, (T, Ṣ, and Ḳ in art. اور,) inf. n. أَيْرٌ; (T, TA;) or آرَهَا, aor. يَؤُورُ; (ISk, T;) or *both*; (Ḳ ubi supra;) *Inivit eam; he compressed her.* (ISk, T, Ṣ, Ḳ.)

أَيْرٌ The *membrum virile*; *penis*; *veretrum:* (TA:) pl. [of pauc.] آيُرٌ and آيَارٌ (Ṣ, M, Ḳ) and [of mult.] أُيُورٌ (Ṣ, Ḳ) and أُيْرٌ. (L.) — كَانَ أَيْرُهُ طَوِيلًا is a phrase meaning ‡ *He had many male children.* (T, TA.)

أُيَارِىٌّ *Having a large membrum virile*, or *penis*; (T, Ṣ, M, Ḳ;) like أُنَافِىٌّ signifying "having a large nose." (T.)

أَيَّارُ *The* [*Syrian*] *month* [*corresponding to May, O. S.*;] preceding حَزِيرَانُ, or (as written by Saạdee Efendee, TA) حُزَيْرَانُ. (So in different copies of the Ḳ.)

آيِرٌ *Iniens.* (T, Ṣ, TA.)

مُثِيرٌ pass. part. n. of 1, (T, Ṣ, TA,) of the same measure as مُصِيرٌ; *i. q.* مَنْيُوكٌ. (TA.)

مِثْيَرٌ (Ḳ, TA, [in the CḲ مَثِير, and in Gol. Lex. مِثْيَر,]) *Qui multum coit.* (Ḳ.)

ايس

1. أَيِسَ مِنْهُ, (Ṣ, M, Mgh, Mṣb, Ḳ,) aor. يَأْيَسُ (Ṣ, Mṣb, Ḳ) and يَأْيِسُ, (Mṣb,) inf. n. أَيْسٌ, (Mṣb,) or إِيَاسٌ, (Ḳ,) or it has the same inf. n. as يَئِسَ, namely يَأْسٌ, (Ṣ,) with which ▼ إِيَاسٌ is syn., (Mgh,) but this last is a contraction of إِيْآسٌ, of the measure إِيعَاسٌ, as determined by Az, and is not an inf. n. of أَيِسَ as some think it to be, (Mgh, art. يئس,) *He despaired of it;* syn. قَنِطَ: (Ḳ:) a dial. var. of يَئِسَ: (ISk, Ṣ, TA:) or it is not so, but is formed by transposition from يَئِسَ, because it has no [proper] inf. n.; and إِيَاسٌ, the proper name of a man, is not to be adduced in evidence, for it is of the measure فِعَالٌ from الأَوْسُ, "the act of giving:" (Preface to the M, quoted in the TA:) if it were a dial. var. of يَئِسَ, they would say إِسْتُ for أَيِسْتُ: (M, TA:) and أَيِسَ, incorrectly written أُويِسَ, also signifies the same. (Mgh.) — أَيِسَ: see يَئِسَ.

2: see 4.

4. آيَسَهُ *He made him to despair;* (Ḳ;) like أَيْأَسَهُ; (Ṣ, Mgh;) and so ▼ أَيَّسَهُ, (Ṣ,* Ḳ,) inf. n. تَأْيِيسٌ. (Ṣ.)

أَيِسٌ and ▼ آيِسٌ [*Despairing*]; part. ns. of أَيِسَ. (Mṣb.) — [Hence,] آيِسَةٌ [and accord. to Golius ▼ أَيْسَآءُ, both properly meaning *Despairing* of the recurrence of the menstrual flux;] *who has not menstruated in a period of five and fifty years.* (KT.)

أَيْسَآءُ: see أَيِسٌ.

إِيَاسٌ: see 1.

آيِسٌ: see أَيِسٌ.

ايش

أَيْشٍ, for أَىُّ شَىْءٍ: see أَىٌّ, in art. اى.

ايض

1. آضَ, aor. يَئِيضُ, inf. n. أَيْضٌ, *i. q.* عَادَ; (ISk, Ṣ, M, Mṣb,* Ḳ;) as in the phrase آضَ إِلَى الشَّىْءِ [*He returned to the thing,* i. e. *to the doing of the thing; he did the thing again, or a second time*]. (Ḳ.) — And *i. q.* رَجَعَ; (Ṣ, M, Mṣb, Ḳ;) as in the phrase آضَ إِلَى أَهْلِهِ [*He returned to his family*]. (Ṣ, M.) — In the phrase فَعَلْتُ كَذَا ▼ أَيْضًا, the last word is the inf. n. of آضَ in the sense of عَادَ, (ISk, IDrd, Ṣ, M, Mṣb,*) and in the sense of رَجَعَ: (IDrd, M:) and the meaning is, [*I did such a thing again, or a second time;*] *I returned to the doing of such a thing:* (IDrd, M:) or *I did such a thing returning to what had preceded.* (Mṣb, Ḳ.*) [It also, and more commonly, signifies *I did such a thing also.*] When one says, ▼ فَعَلْتُ ذٰلِكَ أَيْضًا [*I did that again, &c.*], you say, ▼ قَدْ أَكْثَرْتَ مِنْ أَيْضٍ [*Thou hast made much use of the expression* أَيْضًا], and ▼ دَعْنِى مِنْ أَيْضٍ [*Let me alone and cease from using the expression* أَيْضًا]. (ISk, Ṣ.) — أَيْضٌ also signifies ‡ *A thing's becoming another, or a different, thing; and being changed from its state or condition* [*to another and a different state or condition*]: (Lth, Ḳ:*) so says Kh. (Ḥam p. 356.) And آضَ كَذَا ‡ *He, or it, became such a thing.* (Lth, Ṣ, M,* Ḳ.) You say, آضَ سَوَادُ شَعَرِهِ بَيَاضًا (A, TA) ‡ *The blackness of his hair became whiteness.* (TA.) And Zuheyr says, speaking of a land which he traversed,

* قَطَعْتُ إِذَا مَا الآلُ آضَ كَأَنَّهُ *
* سُيُوفٌ تُنَحَّى سَاعَةً ثُمَّ تَلْتَقِى *

[*I traversed, when the mirage,* or *the mirage of the morning, became as though it were swords which were removed a while, then met*]. (Ṣ.)

أَيْضٌ and أَيْضًا: see above, in four places.

ايك

1. أَيِكَ الأَرَاكُ, aor. ـَ, *The* [*trees called*] اراك *became what is termed* أَيْكَة [n. un. of أَيْكٌ, q. v.]; as also ▼ استأيك. (Ḳ.) The former occurs in poetry contracted into أَيْكَ. (ISd, Ṣgh.)

10: see 1.

أَيْكٌ *Numerous, luxuriant* or *tangled* or *dense, trees:* (Ṣ, Ḳ:) or *a place where water collects and sinks into the ground* (غَيْضَةٌ) *producing* [*trees of the kinds called*] سِدْر *and* أَرَاك (Lth, Ḳ) *and similar soft trees:* (Lth:) or *a collection of any trees;* even, *of palm-trees:* (Ḳ:) or, as some say, *a place where* [*trees of the kind called*] أَثْل *grow, and where is a collection of them:* or, accord. to AḤn, *an abundant collection of* أَرَاك *in one place:* (TA:) or *trees;* said to be *of the* [*kind called*] أَرَاك: (Mṣb:) n. un. with ة: (Ṣ, Mṣb, Ḳ, &c.:) IAạr says, [you say,] أَيْكَةٌ مِنْ أَثْلٍ and رَهْطٌ مِنْ عُشَرٍ and قَصِيمَةٌ مِنْ غَضًا. (Sh.) أَصْحَابُ الأَيْكَةِ occurs in the Ḳur in four chapters: [xv. 78 and xxvi. 176 and xxxviii. 12 and l. 13:] (Ṣgh:) he who reads thus means, by the latter word, الغَيْضَة [explained above, and also signifying *the thicket,* or *collection of tangled trees,* &c.]; (Ṣ, Ḳ;) or *the tangled,* or *luxuriant,* or *abundant and dense, trees:* (TA:) another reading is لَيْكَةَ; accord. to which, this is the name of the town [in which the people here mentioned dwelt]: (Ṣ, Ḳ:) or, as some say, the two words are [applied to the same place,] like بَكَّةُ and مَكَّةُ: (Ṣ:) but Zj says that another reading is allowable, and very good; i. e. أَصْحَابُ لَيْكَةِ, as being originally الأَيْكَةِ; for the Arabs say, الأَحْمَرُ قَدْ جَآءَنِى and لَحْمَرُ جَآءَنِى for الأَحْمَرُ; so that لَيْكَة is like لَحْمَر. (TA.)

أَيْكٌ أَيِكٌ, (Ḳ, TA,) like كَتِفٌ, (TA, [agreeably with the verb, but in the CḲ أَيْكٌ,]) is a phrase in which the latter word signifies مُثْمِرٌ [*Putting forth fruit;* &c.]: (Ḳ, TA:) or, as some say, it is an intensive epithet [signifying *very abundant* or *luxuriant* or *tangled* &c.]. (M, TA.)

ايل

إِيلُ a name of *God;* (Lth, T, Ṣ, M, Ḳ;) a Hebrew word; (Lth, Ṣ;) or Syriac: (Ṣ:) it is a dial. var. of إِلٌّ [q. v.]: or the latter may be an arabicized form of the former: (Az, TA:) Ibn-El-Kelbee says that جَبْرَئِيلُ and مِيكَائِيلُ and the like are similar to عَبْدُ ٱللّٰهِ and عَبْدُ الرَّحْمٰنِ; (M;) [and J says,] they are like عَبْدُ ٱللّٰهِ and تَيْمُ ٱللّٰهِ: (Ṣ:) so that جَبْر signifies "servant," and is prefixed to ايل, governing it in the gen. case: (M:) but this is not a valid assertion; for were it so, such names would be perfectly decl.: (M in art. ال:) Suh says, in the R, that جبرئيل is Syriac, and means عَبْدُ الرَّحْمٰنِ, or عَبْدُ العَزِيزِ, as is related on the authority of I 'Ab: that most persons hold ايل in this case to be a name of God: but that some hold names of this kind to be constructed inversely, after the manner of the language of the 'Ajam; ايل meaning *servant.* (TA. [See what is said of إِلٌّ.])

إِيلَةٌ: see art. اول.

أَيْلُولُ [written by some إِيلُولُ] *One of the Greek* [or *Syrian*] *months;* (T,* M, Ḳzw;) *the last thereof* [*corresponding with September, O. S.*]. (Ḳzw.)

إِيَالٌ : إِيَالَةٌ : أَيِّلٌ : أُيَّلٌ : إِيَّلٌ: see art. اول.

ايم

1. آمَتْ, (T, M, Mgh, Ḳ,) aor. تَئِيمُ, (T, Ḳ,) inf. n. أَيْمَةٌ, (T, M, Mgh, Ḳ,) or this is a simple subst., (Mṣb,) and إِيمَةٌ and أَيْمٌ and أُيُومٌ, (M, Ḳ,) *She had no husband;* said of a virgin and of one who is not a virgin; (IAạr, T, M, Mgh, Ḳ;) as also ▼ تَأَيَّمَت (Lth, T, M) and ▼ ائتامت: (M:) or, as some say, ▼ تأيّمت signifies *she lost her husband by his death, she being still fit for husbands, having in her a remaining force of youth:* (T:) and you say, آمَتْ مِنْ زَوْجِهَا, aor. تَئِيمُ, inf. n. أَيْمَةٌ and أَيْمٌ and أُيُومٌ, (Ṣ, TA, [accord. to the former app. signifying the same as آمَتْ alone as explained above: or]) meaning *she became bereft of her husband by his death, or by his being slain, and remained without marrying.* (TA.) And آمَ, (T, Ṣ, Mṣb,) aor. يَئِيمُ, (T, Mṣb,) inf. n. أَيْمَةٌ, (T,) *He had no wife:* (T, Mṣb:) or *he lost his wife by her death:* (Ṣ,* Ḳ,* and Ḥam p. 650:) and *he did not marry;* as also ▼ تأيّم. (Ḥam ubi suprà.) It is said of the Prophet, in a trad., كَانَ يَتَعَوَّذُ مِنَ الأَيْمَةِ (T, Ṣ) *He used to pray for preservation from remaining long without a wife.* (T.) And Yezeed Ibn-El-Ḥakam Eth-Thakafee says,

* كُلُّ آمْرِئٍ سَتَئِيمُ مِنْــــهُ العِرْسُ أَوْ مِنْهَا يَئِيمُ *

(Ṣ) i. e. *Every man, the wife will be bereft of him by his death, or he will be bereft of her by her death.* (Ḥam p. 531.) One says also,

مَا لَهُ آمَ وَعَامَ, meaning [*What aileth him?*] *May his wife and his cattle die*, or *perish, so that he shall have no wife* (حَتَّى يَئِيمَ) *and be vehemently desirous of milk* (يَعِيمَ). (Ṣ, Ḳ: [in the CḲ, erroneously, أَمْ وعامْ; and in a MS. copy of the Ḳ, آمْ ولاعامْ.])

2. أَيَّمَهُ ٱللّٰهُ inf. n. تَأْيِيمٌ, *God made him to have no wife.* (Ḳ,* TḲ.) And أَيَّمْتُ المَرْأَةَ, inf. n. as above; (Ḥam p. 11, and TA;*) or ↓ آمْتُهَا, like أَعَمْتُهَا; (T, Ṣ;) *I made the woman to be a widow, by slaying her husband.* (T,* Ṣ, and Ḥam ubi suprà.) Taäbbaṭa-sharrà says,

* فَأَيَّمْتُ نِسْوَانًا وَأَيْتَمْتُ إِلْدَةً *

[*And I have made women widows, by slaying their husbands; and children fatherless*]. (TA.)

4. أَأَمْتُ المَرْأَةَ: see 2.

5. تَأَيَّمَتْ and تَأَيَّمَ: see 1, in three places. The former is also explained as signifying *She became forlorn* (تَحَوَّشَتْ) *of her husband.* (Ḳ in art. حوش.) And also, (TA,) or تَأَيَّمَتْ زَمَانًا, (ISk, T, Ṣ,) *She remained some time without marrying.* (ISk, T, Ṣ, TA.) And تَأَيَّمَ, (Mṣb, Ḳ,) or تَأَيَّمَ زَمَانًا, (ISk, T, Ṣ,) *He remained some time without marrying.* (ISk, T, Ṣ, Mṣb, Ḳ.)

8. اِئْتَامَتْ, written with the disjunctive alif ايتامت: see 1. — اِئْتَمْتُهَا, (M, Ḳ,) like اِعْتَمْتُهَا, (TA,) *I took her as my wife, she being what is termed* أَيِّم [*without a husband*]. (M, Ḳ.)

أَيْمَ is a contraction of أَىُّ مَا, meaning أَىُّ شَىْءٍ: it is thus in the saying, أَيْمَ هُوَ يَا فُلَانُ [*What thing is it, O such a one?*]: and أَيْمَ تَقُولُ [*What thing sayest thou?*]. (TA.) — أَيْمُ ٱللّٰهِ [for أَيْمُنُ ٱللّٰهِ]: see in art. يمن. (Ḳ.)

أَيْمٌ, for أُمٌّ: see art. ام.

أَيْمَا: see أَمَّا — and إِمَّا.

إِيمَا: see إِمَّا.

أَيْمَانُ A man *whose wife has died:* and أَيْمَى A woman *whose husband has died:* pl. أَيَامَى, of both; like as سَكَارَى is pl. of سَكْرَانُ: accord. to ISk, أَيَامَى is originally أَيَائِمُ. (Mṣb.) [See also أَيِّمٌ.] أَيْمَانُ عَيْمَانُ are epithets applied to a man, (M, Ḳ, TA,) meaning *Whose wife* [*and cattle*] *have died* or *perished* [*so that he has no wife and is vehemently desirous of milk;* as shown above; see 1, last signification]: (TA:) the former relates to wives; and the latter, to milk: (Ṣ, Ḳ, TA:) fem. أَيْمَى عَيْمَى, applied to a woman. (M, Ḳ.)

أَيِّمٌ A woman *having no husband;* (Lth, T, Ṣ, M, Mgh, Mṣb, Ḳ;) *whether she be a virgin or not;* (IAạr, T, Ṣ, M, Mgh, Ḳ;) or *whether she have married before or not;* (Ṣgh, Mṣb;) as also أَيِّمَةٌ; (Mṣb;) [said to be] applied to one *who has not married:* (IAạr, T:) or *if not a virgin;* accord. to [the Imám] Moḥammad; agreeably with a reading of a trad. by which the أَيِّم is distinguished from the virgin: (Mgh:) also, the former, a man *having no wife;* (Ṣ, M, Mgh, Mṣb, Ḳ;) *whether he have married before or not:* (Ṣ, Ṣgh, Ḳ:) or *who has not married:* (IAạr, T:) pl. أَيَامَى (Ṣ, M, Ḳ) and أَيَائِمُ; (M, Ḳ;) the latter of which is the original form: (Ṣ, M:) [or both, accord. to the Mṣb, are pls. of أَيْمَانُ, q. v.:] and أَيِّمُونَ is a pl. applied to men, and أَيِّمَاتٌ applied to women: and آمَةٌ, also, signifying men *having no wives*, is pl. of ↓ آئِمٌ for أَيِّمٌ. (TA.) — Also A *free* woman: (Ḳ:) pl., in this sense also, أَيَامَى, used in this sense in the Ḳur xxiv. 32, (T, TA,) accord. to some. (TA.) — And *A female relation;* (Ḳ;) in which sense also أَيَامَى is pl.; (T, TA;) meaning *such as the daughter and the sister and the maternal aunt.* (T, Ḳ.)

آئِمٌ: see أَيِّمٌ.

الحَرْبُ مَأْيَمَةٌ (T, Ṣ, M, Mṣb, Ḳ) لِلنِّسَآءِ (M, Ḳ) *War is a cause of widowing to women; it slays the men, and leaves the wives without husbands.* (T, Ṣ, M, Mṣb.)

مُؤْيِمَةٌ A *rich*, or *wealthy, woman*, or one *possessing competence* or *sufficiency, having no husband.* (Ṣgh, Ḳ.)

مَأْتَمٌ: see آمَةٌ, in art. ام.

اين

1. آنَ, [aor. يَئِينُ,] inf. n. أَيْنٌ, [in a copy of the Mṣb, أَيِنَ, aor. يَأْيَنُ, inf. n. أَيْنٌ, but as this is at variance with all other authorities known to me, I regard it as a mistranscription,] *He was*, or *became, fatigued*, or *tired:* (T, M:) so says IAạr: (T:) and Aṣ says the like: (TA, from a marginal note in a copy of the Ṣ:) [see also what I have cited from the Mughnee voce إِنَّ, last sentence:] in proof of this, IAạr cites the following ex., from a poet:

* إِنَّا وَرَبِّ القُلُصِ الضَّوَامِرِ *

[*We were, or have become, fatigued, by the Lord of the lean and lank-bellied youthful she-camels*]: but Lth says that there is no verb derived from أَيْنٌ, in this sense, except in poetry: (T:) Aboo-Moḥammad says that the only instance is that cited above: (TA:) [it is not disputed that] أَيْنٌ signifies *fatigue*, or the *being fatigued* or *tired:* (Ṣ, Ḳ:) AZ says that it has no verb formed from it; but on this point he has been contradicted: (Ṣ:) A'Obeyd also says that it has no verb. (M.) — آنَ, aor. يَئِينُ, inf. n. أَيْنٌ, (Ṣ, M, Mṣb, Ḳ, &c., [but see what follows,]) also signifies *Its time came;* (أَتَى وَقْتُهُ;) as also أَنَى: (Bḍ lvii. 15:) *it was*, or *became, present: it came*, or *attained, to its time; to its full*, or *final, time*, or *state; to maturity: it was*, or *became*, or *drew, near:* syn. أَنَى: (M:) and أَدْرَكَ; like أَنَى: (Ḥam p. 455:) and حَانَ: (Ṣ, M, Mṣb, Ḳ:) and قَرُبَ. (Mughnee voce إِنَّ.) You say, آنَ لَكَ أَنْ تَفْعَلَ كَذَا, aor. and inf. n. as above, (AZ, Ṣ,) i. e. حَانَ [*The time has come, or has drawn near, for thee to do, or that thou shouldst do, such a thing*]; like أَنَى: and it is formed from it by transposition: (Ṣ:) [i. e.] أَنَى is formed by transposition from آنَ: (Mṣb:) or آنَ is a dial. var. of أَنَى; not formed from it by transposition, [nor is the reverse the case,] because of the existence of the inf. n. [of each]: (M:) or آنَ is formed by transposition from أَنَى, because the latter has an inf. n. and the former has not: so says Aṣ: for أَيْنٌ does not belong to this; its meaning being only إِعْيَآءٌ and تَعَبٌ: or, accord. to AZ, آنَ has an inf. n., namely أَيْنٌ; and if the case be so, the two [verbs] are equal; neither being the original of the other: (IJ in the Khaṣáïṣ:) Suh, in the R, asserts that آنَ is formed by transposition from أَنَى: (TA:) the assertion of El-Bekree, that آنَ is originally with و [for its medial radical letter], and that it is of the class of وَلِىَ, aor. يَلِى, requires consideration, and involves what is contrary to rule. (MF.) You say also, آنَ أَيْنُكَ, (Ṣ, M, Ḳ,) and إِينُكَ, (M, Ḳ,) and آنُكَ, (Ṣ, Ḳ,) i. e. حَانَ حِينُكَ [*Thy time*, or *season, came*, or *hath come:* or *drew near*, or *hath drawn near*]. (Ṣ, M, Ḳ.)

آنَ: see أَيْنٌ. — آلْآنَ is a noun denoting the present time; (Ṣ, M, Mṣb, Ḳ;) [signifying *At the present time; now;* for] it is an adverbial noun; (Ṣ, Mṣb, Ḳ;) one which, in a place where it is fitting to be used as such, may not be used otherwise; occurring in a determinate sense; (Ṣ, Ḳ;) the ال being inseparable from it; (IJ, M, Mṣb;) not prefixed to it for the purpose of rendering it determinate, because it has not that which participates in its meaning: (Ṣ, Mṣb, Ḳ:) as Ibn-Es-Sarráj says, there is not one آن and another آن: (Mṣb:) [accord. to ISd, who quotes a long disquisition by IJ on this word,] the ال which is expressed in this case is redundant, because the noun is determinate without it, but it is rendered so by another ال, which is understood, as in the case of أَمْسِ: so says IJ, following Aboo-'Alee; and his is the correct opinion: (M:) Fr says that it is a particle, compounded with ال, which is inseparable from it; and that it is originally أَوَانَ [or آلْأَوَانَ]: or that it may have originated from the phrase آنَ لَكَ أَنْ تَفْعَلَ [explained above], and is therefore manṣoob, like قِيلَ and قَالَ when used as nouns: but Zj disallows its originating from آنَ; and says that the right opinion is that of Kh, that آلْآنَ is indecl. with fet-ḥ for its termination, and that the ال is prefixed because the meaning is هٰذَا الوَقْتَ; and this is the opinion of Sb. (T.) You say, أَنَا آلْآنَ أَفْعَلُ كَذَا [*I, at the present time*, or *now, do*, or *will do, thus*, or *such a thing*]. (M.) And كُنْتُ آلْآنَ عِنْدَهُ, meaning *I was, in this time, of which part is present and some portions have passed, with him*, or *in his presence.* (IJ, M.) And when you mean the kind of expression which is used in this saying, you say, آلْآنُ حَدُّ الزَّمَانَيْنِ [*The term "now" is the limit of the two times;* namely the past and the future]; thus pronounced, marfooạ: so says IJ: but in the Book of Sb we read, الآنَ حَدُّ الزَّمَانَيْنِ, with naṣb: and in like manner, in the same, الآنَ آنُكَ [*Now is thy time*]; the former with naṣb and the latter with refa. (M.) You say also, هٰذَا أَوَانُ ٱلْآنَ [*This is the present time*]: and مَا جِئْتُ إِلَّا أَوَانَ ٱلْآنَ, meaning *I came not save at the present time*, or *now*: with the last word manṣoob in both instances. (ISh, T.) [And حَتَّى ٱلْآنَ and إِلَى ٱلْآنَ *To the present time* and *until the present time*; i. e. *hitherto*. And مِنَ ٱلْآنَ *From the present time; henceforward*.] Sometimes the hemzeh [after the ل] is suppressed, and its vowel is transferred to the ل; so that you say ٱلَانَ. (Bḍ ii. 66.) And sometimes also the ل is pronounced with fet-ḥ and both the hemzehs are suppressed; so that you say لَانَ. (Ṣ, Ḳ.) And sometimes تَ is prefixed to it, like as it is to حِينَ; so that you say تَلَانَ, like as you say تَحِينَ. (El-Umawee, A 'Obeyd. [See art. تلن.])

أَيْنٌ *Fatigue*. (Ṣ, Ḳ, &c.) [Whether it be a simple subst., or an inf. n., and, if the latter, whether it be an inf. n. of آنَ only in the former of the two senses assigned to that verb above, or in both these senses, is doubted: see 1, throughout.] —— *A time; a season*; syn. حِينٌ; (Ṣ, M, Ḳ;) as also ↓ إِينٌ (M, Ḳ) and ↓ آنٌ. (Ṣ, Ḳ.) [See 1, last sentence.]

أَيْنَ is an adverbial noun, (Mṣb,) an interrogative respecting a place: (Ṣ, M, Mṣb, Ḳ:) [signifying *Where? in what place?*]: Zj says that it is an interrogative particle, like كَيْفَ: (T:) [ISd says,] it is a noun, because you say, مِنْ أَيْنَ [meaning *From what place? whence?*]: (M:) [and you say also, إِلَى أَيْنَ *To what place? whither?*]: it is always manṣoob, unless you prefix the article to it, saying ٱلْأَيْنُ [which means *The place where*]: (Lth, T:) it is fem.; but may be made masc. (Lḥ, M.) You say, أَيْنَ زَيْدٌ *Where*, or *in what place, is Zeyd?* (Ṣ, Mṣb.) And أَيْنَ بَيْتُكَ [*Where is thy house*, or *tent?*]. (M.) And أَيْنَ يُذْهَبُ بِكَ, which may mean *Where*, or *whither, wilt thou be taken away, and what will be done with thee and made to come to pass with thee*, if this be thine intellect? or, accord. to Mṭr, it is a saying of the people of Baghdád, addressed to him whom they charge with foolish judgment or opinion, as meaning أَيْنَ يُذْهَبُ بِعَقْلِكَ [*Where*, or *whither, is thine intellect taken away?*]. (Ḥar p. 574.) [And أَيْنَ هٰذَا مِنْ ذَاكَ and عَنْ ذَاكَ and وَذَاكَ *What place does this hold in relation to that*, or *in comparison with that? what is this in relation to that*, or *in comparison with that? what has this to do with that? what has this in common with that?*] —— It also denotes a condition: when you say, أَيْنَ تَجْلِسْ أَجْلِسْ [*Where thou sittest, I will sit*], the sitting must be in one place: and مَا is added to it; so that you say, أَيْنَمَا تَقُمْ أَقُمْ [*Wherever thou standest, I will stand*]. (Mṣb.) —— It also occurs used as a proper name of a particular place: thus the poet Ḥomeyd Ibn-Thowr speaks of his companions as being بِأَيْنَ وَأَيْنَمَا [app. meaning *In certain places: where and wherever those places were*, there were my companions]: in which case it is divested of the meaning of an interrogative, and is imperfectly decl. because determinate and of the fem. gender. (M, L. [In one copy of the former, بِأَنَّى وَأَيْنَمَا, which may mean the same; and voce أَىٌّ, q. v., بِأَىٍّ وَأَيْنَمَا.])

أَيْنَ : see إِينٌ.

أَيَّانَ, (T, Ṣ, M, &c.,) of the measure فَعَّالٌ, or it may be of the measure فَعْلَانُ, (Mṣb,) also pronounced ↓ إِيَّانَ, (T, Ṣ, M, Ḳ,) the latter of the dial. of Suleym, mentioned by Fr, (T, Ṣ,) and by Zj, (M,) is an interrogative respecting a time, (T, Ṣ, Mṣb,) but only respecting a time not come: (T:) signifying *When?* (Ṣ, M, Mṣb;) *at what time?* (Mṣb, Ḳ:) it is fem.; but may be made masc.: (Lḥ, M:) and it may be pronounced with imáleh, though not belonging to a class of words regularly subject to imáleh. (TA.) It is said in the Ḳur [xvi. 22 and xxvii. 67], accord. to different readings, أَيَّانَ يُبْعَثُونَ or ↓ إِيَّانَ [*When they shall be raised to life*]; (T, Ṣ, M;) i. e. when shall be the resurrection. (Aboo-Is-ḥáḳ, T.) But you may not say, أَيَّانَ فَعَلْتَ ذَاكَ as meaning *When didst thou that?* (T.) —— IJ says that, were it syn. with مَتَى, it would be conditional; whereas it was not mentioned by his colleagues among the adverbs used conditionally, as مَتَى and أَيْنَ &c.: but sometimes it has a conditional meaning, though that meaning be not explicit. (M.) A poet says,

• أَيَّانَ نُؤْمِنْكَ تَأْمَنْ غَيْرَنَا وَإِذَا •
• لَمْ تُدْرِكِ الأَمْنَ مِنَّا لَمْ تَزَلْ حَذِرَا •

[*When we grant thee security, thou wilt be secure from others than us; and when thou obtainest not security from us, thou wilt not cease to be in a state of fear*]. (I 'Aḳ p. 300.)

إِيَّانَ : see أَيَّانَ, in two places.

آئِنٌ part. n. of آنَ in both its senses.

آيِنَةٌ : see أَوَانٌ.

ايه

2. أَيَّهَ بِهَا, (Ṣ, TA,) and, accord. to some, بِهِمْ, (TA,) and بِهِ, (Ḳ,* TA,) inf. n. تَأْيِيهٌ, (Ṣ, Ḳ,) *He cried out to*, or *shouted to, and called*, (Ṣ, Ḳ, TA,) *them*, namely, camels, (Ṣ, TA,) and, accord. to some, horses, and men, (TA,) and *him*, (Ḳ, TA,) namely, a camel: (TA:) or ايّه به signifies *he said to him*, namely, a man, and a horse, يَا وَيْهَاهْ [*Ho! On!*]: (A 'Obeyd:) and *he said to him*, namely, a man, يَا أَيُّهَا الرَّجُلُ [*O thou man*]: (Ḳ:) or *he called him*, namely, a man, *as though he said to him*, يا ايّها الرجل: (IAth:) and *he cried out to him*, or *at him*; or *drove him away with crying* or *a cry*; namely, an object of the chase. (TA.)

[أَيَّهْ would seem to be a dial. var. of وَيْهْ; for it is said that] أَيْهَكَ is syn. with وَيْهَكَ. (Ḳ: [but see وَيْهْ.]) —— أَيْهَا : see أَيْهَاتَ.

إِيهْ, with the ه quiescent, is a word used in chiding, or checking; meaning حَسْبُكَ [*Sufficient for thee* is such a thing; &c.]. (ISd, Ḳ.) —— إِيهًا signifies, (Ṣ, Ḳ,) as also إِيهَ, (Ḳ,) a command to be silent, (Ṣ, Ḳ,) and to abstain; (Ṣ, TA;) i. e. *Be silent; and abstain*, or *desist*: (TA:) both are used in chiding, or checking: and هِيهَ is used in the place of إِيهَ. (Lth, TA.) You say [also,] إِيهًا عَنَّا *Be silent, and abstain from* [*troubling*] *us*. (Ṣ, TA.) And إِيهًا عَنِّى ٱلْآنَ *Abstain thou from* [*troubling*] *me now*. (AZ, TA.) —— إِيهًا also occurs as meaning *I hold that to be true, and approve it*. (IAth, TA.) ═══ إِيهِ, as also إِيهَ and إِيهٍ, is a word denoting a desire, or demand, for one to add, or to give, or do, more; (Lth, Ḳ;) and a desire for one to speak: (Ḳ:) it (i. e. إِيهِ) is an imperative verbal noun, (Ṣ,) indecl., with kesr for its termination: (Ḳ:) you say to a man, when you desire, or demand, his telling or saying more of a [certain] story or subject of discourse, or his doing more of a [certain] deed, إِيهِ, with kesr. to the ه; (Ṣ;) [i. e. *Tell me*, or *say, more of this; say on; go on*, or *proceed, with this; or do more of this*;] and إِيهِ ٱفْعَلْ [*Go on*, or *proceed, with this; do it*]; (AZ;) and for إِيهِ, you say, هِيهِ: (Lth:) but when you make no interruption after it, you pronounce it with tenween, (ISk, Ṣ, Ḳ,) and say إِيهٍ, (ISk, Ṣ,) which means حَدِّثْنَا [i. e. *Tell us*, or *relate to us, something*]; (Ks, Lḥ, ISk,* Ṣ;*) and for this one says هِيهٍ, by substitution of one letter for another: (Ks, Lḥ:) or it means زِدْ [i. e. *tell*, or *say*, or *do, something more*]; and هَاتِ [i. e. *give*, or *relate, something*]; (Ḥar p. 592;) and تَكَلَّمْ [i. e. *speak*]. (Idem p. 419.) In the following saying of Dhu-r-Rummeh,

• وَقَفْنَا وَقُلْنَا إِيهِ عَنْ أُمِّ سَالِمٍ •
• وَمَا بَالُ تَكْلِيمِ الدِّيَارِ الْبَلَاقِعِ •

[*We stopped, and we said, Tell us some tidings: inform us* (أَخْبِرْنَا being app. understood) *respecting Umm-Sálim: but what is the case* (meaning what is the use) *of speaking to the vacant dwellings?*], he has used the word without tenween, though making no interruption after it, because he intended a pause. (ISk, Ṣ.) Ibn-Es-Seree says, When you say, إِيهِ يَا رَجُلُ, you only command him to tell you more of the subject of discourse known to you and him, as though you said, هَاتِ الحَدِيثَ [*Give*, or *relate, the story*, or *narrative, O man*]: but if you say, إِيهٍ, with tenween, it is as though you said, هَاتِ حَدِيثًا مَّا [*Give*, or *relate, some story* or *narrative*], because the tenween renders indeterminate: and Dhu-r-Rummeh meant the tenween, but omitted it through necessity. (Ṣ.) Aṣ says that Dhu-r-Rummeh has committed a mistake; the expression of the Arabs being only إِيهٍ [in a case of this kind]: ISd says, the truth is, that it is without tenween when determinate, and with tenween when indeterminate; and that Dhu-r-Rummeh asks the ruins to tell him more of a known story, as though he said, *Relate to us the story*, or *tell us the tidings*: (TA:) Aboo-Bekr Ibn-Es-Sarráj says, citing this verse, that ايه is not known in a case of this kind without tenween in any of the dialects; meaning that it is never conjoined with a following word unless it be with tenween. (IB, TA.)

أَيْهَا : see what next follows.

أَيْهَاتَ *i. q.* هَيْهَاتَ [*Far*, or *far from being believed* or *from the truth*, is such a thing: or *remoteness*, or *remoteness from being believed* or *from the truth*, is to be attributed to such a thing]: as also ▾ أَيْهَانِ, (Ṣ, Ḳ,) and ▾ أَيْهَانَ, (Ḳ, TA, in the CḲ أَيْهَانُ,) [and several other dial. vars., for which see هَيْهَاتَ,] and ▾ أَيْهَا, (TA; and so in some copies of the Ṣ and Ḳ; in other copies of these, ▾ أَيْهًا; [but the former is app. the right;]) with the ن [or the ت] suppressed, (TA,) which is said in pronouncing [a thing] to be remote [whether in a proper or a tropical sense]: (Ṣ, TA:) Th explains ▾ أَيْهَانِ as meaning بَعِيدٌ ذٰلِكَ: AA explains it as meaning بُعْدَ ذٰلِكَ, making it a verbal noun; and this is the correct explanation: (TA:) or the meaning is البُعْدُ, [as I have indicated above,] (Ḳ in art. هيه,) but this is only when لِ is prefixed to what follows it, as Sb says. (TA. [See هَيْهَاتَ.])

أَيْهَانِ and أَيْهَانَ : see أَيْهَاتَ, in three places.

أَيِّهٌ *Having a strong*, or *loud, voice; and vigilant*, or *wary*. (Ḥam p. 675.)

أَيُّهَا : see أَىٌّ ; last portion of the paragraph.

ب

The second letter of the alphabet: called بَآءٌ and بَا; (TA in باب الالف الليّنة;) the latter of which forms is used in spelling; like as are its analogues, as تا [and ثا] and حا [and خا and را] and طا [and ظا and فا and ها] and يا; because in this case they are not generally regarded as nouns, but as mere sounds: (Sb, M:) [these are generally pronounced with imáleh, i. e. bé, té, &c., with the exception of حا, خا, طا, and ظا; and when they are regarded as nouns, their duals are بَيَانِ, تَيَانِ, &c.:] the pl. of بَآءٌ is بَآءَاتٌ; and that of بَا is أَبْوَآءٌ. (TA ubi suprà.) It is one of the letters termed مَجْهُورَة [or vocal, i. e. pronounced with the voice, and not with the breath only]; and of those termed شَفَهِيَّة [or labial]; and of those termed ذُلْق [or pronounced with the extremity of the tongue or the lips]: Kh says that the letters of the second and third classes above mentioned [the latter of which comprises the former] are those composing the words رُبَّ مَنْ لَفَّ; and on account of their easiness of utterance, they abound in the composition of words, so that no perfect quinqueliteral-radical word is without one or more of them, unless it is of the class termed مُوَلَّد, not of the classical language of the Arabs. (TA at the commencement of باب الباء.) —— In the dial. of Mázin, it is changed into م; (TA ubi suprà;) as in بَكَّةُ, which thus becomes مَكَّةُ [the town of Mekkeh]. (TA in باب الالف الليّنة.) —— بِ is a preposition, or particle governing the gen. case; (Ṣ, Mughnee, Ḳ;) having kesr for its invariable termination because it is impossible to begin with a letter after which one makes a pause; (Ṣ;) or, correctly speaking, having a vowel for its invariable termination because it is impossible to begin with a quiescent letter; and having kesr, not fet-ḥ, to make it accord with its government [of the gen. case], and to distinguish between it and that which is both a noun and a particle. (IB.) It is used to denote adhesion (Sb, T, Ṣ, M, Mughnee, Ḳ) of the verb to its objective complement, (Ṣ,) or of a noun or verb to that to which it is itself prefixed; (TA;) and adjunction, or association: (Sb, T:) and some say that its meaning of denoting adhesion is inseparable from it; and therefore Sb restricted himself to the mention of this meaning: (Mughnee:) or Sb says that its primary meaning is that of denoting adhesion and mixture. (Ibn-Eṣ-Ṣáigh, quoted in a marginal note in a copy of the Mughnee.) It denotes adhesion [&c.] in the proper sense; (Mughnee, Ḳ;) as in أَمْسَكْتُ بِزَيْدٍ, (M, Mughnee, Ḳ,) meaning *I laid hold upon,* or *seized,* [*Zeyd,* or] *somewhat of the body of Zeyd,* or *what might detain him, as an arm or a hand, or a garment, and the like;* whereas أَمْسَكْتُهُ may mean I withheld him, or restrained him, from acting according to his own free will: (Mughnee:) and it denotes the same in a tropical sense; (Mughnee, Ḳ;) as in مَرَرْتُ بِزَيْدٍ [*I passed by Zeyd*]; (Ṣ, Mughnee, Ḳ;) as though meaning *I made my passing to adhere to Zeyd;* (Ṣ;) or *I made my passing to adhere to a place near to Zeyd:* accord. to Akh, it is for مَرَرْتُ عَلَى زَيْدٍ; but مَرَرْتُ بِهِ is more common than مَرَرْتُ عَلَيْهِ, and is therefore more properly regarded as the original form of expression: (Mughnee:) accord. to F, the vowel of this preposition is kesr [when it is prefixed to a noun or a pronoun]; or, as some say, it is fet-ḥ when it is with a noun properly so called; as in مَرَّ بَزَيْدٍ: so in the Ḳ; this being the reverse of what they have prescribed in the case of [the preposition] لِ: but in the case of بِ, no vowel but kesr is known. (MF.) It denotes the same in the saying بِهِ دَآءٌ [*In him is a disease;* i. e. *a disease is cleaving to him*]: and so [accord. to some] in أَقْسَمْتُ بِٱللّٰهِ [*I swore,* or, emphatically, *I swear, by God;* and similar phrases, respecting which see a later division of this paragraph]. (L.) So, too, in أَشْرَكَ بِٱللّٰهِ, because meaning *He associated another with God:* and in وَكَّلْتُ بِفُلَانٍ, meaning *I associated a* وَكِيل [*or factor* &c.] *with such a one.* (T.) [And so in other phrases here following.] عَلَيْكَ بِزَيْدٍ *Keep thou to Zeyd:* or *take thou Zeyd.* (TA voce عَلَى.) عَلَيْكَ بِكَذَا *Keep thou to such a thing:* (El-Munáwee:) or *take thou such a thing.* (Ḥam p. 216.) فَبِهَا وَنِعْمَتْ *Keep thou to it,* فبها meaning فَعَلَيْكَ بِهَا, (Mgh in art. نعم,) [or *let him keep to it,* i. e. فَعَلَيْهِ بِهَا,] or *thou hast taken to,* or *adopted and followed,* or *adhered to, the established way,* or *the way established by the Prophet,* i. e. فَبِٱلسُّنَّةِ أَخَذْتَ, (Mgh,) or *he hath taken to,* &c., i. e. فَبِٱلسُّنَّةِ أَخَذَ, (IAth, TA in art. نعم,) or *by this practice,* or *action, is excellence attained,* or *he will attain excellence,* i. e. فَبِهٰذِهِ ٱلخَصْلَةِ أَوِ ٱلفَعْلَةِ يَنَالُ ٱلفَضْلَ, or يُنَالُ ٱلفَضْلُ; (IAth ubi suprà;) *and excellent is the practice, the established way,* or *the way established by the Prophet,* ونعمت meaning وَنِعْمَتِ ٱلخَصْلَةُ ٱلسُّنَّةُ, (Mgh,) or *and excellent is the practice,* or *the action,* i. e. وَنِعْمَتِ ٱلخَصْلَةُ, (Ṣ and Ḳ in art. نعم,) or وَنِعْمَتِ ٱلخَصْلَةُ أَوِ ٱلفَعْلَةُ; (IAth ubi suprà:) and it also occurs in a trad., where the meaning is [He who hath done such a thing *hath adhered to the ordinance of indulgence; and excellent is the practice,* or *action,* &c.: for here فبها is meant to imply] فَبِٱلرُّخْصَةِ أَخَذَ. (TA in the present art. See also art. نعم.) —— It is also used to render a verb transitive; (Mughnee, Ḳ;) having the same effect as hemzeh [prefixed], in causing [what would otherwise be] the agent to become an objective complement; as in ذَهَبْتُ بِزَيْدٍ syn. with أَذْهَبْتُهُ [*I made Zeyd to go away;* or *I took him away*]; (Mughnee;) and hence, [in the Ḳur ii. 16,] ذَهَبَ ٱللّٰهُ بِنُورِهِمْ [*God taketh away their light*]; (Mughnee, Ḳ;) which refutes the assertion of Mbr and Suh, that ذَهَبْتُ بِزَيْدٍ means [*I went away with Zeyd;* i. e.] *I accompanied Zeyd in going away.* (Mughnee.) J says that any verb that is not trans. you may render so by means of ب and ا [prefixed] and reduplication [of the medial radical letter]: you say, طَارَ بِهِ and أَطَارَهُ and طَيَّرَهُ [as meaning *He made him to fly,* or *to fly away*]: but IB says that this is not correct as of common application; for some verbs are rendered trans. by means of hemzeh, but not by reduplication; and some by reduplication, but not by hemzeh; and some by ب, but not by hemzeh nor by reduplication: you say, دَفَعْتُ زَيْدًا بِعَمْرٍو [as meaning *I made 'Amr to repel Zeyd,* lit. *I repelled Zeyd by 'Amr*], but not دَفَّعْتُهُ nor أَدْفَعْتُهُ. (TA.) —— It also denotes the employing a thing as an aid or instrument; (Ṣ, M,* Mughnee, Ḳ;*) as in كَتَبْتُ بِٱلقَلَمِ [*I wrote with the reed-pen*]; (Ṣ, Mughnee, Ḳ;) and نَجَرْتُ بِٱلقَدُومِ [*I worked as a carpenter with the adz*]; (Mughnee, Ḳ;) and ضَرَبْتُ بِٱلسَّيْفِ [*I struck with the sword*]. (M.) And hence the ب in بِسْمِ ٱللّٰهِ, (Mughnee, Ḳ,) accord. to some, because the action [before which it is pronounced] is not practicable in the most perfect manner but by means of it: (Mughnee:) but others disallow this, because the name of God should not be regarded as an instrument: (MF, TA:) and some say that the ب here is to denote beginning, as though one said, أَبْتَدِئُ بِسْمِ ٱللّٰهِ [*I begin with the name of God*]. (TA.) —— It also denotes a cause; as in إِنَّكُمْ ظَلَمْتُمْ أَنْفُسَكُمْ بِٱتِّخَاذِكُمُ ٱلعِجْلَ [*Verily ye have wronged yourselves by,* i. e. *because of, your taking to yourselves the calf* as a god (Ḳur ii. 51)]; and in فَكُلًّا أَخَذْنَا بِذَنْبِهِ [*And every one of these we have punished for,* i. e. *because of, his sin* (Ḳur xxix. 39)]; (Mughnee, Ḳ;) and in لَنْ يَدْخُلَ أَحَدُكُمُ ٱلجَنَّةَ بِعَمَلِهِ [*Not any of you shall enter Paradise by,* or *for,* or *because of, his works*]. (TA from a trad.) And so in لَقِيتُ بِزَيْدٍ ٱلأَسَدَ *I met,* or *found, by reason of* my meeting, or finding, *Zeyd, the lion:* (Mughnee:) or the ب in this instance denotes comparison; [i. e. *I met,* or *found, in Zeyd* the like of *the lion;*] as also in رَأَيْتُ بِفُلَانٍ ٱلقَمَرَ [*I saw in such a one* the like of *the moon*]. (TA.) Another ex. of the same usage is the saying [of a poet],

• قَدْ سُقِيَتْ آبَالُهُمْ بِالنَّارِ •

• وَالنَّارُ قَدْ تَشْفِى مِنَ الْأُوَارِ •

[*Their camels had been watered because of the brand* that they bore: *for fire*, or *the brand*, *sometimes cures of the heat of thirst*]; i. e., because of their being branded with the names [or marks] of their owners, they had free access left them to the water. (Mughnee. See also another reading of this verse voce نَارٌ.) [In like manner] it is used in the sense of مِنْ أَجْلِ [which means بِسَبَبِ (Msb in art. اجل)] in the saying of Lebeed,

• غُلْبٌ تَشَذَّرُ بِالذُّحُولِ كَأَنَّهَا •

• جِنُّ الْبَدِىِّ رَوَاسِيًا أَقْدَامُهَا •

(Ṣ) *Thick-necked* men, like lions, *who threatened* one another *because of rancorous feelings, as though they were the Jinn of* the valley *El-Bedee*, [or *of the desert*, (TA in art. بدو,)] *their feet standing firm* in contention and obstinate altercation. (EM pp. 174 and 175.) It is also used to denote a cause when prefixed to أَنَّ, and to مَا; as in ذٰلِكَ بِأَنَّهُمْ كَانُوا يَكْفُرُونَ بِآيَاتِ ٱللّٰهِ [*That was because they used to disbelieve in the signs of God*]; and in ذٰلِكَ بِمَا عَصَوْا [*That was because they disobeyed*]: both instances in the Ḳur ii. 58. (Bḍ.) — It is also used to denote concomitance, as *syn. with* مَعَ; (Mughnee, Ḳ;) as in اِشْتَرَيْتُ الْفَرَسَ بِلِجَامِهِ وَسَرْجِهِ [*I bought the horse with his bit and bridle and his saddle*]; (TA;) and in لَمَّا رَآنِى بِالسِّلَاحِ هَرَبَ, i. e. *When he saw me advancing with the weapon*, [he fled;] or *when he saw me possessor of a weapon;* (Sh, T;) and in اِهْبِطْ بِسَلَامٍ [*Descend thou with security*, or *with greeting* (Ḳur xi. 50)]; and in وَقَدْ دَخَلُوا بِالْكُفْرِ [*They having entered with unbelief* (Ḳur v. 66)]; (Mughnee, Ḳ;) بالكفر being a denotative of state. (Bḍ.) Authors differ respecting the ب in the saying, فَسَبِّحْ بِحَمْدِ رَبِّكَ, in the Ḳur [xv. 98 and cx. 3]; some saying that it denotes concomitance, and that حمد is prefixed to the objective complement, so that the meaning is, سَبِّحْهُ حَامِدًا لَهُ [*Declare thou his* (*thy Lord's*) *freedom from everything derogatory from his glory, praising Him*], i. e. declare thou his freedom from that which is not suitable to Him, and ascribe to Him that which is suitable to Him; but others say that it denotes the employing a thing as an aid or instrument, and that حمد is prefixed to the agent, so that the meaning is, سَبِّحْهُ بِمَا حَمِدَ بِهِ نَفْسَهُ [*declare thou his* (*thy Lord's*) *freedom from everything derogatory from his glory by means of* ascribing to Him *that wherewith He hath praised himself*]: and so, too, respecting the saying, سُبْحَانَكَ ٱللّٰهُمَّ وَبِحَمْدِكَ; some asserting that it is one proposition, the و being redundant; but others saying, it is two propositions, the و being a conjunction, and the verb upon which the ب is dependent being suppressed, so that the meaning is, [*I declare thy freedom from everything derogatory from thy glory, O God*,] وَبِحَمْدِكَ سَبَّحْتُكَ [*and with the praising of Thee*, or *by means of the praise that belongeth to Thee, I declare thy freedom* &c.]. (Mughnee. [Other explanations of these two phrases have been proposed; but those given above are the most approved.]) You also say, عَلَىَّ بِهِ, meaning *Bring thou him*, [i. e.] *come with him, to me*. (Ḥar p. 109.) ضَاقَتْ عَلَيْهِمُ الْأَرْضُ بِمَا رَحُبَتْ, in the Ḳur ix. 119, means بِرُحْبِهَا [i. e. *The earth became strait to them, with*, meaning *notwithstanding, its amplitude*, or *spaciousness*]. (Bḍ.) Sometimes the negative لا intervenes between ب [denoting concomitance] and the noun governed by it in the gen. case; [so that بِلَا signifies *Without;*] as in جِئْتُ بِلَا زَادٍ [*I came without travelling-provision*]. (Mughnee and Ḳ in art. لا.) — It is also *syn. with* فِى before a noun signifying a place or a time; (Mughnee,* Ḳ,* TA;) as in جَلَسْتُ بِالْمَسْجِدِ [*I sat in the mosque*]; (TA;) and وَلَقَدْ نَصَرَكُمُ ٱللّٰهُ بِبَدْرٍ [*And verily God aided you against your enemies at Bedr* (Ḳur iii. 119)]; and نَجَّيْنَاهُمْ بِسَحَرٍ [*We saved them a little before daybreak* (Ḳur liv. 34)]: (Mughnee, Ḳ, TA:) and so in بِأَيِّكُمُ الْمَفْتُونُ, (T, Ḳ,) in the Ḳur [lxviii. 6], (TA,) accord. to some, (T, Mughnee,) i. e. *In which of you is madness;* or *in which* of the two parties *of you is the mad:* (Bḍ:) or the ب is here redundant; (Sb, Bḍ, Mughnee;) the meaning being *which of you is he who is afflicted with madness*. (Bḍ. [See also a later division of this paragraph.]) — It also denotes substitution; [meaning *Instead of*, or *in place of;*] as in the saying [of the Ḥamásee (Mughnee)],

• فَلَيْتَ لِى بِهِمْ قَوْمًا إِذَا رَكِبُوا •

• شَنُّوا الْإِغَارَةَ فُرْسَانًا وَرُكْبَانَا •

[*Then would that I had, instead of them, a people who, when they mounted* their beasts, *poured the sudden attack, they being horsemen and camel-riders*]; (Ḥam p. 8, Mughnee, Ḳ;) i. e., بَدَلًا بِهِمْ: (TA:) but some read شَدُّوا الْإِغَارَةَ, [and so it is in some, app., the most correct, of the copies of the Mughnee,] for شَدُّوا لِلْإِغَارَةِ [*hastened for the making a sudden attack*]. (Ḥam, Mughnee.) So, too, in the saying, اِعْتَضْتُ بِهٰذَا الثَّوْبِ خَيْرًا مِنْهُ [*I received, in the place of this garment*, or *piece of cloth, one better than it*]; and لَقِيتُ بِزَيْدٍ بَحْرًا [*I found, in the place of Zeyd, a man of abundant generosity* or *beneficence*]; and هٰذَا بِذَاكَ [*This is instead*, or *in the place, of that;* but see another explanation of this last phrase in what follows]. (The Lubáb, TA.) — It also denotes requital; or the giving, or doing, in return; (Mughnee, Ḳ;) and in this case is prefixed to the word signifying the substitute, or thing given or done in exchange [or return; or to the word signifying that for which a substitute is given, or for which a thing is given or done in exchange or return]; (Mughnee;) as in the saying, اِشْتَرَيْتُهُ بِأَلْفِ دِرْهَمٍ [*I purchased it for a thousand dirhems*]; (Mughnee, Ḳ;*) [and in the saying in the Ḳur ix. 112, إِنَّ ٱللّٰهَ ٱشْتَرَى مِنَ ٱلْمُؤْمِنِينَ أَنْفُسَهُمْ وَأَمْوَالَهُمْ بِأَنَّ لَهُمُ ٱلْجَنَّةَ *Verily God hath purchased of the believers their souls and their possessions for* the price of *their having Paradise;*] and كَافَأْتُ إِحْسَانَهُ بِضِعْفٍ [*I requited his beneficence with a like* beneficence, or *with double*, or *more*], (Mughnee,) or كَافَأْتُهُ بِضِعْفِ إِحْسَانِهِ [*I requited him with the like*, or *with double the amount*, or *with more than double the amount, of his beneficence*], (Ḳ,) but the former is preferable; (TA;) [and خَدَمَ بِطَعَامِ بَطْنِهِ (Ṣ and A &c. in art. وغد) *He served for*, meaning *in return for, the food of his belly;*] and

• هٰذَا بِذَاكَ وَلَا عَتْبٌ عَلَى الزَّمَنِ •

[*This is in return for that*, (an explanation somewhat differing from one in the next preceding division of this paragraph,) *and no blame is imputable to fortune*]: and hence, اُدْخُلُوا ٱلْجَنَّةَ بِمَا كُنْتُمْ تَعْمَلُونَ [*Enter ye Paradise in return for that which ye wrought* (Ḳur xvi. 34)]; for the ب here is not that which denotes a cause, as the Moatezileh assert it to be, and as all [of the Sunnees] hold it to be in the saying of the Prophet, لَنْ يَدْخُلَ أَحَدُكُمُ الْجَنَّةَ بِعَمَلِهِ [before cited and explained]; because what is given instead of something is sometimes given gratuitously; and it is evident that there is no mutual opposition between the trad. and the verse of the Ḳur-án. (Mughnee.) — It is also *syn. with* عَنْ; and is said to be peculiar to interrogation; as in فَاسْأَلْ بِهِ خَبِيرًا [*And ask thou respecting Him*, or *it, one possessing knowledge* (Ḳur xxv. 60)]; (Mughnee, Ḳ;) and accord. to IAạr in the Ḳur lxx. 1; (T;) and in the saying of 'Alḳameh,

• فَإِنْ تَسْأَلُونِى بِالنِّسَآءِ فَإِنَّنِى •

• بَصِيرٌ بِأَدْوَآءِ النِّسَآءِ خَبِيرُ •

[*And if ye ask me respecting* the diseases of women, *verily I am knowing in the diseases of women, skilful*]: (A'Obeyd, TA:) or it is not peculiar to interrogation; as in وَيَوْمَ تَشَقَّقُ ٱلسَّمَآءُ بِٱلْغَمَامِ [*And the day when the heavens shall be rent asunder from the clouds* (Ḳur xxv. 27)]; (Mughnee, Ḳ;) and مَا غَرَّكَ بِرَبِّكَ (Ḳ) i. e. *What hath beguiled thee from thy Lord*, and from believing in him? in the Ḳur lxxxii. 6; and so in the same, lvii. 13: (TA: [but see art. غر:]) or, accord. to Z, the ب in بالغمام means *by, as by an instrument;* (Mughnee;) or it means *because of*, or *by means of*, the rising of the clouds therefrom: (Bḍ:) and in like manner the Baṣrees explain it as occurring in فَاسْأَلْ بِهِ خَبِيرًا, as denoting the cause; and they assert that it is never syn. with عَنْ; but their explanation is improbable. (Mughnee.) — It is also *syn. with* عَلَى; as in إِنْ تَأْمَنْهُ بِقِنْطَارٍ (Mughnee, Ḳ*) or بِدِينَارٍ (Ṣ) [*If thou give him charge over a hundredweight* or *over a deenár* (Ḳur iii. 68)]; like as عَلَى is sometimes put in the place of بِ, as after the verb رَضِىَ: (Ṣ, TA:) and so in لَوْ تُسَوَّى بِهِمُ ٱلْأَرْضُ [*That the ground were made even over them*], in the Ḳur [iv. 45], (TA,) i. e. *that* *they were buried;* (Bḍ;) and in مَرَرْتُ بِزَيْدٍ [*I passed by Zeyd*], accord. to Akh, as before mentioned; (Mughnee, in the first division of the art. on this preposition;) and in زَيْدٌ بِالسَّطْحِ [*Zeyd is on the roof*]; (TA;) and in a verse cited in this Lex. voce ثَعْلَبٌ. (Mughnee.) — It also denotes part of a whole; (Mṣb in art. بعض, Mughnee, Ḳ;) so accord. to Aṣ and AAF and others; (Mṣb, Mughnee;) as *syn. with* مِنْ: (Mṣb, TA:) IḲt says, the Arabs say, شَرِبْتُ بِمَآءِ كَذَا, meaning مِنْهُ [*I drank of such a water*]; and AZ mentions, as a saying of the Arabs, سَقَاكَ ٱللّٰهُ مِنْ مَآءِ كَذَا, meaning بِهِ [*May God give thee to drink of such a water*], thus making the two prepositions syn.: (Mṣb: [in which five similar instances are cited from poets; and two of these are cited also in the Mughnee:]) and thus it signifies in عَيْنًا يَشْرَبُ بِهَا عِبَادُ ٱللّٰهِ [*A fountain from which the servants of God shall drink,* in the Ḳur lxxvi. 6; and the like occurs in lxxxiii. 28]; (Mṣb, Mughnee, Ḳ;) accord. to the authorities mentioned above; (Mughnee;) or the meaning is, *with which the servants of God shall satisfy their thirst* (يَرْوَى بِهَا); (T, Mughnee;) or, accord. to Z, *with which the servants of God shall drink wine:* (Mughnee:) if the ب were redundant, [as some assert it to be, (Bḍ,)] the meaning would be, that they shall drink the whole of it; which is not right: (Mṣb:) thus, also, it is used in وَٱمْسَحُوا بِرُؤُسِكُمْ [in the Ḳur v. 8], (Mṣb, Mughnee, Ḳ,) accord. to some; (Mughnee;) i. e. [*And wipe ye*] *a part of your heads;* and this explanation has been given us on the authority of Esh-Sháfi'ee; but he is said to have disapproved it, and to have held that the ب here denotes adhesion: (TA:) this latter is its apparent meaning in this and the other instances: or, as some say, in this last instance it is used to denote the employing a thing as an aid or instrument, and there is an ellipsis in the phrase, and an inversion; the meaning being, امْسَحُوا رُؤُسَكُمْ بِالْمَآءِ [*wipe ye your heads with water*]. (Mughnee.) — It is also used to denote swearing; (Mughnee, Ḳ;) and is the primary one of the particles used for this purpose; therefore it is peculiarly distinguished by its being allowable to mention the verb with it, (Mughnee,) as أُقْسِمُ بِٱللّٰهِ لَأَفْعَلَنَّ [*I swear by God I will assuredly do* such a thing]; (Mughnee, Ḳ;) and by its being prefixed to a pronoun, as in بِكَ لَأَفْعَلَنَّ [*By thee I will assuredly do* such a thing]; and by its being used in adjuring, or conjuring, for the purpose of inducing one to incline to that which is desired of him, as in بِٱللّٰهِ هَلْ قَامَ زَيْدٌ, meaning I adjure thee, or conjure thee, *by God,* to tell me, *did Zeyd stand?* (Mughnee.) [See also the first explanation of this particle, where it is said, on the authority of the L, that, when thus used, it denotes adhesion.] — It is also *syn. with* إِلَى, as denoting the end of an extent or interval; as in أَحْسَنَ بِى, meaning *He did good,* or *acted well, to me:* (Mughnee, Ḳ:) but some say that the verb here imports the meaning of لَطَفَ [which is trans. by means of ب, i. e. *he acted graciously,* or *courteously, with me*]. (Mughnee.) — It is also redundant, (Ṣ, Mughnee, Ḳ,) to denote corroboration: (Mughnee, Ḳ:) and is prefixed to the agent: (Mughnee:) first, necessarily; as in أَحْسِنْ بِزَيْدٍ; (Mughnee, Ḳ;) accord. to general opinion (Mughnee) originally أَحْسَنَ زَيْدٌ, i. e. صَارَ ذَا حُسْنٍ [*Zeyd became possessed of goodness,* or *goodliness,* or *beauty*]; (Mughnee, Ḳ;*) or the correct meaning is حَسُنَ زَيْدٌ [*Good,* or *goodly,* or *beautiful,* or *very good* &c., *is Zeyd!* or *how good,* or *goodly,* or *beautiful, is Zeyd!*], as in the B: (TA:) secondly, in most instances; and this is in the case of the agent of كَفَى; as in كَفَى بِٱللّٰهِ شَهِيدًا [*God sufficeth, being witness,* or *as a witness* (Ḳur xiii., last verse; &c.)]; (Mughnee, Ḳ; [and a similar ex. is given in the Ṣ, from the Ḳur xxv. 33;]) the ب here denoting emphatic praise; but you may drop it, saying, كَفَى ٱللّٰهُ شَهِيدًا: (Fr, TA:) thirdly, in a case of necessity, by poetic licence; as in the saying,

أَلَمْ يَأْتِيكَ وَٱلْأَنْبَآءُ تَنْمِى
بِمَا لَاقَتْ لَبُونُ بَنِى زِيَادِ

[*Did not what the milch camel of the sons of Ziyád experienced come to thee* (يَأْتِيكَ being in like manner put for يَأْتِكَ) *when the tidings were increasing?*]. (Mughnee, Ḳ.) It is also redundantly prefixed to the objective complement of a verb; as in وَلَا تُلْقُوا بِأَيْدِيكُمْ إِلَى ٱلتَّهْلُكَةِ [*And cast ye not yourselves* (بأيديكم meaning بِأَنْفُسِكُمْ) *to perdition* (Ḳur ii. 191)]; and in وَهُزِّى إِلَيْكِ بِجِذْعِ ٱلنَّخْلَةِ [*And shake thou towards thee the trunk of the palm-tree* (Ḳur xix. 25)]: but some say that the former means *and cast ye not yourselves* (أَنْفُسَكُمْ being understood) *with your hands to perdition;* or that the meaning is, *by means,* or *because, of your hands:* (Mughnee:) and ISd says that هُزِّى, in the latter, is made trans. by means of ب because it is used in the sense of جُرِّى: (TA in art هز:) so, too, in the saying,

نَضْرِبُ بِالسَّيْفِ وَنَرْجُو بِالْفَرَجْ

[*We smite with the sword, and we hope for the removal of grief*]: (Ṣ, Mughnee:) and in the trad., كَفَى بِالْمَرْءِ كَذِبًا أَنْ يُحَدِّثَ بِكُلِّ مَا سَمِعَ [*It suffices the man in respect of lying that he relate all that he has heard*]. (Mughnee.) It is also redundantly prefixed to the inchoative; as in بِحَسْبِكَ [when you say, بِحَسْبِكَ دِرْهَمٌ meaning *A thing sufficing thee is a dirhem;* a phrase which may be used in two ways; as predicating of what is sufficient, that it is a dirhem; and as predicating of a dirhem, that it is sufficient; in which latter case, بحسبك is an enunciative put before its inchoative, so that the meaning is, *a dirhem is a thing sufficing thee,* i. e. *a dirhem is sufficient for thee;* as is shown in a marginal note in my copy of the Mughnee: in the latter way is used the saying, mentioned in the Ṣ, بِحَسْبِكَ قَوْلُ ٱلسُّوْءِ *A thing sufficing thee is the saying what is evil:* and so, app., each of the following sayings, mentioned in the TA on the authority of Fr; حَسْبُكَ بِصَدِيقِنَا *A person sufficing thee is our friend;* and نَاهِيكَ بِأَخِينَا *A person sufficing thee is our brother:* the ب is added, as Fr says, to denote emphatic praise]: so too in خَرَجْتُ فَإِذَا بِزَيْدٍ [*I went forth, and lo, there,* or *then, was Zeyd*]; and in كَيْفَ بِكَ إِذَا كَانَ كَذَا [*How art thou,* or *how wilt thou be, when it is thus,* or *when such a thing is the case?*]; and so, accord. to Sb, in بِأَيِّكُمُ ٱلْمَفْتُونُ [mentioned before, in explanation of ب as syn. with فِى]; but Abu-l-Ḥasan says that بأيكم is dependent upon اسْتِقْرَار suppressed, denoting the predicate of المفتون; and some say that this is an inf. n. in the sense of فِتْنَةٌ; [so that the meaning may be, بِأَيِّكُمُ ٱلْمَفْتُونُ مُسْتَقِرٌّ *In which of you is madness residing?*]; or, as some say, ب is here syn. with فِى [as I have before mentioned]. (Mughnee.) A strange case is that of its being added before that which is originally an inchoative, namely, the noun, or subject, of لَيْسَ, on the condition of its being transferred to the later place which is properly that of the enunciative; as in the reading of some, لَيْسَ ٱلْبِرُّ بِأَنْ تُوَلُّوا وُجُوهَكُمْ قِبَلَ ٱلْمَشْرِقِ وَٱلْمَغْرِبِ [*Your turning your faces towards the east and the west is not obedience* (Ḳur ii. 172)]; with البرّ in the accus. case. (Mughnee.) It is also redundantly prefixed to the enunciative; and this is in two kinds of cases: first, when the phrase is not affirmative; and cases of this kind may be followed as exs.; as لَيْسَ زَيْدٌ بِقَائِمٍ [*Zeyd is not standing*]; and وَمَا ٱللّٰهُ بِغَافِلٍ عَمَّا تَعْمَلُونَ [*And God is not heedless of that which ye do* (Ḳur ii. 69, &c.)]: secondly, when the phrase is affirmative; and in cases of this kind, one limits himself to what has been heard [from the Arabs]: so say Akh and his followers; and they hold to be an instance of this kind the phrase, جَزَآءُ سَيِّئَةٍ بِمِثْلِهَا [*The recompense of an evil action is the like thereof* (Ḳur x. 28)]; and the saying of the Ḥamáseh,

وَمَنْعُكَهَا بِشَىْءٍ يُسْتَطَاعُ

[*And the preventing thee from having her* (referring to a mare) *is a thing that is possible*]: but it is more proper to make بمثلها dependent upon اسْتِقْرَار suppressed, as the enunciative; [the meaning being, جَزَآءُ سَيِّئَةٍ مُسْتَقِرٌّ بِمِثْلِهَا, or يَسْتَقِرُّ بِمِثْلِهَا, i. e. *the recompense of an evil action is a thing consisting in the like thereof*]; and to make بشىء dependent upon منعكها; the meaning being, وَمَنْعُكَهَا بِشَىْءٍ مَا يُسْتَطَاعُ [i. e. *and the preventing thee from having her, by something, is possible:* see Ḥam p. 102]: Ibn-Málik also [holds, like Akh and his followers, that ب may be redundant when prefixed to the enunciative in an affirmative proposition; for he] says, respecting بِحَسْبِكَ زَيْدٌ, that زيد is an inchoative placed after its enunciative, [so that the meaning is, *Zeyd is a person sufficing thee,*] because زَيْدٌ is determinate and حَسْبُكَ is indeterminate. (Mughnee. [See also what has been said above respecting the phrase بِحَسْبِكَ دِرْهَمٌ, in treating of ب as added before the inchoative.]) It is also redundantly prefixed to the denotative of state of which the governing word is made negative; as in

• فَمَا رَجَعَتْ بِخَائِبَةٍ رِكَابٌ •
• حَكِيمُ بْنُ الْمُسَيَّبِ مُنْتَهَاهَا •

[*And travelling-camels* (meaning their riders) *returned not disappointed, whose goal, or ultimate object, was Hakeem the son of El-Museiyab*]; and in

• فَمَا ٱنْبَعَثْتَ بِمَزْؤُودٍ وَلَا وَكِلِ •

[*And thou didst not, being sent, or roused, go away frightened, nor impotent, committing thine affair to another*]: so says Ibn-Málik: but AHei disagrees with him, explaining these two exs. as elliptical; the meaning implied in the former being, بِحَاجَةٍ خَائِبَةٍ [*with an object of want disappointed, or frustrated*]; and in the second, بِشَخْصٍ مَزْؤُودٍ, i. e. مَذْعُورٍ [*with a person frightened*]; the poet meaning, by the مزؤود, himself, after the manner of the saying, رَأَيْتُ مِنْهُ أَسَدًا; and this is plain with respect to the former ex., but not with respect to the second; for the negation of attributes of dispraise denoted as intensive in degree does not involve the negation of what is simply essential in those attributes; and one does not say, لَقِيتُ مِنْهُ أَسَدًا, or بَحْرًا, [or رَأَيْتُ مِنْهُ أَسَدًا, as above, or بَحْرًا,] but when meaning to express an intensive degree of boldness, or of generosity. (Mughnee.) It is also redundantly prefixed to the corroborative نَفْس and عَيْن: and some hold it to be so in يَتَرَبَّصْنَ بِأَنْفُسِهِنَّ [as meaning *Shall themselves wait* (Kur ii. 228 and 234)]: but this presents matter for consideration; because the affixed pronoun in the nom. case, [whether expressed, as in this instance, in which it is the final syllable نَ, or implied in the verb,] when corroborated by نَفْس, should properly be corroborated first by the separate [pronoun], as in قُمْتُمْ أَنْتُمْ أَنْفُسُكُمْ [Ye stood, ye, yourselves]; and because the corroboration in this instance is lost, since it cannot be imagined that any others are here meant than those who are commanded to wait: [the preferable rendering is, *shall wait to see what may take place with themselves*:] بِأَنْفُسِهِنَّ is added only for rousing them the more to wait, by making known that their minds should not be directed towards the men. (Mughnee.) Accord. to some, it is also redundantly prefixed to a noun governed in the gen. case [by another preposition]; as in

• فَأَصْبَحْنَ لَا يَسْأَلْنَهُ عَنْ بِمَا بِهِ •

[*And they became in a condition in which they asked him not respecting his father*; which may perhaps be regarded by some as similar to the saying,

• يَضْحَكْنَ عَنْ كَالْبَرَدِ الْمُنْهَمِ •

but in this instance, كَ is generally held to be a noun, syn. with مِثْل]. (The Lubáb, TA.) — Sometimes it is understood; as in اللّٰهِ لَأَفْعَلَنَّ [i. e. بِاللّٰهِ لَأَفْعَلَنَّ] and أَللّٰهِ لَأَفْعَلَنَّ *By God, I will assuredly do* such a thing; in the latter as well as the former, for a noun is often put in the accus. case because of a preposition understood; or, accord. to Bd, in ii. 1, a verb significant of swearing is understood]: and in خَيْرٍ [for بِخَيْرٍ *In a good state*], addressed to him who says, كَيْفَ أَصْبَحْتَ [How hast thou entered upon the time of morning? or How hast thou become?]. (TA.) — [It occurs also in several elliptical phrases; one of which (فَبِهَا وَنِعْمَتْ) has been mentioned among the exs. of its primary meaning: some are mentioned in other arts.; as بِأَبِي and بِنَفْسِي, in arts. ابو and نفس: and there are many others, of which exs. here follow.] Mohammad is related, in a trad., to have said, after hitting a butt with an arrow, أَنَا بِهَا أَنَا بِهَا, meaning أَنَا صَاحِبُهَا [*I am the doer of it! I am the doer of it!*]. (Sh, T.) And in another trad., Mohammad is related to have said to one who told him of a man's having committed an unlawful action, لَعَلَّكَ بِذٰلِكَ, meaning لَعَلَّكَ صَاحِبُ الأَمْرِ [*May-be thou art the doer of that thing*]. (T.) And in another, he is related to have said to a woman brought to him for having committed adultery or fornication, مَنْ بِكِ, meaning مَنْ صَاحِبُكِ [*Who was thine accomplice?*]: (T:) or مَنِ الفَاعِلُ بِكِ [*Who was the agent with thee?*]. (TA.) أَنَا بِكَ وَلَكَ, occurring in a form of prayer, means *I seek, or take, refuge in Thee; or by thy right disposal and facilitation I worship; and to Thee*, not to any other, *I humble myself*. (Mgh in art. بوأ.) One says also, مَنْ لِي بِكَذَا, meaning *Who will be responsible, answerable, amenable, or surety, to me for such a thing?* (Har p. 126: and the like is said in p. 191.) And similar to this is the saying, كَأَنِّي بِكَ, meaning كَأَنِّي أَبْصُرُ بِكَ [It is *as though I saw thee*]; i. e. I know from what I witness of thy condition to-day how thy condition will be to-morrow; so that it is as though I saw thee in that condition. (Idem p. 126.) [You also say, كَأَنَّكَ بِهِ, meaning Thou art so near to him that it is *as though thou sawest him*: or it is *as though thou wert with him*: i. e. thou art almost in his presence.] — The Basrees hold that prepositions do not supply the places of other prepositions regularly; but are imagined to do so when they admit of being differently rendered; or it is because a word is sometimes used in the sense of another word, as in شَرِبْنَ بِمَاءِ الْبَحْرِ meaning رَوِينَ, and in أَحْسَنَ بِي meaning لَطَفَ; or else because they do so anomalously. (Mughnee.) ═ [As a numeral, ب denotes *Two*.]

با

بَا and بَآءٌ: see the letter ب, and arts. بوأ and بى.

بأ

R. Q. 1. بَأْبَأَهُ, (Lth, T, S, M, K,) and بَأْبَأَ بِهِ, (Fr, M, K,) inf. n. بَأْبَأَةٌ (Lth, T, M) and بِئْبَآءٌ; (Fr, M;) [as also أَبَّاهُ; see art. ابو;] *He said to him*, بِأَبِي, (Fr, M,) or بِأَبَا, (M,) or بِأَبِي أَنْتَ, (Lth, T, K,) [all meaning *With my father mayest thou be ransomed!* or] meaning أَفْدِيكَ بِأَبِي [*I will ransom thee with my father*]; (Lth, T;) or *he said to him*, بِأَبِي أَنْتَ وَأُمِّي [*With my father mayest thou be ransomed, and with my mother!* or *I will ransom thee* &c.; see art. ابو]; (S;) the current phrase of the Arabs being that which includes both parents: (TA:) i. e., a man said so to another man, (Lth, T, M,) or to a child; (Fr, S, M;) and in like manner to his horse, for having saved him from some accident: (IAar, T:) the verb is derived from بِأَبِي. (Lth, T, M.) Hence البَأْبُ, in an ex. cited voce أَبٌ, in art. ابو, q. v.; (M;) or البِئْبُ; (TA in art. ابو;) or البِيبُ. (S in that art.) — And [hence,] بَأْبَؤُوهُ *They made a show of treating him with graciousness, courtesy, or blandishment*; as also ✝ تَبَأْبَؤُوا عَلَيْهِ. (M.) — [Hence also,] ✝ بِأْبَآءٌ, with medd, [used as an inf. n.,] A woman's *dandling*, or *dancing*, of her child. (AA, T.) ═ بَأْبَأَ also signifies *He* (a child) *said* ✝ بَأْبَأْ (M, K) [in some copies of the K written بَابَا, both meaning *Papa*, or *Father*,] to his father. (M.) [Accord. to the TA, the verb is trans. in this sense, as in the senses before explained; but I think that بَأْبَأَهُ has been there erroneously put for بَأْبَأَ.] — And *He* (a stallion [meaning a stallion-camel]) *reiterated the sound of the letter* ب [or *b*] *in his braying*. (M.) — [And hence, perhaps,] ✝ بَأْبَأْ [or, more probably, ✝ بَأْبَآءٌ, with medd, agreeably with analogy, used as an inf. n.,] The *chiding of the cat*, or *act of chiding the cat*; (AA, T, Sgh;) also termed غَسٌّ. (AA, T.) ═ Also *He hastened, made haste*, or *sped*: and ✝ تَبَأْبَأْنَا *we hastened*, &c.: (marginal note in a copy of the S:) or ✝ تَبَأْبَأَ signifies *he ran*. (El-Umawee, T, K.)

R. Q. 2: see above, in three places.

بَأْبَأْ and بَأْبَآءٌ: see R. Q. 1, in two places.

بُؤْبُؤٌ The *source, origin, race, root*, or *stock*, syn. أَصْلٌ, (AA, Sh, T, S, M, K,) of a man, (Sh, T,) *whether noble or base*. (AA, T.) You say, هُوَ كَرِيمُ الْبُؤْبُؤِ *He is of generous*, or *noble, origin*; lit., *generous*, or *noble, of origin*. (TK.) And فُلَانٌ فِي بُؤْبُؤِ الْكَرَمِ *Such a one is of* [a race] *the source* (أَصْل) *of generosity*, or *nobleness*. (S. [In the PS, مِن is here put in the place of فِي: but فِي is often used in phrases of the same kind and meaning as that above, in the sense of مِنْ.]) IKh cites from Jereer,

• فِي بُؤْبُؤِ الْمَجْدِ وَبُحْبُوحِ الْكَرَمْ •

[*Of* a race *the source of glory, and the very heart of generosity*, or *nobleness*]: but Aboo-'Alee El-Kálee quotes the words thus;

• فِي ضِئْضِئِ الْمَجْدِ وَبُؤْبُؤِ ✝ الْكَرَمْ •

[which may be rendered, *of* a race *the source of glory, and the very root of generosity*]; whence it appears that ✝ بُؤْبُؤٌ is a dial. var. of بُؤْبُؤٌ in the sense here given. (TA.) — The *middle* of a thing; (K;) [and app. the *heart*, or *very heart*, thereof; the *middle* as being the *best part* of a thing;] like بُحْبُوحٌ. (TA.) — [Hence, perhaps,]

The *pupil*, or *apple*, or the *image that is seen reflected in the black*, (عَيْر AA, T, or إِنْسَان Ḳ,) of the eye. (AA, T, Ḳ.) Whence the saying, هُوَ أَعَزُّ عَلَىَّ مِنْ بُؤْبُؤِ عَيْنِى [*He is dearer to me than the apple of my eye*; a saying common in the present day, with the substitution of إِنْسَان for بُؤْبُؤ]. (TA.) —— *A generous*, or *noble*, (ISk, T,) or *a clever, an ingenious*, or *an accomplished*, or *a well-bred*, or *an elegant*, (M, Ḳ,) *and a light, an active*, or *a sprightly*, (M,) *lord, master, chief*, or *personage*: (ISk, T, M, Ḳ:) fem. with ة. (IKh, TA.) —— Also, (AA, T, Ṣ,* [but I find it only in one of three copies of the Ṣ,]) or ↓ بُؤْبُوْء, and ↓ بَأْبَأ, (Ḳ,) the last from the M, (TA, [but it is not in the M as transcribed in the TT,]) A *learned* man (AA, T, Ṣ, Ḳ) *who teaches*; (AA, T;) but the teaching of others is not a condition required in the application of the epithet; (TA;) like سُرْسُور. (Ṣ [in which this last word is evidently given as a syn.: but in the Ḳ it is given to show the form, only, of بُؤْبُؤ].) —— Also The *body of a locust*, (Ḳ,) *without the head and legs*. (TA.) —— And, accord. to the Ḳ, The *head*, or *uppermost part, of a vessel in which* [*the collyrium called*] كُحْل *is kept*: but it will appear, in art. يأ, that this is [perhaps] a mistranscription for يُؤْيُؤ. (TA.)

بَأْبَأ: see R. Q. 1, in two places: —— and see بُؤْبُؤ.

بُؤْبُوْء: see بُؤْبُؤ, in two places.

بأب

البَئْبُ: see أَبٌ, in art. ابو.

بابل

بَابِلِىٌّ *Of*, or *belonging to*, or *relating to*, بابل [i. e. *Babel*], *a place* [*well known*] *in El-'Irák*: it is an epithet applied to enchantment, [which is said to have been there taught by two fallen angels, Hároot and Mároot, (see the Ḳur ii. 96,)] and to wine. (Ṣ, Ḳ, TA.) —— And hence, (TA,) *Poison*: [and, accord. to the CḲ, *wine*;] as also ↓ بَابِلِيَّة. (Ḳ, TA.) —— In the original language of the place above mentioned, البَابِلِىُّ is a name of المُشْتَرِى [*The planet Jupiter*]. (TA.)

بَابِلِيَّة: see above.

بابونج

بَابُونَج [from the Persian بَابُونَه *Chamomile*; or *chamomile-flowers*: both called by these names in the present day]: *a certain herb, of several different colours; yellow-flowered*, and *white-flowered*, and *purple-flowered*: (Avicenna [Ibn-Seenà] i. 130:) *i. q.* أُقْحُوَان: (Ṣ, Mṣb, Ḳ, all in art. قحو:) i. e. the اقحوان is the بابونج with the Persians: (Mṣb in that art.:) or the *flower of the* اقحوان: (Ṣ in art. قرص:) or *of the yellow* اقحوان, (TA in art. قرص,) *when it has become dry*: (Ṣ, TA, both in art. قرص:) *a well-known flower, of great utility*, (Ḳ, TA,) or *of which the oil is of great utility*: (CḲ:) *commonly known in El-Yemen by the name of* مونس [app. مُؤْنِس, because of its pleasant odour, or its medical properties]. (TA.)

باج

بَأْج, also pronounced بَاج, without ء, (IAạr, Ṣ, Mṣb, Ḳ,) but the former alone is mentioned by Th in the Fṣ, and is the chaste word, (TA,) arabicized, from the Persian بَاهَا, (Ṣ,) *A sort*, or *species*, (Ṣ, Ḳ,) of food, or viands. (Ṣ.) Hence the saying, اجْعَلِ البَأْجَات بَأْجًا وَاحِدًا [*Make thou the sorts*, or *species*, of food, or viands, to be *one sort*, or *species*]: (Ṣ, Ḳ:) occurring in a trad., in which it is without ء in each case, accord. to IDrst: several different sorts of food being brought to 'Omar, he asked respecting them, and it was said, [They are] سِكْبَاج and زِرْبَاج and إِسْفِيذْبَاج; whereupon he ordered that the bowls should be brought, and their contents were emptied into one; he saying the words above. (Marginal note in a copy of the Ṣ.) IKh says that a man would bring various sorts [of food], and one would say, اجْعَلْهَا بَأْجًا وَاحِدًا [*Make thou them* to be *one sort*]. (TA.) The pl. is [بَأْجَات, as shown above, as though the sing. were بَأْجَة, and] أَبْوَاج. (Mṣb, TA.) لَأَجْعَلَنَّ النَّاسَ كُلَّهُمْ بَأْجًا وَاحِدًا is [likewise] a saying of 'Omar, (Mṣb, TA,) meaning [*I will assuredly make the people, all of them, to be*] *one body* or *assemblage*; بَأْج signifying *a state of assembling*, or *collecting together*: (Ḳz, TA:) or [*of*] *one uniform way* or *mode* or *manner*, (Mṣb, TA,) as El-Fihree says in the Expos. of the Fṣ, on the authority of ISd in the book entitled El-'Aweeṣ; (TA;) i. e., in respect of gifts, or allowances: (Mṣb:) accord. to IAạr, it is from بَأْج or بَاج signifying *a uniform line of road*. (TA.) You say also, النَّاسُ بَأْجٌ وَاحِدٌ *The people are* [*as*] *one thing*. (TA.) And هُمْ فِى أَمْرٍ بَأْجٍ *They are* [*in one and the same*, or] *in an equal*, or *a uniform, case*. (Ḳ.) And جَعَلَ الكَلَامَ بَأْجًا وَاحِدًا *He made the speech*, or *language, to be* [*uniform*, or] *of one mode*, or *manner*. (TA.) And اجْعَلْ هٰذَا الشَّىْءَ بَأْجًا وَاحِدًا *Make thou this thing to be* [*uniform*, or] *of one way*, or *mode*, or *manner*. (ISk.) And اجْعَلِ الأَمْرَ بَأْجًا وَاحِدًا *Make thou the affair*, or *case*, [*uniform*, or] *one uniform thing*. (Fr.)

باذنجان

بَاذَنْجَان, [or بَاذِنْجَان, commonly pronounced in the present day بَادِنْجَان and بَيْدِنْجَان and بِيدِنْجَان, from the Persian بَادِنْگَان,] a word of well-known meaning, often mentioned by the author of the Ḳ, [in explaining the words أَنَبٌ and حَدَقٌ and مُغْدٌ and وَغْدٌ,] but not in its proper place in the lexicon. (TA.) [It signifies The *solanum melongena, mad-apple*, or *egg-plant*; both the *black*, distinguished by the epithet أَسْوَد, and the *white*, distinguished by the epithet أَبْيَض. And the *solanum lycopersicum*, or *solanum Aethiopicum*; also called *love-apple*, and so by the Arabs, تُفَّاحُ الحُبِّ; and *golden apple*, تُفَّاحٌ ذَهَبِىٌّ; and *tomato*; and distinguished from the former species by the epithet أَحْمَر, and by the appellation باذنجان قُوطَة. —— بَاذِنْجَانٌ تِرْيَاقِىٌّ *Xanthium*.]

بأر

1. بَأَرَ, (Ṣ, M, Ḳ,) aor. َ, (M, Ḳ,) *He sunk*, or *dug*, (Ṣ, M, Ḳ,) a well; (Ṣ, M;) as also ↓ ابتأر. (M, Ḳ.) —— Also, aor. as above, inf. n. بَأْرٌ, *He dug a* [*hollow such as is termed*] بُؤْرَة, (AZ, Ṣ, M,) *in which to cook*. (AZ, Ṣ.) —— Also, (T, Ṣ, M, Ḳ,) aor. as above, (M, Ḳ,) and so the inf. n.; (M;) and ↓ ابتأر; (T, Ṣ, M, Ḳ;) *He hid*, or *concealed*, a thing: (T, M, Ḳ:) and *he stored* it, or *laid it up, for a time of need*. (T, Ṣ, Ḳ.) Hence a hollow dug in the ground is termed بُؤْرَة. (T.) —— You say also, ابتأر خَيْرًا, (T, M, Ḳ,) and بَأَرَهُ, (M, Ḳ,) *He did good beforehand*: (T, M, Ḳ:) or, accord. to some, *he, as it were, did good beforehand for himself, having laid it up*, or *concealed it, for himself*: (T, TA:) so says El-Umawee: or *he laid up for himself in store concealed good*: (TA:) or *he did good concealedly*: (M, Ḳ:) and ائتبر signifies the same. (T, TA.)

4. ابأر فُلَانًا *He made*, or *he assigned*, or *appointed*, (جَعَلَ,) *for such a one, a well*. (Ḳ.)

8: see 1, in three places.

بِئْرٌ (T, Ṣ, M, &c.) and بِيرٌ, (Mṣb,) of the fem. gender, (Ṣ, M, Mṣb, Ḳ,) and ↓ بِئْرَة, (M,) *A well*: (M, TA:) pl. (of pauc., Ṣ, Mṣb) أَبْؤُرٌ (Ṣ, M, Mṣb, Ḳ) and (by transposition, Fr, Mṣb) آبُرٌ (Fr, Mṣb, Ḳ) and أَبْآرٌ and (by transposition, Yaạḳoob, T, Ṣ, M) آبَارٌ and (of mult., Ṣ, Mṣb) بِئَارٌ; (T, Ṣ, M, Mṣb, Ḳ;) and pl. of pauc. [of بِيرٌ] أَبْيَارٌ. (Mṣb.) The dim. is ↓ بُؤَيْرَة. (Mṣb.)

بُؤْرَةٌ *A hollow*, or *hole, dug in the ground*, (AZ, Ṣ, M, Ḳ,) *in which to cook*; also called إِرَةٌ: (AZ, Ṣ:) or (M) *a place in which fire is lighted*. (M, Ḳ.) [See 1.] —— See also بَئِيرَة.

بِئْرَة: see بِئْرٌ: —— and see بَئِيرَة.

بُؤَيْرَة: see بِئْرٌ.

بَئِيرَةٌ (T, Ṣ, M, Ḳ) and ↓ بِئْرَة and ↓ بُؤْرَة (M, Ḳ) *A thing stored*, or *laid up, for a time of need*. (T, Ṣ, M, Ḳ.)

بَأَّارٌ, (T, TA, and so in some copies of the Ḳ,) or أَبَّارٌ, (as in other copies of the Ḳ, and so in the CḲ,) the latter formed by transposition, and the former [said to have been] not heard, (M,) *A well-sinker*, or *well-digger*. (T, M, Ḳ.)

باز

بَأْزٌ *i. q.* بَازٌ [which see in art. بزو; and بَازٍ]: pl. [of pauc.] أَبْؤُزٌ, and [of mult.] بُؤُوزٌ and بِئْزَانٌ. (Ḳ.) IJ holds that the أ is substituted for ا, and that it remains in ابؤز and بئزان like as is the case in أَعْيَاد [in which the ى is substituted for و

and remains in the pl. because it is substituted for و in the sing. عِيدٌ]. (TA.)

بأس

1. بَؤُسَ, aor. يَبْؤُسُ, (Ṣ, M, Mṣb, Ḳ,) inf. n. بَأْسٌ, (Ṣ, Mṣb, Ḳ,) or بَآسَةٌ; (M; [so I find in a copy of the M, but perhaps it is a mistranscription for بَأَسَةٌ;]) and بَئِسَ, [aor. يَبْأَسُ,] inf. n. بَأْسٌ; (M;) *He was, or became, mighty,* or *strong, in war* or *fight;* (Ḳ;) *courageous,* or *valiant:* (M, Mṣb, Ḳ:) or *very mighty* or *strong in war* or *fight.* (AZ, Ṣ.) —— بَئِسَ, (Ṣ, M, Mṣb, Ḳ,) aor. يَبْأَسُ (Ṣ, M, Ḳ) and يَبْئِسُ, the latter extr., like يَنْعِمُ aor. of نَعِمَ, (M,) [and some other instances, (see حَسِبَ,)] inf. n. بُؤْسٌ (Ṣ, Mṣb,* Ḳ) and بُؤُوسٌ and بُؤْسَى (Ḳ) and بَأْسٌ (TA) and بَئِيسٌ, (Ṣ, Ḳ,) [in measure] like أَمِيرٌ, (TA,) [accord. to the CḲ بِئْسٌ, which is a mistake,] and بَئِيسَى, (TṢ, TA,) incorrectly written in the copies of the Ḳ بُئْسَى; (TA;) or بُؤْسٌ; (A;) or both these forms; (M;) *He was,* or *became, in a state of distress; straitened in his means of subsistence,* or *in the conveniences of life;* (M, Mṣb;) *in a state of poverty:* (M, A, Mṣb,* TA:) or *in a state of pressing want:* (Ṣ, Ḳ, TA:) and بَؤُسَ, inf. n. بَآسَةٌ and بَئِيسٌ, whence the subst. بُؤْسَى, *he was,* or *became, in a state of trial,* or *affliction:* (M:) and [in like manner,] ▼ أَبْأَسَ, (inf. n. إِبْآسٌ, Ṣ,) *distress,* or *poverty,* or *misfortune,* or *calamity,* (البَأْسَآءُ,) *befell him.* (IAạr, Ṣ,* M, TA.) —— بِئْسَ, also written بَئْسَ and بِئِسَ and بَأْسَ, (Ṣ, Ḳ,) is a word of dispraise or blame, (Ṣ,) implying all kinds of dispraise or blame, (TA,) [or superlative dispraise or blame; signifying, *Very evil* or *bad is he,* or *it:* or *superlatively evil* or *bad is he,* or *it:*] *contr. of* نِعْمَ: (Ṣ, M, TA:) a pret. verb, imperfectly inflected, (Ṣ, Ḳ,) like نِعْمَ, (Ṣ,) [having only one variation of form, namely, the fem. بِئْسَتْ, though the masc. is more commonly used even when the agent is fem. or pl.,] because it is translated from its original application, (Ṣ, Ḳ,) i. e. from بَئِسَ فُلَانٌ signifying أَصَابَ بُؤْسًا [he found, met with, or experienced, distress, &c.], to signify dispraise or blame. (Ṣ, TA.) When it is accompanied by a gen. n. without the article ال, this is always in the accus. case: but when the n. has the article ال, it is always in the nom. case: (TA:) you say, بِئْسَ رَجُلًا زَيْدٌ [*Very evil* or *bad,* or *superlatively evil* or *bad, as a man, is Zeyd;* رجلا being a specificative]: (Ḳ:) and بِئْسَ الرَّجُلُ زَيْدٌ [*Very evil,* &c., *is the man, Zeyd*]; and بِئْسَتِ المَرْأَةُ هِنْدٌ [or more commonly بِئْسَ in this case also, *Very evil,* &c., *is the woman, Hind*]. (Ṣ.) Some argue that it is a noun, from the saying, نِعْمَ السَّيْرُ عَلَى بِئْسَ العَيْرُ, because it has a prep.; but this is explained as elliptical, and meaning, نِعْمَ السَّيْرُ عَلَى عَيْرٍ مَقُولٍ فِيهِ بِئْسَ العَيْرُ [*Excellent is the journeying upon an ass of which it is said Very evil,* &c., *is the ass*]. (I 'Aḳ p. 232.) Zj says that when it is followed by مَا, then مَا, with it, is regarded as occupying the place of an indeterminate noun; [namely, شَيْئًا, as a specificative; as in the Ḳur ii. 84, بِئْسَمَا ٱشْتَرَوْا بِهِ أَنْفُسَهُمْ, or بِئْسَ مَا, &c., *Very evil,* &c., *as a thing, is that for which they have sold,* or *exchanged, themselves:*] (TA:) but some say that it is the agent, and is a determinate noun; and this is the opinion of Ibn-Kharoof, which he ascribes to Sb. (I 'Aḳ ubi suprà.) [For further illustration, see نِعْمَ.]

4: see بَئِسَ.

5: see 6.

6. تَبَاءَسَ *He feigned the lowliness,* or *submissiveness, of poverty, humbling,* or *abasing, himself,* (Ḳ,* TA,) with men; and ▼ تَبَأَّسَ is allowable in the same sense. (TA.)

8. ابتأس به, (M, A,) and مِنْهُ, (Ṣ, TA,) *He was distressed by it,* or *at it;* it does not signify dislike: (IB, TA:) or *he grieved at it,* (Ṣ, M, A,) *and humbled and abased himself:* so in the Ḳur xi. 38 and xii. 69. (M, A, TA.) It is said of a man when a thing that he dislikes becomes known to him. (AZ, TA.)

بَأْسٌ *Might,* or *strength,* (Ṣ, A, Mṣb, Ḳ,) *in war* or *fight:* (Ṣ, A, Ḳ:) *courage; valour,* or *valiantness; prowess.* (M, Ḳ.) —— *War,* or *fight;* (M, Mṣb;) as also ▼ بَئِيسٌ (M) and ▼ بَأْسَآءُ: (TA:) pl. of the first, أَبْؤُسٌ. (Mṣb.) —— Hence, (M,) † *Fear,* (M, TA,) in the saying, لَا بَأْسَ عَلَيْكَ, (M, TA,*) and بِكَ, (M,) [† *There is no fear for thee:* lit., *there is no war against thee,* or *with thee*]: the saying of which to an enemy implies the granting him security, or protection: and in the same sense it is used in a trad., in the phrase اشْتَدَّ البَأْسُ [† *Fear became vehement*]. (TA.) —— *I. q.* ضَرَرٌ † [*Harm, injury,* &c.]: so in the phrase لَا بَأْسَ [*There is,* or *will be, no harm,* &c.; and لَا بَأْسَ بِكَذَا, and فِى كَذَا, † *There is,* or *will be, no harm in such a thing*]. (Ḥar p. 311.) It is said in a trad., لَا بَأْسَ بِٱلْغِنَى لِمَنِ ٱتَّقَى [*There is no harm in wealth to him who is pious*]. (El-Jámi' eṣ-Ṣagheer of Es-Suyootee.) بَاس also occurs for بَأْس; the ء being suppressed, agreeably with analogy; not altered by permutation. (M, TA.) —— *Punishment:* (Ṣ, A, Ḳ:) or *severe punishment;* (TA;) as also ▼ بَئِسٌ, in measure like كَتِفٌ. (IAạr, TA.) —— See also بُؤْسٌ, in two places.

بُؤْسٌ (also written بُوسٌ, with the ء suppressed, Mṣb) *Distress; straitness of the means of subsistence,* or *of the conveniences of life; poverty:* (M, Mṣb,* TA:*) or *a state of pressing want:* (Ṣ, Ḳ:) or *misfortune; calamity:* (A:) and ▼ بُؤُوسٌ and ▼ بُؤْسَى (Ḳ, TA) and ▼ بَأْسَآءُ (M, A) and ▼ بَأْسٌ (TA) and ▼ بَئِيسٌ (Ṣ, Ḳ) and ▼ بَئِيسَى (TA) and ▼ مَبْأَسَةٌ (M, TA) [all of which, except بَأْسَآءُ and ▼ مَبْآسَةٌ, are said to be inf. ns. (see بَئِسَ)] signify the same as بُؤْسٌ: (Ṣ, M, A, Ḳ, TA:) ▼ بُؤْسَى and ▼ بَأْسَآءُ are both from بُؤْسٌ [with which they are syn. accord. to authorities indicated above]; (Zj, IDrd, TA;) the former is *contr. of* نُعْمَى, (Ṣ, TA,) and in like manner the latter is *contr. of* نَعْمَآءُ: (TA:) the latter is of the measure فَعْلَآءُ without any أَفْعَلُ, because it is a subst.; like as أَفْعَلُ occurs among substs. without any فَعْلَآءُ, as in the instance of أَحْمَدُ: (Akh, Ṣ:) or ▼ بُؤْسَى signifies *a state of trial* or *affliction,* and is a subst.; and ▼ بَئِيسٌ and ▼ بَآسَةٌ signify the same, but are inf. ns.: (M:) and ▼ بَأْسَآءُ is syn. with شِدَّةٌ [like بُؤْسٌ in the first of the senses explained above]; (Ṣ, TA;) and مَشَقَّةٌ [meaning *distress,* or *difficulty*]: (TA:) or it signifies *misfortune,* or *calamity,* (A, Ḳ,) like بُؤْسٌ; (A;) and so أَبْؤُسٌ: (Ṣ, Ḳ:) or rather this last signifies *misfortunes,* or *calamities;* for it is pl. of ▼ بَأْسٌ, i. e., a pl. of pauc.; not of بُؤْسٌ, as J asserts it to be; for the pl. of pauc. of بُؤْسٌ is أَبْآسٌ: (IB, TA:) but أَبْؤُسٌ may be used as pl. of ▼ بَأْسَآءُ. (Fr, in Ṣ, voce ضَرَّآءُ, q. v.) [See exs. of these two pls. in what follows.] You say يَوْمُ بُؤْسٍ وَيَوْمُ نُعْمٍ [*A day of distress,* or *poverty,* &c., *and a day of ease and plenty*]. (Ṣ, TA.) And بُؤْسًا لَهُ [*May distress,* or *poverty,* &c., *befall him*]: a form of imprecation. (Sb, M, TA.) And بُؤْسَ ٱبْنِ سُمَيَّةَ, app. an expression of pity [meaning *Alas for the distress,* &c., *of Ibn-Sumeiyeh!*]. (TA, from a trad.) And عَسَى الغُوَيْرُ أَبْؤُسًا *Perhaps the little cave* [*may be attended with*] *calamities;* not calamity, as in the Ṣ [and Ḳ]: (IB:) a prov.; (Ṣ;) originating from a cave's having collapsed upon some men in it; or from an enemy's having come to some men in a cave, and slain them; wherefore it is applied to anything whence evil is feared: (Aṣ, Ṣ, Ḳ, in art. غور:) or it is applied to him who is suspected of a thing: (IAạr, TA:) or الغُوَيْرُ was the name of a certain water, which belonged to the tribe of Kelb, and the words of this prov. were said by Ez-Zebbà, when Ḳaseer turned aside from the plain road, and took the way to الغُوَيْرُ: (Ibn-El-Kelbee, Ṣ, Ḳ, in art. غور:) ابؤسا is in the accus. case by reason of يَكُونُ understood. (Mughnee.) [See Freytag's Arab. Prov. ii. 94.] El-Kumeyt also says,

* قَالُوا أَسَآءَ بَنُو كُرْزٍ فَقُلْتُ لَهُمْ *

* عَسَى الغُوَيْرُ بِأَبْآسٍ وَأَغْوَارِ *

[*They said, Benoo-Kurz have done evil: and I said to them, Perhaps the little cave may be attended with calamities and connected with other caves*]: أَبْآسٌ is here pl. of بُؤْسٌ. (IB, TA.) [In the Ṣ, the last words are written بِأَبْآسٍ وَإِغْوَارِ, in one copy: in another, بِأَبْؤُسٍ وَإِغْوَارِ, both of which are app. wrong.] —— See also بَائِسٌ.

بَئِيسٌ and بَئِسٌ and بِئِيسٌ and بِئْسٌ: see بَئِيسٌ. —— بَنَاتُ بِئْسٍ *Calamities; misfortunes.* (Ḳ.)

بَئِسٌ: see بَأْسٌ, last signification: —— and see بَئِيسٌ.

بُؤْسَى: see بُؤْسٌ, in three places.

بَأْسَآءُ: see بَأْسٌ: and بُؤْسٌ: the latter, in five

places. — Zj explains it as signifying, in the Ḳur vi. 42, *Hunger.* (M, TA.*) — Also The *act of beating,* or *striking.* (Lth, TA.)

بَؤُوسٌ One *in whom* بُؤْسٌ [i. e. *distress* &c.] *is apparent,* or *manifest.* (M, TA.)

بُؤُوسٌ : see بُؤْسٌ.

بَئِيسٌ : see بَأْسٌ : and بُؤْسٌ : the latter, in two places. — *Mighty,* or *strong, in war* or *fight;* (A;) *courageous,* or *valiant.* (Ṣ, M, Mṣb, Ḳ.) — عَذَابٌ بَئِيسٌ, (Ṣ, M, Ḳ,) and ▼ بِئِيسٌ, agreeably with a general rule applying to words of this description, (M,) and ▼ بِئْسٌ, (M, Ḳ,) and ▼ بَئْسٌ, (M,) and ▼ بَيْئَسٌ, (M, Ḳ,) and ▼ بَيْئِسٌ, (M,) and ▼ بَيْئَسٌ, and ▼ بَيِّسٌ, which last, however, is of no authority, (M,) or ▼ بِيسٌ, and بَيِيسٌ, with the ء changed into ى, (TA,) *A vehement punishment:* (Ṣ, M, Ḳ:) so in the Ḳur vii. 165. (TA.)

بِئِيسٌ : see بَئِيسٌ.

بَآسَةٌ : } see بُؤْسٌ.
بَئِيسَى : }

بَائِسٌ *Distressed; straitened in his means of subsistence,* or *in the conveniences of life;* (Mṣb;) or *poor:* (A, Mṣb:*) or one *who is in want, and an object of pity for what he suffers:* (TA:) or *in a state of pressing want:* (Ṣ:) or *in a state of trial,* or *affliction:* (M, TA:) or one *who is crippled,* or *deprived of the power of motion, by disease,* or *who suffers from a protracted disease, and is in need:* (Mgh:) an epithet denoting pity, (Sb, M, TA,) or grief: (Mgh:) ▼ بُؤْسٌ occurs as its pl.; (M, TA;) or is for ذَوُو بُؤْسٍ. (M.)

بَيْأَسٌ and بَيْئَسٌ : see بَئِيسٌ. — The former also signifies *Strong.* (Ḳ, TA.) — And hence, (TA,) البَيْأَسُ *The lion.* (Ḳ, TA.)

الإِبَآءُ الأَبْأَسُ *The most vehement refusal.* (Th, M.)

مَبْأَسَةٌ : see بُؤْسٌ, in two places.

مُبْتَئِسٌ *Disliking,* or *hating:* (Ṣ, M, Ḳ:) and *grieving:* (Ṣ, Ḳ:) or rather, *distressed,* by, or at, a thing; not disliking, or hating: (IB, TA:) or *grieving, and humbling and abasing himself.* (Zj, M, TA.)

باه

بَهًا : see مَا بَأَهْتُ لَهُ.

ببر

بَبْرٌ *A certain beast of prey,* (M, Ḳ,) *well known;* (Ḳ;) *a certain animal,* (Mṣb,) namely, the فُرَانِق [or *lion's provider*], (Ṣ,) *that emulates,* or *vies with, the lion in running,* or *that is hostile to the lion:* [so may be rendered the words يُعَادِى الأَسَدَ ; and in the uncertainty that exists respecting the animal in question, the meaning of this expression is doubtful: an animal may be called (as the jackal is) the lion's provider merely because the lion follows it and deprives it of its prey:] (Ṣ, Mṣb:) or *a certain Indian animal, stronger than the lion, between which and the lion and leopard,* or *panther,* (نَمِر,) *exists hostility* (مُعَادَاة); *when it attacks the leopard,* or *panther,* (نمر,) *the lion aids the latter; but the scorpion is on friendly terms with it, and sometimes makes its abode in its hair:* (Ḳzw:) the word is foreign, or Persian, (أَعْجَمِىّ,) [app. the Persian بَبْر, which is said to be applied to the *tiger, leopard,* and *lion,*] arabicized: (M, Ḳ:) Az thinks it to be a foreign word introduced into the Arabic language: (Mṣb:) pl. بُبُورٌ. (Ṣ, Mṣb, Ḳ.)

ببغ

بَبْغَآءُ (Mṣb, Ḳ) and بَبَّغَآءُ (Ḳ, Ḳzw) [in modern vulgar Arabic بَبَّغَان, The *parrot;*] *a certain well-known bird;* (Mṣb;) *a certain green bird,* (Ṣgh, Ḳ, TA,) *well known;* (TA;) the *bird called in Persian* طُوطِى, *beautiful in colour and form, mostly green, but in some instances red, and yellow, and white; having a thick bill and tongue: it hears the speech of men and repeats it, without knowing its meaning; and utters letters rightly:* when they desire to teach it, they put a mirror in its cage, so that it sees therein its own form, and they speak to it from behind the mirror, and when it hears, it repeats, desiring to do as its like; and thus it learns quickly: one of the wonders relating to it is [said to be this], that it never drinks water; for if it drank, it would die: (Ḳzw:) the affix renders fem. the word, but not the thing named thereby, like the ة in حَمَامَةٌ and نَعَامَةٌ ; for the word applies to the male and the female, so that one says, بَبْغَآءُ ذَكَرٌ [*a male parrot*] and بَبْغَآءُ أُنْثَى [*a female parrot*]: and the pl. is بَبْغَاوَاتٌ [or بَبَّغَاوَاتٌ], like as صَحْرَاوَاتٌ is pl. of صَحْرَآءُ. (Mṣb.)

بت

1. بَتَّهُ, (Lth, T, Ṣ, M, &c.,) aor. ـُ and ـِ, (Ṣ, M, Mṣb,) the latter anomalous, because a reduplicative verb [of this kind] having the aor. with kesr is not trans., except in certain instances, of which this is one; the other instances being عَلَّهُ, in relation to drinking, aor. ـُ and ـِ, and نَمَّ الحَدِيثَ, aor. ـُ and ـِ, and شَدَّهُ, aor. ـُ and ـِ, and حَبَّهُ, aor. ـِ; the last having but one form [of aor.]; (Ṣ;) inf. n. بَتٌّ: (Lth, T, Ṣ, M, A, &c.:) and ▼ اِبْتَهُ, (M,) inf. n. إِبْتَاتٌ: (Mgh, Ḳ:) *He cut it off, severed it, separated it,* or *disunited it,* (Lth, T, Ṣ, M, A,* Mgh,* Mṣb, Ḳ,*) *entirely,* or *utterly;* (Lth, T, M;) namely, a thing; (M;) a rope, or cord; (Lth, T;) and a tie, or bond, of union between two persons. (M.) — [بَتَّهُ and ▼ اِبْتَهُ, accord. to the TA, app. signify also *He,* or *it, caused him* (a man) *to become unable to proceed in his journey, his camel that bore him breaking down,* or *stopping from fatigue,* or *perishing:* for انبتّ as signifying "he became so" is there said to be quasi-pass. of those two verbs when it has this sense. Hence,] بَتَّهُ السَّفَرُ [*The journey caused him to become cut off,* &c.]. (A.) And سَاقَ دَابَّتَهُ حَتَّى بَتَّهَا [*He urged on his beast so that,* or *until, he caused it to become cut off,* &c.]: (A:) and ▼ أَبَتَّ بَعِيرَهُ *He caused his camel to become cut off,* &c., (قَطَعَهُ,) *by travel:* (M, TA:) this is not said but of a man who has forced on his camel at a hard pace, or by laborious journeying. (TA.) — بَتَّ طَلَاقَ آمْرَأَتِهِ, (T, Mṣb, TA,) or طَلَاقَ المَرْأَةِ, (Mgh,) and ▼ أَبَتَّهُ, (Lth, T, Mgh, Mṣb,) *He made the divorce of his wife,* or *of the woman, to be absolutely separating,* (Lth, T, Mgh, Mṣb, TA,) *so as to cut her off from return.* (Mṣb.) Lth, with whom AZ agrees, has erred in asserting that بَتَّ is intrans. and ▼ أَبَتَّ trans.: (T, TA:) both are trans. and intrans., (T, Mṣb, TA,) as En-Nawawee asserts in the Tahdheeb el-Asmà wa-l-Loghát. (TA.) You say, الطَّلْقَةُ الوَاحِدَةُ تَبُتُّ, and ▼ تُبِتُّ, i. e. *The single divorce cuts the matrimonial tie,* or *bond, of the woman,* (تَقْطَعُ عِصْمَةَ النِّكَاحِ, T, Mgh,*) *when the period during which she must wait before contracting a new marriage has ended.* (T.) [See also بَتٌّ.] — بَتَّ عَلَيْهِ القَضَآءَ, (T, Ṣ, M, A,) inf. n. بَتٌّ; (M;) and ▼ أَبَتَّهُ; (T, Ṣ, M;) *He* (the judge, T) *decided the judgment,* or *sentence, against him.* (T, Ṣ,* M.) — بَتَّ عَلَيْهِ الشَّهَادَةَ, and ▼ أَبَتَّهَا, *He decided against him by the testimony,* [or *pronounced the testimony decisive against him,*] *and compelled,* or *constrained, him to admit it.* (M.) — بَتَّ شَهَادَتَهُ, and ▼ أَبَتَّهَا, *He gave his testimony decisively.* (Mṣb.) — أَبُتُّ أَنَّهُ قَالَ *I know,* or *declare, decidedly,* not [merely] thinking it, *that he said thus.* (Ṣaheeḥ of Muslim.) — بَتَّ النِّيَّةَ *He made the intention decided;* or *fixed it decidedly.* (A.) It is said in a trad., لَا صِيَامَ لِمَنْ لَمْ يَبُتَّ الصِّيَامَ مِنَ اللَّيْلِ, or ▼ لَمْ يُبِتَّ, (T, Ṣ, Mgh,) accord. to different recitals, (Mgh,) i. e. *There is no fasting to him* [meaning *his fasting is null*] *who does not decisively impose it upon himself, by intention, from the night:* (Ṣ,* Mgh:) or, *who does not form the intention of fasting before daybreak, and thus cut it off from the time in which there is no fasting, namely, the night:* the intention is termed بَتٌّ [and إِبْتَاتٌ] because it makes a division between non-fasting and fasting: (T, TA:) لم يُبَيِّت, from الإِبَاتَةُ, is a mistake; but لَمْ يُبَيِّت, from التَّبْيِيتُ, [see بَيَّتَ,] is correct. (Mgh.) And it is said in another trad., ▼ أَبِتُّوا نِكَاحَ هٰذِهِ النِّسَآءِ, i. e. *Decide ye the affair respecting the marriage of these women, and confirm it by its* [*proper*] *conditions:* an oblique prohibition of the kind of marriage termed نِكَاحُ المُتْعَةِ, because it is a marriage not [absolutely or lawfully] decided, [being] made definite as to duration. (TA.) — بَتَّ also signifies *He made to have,* or *take, effect; he executed,* or *performed;* (Har p. 210;) and so ▼ ابتّ, as in the phrase, ابتّ يَمِينَهُ *He made his oath to have,* or *take, effect; he executed,* or *performed, it.* (M.) — سَكْرَانُ مَا يَبُتُّ كَلَامًا, (Ks, T, M,) and مَا يَبُتُّ, (M,) and ▼ مَا يُبِتُّ, (Ks, T, M,) *One who is drunk, who does not speak plainly,* or *distinctly;* lit., *who does not make speech plain,* or *distinct;* (Ks, T;) or *who does not articulate speech;* syn. مَا يَقْطَعُهُ: (M:) or,

as Aṣ says, (T,) سَكْرَانُ مَا يَبُتُّ, (T, A,) or لَا يَبِتُّ, (Ṣ, Ḳ,) and لَا يُبِتُّ, and ▼لَا يُبِتُّ, (Ḳ,) which last form of the verb is disallowed by Aṣ, but both are correct accord. to Fr, (T, Ṣ,) meaning *one who is drunk, who does not,* or *will not,* [i. e. *cannot,*] *decide an affair.* (Aṣ, T, Ṣ, Ḳ.) [See also بَاتٌّ.] ═ See also 7. — [Hence,] بَتَّتْ يَمِينُهُ, (M, Mṣb,) aor. ـِ only, inf. n. بُتُوتٌ, (Mṣb,) *His oath had,* or *took, effect; was executed,* or *performed;* syn. وَجَبَتْ: (M:) *it was,* or *proved, true:* (Mṣb:) a phrase mentioned by AZ, and, if correct, not needing any explanation. (M.) [See ابتّ يمينه, above.] ═ بَتَّ, aor. ـِ, inf. n. بُتُوتٌ, *He was,* or *became, lean,* or *meagre.* (M, Ḳ.) [See بَاتٌّ.] ═ بَتٌّ [inf. n. of بَتَّ] also signifies The *selling,* and the *weaving,* a [*garment of the kind called*] طَيْلَسَان [or بَتّ, q. v.]. (KL.)

2. بتّتهُ, inf. n. تَبْتِيتٌ, *He cut it off,* or *severed it,* [*entirely,* or *utterly, and*] *much,* or *with extraordinary energy* or *effectiveness;* the teshdeed denoting intensiveness of signification. (Ṣ.) ═ بَتَّتُوهُ *They furnished him with* [بَتَات, or] *travelling-provisions.* (M, Ḳ.) ═ بَتِّتْهُمْ *Give thou to them* [*garments called*] بُتُوت [pl. of بَتّ, q. v.]. (TA, from a trad.)

4: see 1, passim: ═ and see 7.

5. تبتّت *He became furnished with* [بَتَات, or] *travelling provisions:* and *he became provided with* [بَتَات, or] *utensils and furniture of the house* or *tent;* or *household goods.* (M, Ḳ, TA.)

7. انبتّ *It was,* or *became, cut off, severed, separated,* or *disunited,* (Lth, T, Ṣ, M, Mṣb, Ḳ,) *entirely,* or *utterly;* (Lth, T, M;) namely, a thing; (M;) a rope, or cord; (Lth, T;) and a tie, or bond, of union between two persons: (T, M:*) as also ▼بَتَّ, (Lth, AZ, T, M, Mṣb,) aor. ـِ and ـُ, (M, [so accord. to a copy of that work, but it seems to be indicated in the Mṣb (see 1, near the close of the paragraph,) that it is ـِ only, in this case,]) inf. n. بَتٌّ; (Lth, AZ, T, M, Ḳ;) and ▼ابتّ, (T, Mṣb, TA,) inf. n. إِبْتَاتٌ; (T, TA;) the last said by Lth and AZ to be trans. only; (T, TA;) but it is both trans. and intrans., like the second: (T, Mṣb, TA:) so says En-Nawawee, as mentioned above: see 1. (TA.) You say, اِنْقَطَعَ فُلَانٌ عَنْ فُلَانٍ فَانْبَتَّ حَبْلُهُ عَنْهُ [*Such a one broke off,* or *disunited himself, from such a one, and his tie,* or *bond, of union became severed from him*]. (T, TA, [but in a copy of the former, for عن فلان, is put عَنْ مَالِهِ *from his property.*]) — *He became unable to proceed in his journey, his camel that bore him breaking down, or stopping from fatigue, or perishing:* (A,* Mgh,* TA:) quasi-pass. of بَتَّهُ and أَبَتَّهُ. (TA.) You say, سَارَ حَتَّى ٱنْبَتَّ *He journeyed until he was unable to proceed* &c. (A, Mgh, TA.) [See also مُنْبَتٌّ.] — *His* مَآء, (A,) *the* مَآء *of his back,* (Ks, T, Ḳ,) [i. e. *his seminal fluid,*] *became cut off,* or *stopped,* or *ceased,* (Ks, T, A, Ḳ,) *by reason of age:* (A:) said of a man. (Ks, T, A.)

بَتٌّ inf. n. of 1, q. v. (Lth, T, Ṣ, M, &c.) [It is sometimes used as an inf. n.; as also ▼بَتَّةٌ and ▼بَتَاتٌ, explained in the M as syn. with قَطْعٌ: and sometimes, as is often the case with inf. ns., in the sense of the act. part. n. of its verb, namely ▼بَاتٌّ, trans. and intrans.; as also ▼بَتَاتٌ; both of which are masc. and fem., because originally inf. ns.; but بَتٌّ has also بَتَّةٌ for its fem. The following are exs.] — أَعْطَيْتُهُ هٰذِهِ العَطِيَّةَ بَتًّا بَتْلًا [*I gave him this gift, cutting it off from my property so as to make it irrevocable;* or, *it being cut off* &c.]. (Lth, T.) And تَصَدَّقَ صَدَقَةً بَتَّةً بَتْلَةً, and فُلَانٌ صَدَقَةً بَتَاتًا ▼, (T, Ṣ,) *Such a one bestowed an alms,* or *a gift for the sake of God, cut off from his property;* (T, TA;) and therefore, (TA,) *parted from himself.* (Ṣ, TA.) Such a gift is termed صَدَقَةٌ بَتَّةٌ, (A,* Nh,) and صدقة بَتَّةٌ بَتْلَةٌ. (M.) — طَلَّقَهَا بَتَّةً, (Mgh, Ḳ,) and ▼بَتَاتًا, (Ḳ,) and ٱلْبَتَّةَ, (T,) and طَلَّقَهَا بَتَّةً, (Mṣb,) and ▼طَلَاقًا بَاتًّا, (Lth, T, Mṣb,* TA, [in one copy of the T simply بَاتًّا,]) *He divorced her by a separating divorce;* (Ḳ;) *by a divorce cutting her off from returning:* and such a divorce is also termed ▼طلاق مُبِتٌّ: (Mṣb:) or the first of these phrases signifies *he divorced her by a divorce* either *cut off,* [meaning *decided and irrevocable,*] or *cutting off.* (Mgh.) And طَلَّقَهَا ثَلَاثًا بَتَّةً, (Aṣ, T, Ṣ, M, Mṣb,) and ▼بَتَاتًا, (M,) *He divorced her by three divorces so as to cut her off from returning:* (M, Mṣb:) or *by three divorces cut off from himself* [*so as to be irrevocable*]: (Ṣ:) or *by three divorces cutting off* [*from returning*]. (TA.) — حَلَفَ بَتًّا, and بَتَّةً, and ▼بَتَاتًا, [may mean *He swore decidedly,* or *decisively;* or *irrevocably:* or] *he swore with effect,* or *execution,* or *performance;* [see 1, near the end of the paragraph;] from the signification of "cutting," or "cutting off," &c.: (M:) [or, as also] حَلَفَ يَمِينًا بَتًّا, and بَتَّةً, (Mṣb, TA,) and ▼بَاتَّةً, (Mgh,* Mṣb,) and ▼بَتَاتًا, (TA,) *he swore an oath that was,* or *proved, true.* (Mṣb.) — طَحَنَ بِالرَّحَى بَتًّا *He ground with the mill, turning it,* (AZ, T,) or *beginning the turning,* (Ṣ,) *from his left:* (AZ, T, Ṣ:) [i. e., making it to turn in the contrary way of the hands of a watch: the last word is app. an inf. n.; as though meaning *effectually;* for this is the general and easier or more powerful way of turning the hand-mill:] the contrary way is termed شَزْرًا: (AZ, T, Ṣ:*) or طَحَنَ بَتًّا signifies *he began in the turning* [*of the mill*] *with the left* [*hand*]. (Ḳ: [but بِالْيَسَارِ is here evidently put by mistake for عَنِ ٱلْيَسَارِ.]) ═ *A kind of* طَيْلَسَان [q. v.] *called* سَاج, (Lth, T,) or a [*garment of the kind called*] كِسَآء, (M, Mgh,) *square,* or *four-sided,* (Lth, T, M,) *thick,* (Lth, T, M, Mgh,) *loose,* or *uncompact, in texture,* (M,) *and green* [or rather *of a dingy ash-colour,* or *dark dust-colour,* for such is the general meaning of أَخْضَرُ, the term here used, when applied to a garment of this kind]; (Lth, T, M;) or, as some say, (M,) *of* [*the soft hair termed*] وَبَر, and *of wool;* (M, Mgh;) and thus described in the Kifáyet el-Mutaḥaffidh: (TA:) or a طيلسان *of* [*the material termed*] خَزّ, (Ṣ, Mgh, Ḳ,) and *the like:* (Ṣ, Ḳ:) pl. بُتُوتٌ, (Lth, T, Ṣ, Mgh,) or بِتَاتٌ, (M,) but the former occurs in trads. [&c.], (TA,) and [pl. of pauc.] أَبُتٌّ. (M.)

بَتَّةٌ: see بَتٌّ. — لَا أَفْعَلُهُ ٱلْبَتَّةَ, (Ṣ, M, Ḳ,) as also بَتَّةً, (Ṣ, Ḳ,) the latter mentioned by IF, (Mṣb,) but IB says that Sb and his companions allow only the former, and that only Fr allows the latter, (TA,) and some say that the former has been heard pronounced with the disjunctive ء [أَلْبَتَّةَ], (MF,) and thus it is written in a copy of the Ḳ, (TA,) but others greatly disapprove of this, (MF,) [meaning *I will not do it, decidedly,* or *absolutely,*] is said of anything in respect of which there is no returning, or revoking; (Ṣ, IF, M, Mṣb, Ḳ;) ٱلْبَتَّةَ being said of a thing to be done, or performed, irrevocably, and from which there is no abstaining by reason of sluggishness; (T;) as though the speaker cut off the doing of the thing: (M:) the last word is in the accus. case as an inf. n.: (Ṣ:) Sb says, it is a corroborative inf. n., and is not used without ال. (M.) It is said in a trad., أَحْسِبُهُ قَالَ جُوَيْرِيَةَ أَوِ ٱلْبَتَّةَ قَالَ [*I think he said Juweyriyeh, or decidedly he said so*]; as though the speaker doubted of the female's name, and said, "I think it was Juweyriyeh;" then corrected, and said, "or I know," or "declare," "decidedly, (أَبُتُّ, i. e. أَقْطَعُ,) that he said Juweyriyeh: I do not [merely] think." (Ṣaheeḥ of Muslim.)

بَتَاتٌ: see بَتٌّ, in seven places. — A man is said to be عَلَى بَتَاتِ أَمْرٍ, meaning *On the point of* [*accomplishing,* or *deciding,*] *an affair.* (Ṣ, A, Ḳ.) A rájiz says,

وَحَاجَةٍ كُنْتُ عَلَى بَتَاتِهَا

[*Many a needful affair I was on the point of accomplishing*]. (Ṣ.) ═ *Travelling provisions:* (Ṣ, M, A, Ḳ:) and *requisites, equipments,* or *furniture;* syn. جَهَازٌ: (Ṣ, Ḳ:) pl. أَبِتَّةٌ. (Ṣ.) A verse of Ṭarafeh cited voce بَاعَ exhibits an ex. of the former signification. (TA.) — Also The *utensils and furniture of the house* or *tent;* or *household goods:* (Ṣ, M, Ḳ:) pl. as above. (Ḳ.) It is said in a trad., لَا يُؤْخَذُ مِنْكُمْ عُشْرُ البَتَاتِ [*The tithe of the utensils* &c. *of the house or tent shall not be taken from you*]: (Ṣ:) i. e., no poor-rate shall be levied upon such utensils &c. that are not for traffic. (A 'Obeyd.)

بَتِّيٌّ: see what next follows.

بَتَّاتٌ (Ṣ, Mgh, Ḳ) and ▼بَتِّيٌّ (Ṣ, Ḳ) *A maker,* (Ṣ,) or *seller, of the kind of garment called* بَتّ. (Ṣ, Mgh, Ḳ.)

بَاتٌّ: see بَتٌّ, in three places. — *Cut off from* [*the possession of*] *reason,* or *intellect, by drunkenness:* (AḤn, M:) or *drunken:* (Ḳ:) and *stupid,* or *foolish:* (Ṣ, Ḳ:) and أَحْمَقُ بَاتٌّ signifies *very stupid* or *foolish,* (T, M,) accord. to Lth; but [Az adds,] what we remember to have heard from those deserving of confidence is تَابٌّ, from ٱلتَّبَابُ, meaning ٱلْخَسَارُ; like as one says, أَحْمَقُ

خَاسِرٌ دَابِرٌ دَامِرٌ [explained in art. خسر]. (T.) [See also 1, near the end of the paragraph.] —— Also *Lean*, or *meagre*, (Ṣ, M, Ḳ,) *and unable to rise*, or *stand*. (TA.)

طَلَاقٌ مُبِتٌّ : see بَتٌّ.

مَبْتُوتَةٌ A woman *absolutely separated by divorce, so as to be cut off from return*: originally مَبْتُوتٌ طَلَاقُهَا. (Mgh, Mṣb.)

مُنْبَتٌّ A man *unable to proceed in his journey, his camel that bore him having broken down, or stopped from fatigue, or perished*; (T, M,* TA;) syn. مُنْقَطِعٌ بِهِ: (Ṣ, Mgh, TA:) or *who remains on his road unable to attain the place to which he is directing his course, the beast* or *camel that bore him* (ظَهْرُهُ) *having broken down, or stopped from fatigue, or perished*. (TA.)

بتر

1. بَتَرَ, (T, Ṣ, M, &c.,) aor. ُ, (M, Mgh, Mṣb,) inf. n. بَتْرٌ; (T, Ṣ, M, &c.;) and ↓ ابتر; (T;) *He cut*, or *cut off*, a thing *before it was complete*: (Ṣ, A, L, Mṣb:) or *he cut*, or *cut off*, (M, Mgh, Ḳ,) *in any manner*: (M:) or *he cut off* (a tail or the like, T) *entirely*, or *utterly*. (Aboo-Is-ḥáḳ, T, M, Ḳ.) —— بَتَرَهُ, (Ḳ,) aor. and inf. n. as above; (TA;) or ↓ ابترهُ; (M, L;) *He cut off his tail*: (Ḳ:) or *he cut*, or *amputated*, *his tail in any place*. (M, L.) —— بَتَرَ رَحِمَهُ, (M,) aor. as above, (M, Ḳ,) and so the inf. n., (M,) †*He cut*, or *severed*, *the ties*, or *bonds*, *of his relationship*; *he disunited himself from his relations*. (M, Ḳ.*) ═══ بَتِرَ, aor. َ, (Ṣ, Mṣb, Ḳ,) inf. n. بَتَرٌ, (Ṣ, Mṣb,) *He* (any beast, M) *had his tail cut off*: (Ṣ, Mṣb, Ḳ:) or [*had either the whole* or *a part of his tail cut off*;] *had his tail cut*, or *amputated*, *in any place*. (M.)

4: see 1, in two places. —— [Hence,] ابترهُ said of God, *He made him to be*, or *become*, أَبْتَر, (Ṣ, Ḳ,) i. e., *without offspring*, or *progeny*. (TA.)

5: see 7.

7. انبتر *It* (a tail or the like, T) *became cut*, or *cut off*, (T, Ṣ, M, Ḳ, TA,) *in any place*, (M,) or *entirely*; (T, M;) and ↓ تبتّر signifies the same. (TA.)

بَتَّارٌ : / بَتُورٌ : } see بَاتِرٌ.

بُتَيْرَاءُ : see أَبْتَرُ.

بُتَارٌ : see بَاتِرٌ.

بَاتِرٌ A *cutting*, or *sharp*, sword; (T, Ṣ, M, Ḳ;) as also ↓ بَتَّارٌ (T, M, Ḳ) and ↓ بَتُورٌ (M) and ↓ بُتَارٌ. (Ḳ.) [But all of these except the first are app. intensive epithets, signifying *very sharp*.] —— See also أُبَاتِرٌ.

أَبْتَرُ A tail *cut off entirely*. (T, L.) —— Any beast (M) *having the tail cut off*: (T, Ṣ, A, Mṣb, Ḳ:) or [*having* either *the whole* or *a part of the tail cut off*;] *having the tail cut*, or *amputated*, *in any place*: (M:) fem. بَتْرَاءُ; with which ↓ مَبْتُورَةٌ is syn.: (Mgh, Mṣb:) pl. بُتْرٌ. (A, Mṣb.) —— †*A certain malignant*, or *noxious*, *serpent*: (Ḳ:) or *a short-tailed serpent*: (Mgh; and Ed-Durr en-Netheer, an abridgment of the Nh of IAth, by El-Jelál:) or *a certain species of blue serpent, having its tail* [*as it were*] *cut off, which none in a state of pregnancy sees without casting her burden*: (ISh:) or the *kind of serpent called* شَيْطَان, *having a short tail*: *no one sees it without fleeing from it, and no one in a state of pregnancy beholds it without casting her young*: it is thus called only because of the shortness of its tail, as though its tail were cut off. (M.) —— † A leathern water-bag, and a bucket, *having no loop*. (M, Ḳ.) —— †*Defective, deficient, incomplete*, or *imperfect*. (Mgh.) —— † *In want*, or *poor*. (M, Ḳ.) —— † *Suffering loss*; syn. خَاسِرٌ. (M, Ḳ.) —— † One *from whom all good*, or *prosperity*, *is cut off*. (M.) —— † *Having no offspring*, or *progeny*; (Aboo-Is-ḥáḳ, T, Ṣ, M, IAth, Ḳ;) as also ↓ أُبَاتِرٌ (M, Ḳ) and ↓ مُنْبَتِرٌ. (IAth.) [The dim., ↓ أُبَيْتِرٌ, occurs in a trad., in this sense, or in some other sense implying contempt.] —— † Anything *cut off*, (Ḳ,) or anything *of which the effect is cut off*, (Ṣ,) *from good*, or *prosperity*. (Ṣ, Ḳ.) [See an ex. in a trad. cited voce بَالٌ.] —— خُطْبَةٌ بَتْرَاءُ †*A* خطبة [q. v.] *in which the speaker does not praise God nor bless the Prophet*: (Ṣ, A, Ḳ:) particularly applied to a certain خطبة of Ziyád. (Ṣ, A.) —— رَكْعَةٌ بَتْرَاءُ, (TA,) and [its dim.] ↓ بُتَيْرَاءُ, (Ṣ, TA,) †*A single* ركعة [q. v.] *performed instead of the complete performance of the prayer called* الوِتْر: or *a* ركعة *cut short*, or *cut off*, *after the completion of one* ركعة, *when both were to have been performed*. (TA.) —— الأَبْتَرَانِ † *The ass* (العَيْرُ) *and the slave*: (ISk, Ṣ, A, Ḳ:) so called because of the little good that is in them: (ISk, Ṣ:) each is called الأَبْتَرُ. (Ḳ.)

أُبَاتِرٌ † *Short*; (M, Ḳ;) as though cut off from completion. (M.) —— See also أَبْتَرُ. —— Also † A man *who cuts*, or *severs*, *the ties*, or *bonds*, *of his relationship*; *who disunites himself from his relations*; (Ṣ, M, Ḳ;) as also ↓ بَاتِرٌ: (A:) or *quick to cut*, or *sever*, *the ties*, or *bonds*, *between him and his friend*. (IAạr.)

أُبَيْتِرٌ : / مَبْتُورَةٌ : / مُنْبَتِرٌ : } see أَبْتَرُ.

بتع

1. بَتِعَ, (Ṣ, Ḳ,) aor. َ, (Ḳ,) inf. n. بَتَعٌ, (ISh, Ṣ, Ḳ,) *He* (a horse, Ḳ) *was*, or *became*, *long in the neck, and at the same time strong in its base*: (Ṣ, Ḳ:) or *thick and fleshy in the neck*: or *strong in the neck*. (ISh.) —— *It*, (the body,) and *he*, (a man,) *was*, or *became*, *strong in the joints*. (Ḳ, TA.) ═══ بَتَعَ, aor. َ, *He prepared*, and *made*, the beverage called نَبِيذ. (Ibn-'Abbád, Ḳ.) [See بِتْعٌ.]

بَتْعٌ, with fet-ḥ, [perhaps a mistake for بَتَعٌ, (see 1,)] *Strength*. (TA.)

بِتْعٌ (Ṣ, Mgh, Ḳ) and ↓ بِتَعٌ (Ṣ, Ḳ) [*Hydromel*, or] نَبِيذ *of honey*, (Ṣ, Ḳ,) *that has become strong*; (Ḳ;) نبيذ *made of honey, as though it were wine in strength, the drinking of which is disapproved*; (El-'Eyn;) *an intoxicating beverage made of honey, in El-Yemen*: (Mgh:) or *wine made of fresh dates*: (Ibn-El-Beyṭár, cited by Golius:) or the *pure juice of grapes*; (Ibn-'Abbád, Ḳ;) said by some to be so called by reason of the strength therein, from بَتَعٌ, [inf. n. of بَتِعَ,] meaning "strength of the neck:" (TA:) or the former signifies *wine*: (Ḳ:) or *wine made of honey*: (AḤn:) a word of the dial. of El-Yemen: (TA:) the wine of El-Medeeneh is from unripe dates, and from ripe dates; that of the Persians, from grapes; that of the people of El-Yemen is بِتْعٌ, and is from honey; and that of the Abyssinians is سُكُرْكَة. (Aboo-Moosà El-Ash'aree.) [See مِزْرٌ.] ═══ See also بَتِعٌ.

بَتِعٌ A horse *long in the neck, and at the same time strong in its base*: fem. with ة: (Aṣ, Ṣ, Ḳ:) or *long in the neck*. (IAạr.) You say also عُنُقٌ بَتِعٌ (ISh, TA) and بَتِعَةٌ (TA) *A strong neck*: or *an excessively long neck*: (TA:) or *a thick and fleshy neck*: (ISh:) and ↓ أَبْتَعُ [in like manner] signifies *full*, applied to a رُسْغ [app. here meaning a pastern], (Ḳ,) accord. to Lth, who cites, from Ru-beh, the phrase رُسْغًا أَبْتَعَ: but IB thinks that the right reading is جِيدًا أَبْتَعَ [*a full neck*]. (TA.) —— Also A *tall* man: (L, TA:) in this sense, accord. to the Ḳ, ↓ بِتْعٌ, which is a mistake: (TA:) fem. with ة. (L, TA.) —— And *Strong in the joints*, applied to a body, (Lth, Ḳ,) and to a man; as also ↓ أَبْتَعُ: (Ḳ:) fem. of the former with ة: (TA:) and of ↓ the latter, بَتْعَاءُ: and pl. of the latter, بُتْعٌ. (Ḳ.)

بُتْعٌ pl. of بَتْعَاءُ, fem. of أَبْتَعُ, q. v.

بِتَعٌ : see بِتْعٌ.

بَتَّاعٌ *A vintner*, in the dial. of El-Yemen. (TA.) [See بِتْعٌ.]

بَاتِعٌ *Strong*. (TA.)

أَبْتَعُ : see بَتِعٌ, in three places. ═══ It is also a word used as a corroborative: you say, جَاؤُوا أَجْمَعُونَ أَكْتَعُونَ أَبْتَعُونَ [*They came, all of them*, or *all together*]: (Ṣ:) and جَآءَ القَوْمُ أَكْتَعُونَ أَبْتَعُونَ أَبْصَعُونَ [*the people*, or *company of men*, *came, all of them*, or *all together*]: (AHeyth:) and جَاؤُوا كُلُّهُمْ أَجْمَعُونَ أَكْتَعُونَ أَبْصَعُونَ أَبْتَعُونَ [*they came, all of them, all together*]: these words which follow اجمعون being imitative sequents to it, not occurring save after it [in the order above]: (O, Ḳ:) or one may begin with whichsoever of them he will, after it. (Ibn-Keysán, Ḳ.) And [the fem. is بَتْعَاءُ:] you say القَبِيلَةُ كُلُّهَا جَمْعَاءُ كَتْعَاءُ بَصْعَاءُ بَتْعَاءُ [*The tribe, all of it, all together*: in the CḲ, erroneously, كُتْعَة (with ḍamm and ث) and بُصْعَة and بُتْعَة]. (Ḳ.) And [the pl. of بَتْعَاءُ is ↓ بُتَعٌ, originally بَتْعَاوَاتٌ:] you say النِّسَآءُ

كُلُّهُنَّ جُمَعُ كُتَعُ بُصَعُ بُتَعُ [The women, all of them, all together: in the CḲ, erroneously, جُمَعٌ كُتَعٌ بُصَعٌ بُتَعٌ, though it is well known that each of these is determinate, and imperfectly declinable]. (Ḳ.) It is only necessary that he who mentions all these words should mention first كُلّ, and follow it with the word formed from ج م ع, then add the rest in whatsoever order he will; but the more approved way is to put the word formed from ك ت ع before the rest. (TA.) Fr mentions the phrases أَعْجَبَنِى القَصْرُ أَجْمَعَ [The palace pleased me, all of it, or altogether], and الدَّارُ جَمْعَآءَ [the house, all of it, or altogether], with the accus. case, as denotative of state; but does not allow أَجْمَعُونَ nor جُمَعُ to be used otherwise than as corroboratives: IDrst, however, allows أَجْمَعِين to be used as a denotative of state; and this is correct; and accord. to both these ways is related the trad., فَصَلُّوا جُلُوسًا أَجْمَعِين and أَجْمَعُونَ [And pray ye sitting, all of you, or all together]; though some make اجمعين [here] to be a corroborative of a pronoun understood in the accus. case, as though the speaker said, أَعْنِيكُمْ أَجْمَعِين [I mean you, all of you, or all together]. (Ḳ.) [But see أَجْمَعُ.]

بتك

1. بَتَكَهُ, aor. ـُ and ـِ, (Ṣ, Ḳ,) inf. n. بَتْكٌ, (Ṣ,) *He cut it; or severed it, or cut it off,* (Ṣ, Ḳ,) *entirely,* or *from its root;* (TA;) and in like manner, ↓ بَتَّكَهُ, (Ḳ,) inf. n. تَبْتِيكٌ; (TA;) but بتّك is with teshdeed to denote muchness, or frequency, of the action, or its application to many objects. (Ṣ, TA.) فَلَيُبَتِّكُنَّ ↓ آذَانَ الأَنْعَامِ, in the Ḳur [iv. 118], accord. to Abu-l-'Abbás, (TA,) means *And they shall assuredly cut,* or *cut off, the ears of the cattle:* (Ṣ,* TA:) or, as Az thinks, *slit the ears of the cattle,* as they did in the time of ignorance. (TA.) — Also *He plucked it out; he laid hold upon it and pulled it towards him so that it became severed from its root and plucked out;* (Lth, Ṣ,* TA;) namely, a hair, or feather, or the like. (Lth, TA.)

2: see 1, in two places.

5: see 7.

7. انبتك *It became cut;* or *became severed,* or *cut off,* (Ṣ,* Ḳ,) *entirely,* or *from its root;* (TA;) and in like manner, ↓ تبتّك. (Ḳ.) — Also *It became plucked out.* (Lth, TA.)

بِتْكَةٌ (Ṣ, Ḳ) and بَتْكَةٌ (Ḳ) *A piece,* or *portion, of a thing, cut off,* or *severed:* pl. بِتَكٌ. (Ṣ, Ḳ.) Hence the saying of the poet, (Ṣ,) namely, Zuheyr, (TA,)

• حَتَّى إِذَا مَا هَوَتْ كَفُّ الغُلَامِ لَهَا •
• طَارَتْ وَفِى كَفِّهِ مِنْ رِيشِهَا بِتَكُ •

[*Until, when the hand of the boy descends to her, she flies, while portions of her feathers, plucked out, are in his hand*]. (Ṣ, TA.) — And [hence,] i. q. جُهْمَةٌ مِنَ اللَّيْلِ [i. e. *A portion at the commencement of the latter parts of the night,* accord. to the Ṣ and Ḳ in art. جهم; or *a remaining portion of darkness in the latter part of the night,* accord. to the Ḳ in that art.]: (Ṣ, Ḳ:) as though it were a division [or portion cut off] of the night. (TA.)

بَتُوكٌ: see what next follows.

بَاتِكٌ (applied to a sword, Ṣ) *Sharp,* or *cutting;* (Ṣ, Ḳ;) as also ↓ بَتُوكٌ: (Ḳ:) [but the latter is an intensive epithet, signifying *very sharp;* or *cutting much,* or *keenly*]: the pl. [of the former] is بَوَاتِكُ. (TA.)

بتل

1. بَتَلَهُ, (T, Ṣ, M, &c.,) aor. ـِ, (Ṣ,) or ـُ, (Mṣb,) or both, (M, Ḳ,) inf. n. بَتْلٌ, (Lth, T, Ṣ, &c.,) *He cut it off,* or *severed it;* (M, Mṣb, Ḳ;) as also ↓ بَتَّلَهُ, (M, Ḳ,) inf. n. تَبْتِيلٌ: (TA:) *he separated it* (Lth, T, Ṣ, M, Mṣb, Ḳ) from another thing. (Lth, T, Ṣ, M, Ḳ.) — [Hence,] بَتَلَ العُمْرَةَ *He made the performance of the* عمرة [or *minor pilgrimage*] *to be obligatory, by itself.* (A, TA.) And بتّل ↓ العُمْرَى *He made the* عمرى *to be obligatory* [*upon himself*]; i. e., *the saying, I have assigned to thee my house that thou mayest inhabit it to the end of my life.* (TA.) = بَتِلَ, aor. ـَ, inf. n. بَتَلٌ, [but accord. to analogy, this should rather be بَتَلٌ,] *He* (a man) *was,* or *became, wide between the shoulders.* (T.)

2: see 1, in two places: = and see also 5: = and مُبَتَّلٌ.

5. تبتّل: see 7, in two places. — [Hence,] *He was,* or *became, alone.* (TA.) — Also, (Ṣ,) or تبتّل إِلَى اللّٰهِ, (M, Ḳ,) and ↓ بتّل, (Ṣ,* Ḳ,) inf. n. تَبَتُّلٌ, (Ṣ,) *He detached himself from worldly things, and devoted himself to God:* (Ṣ:) or *he devoted himself to God exclusively, and was sincere,* or *without hypocrisy, towards Him:* (M, Ḳ:) *he forsook every other thing, and applied himself to the service of God:* (Fr, T:) *he devoted himself exclusively to the service of God:* (Aboo-Is-ḥáḳ, T:) or *he abstained from sexual intercourse:* (Ḳ:) or تبتّل [alone] has this signification; (M, TA;) or *he separated himself from women, and abstained from sexual intercourse:* and hence, is metaphorically employed to denote exclusive devotion to God. (TA.) Hence, in the Ḳur [lxxiii. 8], وَتَبَتَّلْ إِلَيْهِ تَبْتِيلًا, (T, Ṣ, M,) for تبتّل اليه تَبَتُّلًا. (T.) You say also, تبتّل إِلَى العِبَادَةِ *He applied himself exclusively to the service of God.* (Mṣb.) — تَبَتَّلَتْ, said of a woman, *She adorned and beautified herself.* (TA.)

7. انبتل *It was,* or *became, cut off,* or *severed;* (Ṣ, M, Ḳ;) as also ↓ تبتّل. (M, Ḳ.) You say, انبتلت الفَسِيلَةُ, (Ḳ, [in a copy of the M ↓ ابتتلت, probably a mistranscription,]) *The shoot,* or *offset, of the palm-tree was cut off,* or *severed,* مِنْ أُمِّهَا [*from its mother-tree*]; as also ↓ تبتّلت and ↓ استبتلت. (M, Ḳ.) — انبتل فِى سَيْرِهِ *He strove, laboured,* or *exerted himself, and made much progress, in his journeying,* or *pace.* (TA.)

8: see 7.

10: see 7.

عَطَآءٌ بَتْلٌ *A gift that is* [as it were] *cut off;* i. e., *of which there is not the like;* or *after which another is not given.* (M, Ḳ.) And صَدَقَةٌ بَتْلَةٌ, (M, Ḳ,) and صدقة بَتَّةٌ بَتْلَةٌ, (TA,) *An alms,* or *a gift for the sake of God, cut off from its giver:* (M, Ḳ:) or *cut off from all the property* [*irrevocably*], *to be devoted to the cause of God.* (O, TA. [See also art. بت.]) You say also, أَعْطَيْتُهُ هٰذِهِ العَطِيَّةَ بَتًّا بَتْلًا: see art. بت. And طلّقها طَلْقَةً بَتَّةً بَتْلَةً; (Ṣ;) or طَلَّقَهَا بَتَّةً بَتْلَةً; (Mṣb;) [*He divorced her by a separating divorce;* or *by a decided and irrevocable divorce;* (see art. بت;)] the last word being a corroborative of that next preceding it. (TA.) And حَلَفَ يَمِينًا بَتْلَةً *He swore a decided* [or *an irrevocable*] *oath.* (M, TA. [See also a similar phrase voce بَتٌّ.]) — Also *Truth;* or *true:* whence بَتْلًا *in truth;* or *truly.* (TA.)

بَتُولٌ *A shoot,* or *an offset, of a palm-tree, cut off from its mother-tree, and independent thereof;* as also ↓ بَتِيلَةٌ, (Aṣ, T, Ṣ, M, Ḳ,) and ↓ بَتِيلٌ. (M, Ḳ.) — *A virgin, that is cut off from husbands:* (Ṣ:) *a woman that withholds herself from men,* (T,) or *that is cut off from men,* (M, Ḳ,) *having no desire for them,* (T, M, TA,) *nor need of them;* (T;) and, with the art. ال, applied to the Virgin Mary; (M, Ḳ;) as also ↓ بَتِيلٌ: (M, Ḳ:) with the art. ال, it is applied also to Fáṭimeh, the daughter of Moḥammad, because she was separated from the [other] women of her age and nation by chasteness and excellence and religion and [other] grounds of pretension to respect: (Aḥmad Ibn-Yaḥyà, T, Ḳ:*) or it signifies, (Ṣ,) or signifies also, (Ḳ,) *a woman detached from worldly things, and devoted to God;* (Ṣ, Ḳ;) as also ↓ بَتِيلٌ and ↓ بَتِيلَةٌ. (Ibn-'Abbád, Ḳ.)

بَتِيلٌ: see بَتُولٌ, in three places. — Also *Slender;* (Ḥam p. 589;) applied to a waist; (Ḥam, TA;) as also ↓ مُبَتَّلٌ. (TA.) — *A tree having its racemes pendulous.* (Ḳ. [See also مُبَتَّلٌ.]) — *A watercourse* (Ibn-'Abbád, M, Ḳ) *in the lower part of a valley:* pl. بُتُلٌ. (M, Ḳ.)

بَتِيلَةٌ: see بَتُولٌ, in two places. — Also *Any limb,* or *member,* (Lth, T, Ṣ, M, Ḳ,) *with its flesh,* (Lth, T, Ṣ,) *separate from others,* (M, Ḳ,) or *by itself:* (Lth, T:) pl. بَتَائِلُ. (Lth, T, Ṣ, &c.) — In one dial., (M,) *The posteriors;* (M, Ḳ;) because divided [or distinct] from the back. (M.) — مَرَّ عَلَى بَتِيلَةٍ مِنْ رَأْيِهِ, and ↓ بَتْلَآءَ من رأيه, [*He proceeded according to*] *an irrevocable determination* or *resolution.* (Ibn-'Abbád, Ḳ.)

أَبْتَلُ; fem. بَتْلَآءُ: for the latter, see what next precedes. — عُمْرَةٌ بَتْلَآءُ [*A minor pilgrimage*] *not conjoined with another.* (Ḳ.) — And أَبْتَلُ, applied to a man, *Wide between the shoulders.* (T.)

مُبَتَّلٌ, (Aṣ, T, Ṣ,) or مُبَتَّلَةٌ, (M, Ḳ, TA, [in the CK, erroneously, مُبْتَلَةٌ,]) the first being [in the opinion of ISd] pl. [or rather coll. gen. n.] of the second, like as تَمْرٌ is of تَمْرَةٌ, (M,) *A palm-tree* (نَخْلَةٌ) *having a shoot, or an offset, cut off from it and independent of it;* (Aṣ, T, Ṣ, M, Ḳ;) and used in like manner as a pl.; i. e., the first is also used as a pl.: (Ṣ:) or the first signifies *solitary*, or *isolated*: (Ibn-Ḥabeeb, TA:) or *of which the racemes are pendulous.* (TA. [See also بَتِيلٌ.])

مُبَتَّلٌ: see بَتِيلٌ.—مُبَتَّلَةٌ, applied to a woman, *Beautiful, elegant,* or *pretty*; (Ḳ;) *as though her beauty were divided into portions* (بُتِّلَ ▼, i. e. قُطِّعَ,) *[and distributed in due proportions] upon her limbs*: (M,* Ḳ:) or *perfect in make*, (Ṣ,) *whose flesh is not accumulated, one portion upon another*, (Ṣ, M, Ḳ,) *but distinctly disposed*; this latter being said by some to be the meaning: (M:) or, accord. to Lḥ, (M, TA,) *having a lankness*, or *looseness, in her limbs*; (M, Ḳ, TA;) *not having them compressed, one upon another*; (M:) or *as though the flesh were cut off from them*: (TA:) and in like manner, مُبَتَّلٌ applied to a camel: (M, Ḳ:) not applied as an epithet to a man: (Ṣ, M, Ḳ:) or مُبَتَّلَةُ الخَلْقِ signifies *distinct in make from the generality of women; excelling them [therein]*: (Aboo-Sa'eed, T, TA:) or *perfect in make*: or *having every part beautiful in itself; not dependent [for its beauty] upon another part*: (T:) or *beautiful in make; not with one part falling short of another [in beauty]; not being beautiful in the eye and ugly in the nose, nor beautiful in the nose and ugly in the eye; but perfect.* (IAạr, TA.)

مُنْبَتِلٌ *Cut off,* or *severed.* (Ṣ.)—[And hence,] عَزِيمَةٌ مُنْبَتِلَةٌ *An irrevocable determination* or *resolution.* (TA.)

بث

1. بَثَّهُ, (Lth, T, Ṣ, M, A, Ḳ,) aor. ـُ (Lth, T, M, L, Ḳ) and ـِ, (M, L, Ḳ,) the latter [anomalous, and therefore] thought by MF to be a mistake, arising from confounding بَثَّ with بَتَّ, he not knowing any authority for it except the Ḳ, (TA,) inf. n. بَثٌّ; (Lth, T, M, L;) and ▼ ابثّه, (Ṣ, M, Ḳ,) inf. n. إِبْثَاثٌ; (TA;) and ▼ بثّثه, (Ḳ,) or this has an intensive signification; (Ṣ;) and ▼ بَثْبَثَهُ, (Ṣ, Ḳ,) inf. n. بَثْبَثَةٌ; (Ṣ;) *He spread it*; (Ṣ, A, Ḳ;) *he dispersed it, scattered it,* or *disseminated it*; (Lth, T, Ṣ,* M, A, Ḳ;) namely, a thing; (Lth, T, M, A,* L;) or ‡ news, tidings, or information. (Ṣ, A, L, Ḳ.) You say, بَثُّوا الخَيْلَ فِى الغَارَةِ *They spread,* or *dispersed, the horses,* or *horsemen, in the hostile incursion.* (T, M,* A, L.) And بَثَّ الجُنْدَ فِى البِلَادِ *He* (the Sulṭán) *spread,* or *dispersed, the army in the provinces.* (Mṣb.) And بَثَّ كِلَابَهُ *He* (the hunter, A, L) *spread,* or *dispersed, his dogs* (T, A, L) عَلَى الصَّيْدِ *[against the chase, or game].* (A.) And بَثَّ ٱللّٰهُ الخَلْقَ, (aor. ـُ, inf. n. بَثٌّ, Mṣb,) *God spread,* or *dispersed, mankind,* or *the beings whom He created,* فِى الأَرْضِ *[in the earth]*: (T, A:) or *God created them.* (Mṣb.) وَبَثَّ مِنْهُمَا رِجَالًا كَثِيرًا وَنِسَآءً, in the Ḳur [iv. 1.], means *And spread,* or *dispersed, and multiplied, from them two, many men, and women.* (T.) You say also, بُثَّتِ البُسُطُ *The carpets were spread.* (T.) And بَثَّ المَتَاعَ بِنَوَاحِى البَيْتِ *He spread out the furniture,* or *utensils, in the sides of the tent,* or *house,* or *chamber.* (A.) And بَثَّ الغُبَارَ, (Ḳ,) and ▼ بَثْبَثَهُ, (Ṣ, Ḳ,) *He,* or *it, raised the dust.* (Ṣ, Ḳ.) And ▼ بَثْبَثَ التُّرَابَ *He,* or *it, raised the dust,* or *earth, and removed it from that which was beneath it.* (M.) And ▼ بَثْبَثُوهُ *They uncovered him.* (Hr, M, L, from a trad. respecting a dying Jew.) And بَثَّ الحَدِيثَ † *He spread, published,* or *revealed, the discourse, narration,* or *information.* (Mṣb.) And, accord. to IF, بَثَّ السِّرَّ and ▼ ابثّه † *[He spread, published, or revealed, the secret].* (Mṣb.) And بَثَثْتُهُ مَا فِى نَفْسِى, aor. ـُ; and ▼ أَبْثَثْتُهُ إِيَّاهُ; ‡ *I revealed,* or *showed, to him what was in my mind.* (A.) And ▼ أَبْثَثْتُكَ سِرِّى, (Ṣ,) or السِّرَّ; (Ḳ;) and بَثَثْتُكَ السِّرَّ, (Ḳ,) inf. n. بَثٌّ; (TA;) † *I revealed,* or *showed, to him my secret,* or *the secret*: (Ṣ, Ḳ:) or ▼ أَبْثَثْتُهُ سِرِّى (T) and ▼ بَاثَثْتُهُ سِرِّى (A) ‡ *I acquainted him with my secret*: (T, A:) and ▼ ابثّه الحَدِيثَ † *he acquainted him with the discourse, narration,* or *information.* (M.) And بَثَّهُ شُقُورَهُ † *He complained to him of his state,* or *condition.* (M, in art. شقر.)

2. بَثَّثَ الخَبَرَ *He spread,* or *disseminated, the news, tidings,* or *information, much*: (Ṣ:) or *i. q.* بَثَّهُ, q. v. (Ḳ.)

3. بَاثَثْتُهُ سِرِّى: see 1; last sentence but one.—بَيْنَهُمَا مُبَاثَّةٌ ‡ *[Between them two is a mutual revealing of secrets*: see 6]. (A.)

4: see 1, in six places.—أَبْثَثْتُكَ [without a second objective complement,] † *I revealed,* or *showed,* or *have revealed* or *shown, to thee my* بَثّ, (Ṣ, TA,) whence the verb in this sense is derived; (TA;) i. e., my *state,* (Ṣ,) or my *grief,* or *sorrow.* (Ṣ, TA.)

6. تَبَاثُّوا † *[They revealed secrets, one to another*: see 3]. (Ḳ, in art. نجث.)

7. انبثّ *It spread*; (Ṣ, A, Ḳ;) *it became dispersed, scattered,* or *disseminated*; (Ṣ,* M, A, Ḳ;) namely, a thing; (M, L;) or ‡ news, tidings, or information. (Ṣ, A, L, Ḳ.) You say, انبثّت الخَيْلُ *The horses,* or *horsemen, spread,* or *became dispersed,* or *dispersed themselves,* (M, L,) in a hostile incursion. (L.) And انبثّ الجَرَادُ فِى الأَرْضِ *The locusts spread,* or *became dispersed,* or *dispersed themselves, in the land.* (M, A, L.)

10. استبثّه إِيَّاهُ † *He asked him,* or *petitioned him, to reveal it to him.* (M, L, Ḳ.)

R. Q. 1. بَثْبَثَ, inf. n. بَثْبَثَةٌ: see 1, in four places.—بَثْبَثَ الأَمْرَ † *He inquired respecting the affair* or *event, scrutinized it, and sought information respecting it.* (T, L.)

بَثٌّ (Aṣ, Ṣ, M, A, Ḳ) and ▼ مُنْبَثٌّ, (A, TA,) both applied to dates, (تَمْرٌ, Aṣ, Ṣ, &c.,) *Scattered, strewn, dispersed, and separate,* (Aṣ, Ṣ, Ḳ,) *one from another*: (Aṣ, Ṣ:) or *separate,* or *disunited, not being packed,* or *not compact*: (A:) or *not well packed,* (Ṣ, M,) *so that they are separated,* or *disunited*: (M:) or *scattered*; *not in the bag or other receptacle*; like فَثٌّ: (M:) تَمْرٌ بَثٌّ being a phrase [in which the latter word is an inf. n. used in the sense of a pass. part. n.,] like مَآءٌ غَوْرٌ. (Ṣ.)=*A state,* or *condition.* (Ṣ, Ḳ.)—*Grief,* or *sorrow,* (T, Ṣ, M,) *which one makes known to his companion or friend*: (T:) or *violent,* or *intense, grief* or *sorrow*; and *violent,* or *severe, disease* or *sickness*; as though, in consequence of its violence, one made it known to his companion or friend: (T, TA:) or the *most violent* or *intense grief* or *sorrow.* (Ḳ.) حَضَرَنِى بَثِّى, occurring in a trad., means *My grief,* or *sorrow, became violent,* or *intense.* (TA.)

زَرَابِىُّ مَبْثُوثَةٌ [in the Ḳur lxxxviii. 16] means *Goodly carpets,* or *the like,* (Bḍ,) *spread*: (A, Bḍ:) or, accord. to Fr, *many in number.* (T.)

مُنْبَثٌّ: see بَثٌّ.—*Scattered* dust: so in the Ḳur [lvi. 6]. (T.)—† *Swooning* (Ḳ) *from grief,* or *sorrow.* (TA.)

بثر

1. بَثَرَ, (Ṣ, M, A, Mṣb, Ḳ,) aor. ـُ, (Mṣb,) inf. n. بَثْرٌ; (M, Mṣb, Ḳ;) and بَثِرَ, (Ṣ, M, Mṣb, Ḳ,) aor. ـَ, (Ṣ, M, Mṣb,) inf. n. بَثَرٌ (M, Mṣb, Ḳ) and بُثُورٌ; (M, Ḳ;) and بَثُرَ, aor. ـُ; (Ṣ, Mṣb, Ḳ;) *It* (a man's face, Ṣ, M, Ḳ, or the skin, M, A, Mṣb) *broke out with pimples,* or *small pustules*; (Ṣ, M, A, Mṣb, Ḳ;) as also ▼ تبثّر: (M, A, and some copies of the Ḳ:) or this last signifies *it* (a man's skin) *became blistered,* or *vesicated.* (Ṣ, Mṣb.)

2. بثّر *It* (tar) [*made* a camel *to break out with small pustules*; or] *excoriated* a camel, *and made* him *to bleed.* (Ibn-'Abbád, TA in art. حرش.)

5: see 1.

بَثْرٌ (Ṣ, M, Mṣb, Ḳ) and ▼ بَثَرٌ, (M, Mṣb, Ḳ,) coll. gen. ns., (Mṣb,* MF,) originally inf. ns., (Mṣb,) *Pimples,* or *small pustules*; (Ṣ, M, Mṣb, Ḳ;) accord. to some, specially upon the face; (M, TA;) as also بُثُورٌ; (Ṣ, Mṣb;) which is the pl. of بَثْرٌ: (Mṣb:) ns. un. بَثْرَةٌ (Ṣ, M, Mṣb) and بَثَرَةٌ: (M, Mṣb:) and pl. of this last بَثَرَاتٌ: (Mṣb:) or بُثُورٌ, pl. of بَثْرٌ, signifies *purulent pustules like the small-pox, upon the face and other parts of the person of a man.* (T.) You say, خَرَجَتْ بِهِ بَثْرَةٌ فَعَصَرَهَا *[A pimple, or small pustule, or purulent pustule, came forth on him, and he squeezed it].* (A.) And بِجِلْدِهِ بَثْرٌ شَتَّى *[In his skin are scattered, or sundry, pimples, &c.].* (A.)

بَثِرٌ: see بَثْرٌ.

بثق

1. بَثَقَ المَآءَ, (Mgh, Mṣb,) aor. ـُ and ـِ, (Mṣb,) inf. n. بَثْقٌ, (Mgh, Mṣb,) *He made an opening for the water by breaking through the bank, or the dam that confined it.* (Mgh, Mṣb.*) And بَثَقَ النَّهْرَ, inf. n. بَثْقٌ (Lth, Ḳ) and بِثْقٌ, (Ḳ, TA,) in some of the copies of the Ṣ [and in the CḲ] بَثَقٌ, but this is wrong, though Ru-beh has used it by poetic license, (TA,) and تَبْثَاقٌ, (Ḳ,) *He broke [through] the bank of the river,* or *rivulet, in*

order that the water might pour out, or *flow forth*; (Lth, Ḳ, TA;) as also ▼ بَثَّقَ, (Ḳ,) inf. n. تَبْثِيق; the latter not commonly mentioned. (TA.) And بَثَقَ السَّيْلُ مَوْضِعَ كَذَا, aor. ـُ, inf. n. بَثْق and بِثْق, on the authority of Yaḳoob, *The torrent broke through, and clave, such a place.* (Ṣ.) ═ See also 7. — بَثَقَتِ العَيْنُ, (Ḳ,) aor. ـُ, inf. n. بَثْق and تَبْثَاق, (TA,) *The eye shed tears quickly.* (AA, Ḳ.) — بَثَقَتِ الرَّكِيَّةُ, (AZ, Ḳ,) aor. ـُ, (AZ, TA,) inf. n. بُثُوق *The well became full, and abundant in water.* (AZ, Ḳ.) ═ بَثِقَ, aor. ـَ, [inf. n., by rule, بَثَق,] *It* (seed-produce) *became affected with the disease termed* بَثْق. (TA.)

2: see 1.

7. انبثق *It* (water) *had vent*; or *it poured out*, or *flowed forth*: (Ṣ, Mṣb,* Ḳ:) or *it ran*, or *flowed, of itself, without the breaking through of a dam or the like.* (Mgh.) [For اِنْفَجَرَ, in the Ṣ, Golius appears to have found اِنْفَرَجَ, which is a mistake. — The Christians, as Golius has observed, use this verb to denote the procession of the Holy Spirit.] — انبثق السَّيْلُ عَلَيْهِمْ ‡ *The torrent came upon them without their expecting it*, or *thinking it.* (Ḳ,* TA.) And بَثَقَ ▼ المَآءُ عَلَيْهِمْ † *The water came upon them.* (TA.) — انبثق عَلَيْهِمْ بِالكَلَامِ ‡ *He came upon them with speech without their expecting it.* (Ḳ,* TA.) — انبثقت الأَرْضُ ‡ *The land became abundant in herbage*, or *fruitful.* (TA.)

بَثْق and ▼ بِثْق *An opening made for water by breaking through the bank*, or *the dam that confined it*: (Mgh, Mṣb:*) or the *place where the bank of a river*, or *rivulet, is broken* [*through*] *in order that the water may pour out*, or *flow forth*: *a place where water has vent*, or *pours out*, or *flows forth*: (Ḳ:) or the latter signifies *a place furrowed*, or *hollowed out, by water*: (JK:) pl. بُثُوق. (JK, Ḳ.) ═ Also the former, *A disease that affects seed-produce, occasioned by rain.* (TA.)

بِثْق: see بَثْق.

بَاثِق [act. part. n. of 1]. — رَكِيَّةٌ بَاثِقَةٌ *A well full, and abundant in water.* (Ḳ.) And مِيَاهٌ بُثَّق [pl. of بَاثِق], like رُكَّع [pl. of رَاكِع, app. *Waters flowing forth abundantly*]. (TA.) — [Hence,] هُوَ بَاثِقُ الكَرَمِ † *He is abundant in generosity.* (Ḳ.)

بجح

1. بَجِحَ, [aor. and inf. n. as below,] *He rejoiced*; or *was joyful, glad*, or *happy*; (Ṣ, A;) as also ▼ تبجّح: (Ṣ, Mgh, Ḳ:) and ▼ the latter signifies also *he magnified himself*; and *gloried*, or *boasted*: (Mgh:) or, accord. to Lḥ, this verb signifies *he gloried*, or *boasted*; and *vied with others*, or *contended with them for superiority, in beauty*, or *goodliness, in respect of something*; as also تمجّح: or, as some say, *he magnified himself*: and بَجِحَ is said to signify *he was*, or *became, great in his own estimation.* (TA.) You say also, بَجِحَ بِهِ, (Ṣ, Mṣb, Ḳ,) aor. ـَ, (Mṣb, Ḳ,) inf. n. بَجَحٌ; (Ṣ, Ḳ, TA;) and بَجَحَ بِهِ, (Ṣ, Mṣb, Ḳ,) aor. ـَ; (Mṣb, Ḳ;) but the latter is of weak authority; (Ṣ, Ḳ;) *He rejoiced in it*, or *at it*; (Ṣ, Ḳ;) namely, a thing; (Ṣ;) as also ▼ تبجّح and ▼ ابتجح: (TA:) or *he gloried in it*, or *boasted of it*; and so ▼ تبجّح. (Mṣb.) And فُلَانٌ يَتَبَجَّحُ ▼ عَلَيْنَا, and يَتَمَجَّحُ علينا, *Such a one talks foolishly*, or *irrationally*, [*to us, assuming superiority over us*,] *by reason of self-conceitedness*: and so one says in speaking of a person in jest. (TA.) ═ See also 2.

2. بجّحهُ *It* (a thing, or an affair, TA) *rejoiced him*; *made him joyful, glad*, or *happy*; (A, TA;) as also ▼ ابجحهُ. (TA.) And بَجَّحْتُهُ, (inf. n. تَبْجِيح, Ṣ, Ḳ,) *I rejoiced him*; *made him joyful*, &c.: (Ṣ, Mgh, Ḳ:) or, as some say, *magnified him*: (TA:) and ▼ بَجَحْتُهُ, aor. ـَ, *I magnified it*; namely, a thing. (Mṣb.)

4: see 2.

5: see 1, in five places.

6. النِّسَآءُ يَتَبَاجَحْنَ *Women*, or *the women, vie*, or *contend for superiority, one with another, in beauty*, or *goodliness*, and *in glorying*, or *boasting.* (A, TA.)

8: see 1.

بَجِحٌ *Rejoicing, glad*, or *happy*; as in the phrase, أَنَا بَجِحٌ بِمَكَانِ كَذَا [*I am rejoicing in such a place*]; and so ▼ مُتَبَجِّحٌ بِهِ. (A.)

بَجَّاحٌ *Joyful*; [an intensive epithet] applied to a man. (TA.)

بَاجِحٌ *Great in estimation*; applied to a man: pl. بُجَّحٌ and بُجُحٌ. (TA.)

مَبَاجِحُ [a pl. of which the sing. is app. مَبْجَحَةٌ, meaning, accord. to analogy, *A cause of joy* or *gladness* or *happiness*]. You say, لَقِيتُ مِنْهُ المَنَاجِحَ وَالمَبَاجِحَ [app. *I experienced from it*, or *him*, *the causes of success, and the causes of joy* &c.]. (A, TA.)

مُتَبَجِّحٌ: see بَجِحٌ.

بجد

1. بَجَدَ بِالمَكَانِ, (Ṣ, A, L, Ḳ,*) aor. ـُ, (L,) inf. n. بُجُودٌ (Ṣ, L, Ḳ) and بَجْدٌ; (Kr;) and ▼ بجّد, inf. n. تَبْجِيدٌ; (L, Ḳ;) *He remained, stayed, abode*, or *dwelt*, (Ṣ, A, L, Ḳ,) *in the place*; (Ṣ, A, L;) *settled*, or *remained fixed, in it*; *not quitting it.* (A.) — بَجَدَتِ الإِبِلُ, (L, Ḳ,) inf. n. بُجُودٌ; and ▼ بجّدت; (L;) *The camels kept to the place of pasturing.* (L, Ḳ.)

2: see 1, in two places.

بَجْدٌ *A company*, or *an assembly*, of men: and *a hundred*, and *more*, of horses: (L, Ḳ:) on the authority of El-Hejeree: (TA:) pl. بُجُودٌ. (L.)

بَجْدَةٌ i. q. أَصْلٌ [The *root, basis*, or *foundation*; or the *origin*, or *source*; or the *most essential part*, or *very essence*; of a thing]. (Ḳ.) — And [hence, app.,] The *inward*, or *intrinsic, state* or *circumstances* of a case or an affair; as also ▼ بُجْدَةٌ and ▼ بُجُدَةٌ: (Ṣ, L, Ḳ:) or the *true*, or *real, state* or *circumstances* thereof; the *positive*, or *established, truth* thereof; from بَجَدَ بِالمَكَانِ. (A.) You say, هُوَ عَالِمٌ بِبَجْدَةِ أَمْرِكَ, (Ṣ, A, L,) and ▼ بِبُجْدَتِهِ, and ▼ بِبُجُدَتِهِ, (Ṣ, L,) *He is acquainted with the inward*, or *intrinsic, state* or *circumstances of thy case* or *affair*: (Ṣ, L:) or, *with the true*, or *real, state* or *circumstances thereof*; *with the positive*, or *established, truth thereof.* (A.) And عِنْدَهُ بَجْدَةُ ذٰلِكَ, (Ṣ, Ḳ,) with fet-ḥ, (Ṣ,) *He possesses the knowledge of that.* (Ṣ, Ḳ.) And hence, (Ṣ,) هُوَ ٱبْنُ بَجْدَتِهَا, (Ṣ, Ḳ,) *contr. of* هو ابن نَجْدَتِهَا, (A in art. نجد,) or, as in the books of proverbs, أَنَا ٱبْنُ بَجْدَتِهَا, the [affixed] pronoun referring to الأَرْض [understood], as is said by Meyd and Z, (TA,) applied to [signify *He is*, or *I am*,] *the person acquainted with the thing*; (Ṣ, L, Ḳ;) *possessing*, or *exercising, the skill requisite for it*; (Ṣ, L;) *the discriminator*, or *discerner, thereof*; (L;) and one says likewise, هُوَ ٱبْنُ مَدِينَتِهَا وَٱبْنُ بَجْدَتِهَا: (TA:) it is also applied to [signify *he is*, or *I am*,] *the skilful guide of the way* [*thereof*]: (L, Ḳ:) and hence, [accord. to some,] it is proverbially applied to any one acquainted with an affair; skilful therein: (TA:) and to [signify *he is*, or *I am*,] *the person who will not quit*, or *depart from, his place*; from the saying بَجَدَ بِالمَكَانِ: (L:) or *the person who will not depart from his saying*: (Ḳ: [there explained by the words لِمَنْ لَا يَبْرَحُ مِنْ قَوْلِهِ: but the TA supplies some apparent omissions in this explanation, making it to agree with that which here immediately precedes it, taken from the L; and adds that, in some copies of the Ḳ, عن قوله is erroneously put for من قوله: also, that he who remains in a place knows that place:]) or, accord. to some, بَجْدَةٌ signifies *dust*, or *earth*; so that أَنَا ٱبْنُ بَجْدَتِهَا is as though it meant *I am created of its dust, or earth.* (TA.) — Also *A* [*desert, such as is termed*] صَحْرَآء. (Ḳ.) Kaab Ibn-Zuheyr uses the phrase ٱبْنُ بَجْدَتِهَا as meaning *Its male chameleon*; the pronoun referring to a desert (فَلَاة) which he is describing. (TA.) And you say of a land covered with black locusts, أَصْبَحَتِ الأَرْضُ بَجْدَةً وَاحِدَةً [*The land became*, or *has become, one desert, destitute of vegetable produce*]. (L.)

بُجْدَةٌ and بُجُدَةٌ: see بَجْدَةٌ; each in two places.

بِجَادٌ *A striped garment of the kind called* كِسَآء, (Ṣ, A, L, Ḳ,) being *one of the kinds of* كِسَآء *worn by the Arabs of the desert*: (Ṣ, L:) or, *of which the wool has been spun*, or *twisted, in the manner termed* يَسْرَة [app. a mistranscription for يَسْرًا (see فَتْلٌ يَسْرٌ in art. يسر)], *and woven with the instrument called* صِيصَة: pl. بُجُدٌ: a single oblong piece thereof is called فَلِيجٌ, of which the pl. is فُلُجٌ. (L, TA.) — Also *A kind of tent, of* [*the soft hair called*] وَبَر. (Ibn-El-Kelbee, TA voce بَيْتٌ, q. v.)

بَاجِدٌ *Remaining, staying, abiding*, or *dwelling*,

in a place; (L;) *settled*, or *remaining fixed*, in a land. (A.)

بجر

1. بَجِرَ, aor. ـَ, (M, K,) inf. n. بَجَرٌ, (Ṣ, M,) *He* (a man, Ṣ) *had his navel, or the part remaining of the navel-string after it had been cut, protruding,* (Ṣ, K,) *elevated, and hard,* (TA,) *and thick at the base,* (Ṣ, M,) *and fleshy at the neck, or slender part, with wind remaining in the enlarged part.* (M.) — *He was, or became, large in the belly.* (K.) — *His* (a man's, TA) *belly became full of milk,* (K,) or *pure milk,* (TA,) and *of water, and he was not satiated;* (K;) as also مَجِرَ: (TA:) or *he drank much milk, or water, and was hardly, or not at all, satiated.* (Lḥ, TA.)

بُجْرٌ: see بُجْرٌ, in three places.

بُجْرٌ *A swelling, or inflation, of the belly;* as also ▼بَجَرٌ: (Fr, TA:) or *prominence in the belly.* (Ḥar p. 639.) = *Evil; mischief: a great, terrible, or momentous, thing or case;* (AZ, Ṣ, K;) as also ▼بَجْرٌ and ▼بُجْرِىٌّ: (TA:) *a wonderful thing:* (K:) *a calamity,* or *misfortune;* (Ṣ;) as also ▼بَجْرٌ (TA) and ▼بُجْرِىٌّ (Ṣ, K) and ▼بُجْرِيَّةٌ: (K:) pl. of بُجْرٌ [or pl. pl., being app. pl. of the pl. of pauc. أَبْجُرٌ,] أَبَاجِرُ; and pl. (as though pl. of the pl. أَبْجَارٌ, T) أَبَاجِيرُ: (K:) and pl. of ▼بُجْرِىٌّ (Ṣ, K) and of ▼بُجْرِيَّةٌ (K) بَجَارِىُّ. (Ṣ, K.) You say أَمْرٌ بُجْرٌ *A great, terrible, or momentous, thing or case.* (TA.) And قَالَ هُجْرًا وَبُجْرًا [*He said a foul and*] *a wonderful thing.* (TA.) And إِنَّهُ لَيَجِىْءُ بِالأَبَاجِرِ *Verily he brings to pass calamities, or misfortunes.* (A.) And لَقِيتُ مِنْهُ البَجَارِىَّ *I experienced from him calamities, or misfortunes.* (AZ, Ṣ.) And إِنَّمَا هُوَ ▼الفَجْرُ أَوِ البُجْرُ or البَحْرُ [*It is only the daybreak or misfortune*]: a saying of Aboo-Bekr; meaning, if thou wait until the daybreak shine, thou wilt see the way; but if thou journey without a guide in the darkness, it will lead thee to evil: but the saying is recited differently; with البحر in the place of البجر. (L. [See بَحْرٌ.]) — [See also بُجْلٌ.]

بَجَرٌ inf. n. of 1 [q. v.]. (M.) — See also بُجْرٌ.

بَجِرٌ A man (TA) *having his belly full of milk,* (K,) or *pure milk,* (TA,) and *of water, without being satiated:* (K:) or *drinking much milk, or water, and being hardly, or not at all, satiated.* (Lḥ, TA.)

بَجْرَةٌ *Prominence,* or *protrusion, in the navel:* (Mgh:) or *largeness of the belly:* pl. بَجَرَاتٌ. (Yáḳoot, TA.) [See what next follows.]

بُجْرَةٌ *A tumour,* or *swelling,* or *an inflation, in the navel;* the like of which in the back is termed عُجْرَةٌ: (IAar, IAth:) or the *part of the navel-string which remains after it has been cut, when it is thick at the base, and fleshy at the neck,* or *slender part, with wind remaining in the enlarged part;* as also ▼بَجْرَةٌ: (ISd, L:) or the *navel,* (L, K,) of a man and of a camel, (L,) *whether large or not:* (L, K:) and *a knot in the belly:* (L, K:) or *a knotted vein in the belly;* the like of which in the back is termed عُجْرَةٌ: (L:) and (as some say, L) *a knot in the face,* and *in the neck:* (L, K:) pl. بُجَرٌ. (L.) [See also عُجْرَةٌ.] — [Hence,] ذَكَرَ عُجَرَهُ وَبُجَرَهُ ‡ *He mentioned his vices, or faults,* and *his whole state* or *case:* (K:) or *all his affairs; those which were apparent and those which were hidden:* or *his secrets:* or *his vices,* or *faults.* (TA.) And أَفْضَيْتُ إِلَيْكَ بِعُجَرِى وَبُجَرِى ‡ *I have revealed to thee my vices, or faults;* meaning, *my whole state* or *case.* (Ṣ.) And أَخْبَرْتُهُ بِعُجَرِى وَبُجَرِى ‡ *I acquainted him with my vices, or faults, which I conceal from others,* by reason of my confidence in him. (Aṣ.) And أَشْكُو إِلَى ٱللّٰهِ عُجَرِى وَبُجَرِى, said by 'Alee, ‡ *I complain unto God of my sorrows and my griefs;* (IAar, IAth;) meaning, *all my affairs* or *circumstances; those which are apparent and those which are hidden.* (IAth.) [See, again, عُجْرَةٌ.] — It is said in a prov., ▼عَيَّرَ بُجَيْرٌ بُجَرَهُ نَسِىَ بُجَيْرٌ خَبَرَهُ, meaning †[*Bujeyr cast reproach upon*] *his vices, or faults:* [*Bujeyr forgot his own state* or *condition:*] or, as some say, they were two men: [so that the meaning is, *Bujeyr reproached Bujarah:* &c.:] (Ṣ:) accord. to El-Mufaddal, Bujeyr and Bujarah were two brothers, in an ancient age: but accord. to the lexicologists, the meaning is, that *one affected with what is termed a* بُجْرَة *in his navel reproached another for that which was in him.* (Az, TA.)

بَجْرَةٌ: see بُجْرَةٌ.

بُجْرِىٌّ: see بُجْرٌ, in three places.

بُجْرِيَّةٌ: see بُجْرٌ, in two places.

بَجِيرٌ is an imitative sequent to كَثِيرٌ. (Fr, Ṣ, K.) Accord. to AA, it signifies *Abundant,* or *much, wealth:* [or rather this seems to be the meaning of the phrase مَالٌ بَجِيرٌ: for it is added,] and in like manner [it is used in the phrase], مَكَانٌ عَمِيرٌ بَجِيرٌ [*A place inhabited, peopled, well stocked with people and the like,* or *in a flourishing state,* and *large,* or *ample*]. (TA.)

بُجَيْرٌ: see بُجْرَةٌ.

بَاجِرٌ: see what follows.

أَبْجَرُ A man (Ṣ) *having his navel, or the part remaining of the navel-string after its having been cut, protruding,* (Ṣ, Mgh, K,) *and elevated, and hard,* (TA,) *and thick at the base,* (Ṣ, M,) *and fleshy at the neck, or slender part, with wind remaining in the enlarged part:* (M:) fem. بَجْرَآءُ: (Ṣ:) pl. بُجْرٌ (Ṣ, K) and بُجْرَانٌ. (K.) — *Large in the belly:* pl. as above: and ▼بَاجِرٌ signifies the same: (TA:) or this latter, *having a swollen, or an inflated, belly:* (IAar, K:) or *having a large belly and a protruding navel:* and its pl. is بَجَرَةٌ, occurring in a trad., in which the tribe of Ḳureysh are described as أَشِحَّةٌ بَجَرَةٌ: or بجرة may here mean ‡*hoarders and acquirers of wealth.* (L.) — One says also حَقِيبَةٌ بَجْرَآءُ †*A full* [*receptacle of the kind called*] حقيبة; and صُرَرٌ بُجْرٌ †*full purses;* and كِيسٌ أَعْجَرُ [or أَعْجَرُ ?]: but they did not say, حَقِيبَةٌ عَجْرَآءُ [or عَجْرَآءُ ?]; nor كِيسٌ أَبْجَرُ; though analogy does not disagree to it: it is from بُجْرٌ signifying "prominence in the belly." (Ḥar p. 639.) — And أَرْضٌ بَجْرَآءُ †*Ground,* or *land, that is elevated,* (K,* TA,) *and hard.* (TA.) — أَبْجَرُ also signifies †The *rope of a ship;* (K;) because of its greatness in relation to ropes in general. (TA.)

بجس

1. بَجَسَ المَآءَ, (Ṣ, A, Mṣb, K,) aor. ـُ (Ṣ, Mṣb, K) and ـِ, (A, K,) inf. n. بَجْسٌ, (Mṣb, TA,) *He opened a way, passage, vent, or channel, for the water to flow forth; gave vent to it; made it to flow;* syn. فَجَرَهُ, (Ṣ,) or فَتَحَهُ, (Mṣb,) or شَقَّهُ: (A, K:) [all of which, in this case, signify the same:] and in like manner one says of a wound; (A, K;) but in this case, the phrase is tropical: (TA:) and ▼بَجَّسَ المَآءَ, inf. n. تَبْجِيسٌ, *He* (namely, God, TA) *made the water to flow forth,* or *to flow forth copiously,* syn. فَجَّرَهُ, (K, TA,) from the cloud or clouds, and from the spring. (TA.) = See also 7, in two places.

2: see 1.

5: see 7, in three places.

7. انبجس *It* (water) *had a way, passage, vent, or channel, opened for it to flow forth; it had vent; it poured forth;* (Ṣ, A, Mṣb, K;) [*it burst forth;*] from a cloud or clouds, and from a spring; (A;) and from a rock; (Ḳur vii. 160;) as also ▼بَجَسَ, aor. ـُ; (Ṣ, TA;) and ▼تبجّس: (Ṣ, K:) syn. of the first, (Ṣ, A, K,* TA,) and last, (Ṣ,) اِنْفَجَرَ: (Ṣ, A, TA:) or of the last, تَفَجَّرَ [properly signifying *it poured forth copiously*]: (A, TA:) اِنْبِجَاسٌ signifies particularly the *welling forth* [of water] *from a spring:* or it has a general application: (K:) and ▼بَجْسٌ signifies *cracking* in a water-skin, or stone, or earth, *so that water issues* from it. (TA.) You say, السَّحَابُ يَتَبَجَّسُ بِالمَطَرِ [*The clouds pour with rain*]. (TA.) And أَتَانَا بِثَرِيدٍ ▼يَتَبَجَّسُ ▼أُدْمًا, (A,) or يَتَبَجَّسُ, (TA,) [*He brought us crumbled bread moistened with broth, which streamed with seasoning,*] meaning, by reason of the abundance of grease [in it]. (A, TA.)

مَآءٌ بَجْسٌ *Water having a way, passage, vent, or channel, opened for it to flow forth; having a vent;* or *pouring forth:* (K:) and in like manner, سَحَابٌ بَجْسٌ [*clouds pouring forth rain*]; (TA;) and [so] سَحَائِبُ بُجْسٌ [pl. of ▼بَاجِسٌ and ▼بَاجِسَةٌ]: (Ṣ:) and ▼مَآءٌ بَجِيسٌ *flowing water:* (Kr, TA:) and ▼عَيْنٌ بَجِيسٌ *a copious spring.* (K,* TA.)

بَجِيسٌ: see بَجْسٌ, in two places.

بَاجِسٌ; pl. بُجْسٌ: see بَجْسٌ.

بجل

1. بَجُلَ, aor. ـُ, inf. n. بَجَالَةٌ and بُجُولٌ, *He* (a man) *was, or became, such as is termed* بَجَالٌ *and*

بَجِيل [i. e. *magnified, honoured,* &c.]. (Ḳ.) ═ بَجَلَ, aor. ـُ; and بَجِلَ, aor. ـَ; inf. n. بَجَلٌ and بُجُولٌ; *He was,* or *became, in a good state* or *condition; having abundance of herbage,* or *of the goods* or *conveniences* or *comforts of life.* (Ḳ.) — And *He was,* or *became, joyful, glad,* or *happy.* (Ḳ.) ═ [بَجَلَهُ *He bled him* (namely, a horse, or a camel,) *by opening the vein called* الأَبْجَل: so accord. to analogy; like وَدَجَهُ, meaning "he bled him by opening the vein called الوَدَج," &c.] لَمْ يُبْجَلْ means *He had not been bled in the* أَبْجَل. (TA.)

2. بَجَّلَهُ, (Mṣb, Ḳ,) inf. n. تَبْجِيلٌ, *He magnified, honoured, revered, venerated,* or *respected, him:* (Ṣ, Mṣb, Ḳ:) or *he said to him* بَجَلْ, meaning *Sufficient for thee* (حَسْبُكَ) *is the place* [or *condition* or *rank*] *which thou hast attained.* (Ḳ.)

4. ابجلهُ *It sufficed,* or *contented, him.* (Ṣ, Ḳ.) — *It rejoiced him.* (TA.)

بُجْلٌ: see بَجَلٌ.

بَجَلْ is a noun (Mughnee) *syn. with* حَسْبُ: (Ṣ, Mughnee, Ḳ:*) and is also a verbal noun *syn. with* يَكْفِى. (Mughnee, Ḳ.*) You say بَجَلِى (Ṣ, Mughnee, Ḳ) and بَجْلِى, (Ṣ, Ḳ,) meaning حَسْبِى [*My sufficiency,* or *a thing sufficing me,* i. e. *sufficient for me,* is such a thing]: (Ṣ, Mughnee, Ḳ:) [it is said in the Ḥam, p. 145, as on the authority of Akh, that they do not say بَجَلِى; but this is a mistranscription for بَجَلْنِى, as will be seen from what follows:] and, using it as a verbal noun, (Mughnee, Ḳ,) but this is rare, (Mughnee,) you say بَجَلْنِى, meaning يَكْفِينِى [*It suffices me,* or *will suffice me*]; (Mughnee, Ḳ;) and بَجَلْكَ, meaning يَكْفِيكَ [*It suffices thee,* or *will suffice thee*]: (Ḳ:) or, accord. to Akh, they say بَجَلْكَ, like as they say, قَطْكَ; but not بَجَلْنِى, like قَطْنِى: (Ṣ:) or the ن in بَجَلْنِى is absolutely necessary accord. to him who says that بَجَلْ is a verbal noun; and accord. to him who says that this word is syn. with حَسْبُ, the ن is allowable. (MF.) [See, under the words قَدْ and قَطْ, what is said respecting قَدْنِى and قَطْنِى.] In the saying of Jábir Ibn-Ra-lán Es-Simbisee,

• لَمَّا رَأَتْ مَعْشَرًا قَلَّتْ حَمُولَتُهُمْ •
• قَالَتْ سُعَادُ أَهٰذَا مَالُكُمْ بَجَلَا •

[*When she saw a company whose beasts of burden were few, So'ád said, Is this your property, sufficing* you?] meaning, when she saw the fewness of our camels: the last word occupies the place of a denotative of state, and is made to end thus by poetic license: Abu-l-'Alà says that this word may be put in the accus. case as meaning *not exceeding what I see;* or it may be for بَجَلِى, after the manner of some of the Arabs who are related, by Akh and others, to have said غُلَامَا for غُلَامِى. (Ḥam pp. 299 and 300.) [See also 2: and see بَجَلْ.] ═ It is also a particle, (Mughnee,) meaning نَعَمْ [*Yes; yea;* or *even so*]. (Mughnee, Ḳ.)

بَجْلٌ *Calumny, slander,* or *false accusation:* or this is with damm; (Ḳ;) i. e. ▼بُجْلٌ; (T, TA;) meaning *a great calumny* &c.; (Ḳ,* TA;) and Az thinks that this may be a dial. var. of بُجْرٌ, with which it is syn.; because ل and ر are interchanged in many instances. (TA.) — *A wonderful* thing; syn. عَجَبٌ. (Ḳ.) — ذُو البَجَلِ denotes dispraise; meaning *Content with mean things; not desirous of the means of acquiring eminence:* (Ḳ:) or *content that another should manage affairs in his stead, and that he should be a burden upon others, saying, Sufficient for me* ([بَجَلِى [or حَسْبِى]) *is that* [*state* or *condition*] *wherein I am:* (O, TA:) from a saying of Luḳmán Ibn-'Ád; (O, Ḳ;) as is also ذُو البَجْلَةِ, which denotes praise. (O, TA.)

بَجْلَةٌ *A goodly,* or *beautiful, form* or *appearance, figure, person, mien,* or *external state* or *condition:* (Sh, Ḳ:) *a pleasing aspect; goodliness,* or *beauty; grounds of pretension to respect;* and *excellence;* or *sharpness,* or *quickness, of intellect.* (TA.) You say, إِنَّهُ لَذُو بَجْلَةٍ [*Verily he has a goodly,* or *beautiful, form* &c.]. (Sh, TA.) [See the end of the next preceding paragraph.] — *A small tree:* pl. بَجَلَاتٌ. (Ḳ.)

بَجَالٌ and ▼بَجِيلٌ, applied to a man, *i. q.* ▼مُبَجَّلٌ [*Magnified, honoured, revered, venerated,* or *respected*]: (Sh, Ḳ:) or *bulky,* or *corpulent;* (Aṣ, Ṣ;) applied to a man; (Aṣ, TA;) or to an old man: (Ṣ:) or the former signifies *an old,* or *aged, lord* or *chief:* (AA, Ṣ:) or *a bulky,* or *corpulent, old man:* or, as some say, one *beyond the middle age, in whom one sees goodliness of form* or *appearance, and advancement in years:** (Mgh:) or both signify *an old man, who is a great lord* or *chief, endowed with goodliness, and with excellence,* or *sharpness of intellect:* (Ḳ:) not applied to a woman; (TA;) i. e., a woman is not termed بَجَالَةٌ. (Mgh.)

بَجِيلٌ: see بَجَالٌ. — Also *Gross, big, thick, coarse,* or *rough;* applied to anything. (Ḳ.) — أَمْرٌ بَجِيلٌ *An affair, an event,* or *a case, deemed strange,* or *evil, and great,* or *formidable.* (TA.) خَيْرٌ بَجِيلٌ *Ample, abundant, good* or *wealth* or *prosperity.* (TA.)

بَاجِلٌ *Being in a good state* or *condition; having abundance of herbage,* or *of the goods* or *conveniences* or *comforts of life;* (Ḳ;) applied to a man and to a camel: (TA:) or, as Yaḳoob says, on the authority of Abu-l-Ghamr El-'Oḳeylee, *having much fat;* applied to a man and a she-camel and a he-camel. (Ṣ.) — Also *Joyful, glad,* or *happy.* (Ḳ.)

أَبْجَلُ *A certain vein,* (Ṣ,) *a thick vein,* (Ḳ, Ḥam p. 417,) *of the horse and of the camel,* (Ṣ, TA,) *in the thigh and the shank,* (Ḥam ubi suprà,) or *in the hind leg* or *the fore leg,* (TA,) *corresponding to the* أَكْحَل (Ṣ, Ḳ) *of man:* (Ṣ:) pl. أَبَاجِلُ. (Ḥam ubi suprà, TA.) You say, فَصَدَ أَبْجَلَهُ [*He opened his* ابجل]; i. e., the horse's or the camel's. (TA.) And one says of a swift horse, هُوَ وَاهِى الأَبَاجِلِ [*He is lax in the* اباجل]. (Ḥam ubi suprà.)

مُبَجَّلٌ: see بَجَالٌ.

بح

1. بَحَّ, (L,) first pers. بَحِحْتُ, aor. يَبَحُّ, (ISk, Ṣ, L, Ḳ,) and ISd says, I see, or think, that Lḥ has mentioned يَبْحَحُ, which is extr. with respect to rule, (TA,) inf. n. بَحَحٌ; (ISk, Ṣ, L, Ḳ;) and first pers. بَحَحْتُ, (AO, T, Ṣ, Ḳ,) but the former is the more chaste, (T, TA,) aor. يَبُحُّ (AO, Ṣ, Ḳ) and يَبِحُّ and يَبَحُّ, [which last is contr. to analogy,] (L,) inf. n. بَحٌّ (AO, Ṣ, Ḳ) and بُحُوحٌ and بُحَاحٌ and بَحَاحَةٌ and بُحُوحَةٌ; (Ḳ;) *He had a hoarse, rough, harsh,* or *gruff, voice;* (L;) *he was taken with a hoarseness, harshness, roughness,* or *gruffness, of the voice.* (Ḳ.) — It is tropically used in speaking of inanimate things; as in بَحَّ العُودُ, meaning ‡ [*The lute*] *was rough* [*in sound:* see أَبَحُّ]. (A.)

4. ابحّهُ *It* (crying out, or vociferating,) *rendered him hoarse, rough, harsh,* or *gruff, in voice.* (Ṣ,* Ḳ.)

8. هُمْ فِى ٱبْتِحَاحٍ *They are in a state of amplitude, and of plenty,* or *of abundance of herbage* or *of the goods* or *conveniences* or *comforts of life.* (Ḳ.)

R. Q. 1. بَحْبَحَ: see R. Q. 2, in two places.

R. Q. 2. تَبَحْبَحَ الدَّارَ, (Ḳ,) and ▼بَحْبَحَهَا, (TA,) † *He was,* or *became,* [*established*] *in the middle,* or *midst,* [which is the *best part,*] *of the* دار [i. e. *abode,* or *district,* or *country,* &c.], (Ḳ, TA,) *and became possessed of mastery, dominion,* or *authority, and power, over it.* (TA.) Fr, however, makes تَبَحْبَحَ to be from البَاحَةُ [q. v.], not from a reduplicative root. (TA.) — تبحبح also signifies † *He was,* or *became, settled,* or *established, in authority and power,* (syn. تَمَكَّنَ,) in alighting, and taking up his abode, or sojourning; (Ṣ, Ḳ, TA;) and *was,* or *became,* [*established*] *in the middle,* or *midst,* [or *best part,*] *of the place of abode;* (TA;) and so ▼بحبح. (Ḳ, TA.) — Also ‡ *He took a wide, an ample,* or *a large, range.* (A.) — [Hence,] تَبَحْبَحَ الحَيَا † *The rain became of wide extent, and had influence upon the land.* (TA, from a trad.) — And تَبَحْبَحَتِ العَرَبُ فِى لُغَاتِهَا ‡ *The Arabs were copious,* or *took a wide range, in their dialects.* (A.) — And تبحبح فِى المَجْدِ † *He became in an ample state of glory, honour,* or *dignity.* (TA.) — An Arab of the desert said, of a woman in labour, تَرَكْتُهَا تَبَحْبَحُ عَلَى أَيْدِى القَوَابِلِ [app. † *I left her obtaining delivery by the hands of the midwives*]. (AZ, TA.)

بَحَّةٌ: see أَبَحُّ.

بُحَّةٌ (Ṣ, A, L, Ḳ) and ▼بُحَاحٌ (L) *Hoarseness, roughness, harshness,* or *gruffness, of the voice;* (L, Ḳ;) which is sometimes natural: or the former is applied absolutely, and the latter to that which arises from disease. (L.) You say, فِى صَوْتِهِ بُحَّةٌ [*In his voice is hoarseness*, &c.]. (Ṣ, A.)

بُحَاحٌ : see بُحَّةٌ.

بَحْبَحِىٌّ † *Ample in expenditure*: and *having an ample place of abode.* (Fr, Ḳ.)

بُحْبُوحٌ : see what next follows.

بُحْبُوحَةٌ † The *middle*, or *midst*, [or *best part*,] syn. وَسَطٌ, (A'Obeyd, Ṣ, A, Ḳ,) of an abode, or a district, or country, (Ṣ, A,) or a place, (Ḳ,) and of a place where one alights and abides, (TA,) and of Paradise, and of anything, and the *best part* thereof; (A'Obeyd, TA;) [like وَسَطٌ, by which it is explained; because what is between the two extremes is generally the best: it may be well rendered the *heart*, or *very heart*, of a thing;] and ▼بُحْبُوحٌ, also, has the former of these significations [and by implication the other likewise]. (TA, voce بُؤْبُؤٌ, where see an ex.) Jereer says,

قَوْمِى تَمِيمٌ هُمُ القَوْمُ الَّذِينَ هُمُ
يَنْفُونَ تَغْلِبَ عَنْ بُحْبُوحَةِ الدَّارِ

[*My people are Temeem: they are the people who drive away Teghlib from the middle*, or *best part, of the country*]. (Ṣ.) [It is said in the A, that this word, as syn. with وَسَطٌ, in relation to an abode or the like (دار), is tropical; but I see no reason for this, unless by وسط be meant the "best part."]

أَبَحُّ, applied to a man, (Ṣ, L, Ḳ,) or أَبَحُّ الصَّوْتِ, (A,) *Having a hoarse, rough, harsh*, or *gruff, voice*: (L, Ḳ:) fem. بَحَّآءُ; with which ▼بَحَّةٌ is syn.: (Ṣ, Ḳ:) pl. بُحٌّ. (Ṣ.) بَاحٌّ is not allowable. (Ṣ.) — And أَبَحُّ applied to a lute (عُودٌ), † *Rough* (Ḳ, TA) *in sound.* (TA.) — Also † The *base*, or *thick, chord of a lute*; syn. بَمٌّ; because of its rough sound. (TA.) — † *A* [*gold coin of the kind called*] دِينَار; (Ḳ, TA;) because of its harsh sound [when one rings it]. (TA.) — † *A* قِدْح [or *gaming-arrow*] (Ṣ, Ḳ, TA) *by means of which lots*, or *portions, are divided*: (Ṣ, TA:) pl. بُحٌّ: (Ṣ, Ḳ:) or *such an arrow that has no sound.* (TA.) Khufáf Ibn-Nudbeh says,

قَرَوْا أَضْيَافَهُمْ رَبَحًا بِبُحٍّ
يَعِيشُ بِفَضْلِهِنَّ الحَىُّ سُمْرِ

[*They entertained their guests with young weaned she-camels, on the superabundant remains of which the tribe lived, by means of tawny-coloured gaming-arrows whereby the lots* that determined who should afford the entertainment *were divided*: or, accord. to the TA, ربحا here signifies *fat*, as a subst.; but this is inconsistent with the affixed pronoun relating to it]. (Ṣ.) — † *Fat*, as an epithet, not a subst. (Ḳ.) — كِسْرٌ أَبَحُّ † [*A portion of a limb*, &c.,] *having much fat.* (TA.)

بحت

1. بَحُتَ, aor. ـُ, (Ṣ, Mṣb, Ḳ,) inf. n. بُحُوتَةٌ, (Ḳ,) or بَحْتٌ, (Mṣb,) *It* (a thing) *was*, or *became, unmixed, free from admixture*, or *pure*: (Ṣ, Ḳ:) [and] *he was unmixed*, or *pure, in race, lineage*, or *parentage.* (Mṣb.)

3. باحت المَآءَ, (A,) inf. n. مُبَاحَتَةٌ, (TA,) *He drank water*, or *the water, not upon* ثُفْل [i. e. *without having eaten anything such as flesh-meat* or *bread* or *dates* or *grain*]: (A:) or *he drank water*, or *the water, not mixed with honey* or *any other thing.* (TA.) And باحت الشَّرَابَ *He drank the wine*, or *beverage, pure, without any mixture.* (A.) And باحت الرِّمْثَ [*He* (a camel) *ate of the shrub called* رمث *without any other pasture*]. (T in art. طلح.) And باحت دَابَّتَهُ بِالضَّرِيعِ وَنَحْوِهِ *He fed his beast with* ضريع, (i. e. *dry herbage*, TA,) *and the like, unmixed* [*with other pasture*]. (Ḳ.) — باحته الوُدَّ *He regarded him*, or *acted towards him, with reciprocal purity*, or *sincerity, of love*, or *affection*: (Ṣ, A, Ḳ:) or *he was pure*, or *sincere, to him in love*, or *affection.* (M.) And باحت القِتَالَ *He fought with earnestness and energy, unmixed with lenity.* (A,* TA.) And باحت فُلَانًا (inf. n. as above, TA) *He acted openly*, or *undisguisedly, with*, or *towards, such a one.* (Ḳ, TA.)

بَحْتٌ *Unmixed, free from admixture*, or *pure*; (Ṣ, A, Mgh, Ḳ;) applied to anything: (A, Ḳ:) anything *that is eaten alone, without seasoning* or *condiment* or *any savoury food*: and in like manner, seasoning, or condiment, or any savoury food, *without bread*: (Aḥmad Ibn-Yaḥyà:) *unmixed*, or *pure, in race, lineage*, or *parentage*; (Ṣ, A, Mṣb;) applied [for instance] to an Arab, (Ṣ, A,) and to an Arab of the desert: (TA:) originally an inf. n.; (Mṣb;) [and therefore] the same as masc. and fem. and dual and pl.: but if you will, you may use بَحْتَةٌ as a fem. epithet, applied [for instance] to an Arab woman; and may use the dual and pl. forms: (Ṣ:) or the fem. is [properly] with ة; or, as some say, the word has no dual nor pl. nor dim. form. (Ḳ.) You say شَرَابٌ بَحْتٌ *Unmixed wine* or *beverage*: (Ṣ:) and خَمْرٌ بَحْتٌ and بَحْتَةٌ and خُمُورٌ بَحْتَةٌ [*unmixed wine* and *wines*]. (TA.) And خُبْزٌ بَحْتٌ *Bread without anything else* [*to season it*]. (Ṣ.) And أَكَلَ الخُبْزَ بَحْتًا, and اللَّحْمَ بَحْتًا, *He ate the bread without any seasoning* or *condiment* or *savoury food*, and *the flesh-meat without bread.* (TA.) And قَدَّمَ إِلَيْهِ قَفَارًا بَحْتًا *He presented to him food without any seasoning* or *condiment.* (A.) And ادَّهَنَ بِدُهْنٍ بَحْتٍ *He anointed himself with ointment unmixed with any perfume.* (Mgh.) And مِسْكٌ بَحْتٌ (A, Mṣb) [*Unmixed*, or *unadulterated, and* therefore] *strong* [*-scented,*] *musk.* (Mṣb.) And بَرْدٌ بَحْتٌ لَحْتٌ *Vehement*, or *intense, cold*; (TA;) [*as though unmixed with any degree of warmth*;] syn. صَادِقٌ: (Ḳ in art. لحت:) the last word is an imitative sequent. (TA in that art.)

بحث

1. بَحَثَهُ, aor. ـَ, inf. n. بَحْثٌ, *He scraped it up*; [as one who seeks to find a thing therein;] namely, the dust, or earth: (L:) and *he searched*, or *sought, for it*, or *after it*, (namely, a thing,) *in the dust*, or *earth*; as also ▼ابتحثهُ: (L, TA:) thus each is made trans. by itself: and authors often say, بَحَثَ فِيهِ [meaning *he searched*, or *inquired, into it*; *investigated, scrutinized*, or *examined, it*]: (TA:) one says, بَحَثَ فِى الأَرْضِ *he dug up the earth*; and thus it is used in the Ḳur v. 34: (Mṣb:) but accord. to the usage commonly known and obtaining, (TA,) you say, بَحَثَ عَنْهُ, (Ṣ, A, L, Mṣb, Ḳ,) aor. as above, (L, Mṣb, Ḳ,) and so the inf. n.; (L, Mṣb;) as well as بَحْثَةٌ; (L;) and ▼ابتحث عنه; (T, Ṣ, L, Ḳ;) [in some copies of the Ḳ انبحث, which is said in the TA to be a mistake; and ▼ابتحثهُ; (see above;)] and ▼تبحّث عنه; (T, L, Ḳ;) and ▼استبحث عنه; (L, Ḳ;) and ▼استبحثهُ; (L;) [*he scraped up the dust*, or *earth, from over it*: and hence,] *he searched*, or *sought, for it, after it*, or *respecting it*; *he inquired, and sought for information, respecting it*; *he searched*, or *inquired, into it*; *investigated, scrutinized*, or *examined, it*; *he inquired respecting it, and searched to the utmost after it*; (Ṣ,* A,* L, Mṣb,* Ḳ;*) namely, a thing, (Ṣ, L,) or an affair, or event. (Mṣb.) You say also, ▼استبحث أَخَاهُ عَنْ سِرِّهِ *He examined his brother respecting his secret.* (A in art. نبث.)

3. [باحثهُ عَنْ أَمْرٍ], inf. n. مُبَاحَثَةٌ, *He searched*, or *inquired, with him into a thing*; or *investigated, scrutinized*, or *examined, with him a thing*, or *an affair*: and particularly, *in the way of disputation.*] — عَادَتُهُ أَنْ يُبَاحِثَ وَيُبَاهِتَ [*His custom is to engage with another in mutual scrutiny* of secrets, or faults, or the like, *and in mutual calumniation*, &c.: see 6]. (A in art. بهت.)

5. see 1.

6. تَبَاحَثُوا عَنِ الأَسْرَارِ *They searched*, or *inquired, into each other's secrets.* (A in art. نبث.)

8: see 1, in three places. — ابتحث also signifies *He played with the dust*, or *earth, termed* بحاثة; or *at the game called* البحثة. (Ḳ.) In a copy of the Ḳ, the verb is here incorrectly written انبحث. (TA.)

10: see 1, in three places.

بَحْثٌ, (so in the Ḳ,) or ▼بَحِيثٌ, (so in the L,) accord. to Sh, (L,) *A mine* (L, Ḳ) *in which one searches for gold and silver.* (L.) — Also the former, *A great serpent*; (Ḳ;) because it scrapes up the dust or earth. (TA.)

البُحْثَةُ, (as written in the L,) or البَحْثَةُ, (as in the Ḳ,) accord. to Sh, (L,) and ▼البُحَيْثَى, (L, Ḳ,) accord. to ISh, (L,) *A certain game with* ▼بُحَاثَة, i. e., *dust*, or *earth.* (L, Ḳ.) You say, لَعِبَ البُحْثَةَ *He played the game thus called.* (L.)

إِبِلٌ بَحُوثٌ *Camels that scrape up the dust*, or *earth, with their fore feet, backwards*, (AA, T, L, Ḳ,) *in going*; i. e., *throwing it behind them*; or, as some say, *with their feet.* (TA.) — البَحُوثُ, (Ḳ,) or سُورَةُ البَحُوثِ, (L,) thus written in the Fáïk, and if so, بَحُوثٌ is an intensive epithet, applying alike to a masc. and a fem. noun, like صَبُورٌ; (TA;) or, accord. to some, سُورَةُ البُحُوثِ, (L,) pl. of بَحْثٌ; (TA;) a name of *The chapter of the Ḳur-án called* سُورَةُ التَّوْبَةِ, (L, Ḳ,) *and* البَرَآءَةُ; (L;) [chap. ix.;] given to it because it inquires respecting the hypocrites and their secrets. (L.)

بَحِيثٌ: see بَحْثٌ. — *A secret:* whence the prov., بَدَا بَحِيثُهُمْ [*Their secret became apparent, or revealed*]. (TA. [But in the Ṣ, in art. نجث, q. v., we find بَدَا نَجِيثُ القَوْمِ; and so in Freytag's Arab. Prov. i. 159.])

بُحَاثَةٌ *Dust, or earth,* (Az, Ḳ,) *which is scraped up from what is searched for therein.* (Az, TA.) See البُحْثَةُ.

البُحْثَةُ: see البُحَّيْثَى.

بَاحِثٌ [act. part. n. of 1; *Scraping up* dust or earth: &c.]. كَالبَاحِثِ عَنِ الشَّفْرَةِ [*Like him who is scraping up the dust, or earth, from over the great knife* with which he is to be slaughtered,] is a prov.: (Ṣ, L:) and so كَبَاحِثَةٍ عَنْ حَتْفِهَا بِظِلْفِهَا [*Like one searching for her death with her hoof*]: originating from the fact of a ewe's digging up a knife in the dust, or earth, and then being slaughtered with it. (L.)

بَاحِثَآءُ *Dust, or earth,* (L, Ḳ,) *of the burrow of the Jerboa,* (L,) *resembling the* [*hole termed*] قَاصِعَآء; (L, Ḳ;) *but it is not this:* pl. بَاحِثَاوَاتٌ. (L.)

مَبْحَثٌ *A place,* and *a time, of scraping up* or *digging; of searching, inquiring, investigating, scrutinizing,* or *examining:* pl. مَبَاحِثُ. (KL.) You say, تَرَكْتُهُ بِمَبَاحِثِ البَقَرِ (Ṣ, Ḳ*) [*I left him in the places where the* wild *oxen scrape up the ground*]; meaning, *in a desert place, destitute of herbage, or of human beings;* (Ṣ, Ḳ;) *in an unknown place;* (Ḳ;) i. e., *so that it was not known where he was.* (Ṣ.)

بحثر

Q. 1. بَحْثَرَ, [inf. n. بَحْثَرَةٌ,] *He took, drew,* or *pulled,* a thing *out,* or *forth;* and *uncovered* it, *laid it open,* or *exposed* it; (Abu-l-Jarráḥ, Ṣ, Ḳ;) as also بَعْثَرَ. (Abu-l-Jarráḥ, Ṣ.) It is said in the Ḳur [c. 9], accord. to one reading, إِذَا بُحْثِرَ مَا فِى القُبُورِ, [instead of بُعْثِرَ,] meaning [*When that which is in the graves is taken forth and uncovered;* i. e.,] *when the dead are raised to life;* syn. بُعِثَ; and it is not improbable that بَحْثَرَ may be composed of بَحَثَ and أَثَرَ [app. a mistranscription for أَثَارَ], accord. to the opinion of those who hold that quadriliteral and quinqueliteral words are composed of two. (TA.) — *He searched,* or *sought, for,* or *after,* a thing *in the dust* or *earth,* or *the like;* syn. بَحَثَ [which Ibr D thinks may be a mistake for بَعَثَ: but see بَعْثَرَ]. (L, Ḳ, and Bḍ in c. 9.) — *He separated, disunited, scattered, dispersed,* or *dissipated,* (Ṣ, Ḳ,) a thing. (Ṣ.) *He scattered,* or *dispersed,* his household goods, or his commodities, *and turned* them *over, one upon another;* as also بَعْثَرَ. (Fr, Ṣ.) — *It* (milk) *curdled,* or *coagulated, and formed little clots of curd;* syn. تَقَطَّعَ وَتَحَبَّبَ. (Ṣ, Ḳ.)

Q. 2. تَبَحْثَرَ *It* (a thing, Ṣ) *became separated, disunited, scattered, dispersed,* or *dissipated.* (Ṣ, Ḳ.)

لَبَنٌ مُبَحْثَرٌ *Milk curdling,* or *coagulating, and forming little clots of curd.* (Ḳ. [See Q. 1.]) When the upper portion is thick and the lower thin, it is termed هَادِرٌ. (TA.)

بحر

1. بَحَرَ, (TA,) [aor. ـَ,] inf. n. بَحْرٌ, (Ḳ,) *He slit; cut,* or *divided, lengthwise; split;* or *clave;* (Ḳ, TA;) *and enlarged,* or *made wide.* (TA.) Hence the term بَحْرٌ [as meaning "a sea" or "great river"] is said to be derived, because what is so called is cleft, or trenched, in the earth, and the trench is made the bed of its water. (TA.) — بَحَرَهَا, (M,) or بَحَرَ أُذُنَهَا, (Ṣ, A, Mṣb,) aor. ـَ, (M, Mṣb,) inf. n. بَحْرٌ, (Ṣ, M, Mṣb, Ḳ,) *He slit her* (a camel's, Ṣ, M, A, Mṣb, and a sheep's or goat's, M) *ear,* (Ṣ, M, A, Mṣb, Ḳ,) *in halves,* or *in halves lengthwise,* (M, TA,) *widely;* (B;) and in like manner, بَحَرَهُ *he slit his* (a camel's) *ear widely:* (B:) and ↓ بَحَّرَ آذَانَ الأَنْعَامِ, inf. n. تَبْحِيرٌ, *He slit* [&c.] *the ears of the cattle.* (Az, TA in art. بتك.) — بَحِرَ, aor. ـَ, inf. n. بَحَارَةٌ, *It was,* or *became, wide,* or *spacious.* The inf. n. is mentioned in the A: see بَحْرٌ: and see also 10.]

2: see 1.

4. ابحر *He embarked* [or *voyaged*] *upon the sea* or *a great river.* (Yaạḳoob, Ṣ, M, Ḳ.) [Opposed to أَبَرَّ.] — ‡ *It* (water, Ḳ, sweet water Ṣ, A) *was,* or *became, salt.* (Ṣ, A,* Ḳ.) — أَبْحَرَتِ الأَرْضُ *The land abounded with places where water stagnated.* (T, Ḳ.* [In the latter, مَنَافِعُهَا is put by mistake for مَنَاقِعُهَا. See بَحْرَةٌ.]) — † *He found water to be salt; not easy,* or *pleasant, to be drunk.* (Ḳ, TA. [In some copies of the Ḳ, for لَمْ يَسُغْ, we find لَمْ يَمْتَنِعْ, which is evidently a mistake.]) — *He met,* or *met with,* a man *unintentionally:* (M, Ḳ:) from the phrase, لَقِيتُهُ صَحْرَةً بَحْرَةً. (TA.)

5. تبحّر: see 10. — Also † *He* (a pastor) *took a wide range* in abundant pasturage. (TA.) — تبحّر فِى المَالِ ‡ *He enlarged himself,* or *he became,* or *made himself, ample,* or *abundant, in wealth,* or *camels,* or *the like;* (Ḳ,* TA;) as also ↓ استبحر فيه. (TA.) — تبحّر فِى العِلْمِ ‡ *He went deep into science,* or *knowledge, and enlarged himself,* or *took a wide range, therein,* (Ṣ, A, Ḳ,) *wide as the sea;* (TA;) and in like manner one says with respect to other things: (Ṣ:) and so ↓ استبحر فيه. (A, TA.)

10. استبحر ‡ *It* (a place) *became wide,* or *spacious, like the sea:* (A:) *it spread wide; became expanded;* (Ḳ;) as also ↓ تبحّر. (TA.) [See also بَحِرَ.] — ‡ *He* (a poet, A, Ḳ, and a خَطِيب, [i. e. a speaker, an orator, or the like,] A) *expatiated in speech; was,* or *became, diffuse therein.* (M, A, Ḳ.) — See also 5, in two places.

بَحْرٌ [*A sea:* and *a great river:*] *a spacious place comprising a large quantity of water;* (B;) *a large quantity of water,* (Ḳ, TA,) *whether salt or sweet;* (TA;) contr. of بَرٌّ; (Ṣ, A;) so called because of its depth (Ṣ, TA) and large extent; (Ṣ, Mṣb, TA;) from البَحَارَةُ; (A;) or because its bed is trenched in the earth; see 1: (TA:) or *a large quantity of salt water,* only; (Ḳ;) and so called because of its saltness: (El-Umawee, TA: [but accord. to the A, this word as an epithet meaning "salt" is tropical:]) or rather this is its general meaning: (TA:) for it signifies also *any great river;* (Ṣ, M, TA;) *any river of which the water does not cease to flow;* (Zj, T, TA;) *such as the Euphrates,* for instance; (Ṣ;) or *such as the Tigris, and the Nile, and other similar great rivers of sweet water; of which the great salt* بَحْر *is the place of confluence;* so called because trenched in the earth: (T, TA:) pl. [of pauc.] أَبْحُرٌ and [of mult.] بِحَارٌ and بُحُورٌ. (Ṣ, Mṣb, Ḳ.) The dim. is ↓ أُبَيْحِرٌ, (Ḳ,) which is anomalous; and ↓ بُحَيْرٌ, which is the regular form: accord. to the Ḳ, the latter is not used; but this is untrue; for it is sometimes used, though rare. (MF.) — Hence its application in the saying of the Arabs, يَا هَادِىَ اللَّيْلِ جُرْتَ إِنَّمَا هُوَ البَحْرُ أَوِ الفَجْرُ, which Th explains by saying that the meaning is, ‡ [*O guide of the night, thou hast deviated from the right way:*] *it is only destruction or* thou wilt see *the daybreak:* the night is here likened to the sea [and with the night is associated the idea of destruction]: but accord. to one recital, it is البَجْرُ, instead of البَحْرُ. (TA. [See art. بجر.]) — Also ‡ *Salt;* as an epithet, applied to water. (Ṣ, A.) — ‡ *A fleet,* or *swift, and excellent, horse;* (Aṣ, Ḳ;) *that runs much;* (Aṣ, TA;) *that takes a wide range in his running;* (Ṣ, A, Mṣb, B;) *that runs like the sea,* or *a great river;* or *like the sea,* or *a great river, when it rolls wave over wave.* (Niftaweyh, TA.) — ‡ *A generous man;* (Ḳ, TA;) *one who takes a wide range in his beneficence, bounty,* or *kindness; who abounds therein.* (TA.) You say, لَقِيتُ بِزَيْدٍ بَحْرًا ‡ [*I found, in the place of Zeyd, a man of abundant generosity* or *beneficence*]: ب here denoting substitution. (The Lubáb cited in the TA voce ب.) And لَقِيتُ مِنْهُ بَحْرًا ‡ [*I found him to be a man of exceeding generosity*]; a phrase expressing an intensive degree of generosity: and رَأَيْتُ مِنْهُ بَحْرًا [signifies the same]. (Mughnee in art. ب.) — ‡ *A man of extensive knowledge* or *science; one who takes a wide range in his knowledge* or *science.* (B.) — ‡ *Any person,* or *thing, that takes a wide range in a thing.* (B.) — † *Land of seed-produce and fruitfulness;* or *a tract,* or *region, in which are green herbs* or *leguminous plants, and waters;* or the *part of a country near to water;* syn. رِيفٌ: (Aboo-'Alee, Ḳ:) and the dim. ↓ بُحَيْرٌ is used in the same sense; or, by poetic licence, for ↓ بُحَيْرَةٌ. (TA.) So in the Ḳur [xxx. 40], ظَهَرَ الفَسَادُ فِى البَرِّ وَالبَحْرِ † [*Corruption hath appeared in the desert,* or *deserts, and in the land of seed-produce and fruitfulness;* &c.]: (Aboo-'Alee, TA:) or the meaning here is, [*in the desert*, or *deserts, and in the towns*, or *villages, in which is water*: (see بِرّ:) or *in the open country and*] *in the cities* [or *towns*] *upon the rivers;* by sterility in the former, and scarcity in the latter: (Zj, TA, and T in art. بر:) or *in the land and the sea;* i. e., the land has become sterile, or unfruitful, and the supply of the sea has become cut off. (Az, TA.) See also بَحْرَةٌ. — Also, البَحْرُ, (Ṣ, Ḳ,) or بَحْرُ الرَّحِمِ, (A, Mgh,) † *The bottom* (عُمْق, Ṣ, A, Mgh, Ḳ, or قَعْر, IAth, TA) *of the womb; fundus uteri:* (Ṣ, A, Mgh, Ḳ:) whence blood of a pure red colour, (Ṣ,) or intensely red, (Mgh,) is termed بَحْرَانِىٌّ (Ṣ, Mgh) and ↓ بَاحِرٌ. (Ṣ.)

بَحْرَةٌ *A wide tract of land:* so accord. to Aboo-Naṣr: but in one place he says, *a small valley in rugged land:* pl. بِحَارٌ. (TA.) — *A land, country,* or *territory, belonging to,* or *inhabited by, a people;* syn. بَلْدَةٌ. (Ṣ, Ḳ.) One says, هٰذِهِ بَحْرَتُنَا *This is our land,* &c.; syn. أَرْضُنَا. (Ṣ.) It occurs also in the dim. form [↓ بُحَيْرَةٌ], as in the Towsheeḥ of El-Jelál. (TA.) — *Any town,* or *village, that has a running river and wholesome water:* (Ḳ:) and [absolutely] *any town,* or *village:* of such the Arabs say, هٰذِهِ بَحْرَتُنَا *This is our town,* or *village:* and the pl. بِحَارٌ they apply to *cities,* as well as *towns,* or *villages.* (TA.) — *Low,* or *depressed, land:* (IAạr, Ḳ:) occurring also in the dim. form [↓ بُحَيْرَةٌ]. (TA.) — *A meadow;* or *a garden;* syn. رَوْضَةٌ: (T, TA:) or *one that is large,* (Ḳ,) *and wide.* (TA.) — *A place where water stagnates.* (Sh, Ḳ.) — The pl. is ↓ بَحْرٌ, (as in some copies of the Ḳ, [or this is a coll. gen. n. of which بَحْرَةٌ is the n. un.,]) or بِحَرٌ, (as in other copies of the Ḳ and in the TA,) or بُحَرٌ, (as in the CḲ,) and بِحَارٌ. (Ḳ.) = لَقِيتُهُ صَحْرَةً بَحْرَةً, (Ṣ, Ḳ,) and ↓ صُحْرَةً بُحْرَةً, as in the Expositions of the Tesheel, &c., (MF,) and صَحْرَةً بَحْرَةً, (Ḳ,) and ↓ صَحْرَةَ بَحْرَةَ, (MF,) *I met him out, with nothing intervening between me and him;* (Ṣ, L;) *both of us being exposed to open view;* (TA;) *without anything concealing,* or *intervening.* (Ḳ, TA.) صحرةَ بحرةَ, without tenween, is a compound denotative of state; not, as some say, consisting of two inf. ns.: and sometimes نَحْرَةً is added; in which case each of the three words is with tenween, decl.; and they do not form a compound. (MF. [But see صَحْرَةٌ.)]

صُحْرَةً بُحْرَةً and صَحْرَةَ بَحْرَةَ: see بَحْرَةٌ.

بَحْرِىٌّ *Of,* or *relating to,* or *belonging to, the sea,* or *a great river;* rel. n. of بَحْرٌ. (Ṣ, Ḳ.) — *A seaman; a sailor;* (TA;) as also ↓ بَحَّارٌ: (Ḳ:) and [↓ بَحْرِيَّةٌ and] ↓ بَحَّارَةٌ *seamen; sailors* (Ḳ, TA.) — [In the dial. of Egypt, *North; northern;* because the Mediterranean Sea lies on the north of that country: like as, in Hebrew, יָם signifies "west;" because that sea lies on the west of Palestine.]

بَحْرِيَّةٌ: see بَحْرِىٌّ.

بُحْرَانٌ, a post-classical word, (Ṣ, Ḳ,) used by the physicians, signifying The *crisis of a disease;* the *sudden change which happens to a sick person,* (Ṣ, TA,) and the *commencement of convalescence,* (TA,) *in acute diseases;* (Ṣ, TA;) *at a time fixed by some motion in the heavenly bodies, mostly by a motion of the moon;* being *a change to health or to the contrary:* a word [said to be] of Greek origin. (The Nuzheh of the sheykh Dáwood El-Anṭákee, cited in the TA.) [Pl. بَحَارِينُ.] They say, هٰذَا يَوْمُ بُحْرَانٍ and يَوْمٌ ↓ بَاحُورِىٌّ [*This is the day of a crisis of a disease*]: بَاحُورِىٌّ being anomalous: (Ṣ, Ḳ:) [perhaps from البَاحُورُ signifying "the moon," because the crisis of a disease is thought to be mostly fixed by a motion of the moon: or] as though it were a rel. n. of بَاحُورٌ and بَاحُورَآءُ meaning the "vehemence of heat in [the month of] تَمُّوز." (Ṣ.)

دَمٌ بَحْرَانِىٌّ † *Blood of the menses;* accord. to El-Ḳutabee: or † *intensely red blood:* (Mgh:) or † *intensely red, and thick, and abundant, menstrual blood:* (IAth:) or † *black blood:* (A:) or, as also ↓ دَمٌ بَاحِرٌ, (Ṣ, M, Mṣb, Ḳ,) † *blood of the womb:* (Ḳ:) or † *blood of a pure red colour:* (Ṣ, M, Ḳ:) or † *such blood from the belly:* (M:) or † *pure blood of an intensely red colour:* (Mṣb:) both from البَحْرُ signifying "the bottom of the womb:" (Ṣ:) the former is a rel. n. therefrom, (A, IAth, Mṣb,) in which the ا and ن are added to give intensiveness to the signification, (IAth,) or to distinguish it from the rel. n. of البَحْرُ [in its most common sense]: (Mṣb:) or it is a rel. n. of البَحْرُ [in its most common sense], because of its abundance. (IAth.) — أَحْمَرُ بَحْرَانِىٌّ, and ↓ بَاحِرٌ, (TA,) and ↓ بَاحِرِىٌّ, (IAạr, TA,) † *Intense red.* (TA.)

بُحَيْرٌ dim. of بَحْرٌ, which see, in two places.

بَحِيرَةٌ A she-camel *having her ear slit:* (Ṣ,* A, Mṣb, Ḳ*:) [and, as a subst., or an epithet in which the quality of a subst. is predominant,] *a she-camel of which the mother was a* سَائِبَة; (Fr, Ṣ, Mgh, Mṣb, Ḳ;) i. e., *of which the mother had brought forth ten females consecutively before her, and of which the ear was slit;* (Mgh;) or *of which the mother had brought forth five, of which five the last, if a male, was slaughtered and eaten, but if a female, her ear was slit and she was left with her mother;* (Mgh,* Mṣb;) *the predicament of which was the same as that of her mother;* (Fr, Ṣ, Ḳ;) i. e., *what was unlawful with respect to her mother was unlawful with respect to herself:* (TA:) or *a she-camel,* or *ewe,* or *she-goat, that had brought forth five young ones, and of which the fifth, if a male, was slaughtered, and its flesh was eaten by the men and women; but if a female, her ear was slit, and it was unlawful to the Arabs to eat her flesh and to drink her milk and to ride her; but when she died, her flesh was lawful to the women:* (Ḳ:) so says Az, on the authority of Ibn-'Arafeh: (TA: [but it appears from the explanation in the Mṣb, quoted above, that it was the slit-eared young she-camel here mentioned, not the mother, that was thus termed:]) or *a she-camel,* or *ewe,* or *she-goat, which, having brought forth ten young ones, had her ear slit,* (Ḳ,) *and no use was made of her milk nor of her back,* (TA,) *and she was left at liberty to pasture,* (Ḳ,) *and to go to water,* (TA,) *and her flesh, when she died, was made unlawful to the women of the Arabs, but was eaten by the men:* (Ḳ:) or *one that was left at liberty, without a pastor:* (Ḳ:) or, as some say, *syn. with* سَائِبَة; i. e., say they, *a she-camel which, having brought forth seven young ones, had her ear slit, and was not ridden, nor used for carrying:* (Mṣb:) or *a she-camel that had brought forth five young ones, the last of which was a male, in which case her ear was slit, and she was exempted from being ridden and from carrying and from being slaughtered, and not prevented from taking of any water to which she came, nor from any pasturage, nor even ridden by a weary man who, having become unable to proceed in his journey, his means having failed him, or his camel that bore him stopping with him from fatigue or breaking down or perishing, might chance to find her:* (Aboo-Is-ḥáḳ the Grammarian, TA: [and the like, but less fully, is said in the Mgh:]) or, applied specially to a ewe, or she-goat, *one that, having brought forth five young ones, had her ear slit:* (L, Ḳ, TA: [in the CḲ, for بُحِرَتْ is put نُحِرَتْ:]) it also signifies a she-camel (L) *abounding in milk:* (L, Ḳ:) the pl. is بَحَائِرُ and بُحُرٌ; (L, Ḳ;) the latter a strange form of pl. of a fem. sing. such as بحيرة; and said to be the only instance of the kind except صُرُمٌ pl. of صَرِيمَةٌ, meaning "having her ear cut off." (TA.) It is said in a trad., that the person who instituted the practices relative to the بحيرة and the حَامِى, and the first who altered the religion of Ishmael, was 'Amr the son of Loḥei the son of Ḳama'ah the son of Jundab; and these practices are forbidden in the Ḳur v. 102. (TA.)

بُحَيْرَةٌ *A small sea; a lake:* as though they imagined the word بَحْرَةٌ [as syn. with بَحْرٌ]: otherwise there is no reason for the ة. (M, TA.) — See also بَحْرٌ: and see بَحْرَةٌ, in two places.

بَحَّارٌ: } see بَحْرِىٌّ.
بَحَّارَةٌ: }

بَاحِرٌ: } see بَحْرَانِىٌّ, in three places.
بَاحِرِىٌّ: }

بَاحُورٌ and ↓ بَاحُورَآءُ The *vehemence of heat in* [*the Syrian month of*] تَمُّوز or تَمُوز [corresponding to *July, O. S.*]: (Ṣ, Ḳ:) [pl. of the former بَوَاحِيرُ:] both are [said to be] post-classical words: (Ṣ:) but they are [classical words,] arabicized; for they occur in verses of the kind called رَجَز of some of the [early] Arabs. (MF.) = البَاحُورُ *The moon.* (Aboo-'Alee, Ḳ.)

بَاحُورَآءُ: see بَاحُورٌ.

بَاحُورِىٌّ: see بُحْرَانٌ.

أُبَيْحِرٌ: dim. of أَبْحَرُ, q. v. (Ḳ.)

بخ

R. Q. 1. بَخْبَخَ, (Ṣ, Ḳ,) inf. n. بَخْبَخَةٌ and بِخْبَاخٌ, (TA,) [a verb imitative of the sound which it signifies,] *He* (a camel [in a state of excitement]) *brayed*, (Ṣ, Ḳ,) *so that his* شِقْشِقَة [or *faucial bag*] *filled his mouth*: (Ṣ:) or, as some say, *began to bray*. (TA.) — [Hence, perhaps,] *He* (a man) *said* [بَخٍ] or بَخٍ بَخٍ [&c.]. (TA, and Ḥar p. 556.) — And [hence,] بَخْبَخَ بِصُحْبَتِى *He rejoiced in my company*. (Ḥar ubi suprà.) — And بَخْبَخَ الرَّجُلَ *He said* بَخٍ or بَخٍ بَخٍ &c. *to the man*. (Ṣ.)

بَخٍ, (Ṣ, A, Ḳ, &c.,) [in some copies of the Ḳ written بَخَّ, which is wrong, for it is] like بَلْ, (A,) [i. e.] like قَدْ, (TA,) [perhaps, as I have suggested above, from the sound made by a he-camel in a state of excitement,] a word used on the occasion of praising; (Ṣ, A;) on praising one from whom has proceeded a good and wonderful action; (Ḥar p. 142;) on approving a thing; (T, Ṣ, Mṣb, Ḳ;) on being pleased with it, or having one's admiration excited by it; (A, Ḳ;) or on the occasion of glorying and of praising; (Ḳ;) in pronouncing a thing great in estimation, (IAmb,) or excellent; (AHeyth;) in deeming a thing great in estimation, (AḤei,) or good; (Mgh;) or it means wonder, or admiration; (R;) and sometimes it is used [ironically] to denote disapproval; also, as an exhortation to gentleness with a thing, and to taking extraordinary pains; (TA;) and in a case of expertness, or skilfulness: (AḤei:) it means نِعْمَ الفِعْلُ and نِعْمَ الرَّجُلُ [*Excellent*, or *most excellent, is the man!* and, *the deed!*]; (Ḥar p. 142;) [or simply, *excellent!* or *most excellent! how good! how goodly! well done! bravo!* and the like;] or عَظُمَ الأَمْرُ and فَخُمَ [*great in estimation is the thing*, or *affair*, or *event*, or *case!*]: (Ḳ:) MF observes, [probably from finding بَخَّ in the place of بَخٍ in his copy or copies of the Ḳ,] that this explanation is like an express assertion that it is a verb in the pret. tense, which requires consideration. (TA.) It is used alone; and in this case you say, بَخْ, (Ḳ,) and بَخِ, (Mṣb, Ḳ,) with kesr for its invariable termination, (Mṣb,) and بَخٍ, and بَخٌ; (Ḳ, TA; [but in the CḲ, in the place of بَخٍ and بَخٌ, we find بَخٍّ;]) without teshdeed, (T, Mṣb,) in most cases; (Mṣb;) but also with teshdeed, (T, Ṣ, A,) like a noun; so that one says, بَخٍ لَكَ and بَخٍّ [&c., meaning I say *excellent!* &c., *to thee*]: (Ṣ:) and one repeats it, (Ṣ, A, Ḳ, &c.,) for the sake of emphasis; (Ṣ, A;) saying, بَخْ بَخْ, (IAmb, Ṣ, A, Ḳ, &c.,) with the خ quiescent like the ل in هَلْ and بَلْ, (IAmb,) and بَخٍ بَخٍ, (Ṣ, A, R, Ḳ,) pronounced in the latter manner, with tenween, when in connexion with a following word, [and in this case only, whereas it is pronounced in the former manner in any case,] (Ṣ, A,) and بَخٍّ بَخٍّ, (Ṣ,* A,* R, Ḳ,) and بَخٍ بَخٍ, (Ḳ,) and بَخٌ بَخٌ. (R.)

جَمَلٌ بَخْبَاخُ الهَدِيرِ *A camel that fills his mouth with his* شِقْشِقَة [or *faucial bag*] *when he brays*. (Ṣ.)

إِبِلٌ مُبَخْبَخَةٌ *Camels to which one says* بَخْ بَخْ; being pleased with them: (ISd, TA:) or *large-bellied camels*; (Ḳ;) as also مُخَبْخَبَةٌ, which is formed from the former by transposition; from بَخْ بَخْ, or بَخٍ بَخٍ, which is said by the Arabs in praising a thing; as though, by reason of their greatness, the people, seeing them, said, How goodly are they! (TA.)

بخت

1. بَخَتَهُ *He beat, struck*, or *smote, him*; (JK, Ḳ;) namely, a man. (JK.) [See also بَكَتَهُ.]

2. تَبْخِيتٌ [inf. n. of بَخَّتَهُ] The *overcoming* another *with an argument* or *the like*; or *reducing* him *to silence, through inability to reply*; i. q. تَبْكِيتٌ: and the *addressing* an adversary in a dispute or litigation *with speech so as to put a stop to his plea*, or *allegation*: from the author of the Tekmileh. (Mgh.) — Also, as a term of the theologians, The *believing at first view, without consideration of a thing*: so in صَلَّى عَلَى التَّبْخِيتِ [*he prayed according to the belief which he formed at first view, without consideration*]; said of a person when the ḳibleh is doubtful, and he cannot work out a solution of the difficulty. (Mgh.)

Q. Q. 2. تَبَخْتَى: see تَبَخْتَرَ.

بَخْتٌ *Fortune*; or particularly *good fortune*; syn. جَدٌّ, (Ṣ, A, Ḳ,) and حَظٌّ: (Mṣb, TA:) a foreign, or Persian, word, (Mṣb,) arabicized: (Ṣ, Ḳ:) or post-classical: accord. to the 'Ináyeh, not a chaste Arabic word: but in the Shifá el-Ghaleel said to have been used by the Arabs in ancient times; and the like is said in the L: Az says, "I know not if it be Arabic or not." (TA.)

بُخْتٌ [a coll. gen. n.] *A species of camels*; (Ṣ,* Mṣb;) the *Khurásánee* [or *Bactrian*] *camels*; (Ḳ;) *begot between an Arabian she-camel and a* فَالِج [which is a *large two-humped camel brought from Es-Sind for the purpose of covering*]; (TA;) *long-necked*; (Nh;) [*large and strong*, accord. to Ibn-Maaroof; *and two-humped*, accord. to Leo Africanus: the Mauritanian Arabs call thus all camels promiscuously; but accord. to the more common use of the word are to be understood *hairy camels, fit for winter-work; generally of Turkumán or Bactrian breed*; distinct from the Arabian, which are accustomed to bear burdens in winter and summer: (Golius:)] they are also called ▼بُخْتِيَّةٌ: (Ḳ:) n. un. ▼بُخْتِىٌّ; (Ṣ, Mṣb;) fem. ▼بُخْتِيَّةٌ: (Ṣ:) pl. بَخَاتِىُّ, (Ṣ, Mṣb, Ḳ,) imperfectly decl., (Ṣ,) and بَخَاتِى (Ḳ, TA [in the CḲ بَخَاتِي]) and بَخَاتٌ, (Ḳ,) and you may say [with the article] البَخَاتِى, without tenween: (Ṣ, Mṣb:) it is a foreign, or Persian, word, (TA,) arabicized: but some say, it is Arabic: (Ṣ, TA:) some hesitate as to its being Arabic because بَخْتٌ, meaning حَظٌّ, is not. (Mṣb.)

بُخْتِىٌّ and بُخْتِيَّةٌ: see بُخْتٌ; for the latter, in two places.

بَخِيتٌ, not thought by IDrd to be a chaste word, (TA,) *Fortunate*; *possessed of good fortune*; (A, Ḳ, TA;) as also ▼مَبْخُوتٌ. (Ṣ, A, Ḳ.)

بَخَّاتٌ One *who acquires, as his permanent property, camels such as are termed* بُخْتٌ: (Ḳ:) and one *who makes use of such camels*. (TA.)

بَخِيتٌ : see مَبْخُوتٌ.

بختر

Q. 1. بَخْتَرَ: see what next follows.

Q. 2. تَبَخْتَرَ, (L,) inf. n. تَبَخْتُرٌ; (JK, Ṣ, L, Ḳ;) and ▼بَخْتَرَ, (L,) inf. n. بَخْتَرَةٌ; (L, Ḳ;) *He walked in a certain manner*; (Ṣ;) *with an elegant gait*; (JK, Ḳ;) *with an elegant and a proud and self-conceited gait*, (L, TA, TḲ,) *with an affected inclining of the body from side to side*; (TḲ;) or *with a twisting of the back*, (Fr, in TA, voce تَمَطَّطَ, and Bd in lxxv. 33,) *and with extended steps*. (Bd ibid.) You say also, فُلَانٌ يَتَبَخْتَرُ فِى مِشْيَتِهِ and يَتَبَخْتَى [*Such a one carries himself in an elegant and a proud and self-conceited manner, with an affected inclining of his body from side to side, in his gait; or with a twisting of his back, and with extended steps*]. (L.)

بَخْتَرِىٌّ and ▼بَخْتِيرٌ *Elegant*, or *beautiful, in gait and in body*; (L, Ḳ: in [some of] the copies of the Ḳ, instead of وَالجِسْمِ, is erroneously put وَالجَسِيمُ: TA:) applied to a man: (L:) or (so accord. to the L and TA, but in the Ḳ "and") *proud and self-conceited*: (L, Ḳ:) or *who walks in the manner termed* تَبَخْتُرٌ [see Q. 2]: (JK, L:) the former epithet is also applied to a camel: (L:) the fem. of the former is with ة. (JK, L.)

بَخْتَرِىٌّ a subst. signifying The *gait denoted by* التَّبَخْتُرُ [inf. n. of Q. 2]: (JK:) [and so ▼بَخْتَرِيَّةٌ: whence the phrase] فُلَانٌ يَمْشِى البَخْتَرِيَّةَ *Such a one walks in the manner termed* تَبَخْتُرٌ. (Ṣ, L.)

بَخْتَرِيَّةٌ: see what next precedes.

بَخْتِيرٌ: see بَخْتَرِىٌّ.

بخر

1. بَخَرَتِ القِدْرُ, (Mṣb, Ḳ,) aor. ـَ, (Mṣb,) or ـُ, (Ḳ,) inf. n. بَخْرٌ (Mṣb, Ḳ) and بُخَارٌ, (TA,) *The cooking-pot sent up fume, vapour, steam*, or *an exhalation*. (Mṣb, Ḳ.*) — بَخِرَ, (Ṣ, Ḳ,) aor. ـَ, (Ḳ,) inf. n. بَخَرٌ, (TA,) *He had a stinking mouth* [or *breath*; *he exhaled a stinking*, or *fetid, odour from his mouth*]. (Ṣ, L, Ḳ.) You say, بَخِرَتْ عَلَيْنَا *She exhaled a stinking*, or *fetid, odour upon us from her mouth*. (A. [But in my copy of that work, and in the TA, it is erroneously written بَخَرَتْ.]) And بَخِرَ الفَمُ, aor. and inf. n. as above, *The mouth stank*; *exhaled a stinking*, or *fetid, odour*. (Mṣb.) [See بَخَرٌ, below.]

2. بخّرت *She perfumed* [or rather *fumigated* her own or another's person or clothes &c. with بَخُور]. (A.)

4. ابخرهُ *It* (a thing) *caused him to have a stinking mouth* [or *breath*]. (Ḳ,* TA.)

5. تبخّر (Ṣ, Ḳ, &c.) *He fumigated himself* with perfume or the like; (TA;) with بَخُور. (Ṣ, A,

Ḳ.) One says, فُلَانٌ يَتَبَخَّرُ وَيَتَبَخْتَرُ [*Such a one fumigates himself* with perfume, *and walks with an elegant and a proud and self-conceited gait, with an affected inclining of his body from side to side*]. (A.)

بَخْرٌ *Stench,* or *fetor, of the mouth* [or *breath*] (Ṣ, A, Ḳ) &c.: (AḤn, Ḳ:) and *any odour that rises and diffuses itself,* (Ḳ, TA,) *whether stinking or not;* as also ▼ بُخَارٌ. (TA.)

بُخَارٌ [*Fume, vapour, steam,* or *exhalation;*] *what rises from water, like smoke;* (Ṣ;) *any fume* (Ḳ, TA) *that rises and diffuses itself* (TA) *from what is hot,* (Ḳ, TA,) or *from hot water;* (TA;) *anything that rises and diffuses itself from hot water* or *from damp earth:* pl. أَبْخِرَةٌ and بُخَارَاتٌ. (Mṣb.) — Also The *stench* of a noiseless emission of wind from the anus. (TA.) — See also بَخْرٌ.

بَخُورٌ *Incense,* or *a substance for fumigation;* syn. دُخْنَةٌ; (Mṣb;) *that with which one fumigates himself:* (Ṣ, A, Mṣb, Ḳ:) *aloes-wood used for that purpose.* (TA in art. قتر.) — بَخُورُ مَرْيَمَ [*Arthanita,* or *sow-bread; the common cyclamen;* also called الوَلْفُ; the latter name, accord. to Golius, on the authority of Zeyn El-'Aṭṭár, given to it by the Syrians;] *a certain plant,* (Ḳ,) *originally called* عَرْطَنِيثَا; *hot; dry;* (TA;) *having the property of clearing the complexion,* or *skin; aperient; diuretic;* (Ḳ;) *laxative;* (TA;) *and very useful:* (Ḳ:) it is a laxative when used in the form of a suppository, or applied as a liniment below the navel. (TA.)

أَبْخَرُ *Having a stinking mouth* [or *breath*]: (Ṣ, Mṣb, Ḳ:) fem. بَخْرَآءُ: and pl. بُخْرٌ. (Mṣb.)

مَبْخَرَةٌ *A thing that occasions one's knowing,* or *inferring,* or *suspecting, stench,* or *fetor, of the mouth* [or *breath; a cause of stench,* or *fetor, of the mouth* or *breath*]: such is said to be the sleeping between daybreak and sunrise, or in the first part of the day. (TA.)

مِبْخَرَةٌ *A vessel for fumigation; a censer;* syn. مِجْمَرَةٌ [q. v.: pl. مَبَاخِرُ]. (Mṣb in art. جمر.)

مُبَخَّرٌ A garment *perfumed* [or rather *fumigated* with perfume]. (A.)

مَبْخُورٌ [*Affected by the fumes of wine* &c.; or] *affected with pain and headache occasioned by wine,* or *with the remains of intoxication.* (IAạr, Ḳ.)

بخس

1. بَخَسَهُ, aor. ـَ, inf. n. بَخْسٌ, *He diminished it; lessened it; made it deficient,* or *defective:* (Ṣ, A, Mṣb, Ḳ:) or *he made it faulty.* (Mṣb.) You say, بَخَسَ الكَيَّالُ الكَيْلَ [for *The measurer made defective measure*]. (A.) And of a just sale, لَا بَخْسَ فِيهِ وَلَا شَطَطَ, (Ṣ,) or وَلَا شُطُوطَ, (T, TA,) [*There is no deficiency in it nor excess.*] And it is said in the Ḳur [lxxii. 13], فَلَا يَخَافُ بَخْسًا وَلَا رَهَقًا *He shall not fear diminution* of the reward of his actions, *nor wrong,* or *injustice.* (TA.) And in this sense, [as also in the next,] the verb is doubly trans. (Mṣb.) You say, بَخَسَهُ حَقَّهُ *He diminished to him his right,* or *due; deprived him,* or *defrauded him, of a part of it.* (Ṣ, A.) And it is said in the Ḳur [vii. 83 and xi. 86 and xxvi. 183], وَلَا تَبْخَسُوا النَّاسَ أَشْيَآءَهُمْ [*And ye shall not diminish unto men their things*]: (Mṣb:) or the verb in this instance has the signification next following. (TA.) — *He wronged him; acted wrongfully,* or *unjustly, towards him.* (A, Ḳ.) = بَخَسَ عَيْنَهُ: see بَخَصَ.

6. تباخسوا *They defrauded one another in a sale.* (Ḳ.)

بَخْسٌ *Deficient; defective.* (Ṣ.) It is said in the Ḳur [xii. 20], وَشَرَوْهُ بِثَمَنٍ بَخْسٍ *And they sold him for a deficient,* or *defective, price:* (Ṣ,* Mṣb,* TA:) or *for a price less than was incumbent:* or *for an insufficient price:* or *for an unjust price;* accord. to Zj; because the sale of a man that has been found is unlawful. (TA.) = *Land that produces herbage without being* [*artificially*] *watered:* (JK, Ṣ, Ḳ:) or *land which is watered by the rain;* because it has deficient watering: (Mgh:) pl. بُخُوسٌ. (JK, TA.) — Also, (TA, as from Ibn-Málik,) or ▼ بَخْسِىٌّ, [which is more probably the correct form,] a rel. n. from بَخْسٌ in the sense immediately preceding, explained in the T as signifying, (Mgh,) Seed-produce *that is not irrigated with water from a spring or well or the like, but only by the rain.* (Mgh, and TA from Ibn-Málik.)

بَخْسِىٌّ: see بَخْسٌ.

بَاخِسٌ Any one *who acts wrongfully,* or *unjustly.* (TA.) It is said in a prov., تَحْسِبُهَا حَمْقَآءَ وَهِىَ بَاخِسٌ; (Ṣ, A, Ḳ;) so runs the prov.; but accord. to Th, (Ṣ,) you may also say بَاخِسَةٌ; (Ṣ, Ḳ;) i. e., [*Thou thinkest her stupid,*] *but she is wrongful,* or *unjust:* applied to him who feigns himself to be of weak understanding when he is crafty and cunning. (Ḳ, TA.) The origin of the prov. was this: a man of the Benu-l-'Ambar, of Temeem, mixed his property with that of a woman, coveting the possession of it, and thinking that she was stupid, and that she did not take care of her property nor know it: then he made a division with her, after he had mixed; but she was not content with the division until she took her property: she complained of him to those in authority, so that he released himself from her by giving her what she desired of the property: and the man was reproved for his conduct; it being said to him, "Thou cheatest a woman: is not this wrongful conduct (بَخْس)?" whereupon he replied in the words above, which became a proverb. (Th, Ḳ,* TA.)

بخص

1. بَخَصَ عَيْنَهُ, (Ṣ, A, Mgh, Mṣb, Ḳ, &c.,) aor. ـَ, (Ṣ, Mgh, Ḳ,) inf. n. بَخْصٌ, (Ṣ, Mgh,) *He put out his eye;* syn. فَقَأَهَا, (Mgh,) and عَوَّرَهَا: (A, Mgh:) or *he pulled out his eye* [*altogether,* i. e.,] *with its bulb:* (Ṣ, Ḳ: [in the former, مَعَ شَحْمَتِهَا: in the latter, not so well, بِشَحْمِهَا:]) or *he put his finger into his eye:* (Mṣb:) Yaạḳoob says that you should not say بَخَسَ; (Ṣ;) and so says ISk: (TA in art. بخس:) but accord. to Aṣ, as related by Aboo-Turáb, you say بَخَصَ عَيْنَهُ and بَخَزَهَا and بَخَسَهَا, all as meaning *he put out his eye;* syn. فَقَأَهَا: (TA:) and IAạr says that بَخَسَهَا and بَخَصَهَا signify alike: (Mṣb:) the former of these two is a dial. var. of the latter; (TA in art. بخس;) and signifies *he put it out* (فَقَأَهَا) *with his finger* or *some other thing:* (Lth, Aṣ, and Ḳ in art. بخس:) but بَخَصَ is the better word. (Lḥ, IAạr, Mṣb.)

بخع

1. بَخَعَ الذَّبِيحَةَ, (Z, in the Fáïḳ,) or الشَّاةَ, (Z, in the A,) or بِالشَّاةِ, (O, Ḳ,) [aor. ـَ, inf. n. بَخْعٌ,] *He slaughtered the beast for slaughter,* or *the sheep* or *goat, with much,* or *extraordinary, effectiveness,* or *energy,* (Z, Ḳ,) *so that he reached the back of the neck,* (Z, in the A,) or *so that he reached the* بِخَاع, (Ḳ, TA, [in the CḲ نُخَاع,]) *cutting the bone of the neck.* (TA.) This is the primary signification; and hence the verb is used to denote the doing anything to a great extent, in a great degree, egregiously, or with much or extraordinary effectiveness or energy or the like. (Z, Ḳ.) — [Hence you say,] بَخَعَ نَفْسَهُ, (Ṣ, Mṣb, Ḳ,) aor. ـَ, (Mṣb, Ḳ,) inf. n. بَخْعٌ (Ṣ, Mṣb) and بُخُوعٌ, (TA,) ‡ *He killed himself with grief,* (Ṣ, Mṣb, Ḳ, TA,) or *with wrath,* or *rage.* (Mṣb, TA.) — And بَالَغُوا فِى بَخْعِ أَنْفُسِهِمْ ‡ *They exceeded the ordinary bounds in subduing and abasing themselves by obedience.* (TA.) — And بَخَعْتُ لَكَ نَفْسِى وَنُصْحِى, aor. ـَ, inf. n. بُخُوعٌ, ‡ *I exerted for thee myself and my good advice,* or *counsel, laboriously, earnestly,* or *with energy:* (TA:) and بَخَعَ لَهُ نُصْحَهُ, (Ḳ, TA,) inf. n. بَخْعٌ, (TA,) ‡ *He acted sincerely towards him, and took extraordinary pains, in giving him good advice,* or *counsel.* (Ḳ, TA.) — And بَخَعَ لَهُ بِالحَقِّ, (Ṣ,* Ḳ,* TA,) inf. n. بُخُوعٌ; and بَخِعَ, inf. n. بُخُوعٌ and بَخَاعَةٌ; ‡ *He confessed,* or *acknowledged, to him the right,* or *due, and humbled himself to him:* (Ṣ, Ḳ, TA:) or you say, بَخَعَنِى بِالحَقِّ, inf. n. بُخُوعٌ, meaning † *he submitted himself to me, and gave the right,* or *due, freely:* (Mṣb:) and بَخَعْتُ لَهُ † *I became submissive and obedient, and made confession,* or *acknowledgment, to him:* or, accord. to the A, بَخَعَ signifies ‡ *he made confession,* or *acknowledgment, with the utmost submissiveness.* (TA.) — And بَخَعَ فُلَانًا خَبَرَهُ ‡ *He related his information,* or *news, truly to such a one.* (Ḳ.) — Also, بَخَعَ الرَّكِيَّةَ, aor. ـَ, inf. n. بَخْعٌ, † *He dug the well until its water appeared.* (Ks, Ḳ.) — And hence the saying of 'Áïsheh, speaking of 'Omar, بَخَعَ الأَرْضَ فَقَاءَتْ أُكُلَهَا, meaning † *He subdued and abased the people of the earth,* [*so that it disclosed*] and he drew forth *the treasures that it contained,* and *the possessions of the kings.* (TA.) And بَخَعَ الأَرْضَ بِالزِّرَاعَةِ, (Ḳ,) inf. n. بَخْعٌ, (TA,) ‡ *He exhausted the strength of the land by sowing,*

tilling it continuously, and not giving it rest for a year. (Ḳ, TA.)

البِخَاعُ *A certain vein, or nerve,* (عِرْق,) *in the* صُلْب [or *back-bone*], (Z in the Fáïḳ and Ksh, and Ḳ,) *lying within the* قَفَا [or *back of the neck*]; (Z in the Ksh, and TA;) Bḍ says, *lying within the* فَقَار [or *vertebræ*]; but it is said that this is a mistranscription, and that the right reading is the قفا, as in the Ksh; and it is said in the Ḳ to be *running into the bone* [or, as in the CḲ, *bones,*] *of the neck*; but this is a mistake: (TA:) accord. to an assertion of Z, (Ḳ,) in his Fáïḳ and Ksh, (TA,) it is different from the نُخَاع, with ن, which is the white cord in the interior of the bone of the neck, extending to the back-bone: but IAth says, I have searched long in lexicons, and in books of medicine and anatomy, but have not found البخاع, with ب, mentioned in any of them. (TA.)

فَلَعَلَّكَ بَاخِعٌ نَفْسَكَ, in the Ḳur [xviii. 5], (Ṣ,) means ‡ *And may-be thou wilt kill thyself* (Ṣ, Ḳ) *with grief,* (Ṣ,) being beyond measure eager for their becoming Muslims. (Ḳ, TA.) These words imply an incitement to abstain from regret. (B.)

أَبْخَعُ [*More, and most, effectual to kill,* and *destroy*]. (Ḳ voce أَمْنَعُ, q. v.) — هُمْ أَبْخَعُ طَاعَةً ‡ *They are more sincere and more energetic in obedience* than others; as though they exceeded the ordinary bounds in subduing and abasing themselves by obedience. (TA, from a trad.)

بخق

1. بَخِقَ, aor. ـَ; and بَخَقَ, aor. ـُ; *He had that affection of an eye which is termed* بَخَق, explained below. (Ḳ.) [And,] accord. to ISd, بَخِقَتْ عَيْنُهُ, and بَخَقَتْ, *His eye went away;* or *perished:* and i. q. عَارَتْ [*his eye became blind;* or *became wanting;* or *sank in its socket*]: the more approved form is [بَخِقَتْ,] with fet-ḥ [to the medial radical]: and it is also explained as meaning فُقِئَتْ [*it was put out;* or *was blinded;* &c.]: (TA:) or, accord. to the Mj, بَخِقَتِ العَيْنُ signifies *the flesh* [app. meaning *the bulb,* which is also termed the شَحْمَة,] *of the eye disappeared:* and the epithet applied to the eye in this case is ▼ بَخْقَآءُ. (Mgh.) ═ بَخَقَ عَيْنَهُ, aor. ـَ, (Ṣ, Ḳ,) inf. n. بَخْقٌ, (Ṣ,) i. q. عَوَّرَهَا [*He put out his eye;* or *made it to sink in its socket*]; (Lth, Ṣ, Ḳ;) as also ▼ أَبْخَقَهَا: (TA:) or the former, (Mgh,) and ▼ the latter, (AA, Ḳ, TA,) i. q. فَقَأَهَا [*he put it out;* or *blinded it;* &c.]. (AA, Mgh, Ḳ.)

4: see 1, in two places: ═ and see also 7.

7. اِنْبَخَقَتِ العَيْنُ, so in the Moheet; accord. to the Ḳ, ▼ أَبْخَقَتْ, but this is wrong; i. q. نَدَرَتْ [*The eye fell out from its place;* or *became displaced*]; as in the Ḳ. (TA.)

بَخَقٌ [app. inf. n. of بَخِقَ: and, as a simple subst.,] The *worst,* or *most unseemly, kind of* عَوَر [or *blindness of one eye,* or *loss thereof,* &c.], *and that in which there is most* [*of the foul matter termed*] غَمَص: [in the CḲ, for أَكْثَرُهُ غَمَصًا, is erroneously put أَكْثَرُهُ غَمْضًا; and so I find in the JK:] or the *state in which the edge of one's eyelid* (شُفْرُ عَيْنِهِ [in the CḲ شُفُرُ عَيْنَيْه]) *will not meet the black,* or *part surrounded by the white:* (Lth, Ḳ:) or *blindness of one eye* (عَوَر) *by the disappearance, in the head, of the black,* or *part surrounded by the white:* (Ṣ:) or the *disappearance of that part of the eye, in the head, after blindness of the eye:* (Sh, TA:) or the *having the sight gone, but the eye remaining open, blind,* or *white and blind, but still whole.* (IAạr, TA.)

بَخِيقٌ, and with ة: see أَبْخَقُ, in three places.

بَاخِقُ العَيْنِ: and عَيْنٌ بَاخِقَةٌ: see أَبْخَقُ, in two places.

رَجُلٌ أَبْخَقُ and ▼ بَخِيقٌ and ▼ بَاخِقُ العَيْنِ and ▼ مَبْخُوقُ العَيْنِ all signify the same; (Ḳ;) i. e. *A man blind of one eye;* or *wanting one eye;* or *having one of his eyes sunk in its socket;* or *having one of his eyes dried up;* syn. أَعْوَرُ: (TA:) [or *having that affection of an eye which is termed* بَخَق:] and in like manner بَخْقَآءُ applied to a sheep or goat for sacrifice on the occasion of the pilgrimage signifies عَوْرَآءُ [*blind of one eye;* &c.]; (Mgh, TA;) or, as some say, *having an eye of which the black,* or *part surrounded by the white, has disappeared in the head.* (Mgh.) And عَيْنٌ بَخْقَآءُ and ▼ بَخِيقَةٌ and ▼ بَخِيقٌ and ▼ بَاخِقَةٌ i. q. عَوْرَآءُ [*An eye that is blind;* &c.]: (Ḳ:) see also 1.

مَبْخُوقُ العَيْنِ: see أَبْخَقُ.

بخل

1. بَخِلَ, (JK, Ṣ, Mṣb, Ḳ,) aor. ـَ, inf. n. بَخَلٌ; (JK, Mṣb, Ḳ;) and بَخُلَ, aor. ـُ, inf. n. بُخْلٌ; (Mṣb, Ḳ;) *He was, or became, niggardly, tenacious, stingy, penurious,* or *avaricious:* see بُخْل, below. (Ḳ, TA.) You say, بَخِلَ بِكَذَا, (Ṣ, TA,) and بَخِلَ بِهِ, *He was, or became, niggardly,* &c., *of such a thing.* (TA.) And بَخِلَ عَنْهُ [*He withheld, with niggardliness, from him*]: and بَخِلَ عَلَيْهِ [*he was niggardly to him*]. (Bḍ and Jel in xlvii. last verse.)

2. بَخَّلَهُ, (Ṣ, Ḳ,) inf. n. تَبْخِيلٌ, (Ḳ,) *He attributed,* or *imputed, to him* بُخْل [or *niggardliness,* &c.]: (Ṣ:) or *he accused him thereof:* (Ḳ:) or *he called him* بَخِيل [or *niggardly,* &c.]. (TA.)

4. ابخلهُ *He found him to be* بَخِيل [or *niggardly,* &c.]. (Ṣ, Mṣb, Ḳ.)

بَخْلٌ: see what next follows.

بُخْلٌ and ▼ بَخَلٌ, [both of which are properly inf. ns.,] (JK, Ṣ, Ḳ,) and ▼ بَخْلٌ, (Ks, Ṣ, Mṣb, Ḳ,) which is a simple subst., (Mṣb,) and ▼ بُخُلٌ (Ḳ) and ▼ بَخَلٌ and ▼ بُخْلٌ (TA) and ▼ بُخُولٌ, (Ḳ,) of all which, the first is that which commonly obtains, (TA,) are syn., (JK, Ṣ,) signifying *Niggardliness, tenaciousness, stinginess, penuriousness,* or *avarice;* contr. of كَرَمٌ (Ḳ, TA) and جُودٌ; and its definition is the *withholding of acquired articles of property from that wherefrom it is not lawful to withhold them:* (TA:) or the *debarring the asker,* or *beggar, from what one has that is superabundant:* (Mṣb:) and in the law, the *refusal of what is incumbent,* or *obligatory.* (Mṣb, TA.)

بُخُلٌ: see what next precedes.

بَخَلٌ: see بُخْلٌ: — and see also بَخِيلٌ.

بَخِلٌ: } see بُخْلٌ.
بُخُلٌ: }

بَخْلَةٌ *A single act,* or *instance, of* بُخْل [or *niggardliness* &c.]. (JK, TA.)

بَخَالٌ: see what next follows.

بَخِيلٌ (JK, Ṣ, Mṣb, Ḳ) and ▼ بَاخِلٌ (Ṣ, Mṣb, Ḳ) *Niggardly, tenacious, stingy, penurious,* or *avaricious;* (Ḳ;) i. e. ذُو بُخْلٍ; (Mṣb;) epithets from 1: (Ṣ, Mṣb:*) or one *from whom niggardliness is experienced much* or *often:* (TA: [app. in explanation of the former:]) and so ▼ بَخَلٌ, an inf. n. used as an epithet [and therefore implying more than the possession of the simple attribute of niggardliness &c., being a kind of personification]; (Abu-l-'Omeythil El-Aạrábee, Ḳ;) and ▼ بَخَّالٌ (Ṣ, Ḳ) and ▼ بَخَالٌ (Ḳ) and ▼ مُبَخَّلٌ (JK, Ḳ) i. e. شَدِيدُ البُخْلِ [*very,* or *vehemently, niggardly* &c.]: (Ṣ, TA:) pl. of the first, بُخَلَآءُ; (Mṣb, Ḳ;) and of the second, بُخَّلٌ (Ḳ) and بُخَّالٌ. (TA.)

بُخُولٌ: see بُخْلٌ.

بَخَّالٌ: } see بَخِيلٌ.
بَاخِلٌ: }

مَبْخَلَةٌ *A cause of,* or *a thing that incites to,* بُخْل [or *niggardliness* &c.]: (Ḳ:) a word of the same class as مَجْبَنَةٌ and مَهْلَكَةٌ and مَعْطَشَةٌ and مَفَازَةٌ &c. (TA.) So explained as occurring in the trad., (TA,) الوَلَدُ مَبْخَلَةٌ مَجْبَنَةٌ [*Children are a cause of niggardliness* and *a cause of cowardice*]; (Ṣ, TA;) because on account of them one loves property, and continuance of life. (Ṣ in art. جبن.)

مُبَخَّلٌ: see بَخِيلٌ.

بد

1. بَدَّ, aor. ـُ, inf. n. بَدٌّ: see 2. — بَدَّ رِجْلَيْهِ *He parted his legs,* or *straddled,* (Ṣ, M, Ḳ,) in the stocks, or otherwise. (M.) — بَدَّهُ, (M, Ḳ,) aor. and inf. n. as above, (M,) *He removed with it, withdrew with it, drew away with it,* [or *drew it away,* from its place,] (M, Ḳ,) namely, a thing. (M.) — *He made him* (namely, his companion, M) *to retire,* or *withdraw, far away;* and *to refrain, forbear,* or *abstain;* (M, Ḳ;) عَنِ الشَّىْءِ *from the thing.* (M.) — أَنَا أَبُدُّ بِكَ عَنْ ذٰلِكَ الأَمْرِ *I will defend thee from that thing,* or *event, by repelling it,* or *averting it, from thee.* (M, L.) — بُدَّ عَنْ دَبَرِ الدَّابَّةِ *It* (a felt cloth) *was cut,* or *slit, so as to be clear of the galls,* or *sores, on the back of the beast.* (M, TA.) ═ بَدَّ, (M,) second pers. بَدِدْتَ, (Ṣ, Ḳ,) aor. يَبَدُّ, (M,) inf. n. بَدَدٌ, (T, Ṣ, M, Ḳ,) *He* (a man) *was,* or *became,*

wide between the thighs, (ISk, T, Ṣ, M, Ḳ,) *by reason of abundance of flesh:* (ISk, Ṣ, M:) or *wide between the arms;* (Ḳ;) *having the arms far from the sides:* (M:) or *wide between the shoulder-joints:* (M:) or *large in make, having one part far from another.* (M, Ḳ.) — Also *He* (a quadruped, ISk, T, Ṣ, or a horse, M) *had his fore legs far apart:* (ISk, T, Ṣ, M:) or *he* (a horse) *had his fore legs far from his sides:* (Lth, T:) and *he* (a camel) *had his elbows far from his sides.* (T.) = بَدَّ قَتَبَهُ, aor. ُ, *He furnished his camel's saddle with what are called* بِدَادَانِ *and* بَدِيدَانِ. (Ṣ.) [See بِدَادٌ.]

2. بدّد, inf. n. تَبْدِيدٌ, *He separated, disunited, dispersed,* or *dissipated;* (Ṣ, M, A, Mgh, L, Ḳ;) as also ▼بَدَّ, aor. ُ, inf. n. بَدٌّ: (Ṣ, L:) or the latter has this meaning, and the former signifies *he separated, disunited, dispersed,* or *dissipated, much.* (Mṣb.) — *He* (a man) *gave his equal share of the expenses for a journey.* (IAạr, T.) [See also 3.] = *He* (a man) *was,* or *became, weary, tired,* or *fatigued:* (IAạr, T, M, Ḳ:) or *he drowsed,* or *slumbered, while sitting, without sleeping.* (Ḳ.)

3. بَادَّ القَوْمُ, (T, Ḳ,) inf. n. مُبَادَّةٌ (M, Ḳ) and بِدَادٌ, (T, M, Ḳ,) with which the subst. ▼بَدَادٌ is syn., (M, and mentioned also in a MS. copy of the Ḳ, and in the CḲ, and in the TA, but not as from the Ḳ,) as also ▼بَدَادَةٌ, (TA, as from the Ḳ, but not in the CḲ nor in my MS. copy of the Ḳ,) *The people,* or *company of men, contributed what was necessary to be expended* (*in a journey,* T, M, L), *each man giving something, and then collected the sum, and expended it among themselves.* (T, M, L, Ḳ.) In a copy of the Ḳ, for يُنْفِقُونَهُ, is erroneously put يُبْقُونَهُ. (TA. [In the CḲ, يَبْقُونَهُ.]) Accord. to IAạr, بِدَادٌ signifies The *contributing equally for the purchasing of corn,* or *food, to eat:* and also a people's *having money,* or *property, divided into lots,* or *portions, and distributed in shares among them:* (L:) [and] accord. to the same, the *dividing property among a people in shares.* (T. [See also 4.]) — Also, بَادَّهُ, (M, A, Ḳ,) or بَادَّهُ فِى البَيْعِ, (Ṣ,) inf. n. مُبَادَّةٌ, (Ṣ, A, Ḳ,) or مُبَادَدَةٌ, (TA,) and بِدَادٌ; (Ṣ, M, A, Ḳ;) and so ▼بَايَعَهُ بَدَدًا, (Ṣ, M, Ḳ,) or مُبَادَّةً; (A;) *He bartered,* or *exchanged commodities, with him;* syn. عَارَضَهُ بِالبَيْعِ, (M, A,* L,) and بَاعَهُ مُعَارَضَةً: (Ṣ, Ḳ:) from the saying, هٰذَا بُدُّهُ, and بَدِيدُهُ, "this is the like of it:" (L:) from IAạr. (M.) — [See also بُدٌّ.]

4. ابدّ بَيْنَهُمُ العَطَآءَ, (Aṣ, T,) and ابدّ فِيهِمُ العَطَآءَ, (Ṣ, M, L, Ḳ,) and أَبَدَّهُمُ العَطَآءَ, (M, A, Mgh,) *He divided among them the gift, giving to each of them his lot,* or *share,* or *portion,* (Ṣ, M, A, Mgh, L, Ḳ,) *singly, not giving a portion to be shared by two:* (Aṣ, T, M,* Mgh, L:) said with respect to food and property and any other thing. (M.) You say, أَبْدَدْتُهُمُ المَالَ وَالطَّعَامَ *I divided among them, in shares, the property and the food.* (IAạr, T.) [Hence,] أَبِدِّيهِمْ تَمْرَةً تَمْرَةً (T, Ṣ, A, Mgh, from a trad.) [*Give thou to each of them a date;* or] *distribute thou among them to each a date:* (T:) said by Umm-Selemeh, (T, A, Mgh,) to a slave-girl, when beggars had become numerous. (A.) إِبْدَادٌ in relation to a gift signifies The *giving* [persons] *one by one;* and قِرَانٌ, the "giving two by two." (A'Obeyd, T.) [See also 3.] — يُبِدُّهُمْ is used by a poet, referring to a saying, and is explained by IAạr as meaning *It* (the saying) *shall be distributed among them* (يُفَرَّقُ فِيهِمْ); opposed to يَجْمَعُ [i. e. يَجْمَعُهُمْ; which shows that the former means *it shall be addressed to them one by one,* or *separately*]. (M, TA. [The author of the former adds, "I know not, in discourse, أَبْدَدْتُهُ as meaning فَرَّقْتُهُ:" but this is not what IAạr means.]) — أَبِدَّهُمَا نَعْجَتَيْنِ *Allot thou to them* (namely, two lambs,) *two ewes, to each lamb a ewe,* to suckle it: said when one ewe is not sufficient for both the lambs. (T,* Ṣ.) — ابدّ ضَبْعَيْهِ *He extended his upper arms, separating them from his sides,* in prostrating himself in prayer. (T, A, Mgh, L.) — ابدّ يَدَهُ إِلَى الأَرْضِ *He extended his arm,* or *hand, to the ground,* or *earth,* (T, Ṣ, Mgh, L,) as one does when he takes up something from it. (L.) — ابدّ نَظَرَهُ *He prolonged his look.* (T, L.) And ابدّهُ بَصَرَهُ (T, A, L) *He prolonged his look at him,* or *it;* as one does when he sees a thing that he dislikes. (T, L.)

5. تبدّد *It* (a thing, Ṣ, M, L, and a people, or company of men, T, L) *became separated, disunited, dispersed,* or *dissipated;* (T, Ṣ, M, L, Ḳ;) [as also ▼بَدْبَدَ, for its inf. n.] بَدْبَدَةٌ likewise signifies the *being separated, disunited,* &c. (AA, T.) = تبدّدوا شَيْئًا *They divided a thing among themselves in lots, shares,* or *portions,* (Ḳ,) *equally.* (TA.) — تبدّد صَدْرَ الجَارِيَةِ *It* (an ornament) *occupied the two sides,* (A,) or *the whole,* (Ḳ,) *of the bosom of the girl.* (A, Ḳ.) [See an ex. voce جَلِيفٌ.]

6. تبادّوا *They removed to a distance, one from another.* (Ḥam p. 823.) — *They went,* or *passed, two by two, each one of a pair removing,* or *withdrawing, with the other,* or *making the other to retire,* or *withdraw, far away.* (M.) — *They went forth into the field* [*of battle*], *one to another:* (A:) or *they took their adversaries,* or *opponents,* [*with whom to fight,*] (T, Ṣ, Ḳ,) *each man his man;* as also ▼لَقُوا بَدَادَهُمْ: (Ḳ:) or this latter signifies *they met their numbers, to each man a man.* (T, Ṣ.)

8. ابتدّاهُ بِالضَّرْبِ *They two took him on both sides of him,* (T, Ṣ, Ḳ,) or *came to him on both sides of him,* (Ḳ,) *with beating.* (T, Ṣ.) — السَّبُعَانِ يَبْتَدَّانِ الرَّجُلَ *The two wild beasts come upon both sides of the man.* (Ṣ, A.) — الرَّضِيعَانِ يَبْتَدَّانِ أُمَّهُمَا (T, Ṣ, A*) *The two sucklings suck their mother on either side, one from one breast and the other from the other breast.* (T, A,* TA.) You do not say, يَبْتَدُّهَا ٱبْنُهَا, but يَبْتَدُّهَا ٱبْنَاهَا. (T, Ṣ.)

10. استبدّ *He was,* or *became, alone; independent of others;* (Ṣ, M, L, Mṣb, Ḳ; in the first and last expl. by تَفَرَّدَ; and in the others, by إِنْفَرَدَ;) *exclusively of others;* (L;) *without any to share,* or *participate, with him;* or *he had none to share,* or *participate, with him:* (Mṣb:) بِهِ [*in it;* i. e. *he had it,* or *kept it, to himself, exclusively, with none to share with him in it*]: (Ḳ:) and بِكَذَا [*in such a thing*]: (Ṣ, L:) and بِرَأْيِهِ [*in his opinion;* i. e. *he followed his own opinion only, with none to agree with him;* or *he was singular in his opinion*]: (M, L:) and بِأَمْرٍ [*in a thing,* or *an affair*]: (L, Mṣb:) and بِأَمْرِهِ [*in his affair*]; meaning *he obtained* [*absolute*] *predominance,* or *control, over his affair, so that people would not hear* [or *obey*] *any other.* (A.) It is said in a trad., كُنَّا نَرَى أَنَّ لَنَا فِى هٰذَا الأَمْرِ حَقًّا فَٱسْتَبْدَدْتُمْ عَلَيْنَا [*We used to opine that we had a right* to act *in this affair, and ye have been alone* the actors, predominant *over us*]. (L.) And you say, استبدّ الأَمْرُ بِفُلَانٍ, meaning ‡ *The thing,* or *affair, overcame such a one, so that he could not manage it well,* or *thoroughly.* (A.)

R. Q. 1. بَدْبَدَ, inf. n. بَدْبَدَةٌ: see 5.

بُدٌّ as signifying *A separating oneself,* or *an artifice whereby one may avoid* a thing or *escape* from it, (MF,) or *an avoiding* a thing, (Mṣb,) is not used but in negative phrases, (Mṣb, MF,) except by post-classical writers. (MF.) You say, لَا بُدَّ مِنْ كَذَا (T, Ṣ, M, &c.) *There is no separating oneself from such a thing:* (AA, T, Ṣ, A, Ḳ:) or *there is no artifice whereby one may avoid it,* or *escape from it:* (M, Ḳ:) or *there is no avoiding it:* (Mṣb:) *it is absolutely necessary: it is not possible to separate oneself from it, nor is there anything that can serve in its stead.* (TA.) And مَا لَكَ مِنْهُ بُدٌّ [*Thou hast not any means,* or *way, of separating thyself from it,* or *avoiding it*]. (M, L.) And لَيْسَ لِهٰذَا الأَمْرِ بُدٌّ *There is no artifice for this affair.* (T.) [It is also said, with reference to the first of these phrases, that] بُدٌّ signifies *Amplitude;* from أَبَدُّ meaning "wide between the legs." (Ḥam p. 348.) = Also, (M, Ḳ,) and ▼بِدٌّ (M) and ▼بِدَادٌ (IAạr, T, M, Ḳ) and ▼بُدَادٌ, (Ḳ, TA,) or ▼بَدَادٌ, (CḲ,) and ▼بُدَّةٌ, (IAạr, T, M, Ḳ,) or ▼بِدَّةٌ, (Ṣ, A, IAth, and mentioned also in a copy of the Ḳ,) but J has been charged with error in writing it thus, (Ḳ,) by Ṣgh, (TA,) *A lot, share, portion,* or *set portion;* (T, Ṣ, M, A, IAth, Ḳ;) of anything: (M, Ḳ:) [or] the last signifies *a piece,* or *portion, separated, disunited,* or *dispersed:* (Ḥam p. 823:) the pl. of بِدَادٌ is بُدُدٌ; and of بُدَّةٌ, بُدَدٌ; (IAạr, T, M;) and of بِدَّةٌ, بِدَدٌ. (IAth, and Ḥam p. 823.) — Also the first, *A substitute; a thing given,* or *received,* or *put,* or *done, instead of, in the place of,* or *in exchange for, another thing; a compensation;* syn. عِوَضٌ: (Ṣ, L, TA:) it is said to have this signification. (Ṣ.) [In the copies of the Ḳ, البُعُوضُ is put in the place of العِوَضُ: but this is said in the TA to be a mistake.] = بُدٌّ is also an arabicized word, from بُتْ, (T, Ṣ, M, Ḳ, [in a copy of the M, بُتّ,]) which is Persian; (T, Ṣ;) meaning *An idol;* (IDrd, Ṣ, M, Ḳ;) pl. بِدَدَةٌ (Ṣ, Ḳ) and أَبْدَادٌ: (Ḳ:) and (or accord. to some,

TA) the *house of an idol*: (Ḳ:) or *a house in which are idols and images* or *pictures*. (M.)

بِدٌّ: see بُدٌّ. — Also, and ↓ بَدِيدٌ (T, Ḳ) and ↓ بَدِيدَةٌ, (Ḳ,) *A like; a fellow; an equal.* (T, Ḳ.) You say, هُوَ بِدُّهُ and ↓ بَدِيدُهُ *He, or it, is the like, &c., of him, or it.* (T.) And هُمَا بِدَّانِ *They two are likes, or fellows, or equals.* (TA.) And مَا أَنْتَ لِى بِبَدِيدٍ↓ فَتُكَلِّمَنِى *Thou art not my like, or fellow, or equal, that thou shouldst speak to me.* (TA.)

بُدَّةٌ: see بَدَدٌ.

بُدَّةٌ: see بُدٌّ. — Also *A distance; a space; an interval; an extent, or an extreme extent; a long space, or any space, of time.* (M, Ḳ, * TA.) So in the saying, بَيْنِى وَبَيْنَكَ بُدَّةٌ [*Between me and thee is a distance*, &c.]. (M, TA.)

بِدَّةٌ: see بُدٌّ, and بَدَادِ: — and see also بَدَدٌ.

بَدَدَ and بَدَدًا: see بَدَادِ, in three places: — بَدَدَ and see also 3. — مَا لَكَ بِهِ بَدَدٌ and ↓ بُدَّةٌ and ↓ بِدَّةٌ *Thou hast not power, or ability, to do it, or to bear it, or to cope with him.* (Ṣ, M, Ḳ.)

جَآءَتِ الخَيْلُ بَدَادِ; (T, Ṣ;) in which بداد is indecl., with kesr for its termination because it deviates from its original form, i. e., the inf. n. بَدَدٌ; and it is indecl. because it deviates from its original form and is of the fem. gender and has the quality of an epithet; for two of these causes render it imperfectly decl., and the three render it indecl.; (Ṣ;) or بَدَادِ بَدَادِ, and بَدَادَ بَدَادَ, (Lḥ, M, Ḳ,) the last indecl. with fet-ḥ for its termination, (TA,) and ↓ بَدَدَ بَدَدَ, (Lḥ, M, Ḳ,) also indecl., with fet-ḥ, (TA,) and composed in the same manner as خَمْسَةَ عَشَرَ, (Lḥ, M, TA,) and ↓ بَدَدًا بَدَدًا; (Lḥ, M, Ḳ;) all of these indecl. except the last, and each virtually in the accus. case as a denotative of state, except the last, (MF,) which is literally in the accus. case, as an inf. n.; (M, MF;) *The horses, or horsemen, came in a state of dispersion*: (T, Ṣ, M, Ḳ:) or *one by one; or one after another.* (T, L.) And تَفَرَّقَ القَوْمُ بَدَادِ *The people, or company of men, became separated, in a state of dispersion.* (Ṣ.) And ذَهَبَ القَوْمُ بَدَادِ بَدَادِ *The people, or company of men, went away* [*in a state of dispersion; or*] *one by one; or one after another.* (T, L.) [See also أَبَادِيدُ.] It is said in a form of prayer, اَللّٰهُمَّ أَقْتُلْهُمْ بَدَدًا↓ وَأَحْصِهِمْ عَدَدًا [*O God, slay them one by one, and reckon them by number*]: (M:) or أَحْصِهِمْ عَدَدًا وَٱقْتُلْهُمْ بِدَدًا, or, accord. to one recital, وَٱقْتُلْهُمْ بِدَدًا, pl. of ↓ بِدَّةٌ, the meaning being [*reckon them by number, and*] *curse them, or slay them, with a cursing, or slaughter, distributed among them by shares.* (Mgh.) — يَا قَوْمِ بَدَادِ بَدَادِ means *O my people, take each one of you his adversary, or opponent* [*with whom to fight*]. (Aṣ, T, Ṣ, Ḳ.*) Here بداد is indecl., with kesr for its termination, because it is an imperative verbal noun, and the imperative is alike uninfluenced with respect to its termination by any governing word; and it is said to be with kesr because two quiescent letters would otherwise occur together, [and] because it occupies the place of an imperative verb [which in like manner is terminated with kesr when it is necessary to prevent the occurrence of two quiescent letters together]. (Ṣ.) — With the article, you say, البَدَادُ, (Aṣ, T,) which signifies The *going forth to encounter another in fight, or to single combat*; as in the saying, لَوْ كَانَ البَدَادُ لَمَا أَطَاقُونَا *Had we gone forth to encounter them in fight*, (Aṣ, T, Ṣ, Ḳ,) *man to man*, [*they had not been able to cope with us*;] (Aṣ, T;) or *man by man.* (Ṣ, Ḳ.) You say also, لَقُوا بَدَادَهُمْ, explained above: see 6. — See also بُدٌّ. — And see 3.

بُدَادٌ: see بُدٌّ.

بِدَادٌ: see بُدٌّ. — Also *A stuffed lining put beneath a* [*camel's saddle of the kind called*] قَتَب, *to defend the animal's back from being hurt thereby*: there is one such on each side: (T:) or, of a horse's saddle, and of a قَتَب, (Ṣ, M, Ḳ,) the *stuffed thing, or pad, that is placed beneath, in order that it may not gall the animal's back*; (M, Ḳ;) as also ↓ بَدِيدٌ: (Ḳ:) or the بِدَادَانِ and ↓ بَدِيدَانِ are *two bags* (خُرَيطَتَانِ), *which are stuffed, and placed under the curved pieces of wood, in order that the wood may not gall the animal's back*; derived from بَدَّ رِجْلَيْهِ "he parted his legs:" (Ṣ:) [see also بَدِيدٌ:] or the بِدَادَانِ of a قَتَب are *two things like provender-bags, which are stuffed, and bound with strings, or cords, to the pieces of wood called the* أَحْنَآء *and* ظَلِفَات: (T:) or they are, *to the* قَتَب, *like the* كَرّ *to the* رَحْل, *except that they do not appear before the* ظَلِفَة, *being only within* [*it*]: (M:) [see also حِدْج:] pl. [of pauc.] أَبِدَّةٌ (T, Ṣ) and [of mult.] بَدَائِدُ. (Ṣ.) — Also *A piece of felt cloth, that is bound upon a beast which has a galled, or sore, back*, (L, Ḳ,) *cut, or slit, so as to be clear of the galls, or sores.* (L.)

بَدِيدٌ: see بِدٌّ, in three places. — Also *A saddle-bag*; syn. خُرْجٌ: (Ḳ:) [and] بَدِيدَانِ *a pair of saddle-bags*; syn. خُرْجَانِ. (Ṣ.) — See also بِدَادٌ, in two places. — Also *A wide* [*desert such as is termed*] مَفَازَة: (Ṣ, Ḳ:) or فَلَاةٌ بَدِيدٌ [*a desert, or waterless desert*,] *in which is no one.* (T, L. [In a copy of the former written بَدْبَدٌ.])

بَدَادَةٌ: see 3.

بَدِيدَةٌ: see بِدٌّ.

بَادٌّ The *inner side of the thigh*: (M, A, Ḳ:) or the *part of the* horseman's *thigh that is next the saddle*: (T, M, A, L:) or the *part between the legs*: (M, L:) the *inner sides of the two thighs are called the* بَادَّانِ, (Ṣ,) because the saddle separates them; (IAar, M;) and if so, بَادٌّ is of the measure فَاعِلٌ in the sense of the measure مَفْعُولٌ; or it may be a possessive epithet [meaning ذُو بَدٍّ]. (M, L.) You say, هُوَ حَسَنُ البَادِّ عَلَى السَّرْجِ, meaning *He is a good rider upon the saddle.* (A.) — Also The *part* of a horse's back *upon which the thigh of the rider presses.* (Ḳt, T, L.)

أَبَدُّ A man *wide between the thighs*, (ISk, Ṣ, M, Ḳ,) *by reason of abundance of flesh*: (ISk, Ṣ, M:) or *wide between the arms*; (Ḳ;) *having the arms far from the sides*: (M:) or *wide between the shoulder-joints*: (M:) or (so in the Ḳ; but accord. to the Ṣ, "and") *large in make*, (T, Ṣ, M, Ḳ,) *having one part far from another*: (M, Ḳ:) and *wide in the breast*: (Aboo-Málik, T:) fem. بَدَّآءُ: (Ṣ:) which also signifies a woman (M, L) *large in the* إِسْكَتَانِ [*or labia majora of the vulva*], (M, L, Ḳ,) *having their edges far apart*: (M, L:) or *having much flesh in the thighs.* (T, L.) الأَبَدُّ is used to signify *The weaver*, (T, M, Ḳ,) because of the distance between his thighs. (M.) The following saying, (Ḳ,) quoted by J, from the rájiz Aboo-Nukheyleh Es-Saadee,

* أَلَدُّ يَمْشِى مِشْيَةَ الأَبَدِّ *

is incorrect, and should be thus,

* بَدَّآءُ تَمْشِى مِشْيَةَ الأَبَدِّ *

[*A woman of large make, walking in the manner of the man of large make; or a woman wide between the thighs*, &c.]; (Ḳ;) for it is descriptive of a woman, as IB and Aboo-Sahl El-Harawee have observed before the author of the Ḳ. (TA.) — Also A horse [or any quadruped (see بَدَّ)] *having the fore legs far apart*: (M, Ḳ:) or *having the fore legs far from the sides*: (TA:) or *wide between the legs*: (Ḥam p. 348:) and a camel *having the elbows far from the sides*: (TA:) and the fem. بَدَّآءُ, a cow *having her fore legs far apart.* (Ṣ.) [Hence,] الأَبَدُّ الزَّنِيمُ [in the CḲ الزَّنِيمِ] *The lion*; (M, Ḳ;) the former epithet being applied to him because his fore legs are far apart, and the latter because he is [often] alone. (M.) — كَتِفٌ بَدَّآءُ *A broad shoulder-blade, the sides of which are distant, one from another.* (M, L.)

طَيْرٌ أَبَادِيدُ, (Fr, Ṣ, Ḳ,) and ↓ تَبَادِيدُ, (Ḳ, TA,) [in the CḲ تَبَادِيدُ,] erroneously written by J ↓ يَبَادِيدُ, (Ḳ,) [but see what follows; like أَنَادِيدُ and يَنَادِيدُ;] *Birds in a state of dispersion.* (Ṣ, Ḳ.) In the following verse of 'Otárid Ibn-Ḳurrán, quoted by J,

* كَأَنَّمَا أَهْلُ حَجْرٍ يَنْظُرُونَ مَتَى *

* يَرَوْنَنِى خَارِجًا طَيْرٌ يَبَادِيدُ *

[*As though the people of Hajr, watching when they should see me going forth, were birds in a state of dispersion*], (Ḳ,) thus related also by Yaạḳoob, and thus in the handwriting of Az, (TA,) the last two words should be طَيْرُ اليَنَادِيدِ, the latter with ن, and governed by the former in the gen. case, the rhyme being with kesr: (Ḳ:) so says Aboo-Sahl El-Harawee. (TA.) — ذَهَبُوا أَبَادِيدَ, (M, Ḳ,) and ↓ تَبَادِيدَ, (Ḳ,) or ↓ يَبَادِيدَ, (as in the T, from Fr, and in the M and L, and in some copies of the Ḳ, [but see above,]) [as also تَنَادِيدَ, يَنَادِيدَ, and أَنَادِيدَ,] *They went away in a state of dispersion.* (M, L, Ḳ.)

تَبَادِيدُ: see أَبَادِيدُ, in two places.

مُبِدٌّ [act. part. n. of 4, q. v.]. The following words of 'Omar Ibn-Abee-Rabee'ah,

* أَمُبِدٌّ سُؤَالَكَ العَالَمِينَ *

are said to signify *Dost thou distribute thy petition*

among mankind one by one, so as to include them universally? or dost thou constrain them by thy petition? from the saying, مَا لَكَ مِنْهُ بُدٌّ ["thou hast no means," or "way," "of separating thyself from it," or "avoiding it"]. (M, L.)

شَمْلٌ مُتَبَدِّدٌ *[A united state of affairs] become disunited* [or *discomposed* or *disorganized*]. (Ṣ, L.)

اِمْرَأَةٌ مُتَبَدِّدَةٌ *An emaciated woman,* [*as though*] *having one part far from another.* (M, L.)

يَبَادِيدُ : see أَبَادِيدُ, in two places.

بدأ

1. بَدَأَ بِهِ, (T, Ṣ, M, &c.,) aor. ـَ , (Mgh, Ḳ,) inf. n. بَدْءٌ, (T, Ṣ, M, Mṣb,) i. q. ▼ ابتدأ به; (Ṣ, Mṣb, Ḳ;) [*He began with it;*] *he made it to have precedence,* or *to be first; gave precedence to it;* syn. قَدَّمَهُ: (Mgh, Mṣb:) in the dial. of the Anṣár, بَدِئَ بِهِ is used in this sense of قدّمه; (M;) or بَدَى بِهِ [without ء]; (IḲṭṭ, TA; [see بَدْءٌ;]) [and بَدَى بِهِ; see art. بدى;] and ▼ ابدأ به signifies the same. (Mṣb.) [So in the Ḳur xii. 76, فَبَدَأَ بِأَوْعِيَتِهِمْ قَبْلَ وِعَاءِ أَخِيهِ *And he began with their bags, before the bags of his brother.* And بَدَأَهُ is sometimes used in the sense of بَدَأَ بِهِ; whence, in the Ḳur ix. 13, وَهُمْ بَدَؤُوكُمْ أَوَّلَ مَرَّةٍ *And they,* it was, *began with you the first time;* i. e., as Bḍ says, by acting with hostility, and fighting.] You say also, بَدَأَ ثُمَّ عَادَ *He began,* or *did a first time,* or *the first time: then repeated,* or *did a second time.* (Az, TA in art. عود.) And بَدَأَ فِى الأَمْرِ [*He began,* or *made a beginning, in the affair.*] (M.) — بَدَأَ also signifies *It* (a thing) *began; began to be; originated;* or *came into existence.* (Mṣb.) [See also 5.] = بَدَأَ الشَّىْءَ, (Ṣ, M, Ḳ,) aor. and inf. n. as above, (M,) [*He began the thing; commenced it; set about it;* as also ▼ ابتدأه: accord. to the Mgh, the latter has this meaning, or, agreeably with the authority of the M and Ḳ, the meaning which here next follows:] *he did the thing first, for the first time, by way of beginning,* or *originally;* (Ṣ, M, Ḳ;) as also ▼ ابدأه and ▼ ابتدأه; (M, Ḳ;) i. e., *not after the example of anything preceding.* (TA. [But this addition seems rather to belong to another explanation to be mentioned below.]) One does not say, ▼ ابتدأ زَيْدًا nor بَدَأَهُ, because these two verbs [signifying as last explained above] do not have for their objects corporeal things. (Mgh.) [El-Mutanakhkhil El-Hudhalee uses the phrase سَأَبْدَؤُهُمْ بِمَشْمَعَةٍ *I will begin with them* (meaning his guests) *by sporting and jesting;* like the phrase in the Ḳur ix. 13 cited above: but different from these is the saying in the Ḳur xxxii. 6, وَبَدَأَ خَلْقَ الإِنْسَانِ مِنْ طِينٍ *And He began the creation of man from clay.*] The saying, فَإِنْ كَانَ السَّبُعُ ٱبْتَدَأَهُ ابتدأ أَخْذَهُ أَوْ عَضَّهُ [*But if the beast, or bird, of prey has begun the seizing of him, or the biting of him*]; the noun that is prefixed [to the pronoun] being suppressed. (Mgh.) You say also, كَانَ ذٰلِكَ فِى ▼ ٱبْتِدَاءِ الأَمْرِ *That was in the beginning, or first, of the affair.* (Mṣb.) [See also بَدْءٌ, below.] — *He originated the thing; brought it into being* or *existence; made it,* or *produced it, for the first time, it not having been before;* (Mgh;) [and] so ▼ ابدأه, said [of God, and] of a man, as the agent; (Mṣb;) and ▼ ابتدأه. (Mgh in art. بدع.) [Hence,] بَدَأَ ٱللّٰهُ الخَلْقَ, and ▼ أَبْدَأَهُمْ, *God created,* or *brought into existence, mankind,* or *the created beings:* (M, Mṣb, Ḳ:) both signify the same. (Ṣ.) مَا يُبْدِئُ ▼ البَاطِلُ وَمَا يُعِيدُ [in the Ḳur xxxiv. 48, means *What doth that which is false,* or *the Devil, originate,* or *produce in the first instance? and what doth it,* or *he, reproduce* after it hath perished?]: Zj says that مَا, here, is in the place of an accus., meaning in each instance أَىَّ شَىْءٍ: or it may be a negative; and الباطل here is Iblees; i. e., *Iblees createth not, nor raiseth to life* after death. (M.) You say also, مَا يُبْدِئُ وَمَا يُعِيدُ, meaning مَا يَتَكَلَّمُ بِبَادِئَةٍ وَلَا عَائِدَةٍ, (Ṣ, Ḳ,) i. e. *He does not say anything for the first time, nor anything for the second time;* or *anything original, nor anything in the way of repetition;* ▼ بَادِئَةُ الكَلَامِ signifying *what is said for the first time;* and عَائِدَةُ الكَلَامِ, *what is said for the second time, afterwards:* (TA:) or *he says not anything:* (A in art. عود:) and *he has no art, artifice,* or *cunning.* (IAạr, TA in art. عود; and A in the present art.) — بَدَأَ البِئْرَ *He dug the well* [*for the first time:* see بَدِىٌّ]. (Mṣb.) = بَدَأَ مِنْ أَرْضٍ إِلَى أَرْضٍ, (T,) or مِنْ أَرْضِهِ, (Ḳ,) *He went forth from a land to a land,* or *from his land;* as also ▼ ابدأ. (T, Ḳ.) = بُدِئَ, (inf. n. as above, Ṣ, M, Ḳ,) *He* (a man, Ṣ, M) *had the small-pox:* (AZ, Aṣ, T, Ṣ, M, Ḳ:) or *the* حَصْبَة [i. e. *measles,* or *spotted fever*]: (Ṣ, M, Ḳ:) or, as AZ says, and *the* حصبة: (T:) or, as Lḥ says, *there came forth upon him pustules resembling the small-pox:* but he adds, some say, *the small-pox itself:* (M:) the epithet applied to a person affected therewith is ▼ مَبْدُوْءٌ. (AZ, Aṣ, Lḥ, T, Ṣ, M.) — Also *He fell sick.* (IAth, TA.) In a trad. of 'Áïsheh occur the words, فِى اليَوْمِ الَّذِى بُدِئَ فِيهِ رَسُولُ ٱللّٰهِ [meaning *In the day in which the Apostle of God fell sick*]: and IAth says, مَتَى بُدِئَ فُلَانٌ meaning *When did such a one fall sick?* is a phrase used in inquiring respecting the living [who has been attacked by illness] and respecting the dead. (TA.)

4. ابدأ: see 1, in seven places. — Also *He did a new thing; a thing unknown before;* or *a strange,* or *wonderful, thing.* (Ṣ,* TA.) — And *He voided excrement,* or *ordure;* or *broke wind;* syn. نَجَا; [as also أَبْدَى;] said of a man. (M.) — And *He put forth his second teeth;* said of a child; (M;) and of a colt. (TA voce أَحْفَرَ, q. v.)

5. تبدّأ *He,* or *it, began,* or *made a beginning.* (KL.) [See also 1. Golius mentions, but without giving the authority, and without the vowel-signs, the saying, هَاتِ القِصَّةَ مِنْ ذِى تُبُدِّئَتْ; but writing the last word تبديت, stating only that it is in the passive form; as meaning *Relate thou the story,* or *history, from the beginning.*]

8: see 1, in seven places. — ابتدأه بِوَعْدٍ *He made him a promise in anticipation; without his asking it of him.* (M in art. انف.)

بَدْءٌ inf. n. of 1; (T, Ṣ, M, Mṣb;) [The act of *beginning;*] or the *doing* a thing *first.* (M.) You say, لَكَ البَدْءُ, (M, Ḳ,) and ▼ البُدْءُ, (Aṣ, TA,) and ▼ البَدْأَةُ, (Ṣ, M, Mṣb, Ḳ,) and ▼ البُدْأَةُ, (Ṣ, M, Ḳ,) and ▼ البِدْأَةُ, (L,) and ▼ البَدَاءَةُ, (M, Ḳ,) and ▼ البُدَاءَةُ, (Ṣ, M, Ḳ,) and البُدَاهَةُ, with ه substituted for ء, (M, Mṭr,) and ▼ البِدَاءَةُ, (Mṭr, TA,) and, accord. to IḲṭṭ, البِدَايَةُ, but see what follows, (TA,) and ▼ البَدِيْئَةُ, (M, Ḳ,) and ▼ البُدَّاءَةُ, (AZ, TA,) *It is for thee to begin,* (Ṣ, M, Mṣb, Ḳ,) *before any other,* in shooting or casting, &c.: (Ṣ:) as to البِدَايَةُ, mentioned above, accord. to Mṭr [and Fei], (TA,) it is a vulgar word, (Mgh, Mṣb, TA,) as IB and several others have stated, (Mṣb, TA,*) a corruption of ▼ البِدَاءَةُ, (Mgh, Mṣb,) signifying *the first;* as also ▼ البَدَاءَةُ; and ▼ البُدْأَةُ: (Mṣb:) but IḲṭṭ says that it is a word of the dial. of the Anṣár; بَدِيتُ بِالشَّىْءِ and بَدَأْتُ بِهِ signifying قَدَّمْتُهُ: [see 1:] and he cites the following verse of Ibn-Rawáḥah:

• بِٱسْمِ ٱلْإِلٰهِ وَبِهِ بَدِينَا • وَلَوْ عَبَدْنَا غَيْرَهُ شَقِينَا •

[*In the name of God, and with it we begin; and if we worshipped any other than Him, we should be miserable*]: see art. بدى. (TA. [This verse is also cited in the Ṣ in art. بدو, where, in one copy I find it as above; in another, with بَدَيْنَا instead of بَدِينَا.]) And you say, فَعَلَهُ عَوْدًا وَبَدْءًا, (T, Ṣ,) and عَوْدَهُ عَلَى بَدْئِهِ, (M,) and فِى عَوْدِهِ وَبَدْئِهِ, and ▼ فِى عَوْدَتِهِ وَبَدْأَتِهِ, (Ṣ, M,) [*He did it returning and beginning* again; or *returning to his beginning;* i. e. *he did it again from the beginning; he recommenced it:* or you say this] meaning like as is meant by the saying next following. (TA.) رَجَعَ عَوْدَهُ عَلَى بَدْئِهِ, (Ṣ, Ḳ,) and عَوْدًا عَلَى بَدْءٍ, in both of which [and in the last following] the verb may be trans., and the noun following therefore in the accus. case, (TA,) and فِى عَوْدَتِهِ وَبَدْأَتِهِ ▼, and فِى عَوْدِهِ وَبَدْئِهِ, [in both of which, if correct, the verb must be intrans.,] and عَوْدًا وَبَدْءًا, [as though meaning عَائِدًا وَبَادِئًا, used as a phrase denotative of state,] (Ḳ,) [but in this last, and the two next preceding, accord. to the TA, the verb should be فَعَلَهُ, as in the next preceding sentence, instead of رَجَعَ, and this is confirmed by what is said in the Ḳ in art. عود,] *He returned in the way whence he had come:* (Ṣ, Ḳ:) [accord. to the TA, the literal meaning of the first and second may be *he made his returning to revert to his beginning,* and *he made a returning to revert to a beginning:*] or the meaning of the first, (Sb, TA in art. عود, and Ḳ in that art.,) and of the second, (Ḳ in that art.,) is, *he returned without stopping after he had gone away:* (Sb, Ḳ:) and sometimes it signifies the stopping in one's coming and then returning: (Sb:) [and *it returned to its first state; it recommenced:*] and you say, رَجَعْتُ عَوْدِى عَلَى بَدْئِى, meaning *I returned like as I had come.*

(Sb ubi suprà.) — Also *First*, or *former*; *preceding all others*, or *preceding another*; as also ▼ بَدِىْءٌ; البَدْءُ and البَدِىْءُ being syn. with الأَوَّلُ. (Ṣ, Ḳ.) Hence the saying, اِفْعَلْهُ بَادِىَ بَدْءٍ, and ▼ بَادِىَ بَدِىْءٍ, meaning *Do thou it the first thing*, or *the first of everything*; [accord. to different copies of the Ṣ;] the ى in بادى being quiescent, in the place of the accus. case, accord. to usage; and sometimes they omit the ء [altogether], on account of frequent use [of the phrase], as will be stated in art. بدو, (Ṣ in the present art.,) saying بَادِى بَدٍ, and بَادِى بَدِى. (Ṣ in art. بدو.) You say also, اِفْعَلْهُ بَدْءًا, and أَوَّلَ بَدْءٍ, (Th, M, Ḳ,) and بَدْءَ بَدْءٍ, (CḲ,) and بَدَا بَدْءٍ, (M, Ḳ,) and ▼ بَادِئَ بَدْءٍ, (A'Obeyd, T, Ṣ, M, Ḳ,) and بَادِى بَدْءٍ, (Ḳ,) and بَادِى بَدٍ, (M, Ḳ, [in the CḲ بَادِئَ بَدٍ,]) and ▼ بَادِئَ بَدَا, (M,) and ▼ بَادِىْ بَدَا, (Ḳ,) and بَادِىْ بَدَا, (M, Ḳ,) and ▼ بَادِئَ ▼ بَدِىْءٍ, (A'Obeyd, T, Ṣ, M, CḲ,) and ▼ بَادِئَ بَدِىٍّ, which is anomalous, (M,) or بَادِىَ بَدِىٍّ, (Ḳ,) and ▼ بَادِئَ ▼ بَدِىٍّ, (Fr, A'Obeyd, T, Ṣ, M,) and بَادِئَ بَدِىٍّ, (Ṣ, CḲ,) or ▼ بَادِىَ بَدِىٍّ, (Ḳ, TA,) and بَادِئَ ▼ بَدْأَةٍ, (M, Ḳ, TA,) the former word being the act. part. n. of بَدِىَ, which is of the dial. of the Anṣár, as mentioned above, and the latter being indecl., with fet-ḥ for its termination, (TA, [in the CḲ the latter word is written بَدْءَةً,]) and ▼ بَدْءَ ▼ بَدْأَةٍ, (CḲ,) and بَدْأَةَ ▼ بَدْأَةٍ, (M, Ḳ,) and ▼ بَدْأَةَ ▼ بَدِىْءٍ, (Ṣ,) and ▼ بَدِىْءَ ▼ بَدْءٍ, (Ṣ, CḲ,) and بَدْءَ ذِى بَدْءٍ, (Fr, T,) and ▼ بَدْأَةَ ذِى بَدْءٍ, (Fr, T, Ṣ, Ḳ,) and ▼ بَدْأَةَ ذِى بَدِىْءٍ, and ▼ بَدْأَةَ ذِى بَدْأَةٍ, (Ṣ, Ḳ,) and ▼ بَدْأَةَ ▼ ذِى بَدَاءَةٍ, (Ḳ, TA,) not بداءة [as in the CḲ], (TA,) and بَدِىْءَ ذِى بَدِىْءٍ, (Ṣ, Ḳ, TA, [in the CḲ the last word is written بَدْءٍ,]) and ▼ بَدَاءَةَ ▼ ذِى بَدِىْءٍ, (Ḳ,) meaning *Do thou it the first thing*; (Fr, T, Ḳ;) so in a correct copy [of the Ḳ, and so I find in a MS. copy of the Ḳ and in the CḲ]: accord. to another copy, *the first of everything*: (TA:) or *the first of first*; (Ṣ;) thus in the L: (TA:) the words here put in the accus. case [literally or virtually] are so put [in some instances] as adverbial nouns; or, accord. to MF, they may be [in some instances] denotatives of state, with respect to the agent; the meaning being اِفْعَلْهُ حَالَةَ كَوْنِكَ بَادِئًا, i. e. مُبْتَدِئًا بِهِ [lit. *do thou it in the state of thy being beginning it*]. (TA.) [In like manner,] you also say, بَادِئَ ▼ الرَّأْىِ, بَدْءَ الرَّأْىِ, and [more commonly] *At first thought*; or *on the first opinion*: (Lḥ, M:) [بَادِئَ ▼ الرَّأْىِ and بَدْءَ الرَّأْىِ] signifying *the first*, and *beginning, of the idea, thought, opinion*, or *judgment*; or *what is perceived before considering well* or *thoroughly*: (M:) [and بَدْءٌ alone signifying *a first idea, thought, opinion*, or *judgment*; as is implied in the A, voce صُيُورٌ, q. v.:] hence, فَعَلَهُ فِى بَادِئِ ▼ الرَّأْىِ [*He did it at first thought*, &c.]: (M:) and أَنْتَ بَادِئَ ▼ الرَّأْىِ تُرِيدُ ظُلْمَنَا, and مُبْتَدَأَ ▼ الرأى, i. e. *Thou at first thought, &c., desirest to wrong us*: and one says also, بَادِىَ الرأى, without ء; meaning *on the occasion of what appeared of opinion*; i. e. *at the first of what appeared thereof*; [or *at the first opinion's presenting itself*;] in which case, the phrase does not belong to this art. [but to art. بدو]: it occurs in the Ḳur xi. 29: (M:) AA alone there read بَادِئَ, with ء; all the other readers pronounced it without ء. (TA.) — Also *A chief*, or *lord*, (Ṣ, M, Mṣb, Ḳ,) *who occupies the first place in chieftainship* or *lordship*: (Ṣ:) or, as some say, *a youth*, or *young man, whose judgment*, or *opinion, is deemed good, and who is consulted*: (M:) or it signifies also *an intelligent youth* or *young man*: (Ḳ:) pl. بُدُوءٌ. (M.) A poet (namely, Ows Ibn-Maghrà Es-Saạdee, TA) says,

ثُنْيَانُنَا إِنْ أَتَاهُمْ كَانَ بَدْأَهُمْ
وَبَدْؤُهُمْ إِنْ أَتَانَا كَانَ ثُنْيَانَا

[*Our second chief, if he came to them, would be their first chief; and their first chief, if he came to us, would be a second chief*]. (Ṣ.) — Also, and ▼ بَدْأَةٌ, *A share*, or *portion*, of a slaughtered camel: (Ṣ, Ḳ:) or the *best share* or *portion* thereof: (T:) or the former word has the latter signification; and the latter word, the former signification: and the former signifies also *a bone with the meat*, or *flesh, that is on it*: (M:) and *a joint*; syn. مَفْصِلٌ; (AA, T, M;) and so بَدًا q. v.: (AA, T:) the pl. [of pauc.] of بَدْءٌ is أَبْدَآءٌ (Ṣ, M, Ḳ) and [of mult.] بُدُوءٌ; (Ṣ, Ḳ;) the former of which is the more common: (TA:) or this is pl. of بَدًا. (AA, T.) The shares above-mentioned [as commonly divided for the game called المَيْسِر q. v.] are ten; namely, the two haunches, the two thighs properly so called, the two thighs commonly so called (i. e. the tibiæ), the two shoulders, and the two arms; which last are the worst, because of the many veins [therein]. (TA.) — See also بَدِىْءٌ.

بَدْءٌ: see بَدْءٌ; second sentence.

بَدِىْءٌ: see بَادِئَ بَدِىٍّ, or بَادِىَ بَدِىٍّ, voce بَدْءٌ.

بَدْأَةٌ: see بَدْءٌ, in thirteen places. — Also The *beginning*, or *outward course, of a military expedition*; opposed to رَجْعَةٌ, meaning the returning, or homeward course, thereof: occurring in a trad., in which it is said that the Prophet gave, in the case of the former, a fourth [of the spoil], and in the case of the latter, a third; i. e., when a troop went forth from the main body of the army and attacked a party of the enemy, they were to have a fourth of the spoil that they took, and the rest of the army was to share with them the remaining three fourths; and if a troop did so in returning, they were to have a third of all the spoil that they took, because of the greater difficulty and danger attending this case. (T, Mgh.) — كَانَ ذٰلِكَ فِى بَدْأَتِنَا, and ▼ بُدْأَتِنَا, and ▼ بُدْأَتِنَا, (Ḳ,) and ▼ بَدَاءَتِنَا, (Lḥ, M, TA,) and ▼ بَدَآءَتِنَا, and ▼ بُدَآءَتِنَا, (TA,) and ▼ بَدْأَتِنَا, (Lḥ, M, Ḳ,) but [ISd says,] I know not how that is, (M,) and ▼ مَبْدَئِنَا, and ▼ مُبْدَئِنَا, (Ḳ,) and ▼ مَبْدَأَتِنَا, (Lḥ, M, and so in some copies of the Ḳ,) or مَبْدَاتِنَا, (so in other copies of the Ḳ,) thus in the بَاهِر of Ibn-'Odeys [in the CḲ Ibn-'Adebbes], (Ḳ,) which is said to indicate that we should hesitate respecting them [before admitting them to be of classical authority], are phrases meaning *That was in the first of our state*, and *in our adolescence*. (TA.) — Also, (so in a copy of the M, there written بُدَاةٌ,) or ▼ بُدْأَةٌ, with ḍamm, (Ḳ,) *A certain plant*; (M;) *a black thing, resembling a truffle* (كَمْء), *of which no use is made*: so says AḤn. (M.)

بُدْأَةٌ: see بَدْءٌ; second sentence: and see بَدْأَةٌ, in two places.

بُدَاةٌ: see بَدْءٌ; second sentence: and see بَدْأَةٌ.

بُدَاءَةٌ: see بَدْأَةٌ.

بَدَآءٌ, with medd; [*Excrement from the anus*; as also بَدًا;] a subst. from أَبْدَأَ, as meaning نَجَا. (M.)

بَدِىْءٌ: see بَدْءٌ, as signifying *First*, or *former*; in eight places. — Also, applied to a thing, or an affair, *i. q.* بَدِيعٌ, (Ṣ, and so in a copy of the Ḳ,) or مُبْدَعٌ: (so in other copies of the Ḳ:) [thus it signifies] *Originated; brought into being* or *existence; made*, or *produced, for the first time, not having been before*, or *not after the similitude of any former thing*: (TA:) and *created*: (M, Ḳ:) and *wonderful*: (M, Mṣb, TA:) and *strange*, or *extraordinary, as not being after the similitude of any former thing*. (TA.) — [Hence, as is implied in the Mgh,] بِئْرٌ بَدِىْءٌ *A well newly dug*; (T, Mgh, Mṣb;) *i. q.* بَدِيعٌ; (M;) or *dug since the era of El-Islám*; (Ṣ, Ḳ;) *not ancient*; (Ṣ, Mgh, Mṣb;) as also ▼ بَدْءٌ: (Ṣ:) the former epithet [in this sense] is generally pronounced [بَدِىٌّ] without ء: (T:) the well thus called is one *dug in a waste land that has no owner*: (TA:) AO says, (TA,) this epithet, and بَدِيع, are applied to a well when thou hast dug it; but if thou findest it to have been dug before thee, it is termed خَفِيَّةٌ; and thus the well of Zemzem is termed خَفِيَّة, because it was Ismá'eel's, and was filled up or covered over [after his time]: (T, TA:) the term قَلِيب is [said to be] applied to an ancient well of which neither the owner nor the digger is known: (TA:) it is said in a trad., that the حَرِيم of a well such as is termed بدىء [i. e. the space surrounding it and belonging to it] is five-and-twenty cubits: (T, Ṣ: [but see حَرِيم:]) the pl. is بُدُوءٌ: (M:) and AO says that بُودَانٌ is pl. of بَدِىْءٌ applied to a well, and is syn. with قُلْبَانٌ [a pl. of قَلِيب which I have not found elsewhere] and رَكَايَا, being formed by transposition of letters from بُدْيَانٌ [which is for بُدْدَانٌ, as بَدِىٌّ is for بَدِىْءٌ; the د and ى being transposed, the word becomes بُيْدَانٌ, and this, by a rule of permutation, becomes بُودَانٌ]. (TA.)

بَدْأَةٌ: see بَدْءٌ, in three places: and see بُدْأَةٌ: and بَدِيئَةٌ, in two places.

بُدَاءَةٌ: } see بَدْءٌ, in two places: and see بَدْأَةٌ:
بِدَاءَةٌ: } and for the former, see also بَدِيئَةٌ.

بَدِيئَةٌ: see بَدْءٌ; second sentence. — Also, (M, Ḳ,) and ▼ بَدَاءَةٌ, (Ḳ,) or ▼ بُدَاءَةٌ, (M,) *i. q.* بَدِيهَةٌ, (Ḳ,) and بَدَاهَةٌ, (TA,) or بُدَاهَةٌ, i. e. The *first occurrence* of a thing, *that happens to one unexpectedly:* (M:) [or the *first* of anything: and *an occurrence thereof by which one is taken unawares:* accord. to explanations in the Ḳ in art. بده:] pl. of the first, بَدَايَا. (TA.) — [And all app. signify The *faculty of extemporizing*; like بَدِيهَةٌ (q. v.) &c.] You say, فُلَانٌ ذُو بَدَاءَةٍ ▼ جَيِّدَةٍ, i. e. بَدِيهَةٍ حَسَنَةٍ, [meaning] *Such a one has a good faculty of extemporizing;* or *of uttering,* or *relating, things by means of the promptness of his intelligence.* (TA.)

بَدَاءَةٌ: see بَدْءٌ; second sentence.

بَادِئٌ [act. part. n. of 1]: see بَدْءٌ, in nine places.

بَادِئَةٌ: see 1, in two places.

مَبْدَأٌ [originally noun of place and of time from 1; *A place,* and *a time, of beginning,* &c. —] See بَدْأَةٌ. — [Also *A principle,* or *first rule,* of a science &c.: pl. مَبَادِئُ. — And The *primary import* of a word; opposed in this sense to غَايَةٌ.]

مُبْدَأٌ: see بَدْأَةٌ.

الْمُبْدِئُ, applied to God, *The Creator,* or *Originator, of the things* [*that exist*], *who hath produced them at the beginning, not after the similitude of anything pre-existing.* (Nh.) And الْمُبْدِئُ الْمُعِيدُ, so applied, *He who createth mankind, and who returneth them after life to death in the present world and after death to life on the day of resurrection.* (TA in art. عود.) — مُبْدِئٌ مُعِيدٌ A man *who has gone on warring,* or *warring and plundering, expeditions, time after time, and is experienced in affairs:* (A'Obeyd, and Ḳ in art. عود:) and a horse *upon which the owner has gone time after time on warring,* or *warring and plundering, expeditions;* (TA in that art.;) or *well trained and exercised,* (Ḳ and TA in that art.,) *so as to be obedient to his rider.* (TA in that art.) — [For other significations of مُبْدِئٌ, see its verb (4); and see أَحْفَرَ.]

مَبْدَاةٌ: see بَدْأَةٌ.

مَبْدُوءٌ [pass. part. n. of 1; *Begun,* &c. —] See بَدِئٌ.

مُبْتَدَأٌ: see بَدْءٌ. — [In grammar, as correlative of خَبَرٌ, *An inchoative.*]

بدر

1. بَدَرَ, aor. ـُ, inf. n. بَدْرٌ, *It* (the moon) *became full.* (Mṣb.) — ‡ *He* (a boy) *became full-grown and round;* implying comparison to the full moon. (TA.) — †*It* (fruit) *attained to maturity.* (TA, from a trad.) [See also 4.] — *It rose like the full moon.* (Er Rághib.) ═ See also 3, in six places. — بَدَرَتْ بَوَادِرُ: and بَدَرَتْ مِنْهُ بَوَادِرُ غَضَبٍ: see بَادِرَةٌ. — بَدَرَتِ الْإِبِلُ الْخَيْلَ: *She* (a camel) *brought forth at an earlier period of the year than the other camels.* (TA.) [See بَدْرِيَّةٌ, voce بَدْرِيٌّ.] — خَرَجْتُ أَبْدُرُ ‡ *I went forth to make water.* (A.)

3. بَادَرَهُ, inf. n. مُبَادَرَةٌ and بِدَارٌ; and ▼ ابتدرهُ; *He hastened,* or *made haste,* or *strove to be first* or *beforehand, in doing* [or *attaining* or *obtaining*] *it;* (M, Ḳ, TA, TḲ;) namely, a thing: (M:) and بَدَرَ ▼ غَيْرَهُ إِلَيْهِ, (M, Ḳ,) aor. ـُ; and بادرهُ اليه; (M;) *He hastened with another,* or *vied* or *strove with him in hastening, to it* [or *to do* or *attain* or *obtain it*]: syn. عَاجَلَهُ, (M, Ḳ, TA,) and أَسْرَعَ إِلَيْهِ. (TA.) بادر [as well as ▼ بَدَرَ and ▼ ابتدر] denotes mutual effort only when it is immediately trans.: when it is trans. by means of إِلَى [or بِ (the former in the TA written by mistake على)], there is nothing to show that it denotes this. (MF.) [But it is often immediately trans. without its denoting such effort.] One says, بادرهُ *He hastened to do it* [&c., as explained above]; meaning, a thing that he desired, or wished for: (TA:) [and بادر به signifies *the same;* or *he hastened with it:* and the former signifies also *he betook himself early to him* or *it:*] and بادر إِلَيْهِ *he hastened to it;* (Ṣ, A;) as also ▼ بَدَرَ اليه, (Ṣ, Mgh, Mṣb,) aor. ـُ, (Ṣ,) inf. n. بُدُورٌ: (Ṣ, Mṣb:) or, accord. to Zj, agreeably with its derivation, [see بَدْرٌ] *he employed the fulness of his power,* or *force, to hasten* [*to it*]: (TA:) and بَدَرَهُ ▼ الأَمْرُ, and ▼ بَدَرَ إِلَيْهِ, (aor. ـُ, inf. n. بَدْرٌ, TA, [or بُدُورٌ, as above,]) *the thing,* or *event, came to him,* or *happened to him, hastily, quickly,* or *speedily;* and, *beforehand* [or *before he expected it*]; syn. عَجِلَ, (M, Ḳ,) and سَبَقَ, (M,) or اسْتَبَقَ: (Ḳ:) [and بَدَرَ مِنْهُ قَوْلٌ, and فِعْلٌ, *a saying,* and *an action, proceeded from him hastily, without premeditation:* see بَادِرَةٌ.] It is said in a trad., بَادِرُوا بِالْأَعْمَالِ هَرَمًا [*Strive ye to be before decrepitude with good works;* i. e., *to perform them before decrepitude*]. (El-Jámi' eṣ-Ṣagheer.) And in another, بَادِرُوا الصُّبْحَ بِالْوِتْرِ [*Strive ye to be before daybreak with the prayers* termed وتر; i. e., *to perform them before daybreak*]. (Idem.) And in another, بَادِرُوا بِصَلَاةِ الْمَغْرِبِ قَبْلَ طُلُوعِ النَّجْمِ [*Hasten ye with,* or *to perform, the prayer of sunset before the rising of the star*]. (Idem.) You say also, فُلَانٌ يُبَادِرُ فِى أَكْلِ مَالِ الْيَتِيمِ [*Such a one hastens in consuming the property of the orphan* before the latter is of full age]. (A.) And بَادَرَ كِبَرَ الْيَتِيمِ [*He hastened to be before the orphan's attaining to full age* in expending his property]; said of a guardian; *i. q.* ▼ أَبْدَرَ فِى مَالِ الْيَتِيمِ: (Ḳ:) and thus, بِدَارًا أَنْ يَكْبَرُوا, in the Ḳur [iv. 5], means *hastening to be before their attaining to full age* in expending their property. (Bḍ,* Jel.) And بادرهُ الغَايَةَ and إِلَى الغَايَةِ [*He strove with him in hastening,* or *strove to get before him, to the goal*]. (A.) And ▼ ابتدر الغَايَةَ and إِلَى الغَايَةِ [*He strove in hastening,* or *strove to get first, to the goal*]. (Ḥam p. 46.) And بَادَرَ بَعْضُهُمْ بَعْضًا إِلَى أَمْرٍ, and ▼ تبادروهُ, and ▼ ابتدروا أَمْرًا, *They vied,* or *strove, one with another, in hastening to a thing,* or *an affair, trying which of them would be first.* (T.)

4. ابدر *He had the full moon rising to him,* (Ṣ, M, Ḳ,) or *upon him:* (A:) a verb similar to أَقْمَرَ and أَشْرَقَ: (A:) or *he journeyed during a night of full moon.* (T, Ḳ.) ═ *It* (an unripe date) *became red.* (TA.) [See also 1.] ═ ابدر فِى مَالِ الْيَتِيمِ: see 3.

6. تبادروا *They hastened together;* *vied,* or *strove, one with another, in hastening;* *made haste to be,* or *get, before one another;* *strove, one with another, to be first,* or *beforehand.* (Ṣ, TA.) You say, تبادروا إِلَى أَخْذِ السِّلَاحِ, (TA,) and ▼ ابتدروا السِّلَاحَ, (Ṣ, TA,) *They hastened together,* &c., *to take the weapons.* (Ṣ.) And تبادروا البَاعَ [*They hastened together;* or *vied,* or *strove, one with another, in hastening; to attain power,* or *eminence,* or *nobility*]; as also ▼ ابتدروهُ. (A.) And تبادروا أَمْرًا: see 3, last sentence. — هٰذَا مَا يَتَبَادَرُ مِنْهُ † [*This meaning is what appears from it* (namely, the phrase, or sentence,) *at first sight*]. (A phrase of frequent occurrence in the TA &c.)

8: see 3, in four places; and see 6, in two places. — ابْتَدَرَتْ عَيْنَاىَ *My eyes flowed with tears.* (TA, from a trad.)

Q. Q. 1. بَيْدَرَ *He heaped up* wheat. (Ḳ.)

بَدْرٌ, (Ṣ, A, Mṣb, Ḳ, &c.,) originally an inf. n., (Mṣb,) The *full moon;* (M, A, Mṣb, Ḳ;) as also ▼ بَادِرٌ; (L, Ḳ;) the *moon in its fourteenth night:* (Ṣ:) or the latter signifies [simply] the *moon:* (IAạr, T:) the moon in its fourteenth night is called بدر because it hastens to rise before the sun sets; (Ṣ, M;) and to set before the sun rises: (TA:) or because of its fulness; (Ṣ, TA;) as being likened to a بَدْرَة: or, as Er-Rághib thinks to be most probable, it is itself a primitive word: (TA:) pl. بُدُورٌ. (M, A.) Hence, لَيْلَةُ الْبَدْرِ [*The night of the full moon;* which is] *the fourteenth night* [*of the lunar month*]. (Ṣ.) — ‡ *A lord, master,* or *chief,* (M, Ḳ,) of a people: so called as being likened to the full moon. (M.) — Applied to a boy, (Zj, M, Ḳ,) ‡ *Full of youthful vigour and of flesh:* (Zj:) or *full,* or *plump:* (M:) or *i. q.* ▼ مُبَادِرٌ [*precocious*]. (T, Ḳ.) [In this sense, an epithet; and so its fem. بَدْرَةٌ (q. v.), applied to an eye.] — ‡ *A cover;* or *a dish* or *plate;* syn. طَبَقٌ: (Ibn-Wahb, Ḳ:) because resembling the full moon, being round: so Az thinks. (TA.) — See also بَدْرَةٌ, in two places.

بَدْرَةٌ, applied to an eye (عَيْنٌ), *Quick-sighted;* or *that sees before others:* (Aṣ, T, Ṣ, Ḳ, TA:) or *that sees before* [*the eyes of*] *other horses;* applied to a horse's eye: (IAạr, T, M:) or *sharp-sighted:* or *round and large:* (M:) or *full like the full moon:* (Ṣ, Ḳ:) but the correct meaning is [said to be] that [mentioned above as] given by IAạr: (M:) or, accord. to IAạr, *full; not defective.* (T.) ═ Also, (Ṣ, M, Ḳ,) and ▼ بَدْرٌ, (Ḳ,) The *skin of a lamb or kid* (Ṣ, M, Ḳ) *when it has been weaned,* (AZ, Ṣ, M,) *used for milk:* for [when it is killed] while it continues sucking, its skin, if used for milk, is called شَكْوَةٌ; and for clarified butter, عُكَّة: when it has been weaned, its skin for milk is called بَدْرَة; and for clarified butter, مِسْأد: and when it is in its second year, its skin for milk is called وَطْب; and for clarified butter, نِحْي: (AZ, Ṣ:) pl. (of the former, M) بِدَرٌ and بُدُورٌ: (M, Ḳ:) the former said by El-Fárisee to be the only instance of the kind except هِضَبٌ pl. of هَضْبَةٌ, and بِضَعٌ pl. of بَضْعَةٌ [or this may be pl. of بِضْعَةٌ]. (M. [But the assertion of El-Fárisee is incorrect (see حَيْضَةٌ), unless it be meant to apply only to sound words; and in this case, at least one addition should be made, namely قِصَعٌ pl. of قَصْعَةٌ.]) — Hence, (M,) the former word, (Ṣ, M, A, Ḳ, &c.,) and ▼the latter also, (Ḳ,) The *sum of ten thousand dirhems:* (Ṣ, A:) or *a purse containing a thousand,* (T, M, Ḳ,) or *ten thousand, dirhems,* (T, M,* A, Ḳ,) or *seven thousand deenárs:* (Ḳ:) pl. بُدُورٌ, (TA,) and pl. of pauc. بَدَرَاتٌ. (T.)

اِسْتَبَقْنَا البَدَرَى *We strove to outrun one another, vying, one with another, in haste.* (M, Ḳ.)

بَدْرِىٌّ Rain *that is before* (قَبْلَ), or *a little before* (قُبَيْلَ), or *in the first part of* (قُبُلَ), *winter.* (Ḳ, accord. to different copies: the second reading is that followed in the TA.) — A بَدْرِيَّةٌ A she-camel *whose mother has brought her forth at an earlier period of the year than that when the others brought forth, and therefore more abundant in milk than others, and of a more generous quality.* (M.) — And the former, A *fat* young camel weaned from its mother. (Ḳ.)

بَدَارِىٌّ A lamb *brought forth a little before winter.* (TA.)

بَادِرٌ: see بَدْرٌ.

بَيْدَرٌ a word of the dial. of El-'Irák, (A'Obeyd in art. ربد in the TA,) *A place in which wheat,* (Ṣ, Mgh, Ḳ,) or *grain,* (Mṣb,) *is trodden out.* (Ṣ, Mgh, Mṣb, Ḳ.) — It may also mean, tropically, ‡ The *wheat and straw therein:* (Mgh:) or rather, as Az says, on the authority of IAạr, it signifies [also] (Mgh) *reaped grain collected together;* or *wheat collected together in the place in which it is trodden out;* syn. كُدْسٌ, (M, Mgh, Ḳ,) and عَرَمَةٌ: (Mgh:) Kr restricts it to wheat. (M.) — Accord. to the Towsheeḥ, it is [*A place*] *for* [*drying*] *dates.* (TA in art. جرن.)

بَادِرَةٌ *Hastiness of temper; passionateness:* (Ṣ:) or *a hasty saying,* or *action, that suddenly proceeds* (يَبْدُرُ, in the CḲ يَبْدُو,) *from one in anger:* (M, A,* Mgh,* Mṣb,* Ḳ:) and *a slip; a mistake; an error;* (Ṣ, Mṣb;) *on an occasion of one's being angry:* (Ṣ:) or *a bad, an abominable,* or *a foul, word* or *saying:* and *a quick fit of anger:* (IAạr, T:) pl. بَوَادِرُ. (Ṣ, A.) You say, أَخْشَى عَلَيْكَ بَادِرَتَهُ *I fear for thee his hastiness of temper,* or *passionateness:* (Ṣ:) or *what may hastily proceed from him in his anger.* (A.) And بَدَرَتْ ▼ مِنْهُ بَوَادِرُ غَضَبٍ *Slips, mistakes,* or *errors, on an occasion of his being angry, hastily proceeded from him.* (Ṣ.) And بَادِرَةُ الشَّرِّ signifies *What hastily,* or *suddenly, befalls one, of evil,* or *mischief.* (M.) — *An intuitive knowledge, notion,* or *idea;* or *a faculty of judging rightly at the first of an unexpected occurrence;* or *a faculty of extemporizing;* syn. بَدِيهَةٌ. (Ṣ, Ḳ.) You say, فُلَانٌ حَسَنُ البَادِرَةِ *Such a one has a good intuitive knowledge,* &c. (TA.) — The *point* of a sword. (M, Ḳ.) — The *extremity* of an arrow, *next the head.* (A.) — The *head* of a plant; (M;) the *first part* thereof *from which the earth cleaves asunder.* (M, Ḳ.*) — The *first that appears* of the [plant called] حِنَّآء. (M.) — The *leaves of the* [*herb called*] حُوَّاءَة. (Ḳ.) — The *best, and freshest in growth, of the* [*plant called*] وَرْس. (M, Ḳ.*) — Also, (M, Ḳ,) or بَوَادِرُ, (Ṣ, A,) which is the pl., (Ḳ,) of a man &c., (Ṣ, M,) The *portion of flesh,* (Ṣ, M, Ḳ,) or the *portions thereof,* (A,) *between the shoulder-joint and the neck,* (Ṣ, M, Ḳ,) or *between the necks and the shoulder-joints:* (A:) or the former, (Ḳ,) or its dual, (M,) of a man, the *two portions of flesh that are above the* رُغَثَاوَانِ *and below the* تَنْدُوَة: (M, Ḳ:) or the dual, [relating to a camel, signifies] the *two sides of the* كِرْكِرَة [or *callous lump on the breast*]: or *two veins on either side thereof.* (M.) — بَدَرَتْ ▼ بَوَادِرُ الخَيْلِ *The first,* or *fore parts,* (أَوَائِل,) *of the horses appeared* [or *suddenly came in view*]. (Mṣb.)

بَدْرَةٌ مُبَدَّرَةٌ [*A sum such as is termed* بدرة *aggregated, made up,* or *completed*]: the latter word is a corroborative; like the latter in قَنَاطِيرُ مُقَنْطَرَةٌ, (Ksh and Bḍ in iii. 12,) and in أَلْفٌ مُؤَلَّفَةٌ. (Ksh ibid.)

مُبَادِرٌ applied to a boy: see بَدْرٌ.

بدع

1. بَدَعَهُ: see 4, in two places. ═ بَدُعَ, aor. ـُ, inf. n. بَدَاعَةٌ and بُدُوعٌ, *He became superlative in his kind;* or *it became so in its kind;* (Ks, Ḳ;) in good or in evil. (Ks.) ═ بَدُعَ, aor. ـُ, *He was,* or *became, fat.* (Aṣ, Ḳ.)

2. بَدَّعَهُ, (Ṣ, Ḳ,) inf. n. تَبْدِيعٌ, (Ḳ,) *He attributed to him, imputed to him, charged him with,* or *accused him of, innovation,* or *what is termed* بِدْعَة; expl. by نَسَبَهُ إِلَى البِدْعَةِ [which means نَسَبَ إِلَيْهِ البِدْعَةَ]. (Ṣ, Ḳ.)

4. ابدعهُ *He originated it; invented it; devised it; excogitated it; innovated it; made it, did it, produced it, caused it to be or exist,* or *brought it into existence, newly, for the first time, it not having been or existed before, and not after the similitude of anything pre-existing;* syn. اخْتَرَعَهُ لَا عَلَى مِثَالٍ, (Ṣ,) and اِسْتَخْرَجَهُ, and أَحْدَثَهُ, (Mṣb,) and أَبْدَأَهُ; (Ḳ, TA; but in both without the pronoun;) as also ▼ ابتدعه; (Mṣb;) syn. اِبْتَدَأَهُ, and أَحْدَثَهُ, (Mgh,) and أَنْشَأَهُ, (Ḳ,) and بَدَأَهُ; (TA;) and so ▼ بَدَعَهُ, aor. ـَ, (Ḳ, TA,) inf. n. بَدْعٌ; (TA;) but أَبْدَعَ is more commonly used than بَدَعَ. (TA.) You say, ابدع اللّٰهُ الخَلْقَ *God created the creation, not after any similitude.* (Mṣb.) And in the Ḳur [lvii. 27], we find, وَرَهْبَانِيَّةً ▼ ٱبْتَدَعُوهَا *And monkery which they originated,* or *innovated.* (TA.) And you say, بَدَعَ ▼ الرَّكِيَّةَ, (IDrd, Ḳ,) inf. n. بَدْعٌ, (IDrd,) *He produced,* or *fetched out, by his labour in digging, the water of the well;* (IDrd, Ḳ;) and *originated it;* or *made it to be for the first time, it not having been before.* (IDrd.) And ابدع الرَّجُلُ *The man introduced an innovation,* or *what is termed a* بِدْعَة; [the object being understood;] as also ▼ ابتدع. (TA.) And ابدع الشَّاعِرُ *The poet produced a new saying,* or *new poetry, not after the similitude of anything preceding.* (Ṣ,* Ḳ,* TA.) — ابدعت الرَّاحِلَةُ, (Ṣ, Ḳ,) or الرِّكَابُ, (Ks, Mgh,) *The ridden camel,* or *travelling camel, became fatigued,* or *jaded, and broke down,* or *perished;* (Ks, Ṣ, Mgh, Ḳ;) *as though doing a new thing:* (Ks, Mgh:) or the former phrase, (Ḳ,) followed by بِهِ, (TA,) *she limped* [*with him*], *halted,* or *was slightly lame:* (Ḳ, TA:) or *she lay down upon her breast in the road, by reason of emaciation or disease:* or *she ceased from going on, by reason of fatigue, or of limping, or halting, or slight lameness; as though she did a new and unaccustomed thing:* (TA:) or ابداع is not without limping, or halting, or slight lameness, (Ḳ, TA,) accord. to certain of the Arabs of the desert; but, says AO, this is not at variance with the explanations given. (TA.) And أُبْدِعَ بِالرَّجُلِ *The man's camel which he rode became fatigued,* or *jaded:* (Ṣ:) or أُبْدِعَ بِفُلَانٍ (Mgh, Ḳ) *such a one's camel which he rode ceased from going on, by reason of fatigue or lameness:* (Mgh:) or *broke down,* or *perished,* (Ḳ, TA,) or *became fatigued,* or *jaded,* (TA,) *and he became unable to prosecute his journey;* (Ḳ, TA;) and *his beast became so fatigued that it was left to remain where it was;* or *stood still with him.* (TA.) [See also أُعْبِدَ بِهِ.] It is said in a proverb, إِذَا طَلَبْتَ البَاطِلَ أُبْدِعَ بِكَ [*When thou seekest what is vain, or false, thou wilt be prevented from attaining thine object*]. (TA.) — أَبْدَعَ فُلَانٌ بِفُلَانٍ ‡ *Such a one prevented such a one from attaining his wish,* (قَطَعَ بِهِ,) *and abstained from aiding,* or *assisting, him, and did not undertake the accomplishment of his want,* (Lḥ, Ḳ, TA,) *and was not* [*at hand*] *when he thought he would be.* (TA.) — أَبْدَعَتْ حُجَّتُهُ ‡ *His argument,* or *plea,* or *the like, was,* or *became, vain,* or *false,* or *ineffectual:* (Aboo-Sa'eed, Ḳ:) or *was,* or *became, weak.* (A, TA.) And أُبْدِعَتْ حُجَّتُهُ ‡ *His argument,* or *plea,* &c., *was rendered vain,* or *ineffectual.* (Aboo-Sa'eed, Ḳ,* TA.) أَبْدَعَ بِرُّهُ بِشُكْرِى وَفَضْلُهُ وَإِيجَابُهُ بِوَصْفِى † [*His kindness has crippled my power of thanking, and his bounty, and the obligation which he has imposed, my power of description*]: so in the L; but in the O and Ḳ, قَصْدُهُ [*his intention*] is put in the place of فضله; and in the Ḳ, وايجابه is omitted: (TA:) said when one thanks another for his beneficence, acknowledging that his thanks are inadequate to his beneficence. (Ḳ.) ═ ابدع بِالحَجِّ, and بِالسَّفَرِ, *He determined,*

resolved, or *decided*, *upon pilgrimage*, and *upon journeying*. (TA.) — ابدع يمينًا *He rendered an oath binding*, or *obligatory*. (IAạr.) = ابدعوا به *They beat him*, or *struck him*. (TA.)

5. تبدّع *He turned innovator*. (O, Ḳ.) Ru-beh says,

إِنْ كُنْتَ لِلّٰهِ التَّقِيَّ الأَطْوَعَا
فَلَيْسَ وَجْهَ الحَقِّ أَنْ تَبَدَّعَا

[*If thou be, towards God, the pious, the very obedient, it is not the right way that thou shouldst turn innovator*]. (TA.)

8: see 4, in three places.

10. استبدعهُ *He reckoned it* بَدِيع [i. e. *new, wonderful, unknown before*]. (Ṣ, Ḳ.)

بِدْعٌ *i. q.* ▼ بَدِيعٌ, q. v., and ▼ مُبْتَدَعٌ; (Ṣ;) [but generally used as an epithet in which the quality of a subst. is predominant; signifying] *A novelty*; or *thing existing for the first time*: (Ḳ:) and *i. q.* ▼ بَدِيعٌ and ▼ مُبْتَدِعٌ, *a first doer*; as though meaning *one who has none among his fellows to share, or participate, with him* in a thing, or an affair: (Mṣb:) pl. أَبْدَاعٌ. (Akh, Ṣ.) You say, فُلَانٌ بِدْعٌ فِي هٰذَا الأَمْرِ, (Ṣ, Mṣb,) i. e. ▼ بَدِيعٌ, (Ṣ,) meaning *Such a one is the first doer in this affair*; *the first who has done it*. (Mṣb.) And hence the saying in the Ḳur [xlvi. 8], قُلْ مَا كُنْتُ بِدْعًا مِنَ الرُّسُلِ (Ṣ, Mṣb, TA) *Say thou, I am not the first who has been sent of the apostles*: (Mṣb, TA:) or the meaning is, *I am not an innovator among the apostles*; inviting you to that to which they do not invite you; or able to do that which they were not able to do: and accord. to one reading, it is ▼ بِدَعًا; as being [a sing. epithet] like قِيَمٌ; or for ذَا بِدَعٍ [in which the latter word is pl. of بِدْعَةٌ]. (Bḍ.) — Applied to a man, (TA,) *Superlative* (Ks, Ḳ) *in his kind* (Ks) in anything; (Ḳ;) in good and in evil; (Ks;) or in knowledge, or courage, or nobility: (Ḳ:) fem. with ة: pl. of the masc. أَبْدَاعٌ [a pl. of pauc., which is also, as is said in the L, applied to women,] and بُدُعٌ [a pl. of mult.]; and pl. of the fem. بِدَعٌ. (Ḳ.) — *A man liberal in disposition*; syn. غُمْرٌ. (IAạr, Ḳ.) — *A full* body. (Ḳ.)

بِدَعٌ: see بِدْعٌ. — It is also pl. of بِدْعَةٌ, [both as a subst. and] as fem. of بِدْعٌ. (Ḳ.)

بِدْعَةٌ *An innovation*; *a novelty*; *anything originated, invented*, or *innovated*; *anything made, done, produced, caused to be* or *exist*, or *brought into existence, newly, for the first time, it not having been* or *existed before, and not after the similitude of anything pre-existing*: (ISk:) *a dissentient state* or *condition*: (Mṣb:) a subst. from اِبْتِدَاعٌ, like رِفْعَةٌ from اِرْتِفَاعٌ, (Mgh, Mṣb,) and خِلْفَةٌ from اِخْتِلَافٌ: (Mgh:) subsequently and generally applied to *an addition*, or *an impairment, in religion*: (Mgh, Mṣb:) or *a novelty*, or *an innovation, in religion, after the completion* [*thereof*]: (Ṣ, Ḳ:) or *an opinion declining*, or *swerving, from the right way*, and *an action, innovated after* [*the time of*] *the Prophet*: (Lth, Ḳ:) or *an action at variance with the Sunneh*: (KT:) [generally *a heretical innovation*; or *a new heresy*: but] there is a بدعة not disapproved, termed بِدْعَةٌ مُبَاحَةٌ [*an allowed*, or *allowable, innovation*]; which is that whereof the goodness is attested by some principle in the law, or which is required to prevent some cause of evil; such as the Khaleefeh's seclusion of himself from the promiscuous classes of the people: (Mṣb:) there are two kinds of بدعة; namely بِدْعَةُ هُدًى [*an innovation of a right kind*], and بِدْعَةُ ضَلَالٍ [*an innovation of an erroneous kind*]. (IAth.)

بَدِيعٌ *i. q.* بِدْعٌ, which see in three places, (Ṣ, Mṣb,) and ▼ مُبْتَدَعٌ; [i. e. *Originated*; *invented*; *innovated*; *made, done, produced, caused to be* or *exist*, or *brought into existence, newly, for the first time, not having been* or *existed before, and not after the similitude of anything pre-existing*;] (Ṣ, Mṣb, Ḳ;) *new*; *wonderful*; *unknown before*. (TA.) You say, جِئْتَ بِأَمْرٍ بَدِيعٍ *Thou hast done a new thing*; *a wonderful thing*; *a thing unknown before*: and ▼ أَمْرٌ بَادِعٌ signifies *the same as* أَمْرٌ بَدِيعٌ. (TA.) And جَآءَ بِالبَدِيعِ, (Ṣ,) or أَتَى بِالبَدِيعِ, (Ḳ,) said of a poet, (Ṣ, Ḳ,) *He produced a new saying*, or *new poetry, not after the similitude of anything preceding*. (TA.) And حَبْلٌ بَدِيعٌ *A new rope*: (AḤn:) or *a rope begun to be twisted, not being yet a rope, but undone, then spun, then twisted again*. (Ḳ.) And زِمَامٌ بَدِيعٌ *A new nose-rein of a camel*. (TA.) And رَكِيَّةٌ بَدِيعٌ *A newly-dug well*. (TA.) [See also بَدِىٌّ.] And بَدِيعٌ alone, *A skin for wine &c.*: (Ṣ:) or *a new skin for wine &c.*: (Ḳ:) and *a new skin for water or milk*: an epithet in which the quality of a subst. is predominant. (TA.) Hence the trad., إِنَّ تِهَامَةَ كَبَدِيعِ العَسَلِ حُلْوٌ أَوَّلُهُ حُلْوٌ آخِرُهُ [*Verily Tihámeh is like the skin*, or *new skin, of honey*: *the first part thereof is sweet*: *the last part thereof is sweet*]: (Ṣ, Ḳ*:) because honey does not change in flavour, whereas milk does change. (Ṣ.) — *Fat*; as an epithet: (Aṣ, Ḳ:) pl. بُدُعٌ. (Ḳ.) = Also *i. q.* ▼ مُبْتَدِعٌ [*An originator, inventor*, or *innovator*; *one who makes, does, produces, causes to be or exist, or brings into existence, newly, for the first time, and not after the similitude of anything pre-existing*]: (Ṣ, Ḳ:) of the measure فَعِيلٌ in the sense of the measure فَاعِلٌ, like قَدِيرٌ in the sense of قَادِرٌ; from بَدَعَ. (TA.) [See also بِدْعٌ.] You say, اللّٰهُ بَدِيعُ السَّمٰوَاتِ وَالأَرْضِ *God is the Creator of the heavens and the earth, not after the similitude of anything pre-existing*. (Aboo-Is-ḥáḳ, Ṣ.*) And hence البَدِيعُ is a name of God, meaning *The Originator of the creation, according to his own will, not after the similitude of anything pre-existing*. (TA.)

[بَدِيعَةٌ *A new, and an admirable*, or *a wonderful, thing*; and especially such in speech, or language, in poetry, and in answering, or replying: pl. بَدَائِعُ: see an ex. voce بَدِيهَةٌ.]

بَادِعٌ: see بَدِيعٌ.

مُبْتَدَعٌ: } see بِدْعٌ and بَدِيعٌ, each in two places.
مُبْتَدِعٌ: }

بدل

1. بَدَلَ, inf. n. بَدَالٌ: see 2, in three places.

2. تَبْدِيلٌ properly signifies [The *changing*, or *altering*, a thing; or] the *changing*, or *altering, the form*, or *fashion*, or *semblance*, or *the quality*, or *condition*, [of a thing,] *to another form*, &c., *while the substance remains the same*; (Th, T, TA;) or the *changing* a thing *from its state*, or *condition*; (Ibn-'Arafeh, TA;) or the *changing* a thing *without substitution*: (Ṣ:) but the Arabs have used it also in the sense of ▼ إِبْدَالٌ, (Mbr, T, TA,) which signifies [the *changing* a thing *by substitution*; *exchanging* it; *replacing* it *with another thing*; or] the *removing*, or *displacing, the substance* [of a thing], *and introducing anew another substance*. (Th, T, TA.) You say, بَدَّلْتُهُ, inf. n. تَبْدِيلٌ, (M,* Mṣb, Ḳ,) meaning *I changed it*, or *altered it*; (M, Ḳ;) or *I changed*, or *altered, the form*, or *fashion*, or *semblance*, or *the quality*, or *condition, of it*; (Mṣb;) as in the phrase, بَدَّلْتُ الخَاتَمَ بِالحَلْقَةِ [*I changed*, or *altered, the signet-ring into the simple ring*], said when one has melted the former and made of it a simple ring; (Fr, T, TA;) and بَدَّلَ اللّٰهُ السَّيِّئَاتِ حَسَنَاتٍ [*God changed the evil deeds into good deeds*]; the verb being doubly trans. by itself because it has the meaning of جَعَلَ and صَيَّرَ. (Mṣb. [But see what follows.]) ▼ أَبْدَلْتُهُ بِكَذَا, [in the Ṣ, أَبْدَلْتُ الشَّىْءَ بِغَيْرِهِ,] without explanation,] inf. n. إِبْدَالٌ, [*I changed it by substituting for it such a thing*, or *exchanged it for such a thing*, or *replaced it with such a thing*,] is said when one has removed the first, and put the second in its place; (Mṣb;) as in the phrase, أَبْدَلْتُ الخَاتَمَ بِالحَلْقَةِ [*I changed the signet-ring by substituting for it the simple ring*; *exchanged the signet-ring for the simple ring*; or *replaced the signet-ring with the simple ring*]; said when one removes the one, and puts the other in its place: (Fr, T, TA:) and this verb is also made doubly trans. by itself, like بَدَّلْتُ, (Mṣb,) which is used in the sense of أَبْدَلْتُ [as shown above]; (Mbr, T, TA;) for instance, where it is said, [in the Ḳur lxvi. 5,] عَسَى رَبُّهُ إِنْ طَلَّقَكُنَّ أَنْ يُبْدِلَهُ أَزْوَاجًا خَيْرًا مِنْكُنَّ [*May-be, his Lord, if he divorce you, will give him in exchange wives better than you*]; accord. to one reading, يُبَدِّلَهُ. (Mṣb.) An ex. of the latter of these two verbs in the sense of the former is the saying in the Ḳur [xxv. 70], يُبَدِّلُ اللّٰهُ سَيِّئَاتِهِمْ حَسَنَاتٍ [*God will change their evil deeds by substituting for them good deeds*]; i. e. will cancel the evil deeds and put in their place good deeds: but in the saying in the Ḳur [iv. 59], كُلَّمَا نَضِجَتْ جُلُودُهُمْ بَدَّلْنَاهُمْ جُلُودًا غَيْرَهَا [*Whenever their skins are thoroughly burned, we will change the condition thereof to them into the condition of other skins*], the meaning is, that the first condition of their skins shall be restored;

so that the substance is one, but the condition is different. (Mbr, T, TA.) You say also, بَدَّلَهُ ٱللّٰهُ مِنَ الخَوْفِ أَمْنًا [*God gave him in exchange for fear, or in lieu of fear, security*]. (Ṣ.) [And بَدَّلَهُ بِهِ كَذَا *He gave him in exchange for it, or in lieu of it, such a thing:* see Ḳur xxxiv. 15. And بَدَّلَ مَكَانَهُ كَذَا *He gave in exchange for it, or in lieu of it, such a thing:* see Ḳur vii. 93 and xvi. 103.] بَدَّلَ حُسْنًا بَعْدَ سُوْءٍ, in the Ḳur [xxvii. 11], means *He hath done good* [*by way of exchange after evil*]; i. e., *repented;* (Jel;) or بَدَّلَ ذَنْبَهُ بِالتَّوْبَةِ [*hath exchanged his sin for repentance*]. (Bḍ.) تَبْدِيلٌ and ↓ إِبْدَالٌ both signify The act of *exchanging* [a thing for another thing]; or *making* [a thing] *to be a substitute* [for another thing]; (KL, PṢ;) and so does ↓ بَدَالٌ. (KL.) You say, بَدَّلَ الشَّىْءَ مِنَ الشَّىْءِ, (M, Ḳ,*) and ↓ ابدلهُ منهُ, i. e. اِتَّخَذَهُ مِنْهُ بَدَلًا [here meaning *He exchanged the thing for the thing;* or, more literally, *he made the thing a substitute for the thing*]. (M, Ḳ. [In the text of the former of these, as given in the TT, instead of اِتَّخَذَهُ, I find تَخِذَ (a dial. var. of اِتَّخَذَ) without the affixed pronoun, which is meant to be understood or is omitted inadvertently by the transcriber: and here it should be observed, that the explanation which I have rendered as above admits of another meaning, namely, أَخَذَهُ مِنْهُ بَدَلًا "he took it as a substitute for it:" in the M, immediately before, أَخَذَ مِنْهُ بَدَلًا is given as the explanation of the phrases تبدّل الشَّىْءَ and بِالشَّىْءِ, and استبدلهُ and بِهِ: see 10.]) You say also, ↓ بَدَلْتُ الثَّوْبَ بِغَيْرِهِ, aor. ـُ, [inf. n. بَدَالٌ, mentioned and explained above, *I exchanged the garment, or piece of cloth, for another;* or *made it to be a substitute for another;*] and ↓ اِسْتَبْدَلْتُهُ بِغَيْرِهِ signifies the same. (Mṣb. [But the latter phrase has more frequently another meaning, explained below: see 10.]) [↓ ابدلهُ in the phrases ابدلهُ كَذَا as meaning *He changed it into,* or *substituted for it, such a thing,* and ابدلهُ مِنْ كَذَا as meaning *he changed it from,* or *substituted it for, such a thing,* is more common than بَدَّلَهُ, which is used in the same sense; as ↓ بَدَلَهُ is also; for] AO applies the term ↓ مَبْدُولٌ [in lieu of the more common term ↓ مُبْدَلٌ] to a letter that is *changed* from another letter, as in مَدَهْتُهُ for مَدَحْتُهُ; and this shows that بَدَلْتُ is trans. [and signifies *I changed,* &c.]. (Az, TA.)

3. مُبَادَلَةٌ and ↓ تَبَادُلٌ signify the same, (Ṣ,) namely, The act of *exchanging with another* or *others.* (PṢ.) You say, بادلهُ, inf. n. مُبَادَلَةٌ and بِدَالٌ [in the CḲ erroneously written with fet-ḥ to the ب], *He exchanged,* or *made an exchange, with him;* or] *he gave him the like of that which he took, or received, from him;* (IDrd,* M, Ḳ;) for instance, a garment, or piece of cloth, in the place of another; (Lth, T, Mṣb,* in explanation of the former inf. n.;) and a brother in the place of a brother. (Lth, T.) And ↓ تَبَادَلَا *They exchanged,* or *made an exchange, each with the other;* or *each gave to the other the like of that which he took,* or *received, from him.* (TA.) نُبَادِلُهْ, ending a verse of El-Ḳulákh, means *for whom we would take a substitute:* El-Marzooḳee says, it is for نُبَادِلُ بِهِ النَّاسَ [*for whom we would make an exchange with the people*]; the preposition being suppressed. (Ḥam p. 465.)

4. ابدلهُ, inf. n. إِبْدَالٌ: see 2, in five places.

5. تبدّل *It* (a thing, M) *became changed,* or *altered.* (M, Ḳ.) — In the saying of the rájiz,

* فَبُدِّلَتْ وَالدَّهْرُ ذُو تَبَدُّلِ *

the meaning is, ذو تبديل [i. e. the meaning of the whole is, *And,* or *but, she was changed,* or *altered; for time has the property of changing,* or *altering*]. (M.) — See also 10, in three places.

6: see 3, in two places.

10. استبدل الشَّىْءَ, and بِالشَّىْءِ, and ↓ تبدّلهُ and بِهِ, (M, Ḳ,*) *He took a substitute,* or *a thing in exchange, for the thing.* (M.) You say, استبدل الشَّىْءَ بِغَيْرِهِ, and ↓ تبدّلهُ بِهِ, *He took the thing* [*as a substitute,* or *in exchange, for another;* or] *in the place of another.* (Ṣ.) And استبدل ثَوْبًا مَكَانَ ثَوْبٍ [*He took a garment, or piece of cloth, in the place,* or *in lieu, of a garment,* &c.]; and أَخًا مَكَانَ أَخٍ [*a brother in the place,* or *in lieu, of a brother*]. (Lth, T.) It is said in the Ḳur [ii. 58], أَتَسْتَبْدِلُونَ ٱلَّذِى هُوَ أَدْنَى بِٱلَّذِى هُوَ خَيْرٌ *Will ye take in exchange that which is worse for that which is better?* (Jel. [See also other exs. in the Ḳur ix. 39 and xlvii. last verse.]) And مَنْ يَتَبَدَّلِ ↓ الكُفْرَ بِالإِيمَانِ [*Whoso adopteth infidelity in lieu of faith*]. (Ḳur ii. 102. [See also other exs. in the Ḳur iv. 2 and xxxiii. 52.]) — See also 2, last sentence but one.

بِدْلٌ: see the next paragraph, in four places.

بَدَلٌ and ↓ بِدْلٌ, (Fr, T, Ṣ, M, Mṣb, Ḳ,) like مَثَلٌ and مِثْلٌ, and شَبَهٌ and شِبْهٌ, (Fr, T, Ṣ,) and نَكَلٌ and نِكْلٌ, the only other instances of the kind, i. e. of words of both these measures, that have been heard, accord. to AO, (Ṣ, TA, [but in one copy of the Ṣ, I find A'Obeyd,]) and ↓ بَدِيلٌ, (Ṣ, M, Mgh, Mṣb, Ḳ,) all signify the same; (Ṣ, M, Mṣb, Ḳ;) namely, *A substitute; a thing given,* or *received,* or *put,* or *done, instead of, in place of, in lieu of,* or *in exchange* for, another thing; *a compensation;* syn. خَلَفٌ, (M, Ḳ,) and عِوَضٌ: (Kull:) [and البَدَلُ مِنَ الشَّىْءِ] بَدَلُ الشَّىْءِ and ↓ بِدْلُهُ and ↓ بَدِيلُهُ meaning الخَلَفُ مِنْهُ [*the substitute for the thing;* &c.]; (M, Ḳ;) i. e., another thing: (Ṣ:) pl. أَبْدَالٌ, (IDrd, Mṣb, Ḳ,) which, as pl. of ↓ بَدِيلٌ, has few parallels. (IDrd, TA.) Sb says, [making a distinction between بَدَلٌ and ↓ بَدِيلٌ,] you say, إِنَّ بَدَلَكَ زَيْدًا, i. e. *Verily Zeyd is in thy place:* but if you put بَدَل in the place of بديل, you say, إِنَّ بَدَلَكَ زَيْدٌ, i. e. ↓ إِنَّ بَدِيلَكَ زَيْدٌ [*Verily thy substitute is Zeyd*]: and a man says to another, Go thou with such a one; and he replies, مَعِى رَجُلٌ بَدَلُهُ, i. e. *With me is a man who stands in his stead,* and is *in his place,* or who will stand &c. (M.) You say also, بَدَلَ كَذَا [and بَدَلًا مِنْ كَذَا], meaning *Instead of, in the place of, in lieu of,* or *in exchange for, such a thing.* (Kull.) [And بَدَلَ أَنْ تَفْعَلَ كَذَا *Instead of thy doing thus.*] — الأَبْدَالُ (IDrd, Ṣ, M, Ḳ, &c.) and البُدَلَآءُ (TA) [*The Substitutes,* or *Lieutenants;*] *certain righteous persons, of whom the world is never destitute; when one dies, God substituting another in his place:* (Ṣ:) *certain persons by means of whom God rules the earth;* (M, Ḳ;) *consisting of seventy men,* (IDrd, M, Ḳ,) *according to their assertion, of whom the earth is never destitute;* (IDrd, TA;) *forty of whom are in Syria, and thirty in the other countries;* (IDrd, M, Ḳ;) *none of them dying without another's supplying his place,* (M, Ḳ,) *from the rest of mankind;* (Ḳ;) *and therefore they are named* ابدال: (M:) accord. to Abu-l-Baḳà, as stated by El-Munáwee, it seems that they meant [by this appellation] *the substitutes and successors of the prophets;* and accord. to some, they were *seven, neither more nor fewer, by means of whom God takes care of the seven climates; one being successor of Abraham* (*El-Khaleel*), *and to him pertains the first climate; the second, of Moses* (*El-Keleem*); *the third, of Aaron; the fourth, of Idrees; the fifth, of Joseph; the sixth, of Jesus; and the seventh, of Adam:* (TA: [in which is also mentioned a treatise denying their existence, and disapproving of the assertion that by means of them God takes care of the earth:]) the sing. is بَدَلٌ and ↓ بِدْلٌ, (T,) or ↓ بَدِيلٌ. (IDrd, Ṣ.) — حُرُوفُ البَدَلِ (M, Ḳ) *The letters of substitution; those which are substituted for other letters; not those which are substituted in consequence of idghám.* (M.) [The letters included under this appellation differ accord. to different authors: see De Sacy's Gram. Ar. 2nd ed. i. 33.] — ↓ بِدْلٌ (Kr, M, Ḳ) and بَدَلٌ, (M, Ḳ,) applied to a man, also signify *Generous,* and *noble:* (Kr,* M, Ḳ:) and used in these senses, [says ISd,] they are, in my opinion, not devoid of implication of the meaning of a substitute: (M:) the pl. is أَبْدَالٌ. (M, Ḳ.)

بَدِيلٌ: see بَدَلٌ, in six places.

بَدَّالٌ *A seller of eatables* (AHeyth, T, Ḳ) *of every kind:* thus he is called by the Arabs; (AHeyth, T;) because he changes one sale for another; selling one thing to-day and another to-morrow: (AḤát, TA:) the vulgar say, بَقَّالٌ. (AHeyth, T, Ḳ.) — Also *One who has no more property than is sufficient for his purchasing one thing, and who, when he sells this, buys another thing in exchange for it.* (TA in art. جدل.) [Hence,] هٰذَا رَأْىُ الجَدَّالِينَ وَالبَدَّالِينَ is a phrase used as meaning *This is a flimsy opinion.* (TA in the present art. and in art. جدل, [but in the latter without the و,] on the authority of AHeyth.)

مُبْدَلٌ :
مَبْدُولٌ : } see 2.

بدن

1. بَدُنَ, (T, Ṣ, M, Mgh, Mṣb, Ḳ,) aor. ـُ; (T, Ṣ;) and بَدَنَ, aor. ـُ; (T, Ṣ, M, Mṣb, Ḳ;) inf. n.

بَدَانَةٌ, (T, Ṣ, M, &c.,) of the former, (ISk, T, Ṣ, &c.,) and بُدْنٌ, (T, Ṣ, M, Ḳ,) also of the former, (ISk, T,) or of the latter, (Ṣ,) and بَدَنٌ, (M, Ḳ,) accord. to AZ, (T,) and بَدَانٌ, (M, Ḳ,) or بُدُونٌ is the inf. n. of the latter verb; (Mṣb;) said of a man, (ISk, T, Ṣ,) and of a camel; (Mṣb;) and بَدُنَتْ and بَدَنَتْ, said of a woman, (AZ, T, M, Ḳ,) and of a بَدَنَة, q. v.; (Zj, T, &c.;) *He, and she, was, or became, big, bulky, big-bodied,* or *corpulent;* (ISk, T, Ṣ, M, Mgh, Mṣb, Ḳ;) *abounding in flesh;* (T;) *fat:* (Zj, T, M:) or the former verb has this last signification, that of fatness; and the latter verb is syn. with بَدَّنَ, q. v. (Ḥam p. 158.) [See also بُدْنٌ, below.]

2. بَدَّنَ, inf. n. تَبْدِينٌ, *He* (a man, T, Ṣ, M) *was,* or *became, aged,* (T, Ṣ, M, Mgh, Mṣb, Ḳ,) *and weak:* (M, Ḳ:) or *he was,* or *became, heavy by reason of age;* as also ▼ بَدَنَ. (Ḥam p. 158.) ═ *He clad* a man *with a* بَدَن, i. e. a دِرْع [or *coat of mail*]. (Ḳ,* TA.)

بُدْنٌ [properly an inf. n.; see 1:] *Fatness and compactness;* as also ▼ بُدُنٌ. (Ṣ.) — And *Fat;* i. e. the *substance termed* شَحْمٌ. (M, TA.) ═ It is also a pl. of بَدَنَةٌ: (T, Ṣ, &c.:) — and of بَادِنٌ. (M, TA.)

بَدَنٌ The *body, without the head and arms and legs;* (M, Mṣb, Ḳ;) so says Az: (Mṣb:) or the *body without the arms and legs:* (Mgh:) or [the *part*] *from the shoulder-joint to the posteriors* [*inclusive*]: (TA [as from the Mgh, in my copy of which it is not found]:) or the جَسَد [generally meaning the *body together with the members*] of a man; (Ṣ;) often applied to the *whole of the* جَسَد; (Az, TA;) and in the Ḳur x. 92 it is said to mean the *body without soul:* (Ṣ:) pl. أَبْدَانٌ; (M, Mṣb;) whence the phrase, mentioned by Lḥ, إِنَّهَا لَحَسَنَةُ الأَبْدَانِ [meaning *Verily she is beautiful in respect of the body*], as though the term بَدَنٌ were applied to every portion of her. (M.) شَرِكَةُ الأَبْدَانِ is originally شَرِكَةٌ بِالأَبْدَانِ, meaning *Copartnership in bodily labours for the acquirement of gains.* (Mṣb.) — And hence, ‡ The *part* of a shirt, (Mgh, Mṣb,) and of a [garment of the kind called] جُبَّة, (Mgh,) *that lies against the back and the belly,* [i. e. the *body* thereof,] *without the sleeves and the* دَخَارِيص [or *gores with which it is widened*]: (Mgh, Mṣb:) pl. as above. (Mṣb.) — Also † *A short* دِرْع [or *coat of mail*], (Ṣ, M, Ḳ,) *of the measure of the body:* (M:) or it is [*a coat of mail*] *like a* دِرْع, *except that it is short, only such as covers the body, with short sleeves:* (T:) or, as some say, *any* دِرْع: (M:) and so it is said to mean in the Ḳur x. 92 by IAạr (T) and by Th; (M;) but Akh says that this assertion is of no account: (Ṣ:) pl. as above. (M, Ḳ.) — And † *A small* [*garment of the kind called*] جُبَّة; as being likened to a coat of mail. (TA.) — Accord. to Kr, (M,) *A limb,* or *member:* or, specially, the *limbs,* or *members, of a slaughtered camel:* (M, Ḳ: [in the latter of which, the former of these two explanations is improperly connected with the first in this paragraph by the conjunction او:]) to these he specially applies it in one instance: pl. as above. (M.) — Also *An old,* or *aged, man:* (Ḳ:) or so رَجُلٌ بَدَنٌ. (T, Ṣ, M.) [In like manner, ▼ بَادِنٌ and ▼ بَدِنٌ are said by Golius, as on the authority of the Ṣ, to signify *annosus et senior,* applied to a man, and also to a woman; but this explanation is wrong; and the latter word I do not find in any lexicon.] — And *An old mountain-goat:* (M, Ḳ:) or so وَعِلٌ بَدَنٌ: (Ṣ:) [in the present day, بَدَن is applied to the *wild goat of the Arabian and Egyptian deserts and mountains;* the *capra jaela* of Hamilton Smith; called by some an *ibex;* as is also تَيْتَل, properly تَيْتَلٌ:] pl. [of pauc.] أَبْدُنٌ (M, Ḳ [in the CḲ, erroneously, أَبْدَنٌ]) and [of mult.] بُدُونٌ, which is extr. [with respect to rule], on the authority of IAạr. (M, TA.) The rájiz says, describing a bitch (Ṣ, M) and a mountain-goat, (M, TA,)

قَدْ قُلْتُ لَمَّا بَدَتِ العُقَابُ •
وَضَمَّهَا وَالبَدَنَ الحِقَابُ •
جِدِّى لِكُلِّ عَامِلٍ ثَوَابُ •
اَلرَّأْسُ وَالأَكْرُعُ وَالإِهَابُ •

(Ṣ,* M,* TA,) [*I had said, when El-'Iḳáb appeared, and El-Ḥiḳáb comprised her and the old mountain-goat,* "*Exert thyself: for every worker there is a recompense: the head and the shanks and the hide* shall be thine"]: العقاب is the name of a bitch, and الحقاب is a certain mountain: he says, "Catch thou this goat, and I will make thy recompense to be the head and the shanks and the hide." (TA.) [Hence Golius has been led to mistake الحِقَابُ for a signification of البَدَنُ.] — † The *lineage,* or *parentage,* of a man, *and his grounds of pretension to respect* or *honour.* (M, Ḳ.)

بَدِنٌ: see بَدَنٌ.

بُدُنٌ: see بُدْنٌ. ═ It is also a pl. of بَدَنَةٌ. (M, Ḳ, &c.)

بَدَنَةٌ *A she-camel,* (T, Ṣ, M, Mgh, Mṣb, Ḳ,) and *a male camel,* (T, M, Mgh, Ḳ,) and *a cow,* (T, Ṣ, M, Mgh,* Mṣb, Ḳ,) and *a bull,* (M, Ḳ,) accord. to some, (Mṣb,) or properly the first of these, (Mgh, Mṣb,) and the second, (Mgh,) but made by the Sunneh to apply to a cow also, (Mgh,* Mṣb,) *that is slaughtered at Mekkeh,* (Ṣ,) or that is, (M, Ḳ,) or may be, (T,) *brought thither for sacrifice;* (T, M, Ḳ;) so called because they used to fatten them, (Ṣ,) or because of their greatness, or bulkiness: (T, Mgh, Mṣb:) not applied to a sheep or goat: (T, Mṣb, TA:) En-Nawawee erroneously cites the T as asserting that it is thus applied; misled, it is said, by an omission in his copy: (MF, TA:) pl. بَدَنَاتٌ, (T, Mgh, Mṣb,) a pl. of pauc., (Mgh,) and بُدْنٌ, (T, Ṣ, M, Mṣb,) or بُدُنٌ, (Mgh, Ḳ,) or both, (M, Mṣb, TA,) the former being a contraction of the latter, which seems to be pl. of بَدِينٌ: (Mṣb:) one should not use بَدَنٌ as a pl. of بَدَنَةٌ; though they used to say خَشَبٌ and أَجَمٌ &c. (M, TA.)

[بَدَنِيٌّ *Of,* or *relating to, the* بَدَن, or *body corporeal.* — See also بَادِنٌ.]

بَدِينٌ: see بَادِنٌ, in four places.

بَادِنٌ, applied to a man, *Big, bulky, big-bodied,* or *corpulent;* (ISk, T, Ṣ, M, Mgh, Mṣb, Ḳ;) as also ▼ بَدِينٌ (Mṣb, Ḳ) and ▼ مُبَدَّنٌ (M, Ḳ) [and ▼ بَدَنِىٌّ]: and *fat;* as also ▼ مُبَدَّنٌ: (T, M:) or *heavy in body; heavy by reason of age:* and ▼ بَدِينٌ signifies *fat:* (Ḥam p. 158:) بَادِنٌ is likewise applied to a woman, (Ṣ, M, Mṣb, Ḳ,) as are also بَادِنَةٌ (M, Mgh, Ḳ) and ▼ بَدِينٌ (Ṣ, Ḳ) and ▼ مُبَدَّنَةٌ: (T, M:) the pl. is بُدْنٌ (M, Mṣb, Ḳ) and بُدُنٌ (M, TA) and بُدَّنٌ; (Mṣb, Ḳ;) the first of these being pl. of بَادِنٌ, (M, Mṣb,) and so the second; (M;) and the third being pl. of ▼ بَدِينٌ. (Mṣb.) See also بَدَنٌ.

مُبَدَّنٌ, and with ة: see بَادِنٌ, in three places.

مِبْدَانٌ *That becomes fat quickly, with little fodder* [or *food*]. (M, Ḳ.)

بده

1. بَدَهَهُ, (JK, Ṣ, Mṣb, Ḳ,) aor. َ, (Ṣ, Mṣb, Ḳ,) inf. n. بَدْهٌ, (JK, Ṣ, Mṣb,) *He,* or *it, came upon him,* or *happened to him, suddenly, unexpectedly,* or *without his being aware of it; surprised him,* or *took him unawares;* (JK, Ṣ, Mṣb, Ḳ;) as also ▼ بَادَهَهُ, inf. n. مُبَادَهَةٌ: (JK, Mṣb:) the former verb has this signification said of an affair, or event. (Ṣ, Ḳ.) And بَدَهَهُ بِأَمْرٍ, (Ṣ, Ḳ,) aor. as above, (Ḳ,) and so the inf. n., (JK, TA,) signifies اِسْتَقْبَلَهُ بِهِ, (JK, T, Ṣ, Ḳ,) i. e. *He met him,* or *encountered him, with a thing,* or *an affair,* or *an action,* (TḲ,) *suddenly, unexpectedly,* or *without his being aware of it:* (T, TA:) or *he began with him by it,* or *with it;* syn. بَدَأَهُ بِهِ; (Ḳ;) the ه being a substitute for the أ: (TA:) and بَدَاهُ, (Ṣ,* Ḳ,) بَادَهَهُ بِهِ ▼ inf. n. مُبَادَهَةٌ and بِدَاهٌ, (Ḳ,) *he came upon him suddenly, unexpectedly,* or *without his being aware of it; surprised him,* or *took him unawares;* (Ṣ, Ḳ;) *with it.* (Ḳ.) — See also 2.

2. بَدَّهَ, inf. n. تَبْدِيهٌ, *He answered,* or *replied, quickly:* (IAạr, TA:) and ▼ بَدَهَ *he answered,* or *replied,* or *he spoke, extempore; without premeditation.* (Ḥar p. 64.)

3: see 1, in two places.

6. هُمَا يَتَبَادَهَانِ بِالشِّعْرِ (Ṣ, TA) *They two dispute,* or *contend together* [*extemporaneously,* or *extemporizing, with verses* or *poetry*]. (TA.) — See also 8.

8. ابتده الخُطْبَةَ (Ḳ, TA) *He extemporized the discourse,* or *sermon,* or *oration; spoke it,* or *composed it, extemporaneously, impromptu, without premeditation.* (TA.) And ▼ هُمْ يَتَبَادَهُونَ الخُطَبَ (Ḳ, TA) *They extemporize discourses,* &c.: here the measure تَفَاعَلَ has not its proper quality [of denoting participation in the manner of contention, though it has in a phrase mentioned before]. (TA.)

بَدْهٌ and بُدْهٌ : see بُدَاهَةٌ.

بَدِيهَةٌ, بَدِيهًا, and عَلَى بَدِيهٍ : see بَدِيهَةٌ.

بَدَاهَةٌ : see بُدَاهَةٌ, in two places.

بَدِيهَةٌ (Ṣ, Ḳ) and ▼ بَدَاهَةٌ (Ṣgh, Ḳ) and ▼ بُدَاهَةٌ (JK, Ṣ, Ḳ) and ▼ بَدْهٌ and ▼ بُدْهٌ (Ḳ) substs. from بَدَهَهُ بِأَمْرٍ, (JK, Ṣ,) meaning The *first* of anything; and *an occurrence* thereof *by which one is taken unawares:* (Ḳ:) or the *first occurrence* of a thing, *that happens to one unexpectedly.* (M, in explanation of the first word, in art. بدأ.) —— Also the first (Ṣ, TA) and ▼ second (JK) and ▼ third (TA) The *first part of the running* of a horse; (JK, Ṣ, TA;) opposed to عُلَالَةٌ, signifying [the "remaining part of the running," or "an after-running," or] "a running after a running." (TA.) You say, هُوَ ذُو بَدِيهَةٍ ▼ وَعُلَالَةٍ, and بُدَاهَةٍ, [*He has a first running and an after-running,* differing, the one from the other]. (Aẓ, TA.) And لَحِقَهُ فِى بُدَاهَةِ جَرْيِهِ [*He overtook him in the first part of his running*]. (Z, TA.) ISd thinks that in all these cases the ه is a substitute for ء. (TA.) [Hence,] ▼ غَمْرُ البَدِيهَةِ [properly *Fleet in the first part of his running;* meaning] ‡a man *who takes by surprise with large bounty.* (TA, in art. غمر.) —— See also the next paragraph, in three places.

بَدِيهَةٌ : see بُدَاهَةٌ, in four places. You say, لَكَ البَدِيهَةُ, (Ḳ,) in which ISd thinks the ه to be a substitute for ء, (TA,) *It is for thee to begin;* (Ḳ;) and so ▼ لك البُدَاهَةُ, with ه substituted for ء. (M, Mbr, TA art. بدأ.) And أَجَابَ عَلَى البَدِيهَةِ (Ḳ) *He answered,* or *replied, on the first of his being taken unawares.* (TA.) [▼ عَلَى بَدِيهٍ is mentioned by Freytag, but on what authority he does not say, as meaning *Unpreparedly, suddenly,* or *unexpectedly;* and so ▼ بَدِيهًا by Golius, as on the authority of J, but I do not find it in the Ṣ in the present article.] And رَآهُ بَدِيهَةً signifies *He saw him suddenly,* or *unexpectedly.* (TA.) And بَدِيهَةُ الرَّأْىِ, *Suddenly formed, unpremeditated, judgment* or *opinion.* (Mṣb.) —— بَدِيهَةٌ and ▼ بُدَاهَةٌ both signify The *coming, of speech, without premeditation:* and the *coming suddenly, unexpectedly,* or *unawares.* (KL.) —— And ▼ the latter, [and more commonly the former,] *An intuitive knowledge, notion,* or *idea; such as that one is the half of two;* being, *with respect to knowledge, like* بَدِيعٌ *with respect to intellect:* (Kull:) [or] the former signifies the *faculty of judging rightly at the first of an unexpected occurrence:* [*intuition,* or *intuitive perception:*] accord. to 'Alee-Ibn-Ḍháfir El-Ḥaddád, it signifies primarily اِرْتِجَالٌ فِى الكَلَامِ [i. e. the *faculty of extemporizing;* or *speaking,* or *composing, extemporaneously, impromptu, without premeditation*]: and predominantly, the *poetizing,* or *versifying, impromptu, without premeditation* or *consideration: except that* ارتجال *is quicker than* بديهة. (TA.) You say, هُوَ ذُو بَدِيهَةٍ (Ḳ) *He has a faculty of judging rightly at the first of an unexpected occurrence.* (TA.) And فُلَانٌ ذُو بَدِيهَةٍ حَسَنَةٍ *Such a one has a good faculty of extemporizing;* or *of uttering,* or *relating, things by means of the promptness of his intelligence.* (TA, in art. بدأ: see بَدِيئَةٌ.) And هٰذَا مَعْلُومٌ فِى بَدَائِهِ العُقُولِ [*This is known among the intuitive notions of intellects;* i. e., *intuitively*]. (Ḳ,* TA.) بَدَائِهُ seems to be pl. of بَدِيهَةٌ, as in the phrase, (TA,) لَهُ بَدَائِهُ, i. e. بَدَائِعُ [*He has new,* or *admirable, things that he utters*], (Ḳ, TA,) in speech, or language, and poetry, and in answering, or replying: but here it is not improbable that the ه may be a substitute for the ع. (TA.)

بَدِيهِىٌّ [*Intuitive* knowledge,] *such that its origination does not rest upon speculation, and acquisition by study, whether it do, or do not, require some other thing, as conjecture or experience &c.;* (KT, Kull;) *so that it is* [sometimes] syn. with ضَرُورِىٌّ [and opposed to نَظَرِىٌّ]: and sometimes it means *such as does not require anything whatever after the intellect has directed itself; so that it is more particular than* ضَرُورِىٌّ: (KT:) *as the conception of heat and cold, and the assent of the mind to the position that negation and affirmation cannot be co-existent, nor be simultaneously non-existent, in the same instance.* (KT, Kull.) —— [And hence,] *A mere simpleton* or *fool:* but this is post-classical. (TA.)

رَجُلٌ مِبْدَهٌ (Ṣ) *A man possessing in a large degree the faculty of extemporizing,* or *of judging rightly at the first of an unexpected occurrence; firm,* or *steady, in speech* or *discourse,* or *whose tongue makes no slip in contentions, when he is taken unawares.* (Ḥar p. 64.)

بدو

1. بَدَا, (T, Ṣ, M, &c.,) aor. يَبْدُو, (Ṣ, Mṣb,) inf. n. بُدُوٌّ (Ṣ, M, Mṣb, Ḳ) and بَدْوٌ and بَدَآءٌ (M, Ḳ) and بَدَاءَةٌ (Ḳ) and بَدًا, (M, on the authority of Sb,) for which last we find, in [some of] the copies of the Ḳ, بُدُوٌّ, a repetition, (TA,) or بُدُوٌّ, (so in other copies of the Ḳ,) *It appeared; it became apparent, open, manifest, plain,* or *evident:* (T, Ṣ, M, Mṣb, Ḳ:) and ▼ تَبَدَّى [signifies the same; or *he showed himself,* or *it showed itself;* (see an ex. in art. جيش, voce جَاشَ, last sentence;) or] *he,* or *it, came in sight,* or *within sight.* (KL.) —— بَدَا لَهُ فِى الأَمْرِ, (T, M, Mṣb, Ḳ, and Ḥar p. 665,) inf. n. بَدْوٌ (M, Ḳ) and بَدًا (M, and so in a copy of the Ḳ) and بَدَآءٌ, (T, M, and so in the CḲ,) or بَدَاةٌ and بَدَاءَةٌ; (as in some copies of the Ḳ;) or ▼ بَدَا لَهُ فِى الأَمْرِ بَدَآءٌ, (Ṣ, IB,) the last word being in the nom. case because it is the agent; (IB, TA;) *An opinion presented itself,* or *occurred, to him,* or *arose in his mind,* syn. نَشَأَ, (Ṣ, Ḳ, and Ḥar ubi suprà,) or *appeared to him,* (M,) [*respecting the affair,* or *case,*] *different from his first opinion, so that it turned him therefrom:* (Ḥar ubi suprà:) or *there appeared to him, respecting the affair,* or *case, what did not appear at first:* (Mṣb:) accord. to Fr, ▼ بَدَا لِى بَدَآءٌ means *another opinion appeared to me:* accord. to Az, بَدَا لِى بَدًا means *my opinion changed from what it was.* (TA.) Esh-Shemmákh says,

• لَعَلَّكَ وَالمَوْعُودُ حَقٌّ وَفَاؤُهُ •
• بَدَا لَكَ فِى تِلْكَ القَلُوصِ بَدَآءُ ▼ •

[*May-be (but it is right that the promise be fulfilled) an opinion different from thy first opinion hath arisen in thy mind respecting that youthful she-camel*]. (M, TA.) ثُمَّ بَدَا لَهُمْ مِنْ بَعْدِ مَا رَأَوُا الآيَاتِ لَيَسْجُنُنَّهُ, in the Ḳur [xii. 35], means بَدَا لَهُمْ بَدَآءٌ ▼ وَقَالُوا لَيَسْجُنُنَّهُ, [i. e. *Then an opinion arose in their minds, after they had seen the signs of his innocence, and they said that they should certainly imprison him,*] because ليسجننّه, being a proposition, cannot be the agent: so says Sb. (M.) بَدَا لِلّٰهِ أَنْ يَقْتُلَهُمْ, occurring in a trad., means ‡ *God determined that He would slay them:* for, as IAth says, بَدَآءٌ signifies the *deeming to be right a thing that is known after its having been not known;* and this may not be attributed to God: but, as is said by Suh, in the R, one may say, [of God,] بَدَا لَهُ أَنْ يَفْعَلَ كَذَا, [properly signifying *It occurred to him,* or *appeared to him, that he should do such a thing,*] as meaning ‡ *He desired to do such a thing;* [as also بَدَا لَهُ فِى فِعْلِ كَذَا;] and thus the phrase in the trad., here mentioned, has been explained. (TA.) [One says also, اِفْعَلْ كَذَا مَا بَدَا لَكَ *Do thou thus as long as it seems fit to thee:* see a verse of El-Aḥmar cited voce جَلَّ.] —— بَدَا القَوْمُ, (T, Ṣ, M, Ḳ,) inf. n. بَدْوٌ, (Ṣ,) or بَدَآءٌ; (M, Ḳ;) [the latter of which is said in the TA to be the right;] or بَدَا إِلَى البَادِيَةِ, inf. n. بَدَاوَةٌ and بِدَاوَةٌ; (Mṣb;) *The people,* or *company of men, went forth to the* بَادِيَة [or *desert*]: (M, Mṣb, Ḳ:) or, the former, *went forth to their* بَادِيَة: (Ṣ:) or *went forth from the region,* or *district, of towns or villages or of cultivated land, to the pasturing-places in the deserts:* (T:) [ISd says,] بَدْوٌ may be used as meaning بَدَاوَةٌ which is the *contr. of* حَضَارَةٌ: (M:) [J says,] بَدَاوَةٌ and بِدَاوَةٌ signify the *dwelling,* or *abiding, in the* بَادِيَة [or *desert*]; the *contr. of* حِضَارَةٌ: but Th says, I know not بَدَاوَةٌ, with fet-ḥ, except on the authority of AZ alone: (Ṣ:) Aṣ says that بداوة and حضارة are with kesr to the ب and fet-ḥ to the ح; but AZ says the reverse, i. e. with fet-ḥ to the ب and kesr to the ح: (T:) both are also explained as signifying the *going forth to the* بَادِيَة: and some mention بُدَاوَةٌ, with ḍamm; but this is not known: (TA:) ▼ تَبَدَّى likewise signifies *he went forth from the constant sources of water to the places where herbage was to be sought* [*in the desert*]; (T;) or *he dwelt,* or *abode, in the* بَادِيَة. (Ṣ, Ḳ.) It is said in a trad., مَنْ بَدَا جَفَا, i. e. *He who abides in the desert becomes rude, rough, coarse,* or *uncivil, like the desert-Arabs.* (Ṣ.) And in another, كَانَ يَبْدُو إِلَى هٰذِهِ التِّلَاعِ [*He used to go forth to these water-courses in the desert,* or *these high grounds,* or *low grounds,* &c.]. (TA.) —— [Hence,] بَدَا *He voided his excrement,* or *ordure;* (M, Ḳ;) as also ▼ ابدى (T, Ḳ) [and ابدأ]: because he who does so goes forth from the tents or houses into the open country. (T.) —— بَدَانِى بِكَذَا, aor. يَبْدُو, is like بَدَأَنِى [i. e. *He began with me by* doing *such a thing*]. (M, TA.) ═ بَدِيَتِ الأَرْضُ *The land produced*, or *abounded with*, بَدَاة, i. e. *truffles:* (Ḳ,* TA:) or *had in it truffles.* (TḲ.) — And *The land had in it* بَدَاة, meaning *dust*, or *earth.* (Ḳ,* TḲ.)

2. بدّى, inf. n. تَبْدِيَةٌ, *He showed*, or *made apparent, a want that occurred*, or *presented itself, to him.* (TA.) [See بَدَاءَةٌ.] — *He sent forth* a horse [or beast] *to the place of pasture* [app. *in the* بَادِيَة, or *desert*]. (TA, from a trad.)

3. مُبَادَاةٌ The *going*, or *coming, out*, or *forth, in the field, to encounter another in battle*, or *war.* (TA.) — And [more commonly] The *showing open enmity*, or *hostility, with any one:* (KL, TA:) [a meaning more fully expressed by the phrase مُبَادَاةٌ بِالعَدَاوَةِ: for you say,] بَادَى بِالعَدَاوَةِ *He showed open enmity*, or *hostility*, [*with another;*] syn. جَاهَرَ بِهَا; (Ṣ, Ḳ;*) as also ▼ تبادى: (Ḳ:) or you say, ▼ تبادوا بالعداوة *they showed open enmity*, or *hostility, one with another;* syn. تَجَاهَرُوا بِهَا. (Ṣ.) You say also, بادى النَّاسَ بِأَمْرِهِ *He showed*, or *revealed, to the people*, or *to men, his affair*, or *case.* (TA.) [Thus, باداهُ بِالأَمْرِ and ▼ ابدى لَهُ الأَمْرَ signify the same; i. e. *He showed*, or *revealed, to him the affair*, or *case.*] — And بادى بَيْنَهُمَا *He measured*, or *compared, them both together, each with the other.* (A, TA.)

4. ابداهُ *He made it apparent, open, manifest, plain*, or *evident; he showed, exhibited, manifested, evinced, discovered*, or *revealed, it;* (Ṣ, M, Mṣb, Ḳ;) and it has been said [correctly, as will be seen below,] that ابدى عَنْهُ signifies the same. (MF, TA.) It is said in a trad., مَنْ يُبْدِ لَنَا صَفْحَتَهُ نُقِمْ عَلَيْهِ كِتَابَ ٱللّٰهِ, i. e. ‡ *Whoso showeth*, or *revealeth, to us his deed* [or *crime*] *which he was concealing*, [*the book of God shall execute vengeance upon him*, meaning] *we will inflict upon him the punishment ordained by the book of God.* (TA.) ابدى لَهُ صَفْحَتَهُ also means ‡ *He showed open enmity*, or *hostility, with him.* (A and TA in art. صفح.) And ابدى عَنْ قَعْرِهِ, said of water, means *It showed its bottom*, by reason of its clearness. (L in art. مكد.) See also **3.** — أَبْدَيْتَ فِي مَنْطِقِكَ *Thou deviatedst*, or *hast deviated, from the right way in thy speech.* (Ṣ.) — See also **1.**

5. تبدّى: see **1**, in two places. ═ In the common dial. of the people of El-Yemen, it signifies *He ate the morning-meal;* syn. تَغَدَّى. (TA.)

6. تبادى: see **3**, in two places. — Also *He affected to be like*, or *imitated, the people of the* بَادِيَة [or *desert*]. (Ṣ, Ḳ.)

بَدٌ: see بَدْوٌ, in two places.

بَدًا The *excrement from the anus* (M, Ḳ*) of a man. (M.) [And بَدَآءٌ, from أَبْدَأَ, signifies the same.] — *A joint* (مَفْصِل) of a man; (AA, M, Ḳ;) as also بَدْءٌ: (AA, M:) pl. أَبْدَآءٌ. (AA, M, Ḳ.) ═ بَدًا for بَدْ: see بَدْوٌ, in two places.

بَدْوٌ: see بَادِيَةٌ: ═ and see also بَادٍ. ═ Also The *first* of a thing; originally [بَدْءٌ,] with hemzeh: (Ḥar p. 583:) and ▼ بَدِيٌّ, also, [originally بَدِيءٌ,] signifies the *first:* (TA:) [and ▼ بَدٍ and ▼ بَدًا, the latter for بَدَأَ, are used for بَدْءٌ: Hence,] one says, ▼ اِفْعَلْ ذٰلِكَ بَادِيَ بَدٍ, (Ṣ,) or بَادِيَ بَدٍ, (M, Ḳ,) and ▼ بَادِيَ بَدِيٍّ, (Fr, Ṣ, M,) or بَادِيَ بَدِي, (as in some copies of the Ḳ,) or ▼ بادى بَدِيّ, (as in other copies of the Ḳ and in the TA,) and ▼ بَادِيَ بَدَا, (M, Ḳ,) mentioned by Sb, who says that it is without tenween, though analogy does not forbid its being with tenween, (M,) meaning *Do thou that first;* (Ṣ, TA;) or, *the first thing:* (Fr, TA:) originally [بَادِئَ بَدْءٍ, &c.,] with hemz. (Ṣ, Ḳ. [See بَدْءٌ.]) Hence also the phrase, ▼ الحَمْدُ لِلّٰهِ بَدِيًّا [*Praise be to God in the first place*]. (TA.)

بَدٍ for بَدِى: see بَدْوٌ.

بَدَاةٌ: see بَدَآءٌ: — and see also بَادِيَةٌ. ═ Also, (Ḳ, TA,) like قَطَاةٌ, (TA, [but in the CḲ بَدْأَة, q. v.,]) *Truffles;* syn. كَمْأَةٌ. (Ḳ.) — And *Dust*, or *earth.* (Ḳ.)

بَدْوَةٌ Either *side* of a valley. (AḤn, M, Ḳ.)

بَدَوِيٌّ [*Of*, or *belonging to*, or *relating to, the* بَدْو, or *desert:* and, used as a subst., *a man*, and particularly *an Arab, of the desert:*] a rel. n. from بَدْوٌ, (Ṣ, M, Ḳ,) extr. [with respect to rule], (M, Ḳ,) for by rule it should be بَدْوِيٌّ; (El-Tebreezee, TA;) or it is an irregular rel. n. from بَادِيَة: (Mṣb:) and ▼ بَدَاوِيٌّ and ▼ بِدَاوِيٌّ are similar rel. ns., (M, Ḳ,) from بَدَاوَةٌ and بِدَاوَةٌ, as syn. with بَدْوٌ and بَادِيَةٌ, agreeably with rule; or the former of these two may be a rel. n. from بَدْوٌ and بَادِيَة, and therefore extr. [with respect to rule]; but it is said that when a rel. n. may be regarded as regular or irregular, it is more proper to regard it as regular; (M;) or the former is a rel. n. signifying *of*, or *belonging to*, or *relating to*, البَدَاوَة as meaning *the dwelling*, or *abiding, in the desert*, (Ṣ, TA,) accord. to the opinion of AZ; and the latter is a rel. n. from البِدَاوَة accord. to the opinion of Aṣ and others; and is held by Th to be the chaste form: (TA:) but بَدَوِيٌّ is the only one of these rel. ns. that is known to the common people: (M:) it is opposed to a townsman or villager. (TA.) [The pl. is بَدَاوَى, and vulg. بِدْوَان. See also بَادٍ, often applied to a man as syn. with بَدَوِيٌّ.]

بَدَوَاتٌ: see بَدَآءٌ, in three places.

بَدَآءٌ [*An opinion that occurs to one*, or *arises in the mind;* and particularly *one that is different from a former opinion;*] a subst. from بَدَا in the phrase بَدَا لَهُ فِي الأَمْرِ. (Mṣb.) See **1**, in four places. One says also, ▼ هُوَ ذُو بَدَوَاتٍ *He is one who has various opinions occurring to him*, or *arising in his mind*, (IDrd, Ṣ,* Ḳ,* and Ḥar p. 665,) *of which he chooses some and rejects others:* (IDrd, TA:) it is said in praise, (IDrd, TA, and Ḳzz in Ḥar ubi suprà,) and sometimes in dispraise: (Ḳzz in Ḥar ubi suprà:) بَدَوَاتٌ is pl. of ▼ بَدَاةٌ, [which is therefore syn. with بَدَآءٌ,] like as قَطَوَاتٌ is pl. of قَطَاةٌ. (IDrd, TA, and Ḥar ubi suprà.) One says likewise ▼ أَبُو البَدَوَاتِ, meaning *The father* [i. e. *originator*] *of opinions that present themselves to him.* (IDrd, TA.) And ▼ السُّلْطَانُ ذُو عَدَوَاتٍ وَذُو بَدَوَاتٍ (Ṣ, [in which the context indicates it to mean *The Sultán is characterized by deviations from the right way:*] but accord. to SM, it is) a trad., meaning *the Sultán ceases not to have some new opinion presenting itself to him.* (TA.)

بَدَآءٌ, in the common dial. of the people of El-Yemen, signifies The *morning-meal;* syn. غَدَآءٌ. (TA.)

بَدِيٌّ: see بَادِيَةٌ: — and see بَدْوٌ, in three places. — Also, [or بِئْرٌ بَدِيٌّ,] originally بَدِيءٌ, q. v. in art. بدأ, (TA,) *A well:* (T:) or *a well that is not ancient:* (TA:) pl. بُودَانٌ, formed by transposition from بُدْيَانٌ. (T.)

بَدَاءَةٌ *What appears*, or *becomes apparent*, of wants, or needful things: pl. بَدَاآتٌ; for which one may also say, بَدَاوَاتٌ. (T.) These two pls. also signify *Wants that appear*, or *become apparent, to one.* (TA.) [The latter of them is likewise pl. of what next follows.]

بَدَاوَةٌ and بِدَاوَةٌ: see بَادِيَةٌ. — The former also signifies The *first that appears*, or *becomes apparent*, of a thing. (Lḥ, M, Ḳ.) [See بَدَاءَةٌ.]

بَدَاوِيٌّ and بِدَاوِيٌّ: see بَدَوِيٌّ.

بَادٍ *Appearing*, or *apparent;* or *becoming*, or *being, apparent, open, manifest, plain*, or *evident.* (Mṣb.) [Hence,] بَادِيَ الرَّأْيِ *At the* [*first*] *appearance of opinion;* (Fr, Lḥ, M;) or *according to the appearance of opinion;* (Zj, Ṣ, Ḳ;*) which may mean either *insincerely* or *inconsiderately:* (Zj, TA:) so in the Ḳur xi. 29; (Zj, Ṣ;) where only AA read it with hemz: (TA:) if with hemz, it is from بَدَأْتُ, and means *at first thought*, or *on the first opinion.* (Ṣ; and Lḥ in M, art. بدأ: see بَدْءٌ.) For بَادِيَ بَدٍ, or بَادِيَ بَدٍ, and بَادِي بَدِي, &c., see بَدْوٌ, in four places. — بَادِي بَدِي is sometimes used as a name for *Calamity*, or *misfortune:* it consists of two nouns made one, like مَعْدِي كَرِبَ. (Ṣ.) — بَادٍ also signifies A man *going forth to the* بَادِيَة [or *desert*]: (M,* Mṣb, Ḳ,* TA:) or one *who is in the* بَادِيَة, *dwelling in the tents, and not remaining in his place:* (TA:) pl. بَادُونَ and بُدًّا [in the TA erroneously said to be like هُدًى بُدًى] and بُدَّآءٌ: (M, Ḳ:) and ▼ بَدْوٌ is a quasi-pl. n. of بَادٍ; (M, TA;) or is for أَهْلُ بَدْوٍ, meaning *people who go forth to the desert;* (M;) or it means *dwellers in the desert*, or *people of the desert:* (MF:) ▼ بَادِيَةٌ also signifies the same as بَادُونَ, i. e. people *migrating from the constant sources of water, and going forth to the desert, seeking the vicinity of herbage; contr. of* حَاضِرَة; and بَوَادِي [or بَوَادٍ] is pl. of بَادِيَة. (T.)

بَادَاةٌ: see what next follows.

بَادِيَةٌ (T, Ṣ, &c.) *A desert*; so called because of its being open, or uncovered; (TA;) *contr. of* حَضَرٌ; (M, Ḳ;) as also ↓ بَدْوٌ, (Ṣ,* M, Mṣb, Ḳ,) and ↓ بَادَاةٌ, (M, Ḳ,) or ↓ بَدَاةٌ, (TA, [thought by SM to be the correct form because found by him in the M, in which I find بادات,]) and ↓ بَدِىٌّ, said to be used as syn. with بَادِيَةٌ in a verse of Lebeed cited among the exs. of the preposition بِ, p. 142, (TA,) and ↓ بَدَاوَةٌ (M, Ḳ) and ↓ بِدَاوَةٌ; (M;) [of which the last two and the second (namely, بَدْوٌ,) seem to be originally inf. ns.; see 1:] or *a land in which are no towns or villages or cultivated soil*: (Lth, T:) or the *places to which people migrate from the constant sources of water, when they go forth to the desert, seeking the vicinity of herbage*; also termed مَبَادٍ, which is *syn. with* مَنَاجِعُ, *contr. of* مَحَاضِرُ, and pl. of ↓ مَبْدًى, (T,) this last signifying the *contr. of* مَحْضَرٌ: (Ṣ:) the pl. of بَادِيَةٌ is بَوَادٍ. (T, Mṣb.) — See also بَادٍ.

مَبْدًى: pl. مَبَادٍ: see بَادِيَةٌ.

رَكِىٌّ مُبْدٍ *Wells showing their water; having it uncovered by dust or earth; contr. of* رَكِىٌّ غَامِدٌ. (A in art. غمد.)

بدى

1. بَدِيتُ بِالشَّىْءِ and بَدَيْتُ بِهِ, i. q. [بَدَأْتُ and] اِبْتَدَأْتُ [*I began with the thing; or made it to have precedence, or to be first*]; (M, Ḳ;) of the dial. of the Anṣár: (M:) the people of El-Medeeneh say, بَدَيْنَا, or بَدِينَا, [accord. to different copies of the Ṣ,] in the sense of بَدَأْنَا: (Ṣ:) [the right reading seems to be بَدِينَا; for] IKh says, none says بَدِيتُ in the sense of بَدَأْتُ, except the Anṣár: all others say, بَدِيتُ and بَدَأْتُ; when the hemzeh is suppressed, the د is pronounced with kesr, and therefore the hemzeh is changed into ى. (IB, TA.) [See a verse of Ibn-Rawáḥah cited voce بَدْءٌ.]

بِدَايَةٌ, said by Mṭr to be a vulgar word, and by IB to be erroneous, but by IḲṭṭ to be of the dial. of the Anṣár: see art. بدأ [voce بَدْءٌ, second sentence, in two places]. (TA.)

بذ

1. بَذَّ, (M,) sec. pers. بَذِذْتَ, (Ṣ, Mgh, Ḳ,) aor. يَبَذُّ, (L, Ḳ,) inf. n. بَذَاذَةٌ (Ṣ, M, Mgh, Ḳ) and بُذُوذَةٌ (Ṣ, M, Ḳ) and بَذٌّ (M, Mgh, Ḳ) and بَذَاذٌ, (Ḳ,) or بِذَاذٌ, with kesr, (TA,) [of all which, the third is the regular form,] *He* (a man) *was, or became, threadbare, and shabby,* or *mean, in the state of his apparel,* (Ks, Ṣ, M, Mgh, L,) and *in an evil condition*; (M, L, Ḳ;) *slovenly with respect to his person*: (Ks, M, L:) or *he neglected the constant adornment of himself*: or *he adorned himself one day, and another day left his hair in a shaggy* or *dishevelled,* or *matted and dusty, state*: (T, L:) or *he was humble in his apparel, not taking pleasure therein.* (IAth, L.) بَذَاذَةٌ is said in a trad. to be a part of religion; (Ks, T, M, Mgh, L;) meaning, in this instance, The *being humble in dress, and wearing that which is not conducive to self-conceit and pride.* (Mgh.) — بَذَّهُ, aor. يَبُذُّ, (T, Ṣ, M, L,) inf. n. بَذٌّ (Ṣ, M, L, Ḳ) and ↓ بَذِيذَةٌ, (Ḳ,) [or this may be a simple subst.,] *He overcame him*; (T, Ṣ, M, L, Ḳ;) *he surpassed him* in goodliness or beauty, or in any deed: (T, L:) *he outstripped him.* (M, L.) It is said in a trad., بَذَّ القَائِلِينَ *He outstripped,* or *surpassed, and overcame, the speakers.* (L.)

3. بَاذَّهُ *He hastened with him; made haste,* or *strove, to be,* or *get, before him*: (Ḳ,* TA:) *he vied with him in glory* or *excellence.* (TA.)

8. ابتذّ حَقَّهُ *He took his* (i. e. his own) *right,* or *due.* (Ḳ.)

10. استبذّ بالأَمْرِ *He was alone, with none to share, or participate, with him, in the affair*; (Ḳ,* TA;) *i. q.* استبدّ (Ḳ) *and* استقلّ. (TA.)

بَذٌّ [perhaps from the Persian بَدْ] A man *slovenly with respect to his person, and poor.* (IAạr, T, L.) And بَذُّ الهَيْئَةِ, and ↓ بَاذُّ الهَيْئَةِ, A man *threadbare, and shabby,* or *mean, in the state of his apparel*; (Ks, T,* Ṣ, Mgh, L;) and *in an evil condition with respect to it*; (L, Ḳ;) *slovenly with respect to his person*: (Ks, L:) or one *who neglects the constant adornment of his person*: or *who adorns himself one day, and another day leaves his hair in a shaggy* or *dishevelled,* or *matted and dusty, state*: (T, L:) or *humble in his apparel, not taking pleasure therein.* (IAth, L.) — بَذُّ البَخْتِ A man *having evil fortune.* (Kr, M, L.) — هَيْئَةٌ بَذَّةٌ *A threadbare, and shabby,* or *mean, state of apparel.* (M.) — حَالٌ بَذَّةٌ, (Ṣ,) and حَالَةٌ بَذَّةٌ, (TA,) *An evil state or condition.* (Ṣ, TA.) — تَمْرٌ بَذٌّ *Dates that are separate, each one from another, not sticking together*; like فَذٌّ: (IAạr, M:) or *that are scattered.* (Ḳ.) — فَذٌّ بَذٌّ *Single; sole; that is alone, or apart from others*: (IAạr, Ḳ:) and so أَحَذُّ ↓ أَبَذُّ. (Ḳ.)

فِى هَيْئَتِهِ بَذَّةٌ, and بَذَاذَةٌ, [the latter an inf. n. (of بَذَّ) used as a simple subst.,] *In his state of apparel is slovenliness, and threadbareness, and shabbiness,* or *meanness.* (T.) بَذِيذَةٌ, also, (sometimes written ↓ بُذَيْذَةٌ, TA, and so in the TT but without vowel-signs,) signifies *Slovenliness with respect to one's person; or neglect of cleanliness.* (T, L, Ḳ.)

بَذِيذَةٌ, or بُذَيْذَةٌ: see بَذَّةٌ. — And for the former, see also بَذَّهُ.

بَاذٌّ: see بَذٌّ. — Also Any one *overcoming,* or *surpassing.* (M, L.)

أَبَذُّ: see بَذٌّ.

بذأ

1. بَذُؤَ, (T, M, Ḳ,) with and without ء, (Mgh,) aor. ـُ, (T,) inf. n. بَذَآءٌ and بَذَاءَةٌ, (M, Ḳ,) the former written in one copy of the Ḳ بَذَأٌ, and the latter in some copies written بَذَاةٌ; (TA;) and بَذَأَ, and بَذِئَ, (Ḳ,) aor. of both ـَ; (TA;) and some say بَذِىَ, aor. يَبْذَى, inf. n. بَذَآءٌ; (T;) or, accord. to the Mṣb, only بَذُأَ is with ء, and the others are properly written بَذِىَ and بَذُوَ; (TA;) *He* (a man) *was,* or *became, foul, unseemly,* or *obscene,* (T, M, Ḳ, TA,) *in tongue*; (TA;) *evil in speech.* (T.) And بَذَأَ عَلَى القَوْمِ, aor. ـَ, inf. n. بَذْءٌ and بَذَآءٌ, *He behaved in a lightwitted, weak, stupid,* or *foolish, manner,* or *ignorantly, towards the people,* or *company of men*; and *uttered foul, unseemly,* or *obscene, language against them*; and *so though with truth.* (Mṣb.) — بَذُأَ also signifies *He was,* or *became, evil in disposition.* (Fr, T.) — And, said of a place, *It became devoid of pasture, barren,* or *unfruitful.* (TA.) — بَاذَأَهُ فَبَذَأَهُ: see 3. — بَذَأَهُ, (T, Ṣ, M, Ḳ,) aor. ـَ, (T,) inf. n. بَذْءٌ, (T, Ṣ,) also signifies *He dispraised it; discommended it*; (T, M, Ḳ;) namely, a thing: (M:) and *he despised him*: (T, Ḳ:) and *he saw in him* (a man, Ṣ) *a state,* or *condition, that he disliked,* or *hated*: (Ṣ, Ḳ:) *he did not approve him*; and *was not pleased with his aspect.* (TA.) And بَذَأَتْهُ عَيْنِى, (T, Ṣ, M, Mṣb,*) aor. as above, (M,) and so the inf. n., (Ṣ, M,) *My eye did not approve him,* or *it*; (T, Ṣ;) *I was not pleased with his,* or *its, aspect*; (Ṣ;) and *I saw in him,* or *it, a state,* or *condition, that I disliked,* or *hated*: (T:) or *my eye despised,* or *regarded as of light estimation, him,* or *it*: (M, Mṣb:) accord. to AZ, this is said when a thing has been praised, or greatly praised, to thee, and in thy presence, and then thou dost not see it to be as it has been described: but when thou seest it to be as it has been described, thou sayest, مَا تَبْذَؤُهُ العَيْنُ. (T.) One says also, بَذَأَ الأَرْضَ *He dispraised,* or *discommended, the pasture of the land.* (Ṣ, M, Ḳ.) And in like manner, بَذَأَ المَوْضِعَ (Ṣ) *He did not praise the place.* (TA.)

3. بَاذَأَهُ, (T,) inf. n. مُبَاذَأَةٌ, (T, Ḳ,) in some copies of the Ḳ without ء, (TA,) and بِذَآءٌ, (T, Ḳ,) [*He vied with him, or strove to surpass him, in foul, unseemly,* or *obscene, speech* or *language*: and *he held such discourse with him*: these significations being indicated by the following exs., and by the saying that] the inf. ns. are *syn. with* مُفَاحَشَةٌ. (T, Ḳ.) You say, ↓ بَاذَأَهُ فَبَذَأَهُ [*He vied with him, or strove to surpass him, in foul, unseemly,* or *obscene, speech* or *language, and he surpassed him therein*: in this case, the aor. of the latter verb is ـُ, notwithstanding the final faucial letter]. (TA.) And Esh-Shaabee says, إِذَا عَظُمَتِ الحَلْقَةُ فَإِنَّمَا هُوَ بِذَآءٌ وَنِجَآءٌ [i. e. *When the ring of people becomes large, it is only* an occasion of *holding foul, unseemly,* or *obscene, and secret, discourse*]: it is said that بذآء here signifies مفاحشة: (T:) the meaning is, that there is much بذاء and نجاء, i. e. مُنَاجَاة, therein. (TA in art. نجو. [But there, in the place of فَإِنَّمَا هُوَ, I find فَهِىَ; and in the TA in the present art., فَإِنَّمَا بِهِ.]) — Also *He contended with him in an altercation.* (T.)

4. ابذأ *He uttered foul, unseemly,* or *obscene, speech* or *language.* (TA.)

بَذِىٌّ A man *foul, unseemly,* or *obscene,* (T,

M, Ḳ, TA,) *in tongue*; (TA;) *evil in speech.* (T.) [See also art. بذو.] — A place *in which is no pasture*: (Ḳ:) and أَرْضٌ بَذِيَّةٌ *a land in which is no pasture.* (Ṣ, M.)

بذخ

1. بَذِخَ, aor. َ, inf. n. بَذَخٌ; (Mṣb;) and بَذَخَ, [aor. َ and ُ, (see what follows,)] inf. n. بُذُوخٌ; (L;) *It* (a mountain) *was high*, or *lofty*. (L, Mṣb.) — And hence, (Mṣb,) بَذِخَ, (Ṣ, Mṣb, Ḳ,) aor. َ, (Ḳ,) inf. n. بَذَخٌ; (Ṣ, Ḳ;) and بَذَخَ, aor. َ and ُ, but the former is the more approved, inf. n. بَذْخٌ and بُذُوخٌ; (L;) † *He was*, or *became, proud*, and *lofty*, or *haughty*; (Ṣ, Mṣb,* Ḳ;) as also ▼ تبذّخ: (Ṣ, Ḳ:) ‡ *he exalted himself above others*, (L, TA,) as also ▼ تبذّخ, (A,) *by his speech, and his glorying*, or *boasting*. (L, TA.) — And بَذَخَ, aor. َ, inf. n. بَذَخَانٌ, ‡ *He* (a camel) *brayed in the most vehement manner*, (L, TA,) *and put forth his* شِقْشِقَة [or *faucial bag*]. (TA.) — بَذَخَ, aor. َ, inf. n. بَذْخٌ, *He split, clave, rifted, slit*, or *rent*, a thing. (Mṣb.)

3. باذخهُ † *He vied*, or *competed*, or *contended, with him in glorying* or *boasting*, or *in glory* or *excellence*, or *for superiority in nobleness.* (L, TA.)

5: see 1, in two places.

بَذْخٌ: see بَاذِخٌ.

بَذِخْ and بَذَخْ [for the latter of which, in the CḲ, we find بَذِخْ,] *i. q.* بَخْ [*Excellent!* &c.]; (JK, T, Ḳ, TA;) and *wonderful!* (T, TA.) — بَذِخْ بَذِخْ is also said in chiding a camel that brays in the most vehement manner, (see بَذَخَ,) or in imitating his braying. (L.)

بَذِخٌ: see بَاذِخٌ.

بُذَاخِيٌّ *Great*; syn. عَظِيمٌ. (Ḳ.)

بَذَّاخٌ: see what next follows, in four places.

بَاذِخٌ *High*, or *lofty*; (JK, A, Mṣb;) applied to a mountain: (JK, Mṣb:) [and] *a high*, or *lofty, mountain*; an epithet in which the quality of a subst. is predominant: (L, TA:) pl. بَوَاذِخُ (JK, Ṣ, A, L, Mṣb) and بَاذِخَاتٌ [both fem. forms]: (JK:) and the former pl. applied as an epithet to mountains. (Ṣ, A, Ḳ.) — [Hence,] رَجُلٌ بَاذِخٌ, (JK, L,) and ▼ بَذَّاخٌ, (JK, A, L,) [the latter an intensive epithet,] ‡ *A proud, and lofty*, or *haughty, man, who exalts himself above others*, (JK, A, L,) *by his speech, and his glorying*, or *boasting*: (JK, L:) pl. of the former بُذَخَاءُ, like as عُلَمَاءُ is pl. of عَالِمٌ, and بُذَّخٌ. (L.) You say, In speech, he is ▼ بَذَّاخٌ; and in poetry, بَاذِخٌ. (L.) — And شَرَفٌ بَاذِخٌ ‡ *High*, or *exalted, nobility.* (Ṣ, Ḳ, TA.) — بَعِيرٌ بَاذِخٌ, (L,) and ▼ بَذَّاخٌ, (L, Ḳ,) or ▼ بَذَّاخٌ البَذِيرِ, (A,) and ▼ بِذْخٌ, and ▼ بَذِخٌ, (Ḳ,) ‡ *A camel that brays much*, (Ḳ,) or *in the most vehement manner*, (L,) *and puts forth his* شِقْشِقَة [or *faucial bag*]. (Ḳ.)

بَيْذَخٌ A *large-bodied*, or *corpulent*, woman; (Ṣ, Ḳ;) as also بَيْذَخٌ. (TA.)

بذر

1. بَذَرَ, (T, Ṣ, A, Mṣb,) aor. ُ, (Mṣb,) inf. n. بَذْرٌ, (T, Mṣb, Ḳ,) *He sowed* seed; (Ṣ, TA;) *he cast* grain *upon the ground to sow it*; (Mṣb;) *he cast* grain upon the ground, *scattering it*; (A;) *he scattered* seed (T, MF) *upon the ground*; as also ▼ بذّر, [but app. in an intensive sense,] (MF,) inf. n. تَبْذِيرٌ (T, MF) and تَبْذِرَةٌ: (T:) this is the primary signification. (MF.) — Also, (M,) inf. n. as above, (M, Ḳ,) *He sowed* land; (M, L, Ḳ;) and so ▼ بذّر, (M, L,) inf. n. تَبْذِيرٌ. (L, Ḳ.) — Also, (M,) inf. n. as above, (M, Ḳ,) *He scattered*, or *dispersed*, (M, Ḳ,) a thing; (M;) and so ▼ بذّر, [or rather *he scattered*, or *dispersed, much*,] inf. n. تَبْذِيرٌ. (Ḳ.) — بَذَرَ اللّٰهُ الخَلْقَ, (M, A,) inf. n. as above, (M,) *God scattered*, or *dispersed, mankind* (M, A) in the earth. (A.) — بَذَرَ الكَلَامَ ‡ *He disseminated, scattered*, or *diffused, talk*, or *speech*, (Mṣb, TA,) بَيْنَ النَّاسِ *among the people*, or *mankind*, like as seed is scattered: (TA:) and ▼ بذّرهُ *he did so much.* (Mṣb.) — بَذَرَتِ الأَرْضُ, (M, A,) aor. as above, (M,) and so the inf. n., (M, Ḳ,) ‡ *The land put forth its plants*, or *herbage*, (Aṣ, M, A, Ḳ,) *in a scattered state*: (Aṣ, M, A:) or *put forth its* بَذْر. (M.) — بَذُرَ, aor. ُ, inf. n. بَذَارَةٌ, ‡ *He divulged what was secret*; *he revealed what he had heard.* (T, L.) — بَذِرَ, [aor. َ,] inf. n. بَذَرٌ, *He talked much*; *was loquacious.* (M.)

2: see 1, in four places. — بذّر, inf. n. تَبْذِيرٌ, also signifies *He was extravagant in expenditure*; and so ▼ باذر, inf. n. مُبَاذَرَةٌ: (TA:) or the former, *he dissipated*, or *squandered*, (his wealth, or property, Ṣ, M, and any other thing, M, TA,) *by extravagant expenditure*, (Ṣ, M, Ḳ, TA,) *and destroyed, consumed, wasted*, or *ruined, it*: (M, Ḳ, TA: [in the CḲ, جَرَّبَهُ is here put for خَرَّبَهُ: in the M it is أَفْسَدَهُ:]) or *he expended* his wealth, or property, *so largely as not to leave of it that whereby he might subsist*: or *he expended* it *in acts of disobedience*: (TA:) or *he dissipated*, or *squandered*, his wealth, or property, *in a way that was not right*: (Mṣb:) or *in a way that did not behoove*: it includes the meaning of أَسْرَفَ in common, or conventional, acceptation, and is used in the proper sense of this latter verb: or, as some say, تَبْذِيرٌ denotes excess in respect of the right objects of expenditure, which is ignorance of the [right] manner, and of things that should prevent it; and إِسْرَافٌ denotes excess with respect to quantity, and is ignorance of the values of the right objects. (MF.) [See also بَذَارَةٌ.]

3: see 2.

5. تبذّر *It became scattered* or *dispersed*; or *much scattered* or *dispersed.* (A.) — ‡ *It* (talk, or speech,) *became much disseminated* or *scattered* or *diffused.* (Mṣb.)

بَذْرٌ (Ṣ, M, Mṣb, Ḳ, &c.) and ▼ بُذْرٌ, (M,) the former either an inf. n. used as a proper subst. or of the measure فَعْلٌ in the sense of the measure مَفْعُولٌ, (Mṣb,) *Grain that is set apart for sowing*; (Lth, M, Ḳ;) *any seed*, or *grain that is sown*; as also بَزْرٌ or بِزْرٌ: (Kh, Mṣb:) or *grain such as wheat, that is sown*; distinguished from بزر, which is applied to the seed of sweet-smelling plants and of leguminous herbs: and this distinction commonly obtains: (Mṣb:) or [so accord. to the M, but in the Ḳ "and,"] the *first that comes forth, of seed-produce and of leguminous and other plants*, (M, Ḳ,*) *as long as it has but two leaves*: (M:) or بَذْرٌ signifies *any plant*, or *herbage, when just come forth from the earth*: (M:) or *such as has assumed a colour*, (M, Ḳ,) or *shown its kind* or *species*: (M:) pl. بُذُورٌ and بِذَارٌ. (M, Ḳ.) — [Hence,] بَذْرٌ signifies also ‡ *Progeny*; (T, M, Ḳ;) and so ▼ بُذَارَةٌ. (M, Ḳ.) One says, إِنَّ هٰؤُلَاءِ لَبَذْرُ سَوْءٍ ‡ *Verily these are a progeny of evil*, or *an evil progeny.* (T, A.*)

بُذْرٌ: see بَذْرٌ.

تَفَرَّقُوا شَذَرَ بَذَرَ and ▼ شِذَرَ بِذَرَ *They dispersed*, or *became dispersed, in every direction*: (Ṣ, M, Ḳ:) [namely, men: and] the like is said of a man's camels: (Ṣ:) بذر is an imitative sequent to شذر: (Ṣ:) some say that the ب in the former is a substitute for م [in مَذَرَ or مِذَرَ]; but others hold that in each case the word is an original. (TA.)

بَذِرٌ: see تِبْذَارَةٌ. — Also, (M, Ḳ,) and ▼ تِبْذَارٌ and ▼ بَيْذَارَةٌ and ▼ تِبْذَارٌ and ▼ بَيْذَرَانِيٌّ, (Ḳ,) ‡ A man *who talks much*; *loquacious*; (M, Ḳ;) and so ▼ بَذَرَةٌ هُذَرَةٌ (IDrd, M) and ▼ هَيْذَارَةٌ بَيْذَارَةٌ: (M:) *irrationally*, or *vainly*, or *frivolously, loquacious*; *a great babbler.* (TA.) — See also بَذُورٌ. — طَعَامٌ بَذِرٌ [*Wheat*, or *food*,] *in which is* بُذَارَة, i. e. *increase, redundance, exuberance, plenty*, or *abundance.* (T,* M, L, Ḳ.*)

شِذَرَ بِذَرَ: see شَذَرَ بَذَرَ, above.

هُذَرَةٌ بُذَرَةٌ: see بَذِرٌ.

البُذَّرَى *What is false, vain*, or *ineffectual*; syn. البَاطِلُ: (Seer, M, L, Ḳ:) [like الحُذُّرَى:] the radical idea denoted by it is that of dispersion. (M, L.)

بَذُورٌ (Ṣ, M, A, Ḳ) and ▼ بَذِيرٌ (M, Ḳ) ‡ A man *who divulges secrets*; (Ṣ, M, A;) as also ▼ بَذِرٌ, of which the fem. is with ة: (L:) or one *who cannot keep his secret*: (T, Ḳ:) pl. of the first بُذُرٌ. (T, Ṣ, M.) — Also, both the first and second, ‡ *A calumniator*; *a slanderer*: (Ḳ, TA:) pl. of the former as above. (TA.)

بَذِيرٌ is [said to be] an imitative sequent to كَثِيرٌ; (M, Ḳ;) like بَثِيرٌ, of which it is [held to be] a dial. var., or a corruption occasioned by mispronunciation. (Fr, Ṣ.) [But I think it is more probably syn. with ▼ مَبْذُورٌ, as signifying *Scattered*, or *dispersed*, like نَثِيرٌ in the sense of مَنْثُورٌ, &c.; and that for this reason it is used as a corroborative of كَثِير.] — See also بَذُورٌ.

بَذَارَّةٌ : see بَذَارَةٌ.

بُذَارَةٌ *Increase, redundance, exuberance, plenty*, or *abundance*, in wheat, or food. (Lḥ,* T,* M, L, Ḳ.*) You say, طَعَامٌ كَثِيرُ البُذَارَةِ *Wheat*, or *food, in which is much increase*, &c. (T, TA.) — See also بَذْرٌ.

بَذَارَةٌ, and sometimes ▾ بَذَارَّةٌ, (Lḥ, M, Ḳ,) and ▾ بَيْذَرَةٌ, (AA,) and ▾ نَبْذَرَةٌ, with ن, (T, Ḳ,) *i. q.* تَبْذِيرٌ, (M, Ḳ,) The *dissipating*, or *squandering, of wealth*, or *property, in a way that is not right*. (T, TA.)

بَيْذَرَةٌ : see what next precedes.

بَيْذَرَانِىٌّ : see بَذْرٌ.

بَيْذَارٌ : see بَذْرٌ.

تَبْذَارَةٌ : see تِبْذَارَةٌ :— and see also بَذْرٌ, in two places.

تِبْذَارٌ : see بَذْرٌ.

تِبْذَارَةٌ A man *who dissipates*, or *squanders, his wealth*, or *property, by extravagant expenditure, and consumes, destroys, wastes*, or *ruins, it*; (AZ, Ṣ, M, Ḳ;) as also ▾ مُبَذِّرٌ and ▾ مُبَاذِرٌ and ▾ بَذِرٌ and ▾ تَبْذَارَةٌ. (TA.)

مُبَذِّرٌ : see what next precedes.

مِبْذَارٌ أَرْضٌ مِبْذَارُ النَّبَاتِ [or more probably لِلنَّبَاتِ] ‡ *Land that yields increase*. (A.)

مَبْذُورٌ : see بَذِيرٌ. — ‡ *Many; much; abundant*: (Ḳ, TA:) water that is *abundant*; or *blessed with abundance, plenty*, or *increase*. (A.)

مُبَاذِرٌ : see تِبْذَارَةٌ.

نَبْذَرَةٌ : see بَذَارَةٌ.

بذق

بَذْقٌ : see بَيْذَقٌ, in two places.

بَاذَقٌ (Mgh, Ḳ) and ▾ بَاذِقٌ (Ḳ) [in my copy of the Mṣb erroneously written بَاذِيق] a Persian word, arabicized; originally بَادَهْ, which signifies *Wine*: (A'Obeyd, TA:) or *juice of grapes cooked in the least degree, so as to be strong* (Mgh, Mṣb, Ḳ) *and intoxicating*; an arabicized word; (Mṣb;) said to have been introduced by the Benoo-Umeiyeh, (TA,) and to have been unknown to the Prophet; (Mgh;) but there is a trad. of I 'Ab which is understood to mean that the Prophet forbade what is thus called: (Mgh, TA:) some assert it to mean that it existed not in his time; (TA;) but this latter assertion is weak. (Mgh.)

بَاذِقٌ : see above. — It is also an imitative sequent to حَاذِقٌ. (Ḳ.)

بَيْذَقٌ [meaning *A pawn*] *in the game of chess* is from ▾ بَيَاذِقَةٌ; (TA;) which latter signifies *footmen, as opposed to horsemen*, (AO, Ḳ, TA,) and is an arabicized word, from the Persian, (AO, TA,) originally پِيَادَهْ : (TA:) the pl. of بيذق is بَيَاذِقُ; for which a poet uses بُذُوقٌ, as though he suppressed the ى [in the sing.], making بيذق to become ▾ بَذْقٌ : (Ibn-Buzurj, TA:) or, accord. to El-Khárzenjee, (JK, TA,) ▾ بَذْقٌ signifies *a guide in a journey*; as also بَيْذَقٌ : (JK, Ḳ, TA:) or [in the CḲ "and"] *small and light* or *active*: (Ḳ, TA:) or, as in the Tekmileh, (TA,) *short and light* or *active*: (JK, TA:) and its pl. is بُذُوقٌ. (JK, Ḳ.)

بَيَاذِقَةٌ : see بَيْذَقٌ.

بذل

1. بَذَلَهُ, aor. ـُ (Ṣ, M,* Mṣb, Ḳ) and ـِ, (M, Ḳ,) inf. n. بَذْلٌ, (Ṣ, M, Mṣb, Ḳ,) *He gave it, and was liberal*, or *bountiful, with it; he gave it liberally, bountifully, unsparingly*, or *freely*; (Ṣ, Mṣb, Ḳ, TA;) *he gave it willingly, of his own free will* or *good pleasure*: (TA:) and *he made it allowable*, or *lawful, to be taken* or *possessed* or *done, willingly*, or *of his own free will* or *good pleasure*: (Mṣb:) بَذْلٌ is the *contr. of* مَنْعٌ. (M.) [Hence,] سَأَلْتُهُ فَأَعْطَانِى بَذْلَ يَمِينِهِ *I asked him, and he gave me what he was able to give*. (TA.) [And بَذَلَ لَهُ نَفْسَهُ ‡ *He gave up himself to*, or *spent himself for, him* or *it*; *he gave*, or *applied, himself*, or *his mind, unsparingly to it*, namely, an undertaking &c.: a phrase of frequent occurrence. And بَذَلَ جُهْدَهُ, and مَجْهُودَهُ, ‡ *He exerted*, or *put forth*, or *expended, unsparingly*, or *freely, his power*, or *ability*, or *his utmost power* or *ability* or *endeavour*: also of frequent occurrence.] And فَرَسٌ لَهُ صَوْنٌ وَبَذْلٌ ‡ *A horse that reserves a portion of his run, and is unsparing with a portion thereof; not putting forth the whole at once*: (TA:) or *that has a run which he reserves* [*for the time of need*], *and a run which he performs unsparingly*: (A in art. شهد: see شَاهِدٌ:) and فَرَسٌ ذُو صَوْنٍ وَٱبْتِذَالٍ ▾ *a horse that has a running pace* (حُضْرٌ) *which he has reserved for the time of need, and a run* (عَدْوٌ) *less quick which he has performed freely*, or *without reservation* (قَدِ ٱبْتَذَلَهُ). (T.) [In the Ḳ these phrases are given in a mutilated state, and with a mutilated explanation.]) And صَوْنُهُ خَيْرٌ مِنْ بَذْلِهِ ‡ *His interior state*, or *disposition of mind, is better than his apparent state* &c. (TA.) — See also 8.

5. تبذّل *He neglected the preserving of himself* or *his honour* or *reputation* [from disgrace]; *i. q.* تَرَكَ التَّصَاوُنَ (Ṣ) or التَّصَوُّنَ; (TA;) *he was careless of himself* or *his honour* or *reputation*; *contr. of* تَصَاوَنَ; (Mṣb in the present art.;) as also ▾ ابتذل. (Mṣb in art. صون.) You say, كَرُمَ وَلَمْ يَتَبَذَّلْ [*He was generous, and was not careless of his honour* or *reputation*]. (M and L in art. وفر.) And ▾ ابتذل نَفْسَهُ فِيهِ, and تبذّل فِى عَمَلِ كَذَا — بِهِ, *He employed his own self in the doing of such a thing*. (T.)

8. اِبْتِذَالٌ is the *contr. of* صِيَانَةٌ; (M, Ḳ;) [i. e.] ابتذلهُ signifies *He held it in mean estimation*; namely, a garment or other thing; (TA;) [*he was careless of it; he used it*, or *employed it, on*, or *for, ordinary, mean*, or *vile, occasions*, or *purposes*;] *he used it for service and work*; namely, a garment &c.; syn. اِمْتَهَنَهُ; (Ṣ, Mṣb;) *he wore it* (a garment) *in times of service and work*; as also ▾ بَذَلَهُ; (Mṣb, TA;) or, as IḲooṭ says, بَذَلَهُ, [aor. ـُ and ـِ,] inf. n. بَذْلَةٌ and بِذْلَةٌ, signifies *he did not preserve it, lay it up, take care of it*, or *reserve it*; namely, a garment. (Mṣb.) See also 5, in two places. You say also, ابتذل عَدْوَهُ ‡ [*He* (a horse) *performed his run freely*, or *without reservation*; opposed to صَانَهُ]. (T.) See 1.

10. استبذلهُ *He sought*, or *demanded, of him a liberal, free*, or *willing, gift*. (TA.) And اِسْتَبْذَلْتُ فُلَانًا شَيْئًا *I asked of such a one that he would liberally, freely*, or *willingly, give me a thing*. (T.)

بَذْلٌ *A thing that is given liberally, freely*, or *willingly*: an inf. n. [of 1, q. v.], used as a proper subst.: pl. بُذُولٌ. (Ḥar p. 206.)

بَذْلَةٌ : see what next follows, in two places.

بِذْلَةٌ *A garment that is worn* (T, Ṣ, Mṣb) *in service*, or *work*; (Ṣ, Mṣb;) *that is not preserved, laid up, taken care of*, or *reserved*; (T, M, Ḳ;) as also ▾ بَذْلَةٌ (Mṣb) and ▾ مِبْذَلٌ, (T,) or ▾ مِبْذَلَةٌ, (Ṣ, M, Ḳ,) the pl. of which is مَبَاذِلُ : (Ṣ:) and *an old and worn-out garment*; (TA;) as also ▾ مِبْذَلٌ and ▾ مِبْذَلَةٌ; (M, Ḳ;) the last of which is mentioned on the authority of AZ, but is disapproved by 'Alee Ibn-Ḥamzeh, who asserts it to be without ة: (IB, TA:) بِذْلَةٌ sometimes has بِذَلٌ as pl. (TA.) You say, جَآءَنَا فُلَانٌ فِى مَبَاذِلِهِ ▾, i. e. فِى ثِيَابِ بِذْلَتِهِ or ▾ بَذْلَتِهِ [*Such a one came to us in his garments that he wore in service*, or *work*]. (Ṣ, accord. to different copies. [I have shown that بِذْلَةٌ and بَذْلَةٌ are dial. vars., both as inf. ns. (see 8) and as proper substs.]) The word بَدْلَةٌ, with fet-ḥ, and with the unpointed د, applied by the vulgar to [a suit of] new clothes, is a mistake for بِذْلَةٌ, and this is correctly a name for old and worn-out clothes. (TA. [But this is doubtful; for بَدْلَةٌ commonly signifies, in modern Arabic, a change of clothes; and hence, a suit of clothes, whether new or old.]) — IJ uses it metaphorically, in relation to poetry; saying, الرَّجَزُ إِنَّمَا يُسْتَعَانُ بِهِ فِى البِذْلَةِ وَعِنْدَ الاِعْتِمَالِ وَالحُدَآءِ وَالمِهْنَةِ ‡ [*The metre termed rejez is only used as an aid in the ordinary, or meaner, business of life, and on the occasion of doing one's work, and singing to camels for the purpose of urging them on, and performing service of any kind*: but in this case it may be regarded as an inf. n.: see 8]. (M.)

بَذَّالٌ : see بَذُولٌ.

بَذَالَةٌ *i. q.* بَذْلٌ [inf. n. of 1, The *act of giving liberally*, &c.]. (TA.)

بَذَّالٌ A man *wont to give property liberally, freely*, or *willingly*; or *who so gives it much*, or *frequently*; as also ▾ بَذُولٌ (T, TA) [and app. ▾ مِبْذَالٌ, (like مِسْمَاحٌ &c.,) of which the pl. occurs in the following saying]. هُمْ مَبَاذِيلُ ▾ لِلْمَعْرُوفِ [*They are very liberally disposed to the exercise of beneficence*, or *bounty*]. (TA.)

بَاذِلٌ Any one *who gives* [*liberally*,] *freely*, or *willingly*. (M.)

مِبْذَلٌ : see بِذْلَةٌ, in two places.

مِبْذَلَةٌ ; and its pl. مَبَاذِلُ : see بِذْلَةٌ, in three places.

مِبْذَالٌ ; pl. مَبَاذِيلُ : see بَذَّالٌ.

مُبْتَذَلٌ *Held in mean estimation*: as in the saying, مَالُهُ مَصُونٌ وَعِرْضُهُ مُبْتَذَلٌ [*His wealth is preserved*, or *taken care of, and his honour*, or *reputation, is held in mean estimation*]. (TA.) — † Language, and a proverb, *which one is wont to speak* or *mention*, or *which one is fond of speaking* or *mentioning*. (TA.) — فُلَانٌ صَدْقُ المُبْتَذَلِ *Such a one is strong*, or *sturdy, in the work in which he employs himself*: (T:) or *sharp, vigorous*, or *effective, in nature*, or *disposition; one who, when employed in a work, is found to be strong*, or *sturdy*. (TA.) And سَيْفٌ صَدْقُ المُبْتَذَلِ ‡ *A sword sharp*, or *penetrating, in the part with which one strikes*. (Ḳ, TA.)

مُبْتَذِلٌ, (Ḳ,) or ↓ مُتَبَذِّلٌ, (M, [so in a copy of that work, accord. to the TT, but this is probably a mistranscription,]) *Wearing a* مِبْذَل, i. e. [*a garment used in service* or *work*, or] *an old and worn-out garment*: (M, Ḳ:) and the latter, [if not a mistranscription for the former,] *neglecting the adorning of himself, by way of humility*. (TA, from a trad.) — See also what follows.

مُتَبَذِّلٌ (T, M, Ḳ) and ↓ مُبْتَذِلٌ (M, Ḳ) *A man who employs his own self in doing a thing*; (T;) *a man who performs his own work*. (M, Ḳ.) — See also what next precedes.

بذو

1. بَذُوَ, (T, Ṣ, M, &c.,) aor. يَبْذُو, (T, Ṣ,) inf. n. بَذَآءٌ (Ṣ, M, Mṣb, Ḳ) and بَذَاءَةٌ, (Ḳ,) or the latter is the original form, but the ة is elided, as in جَمَالٌ, inf. n. of جَمُلَ, (Ṣ,) or بَذَاءَةٌ is an inf. n. of the verb with ء, but that of بذو is بَذَاوَةٌ; (IB;) and some say, بَذِىَ, (T,) which is a dial. var. of the former, (Mṣb,) aor. يَبْذَى, inf. n. بَذَآءٌ; (T in art. بذأ;) *He* (a man) *was*, or *became, foul, unseemly*, or *obscene* [*in tongue*]; (T, Ṣ, M, Ḳ;) *evil in speech*; (T in art. بذأ;) as also بَذُؤَ, (T, M, Ḳ, in that art.,) and بَذَأَ, (Mṣb and Ḳ in art. بذأ,) and بَذِىَ: (Ḳ in that art.:) and ↓ ابذى *he uttered foul, unseemly*, or *obscene, speech* or *language*. (TA.) And بَذَوْتُ عَلَى القَوْمِ, (Ṣ, M, Mṣb,* Ḳ,) aor. ـُ, inf. n. بَذَآءٌ; (Mṣb;) and ↓ أَبْذَيْتُ عَلَيْهِمْ, (Ṣ, Mṣb,*) or أَبْذَيْتُهُمْ, (M, IB, Ḳ,) or both, (TA,) *I uttered foul, unseemly*, or *obscene, language against the people*, or *company of men*: (Ṣ, M, Ḳ, TA:) or *behaved in a lightwitted, weak, stupid*, or *foolish, manner*, or *ignorantly, towards them; and uttered foul, unseemly*, or *obscene, language against them*; and *so though with truth*. (Mṣb.) And بَذَا also signifies *He* (a man) *was*, or *became, evil in disposition*. (TA.)

3. بَاذَى, (Ṣ, TA,) inf. n. مُبَاذَاةٌ, (TA,) [*He vied with another*, or *strove to surpass him, in foul, unseemly*, or *obscene, speech* or *language*: or *he held such discourse with another*:] the inf. n. is syn. with مُفَاحَشَةٌ. (TA.)

4: see 1, in two places.

بَذَآءٌ [inf. n. of 1, used as a subst.,] *Foul, unseemly*, or *obscene, speech* or *language*. (Ṣ, M, Ḳ.)

بَذِىٌّ, (T, M, Mṣb, Ḳ,) or بَذِىُّ اللِّسَانِ, (Ṣ,) A man *foul, unseemly*, or *obscene, in tongue*: (T, Ṣ, M,* Ḳ:*) or *lightwitted, weak, stupid*, or *ignorant, in behaviour; and foul, unseemly*, or *obscene, in speech*; and *so though speaking truth*: (Mṣb:) fem. with ة: (Ṣ, Mṣb:) and pl. أَبْذِيَآءُ. (T.)

بر

1. بَرَّ, [first pers. بَرِرْتُ,] aor. يَبَرُّ, (T, M, Mṣb,) inf. n. بِرٌّ, (M, Mṣb, Ḳ,) *He was pious* [*towards his father* or *parents*, and ‡ *towards God*; (see the explanations of the verb as used transitively;)] and *was kind*, or *good and affectionate and gentle in behaviour, towards his kindred*; and *kind*, or *good, in his dealings with strangers*]: (Mṣb:) *he was good, just, righteous, virtuous*, or *honest*: (T, Mṣb:) [or *he was amply, largely*, or *extensively, good* or *beneficent*:] and *he was true*, or *veracious*. (M, Mṣb, Ḳ.) [Authorities differ as to the primary signification of this verb, and as to the subordinate meanings: see بِرٌّ below.] You say also, بَرَّ فِى قَوْلِهِ, (Mṣb, TA,) and فِى يَمِينِهِ, (Ṣ, M, Mgh, Mṣb, Ḳ,) first pers. بَرِرْتُ (T, A, Mgh, Ḳ) and بَرَرْتُ, (Ḳ,) aor. يَبَرُّ (M, Mṣb) and يَبِرُّ, (M,) inf. n. بِرٌّ (Ṣ, M, Ḳ) and بَرٌّ, (Ḳ,) or بُرُورٌ, (Mṣb,) *He was true*, or *veracious*, (Ṣ, Mgh, Mṣb, Ḳ, TA,) *in his saying*, (Mṣb, TA,) and *in his oath*. (Ṣ, Mgh, Mṣb, Ḳ.) — بَرَّ عَمَلُهُ and بُرَّ, inf. n. بِرٌّ and بُرُورٌ; and ↓ أُبِرَّ; [*His deed*, or *work, was*, or *proved, good*; or *was well*, or *sinlessly, performed*;] all signify the same. (M.) And بُرَّ العَمَلُ, i. e. الحَجُّ, a form of benediction, said to a person come from pilgrimage, *May the deed*, or *work*, i. e. the pilgrimage, *have been sinlessly performed*. (TA.) And بَرَّ حَجُّهُ, (T, Ṣ, A, Mṣb, Ḳ,) aor. يَبَرُّ, (T,) inf. n. بِرٌّ, (Ṣ, Mṣb,) or بُرُورٌ; (T;) and بُرَّ حَجُّهُ, (Fr, T, Ṣ, M, Ḳ,) aor. يُبَرُّ, inf. n. بِرٌّ; (T;) *His pilgrimage was sinlessly performed*: (Sh, T:) or *was characterized by the giving of food, and by sweetness of speech*; as explained by Mohammad himself: *was accepted*: *was rewarded*. (TA.) — بَرَّ, (A, Mṣb, Ḳ,) aor. يَبَرُّ (T, M, Ḳ) and يَبِرُّ, (M, Ḳ,) inf. n. بِرٌّ (M, Mṣb, Ḳ) and بَرٌّ and بُرُورٌ, (M, Ḳ,) *It* (a saying, Mṣb, and an oath, T, A, M, Mṣb, Ḳ) *was*, or *proved, true*. (M, A,* Mṣb,* Ḳ,* TA.) [See an ex. voce أَلِيَّةٌ, in art. الو.] — بَرَّتْ بِى سِلْعَتُهُ, inf. n. بِرٌّ, ‡ *His commodity*, or *article of merchandise, was easy of sale to me*, (Aboo-Sa'eed, T, A,*) *and procured me gain*: (A:) originally meaning *it recompensed me*, by its high price, for my care of it. (T.) [See also بَرَّهُ, below.] ═ بَرَّ وَالِدَهُ, (M,) [and app. بِوَالِدِهِ, (see بِرٌّ,)] first pers. بَرِرْتُ (Ṣ, M, Mṣb, Ḳ) and بَرَرْتُ, (M, Ḳ,) aor. يَبَرُّ (Ṣ, M, Mṣb, Ḳ) and يَبِرُّ, (M, Ḳ,) inf. n. بِرٌّ (Ṣ, M, Mṣb, Ḳ) and مَبَرَّةٌ (Ṣ, Ḳ, Mṣb*) and بُرُورٌ, (Mṣb,) *He treated*, or *behaved towards, his father with filial piety, duty*, or *obedience*; (TA;) or *with ample obedience*; (B;) the inf. ns. signifying the *contr. of* عُقُوقٌ: (Ṣ, M, A, Ḳ:) *he treated*, or *behaved towards, his father with good obedience, and with gentleness*, or *courtesy, striving to do the things that were pleasing to him, and to avoid what were displeasing to him*. (Mṣb.) And [hence, app., for accord. to the A it is tropical,] بَرَّ خَالِقَهُ, (Ṣ,) or رَبَّهُ, (A,) aor. يَبَرُّ, (Ṣ, A,) inf. n. بِرٌّ; (T, Ṣ, M, Ḳ;) and ↓ تَبَرَّرَهُ; (Ṣ, Ḳ;*) ‡ *He obeyed his Creator*, or *his Lord*; (Ṣ, M,* A, Ḳ;*) [*was pious towards Him*;] *served Him*; *rendered religious service to Him*: (TA:) or *rendered Him ample obedience*: the obedience here meant is of two kinds; namely, that of belief and that of works; and both these kinds are meant by البِرّ in the Ḳur ii. 172. (B.) [And app. بَرَّتْ وَلَدَهَا, or بِوَلَدِهَا, *She behaved with maternal affection towards her child*, or *offspring*. (See بِرٌّ.)] And بَرَّهُ, (M,) and بَرَّ رَحِمَهُ, (T,) first pers. بَرِرْتُ, (T, M,) inf. n. بِرٌّ, (T, M, Ḳ,) *He behaved towards him, and towards his kindred*, or *relations, with kindness*, or *goodness and affection and gentleness, and regard for his*, or *their, circumstances*; syn. وَصَلَهُ [and وَصَلَهُمْ]: (T, M, Ḳ:) such is said to be the signification of the verb as use in the Ḳur lx. 8. (M, B, TA. [See also 3.]) And اَللّٰهُ يَبَرُّ عِبَادَهُ † *God is merciful to his servants*: (M, TA:) or بَرَّهُ, inf n. بِرٌّ, said of God, means *He recompensed him*, or *rewarded him, for his obedience*. (B, TA.) [بَرَّهُ بِكَذَا (occurring in the Ṣ and Ḳ in explanation of أَلْطَفَهُ بِكَذَا) may be rendered *He showed kindness*, &c., *to him by such a thing*, or *such an action*, &c.: and also *he presented him with such a thing*; like وَصَلَهُ بِكَذَا.] — بَرَّ اللّٰهُ حَجَّهُ, (T, Ṣ, Mṣb,) aor. يَبَرُّ, (Mṣb,) inf. n. بِرٌّ, (Ṣ,) or بُرُورٌ, (Mṣb,) *God accepted his pilgrimage*; (Ṣ, Mṣb;) as also ↓ ابرّه: (T, Ṣ, M, Mṣb:) the latter alone is allowed by Fr: (M, TA:) [though بُرَّ حَجُّهُ and عَمَلُهُ, mentioned above, are well known; as is the pass. part. n. مَبْرُورٌ, which see below:] and one says, [in like manner,] ↓ ابرّ اللّٰهُ عَمَلَهُ [*God accepted his deed*, or *work, as good*; *approved it*]. (M.) — See also 4, in three places. ═ بَرَّ, (TḲ,) inf. n. بِرٌّ, (Ṣ, Ḳ,) *He drove* sheep or goats: (IAạr, Ṣ, Ḳ:) or *he called* them. (Yoo.) [See also بِرّ below.]

3. بَارَّهُ, inf. n. مُبَارَّةٌ, *He behaved towards him with kindness*, or *goodness and affection and gentleness, and regard for his circumstances*; or *he did so, experiencing from him the same behaviour*; syn. of the inf. n. مُلَاطَفَةٌ. (Ṣ and Ḳ in art. لطف: but only the inf. n. is there mentioned. [See also 1.])

4. ابرّ عَمَلَهُ : see 1. ═ ابرّ حَجَّهُ, and عَمَلَهُ: see 1, near the end of the paragraph. — ابرّ القَوْلَ,

(Mṣb,) and اليَمِينَ, (T, M, A, Mgh, Mṣb, Ḳ,) *He executed*, or *performed, the saying*, and *the oath, truly.* (M, A, Mgh, Mṣb, Ḳ.) Accord. to El-Aḥmar, one also says, بَرَرْتُ ♦ قَسَمِى; but none other asserts this. (T, TA.) — ابرّ ٱللّٰهُ قَسَمَهُ, (T, TA,) inf. n. إِبْرَارٌ; and ♦ بَرَّهُ, inf. n. بِرٌّ; *God verified his oath.* (TA.) — ابرّ فُلَانٌ قَسَمَ فُلَانٍ *Such a one assented, or consented, to the conjurement of such a one:* أَحْنَثَهُ signifies "he assented not," or "consented not, thereto." (T, TA.) — ابرّ عَلَيْهِمْ, (Ṣ, M, Ḳ,) inf. n. as above, (T, TA,) *He overcame them:* (T, Ṣ, M, Ḳ:) *he subdued them, or overcame them, by good or other actions;* (TA;) *by actions or sayings;* (TA;) as also ♦ بَرْهَرَهُمْ, aor. يُبَرْهِرُ: (T, Ḳ, TA:) *he was refractory, or stubborn, and overcame them.* (TA, from a trad.) You say, ابرّ عَلَى خَصْمِهِ [*He overcame his adversary*]. (A.) And ابرّ عَلَيْهِمْ شَرًّا [*He overcame them in evil*]: and hence ابرّ is used in the sense of فَجَرَ [*he transgressed*, &c.]; as in the saying of a poet,

فَلَسْتُ أُبَالِى مَنْ أَبَرَّ وَمَنْ فَجَرْ

[*Then I care not who acts wickedly and who transgresses*]. (IAạr, M.) — ابرّ [from بَرٌّ] *He rode, or journeyed, upon the land.* (ISk, Ṣ, A, Ḳ.) Opposed to أَبْحَرَ. (A.)

5. تبرّر [*He affected, or endeavoured to characterize himself by,* بِرّ, i. e. *filial piety,* &c.]. — قَدْ تَبَرَّرْتَ فِى أَمْرِنَا *Thou hast abstained from crime, or sin, or the like, in our affair, or business, or case.* (T, TA.) — تبرّر خَالِقَهُ: see 1.

6. تبارّوا *They practised mutual* بِرّ [meaning *kindness, or goodness and affection and gentleness, and regard for each other's circumstances*]. (Ṣ.)

R. Q. 1. بَرْبَرَ, inf. n. بَرْبَرَةٌ, *He talked much, and raised a clamour, or confused noise,* (M, Ḳ,) *with his tongue:* (M:) *he cried, or cried out,* (Ṣ, Ḳ,) *and talked in anger,* (Ṣ,) or *talked confusedly, with anger and aversion.* (TA.) And بَرْبَرَ فِى كَلَامِهِ *He was profuse and unprofitable in his talk.* (Fr.) — Also, inf. n. as above, *He* (a goat) *uttered a cry or cries,* [or *rattled,*] (M, Ḳ,) *being excited by desire of the female.* (M.)

بَرٌّ [originally بَرِرٌ] (M, Mṣb, Ḳ) and ♦ بَارٌّ (Mṣb) *Pious* [*towards his father* or *parents*, and ‡ *towards God;* ‡ *obedient to God, serving God,* or *rendering religious service to God;* (see 1;) and *kind,* or *good and affectionate and gentle in behaviour, towards his kindred;* and *good in his dealings with strangers*]; *good, just, righteous, virtuous,* or *honest:* (Mṣb:) *true,* or *veracious:* (M, Mṣb, Ḳ:) and both signify also *abounding in* بِرّ [or *filial piety,* &c.]: (Ḳ:) the former is [said to be] a stronger epithet than the latter, like as عَدْلٌ is stronger than عَادِلٌ: (B:) [but its pl. shows that it is not, like عَدْلٌ, originally an inf. n.: it is a regular contraction of بَرِرٌ, like as بَارٌّ is of بَارِرٌ:] the fem. of each is with ة: (Lḥ, M:) the pl. (of the former, Ṣ, M, Mṣb, or of the latter, B) is أَبْرَارٌ; and (of the latter, Ṣ, M, Mṣb, or of the former, B) بَرَرَةٌ: (Ṣ, M, Mṣb, Ḳ:) the former pl. is often specially applied to saints, those who abstain from worldly pleasures, and devotees; and the latter, to the recording angels. (B.) You say, أَنَا بَرٌّ بِوَالِدِى, and ♦ بَارٌّ, *I am characterized by filial piety, dutifulness,* or *obedience, to my father:* (Ṣ, M, A:*) the latter is mentioned on the authority of Kr; but some disallow it. (M, TA.) And الأُمُّ بَرَّةٌ بِوَلَدِهَا [*The mother is maternally affectionate to her child,* or *offspring*]. (Ṣ.) And رَجُلٌ بَرٌّ بِذِى قَرَابَتِهِ, and ♦ بَارٌّ, *A man who behaves towards his kindred with kindness,* or *goodness and affection and gentleness, and regard for their circumstances.* (T.) And رَجُلٌ بَرٌّ سَرٌّ *A man who treats with goodness and affection and gentleness, and rejoices,* or *gladdens, his brethren:* pl. بَرُّونَ سَرُّونَ. (Ṣ,* Ḳ,* TA, in art. سر.) And بَرٌّ فِى قَوْلٍ, and فِى يَمِينٍ, and ♦ بَارٌّ, *True,* or *veracious, in a saying,* and *in an oath.* (Mṣb.) And يَمِينٌ بَرَّةٌ and ♦ بَارَّةٌ [*A true oath;* or *an oath that proves true*]. (Ḥam p. 811.) البَرُّ is also a name of God; (M, Ḳ;) meaning † *The Merciful,* or *Compassionate:* (M:) or *the Very Benign to his servants;* (IAth;) *the Ample in goodness* or *beneficence:* (B:) البَارُّ is not so used. (IAth.) It is said in a trad., تَمَسَّحُوا بِالأَرْضِ فَإِنَّهَا بِكُمْ بَرَّةٌ † *Wipe yourselves with the dust,* or *earth,* [in performing the ceremony termed التَّيَمُّم,] *for it is benignant towards you,* like as the mother is to her children; meaning, ye are created from it, and in it are your means of subsistence, and to it ye return after death: (IAth:) or the meaning is, that your tents, or houses, are upon it, and ye are buried in it. (M.) — بَرٌّ *Land;* opposed to بَحْرٌ [as meaning "sea" and the like]: (Ṣ, Mṣb, Ḳ:) from بِرٌّ signifying "ampleness," "largeness," or "extensiveness;" (Esh-Shiháb [El-Khafájee], MF;) or the former word is the original of the latter. (B, TA. [See the latter word.]) [Hence, بَرًّا وَبَحْرًا *By land and by sea.*] — *A desert,* or *deserts;* a *waste,* or *wastes.* (T, TA. [See also بَرِّيَّةٌ, voce بَرِّىٌّ.]) So, accord. to Mujáhid [and the Jel] in words of the Ḳur [vi. 59], وَيَعْلَمُ مَا فِى البَرِّ وَالبَحْرِ *And He knoweth what is in the desert, or deserts, and the towns, or villages, in which is water,* (T, TA,) or *which are upon the rivers.* (Jel.) [So too in the phrase نَبَاتُ البَرِّ *The plants,* or *herbage, of the desert* or *waste; the wild plants* or *herbage.* And عَسَلُ البَرِّ *Honey of the desert; wild honey.* And حَيَوَانُ البَرِّ *The animal,* or *animals, of the desert; the wild animal* or *animals.*] — *A wide tract of land.* (Bḍ in ii. 41.) — [The *open country;* opposed to بَحْرٌ as meaning the "cities," or "towns," "upon the rivers:" see the latter word.] — *Elevated ground, open to view.* (T.) — *The tract,* or *part, out of doors,* or *where one is exposed to view; contr. of* كِنٌّ: used by the Arabs indeterminately; [without the article ال;] as in the phrase, جَلَسْتُ بَرًّا (Lth, T) meaning *I sat outside the house;* (A;) and خَرَجْتُ بَرًّا (Lth, T) meaning *I went forth outside the* [*house* or] *town,* (A,) or *into the desert:* (TA:) but [Az says,] these are post-classical phrases, which I have not heard from the chaste-speaking Arabs of the desert. (T.) — You say also, أُرِيدُ جَوًّا وَيُرِيدُ بَرًّا *I desire concealment,* or *secrecy, and he desires publicity.* (A.)

بُرٌّ *Wheat;* and the *grain of wheat;* syn. قَمْحٌ, (Ṣ,* Mṣb,) or حِنْطَةٌ; (M, Ḳ;) but it is a more chaste word than قَمْحٌ and حِنْطَةٌ: (M:) pl. of بُرَّةٌ; (Ṣ, M;) or [rather] بُرَّةٌ is the n. un. [signifying *a grain of wheat,* like قَمْحَةٌ]: (IDrd, Mṣb:) the pl. of بُرٌّ is أَبْرَارٌ: (Ḳ;) or this pl. is allowable on the ground of analogy, accord. to Mbr, but is disallowed by Sb. (Ṣ.) It is said in a prov., (TA,) هُوَ أَقْصَرُ مِنْ بُرَّةٍ [*He, or it, is shorter than a grain of wheat*]. (A, TA.) And you say, أَطْعَمَنَا ٱبْنَ بُرَّةٍ *He fed us with bread.* (A.)

بِرٌّ inf. n. of 1: (T, Ṣ, M, &c.:) it is said by some to signify primarily *Ampleness, largeness,* or *extensiveness;* whence بَرٌّ as opposed to بَحْرٌ: then, — *Benevolent and solicitous regard* or *treatment* or *conduct* [*to parents and others;* i. e. *piety to parents;* and ‡ *towards God*]: and *goodness,* or *beneficence:* and *kindness,* or *good and affectionate and gentle behaviour, and regard for the circumstances of another:* (Esh-Shiháb [El-Khafájee], MF:) or بَرٌّ, as opposed to بَحْرٌ, [or as signifying "a wide tract of land," (Bḍ in ii. 41,)] is the original of بِرٌّ, (Bḍ in ii. 41, B, TA,) which signifies *ample, large,* or *extensive, goodness* or *beneficence,* (Z, in the Ksh, ii. 41, [but he regards it as the original of بَرٌّ,] and Bḍ on the same passage, and B, Ḳ, TA,) *to men;* (TA;) or *comprehending every kind of goodness:* (Ksh and Bḍ ubi suprà:) and hence it is said to be in three things: *in the service of God: in paying regard to relations; acting well to them:* and *in dealing with strangers:* (Bḍ ubi suprà:) or *every deed that is approved:* (Ksh and Bḍ in ii. 172:) and [particularly] *obedience to God:* (T, Ṣ, M, &c.: [see also بَرَّةٌ:]) [and *every incumbent duty:* and hence,] the *pilgrimage to Mekkeh:* (Ḳ:) and *fidelity to an engagement:* (TA:) also *a gratuitous gift,* or *favour;* and *a bounty,* or *benefit;* syn. فَضْلٌ; (Mṣb;) and إِحْسَانٌ; as also ♦ مَبَرَّةٌ [an inf. n., but when used as a simple subst. its pl. is مَبَارُّ and مَبَرَّاتٌ]. (Ḥar p. 94.) In the Ḳur [ii. 172], where it is said, لٰكِنَّ البِرَّ مَنْ آمَنَ بِٱللّٰهِ, by البِرّ is meant ذَا البِرِّ [i. e. *But the pious,* or *obedient* to God, *is he who believeth in God*]; (T, M, Ksh, Bḍ, Jel;) and some read البَارَّ: (Ksh, Bḍ, Jel:) or the meaning is, لٰكِنَّ البِرَّ بِرُّ مَنْ آمَنَ بِٱللّٰهِ i. e. *but the obedience* of which it behooveth one to be mindful *is the obedience of him who believeth in God:* (Sb, T, IJ, M, Ksh, Bḍ:) and this explanation is preferable to the former. (Bḍ.) It is said in a prov., (T, Ṣ,) لَا يَعْرِفُ هِرًّا مِنْ بِرٍّ, (Ṣ, A, Ḳ, but in the T and M مَا is put in the place of لَا,) meaning *He knows not him who dislikes him,* or *hates him, from him who behaves towards him with kindness*, or *goodness and affection and gentleness, and regard for his circumstances*: (Ṣ, M, A, Ḳ,* TA:) or *undutiful conduct to a parent from gentleness*, or *courtesy*: (El-Fezáree, T, Ḳ:) or *altercation*, (T,) or *dislike*, or *hatred*, (Ḳ,) *from honourable treatment*: (T, Ḳ:) or *the calling of sheep*, or *goats*, *from the driving of them*: (IAạr, Ṣ, Ḳ:) or *the driving of sheep*, or *goats, from the calling of them*: (Yoo, T:) or *the calling of them to water from the calling of them to fodder*; (Ḳ;) which last rendering is agreeable with an explanation of بِرّ by IAạr [mentioned in the T]; (TA;) and ▼بَرْبَرٌ, also, has the signification here assigned to بِرّ: (Ḳ,* TA:) or البَرْبَرَة *from* الهَرْهَرَة; (A'Obeyd, T, Ḳ;) i. e. *the crying of sheep from the crying of goats*: (A'Obeyd, T:) or *the cat from the rat*, or *mouse*: (IAạr, T, M, Ḳ:) and بِرّ also signifies the [*species of rat called*] جُرَذ: (Aboo-Ṭálib, T, Ḳ:) or *a small animal resembling the rat* or *mouse*: (M:) and the *young of the fox*. (Ḳ.) — Also *Good*, as a subst., not an adj.; syn. خَيْر; (Sh, T, Mgh, Mṣb, Ḳ;) which comprises all that has been said in explanation of بِرّ (Sh, T, Mgh) as used in the saying of Moḥammad, عَلَيْكُمْ بِالصِّدْقِ فَإِنَّهُ يَهْدِى إِلَى البِرِّ [*Keep ye to truth; for it guides to good*, or *to a good*, or *right, state*]: some render it in this instance by الخَيْر; and some, by الصَّلَاح. (Sh, T.) It signifies also The *good of the present life, consisting in spiritual and worldly blessings, and of that which is to come, consisting in everlasting enjoyment in Paradise*: so in the Ḳur iii. 86: (T:) or [simply] *Paradise*. (Ḳ.) — Also The *heart*; or the *mind*. (Ḳ.) So in the saying, هُوَ مُطْمَئِنُّ البِرِّ [*He is quiet*, or *at rest, in heart*, or *mind*]. (TA.)

بَرَّةُ a subst. in the sense of البِرُّ, (Ṣ, M, Ḳ,) meaning *Obedience* [&c.]; (Ḳ;) determinate, (Ṣ, Ḳ,) being a proper name; for which reason, combined with its being of the fem. gender, it is imperfectly decl. (M.) [It is opposed to فَجَارِ. See a verse of En-Nábighah in the first paragraph of art. حمل.]

بُرْبُرٌ [a coll. gen. n.] The *fruit of the* أَرَاك [q. v.], (Ṣ, M,) *in a general sense*: (M:) or the *first thereof*; (Ḳ;) [i. e.] the *first that appears*, or *when it first appears, and is sweet*: (M:) or *when it has become hard*: (Mṣb:) or *when it is larger in its berries* (حَبّ) *than such as is termed* كَبَاث, *and smaller in its clusters; having a round, small, hard stone, a little larger than the* حِمَّص; *its cluster filling the hand*: (AḤn, M:) n. un. with ة. (AḤn, Ṣ, M, Mṣb.)

بَرِىٌّ *A good, sweet*, or *pleasant, word* or *expression* or *saying*: (Ḳ:) from بِرّ signifying "benevolent and solicitous regard or treatment or conduct." (TA.)

[بَرِّىٌّ *Of*, or *belonging to*, or *relating to*, the *land* as opposed to the sea or a great river. — And *Of*, or *belonging to*, or *relating to, the desert* or *waste*; *growing*, or *living*, or *produced, in the desert* or *waste*; *wild*, or *in an uncultivated state*. — And hence,] أَرْضٌ بَرِّيَّةٌ *Uncultivated land; without seed-produce, and unfruitful; without green herbs* or *leguminous plants and without waters*; *contr. of* رِيفِيَّةٌ. (IAạr, M, Ḳ.*) And, simply, ▼بَرِّيَّةٌ, (Ṣ, M, A, Mṣb, Ḳ,) and ▼بَرِّيتٌ, (A'Obeyd, IAạr, Sh, Ṣ, Ḳ,) the latter a variation of the former, the ى being made quiescent, and the ة therefore being changed into ت, as in عِفْرِيتٌ, originally عِفْرِيَةٌ, (Ṣ,) a rel. n. from بَرٌّ, (Sh, T, Mṣb,) *A desert; a waste; a spacious tract of ground without herbage*; syn. صَحْرَآءُ: (Ṣ, M, A, Mṣb, Ḳ:) [see also بَرّ:] or *a tract nearer to the desert* (البَرّ) *than it is to water*: (Sh, T:) [but some write the latter word ▼بَرِيتٌ; and it is said that] بَرِيتٌ, (T and Ḳ in art. برت,) of the same measure as سِكِّيتٌ, (Ḳ in that art.,) signifies *flat, even*, or *level, land*: (T, Ḳ:) or *a barren, flat, even*, or *level, land*: a poet says,

بَرِّيتُ أَرْضٍ بَعْدَهَا بَرِّيتُ

[*A barren, flat land, after which is a* second *barren, flat land*]: (T:) ISd says that بَرِّيتٌ, in a poem of Ru-beh, [from which the ex. given above is probably taken,] is of the measure فِعْلِيتٌ from البَرّ; and that art. برت is not the place in which it should be mentioned: (TA:) Lth says, البَرِّيتُ is a noun derived from البَرِّيَّة; the ى becoming quiescent, and the ة becoming an inseparable ت, as though it were a radical letter, as in the case of عِفْرِيَةٌ, which thus becomes عِفْرِيتٌ: (T, TA:) the pl. of بَرِّيَّة is بَرَارِىُّ; and that of بَرِّيت is بَرَارِيتُ. (Ṣ.)

بَرِّيَّةٌ and بَرِّيتٌ and بَرِيتٌ: see بَرِّىٌّ.

بَرَّارٌ as signifying *A possessor of* بُرّ, i. e. *wheat*, though agreeable with prevailing analogy, is not allowable, not being sanctioned by usage. (Sb, M.)

بَرَّانِىٌّ *External*; or *outward*: *apparent*; *public*. (T.) Hence the saying of Selmán, (T,) مَنْ أَصْلَحَ جَوَّانِيَّهُ أَصْلَحَ ٱللّٰهُ بَرَّانِيَّهُ (T, A, Ḳ) *Whoso maketh his inner man* (سَرِيرَتَهُ) *to be good, God will make his outward man* (عَلَانِيَتَهُ) *to be good*. (T.) بَرَّانِىٌّ is a rel. n., irregularly formed, (Ḳ,) from بَرّ signifying "elevated ground, open to view;" and جَوَّانِىٌّ, from جَوّ signifying "any low, or depressed, part of the ground." (T.) You say, اِفْتَتَحَ البَابَ البَرَّانِىَّ *He opened the outer door*. (A.)

بَرْبَرُ, (Ṣ, Ḳ,) or البَرْبَرُ, (Mgh, Mṣb,) [a coll. gen. proper name, of which the n. un., or rel. n., is ▼بَرْبَرِىٌّ,] a foreign word, (Ṣ,) [probably of African origin, the primary form of which is the source of Βάρβαρος, &c.,] arabicized; (Mṣb;) or, as some say, from بَرْبَرَة in speech; (TA; [see R. Q. 1;]) and البَرَابِرَةُ, (Ṣ, M, Mṣb, Ḳ,) the pl. of بَرْبَرُ, (Ḳ,) or of البَرْبَرُ, (Mṣb,) [or of بَرْبَرِىٌّ, agreeably with what follows and with analogy,] the ة being added because the sing. is a foreign word, or [so in the M and TA, but in the Ṣ "and,"] a rel. n., (Ṣ, M,) but it may be elided; [so that one may say البَرَابِرُ;] (Ṣ;) *A certain people*, (Ṣ, M, Mgh, Mṣb, Ḳ,) *of the inhabitants of El-Maghrib* [or *Northern Africa west of Egypt*], (Mgh,* Mṣb, Ḳ,*) *like the Arabs of the desert in hardness, and coarseness*, or *rudeness*, (Mgh,* Mṣb,) *and in slightness of religion, and littleness of knowledge*: (Mgh:) and *another people*, [*the Colobi* mentioned by Diodorus Siculus and Strabo,] *between the Abyssinians and the Zinj, who amputate* [*the glans of*] *the penis, and make it a dowry for a wife*. (Ḳ.) [There are various opinions of the origins of these races. The appellation of البَرَابِرَة, sing. ▼بَرْبَرِىٌّ, is also applied by late historians, and in the present day, to *The races inhabiting the portion of the valley of the Nile which we commonly call Nubia*.]

بَرْبَرٌ: see بَرْبَارٌ.

بَرْبَرٌ: see بِرّ.

بَرْبَرِىٌّ: see بَرْبَارٌ: — and see also بَرْبَرُ, in two places.

بَرْبَارٌ One *who talks much, and raises a clamour*, or *confused noise*, (M, Ḳ,) *with his tongue*: (M:) *who cries*, or *cries out*, (Ṣ, Ḳ,) *and talks in anger*, (Ṣ,) or *talks confusedly, with anger and aversion*: (TA:) *who vociferates much*; (TA;) as also ▼بَرْبَرٌ: (Ḳ:) and بَرْبَرِىٌّ signifies one *who talks much and unprofitably*. (Fr.) — البَرْبَارُ *The lion*; as also ▼المُبَرْبِرُ: (Ḳ:) because of the confused noise that he makes, and his aversion and anger. (TA.) — دَلْوٌ بَرْبَارٌ *A bucket that makes a noise* (M, Ḳ) *in the water*. (M.)

بُرْبُورٌ *What is termed* جَشِيش [i. e. *coarsely-ground flour*, &c.], (M, CḲ, [in MS. copies of the Ḳ, and of the Ṣ also, حَشِيش, which is evidently a mistranscription,]) *of wheat*. (Ṣ, M, Ḳ.)

بَارٌّ; fem. with ة: see بَرّ, in five places.

أَبَرُّ [accord. to analogy signifies *More*, and *most, pious* &c.: see بَرّ. But the only meaning that I find assigned to it in any of the lexicons is that here following. —] *More*, and *most, distant in the desert*, (T, Ḳ,) *as to habitation*. (T.) So in the saying, أَفْصَحُ العَرَبِ أَبَرُّهُمْ *The most chaste in speech of the Arabs are the most distant of them in the desert, as to habitation*. (T, Ḳ.* [In the latter, instead of أفصح, we find أَصْلَحُ.])

مُبِرٌّ One *who overcomes*. (TA.) [See 4.] — إِنَّهُ لَمُبِرٌّ بِذٰلِكَ means *Verily he is a prudent*, or *sound, manager of that*; syn. ضَابِطٌ لَهُ. (M, Ḳ.*)

مَبَرَّةٌ: see بِرّ.

مَبْرُورٌ, applied to a pilgrimage, *Sinlessly performed*: (Sh, T, Mgh:) or *characterized by the giving of food and by sweetness of speech*; as explained by Moḥammad himself: *accepted*: *rewarded*. (TA.) مَبْرُورٌ مَأْجُورٌ [Thou art *accepted*, or *approved, and rewarded*] and مَبْرُورًا مَأْجُورًا [Go thou *accepted*, or *approved, and rewarded*] are forms of benediction: the former, of the dial.

of Temeem; أَنْتَ being understood: the latter, of the dial. of the people of El-Ḥijáz; اِذْهَبْ being understood. (M.) — Applied to a sale, *Truly and honestly executed.* (Sh, T, Mgh.)

بَرْبَارٌ: see المُبَرْبِرُ.

برأ

1. بَرِئَ, [aor. َ, inf. n. generally بُرْءٌ or بَرَاءَةٌ,] *He was,* or *became, clear,* or *free,* of, or from, a thing; in the manners which will be explained below: (Bḍ ii. 51:) *he was,* or *became, in a state of freedom* or *immunity, secure,* or *safe.* (T.) [Hence,] بَرِئَ مِنَ المَرَضِ, and بَرَأَ, (T, Mṣb,) aor. َ; and بَرُؤَ, aor. ُ; (Mṣb;) inf. n. بُرْءٌ: (T, Mṣb:) or بَرِئَ من المرض, inf. n. بُرْءٌ, with damm; and the people of El-Ḥijáz say بَرَأَ, inf. n. بَرْءٌ, with fet-ḥ: (Ṣ:) accord. to Aṣ, بَرِئَ من المرض is of the dial. of Temeem; and بَرَأَ of the dial. of the people of El-Ḥijáz: or, accord. to AZ, the people of El-Ḥijáz say بَرَأَ; and the rest of the Arabs say بَرِئَ: (T:) or بَرَأَ [alone], said of a sick man, aor. ُ and َ; and بَرِئَ; and بَرُؤَ; inf. n. بُرْءٌ [probably a mistranscription for بَرْءٌ] and بُرُوْءٌ: or, accord. to Lḥ, the people of El-Ḥijáz say بَرَأَ, aor. َ, inf. n. بَرْءٌ and بُرُوْءٌ [i. e. بُرُوْءٌ]; and the people of El-'Áliyeh, [بَرَأَ,] aor. َ, inf. n. بُرْءٌ and بُرُوْءٌ; and Temeem, بَرِئَ, [aor. َ,] inf. n. بُرْءٌ and بُرُوْءٌ: (M:) or بَرَأَ, (Ḳ,) said by IḲṭṭ to be the most chaste form, (TA,) aor. َ, (Ḳ,) agreeably with analogy, (TA,) and ُ, (Ḳ,) said by Zj to be the only instance of a verb of the measure فَعَلَ with ء for its last radical letter having its aor. of the measure يَفْعُلُ, [though others mention also قَرَأَ, aor. يَقْرُؤُ, and هَنَأَ, aor. يَهْنُؤُ,] and asserted to be a bad form, (TA,) inf. n. بُرْءٌ and بُرُوْءٌ; and بَرُؤَ, (Ḳ,) not a chaste form, (TA,) aor. ُ; and بَرِئَ, (Ḳ,) a chaste form, (TA,) [and the most common of all,] aor. َ, inf. n. بُرْءٌ and بُرُوْءٌ, (Ḳ, TA,) or بُرْءٌ, (CḲ,) and بُرُوْءٌ; (Ḳ, TA;) *He became free from the disease, sickness,* or *malady:* (T:) or [*he recovered from it:*] *he became convalescent;* or *sound,* or *healthy, at the close of disease, but was yet weak;* or *he recovered, but not completely, his health and strength;* syn. نَقِهَ; (M, Ḳ;) i. e., *he acquired that slight degree of soundness,* or *health, which comes at the close of disease, but with disease remaining in him.* (TA.) [And بَرِئَ الجُرْحُ, or بَرَأَ, *The wound healed;* or *became in a healing state:* of frequent occurrence.] And بَرِئَ مِنَ الأَمْرِ, [the only form of the verb used in this case, and in the other cases in which it is mentioned below,] aor. َ and ُ, the latter extr., (M, Ḳ,) or rather it is very strange, for IḲooṭ says that نَعِمَ, aor. يَنْعُمُ, and فَضِلَ, aor. يَفْضُلُ, are the only instances of this kind, (TA,) inf. n. بَرَاءَةٌ (M, Ḳ) and بَرَآءٌ (Lḥ, M, Ḳ) and بُرُوْءٌ, (M,) or بُرْءٌ, (Ḳ, TA,) or بُرُوْءٌ; (CḲ;) and ▼تَبَرَّأَ; (Ṣ,* M, Ḳ, Mgh;*) [*He was,* or *became, free from the thing,* or *affair;* or *clear,* or *quit, thereof; clear of having* or *taking,* or *of having had* or *taken, any part therein; guiltless of it:* and also, *irresponsible for it;* as in an ex. q. v. voce عِضَاضٌ:] said in relation to [a fault or the like, and] a debt, and a claim, and religion [&c.]. (Lḥ, M.) You say, بَرِئَ مِنَ العَيْبِ, (Mgh, Mṣb,) or العُيُوبِ, (Ṣ,) inf. n. بَرَاءَةٌ, (Mgh,) *He was,* or *became, free* (Mṣb) [*from the fault, defect, imperfection, blemish,* or *vice*], (Mgh, Mṣb,) [or *faults,* &c.]. (Ṣ.) And بَرِئَ مِنَ الدَّيْنِ, (T, Mgh, Mṣb,) or الدُّيُونِ, (Ṣ,) aor. َ, (T, Mṣb,) inf. n. بَرَاءَةٌ, (T, Mgh, Mṣb,)* *He was,* or *became, clear,* or *quit, of the debt;* (or *debts;* Ṣ;) *irresponsible for it* [or *them*]: or *in a state of immunity with respect to it* [or *them*]; i. e., *exempt from the demand thereof.* (Mṣb.) And بَرِئَ إِلَيْكَ مِنْ حَقِّكَ, inf. n. بَرَاءَةٌ and بَرَآءٌ (Lḥ, M) and بُرُوْءٌ, [*He was,* or *became, clear,* or *quit, to thee, of thy claim,* or *due,* or *right;* or *exempt from the demand thereof;*] as also ▼تَبَرَّأَ. (M.) And بَرِئْتُ إِلَيْكَ مِنْ فُلَانٍ, inf. n. بَرَاءَةٌ, [*I was,* or *became,* or *have become, clear, to thee, of having* or *taking,* or *of having had* or *taken, any part with such a one;* or, *irresponsible to thee for such a one:*] (AZ, T, Ṣ:* [in one copy of the Ṣ, I find the phrase بَرِئْتُ مِنْكَ, commencing the art.; but not in other copies:]) this is the only form of the verb used in this case, and in relation to debt [and the like]. (AZ, T.) — *He removed himself,* or *kept, far,* or *aloof,* [from unclean things, or things occasioning blame; followed by مِنْ, with which it may be rendered *he shunned,* or *avoided;*] syn. تَنَزَّهَ and تَبَاعَدَ. (T.) [You say, بَرِئَ مِنَ الأَقْذَارِ *He removed himself,* or *kept, far,* or *aloof, from unclean things.*] — *He manifested an excuse,* [or *asserted himself to be clear* or *quit* or *irresponsible,* like ▼تَبَرَّأَ,] *and gave warning;* syn. أَعْذَرَ and أَنْذَرَ. (T.) Hence, in the Ḳur [ix. 1], بَرَاءَةٌ مِنَ ٱللّٰهِ وَرَسُولِهِ *A manifestation of excuse, and a warning, from God and his apostle.* (T.) — بَرَأَ ٱللّٰهُ الخَلْقَ, (Fr, T, Ṣ, M, Ḳ,) or الخَلِيقَةَ, (Mṣb,) aor. َ, (T, M, &c.,) inf. n. بَرْءٌ (T, Ṣ, M, Ḳ) and بُرُوْءٌ, (AZ, Lḥ, M, Ḳ,) *God created mankind,* or *the beings,* or *things, that are created,* syn. خَلَقَ, (Fr, T, M, Mṣb, Ḳ,) *after no similitude,* or *model,* (TA,) [*but,* properly, though not always meaning so, *out of pre-existing matter;* for] Bḍ says [in ii. 51] that the primary meaning of the root برء is to denote a thing's becoming clear, or free, of, or from, another thing; either by being released [therefrom], as in بَرِئَ المَرِيضُ مِنْ مَرَضِهِ and المَدْيُونُ مِنْ دَيْنِهِ [both sufficiently explained above]; or by production [therefrom], as in بَرَأَ ٱللّٰهُ آدَمَ مِنَ الطِّينِ [*God produced,* or *created, Adam, from,* or *out of, clay*]. (TA.) This verb relates to substances [as in the exs. given above] and to accidents; and hence, [in the Ḳur lvii. 22,] مِنْ قَبْلِ أَنْ نَبْرَأَهَا [*Before our creating it,* if ها refer to مُصِيبَة, preceding it; but, as Bḍ says, it may refer to this, or to الأَرْض, or to الأَنْفُس]: (M:) but البَرْءُ has a more particular application than الخَلْقُ; the former being particularly applied to the creation of animate beings, with few exceptions: you say, بَرَأَ ٱللّٰهُ النَّسَمَةَ وَخَلَقَ السَّمٰوَاتِ وَالأَرْضَ [*God created,* or *produced, man,* or *the soul, and He created the heavens and the earth*]. (TA.) [To this verb, or perhaps to بَرِئَ, or to both, בָּרָא is the Hebrew equivalent, properly (though not necessarily always) signifying "he created out of pre-existing matter," or "he fashioned."]

2. بَرَّأَهُ, inf. n. تَبْرِئَةٌ: see 4, in four places. [Hence,] لَا التَّبْرِئَةِ *The* لا *that denies in a general manner, absolutely,* or *to the uttermost;* i. e. *the* لا *that is a universal negative.* (Mughnee &c.) — Also *He verified his being free* [from a thing], *clear,* or *quit,* [of it,] *guiltless* [of it], or *irresponsible* [for it]. (Mgh, TA.)

3. بَارَأَهُ, (T, Ṣ, M, Mgh, Ḳ,) inf. n. مُبَارَأَةٌ (T, M, Mgh) and بِرَآءٌ, (M,) *He made him* (his copartner) *free, clear, quit,* or *irresponsible, the latter doing to him the same:* (Mgh:) *he compounded,* or *made a compromise, with him* (his hired man, T, M) *for their mutual separation:* (M:) *he separated himself from him* (his copartner, Ṣ, O), *the latter doing the same.* (Ṣ, O, Ḳ.) And بَارَأْتُ الرَّجُلَ *I became free, clear, quit,* or *irresponsible, to the man, he becoming so to me.* (M.) And بَارَأَ المَرْأَةَ, (T, M, Ḳ,) or ٱمْرَأَتَهُ, (Ṣ,) inf. n. as above, (M,) *He compounded,* or *made a compromise, with the woman* (or *his wife,* Ṣ) *for their mutual separation;* (M, Ḳ;) i. e. *he divorced her for a compensation* [*which she was to make him,* such as her giving up a portion of her dowry remaining due to her, *in order that they might be clear, each of the other*]: it occurs also [without ء] in art. برى. (TA.)

4. ابرأهُ *He* (God, Ṣ, M, Ḳ) [*recovered him,* or] *restored him to convalescence,* (M, Ḳ,) مِنَ المَرَضِ [*from the disease, sickness,* or *malady*]. (Ṣ.) — أَبْرَأَكَ مِنَ الأَمْرِ and ▼بَرَّأَكَ (M, Ḳ*) *He* (i. e. God, TA) *made thee, pronounced thee,* or *held thee,* or *hath made thee,* &c., or *may He make thee,* &c., *to be free from the thing* or *affair,* or *clear* or *quit thereof,* or *guiltless thereof,* or *irresponsible for it;* (TA;) [or *He acquitted thee,* or *hath acquitted thee,* or *may He acquit thee, thereof;* or *He showed thee,* or *hath showed thee,* or *may He show thee, to be free from it,* &c.: see also 2, above:] said in relation to [a fault or the like, and] a debt, and a claim, and religion [&c.]. (M.) You say, ▼بَرَّأْتُهُ مِنَ العَيْبِ *I made him, pronounced him,* or *held him, to be free from the fault, defect, imperfection, blemish,* or *vice.* (Mṣb.) It is said in the Ḳur [xxxiii. 69], ▼فَبَرَّأَهُ ٱللّٰهُ مِمَّا قَالُوا (M) *But God showed him to be clear of that which they said.* (Bḍ.) You say also, أَبْرَأْتُهُ مِنَ الدَّيْنِ *I made him, pronounced him,* or *held him, to be clear,* or *quit, of the debt; irresponsible for it;* or *in a state of immunity with respect to it;* i. e., *exempt from the demand thereof:* (Mṣb:) and أَبْرَأْتُهُ مِمَّا لِي عَلَيْهِ; and ▼بَرَّأْتُهُ, inf. n. تَبْرِئَةٌ; [*I acquitted him of that which he owed me:*] (Ṣ:) and أَبْرَأْتُهُ [alone] *I made him, pronounced him,* or *held him, to be clear,* or *quit, of a claim that I had* upon him, or a due or right that he owed me. (Mgh.) —— ابرأ [in the T (as on the authority of Aboo-'Amr Esh-Sheybánee) أَبْرَى] *He entered upon* [*the night*, or *day, called*] البَرَآء, q. v. (Ḳ.)

5: see 1, in three places. تبرّأ منْهُ also signifies *He asserted himself to be free from it;* or *clear*, or *quit, of it;* namely, a fault, or the like. (Mgh.) [And *He declared himself to be clear of him; to be not connected*, or *implicated, with him; he renounced him:* see Ḳur ii. 161 and 162, &c:]

6. تَبَارَأْنَا *We separated ourselves, each from the other.* (TA.) [See 3.]

10. استبرأ, (T,) or استبرأ مِنَ البَوْلِ, (Mṣb,) *He took extraordinary pains*, or *the utmost pains, in cleansing the orifice of his penis from the remains of urine, by shaking it and pulling it and the like, until he knew that nothing remained in it:* (T:) or *he purified*, or *cleansed, himself from urine;* syn. تَنَزَّهَ عَنْهُ: (Mṣb:) or استبرأ, (M,) or استبرأ الذَّكَرَ, (Ḳ, TA,) signifies *he took extraordinary pains*, or *the utmost pains, in cleansing the penis from urine;* or *he cleansed it entirely from urine;* (M,* Ḳ,* TA;) and so استبرأ الفَرْجَ: and in like manner, استبرأت الفرج said of a woman: (El-Munáwee, TA:) but the lawyers make a distinction between اِسْتِبْرَآء and اِسْتِنْقَآء [which are made syn. in the M and Ḳ]: see the latter word. (TA.) —— And استبرأ الجَارِيَةَ, (T, Ṣ, Mgh,) or المَرْأَةَ, (M, Mṣb, Ḳ,) *He abstained from sexual intercourse* (T, M, Ḳ) *with the girl* whom he had purchased or whom he had taken captive, (T,) or *with the woman,* (M, Ḳ,) *until she had menstruated* (T, M, Ḳ) *at his abode, once, and then become purified:* (T:) the meaning is, (T,) *he sought to find her free from pregnancy.* (T, Mgh, Mṣb.) —— Hence, (Mgh,) استبرأ الشَّىْءَ, (Z, Mgh, Mṣb,) or الأَمْرَ, (TA,) *He searched, searched out*, or *sought to find* or *discover, the uttermost of the thing*, or *affair,* (Z, Mgh, Mṣb, TA,) *in order that he might know it,* (Mgh,) *to put an end to his doubt.* (Z, Mgh, Mṣb, TA.) You say, اسْتَبْرَأْتُ مَا عِنْدَكَ [*I searched*, or *sought to find* or *discover*, or *I have searched*, &c., *the uttermost of what thou hast*, of knowledge &c.]. (Ṣ, TA.) And استبرأ أَرْضَ كَذَا فَمَا وَجَدَ ضَالَّتَهُ [*He searched the uttermost of such a land and found not his stray beast*]. (TA.) It is said in the Expos. of the Jámi' eṣ-Ṣagheer that اِسْتِبْرَآء is an expression denoting *The seeking*, or *seeking leisurely and repeatedly, to obtain knowledge* of a thing, *until one knows it; considering it with the endeavour to obtain a clear knowledge of it; taking, in doing so, the course prescribed by prudence, precaution, or good judgment.* (Mgh.)

بُرْأَةٌ *A hunter's lurking-place* or *covert:* (T, Ṣ, M, Ḳ:) pl. بُرَأٌ. (T, Ṣ, M.) El-Aạshà says,

* بِهَا بُرَأٌ مِثْلُ الفَسِيلِ المُكَمَّمِ *

[*At it* (a source of water mentioned in the context) *were hunters' lurking-places, like young palm-trees covered over:* for tender young palm-trees are often covered over with a kind of coarse matting]. (T, Ṣ, M.)

بَرَآءٌ: see بَرِىْءٌ, in six places. —— البَرَآءُ *The first night of the* [*lunar*] *month;* (El-Mázinee, T, Ṣ, Ḳ;) called thus, (Ṣ,) or لَيْلَةُ البَرَآءِ, (M,) because the moon has then become clear of the sun: (Ṣ, M:) or *the first day of the month:* (AA, T, Ḳ:) or *the last night thereof:* (Aṣ, T, Ḳ:) or *the last day thereof;* (IAạr, T, Ḳ;) *a fortunate day; every event happening therein being regarded as a means of obtaining a blessing;* (IAạr, T;) but most hold that the last day of the month is termed النَّحِيرَةُ; (TA;) as also ابْنُ البَرَآءِ: (Ḳ:) or this is *the first day of the month:* (IAạr, T, TA:) pl. أَبْرِئَةٌ. (Th, M.)

بُرَآءٌ: see بَرِىْءٌ, in two places.

بَرِىْءٌ *Free,* (Mṣb,) مِنْهُ *from it;* namely a fault, defect, imperfection, blemish, or vice; (Mgh, Mṣb;) and, also followed by مِنْهُ, *clear*, or *quit, of it; irresponsible for it;* or *in a state of immunity with respect to it;* i. e. *exempt from the demand thereof;* namely a debt, (Mṣb,) or a claim, or due, or right; (Mgh;) as also ↓ بَارِئٌ and ↓ بَرَآءٌ. (Mṣb.) You say, أَنَا بَرِىْءٌ مِنْهُ [*I am free from it*, &c.]; (T,* Ṣ, M, Ḳ;*) and ↓ بَرَآءٌ, used alike as sing. and dual and pl. (Fr, T, Ṣ, M, Ḳ) and masc. and fem., (Fr, T, M, Ḳ,) because it is originally an inf. n.; (Fr, T, Ṣ;) and ↓ بُرَآءٌ: (Ṣ, M:) the pl. of بَرِىْءٌ is بَرِيؤُونَ (T Ṣ, Ḳ) and بُرَآءُ (T, Ṣ, M, Ḳ) and بُرَآءٌ, (T, M, Ḳ,) of the measure فُعَالٌ, (T,) like رُخَالٌ, (M, Ḳ,) of an extr. measure, disapproved by Suh, who says, in the R, that it is a contraction of بُرَآءُ, and has tenween because it resembles [words originally of the measure] فُعَالٌ, and that the rel. n. formed from it is ↓ بُرَاوِىٌّ, (TA,) but it is mentioned by AAF as a pl. of بَرِىْءٌ, and as being like رُخَالٌ, and Fr mentions بُرَآءُ as a pl. of the same, imperfectly decl., with one of the two hemzehs suppressed, (M,) and بِرَآءٌ (Ṣ, M, Ḳ) and أَبْرَآءٌ (Ṣ, Ḳ) and أَبْرِئَآءُ, (T, Ṣ, Ḳ,) the last two anomalous: (TA:) the fem. of بَرِىْءٌ is بَرِيْئَةٌ; pl. بَرِيْئَاتٌ (T, Ṣ, M, Ḳ) and بَرِيَّاتٌ (Lḥ, M, Ḳ) and بَرَايَا. (T, Ṣ, M, Ḳ.) You say, أَنَا بَرِىْءٌ مِنْهُ and خَلِىٌّ مِنْهُ [*I am free from it;* or, more commonly, *I am clear*, or *quit, of it*, or *him*]; and أَنَا بَرَآءٌ ↓ مِنْهُ and خَلَآءٌ مِنْهُ; (Ṣ;) and نَحْنُ مِنْكَ البَرَآءُ ↓: (M:) and أَنَا البَرَآءُ ↓ مِنْهُ and الخَلَآءُ [*We are clear*, or *quit, of you*]; (Fr, T;) i. e., ذَوُو البَرَآءِ: so says Aboo-Is-ḥáḳ; and Aṣ says the like of what Fr says. (T.) It is said in the Ḳur [xliii. 25], إِنَّنِى بَرَآءٌ ↓ مِمَّا تَعْبُدُونَ [*Verily I am clear of that which ye worship*]; (T, M;) or بَرِىْءٌ, or ↓ بُرَآءٌ; accord. to different readers. (Bḍ.) بَرِىْءٌ occurs in several places in the Ḳur. (M.) Accord. to IAạr, it signifies *Clear of evil qualities* or *dispositions; shunning what is vain and false; remote from actions that occasion suspicion; pure in heart from associating any with God:* and it signifies *sound in body and intellect.* (T.) See also بَارِئٌ, in two places.

بَرَآءَةٌ *A writing of* [i. e. *conferring*] *immunity* or *exemption:* from بَرِئَ مِنَ الدَّيْنِ and العَيْبِ, of which it is the inf. n.: pl. بَرَآءَاتٌ, with medd: بَرَاوَاتٌ is [pl. of بَرَاةٌ, and both of these are] vulgar. (Mgh.)

بُرَاوِىٌّ: see بَرِىْءٌ.

البَرِيَّةُ *The creation;* as meaning *the beings*, or *things, that are created;* or, particularly, *mankind;* syn. الخَلْقُ: (T, Ṣ, M:) pronounced without ء; (T, Ṣ;) originally with ء, like نَبِىٌّ and ذُرِّيَّةٌ; (M;) and the people of Mekkeh differ from the other Arabs in pronouncing these three words with ء: (Yoo, T, M:) Lḥ says that the Arabs agree in omitting the ء in these three instances; and he does not except the people of Mekkeh: (M:) it is of the measure فَعِيلَةٌ in the sense of مَفْعُولَةٌ, (Mṣb,) from بَرَأَ اللّٰهُ الخَلْقَ, meaning خَلَقَهُمْ: (Fr, T:) or, if derived from البَرَى ["earth" or "dust"], it is originally without ء: (Fr, T, Ṣ:) pl. بَرَايَا and بَرِيَّاتٌ. (Ṣ in art. برو and برى.)

بَارِئٌ, (Ḳ,) or بَارِئٌ مِنْ مَرَضِهِ, (Lḥ, Ṣ, M,) [*Recovering from his disease, sickness*, or *malady:* or] *convalescent;* or *becoming sound*, or *healthy, at the close of his disease, but being yet weak;* or *recovering, but not completely, his health and strength:* [see 1:] (M, Ḳ:) as also ↓ بَرِىْءٌ: (Lḥ, M, Ḳ:) but whether the latter be properly used in this sense is disputed; while the former is said to be the act. part. n. of 1 in all its senses: (TA:) pl. بِرَآءٌ, (M, Ḳ,) like as صِحَاحٌ is pl. of صَحِيحٌ, accord. to Lḥ, so that he holds it to be pl. of بَرِىْءٌ; or it may be pl. of بَارِئٌ, like as جِيَاعٌ is pl. of جَائِعٌ, and صِحَابٌ of صَاحِبٌ. (M.) ↓ بَرِىْءٌ is sometimes written and pronounced بَرِىٌّ [in all its senses]. (Kz.) —— See also بَرِىْءٌ. —— البَارِئُ, applied to God, *The Creator;* (T, Ṣ, Mṣb;) *He who hath created the things that are created, not after any similitude*, or *model;* (Nh;) or *He who hath created those things free from any incongruity*, or *faultiness,* (Mgh, and Bḍ in ii. 51,) *and distinguished, one from another, by various forms and outward appearances:* (Bḍ:) or *the Former*, or *Fashioner;* syn. المُصَوِّرُ [q. v.]. (M.)

بربخ

بَرْبَخٌ The *passage*, or *conduit, of water, called* بَالُوعَة *and* إِرْدَبَّة [q. v.], *made of baked clay:* (Ḳ:) or بَرَابِخ [the pl.] signifies the *baked-clay conduits of privies, which convey* [*the water &c.*] *from the house-top to the ground.* (Ṣ, but omitted in some copies.) —— بَرْبَخُ البَوْلِ *The canal of the urine* [*from the kidney to the bladder;* i. e. *the ureter*]: (L, KL, TA:) of the dial. of Egypt. (TA.)

بربط

بَرْبَطٌ [The *Persian lute;*] *a certain musical instrument* (Lth, Mṣb) *of the* عَجَم [or *Persians*]; (Mṣb;) i. q. عُودٌ: (Lth, Ḳ:) an arabicized word, (Ḳ,) from بَرِبَتْ, (IAth,) or بَرْبَطْ; meaning "the breast of the duck, or goose;" because of its resemblance thereto; (Ḳ;) for بَرْ, in Persian, signifies the "breast;" (TA;) [and بَتْ and بَطْ or بَطّ, like the Arabic بَطّ, "a duck," or "goose;"] or because the player upon it places it against his breast: (IAth:) or it is said to be arabicized because it is the name of a musical instrument of the عجم. (Mṣb.)

برثن

بُرْثُنٌ, of the lion, (AZ, T,) and of any animal of prey, (AZ, Aṣ, T, Ṣ, M, Ḳ,) and of birds, (Aṣ, Ṣ,) [The *toe;* i. e.] *what corresponds to the* إِصْبَع *of a man;* (AZ, Aṣ, T, Ṣ, M, Ḳ;) [in the Lex. of Golius, as on the authority of the Ṣ, and in that of Freytag, *idem quod* انملة *in homine;* but this is a mistake, app. occasioned by a mistranscription in a copy of the Ṣ;] and the مِخْلَب is its claw, i. e., nail: (AZ, Aṣ, T, Ṣ:) or the *paw* (كَفّ), (M, Ḳ,) *altogether,* (M,) *with the* أَصَابِع [or *toes*]: (M, Ḳ:) or the *claw,* i. e. *nail,* of the lion, (Lth, T, M, Ḳ,) likened to the instrument for perforating leather; (Lth, T;) and of [all] animals of prey, and of birds that do not prey, *corresponding to the* ظُفُر *of man:* Th says, of man, it is [termed] the ظُفْر; of animals having the kind of foot called خُفّ, the مَنْسِم; of solid-hoofed animals, the حَافِر; of cloven-hoofed animals, the ظِلْف; of beasts and birds of prey, the مِخْلَب; and of birds that do not prey, and of dogs and the like, the بُرْثُن; though it may be also used [in like manner] of all animals of prey: (Mṣb:) [but properly] it is of birds that do not prey, as the crow-kind, and the pigeon; (M;) and sometimes, of the [lizard called] ضَبّ, (Ṣ, M,) and of the rat, or mouse, and of the jerboa: (M:) and is, in the pl. form, (M, TA,) which is بَرَاثِنُ, (T, Ṣ, M, TA,) metaphorically applied, by Sá'ideh Ibn-Ju-eiyeh, to the *fingers* of a man gathering honey [deposited by wild bees in a hollow of a rock]. (M,* TA.) — بُرْثُنُ الأَسَدِ also signifies †*A certain brand, or mark made with a hot iron, upon camels,* (Ḳ, TA,) *in the form of the claw of the lion.* (TA.) — This, also, is the name of a sword of Marthad Ibn-'Alas. (Ḳ.) — [بُرْثُنَةٌ seems to signify the same as بُرْثُن or بَرَاثِن: for] Temeem are termed in a trad. the بُرْثُنَة and بُرْجُمَة of the tribes of Mudar; and El-Khattábee says that it should be the بُرْثُنَة, i. e. † [The *claw,* or] the *claws;* meaning thereby their impetuous valour, and strength: but برثمة may be a dial. var. of برثنة, or the م may be substituted for the ن for the purpose of assimilation [to برجمة]. (TA.)

برج

1. بَرَجَ [written in the TA without the vowel-signs, but the context seems to show that it is thus, and that the inf. n. is بُرُوجٌ,] *It* (anything) *was,* or *became, apparent, manifest,* or *conspicuous,* and *high,* or *elevated:* whence بُرْجٌ, applied to a certain kind of structure. (TA.) — بَرِجَ, [aor. ـَ,] inf. n. بَرَجٌ, [also signifies] *He had that quality of the eye which is termed* بَرَجٌ, explained below. (M, TA.) — Also, (Ḳ,) or بَرِجَ أَمْرُهُ, (TA,) aor. ـَ, *His state, condition,* or *case, became ample in respect of eating and drinking.* (IAar, Ḳ, TA.)

2: see 4.

4. ابرج *He* (a man, TA) *built a* بُرْج [or *tower,* &c.]; as also ↓ برّج, inf. n. تَبْرِيجٌ. (Ḳ.)

5. تَبَرَّجَتْ *She* (a woman) *showed,* or *displayed, her finery,* or *ornaments,* (Ṣ, Mṣb, Ḳ,) *and beauties of person* or *form* or *countenance,* (Ṣ, Mṣb,) *to men,* (Ṣ, Ḳ,) or *to strangers,* or *men distantly related to her;* (Mṣb;) to do which is culpable; but to do so to the husband is not: (TA:) or *she showed her face:* or *she showed the beauties of her neck and face:* or *she did so exhibiting a pretty look:* (TA:) or *she showed,* or *displayed, her finery,* or *ornaments, and what excites a man's lust.* (Aboo-Is-ḥáḳ, TA.) Fr, referring to verse 33 of ch. xxxiii. of the Ḳur, says that in the time when Abraham was born, the women used to wear a shirt of pearls, not sewed at the two sides; or, as some say, they used to wear garments which did not conceal their persons. (TA.)

بُرْجٌ [Gr. πύργος, (Golius,) *A tower;*] *an angle,* syn. رُكْن, (Ṣ, Ḳ,) of a fortress, (Ṣ,) or of a city: (TA:) and sometimes *a fortress itself:* (Ṣ, Ḳ:) so called from its conspicuousness and construction and height: (TA: [see 1:]) or the primary signification of برج is *strength;* whence أَبْرَجُ in a sense explained below: (Ḥar p. 286:) pl. [of mult.] بُرُوجٌ and [of pauc.] أَبْرَاجٌ: (Ṣ:) the بُرُوج of the wall of a city or fortress are *chambers* (بُيُوت [meaning *towers*]) *built upon the wall:* and *such chambers* (بيوت) *built upon the sides of the angles of a* قَصْر [i. e. *pavilion* or *palace* &c.] are sometimes thus called. (Lth.) [Hence,] بُرْجُ حَمَامٍ [*A pigeon-turret; a pigeon-house;* being generally constructed in the form of a turret, or of a sugar-loaf;] *a lodging-place of pigeons:* pl. as above. (Mṣb.) — Also † [*A sign of the Zodiac;*] *one of the* بُرُوج *of the heaven;* (Ṣ, Ḳ;) *which are twelve in number;* every one having a distinct name: (TA:) the Arabs in ancient times did not know them: (Ḥam p. 560:) pl. أَبْرَاجٌ as well as بُرُوجٌ: (Mṣb, TA:) these are meant by the بروج mentioned in the Ḳur xv. 16 and xxv. 62 and lxxxv. 1: (Bḍ, Jel:) or in the last of these instances, (Bḍ,) by the بروج in the heaven are meant the *Mansions of the Moon:* (Bḍ, Mṣb:) or the *stars* or *asterisms* or *constellations:* (TA:) or the *great stars* or *asterisms* or *constellations;* (Bḍ, Mṣb;) and so, accord. to Zj, in the second of the said passages of the Ḳur: (TA:) or the *gates of heaven:* (Bḍ, Mṣb:) or, as some say, i. q. قُصُور [i. e. *pavilions* &c.]. (TA.)

بَرَجٌ *Such a constitution of the eye that the white entirely surrounds the black,* (Ṣ, M, Ḳ,) *no part of the black being concealed:* (Ṣ, M:) or *width of the eye:* or *width of the white of the eye, and largeness of the eyeball, and beauty of the black part:* or *clearness of the white and black parts thereof:* (M, TA:) or *width of the eye, and largeness of the eyeball:* (Ḥam p. 560:) or *width of the eye with intense whiteness of the person:* (TA:) and *distance between the eyebrows.* (L, TA.) [See also بَلَج.] = *Goodly, elegant,* or *pretty; beautiful of face:* or [so in copies of the Ḳ, and in the TA, but in the CḲ "and"] *shining,* or *splendid; conspicuous; and well known.* (Ḳ.)

خُلُقٌ بَارِجٌ *A large,* or *liberal, disposition;* syn. وَاسِعٌ. (Ḥam p. 560.)

أَبْرَجُ A man *having that quality of the eye which is termed* بَرَجٌ: (M, TA:) fem. بَرْجَآءُ; applied to a woman; (Ṣ;) and also to an eye (عَيْنٌ) *having the quality termed* بَرَجٌ: (M, TA:) pl. بُرْجٌ. (Ḥam p. 560.) = هٰذَا أَبْرَجُ مِنْ هٰذَا *This is stronger than this.* (Ḥar p. 286.)

إِبْرِيجٌ The *vessel,* or *receptacle,* [generally *a skin,*] *in which milk is churned,* or *beaten and agitated,* or *in which the butter of the milk is extracted,* or *fetched out, by putting water in it, and agitating it;* syn. مِمْخَضَةٌ. (Ṣ, Ḳ.)

ثَوْبٌ مُبَرَّجٌ *A garment whereon are figures of* بُرُوج [or *towers*]: (Zj, TA:) or *whereon are depicted figures resembling the* بُرُوج [or *towers*] *of the wall of a city or the like:* (T, A, TA:) or *figured with eyes, of the garments termed* حُلَل; from البَرَجُ. (Ṣ.)

برجم

بُرْجُمَةٌ (in the Ḥam p. 352 بُرْجُمٌ) is the sing. of بَرَاجِمُ (Ṣ, Mgh, Mṣb, Ḳ) and بُرْجُمَاتٌ; (T, TA;) and signifies [*A knuckle,* or *finger-joint;*] the *outer,* or the *inner, joint,* or *place of division, of the fingers:* and (as some say, TA) the *middle toe of any bird:* (Ḳ:) or بَرَاجِمُ signifies all the *finger-joints;* (A'Obeyd, Ḳ;) as also رَوَاجِمُ [a mistranscription for رَوَاجِب]: (A'Obeyd, TA:) or the *parts of the fingers that are protuberant when one clinches his hand:* (Ḥam ubi suprà:) or the *backs of the finger-bones:* (Ḳ:) or the *finger-joints* (Ṣ, Mgh) *that are between the* أَشَاجِع *and the* رَوَاجِب; (Ṣ;) i. e. (Ṣ, Mgh) [the *middle knuckles;* (see أَشْجَعُ and رَاجِبَةٌ;)] the *heads of the* سُلَامَيَات, (Ṣ, Mgh, Mṣb, Ḳ,) *on the back,* or *outer side, of the hand,* (Ṣ, Mṣb,) *which become protuberant when one clinches his hand:* (Ṣ, Mgh, Mṣb, Ḳ:) or, as in the Kf, the *heads of the* سلاميات; and their inner and outer sides are termed the رَوَاجِب: (Mṣb:) accord. to the T, the *wrinkled parts at the joints of the fingers;* the smooth portion between which is called رَاجِبَة: or, as in another place, *in the backs of the fingers;* the parts between them being called the رَوَاجِب: *in every finger are three* بُرْجُمَات, *except the thumb:* or, as in another place, *in every finger are two of what are thus termed:* it is also explained as signifying the *joints in the backs of the fingers, upon which the dirt collects.* (TA.) The phrase الأَخْذُ بِالبَرَاجِمِ, meaning *The seizing with the hand*, is one requiring consideration [as of doubtful character]. (Mgh.) [See also بُرْثُنٌ.]

برح

1. بَرِحَ is *syn. with* زَالَ [in two senses; i. e. as an attributive verb, and also as a non-attributive verb; as will be shown by what follows]. (Ṣ, A, Mgh.) [Using it as an attributive verb,] you say, لَا أَبْرَحُ حَتَّى تَقْضِىَ حَاجَتِى *I will not go away*, or *depart*, or *withdraw*, (لَا أَزُولُ,) and (لَا أَتَنَحَّى,) *until thou accomplish my want*: from بَرِحَ المَكَانَ, inf. n. بَرَاحٌ, *he went away*, or *departed*, *from the place*; syn. زَالَ مِنْهُ: and to be distinguished from the phrase in the Ḳur [xviii. 59, similar as to words,] mentioned below. (Mgh.) You say, بَرِحَ مَكَانَهُ, (Ṣ, A, L, Ḳ,) aor. َ, (Ḳ,) inf. n. بَرَاحٌ (Ṣ, L, Ḳ) and بُرُوحٌ (L, TA, and Ḥam p. 250) and بَرْحٌ, (L,) or بَرَحٌ, (as in a copy of the TA,) *He went away*, or *departed*, *from his place*; (Ṣ, L, Ḳ, and Ḥam ubi suprà;) and *he became in the* بَرَاح [or *wide*, *uncultivated*, or *uninhabited*, *tract*]. (Ṣ, L, Ḳ.) And مَا بَرِحَ مَكَانَهُ *He did not quit his place.* (Mṣb.) And بَرِحَ [alone], aor. َ, inf. n. بَرَاحٌ, *It* (a thing) *went away*, or *departed*, (زَالَ,) *from its place*; (Mṣb;) as also ▼ تبرّح. (L.) In the phrase لَا بَرَاحَ [*There is*, or *shall be*, *no quitting of place*, or *going away*, or *departing*], the noun is in the accus. case, as in لَا رَيْبَ: but it is allowable to put it in the nom. case, so that لا is used in the manner of لَيْسَ; (Ṣ, Ḳ;) as in the following saying of Saạd Ibn-Málik, [in the TA, in one place, Ibn-Náshib,] in a poem of which the rhyme is with refạ, (Ṣ, IAth,) alluding to El-Ḥárith Ibn-'Abbád, who had withdrawn himself from the war of Teghlib and Bekr the sons of Wáïl: (IAth, TA:)

* مَنْ فَرَّ عَنْ نِيرَانِهَا * فَأَنَا ٱبْنُ قَيْسٍ لَا بَرَاحُ *

[*Whoso fleeth from its fires*, (i. e. نِيرَانِ الحَرْبِ *the fires of the war*,) let him do so: *but* as for me, *I am the son of Keys*: to me *there is not*, or *shall not be*, *any quitting of place*]. (Ṣ, IAth. [See also Ḥam p. 250, where, for مَنْ فَرَّ, we find مَنْ صَدَّ *whoso turneth away*.]) [Hence,] بَرِحَتِ الرِّيحُ بِالتُّرَابِ *The wind carried up*, *raised*, or *swept up and scattered*, [lit. *went away with*,] *the dust*. (Mṣb.) [Hence also, accord. to some,] بَرِحَ الخَفَآءُ, (T, Ṣ, Ḳ, &c.,) and بَرَحَ, (Ibn-El-Liḥyánee, Z, and TA, [thus written in a copy of the A,]) ‡ *The state of concealment departed*, or *ceased*: or ‡ *what was in a state of concealment became apparent*; from بَرَاح meaning "what is open and apparent" of land: or ‡ *what I was concealing became apparent*: (T, TA:) or ‡ *the affair*, or *case*, *became manifest*, (Ṣ, A, Ḳ,) and *its concealment ceased*, (A,) [or] *as though the secret departed*, *and ceased*: (Ṣ:) or, as some say, † *the secret became apparent*: (TA in art. خفى:) or, lit., *the low ground became high and apparent*; meaning † *what was concealed became revealed*: (Ḥar pp. 133—4:) the first who said it was Shiḳḳ the Diviner. (IDrd, TA.) — [Using it as a non-attributive verb,] you say, لَا أَبْرَحُ أَفْعَلُ ذٰلِكَ *I will not cease*, or *I will continue*, *to do that*: (Ṣ, A:*) and (لَا أَزَالُ,) مَا بَرِحَ يَفْعَلُ كَذَا [*he ceased not to do thus*; or] *he persevered in*, or *kept to*, *doing thus*: (Mṣb:) and مَا بَرِحَ زَيْدٌ قَائِمًا [*Zeyd ceased not to be*, or *he kept*, or *continued*, *standing*]: in this case, the verb is of the category of كَانَ; (Mgh;) relates to time; and requires a predicate: and its inf. n. is بَرَاحٌ. (Ḥam p. 250.) Hence the saying in the Ḳur [xviii. 59], لَا أَبْرَحُ حَتَّى أَبْلُغَ مَجْمَعَ البَحْرَيْنِ, but the predicate is suppressed: it may be مَا نَحْنُ فِيهِ كَذٰلِكَ [i. e. *I will not cease in that wherein we are thus engaged until I reach the place of meeting of the two seas*]: (Mgh:) or it means لَا أَزَالُ أَسِيرُ [*I will not cease journeying*]: (Bḍ, Jel:) or لا ابرح here may mean *I will not depart* (لَا أَزُولُ) *from that upon which I am intent*, namely journeying and seeking; and *I will not relinquish it*; so that it does not require the predicate. (Bḍ. [He gives a third explanation, paraphrastic and strained, which I omit.]) = بَرَحَ, (Ṣ, Ḳ,) aor. َ, (L, TA, [but it is implied in the Ḳ that it is ُ, which is contr. to rule,]) inf. n. بُرُوحٌ, *It* (a gazelle, Ṣ, Ḳ, and a bird, and any wild animal, that is hunted or shot, TA) *turned its left side towards the spectator*, *passing by* (Ṣ, Ḳ*) *from the direction of his right hand towards that of his left hand*: (Ṣ:) or *passed by from the direction of the spectator's left hand towards that of his right hand*: (Aboo-'Amr Esh-Sheybánee, IF, L, Mṣb, in art. سنح:) [the former appears to be accord. to the usage of the Ḥijázees; and the latter, accord. to that of the Nejdees, in general: see بَارِحٌ:] contr. of سَنَحَ. (Ṣ.) = بَرِحَ, aor. َ, [contr. to rule,] (Ḳ,) inf. n. بَرْحٌ, (TA,) *He was angry*. (Ḳ.) When a man has been angry with his companion, one says, مَا أَشَدَّ مَا بَرِحَ عَلَيْهِ [*How violently angry was he with him!*]. (L.)

2. بَرَّحَتْ بِىَ الحُمَّى *The fever affected me with its severity*, *violence*, or *sharpness*, termed بُرَحَآء. (TA.) — Hence, (TA,) from بُرَحَآء, (Ṣ, Ḳ,) بَرَّحَ بِهِ, inf. n. تَبْرِيحٌ, *It* (an affair, an event, or a case,) *affected him severely*; *afflicted*, *distressed*, or *harassed*, *him*: (Ṣ, Ḳ:) said also of anxiety; or disquietude, or trouble, of mind: (A:) and of a beating, meaning *it hurt him severely*, or *greatly*. (Mṣb.) Also said of a man, meaning *He importuned him*, or *pressed him*, *with annoyance*, or *molestation*: (A, TA:) *he annoyed him*, or *molested him*, *by importuning* or *pressing*; as also ▼ ابرح: (TA:) *he annoyed him*, or *molested him*, *by distressing importunity* or *pressing*: (T, TA:) and *he punished*, *tormented*, or *tortured*, *him*. (TA.) تَبْرِيحٌ signifies The act of *annoying*, *molesting*, or *hurting*: (Mgh:) and in a trad., (in which it is forbidden, TA,) the *killing*, or *putting to death*, *in an evil* [or *a cruel*] *manner*; *such as throwing live fish*, *and lice*, *into the fire*. (Mgh, TA.) = بَرَّحَ ٱللّٰهُ عَنْكَ *May God remove from thee* البَرْحُ [i. e. *difficulty*, *distress*, *affliction*, &c., or *the difficulty*, &c.]. (A, TA.)

4. ابرحهُ *He made him*, or *caused him*, *to go away from*, *depart from*, or *quit*, *his place*. (A,* L.) = *He*, or *it*, *pleased*, or *rejoiced*, *him*; *excited his admiration and approval*: *induced in him wonder*, or *admiration*, *and pleasure*, or *joy*. (Ṣ, Ḳ.) One says also, مَا أَبْرَحَ هٰذَا الأَمْرَ *How greatly does this affair*, or *event*, *please*, or *rejoice! how greatly does it excite admiration and approval!* or *how greatly does it induce wonder*, or *admiration*, *and pleasure*, or *joy!* (Ṣ.) — *He treated him with honour*, or *honoured him*, and *magnified him*: (Ṣ, Ḳ:) or, as some say, *he found him to be generous*, or *noble*. (TA.) — *He judged him*, or *it*, i. e. a man, (A, TA,) and a horse, (A,) or anything, (TA,) *to be excellent*, or *to excel*, (A, TA,) *and wondered at*, or *admired*, *him*, or *it*. (A.) = ابرح also signifies *He exceeded the usual bounds*, *degree*, or *mode*. (Aṣ, Ṣ,* TA.) You say, أَبْرَحْتَ كَرَمًا, and لُؤْمًا, (A, TA,) *Thou hast done a thing exceeding the usual bounds* [*in generosity*, or *nobleness*, and *in meanness*, or *ignobleness*]; or *extravagant*; or *excessive*. (TA.) — See also 2.

5: see 1.

بَرْحٌ *Difficulty*, *distress*, *affliction*, or *adversity*; *evil*, or *mischief*; (Ḳ, TA;) *annoyance*, *molestation*, or *hurt*; *severe punishment*; *trouble*, *inconvenience*, or *fatigue*; (TA;) *a difficult*, *a distressing*, *an afflictive*, or *adverse*, *and a wonderful*, *thing* or *event*: (Ḥam p. 135:) and *annoyance*, or *molestation*, *by distressing importunity* or *pressing*; a subst. from 2: (T, TA:) and بِنْتُ بَرْحٍ, [and app. ٱبْنُ بَرْحٍ also,] *a calamity*, *misfortune*, or *disaster*; or *a great*, or *terrible*, *thing*, *affair*, or *case*; (TA;) as also ▼ بِنْتُ بَارِحٍ, and ▼ ٱبْنُ بَرِيحٍ; (Ḳ;) pl. بَنَاتُ بَرْحٍ and بَنُو بَرْحٍ. (TA.) [See also تَبْرِيحٌ.] You say, لَقِيتُ مِنْهُ بَرْحًا ▼ بَارِحًا *I experienced from him*, or *it*, [*great*] *difficulty*, *distress*, *affliction*, or *adversity*; [*great*] *annoyance*, *molestation*, or *hurt*; (Ṣ, A,* Ḳ;*) a phrase having an intensive signification, (Ḳ, TA,) like لَيْلٌ لَائِلٌ [and لَيْلٌ أَلْيَلُ]; and so بَرْحًا ▼ مُبَرِّحًا. (TA.) When used as an imprecation, the more approved way is to put the two words in the accus. case: but sometimes they are put in the nom. case; as in the saying of a poet, بَرْحٌ لِعَيْنَيْكَ ▼ بَارِحٌ [*May great difficulty*, &c., *befall thy two eyes!*]. (TA.) You say also, لَقِيتُ مِنْهُ بَنَاتِ بَرْحٍ, (Ṣ, A,) and بَنِى بَرْحٍ, (Ṣ,) *I experienced from him*, or *it*, *difficulties*, *distresses*, *afflictions*, or *adverse events*; and *calamities*, *misfortunes*, or *disasters*: (Ṣ:) and, in the same sense, ▼ لقيت منه البرحين, and ▼ البُرَحِين, (Ṣ, Ḳ,) and ▼ البِرَحِينَ; (Ḳ;) or, accord. to some copies of the Ḳ, ▼ البُرْحَيْنِ, and ▼ البِرْحَيْنِ, as duals; but the former reading is the more correct: (TA:) [MF disapproves of the form بِرَحِين, and it is not mentioned in the

L; but the dual form بُرَحَيْنِ is there mentioned:] it seems as though the sing. of بَرَحِينَ [or بُرَحِينَ] were بَرَحَةٌ [or بُرَحَةٌ], and that the pl. is formed by the termination ون to compensate for the rejection of the ة, as is virtually the case in أَرَضُونَ; [or because the signification is regarded as that of a personification;] and that the pl. only is used. (L.) It is said in a prov., بِنْتُ بَرْحٍ شَرَكٌ عَلَى رَأْسِكَ [Calamity is, or be, a snare upon thy head]. (TA.)

مُبَرِّح: see بَرْحٌ.

صَرْحَةٌ بَرْحَةٌ, or صَرْحَةُ بَرْحَةَ, &c.: see art. صرح.

بُرْحَةٌ The best of anything: (TA:) and [particularly] one of the best of she-camels: (Ṣ, Ḳ:) or, of he-camels: (T:) pl. بُرَحٌ. (T, Ṣ, Ḳ.) You say, هٰذِهِ بُرْحَةٌ مِنَ البُرَحِ, (Ṣ, Ḳ,*) or هُوَ بُرْحَةٌ مِنَ البُرَحِ, (T,) This is a she-camel, (Ṣ, Ḳ,*) or he is a camel, (T,) of the best of camels. (T, Ṣ, Ḳ.)

بَرْحَى a word that is said when one misses the mark in shooting or casting; like as مَرْحَى is said when one hits the mark. (Ṣ, ISd, A, Ḳ.)

بُرَحَآءُ Severity, violence, or sharpness, (Aṣ, A, TA,) or vehement molestation, (Ṣ, Ḳ,) of a fever (Aṣ, A, Ṣ, Ḳ) &c.: (Ṣ, Ḳ:) [a paroxysm; used in this sense by modern physicians:] and vehement distress of mind arising from the oppression caused by inspiration or revelation; such as is said to have affected the Prophet; [but most probably a paroxysm of that species of catalepsy which physicians term ecstasy;] occurring in a trad. (TA.) You say of one suffering from fever, when it is intense, أَصَابَتْهُ البُرَحَآءُ [The paroxysm, or severe fit, has befallen him]. (TA.)

البَرَحِينَ and البُرَحِينَ &c.: see بَرْحٌ.

بَرَاحٌ inf. n. of بَرِحَ, q. v.; whence the phrase لَا بَرَاحَ, explained above. (Ṣ, L, Ḳ.) = A wide, or spacious, tract of land, (Ṣ, A, Ḳ,) having in it no seed-produce nor trees: (Ṣ, Ḳ:) or land having in it no building nor habitation: (Ḥam p. 237:) and applied as an epithet to land, signifying wide, or spacious, open, or conspicuous, and having in it no herbage nor habitation: and what is open, uncovered, and wholly apparent, of land: (TA:) or a place having no trees nor other things to cover or conceal it; as though such things had departed; (Mgh;) a place free from trees &c.: (Mṣb:) or an elevated and open tract of land. (Ḥar p. 134.) — حَبِيلُ بَرَاحٍ is an appellation given to †A lion: and †a courageous man: as though each of them were bound with ropes, (Ḳ, TA,) and did not quit his place. (TA.) = An affair, a thing, or a case, that is plain, evident, or manifest; (Ḳ, TA;) or open, or public. (TA.) You say, جَآءَنَا بِالأَمْرِ بَرَاحًا [He told us, or did to us, the thing] plainly [or openly]. (Ṣ.) And جَآءَ بِالكُفْرِ بَرَاحًا وَبِالشَّرِّ صُرَاحًا [He uttered, or committed an act of, infidelity plainly, or openly, and evil, or mischief, unmixedly]. (A, TA.) — Counsel, or an opinion, that is disapproved, or deemed evil. (Ḳ.) = بَرَاحِ, (El-Mufaḍḍal, Ṣ, A, &c.,) and بَرَاحُ, with ḍamm and without tenween, (AZ, El-Mufaḍḍal,) a name of The sun: (Ṣ, A, &c.:) determinate [and the former indecl.]: the sun is so called because of the spreading of its light, and its conspicuousness; or, being applied to the sun when it sets, براح means بَارِحَةٌ; like as كَسَابِ, a name applied to a hunting-bitch, means كَاسِبَةٌ. (TA.) You say, دَلَكَتْ بَرَاحِ The sun set [or declined from the meridian]. (A, TA.) For this phrase, occurring at the end of a verse cited by Ḳṭr, Fr reads دَلَكَتْ بِرَاحِ; راح being pl. [or rather a quasi-pl. n.] of رَاحَةٌ, meaning the "hand" [or "palm of the hand"]: (Ṣ, TA:) accord. to which reading, the poet means The sun had set, or had declined from the meridian, while they put their hands, or the palms of their hands, over their eyes, looking to see if it had set, or had declined from the meridian: or he who says, دَلَكَتِ الشَّمْسُ بِرَاحِ means the sun had almost set: the two readings بَرَاحِ and براح are mentioned by A'Obeyd and Az and Hr and Z and others: AZ says, دلكت براحِ, with tenween, and بَرَاحُ, without tenween. (TA.) [See also رَاحَةٌ, in art. روح.]

بَرُوحٌ: see بَارِحٌ.

بَرِيحٌ: see بَارِحٌ. = Also The croaking of the غُرَاب [or crow, of whatever species, as raven, carrion-crow, &c.]. (L.) — [Hence,] ابْنُ بَرِيحٍ: so in the Ḳ: in the Ṣ, أُمُّ بَرِيحٍ; but IB and Aboo-Zekereeyà say that only the former is right: (TA:) [in one copy of the Ṣ, however, I find both of these:] The غُرَاب [or crow, as a generic term, applying to the raven, carrion-crow, &c.]: (Ṣ, Ḳ, &c.:) so called because of its cry: a determinate appellation: for the pl., the expression used is بَنَاتُ بَرِيحٍ. (TA.) — See also بَرْحٌ. = قَوْلٌ بَرِيحٌ A saying by which one pronounces a person to have said, or done, right. (L.)

بَارِحٌ, (Ṣ, Ḳ, &c.,) as also ▼بَرُوحٌ and ▼بَرِيحٌ, (Ḳ,) applied to a gazelle, (Ṣ,) or what is hunted or shot, (Ḳ, TA,) of gazelles and birds and wild animals [in general], (TA,) Turning his left side towards the spectator, (Ṣ,) passing from the direction of the right hand of the latter towards the direction of his left hand: (Ṣ, Ḳ:) or turning his right side towards the spectator, passing from the direction of the latter's left hand towards that of his right: (Aboo-'Amr Esh-Sheybánee, IF, A,* L, Mṣb,* in art. سنح:) contr. of سَانِحٌ: (Ṣ,* TA:) pl. بَوَارِحُ. (L in art. سنح.) The Arabs [who apply the epithet in the latter sense] regard the بارح as an evil omen, and the سانح as a good omen; because one cannot shoot at the former without turning himself: (Ṣ:) but some of them hold the reverse: (Aboo-'Amr Esh-Sheybánee and L in art. سنح:) the people of Nejd hold the سانح to be a good omen; but sometimes a Nejdee adopts the opinion of the Ḥijázee [which is the contrary]. (IB in that art.) The first of these epithets is also applied to a bird as meaning Inauspicious; ill-omened. (A.) It is said in a prov., مَنْ لِى بِالسَّانِحِ بَعْدَ البَارِحِ (TA) i. e. [Who will be responsible to me] for a fortunate, or lucky, event, after an unfortunate, or unlucky? (Ḳ in art. سنح:) applied in the case of a man's doing evil, and its being said, "He will at a future time do good to thee:" originally said by a man on the occasion of gazelles' passing before him in the manner of such as are termed بَارِحَة, and its being said to him, "They will present themselves to thee in the manner of such as are termed سَانِحَة." (TA.) And in another prov. it is said, إِنَّمَا هُوَ كَبَارِحِ الأَرْوَى [It, or he, is only like the mountain-goat passing in the manner of such as is termed بارح]: for it dwells on the tops of the mountains, and men scarcely ever see it passing with the right or left side towards them save once in the course of ages: (Ṣ, Ḳ:) applied in the case of an extraordinary occurrence: (Ḳ:) [or in the case of a benefit conferred by a man who very rarely confers benefits on others: (Freytag's Arab. Prov. i. 35:)] or when a man has delayed, or been tardy in, visiting [but has come at last]. (TA.) — Hence, فَتْلَةٌ بَارِحَةٌ i. q. شَزْرَةٌ [i. e. ‡A manner of twisting contrary to that which is usual: see شَزَرَ]. (A.) — And هٰذِهِ فَعْلَةٌ بَارِحَةٌ ‡This is an action that has not happened rightly. (A.) — [Hence,] بِنْتُ بَارِحٍ: and [perhaps] لَقِيتُ مِنْهُ بَرْحًا بَارِحًا and بَرْحٌ لِعَيْنَيْكَ بَارِحٌ: see بَرْحٌ. — [And hence, perhaps, because of its evil effect; or because it comes, accord. to some, from the left, i. e. northerly direction, or, accord. to others, from the right, i. e. southerly direction; or] from بَرْحٌ as signifying "a difficult, a distressing, an afflictive, or adverse, and a wonderful, thing, or event;" (Ḥam p. 135;) بَارِحٌ signifies also A hot wind: (Ṣ:) or a hot wind in the صَيْف [i. e. summer or spring]: (Ḳ:) or a hot wind coming from the direction of El-Yemen: (Ḥam p. 135:) or a wind that carries up, raises, or sweeps up and scatters, the dust: (Mṣb:) pl. بَوَارِحُ: (Ṣ, Ḳ, &c.:) or the بوارح are hot north, or northerly, winds in the صَيْف: (AZ, Az, Ṣ:) this Az found to be the sense in which the term was used by the Arabs in his time: (TA:) or violent winds that carry with them the dust by reason of their violence: (TA:) or this name (the pl.) was given by the Arabs to all winds in the time of the stars of the قَيْظ [or summer]: they mostly blow in the time of the stars of Libra; [app. meaning when Libra is on, or near, the meridian at nightfall, agreeably with a statement in modern Arabic almanacs, that the periods of the beginning and end of the winds thus called are the 30th of May and the 9th of July;] and these winds are what are termed the سَمَائِم [pl. of سَمُومٌ]. (Ibn-Kunáseh, TA.) — البَوَارِحُ is also said by some to signify الأَنْوَآءُ [pl. of نَوْءٌ, q. v.]; as mentioned by AḤn; but he repels their assertion. (TA.)

البَارِحَةُ The next, or nearest, past, or preceding, night; yesternight: (Ṣ, A, Mgh,* Mṣb,* Ḳ:) from بَرِحَ signifying زَالَ ["he, or it, went away" &c.].

(Ṣ, A.) [In modern Arabic, *Yesterday*; as also البَارِح.] It has no dim. formed from it. (Sh, in Ṣ, in art. أمس; and TA.) You say, لَقِيتُهُ البَارِحَةَ [*I met, or met with, him, or it, last night, or yesternight*]: and لَقِيتُهُ البَارِحَةَ الأُولَى [*I met, or met with, him, or it, the night before last*; this being the sense in which the phrase is now used by the learned: but the vulgar expression is أَوَّلَ البَارِحَةِ, generally pronounced أَوَّلَ أَمْبَارِحْ or أَوَّلَ أَمْبَارِحَةْ, agreeably with a peculiarity of the dial. of the people of El-Yemen, or of Ṭeiyi and Ḥimyer, by the substitution of أَمْ for أَلْ: see art. ام]. (Ṣ.) From daybreak to the time when the sun declines from the meridian, one says, رَأَيْتُ اللَّيْلَةَ فِى مَنَامِى [I saw to-night in my sleep (such a thing)]; but when the sun has declined, one says, رَأَيْتُ البَارِحَةَ [*I saw last night, or yesternight*]: (AZ, Th: [and the like is said in the Mgh and Mṣb:]) or one says, كَانَ كَذَا وَكَذَا اللَّيْلَةَ [*Such and such things happened to-night*] until the sun is somewhat high and the day has become bright; but after this, one says, كَانَ البَارِحَةَ [*It happened last night, or yesternight*]. (Yoo, Seer.) The Arabs say,

مَا أَشْبَهَ اللَّيْلَةَ بِالبَارِحَهْ

How like is this night wherein we are to the former night that has departed! (TA:) [or, *this night to yesternight!*]: originally occurring in a poem of Ṭarafeh: used as meaning "how like is the child to the father!" and applied to [any] two things resembling each other. (Ḥar p. 667.)

أَبْرَحُ is formed [from بَرَحَ for بَرَّحَ] by the rejection of the added letter: [for a word of this kind is regularly formed only from an unaugmented triliteral-radical verb:] or it is like أَحْنَكُ, having no proper verb. (L.) You say, هٰذَا أَبْرَحُ عَلَىَّ مِنْ ذَاكَ (A,* L, Mṣb*) *This is more difficult, distressing,* or *afflicting, to me than that.* (L, Mṣb.*) And هٰذَا الأَمْرُ أَبْرَحُ مِنْ هٰذَا *This affair, event,* or *case, is more difficult,* or *distressing, than this.* (Ṣ.) And قَتَلُوهُمْ أَبْرَحَ قَتْلٍ [*They slew them with a most severe slaughter*]. (Ṣ.)

تَبْرِيحٌ [inf. n. of 2, used as a simple subst.,] is said by some to be sing. of تَبَارِيحُ, and has been used as such by post-classical authors, but is not of established authority: accord. to others, the latter has no sing.: (MF:) the pl. signifies *Difficulties, distresses, afflictions,* or *adversities*: [see also بَرْحٌ:] or the *difficulties,* or *obligations, incurred by troublesome,* or *inconvenient, means of obtaining subsistence*: (TA:) and تَبَارِيحُ الشَّوْقِ *the burning,* or *fierce burning,* [or *the burnings,* &c.,] *of the yearning,* or *longing, of the soul,* or *of longing desire.* (Ṣ, Ḳ.)

أَنَا مُبَرَّحٌ بِى *I am importuned,* or *pressed, with annoyance,* or *molestation.* (A, TA.) [See the verb (2).]

مُبَرِّحٌ and ▼ بَرْحٌ, applied to an affair, an event, or a case, signify the same; (Ḳ, TA;) i. e. *Severe, afflicting, distressing,* or *harassing*: (TA:) and the former, to a beating, (Ṣ, A, Mgh, TA,) meaning *the same*; (TA;) or *hurting* (Ṣ, Mgh) *severely*: (Ṣ:) and to a man, meaning *annoying,* or *molesting, by importuning,* or *pressing.* (TA.) [See 2.] لَقِيتُ مِنْهُ بَرْحًا مُبَرِّحًا: see بَرْحٌ.

يَبْرُوحٌ, (Ḳ,) thus correctly written, with the ى before the ب; [not بيروح, as in the CḲ; in Chald. יַבְרוּחַ, the word corresponding to the sing. of the Hebr. דּוּדָאִים in Gen. xxx. 14 and 16, accord. to the paraphrase of Onkelos;] or يَبْرُوحٌ صَنَمِىٌّ [the *idol-like* يبروح]; (TA;) The *root,* or *lower part, of the wild* لُفَّاح [or *mandrake,* not to be confounded with another plant to which the name of لُفَّاح, q. v., is also applied], (Ḳ,) *which is known by the names of* فَاوَانِيَا *and* عُودُ الصَّلِيبِ [names now given to the peony], and called by MF تُفَّاحُ البَرِّ, [or *the wild apple,* but perhaps this is a mistranscription for لُفَّاحُ البَرِّ,] said by him to be an appellation used by the vulgar; (TA;) *resembling the form of a man*; (Ḳ;) *and of two sorts, male and female; called by the people of Greece* عَبْدُ السَّلَامِ: (TA:) *it torpifies,* (Ḳ,) *and strengthens the two appetites* [namely that of the stomach and that of the generative organ): (TA:) *if ivory is cooked with it for six hours, it renders it soft; and if a part affected by* [*the disease termed*] بَرَش *is rubbed with its leaves for a week,* (Ḳ,) *without interruption,* (TA,) *it removes it without causing ulcers,* or *sores*: (Ḳ:) the root of the wild لُفَّاح is the يَبْرُوح: *it has the form of a human being; the male like the male, and the female like the female; and they pretend that he who pulls it up dies; wherefore, when they desire to do so, they tie a dog or some other animal to it.* (Ḳzw, voce لُفَّاح.)

برد

1. بَرُدَ, aor. ـُ, inf. n. بُرُودَةٌ; (Ṣ, M, Mgh, Mṣb, Ḳ;) and بَرَدَ, aor. ـُ, (M, Mṣb, Ḳ,) inf. n. بَرْدٌ; (M, Mṣb;) *It* (a thing, Ṣ, Mṣb, and the latter said of water, Mṣb) *was,* or *became, cold, chill,* or *cool*; [see بَرْدٌ below;] (Ṣ, M;) *its heat became allayed.* (Mṣb.) The latter verb is also used transitively, as will be shown below. (Mṣb.) — [Hence,] بَرَدَ مَضْجَعُهُ [lit. *His bed,* or *place of sleep, became cold*; meaning] ‡ *he went on a journey.* (A.) — بَرَدَ also signifies ‡ *He died*; (Aṣ, T, Ṣ, A, Ḳ;) because death is the non-existence of the heat of the soul; (L;) or it is allusive to the extinction of the natural heat; or to the cessation of motion. (MF.) For — بَرَدَ, (MF,) aor. ـُ, (Mgh,) inf. n. بُرُودٌ, (MF,) likewise signifies † *It was,* or *became, still, quiet,* or *motionless*; (Mgh, MF;) for instance, a slaughtered sheep or goat [&c.]. (Mgh.) And † *It* (beverage of the kind called نَبِيذ) *became still, and without briskness.* (TA, from a trad.) You say, رُعِبَ فَبَرَدَ مَكَانَهُ [† *He became frightened, and remained motionless in his place*; مَكَانَهُ meaning فِى مَكَانِهِ: and hence,] ‡ *he became amazed,* or *stupified.* (A.) And بَرَدَتْ عَيْنُهُ † *The pain in his eye became allayed,* or *stilled.* (L.) And بَرَدَ أَمْرُنَا † *Our affair,* or *case, became easy.* (TA, from a trad. [See also بَارِدٌ.]) — Also, inf. n. بَرْدٌ, [which see below,] † *He slept.* (T.) — And hence, ‡ *It remained,* or *became permanent,* or *fixed,* or *settled.* (T.) So in the saying, لَمْ يَبْرُدْ بِيَدِى مِنْهُ شَىْءٌ ‡ *There did not remain,* or *become permanent* or *fixed* or *settled, in my hand, thereof, anything.* (T, L.*) You say also, بَرَدَ أَسِيرًا فِى أَيْدِيهِمْ ‡ *He remained safely a captive in their hands.* (A.) And بَرَدَ فِى أَيْدِيهِمْ سَلَمًا ‡ *He became a permanent captive, remaining in their hands, not to be ransomed nor liberated nor demanded.* (L.) And بَرَدَ المَوْتُ عَلَى مُصْطَلَاهُ ‡ *Death fixed,* or *settled,* [*upon his face and extremities,* or] *upon his limbs,* or *upon his arms and legs and face and every prominent part,* which become cold at the time of death, and which are warmed at the fire. (AHeyth, L.) And بَرَدَ المَوْتُ عَلَيْهِ [‡ *Death became impressed upon him*;] *the marks,* or *signs, of death became apparent upon him.* (A.) — [And hence, app.,] ‡ *It* (a right, or due,) *became incumbent,* or *obligatory,* (M, Ḳ, TA,) *and established.* (TA.) You say, بَرَدَ لِى حَقِّى عَلَى فُلَانٍ ‡ *My right,* or *due, became incumbent,* or *obligatory, on such a one, and established against him.* (M,* A,* TA.) And مَا بَرَدَ لَكَ عَلَى فُلَانٍ ‡ *What hath become incumbent,* or *obligatory, to thee, on such a one, and established against him? or what hath become owed,* or *due, to thee, by,* or *from, such a one?* as also مَا ذَابَ لَكَ عَلَيْهِ. (Ṣ.) And بَرَدَ لِى عَلَيْهِ كَذَا مِنَ المَالِ ‡ *Such an amount of the property,* or *of property, became incumbent,* or *obligatory, to me, on him, and established against him*; or *became owed,* or *due, to me, by,* or *from, him.* (Ṣ.) — Also, (Ḳ,) aor. ـُ, inf. n. بَرْدٌ, (TA, [but see the next sentence,]) † *He* (a man) *was,* or *became, weak*; and so بَرُدَ, a verb like غَنِىَ. (Ḳ.) And, inf. n. بُرَادٌ and بُرُودٌ, (M, Ḳ,) † *He was,* or *became, languid,* (Ḳ,) or *weak and languid, from leanness or disease*: (M:) or *weak in the legs, from hunger* or *fatigue.* (Ibn-Buzurj, T.) And بَرَدَ مُخُّهُ, (A, Ḳ,) aor. ـُ, inf. n. بَرْدٌ, (TA,) ‡ *He was,* or *became, lean,* or *emaciated*; (A, Ḳ;) and so بَرَدَتْ عِظَامُهُ. (A, TA.) — † *It* (a sword [or the like]) *was,* or *became, blunt.* (M, Ḳ.) = بَرَدَهُ, (Ṣ, Mṣb, Ḳ,) aor. ـُ, (Mṣb,) inf. n. بَرْدٌ; (Ḳ;) and ▼ بَرَّدَهُ, (Ṣ, M, Mṣb, Ḳ,) inf. n. تَبْرِيدٌ; (Ṣ;) *He made it,* or *rendered it,* (for ex., water, M, Mṣb, Ḳ,) *cold, chill,* or *cool*: (Ṣ, &c.:) but the latter has an intensive signification [*he made it,* or *rendered it, very cold,* or *very cool*]: (Mṣb:) or both signify, (Ḳ,) or the former signifies, (M, TA,) *he mixed it with snow*: (M, Ḳ:) one does not say ▼ أَبْرَدَهُ, except in a bad dialect. (Ṣ.) بَرِّدِيهِ, being used by a poet for بَلْ رِدِيهِ, has been erroneously supposed to mean "Make thou it hot." (M.) You say, بَرَدَنَا اللَّيْلُ, (aor. and inf. n. as above, M,) and بَرَدَ عَلَيْنَا, *The night affected us with its cold.* (M, Ḳ.) And سَقَيْتُهُ شَرْبَةً بَرَدَتْ فُؤَادَهُ, (Ṣ, M,*) aor. and inf. n. as above, (Ṣ,) *I gave him to drink a draught*

that cooled his heart: (Ṣ, M:) or بَرَدْتُ بِهَا فُؤَادَهُ [*with which I cooled his heart*]. (So in the T.) And بَرِّدْ ▾ فُؤَادَكَ بِشَرْبَةٍ *Cool thy heart by a draught.* (A.) And اِسْقِنِى سَوِيقًا أَبْرُدْ بِهِ كَبِدِى [*Give thou me to drink* سويق *with which I may cool my liver*]. (T.) And بَرَدَ عَيْنَهُ بِالْكُحْلِ, (A'Obeyd, T, M,) or بِالْبَرُودِ, (Ṣ, Mṣb, Ḳ,) aor. and inf. n. as above, (M,) [*He cooled his eye with the collyrium,* or] *he applied the cooling collyrium to his eye,* (T,* Ṣ, M,* Mṣb, Ḳ,*) *and allayed its pain.* (M.) The following words, cited by IAạr,

بَرَدُوا غَوَارِبَ أَيْنُقٍ حُدْبِ

[lit. *They cooled the fore parts of the humps,* or *the backs, of humped she-camels*], mean ‡ *they put off from them their saddles, that their backs might become cool.* (M.) You say also, ▾ بَرِّدْ ظَهْرَ فَرَسِكَ سَاعَةً ‡ *Relieve thy horse from riding* [lit. *cool his back*] *awhile.* (A.) And ▾ لَا تُبَرِّدْ عَنْ فُلَانٍ ‡ *Do not thou alleviate the punishment* [*in the world to come*] *due to the offence of such a one by thy reviling him,* or *cursing him,* when he has acted injuriously to thee. (T, Ṣ,* M,* A,* L.) And بَرَدَ الخُبْزَ بِالْمَآءِ, (T, L, Ḳ,) (T,) *He poured* [*cold*] *water upon the bread,* (T, L, Ḳ,) and *moistened it* [*therewith:* see بَرُودٌ]. (T, L.) — بُرِدَ (a verb like عُنِىَ, Ḳ) *It* (a company of men) *was hailed upon.* (Ṣ, M, Ḳ.) And بُرِدَتِ الأَرْضُ *The land,* or *ground, was hailed upon.* (Ṣ.) = بَرَدَ, (Ṣ, M, &c.,) aor. ـُ, (TA,) inf. n. بَرْدٌ, (Mgh, TA,) also signifies *He filed* (M, Mgh, Ḳ) iron, (Ṣ, M, &c.,) and the like, (M,) with a مِبْرَد. (Ṣ, M, Mgh, Mṣb, Ḳ.) = بَرَدَهُ and ▾ ابردهُ *He sent him as a* بَرِيد [or *messenger on a post-mule* or *post-horse*]. (Ḳ.) And بَرَدَ بَرِيدًا, (M,) and ▾ ابردهُ, (A,) *He sent a* بريد. (M, A.) And ▾ ابرد اليه بَرِيدًا, (Ṣ,) or ▾ ابرد إِلَيْهِ, (T, TA.) *He sent to him a* بريد. (T, Ṣ.)

2: see بَرَدَهُ, in four places. — بَرَّدَهُ عَلَيْهِ ‡ *He made it incumbent,* or *obligatory, on him.* (M, A.) — And بَرَّدَهُ, (Ḳ, TA, but omitted in the CḲ,) inf. n. تَبْرِيدٌ; (TA;) and ▾ ابردهُ; (M, Ḳ;) † *It* (a thing, M) *made him,* or *rendered him, weak; weakened him;* (Ḳ;) or *made him,* or *rendered him, weak and languid.* (M.) = بَرَّدَ also signifies, as is indicated in the TA voce حُبَاحِبٌ, *It* (a locust) *spread forth its wings;* which are termed its بُرْدَانِ: see بُرْدٌ.]

4. ابرد *He entered upon a cold,* or *cool, time:* (Mgh, Mṣb:) *he entered upon the last part of the day:* (M, Ḳ:) *he entered upon the time when the sun had declined:* (Moḥammad Ibn-Kaạb, T:) and *he entered upon the cool season, at the end of the summer.* (Lth, T.) [Hence,] أَبْرِدُوا بِالطَّعَامِ *Delay ye to eat food until it is cool:* occurring in a trad. (El-Munáwee.) And أَبْرِدُوا بِالظُّهْرِ (T, A, Mgh, Mṣb) *Defer ye the noon-prayers until the cooler time of the day, when the vehemence of the heat shall have become allayed.* (Mgh, Mṣb.) And أَبْرِدْ عَنْكَ مِنَ الظَّهِيرَةِ *Stay thou until the mid-day heat shall have become assuaged, and the air be cool.* (M, and L in art. فيح.) — ابرد لَهُ *He gave him to drink what was cold,* or *cool.* (M, Ḳ.) You say also, سَقَيْتُهُ فَأَبْرَدْتُ لَهُ, meaning *I gave him to drink what was cold,* or *cool.* (A'Obeyd, Ṣ.) — ابردهُ *He brought it cold,* or *cool.* (M, Ḳ.) — See بَرَدَهُ, first sentence. — And see 2. = See also 1, in four places; last three sentences.

5. تبرّد فيه *He descended into it,* (i. e., into water, TA,) *and washed himself in it, to refresh himself by its coolness.* (M, Ḳ.) See also 8. — تبرّد also signifies † *He became weakened.* (TA.)

8. ابترد *He washed himself with cold water:* (Ṣ:) and likewise, (Ṣ,) or ابترد المَآءَ, (Ḳ,) *he drank water to cool his liver:* (Ṣ, Ḳ:) or the latter signifies *he poured the water cold upon himself,* (M, Ḳ,) meaning, *upon his head:* (M:) and ▾ تبرّد بِالمَآءِ, (T, A,) and ابترد, (A,) *he washed himself with water,* or *with the water.* (T.)

10. استبرد عَلَيْهِ لِسَانَهُ ‡ *He let loose his tongue and used it like a file against him.* (A.)

بَرْدٌ and ▾ بُرُودَةٌ [originally inf. ns.] *Cold; coldness; chill; chilness; cool,* as a subst.; *coolness;* the former, *contr. of* حَرٌّ; (Ṣ, M, A, Mṣb;) and the latter, *of* حَرَارَةٌ. (Ṣ.) — And [hence] the former, ‡ *Pleasantness; enjoyment; ease; comfort:* as in the saying, نَسْأَلُكَ الجَنَّةَ وَبَرْدَهَا ‡ *We ask of Thee Paradise and its pleasantness,* &c. (L.) — Also † *Sleep:* (T, Ṣ, M, A, Ḳ:) [an inf. n. used as a subst.:] so in the Ḳur lxxviii. 24: (Ṣ, M, Ḳ:) for sleep cools a man: (TA:) or, accord. to I 'Ab, it there means the *coldness,* or *coolness,* of beverage. (T.) You say, مَنَعَ البَرْدُ البَرْدَ † *The hail prevented sleep.* (A.) — And † *Saliva:* (Th, T, M, Ḳ:) so, accord. to Th, in the saying of El-'Arjee,

وَإِنْ شِئْتِ لَمْ أَطْعَمْ نُقَاخًا وَلَا بَرْدَا

And if thou desire, I will not taste sweet water, nor saliva [from any lips but thine]. (T, M,* TA. [But this is cited in the Ṣ as an ex. of بَرْدٌ signifying *sleep.*]) — See also بَارِدٌ. — [Hence,] البَرْدَانِ: see الأَبْرَدَانِ, voce أَبْرَدُ.

بُرْدٌ *A kind of garment;* (Ṣ;) *a kind of striped garment:* (M, Ḳ:) accord. to some, *of the description termed* وَشْىٌ [or *variegated*]: (M:) or particular kinds thereof are distinguished by such terms as بُرْدُ عَصْبٍ and بُرْدُ وَشْىٍ: (Mṣb:) also, (as a coll. gen. n., TA,) *garments of the kind called* أَكْسِيَةٌ, [pl. of كِسَآءٌ,] *which are wrapped round the body;* (Ḳ;) *one of which is called* ▾ بُرْدَةٌ: (M, Ḳ:) or, as Lth says, the بُرْد is [*a*] *well-known* [*garment*], *of the kind called* بُرُودُ العَصْبِ *and* بُرُودُ الوَشْىِ; (T;) but the ▾ بُرْدَة is *a garment of the kind called* كِسَآء*, four-sided, black, and somewhat small, worn by the Arabs of the desert:* (T, Ṣ, Mgh,* Mṣb,* TA:) or this latter (the بردة) is *a striped garment of the kind called* شَمْلَة: (T:) or it is *an oblong piece of woollen cloth, fringed:* (M:) Sh says, I saw an Arab of the desert wearing *a piece of woollen cloth resembling a napkin, wrapped round the body like an apron;* and on my saying to him, What dost thou call it? he answered, بُرْدَة: (T:) [the modern بردة, in every case in which I have seen it, I have observed to be *an oblong piece of thick woollen cloth, generally brown or of a dark or ashy dust-colour, and either plain, or having stripes so narrow and near together as to appear, at a little distance, of one colour; used both to envelop the person by day and as a night-covering:* the بردة of Moḥammad is described as about seven feet and a half in length, and four and a half in width, and in colour either أَحْمَر or أَخْضَر, i. e. of a dark or ashy dust-colour or brown; for such are the significations of these two epithets when applied to a garment of this kind, and in some other cases:] the pl. of بُرْدٌ is أَبْرُدٌ (M, Ḳ) and بُرُودٌ (Ṣ, M, Ḳ) and أَبْرَادٌ [both pls. of pauc.] and بُرَدٌ, (IAạr, T,) or this last is pl. of بُرْدَةٌ, (Ṣ, M,) and بِرَادٌ, like as قِرَاطٌ is pl. of قُرْطٌ, or this, also, is pl. of بُرْدَةٌ, like as بِرَامٌ is pl. of بُرْمَةٌ. (M.) — ذُو بُرْدٍ, as opposed to ذُو كِسَآءٍ, means † *A rich man.* (Ṣ in art. عج.) — وَقَعَ بَيْنَهُمَا قَدُّ بُرُودٍ يُمْنَةٍ, (so in copies of the Ḳ, in the TA يَمَنِيَّةٍ,) or بُرُودٍ ثَمِينَةٍ, (so in a copy of the A,) ‡ [*There happened between them two the rending of* بُرُود *of the fabric of El-Yemen,* accord. to the reading in the Ḳ, or *of costly* بُرُود, accord. to the reading in the A,] means *they arrived at a great,* or *severe, state of affairs;* (Ḳ;) or is said of two men who have contended together in vehement altercation so that they have rent each other's garments; (A;) [accord. to the reading in the Ḳ,] because يُمْنٌ, [in the CḲ يُمَنٌ,] which are بُرُود of El-Yemen, are not rent save on account of some great, or severe, thing, or affair. (Ḳ.) — ▾ هُمَا فِى بُرْدَةٍ أَخْمَاسٍ means † *They two do one deed;* or *act alike;* (IAạr, M, Ḳ;) *and resemble each other, as though they were in one* بُرْدَة: (IAạr, M:) or *they two have become near together, and in a state of agreement.* (Ḳ in art. خمس, q. v.) — And ▾ سَلَبَ الصَّهْبَآءَ بُرْدَتَهَا ‡ *He, or it, deprived the wine of its colour.* (A.) — And بُرْدَا الجَرَادِ, (T,) or الجُنْدَبِ, (Ṣ,) † *The two wings* [*of the locust,* or *of the species called* جندب]. (T, Ṣ.) — And ▾ بُرْدَةُ الضَّأْنِ † *A certain sort of milk.* (Ḳ.)

بَرَدٌ *Hail; what descends from the clouds, resembling pebbles;* (M, Mṣb;) *frozen rain;* (Lth, T;) *what is called* حَبُّ الغَمَامِ (Ṣ, A, Mṣb, Ḳ) *and* حَبُّ المُزْنِ (Mṣb) [i. e. *the grains,* or *berries, of the clouds:* a coll. gen. n., of which the n. un. is with ة, signifying *a hailstone*].

بَرِدٌ *Possessing coldness* or *coolness:* an epithet applied to the [plant called] صِلِّيَان. (Ṣ.) — سَحَابٌ بَرِدٌ, (T, Ṣ, M, Ḳ,) and ▾ أَبْرَدُ, (Ṣ, Ḳ,) *Clouds containing hail* (T, Ṣ, M, Ḳ*) *and cold.* (T.) You say also سَحَابَةٌ بَرِدَةٌ *A cloud containing hail* (T, Ṣ, M, A*) *and cold;* (T;) but not سحابة بَرْدَآءُ. (M.)

بَرْدَةٌ: see بَارِدٌ: = and see also بُرْدَةٌ. = هِىَ لَكَ بَرْدَةً نَفْسُهَا *She is purely thine;* (Fr, A'Obeyd, T, Ṣ, M;) syn. خَالِصَةٌ: (M:) A'Obeyd explains it by خَالِصًا, (T, Ṣ, M,) not in the fem. form, (TA,) on the authority of Fr. (T.) — هُوَ لِى بَرْدَةُ يَمِينِى,

(A'Obeyd, M,) or هُوَ بُرْدَةُ يَمِينِى, (Ṣ,) *He, or it, is known to me.* (A'Obeyd, Ṣ, M.) — بُرْدَةٌ a proper name applied to *The ewe.* (Ḳ.)

بُرْدَةٌ : see بُرْدٌ, in five places.

بَرْدَةٌ (T, Ṣ, M, A, &c.) and † بَرَدَةٌ (T, M, Ḳ) *Indigestion; a malady arising from unwholesome food:* (Ṣ, M, A, L, Mṣb, Ḳ:) or *heaviness of food to the stomach:* (IAạr, T, L:) so termed because it makes the stomach cold. (T, L, Mṣb.) It is said in a trad., أَصْلُ كُلِّ دَآءٍ البَرَدَةُ [*The origin of every disease is indigestion*]. (T, Ṣ, M,* A.) — Also, the former, The *middle* of the eye. (Ḳ.)

بُرَدَآءُ *An ague;* i. e. *a fever attended by a cold fit,* (Ḳ,) or *by shivering.* (TA.)

بَرْدِىٌّ *A well-known kind of plant,* (Ṣ, M,* Ḳ,) *of which the kind of paper termed* قِرْطَاس *is made;* (TA in art. قرطس, q. v.;) [namely, *papyrus;* and] *of which mats are made;* (Mṣb;) [app. meaning *rushes* in general: but the former is generally meant by it in the present day, and is probably the proper signification: anciently, mats, as well as ropes and sails &c., were made of the rind of the papyrus; and even small boats were constructed of its stalks bound together; and of such, probably, was the ark in which the infant Moses was exposed: it is a coll. gen. n.:] n. un. بَرْدِيَّةٌ. (M, TA.) Hence, قُطْنُ البَرْدِىِّ *The cotton of the papyrus, which, resembling wool, is gathered from the stalk, and, mixed with lime, composes a very tenacious kind of cement.* (Golius, from Ibn-Maạroof.) — [Also, a rel. n. from the same, meaning *Of,* or *belonging to,* or *resembling,* the *plant so called.* Hence the saying,] لَهَا سَاقٌ بَرْدِيَّةٌ [*She has a shank like a papyrus-stalk*]. (A.)

بُرْدِىٌّ *One of the most excellent sorts of dates:* (Ṣ, Mṣb:) *an excellent sort of dates,* (AḤn, M, Ḳ,) *resembling the* بَرْنِىّ: (AḤn, M:) or *a sort of dates of El-Hijáz.* (TA.)

[بَرْدَانُ *Feeling cold* or *chilly* or *cool:* fem. with ة: perhaps post-classical; for I have not found it mentioned in any of the lexicons.]

بُرَادٌ : see بَارِدٌ. — Also *Weakness of the legs, from hunger or fatigue.* (Ibn-Buzurj, T.) [See also 1.]

بَرُودٌ : see بَارِدٌ. — Beverage *that cools the heat of thirst.* (T.) — Also, (T, L, Ḳ,) and † مَبْرُودٌ, (T, M, A, L, Ḳ,) Bread *upon which water is poured;* (T, L, Ḳ;) *which is moistened with cold water:* (A:) eaten by women to make them fat. (M, A, L.) The subst. applied to such bread is † بَرِيدٌ (A.) — بَرُودٌ [as an epithet in which the quality of a subst. predominates] also signifies *Cold water which one pours upon his head.* (M.) — *Anything with which a thing is rendered cold,* or *cooled.* (Ṣ, M.) — *A collyrium which cools the eye;* (Lth, T, M, Mṣb;) also termed بَرُودُ العَيْنِ. (T, Ṣ.) — بَرُودُ الظِّلِّ †*Pleasant in social intercourse:* applied alike to the male and the female. (TA, from a trad.) — ثَوْبٌ بَرُودٌ *A garment without nap:* (Ḳ:) and *a garment that is not warm nor soft.* (TA.)

بَرِيدٌ : see بَرُودٌ. — Also *A mule appointed* [*for the conveyance of messengers*] *in a* رِبَاط [or *public building for the accommodation of travellers and their beasts, or in a* سِكَّة, which is *a house or the like specially appropriated to messengers and the beasts that carry them:* thus it signifies *a post-mule:* afterwards, it was applied also to *a post-horse,* and *any beast appointed for the conveyance of messengers*]: (Mgh:) [this is what is meant by the words in the Ṣ and Ḳ, البَرِيدُ المُرَتَّبُ:] it is a word of Persian origin, (Z in the Fáïḳ,) arabicized, from بُرِيدَهْ دُمْ, (Z in the Fáïḳ, and Mgh,) i. e. "docked," or "having the tail cut off;" for the post-mules (بِغَالُ البَرِيدِ) had their tails cut off in order that they might be known: (Z in the Fáïḳ:) [or perhaps it is from the Hebrew פֶּרֶד "a mule:"] or it is applied to the *beast appointed for the conveyance of messengers* (دَابَّةُ البَرِيدِ) because he traverses the space called بَرِيد [defined below: but the reason before given for this appellation is more probable: it is like the Lat. "veredus"]: (T, Mṣb:) pl. بُرُدٌ (Z, Mgh, Mṣb) and بُرْدٌ, which is a contraction of the former, like as رُسْلٌ is of رُسُلٌ. (Z.) You say, حُمِلَ فُلَانٌ عَلَى البَرِيدِ [*Such a one was borne on the post-mule* or *post-horse*]. (Ṣ.) Imra-el-Ḳeys speaks of a بريد of the horses of Barbar. (Ṣ.) — Having been originally used in the sense first explained above, it was afterwards applied to *A messenger borne on a post-mule* [or *post-horse*]: (Z in the Fáïḳ, and Mgh:) or *messengers on beasts of the post:* (M, Ḳ:) or *a messenger that journeys with haste:* (A:) or [simply] *a messenger:* (Ṣ, Mṣb, Ḳ:) pl. as above. (M,* Z.) Hence the saying, الحُمَّى بَرِيدُ المَوْتِ *Fever is the messenger of death:* (T, Mṣb:) because it gives warning thereof. (T.) Hence also البَرِيدُ applied to *The animal called* الفُرَانِقُ, (said to be *the jackal,* but some say otherwise, TA,) because he gives warning before [the approach of] the lion. (T, Ṣ, Ḳ.) And صَاحِبُ البَرِيدِ [*The master of the messengers that journey on post-mules or post-horses*]. (Ṣ.) [And خَيْلُ البَرِيدِ, occurring in many histories &c., *The post-horses, that carry messengers and others.*] — Also, having been applied to a messenger on a post-mule [or post-horse], it then became applied to The *space,* or *distance, traversed by the messenger thus called;* (Mgh, Mṣb;*) the *space,* or *distance, between each* سِكَّة *and the* سِكَّة *next to it;* the سِكَّة being a structure of either of the kinds called بَيْت and قُبَّة, or a رِبَاط [explained above], in which the appointed messengers lodge; (Z in the Fáïḳ;) the *space,* or *distance, between two stations,* or *places of alighting;* or *two parasangs,* or *leagues;* (M, Ḳ;) [*six miles;*] each parasang, or league, being three miles, and each mile being four thousand cubits: (TA:) or *twelve miles;* (Ṣ, A, Mṣb, Ḳ;) i. e. *four parasangs, or leagues:* (Mgh, TA:) [for] the space, or distance, between each station termed سِكَّة and the next to it is either two parasangs or four: (Z in the Fáïḳ:) the distance of *twelve miles* is [also] termed سِكَّةُ البَرِيدِ: (T:) the pl. is as above. (T, Z.) A journey of four بُرُد, or forty-eight miles, renders it allowable to shorten prayers; which miles are of the Háshimee measure, such as are measured on the road to Mekkeh. (T.) — Also The *course,* or *pace,* of a camel *along the space thus called:* so in the following verse of Muzarrid, in praise of 'Arábeh El-Owsee:

فَدَتْكَ عَرَابَ اليَوْمَ أُمِّى وَخَالَتِى
وَنَاقَتِىَ النَّاجِى إِلَيْكَ بَرِيدُهَا

[*May my mother, and my maternal aunt, and my she-camel that is swift in her course to thee from one station to another, be ransoms for thee, O 'Arábeh,* (the name being contracted,) *this day!*]. (Ṣ.)

بُرَادَةٌ *Filings;* (M, Mgh, Ḳ;) *what falls from iron* [&c.] *when filed.* (Ṣ.)

بُرُودَةٌ : see بَرْدٌ.

بَرَّادَةٌ *A vessel which cools water:* (M, Ḳ:) or *a* كُوَارَة [app. meaning either a *stand,* or a *shelf, upon which mugs* (كِيزَان, pl. of كُوز,) *are placed;* erroneously in the Ḳ, كُوَّارَة, and كُوَارَة, as I find it in different copies;] *upon which water is cooled:* (Lth, T, Ḳ:*) but [Az says,] I know not whether it be a classical or a post-classical word. (T.) Hence the saying, بَاتَتْ كِيزَانُهُمْ عَلَى البَرَّادَةِ *Their mugs passed the night upon the* برّادة. (A, TA.)

بَارِدٌ (Ṣ, M, Mṣb, Ḳ) *Cold; chill; cool;* (Ṣ, Mṣb;) applied to water [&c.]; (M, Ḳ;) as also † بَرْدٌ, [originally an inf. n., like عَدْلٌ, used as an epithet,] (M, Ḳ,) and † بَرُودٌ, (Ṣ, M, Ḳ,) and † بُرَادٌ; (M, Ḳ;) but the last two are intensive forms [signifying *very cold* or *chill* or *cool*]. (TA.) — ‡ Anything *loved, beloved, liked,* or *approved.* (TA.) [Hence,] عَيْشٌ بَارِدٌ ‡ *An easy and a pleasant life,* or *state of life.* (ISk,* T,* M, A, L, Ḳ.) And لَيْلَةٌ بَارِدَةُ العَيْشِ, and † بَرْدَةُ العَيْشِ, [the latter written in the TT بَرِدَةُ العيش,] ‡ *A night of easy and pleasant life.* (M, L.) And غَنِيمَةٌ بَارِدَةٌ : see the latter word. — سَمُومٌ بَارِدٌ ‡ *A hot wind that is constant, continual, permanent, settled,* or *incessant.* (Ṣ, L.) — لِى عَلَيْهِ أَلْفٌ بَارِدٌ ‡ *A thousand* [pieces of money &c.] *are incumbent,* or *obligatory, on him, to me, and established against him;* or *are owed,* or *due, to me, by,* or *from, him.* (Ṣ, M.*) — جَآءَ فُلَانٌ بَارِدًا مُخُّهُ, and بَارِدَ العِظَامِ, ‡ *Such a one came in a lean,* or *an emaciated, state:* in the contr. case, one says, حَارًّا مُخُّهُ, and حَارَّ العِظَامِ. (A, TA.) — بَارِدٌ also signifies †*Blunt;* applied to a sword and the like: see 1. — And, contr., †*Sharp:* for you say,] مُرْهَفَاتٌ بَوَارِدُ [pl. of بَارِدَةٌ, meaning] †*Sharp,* or *cutting, swords:* (TA:) or *slaying swords.* (Ṣ.)

بَارِدَةٌ †*Spoil acquired without fatigue;* (IAạr, T;) also termed غَنِيمَةٌ بَارِدَةٌ; and to this is likened, by the Prophet, fasting in winter. (T.) Also † *Gain made by merchandise at the time of one's buying it.* (IAạr, T.)

أَبْرَدُ [*More,* and *most, cold,* or *chill,* or *cool*]. — [Hence,] الأَبْرَدَانِ and † البَرْدَانِ *The morning between daybreak and sunrise, and the evening, between sunset and nightfall*; (T, Ṣ, M, Ḳ;) also called الْعَصْرَانِ (Ṣ, Ḳ) and الصَّرْعَانِ and الرِّدْفَانِ: (T:) or (as in the Ṣ, but in the M and Ḳ "and") *the morning-shade and evening-shade*: (Ṣ, M, Ḳ:) so called because of their coldness, or coolness. (TA.) —— See also بَرْدٌ —— ثَوْرٌ أَبْرَدُ *A bull upon which are spots, or patches, of white and black*: (Ṣ, M:) of the dial. of El-Yemen. (M.) —— And الأَبْرَدُ *The leopard*: fem. with ة: (T, Ḳ: [but in the TT, the fem. is written like the masc.:]) pl. الأَبَارِدُ. (T, Ḳ.) The female is also called الخَيْثَمَةُ. (T.)

إِبْرِدَةٌ, (Ṣ, M, &c.,) with kesr (Ṣ, Mgh, Ḳ) to the ء and the ر, (Mgh, TA,) [in the CḲ إِبْرَدَة,] *Cold in the belly*, or *inside*; (M, Ḳ;) *a well-known malady, arising from the prevalence of cold and humidity, and preventing one, by languor, from performing the act of coition*: (Ṣ, Mgh:) and *a dripping of the urine, which prevents a man's taking pleasure in women*. (T, L.) —— Also *Coldness* of the damp earth, and of rain. (M, L.) An Arab says, إِنَّهَا لَبَارِدَةُ اليَوْمَ [*Verily it* (the morning, الغَدَاةُ, L) *is cold to-day*]; and another says to him, لَيْسَتْ بِبَارِدَةٍ إِنَّمَا هِىَ إِبْرِدَةُ الثَّرَى [*It is not cold: it is only the coldness of the damp earth*]. (Ṣ, L.)

مُبْرَدٌ [pass. part. n. of 4]. You say, أَرْضٌ مُبْرَدَةٌ: see مَبْرُودٌ.

مُبْرِدٌ [act. part. n. of 4]. You say, جِئْنَاكَ مُبْرِدِينَ *We came to thee when the heat had become allayed*. (T.) ═ Also One *sending*, or *who sends*, a بَرِيد [or بُرُد, i. e., *a messenger on a post-mule* or *post-horse*, or *messengers on post-mules* or *post-horses*]. (Ṣ.)

مِبْرَدٌ (Ṣ, Ḳ, &c.) *A file*; (M;) syn. سُوهَانٌ; (M, Ḳ;) which is a Persian word: (M:) pl. مَبَارِدُ. (Mṣb.) —— [Hence,] جَعَلَ لِسَانَهُ عَلَيْهِ مِبْرَدًا ‡ [*He made his tongue like a file upon him*; i. e.] *he annoyed him*, or *hurt him, with his tongue, and vituperated him*. (A.) [See a saying of Moosà Ibn-Jábir voce جِنٌّ.]

مَبْرَدَةٌ [*A cause of coldness* or *coolness*]. You say, هٰذَا الشَّىْءُ مَبْرَدَةٌ لِلْبَدَنِ [*This thing is a cause of coldness*, or *coolness, to the body*]: and Aṣ relates that he said to an Arab of the desert, "What induceth thee to take a sleep in the morning while the sun is yet low?" and he answered, إِنَّهَا مَبْرَدَةٌ فِى الصَّيْفِ مَسْخَنَةٌ فِى الشِّتَآءِ [*Verily it is a cause of coolness in the summer*, and *a cause of warmth in the winter*]. (Ṣ, A.)

مُبَرَّدٌ: see what follows.

مَبْرُودٌ *Made*, or *rendered, cold* or *chill* or *cool*: (Ṣ, Mṣb, Ḳ:) [and ↓ مُبَرَّدٌ signifies the same in an intensive manner:] applied to water [&c.: or signifying *mixed with snow*: see بَرَدَهُ]. (Ḳ.) —— شَجَرَةٌ مَبْرُودَةٌ *A tree deprived of its leaves by the cold*. (AḤn, M.) —— أَرْضٌ مَبْرُودَةٌ (M, A, Ḳ) and ↓ مُبْرَدَةٌ (Ḳ) *Land*, or *ground, hailed upon*: (M, Ḳ:) or *snowed upon*. (A, TA.) —— See also بُرُودٌ.

بردع

بَرْدَعَةٌ: see بَرْذَعَةٌ.

برذع

بَرْذَعٌ: see what next follows.

بَرْذَعَةٌ (Ṣ, Mgh, Mṣb, Ḳ) and بَرْدَعَةٌ (Mṣb, Ḳ) *A* [*cloth of the kind called*] حِلْس *which is put beneath the* [*saddle called*] رَحْل (Ṣ, Mgh, Mṣb, Ḳ) *of the camel*: (Mgh:) pl. بَرَاذِعُ (Mgh, Mṣb) and بَرَادِعُ. (Mṣb.) Ru-beh says, [using the sing. without the ة as a coll. gen. n.,]

• وَتَحْتَ أَحْنَآءِ الرِّحَالِ البَرْذَعُ •

[*And beneath the curved pieces of wood of the camels' saddles are the bardha'ahs*]. (TA.) —— This is the primary signification: but in the conventional language of our time, it is applied to *An ass's saddle*; *the thing upon which one rides on an ass, like the* سَرْج *to the horse*; (Mṣb;) [i. e. *a pad*, or *stuffed saddle*; *generally stuffed with straw*; *and used for a mule as well as for an ass*;] or an ass's بردعة is *a saddle like the* رَحْل *and* قَتَب. (TA voce إِكَافٌ, q. v.) ═ بَرْذَعَةٌ also signifies *Land which is neither hard nor soft*: (Ḳ:) pl. as above. (TA.)

بَرَاذِعِىٌّ *A maker of* بَرَاذِع, pl. of بَرْذَعَةٌ: a rel. n. similar to أَنْمَاطِىٌّ. (TA.)

برذن

Q. 1. بَرْذَنَ, (M, Ḳ,) inf. n. بَرْذَنَةٌ, (T,) *He* (a horse) *went in the manner of the* بِرْذَوْن, q. v. (T, M, Ḳ.) —— *He* (a man) *was*, or *became, heavy*, or *sluggish*: whence IDrd thinks بِرْذَوْنٌ to be derived: (M, Mṣb:*) but this opinion is of no account. (M.) —— *He was unable to reply*, (T, Ḳ,) when asked respecting a thing. (T.) —— *He subdued, overpowered*, or *overcame*: (Ḳ: [expl. by قَهَرَ and غَلَبَ; but I think that the right reading may be قُهِرَ and غُلِبَ, meaning *he was*, or *became, subdued*, &c.:]) said of a man. (TA.)

بِرْذَوْنٌ [*A horse of mean breed*, or *of coarse make*; *a jade*: but commonly applied to *a hack*, or *hackney*; *a horse for ordinary use*, and *for journeying*:] *a* دَابَّة, (Ṣ, Ḳ,) not in an absolute sense, but *of a particular sort*, namely, (MF,) *a horse that is not of Arabian breed*: (T, MF:) or *a heavy*, or *sluggish*, دابّة: (so in a copy of the Ṣ:) or *a coarse horse*: (Towsheeḥ, TA:) or *a horse of coarse make, hardy so as to endure travel upon the mountain-roads and rugged ground, not of Arabian breed, mostly brought from Er-Room* [meaning *Asia Minor* or *Greece*]: (TA, from the Expos. of the 'Irákeeyeh of Es-Sakháwee:) or *a horse of large and coarse make, with thick limbs*; whereas those of Arabian breed are light of flesh, lank in the belly, and more slender in the limbs: (El-Bájee, TA:) or *a Turkish horse*; *opposed to Arabian*: (Mgh, Mṣb:) or *a pacing-horse*; syn. رَهْوَانٌ: (TA voce هِمْلَاجٌ:) fem. with ة; (Ks, Ṣ, M, Mgh, Mṣb, Ḳ;) sometimes; but without ة it is applied to the female as well as the male: (IAmb, Mṣb:) pl. بَرَاذِينُ. (T, Ṣ, Mgh, Ḳ.)

مُبَرْذِنٌ *An owner of a* بِرْذَوْن: (Ḳ:) or *a rider thereon*. (TA.)

برز

1. بَرَزَ, (Ṣ, A, Mṣb, Ḳ,) aor. ـُ, (Ṣ, TA,) inf. n. بُرُوزٌ, (Ṣ, Mṣb, TA,) *He* (a man, Ṣ) *went*, or *came*, or *passed, out*, or *forth*; *he issued*. (Ṣ, A.) *He* (a man, TA) *went*, or *came*, or *passed, out*, or *forth, into the field, plain*, or *open tract* or *country*: (Ḳ:) or *did so to satisfy a want of nature*: (TṢ, TA:) as also, in the former sense, (Ḳ,) or in the latter, (Ṣ,) ↓ تبرّز; (Ṣ, Ḳ, TA;) and بَرِزَ; (Ṣgh, TA;) and so, in the former sense, ↓ برّز, inf. n. تَبْرِيزٌ; (Ḥar p. 510;) [and in the latter sense, ↓ بارز, accord. to an explanation of its part. n. مُبَارِزٌ in Ḥar p. 566:] or ↓ تبرّز signifies *he voided his excrement*, or *ordure*. (Mgh, Mṣb.) You say, بَرَزَ إِلَى القِرْنِ فِى الحَرْبِ *He went*, or *came, out*, or *forth, into the field to his adversary in battle or war*. (TA.) —— *He*, or *it*, (a man, TA, or thing, Mṣb, or anything, Fr,) *appeared*, or *became apparent*, (Fr, Ṣgh, Mṣb, Ḳ,) *after concealment*, (Fr, Ḳ,) or *after obscurity*; (Ṣgh;) as also بَرِزَ. (Ṣgh, Ḳ.) —— [*It was*, or *became, prominent*, or *projecting*: often used in this sense.] ═ بَرُزَ, (Mṣb, Ḳ,) inf. n. بَرَازَةٌ, (Mṣb,) *He* (a man) *was*, or *became, such as is termed* بَرْزٌ, q. v.: (Mṣb, Ḳ:) and in like manner, بَرُزَتْ, inf. n. as above, *she* (a woman) *was*, or *became, such as is termed* بَرْزَةٌ. (A.)

2. برّزهُ, (inf. n. تَبْرِيزٌ, Ṣ, Ḳ,) *He made it apparent, manifest, plain*, or *evident*; *he showed*, or *manifested, it*; (Ṣ, A, Ḳ;) namely, a writing, or book, (A,) or other thing; (Ṣ, A;) as also ↓ ابرزهُ: (A, Mṣb:) or ↓ ابرز الكِتَابَ signifies *he put forth*, or *produced, the writing*, or *book*; syn. أَخْرَجَهُ: (TA:) and [as it often signifies in the present day,] *published, it*; syn. نَشَرَهُ. (Ḳ, TA.) [See also 4 below.] It is said in the Ḳur [xxvi. 91 and lxxix. 36], وَبُرِّزَتِ الجَحِيمُ, meaning *And Hell shall be uncovered*. (A.) —— برّز رَاكِبَهُ *He* (a horse) *saved his rider*. (Ḳ.) ═ See also 1. —— [Hence,] برّز الفَرَسُ, (Ṣ, Mṣb,) or برّز عَلَى الخَيْلِ, (Ḳ,) inf. n. تَبْرِيزٌ, (Mṣb,) *The horse outstripped* (Ṣ, Mṣb, Ḳ) *the* [*other*] *horses* (Mṣb, Ḳ) *in the race-ground*: (Mṣb:) it is said of a horse that outstrips in a race: and, accord. to some, the like is said of whatever outstrips: (TA:) and برّز عَلَى الغَايَةِ [*He* (a horse) *passed beyond the goal*]. (A.) —— Hence, برّز فِى العِلْمِ, inf. n. as above, *He surpassed*, or *excelled, his fellows in knowledge*. (Mṣb.) And [simply] برّز *He surpassed his companions* (Ṣ, Ḳ) *in excellence*, or *in courage*. (Ḳ.) And برّز عَلَى أَقْرَانِهِ [*He surpassed*, or *excelled, his fellows*, or *his opponents*]. (A.) ═ See also 4, last signification.

3. بارزهُ فِى الحَرْبِ, (A, Mṣb,* Ḳ,*) inf. n.

مُبَارَزَةٌ and بِرَازٌ, (Ṣ, A, Mṣb, Ḳ,) *He went, or came, out, or forth, in the field, to [encounter] him* (i. e. his adversary) *in battle, or war.* (Ḳ,* TA.) —— See also 1.

4. ابرزهُ *He made, or caused, him* (a man) *to go, or come, or pass, out, or forth:* (Ṣ:) [or *to go, or come, or pass, out, or forth, into the field, plain, or open tract or country:* (see 1:)] and *he made, or caused, it* (a thing) *to go, or come, or pass, out, or forth; or he put it, or took it, or drew it, out, or forth;* syn. أَخْرَجَهُ; as also ↓استبرزهُ. (Ḳ.) See also 2, in two places. —— ابرز *He determined, resolved, or decided, upon journeying:* (IAạr, Ḳ:) the vulgar say ↓بَرَّزَ. (TA.)

5: see 1, in two places.

6. هُمَا يَتَبَارَزَانِ *They two* (meaning two adversaries) *go, or come, out, or forth, into the field, each to [encounter] the other,* in battle or war. (Ḳ,* TA.) —— تبارزا *They both separated themselves, each from his company, and betook themselves each to the other.* (Ḳ.)

10: see 4.

بَرْزٌ A man *characterized by pleasing or goodly aspect, and by intelligence:* fem. with ة: (Ṣ, TA:) or a man *of open condition or state:* (TA:) or *pure in disposition;* (TA;) *abstaining from what is unlawful and indecorous;* (Ṣ, A, Mṣb:) *of great dignity* or *estimation:* (Mṣb:) fem. with ة: (A, Mṣb:) pl. fem. بَرْزَاتٌ: (A:) or, as also ↓بَرْزِيٌّ, a man *who abstains from what is unlawful and indecorous, and in whose intelligence,* (Ḳ,) or, as in some copies of the Ḳ, *in whose excellence,* بفضله, but this is app. a mistranscription, or, as some say, *in whose abstinence from what is unlawful and indecorous,* (TA,) *and his judgment, confidence is placed:* (Ḳ:) and بَرْزَةٌ a woman *whose good qualities or actions, or whose beauties, are apparent:* (Ḳ:) or *open in her converse;* syn. مُتَجَاهِرَةٌ: or, as in some correct lexicons, *disdainful of mean things;* syn. مُتَجَالَّةٌ: or *of middle age,* (كَهْلَةٌ,) *who is not veiled or concealed like young women:* (TA:) or *of great dignity or estimation:* (AO, TA:) or *who goes or comes forth to people, and with whom they sit, and of whom they talk, and who abstains from what is unlawful and indecorous, and is intelligent:* (TA:) or *who abstains from what is unlawful and indecorous, and goes or comes forth to men, and talks with them, and is advanced in age beyond those women who are kept concealed:* (Mgh, Mṣb:) or *open in her converse,* (مُتَجَاهِرَةٌ,) *of middle age,* (كَهْلَةٌ,) *of great dignity or estimation, who goes or comes forth to people, and with whom they sit and talk, and who abstains from what is unlawful and indecorous:* (Ḳ:) or *in whose judgment, and her abstaining from what is unlawful and indecorous, confidence is placed:* (TA:) or *who does not veil her face from a man and bend her head down towards the ground.* (IAạr, on the authority of Ibn-Ez-Zubeyr.)

بَرْزِيٌّ: see بَرْزٌ.

بَرَازٌ *A field, plain, or wide expanse of land,* (Ṣ, Mṣb, Ḳ,) *without trees;* (Mṣb;) as also ↓بِرَازٌ; but this latter form is rare: (Mṣb:) or *an open tract of land destitute of herbage and trees and without hills or mountains:* (Mgh, Mṣb:) or *a place in which is no covert of trees or other things:* (Fr, Ṣ:) *an open place in which is no covert.* (TA.) —— [Hence,] خَرَجَ إِلَى البَرَازِ ‡ *He went forth to satisfy a want of nature.* (A.) And إِذَا أَرَادَ البَرَازَ أَبْعَدَ ‡ [*When he desired to satisfy a want of nature, he went far off*]: a trad.; respecting which El-Khaṭṭábee says that the relaters of traditions err respecting the word, pronouncing it with kesr, for ↓بِرَازٌ is an inf. n.: but (SM says that) authorities differ as to this point. (TA.) —— [It is further said,] بَرَازٌ, (Mgh, Mṣb,) or ↓بِرَازٌ, (Ṣ, Ḳ,) is metonymically applied to ‡ *Excrement; human ordure;* (Ṣ, Mgh, Mṣb, Ḳ;) the *feces of food.* (Ṣ.)

بِرَازٌ: see بَرَازٌ, in three places.

بَارِزٌ act. part. n. of بَرَزَ [q. v.]. —— *Wholly,* or *entirely, apparent* or *manifest.* (TA.) —— أَرْضٌ بَارِزَةٌ *Land that is apparent, open,* or *uncovered,* (Bḍ and Jel in xviii. 45, and TA,) *upon which is no mountain nor any other thing,* (Jel,) or *that has no hill nor mountain nor sand.* (TA.)

إِبْرِزِيٌّ: see what next follows.

إِبْرِيزٌ (Sh, IAạr, A, Mṣb, Ḳ) and ↓إِبْرِزِيٌّ, (Sh, IAạr, Ḳ,) the latter of which is incorrectly written in [some of] the copies of the Ḳ إِبْرِيزِيٌّ, (TA,) *Pure* gold: (Sh, Mṣb, Ḳ:) or *an ornament of pure gold:* (IAạr:) the former an arabicized word [app. from the Greek ὄβρυζον, as also the latter]: (Mṣb:) of the measure إِفْعِيلٌ; the ء and ى being augmentative. (IJ.)

مُبْرَزٌ [lit. *A place to which one goes forth in the field, or plain, or open tract or country;*] *a privy,* or *place where one performs ablution;* syn. مُتَوَضَّأٌ; (Ṣ;) [as also ↓مُتَبَرَّزٌ, occurring in the TA in art. جوز.]

كِتَابٌ مُبْرَزٌ, (Ḳ,) and ↓مَبْرُوزٌ, (Ṣ, Mṣb, Ḳ,) *A writing,* or *book, put forth,* or *published;* syn. مَنْشُورٌ: (Ṣ, Ḳ:) or *made apparent, shown,* or *manifested:* (Mṣb:) ↓ the latter anomalous; (Ṣ, Mṣb;) being from أَبْرَزَ; (Mṣb;) and AḤát disapproved it; and thought that it might be a mistake for مَزْبُور, meaning "written;" but it [is said that it] occurs in two poems of Lebeed: (Ṣ:) in one of these instances, however, for المَبْرُوزُ, some read المُبْرَزُ; and Ṣgh says that he found not the other instance in the poems of Lebeed: IJ says that ↓المَبْرُوزُ is for المَبْرُوزُ بِهِ. (TA.) You say, قَدْ أَعْطَوْهُ كِتَابًا مَبْرُوزًا ↓ *They had given him a writing,* or *book, published;* i. e., مَنْشُورًا. (TA.)

مَبْرُوزٌ: see مُبْرَزٌ, throughout.

مُتَبَرَّزٌ: see مُبْرَزٌ.

برزخ

بَرْزَخٌ *A thing that intervenes between any two things:* (L:) or *a bar, an obstruction,* or *a thing that makes a separation, between two things:* (Ṣ, A, L, Ḳ:) so in the Ḳur lv. 20: pl. بَرَازِخُ. (L.) —— The *interval between the present life and that which is to come,* (Ṣ, A,) *from the period of death to the resurrection,* (Ṣ, A, Ḳ,) *upon which he who dies enters;* (Ṣ, Ḳ;) the *period,* or *state, from the day of death to the day of resurrection:* so in the Ḳur xxiii. 102. (Fr.) —— بَرَازِخُ الإِيمَانِ *What is between the beginning of faith,* (L, Ḳ,) which is the acknowledgment, or confession, of God, (L,) *and the end thereof,* (L, Ḳ,) which is the removal of what is hurtful from the road: (L:) or *what is between doubt and certainty.* (L, Ḳ.)

برسم

Q. 1. بُرْسِمَ *He* (a man) *was affected with the disease termed* بِرْسَام; (Ṣ, Mgh, Mṣb, Ḳ;) as also بُلْسِمَ. (TA.)

بِرْسَامٌ, (in the T with fet-ḥ, [بَرْسَامٌ,] Mgh,) *A certain malady,* or *disease,* (Ṣ, Mṣb, Ḳ,) *well known,* (Ṣ, Mṣb,) *attended by delirium:* (Ḳ:) [in the present day, this term is applied to the *pleurisy,* as also ذَاتُ الجَنْبِ; and so it is explained by Golius and Freytag; or, as the latter adds, accord. to Avicenna, *pleurodyne:* but] in some of the books of medicine, it is said to be *a tumour,* (Mṣb,) or *a hot tumour,* (TA,) *that is incident to the septum which is between the liver and the bowels,* [app. meaning *the upper parts of the greater and lesser omentum,*] *and then reaches to the brain:* (Mṣb, TA:) also pronounced بِلْسَامٌ: (ISk, Mṣb:) i. q. مُومٌ: (M, TA:) it is an arabicized word; (IDrd, Mgh, Mṣb;) or seems to be so; composed of بَرْ and سَامْ; the former of these, in Persian, signifying the "breast," or "chest;" and the latter, "death" [and "fire" and "a swelling;" of which three meanings, the second and third are agreeable with the two explanations of برسام given above]: so says Az. (TA.)

بِرْسِيمٌ, with kesr, (Ḳ,) vulgarly pronounced with fet-ḥ to the ب, [بَرْسِيمٌ,] (TA,) [*Alexandrian trefoil* or *clover; trifolium Alexandrinum;* described by Forskål in his Flora Aegypt. Arab. p. 139; *the most common and the best kind of succulent food for cattle grown in Egypt: it is sown when the waters of the inundation are leaving the fields; and yields three crops; the second of which is termed* رِبَّة; *and so is the third; but this is generally left for seed: when dry, it is termed* دَرِيس: if his words have not been perverted by copyists, F explains it as] the *grain of the* قُرْط, (حَبُّ القُرْطِ) [but I think it probable that this is a mistranscription, for خَيْرُ القُرْطِ, i. e., *the best of the (species of trefoil, or clover, called)* قُرْط,] *resembling the* رَطْبَة [or رُطْبَة], *or superior to this latter in size, or quality* (أَجَلُّ مِنْهَا): (Ḳ:) the قُرْط resembles the رطبة, [written in the TA without the vowel signs,] but is superior to this latter in size, or quality (اجلّ منها), and larger in the leaves, and is what is called in Persian شَبْذَر [or شُبْدُر]: (AḤn, TA:)

it is one of the best kinds of herbage for horses and the like, which fatten upon it. (TA.)

إِبْرِيسَمٌ, (M, [and thus written in copies of the Ḳ,]) with kesr to the ر [as well as the ء], accord. to IAạr., (M,) [and] with fet-ḥ to the س; (Ḳ;) or إِبْرِيسِمٌ; (M;) and [app. أُبْرِيسَمٌ,] with ḍamm to the س; (Ḳ;) or it has three dial. forms; accord. to ISk, it is ابريسم [app. إِبْرِيسِمٌ]; others say that it is ابريسم [app. أَبْرَيْسَمٌ], with fet-ḥ; IAạr says that it is إِبْرِيسَمٌ, with kesr to the ء and the ر, and with fet-ḥ to the س, and he says that there is not in the language an instance of إِفْعِيلِلٌ, with kesr, but there are instances of إِفْعِيلَلٌ, as إِهْلِيلَجٌ [q. v.] and إِبْرِيسَمٌ; (Ṣ; [but I find that in two copies of that work, and in the L, this passage is mutilated; for it runs thus; "ISk says that it is إِبْرِيسَمٌ, with kesr to the ء and ر, and with fet-ḥ to the س," &c.;]) or one of its dial. forms is إِبْرِيسِمٌ, with kesr to the ء and the ر and the س; but ISk disallows this, [or, probably, as appears from what has been said above, we should read here, "accord. to ISk, but others disallow this,"] saying that there is not in the language an instance of افعيلل with kesr to the [former] ل, but with fet-ḥ, as إِهْلِيلَجٌ and إِطْرِيفَلٌ; and the second form is أَبْرَيْسَمٌ, with fet-ḥ to those three letters; and the third is إِبْرَيْسَمٌ, with kesr to the ء, and fet-ḥ to the ر and the س; (Mṣb;) and IB [appears to indicate the second and third of these forms, for he] says that some pronounce ابريسم with fet-ḥ to the ء and the ر, and some pronounce it with kesr to the ء, and with fet-ḥ to the س; (TA;) *Silk;* syn. حَرِيرٌ: (M, Ḳ:) or, accord. to some, specially, *raw silk:* (TA:) [it is said that] حرير is the same as ابريسم: (Mṣb in art. حر:) or *dressed silk;* syn. ابريسم مَطْبُوخٌ: (Mgh and Mṣb in that art.:) or *stuff wholly composed of silk:* or *of which the woof is silk:* (Mgh in that art., from the Jemạ et-Tefáreeḳ:) [and it is also said that] قَزٌّ is the same as ابريسم: (Ḳ in art. قز:) or a kind thereof: (Ṣ in that art.:) or that whereof ابريسم is made: (Lth, Az, Mṣb, TA, all in that art.:) [medicinal properties are ascribed to it: it is said that] *it is exhilarating, warming to the body, moderate in temperament, and strengthening to the sight when used as a collyrium:* (Ḳ:) the word is arabicized, (Ṣ, Mṣb, Ḳ, [but in the last it is said, after the explanation of the meaning, "or it is arabicized,"]) from [the Persian] ابريشم [i. e. أَبْرِيشُمْ]: (TA:) and is perfectly decl., even if used as a proper name, in the manner of a surname, because it was arabicized in its indeterminate state, not like إِسْحَاقُ &c., which were arabicized in their determinate state, and are not used by the Arabs indeterminately. (Ṣ.)

إِبْرِيسَمِىٌّ or إِبْرِيسَمِىٌّ [&c.] *A manufacturer* [or *seller*] *of* ابريسم. (TA.)

مُبَرْسَمٌ A man *affected with the disease termed* بِرْسَامٌ; (Mgh, Mṣb, Ḳ;) as also مُبَلْسَمٌ. (Mṣb, TA.)

برش

1. بَرِشَ, aor. ـَ, inf. n. بَرَشٌ, i. q. بَرِصَ, aor. ـَ, inf. n. بَرَصٌ: (Mṣb:) [or rather, used allusively for the latter verb: see أَبْرَشُ. See also بَرَشٌ, below.]

9. ابرشّ, inf. n. إِبْرِشَاشٌ, *He* (a horse) *was,* or *became, marked with small specks, called* بَرَشٌ, *differing from the rest of his colour.* (Ṣ.)

بَرَشٌ, in the hair of a horse, *Small specks, differing from the rest of the colour;* (Ṣ, Ḳ;) as also ↓ بُرْشَةٌ: (Ḳ:) or both signify *a colour in which one speck is red and another black* or *dust-coloured* or *the like.* (TA.) — And hence, (TA,) the former, (A, TA,) or ↓ both, (Ḳ,) *A whiteness that appears upon the nails.* (Ibráheem El-Ḥarbee, A, Ḳ.) — And the former, *White specks in the skin.* (A.) — [See also 1.]

بُرْشَةٌ: see بَرَشٌ, in two places.

بَرِيشٌ: see أَبْرَشُ.

أَبْرَشُ, applied to a horse, (Ṣ, Ḳ,) or to one of the sort termed بِرْذَوْن, (Lḥ,) *Marked with the small specks termed* بَرَش; (Lḥ, Ṣ, K;) as also ↓ بَرِيشٌ. (Ḳ.) Also, شَاةٌ بَرْشَآءُ *A ewe,* or *she-goat, marked with specks of various colours.* (TA.) And حَيَّةٌ بَرْشَآءُ *A serpent black speckled with white,* or *white speckled with black.* (TA.) — [Hence,] i. q. أَبْرَصُ: fem. بَرْشَآءُ: pl. بُرْشٌ: (Mṣb:) [or rather, used allusively for أَبْرَص; for] Jedheemeh (Ṣ, A, Ḳ) Ibn-Málik (Ṣ, TA) Ibn-Fahm, (TA,) the king [of El-Ḥeereh], (Ḳ,) was surnamed الأَبْرَشُ in allusion to his being أَبْرَص; (Ṣ, A, Ḳ;) the Arabs fearing to apply to him this latter epithet: (Ḳ:) or he was thus called because he was marked with black or red specks caused by a burn. (Kh.) — مَكَانٌ أَبْرَشُ *A place of various colours, abounding in plants* or *herbage:* (Ḳ:) and أَرْضٌ بَرْشَآءُ, and سَنَةٌ بَرْشَآءُ, *land,* and *a year, in which is abundance of herbage* (Ks, Ḳ) *of various colours;* (Ks;) as also رَمْشَآءُ and رَشْآءُ. (TA.)

برص

1. بَرِصَ, (Ṣ, [so in two copies, in one mentioned by Freytag بَرُصَ, which is a mistake,] M, Mṣb, Ḳ,) aor. ـَ, (Mṣb, Ḳ,) inf. n. بَرَصٌ, (M, Mṣb,) *He* (a man, Ṣ) *was,* or *became, affected with* بَرَص [or *leprosy* (see بَرَص below)]. (Ṣ, M, Mṣb, Ḳ.) [See also بَرِشَ.]

2. بَرَّصَ رَأْسَهُ, (A,) inf. n. تَبْرِيصٌ, (Ḳ,) ‡ *He shaved his head.* (Ibn-'Abbád, A, Ṣgh, Ḳ.) — بَرَّصَ المَطَرُ الأَرْضَ, (TḲ,) inf. n. as above, (Ḳ,) † *The rain fell upon the land before it was ploughed,* or *tilled.* (Ibn'-Abbád, Ṣgh, Ḳ.)

4. ابرص *He begot a child that was* أَبْرَص [or *leprous*]. (Ḳ.) — ابرصهُ اللّٰهُ *God rendered him,* or *caused him to be* or *become,* أَبْرَص [or *leprous*]. (Ṣ, Ḳ.)

5. تبرّص الأَرْضَ ‡ *He* (a camel, A, TA) *found no pasture in the land without depasturing it;* (Ṣgh, Ḳ;) *left no pasture in the land.* (A.)

بَرْصٌ, with fet-ḥ, *A certain small reptile* (دُوَيْبَّةٌ) *that is in the well.* (Ibn-'Abbád, Ṣgh, Ḳ. [In the CḲ, فى البَعِيرِ is put by mistake for فى البِئْرِ.]) [Perhaps it is the same as is called بُرْص, (see this word below,) which may be a vulgar pronunciation; and if so, this may be the reason why the author of the Ḳ has added, contr. to his usual rule, "with fet-ḥ."]

بُرْصٌ i. q. وَزَغَةٌ [*A lizard of the species called gecko, of a leprous hue,* as its name برص indicates; so applied in the present day]; (TA;) and أَبُو بَرِيصٍ, ↓ (M,) or ↓ أَبُو بُرَيْصٍ, (TA,) is *a surname of the same.* (M, TA.) [See also بَرْص; and see سَامُّ أَبْرَصَ, voce أَبْرَصُ; and بُرَيْصَةٌ.]

بَرَصٌ [*Leprosy;* particularly the *malignant species thereof termed "leuce;"*] *a certain disease,* (Ṣ, TA,) *well known,* (TA,) *which is a whiteness;* (Ṣ;) *a whiteness incident in the skin;* (M;) *a whiteness which appears upon the exterior of the body, by reason of a corrupt state of constitution.* (A, Ḳ.) — ‡ *What has become white, in a beast, in consequence of his being bitten.* (Ḳ, TA.)

بُرْصَةٌ † i. q. بَلُّوقَةٌ; (ISh;) pl. بِرَاصٌ, (ISh, Ḳ,) which signifies *White places,* (ISh,) or *portions distinct from the rest,* (Ḳ,) *in sand, which give growth to nothing.* (ISh, Ḳ.) — The pl. also signifies † *The alighting-places of the jinn,* or *genii:* (Ḳ:) [reminding us of our fairy-rings:] in which sense, also, it is pl. of بَرْصَةٌ. (TA.) — Also, the sing., † *An aperture in clouds,* or *mist, through which the face of the sky is seen.* (M, TA.)

بَرَصَةٌ: see سَامُّ أَبْرَصَ, voce أَبْرَصُ.

بَرِيصٌ *A shining,* or *glistening;* syn. بَصِيصٌ (A, Ḳ) and بَرِيقٌ. (A.) — Also *A certain plant, resembling the* سُعْد [or *cyperus*], (AA, Ḳ,) *growing in channels of running water.* (AA.) — أَبُو بَرِيصٍ: see بُرْص.

بُرَيْصٌ dim. of أَبْرَصُ, q. v. — أَبُو بُرَيْصٍ: see بُرْص. — أَبُو بُرَيْصٍ is also the name of *A certain bird, otherwise called* بلعة, [so written in the TA, without any syll. signs,] accord. to IKh, and mentioned in the Ḳ in art. بلص. (TA.)

بُرَيْصَةٌ *A certain small reptile* (دَابَّةٌ صَغِيرَةٌ), *smaller than the* وَزَغَة; *when it bites a thing, the latter is not cured.* (M, TA.) [See also بُرْص; and see سَامُّ أَبْرَصَ, voce أَبْرَصُ.]

أَبْرَصُ [*Leprous;*] *having the disease called* بَرَص: (Ṣ, M, Ḳ:) fem. بَرْصَآءُ: (M, Mṣb:) pl. بُرْصٌ (Mṣb, TA) and بُرْصَانٌ. (TA.) — سَامُّ أَبْرَصَ, (Ṣ, M, Mṣb, Ḳ,) the former word being decl., prefixed to the latter as governing it in the gen. case; (Ṣ, Mṣb;) and سَامَّ أَبْرَصَ, as one word, the former being indecl. with fet-ḥ for its termination, and the latter being imperfectly decl., (Ṣ, Mṣb,) in this and in the former instance; (Mṣb;) and سِمُّ أَبْرَصَ; (as in some copies of the Ḳ in art. سم;) i. q. الوَزَغَةُ [*The species of lizard described above, voce* بُرْص]: (M, and so in the JK and Ḳ in art.

وزغ:) or *such as are large, of the* وَزَغ [whereof وَزَغَةٌ is the n. un.]: (A, Mṣb:) or [*one*] *of the large* [*sorts*] *of the* وَزَغ: (Ṣ, Ḳ:) determinate, as a generic appellation: (Ṣ, TA:) Aṣ says, I know not why it is so called: (TA:) [the reason seems to be its leprous hue: see بَرَصٌ:] its blood and its urine have a wonderful effect when put into the orifice of the penis of a child suffering from difficulty in voiding his urine, (Ḳ, TA,) relieving him immediately; (TA;) and its head, pounded, when put upon a member, causes to come forth a thing that has entered into it and become concealed therein, such as a thorn and the like: (Ḳ:) the dual is سَامَّا أَبْرَصَ: (Ṣ, M, Mṣb, Ḳ:) and the pl. is سَوَامُّ أَبْرَصَ, (Ṣ, M, A, Mṣb, Ḳ,) ابرص having no dual form nor pl.; (M;) or, (Ḳ,) or sometimes, (Mṣb,) or if you will you may say, (Ṣ,) السَّوَامُّ, without mentioning ابرص; and ↓البِرَصَةُ; (Ṣ, Mṣb, Ḳ;) and الأَبَارِصُ; (Ṣ, M, A, Mṣb, Ḳ;) without mentioning سَامّ; (Ṣ, Mṣb, Ḳ;) the last of these pls. being as though formed from a rel. n., [namely, أَبْرَصِىٌّ,] although without [the termination] ة, like as they said المَهَالِبُ [for المَهَالِبَةُ]. (M.) — الأَبْرَصُ *The moon.* (A, Ṣgh, Ḳ.) [So called because of its mottled hue.] You say, بِتُّ لَا مُؤْنِسِى إِلَّا الأَبْرَصُ [*I passed the night, none but the moon cheering me by its presence*]. (A, TA.) — حَيَّةٌ بَرْصَآءُ *A serpent having in it,* (Ḳ,) i. e., *in its skin,* (M, TA,) *white places, distinct from the general colour.* (M, Ḳ, TA.) — أَرْضٌ بَرْصَآءُ ‡ *Land bare of herbage;* (A;) *of which the herbage has been depastured* (Ḳ, TA) *in some places, so that it has become bare thereof.* (TA.)

برطل

Q. 1. بَرْطَلَ, (inf. n. بَرْطَلَةٌ, TḲ,) *He placed a long stone* (بِرْطِيل) *in the fore part* (إِزَآء, q. v.,) *of his watering-trough.* (Lth, Ḳ.) = [*He gave him a* بِرْطِيل, or *bribe;*] *he bribed* him. (Ḳ.) And بُرْطِلَ *He was bribed.* (TA.)

Q. 2. تَبَرْطَلَ *He received a* [بِرْطِيل, or] *bribe.* (Ḳ.)

بِرْطِيلٌ *A long stone:* pl. بَرَاطِيلُ: (Ṣ:) or *a broad stone:* (TA in art. برم:) or *a stone* (Seer, A, Ḳ) *of an oblong form* (A, TA) *a cubit in length,* (Seer, TA,) or *an iron, long, broad, and hard by nature,* (Ḳ,) *not such as is made long, or sharpened* or *made sharp-pointed, by men,* (TA,) *with which the millstone is pecked* (تُنْقَرُ) [i. e., *wrought into shape, and roughened in its surface, by pecking*]): so says Lth: (TA:) to this is sometimes likened the muzzle, or fore part of the nose and mouth, of a she-camel of high breed: (Lth, TA:) [and hence,] it signifies also † the *muzzle,* or *fore part of the nose and mouth, of an old bear:* (TA:) some say that the dual signifies *two elongated stones, of the hardest kind, slender, and sharp-pointed, with which the millstone is pecked* (تُنْقَرُ [explained above]). (TA.) Also, (Ḳ,) accord. to Sh, (TA,) *A pickaxe,* or *stonecutter's pick;* syn. مِعْوَل: (Sh, Mṣb, Ḳ:) pl. as above: accord. to IAạr, *what is called in Persian* اسكنه [app. a mistranscription, or a dial. var., of إِسْكَنَك]. (TA.) = *A bribe;* syn. رِشْوَةٌ: (Mṣb, Ḳ:) app. mentioned in the Ḳ as an Arabic word; and if so, the pronunciation with fet-ḥ to the ب is a vulgarism, since there is no such measure as فَعْلِيلٌ: Abu-l-'Alà El-Ma'arree says that it is not known in this sense in the [classical] language of the Arabs; and it seems as though it were taken from the same word signifying "an oblong stone;" as though the bribe were likened to a stone that is thrown: (TA:) or it seems as though it were taken from the same word signifying a مِعْوَل; because therewith a thing is got out; (Mṣb;) and so El-Munáwee asserts it to be: (TA:) pl. as above. (Mṣb, Ḳ.) Hence the phrase, أَلْقَمَهُ البِرْطِيلَ [*He tipt him the bribe; conveyed it to him in like manner as one puts a morsel into another's mouth;* somewhat like our phrase *he greased his fist*]. (TA.) And the saying, البَرَاطِيلُ تَنْصُرُ الأَبَاطِيلَ [*Bribes render victorious false allegations*]: (Mṣb, TA:) a prov. (Mṣb.)

مُبَرْطَلُ الرَّأْسِ A man *having a long head.* (A in art. كوز.)

برع

1. بَرَعَ الجَبَلَ *He ascended,* or *ascended upon, the mountain.* (TA.) — And بَرَعَ صَاحِبَهُ *He was,* or *became, superior to his companion; he excelled him;* (IAạr;) *he overcame him.* (Ḳ.) = بَرَعَ, (Ṣ, Mṣb, Ḳ,) aor. ـَ; (Mṣb, MṢ, PṢ, [accord. to the TA, which is followed in the TḲ, ـُ, which is evidently a mistake,]) and بَرُعَ, aor. ـُ; (Ṣ, Mṣb, Ḳ;) and بَرِعَ, aor. ـَ; (Ṣgh, Ḳ;) inf. n. بُرُوعٌ, (M, Ḳ,) which is of بَرَعَ, (TA,) and بَرَاعَةٌ, (Ṣ, M, Mṣb, Ḳ,) which is of بَرُعَ [and is the more common]; (Mṣb, TA;) *He excelled in knowledge,* or *courage,* or *other qualities:* (Mṣb:) or *he excelled his companions in knowledge &c.:* (Ṣ, Ḳ:) or *he was,* or *became, accomplished, perfect,* or *complete, in every excellence,* and *in goodliness.* (M, Ḳ.)

5. تبرّع بِالعَطَآءِ *He gave what was not incumbent,* or *obligatory, on him; he gave supererogatorily:* (Ḳ:) or *he gave gratuitously, unasked,* or *unbidden:* (TA:) *as though he affected* بَرَاعَة [or *excellence*] *therein, and generosity.* (Z, TA.) And تبرّع بِالأَمْرِ *He did,* or *performed, the thing,* or *affair, disinterestedly; not seeking,* or *desiring, a compensation.* (Mṣb.) And تبرّع بِالجِهَادِ [*He engaged unbidden,* or *disinterestedly, in war against unbelievers*]. (Mṣb in art. طوع.)

بَرِيعَةٌ: see بَارِعٌ.

بَارِعٌ Anything *overtopping.* (IAạr.) — *Excelling in knowledge,* or *courage,* or *other qualities:* (Mṣb:) or *excelling his companions in knowledge &c.:* (Ṣ, Ḳ:) or *accomplished, perfect,* or *complete, in every excellence,* and *in goodliness:* (Ḳ:) fem. with ة. (Ḳ.) And ↓بَرِيعَةٌ, applied to a woman, (IAạr,) *Excelling in goodliness,* or *beauty,* and *in intelligence.* (IAạr, Ḳ.) And بَارِعَةٌ, applied to a girl, *Goodly,* or *beautiful.* (TA.) — أَمْرٌ بَارِعٌ *A case, a state,* or *condition,* or *an affair, exalted,* or *of high estimation;* (TA;) *goodly,* or *comely.* (Ḳ, TA.) — سَعْدُ البَارِعِ *A certain* نَجْم [or *asterism*]. (TA, [in which it is here said to be "of the Mansions," i. e., of the Mansions of the Moon; but it seems that لَيْسَ, or the like, has been omitted by a copyist; for it is said in art. سعد, (q. v.,) on several authorities, to be not of the Mansions of the Moon.])

هٰذَا أَبْرَعُ مِنْهُ *This is larger, bigger,* or *more bulky, than he,* or *it.* (Ḳ, TA.)

فَعَلَهُ مُتَبَرِّعًا *He did it without its being incumbent,* or *obligatory, on him; supererogatorily:* or *gratuitously, unasked,* or *unbidden:* or *disinterestedly; not seeking,* or *desiring, a compensation:* syn. مُتَطَوِّعًا. (Ṣ, Ḳ.)

برعم

Q. 1. بَرْعَمَتِ الشَّجَرَةُ *The tree put forth its* بَرَاعِيم [pl. of بُرْعُومٌ], (Ṣ,) or *its* بُرْعُمَة. (M, Ḳ.)

بُرْعُمٌ: and بُرْعُمَةٌ: see what next follows.

بُرْعُومٌ and ↓بُرْعُمٌ (Ṣ, Ḳ) and ↓بُرْعُومَةٌ and ↓بُرْعُمَةٌ (Ḳ) The *calyx of the fruit,* or *produce, of a tree:* (Ḳ:) and *blossoms,* or *white blossoms,* syn. نَوْرٌ, (Ḳ, TA,) *before they open:* (TA:) or *flowers,* (Ṣ, and Mṣb in explanation of the first word in art. زهر,) or the *flower of a tree,* (Ḳ,) *before the opening thereof:* (Ṣ, Mṣb ubi suprà, Ḳ:) pl. بَرَاعِيمُ. (Ṣ, TA.) — بَرَاعِيمُ also signifies The *heads,* or *tops;* or *round, high, slender tops;* or *peaks;* (شَمَارِيخ;) of mountains: (AZ, Ḳ:) sing. ↓بُرْعُومَةٌ. (AZ, TA.)

بُرْعُومَةٌ: see بُرْعُومٌ, in two places.

برغث

بُرْغُوثٌ, (Ṣ, Ḳ,) also, accord. to Es-Suyooṭee, with fet-ḥ and with kesr to the first letter, and Dmr says the like; [so that it is app. written also بَرْغُوثٌ, as it is commonly pronounced by the vulgar, though it is generally said that there is no word of this measure except صَعْفُوق; and بِرْغَوْثٌ, like بِرْذَوْنٌ, for there is no word of the measure فِعْلُول;] but each of these two forms requires proof; (MF;) [like the Hebr. פַּרְעֹשׁ which, accord. to Gesenius, is undoubtedly from an Æthiopic root signifying "to spring," "to dance;" The *flea;*] *a certain insect* (دُوَيْبَّة), *resembling the* حُرْقُوص; (TA;) *well known:* (Ḳ:) [a coll. gen. n.: n. un. with ة:] pl. بَرَاغِيثُ. (Ṣ.)

برق

1. بَرَقَ, (Ṣ, Mgh, Ḳ,) aor. ـُ, (Ṣ, Mgh,) inf. n. بُرُوقٌ, (Ṣ,) or بَرِيقٌ, (Mgh, Ḳ,) or this is a simple subst., (Ṣ,) and بَرْقٌ and بَرَقَانٌ, (Ḳ, TA, but in

the CK بَرُوق, as in the Ṣ,) *It* (a thing, Mgh, Ḳ, a sword, &c., Ṣ, and the dawn, Ḳ, TA) *shone, gleamed,* or *glistened.* (Ṣ, Mgh, Ḳ, TA.) — Also said of a cloud, aor. as above, inf. n. بَرِيق and بَرْق and بَرَقَان, *It gleamed* or *shone* [*with lightning*]; and so ▼ ابرق, (JK,) and ▼ تبرّق. (Ḳ in art. حلج.) And بَرَقَتِ السَّمَآءُ, (Ṣ, Mṣb, Ḳ,) aor. as above, (Mṣb, TA,) inf. n. بَرَقَان (Aṣ, Ṣ, Mṣb, Ḳ) and بَرْق (Mṣb, TA) and بُرُوق, (Ḳ,) *The sky lightened;* (Mṣb, Ḳ;) as also ▼ ابرقت: (AO, AA, Ḳ:) or *gleamed* or *shone* [*with lightning*]: (Ṣ, Ḳ:) or *lightened much* before rain; as also ▼ ابرقت. (TA in art. رعد.) And بَرَقَ البَرْقُ *The lightning appeared.* (Ḳ.) — And [hence] said of a man, (JK, Mṣb, Ḳ,) or رَعَدَ وَبَرَقَ, (Ṣ,) ‡ *He threatened;* (JK, Ṣ, Ḳ;) or *he threatened with evil;* (Mṣb;) [or *he threatened and menaced;*] or *he frightened* (Ṣ and Ḳ in art. رعد) *and threatened;* (Ṣ in that art.;) and ▼ ابرق signifies the same; (JK, Mṣb, Ḳ;) and so أَرْعَدَ وَأَبْرَقَ: (Ḳ:) or, accord. to Aṣ, ارعد and ابرق are not allowable. (TA, and Ṣ in art. رعد, q. v.) But بَرَقَتْ, inf. n. بَرْق, said of a woman, (Ḳ,) or رَعَدَتْ وَبَرَقَتْ, (Ṣ,) means ‡ *She beautified* (Ṣ and A in art. رعد, and Ḳ) *and adorned herself,* (Ṣ, Ḳ,) [as also ▼ تبرّقت, (occurring in the Ḳ in art. الق, coupled with its syn. تَزَيَّنَتْ,)] *and showed,* or *presented, herself,* (A in art. رعد, and TA,) لِى *to me:* (A in art. رعد:) or *she exhibited her beauty intentionally:* (TA:) and ▼ برّقت means the same, (Lḥ, Ḳ,) inf. n. تَبْرِيق; (TA;) and so ▼ ابرقت: (Ḳ:) you say, ▼ ابرقت بِوَجْهِهَا وَسَائِرِ جِسْمِهَا ‡ *She beautified herself in her face and the rest of her person:* (Lḥ, TA:) and ▼ ابرقت عَنْ وَجْهِهَا ‡ *She showed her face.* (JK, Ibn-'Abbád, Ḳ.) — Also, said of a star, or an asterism, *It rose.* (Lḥ, Ḳ.) One says, لَا أَفْعَلُهُ مَا بَرَقَ النَّجْمُ فِى السَّمَآءِ *I will not do it as long as the star,* or *asterism,* [by which may be meant *the asterism of the Pleiades,*] *rises in the sky.* (Lḥ, TA.) — بَرِقَ البَصَرُ, (Ṣ,) or بَصَرُهُ, (Ḳ,) *The eye or eyes,* or *his eye* or *eyes, glistened,* (Ṣ, Ḳ,) *being raised,* or *fixedly open:* (Ṣ:) or *became raised,* or *fixedly open:* occurring in the Ḳur [lxxv. 7], accord. to one reading: (Fr, TA:) or *the eye,* or *his eye, became open by reason of fright.* (TA.) بَرِقَ has a different meaning, which see below. (Ṣ.) — بَرَقَتْ, said of a she-camel, *She put her tail between her thighs, making it to cleave to her belly, without being pregnant:* (IAạr, TA:) or *she raised her tail, and feigned herself pregnant, not being so;* as also ▼ ابرقت, (Lḥ, Ṣ, Ḳ,) and ابرقت بِذَنَبِهَا: (TA:) or ابرقت signifies *she smote with her tail at one time upon her vulva and another time upon her buttocks;* and also, *she feigned herself pregnant, not being so.* (JK.) — بَرِقَ *He feared, so that he was astonished* or *amazed* or *stupified, at seeing the gleam of lightning:* (TA voce بَحِرَ:) or *his* (a man's) *sight became confused in consequence of his looking at lightning.* (Bḍ in lxxv. 7.) And hence, (Bḍ ibid.,) بَرِقَ البَصَرُ, (Ṣ, Bḍ,) or بَصَرُهُ, (Ḳ,) aor. ـَ; (Ṣ, Ḳ;) and بَرَقَ, aor. ـُ; (Ḳ;) or the latter has [only] a meaning explained above; (Ṣ;) inf. n. بَرَق, which is of the former verb; (Ṣ;) accord. to the Ḳ, بَرْق; but this is wrong; (TA;) and [of the latter verb,] بُرُوق; (Lḥ, Ḳ;) *The eye or eyes,* or *his eye* or *eyes, became dazzled, so as not to close,* or *move, the lid,* or *lids:* (Ṣ, Ḳ:) or *became confused, so as not to see.* (Ḳ.) بَرِقَ بَصَرُهُ signifies also *His eye* or *eyes,* or *his sight, became weak:* whence بَرِقَتْ قَدَمَاهُ *His two feet became weak.* (TA.) Also بَرِقَ alone, (TA,) inf. n. بَرَق, (Fr, Ḳ, TA,) *He* (a man, TA) *was frightened;* or *he feared,* or *was afraid:* (Fr, Ḳ, TA:) and *he became confounded,* or *perplexed, and unable to see his right course.* (Ḳ.) — بَرِقَ said of a skin, aor. ـَ, (JK, Ḳ,) inf. n. بَرَق, (JK,) so in the O, in which, as in the Ḳ, the part. n., being بَرِق, indicates that the verb is like فَرِحَ; (TA;) and بَرَقَ, (Ḳ,) so in the L, (TA,) aor. ـُ, (Ḳ,) inf. n. بَرْق and بُرُوق; thus in the L, which indicates that the verb is like نَصَرَ; (TA;) *It became affected by the heat so that its butter melted and became decomposed,* (Aṣ, JK, Ḳ,) *and did not become compact.* (Ḳ.) — بَرَقَهُ بِزَيْتٍ أَوْ سَمْنٍ, (Ṣ, Ḳ,) or بَرَقَ طَعَامًا, (JK,) aor. ـُ, (JK,) inf. n. بَرْق (JK, Ṣ) and بُرُوق, (L,) *He poured upon the food,* (JK,) or *put into it,* (Ṣ,* Ḳ,) *somewhat,* (JK,) or *a small quantity,* (Ṣ, Ḳ,) *of olive-oil* (JK, Ṣ, Ḳ) or *of clarified butter.* (Ṣ, Ḳ.) And بَرَقْتُ لَهُ *I made his food* [*somewhat*] *greasy for him with clarified butter.* (TA.) And أَبْرِقُوا المَآءَ بِزَيْتٍ *Pour ye upon the water a little olive-oil.* (Ṣ.) — بَرِقَتِ الغَنَمُ, aor. ـَ, (Ṣ, Ḳ,) inf. n. بَرَق, (Ṣ,) *The sheep,* or *goats, had a complaint in their bellies from eating the* بَرْوَق: (Ṣ, Ḳ:) and in like manner, الإِبِلُ *the camels.* (TA.)

2. برّق بِعَيْنَيْهِ, (JK,) or بَصَرَهُ, (TA,) *He glistened with his eyes by reason of looking hard,* or *intently.* (JK, TA.*) And برّق عَيْنَيْهِ, inf. n. تَبْرِيق, *He opened his eyes wide, and looked sharply,* or *intently.* (Lth, Ṣ, Ḳ.) — برّقت, said of a woman: see 1. — And برّق *He decorated,* or *adorned,* his place of abode. (El-Muärrij, Ḳ.) — بَرَّقْتَ وَعَرَّقْتَ *Thou madest a sign with a thing, that had nothing to verify it,* [app. meaning *thou madest a false display,* or *a vain promise,*] *and didst little.* (IAạr.) — Also برّق, (inf. n. as above, TA,) *He* (a man) *journeyed far.* (El-Muärrij, Ḳ.) — برّق فِى المَعَاصِى *He persisted,* or *persevered, in acts of disobedience.* (El-Muärrij, Ḳ.) — برّق بِىَ الأَمْرُ *The affair was unattainable,* or *impracticable, to me.* (Ḳ.)

4: see 1, in eight places. — ابرق, (Aboo-Naṣr, Ṣ, Ḳ,) or ابرق بِسَيْفِهِ, (JK,) said of a man, (Aboo-Naṣr, JK, Ṣ,) *He made a sign with his sword* [*by waving it about so as to make it glisten*]. (Aboo-Naṣr, JK, Ṣ, Ḳ.) — And ابرق *He betook himself,* or *directed his course, towards the lightning.* (TA.) — *He entered into* [*a tract wherein was*] *lightning.* (TA.) — *He saw lightning.* (TA.) Ṭufeyl uses the phrase أَبْرَقْنَ الخَرِيفَ as meaning *They* (women borne in vehicles upon camels) *saw the lightning of* [*the season,* or *the rain, called*] *the* خريف. (AAF, TA.) — *He was smitten,* or *assailed,* or *affected, by lightning.* (Ṣ, Ḳ.) — ابرقهُ الفَزَعُ [app. *Fright,* or *fear, made him to be confounded,* or *perplexed, and unable to see his right way:* see بَرِقَ.]. (TA.) — [And hence, perhaps,] ابرق الصَّيْدَ *He roused the game,* or *chase.* (Ḳ.)

5: see 1, in two places.

10. استبرق *It* (a place, and the horizon,) *shone,* or *gleamed, with lightning.* (TA.)

بَرْقٌ [*Lightning;*] *what gleams in the clouds,* (TA,) or, *from the clouds;* from بَرَقَ [in the first of the senses explained above], said of a thing, inf. n. [بَرْق and] بَرِيق: (Bḍ in ii. 18:) or *an angel's smiting the clouds, and putting them in motion, in order that they may become propelled, so that thou seest the fires* [*issue from them*]: (Mujáhid, Ḳ:) or *a whip of light with which the angel drives the clouds:* (I 'Ab, TA:) sing. of بُرُوق, i. e., of the بروق of the clouds: (Ṣ, Ḳ:) or it has no pl., being originally an inf. n. (Bḍ ubi suprà.) بَرْقُ خُلَّبٍ and بَرْقُ الخُلَّبِ and بَرْقٌ خُلَّبٌ signify *That* [*lightning*] *which is without rain.* (Ṣ. [See also art. خلب.])

بُرْقٌ [*Lizards of the species called*] ضِبَاب, pl. of ضَبّ. (IAạr, Ḳ.) It is app. pl. of بَرُوق or of أَبْرَق: more probably, I think, of the former; from the raising of the tail, which is a habit of those lizards.] — See also بُرْقَة.

بَرَقٌ *A lamb;* syn. حَمَلٌ [q. v.]: (Ṣ, Ḳ:) a Persian word, (Ṣ,) arabicized; (Ṣ, Ḳ;) originally بَرَه: (Ḳ:) pl. [of mult.] بُرْقَان (Ṣ, Ḳ) and بِرْقَان and [of pauc.] أَبْرَاق. (Ḳ.)

بَرِقٌ [part. n. of بَرِقَ: and particularly explained as meaning] A skin *affected by the heat so that its butter melts and becomes decomposed,* (JK, O, Ḳ,) *and does not become compact.* (Ḳ.)

بَرْقَةٌ [app. an inf. n. of un., signifying *A flash of lightning*]. (M, TA in art. وبص.) — *A fit of confusion,* or *perplexity, affecting one in such a manner that he is unable to see his right course.* (Ḳ,* TA.)

بُرْقَةٌ *A quantity of lightning:* (Bḍ in xxiv. 43, TA:) pl. ▼ بُرْق; (TA;) or [this is a coll. gen. n., of which the former is the n. un.; or, probably, it is a mistranscription, and] the pl. is بُرَق, also pronounced بُرْق. (Bḍ ubi suprà.) — *Rugged ground in which are stones and sand and earth mixed together,* (Ṣ, Ḳ, TA,) *the stones thereof mostly white, but some being red, and black, and the earth white and of a whitish dust-colour, and sometimes by its side are meadows* (رَوْض); (TA;) as also ▼ أَبْرَق and ▼ بَرْقَآءُ: (Ṣ, Ḳ, TA:) or *a portion of such land* (أَرْض) *as is termed* ▼ بَرْقَآءُ, *which consists of tracts containing black stones mixed with white sand, and which, when spacious, is termed* ▼ أَبْرَق: (JK:) [and] *a mountain mixed with sand;* as also ▼ أَبْرَق: (IAạr, TA:) the pl. of بُرْقَة is بُرَق (Ḳ, TA) and بِرَاق; (JK, Ṣ;) and that of ▼ ابرق is أَبَارِق, (JK, Ṣ, Ḳ,) after the manner of a subst., because the quality of a subst. is predominant in it; (TA;) and that of ▼ برقآء is بَرْقَاوَات. (Aṣ, IAạr, Ṣ, Ḳ.) The بُرْق of the country of the Arabs are more than a hundred; and are distinguished by particular adjuncts, as بُرْقَةُ الأَثْمَادِ and بُرْقَةُ الأَجَاوِلِ &c. (Ḳ.) One says قُنْفُذُ بُرْقَةٍ [*A hedge-hog of a* برقة], like as one says ضَبُّ كُدْيَةٍ. (Ṣ.) —— [The *colour denoted by the epithet* أَبْرَقُ: in a mountain, *a mixture of blackness and whiteness*: see حُقْبَةٌ, voce أَحْقَبُ.] ═ *Paucity of grease or gravy* (JK, TA) *in food.* (TA.)

بُرْقَانٌ *Shining much in the body*: (JK, Ḳ:) applied to a man. (JK.) ═ *Locusts when they become yellow, and have variegated stripes* or *streaks*: (JK:) or *locusts that are variegated* (Ḳ, TA) *with white and black*: (TA:) [a coll. gen. n.:] n. un. with ة. (Ḳ.) —— [See also بُرُقٌ, of which it is a pl.]

بَرْقُوقٌ, (Ḳ,) with ḍamm, (TA,) [vulg. بُرْقُوق, The *plum*; or] *small* إِجَّاص [or *plums*]; (Ḳ;) *known in Syria by the name of* جانرك: (TA:) and (as some say, TA) the مِشْمِش [or *apricot*]: a post-classical word [probably arabicized from the Persian بَرْقُوق, which is applied to both the fruits above mentioned]. (Ḳ.)

البُرَاقُ *A certain beast which Mohammad rode on the night of the ascension* [*to heaven*]; (Ṣ, Mṣb,* Ḳ;) or *which the apostles ride in ascending to heaven; resembling a mule*; (Mṣb;) or *less than the mule, but greater than the ass*: (Ḳ:) so called because of the intense whiteness of his hue, and his great brightness; or because of the quickness of his motion; in respect of both of which he is likened to lightning. (TA.)

بَرُوقٌ A she-camel *raising her tail, and feigning herself pregnant, not being so*; as also ↓ مُبْرِقٌ: (Ṣ, Ḳ:) and ↓ بَارِقٌ a she-camel *putting her tail between her thighs, making it to cleave to her belly, not being pregnant*: (IAạr, TA:) pl. of the first بُرُقٌ; (TA;) and of the second مَبَارِيقُ. (Ṣ, Ḳ.) The Arabs say, دَعْنِى مِنْ تَكْذَابِكَ وَتَأْثَامِكَ شَوْلَانَ البَرُوقِ [*Let me alone and cease from thy lying and thy sin like the she-camel's raising of her tail and feigning herself pregnant when she is not so*]: شولان being in the accus. case as an inf. n.: i. e., thou art in the predicament of the she-camel that raises her tail so as to make one imagine her to be pregnant when she is not so. (TA.) The pl. بُرُقٌ is also applied to scorpions, as meaning *Raising their tails like the she-camel termed* بروق. (TA.) —— Also, applied to a man, *Fearful*, or *timid*; (JK;) or *cowardly*. (TA.)

بَرْوَقٌ *A certain kind of plant* (JK, Ṣ) *which camels do not feed upon except in cases of necessity*; (JK;) *a small, feeble tree, which, when the sky becomes clouded, grows green*: (Ḳ:) n. un. with ة: (Ṣ, Ḳ:) it was described by an Arab of the desert to AḤn as follows: *a feeble, juicy plant, having slender branches, at the heads of which are small envelopes* (قَمَاعِيلُ صِغَارٌ) *like chick-peas, in which is a kind of black grain: its feebleness is such that it withers on the spot when the sun becomes hot upon it: and nothing feeds upon it; but men, when they are afflicted with dearth*, or *drought, express from it a bitter juice, then work it together*, or *knead it, with* هَبِيد [or *colocynths*, or the *pulp*, or *seeds, thereof*], *or some other thing, and eat it; but it is not eaten alone, because it occasions excitement: it is one of the plants that are plentiful in time of drought and scarce in time of fruitfulness; when copious rain falls upon it, it dies; and when we see it to have become abundant, and coarse*, or *rough, we fear drought*: accord. to another of the Arabs of the desert, the بَرْوَقَة *is a bad kind of herb*, or *leguminous plant, that grows among the first of the herbs*, or *leguminous plants: it has a reed like the* سباط [so I render لها قصبة مثل السباط, but I think that the right reading is, لَهَا قُضُبٌ مِثْلُ السِّيَاطِ *it has twigs like whips*, agreeably with the description next preceding, in which it is said to have slender branches,] *and a black fruit*, or *produce*. (TA.) Hence, أَشْكَرُ مِنْ بَرْوَقَةٍ [*More grateful than a barwakah*]; (Ṣ, Ḳ;) because it grows green when it sees the clouds, (Ṣ,) or by means of the least moisture falling from the sky: (TA:) a prov. (Ṣ.) And أَضْعَفُ مِنْ بَرْوَقَةٍ [*Weaker than a barwakah*]. (TA.)

بَرِيقٌ [accord. to the Mgh and Ḳ an inf. n. of بَرَقَ, but accord. to the Ṣ a simple subst.,] *A shining, gleaming, glistening, glitter, lustre, brilliancy*, or *splendour*. (Ṣ, Ḳ, TA.)

بَرِيقَةٌ *Milk upon which is poured a little grease* or *clarified butter*: (ISk, Ṣ, Ḳ:) or *food in which is milk*: and such as has *a little clarified butter, and grease, put into it*: (TA:) or *food that has a little olive-oil poured upon it*: (JK:) or *condiment in which is put a little olive-oil* or *grease*: (L:) pl. بَرَائِقُ; (JK, Ṣ, L, Ḳ;) with which ↓ تَبَارِيقُ [pl. of ↓ تَبْرُوقٌ] is syn., (L, TA,) applied to food (Ṣ, TA) in which is put a little olive-oil or clarified butter: (Ṣ:) or ↓ تَبْرُوقٌ signifies the *grease in a cooking-pot*: and *water with a little olive-oil poured upon it*: and ↓ تَبَارِيقُ is its pl. (JK.)

بَرَّاقٌ *Shining, gleaming*, or *glistening, much*, or *intensely*. (TA.) See also إِبْرِيقٌ, and بَارِقٌ. —— فَتًى بَرَّاقُ الثَّنَايَا *A young man whose middle pairs of teeth are beautiful and bright, glistening, when he smiles, like lightning*: meant to imply cheerfulness of countenance. (TA.) —— بَرَّاقَةٌ A woman *characterized by beauty and splendour* or *brilliancy* [*of complexion* or *skin*]: (Ḳ,* TA:) or, as some say, *who shows her beauty intentionally*. (TA.) [See إِبْرِيقٌ.]

بَرْوَاقٌ *A certain plant also called* خُنْثَى [i. e. the *asphodel*, called by both these names in the present day]: *the eating of its fresh, juicy stalk, boiled with olive-oil and vinegar, counteracts jaundice; and the smearing with its root*, or *lower part, removes the two kinds of* بَهَق [q. v.]. (Ḳ.)

بَارِقٌ *Shining, gleaming*, or *glistening*. (Mgh.) —— Clouds (سَحَابٌ) *having*, or *containing*, [or *emitting*,] *lightning*. (Ṣ.) You say also سَحَابَةٌ بَارِقَةٌ [*A cloud having*, or *emitting, lightning*]: (Ṣ, TA:) and ↓ سحابة بَرَّاقَةٌ signifies the same [but in an intensive manner: see بَرَّاقٌ]. (TA.)

—— بَارِقَةٌ ‡ *Swords*: (Ṣ, Ḳ, TA:) so called because of their shining, or glistening: (TA:) pl. بَوَارِقُ; (JK, Ḥam p. 306;) applied to *swords* and *other weapons*. (Ḥam ubi suprà.) Hence the trad. of Ammár, الجَنَّةُ تَحْتَ البَارِقَةِ [‡*Paradise is beneath the swords*]; (JK, TA;) meaning, in warring in the cause of God. (JK.) You also say, رَأَيْتُ البَارِقَةَ, meaning *I saw the shining*, or *glistening, of the weapons*. (Lḥ, TA.) —— See also بَرُوقٌ.

بَوْرَقٌ, (JK, Mgh,) with fet-ḥ to the ب, (Mgh,) or بُورَقٌ, with ḍamm, (Ḳ,) *A certain thing*, or *substance, that is put into dough*, (JK, Mgh, TA,) *and causes it to become inflated*; (Mgh;) or *into flour*; (TA voce بَوْرَق;) [or this is a particular kind thereof, as appears from what follows: accord. to Golius, *nitrum* and *aphronitrum*: but] *it is of four kinds*; مَائِىٌّ [or the *water-kind*], and جَبَلِىٌّ [or the *mountain-kind*], and أَرْمَنِىٌّ [or *Armenian*], and مِصْرِىٌّ [or *Egyptian*], *which is the* نَطْرُون [q. v., i. e. *natron*]: (Ḳ:) *the best thereof is the* ارمنى; *and this is said to be meant by the term when it is used absolutely: this is called also* بورقُ الصَّاغَةِ [a term now applied to *borax*, as is بورق alone, and مِلْحُ الصَّاغَةِ], *because it polishes silver well* [*or because of its use in soldering*]: *the dust-coloured kind thereof is called* بورقُ الخَبَّازِينَ [*the* بورق *of the bakers*, or *makers of bread*]: *the* نطرون *is the red kind thereof: and there is a kind thereof having an oily quality: and a kind consisting of thin butyraceous fragments; and this, if light and hard, is the* إِفْرِيقِىّ: *and the best thereof is that which is produced in Egypt*: (TA:) *bruised*, or *powdered, the belly is smeared with it, near to a fire, and it expels worms: and moistened with honey or with oil of jasmine, the male organs of generation are anointed with it, for it is excellent for the venereal faculty*. (Ḳ.) ═ Also *A man in whom one does not trust*, or *confide*: pl. بَوَارِقُ. (JK.)

بُورَقِىٌّ [or بَوْرَقِىٌّ] *A seller of* بُورَق [or بَوْرَق]. (TA.)

أَبْرَقُ A rope (حَبْل) *having two colours*; (Ṣ, O;) *twisted with a black strand and a white strand*: (JK:) and in like manner, (JK,) a mountain (جَبَل, JK, Ḳ) *in which are two colours*, (Ḳ, TA,) *black and white*: (TA:) and (so in the Ṣ, but in the Ḳ "or,") anything *having blackness and whiteness together*. (Ṣ, Ḳ.) You say تَيْسٌ أَبْرَقُ and عَنْزٌ بَرْقَآءُ [*A black and white he-goat* and *she-goat*]: (Ṣ, Ḳ:) and شَاةٌ بَرْقَآءُ *a ewe whose white wool is cleft*, or *divided, by black flocks* [or *streaks*]: (Ḳ:) أَبْرَقُ and بَرْقَآءُ applied to sheep or goats are like أَبْلَقُ and بَلْقَآءُ applied to beasts of the equine kind, and أَبْقَعُ and بَقْعَآءُ to dogs. (Lḥ, TA.) —— بَرْقَآءُ is also a name given to *An eye*; (Ṣ, M;) because it has blackness and whiteness mingled in it: (M, TA:) dual بَرْقَاوَانِ. (TA.) And عَيْنٌ بَرْقَآءُ signifies *An eye black in the iris, with whiteness* [*of the rest*] *of the bulb*. (TA.) —— رَوْضَةٌ بَرْقَآءُ *A meadow*, or *garden, in which are two colours.* (TA.) — See also بُرْقَةٌ, in seven places. — أَبْرَقُ also signifies *A certain bird.* (Tekmileh, Ḳ.) — And [the pl.] بُرْقٌ is used as a name for The [*locusts, or crickets, termed*] جَنَادِب. (IB, TA.) == Also *A certain Persian medicine, good for the memory.* (Ṣgh, Ḳ.)

إِبْرِيقٌ, a Persian word, (Ṣ, Mṣb,) arabicized, (Ṣ, Mṣb, Ḳ,) originally آبْ رِيزْ; (CḲ; [in a MS. copy of the Ḳ and in the TA, incorrectly, آب رى;]) [*A ewer, such as is used for wine,* and also *such as is used for water to be poured on the hands; each having a long and slender spout, and a handle;*] *a well-known vessel;* (TA;) *a vessel having a spout* (Mgh, and Bḍ and Jel in lvi. 18) *and a handle:* (Bḍ and Jel ibid:) accord. to Kr, *a* كُوز; and so says AḤn in one place; but in another he says that it is *like a* كوز: (TA:) [it is *somewhat like a* كوز *with the addition of a spout:*] pl. أَبَارِيقُ (Ṣ, Mṣb) [and sometimes أَبَارِقَةٌ]. == *A sword such as is termed* ♦ بَرَّاق; (Ḳ;) i. e. (TA) *a sword that shines, gleams,* or *glistens, much,* or *intensely:* (Ṣ, Kr:) or simply *a sword:* or, as some say, *a bow:* (JK:) or it signifies also *a bow in which are* تَلَامِيع [or *places differing in colour from the rest, and,* app., *glistening*]: (Ḳ:) thus, accord. to Az, in a verse of 'Amr Ibn-Aḥmar: but correctly, accord. to Ṣgh, it has there the first of the significations explained in this sentence: and it is said, also, that سَيْفٌ إِبْرِيقٌ signifies *a sword having much lustre, and much diversified with wavy marks* or *streaks,* or *in its grain.* (TA.) — *A woman who is beautiful, and splendid,* or *brilliant,* (Lḥ, JK, Ḳ, TA,) *in colour* [or *complexion*]: (Lḥ, TA:) or, as some say, *who shows her beauty intentionally.* (TA.) [See also بَرَّاقَةٌ (voce بَرَّاقٌ).]

أُبَيْرِقٌ dim. of إِسْتَبْرَقٌ, q. v. (Ṣ, Ḳ.)

إِسْتَبْرَقٌ, (IDrd, Ṣ, Ḳ, &c.,) sometimes with the conjunctive ا, (TA,) *Thick* دِيبَاج [or *silk brocade*]: (Eḍ-Ḍaḥḥak, Ṣ, Ḳ, and so Bḍ and Jel in xviii. 30, &c.:) or ديباج *made* [or *interwoven*] *with gold:* (Ḳ:) or *closely-woven, thick, beautiful* ديباج *made* [or *interwoven*] *with gold:* (TA:) or *closely-woven cloths,* or *garments, of silk, like* ديباج: (IDrd, Ḳ:) or *thick silk:* (IAth, TA:) or *a red thong cut from an untanned skin* (قِدَّةٌ حَمْرَآءُ), *as though it were* [*composed of*] *pieces of bow-strings,* or *chords:* (Ibn-'Abbád, Ḳ:) it is an arabicized word, (IDrd, Ṣ, Ḳ,) from إِسْتَرْوَهْ, (IDrd, Ḳ,) which is Syriac; (IDrd, TA;) or from the Persian, (Ṣ, TA,) in which سِتَبْر and إِسْتَبْر signify "thick," absolutely, whence سِتَبْرَهْ and إِسْتَبْرَهْ are particularly applied to signify "thick ديباج," and then the latter is arabicized by substituting ق for the ه: so says Esh-Shiháb El-Khafájee: or the ا and س and ت are augmentative, and it is mentioned in the present art. in the Ṣ and Ḳ as though this were the case, agreeably with the form of its dim., which is said by J and in the Ḳ to be ♦ أُبَيْرِقٌ; for in forming the dim., a word is reduced to its root. (TA.)

تَبْرُوقٌ; pl. تَبَارِيقُ: see بُرَيْقَةٌ, in four places.

مَبْرِقٌ [*A shining, gleaming,* or *glistening:* or *a time thereof*]. You say, جَآءَ عِنْدَ مَبْرِقِ الصُّبْحِ [*He came at the shining,* &c., or *at the time of the shining,* &c., *of the dawn;* or] *when the dawn shone,* or *gleamed,* or *glistened.* (Ḳ, TA. [In the latter, مبرق is said to be here a meemee inf. n.])

مُبْرُوقٌ: see بُرُوقٌ.

برقش

Q. 1. بَرْقَشَهُ, (Ṣ, A, TA,) inf. n. بَرْقَشَةٌ, (TA,) *He variegated it with divers,* or *different, colours;* (Ṣ, TA;) from أَبُو بَرَاقِش, the bird so called: (Ṣ:) or *he adorned him,* or *it.* (A.) [See also بَرْقَشَةٌ, below.] — Hence, بَرْقَشَ قَوْلَهُ †*He embellished his saying.* (Ḥar p. 235.)

Q. 2. تَبَرْقَشَ *He adorned himself* (A, Ḳ) *with various colours.* (Ḳ.) You say, تَبَرْقَشَ لَنَا *He adorned himself with various colours for us:* (Ḳ:) or *with various colours of every kind.* (TA.) And تَبَرْقَشَتْ *She assumed various colours:* or *she varied in dispositions:* syn. تَلَوَّنَتْ. (A.) And تبرقش البَيْتُ *The house,* or *chamber,* or *tent, became variegated.* (TA.) And تبرقشت البِلَادُ *The countries became adorned with various colours;* from أَبُو بَرَاقِش. (TA.)

بِرْقِشٌ *A certain bird,* (Ṣ, Ḳ,) *different from that called* أَبُو بَرَاقِش, (Ḳ, accord. to the TA, [for we there read طَائِرٌ آخَرُ; the bird called ابو براقش having been mentioned before; but in the CḲ, in the place of آخَرُ, we find أَخْضَرُ, i. e., *green;*]) *of small size,* (Ṣ, TA,) *that assumes various colours, of the kind called* حُمَّر, (TA,) *like the sparrow,* (Ṣ, TA,) *and called* شُرْشُورٌ (Ṣ, Ḳ) *by the people of El-Hijáz:* (Ṣ, TA:) but Az states his having heard certain of the Arabs of the desert call it ابو براقش. (TA.)

بَرْقَشَةٌ The *diversity of colour of that which is termed* أَرْقَشُ. (Ḳ.) [See also 1.]

أَبُو بَرَاقِش *A certain bird that assumes various colours;* (Ṣ;) *a small wild bird, like the* قُنْفُذ [or *hedge-hog,* but قنفذ is probably a mistranscription for قُنْبُر, or *lark*], *the upper part of whose feathers is dust-coloured* (أَغْبَرُ), as in the Ḳ, accord. to the TA), or *white* (أَغَرُّ, as in some copies of the Ḳ), *and the middle red, and the lower part black, so that when it is roused,* or *provoked, it ruffles its feathers and becomes variously changed in colour:* (Lth, Ḳ:) or *a certain bird that is found in the trees called* عِضَاه, *and the colour of which is between blackness and whiteness, having six* قَوَادِم [or *primary feathers*], *three on each side, heavy in the rump, that makes a noise with its wings when it flies, and assumes various colours:* (IKh:) *a certain variegated bird.* (TA in art. ابو.) — [Hence,] هُوَ أَبُو بَرَاقِش †*He is varying,* or *variable, in dispositions.* (A, TA.)

الجَارُ البَرَاقِشِىُّ *The neighbour that is variable in his actions;* like الجَارُ اليَرْبُوعِىُّ. (IAạr, TA in art. جور.)

برقع

Q. 1. بَرْقَعَهُ, (Ṣ, Ḳ,) inf. n. بَرْقَعَةٌ, (TA,) *He attired him with a* بُرْقُع: (Ṣ, Ḳ:) and بَرْقَعَ المَرْأَةَ *he attired the woman with a* بُرْقُع. (Mṣb.) — بَرْقَعَ لِحْيَتَهُ [*He veiled his beard with a* بُرْقُع;] *he assumed the guise of such as wear the* بُرْقُع; (TA;) i. e. صَارَ مَأْبُونًا ‡ [*he became effeminate,* or *a catamite*]. (Ḳ, TA.) A poet says,

> أَلَمْ تَرَ قَيْسًا قَيْسَ عَيْلَانَ بَرْقَعَتْ
> لِحَاهَا وَبَاعَتْ نَبْلَهَا بِالمَغَازِلِ

[*Dost thou not see that Keys, Keys-'Eylán, have veiled their beards, and sold their arrows for spindles?*]. (TA.) — بَرْقَعَ فُلَانًا بِالعَصَا, (Ḳ,) inf. n. as above, (TA,) ‡ *He struck such a one with the staff,* or *stick, between his ears,* (Ḳ, TA,) *so that it became like the* بُرْقُع *upon his head.* (TA.)

Q. 2. تَبَرْقَعَ *He attired himself with a* بُرْقُع: (Ṣ, Ḳ:) and تَبَرْقَعَتْ *she* (a woman) *attired herself with a* بُرْقُع. (Mṣb.)

بُرْقَعٌ: see what next follows.

بُرْقُعٌ (IAạr, Ṣ, Mgh, Mṣb, Ḳ) and ♦ بُرْقَعٌ, (IAạr, Ṣ, Mṣb, Ḳ,) but some disallow this latter, (Mṣb,) and ♦ بُرْقُوعٌ, (IAạr, Ṣ, Ḳ,) but AḤát disallows this, as well as the second, (TA,) *A thing pertaining to women and to horses or similar beasts,* (Ḳ,) or *to horses or similar beasts and to the women of the Arabs of the desert;* (Ṣ;) *a thing with which a woman veils her face;* (Mṣb;) *having in it two holes for the eyes:* (Lth:) *a small piece of cloth,* or *rag, pierced for the eyes, worn by horses or similar beasts and by the women of the Arabs of the desert:* (Mgh:) [or, accord. to the general fashion of the present time, *a long strip of cotton or other cloth, black, blue, or of some other colour, or white, concealing the whole of the face of the woman wearing it, except the eyes, and reaching nearly to the feet, suspended at the top by a narrow band, or other fastening, which passes up the middle of the forehead, and which is sewed, as are also the two upper corners, to a band which is tied round the head, beneath the head-veil:* (see my "Manners and Customs of the Modern Egyptians," ch. i.:)] ♦ بُرْقُعَةٌ, if correct, is a more particular term: (Mgh:) the pl. is بَرَاقِعُ. (Lth, Mṣb.) [See نِقَابٌ.] — [البُرْقُعُ *The curtain of the door of the Kaabeh.*] — See also بِرْقِعُ.

بُرْقُوعٌ: see what next follows.

بِرْقِعُ, (Ṣ, Ḳ,* TA,) imperfectly decl., (Ṣ, TA,) and ♦ بُرْقَعُ, (Fr, Az, Ibn-'Abbád,) of a rare form, like هِجْرَع, (Fr, Az,*) or البُرْقَعُ and ♦ البُرْقُعُ, (Ḳ,* TA,) but perhaps this last is a mistranscription, for بِرْقِعُ, (TA,) a name of *The heaven,* or *sky:* (Fr:) or *the seventh heaven:* (AAF, Ṣ, Ḳ:) or *the fourth heaven:* (Lth, Az, Ḳ:) or *the first heaven;* (Ḳ;) i. e. *the lowest heaven:* IDrd says, so they assert; and in like manner says

IF; and he says, the ب is augmentative, the radical letters being ر ق ع, for every heaven is termed رَقِيعٌ, and the heavens [together] are termed أَرْقِعَةٌ: (TA:) or the lowest heaven is termed الرَّقِيعُ. (Ṣ, TA.) [See an ex. voce سَدِرٌ.]

بُرْقُعَةٌ : } see بُرْقُعٌ.
بُرْقُوعٌ :

فَرَسٌ أَغَرُّ مُبَرْقَعٌ, (TA,) or فَرَسٌ مُبَرْقَعٌ, (Mgh,) *A horse having what is termed* غُرَّةٌ مُبَرْقِعَةٌ: (TA:) or *a horse having the whole of his face white.* (Mgh.) And شَاةٌ مُبَرْقَعَةٌ *A sheep, or ewe, having the head white.* (Ṣ, Ḳ.)

غُرَّةٌ مُبَرْقِعَةٌ *A blaze, or whiteness, on the face of a horse, occupying the whole of his face, except that he looks* (يَنْظُرُ [for which يُنْظَرُ is erroneously substituted in the CḲ]) *in blackness;* (Ṣ, L, Ḳ;) [i. e.] *this whiteness passing downwards to the cheeks without reaching to the eyes.* (L, TA.)

برك

1. بَرَكَ, (Ṣ, Mṣb, Ḳ,) aor. ـُ, (Ṣ, TA,) inf. n. بُرُوكٌ (Ṣ, Mgh, Mṣb, Ḳ) and تَبْرَاكٌ, (Ḳ,) said of a camel, (Ṣ, Mgh, Mṣb,) *i. q.* اِسْتَنَاخَ [i. e. *He lay down, or kneeled and lay down, upon his breast, with his legs folded*]; (Ṣ, Ḳ;) *he made his breast to cleave to the ground;* (Mgh;) *he fell upon his* بَرْك, i. e. *breast;* (Mṣb;) *he threw his* برك, i. e. *breast, upon the ground;* (TA;) and in like manner, ↓ برّك, (TA, and so in some copies of the Ḳ,) inf. n. تَبْرِيكٌ. (TA.) And بَرَكَتِ النَّعَامَةُ *The ostrich lay upon its breast.* (TA.) And بَرَكَ is also said of a lion, and of a man. (Ḳ voce ربض.) [Of the latter, one also says, بَرَكَ عَلَى رُكْبَتَيْهِ *He fell, or set himself, upon his knees; he kneeled.*] The بُرُوك of a man praying, which is forbidden, is The *putting down the hands before the knees*, after the manner of the camel [when he lies down; for the latter falls first upon his knees, and then upon his stifle-joints]. (Mgh.) — Hence, i. e., from the verb said of a camel, inf. n. بُرُوكٌ, (TA,) *He, or it,* (i. e. anything, Ṣ,) *was, or became, firm, steady, steadfast, or fixed; continued, remained, or stayed;* (Ṣ, Ḳ;) in a place: (TḲ:) [and so, app., with ـِ for its aor.; for] you say, بَرَكَ لِلْقِتَالِ, aor. ـِ, [*He was, or became, firm,* &c., *for the purpose of fighting,*] and in like manner بَرِكَ, aor. ـَ. (TA. [See also a similar signification of 8.]) — † *It* (the night) *was, or became, long,* or *protracted; as though it did not quit its place.* (A and TA in art. قعس.) — See also 8, in two places.

2: see 1. — تَبْرِيكٌ also signifies The *praying for* بَرَكَة, (Ṣ, Ḳ, TA,) for a man, &c. (TA.) You say, بَرَّكْتُ عَلَيْهِ, inf. n. تَبْرِيكٌ, *I said to him,* بَارَكَ ٱللّٰهُ عَلَيْكَ [or فِيكَ &c., *God bless thee!* &c.]. (TA.) And برّك على الطَّعَامِ *He prayed for, or invoked, a blessing on the food.* (TḲ.)

3. بارك عَلَيْهِ *He kept, or applied himself, constantly, or perseveringly, to it;* (Lḥ, Ḳ;) namely, an affair, (TA in art. حفد,) or commerce, or traffic, &c. (Lḥ, TA.) — بَارَكَ ٱللّٰهُ فِيكَ, (Fr, Ṣ, Mṣb, Ḳ,) and لَكَ, and عَلَيْكَ, (Ṣ, Ḳ,) and بَارَكَكَ, (Fr, Ṣ, Ḳ,) inf. n. مُبَارَكَةٌ, (TḲ,) [*God bless, beatify, felicitate, or prosper, thee;*] *God put in thee,* (TA,) *give thee, make thee to possess,* (T, Ḳ,) بَرَكَة [i. e. *a blessing, good of any kind, prosperity* or *good fortune, increase,* &c.]. (TA, TḲ.) بَارِكْ عَلَى مُحَمَّدٍ وَعَلَى آلِ مُحَمَّدٍ (in a trad., TA,) means *Continue Thou,* or *perpetuate Thou,* (O God,) *to Mohammad and to the family of Mohammad the eminence and honour which Thou hast given them:* (Ḳ, TA:) [or *still bless* or *beatify,* or *continue to bless* or *beatify, Mohammad* &c.: though it may well be rendered simply *bless* or *beatify* &c.:] Az says that it is from بَرَكَ said of a camel, meaning "he lay down upon his breast in a place and clave thereto." (TA.) And اَللّٰهُمَّ بَارِكْ لَنَا فِى المَوْتِ, in another trad., means [*O God, bless us*] *in the state to which death will bring us.* (TA.) The Arabs say to the beggar, بُورِكَ فِيكَ [*Mayest thou be blest;* and, in the present day, الله يُبَارِك فيك *God bless thee*]; meaning thereby to repel him; not to pray for him: and by reason of frequency of usage of this phrase, they have made ↓ بُورِك a noun: a poet [in Ḥar شريش العدوى (app. Sherees, not Shereesh, El-'Adawee), in the TA Aboo-Fir'own,] says,

تَظُنُّ أَنَّ بُورِكًا يَكْفِينِى
إِذَا خَرَجْتُ بَاسِطًا يَمِينِى

[*She imagines that the saying "Mayest thou be blest" will suffice me when I go forth stretching out my right hand* for an alms]. (Ḥar p. 378. [This verse is differently cited in the TA; for there, instead of تظنّ and خرجت, we find تُحِبُّ and غَدَوْتُ.]) — [You also say of a man, بارك فِيهِ, and لَهُ, &c., meaning *He blessed him;* i. e. *he prayed God to bless him.*] — See also 6.

4. ابركهُ *He made him* (namely, a camel,) *to lie down* [or *kneel and lie down*] *upon his breast.* (Ṣ, Ḳ.) You say, أَبْرَكْتُهُ فَبَرَكَ *I made him to lie down upon his breast, and he lay down upon his breast:* but this is rare: the more common phrase is أَنَخْتُهُ فَٱسْتَنَاخَ. (Ṣ.) — See also 8. — مَا أَبْرَكَهُ [*How blessed is he, or it!*] is an instance of a verb of wonder with a passive meaning [and irregularly derived]. (TA.)

5. تبرّك به *i. q.* تَيَمَّنَ بِهِ [*He had a blessing;* and *he was,* or *became, blest; by means of him,* or *it:* so accord. to explanations of تَبَرُّك in the KL: but very often signifying *he looked for a blessing by means of him, or it; he regarded him, or it, as a means of obtaining a blessing; he augured good from him, or it;* تيمّن به being opposed to تَشَاءَمَ به; as in the Ḳ in art. طير, and in Bḍ in xvii. 14, &c.]: (Ṣ, Ḳ:) and ↓ تبارك بِالشَّىْءِ *He augured good from the thing.* (Lth, Ḳ.) One says so of a man. (Ḳ in art. مسح.) And one says, تبرّك بِٱسْمِ ٱللّٰهِ [*He looked for a blessing by means of* uttering *the name of God,* or saying بِسْمِ ٱللّٰهِ]. (Ksh, on the بسملة; &c.)

6. تبارك, accord. to Zj, is an instance of تَفَاعَلَ [as quasi-pass. of فَاعَلَ, i. e., of بَارَكَ, like as تَبَاعَدَ is of بَاعَدَ,] from البَرَكَةُ; and so say the lexicologists [in general]. (TA.) [Hence,] تبارك ٱللّٰهُ means [*Blessed is,* or *be, God;* or] *hallowed is,* or *be, God;* or *far removed is,* or *be, He from every impurity or imperfection, or from everything derogatory from his glory;* (Ḳ;) or *highly to be exalted, or extolled, is God; or highly exalted, or extolled, be He;* (Abu-l-'Abbás, TA;) *greatly to be magnified is God;* or *greatly magnified be He:* (TA:) or i. q. ↓ بَارَكَ, like قَاتَلَ and تَقَاتَلَ, except that فَاعَلَ is trans. and تَفَاعَلَ is intrans.: (Ṣ:) accord. to IAmb, it means [that] one looks for a blessing by means of [uttering] his name (يُتَبَرَّكُ بِٱسْمِهِ) in every affair, or case: accord. to Lth, it is a phrase of glorification and magnification: (TA:) or تبارك signifies *He is abundant in good;* from البَرَكَةُ, which is "abundance of good:" or *He exceeds everything, and is exalted above it, in his attributes and his operations;* because البَرَكَةُ implies the meaning of increase, accession, or redundance: or *He is everlasting;* syn. دَامَ; from بُرُوكُ الطَّيْرِ عَلَى المَآءِ ["the continuing of the birds at the water"]; whence البِرْكَةُ, because of the continuance of the water therein: the verb is invariable [when thus used, being considered as divested of all signification of time, or used in an optative sense]; and is not employed [in any of the senses above] otherwise than in relation to God: (Bḍ in xxv. 1:) it is an attributive peculiar to God. (Ḳ.) — تبارك بِالشَّىْءِ: see 5.

8. ابترك *He* (a man) *threw his* بَرْك [i. e. *breast*] upon the ground (as the camel does in lying down), or upon some other thing]. (Ṣ.) — *He* (a sword-polisher) *leaned upon the polishing-instrument,* (Ḳ,) *on one side.* (TA.) And *He* (a horse) *inclined on one side in his running.* (TA: [accord. to which, this is from what next follows.]) — *He hastened,* or *sped, and strove, laboured,* or *exerted himself, in running:* (Ṣ, Ḳ:) and ↓ بَرَكَ, inf. n. بُرُوكٌ, (Ḳ,) or, as some say, this is a subst. from the former verb, (TA,) *He strove, laboured,* or *exerted himself.* (Ḳ.) — † *It* (a cloud) *rained continually,* or *incessantly:* (TA:) and ابتركت السَّمَآءُ † *the sky rained continually;* as also ↓ بَرَكَتْ, (Ḳ,) and ↓ ابركت; but Ṣgh says that the first of these three is the most correct. (TA.) And ابتركت السَّحَابَةُ ‡ *The cloud rained vehemently.* (Ḳ, TA.) — ابترك فِى عِرْضِهِ, and عَلَيْهِ, ‡ *He detracted from his reputation, censured him,* or *impugned his character, and reviled him,* (Ḳ, TA,) *and laboured in vituperating him.* (TA.) ابتركوا فِى الحَرْبِ ‡ *They fell upon their knees in battle, and so fought one another.* (Ḳ, TA. [See بَرَاكَآءُ, below.]) — ابتركتُهُ *I prostrated him,* or *threw him down prostrate, and put him beneath my* بَرْك [i. e. *breast*]. (Ṣ.)

بَرْكٌ *Many camels:* (Ṣ, Ḳ:) or *a herd of camels lying down upon their breasts:* (Ḳ:) or *any camels, males and females, lying down upon their breasts by the water or in the desert by reason of the heat of the sun* or *by reason of satiety:* (TA:) or *all the camels of the people of an encampment, that return to them from pasture in the evening,* or *afternoon, to whatever number they may amount, even if they be thousands:* (K:) *one thereof* is termed ▼ بَارِكٌ; (K;) the two words being like تَاجِرٌ and تَجْرٌ; (TA;) fem. ▼ بَارِكَةٌ: (K:) pl. بُرُوكٌ, (S, K,) i. e., pl. of بَرْكٌ. (S.) ═ Also, (S, Msb, K,) and ▼ بِرْكَةٌ, which is with kesr, (S, K,) The *breast* (S, Msb, K) of a camel: (Msb, TA:) this is the primary signification: (TA:) as some say, the former signifies the *breast of the camel with which he crushes a thing beneath it:* (TA:) and (K) accord. to Lth, (TA,) the latter is the *part next to the ground of the skin of the breast of the camel;* (or, as in the 'Eyn, *of the skin of the belly of the camel and of the portion of the breast next to it;* TA;) as also the former: (K:) or, as some say, the former is the *middle of the breast, where* [*the two prominences of flesh called*] *the* فَهْدَتَانِ *conjoin at their upper parts:* (Ham p. 66:) or *the latter is pl. of the former,* like as حَلَقٌ is of حَلْقَةٌ: or the former is *of man;* and the latter, *of others:* or the former is the *interior of the breast;* (or, as Yakoob says, the *middle of the breast;* TA;) and the latter, the *exterior thereof:* (K:) or the former is the *breast,* primarily *of the camel,* because camels lie down (تَبْرُكُ) upon the breast; and metaphorically *of others.* (Ham p. 145.) — Hence, بَرْكُ الشِّتَآءِ ‡ *The first part of winter;* (L, TA;*) and *the main part thereof.* (L.) — And hence, (TA,) البُرُوكُ is an appellation applied to ‡ *The stars composing the constellation of the Scorpion,* of which are الزُّبَانَى and الإِكْلِيلُ and القَلْبُ and الشَّوْلَةُ [the 16th and 17th and 18th and 19th of the Mansions of the Moon], which rise [aurorally] in the time of intense cold; as is also الجُثُومُ: (L, TA:*) or, accord. to IF, to *a* نَوْء *of the* أَنْوَآء *of* الجَوْزَآء; because the انواء thereof do not set [aurorally] without there being during their period a day and a night in which the camels lie upon their breasts (تَبْرُكُ) by reason of the vehemence of the cold and rain. (TA.)

بُرْكٌ: see بَرْكٌ.

بِرْكٌ: see بِرْكَةٌ.

بَرِكٌ *Remaining fixed* (▼بَارِكٌ) at, or by, a thing. (IAar, K.) So in the phrase بَرِكٌ عَلَى جَنْبِ الإِنَآءِ [*Remaining fixed at,* or *by, the side of the vessel*], in a verse describing a [gluttonous] man, who swallows closely-consecutive mouthfuls. (IAar.) — †*Incubus,* or *nightmare;* as also ▼بَارُوكٌ. (K.) — ‡*A coward;* and so ▼the latter word. (K, TA.) ═ Also, [and by contraction ▼ بَرْكٌ, as in a verse cited in the M and TA in art. وبص,] *A name of the month* ذُو الحِجَّة; (AA, K;) *one of the ancient names of the months.* (AA.)

بُرْكَةٌ, (S, K,) or ▼ بُرَكَةٌ, (Msb,) *A certain aquatic bird, white,* (S, Msb, K,) *and small:* (K:) [the former applied in Barbary, in the present day, to *a duck:*] pl. بُرَكٌ (S, Msb, K) and بِرْكَانٌ and بُرْكَانٌ and [pl. of pauc.] أَبْرَاكٌ; (K;) or, in the opinion of ISd, ابراك and بركان are pls. of the pl. [بُرَكٌ]. (TA.)

بِرْكَةٌ *A mode,* or *manner, of* بُرُوك [i. e. of a camel's *kneeling and lying down upon the breast*]; (S,* O,* K;) a noun like رِكْبَةٌ and جِلْسَةٌ. (S, O.) One says, مَا أَحْسَنَ بِرْكَةَ هٰذِهِ النَّاقَةِ [*How good is this she-camel's manner of lying down on the breast!*]. (S.) ═ See also بَرْكٌ. ═ *A* حَوْض [i. e. *watering-trough* or *tank*]: (K:) or the *like thereof,* (S, TA,) *dug in the ground, not having raised sides constructed for it above the surface of the ground;* (TA;) and ▼ بِرْكٌ signifies the same: (Lth, K:) said to be so called because of the continuance of the water therein: (S:) pl. بِرَكٌ, (S, Msb, K,) which Az found to be applied by the Arabs to the *tanks,* or *cisterns, that are constructed with baked bricks, and plastered with lime, in the road to Mekkeh, and at its watering-places;* sing. بِرْكَةٌ; and sometimes a بركة is a thousand cubits [in length], and less, and more: but the watering-troughs, or tanks, that are made for the rain-water, and not cased with baked bricks, are called أَصْنَاعٌ, sing. صِنْعٌ: (TA:) [بِرْكَةٌ often signifies *a basin; a pool; a pond;* and *a lake:* and in the present day, also *a bay of the sea:* and *a reach of a river:*] also *a place where water remains and collects,* or *collects and stagnates,* or *remains long and becomes altered.* (ISd, K.)

بَرَكَةٌ [*A blessing; any good that is bestowed by God;* and particularly *such as continues and increases and abounds:*] *good,* (Jel in xi. 50,) or *prosperity,* or *good fortune,* (Fr, K,) *that proceeds from God:* (Fr, in explanation of the pl. as used in the Kur xi. 76:) *increase; accession; redundance; abundance,* or *plenty;* (S, Msb, K, Kull;) whether *sensible* or *intellectual:* and the *continuance of divinely-bestowed good, such as is perceived by the intellect, in,* or *upon, a thing:* (Kull:) or *firmness, stability,* or *continuance, coupled with increase:* (Ham p. 587:) or *increasing good:* (Bd in xi. 50:) and *abundance of good; implying the meaning of increase, accession,* or *redundance:* (Bd in xxv. 1:) or *abundant and continual good:* (so in an Expos. of the Jámi' eṣ-Ṣagheer, cited in the margin of a copy of the MS:) and, accord. to Az, God's *superiority over everything.* (TA.)

بُرَكَةٌ: see بُرْكَةٌ.

بَرَاكِ بَرَاكِ, (S, K,*) like قَطَامِ, (K,) said in war, or battle, (S,) means ابْرُكُوا [*Be ye firm, steady,* or *steadfast:* in the CK, erroneously, أَبْرِكُوا]. (S, K.)

بَرُوكٌ A woman *that marries having a big son* (S, K) *of the age of puberty.* (S.)

بُرُوكٌ *A hasting, speeding, striving, labouring,* or *exerting oneself, in running;* a subst. from ابترك: and inf. n. of بَرَكَ in a sense in which it is explained above with the former verb. (K: but see 8.)

بَرِيكٌ: see مُبَارَكٌ.

بَرَاكَآءُ (S, K) and بُرَاكَآءُ (TA) *Firmness, steadiness,* or *steadfastness, in war,* or *battle;* (IDrd, S;) and *a striving, labouring,* or *exerting oneself* [*therein*]; from البُرُوكُ [inf. n. of بَرَكَ]: (S:) or *a falling upon the knees in battle, and so fighting;* as also ▼ بَرُوكَآءُ. (K.) — Also The *field of battle:* or, accord. to Er-Rághib, بَرَاكَآءُ الحَرْبِ and ▼ بَرُوكَاؤُهَا signify *the place to which the men of valour cleave.* (TA.)

بَرُوكَآءُ: see what next precedes, in two places.

بَرَّكَانٌ and بَرَّكَانِىٌّ (Fr, Mgh, Msb, K) and ▼ بَرْنَكَانٌ, (S, Mgh, Msb, K,) which is the form commonly obtaining, (Msb,) and mentioned by El-Ghooree as well as J, (Mgh,) but disallowed by Fr, (Mgh, TA,) and ▼ بَرْنَكَانِىٌّ, (K,) but this also is disallowed by Fr, (Mgh, TA,) or, accord. to IDrd, ▼ بَرْنَكَآءُ and ▼ كِسَآءُ بَرْنَكَانِىٍّ, but he says that it is not Arabic, (TA,) *A kind of* [*garment such as is called*] كِسَآء, (S, Mgh, Msb,) [*similar to a* بُرْدَة,] *well-known;* (Msb;) the *black* كِسَآء; (Fr, Mgh, K;) *a woollen* كِسَآء *having two ornamental borders:* (Fr, TA in art. برنك:) [in Spanish *barangane:* (Golius:)] pl. [of all except the first two] بَرَانِكُ. (IDrd, K.) بَرَكَانٌ, without teshdeed, is not mentioned by any one. (Mgh.)

بَرْنَكَآءُ and بَرْنَكَانٌ and بَرْنَكَانِىٌّ: see بَرَّكَانٌ, in four places.

بَارِكٌ, fem. with ة: see بَرْكٌ, in two places: — and see بَرِكٌ.

بُورَكٌ i. q. بُورَقٌ; (K;) *that is put into flour,* (TA,) or *into dough.* (JK and Mgh and TA in explanation of the latter word.)

بُورِكَ, as a noun: see 3.

بَارُوكٌ: see بَرِكٌ, in two places.

مَبْرَكٌ *A place where camels lie upon their breasts:* pl. مَبَارِكُ. (Msb.) You say, فُلَانٌ لَيْسَ لَهُ مَبْرَكُ جَمَلٍ [*Such a one has not a place in which a camel lies;* meaning *he does not possess a single camel*]. (S.)

مُبَارَكٌ is originally مُبَارَكٌ فِيهِ [or لَهُ or عَلَيْهِ, accord. to those who know not, or disallow, بَارَكَ as trans. without a preposition; and signifies *Blessed, beatified, felicitated,* or *prospered; gifted with,* or *made to possess,* بَرَكَة, i. e. *a blessing, any good that is bestowed by God, prosperity* or *good fortune, increase,* &c.]; (Msb;) *abounding in good;* (Ksh and Bd in iii. 90;) *abounding in advantage* or *utility:* (Bd in vi. 92 and 156, and xxxviii. 28, and l. 9:) the pl. applied to irrational things is مُبَارَكَاتٌ. (Msb.) You say also ▼ بَرِيكٌ as meaning مُبَارَكٌ فِيهِ: (K:) or طَعَامٌ بَرِيكٌ is as though meaning مُبَارَكٌ [i. e. *Blessed food; or food in which is a blessing,* &c.]. (S.)

مُبْتَرِكٌ, [in the CK مُتَبَرِّكٌ,] applied to a man, ‡ *Leaning,* or *bearing, upon a thing; applying himself* [*thereto*] *perseveringly, assiduously,* or *constantly.* (K, TA.) — Also, applied to a cloud, ‡ *Bearing down* [*upon the earth*], *and paring off the surface of the ground* [*by its vehement rain:* see 8]. (TA.)

مُتَبَارِكٌ [app. applied to God (see its verb)] *High*, or *exalted*. (Th, TA.)

برم

1. بَرَمَهُ: see 4, in two places. ═ بَرِمَ, aor. َ; and ↑تبرّم; *He was, or became, affected with disgust, loathing, or aversion*; (M,* Ḳ;) *he was vexed, grieved, disquieted by grief*, or *distressed in mind*. (M.) You say, بَرِمَ بِهِ, inf. n. بَرَمٌ; (T, Ṣ, M, Mṣb, Ḳ;) and ↑تبرّم به; (T, Ṣ, Mṣb, Ḳ;) *He was*, or *became, disgusted by it*, or *by reason of it; he loathed it*; (T,* Ṣ, M,* Mṣb,* Ḳ;) *he was vexed, grieved, disquieted by grief*, or *distressed in mind, by it*, or *by reason of it*. (T, M, Mṣb, Ḳ.) — بَرِمَ بِحُجَّتِهِ, aor. َ, ‡ [*He was unable to adduce, as he had intended, his argument, allegation, or evidence*,] is said when one has intended to adduce an argument, allegation, or evidence, and it did not present itself to him. (A, Ḳ, TA.)

4. ابرمهُ, (inf. n. إِبْرَامٌ, T,) *He made it* (a rope, AḤn, M, Ḳ, or a thread, or string, T) *of two strands*, or *distinct yarns* or *twists, and then twisted it*; (AḤn, T, M, Ḳ;) as also ↑بَرَمَهُ [aor. ُ, inf. n. بَرْمٌ]: (T:) or *he twisted it well*; namely, a rope. (M.) — And hence, (T, TA,) ‡ *He made it* (a thing, Ṣ, or an affair, T, M, Ḳ, or a compact, Mṣb) *firm, strong, solid*, or *sound; he established it, settled it*, or *arranged it, firmly, strongly, solidly, soundly*, or *thoroughly*; (T, Ṣ, M, Mṣb, Ḳ, TA;) as also ↑بَرَمَهُ, (M, Ḳ,) [aor. ُ,] inf. n. بَرْمٌ. (Ḳ.) — † *He thought*, or *meditated, upon it*; (namely, a thing;) or *did so looking to its end, issue*, or *result*; or *he did it, performed it*, or *executed it, with thought*, or *consideration*. (Mṣb.) ═ *He affected him with disgust, loathing*, or *aversion*; (T,* Ṣ, M,* Mṣb,* Ḳ;) *caused him to be vexed, grieved, disquieted by grief*, or *distressed in mind*. (T, Ṣ, M, Mṣb.) You say, لَا تُبْرِمْنِى بِكَثْرَةِ فُضُولِكَ [*Disgust me not*, or *vex me not, by the abundance of thy meddling*, or *impertinent, speech*]. (T, TA.) ═ ابرم *It* (a vine) *put forth grapes in the state in which they are termed* بَرَم, q. v. (Th, M, Ḳ.)

5: see 1, in two places.

7. انبرم [*It* (a rope, or a thread, or string,) *was made of two strands*, or *distinct twists, and then twisted*: or *was twisted well*: see 4, of which it is quasi-pass. — And hence,] ‡ *It* ([a thing, or an affair, or] a compact, Mṣb) *was*, or *became, firm, strong, solid*, or *sound*; *it was*, or *became, established, settled*, or *arranged, firmly, strongly, solidly, soundly*, or *thoroughly*. (Mṣb, KL.)

بَرَمٌ The *fruit of the* [*trees called*] عِضَاه: (Ṣ, M, Ḳ:) n. un. with ة: (Ṣ, M:) *in its first stage it is termed* فَتْلَة; *then*, بَلَّة; *then*, بَرَمَة: AḤn has erred in saying that the فتلة is above the برمة [in degree]: (M:) *that of every kind of* عضاه *is yellow, except that of the* عُرْفُط, *which is white*, (Ṣ, M,) *as though its filaments*, or *fringe-like appertenances, were cotton, and it is like the button of a shirt, or somewhat larger*: (M:) *that of the* سَلَم *is the sweetest in odour*, (Ṣ, M,) *and this is yellow, and is eaten, being sweet*, or *pleasant*: (M:) accord. to AA, the *fruit of the* طَلْح [or *acacia gummifera*, which is of the trees called عضاه]: n. un. with ة: (T:) sometimes, also, بَرَمَةٌ is applied to *a fruit of the* أَرَاك (M,* Ḳ,* TA) *before it has become ripe and black*; for when ripe, it is called مَرْدٌ; and when black, كَبَاثٌ: (TA:) and the pl. is بِرَامٌ (M, Ḳ) and بُرُمٌ, (M,) or بَرَمٌ. (Ḳ: [but the last is a coll. gen. n.]) — Also *Grapes when they are above*, (M,) or *when they are like*, (Ḳ,) *the heads of young ants*. (M, Ḳ.) ═ ‡ *One who does not take part with others in the game called* المَيْسِر [q. v.], (Aṣ, T, Ṣ, M, Ḳ,) *nor contribute with them anything*, (TA,) *by reason of his avarice*, (Ḥar p. 382,) *though he eats with them of the flesh-meat thereof*; (Aṣ, TA;) *but sometimes he shuffles*, or *deals forth*, (يُفِيضُ,) *the gaming-arrows for the players*: (Ṣ in art. جمد:) likened to the بَرَم of the أَرَاك, because he is of no use: (Ḥar ubi suprà:) and ↑بَرَمَةٌ occurs in the same sense; [the man so termed being likened to a بَرَمَة of the اراك; or] the ة being added to give intensiveness to the meaning: (M:) the pl. is أَبْرَامٌ. (T, Ṣ, M, Ḳ.) And hence, ‡ *Avaricious*, or *niggardly*; *mean*, or *sordid*: (Ḥar ubi suprà:) or *heavy*, or *sluggish*; (Ḳ, TA;) *destitute of good*. (TA.) It is said in a prov., أَبَرَمًا قَرُونًا ‡ [*Art thou* (تَكُونُ being understood after أ) *one taking no part with others in the game of* الميسر, as is implied in the Ṣ, or *art thou*] *heavy*, or *sluggish*, (Ḳ, TA,) *destitute of good*, (TA,) *yet eating two dates at once each time*? (Ṣ, Ḳ, TA.)

بَرِمٌ part. n. of بَرِمَ [and therefore meaning *Affected with disgust, loathing*, or *aversion*; or *vexed, grieved, disquieted by grief*, or *distressed in mind*]. (M, Mṣb.)

بُرْمَةٌ *A cooking-pot* (T, M, &c.) *of stone*, (T, Mgh, Mṣb,) or *of stones*: [see مُبْرِم:] (M, Ḳ:) or [simply] *a cooking-pot*, (Ṣ, TA,) as some say, *in a general sense*, so that it may be *of copper*, and *of iron, &c.*: (TA:) pl. بِرَامٌ (T, Ṣ, M, Mgh, Mṣb, Ḳ) and بُرَمٌ (T, M, &c.) and [coll. gen. n.] بُرْمٌ. (T, M, Ḳ.) ═ Also *A certain thing which women wear upon their arms, like the bracelet*. (TA.)

بَرَمَةٌ [originally n. un. of بَرَمٌ]: see بَرَمٌ.

بَرِيمٌ *A rope composed of two twists twisted together into one*; as also ↑مُبْرَمٌ: (Ṣ:) or *a thread*, or *string, twisted of two distinct yarns* or *twists*: (T:) or *a thread*, or *string, twisted of white and black yarns*: (Ḥam p. 704:) or *a twisted rope in which are two colours*, (A'Obeyd, Ṣ,) or *two threads*, or *strings, of different colours*, (IAạr, T, M, Ḳ,) *red and yellow*, (M,) or *red and white*, (Ḳ,) *sometimes* (A'Obeyd, Ṣ) *bound by a woman upon her waist, and upon her upper arm*: (A'Obeyd, Ṣ, Ḳ:) *a rope of two colours, adorned with jewels, so bound by a woman*: (M, Ḳ:) or *a thread*, or *string*, (Lth, A'Obeyd, T,) *with beads strung upon it*, (Lth, T,) or *of different colours*, (A'Obeyd, T,) *which a woman binds upon her waist*: (Lth, A'Obeyd, T: [see also حَوْطٌ]:) or *a string of cowries, which is bound upon the waist of a female slave*. (Aboo-Sahl El-Harawee in art. بزم of the TA.) — *Anything in which are two colours* (T, M, Ḳ) *mixed together*: (M, Ḳ:) and *any two things mixed together and combined*. (M.) — *An amulet* (M, Ḳ, TA) *that is hung upon a boy*; because of the colours therein. (TA.) — *A garment*, or *piece of cloth, in which are silk* (قَزّ) *and flax*. (T.) — Also, (Ḳ,) or the dual thereof, (AO, T, Ṣ,) which latter is the right, (TA,) The *liver and hump* [*of a camel*], (AO, T, Ṣ, Ḳ,) *cut lengthwise, and tied round with a string* or *thread, or some other thing*, (Ṣ, Ḳ,) in some copies of the Ṣ, *or with a gut*; (TA;) said to be thus called because of the whiteness of the hump and the blackness of the liver. (Ṣ, Ḳ.) So in the phrase, اِشْوِ لَنَا مِنْ بَرِيمَيْهَا [*Roast thou for us some of her liver and hump, cut lengthwise*, &c.]. (AO, T, Ṣ: [in copies of the Ḳ, بَرِيمِهَا: and in the CḲ, بَرِيمَتِهَا.]) — Also, the sing., *Water mixed with other* [*water* &c.]. (TA.) — *Tears mixed with* [*the collyrium termed*] إِثْمِد; (M, Ḳ;) because having two colours. (TA.) — *A mixed company* of people. (M, Ḳ.) — *An army*; (Ṣ, Ḳ;) because comprising a mixed multitude of men; (Ḳ;) or because of the colours of the banners of the tribes therein: (Ṣ, Ḳ, TA:) or *an army in which is a mixed multitude of men*: (M:) or *an army having two colours*: (T:) and the dual, *two armies, Arabs and foreigners*. (IAạr, T.) — *A number of sheep and goats together*. (IAạr, T, M, Ḳ.) — The *light of the sun with the remains of the blackness of night*: (IAạr, T:) or the *dawn*; (M, Ḳ;) because of its combining the blackness of night and the whiteness of day: or, as some say, بَرِيمُ الصُّبْحِ means *the tint* (خَيْط [q. v.]) *of the dawn that is mixed with two colours*. (M.) — † *Inducing suspicion*, or *evil opinion*; [as though of two colours;] (IAạr, T;) *suspected*. (IAạr, T, Ṣgh, Ḳ.)

بَرِّيمَةٌ, with fet-ḥ, and with teshdeed to the ر, which is meksoorah, *A* دَائِرَة [*or feather*, or *portion of the hair naturally curled or frizzled, in a spiral manner, or otherwise*,] *upon a horse, whereby one judges of its goodness or badness*: pl. بَرَارِيمُ. (TA: [and used in this sense in the present day.]) — See also بَيْرَم.

بَيْرَمٌ The [*implement called*] عَتَلَة: or particularly the عتلة *of the carpenter*: (M, Ḳ:) [i. e.,] *an auger, a wimble*, or *a gimlet*; [called in the present day ↑بَرِّيمَة; accord. to Mirḳát el-Loghah, cited by Golius, who writes the latter word without teshdeed, the former signifies *such an implement* ("terebra") *of a large size*;] *that with which the carpenter perforates*: and also said to signify *that with which the saddler perforates leather*: (KL:) also *a well-known kind of* [*implement such as is called in Persian*] تيشة [i. e., *a hatchet*, or *the like*]: (PṢ:) AO said, the بيرم is the عَتَلَة of the carpenter: or he said, the عتلة is the بيرم of the carpenter: (T:) this word, (M,) the بيرم of the carpenter, (Ṣ,) is Persian, (Ṣ, M,) arabicized. (Ṣ.)

مُبْرَمٌ: see بَرِيمٌ. — Also A garment, or piece of cloth, *of which the thread is twisted of two yarns*, or *distinct twists*. (Ṣ, Ḳ.) And hence, (Ṣ,) *A certain kind of garments*, or *cloths*. (Ṣ, Ḳ.) — [† A thing, or an affair, or a compact, *made firm, strong, solid,* or *sound; established, settled,* or *arranged, firmly, strongly, solidly, soundly,* or *thoroughly.* See its verb, 4. — And hence, قَضَآءٌ مُبْرَمٌ †*Ratified destiny; such as is rendered inevitable.*]

مُبْرِمٌ [act. part. n. of 4. — And also] *A gatherer of* بَرَم [q. v.]: (M:) or, *of the* بَرَم *of the* عِضَاه: (Ḳ:) or, specially, *a gatherer of the* بَرَم *of the* أَرَاك. (M.) — *A maker of* بِرَام [or *stone cooking-pots*]: (Ḳ:) or *one who wrenches out the stones of which they are made from the mountain,* (M, Ḳ, TA,) *and fashions them, and hews them out.* (TA.) — And hence, (M,) †*A heavy,* or *sluggish,* man; as though [in the CḲ لأنّه is erroneously put for كَأَنَّهُ] he cut off for himself something from the persons sitting with him: (M, Ḳ:*) or, as some say, [so in the M; but in the Ḳ, "and"] *bad,* or *corrupt, in discourse;* (M, Ḳ;) *who discourses to others of that in which is no profit nor meaning;* (TA;) from the same word as signifying "a gatherer of the fruit of the أراك," (M, TA,) which has no taste nor sweetness nor sourness nor virtue, or efficacy: (AO, TA:) or one *who is a burden upon his companion, without profit and without good; like the* بَرَم *who takes no part with others in the game of* المَيْسِر, *though he eats of the flesh-meat thereof.* (Aṣ, TA.)

مِبْرَمٌ sing. of مَبَارِم, (TA,) which signifies The *spindles with which the twisting termed* إِبْرَام *is performed.* (M, Ḳ, TA.) [See 4.]

برن

بَرْنِىٌّ *A sort of dates,* (T, Ṣ, M, Mṣb, Ḳ,) *well known,* (Ḳ,) *the best of dates,* (M,) or *of the best of dates,* (Mṣb,) *red, intermixed,* or *tinged, with yellow, having much* لِحَآء [i. e. *flesh,* or *pulp*], *and very sweet,* (T,) or *yellow, and round:* (M:) n. un. with ة: (M:) it is an arabicized word, originally بَرْنِيك, i. e. good, or excellent, fruit: (Ḳ:) accord. to AḤn, of Persian origin, i. e., بَارِنِى; بار meaning fruit, and نى denoting egregiousness: (M:) accord. to Suh, a foreign, or Persian, word, meaning blessed [or good or excellent] fruit; بَر meaning fruit; and هِنى, good or excellent [or wholesome]: the Arabs introduced it into their language: (Mṣb:) or, accord. to the Moạjam of El-Bekree, it is from بَرْن, the name of a town, or village. (TA.) It is converted by a rájiz into بَرْنِجّ; the double ى being changed into [double] ج. (Ṣ, M.) — You say also نَخْلَةٌ بَرْنِيَّةٌ and نَخْلٌ بَرْنِىٌّ [*Palm-trees,* and *a palm-tree, of which the dates are of the sort described above*]. (T.)

بَرْنِيَّةٌ n. un. of بَرْنِىٌّ. — Also *A kind of vessel,* (Ṣ, Mgh, Mṣb, Ḳ,) *well known,* (Mṣb,) *of baked clay:* (Ṣ, Mgh, Ḳ:) or, as some say, *of those that are termed* قَوَارِير [i. e. *flasks,* or *bottles,* generally *of glass*]; *such as are used by the seller of perfumes:* (Mgh:) or *a thing like a vessel of baked clay, big,* or *bulky, and green:* and sometimes *of the kind termed* قوارير: (M:) or *a thing like vessels of baked clay, big,* or *bulky, and green; of the kind termed* قوارير *that are thick, with wide mouths:* (Lth, T:) pl. بَرَانِىُّ. (Mgh.) — And *A cock:* (IAạr, T:) or *a young cock,* (M, Ḳ,) *when it attains to maturity,* (M,) or *when it begins to do so:* (Ḳ:) of the dial. of El-'Irák: (M:) pl. as above. (T, M, Ḳ.)

برنس

Q. 2. تَبَرْنَسَ *He wore,* or *clad himself with, a* بُرْنُس. (Ṣ.)

بُرْنُسٌ *A long* قَلَنْسُوَة, (Ṣ, Mṣb, Ḳ,) *which the devotees used to wear in the first age of El-Islám:* (Ṣ:) or *any garment of which the head forms a part,* (M, Ḳ,) *being joined to it,* (M,) *whether it be a* دُرَّاعَة *or a* مِمْطَر *or a* جُبَّة; (M, Ḳ;) and this is said to be the correct explanation: (TA:) [agreeably with the latter explanation, it is applied in the present day to *a hooded cloak,* mostly *of white woollen stuff;* but often, *of cloth of any colour:*] pl. بَرَانِسُ: (Mṣb:) [some say] it is from البِرْسُ, meaning "cotton," and the ن is augmentative: or, accord. to some, it is not Arabic. (TA.) — بُرْنُسُ الحُسْنِ † *Comely,* or *goodly, hair.* (TA in art. ملأ.)

برنك

بَرْنَكَاةٌ and بَرْنَكَانِىٌّ and بَرْنَكَانٌ: see بَرْكَانٌ, in art. برك.

بره

1. بَرِهَ, aor. ـَ, inf. n. بَرَهٌ, or, as in some copies of the Ḳ, بَرَهَانٌ, (TA, [and so I find in an excellent copy of the Ḳ, but in the CḲ بُرْهَانٌ,]) *His body returned to a healthy state,* or *his health of body returned to him,* or *his bodily condition became good, after having been altered by disease.* (IAạr, Ḳ.*) [The ه is perhaps a substitute for ء: see بَرِئَ.] — And *He was,* or *became, white in person,* or *body and members.* (Ḳ.) — See also بَرَهٌ, below.

4. ابره *He adduced the evidence* or *proof:* (Mṣb, Ḳ:) but as to ▼بَرْهَنَ, meaning *he manifested the evidence* or *proof,* it is said, on the authority of IAạr, to be post-classical; the former being the correct word: (AA, T, Z, Mṣb, TA:) or the former signifies *he adduced,* or *uttered,* or *did, wonderful things, and overcame men.* (Ḳ.)

Q. Q., or, as some say, Q., 1. بَرْهَنَ: see 4; and see art. برهن.

بَرَهٌ [perhaps an inf. n., of which the verb is ▼بَرِهَ,] *Softness, thinness of skin, and plumpness,* (Ḳ, TA,) of a woman; as also ▼بَرَهْرَهَةٌ. (TA.)

بُرْهَةٌ: see what next follows.

بُرْهَةٌ and ▼بَرْهَةٌ *A long space* or *period* of time: (JK, Ṣ:) or *a long time:* (ISk, Ḳ:) or they have a more general sense; (Ḳ;) i. e. *a space,* or *period,* of time: pl. of the former بُرَهٌ and بُرُهَاتٌ and بُرْهَاتٌ. (Mṣb.) You say, أَتَتْ عَلَيْهِ بُرْهَةٌ مِنَ الدَّهْرِ and بَرْهَةٌ [*A long space* or *period of time,* or merely *a space* or *period of time, passed over him*]. (Ṣ.)

بُرْهَانٌ: see art. برهن.

بَرَهْرَهَةٌ A *white* (IAạr, JK, Mṣb) girl (IAạr, Mṣb) or female: (JK:) or a woman (Ṣ, Ḳ,) *white and youthful:* or *soft,* or *tender:* (Ḳ:) or *that quivers,* (Ḳ,) or *almost quivers,* (Ṣ,) *from sappiness, softness,* or *tenderness:* (Ṣ,* Ḳ:) or *that shines,* or *glistens, by reason of her clearness* [*of complexion*]: or *thin-skinned; appearing as though water were running upon her, by reason of her softness,* or *tenderness:* (TA:) of the measure فَعَلْعَلَةٌ, (Ṣ, TA,) from بَرَهٌ: (TA:) dim. ▼بُرَيْهَةٌ (JK, TA) and ▼بُرَيْرِهَةٌ, (JK,) or ▼بُرَيْرِيهَةٌ; but ▼بُرَيْهِرَةٌ is bad, and seldom used. (TA.) Imra-el-Ḳeys says,

* بَرَهْرَهَةٌ رُؤْدَةٌ رَخْصَةٌ * كَخُرْعُوبَةِ البَانَةِ المُنْفَطِرْ *

[*White,* or *white and youthful,* &c., *soft,* or *beautiful, tender, like the shoot of the ben-tree breaking forth with leaves:* the last word being made masc. by poetic license, for the sake of the metre.]. (Ṣ.) — [Hence, app.,] it is said to signify also *A white knife, of clear, pure,* or *bright, iron.* (TA.) — See also بَرَهٌ.

بُرَيْهَةٌ and بُرَيْرِهَةٌ:
بُرَيْرِيهَةٌ, or بُرَيْهِرَةٌ: } see بَرَهْرَهَةٌ.

أَبْرَهُ [app.] *Having the body in a healthy state,* or *in good condition, after disease:* and *white in person,* or *body and members:* [but whether it have both these significations, or only the latter of them, is not clear:] fem. بَرْهَآءُ. (Ḳ.)

برهن

Q., or, as some say, Q. Q., 1. بَرْهَنَ *He adduced,* (T, Z, Mṣb,) or *established,* (Ṣ, Ḳ, and Ḥam p. 7,) *the* بُرْهَان, (T, Z, Mṣb, Ḳ,) i. e. the *evidence* or *proof* [&c.]; (T, Ṣ, Mṣb, &c.;) or *he adduced his evidence* or *proof* [&c.]; (T, Mṣb;) عَلَيْهِ [*against him,* or *it,* or (as in اِسْتَدَلَّ عَلَيْهِ) *of it*], (Ṣ, Ḳ, and Ḥam p. 7,) and لَهُ [*to him,* or *for him*]: (Ḥam ubi suprà:) but this verb is said by Az and Z, on the authority of IAạr, to be post-classical; the correct word, they say, being أَبْرَهَ: (Mṣb:) this they assert on the ground of the opinion that بُرْهَانٌ [q. v.] is of the measure فُعْلَانٌ; but J holds the ن to be a radical. (TA.)

بُرْهَانٌ *An evidence,* or *a proof:* (T, Ṣ, Mṣb, Ḳ, and Ḥam p. 7:) and *a demonstration;* i. e. the *manifestation of an evidence* or *proof:* (Mṣb:) or *a decisive and manifest evidence* or *proof:* (TA:) or the *firmest, strongest,* or *most valid, evidence* or *proof;* which is *such as ever necessarily implies truth,* or *veracity, as its consequence,* or *concomitant;* for evidences, or proofs, are of five sorts; whereof this is one; another is that which ever necessarily implies falsity, or falsehood, as its consequence, or concomitant; another, that which is nearer to truth, or veracity; another, that which is nearer to falsity, or falsehood; and another, that which is intermediate between these two: (Er-Rághib, TA:) [pl. بَرَاهِينُ:] some say that the ن in this word is augmentative; (Mṣb, and Ḥam p. 7;) that it is of the measure فُعْلَانٌ, from البره [app. البَرْهُ] signifying the "act of cutting:" (Ḥam ubi suprà:) others, that it is radical: Az mentions both of these opinions: J confines himself to the later opinion: Z, to the former, saying, on the authority of IAar, that the word is derived from بُرْهُرَهَة, meaning "white," [or "fair in complexion,"] applied to a girl: (Msb:) Abu-l-Fet-h [i. e. IJ] says that he holds it to be of the measure فُعْلَال, like قُرْطَاس and قُرْنَاس, the ن not being augmentative, as is shown by the verb above mentioned: (Ham ubi suprà:) but [it has been stated above that] this verb is said, on the authority of IAar, to be post-classical. (Msb, TA.)

برو

1. بَرَوْتُهَا, i. e. النَّاقَةَ: see 4. — بَرَوْتُهُ, (M, Msb, K,) aor. ـُ, (Lth, T,) inf. n. بَرْوٌ, (M,) *I formed it, or fashioned it, by cutting; shaped it out; or pared it;* (K;) namely, a reed for writing, (Lth, T, M, Msb, K,) and a stick, or piece of wood, (M, K,) and an arrow, (K,) [&c.;] a dial. var. of بَرَيْتُهُ, (Lth, T, M, Msb,) used by some, (Lth, T,) but the latter is the more approved: (M, TA:) mentioned by AZ. (TA.) — [Hence, perhaps,] بَرَاهُ, aor. ـُ, inf. n. بَرْوٌ, *He* (i. e. God) *created him,* or *it:* (Fr, S, K:) [but] they affirm that it is originally بَرَأَهُ, with hemz: (MF:) so says IAth: (TA:) or it is from بَرًا or بَرًى, signifying "dust," or "earth." (Fr, S.) — بَرَا, aor. ـُ, is also a bad dial. var. of بَرَأَ [signifying *He,* or *it, recovered* from disease, or *became convalescent,* &c.], aor. يَبْرُؤُ. (TA.)

4. أَبْرَيْتُهَا, (S, M, K,) i. e. النَّاقَةَ, (S, M,) *I put a* [*ring such as is termed*] بُرَة *in her* (a camel's) *nose;* (S, M, K;) as also ▾ بَرَوْتُهَا: (IJ, M, K:) and ابريتهُ, namely, a camel, *I put him a* بُرَة. (Msb.) — ابرى *Dust,* or *earth, came,* or *lighted, upon it.* (K,* TA, in art. برى.)

بُرَةٌ (in which the final radical letter is elided, [and replaced by ة,] Msb) *A ring* (T, S, M, &c.) *of brass,* (Lth, Lh, T, S, M, [in a copy of the Msb, من صوف is erroneously put for مِنْ صُفْرٍ,]) or *of silver,* (Lth, T,) or *of some other material,* (Lh, M,) *slender, and bent at the two ends* [lest it should open at the place where the two ends meet], *that is put in the nose of a she-camel,* (Lth, T,) or *put in the nose of the camel,* (M, Msb, K,) or *in the flesh of the nose of the camel,* (Lh, S, M, K,) or, as As says, *in one of the two sides of the two nostrils,* (S,) app. *either for the purpose of ornament or to render the animal obedient;* (MF;) [*generally for the latter purpose, to attach the rein thereto:*] when the ring is of hair, it is termed خِزَامَةٌ; (As, S, Msb;) and when of wood, خِشَاشٌ: (Msb:) Aboo-'Alee mentions, and explains in like manner, ▾ بَرْوَةٌ and بُرًى; [the latter as pl. of the former;] but this is extr.: (M:) J says, [in the S,] Aboo-'Alee says that بُرَةٌ is originally بَرْوَةٌ, because it has بُرًى for a pl., like as قَرْيَة has قُرًى; but Aboo-'Alee does not say this; he only desires to show that the final radical letter of بُرَة is و by the fact that بَرْوَة is a dial. var. thereof: (IB, TA:) some, however, remarking upon J's saying that the original of بُرَة is بَرْوَة, assert that it is correctly ▾ بُرْوَةٌ: (TA:) بُرَةٌ also signifies *an anklet:* (M, K:) or *any ring; such as a bracelet* and *an earring* and *an anklet* and *the like of these:* (S:) the pl. (in the former and the latter senses, M, TA) is بُرَاتٌ, (S, M, K,) in [some of] the copies of the K erroneously written بُرَاةٌ, (TA,) and بُرًى, (T, S, M,) and بُرُونَ, contr. to analogy, (Msb,) or بُرِينَ (T, S, M, K, [in all of which, except the last, this is in the accus. or the gen. case, but, as it is the nom. case in the K, it may be that بُرُونَ and بُرِينَ are dial. vars., like سِنُونَ and سِنِينَ,]) and بِرِينَ. (M, K: [in a copy of the former of which, accord. to the TT, بُرًى and بِرًى are put in the place of the last two of these pls.])

بَرًا, or بَرًى, *Dust,* or *earth:* (Fr, S, M, Msb, K, mentioned in the M and K in art. برى:) whence بَرَاهُ, [if not originally بَرَأَهُ,] meaning "He (i. e. God) created him." (Fr, S.) Hence the saying, بِفِيهِ البَرَا, or البَرَى, [*In his mouth be dust,* or *earth*], (S, M,) a form of imprecation against a man. (M.)

بُرَوَةٌ *Cuttings, chips, parings,* or *the like,* of a reed for writing, and of a stick, or piece of wood, and of soap, and the like. (TA.) — See also بُرَةٌ.

بَرْوَةٌ: see بُرَةٌ.

البَرِيَّةُ *The creation;* as meaning *the beings,* or *things, that are created;* or, particularly, *mankind;* syn. الخَلْقُ: originally with ء: (S:) but not pronounced with ء: (IAth, TA in art. برى:) or, accord. to Fr, if from بَرًا, or بَرًى, i. e. "dust," or "earth," it is originally without ء: pl. بَرَايَا and بَرِيَّاتٌ. (S.)

مُبْرَاةٌ A she-camel (T, S) *having a* [*ring such as is termed*] بُرَة *put in her nose:* (T, S, K:) pl. مُبْرَيَاتٌ. (TA in art. عرف.)

بُرَةٌ مَبْرُوَةٌ (T, M, K) *A* بُرَة *made,* or *manufactured.* (T, TA.)

برى

1. بَرَى, (T, M, K,) first pers. بَرَيْتُ, (T, S, Msb,) aor. ـِ, (T, K,) inf. n. بَرْىٌ, (T, S, M, Msb, K,) *He formed, or fashioned, by cutting; shaped out; or pared;* (As, T, M, K;) a reed for writing, (Lth, As, ISk, T, S, M, Msb,) and a stick, or piece of wood, (Lth, T, M,) and an arrow, (M, K,) &c.; (M;) as also ▾ ابترى: (M, K:) and بَرَوْتُ, (Msb,) aor. ـُ, (Lth, T,) is a dial. var., (Msb,) used by some, who say, هُوَ يَبْرُو البُرَّ [instead of يَبْرِى]. (Lth, T.) — And hence, (As, T,) aor. and inf. n. as above, (As, T, M, K,) †*He* (a man) *fatigued,* or *jaded, and made to lose flesh,* (As,* T,* S,) a she-camel, (As, T,) or a camel: (S:) or *it* (journeying) *rendered* him *lean,* or *emaciated:* (M, K:) and in like manner one says of a year of dearth or drought. (TA.) And بَرَيْتُ سَنَامَهَا بِسَيْرِى عَلَيْهَا †[*I wasted her hump by my journeying upon her*]: occurring in a poem of El-Aashà. (M.) — See also 3: — and see 5, in two places.

3. بَارَاهُ, (T, S, M, &c.,) inf. n. مُبَارَاةٌ, (T, TA,) *He vied, competed,* or *contended for superiority, with him; emulated,* or *rivalled, him;* or *imitated him;* i. q. عَارَضَهُ; (S, M, Msb, K;) i. e., (TA,) *he did the like of what he* (the latter) *did,* (ISk, T, S, Msb, TA, and EM p. 64,) *striving to overcome him or surpass him;* (EM ubi suprà;) as also ▾ بَرَى لَهُ, aor. ـِ, inf. n. بَرْىٌ; and ▾ انبرى له: (As, T:) and *he vied,* or *competed, with him,* or *contended with him for superiority, in glory,* or *excellence,* or *in beauty,* or *goodliness; he emulated,* or *rivalled, him therein;* syn. بَاهَاهُ: (TA in art. بهج:) and *he vied, competed,* or *contended, with him in running; and strove with him to outstrip him, to be before him, to get before him,* or *to precede him.* (TA.) You say, فُلَانٌ يُبَارِى الرِّيحَ سَخَاءً [*Such a one vies with the wind in bounty*]: (T, S:) [for] the bountiful man whose gifts are common is likened by the Arabs to the wind because it blows upon all in common, not only upon particular persons. (Ham p. 445.) — بارى امرأته *He compounded,* or *made a compromise, with his wife for their mutual separation;* (K;) as also بَارَأَهَا [which is the original]. (TA.)

4. ابرى: see art. برو. — Also *He found,* or *met with, sugar-canes.* (K.) — See also أَبْرَأَ, in art. برأ, last signification.

5. التَّبَرِّى signifies *The coming before* or *forward, presenting oneself, advancing, confronting, encountering, meeting,* or *opposing;* (KL;) and so ▾ الاِنْبِرَآءُ. (KL, PS.) You say, تبرّى لَهُ *He presented, addressed, applied,* or *betook, himself to him,* i. e., one man to another man; *advanced, came forward,* or *went forward, to him;* or *opposed himself to him;* syn. تَعَرَّضَ; as also تبرّاه; and ▾ بَرَى لَهُ, aor. ـِ: (T:) and ▾ انبرى له signifies اِعْتَرَضَ له, (S, K, and Har p. 558,) meaning [as above; or] *he betook himself, and advanced,* or *went forward, to it,* namely, an action; (Har ubi suprà;) and *it presented itself to it,* as a thought to the heart, or mind, syn. تعرّض: (Ham p. 541:) ▾ بَرَى لَهُ, inf. n. بَرْىٌ, is *syn. with* عَرَضَ لَهُ [meaning as above, for it is syn. with تَعَرَّضَ and اِعْتَرَضَ; or *it happened to him, befell him,* or *occurred to him*]: (M:) and ▾ انبرى is also *syn. with* عَرَضَ [meaning *it happened, befell,* or *occurred*]. (Har p. 56.) You say also, تبرّى لِمَعْرُوفِهِ, i. e. تَعَرَّضَ لَهُ (ISk, S, K) or اِعْتَرَضَ له (M) [both of which explanations mean *He presented, addressed, applied,* or *betook, himself,* or *he advanced, came forward, went forward,* or *attempted, to obtain his favour,* or *bounty;* or *he sought it,* or *demanded it*]; as also تبرّى مَعْرُوفَهُ. (M, TA.) And تَبَرَّيْتُ وُدَّهُمْ [*I addressed, applied,* or *betook, myself to obtain their love,* or *affection*]. (S, M.) And ▾ انبرى لِطَيِّ بِسَاطِهِ, *i. q.* اِعْتَرَضَ, meaning, in this instance, *He hastened to cut short his speech.* (Har p. 280.) And ▾ انبرى يُنْشِدُ شِعْرًا, i. e. تَعَرَّضَ لِإِنْشَادِهِ [or لِإِنْشَائِهِ], meaning *He addressed himself to reciting poetry,* or *verses*]. (Har p. 34.) And ▾ انبرى مِنَ الجَمَاعَةِ, *i. q.* اِعْتَرَضَ [*He presented himself,* or *advanced,* or *came forward, from the company*]. (Har p. 647.)

6. تَبَارَيَا *They vied, competed,* or *contended for superiority, each with the other; emulated,* or *rivalled, each other; imitated each other;* (S, K,

TA;) *they did each like as the other did.* (T, Ṣ, TA.) [See the part. n., below.]

7. انبرى, (Ḳ, TA,) or ↓ ابترى, (so in a copy of the M,) *It was,* or *became, formed,* or *fashioned, by cutting; shaped out;* or *pared:* (M, Ḳ:) said of a reed for writing, and of a stick, or piece of wood, (M,) and of an arrow, (M, Ḳ,) &c. (M.) ═ See also 3: — and see 5, in six places.

8: see 1: ═ and see also 7.

بَرًى, or بَرًا: see art. برو.

بَرَاةٌ: see مِبْرَاةٌ. ═ See also بَرَاءَةٌ, in art. برأ.

بُرَآءُ: see مِبْرَاةٌ.

بُرَاءٌ: see بُرَايَةٌ.

بَرِىٌّ, applied to an arrow, *i. q.* ↓ مَبْرِىٌّ [i. e. *Formed,* or *fashioned, by cutting; shaped out;* or *pared*]; (T, M, Ḳ;) or (M, Ḳ) *completely;* (T, M, Ḳ;) *but not feathered, nor headed:* for an arrow when first cut is termed قِطْعٌ; then it is formed, or fashioned, by cutting, or shaped out, or pared, and is termed بَرِىٌّ; and when straightened, and fit to be feathered and headed, it is a قِدْحٌ; and when feathered and headed, it becomes a سَهْمٌ. (T.) ═ It is also sometimes used for بَرِىْءٌ. (Ḳz, TA in art. برأ.)

البَرِيَّةُ: see art. برو.

بُرَايَةٌ (T, Ṣ, M, Ḳ) and ↓ بُرَاءٌ, (Ṣ, M, Ḳ,) in which latter the ء is originally ى, (IJ, M,) *Cuttings, chips, parings,* or *the like;* (Ṣ, M, Ḳ;) *what falls from a thing that is formed,* or *fashioned, by cutting.* (T, Ṣ.*) — [Hence,] مَطَرٌ ذُو بُرَايَةٍ †*Rain that pares and peels the ground.* (TA.) — And هُوَ مِنْ بُرَايَتِهِمْ †*He is of the refuse,* or *lowest* or *meanest sort, of them.* (M, TA.) — But ذُو بُرَايَةٍ, applied to a camel, means †*Enduring travel:* (T, Ṣ, M:) or *having fat and flesh:* (Ṣ:) and ذَاتُ بُرَايَةٍ, applied to a she-camel, has the latter meaning: or the former: (M, Ḳ:) or *strong when fatigued and emaciated by travel:* (TA:) or, as some say, براية in both cases means the *remains of fatness and compactness,* or *of fat, and of strength.* (M, TA.) حَتٌّ البُرَايَةِ is said to mean †*Fleet,* or *swift, when emaciated by travel;* for the subst. براية is said to be here put for the inf. n. بَرْى. (L in art. حت, q. v.)

بِرَايَةٌ a quasi-inf. n. of 1 in the first of the senses assigned to it above: as when it is said that a reed for writing is not called a قَلَم except after the براية [i. e. the *shaping,* or *paring*]. (Mṣb.)

بَرَّآءٌ *A maker of arrows, who forms,* or *fashions, them by cutting; who shapes them out,* or *pares them:* or *who does so completely:* (Ḳ:) and *a maker of spindles, who forms,* or *fashions, them by cutting:* and *a cutter,* or *parer, of aloes-wood, that is used for fumigation:* (TA:) [and in like manner, ↓ بَارِى قِسِىٍّ *a fashioner,* or *shaper, of bows:* whence the saying,] أَعْطِ القَوْسَ بَارِيَهَا [*Give thou the bow to its fashioner*]; meaning †*commit thou thine affair to him who will execute it well:* a prov. (Ḥar p. 68. [See also Freytag's Arab. Prov. ii. 98.])

بَرَّآءَةٌ: see مِبْرَاةٌ.

بَرَّآءٌ: see بَارِى قِسِىٍّ.

بَارِىٌّ and بَارِيَّةٌ and بَارِيَآءُ: see in art. بور.

مَبْرَى القَلَمِ [*The place where the paring is commenced of the reed for writing*]. (Ḳ in art. جلف.)

مِبْرَاةٌ The *iron implement,* (Ṣ,) or *knife,* (AḤn, M, Ḳ,) *with which one forms, fashions, shapes out,* or *pares,* (AḤn, Ṣ, M, Ḳ,) *a bow;* (AḤn, M, Ḳ;) as also ↓ بَرَّآءَةٌ, (Ḳ, TA,) with teshdeed and medd, (TA,) or ↓ بُرَآءُ, (so in a copy of the M,) or ↓ بَرَاةٌ. (CḲ, and so in a MS. copy of the Ḳ.)

مَبْرِىٌّ: see بَرِىٌّ.

مُتَبَارٍ part. n. of 6. It is said in a trad., المُتَبَارِيَانِ لَا يُجَابَانِ وَلَا يُؤْكَلُ طَعَامُهُمَا [*The two persons who vie with each other* in the expensiveness of their entertainments *shall not have their invitations accepted, nor shall their food be eaten*]. (El-Jámi' eṣ-Ṣagheer of Es-Suyooṭee.) The متباريان whose food is forbidden, in a trad., to be eaten, are They *who vie with each other in order that each may render the other unable to equal him in respect of the repast prepared by him for his guests:* and the doing of this is disliked because of the rivalry and ostentation that are involved in it. (TA.) — المُتَبَارِيَانِ is also an appellation of *The night and the day.* (Ḥar p. 377.)

بز

1. بَزَّهُ, aor. ـُ, (Ṣ, TA,) inf. n. بَزٌّ, (Ṣ, Ḳ, TA,) *He took it away;* or *seized it,* or *carried it away, by force;* (Ṣ, TA;) as also ↓ ابتزّه, (Ṣ, Ḳ,) and ↓ بَزْبَزَهُ: (Ḳ:) *he took it away unjustly, injuriously, and forcibly;* as also ↓ ابتزّه: (Ḳ,* TA:) *he gained the mastery over it:* (Ḳ,* TA:) *he pulled it up* or *out* or *off; removed it from its place; displaced it;* (Ḳ,* TA;) as also ↓ ابتزّه, and ↓ بَزْبَزَهُ. (TA.) It is said in a prov., مَنْ عَزَّ بَزَّ *He who overcomes takes the spoil.* (Ṣ, A.) And you say, بَزَّهُ ثَوْبَهُ, and ↓ ابتزّه, *He took away from him,* or *seized* or *carried away from him by force, his garment.* (A.) It is said in a trad., فَيَبْتَزُّنِى ↓ ثِيَابِى وَمَتَاعِى *And he strips me,* or *despoils me, of my clothes and my goods; takes them from me by superior force.* (TA.) You say also, بَزَّهُ ثِيَابَهُ *He pulled off from him his clothes.* (TA.) And ابتزّ ↓ الرَّجُلُ جَارِيَتَهُ مِنْ ثِيَابِهَا *The man stripped his slave-girl of her clothes.* (Mgh,* TA.) — Also بَزَّ ثَوْبَهُ, aor. as above, *He pulled his garment towards him,* or *to him:* so in a verse of Khálid Ibn-Zuheyr El-Hudhalee [cited in art. ريب, but with this difference, that يَجُرُّ is there put in the place of يَبُزُّ]. (Ṣ, TA.) — بَزَّهُ is also explained in the TA by حَبَسَهُ; but without any ex.; and I think it probable that حَبَسَهُ is a mistake for جَذَبَهُ].

8: see 1, in six places. ═ ابتزّت مِنْ ثِيَابِهَا *She stripped herself of her clothes.* (A.)

R. Q. 1. بَزْبَزَهُ: see 1, in two places. — بَزْبَزَةٌ [the inf. n.] also signifies The *being quick and active in wrongful, unjust, injurious,* or *tyrannical, conduct:* and the rel. n. is ↓ بَزْبَزِىٌّ. (TA.)

بَزٌّ inf. n. of 1. (Ṣ, &c.) — [Hence, app.,] جِىْءَ بِهِ عَزًّا بَزًّا *He was brought without any means of avoiding it;* (A, TA;) *willingly or against his will:* (TA in art. عز:) [as though originally signifying *by being overcome and despoiled.*] ═ *Cloths,* or *stuffs,* or *garments;* syn. ثِيَابٌ: (IAmb, Mgh, Ḳ:) [see also بِزَّةٌ:] or *a kind thereof:* (Lth, Mgh, Mṣb:) or *such as are the goods of the* بَزَّاز, (Ṣ, A,) or *of the merchant:* (Mṣb:) or the *furniture of a house or tent, consisting of cloths* or *stuffs* (ثياب, IDrd, Mgh, Mṣb, Ḳ) *and the like:* (Ḳ:) in the dial. of the people of El-Koofeh, *cloths,* or *stuffs,* or *garments,* (ثياب,) *of linen* and *of cotton; not of wool nor of* خَزّ: (Mgh:) pl. بُزُوزٌ; (A;) meaning, in conjunction with خُزُوزٌ, (i. e., خُزُوزٌ وَبُزُوزٌ,) *good cloths* or *stuffs* or *garments.* (A.) [Golius explains it as "Chald. בוּץ *Byssus,* seu potius *pannus lineus, bombacinus,* etiam *sericus:*" as on the authority of the Ṣ and Ḳ (though he omits the explanations in both those lexicons) and Meyd and Ibn-Maaroof (who explains it only by the Persian word جَامَهْ, meaning *cotton* or *linen cloth,* or *a garment,*) and the Mirkát el-Loghah. He seems to have judged from its resemblance in sound to the Chaldee and Latin words with which he identifies it. The things which it signifies, however, may perhaps be so called because they are usual spoils: and hence also, perhaps, the application here next following.] ═ *Weapons,* or *arms;* or *a weapon;* syn. سِلَاحٌ; (Ṣ, Mṣb, Ḳ;) as also ↓ بِزَّةٌ, (Ṣ, A, Mṣb, Ḳ,) and ↓ بَزَزٌ, (Ḳ,) and ↓ بَزْبَزِىٌّ: (TA:) the first of these four words including in its application *coats of mail and the* مِغْفَر *and the sword:* (TA:) or it signifies *a sword:* (IDrd, A, TA:) and ↓ بَزَزٌ, accord. to AA, *complete arms.* (TA.) You say, تَقَلَّدَ بَزًّا حَسَنًا *He hung upon himself a goodly sword, putting its suspensory belt or cord upon his neck.* (A.) And غَزَا فِى بِزَّةٍ ↓ كَامِلَةٍ *He went to war in complete arms.* (A.)

بِزَّةٌ *Constraint,* or *force:* as in the saying, لَنْ يَأْخُذَهُ أَبَدًا بِزَّةً مِنِّى *He will never take it by constraint,* or *force, from me.* (Ks, TA.) ═ *Outward appearance; state with regard to apparel and the like;* syn. هَيْئَةٌ, (Ṣ, A, Mgh, Mṣb, Ḳ, TA,) and شَارَةٌ: (TA:) *garb; mode, manner,* or *fashion, of dress:* (TA:) *apparel.* (A, Mgh.) You say, رَجُلٌ حَسَنُ البِزَّةِ *A man of goodly outward appearance,* or *state of apparel and the like:* (Mgh, Mṣb:) or as some say, *clothes and arms.* (Mgh.) And إِنَّهُ لَذُو بِزَّةٍ حَسَنَةٍ *Verily he has a goodly outward appearance and dress.* (A, TA.) ═ See also بَزٌّ, latter part, in two places.

بَزَزٌ: see بَزٌّ, latter part, in two places.

بِزَازَةٌ The *trade of the* بَزَّاز. (Mgh, Mṣb, Ḳ.)

بَزَّازٌ The *seller of the cloths or stuffs or the like called* بَزّ. (Ṣ,* A,* Mgh,* Ḳ.)

بِزِّيزَى a subst. from بَزَّ in the first of the senses explained above; The *act of taking away*; or *spoliation*; or the *act of seizing*, or *carrying away, by force*: (Ṣ, TA:) the *act of taking*, or *obtaining, by superior power or force*. (Ḳ,* TA.) It is said in a trad., ثُمَّ يَكُونُ بِزِّيزَى وَأَخْذُ أَمْوَالٍ بِغَيْرِ حَقٍّ *Then it shall be by spoliation, and the taking of possessions without right*: or, as some relate this trad., ▼ بَزْبَزِيًّا; but accord. to Az, this is naught. (TA.) You say also, رَجَعَتِ الخِلَافَةُ بِزِّيزَى [*The office of Khaleefeh became reduced to be a thing taken by superior power or force*]; *was not taken by desert*. (A, TA.) ═ See also بَزٌّ, latter part.

بَزْبَزِيٌّ: see R. Q. 1, and بِزِّيزَى.

بزخ

1. بَزِخَ, aor. َ, (L,) inf. n. بَزَخٌ, (Ṣ, L, Ḳ,) *He had a prominent breast and hollow back*: (Ṣ, L, Ḳ:) or *he had the lower part of his belly prominent, and the part between the hips, or haunches*, [*behind*,] *hollow, or depressed*: or *he had the middle of his back hollow, or depressed, and the lower part of his belly prominent*: or *he had his back retiring from his belly*: or *he had his belly depressed, and the* ثُنَّة [here app. meaning the pubes], *and the part next thereto, prominent*: (L:) بَزَخٌ is similar to قَعَسٌ: [see قعس:] (A:) and ▼ انبزخ signifies the same as بَزِخَ. (IAạr, TA.) The epithet applied to a man is ▼ أَبْزَخُ; and to a woman, بَزْخَآءُ. (Ṣ, A, L, Ḳ.) — Also, inf. n. as above, *He* (a horse) [*was saddle-backed*; i. e.,] *had a hollow back, and prominent croup and withers*. (ISd, L.)

6. تبازخ *He walked, or sat, in the manner of him who is termed* أَبْزَخ. (L.) And تبازخت *She* (a woman) *made her posteriors to stick out*: (Ṣ:) or *she had prominent posteriors*: (Ḳ:) or *she* (an old woman, in walking,) *erected her backbone, and made the part between her shoulders to recede, and bent the part above it, next her neck*: (L:) or *she had her posteriors prominent, and the upper part of her back, next the neck, bent*. (TA.) — *He* (a horse) *bent his hoof towards his belly, because of the shortness of his neck, at the time of drinking*. (TA.) — تبازخ عَنِ الأَمْرِ ‡ *He drew back, held back, or hung back, from the thing, or affair; would not go forward in it*. (Ṣ, A, Ḳ.)

7: see 1.

أَبْزَخُ A man *having a prominent breast and hollow back*: &c.: (see 1:) fem. بَزْخَآءُ. (Ṣ, A, L, Ḳ.) — A horse *having a depressed croup and backbone*: (Ṣ:) or [*saddle-backed*; i. e.] *having a hollow back, and prominent croup and withers*. (ISd, L.) It is applied to a horse such as is termed بِرْذَوْنٌ. (L.) — And the fem., A she-camel *having a plain, or even, croup, or rump*. (L.)

مَشَى مُتَبَازِخًا *He* (a man) *walked like an old woman affecting, or constraining herself, to erect her backbone, so that the part between her shoulders recedes*: (A:) or, *like an old woman having her posteriors prominent, and the upper part of her back, next the neck, bent*. (TA.)

بزر

1. بَزَرَ القِدْرَ, (Mṣb,) [aor. ُ or ِ, accord. to the rule of the Ḳ,] inf. n. بَزْرٌ; (Ḳ;) and ▼ بزّرها, (A,) inf. n. تَبْزِيرٌ; (TA;) *He threw, or put*, أَبْزَار, (A,) or إِبْزَار, (Mṣb,) or أَبَازِير, (A, Ḳ,) [i. e. *seeds for seasoning the food*,] *into the cooking-pot*. (A, Mṣb, Ḳ.) — [Hence,] ▼ بزّر كَلَامَهُ ‡ *He seasoned* (تَوْبَلَ [meaning *he embellished*]) *his speech, or language*. (A.) — بَزَرَ, (TḲ,) inf. n. بَزْرٌ, (Ḳ,) also signifies *He sowed* (Ḳ, TḲ) seeds; (TḲ;) *i. q.* بَذَرَ. (Ḳ, TA.)

2: see 1, in two places.

بَزْرٌ: see what next follows, in five places.

بِزْرٌ and ▼ بَزْرٌ, (Ṣ, Mṣb, Ḳ,) the former the more chaste, (T, Ṣ, Mṣb,) or the only form used by persons of chaste speech, (ISk, T, Mṣb,) The *seed of herbs* or *leguminous plants*, (Ṣ, A, Mgh, Mṣb,) *and of other plants*: (Ṣ, A, Mṣb:) or *small seed* or *grain, such as that of herbs* or *leguminous plants and the like*: (TA:) or *any seed*, or *grain, that is sown* (Kh, Mṣb, Ḳ) *for vegetation*; (Ḳ;) as also بِذْرٌ [q. v.]: (Kh, Mṣb:) pl. بُزُورٌ. (Ḳ.) — And *Seeds that are used in cooking, for seasoning food*; syn. تَابَلٌ: pl. ▼ أَبْزَارٌ and أَبَازِيرُ; (Ḳ;) the latter of which is pl. of أَبْزَارٌ; (TA;) or of this word and of ▼ إِبْزَارٌ; both of which are sings.; arabicized [from the Persian أَفْزَارْ]; the former of them anomalous, being of a pl. form: (Mṣb:) أَبْزَارٌ and أَبَازِيرُ are *syn. with* تَوَابِلُ: (Ṣ:) or ابزار and توابل both signify *that with which food is seasoned*; but the former of these is applied to *what is moist* and *what is dry*; and the latter, to what is dry only: this distinction, however, appears to be conventional [and modern]; for the [classical] language of the Arabs does not indicate it. (MF.) — Hence, ▼ أَبَازِيرُ also signifies ‡ *Additions* [or *embellishments*] *in speech*. (A.) — بِزْرٌ and ▼ بَزْرٌ signify also *Oil of* بِزْر [i. e. of *seeds*]. (Ṣ.) بِزْرُ الكَتَّانِ [commonly meaning *Linseed*] signifies *linseed-oil* in the dial. of the people of Baghdád. (Ḳ.) — Also ▼ بَزْرٌ, (Mgh,) or بِزْرُ القَزِّ, (Mṣb,) ‡ *The eggs of the silk-worm*. (Mgh, Mṣb.) — And ▼ the former of these, † *Offspring*. (Ḳ, TA.) One says, ▼ مَا أَكْثَرَ بَزْرَهُ † *How numerous is his offspring!* (TA.)

بَزْرَآءُ: see مَبْزُورٌ.

بَزْرِيٌّ *One who expresses the oil of* بِزْر. (TA.)

بَزَّارٌ *One who sells* بِزْر الكَتَّانِ, i. e., *linseed-oil*, in the dial. of the people of Baghdád. (Ḳ.)

بَازُورٌ ‡ A man *who induces in one, or throws one into, doubt or suspicion*; from the phrase بَزَّرَ كَلَامَهُ. (A.)

أَبْزَار and إِبْزَار: pl. أَبَازِيرُ: see بِزْرٌ, in three places.

إِبْزَارِيٌّ [*One who sells* إِبْزَار or أَبْزَار]. (Ḳ.)

مُبَزَّرٌ *Seasoned with* أَبَازِير, i. e. تَوَابِل. (Mgh.) [See بَزَّرَ.]

مَبْزُورٌ † *Having many children*; applied to a man: and so ▼ بَزْرَآءُ applied to a woman. (Ḳ, TA.)

بزغ

1. بُزُوغٌ [inf. n. of بَزَغَ] signifies The *beginning to rise, or come forth*: this is the primary meaning: mentioned by Zj. (TA.) — Hence, (TA,) بَزَغَ, said of a tush, or tusk, or canine tooth, (A,) or of the tush of a camel, (Ṣ, Mṣb, Ḳ,) [aor. ُ,] inf. n. بُزُوغٌ, (Mṣb,) *It came forth*; (Ṣ, Mṣb, Ḳ;) *it clave the flesh, and came forth*. (A.) — And hence, (A, TA,) بَزَغَتِ الشَّمْسُ, (JK, Ṣ, A, Mṣb, Ḳ,) aor. ُ, (TḲ,) inf. n. as above (JK, Ṣ, Ḳ) and بَزْغٌ, (Ḳ,) *The sun began to rise*; (JK, TA;) *as though it clave the darkness with its light*: (A, TA:) or *rose*, (Ṣ, Mṣb, Ḳ,) *with spreading light*: (TA:) or بُزُوغٌ has the meaning first explained above; the *beginning to rise, or come forth*. (Ḳ.) And in like manner one says, بَزَغَ القَمَرُ [*The moon began to rise*: or *rose*]. (A, TA.) ═ بَزَغَ, (Ṣ, Mgh, Mṣb, Ḳ,) aor. ُ, (Mṣb,) inf. n. بَزْغٌ, (JK, Mṣb,) *He* (a cupper, and a farrier,) *scarified*, (Ṣ, Mṣb, Ḳ,) *and made the blood to flow*: (Mṣb:) *he* (a farrier) *scarified* a beast (JK, Mgh, TA) *in its* أَشْعَر [or *part next the hoof* (in the TA, erroneously, شعر)], (JK,) *with a* مِبْزَغ (JK, Mgh, TA) *of iron*; (JK;) as also ▼ بزّغ, inf. n. تَبْزِيغٌ: (JK,* TA:) Aboo-'Adnán says that تَبْزِيغ and تَعْرِيبٌ signify the same, namely, the *making a slight incision, or stab, such as does not reach the sinews, or tendons*. (TA.) — And *He made* his blood *to flow*. (TA.)

2: see 1.

7. انبزغ الرَّبِيعُ, (Ṣ, and so in a copy of the Ḳ,) or ▼ ابتزغ, (so in other copies of the Ḳ and in the TA,) *The first, or beginning, of the* [*season, or rain, or herbage, called*] ربيع *came*. (Ṣ, Ḳ.)

8: see 7.

قَمَرٌ بَازِغٌ, (TA,) and شَمْسٌ بَازِغَةٌ, (Mṣb,) and نُجُومٌ بَوَازِغُ, (JK, A,) [*A moon, and a sun, and stars*,] *beginning to rise*: (JK, TA:) or *rising*. (Mṣb, TA.)

مِبْزَغٌ *A lancet* (Ṣ, Mgh, Ḳ) *of a cupper* and *of a farrier*. (JK, Mgh, TA.)

بزق

1. بَزَقَ, (Ṣ, Mṣb, Ḳ,) aor. ُ, (Mṣb, TA,) inf. n. بَزْقٌ, (Ṣ, TA,) or بُزَاقٌ, (Mṣb,) [but see the latter below,] *i. q.* بَصَقَ (Ṣ,* Mṣb) or بَسَقَ (Ḳ) [*He spat*: see also 5]: but it is of weak authority, or rare; the most chaste being بصق. (TA in art. بسق.) ═ بَزَقَ الأَرْضَ *He sowed the land*: (Az, Ḳ:) of the dial. of El-Yemen. (TA.) ═ بَزَقَتِ الشَّمْسُ *i. q.* بَزَغَت; (Az, Ḳ;) so in a trad., meaning *The sun rose*: the latter of which is that which is [commonly] known; but the former may be a dial. var.;

though the right reading seems to be بَرَقَتْ. (Az, TA.)

4. ابزقت She (namely, a ewe, JK, or a camel, Ḳ) excerned the milk [or biestings into her udder before bringing forth]; (Yz, JK, Ḳ, TA;) i. q. ابسقت [q. v.]. (TA.)

5. تبزّق He ejected his spittle, as the faster is commanded to do. (Mgh.)

بُزَاقٌ is well known; (Ḳ;) i. q. بُصَاقٌ [Spittle, or saliva, when it has gone forth from the mouth]: (Ṣ:) or saliva that flows. (TA in art. رضب.) [See also 1.]

مِبْزَقَةٌ A spittoon, or vessel in which to spit; syn. مِتْفَلَةٌ. (TA in art. تفل.)

بزل

1. بَزَلَهُ, (Mṣb, Ḳ,) aor. ـُ, (TA,) inf. n. بَزْلٌ, (Mṣb, TA,) He clave it, split it, or slit it; (Ḳ;) as also ▼ بزّلهُ, (Ḳ,) inf. n. تَبْزِيلٌ. (TA. [But the latter verb probably has an intensive or a frequentative sense, or applies to many objects.]) — He broached it, or pierced it, and drew forth what was in it. (Mṣb.) — He broached, or pierced, the vessel containing it, (IDrd, Ḳ, TA,) and drew it forth; (IDrd, TA;) namely wine, &c.; (IDrd, Ḳ, TA;) as also ▼ ابتزله and ▼ تبزّله. (Ḳ,* TA.) You say, ▼ ابْتَزَلْتُ الشَّرَابَ لِنَفْسِى [I broached its vessel, and drew forth the wine, or beverage, for myself]. (TA.) — He removed it, or took it off, namely, the clay [that closed the mouth,] from the head of the دَنّ [or wine-jar]. (Ḥar p. 140.) — He cleared it, or clarified it; namely, wine, or beverage; (Ḳ;) as also ▼ ابتزله: but Az says, I know not البَزْل as signifying "the act of clearing, or clarifying." (TA. [بَزَلْتُ الشَّرَابَ is mentioned, but not explained, in the Ṣ. The meaning there intended may be either the third or the last given above.]) — ‡ He decided it, (Ḳ, TA,) and settled it firmly; (TA;) namely, a case, or an affair; or an opinion: (Ḳ, TA:) and † he decided it; namely, the judicial sentence. (TA.) — † He originated it, or devised it; namely, his opinion. (TA.) — مَا عِنْدَهُ بُلْغَةٌ تَبْزُلُ حَاجَةً † He has not a sufficiency, or a sufficiency of the means of subsistence, that will satisfy a want. (Z, TA.) = بَزَلَ, (Ṣ, Mṣb, Ḳ,) aor. ـُ, (Ṣ, Mṣb,) inf. n. بُزُولٌ (Ṣ, Mṣb, Ḳ) and بَزْلٌ, (Ḳ, TA, [in the CḲ بُزْلٌ,]) It (the ناب [or tush] of a camel) clave the flesh, and came forth: (Ḳ,* TA:) or his (a camel's) ناب [or tush] clave the flesh, and came forth; (Ṣ, Mṣb;) [or he became such as is termed بَازِل; generally] by his entering the ninth year. (Mṣb.) — [And hence, as being likened to a camel that has attained his full strength,] inf. n. بزالة [written without any indication of the syll. signs, but most probably بَزَالَةٌ, though the verb seems to be بَزُلَ, not بَزَلَ,] † It (an opinion, or a judgment,) was, or became, right. (Mṣb.)

2: see 1.

5. تبزّل and ▼ انبزل, (Ḳ, TA,) or ▼ ابتزل, (so the latter is written in the CḲ,) It clave, split, or slit; intrans.: (Ḳ:) or the former signifies it clave, split, or slit, much, in several places, or often; syn. تَشَقَّقَ: and ▼ the second, said of a طَلْع, [app. here meaning a spathe, rather than a spadix, of a palm-tree,] it clave, split, or burst. (Ṣ.) — Also, the first, said of the body, It burst forth, or flowed, with blood: and in like manner one says of a water-skin تبزّل and تبزّل بِالمَآءِ [it burst forth, or flowed, with water, or the water]. (TA.) = See also 1.

7: see 5, in two places.

8: see 1, in three places = and see 5.

10. استبزلهُ He opened it; namely, a دَنّ [or wine-jar]. (Ḥar p. 140.)

أَمْرٌ ذُو بَزْلٍ A distressing, an afflictive, or a calamitous, affair or event or case. (Ṣ, Ḳ.)

سِقَآءٌ فِيهِ بَزْلٌ A water-skin that bursts forth, or flows, with the water: pl. بُزُولٌ. (TA.)

بَزْلَآءُ ‡ A great calamity or misfortune or disaster. (IDrd, Ḳ, TA.) — † Difficulties, distresses, or afflictions. (IDrd, Ḳ.) You say, هُوَ نَهَّاضٌ ▼ بِبَزْلَآءَ † He is one who manages great affairs; (Ṣ, Ḳ, TA;) who has ability and strength to overcome difficulties. (TA.) — † Good judgment or opinion or counsel. (Ṣ, Ḳ.) — مَا لِفُلَانٍ بَزْلَآءُ يَعِيشُ بِهَا † Such a one has not determination, resolution, or decision, of judgment, whereby to live. (TA.) — هُوَ ذُو بَزْلَآءَ † He has a firm, or well-established, way, or manner, of acting, or conducting himself. (TA.) — خُطَّةٌ بَزْلَآءُ ‡ A great event that distinguishes that which is true and that which is false. (Ḳ,* TA.)

بُزَالٌ The place that is broached, or pierced, in a vessel containing wine &c.; (Ḳ;) the place whence issues the thing [or liquid] whereof the containing vessel is broached, or pierced. (IDrd.)

بِزَالٌ An iron instrument with which the مِبْزَل [or مَبْزَل ?] of a wine-jar is opened. (Ṣgh, Ḳ.)

بَزُولٌ: see بَازِلٌ, in two places.

بَزِيلٌ, applied to wine or beverage, i. q. ▼ مُبْتَزَلٌ [which may mean either That whereof the containing vessel has been broached and which has been drawn forth, or that which is cleared or clarified; but more probably the former]. (Ibn-'Abbád.)

بَازِلٌ, applied to a camel, the male and the female, (Ṣ, Mgh, Mṣb, Ḳ,) That has cut its ناب [or tush]; (Ṣ, Mṣb, Ḳ;) by its entering the ninth year; (Mṣb;) or in its ninth year; (Ṣ, Mgh, Ḳ;) for then it cuts that tooth; (Ṣ, Ḳ;) or, as is sometimes the case, in the eighth year; (Ṣ;) and after this there is no age named: (IAạr, Ḳ:) or a she-camel that has completed her ninth year, and attained her full strength: (Ḥam p. 506:) and ▼ بَزُولٌ signifies the same, applied to the male and the female: (IDrd, Ḳ:) or, accord. to AZ, a she-camel is not termed بَازِل; but the epithet ▼ بَزُولٌ is applied to her that has completed a year after cutting the tooth above mentioned, until she is termed ناب: (MF, TA:) the pl. (of بازل, Ṣ, Mṣb) is بَوَازِلُ (Ṣ, Mṣb, Ḳ) and بُزَّلٌ (Ṣ, Ḳ) and بُزُلٌ, (Ṣ,) or بُزْلٌ, like كُتْبٌ. (Ḳ.) بَازِلُ عَامٍ and بَازِلُ عَامَيْنِ signify That has passed a year, and two years, after cutting the tooth above mentioned. (MF, TA.) — Also The tooth that has come forth at the time above mentioned: (Ṣ, Ḳ:) pl. بَوَازِلُ. (IAạr, Ḳ.) — And ‡ A man perfect in his experience and his intellect: (Ḳ, TA:) or rendered firm, or sound, in judgment by age and experience: so says IDrd: likened to the camel thus termed: (TA:) or old: opposed to جَذَعٌ, q. v. (IAạr in art. جذع of the TA.) — And ‡ A case, or an affair, and an opinion, firmly settled or established. (TA.) — خَطْبٌ بَازِلٌ † A difficult, a distressing, or an afflicting, thing, affair, or business. (TA.) You say also, بُلِىَ بِأَشْهَبَ بَازِلٍ † He was afflicted with a difficult and distressing thing or event. (TA. [See also art. شهب.]) — شَجَّةٌ بَازِلَةٌ A wound in the head from which the blood flows: (Ṣ:) or such as is termed حَارِصَةٌ, (Ḳ,) i. e. مُتَلَاحِمَةٌ, (TA,) [but see these two words, and see شَجَّةٌ,] that cleaves the skin, but does not penetrate beyond it: (Ḳ:) the mulct for which is said to be three camels. (TA.) — مَا بَقِيَتْ لَهُمْ بَازِلَةٌ is like the saying مَا بَقِيَتْ لَهُمْ ثَاغِيَةٌ وَلَا رَاغِيَةٌ, i. e. ‡ [There remained not to them] one [sheep or goat, or camel]. (Ṣ, TA.) You say also, مَا عِنْدَهُ بَازِلَةٌ, i. e. † There is not in his possession anything of property, or of camels &c.: (Yaạḳoob, Ṣ, Ḳ:) or, a sufficiency, or a sufficiency of the means of subsistence, that will satisfy a want. (Z, TA.) And لَا تَرَكَ اللّٰهُ عِنْدَهُ بَازِلَةً † [May God not leave in his possession] anything. (Ṣ.) And لَمْ يُعْطِهِمْ بَازِلَةً † [He did not give them] anything. (Ṣ.)

[مَبْزَلٌ app. The mouth of a wine-jar: see بِزَالٌ.]

مِبْزَلٌ A strainer, or thing with which wine, or beverage, is cleared, or clarified; (Ṣ, Ḳ, TA;) as also ▼ مِبْزَلَةٌ. (Ḳ.) — An instrument for broaching, piercing, or perforating. (Mṣb.)

مِبْزَلَةٌ: see مِبْزَلٌ.

مُبْتَزَلٌ: see بَزِيلٌ.

بزم

إِبْزَامٌ: see what follows.

إِبْزِيمٌ (Ṣ, Mgh, Ḳ, &c.) and ▼ إِبْزَامٌ (Ḳ) [A buckle;] the thing that is at the head [or end] of the [zone, or waist-belt, called] مِنْطَقَة (Ṣ, Ḳ) and the like, and that has a tongue, into which [thing] the other extremity [of the منطقة] enters; (Ḳ;) a ring with a tongue, which is at the head of the منطقة and the like, and with which it is fastened; (Mgh;) the ring that has a tongue which enters into the hole in the lowest part of the shoulder-belt of the sword, and upon which the ring then bites, or presses; the ring altogether [with the tongue] being termed ابزيم; (ISh, TA;) the iron thing that is at the end of the girth of the horse's saddle, which is fastened therewith; and sometimes it is at the end of the منطقة: (IB, TA:) pl. أَبَازِيمُ. (Ṣ.) — Also A lock; and so إِبْزِينٌ. (TA.) — You say, إِنَّ فُلَانًا لَإِبْزِيمٌ, meaning † Verily such a one is a niggard. (TA.)

بزو

1. بَزَا, aor. يَبْزُو, i. q. تَطَاوَلَ [app. as meaning He stretched out his neck, looking at a thing far *off*]; and تَأَتَّسَ [here meaning the same, or *he looked, raising his head;* said of a hawk, or falcon]: (Az, ISd, Ḳ:) and hence IJ says that بَازٍ is [originally] of the measure فَلْعٌ from this verb: (TA: [and it is said in the Ḳ that بَازٍ seems to be hence derived:]) [or تطاول may here be used in another sense; for, accord. to Fei,] بَزَا, aor. as above, signifies *he overcame,* or *subdued;* and hence is derived بَازٍ. (Mṣb.) You say also, بَزَا عَلَيْهِ, aor. as above, meaning تطاول [i. e., thus followed by عليه, *He held up his head with an assumption of superiority over him; behaved haughtily towards him; exalted himself above him;* or *overpowered, subdued,* or *oppressed, him*]. (Ṣ.) And بُزِىَ بِالقَوْمِ *The people,* or *company of men, were overcome,* or *subdued.* (TA.) And بَزَاهُ, aor. as above, (Ḳ,) inf. n. بَزْوٌ, (TA,) *He overcame,* or *subdued, him;* and *laid violent hands upon him,* or *assaulted him;* as also ابزى بِهِ: (Ḳ:) or this last signifies *he overcame him, and subdued him:* (Ṣ:) and بَزَاهُ, *he wronged him;* or *treated him wrongfully,* or *injuriously:* and ابزاهُ may signify the same; or this may mean *he induced him to become* أَبْزَى, q. v.: (Ḥam p. 502:) and accord. to Aboo-Riyásh, ابزى signifies *he pressed heavily upon his adversary,* or *imposed on him that which he was unable to do,* or *to bear, in order to treat him wrongfully,* or *injuriously.* (Ḥam pp. 104 and 105.) [It is said that] بَزَوَانٌ [an inf. n. of which the verb, if it have one, is بَزَا,] signifies the act of *Leaping;* syn. وَثْبٌ. (Ṣ: [but I think it not improbable that this may have been taken from a mistranscription of نَزَوَانٌ, an inf. n. of نَزَا.]) ═ بَزِىَ, (Ḳ,) aor. َ; (Ḥam p. 502;) and بَزَا, aor. ُ; (Ḳ;) inf. n. بَزًا (Ṣ,* Ḳ,* TA) and بَزْوٌ, (TA,) *He* (a man, TA) *had what is termed* بَزًا; (Ḳ;) i. e., *prominence of the breast and depression of the back:* (Ṣ, Ḳ, and Ḥam ubi suprà:) or *depression of the back and prominence of the belly:* or, as some say, *prominence of the breast and depression of the lower part of the belly:* (Ḥam ubi suprà:) or *depression of the breast and prominence of the lower part of the belly:* (Ḥam p. 105:) or a *bending in the back next the posteriors:* (Ḳ, TA:) or *a projecting of the middle of the back over the posteriors:* or *a backward bulging of the posteriors:* (Ḳ:) or *he was as though his posteriors projected over the hinder part of the thighs:* or *he had the breast bulging forward and the posteriors backward, so that he appeared unable to straighten his back.* (T, TA.) [See also 4.] The epithet is أَبْزَى: fem. بَزْوَآءُ. (Ṣ, Ḳ.)

4. ابزى: see 1, in three places. ═ Also, (Ṣ, Ḳ,) inf. n. إِبْزَآءٌ, (A 'Obeyd, Ṣ,) *He* (a man, A 'Obeyd, Ṣ) *elevated his posteriors;* (A 'Obeyd, Ṣ, Ḳ;) as also تبازى: (Ṣ, Ḳ:) or the latter signifies *he acted in such a manner in his walk as to cause it to be imagined that he was* أَبْزَى; (Ḥam p. 105;) or *he moved his posteriors in walking, like as does a woman;* or *he bent,* or *bowed, himself to others.* (TA.) Accord. to IAạr, البزاء [probably a mistranscription for الإِبْزَآءُ] signifies الصلف [i. e. الصَّلَفُ, app. meaning *An extravagant affecting of elegance of carriage,* such as is common with women]. (TA.)

6. تبازى: see 4. — Also *He stepped wide.* (Ḳ.) — And *He made a vain,* or *false, boast of abundance,* or *riches;* or *a boast of more than he possessed;* or *invested himself with that which did not belong to him.* (Ḳ.)

بَزْوٌ The *equal, equivalent,* or *like,* of a thing. (Ṣ, Ḳ.) You say, أَخَذْتُ مِنْهُ بَزْوَ كَذَا [*I took from him,* or *of it, the equal, equivalent,* or *like, of such a thing*]. (Ṣ.)

بَازٍ (Ṣ, Mṣb, Ḳ) and بَازٌ [mentioned in art. بوز] (Mṣb, TA, and so in some copies of the Ḳ in this art.) and بَأْزٌ [mentioned in art. باز] and بَازِىٌّ (TA) [*A name given to several varieties of the hawk,* or *falcon;*] *a species of* صَقْر, (Ḳ,) *that preys,* or *hunts or catches game;* (Ṣ;) *the proudest and fiercest of birds of prey, found in the country of the Turks: it is said that this name is only given to the female, and that the male is of another kind, a kite, or a white falcon* (شَاهِين), *and hence the varieties of form &c. in different individuals of the species: that of which the prevailing colour is white is the best, and the fullest in body, and the boldest, and the easiest to train: this variety* (the أَشْهَب) *is found only in the country of the Turks, and Armenia, and the country of the Khazar:* (Ḳzw:) [see also بَاشَقٌ:] respecting the derivation, see 1, in two places: the pl. (of بَازٍ, Ṣ, ISd, Mṣb) is بُزَاةٌ (Ṣ, ISd, Mṣb, Ḳ) and بَوَازٍ; (ISd, Ḳ;) and (of بَازٌ, Mṣb) بِيزَانٌ (Mṣb, Ḳ) and أَبْوَازٌ, (Mṣb,) the former a pl. of mult., and the latter a pl. of pauc., (TA,) or the former is originally بُزْيَانٌ [and therefore a pl. of بَازٍ]; (IKṭṭ, TA in art. ميد;) and (of بَأْزٌ, Ḳ in art. باز) أَبْؤُزٌ [a pl. of pauc.] and بُؤُوزٌ (Ḳ in this art. and in art. باز) and بِئْزَانٌ. (Ḳ in the latter art.)

بَازِىٌّ: see بَازٍ.

أَبْزَى, applied to a man, (Ṣ, Mgh,) *Having what is termed* بَزًا; (Ṣ, Ḳ;) i. e., *prominence of the breast and depression of the back,* (Ṣ, Mgh, Ḳ, and Ḥam p. 105,) or *of the part between the shoulder-blades:* (Ḥam ubi suprà:) &c.: [see 1, latter part:] fem. بَزْوَآءُ: (Ṣ, Ḳ:) the masc. is sometimes coupled with أَبْزَخُ; and the fem., with بَزْخَآءُ, applied to an old woman who, when she walks, is as though she were bowing down her head and body: and the fem. is said by some to signify *sticking out her posteriors to be seen of men.* (TA.)

هُوَ مُبْزٍ بِهٰذَا الأَمْرِ *He is strong,* or *able, to perform this affair; a prudent,* or *sound, manager thereof.* (Ṣ.)

بس

1. بَسٌّ signifies The *act of breaking:* or *breaking in pieces:* syn. حَطْمٌ. (TA.) — [And The *act of mixing:* see بَسِيسَةٌ. This, or the former, is probably the primary signification.] — [And hence, app.,] بَسَّهُ, aor. ُ, inf. n. بَسٌّ, (M, Mṣb,) *He broke it, crumbled it,* or *bruised* or *brayed it;* said of wheat, &c.; *thus making it what is termed* بَسِيسَة: (Mṣb:) or *he mixed it,* namely, سَوِيق [or meal of parched barley or wheat], and flour, &c., *with clarified butter,* or *with olive-oil; thus making it what is termed* بَسِيسَة: (M:) or *he moistened it,* namely, سَوِيق, and flour, *with a little water;* (ISk, Mṣb;) *but making it more moist than one does in the action termed* لَتٌّ: (Yaạḳoob, cited in the Ṣ; and ISk, in the Mṣb:) or بَسٌّ signifies the *making,* or *preparing,* بَسِيسَة, *by stirring about,* or *moistening,* سَوِيق, or *flour,* or *ground* أَقِط, *with clarified butter,* or *with olive-oil;* (Ṣ, Ḳ;) after which it is eaten, without being cooked. (Ṣ.) — [And hence the saying in the Ḳur lvi. 5,] وَبُسَّتِ الجِبَالُ بَسًّا *And the mountains shall be crumbled with a vehement crumbling,* (Lḥ, M, A, Ḳ,) *like flour, and* سَوِيق, (A,) *and become earth:* (Fr, Ḳ:) or *become dust cleaving to the earth:* (AO, M, TA:) or *be levelled:* (M, TA:) or *mixed with the dust:* (Zj, M, TA:) or *reduced to powder and scattered in the wind.* (TA.)

بَسِيسَةٌ *Wheat, &c., broken,* or *crumbled,* or *bruised:* (Mṣb:) or سَوِيق [or *meal of parched barley or wheat*], and *flour, &c., mixed with clarified butter,* or *with olive-oil:* (M:) or *what is stirred about with olive-oil,* or *with clarified butter, and not wetted* [*with water*]: (Lḥ, M:) or سَوِيق, or *flour,* or *ground* أَقِط, *stirred about,* or *moistened, with clarified butter,* or *with olive-oil;* (Ṣ, Ḳ;) *after which it is eaten, without being cooked:* (Ṣ:) or سَوِيق, and *flour, moistened with a little water,* (ISk, Mṣb,) *but more moist than such as is prepared in the manner termed* لَتٌّ; (Yaạḳoob, cited in the Ṣ; and ISk, in the Mṣb;) *and used as travelling-provision:* (TA:) and *bread dried and pounded, and* [*mixed with water so that it is*] *drunk like as* سَوِيق *is drunk:* (M, Ḳ:*) IDrd thinks it to be *what is termed* قُتُوت: also *barley mixed with date-stones, for camels:* (M, TA:) or, accord. to Aṣ, *anything that one mixes with another thing: such as* سَوِيق *with* اقط, *which one then moistens with fresh butter:* and *such as barley with date-stones, which one then moistens, for camels:* (Mṣb,* TA:) pl. بَسَائِسُ, (IAạr, TA,) which is explained in the Ḳ as signifying *messes of* سَوِيق *moistened,* or *stirred about with water, &c.* (أَسْوِقَةٌ مَلْتُوتَةٌ). (TA.)

بسأ

1. بَسَأَ بِهِ, and بَسِئَ; (Ṣ, M, Ḳ;) aor. َ; (M, Ḳ;) inf. n. بَسْءٌ and بُسُوْءٌ (Ṣ, M, Ḳ) and بَسَآءٌ, (M, Ḳ,) all of the former verb; (M;) and بَسَأً, (M, Ḳ,) of the latter; (M;) *He was,* or *became, sociable, friendly,* or *familiar, with him;* (namely, a man, Ṣ, TA;) or *cheered,* or *gladdened, by his company* or *converse,* or *by his presence.* (Ṣ, M, Ḳ.) — بَسَأَ بِالأَمْرِ, inf. n. بَسْءٌ and بُسُوْءٌ, *He was,* or *became, accustomed,* or *habituated, to the affair,* or *case.* (M,* Ḳ,* TA.) — [And hence,] بَسَأَ بِهِ *He despised,* or *made light of, him,* or *it.* (M, Ḳ.)

4. أَبْسَأْتُهُ *I made him sociable, friendly,* or *familiar;* or *cheered him,* or *gladdened him, by my company* or *converse,* or *by my presence.* (Ṣ, Ḳ.)

بَسُوٌّ A she-camel *that offers no opposition to her milker,* (Ṣ, Ḳ,) *being of a good disposition, and accustomed to him.* (TA.)

بست accord. to some: بستان accord. to others.

بُسْتَانٌ [accord. to its etymology (which will be explained below) and to general modern usage, *A garden of sweet-scented flowers and trees:* but accord. to the Arabic Lexicons,] *a* [*garden such as is termed*] جَنَّةٌ: (Mgh, Mṣb:) or *a* [*garden, or walled garden, such as is termed*] حَدِيقَةٌ, (M, Ḳ, TA,) *of palm-trees;* as in a poem of El-Aashà: (TA:) said by Fr to be an Arabic word; (Mṣb, TA;) but this is denied by IDrd: (TA:) and said by some to be رُومِىّ [or Greek]: (Mṣb:) [but correctly] it is an arabicized word, from [the Persian] بُوسْتَانْ [bóstán], (Ḳ, [in which the ن is regarded as a radical letter,] Shifá el-Ghaleel, MF,) meaning "taking odour, or fragrance," or, as some say, "a place where odour, or fragrance, collects, or is collected:" (Shifá el-Ghaleel, MF:) its composition from بو and ستان requires the former meaning to be assigned to it: (TA:) [or rather it signifies "a place of odour, or fragrance:"] afterwards applied to *trees:* (TA:) pl. بَسَاتِينُ (Mṣb, Ḳ) and بَسَاتُونَ, (Ḳ,) like شَيَاطِينُ and شَيَاطُونَ. (TA.)

بُسْتُنْبَانٌ [an arabicized word from the Persian بُسْتَانْبَانْ, *i. q.* ▼ بُسْتَانِىٌّ, which is the more common; *A gardener, or*] *a keeper of a* بُسْتَان. (TA.)

بُسْتَانِىٌّ: see what next precedes.

بسد

بُسَّدٌ an arabicized word, [because س and د do not occur in any one Arabic word, (Mṣb, voce أُسْتَاذٌ,)] *Coral;* syn. مَرْجَانٌ. (Ḳ.)

بسر

1. بَسَرَ *He took* anything *when it was fresh, juicy, moist, or not flaccid;* (TA;) as also ▼ ابتسر [which is more commonly used]. (M, Ḳ,* TA.) [Hence,] بَسَرْتُ النَّبَاتَ, aor. ـُ, inf. n. بَسْرٌ, *I pastured* [*beasts*] *upon the herbage when it was fresh and juicy, I being the first to do so.* (TA.) — Also, (Ḳ,) aor. as above, (TA,) and so the inf. n., (M,) *i. q.* أَعْجَلَ [as meaning † *He was quick, or beforehand,* or *before the proper time, with* a person or thing, or *in doing,* or *seeking,* a thing]. (M, Ḳ.) [Hence,] بَسَرَ النَّاقَةَ, (Aṣ, Ṣ, M, Ḳ,) aor. and inf. n. as above; (M;) and ▼ ابتسرها, (Ṣ, A,) and ▼ تبسّرها; (T;) ‡ *He* (the stallion) *covered the she-camel without her desiring it:* (Aṣ, Ṣ, A:) or *before she desired it.* (M, Ḳ.) And in like manner, بَسَرَ and ▼ تبسّر ‡ *He* (a stallion) *covered* a mare *when she had only begun to feel the excitement of desire.* (TA.) And ▼ ابتسر الجَارِيَةَ ‡ *He deflowered the girl before she had attained to puberty.* (A, and Mṣb in art. قض.) And بَسَرَ and ▼ ابتسر † *He fecundated* a palm-tree *before the proper time for doing so.* (M, Ḳ.) And بَسَرَ السِّقَآءَ, (Ḳ,) inf. n. as above, (Ṣ,) † *He drank the milk of the skin,* (Ḳ,) or *gave it to be drunk,* (Ṣ,) *before it had become thick, and fit for churning.* (Ṣ, Ḳ.) And بَسَرَ, (M, Ḳ,) aor. as above, (M, A,) and so the inf. n., (Ṣ, M,) ‡ *He broke* a pustule: (A:) or *he squeezed* a pustule, or a boil, *before it was ripe:* (TA:) or *he laid it open by peeling off its crust,* or *scab, before it was ripe;* (Ṣ, M, Ḳ;) as also ▼ ابسر. (Ḳ.) And, inf. n. as above, † *He dug rivers when water was scarce:* or *sought for,* or *after, water* [*when it was scarce*]: and so, accord. to Az, ▼ تبسّر. (L. [But for اذا عرا الماء او طابه, as part of the explanation, I read إِذَا عَزَّ المَآءُ أَوْ طَلَبَهُ.]) And بَسَرَ النَّهْرَ † *He dug a well in* [*the bed of*] *the river, it being dry.* (L. [But here, for وهو صاف, I read وهو جَافٌّ.]) Also بَسَرَ, (Ṣ, M, Ḳ,) aor. as above, (M,) and inf. n. as above (Ṣ, M) and بِسَارٌ; (M;) and ▼ ابتسر (M, A, Ḳ) and ▼ تبسّر and ▼ ابسر; (M, Ḳ;) ‡ *He sought, sought for* or *after, demanded,* or *desired,* a thing that he wanted, or needed, *in an improper time:* (M, Ḳ:) or *in an improper place:* (Ṣ, M:) or *in an improper manner:* (Jm:) or *before its time.* (A.) And the first of these verbs, ‡ *He required* a debt *to be paid before the time when it was due.* (Ḳ, TA.) And ‡ *He required* his debtor *to pay a debt before the time when it was due:* from بَسَرَ النَّاقَةَ, explained above. (Sh, TA.) — Also, inf. n. بَسْرٌ, † *He began* a thing; and so ▼ ابتسر. (Ḳ.) And بَسَرَ بِهِ (TḲ) and ▼ ابتسر به (TA, TḲ) † *He began with it.* (TA, TḲ.) = Also, aor. ـُ, inf. n. بَسْرٌ, *He mixed* بُسْر [or *full-grown unripe dates*] *with others, in beverage of the kind called* نَبِيذ: the doing of which is forbidden in a trad.: (Ṣ:) or *he mixed* بُسْر *with fresh ripe dates,* or *with dry dates, and made with them both together that kind of beverage.* (TA.) And بَسَرَ تَمْرًا, (M, Ḳ,) aor. and inf. n. as above; and ▼ بَسَّرَهُ (M) and ▼ ابسره; (Ḳ;) *He made, of dry dates, that kind of beverage, and mixed* بُسْر *with it.* (M, Ḳ.) = Also, (M, Ḳ,) aor. ـُ, inf. n. بَسْرٌ and بُسُورٌ, (M,) *He frowned; contracted his face;* or *grinned,* or *displayed his teeth, frowning,* or *contracting his face,* or *looking sternly, austerely,* or *morosely;* (M, Ḳ;) as also بَسَرَ وَجْهَهُ, inf. n. بُسُورٌ: (Ṣ:) or *he did so excessively:* (Jel in lxxiv. 22:) or *he looked with intense dislike* or *hatred.* (TA.)

2: see 1; last sentence but one.

3. بَاسَرَتْ, inf. n. مُبَاسَرَةٌ, † *She* (a mare) *desired the stallion when she had only begun to feel the excitement of lust.* (AO.)

4. ابسر: see 1, in three places. — Also † *He dug in ground that had not been dug before.* (Ḳ.) = ابسر النَّخْلُ *The palm-trees had dates in the state in which they are called* بُسْر: (Ṣ, M:*) or *produced dates that did not ripen.* (TA.)

5. تبسّر: see 1, in four places. It signifies also † *He sought for,* or *after,* fresh water recently produced by rain. (Ṣ. [See بُسْر.]) And † *He dug for plants before they came forth:* (M, TA:) [or] تبسّر نَبَاتًا has this meaning. (TA.) And † *He* (a [wild] bull) *came to the roots of dry plants, and ate them.* (Ḳ.)

8. ابتسر: see 1, in seven places. = اِبْتَسَرَ لَوْنُهُ ‡ *His colour changed,* (Ḳ, TA,) *and became like that of* بُسْر [or *full-grown unripe dates*]. (TA.)

بُسْرٌ: see بُسْرٌ: = and see also بَاسِرٌ.

بُسْرٌ Anything *fresh, juicy, moist, not flaccid.* (IF, M, Mṣb, Ḳ.) You say نَبَاتٌ بُسْرٌ *A fresh plant:* (Mṣb:) or *a plant that has risen from the surface of the ground, but not grown tall;* because it is then fresh and juicy: (TA:) or such is called بُسْرَةٌ [fem. of بُسْر]; as also *what is fresh, juicy, moist,* or *not flaccid, of the plant called* بُهْمَى. (M.) A plant, or herbage, when it first appears in the ground is termed بَارِضٌ; then, جَمِيمٌ; then, بُسْرَةٌ; then, صَمْعَآءُ; and then, [when it is dry,] حَشِيشٌ. (Ṣ.) — *Fresh water,* (Ṣ, M, Ḳ,) *recently produced by rain;* (Ṣ, M;) as also ▼ بُسُرٌ: (M:) or this latter signifies *cold,* or *cool, water:* (Ḳ:) pl. of the former بِسَارٌ; (Ṣ, Ḳ;) like as رِمَاحٌ is pl. of رُمْحٌ. (Ṣ.) — ‡ A *young,* or *youthful,* man, and woman: (Ḳ, TA:) or *young,* or *youthful,* and *fresh;* fem. with ة: (M, A:) applied, respectively, to a man and a woman; (M;) or to a boy and a girl. (A.) — And, with ة, ‡ The sun *when it has just risen,* (Ṣ, Ḳ, TA,) *and is red, and not yet clear.* (A,* TA.) [Accord. to the A, this meaning seems to be derived from that next following.] — بُسْرٌ and ▼ بُسُرٌ (Ṣ, M, Ḳ) [the former, only, mentioned in the A and Mṣb &c., as the latter is rare; coll. gen. ns., signifying *Full-grown*] *unripe dates; dates before they have become* رُطَب; (M, Ḳ;) *dates that have become coloured, but have not become ripe;* (TA;) *dates that have begun to colour,* i. e., *to become red or yellow;* (Mṣb in art. بلح;) *dates beginning to ripen:* (IAth, TA in art. بلح:) so called because fresh and juicy, and not flaccid: (M:) n. un. بُسْرَةٌ and بُسُرَةٌ: (Ṣ, M, Ḳ:) pl. بُسْرَاتٌ (Ṣ) [or بُسُرَاتٌ] and بُسُرَاتٌ: (M:) Sb says that بُسْرَةٌ [or بُسُرَةٌ or each of these] has no broken pl.; but he allows بُسْرَانِ and تَمْرَانِ, as meaning *two sorts of* بُسْر and *of* تَمْر. (M.) [J says,] بُسْر in their first stage are termed طَلْعٌ; then, خَلَالٌ; then, بَلَحٌ; then, بُسْرٌ; then, رُطَبٌ; then, تَمْرٌ. (Ṣ:) but this saying of J is not good: the original thereof is termed طلع; and when they have become organized and compact (إِذَا انْعَقَدَ), they are termed سَيَابٌ or سَدَّابٌ [accord. to different copies of the Ḳ]; and when they have become green and round, جَدَالٌ and سَرَادٌ and خَلَالٌ; and when they have become somewhat large, بَغْوٌ; and when they have become large, [or full-grown,] بُسْرٌ; then, مُخَطَّمٌ; then, مُوَكِّتٌ; then, تُذْنُوبٌ; then, جُمْسَةٌ [in the CḲ جَمِيسَةٌ]; then, ثَعْدَةٌ and خَالِعٌ and خَالِعَةٌ; and when completely ripe, رُطَبٌ and مَعْوٌ; then, تَمْرٌ. (Ḳ.) — [Hence,] بُسْرَةٌ signifies also ‡ The *head,* or *extremity, of the penis of a dog.* (Ḳ, TA.) — And † *A kind of bead;* syn. خَرَزَةٌ. (Ḳ.)

بُسُرٌ: see بُسْرٌ.

بُسْرَةٌ fem. of بُسْر as an epithet, and n. un. of the same as a subst.: explained with the latter.

بُسُرَةٌ n. un. of بُسُرٌ, a dial. var. of بُسْرٌ, q. v.

بَاسِرٌ and ↓ بُسُورٌ, the latter an inf. n. used as an epithet, A face *frowning*; or *contracted*; or *grinning*, or *displaying the teeth, with a frowning*, or *contraction*, or *a stern, an austere*, or *a morose, look*. (M.) [See 1, last sentence.] وُجُوهٌ يَوْمَئِذٍ بَاسِرَةٌ, in the Ḳur lxxv. 24, means *And faces on that day* shall be *excessively frowning* or *contracted, &c.*: (Jel:) or *expressive of dislike or hatred, and contracted*. (Ḳ.) [See also بَاسِلٌ.]

بَاسُورٌ *A well-known disease*; (Ḳ;) *a swelling, or tumour, which nature drives to every part of the body, from a humour that comes from the anus* (المَقْعَدَة), *and the testicles, and the edges of the labia majora of the pudendum muliebre, and other parts; and when in the anus, attended by a swelling of the veins*; (Mṣb;) sing. of بَوَاسِيرُ; (Ṣ, Ḳ;) which signifies *a certain disease that arises in the anus* (المقعدة), [namely, the *hemorrhoids*, or *piles*, to which this term generally applies when it is used absolutely,] and also *in the inside of the nose*; (Ṣ;) *what resembles boils in the anus*: (Mgh:) sometimes the س is changed into ص: (Mgh, Mṣb:) and it is said that the word is not Arabic. (Mṣb.)

مُبْسِرٌ: see what next follows.

نَخْلَةٌ مِبْسَارٌ, (M, Ḳ,) and ↓ مُبْسِرٌ, without ة, as though a possessive epithet, (M,) *A palm-tree of which the dates do not ripen*. (M, Ḳ.) [See also 4.]

مَبْسُورٌ *Affected by the disease termed* بَوَاسِير, pl. of بَاسُور. (TA.)

مُبَاسِرَةٌ † A mare *desiring the stallion* (AO, Ḳ*) *when she has only begun to feel the excitement of lust*, (AO,) or *before she is fully excited by lust*. (Ḳ.) [See also مُبَاشِرٌ.]

بسط

1. بَسَطَهُ, (M, Mṣb, Ḳ,) aor. ـُ, (M, TA,) inf. n. بَسْطٌ, (Ṣ, M, Mṣb,) contr. of قَبَضَهُ; (M, TA;) as also ↓ بَسَّطَهُ, (M,* TA,) inf. n. تَبْسِيطٌ. (TA.) [As such,] *He spread it; spread it out*, or *forth; expanded it; extended it*; (Ṣ, Mṣb, Ḳ, B;) as also ↓ بَسَّطَهُ: (Ḳ:) and *he made it wide*, or *ample*: these are the primary significations; and sometimes both of them may be conceived; and sometimes, one of them: and the verb is also used, metaphorically, as relating to anything which cannot be conceived as composed or constructed: (B:) and بَصَطَ is the same as بَسَطَ, (Ṣ, and Ḳ in art. بصط,) in all its meanings. (Ḳ.) You say, بَسَطَ الثَّوْبَ [*He spread, spread out, expanded*, or *unfolded, the garment*, or *piece of cloth*]. (Mṣb.) And بَسَطَ رِجْلَهُ ‡ [*He stretched forth*, or *extended, his leg*]. (TA.) And بَسَطَ ذِرَاعَيْهِ, and ↓ بَسَّطَهُمَا, †*He spread his fore arms upon the ground*; the doing of which [in prostrating oneself] in prayer is forbidden. (TA.) And بَسَطَ يَدَهُ (M, Mṣb, Ḳ) ‡ *He stretched forth*, or *extended, his arm*, or *hand*; (M, Ḳ;) as in the saying بَسَطَ إِلَىَّ يَدَهُ بِمَا أُحِبُّ وَأَكْرَهُ ‡ [*He stretched forth*, or *extended, towards me his arm*, or *hand, with*, i. e. *to do to me, what I liked and disliked*]: (M, TA:*) or *he stretched forth his hand opened*. (Mṣb.) It is said in the Ḳur [v. 31], لَئِنْ بَسَطْتَ إِلَىَّ يَدَكَ لِتَقْتُلَنِى ‡ [*Assuredly if thou stretch forth towards me thy hand to slay me*]. (M, TA.) بَسْطُ اليَدِ and الكَفِّ is sometimes used to denote assaulting and smiting: [as in the last of the exs. given above; and] as in the words of the Ḳur [lx. 2], وَيَبْسُطُوا إِلَيْكُمْ أَيْدِيَهُمْ وَأَلْسِنَتَهُمْ بِالسُّوْءِ ‡ [*And they will stretch forth towards you their hands and their tongues with evil*]; (TA;) i. e., by slaying, (Bḍ, Jel,) and smiting, (Jel,) and reviling. (Bḍ, Jel.) And sometimes to denote giving liberally: (TA:) [as in] بَسَطَ يَدَهُ فِى الإِنْفَاقِ ‡ *He* [*stretched forth his hand, opened*, or] *was liberal* or *bountiful* or *munificent* [*in expenditure*]: (Mṣb:) see بَسِيطٌ, below. (TA.) And sometimes to denote taking, or taking possession, or seizing: as in the saying, (TA,) بُسِطَتْ يَدُهُ عَلَيْهِ ‡ [*His hand was stretched forth against him*]; i. e. *he was made to have dominion over him by absolute force and power*. (Ḳ, TA.) And sometimes to denote seeking, or demanding: [as in بَسَطَ كَفَّيْهِ فِى الدُّعَآءِ ‡ *He expanded his two hands in supplication*; a common action, in which the two hands are placed together like an open book upon a desk before the face, in supplicating God:] see بَاسِطٌ, below. (TA.) — [And hence,] بَسَطْتُ لَهُ أَمْرِى ‡ *I displayed*, or *laid open, to him my state*, or *case*, or *affair*; syn. فَرَشْتُهُ إِيَّاهُ: (A in art. فرش:) and أَمْرَهُ [*his state, &c.*]. (TA in that art.) — [Hence also,] اللّٰهُ يَبْسُطُ الأَرْوَاحَ فِى الأَجْسَادِ عِنْدَ الحَيَاةِ † [*God diffuses the souls in the bodies at the time of* their *being animated*]. (TA.) — [Hence also,] بَسَطَ اللّٰهُ الرِّزْقَ † *God multiplied*, or *made abundant, and amplified, enlarged*, or *made ample* or *plentiful, the means of subsistence*. (Mṣb, Ḳ.*) It is said in the Ḳur [ii. 246], وَاللّٰهُ يَقْبِضُ وَيَبْسُطُ. (Mṣb and TA in art. قبض, q. v.) And you say, بَسَطَ عَلَيْهِمُ العَدْلَ ‡ [*He largely extended to them equity*, or *justice*]; as also ↓ بَسَّطَهُ. (TA.) — [Hence also,] فُلَانٌ يَبْسُطُ عَبِيدَهُ ثُمَّ يَقْبِضُهُمْ ‡ [*Such a one enlarges the liberty of his slaves; then abridges their liberty*]. (A in art. قبض.) — [Hence also, بَسَطَ وَجْهَهُ † *It unwrinkled*, as *though it dilated, his countenance*: see 7. And بَسَطَ قَلْبَهُ † *It dilated his heart*: see remarks on قَبْضٌ and بَسْطٌ, as used by certain of the Ṣoofees, near the end of 1 in art. قبض. And] بَسَطَهُ, alone, [signifies *the same*; or] ‡ *it rejoiced him; rendered him joyous*, or *cheerful*: (M, Ḳ, TA:) because, when a man is rejoiced, his countenance becomes unwrinkled (يَنْبَسِطُ), and he becomes changed [and cheerful] in [its] complexion: it is wrongly said, by MF, to be not tropical: that it is tropical is asserted by Z, in the A: MF also says that it is not post-classical; and in this he is right; for it occurs in a saying of Moḥammad: thus in a trad. respecting Fáṭimeh, يَبْسُطُنِى مَا يَبْسُطُهَا *What rejoices her rejoices me*: (TA:) [see also قَبَضَهُ, where this saying is cited according to another relation:] ↓ أَبْسَطَنِى [as signifying ‡ *it rejoiced me*] is a mistake of the vulgar [obtaining in the present-day]. (TA.) — [Hence also,] الغِنَى يَقْبِضُهُ وَالشَّرُّ يَبْسُطُهُ ‡ [*Wealth makes him close-fisted, tenacious*, or *niggardly*; *and poverty makes him open-handed, liberal*, or *generous*]. (A in art. قبض.) — [Hence also,] بَسَطَ مِنْ فُلَانٍ ‡ *He rendered such a one free from shyness*, or *aversion*: (Ṣ, O, Ḳ, TA:) *he emboldened him; incited him to* [*that kind of presumptuous boldness which is termed*] دَالَّة. (Ḥar p. 155.) [In the CḲ, بَسَطَ فُلَانًا من فُلانٍ is erroneously put for بَسَطَ مِنْ فُلَانٍ.] — [Hence also,] بَسَطَ اللّٰهُ فُلَانًا عَلَىَّ ‡ *God made*, or *judged, such a one to excel me*. (Z, Ṣgh, Ḳ, TA.) — [Hence also,] بَسَطَ المَكَانُ القَوْمَ ‡ *The place was sufficiently wide*, or *ample, for the people*, or *company of men*. (Ḳ, TA.) And هٰذَا فِرَاشٌ يَبْسُطُكَ ‡ *This is a bed ample*, (Ṣ, Ḳ,) or *sufficiently wide for thee*. (A.) And فَرَشَ لِى فِرَاشًا لَا يَبْسُطُنِى ‡ *He spread for me a bed* [*not wide enough for me*, or] *that was* [*too*] *narrow* [*for me*], (ISk, Ṣ.) — [Hence also,] بَسَطَ العُذْرَ, (Ḳ,) aor. as above, (TA,) and so the inf. n., (Ṣ, TA,) ‡ *He accepted*, or *admitted, the excuse*. (Ṣ, Ḳ, TA.) — All these significations of the verb are ramifications of that first mentioned above. (TA.) — بَسُطَ, aor. ـُ, (M, Ḳ,) inf. n. بَسَاطَةٌ, (M,) †*He was*, or *became, free*, or *unconstrained*, (مُنْبَسِط,) *with his tongue*. (M, Ḳ.)

2: see 1, in four places.

3. بَاسَطَهُ, inf. n. مُبَاسَطَةٌ and بِسَاطٌ, ‡ [*He conversed*, or *acted, with him without shyness*, or *aversion; boldly; in a free and easy manner*; or *cheerfully*]: (TA:) *he met him laughingly*, or *smilingly, so as to show his teeth*. (So accord. to an expl. of the latter of the two inf. ns. in the TA.) [See كَاشَرَهُ.] You say also, بَيْنَهُمَا مُبَاسَطَةٌ ‡ [*Between them two is conversation*, or *behaviour, free from shyness*, or *aversion; bold; free and easy*; or *cheerful*]. (TA.)

4: see 1, latter half.

5: see 7. — تَبَسَّطَ فِى البِلَادِ † *He journeyed far and wide in the countries*. (Ṣ, TA.) — خَرَجَ يَتَبَسَّطُ † *He went forth betaking himself to the gardens and green fields*: from بَسَاطٌ signifying "land having sweet-smelling plants." (TA.)

7. انبسط quasi-pass. of بَسَطَهُ; as also ↓ تبسّط is of بَسَّطَهُ; both signifying *It became spread* or *spread out* or *forth*, or *it spread* or *spread out* or *forth; it became expanded*, or *it expanded*, or *it expanded itself; it became extended*, or *it extended*, or *it extended itself*: [&c.]. (M, Ḳ, TA.) You say, انبسط الشَّىْءُ عَلَى الأَرْضِ [*The thing became spread or spread out, &c., upon the ground*]. (Ṣ.) And انبسط النَّهَارُ ‡ *The day became advanced, the sun being high: it became long*: (M, Ḳ, TA:) and in like manner one uses the verb in relation to other things. (M, TA.) — [And hence, †*He expatiated*. — And] انبسط وَجْهُهُ † [*His countenance became unwrinkled, as though dilated*; i. e. *it became open*, or *cheerful*; and so انبسط alone; or *he became open*, or *cheerful, in countenance*, as is said in the KL.]. (TA.) [And انبسط, alone, †*He became dilated in heart*; or *he rejoiced*; or

became joyous, or cheerful: see بَسْطَةٌ.] — [Hence also,] انبسط ‡ *He left shyness, or aversion; he became free therefrom*: (Ṣ, TA:) *he was, or became, bold, forward, presumptuous, or arrogant*: (KL, PṢ:) *he became emboldened*, and *incited to* [*that kind of presumptuous boldness which is termed*] دَالَّة. (Ḥar p. 155.) And انبسط إِلَيْهِ ‡ [*He was open, or unreserved, to him in conversation: and he acted towards him, or behaved to him, without shyness or aversion; or with boldness, forwardness, presumptuousness, or arrogance: and he applied himself to it* (namely, an affair,) *with boldness, forwardness, presumptuousness, or arrogance.*] (TA.)

بَسْطٌ, as signifying *A certain intoxicating thing*, [*a preparation of hemp*,] is post-classical. (TA.)

بُسْطٌ: / بِسْطٌ: / بُسُطٌ: } see بَسِيطٌ, in seven places.

بَسْطَةٌ *Width*, or *ampleness*; syn. سَعَةٌ: (Ṣ, Ṣgh, Mṣb:) and *length*, or *height*: (Ṣgh:) pl. بِسَاطٌ: (Ṣgh:) and *increase*: or *redundance*, or *excess*: (TA:) and, (M, Ḳ,) as also ▼ بُسْطَةٌ, (Ḳ,) *excellence*; (M, Ḳ;) in science and in body: (M:) or in science, *expatiation*, or *dilatation*: (Ḳ:) or *profit to oneself and others*: (TA:) and in body, *height*, or *tallness*; and *perfection*, or *completeness*. (Ḳ.) It is said in the Ḳur [ii. 24], وَزَادَهُ بَسْطَةً فِى الْعِلْمِ وَالْجِسْمِ [*And hath increased him in excellence, &c., in respect of science, or knowledge, and body*]: (M, TA:) Zeyd Ibn-'Alee here read ▼ بُسْطَةً. (TA.) — [*An arm's length.*] See بَاسِطٌ. — امْرَأَةٌ بَسْطَةٌ *A woman beautiful and sleek in body*: and in like manner, ظَبْيَةٌ *a gazelle* that is so. (M.)

بُسْطَةٌ: see بَسْطَةٌ, in two places.

أُذُنٌ بَسْطَآءُ ‡ *A wide and large ear.* (M, Ḳ, TA.)

بُسُطِيٌّ *A seller of* بُسُط [or carpets, &c.]: pl. بُسُطِيُّونَ. (TA, but only the pl. is there mentioned and explained.)

بَسْطَانٌ: / بُسْطَانٌ: } see بَسِيطٌ.

بَسَاطٌ Land (أَرْض) *expanded and even*; as also ▼ بَسِيطَةٌ: (M, Ḳ:) and *wide*, or *spacious*; (AO, Ṣ, Ḳ;) as also ▼ بِسَاطٌ, (Fr, Ḳ,) in his explanation of which Fr adds, *in which nothing is obtained*; (TA;) and ▼ بَسِيطٌ; (Ḳ;) and ▼ بَسِيطَةٌ: (AO, Ḳ:) and in like manner, a place; (Ṣ, TA;) as also ▼ بِسَاطٌ; (TA;) and ▼ بَسِيطٌ: (Ṣ, TA:) and *land in which are sweet-smelling plants*: (TA:) or ▼ بَسِيطَةٌ is a subst., (IDrd, M,) as some say, (M,) and signifies the *earth*. (IDrd, M, Mṣb, Ḳ.) You say, نَحْنُ فِى بِسَاطٍ ▼ وَسَعَةٍ ‡ [*We are in an ample and a plentiful state*]. (TA.) And بَيْنَنَا وَبَيْنَ الْمَآءِ مِيلٌ بساط [the last word thus, without any vowel-sign to the ب,] †*Between us and the water is a long mile.* (TA.) [See also بَاسِطٌ.] And مَا عَلَى الْبَسِيطَةِ ▼ مِثْلُ فُلَانٍ *There is not upon the earth the like of such a one.* (TA.) And ▼ ذَهَبَ فِى بُسَيْطَةَ, a dim., imperfectly decl., *He* (a man, TA) *went away in the earth*, or *land*. (A, O, L, Ḳ.) — Also *A great cooking-pot.* (Ṣgh, Ḳ.)

بِسَاطٌ *A thing that is spread* or *spread out* or *forth*; (Ṣ, M, Ḳ, B;) *whatever it be*; a subst. applied thereto: (B:) [and particularly *a carpet*; which is meant by its being said to be] *a certain thing well known*; the word being of the measure فِعَال in the sense of the measure مَفْعُول, like كِتَابٌ in the sense of مَكْتُوبٌ, and فِرَاشٌ in the sense of مَفْرُوشٌ, &c.: (Mṣb:) pl. [of mult.] بُسُطٌ (M, Mṣb, Ḳ) and بُسْطٌ and [of pauc.] أَبْسِطَةٌ. (TA.) — See also بَسِيطٌ; near the middle of the paragraph. — انْبَرَى لِطَىِّ بِسَاطِهِ is a phrase meaning †*He hastened to cut short his speech.* (Ḥar p. 280.) = Also The *leaves of the tree called* سَمُر *that fall upon a garment, or piece of cloth, spread for them, the tree being beaten.* (M, Ḳ.) = See also بَسَاطٌ, in three places.

بَسِيطٌ, and بَسِيطَةٌ: see بَسَاطٌ, in six places. — وَقَعَ الغَيْثُ بَسِيطًا مُتَدَارِكًا *The rain fell spreading widely upon the earth, continuously*, or *consecutively.* (TA.) — فُلَانٌ بَسِيطُ الجِسْمِ † [*Such a one is tall of body*]. (Ṣ, TA.) — بَسِيطُ الوَجْهِ ‡ A man (M) *having the countenance* [*unwrinkled*, or] *bright with joy*: (M, Ḳ, TA:) pl. بُسُطٌ. (M, Ḳ.*) — بَسِيطُ اليَدَيْنِ ‡ A man *large*, or *extensive, in beneficence*; (M, TA;) *liberal, bountiful*: (Ḳ, TA:) pl. بُسُطٌ: (M, Ḳ:) [and so] بَسِيطُ البَاعِ (Ṣ,) [and] ▼ مُنْبَسِطُ البَاعِ. (TA.) And ▼ يَدُهُ بِسْطٌ, (Ṣ, Ḳ,) like طِحْنٌ in the sense of مَطْحُونٌ, and ▼ بُسُطٌ in the sense of قِطْفٌ مَقْطُوفٌ, (TA,) and ▼ بُسُطٌ, (Z, Ḳ,) like أُنُفٌ and سُجُحٌ, (Z,) and (Z, Ḳ) by contraction, (Z,) ▼ بُسْطٌ, (Z, Ḳ,) and ▼ مَبْسُوطَةٌ, (TA,) ‡ *His hand is liberal*; syn. مُطْلَقَةٌ, (Ṣ, Ḳ, TA,) and طَلْقٌ; (TA;) or *he is large in expenditure.* (TA.) It is said in the Ḳur [v. 69], بَلْ ▼ يَدَاهُ مَبْسُوطَتَانِ; (TA;) and accord. to one reading, ▼ بِسْطَانِ; (Ṣ, Ḳ;) and accord. to another, with ḍamm, [as though it were ▼ بُسْطَانِ,] (Z, Ḳ, TA,) [but it is said that] in this case it is used as an inf. n., [and therefore ▼ بُسْطَانٌ, for an inf. n. is applied as an epithet to a dual and a pl. subst. without alteration,] like غُفْرَانٌ and رِضْوَانٌ; or, accord. to some, it is most probably [▼ بَسْطَانٌ,] like رَحْمَانٌ; and Ṭalḥah Ibn-Muṣarrif read ▼ بِسَاطَانِ: (TA:) the meaning is, ‡ *Nay, his hands are liberal*, or *bountiful*; the phrase being a simile; for in this case there is no hand, nor any stretching forth. (TA.) And it is said in a trad., يَدَا ٱللّٰهِ ▼ بُسْطَانِ لِمُسِىْءِ النَّهَارِ حَتَّى يَتُوبَ بِاللَّيْلِ وَلِمُسِىْءِ اللَّيْلِ حَتَّى يَتُوبَ بِالنَّهَارِ, (Ḳ,* TA,) or, accord. to one relation, ▼ بِسْطَانِ, (TA,) meaning ‡ *God is liberal* in forgiveness *to the evil-doer of the day-time until he repent* [*in the night, and to the evil-doer of the night-time until he repent in the day*]: for a king is said to be ▼ مَبْسُوطُ اليَدِ when he is ‡ *liberal in his gifts* by command and by sign, although he gives nothing thereof with his hand, nor stretches it forth with them at all. (Ṣgh, TA.) — بَسِيطٌ also signifies ▼ مُنْبَسِطُ اللِّسَانِ, (Lth,) or مُنْبَسِطٌ بِلِسَانِهِ, (M, Ḳ,) † [*Free*, or *unconstrained, in tongue*, or *with his tongue*,] applied to a man: (M:) fem. with ة. (Ḳ.) — البَسِيطُ is also the name of *A certain kind of metre of verse*; (Ṣ, M,* Ḳ;) namely, *the third*; *the measure of which consists of* مُسْتَفْعِلُنْ فَاعِلُنْ *eight* [a mistake for *four*] *times*: (Ḳ:) so called because of the extension of its أَسْبَاب, commencing with a سَبَب immediately followed by another سَبَب, as is said by Aboo-Is-ḥáḳ. (M.) — [بَسِيطٌ is also used in philosophy as signifying † *Simple*; *uncompounded.*]

بَسِيطَةٌ, as an epithet; and as a subst.: see بَسَاطٌ, in four places. — [In philosophy, † *A simple element*: pl. بَسَائِطُ.]

ذَهَبَ فِى بُسَيْطَةَ: see بَسَاطٌ.

بَاسِطٌ act. part. n. of بَسَطَ. — It is said in the Ḳur [vi. 93], وَالْمَلَائِكَةُ بَاسِطُوا أَيْدِيهِمْ, meaning ‡ *The angels being made to have dominion over them by absolute force and power.* (Ḳ,* TA.) And again, in the Ḳur [xiii. 15], كَبَاسِطِ كَفَّيْهِ إِلَى الْمَآءِ لِيَبْلُغَ فَاهُ ‡ *Like the supplicator of water, making a sign to it* [*with his two hands*], *in order that it may* [*reach his mouth*, and so] answer his prayer; (Ḳ,* TA;) or, but it will not answer his prayer. (O, TA.) — البَاسِطُ † God, *who amplifies*, or *enlarges*, or *makes ample* or *plentiful, the means of subsistence, to whomsoever He will*, (Ḳ, TA,) by his liberality and his mercy: (TA:) or *who diffuses* (يَبْسُطُ) *the souls in the bodies at the time of* [*their*] *being animated.* (TA.) — مَآءٌ بَاسِطٌ ‡ *Water that is distant from the herbage*, or *pasturage*, (M, Ḳ, TA,) *but less so than what is termed* مُطْلِب. (M, TA.) And خِمْسٌ بَاسِطٌ † *A difficult* [*journey of the kind termed*] خِمْس [i. e. *of five days, whereof the second and third and fourth are without water*]; syn. بَائِصٌ. (Ṣgh, Ḳ.) And عُقْبَةٌ بَاسِطَةٌ (ISk, Ṣ, M, Ḳ [in the CK, erroneously, عَقَبَةٌ]) † [*A stage of a journey*, or *march* or *journey from one halting-place to another*,] *that is far*, or *distant*, (ISk, Ṣ,) or *long*: (TA:) or *in which are two nights to the water.* (M, Ḳ.) You say, سِرْنَا عُقْبَةً بَاسِطَةً † [*We journeyed a stage, &c.*,] *that was far*, or *distant*, or *long*. (ISk, Ṣ,* TA.) — رَكِيَّةٌ قَامَةٌ بَاسِطَةٌ, [in the CḲ قَامَةُ بَاسِطَةٍ,] and قَامَةُ بَاسِطَةٍ, as a prefixed n. with its complement imperfectly decl., as though they made it determinate, *i. q.* ▼ قَامَةٌ وَبَسْطَةٌ [*A well measuring*, or *of the depth of, a man's stature and an arm's length*]. (O, Ḳ.) AZ says, حَفَرَ الرَّجُلُ قَامَةً بَاسِطَةً *The man dug to the depth of his stature and his arm's length.* (L, TA.)

مَبْسَطٌ *Width*, or *extent*; syn. مُتَّسَعٌ: (Ḳ:) as in the phrase بَلَدٌ عَرِيضُ الْمَبْسَطِ [*A region wide in extent*]. (TA.) [See also بَسْطَةٌ.]

مَبْسُوطُ اليَدِ : and يَدُهُ مَبْسُوطَةٌ, and يَدَاهُ مَبْسُوطَتَانِ : see بَسِيطٌ.

مُنْبَسِطُ البَاعِ : and مُنْبَسِطُ اللِّسَانِ : see بَسِيطٌ.

بسق

1. بَسَقَ النَّخْلُ, (aor. ـُ, Mṣb,) inf. n. بُسُوقٌ, *The palm-trees were, or became, tall,* (JK, Ṣ, Mṣb, Ḳ,) *and full-grown:* (JK:) or *exceedingly tall.* (Mṣb.) —— بَسَقَ عَلَيْهِمْ, (inf. n. as above, TA,) ‡ *He overcame them, excelled them,* or *was superior to them;* (JK, Ṣ, Ḳ;) namely, his companions: (Ṣ:) *he surpassed them in excellence.* (TA.) And بَسَقَهُمْ † *He became exalted above them in fame,* or *renown.* (TA, from a trad.) —— بَسَقَ فِى عِلْمِهِ † *He was,* or *became, skilled in his science, knowing its abstrusities and niceties,* or *having learned the whole of it.* (Mṣb.) ═ بَسَقَ, (JK, Ṣ, &c.,) [aor. ـُ,] inf. n. بَسْقٌ, (Ṣ, TA,) or بُسَاقٌ, (Mṣb,) [but see the latter below,] *i. q.* بَصَقَ (JK, Ṣ,* Mṣb, Ḳ) and بَزَقَ (TA) [*He spat*]: but some, as on the authority of Kh, disallow it, saying that it has no other signification than that of excessive tallness, as in the case of a palm-tree: (Mṣb:) or the second of these verbs is the most chaste; the first and last being of weak authority, or rare. (TA.) ═ بَسَقَتِ الشَّمْسُ *i. q.* بَزَقَت [and بَزَغَت, i. e. *The sun rose*]. (TA.)

2. لَا تُبَسِّقْ عَلَيْنَا, (JK, Ḳ,) inf. n. تَبْسِيقٌ, (Ḳ,) ‡ *Be not thou prolix,* or *tedious, to us;* syn. لَا تَطَوَّلْ, (JK, Ḳ, TA,) or لَا تَتَطَوَّلْ, (TA,) both of which signify the same. (TḲ.) [بَسَّقَ and ▼ تبسّق are syn.; or] تَبَسُّقٌ signifies † The *being prolix,* or *tedious,* (تَطَوُّلٌ,) *and heavy,* or *sluggish.* (TA.)

4. ابسقت *She* (a camel) *excerned the first milk,* or *biestings, into her udder, before bringing forth:* (Aṣ, Ṣ, Ḳ:) or *she* (a ewe, JK, or a camel, Yz, T) *excerned the milk* (Yz, JK, T) *a month before bringing forth,* (JK, T,) *so that it oozed,* or *flowed;* or, as is sometimes the case, *when she was not pregnant.* (T.) Also *She* (a girl being a بِكْر [which means a virgin, and also one that has not yet brought forth, and one that has brought forth but once,]) *had milk in her breast:* so, says Az, I have heard. (TA.) —— *She* (a ewe) *had a long udder.* (TA.) —— And *She* (a ewe) *was,* or *became, pregnant.* (Bḍ in l. 10.)

5 : see 2.

بَسْقَةٌ *A* [*stony tract such as is termed*] حَرَّة: [or *one that is somewhat elevated;* as also بَصْقَةٌ:] pl. بِسَاقٌ. (Ḳ.)

بُسَاقٌ *i. q.* بُصَاقٌ [*Spittle,* or *saliva, when it has gone forth from the mouth:* or *saliva that flows;* see بُزَاقٌ: see also 1]. (Ṣ, Ḳ.) [بُسَاقَةٌ is app. its n. un. And hence,] —— بُسَاقَةُ القَمَرِ *Stone of a clear white colour, that glistens;* as also with ص. (TA.)

بَسُوقٌ and ▼ مِبْسَاقٌ, both applied to a ewe, (JK, Ḳ,) and to a she-camel, (TA,) *Having a long udder:* (JK, Ḳ:) or *i. q.* ▼ مُبْسِقٌ, applied to a ewe. (JK.)

بَاسِقٌ [act. part. n. of 1]. نَخْلَةٌ بَاسِقَةٌ *A tall palm-tree:* [or *an exceedingly tall palm-tree;* see 1:] pl. بَاسِقَاتٌ and بَوَاسِقُ. (Mṣb.) The former of these pls. occurs in the Ḳur l. 10, meaning *tall:* (Ṣ, Bḍ, TA:) or *bearing fruit;* from أَبْسَقَتْ said of a ewe, as signifying "she was, or became, pregnant;" so that it is an instance of a part. n. of the measure فَاعِلٌ from a verb of the measure أَفْعَلَ: accord. to one reading, it is بَاصِقَات, because of the ق. (Bḍ.) The latter of the pls. also signifies The *first portions* of clouds: (AḤn, TA:) [app. the *portions that first appear above the horizon:*] or *what are elongated of the heads,* or *summits,* (فُرُوع,) of a cloud: and hence, of [the plant called] أُقْحُوَان [or chamomile]. (TA.) And بَاسِقَةٌ signifies *A cloud of a clear white colour* [as being always very high in the sky]. (Ṣgh, Ḳ.*) —— بَاسِقُ الأَخْلَاقِ † *Endowed with elevated,* or *noble, natural dispositions* or *mental qualities.* (Ḥam p. 369.) ═ *A sweet yellow fruit.* (Ṣgh, Ḳ.) [Golius appears to have found تَمْرَةٌ in the place of ثَمَرَةٌ.]

مُبْسِقٌ A she-camel *excerning the first milk,* or *biestings, into her udder before bringing forth:* (Aṣ, Ṣ, Ḳ: [see 4:] and see also بَسُوقٌ:) pl. مَبَاسِيقُ. (Ṣ, Ḳ.) And A girl that is a بِكْر [see 4] *having milk flowing into her breast.* (TA.)

مِبْسَاقٌ : see بَسُوقٌ.

بسل

1. بَسْلٌ (inf. n. of بَسَلَ, M) is The act of *preventing, hindering, withholding, debarring, forbidding,* or *prohibiting;* syn. مَنْعٌ; the primary meaning; (Bḍ in vi. 69;) and إِعْجَالٌ (M, Ḳ) and حَبْسٌ; (AA, Ḳ;) [both syn. with مَنْعٌ;] and ▼ إِبْسَالٌ [inf. n. of 4, q. v. infrà,] signifies the same. (Bḍ ubi suprà.) You say, بَسَلَنِى عَنْ حَاجَتِى, inf. n. as above, *He prevented me from accomplishing my want;* syn. أَعْجَلَنِى. (M.) ═ بَسَلَ, (M, Ḳ,) aor. ـُ, (M,) inf. n. بُسُولٌ, *He* (a man, TA) *frowned, contracted his face,* or *looked sternly* or *austerely* or *morosely;* or, *doing so, grinned,* or *displayed his teeth;* or *contracted the part between his eyes;* (عَبَسَ;) *by reason of courage,* or *of anger;* as also ▼ تبسّل : (M, Ḳ:) and [so in the M, but in the Ḳ "or"] ▼ تبسّل وَجْهُهُ, (M, and so in some copies of the Ḳ,) or ▼ تبسّل [alone], (so in other copies of the Ḳ, and in the TA,) *His face,* or *he, was,* or *became, odious, and excessively foul* or *unseemly* or *hideous, in aspect:* (M, Ḳ:) and ▼ تبسّل لِى *He* (a man) *was displeasing,* or *odious, in aspect to me.* (TA.) —— And [hence], (M, Ḳ,) inf. n. بُسُولٌ, (TA,) said of milk, and of نَبِيذ [or must &c.], ‡ *It was,* or *became, strong:* (Ḳ: [in the CḲ, بَسَّلَ is here erroneously put for بَسَلَ; and وَبَسَّلَهُ, which should next follow, is omitted:]) or, said of the former, *it was,* or *became, displeasing,* or *odious, in taste, and sour;* and, said of the latter, *it was,* or *became, strong, and sour.* (M, TA.) Also, said of vinegar, † *It, having been left long, became altered,* or *corrupted, in flavour.* (Az in art. حذق, TA.) And, said of flesh-meat, † *It stank,* or *became stinking.* (AḤn, M, TA.) ═ بَسُلَ, [aor. ـُ,] inf. n. بَسَالَةٌ (Ṣ, M, Mṣb, Ḳ) and بَسَالٌ, [respecting which latter see what follows in the next sentence,] (M, Ḳ,) *He was,* or *became, courageous,* or *strong-hearted, on the occasion of war,* or *fight:* (Ṣ, M, Mṣb, Ḳ:) from بَسْلٌ meaning "forbidden," or "prohibited;" because he who has this quality defends himself from his antagonist, as though it were forbidden to him [the latter] to do him a displeasing, or an evil, deed. (Ḥam p. 13.) El-Ḥoṭeiah says,

وَأَحْلَى مِنَ التَّمْرِ الجَنِىِّ وَفِيهِمُ •
بَسَالَةُ نَفْسٍ إِنْ أُرِيدَ بَسَالُهَا •

[*And sweeter than fresh-gathered dates, and in them is courageousness of soul, if courageousness thereof be desired*]: but بسالها may be here altered by curtailment from بَسَالَتُهَا. (M.) You say, مَا أَبْيَنَ بَسَالَتَهُ [*How manifest is*] *his courage!* (TA.) —— See also 4.

2. بسّلهُ, (M, Ḳ,) inf. n. تَبْسِيلٌ, (Ḳ,) *He made it* (a thing) *to be an object of dislike, disapprobation,* or *hatred;* syn. كَرَّهَهُ: (M:) or *he disliked it, disapproved of it,* or *hated it;* syn. كَرِهَهُ. (Ḳ.)

3. مُبَاسَلَةٌ [inf. n. of باسل] The act of *assaulting,* or *assailing, in war.* (Ṣ, PṢ.)

4. إِبْسَالٌ [inf. n. of ابسل] *i. q.* بَسْلٌ as explained in the first sentence of this art.; i. e., The act of *preventing, hindering, withholding, debarring,* (Bḍ in vi. 69,) *forbidding,* or *prohibiting.* (Ṣ, Ḳ, and Bḍ ubi suprà.) ═ ابسلهُ (inf. n. as above, TA) *He pledged,* or *gave in pledge, him,* or *it,* (M, Mṣb, Ḳ,) لِكَذَا [and بِكَذَا, as will be shown below, both meaning *for such a thing*]: and *he gave in exchange,* or *as an equivalent, him,* or *it,* لِكَذَا [and app. بِكَذَا also, as above, *for such a thing*]; syn. عَرَّضَهُ: (M, Ḳ:) and *he gave him up, delivered him, delivered him over,* or *consigned him, to destruction,* (Ṣ, Ḳ,) or *to punishment.* (Az, TA.) 'Owf Ibn-El-Aḥwaṣ says,

• وَإِبْسَالِى بَنِىَّ بِغَيْرِ جُرْمٍ • بَعَوْنَاهُ وَلَا بِدَمٍ مُرَاقِ •

[*And my giving in pledge, or as an equivalent,* or *giving up to destruction, my sons, not for a crime that we have committed, nor for blood that has been shed* by us]: (Ṣ, M, TA:) for he had given his sons in pledge for others, seeking peace, or reconciliation. (Ṣ, TA.) أَنْ تُبْسَلَ نَفْسٌ بِمَا كَسَبَتْ, in the Ḳur [vi. 69], means *Lest a soul should be given up,* or *delivered,* &c., (AO, Ṣ, Bḍ, Jel, TA,) *to destruction,* (Bḍ, Jel, TA,) or *to punishment,* (Az, TA,) *for that which it hath done,* (Az, Bḍ, Jel, TA,) of evil: (Bḍ:) or *be given in pledge.* (Bḍ, TA.) And أُولٰئِكَ الَّذِينَ أُبْسِلُوا بِمَا كَسَبُوا, in the same [ubi suprà], means, in like manner, *Those who are given up,* or *delivered,* &c., (*to punishment,* Bḍ,) *for their sins:* (El-Ḥasan, Bḍ,* TA:) or, *who are given in pledge:* (Mṣb, TA:) or *are destroyed:* or, as Mujáhid says, *are disgraced,* or *put to shame, by the* *exposure of their sins*: or, as Katádeh says, *are imprisoned*. (TA.) — ابسلهُ لعَمَلِه and بعَمَلِه *He left him to his work, not interfering with him therein.* (M, K.) — ابسل نَفْسَهُ لِلْمَوْتِ, (M, K,) as also ↓استبسل [alone], (M, K, and Ham p. 291), and ↓تبسّل, and ↓بسل, [which last may be either بَسَلَ or بَسُلَ, or perhaps it is a mistranscription for أَبْسَلَ,] (Ham ibid.,) *He disposed and subjected his mind, or himself, to death,* (M, K, Ham,) *and felt certain, or sure, of it*: (Ham, TA:) and in like manner, لِلضَّرْبِ [*to beating*, i. e., *to being beaten*]: (TA:) and ↓ابتسل لِلْمَوْتِ *He submitted himself to death*: (TA:) and ↓استبسل *He threw himself into war, or battle, or fight, desiring to slay or be slain,* (S, K,) *inevitably.* (S.) = مَا أَبْسَلَهُ *How courageous, or strong-hearted, is he, on the occasion of war, or fight!* (TA.)

5. تبسّل *He affected courage, or strength of heart, on the occasion of war, or fight; emboldened himself; or became like a lion in boldness.* (TA.) — See 4. = See also 1, in four places.

8. ابتسل لِلْمَوْتِ: see 4.

10: see 4, in two places.

بَسْلٌ [an inf. n. (see 1) used as an epithet;] *Forbidden; prohibited; unlawful*: (S, M, K:) and *allowed; permitted; lawful*: (AA, IAar, M, K:) thus having two contr. significations: (AA, K:) used alike as sing. and pl. and masc. and fem. [because originally an inf. n.]. (M, K.) You say, هٰذَا بَسْلٌ عَلَيْكَ *This is forbidden, prohibited, or unlawful, to thee.* (Bd in vi. 69.) And دَمِى لَكُمْ بَسْلٌ *My blood is, or shall be, allowed, permitted, or lawful, to you.* (M.) = See also بَاسِلٌ, in two places.

بَسِلٌ: see بَاسِلٌ.

بِسِلَّى [more commonly written in the present day بِسِلَّة] *A certain kind of grain like the lupine* (تُرْمُس), *or less than this*; [the *pea termed* by Linnæus *pisum arvense*:] a word of the dial. of Egypt. (TA.)

بَسُولٌ: see بَاسِلٌ, in two places.

بَسِيلٌ: see بَاسِلٌ, in three places.

بَسَالَةٌ inf. n. of بَسُلَ, q. v. (S, M, &c.) — Also [i. q. بُسُولٌ, inf. n. of بَسَلَ, q. v.; meaning] *A frowning, contracting the face, or looking sternly or austerely or morosely; or doing so with grinning, or displaying the teeth; or contracting the part between the eyes; by reason of courage, or of anger.* (Ham p. 14.) — And *Dislike, disapprobation, displeasure, or hatred.* (Ham ibid.)

بَاسِلٌ *Courageous, or strong-hearted, on the occasion of war, or fight*; (S, M, Msb, K;) because he who is so defends himself from his antagonist; (Ham p. 13, and Bd in vi. 69;) as also ↓بَسِيلٌ (Msb) and ↓بَسُولٌ: (Ham ubi suprà:) pl. of the first بُسْلٌ (S, M, K) and بُسَلَآءُ. (M, K.) — *Frowning, contracting the face, or looking sternly or austerely or morosely; or doing so with grinning, or displaying the teeth; or contracting the part between the eyes; by reason of courage, or of anger;* (M, K;) as also ↓بَسْلٌ, (M, TA,) in the K ↓بَسِلٌ, but this is incorrect, (TA,) and ↓بَسِيلٌ: (M, K:) and بَاسِرٌ بَاسِلٌ *frowning, &c., much, or vehemently*; applied to the face: (TA:) and ↓بَسْلٌ (IAar, K) and ↓بَسِيلٌ (IAar, S, K) *displeasing, or odious,* (IAar, S, K,) *in face,* (IAar, S,) or *aspect.* (K.) — The *lion*; (M, K;) because of his displeasing, or odious, aspect; (M;) or because his prey does not escape from him; (Bd in vi. 69;) as also ↓بَسُولٌ (TA) and ↓مُتَبَسِّلٌ. (K.) — Applied to a saying, *Hard, or severe, and displeasing, or odious.* (M, K.) — Applied to milk, and to نَبِيذ [or must &c.] ‡ *Strong*: (K:) or, applied to the former, *displeasing, or odious, in taste, and sour*; and applied to the latter, *strong and sour.* (M, TA.) And, applied to vinegar, † *Altered, or corrupted, in flavour, from having been left long*; as also ↓مُبْسَلٌ. (Az in art. حذق, TA.) — Applied to a day, † *Distressing, afflictive, or calamitous.* (M, TA.)

مُبْسَلٌ: } see بَاسِلٌ.
مُتَبَسِّلٌ: }

مُسْتَبْسِلٌ *Disposing and subjecting one's mind, or oneself, to death, or to being beaten*: (S: [see also its verb:]) or, as some say, *falling into a displeasing, an odious, or an evil, case, from which there is no escape.* (TA.)

بسم

1. بَسَمَ: see 5, with which it is syn. — [Hence,] مَا بَسَمْتُ فِى الشَّىْءِ ‡ *I did not taste the thing.* (K, TA.)

5. تبسّم; and ↓ابتسم; and ↓بَسَمَ, aor. ـِ, inf. n. بَسْمٌ (S, M, Msb, K) and مَبْسِمٌ; (K,* TA;) [*He smiled*;] these verbs signify less than ضَحِكَ [so that they are properly explained by the Latin *subrisit*]: (S, Msb:) or *he opened his lips like him who displays to another his teeth*: (Lth, TA:) or *he laughed in the least degree and in the most beautiful manner*: (M, K:) or *he laughed a little without any sound*: (Msb:) or تَبَسُّمٌ is the *beginning of* ضَحِك [or *laughter*]: (Towsheeh, and Neseem er-Riyád, in TA art. ضحك, q. v.:) accord. to Zj, it is the utmost degree of laughing of the prophets. (M.) — [Hence,] ↓ابتسم السَّحَابُ عَنِ البَرْقِ, (M,) or تبسّم عَنْهُ, (TA,) i. q. انْكَلَّ عنه [i. e. ‡ *The clouds displayed a faint flashing of lightning*]. (M, TA.) — And تبسّم الطَّلْعُ ‡ *The extremities of the* طلع [i. e. the *spadix*, or the *spathe, of the palm-tree*,] *burst asunder.* (TA.)

8: see 5, in two places.

بَسَّامٌ (S, M, K) and ↓مِبْسَامٌ (S, K) epithets from بَسَمَ, (M, K,) applied to a man, (S, M,) meaning كَثِيرُ التَّبَسُّمِ [*That smiles much*]. (S.)

بَاسِمٌ part. n. of بَسَمَ [meaning *Smiling*]. (K, TA.)

مَبْسِمٌ i. q. ثَغْرٌ, (S, K,) meaning The *front teeth*: (TK:) [and sometimes, perhaps, the *mouth*:] so called as being the place of التَّبَسُّم [or smiling: pl. مَبَاسِمُ]. (TA.) One says, [of women or girls,] هُنَّ غُرُّ المَبَاسِمِ [*They are white in the front teeth*]. (TA.)

مِبْسَامٌ: see بَسَّامٌ.

بسمل

Q. 1. بَسْمَلَ, (T, S, &c.,) inf. n. بَسْمَلَةٌ, (S, Msb,) *He said,* (S, Msb, K, KL,) or *wrote,* (T, Msb,) بِسْمِ ٱللّٰهِ [*In, or with, the name of God I recite, or read, or I begin, &c.*]: (T, S, Msb, K, KL:) or بِسْمِ ٱللّٰهِ الرَّحْمٰنِ الرَّحِيمِ [*In, or with, the name of God, the Compassionate, the Merciful*]: (KL:) a verb of the kind termed مَنْحُوت, i. e. compounded of two [or more] words; like حَمْدَلَ and حَوْقَلَ and حَسْبَلَ &c.: (Msb, TA:) said by some to be post-classical, not heard from the chaste Arabs; but authorized by many of the leading lexicologists, as ISk and Mtr; and occurring in the poetry of 'Omar Ibn-Abee-Rabee'ah [who is said to have been born in the year of the Flight 23]. (TA.)

مُبَسْمَلٌ Discourse, (TA,) or amorous behaviour, and coquettish boldness, (Msb,) *accompanied by the saying* بِسْمِ ٱللّٰهِ: (Msb, TA:) occurring in a verse of 'Omar Ibn-Abee-Rabee'ah [referred to above]. (TA.)

بسن

4. ابسن, said of a man, *He was, or became good, or beautiful, in respect of his* سَجِيَّة [i. e. *natural disposition*], accord. to the copies of the K, but correctly, as explained by IAar, *his* سَحْنَة [i. e. *aspect, or colour, &c.*]. (TA.)

بَسَنٌ an imitative sequent to حَسَنٌ: (S, M, K:) [or it may signify *Beautiful in aspect* &c., from the verb above; or the verb may be from this word:] or, in the opinion of Aboo-'Alee El-Kálee, originally بَسٌّ, inf. n., used in the sense of the pass. part. n., of بَسَّ السَّوِيقَ, meaning "he moistened, or stirred about, the سويق with clarified butter, or with olive-oil, to complete, or perfect, its goodness;" one of the two س being suppressed, and ن being added; so that it means *complete, or perfect.* (MF. [But this derivation seems to be extremely far-fetched.])

بش

1. بَشَّ, first pers. بَشِشْتُ, aor. يَبَشُّ, (S, K,) and, accord. to a relation of a verse of Ru-beh, يَبِشُّ, so that perhaps بَشَشْتُ was also said, (TA,) inf. n. بَشَاشَةٌ (S, A, K) and بَشٌّ (A, K) and بَشِيشٌ, (TA,) *He was, or became, cheerful in countenance.* (S, A, K.) You say, بَشِشْتُ بِهِ *I was, or became, cheerful in countenance* [*by reason of meeting*] *with him*: (S:) or بَشَّ بِهِ, (TK,) inf. n. بَشٌّ (Lth, K) and بَشَاشَةٌ, (K,) signifies *he rejoiced in him, or was pleased with him,* namely, a friend, (Lth, K,) *at meeting*: (Lth:) or *he showed joy, or pleasure, at meeting him.* (TK.) You say

also, لَقِيتُهُ فَتَبَشْبَشَ ♦ بِى [app. meaning *I met him and he became cheerful in countenance by reason of meeting with me*]; originally ♦ تَبَشَّشَ; the middle ش being changed into ب: (Yaakoob, Ṣ:) or ♦ تَبَشْبَشَ بِهِ signifies *he was, or became, sociable, or companionable, or cheerful, with him; and held loving communion with him*: syn. آنَسَهُ, and وَاصَلَهُ: (Ḳ:) but when said of God, it means ‡ *He regarded him with favour, and honoured him*, (IAmb, Ḳ,) *and received him graciously, and drew him near to Him*. (IAmb.) — Also بَشَّ لَهُ, (TḲ,) inf. n. بَشٌّ (IDrd, Ḳ) and بَشَاشَةٌ, (Ḳ,) *He presented a favourable aspect to him; or met him kindly*, namely, his brother; syn. أَقْبَلَ عَلَيْهِ: (Ḳ:) *he behaved laughingly towards him; without shyness, or aversion; or boldly; or in a free and easy manner; or cheerfully*; syn. ضَحِكَ إِلَيْهِ, (IDrd, Ḳ,) and انْبَسَطَ. (IDrd.) — And بَشَّ لَهُ فِى الْمَسْأَلَةِ, (TḲ,) inf. n. بَشٌّ (IAạr, A, Ḳ) and بَشَاشَةٌ, (A, Ḳ,) *He was courteous, or gracious, to him in asking*. (IAạr, A, Ḳ.) — And بَشَّ لِى بِخَيْرٍ ‡ *He gave me* [*something good*]. (A, TA.)

4. ابشّت الأَرْضُ ‡ *The land had tangled, or luxuriant, plants, or herbage*: (Aṣ, Ḳ:) *or produced its first plants, or herbage*. (Ḳ.)

5: see 1.

R. Q. 2: see 1, in two places.

رَجُلٌ هَشٌّ بَشٌّ *A man* [*brisk, lively, or sprightly; or joyful*; and] *cheerful in countenance; pleasant* [*therein*]; (Ṣ, TA;) as also ♦ بَشَاشٌ. (TA.) [See also art. هش.]

بَشِيشٌ *The face, or countenance*. (Ibn-'Abbád, Ḳ.) You say, فُلَانٌ مُضِىْءُ الْبَشِيشِ *Such a one is bright in countenance*. (Ibn-'Abbád.)

بَشَاشٌ: see بَشٌّ.

أَبَشُّ [*More, and most, cheerful in countenance*]. You say, مَا رَأَيْتُ أَبَشَّ مِنْهُ بِالْلَاقِى [*I have not seen any one more cheerful in countenance than he to the meeter*]. (A.)

بشر

1. بَشَرَ, aor. ـُ, (Ṣ, Mṣb,) inf. n. بَشْرٌ; (Ṣ, Mṣb, Ḳ;) and ♦ ابشر, (A,) inf. n. إِبْشَارٌ; (Ḳ;) *He pared* (Ṣ, A, Mṣb, Ḳ) a hide, (Ṣ, A, Mṣb,) *removing its* بَشَرَة, (Ṣ,) *or face, or surface*, (A, Mṣb,) *or the skin upon which the hair grew*: (TA:) or, as some say, *removing its inner part with a large knife*: or, accord. to Ibn-Buzurj, some of the Arabs say, بَشَرْتُ الأَدِيمَ, aor. ـِ, meaning *I removed from the hide its* بَشَرَة; and ♦ أَبْشَرْتُهُ as meaning *I exposed to view its* بَشَرَة *that was next to the flesh*; and آدَمْتُهُ I exposed to view its أَدَمَة upon which the hair grew. (TA.) [But see أَدَمَةٌ.] — Hence the saying in a trad., مَنْ أَحَبَّ القُرْآنَ فَلْيَبْشُرْ, accord. to him who recites it thus, with ḍamm to the ش; meaning † *Whoso loveth the Ḳur-án, let him make himself light of flesh*, [*by not eating more than will be sufficient*, and so prepare himself] for [reading, or reciting,] it, [like as one prepares a horse for running,] because eating much causes one to forget it. (TA.) — Hence also, بَشَرَ الأَرْضَ, (TA,) inf. n. as above, (Ṣ, Ḳ,) † *It* (a swarm of locusts) *stripped the ground*; (TA;) *ate what was upon the ground*, (Ṣ, Ḳ,) i. e., *upon its surface*; as though the exterior of the ground were its بَشَرَة. (TA.) — And بَشَرَ, aor. ـُ, (TA,) inf. n. as above, (Ḳ,) *He clipped* his mustache *much, so that the* بَشَرَة (i. e. the *exterior of the skin*, TA) *became apparent*. (Ḳ, TA.) This the Muslim is commanded to do. (TA.) — بَشَرَنِى فُلَانٌ بِوَجْهٍ حَسَنٍ *Such a one met me with a cheerful countenance*. (Ṣ.) See also 2, in two places. — And see 3. == بَشِرَ, aor. ـَ; (IAạr, Ṣ, Mṣb, Ḳ;) and بَشَرَ, aor. ـُ, (IAạr, Ḳ,) inf. n. بَشْرٌ and بُشُورٌ; (TA;) and ♦ ابشر, [which is the most common, though extr. in respect of analogy, as being quasi-pass. of بَشَّرَ, like احجم and احنع and اعرض and اقشع and اكبّ and انهج, (mentioned by MF in art. حنع as the only other instances of the kind,) and اخلع, (added in the TA in art. خلع,)] (Ṣ, A, Mgh, Ḳ,) inf. n. إِبْشَارٌ; (Ṣ;) and ♦ استبشر; (Ṣ, A, Mṣb, Ḳ;) and ♦ تبشّر; (A;) [originally, *He became changed in his* بَشَرَة (or *complexion*) *by the annunciation of an event*: see بُشْرَى: and hence,] *he rejoiced, or became rejoiced*; (IAạr, Ṣ, A, Mṣb, Ḳ;) بِكَذَا [*at, or by, such a thing*; or *at, or by, the annunciation of such a thing*]. (IAạr, Ṣ, Ḳ.*) You say, أَتَانِى أَمْرٌ بَشِرْتُ بِهِ *An affair happened to me whereat I rejoiced, or whereby I became rejoiced*. (Ṣ.) And ♦ أَبْشَرَ بِمَوْلُودٍ *He rejoiced* [*at the annunciation of a new-born child*]. (Ṣ.) And ♦ أَبْشِرْ بِخَيْرٍ *Rejoice thou* [*at the annunciation of a good event*]. (Ṣ, Ḳ.) And in the same sense ♦ أَبْشِرُوا is used in the Ḳur xli. 30. (Ṣ.)

2. بشّرهُ, (Ṣ, A, Mṣb, &c.,) the form used by the Arabs in general, (Mṣb,) inf. n. تَبْشِيرٌ; (Ṣ, Mṣb, Ḳ, &c.;) and ♦ بَشَرَهُ, aor. ـُ, (Ṣ, Mgh, Mṣb,) of the dial. of Tihámeh and the adjacent parts, (Mṣb,) inf. n. بَشْرٌ and بُشُورٌ (Ṣ, Ḳ) and بُشْرٌ, (TA,) or this last is a simple subst.; (Mṣb;) and ♦ ابشرهُ; (Ṣ, A, Mgh, Ḳ;) and ♦ استبشرهُ; (Ḳ, TA;) are syn.; (Ṣ, Ḳ, &c.;) originally signifying *He announced to him an event which produced a change in his* بَشَرَة [or *complexion*]: and hence, (El-Fakhr Er-Rázee,) *he announced to him an event which rejoiced him*: (A, El-Fakhr Er-Rázee:) so in common acceptation [when not restricted by an adjunct that denotes its having a different meaning: see بُشْرَى, and an ex. below in this paragraph]: (El-Fakhr Er-Rázee:) or *he rejoiced him* [*by an annunciation*]: (Mṣb:) and *he announced to him an event which grieved him*: [or *he grieved him by an annunciation*:] both these significations are proper. (El-Fakhr Er-Rázee.) You say, بَشَّرَهُ بِالأَمْرِ [generally meaning *He rejoiced him by the annunciation of the event*]; and ♦ بَشَرَهُ بِهِ, aor. and inf. ns. as above; &c. (TA.) And بَشَّرْتُهُ بِمَوْلُودٍ [*I rejoiced him by the annunciation of a new-born child*]. (Ṣ.) And it is said in the Ḳur [iii. 20, &c.], بَشِّرْهُمْ بِعَذَابٍ أَلِيمٍ [*Grieve thou them by the annunciation, or denunciation, of a painful punishment*]. (Ṣ.) You say also, of a she-camel, بَشَّرَتْ بِاللِّقَاحِ, meaning † *She made it known that she had begun to be pregnant*. (TA. [See also 4.])

3. باشر المَرْأَةَ, (Ḳ, &c.,) inf. n. مُبَاشَرَةٌ (Ṣ, Mgh, TA) and بِشَارٌ, (TA,) *He was, or became, in contact with the woman, skin to skin*: (TA:) *he enjoyed* [*contact with*] *her skin*: (Mṣb:) *he became in contact with her, skin to skin, both being within one garment or piece of cloth*: (Ḳ:) *he lay with her*, [*skin to skin*; or *in the sense of*] *inivit eam*: (Ṣ, Ḳ:) i. q. وَطِئَهَا, both فِى الفَرْجِ and خَارِجًا مِنْهُ: (TA:) [and so ♦ بَشَرَهَا, inf. n. بَشْرٌ; for] بَشْرٌ and مُبَاشَرَةٌ are syn. [in the sense of *congressus venereus*, as is shown by an ex. in the Ṣ]. (Ṣ, Ḳ.) — باشرهُ النَّعِيمُ ‡ [*Enjoyment attended him; as though it clave to his skin*]. (A.) — رُوحَ اليَقِينِ, or فَبَاشَرُوا رَوْحَ اليَقِينِ, is a metaphorical expression, [app. meaning ‡ *And they felt the joy and happiness that arise from certainty*,] occurring in a trad. of 'Alee. (TA.) — باشر الأَمْرَ, (Ṣ, A, &c.,) inf. n. مُبَاشَرَةٌ, (Ṣ,) ‡ *He superintended, managed, or conducted, the affair himself, or in his own person*: (Ṣ, Ḳ, TA:) or ‡ *he was present, himself, at the affair*: (A, TA:) or, [properly,] *he managed, or conducted, the affair with his* بَشَرَة, i. e., his *own hand*: (Mgh,* Mṣb:) and hence a later application of the verb in the sense of لَاحَظَ † [*He regarded, or attended to*, the thing, or affair, &c.]. (Mṣb.)

4. ابشر: see 1, first sentence, in two places. — [Hence,] ابشر الأَمْرُ وَجْهَهُ *The affair made his countenance beautiful and bright*: in the Ḳ we read, أَبْشَرَ الأَمْرُ حُسْنَهُ وَنَضْرَهُ; but this is a mistake. (TA.) Agreeably with this explanation, AA renders a reading in the Ḳur [xlii. 22], ذٰلِكَ الَّذِى يُبْشِرُ اللّٰهُ عِبَادَهُ, meaning *That is it with which God will make beautiful and bright* the faces of *his servants*: so in the L. (TA.) — See also 2. — [Hence,] أَبْشَرَتِ النَّاقَةُ † *The she-camel conceived, or became pregnant*: (Ḳ:) as though she rejoiced [her owner] by announcing her conception. (TA. [See 2, last sentence.]) — And أَبْشَرَتِ الأَرْضُ ‡ *The earth put forth its herbage appearing upon its surface*. (Ṣ, Ḳ.) == See also 1, latter part, in four places.

5: see , latter part.

6. تباشر القَوْمُ *The people, or company of men, announced, one to another, a joyful event, or joyful events*. (Ṣ.) And هُمْ يَتَبَاشَرُونَ بِذٰلِكَ الأَمْرِ *They rejoice one another by the annunciation of that event*. (TA.)

10. استبشر: see 1, latter part. == استبشرهُ *He demanded of him a reward for an annunciation of joyful tidings*. (M.) — See also 2.

بَشْرٌ: see بُشْرَى. — It is also a contraction of بُشُرٌ, which is pl. of بَشُورٌ (TA) or بَشِيرٌ. (TA in art. نشر.)

بِشْرٌ *Cheerfulness, or openness and pleasantness,*

of countenance: (Mgh, Mṣb, Ḳ,* TA:) and *happiness, joy,* or *gladness.* (Ḥar p. 192.) You say, هُوَ حَسَنُ البِشْرِ *He is cheerful,* or *open and pleasant, in countenance.* (Ṣ.)

بَشَرٌ: see بَشَرَةٌ. —— [Hence,] البَشَرُ † *Mankind:* (Ṣ, Mṣb, Ḳ:) and *the human being:* (Mṣb, Ḳ:) applied to the male and to the female; and used alike as sing. and pl. (Mṣb, Ḳ, TA) and dual: (TA:) so that you say, هُوَ بَشَرٌ *He is a human being,* and هِىَ بَشَرٌ *She is a human being,* and هُمْ بَشَرٌ *They* (more than two) *are human beings,* and هُمَا بَشَرٌ *They two are human beings:* (TA:) but sometimes it has the dual form; (Mṣb, Ḳ;) as in the Ḳur xxiii. 49; (Mṣb, TA;) though the Arabs may have used the dual form in the sense of the sing.: (MF:) and sometimes it has a pl., namely, أَبْشَارٌ. (Ḳ.) This is a secondary application of the word: (Mṣb:) i. e., this signification is tropical; or, as some say, the word is so much used in this sense as to be, so used, conventionally regarded as proper; the sense not depending upon its having another word connected with it: but in the Ṣ and Ḳ, and by the generality of authors, this signification is given as proper. (MF.) Some say that a human being is thus called because his بَشَرَة is bare of hair and of wool. (MF.) [Hence,] أَبُو البَشَرِ [*The father of mankind;* meaning] *Adam.* (Ḳ.)

بَشَرَةٌ (Lth, Ṣ, M, A, Mgh, Mṣb) and ↓ بَشَرٌ, (Ṣ, Ḳ,) or the latter is pl. of the former, (Mṣb, Ḳ,) [or rather a coll. gen. n., of which the former is the n. un.,] like قَصَبَةٌ and قَصَبٌ, (Mṣb,) and أَبْشَارٌ is pl. of بَشَرٌ, (Ḳ,) [*The external skin;* the *cuticle,* or *scarf-skin;* the *epidermis;*] the *exterior of the skin* (Ṣ, A, Mgh, Mṣb, Ḳ) of a human being; (Ṣ, A, Ḳ;) and, as some say, of other creatures, (Ḳ,) such as the serpent; but this is generally disallowed: (TA:) or بَشَرَةٌ signifies the *exterior of the skin of the head, in which grows the hair;* as also أَدَمَةٌ and شَوَاةٌ: (Aboo-Ṣafwán:) or the *upper skin* (Lth, M) *of the head* (M) *and of the face and body* of a human being; (Lth, M;) *that upon which the hair grows:* (M:) or, as some say, *that which is next the flesh.* (M.) It is said in a prov., إِنَّمَا يُعَاتَبُ الأَدِيمُ ذُو البَشَرَةِ: see أَدِيمٌ. —— بَشَرَةٌ sometimes means The *complexion,* or *hue:* and *fineness,* or *delicacy.* (TA.) ══ بَشَرَةُ الأَرْضِ ‡ *The herbage appearing upon the surface of the earth.* (Ṣ, A, Ḳ.) You say, مَا أَحْسَنَ بَشَرَتَهَا ‡ *How goodly is its herbage appearing upon its surface!* (Ṣ, A.) And بَشَرَةٌ [alone] signifies ‡ *Leguminous plants; herbs,* or *herbage.* (TA.) —— بَشَرَةٌ is used also as signifying † A man's *hand.* (Mṣb.) [See 3, last sentence.]

بُشْرَى (imperfectly decl., because it terminates with a fem. alif which is inseparable from it, Ṣ) and ↓ بِشَارَةٌ and ↓ بُشَارَةٌ [but respecting this last see بُشَارَةٌ below] (Ṣ, Mṣb, Ḳ) and ↓ بُشْرٌ (Mṣb) are substs. from بَشَّرَهُ (Ṣ, Mṣb, Ḳ) [originally signifying *An annunciation which produces a change in the* بَشَرَة (or *complexion*) *of the person to whom it is made:* and hence, *a joyful annunciation; joyful,* or *glad, tidings; good news*]: and ↓ تَبَاشِيرُ [q. v. infrà] signifies the same as بُشْرَى: (Ṣ, Ḳ:) ↓ بِشَارَةٌ, when used absolutely, relates only to good; (Ṣ, Mṣb;) not to evil unless when expressly restricted thereto by an adjunct: [see 2:] (Ṣ:) its pl. is بِشَارَاتٌ and بَشَائِرُ. (A.) يَا بُشْرَاىَ, in the Ḳur [xii. 19, accord. to one reading, (otherwise, as Bḍ mentions, بُشْرَاىَ, or بُشْرَىَّ, which is a dial. var. of the same, or بُشْرَى, which, as some say, was the name of a man,) meaning *O my joyful annunciation,* or *joyful tidings,* or *good news!*], is like عَصَاىَ: and in the dual you say, يَا بُشْرَيَىَّ. (Ṣ.) You say also, تَتَابَعَت البِشَارَاتُ ↓ and البَشَائِرُ [*The joyful annunciations followed consecutively*]. (A.) See another ex. voce بَشِيرٌ. —— See also بِشَارَةٌ.

[بَشَرِىٌّ *Human; of,* or *belonging to,* or *relating to, mankind* or *a human being.*]

بُشَارٌ † The *refuse,* or *lowest* or *basest* or *meanest sort,* of mankind, or of people. (IAạr, Ḳ.)

بَشُورٌ: see what next follows, in three places.

بَشِيرٌ *i. q.* ↓ مُبَشِّرٌ, (Ṣ, Mgh, Ḳ,) [and so ↓ بَشُورٌ, as will be seen by an ex. in what follows,] *One who announces to a people* [or *person*] *an event, either good or evil;* (TA;) but meaning the former oftener than the latter: (Mṣb:) [*an announcer of a joyful event,* or *joyful events: one who rejoices another,* or *others, by an annunciation:*] pl. بُشَرَآءُ (A) and بُشُرٌ, (TA in art. نشر,) or this is pl. of ↓ بَشُورٌ. (TA in the present art.) It is said in the Ḳur [vii. 55], وَهُوَ الَّذِى يُرْسِلُ الرِّيَاحَ بُشُرًا, and بُشْرًا, and ↓ بُشْرَى, and بَشْرًا; [accord. to different readings, meaning †*And He it is who sendeth the winds announcing coming rain;*] in which بُشُرٌ is pl. of ↓ بَشُورٌ, [syn. with بَشِيرٌ and مُبَشِّرٌ, but both masc. and fem.,] (TA,) or of بَشِيرٌ, (Bḍ,) or of بَشِيرَةٌ; (TA in art. نشر;) and بُشْرًا is a contraction of the same; and بُشْرَى is syn. with بِشَارَةٌ; and بَشْرًا is the inf. n. of بَشَرَهُ in the sense of بَشَّرَهُ. (TA. [But the reading commonly followed in this passage is نُشُرًا, with ن: another reading is نَشْرًا: another, نُشْرًا: and another, نَشَرًا.]) And ↓ المُبَشِّرَاتُ, (A,) or مُبَشِّرَاتُ الرِّيَاحِ, (Ṣ,) signifies ‡ *Winds that announce* [*coming*] *rain:* (Ṣ, A:) so in the Ḳur xxx. 45. (TA.) ══ Also *Goodly; beautiful; elegant in form or features;* (Ṣ, Ḳ;) applied to a man, and to a face: (TA:) fem. with ة; (Ṣ, Ḳ;) applied to a woman, and to a she-camel; (Ṣ;) and meaning, when applied to a she-camel, *neither emaciated nor fat:* or, accord. to Aboo-Hilál, *neither of generous nor of ignoble breed:* or, as some say, *half-fattened:* (TA:) pl. of the fem. بَشَائِرُ: (Ṣ:) and ↓ مَبْشُورَةٌ signifies *beautiful in make and colour;* (IAạr, Ḳ;) applied to a girl. (IAạr.)

بَشَارَةٌ *Goodliness; beauty; elegance of form or features.* (Ṣ, Ḳ, TA.)

بُشَارَةٌ *What is pared off from the face of a hide:* what is pared off from its back is called تِحْلِئٌ. (Lḥ.) ══ See also بِشَارَةٌ: —— and see بُشْرَى.

بِشَارَةٌ; pl. بِشَارَاتٌ and بَشَائِرُ: see بُشْرَى, in three places; and see also تَبَاشِيرُ. —— Also *A gift to him who announces a joyful event;* and so ↓ بُشَارَةٌ: (Ḳ,* TA:) or the latter, which is like the عُمَالَة of the عَامِل, has this signification; (IAth;) and so ↓ بُشْرَى; (M;) and ↓ بِشَارَةٌ [has the same meaning accord. to common usage, but, properly,] is a subst. in the sense explained above, voce بُشْرَى. (IAth.) You say, أَعْطَيْتُهُ ثَوْبِى بِشَارَةً *I gave him my garment as a reward for the joyful annunciation.* (TA from a trad.)

هُوَ أَبْشَرُ مِنْهُ *He is more goodly* or *beautiful, more elegant in form* or *features, and more fat, than he.* (Ḳ.)

تُبُشِّرٌ, in the handwriting of J تُبَشِّرٌ, [and so in my copies of the Ṣ,] a word of which there is not the like except in the instances of تُنَوِّطٌ [or تُنَوُّطٌ], a certain bird, and وَادِى تُهُلِّكَ [or تُهَلِّكَ?] and وَادِى تُخُيِّبَ [or تُخَيِّبَ] and تُضُلِّلَ [or تُضَلِّلَ], (TA,) *A certain bird, called the* صُفَارِيَّة: (Ṣ, Ḳ:) n. un. with ة. (Ḳ.)

تَبَاشِيرُ, as though it were pl. of تَبْشِيرٌ, inf. n. of بَشَّرَ; (A;) a word which has not its like except in the instances of تَعَاشِيبُ and تَعَاجِيبُ and تَفَاطِيرُ [and تَبَارِيحُ and تَبَاكِيرُ, and probably a few others]; (TA;) ‡ [*Annunciations; foretokens; foretellers; foreshowers; prognostics; earnests;* of what is good:] the *beginnings* of anything: (Ṣ, Ḳ:) the *first* of blossoms &c.: (TA:) the *beginnings,* (Ṣ, Ḳ,) or *first annunciations,* (A,) of daybreak; (Ṣ, A, Ḳ;) as also ↓ بَشَائِرُ: (TA:) it has no verb: (Ṣ:) and [is said to have] no sing.: but in a trad. of El-Ḥajjáj, تَبْشِيرٌ occurs as meaning † the *commencement* of rain. (TA.) One says, فِيهِ مَخَايِلُ الرُّشْدِ وَتَبَاشِيرُهُ ‡ [*In him are indications of right conduct,* or *belief, and its earnests*]. (A.) See also بُشْرَى. —— †*Streaks of the light of daybreak in the night.* (TA.) —— † *Streaks that are seen upon the surface of the ground, caused by the winds.* (Lth, Ḳ.*) —— † The *colours of palm-trees when their fruit begins to ripen;* (Ḳ;) as also تَبَاكِيرُ. (TA.) —— † *Such as bear fruit early,* or *before others,* of palm-trees. (Ḳ.) —— † *Marks of galls upon the side of a beast.* (Ḳ.)

رَجُلٌ مُؤْدَمٌ مُبْشَرٌ ‡ *A perfect man; as though he combined the softness of the* أَدَمَة [or *inner skin*] *with the roughness of the* بَشَرَة [or *outer skin*]: (Ṣ:) or *a man who combines softness,* or *gentleness, and strength, with knowledge of affairs:* (Aṣ:) and امْرَأَةٌ مُؤْدَمَةٌ مُبْشَرَةٌ ‡ *a woman perfect in every respect.* (TA.) [See also art. ادم.]

مُبَشِّرٌ and مُبَشِّرَاتٌ: see بَشِيرٌ.

مَبْشُورَةٌ: see بَشِيرٌ, last sentence.

حِجْرٌ مُبَاشِرٌ [so in two copies of the Ṣ: in Golius's Lex. مُبَاشِرَةٌ:] *A mare* [so I render حِجْر, which Golius renders "vulva,"] *desiring the stallion.* (Ṣ.) [See also مُبَاسِرَةٌ, with س.]

بشع

1. بَشِعَ, aor. ـَ, (Ḳ, TA,) inf. n. بَشَاعَةٌ (Ṣ, Ḳ) and بَشْعٌ, (Ḳ,) said of a thing, (Ṣ,) or of food, (Ḳ, TA,) *It was, or became, disagreeable in taste, and choking:* (Ṣ:) or *disagreeable,* or *unpleasant, having in it dryness and bitterness.* (Ḳ, TA.) —— بَشِعَ الرَّجُلُ, (Ḳ,* TA,) aor. ـَ, (Ḳ,) inf. n. بَشَعٌ (Ṣ, Ḳ) and بَشَاعَةٌ, (Ḳ,) *The man was,* or *became, disagreeable in the odour of the mouth,* (Ṣ,* Ḳ,) *from eating food disagreeable in taste, and choking;* (Ṣ;) *not removing the remains of food from between his teeth, nor cleaning them with the tooth-stick.* (Ḳ.) You say, بَشِعَ مِنْهُ [*He was,* or *became, disagreeable in the odour of the mouth from it*]; meaning, from eating food such as is described above. (Ṣ.) [Or this phrase in the Ṣ may have another meaning, which see in what follows.] —— And [hence,] ‡ *The man was,* or *became, evil in his disposition, and in his social intercourse.* (Mṣb.) You say also, فِى خُلُقِهِ بَشَاعَةٌ ‡ *In his disposition is evilness.* (TA.) —— بَشَعٌ also signifies, in relation to wood, ‡ The *abounding in knots.* (TA.) —— Also The fauces' *being straitened,* or *choked, by coarse,* or *rough, food.* (TA.) [And بَشِعَ مِنْهُ means *He experienced a straitened state,* or *choking, of the fauces from it;* namely coarse, or rough, food; or food disagreeable in taste, and choking: see 4: and see another meaning of this phrase above.] —— And [hence,] بَشِعَ, [or بَشِعَ بِالْمَآءِ,] aor. ـَ, ‡ *It* (a valley) *was,* or *became, choked, surcharged,* or *overfilled, with the water.* (Ḳ.) And بَشِعَ بِالنَّاسِ ‡ *It* [a place] *was,* or *became, choked,* or *overfilled, with men,* or *the people.* (Z, TA.) —— [Hence also,] بَشِعَ بِالأَمْرِ, (Ḳ,) inf. n. بَشَعٌ and بَشَاعَةٌ, (TA,) ‡ *He was unable to do,* or *accomplish, the thing,* or *affair.* (Ḳ, TA.) ══ بَشَعَ بِالشَّىْءِ, and بَشَعَ بِهِ, inf. n. بَشْعٌ, *He seized the thing in a violent and an abominable manner.* (L, TA.)

4. أَبْشَعَنِى الطَّعَامُ *The food caused me to experience a straitened state,* or *choking, of the fauces,* (حَمَلَنِى عَلَى البَشَعِ,) *by reason of its coarseness,* or *roughness.* (IAạr.) [See 1.]

10. استبشعهُ *i. q.* عَدَّهُ بَشِعًا [*He reckoned it disagreeable in taste, and choking;* or *disagreeable,* or *unpleasant, as having in it dryness and bitterness*]; (Ṣ, Mṣb, Ḳ;) namely, a thing. (Ṣ.) —— And [hence,] استبشع المُقَامَ فِى مَحَلِّ كَذَا ‡ *He reckoned unpleasant,* or *uncomfortable, the remaining in such a place of abode;* syn. اِسْتَخْشَنَهُ. (TA.) ══ اِسْتِبْشَاعٌ also signifies *The being bad, unpleasant,* or *disapproved.* (KL.)

بَشِعٌ A thing *disagreeable in taste, and choking;* or ▼ بَشِيعٌ has this signification: (so accord. to different copies of the Ṣ:) or both, applied to food, have the same signification: (TA:) or the former signifies also *disagreeable,* or *unpleasant,* food, *having in it dryness and bitterness;* (Lth, Z, Ḳ;) *like the taste of the myrobalan:* (TA:) or food *rough,* or *coarse, and disagreeable in taste:* or *dry* food, *in which is no seasoning,* or *condiment:* (TA:) or *rough,* or *coarse;* applied to food; (Nh;) and so ‡ applied to clothing; (IAạr, Nh;) and ‡ to speech, or language; (Nh;) and ▼ بَشِيعٌ applied to speech, or language, signifies ‡ *rough,* or *coarse, and disagreeable.* (IAạr.) —— Applied to a man, (Ṣ, TA,) as is also ▼ بَشِيعٌ, in the same sense, (TA, [but in what sense is not there said,]) it signifies *Disagreeable in the odour of the mouth,* (Mṣb,* Ḳ,) *who does not remove the remains of food from between his teeth, nor clean them with the tooth-stick;* (Ḳ;) fem. with ة: (TA:) and one *who has eaten a thing such as is thus termed,* (Ṣ, Ḳ, TA,) *and not swallowed it easily,* (TA,) *and has become disagreeable in the odour of the mouth from it,* or *has experienced a straitened state,* or *choking, of the fauces from it.* (Ṣ, TA: [the last words of the explanation being فَبَشِعَ مِنْهُ.]) —— Also ‡ One *whose soul is heavy,* or *heaving,* or *agitated by a tendency to vomit.* (ISh, Ḳ, TA.) —— And ‡ *Evil in disposition,* (Ḳ, TA,) *and in social intercourse.* (TA.) You say also, هُوَ بَشِعُ الخُلُقِ ‡ *He is evil in disposition.* (TA.) —— Also, (Ḳ, TA,) or بَشِعُ المَنْظَرِ, (Mṣb,) ‡ *Foul,* or *ugly, in aspect;* (Mṣb, Ḳ;) *not pleasing to the eyes.* (TA.) —— Also, (Ḳ,) or بَشِعُ الوَجْهِ, (ISh, Mṣb,) ‡ *Having a frowning, a contracted, a stern, an austere,* or *a morose, countenance.* (ISh, Mṣb, Ḳ.) —— خَشَبَةٌ بَشِعَةٌ ‡ *A piece of wood abounding in knots.* (Ḳ, TA.)

بَشِيعٌ: see بَشِعٌ, in three places.

بشق

1. بَشَقَ, aor. ـُ; and بَشَّقَ, aor. ـِ; *He struck, smote,* or *beat,* another with a staff or stick. (Nawádir el-Aạráb, Ḳ.) ══ *He looked sharply,* or *intently:* (Ibn-'Abbád, Ḳ:) inf. n. بَشْقٌ. (JK.) ══ Also the former verb, *He hastened,* or *was quick;* as also بَشَكَ. (IDrd, TA.) ══ And the former, [but the aor. is not mentioned,] *He cut* a garment, or piece of cloth, *in a light,* or *prompt, manner;* as also بَشَكَ. (TA.) ══ And بَشَقَ, inf. n. بَشْقٌ, *He took,* or *seized.* (Mṣb.)

نَظَرٌ بَشْقٌ *A sharp,* or *an intent, look.* (JK.)

بَاشَقٌ (JK, Mṣb, Ḳ) and بَاشِقٌ, (Mṣb, Es-Suyootee, TA,) the latter being allowable accord. to some for the sake of conformity to the usual Arabic measure, as in خاتم and دانق and طابع and the like; (Mṣb;) perhaps derived from بَشْقٌ meaning the "looking sharply," or "intently;" (JK;) or from بَشَقَ meaning "he took," or "seized;" (Mṣb;) or it is arabicized, (Mṣb, Ḳ,) from [the Persian] بَاشَهْ; (Ḳ;) *A certain bird;* (Ḳ;) [the *musket,* or *sparrow-hawk; falco nisus;*] *a bird of beautiful form, the smallest of birds of prey, that preys upon sparrows and other birds of their size:* (Ḳzw:) *it is of the birds called* صُقُور, [pl. of صَقْرٌ,] as are also the بَازِى and the شَاهِين and the زُرَّق and the يُؤْيُؤ: (AḤát in "the Book of Birds," TA:) pl. بَوَاشِقُ. (Mṣb.)

بشم

1. بَشِمَ, aor. ـَ, inf. n. بَشَمٌ, *He* (a man, Ṣ, TA, or an animal, Mṣb) *suffered,* or *became affected with, indigestion,* (Ṣ, Mṣb, Ḳ,) in consequence of much eating: (Mṣb:) or *he was heavy* in consequence of food: (Ḥam p. 363:) or *he became distressed,* or *oppressed, by eating much food.* (TA.) You say, بَشِمْتُ مِنَ الطَّعَامِ *I suffered indigestion from the food:* (Ṣ:) or *was heavy in consequence of the food.* (Ḥam ubi suprà.) And بَشِمَ الفَصِيلُ مِنْ كَثْرَةِ شُرْبِ اللَّبَنِ *The young camel suffered indigestion from drinking much milk.* (Ṣ.) Accord. to IDrd, بَشَمٌ specially relates to beasts: accord. to Kh, it specially arises from greasy food. (Ḥar p. 164.) —— Also ‡ *He became affected with disgust, aversion, loathing,* or *nausea.* (Ṣ, Ḳ, TA.) You say, بَشِمْتُ مِنَ الطَّعَامِ, (Ṣ,) or عَنِ الطعام, (TA,) ‡ *I turned away with disgust from the food; was averse from it; loathed it; nauseated it.* (Ṣ, TA.) And بَشِمَ الفَصِيلُ عَنِ اللَّبَنِ † [*The young camel turned away with disgust from the milk; was averse from it;* &c.]. (Ḳ in art. دقع.)

4. ابشمهُ *It* (food) *caused him to suffer,* or *be affected with, indigestion:* (Ṣ, Ḳ,* TA:) or † *loathing,* or *nausea.* (Ḳ.)

بَشِمٌ part. n. of 1, meaning *Suffering,* or *affected with, indigestion.* (Mṣb.) —— [And † *Affected with disgust, aversion, loathing,* or *nausea.*]

بَشَامٌ [The *tree of the balsam of Mekkeh; amyris opobalsamum;* mentioned by Forskål in his Flora Aegypt. Arab. p. cx. as growing in the middle mountainous region of El-Yemen, and described by him in p. 79 of the same work; in both places as being called in Arabic ابو شام, which is a mistake for بشام;] *a certain odoriferous kind of tree,* (Ṣ, Ḳ,) *of sweet taste,* (TA,) *the leaves of which,* (AḤn, Ḳ,) *pounded, and mixed with* الحِنَّآء [or *the leaves of the Lawsonia inermis*], (AḤn,) *blacken the hair;* (AḤn, Ḳ;) it is *a kind of tree having a stem and branches, and small leaves, but larger than the leaves of the* [*species of marjoram called*] صَعْتَر, *and having no fruit;* [*but only,* as Forskål states, *a blackish seed, which is abortive;*] *when its leaf or its branch is cut, it pours forth a white milk;* (AḤn, TA;) *and its twigs are used for cleaning the teeth:* (Ṣ, Ḳ:) n. un. with ة. (TA.) In a trad., mention is made of persons having no food but the leaves of the بشام. (TA.)

بشنين

بَشْنِينٌ, with fet-ḥ, and then sukoon, and then kesr, *I. q.* نيلوفر [i. e. نِيلُوفَرٌ and نَيْلُوفَرٌ or نَيْلُوفَرٌ, the *nymphæa lotus,* or *white lotus:* and the *nymphæa cærulea,* or *blue lotus:* see art. نيلوفر]: a word of the dial. of Egypt. (TA.)

بص

1. بَصَّ, aor. يَبِصُّ, inf. n. بَصِيصٌ (Ṣ, A, Ḳ) and بَصٌّ, (TA,) *It* (a thing, Ṣ, as, for instance, a grain of a pomegranate, TA) *shone,* or *glistened.* (Ṣ, A, Ḳ.) —— هُوَ يَبُصُّ لِى [*He looks at me*] is an expression used by the vulgar [in the present day], and is from البَصَّاصَةُ signifying "the eye." (TA.) [By rule it should be يَبِصُّ.]

2. بَصَّصَ بِسَيْفِهِ *He made a sign with his sword, waving it,* or *moving it about* [*so that it shone,* or *glistened*]. (TA.)

R. Q. 1. بَصْبَصَ, (Ṣ, Ḳ,) or بَصْبَصَ بِذَنَبِهِ, (M,) inf. n. بَصْبَصَةٌ, (TA,) *He* (a dog, Ṣ, M, Ḳ, and a beast of prey, and a gazelle, and a camel when urged on by the driver's singing, TA) *wagged,* or *moved about, his tail;* (Ṣ, Ḳ;) which a dog does by reason of cupidity, or fear; (TA;) as also ▾تَبَصْبَصَ: (Ṣ:) or *he* (a dog) *struck with his tail.* (ISd.) The inf. n. بَصْبَصَةٌ has a pl., namely, بَصَابِصُ; as in the following ex.:

* حَتَّى إِذَا أَبْصَرْنَهُ وَعَلِمْنَهُ *
* حَيَّيْنَهُ بِبَصَابِصِ الأَذْنَابِ *

[*Until, when they see him and know him, they greet him with waggings of the tails*]. (TA.) It is said in a prov., respecting the flight and submissiveness of the coward,

* بَصْبَصْنَ إِذْ حُدِينَ بِالأَذْنَابِ *

[*They wagged the tails when they were urged on by the driver's singing*]. (Aṣ.) — بَصْبَصَتِ الإِبِلُ قَرَبَهَا *The camels performed quickly their night-journey to water.* (Ḳ.) [See بَصْبَاصٌ.]

R. Q. 2. تَبَصْبَصَ: see R. Q. 1.

[بَصٌّ, and بَصُّ نَارٍ, *Live coals;* because they shine, or glisten: n. un. with ة: so in the present day; but probably only post-classical: or, accord. to the TA, in art. بصو, the word بَصَّةٌ is used by the vulgar, for بَصْوَةٌ.]

بَصَّاصٌ [*Shining,* or *glistening:* or rather, *shining,* or *glistening, much*]. — [Hence,] البَصَّاصَةُ *The eye:* (Ṣ, A, Ḳ:) an epithet in which the quality of a subst. predominates: (TA:) said to be so called (TA) because it shines, or glistens. (Ḳ, TA.) — [And hence بَصَّاصٌ is applied in the present day to *An officer employed as an inspector by a police-magistrate.*]

بُصَّانٌ a name of [*The month afterwards called*] رَبِيعٌ الآخِرُ: the former was its name in the Time of Ignorance: thus it is written accord. to the Jm: [or it was called, or was also called, وَبْصَانٌ, and وُبْصَانٌ: (see art. وبص:) or وَبُصَانٌ, and وَبَصَانٌ: (see art. بصن:)] the author of the Ḳ mentions it in art. بصن; [where it is said to be also written بُصَانٌ, i. e., without teshdeed;] but this is its proper place, for it is from البَصِيصُ [inf. n. of بَصَّ]. (TA.)

خِمْسٌ بَصْبَاصٌ, (T, Ḳ,) or قَرَبٌ بَصْبَاصٌ, (Ṣ,) *A laborious,* (T, Ṣ, Ḳ,) *fatiguing,* (T,) *night-journey to water,* (T, Ḳ,) or *journey in which the second and third and fourth days are without water; in which is no flagging:* (Ṣ:) [as also صَبْصَابٌ.] — يَوْمٌ بَصْبَاصٌ *A vehemently-hot day.* (TA.)

بصر

1. بَصُرَ, [aor. ـُ,] (Sb, M, Ḳ,) and بَصِرَ, [aor. ـَ,] (Lḥ, Ḳ,) inf. n. بَصَرٌ and بَصَارَةٌ and بِصَارَةٌ, (M, Ḳ,) [*He saw;* i. e.] *he became seeing;* syn. صَارَ مُبْصِرًا; (Sb, M, Ḳ;) with ب prefixed to the noun following. (Ḳ.) But see 4, in four places. بَصَرٌ is seldom used to signify the sense of sight unless to this meaning is conjoined that of mental perception. (B.) — [Hence,] بَصُرَ, [and بَصِرَ,] inf. n. بَصَارَةٌ [and بَصَرٌ], *He was,* or *became, endowed with mental perception;* or *belief,* or *firm belief;* or *knowledge, understanding, intelligence,* or *skill.* (Ṣ,* M, TA.) And بَصُرَ بِهِ, (Ṣ, Mṣb, B,) and بَصِرَ بِهِ, and sometimes بَصُرَهُ and بَصِرَهُ, but more chastely with ب, inf. n. [بَصَارَةٌ and] بَصَرٌ; (Mṣb;) and ▾ابصرهُ; (B;) *He perceived it mentally;* (B;) *he knew it* [or *understood it*]. (Ṣ, Mṣb.) بَصُرْتُ بِمَا لَمْ يَبْصُرُوا بِهِ, in the Ḳur [xx. 96], means *I knew that which they knew not.* (Ṣ.) — بَصَرَ الأَدِيمَيْنِ, aor. ـُ, (T, Ḳ,) inf. n. بَصْرٌ, (Ṣ, M, Ḳ,) *He put the two hides together, and sewed them, like as the two edges of a garment,* or *piece of cloth, are sewed, one being put upon the other; which* [*mode of sewing*] *is contrary to,* or *different from, that in which a garment,* or *piece of cloth, is sewed before it is sewed the second time:* (Ṣ:) or *he put together the two edges of the two hides, when they were being sewed,* (M, Ḳ,) *like as a garment,* or *piece of cloth, is sewed.* (M.)

2. بَصَّرَ *He* (a whelp) *opened his eyes.* (M, Ḳ.) — بَصَّرَهُ, (Ṣ, Ḳ,) inf. n. تَبْصِيرٌ; (TA;) or ▾ابصرهُ; (accord. to some copies of the Ḳ; [see مُبْصِرٌ, as confirmatory of the latter; but both seem to be correct;]) *It* [or *he*] *made him* [or *caused him*] *to see,* or *to have sight:* or *to have mental perception,* or *knowledge,* or *skill:* syn. جَعَلَهُ بَصِيرًا. (Ṣ, Ḳ.) — And the former, (Ḳ,) inf. n. as above, (Ṣ, Ḳ,) *He made him to know.* (Ṣ, Ḳ.) You say, بَصَّرْتُهُ بِهِ, (A, Mṣb,) inf. n. as above, (Mṣb,) *I made him to know it; acquainted him with it.* (A, Mṣb.) And بَصَّرَهُ الأَمْرَ, inf. n. as above and تَبْصِرَةٌ, *He made him to understand the affair,* or *case.* (M.) — Also *He rendered it apparent,* or *plainly apparent, conspicuous, manifest,* or *evident.* (Ṣ, Ḳ.) — بَصَّرَتْ بِدَمٍ, said of the feathers of an arrow, *They were besmeared* بِالبَصِيرَةِ, i. e. *with blood:* (Ṣ:) or *were strengthened and fastened with glue.* (M.) — Also بَصَّرَ, inf. n. تَبْصِيرٌ; (Ṣ, Ḳ;) and ▾ابصر; (Ḳ;) *He went,* (Ṣ,) or *came,* (M, Ḳ,) *to the city of El-Baṣrah* (البَصْرَةُ). (Ṣ, M, Ḳ.)

3. باصرهُ *He looked with him at a thing, trying which of them two would see it before the other.* (M.) And بَاصَرَا *They two looked, trying which of them would see first.* (Ḳ.) — *He elevated himself,* or *rose up,* or *stood up, so as to be higher than the surrounding objects,* (أَشْرَفَ,) *looking at him,* or *towards him, from afar.* (Ṣ.) — See also 4.

4. ابصرهُ, (Lḥ, Ṣ, M, A, &c.,) inf. n. إِبْصَارٌ, (Mṣb,) *He saw him,* or *it,* (Lḥ, Ṣ, A, Mgh, Mṣb,) بِرُؤْيَةِ العَيْنِ *by the sight of the eye;* (Mṣb;) as also ▾بَصُرَ بِهِ: (A:) or *he looked* (M, Ḳ) *at,* or *towards, him,* or *it,* (M,) *trying whether he could see him,* or *it;* (M, Ḳ;) as also ▾بَصُرَ بِهِ, inf. n. بَصَرٌ and بَصَارَةٌ and بِصَارَةٌ; (M;) and ▾بَصِرَ بِهِ (Lḥ, M;) and ▾تَبَصَّرَهُ; (M, Ḳ;) and ▾بَاصَرَهُ: (M:) or, accord. to Sb, ▾بَصُرَ [is used when no object of sight is mentioned, and] signifies *he* [*saw,* or] *became seeing:* and ابصرهُ is said when one mentions that upon which his eye has fallen. (M.) You say also, أَبْصِرْ إِلَيَّ *Look thou at me:* or *turn thy face towards me.* (Ibn-Buzurj, TA.) — See also 1. — And see 2. — أَبْصِرْ بِهِ وَأَسْمِعْ, in the Ḳur [xviii. 25], means مَا أَبْصَرَهُ وَمَا أَسْمَعَهُ (Jel) ‡ *How clear is his sight! and how clear his hearing!* the pronoun relating to God; (Bḍ, Jel;) and thus used, the phrase is tropical; i. e., nothing escapes his sight and hearing. (Jel.) And أَسْمِعْ بِهِمْ وَأَبْصِرْ, in the same [xix. 39], means مَا أَسْمَعَهُمْ وَمَا أَبْصَرَهُمْ (Ṣ in art. سمع, and Jel) *How clearly shall they hear! and how clearly shall they see!* (Ṣ, Bḍ, Jel:) or the meaning is, *do thou make them to hear, and make them to see,* the threats of that day which is afterwards mentioned, and what shall befall them therein. (Bḍ.) — أَبْصَرَ also signifies *He relinquished infidelity, and adopted the true belief.* (IAạr.) — See also 10. — *He hung upon the door of his dwelling a* بَصِيرَة, i. e. *an oblong piece of cotton or other cloth.* (TA.) — See also 2, last sentence.

5. تبصّرهُ *He looked at it;* namely, a thing: or *looked long at it:* or *glanced lightly at it:* like رَمَقَهُ: (TA:) or *he sought,* or *endeavoured, to see it:* (Mgh:) or i. q. أَبْصَرَهُ, in a sense explained above; see 4. (M.) You say also, تَبَصَّرْ لِي فُلَانًا [*Consider thou,* or *examine thou, for me, such a one, that thou mayest obtain a clear knowledge of him*]. (TA.) And تبصّر فِي شَىْءٍ *He considered a thing, endeavouring to obtain a clear knowledge of it; he looked into it, considered it, examined it,* or *studied it, repeatedly, until he knew it: he sought,* or *sought leisurely,* or *repeatedly, after the knowledge of it, until he knew it.* (Ṣ,* Ḳ,* TA.) And تبصّر فِى رَأْيِهِ signifies the same as ▾استبصر فيه, i. e. *He sought,* or *endeavoured, to see,* or *discover, what would happen to him, of good and evil.* (M.)

6. تباصروا *They saw one another.* (M, Ḳ.) — [تباصر also signifies *He feigned himself seeing,* either *ocularly* or *mentally;* contr. of تَعَامَى.]

10. استبصر [*He sought,* or *endeavoured, to see,* or *to perceive mentally*]. You say, استبصر فِى رَأْيِهِ: see 5, last sentence. — *He had,* or *was endowed with,* [*mental perception,* or] *knowledge,* (Mṣb,) [or *understanding, intelligence,* or *skill:* as in the phrase,] استبصر فِى شَىْءٍ [*He had a mental perception,* or *knowledge,* &c., *of,* or *in relation to, a thing*]. (Ṣ.) [See مُسْتَبْصِرٌ.] — *It* (a road, TA) *was,* or *became, plain, clear, manifest,* or *conspicuous;* (Ḳ,* TA;) as also ▾ابصر. (A.)

بَصْرٌ: see بَصْرَةٌ, in four places: and see بُصْرٌ.

بُصْرٌ *The thickness* of anything; (M;) as of the heaven, (TA,) or of each heaven [of the seven heavens], (Ṣ, A, TA,) and of the earth, [or of each of the seven earths,] and of the skin of a man, (TA,) and of a garment, or piece of cloth. (A.) You say ثَوْبٌ جَيِّدُ البُصْرِ *A thick garment or piece of cloth.* (M.) صُبْرٌ, formed by transposition, signifies the same. (Ṣ in art. صبر.) — *A side:* (Ṣ, M, Ḳ:) the *edge* of anything: (Ṣ, Ḳ:) formed by transposition from صُبْرٌ. (M.) = *Cotton:* (Ḳ:) whence بُصْرَةٌ signifying "an oblong piece of cotton cloth." (TA.) = See also بَصْرَةٌ.

بِصْرٌ: see بَصْرَةٌ, in five places.

بَصَرٌ The *sense of sight,* (Lth, Ṣ,) or *of the eye:* (M, Ḳ:) or the *light whereby the organ* [*of sight*] (الجَارِحَة) *perceives the things seen* (المُبْصَرَات): (Mṣb:) pl. أَبْصَارٌ. (M, Mṣb, Ḳ.) [Hence,] صَلَاةُ البَصَرِ *The prayer of sunset:* or, as some say, *of daybreak:* because performed when the darkness becomes mixed with the light: (TA:) or because performed when the stars are seen: also called صَلَاةُ الشَّاهِدِ: (TA in art. شهد:) or because performed at a time when the eyes see corporeal forms, after the intervention of darkness, or before it. (JM.) And لَقِيَهُ بَصَرًا *He met him when eyes saw one another:* or *at the beginning of darkness, when there remained enough light for objects to be distinguished thereby:* [accord. to some,] the noun is used [in the sense which it here bears] only as an adv. n. [of time]. (M.) And رَأَيْتُهُ بَيْنَ سَمْعِ الأَرْضِ وَبَصَرِهَا ‡ *I saw him in a vacant tract of land, or of the earth, where nothing but it heard or saw me.* (A.) [See also سَمْعٌ, in two places.] — See also بَصِيرَةٌ, first sentence, in four places. — Also The *eye;* [and so ▾ بَاصِرَةٌ;] syn. عَيْنٌ; but of the masc. gender: (TA:) pl. as above: (Ḳur ii. 6, &c.:) but the sing. is also used in a pl. sense [like سَمْعٌ]. (TA in art. سمع.) See two exs. voce بَصِيرَةٌ.

بَصْرَةٌ *Soft stones;* (AA, M, Mṣb;) i. q. كَذَّانٌ; (AA, M;) as also ▾ بِصْرٌ (M, Mṣb) and ▾ بَصْرٌ; or, accord. to Zj, this last is not allowable: (Mṣb:) or *soft stones in which is whiteness:* (Ḳ:) or *in which is some whiteness:* (TA:) or *soft stones inclining to white;* as also ▾ بِصْرٌ, with kesr if without ة: (Ṣ:) [i. e. *whitish soft stones:*] or *soft white stone;* as also ▾ بِصْرٌ (M) and ▾ بُصْرٌ: (TA:) or *glistening stones;* as also ▾ بِصْرٌ: (Fr:) pl. بِصَارٌ. (M:) and *rugged ground:* (Ḳ:) or *stones of rugged ground;* (TA;) as also ▾ بِصْرٌ and ▾ بُصْرٌ and ▾ بَصْرٌ: (Kz, TA:) or these three words, without ة, signify *thick,* or *rough,* or *rugged, stone:* (Ḳ:) or the same three, *hard,* or *strong, and thick,* or *rough,* or *rugged, stone:* (Lḥ, M:) and بَصْرَةٌ signifies, also, *land that is as though it were a mountain of gypsum:* (ISh, L:) or *land of which the stones are gypsum;* (M, TA;) as also ▾ بُصْرَةٌ and ▾ بِصْرَةٌ; (so in a copy of the M, but accord. to the TA ▾ بُصْرَةٌ and ▾ بَصِرَةٌ;) but the last is app. an epithet: (M: [see بَصِرَةٌ, below; and ▾ بَصِرٌ:]) also *tough clay in which is gypsum;* (TA;) and ▾ بَصْرَةٌ signifies *tough clay:* (M, TA:) or بُصْرَةٌ, (M,) or ▾ بُصْرٌ, (TA,) *tough and good clay, containing pebbles.* (Lḥ, M, TA.)

بُصْرَةٌ [in the TA, as on the authority of ISd, ▾ بُصْرٌ,] *Good red land.* (M, Ḳ.) See also بَصْرَةٌ.

بِصْرَةٌ:
بَصِرَةٌ: } see بَصْرَةٌ.

أَرْضٌ بَصِرَةٌ *Land in which are stones that cut the hoofs of beasts.* (TA.) See also بَصْرَةٌ, in two places.

بَصِيرٌ *Seeing;* i. q. ▾ مُبْصِرٌ; (M, Ḳ;) *contr. of* ضَرِيرٌ: (Ṣ:) of the measure فَعِيلٌ in the sense of the measure مُفْعِلٌ, (M,) or of the measure فَاعِلٌ [i. e. ▾ بَاصِرٌ]: (TA:) pl. بُصَرَآءُ. (M, Ḳ.) One says, إِنَّهُ لَبَصِيرٌ بِالعَيْنَيْنِ *Verily he is one who sees with the two eyes.* (Lḥ, M.) [Hence,] البَصِيرُ, as a name of God, *The All-seeing; He who sees all things, both what are apparent thereof and what are occult, without any organ* [*of vision*]. (TA.) And *The dog;* (M;) as also أَبُو بَصِيرٍ: (Mṣb:) because it is one of the most sharp-sighted of animals. (M.) — *Endowed with mental perception;* (B;) *knowing; skilful; possessing understanding, intelligence,* or *skill:* (Ṣ, M, A, Mṣb, Ḳ:) pl. as above. (A.) One says, أَنَا بَصِيرٌ بِهِ *I am knowing in it,* or *respecting it.* (Mṣb.) And إِنَّهُ لَبَصِيرٌ بِالأَشْيَآءِ *Verily he is knowing,* or *skilful, in things.* (Lḥ, M.) And رَجُلٌ بَصِيرٌ بِالعِلْمِ *A man knowing,* or *skilful, in science.* (M.) And هُوَ مِنَ البُصَرَآءِ بِالتِّجَارَةِ *He is of those who are knowing,* or *skilful, in commerce.* (A.) — It is also an epithet applied to *A blind man;* (A'Obeyd, M, B;) and so أَبُو بَصِيرٍ: (TA in art. عور:) so applied as meaning *endowed with mental perception;* (B;) or as meaning *a believer;* (A'Obeyd, M;) or as an epithet of good omen: (M:) and الأَعْشَى is used as meaning أَبُو بَصِيرٍ [*the weak-sighted,* &c.,] for this last reason. (M.) = See also بَصِيرَةٌ.

بَصِيرَةٌ *Mental perception;* the *perceptive faculty of the mind;* as also ▾ بَصَرٌ: (B:) *knowledge;* (Mṣb;) as also ▾ بَصَرٌ (Ṣ, Mṣb) and اِسْتِبْصَارٌ: (Mṣb:) *understanding; intelligence; skill:* (M, Ḳ:) البَصِيرَةُ signifies الاِسْتِبْصَارُ فِى الشَّىْءِ [which implies all the meanings above: see 10]: (Ṣ:) and بَصَرُ القَلْبِ [in like manner] signifies *mental perception* or *vision* or *view; idea,* or *opinion, occurring to the mind:* (M, K:) the pl. of بَصِيرَةٌ is بَصَائِرُ; (M, B;) and the pl. of ▾ بَصَرٌ, as syn. therewith, أَبْصَارٌ. (B.) [Sometimes it is opposed to بَصَرٌ, as in the first and second of the following exs.] عَمَى الأَبْصَارِ أَهْوَنُ مِنْ عَمَى البَصَائِرِ [*Blindness of the eyes is a lighter thing than blindness of the perceptive faculties of the mind*]. (A.) When Mo'áwiyeh said to Ibn-'Abbás, يَا بَنِى هَاشِمٍ تُصَابُونَ فِى أَبْصَارِكُمْ [*O sons of Háshim, ye are afflicted in your eyes*], the latter replied, وَأَنْتُمْ يَا بَنِى أُمَيَّةَ تُصَابُونَ فِى بَصَائِرِكُمْ [*And ye, O sons of Umeiyeh, are afflicted in your perceptive faculties of the mind*]. (M.) And the Arabs say, أَعْمَى ٱللّٰهُ بَصَائِرَهُ *May God blind his faculties of understanding!* And one says, لَهُ فِرَاسَةٌ ذَاتُ بَصِيرَةٍ, and بَصَائِرُ, ‡ *He possesses true intuitive perception.* (A.) And رَأَيْتُ عَلَيْكَ ذَاتَ البَصَائِرِ ‡ [*I saw impressed upon thee the signs of perceptive faculties of the mind*]. (A.) — Also *Belief,* or *firm belief, of the heart,* or *mind.* (M, Ḳ.) And عَلَى بَصِيرَةٍ *According to,* or *agreeably with, knowledge and assurance:* (TA:) and *purposely; intentionally.* (M, TA.) And عَلَى غَيْرِ بَصِيرَةٍ *Without certainty.* (M, TA.) — *Constancy,* or *firmness, in religion.* (TA.) — *An evidence, a testimony, a proof, an argument,* or *the like;* as also ▾ مَبْصَرَةٌ (Ṣ, Ḳ) and ▾ مَبْصَرٌ. (Ḳ.) — [And hence,] *Blood,* (M,) or *somewhat thereof,* (Aṣ, Ṣ, Ḳ,) *by which one is directed to an animal that has been shot, or to the knowledge thereof:* (Aṣ, AA, Ṣ, M, Ḳ:) or *blood upon the ground;* (AZ, Ṣ;) *what sticks upon the ground, not upon the body:* (M:) what adheres to the body is termed جَدِيَّةٌ: (AZ, Ṣ:) or *a portion of blood of the size of a dirhem:* (TA:) or *what is of a round form, like a shield:* or *what is of an oblong form:* or *what is of the size of the* فِرْسِن [or *foot*] *of the camel:* in all these explanations, blood being meant: or *blood not flowing:* or *what flows thereof at one single time:* (M:) or *a portion of blood that glistens:* (B:) and (as some say, M) the *blood of a virgin:* (M, Ḳ:) and *blood-revenge:* and *a fine for homicide:* (TA:) pl. بَصَائِرُ, as above: (Ṣ, M:) and ▾ بَصِيرٌ, which occurs in a verse cited by AḤn, may also be a pl. of بَصِيرَةٌ, applied to blood, [or rather a coll. gen. n., of which بصيرة is the n. un.,] like as شَعِيرٌ is of شَعِيرَةٌ; or it may be for بصيرة, the ة being elided by poetic license; or it may be a dial. var. of بصيرة, like as one says بَيَاضٌ and بَيَاضَةٌ. (M.) El-As'ar El-Joafee says,

• رَاحُوا بَصَائِرُهُمْ عَلَى أَكْتَافِهِمْ •
• وَبَصِيرَتِى يَعْدُو بِهَا عَتَدٌ وَأَى •

[*They went with their blood upon their shoulder-blades; but my blood, a ready and swift and strong horse runs with it*]; meaning, they neglected the blood of their father, and left it behind them; i. e., they did not take revenge for it; but I have sought my blood-revenge: (Ṣ, M:*) but see another explanation in what follows. (Ṣ. [See also Ḥam p. 59.]) — ‡ *A witness:* (Lḥ, Ṣ,* M, Mgh, Ḳ:) *an observer and a witness.* (A.) بَلِ الإِنْسَانُ عَلَى نَفْسِهِ بَصِيرَةٌ, in the Ḳur [lxxv. 14], means ‡ *Nay, the man shall be witness against himself:* (Ṣ, Mgh:) or it means that his arms, or hands, and his legs, or feet, and his tongue, shall be witnesses against him on the day of resurrection: (M:) Akh says that it is like the saying to a man, أَنْتَ حُجَّةٌ عَلَى نَفْسِكَ: (Ṣ:) the ة is added because the members are meant thereby; (B;) or to give intensiveness to the signification, (Mgh, B,) as in عَلَّامَةٌ and رَاوِيَةٌ; (B;) or because the meaning is عَيْنٌ بَصِيرَةٌ. (Mgh.) You say also, اِجْعَلْنِى بَصِيرَةً عَلَيْهِمْ ‡ *Make thou me an observer of them and a witness against them.* (Lḥ,* M,* A.) — *An example by which one is admonished:* (Ḳ:) pl. بَصَائِرُ; which is said to be used agreeably with this interpretation in the Ḳur xxviii. 43. (TA.) You say, أَمَا لَكَ بَصِيرَةٌ فِيهِ ‡ *Hast thou not an example whereby thou shouldst be admonished in him?* (TA.) ═ *A shield:* (AO, Ṣ, M, Ḳ:) or *a glistening shield:* or *an oblong shield:* (TA:) and *a coat of mail:* (AO, Ṣ, M, Ḳ:) and *any defensive armour:* (M, TA:) and بَصَائِرُ السِّلَاحِ *any arms that are worn:* and بِصَارٌ, as well as بَصَائِرُ, is a pl. thereof. (TA.) Accord. to AO, the verse of El-Joạfee cited above commences thus:

حَمَلُوا بَصَائِرَهُمْ عَلَى أَكْتَافِهِمْ

and the meaning is, [*They bore*] *their shields* [*upon their shoulder-blades*]; or *their coats of mail.* (Ṣ.) ═ *An oblong piece of cloth* (Ḳ, TA) *of cotton or other material.* (TA.) [See بُصْر.] Such is hung upon the door of a dwelling. (TA.) And you say, رَأَيْتُ عَلَيْهِ بَصِيرَةً, i. e. شُقَّةً مُلَفَّقَةً [app. meaning *I saw upon him a garment composed of two oblong pieces of cloth joined and sewed together*]. (TA.) — *What is between the two oblong pieces of cloth* [i. e. *between any two of such pieces*] *of a* بَيْت [or tent]; (Ṣ, Ḳ;) and *what is between the two pieces of a* مَزَادَة and *the like; what is sewed, thereof, in the manner termed* بَصْر [inf. n. of بَصَرَ: see 1, last sentence]: (B:) pl. بَصَائِرُ: (Ṣ:) and ▼بَاصِرٌ signifies [in like manner] *what is joined and sewed together* (مُلَفَّق) *between two oblong pieces of cloth* or *two pieces of rag.* (TA.)

بَاصِرٌ: see بَصِيرٌ. — لَمْحٌ بَاصِرٌ ‡ *An intent,* or *a hard, glance:* (M, Ḳ:) or *a very intent* or *hard glance.* (Ṣ.) You say, أَرَيْتُهُ لَمْحًا بَاصِرًا ‡ *I showed him a very intent* or *hard glance:* (Ṣ, M:*) بَاصِرًا being here used for the augmented epithet [مُبْصِرًا]; (M;) or it is a possessive epithet, (Yaạḳoob, M,) like لَابِنٌ and تَامِرٌ, meaning ذُو بَصَرٍ, from أَبْصَرْتُ, like مَوْتٌ مَائِتٌ from أَمَتُّ; and it means *I showed him a severe thing.* (Ṣ.) And لَقِيَ مِنْهُ لَمْحًا بَاصِرًا ‡ *He experienced from him a manifest,* or *an evident, thing.* (M. [See also art. لمح.]) And رَأَى فُلَانٌ لَمْحًا بَاصِرًا ‡ *Such a one beheld a terrible thing.* (Lth, TA.) And أَرَانِي الزَّمَانُ لَمْحًا بَاصِرًا ‡ *Fortune showed me a terrifying thing.* (A.) — It is said in a prov., خَيْرُ الغَدَآءِ بَوَاكِرُهُ وَخَيْرُ العَشَآءِ بَوَاصِرُهُ, [the word بَوَاصِرُ being pl. of ▼بَاصِرَةٌ,] meaning [*The best kinds of morning-meal are those thereof that are early; and the best kinds of evening-meal are those thereof*] *in which the food is seen,* before the invasion of night. (Meyd. See Freytag's Arab. Prov. i. 442.) — بَاصِرَةٌ [as an epithet in which the quality of a subst. predominates]: see بَصَرٌ. ═ See also بَصِيرَةٌ, last sentence.

بَاصِرَةٌ: see بَصَرٌ: and see بَاصِرٌ.

بَاصُورٌ: see بَاسُور.

بِنْصِرٌ: see art. بنصر.

أَبْصَرُ [*More,* and *most, sharp-sighted* or *clear-sighted:* see an ex. voce حَيَّةٌ].

مَبْصَرٌ: see بَصِيرَةٌ.

مَبْصَرٌ and its fem. مَبْصَرَةٌ: see the next paragraph, in three places.

مُبْصِرٌ: see بَصِيرٌ. — [Hence,] ‡ *A watcher,* or *guard,* set in a garden. (A.) — And المُبْصِرُ † *The lion,* which sees his prey from afar, and pursues it. (Ḳ.) ═ [*Making,* or *causing, to see,* or *to have sight:* and hence, *giving light; shining; illumining:* and *conspicuous; manifest; evident; apparent:* also *making,* or *causing, to have mental perception,* or *knowledge,* or *skill.*] وَالنَّهَارَ مُبْصِرًا, in the Ḳur [x. 68, &c. (in the CḲ وَالنَّهَارُ ▼مَبْصَرًا)], means, *And the day* [*causing to see;* or] *in which one sees;* (Ḳ;) *giving light; shining;* or *illumining.* (TA.) And فَلَمَّا جَآءَتْهُمْ آيَاتُنَا مُبْصِرَةً, also in the Ḳur [xxvii. 13], † *And when our signs came to them, making them to have sight,* or *to have mental perception,* or *knowledge,* or *skill;* expl. by تَجْعَلُهُمْ بُصَرَآءَ: (Akh, Ṣ, Ḳ:) or *giving light; shining;* or *illumining:* (Ṣ:) or *being conspicuous, manifest,* or *evident:* or we may read ▼مَبْصَرَةً, meaning *having become manifest,* or *evident.* (Zj, M.) And آتَيْنَا ثَمُودَ النَّاقَةَ مُبْصِرَةً, also in the Ḳur [xvii. 61], † *And we gave to Thamood the she-camel, by means of which they had sight,* or *mental perception,* or *knowledge,* or *skill:* (Akh:) or *a sign giving light, shining,* or *illumining;* (Fr, T;) and this is the right explanation: (T:) or *a manifest,* or *an evident, sign:* (Zj, L, Ḳ:) and some read ▼مَبْصَرَةً, meaning *having become manifest, so as to be seen.* (Zj, L.) And جَعَلْنَا آيَةَ النَّهَارِ مُبْصِرَةً, also in the Ḳur [xvii. 13], ‡ *We have made the sign of the day manifest,* or *apparent.* (Ḳ, TA.) ═ One *who hangs upon his door a* بَصِيرَة, i. e. *an oblong piece of cloth* (Ḳ, TA) *of cotton or other material.* (TA.)

مُبْصَرَةٌ: see بَصِيرَةٌ.

مُسْتَبْصِرٌ One *who seeks,* or *endeavours, to see a thing plainly* or *clearly* [either *with the eyes* or *with the mind*]. (TA, from a trad.) — وَكَانُوا مُسْتَبْصِرِينَ, in the Ḳur [xxix. 37], means, *And they were endowed with perceptive faculties of the mind,* or *of knowledge,* or *of skill:* (Jel:) or *they clearly perceived,* when they did what they did, that the result thereof would be their punishment. (M.) And you say, هُوَ مُسْتَبْصِرٌ فِي دِينِهِ وَعَمَلِهِ *He is endowed with mental perception,* or *knowledge,* or *understanding, intelligence,* or *skill, in his religion and his actions.* (TA.)

بصط

1. بَصْطٌ, [inf. n. of بَصَطَ,] i. q. بَسْطٌ, in all its meanings: (Ḳ:) the س, with ط, is changed into ص because of the nearness of the places of utterance. (L.)

بصع

1. بَصَعَ, aor. ـَ, (Ḳ,) inf. n. بَصْعٌ, (Ṣ,) *He collected:* (Ḳ:) [J says,] I have heard from certain of the grammarians that البَصْعُ is syn. with الجَمْعُ, but I know not what is the truth of the matter. (Ṣ.) Hence what here follows. (TA.)

أَبْصَعُ is a word used as a corroborative, and is pronounced by some with the pointed ض, but this is not of high authority: you say, أَخَذْتُ حَقِّي أَجْمَعَ أَبْصَعَ [*I took my right,* or *due, altogether*]: and [the pl. is أَبْصَعُونَ:] you say, جَآءَ القَوْمُ أَجْمَعُونَ أَبْصَعُونَ [*The people,* or *company of men, came all together*]: and the fem. is بَصْعَآءُ: you say, جَمْعَآءَ بَصْعَآءَ: and [the pl. of بَصْعَآءُ is بُصَعُ: you say,] رَأَيْتُ النِّسْوَةَ جُمَعَ بُصَعَ [*I saw the women all together*]: it is a corroborative occurring in a particular order, never before اجمع. (Ṣ.) [See أَبْتَعُ.]

بصق

1. بَصَقَ, (Lth, JK, Ṣ, Ḳ,) [aor. ـُ,] inf. n. بَصْقٌ, (Ṣ,) i. q. بَزَقَ (Lth, Ṣ,* Ḳ) or بَسَقَ (JK) [*He spat*]: it is the most chaste of these three verbs. (TA in art. بسق.) بَصَقَ فِي وَجْهِهِ [lit. *He spat in his face,*] means † *he held him in contempt,* or *despised him.* (TA.) ═ *He milked* a ewe *when she was with young.* (Ḳ.)

4. ابصقت *She* (a ewe) *excerned the milk* [or *biestings into her udder before bringing forth*]; (JK, Ḳ;) like ابسقت [q. v.]. (TA.) — ابصق is also said of the قَصْد, or small juicy branches, in the [species of mimosa termed] عُرْفُط [app. as meaning *They excerned a matter like spittle*]. (TA.)

بَصْقَةٌ A [*stony tract such as is termed*] حَرَّة *somewhat elevated;* [as also بَسْقَةٌ:] pl. بِصَاقٌ. (AA, Ḳ.)

بُصَاقٌ *Spittle,* or *saliva, that has gone forth from the mouth:* as long as it is in the mouth, it is termed رِيقٌ: (Ḳ:) [or *saliva that flows:* see بُزَاقٌ:] i. q. بُزَاقٌ (Ṣ, Ḳ) and بُسَاقٌ: (Ḳ:) but it is more chaste than either of these. (TA.) [بُصَاقَةٌ is app. its n. un. And hence,] بُصَاقَةُ القَمَرِ *White glistening stone:* (Ṣ:) or *stone of a clear white colour.* (JK, Ḳ.) [Also written with س.] ═ *A species of palm-tree.* (Ṣ, Ḳ.) ═ The *best of camels:* both sing. and pl. (IDrd, Ḳ.)

بَصُوقٌ A ewe *having the least quantity of milk.* (Ḳ, TA.)

بصل

2. تَبْصِيلٌ The act of *stripping,* or *divesting;* [*like as when one strips an* onion (بَصَلَة) *of its coats;*] (Ḳ;) as also ▼تَبَصُّلٌ. (Fr, Ḳ.) You say, بَصَّلْتُ الرَّجُلَ عَنْ ثِيَابِهِ [and ▼تَبَصَّلْتُهُ] *I stripped the man of his clothes.* (TA.)

5. تبصّل *It* (a thing) *was,* or *became, several fold,* or *many fold, like the coats of the* بَصَل [or *onion*]. (Z, TA.) See also مُتَبَصِّلٌ. ═ It is also trans.: see 2, in two places. — [Hence,] تَبَصَّلُوهُ † *They begged of him so much that all that he had became exhausted.* (Ṣgh, Ḳ.)

بَصَلٌ [The *onion; allium cepa:* or *onions,* collectively:] what it signifies is *well known:* n. un. with ة. (Ṣ, M, Mṣb, Ḳ.) Hence the prov., أَكْسَى مِنَ البَصَلِ [*Having more coats,* or *coverings, than the onion*]. (TA.) — [Also *Any kind of bulb, or bulbous plant.*] بَصَلُ الزَّعْفَرَانِ [*The bulb of the saffron*], which is buried in the ground, is like the بَصَل [or onion] commonly known. (Mgh.) بَصَلُ الفَأْرِ is *the same as* الإِسْقِيلُ and العُنْصُلُ and الإِسْقَالُ, (Ḳ in art. سقل,) also written العُنْصُلُ ,بَصَلُ العنصلِ, (Ḳ in art. عصل,) or (KL voce زِيزْ, [and so as written by Golius,]) [*Scilla*, or *squill*; particularly *scilla maritima*, or *officinal squill*; called by all these names, except, perhaps, الاسقال, in the present day;] also called زيز, and البَصَلُ البَرِّىُّ [*the wild onion*; but from what follows, it seems that there is a confusion here]. (KL ubi suprà.) بَصَلُ الذِّئْبِ, and بصل الزير, (Golius on the authority of Zeyn El-Aṭṭár,) or بصل الرند, (so in the TA in art. بلبس,) *i. q.* بلبوس *Bulbus esculentus*, (Golius, from Zeyn El-Aṭṭár,) or البَلْبُوس, with fet-ḥ, [thus generally written, though it would seem to be correctly بُلْبُوس,] *the leaves of which resemble those of the* سَذَاب [or *rue*]: (TA in art. بلبس:) the بَلْبُوس is *the wild onion* (in Pers. پِيَازِ صَحْرَائِى). (KL voce بلبوس. [This last assertion suggests that الزير and الرند may be mistranscriptions for الزِّيز; the زيز mentioned before.]) [بَصَلُ القَىْءِ *Bulbus vomitorius*; mentioned by Golius; and by Dioscorides, (l. ii. c. 201,) as being emetic and diuretic.] — Also, (Ḳ,) or بَصَلَةٌ, (M,) ‡ *A helmet* (M, Ḳ) *of iron*, (Ḳ,) *pointed in the middle*; so called as being likened to what is first mentioned above. (M.) Lebeed likens helmets to بَصَل. (Ṣ.)

مُتَبَصِّلٌ (ISh, Ḳ) and ▾ ذُو تَبَصُّلٍ (ISh, TA) A covering of any kind (قِشْر) *consisting of many coats; thick*; (ISh, Ḳ;) *like the coats of the* بَصَل [or *onion*]. (ISh, TA.)

بصم

بُصْمٌ The *space that is between the extremity of the little finger and that of the third finger* [*when they are extended apart*]: (Ṣ, M,* Ḳ:) mentioned on the authority of AO, (Ṣ,) or on that of Aboo-Málik alone. (M.) The عَتَب is the space between the third finger and the middle finger; the رَتَب, that between the middle finger and the first finger; [but see these two words;] the فِتْر, that between the first finger and the thumb; the شِبْر, that between the thumb and the little finger; and the فَوْت, that between every two fingers, in length. (Ṣ.) — ذُو بُصْمٍ *Thick*, or *coarse*; applied to a man, (M, Ḳ,) or a garment, or piece of cloth: (Ḳ:) or you say ثَوْبٌ لَهُ بُصْمٌ, meaning *a garment*, or *piece of cloth, that is dense*, or *compact*; *close in texture*. (M.)

بصن

بُصَانٌ, (M, Ḳ,) so accord. to Kṭr, (M,) and بُصَّانٌ, (Ḳ,) thus in some of the copies of the Jm of IDrd, (TA,) a name of *The month* رَبِيعُ الآخِرُ, (M, Ḳ,) in the Time of Ignorance: (M:) pl. [of pauc.] أَبْصِنَةٌ (M, Ḳ) and [of mult.] بِصْنَانٌ; (M, TA;) the latter erroneously written in the copies of the Ḳ بُصَانَاتٌ: (TA:) so says Kṭr; but other lexicologists hold that it is وَبْصَانٌ, like سَبْعَانِ, and وِبِصَانٌ, like شُقْرَان; and this is the correct opinion: Aboo-Is-ḥáḳ says that it was so named because of the وبيص, i. e. gleaming, of the weapons therein: (M:) but it is said in art. وبص of the Ḳ to be وَبْصَان and وَبِصَان: and Ṣgh holds بُصَّانٌ to be correct because بَصَّ and وَبَصَ signify the same. (TA.)

بض

1. بَضَضْتَ, and بَضِضْتَ, (Ṣ, TA,) and بَضُضْتَ also, (accord. to one copy of the Ṣ,) [third pers., accord. to rule, بَضَّ, (accord. to Golius and Freytag بَضِضَ or بَضُضَ, but these are irregular forms, and not admissible without authority,)] aor., accord. to rule, of the first يَبِضُّ, and of the second يَبَضُّ, and of the third يَبُضُّ,] inf. n. بَضَاضَةٌ and بُضُوضَةٌ, (Ṣ, TA,) *Thou* (O man) *wast*, or *becamest, such as is termed* بَضّ; i. e. *thin-skinned and plump*; &c.: (Ṣ:) or *very white* or *fair, with fatness*: or *delicate and clear in complexion, and such that the least thing made a mark*, or *an impression, upon thee*. (TA.) — بَضَّ المَآءُ, aor. يَبِضُّ, inf. n. بَضِيضٌ (Ṣ, Ḳ) and بُضُوضٌ and بَضٌّ, (Ḳ,) *The water flowed by little and little*: (Ṣ, Ḳ:) or *exuded* upon a rock or the ground. (TA.) And بَضَّتْ بِمَائِهَا, and بَضَّتِ الرَّكِيَّةُ, *The well had*, or *yielded, little water*; or *its water became little*. (TA.) It is said in a trad. respecting Tabook, وَالعَيْنُ تَبِضُّ بِشَىْءٍ مِنَ المَآءِ [*The source*, or *spring, yielding scantily somewhat of water*]. (TA.) And you say, بَضَّتِ العَيْنُ, aor. as above, inf. n. بَضٌّ and بَضِيضٌ, *The eye shed tears*. (TA.) And, of a man when you characterise him as patient under affliction, مَا تَبِضُّ عَيْنُهُ [*His eye does not shed tears*]. (TA.) And بَضَّتِ الحَلَمَةُ *The nipple streamed with milk*. (TA.) It is said in a trad., مَا تَبِضُّ بِبِلَالٍ *Having no milk dropping from it*, or *her*. (TA.) And in another trad., سَقَطَ مِنَ الفَرَسِ فَإِذَا هُوَ جَالِسٌ وَعُرْضُ وَجْهِهِ يَبِضُّ مَآءً أَصْفَرَ [*He fell from the horse, and lo, he was sitting, with the side of his face exuding yellow water*]. (TA.) One should not say, بَضَّ السِّقَآءُ, nor القِرْبَةُ: but some say so, urging the authority of Ru-beh. (Ṣ.) And you say of a stone, and the like, بَضَّ, aor. as above, meaning *Water flowed from it like sweat*; *water oozed from it*. (TA.) — Hence the saying, مَا يَبِضُّ حَجَرُهُ † *No good is obtained from him*; (TA;) *i. q.* مَا تَنْدَى صَفَاتُهُ: (Ṣ:) a prov. applied to the niggardly. (Ṣ, Ḳ.) [Hence also,] بَضَّ لَهُ, [aor., accord. to the TA, يَبُضُّ, but this is evidently a mistake,] † *He gave him a little*; as also ▾ ابضّ له, (Sh, Ḳ,) inf. n. إِبْضَاضٌ: (TA:) and بَضَّ لَهُ بِشَىْءٍ † *He did him a small benefit*; as also نَضَّ. (Aṣ.)

4. ابضّ لَهُ: see 1, last sentence.

5. تَبَضَّضْتُهُ *I took everything belonging to him*. (Ibn-'Abbád, Ḳ.) — تَبَضَّضْتُ حَقِّى مِنْهُ *I took the whole of my right*, or *due, from him by little and little*: (Ṣ, Ḳ:) [as also تَنَضَّضْتُهُ مِنْهُ.]

10. خُذْ مَا ٱسْتَبَضَّ *Take thou what is easily attainable*; *what offers itself without difficulty*. (AA, TA in art. ندب.)

بَضٌّ A man *thin-skinned*, or *fine-skinned, and plump*: (Ṣ:) or a man *having a thin*, or *fine, and plump, skin, upon which the least thing makes a mark*, or *an impression*: (Mgh:) or a man (Aṣ) *soft*, or *tender, in body*; not particularly implying whiteness: (Aṣ, Ṣ:) or *soft*, or *tender, in body, thin-skinned*, or *fine-skinned, and plump*: (Ḳ:) fem. with ة; (Ṣ, Ḳ, &c.;) signifying *a girl*, (Ṣ,) or *a woman, thin-skinned*, or *fine-skinned, and soft*, or *tender*, or *delicate*, (TA,) *if tawny* or *white*: (Ṣ, TA:) or *soft*, or *tender, in body*; not particularly implying whiteness: (Aṣ, Ṣ:) or *fleshy and white*: (AA:) or *thin-skinned*, or *fine-skinned, in whom the blood appears* [*through the skin*]: (Lḥ:) or *soft*, or *tender*, or *delicate, compact in flesh, and very white* or *fair in complexion*: (Lth:) and ▾ بَضِيضَةٌ and ▾ بَاضَّةٌ and ▾ بُضَاضَةٌ, applied to a girl, signify the same as بَضَّةٌ; (Ḳ, TA;) *compact in flesh, plump*, or *soft and thin-skinned and plump, with a very white* or *fair complexion*: (TA:) and ▾ بَضَاضٌ also is syn. with بَضَّةٌ, applied to a woman. (TA.)

بَضَضٌ *Little water*. (Ṣ, Ḳ.)

بَضَاضٌ: see بَضٌّ, at the end of the paragraph.

بَضُوضٌ, (Ḳ,) or رَكِيَّةٌ بَضُوضٌ, بِئْرٌ, (Ṣ,) *A well having little water*: (Ṣ:) or *of which the water comes forth by little and little*: (Ḳ:) pl., in some copies of the Ḳ, بِضَاضٌ: in others, بَضَائِضُ. (TA.)

بُضَاضَةٌ مِنْ مَآءٍ, (Ḳ,) or مَا فِى السِّقَآءِ بُضَاضَةٌ, (TA,) and ▾ بَضِيضَةٌ, (Ḳ,) *There is not in the skin* [even so much as] *a small quantity of water*: (Ḳ, TA:) from Aboo-Sa'eed. (TA.)

بَضِيضَةٌ: see بَضٌّ, near the end of the paragraph. — *Rain little in quantity*. (Ṣgh, Ḳ.) — See also بُضَاضَةٌ. — *A thing which the hand possesses*. (Ḳ.) You say, أَخْرَجْتُ لَهُ بَضِيضَتِى *I produced to him what my hand possessed*. (TA.)

بُضَاضَةٌ: see بَضٌّ, near the end of the paragraph.

بَاضَّةٌ: see بَضٌّ, near the end of the paragraph.

مَا فِى البِئْرِ بَاضُوضٌ *There is not any moisture in the well*. (Ibn-'Abbád, Ḳ.)

هُوَ أَبَضُّ النَّاسِ *He is the most delicate*, or *fine, in complexion, of men, and the most beautiful of them in external skin*. (TA.)

بضع

1. بَضَعَهُ, (Ṣ, Mṣb,) aor. ـَ, (Mṣb,) inf. n. بَضْعٌ, (Ṣ, Mgh, Mṣb, Ḳ,) *He cut it*; (Ṣ, Mgh, Mṣb, Ḳ;) namely, flesh, or flesh-meat: (Ṣ, TA:) and *it* (a sword) *cut a piece off from it*; namely, a thing: (Aṣ, Ṣ:) and *he cut it in pieces*; namely, flesh, or flesh-meat: (Ḳ, TA:) and ▾ بضّعه, inf. n. تَبْضِيعٌ, has the first of these significations: (Ḳ: [but only the inf. n. is there mentioned:]) or this latter signifies *he cut it much*, or *in several pieces*, or *in many pieces*. (Mṣb, TA.*) — *He slit it*; or *cut it lengthwise*; (Ṣ, Mgh, Mṣb, Ḳ;) namely,

flesh, or flesh-meat, (Mṣb,) or a wound, (Ṣ, TA,) and a vein, and a hide. (Ṣ.) — [And hence,] بَضَعَهَا, (Sb, Mṣb, TA,) aor. ـَ, (Mṣb,) inf. n. بَضْعٌ (Ḳ, TA) and بُضْعٌ, like شُكْرٌ and شُغْلٌ and كُفْرٌ, for فُعْلٌ is not rare as a measure of inf. ns., (Sb, TA,) or accord. to some it is an inf. n. of this verb, (Mṣb,) but accord. to others it is a simple subst., (TA,) ‡ *Inivit eam; he lay with her,* or *compressed her;* (Sb, Mṣb, Ḳ, TA;) as also ▼ باضعها, (Mṣb,) inf. n. مُبَاضَعَةٌ (Ṣ, Mgh, Mṣb, Ḳ) and بِضَاعٌ: (Ṣ, Mṣb, Ḳ:) because in the act which it signifies is a kind of slitting. (Mgh.) You say, مَلَكَ بُضْعَهَا, i. e. جِمَاعَهَا. (Mṣb.) And it is said in a prov., ▼ كَمُعَلِّمَةٍ أُمَّهَا البِضَاعَ ‡ [*Like her who teaches her mother* المُجَامَعَة]. (Ṣ.) — بُضْعٌ also signifies ‡ The *taking in marriage:* (Ḳ, TA:) and بُضْعٌ, as an inf. n., † The *making a contract of marriage.* (Mṣb.)

2: see 1.

3: see 1, in two places.

4. ابضعها, (Mgh, Mṣb, Ḳ,) inf. n. إِبْضَاعٌ, (Mgh, Mṣb,) ‡ *He gave her in marriage.* (Mgh, Mṣb, Ḳ.) It is said in a trad., (TA,) تُسْتَأْمَرُ النِّسَآءُ فِى إِبْضَاعِهِنَّ ‡ *Women shall be consulted respecting the giving them in marriage:* (T, Mgh, Mṣb, TA:) or, accord. to one relation, ▼ أَبْضَاعِهِنَّ, (Mgh, Mṣb,) which [virtually] means the same; (Mṣb;) but this is a pl., namely, of بُضْعٌ. (Mgh, Mṣb.) — ابضع الشَّىْءَ *He made the thing to be* بِضَاعَة [i. e. *an article of merchandise*], (Ṣ, Ḳ, TA,) whatever it was; (TA;) as also ▼ استبضعه: (Ṣ, Ḳ:) or ▼ اِسْتَبْضَعْتُ الشَّىْءَ signifies *I made* [or *took*] *the thing as* بضاعة [*an article of merchandise*] *for myself:* and you say, أَبْضَعْتُهُ غَيْرِى [*I made it, or gave it as, an article of merchandise to another than me*]: (Mgh, Mṣb:) and ابضعه البِضَاعَةَ *he gave him the article of merchandise.* (TA.) Hence the phrase, in a trad. relating to El-Medeeneh, accord. to one relation, تُبْضِعُ طِيبَهَا, meaning † *It gives the good that it possesses* to its inhabitants; as explained by Z; but accord. to the relation commonly known, it is تَنْصَعُ, with ن and with the unpointed ص; [meaning "it purifies;" (L in art. نصع;)] and there are two other relations, which are تنضع and تَنْضَحُ. (TA.)

7. انبضع *It was, or became, cut, or cut off.* (Ḳ, TA.)

8. ابتضع مِنْهُ *He took, or received,* [*merchandise*] *from him.* (TA: [in which the word بِضَاعَةً requires to be supplied in the explanation, and is indicated by the context.])

10. اِسْتِبْضَاعٌ denotes a kind of matrimonial connection practised by people in the Time of Ignorance; i. e., A woman's *desiring sexual intercourse with a man only to obtain offspring by him:* a man of them used to say to his female slave or his wife, أَرْسِلِى إِلَى فُلَانٍ فَاسْتَبْضِعِى مِنْهُ [*Send thou to such a one, and demand of him sexual intercourse to obtain offspring*]; and he used to separate himself from her, and not touch her, until her pregnancy by that man became apparent: and this he did from a desire of obtaining generous offspring. (IAth, TA.) — See also 4, in two places.

بَضْعٌ: see بِضْعٌ, first sentence, and near the end: and see also بَضْعَةٌ.

بُضْعٌ *Initus; sexual intercourse:* (Mgh, Mṣb, Ḳ:) a subst., (Mgh, Mṣb, TA,) accord. to some; but accord. to others, an inf. n.; (Mṣb;) held by Sb to be the latter: (TA:) [see 1:] and *marriage;* or the *taking in marriage;* syn. نِكَاحٌ; (ISk, Ṣ, Mṣb, TA;) [which has also the first of the meanings given above;] as in the phrase مَلَكَ فُلَانٌ بُضْعَ فُلَانَةَ [explained above (see 1)]: (ISk, Ṣ:) or, (Ḳ,) in this phrase, (Mgh,) ‡ the *pudendum muliebre;* the *vulva;* (Az, Mgh, Mṣb, Ḳ,* TA;) and so in the saying, in a trad., عَتَقَ بُضْعُكِ فَاخْتَارِى ‡ *Thy vulva hath become freed, therefore choose thou* whether thou wilt remain with thy husband or separate thyself from him; (TA;) and in the saying, تُسْتَأْمَرُ النِّسَآءُ فِى أَبْضَاعِهِنَّ, accord. to those who thus relate it, others saying إِبْضَاعِهِنَّ; (see 4;) أَبْضَاعٌ being pl. of بُضْعٌ. (Mgh, Mṣb.) — Also ‡ The *marriage-contract.* (Ḳ.) — And ‡ *A dowry;* or *gift given to,* or *for, a bride:* (Ḳ, TA:) pl. بُضُوعٌ. (TA.) So in the saying of 'Amr Ibn-Maadee-Kerib,

وَفِى كَعْبٍ وَإِخْوَتِهَا كِلَابٍ
سَوَامِى الطَّرْفِ غَالِيَةُ البُضُوعِ

[*And among Kaab, and their brethren Kiláb, are females lofty in look,* or] *proud,* and *dear in respect of dowries.* (TA.) — Also † *Divorce:* (Az, Ḳ:) thus having two contr. significations. (Ḳ.) — And † The *authority possessed over a woman by her guardian who affiances her.* (TA.) — And † *An equal;* particularly as a suitor in a case of marriage: as in the saying, in a trad., هٰذَا البُضْعُ لَا يُقْرَعُ أَنْفُهُ † *This equal's marriage shall not be refused,* nor shall it be desired, or wished for; *he shall not be rejected.* (TA.)

بِضْعٌ (Ṣ, Mgh, Mṣb, Ḳ, &c.) and ▼ بَضْعٌ, (Ṣ, Mṣb, Ḳ,) some of the Arabs pronouncing it with kesr, (Ṣ, Mṣb,) [*A number under ten;* and *an odd number,* meaning] *a number between two round,* or *decimal, numbers;* (AZ, Ḳ;) *from one to ten* [*exclusive of the latter*]; and *from eleven to twenty* [*exclusive of the latter*]; so accord. to Mebremán; (Ḳ;) i. e. Moḥammad Ibn-'Alee Ibn-Ismá'eel the Lexicologist, Mebremán being his surname: (TA:) or *from three to nine;* (Ṣ, Mṣb, Ḳ [in the first and last the ns. of number being in the fem. gender; but in the second, masc.];) so accord. to Ḳatádeh; (Mgh;) *from three to less than ten:* (Fr [the ns. of number in the masc. gender]:) or *not less than three nor more than ten;* (Sh [the first n. of number in the fem. gender, and the second masc.];) *from three to ten:* (Mgh [the ns. of number in the masc. gender]:) or *to seven:* (Mujáhid, Mgh:) or *to five:* (AO, Ḳ [the n. of number in the fem. gender]:) or *from one to four:* (AO, O, Ḳ [the ns. of number in the masc. gender]:) or *to five;* an explanation ascribed to AO: (TA:) or *from four to nine;* (ISd, Ḳ [the ns. of number fem.];) and this is the signification preferred by Th: (TA:) or it signifies *five:* (Muḳátil [this n. of number masc.]:) or *seven;* (Muḳátil, Ḳ [in the Ḳ this n. of number being fem.];) so accord. to some: (AO:) or *ten:* (Eḍ-Ḍaḥḥák [this n. of number masc.]:) or *an undefined number;* غَيْرُ مَحْدُودٍ; so says Ṣgh; [and the like is said in the Mṣb;] in the Ḳ, erroneously, غَيْرُ مَعْدُودٍ; (TA;) because it means *a portion,* (Ṣgh, Ḳ,) which is undefined: (Ṣgh, TA:) it also signifies, *with ten,* [in like manner; i. e. *ten and a number under ten;* or the like: as] *from thirteen to nineteen.* (Mṣb.) When used as signifying from three to nine, (Mgh, Mṣb,) or to ten, or to seven, (Mgh,) [or to signify some number under ten, without another n. of number,] it is masc. and fem. without variation: (Mgh, Mṣb:) you say بِضْعُ رِجَالٍ *From three to nine* [&c.] *men:* and بِضْعُ نِسْوَةٍ *from three to nine* [&c.] *women:* (Mṣb:) and بِضْعُ سِنِينَ *from three to nine* [&c.] *years:* (Ṣ:) and فِى بِضْعِ سِنِينَ [*in from three to nine,* &c., *years*]: (Ḳur xxx. 3:) and فَلَبِثَ فِى السِّجْنِ بِضْعَ سِنِينَ [*And he remained in the prison from three to nine,* &c., *years*]. (Ḳur xii. 42.) But when used to denote a number above ten, (Mgh, Mṣb,) with a masc. n. it is with ة, (▼ بِضْعَة,) and with a fem. n. it is without ة: (ISk, Mgh, Mṣb, Ḳ:) you say بِضْعَةَ عَشَرَ رَجُلًا *From thirteen to nineteen* [&c.] *men:* and بِضْعَ عَشْرَةَ آمْرَأَةً *from thirteen to nineteen* [&c.] *women:* (Ṣ, Mgh,* TA:) like as you say ثَلَاثَةَ عَشَرَ رَجُلًا and ثَلَاثَ عَشْرَةَ آمْرَأَةً. (Mgh.) When you have passed the word denoting ten, (Ṣ, Ḳ,) [i. e.] to denote a number above twenty, (Mṣb,) it is not used: (Ṣ, Mṣb, Ḳ:) you do not say بِضْعٌ وَعِشْرُونَ, (Ṣ, Ḳ,) but نَيِّفٌ وَعِشْرُونَ; and so in the cases of the remaining numbers: (Ṣ:) or you do say بِضْعٌ وَعِشْرُونَ: (Ṣgh, Ḳ:) accord. to AZ, (Mṣb,) you say بِضْعَةٌ وَعِشْرُونَ رَجُلًا (Mgh, Mṣb, Ḳ) meaning *Twenty and odd men:* (AZ, TA:) and بِضْعٌ وَعِشْرُونَ آمْرَأَةً (Mgh, Mṣb, Ḳ) meaning *twenty and odd women:* (AZ, TA:) but not the reverse: (Ḳ:) ISd says, we have not heard this, but there is no objection to it: (TA:) and Fr says, بِضْعٌ is not mentioned save with ten and twenty to ninety; (IB, Ḳ;) not with what exceeds this: (IB:) you do not say بِضْعٌ وَمِائَةٌ nor بِضْعٌ وَأَلْفٌ, (IB, Ḳ,) but مِائَةٌ وَنَيِّفٌ [and أَلْفٌ وَنَيِّفٌ]: (IB:) it occurs in trads. with عِشْرُونَ and with ثَلَاثُونَ. (TA.) — بِضْعٌ and ▼ بَضْعٌ also signify *A part,* or *portion,* of the night: (Ḳ:) *a time* thereof. (Lḥ.) You say, مَضَى بِضْعٌ مِنَ اللَّيْلِ [*A part, or portion, of the night passed*]. (TA.) J mentions it with ص [in the place of ض]; and explains it by جَوْشٌ, q. v. (TA.)

بَضْعَةٌ, (Ṣ, Mṣb, Ḳ,) with fet-ḥ, other words of like meaning being with kesr, as فِلْذَةٌ and قِطْعَةٌ and فِدْرَةٌ, (Ṣ,) and sometimes with kesr, [▼ بِضْعَةٌ,]

(Ḳ,) and ↑ بُضْعَةٌ also is mentioned, (TA,) of which the first is the most chaste, though Esh-Shiháb asserts the second to be more common, (TA,) *A piece*, or *lump*, or *portion cut off*; (TA;) particularly *of flesh*, or *flesh-meat*, (Ṣ, Mṣb, Ḳ,) *in a compact*, or *collective*, *state*: (TA:) pl. ↑ بَضْعٌ, [or rather this is a coll. gen. n., of which بَضْعَةٌ is the n. un.,] and بِضَعٌ, (Ṣ, Mṣb, Ḳ,) as some say, (Ṣ,) but this is disallowed by 'Alee Ibn-Ḥamzeh, (TA,) [or it may be a correct pl. of بِضْعَةٌ agreeably with analogy,] and بِضَاعٌ, and بَضَعَاتٌ, (Mṣb, Ḳ,) and [quasi-pl. n.] بَضِيعٌ, which is extr., like رَهِينٌ and كَلِيبٌ and مَعِيزٌ [&c.]. (TA.) Hence the saying [of Moḥammad] in a trad., فَاطِمَةُ بَضْعَةٌ مِنِّى يُرِيبُنِى مَا رَابَهَا وَيُؤْذِينِى مَا آذَاهَا ‡ *Fáṭimeh is a part of me*: [*that displeases and disquiets me which has displeased and disquieted her, and that hurts me which has hurt her*:] or, accord. to one relation, he said بُضَيْعَةٌ [*a little part*]. (TA.) One says also, إِنَّ فُلَانًا لَشَدِيدُ البَضْعَةِ حَسَنُهَا meaning *Verily such a one is corpulent and fat*. (TA.) — See also بَضْعَةٌ.

بُضْعَةٌ: see بَضْعَةٌ.

بِضْعَةٌ: see بَضْعَةٌ: and, as a noun of number, see بِضْعٌ, latter half of the paragraph.

بَضْعَةٌ The *sound of cutting* of swords: occurring in the saying, سَمِعْتُ لِلسِّيَاطِ خَضْعَةً وَلِلسُّيُوفِ بَضْعَةً *I heard a sound of falling of the whips, and a sound of cutting of the swords*: (TA:) but in the Ṣ and A in art. خضع, and by IB, خضعة and بضعة are written خَضَعَةٌ and ↑ بَضَعَةٌ; and IB explains the former as signifying the sounds of swords; and the latter, the *sounds of whips*. (TA in art. خضع.) [See also بَاضِعٌ.]

بِضَاعٌ [The *giving and receiving merchandise*;] a subst. from أَبْضَعَهُ البِضَاعَةَ and اِبْتَضَعَ مِنْهُ; [or rather an inf. n. of which the verb, بَاضَعَ, is not used;] similar to قِرَاضٌ. (TA.)

بَضِيعٌ *Flesh*. (Aṣ, Ṣ.) You say, دَابَّةٌ كَثِيرَةُ البَضِيعِ (Aṣ, Ṣ, TA) *A beast abounding in what is distinct from the rest of the flesh of the thigh*: n. un. with ة. (TA.) And رَجُلٌ خَاظِى البَضِيعِ (Aṣ, Ṣ) *A fat man*. (TA.) And سَاعِدٌ خَاظِى البَضِيعِ [*A fore arm, or an upper arm*,] *full of flesh*. (IB.) [See also بَضْعَةٌ, of which it is a quasi-pl. n.]

بِضَاعَةٌ *Merchandise*; or *an article of merchandise*; (TA;) *a portion of one's property which one sends for traffic*; (Ṣ;) *a portion of property prepared for traffic*, (Mgh,* Mṣb,) or *with which one traffics*; from بَضْعٌ signifying the act of "cutting," or "cutting off;" and vulgarly pronounced بُضَاعَةٌ: (TA:) pl. بَضَائِعُ. (Mṣb, TA.)

بَاضِعٌ A sword *that cuts off a piece of a thing that it strikes*: (Ṣ, TA:) or a *sharp*, or *cutting*, sword: (Ḳ:) or a sword *that cuts everything*: (TA:) pl. بَضَعَةٌ: (Ḳ:) Fr says that بَضَعَةٌ signifies *swords*; and خَضَعَةٌ, whips: but some say the reverse. (TA.) [See also بَضَعَةٌ above.] — [See also the next paragraph.] = [*A broker who acts as an intermediary between the sellers and buyers of camels*;] the same with respect to camels as the دَلَّال with respect to houses: (O, L, Ḳ:) or *one who carries the articles of merchandise of the tribe, and conveys those articles from place to place for sale*: (Ibn-'Abbád, Ṣgh, Ḳ:) it is said in the A that بَاضِعُ الحَىِّ signifies *the person who carries the articles of merchandise of the tribe*. (TA.)

بَاضِعَةٌ *A wound by which the head is broken*, (Ṣ, Mgh, Mṣb, Ḳ,) *which cuts the skin, and cleaves the flesh* (Ṣ, Ḳ) *in a slight degree*, (Ḳ,) *and brings blood, but does not make it to flow*: (Ṣ, Ḳ:) or *which wounds the skin, and cleaves the flesh*: (Mgh:) or *which cleaves the flesh, but does not reach to the bone, nor cause the blood to flow*: (Mṣb:) that from which the blood flows is termed دَامِيَةٌ [app. a mistake for دَامِعَةٌ]. (Ṣ, Mṣb.) = *A large flock* (فِرْقٌ [in the CḲ, erroneously, فَرْق,]) of sheep or goats: (Ṣ, Ṣgh, Ḳ:) or *a portion separated from the rest* of the sheep or goats: (Lth, Ḳ:) pl. بَوَاضِعُ: you say, فِرَقٌ بَوَاضِعُ. (Lth.)

أَبْضَعُ as a corroborative after أَجْمَعُ: see أَبْصَعُ, with the unpointed ص. Az says that it is an evident mistranscription. (TA.)

مِبْضَعٌ *A lancet; an instrument with which a vein is cut*: (Ṣ, Mgh,* Ḳ, TA:) and [*a currier's knife*] *with which leather is cut*: (Ṣ, TA:) [pl. مَبَاضِعُ: accord. to the Mirḳát el-Loghah, as cited by Golius, it signifies *a farrier's fleam*; differing from مِشْرَطٌ, which signifies a surgeon's lancet: but this distinction is probably post-classical; for accord. to the TA, these two words signify the same.]

مَبْضُوعَةٌ [used as a subst.] *A bow: a bow cut from a branch*. (TA.)

مُسْتَبْضِعٌ. It is said in a prov., كَمُسْتَبْضِعِ تَمْرٍ إِلَى هَجَرٍ [*Like the taker of dates as merchandise to Hejer*]; because Hejer is [famous as] the place of production (مَعْدِن) of dates. (Ṣ.) مستبضع is here made trans. by means of الى because it has the meaning of حَامِلٌ. (TA.)

بط

1. بَطَّ, (Ṣ, Mgh, Mṣb, Ḳ,) aor. ـُ, inf. n. بَطٌّ, (Mgh, Mṣb,) *He slit* a wound, (Ṣ, Mgh, Mṣb, Ḳ,) or an ulcer, (Ṣ,) and a purse, (Ḳ,) &c. (TA.) [See also R. Q. 1.]

2. بطّط, inf. n. تَبْطِيطٌ, *He trafficked in the birds called* بَطّ, q. v. (Ḳ.)

4. ابطّ, (IAạr, Ḳ,) inf. n. إِبْطَاطٌ, (IAạr,) *He purchased* [or *became possessed of*] *a* بَطَّة [q. v.] *for oil*, or *of oil*. (IAạr, Ḳ.)

R. Q. 1. ضَرَبَهُ فَبَطْبَطَهُ *He struck him and clave his skin, or his head*. (TA.) [See 1.] = See also بَطْبَطَةٌ, below.

بَطٌّ *A kind of water-fowl*; (Ṣ, O, Mṣb;) [the *duck*, or *ducks*; and the *goose*, or *geese*; but generally the former of these birds; agreeably with a statement in the Jm, that بَطّ is applied by the Arabs to the *small*, and إِوَزّ to the *large*;] *i. q.* إِوَزٌّ, (Ḳ, TA,) both the *small thereof* and the *large*: (TA:) a Persian word (عَجَمِىٌّ), arabicized; [originally بَتْ, or بَطْ, or بَطّ;] or, accord. to IJ, an imitation of its cries: n. un. بَطَّةٌ, (Ṣ, Mṣb, Ḳ,) which is applied to the male and to the female, (Ṣ, Mṣb,) like حَمَامَةٌ and دَجَاجَةٌ: (Ṣ:) pl. بِطَاطٌ. (TA.)

بَطَّةٌ n. un. of بَطّ, q. v. — Also *A kind of bottle*, or *pot, of glass*; syn. دَبَّةٌ; (Ḳ, TA; [in the CḲ, erroneously, دُبَّةٌ;]) in the dial. of the people of Mekkeh; so called because made in the form of a living بَطَّة: (Lth, TA:) or *a vessel like the* [*flask, or bottle, called*] قَارُورَة; (Ḳ;) [*a kind of leathern pot, or bottle, of which the body is nearly globular, with a short and wide neck*;] *in which oil &c. are put*: pl. بُطَطٌ. (TA.)

بَطَّاطٌ *A maker of* بُطَط, pl. of بَطَّة. (TA.)

بَطْبَطَةٌ [app. an inf. n., of which the verb is ↑ بَطْبَطَ,] The *crying*, or *cry*, *of the* بَطّ; (Ḳ;) after which it [the bird] is named, accord. to IJ, as mentioned above: (TA:) or its *diving in water*. (Ḳ.)

مِبَطَّةٌ The مِبْضَع [or *scarifying instrument*] (Ḳ, TA) *with which a wound is slit*. (TA.)

بطأ

1. بَطُؤَ, aor. ـُ, inf. n. بُطْءٌ (Ṣ, Mṣb, Ḳ) and بِطَآءٌ, with fet-ḥ and medd, (Mṣb,) or بِطَآءٌ, like كِتَابٌ; (Ḳ;) and ↑ ابطأ; (Ṣ, Mṣb, Ḳ;) *He was*, or *became, slow, tardy, dilatory, late*, or *backward*; *contr. of* أَسْرَعَ; (Ḳ;) in his going or course, and in his gait [&c.]: (TA:) or the latter is said of a man; (Ṣ, Mṣb;) meaning [as above; or] *his coming was late*, or *backward*; (Mṣb;) [and is app. elliptical, for ابطأ مَشْيَهُ *he made his pace, or going, slow*, &c.; or the like; see اسرع:] and بَطُؤَ [denotes what is as it were an innate quality; see, again, أَسْرَعَ; or] is said of one's coming; [meaning *it was*, or *became, slow*, &c.;] (Ṣ, Mṣb;) بُطْءٌ being the *contr. of* سُرْعَةٌ. (Ṣ.) One should not say ↑ أَبْطَيْتُ for أَبْطَأْتُ. (Ṣ.) [See also 6.] — بَطُؤَ ذَا خُرُوجًا: see بَطْآنَ.

2. بطّأ به [and بطّاه, inf. n. as below, *It made him slow, tardy, dilatory, late, or backward*;] *it kept him*, or *held him, back*; or *put him back*, or *backward*. (TA.) It is said in a trad., مَنْ بَطَّأَ بِهِ عَمَلُهُ لَمْ يُسْرِعْ بِهِ نَسَبُهُ *Him whom his evil deeds keep*, or *hold, back*, or *put back*, or *backward*, *his nobility of lineage will not profit*, [or *advance*, or *put forward*,] in the life to come, or in the world to come. (TA.) مَا بَطَّأَ بِكَ and مَا أَبْطَأَ ↑ بِكَ signify the same [*What made thee*, or *hath made thee, slow?* &c.]; (Ṣ, TA;) and so مَا بَطَّأَكَ. (TA.) And you say, بَطَّأَ عَلَيْهِ بِالأَمْرِ, inf. n. تَبْطِئَةٌ; and

ابطأ ▼ به; *He delayed to him* [*the doing of*] *the thing, or affair.* (Ḳ.)

4: see 1 and 2; each in two places. — أَبْطَؤُوا *Their beasts on which they rode were,* or *became, slow.* (AZ, Ṣ, Ḳ.) — مَا أَبْطَأَهُ *How slow,* or *tardy, &c., is* [*he,* or] *it!* (Ṣ.)

6. تباطأ [accord. to general analogy, *He feigned,* or *affected, to be slow, tardy, &c.:* or] *he was slow,* or *sluggish;* or *he made delay;* in going, or pace: and *he held back* from work, or action. (KL.) You say of a man, تباطأ فِى مَسِيرِهِ [*He feigned,* or *affected, to be slow, &c., in his going, course,* or *pace*]. (Ṣ.)

10. استبطأه (Ṣ, TA) *He deemed him,* or *reckoned him, slow, tardy, &c.* (KL.) You say, كَتَبَ إِلَىَّ يَسْتَبْطِئُنِى [*He wrote to me, deeming me,* or *reckoning me, slow, &c.*]. (TA.)

بُطْءٌ inf. n. of 1. (Ṣ, Mṣb, Ḳ.) — One says, in the dial. of Benoo-Yarbooa, (TA,) لَمْ أَفْعَلْهُ بُطْأً يَا هٰذَا, and ▼بُطْأَى, [*I never did it,* lit.] *I did it not ever, O thou!* i. e. الدَّهْرَ. (Ḳ, TA.)

بُطْأَى: see بُطْءٌ.

بُطْآنَ ذَا خُرُوجًا, and بَطْآنَ, (Ṣ, Ḳ,) but the latter is extr., (TA,) i. q. بَطُؤَ ▼ ذَا خُرُوجًا [*Slow,* or *very slow,* or *how slow, is this in coming forth!*]; (Ṣ, Ḳ;) the fet-ḥah in [the last syllable of] بَطُؤَ is transferred to the ن of بُطْآنَ, and the ḍammeh of the ط [in the former] to the ب [in the latter]; the meaning being one of wonder; i. e. مَا أَبْطَأَهُ. (Ṣ, TA.) [بطآن is an enunciative placed before its inchoative: and, being originally بَطُؤَ, it may be a simple enunciative, or an enunciative having an intensive signification; as that verb signifies simply "it was slow," &c., and may be used as co-ordinate to رَمُوَ, meaning "excellent is he in his shooting!" &c., and قَضُوَ "excellent is he in his judging!" &c.: or it may be equivalent to مَا أَبْطَأَ, as it is said to be in the Ṣ. See also سَرْعَانَ.]

بَطِىْءٌ *Slow, tardy, dilatory, late,* or *backward;* applied to a man, (Ṣ, Mṣb, TA,) and to a horse or the like: (Ṣ, TA:) pl. بِطَآءٌ. (Ṣ, Ḳ, TA.) — Also an imitative sequent to خَطِىْءٌ. (Ṣ in art. خطأ.)

أَبْطَأُ *More,* and *most, slow, &c.* (Meyd, &c.)

البَنْطَأُ for البَنْدَأُ is mentioned by AO. (TA on the letter ط.)

بطح

1. بَطَحَهُ, aor. ـَ, (Mṣb, TA,) inf. n. بَطْحٌ, (Mgh, TA,) *He spread it; spread it out,* or *forth; expanded it; extended it.* (Mgh,* Mṣb, TA.) — Also, (Ṣ, A, Ḳ,) or بَطَحَهُ عَلَى وَجْهِهِ, (Mgh, Mṣb,) aor. as above, (Ḳ,) and so the inf. n., (TA,) *He threw him down upon his face.* (Ṣ, A, Mgh, Mṣb, Ḳ.) — See also 2.

2. بطّح المَسْجِدَ, (TA,) inf. n. تَبْطِيحٌ; (Ḳ;) and ▼ابطحه; (TA;) *He strewed pebbles in the mosque, and made it plain,* or *level* [*in its ground,* or *floor*]: (Ḳ, TA:) and بَطْحَةٌ, [inf. n. of ▼بَطَحَهُ,] occurring in a trad., also signifies the *making it plain,* or *level.* (TA.)

4: see 2.

5. تبطّح: see 7. — Also *It* (a torrent) *flowed widely:* (ISd, A:) or *spread widely in the* بَطْحَآء. (Ṣ, Ḳ.) — Also, [and ▼انبطح,] *It* (a place &c.) *spread; spread out,* or *forth; became expanded* or *extended.* (TA.) = And i. q. اِنْتَصَبَ [*It became set up* or *upright, erected, &c.:* thus the verb bears two contr. significations]. (TA.) = Also *He* (a man) *took the* أَبْطَح *as a place of abode.* (A, TA.)

7. انبطح *It* (water) *went to the right and left* in a place. (AA.) — See also 5. — *He became thrown down upon his face:* (Ṣ, A, Ḳ:) or *he lay,* or *lay as though thrown down* or *extended, upon his face:* (Mgh, Mṣb:) or *he stretched himself;* or *lay, and stretched himself; upon his face, extended upon the ground;* as also ▼تبطّح. (TA.) — *It* (a valley) *became wide;* (Ḳ, TA;) as also ▼استبطح. (TA.)

10: see 7.

بَطْحٌ: see أَبْطَحُ, in two places.

بَطْحَةٌ The *stature* of a man [app. in a lying posture]: as in the phrase هُوَ بَطْحَةُ رَجُلٍ [*It is of the stature of a man*]. (Ḳ.) — بَيْنَهُمَا بَطْحَةٌ بَعِيدَةٌ *Between them two is a far-extending distance* or *space* or *interval.* (L.) — See also أَبْطَحُ.

بَطْحَآءُ: see أَبْطَحُ, in four places.

بِطَاحٌ بُطْحٌ [*Many wide water-courses in which are fine,* or *minute,* or *broken, pebbles:* the former word is pl. of أَبْطَحُ or of بَطْحَآءُ]: a phrase like أَعْوَامٌ عُوَّمٌ. (Aṣ, A 'Obeyd, Ṣ.)

بَطِيحَةٌ: see أَبْطَحُ.

بَاطِحٌ applied to a man, i. q. ▼مُنْبَطِحٌ [part. n. of 7, q. v.]. (Ḥam p. 244.)

أَبْطَحُ, originally an epithet [and therefore imperfectly decl.], (M, TA,) that is, an epithet converted into a subst., and not used as an epithet, (Ḥam p. 21,) *A wide water-course,* or *channel of a torrent, in which are fine,* or *minute,* or *broken, pebbles;* (Ṣ, A, Ḳ, and Ḥam ubi suprà;) so called because the water goes in it to the right and left; [i. e. spreads widely; see 7;] (AA;) as also ▼بَطْحَآءُ, (Ṣ, A, Ḳ, Ḥam,) fem. of the former, and, like it, an epithet converted into a subst.; (Ḥam ubi suprà;) and ▼بَطِيحَةٌ, (Ṣ, Ḳ,) and ▼بَطْحٌ: (Ḳ:) or *a water-course,* or *channel of a torrent, in which are sand and pebbles;* as also ▼بَطْحَآءُ: (Mgh:) or *a wide place* [app. *in a water-course*]; as also ▼بطحة [app. بَطْحَةٌ, which is explained by Freytag, but without his stating on what authority, as signifying *a depressed place through which water flows, abounding with pebbles;* as is also بَطِحَةٌ; and in like manner Golius explains the former, but mentions the latter as a pl. of بطيحة]: (Mṣb:) or, accord. to AḤn, the *bottom of a water-course,* or *channel of a torrent, producing no plants* or *herbage:* (TA:) or ▼بَطْحَآءُ signifies *soft earth* of a valley, *such as has been drawn along by the torrents:* (ISd, TA:) or the *soft pebbles in the bottom of the water-course,* or *channel of a torrent,* of a valley; as also أَبْطَحُ: (IAth, TA:) or the *soft earth, such as has been drawn along by the torrents, in the bottom of a* تَلْعَة [meaning *a water-course* &c.] and *of a valley;* and the أَبْطَح and ▼بَطْحَآء of a valley are its *earth and soft pebbles:* (En-Naḍr, TA:) and accord. to AA, ▼بَطْحٌ signifies *sand in a* بَطْحَآء: (TA:) the pl. is أَبَاطِحُ and بِطَاحٌ (Ṣ, A, Ḳ) and بَطَائِحُ; (Ḳ;) the first of these, and the second also, contr. to analogy, being pls. of ابطح; (Ṣ;) or both are pls. of بطحآء, contr. to analogy; (Ḥam p. 251;) or the first is pl. of ابطح, formed after the manner of the pl. of a subst. of this measure, though the sing. is originally an epithet; (M, TA;) and the second, as is asserted by more than one, is correctly pl. of بطحآء, as is also بَطْحَاوَاتٌ; (TA;) and the third is pl. of بطيحة. (M, TA.)

مُنْبَطِحٌ [part. n. of 7, q. v.: often applied to anything *Spread out, expanded,* or *flat*]: see بَاطِحٌ.

بطخ

4. أَبْطَخُوا *They had abundance of* بِطِّيخ [or *melons,* or *water-melons*]. (Ṣ, A, L, Ḳ.)

5. تبطّخ *He ate* بِطِّيخ. (A, TA.)

رِجَالٌ بَطْخَةٌ, and إِبِلٌ بَطْخَةٌ, ‡ *Large, big, bulky,* or *corpulent, camels,* and *men:* and رَجُلٌ ▼بُطَاخِىٌّ ‡ *a large, big, bulky,* or *corpulent, man.* (Ḳ, TA.)

بُطَاخِىٌّ: see what immediately precedes.

بِطِّيخٌ, (Ṣ, Mṣb, Ḳ, &c.,) vulgarly and incorrectly pronounced بَطِّيخ, (ISk, Mṣb,) and in the dial. of El-Ḥijáz called طِبِّيخٌ, (Mṣb,) *A certain well-known fruit;* (Mṣb;) [the *melon,* absolutely, as is shown by many passages in the lexicons, and expressly stated in law-books: and, particularly, the *water-melon; cucurbita citrullus:* or *a plant*] *of the kind called* يَقْطِين, *that does not grow tall, but extends itself upon the surface of the ground:* (Ḳ, TA:) and also the خِرْبِز [or خُرْبُز, a Persian word, and applied to the *water-melon,* by the Turks termed by this name, and in their own language قَارْپُوز]: (CḲ: [but not found by me in my MS. copy of the Ḳ, nor in the L, nor in the TA:]) or البِطِّيخُ الهِنْدِىُّ [the Indian بطّيخ] is *what is called in Persian the* خُرْبُز: (Mgh:) [the term بطّيخ is applied to many varieties of the water-melon, distinguished by different epithets; as الأَحْمَرُ *the red,* الأَصْفَرُ *the yellow,* الأَبْيَضُ *the white,* الأَجْرَبُ *the mangy,* النَّمِشُ *the speckled,* البُرُلُّسِىُّ *that of El-Burullus,* &c.: it is a coll. gen. n.:] n. un. with ة. (Ṣ, Ḳ.)

مَبْطَخَة (Ṣ, A, Mgh, &c.) and مَبْطُخَة (Ṣ, L, Ḳ) *A place where* بِطِّيخ *grow:* (Ṣ, A, Mgh, &c.:) pl. مَبَاطِخُ. (A, TA.)

بطر

1. بَطِرَ, aor. َ, inf. n. بَطَرٌ, *He exulted; or exulted greatly, or excessively; and behaved insolently and unthankfully, or ungratefully:* or *he exulted by reason of wealth, and behaved with pride and self-conceitedness, and boastfulness, and want of thankfulness:* or *he behaved with the utmost exultation, &c.:* or *he rejoiced, and rested his mind upon things agreeable with natural desire:* syn. of the inf. n. أَشَرٌ, (Ṣ, A, L, Mṣb, TA,) and مَرَحٌ; (L, TA;) the former of which signifies شِدَّةُ المَرَحِ, (Ṣ, A,) and مُجَاوَزَةُ الحَدِّ فِى مَرَحٍ: (A:) *he was, or became, stupified, deprived of his reason, confounded, or amazed,* (Ṣ, Ḳ, Er-Rághib,) *bearing wealth ill, or in an evil manner, performing little of the duty imposed on him by it, and turning it to a wrong purpose:* (Er-Rághib, TA,* TḲ:) this is said to be the primary signification: (TA:) *he was, or became, stupified, or confounded, and knew not what to prefer nor what to postpone:* (TA:) *he was, or became, confounded, perplexed, or amazed, by reason of fright:* (Aṣ, Ṣ voce بَحِرَ:) *he behaved exorbitantly, or insolently, with wealth,* (Ḳ, TA,) or *on the occasion of having wealth:* and this, also, is said to be the primary signification: (TA:) *he had, or exercised, little of the quality of bearing wealth* [*in a becoming, or proper, manner*]: (Ḳ:) *he behaved proudly:* (TA:) *he regarded a thing with hatred, or dislike, without its deserving to be so regarded: he was, or became, brisk, lively, or sprightly:* (Ḳ:) accord. to some, *he walked with an elegant and a proud and self-conceited gait, with an affected inclining of the body from side to side.* (TA.) It is said in a trad., لَا يَنْظُرُ ٱللّٰهُ يَوْمَ القِيَامَةِ مَنْ جَرَّ إِزَارَهُ بَطَرًا [*God will not look, on the day of resurrection, upon him who drags along his wrapper of the lower part of the body in exultation and insolence, or pride:* meaning one who wears too long a wrapper of the lower part of the body]. (TA.) — بَطِرْتَ عَيْشَكَ ‡ [*Thou exultedst, or exultedst greatly, or excessively, and behavedst insolently and unthankfully, or ungratefully, &c., in thy manner of life,*] is a phrase similar to رَشِدْتَ أَمْرَكَ; (Ṣ, TA;) and in like manner بَطِرَتْ مَعِيشَتَهَا, in the Ḳur [xxviii. 58]; in which the verb is not trans., but the subst. is put in the accus. case because of فِى understood before it. (Aboo-Is-ḥáḳ.) — لَا أَبْطَرُ الغِنَى † *I do not, or will not, domineer, or assume superiority, over others when I am rich.* (Ḥam p. 517.) — بَطِرَ النِّعْمَةَ ‡ *He held wealth, or the favour, or benefit, in light estimation, and was unthankful, or ungrateful, for it.* (A.) — بَطِرَ هِدَايَةَ أَمْرِهِ † *He refused the right direction as to the management of his affair, and was ignorant of it.* (TA.) — It is said in a trad., that pride is بَطَرُ الحَقِّ, which means ‡ *The considering as false, or vain, what God has pronounced to be the truth, or our duty;* namely, the confession of his unity, and the obligation of rendering Him religious service: or *the being confounded at considering truth, or duty, and not seeing it to be true, or incumbent:* (TA:) or *the disdaining the truth, or right, and not accepting it or not admitting it.* (Ḳ.) = بَطَرَهُ, aor. ُ (Ṣ, Ḳ) and ِ, (Ḳ,) inf. n. بَطْرٌ, (Ṣ, Mṣb,) *He cut it, or divided it, lengthwise; slit it; split it.* (Ṣ, Mṣb, Ḳ.) Hence the appellation بَيْطَارٌ. (Ṣ, Mṣb.)

4. ابطرهُ *It rendered him such as is termed* بَطِر; *it* (wealth) *caused him to exult, or to exult greatly, or excessively, and to behave insolently and unthankfully, or ungratefully:* &c.: [see بَطِرَ:] (Ṣ, A:) *it stupified him, deprived him of his reason, confounded him, or amazed him.* (Ṣ, Ḳ.) You say, مَا أَمْطَرَتْ حَتَّى أَبْطَرَتْ *It* (the sky) *rained not until it caused* [men] *to exult, or to exult greatly, &c.* (A.) — ابطر حِلْمَهُ ‡ *It* (the ignorance of a person) *caused his* (another's) *clemency, moderation, or gravity, to become converted into inordinate exultation, and insolence, or the like, and levity.* (A.) — ابطرهُ حِلْمَهُ ‡ *It stupified, confounded, or amazed, him, so as to turn him from his clemency, moderation, or gravity.* (TA.) — ابطرهُ ذَرْعَهُ ‡ *He imposed upon him more than he was able to do;* (Ṣ;) *what was above his power:* (Ḳ:) ذرعه is here a substitute for its antecedent to indicate an implication therein: (A:) you say this when a slow-paced camel has endeavoured in vain to keep pace with another camel; and when any man has imposed upon another a difficulty beyond his power: (TA:) or the meaning is, *he cut off his means of subsistence, and wasted his body:* (IAṭr, Ḳ:) ذرع signifying the "body." (IAṭr.)

Q. Q. 1. بَيْطَرَ, inf. n. بَيْطَرَةٌ, *He practised* [*farriery, the veterinary art, or*] *the art of the* بَيْطَار. (Mṣb.) — هُوَ يُبَيْطِرُ الدَّوَابَّ *He treats beasts, or horses and the like, medically, or curatively.* (TA.)

ذَهَبَ دَمُهُ بِطْرًا ‡ *His blood went unrevenged,* (Ks, Ṣ, A, Ḳ,) *being held in light estimation.* (A.)

بَطِرٌ part. n. of بَطِرَ, (Mṣb, TA,) *Exulting, or exulting greatly, or excessively, and behaving insolently and unthankfully, or ungratefully:* or *exulting by reason of wealth, and behaving with pride and self-conceitedness, and boastfulness, and want of thankfulness:* or *behaving with the utmost exultation, &c.:* see its verb. (A, Mṣb, TA.)

بَطِيرٌ *Cut, or divided, lengthwise; slit; split;* (Ḳ;) as also ▼مَبْطُورٌ. (TA.) = See also بَيْطَارٌ.

اِمْرَأَةٌ بَطِيرَةٌ *A woman who behaves with much* بَطَر, i. e. *exultation, and insolence and unthankfulness, or ingratitude, &c.:* [see بَطِرَ.] (A.) [See also what next follows.]

بِطْرِيرٌ *Clamorous; long-tongued:* and one *who perseveres in error:* fem. with ة: (Ḳ:) but it [the former] is mostly used in relation to women, (TA,) and as signifying a woman *who exults, or exults greatly, or excessively, and behaves insolently and unthankfully, or ungratefully,* (تَبْطَرُ,) *and perseveres in error:* (ADḳ:) [it is said in the TA that some say بِطْرِيرٌ, and that this is the more approved; but Az says,] Lth cites, from ADḳ, the phrase اِمْرَأَةٌ بِطْرِيرٌ as meaning *a clamorous, long-tongued woman;* لِأَنَّهَا قَدْ بَطِرَتْ وَأَشِرَتْ [because of her insolent behaviour]: and says that, accord. to Aboo-Kheyreh, it is امرأة بِطْرِيرٌ; her tongue being likened to the بَطْر: but Lth adds, the saying of ADḳ is preferable in my opinion, and more correct. (T in art. بطر.)

بَيْطَرٌ: see بَيْطَارٌ.

بِيَطْرٌ: see بَيْطَارٌ. — [Hence,] *A tailor.* (Sh, Ṣ,* Ḳ.) A poet says, (calling a tailor a بيطر, like as one calls a skilful man an إِسْكَافٌ, Sh, TA,)

شَقَّ البِيَطْرِ مِدْرَعَ الهُمَامِ

[*Like as the tailor cuts lengthwise, or slits, the woollen tunic of the valiant chief*]. (Sh, Ṣ.)

بَيْطَرَةٌ [*Farriery; the veterinary art;*] the *art of the* بَيْطَار. (Ṣ, Ḳ.) [See Q. Q. 1.]

بَيْطَارٌ (Ṣ, Mṣb, Ḳ) and ▼بِيَطْرٌ (Ṣ, Ḳ) and ▼بَيْطَرٌ and ▼بَطِيرٌ (Ḳ) and ▼مُبَيْطِرٌ (Ṣ, Ḳ) [*A farrier; one who practises the veterinary art;*] *one who treats beasts, or horses and the like, medically,* or *curatively:* (Ḳ:) from بَطَرَهُ, explained above. (Ṣ, Mṣb.*) أَشْهَرُ مِنْ رَايَةِ البَيْطَارِ [*More commonly known than the sign of the farrier,* app. meaning a sign which, I suppose, the itinerant farrier carried about with him,] (A, TA) is one of the proverbs of the Arabs. (TA.) — You say, also, هُوَ بِهٰذَا عَالِمٌ بَيْطَارٌ ‡ [*He is knowing and skilful in this:* see also بَيْطَرٌ]. (A.)

مَبْطُورٌ: see بَطِيرٌ.

مُبَيْطِرٌ: see بَيْطَارٌ.

بطرق

بِطْرِيقٌ *A* قَائِد [*or leader of an army*], in the language of the رُوم [or Greeks of the Lower Empire]; (JK;) *one who is to the* روم *like the* قائد *to the Arabs;* (Mgh, Mṣb;) [i. e.] *a leader of an army* (قائد) *of the* روم; (Ṣ, Ḳ;) accord. to Ḳudámeh, (Mgh,) *one who is over ten thousand men:* (Mgh, Ḳ:) next to him is the طَرْخَان [in the CḲ تَرْخان], over five thousand: then, the قُومَس, over two hundred: (Ḳ:) but in art. طرخ in the Ḳ, it is said that طرخان signifies "a headman, or chief, of high, or noble, rank," in the language of Khurásán; and in art. قمس, that قومس signifies "a commander," or the like, syn. أَمِير; and قَمَامِسَةٌ, i. q. بَطَارِقَةٌ, (TA,) which is pl. of بطريق, (Ṣ, Mgh, Mṣb, Ḳ,) as also بَطَارِيقُ, for which بَطَارِقُ is used in a verse of Aboo-Dhueyb: (TA:) it is an arabicized word; (Ṣ, TA;) [app. from the Latin "patricius;"] or, as some say, of the language of the روم and of Syria: or Arabic, agreeing with the foreign word, and of the dial. of the people of El-Ḥijáz: accord. to El-Jawáleeḳee and others, in the language of the روم it is بترك: some say that it signifies *skilled in war and its affairs,* in the language of the روم; and he who is so has rank, or office, and is sometimes made foremost, among them: (TA:) and (some say, TA) a *proud and self-conceited* man; (JK, Ḳ;) so says Ibn-'Abbád: (TA:) and *fat;* applied to a bird (JK, Ḳ) &c.: (JK:) pl. بَطَارِقَةٌ. (Ḳ.) — [See also بَطْرَكٌ, and جَاثَلِيقٌ.]

بطرك

بَطْرَكٌ and بِطْرَكٌ *i. q.* بِطْرِيقٌ, (Aṣ, Ḳ,) i. e. *A leader of the Christians:* (TA:) or the *chief of the Magians:* (Ḳ:) [in the present day, the former is applied to *a Patriarch of a Christian church;* as also † بِطْرِيكٌ: (see جَاثَلِيقٌ:) pl. بَطَارِكَةٌ and بَطَارِيكُ]: adventitious; not Arabic. (Az, TA.)

[بَطْرَكِىٌّ *Patriarchal;* i. e. *of,* or *belonging to,* or *relating to, a Patriarch of a Christian church;* as also † بِطْرِيكِىٌّ: both modern terms.]

[بَطْرَكِيَّةٌ *A patriarchate;* i. e. the *office,* or *jurisdiction, of a Patriarch of a Christian church;* as also † بِطْرِيكِيَّةٌ: both modern terms.]

بِطْرِيكٌ: see بَطْرَكٌ.

بِطْرِيكِىٌّ: see بَطْرَكِىٌّ.

بِطْرِيكِيَّةٌ: see بَطْرَكِيَّةٌ.

بطش

1. بَطَشَ بِهِ, (Ṣ, A, Mgh, Mṣb, Ḳ,) aor. ـِ and ـُ, (Ṣ, Mṣb, Ḳ,) the former of which is that adopted by the seven readers (Mṣb, TA) in chap. xliv. verse 15 of the Ḳur, (TA,) inf. n. بَطْشٌ, (Ṣ, Mgh, Mṣb,) *He seized him violently; laid violent hands upon him:* (Ṣ, Mṣb:) *assaulted him:* (Ṣ:) or *he seized him with violence and assault:* (A, Ḳ:) or *he seized him vehemently, in anger:* (Mgh:) and *he laid hold upon him* (Mgh, TA) *vehemently,* (TA,) *in making an assault:* (Mgh, TA:) and † أَبْطَشَهُ signifies the same as بَطَشَ بِهِ, (Ḳ,) but is rare, occurring in the words [of the Ḳur xliv. 15], يَوْمَ نُبْطِشُ البَطْشَةَ الكُبْرَى, accord. to the reading of El-Ḥasan and Ibn-Rejà, [meaning *On the day when we make the greatest assault:*] or, accord. to AḤát, [and Bḍ says the like,] the meaning is, [*on the day when*] *we give power over them to such as shall assault them* [*with the great assault;* or *make to assault with the great assault*]. (TA.) — Also *He took it,* namely, anything, or *took hold of it,* (Lth, Ḳ,* TA,) or *clung to it,* (TA,) *strongly.* (Lth, Ḳ, TA.) In the saying of El-Ḥulwánee, وَمَا لَا يَقَعُ عَلَيْهِ العَيْنُ وَلَا يَبْطِشُهُ الكَفُّ, [meaning *And that upon which the eye falls not, and of which the hand does not take hold,*] the prep. [بِ] is understood; or the verb is thus used as implying the meaning of الأَخْذُ and التَّنَاوُلُ. (Mgh.) — ‡ بَطَشَتْ بِهِمْ أَهْوَالُ الدُّنْيَا [*The terrors of the world assaulted them*]. (A.) — بَطَشَتِ اليَدُ *The hand worked, wrought,* or *laboured.* (Mṣb.) — ‡ فُلَانٌ يَبْطِشُ فِى العِلْمِ بِبَاعٍ بَسِيطٍ [*Such a one labours in science with extensive ability*]. (A, TA.) — ‡ بَطَشَ مِنَ الحُمَّى *He recovered from the fever, being still weak.* (Aboo-Málik, A,* Ḳ.)

3. بَاطَشَهُ, (Ṣ, TA,) inf. n. مُبَاطَشَةٌ (Ṣ, Ḳ) and بِطَاشٌ, (TA,) *He laboured, strove, struggled, contended,* or *conflicted, with him, to prevail,* or *overcome;* syn. of the inf. n. مُعَالَجَةٌ. (Ḳ, TA.) — بَاطَشَا, (TḲ,) inf. n. مُبَاطَشَةٌ, (Ḳ,) *Each of them two stretched forth his hand towards the other to seize him violently* (Ḳ, TA) *and to assault him quickly.* (TA.)

4: see 1, where two meanings are assigned to it.

5. ‡ الرِّكَابُ تَبَطَّشُ بِأَحْمَالِهَا, [for تَتَبَطَّشُ,] ‡ *The travelling-camels walk with slow steps* (تَزَحَّفُ [for تَتَزَحَّفُ]) *with their burdens, hardly moving.* (Ibn-'Abbád, Z, Ṣgh, Ḳ.)

بَطْشٌ inf. n. of 1 [q. v.]. — Also *Might,* or *strength, in war* or *fight:* or *courage; valour,* or *valiantness; prowess:* syn. بَأْسٌ. (Ḳ.) You say, رَجُلٌ شَدِيدُ البَطْشِ [*A man of great might,* &c.]. (Ḳ,* TA.) — And *Anger.* (Ḥar p. 258.)

البَطْشَةُ *An assault; a violent seizure.* (Ṣ.) البَطْشَةُ الكُبْرَى [*The greatest assault*], in the Ḳur xliv. 15, is applied to the day of resurrection, or to the battle of Bedr. (Bḍ.)

بَطِيشٌ *i. q.* شَدِيدُ البَطْشِ; (Ḳ;) [see بَطْشٌ;] applied to a man; as also † بَطَّاشٌ. (TA.)

بَطَّاشٌ: see بَطِيشٌ.

[مَبْطَشٌ, or مَبْطِشٌ, *A place of assault,* or *the like;* sing. of مَبَاطِشُ, of which the following is an ex.] سَلَكُوا أَرْضًا بَعِيدَةَ المَسَالِكِ قَرِيبَةَ المَهَالِكِ ‡ وَوُقِذُوا بِمَبَاطِشِهَا وَمَا أُنْقِذُوا مِنْ مَعَاطِشِهَا [*They traversed a land whereof the roads were far-extending, whereof the places of destruction were near, and they were prostrated,* or *left sick, in its places of assault, and were not saved from its places of thirst*]. (A, TA.)

بطق

بِطَاقَةٌ *A piece of paper:* (IAạr, M, Ṣgh, TA:) in the Ḳ, الحَدَقَةُ is erroneously put for الوَرَقَةُ: (TA:) *a ticket that is attached to a garment,* or *piece of cloth,* (T, Ṣ, M, L, Ḳ,) *bearing the mark,* or *inscription, of its price;* (T, Ṣ, L, Ḳ;) or *a ticket marked,* or *inscribed, with the weight,* and *the number, of a thing:* (TA:) of the dial. of Egypt (T, Ṣ, L) and the neighbouring parts: (T, L:) so called, (Ḳ,) or said (by Sh, TA) to be so called, (Ṣ,) because it is tied by a twist, or thread, (بِطَاقَة,) of the unwoven end of the cloth: (Ṣ, Ḳ:) but this is a mistake: (ISd, TA:) [in Greek, πιττάκιον, as observed by Freytag; and hence probably derived:] accord. to some, it is [نِطَاقَة,] with ن, because it tells (تَنْطِقُ) what is marked, or inscribed, thereon; but this is strange. (TA.) It is said in a trad., that a man will be brought on the day of resurrection, and ninety-nine scrolls, or records, inscribed with his sins will be produced; and there will be produced for him a بطاقة bearing the testimony that there is no deity but God, and it will outweigh the others. (TA.)

بطل

1. بَطَلَ, (Ṣ, Mṣb, Ḳ,) aor. ـُ, (Ṣ, Mṣb,) inf. n. بُطْلٌ and بُطُولٌ and بُطْلَانٌ, [of which the last seems to be the most common,] (Ṣ, Mṣb, Ḳ, KL, &c.,) *It* (a thing) *was,* or *became,* بَاطِل, as meaning contr. of حَقّ; (Ṣ;) [i. e.,] *it was,* or *became false, untrue, wrong* or *incorrect, fictitious, spurious, unfounded, unsound,* (KL,) *vain, unreal, naught, futile, worthless, useless, unprofitable,* (KL, PṢ,) *devoid of virtue* or *efficacy, ineffectual, null, void, of no force,* or *of no account;* (Mṣb;) *it went for nothing, as a thing of no account,* (Ṣ, Mṣb, Ḳ,) or *as a thing that had perished* or *become lost.* (Ḳ.) [It is said of an assertion or allegation and the like, and of a deed, &c.] Hence the saying in the Ḳur [vii. 115], وَبَطَلَ مَا كَانُوا يَعْمَلُونَ [*And what they were doing became vain,* or *null;* or *went for nothing, as a thing of no account*]. (TA.) And ذَهَبَ دَمُهُ بُطْلًا *His blood went for nothing,* [*unretaliated, and uncompensated by a mulct,*] *as a thing of no account.* (Ṣ, Mṣb.) And بَطَلَ دَمُهُ [signifies the same; or] *He was slain without there being obtained for him either blood-revenge or blood-wit.* (Er-Rághib, TA.) — See also the inf. n. بُطُولٌ below, voce بَطَّالٌ. — بَطَلَ القَوْلُ [*How false, untrue, wrong* or *incorrect,* &c., *is the saying!*] is said in wonder at that which is بَاطِل. (TA.) — بَطَلَ مِنَ العَمَلِ, (Ṣ, Ḳ,) or بَطَلَ, (Mṣb,) aor. ـُ, (TA,) inf. n. بَطَالَةٌ (Ṣ, Mṣb, Ḳ, KL) and بِطَالَةٌ, which is mentioned by one of the expositors of the Mo'allaḳát, and said to be the more chaste, and sometimes one says بُطَالَةٌ, to make it accord with its contr. عُمَالَةٌ, (Mṣb,) *He* (a hired man, or hireling,) *was,* or *became, idle, unoccupied,* or *without work.* (Ṣ, Mṣb,* Ḳ, KL. [See also 5.]) [Hence, يَوْمُ بَطَالَةٍ *A day of idleness; a holiday.*] — بِطَالَةٌ, with kesr, also signifies The *being diverted from that which would bring profit in the present life or in the life to come.* (TA.) — See also 2. — بَطَلَ فِى حَدِيثِهِ, (Ḳ,) aor. ـُ; so it seems to be from the context in the Ḳ, but correctly بَطُلَ, aor. ـُ, as in the Jm; (TA;) inf. n. بَطَالَةٌ (Ḳ) [and app. بُطُولٌ also; see بَطَّالٌ]; *He jested,* or *joked,* or *was not serious* or *in earnest, in his discourse;* as also † ابطل. (Ḳ.) ═ بَطُلَ, aor. ـُ, (Mṣb,) inf. n. بَطَالَةٌ (Ṣ, Mṣb, Ḳ, KL) and بِطَالَةٌ (Lth, Mṣb, TA) and بُطَالَةٌ (TA) and بُطُولَةٌ, (Ṣ, Ḳ, KL,) *He* (a man) *was,* or *became, courageous, brave,* or *strong-hearted, on the occasion of war,* or *fight; such as is termed* بَطَلٌ, q. v.; (Ṣ, Mṣb, Ḳ, KL;) as also † تبطّل: (Ḳ:) or this last signifies *he affected courage,* &c.; *he made himself,* or *constrained himself to be, courageous,* &c.; syn. تَشَجَّعَ. (TA.) — لَبَطُلَ الرَّجُلُ [*How courageous,* &c., *is the man!*] is said in wonder at التَّبَطُّلُ [i. e. courage, &c., or the affecting of courage, &c.]. (TA.)

2. التَّبْطِيلُ [inf. n. of بطّل] signifies † فِعْلُ البِطَالَةِ, [in which the latter word is written in the TA without any indication of the vowel of the ب,] i. e. *The pursuit of vain,* or *frivolous, diversion* or *sport, and foolish,* or *ignorant, conduct.* (TA.) [See بِطَالَةٌ, above, and the phrase next following it.] ═ See also 4.

4. ابطل *He said,* or *spoke, what was false,*

or *untrue;* (Mgh, Mṣb, Ḳ;) [*contr. of* أَحَقَّ;] *he lied:* (Mgh:) *he made a false,* or *vain, claim* or *demand; he claimed,* or *demanded, for himself that which was not right,* or *just.* (Lth, TA.) — See also 1. ═ ابطلهُ [and vulgarly ▼بطّلهُ] *He made it,* or *rendered it,* [and *he proved it to be,*] بَاطِلٌ, i. e. *false, untrue, wrong* or *incorrect, fictitious, spurious, unfounded, unsound, vain, unreal, naught, futile, worthless, useless, unprofitable,* (Ṣ,* L, K, TA,) *devoid of virtue* or *efficacy, ineffectual, null, void, of no force,* or *of no account;* (Mṣb, TA;) *he nullified it, annulled it, abolished it, cancelled it;* whether it was true or false, right or wrong, authentic or spurious, valid or null; (TA;) *he made it to go for nothing, as a thing of no account,* or *as a thing that had perished* or *become lost.* (Ḳ.) Hence, ابطل شَهَادَتَهُ *He annulled his testimony.* (TA in art. زور.) And لِيُحِقَّ الحَقَّ وَيُبْطِلَ البَاطِلَ, in the Ḳur [viii. 8, meaning *That He might establish that which is true, and annul that which is false*]. (TA.)

5. تبطّلوا بَيْنَهُمْ *They took it by turns to say,* or *to do, that which was false, wrong, vain, futile,* or *the like;* syn. تَدَاوَلُوا البَاطِلَ. (Az, Ḳ.) — [تبطّل, said in the Mgh to be from البَطَالَةُ, (see بَطَلَ, or بَطَلَ مِنَ العَمَلِ,) app. signifies, as its part. n. (q. v. voce بَطَّالٌ) indicates, *He became unoccupied and lazy.*] ═ See also 1, near the end of the paragraph.

بُطْلٌ [originally an inf. n. of 1, and mentioned therewith, first sentence:] *i. q.* بَاطِلٌ, q. v. (Ḥam p. 114.)

بَطَلٌ, said to be the only epithet of its measure except حَسَنٌ; (TA in art. حسن;) applied to a man, *Courageous, brave,* or *strong-hearted, on the occasion of war,* or *fight;* [commonly used as a subst., meaning *a man of courage* or *valour, a brave man, a hero;*] (Ṣ, Mṣb, Ḳ;) as also ▼بَطَالٌ; (Ḳ;) one *whose wound goes for nothing, so that he does not care for it,* (Lth, Ḳ,) *and it does not withhold him from the exercise of his courage;* (Lth, TA;) or *the blood of whose adversaries goes for nothing with him,* (Ḳ,) *unrevenged:* (TA:) or for this reason he is thus called; (TA;) or because life is annulled, or made to go for nothing, on the occasion of encountering him, and severe misfortunes are annulled by him, (Mṣb,) or by his sword, and made to be of no account: (TA:) and so ▼بَطَلَةٌ applied to a woman; (Ṣ, Mṣb, Ḳ;) accord. to one of the expositors of the Ḥamáseh; (Mṣb;) but AZ says that this is not allowable: (IDrd, TA:) the pl. of بَطَلٌ is أَبْطَالٌ. (Mṣb, Ḳ.)

بَطَلَةٌ: see بَاطِلٌ: ═ and see also بَطَلٌ.

بَطْلَانٌ One *whose powers have become weak:* but this is a vulgar word. (TA.)

بُطْلَاتٌ (pl. of بُطْلٌ, TA) *False,* or *vain, things;* or *unprofitable sayings.* (Ibn-'Abbád, Ḳ.) You say, جَآءَ بِالبُطْلَاتِ *He uttered false,* or *vain things;* &c. (El-Moḥeeṭ, TA.)

بَطَّالٌ, applied to a man, signifies ذُو بَاطِلٍ بَيِّنُ ▼البُطُولِ [app. meaning *Having a vain,* or *false, object* or *pursuit; manifesting the having such an object* or *pursuit:* or, accord. to an explanation of ذو باطل by Bḍ in xxxviii. 26, *i. q.* مُبْطِلٌ and عَابِثٌ, i. e. *jesting,* or *joking;* (see بَطَلَ فِى حَدِيثِهِ, or بَطَلَ;) or *saying what is untrue:* and *playing,* or *sporting,* and *doing that in which is no profit;* as also ▼بَاطِلٌ, q. v.:] (Ḳ:) one *who jests,* or *jokes, in his discourse:* one *who is diverted from that which would bring profit in the present life or in that which is to come:* (TA:) *idle; unoccupied:* (Ṣ, Mṣb:) or *exceedingly,* or *extremely, idle:* (KL:) or *unoccupied and lazy;* as also ▼مُتَبَطِّلٌ. (Mgh.) [In the present day it is commonly used as signifying *Bad, worthless,* and *useless;* applied to a man and to anything.] ═ See also بَطَلٌ.

بَاطِلٌ *contr. of* حَقٌّ; (Ṣ, Ḳ;) i. e. *False, untrue, wrong* or *incorrect, fictitious, spurious, unfounded, unsound,* (KL,) *vain, unreal, naught, futile, worthless, useless, unprofitable,* (KL, PṢ,) *devoid of virtue* or *efficacy, ineffectual, null, void, of no force,* or *of no effect;* (Mṣb;) *that proves, when inquired into,* or *investigated, to be false, wrong, unfounded, unsound,* or *not established;* applying to a saying, and [sometimes] to a deed: (TA:) [*going for nothing, as a thing of no account,* or *as a thing that has perished* or *become lost:* (see the verb, 1, first sentence:) often used as a subst., meaning *a false,* or *vain, saying,* or *assertion,* or *allegation; a lie; a falsehood:* and *a false,* or *vain, deed,* or *action,* or *affair,* or *thing;* &c.:] and ▼بُطْلٌ is syn. therewith, (Ḥam p. 114,) and so are ▼أُبْطُولَةٌ and ▼إِبْطَالَةٌ: (Ḳ:) the *pl. of بَاطِلٌ is بَوَاطِلُ; (Mṣb;) and بُطُلٌ occurs as a pl. of the same; (Ḥam p. 360;) or its pl. is أَبَاطِيلُ, contr. to analogy, (Ṣ, Mṣb,) as though the sing. were إِبْطِيلٌ; (Ṣ;) or, accord. to AḤát, this is pl. of ▼أُبْطُولَةٌ, or, as some say, of ▼إِبْطَالَةٌ, (Mṣb,) or, accord. to Aṣ and AḤát and IDrd, of both these; (TA;) and signifies *false,* or *vain, sayings* and *actions* or *deeds.* (Ḳ in art. هتر, &c.) You say, قَدْ قُلْتَ بَاطِلًا [*Thou hast said a false,* or *vain, saying; a lie; a falsehood*]; like as you say, قَدْ قُلْتَ حَقًّا. (Ḥam p. 360.) And يَأْكُلُونَ أَمْوَالَ النَّاسِ بِالبَاطِلِ [*They devour the possessions of men by false pretence*]. (Ḳur ix. 34.) And بَيْنَهُمْ ▼أُبْطُولَةٌ and ▼إِبْطَالَةٌ [*Between them is false, or vain, speech, or discourse, &c.*]; syn. بَاطِلٌ. (Ḳ.) — The *belief in a plurality of Gods:* so explained as occurring in the Ḳur xlii. 23. (TA.) — See also بَطَّالٌ, in two places. [Hence,] بَاطِلًا *In play,* or *sport; acting unprofitably;* or *aiming at no profit.* (Jel in iii. 188 and xxxviii. 26.) — البَاطِلُ *Iblees:* so in the Ḳur [xxxiv. 48], where it is said, مَا يُبْدِئُ ٱلْبَاطِلُ وَمَا يُعِيدُ [explained in art. بدأ]: (Ḳatádeh, Ḳ:) and again [xli. 42], where it is said, لَا يَأْتِيهِ ٱلْبَاطِلُ مِنْ بَيْنِ يَدَيْهِ وَلَا مِنْ خَلْفِهِ, [accord. to some,] meaning that Iblees shall not add to the Ḳur-án nor diminish therefrom: (TA:) ▼بَطَلَةٌ [is its pl., and] signifies *devils:* (A, TA:) or *enchanters.* (O, Ḳ.)

إِبْطَالَةٌ: } see بَاطِلٌ; for each in three places.
أُبْطُولَةٌ: }

مُبْطِلٌ One *who says a thing in which is no truth,* or *reality:* (Er-Rághib, TA:) one *who embellishes speech with lies:* (Bḍ in xxx. 58:) one *who says,* or *does, false,* or *vain, things.* (Jel ibid.) [See also its verb, 4.]

مُتَبَطِّلٌ: see بَطَّالٌ.

بطم

بُطْمٌ (Ṣ, Ḳ) and بُطُمٌ, (Ḳ,) the latter allowable accord. to IAạr, (TA,) The حَبَّةٌ خَضْرَآءُ [or *fruit of the terebinth-tree,* to which this latter appellation is given in the present day, i. e., *of the pistacia terebinthus of the botanists*]; (Ṣ, Ḳ;) so accord. to the people of El-'Áliyeh; and the like is said on the authority of Aṣ: (TA:) or the *tree thereof;* (Ḳ;) [which is called بُطْم in the present day;] so accord. to AḤn; and he says, but no one has told me that it grows in the land of the Arabs; but they assert that *the* ضِرْو [meaning the *cancamum-tree,* also called كَمْكَام, but said by IAạr to be the حَبَّة خضراء,] *is nearly like it:* (TA:) *its fruit is heating, diuretic, strengthening to the venereal faculty, good for the cough, and for the* [*disease of the face called*] لَقْوَة, *and for the kidney; and the overspreading of the hair with its dry and sifted leaves causes it to grow, and beautifies it.* (Ḳ.)

بطن

1. بَطَنَ, aor. ـُ, (Ḳ,) inf. n. بَطَانَةٌ, (TA,) *He* (a man) *was,* or *became, big,* or *large, in the belly,* (Ḳ, TA,) *in consequence of much eating.* (TA.) — And بَطِنَ, aor. ـَ, inf. n. بَطَنٌ, *He* (a man) *was,* or *became, big,* or *large, in the belly, in consequence of satiety,* (Ṣ, TA,) *and disordered therein:* (TA:) *he was,* or *became, in a state of repletion,* or *much filled with food.* (TA.) — And [hence,] بَطِنَ signifies also ‡ *i. q.* أَشِرَ and بَطِرَ [*He exulted,* or *exulted greatly,* or *excessively, and behaved insolently and unthankfully,* or *ungratefully:* &c.]. (TA.) — بُطِنَ *He* (a man, Ṣ, TA) *had a complaint of,* or *a disease in,* or *a pain in, his belly.* (Ṣ, Mṣb, TA.) ═ بَطَنَهُ, (Ṣ, Ḳ,) aor. ـُ, (Ṣ, TA,) inf. n. بَطْنٌ, (TA,) *He struck,* or *beat, his belly;* as also بَطَنَ لَهُ, (Ṣ, Ḳ,) accord. to some, or the ل is added [only] in verse; (Ṣ;) and ▼بطّنهُ, (Ḳ,) inf. n. تَبْطِينٌ. (TA.) — *It* (a disease) *entered into him:* [as though it penetrated into his belly: see 10:] in this sense it has for its inf. n. بُطُونٌ. (TA.) And بَطَنَتْ بِهِ الحُمَّى *The fever produced an effect within him.* (TA.) — *He entered into it;* namely, a valley; (Ṣ, TA;) in which sense it has for its inf. n. بُطُونٌ; and ▼تبطّنهُ signifies the same: or the latter, *he went about in it;* namely, the valley; as also ▼استبطنهُ. (TA.) — ‡ [*He penetrated into it mentally;*] *he knew it;* (Mṣb, Ḳ, TA;) namely, the news or story, or the state or case, of another: (Ḳ, TA:) ‡ *he knew the inward,* or *intrinsic, state or circumstances thereof;* (Ṣ, Mṣb, TA;) i. e., of a case, or an affair; (Ṣ,

TA;) as also ♦استبطنهُ: (Ḳ, A, TA:) and ♦تبطّنهُ † *he entered into it so that he knew its inward, or intrinsic, state or circumstances.* (Ḥam p. 688.) — بَطَنَ بِفُلَانٍ, accord. to the Ṣ and M, but in the Ḳ مِنْ فُلَانٍ, (TA,) ‡ *He became one of his particular, or special, intimates, friends, or associates,* (Ṣ, Ḳ, TA,) *entering into his affair* [or *affairs*]: (TA:) or بَطَنَ بِهِ, aor. ـُ, inf. n. بُطُونٌ and بِطَانَةٌ, means † *he entered into his affair* [or *affairs*]. (TA.) — And بَطَنَ, (Mṣb, Ḳ,) aor. ـُ, said of a thing, (Mṣb,) *It was,* or *became, unapparent, hidden, concealed,* or *covert;* (Ḳ, TA;) *contr. of* ظَهَرَ. (Mṣb.) — See also 4.

2. بطّنهُ, inf. n. تَبْطِينٌ: see 1. — See also 4. — *He put a* بِطَانَة, i. e. a *lining, to it;* namely, a garment, or piece of cloth; (Ṣ, Ḳ;) as also ♦ابطنهُ. (Ḳ.) — بطّن لِحْيَتَهُ, inf. n. as above, *He took,* or *cut off, from that part of his beard which was beneath the chin and lower jaw.* (Sh, Nh, TA.) Accord. to the copies of the Ḳ, تَبْطِينُ اللِّحْيَةِ signifies the *not* doing so: but this is wrong. (TA.)

3. بَاطَنْتُ صَاحِبِى i. q. شددته [app. a mistranscription for شَاوَرْتُهُ, meaning † *I consulted with my companion in order to know what was in his mind*]. (TA.)

4. ابطن البَعِيرَ, (IAạr, Ṣ, Ḳ,) inf. n. إِبْطَانٌ, (Ṣ,) *He bound,* or *made fast, the camel's* بِطَان [or *belly-girth*]; (Ṣ, Ḳ;) as also ♦بطّنهُ, accord. to the copies of the Ḳ; but this is a mistake for ♦بَطَنَهُ, aor. ـُ, inf. n. بَطْنٌ; which last verb, however, though said by Az to be a dial. var., is disallowed by IAạr and by AHeyth. (TA.) — أَبْطَنْتُ السَّيْفَ كَشْحِى (Ṣ, TA) *I put the sword beneath my waist.* (TA.) And ابطن كَشْحَهُ سَيْفَهُ † *He made his sword to be his* ♦بطانة [app. meaning his *secret companion*]. (TA.) [This seems to be from the phrase next following.] — أَبْطَنْتُ الرَّجُلَ † *I made the man to be one of my particular,* or *special, intimates, friends,* or *associates;* (Ṣ, TA;*) *took him as a* بِطَانَة. (TA.) One says also, ♦اِسْتَبْطَنْتُ فُلَانًا دُونَكَ, (Ḥam p. 688; [there rendered by خاصصته, app. a mistranscription for خَصَصْتُهُ;] meaning † *I took,* or *chose, such a one particularly,* or *specially, for my companion, in preference to thee:* it is said in explanation of the phrase مُسْتَبْطِنًا سَيْفِى, which seems to mean † *taking my sword as my special companion,* or *putting it beneath my waist;* so that ♦استبطن سَيْفَهُ is similar to one, or both, of two phrases mentioned above in this paragraph.]) — See also 2.

5. تبطّن *He filled the* [meaning *his*] *belly.* (Ḥar p. 176.) — تبطّن جَارِيَةً (Sh, Ṣ, TA) *He made his* بَطْن *to be in contact with that of a girl, skin to skin:* (Sh, TA:) or *inivit puellam;* i. e. أَوْلَجَ ذَكَرَهُ فِيهَا. (TA.) — تبطّن الكَلَأَ *He was,* or *became, in the middle,* or *midst, of the herbage:* (TA:) or *he went round about in the herbage.* (Ṣ.) See also 1, in two places.

6. تباطن *It* (a place) *was far-extending; one part thereof being remote from another.* (TA.)

8. ابْتَطَنْتُ النَّاقَةَ عَشَرَةَ أَبْطُنٍ *I assisted the she-camel in bringing forth,* or *delivered her of her young, ten times.* (Ṣ, TA. [Golius and Freytag render the verb by "ventre enixa fuit:" and the former renders the phrase above (incorrectly printed in his Lex.) by "peperit camela decem vicibus."])

10. استبطن الفَرَسَ *He sought to find what young was in the belly of the mare.* (TA.) — استبطن الفَحْلُ الشُّوَّلَ *The stallion covered the she-camels raising their tails, so that they conceived,* or *received his seed into their wombs;* as though [meaning] *he deposited his seed in their bellies.* (TA.) — استبطنهُ *He,* or *it, entered* [or *penetrated*] *into his,* or *its, belly,* or *interior;* [or *was,* or *became,* or *lay, within it;*] *like as the vein enters* [or *penetrates*] *into* [or *lies within*] (يَسْتَبْطِنُ) *the flesh.* (A, TA.) You say, اِسْتَبْطَنْتُ الشَّىْءَ [*I entered,* or *penetrated, into the thing,* whether *actually* or *mentally*]. (Ṣ.) See 1, in two places. — See also 4, in two places. — اِسْتِبْطَانٌ also signifies The *having,* or *holding,* [a thing] *concealed within.* (PṢ.) [This explanation seems to be given to show that, in the opinion of the author of the PṢ, اِسْتَبْطَنْتُ الشَّىْءَ in the Ṣ means *I had,* or *held, the thing concealed within.*]

بَطْنٌ The *belly,* or *abdomen;* i. e. the *part of the body which is separated from the* جَوْف [i. e. *chest,* or *thorax,*] *by the* حِجَاب [i. e. *midriff,* or *diaphragm*]; *containing the liver and the spleen and the stomach and the lower intestines &c.;* (Zj in his "Khalḳ el-Insán;" [in which it is erroneously said to comprise also the lungs;]) *contr. of* ظَهْر; (Ṣ, Mṣb, Ḳ;) of a man and of any animal: (TA:) of the masc. gender, (Ṣ, Ḳ,) and, accord. to AO, fem. also: (AḤát, Ṣ:) pl. أَبْطُنٌ and بُطُونٌ (Az, Mṣb, Ḳ) and بُطْنَانٌ; (Ḳ;) the first a pl. of pauc.; and the second [as also the third] a pl. of mult., applied to more than ten. (Az, TA.) [Hence,] ذُو البَطْنِ [*What is in the belly:* but generally meaning] *excrement, ordure,* or *dung.* (Ḳ, TA.) You say, أَلْقَى ذَا بَطْنِهِ *He* (a man) *ejected his excrement,* or *ordure.* (TA.) And أَلْقَتْ ذَا بَطْنِهَا *She* (a woman, TA) *brought forth;* (Ḳ;) as also وَضَعَتْ ذَاتَ بَطْنِهَا: (TA in art. ذو:) and *she* (a hen) *laid an egg.* (Ḳ.) And نَثَرَتْ ذَا بَطْنِهَا, (T and Mgh in art. نثر,) and [elliptically] نَثَرَتْ بَطْنَهَا, (T and A and Mgh in that art.,) *She* (a woman) *brought forth many children.* (T in that art.) And it is said in a prov., (TA,) الذِّئْبُ يُغْبَطُ بِذِى بَطْنِهِ [*The wolf is envied for what is in his belly*]: for one never thinks him to be hungry, but only thinks him to be in a state of repletion, because of his hostility to men and cattle, (A'Obeyd, Ḳ,) though he is sometimes distressed by hunger. (A'Obeyd. [See various readings of this prov. in Freytag's Arab. Prov. i. 500 and 501.]) مَاتَتْ فِى بَطْنٍ, a phrase occurring in a trad., means *She* (a woman) *died in childbirth.* (TA.) See also بَطِن. فُلَانٌ اَبْنُ بَطْنِهِ means † *Such a one is solicitous for his belly.* (Er-Rághib, TA in art. بنى.) [Many phrases in which the word بَطْن occurs will be found explained under other words of those phrases; as ظَهْر, and أَخَذَ, and عُصْفُور, &c.] بَطْنُ الحُوتِ: see الرِّشَاءُ. — Also The *inside,* or *interior,* of anything; syn. جَوْف: and so ♦بَاطِنٌ; syn. دَاخِلٌ: (Ḳ:) pl. of the former as above. (TA.) Thus بَطْنُ وَادٍ means *The interior of a water-course* or *river-bed* [or *valley;* i. e. *its bottom, in which flows, occasionally* or *constantly, its torrent* or *river*]. (MA.) And بَطْنُ مَكَّةَ means *The interior of Mekkeh.* (Bḍ in xlviii. 24.) [Hence,] it is said of the Ḳur-án, لِكُلِّ آيَةٍ مِنْهَا ظَهْرٌ وَبَطْنٌ, meaning † *To every verse thereof is an apparent sense and a sense requiring development.* (TA.) [See ظَهْر.] See also بَاطِنٌ. [And its pl. بُطْنَانٌ is also used as a sing., meaning The *middle,* or *midst,* of a thing: and the *lower,* or *lowest, part,* or the *foundation.* Thus,] بُطْنَانُ الجَنَّةِ means *The middle,* or *midst, of Paradise:* (Ṣ, TA:) and بُطْنَانُ العَرْشِ, *The lower,* or *lowest, part,* or *the foundation, of the* عرش [vulgarly held to be the *throne of God*]. (TA.) You say also [بَطْنُ الكَفِّ and] ♦بَاطِنُ الكَفِّ † *The palm of the hand* [opposed to ظَهْرُهَا and ظَاهِرُهَا]: and [بَطْنُ القَدَمِ and] ♦بَاطِنُ القَدَمِ † *The sole of the foot* [likewise opposed to ظَهْرُهَا and ظَاهِرُهَا]: (Zj in his "Khalḳ-el-Insán:") and بَطْنُ الحَافِرِ (Ṣ in art. نسر) and ♦بَاطِنُ الحَافِرِ (M and Ḳ in that art.) † [*The sole of the solid hoof;*] *the part of the solid hoof in which is the* نَسْر, q. v. (Ṣ and M and Ḳ in that art.) بَطْنُ الرَّاحَةِ is well known [as another name for بَطْنُ الكَفِّ, explained above; for الرَّاحَة is often used as syn. with الكَفّ]: and ♦بَاطِنُ الخُفِّ is [said to be] † *The part of the foot of a camel or the like that is next the leg:* and one says, ♦بَاطِنُ الإِبْطِ, [meaning † *The armpit,* or *hollow of the inner side of the shoulder-joint,*] but not بَطْنُ الإِبْطِ: (TA:) [and ♦بَاطِنُ العُنُقِ *the throat.*] The بَطْن of a feather is ‡ The *long,* (Ṣ,) or *longer,* (Ḳ,) [or *wider,* i. e. *inner,*] *lateral half:* pl. بُطْنَانٌ; (Ṣ, Ḳ, TA;) which is explained as signifying the *parts beneath the shaft:* opposed to ظُهْرَانٌ, pl. of ظَهْر [q. v.]. (TA.) — Also *A low,* or *depressed, tract,* or *portion,* of land, or ground; (Ṣ, TA;) and so ♦بَاطِنٌ: (TA:) [or *a bottom,* or *low land;* or *a low, soft flat;* i. e.] *soft, plain, fine, low land* or *ground;* opposed to ظَهْر [q. v.]: (TA in art. ظهر:) pl. of the former, (Ṣ,) or of the latter, (Ḳ,) بُطْنَانٌ, (Ṣ, Ḳ,) a pl. of mult., (TA,) and أَبْطِنَةٌ, (Ḳ,) a pl. of pauc., and anomalous [as pl. of either]: (TA:) the former pl., in relation to land, is also used as a sing., like بَطْن: (AḤn, TA:) and accord. to ISh, بُطْنَانُ الأَرْضِ signifies *the low,* or *depressed, tract,* or *tracts, of land, of the plain,* or *soft, parts thereof, and of the rugged, and of the meadows, where water rests and stagnates:* and such tracts are also called بَوَاطِنُ and بُطُونٌ. (TA.) — بَطْنُ السَّمَآءِ and ظَهْرُ السَّمَآءِ both signify † *The apparent, visible, part of the sky.* (Fr, T voce ظَهْر [q. v.].) — Also

‡ *A tribe below that which is termed* قَبِيلَة: (Ṣ, Mṣb, Ḳ, TA:) or *next below the* عِمَارَة: (Ṣ and TA voce شَعْب, &c.:) or *below the* فَخِذ *and above the* عِمَارَة: (Ḳ: [but for this I have found no other authority:]) of the masc. gender: (TA:) or [properly] fem.: but if حَىّ [said by some to signify *a tribe*, absolutely,] be meant thereby, it is masc.: (Mṣb:) or fem. if used in the sense of قَبِيلَة: (TA:) pl. [of pauc.] أَبْطُنٌ and [of mult.] بُطُونٌ. (Mṣb, Ḳ.) [See شَعْب.]

بَطَنٌ *Disease of the belly,* (Ḳ, TA,) *being a state of enlargement thereof arising from satiety;* and so ▾بُطْنٌ; whence the phrase مَاتَ بِالبَطَنِ *He died by the disease of the belly.* (TA.)

بَطِنٌ One *whose object of care,* or *anxiety, is his belly:* (Ḳ:) or *who has an inordinate desire,* or *appetite, for food;* (Ṣ;) *whom nothing causes care,* or *anxiety, but his belly;* (Ṣ, TA;) as also ▾مِبْطَانٌ: (TA:) or the former, (TA,) or ▾the latter, (Ṣ,) *ever large,* or *big, in the belly in consequence of much eating:* (Ṣ, TA:) or ▾both signify *voracious; not ceasing from eating.* (Ḳ.) — And [hence,] ‡ One *who exults,* or *exults greatly,* or *excessively, and behaves insolently and unthankfully,* or *ungratefully:* (TA:) or *who does so, being abundant in wealth.* (Ḳ, TA.)

بِطْنَةٌ *Repletion;* the *state of being much filled with food* (Ṣ, Ḳ) *and drink.* (So in a copy of the Ṣ.) It is said in a prov., البِطْنَةُ تُذْهِبُ الفِطْنَةَ [*Repletion banishes intelligence*]. (TA.) — And [hence,] ‡ *Exultation,* or *great or excessive exultation, and insolent and unthankful,* or *ungrateful, behaviour.* (Ḳ, TA.) — [Hence also,] مَاتَ فُلَانٌ بِبِطْنَتِهِ †*Such a one died with his wealth complete, not having expended,* or *dispensed, anything thereof:* or, accord. to A'Obeyd, this prov. relates to religion, and means † *he went forth from the present world in a state of integrity, without any infringement of his religion.* (TA.) [See also تَغَضْغَضَ, in two places.] [Hence also,] نَزَتْ بِهِ البِطْنَةُ †*Richness caused him to exult,* or *exult greatly,* or *excessively, and to behave insolently and unthankfully,* or *ungratefully.* (TA.)

البَطْنَةُ *i. q.* الدُّبُرُ [*The back, hinder part, posteriors, &c.*]. (TA.) — بَطِنَاتُ الوَادِى *The roads,* or *beaten tracks, of the valley.* (TA.)

بِطَانٌ [The *belly-girth* of a camel: or] the *girth of the* [*kind of saddle called*] قَتَب, (Ṣ, Ḳ,) *which is put beneath the belly of the camel, and is like the* تَصْدِير *to the* رَحْل: (Ṣ:) or the *girth of the* [*saddle called*] رَحْل: (Mṣb:) pl. [of pauc.] أَبْطِنَةٌ and [of mult.] بُطُنٌ. (Ḳ.) [Hence,] الْتَقَتْ حَلْقَتَا البِطَانِ [*The two rings of the belly-girth met*]: said of a case, or an affair, that has become severe, strait, or distressing. (Ṣ.) And رَجُلٌ عَرِيضُ البِطَانِ ‡ *A man in ample and easy circumstances;* or *in an easy,* or *a pleasant, state* or *condition;* or *easy,* or *unstraitened, in mind.* (Ḳ, TA. [See also art. عرض.]) And مَاتَ فُلَانٌ وَهُوَ عَرِيضُ البِطَانِ, meaning, accord. to A'Obeyd, †*Such a one died broad in the fleshy parts* (المَلَاحِمِ); *nothing of him having gone.* (TA. [But this seems to be said of a man's dying in a state of opulence: see Freytag's Arab. Prov. ii. 601.])

بَطِينٌ, applied to a man, (Ḳ,) *Big,* or *large, in the belly;* (Ṣ, Ḳ;) as also ▾مِبْطَانٌ: the former occurs, in a description of 'Alee, used as an epithet of praise: and signifies also *big,* or *large, in the belly in consequence of much eating:* and *having the belly full;* as also ▾the latter: pl. of the former بِطَانٌ. (TA.) — Hence, ‡ *Full;* applied to a purse [&c.]. (TA.) You say رَجُلٌ بَطِينُ الكُرْزِ † [lit. *A man having the pair of provision-bags full*]; meaning † *a man who conceals his travelling-provision in a journey, and eats that of his companion.* (TA.) — †*Far; far-extending.* (Ṣ, Ḳ, TA.) So in the phrase شَأْوٌ بَطِينٌ † [*A far-extending heat,* or *single run to a goal* or *limit*], (Ṣ, TA,) and شَوْطٌ بَطِينٌ [signifying the same]. (TA.) — † *Wide, and low,* or *depressed;* applied to a tract of land or ground. (Ḥam p. 506.)

البُطَيْنُ *One of the Mansions of the Moon;* (Ṣ, Ḳ;) namely, *the Second;* (Ḳzw, &c.;) *three small stars* [ε and π and ν], (Ṣ, Ḳ,) *disposed in the form of an equilateral triangle,* (Ṣ,) *as though they were three stones whereon a cooking-pot is placed, and forming the belly of the Ram;* (Ṣ, Ḳ;) the appellation being made a diminutive because the Ram consists of many stars in the form of a ram; [so I here render حَمَل though it properly signifies a lamb;] the شَرَطَانِ being its two horns; and the بُطَيْن, its belly; [or, accord. to our configuration of Aries, the rump;] and the ثُرَيَّا, its rump, or tail; (Ṣ;) *three obscure stars, forming the points of a triangle, in the belly of the Ram, between the* شَرَطَانِ *and the* ثُرَيَّا; (Ḳzw, Mir-át ez-Zemán, &c.;) *the three stars of which two are on the tail and one on the thigh of the Ram, forming an equilateral triangle.* (Ḳzw in his description of Aries.) [See مَنَازِلُ القَمَرِ, in art. نزل.] The Arabs assert that it has no نَوْء [here meaning effect upon the weather], except wind. (TA.)

بِطَانَةٌ The *lining,* or *inner covering,* of a garment, or piece of cloth [&c.]; *contr. of* ظِهَارَةٌ; (Ṣ, Mṣb, Ḳ;) as also ▾بَاطِنَةٌ: (JK in art. ظهر:) pl. of the former بَطَائِنُ. (TA.) — †*A secret* (Ḳ, TA) *that a man conceals.* (TA.) One says, هُوَ ذُو بِطَانَةٍ بِفُلَانٍ, i. e. †*He is one who possesses knowledge of the inward,* or *intrinsic, state* or *circumstances of the case,* or *affair, of such a one.* (TA.) — ‡ *A particular,* or *special, intimate, friend,* or *associate;* (Ṣ, Ḳ, TA;) *one who is particularly distinguished by entering into, and becoming acquainted with, the inward,* or *intrinsic, state* or *circumstances of one's case* or *affair;* (TA;) *an intimate and familiar friend* or *associate;* (Zj, TA;) *a confidential friend, who is consulted respecting one's circumstances:* (TA:) it is from the same word in the sense first explained above, relating to a garment, or piece of cloth: (Mgh, Er-Rághib:) and is used in a pl. sense, as meaning *intimate and familiar friends* or *associates, to whom one is open,* or *unreserved, in conversation, and who know the inward state* or *circumstances* [*of one's case* or *affair*]: (Zj, TA:) or one's *family;* and one's *particular,* or *special, intimates, friends,* or *associates.* (Mgh.) You say, هُوَ بِطَانَتِى ‡ [*He is my particular,* or *special, intimate, &c.*]: and هُمْ بِطَانَتِى and أَهْلُ بِطَانَتِى ‡ [*They are my particular,* or *special, intimates, &c.*]. (A, TA.) See also 4. — Coupled with عِلَاوَة, it signifies *What is put beneath* [*the things that compose the main load of a camel*], *such as a water-skin and the like.* (TA.) — See also بَاطِنَةٌ.

بَاطِنٌ *Unapparent; hidden; concealed; covert:* (Ḳ, TA:) [and *inward; inner; interior; internal; intrinsic; esoteric:* in all these senses] *contr. of* ظَاهِرٌ. (Mṣb, TA.) — بَاطِنُ أَمْرٍ [*The inward,* or *intrinsic, state* or *circumstances, of a case* or *an affair*]; (TA, &c.;) [and so ▾بَطْنُ أَمْرٍ; whence the phrases,] أَفْرَشَنِى ظَهْرَ أَمْرِهِ وَبَطْنَهُ † [*He displayed,* or *laid open, to me the outward state* or *circumstances of his case* or *affair, and the inward state* or *circumstances thereof*]; and هُوَ مُجَرِّبٌ بَطْنَ الأُمُورِ † [*He is one who possesses experience of the inward,* or *intrinsic, state* or *circumstances of affairs*], as though he hit their bellies by his knowledge of their true, or real, states or circumstances. (TA.) — البَاطِنُ [*The internal, inward,* or *intrinsic, state, condition, character,* or *circumstances,* of a man: and *the heart,* meaning *the secret thoughts; the recesses of the mind; the state of mind; the inward,* or *secret, disposition of the mind:* opposed to الظَّاهِرُ. — Also,] an epithet applied to God, meaning *He who knows the inward,* or *intrinsic, states* or *circumstances of things:* (Ṣ:) or *He who knows the secret and hidden things:* or *He who is veiled from the eyes and imaginations of created beings.* (TA.) — [بَاطِنًا *Covertly; secretly.*] — See also بَطْنٌ, in eight places. — بَاطِنٌ also signifies *A water-course,* or *place in which water flows, in rugged ground:* pl. بُطْنَانٌ (Ḳ) and بُطُنٌ. (TA.)

بَاطِنَةٌ: see بِطَانَةٌ. — Also The *middle,* and the *retired part,* of a كُورَة [i. e. province, or district, or city]: in the copies of the Ḳ erroneously written ▾بِطَانَة, and explained as meaning the "middle of a كُورَة." (TA.)

الأَبْطَنُ *A certain vein in the interior of the arm of the horse; one of two veins which are called* الأَبْطَنَانِ: (Ṣ:) accord. to AO, these are *two veins that penetrate into the interior of the arm until they become hidden among the sinews of the shank.* (TA.)

مُبَطَّنٌ, applied to a man, *Lank in the belly:* (Ṣ, Ḳ, TA:) fem. with ة. (Ṣ.) — Applied to a horse, *White in the back and belly.* (Ḳ.) — *Lined; having a* بِطَانَة *put to it.* (TA.)

مِبْطَانٌ: see بَطِينٌ, in two places: and see بَطِنٌ, in three places.

مَبْطُونٌ *Having a complaint of,* or *a disease in,* or *a pain in, his belly:* (Ṣ, Mgh, Mṣb, Ḳ:) one *who dies of disease of his belly, as dropsy and the like:* such is reckoned a martyr. (TA.)

بطو or بطى

1. بَطَا, aor. يَبْطُو, is said by Z and Meyd to signify *He, or it, was,* or *became, wide:* and hence بَاطِيَةٌ, meaning a نَاجُود. (TA.)

4: see what next follows.

بِطْيَةٌ, with kesr, is a word mentioned by Sb; (Ḳ;) but ISd says, "I know not to what it is applied, unless ↓ أَبْطَيْتُ be a dial. var. of أَبْطَأْتُ, (Ḳ, TA,) like as اِحْبَنْطَيْتُ is of اِحْبَنْطَأْتُ; in which case it is thence derived as meaning The *state* [*of being slow, &c.*]; and is not to be regarded as formed by substitution [of ى for ء], because that would be extr.:" so in the M: (TA:) it is asserted, however, in the Ṣ and the Fṣ and the Jámi' el-Loghah of Ḳz and in other lexicons, that one should not say, ابطيت, with ى, but ابطأت, with ء. (MF, TA.)

بَاطٍ part. n. of بَطَا, mentioned above, accord. to Z and Meyd. (TA.)

بَاطِيَةٌ *A certain vessel;* (Ṣ;) *a* نَاجُود [or *vessel into which wine is put*]; (AA, Ṣ, Mgh, Ḳ;) *a large vessel of glass, which is filled with wine, or beverage, and placed amid the drinkers, who ladle out from it* [*into their cups*], (Az, Mgh, TA,) *and drink:* (Az, TA:) [*a wine-vase, of glass* or *of earthenware; an amphora; an earthen jar;* now applied to *a vessel of this kind into which wine and oil &c. are put:*] said to be an arabicized word: (TA:) [J says,] "I think it to be arabicized:" (Ṣ:) but accord. to Z and Meyd, it is from 1, as mentioned above. (TA.)

بظر

1. بَظِرَتْ, [aor. ـَ, inf. n. بَظَرٌ,] said of a woman, [*She had a* بَظْر (q. v.), or *a long* بظر; or] *she was uncircumcised.* (Mṣb.) [But see بَظْرٌ, below.] —— And بَظِرَ, inf. n. بَظَرٌ, *He had what is termed a* بُظَارَة [q. v.] *in his upper lip.* (Ṣ.)

2. بَظَّرَتْ, inf. n. تَبْظِيرٌ, *She circumcised* a female. (Ḳ.) —— هُوَ يُمِصُّهُ وَيُبَظِّرُهُ (M, Ḳ) *He says to him,* أُمْصُصْ بَظْرَ فُلَانَةَ: (Ḳ:) a prov. of the Arabs. (TA.)

بَظْرٌ, (Lḥ, T, Ṣ, M, &c.,) also pronounced بَضْرٌ, (T,) and ↓ بُظَارَةٌ [which see below] (Lḥ, T, Ṣ, M, Ḳ) and ↓ بَظَارَةٌ (M, Ḳ) and ↓ بَيْظَرٌ (Lḥ, T, M, Ḳ) and ↓ بُنْظُرٌ, (Ḳ,) *A certain thing,* (Ṣ, M, Mgh, Ḳ,) or *piece of flesh,* (A,) *between the two sides of the vulva* (الإِسْكَتَانِ, Ṣ, M, Ḳ, or الشُّفْرَانِ, A, or شُفْرَا الفَرْجِ, Mgh) *of a woman,* (M, A, Mgh, Ḳ,) *which is cut off in circumcision,* (A,) *not yet cut off;* (Ṣ;) *a piece of flesh between the two sides of the vulva* (الشُّفْرَانِ) *of a woman;* i. e. the *prepuce* (قُلْفَة) *that is cut off in circumcision;* (Mṣb;) *also called* عُنْبُل and رَفْرَف and نَوْف (Lḥ, T) *and* قُنْب [which last properly signifies the "prepuce," or "sheath," of a beast or horse or the like]; (A and Ḳ in art. قنب;) *and likened to a cock's comb:* (Mṣb in art. عرف:) [the last of these explanations plainly shows that what is meant thereby is the *prepuce of the clitoris;* which, it seems, in the Arabian and Egyptian races, and others throughout Eastern Africa, and still more so in the Hottentot race, grows to an extraordinary size; and this may be the reason why the بظر is described by some travellers as a caruncle for which we have no name: or it may, perhaps, be *a distinct excrescence from the prepuce of the clitoris:* it has been described to me as *a caruncle a little in front of the meatus urinarius:* many of the Egyptians assert that it is the *clitoris itself* that is amputated, (as Ludolph also does in his Comment. to his Ethiop. Hist. p. 273, finding fault with those who say otherwise;) and they affirm that this is done for the purpose of lessening the libidinous passion: such, indeed, appears to be the case in some instances, but not generally; and it may have led to a misapplication of the term بظر in post-classical times: an analogous practice, one still more barbarous, is said to have obtained among an African race hence called the Colobi: see بُرْبُرٌ: Abu-l-Ḳásim Ez-Zahráwee speaks of the amputation of the redundance of the بظر when preternaturally large, and also of an excrescence in the vulva: the former he describes in such a manner as plainly shows that he means thereby the *clitoris:* the latter, in terms apparently indicating a preternatural elongation of the lower part of the prepuce of the clitoris; as "an excrescence of flesh at, or in, the mouth of the vulva, such as fills it up, and sometimes protrudes externally, like a tail, wherefore the ancients term it the caudal disease (المرض الذنبى); and this," he says, "should be amputated, like as the بظر is amputated" when preternaturally large: (Albucasis de Chirurgia, pp. 314 and 316:) in some of our medical books, the term "caudatio" is defined as "an elongation of the clitoris;" inconsistently with the foregoing description of "the caudal disease:"] the pl. [of mult.] of بَظْر is بُظُورٌ, (M, Mṣb, Ḳ,) and [pl. of pauc.] أَبْظُرٌ. (Mṣb.) يَا ٱبْنَ مُقَطِّعَةِ البُظُورِ [*O son of her who amputates* بظور!] is an expression of contumely employed by the Arabs whether the mother of the person addressed be really a circumciser of females or not. (TA.)

بَظَرٌ The *having a* بَظْر: (T, Ṣ:) or the *having a long* بَظْر: (Ḳ:) a subst., (Ḳ,) or an inf. n., (T,) having no verb, (T, M,*) because it denotes an inherent quality, not one that is accidental. (T.) [But see بَظِرَتْ.]

بُظَارَةٌ, or بَظَارَةٌ: see بُظَارَةٌ.

بَظْرٌ: see بُظَارَةٌ.

بُظَارَةٌ The *lower extremity,* (M,) or *a thing in the extremity,* (Ṣ, Ḳ,) or *a protuberant,* or *prominent, thing in the lower part,* (Lḥ, T, M,) *of the vulva* (Lḥ, T, Ṣ, M) of a ewe or goat, (Lḥ, T, Ṣ, M, Ḳ,) or camel, (Lḥ, T,) and any animal. (M.) It is metaphorically used by Jereer in relation to a woman. (M.) See بَظْرٌ. —— Also, (Lḥ, Ṣ, T, M, &c.,) and ↓ بُظْرَةٌ, (M, Ḳ,) or ↓ بَظْرَةٌ, (IAạr, T,) The *thing* (M, Ḳ) *protuberant,* (M,) or *a protuberant thing,* (Ṣ, A, Mgh,) *in the upper lip,* (Ṣ, M, A, Mgh, Ḳ,) *in the middle thereof,* (M, A, Mgh, Ḳ,) *when it is somewhat long,* (Ṣ,) or *somewhat large:* (M:) or *a protuberance in the lip:* (IAạr, T:) when not long, it is called حُثْرُمَةٌ: (Ṣ:) it is not every one that has it: (Mgh:) dim. ↓ بُظَيْرَةٌ. (T.)

بُظَيْرَةٌ: see what next precedes.

بِظْرِيرٌ † A *long-tongued,* (M,) *clamorous* woman: (M, Ḳ: [in the CḲ, erroneously, with ة:]) but some say بِطْرِيرٌ [q. v.]. (M.) [See أَبْظَرُ.]

بُنْظُرٌ: see بَظْرٌ.

بَيْظَرٌ: see بَظْرٌ. —— يَا بَيْظَرُ is an expression of contumely addressed to a female slave. (Ḳ.)

أَبْظَرُ A man *uncircumcised.* (M, Ḳ.) And the fem., بَظْرَآءُ, A woman, (T, Ṣ, Mṣb,) or a female slave, (M, Ḳ,) *having a* بَظْر; (T, Ṣ, Mṣb;) or *having a long* بَظْر: (M, Ḳ:) or a woman *uncircumcised:* (Mgh:) pl. بُظْرٌ. (T.) يَا ٱبْنَ البَظْرَآءِ *O son of the uncircumcised woman!* is an expression of contumely. (Mgh.) —— A man *having what is termed a* بُظَارَة *in his upper lip;* (Ṣ, A, Mgh;) [i. e.] *having a* حُثْرُمَة *somewhat long;* (Ṣ in art. حثرم;) *having a long* (T, M) *and projecting* (M) *upper lip, with a protuberance in the middle of it.* (T, M.) —— Accord. to some, † *Clamorous; long-tongued.* (Mgh.) [See بِظْرِيرٌ.]

مُبَظِّرٌ *A circumciser:* (M, L:) and مُبَظِّرَةٌ *a woman who circumcises females.* (Ḳ.)

بعث

1. بَعْثٌ signifies The *removing of that which restrains one from free action.* (TA.) [And hence,] —— بَعَثَهُ, (Ṣ, A, &c.,) aor. ـَ, (A, Ḳ,) inf. n. بَعْثٌ (Mgh, L, Mṣb, TA) and بَعَثٌ, (L, TA,) *He sent him;* (Ṣ, A, Mgh, Mṣb, Ḳ;) namely, a messenger; (Mṣb;) and, when said of God, an apostle; (A;) [and when said of a man, a letter, &c.;] as also ↓ ابتعثه: (Ṣ, A, Mṣb, Ḳ:) [or] the former is said of anything that goes, or is sent, by itself; and of anything that will not go, or be sent, by itself, as a letter, and a present, one says, بَعَثَ بِهِ: (Mṣb:) [thus,] بَعَثَهُ signifies *he sent him,* or *it, alone, by himself,* or *by itself;* and بَعَثَ بِهِ, *he sent him,* or *it, by,* or *with, another,* or *others:* (L:) but El-Fárábee says that the former of these two has another signification, which will be found below; and that the latter signifies *he sent him,* or *it.* (Mṣb.) Hence, ضُرِبَ عَلَيْهِمُ البَعْثُ *The being sent to the war was appointed them and imposed upon them as an obligation.* (Mṣb.) You say, بَعَثَهُ لِكَذَا [*He sent him for such a thing* or *purpose*]. (A, TA.) [And بَعَثَ إِلَيْهِ بِكَذَا *He sent to him such a thing;* lit., *he sent to him* a messenger *with such a thing.*] And بَعَثَ الجُنْدَ إِلَى الغَزْوِ [*He sent the army to the war*]. (TA.) And بَعَثَ عَلَيْهِمُ البَلَآءَ [*He sent upon them trial,* or *affliction;*] *he caused trial,* or *affliction, to befall them.* (TA.) —— Also, (A, L, TA,) inf. n. بَعْثٌ (Mgh, L, TA) and بَعَثٌ (L) and تَبْعَاثٌ [an intensive form], (TA,) *He roused him, excited him,* or *put him in motion* or *action;* (A, L, Mgh, TA;) namely, anything; (TA;) [i. e. any person or animal; and particularly,] an animal lying down, or a person sitting. (L, TA.) You say, بَعَثَ النَّاقَةَ

He roused, or *put in motion* or *action, the she-camel;* (Ṣ, Mgh, Ḳ, TA;) i. e., *loosed the cord that bound her shank to her arm, and dismissed her;* or *he roused her,* or *made her to rise, she being lying down.* (TA.) It is said in a trad. respecting 'Áïsheh, فَبَعَثْنَا البَعِيرَ فَإِذَا العِقْدُ تَحْتَهُ [*And we made the camel to rise, and lo, the necklace was beneath him*]. (TA.) You say also, بَعَثَهُ عَلَى الأَمْرِ, (A,) or الشَّىْءِ, (L,) *He roused him, excited him,* or *put him in motion* or *action, to do the affair,* or *thing:* (A:) or *he incited him, urged him,* or *instigated him, to do the thing.* (L.) — Also, accord. to El-Fárábee, (Mṣb,) or بَعَثَهُ مِنْ مَنَامِهِ, (Ṣ, A, Ḳ,) inf. n. بَعْثٌ and بَعَثٌ, (TA,) *He roused him,* or *awoke him, from his sleep;* (Ṣ, A, Mṣb, Ḳ;) as also ▼ ابتعثهُ. (TA, from a trad.) — بَعْثٌ (Ṣ, Ḳ, TA) and بَعَثٌ (TA) also signify The *quickening, vivifying,* or *revivifying,* of the dead; the *raising* of the dead *to life;* (Ṣ, Ḳ,* TA;) by God, (TA,) *on the day called* يَوْمُ البَعْثِ (Ṣ, TA) *the day* [*of resurrection,*] *when those who are in the graves shall be raised.* (A, Mgh.) You say, بَعَثَ ٱللّٰهُ الخَلْقَ, and المَوْتَى, *God quickened, vivified, revivified,* or *raised to life, mankind,* and *the dead.* (TA.) ═ بَعِثَ, aor. ـَ, (inf. n. بَعَثٌ, TḲ,) *He* (a man, TA) *was sleepless,* or *wakeful.* (Ḳ,* TA.) [See بَعِثٌ.]

5: see 7, in two places.

6. تَبَاعَثُوا [*They roused, excited, incited, urged,* or *instigated, one another;* or *put one another in motion* or *action;* to do a thing]. One says, تَوَاصَوْا بِالخَيْرِ وَتَبَاعَثُوا عَلَيْهِ [*Enjoin ye,* or *charge ye, one another to do good, and rouse ye,* or *excite ye,* &c., *one another to do it*]. (A.)

7. انبعث *He became sent;* [i. e. *he went, being sent;*] quasi-pass. of بَعَثَهُ, as signifying "he sent him:" (Ṣ, Mṣb, Ḳ:) *he rose, and went away:* (TA:) *he rose to go forth.* (Bḍ in ix. 46.) You say, انبعث لِكَذَا [*He went, being sent,* or *he rose, and went away,* or *he rose to go forth, for such a thing* or *purpose*]. (A, TA.) And انبعث فُلَانٌ لِشَأْنِهِ *Such a one rose, and went away, to perform his affair.* (TA.) And انبعث فِى السَّيْرِ *He hastened, made haste, sped,* or *was quick* or *swift, in going, journeying,* or *pace.* (Ṣ.) And انبعث الشَّىْءُ, i. e. اِنْدَفَعَ [*The thing became impelled,* or *propelled;* or *went quickly,* or *swiftly, as though impelled* or *propelled;* &c.]; as also ▼ تبعّث. (TA.) [Thus] you say, انبعث المَآءُ [*The water poured out,* or *forth, as though impelled* or *propelled*]. (TA in art. فجر; &c.) And [hence,] ▼ تبعّث مِنِّى الشِّعْرُ, i. e. انبعث [*The poetry issued quickly from me*], as though it flowed (كَأَنَّهُ سَالَ): so in the Ṣ and Ḳ: but in some of the copies of the Ṣ, in the place of سَالَ, we find سَارَ. (TA.) And انبعث بِشَرٍّ [*He broke forth with evil,* or *mischief*]. (JK in art. بوق.) — [*He became roused, excited, incited, urged, instigated,* or *put in motion* or *action.*] You say, انبعثت النَّاقَةُ *The she-camel became roused,* or *put in motion* or *action, and rose:* (L, Mgh, TA:*) quasi-pass. of بَعَثَ النَّاقَةَ [q. v.]. (Mgh, TA.) And فُلَانٌ كَسْلَانُ لَا يَنْبَعِثُ [*Such a one is sluggish, lazy,* or *indolent: he will not become roused,* &c.]. (A.) — *He became roused,* or *awakened, from his sleep;* or *he awoke from his sleep.* (TA.)

8: see 1, in two places.

بَعْثٌ an inf. n. used as a pass. part. n.; *Sent;* as also ▼ بَعِيثٌ and ▼ مَبْعُوثٌ: pl. of the first بُعُوثٌ; and of the second بُعُثٌ. (L, TA.) — And [used as a subst., signifying] *A person sent; a messenger:* pl. بُعْثَانٌ. (L.) You say also, مُحَمَّدٌ خَيْرُ ▼ مُبْتَعَثٍ and ▼ مَبْعُوثٍ [*Moḥammad is the best person that has been sent*]. (A.) And ▼ بَعِيثُكَ نِعْمَةً, i. e. ▼ مَبْعُوثُكَ [*He whom Thou* (O God) *hast sent* (namely Moḥammad) *as a boon,* or *benefit,* or *favour*]. (L, from a trad. [The latter word (نعمة) is written in the L without any syll. signs; but the context shows that it is in the accus. case as a specificative.]) — *A people sent from one place to another;* as also ▼ بَعَثٌ: (L, TA:) *a people sent in any direction;* a word similar to سَفْرٌ and رَكْبٌ. (TA.) بَعْثُ النَّارِ, occurring in a trad., means *The people sent to the fire* [*of Hell*]. (L.) — *An army;* (Ṣ, Mgh, Mṣb, Ḳ;) because sent; (Mgh;) as also ▼ بَعَثٌ (Ḳ) and ▼ بَعِيثٌ: (TA:) pl. of the first بُعُوثٌ; (Ṣ, A, Mgh, Mṣb, Ḳ;) and of the last بُعُثٌ: (TA:) the first, [as also the second,] an inf. n. used as a subst. (Mṣb.) You say, كُنْتُ فِى بَعْثِ فُلَانٍ *I was in the army of such a one, that was sent with him.* (Ṣ.) And خَرَجَ فِى البُعُوثِ *He went forth among the forces that were sent to the frontiers.* (A.) — See also بَعِثٌ.

بُعْثٌ: see بَعِثٌ.

بَعَثٌ: see بَعْثٌ, in two places: — and see what next follows.

بَعِثٌ (A, L, Ḳ) and ▼ بَعْثٌ (L, TA) and ▼ بُعْثٌ, (L,) or ▼ بَعَثٌ, (TA,) *Sleepless,* or *wakeful:* (Ḳ:) a man *incessantly,* (A,) or *often,* (TA,) *awaking from his sleep:* (A, TA:) a man *whose anxieties,* or *griefs, incessantly render him sleepless,* or *wakeful, and awake him from his sleep:* pl. أَبْعَاثٌ. (TA.)

بَعْثَةٌ [inf. n. of un. of 1; and particularly signifying] *An occasion,* or *occurrence, of raising, rousing, exciting, stirring up,* or *provoking,* of sedition, or the like: pl. بَعَثَاتٌ. (TA, from a trad.)

بَعِيثٌ: see بَعْثٌ, in three places.

بَاعِثٌ [act. part. n. of 1; *Sending:* &c. — And hence, *Occasioning,* or *causing: an occasion,* or *a cause;* and *a motive*]. — البَاعِثُ one of the names [or epithets] of God; *The Quickener of mankind after death, on the day of resurrection.* (TA.)

البَاعُوثُ, (L, Ḳ,) or, accord. to some, البَاغُوثُ, q. v., with the pointed غ and the double-pointed ت, (TA,) [*The Christian festival of Easter;*] *the* اِسْتِسْقَآء *of the Christians;* (Ḳ;) or [rather] *what is to the Christians as the* استسقاء *is to the Muslims:* a Syriac word. (L.)

مَبْعَثٌ [a noun of place and of time from 1; *A place,* and *a time, of sending:* &c. Hence, المَبْعَثُ is particularly applied to *The time of the mission of Moḥammad:* and it is also applied to *the mission* itself]. (A, TA.)

مَبْعُوثٌ: see بَعْثٌ, in three places.

مُبْتَعَثٌ: see بَعْثٌ.

بعثر

Q. 1. بَعْثَرَ, [inf. n. بَعْثَرَةٌ,] *He took, drew,* or *pulled,* a thing *out,* or *forth, and uncovered* it, *laid* it *open,* or *exposed* it; (Ṣ, Ḳ;) as also بَحْثَرَ: (Ṣ:) *he raised* what was in a thing, (Ṣ, Ḳ,) *and caused it to come forth.* (Ṣ.) Hence, in the Ḳur [c. 9], إِذَا بُعْثِرَ مَا فِى ٱلْقُبُورِ *When that which is in the graves is raised, and caused to come forth:* (AO, Ṣ:) [see also بَحْثَرَ:] or the meaning is, *when the dust,* or *earth, in the graves is turned over, and the dead in them are raised:* (Zj:) or *when what is in the graves,* of gold and silver, *comes forth;* after which the dead are to come forth. (Fr.) — Also *He examined; he searched.* (Ḳ.) — *He searched for,* or *after,* or *into,* news, or tidings. (TA.) — *He scattered,* or *dispersed,* a thing, *and turned it over, one part upon another:* (Ḳ:) *he scattered,* or *dispersed,* his household goods, or his commodities, (Fr, Ṣ,) *and turned them over, one upon another;* (Fr, Zj, Ṣ;) as also بَحْثَرَ, (Fr, Ṣ,) and بَغْثَرَ. (Yaạkoob.) — *He demolished* a watering-trough or tank, *and turned* it *upside-down.* (AO, Ṣ, Ḳ.)

بعج

1. بَعَجَهُ, aor. ـَ, (T, Ṣ, A, Ḳ,) inf. n. بَعْجٌ, (T, Ṣ,) *He slit, ripped,* or *rent, it,* (T, Ṣ, A, Ḳ,) namely, a belly, with a knife, (T, Ṣ, A, TA,) *and moved about the knife in it,* (T,) *so that what was in it became displaced and apparent, hanging down;* (TA;) as also ▼ بعّجهُ. (Ḳ.) — بَعَجَتْ بَطْنَهَا لِزَوْجِهَا † [*She brought forth many children to her husband; i. q.* نَثَرَتْ: see بَعِيجٌ]. (Ḳ.) — بَعَجْتُ لَهُ بَطْنِى ‡ *I disclosed,* or *revealed, to him my secret* [or *my whole mind*]. (A.) Esh-Shemmákh uses the phrase بَعَجْتُ إِلَيْهِ البَطْنَ [meaning the same]. (TA.) — بَعَجَ بَطْنَهُ لَكَ signifies [also] ‡ *He took extraordinary pains,* or *exceeded the usual bounds, in giving thee sincere, honest,* or *faithful, advice,* or *counsel.* (Ḳ, TA.) — بَعَجَ أَرْضَهُ ‡ *He clave,* or *furrowed,* or *trenched, his land.* (A.) — بَعَجَ الأَرْضَ آبَارًا ‡ *He dug many wells in the ground.* (A.) — بَعَجَ الأَرْضَ وَبَجَّهَا ‡ *He clave the earth,* or *land, and subdued it:* said of 'Omar, in a trad., alluding to his conquests. (TA.) — بَعَجَتْ لَهُ الدُّنْيَا مِعَاهَا ‡ *The world disclosed to him what it contained, of treasures, and other possessions, and spoil:* also said of 'Omar, in another trad. (TA.) — بَعَجَتْ هٰذِهِ الأَرْضَ غَدَاةٌ طَيِّبَةُ الأَرْضِ † *A tract of good land intervened in the middle of this land* [*as though cleaving it*]. (L.) — بَعَجَهُ الحُبُّ ‡ *Love threw him into mourning,* or *sorrow; brought grief to him:*

(Ḳ, TA:) [or *occasioned him intense grief:* for] you say, بَعَجَهُ حُبُّ فُلَانٍ meaning ‡ *the love of such a one occasioned him intense grief, and he mourned for him:* Az says that لَعَجَهُ الحُبُّ is more correct than بَعَجَهُ: but he afterwards mentions بَعَجَهُ الأَمْرُ as meaning † *the affair caused him to mourn,* or *sorrow.* (L, TA.)

2: see 1. — بَعَّجَ المَطَرُ الأَرْضَ, (Ṣ,) or فِى الأَرْضِ, (L, TA,) inf. n. تَبْعِيجٌ, † *The rain dug up the stones of the earth by its vehemence.* (Ṣ, L, TA.)

5. تَبَعَّجَ السَّحَابُ, (Ṣ, A, Ḳ,) and ▼انبعج, (Ḳ,) بِالمَطَرِ, (TA,) ‡ *The clouds clave asunder, with,* or *by reason of, rain,* (Ṣ, A, Ḳ, TA,) and *vehement rain.* (TA.)

7. انبعج *It* [a belly] *became slit, ripped,* or *rent.* (Ṣ, Ḳ, TA.) — *He had his belly slit,* or *ripped,* or *rent,* with a knife, *so that what was in it became displaced and apparent, hanging down.* (TA.) — See also 5. — † *It* (anything, as, for instance, a valley,) *became wide,* or *ample.* (TA.) اِنْبَعَجَتْ دُفْعَةٌ مِنَ المَطَرِ ‡ [*A fall of rain burst forth*]. (A.) And انبعج السَّيْلُ ‡ [*The torrent burst forth*]. (A.)

بَعْجٌ: see بَعِيجٌ. — Also † A man *who walks weakly, as though his belly were slit,* or *ripped,* or *rent.* (Ṣ, Ḳ.)

بَعِيجٌ A belly (Ṣ) *slit, ripped,* or *rent,* (Ṣ, Ḳ,) with a knife, (Ṣ,) *so that what was in it is displaced and apparent, hanging down;* (TA;) as also ▼بَعِجٌ, thought to be after manner of a rel. n.; (L, TA;) and ▼مَبْعُوجٌ. (Ṣ, Ḳ.) — Hence, بَطْنِى لِلْكِرَامِ بَعِيجٌ, an expression used by Aboo-Dhu-eyb, meaning ‡ *My sincere, honest,* or *faithful, advice,* or *counsel, is liberally,* or *freely, given to the generous.* (TA. [In a reading given in the Ṣ, بالكرام is substituted for للكرام]) [Or it may mean ‡ *My secret is disclosed,* or *revealed, to the generous:* or *my whole mind.*] — بَعِيجٌ is also applied to a man, and, without ة, to a woman, as signifying *Having the belly slit, ripped,* or *rent,* with a knife, *so that what was in it is displaced and apparent, hanging down:* pl., masc. and fem., بَعْجَى. (TA.) — And [hence,] † A woman *who has brought forth many children* (بَعَجَتْ بَطْنَهَا, and نَثَرَتْ, [see 1, and see art. نثر,]) *to her husband.* (Ḳ.)

بَاعِجَةٌ † The *wide part of a valley;* (Ṣ, Ḳ;) the *place where it becomes wide.* (TA.) — Also † *Plain,* or *soft, land, that produces* [*the plant called*] نَصِىّ: or the *extremity of a tract of sand,* and *of plain,* or *soft, land,* [*extending*] *to what is termed* قُفّ [or *high,* or *high and rugged, ground*]: and [the pl.] بَوَاعِجُ signifies *places, in sand, which are of little depth* [*of sand*], *and which, if* نَصِىّ *grow therein, are of least depth, and best.* (TA.)

مَبْعُوجٌ: see بَعِيجٌ.

بعد

1. بَعُدَ, aor. ـُ, inf. n. بُعْدٌ; (Ṣ, L, Mṣb, Ḳ;) and بَعِدَ, aor. ـَ, inf. n. بَعَدٌ; (L, Ḳ;) and ▼ابعد, inf. n. إِبْعَادٌ, which is also trans.; (Mṣb;) and ▼تباعد; (Ṣ, Mṣb, Ḳ;) and ▼استبعد; (Ṣ, Ḳ, &c.;) *He,* or *it, was,* or *became, distant, remote, far off,* or *aloof: he went,* or *removed,* or *retired,* or *withdrew himself, to a distance,* or *far away,* or *far off: he alienated,* or *estranged, himself: he stood,* or *kept, aloof: contr. of* قَرُبَ: (Ṣ, L:) [but بَعُدَ generally has the first of these significations; and ▼ابعد, the others, as also ▼تباعد and ▼استبعد:] it is the general opinion of the leading lexicologists that بَعِدَ, as well as بَعُدَ, is thus used; but some deny this; and some assert that they may be employed alike, but that بَعُدَ is more chaste than بَعِدَ thus used. (TA.) [You say also, of a desert, and a tract of country, and the like, بَعُدَ, meaning *It extended far.*] And ▼ابعد زَيْدٌ عَنِ المَنْزِلِ, meaning ▼تباعد [i. e. *Zeyd went,* or *removed, to a distance,* or *far, from the place of alighting* or *abode*]. (IḲt, Mṣb.) And ▼تباعد مِنِّى, and ▼ابتعد, and ▼تبعّد, [*He went,* or *removed, to a distance,* or *far, from me; he alienated,* or *estranged, himself from me; he shunned,* or *avoided, me;*] (A;) and ▼تباعد عَنِّى [and بَعُدَ عَنِّى signify the same]. (Mṣb in art. كشح.) And إِذَا أَرَادَ أَحَدُكُمْ قَضَآءَ الحَاجَةِ ▼أَبْعَدَ, (L, Mṣb,) a trad., (Mṣb,) meaning *When one of you desires to accomplish that which is needful,* (i. e. to ease nature,) *he goes far,* or *to a great distance.* (L.) And ▼أَبْعَدْتُ فِى المَذْهَبِ, meaning ▼تَبَاعَدْتُ, (Mṣb,) *I went far,* or *to a great distance, to the place of ease,* i. e., to ease nature. (L.) — [بَعُدَ, referring to a saying or the like, and an event, means *It was far from being probable* or *correct; it was improbable, extraordinary,* or *strange:* (see بَعِيدٌ, and see also 10:) often occurring in these senses.] And ▼ابعد فِى نَوْعِهِ *It reached the utmost point,* or *degree, in its kind,* or *species.* (IAth.) And ▼ابعد فِى السَّوْمِ *He exceeded the due bounds in offering a thing for sale and demanding a price for it,* or *in bargaining for a thing.* (A.) — أَخَذَهُ مَا قَرُبَ وَمَا بَعُدَ *Recent and old griefs took hold upon him:* a saying similar to أَخَذَهُ مَا قَدُمَ وَمَا حَدُثَ. (Mgh in art. قدم.) — [بَعُدَ is often used, agreeably with a general rule, in the manner of a verb of praise or dispraise; and in this case is commonly contracted into بُعْدَ, like حُسْنَ; as in the phrase, in a verse of Imra-el-Ḳeys, بُعْدَ مَا مُتَأَمَّلِى (in which ما is redundant) *Distant,* or *far distant, was the object of my contemplation!* or (as explained in the EM p. 52) *how distant,* &c.!] — بَعِدَ, aor. ـَ, inf. n. بَعَدٌ; (Ṣ, L, Mṣb, Ḳ;) and بَعُدَ, aor. ـُ, inf. n. بُعْدٌ; (L, Ḳ;) also signify *He,* or *it, perished:* (Ṣ, L, Mṣb:) *he died:* (Ḳ:) it is the general opinion of the leading lexicologists that both these verbs are used as signifying "he perished," and both occur in different readings of v. 98 of ch. xi. of the Ḳur: the former is said to be used in this sense by some of the Arabs; and the latter, by others; but some disallow the latter in this sense; and some say that the former is more chaste than the latter thus used: (TA:) or both signify *he became far distant from his home* or *native country; became a stranger,* or *estranged, therefrom:* (L, TA:) or the Arabs say, بَعُدَ الرَّجُلُ and بَعِدَ in the sense of تباعد, when not reviling; but when reviling, they say, بَعِدَ, only. (Yoo, TA.) You say, لَا تَبْعَدْ وَإِنْ بَعُدْتَ عَنِّى [*Mayest thou not perish though thou be distant from me!*] (A.) [And as an imprecation against a man, you say, بَعِدْتَ, meaning *Mayest thou perish!* (See the printed edition of the Ḥam, pp. 89 and 90, where بَعُدْتَاىَ هلكت is an evident mistake for بَعِدْتَ أَىْ هَلَكْتَ.)] And بُعْدًا لَهُ *May God alienate him,* or *estrange him, from good,* or *prosperity!* or, *curse him!* (A,* Ḳ, TA;) i. e. may he not be pitied with respect to that which has befallen him! like سُحْقًا لَهُ: the most approved way being to put بعد thus in the accus. case as an inf. n.; but the tribe of Temeem say, ▼بُعْدٌ لَهُ, and سُحْقٌ, like غُلَامٌ لَهُ. (TA.) = بَعُدَ is made trans. by means of [the preposition] ب: see 4. (Mṣb.)

2: see 4, in four places. — [You say also, بَعَّدَهُ عَنِ السُّوْءِ *He declared him,* or *pronounced him, to be far removed from evil.*]

3. باعده *He was,* or *became,* [*distant, remote, far off,* or *aloof, from him;* or] *in a part, quarter,* or *tract, different from that in which he* (the other) *was.* (TA in art. جنب.) — See also 4, in seven places.

4. ابعد, inf. n. إِبْعَادٌ: see 1, in seven places. = ابعدهُ; (Ṣ, Mṣb, Ḳ;) and ▼باعدهُ, (Ṣ, Ḳ,) inf. n. مُبَاعَدَةٌ and بِعَادٌ; (Ḳ;) and ▼بعّدهُ, (Ṣ, Ḳ,) inf. n. تَبْعِيدٌ; (Ṣ;) and ▼بَعُدَ بِهِ; (Mṣb;) *He made,* or *caused, him,* or *it, to be,* or *become, distant, remote, far off,* or *aloof;* or *to go, remove, retire,* or *withdraw himself, to a distance, far away,* or *far off; he placed,* or *put, at a distance,* or *he put,* or *sent, away,* or *far away,* or *far off,* or *he removed far away, alienated,* or *estranged, him,* or *it.* (Ṣ, Mṣb.) You say, ▼بَاعِدْ نَفْسَكَ عَنْ زَيْدٍ [*Remove thyself far from,* or *avoid thou, Zeyd*]: and ▼بَاعِدْ زَيْدًا عَنْكَ [*Remove thou Zeyd far from thee*]. (TA, voce إِيَّا.) And ▼بَعَّدْتُ بَيْنَهُمَا, inf. n. تَبْعِيدٌ, [*I made a wide separation between them two*]; as also ▼بَاعَدْتُ, inf. n. مُبَاعَدَةٌ. (Mṣb.) And ▼بَاعَدَ اللّٰهُ مَا بَيْنَهُمَا [*May God make the space between them two far extending! may He make a wide separation between them two!*]; as also ▼بَعَّدَ. (TA.) And رَبَّنَا ▼بَاعِدْ, or ▼بَعِّدْ, بَيْنَ أَسْفَارِنَا [*O our Lord, make to be far-extending the spaces between our journeys!* or, *put wide distances between our journeys!*] accord. to different readings [in the Ḳur xxxiv. 18]: the former of these is the common reading: Yaḳoob El-Ḥadramee read ▼رَبُّنَا بَاعَدَ [*Our Lord, He hath made to be far extending* &c.]. (TA.) — أَبْعَدَهُ اللّٰهُ means *May God alienate him,* or *estrange him, from good,* or *prosperity!* or, *curse him!* (Ḳ;) i. e., may he not be pitied with respect to that which has befallen him! (TA.) [You say also, أَبْعَدَ اللّٰهُ الأَخِرَ: see أَخِرٌ.] — See also 10. = مَا أَبْعَدَهُ مِنَ الصَّوَابِ [*How far is it* (namely the saying) *from what is right,* or *correct!*]. (A.)

5: see 1.

6. تباعد : see 1, in six places. — [It also signifies *He became alienated*, or *estranged*, from his family or friends. — And تباعدوا *They became distant*, or *remote, one from another; they went, removed, retired*, or *withdrew themselves, to a distance, far away*, or *far off, one from another; they removed themselves far*, or *kept aloof, one from another*.] You say, كَانُوا مُتَقَارِبِينَ فَتَبَاعَدُوا [*They were near, one to another, and they became distant*, or *remote, one from another*]. (A.)

8 : see 1.

10. استبعدهُ *He reckoned it*, or *esteemed it*, (namely, a thing, Ḳ, or a saying, A,) بَعِيد [i. e. *distant*, or *remote*; or, if a saying or the like, *far from being probable* or *correct, improbable, extraordinary*, or *strange*]; (Ṣ, A, Ḳ;) as also ▼ابعدهُ. (A.) ═ See also 1, first sentence, in two places.

بَعْدُ an adv. n. of time, signifying *After*, or *afterwards*: and allowable also, accord. to some of the grammarians, as an adv. n. of place, signifying *after*, or *behind*: (TA:) contr. of قَبْلُ: (Ṣ, A, Ḳ:) it is a vague adv. n., of which the meaning is not understood without its being prefixed to another noun [expressed or implied]; denoting after-time. (Mṣb.) When it occurs without any complement, (Ṣ, Ḳ,) a noun or the like which should be its complement being intended to be understood as to the meaning thereof but not as to the letter, (Ṣ,* TA,) it is indecl., (Ṣ, Ḳ,) because it resembles a particle, (TA,) and has ḍamm for its termination to show that it is indecl., since it cannot have ḍamm by any rule of desinential syntax because it cannot occur as an agent nor as an inchoative or enunciative. (Ṣ.) Sb, however, mentions [as exceptions to this rule] the phrases مِنْ بَعْدٍ [*Afterwards*] and أَفْعَلُ هٰذَا بَعْدًا [*I will do this afterwards*], as having been used by the Arabs. (Ḳ,* TA.) [The latter of these phrases is common in the present day. Another exception to the rule above-mentioned will be found in what follows.] Accord. to the primary rule, it is used as a prefixed n. governing its complement in the gen. case; (Ṣ;) [i. e., it is used in the manner of a preposition;] and when thus used, it is decl., (Ḳ,) because it does not in this case [always] resemble a particle. (TA.) You say, جَآءَ زَيْدٌ بَعْدَ عَمْرٍو *Zeyd came after 'Amr*. (Mṣb.) And رَأَيْتُهُ بَعْدَكَ and مِنْ بَعْدِكَ [*I saw him after thee*]. (L.) The words of the Ḳur [xxx. 3], لِلّٰهِ ٱلْأَمْرُ مِنْ قَبْلُ وَمِنْ بَعْدُ, meaning *To God* belonged *the command before* that the Greeks were overcome *and after* that they had been overcome, [thus read when the complements of قبل and بعد are intended to be understood as to the meaning thereof but not as to the letter,] are also read مِنْ قَبْلِ وَمِنْ بَعْدِ, when each complement is intended to be understood as to the meaning and the letter, and also مِنْ قَبْلٍ وَمِنْ بَعْدٍ, meaning To God belongeth the command *first and last*, [when neither complement is intended to be understood either as to the letter or as to the meaning,] but the first of these readings is the best. (L.) [You say also, بَعْدَ ذٰلِكَ and مِنْ بَعْدِ ذٰلِكَ *After that*: and بَعْدَ أَنْ فَعَلْتُ and مِنْ بَعْدِ أَنْ فَعَلْتُ and بَعْدَ مَا فَعَلْتُ and مِنْ بَعْدِ مَا فَعَلْتُ *After I did*, or *after my doing*, such a thing: &c.] Also جِئْتُ بَعْدَيْكُمَا, meaning بَعْدَكُمَا, *I came after you two*. (Ḳ.) And هٰذَا مِمَّا لَيْسَ بَعْدَهُ غَايَةٌ فِى الجَوْدَةِ, and فِى الرَّدَآءَةِ, *This is of the things after*, or *beyond, which there is not any extreme degree in respect of goodness*, and *in respect of badness*: and, by way of abridgment, لَيْسَ بَعْدَهُ [with nothing following this]: and hence, app., the saying of Moḥammad, وَإِنْ كَانَ لَيْسَ بِالَّذِى لَا بَعْدَ لَهُ, meaning [*And though*] *it be not in the utmost degree* in respect of goodness: بعد being thus used as a decl. noun. (Mgh.) [بَعْدِى and the like are also frequently used as meaning بَعْدَ عَهْدِى بِكَ and the like; as in the phrase, قَدْ تَغَيَّرْتَ بَعْدِى *Thou hast become altered since I knew thee*, or *saw thee*, or *met thee*, or *was with thee*. And similar to this are many phrases in the Ḳur; as, for instance, in ii. 48,] ثُمَّ ٱتَّخَذْتُمُ ٱلْعِجْلَ مِنْ بَعْدِهِ *Then ye took to yourselves the calf* as a god, or an object of worship, *after him*, namely Moses, i. e., *after his having gone away*. (Bḍ.) أَمَّا بَعْدُ (Ṣ, Ḳ, &c.) is [an expression denoting transition;] an expression by which an address or a discourse is divided; (Ṣ;) used without any complement to بعد, which in this case signifies the contr. of قَبْلُ: (TA:) you say, أَمَّا بَعْدُ فَقَدْ كَانَ كَذَا, meaning [*Now, after these preliminary words*, (Abu-l-'Abbás in TA voce خِطَابٌ,) I proceed to say, that *such a thing has happened*: or] *after my prayer for thee*: (Ḳ:) or *after praising God*: (TA:) the first who used this formula was David; (Ḳ;) or Jacob; (TA;) or Kaab Ibn-Lu-ei; (Ḳ;) or Ḳuss Ibn-Sá'ideh; or Yaarub Ibn-Ḳaḥṭán. (TA.) — You also use the dim. form, saying ▼بُعَيْدَهُ [*A little after him*, or *it*], when you mean by it to denote a time near to the preceding time. (Mṣb.) You say also, رَأَيْتُهُ ▼بُعَيْدَاتِ بَيْنٍ, (Ṣ, Ḳ,) and ▼بُعَيْدَاتِهِ, (Ḳ, TA, [in the CḲ بَعِيدَاتِهِ,]) *I saw him a little after a separation*: (Ṣ, Ḳ:) or, *after intervals of separation*: (Ṣ, L:) or, *after a while*. (A'Obeyd, A.) And إِنَّهَا لَتَضْحَكُ بُعَيْدَاتِ ▼بَيْنٍ *Verily she laughs after intervals*. (L.) [See also art. بين.] ▼بُعَيْدَاتٌ is used only as an adv. n. of time. (Ṣ, L.) — بَعْدُ also sometimes means *Now; yet; as yet*. (TA.) [It is used in this sense mostly in negative phrases; as, for instance, in لَمْ يَمُتْ بَعْدُ *He has not died yet*. The following is one of the instances of its having this meaning in affirmative phrases: سُمِّىَ الحَوْلِىُّ مِنْ أَوْلَادِ البَقَرِ تَبِيعًا لِأَنَّهُ يَتْبَعُ أُمَّهُ بَعْدُ *The yearling of the offspring of cows is called* تبيع *because he yet follows his mother*: occurring in the Mgh &c., in art. تبع.] — It occurs also in the sense of مَعَ; as in the words of the Ḳur [ii. 174 and v. 95], فَمَنِ ٱعْتَدَى بَعْدَ ذٰلِكَ, i. e., (as some say, MF,) مَعَ ذٰلِكَ [*And whoso transgresseth notwithstanding that*; lit., *with that*]. (Mṣb.) — It has been said that it also means *Before, in time*; thus bearing two contr. significations: that it has this meaning in two instances; in the Ḳur [lxxix. 30], where it is said, وَٱلْأَرْضَ بَعْدَ ذٰلِكَ دَحَاهَا [as though signifying *And the earth, before that, He spread it forth*]; and [xxi. 105] where it is said, وَلَقَدْ كَتَبْنَا فِى ٱلزَّبُورِ مِنْ بَعْدِ ٱلذِّكْرِ [as though meaning *And verily we wrote in the Psalms before the Ḳur-án*]: (MF, TA:) but Az says that this is a mistake; that God created the earth not spread forth; then created the heaven; and then spread forth the earth: (L, TA:) and الذكر in the latter of these instances means *the Book of the Law revealed to Moses*: (Bḍ:) or الزبور means *the revealed Scriptures*; (Bḍ, Jel;) and الذكر, *the Preserved Tablet*, (Bḍ,) [i. e.] *the Original of the Scriptures*, which is with God. (Jel.)

بُعْدٌ [as an inf. n. used in the manner of a subst. signifies] *Distance*, or *remoteness*; (Ṣ, A, L, Ḳ;*) and so ▼بَعَدٌ, (L, Ḳ,) accord. to most of the leading lexicologists, (TA, [see بَعُدَ,]) [and ▼بُعْدَةٌ, for] you say, بَيْنَنَا بُعْدَةٌ, meaning [*Between us two is a distance*] of land or country, or of relationship. (Ṣ, Ḳ.) — [*Remoteness from probability* or *correctness*; *improbability*, or *strangeness*: see بَعُدَ. Hence the phrase, هٰذَا مِنَ البُعْدِ بِمَكَانٍ *This is improbable*, or *extraordinary*, or *strange*: often occurring in the TA &c.] — Also i. q. ▼بَعَدٌ: (L, Ḳ:) this latter (Ṣ, L, Mṣb, Ḳ) and بُعْدٌ, (L, Ḳ,) accord. to most of the leading lexicologists, as, for instance, in the Ḳur xi. 98, (TA, [see بَعِدَ,]) signifying *Perdition*; (Ṣ, L, Mṣb;) or *death*. (Ḳ.) — *Judgment and prudence*; as also ▼بُعْدَةٌ: so in the phrase, إِنَّهُ لَذُو بُعْدٍ, and بُعْدَةٍ, *Verily he is possessed of judgment and prudence*: (Ḳ:) or *penetrating*, or *effective, judgment*; *depth*, or *profundity*; *far-reaching judgment*. (TA.) [See also أَبْعَدُ.] ▼ذُو البُعْدَةِ also signifies A man *who goes to a great length*, or *far, in hostility*. (L.) — *A cursing; execration; malediction*; as also ▼بِعَادٌ. (Ḳ.) You say, بُعْدًا لَهُ, as well as بُعْدٌ لَهُ: see 1, last sentence but one. (TA.)

بَعَدٌ : see بُعْدٌ, in two places: ═ and بَعِيدٌ, in five places.

بُعْدَى : see أَبْعَدُ, in two places.

بُعْدَةٌ : see بُعْدٌ, in three places.

بُعَادٌ : see بَعِيدٌ: — and see also بَاعِدٌ.

بِعَادٌ : see بُعْدٌ.

بَعِيدٌ *Distant; remote; far; far off*; (Ṣ, L, Ḳ;*) as also ▼بُعَادٌ, and ▼بَاعِدٌ: (L, Ḳ:) pl. (of the first, Ṣ, L) بُعْدَانٌ (Ṣ, L, Ḳ) and (of the first also, L, TA) بُعُدٌ (L, Ḳ) and بِعَادٌ (TA) and (of the first and second, L) بُعَدَآءُ (L, Ḳ) and of the third, ▼بَعَدٌ, [but this (which is also used as a sing. epithet, as will be shown in what follows,) is properly a quasi-pl. n.,] like as خَدَمٌ is of خَادِمٌ. (Ṣ.) As signifying *Distant with respect to place*, it is correctly used alike as masc. and fem. and sing. and dual and pl.; (L, and TA in this art. and in art. قرب, in which latter see the authorities;) but not necessarily; like its contr. قَرِيبٌ: (L:) you say, هِىَ بَعِيدٌ مِنْكَ [*She is distant from thee*; or it is] as though you said, مَكَانُهَا بَعِيدٌ:

(L:) also مَا أَنْتَ مِنَّا بِبَعِيدٍ [*Thou art not distant from us*], and مَا أَنْتُمْ مِنَّا بِبَعِيدٍ [*Ye are not distant from us*]: and in like manner, مَا أَنْتَ مِنَّا بِبَعَدٍ ▼, and ▼ مَا أَنْتُمْ مِنَّا بِبَعَدٍ. (Ṣ, TA.) [But it receives, sometimes, the fem. form when used in this sense; for] جَلَسْتُ بَعِيدًا مِنْكَ and بَعِيدَةً مِنْكَ are phrases mentioned as signifying *I sat distant*, or *remote in place*, or *at a distance*, or *aloof, from thee;* مَكَانًا [and نَاحِيَةً or the like] being understood. (L.) You say also, ▼ مَنْزِلٌ بَعَدٌ *A distant*, or *remote, place of alighting* or *abode.* (Ḳ.) And تَنَحَّ غَيْرَ بَعِيدٍ (Ṣ, Ḳ) and ▼ غَيْرَ بَاعِدٍ and ▼ غَيْرَ بَعَدٍ (Ḳ) [*Retire thou not far;*] meaning *be thou near:* (Ṣ, Ḳ:) [or] the second and third of these phrases mean *retire thou not in an abject*, or *a mean*, or *contemptible*, or *despicable, state.* (Ṣ, A.) And ▼ اِنْطَلِقْ يَا فُلَانُ غَيْرَ بَاعِدٍ [*Depart thou, O such a one, not far;*] meaning *mayest thou not go away!* (L.) [And رَأَيْتُهُ مِنْ بَعِيدٍ *I saw him, or it, from afar:* and جَآءَ مِنْ بَعِيدٍ *He came from afar:* and the like. And بَعِيدٌ as applied to a desert and the like, meaning *Far extending.*] And ▼ بُعْدٌ بَاعِدٌ *A far distance.* (Ḳ.) [And نِيَّةٌ بَعِيدَةٌ *A distant, far-reaching*, or *far-aiming, intention, purpose*, or *design.*] And فُلَانٌ بَعِيدُ الهِمَّةِ [*Such a one is far-aiming*, or *far-aspiring, in purpose, desire*, or *ambition*]. (A.) And هِىَ بَعِيدَةُ العَهْدِ [*She was known*, or *seen*, or *met, a long time ago*]: in this case, the fem. form, with ة, must be used. (L.) And قَوْلٌ بَعِيدٌ [*A saying far from being probable* or *correct; improbable; far-fetched; extraordinary*, or *strange*]. (A.) And أَمْرٌ بَعِيدٌ *An extraordinary thing* or *affair* or *case, of which the like does not happen* or *occur.* (L.) — Also *Distant with respect to kindred* or *relationship:* in which sense, the word receives the fem. form, [as well as the dual form, and pl. forms, like its contr. قَرِيبٌ,] by universal consent. (TA.) [Its pl.] بُعَدَآءُ signifies *Strangers, that are not relations.* (IAth.) You say also, فُلَانٌ مِنْ بُعْدَانِ الأَمِيرِ [meaning *Such a one is of the distant dependents*, or *subjects, of the governor*, or *prince*]. (Ṣ.) And إِذَا لَمْ تَكُنْ مِنْ قُرْبَانِ الأَمِيرِ فَكُنْ مِنْ بُعْدَانِهِ [*If thou be not of the particular companions*, or *familiars, of the governor*, or *prince, then be of his distant dependents*, or *subjects*]; i. e., be distant from him, that his evil may not affect thee. (AZ, A.) — رَأَيْتُهُ بُعَيْدَاتِ بَيْنٍ: see بُعْدٌ, in the latter half of the paragraph. — See also بَاعِدٌ.

بُعُدٌ and بُعَيْدَاتٌ: see بُعْدٌ, in four places.

بَاعِدٌ: see بَعِيدٌ, in four places. — Also *Perishing:* (Ṣ, L: [in the Ḳ it is implied that it signifies *dying;* and so ▼ بَعِيدٌ and ▼ بُعَادٌ:]) or *far distant from his home*, or *native country; in a state of estrangement therefrom.* (L.)

أَبْعَدُ *More*, and *most, distant* or *remote; further*, and *furthest:* by poetic licence written أَبْعَدُّ: (L:) [pl. أَبَاعِدُ; as in the saying,] فُلَانٌ يَسْتَجِرُّ الحَدِيثَ مِنْ أَبَاعِدِ أَطْرَافِهِ [*Such a one draws forth talk*, or *discourse*, or *news*, or *the like, from its most remote sources*]. (A.) — *More*, and *most, extreme, excessive, egregious*, or *extraordinary*, in its kind. (IAth.) [Hence, perhaps,] إِنَّهُ لَغَيْرُ أَبْعَدَ [in the CḲ أَبْعَدٍ] and ▼ بُعْدٍ *Verily there is no good in him:* (Ḳ:) or, *no depth in him in anything:* (IAar:) [or, *he is not extraordinary* in his kind: see also بُعْدٌ:] said in dispraising one. (TA.) And مَا عِنْدَهُ أَبْعَدُ and ▼ بُعْدٌ [*He has not what is extraordinary* in its kind: or] *he possesses not excellence*, or *power*, or *riches:* or *he possesses not anything profitable:* (L, Ḳ:) said only in dispraising one: (AZ:) or it may mean *he possesses not anything which one would go far to seek;* or, *anything of value:* or *what he possesses, of things or qualities that are desirable, is more extraordinary than what others possess.* (MF.) — *Remote from good:* [which is the meaning generally intended in the present day when it is used absolutely as an epithet applied to a man; but meaning also *remote* from him or those in whose presence this epithet is used, both *as to place and as to moral condition:*] and, *from continence:* (L:) and *stupid; foolish;* or *having little*, or *no, intellect* or *understanding;* syn. خَائِنٌ: (so in a copy of the Ṣ and in the L and TA:) or *treacherous*, or *unfaithful;* syn. خَائِنٌ. (So in two copies of the Ṣ and in a copy of the A.) It is used as an allusion to the name of a person whom one would mention with dispraise; as when one says, هَلَكَ الأَبْعَدُ [*May such a one, the remote from good, &c., perish!*]: with respect to a woman, one says, هَلَكَتِ البُعْدَى. (En-Naḍr, Az.) One says also, كَبَّ اللّٰهُ الأَبْعَدَ لِفِيهِ, meaning [*May God cast down prostrate such a one, the remote from good, &c., upon his mouth!* or,] *cast him down upon his face!* (Ṣ.) [It is a rule observed in decent society, by the Arabs, to avoid, as much as possible, the mention of opprobrious epithets, lest any person present should imagine an epithet of this kind to be slily applied to himself: therefore, when any malediction or vituperation is uttered, it is usual to allude to the object by the term الأَبْعَدُ, or البَعِيدُ, as meaning the remote from good, &c., and also the remote from the person or persons present. See also الآخِرُ, which is used in a similar manner.] — *A more distant*, or *most distant*, or *very distant, relation;* (Lth;) *contr. of* أَقْرَبُ: (Mṣb:) pl. أَبَاعِدُ (Lth, Ṣ, A, Mṣb, Ḳ) and أَبْعَدُونَ; (Lth;) *contr. of* أَقَارِبُ (Lth, Ṣ, Ḳ) and أَقْرَبُونَ. (Lth.)

مُبْعِدٌ A man *who makes far journeys.* (Ḳ.)

بعر

1. بَعَرَ, aor. ـَ, (Ṣ, Mgh, Mṣb, Ḳ,) inf. n. بَعْرٌ, (Ṣ, Mṣb,) said of an animal having the kind of foot called خُفّ, (Mgh, Mṣb, Ḳ,) [i. e.,] of a camel, and also of a sheep and goat, (Ṣ,) and of a cloven-hoofed animal (Mgh, Mṣb, Ḳ) of the wild kind of bull or cow, but not of the domestic kind, and of the gazelle-kind, beside the other two cloven-hoofed kinds mentioned before, and of the hare or rabbit, (TA,) *He voided dung.* (Ṣ,* Mgh, Mṣb, Ḳ.) — بَعَرَهُ *He threw at him a piece of* بَعْر. (A.) — بَعَرَتْ, said of a widow, *She threw the piece of* بَعْر; *i. q.* ▼ رَمَتْ بِالبَعْرَةِ; meaning *she ended the number of days during which she had to wait after the death of her husband before she could marry again.* (A.) [It seems to have been customary for the widow to collect a number of pieces of بَعْر, as many as the days she had to wait before she could marry again, and to throw away one each day: so that the saying means She threw the last piece of بعر.] = بَعِرَ, aor. ـَ, (Ḳ,) inf. n. بَعَرٌ, (TA,) *He* (a camel) *became a* بَعِير. (Ḳ.)

2: see 4.

3. بَاعَرَتْ حَالِبَهَا, [inf. n., app., بِعَارٌ, q. v.,] said of a ewe or she-goat, (Ḳ,) and of a she-camel, (TA,) *She befouled her milker with her dung.* (TA voce بِعَارٌ.) = بَاعَرَتْ إِلَى حَالِبِهَا *She* (a ewe or goat, and a camel,) *hastened to her milker.* (TA.)

4. ابعر *He cleansed* an intestine, or a gut, *of its* بعر; as also ▼ بعّر, inf. n. تَبْعِيرٌ. (Ḳ.)

بَعْرٌ (Ṣ, A, Ḳ) and ▼ بَعَرٌ (Mṣb, Ḳ) [coll. gen. ns. signifying *Camels'*, and *sheeps'*, and *goats'*, and *similar, dung;*] *dung* (Mṣb, Ḳ) *of animals having the kind of foot called* خُفّ, (A, Mgh, Mṣb, Ḳ,) [i. e.,] *of the camel*, and also *of the sheep* and *goat*, (Ṣ,) and *of cloven-hoofed animals* (A, Mgh, Mṣb, Ḳ) *of the wild kind of bull and cow, but not of the domestic kind*, and *of the gazelle-kind*, beside the two other cloven-hoofed kinds, and *of the hare* or *rabbit:* (TA:) n. un. with ة: (Ṣ, Mgh, Ḳ:) and pl. أَبْعَارٌ. (Ṣ, Mṣb, Ḳ.) One says, هُوَ أَهْوَنُ عَلَىَّ مِنْ بَعْرَةٍ يُرْمَى بِهَا كَلْبٌ [*He is a lighter thing to me than a piece of* بعر *that is thrown at a dog*]. (A.) And it is said in a prov., أَنْتَ كَصَاحِبِ البَعْرَةِ [*Thou art like the owner of the piece of* بعر], or أَنْتَ فِى مِثْلِ صَاحِبِ البَعْرَةِ *Thou art in a condition like that of the owner of the piece of* بعر; (meaning the person for whom it was intended;) applied to him who reveals a thing relating to himself; (see Freytag's Arab. Prov. i. 85;)] originating from the fact that a man had a suspicion respecting some one among his people; so he collected them to search out from them the truth of the case, and took a piece of بعر, and said, "I am about to throw this my piece of بعر at the person whom I suspect;" whereupon one of them withdrew himself quickly, and said, "Throw it not at me;" and confessed. (TA.) See also بَعَرَتْ, above.

بَعَرٌ: see بَعْرٌ.

بِعَارٌ, a subst., [or inf. n. of 3,] *The befouling of her milker with her dung*, by a ewe or she-goat, (Ḳ,) or a camel: (TA:) it is reckoned a fault, because the animal that does so sometimes casts her dung into the milking-vessel. (TA.)

بَعِيرٌ, (Ṣ, Mṣb, Ḳ, &c.,) sometimes pronounced بِعِيرٌ, (Ḳ,) which latter is of the dial. of Benoo-Temeem, but the former is the more chaste, (TA,) *A camel, male or female;* (Ṣ, Mṣb, Ḳ;) as applied to a camel, like إِنْسَانٌ applied to a human being; (Ṣ, Mṣb;) whereas جَمَلٌ is applied only to a male camel, and نَاقَةٌ to a she-camel;

بَكْرٌ and بَكْرَةٌ are respectively terms like فَتًى and فَتَاةٌ; and قَلُوصٌ is like the term جَارِيَةٌ; so say, among others, ISk and Az and IJ; and it is added in the Mutahaffidh, that the terms جمل and ناقة are applied only when the animal has entered the seventh year: (Mṣb:) but بعير is more commonly applied to the *male camel;* (Mṣb, Ḳ;) and only to *one that has entered its fifth year;* (Ṣ, Ḳ;) or *that has entered its ninth year:* (Ḳ:) the pl. is أَبْعِرَةٌ [a pl. of pauc.] and بُعْرَانٌ (Ṣ, Mṣb, Ḳ) and بِعْرَانٌ (Ḳ) and بُعُرٌ (TA) and (pl. of أَبْعِرَةٌ TA) أَبَاعِرُ (Ṣ, Mṣb, Ḳ) and أَبَاعِيرُ. (Ḳ.) If one say, أَعْطُونِى بَعِيرًا [*Give ye to me a* بعير], the persons so addressed, accord. to Esh-Sháfi'ee, are not to give a she-camel: (Mṣb:) but the following phrases are transmitted from the Arabs: صَرَعَتْنِى بَعِيرِى *My she-camel threw me down prostrate:* (Ṣ, A:) and حَلَبْتُ بَعِيرِى *I milked my camel:* (A, Mṣb:) and شَرِبْتُ مِنْ لَبَنِ بَعِيرِى *I drank of the milk of my camel:* (Ṣ:) and كِلَا هٰذَيْنِ البَعِيرَيْنِ نَاقَةٌ *Each of these two camels is a she-camel.* (A.) لَيْلَةُ البَعِيرِ [*The night of the camel*], mentioned in a trad. of Jábir, means the night in which the Prophet purchased of him his camel. (TA.) —— Also *An ass:* (IKh, Ḳ:) so in the Ḳur xii. 72; but this signification is of rare occurrence: (IKh:) and *anything that carries:* (IKh, Ḳ:) so in the Hebrew language [בְּעִיר (see Gen. xlv. 17)]. (TA.)

بَاعِرٌ A widow *throwing the piece of* بَعَر; meaning *ending the number of days during which she has had to wait after the death of her husband previously to her being allowed to marry again.* (A.) [See 1.]

مَبْعَرٌ and ▼مَبْعِرٌ [and ▼مَبْعَرَةٌ (occurring in the Ḳ in art. خور)] The *place* [or *passage* (as is shown in the Lexicons in many places)] *of the* بَعَر; [i. e. the *rectum;* the *intestine,* or *gut, containing the* بَعَر;] of any quadruped: (Ḳ:) pl. مَبَاعِرُ. (TA.) It is said in a prov., إِنَّ هٰذَا الدَّاعِرَ مَا زَالَ يَنْحَرُ الأَبَاعِرَ وَيَنْثُلُ المَبَاعِرَ [*Verily this bad man has not ceased to slaughter camels and to cleanse the intestines containing the dung*]. (A, TA.)

مَبْعِرٌ: } see مَبْعَرٌ.
مَبْعَرَةٌ:

مِبْعَارٌ A ewe or she-goat, (Ḳ,) or a she-camel, (TA,) *that befouls with her dung* (تُبَاعِرُ) *her milker.* (Ḳ, TA.) [See بِعَارٌ.]

بعض

1. بَعَضَهُ البَعُوضُ, [aor. ـَ,] inf. n. بَعْضٌ, *The* بَعُوض [or *gnats,* or *musquitoes,*] *bit him; and annoyed,* or *molested, him.* (TA.) And بُعِضُوا *They were bitten by the* بَعُوض: (A:) or *were annoyed,* or *molested, thereby.* (Ḳ.) بَعَضَهُ is not used in relation to anything but بَعُوض. (TA.) A poet says, praising a man who passed the night within a كِلَّة [or thin curtain used for protection from gnats, or musquitoes], which is also called أَبُو دِثَارٍ,

• لَنِعْمَ البَيْتُ بَيْتُ أَبِى دِثَارٍ •
• إِذَا مَا خَافَ بَعْضُ القَوْمِ بَعْضَا •

[*Excellent indeed is the tent, the tent of Aboo-Dithár, when some of the people fear biting, and annoyance,* or *molestation, from gnats,* or *musquitoes*]: by بعضا meaning عَضًّا. (TA.)

2. بَعَّضَهُ, inf. n. تَبْعِيضٌ, *He divided it into parts,* or *portions,* (Ṣ, A, Mṣb, Ḳ,) *distinct,* or *separate, one from another.* (Mṣb.) You say, أَخَذُوا مَالَهُ فَبَعَّضُوهُ *They took his property and divided it into parts,* or *portions.* (A, TA.) And عَضَّى الشَّاةَ وَبَعَّضَهَا [*He limbed,* or *dismembered, the sheep,* or *goat, and divided it into parts,* or *portions*]. (A, TA.) [Hence,] مِنْ in certain cases, and بِ in the like cases, as in the saying شَرِبْتُ بِمَآءِ كَذَا ["I drank of," i. e. "some of, such water"], are said to be لِلتَّبْعِيضِ [*For the purpose of dividing into parts,* or *portions*]. (Mṣb.)

4. ابعضوا *They had* بَعُوض [or *gnats,* or *musquitoes*], (Ḳ,) or *abundance thereof,* (A,) *in their land.* (A, Ḳ.)

5. تبعّض *It was,* or *became, divided into parts,* or *portions.* (Ṣ, Ḳ.)

بَعْضٌ *Some,* or *somewhat* or *some one,* (lit. *a thing,*) of things, or of a thing: Th says that it signifies thus accord. to all the grammarians; (Mṣb, TA;) except Hishám, as will be seen hereafter: (TA:) or *a part,* or *portion,* (A, Mṣb, Ḳ,) of a thing, (Mṣb,) or of anything; (A, Ḳ;) whether little or much: (TA:) accord. to both these explanations, it may denote the greater part; as eight of ten: (Mṣb:) [thus it signifies *some one* or *more;* and it relates to persons and to other things:] pl. أَبْعَاضٌ; (Ṣ, IJ, Ḳ;) but ISd doubts whether IJ had an authority for this. (TA.) You say, بَعْضُ الشَّرِّ أَهْوَنُ مِنْ بَعْضٍ [*Some kinds of evil are easier to be borne than some*]. (A.) And جَارِيَةٌ حُسَّانَةٌ يُشْبِهُ بَعْضُهَا بَعْضًا [*A very beautiful girl, parts of whom resemble other parts*]. (A.) [And ضَرَبَ بَعْضُهُمْ بَعْضًا *Some of them beat some;* i. e. *they beat one another.*] And لَبِثْنَا يَوْمًا أَوْ بَعْضَ يَوْمٍ [*We have tarried a day or part of a day*]. (Ḳur xviii. 18.) And one says to a man of a company of men, "Who did this?" and he answers, أَحَدُنَا or بَعْضُنَا [*Some one of us*]; meaning himself. (A.) The article ال should not be prefixed to it, (Ḳ,* TA,) because it is originally a prefixed n., and as such determinate either literally or virtually, so that it does not admit another cause of being determinate; (TA;) contr. to what is said by IDrst (Ḳ, TA) and Ez-Zejjájee; for they said البَعْض and الكُلّ; which, properly, as ISd says, is not allowable; and it is said in the O that IDrst, in this matter, was at variance with all the people of his age: (TA:) AḤát says that the Arabs did not say الكُلّ nor البَعْض, but that people used these expressions, even Sb and Akh in their two books, by reason of their little knowledge in this way: (Ḳ,* TA:) a remark, says MF, which is extr., and needs no comment: (TA:) [for who surpassed Sb and Akh in knowledge respecting matters of this kind?] AḤát also relates his having told Aṣ that he had seen in the book of [that celebrated and chaste author] Ibn-El-Muḳaffa', العِلْمُ كَثِيرٌ وَلٰكِنَّ أَخْذَ البَعْضِ خَيْرٌ مِنْ تَرْكِ الكُلِّ [*Science is large; but the acquiring of part is better than the neglecting of the whole*]; and that Aṣ disapproved of it most strongly, saying that the article ال is not prefixed to بَعْض and كُلّ because they are determinate without it: (TA:) Az, however, says that the grammarians allow its being prefixed to these two words, (Mṣb, TA,) though Aṣ disallows it, (TA,) because they are meant to be understood as prefixed ns.; (Mṣb;) or because the article is meant to be a substitute for the noun to which they should be prefixed; or, in the case of بَعْض, because this word is equivalent to جُزْء, which receives the article ال. (MF.) It is related of AO, that he assigned also to بَعْض the contr. meaning of *All;* or *the whole:* adducing as a proof thereof the words of the Ḳur [xl. 29], يُصِبْكُمْ بَعْضُ ٱلَّذِى يَعِدُكُمْ as meaning *All of that with which he threateneth you will befall you:* and the saying of Lebeed,

• أَوْ يَعْتَلِقْ بَعْضَ النُّفُوسِ حِمَامُهَا •

[as meaning *Or their death shall cling to all living creatures:* or, accord. to another relation, او يَرْتَبِطْ, which means the same as او يعتلق]: thus also AHeyth explains the above-cited verse of the Ḳur; and thus Hishám explains the saying of Lebeed, erroneously asserting that بعض is here a pl.: (TA:) but with respect to the former instance, the Prophet had threatened them with two things, the punishment of the present world and that of the world to come; so he says, "This punishment will befall you in the present world;" which is part (بعض) of the two threats; without denying the punishment of the world to come: or, as Aboo-Is-ḥáḳ says, he mentions the part to indicate the necessary consequence of the whole: and as to the saying of Lebeed, by بعض النفوس he means himself. (TA [app. from ISd].)

أَرْضٌ بَعِضَةٌ *A land abounding with* بَعُوض [or *gnats,* or *musquitoes*]; (Ḳ;) as also ▼مَبْعَضَةٌ, like as you say مَبَقَّةٌ. (TA.) And لَيْلَةٌ بَعِضَةٌ *A night in which are many* بَعُوض; as also ▼مَبْعُوضَةٌ. (A, Ḳ.)

بَعُوضٌ [*Gnats,* or *musquitoes;*] i. q. بَقٌّ [which signifies both gnats, or musquitoes, (called in Egypt نَامُوس,) and also bugs]: n. un. with ة: (Ṣ:) or pl. of بَعُوضَةٌ, (Ḳ,) which signifies i. q. بَقَّةٌ. (A, Ḳ.) A poet speaks of the humming of the بعوض of the water. (TA.) The author of the Ḳ says, in the B, that the word is taken from بَعْض, because of the smallness of the body of the بعوضة in comparison with other living things. (TA.) You say, كَلَّفَنِى مُخَّ البَعُوضِ ‡ *He imposed upon me a difficult thing:* (A:) or *an impossible thing.* (TṢ, Ḳ.)

أَرْضٌ مَبْعَضَةٌ: } see بَعِضَةٌ.
لَيْلَةٌ مَبْعُوضَةٌ:

بعق

1. بَعَقَ, (TA,) [aor. ـَ,] inf. n. بُعَاقٌ, (Lth, Ḳ, TA,) said of a man, and a camel, &c., (TA,) *He uttered a vehement sound*, or *cry*. (Lth,* Ḳ,* TA.) — Also, inf. n. as above, said of a vehement rain, descending in large drops, *It clave*, or *furrowed*, the ground, *and made it to flow*. (Ḳ,* TA.) — And, inf. n. بَعْقٌ, *He stabbed*, or *stuck*, a camel *in the* نَحْر, or *throat*, or *uppermost part of the breast*, (Ḳ, TA,) *making the blood to flow*; (TA;) and (TA) so ↓ بعّق. (A'Obeyd, Ṣ, L, TA, all of which, except the last, mention only the latter verb in this sense.) — Also, (Ḳ,) inf. n. بَعْقٌ, (TA,) *He dug* a well. (Z, Ḳ.) — بَعْقٌ also signifies The act of *slitting*, *ripping*, or *rending*; like بَعْجٌ: (TA:) and ↓ تَبْعِيقٌ the same; (Ṣ;) or the *doing so much*. (Ḳ.) You say, بَعَّقْتُ ↓ زِقَّ الخَمْرِ, inf. n. تَبْعِيقٌ, *I slit*, or *ripped*, or *rent*, *the wine-skin*. (Ṣ.) — بَعَقَهُ عَنْ كَذَا, (Ḳ,) inf. n. بَعْقٌ, (TA,) *He removed it, took it off*, or *stripped it off, from over*, or *before, such a thing, which it covered*, or *concealed*. (Ibn-'Abbád, Ḳ.)

2: see 1, in three places.

5: see 7, in two places.

7. انبعق *It came upon one suddenly, unexpectedly, without his knowledge*. (Ṣ, Ḳ, TA.) — انبعق المُزْنُ ‡ [*The clouds*, or *white clouds*, or *clouds containing water*,] *clave asunder, with*, or *by reason of, rain*, or *violent rain*; syn. اِنْبَعَجَ بِالمَطَرِ; (Ṣ, Ḳ, TA;) or *opened vehemently with rain*; (Z, TA;) and ↓ تبعّق signifies the same. (Ṣ.) — انبعق فُلَانٌ بِالجُودِ وَالكَرَمِ ‡ [*Such a one was profuse in bounty and generosity*]. (TA.) — انبعق فى الكَلَامِ (Ṣ, Ḳ) † *He was profuse in speech*; (Ḳ,* TA;) as also ↓ تبعّق (Ḳ) and ↓ ابتعق. (Ṣgh, Ḳ.)

8: see 7.

بَعَاقٌ: see what next follows, in two places.

بُعَاقٌ † Clouds (سَحَابٌ) *pouring forth* [rain] *with vehemence*. (Ṣ.) — Also, and ↓ بَعَاقٌ and ↓ بِعَاقٌ and ↓ بَاعِقٌ, ‡ Rain *coming suddenly*, or *unexpectedly*, *with vehemence, in large drops*. (Ḳ, TA.) جُمُّ البُعَاقِ, in a trad. respecting prayer for rain, means † *Copious, abundant, extensive rain*. (TA.) — And ↓ all these four words, † A torrent *vehemently driving*; (Ḳ, TA;) *that carries away everything*. (AḤn, TA.)

بِعَاقٌ: } see بُعَاقٌ, in two places.
بَاعِقٌ: }

أَرْضٌ مَبْعُوقَةٌ *Land upon which what is termed* بُعَاقٌ [i. e. either the rain or torrent so termed] *has fallen*, or *descended*. (Nawádir el-Aạráb, TA.)

بعل

1. بَعَلَ, (Ṣ, Mṣb, Ḳ,) aor. ـَ, (Ḳ,) or ـُ [contr. to rule]; (Mṣb;) or the pret. is بَعُلَ; (so in the Ḥam p. 337;) inf. n. بُعُولَةٌ (Mṣb, Ḳ) and بَعَالَةٌ also (Ḥam ubi suprà) [and app. بَعْلٌ, for it is said in the Ḥam p. 359 that the primary signification of بَعْلٌ is النِّكَاحُ]; *He* (a man, Ṣ) *became a husband*; (Ṣ, Ḳ;) as also ↓ استبعل: (Ḳ:) *he married*, or *took a wife*. (Mṣb.) And in like manner, بَعَلَتْ, inf. n. بُعُولَةٌ, *She became a wife*: (TA:) [and it seems to be indicated in the Ḥam p. 359 that ↓ ابتعلت and ↓ تبعّلت signify the same:] and ↓ باعلت *she took to herself a husband*. (Ḳ.) — بَعِلَ عَلَيْهِ [as though originally signifying *He became a* بَعْل, or *lord, over him*:] *he was incompliant*, or *unyielding, to him*; *he resisted him*, or *withstood him*. (Ḳ.) Hence, in a trad., فَمَنْ بَعِلَ عَلَيْكُمْ أَمْرَكُمْ فَاقْتُلُوهُ *And whoso resisteth and disobeyeth your command, slay ye him*. (TA.) — بَعِلَ, (Ṣ, Ḳ,) بِأَمْرِهِ, aor. ـَ, (Ḳ,) † *He became confounded*, or *perplexed, so that he was unable to see his right course*, (Ṣ, Ḳ,) *by his affair*, or *case, and feared, and was disgusted*, (Ḳ,) *and remained fixed in his place like as do the palm-trees termed* بَعْل, (TA,) *not knowing what to do*. (Ḳ.)

3. باعلت: see 1. — باعل القَوْمُ قَوْمًا *The people intermarried with a people*. (Ḳ.) You say also, بَنُو فُلَانٍ لَا يُبَاعَلُونَ *The sons of such a one, none is married to them, nor are they married* [*to any but persons of their own tribe*]. (Ḥam p. 337.) — [The inf. n.] بِعَالٌ signifies also The *playing*, or *toying, together*, of a man with his wife; (Ṣ, Mgh, Mṣb, Ḳ;) and so مُبَاعَلَةٌ [also an inf. n. of the same verb], (Mṣb, Ḳ,) and ↓ تَبَاعُلٌ [inf. n. of 6]. (Ḳ.) You say, باعل آمْرَأَتَهُ *He played*, or *toyed, with his wife*. (Mṣb.) And تُبَاعِلُ زَوْجَهَا *She plays*, or *toys, with her husband*. (Ṣ.) And بَيْنَهُمَا مُبَاعَلَةٌ *Between them two is playing*, or *toying*. (TA.) And ↓ هُمَا يَتَبَاعَلَانِ *They two play*, or *toy, together, each with the other*. (TA.) — And metonymically, (TA,) بِعَالٌ signifies also ‡ *I. q.* جِمَاعٌ; (Az, Ḳ, TA;) and so مُبَاعَلَةٌ. (TḲ.) You say, بَاعَلَهَا, meaning ‡ *He lay with her*. (TḲ.) — And باعل فُلَانٌ فُلَانًا ‡ *Such a one sat with such a one*: (Ḳ, TA:) the idea of playing, or toying, being imagined to be implied. (TA.)

5. تبعّلت: see 1. — Also *She was obedient to her husband*; (Ḳ;) [so too ↓ ابتعلت, as will be seen from what follows;] and so تبعّلت زَوْجَهَا: (TA:) or *she adorned herself for her husband*. (Ḳ.) You say ↓ آمْرَأَةٌ حَسَنَةُ الاِبْتِعَالِ *A woman who is good in obedience to her husband*. (TA.)

6: see 3, in two places.

8: see 1: — and see also 5, in two places.

10. استبعل: see 1. — Also, said of palm-trees (نَخْل), *They became what are termed* بَعْل, q. v., (Ṣ, TA,) *and great*. (TA.) — And, said of a place, *It became what is termed* بَعْل: (Ḳ:) or *it became elevated*. (TA.)

بَعْلٌ *A husband*: (Ṣ, Mgh, Mṣb, Ḳ:) pl. بُعُولَةٌ (Ṣ, Mṣb, Ḳ) and بُعُولٌ and بِعَالٌ. (Ḳ.) And *A wife*; as also بَعْلَةٌ; (Ṣ, Mṣb, Ḳ;) like زَوْجٌ and زَوْجَةٌ. (Ṣ, Mṣb.*) — *A lord, a master, an owner*, or *a possessor*, (Ṣ, Mṣb, Ḳ,) of a thing, (Ḳ,) such as a house, and a beast, (TA,) or a she-camel: (Ṣ:) *a head, chief, ruler*, or *person of authority*. (El-Khaṭṭábee, TA.) — [And hence,] *A certain idol*, (Ṣ, Ḳ,) *of gold*, (TA,) *belonging to the people of Ilyás*, (Ṣ, Ḳ,) who is said to be the same as Idrees, the grandfather, or an ancestor, of Noah, or to have been a grandson of Aaron, (Bḍ in vi. 85,) or the son of the brother of Aaron: (Jel ibid.:) it is mentioned in the Ḳur xxxvii. 123: accord. to one copy of the Ḳ, *it belonged to the people of Jonas*; and so in the Kitáb el-Mujarrad of Kr: accord. to Mujáhid, it means *a deity that is not God*: (TA:) or *a certain king*: (IAạr, Ḳ:) but [SM says,] the correct explanation is the first: (TA:) or *a certain idol belonging to the people of Bekk, in Syria*; i. e., *of the town now called Baala-Bekk*: so in the Ḳur: (Bḍ, Jel:*) or it means in the dial. of El-Yemen *a lord*; and so in the Ḳur. (Bḍ.) — Also *One whom it is a necessary duty to obey*; as *a father*, and *a mother*, and *the like*. (TA.) — And *A family*, or *household, whose maintenance is incumbent on a man*. (TA.) — And it may be a contraction of بَعِل, as meaning *Lacking strength*, or *power*, or *ability*; *unable to find the right way to accomplish his affair*. (TA.) — Also ‡ *A weight*, or *burden*. (Ḳ, TA.) You say, أَصْبَحَ فُلَانٌ بَعْلًا عَلَى أَهْلِهِ ‡ *Such a one became a weight*, or *burden, upon his family*; because of his ascendency over them. (Er-Rághib, TA.) — † *Elevated land*, (Ṣ, Ḳ,) *upon which comes neither running water nor torrent*, (Ṣ,) or *that is not rained upon more than once in the year*: (Ḳ:) or ‡ *land elevated above other land*; as being likened to the man who is thus termed. (Er-Rághib, TA.) — † *Any palm-trees, and other trees, and seed-produce, not watered*: or *such as are watered by the rain*: (Ḳ:) or ‡ *palm-trees* (نَخْل) *that imbibe with their roots, and so need not to be watered*: (Ṣ, Mgh, Mṣb, Ḳ:) metaphorically so applied: (Mgh:) AA says that it is *syn. with* عِذْىٌ, meaning *what is watered by the rain*: but Aṣ says that this latter word has the meaning just given, whereas بعل signifies *what imbibes with its roots, without irrigation or rain*: (Ṣ, Mṣb:) or *palm-trees growing in land whereof the supply of water is near* [*to the surface*], *so that it suffices without their having irrigation or rain*: (TA:) or *large, so as to imbibe with the roots*: (Er-Rághib, TA:) and ‡ *a male palm-tree*; (Ḳ, TA;) likened to the man who is thus termed: (TA:) and Az says that it is used as meaning † [*dates such as are termed*] قَسْب. (TA.) — And † The *tax*, or *impost, that is given for the watering of palm-trees*. (Ḳ.)

بَعِلٌ part. n. of بَعِلَ, *Confounded*, or *perplexed*, &c. (Ḳ.) And *Lacking strength*, or *power*, or *ability*; *unable to find the right way to accomplish his affair*. (TA.) — With ة, applied as an epithet to a woman, (Ṣ,) and meaning One *who does not dress*, or *wear clothes, well*, (Ḳ, TA,) *nor well adjust her personal state or condition*. (TA.)

بغت

1. بَغَتَهُ, (Ṣ, A, &c.,) aor. ـَ, (A, Mṣb, Ḳ,) inf. n. بَغْتٌ and بَغْتَةٌ (Ṣ, A, Mṣb, Ḳ) and بَغَتٌ (MF) and بَغَتَةٌ (Ḳ) and بَغَّتَةٌ, with teshdeed to the ت, of the same measure as جَرَّبَةٌ, accord. to AA's

reading of the Ḳur in a passage which will be found below, without a parallel among inf. ns., (Z,) [and said by some to have an intensive signification,] *He, or it, came upon him, or happened to him, suddenly, unexpectedly, without his being aware of it, or without any previous cause; surprised him; took him by surprise, or unawares;* (Ṣ, A, Mṣb, Ḳ;) as also ↓ بَاغَتَهُ, (A, Mṣb,) inf. n. مُبَاغَتَةٌ (Ṣ, Ḳ) and بِغَاتٌ. (TA.) It is said in the Ḳur vi. 31, accord. to the reading mentioned above, إِذَا جَآءَتْهُمُ ٱلسَّاعَةُ بَغَتَةً [*When the hour of the resurrection shall come upon them suddenly, unexpectedly,* &c.]. (Z.) And you say, جَآءَهُ بَغْتَةً *He, or it, came to him suddenly,* &c. (A, Mṣb.) And لَقِيَهُ بَغْتَةً *He met,* or *found, him,* or *it, suddenly,* &c. (Ṣ.) And لَسْتُ آمَنُ بَغَتَاتِ العَدُوِّ *I am not secure from,* or *free from fear of, the enemy's comings* [upon me] *unawares.* (Ṣ.)

3: see 1.

البَاغُوثُ *The festival,* (A,) or *a certain festival,* (IAth, Ḳ,) *of the Christians;* (A, IAth, Ḳ;) [namely, *Easter;*] thus called accord. to some; but accord. to others, الباعوث [q. v.], with the unpointed ع and the three-pointed ث. (IAth.)

مَبْغُوتٌ i. q. مَبْهُوتٌ [*Confounded,* or *perplexed, and unable to see his right course*]: so in the saying, لَا رَأْىَ لِمَبْغُوتٍ [*There is no judgment to one who is confounded,* &c.]. (A.)

بغث

1. بَغِثَ, (Mṣb, Ḳ,) aor. ـَ, (Ḳ,) inf. n. بُغْثَةٌ, (Mṣb,) or this is a simple subst., and the inf. n. is بَغَثٌ, (TA,) *He* (a bird) *was,* or *became, of a colour resembling that of ashes:* (Mṣb:) or *he* (a sheep or goat) *was of the mixed colours of those to which the epithet* بَغْثَآءُ *is applied.* (Ḳ, TA.) [See أَبْغَثُ, and بُغْثَةٌ, and بَغَثٌ.]

بَغَثٌ *Dust-colour.* (A.) [But see بُغْثَةٌ. Accord. to the TA, the former is the inf. n. of 1, q. v.]

بُغْثَةٌ *Whiteness inclining to* خُضْرَة [which here app. means *a dark,* or *ashy, dust-colour*]: (T:) [or, in a bird, *a colour resembling that of ashes:* (see 1:)] or the *colour of sheep or goats to which the epithet* بَغْثَآءُ *is applied.* (Ḳ, TA.) [See أَبْغَثُ.]

بَغْثَآءُ: see أَبْغَثُ, of which it is the fem.

بَغَاثٌ (T, Ṣ, A, Mgh, Mṣb, Ḳ) and بُغَاثٌ and بِغَاثٌ; (A, Mgh, Ḳ;) only the second of these three mentioned by Sb; (TA;) but the second and third asserted to be correct by Yoo; (AZ, TA;) and the last heard by Az; (TA;) or neither of these two is allowable; (Mṣb;) *A bird that does not prey, and such as one does not desire to make an object of prey because it is not eaten:* (T, Mṣb:) or *small birds that do not prey, such as sparrows and the like;* [a coll. gen. n.;] n. un. with ة: (Mgh:) or [accord. to Lth,] *a certain dust-coloured bird,* (T, A, Ḳ,) *of the birds of the water, ash-coloured, and long-necked;* as also ↓ أَبْغَثُ; pl. [of the latter] بُغْثٌ and أَبَاغِثُ: (T:) [but this appears to be wrong; for AM says, in the T,] Lth makes the بغاث and the ابغث to be one, asserting them to be of aquatic birds; but in my opinion, the former is different from the latter: as to the latter, it is *a well-known kind of aquatic bird,* so called because it is *of the colour termed* بُغْثَة, i. e. *white inclining to* خُضْرَة [explained above, voce بُغْثَةٌ]: but as to the بغاث, it is *any bird that is not one of prey:* and the word is said to be a coll. gen. n., signifying the *class of birds that are objects of prey:* (TA:) ISk says that the بَغَاث is *a bird of a colour inclining to that of dust,* (Ṣ, Mṣb,*) *a little less than the* رَخَمَة [or *vultur percnopterus*], (Ṣ,) or *less than the* رخمة, (Mṣb,) *slow in flight:* (Ṣ, Mṣb:) but IB says that this is a mistake in two points of view; first, because بغاث is a [coll.] gen. n., of which the n. un. is with ة, like as is that of حَمَامٌ; and secondly, because it applies to the *class of birds that do not prey;* but the ↓ أَبْغَثُ is *a bird of the colour of dust,* and this may be *a bird of prey,* and it may be *not a bird of prey:* (TA:) AZ says that بغاث signifies the [*species of vulture called*] رَخَم; and the n. un. is with ة: others, the *young ones of the* رخم and *birds of the crow-kind:* or [*birds*] *like the* [*hawks called*] سَوَادِق [pl. of سَوْذَق], *not predaceous:* in the T, it is said to be [*a kind of bird*] *like the* [*hawk called*] بَاشَق, *that does not prey upon any other bird:* (TA:) or بُغَاثٌ and بَغَاثٌ (ISd, Ḳ) and بِغَاثٌ (Ḳ) signify the *worst* [or *most ignoble*] *of birds,* (ISd, Ḳ, [the latter giving this as a second and distinct signification,]) and *such as do not prey:* (ISd, TA:) Fr says, بُغَاثُ الطَّيْرِ signifies *the worst of birds,* and *such as do not prey;* and بُغَاثٌ and بِغَاثٌ are dial. vars.: (Ṣ:) the pl. is بِغْثَانٌ, (Sb, T, Ṣ, Mṣb, Ḳ,) accord. to those who make بغاث a sing., (Yoo, Ṣ, Mṣb, TA,) or accord. to those who make the sing. to be with ة; (T, TA;) or those who apply بَغَاثَةٌ [as a n. un.] to the male and the female make بَغَاثٌ to be pl. [or rather a coll. gen. n.]; (Yoo, Ṣ, Mṣb;) as is done in the case of نَعَامَةٌ and نَعَامٌ: (Yoo, Ṣ:) ISd says that بَغَاثَةٌ, with fet-ḥ, is the n. un., applied alike to the male and the female: (TA:) [and Fei says,] it is not allowable to pronounce this with ḍamm or with kesr to the first letter: (Mṣb:) but Yoo asserts both of these forms to be used: (AZ, TA:) and بغاثة is said to signify *a weak bird.* (TA.) It is said in a prov., إِنَّ البَغَاثَ بِأَرْضِنَا يَسْتَنْسِرُ (Ṣ, A, Mṣb, Ḳ*) *Verily the* بغاث *in our land becomes* [*like*] *a vulture,* or *become* [*like*] *vultures:* (Mṣb:) applied to the low person who becomes of high rank: (A:) meaning ‡ *the weak in our land becomes strong:* (Mṣb:) or *he who makes himself our neighbour becomes mighty, strong,* or *of high rank, by our means,* (Ṣ, Ḳ, TA,) *acquiring the might,* or *strength, of the vulture, after having been low,* or *mean, in condition.* (TA.)

بَغِيثٌ *Wheat* (حِنْطَةٌ and طَعَامٌ [both of which signify the same, though the latter, q. v., has a larger application,]) *adulterated by being mixed with barley;* (Th, Ḳ;) as also غَلِيثٌ and لَغِيثٌ. (Th, TA.)

بُغَيْثَآءُ [dim. of بَغْثَآءُ fem. of أَبْغَثُ, q. v.,] The *place of the* حَقِيبَة [q. v.] in a camel. (Ḳ.) [So called because of its colour, produced by chafing.]

أَبْغَثُ *Of a white colour inclining to* خُضْرَة [which here app. means *a dark,* or *ashy, dust-colour*]: (T:) [or *of a colour resembling that of ashes:* (see 1:)] or *dust-coloured:* (A:) or *of a colour near to that of dust:* (Ṣ:) an epithet, like أَحْمَرُ: [fem. بَغْثَآءُ: and] pl. بُغْثٌ: and sometimes, when used as a subst., it has for pl. أَبَاغِثُ. (IB, TA.) You say طَائِرٌ أَبْغَثُ *A bird of the colour above described:* (T, Ṣ:) whether it be a bird of prey or not: see بَغَاثٌ in two places: (IB, TA:) and صَقْرٌ أَبْغَثُ [*a hawk of that colour*]; (ISh, A;) as well as أَحْوَى and أَبْيَضُ; i. e., that wherewith men take game. (ISh, TA.) بَغْثَآءُ applied to sheep or goats, (Ṣ, Ḳ,) or, as in some lexicons, to sheep, (TA,) is like رَقْطَآءُ; (Ṣ, Ḳ;) [*Black speckled with white; or the reverse;*] or *in which are blackness and whiteness, with predominance of the latter colour:* (TA:) or شَاةٌ بَغْثَآءُ and غَنَمٌ بُغْثٌ signify *a sheep* or *goat,* and *sheep* or *goats, in which are blackness and whiteness.* (A.)——Also, [as a subst.,] *A certain bird,* (Ḳ, TA,) *dust-coloured,* in truth *different from the* بَغَاث, as shown above: see the latter word: (TA:) pl. بُغْثٌ and أَبَاغِثُ. (T, TA.) You say, هُوَ مِنْ أَبَاغِثِ الطَّيْرِ [*He is of the birds thus called*]. (A.)——And الأَبْغَثُ signifies *The lion;* (TṢ, Ḳ;) because he is of the colour termed بُغْثَة. (TA.)——And البَغْثَآءُ ‡ *The medley,* or *mixed* or *promiscuous multitude* or *collection, of men* or *people;* or *of the lowest* or *basest* or *meanest sort,* or *refuse,* or *riffraff, thereof;* (Ṣ, A, Ḳ;) *the commonalty,* or *vulgar,* and *collective body, of the people.* (Ṣ.) One says, خَرَجَ فُلَانٌ فِى البَغْثَآءِ and الغَثْرَآءِ ‡ *Such a one went forth among the medley,* &c., *of the people.* (A.) And دَخَلْنَا فِى البَغْثَآءِ ‡ *We entered among the commonalty,* or *vulgar,* and *the collective body, of the people.* (Ṣ.)

بغش

1. بَغَشَتِ السَّمَآءُ, aor. ـُ, (Ṣ, Ḳ,) inf. n. بَغْشٌ, (Ṣ,) *The sky rained a rain such as is termed* بَغْشَة, q. v. (Ṣ, Ḳ.)——بُغِشَتِ الأَرْضُ *The land was watered by a rain such as is termed* بَغْشَة, (Ṣ,) or بَغْش. (TA.)

بَغْشٌ: see what next follows.

بَغْشَةٌ *A weak shower of rain;* (Ṣ, Ḳ:) *above what is called* طَشَّة: (Ṣ:) or *weak rain, small in its drops;* as also ↓ بَغْشٌ [originally an inf. n.]: or both signify *a cloud that pours forth its rain in one shower:* Aṣ says that the lightest and weakest of rain is that called طَلّ; then, the رَذَاذ; then, the بَغْش: the dim. of the last is بُغَيْشٌ. (TA.)

مَطَرٌ بَاغِشٌ *Weak rain.* (Ṣ, Ḳ.)

أَرْضٌ مَبْغُوشَةٌ *Land watered by a rain such as is termed* بَغْشَة, (Ṣ,) or بَغْش. (TA.)

بغض

1. بَغُضَ; (Ṣ, A, Mṣb, Ḳ;) and بَغِضَ; aor. [of

both] ؛; and بَغُضَ, aor. ؛; (K;) inf. n. بَغَاضَةٌ, (S, A, Msb, K,) inf. n. of the first; (TA;) *He,* or *it,* (a man, S, or a thing, Msb,) *was,* or *became, hateful, odious,* or *an object of hatred.* (S, A, K.) — بَغُضَ جَدُّهُ ‡ *His fortune,* or *good fortune, fell;* syn. عَثَرَ. (A.) And بَغُضَ جَدُّكَ, (L, K, TA,) or بَغِضَ, (as in one copy of the K,) or بَغَضَ, (as in the CK,) ‡ *May thy fortune,* or *good fortune, fall:* syn. تَعَسَ, (K, TA,) and عَثَرَ: (TA:) a phrase ascribed by IB to the people of El-Yemen. (TA.) = See also 4, in three places.

2. بَغَّضَهُ ٱللّٰهُ إِلَى ٱلنَّاسِ, (S, TA,) or لِلنَّاسِ, (Msb,) [but this I think doubtful, from what is said in explanation of the verb of wonder, (see 4,)] inf. n. تَبْغِيضٌ, (S, K,) *God rendered him hateful, odious,* or *an object of hatred, to men;* (S, Msb;*) تَبْغِيضٌ being the *contr. of* تَحْبِيبٌ: (K:) or *very hateful* or *odious.* (TA.) You say also, حُبِّبَ إِلَىَّ زَيْدٌ وَبُغِّضَ إِلَىَّ عَمْرٌو [*Zeyd was rendered an object of love to me, and 'Amr was rendered an object of hatred,* or *of much hatred, to me*]. (A, TA.)

3. بَاغَضْتُهُ, inf. n. مُبَاغَضَةٌ, *I rendered him* [*hatred,* or] *vehement hatred, reciprocally.* (A,* TA.) You say also, بَيْنَهُمَا مُبَاغَضَةٌ [*Between them two is reciprocal hatred,* or *vehement hatred*]. (A.)

4. ابغضهُ, (S, A, Msb, K,) inf. n. إِبْغَاضٌ, (Msb,) *He hated him.* (S, A,* Msb,* K.) It is said that ▼بَغَضَهُ is not allowable: (Msb:) or يَبْغُضُنِى is a bad form; (AHát, K;) used by the lower class; and sanctioned by Th only; for he explains قَالِينَ, as occurring in the Kur [xxvi. 168], by بَاغِضِينَ, which shows that he held بَغَضَ to be a dial. var.; for otherwise he would have said مُبْغِضِينَ: (AHát:) but the epithet بَغُوضٌ affords a strong evidence in favour of the opinion of Th here mentioned; for فَعُولٌ is mostly from فَاعِلٌ, not from مُفْعِلٌ. (TA.) = مَا أَبْغَضَهُ إِلَىَّ, (S,) or لِى, (K,) is [said to be] anomalous; (S, K;) because the verb of wonder is not regularly formed from a verb of the measure أَفْعَلَ; but this is not anomalous; for it is from بَغُضَ فُلَانٌ إِلَىَّ ["such a one was, or became, hateful, or odious, to me:" ما ابغضه الىّ signifying *How hateful,* or *odious, is he to me!* but ما ابغضه لى, *How he hates me!* for] the lexicologists and grammarians relate that مَا أَبْغَضَنِى لَهُ is said when thou hatest him; and ما ابغضنى إِلَيْهِ, when he hates thee: (IB:) ISd says, on the authority of Sb, that ما ابغضنى له means that thou art an object of hatred (مُبْغَضٌ [so in the TA, but this is evidently a mistake for مُبْغِضٌ, a hater,]) to him; and ما ابغضه الىّ, that he is an object of hatred with thee, or in thine estimation. (TA.) = أَنْعَمَ ٱللّٰهُ بِكَ عَيْنًا وَأَبْغَضَ بِعَدُوِّكَ عَيْنًا, (so in the A, and the latter verb thus in the JK and in the L,) or the former verb is نَعِمَ, (L, K,) and the latter ▼بَغَضَ, (K, TA,) like نَصَرَ, (TA,) or ▼بَغِضَ, (CK,) is a form of imprecation (TA) ‡ [app. meaning *May God make thine eye to be refreshed by the sight of him whom thou lovest, and make the eye of thine enemy to be pained by the sight of him whom he hateth:* or *may God make an eye to be refreshed by the sight of thee, and make an eye to be affected with hatred by the sight of thine enemy*].

5. تبغّض *He manifested,* or *showed, hatred;* or *he became,* or *made himself, an object of hatred; contr. of* تَحَبَّبَ. (K.) You say, تَحَبَّبَ لِى فُلَانٌ وَتَبَغَّضَ لِى أَخُوهُ [*Such a one manifested love to me, or made himself an object of love to me, and his brother manifested hatred to me, or made himself an object of hatred to me*]. (A, TA.)

6. تباغض القَوْمُ *The company of men hated one another:* (Msb:) تَبَاغُضٌ is the *contr. of* تَحَابٌّ. (S, K.) You say, مَا رَأَيْتُ أَشَدَّ تَبَاغُضًا مِنْهُمَا [*I have not seen any more vehement in mutual hatred than they two*]. (A, TA.)

بُغْضٌ *Hatred; contr. of* حُبٌّ: (S, A, K:) a subst. from أَبْغَضَهُ. (Msb.)

بِغْضَةٌ *Vehement hatred;* as also ▼بَغْضَآءُ, (S, A, Msb, K,) and ▼بَغَاضَةٌ [but see 1]. (TA.) = See also بَغِيضٌ.

بَغْضَآءُ: see what next precedes.

بَغُوضٌ: see what next follows.

بَغِيضٌ *Hateful; odious; an object of hatred:* (S, A, Msb,* K:) *hated;* as also ▼بَغُوضٌ (TA) and ▼مُبْغَضٌ: (Msb,* TA:) pl. of the first, بُغَضَآءُ. (A, TA.) — Some say that it has also the contr. signification of *Hating; i. q.* ▼مُبْغِضٌ: (TA:) and Skr explains ▼بِغْضَةٌ as signifying people *hating* thee. (L, TA.*)

بَغَاضَةٌ: see بِغْضَةٌ.

مُبْغَضٌ: } see بَغِيضٌ.
مُبْغِضٌ: }

مَبْغَضَةٌ [*A cause of hatred:* a word of the same class as مَبْخَلَةٌ and مَجْبَنَةٌ]. (A.)

بغل

1. بَغَلَ, aor. ؛, inf. n. بُغُولَةٌ, said of a man, *i. q.* تَبَلَّدَ [i. e. † *He affected stupidity, dulness,* or *want of intelligence;* or *he became submissive, and humble;* &c.]. (TA.) [See also 2.] = بَغْلَهَرَ: see 2.

2. تَبْغِيلٌ, the inf. n., signifies † The *being big, thick,* or *rude, and hard, strong,* or *sturdy, in body;* or said of the body: and hence, accord. to some, is derived ▼بَغْلٌ. (TA.) — بَغَّلَ, inf. n. as above, ‡ *He was impotent and weak,* or *languid, and fatigued,* (JK, K, TA,) *in going,* or *pace.* (TA.) — بَغَّلَتِ الإِبِلُ, (K,) inf. n. as above, (S, K,) ‡ *The camels went a pace between that termed* هَمْلَجَة *and that termed* عَنَق: (S,* K, TA:) and hence ▼بَغْلٌ is derived accord. to IDrd: (TA:) or *they went in a certain manner, with wide step:* (JK:) [see also 5:] or the inf. n. signifies the *going in a gentle manner:* and one says, أَعْيَا فَبَغَّلَ, i. e. [*he was fatigued, so*] *he went an easy, but a quick, pace;* syn. هَمْلَجَ. (TA.) = بَغْلَهَرَ, (inf. n. as above, TA,) ‡ *He made their children to be base-born,* or *ignoble,* (K, TA,) by marrying among them; (IDrd, TA;) as also ▼بَغَلَهُمْ, aor. ؛: (K:) from بَغْلٌ; because the بغل [or mule] is unable to equal the heat, or course, of the horse. (TA.)

5. تبغّل *He* (a camel) *became like the* بَغْل [or *mule*] *in the width of his step.* (TA.) [See also 2.]

بَغْلٌ The *mule;* i. e. the *animal generated between the he-ass and the mare* [or sometimes *between the horse and the she-ass*]; (TA;) also called ▼بَغَّالٌ; so in a verse of Jereer: (S, Sgh:) pl. أَبْغُلٌ [a pl. of pauc.] (JK) and أَبْغَالٌ, [also] a pl. of pauc., (Msb,) and بِغَالٌ, (JK, S, Msb, K,) a pl. of mult.; (Msb;) and quasi-pl. n. ▼مَبْغُولَآءُ, (K,) meaning *a number of mules* (بغال) *together:* (JK,* S:) the female is termed بَغْلَةٌ; (S, Msb, K;) pl. بَغَلَاتٌ and بِغَالٌ. (Msb.) See 2, in two places. You say طَرِيقٌ فِيهِ أَبْوَالُ البِغَالِ [*A road in which is the urine of mules*]; meaning † *a difficult road.* (TA.) And فُلَانَةُ أَعْقَرُ مِنْ بَغْلَةٍ [*Such a woman is more barren than a she-mule*]. (TA.) And البَغْلُ نَغْلٌ وَهُوَ لَهُ أَهْلٌ [*The mule is a bastard, and he is a relation to him*]; meaning † *he is a bastard.* (TA.) And as the mule suggests the idea of evil disposition, or perverseness, and roughness, you say, in describing him who is low, or ignoble, هُوَ بَغْلٌ نَغْلٌ † [*He is a mule, a bastard*]. (Er-Rághib, TA.) The people of Egypt say, اِشْتَرَى فُلَانٌ بَغْلَةً حَسْنَآءَ, meaning ‡ [*Such a one bought a beautiful*] *female slave:* and فِى بَيْتِ بَنِى فُلَانٍ بِغَالٌ ‡ [*In the house of the sons of such a one are slaves,* or *female slaves*]: and اِشْتَرَيْتُ مِنْ بِغَالِ اليَمَنِ وَلٰكِنْ بِغَالِى الثَّمَنِ ‡ [*I bought of the slaves,* or *female slaves, of El-Yemen, but for a high price*]. (TA.)

بَغَّالٌ [n. un. of ▼بَغَّالَةٌ, which is a coll. gen. n., like حَمَّارَةٌ and جَمَّالَةٌ, but explained by Freytag as meaning "he who possesses many mules;"] *An owner,* or *attendant,* (Sb, S,) *of mules,* (Sb, TA,) or *of the mule.* (S.) = See also بَغْلٌ, with which it is syn.

بَغَّالَةٌ: see what next precedes.

هُوَ مِنَ الثَّوْرِ أَبْغَلُ وَمِنَ الحِمَارِ أَثْقَلُ † [*He is more mulish than the bull, and more heavy,* or *sluggish, than the ass*]. (TA.)

مَبْغُولَآءُ: see بَغْلٌ.

بغم

1. بَغَمَتْ, aor. ـَ (S, K) and ـِ and ـُ, (K,) inf. n. بُغَامٌ (JK, S, K) and بُغُومٌ; (JK, K;) and ▼تبغّمت; (K;) *She* (a gazelle) *uttered a cry:* (S:) or *uttered her softest,* or *gentlest, cry* (JK, K) *to her young one:* (K:) and sometimes it is said of a [wild] cow: (TA:) so too بَغَمَ said of a male gazelle: and the verb is also used transitively, said of a female gazelle uttering this cry to her young one. (JK.) Also, (S, K,) ▼ both verbs, (K,) *She* (a camel) *uttered a cry without clearness:* (S:) or *uttered a broken,* or *an interrupted, not a prolonged, yearning cry, to,* or *for,*

her young one: (Ḳ:) or *uttered a weak cry, below that* [*grumbling cry*] *which is termed* رُغَآء. (Ḥam p. 233.) [See an ex. in a verse of Dhu-r-Rummeh cited voce إِلَّا.] And بَغَمَ and ▼تبغّم said of the ثَيْتَل and إِيَّل and وَعِل, [all of which words are said to signify the mountain goat,] *He uttered a cry.* (Ḳ.) —— بَغَمَهُ, (Ṣ, Ḳ,) and بَغَمَ لَهُ, (TA,) † *He spoke to him obscurely, not expressing clearly to him the meaning of his speech to him;* (Ṣ, Ḳ;) taken from the بُغَام of the she-camel; because it is a cry not uttered clearly. (TA.)

3: باغمهُ, (Ḳ,) inf. n. مُبَاغَمَةٌ, (Ṣ,) ‡ *He talked with him with a soft, or gentle, voice:* (Ṣ, Ḳ, TA:) or المُبَاغَمَةُ is like المُنَاغَمَةُ, and means *the speaking* [*with another*] *faintly;* taken from the بُغَام [see 1] of the gazelle and the she-camel: (Ḥam p. 233:) or *the holding amatory and enticing talk, or conversation, with another, with a soft, or gentle, voice.* (TA.)

5: see 1, in three places.

6. [تَبَاغَمَتْ *They* (gazelles) *uttered cries,* or *their softest or gentlest cries, one to another.*] One says, مَرَرْتُ بِرَوْضَةٍ تَتَبَاغَمُ فِيهَا الظِّبَآءُ [*I passed by a meadow in which the gazelles were uttering cries,* &c., *one to another*]: and بغزلان يَتَبَاغَمْنَ [*by gazelles uttering cries,* &c., *one to another*]. (TA.)

بُغْمَةٌ *A thing like the* قِلَادَة, [*a necklace,*] *with which women ornament themselves.* (TA.) [But this is apparently post-classical, from the Turkish بُوغْمَقْ. In the present day, it is applied to *A necklace of pearls.*]

بُغَامٌ The *crying,* or *cry, of the female gazelle,* and *of the she-camel, as explained above:* see 1. (Ṣ.)

بَغُومٌ A female gazelle *uttering,* or *that utters, the cry termed* بُغَام. (Ṣ, Ḳ.) —— † A woman *having a soft, or gentle, voice.* (JK, TA.)

مَبْغُومٌ A young gazelle, and a young camel, *to which the cry termed* بُغَام *is addressed by its mother.* (JK.) —— One says, also, بُغَامٌ مَبْغُومٌ [*A cry* &c. *uttered*]; like as one says, قَوْلٌ مَقُولٌ. (TA.)

بغو

1. بَغَا الشَّىْءَ, inf. n. بَغْوٌ, *He looked at the thing* [*to see*] *how it was;* (Ḳ;) as also بَغَى, (Ḳ in art. بغى,) inf. n. بَغْىٌ. (TA in that art.)

بغى

1. بَغَى, (Ṣ, Ḳ, &c.,) aor. ـِ, (Mṣb, Ḳ,) inf. n. بُغَآءٌ, (Ṣ, Mgh, Ḳ, &c.,) or this is a simple subst., and the inf. n. is بَغْىٌ, (Mṣb,) [but, if this be correct, the former is generally used for the latter,] and بُغًى, (Lḥ, Ḳ,) but the first is better known, and is the chaste form, and some say, بِغًى, (TA,) and بُغْيَةٌ and بِغْيَةٌ, (Ḳ,) accord. to Th, but others hold these two to be simple substs., and some mention also بَغْيَةٌ, with fet-ḥ, (TA,) and بُغَايَةٌ, (Aṣ, Ṣ, TA,) *He sought; sought for,* or *after; sought, desired,* or *endeavoured, to find, and take,* or *get;* (Ṣ, Mgh, Mṣb, Ḳ, &c.;) a stray-beast, (Aṣ, Ṣ, TA,) or any other thing, (Ṣ, Mgh,* Mṣb,* Ḳ,* TA,) good or evil; (Lḥ, TA;) as also ▼ابتغى and ▼تبغّى (Ṣ, Mṣb, Ḳ) and ▼استبغى: (Ḳ:) or ▼ابتغى signifies *he sought,* &c., *diligently, studiously, sedulously,* or *earnestly:* (Er-Rághib, TA:) and بَغَى signifies also *he loved,* or *affected,* a thing: (MF, TA:) or, accord. to Er-Rághib, the inf. n. signifies the *seeking to exceed the just bounds in respect of that which one aims at,* or *endeavours after, whether one actually exceed or do not;* and sometimes it is considered *in relation to quantity;* and sometimes, *in relation to quality.* (TA.) You say, بَغَاهُ بِشَرٍّ [*He sought him with an evil purpose;* or *sought to do him evil*]. (Ṣ and Ḳ in art. عقب.) —— And بَغَاهُ *He sought,* &c., a thing *for him;* like بَغَى لَهُ. (Lḥ, Mgh,* Ḳ.*) You say, بَغَاهُ الشَّىْءَ *He sought,* &c., *the thing for him;* (Ṣ, Ḳ;) as also ▼ابغاهُ الشَّىْءَ: (Ḳ:) thus you say, اِبْغِ لِى كَذَا or ▼أَبْغِنِى كذا and اِبْغِنِى كَذَا *Seek thou for me such a thing;* (TA;) and ▼أَبْغِنِى ضَالَّتِى *Seek thou for me my stray-beast:* (Mgh:) or ▼ابغاهُ الشَّىْءَ signifies *He aided,* or *assisted, him to seek the thing:* (Ks, Ḳ:) or ▼أَبْغِنِى كَذَا signifies *Seek thou for me such a thing;* and also *Aid thou me to seek such a thing.* (JK.) It is said in the Ḳur [ix. 47], يَبْغُونَكُمُ الفِتْنَةَ *They seek,* or *desire, for you discord,* or *dissension;* or *they seeking,* &c.: and in the same [iii. 94], تَبْغُونَهَا عِوَجًا *Ye seek,* or *desire, for it,* namely, the way [of God], *crookedness;* or *ye seeking,* &c.: the first objective complement of the verb being in the accus. case because of the suppression of the preposition ل. (TA.) —— [Hence, app.,] بَغَانِى دَآءٌ *It procured to me disease; it caused disease to befall me.* (Ḥam p. 794.) And إِنَّهُ لَذُو بُغَايَةٍ *Verily he is one who makes much gain:* (JK, Ḳ:) but in the M, ذُو بُغَايَةٍ لِلْكَسْبِ, meaning *a seeker of gain.* (TA.) And مَا بُغِىَ لَهُ *Good was not appointed to betide him.* (TA.) —— بَغَى عَلَى أَخِيهِ, inf. n. بَغْىٌ, *He envied his brother; he wished that a blessing, or cause of happiness, or an excellence, might become transferred from his brother to himself:* so says Lḥ, who holds this to be the primary signification of the verb. (TA.) It is said in a prov., البَغْىُ عِقَالُ النَّصْرِ [*Envy is the shackle of aid* from God against an enemy or a wrongdoer]. (TA.) —— Hence, (Lḥ, TA,) بَغْىٌ signifies The *acting wrongfully, injuriously,* or *tyrannically;* (Lḥ, Ṣ, TA;) because the envier so acts towards the envied; his endeavour being to cause, by guile, the blessing of God upon him to depart from him: (Lḥ, TA:) or the *seeking,* or *endeavouring, to act corruptly, wrongly,* or *unjustly:* (Az, TA:) or the *exceeding the due bounds,* or *just limits, in any way:* (Ṣ:) accord. to Er-Rághib, it is of two kinds: one of these is approved, and this is the *passing beyond the bounds of equity to exercise beneficence, and beyond the bounds of obligatory duties to do what is not obligatory:* the other is disapproved, and this is the *passing beyond the bounds of that which is true,* or *right, to do that which is false,* or *wrong,* or *to do acts of a doubtful nature:* but in most instances it is that which is disapproved. (TA.) You say, بَغَى عَلَيْهِ, (Ṣ, Ḳ,) and بغى عَلَى النَّاسِ, (Az, Mṣb,) aor. ـِ, (Ḳ,) inf. n. بَغْىٌ, (Mṣb, Ḳ,) *He exalted himself against him,* or *above him; overpowered,* or *oppressed, him;* (Fr, Ṣ, Ḳ;) *acted wrongfully, injuriously,* or *tyrannically, towards him; and deviated from the right way:* (Ḳ:) and *he acted wrongfully, injuriously,* or *tyrannically, towards men,* or *the people,* (Az, Mṣb,) *and sought to annoy them,* or *hurt them.* (Az, TA.) Lḥ mentions, on the authority of Ks, the saying, مَا لِى وَلِلْبَغِ بَعْضِكُمْ عَلَى بَعْضٍ [*What have I to do with wrongful conduct,* the wrongful conduct *of one of you towards another?*], for وَلِلْبَغْىِ; ISd thinks, because of the difficulty found in pronouncing the kesreh after the ى. (TA.) بَغَى also signifies *He occupied himself with corrupt, wrong,* or *unjust, conduct:* [accord. to Fei,] from the same verb [in a sense to be mentioned below,] said of a wound. (Mṣb.) Also, aor. ـِ, (TA,) inf. n. بَغْىٌ, (Az, TA,) *He magnified himself;* or *behaved proudly, haughtily,* or *insolently:* (Az, TA:) because he who does so passes beyond the bounds of his proper station to a station that does not belong to him. (TA.) —— And [hence,] بَغَى فِى مِشْيَتِهِ, (Ḳ,) inf. n. بَغْىٌ, (TA,) *He* [app. a horse, and perhaps a man also,] *was proud,* or *self-conceited, and quick, in his gait:* (Ḳ:) or بَغْىٌ in a horse, (Ṣ, TA,) or in the running of a horse, (JK, TA,) is the *being proud,* or *self-conceited, with exceeding briskness* or *liveliness* or *sprightliness.* (JK, Ṣ, TA.) —— And بَغَتِ السَّمَآءُ, (Ṣ, Ḳ,) inf. n. بَغْىٌ, (TA,) *The sky rained vehemently:* (A'Obeyd, Ṣ, Ḳ:) or *exceeded, in rain, the limit of what was wanted.* (Er-Rághib, TA.) And بَغَى الوَادِى *The valley flowed with water reaching to a place to which it had not reached before.* (Ṣ, TA.) —— بَغَتْ, (Ṣ, Mgh, Mṣb, Ḳ,) said of a woman, (Th, IKh, Ṣ, Mṣb, and so in some copies of the Ḳ,) or of a female slave, (so in other copies of the Ḳ,) but it is not restricted to the latter, (TA,) aor. ـِ, (JK, Mṣb,) inf. n. بِغَآءٌ, (IKh, JK, Ṣ, Mgh, Mṣb, TA,) or بَغْىٌ, (ISd, Ḳ,) [but the former, only, is commonly known,] *She committed fornication,* or *adultery; she prostituted herself;* (JK, Ṣ, Mgh, Mṣb, Ḳ;) because she who does so transgresses her proper bounds; (TA;) as also ▼بَاغَتْ, (IKh, Ṣ,* Mṣb, Ḳ,) inf. n. بِغَآءٌ (IKh, Ḳ) and مُبَاغَاةٌ, (Ḳ,) said of a female slave: (Mṣb:) or مباغاة signifies the *committing fornication,* or *adultery, with another.* (KL.) It is said in the Ḳur [xxiv. 33], وَلَا تُكْرِهُوا فَتَيَاتِكُمْ عَلَى البِغَآءِ [*And compel not ye your young women to prostitute themselves*]. (Mgh.) And you say, خَرَجَتِ المَرْأَةُ ▼تُبَاغِى [*The woman went forth for prostituting herself*]. (Ṣ.) Accord. to the Jemṛ et-Tefáreeḳ, بِغَآءٌ signifies The *knowing of a woman's committing fornication* or *adultery,* or *prostituting herself, and approving,* or *being content:* but this, if correct, is an amplification in speech. (Mgh.) —— بَغَى الجُرْحُ, (JK, Ṣ, Mṣb,) aor. ـِ, inf. n. بَغْىٌ, (JK,) *The wound swelled,* (Ṣ,) *and became in a corrupt state,* (JK, Ṣ, Mṣb,) *and produced thick*

purulent matter. (JK.) And بَرَأَ جُرْحُهُ عَلَى بَغْيٍ *His wound healed having somewhat of corruption in it.* (Ṣ.) — بَغَى, (Ḳ,) aor. ـِ , inf. n. بَغْىٌ, (TA,) also signifies *He lied; said what was untrue.* (Ḳ.) مَا نَبْغِى, in the Ḳur [xii. 65], is said to mean *We do not lie:* and *we do not act wrongfully:* or it may mean *what do we seek,* or *desire?* (TA.) — Also, (Ḳ,) inf. n. بُغْىٌ, (TA,) *He looked at* a thing [*to see*] *how it was;* (Ḳ;) and so بَغَا, inf. n. بَغْوٌ: mentioned by Kr. (TA.) — And, (Ḳ,) with the same inf. n., (TA,) *He looked, watched,* or *waited, for* a person or thing. (Kr, Ḳ.)

3: see 1, latter part, in two places. — Lḥ mentions the saying, addressed to a pretty woman, إِنَّكِ لَجَمِيلَةٌ وَلَا تُبَاغِى, as meaning *Verily thou art pretty, and mayest thou not be smitten by the* [*evil*] *eye:* (TA in this art.:) but accord. to some, the verb in this instance belongs to art. بوغ or art. بيغ. (TA in art. بوغ.)

4: see 1, in five places. — ابغاهُ الشَّىْءَ also signifies *He made him,* or *caused him, to seek the thing; to seek for it,* or *after it; to seek,* or *desire,* or *endeavour, to find, and take,* or *get, it.* (Ṣ.)

5: see 1, first sentence.

6. تَبَاغَوْا *They acted wrongfully, injuriously,* or *tyrannically, one towards another; exalted themselves, one against,* or *above, another; overpowered,* or *oppressed, one another.* (Ṣ, TA.)

7. انبغى is said in the Ṣ to be quasi-pass. of بَغَيْتُهُ, like as انْكَسَرَ is of كَسَرْتُهُ; and Esh-Shiháb says of the aor. that it is quasi-pass. of بَغَاهُ, aor. يَبْغِيهِ, in the sense of طَلَبَهُ: (TA:) [Fei says,] it has been asserted that انبغى is quasi-pass. of بَغَى; but a verb of the measure انفعل is not used as a quasi-pass. unless it implies effort, and the consequence of an action, as in the case of كَسَرْتُهُ, of which the quasi-pass. is انْكَسَرَ; which انبغى does not: some, however, allow its being thus used: (Mṣb:) accord. to Zj, it is as though it were syn. with انْطَلَبَ, as quasi-pass. of طَلَبَ, and means *It was,* or *became, suitable, fit, meet,* or *proper;* (Zj, TA;) [or *right,* and *allowable;* and *good:* or *very requisite:* (see explanations of exs. following:) or *it behooved:* and] *it was,* or *became, facilitated,* or *easy;* (Er-Rághib, Ḳ;) and *practicable,* or *manageable.* (Er-Rághib, TA.) Accord. to some, this verb is not used in the pret. tense, but only in the aor.: it is reckoned among verbs imperfectly inflected: (Mṣb, TA:) but the pret. is mentioned by AZ and Sb and Zj, and by El-Khaṭṭábee on the authority of Ks; and was often used by Esh-Sháfi'ee: it is, however, very rare. (TA.) You say, يَنْبَغِى لَكَ أَنْ تَفْعَلَ كَذَا [*It is suitable to thee, or is fit, meet,* or *proper,* &c., *for thee,* or *it behooveth thee, that thou shouldst do such a thing*]. (Ṣ, TA.) And, accord. to Zj, انْبَغَى لِفُلَانٍ أَنْ يَفْعَلَ, as meaning *It was,* or *became, suitable to such a one,* or *fit, meet,* or *proper, for him, that he should do,* or *to do,* such a thing. (TA.) And مَا يَنْبَغِى لَكَ أَنْ تَفْعَلَ هٰذَا, (Lḥ, Ḳ,) and مَا يُنْبَغَى ↓, (Ḳ, TA,) with fet-ḥ to the غ, (TA,) and مَا ٱنْبَغَى, and مَا ٱبْتُغِىَ ↓; (Lḥ, Ḳ;) of which four phrases, the first is given by Lḥ as explanatory of the third and fourth, and means, accord. to Esh-Shiháb, *It is not right, proper, fit,* or *meet, nor allowable, for thee that thou shouldst do this,* or *to do this;* and *it is not good for thee* &c.; but he adds that only the aor. has been heard from the Arabs in this sense. (TA.) And يَنْبَغِى أَنْ يَكُونَ كَذَا *It is very requisite that it should be so, or that such a thing should be;* [*or it ought to be so, or such a thing ought to be; it behooves that it should be so,* or *such a thing behooves;*] *it is not well that such a thing should be neglected,* or *left undone.* (Mṣb.) And Ks is related to have heard, from the Arabs, the phrase, مَا يَنْبَغِى أَنْ يَكُونَ كَذَا, meaning *It is not right that it should be so,* or *that such a thing should be:* or *it is not good* &c. (Mṣb.) It is said in the Ḳur [xxxvi. 69], وَمَا عَلَّمْنَاهُ ٱلشِّعْرَ وَمَا يَنْبَغِى لَهُ, i. e. [*And we have not taught him poetry,* or *versification*], *nor is it right, proper, fit,* or *meet, for him:* (Bḍ:) or *nor is it easy to him,* (Bḍ, Jel, Er-Rághib,) or *practicable to him.* (Bḍ, Er-Rághib.)

8: see 1, first sentence, in two places: — and see also 7, in two places.

10: see 1, first sentence. — You say also, استبغى القَوْمَ فَبَغَوْهُ and بَغَوْا لَهُ [*He asked the people,* or *company of men, to seek* a thing for him, *and they sought* it *for him*]. (Lḥ, Ḳ.)

بَغْىٌ [originally an inf. n. (see 1)] *Much* of rain; or *much rain:* in [some of] the copies of the Ḳ, البطر is erroneously put for المطر: (TA:) [and in some, البَغْىُ for البَغْىُ: in a MS. copy, I find البَغْىُ الكَثِيرُ مِنَ المَطَرِ: and in the CḲ, البَغْىُ الكَثِيرُ من النَّظَرِ:] or بَغْىُ السَّمَآءِ signifies *the main portion,* (Aṣ, Ṣ,) or *the vehemence, and the main portion,* (Lḥ, JK, TA,) *of the rain of the sky.* (Aṣ, Lḥ, JK, Ṣ, TA.) Hence the saying, دَفَعْنَا بَغْىَ السَّمَآءِ خَلْفَنَا (Aṣ, Ṣ, TA) or عَنَّا (Lḥ, TA) [lit. *We drove away the main portion,* or *the vehemence, and the main portion, of the rain of the sky behind us* or *from us;* meaning *it was driven away behind us* or *from us,* or *it departed;* as is shown in art. دفع].

بَغْيَةٌ: see what next follows.

بُغْيَةٌ and بِغْيَةٌ ↓ (JK, Ṣ, Mṣb, Ḳ) and بَغْيَةٌ ↓ (Ḳ) *A thing sought;* (JḲ, Ḳ;) as also بُغَايَةٌ ↓ [originally an inf. n. (see 1)]: (JK:) or *a thing wanted, needed,* or *required; an object of want* or *need; a want,* or *needful* or *requisite thing* or *affair:* (Ṣ, Mṣb:) as in the saying, لِى فِى بَنِى فُلَانٍ بُغْيَةٌ and بِغْيَةٌ [*I have among the sons of such a one an object of want*]: (Ṣ:) or the first signifies *a state that one seeks;* and the second, *a thing itself that one wants:* (Aṣ, Ṣ, Mṣb:*) and the first, (JK,) or third, (Ḳ,) signifies also *a stray beast that is sought:* (JK, Ḳ:) the pl. of the second is بُغًى. (JḲ.) ارْتَدَّتْ عَلَى فُلَانٍ بُغْيَتُهُ [*The thing that he sought was refused to such a one*] is said of one who finds not what he seeks. (TA.)

بَغُوٌّ: see what next follows.

بَغِىٌّ, accord. to some, of the measure فَعِيلٌ; accord. to others, of the measure فَعُولٌ, originally بَغُوىٌ; [if of the former, originally meaning "sought;" and if of the latter, originally meaning "seeking;"] and therefore [in either case] not admitting the affix ة: (TA:) *A fornicatress, an adulteress,* or *a prostitute;* (JK, Ṣ, Mgh, Mṣb, Ḳ;) as also بَغُوٌّ ↓ [of the measure فَعُولٌ, and therefore anomalous, like نَهُوٌّ]: (M, Ḳ:) بَغِىٌّ is not applied to a man, (Lḥ, Mṣb,) nor بَغِيَّةٌ to a woman: (Lḥ, TA:) pl. بَغَايَا. (Ṣ, Mgh, Mṣb.) [See an ex. voce مَهْرٌ.] — Also *A female slave,* (JK, Ṣ, Ḳ,) *whether she be a fornicatress* or *an adulteress* or *a prostitute* or *not;* (TA;) not meant to imply revilement, though originally applied to female slaves because of their prostitution of themselves: (Ṣ:) or *a free woman who is a fornicatress* or *an adulteress* or *a prostitute:* so in the Ḳ: but correctly, or *a fornicatress* or *an adulteress* or *a prostitute, whether free* or *a slave:* (TA:) and *a female singer, though chaste;* because of fornication's being originally attributable to such a person: (Mṣb:) pl. as above. (JK, Ṣ, TA.) One says, قَامَتْ عَلَى رُؤُوسِهِمُ البَغَايَا [*The female slaves stood over their heads*]. (Ṣ.) — بَغَايَا also signifies The *scouts,* or *companies of scouts, that precede an army:* (Ṣ, Ḳ, TA:) but the sing. of this is بَغِيَّةٌ ↓. (TA.)

بَغِيَّةٌ: see بُغْيَةٌ. — Also, pl. بَغَايَا: see بَغِىٌّ, last sentence.

بُغَايَةٌ: see بُغْيَةٌ.

بَاغٍ *Seeking; seeking for,* or *after; seeking, desiring,* or *endeavouring, to find, and take,* or *get:* pl. بُغَاةٌ and بُغْيَانٌ (Ḳ) and بُغَّآءٌ. (TA: [there mentioned as a pl., but not said to be of بَاغٍ, nor explained.]) بَاغٍ وَهَادٍ, lit. *A seeker* of [stray] camels *and a guide* of the way, mentioned in a trad. respecting the Hijreh (as said by Aboo-Bekr to a man who asked him "Who are ye?"), alludes to the seeking of religion and the guiding from error. (TA.) One says, فَرِّقُوا لِهٰذِهِ الإِبِلِ بُغْيَانًا يُضِبُّونَ لَهَا, i. e. [*Disperse ye, for these camels, seekers*] *to scatter themselves in search thereof.* (Ṣ.) — *Acting wrongfully, injuriously,* or *tyrannically,* [&c.,] towards others: pl. بُغَاةٌ. (Mṣb. [See 1.]) غَيْرَ بَاغٍ, in the Ḳur ii. 168, [&c.,] means *Not being a revolter from the Muslims,* (Jel,) or, *against the Imám:* (TA:) or it means *not desiring to eat for the sake of enjoyment:* or *not seeking to exceed the limit of his want:* (Az, TA:) or *not seeking what he should not seek.* (Er-Rághib, TA.) فِئَةٌ بَاغِيَةٌ *A company of men revolting from the just Imám.* (Ḳ.) فِرْقَةٌ بَاغِيَةٌ *A party occupying itself with corrupt, wrong,* or *unjust, conduct.* (Mṣb.) — *A camel that does not impregnate,* or *get with young.* (Kr, Ḳ.) — *A horse that is proud,* or *self-conceited, with exceeding briskness* or *liveliness* or *sprightliness:* (JK, Ḥam p. 210:) [but] Kh disallows its being thus used. (Ṣ.) — [The pl.] بُغْيَانٌ also signifies *What the sportsman,* or *hunter, seeks,* of *game,* or *objects of the chase.* (JK.)

مَبْغًى [*A place where a thing is sought:* and

hence, *a way*, or *manner*, *in which a thing is*, or *should be, sought*]: this is meant in the saying, ▾بَغَيْتُ الْمَالَ مِنْ مَبْغَاتِهِ [*I sought wealth by the way*, or *manner, whereby it should be sought*]; like as مَأْتَى is meant in the saying, أَتَيْتُ الأَمْرَ مِنْ مَأْتَاتِهِ. (Ṣ.)

مَبْغَاةٌ: see what next precedes.

المُبْتَغِى, (Ḳ,) or, as in the Tekmileh, المُتَبَغِّى, (TA,) *The lion:* (Ḳ:) because he is always seeking prey. (TA.)

المُتَبَغِّى: see what next precedes.

بق

1. بَقَّ, (JK, M,) aor. يَبِقُّ; and بَقَّ, [first pers. بَقِقْتُ,] aor. يَبَقُّ [in the TA يَبُقُّ, which, being anomalous, is probably a mistake,] inf. n. بَقٌّ and بَقَقٌ [which is of the latter verb accord. to analogy] and بَقِيقٌ; (M;) *He spoke*, or *talked, much; was*, or *became, loquacious;* (JK, M, TA;) as also ▾ابقّ (JK, Ṣ, M, TA) and ▾بَقْبَقَ. (M, TA.) And بَقَّ كَلَامًا [in which case the aor., accord. to rule, unless the noun be a specificative, is يَبُقُّ,] and بَقَّ بِكَلَامٍ [*He was*, or *became, profuse in speech*]. (M.) And بَقَّ عَلَى القَوْمِ, (Zj, Ḳ,) or بَقَّ كَلَامَهُ, (M,) inf. n. بَقٌّ and بَقَاقٌ, (Ḳ,) *He spoke*, or *talked, much against the people*, or *company of men;* (Zj, M,* Ḳ;) as also ▾ابقّ. (Ḳ.) Hence, (TA,) قَدْ مَلَأْتَ الأَرْضَ بَقَاقًا [*Thou hast filled the earth*, or *land, with much discoursing*], said, in dispraise, to a voluminous writer. (M, TA.) — بَقَّتْ and ▾ابقّت, said of a woman, *She had many children:* (JK, Ṣ, M, Ḳ:) or, as Sb says, بَقَّتْ وَلَدًا *she brought forth many children.* (M, TA.) — بَقَّتِ السَّمَآءُ, (Ṣ, M, Ḳ,) and ▾ابقّت, (M, TA,) *The sky rained much, and consecutively*, or *uninterruptedly:* (M, TA:*) or *rained vehemently.* (Ṣ, M, Ḳ.) — بَقَّ, (M, Ḳ,) aor. يَبِقُّ, (M,) or يَبُقُّ, (TA,) inf. n. بَقٌّ, (M, TA,) *He gave largely*, or *amply:* (IF, M, Ḳ,* TA:) in some of the copies of the Ḳ, العَظَمَة is erroneously put for العَطِيَّة. (TA.) And بَقَّ لَنَا العَطَآءَ *He made the gift large*, or *ample, to us.* (M.) — بَقَّ مَالَهُ *He distributed*, or *dispersed*, or *scattered, his property;* (Ḳ;) as also ▾بَقْبَقَهُ. (JK,* Ḳ.) — بَقَّ الخَبَرَ, inf. n. بَقٌّ, *He spread, and sent forth, the news*, or *information.* (M.) — بَقَّ الشَّىْءَ, aor. يَبُقُّ, *He put forth*, or *took forth, what was in the thing.* (M, TA.) Hence, (M,) بَقَّ عِيَابَهُ, (M, L, TA,) in the Ḳ, erroneously, عِيَالَهُ, (TA,) *He spread out* (Ḳ, TA) *his* [*receptacles of skin*, or *leather, termed*] عياب, *and put forth*, or *took forth, what was in them.* (TA.) — *He clave, slit, ripped*, or *rent, the thing.* (JK.) So in the phrase بَقَّ الجِرَابَ [*He slit, ripped*, or *rent, and opened*, (see مَبْقُوقٌ,) *the bag*, or *receptacle, for travelling-provisions &c.*]. (Ḳ.) — بَقَّ, (IF, Ḳ,) inf. n. بُقُوقٌ, (TA,) said of a plant, [app. from its cleaving the earth,] *It came forth.* (IF, Ḳ, TA.) — بَقَّ المَكَانُ, [aor., app., يَبَقُّ, or يَبِقُّ,] *The place abounded with* بَقّ [i. e. *gnats*, or *musquitoes;* or *bugs*]; as also ▾ابقّ. (M, TA.)

2: see 1.

4: see 1, in five places. — ابقّ وَلَدُ فُلَانٍ, inf. n. إِبْقَاقٌ, *The children of such a one multiplied; became many*, or *numerous.* (TA.) — أَبَقَّتِ الغَنَمُ فِى الجَدْبِ, accord. to the Ḳ, (TA,) or ▾انبقّت الغَنَمُ فِى عَامٍ جَدْبٍ, (JK, and thus in the O, TA,) *The ewes*, or *she-goats, being lean*, or *meagre, brought forth* [*in drought*, or *scarcity*, or *in a year of drought* or *scarcity*]. (JK, O, Ḳ, TA.) — ابقّ الوَادِى *The valley put forth its plants*, or *herbage.* (O, L, TA.) In the Ḳ, خَرَجَ بَقَاقَةُ is erroneously put for خَرَجَ نَبَاتُهُ. (TA.) — ابقّه خَيْرًا, or شَرًّا, *He did to him much*, or *ample, good*, or *evil.* (Ibn-'Abbád, JK, Ḳ.)

7: see 4.

R. Q. 1. بَقْبَقَ الكُوزُ, (Ṣ, M,) بِالمَآءِ, (M,) [inf. n. بَقْبَقَةٌ, q. v. infrà,] *The mug made a* [*guggling* or *gurgling*] *sound with the water* [*on being dipped into it or on one's pouring out from it*]. (Ṣ,* M.) And بَقْبَقَتِ القِدْرُ *The cooking-pot boiled* [*so as to make a sound of bubbling*]. (M.) — See also 1. — بَقْبَقَ عَلَيْنَا الكَلَامَ i. q. فَرَّقَهُ [lit. *He scattered speech* (app. meaning *he jabbered*) *at us*, or *against us:* compare بَقَّ عَلَى القَوْمِ, or بَقَّ كَلَامَهُ, above]. (Ḳ.)

بَقٌّ: see بَقَاقٌ. — بَقَّةٌ A woman *having many children:* (Ibn-'Abbád, JK, Ḳ:) and ▾مِبَقَّةٌ a woman *that brings forth many children.* (M, TA.) — أَثَرٌ بَقٌّ [*A trace, mark, track, impression*, or *the like*,] *that is plainly apparent*, or *conspicuous.* (JK, TA.) — Also, a pl. n.; (Ṣ, TA;) [or rather a coll. gen. n.;] sing., (Ṣ, TA,) or n. un., (JK, M, Mṣb, Ḳ,*) بَقَّةٌ; (JK, Ṣ, M, &c.;) *Gnats*, or *musquitoes;* syn. بَعُوضٌ: (Ṣ, M, Ḳ:*) or *large* بَعُوض: (JK, M, Mṣb:) the poet 'Abd-er-Rahmán Ibn-El-Ḥakam, cited by IB, speaks of their singing [or humming]. (TA.) يَا عَيْنَ بَقَّةٍ [*O eye of a gnat or musquito*] denotes smallness of the person of him to whom it is said; or of the eye, as being likened to the eye of the gnat or musquito. (Ḥar p. 619. [See an ex. voce حُزُقٌّ.]) — Also, [in the M is here added "it is said," but this implies uncertainty where none exists,] *A kind of insect*, [namely, *bugs*,] (M, Ḳ,) *resembling the louse*, (M, TA,) [*but larger*,] *wide*, (Ḳ,) *red, and stinking*, (M, Ḳ,) [and hence termed بَقٌّ مُنْتِنٌ,] *found in bed-frames*, or *couch-frames, and in walls*, [and therefore termed بَقُّ الحِيطَانِ and بَقُّ الخَشَبِ,] (M, TA,) *called also* بَنَاتُ الحَصِيرِ [from being found in mats]; (TA;) *when one kills them, he smells* [*what resembles*] *the odour of bitter almonds proceeding from them.* (M, TA.) — شَجَرَةُ البَقِّ [*The elm-tree*]: see دِرْدَارٌ.

بَقَقَةٌ: see what next follows.

بَقَاقٌ A man *who speaks*, or *talks, much; loquacious; talkative; garrulous; a great talker;* (Ṣ, Ḳ;) *whether incorrectly or correctly;* (M;) or such is termed ▾بَقَّاقٌ; (so written in a copy of the M;) as also ▾بَقَاقَةٌ, (JK, Ṣ, Ḳ,) but this has a more intensive signification, (Ṣ, TA,) and ▾مِبَقٌّ, (M, Ṣgh, Ḳ,) and ▾بَقْبَاقٌ, (JK, Ṣ, M,) or ▾لَقْلَاقٌ بَقْبَاقٌ, (Ḳ,) and ▾لَقٌّ بَقٌّ, (Ḳ,) which last occurs in a trad., but accord. to one recital it is لَقًى بَقًى, in which the former word signifies "cast away," and the latter is an imitative sequent thereto: (TA:) ▾بَقَقَةٌ, also, [app. pl. of بَاقٌّ,] is syn. with ثَرْثَارُونَ [*great talkers, &c.*]: (IAạr, TA:) and بَقَاقٌ [thus written without teshdeed] signifies *a babbler; nonsensical, irrational, foolish*, or *delirious, in his talk;* one *who speaks confusedly and improperly;* or *who speaks*, or *talks, much and badly*, or *erroneously.* (M.) [See also 1, of which it is an inf. n.] — Also, (Ḳ,) n. un. with ة, (JK, Ḳ,) *A kind of clamorous bird:* (JK, Ḳ:) but Ṣgh writes it [▾بَقَّاقٌ,] with teshdeed. (TA.) — Also The *worthless*, or *mean*, or *vile, articles of the furniture or utensils of a house or tent*, or *of household-goods.* (M, Ḳ.)

بَقَاقَةٌ: see بَقَاقٌ.

بَقَّاقٌ: see بَقَاقٌ, in two places.

بَقْبَقَةٌ a word imitative of The [*guggling* or *gurgling*] *sound of a mug* (JK, Ṣ, Ḳ) [*when dipped*] *in water*, (JK, Ḳ,) and *the like:* (Ḳ:) and *of a cooking-pot in its boiling.* (TA.) [See also R. Q. 1.]

بَقْبَاقٌ: see بَقَاقٌ, in two places. — Also The *mouth.* (Ḳ.)

مِبَقٌّ: see بَقَاقٌ. — مِبَقَّةٌ [its fem.]: see بَقٌّ.

أَرْضٌ مَبَقَّةٌ *A land abounding with* بَقّ [i. e. *gnats*, or *musquitoes;* or *bugs*]; (M, TA;) like as you say مَبْعَضَةٌ. (TA in art. بعض.)

جِرَابٌ مَبْقُوقٌ [*A bag, or receptacle, for travelling-provisions &c.*] *opened:* (JK:) or *slit, ripped*, or *rent, and opened.* (Ibn-'Abbád, TA.)

بقر

1. بَقَرَ, (Ṣ, Ḳ, &c.,) aor. ـُ, (JK, Ṣ, A, Mgh, Mṣb,) or ـَ, (Ḳ,) [but this seems to be a mistake,] inf. n. بَقْرٌ, (Ṣ, Mṣb,) *He slit; ripped; split; cut*, or *divided, lengthwise.* (Ṣ, Mṣb, Ḳ, &c.) *He slit*, or *ripped open*, an animal's belly. (A, Mgh.) One says, اُبْقُرْهَا عَنْ جَنِينِهَا *Rip thou open her* [a camel's] *belly so as to disclose her fœtus.* (Ṣ.) [See بَقِيرٌ.] — *He opened*, or *laid open.* (Ṣ, A, Mṣb.) — *He widened; made wide*, or *ample.* (Ṣ, Ḳ.) — *He opened, and widened*, or *made wide*, a house, or tent. (TA, from a trad.) — *He opened and revealed* to a person a story. (TA, from a trad.) — بَقَرَ الأَرْضَ, said of a هُدْهُد [or hoopoe], *It looked for the place of water and saw it:* (Ḳ:) [or *it clave the ground and discovered water:*] occurring in a trad. respecting the هدهد of Solomon [mentioned in the Ḳur ch. xxvii.] (T.) — بَقَرَ فِى بَنِى فُلَانٍ *He knew the state, condition, case*, or *affair, of the sons of such a one, and examined*, or *inspected, them.* (Ḳ.) — بَقَرَ عَنِ العُلُومِ *He inquired, and searched*

to the utmost, after sciences. (A.) — بَقَّرَ العِلْمَ: see 5. ═ بَقِرَ, aor. ـَ, *He* (a dog) *became confounded,* (Ṣ, Ḳ,) *and stupified,* (TA,) *with joy,* (Ḳ,) *at seeing* بَقَر, (Ṣ, Ḳ,) i. e., بَقَر الوَحْش [*wild oxen,* or *wild bulls* or *cows*]; (TA;) like as one says غَزِلَ meaning "he sported," or "played," "at seeing a gazelle," or "a young gazelle;" as also ▼بَيْقَرَ: or the former, *he feared, so that he was astonished, amazed,* or *stupified, at seeing many* بَقَر: (TA voce بَحِرَ:) and ▼the latter signifies also [simply] *he became confounded,* or *perplexed:* (IAạr, TA:) and *he doubted respecting a thing.* (Ḳ.) — Also, aor. as above, inf. n. بَقَرٌ (Ṣ, Ḳ) and بَقْرٌ; (Ḳ;) but Az says, El-Mundhiree has informed me that AHeyth disallowed بَقْرٌ, saying that it is accord. to analogy بَقَرٌ, as the verb is intrans.; (TA;) *He* (a man) *became tired,* or *fatigued,* (Ṣ, Ḳ,) *so that he could hardly see;* (Ḳ;) and *he became weary,* or *jaded;* (Ṣ, Ḳ;) as also ▼بَيْقَرَ. (Ṣ, Ḳ.*)

2. بقّر القَوْمُ مَا حَوْلَهُمْ *The people dug the tract around them, and made wells.* (Aṣ.)

5. تبقّر *It* (a she-camel's belly) *became ripped open;* as also ▼ابتقر and ▼انبقر. (TA.) — *It became open.* (Aṣ.) — And *i. q.* توسّع; (Aṣ, Ḳ;) as also ▼تَبَيْقَرَ. (Ḳ.) So in the phrase تبقّر فِى العِلْمِ [*He enlarged himself,* or *took a wide range, in science,* or *knowledge*]; (Ṣ, A, Mṣb;) and بَقَّرَ العِلْمَ, inf. n. بَقْرٌ, signifies the same. (TA.) And so in the phrase تبقّر فِى المَالِ, (Ṣ, A, Mṣb,) and فِى الأَهْلِ, (TA,) i. e., *He enlarged himself,* or *he became,* or *made himself, large,* or *abundant, in wealth,* or *camels* or *the like,* and *in family;* as explained by Aṣ. (A'Obeyd.) You say also, تبقّر الكَلَامَ, [meaning فِى الكَلَامِ,] i. e., *He was diffuse,* or *profuse, in speech;* syn. تَفَتَّقَ بِهِ. (A.)

7: see 5.

8: see 5.

Q. Q. **1**: see 1, in three places.

Q. Q. **2**: see 5.

بَقَرٌ a gen. n., (Ṣ, Mṣb,) a word of well-known meaning, (Ṣ, Mṣb, Ḳ,) [The *bovine genus;* the *ox,* or *bull, and cow;* and *oxen,* or *bulls,* and *cows; neat; black cattle;*] applied to the *domestic* and the *wild:* (TA:) [but the wild have also distinctive appellations, as will be seen below:] n. un. بَقَرَةٌ, (Ṣ, Mṣb, Ḳ, [but in the Ḳ it is said that بَقَرٌ is pl. of بَقَرَةٌ,]) which is applied to the *male* and the *female;* (Ṣ, Mṣb, Ḳ;) the ة being added only to restrict it to unity: (Ṣ, Mṣb:) the pl. of بَقَرٌ is أَبْقُرٌ [a pl. of pauc.]; (M,) and أَبْقَارٌ, meaning *herds of oxen,* or *bulls,* or *cows:* (Mṣb and TA in art. ابل:) and the pl. of بَقَرَةٌ is بَقَرَاتٌ (Ṣ, Mṣb, Ḳ) and بُقُرٌ and بُقَّارٌ (Ḳ) and بَوَاقِرُ (Aṣ, T, Ḳ) and ▼أُبْقُورٌ; (Ḳ;) [or rather this last is a quasi-pl. n.;] and the following [also] are quasi-pl. ns., namely, ▼بَيْقُورٌ, (Ḳ,) which is syn. with بَقَرٌ, (Ṣ,) and ▼بَقِيرٌ, (Ḳ,) or this signifies *a collection,* or *herd, of* بَقَر, (Ṣ,) and ▼بَاقِرٌ, (Ḳ,) or this signifies *a collection,* or *herd, of* بَقَر *with their pastors,* (Lth, Ṣ,) and ▼بَاقُورٌ, and ▼بَاقُورَةٌ, (Ḳ,) or this last is syn. with بَقَرَةٌ in the dial. of the people of El-Yemen: (Ṣ:) or ▼بَاقُورٌ and ▼بَيْقُورٌ and ▼أُبْقُورٌ are all syn. with بَقَرٌ; and so, accord. to Ḳṭr, is ▼بَاقُورَةٌ. (Mgh.) — بَقَرُ الوَحْشِ [and البَقَرُ الوَحْشِىُّ signify *The wild ox,* or *bull,* and *cow;* and *wild oxen,* or *bulls,* and *cows,* collectively: n. un. بَقَرَةُ الوَحْشِ and البَقَرَةُ الوَحْشِيَّةُ; masc. and fem.: in Egypt, these appellations are applied to the *antilope defassa* of modern zoologists: so says Sir Gardner Wilkinson; and to this, I believe, they generally apply in the poems &c. of the early Arabs: it is a *species of bovine antelope:* in Barbary, it seems that the animal thus called is another species of bovine antelope, or perhaps a variety of the former; it is said to be what is termed by Pallas *antilope bubalis;* by others, *alcephalus bubalis,* or *acronotus bubalis;* and this is said to come occasionally to the Nile: but the Arabic appellations given above are employed with much laxity: thus we find بَقَرُ الوَحْشِ explained as meaning] *a kind of animal of which there are four different species: the first called* مها [i. e. مَهًا, a coll. gen. n. of which the n. un. is مَهَاةٌ]; *the second,* ايل [i. e. إِيَّلٌ]; *the third* يحمور [i. e. يَحْمُورٌ], or يامور [i. e. يَامُورٌ]; *the fourth,* ثيتل [or ثَيْتَلٌ], *and also* وعل [i. e. وَعِلٌ]: (Ed-Demeeree, cited by De Sacy, erroneously written by him "Domaïri," in his Chrest. Ar. sec. ed. ii. 435 et seq.:) or *what is called in Persian* كوزن [or گَوَزْنْ (see also إِيَّلٌ in art. اول)]; *it has a great horn, with branches; an additional branch growing upon its horn every year; and its horn is solid, thus differing from the horns of other animals, for their horns are hollow: when it hears singing, and the sounds of musical instruments, it listens thereto, and then it takes no care to guard itself from the arrows, by reason of its intense delight therein: when it raises its ear, it hears sounds; and when it relaxes it, it hears not anything.* (Ḳzw: also cited by De Sacy, ubi suprà.) The Arabs regard بَقَر [meaning بقر الوحش] as ominous of evil, because of the sharpness of their horns. (Ḥam p. 285.) — مِلْءُ مَسْكِ البَقَرَةِ [*The quantity that fills the hide of the bull,* or *cow,*] means ‡ *a large quantity.* (A.) — الظِّبَآءَ عَلَى البَقَرِ [or الكِلَابَ, and الكِرَابَ عَلَى البَقَرِ [or الظِّبَآءَ or الكِلَابَ,] are provs. of the Arabs. (TA.) [See arts. ظبى and كرب and كلب.] — عَيْنُ البَقَرِ †[*The buphthalmum,* or *ox-eye;*] *i. q.* بَهَارٌ, q. v. (Ṣ in art. بهر.) — عُيُونُ البَقَرِ ‡ *A species of grape, black, large, round, and not very sweet.* (Ḳ, TA.) In Palestine, applied to ‡ *A species of* إِجَّاص [or *plum*]. (Ḳ, TA.) — بَقَرٌ is also applied to ‡ *A family,* or *household; those who dwell with a man, and whose maintenance is incumbent on him.* (TA.) You say, جَآءَ فُلَانٌ يَجُرُّ بَقَرَهُ ‡ *Such a one came dragging along his family,* or *household.* (A,* TA.) And عَلَى فُلَانٍ بَقَرَةٌ مِنْ عِيَالٍ وَمَالٍ ‡ *Upon such a one is dependent a troop,* or *large number, of his family, and of camels* or *the like;* (A,* TA;) and in like manner you say, فُلَانٌ فِى بَقَرٍ مِنَ النَّاسِ. (A.) And كَرِشٌ مِنْ عِيَالٍ ‡ *Such a one is among a large company of men.* (A.)

بَقِيرٌ *Slit; ripped; split; cut,* or *divided, lengthwise;* as also ▼مَبْقُورٌ. (Ḳ.) — A she-camel *having her belly ripped open so as to disclose her fœtus.* (Ṣ.) — A mare's colt or foal *that is born in a* [*membrane such as is called*] مَاسِكَةٌ or سَلًى: (Ḳ:) so termed because this is ripped open over it. (TA.) — Also, and ▼بَقِيرَةٌ, *A garment of the kind called* بُرْد, *which is slit* [*in the middle*], *and worn* (Aṣ, Ḳ) *by a woman, who throws it upon her neck,* [*putting her head through the slit,*] (Aṣ,) *without sleeves,* (Aṣ, Ḳ,) *and without a* جَيْب [or *an opening at the bosom*]; (Aṣ;) *i. q.* إِتْبٌ [q. v.], which is *a kind of shirt without sleeves, worn by women.* (Ṣ.) ═ See also بَقَرٌ.

بَقِيرَةٌ: see بَقِيرٌ.

بَقَّارٌ *A grave-digger;* syn. حَفَّارٌ. (TA.) — *A worker in iron; a blacksmith.* (Ḳ.) ═ *An owner,* or *a possessor,* [or *an attendant,*] *of* بَقَر [or *oxen,* or *bulls,* or *cows*]. (Ḳ.)

عَصًا بَقَّارِيَّةٌ *A strong staff* or *stick* [*such,* app., *as is used for driving oxen or bulls or cows*]. (Ḳ.)

البَاقِرُ *The lion:* (Ḳ:) because, when he catches his prey, he rips open his belly. (TA.) — بَاقِرٌ and ▼بَاقِرَةٌ, [the latter an intensive epithet,] *A man who inquires, and searches to the utmost, after sciences.* (A.) And بَاقِرُ عِلْمٍ *One who enlarges himself,* or *takes a wide range, in science,* or *knowledge.* (Mṣb.) — فِتْنَةٌ بَاقِرَةٌ, (Ṣ, Ḳ,) occurring in a trad., (TA,) †*A sedition, discord, dissension,* or *the like, that severs society;* (Ḳ;) *that corrupts religion, and separates men:* or *that is wide-spreading and great:* (TA:) it is likened to the disease of the belly; meaning the yellow water or fluid: (Ṣ:) or to pain of the belly; because its exciting cause and its cure are unknown. (TA.) ═ See also بَقَرٌ.

بَاقِرَةٌ: see بَاقِرٌ.

بَيْقَرَةٌ *Abundance of wealth,* or *of camels* or *the like,* and *of commodities,* or *household goods* or *utensils and furniture.* (Ḳ.)

بَاقُورٌ:
بَيْقُورٌ:
بَاقُورَةٌ:
أُبْقُورٌ:
} see بَقَرٌ; each in two places.

مَبْقُورٌ: see بَقِيرٌ.

بقس

بَقْسٌ and ▼بَقْسِيسٌ, (Ḳ,) the latter written, in some copies of the Ḳ, بقبيس, (TA,) [The *box-tree;* Greek πυξος;] *a certain kind of tree, resembling the* آس [or *myrtle*] *in leaves and berries:* or *i. q.* شَمْشَاد [a Persian word, also applied to the *box-tree*]: (Ḳ:) *it grows in the country of the Greeks; and spoons and doors are made of it, because of its hardness:* and it may be with ش [بَقْشٌ, which is explained by Ṣgh and in the Ḳ as a kind of tree called in Persian خُوشْ سَائ; and this, also, is a name of the *box-tree*]: (TA:) it is astringent, having the property of drying up the moisture of the intestines; and its saw-dust, kneaded with honey, strengthens the hair, and makes it abundant, and is good for (or prevents, as in the CḲ,) the headache, and with the white of the egg is good for what is termed وَثْىٌ, (Ḳ,) i. e., a fracture [of the flesh]. (TA.)

بَقْسِيسٌ: see بَقْسٌ, above.

بقش

بَقْشٌ *A certain kind of tree, called in Persian* خُوشْ سَائ, (Ṣgh, Ḳ,) which means "good in shade;" [and also is applied to the *box-tree*;] as has been said before, voce بَقْسٌ, which may be the same: IDrd says that بَقْشٌ is a post-classical word. (TA.)

بقع

1. بَقِعَ, aor. َ, (Mṣb, Ḳ,) inf. n. بَقَعٌ, (Ṣ, Mṣb, Ḳ,) *It* (a bird, and a dog,) *was black and white*; syn. بَلِقَ; (Ḳ;) [or rather] بَقَعٌ in birds and dogs is like بَلَقٌ in beasts that are ridden, or horses and the like: (Ṣ, Ḳ:) or *it* (a crow, &c.,) *was party-coloured*, or *pied*. (Mṣb.) —— *He* (a drawer of water, L, Ḳ, from a well, by means of a pulley and rope and bucket, L) *had his body sprinkled with the water, so that some parts of it became wetted.* (L, Ḳ.) ═ مَا أَدْرِى أَيْنَ بَقَعَ *I know not whither he went*; (Ṣ, Ḳ;) as though one said, to what بُقْعَة of the بِقَاع of the earth he went; (Ṣ;) not used except negatively; (TA;) as also ↓ بَقَّعَ. (Fr, Ḳ.) —— بَقَعَتْهُمُ الدَّاهِيَةُ *The calamity*, or *misfortune, befell them.* (TA.) ═ بُقِعَ, (Ṣ, Ḳ,) like عُنِىَ, (Ḳ,) *He was assailed with bad*, or *foul, speech*, or *language*: (Ṣ, O, Ḳ:) or *with calumny, slander*, or *false accusation.* (Ṣ.) And بُقِعَ بِقَبِيحٍ *He was assailed with foul, evil*, or *abominable, speech*, or *language.* (L.)

2. بقّع الثَّوْبَ *He* (a dyer) *left spots*, or *portions, of the garment*, or *piece of cloth, undyed.* (Mgh, TA.) —— بقّع ثَوْبَهُ *He* (a waterer) *sprinkled the water upon his garment, so that spots*, or *portions, of it became wetted.* (Mgh.) —— بقّع المَطَرُ فِى مَوَاضِعَ مِنَ الأَرْضِ, inf. n. تَبْقِيعٌ, *The rain fell in places of the land, not universally.* (TA.) ═ مَا أَدْرِى أَيْنَ بَقَّعَ: see 1.

7. انبقع *He went away quickly*; (Ḳ;) and *ran.* (TA.)

8. اُبْتُقِعَ لَوْنُهُ, with ḍamm, i. q. اُنْتُقِعَ, and اُمْتُقِعَ; (the former in some copies of the Ḳ; the latter in others; and both in the TA;) i. e. *His colour changed*, (TA,) *by reason of grief*, or *sorrow.* (Ḥar p. 244.) The last of these three verbs is the best. (Ḥar ubi suprà.)

بَقْعَةٌ *A place in which water remains and stagnates*; (Ḳ;) [and *which is not a usual place of watering*: (see بَاقِعَةٌ:) this is what is meant, app., by its being said that] بِقَاعٌ, which is its pl., signifies the *contr. of* مَشَارِعُ [or watering-places to which men and beasts are accustomed to come]. (TA.) —— See also what next follows.

بُقْعَةٌ (Ṣ, Mgh, Mṣb, Ḳ) and ↓ بَقْعَةٌ, (AZ, Mṣb, Ḳ,) but the former is the more common, (Mṣb,) and more chaste, (TA,) *A piece, part, portion*, or *plot*, (Mgh, Mṣb, Ḳ,) of land, or ground, (Ṣ, Mgh, Mṣb, Ḳ,) *differing* [*in any manner*,] *in colour*, (Mgh,) or *in appearance*, or *external state or condition*, (Ḳ,) *from that which adjoins it*, or *is next to it*: (Mgh, Ḳ:) this is the primary signification: (Mgh:) [*a patch of ground*:] pl. بِقَاعٌ, (Ṣ, Ḳ,) or this is pl. of بَقْعَةٌ, (Mṣb, TA,) and the pl. of بُقْعَةٌ is بُقَعٌ. (Mgh, Mṣb, TA.) You say أَرْضٌ فِيهَا بُقَعٌ مِنَ الجَرَادِ [meaning *Land in which are bare places occasioned by the locusts*]. (Lḥ, Ḳ.) And فِى الأَرْضِ بُقَعٌ مِنْ نَبْتٍ *In the land are small portions of herbage.* (AḤn.) And بُقْعَةٌ مِنْ كَلَإٍ *A patch of herbage.* (TA in art. بقط.) —— [The former also signifies *A spot*; or *small portion of any surface, distinct from what surrounds it.*] And the pl. بُقَعٌ *Places* in a garment, or piece of cloth, which has been dyed, *remaining undyed.* (Mgh.) And بُقَعُ المَآءِ *Places* in a garment, or piece of cloth, which has been washed, *in which the water remains, undried.* (Mgh.) —— هُوَ حَسَنُ البُقْعَةِ عِنْدَ الأَمِيرِ ‡ *He has a good station with the prince*, or *commander.* (TA.) [See also جُلْبَةٌ.]

أَرْضٌ بَقِعَةٌ *Land in which are* بُقَعٌ مِنَ الجَرَادِ [meaning *bare places occasioned by the locusts*]: (Lḥ, Ḳ:) and *land of which the herbage is unconnected* [or *in patches*]. (TA.)

أَصَابَهُ خُرُّ بَقَاعِ, like قَطَامِ, [indecl.,] and decl., (Ḳ,) and imperfectly decl., so that you say also بَقَاعٍ, and بَقَاعَ, (AZ, TA,) *Dust and sweat came upon him, and discolorations produced thereby remained upon his body*: (AZ, Ḳ:) by بقاع is [lit.] meant *land*, or *a land*: so says AZ: and عَلَيْهِ خُرُّ بَقَاعِ is said to mean *upon him is sweat which has become white upon his skin, like what are termed* لُمَع. (TA.)

بَقِيعٌ *A place in which are roots of trees of various kinds*: (Ṣ, Ḳ:) or *a wide*, or *spacious, place*: or *a place in which are trees*: (Mṣb:) or *a wide*, or *spacious, piece of land*; but not so called unless *containing trees*; (TA;) though بَقِيعُ الغَرْقَدِ continued to be the name of a burial-ground of El-Medeeneh after the trees therein had ceased to be. (Mṣb,* TA.)

بَاقِعَةٌ *A bird* (Ḳ, TA) *that is cautious*, or *wary, and cunning*, or *wily, that looks to the right and left when drinking*, (TA,) *that does not come to drink to the* مَشَارِع [or *watering-places to which men and beasts are accustomed to come*], (Ḳ, TA, [but in the CḲ, for مشارع is put مَشَارِب,]) *and the frequented waters*, (TA,) *from fear of being caught, but only drinks from the* بَقْعَة, i. e., the *place in which water remains and stagnates.* (Ḳ, TA.) —— Hence, as being likened thereto, ‡ *Any one that is cautious*, or *wary, cunning*, or *wily, and skilful*: (TA:) ‡ *a man possessing much cunning*: (Ḳ, TA:) [accord. to some] so called because he alights and abides in [various] parts (بِقَاع) of the earth, and often traverses countries, and possesses much knowledge thereof: to such, therefore, is likened ‡ *a man knowing*, or *skilful, in affairs, who investigates them much, and is experienced therein*; the ة being added to give intensiveness to the signification: (TA:) and ‡ *sharp*, or *quick, in intellect; knowing; whom nothing escapes, and who is not to be deceived, beguiled*, or *circumvented*: (Ḳ, TA:) pl. بَوَاقِعُ. (TA.) You say, مَا فُلَانٌ إِلَّا بَاقِعَةٌ مِنَ البَوَاقِعِ ‡ *Such a one is none other than a very cunning man of the very cunning.* (TA.) —— Also † *A calamity*, or *misfortune*, (Ṣ, TA,) *that befalls a man.* (TA.)

أَبْقَعُ, applied to a غُرَاب [or bird of the crow-kind], *In which is blackness and whiteness*; (Ṣ, TA;) and so applied to a dog: (Lḥ, TA voce أَبْرَقُ, q. v.:) or, applied to the former, *having whiteness in the breast*; and this is the worst [or most ill-omened] of the crow-kind: (TA:) [it is this species, accord. to some, which is called غُرَابُ البَيْنِ: (see art. بين:)] or, applied to a غراب &c., *party-coloured*, or *pied*: (Mṣb:) or the *white-winged* غراب: (ISh, TA in art. حذف:) pl., when thus applied, بُقْعَانٌ, (TA,) or بِقْعَانٌ, with kesr; the quality of a subst. being predominant in it; but when it is regarded as an epithet, [in which case the fem. is بَقْعَآءُ,] its pl. is بُقْعٌ. (Mṣb.) —— Hence, as being likened to such a bird, ‡ *Anything bad, evil, wicked, mischievous*, [*ill-omened*,] or *the like.* (TA.) —— And † *Leprous.* (IAạr, Ḳ.) —— بُقْعَانُ الشَّأْمِ, (Ṣ, Ḳ,) with ḍamm, (Ḳ,) mentioned in a trad., (Ṣ,) † *The servants and slaves of Syria*; because of their whiteness and redness, (Ṣ, Ḳ,) or blackness; (Ṣ;) or because of their whiteness and redness and blackness likened to a thing such as is termed أَبْقَع; (TA;) or (Ḳ) because they are of the Greeks and the Negroes: (Ṣ, Ḳ:) or so called because of the mixture of their colours; their predominant colours being white and yellow: A'Obeyd says that what is meant is whiteness and yellowness, and they are thus called because of their difference of colours and their being begotten of two races: but Ḳt says, البُقْعَانُ signifies † *those in whom is blackness and whiteness*; and one who is white without any admixture of blackness is not called ابقع: how then should the Greeks be called بقعان when they are purely white? and he adds that he thinks the meaning to be, the *offspring of Arabs, who are black*, [which is not to be understood literally, but rather in the sense of *swarthy*,] *by female slaves of the Greeks, who are white.* (TA.) —— بُقْعٌ is also applied to *Waterers* (سُقَاة); because their bodies become sprinkled with the water, so that some parts thereof are wetted. (Ḳ.) —— رَأَيْتُ قَوْمًا بُقْعًا ‡ *I saw a people wearing patched garments*; said by El-Ḥajjáj; (Ḳ, TA;) and thus explained by him; i. e., by reason of their evil condition. (TA.) —— ذَوْدٌ بُقْعُ الذُّرَى *A herd of camels having white humps.* (TA.) —— الأَبْقَعُ *The mirage*; because of its varying, or assuming different hues.

(TA.) —— أَرْضٌ بَقْعَآءُ *Land containing* [or *diversified with*] *small pebbles.* (TA.) —— سَنَةٌ بَقْعَآءُ ‡ *A barren*, or *an unfruitful, year:* (Ṣ, Ḳ:) or *a year in which is fruitfulness and barrenness.* (Ṣ, Mṣb, Ḳ.) And عَامٌ أَبْقَعُ ‡ *A year in which the rain falls in places of the land, not universally.* (TA.) And عَامٌ أُبَيْقِعُ, (Ḳ,) the dim. form being used to denote terribleness, (TA,) ‡ *A year of little rain.* (Ḳ, TA.)

أُبَيْقِعُ, dim. of أَبْقَعُ, which see, last sentence.

هُوَ مُبَقَّعُ الرِّجْلَيْنِ *He has his legs wetted by water in some places, so that their* [*general*] *colour is different from the colour of those places.* (TA.)

بقل

1. بَقَلَ: see 4, in two places. —— [Hence,] said of a boy's face, (Ṣ, Mgh, Ḳ,) aor. ُ, inf. n. بُقُولٌ, (Ṣ,) ‡ *It put forth its beard,* (Ṣ, TA,) or *hair;* (Ḳ;) as also ابقل and بَقَّلَ; (Ḳ;) or this last is not allowable: (Ṣ:) similar to اِخْضَرَّ said of a boy's mustache. (Mgh.) —— And said of a camel's tush, ‡ *It cut*, or *came forth.* (ISk, Ṣ, TA.) —— † *It* (a thing, TA) *appeared:* (Ḳ, TA:) derived from بَقْلٌ, q. v. (TA.) ═ *He collected* [*plants*, or *herbs, of the kind termed*] بَقْل for his camel. (Fr, Ḳ.) —— بَقَلَ البَقْلَ *He cut the* بقل: so in the "Mufradát." (TA.)

2. بقّل, inf. n. تَبْقِيلٌ, *He* (a pastor) *left* camels *to pasture upon* بَقْل. (TA.) —— And, [hence, app.,] inf. n. as above, *i. q.* سَاسَ. (Ṣgh, Ḳ.) You say, بقّل الدَّابَّةَ, i. e. سَاسَهَا, meaning *He tended*, or *took care of, the beast well.* (TḲ.) ═ See also 1.

4. ابقلت الأَرْضُ *The land produced* [*plants*, or *herbs, of the kind termed*] بَقْل: (Mṣb:) or *produced its* بقل: (Ṣ:) or *produced plants*, or *herbage:* (Ḳ:) or *became green with plants*, or *herbage:* (Mgh:) and بَقَلَتْ signifies the same: (IDrd, Ḳ:) both are chaste words. (IDrd, TA.) In like manner one says also of a place, ابقل, (JK, Mṣb,) from بَقْل. (Mṣb.) —— ابقل الرِّمْثُ *The* [*tree*, or *shrub, called*] رمث *became green;* as also بَقَلَ: (Ḳ:) or *it put forth what resembled young wingless locusts, and the greenness of its leaves became apparent.* (Ṣ. [See also حَنَطَ.]) And ابقل الشَّجَرُ *The trees put forth their* بَاقِل [q. v., app. *buds,*] *in the days of the* ربيع [or *spring*], *before their leaves became apparent:* (JK:) or *they put forth, in the time of the* ربيع, *in their sides, what resembled the necks of locusts.* (TA.) —— See also 1. ═ ابقل القَوْمُ *The people*, or *company of men, found* [*plants*, or *herbs, such as are termed*] بَقْل. (Mṣb.) —— See also 8. ═ ابقل وَجْهَهُ ‡ *He* (God) *made his* (a boy's) *face to put forth its hair,* (Ḳ, TA,) meaning, *its beard.* (TA.)

5. تبقّل *He went forth seeking* [*plants*, or *herbs, of the kind called*] بَقْل. (Ḳ.) —— See also 8, in three places.

8. ابتقل الحِمَارُ, and تبقّل; (Ṣ;) or ابتقلت الماشِيَةُ, (Ḳ,) or الإِبِلُ, (JK,) and تبقّلت; (JK, Ḳ;) *The ass,* or *the beasts,* or *camels, pastured upon* [*plants*, or *herbs, of the kind called*] بَقْل: (Ṣ, Ḳ:) or *became fat from pasturing upon* بقل. (JK.) —— And ابتقل القَوْمُ *The people*, or *company of men, had their cattle pasturing upon* بَقْل; as also تبقّلوا and ابقلوا: (Ḳ:) or *they pastured their cattle upon* بقل. (JK.)

بَقْلٌ a word of which the meaning is well known; (Ṣ;) [*Leguminous*, or *tender, plants; such as we term herbs;* i. e. *plants*, or *vegetables, that may be gathered with the hand, or depastured down to the ground, and that are only annuals;*] *plants which are neither shrubs nor trees;* (Lth, JK,* Mgh;) *such as, when depastured, have no stem remaining; thus differing from trees and shrubs, which have stems remaining* [*when they have been depastured*]: (Lth, Mgh:) or the *herbs*, or *herbage, produced by* [*the rain*, or *the season, called*] *the* رَبِيع: (Mgh:) or *whatever herbs*, or *plants, grow from seed,* (AḤn, Mgh, Ḳ,*) *not upon a permanent* أَرُومَة [i. e. *root-stock*, or *root*]: (AḤn, Ḳ:) and accord. to this definition may be explained the saying that the cucumber is of the things termed بُقُول [pl. of بَقْلٌ, meaning *sorts*, or *species, of* بَقْل], not of those termed فَوَاكِهُ: (Mgh:) or the *kind of which the root and branch do not last in the winter:* (Er-Rághib, TA:) or, it is said, (Ṣ, Mgh,) *any plants*, or *herbs, whereby the earth becomes green:* (Ṣ, IF, Mgh, Mṣb:) [pl. of pauc. أَبْقَالٌ: the pl. of mult. has been mentioned above:] the n. un. is with ة, i. e. بَقْلَةٌ. (Ṣ, Ḳ.) Hence the prov., لَا تُنْبِتُ البَقْلَةَ إِلَّا الحَقْلَةُ [*Nothing produces the leguminous*, or *tender, plant*, or *herb, but the clear and open piece of good land*]: (TA:) [i. e., only a good parent produces good offspring: (see Freytag's Arab. Prov. ii. 516:)] it is said to be applied to the case of a vile saying proceeding from a vile man. (TA in art. حقل.) The saying بَاعَ الزَّرْعَ وَهُوَ بَقْلٌ means [*He sold the seed-produce*] *when it was green, not yet ripe.* (Mgh.) بَقْلَةُ الحَمْقَآءِ, also, and البَقْلَةُ الحَمْقَآءُ, (Ṣ,) or البَقْلَةُ الحَمْقَآءُ, (Ḳ,) or all these, (TA,) signify the same as الرِّجْلَةُ [i. e. *Purslane;* called by these names in the present day]; (Ṣ, Ḳ;) and so البَقْلَةُ اللَّيِّنَةُ and البَقْلَةُ المُبَارَكَةُ: or this last, *i. q.* الهِنْدَبَآءُ [i. e. *wild and garden succory*, or *endive*]. (Ḳ.) —— بَقْلَةُ الأَنْصَارِ *i. q.* الكُرُنْبُ [or الكَرَنْبُ, q. v., the name now given to *Cabbage:* in the CḲ الكُرُنْبُ]. (Ḳ.) —— بَقْلَةُ الخَطَاطِيفِ [*Chelidonium*, or *celandine;* thus called in the present day;] *i. q.* العُرُوقُ الصُّفْرُ. (Ḳ.) —— بَقْلَةُ المَلِكِ *i. q.* الشَّاهْتَرَجُ [*Fumaria officinalis*, or *common fumitory*]. (Ḳ.) —— البَقْلَةُ البَارِدَةُ *i. q.* اللَّبْلَابُ [now commonly applied to the *Dolichos lablab* of Linnæus; but Golius explains the former appellation by *hedera*, i. e. *ivy*, though only as on the authority of the Ḳ]. (Ḳ.) —— البَقْلَةُ الذَّهَبِيَّةُ *i. q.* القَطَفُ [or القُطْفُ, a name now given to *Atriplex*, or *orache:* Golius explains the former appellation by *spinachium seu atriplex;* and the latter, in its proper art., by *atriplex herba*, and *androsæmum*]. (Ḳ.) —— البَقْلَةُ اليَهُودِيَّةُ [*Sonchus*, or *sow-thistle;* thus called in the present day]. (TA voce خُبَّازٌ, q. v.) —— البَقْلَةُ اليَمَانِيَّةُ [*Blitum*, or *blite;* and particularly the species called *strawberry blite;*] *a certain herb.* (Ḳ.) —— البَقْلَةُ الأُتْرُجِّيَّةُ [*Citrago*, or *balm-gentle;*] *a certain herb.* (Ḳ.) —— بَقْلَةُ الضَّبِّ and بَقْلَةُ الرَّمْلِ and بَقْلَةُ الرُّمَاةِ and [in the CḲ "or"] البَقْلَةُ الحَمْضَآءُ and بَقْلَةُ البَرَارِى, (Ḳ, TA,) or البَقْلَةُ الحَامِضَةُ, (CḲ,) are also *Certain herbs.* (Ḳ.) —— بُقُولُ الأَوْجَاعِ *A certain plant proved by experience to remove pains from the belly.* (Ḳ, TA.)

بَلَدٌ بَقِلٌ and مُبْقِلٌ [*A country*, or *region*, or *district, producing plants*, or *herbs, of the kind termed* بَقْل]. (JK.) And أَرْضٌ بَقِلَةٌ, (Mṣb, Ḳ,) [in the CḲ بَقْلَةٌ, but it is] like فَرِحَةٌ, (TA,) and بَقِيلَةٌ and مُبْقِلَةٌ, (JK, Mṣb, Ḳ,) *Land producing* بَقْل: (Mṣb:) or *producing plants*, or *herbage:* (Ḳ:) and the first and second of these, (Ḳ,) and بَقَّالَةٌ, erroneously written in the copies of the Ḳ بَقَالَةٌ, without teshdeed, (TA,) and مَبْقَلَةٌ and مُبْقَلَةٌ, (Ḳ,) *land having*, or *containing,* بَقْل (Ḳ,* TA) *of* [*the rain*, or *season, called*] *the* رَبِيع: (Ḳ:) or مَبْقَلَةٌ [used alone, as a subst.,] signifies *a land having*, or *containing,* بَقْل; (JK;) or *a place of* بَقْل: (Ṣ:) and بَاقِلٌ [app. as meaning *producing* بَقْل] is applied as an epithet to a place; (JK, Mṣb;) but not مُبْقِلٌ; (JK;) or this last sometimes occurs, thus applied. (IJ, IB.)

بُقْلَةٌ The [*plants*, or *herbs, termed*] بَقْل *of* [*the rain*, or *season, called*] *the* رَبِيع. (JK, Ḳ, TA.)

أَرْضٌ بَقِيلَةٌ: see بَقِلٌ, in two places.

[بُقُولِىٌّ *Of*, or *relating to, the plants*, or *herbs, termed* بَقْل: from the pl. بُقُولٌ.]

بَقَّالٌ [properly *A green-grocer;* i. e.] *a seller of* تَرَه [Persian for بَقْل]: and [by extension of its application] *a shop-keeper:* (KL:) or *a seller of dry fruits:* (Ibn-Es-Sem'ánee, TA:) vulgarly, *a seller of eatables* [*of various kinds*, and particularly *of dried and salted provisions, cheese, &c.;* *a grocer*]; correctly, بَدَّالٌ. (AHeyth, T in art. بدل, Ḳ.) —— أَرْضٌ بَقَّالَةٌ: see بَقِلٌ.

بَاقِلٌ: see بَقِلٌ. —— Also, as an epithet applied to the [tree, or shrub, called] رِمْث, (Ṣ, Ḳ,) *Becoming green:* (Ḳ:) or *putting forth what resemble young wingless locusts, and showing the greenness of its leaves:* they did not say مُبْقِلٌ [in this sense], in like manner as [it is commonly asserted that] they did not say مُورِسٌ, from أَوْرَسَ, but وَارِسٌ. (Ṣ.) —— Also *What comes forth*, or *come forth, in the sides of trees, in the days of the* رَبِيع [or *spring*], *before their leaves become apparent.* (JK.) [See 4.]

بَاقِلَّى and بَاقِلَآءُ, (JK, Ṣ, Mgh, Mṣb, Ḳ,) the former with teshdeed and the latter without teshdeed, (Ṣ, Mgh, Mṣb,) and بَاقِلَى, (Ḳ,) [every one with tenween when it has not the article ال,

for] the n. un. is with ة, (Ṣ, Mgh, Mṣb, Ḳ,) i. e. بَاقِلَّاةٌ and بَاقِلَاةٌ (Ṣ, Mgh, Mṣb) [and بَاقِلَّى; or the sing. and pl. are alike, (El-Aḥmar, Ḳ,) [and if so, the word may be fem., as Ibn-Buzurj, cited in the TA voce هِنْدَبٌ, asserts بَاقِلَاء to be, and therefore in every case without tenween,] *i. q.* فُولٌ [*Beans;* or the *bean; faba sativa* of Jussieu; *vicia faba* of Linnæus]; (JK, Ḳ;) a name of the dial. of the Sawád [of El-'Irák]; *its produce is called* الجرجر; (TA; [but see جِرْجِيرٌ; and see تُرْمُسٌ;]) [or it is applied to the plant and to its produce;] *a certain well-known* حَبّ [or *grain*]: (Mgh:) *the eating of it produces exhalations* (Ḳ) *of a gross kind,* (TA,) *and bad dreams, and* سَدَر, (Ḳ,) i. e. *vertigo,* (TA,) *and anxiety, and gross humours; but it is good for the cough, and for rendering the body fruitful* (تَخْصِيب البَدَن); *when properly qualified* [app. *by seasoning* or *by some admixture*] (إِذَا أُصْلِحَ), *it preserves the health; and in its green state, together with ginger, it has the utmost effect in strengthening the venereal faculty:* (Ḳ:) the pl. is بَوَاقِلُ: and the dim. of باقلّى is ▼ بُوَيْقِلَةٌ and ▼ بُوَيْقِلِيَةٌ, the latter with the ل quiescent because kesreh is disapproved in so long a word; [both forms indicating that باقلّى is held to be fem.;] and that of بَاقِلَاء is بُوَيْقِلَاء [with or without tenween accord. as it is held to be masc. or fem.], or, if one will, he [who holds باقلاء to be fem.] may say ▼ بُوَيْقِلَةٌ, suppressing the augmentative meddeh, and adding ة to indicate the fem. gender; and that of باقلّاة is ▼ بُوَيْقِلَاةٌ. (TA.) — البَاقِلَّى القِبْطِىُّ [app. the same as الباقلّى المِصْرِىّ mentioned in the Ḳ voce تُرْمُسٌ, &c., i. e. *The Egyptian bean;* an appellation said to be applied by some in the present day to *the colocasia;* but what it properly denotes is doubtful;] *a certain plant, the grain of which is smaller than the* فُول [or *bean*]: (Ḳ:) *the people of Egypt know it by the name of* الجَامِسَة, with جيم, and with the unpointed سين: he who says that it is the تُرْمُس is in error. (Ibn-Beyṭár, cited by De Sacy in his "Relation de l'Égypte par Abd-allatif," q. v., p. 97.)

بَاقِلِّىٌّ and بَاقِلَانِىٌّ rel. ns. of بَاقِلَّى and بَاقِلَاء, respectively. (Mgh.)

بَاقُولٌ, (JK, A, O,) or ▼ بُوقَالٌ, (Ḳ,) *A mug* (كُوز) *having no* عُرْوَة [or *handle*]; (JK, O, Ḳ;) *i. q.* كُوب: (A, TA:) [in Spanish *bokal,* (Golius,) which favours the form in the Ḳ; but the Spanish word may be from بُوقَالَة, if from the Arabic:] pl. بَوَاقِيلُ. (JK, A, TA.)

بُوقَالٌ: see what next precedes.

بُوقَالَةٌ *A kind of drinking-vessel, like a* طَاس, or *like a* كَأْس; syn. طَرْجِهَارَة. (IAạr, TA.) [See also بَاقُولٌ.]

بُوَيْقِلَةٌ: } بُوَيْقِلَاةٌ: } see بَاقِلَّى, in four places. بُوَيْقِلِيَةٌ: }

مُبْقِلٌ: see بَقْلٌ, in three places: — and see بَاقِلٌ.

مَبْقَلَةٌ: } مَبْقُلَةٌ: } see بَقْلٌ, in three places.

بقم

بَقَّمٌ [*Brazil-wood;* the *wood of the Brazil-tree, a species of Cæsalpinia;*] *a well-known dye;* (Ṣ, Mṣb;) *i. q.* عَنْدَمٌ; (Ṣ;) [or rather the *wood from which a well-known dye is prepared;*] the *wood of a certain great tree, the leaves of which are like those of the almond, and having a red stem, the decoction of which is used as a dye: it consolidates wounds, stops a flow of blood from any member, and dries up ulcers; and its root,* or *lowest part, is an instantaneous poison:* (Ḳ:) the word is said by some to be Arabic; (Mṣb;) others say that it is arabicized; (Ṣ, Mṣb, TA;) [perhaps from the Persian بَقَمْ, or بَكَمْ;] and that the only other words of the same measure in the Arabic language are proper names, and four in number, (Ṣ, TA,) or seven: (TA:) if used as a proper name, it is imperfectly decl., because determinate and of the measure of a verb. (Ṣ.)

بقو

1. بَقَاهُ بِعَيْنِهِ, [aor. ـُ,] inf. n. بَقَاوَةٌ [and بَقْوَةٌ, as will be seen from what follows, like رَحْمَةٌ], *He looked,* (Lḥ, JK, ISd, Ḳ,) or *looked long,* or *glanced lightly,* (JK,) *at him,* or *it;* (Lḥ, JK, ISd, Ḳ;) and so with ى for the last radical: (JK:) and بَقَاهُ [alone], with و and with ى for the last radical, (Ḳ in art. بقى,) first pers. بَقَوْتُهُ and بَقَيْتُهُ, (Lḥ, TA,) *he looked at him,* or *it:* (Lḥ, Ḳ:) or *he watched,* or *observed, him,* or *it:* (Ḳ in art. بقى:) and بَقَوْتُهُ *I looked, watched,* or *waited, for him,* or *it:* (Ḳ:) a dial. var. of بَقَيْتُهُ, which is the more approved. (TA.) [Hence,] اُبْقُهْ بَقْوَتَكَ مَالَكَ and بَقَاوَتَكَ مَالَكَ *Guard thou,* or *preserve thou, him,* or *it, as thou guardest,* or *preservest, thy property.* (M, Tekmileh, Ḳ.)

بَقْوَى and بُقْوَى: see art. بقى.

بقى

1. بَقِىَ, aor. يَبْقَى, inf. n. بَقَآءٌ (JK, Ṣ, Mṣb, Ḳ) and بَاقِيَةٌ; (Mṣb; [but see this latter below;]) [and accord. to the CḲ, بَقِىَ and بُقْىٌ; but this is a mistake; وبَقِىَ وبُقْيًا being there erroneously put for وَبَقَى بَقْيًا, explained by what here follows;] and بَقَى, [by some written بَقَا,] (JK, Ṣ, Mṣb, Ḳ,) aor. as above, (JK,) inf. n. بُقْىٌ, (Ḳ,) of the dial. of Belḥárith Ibn-Kaab, (TA,) or of that of Ṭeiyi, (JK, Ṣ, TA,) who in like manner say بَقَتْ instead of بَقِيَتْ, (Ṣ, TA,) and the like is done in other verbs of the same class, (Ṣ, Mṣb,) whether the kesreh and the ى be original, as in بَقِىَ and نَسِىَ, or accidental, as in the pass. verbs هُدِىَ and فُنِىَ, and بُنِىَ; (Mṣb;) [*He,* or] *it,* namely, a thing, *remained, continued, lasted, endured:* and *was,* or *became, permanent,* or *perpetual;* or *continued, lasted,* or *existed, incessantly, always, endlessly,* or *for ever:* syn. دَامَ, and ثَبَتَ; (Mṣb;) *contr. of* فَنِىَ: (Ḳ:) بَقَآء signifies a thing's *remaining, continuing, lasting,* or *enduring, in its first state, to a period determined by the will of God, either with respect to its corporeal substance,* as in the case of a heavenly orb, *or with respect to its kind only,* as in the case of the human and other animal races; and the *continuing, lasting,* or *existing, for ever, either by self,* as in the instance of God alone, *or otherwise,* and thus *either with respect to the corporeal substance,* as in the case of an inhabitant of Paradise, *or with respect to kind only,* as in the case of the fruits of the inhabitants of Paradise. (Er-Rághib, TA.) [Hence,] دَارُ البَقَآءِ [*The abode of everlasting existence;*] *the world to come.* (T in art. دور.) The verb is said of a thing; and in like manner of a man, as in بَقِىَ زَمَانًا طَوِيلًا, i. e. *He lived* [or *continued in life*] *a long time.* (Ṣ.) [You say also, بَقِىَ عَلَى حَالِهِ *He,* or *it, remained,* or *continued, in his,* or *its, state,* or *condition;* i. e., *as he,* or *it, was.* And بَقِىَ عَلَى الشِّدَّةِ *He endured,* or *bore up against, difficulty, distress,* or *adversity.*] And بَقِىَ مِنَ الشَّىْءِ بَقِيَّةٌ [*A remain, remainder, remnant, relic,* or *residue, of the thing remained.*] (Ṣ.) And بَقِىَ مِنْهُ كَذَا *Such a thing remained, over and above,* and *behind, thereof;* as also ▼ تبقّى. (Mṣb.) — بَقَاهُ, with ى and with و for the last radical, (Ḳ,) first pers. بَقَيْتُهُ (Lḥ, Ṣ) and بَقَوْتُهُ, (Lḥ, TA,) aor. of the former ـِ, (Ṣ,) inf. n. بَقْىٌ, [of the former verb,] (Ḳ,) *He looked at him,* or *it:* (Lḥ, Ṣ, Ḳ:) or [so in the Ḳ, but in the Ṣ "and,"] *he watched,* or *observed, him,* or *it:* (Ṣ, Ḳ:) and بَقَيْتُهُ *I looked, watched,* or *waited, for him,* or *it;* (TA in art. بقو;) as also بَقَوْتُهُ; (Ḳ in that art.;) but the former is the more approved. (TA in that art.) [See also art. بقو.] You say also, فُلَانٌ يَبْقِى الشَّىْءَ بِبَصَرِهِ *Such a one looks at the thing,* and *watches,* or *observes, it.* (JK.) And it is said in a trad., بَقَيْنَا رَسُولَ ٱللّٰهِ *We looked, watched,* or *waited, for the Apostle of God.* (Ṣ.)

2: see 4, in two places.

4. ابقاهُ (Ṣ, Mṣb, Ḳ) and ▼ بقّاهُ and ▼ تبقّاهُ (Ṣ, Ḳ) all signify the same, (Ṣ,) and ▼ استبقاهُ likewise, (Ḳ,) *He made,* or *caused,* [and *he suffered,*] *him,* or *it, to remain, continue, last; to be,* or *become, permanent,* or *perpetual; to continue, last,* or *exist, incessantly, always, endlessly,* or *for ever; he continued it; he perpetuated it.* (Mṣb, Ḳ.*) You say, ابقاهُ ٱللّٰهُ [*God preserved him,* or *prolonged his life;* or *may God preserve him,* or *prolong his life;* or] *God made him,* or *caused him,* or *may God make him,* or *cause him, to continue in life.* (Ṣ.) And أَبْقَى أَصْلَ الشَّىْءِ وَجَعَلَ ثَمَرَهُ فِى سَبِيلِ ٱللّٰهِ *He made the thing itself to remain unalienable, not to be inherited nor sold nor given away, and assigned the profit arising from it to be employed in the cause of God,* or *of religion.* (TA in art. حبس.) And أَبْقَيْتُ مَا بَيْنَنَا *I was sparing of marring,* i. e., *forbore from marring much,* or *exceedingly, that* [*state of union* or *amity*] *which subsisted between us.* (Ḳ.) And بَقِّ ▼ نَعْلَيْكَ وَٱبْذُلْ قَدَمَيْكَ [*Pre-*

serve thou, or *spare thou, thy sandals, and use freely*, or *unsparingly, thy feet*]: a prov. (Meyd. See Freytag's Arab. Prov. i. 149.) And ▼ تَبَقَّهْ وَتَوَقَّهْ *Preserve thou the soul* (اِسْتَبْقِ ▼ النَّفْسَ), *expose it not to destruction*, [meaning *preserve thyself*,] *and guard against evils*, or *calamities*: a trad.: the ه in each verb is that of pausation. (TA.) [And ابقى مِنَ الشَّىْءِ بَقِيَّةً *He left*, or *reserved, of the thing, a remain, remainder, remnant*, &c.:] and استبقى ▼ مِنَ الشَّىْءِ *He left a portion of the thing*; (Ṣ, Ḳ;) as also ▼ تبقّى; whence the prov., used to incite to liberality, لَا يَنْفَعُكَ مِنْ زَادٍ تَبَقٍّ ▼ *Leaving a portion of travelling-provision will not profit thee*. (JK.) [And ابقى الشَّىْءَ and ▼ استبقاهُ *He reserved the thing* for a future time or use &c.] And ▼ استبقاهُ as meaning [*He spared him; he let him live*;] *he left him alive*; (Ṣ, Ḳ;) [as also ابقاهُ; for] men say to their enemies when the latter have overcome, أَبْقُونَا وَلَا تَسْتَأْصِلُونَا [*Spare ye us, and destroy us not entirely*]: (TA:) [or ابقاهُ, in a case of this kind,] and ابقى عَلَيْهِ and ▼ استبقاهُ signify *He pardoned him*, [*and forbore to slay him*,] *when slaughter was his due*: (TA:) and ▼ استبقاهُ signifies also *He pardoned*, or *forgave, his fault, wrong action*, or *lapse into sin, and preserved his love*, or *affection*. (JK, TA.*) And [hence,] أَبْقَيْتُ عَلَى فُلَانٍ signifies also *I showed mercy to such a one* [*by sparing him*, or *letting him live*, or *by pardoning him*, or *otherwise*]; *had mercy on him*; *pitied*, or *compassionated, him*; syn. رَحِمْتُهُ and أَرْعَيْتُ عَلَيْهِ. (Ṣ.) One says, لَا أَبْقَى ٱللّٰهُ عَلَيْكَ إِنْ أَبْقَيْتَ عَلَىَّ [*May God not show mercy to thee if thou show mercy to me*: a prov., said in derision to one who affects to show mercy when unable to take revenge]. (Ṣ, Meyd.) And لَا تُبْقِ إِلَّا عَلَى نَفْسِكَ [*Show not mercy save to thyself*: another prov., similar to the former]. (Meyd.) And it is said, in a trad., of the fire [of Hell], لَا تُبْقِى عَلَى مَنْ تَضَرَّعَ إِلَيْهَا, i. e. *It will not pity* [*him who abases himself to it*: or rather *it will not spare* &c.: and in like manner, لَا تُبْقِى وَلَا تَذَرُ, in the Ḳur lxxiv. 28, is generally understood as meaning *It* (namely, Hell,) *will not spare, nor leave* unburned]. (TA.)

5: see 1: — and see also 4, in four places.

6. تَبَاقٍ *The remaining together*. (KL.) [You say, app., تَبَاقَوْا, and تَبَاقَيَا, *They*, and *they two, remained together*.]

10: see 4, in seven places. [See also a usage of this verb in art. حى, conj. 10, second sentence.]

بَقَاقِ: see لَقَى بَقَى.

بَقِيَّةٌ: see بَقِيَّةٌ.

بَقْوَى: see بُقْيَا, in five places.

بُقْوَى: see بُقْيَا, in two places.

بَقْيَا: see what next follows.

بُقْيَا (JK, Ṣ, Mṣb, Ḳ, &c.) and ▼ بَقْيَا (TA) and ▼ بَقْوَى (JK, Ṣ, Mṣb, Ḳ) and ▼ بُقْوَى (Th, Ḳ) and ▼ بَقِيَّةٌ, (JK, Ḳ,) the ▼ third and ▼ fourth with و changed into ى, like as ى is changed into و in دُنْيَا and عُلْيَا and قُصْيَا, (ISd, TA,) [substs. in the sense of إِبْقَآءٌ, inf. n. of 4, signifying The *making*, or *causing*, and *suffering, to remain, continue, last*, &c.; *preservation* of a person *in life*, and of a thing *in being*; and the *sparing, letting live*, or *leaving alive*;] substs. from أَبْقَاهُ: (Mṣb, Ḳ:) or [the *showing mercy by sparing* or *letting live*, or *by pardoning*, or *otherwise*; *having mercy*; *pitying*, or *compassionating*;] substs. from أَبْقَيْتُ عَلَى فُلَانٍ. (Ṣ.) Thus one says of a pilgrim, that he put gum, or something glutinous, upon his head, and so caused his hair to become compacted, بُقْيَا عَلَيْهِ *to preserve it in the state in which it was* (expl. by إِبْقَآءً عليه), lest it should become shaggy, or dishevelled, &c. (L in art. لبد.) And one says, نَشَدْتُكَ ٱللّٰهَ وَالْبُقْيَا and ▼ الْبَقْوَى [*I conjure*, or *beg*, or *beseech, thee by God and by the preservation of* thy *life*]. (JK.) And مَا لِى عَلَيْهِ رَعْوَى وَلَا بَقْوَى ▼ [*I have no mercy nor pity* to bestow *upon him*]. (JK. [There expl. by the words أَىْ أَرْعَيْتُ عَلَيْهِ وَأَبْقَيْتُ; but أَىْ is evidently a mistranscription for مِنْ, i. e. from.]) A poet (El-La'een El-Minkaree, TA) says,

• فَمَا بُقْيَا عَلَىَّ تَرَكْتُمَانِى •
• وَلٰكِنْ خِفْتُمَا صَرَدَ النِّبَالِ •

[*And it was not to show mercy by sparing me that ye two left me; but ye feared the transpiercing of the arrows*]. (Ṣ.) And another says, on his having refused to accept an offer of seven bloodwits,

• أُذَكَّرُ بِالْبُقْيَا عَلَى مَنْ أَصَابَنِى •
• وَبُقْيَاىَ أَنِّى جَاهِدٌ غَيْرُ مُؤْتَلِى •

i. e. *Am I required* [or *exhorted* or *reminded*] *to show mercy to him who slew my relation, when the mercy that I show* to him *is that I am labouring* to slay him, and *not falling short*, or *being remiss*: by بقياى is meant إِبْقَائِى عَلَيْهِ; though الْإِبْقَآءُ is not الْجَهْدُ: the meaning is, that this is done by me in lieu of that: الْبُقْيَا is a subst. from الْإِبْقَآءُ, syn. therewith; and the و prefixed to it is a denotative of state. (Ḥam p. 119. [This verse is also cited in the TA, but with the substitution of ▼ بِالْبَقْوَى and وَبَقْوَاىَ for the corresponding words above.] ▼ الْبَقِيَّةَ is said by men to their enemies when the latter have overcome; meaning [We ask, or beg, *the being spared*, or *mercy*, or *quarter*; a verb, whereby it is governed, being understood: or] أَبْقُونَا وَلَا تَسْتَأْصِلُونَا [*spare ye us, and destroy us not entirely*]. (TA.)

بَقِيَّةٌ *A remain, remainder, remaining portion, remnant, relic, residue*, or the *remains*, or *rest*, of a thing; (KL, PṢ, &c.;) a subst. from بَقِىَ as signifying "it remained over and above," and "it remained behind:" pl. بَقَايَا and بَقِيَّاتٌ: (Mṣb:) ▼ بَاقِيَةٌ, also, [pl. بَاقِيَاتٌ and بَوَاقٍ,] has the same meaning as بَقِيَّةٌ; (TA;) [i. e., as explained above; and so has بَاقٍ, for شَىْءٌ بَاقٍ &c.] You say, بَقِىَ مِنَ الشَّىْءِ بَقِيَّةٌ [explained before: see 1]. (Ṣ.) [And هُمْ بَقِيَّةُ السَّيْفِ, and بَقَايَا السَّيْفِ, *They are those who have been spared by the sword*]. — [Hence,] فُلَانٌ مِنْ بَقِيَّةِ الْقَوْمِ *Such a one is of the best of the people*, or *company of men*: because a man reserves the most excellent of the things that he produces. (Bḍ in xi. 118.) And فُلَانٌ مِنْ بَقِيَّةِ أَهْلِهِ *Such a one is of the most excellent of his people*, or *family*. (Ḥam p. 78.) And فُلَانٌ بَقِيَّةُ الْقَوْمِ *Such a one is the best of the people*, or *company of men*: pl. بَقَايَا. (Kull p. 96.) — أُولُو بَقِيَّةٍ, in the Ḳur xi. 118, hence means *Persons possessed of excellence*: [see a phrase mentioned voce بَلَلٌ:] or *possessing a relic of judgment and intelligence*: (Bḍ:) or *persons of religion and excellence*: (Jel:) or *persons of understanding* (Ḳ, TA) *and discrimination*: (TA:) or *persons of obedience*: (TA:) or *having the quality of preserving themselves* (Az, Bḍ, Ḳ*) *from punishment*, (Bḍ,) *by their holding the approved religion*: (Az, TA:) and this last explanation is confirmed by another reading, which is اولو بَقْيَةٍ ▼ [*possessing a quality of watching*, or *observing*, and hence, *of guarding*, or *preserving*]; بَقْيَةٌ being the inf. n. of un. of بَقَاهُ, aor. يَبْقِيهِ, signifying "he watched," or "observed," &c., "him," or "it." (Bḍ.) See also بُقْيَا, in two places. بَقِيَّةٌ is also a subst. from أَبْقَيْتُ مَا بَيْنَنَا [explained before: see 4: app. meaning *Forbearance from marring much*, or *exceedingly, the state of unity*, or *of amity, subsisting between two persons*, or *parties*: and such may be its meaning in the phrase above-mentioned (اولو بقية)]. (Ḳ.) — بَقِيَّةُ ٱللّٰهِ, in the Ḳur xi. 87, [after the command, in the next preceding verse, to give full measure and weight,] means *God's sustenance that remains for you* after your giving full measure [and weight]: (Jel:) or *that which God has preserved for you, of what is lawful*, (Fr, Bḍ,) after [your] keeping aloof from that which he has forbidden you: (Bḍ:) or *the good state*, or *condition, remaining for you*: (Zj, Ḳ:) or *the fear* (مُرَاقَبَة) *of God*; accord. to some: (Fr, TA:) or *the obedience of God, and* (as Aboo-'Alee says, TA) *the looking for his recompense*: (Ḳ, TA:) or بَقِيَّةٌ and ▼ بَاقِيَةٌ signify *any religious service whereby one seeks to obtain the recompense of God*; and such is the meaning of the former in this instance. (Er-Rághib, TA.) — See also بَاقِيَةٌ.

بَاقٍ part. n. of بَقِىَ [in all its senses; *Remaining, continuing, lasting*, or *enduring*: and *permanent*, or *perpetual*; or *continuing, lasting*, or *existing, incessantly, always, endlessly*, or *for ever*: &c.: see 1]. (Er-Rághib, TA.) الْبَاقِى, a name of God, [as also, pleonastically, الْبَاقِى الْأَبَدِىُّ, means *The Everlasting*, or] *He whose existence will have no end*. (TA.) See also بَقِيَّةٌ. — الْبَاقِى also signifies *The* حَاصِل [or *net produce*, or perhaps simply the *produce*,] *of the* [tax termed] خَرَاج, *and the like*. (Lth, JK, TA.)

بَاقِيَةٌ: see بَقِيَّةٌ, first sentence. — الْبَاقِيَاتُ الصَّالِحَاتُ [in the Ḳur xviii. 44, and xix. 79,] means *Any righteous*, or *good, work*, (Ḳ, TA,) *of which the recompense remains*: (TA:) or *acts of obedience*,

(Bd and Jel in xix. 79,) or *good works,* (Bd in xviii. 44,) *of which the fruit remains for ever:* (Bd in both those places, and Jel* in the former:) and, as included therein, [so Bd, but in the Ḳ "or,"] *the five prayers;* (Bd, Ḳ;) and *the performance of the pilgrimage;* and *the keeping the fast of Ramadán;* (Bd in xviii. 44;) and [so Bd, but in the Ḳ "or,"] *the saying,* سُبْحَانَ ٱللّٰهِ وَٱلْحَمْدُ لِلّٰهِ وَلَا إِلٰهَ إِلَّا ٱللّٰهُ وَٱللّٰهُ أَكْبَرُ; (Bd and Jel in xviii. 44, and Ḳ;) to which some add, وَلَا حَوْلَ وَلَا قُوَّةَ إِلَّا بِٱللّٰهِ: (Jel ibid.:) or, accord. to Er-Rághib, the correct meaning is *any religious service whereby one seeks to obtain the recompense of God:* see also بَقِيَّةٌ, last explanation. (TA.) —— بَاقِيَةٌ is sometimes put in the place of an inf. n.; (Ṣ, Ḳ;) or it is an inf. n.; (Mṣb;) *syn. with* بَقَآءٌ; (Ṣ, Mṣb, TA;) with which ▼بَقِيَّةٌ, also, is syn. (TA in art. سرع.) So in the Ḳur [lxix. 8], فَهَلْ تَرَى لَهُمْ مِنْ بَاقِيَةٍ [*And dost thou see them to have any continuance?*]; (Ṣ, TA;) so says Fr: (TA:) or, as some say, the meaning is, بَقِيَّة [i. e. *a remnant*]: (TA:) or جَمَاعَة بَاقِيَة [*a company remaining*]: (Er-Rághib, TA:) or نَفْس بَاقِيَة [*a soul,* or *person, remaining*]: (Bd, Jel:) or the ة is an intensive affix; (Jel;) [or a restrictive to unity;] i. e. *one remaining;* (Jel, TA;) and this is also allowable and good: one says, likewise, مَا بَقِيَتْ بَاقِيَةٌ وَلَا وَقَاهُمْ مِنَ ٱللّٰهِ وَاقِيَةٌ [*One remaining remained not, nor did one preserver preserve them from God*]. (TA.)

أَبْقَى *Longer continuing.* (Bd and Jel in xx. 74, &c.) —— هُوَ أَبْقَى ٱلرَّجُلَيْنِ means أَكْثَرُ إِبْقَآءً عَلَى قَوْمِهِ [*He is the more merciful,* or *pitiful,* or *compassionate, of the two men, towards his people*]. (TA.)

نَاقَةٌ مُبْقِيَةٌ *A she-camel* [*that retains some milk;*] *that does not exhaust her copious supply of milk.* (JK.) —— مُبْقِيَاتُ ٱلْخَيْلِ, (Ḳ,) or rather ٱلْمُبْقِيَاتُ مِنَ ٱلْخَيْلِ, (TA,) *The horses whose running continues after the running of other horses has ceased:* (M, Ḳ:) or, *that reserve somewhat of their running.* (T, TA.) —— And ٱلْمُبْقِيَاتُ *The places that retain some of the pools in which water has collected, and do not drink it up.* (TA.)

بكأ

1. بَكَأَتْ, aor. ـَ; and بَكُؤَتْ, aor. ـُ; inf. n. بَكْءٌ (Ṣ, Ḳ) and بُكْءٌ (AZ, TA) and بَكَآءَةٌ, or بَكَاءَةٌ, (accord. to different copies of the Ḳ,) or بَكَآءَةٌ, (as in the O and CḲ,) and بُكُوْءَةٌ, (Ṣ, Ḳ,) which is inf. n. of بَكُؤَ, (Ṣ, TA,) as is also that next preceding it, (TA,) and بَكَآءٌ, (AZ, Ḳ, TA,) in some copies of the Ḳ بُكْءٌ, (TA,) *She* (a camel, Ṣ, Ḳ, or a ewe or goat, Ṣ) *had little milk; her milk became little:* (Ṣ, Ḳ, TA:) or, as some say, *her milk ceased,* or *stopped.* (TA.) —— And [hence,] بَكَأَتْ عَيْنِى †*My eye had few tears.* (TA.) —— And بَكُؤَ, inf. n. بَكَآءَةٌ, [app. †*He became poor; had little wealth;* being] said of a man. (TA.) [See also 4.] —— And بَكِئَ †*He failed of attaining the object of his want.* (TA.)

4. قَدْ أَبْكَأَ ٱلدَّرَّ, occurring in a verse, [see Ḥam p. 758,] is asserted by Aboo-Riyásh to mean *He* (the milker) *has found the milk to be little in quantity;* like as أَحْمَدَهُ signifies "he found him to be such as is praised:" ISd holds that it may signify *he has made the milk to be little in quantity* [app. by his niggardness]; but he confesses his not having heard the verb used in this sense by any one. (TA.) —— ابكأ also signifies †*He* (a man) *became poor;* or *in the condition of having little,* or *no, wealth.* (TA.) [See also بَكُؤَ.]

بَكْءٌ [originally inf. n. of 1, q. v.: and hence,] †*Poverty;* or *paucity of wealth.* (TA.) —— And †*Paucity of speech, except as to things requiring speech.* (TA.)

بَكِئٌ and بَكِيئَةٌ A she-camel, (Ṣ, Ḳ,) or a ewe or she-goat, (Ṣ,) *having little milk; whose milk has become little:* (Ṣ, Ḳ, TA:) or, as some say, *whose milk has ceased,* or *stopped:* (TA:) pl. بِكَآءٌ (Ṣ, Ḳ) and بَكَايَا. (Ḳ.) —— And [hence,] دَرٌّ بَكِئٌ †[*Milk,* or *a flow of milk, little in quantity*]. (TA.) —— And رَكِيَّةٌ بَكِيَّةٌ †*A well of which the water has sunk into the earth;* or *become low:* the latter word having its ء changed into ى to assimilate it to the former. (TA.) —— And عُيُونٌ بِكَآءٌ †*Eyes having few tears.* (TA.) —— And أَيْدٍ بِكَآءٌ †*Hands of which the gifts are few.* (TA.) And رَجُلٌ بَكِئٌ †[app. *A poor man; a man having little wealth:* or *of few words:* or *unable to speak:* see بَكْءٌ; and see بَكِىٌّ, in art. بكى]: pl. بِكَآءٌ. (TA.)

بكت

1: see 2, in four places.

2. بَكَّتَهُ, inf. n. تَبْكِيتٌ, *He reprehended, reproved, blamed, chid,* or *reproached, him, for an affair,* or *for a crime or the like;* (Ṣ, A, Mṣb, Ḳ;) accord. to some, *with justice;* (TA;) or *he did so severely;* (Ṣ,* TA;) *and threatened him;* (TA;) *and declared his deed to be evil;* (Mṣb;) *as when one says, "O wicked man! wast thou not ashamed? didst thou not fear God?"* (TA:) and sometimes this is done *by using an enunciative phrase, such as the saying of Abraham,* [mentioned in the Ḳur xxi. 64,] *"Nay, the chief of them, this, did it;"* for thus he said to reprove their worship of idols; (Mṣb;) and it may be *by means of the hand,* and *a staff* or *stick,* and *the like.* (Hr, TA.) —— *He accused him, to his face,* (اِسْتَقْبَلَهُ, q. v.,) *of that which he disliked,* or *hated;* (Aṣ, A, Ḳ;) as also ▼بَكَتَهُ, (Aṣ, Ḳ,) aor. ـُ, inf. n. بَكْتٌ. (TA.) —— *He overcame him,* بِٱلْحُجَّةِ [*with the argument, allegation,* or *plea*]; (Ṣ, A, Ḳ;) as also ▼بَكَتَهُ; (A, TA;) and both, *he obliged him to be silent by reason of his inability to reply.* (A,* TA.) You say, بَكَّتَهُ حَتَّى أَسْكَتَهُ, and ▼بَكَتَهُ, *He overcame him* [by an argument, &c.,] *so that he silenced him.* (A, TA.) —— Also, (Lth, TA,) and ▼بَكَتَهُ, (Ḳ, TA,) aor. and inf. n. as above, (TA,) *He beat, struck,* or *smote, him* (Ḳ, TA) with a staff or stick, and a sword, (Lth, Ḳ, TA,) and the like. (Lth, TA.)

مُبْكِتٌ A woman *who usually brings forth a male child after a female.* (Ḳ, TA.) [Such a woman is app. thus called because supposed to reproach her husband for his having been displeased with her on her bringing forth a female.]

بكر

1. بَكَرَ and غَدَا both [properly] relate to the beginning of the day: (AZ, Mṣb:) the former of these verbs, (T, Ṣ, A,) aor. ـُ, inf. n. بُكُورٌ; (T, Ṣ;) and ▼بكّر, (T, Ṣ, A,) inf. n. تَبْكِيرٌ; (T, Ṣ;) and ▼ابكر, and ▼ابتكر, (Ṣ, A,) and ▼باكر; (Ṣ;) all signify the same; (Ṣ;) *He* (a traveller, A) *went forth early in the morning, in the first part of the day;* or *between the time of the prayer of daybreak and sunrise;* syn. خَرَجَ فِى ٱلْبُكْرَةِ: (T, A:) or ▼ابكر, inf. n. إِبْكَارٌ, signifies *he entered upon that time:* (T:) one should not say بَكُرَ nor بَكِرَ in the sense of بكر [&c.]. (Ṣ.) —— You say also, بَكَرَ إِلَيْهِ, and عَلَيْهِ, and فِيهِ, inf. n. as above; and ▼بكّر, and ▼ابكر, and ▼ابتكر; and ▼بَاكَرَهُ; meaning أَتَاهُ بُكْرَةً [i. e. *He came to him,* or *it, early in the morning, in the first part of the day;* or *between the time of the prayer of daybreak and sunrise:* and *he did it at that time:* or بكر &c. with فيه following may be rendered *he occupied himself at that time in doing it*]. (Ḳ.) —— And [hence,] بَكَرَ إِلَيْهِ, [and عَلَيْهِ,] aor. and inf. n. as above; (Mṣb;) and بَكِرَ اليه, aor. ـَ; (ISd, Ḳ;* [but see a remark respecting this verb above;]) and ▼بكّر اليه, (Ṣ, Mṣb, TA,) and عليه; (TA;) and ▼ابكر اليه, (Ṣ, Ḳ,) and عليه; [and ▼ابكره;] and ▼باكره; (TA;) signify also † *He hastened* [or *betook himself early*] *to it,* or *to do it,* at any time, (Ṣ, Mṣb, Ḳ, TA,) morning or evening. (TA.) You say, بَكَرْتُ عَلَى ٱلْحَاجَةِ †[*I hastened to do, or accomplish, or attain, the thing needed*], inf. n. as above: and in like manner, ▼أَبْكَرْتُ عَلَى ٱلْوِرْدِ †[*I hastened to come to water*]: (AZ, Ṣ:) and ▼ابكر ٱلْوِرْدَ, (TA,) and ٱلْغَدَآءَ, (AZ, Ṣ, TA,) †*He hastened to come to water,* and *to take the morning-meal.* (TA.) Lebeed says,

* ▼بَاكَرْتُ حَاجَتَهَا ٱلدَّجَاجَ بِسُحْرَةٍ *

meaning †*I hastened to be before the crowing of the cock, at the close of night, in obtaining what was wanted* [*of it,* namely, *of wine,*] *by me:* (TA:) حاجتها being for حَاجَتِى إِلَيْهَا, i. e., إِلَى ٱلْخَمْرِ. (EM p. 170: but the first word is there written بَادَرْتُ.) [See also 2, below.] —— [It is also said that] بكر, [app. بَكُرَ,] inf. n. بكر, [app. بَكْر,] signifies †*He possessed the quality of applying himself early,* or *of hastening;* expl. by كَانَ صَاحِبَ بُكُورٍ. (Mṣb.) [But see بَكُرَ.]

2. بكّر, inf. n. تَبْكِيرٌ: see 1, in three places: and see 8. You say also, بكّر إِلَى ٱلْجُمُعَةِ ‡ *He went forth to the* [*prayers of*] *Friday at the commencement of the time thereof.* (A.) And بكّر [alone], inf. n. as above, ‡ *He came to prayer at the commencement of its time.* (Ḳ, TA.) And بكّر بِٱلصَّلَاةِ ‡ *He performed the prayer at the commencement of its time:* (A, Mgh, Mṣb, TA:) *he was regardful of it, and performed it early.* (TA.) And بَكِّرُوا بِصَلَاةِ ٱلْمَغْرِبِ ‡ *Perform ye*

the prayer of sunset at the setting of the [*sun's*] *disc.* (Ṣ.) And بَكَّرَتِ النَّخْلَةُ بِحَمْلِهَا ‡ [*The palm-tree was early with its fruit*]. (A.) —— Also ‡ *He was,* or *became,* or *went, before; preceded; had,* or *took, precedence;* syn. تَقَدَّمَ; and so ▼ ابكر and ▼ تبكّر. (Ḳ, TA.) You say, بَكَّرْتُ فِى كَذَا ‡ *I was,* or *became,* or *went, before,* &c., *in such a thing;* syn. تَقَدَّمْتُ. (IJ, IB, TA.) And بكّر عَلَى أَصْحَابِهِ † [*He was,* or *became,* or *went, before his companions; preceded them;* or *had,* or *took, precedence of them*]. (M, Ḳ.) ═ بكّره عَلَى أَصْحَابِهِ signifies جَعَلَهُ يُبَكِّرُ عَلَيْهِمْ † [*He made him to be,* or *become,* or *go, before his companions; to precede them;* or *to have,* or *take, precedence of them*]; and so ▼ ابكره عَلَيْهِمْ. (M, Ḳ.) —— See also 4. —— بكّر الفَاكِهَةَ: see 8.

3: see 1, in four places.

4: see 1, in seven places: and see 2 as meaning تَقَدَّمَ. —— ابكر also signifies *He had camels coming to water early in the morning, in the first part of the day;* or *between the time of the prayer of daybreak and sunrise.* (Ṣ, Ḳ.) ═ It is also trans. of بَكَرَ: (Ṣ, Ṣgh, Mṣb:) you say, أَبْكَرْتُ غَيْرِى [*I made another to go forth early in the morning, in the first part of the day;* or *between the time of the prayer of daybreak and sunrise:* and *I made another to go* to a person &c. *at that time;* and *to betake himself* to an action *at that time:* and † *to hasten,* or *betake himself early,* to a thing at any time, morning or evening: and بَكَّرْتُ ▼ غَيْرِى app. signifies the same]. (Ṣ.) —— You say also, ابكره عَلَى أَصْحَابِهِ: see 2.

5: see 2.

8. ابتكر: see 1, in two places. —— Also ‡ *He arrived* [at the mosque on the occasion of the Friday-prayers] *in time to hear the first portion of the* خُطْبَة: (Ṣ, Ḳ:) or *he heard the first portion of the* خُطْبَة; (A, Mṣb;) [and] ابتكر الخُطْبَةَ has this meaning. (Mgh.) مَنْ بَكَّرَ ▼ وَٱبْتَكَرَ, occurring in a trad., (Ṣ, Mṣb,) respecting [the prayers of] Friday, (Ṣ,) means ‡ *Whoso hasteneth,* (Ṣ, Mṣb,) *and arriveth in time to hear the first portion of the* خُطْبَة, (Ṣ,) or *heareth the first portion thereof:* (Mṣb:) or *whoso hasteneth, going forth to the mosque early, and performeth the prayer at the first of its time:* or, accord. to Aboo-Sa'eed, *whoso hasteneth to the Friday-prayers, before the call to prayer, and arriveth at the commencement of their time:* or both the verbs signify the same, and the [virtual] repetition is to give intensiveness and strength to the meaning. (TA. [See 2.]) —— You say also, ابتكره, meaning ‡ *He took,* (A, Mṣb,) or *obtained possession of,* (Ṣ, TA,) *its* بَاكُورَة, (Ṣ, TA,) i. e., (TA,) *the first of it:* (A, Mṣb, TA:) which is the primary signification [of the trans. verb]. (TA.) —— And ابتكر, (Ḳ,) or ابتكر الفَاكِهَةَ, (A, Mgh, Mṣb,) and ▼ بَكَّرَهَا, (TA,) ‡ *He ate the first that had come to maturity of fruit,* or *of the fruit.* (A, Mgh, Mṣb, Ḳ.) —— And hence, (Mgh,) ابتكر الجَارِيَةَ ‡ *He took the girl's virginity:* (A, Mgh:) or *he did so before she had attained to puberty.* (Mṣb in art. قض, and TA in art. خضر.) —— And ابتكر عَجِينًا † [*He took,* or *made use of, fresh dough* for preparing bread]. (Ḳ in art. غرض.) ═ And اِبْتَكَرَتْ, (Abu-l-Beydà,) or ابتكرت بِوَلَدِهَا, (AHeyth,) *She brought forth her first offspring:* (AHeyth, Abu-l-Beydà:) or the former signifies *she* (a woman) *brought forth a male at her first birth.* (Ḳ.)

بَكْرٌ (Ṣ, Mgh, Mṣb, Ḳ, &c.) and ▼ بُكْرٌ, (Ḳ,) but this latter is hardly to be found in any of the lexicons, (MF,) and ▼ بِكْرٌ, (ISd, TA,) *A youthful he-camel; one in a state of youthful vigour:* fem. with ة; (Ṣ, Mgh, Mṣb, Ḳ;) and also بَكْرٌ, without ة: (TA:) the term بَكْرٌ, applied to a camel, corresponds to فَتًى, applied to a human being; and بَكْرَةٌ, to فَتَاةٌ; and قَلُوصٌ, to جَارِيَةٌ; and بَعِيرٌ, to إِنْسَانٌ; and جَمَلٌ, to رَجُلٌ; and نَاقَةٌ, to مَرْأَةٌ: (AO, Ṣ:) or the *offspring,* or *young one, of a she-camel;* (Ḳ;) thus indefinitely explained: (TA:) or *a camel in his sixth year* (ثَنِىٌّ) [and] *until he becomes a* جذع: [but it seems that the reverse must be meant; for a جذع, of camels, is one in his fifth year:] or *a camel in his second year* [and] *until he enters his sixth year:* or *a camel in his second year,* or *that has entered his third year,* or *that has completed his second year and entered his third year;* syn. اِبْنُ لَبُونٍ: (Ḳ:) and *a camel that has just entered upon his fourth year:* and *a camel in his fifth year:* (IAạr, Az:) or *a camel that has not entered his ninth year:* (Ḳ:) and sometimes it is metaphorically applied to a human being; [meaning ‡ *a young man;*] and بَكْرَةٌ to ‡ *a young woman:* (TA:) the pl. (of pauc., Ṣ) is أَبْكُرٌ; (Ṣ, Ḳ;) and ▼ أُبَيْكِرُونَ occurs as pl. of the dim. of أَبْكُرٌ; (Ṣ, TA;) and (pl. of mult., Ṣ, TA) بِكَارٌ, (Ṣ, Mṣb,) like as فِرَاخٌ is pl. of فَرْخٌ; (Ṣ;) or this is pl. of بَكْرَةٌ; (Mṣb, Ḳ;) and there are other pls. of بَكْرٌ, namely, بُكْرَانٌ (Ḳ) and بِكَارَةٌ; (Ṣ, Mṣb, Ḳ;) and [quasi-pl. n.] ▼ بَكَارَةٌ. (Ḳ.) Hence the well-known prov., (TA,) صَدَقَنِى سِنَّ بَكْرِهِ, and سِنُّ بَكْرِهِ, meaning *He hath told me what is in his mind, and what his ribs infold:* a saying originating from the following fact: a man bargained with another for a youthful camel (بَكْر), and said, "What is his age (سِنُّهُ)?" the other answered, "He is in his ninth year:" then the young camel took fright and ran away: whereupon his owner said to him, هِدَعْ هِدَعْ; and this is an expression by which are quieted young ones, (Ḳ,) of the camel; (TA;) so when the purchaser heard it, he said, صدقنى سنّ بكره [*He hath told me truly the age,* or *as to the age, of his youthful camel:* or *the age of his youthful camel has spoken truly to me*]: if سنّ is in the accus. case, the meaning [of the verb] is عَرَّفَنِى, (Ḳ,) and سنّ is in the accus. case as a second objective complement; (TA;) or خَبَرَ سِنِّ is meant; [in the CḲ, erroneously, خَبَرِ سِنِّ;] or فِى سِنِّ; the prefixed noun [خَبَرَ] or the proposition [فِى] being suppressed [and سنّ being therefore in the accus. case]: but if سنّ is in the nom. case, veracity is attributed to the [animal's] age, by an amplification: (Ḳ:) or, as some say, the buyer said to the owner of the camel, "How many years has he?" and he told him; and he looked at the teeth of the camel, and found him to be as he had said; whereupon he said, صدقنى سِنُّ بكره. (Har p. 95.)

بُكْرٌ: see بَكْرٌ.

بِكْرٌ *A virgin;* (Ṣ, Ḳ;) and *a man who has not yet drawn near to a woman;* (TA;) *contr. of* ثَيِّبٌ, *applied to a man as well as to a female:* (Mgh, Mṣb:) pl. أَبْكَارٌ. (Ṣ, Mṣb, Ḳ.) —— And [hence,] † *A pearl unpierced.* (MF.) And † *A bow when one first shoots with it.* (TA.) And ‡ *A cloud abounding with water:* (Ḳ, TA:) likened to a virgin, because her blood is more than that of her who is not a virgin: and the phrase سَحَابٌ بِكْرٌ is sometimes used. (TA.) And نَارٌ بِكْرٌ ‡ *Fire not lighted from another fire.* (Aṣ, A.) —— Also *She that has not yet brought forth offspring:* (AHeyth:) and *a cow that has not yet conceived:* (Ḳ:) or *a heifer* (Ḳ, TA) *that has not yet conceived:* (TA:) and *a woman,* (Ṣ, Ḳ,) and *a she-camel,* (Aṣ, Ḳ,) *that has brought forth but once:* pl. أَبْكَارٌ and بِكَارٌ: (TA:) or *a she-camel in her first state* or *condition.* (Ham p. 340.) —— And [hence,] ‡ *A grape-vine that has produced fruit but once:* (A, Ḳ:) pl. أَبْكَارٌ. (A.) —— Also *i. q.* بَكْرٌ, q. v. (ISd, TA.) And [hence,] أَبْكَارُ الأَوْلَادِ † *Young children.* (TA, from a trad.) And أَبْكَارُ النَّحْلِ † *Young bees.* (TA.) Whence, عَسَلُ أَبْكَارٍ ‡ *Honey produced by young bees:* or this means *honey of which the preparation has been superintended by virgin-girls.* (A,* TA.) —— Also ‡ The *first-born of his,* or *her, mother* (Ṣ, Mṣb, Ḳ) *and father;* (Mṣb, Ḳ;) applied alike to the *male* and the *female:* (Ṣ:) and sometimes to that which is not the offspring of human beings; (TA;) the *first-born* of camels; (Ṣ;) and of a serpent: (TA:) pl. أَبْكَارٌ. (TA.) You say, هٰذَا بِكْرُ أَبَوَيْهِ ‡ *This is the first-born of his parents.* (TA.) And أَشَدُّ النَّاسِ بِكْرُ ٱبْنِ بِكْرَيْنِ (A) or بِكْرُ بِكْرَيْنِ (M, TA) ‡ [*The strongest of men is the first-born of a man and woman each a first-born*]. —— † The *first* of anything; (Ḳ;) as also ▼ بَاكُورَةٌ: (TA:) and † *an action that has not been preceded by its like.* (Ḳ.) You say, مَا هٰذَا الأَمْرُ مِنْكَ بِكْرًا وَلَا ثِنْيًا ‡ *This thing,* or *affair, is not thy first nor thy second.* (A, TA.) —— حَاجَةٌ بِكْرٌ ‡ *A want,* or *needful thing, recently sought to be accomplished* or *attained:* (TA:) or *that is the first in being referred to him of whom its accomplishment is sought.* (A, TA.) —— ضَرْبَةٌ بِكْرٌ ‡ *A cutting blow* or *stroke,* (Ṣ, Ḳ,) *that kills* (Ḳ) *at once,* (TA,) *not requiring to be struck a second time:* (Ṣ, A:) pl. ضَرَبَاتٌ أَبْكَارٌ; occurring in a trad., in which it is said that such were the blows of 'Alee; (Ṣ, TA;) but in that trad., as some recite it, the latter word is ▼ مُبْتَكَرَاتٌ. (TA.)

بَكَرٌ: see بُكْرَةٌ, in three places: ═ and see also بَكْرَةٌ.

رَجُلٌ بَكُرٌ فِى حَاجَتِهِ, [in the CḲ, erroneously, بَكْرٌ,] and ▾بَكِرٌ, (Ṣ, Ḳ,* TA,) like حَذُرٌ and حَذِرٌ, (Ṣ,) and ▾بَكِيرٌ, (TA,) †*A man possessing the quality of applying himself early, or of hastening, or having strength to apply himself early, or to hasten,* (صَاحِبُ بُكُورٍ, Ṣ, or قَوِىٌّ عَلَى البُكُورِ, Ḳ,) *to do, or accomplish, the thing that he needs,* or *wants:* (Ṣ:) بَكُرٌ and بَكِرٌ [and بَكِيرٌ] are [said to be] possessive epithets; for they have no simple triliteral verb. (TA.) [But see 1, last sentence.]

بَكُرٌ: see what next precedes.

بَكْرَةٌ (Ṣ, Mṣb, Ḳ) and ▾بَكَرَةٌ (Mṣb, Ḳ) The *thing upon which [passes the rope wherewith] one draws water* (Ṣ, Mṣb, Ḳ) *from a well [or the like]*; (Ṣ;) [i. e. the *sheave of a pulley;*] *a round piece of wood, in the middle [of the circumference] whereof is a groove* (Ḳ, TA) *for the rope, and in the interior [or centre] whereof is an axis upon which it turns:* (TA:) or *a quick* مَحَالَة [or *large sheave of a pulley*]: (M, Ḳ:) [but MF disapproves of this last explanation: sometimes, by a synecdoche, it is used to signify *a pulley complete*:] the pl. is ▾بَكَرٌ, (Ṣ, Mṣb, Ḳ,) a pl. of the former, anomalous, like حَلَقٌ pl. of حَلْقَةٌ, and حَمًا pl. of حَمَاةٌ, (Ṣ,) or of the latter; (Mṣb;) or a coll. gen. n., of which بَكَرَةٌ is the n. un.; (MF;) and بَكَرَاتٌ, (Ṣ, Mṣb, Ḳ,) a pl. of the former [as well as of the latter]. (Ṣ, Mṣb.) —— Hence, app., the former signifies also †*A small ring, like a bead, in the ornamental part of a sword:* (Mgh:) [and the pl.] بَكَرَاتٌ signifies †the *rings that are attached to the ornamental part [of the scabbard] of a sword,* (Ḳ,) *resembling the [rings called]* فَتَخ *[which are worn upon the fingers or toes] of women.* (TA.) —— [And hence, perhaps,] †*An assembly, a company,* or *a congregated body.* (IAạr, Ḳ.) —— جَاؤُوا عَلَى بَكْرَةِ أَبِيهِمْ is a prov., (TA,) meaning ‡*They came together, not one remaining behind,* (Ṣ, TA;) *they came all of them,* (AA, IJ, A, TA,) *without exception:* (TA:) or *they came in a multitude, and all together, none remaining behind:* (TA:) or *they came in succession, one after,* or *at the heels of, another:* (AO:) or *they came in one way,* or *manner:* (Aṣ:) [accord. to some, from بكرة as explained in the next preceding sentence; and, if so, على is used in the sense of مَعَ, or مُشْتَمِلِينَ is understood before it: or it is from بكرة signifying "a youthful she-camel;" and thus implies that they were few: (see Freytag's Arab. Prov. i. 312:) or] from بَكَرْتُ فِى كَذَا meaning "I was," or "became," or "went," "before in such a thing;" so that it signifies that they came from first to last: (IJ:) or from بكرة in the first of the senses explained in this paragraph; though in this case there is no بكرة in reality. (AO, Ṣ.*)

بُكْرَةٌ and ▾بُكَرٌ The *early morning,* or *first part of the day;* (Bḍ and Jel in xix. 12 and xxxiii. 41 and xlviii. 9, as relating to the former word; and Ḳ;*) *between the time of the prayer of daybreak and sunrise;* syn. غُدْوَةٌ; and ▾إِبْكَارٌ is a subst. in the same sense, (Ḳ,) accord. to the lexicologists, as Sb says; but he adds that he holds it to be [only] the inf. n. of أَبْكَرَ: (TA: [and the like is said in the Ṣ with reference to its occurrence in the Ḳur iii. 36 and xl. 57:]) pl. [of pauc.] of the first, أَبْكَارٌ, and [of mult.] بُكَرٌ. (T, Mṣb.) You say, أَتَيْتُهُ بُكْرَةً (Ṣ, A, Mṣb) and ▾بُكَرًا, (A,) meaning ▾بَاكِرًا [*I came to him early in the morning,* &c.]. (Ṣ, A, Mṣb.) But if you mean the بُكْرَة of a particular day, you say, أَتَيْتُهُ بُكْرَةَ, making the noun imperfectly decl.; [meaning *I came to him early in the morning,* &c., *of this day;*] and in this case it is not to be used otherwise than as an adv. n. of time. (Ṣ.) If you say ▾بَاكِرًا, using this word as an epithet, you use بَاكِرَة for the fem. (TA.) You say also, سِرْ عَلَى فَرَسِكَ بُكْرَةً and ▾بُكَرًا [*Go thou on thy horse early in the morning,* &c.]; like as you say, سَحَرًا. (Ṣ, TA. [But in two copies of the Ṣ, for سِرْ, I find سِيرَ.])

بَكَرَةٌ: see بَكْرَةٌ.

بَكُورٌ (A, Ḳ) and ▾بَاكُورٌ (Ḳ) and ▾بَاكِرٌ (A) and ▾مِبْكَرٌ (Ḳ) ‡Rain *that falls in the first of its season:* (A:) or *that comes* (TA) *in the commencement of [the season of] the* وَسْمِىّ [q. v.]: (Ḳ, TA:) and *that comes in the end of the night,* or *the beginning of the day.* (TA.) You say also سَحَابَةٌ مِدْلَاجٌ بَكُورٌ ‡[*A cloud that comes in the latter part of the night, in the first of its season, bringing rain*]: (A:) and ▾سَحَابَةٌ مِبْكَارٌ *a cloud that comes in the end of the night.* (TA.) —— Also بَكُورٌ (Ṣ, A, Mṣb, Ḳ) and ▾بَكِيرَةٌ (Ṣ, Ḳ) and ▾بَاكُورَةٌ (Mṣb, Ḳ) and ▾بَاكِرٌ (A) and ▾مِبْكَارٌ (A in art. اخر, and Ḳ) ‡ A palm-tree (نَخْلَةٌ, A) *that comes to maturity first,* (Ṣ, Mṣb, Ḳ,) *before the other palm-trees:* (Ṣ:) or *that produces its fruit early;* (A;) *contr. of* مِئْخَارٌ: (A in art. اخر:) pl. (of the first, Mṣb, Ḳ) بُكُرٌ; (Ṣ, Mṣb, Ḳ; [in the CḲ بُكْرٌ;]) and [pl. of ▾بَاكِرٌ or بَاكِرَةٌ] بَوَاكِرُ. (Ḳ voce تَبَاشِيرُ.) ▾بَاكُورَةٌ is fem. of بَاكُورٌ, (Ḳ, TA,) which signifies †Anything *that hastens its coming* (TA) *and its attaining to maturity.* (Ḳ, TA.) You say also أَرْضٌ ▾مِبْكَارٌ †*Land that produces plants,* or *herbage, quickly.* (Ḳ.)

بَكِيرٌ, and its fem., with ة: see بَكُرٌ and بَكُورٌ.

بَكَارَةٌ *Virginity:* (Ṣ, Ḳ:) the *virginity,* or *maidenhead,* of a woman. (Mgh, Mṣb.) ═ See also بِكْرٌ.

بَاكِرٌ [part. n. of بَكَرَ]: see بُكْرَةٌ, in two places: ═ and see بَكُورٌ, in three places: —— and see an ex. of the pl. of its fem. بَاكِرَةٌ, i. e. بَوَاكِرُ, voce بَاصِرٌ. —— Also †Fruit when *first ripe:* pl. بِكَارٌ, like as صِحَابٌ is pl. of صَاحِبٌ. (TA.)

بَاكُورٌ, and its fem. بَاكُورَةٌ: see بَكُورٌ, in three places.

بَاكُورَةٌ [as a subst.]: see بِكْرٌ. —— Also, (Ṣ, Ḳ,) or بَاكُورَةُ الفَاكِهَةِ, (A, Mṣb,) ‡The *first of fruit:* (Ṣ:) or the *first that comes to maturity, of fruit:* (A, Mṣb, Ḳ:) or *fruit that hastens to come forth:* (AHát, Mṣb:) pl. بَوَاكِيرُ and بَاكُورَاتٌ. (Mṣb.) —— The pl. بَوَاكِيرُ also signifies †*Winds that announce [coming] rain.* (A in art. بشر.)

إِبْكَارٌ: see بُكْرَةٌ.

أُبَيْكِرٌ dim. of أَبْكُرٌ, pl. of pauc. of بَكْرٌ: see its pl. أُبَيْكِرُونَ voce بَكْرٌ.

تَبَاكِيرُ †The *colours of palm-trees when the fruit begins to ripen.* (TA voce تَبَاشِيرُ.)

مِبْكَرٌ: see بَكُورٌ.

مِبْكَارٌ: see بَكُورٌ, in three places.

ضَرَبَاتٌ مُبْتَكِرَاتٌ: see بِكْرٌ, last sentence.

بكم

1. بَكِمَ, aor. ـَ, (Mṣb, Ḳ,) inf. n. بَكَمٌ, (Ṣ, Ḳ,) *He was* أَخْرَس [meaning *dumb,* either *by natural conformation* or *from inability to find words to express what he would say*]; (Ṣ, Mṣb, Ḳ;*) بَكَمٌ being *syn.* with خَرَسٌ, as is also بَكَامَةٌ [accord. to rule an inf. n. of بَكُمَ, which may also have the same signification as بَكِمَ, as well as another to be explained below]: (Ḳ:) or *he had not understanding to reply,* (T, Mṣb, TA,) *nor ability to frame speech well,* (T, TA,) *though possessing the faculty of speech:* [see أَبْكَمُ:] (T, Mṣb, TA:) or *he was dumb, and moreover unable to find words to express what he would say, and weak in understanding, silly,* or *stupid:* (Ḳ:) or *he was dumb and deaf and blind by birth.* (Th, Ḳ.) —— بَكُمَ, aor. ـُ, (inf. n. بَكَامَةٌ, TḲ,) *He refrained,* (Lth, Ḳ,) or, as some say, *broke off,* or *ceased,* (TA,) *from speaking, intentionally,* (Lth, Ḳ, TA,) or *from ignorance.* (Lth, TA.) —— ‡*He cut himself off,* or *desisted, from marriage,* or *sexual intercourse,* either *from ignorance* or *intentionally.* (Ḳ, TA.)

5. تبكّم عَلَيْهِ الكَلَامُ *His speech was,* or *became, impeded; he was unable to speak freely.* (A, Ḳ.)

بَكِيمٌ: see what follows, in two places.

أَبْكَمُ (T, Ṣ, Mṣb, Ḳ, &c.) and ▾بَكِيمٌ (Ṣ, Ḳ) *i. q.* أَخْرَسُ [meaning *Dumb,* either *by natural conformation* or *from inability to find words to express what he would say*]: (Ṣ, Mṣb, Ḳ:) or *not having understanding to reply,* (IAạr, T, Mṣb, TA,) *nor ability to frame speech well,* (T, TA,) *though possessing the faculty of speech;* whereas اخرس signifies speechless, or destitute of the faculty of speech, by natural conformation, (T, Mṣb, TA,) like the beast that lacks the faculty of articulation; (T, TA;) *unable to find words to express what he would say; unable to reply:* (AZ, TA:) or *dumb by natural conformation:* (IAth, TA:) fem. بَكْمَاءُ: (TA:) pl. بُكْمٌ (Mṣb, Ḳ) and بُكْمَانٌ, (Ḳ,) both pls. of أَبْكَمُ, like as صُمٌّ and صُمَّانٌ are pls. of أَصَمُّ; and the pl. of ▾بَكِيمٌ is أَبْكَامٌ. (TA.) In the Ḳur ii. 166, بُكْمٌ means persons *in the condition of him who has been born dumb:* or, as some say, *deprived of their intellects:* (Zj, TA:) or *ignorant and ignoble;* because not profiting much by the faculty of speech, so that they are as though they had been deprived of it. (IAth, TA.) The phrase فِتْنَةٌ صَمَّآءُ بَكْمَآءُ عَمْيَآءُ, occurring in a trad., [lit.] meaning [*A sedition*, or the like,] *deaf, dumb, blind*, applies to a فتنة that does not withdraw, or become removed: or, as some say, to one which, by reason of the confusion attending it, and the perishing of the sound and the sick therein, is likened to the deaf and dumb and blind who does not pursue the right course to a thing, but goes at random like the weak-sighted she-camel. (TA.)

بكى

1. بَكَى, aor. يَبْكِى, (Mṣb, Ḳ,) inf. n. بُكَآءٌ and بُكًا (Ṣ, Mṣb, Ḳ) and مَبْكًى, (Ḥar p. 11,) *He wept*; i. e. *he lamented*, or *grieved, shedding tears at the same time*; and *he lamented*, or *grieved*, alone; and *he shed tears* alone: (Er-Rághib, TA:) accord. to some, the preferable opinion is, that there is no difference between بُكَآءٌ and بُكًا: (TA:) or the former means the *crying*, or *uttering of the voice* [*of lamentation*], (Ṣ, IḲṭṭ, Mṣb, TA, &c.,) *that accompanies* البُكَآء [so in copies of the Ṣ and in the TA, but correctly البُكَا]; (Ṣ, IḲṭṭ, TA;) and the latter (بُكًا), the *shedding of tears*: (Ṣ, IḲṭṭ, Mṣb, TA, &c.:) or the former, i. e. with medd, means the *shedding of tears by reason of lamentation*, or *grief, and raising of the voice*, or *crying*, [*at the same time*,] *when the voice is predominant*, being like رُغَآءٌ and ثُغَآءٌ and other words of the same form applied to denote the uttering of a cry or of the voice; and the latter, [the *shedding of tears* &c.] *when lamentation*, or *grief, is predominant*: (Er-Rághib, TA:) or by the former is meant the *crying*, or *uttering of the voice* [*of lamentation*]; and by the latter, the *lamenting*, or *grieving*. (Kh, TA.) تَبْكَآءٌ and تِبْكَآءٌ [may be inf. ns. of بَكَى or of ▼بَكَّى, and] signify *the same as* بُكَآءٌ: or *much* بُكَآء [or *weeping*, &c.]: (Ḳ:) MF asserts that تِبْكَآءٌ (with kesr) and the former of these explanations are unknown; but both the word and the explanation are mentioned by Lḥ, as used in a form of words uttered by Arab women of the desert to fascinate men: ISd, however, says that it should be تَبْكَآء, because it is an inf. n. of a class formed to denote muchness [of the attribute signified by the verb], like تَهْذَارٌ and تَلْعَابٌ &c.; and IAạr says that تَبْكَآءٌ, with fet-ḥ, has the latter of the two significations assigned to it above. (TA.) [See what is said of the measure تفعال voce بَيَّنَ.] You say, بَكَى لَهُ (MF, TA) and بَكَى عَلَيْهِ, (Ṣ, Mṣb, Ḳ, MF,) meaning [*He wept*] *for*, or *over, him*, or *it*: and only بَكَى بِهِ [or thus and also بَكَى مِنْهُ as appears from what follows] when meaning [*He wept*] *because*, or *in consequence, of it*: ('Ináyeh, MF, TA:) and بَكَاهُ and ▼بَكَّاهُ, (Aṣ, AZ, Ṣ, Mṣb, Ḳ,) inf. n. of the former بُكَآءٌ (Ḳ) [and بُكًا], and of the latter تَبْكِيَةٌ, (TA,) signify *the same as* بَكَى عَلَيْهِ; (Aṣ, AZ, Ṣ, Mṣb,* Ḳ;) the object being a man: (Aṣ, Ṣ:) and (or as some say, TA) *he wept for*, or *over, him*, i. e., one dead; or *did so, and enumerated his good qualities* or *actions*; syn. رَثَاهُ: (Ḳ:) or, as some say, بَكَاهُ means [*he wept because*, or *in consequence, of it*, i. e.,] *on account of being pained*: and بَكَى عَلَيْهِ, [*he wept for*, or *over, him*,] *by reason of tenderness of heart*, or *compassion*: and [hence] it is said that بَكَيْتُهُ is originally بَكَيْتُ مِنْهُ: (TA:) [and ▼بَكَّاهُ may have an intensive, or a frequentative, meaning; for it is said that] بَكِّى, addressed to the eye, signifies *weep thou much*, and *repeatedly*. (Ḥam p. 461.) — [Hence,] بَكَتِ السَّحَابَةُ † *The cloud rained*. (Mṣb.) — بَكَى also means *He sang*: [in the CḲ, وبَكَى غَنّى is erroneously put for وبَكَى غَنَّى:] thus it has two contr. significations: (Ḳ, TA:) accord. to MF, it has this meaning only in relation to the pigeon and the like; but it is also used in this sense when said of a man, as in a verse cited voce جَنَازَةٌ, q. v.: and he observes that the assertion of its having two contr significations requires consideration, seeing that it is also said to signify رَثَى; [for in the performance of رِثَآء, it is a common practice to sing;] but رِثَآء is generally accompanied by lamentation, and غِنَآء by rejoicing. (TA.) — بَاكَيْتُهُ فَبَكَيْتُهُ: see 3.

2: see 1, in three places: = and see also 4.

3. بَاكَيْتُهُ فَبَكَيْتُهُ, (Ṣ, TA,) aor. of the latter أَبْكُوهُ, (TA,) or أَبْكِيهِ, retaining its original form, accord. to a rule observed in the case of a verb having an infirm letter [for its second or third radical] lest a verb with a radical ى should be confounded with one having a radical و, (Ḥam p. 670,) i. e. [*I vied with him*, or *strove to exceed him, in weeping, and I exceeded him therein*, or] *I was a greater weeper* (أَبْكَى) *than he*. (Ṣ, TA.)

4. ابكاه [*He made him*, or *caused him, to weep*; or] *he did to him what made him to weep*; (Ṣ, Ḳ;) as also ▼استبكاه. (Ṣ.) And ▼بَكَّاهُ عَلَيْهِ, inf. n. تَبْكِيَةٌ, *He excited him to weep for him*, or *it*; (Ḳ, TA;) namely, a person dead, (Ḳ,) or a thing lost. (TA.)

6. تباكى signifies تَكَلَّفَ البُكَآءَ [i. e. *He affected weeping*; or *endeavoured*, or *constrained himself, to weep*]. (Ṣ, Ḳ.) Hence, in a trad., فَإِنْ لَمْ تَجِدُوا بُكَآءً فَتَبَاكَوْا [*And if ye experience not weeping, endeavour to weep*]: (TA:) [or the words of the trad. are] اُتْلُوا القُرْآنَ وَٱبْكُوا فَإِنْ لَمْ تَبْكُوا فَتَبَاكَوْا [*Peruse ye the Ḳur-án, and weep*; *or, if ye weep not, endeavour to do so*]. (Bḍ in xix. 59.) — And *He feigned*, or *made a show of, weeping*. (Ḥar p. 602.)

10. استبكاه: see 4. — Also *He desired*, or *required, of him weeping*. (TA.)

بَكِىٌّ One *who weeps much*; (Ṣ, Ḳ;) as also ▼بَكَّآءٌ. (Ḳ, but omitted in some copies and in the TA.) = رَجُلٌ عَيِىٌّ بَكِىٌّ *A man unable to speak*. (Mbr, TA.) [But perhaps this should be بَكِىٌّ: see art. بكأ.]

بَكَّآءٌ: see بَكِىٌّ.

بَاكٍ part. n. of بَكَى [i. e. *Weeping*, &c.]: (Ḳ:) pl. بُكِىٌّ, (Ṣ, Ḳ,) of the measure فُعُولٌ, with the و changed into ى [and the second ḍammeh consequently into a kesreh, wherefore it is also, sometimes, pronounced بِكِىٌّ], (Ṣ,) and بُكَاةٌ, (Ḳ,) which is agreeable with analogy and usage, though said by Es-Semeen to have not been heard. (TA.) [The pl. of the fem., i. e. of بَاكِيَةٌ, is بَاكِيَاتٌ and بَوَاكٍ.]

أَبْكَى [*A greater weeper*, or one *who weeps more*, than another: see 3]. (Ṣ, TA.)

بل

1. بَلَّهُ (Ṣ, M, &c.,) aor. يَبُلُّ, (Ṣ, M,) inf. n. بَلٌّ (M, Mṣb, Ḳ) and بِلَّةٌ, (M, Ḳ,) *He moistened it* (Ṣ, M, Ḳ) with water (M, Mṣb, Ḳ) &c.; (M;) and in like manner, ▼بلّله, (Ṣ, M, Ḳ,) but signifying *he moistened it much*. (Ṣ, TA.) — [Hence,] بَلَّتِ الإِبِلُ أَغْمَارَهَا [*The camels damped their thirst*;] i. e., *drank a little*. (TA in art. غمر.) — [Hence also,] بَلَّ رَحِمَهُ, (T, Ṣ, M, Ḳ,) aor. يَبُلُّ, (T, M,) inf. n. بَلٌّ (with fet-ḥ, TA [in the CḲ it has kesr]) and بِلَالٌ, (M, Ḳ,) ‡ *He made close* [or *he refreshed*] *his ties of relationship by behaving with goodness and affection and gentleness to his kindred*; syn. وَصَلَهَا, (T, Ṣ, M, Ḳ,) and نَدَّاهَا: (T:) for, as some things are conjoined and commixed by moisture, and become disunited by dryness, بَلٌّ is metaphorically used to denote conjunction, as above, and يُبْس to denote the contrary. (TA.) A poet says,

• وَالرَّحْمَ فَابْلُلْهَا بِخَيْرِ البُلَّانْ •
• فَإِنَّهَا ٱشْتُقَّتْ مِنِ ٱسْمِ الرَّحْمٰنْ •

[‡ *And the ties of relationship, make thou them close* &c. *by the best mode*, or *modes, of doing so*; *for the name thereof is derived from the name of the Compassionate*]: here ▼البُلَّانِ may be a noun in the sing. number, like غُفْرَانٌ, or it may be pl. of بَلَلٌ, which may be either a subst. or an inf. n., for some inf. ns. have pls., as شُغْلٌ and مَرَضٌ and عَقْلٌ. (M.) And it is said in a trad., بُلُّوا أَرْحَامَكُمْ وَلَوْ بِالسَّلَامِ ‡ *Make ye close* [or *refresh ye*] *your ties of relationship* &c., *though but*, or *if only, by salutation*; syn. صِلُوهَا, (M,) or نَدُّوهَا بِالصِّلَةِ. (Ṣ.) And hence the saying in another trad., إِذَا ٱسْتَشَنَّ مَا بَيْنَكَ وَبَيْنَ ٱللّٰهِ فَٱبْلُلْهُ بِالإِحْسَانِ إِلَى عِبَادِهِ ‡ [*When the tie between thee and God wears out, repair thou it*, or *refresh thou it, by beneficence to his servants*]. (TA.) [See also بِلَالٌ.] — بَلَّكَ ٱللّٰهُ بِٱبْنٍ, (Ṣ, M, Ḳ,) and ٱبْنًا, (M, Ḳ,) † *May God give thee a son*. (Ṣ, M, Ḳ, TA.) Hence, perhaps, the phrase, بُلَّتْ يَدَاكَ بِهِ as meaning † *Thou was given it*. (Ḥar p. 479.) You say also, بَلَلْتُهُ, meaning † *I gave to him*. (T.) And لَا تَبُلُّكَ عِنْدِى ▼بَالَّةٌ, and ▼بَلَالِ, (T, Ṣ, M, Ḳ, [but in the Ḳ عِنْدَنَا, and "or" for "and," and in the CḲ لا تَبُلُّكَ,]) ‡ *No bounty*, (Ṣ,) *no good*, or *no benefit, shall betide thee from me*, (T, Ṣ, Ḳ, TA,) *nor will I profit thee, nor believe thee*. (T.) — بَلُّوا *They sowed* land. (ISh, T, Ḳ.) = [بَلَّ as an intrans. verb perhaps primarily signifies

It was, or became, moist; and has for its sec. pers. بَلِلْتَ or بَلَلْتَ, and for its aor. َ or ِ, and for its inf. n. بَلَلٌ, and probably بِلَّةٌ &c. mentioned with that noun below. — And hence,] بَلَّتِ الرِّيحُ, aor. ِ, inf. n. بُلُولٌ, *The wind was cold and moist.* (M, Ḳ.) [See بَلِيلٌ.] — [And hence, probably, as though originally said of one who had had a fever,] بَلَّ مِنْ مَرَضِهِ, aor. ِ, inf. n. بَلٌّ (Ṣ, M, Ḳ) and بَلَلٌ and بُلُولٌ; (M, Ḳ;) and ↓ابلّ, and ↓استبلّ; (Ṣ, M, Ḳ;) *He recovered from his disease:* (Ṣ, M:) and ↓ابتلّ and ↓تبلّل *he became in a good condition after leanness,* or *meagerness:* (M, Z:) or all have this latter signification: and the second (ابلّ) has the former also. (Ḳ.) — And بَلَّ, (M, Ḳ,) aor. ِ, (M,) inf. n. بُلُولٌ; and ↓ابلّ; *He* (a man, TA) *escaped,* or *became safe* or *secure,* (M, Ḳ,) *from difficulty, distress,* or *straitness.* (TA.) — بَلَّ فِى الأَرْضِ, (Mṣb, Ḳ,* TA,) aor. ِ, inf. n. بَلٌّ; (Mṣb;) and ↓ابلّ; (M, Ḳ;) *He* (a man, M) *went away in,* or *into, the land,* or *country.* (M, Mṣb, Ḳ.) And بَلَّتْ نَاقَتُهُ *His she-camel went away.* (TA.) And بَلَّتْ مَطِيَّتُهُ عَلَى وَجْهِهَا, (Fr, T, TA,) and ↓ابلّت على وجهها, (Ḳ,) *His camel,* or *riding-camel, ran away,* or *went away, at random, to pasture, straying;* syn. هَمَتْ ضَالَّةً. (Fr, T, Ḳ, TA. [In the CḲ, همت, which, as is said in the TA, is without teshdeed, is written هَمَّتْ.]) ═ بَلِلْتُ بِهِ, (Aṣ, T, Ṣ, &c.,) inf. n. بَلَلٌ, (M,) *I got him; got possession of him;* (Aṣ, T, Ṣ, M, Ḳ;) *got him in my hand.* (Ṣ.) One says, لَئِنْ بَلَّتْ بِكَ يَدِى لَا تُفَارِقُنِى أَوْ تُؤَدِّىَ حَقِّى [*Assuredly if my hand get hold of thee, thou shalt not quit me unless thou give up,* or *pay, my right,* or *due*]. (Ṣ.) And hence the prov., مَا بَلِلْتُ مِنْ فُلَانٍ بِأَفْوَقَ نَاصِلٍ [*I did not get, in such a one, a man like an arrow with a broken notch and without a head*]; meaning I got a perfect man; one sufficient. (Sh, T.) — Also, (T,) or بَلِلْتُهُ, (M, Ḳ,) *I kept,* or *clave, to him,* (T, M, Ḳ,) namely, a man, (T, Ḳ,) *and constantly associated with him.* (T.) And بَلَّ بِالشَّىْءِ, inf. n. بَلٌّ, *He became devoted,* or *attached, to the thing, and kept to it constantly.* (TA.) — And بَلِلْتُ بِهِ, (M, Ḳ,) aor. َ, (TA,) inf. n. بَلَلٌ and بَلَالَةٌ and بُلُولٌ, *I was tried by him* (مُنِيتُ بِهِ [app. meaning بِحُبِّهِ *by love of him*]), *and loved him* (عَلِقْتُهُ [in the CḲ عَلَقْتُهُ]); as also بَلَلْتُ بِهِ, (AA, M, Ḳ,) aor. ُ, inf. n. بُلُولٌ. (AA, TA.) And بَلِلْتُ بِهِ *I was tried by him, as though by fire,* (صَلِيتُ بِهِ, [in the CḲ صَلَيْتُ بِهِ,]) *and suffered distress,* or *misery,* or *fatigue* (شَقِيتُ, for which شُفِيتُ is erroneously put in the copies of the Ḳ: TA). (M, Ḳ.*) — مَا بَلِلْتُ بِهِ, (Ḳ,) aor. َ, inf. n. بَلَلٌ, (TA,) *I did not light on,* or *meet with,* or *find, nor know, him,* or *it;* expl. by مَا أَصَبْتُهُ وَلَا عَلِمْتُهُ. (Ḳ.) ═ بَلَّ, (Th, M, Ḳ,) inf. n. بَلَلٌ, (Th, Ṣ, M, Ḳ,) *He* (a man) *was,* or *became, such as is termed* أَبَلُّ [which epithet see below]. (Th, Ṣ, M, Ḳ.)

2: see 1, first sentence.

4. ابلّ *It* (wood, or a branch or twig,) *had the sap,* (المَآءُ, Ḳ,) or *the produce of the rain,* (O,) *flowing in it.* (O, Ḳ.) — See also بَلَّ, in four places. ═ *He* (a man) *resisted,* or *withstood, and overcame.* (Aṣ, T, Ṣ. [See also أَبَلُّ.]) And ابلّ عَلَيْهِ *He overcame him.* (M, Ḳ.) [See an ex. in a verse of Sá'ideh, cited voce خَسَفَ.] — *He wearied by badness,* or *wickedness:* (M, Ḳ:) or *he wearied another in aiding him to accomplish his desire.* (TA. [See مُبِلٌّ.]) ═ أَبْلَلْتُهُ *I made him to go away.* (Mṣb.)

5: see 8: — and see also بَلَّ.

8. ابتلّ *It became moist* or *moistened* (Ṣ, M, Mṣb,* Ḳ) with water (M, Mṣb, Ḳ) &c.; (M;) and in like manner, [but signifying *it became much moistened,* being quasi-pass. of بلّلهُ,] ↓تبلّل. (M, Ḳ.) — See also بَلَّ.

10: see بَلَّ.

R. Q. 1. بَلْبَلَ, inf. n. بَلْبَلَةٌ and بِلْبَالٌ, (M, Ḳ,) the latter with kesr, (TA,) [but written in the CḲ with fet-ḥ,] *He put* people *in motion;* and *roused,* or *excited,* them. (M, Ḳ.) — Also, (T,) inf. n. بَلْبَلَةٌ, (Ḳ,) *He scattered, dispersed,* or *put asunder,* his goods, commodities, or household-utensils and furniture. (IAạr, T, Ḳ.* [In the CḲ, والمَتَاعُ is erroneously put for وَالمَتَاعِ.]) — And *He divided,* or *disunited,* opinions. (Fr, T, Ḳ; but only the inf. n. of the verb in this sense is mentioned.) — And *He* (God) [*mixed* or *confounded* or] *made discordant* the tongues, or languages, of a people. (T.) — [See also بَلْبَلَةٌ below.]

R. Q. 2. تَبَلْبَلَ *He* (a man) *was moved by grief* [or *anxiety:* see بَلْبَلَةٌ, below]. (Ḥar p. 94.) — تَبَلْبَلَتِ الأَلْسُنُ *The tongues,* or *languages, became mixed,* or *confounded.* (Ṣ, Ḳ.) ═ تَبَلْبَلَتِ الإِبِلُ الكَلَأَ *The camels went on seeking the herbage,* or *pasture, and left not of it aught.* (Ṣ, Ḳ.)

بَلْ is a particle of digression: (Mughnee, Ḳ:) or, accord. to Mbr, it denotes emendation, wherever it occurs, in the case of a negation or an affirmation: (T, TA:) or it is a word of emendation, and denoting digression from that which precedes; as also بَنْ, in which the ن is a substitute for the ل, because بل is of frequent occurrence, and بن is rare; or, as IJ says, the latter may be an independent dial. var. (M.) When it is followed by a proposition, the meaning of the digression is either the cancelling of what precedes, as in وَقَالُوا ٱتَّخَذَ ٱلرَّحْمٰنُ وَلَدًا سُبْحَانَهُ بَلْ عِبَادٌ مُكْرَمُونَ [*And they said, "The Compassionate hath gotten offspring:" extolled be his freedom from that which is derogatory from his glory! nay,* or *nay rather,* or *nay but, they are honoured servants* (Ḳur xxi. 26)], or transition from one object of discourse to another, as in قَدْ أَفْلَحَ مَنْ تَزَكَّى وَذَكَرَ ٱسْمَ رَبِّهِ فَصَلَّى بَلْ تُؤْثِرُونَ ٱلْحَيَاةَ ٱلدُّنْيَا [*He hath attained felicity who hath purified himself, and celebrated the name of his Lord, and prayed: but ye prefer the present life* (Ḳur lxxxvii. 14—16)]: (Mughnee, Ḳ:*) and in all such cases it is an inceptive particle; not a conjunctive. (Mughnee.) When it is followed by a single word, it is a conjunction, (Ṣ,* Mṣb,* Mughnee, Ḳ,) and requires that word to be in the same case as the word before it: (Ṣ:) and if preceded by a command or an affirmation, (Mughnee, Ḳ,) as in اِضْرِبْ زَيْدًا بَلْ عَمْرًا [*Beat thou Zeyd: no, 'Amr*], (Mṣb, Mughnee, Ḳ,) and قَامَ زَيْدٌ بَلْ عَمْرٌو [*Zeyd stood: no, 'Amr*], (M, Mughnee, Ḳ,) or جَآءَنِى أَخُوكَ بَلْ أَبُوكَ [*Thy brother came to me: no, thy father*], (Ṣ,) it makes what precedes it to be as though nothing were said respecting it, (Ṣ,* Mṣb,* Mughnee, Ḳ,) making the command or affirmation to relate to what follows it: (Ṣ,* Mṣb,* Mughnee:) [and similar to these cases is the case in which it is preceded by an interrogation: see أَمْ as syn. with this particle:] but when it is preceded by a negation or a prohibition, it is used to confirm the meaning of what precedes it and to assign the contrary of that meaning to what follows it, (Mughnee, Ḳ,) as in مَا قَامَ زَيْدٌ بَلْ عَمْرٌو [*Zeyd stood not, but 'Amr* stood], (Mughnee,) or مَا رَأَيْتُ زَيْدًا بَلْ عَمْرًا [*I saw not Zeyd, but* I saw *'Amr*], (Ṣ,) and لَا يَقُمْ زَيْدٌ بَلْ عَمْرٌو [*Let not Zeyd stand, but* let *'Amr* stand]. (Mughnee.) Mbr and 'Abd-El-Wárith allow its being used to transfer the meaning of the negation and the prohibition to what follows it; so that, accord. to them, one may say, مَا زَيْدٌ قَائِمًا بَلْ قَاعِدًا [as meaning *Zeyd is not standing: no,* is not *sitting*], and بَلْ قَاعِدٌ [*but is sitting*]; the meaning being different [in the two cases]. (Mughnee, Ḳ.*) The Koofees disallow its being used as a conjunction after anything but a negation [so in the Mughnee, but in the Ḳ a prohibition,] or the like thereof; so that one should not say, ضَرَبْتُ زَيْدًا بَلْ إِيَّاكَ [*I beat Zeyd: no, thee*]. (Mughnee, Ḳ.) Sometimes لَا is added before it, to corroborate the meaning of digression, after an affirmation, as in the saying,

وَجْهُكَ البَدْرُ لَا بَلِ الشَّمْسُ لَوْ لَمْ
يُقْضَ لِلشَّمْسِ كَسْفَةٌ وَأُفُولُ

[*Thy face is the full moon: no, but* it would be *the sun, were it not that eclipse and setting are appointed to happen to the sun*]: and to corroborate what precedes it, after a negation, as in

وَمَا هَجَرْتُكَ لَا بَلْ زَادَنِى شَغَفًا
هَجْرٌ وَبُعْدٌ تَرَاخَى لَا إِلَى أَجَلِ

[*And I did not abandon thee,* or *have not abandoned thee: no, but abandonment and distance, protracted, not to an appointed period, increased,* or *have increased, my heart-felt love*]. (Mughnee, Ḳ.*) — Sometimes it is used to denote the passing from one subject to another without cancelling [what precedes it], and is *syn. with* وَ, as in the saying in the Ḳur [lxxxv. 20 and 21], وَٱللّٰهُ مِنْ وَرَائِهِمْ مُحِيطٌ بَلْ هُوَ قُرْآنٌ مَجِيدٌ [*And God from behind them is encompassing: and it is a glorious Kur-án:* or here it may mean إِنَّ, as in an ex. below]: and to this meaning it is made to accord in the saying, لَهُ عَلَىَّ دِينَارٌ بَلْ دِرْهَمٌ [*I owe him a deenár and a dirhem*]. (Mṣb.) — In the following saying in the Ḳur [xxxviii. 1], وَٱلْقُرْآنِ ذِى ٱلذِّكْرِ بَلِ ٱلَّذِينَ كَفَرُوا فِى عِزَّةٍ وَشِقَاقٍ, it is said to signify إِنَّ; [so that the meaning is, *By the Ḳur-án possessed of eminence, verily they who have disbelieved are in a state of pride and opposition;*] therefore the oath applies to it. (Akh, Ṣ.) — Sometimes the Arabs use it in breaking off a saying and commencing another; and thus a man commences with it a citation, or recitation, of verse; in which case, it does not form any part of the first verse, but is a sign of the breaking off, or ending, of what precedes. (Akh, Ṣ.) — Sometimes it is put in the place of رُبَّ, (Ṣ, Mughnee,) as in the saying of the rájiz,

* بَلْ مَهْمَهٍ قَطَعْتُ بَعْدَ مَهْمَهِ *

[*Many a far-extending desert have I traversed, after a far-extending desert*]. (Ṣ: [and a similar ex. is given in the Mughnee.]) — What is deficient in this word [supposing it to be originally of three letters] is unknown; and so in the cases of هَلْ and قَدْ: it may be a final و, or ى; or they may be originally بَلَّ and هَلَّ and قَدَّ. (Akh, Ṣ.)

[بَلٌّ *Moist*, or *containing moisture*: or rather *moistened*; being, app., an inf. n. used in the sense of a pass. part. n.; like خَلْقٌ in the sense of مَخْلُوقٌ. Hence,] رِيحٌ بَلَّةٌ and ▼بَلِيلٌ and ▼بَلِيلَةٌ *A wind in which is moisture*: (Ṣ:) or the last, *a wind mixed with feeble rain*: (T:) and the second, *a wind cold with moisture*; (M, Ḳ;) or the same, *a wind cold with rain*; (A, TA;) the *north wind*, as though it sprinkled water by reason of its coldness: (TA:) and بَلِيلٌ also signifies *a cold north wind*: (Ibn-'Abbád, TA:) بَلِيلٌ is used alike as sing. and pl.: (Ḳ:) it has no pl. (M.) — بَلٌّ بِشَىْءٍ A man (M) *devoted*, or *attached, to a thing, and keeping to it constantly*. (M, Ḳ. [In the CḲ and in my MS. copy of the Ḳ, اللَّبِجُ is erroneously put for اللَّهِجُ.]) — And بَلٌّ, alone, *Much given to the deferring of payment to his creditors, by repeated promises*; (T;) *withholding, by swearing, what he possesses of things that are the rightful property of others*. (IAạr, T, Ḳ.) See also أَبَلُّ, in two places.

بِلٌّ *Allowable*, or *lawful*; i. e., *to be taken*, or *let alone*, or *done*, or *made use of*, or *possessed*: (T, Ṣ, M, Ḳ:) so in the dial. of Ḥimyer: (T, Ṣ, M:) or *a remedy*; (A'Obeyd, T, Ṣ, M, Ḳ;) from the phrase بَلَّ مِنْ مَرَضِهِ [q. v.]: (A'Obeyd, T, Ṣ, M:) or it is an imitative sequent to حِلٌّ, (M, Ḳ,) as some say: (M:) so Aṣ thought until he heard that it was said to be of the dial. of Ḥimyer in the first of the senses explained above: (Ṣ, M:) A'Obeyd and ISk say that it may not be so because it is conjoined with حِلٌّ by وَ: (T:) and A'Obeyd says, We have seldom found an imitative sequent conjoined by و. (TA.) Hence the phrase, هُوَ لَكَ حِلٌّ وَبِلٌّ *It is to thee lawful and allowable*: or *lawful and a remedy*. (M, Ḳ.*) And hence the saying of El-'Abbás the son of 'Abd-El-Muttalib, respecting [the well of] Zemzem, هِىَ لِشَارِبٍ حِلٌّ وَبِلٌّ *It is to a drinker lawful* &c. (T, Ṣ, M.)

بَلَّةٌ [*A single act of moistening*. — And hence,] The *least sprinkling* (أَدْنَى بَلَلٍ lit. the *least moisture*) *of good*. (TA in art. هل.) You say, فُلَانٌ فَلَمْ يَأْتِنَا بِهَلَّةٍ وَلَا بَلَّةٍ جَآءَنَا [*Such a one came to us and did not bring us anything to rejoice us nor the least sprinkling of good*]: هَلَّةٌ, accord. to ISk, being from الفَرَحُ and الاِسْتِهْلَالُ, and بَلَّةٌ from البَلَلُ and الخَيْرُ. (Ṣ.) And مَا أَصَابَ هَلَّةً وَلَا بَلَّةً *He did not obtain*, or *has not obtained, anything*. (Ṣ.) — *Wealth*, or *competence*: (Fr, TA:) or *wealth*, or *competence, after poverty*; (Fr, T, Ḳ, TA;) as also ▼بُلَّى. (Ḳ.) — *Remains of herbage* or *pasture*; (Ḳ;) as also ▼بُلَّةٌ. (Fr, T, Ḳ.) — The *freshness* of youth; as also ▼بُلَّةٌ; (M, Ḳ;*) but the former word is the more approved. (M.) — See also an ex. voce بَلَلٌ.

بُلَّةٌ: see بَلَلٌ, in two places: — and see also بَلَّةٌ, in two places. — Also *A state of moisture*. (M.) — The *moisture of fresh pasture*. (Ṣ, M, Ḳ.) The rájiz (Ihâb Ibn-'Omeyr, TA) says, describing [wild] asses,

* حَتَّى إِذَا أَهْرَأْنَ بِالْأَصَائِلِ * وَفَارَقَتْهَا بُلَّةُ الْأَوَابِلِ *

meaning that they went in the cool of the evening to the water after that the herbage had dried up: الاوابل means the wild animals that are satisfied with green pasture, so as to be in no need of water. (Ṣ.)

بِلَّةٌ: see بَلَلٌ, in two places. — Also *Good, good fortune, prosperity*, or *wealth*: and *sustenance*, or *means of subsistence*. (M, Ḳ.) — *Health; soundness*; or *freedom from disease*. (T, Ḳ, TA.) — *A repast prepared on the occasion of a wedding*, or *on any occasion*. (Fr, Ḳ.) — ‡The tongue's *fluency, and chasteness of speech*: (Ḳ, TA:) or its *readiness of diction* or *expression, and facility*; (M;) *and* [so in the M, but in the Ḳ "or,"] *its falling upon the* [*right*] *places of utterance of the letters*, (T, M, A, Ḳ,) *and its regular and uniform continuance of speech*, (T, M, Ḳ,) *and its facility*. (Ḳ.) You say, مَا أَحْسَنَ بِلَّةَ لِسَانِهِ ‡[*How good is the fluency*, &c., *of his tongue!*]. (T, M, TA.)

بَلَلٌ *Moisture*; (Ṣ, M, Mṣb, Ḳ;) as also ▼بِلَّةٌ (Ṣ, M, Ḳ) and ▼بِلَالٌ and ▼بُلَالَةٌ (M, Ḳ) [and several other dial. vars. occurring in phrases in this paragraph]: or ▼بِلَّةٌ signifies *an inferior*, or *inconsiderable, degree of moisture*; (Lth, T, Ḳ; [an ambiguity in the Ḳ in this place has occasioned several mistakes in Freytag's Lex. voce بَلَلٌ;]) and ▼بِلَالٌ is an anomalous pl. of this word; (M, TA;) and is pl. also of ▼بُلَّةٌ: (Ṣ, TA:) and بَلَالٌ, occurring in a verse cited above (see 1) may be pl. of بَلَلٌ. (M.) [Using syns. of بَلَلٌ in the sense explained above,] you say, طَوَيْتُ السِّقَآءَ عَلَى بُلُلَتِهِ, (Ṣ, Ḳ,) and ▼بُلَلَتِهِ, (Ḳ,) or ▼بَلَلَتِهِ, (T, M,) *I folded the skin while it was moist*, (T, Ṣ, M, Ḳ,) before it should break in pieces, (T,) or lest it should break in pieces. (M.) And [hence,] طَوَيْتُ فُلَانًا عَلَى بُلُلَتِهِ, (T,* Ṣ, M,* Ḳ,*) and ▼بُلَّتِهِ, (T, Ṣ, Ḳ,) and ▼بَلَلَتِهِ, and ▼بُلَلَاتِهِ, and ▼بِلَّتِهِ, and ▼بَلَلَاتِهِ, (Ḳ,) and ▼بَلَّتِهِ, (Ṣ, Ḳ,) and ▼بِلَّتِهِ, (M, Ḳ,) and ▼بُلَالَتِهِ, (Ṣ, Ḳ,) and ▼بِلَالَتِهِ, (Ḳ,) and ▼بُلُولَتِهِ, (Ṣ, Ḳ,) which is of the dial. of Temeem, (TA,) and ▼بُلُولِهِ, (Ḳ,) ‡*I bore with, suffered*, or *tolerated, such a one*, (Ṣ, Ḳ,) *notwithstanding his vice*, or *fault*, (T, Ṣ, M, Ḳ,) *and evil conduct*: (Ṣ:) or [so in the M and Ḳ, but in the Ṣ "and,"] *I treated him with gentleness*, or *blandishment*, (Ṣ, Ḳ,) *while some love*, or *affection, remained in him*; (Ṣ, M, Ḳ;) and this is the true meaning; (M;) and in like manner, عَلَى بِلَالِ▼ نَفْسِهِ. (Ṣ, TA.) And ▼طَوَاهُ عَلَى بِلَالِهِ, and ▼بُلُولِهِ, ‡*He feigned himself heedless of*, or *inattentive to, his vice*, or *fault*; like as one folds a skin upon its fault [to conceal that fault]. (T.) And ٱنْصَرَفَ الْقَوْمُ ▼بِبَلَلَتِهِمْ, and ▼بِبُلُولَتِهِمْ, and ▼بِبُلُلَتِهِمْ, †*The people*, or *company of men, turned away*, or *back, having some good*, or *somewhat good, remaining, in them*, or *among them*; expl. by وَفِيهِمْ بَقِيَّةٌ [in which the last word generally implies something good; as, for instance, in the Ḳur xi. 118]: (M, Ḳ:) or, *in a good state*, or *condition*: (Ḳ:) or this latter is meant when one says, بِبُلُلَتِهِمْ. (T.) — *Abundance of herbage*; or *of the goods, conveniences*, or *comforts, of life*. (TA.) — See also بَلَلٌ — مَا أَحْسَنَ بَلَلَهُ *How good is his adornment of himself!* or *his manner of undertaking a task*, or *taking upon himself a responsibility!* (Ḳ: expl. in some copies by تَجَمُّلَهُ; and so in the TA: in others by تَحَمُّلَهُ.)

بُلُلٌ, like صُرَدٌ, (Ḳ,) or بُلُلٌ, (so in a copy of the T, accord. to the TT,) *Seed; grain for sowing*. (ISh, T, Ḳ.)

بَلَلَةٌ and its pl.: see four exs. voce بَلَلٌ.

بُلُلَةٌ and its pl.: see three exs. voce بَلَلٌ. — The sing. also signifies *Garb, guise, aspect* or *appearance, external state* or *condition*. (Ibn-'Abbád, Ḳ.) You say, إِنَّهُ لَحَسَنُ الْبُلُلَةِ *Verily he is goodly*, or *beautiful, in garb*, &c. (Ibn-'Abbád, TA.) — You say also, كَيْفَ بُلُلَتُكَ, and ▼بُلُولَتُكَ, meaning *How is thy state, or condition?* (Ibn-'Abbád, Ḳ.)

بُلَلَةٌ: see three exs. voce بَلَلٌ.

بِلَالٌ a subst. signifying *The making close the ties of relationship by behaving with goodness and affection and gentleness to one's kindred*: (Ḳ:) changed in form from بَالَّةٌ; q. v. (TA.) [See also بِلَالٌ.]

بَلَالٌ: } see what next follows.
بُلَالٌ:

بِلَالٌ: see بَلَلٌ, in four places. — Also *Water*; (T, Ṣ, M, Ḳ;) and so ▼بُلَالٌ and ▼بَلَالٌ. (Ḳ.) You say, مَا فِى سِقَائِهِ بِلَالٌ *There is not in his skin any water*: (T, Ṣ:) or *anything whatever*: (so in a copy of the Ṣ:) and in like manner one says of a well. (T.) And ▼ مَا فِى البِئْرِ بَالُولٌ *There is not any water in the well.* (Ḳ.) — And *Anything with which one moistens the fauces, of water or of milk:* (Ṣ, Mṣb, Ḳ:) such is said to be its meaning. (Mṣb.) — And hence the saying, صِلُوهَا بِصِلَتِهَا, اِنْضَحُوا الرَّحِمَ بِبِلَالِهَا, i. e. [*Make ye close the ties of relationship by behaving with that goodness and affection and gentleness to kindred which those ties require:* see بَلَّ رَحِمَهُ; and see also بِلَالٌ]. (Ṣ.)

بَلُولٌ: see two exs. voce بَلَلٌ.

بَلِيلٌ: see بَلٌّ.

بَلَالَةٌ: see an ex. voce بَلَلٌ.

بُلَالَةٌ: see بَلَلٌ, in two places. — Also The *quantity with which a thing is moistened.* (Ḥar p. 107.) — And *A remain,* or *remainder;* (T, and Ḥar ubi suprà;) as also عُلَالَةٌ. (Ḥar ubi suprà.) You say, مَا فِيهِ بُلَالَةٌ وَلَا عُلَالَةٌ *There is not in it anything remaining.* (T, and Ḥar ubi suprà.)

بُلُولَةٌ: see two exs. voce بَلَلٌ: — and see an ex. voce بَلَلَةٌ.

بَلِيلَةٌ: see بَلٌّ. — Also *Wheat boiled in water,* [in the present day, *with clarified butter, and honey,*] *and eaten.* (TA.) ═ And *i. q.* صِحَّةٌ [*Health,* or *soundness,* &c.]. (TA.)

بَلِّى: see بَلَّةٌ.

بَلَّانٌ *A hot bath:* (Ḳ:) the ا and ن are augmentative: for the hot bath is thus called because he who enters it is moistened by its water or by his sweat: (TA:) pl. بَلَّانَاتٌ, (Ḳ,) occurring in a trad., and said by IAth to be originally بَلَّالَاتٌ. (TA in art. بلن; in which, as well as in the present art., it is mentioned in the Ḳ.) — It is now applied to *A man who serves* [*the bathers, by washing them* &c.,] *in the hot bath:* [fem. with ة:] but this is a vulgar application of the word. (TA.)

بُلَّانٌ: see 1.

بُلْبُلٌ [The *nightingale:* and *a certain melodious bird resembling the nightingale:* both, in the present day, vulgarly called بِلْبِل:] the عَنْدَلِيب [q. v.]: and the كُعَيْت [q. v.]: (T:) *a certain bird,* (Ṣ, M, Ḳ,) *well known,* (Ḳ,) *of beautiful voice, that frequents the Ḥaram* [or *Sacred Territory of Mekkeh*], *and is called by the people of El-Ḥijáz the* نُغَر [q. v.]. (M.) — A man *light,* or *active:* (Ṣ:) or *clever, well-mannered,* or *elegant, and light,* or *active:* (T:) or a man (M) *light,* or *active, in journeying, and very helpful;* (M, Ḳ;) and so ▼ بُلَابِلٌ, (M,) or ▼ بُلْبُلِىٌّ: (Ḳ:) or, accord. to Th, a boy *light,* or *active, in journeying:* (M:) and a man *light,* or *active, in that which he sets about;* (TA;) as also ▼ بُلَابِلٌ; (Ḳ;) or this last signifies a man *active in intellect, to whom nothing is unapparent:* (T:) pl. of the first, (Ṣ,) and of the last, (Ḳ,) بَلَابِلُ. (Ṣ, Ḳ.) ═ *A certain fish, of the size of the hand.* (Ibn-'Abbád, Ḳ.) ═ The *spout* (قَنَاة) *of a mug* (كُوز), *that pours forth the water.* (M, Ḳ.)

بَلْبَلَةٌ inf. n. of بَلْبَلَ [q. v.]. (M, Ḳ.) ═ *A state of confusion,* or *mixture, of tongues,* or *languages.* (M, Ḳ.*) In the copies of the Ḳ, الأَلْسِنَة is here erroneously put for الأَلْسُنَة. (TA.) — Also, and ▼ بَلْبَالٌ, The *vain,* or *unprofitable,* or *evil, suggestion of anxieties in the bosom:* (T:) or *anxiety, and vain,* or *unprofitable,* or *evil, suggestion of the mind:* (Ṣ:) or *intense anxiety, and vain,* or *unprofitable,* or *evil, suggestions* or *thoughts;* (M, Ḳ;) as also ▼ بُلَابِلٌ, (so in the M, accord. to the TT,) or ▼ بَلَابِلُ: (so in copies of the Ḳ:) this last [however] is pl. of ▼ بَلْبَالٌ; (T;) which also signifies *vehement distress in the bosom;* (M, Ḳ;) and so does ▼ بَلْبَالَةٌ: (IJ, M:) or ▼ بِلْبَالٌ signifies *anxiety* and *grief:* and, as also بَلْبَلَةٌ, *a motion,* or *commotion, in the heart, arising from grief* or *love.* (Ḥar p. 94.)

بُلْبُلَةٌ *A mug* (كُوز) *having a spout* (بُلْبُل) *by the side of its head,* (M, Ḳ, TA,) *from which the water pours forth:* (TA:) or *a ewer, as long as it contains wine.* (Kull p. 102.)

بُلْبُلِىٌّ: see بُلْبُلٌ.

بَلْبَالٌ: see بَلْبَلَةٌ, in three places. ═ Also *A putting* people *in motion;* and *rousing,* or *exciting,* them: a subst. from R. Q. 1. (M, Ḳ.)

بَلْبَالَةٌ: } see بَلْبَلَةٌ.
بَلَابِلُ: }

بُلَابِلٌ: see بُلْبُلٌ, in two places: ═ and see بَلْبَلَةٌ.

بَلَالٌ [properly *A thing that moistens.* — And hence,] ‡ *Bounty,* or *liberality;* or *a gift;* as also ▼ بِلَالٌ: (T, Ṣ, TA:) and both these words, *good,* or *benefit:* (T, Ṣ, M, TA:) so in a phrase mentioned above; see 1: (T, Ṣ, Ḳ:) the latter word is changed in form from the former. (T.) [See also بِلَالٌ above.]

بَالُولٌ: see بِلَالٌ.

[أَبَلُّ *More,* and *most, moist:* fem. بَلَّآءُ: and pl. بُلٌّ. Hence,] الجَنُوبُ أَبَلُّ الرِّيَاحِ [*The south is the most moist of the winds.* (Ṣ.) — [Hence, also,] مَا شَىْءٌ أَبَلَّ لِلْجِسْمِ مِنَ اللَّهْوِ *Nothing is more healthful and suitable to the body than sport.* (TA.) — And صَفَاةٌ بَلَّآءُ *A smooth stone* or *rock.* (Ṣ.) — And أَبَلُّ, applied to a man, (T, Ṣ, &c.,) *Violent,* or *vehement, in contention, altercation,* or *dispute;* (T, M, Ḳ;) as also ▼ بَلٌّ: (Ḳ:) or (M) one *who has no sense of shame:* (M, Ḳ:) or (TA) one *who resists,* or *withstands,* (Ḳ, TA,) *and overcomes:* (TA:) or (M) *very mean,* (M, Ḳ,) *from whom that which he possesses cannot be obtained,* (Ks, T, Ṣ, M, Ḳ,) *by reason of his meanness;* (Ks, T, Ṣ;) and so بَلَّآءُ applied to a woman: (Ks, Ṣ:) or *mean,* (TA,) *much given to the deferring of payment to his creditors,* (IAạr, M, Ḳ,) *much given to swearing* (T, Ṣ, Ḳ) *and to wronging,* (Ṣ, Ḳ,) *withholding the rightful property of others;* (TA;) as also ▼ بَلٌّ [q. v.]: (IAạr, M, [but referring only to what is given above on the authority of the former,] Ḳ, [referring to the same and to what follows except the addition in the TA,] and TA:) or, (Ṣ, M,) accord. to AO, (Ṣ,) *i. q.* فَاجِر [i. e. *vicious, immoral, unrighteous,* &c.]: (Ṣ, M, Ḳ:) fem. بَلَّآءُ: (M, Ḳ:) and pl. بُلٌّ: (Ḳ:) or it signifies one *who pursues his course at random, not caring for what he meets.* (Ḥam p. 383.)

مُبِلٌّ One *whose aiding thee to accomplish thy desire wearies thee.* (A'Obeyd, T, Ḳ, TA. [In the CḲ, for مَنْ يُعْيِيكَ أَنْ يُتَابِعَكَ عَلَى مَا تُرِيدُ, we find مَنْ يُعِينُكَ أَىْ يُتَابِعُكَ على ما تُرِيدُ.])

خَصْمٌ مُبِلٌّ *A constant, firm,* or *steady, adversary in a contention, dispute,* or *litigation.* (M, Ḳ.)

بلج

1. بَلِجَ, aor. ـَ, (ISh, TA,) inf. n. بَلَجٌ, (Ṣ, Ḳ, TA,) *He* (a man) *had a clear, a conspicuous,* or *a white, space between the eyes, not having the eyebrows joined;* (ISh, TA;) *he had a clear space between the eyebrows;* (Ṣ, Ḳ, TA;) *he had a wide space,* or *a space clear of hair, between the eyebrows.* (TA.) — [Hence, *He* (a man) *was,* or *became, bright* in countenance: or *fair, beautiful, and wide in countenance:* or † *open and pleasant,* or *cheerful, in countenance:* or † *liberal with acts of beneficence:* or ‡ *generous, beneficent, and open and pleasant,* or *cheerful, in countenance:* see the part. n. أَبْلَجُ, below.] — And [hence,] aor. as above, (Ḳ,) and so the inf. n., (TA,) ‡ *He* (a man, TA) *was,* or *became, joyful, glad,* or *happy.* (Ḳ, TA.) You say, بَلِجَ بِالشَّىْءِ ‡ *He rejoiced at the thing;* or *was rejoiced by it;* as also ثَلِجَ. (Aṣ, TA.) And بَلِجَ بِهِ الصَّدْرُ فَرَحًا ‡ *The bosom became dilated with joy thereat.* (A.) And بَلِجَ بَعْدَ مَا حَرِجَ ‡ [*It* (the bosom) *became dilated* with joy *after it had been contracted* with grief]. (TA.) — [And hence,] aor. and inf. n. as above; (Mṣb;) and بَلَجَ, (Ṣ, A, Mṣb, Ḳ,) aor. ـُ, inf. n. بُلُوجٌ; (Ṣ, Mṣb;) and ▼ انبلج, (Ṣ, Ḳ,) or ▼ ابتلج; (so in copies of the A and Mṣb;) and ▼ تبلّج; (Ṣ, A, Ḳ;) and ▼ ابلج; (Mṣb, Ḳ;) † *It* (the dawn, or daybreak,) *shone, was bright,* or *shone brightly.* (Ṣ, A, Mṣb, Ḳ.) And ▼ أَبْلَجَتِ الشَّمْسُ † *The sun shone, was bright,* or *shone brightly.* (TA.) And ▼ ابلاجّ الشَّىْءُ †*The thing shone, was bright,* or *shone brightly.* (TA.) — And hence, (Mṣb,) بَلِجَ الحَقُّ, and بَلَجَ; (Mṣb;) or ▼ ابلج; (A, TA;) ‡ *The truth became apparent,* (A, Mṣb, TA,) *manifest, evident,* or *clear.* (A, Mṣb.) And ▼ ابلاجّ, inf. n. اِبْلِيجَاجٌ, (Ṣ, and so the inf. n. is written in a copy of the Ḳ: in another copy of the Ḳ it is written اِبْلِجَاجٌ [inf. n. of ▼ ابلجّ], and the verb is written ابلجّ in a copy of the Ṣ: accord. to the CḲ, the inf. n. is اِبْلِيلَاجٌ [of which the verb is ▼ ابلولج]:) said of anything, (Ṣ, TA,) signifies ‡ *It was,* or *became, apparent, manifest, evident,* or *clear.* (Ṣ, Ḳ,

TA.) ═ بَلَجَ, aor. ـُ, (Ḳ,) inf. n. بَلْجٌ, (TA,) *He opened;* syn. فَتَحَ. (Ḳ.)

4: see 1, in three places. ═ ابلجهُ †*He made it apparent, manifest, evident,* or *clear.* (Ḳ.) — And †*He made him joyful, glad,* or *happy;* syn. فَرَّحَهُ: (Ḳ accord. to the TA [and so in a MS. copy of the Ḳ in my hands]:) or †*he removed it,* or *cleared it away;* syn. فَرَّجَهُ. (So accord. to the CḲ.)

5. تبلّج †*He laughed, and was cheerful, brisk, lively,* or *sprightly.* (Ṣ.) — See also 1.

7: see 1.

8: see 1.

9: see 1.

11: see 1, in two places.

12: see 1.

بَلْجٌ: see أَبْلَجُ, in four places.

بَلَجٌ: see بُلْجَةٌ.

بَلِجٌ ‡ *Joyful, glad,* or *happy.* (TA.) [See also أَبْلَجُ.]

بُلُجٌ, with two ḍammehs, Men *clear of hair in the* [*parts of the face called the*] قَسَمَات. (IAạr, Ḳ.)

بَلْجَةٌ: see what next follows.

بُلْجَةٌ *Clearness of the space between the eyebrows:* (Ṣ, A, Ḳ:) or *width of the space between the eyebrows;* or [*of*] *the space between the eyebrows when clear of hair;* as also ▾بَلَجٌ [which is the inf. n. of بَلِجَ]. (TA.) One says, مَا أَحْسَنَ بُلْجَتَهُ *How beautiful is the clearness of the space between his eyebrows!* (A.) — The *part behind the* عَارِض [or *side of the cheek* or *face*], *to the ear, when there is no hair upon it.* (TA.) — Also, and ▾بَلْجَةٌ, †The *light* (Ṣ, L, Ḳ) of the dawn, or daybreak, (Ṣ, L,) *in the last part of the night,* (Ṣ, TA,) *at the breaking of the dawn.* (TA.) You say, رَأَيْتُ بُلْجَةَ الصُّبْحِ †*I saw the light of the dawn.* (Ṣ.) And لَقِيتُهُ عِنْدَ البُلْجَةِ †[*I met,* or *found, him,* or *it, at the break of the dawn*]. (A.) And سَرَيْتُ الدُّلْجَةَ وَالبُلْجَةَ حَتَّى وَصَلْتُ †[*I journeyed during the whole night,* or *from the beginning of the night,* or *during the latter part of the night, and the breaking of the dawn, until I arrived*]. (A.) And it is said in a trad., لَيْلَةُ القَدْرِ بُلْجَةٌ †*The night of* القدر *is bright* [*like the dawn*]. (TA.)

بَلِيجٌ: see أَبْلَجُ, in two places.

بِلِيلَجٌ, with kesr to the ب and to the first ل, and with fet-ḥ to the second ل; (Mṣb;) or بَلِيلَجٌ; (so written in some copies of the Ḳ, in other copies of which it is omitted;) [*Myrobalana Bellerica:* (Golius and Freytag:) *Terminaria Chebula:* Sprengel. hist. rei herb. p. 262: (Freytag:)] *a certain well-known Indian medicine;* (Mṣb;) *very beneficial to the stomach and to the intestinum rectum.* (Ḳ.) [For other properties &c. assigned to it, see Ibn-Seenà (Avicenna), book ii. p. 144. See also إِهْلِيلَجٌ, in art. هلج.]

أَبْلَجُ A man *having a clear, a conspicuous,* or *a white, space between the eyes, not having the eyebrows joined:* (ISh, TA:) or *having such a space between the eyebrows,* (Ḳ,* TA,) *not having the eyebrows joined:* (Ṣ, TA:) or *having a wide space,* or *a space clear of hair, between the eyebrows:* fem. بَلْجَآءُ. (TA.) — [Hence,] *Bright* of countenance; the Prophet being said by Umm-Maạbad to have been أَبْلَجُ الوَجْهِ; by which she did not mean the بَلَج of the eyebrows, for she described him as having joined eyebrows: (A'Obeyd, Ṣ, TA:) or *fair, beautiful, and wide in countenance,* whether long or short: or [alone, or] followed by ▾بَلْجٌ, †*open and pleasant,* or *cheerful, in countenance;* (TA;) and so ▾the latter alone: (Ḳ:) or ▾the latter, ‡*open and pleasant,* or *cheerful, in countenance, with beneficence:* (TA:) or the former, and ▾the latter, and ▾بَلِيجٌ, †*liberal with acts of beneficence:* (TA:) or the first, ‡*generous, beneficent, and open and pleasant,* or *cheerful, in countenance;* although having joined eyebrows. (A, TA.) — Also †*Shining, bright,* or *shining brightly;* applied to the dawn, or daybreak; (Ṣ, A, Mṣb;) and so ▾بَلِيجٌ, applied to a thing [of any kind]: (TA:) and the former, anything †*apparent, manifest, evident,* or *clear;* (Ḳ;) thus applied to a face, and to the dawn, (TA,) and to the truth, (Mṣb, TA,) and to an affair or event, or a case, &c. (TA.) It is an act. part. n. of بَلِجَ. (Mṣb.) You say, الحَقُّ أَبْلَجُ والبَاطِلُ لَجْلَجٌ ‡*The truth is apparent, manifest, evident,* or *clear;* [*and falsity is a cause of embarrassment,* or *hesitation, to the speaker;*] (Ṣ, A;*) i. e., the latter is agitated to and fro, without having utterance: (Ṣ in art. لج:) or *the truth is lucid and direct; and falsity is confused and indirect.* (TA in that art.) And حُجَّةٌ بَلْجَآءُ †*A manifest, an evident,* or *a clear, proof* or *argument.* (Mṣb.)

أُبْلُوجُ السُّكَّرِ, with ḍamm, [meaning *Sugar-candy,* and *loaf-sugar,* thus applied in the present day,] is an arabicized term [from the Persian آبْلُوج]: (Ḳ, TA:) in one copy of the Ḳ, it is said that أُبْلُوجٌ, with ḍamm, is [syn. with] السُّكَّرُ [*sugar*]: by the people [who are makers] of الحَلْوَا and القَطِيف, [see these words, the latter of which is a coll. gen. n., of which the n. un. is with ة, pl. قَطَائِف,] it is called أُمْلُوجٌ. (TA.)

بلح

4. ابلح *It* (a palm-tree) *bore,* or *had, dates in the state in which they are termed* بَلَح. (Ṣ, A, Ḳ.)

بَلَحٌ *Dates,* or the *fruit of the palm-tree, while continuing green* (Mṣb, TA) *and small;* (TA;) a term like حِصْرِم applied to grapes; (Mṣb, TA;) *called by the people of El-Baṣrah* خَلَال: when they have begun to colour, i. e., to become red or yellow, they are termed بُسْر: (Mṣb:) or *dates in the state between that in which they are called* خلال *and that in which they are called* بسر; (Ṣ, Mgh, Ḳ;) for dates in their incipient state are termed طَلْع; then, خلال; then, بلح; then, بسر; then, رُطَب; and then, تَمْر: (Ṣ, IAth:) or i. q. سَيَاب: (Aṣ, and Ṣ and Ḳ in art. سيب:) [by many of the Arabs in the present day, it is applied to *fresh ripe dates,* and to *dried dates:* it is a coll. gen. n.:] n. un. with ة. (Ṣ, Mṣb.)

بلد

1. بَلَدَ, aor. ـُ, [inf. n. بُلُودٌ,] *He* (a man) *remained, stayed, abode,* or *dwelt, in the* بَلَد [i. e. *country,* or *town,* &c.]: (Mṣb:) or بَلَدَ بِالمَكَانِ, (T, Ṣ, M, L, Ḳ,) aor. ـُ, (M, L,) inf. n. بُلُودٌ, (T, M, L, Ḳ,) *he remained, stayed, abode,* or *dwelt, in the place,* (AZ, T, Ṣ, L, Ḳ,) *and kept to it:* (Ḳ:) or *he took it as his* بَلَد [or *country,* or *town,* &c.], (M, L, Ḳ,) *and kept to it.* (M, L.) — And بَلَدُوا, aor. ـُ; (M, Ḳ;) and بَلِدُوا, aor. ـَ; (Ḳ;) or the latter is correctly ▾بلّدوا; (M,* TA;) *They kept to the ground, fighting upon it:* (M, Ḳ:) said to be derived from بِلَادُ الأَرْضِ. (TA.) ═ بَلِدَ, aor. ـَ, *His skin had* أَبْلَاد, or *marks,* [pl. of بَلَدٌ,] *remaining upon it.* (M, L.) — Also, (M, Ḳ,) inf. n. بَلَدٌ, (Ṣ, M,) *He* (a man, M) *had a space clear from hair between his eyebrows:* (Ṣ, M, Ḳ:) or *had eyebrows not joined.* (M.) ═ بَلُدَ, aor. ـُ, (Ṣ, M, Mṣb, Ḳ,) inf. n. بَلَادَةٌ, (T, Ṣ, M, A, Mṣb,) *He was,* or *became, stupid, dull, wanting in intelligence:* (Ṣ, A, Mṣb:) *inert; wanting in vigour; not penetrating, sharp, vigorous,* or *effective, in the performance of affairs;* (T, M, Ḳ,* TA;) [or *soft, weak, feeble, wanting in endurance,* or *patience;* (see بَلِيدٌ;)] as also بَلِدَ, aor. ـَ, (Ḳ, TA,) inf. n. بَلَدٌ. (TA.) — Also, inf. n. as above, said of a horse, meaning *He lagged behind those that outstripped in running.* (T, TA.) [See also 2.] — بَلَدَ السَّحَابُ: see 2.

2. بلّد, inf. n. تَبْلِيدٌ, *He remained, stayed,* or *abode;* [like بَلَدَ;] or *cast,* or *laid, himself down upon the ground;* syn. ضَرَبَ بِنَفْسِهِ الأَرْضَ: (Ṣ, Ḳ:) or *he did so by reason of fatigue.* (TA. [See 5.]) See also بَلَدُوا. — *He became languid, and affected laziness,* after being brisk, lively, or sprightly. (A.) — *He* (a man) *was impotent* in work, and *was weak;* (T, L;) and so even in bounty, or liberality, (T,) or in running. (T,* L.) — *He* (a horse) *failed to outstrip in running.* (M, Ḳ.) [See also بَلُدَ.] — *He was niggardly,* or *avaricious; was not liberal, nor generous.* (M, Ḳ.) [And hence,] بَلَّدَتِ السَّحَابَةُ, (Ḳ,) or بَلَّدَ السَّحَابُ, (M,) [but the latter is probably imperfectly transcribed,] *The cloud,* or *clouds, gave no rain.* (M, Ḳ.) — *He did not apply himself rightly to anything.* (M, Ḳ.) ═ بَلَّدَتِ الجِبَالُ ‡*The mountains appeared low to the eye by reason of the darkness of the night:* so in the L, confirmed by a citation from a poet: in the A, تَبَلَّدَتِ ▾ البِلَادُ ‡*The countries,* or *regions,*

appeared short [*in extent*] *to the eye by reason of the darkness of the night.* (TA.)

3. مُبَالَدَةٌ [inf. n. of بَالَدَ] The *contending with another,* or *others, in fight,* (i. q. مُبَالَطَةٌ, T, Ṣ, M, Ḳ,) *with swords and staves.* (T, M, Ḳ.)

4. ابلد *He clave to the ground,* (Ṣ, Ḳ,) *in submissiveness.* (TA.) [Perhaps formed by transposition from أَلْبَدَ: see مُبْلِدٌ.] — See also 5. — *His beast became dull; not to be rendered brisk, lively,* or *sprightly, by being put in motion.* (AZ, Ṣ,* Ḳ.) ═ ابلدهُ مَكَانًا *He made him to keep to a place.* (Ḳ.) ═ ابلد, inf. n. إِبْلَادٌ, *It* (a watering-trough or tank) *was,* or *became, abandoned, and no longer used, so that it threatened to fall to ruin.* (T.) ═ [And] ابلدهُ الدَّهْرُ *Time caused it* (a watering-trough or tank) *to become abandoned, and worn, and no longer used, so that it threatened to fall to ruin.* (TA.) [See مُبْلِدٌ.]

5. تبلّد *He obtained,* or *exercised, dominion over a* بَلَد [i. e. *country,* or *town,* &c.,] *belonging to others.* (Ḳ.) — *He alighted,* or *sojourned, in a* بَلَد [or *country,* &c.,] *wherein was no one,* (L, Ḳ,) *saying within himself, O my grief,* or *sorrow,* or *regret!* (L.) — *He was,* or *became, confounded,* or *perplexed, and unable to see his right course;* (M, Ḳ;) *he went backwards and forwards in confusion or perplexity, unable to see his right course:* (T,* Ṣ:) because he who is in this state is like one in a بَلْدَة, meaning a desert in which he cannot find his way: (T, L:) *he was overtaken by confusion,* or *perplexity, such that he was unable to see his right course;* as also ↓ أَبْلَدَ. (TA.) — *He fell to the ground,* (Ḳ,) *by reason of weakness.* (TA.) [See also 2.] — *He became submissive, and humble;* (T, TA;) contr. of تَجَلَّدَ. (T, M, Ḳ.) — *He affected* بَلَادَة [i. e. *stupidity, dulness, want of intelligence,* &c.]. (Ṣ.) — † *He turned his hands over,* or *upside-down:* (Ḳ:) [thus one does in sorrow, or regret, or in perplexity: see Ḳur xviii. 40:] or the meaning is that which here next follows: (TA:) † *he clapped his hands;* or *smote palm upon palm;* syn. صَفَّقَ بِالكَفِّ. (M, Ḳ) (TA.) [See بَلْدَة.] — [And hence, app.,] ‡ *He felt,* or *expressed, grief, sorrow,* or *regret.* (M, A, L, Ḳ.) ═ تَبَلَّدَتِ البِلَادُ: see 2. ═ Accord. to AAF, تبلّد also signifies *It* (the dawn, or daybreak,) *shone, was bright,* or *shone brightly;* i. q. تبلّج. (M.)

بَلَدٌ (which is masc. and fem., Mṣb) and ↓ بَلْدَةٌ both signify the same; (M, A, Mṣb, Ḳ;) namely, [*A country, land, region, province, district,* or *territory:* and *a city, town,* or *village:* or] *any portion of the earth,* or *of land, comprehended within certain limits,* [thus I render مُسْتَحِيزَة, and in like manner it is rendered in the TḲ,] *cultivated,* or *inhabited,* or *uncultivated,* or *uninhabited:* (M, Mṣb,* Ḳ:) or the former signifies *any place of this description;* and the latter, *a portion thereof:* (T:) or the former is a generic name of *a place* [or *country* or *region* or *province*] *such as El-'Irák and Syria;* and the latter signifies *a particular portion thereof such as* [*the city or town of*] *El-Basrah and Damascus;* (M, Ḳ;) or these are post-classical applications: (TA:) or the former, *a tract of land,* or *district, which is an abode,* or *a place of resort, of animals,* or *genii, even if containing no building:* (Nh:) or *a land,* or *country,* absolutely: and also *a town,* or *village,* syn. قَرْيَة: but this latter is a conventional adventitious application: ('Ináyeh, TA:) and the latter, *a land, country,* or *territory,* [*belonging to,* or *inhabited by, a people,*] syn. أَرْض: (Ṣ, TA: [a meaning assigned in the Ḳ to بَلَد; but this appears to be a mistake occasioned by the accidental omission of the word البَلْدَة:]) you say, هٰذِهِ بَلْدَتُنَا [*This is our land,* &c.] like as you say, هٰذِهِ بَحْرَتُنَا: (Ṣ, TA:) the pl. (of the former, Ṣ, Mṣb) is بُلْدَانٌ (Ṣ, M, Mṣb) and (of the same, Ṣ, or of the latter, Mṣb) بِلَادٌ: (T, Ṣ, M, Mṣb:) [which latter, regarded as pl. of بَلْدَة in a more limited sense than بَلَد, is often used as meaning *provinces collectively;* i. e. *a country:*] بُلْدَانٌ is *syn. with* كُوَرٌ [which signifies *districts,* or *tracts of country; quarters,* or *regions;* and also, *cities, towns,* or *villages*]. (T.) البَلَدُ and ↓ البَلْدَةُ are names applied to *Mekkeh;* (M, Ḳ;) in like manner as النَّجْمُ is a name applied to the Pleiades. (M.) [So too البَلَدُ الأَمِينُ and البَلَدُ الحَرَامُ &c.] بَلَدٌ مَيِّتٌ means *A tract of land without herbage,* or *pasture:* (Mṣb:) and بَلَدٌ alone, *a* [*desert, a waterless desert,* or *such as is termed*] مَفَازَة. (TA voce لا; under which see an ex.) — بَلَدٌ also signifies *Land which has not been dug, and upon which fire has not been kindled.* (M, Ḳ.) — *A* [*house,* or *dwelling, such as is termed*] دار: (M, Ḳ:) of the dial. of El-Yemen. (M.) Sb mentions the saying, هٰذِهِ الدَّارُ نِعْمَتِ البَلَدُ [*This house, excellent,* or *most excellent, is the dwelling!*]; in which البلد is made fem. because it is syn. with الدار. (M.) — *A burial-ground:* (M, Ḳ:) or, as some say, (M, but in the Ḳ "and,") *a grave,* or *sepulchre:* (M, Ḳ:) pl. as above. (M.) — *Dust,* or *earth;* and so ↓ بَلْدَةٌ. (T, M, Ḳ.) — The *place in which an ostrich lays its egg, in sand.* (Ṣ, M, L, Ḳ.) And hence, بَيْضَةُ البَلَدِ *The egg of the ostrich, which it abandons in the place where it lays it, in the sand,* or *in a desert:* (M, L:) also called ↓ البَلَدِيَّةُ and ذَاتُ البَلَدِ. (M.) You say, فُلَانٌ بَيْضَةُ البَلَدِ [‡ *Such a one is* like *the egg of the ostrich,* &c.], meaning *such a one is unequalled,* or *unparalleled:* said in dispraise and in praise: (M,* L:) allowed by A'Obeyd to be used in praise: and said by El-Bekree to be applied to him who is separated from his family and near relations. (TA.) [See also art. بيض.] You also say, هُوَ أَذَلُّ مِنْ بَيْضَةِ البَلَدِ (Ṣ, M, A) ‡ *He is more abject,* or *vile, than the egg of the ostrich, which it abandons* (Ṣ, TA) *in the desert, and to which it does not return.* (TA.) [See again art. بيض.] Also هُوَ أَعَزُّ مِنْ بَيْضَةِ البَلَدِ ‡ [*He is more highly esteemed than the egg of the ostrich, which it lays in the sand*]; because the ostrich spreads its wings over it and sits upon it. (A in art. فرخ.) [See more in art. بيض.] — *A trace, mark,* or *vestige,* (T, Ṣ, M, Ḳ, [in the Ḳ mentioned in two places, but in the latter of these omitted in the CḲ,]) *of a house,* or *dwelling:* (TA:) and *a mark remaining upon the body:* (A'Obeyd, T:) pl. أَبْلَادٌ. (Ṣ, A'Obeyd, M, Ḳ.) — The *origin,* or *an element,* (عُنْصُر,) of a thing. (Th, M, Ḳ.) — See also the next paragraph, in three places: — and see بَلْدَة.

بَلْدَةٌ: see بَلَدٌ, in three places. You say, إِنْ لَمْ تَفْعَلْ كَذَا فَهِىَ بَلْدَةٌ بَيْنِى وَبَيْنَكَ ‡ *If thou do not thus, it will be* [a cause of] *separation between me and thee;* (M,* A, TA;) i. e., I will alienate thee from me so that a country, or region, shall separate us, each from the other. (A, TA.) — Also *A desert,* or *waterless desert, in which one cannot find his way:* and *any extensive tract of land.* (T, L.) [Hence,] لَقِيتُهُ بِبَلْدَةٍ إِصْمِتَ *I found him,* or *met him, in a desert,* or *desolate, place, in which there was no one beside.* (M.) [See also art. صمت.] — And [hence, app.,] البَلْدَةُ *One of the Mansions of the Moon,* (M, Ḳ,) [namely, *the Twenty-first Mansion,*] *a patch of the sky,* (Ḳ,) *containing no stars,* (M, Ḳ,) or *containing only small stars,* (T,* M,) *between the* نَعَائِم *and* سَعْدُ الذَّابِحِ: (M, Ḳ:) sometimes the moon declines from it, and takes as its mansion the قِلَادَة: it [app. القلادة, accord. to the Ḳ, but accord. to the TA البلدة,] consists of six stars resembling a bow, (Ḳ,) in the sign of Sagittarius (القوس): (T:) or البلدة is *one of the Mansions of the Moon, consisting of six stars of Sagittarius* (القوس), *which the sun enters on the shortest day of the year:* (Ṣ:) [see مَنَازِلُ القَمَرِ, in art. نزل: in the Ḳ it is also said that ↓ البَلَدُ is a Mansion of the Moon; but this appears to be a mistake, occasioned by the accidental omission of the word البَلْدَة; though البَلَدُ would seem to be an appropriate name for the mansion next after the نعائم:] IF says that البَلْدَةُ is *a star,* or *an asterism,* (نَجْم,) *said to be the* بَلْدَة, i. e. *breast, of the Lion;* not meaning the mansion thus called in the sign of Sagittarius: El-Hareeree finds fault with him for using this expression, [the بلدة of the Lion,] but Ibn-Dhafr replies that it occurs in the language. (TA.) — بَلْدَةٌ also signifies The *earth,* or *ground.* (Ṣ.) — Also (Ṣ, M, L, TA, [in the Ḳ ↓ بَلَد, by the accidental omission of the word البَلْدَة,]) The *pit between the two collar-bones, with the part around it:* or the *middle thereof,* i. e., *of that pit:* (M, Ḳ:) or the *third of the* فَلْك (which are six in number) *of that part of a horse's breast which is called the* زَوْر: or the *part called* رَحَى الزَّوْرِ: (M:) or [so accord. to the M, but accord. to the Ḳ "and,"] the *breast,* syn. صَدْر, (Ṣ, M, A, Ḳ,) of a camel, (M, A,) or of that which has a foot like the camel's, and of a solid-hoofed animal, (M,) and of a man: (A:) and the *part immediately beneath the two prominent portions of flesh of the breast* of a horse, *extending to the arms.* (M, L.) Dhu-r-Rummeh says,

أُنِيخَتْ فَأَلْقَتْ بَلْدَةً فَوْقَ بَلْدَةٍ

She (the camel) *was made to lie down, and threw* her *breast upon* [*a tract of*] *ground.* (Ṣ, M.) And you say, فُلَانٌ وَاسِعُ البَلْدَةِ *Such a one is wide in the breast.* (Ṣ.) — Also ‡ The *palm of the*

hand. (M, A, TA. [In the Ḳ, by the accidental omission of the word البُلْدَةُ, this meaning is assigned to ↑بَلْدٌ.]) You say, ضَرَبَ بُلْدَتَهُ عَلَى بُلْدَتِهِ ‡ *He smote the palm of his hand upon his breast.* (A.) ═ See also بَلْدَةٌ, in two places: ═ and see بَلَادَةٌ.

بُلْدَةٌ (Ṣ, M, L, Ḳ) and ↑بُلْدَةٌ (Ṣ, M, L) and ↑بَلَدٌ [which is an inf. n. of بَلِدَ] (Ṣ, Ḳ) *Clearness, from hair, of the space between the eyebrows:* (Ṣ, L, Ḳ:) *i. q.* بُلْجَةٌ: or *more than* بُلْجَةٌ: or the *having the eyebrows not joined:* (M:) or ↑the second signifies the *space between the eyebrows.* (M.) — And the first, The *form, aspect, appearance,* or *lineaments,* of the face. (Ḳ.) ═ See also بَلَادَةٌ.

بَلَدِىٌّ : البَلَدِيَّةُ : see بَلَدٌ.

بَلِيدٌ (Ṣ, M, Ḳ) and ↑أَبْلَدُ (M, Ḳ) *Stupid, dull, wanting in intelligence;* (Ṣ, Mṣb;) *inert; wanting in vigour; not penetrating, sharp, vigorous,* or *effective, in the performing of affairs:* (T, M, Ḳ:*) [*soft, weak, feeble; wanting in endurance,* or *patience:*] *contr. of* جَلِيدٌ. (Ḳ.) — Also the former, A horse *that lags behind those that outstrip in running:* (T, TA:) and a camel (TA) *not to be rendered brisk, lively,* or *sprightly, by being put in motion.* (M, Ḳ, TA.) — See also مَبْلُودٌ.

بَلَادَةٌ [an inf. n. (of بَلُدَ) used as a subst.] (Ṣ, M, A) and ↑بُلْدَةٌ and ↑بَلْدَةٌ (M, TA) *Stupidity, dulness, want of intelligence,* (Ṣ, A,) or *of penetration, sharpness, vigour,* or *effectiveness, in the performing of affairs.* (M, TA.)

بَالِدٌ *Remaining, staying, abiding,* or *dwelling,* (Ṣ, Mṣb,) *in a* بَلَد [i. e. *country,* or *town,* &c.], (Mṣb,) or in a place. (Ṣ.) — تَالِدٌ بَالِدٌ *Lasting; that does not cease,* or *fail,* or *pass away:* the former word signifies *old;* and the latter is [said to be] an imitative sequent. (TA.)

أَبْلَدُ A man *having a space clear from hair between his eyebrows:* or *having eyebrows not joined: i. q.* أَبْلَجُ. (Ṣ, M.) ═ [*More,* and *most, stupid, dull, wanting in intelligence,* or *in penetration, sharpness, vigour,* or *effectiveness, in the performing of affairs:* see بَلِيدٌ.] You say, أَبْلَدُ مِنْ ثَوْرٍ [*More stupid, &c., than a bull*]. (A.) — See also بَلِيدٌ. — A man (Ṣ) *of large,* (Ṣ, Ḳ,) *big, gross, rude,* or *coarse,* (M,) *make.* (Ṣ, M, Ḳ.)

مُبْلِدٌ, (Ḳ,) or مُبْلَدٌ, (T,) *Old;* applied to a watering-trough or tank. (T, Ḳ.) So in the words of a poet, describing a watering-trough or tank,

* وَمُبْلِدٍ بَيْنَ مَوْمَاةٍ بِمَهْلَكَةٍ *

formed by transposition from مُلْبِدٌ, which [properly] means *cleaving to the ground:* (IAạr, T, TA:) or it is مُبْلِدٌ, (TA,) or مُبْلَد, (T,) which means *abandoned, and worn, and no longer used, so that it threatens to fall to ruin.* (T, TA.)

مَبْلُودٌ *Confounded,* or *perplexed, and unable to see his right course:* [a pass. part. n., but] it has no verb answering to it: (M, TA:) or *idiotic; deficient,* or *wanting, in intellect;* or *bereft thereof:* (Esh-Sheybánee, M, Ḳ:) or *unable to proceed in,* or *prosecute, his journey, his means having failed him, or his camel that bore him stopping with him from fatigue or breaking down or perishing, or an event befalling him so that he cannot move:* (Aṣ, M:) all of these significations refer to confusion or perplexity: (M, L:) or one *whose modesty,* or *shame,* or *whose intellect, has quitted him;* as also ↑بَلِيدٌ. (TA.)

بلز

طِينُ الْإِبْلِيزِ *The mud of Egypt;* (Ḳ;) *what the Nile leaves behind it after retiring from the surface of the ground:* (TA:) a foreign word [arabicized, perhaps from the Greek πηλὸς, as suggested by De Sacy; who also remarks that it might be derived from the Greek ἰλὺς with the Egyptian masc. art. πι, were it not that ἰλὺς is fem.: (see his "Abd-allatif," p. 8:) if we might suppose ابليز to be an old mistranscription for ايليز, we might with good reason derive it from ἰλὺς, which, as pronounced by the modern Greeks, very nearly resembles إيليز in sound]: (Ḳ:) [some of] the vulgar pronounce it with س. (TA.) — [Also applied to *Clay; plastic clay;* or *potters' earth.*]

بلس

4. ابلس, (inf. n. إِبْلَاسٌ, Ṣ, &c.,) *He despaired,* (Aboo-Bekr, Ṣ, M, Mṣb, Ḳ,) or *gave up hope,* (Aboo-Bekr, TA,) مِنْ رَحْمَةِ ٱللّٰهِ *of the mercy of God.* (Aboo-Bekr, Ṣ, TA.) — *He became broken* [*in spirit*], *and mournful.* (Ṣ, TA.) — *He was,* or *became, silent,* (Ṣ, M, A, Mṣb,) *returning no reply, or answer,* (TA,) *by reason of grief,* (Ṣ,) or *of despair.* (A.) — *He was,* or *became, confounded,* or *perplexed, and unable to see his right course.* (Ibn-'Arafeh, Ḳ.) — *He was,* or *became, cut short,* or *stopped,* (Ḳ, TA,) فِى حُجَّتِهِ [*in his argument,* or *plea*]. (TA.) — *He became unable to prosecute his journey:* or *was prevented from attaining his wish:* syn. قُطِعَ بِهِ. (Th, M, TA.) — *He repented;* or *grieved for what he had done.* (M.) ═ *He caused* a person *to despair.* (Ḥar p. 138.)

مُبْلِسٌ *Despairing,* (مُبْلِس,) *and silent respecting what is in his mind,* (Ḳ, TA,) *by reason of grief* or *fear.* (TA.)

بَلَاسٌ, (Ṣ, Mṣb, Ḳ,) like سَلَامٌ, (Mṣb,) and سَحَابٌ, (Ḳ,) [in a copy of the M written بِلاس,] *A* [*garment, or piece of stuff, of the kind called*] مِسْح [i. e. *of hair-cloth*]: (Ṣ, M, Mṣb, Ḳ:) used in this sense by the people of El-Medeeneh: (Ṣ:) a Persian word; (AO, Ṣ, Mṣb;) originally پَلَاس, without ال: (TA:) arabicized: (Ṣ, Mṣb:) also called by the Arabs پَلَاس, with the پ termed مُشَبَّع: (TA:) pl. بُلُسٌ. (M, Mṣb, Ḳ.) [The pl.] بُلُسٌ is also applied to *Large sacks of* مُسُوح [i. e. *hair-cloths*], *in which figs are put,* [or, more probably, *in which straw is put,* for التِّبْنُ, which I find in two copies of the Ṣ and in the TA, can hardly be doubted to be a mistranscription of التِّبْنُ], *and upon which is paraded he who is made a public example that others may take warning from him, and the subject of a proclamation* [*acquainting the spectators with his offence*]: whence the imprecation, أَرَانِيكَ ٱللّٰهُ عَلَى البُلُسِ [*May God show me thee upon the large hair-cloth-sacks*]. (Ṣ, TA.)

بَلَسَانٌ [The *balsam-tree;* or the *species that produces the balsam of Mekkeh;* i. e., the *amyris opobalsamum;*] *a certain kind of tree,* (M,) or *shrub, resembling the* حِنَّآء, (Ḳ,) *having many leaves, inclining to white, in odour resembling the* سَذَاب [or *rue*], (TA,) *the berry of which has an unguent,* (Lth, M, TA,) *which is hot,* (Lth, TA,) *and its unguent is in great request:* (Lth, Ḳ, TA:) *its unguent* [*opobalsamum*] *is more potent than its berry* [*carpobalsamum*], *and its berry is more so than its wood* [*xylobalsamum*]: *the best of its wood is the smooth, tawny-coloured, pungent and sweet in odour: it is hot and dry in the second degree; and its berry is a little hotter than it: its wood opens stoppages of the nose, and is good for the sciatica and vertigo and headache, and clears cloudiness of the eye, and is good for asthma and oppression of the breath, and for flaccidity of the womb, used by fumigation; it is also beneficial in cases of barrenness, and counteracts poisons and the bite of vipers:* (the Minháj, TA:) it is said in the Ḳ and in the Minháj, and by most of the physicians and those who treat of drugs, that it grows only at 'Eyn-Shems, in the neighbourhood of El-Ḳáhireh, the place called El-Maṭareeyeh; but MF observes that this is strange, as it is well known that it is mostly found in the district of El-Ḥijáz, between the Ḥarameyn and El-Yembo', whence it is conveyed to all countries: the truth, however, is, that it ceased to grow at 'Eyn-Shems in the latter part of the eighth century [of the Flight], and it was endeavoured [successfully] to be made to grow in El-Ḥijáz. (TA.) [See also De Sacy's "Abd-allatif," p. 89.]

بَلَّاسٌ *One who sells what is termed* بَلَاس. (Ḳ.)

إِبْلِيسُ [A name of *Satan*]; from أَبْلَسَ, (Ṣ, M, Mṣb, Ḳ,) in the first of the senses assigned to it above, (Ṣ, M, Mṣb,) accord. to some; (M, Mṣb, Ḳ;) his former name being عَزَازِيلُ: (Ṣ, TA:) or it is a foreign word, (Aboo-Is-ḥáḳ, M, Mṣb, Ḳ,) and for this reason, (Aboo-Is-ḥáḳ, M, Mṣb, TA,) and its being also determinate, (Aboo-Is-ḥáḳ, M, TA,) or a proper name, (Mṣb,) it is imperfectly decl.; (Aboo-Is-ḥáḳ, M, &c.;) for if it were an Arabic word, it would be perfectly decl., like إِخْرِيطٌ and إِجْفِيلٌ. (Mṣb.)

بلسان

بَلَسَانٌ: see art. بلس.

بلط

1. بَلَطَ, (IDrd, Ḳ,) [aor., accord. to a rule observed in the Ḳ, ـُ,] inf. n. بَلْطٌ, (IDrd, TA,) *He spread,* or *paved,* (Ḳ, TA,) a house, (Ḳ,) and the ground, (TA,) *with* بَلَاط [or *flag-stones*], (Ḳ, TA,) or *with baked bricks;* (TA;) as also ↑بلّط, (Ḳ,) inf. n. تَبْلِيطٌ; (TA;) and ↑ابلط:

(Ḳ:) or, as also ↓ the second, *he made* [or *constructed*] a wall *with* بَلَاط: (IDrd, TA:) or ↓ the second, *he made* a house *plain*, or *even*. (TA.) ═ *He struck* him, or it, *with the* بَلْط [q. v.]. (TA.)

2: see 1, in three places. ═ The vulgar phrase بَلِّطِ السَّفِينَةَ signifies *Make thou fast the ship*; as though it were an order to make it cleave to the ground. (TA.) [You say, بَلَّطَ السَّفِينَةَ فِى الرَّمْلِ, meaning *He ran the ship aground upon the sand.*]

3. بالط القَوْمُ بَنِى فُلَانٍ *The people, or company of men, alighted with the sons of such a one, each party to oppose the other, upon the ground:* (Ḳ,* TA:) from بَلَاطٌ signifying the "earth," or "ground;" or "even, smooth ground." (TA.) بالط القَوْمُ, (Ḳ,) inf. n. مُبَالَطَةٌ, (Ṣ,) *The people, or company of men, contended, one with another, in fight with swords,* (Ṣ,* Ḳ, TA,) *upon their feet;* (TA;) as also ↓ تبالطوا: (Ṣ, Ḳ:) مبالطة is only upon the ground; (Z, TA;) and you do not say تبالطوا when the people are riders. (TA.) — بَالَطَنِى *He fled from me,* (AḤn, Ḳ,) *and went away in the land:* (AḤn, TA:) or *he left me; quitted me.* (TA.)

4. أَبْلَطَ *He clave to the* [بَلَاط, i. e.] *earth,* or *ground;* (Ḳ;) said of a man: (TA:) *he became bankrupt,* or *insolvent,* or *reduced to a state of difficulty* or *poverty,* or *without any property, and clave to the* بَلَاط: (AHeyth:) *he became poor, and his property went away;* as also أُبْلِطَ: (Ṣ, Ḳ:) so says Ks; and AZ says the like: (Ṣ:) or *he became poor;* or *had little property.* (TA.) ═ أَبْلَطَ اللِّصُّ القَوْمَ *The robber left the people, or company of men, upon the surface of the ground, and left them not anything:* (Lḥ, TA:) or simply, *left them not anything.* (Ḳ.) — ابلط المَطَرُ الأَرْضَ *The rain fell upon the* بَلَاط [or *surface*] *of the earth,* (Ḳ, TA,) *so that no dust was seen upon it.* (TA.) — See also 1.

6: see 3.

بَلْطٌ and ↓ بُلْطٌ [*An axe;*] *i. q.* مِخْرَطٌ; (Ḳ, TA;) i. e. the *iron instrument with which the* خَرَّاط *barks and planes* (يَخْرِطُ) [*a branch of a tree*]: an Arabic word: the vulgar call it ↓ بَلْطَة [now mostly applied to *a battle-axe;* in Turkish بَالْتَهْ]. (TA.) AḤn says, An Arab of the desert quoted to me,

فَالْبَلْطُ يَبْرِى حِيَدَ الفَرْفَارِ

[*And the axe pares off the knobs, or knots, of the tree called farfár*]: حَيْدَةٌ [the sing. of حِيَدٌ] signifying a knob (سِلْعَة) in a tree; or a knot; which is cut off, and whereof vessels are shaped out, so that they are variegated and beautiful. (TA.)

بُلْطٌ: } see بَلْطٌ.
بَلْطَةٌ:

بُلْطِىٌّ [The *labrus Niloticus;*] *a kind of fish that is found in the Nile, said to eat of the leaves of Paradise: it is the best of fish:* and they liken to it him who is rising out of childhood, in a state of youthfulness and tenderness or delicateness. (TA.)

بَلَاطٌ The *earth,* or *ground:* (TA:) or *even, smooth ground.* (Ḳ, TA.) — The *face,* or *surface,* of the earth, or ground: (Ḳ:) or the *part where what is hard,* thereof, i. e. of the earth or ground, *ends:* (AḤn, Ḳ:) or the *hard part of the exterior* thereof. (A, TA.) — [*Flag-stones,* or *flat stones for pavement;* and *baked bricks for pavement;* (a coll. gen. n., of which the n. un. is with ة;)] *stones,* (Ṣ, Mṣb, Ḳ,) and *any other things,* (Mṣb,) *which are spread in a house* (Ṣ, Ḳ) *&c.,* (Ṣ,) or *with which a house is spread* or *paved.* (Mṣb.) — *Any ground,* or *floor, paved with such stones, or with baked bricks;* (Ḳ;) [*a pavement.*] — You say with respect to a niggardly and mean man, مَا ذَا يَأْخُذُ الرِّيحُ مِنَ البَلَاطِ [*What will the wind take from the pavement?*]. (TA.) — And رَجُلٌ بَلَاطٌ † *A man poor,* or *in want.* (TA.) — And إِنَّهَا حَسَنَةُ البَلَاطِ إِذَا جُرِدَتْ ‡ *Verily she is goodly,* or *beautiful, in skin when she is stripped.* (TA.)

بَلُّوطٌ [The *acorn;*] *a certain thing well known;* (Ṣ;) the *fruit,* or *produce, of a kind of tree,* [namely, *the oak,*] *which is eaten,* (Mgh, Mṣb,) *sometimes,* (Mṣb,) *and with the bark of which one tans,* (Mgh, Mṣb,) *sometimes:* (Mṣb:) or [the *oak;* or this kind of tree is properly called شَجَرُ البَلُّوطِ;] *a kind of tree; the fruit,* or *produce, whereof they used as food, in ancient times; cold and dry* (Ḳ, TA) *in the second degree, or, as some say, in the first; or its dryness is in the third degree; or it is hot in the first degree;* (TA;) *heavy, coarse,* (Ḳ, TA,) *slow of digestion, bad for the stomach, occasioning headache, injurious to the bladder, but rendered good by its being roasted and having sugar added to it;* (TA;) *suppressing the urine,* (Ḳ, TA,) *and rendering it difficult; preventing exhaustion by loss of blood, and the emission of blood* [*from a wound*]; *good for hardnesses, with the fat of a kid; preventing the progress of* [*the disease in the mouth called*] قُلَاع, *and* فروع [app. a mistake for قُرُوح, or *wounds*], *when it is burnt; preventing also excoriation, and poisons, and looseness of the bowels; and very nutritious when easily digested.* (TA.) [See also عَفْص. — Forskål, in his Flora Aegypt., p. lvi., mentions this name as applied to The *common ash-tree; fraxinus excelsior.*] — بَلُّوطُ المَلِكِ, according to some, The *walnut:* accord. to others, the شَاهْبَلُّوط [a Persian word, and also used by Arabs in the present day, applied to the *chestnut*]: as is said in the Minháj. (TA.) — بَلُّوطُ الأَرْضِ [applied in the present day to The herb *germander,* or *chamædrys;*] *a certain plant, the leaves of which resemble the* هِنْدِبَآء [or *endive*]: it is *diuretic; aperient; and wasting to the spleen.* (Ḳ.)

بَلَالِيطُ *Level,* or *even, lands,* or *tracts of ground:* (Ḳ:) no sing. to it is known. (Seer.) [See also بَلَاطٌ.]

[مَبْلِطٌ and مُبْلَطٌ, as epithets applied to a man, part. ns. of أَبْلَطَ and أُبْلِطَ, which see above.]

بلع

1. بَلِعَهُ, (Ṣ, Mṣb, Ḳ,) aor. ـَ, (Mṣb, Ḳ,) inf. n. بَلْعٌ, (TA, [and the same is indicated in the Ḳ,]) or بَلْعٌ when the object is food, but بَلَعٌ when it is water or spittle; (Mṣb;) and بَلَعَهُ, aor. ـَ, inf. n. بَلْعٌ; (Mṣb;) and ↓ ابتلعهُ; (Ṣ, Mṣb, Ḳ;) and ↓ تبلّعهُ; (IAạr;) and ↓ بَلْعَمَهُ, inf. n. بَلْعَمَةٌ; (Ṣ* and TA in art. بلعم;) *He swallowed it.* (IAạr, TA.) It is said in a proverb, لَا يَصْلُحُ رَفِيقًا مَنْ لَمْ يَبْتَلِعْ ↓ رِيقًا [*He is not suitable,* or *fit, for being a companion who does not swallow* his *spittle;* meaning, † *who does not restrain his anger*]. (TA.) You say also, ↓ بَلْعَمَ اللُّقْمَةَ meaning *He ate the morsel.* (TA in art. بلعم.) And بَلَعَ الطَّعَامَ and ↓ ابتلعهُ also signify [*He swallowed the food without chewing it;*] *he did not chew the food.* (TA.)

2. بلّع الشَّيْبُ فِيهِ, (Ḳ,) or فِى رَأْسِهِ, (Ṣ, TA,) inf. n. تَبْلِيعٌ, (Ṣ, Ḳ,) *Hoariness began to appear* (Ṣ, Ḳ) *upon him,* (Ḳ,) or *upon his head:* (Ṣ:) or *rose:* (A, TA:) or *spread much.* (TA.) [See also بُلَّعٌ.] Ḥassán says,

قَدْ بَلَّعَتْ بِى ذَرْأَةٌ فَأَلْحَقَتْ

[*Hoariness, or grayness, or the like, had begun to appear, &c., upon me, and marred me*]; making the verb trans. by بِ because it has the meaning of قَدْ آلَمَتْ [*it had given pain,* and this verb is thus made trans.]; or substituting بِى for فِىَّ on account of the measure, which would not be right if he said فِىَّ. (TA.) You say also, ↓ تبلّع فِيهِ الشَّيْبُ *Hoariness appeared upon him.* (IAạr.)

4. ابلعهُ الشَّىْءَ (Ṣ, Ḳ,* TA) *He made him to swallow the thing:* (Ṣ, TA:) or *he enabled him to swallow the thing.* (Ḳ,* TA.) You say, أَبْلِعْنِى رِيقِى [*Suffer thou me to swallow my spittle;*] *give thou me time to swallow my spittle.* (Ḳ, TA.)

5: see 1: ═ and 2.

8: see 1, in three places.

Q. Q. 1. بَلْعَمَ: see 1, in two places. [The م in this word is generally held to be augmentative: see بَلْعَمٌ.]

بُلَعٌ, applied to a man, *Voracious; a great eater;* as also ↓ بُلَعَةٌ and ↓ مِبْلَعٌ (Ḳ) and ↓ بُولَعٌ: (IAạr, Ḳ:) [↓ بَلَّاعٌ signifies the same:] and ↓ هُبَلِعٌ, (Ṣ and Ḳ in art. هبلع,) in which the ه is said by some to be augmentative, (TA,) and ↓ هُبَلَعٌ (Lth, Ḳ) and ↓ هِبْلَاعٌ, (IDrd, Ḳ,) also signify the same; (Ṣ in art. هبلع;) or *voracious,* or *a great eater, who takes large mouthfuls, and is wide in the* حُنْجُور [app. here meaning the *fauces*]: (Lth, and Ḳ in art. مبلع:) and ↓ بُلَعَةٌ, applied to a woman, one *who swallows everything.* (Fr.) يَا بَلَاعِ ↓ الأَيْرِ [app. meaning يَا مَأْبُونُ] is an expression of vituperation used by the people of Syria. (TA.) — سَعْدُ بُلَعَ, (Lth, Ṣ, Ḳ,) determinate, (Lth, Ḳ,) [the latter word imperfectly decl.,] *One of the Mansions of the Moon;* (Ṣ, Ḳ;) [namely, *the Twenty-third;*] which rose [aurorally], (Ṣ, Ḳ,) as they assert, (Ṣ,) when God said, يَا أَرْضُ ٱبْلَعِى مَآءَكِ [Ḳur xi. 46]; (Ṣ, Ḳ;) *consisting of two stars near together;* (Ṣ;) or *two stars, straight* (مُسْتَوِيَانِ) *in course,* (IḲt, Ḳ,) or *near together and oblique;* (TA;) *one of them dim, and the other bright, and called* ▼بَالِع, as though it swallowed the former, (IḲt, Ḳ, TA,) namely, the dim one, and took its light: (TA:) it rises [aurorally] in the last night but one [lit. one night remaining] of كَانُونُ الآخِر [Jan., O. S.], and sets [aurorally] when one night has passed of آب [Aug., O. S.]. (IḲt, Ḳ.) [Accord. to my calculation, it thus rose in Arabia about the commencement of the era of the Flight, on the 29th of Jan., O. S., and set aurorally on the 30th of July. See مَنَازِلُ القَمَرِ, in art. نزل: and see also سَعْد.] The rhyming-proser of the Arabs says, إِذَا طَلَعَ سَعْدُ بُلَعْ ٱقْتَحَمَ الرُّبَعْ وَلَحِقَ الهُبَعْ وَصِيدَ المُرَعْ وَصَارَ فِى الأَرْضِ لُمَعْ [*When Saad-Bula' rises* aurorally,] *the* رُبَع [or *young camel brought forth in the season called* رَبِيع, which is the beginning of the breeding-time,] *becomes strong in his walk, and quick, but not strong to labour, and the* هُبَع [or *young camel brought forth in the end of the breeding-time*] *acquires some strength, and attains to him, and the* مُرَع, a kind of bird, *is then,* it seems, *caught,* or *snared,* [*and parts differing in colour from the rest become apparent in the earth.*] (TA.) — Also The *hole,* or *perforation,* of the بَكْرَة [or sheave of a pulley]: n. un. with ة: (Ḳ:) or the *hole,* or *perforation, in the* قَامَة *of the* بَكْرَة [which here means *the pulley,* or *sheave with its apparatus*]: (Ṣ:) or ▼بُلَعَة has this latter signification; and بُلَع is its pl.; [or is a coll. gen. n.;] so explained by Az; and this is the correct explanation. (Marginal note in a copy of the Ṣ.)

بُلْعَة *A gulp,* or *as much as one swallows at once,* of beverage; like جُرْعَة. (TA.)

بُلَعَة, as an epithet: see بُلَع, in two places: — and as a subst.: see the same, last sentence.

بُلْعُم, applied to a man, (Ṣ,) *That eats much, and swallows food vehemently.* (Ṣ, Ḳ.*) The م is augmentative, (Ṣ,) accord. to most authorities. (TA.)

بُلْعُمٌ: see what next follows.

بُلْعُومٌ and ▼بُلْعُمٌ; (Mṣb, and Ṣ and Ḳ in art. بلعم;) the latter a contraction of the former; the م augmentative; (Mṣb;) The *place of passage of the food in the* حَلْق; (Ṣ, Mṣb, Ḳ, TA;) the *gullet,* or *œsophagus;* (Ṣ, Mṣb;) as also ▼مَبْلَع: (TA:) or this last, *i. q.* حَلْق [which is properly the *fauces;* but by a synecdoche, the *throat,* or *gullet*]. (Ḳ.) [See an ex. voce سُوْرٌ.] — Also, the first, *A torrent, in ground such as is termed* قُفّ, *entering into the earth.* (AḤn, and Ḳ in art. بلعم.) — And The *whiteness that is upon the lip of the ass,* (Ḳ in art. بلعم,) *at the extremity of the mouth.* (TA in that art.)

بَلُوع a subst. signifying *A medicine which is swallowed.* (TA.) — *Beverage:* or *wine:* syn. شَرَاب. (TA.) — قِدْرٌ بَلُوعٌ ‡ *A wide cooking-pot,* (A, Ḳ, TA,) *that swallows what is thrown into it.* (A, TA.)

بَلَّاع: see بُلَع, in two places.

بَلَّاعَة: \
بَلُوعَة: \} see بَالُوعَة. \
بَلِّيعَة: \

بَالِع: \
بَوْلَع: \} see بُلَع.

بَالُوعَة, (Ṣ, Mṣb, Ḳ,) of the dial. of El-Baṣrah, (TA,) and ▼بَلُوعَة, (Ṣ, Mṣb, Ḳ,) and ▼بَلَّاعَة, (Ḳ,) and ▼بَلِّيعَة, (TA,) *A hole,* or *perforation, in the midst of a house;* (Ṣ;) *a sink-hole; a hole,* or *perforation, into which water descends:* (Mṣb:) or *a well that is dug* (Ḳ, TA) *in the midst of a house,* (TA,) *narrow at the head, into which run the rain-water and the like:* (Ḳ, TA:) pl. [of the first] بَوَالِيعُ (Ṣgh, Ḳ) and [of the others] بَلَالِيعُ. (Ṣ, Ṣgh, Ḳ.)

مَبْلَع: see بُلْعُوم.

مِبْلَع: see بُلَع.

مُبْلَعَة A well (رَكِيَّة) *cased with stones,* or *with baked bricks, from the bottom to the brink:* (O, TṢ, Ḳ:) from Ibn-'Abbád. (TA.)

هِبْلَع: \
هَبْلَع: \} see بُلَع. \
هِبْلَاع: \

بلعم

بَلْعَم: \
بَلْعَمٌ: \} see art. بلع. \
بُلْعُمٌ: \
بُلْعُومٌ: \

بلغ

1. بُلُوغٌ [inf. n. of بَلَغَ] and إِبْلَاغٌ [inf. n. of ▼أَبْلَغَ, but it seems that ابلاغ is here a mistranscription for بَلَاغٌ, which is, like بُلُوغٌ, an inf. n. of بَلَغَ, and this observation will be found to be confirmed by a statement immediately following this sentence,] signify The *reaching, attaining, arriving at,* or *coming to, the utmost point of that to which,* or *towards which, one tends* or *repairs* or *betakes himself, to which one directs his course,* or *which one seeks, pursues, endeavours to reach, desires, intends,* or *purposes; whether it be a place, or a time, or any affair or state or event that is meditated or intended or determined or appointed:* and sometimes, the *being at the point thereof:* so says Abu-l-Ḳásim in the Mufradát. (TA: [in which it is said, in the supplement to the present art., that بَلَاغٌ signifies The *reaching, attaining, arriving at,* or *coming to, a thing.*]) You say, بَلَغَ المَكَانَ, (Ṣ, Ḳ,) and المَنْزِلَ, (Mṣb,) [aor. ـُ,] inf. n. بُلُوغٌ (Ṣ, Ḳ) [and بَلَاغٌ, as shown above], *He reached, attained, arrived at,* or *came to,* (Ṣ, Mṣb, Ḳ,) *the place,* (Ṣ, Ḳ,) and *the place of abode:* (Mṣb:) and (so in the Ṣ, but in the Ḳ "or,") *he was,* or *became, at the point of reaching it, attaining it,* &c. (Ṣ, Ḳ.) فَبَلَغْنَ أَجَلَهُنَّ, in the Ḳur [ii. 232], means *And they have fully attained,* or *ended, their term.* (Mṣb.) But فَإِذَا بَلَغْنَ أَجَلَهُنَّ, in the same [lxv. 2], means *And when they are near to attaining,* or *ending, their term:* (Ṣ, TA:) or *are at the point of accomplishing their term.* (Mṣb, TA.) It has the first of the meanings explained above in the phrase, بَلَغَ أَشُدَّهُ [Ḳur xii. 22 &c., *He attained his manly vigour,* or *full maturity,* &c.]. (TA.) And in بَلَغَ أَرْبَعِينَ سَنَةً [Ḳur xlvii. 14, *He attained* the age of *forty years*]. (TA.) And in بَلَغَ مَعَهُ السَّعْىَ [Ḳur xxxvii. 100, *He attained to working with him*]. (TA.) In the Ḳur [iii. 35], occurs the phrase, وَقَدْ بَلَغَنِىَ الكِبَرُ [*When old age hath come to me,* or *overtaken me*]: and in another place [xix. 9], وَقَدْ بَلَغْتُ مِنَ الكِبَرِ عُتِيًّا [*And I have reached the extreme degree of old age:* so explained in the Expos. of the Jel]: phrases like أَدْرَكَتْهُ الجَهْدُ and أَدْرَكَنِىَ الجَهْدُ. (Er-Rághib, TA.) You say also, لَزِمَهُ ذٰلِكَ بَالِغًا مَا بَلَغَ with the accus. case as a denotative of state; meaning [*That clave to him,* or *adhered to him,* &c.,] *rising to its highest degree* or *point;* from بَلَغَ المَنْزِلَ, explained above. (Mṣb.) [But ▼بَالِغًا مَا بَلَغ more frequently means *Whatever point, degree, amount, sum, quantity, number,* or *the like, it may reach, attain, arrive at, come to,* or *amount to.*] And ▼بَلَغَ فُلَانٌ مَبْلَغَهُ and ▼مَبْلَغَتَهُ [*Such a one reached,* or *attained, his utmost point* or *scope* or *degree*]. (TA.) And ▼بَلَغَ فِى العِلْمِ المَبَالِغَ [*He attained, in knowledge,* or *science, the utmost degrees of proficiency*]. (TA.) And بَلَغَ فِى الجَوْدَةِ مَبْلَغًا ▼ [*It reached a consummate degree in goodness*]. (Ṣ, Ḳ,* TA.) And بَلَغَ مِنَ الجَوْدَةِ مَبْلَغًا ▼ [*He attained a consummate degree of goodliness*]: said of a boy that has attained to puberty. (O, TA.) And بَلَغَ غَايَتَهُ فِى الطَّلَبِ [*He did his utmost,* or *used his utmost power* or *ability, in seeking to attain an object*]. (Mṣb in art. جهد.) And بَلَغَ أَقْصَى مَجْهُودِ بَعِيرِهِ فِى السَّيْرِ [*He exerted the utmost endeavour,* or *effort,* or *power,* or *strength, of his camel, in journeying*]. (Ṣ in art. نكث.) And بَلَغَ جَهْدَ دَابَّتِهِ *i. q.* جَهَدَهَا [*He jaded, harassed, distressed, fatigued,* or *wearied, his beast*]: (Ḳ in art. جهد:) and in like manner, بَلَغَ مَشَقَّتَهُ and بَلَغَ مِنْهُ المَشَقَّةَ *i. q.* جَهَدَهُ [and شَقَّ عَلَيْهِ, i. e. *He,* or *it, jaded him, harassed him,* &c.; *distressed him, afflicted him, oppressed him, overpowered him:* thus in each of these instances, as in many similar cases, the verb with the inf. n. that follows is equivalent to the verb of that inf. n.]. (Mṣb in art. جهد.) [And, elliptically, بَلَغَ مِنْهُ *i. q.* بَلَغَ مِنْهُ المَشَقَّةَ, explained above: and often meaning *It took,* or *had, an effect upon him; it affected him:* frequently said of wine and the like: and of a saying; as in the Ksh and

Bd in iv. 66, where يَبْلُغْ مِنْهُمْ is followed by وَيُؤَثِّرْ فِيهِمْ as an explicative: see also بَلِيغٌ.] And كُلَّ البُلَغِينَ, بَلَغْتَ مِنَّا البَلْغِينَ, (Ṣ, Ḳ,) and البِلَغِينَ, and بَلَغْتُ مِنَ: (Ḳ:) see البُلَغِينَ below. And مَبْلَغٌ الأَمْرِ المَشَقَّةَ [I experienced distress from the affair, or event]. (TA in art. مضّ.) [See also an ex. voce ابد.] بَلَغَنِى also signifies It has come to my knowledge, or been related to me, or been told me; or it came to my knowledge, &c.: and in this case it is generally followed by أَنَّ, or by أَنْ as a contraction of أَنَّ: for exs., see these two particles. And in like manner, بَلَغَنِى عَنْهُ Information has come to me, or information came to me, from him, or concerning him, that such a thing has happened, or had happened.] And بَلَغَ said of a letter or writing, inf. n. بَلَاغٌ and بُلُوغٌ, It reached, arrived, or came. (Mṣb.) And said of a plant, or of herbage, It attained its full growth: (TA:) and of a tree, such as a palm-tree &c., its fruit became ripe: (AḤn, TA:) and of fruit, it became ripe. (Mṣb.) Also, said of a boy, (T, Ṣ, M, &c.,) aor. ـُ, inf. n. بُلُوغٌ, or, as IḲooṭ says, بَلَاغٌ, (Mṣb,) He attained to puberty, virility, ripeness, or maturity; syn. أَدْرَكَ, (T, Ṣ, Mṣb, Ḳ,) and اِحْتَلَمَ; (M, Mṣb;) and attained a consummate degree of goodliness (بَلَغَ مِنَ الجَوْدَةِ مَبْلَغًا): (O, TA:) as though he attained the time of the writing of his marriage-contract, and of his having duties or obligations imposed upon him: (TA:) and in like manner one says of a girl, بَلَغَتْ, (T, TA,) or بَلَغَتْ. (TA.) — بَلَغَ ٱللّٰهُ بِهِ [God caused him to reach, attain, arrive at, or come to, his appointed end, or term of life; أَجَلَهُ, or the like, being understood]. (TA.) You say, بَلَغَ ٱللّٰهُ بِكَ أَكْلَأَ العُمُرِ, i. e. [May God cause thee to reach, or attain,] the extreme, or most distant, period of life! (Ṣ and TA in art. كلأ.) And فَعَلْتُ بِهِ مَا بَلَغَ بِهِ الأَذَى وَالمَكْرُوهَ [I did with him that which caused him to come to what was annoying, or hurtful, and evil]. (TA.) And بَلَغَ بِهِ البِلَغِينَ: see the last word of this phrase below. — بَلِغَ, like عَنِىَ, He (a man) was, or became, jaded, harassed, distressed, fatigued, or wearied. (Ḳ.) — بَلُغَ, [aor. ـُ,] (Ṣ, Mṣb, Ḳ,) inf. n. بَلَاغَةٌ, (Ṣ, Mṣb,) He was, or became بَلِيغ, i. e. فَصِيح [more properly signifying chaste, or perspicuous, in speech, but here meaning eloquent]; (Ṣ,* Mṣb, Ḳ;) and sharp, or penetrating, or effective, in tongue; (Mṣb;) attaining, by his speech, or diction, the utmost scope of his mind and desire. (Ḳ,* TA.) The difference between بَلَاغَةٌ and فَصَاحَةٌ is this: that the latter is an attribute of a single word and of speech and of the speaker; but the former is an attribute only of speech and the speaker: (Ḳull:) بلاغة in the speaker is A faculty whereby one is enabled to compose language suitable to the exigency of the case, i. e., to the occasion of speaking [or writing], with chasteness, or perspicuity, or eloquence, thereof: in language, it is suitableness to the exigency of the case, i. e., to the occasion of speaking [or writing], with chasteness or perspicuity, or eloquence, thereof. (KT.)

2. تَبْلِيغٌ and ↓ إِبْلَاغٌ [inf. ns. of بلّغ and ابلغ] signify The causing to reach, attain, arrive, or come; bringing, conveying, or delivering: (Ṣ, Ḳ, TA:) the former is the more common. (Er-Rághib, TA.) [You say, بلّغهُ المَكَانَ He caused him, or it, to reach, attain, arrive at, or come to, the place. And بلّغهُ مَقْصُودَهُ He caused him to attain his object of aim or endeavour &c.] And بَلَّغْتُ الرِّسَالَةَ [I brought, conveyed, or delivered, the message]. (Ṣ.) And بلّغهُ السَّلَامَ, (Mṣb,) and الخَبَرَ, (TA,) as also ↓ ابلغهُ, (Mṣb, TA,) He brought, conveyed, delivered, or communicated, to him the salutation, (Mṣb,) and he brought, &c., or told, to him the news, or information. (TA.) [And بَلَّغَنِى عَنْ فُلَانٍ He told me from such a one, or on the part of such a one, some piece of information, or that some event had happened, &c.] — بلّغ الفَارِسُ, (Ṣ, A, Ḳ,) inf. n. تَبْلِيغٌ, (Ḳ,) The horseman stretched forth, or extended, his hand, or arm, with the rein of his horse, [or gave the rein to his horse,] in order that he might increase in his running. (Ṣ, A, Ḳ.) — بلّغ الشَّيْبُ فِى رَأْسِهِ Hoariness began to appear on his head; accord. to IAạr; as also بلّع, with the unpointed ع: the Baṣrees assert that the former is a mistranscription; but it is related as heard from Th, by Aboo-Bekr Eṣ-Ṣoolee. (TA.)

3. بالغ, (Ṣ, Mṣb, Ḳ, &c.,) inf. n. مُبَالَغَةٌ (JK, Ḳ, &c.) and بِلَاغٌ, (Ḳ,) He exceeded the usual, or ordinary, or the just, or proper, bounds, or degree, in a thing; acted egregiously, or immoderately, or extravagantly, therein: (KL:) he strove, or laboured; exerted himself, or his power or efforts or endeavours or ability; employed himself vigorously, strenuously, laboriously, sedulously, earnestly, with energy or effectiveness; took pains, or extraordinary pains: (Ḳ, TA:) he did not fall short of doing what was requisite, or what he ought; did not flag, or was not remiss: (Ṣ, Ḳ, TA:) he exerted unsparingly his power or ability, or effort or endeavour, or the utmost thereof: (Mṣb:) he accomplished, or did, or attained, the utmost of his power or ability, or effort or endeavour; he did his utmost: (JK:) فِى أَمْرٍ [in an affair]: (Ṣ, Ḳ, TA:) or فِى كَذَا, meaning in the pursuit of such a thing. (Mṣb.) [بالغ فِى كَذَا may be rendered as above, or He did such a thing much, exceedingly, egregiously, extraordinarily, immoderately, extravagantly, excessively, vehemently, energetically, superlatively, excellently, consummately, thoroughly. Hence مُبَالَغَةٌ in explanations of words; meaning Intensiveness; muchness; extraordinariness; excessiveness; vehemence; energy; emphasis; hyperbole; &c.; and sometimes, frequentative signification. Thus, اِسْمُ مُبَالَغَةٍ means A noun of intensiveness; or an intensive epithet: as شَكُورٌ "very thankful," or "very grateful;" and حَمَّادٌ "a great praiser," or "a frequent praiser."]

4. ابلغ, inf. n. إِبْلَاغٌ: see 2, in two places. [Hence,] ابلغ الأَمْرَ جُهْدَهُ [He brought his utmost power or ability, or effort or endeavour, to the performance, or accomplishment, of the affair]. (TA.) And فَعَلْتُ بِهِ مَا بَلَغَ بِهِ i. e. أَبْلَغْتُ إِلَيْهِ الأَذَى وَالمَكْرُوهَ [I did with him that which caused him to come to what was annoying, or hurtful, and evil]. (TA.) — See also 1, first sentence; where it is said that إِبْلَاغٌ is syn. with بُلُوغٌ; but this is app. a mistake. — [مَا أَبْلَغَهُ, and أَبْلِغْ بِهِ, How eloquent is he!].

5. تبلّغ المَنْزِلَ He constrained himself to reach, or attain, the place of abode, until, or so that, he did reach [it], or attain [it]. (Ḳ.) — تبلّغ بِهِ He was satisfied, or content, with it, (Ṣ, Mṣb, Ḳ,) and attained his desire [thereby]. (TA.) — تَبَلَّغَتْ بِهِ العِلَّةُ The disease, or malady, distressed him; afflicted him; became vehement, or severe, in him. (Ṣ, Z, Ṣgh, Ḳ.)

6. تبالغ الدِّبَاغُ فِى الجِلْدِ The tan attained its utmost effect in the skin. (AḤn.) And تبالغ فِيهِ الهَمُّ, and المَرَضُ, Anxiety, or disquietude of mind, or grief, attained its utmost degree in him, and so disease, or the disease. (TA.) [This verb seems properly to signify It reached, or attained, by degrees.] — تبالغ فِى كَلَامِهِ He affected eloquence (بَلَاغَة) in his speech, not being of those characterized thereby: [whence] one says, مَا هُوَ بِبَلِيغٍ وَلٰكِنْ يَتَبَالَغُ [He is not eloquent, but he affects eloquence]. (TA.)

بَلْغٌ: see what next follows, in three places: — and see بَالِغٌ, in two places: — and بَلِيغٌ, in two places.

اَللّٰهُمَّ سِمْعٌ لَا بِلْغٌ, and ↓ سَمْعٌ لَا بَلْغٌ, (Ks, Fr, Ṣ, Ḳ,) and ↓ سَمْعًا لَا بَلْغًا, (Ks, Ṣ, Ḳ,) and سِمْعًا لَا بِلْغًا, (Ḳ,) O God, may we hear of it (or may it be heard of, IB) but may it not be fulfilled; (Fr, Ṣ, Ḳ;) or, may it not reach us, or come to us: said on hearing of a displeasing, or hateful, or an evil, event: (L:) or on hearing tidings not pleasing to one: (Ks, Ṣ, Ḳ:) or on the coming of tidings not held to be true. (TA.) [See also art. سمع.] — أَحْمَقُ بِلْغٌ, (Ṣ, Ḳ,) and ↓ بَلْغٌ, and بِلْغَةٌ, (Ḳ,) Stupid, or foolish, but, notwithstanding his stupidity, or foolishness, attaining his desire: (Ṣ, Ḳ:) or stupid, or foolish, in the utmost degree: (Ḳ, TA:) fem. حَمْقَآءُ بِلْغَةٌ. (TA.) — رَجُلٌ بِلْغٌ مِلْغٌ (Ṣ,* Ḳ) A man who is bad, evil, or wicked, (Fr, Ḳ,) in the utmost degree. (Fr, TA.) — See also بَلِيغٌ.

بُلْغٌ: see بِلْغٌ.

بَلْغَةٌ: see بِلْغٌ.

بُلْغَةٌ A sufficiency of the means of subsistence, (T, Ṣ, Mṣb, Ḳ,) such that nothing remains over and above it: (T, Mṣb:) and simply a sufficiency; enough; (JK, Mṣb, TA;) as also ↓ بَلَاغٌ, (JK, Ṣ, Mṣb, Ḳ,) meaning a thing that suffices, or contents, and enables one to attain what he seeks; (TA;) and ↓ تَبَلُّغٌ. (JK, Mṣb, TA.) You say, فِى هٰذَا بُلْغَةٌ, and ↓ بَلَاغٌ, and ↓ تَبَلُّغٌ, In this is a sufficiency, or enough. (Mṣb, TA.) And it is said in the Ḳur [xxi. 106], إِنَّ فِى هٰذَا لَبَلَاغًا لِقَوْمٍ عَابِدِينَ *Verily in this is a sufficiency* [*for a people serving* God]: (Bḍ, TA:) or *a means of attaining the object sought after*, or *desired*. (Bḍ.)

بِلَغْنٌ: see بَلَاغَةٌ. — Also *A calumniator*, or *slanderer*: (Kr, TA:) or *one who conveys people's discourse to others*. (TA.)

البُلَغِينَ, (Ṣ,) or البِلَغِينَ, (JK,) or both, (Ḳ,) *Calamity, misfortune*, or *disaster*: (Ṣ, Ḳ:) or *distress*, or *affliction*. (JK.) Hence the saying of 'Áisheh to 'Alee, (Ṣ, Ḳ,) when she was taken prisoner [by him], (Ṣ,) بَلَغْتَ مِنَّا البُلَغِينَ, (Ṣ, Ḳ,) and البِلَغِينَ, (Ḳ,) i. e., الدَّاهِيَةَ; meaning بَلَغْتَ مِنَّا كُلَّ مَبْلَغٍ [*Thou hast distressed us*, or *afflicted us, in the utmost degree*]: (Ḳ:) it is said to mean that the war harassed her, and distressed her in the utmost degree. (TA.) It is like البُرَحِينَ [and البِرَحِينَ] and الأُقْوَرِينَ; all meaning *calamities, misfortunes*, or *disasters*: (A'Obeyd, TA:) and is as though they said خَطْبٌ بُلَغٌ [and بُلَغٌ], meaning بَلِيغٌ, and then formed the pl. thus because they considered calamities [as personified, i. e.,] as rational beings having purpose, or design. (IAth, TA.) It is invariably thus, terminating with ى and ن: or one may say in the nom. case البُلَغُونَ, and in the accus. and gen. البُلَغِينَ. (O, Ḳ.*) You say also, بَلَغَ بِهِ البِلَغِينَ [lit. *He caused him to come*, i. e. *he brought him, to calamity, misfortune*, or *disaster*, or *to distress*, or *affliction*]; meaning *he went to the utmost point in reviling him, and annoying him*, or *molesting him*. (IAạr, TA.)

بَلَاغٌ is a subst. from تَبْلِيغٌ and إِبْلَاغٌ, meaning The *bringing, conveyance, delivery*, or *communication*, (Ṣ, Ḳ, &c.,) of a message [&c.]. (Jel in iii. 19, &c.) [It often occurs in the Ḳur as meaning The *communication*, or *announcement*, of what is revealed.] — In a trad., in which it is said, كُلُّ رَافِعَةٍ رَفَعَتْ إِلَيْنَا مِنَ البَلَاغِ, [in the CḲ رفعتْ علينا,] it means *What is communicated*, or *announced*, (مَا بُلِّغَ,) *of the Ḳur-án and of the* [*statutes*, or *ordinances*, &c., *termed*] سُنَن: or the meaning is, مِنْ ذَوِى البَلَاغِ, i. e., التَّبْلِيغ, [*of those who have the office of communicating*, or *announcing*,] the simple subst. being put in the place of the inf. n.: (Ḳ, TA:) but some relate it differently, saying مِنَ البُلَّاغِ [*of the communicators*, or *announcers*,] like حُدَّاث in the sense of مُحَدِّثُون: (TA:) and some say, مِنَ البِلَاغِ, meaning مِنَ المُبَالِغِينَ فِى التَّبْلِيغِ, i. e. *of those who do their utmost in communicating*, or *announcing*. (Hr, Ḳ.) [See this trad. cited and explained more fully in the first paragraph of art. رفع.] — هٰذَا بَلَاغٌ لِلنَّاسِ, in the Ḳur [xiv. last verse], means *This Ḳur-án contains a sufficient exposition*, or *demonstration, for men*. (TA.) — See also بُلْغَةٌ, in three places.

بِلَاغٌ: see بَلَاغٌ.

بَلِيغٌ i. q. فَصِيحٌ [properly signifying *Chaste in speech*, but here meaning *eloquent*]; (Ṣ,* Mṣb, Ḳ;) *sharp*, or *penetrating*, or *effective, in tongue*; (Mṣb;) one *who attains, by his speech*, or *diction, the utmost scope of his mind and desire*; (Ḳ,* TA;) [*possessing the faculty of* بَلَاغَة; (see بَلُغَ;)] as also بَلْغٌ, and بِلْغٌ, and بُلَغٌ, and بَلَاغِىّ, like سَكَارَى, [in the CḲ like سُكَارَى,] and بُلَاغِىّ, like حُبَارَى: (Ḳ:) or بَلْغٌ signifies a man *who does not commit mistakes often in his speech*: (JK:) the pl. of بَلِيغٌ is بُلَغَآءُ. (TA.) Applied to a saying, [&c.,] it also signifies *Effectual*, or *producing an effect*. (Ksh and Bḍ and Jel in iv. 66.) — [Also *Surpassing* in any quality: and *superlative*.] It is also applied to a calamity or the like [as meaning *Great, severe, distressing*, or *afflictive*]. (IAth.)

بَلَاغَةٌ i. q. فَصَاحَةٌ, [as meaning *Eloquence*; (see بَلُغَ, of which it is the inf. n.;)] (Ṣ, Mṣb,*) as also بِلَغْنٌ. (Seer, TA.) — And [the pl.] بَلَاغَاتٌ *Slanders*, or *calumnies*. (Ṣ, Ḳ.)

بَلَاغِىّ and بُلَاغِىّ: see بَلِيغٌ.

بُلَّاغٌ: see بَلَاغٌ.

بَالِغٌ *Reaching, attaining, arriving at*, or *coming to*, a place [or time, or an affair or a state or an event that is meditated or intended or determined or appointed; *reaching*, &c., *to the utmost point* or *degree*: and sometimes, *being at the point of reaching* &c.: see 1, first sentence]. (TA.) You say also, جَيْشٌ بَلْغٌ, meaning بَالِغٌ [*An army reaching*, or *arriving at, its appointed place*]. (Ḳ, TA.) And أَمْرُ ٱللّٰهِ بَلْغٌ, i. e. بَالِغٌ, (Ṣ, Ḳ,) meaning [*The decree of God*] *reacheth*, or *attaineth, its intended object*: (Ḳ:) from the saying in the Ḳur [lxv. 3], إِنَّ ٱللّٰهَ بَالِغُ أَمْرِهِ (Ṣ) *Verily God attaineth his purpose*. (Bḍ, Jel.) And بَالِغٌ فِى الحُمْقِ *Reaching the utmost point*, or *degree, in stupidity*, or *foolishness*. (TA.) And لَزِمَهُ ذٰلِكَ بَالِغًا مَا بَلَغَ: see 1: and see the sentence there next following it. (Mṣb.) أَيْمَانٌ بَالِغَةٌ, in the Ḳur lxviii. 39, means *Firm covenants*: (Jel:) or *covenants confirmed by oaths in the utmost degree*: (Bḍ:) or *rendered obligatory for ever; sworn to, that they shall be constantly observed*: or *that have reached their utmost point*: (Th, TA:) or يَمِينٌ بَالِغَةٌ means [*an oath*, or *a covenant*,] *confirmed*. (TA.) — *Attaining*, or *having attained, to puberty, virility, ripeness*, or *maturity*; applied to a boy: (T, IḲooṭ, IḲṭṭ, Mṣb:) and in like manner, without ة, applied to a girl; (T, IAmb, Mṣb, Ḳ;) thus applied, with the mention of the noun qualified by it, by Esh-Sháfi'ee (T, Mṣb) and other chaste persons, of the Arabs; (T, TA;) or بَالِغَةٌ; (IḲooṭ, Mṣb;) or the latter is also thus applied, with the mention of the noun which it qualifies, (T, Mṣb, Ḳ,) not being wrong because it is the original form; (T, TA;) and seems to be necessarily used when the noun which it qualifies is not mentioned, to prevent ambiguity. (Mṣb.) — *A good*, a *goodly*, or an *excellent*, thing. (Ṣ, Ḳ.)

أَبْلَغُ [*More*, and *most, effectual* or *efficacious*: see بَلِيغٌ.] — ثَنَآءٌ أَبْلَغُ i. q. مُبَالِغٌ فِيهِ [*Praise*, or *eulogy*, or *commendation, in which the usual*, or *ordinary*, or *the just*, or *proper, bounds are exceeded; such as is egregious*, or *immoderate*, or *extravagant*; &c.: see 3]. (Ḳ.)

تَبْلِغَةٌ *A rope*, or *cord, with which the main well-rope* (الرِّشَآء) *is joined to* [*that which is called*] *the* كَرَب: (Ḳ:) or *a rope*, or *cord, that is joined to the* رِشَآء *so that it may reach the water*: (Z, TA:) pl. تَبَالِغُ. (Ḳ.) — Also *A thong that is wound upon the curved extremity of a bow, where the bow-string ends, three times*, or *four, in order that the bow-string may become firm*, or *fast*. (AḤn, TA.)

تَبَلُّغٌ [an inf. n. (of 5, q. v.,) used as a subst.]: see بُلْغَةٌ, in two places.

مَبْلَغٌ [The *place*, and the *time, which a person*, or *thing, reaches, attains, arrives at*, or *comes to*: the *utmost point to which*, or *towards which, one tends*, or *repairs*, or *betakes himself*; *to which one directs his course*; or *which one seeks, pursues, endeavours to reach, desires, intends*, or *purposes*; *whether it be a place, or a time, or any affair or state or event that is meditated or intended or determined or appointed*: (see 1, first sentence:)] the *utmost point*, or *scope*, or *degree*, of knowledge [and of any attainment]: (Bḍ and Jel in liii. 31:) [the *utmost degree of proficiency*: *a consummate degree* of goodness and of any other quality: the *age of puberty, virility, ripeness*, or *maturity*: the *sum, amount*, or *product, resulting from addition* or *multiplication*: *a sum of money*: and particularly *a considerable sum thereof*: and] *cash*, or *ready money, consisting of dirhems* and *of deenárs*: in this sense, post-classical: pl. مَبَالِغُ. (TA.) You say, بَلَغَ فُلَانٌ مَبْلَغَهُ and مَبْلَغَتَهُ: and بَلَغَ فِى العِلْمِ المَبَالِغَ, and بَلَغَ فِى الجَوْدَةِ مَبْلَغًا and مِنَ الجَوْدَةِ: for explanations of all which, see 1. And بَلَغْتَ مِنَّا كُلَّ مَبْلَغٍ: see البُلَغِينَ.

مَبْلَغَةٌ: see 1.

[مُبَلِّغٌ *One whose office it is, with other persons each of whom is thus called, to chant certain words, as the* إِقَامَة *&c., in a mosque*. (See my "Modern Egyptians," ch. iii.)]

هُوَ مَبْلُوغٌ بِهِ [*He is caused to reach, attain, arrive at*, or *come to, his appointed end*, or *term of life*, (أَجَلَهُ, or the like, being understood,)] is said of the object of the phrase بَلَغَ ٱللّٰهُ بِهِ [which see, and the phrase next following it]. (TA.)

مُبَالِغٌ: see أَبْلَغُ: ثَنَآءٌ مُبَالِغٌ فِيهِ.

بلغم

بَلْغَمٌ [*Phlegm*;] *one of the four* [*natural constituents termed*] طَبَائِع; (Ṣ;) [i. e.] *one of the humours* (أَخْلَاط) *of the body*. (Ḳ.) — And hence, ‡ *A heavy*, or *sluggish, person, who is a great talker*, or *babbler*. (TA.)

[بَلْغَمِىٌّ *Of, or relating to, phlegm; phlegmatic*.]

بلق

1. بَلِقَ and بَلُقَ: see 9. — بَلَقَ, (Ṣ, Ḳ, &c.,) aor. ِ, (MṢ, TA,) inf. n. بَلْقٌ, (TA,) *He opened* a door *wholly:* (JK, Ṣ, Ḳ:) or *opened* it *vehemently:* (Ḳ:) and ▼ ابلق signifies the same. (JK, Ṣ, Ḳ.) — And [hence,] *He devirginated,* or *deflowered,* a girl. (AA, Ḳ.) — Also *He shut,* or *closed,* a door. (IF, Ḳ.) Thus it bears two contr. significations. (Ḳ.)

4. ابلق *He* (a stallion) *begot offspring such as are termed* بُلْق [pl. of أَبْلَقُ, q. v.]. (Zj, Ḳ.) — See also 1.

7. انبلق *It* (a door) *became opened wholly:* (JK, Ṣ, Ḳ:) or *became opened with vehemence.* (Ḳ.)

9. ابْلَقَّ, inf. n. اِبْلِقَاقٌ; (IDrd, Ṣ, Ḳ;) and ▼ ابلاقّ, (IDrd, Ḳ,) inf. n. اِبْلِيقَاقٌ; (IDrd, TA;) and ▼ ابلولق, inf. n. اِبْلِيلَاقٌ; (TA;) and ▼ بَلِقَ, aor. َ, (JK, Ḳ,) inf. n. بَلَقٌ; (Ḳ,* TA; [accord. to the CḲ بَلْقٌ, but this is a mistake;]) and ▼ بَلُقَ, aor. ُ; (Ḳ;) but IDrd asserts only the first and second of these verbs to be known; (TA;) *He* (a horse) *was,* or *became,* ابلق, i. e., *black and white:* (Ṣ, Ḳ:) or *white in the hind legs as high as the thighs.* (Ḳ.)

11: } see 9.
12: }

بَلَقٌ and ▼ بُلْقَةٌ, (Ṣ, Ḳ,) the former an inf. n. of بَلِقَ, (Ḳ,* TA,) *Blackness and whiteness* [*together,* generally in horses]: (Ṣ, Ḳ:) or the *extension of whiteness in the hind legs* of a horse *as high as the thighs:* (ISd, Ḳ:) and the latter, *any colour with which white is mixed.* (Golius on the authority of Meyd.)

بُلْقَةٌ: see what next precedes.

بُلَيْقٌ a contracted dim. of أَبْلَقُ. (TA.)

بَلُوقٌ: see what next follows.

بَلُوقَةٌ, (JK, Ṣ, &c.,) [said to be] like عَجُوزَةٌ, (Ḳ,) [but this is wrong, and is probably a mistranscription, for عَجُّورَةٌ, with teshdeed and the unpointed ر, n. un. of عَجُّور,] and with ḍamm, [▼ بُلُّوقَةٌ,] (IDrd, Ḳ,) both mentioned by AA, (TA,) but more commonly with fet-ḥ [to the ب], (IDrd, TA,) *A* [*desert such as is termed*] مَفَازَة: (AA, Ṣ, Ḳ:) or *a tract of sand that gives growth to nothing except the* [*plant or tree called*] رُخَامَى, (Aṣ, Ḳ,* TA,) *of which the* [*wild*] *bulls are fond, and the roots of which they dig up and eat:* (TA:) or *a wide tract of fertile land in which no one shares with thee:* (Fr, TA:) or *a hard place among sands, as though it were swept, asserted by the Arabs of the desert to be of the dwelling-places of the Jinn:* (Aboo-Kheyreh, TA:) or *a desert land, destitute of vegetable produce and of water,* or *of human beings, inhabited by none but Jinn:* (TA:) or *a level, soft land:* (Ḳ:) or *a place in which no trees grow:* (JḲ:) or *white places in sand, which give growth to nothing:* (ISh, TA in art. برص:) or *a piece of ground differing in colour or appearance from that which is next to it, that produces nothing whatever:* as also ▼ بَلُّوق, like تَنُّور: and, with the art. ال, particularly applied to a place in the district of El-Baḥreyn, asserted (as IDrd says, TA) to be of the dwelling-places of the Jinn: (Ḳ:) pl. بَلَالِيقُ; (JK, Ṣ, Ḳ;) which is *syn. with* مَوَامٍ (A'Obeyd, Ṣ) and سَبَارِيتُ, meaning *lands wherein is nothing:* (A'Obeyd, TA:) in poetry, بَلَالِقُ occurs as its pl. (Ḳ, TA.)

بُلُّوقَةٌ: see what next precedes.

أَبْلَقُ, applied to a horse, fem. بَلْقَآءُ, *Black and white:* (Ṣ, Ḳ:) or *white in the hind legs as high as the thighs:* (ISd, Ḳ:) pl. بُلْقٌ: which is applied by Ru-beh to mountains: but the Arabs apply the epithet ابلق to a beast of the equine kind, and أَبْرَقُ to a mountain (TA) and to a sheep or goat: (Lḥ, TA in art. برق:) the former is also applied to a rope. (JK.) طَلَبَ الأَبْلَقَ العَقُوقَ (which is a prov., TA) means *He sought an impossible thing;* because ابلق is applied to a male, and عقوق means pregnant: or الابلق العقوق means *the dawn;* because it breaks, (lit., cleaves,) from عَقَّهُ signifying شَقَّهُ. (Ḳ.)

بلقع

Q. 1. بَلْقَعَ, (Ḳ,) inf. n. بَلْقَعَةٌ, (TA,) *It* (a country, or region,) *was,* or *became, vacant,* or *void; destitute of herbage* or *pasturage, and of human beings, &c.* (Ḳ.)

Q. 3. اِبْلَنْقَعَ *It* (sorrow, grief, or anxiety, such as is termed كَرْبٌ,) *became removed,* or *cleared away.* (Ḳ.) — *It* (the dawn) *shone,* or *shone brightly.* (Ḳ.) — *It* (a thing) *appeared, and came forth.* (TA.)

بَلْقَعٌ and ▼ بَلْقَعَةٌ *A land that is vacant,* or *void; destitute of herbage* or *pasturage, and of human beings, &c.;* (Ṣ, Ḳ;) *in which is nothing:* (Ṣ:) or the former signifies *a vacant,* or *void, place:* (Mgh:) [or instead of using the former alone, you say أَرْضٌ بَلْقَعٌ; for] you say مَنْزِلٌ بَلْقَعٌ [*a vacant,* or *void, place of alighting* or *abiding*], (Ṣ, TA,) and دَارٌ بَلْقَعٌ [*a vacant,* or *void, house* &c.], without ة, when it is an epithet, (Ṣ, TA,) applied to a masc. subst. and to a fem.; (TA;) but if it be a subst., you say, اِنْتَهَيْنَا إِلَى ▼ بَلْقَعَةٍ مَلْسَآءَ [*we came at last to a smooth, vacant,* or *void, land*]: (Ṣ, TA:) and ▼ بَلْقَعَةٌ also signifies *a land in which are no trees, either in sands or in plain or level tracts:* (TA:) or *a vacant land, in which is no one, whether there be in it herbage or not, and whether plain or not:* (Ḥam p. 445:) pl. بَلَاقِعُ. (Ṣ, Mgh, Ḳ.) It is said in a trad., اليَمِينُ الفَاجِرَةُ تَذَرُ الدِّيَارَ بَلَاقِعَ (Ṣ, Mgh, TA; but in the second and third of these, in the place of تَذَرُ, we find تَدَعُ;) *The false oath causes the places of abode to become void,* or *vacant;* i. e., by reason of its evil influence, the possessions and their possessors perish; (Mgh;) or the [false] swearer becomes poor, and the property that was in his house goes away; (Sh;) or God renders him in a state of disunion, and changes the blessings which He had conferred upon him: (TA:) accord. to another relation, the words of the trad. are اليَمِينُ الغَمُوسُ الخ. (Mgh.) You say also, دِيَارٌ بَلْقَعٌ [*Vacant,* or *void, places of abode*]; as though the places were one place: (TA:) and Ru-beh says,

• فَأَصْبَحَتْ دَارُهُمُ بَلَاقِعَا •

[*And their abode became vacant*]: (TA:) and it is said in a trad., أَصْبَحَتِ الأَرْضُ بَلَاقِعَ [as though meaning *the land became altogether vacant*]; the pl. being used to render the meaning intensive, as in the phrases ثَوْبٌ أَخْلَاقٌ and أَرْضٌ سَبَاسِبُ; (IAth, TA;) or because every portion thereof is considered as being بلقع. (TA.) — Also, without ة and ▼ with ة, ‡ A woman *devoid of every good quality.* (Ḳ, TA.) — IF says that the ل in بَلْقَع is augmentative. (TA.)

بَلْقَعَةٌ: see بَلْقَعٌ, in four places.

بَلْقَعِىٌّ An arrow, or a spear-head, *bright,* or *free from rust, in the point.* (Ḳ.)

صَلَنْقَعٌ بَلَنْقَعٌ is an expression applied to *A road* [as though meaning *made bare* by the feet of men and beasts]. (I'Abbád, Ḳ.)

بلن

بَلَانٌ: see art. بل.

بله

1. بَلِهَ, (Ṣ, Mṣb, Ḳ,) aor. َ, (Mṣb, Ḳ,) inf. n. بَلَهٌ, (Ṣ,* Mṣb, Ḳ,* TA,) [and irregularly بَلَاهَةٌ and بُلْهْنِيَةٌ, (see بَلَهٌ, below,)] *He was,* or *became,* أَبْلَه [q. v.]; as also ▼ تبلّه; (Ṣ, Ḳ;) and ▼ ابتله: (TA:) or *he was,* or *became, weak in intellect.* (Mṣb.) — Also *He was unable to adduce his argument, proof,* or *evidence,* (Ḳ, TA,) *by reason of his heedlessness, and his smallness,* or *lack, of discrimination.* (TA.)

3. مُبَالَهَةٌ The *showing stupidity* [*in an action* or *in one's actions,* i. e. the *acting stupidly,*] *with any one.* (KL.) [You say, بالهه *He acted stupidly,* or *in the manner of him who is termed* أَبْلَه, *with him.*]

4. ابلهه *He found him,* or *knew him by experience, to be* أَبْلَه [q. v.]. (Ḳ.)

5. تبلّه: see 1. — And see 6. — Also ‡ *He journeyed,* or *proceeded,* or *pursued his way, without any sign of the road,* or *any track, to guide him,* (Az, Ḳ, TA,) *without following the right course,* (Az, TA,) *and without asking* [*to be directed*]. (Ḳ, TA.) — And † *He prosecuted a search after a stray,* or *lost, beast.* (JK, Ḳ.)

6. تباله *He feigned* بَلَه, or *the attribute denoted by the term* أَبْلَه: (Ṣ:) or *he made use of that attribute* [*as a mask*]; *i. q.* اِسْتَعْمَلَ البَلَهَ; as also ▼ تبلّه. (Ḳ.)

8: see 1.

بَلْهَ is an indecl. word with fet-ḥ for its termination, like كَيْفَ, and means دَعْ [*Let alone,* or *say nothing of*]; (Ṣ;) [i. e.] it is a noun for دَعْ; indecl.; (Mughnee, Ḳ;) a verbal noun, meaning دَعْ and اُتْرُكْ; (IAth, TA;) and the noun that follows it, when it is thus used, is in the accus. case; (Mughnee, Ḳ;) i. e. it is indecl., with fet-ḥ for its termination, when the noun following it is in the accus. case; so that you say, بَلْهَ زَيْدًا [*Let alone Zeyd*, or *say nothing of Zeyd*]; like as you say, رُوَيْدَ زَيْدًا: (IB, TA:) and it is also an inf. n. in the sense of اَلتَّرْكُ; likewise with fet-ḥ for its termination, but decl.; and when it is thus used, the noun that follows it is in the gen. case; (Mughnee, Ḳ;) or it is put in the place of an inf. n., meaning تَرْكَ [which is virtually the same as اُتْرُكْ and دَعْ], and is prefixed to a noun in the gen. case; so that you say, بَلْهَ زَيْدٍ, i. e. تَرْكَ زَيْدٍ [which is virtually the same as بَلْهَ زَيْدًا explained above; for تَرْكَ زَيْدٍ is originally اُتْرُكْ زَيْدًا تَرْكًا, like as فَضَرْبَ الرِّقَابِ in the Ḳur xlvii. 4 is originally فَاضْرِبُوا الرِّقَابَ ضَرْبًا]; (IAth, TA;) for in this case it cannot be regarded as a verbal noun, since verbal nouns are not prefixed to other nouns, governed by them in the gen. case: (IB, TA:) and it is also a noun syn. with كَيْفَ [*How?*]; likewise with fet-ḥ for its termination, indecl.; and when it is thus used, the noun that follows it is in the nom. case. (Mughnee, Ḳ.) A poet says, describing swords, (Ṣ, Mughnee,) namely, Kaab Ibn-Málik, (Ṣ,)

تَذَرُ الجَمَاجِمَ ضَاحِيًا هَامَاتُهَا
بَلْهَ الأَكُفِّ كَأَنَّهَا لَمْ تُخْلَقِ

[*They leave the skulls with their crowns lying open to the sun* (*let alone*, or *say nothing of*, *the hands*) *as though they had not been created*]: (Ṣ, Mughnee:) he says, when they cut, or cut off, the crowns, then let alone, or say nothing of, the hands (فَدَعِ الأَكُفَّ): i. e., they are more fit for cutting off the hands: (TA:) Akh says that بله is here in the place of an inf. n.; that it is as when you say, ضَرْبَ زَيْدٍ: but الاكف may be in the accus. case; so that the meaning may be دَعِ الأَكُفَّ: (Ṣ:) the verse is thus recited in two different ways: and also بَلْهَ الأَكُفُّ [*how then must be the case of the hands?*]. (Mughnee.) And hence the prov., تُحْرِقُكَ النَّارُ إِنْ تَرَاهَا بَلْهَ أَنْ تَصْلَاهَا, i. e. *The fire will burn thee if thou see it from a distance: then let alone*, or *say nothing of*, (فَدَعْ,) *thy entering into it*. (TA.) A strange instance occurs in the Ṣaḥeeḥ of El-Bukhárec, in the explanation of the الٓمٓ of the chapter of السَّجْدَة [the 32nd ch. of the Ḳur]: he says, God says [by these three letters], أَعْدَدْتُ لِعِبَادِى الصَّالِحِينَ مَا لَا عَيْنٌ رَأَتْ وَلَا أُذُنٌ سَمِعَتْ وَلَا خَطَرَ عَلَى قَلْبِ بَشَرٍ ذُخْرًا مِنْ بَلْهِ مَا أَطْلَعْتُمْ عَلَيْهِ: (Mughnee, Ḳ:*) or مَا أَطْلَعْتُهُمْ عَلَيْهِ: (so in some copies of the Ḳ:) thus بله is used as a decl. word, governed in the gen. case by مِن, and deviating from the three meanings [explained above]: (Mughnee, Ḳ:) but the reading commonly known is, على قلب بشر بَلْهَ مَا أَطْلَعْتُهُمْ عليه; and this is the reading in the work of J, [the Ṣ,] and in the Nh, and other lexicological works: (TA:) it has been explained by غَيْر; [so that the meaning of the sentence as first related above is, *I have prepared for my righteous servants what eye hath not seen, nor ear heard, nor hath it occurred to the mind of man, as a treasure for the future*, (obviously taken from Isaiah lxiv. 4, quoted by St. Paul in 1 Cor. ii. 9,) *save*, or *except, that with which ye have become acquainted*, or *that with which I have acquainted them*; and the same, with the omission of "as a treasure for the future," is the meaning of the sentence as related in the Ṣ and Nh &c.;] (Mughnee, Ḳ;) i. e. سِوَى, as in the Ṣ; (TA;) and this corroborates, (Mughnee,) or is agreeable with, (Ḳ,) the opinion of those who reckon بله as an exceptive word: (Mughnee, Ḳ:) and as meaning أَجَلْ [app. a mistranscription for أَجْلِ; i. e., it has been explained also as meaning I have done all this because of my promise to them; مِنْ أَجْلِ مَا أَطْلَعْتُهُمْ عَلَيْهِ *because of that with which I have acquainted them*;) and thus it may have been read by SM, for he has written اجل without any syll. signs; and has given no other ex. of بله in the sense here intended except one commencing with the words, بَلْهَ أَنِّى لَمْ أَخُنْ عَهْدًا, which may mean *because I have not broken a covenant*, or *yea, verily I have not* &c., accord. as we read أَنِّى or إِنِّى]: or as meaning كَفَّ [or rather كُفَّ عَنْ] and دَعْ [*let alone*, or *say nothing of*; but this explanation must relate to the sentence as given in the Ṣ and Nh]: (Ḳ, but omitted in an excellent copy of that work:) or, accord. to El-Aḥmar, it means, in this trad. [as commonly known], كَيْفَ [*how?* which seems to be the least suitable of all these explanations]. (TA.) IAmb relates, on the authority of others, that بَلْهَ is also *syn. with* عَلَى: [but I think that this is a mistake, arising from a misunderstanding of what here follows:] Fr says that he who makes it to govern a gen. case regards it as used in the manner of عَلَى, and similar particles governing the gen. case. (TA.) — مَا بَلْهُكَ means مَا بَالُكَ [*What is thy state*, or *condition*, or *case?*]: (Ḳ, TA:) or مَا لَكَ [which often has this meaning: see the letter ل]. (So in some copies of the Ḳ.)

بَلَهٌ and ↓ بَلَاهَةٌ [both properly inf. ns.; see 1;] The *attribute*, or *quality, denoted by the epithet* أَبْلَهُ [q. v.]; (Ṣ, Ḳ;) i. e. *heedlessness*: (Ḳ:) or *heedlessness of evil*; (JK in explanation of the former, and Ḳ;) &c.; (Ḳ;) and ↓ بُلَهْنِيَةٌ signifies the same; and *stupidity and languor*. (JK.)

بُلْهَآءُ: see أَبْلَهُ.

بُلَهْنِيَةٌ, (Ḳ,) or بُلَهْنِيَةُ العَيْشِ, (JK,) or بُلَهْنِيَةٌ مِنَ العَيْشِ, (Ṣ,) ‡ *An easy and a plentiful*, (Ṣ, Ḳ, TA,) or *a pleasant and heedless*, (JK, TA,*) *state*, or *condition, of life*: (JK, Ṣ, Ḳ, TA:) from عَيْشٌ أَبْلَهُ [q. v.]: (Har p. 216:) the word بلهنية is rendered quasi-coordinate to the quinqueliteral-radical class by ا at the end, which is changed into ى because of the kesreh before it: (Ṣ in art. بلهن:) it is like رُفَهْنِيَةٌ and رُفَغْنِيَةٌ: IB says that it should be mentioned in art. بله, and means عَيْشٌ أَبْلَهُ; the ن and ى being augmentative, to render it quasi-coordinate to خُبَعْثِنَةٌ: it is mentioned in the Ḳ [and Ṣ] in arts. بلهن and بله: (TA in art. بلهن:) the ن is augmentative accord. to Sb. (Ṣ in the present art.) One says, لَا زِلْتَ مُلَقًّى بِتَهْنِئَةٍ مُبَقًّى فِى بُلَهْنِيَةٍ ‡ [*Mayest thou not cease to be greeted with congratulation*, and *made to continue in an easy and a plentiful state of life*]. (A, Ḳ.) — See also بَلَهٌ.

بَلَاهَةٌ: see بَلَهٌ.

أَبْلَهُ *Heedless*: (Ḳ:) or *heedless of evil* (Ḳ, TA) *by reason of his goodness*: (TA:) or *simple, foolish*, or *of little sense, without discrimination*: (Ḳ:) or *weak in intellect*: (Mṣb:) accord. to En-Naḍr, (TA,) one *whose evilness is dead*, (Ḳ, TA,) *so that he is not cognizant of it*: (TA:) *good in disposition; having little cognizance*, or *understanding, of subtilties*; or *having little skill therein*: (Ḳ:) or one *whose predominant quality is freedom of the bosom*, or *heart*, or *mind, from evil affections*; (Ṣ, Ḳ, TA;) *and good opinion of men*: (TA:) *simple-hearted*: (TḲ:) *naturally disposed to goodness, and therefore heedless of evil, not knowing it*: (T, TA:) or *heedless with respect to the present world and its people and their corruptness and malevolence, but intelligent and skilled in the law with respect to that which is commanded and that which is forbidden*: (Aḥmad Ibn-Ḥambal, TA:) fem. بَلْهَآءُ: (Ṣ, Mṣb, Ḳ:*) pl. بُلْهٌ: (Ṣ, Mṣb:) and ↓ بُلْهَآءُ, a pl., [as though the sing. were بَلِيهٌ,] signifies *dull, stupid*, or *wanting in intelligence*: but this is post-classical. (TA.) Hence, شَابٌّ أَبْلَهُ [*A youth*, or *young man, who is heedless*, &c.], because of his inexperience in affairs: the epithet is applied to a youth in like manner as freedom from care, or thought, and like as insanity, are attributed to him. (Ṣ.) And خَيْرُ أَوْلَادِنَا الأَبْلَهُ العَقُولُ ‡ [*The best of our children is the heedless*, &c., *that has much intelligence*]; (Ṣ, Mṣb;) a saying of Ez-Zibriḳán Ibn-Bedr; (Ṣ;) meaning such as, by reason of his bashfulness, is like the ابله, (Ṣ, Mṣb,) so that he feigns heedlessness, and passes over things, (Mṣb,) though he has much intelligence; (Ṣ;) or such as is thought to be stupid, but, when examined, is found to be [very] intelligent. (IAth, TA in art. عقل.) And أَكْثَرُ أَهْلِ الجَنَّةِ البُلْهُ, a trad., meaning *Most of the people of Paradise are the* بُلْه [or *heedless*, &c.,] with respect to the present world, because of their being little concerned thereby, while they are intelligent with respect to the world to come; (Ṣ;) or they are thus termed because they are heedless of their affairs in the present world, and unskilful in the management thereof, and busy themselves with their affairs relating to the world to come. (TA.) — بَلْهَآءُ, applied to a woman, *Generous, strong-hearted*, (مَزِيرَةٌ, for المَرِيرَةُ in the copies of the Ḳ is a mistake for المَزِيرَةُ, with زاى, TA, [app. here meaning *bold*,]) *inexperienced in affairs, and simple*, or *unintelligent*. (Ḳ,* TA.) ISh cites a poet as applying this epithet to a young girl with whom he had sported, and who acquainted him with her secrets, by reason of her inexperience, and want of cunning, not knowing what that implied against her. (TA.) — Also, applied to a she-camel, ‡ *That does not take fright, and flee from a thing*, (ISh, A, Ḳ,) *by reason of staidness*,

(ISh, Ḳ,) or *heaviness*, (A,) *as though she were stupid*. (ISh, A, Ḳ.) One does not say جَمَلٌ أَبْلَهُ. (ISh, TA.) —— شَبَابٌ أَبْلَهُ ‡ *Soft*, or *delicate, youth*; (T, A, Ḳ;) as though he who enjoys it were heedless of nocturnal accidents or calamities. (A, Ḳ.) —— And عَيْشٌ أَبْلَهُ ‡ *A soft*, or *delicate*, or *pleasant*, or *plentiful and easy, life*: (Ḳ, TA:) or *a life in which are few anxieties*: (CḲ:) or *a life in which are few griefs*, or *sorrows*. (Ṣ.) [See also بُلَهْنِيَةٌ.]

بلو

1. بَلَاهُ, (T, Ṣ, Mgh, Mṣb,) aor. ـُ, (T, Mṣb,) inf. n. بَلَآءٌ, (Ṣ,) or this is a simple subst., and the inf. n. is بَلْوٌ, (T, Mṣb,) *He* (God) *tried, proved*, or *tested, him*, (T, Ṣ, Mṣb,) بِخَيْرٍ [*by*, or *with, good*], or بِشَرٍّ [*by*, or *with, evil*]; (Mṣb;) for God tries his servant (يَبْلُوهُ) by, or with, a benefit, to test his thankfulness; and by, or with, a calamity, to test his patience; (T;) [wherefore it often means *He afflicted him*;] as also ↓ ابلاهُ, (T, Ṣ, Mṣb,) inf. n. إِبْلَآءٌ; (T, Ṣ; [in both restricted to good; but in the Mṣb it seems to be common to good and evil;]) and ↓ ابتلاهُ: (T, Ṣ, M, Mṣb:) and بَلَوْتُهُ, inf. n. بَلْوٌ (Ṣ, M, Ḳ) and بَلَآءٌ, (M, Ḳ,) [but from what has been said above, it seems that the latter is used only when the agent is God, and that it is properly a simple subst.,] *I tried, proved*, or *tested, him*; (Ṣ, M, Mgh,* Ḳ;) as also ↓ اِبْتَلَيْتُهُ: (M, Ḳ:) each of these verbs implying two things; one of which is the learning the state, or condition, of the object, and becoming acquainted with what was unknown of the case thereof; and the other, the manifesting of the goodness or badness thereof; both of these things being sometimes meant, and sometimes only one of them, as when God is the agent, in which case only the latter is meant: (Er-Rághib, TA:) and ↓ التَّبَالِى, also, signifies *the act of trying, proving*, or *testing*. (Ṣ.) It is said in the Ḳur [xxi. 36], وَنَبْلُوكُمْ بِالشَّرِّ وَالْخَيْرِ فِتْنَةً [*And we try you by*, or *with, evil and good, by way of probation*]. (TA.) And in the same [ii. 118], ↓ وَإِذِ ٱبْتَلَى إِبْرَاهِيمَ رَبُّهُ بِكَلِمَاتٍ [*And when his Lord tried Abraham by* certain *words*, meaning commands and prohibitions]. (TA.) And you say, ↓ لَا تُبْلِنَا إِلَّا بِٱلَّتِى هِىَ أَحْسَنُ [*Try Thou not us save by those things that are best*]; (T;) from a trad. (TA.) [See also 4 and 8 below.] —— [Hence,] بَلَوْتُهُ also signifies ‡ *I smelt it*. (T in art. بول, and A and TA.) —— [And بَلَاهُ *He knew it*, or *became acquainted with it*. (See بَالٌ.)] —— See also 4, in the latter half of the paragraph. ═══ بَلِىَ, aor. ـَ, inf. n. بِلًى, or بِلَى, [in the CḲ, erroneously, بَلَى,] and بَلَآءٌ, [in the CḲ, erroneously, بِلاء,] (T, Ṣ, M, Mṣb, Ḳ,) the former with kesr and the latter with fet-ḥ, (T, Ṣ, Mṣb,) said of a garment, (T, Ṣ, M, &c.,) *It was*, or *became, old, and worn out*: (Mṣb:) belonging to the present art. and to art. بلى. (M.) [The inf. n., used as a subst., signifies *Wear; attrition; wear and tear*: see an ex. in a hemistich cited near the end of the first paragraph of art. الا, where a dwelling is likened to a garment.] —— Also said of a plant [as meaning *It became old and withered*, or *wasted*]. (Ḳ in art. عنث, &c.) —— And of a corpse, meaning *It became consumed by the earth*. (Mṣb.) —— And of a bone, meaning *It became old*, and *decayed*; syn. رَمَّ. (Ṣ and Ḳ &c. in art. رم.) —— And of a man's reputation, meaning †*It became worn out of regard or notice*. (TA in art. دثر.) —— And [hence,] بَلِيَتْ, (M,) or بُلِيَتْ, (Ḳ,) *She* (a camel, M, Ḳ, or a mare, or beast of the equine kind, M) *was*, or *became, a* بَلِيَّة; i. e., *was tied at her dead master's grave* (M, Ḳ) *without food or water* (M) *until she died* (M, Ḳ) *and wasted away*. (M in art. بلى.)

2: see 4, in six places, in the latter half of the paragraph.

3. لَا أُبَالِيهِ is from البَلَآءُ, [inf. n. of بَلَاهُ,] so that it signifies [properly] *I shall not*, or *I do not, care for him, mind him, heed him*, or *regard him, so as to share with him my trial and his trial*: (Ḥam p. 94:) [and hence,] one says thus, (Ṣ, Mgh, Mṣb,) or مَا أُبَالِيهِ, (M, Ḳ,) and لَا أُبَالِى بِهِ, (Mgh, Mṣb,) or مَا أُبَالِى بِهِ, (MF, TA,) but the verb is more chastely made trans. without the preposition بِ, (A, TA,) inf. n. مُبَالَاةٌ (M, Mgh, Mṣb, Ḳ) and بِلَآءٌ (M, Ḳ, TA [in the CḲ, erroneously, بَلاء,]) and بَالَةٌ; (T, Ṣ, M, Mgh, Mṣb, Ḳ,) said by some to be a quasi-inf. n. and by others to be an inf. n., (MF, TA,) [in the T it is said to be a subst., from المُبَالَاةُ,] originally بَالِيَةٌ, like عَافِيَةٌ from عَافَاهُ, (T, Ṣ, Mgh, Mṣb,) and بَالٌ, [which is more strange,] (M, Ḳ,) meaning [merely] *I shall not*, or *I do not, care for, mind, heed*, or *regard, him*, or *it*; (Ṣ, Mgh, Mṣb, Ḳ;) *I shall not be*, or *I am not, disquieted by him*, or *it*: (Mgh, Mṣb:) or, as some say, لَا أُبَالِيهِ is formed by transposition from لَا أُبَاوِلُهُ, from البَالُ, i. e. *I will not*, or *I do not, cause him*, or *it, to move*, or *occur to, my mind; nor give*, or *pay, any attention to him*, or *it*: (Z, TA: [and the like is said in the T:]) or the proper [or literal] meaning is, *I will not*, or *I do not, contend with him for superiority in goodness*, or *excellence, by reason of my little care*, or *regard, for him*: (Mgh:) or it was employed to denote the contending with another for superiority in glory, or excellence, as will be shown by the citation of a verse in the latter portion of this paragraph; and then, in consequence of frequency of usage, came to denote contempt, or mean estimation: (Ḥam p. 31:) or its original meaning is, *I will not*, or *I do not, strive with him to be first; neglecting him*, or *leaving him to himself*; from تَبَالَى القَوْمُ as explained below; see 6. (Mṣb.) It is said in a trad., لَا يُبَالِيهِمُ ٱللّٰهُ بَالَةً, or, accord. to one reading, لَا يُبَالِى بِهِمْ بَالَةً, meaning *God will not hold them to be of any value or weight*. (TA.) And in another, هٰؤُلَآءِ فِى الجَنَّةِ وَلَا أُبَالِى وَهٰؤُلَآءِ فِى النَّارِ وَلَا أُبَالِى, said to mean [*These will be in Paradise*, and] *I shall not disapprove*; [*and these will be in the fire* of Hell,] *and I shall not disapprove*. (Az, TA.) And one says, لَا أُبَالِى مَا صَنَعْتَ [*I shall not*, or *I do not, care for what thou didst*, or *hast done*]. (IDrd, TA.) And مَا أُبَالِى أَقُمْتَ أَمْ قَعَدْتَ [*I care not whether thou stand or sit*]: and مَا أُبَالِى بِقِيَامِكَ وَعَدَمِهِ [*I care not for thy standing and thy not doing so*]. (Mughnee in art. أ.) And مَا بَالَيْتُ بِهِ (AZ, Mṣb, TA) *I did not care for, mind*, or *regard, him*, or *it*. (TA.) And بَالَى بِالشَّىْءِ [*He cared for the thing*; or] *he was disquieted by the thing*. (T.) The verb is sometimes thus used, in an affirmative manner; (Ḥam p. 94; [and the like is said in the TA;]) though some say that it is not; (Mṣb;) but it is not unless it occurs with a negative in the former part of the sentence or in the latter part thereof; as when one says, مَا بَالَى بِكَ صَدِيقُكَ وَلٰكِنْ بَالَى عَبْدُكَ [*Thy friend cared not for thee, but thy slave cared*]; and as in the saying of Zuheyr,

* لَقَدْ بَالَيْتُ مَظْعَنَ أُمِّ أَوْفَى *
* وَلٰكِنْ أُمُّ أَوْفَى لَا تُبَالِى *

[*Verily I cared for the departure of Umm-Owfà, but Umm-Owfà cares not*]. (Ḥam p. 94.) One says also, لَمْ أُبَلْ and لَمْ أُبَالِ [*I did not care*, &c.]: (T, Ṣ, M, Mgh, Mṣb, Ḳ: [but in the CḲ the latter of these is omitted:]) in the latter the ا [of prolongation] is suppressed for the purpose of alleviating the utterance, like as ى is suppressed in the inf. n. [or quasi-inf. n.] بَالَةٌ, (Ṣ, Mgh, Mṣb,) originally بَالِيَةٌ, (Ṣ, Mṣb,) and in لَا أَدْرِ: (Ṣ:) or the ا is suppressed in this case to avoid the concurrence of two quiescent letters; (Kh, Sb, M, IB;) not for the purpose of alleviating the utterance; (IB, TA;) for this is done because the ل is made quiescent. (Kh, Sb, M.) And, accord. to Kh, (Sb, M,) some of the Arabs say, لَمْ أُبَلِهِ [*I did not care for him*, or *it*], (Sb, M,) or لَمْ أُبَلِ, [in the CḲ, erroneously, لم أبَلِ,] with kesr to the ل; (Ḳ, TA;) [for لم أُبَالِ, or لم أُبَالِهِ;] only suppressing the ا, as they do in عُلَبِط [for عُلَابِط]. (Sb, Ṣ, M.) —— IAar says that بَالَى, inf. n. مُبَالَاةٌ, is like ↓ أَبْلَى meaning *He exerted himself in a description of a war*, or *battle, or of generous conduct*; as when one says, أَبْلَى ذٰلِكَ اليَوْمَ بَلَآءً حَسَنًا [*He exerted himself well, that day, in a description of war*, &c.]: and he cites the following verse [to which reference has been made above]:

* مَا لِى أَرَاكَ قَائِمًا تُبَالِى * وَأَنْتَ قَدْ مُتَّ مِنَ الهُزَالِ *

[*What hath happened to me that I see thee standing exerting thyself in a description of generous qualities, when thou hast become like one dead by reason of leanness*?]: he says that he [the poet] heard him [whom he thus addresses] saying, "We have eaten and we have drunk [with guests], and we have done [such and such things];" enumerating, or recounting, generous qualities or actions, and lying in doing so: (T, TA:) in another place he says that تُبَالِى means *looking to see which of them* [or *of thee and others*] *is best in* بال [i. e. *state*, or *condition*], *while thou art dying*: (TA:) he says, also, that بَالَاهُ, inf. n. مُبَالَاةٌ, signifies *he contended with him for superiority in glory*, or *excellence*; (T, TA;*) and [it is said that] تبالى

in the verse here cited means *thus contending;* syn. تَفَاخُرٌ: (Ham p. 31:) and accord. to IAạr, بَالَاهُ also signifies *he contended with him in contradiction.* (T, TA.)

4. ابلاهُ, inf. n. إِبْلَآءٌ: see 1, in two places. — [Hence,] ابلاهُ ٱللّٰهُ إِبْلَآءً حَسَنًا, (T,) or بَلَآءً حَسَنًا, (Ṣ,) *God did to him a good deed.* (T.) [And hence,] it is said in the Ḳur [viii. 17], وَلِيُبْلِىَ ٱلْمُؤْمِنِينَ مِنْهُ بَلَآءً حَسَنًا (TA) *And that He might confer upon the believers a great benefit,* or *favour,* or *blessing:* (Bḍ:) or *a good gift;* meaning spoil. (Jel.) And أَبْلَيْتُهُ مَعْرُوفًا [*I conferred upon him a favour,* or *benefit*]. (Ṣ.) Zuheyr says,

جَزَى ٱللّٰهُ بِٱلْإِحْسَانِ مَا فَعَلَا بِكُمْ
وَأَبْلَاهُمَا خَيْرَ ٱلْبَلَآءِ ٱلَّذِى يَبْلُو

(T,* Ṣ,) meaning, ٱلَّذِى يَبْلُو بِهِ عِبَادَهُ, (T,) or ٱلَّذِى يَخْتَبِرُ بِهِ عِبَادَهُ, (Ṣ,) i. e. [*May God recompense with beneficence what they two have done to you,*] *and do to them two the best of the deeds wherewith He tries* [the thankfulness of] *his servants.* (T.) — ابلاهُ also signifies *He made him to swear;* [as though he tried his veracity by so doing;] (M, Ḳ;) or so ابلاهُ يَمِينًا. (TA.) [See also 8.] — And *He swore to him:* (M, Ḳ:) or this, (TA,) or ابلاهُ يَمِينًا, [as above,] (T, Ṣ,) *he swore* [or *swore an oath*] *to him, and thereby soothed,* or *placated, his mind.* (T, Ṣ,* TA.) — And hence, (TA,) *He informed him, acquainted him,* or *told him.* (IAạr, M, Ḳ, TA.) — [And hence, *He manifested it; revealed it; made it manifest, apparent, evident, clear,* or *plain;* whence a phrase in a verse cited voce مُضْمَرٌ; and the phrase] مَا لَمْ يُبْلِ ٱلْعُذْرَ, i. e. *As long as he does not manifest, show,* or *make apparent, the excuse:* but the verb [in this sense] is originally doubly trans.: one says, أَبْلَيْتُ فُلَانًا عُذْرًا, meaning *I manifested to such a one an excuse so that I was not to be blamed after it;* properly signifying *I made such a one to be acquainted with my excuse, and to know the manner thereof;* (Mgh;) and thus it is explained in the A: (TA: [in like manner, also, it is explained in the T:]) [or] ابلاهُ عُذْرًا signifies *He gave him an excuse which he accepted:* (M, Ḳ:) and in like manner, ابلاهُ جُهْدَهُ [*He gave him his endeavour,* or *energy, in an acceptable manner*]; and نَائِلَهُ [*his gift*]. (M.) Hence, ابلى عُذْرَهُ signifies also *He strove, laboured,* or *exerted himself,* [and thus manifested his excuse,] *in work.* (Mgh.) And hence, ابلى فِى ٱلْحَرْبِ *He manifested,* or *showed, his might, valour,* or *prowess, in war,* or *fight,* [and *he strove, laboured,* or *exerted himself, therein,* (عُذْرَهُ being understood,)] *so that men proved him and knew him.* (Mgh.) See also 3, where another explanation of ابلى is given, in the latter portion of the paragraph. = ابلى ٱلثَّوْبَ [*He wore out the garment;*] trans. of بَلِىَ; (T, Ṣ, M, Ḳ;) as also ▼ بَلَّاهُ; (M, Ḳ;) belonging to the present art. and to art. بلى. (M.) One says to the مُجِدّ [i. e. him who makes, or puts on, a new garment], أَبْلِ وَيُخْلِفُ ٱللّٰهُ [*Wear out* thy garment, *and God will replace* it *with another;* or, *may God replace* &c.]. (Ṣ.) And أَبْلِ وَأَجِدَّ وَٱحْمَدِ ٱلْكَاسِى *Wear out, and make new,* [or *put on new,*] *and praise the Clother* [meaning God]. (Ṣ in art. جد.) — [Hence,] بَلَّاهُ ▼ ٱلسَّفَرُ [*Journeying,* or *travel, wore him,* or *wasted him*]; namely, a man; (M, Ḳ; but in the copies of the latter, ▼ بَلَاهُ [which I think an evident mistranscription];) as also ▼ بلّى عَلَيْهِ; and ابلاهُ: (M:) and so ٱلْهَمُّ [*anxiety*], (M, Ḳ,) and the like, (M,) and ٱلتَّجَارِبُ [*tryings,* or *trying events*]: (Ḳ:) and ابلاها ٱلسَّفَرُ (T, Ṣ) or ▼ بلّاها (thus in a copy of the Ṣ) [*journeying,* or *travel, wore her,* or *wasted her*]; namely, a she-camel. (T, Ṣ.) El-'Ajjáj says,

وَٱلْمَرْءُ يُبْلِيهِ بَلَآءَ ٱلسِّرْبَالْ
كَرُّ ٱللَّيَالِى وَٱخْتِلَافُ ٱلْأَحْوَالْ

[*And man, the returning of the nights time after time, and the alternation of states of being, wear him out as the wearing out of the shirt*]: (Ṣ, M:*) he means, إِبْلَآءَ ٱلسِّرْبَالِ, or فَيَبْلَى بَلَآءَ ٱلسِّرْبَالِ. (M.) And Ibn-Aḥmar says,

لَبِسْتُ أَبِى حَتَّى تَمَلَّيْتُ عُمْرَهُ
وَبَلَّيْتُ ▼ أَعْمَامِى وَبَلَّيْتُ خَالِيَا

he means *I lived the period that my father lived* [*so that I had long enjoyment of his life, and I outwore my paternal uncles, and I outwore my maternal uncle*]: or, as some say, *I lived with my father for the length of his life* &c. (M, TA.* [In the latter, ▼ تَبَلَّيْتُ is put in the place of تَمَلَّيْتُ; and hence it is there said that تَبَلَّاهُ is like بَلَّاهُ: but I think that تبلّيت is a mistranscription.]) — أَبْلَيْتُ and ▼ بَلَّيْتُ also signify *I bound the foreshank of a she-camel to her arm at the grave of her* [*dead*] *master, and left her without food or water until she died;* or *I dug for her a pit, and left her in it until she died.* (Ṣ, TA. [See بَلِيَّةٌ, and مُبَلًّى.])

5: see 4, near the end of the paragraph.

6. تَبَالَى [inf. n. of التَّبَالِى] : see 1. = تبالى القومُ *The people,* or *company of men, vied,* or *strove, one with another, in hastening to a little water, and drew from it.* (Mṣb.)

8. ابتلاهُ: see 1, in three places. [Hence, اُبْتُلِىَ بِكَذَا (vulg. اِبْتَلَى) *He was tried, proved,* or *tested, by,* or *with, such a thing;* generally meaning *he was afflicted thereby,* or *therewith;* as, for instance, by, or with, a disease.] — Also *He asked,* or *sought,* or *desired, of him information,* or *news,* or *tidings.* (M, Ḳ.) And ابتلى signifies also *He conjured,* or *adjured, and asked if any had knowledge;* syn. اِسْتَحْلَفَ and اِسْتَعْرَفَ [explained by what here follows]. (M, Ḳ, TA. [In the CḲ, both the verb and the explanation are here wrong: the former is written أَبْلَى; and the latter, اسْتَحْلَفَ واسْتَعْرَفَ.]) A poet says,

تَبَغَّى أَبَاهَا فِى ٱلرِّفَاقِ وَتَبْتَلِى
وَأَوْدَى بِهِ فِى لُجَّةِ ٱلْبَحْرِ تِمْسَحُ

[*She seeks for her father among the travelling-companions, and conjures,* or *adjures, and asks if any have knowledge, when a crocodile has destroyed him in the depth of the great river:* تبغّى is for تَتَبَغَّى]: he means that she says to them, "I conjure you, or adjure you, by God, (نَاشَدْتُكُمُ ٱللّٰهَ,) [tell me,] do ye know any tidings of my father?" (M, TA.) But Aboo-Sa'eed says that تبتلى here means *tries, proves,* or *tests;* and that ٱلاِبْتِلَآءُ signifies *the trying, proving,* or *testing, whether by an oath or otherwise.* (TA.) — [Also *He desired it; he sought it.*] It is said in a trad., ٱلنَّذْرُ مَا ٱبْتُلِىَ بِهِ وَجْهُ ٱللّٰهِ, i. e. [*The vow that a man makes to be binding,* or *obligatory, on himself is that whereby the recompense of God*] *is desired,* or *sought.* (TA.) — And *He chose him, made choice of him,* or *elected him.* (Sh and T, from a trad.)

12. اِبْلَوْلَى *It* (herbage) *became tall, so that the camels were able to avail themselves of it.* (Ḳ.)

بِلْوُ سَفَرٍ, (T, Ṣ, M, A,) with kesr to the ب, (Ṣ,) and بِلْىُ سَفَرٍ, (Ṣ, A,) *Worn,* or *wasted, by journeying,* or *travel;* applied to a she-camel, (T, Ṣ, M, A,) and in like manner to a man, and to a he-camel: (M:) and بِلْىُ أَسْفَارٍ (M, Ḳ) and بِلْوُ أَسْفَارٍ, (Ḳ, TA,) with kesr to the ب in both, (TA, [in the CḲ written with fet-ḥ,]) a man *worn,* or *wasted, by journeyings,* or *travels, and anxiety,* (M, Ḳ,*) *and the like,* (M,) *and tryings,* or *trying events:* (Ḳ:) pl. أَبْلَآءٌ. (Ṣ, M.) And بِلْوُ شَرٍّ and بِلْىُ شَرٍّ [both written in the CḲ with fet-ḥ to the ب] A man *having strength,* or *power, to endure evil; tried, proved,* or *tested, thereby:* (M, Ḳ:) and in like manner, بِلْوُ خَيْرٍ and بِلْىُ خَيْرٍ [*tried,* &c., *by good,* or *prosperity*]. (TA.) And إِنَّهُ بِلْوُ مِنْ أَبْلَآءِ ٱلْمَالِ and بِلْىُ [both written in the CḲ with fet-ḥ to the ب as before] *Verily he is one of those who manage,* or *tend, camels,* or *the like, well.* (M,* Ḳ,* TA.) The ى in بِلْىٌ, in all these instances, is originally و, changed into ى because of the kesreh, and the weakness of the intervening letter, ل; as is the case in عِلْيَةٌ: so says IJ. (M.)

بَلَى: see art. بلى.

بِلْوَةٌ, بِلْيَةٌ, بَلْوَى: see what next follows.

بَلَآءٌ (T, Ṣ, Mṣb) and ▼ بَلْوَى (T, Ṣ, M, Mṣb, Ḳ) and ▼ بِلْيَةٌ (Ṣ, M, Mṣb, Ḳ) and ▼ بِلْوَةٌ, (Ṣ, M, Ḳ,) with kesr, (Ṣ, Ḳ,) and ▼ بَلِيَّةٌ, (so in a copy of the Ṣ, beside the third,) thus in the handwriting of Aboo-Zekereeyà, in the place of the third, (TA,) substs. (T, M, Mṣb, Ḳ) from بَلَاهُ ٱللّٰهُ, (T, Mṣb,) or from ٱبْتَلَاهُ ٱللّٰهُ, [which is the same in meaning,] (M,) or from بَلَوْتُهُ, (Ḳ,) are one [in their signification; which is *A trial,* as meaning *a probation,* or *a test;* and as meaning particularly *a trouble* or *an affliction of any kind by which one's patience or any other grace or virtue is tried, proved,* or *tested*]; (Ṣ;) and the pl. (Ṣ, TA) of ▼ بَلِيَّةٌ (TA) is بَلَايَا, of the measure فَعَائِلُ

changed to فَعَالَى: (Ṣ, TA:) [or] بَلَآءٌ is [properly, or originally,] an inf. n., (Ṣ, M, Ḳ,) and signifies the *act of trying, proving,* or *testing, by,* or *with, good,* and *by,* or *with, evil:* (Ṣ, M:) it is *evil* and *good:* (T, M:*) *a trial,* or *an affliction,* (T, Ḳ,) which is its original meaning; (T;) and *a [probationary] benefit, favour,* or *blessing,* (T,) or *a [probationary] gift;* (Ḳ;) the former of these requiring patience, and the latter being the greater of the two [as being commonly the more dangerous to the soul]; (TA;) [but the latter meaning is generally indicated only by the addition of an epithet: thus] بَلَآءٌ حَسَنٌ means *a great benefit,* or *favour,* or *blessing,* of God; (Bḍ in viii. 17;) or *a good gift* of God: (Jel ibid.:) بَلَآءٌ also means *grief;* as though it tried the body: (Er-Rághib, Ḳ:) and the *imposition of a difficult,* or *troublesome, thing; a requirement; an exaction;* because it is difficult, or distressing, to the body; or because it is a trying. (Ḳ.) بَلَآءِ (like قَطَامِ, Ṣ, Ḳ) is *syn. with* البَلَآءُ: (Ṣ, M, Ḳ:) occurring in the saying, نَزَلَتْ بَلَآءِ عَلَى الكُفَّارِ [*Trial,* or *affliction, befell the unbelievers*]: (Ṣ, M,* Ḳ:*) mentioned by El-Aḥmar, as heard by him from the Arabs. (Ṣ.)

بِلَآءٌ, like كِتَابٌ in form, [is an inf. n. of 3, q. v.: = and also signifies] *Anxiety respecting which one talks to himself,* or *soliloquizes.* (Mṣb. [Compare a meaning of بَلَآءٌ, above.])

بَلِىٌّ: see the paragraph next following; last sentence.

بَلِيَّةٌ: see بَلَآءٌ, in two places. = Also *A she-camel that has her fore shank bound to her arm at the grave of her master, and is left without food until she dies:* (T:) or *a she-camel,* (M in arts. بلو and بلى, and Ḳ,) or *a mare,* or *beast of the equine kind,* (M in art. بلو,) *that is bound at the grave of her master,* (M, Ḳ,) *he being dead, and is left without food or water* (M) *until she dies* (M, Ḳ) *and wastes away;* for they used to say that her master would be raised from the dead upon her: (M:) or *a she-camel which, in the Time of Ignorance, had her fore shank bound to her arm at the grave of her master, and was left without food or water until she died:* or *for which was dug a pit, wherein she was left until she died:* for they used to assert that men would be raised from the dead riding upon the بَلَايَا, [pl. of بَلِيَّةٌ in the sense above explained, (T, TA,)] or walking if their beasts whereon they rode were not bound, with the head turned backwards, at their graves: (Ṣ:) or *a cow,* or *she-camel,* or *sheep,* or *goat, which, in the Time of Ignorance, they used to hamstring,* or *slaughter, at the grave:* so in a trad. (TA.) Suh says that this custom proves that, in the Time of Ignorance, they held the doctrine of the resurrection of the body: but they who held it were the fewer number. (TA.) It is said that بَلِيَّةٌ is originally مُبْلَاةٌ or مُبْلَاةٌ. (TA.) Eṭ-Ṭirimmáḥ says,

* مَنَازِلُ لَا تَرَى الأَنْصَابَ فِيهَا *
* وَلَا حُفَرَ المُبْلَّى لِلْمَنُونِ *

[*Places of abode in which thou wilt not see the stones,* or *other things, that have been set up to be worshipped, nor the pits of the beast left by the grave of the master to die*]; meaning places of abode of the people of El-Islám, exclusively of the pagans. (Ṣ.) IAạr says that بَلِىٌّ and بَلِيَّةٌ signify *Such as is wearied,* or *jaded, and emaciated, and dying.* (TA.)

بَالٍ [act. part. n. of بَلَاهُ; *Trying, proving,* or *testing.* — And hence,] *Knowing,* or *being acquainted* [with a thing]; as in the phrase, جَعَلْتُهُ بَالِيًا بِعُذْرِى *I made him to be acquainted with my excuse, and to know the manner thereof.* (Mgh.) = Also *Old, and wearing out* [or *worn out*]; applied to a garment. (Mṣb.) — [Hence,] بَالِيَاتٌ is used as meaning The *places of tents.* (Ḥam p. 492.)

مُبْلَاةٌ, fem. of مُبْلًى: } see بَلِيَّةٌ.
مُبَلًّى, and its fem. مُبَلَّاةٌ: }

مُبَلِّيَاتٌ *Women that stand around a man's riding-camel* [*which they bind,* or *place in a pit, by his grave, to die of hunger and thirst,*] *when he has died or been slain, wailing for him.* (T, Ṣ.*) You say, قَامَتْ مُبَلِّيَاتُ فُلَانٍ يَنُحْنَ عَلَيْهِ [*The women that bound,* or *placed, the* بَلِيَّة *by the grave of such a one stood around it wailing for him*]. (T, Ṣ.)

بلور

بِلَّوْرٌ (M, Mṣb, Ḳ) and بَلُّورٌ (Mṣb, Ḳ) and بِلْوَرٌ, (Ḳ,) or the last only, (IAạr, T,) [a coll. gen. n., signifying *Crystal;*] the *kind of stone called* مَهًا, (M,) *which shines by reason of its whiteness and clearness;* (TA in art. مهو;) *a well-known kind of stone, the best of which is brought from the islands of the Zinj* (الزَّنْج); (Mṣb;) *a well-known kind of precious stone,* (Ḳ, TA,) *white and transparent:* (TA:) [Golius says, but I know not on what authority, if on any better ground than the resemblance of the name, "Græc. Βήρυλλος, *beryllus,* lapidis genus: de quo vide Plin. xxxvii. 5: aut potius, quo illum lapidem adulterari idem scribit, *crystallum:*"] n. un. with ة: (M:) some say that it is *a kind of glass* [or *factitious crystal;* what we term *crystal-glass;* and to this the word is commonly applied in the present day; though still also applied to *rock-crystal*]. (TA.)

بلى

1. بَلِىَ: }
4. ابلى الثَّوْبَ: } see art. بلو.
بِلًى: and بِلَى سَفَرٍ: &c.: }

بَلَى is a particle; (Ṣ, Mṣb, Mughnee;) *contr. of* لَا: (Ṣ:) not a noun: (Sb, Ṣ:) it is a replicative; (Ṣ, Mughnee;) an affirmative of what is said [in that to which it is a reply]; (Ṣ, Mṣb;) [with very few exceptions] relating only to a negation, which it annuls: (Mṣb, Mughnee:) the final letter is a radical: or, accord. to some, the word is originally بَلْ, [after which an affirmation is to be understood,] and the final letter is augmentative: and some of these say that this letter is a denotative of the fem. gender, because it is [often] pronounced with imáleh. (Mughnee.) It is a reply to an interrogation in which is a negative, (T, M, Mṣb, Mughnee, Ḳ,) and affirms what is said to thee [in that interrogation]; (M, Ḳ;) whether it be an interrogation in the proper sense, (Mughnee,) as when you say to another, أَلَمْ تَفْعَلْ كَذَا [*Didst thou not such a thing?*], and he replies, بَلَى [meaning *Yes,* or *yea,* or *ay,* I did], (T,) or as when one says, أَلَيْسَ زَيْدٌ بِقَائِمٍ [*Is not Zeyd standing?*], and you reply, بَلَى [*Yes,* he is]; or be meant to convey reproof, (Mughnee,) as in the Ḳur [lxxv. 3 and 4], أَيَحْسَبُ الإِنْسَانُ أَنْ لَنْ نَجْمَعَ عِظَامَهُ بَلَى [*Doth man think that we will not collect his bones? Yes*], (Mṣb, Mughnee,) i. e., we will collect them; (Mṣb;) or be meant to make a person confess, or acknowledge, a thing, (Mughnee.) as in the Ḳur [vii. 171], أَلَسْتُ بِرَبِّكُمْ قَالُوا بَلَى [*Am I not your Lord? They said, Yea*]. (M, Mughnee.) It is also a reply to a simple negation, (Mṣb, Mughnee,) as when I say, مَا قَامَ زَيْدٌ [*Zeyd did not stand,* or *has not stood*], and you reply, بَلَى as an affirmative [meaning *Yes,* he did, or he has]. (Mṣb.) It occurs in the Ḳur [xxxix. 60], where it is said, بَلَى قَدْ جَآءَتْكَ آيَاتِى [*Yea, my signs have come to thee*], preceded by that which is not literally a negation, but which has the force of a negation; for the preceding saying, لَوْ أَنَّ ٱللّٰهَ هَدَانِى [*If God had directed me aright,* or *would that God* &c.], is like the saying, مَا هُدِيتُ [*I was not directed aright*]. (M.) It also occurs in the books of traditions, in some instances, as a reply to an interrogation without a negative; but these instances are rare, and not to be followed in rendering revelation. (Mughnee.) Az says that when a man says to another, أَلَا تَقُومُ [*Wilt thou not stand?*], and the latter replies, بَلَى, he means بَلْ أَقُومُ [*Nay, I will stand*], adding the alif [written ى] to make the pause good; for if he said, بَلْ, the other would expect something more to be said after it. (TA.) It is said that the pronunciation termed imáleh is allowable in the case of بَلَى; and if so, its final radical letter is ى: and some of the grammarians say that this pronunciation of بلى is because, by reason of its completeness and independence of meaning, so that it requires nothing after it, it resembles independent nouns, in the cases of which this pronunciation is allowable. (M.)

بِلْيَةٌ and بَلِىٌّ and بَلِيَّةٌ: see art. بلو.

بم

بَمٌّ [The *bass* in music; used in this sense in the present day: or particularly the *bass notes* of the lute: in this sense F seems to have understood the saying of ISd that] the بَمّ of the lute is well known: (M, Ḳ: [in the CḲ, البَمُّ مِنَ العُوْدِ او الوَتَرِ الخ is erroneously put for البَمُّ مِنَ العُودِ مَا أَوِ الوَتَرُ الخ:]) or (so in the Ḳ) it is the *thick* [or *bass*] *chord of the lute:* (Ṣ, Ḳ:) the word is foreign: (M:) [in Persian بُر:] Az says that it is not Arabic. (TA.)

بُر i. q. بُورَ, q. v. (K.)

بن

1: see 4.

2. بَنَّنَ, (K,) inf. n. تَبْنِينٌ, (TA,) *He tied a sheep, or goat, in order to fatten it*: (K:) from بَنَّ بِالْمَكَانِ. (TA.)

4. ابنّ بالْمَكَانِ, (T, Ṣ, M, Mṣb, K,) inf. n. إِبْنَانٌ; (Lth, T;) and بَنَّ ♦ بِهِ, aor. يَبِنُّ, (M, K,) inf. n. بَنٌّ; (M, TA;) but Aṣ allows only the former verb; (M, TA;) *He remained, continued, stayed, dwelt, or abode, in the place*; (T, Ṣ, M, Mṣb, K;) *he kept, or clave, to the place*. (Lth, T, TA.) Accord. to Z, it is a tropical meaning, from the بَنَّة [i. e. odour] of the camels or cattle [of a stationary people]. (TA.) — And أَبَنَّتِ السَّحَابَةُ † *The cloud remained, or continued raining*, (M, TA,) *some days*, (TA,) *and kept its place*. (M.)

5. تبنّن *He acted, or proceeded, deliberately, not hastily*. (T, TA.) An Arab of the desert said to Shureyḥ, on his desiring to pronounce judgment against him hastily, تَبَنَّنْ, meaning *Act thou deliberately, not hastily*. (T.)

بَنْ is a dial. var. of بَلْ, (M, K,) and so is لَا بَنْ of لَا بَلْ; or, as some say, formed by substitution [of ن for ل; not peculiar to any dialect]. (M.) One says, بَنْ وَٱللّٰهِ لَا آتِيكَ [*Nay, by God, I will not come to thee*]: Fr says that it is of the dial. of Benoo-Saad and Kelb; and that he had heard the Báhilees say, لَا بَنْ, meaning بَلْ [or لَا بَلْ]: but IJ says, I do not trace up بَنْ [to any authority] as being an independent word of a particular dialect. (TA.) — [ابْنُ and بِنْ and بُنْ, for ابَنَ &c.: see art. بنى.]

بُنٌّ [*Coffee-berries*, whether *green* or *roasted, whole* or *reduced to powder by pounding or grinding*;] expl. in the K as شَىْءٌ يُتَّخَذُ كَٱلْمُرِّىِّ [*a certain thing that is taken like the condiment termed* مُرِّىّ, which is used to give relish to food or to quicken the appetite]; Ibn-Es-Sim'ánee says, هُوَ شَىْءٌ فِى الكَوَامِيخِ [app. meaning *it is a thing reckoned among what are termed* كواميخ, pl. of كَامَخ, which signifies the same as مُرِّىّ, for it seems that فى is here used in the sense of مِنْ, or it may be a mistranscription for مِنْ]; the physician Dáwood says, it is *the produce of certain trees in El-Yemen; the berries thereof are put into the earth in* آذار [the Syrian month corresponding to March, O. S.], *and it increases, and is gathered in* أَبِيب [the Coptic month commencing on the 25th of June, O. S.; the 7th of July, N. S.]; *it grows to the height of about three cubits, on a stem of the thickness of the thumb, and has a white flower, which is succeeded by a berry like the hazel-nut; sometimes it is cut like beans; and sometimes, when it is divested of its covering, it divides into two halves: it has been proved to be good for alleviating humidities, and cough, and phlegm, and defluxions, and for opening obstructions, and causing a flow of the urine: when roasted*, [and pounded or *ground*,] *and well cooked*, [i. e. *boiled in water*,] *it is now commonly known by the name of* قَهْوَة. (TA.) [Golius, I think, has misunderstood the explanation of this word in the K: after having given that explanation, and rendered it by "res quæ sumitur instar المرى *Múrriji*," he adds, "Pers. ابكامه Abcâma dictæ: hæc sorbitio est rei ex hordeo et frumento paratæ multa cura et arte, quam Malajesa et Halimæus describunt." He then mentions the signification of coffee-berries as a second and distinct meaning.]

بِنٌّ *A place having a fetid odour*. (Fr, T, K.) — It also signifies طِرْقٌ مِنَ الشَّحْمِ (T, K) and السَّمْنِ (K, TA: in the CK السِّمَنِ:) [said in the TA to mean قُوَّةٌ مِنْهُمَا, i. e. *Strength* arising *from fat* and *from fatness*: but I think that وَالسِّمَنِ has been added in the K in consequence of a misunderstanding, and that the meaning is *a layer of fat*; this meaning seeming to be indicated by the ex. here following, and corroborated by significations of several conjugates of طِرْق, as طَرِيقَة and طَرْق and طِرَاق &c.] One says (T, K) of a beast (دَابَّة) when it has become fat, (T,) رَكِبَهَا بِنٌّ (T, K*) and طِرْقٌ عَلَى طِرْقٍ (T) [clearly I think, meaning *Layer upon layer, of fat, has accumulated upon it*.]

بَنَّةٌ *A sweet, or pleasant, odour*; (Aṣ, AA, T, Ṣ, M, K;) *such as that of the apple* (T, M) *and the like*, (M,) *or the quince*: (T:) Sb says that it is a name for *a sweet*, or *pleasant, odour, like* خَمْطَة: (M,* TA:) and *an unpleasant odour*; (Aṣ, T, Ṣ;) *a fetid odour*; (M, K;) whence بَنَّةُ الغَزْلِ [*the odour of the yarn*] occurring in a saying of 'Alee, respecting a weaver; (M;) which shows that A'Obeyd erred in asserting it to have only the first of the foregoing significations; (IB, TA;) which Suh, in the R, assigns also to ♦ بُنَانَةٌ: (TA:) the *odour of sheep, or goats*, (Ṣ, M,) or *of camels or cattle*; (Z, TA;) and *of the dung of gazelles*; (Ṣ, K;) and *of the lodging-places of sheep or goats* and *of oxen or bulls or cows* and *of gazelles*: (T, M:) and sometimes the *lodging-places themselves, of sheep or goats*: (M, TA:) pl. (in all the senses, M) بِنَانٌ. (T, Ṣ, M, K.)

بُنِّىٌّ *A seller of* بُنّ [or *coffee-berries*]. (TA.) — Also, [vulgarly pronounced بِنِّى,] *A species of fish*; (K;) [the *cyprinus Bynni* of Forskål; described by him in his Descr. Anim. p. 71;] it is *white*, and is *the best kind* [*of fish*], and *abundant in the Nile*. (TA.)

بَنَانٌ The *fingers*; syn. أَصَابِعُ: (M, Mṣb, K:) but whether it means peculiarly the اصابع of the hand, or those of the foot also, [i. e. the *toes*,] is disputed: (TA:) or the *ends*, or *extremities, thereof*: (Ṣ, M, Mṣb, K:) said to be so called because by their means are ordered those circumstances whereby man continues in existence; from أَبَنَّ بِالْمَكَانِ: (Mṣb:) mentioned in the Kur viii. 12 because therewith one fights, and defends himself: (Er-Rághib, TA:) or it there signifies all the *limbs*, or *members, of the body*: (Aboo-Is-ḥák, M:) or the *fingers*, or *toes, and any other parts of all the limbs*, or *members*: (Zj, TA:) or it means in the Kur the شَوَى; (Lth, T, TA;) so in lxxv. 4; (M;) i. e. the *arms* or *hands* and the *legs* or *feet*: (Lth, T, TA:) accord. to El-Fárisee the meaning of the words in the Kur lxxv. 4 is, we are able to make their extremities like those of the camel, so that they should not profit by them in handicraft: (M, TA:) the n. un. is with ة; (Lth, T, Ṣ, M, K;) meaning, accord. to Lth, *a single* إِصْبَع [i. e. *finger*, or *toe*]; or, accord. to AlHeyth, the *whole* اصبع; or, as some say, the *highest* عُقْدَة [or *joint*] *of the* اصبع: (T:) the pl. of pauc. is بَنَانَاتٌ; but a pl. of mult. is sometimes used as one of pauc.; and hence the saying of the rájiz,

• خَمْسَ بَنَانٍ قَانِىِ الأَظْفَارِ •

[*Five fingers*, or *ends of fingers, intensely red* from the dye of ḥinnà *in the nails*], meaning بَنَانٌ مُخَضَّبٌ: and one says, خَمْسًا مِنَ البَنَانِ [*Fingers*, or *ends of fingers, dyed*, or *much dyed*, with ḥinnà]; for every pl. [or rather coll. gen. n.] between which and its sing., or n. un., there is no difference but ة [added in the latter] may be treated as sing. and masc. (Ṣ.) Lth cites as an ex. of the n. un.,

• لَاهُمَّ أَكْرَمْتَ بَنِى كِنَانَهْ • لَيْسَ لِحَىٍّ فَوْقَهُمْ بَنَانَهْ •

meaning [*O God, Thou hast honoured the sons of Kinánch: there belongs not to any tribe*] excellence of the measure of *a finger above them*. (T, TA.)

بَنِينٌ *Deliberate and intelligent*: (AA, T, K:) from بَنَّ بِالْمَكَانِ. (TA.)

بَنَانَةٌ n. un. of بَنَانٌ. (Lth, T, Ṣ, M, K.) — See also what next follows.

بُنَانَةٌ: see بَنَّةٌ. — Also *A meadow*, or *verdant tract of land somewhat watery*, (AA, T, M, K,) *producing herbage*, (M, K,) *and adorned with flowers*; (TA;) and so ♦ بَنَانَةٌ. (M.)

مُبِنٌّ *Remaining, continuing, staying, dwelling*, or *abiding*, in a place. (T, TA.) Applied to a mixture of urine and dung (عَبَس) upon the tail [of a camel &c.], it may mean *Cleaving*, and *sticking*: or it may be from بَنَّةٌ signifying "a fetid odour" [so as to mean *having a fetid odour*]: thus, in this case, it may be either a part. n. or a possessive epithet. (M, TA.) It signifies also *Having the odour of the dung of gazelles*; applied to a covert, or hiding-place, of those animals, among trees. (Ṣ, K.*)

بنج

2. بَنَّجَهُ, inf. n. تَبْنِيجٌ, [*He dosed him, or stupified him, with* بَنْج, q. v.;] *he gave him* بَنْج *to eat*. (K.) [See the act. part. n. below.]

بَنْجٌ [*Hyoscyamus*, or *henbane*;] an arabicized word, [said to be] from [the Persian] بَنْگ; [but see a quotation from Hammer-Purgstall, near the close of this paragraph;] *a certain plant*, (Mgh, and Ḥar p. 365,) *having an intoxicating kind of grain*, or, as some say, (Mgh,) *of which the leaves and peel and seeds torpify:* (Mgh, Ḥar:) it is said, in the Ḳánoon, (Mgh,) by Aboo-'Alee [Ibn-Seenà, or Avicenna], (Ḥar,) that *it is a poison which confuses the intellect, and annuls the memory, and occasions insanity and* [*the disorder termed*] خُنَاق [or *quinsy*]; (Mgh, Ḥar;) *and it is red, and white:* (Ḥar:) *a certain plant having a kind of grain that confuses the intellect, and occasions alienation of the mind*, or *insanity; and sometimes it intoxicates, when a man drinks it after it has been dissolved; and it is said to occasion forgetfulness:* (Mṣb:) *a certain torpifying plant, well known; different from* حَشِيشُ الحَرَافِيشِ; *disordering the intellect* (مُخَبِّطٌ لِلْعَقْلِ), *rendering insane, allaying the pains of humours and pustules, and the earache*, (Ḳ, TA,) *applied as a liniment or as a poultice;* (TA;) *the worst kind* (Ḳ, TA) *for use* (TA) *is the black; then, the red; and the safest kind is the white.* (Ḳ, TA.) [Ḳzw says that the leaves of the garden-hemp (شَهْدَانِج, or قِنَّبٌ بُسْتَانِىٌّ, the latter of which properly signifies hemp-seed,) are the بَنْج which, when eaten, disorders the intellect. And El-Idreesee applies the appellation حَشِيشِيَّة to the "Assassins." This establishes the correctness of De Sacy's opinion, that the appellation "Assassins" is derived from the vulgar pl. حَشَّاشِين, (hemp-eaters, or persons who intoxicate themselves with hemp,) for حَشَّاشِين is syn. with حَشِيشِيَّة, and the sect called by us the "Assassins" are expressly said by the Arabs to have made frequent use of بَنْج. Baron Hammer-Purgstall, correctly regarding بَنْج as hyoscyamus (or henbane), makes the following important observations, "'Bendj,' the pl. of which in Coptic is 'nibendj,' is without doubt the same plant as the 'nepenthe,' which has hitherto so much perplexed the commentators of Homer. Helen evidently brought the nepenthe from Egypt, and bendj is there still reputed to possess all the wonderful qualities which Homer attributes to it." (Trébutien, "Contes Inédits des Mille et une Nuits," tome i. p. 12, note.)] The phrase شَرِبَ البَنْجَ is used by El-Karkhee [as meaning *He drank the* بنج] because it is mixed with water; or [as meaning *he took*, or *swallowed, the* بنج,] according to the conventional language of the physicians. (Mgh.)

مُبَنِّج One *who employs a stratagem by means of food containing* بَنْج [*in order to obtain some advantage over another, by stupifying him therewith;* as the "Assassins" used to do]. (Mgh.)

بند

بَنْدٌ is a Persian word arabicized, originally signifying *A knot*, or *tie*. (TA.) — Hence, (TA,) ‡ [*Any of*] *the stops that are put between the beads of the* سُبْحَة *to mark the place where the performer of* تَسْبِيح *pauses on the occasion of a thing's diverting his attention:* so in the Comm. on the Toḥfeh by the seyyid 'Omar El-Baṣree: (MF, TA:) app. post-classical and recent. (TA.) — *A dam; a thing that stops*, or *dams*, [*water*, or] *from water* (الَّذِى يُسْكِرُ مِنَ المَآءِ). (Ḳ. [In the CḲ, يُسْكَرُ is put in the place of يُسْكِرُ. In this sense, also, it is of Persian origin.]) — *A stratagem, a trick*, or *an expedient, of which one makes use:* (T, Ḳ:) *a snare by which one snares men:* (TA in art. قمط:) pl. بُنُودٌ. (T.) You say, فُلَانٌ كَثِيرُ البُنُودِ *Such a one abounds in*, or *practises much, stratagems, tricks*, or *expedients*, (Lth, T, A,) *and mischievous*, or *calamitous, acts*. (A.) In this sense, also, it is an arabicized Persian word. (TA.) — *An enigma.* (TA.) — *A pawn that is tied* (مُنْعَقِدٌ, in the CḲ مُتَعَقِّدٌ,) *by a queen in the game of chess:* as though it confined and tied itself. (TA.) — Also a Persian word, arabicized, (Ṣ, A,) signifying *A large banner, standard*, or *ensign:* (En-Naḍr, Ṣ, A, Ḳ:) or *a banner*, or *standard*, or *an ensign, of a general*, or *leader*, (T, M,) *of the Greeks*, (M,) *under which are ten thousand men*, (T, M,) or *less*, or *more:* (T:) or *a banner*, or *standard*, or *an ensign, of horsemen:* (El-Hujeymee, T:) [in barbarous Latin *bandum;* and in Spanish, *bandera;* as mentioned by Golius; and in modern Arabic بَنْدِيرَة:] pl. as above: (Ṣ, M:) it has no pl. of pauc. (M.) — [The pl.] بُنُودٌ also signifies, in Greece, [*Provinces*, or *districts;*] *what are called* أَجْنَادٌ *in Syria, and* أَعْرَاضٌ *in El-Ḥijáz, and* كُوَرٌ *in El-'Irák, and* مَخَالِيفُ *in El-Yemen.* (Yáḳoot.)

بندر

بَنْدَرٌ [app. from the Persian بَنْدَرْ,] *A place where ships or boats anchor or moor; a port* [or *port-town:* pl. بَنَادِرُ]. (Ḳ, TA.)

بندق

Q. 1. بَنْدَقَ *He made* a thing *into* بَنَادِق [meaning *bullets*, or *little balls*], (Mgh, Ḳ,) or *like* بنادق. (TA.) ═ [In post-classical Arabic, *He shot a bullet*, or *bullets*, from a cross-bow or other weapon.] — بندق إِلَيْهِ † *He looked sharply*, or *intently, at him*, or *it*. (Ibn-'Abbád, Ḳ.)

بُنْدُقٌ [The *hazel-nut;* or *hazel-nuts;* so in the present day;] *a certain thing that is eaten;* (Mṣb;) *i. q.* جِلَّوْزٌ: (IDrd, Ḳ:) or, as some say, *like* جلّوز; *brought from an island; the best whereof is the fresh, heavy, white, and sweet in taste; the old being bad: it is beneficial as a remedy for palpitation, parched with anise-seed; and for poisons, and wasting of the kidneys, and burning of the urine; and with pepper, it excites the venereal faculty; with sugar, it removes cough; and the shell thereof, burnt, and applied as a collyrium, sharpens the sight:* (TA:) *they assert that the suspending it upon the upper arm preserves from scorpions*, (Ḳ,) i. e., *from their stinging:* (TA:) *the moistening of the top of the head of a child with the powder of it when burnt, together with oil, removes the blueness of its eyes and the redness of its hair: and the Indian kind thereof is an antidote very beneficial to the eyes:* (Ḳ, TA:) but in some copies of the Ḳ, [and so in the CḲ,] instead of لِلْعَيْنَيْنِ, we here find لِلْعِنِّينِ [*for the impotent in respect of the venereal faculty*]: (TA:) [it is said in the Mṣb that most hold the ن to be augmentative: but this is not the case; for] the word is Persian [arabicized, from فُنْدُقْ]: (Ḳ:) [it is a coll. gen. n.:] n. un. with ة: pl. بَنَادِقُ. (Mṣb.) — [Hence, *Bullets*, i. e.] *certain things that one shoots*, (Ṣ, Mṣb, Ḳ,) *made of clay:* (Mṣb:) n. un. with ة: (Ṣ, Mṣb, Ḳ:) the latter signifies *a piece of clay, made round, which one shoots*, or *casts;* or *i. q.* جُلَاهِقٌ: (Mgh:) it is said in the Shifá el-Ghaleel to be an arabicized word: (TA:) pl. as above. (Ṣ, Mṣb.) [See a prov. voce حِدَأَةٌ. Hence قَوْسُ البُنْدُقِ *The cross-bow*. In modern Arabic, بُنْدُق is also applied to *Balls of any kind of the size of hazel-nuts:* n. un. with ة.]

بُنْدُقِىٌّ *A garment*, or *piece of cloth, of fine, delicate*, or *thin, linen*. (Ṣgh, Ḳ.) [SM says,] It is most probably, in my opinion, so called in relation to the land of البُنْدُقِيَّة [or Venice]. (TA.) [In modern Arabic, *A Venetian sequin:* pl. بَنَادِقَة.]

بُنْدُقَانِىٌّ [app. a post-classical word,] *A maker of cross-bows* (قِسِىّ البُنْدُق). (El-Maḳreezee's Khiṭaṭ, art. خط البندقانيين.)

بنصر

بِنْصِرٌ The *finger that is next to the little finger;* (Ṣ in art. بصر;) [*the third finger;*] *that which is between the little and middle fingers:* (Mṣb in art. بصر, and Ḳ:) of the fem. gender: (Ḳ:) pl. بَنَاصِرُ, (Ṣ,) or بَنَاصِرَةٌ. (Mṣb.) Accord. to the author of the Ḳ, the ن is a radical letter, and therefore the mention of this word in art. بصر is wrong. (TA.)

بنفسج

بَنَفْسَجٌ, of the measure فَعَلَّلٌ, like سَفَرْجَلٌ, (Mṣb,) [an arabicized word, from the Persian بَنَفْشَه; The *violet; viola odorata* of Linn: and accord. to Forskål (Flora AEgypt. Arab. p. ciii.) applied in El-Yemen to the "*iris:*" and (p. cxx.) "*tagetes dubia?*"] what is thus called is well known: *the smelling it in its fresh state is beneficial to those who are heated by wrath* (المَحْرُورِين), *and the continual smelling of it induces good sleep: the conserve made of it is beneficial for the pleurisy* (ذَاتُ الجَنْبِ), *and for inflammation of the lungs* (ذَاتُ الرِّئَةِ), *and for cough, and for headache.* (Ḳ.)

بنق

1. بَنَقَ, (Ḳ,) aor. ـُ, inf. n. بَنْقٌ, (TḲ,) *He joined* [a thing to another thing, like as the بَنِيقَة of a shirt is joined: see the pass. part. n., below]; syn. وَصَلَ. (Ḳ.)

2. بَنَّقَ القَمِيصَ, inf. n. تَبْنِيقٌ, *He put a* بَنِيقَة *to the shirt.* (Ḳ.) — بَنَّقَ الجَعْبَةَ ‡ *He made the upper part of the quiver wide* [*by adding to it*

the like of a بَنِيقَة (see the pass. part. n., below,)], *and the lower part narrow:* (Ḳ, TA:) or *he widened its upper part, the lower part being* [or *remaining*] *narrow.* (JK.)

بَنَق : / بَنَقَة : / بَنِيق : } see what next follows.

بَنِيقَة The لِبْنَة, (AZ, Abu-l-Ḥajjáj El-Aạlam, JK, Ṣ, Ḳ,) or دِخْرِصَة, (Abu-l-'Abbás El-Aḥwal, TA,) [both of which signify the *gore*,] of a shirt, (AZ, Ṣ, Ḳ,) or of a garment; (JK;) or the دخرصة is longer than the لبنة: (Seer, TA:) and *any piece that is added in a garment or a leathern bucket to widen it:* (Abu-l-Ḥajjáj El-Aạlam, TA:) or, accord. to IDrd, the دخاريص of a shirt: (TA: [but this is app. a mistranscription for its sing. دِخْرِيص, q. v., a dial. var. of دِخْرِصَة:]) or the جُرُبَّان [or *opening at the neck and bosom*] of a shirt: (Ḳ:) جربّان is prefixed to البنيقة in a verse of Jereer, governing the latter in the gen. case, to show that both these words have the same meaning: (TA:) ↓ بَنَقَة, also, signifies the same as بنيقة; (JK, Ḳ; [in the latter of which it is mentioned in such a manner as perhaps to denote that it has only the last of the significations above; but I think that this restriction is not meant;]) and its pl. [or rather the coll. gen. n.] is ↓ بَنَق: (Ibn-'Abbád, TA:) Th mentions بَنَائِق and بُنُق, and says that the latter is a pl. pl.; [i. e., pl. of the former;] but this is unintelligible: (TA:) بَنَائِق is pl. of بَنِيقَة, (JK, Ṣ, &c.,) and syn. with دَخَارِيص. (JK.) AZ cites, from Mejnoon,

• كَمَا ضَمَّ أَزْرَارَ القَمِيصِ البَنَائِقُ •

(Ṣ, IB,) which is an inverted phrase; the meaning being,

• كَمَا ضَمَّ أَزْرَارُ القَمِيصِ البَنَائِقَا •

[*Like as the buttons of the shirt draw together the gores:* if the last word mean *the gores*]: or, if the بنيقة of the shirt be really its جربّان, the meaning is intelligible [without inversion]; for its جربّان is the *part around the neck, upon which are sewed the buttons;* and when one desires to draw it together, he puts its buttons into the loops, and so draws together the bosom [of the shirt, with its buttons,] to the uppermost part of the chest. (IB, TA.) Aboo-'Amr Esh-Sheybánee explains البنائق, here, as meaning the *loops into which the buttons are inserted;* and accord. to this explanation the meaning is plain, not requiring the supposition of inversion nor of deviation from the usual way: but the first explanation is that which is generally given. (TA.) In the saying,

• قَدْ أَغْتَدِي وَالدَّهْرُ ذُو بَنِيقِ ↓ •

[in the last word of which, ة is elided; lit., *Sometimes I go forth early in the morning, when the time has a* بَنِيقَة;] Lth says that the whiteness of the dawn is likened to the whiteness of the بنيقة; citing another verse, in which a shirt is described as having white بنائق. (TA.)

جَعْبَةٌ مُبَنَّقَةٌ ‡ *A quiver that is widened:* (Ibn-'Abbád, TA:) or *in the upper part of which is added what resembles a* بَنِيقَة, *to enlarge it.* (A, TA.) — طَرِيقٌ مُبَنَّقٌ ‡ *A wide road.* (TA.)

أَرْضٌ مَبْنُوقَةٌ † *Land joined* (مَوْصُولَة) *to other land, like as the* بَنِيقَة *of a shirt is joined.* (ISd, TA.) And مَفَازَةٌ مَبْنُوقَةٌ, (JK,) or مَبْنُوقَةٌ بِأُخْرَى, (TA,) †[*A desert,* or *a desert in which is no water, &c.,*] *joined to another.* (JK, TA.)

بنم

اِبْنِمٌ or اَبْنُمٌ, and اِبْنَمٌ or اَبْنَمٌ; and اِبْنِمَا for اَبْنُمَا: see اِبْنٌ, in art. بنى.

بنو

1. بَنَا, aor. يَبْنُو: see art. بنى.

اِبْنٌ, held by some to be originally بَنَوٌ: see art. بنى.

بُنُوَّة : / بَنَوِيّ : } see art. بنى.

بنى

1. بَنَاهُ, (T, Ṣ, M, &c.,) aor. يَبْنِى, (M, Mṣb,) and يَبْنُو, but the former is the more common, (M,) [or rather the only form commonly known,] inf. n. بِنَآءٌ (T, Ṣ, M, Mgh, Ḳ) and بِنًا (T, and TA as from the M [but it is not in the transcript of the M in the TT]) and بَنْىٌ and بُنْيَانٌ and بِنْيَةٌ and بِنَايَةٌ, (M, Ḳ,) *He built it; framed it; constructed it; contr. of* هَدَمَهُ; (M, Ḳ;) namely, a house, (Ṣ, Mgh, Mṣb,) or tent, (Ṣ,* Mṣb,) &c.; (Mṣb;) as also ↓ ابتناه, (Ṣ, M, Mṣb, Ḳ,) and ↓ بنّاه; (M, Ḳ;) or the last has teshdeed given to it to denote muchness, or frequency, or repetition, of the action, or its application to many objects; and hence you say, بَنَّى قُصُورًا [*He built palaces,* or *pavilions:* or *he raised them high:* see the pass. part. n. below]. (Ṣ, TA.) AḤn speaks of a kind of plank as being used فِى بِنَآءِ السُّفُنِ [*in the construction of ships*]: but بِنَآءٌ is originally used only in relation to that which does not grow; as stone, and clay, and the like. (M.) You say also, بَنَى أَرْضًا, for بَنَى فِى أَرْضٍ [*He built in,* or *upon, land*]. (Mgh.) — [Hence,] بَنَى عَلَى أَهْلِهِ, (T, Ṣ, M, Mṣb, Ḳ,) or عَلَى ٱمْرَأَتِهِ, (Mgh,) and بَنَى بِهَا also, (M, Mgh, Mṣb, Ḳ,) accord. to IDrd (Mgh, Mṣb) and IJ, (M,) and occurring in traditions and elsewhere, though said in the Ṣ to be vulgar, (IAth, MF,) and said to be so by ISk, (T, Mṣb,) and by some said to be not allowable, (M,) but the former is the more chaste, (Mṣb,) inf. n. بِنَآءٌ; (Ṣ, TA;) as also ↓ ابتنى, (Ḳ,) i. e. ابتنى عليها, (ISk, Mṣb,) or ابتنى بها, (IJ, M,) *He had his wife conducted to him on the occasion of the marriage:* (ISk, T, Ṣ, Mṣb, Ḳ:) or *he went in to his wife* [*for the first time*]: (Mgh, Mṣb:) originating from the fact that the bridegroom used, on that occasion, to pitch a tent for her, (ISk, T, Ṣ, Mgh, Mṣb,) a new tent, (Mgh, Mṣb,) and furnish it with what was requisite, (Mṣb,) or a new tent was set up for him, (Mgh, Mṣb,) in honour of him. (Mṣb.) [See also بَيْتٌ.] — بِنَايَةٌ is sometimes used in relation to nobility: (M, Ḳ:) and the verb thus used is بَنَى, as above, (T, M,) having [also] بُنًى for its inf. n., (IAạr, T,) and بِنَآءٌ; held by many to be tropical, but by some to be proper. (MF.) Lebeed says,

• فَبَنَى لَنَا بَيْتًا رَفِيعًا سَمْكُهُ • فَسَمَا إِلَيْهِ كَهْلُهَا وَغُلَامُهَا •

(M) *And He* (namely, God,) *hath built for us a house of nobility of lofty pitch, and its* (the tribe's) *middle-aged and its youth have risen to it:* i. e., all of them have attained to high degrees. (EM, p. 180.) — بَنَى بَدَنَهُ *It* (food) *fattened his body,* (Ḳ,) *and made it large:* (TA:) and بَنَى لَحْمَهُ, (T, M, Ḳ,) aor. يَبْنِى, (TA,) inf. n. بِنَآءٌ, (M,) or بَنْىٌ, (TA,) *It* (food) *made his flesh to grow,* (T, M, Ḳ,) *and to become large.* (T, TA.) — بَنَى الرَّجُلَ *He reared, brought up,* or *educated, the man;* (M, Ḳ;) as also ↓ ابتناه. (M.) — [بَنَى كَلِمَةً, inf. n. بِنَآءٌ, *He formed a word.* — And *He made a word indeclinable, so as to end invariably with a quiescent letter* or *with a particular vowel.*] بِنَآءُ كَلِمَةٍ [when the former word is considered as the inf. n. of the pass. form بُنِىَ, generally] signifies *A word's keeping always the same mode of termination, ending with a quiescent letter* or *with a particular vowel, not by reason of any governing word:* (M, Ḳ:) as though the word resembled a fixed, immoveable building. (M.) [You say, بُنِيَتْ عَلَى السُّكُونِ *It was made indeclinable, with a quiescent letter for its termination;* and عَلَى الفَتْحِ *with fet-ḥ for its termination;* &c. — And in like manner you say, بَنَى القَصِيدَةَ عَلَى البَآءِ, &c., *He made the* قصيدة *to have* ب, &c., *for its rhyme-letter,* or *its chief rhyme-letter.*] — بَنَتِ القَوْسُ عَلَى وَتَرِهَا *The bow clave to its string* (T, Ṣ, Ḳ) *so that it* (the latter) *almost broke.* (T, Ṣ.) [See the part. n. below.]

2: see 1, first sentence.

4. ابناه *He made him to build, frame,* or *construct, a house,* or *tent:* (Ṣ:) or *he gave him a building:* or *he gave him that wherewith to build a house:* (M, Ḳ:) and ابناه بَيْتًا *he gave him a house,* or *tent, to build* or *frame* or *construct.* (T.) It is said in a prov., المِعْزَى تُبْهِى وَلَا تُبْنِى [*Goats rend,* or *make holes, and render vacant, and do not afford materials for fabricating tents*]; i. e., they do not yield hair of which a tent is fabricated; (T, Ṣ;*) for the tents of the Arabs [of the desert] are of the kind called طِرَاف, made of skin, and أَخْبِيَة, made of wool or of camels' fur, and not of شَعَر [by which is especially meant goats' hair], (Ṣ,) or, as is found in the handwriting of Aboo-Sahl, of wool or of skin: (TA:) or the meaning is, *goats rend* tents, or *pierce them with holes,* by their leaping upon them, (T and Ṣ in art. بهو,) so that they cannot be inhabited, (Ṣ in that art.,) *and do not aid in the fabrication of tents;* for the goats of the Arabs of the desert

have short hair, not long enough to be spun; whereas the goats of the cold countries, and of the people of the fertile regions, have abundant hair, and of this the Akrád [or Kurdees] fabricate their tents. (T.) — [Hence,] *He introduced him to his wife* [*on the occasion of his marriage*]: whence the saying of 'Alee, مَتَى تُبْنِينِي, accord. to IAth properly meaning مَتَى تَجْعَلُنِي أَبْنِي بِزَوْجَتِي [*When wilt thou make me to have my wife conducted to me?* or, *to go in to my wife?*]. (TA.)

5. تَبَنَّتْ, said of a woman sitting, (T, TA,) *She became like a tent* (T, IAth, Ḳ,* TA) *of the kind called* مِبْنَاةٌ, (T, TA,) i. e., *a* قُبَّة *of skin; by reason of her fatness,* (T, IAth, TA,) *and largeness,* (T, TA,) or *fleshiness:* (IAth, TA:) or *she parted her legs;* as though from مِبْنَاةٌ, i. e. a قُبَّة of skin, which, when pitched, is spread out by the ropes: so this woman, sitting cross-legged, spread apart her legs. (T, TA.) And تَبَنَّى, said of a camel's hump, *It became fat.* (M.) — تبنّاهُ *He adopted him as a son:* (Ṣ, Ḳ:) or *he asserted him to be,* or *claimed him as, a son:* (M:) and تَبَنَّى بِهِ signifies the same. (Zj, TA.)

8. ابتنى: see 1, in three places. — Also *It became built, framed,* or *constructed.* (Mṣb.)

بِنْتٌ; pl. بَنَاتٌ: fem. of اِبْنٌ, which see, in three places.

بُنًى : } see بِنَآءٌ.
بِنًى : }

بَنَاةُ اللَّحْمِ, (IB, TA,) the former of which words is incorrectly written in the Ḳ بنات, (TA,) A girl *whose flesh has been made to grow and become large:* (IB, Ḳ, TA: [in the CḲ, مَبْنِيَّةٌ is erroneously put for مُبْنِيَتُهُ:]) or, accord. to a learned scholiast, this is a mistake of IB, and the meaning is *sweet in odour;* i. e. *sweet in the odour of the flesh.* (TA.)

بَنَاتٌ: pl. of بِنْتٌ; and sometimes of اِبْنٌ: see اِبْنٌ.

بَنُونَ: pl. of اِبْنٌ, which see below.

بُنْيَةٌ: see بِنَآءٌ.

بِنْيَةٌ *A form, mode,* or *manner, of building* or *framing* or *construction;* a word like مِشْيَةٌ and رِكْبَةٌ. (T, TA.) [The *form,* or *mode of formation,* of a word.] *Natural constitution:* as in the phrase, فُلَانٌ صَحِيحُ البِنْيَةِ [*Such a one is sound in natural constitution*]. (Ṣ.) — See also بِنَآءٌ.

بِنْتِىٌّ: see what next follows.

بَنَوِىٌّ *Of,* or *relating to, a son;* rel. n. of اِبْنٌ; as also ↓ اِبْنِىٌّ [with ا when connected with a preceding word]: (Ṣ, Mṣb:) the latter is allowable, (Mṣb,) and used by some. (Ṣ.) And *Of,* or *relating to, a daughter;* rel. n. of بِنْتٌ; as also ↓ بِنْتِىٌّ: (Ṣ, M, Mṣb, Ḳ:) the latter accord. to Yoo; (Ṣ, M;) but rejected by Sb. (TA.) — Also *Of,* or *relating to, what are termed* بُنَيَّاتُ الطَّرِيقِ, i. e., *the small roads that branch off from the main road.* (Ṣ.)

بُنْيَانٌ and بُنْيَانَةٌ: see what next follows.

بِنَآءٌ [originally an inf. n.: (see 1, first sentence:) then applied to *A building; a structure; an edifice;*] *a thing that is built,* or *constructed;* pl. أَبْنِيَةٌ, and pl. pl. أَبْنِيَاتٌ: (M, Ḳ:) and ↓ بُنْيَانٌ [also] has this meaning; (Mṣb;) [and is likewise originally an inf. n.;] or this signifies *a wall;* syn. حَائِطٌ; (Ṣ;) or it may be a pl., [or rather a coll. gen. n., meaning *buildings, structures, edifices,* or *walls,*] of which the sing. [or n. un.] is ↓ بُنْيَانَةٌ, and as such may be masc. and fem.: (Er-Rághib, TA:) ↓ بِنْيَةٌ and ↓ بُنْيَةٌ also signify [the same as بِنَآءٌ as explained above; or] *a thing that one has built, framed,* or *constructed;* (M, Ḳ;) or, accord. to some, the former of these two relates to objects of the senses, and the latter to objects of the mind, to glory or honour or the like; (MF, TA;) and their pls. are ↓ بِنًى and ↓ بُنًى; (Ḳ;) or, accord. to the Ṣ and M, these two appear to be sings.; (TA;) [or they may be pls. or sings.; for J says that] البُنَى is like البِنَى; one says, بُنْيَةٌ and بُنًى, and بِنْيَةٌ and بِنًى; (Ṣ;) [and ISd says that] بِنْيَةٌ and بُنْيَةٌ signify as above, and so بِنًى and بُنًى; or, accord. to Aboo-Is-ḥáḳ, بِنًى is pl. of بِنْيَةٌ; or it may be used by poetic licence for بِنَآءٌ: (M:) accord. to IAạr, بِنًى signifies *buildings,* or *structures, of clay:* and also [*tents*] *of wool;* (T;) and بِنَآءٌ likewise signifies *a tent* (M, TA) *in which the Arabs of the desert dwell, in the desert,* (TA,) *such as is called* خِبَآءٌ; (M, TA;*) and طِرَافٌ and قُبَّةٌ and مِضْرَبٌ are names applied to dwellings of the same kind; (TA;) pl. أَبْنِيَةٌ: (M:) the *moveable dwelling, such as the* خَيْمَة *and* مِظَلَّة *and* فُسْطَاط *and* سُرَادِق *and the like,* is called بِنَآءٌ as being likened to the building of burnt bricks and of clay and of gypsum. (M.) [See also بِنْيَةٌ.] — Also The *roof,* or *ceiling,* of a house or chamber or the like; as in the Ḳur [ii. 20], الَّذِى جَعَلَ لَكُمُ الأَرْضَ فِرَاشًا وَالسَّمَآءَ بِنَآءً [*Who hath made for you the earth as a bed, and the heaven as a roof,* or *ceiling*]: (Ṣ, [but wanting in some copies,] and Jel:) so says AZ: (Ṣ:) or the meaning here is, *as a tent* (قُبَّة) pitched over you. (Bḍ.) — And The *body, with the limbs* or *members.* (TA.) — And *i. q.* نِطْعٌ [*A thing that is spread on the ground to serve as a table for food &c., made of leather;* like مِبْنَاةٌ]: occurring in a trad., where it is mentioned as spread on the ground, on a day of rain, for Moḥammad to pray upon: so says Sh. (T.)

بُنَىٌّ, [said to be] originally بُنَيْوٌ, *A little son;* [used as a term of endearment;] (Mṣb;) dim. of اِبْنٌ. (Ṣ, Mgh, Mṣb.) You say, يَا بُنَىِّ and يَا بُنَىَّ [*O my little son,* or *O my child*], with kesr to the ى and with fet-ḥ also; like as you say, يَا أَبَتِ and يَا أَبَتَ [which see in art. ابو, voce أَبٌ]. (Fr, Ṣ, Ḳ.) [The fem. is بُنَيَّةٌ *A little daughter;* dim. of بِنْتٌ. And hence,] — بُنَيَّاتُ الطَّرِيقِ *The small roads that branch off from the main road;* (Ṣ;) *what are termed* التُّرَّهَاتُ. (Ṣ, Ḳ.) — The Arabs say, الرِّفْقُ بُنَىُّ الحِلْمِ, meaning الرفق *is like* الحلم. (IAạr, ISd.)

بُنُوَّةٌ *Sonship:* (Lth, Zj, Ṣ, M, Mṣb, Ḳ:) [it may be originally بُنُويَةٌ, for Az says, app. on the authority of Zj,] it is not a decisive proof that the last radical is و, since they say فُتُوَّةٌ, though the dual [of the word from which this is derived] is فَتَيَانِ; (T;) [and ISd says that] بُنُوَّةٌ is thus because of the ḍammeh. (M.)

البَنِيَّةُ [properly *The building,* like البِنَآءُ &c.: but particularly applied to] *the Kaạbeh;* (Ṣ, M, Ḳ;) because of its nobleness. (M, Ḳ.) One says, لَا وَرَبِّ هٰذِهِ البَنِيَّةِ مَا كَانَ كَذَا وَكَذَا [*No, by the Lord of this building* (the Kaạbeh), *such and such things were not*]: (Ṣ, TA:) and this was a common form of oath. (TA.) The Kaạbeh is also called بَنِيَّةُ إِبْرَاهِيمَ [*The building of Abraham*]; because he built it. (TA.)

بَنَّآءٌ *A builder;* [meaning *one whose business is that of building;*] *an architect.* (M.) [See also what next follows.]

بَانٍ [*Building, framing,* or *constructing*]: accord. to A'Obeyd, its pl. is أَبْنَآءٌ; and in like manner, أَجْنَآءٌ is pl. of جَانٍ: and hence the prov., أَبْنَاؤُهَا أَجْنَاؤُهَا, (M,) or أَجْنَاؤُهَا أَبْنَاؤُهَا, i. e. *The injurers thereof,* meaning this house (هٰذِهِ الدَّار), *by demolishing it, are the builders thereof.* (Ṣ in art. جنى.) ISd says, I am of opinion that these two pls. are not used except in this prov.: and J says, in art. جنى, I think that the prov. is originally جُنَاتُهَا بُنَاتُهَا; but IB affirms that it is not so: and he says that the prov. is applied to him who does, or makes, a thing without consideration, and commits a fault therein, which he repairs by undoing what he has done or made: it originated from the fact that the daughter of a certain king of El-Yemen, during his absence on a military expedition, built, by the advice of others, a house, which he, disliking it, commanded them to demolish. (TA in art. جنى. [See also Freytag's Arab. Prov. i. 294.]) — *A bridegroom:* from بَنَى عَلَى أَهْلِهِ [q. v.]. (TA.) And hence, *Any one going in to his wife.* (Ṣ, TA.) — قَوْسٌ بَانِيَةٌ *A bow cleaving to its string* (T, Ṣ, M, Ḳ) *so that it* (the latter) *almost breaks;* (T, Ṣ, M;) the doing of which is a fault; (M;) *contr. of* بَائِنَةٌ [q. v.]: (Ṣ and M in art. بين:) and so ↓ بَانَاةٌ (T, M, Ḳ) in the dial. of Ṭeiyi: (T, M:) or the latter signifies *widely separate from its string* [like بَائِنَةٌ]. (TA.)

بَانَاةٌ: see بَانٍ. — Also, (in [some of] the copies of the Ḳ erroneously written بانات, TA,) A man *bending himself over his bow-string when shooting.* (M, Ḳ.) — And *Small* نَبْل [or *arrows*]. (M and TA in art. بين.)

بَانِيَةٌ fem. of بَانٍ [q. v.]. — Also sing. of بَوَانٍ, (TA,) which signifies The *ribs of* [*the breast,* or *of the part thereof called*] *the* زَوْر: (M, Ḳ:) or the *bones of the breast:* or the *shoulder-blades and the four legs:* (TA:) and the *legs* of a she-camel. (M, Ḳ.) One says, [likening a man to a camel lying down,] أَلْقَى بَوَانِيَهُ, meaning *He took up his abode, and settled,* (T, M, Ḳ,) in a place; like أَلْقَى عَصَاهُ. (T, M.) أَلْقَى الشَّأْمُ بَوَانِيَهُ [meaning *Syria became in a settled state*] occurs in a trad. as related by A'Obeyd: and if he said بَوَانَهُ, it would be allowable; بَوَائِنُ being pl. of بُوان, [i. e. بُوَانٌ or بِوَانٌ,] which is a name for any tent-pole except in the middle of the بَيْت, which has three poles. (T.) And it is said in another trad., أَلْقَتِ السَّمَآءُ بَرَكَ بَوَانِيهَا, meaning *The sky cast down the rain that it contained.* (TA.)

اِبْنٌ, meaning *A son;* (M, Mgh, Ḳ;) because he is the father's building, made to be so by God; (Er-Rághib, TA;) and ‡ *a son's son;* and ‡ *a descendant more remote;* (Mṣb;) is with a conjunctive ا [when not immediately preceded by a quiescence, written آبْنٌ]; (Zj, T, M;) [and when immediately preceded by the proper name of a man and immediately followed by the proper name of his parent, written without the ا, as in زَيْدُ بْنُ عَمْرٍو *Zeyd the son of 'Amr* (in which case it should also be observed that the former proper name is without tenween); unless the words compose a proposition, as in زَيْدٌ آبْنُ عَمْرٍو *Zeyd is the son of 'Amr;* or in the case of an interrogation, as in هَلْ زَيْدٌ آبْنُ عَمْرٍو *Is Zeyd the son of 'Amr?*]: the pl. is ▼ بَنُونَ (T, Ṣ, Mgh, Mṣb) in the nom. case, and بَنِينَ in the accus. and gen.; (Mgh;) and أَبْنَآءٌ, (T, Ṣ, M, Mgh, Mṣb, Ḳ,) which is a pl. of pauc.: (Mṣb:) [and hence it is argued that] the sing. is of the measure فَعَلٌ with the final radical letter elided and the conjunctive ا prefixed; (M;) originally بَنَيٌ, (M, Ḳ,) with ى, as we judge, because [the aor.] يَبْنِي is more common than يَبْنُو: (M:) or originally بَنَوٌ, (Ṣ, Mṣb, Ḳ,) with two fet-ḥahs, because it has بَنُونَ for a pl., and the perfect pl. does not admit of change [in its vowels beyond that which is here made in بَنُونَ for بَنَوُونَ]; (Mṣb;) and because it has for a pl. أَبْنَآءٌ, like as جَمَلٌ has أَجْمَالٌ; (Ṣ;) and the elided letter is و, (Akh, T, Ṣ,) as in أَبٌ and أَخٌ, (Ṣ,) because و is more commonly elided than ى; (Akh, T;) or because the fem. is بِنْتٌ and [that of أَخٌ is] أُخْتٌ; for we do not see this ه [or ت] affixed in the fem. except when و is elided in the masc., as is shown by هَنَوَاتٌ and أَخَوَاتٌ; (Ṣ;) though بُنُوَّةٌ is not a decisive proof that the last radical is و, for a reason stated above in the explanation of it: (T:) or, as some say, it is originally بِنْوٌ, with kesr to the ب, like حِمْلٌ, because they say بِنْتٌ, and a change [of a vowel] in a case of this kind is rare: (Mṣb:) [but J says,] it may not be of the measure فِعْلٌ nor فُعْلٌ, because it has بَنُونَ, with fet-ḥ to the بَ, for a pl.; nor of the measure فَعْلٌ, because this has [generally] for its [broken] pl. أَفْعُلٌ or فُعُولٌ: (Ṣ:) Zj says that it is originally بَنَيٌ or بَنَوٌ, or it may be originally بَنًا; that it is app. the last accord. to those who say بَنُونَ; and that أَبْنَآءٌ may be pl. of the measure فَعَلٌ and of فِعْلٌ; that بِنْتٌ favours its being of the latter; but that it may be of the measure فَعَلٌ changed to فِعْلٌ, as فَعَلٌ is changed to فُعْلٌ in the case of أُخْتٌ. (T.) Beside the pls. mentioned above, اِبْنٌ has a quasi-pl. n., namely ▼ أَبْنَى, of the same measure as أَعْمَى; (Mgh, TA;*) a sing. denoting the pl.: or, as some say, اِبْنٌ has for pls. أَبْنَآءٌ and أَبْنَى. (TA.) Lḥ mentions the phrase, هٰؤُلَآءِ أَبْنَا أَبْنَائِهِمْ [or أَبْنَى ابنائهم *These are the sons of their sons*]. (M.) Sometimes م is affixed to اِبْنٌ [so that it becomes ▼ اِبْنَمٌ or اِبْنُمٌ at the beginning of a sentence, and ▼ آبْنَمٌ or آبْنُمٌ in other cases]: the word is then doubly declinable [like آمْرُؤٌ or آمْرَأٌ]: you say, هٰذَا آبْنُمٌ [*This is a son*], and رَأَيْتُ آبْنَمًا [*I saw a son*], and مَرَرْتُ بِآبْنِمٍ [*I passed by a son*]; making the ن similarly declinable to the م; and the ا is with kesr in every case [when the word commences a sentence, whether you make the word doubly declinable or not]: (AHeyth,* Ṣ:) [for] some make it singly declinable, leaving the ن with fet-ḥ in every case [as the ر in امْرَأٌ or آمْرَأٌ]; saying, هٰذَا آبْنَمُكَ [*This is thy son*], and رَأَيْتُ آبْنَمَكَ [*I saw thy son*], and مَرَرْتُ بِآبْنَمِكَ [*I passed by thy son*]. (AHeyth, TA.) Ḥassán says,

* وَلَدْنَا بَنِى العَنْقَآءِ وَٱبْنَىْ مُحَرِّقٍ *
* فَأَكْرِمْ بِنَا خَالًا وَأَكْرِمْ بِنَا ٱبْنَمَا ▼ *

[*We begot the sons of El-'Anḳà, and the two sons of Moḥarriḳ; and how generous are we as a maternal uncle! and how generous are we as a son!*], (Ṣ, Ḳ,*) i. e., آبْنًا: the م is augmentative, and the hemzeh [or rather ا] is that of conjunction. (Ḳ.) And Ru-beh says,

* بُكَآءَ ثَكْلَى فَقَدَتْ حَمِيمَا * فَهْىَ تُنَادِي بِأَبِي وَٱبْنِيمَا ▼ *

[*As the weeping of a bereft woman, who has lost a relation, therefore she calls out, With my father would I ransom thee, and a son*]; meaning آبْنِمَا. (TA.) The fem. of اِبْنٌ is ▼ اِبْنَةٌ or آبْنَةٌ [with the conjunctive ا when not commencing a sentence] and ▼ بِنْتٌ [meaning *A daughter;* and † *any female descendant*]: (T, Ṣ, M, Mgh, Mṣb, Ḳ:) accord. to Sb, (M,) اِبْنَةٌ is formed from اِبْنٌ by affixing ه [or ة]; but not so بِنْتٌ; for this is formed by affixing ى as a letter of quasi-coordination, and then substituting for it ت: (M, Ḳ:) [but if the ت be substituted for ى, it seems more probable that the ى is the final radical:] or, as some say, the ت is substituted for و: (M:) [Mṭr says,] the ت is substituted for the final radical: (Mgh:) accord. to Ks, it is originally with ه [or ة], because it has a fem. meaning: (IAạr, Mṣb:) [my own opinion is most agreeable with this of Ks; and with that of Zj, which will be mentioned below; or, perhaps, is identical with that of Zj: I think it most probable that, as اِبْنٌ is generally held to be originally بَنَوٌ or بَنَيٌ, so اِبْنَةٌ and بِنْتٌ are both originally بَنَوَةٌ or بَنَيَةٌ, and that بِنْتٌ is formed from اِبْنَةٌ by suppressing the alif, transferring its kesreh to the ب, making the ن quiescent, and changing the ة into ت, which is therefore said to be not the sign of the fem. gender, either because it is not ة, but is a substitute for ة, or because it is preceded by a quiescent letter:] AḤn says that the ت is substituted for the final radical letter, which is و; and that it is not the sign of the fem. gender, because the letter [next] before it is quiescent: this [he says] is the opinion of Sb, and is the right opinion; for he says that if you were to use it as the proper name of a man, you would make it perfectly decl.; and if the ت were to denote the fem. gender, the name would not be perfectly decl.: (TA:) and the same is said respecting the ت in أُخْتٌ: (TA in art. اخو:) this ت remains in a case of pause (Ks, IAạr, Ṣ, Mṣb) as in the case of the connexion of the word with a word following: (Ṣ:) but one should not say اِبْنَتٌ, (Th, T, Ṣ,) because the ا is required only on account of the quiescence of the ب, and is therefore dropped when this is made movent: (Ṣ:) Zj says that, in forming the pl. of بِنْتٌ [and of اِبْنَةٌ], the sing. is reduced to its original form, which is فَعْلَةٌ [as I find it written in the transcript from the T in the TT, but it may be a mistake for فَعَلَةٌ,] with the last radical letter suppressed: (T in TT:) the pl. is بَنَاتٌ (T, Ṣ, Mṣb) alone: (Ṣ:) [and this is generally treated as a fem. pl. of the perfect, or sound, kind, although the ت in بِنْتٌ is said to be not a sign of the fem. gender; so that you say, رَأَيْتُ بَنَاتِكَ *I saw thy daughters;* but sometimes] one says, رَأَيْتُ بَنَاتَكَ, with fet-ḥ [as the case-ending], treating the ت as a radical letter. (Ṣ.) It is said in the Bári' that when men and women are mixed together, the masc. pl. is made predominant; so that one says, بَنُو فُلَانٍ [meaning *The sons and daughters,* or *the children, of such a one*]; and even, اِمْرَأَةٌ مِنْ بَنِى تَمِيمٍ [*A woman of the children of Temeem*]; and accordingly, if بَنُو فُلَانٍ is applied to denote the persons to whom a legacy is left, the males and the females are included therein. (Mṣb.) —— When اِبْنٌ is applied to that which is not a human being, (IAmb, Mṣb,) to an irrational being, (Mṣb,) it has for its pl. بَنَاتٌ: (IAmb, Mṣb:) thus the pl. of اِبْنُ مَخَاضٍ [*A young male camel in his second year*] is بَنَاتُ مَخَاضٍ: (Mgh, Mṣb:) that of اِبْنُ لَبُونٍ [*A male camel that has entered upon his third year*] is بَنَاتُ لَبُونٍ: (Mṣb:) and that of اِبْنُ نَعْشٍ [*Any one of the stars of the tail of Ursa Major* or *of that of Ursa Minor*] is بَنَاتُ نَعْشٍ; but sometimes, by poetic licence, بَنُو نَعْشٍ: and hence, or to make a distinction between the males and the females, the lawyers say, بَنُو اللَّبُونِ. (IAmb, Mṣb.) —— ▼ بَنَاتٌ also signifies ‡ *Dolls with which young girls play:* (Ṣ, Mgh, Ḳ:) sing. بِنْتٌ. (Mgh.) It occurs in this sense in a trad., in which 'Áïsheh speaks of her playing therewith (Ṣ, Mgh) when, being nine years of age, she was conducted as a bride to Moḥammad. (Mgh.) —— اِبْنٌ is often prefixed to some other noun (T, M, Mṣb) that particularizes its signification, because of a close connexion between the two meanings: (Mṣb:) and so is ▼ بِنْتٌ. (T, M.) [Most of the compounds thus formed will be found explained in the arts. to which belong the nouns that occupy the second place. The following are among the more common, and are therefore here mentioned, as exs. of different kinds.] — اِبْنُ الطِّينِ [*The son of earth*, or *clay*, meaning] *Adam.* (T.) اِبْنُ الطَّرِيقِ and اِبْنُ اللَّيْلِ *The thief*, or *robber.* (T.) Also the former, *The wayfarer*, or *traveller;* (Er-Rághib, TA;) and so اِبْنُ السَّبِيلِ. (Mṣb, Er-Rághib.) اِبْنُ حَرْبٍ *A warrior:* (Er-Rághib, TA:) and اِبْنُ الحَرْبِ [*the warrior;* or] *he who suffices for war, and who defends.* (Mṣb.) اِبْنُ الدُّنْيَا *The rich man.* (Mṣb.) — اِبْنُ آوَى [*The jackal;*] *a certain beast of prey.* (TA.) اِبْنُ عِرْسٍ *The* سُرْعُوب [or *weasel*]. (TA.) — اِبْنُ أَدِيمٍ *A skin for water or milk made of one hide;* and اِبْنُ أَدِيمَيْنِ *one made of two hides;* and اِبْنُ ثَلَاثَةِ آدِمَةٍ *one made of three hides.* (T.) — اِبْنَةُ الجَبَلِ *The echo.* (T.) — بَنَاتُ بِئْسٍ and بَنَاتُ طَبَقٍ and بَنَاتُ أَوْدَكَ and بَنَاتُ بَرْحٍ *Calamities*, or *misfortunes.* (T.) — Ru-beh said of a man who was mentioned to him, كَانَ إِحْدَى بَنَاتِ مَسَاجِدِ ٱللّٰهِ; as though he asserted that *He was one of the pebbles of the mosque* [or rather *of the mosques of God*]. (Ṣ.)

اِبْنَةٌ or اَبْنَةٌ: fem. of اِبْنٌ, which see.

اِبْنَمٌ and اِبْنُمٌ, or اَبْنَمٌ and اَبْنُمٌ: see اِبْنٌ, in three places.

أَبْنَى: quasi-pl. n. of اِبْنٌ, which see.

اِبْنِىٌّ: see بَنَوِىٌّ.

اِبْنِيمَا, for اَبْنِمَا: see a verse cited voce اِبْنٌ.

أُبَيْنٌ [an unused, or unusual, dim. of اِبْنٌ]: see what next follows.

أُبَيْنٌ, of the same measure as أُعَيْمٍ, is the dim. of أَبْنَى, which is like أَعْمَى, (Sb, IB, Mgh,) and is quasi-pl. of اِبْنٌ. (Mgh.) Mohammad is related, in a trad., to have said, أُبَيْنِى لَا تَرْمُوا جَمْرَةَ العَقَبَةِ حَتَّى تَطْلُعَ الشَّمْسُ [*O little* (meaning *dear*) *sons, cast not ye the pebble of the 'Akabeh* (see جَمْرَةٌ) *until the sun rise*], (TA,) or أُبَيْنِىَّ الخ [*O my little sons* &c.]: (Mgh, TA:) IAth says that the hemzeh is augmentative; and that there are differences of opinion respecting the form of the word and its meaning: some say that it is the dim. of أَبْنَى, like أَعْمَى, a sing. word denoting a pl. meaning, or, accord. to some, a pl. of اِبْنٌ, as well as أَبْنَآءٌ: some say that it is the dim. of اِبْنٌ; [and if so, we must read أُبَيْنِى *my little son;*] but this requires consideration [more especially as it is followed by a pl. verb]: AO says that it is the dim. of بَنِىَّ, pl. of اِبْنٌ with the affixed pronoun of the first pers. [sing.]; and this requires us to read أُبَيْنِىَّ. (TA.) J says, in the Ṣ, that the dim. of أَبْنَآءٌ [pl. of اِبْنٌ] is ↓ أُبَيْنَآءٌ, and, if you will, ↓ أُبَيْنُونَ; and he cites a verse in which occurs the expression أُبَيْنِيكَ, [in the gen. case, meaning *thy little sons*,] and adds, it is as though its sing. were إِبْنٌ, with the disjunctive ا, whence the dim. ↓ أُبَيْنٌ, in the pl. أُبَيْنُونَ: but he should have said, as though its sing. were أَبْنَى, like أَعْمَى, originally أَبْنَوُ. (IB, TA.)

أُبَيْنَآءٌ: } see what next precedes.
أُبَيْنُونَ: }

مِبْنَاةٌ (T, Ṣ, M, Ḳ) and مَبْنَاةٌ (M, Ḳ) *A* نِطْع [like بِنَآءٌ, which see for an explanation]: (Ṣ, M, Ḳ:) and *a* سِتْر [i. e. *curtain* or *the like*]: (Ḳ:) or *a thing in the form of a* سِتْر: (M:) or *a* [*tent of the kind called*] قُبَّة, *made of skins*, or *hides:* (IAạr, T:) or *a thing of skins*, or *hides, of like form to the* قُبَّة, *which a woman places in*, or *at, the side of her tent* (فِى كِسْرِ بَيْتِهَا), *and in which she dwells;* and may-be she has sheep, or goats, and is content with the possession of these, exclusively of the other sheep, or goats, for herself and her garments [and app. for making of their skins her مبناة]; and she has a covering (إِزَار) [extended] in the middle of the بَيْت [or tent], within, to protect her from the heat, and from the violent rain, so that she and her clothes are not wetted: (Aboo-'Adnán, T:) or, accord. to Aṣ, *a mat* (حَصِير), or *a* نِطْع, *which the trafficker spreads upon the things that he sells:* and they used to put the mats (الحُصُر) upon the أَنْطَاع [pl. of نِطْع], and go round about with them [in the market]: the مبناة is thus called because it is made of skins joined together: (T:) also *a receptacle of the kind called* عَيْبَة: (M, Ḳ:) such is said to be its meaning: (Ṣ:) pl. مَبَانٍ. (T.)

مَبْنِىٌّ [*Built*, &c.: see 1]. أَرْضٌ مَبْنِيَّةٌ means أَرْضٌ مَبْنِىٌّ فِيهَا [*Land built in* or *upon*]; and is deemed a chaste phrase. (Mgh.)

مُبَنًّى *Raised high;* applied to a palace, or pavilion. (M, TA.)

مُبْتَنًى [pass. part. n. of اِبْتَنَاهُ] is used in the place of the inf. n. [of that verb, agreeably with many other instances, or accord. to a common licence], meaning The act of *building, framing*, or *constructing.* (TA.)

بهأ

1. بَهَأَ بِهِ, and بَهِئَ, (AZ, Ṣ, Mgh, Ḳ,) [aor. َ,] and بَهُؤَ, (Ḳ,) [aor. ُ,] inf. n. بَهْءٌ and بُهُوْءٌ (AZ, Ṣ, Ḳ) and بَهَآءٌ; (Ḳ;) and ↓ ابتهأ به; (Aboo-Sa'eed, TA;) *He was*, or *became, sociable, friendly*, or *familiar, with him*, or *it;* (AZ, Ṣ, Mgh, Ḳ;) namely, a man, (AZ, Ṣ,) or a thing; (Mgh;) *and loved*, or *liked, his*, or *its, nearness:* (Aboo-Sa'eed, TA:) and *he became familiar with it so as to have little*, or *no, reverence for it*, or *awe of it.* (Mgh, TA.) بَهُوا بِهِ occurs in a trad., as they relate it, for بَهَؤُوا بِهِ: (A'Obeyd, TA:) and ↓ يَبْتَهِى, in a verse of El-Aạshà, for يَبْتَهِئُ. (Aṣ, O, TṢ, L.) — مَا بَهَأْتُ لَهُ *I did not understand it;* or *I did not know it;* (ISk, Ṣ, Ḳ;) as also مَا بَأَهْتُ لَهُ. (ISk, Ṣ.)

8: see 1, in two places.

نَاقَةٌ بَهَآءٌ *A she-camel familiar with*, or *accustomed to, her milker;* (Aṣ, Ṣ;) *that offers no opposition to him.* (Ḳ.) — بَهَآءٌ as syn. with حُسْنٌ belongs to art. بهو. (Ṣ, &c.)

بهت

1. بُهِتَ, (Ṣ, Mṣb, Ḳ, &c.,) the most chaste form of the verb in the sense here following, (Ṣ, TA,) and that which most commonly obtains, and the only form allowed by Th and IḲt; (TA;) and بَهِتَ, (Ṣ, L, Mṣb, Ḳ,) aor. َ; (Mṣb, Ḳ;) and بَهُتَ, (Ṣ, L, Mṣb, Ḳ,) in which the ḍammeh is said to give intensiveness to the signification, as in قَضُوَ الرَّجُلُ, (TA,) aor. ُ; (Mṣb, Ḳ;) and بَهَتَ, aor. َ (Ḳ) and ِ; (TA;) inf. n. بَهْتٌ; (JK, Ḳ;) *He was*, or *became, confounded, perplexed*, or *amazed, and unable to see his right course;* (JK, Ṣ, Mṣb, Ḳ;) *not knowing what to prefer nor what to postpone:* (TA in art. اشر:) *he looked* at a thing that he saw *with a look of wonder:* (A, TA:) *he was*, or *became, affected with wonder:* (JK:) *he was*, or *became, cut short*, (اِنْقَطَعَ, Ḳ, TA,) *and was silent, being confounded*, or *perplexed, and unable to see his right course:* (TA:) *he* (an adversary in a dispute or litigation) *was overcome by an argument, an allegation*, or *a plea.* (L.) All these forms occur in different readings of the saying in the Ḳur [ii. 260], فَبُهِتَ ٱلَّذِى كَفَرَ and فَبَهِتَ &c., (IJ, TA,) explained in the Wá'ee as meaning, *And he who disbelieved remained in confusion*, or *perplexity, not seeing his right course, looking as one in wonder:* (Lb, TA:) but accord. to him who reads فَبَهَتَ, the word الذى may hold the place of a noun in the accus. case [as will be seen from what follows]. (IJ, TA.) — بَهَتَهُ, aor. َ, (Ṣ, Mṣb,) inf. n. بَهْتٌ, (Ṣ, Ḳ,) *He*, or *it, caused him to become confounded, perplexed*, or *amazed, not seeing his right course:* (Zj, Mṣb: [Golius, on the authority of Ibn-Maạroof, assigns this meaning to ↓ بهّته:]) or *took him unawares*, or *by surprise*, or *unexpectedly*, or *suddenly.* (Ṣ, Ḳ.) Zj cites as an ex. of the former meaning the saying in the Ḳur [xxi. 41], تَأْتِيهِمْ بَغْتَةً فَتَبْهَتُهُمْ, i. e., *It shall come upon them suddenly*, or *unawares, and cause them to become confounded*, &c.: (TA: and so Bḍ and Jel explain it:) or, *and shall overcome them:* (Bḍ:) J cites the same as an ex. of the latter of the two meanings in the preceding sentence; but his doing so requires consideration; for the meaning which he gives is taken from the word بغتة; not from البَهْت. (MF, TA.) [But it is said also that] مُبَاهَتَةٌ [inf. n. of ↓ باهته] signifies The *taking*, or *coming upon*, [one] *unawares, by surprise*, or *unexpectedly.* (JK.) — بَهَتَهُ, aor. َ, (Ṣ, A, Ḳ, &c.,) inf. n. بَهْتٌ and بُهْتٌ and بُهْتَانٌ, (Ṣ, Ḳ,) or the last is a simple subst., (Mṣb,) *He calumniated him; slandered him; accused him falsely; said against him that which he had not done:* (Ṣ, A, Ḳ:) [or *he did so in such a manner as to make one to be confounded*, or *perplexed*, or *amazed, at the falsity*

of the charge, and not to see his right course: (see بُهْتَانٌ, below:)] *he lied against him; forged a lie, or lies, against him;* and i. q. قَابَلَهُ بِالكَذِبِ [*he accused him to his face falsely, or with falsehood*]; (TA;) اِسْتِقْبَالُكَ أَخَاكَ بِمَا لَيْسَ فِيهِ signifies البَهْتُ [*thy accusing thy brother, or fellow, to his face, of that which is not in him*]: (JK:) and بَهْتًا, aor. ـَ, inf. n. بَهْتٌ, *he accused her falsely of adultery; and forged a lie against her.* (Mṣb.) [See also اِغْتَابَهُ.] In the saying of Abu-n-Nejm,

سُبِّى الحَمَاةَ وَٱبْهَتِى عَلَيْهَا •

[*Revile thou the mother-in-law, and calumniate her, or forge lies against her*], على is [said by J to be] redundant, or pleonastic; for one does not say, بَهَتَ عَلَيْهِ, but only بَهَتَهُ. (Ṣ.) Upon this, F says, in the Ḳ, that فَٱبْهَتِى عليها [thus in the Ḳ] is a mistake; that J is in error, and that the right reading is فَٱنْهَتِى عليها, with ن: but this assertion made by F depends upon the authority of relaters of the verse in which the word in question occurs. (MF.) IB says that ابهتى may be here rendered trans. by means of على because it is syn. with اِفْتَرِى, which is so rendered trans., in like manner as is done in other instances, of which he gives an ex. from the Ḳur [xxiv. 63], يُخَالِفُونَ عَنْ أَمْرِهِ, meaning يَخْرُجُونَ عن امره: he adds that, accord. to J, عن in this ex. should be considered redundant; but that عن and على are not used redundantly like ب. (TA.) — بَهَتَ الفَحْلَ عَنِ النَّاقَةِ *He removed the stallion from the she-camel in order that a stallion of more generous race might cover her.* (TA.)

2: see 1.

3. باهتهُ, inf. n. مُبَاهَتَةٌ: see 1. — [Also *He engaged with him in mutual calumny, slander, or false accusation:* a meaning indicated, but not expressed, in the A.] You say, بَيْنَهُمَا مُبَاهَتَةٌ [*Between them two is mutual calumniation, &c.*]: and عَادَتُهُ أَنْ يُبَاحِثَ وَيُبَاهِتَ [*His custom is to engage with another in mutual scrutiny* of secrets, or faults, or the like, *and in mutual calumniation, &c.*]: and لَا تَبَاهَتُوا ♦ وَلَا تَمَاقَتُوا [*Calumniate ye not one another, &c., nor hate ye one another on account of any foul, or evil, affair*]. (A.) — And *He confounded, perplexed, or amazed, him* (namely, his hearer,) *by what he forged against him.* (TA.)

6: see 3.

بَهْتٌ: see بُهْتَانٌ. — *A certain well-known kind of stone.* (Ḳ.)

بُهُتٌ: see بُهْتَانٌ, in two places. — *A certain sidereal computation, or calculation;* being [that of] *the direct course of stars in a day:* [in Persian, *a planet's motion in any given time:* (Johnson's Pers. Arab. and Engl. Dict.:)] thought by Az to be not Arabic. (TA.)

بُهْتَانٌ and ♦ بَهِيتَةٌ signify the same [when the former is used as a subst.; i. e. *A calumny, slander, or false accusation*]: (Ṣ, A, Mṣb: [see 1:]) or both signify, the former as explained by Aboo-Is-ḥáḳ, and the latter as explained in the Ḳ, *a falsehood by reason of which one is confounded, or perplexed, and unable to see his right course;* (TA; [in which it seems to be indicated that ♦ بُهْتٌ signifies the same;]) from البَهْتُ as meaning "the being confounded" &c.: (Aboo-Is-ḥáḳ, TA:) the former is a subst. signifying [also] *a false accusation of adultery* against a woman; and *a forgery of a lie* against her: (Mṣb:) and ♦ the latter, [and the former also, simply,] *a lying,* or *lie,* or *falsehood;* (Ḳ;) and so ♦ بَهْتٌ (Ḳ) and ♦ بُهُتٌ. (TA.) بُهْتَانًا وَإِثْمًا مُبِينًا, in the Ḳur iv. 24, is said to mean *Falsely accusing of adultery, and acting in a manifestly sinful* or *criminal manner:* (Bḍ:) or it means *acting wrongfully* &c. (Bḍ, Jel.) You say, رَمَاهُ ♦ بِالبَهِيتَةِ [*He accused him with,* or *of, calumny, &c.*]. (A.) And يَا ♦ لِلْبَهِيتَةِ, with kesr to the [prep.] ل, [i. e., *O, come to my aid,* or *succour, on account of the calumny!* &c.; for it is] a phrase used in calling for aid, or succour. (Ṣ.) [And if you would express wonder, you say, يَا ♦ لَلْبَهِيتَةِ, with fet-ḥ to the prep. ل, i. e. *O the calumny!* &c.]

بَهُوتٌ [*A great, or frequent, calumniator, slanderer,* or *false-accuser;* as also ♦ بَهَّاتٌ, mentioned in the Ṣ only as an epithet applied to him *who calumniates, slanders,* or *accusely falsely;*] an intensive epithet from البَهْتُ; (IAth;) [i. e.] an intensive form of the act. part. n. from البُهْتَانُ [inf. n. of بَهَتَهُ]: (Mgh:) or i. q. ♦ مُبَاهِتٌ; (Ḳ;) i. e., one *who confounds,* or *perplexes,* or *amazes, the hearer, by what he forges against him:* (TA:) and one *who falsely accuses a woman of adultery, and forges a lie against her:* (Mṣb:) pl. بُهُتٌ (IAth, Mgh, Mṣb, Ḳ) and بُهْتٌ, and, accord. to the Ḳ, also بُهُوتٌ; but ISd and MF hold it to be pl. of بَاهِتٌ, not of بَهُوتٌ; the former observing, that a word of the measure فَاعِلٌ is one of those which have a pl. of the measure فُعُولٌ, but not so one of the measure فَعُولٌ; and that, as to the saying of A'Obeyd, that عُذُوبٌ is pl. of عَذُوبٌ, it is a mistake; for it is only pl. of عَاذِبٌ, and the pl. of عَذُوبٌ is عُذُبٌ. (TA. [But see art. عذب.])

بَهِيتٌ, see مَبْهُوتٌ, in two places.

بَهِيتَةٌ: see بُهْتَانٌ, in five places.

بَهَّاتٌ: see بَهُوتٌ: — and see مَبْهُوتٌ.

بَاهِتٌ: see مَبْهُوتٌ, in two places. — Also act. part. n. [of بَهَتَهُ; signifying *Causing to become confounded, &c.:* and *calumniating, &c.:*] from البُهْتَانُ: (Mgh:) بُهُوتٌ, as mentioned above, is held by ISd and MF to be a pl. of this word; not of بَهُوتٌ, q. v. (TA.)

مَبْهُوتٌ *Confounded, perplexed,* or *amazed, and unable to see his right course:* (Ṣ, Ḳ:) [other (similar) meanings may be seen from explanations of بُهِتَ:] accord. to Ks and the Ṣ and Ṣgh and the Ḳ, one should not say ♦ بَاهِتٌ nor ♦ بَهِيتٌ; but there is no reason in analogy why he who says بَهَتَ, like نَصَرَ and مَنَعَ, should not say thus: (TA:) Lb says, in the Expos. of the Fṣ, that they said ♦ بَاهِتٌ and ♦ بَهَّاتٌ [which latter is an intensive form] and ♦ بَهِيتٌ, which [last] may be considered as having the meaning of the measure مَفْعُولٌ, like مَبْهُوتٌ, or that of the measure فَاعِلٌ, like بَاهِتٌ; but the former is the more agreeable with analogy, and the more probable. (MF, TA.) — Also *Calumniated, slandered,* or *falsely accused.* (Ṣ.)

مُبَاهِتٌ: see بَهُوتٌ.

بهج

1. بَهُجَ, aor. ـُ, (AZ, Ṣ, Mṣb, &c.,) inf. n. بَهَاجَةٌ (AZ, Ṣ, L, Ḳ) and بَهْجَةٌ (AZ, L, [but some seem to regard this as a simple subst.,]) and بُهْجَانٌ, (L,) *He,* or *it, was,* or *became, beautiful,* or *goodly:* (AZ, Ṣ, L, Mṣb, Ḳ:) or *beautiful in colour:* or *beautiful and bright* or *splendid:* or *it* (a plant) *was,* or *became, beautiful and bright;* and *he* (a man) *was,* or *became, characterized by a laughing,* or *happy, appearance of the beautiful parts of the face, as the cheeks, and the lines of the forehead:* or *by the appearance of joy, gladness,* or *happiness;* or *by a joyful, glad,* or *happy, aspect,* or *appearance.* (L.) You say also, بَهِجَ النَّبَاتُ, with kesr, meaning †*The plant,* or *herbage, was,* or *became, beautiful* [&c.]. (TA, [but this is probably a tropical signification, from بَهِجَ in the sense here following.]) — بَهِجَ, (Ṣ, A, L, Ḳ,) with kesr, (Ṣ,) aor. ـَ, (Ḳ,) inf. n. بَهَجٌ; (L;) and ♦ ابتهج; (Ṣ, A, L, Mṣb, Ḳ;) *He was,* or *became, joyful, glad,* or *happy.* (Ṣ, A, L, Mṣb, Ḳ.) You say, بَهِجَ بِهِ, (Ṣ, A,) and لَهُ; (TA;) and ♦ ابتهج بِهِ; (A, Mṣb;) *He rejoiced in it,* or *at it;* or *became rejoiced by it,* or *at it.* (Ṣ, A, Mṣb, TA.) [See also 10.] — بَهَجَ, (Ṣ, Ḳ,) aor. ـَ; (Ḳ;) and ♦ ابهج; (Ṣ, A, Ḳ;) the latter of which is the more approved; (TA;) *It* (a thing, TA, or an affair or event, Ṣ, A) *rejoiced;* or *made joyful, glad,* or *happy;* (Ṣ, A, Ḳ;) a person. (Ṣ, A.)

2. بهّج, (ISd, L,) inf. n. تَبْهِيجٌ, (Ḳ,) *He beautified; rendered beautiful,* or *goodly.* (ISd, L, Ḳ.) ISd says, I have not heard this, except in the saying of El-'Ajjáj,

دَعْ ذَا وَبَهِّجْ حَسَبًا مُبَهَّجَا •

as though meaning [*Leave thou this subject, and*] *beautify,* or *adorn,* the more this *nobility* [*already beautified,* or *adorned,*] *by thy describing it.* (L.)

3. باهجهُ, (A, Ḳ,) inf. n. مُبَاهَجَةٌ, (A,) *He vied,* or *competed, with him,* or *contended with him for superiority, in beauty,* or *goodliness;* [as expl. in the TḲ; or *in glory,* or *excellence;*] syn. بَاهَاهُ (A, Ḳ) and بَارَاهُ, (Ḳ,) both of these meaning the same. (TA.)

4: see 1, last sentence. — أَبْهَجَتِ الأَرْضُ *The land,* or *earth, became beautiful,* or *goodly,* (Ṣ, L, Ḳ,) or *beautiful and bright* or *splendid,* (L,) *in its plants,* or *herbage.* (Ṣ, L, Ḳ.)

6. تباهج الرَّوْضُ †*The meadows,* or *gardens, became abundant in blossoms* or *flowers* [*as though vying, one with another, in beauty,* or *goodliness:* see 3]. (Ḳ, TA.)

8: see 1, in two places.

10. استبهج *i. q.* اِسْتَبْشَرَ [i. e. *He rejoiced*, or *became rejoiced*; بِهِ *at it*, or *by it*; or *at*, or *by*, *the annunciation of it*]. (Ḳ.) [See also بَهِجَ.]

بَهْجٌ, fem. with ة: see بَهِيجٌ, in two places.

بَهِجٌ *Joyful, glad*, or *happy*; (Ṣ, Ḳ;) as also ♦ بَهِيجٌ (Ṣ, A, Ḳ) and ♦ مُبْتَهِجٌ. (A, TA.) — See also بَهِيجٌ.

بَهْجَةٌ *Beauty*, or *goodliness*: (Ṣ, A, L, Mṣb, Ḳ:) or *beauty of colour* of a thing: or its *beauty and brightness* or *splendour*: or in plants or herbage, *beauty and brightness* or *splendour*; and in a man, the *laughing*, or *happy*, *appearance of the beautiful parts of the face, as the cheeks, and the lines of the forehead*: or the *appearance of joy, gladness*, or *happiness*; or *joyfulness, gladness*, or *happiness, of aspect* or *appearance*. (L.) You say رَوْضَةٌ ذَاتُ بَهْجَةٍ غَالِبَةٍ [*A meadow*, or *garden, of surpassing beauty*, &c.]. (A.) And رَجُلٌ ذُو بَهْجَةٍ *A man possessed of beauty*, or *goodliness*: (Ṣ:) or *of beauty and brightness*, &c. (L.) — Also *Happiness, joy*, or *gladness*. (Ḥam p. 403.)

بَهِيجٌ *Beautiful*, or *goodly*; (Ṣ, A, L, Mṣb, Ḳ;) as also ♦ بَهْجٌ (Ḥam p. 403) and ♦ بَهِجٌ: (AZ, TA:) or *beautiful in colour*: or *beautiful and bright* or *splendid*: or, applied to a plant, it has this last meaning; and, applied to a man, *characterized by a laughing*, or *happy*, *appearance of the beautiful parts of the face, as the cheeks, and the lines of the forehead*: or *characterized by the appearance of joy, gladness*, or *happiness*; *having a joyful, glad*, or *happy, aspect* or *appearance*: (L:) the fem. epithet is ♦ مِبْهَاجٌ. (A, Ḳ, TA: [in the CḲ مُبْهاجٌ.]) It is applied to a plant, or herbage, (Ṣ, A,) in the Ḳur xxii. 5 and l. 7. (Ṣ.) And ♦ مِبْهَاجٌ is applied to a woman, as meaning *One in whom beauty*, or *goodliness*, &c., *predominates*; (L, TA;) as also ♦ بَهْجَةٌ; (TA;) pl. of the former, مَبَاهِيجُ: (A, TA:) and to a camel's hump, meaning ‡ *fat*; (A, Ḳ;) because beauty, or goodliness, is combined [in this case] with fatness; pl. as above. (A, TA.) — See also بَهِجٌ.

مِبْهَاجٌ: see بَهِيجٌ, in two places.

مُبْتَهِجٌ: see بَهِجٌ.

بهر

1. بَهَرَهُ, (Ṣ, A, Mṣb,) aor. ـَ, (Mṣb,) inf. n. بَهْرٌ, (Ṣ, Mṣb, Ḳ,) *He overcame him*: (Ṣ, A, Mṣb, Ḳ:) *he overpowered him; subdued him*: (TA:) *he surpassed him; excelled him*. (Mṣb.) See also 3. You say, بَهَرَتْ فُلَانَةُ النِّسَآءَ *Such a woman surpassed the* [other] *women in beauty*. (Ṣ.) And بَهَرَ [alone] *He excelled in knowledge &c.*; or *he was*, or *became, accomplished*, or *perfect, in every excellence*, and *in goodliness*. (Ṣ, Ḳ.) And بَهَرَ القَمَرُ, (Ṣ, Ḳ,) or بَهَرَ القَمَرُ النُّجُومَ, (TA,) aor. ـَ, (Ḳ,) inf. n. بُهُورٌ, (TA,) ‡ *The moon overcame with its light the light of the stars*. (Ṣ, Ḳ, TA.) And بَهَرَتِ الشَّمْسُ الأَرْضَ † *The light of the sun overspread the earth*. (TA.) — [Hence,] بَهَرَ, aor. ـَ, (TA,) inf. n. بَهْرٌ and بُهُورٌ, (Ḳ,) ‡ *It shone*, or *shone brightly*: (Ḳ, TA:) and ♦ تَبَهَّرَتِ السَّحَابَةُ ‡ *The cloud shone*, or *shone brightly*. (Ḳ.) — بَهَرَهُ, (Ṣ, A,) aor. ـَ, inf. n. بَهْرٌ, (Ṣ,) also signifies ‡ *It* (a load, or burden, Ṣ, A, and running, A) [*caused him to be out of breath; interrupted his breathing*; (see بُهْرٌ;)] *caused to pant*, or *breathe* [*shortly* or] *uninterruptedly*. (Ṣ, A.) — Also, (ISh, JK, TA,) inf. n. بَهْرٌ, (Ḳ, TA,) † *He stopped his breath* by beating, or by squeezing his throat, or throttling him, or by any other means: (ISh, TA:) † *he plied him*, or *worked him*, (عَالَجَهُ,) *until he became out of breath*, or *until he panted*: (JK, TA:) † *he imposed upon him a thing that was above his power*, or *ability*. (Ḳ, TA.) A poet says,

إِنَّ البَخِيلَ إِذَا سَأَلْتَ بَهَرْتَهُ

Verily the niggardly, when thou askest of him, *thou stoppest his breath*. (ISh, TA.) — [Hence,] بَهَرَ, *i. q.* انبهر, as explained below. (Ḳ.) — بَهَرَهَا, (JK,) or بَهَرَهَا بِبُهْتَانٍ, (TA,) inf. n. بَهْرٌ, (Ḳ,) *He reproached her*, or *accused her, falsely*; (JK;) *he aspersed her; calumniated her*; or *brought a false accusation against her*. (Ḳ,* TA.) You say, بَهَرَهَا بِكَذَا *He reproached her falsely with*, or *accused her falsely of, such a thing*. (JK.) [See also 8.]

3. ♦ باهر صَاحِبَهُ فَبَهَرَهُ, (Ḳ,* TA,) inf. n. مُبَاهَرَةٌ and بِهَارٌ, (TA,) [aor. of the latter verb, accord. to rule, ـُ, not ـَ,] *He contended*, or *disputed*, or *vied, with his companion for glory*, or *superiority*, or *excellence, and overcame him*. (Ḳ,* TA.)

4. ابهر *He did*, or *effected*, or *he said*, or *uttered, what was wonderful*; syn. جَآءَ بِالعَجَبِ. (Ḳ.)

5: see 1.

7. انبهر, (Ṣ, A, Ḳ,) and ♦ ابتهر, (TA,) and ♦ بُهِرَ, like عُنِىَ, (Ḳ,) ‡ *He was*, or *became, out of breath*; *his breath became interrupted*, by reason of fatigue [or running, or by hard work, or bearing a heavy load; see 1]: (Ḳ:) *he panted*, or *breathed* [*shortly* or] *uninterruptedly*. (Ṣ, A.)

8. ابتهر *He arrogated to himself*, or *professed, a thing falsely*. (Ṣ, Ḳ.) El-Akhṭal says,

وَمَا بِى إِنْ مَدَحْتُهُمُ ٱبْتِهَارُ

And there is not in me, if I praise them, false profession: (Ṣ:) or ابتهر signifies *he said what was false, and swore to it*. (TA.) — *He said that he had transgressed*, or *acted viciously*, or *committed adultery* or *fornication*, *when he had not done so*. (Ḳ.) And ابتهر بِذَنْبٍ *He asserted himself to have committed a crime*, or *sin*, *when he had not done so*. (TA, from a trad.) — ابتهرها *He asserted falsely that he had had sexual intercourse with her*: (M, TA:) ابتارها signifies "he asserted the same with truth:" (TA:) or ابتهر signifies *he charged*, or *upbraided*, a person *with that which was in him*; (Ḳ, TA;) and ابتار, "he charged, or upbraided, with that which was not in him." (TA.) See an ex. voce بَارَ in art. بور. — Also *He* (a poet) *mentioned her* (a girl) *in his poetry*. (JK.) ابْتُهِرَ بِفُلَانَةَ *He became*, or *was rendered, notorious*, or *infamous, on account of such a woman* [*with whom he was said to have had an illicit connexion*]. (Ṣ, Ḳ.) — See also 7.

11. ابهارّ اللَّيْلُ, (Ṣ, A, Ḳ,) inf. n. اِبْهِيرَارٌ, (Ṣ,) *The night reached its middle point*; (Aṣ, Ṣ, A, Ḳ;) from بُهْرَةٌ signifying the "middle" of a thing: (A:) or *reached the point when all its stars appeared and shone*: (Aboo-Sa'eed Eḍ-Ḍareer:) or *became thickly dark*: (Ḳ:) or *for the most part passed*: (Ṣ, Ḳ:) or *reached the point when about one third of it remained*. (Ḳ.) And ابهارّ عَلَيْنَا اللَّيْلُ *The night became long to us*. (Ṣ.) And ابهارّ النَّهَارُ *The day reached the point when the sun had become high*. (TA.)

بَهْرٌ inf. n. of 1 [q. v.]. (Ṣ, Mṣb, Ḳ.) You say, بَهْرًا لَهُ, an imprecation, meaning *May he be overcome!* (A:) or *i. q.* تَعْسًا لَهُ [*may he fall, having stumbled!* or *stumble and fall!* &c.]: (AA, Ṣ, Ḳ:) and thus used [app. in the latter sense] as an imprecation, accord. to Sb, it has no verb, but is put in the accus. case on the supposition of a verb. (TA.) One says also, ♦ قُهْرًا وَبُهْرًا, with ḍamm to each. (TA in art. قهر.) And بَهْرًا مَا أَسْخَاهُ [*May he fall, having stumbled!* &c.: *how bountiful is he!*], like as one says تَعْسًا لَهُ [when not meaning it to be understood as an imprecation]. (A.) — It also signifies *Distance*, or *remoteness*: (Ḳ:) and *remoteness from good* or *prosperity*. (TA.) — *Disappointment*. (IAạr, TA.) — *Wonder*; syn. عَجَبٌ. (Ḳ.) One says, بَهْرًا meaning عَجَبًا [for أَعْجَبُ عَجَبًا *I do wonder*: or *wonderful!*]. (Ṣ.) So [sometimes] in the phrase بَهْرًا لَهُ [*I do wonder at him*, or *it*]. (IAạr, TA.) — *Love*. (Ḳ.) Accord. to some, بَهْرًا لَكُمْ means *Love to you*. (JK.) — الأَزْوَاجُ ثَلَاثَةٌ زَوْجُ بَهْرٍ وَزَوْجُ دَهْرٍ وَزَوْجُ مَهْرٍ is a saying of the Arabs, meaning *Husbands are three: a husband who overcomes the eyes by his goodliness*, (Ṣ,) or *a husband of noble race, though he may be of little wealth*; (TA;) *and a husband prepared for the accidents*, or *calamities, of fortune*; *and a husband from whom a dowry is got*, (Ṣ,) or *a husband who has not nobility of race, and who therefore doubles the dowry to make himself desired*. (TA.) — † *Distress that affects the breath or respiration*, syn. كَرْبٌ, (Ḳ, TA,) [particularly] *of a camel when he is spurred on*, or *of a man when a labour above his power is imposed upon him*. (TA.)

بُهْرٌ: see بَهْرٌ. — Also ‡ The *state of being out of breath; interruption of the breath, by reason of fatigue*, (Ḳ, TA,) [or *by bearing a heavy load*, (see 1,)] or *by hard work*, and *by running*: (TA:) *a panting*, or *breathing* [*shortly* or] *uninterruptedly*. (Ṣ, A, TA.) — *Wide-spreading land*; *a wide tract of land*; as also ♦ بُهْرَةٌ [q. v.]. (Ḳ.) — *A country*, or *district*; or *a city*, or *town*; syn. بَلَدٌ: (Ḳ:) or the *middle thereof*. (TA.) — The *middle*, and *best part*, (سِرّ, and خَيْر, for the former of which words we find شَرّ erroneously put in the copies of the Ḳ, TA,) *of a valley*; as also ♦ بُهْرَةٌ [q. v.]. (Ḳ, TA.)

بُهْرَةٌ *Plain*, or *even*, or *soft, land* or *ground:* or *a wide tract of land between mountains.* (L.) — See also بُهْرٌ, in two places. — The *middle* (Ṣ, A, Ḳ) of a valley, and of the night, and of a horse, (Ṣ, Ḳ,) and of a camel's saddle, (TA,) and of a ring, (Ḳ,) or of a thing. (A.)

بَهَارٌ *A certain plant, of sweet odour;* (Ḳ;) the [*plant called*] عَرَار, *which is also called* عَيْنُ البَقَرِ; [*buphthalmum*, or *ox-eye;*] it is the بَهَارُ البَرِّ, *a crisping*, or *curling, plant, having a yellow flower; growing in the days of the spring* (الرَّبِيع), *and called* عَرَارَةٌ: (Ṣ:) Aṣ says, The عَرَار is the بَهَارُ البَرِّ: and Az says, The عَرَارَة is the خَشْوَة; and I regard بهار as a Persian word. (TA.) — *Perfume.* (Mṣb.) — And hence applied to The *flowers of the desert.* (Mṣb.) — And *Anything goodly*, or *beautiful, and bright*, or *shining.* (Ḳ, TA.)

بُهَارٌ *A certain thing with which one weighs;* (Ṣ, Mṣb, Ḳ;) the *weight of three hundred pounds:* (Fr, IAạr, A'Obeyd, Ṣ, Ḳ:) thought by A'Obeyd to be not Arabic, but Coptic; (Ṣ;) having this signification in Coptic; (JK;) but thought by Az to be pure Arabic: (TA:) or *four hundred pounds:* or *six hundred:* or *a thousand:* (Ḳ:) and, (Ḳ,) or as some say, (TA,) *one half of a load* (Ḳ, TA) *borne by a camel,* (TA,) *containing four hundred pounds,* (Ḳ, TA,) in the dial. of Syria: (TA:) or *a load borne by a camel:* (Ḳt:) or *a camel-load of household-goods or furniture and utensils:* (Aṣ:) and *commodities*, or *utensils*, or *the like, of the sea;* expl. by مَتَاعُ البَحْرِ [perhaps a mistranscription for مَتَاعُ التُّجْرِ or التُّجْرِ, *commodities*, or *goods, of the merchants:* the poet Bureyḳ El-Hudhalee speaks of camels bearing أَبْهَار]. (JK, Ḳ.) It is said that Ṭalḥah the son of 'Obeyd-Allah left a hundred بُهَار, in each بهار of which was three hundred-weight of gold (Ṣ, TA) and silver; (TA;) بهار being thus made to signify a receptacle: (Ṣ, TA:) accord. to Aṣ and Ḳt, the meaning is, a hundred camel-loads. (TA.)

بَهِيرٌ and ▼مَبْهُورٌ (A, Ḳ) and ▼مُنْبَهِرٌ (A) [and ▼مُبْتَهِرٌ] ‡ *Out of breath; having his breath interrupted*, by reason of fatigue [or running, or by hard work, or bearing a heavy load; see 1 and 7]; *panting*, or *breathing* [*shortly* or] *uninterruptedly.* (A.)

بَاهِرٌ [act. part. n. of 1, *Overcoming;* &c. And particularly,] † *Overcoming in light.* (JK.) [Hence,] قَمَرٌ بَاهِرٌ ‡ *A moon that overcomes with its light the light of the stars.* (Ṣ, A.) And البَاهِرُ ‡ *The moon;* because it outshines the stars: (Mṣb:) or *the full moon.* (JK.)

أَبْهَرُ [The *aorta;* so in the present day;] *a certain vein* [or *artery*], (Ṣ, A, Ḳ,) *in the back,* (Ḳ,) *lying within*, or *at the inner side of, the back-bone* (A'Obeyd, A, TA) *and the heart,* (A'Obeyd, TA,) *the severing of which causes death:* (A'Obeyd, Ṣ, A:) it is a name given to *each of two veins* [or *arteries*, or *the two portions of the aorta which are called the aorta ascendens and aorta descendens,*] *which issue from the heart, and from which then branch off all the other arteries:* (Ṣ:) and, (Ḳ,) or as some say, (TA,) the وَرِيد [i. e. either the *carotid artery* or the *external jugular vein*] *of the neck:* (Ḳ:) and, (Ḳ,) or as some say, (TA,) [the *vein in the arm called*] *the* أَكْحَل: (Ḳ:) or, accord. to the more full description of IAth, *a certain vein* [or *artery*] *arising from the head, and extending to the foot, and having arteries which communicate with most of the extremities and the body: what is in the head is called the* نَامَّة; and hence the saying, أَسْكَتَ ٱللّٰهُ نَامَّتَهُ, meaning "God killed him," or "may God kill him!" *and it extends to the throat, and is there called the* وَرِيد; *and to the chest, and is there called* [*especially*] *the* أبهر [meaning the *aorta ascendens*]; *and to the back, and is there called the* وَتِين [meaning the *aorta descendens*]; *and the heart is suspended to it; and it extends to the thigh, and is there called the* نَسَا; *and to the shank, and is there called the* صَافِن: the ء in it is augmentative. (TA.) You say, قَطَعَ أَبْهَرَهُ [*It severed his aorta*]; meaning ‡ *it* (pain) *destroyed him.* (A.) — Also The *back:* (Ḳ:) or the *place of the vein* [or *artery*] *so called.* (Aṣ, in art. خدع of the Ṣ.) One says, فُلَانٌ شَدِيدُ الأَبْهَرِ *Such a one is strong in the back:* (TA:) or *strong in the place of the vein* [or *artery*] *called the* ابهر. (Aṣ, ubi suprà.) — And The *back of the curved part of the extremity* of a bow: (Ḳ:) or the *part between the* طَائِف *and the* كُلْيَة: (Ṣ, Ḳ:) in the bow is its كَبِد, which is the part between the two extremities of its string or the like; then, next to this, the كُلْيَة; then, next to this, the أَبْهَر; then, the طَائِف; then, the سِئَة, which is the curved part of the extremity. (Aṣ.) — And *A tent-pole.* (JK.) — And The *shorter side of a feather:* (Ḳ:) [or] so أَبَاهِرُ [which is the pl.]: (JK:) [or] the latter signifies the *feathers* (Lḥ, Ṣ) *of the wing* (Lḥ) of a bird (Lḥ, Ṣ) *next after those called* الخَوَافِي, (Lḥ,) [*and*] *next* [*before*] *those called* الكُلَى: (Ṣ:) the first of them are those called القَوَادِمُ, (Ṣ,) four in number, in the fore part of the wing; (Lḥ;) the next, المَنَاكِبُ, (Lḥ, Ṣ,) also four; (Lḥ;) the next, الخَوَافِي, (Lḥ, Ṣ,) also four; (Lḥ;) the next, الأَبَاهِرُ, (Lḥ, Ṣ,) also four; (Lḥ;) and the next, الكُلَى [which are also four]. (Ṣ.)

مَبْهُورٌ :
مُبْتَهِرٌ : } see بَهِيرٌ.
مُنْبَهِرٌ :

بهرج

Q. 1. بُهْرِجَ, in the pass. form, (Ḳt, Mṣb,) inf. n. بَهْرَجَةٌ, (Ḳ,) † *It* (a thing) *was taken otherwise than by*, or *in, the right way:* (Mṣb:) or ‡ *it was turned away*, or *conveyed by turning away,* (Ḳt, Ḳ, TA,) *from the beaten way* or *road,* (Ḳt, TA,) or *from the direct*, or *right, main road.* (Ḳ, TA.) And بُهْرِجَ بِهِمْ ‡ *It* (the road, A) *lead them otherwise than in the beaten track.* (T, A, TA.) [See بَهْرَجٌ, from which the verb is derived.] — ‡ *It* (a man's blood) *was made to be of no account, to go for nothing, unretaliated*, or *uncompensated by a mulct; was made allowable to be taken* or *shed.* (Mgh.) And بَهْرَجَ دَمَهُ ‡ *He made his blood to be of no account,* &c. (TA.) — Hence, (TA,) أَمَا إِذْ بَهْرَجْتَنِى فَلَا أَشْرَبُهَا أَبَدًا (Ḳ,* TA) ‡ *Verily, since thou hast made me* [meaning my offence] *to pass unnoticed*, or *hast taken no account of me,* (هَدَرْتَنِى,) by annulling in respect of me the prescribed castigation, (Ḳ, TA,) *I will not drink it* (i. e. wine) *henceforth:* (TA:) said by Aboo-Mihjen (Ḳ, TA) Eth-Thaḳafee, (TA,) to Ibn-Abee-Waḳḳáṣ. (TA.) — You say also, بَهْرَجَ المَكَانَ † *He made the place free to the people in general to pasture their beasts in it.* (IAạr, L.)

Q. 2. تَبَهْرَجَ † *It* (a place) *became*, or *was made, free to the people in general to pasture their beasts in it.* (IAạr, L.)

بَهْرَجٌ an arabicized word, (T, Ṣ, Mgh, L, TA,) from نَبَهْرَه, (T, Mgh, L, TA,) which is Persian; (L, TA;) or, as some say, it is an Indian word, originally نَبَهْلَه, meaning *Bad*, whence the Persian نَبَهْرَه, and hence the arabicized نَبَهْرَج; (TA;) applied to a dirhem, as meaning *bad;* (Kr, Ṣ;) *false;* (Ṣ, El-Marzooḳee;) *adulterated;* (Shifá el-Ghaleel, El-Marzooḳee;) *of bad silver;* (A, Mgh, L, Mṣb;) *with which one cannot buy:* (IAạr, TA:) or, as some say, *in which the silver is predominant:* or, accord. to IAạr, *of which the die has been falsified:* (Mgh:) or *not coined in the government-mint:* (Lḥ, TA:) and ▼مُبَهْرَجٌ signifies the same, applied to a dirhem; (Lḥ, A, Mgh;) and so ▼نَبَهْرَجٌ; (Lḥ, El-Marzooḳee;) but [Mṭr says,] I have not found it with ن, except on the authority of Lḥ; (Mgh;) and IKh says that it is a word of the vulgar: (TA:) the pl. [of بهرج] is بَهَارِجُ, and [of نبهرج] نَبَهْرَجَاتٌ. (TA.) — Hence, metaphorically, (Mgh,) ‡ *Bad;* (Ṣ, A, Mgh, L, Mṣb, Ḳ;) and *false*, or *of no account;* (Ṣ, A, Mgh, Ḳ;) applied to a thing (Ṣ, A, Mgh, L, Mṣb) of any kind: (A, Mgh, L:) anything *rejected; not received* or *accepted; rejected as wrong* or *bad;* as also ▼نَبَهْرَجٌ: (TA:) and a thing is termed ▼مُبَهْرَجٌ when it is *as though it were cast away, and not an object of emulous desire* or *envy*, or *not in request.* (El-Marzooḳee, TA.) You say, كَلَامٌ بَهْرَجٌ ‡ *Bad language.* (A, L.) And عَمَلٌ بَهْرَجٌ ‡ *A bad action.* (A, L.) — † *Allowed* or *allowable* [*to any person, to be taken* or *let alone*, or *to be possessed* or *made use of* or *done*]; *made allowable, free*, or *lawful.* (Ḳ.) You say, دَمٌ بَهْرَجٌ ‡ *Blood made to be of no account, to go for nothing, unretaliated*, or *uncompensated by a mulct; allowed to be taken* or *shed;* (A, L;) as also ▼مُبَهْرَجٌ. (Ḳ.) And مَكَانٌ بَهْرَجٌ † *A place free to the people in general to pasture their beasts in it.* (IAạr, L.) And ▼مَآءٌ مُبَهْرَجٌ ‡ *A water left free to those who come to water at it.* (A, Ḳ,* TA.)

مُبَهْرَجٌ : see بَهْرَجٌ, in four places.

نَبَهْرَجٌ : see بَهْرَجٌ, in two places.

بهظ

1. بَهَظَهُ, aor. ـَ, inf. n. بَهْظٌ, *It* (a load, or burden,) *oppressed him by its weight, and he was unable to bear it:* (Ṣ, M, TA:) or *pressed heavily upon him, and distressed him.* (T, TA.) [And hence,] ‡ *It* (an affair, M, Ḳ, or anything, T) *oppressed him by its weight,* (T, M,) *and he was unable to bear it:* (M:) or *overpowered him, and pressed heavily upon him, and distressed him;* (Jm, Ḳ;) and so بَهَضَهُ, as heard by Aboo-Turáb from an Arab of the desert; but no one has followed him in this. (Az, TA.) You say also, بَهَظَ الرَّاحِلَةَ *He loaded the riding-camel heavily, and fatigued it.* (Ḳ.)

أَمْرٌ بَاهِظٌ ‡ *A distressing, grievous,* or *difficult, affair.* (Ṣ, CḲ, but wanting in two MS. copies of the Ḳ.) And بَاهِظٌ [alone], (CḲ, but wanting in two MS. copies of the Ḳ,) or ▾ بَاهِظَةٌ, (O, TA,) ‡ *A calamity,* or *misfortune.* (O, Ḳ, TA.)

بَاهِظَةٌ : see بَاهِظٌ.

مَبْهُوظٌ *Oppressed by the weight of a load, and unable to bear it.* (Ṣ.) [And hence,] † *Any one having a thing required of him which he is unable to do,* or *which he cannot find.* (TA.) And قِرْنٌ مَبْهُوظٌ † *An opponent,* or *an adversary, overcome,* or *vanquished.* (TA.)

بهق

1. بَهِقَ, aor. ـَ, inf. n. بَهَقٌ, *It* (the body) *was,* or *became, affected with* [*the disease termed*] بَهَقٌ. (Mṣb.)

بَهَقٌ [The *mild species of leprosy termed* "*alphus,*" or "*vitiligo alba;*" in Hebrew בֹּהַק;] *a whiteness, less than what is termed* بَرَصٌ, *that comes upon the external skin of a man;* (JK;) *a whiteness that affects the skin,* (Ṣ,) or *body,* (Mgh, Mṣb,) *differing from the colour of the latter;* (Ṣ, Mṣb;) *not from what is termed* بَرَص, (Ṣ, Mgh,) or *not* بَرَص: (Mṣb:) and, accord. to IF, *a blackness that affects the skin;* [i. e. the *species of leprosy termed* "*melas,*" or "*lepra maculosa nigra;*"] or *a colour differing from that of the skin:* (Mṣb:) *a thin whiteness that affects the exterior of the cuticle, by reason of a bad state of the temperament of the part, inclining to coldness, and the predominance of the phlegm over the blood: the black* [*species*] *thereof alters* (يُغَيِّرُ, in the CḲ يَعْتَرِى,) *the skin to blackness, by reason of the mixing of the black bile with the blood.* (Ḳ, TA.) — [Hence,] بَهَقُ الحَجَرِ † [*Lichen,* or *liverwort;*] *a certain plant;* (Ḳ;) i. e. حَزَازُ الحَجَرِ [more commonly called حَزَازُ الصَّخْرِ]: (TA:) or *i. q.* الجَوْزُ جَنْدَمُ, (Ḳ, TA,) or الجَوْزَ جَنْدَمُ, (CḲ,) [evidently from the Persian جوز كندم explained in Johnson's Pers. Ar. and Engl. Dict. as "sandix-gum, juniper:" but SM says that] this is *a certain plant, the body* [or *substance*] *of which is* مُحَبَّب [app. meaning *composed of globules* or *the like;* probably *a particular species of lichen, with spherical cells*]. (TA.)

أَبْهَقُ, applied to a man, *Affected with* [*the disease termed*] بَهَقٌ: (JK, Mṣb:) fem. بَهْقَآءُ. (Mṣb.) — [And hence,] so applied, † *Very white.* (TA.)

بهل

1. بَهَلَ النَّاقَةَ, [aor. ـَ, inf. n. بَهْلٌ,] *He left the she-camel without a* صِرَار [*bound upon her udder to prevent her being sucked*]; (Bḍ in iii. 54;) as also ▾ ابهلها: (Ṣ:) or *he left her to be milked;* or *allowed her being milked:* (Z, TA:) and ▾ the latter, *he loosed her* صِرَار, *and left her young one at liberty to suck her;* (Ḳ;) and *he left her to herself* (Ḳ, TA) *to be milked by any one who pleased.* (TA.) — And بَهَلَهُ, (Ṣ, Ḳ,) aor. ـَ, (Ḳ,) [inf. n. بَهْلٌ,] *He left him* (Ṣ, Ḳ) *to his own will,* or *wish,* (Ṣ,) or *to his own opinion,* or *judgment;* (Ḳ;) as also ▾ ابهلهُ: (Ṣ, Ḳ:) or the former is said in relation to the free man; and ▾ the latter, in relation to the slave; (Zj, Ḳ;) and signifies also [simply] *he left him to himself.* (Ḳ,* TA.) — Hence, (TA,) بَهْلٌ signifies [also] The *act of cursing.* (Ṣ, Mṣb, Ḳ.) You say, بَهَلَهُ, aor. ـَ, inf. n. بَهْلٌ, *He cursed him.* (Mṣb.) And بَهَلَ ٱللّٰهُ فُلَانًا *May God curse such a one!* (Ḳ, TA.) — بَهِلَتْ, aor. ـَ, inf. n. بَهَلٌ, *She* (a camel) *had her* صِرَار *loosed, and her young one left to suck her.* (Ḳ.)

3. مُبَاهَلَةٌ The *act of cursing each other:* (Ṣ, Mgh, Mṣb:) inf. n. of باهلهُ *He cursed him, being cursed by him:* (Mṣb:) [or rather] بَاهَلْتُهُ signifies *I joined with him in imprecating the curse of God upon whichever of us did wrong.* (JK.) Hence the saying of Ibn-Mes'ood, مَنْ شَآءَ بَاهَلْتُهُ أَنَّ سُورَةَ النِّسَآءِ القُصْرَى نَزَلَتْ بَعْدَ البَقَرَةِ [*Whosoever will, I will contend with him by imprecating the curse of God upon whichever of us is wrong, that the shorter chapter of* "*Women*" came down from heaven *after* the chapter of "*The Cow*"]: or, accord. to one recital, he said لَاعَنْتُهُ: for when they differed respecting a thing, they used to come together, and say, ▾ بَهْلَةُ ٱللّٰهِ عَلَى الظَّالِمِ مِنَّا [*The curse of God be upon such of us as is the wrongdoer!*]. (Mgh.) باهل بَعْضُهُمْ بَعْضًا and ▾ تبهّلوا and ▾ تباهلوا all signify *They cursed one another:* (Ḳ:) [or] *they joined in imprecating a curse upon such of them as was the wrongdoer:* (TA:) and ▾ ابتهلوا signifies the like: whence, ثُمَّ نَبْتَهِلْ, in the Ḳur [iii. 54], (Bḍ, TA,) as some explain it, (TA,) meaning ▾ ثُمَّ نَتَبَاهَلْ, i. e., *Then let us imprecate a curse upon such of us as is the liar.* (Bḍ. [But see also 8 below.])

4: see 1, in four places. — [The inf. n.] إِبْهَالٌ also signifies The *sending forth,* or *letting flow, the water upon what has been sown,* (JK, Ḳ, TA,) *after having finished the sowing.* (JK, TA. [In the CḲ, نَذْرَتَهُ is erroneously put for بَذْرَتَهُ.])

5: see 3.

6: see 3, in two places.

8: see 3. — [Hence,] ابتهل, (Ṣ, Mṣb, Ḳ,) or ابتهل فِى الدُّعَآءِ, (JK,) ‡ *He humbled,* or *abased, himself;* or *addressed himself with earnest,* or *energetic, supplication;* syn. تَضَرَّعَ; (Ṣ, Mṣb, Ḳ;) إِلَى ٱللّٰهِ *to God:* (Mṣb:) *he strove,* or *was earnest,* or *energetic, in prayer,* or *supplication;* (JK, Ḳ;) *and was sincere,* or *without hypocrisy, therein;* (Ṣ, Ḳ;) *with a striving,* or *an earnestness,* or *energy, like that of the* مُبْتَهِلُون [properly so called, i. e., *persons who join in imprecating a curse upon such of them as is the wrongdoer*]. (TA.) It is said that ثُمَّ نَبْتَهِلْ, in the Ḳur [iii. 54, of which one explanation has been given above, (see 3,)] means ‡ *Then let us be sincere,* or *without hypocrisy, in prayer,* or *supplication;* (Ṣ, TA;) *and let us strive,* or *be earnest,* or *energetic:* (TA:) or *let us humble,* or *abase, ourselves;* &c.; syn. نَتَضَرَّعْ. (Jel.)

10. استبهلها *He milked her* (namely, a camel,) *without a* صِرَار. (Ḳ. [See 1, first sentence.]) — *He* (a young camel) *pulled off her* أَصِرَّة [pl. of صِرَار] *to suck her,* namely, his mother. (JK.) — استبهل الرَّعِيَّةَ *He* (the ruler) *left the people,* or *subjects, to themselves,* (Lḥ, Ḳ,) *to do what they would; not restraining them.* (Lḥ, TA.) — استبهلتهم البَادِيَةُ (Ḳ) and اِسْتَبْهَلَتْهَا السَّوَاحِلُ (Ṣ) † *The shores, and the desert, left them at liberty in their abodes therein, no Sulṭán reaching them, so that they did what they pleased.* (Ṣ,* Ḳ.)

بَهْلَةٌ (Ṣ, Mgh, Ḳ) and ▾ بُهْلَةٌ (Ṣ, Mṣb, Ḳ) *A curse:* (Ṣ, Mgh, Mṣb, Ḳ:) from بَهَلَ النَّاقَةَ in the sense first explained above. (Bḍ in iii. 54.) You say, عَلَيْهِ بَهْلَةُ ٱللّٰهِ and ▾ بُهْلَتُهُ *The curse of God be on him!* (Ṣ.) For another ex., see 3.

بُهْلَةٌ : see what next precedes, in two places.

بَهْلَلَةٌ The *quality of shrinking from foul things, and of generosity,* or *nobleness.* (JK.)

بُهْلُولٌ One *that shrinks from foul things, and is generous,* or *noble;* applied to a man (Ibn-'Abbád, JK) and to a woman: (JK:) pl. بَهَالِيلُ. (Ibn-'Abbád, JK.) *A lord, chief,* or *prince, combining all good qualities.* (Seer, Ḳ.) — *A great,* or *frequent, laugher.* (Ṣ, Ḳ.)

بَاهِلٌ A she-camel *having no* صِرَار *upon her,* (Ṣ, Ḳ, TA,) *so that any one who will may milk her:* (TA:) or one *having no nose-rein upon her,* (Ḳ, TA,) *so that she pastures where she will:* (TA:) or also one *having no* عِرَان [which is a *piece of wood inserted in the partition between the nostrils*]: (Ṣ:) and (so in the Ṣ, but in the Ḳ "or") one *having no mark,* or *brand, upon her:* (JK, Ṣ, Ḳ:) pl. بُهَّلٌ (JK, Ṣ, Ḳ) and بُهْلٌ: (JK, Ḳ, TA: [the latter in the CḲ like بُرْدٌ:]) and ▾ مُبْهَلَةٌ signifies *left in the state of her that is termed* بَاهِل, (Ṣ,) or *having her* صِرَار *loosed, and her young one left at liberty to suck her:* (Ḳ:) and ▾ مَبَاهِيلُ is applied in the same sense [as its pl.]. (Ṣ, Ḳ. [In the CḲ the latter is written مُبَاهِل, as a sing.]) — [Hence,] أَتَيْتُكَ بَاهِلًا غَيْرَ ذَاتِ صِرَارٍ, said by an Arab woman to her husband; (Ṣ;) by the wife of Dureyd Ibn-Eṣ-Ṣimmeh, to him, on his desiring to divorce her; meaning † *I made my property lawful to thee.* (TA.) — بَاهِلُونَ † *People at liberty in their place of abode, no Sultán reaching them, so that they do what they please.* (K.) — And the sing., ‡ *Going to and fro without work.* (Ibn-'Abbád, Z, K.) — ‡ *A pastor without a staff:* (JK, K:) or, *walking without a staff.* (TA.) — † *A man without a weapon.* (IAar, TA.) — And بَاهِلَةٌ † *A woman having no husband;* (JK;) syn. أَيِّمٌ. (K.)

أَيْهُلٌ *The produce,* or *fruit, of a certain tree, which is the* عَرْعَر [a name applied to the *cypress* and to the *juniper-tree*]: (S:) so says Ibn-Seenà [Avicenna] in the Kánoon; and he adds that *it is of two species, small and great, both brought from the country of the* رُوم: *one species of the tree thereof has leaves like those of the* سَرْو [or *common, evergreen, cypress*], *has many thorns, and grows,* or *spreads, wide,* (يَشْتَعْرِضُ,) *not growing tall: the leaves of the other are like those of the* طَرْفَآء [or *tamarisk*], *the taste thereof is like* [*that of*] *the* سَرْو, *and it is drier, and less hot:* (TA:) or it is *the produce of a kind of great tree, the leaves of which are like* [*those of*] *the* طرفاء, *and the fruit of which is like the* نَبِق [or *fruit of the lote-tree called* سِدْر]; *and it is not* [*the fruit of*] *the* عرعر, *as J imagined it to be: the smoke thereof expels quickly the young in the womb: used as a liniment, with vinegar, it cures what is termed* دَآءُ الثَّعْلَبِ [*alopecia*]: *and with honey, it cleanses foul ulcers.* (K.) [In the present day, it is applied to the *juniper-tree;* as is also عَرْعَر; and particularly to the species thereof called the *savin.* See قَطِرَانٌ.]

مُبْهَلَةٌ and مَبَاهِلُ [its pl.]: see بَاهِلٌ.

بهم

2. بَهَّمُوا البَهْمَ, inf. n. تَبْهِيمٌ, *They separated the* بهم [i. e. *lambs,* or *kids,* or both,] *from their mothers,* (S, K,) *and pastured them alone.* (S.) — بَهَّمُوا بِالْمَكَانِ, inf. n. as above, *They stayed,* or *remained, in the place;* (K, TA;) *did not quit it.* (TA.) — Also بَهَّمَ, said of a man, † *He continued looking at a thing without his being relieved by doing so.* (JK.) — † *He was silent, and confounded,* or *perplexed, when asked respecting a thing.* (JK.) — † *He did not fight,* or *engage in conflict.* (JK.)

4. ابهم, (K,) inf. n. إِبْهَامٌ, (JK,) † *It* (a thing, or an affair,) *was,* or *became, dubious, confused,* or *vague,* (JK, K, TA,) *so that one knew not the way,* or *manner, in which it should be engaged in, done, executed,* or *performed;* (JK, TA;) as also ▼استبهم; (JK, K, TA;) for which grammarians often use ▼انبهم; but this has not been heard in the [classical] language of the Arabs: (MF, TA:) [said to be] from بَهِيمٌ denoting a colour, whatever it be, except that which is termed شِيَةٌ, in which is no colour differing therefrom. (Har p. 50.) — *He closed,* or *locked,* a door; (S, Mgh, TA;) [or, *so that one could not find the way to open it;* (see مُبْهَمٌ;)] and *stopped it up.* (TA.) [And hence,] one says of the thumb, تُبْهِمُ الكَفَّ, meaning *It closes upon* [the palm of] *the hand, as a cover.* (TA.) — [Hence also,] † *He made a thing,* or *an affair, to be dubious, confused,* or *vague,* (JK, TA,*) *so that there was no way,* or *manner, of knowing it,* (TA,) or *so that one knew not the way,* or *manner, in which it should be engaged in, done, executed,* or *performed:* (JK:) [in the former sense, or meaning † *he made it to be dubious, confused,* or *vague,*] said of speech, or language, (K in art. غمض, &c.,) and of information, or news, or a narration; (Msb;) contr. of أَوْضَحَ; (TA in art. غمض;) i. q. لَمْ يُبَيِّنْ. (Msb.) — † *He made,* or *held,* a thing *to be vague,* or *indefinite.* (Mgh.) — And, said of a prohibited thing, † *He made it,* or *held it, to be not allowable in any manner, nor for any cause:* (Az, TA:) or *to be prohibited unconditionally.* (Mgh.) [See مُبْهَمٌ.] — † *He made* a man *to turn away,* or *withdraw,* or *retire,* (JK, K,) عَنْ كَذَا *from such a thing,* (JK,) or عَنِ الأَمْرِ *from the affair.* (K.) — ابهمت الأَرْضُ *The land produced what is termed* بُهْمَى: (JK, K:) or *produced much thereof.* (S.)

5: see 10.

7: see 4.

10: see 4. — You say, استبهم عَلَيْهِ الأَمْرُ ‡ *The affair was as though it were closed against him, so that he knew not the way in which to engage in it,* or *execute it;* syn. أُرْتِجَ عَلَيْهِ. (TA.) And استبهم عليه الكَلَامُ, (S, TA,) or استبهم عَلَيْهِ, (K,) † *Speech was as though it were closed against him;* or *he was,* or *became, impeded in his speech, unable to speak,* or *tongue-tied;* (S,* K, TA;) syn. اِسْتَغْلَقَ; (S;) and تبهّم ▼ عليه كَلَامُهُ [signifies the same]; syn. أُرْتِجَ; (JK, S;*) on the authority of AZ. (S.) And استبهم الخَبَرُ † *The information,* or *narration, was dubious, confused, vague,* or *difficult to be understood* or *expressed;* or *was not to be understood* or *expressed; as though it were closed* [*against the hearer* or *speaker*]; syn. اِسْتَغْلَقَ, and اِسْتَعْجَمَ. (Msb.)

بَهْمٌ is pl. of ▼ بَهْمَةٌ, (S, Msb, K,) as are also ▼ بُهُمٌ and بِهَامٌ, (K,) [or rather بَهْمٌ is a coll. gen. n., and ▼ بَهْمَةٌ is its n. un., and ▼ بُهُمٌ is a quasi-pl. n., and] بِهَامٌ is pl. of بَهْمٌ, (S, Msb,) and بِهَامَاتٌ is a pl. pl. [i. e. pl. of بِهَامٌ]: (K:) ▼ بَهْمَةٌ signifies *A lamb,* and is applied to the *male* and the *female;* (S, Msb;) or, accord. to a trad. in which it occurs, it is a name for the *female;* (IAth, TA;) but بِهَامٌ, which is applied to *lambs when they are alone,* as سِخَالٌ is to kids when they are alone, is also applied to *lambs and kids together:* (S,* Msb:) or, accord. to IF, بَهْمٌ signifies *young lambs* or *goats:* (Msb:) and accord. to AZ, (Msb,) or A'Obeyd, (TA,) ▼ بَهْمَةٌ is applied to *a lamb* or *goat, whether male or female, after the period when it is termed* سَخْلَةٌ, *which is when it is just brought forth;* (Msb, TA;) and its pl. is ابهم: (Msb: [so in my copy of that work, as though meant for أَبْهُمٌ; but perhaps a mistranscription for البَهْمُ:]) or it is applied to *a lamb* or *goat when just brought forth,* i. e., *before it is termed* سَخْلَةٌ: (Mgh: [and this is agreeable with its application in a trad. cited by IAth:]) or to the *young one,* not, as in the K, *young ones,* (TA,) *of the sheep,* and *of the goat,* and *of an animal of the bovine kind* (K, TA) both *wild* and *not wild,* alike to the *male* and the *female, while small;* or, as some say, *when it has attained to youthful vigour:* (TA:) Lebeed applies بِهَامٌ to the *young ones of* [*wild*] *animals of the bovine kind:* (S, TA:) accord. to Th, بَهْمٌ signifies *young kids.* (TA.) — سَعْدُ البِهَامِ *One of the Mansions* (K, TA) *of the Moon:* (TA:) or *two stars which are not of the Mansions of the Moon.* (S and L and K in art. سعد, q. v.)

بُهُمٌ: see بَهْمٌ, in two places.

[بُهْمٌ an epithet of which only the fem. form is mentioned. You say] أَرْضٌ بَهْمَةٌ *Land abounding with what is termed* بُهْمَى: (AHn, K:) the word بهمة is a possessive epithet. (TA.)

بَهْمَةٌ: see بَهْمٌ, in four places.

بُهْمَةٌ *A rock,* or *great mass of stone* or *of hard stone,* (K, TA,) *that is solid, not hollow.* (TA.) — And hence, accord. to some, (TA,) or because his condition is such that one knows not how to prevail with him, (Ham pp. 334 and 610,) *A courageous man,* (K, and Ham ubi suprà,) or *a horseman,* (AO, S,) *to whom one knows not the way whence to gain access,* or *whence to come,* (AO, S, K,) *by reason of his great might,* or *valour:* (AO, S:) or, as in the Nawádir, رَجُلٌ بُهْمَةٌ signifies *a man who will not be turned from a thing that he desires to do:* (TA:) it is not applied as an epithet to a woman: (IJ, TA:) pl. بُهَمٌ. (S, A.) You say, هُوَ بُهْمَةٌ مِنَ البُهَمِ, meaning † *He is a courageous man, of those to whom the approach is as though it were closed against his adversaries.* (A, TA.) Accord. to IJ, it is an inf. n. used as an epithet, though having no verb. (TA.) [Hence,] it applies to one and to a number of persons. (Ham p. 494.) [For] it signifies also — † *An army:* (S, K:) or *courageous men,* or *courageous men clad in armour;* because one knows not the way in which to fight with them: or, as some say, *a company of horsemen:* (TA:) pl. as above. (K.) — † *A difficult affair* or *case;* (K, TA;) *such that one cannot find the way to perform it,* or *manage it:* pl. as above. (TA.) You say, وَقَعَ فِي بُهْمَةٍ لَا يَتَّجِهُ لَهَا † [*He fell into a difficult,* or *an embarrassing, case, which one knew not the way to manage*]. (TA.) The pl. is also explained as meaning † *Dubious, confused,* or *vague, affairs* or *cases.* (TA.) — † *Blackness.* (TA.) — And البُهَمُ † *The three nights in which the moon does not* [*visibly*] *rise.* (TA.)

بُهْمَى, a word both sing. and pl., (Sb, S, K,) its alif [written ى] being a denotative of the fem. gender, wherefore it is without tenween; (Sb, S;) or [it is written بُهْمًى, with tenween, for it is a coll. gen. n., and] its n. un. is بُهْمَاةٌ, (S, K, and so in the JK,) its alif, some say, being a letter of quasi-coordination; but Mbr says that this is not known, and that the alif in a word of the measure فُعْلَى is nought but a denotative of the fem. gender; (S;) and the n. un. بهماة is anomalous; (El-'Ashmoonee's Expos. of the Alfeeyeh of Ibn-Málik, (التَّأْنِيث ;) [*A species of barley-grass; app. hordeum murinum, or common wall-barley-grass;*] *a certain plant*, (Lth, JK, Ṣ, Ḳ,) *well known*; (Ḳ;) *the sheep and goats*, (Lth, TA,) or *the camels*, (JK,) *are vehemently fond of it as long as it is green*; (Lth, JK, TA;) *but when it dries up, its prickles bristle out, and it repugns*; (Lth, TA;) *it is of the herbs* (بُقُول) *that are termed* أَحْرَار [app. here meaning *slender and sweet*] *when fresh and when dry, and comes forth at first undistinguishably as to species, from the earth, like as does corn; then it becomes like corn, and puts forth prickles like those* [*that compose the awn, or beard,*] *of the ear of corn, which, when they enter the noses of the sheep or goats and the camels, cause pain to their noses, until men pull them out from their mouths and their noses; and when it becomes large, and dries up, it is a pasture that is fed upon until the rain of the next year falls upon it, when its seed that has fallen from its ears germinates beneath it.* (AḤn, TA.)

بَهِيمٌ *Black*: (Ḳ:) pl. بُهُمٌ. (TA.) And [app. used also as a subst., signifying] *A black ewe* (Ḳ, TA) *in which is no whiteness*: pl. as above and بُهْمٌ. (TA.) — Applied to a horse, to the male and the female, (Ṣ,* Mgh,* Ḳ,) *Of one, unmixed, colour; in which is no colour differing from the rest*: (Ṣ, Mgh, Ḳ:) pl. بُهُمٌ. (Ṣ.) لَا أَغَرُّ وَلَا بَهِيمٌ [*Not having a star, or blaze, on the forehead or face, nor of one, unmixed, colour*, or *not white nor black*, (some such proposition as "This is a horse" being understood before لا,)] is a prov. applied to a dubious, confused, or vague, affair or case. (TA.) — A colour *of one kind*, (JK,) *in which is no colour differing from the rest*, (JK, and Ḥar p. 50,) *whatever colour it be, except that which is termed* شُهْبَة: (Ḥar ubi suprà:) or a colour *that is clear, pure*, or *unmixed, not resembling any other*, (AA, Ḳ,* TA,) *whether it be black or any other colour*, (AA, TA,) *except*, as Z says, *that which is termed* شُهْبَة. (TA.) — A night *in which is no light* (JK, TA) *until the dawn*. (TA.) — † A sound, or voice, *in which is no trilling*, or *quavering*, or *reiteration in the throat* or *fauces*. (JK, Ḳ,* TA.*) — *Perfect*, or *complete, in make*; as also ↓ مُبْهَمٌ: pl. بُهْمٌ: so in the phrase in a trad. (respecting the day of resurrection, TA), يُحْشَرُ النَّاسُ بُهْمًا, i. e. *Mankind shall be congregated perfect*, or *complete, in make, without mutilation*, or *defect*: (JK:) or the meaning here is, *sound*, or *healthy*: (Ṣ:) or *not having any of the diseases or noxious affections of the present state, as blindness, and elephantiasis, and leprosy, and blindness of one eye, and lameness, &c.*: (A'Obeyd, Ḳ,* TA:) or *naked*; (JK, Ḳ;) *not having upon them anything to conceal them*: (JK:) or *not having with them anything* (Ṣ, TA) *of worldly goods or commodities*. (TA.) — †*Unknown*. (El-Khaṭṭábee, TA.) — See also إِبْهَامٌ.

بَهِيمَةٌ [*A beast; a brute;*] *any quadruped*, (Akh, M, Mṣb, Ḳ,) *even if in the water*, (Akh, M, Ḳ,) [i. e.,] *of the land* and *of the sea*; (Mṣb;) and (so in the Mṣb, but in the Ḳ "or") *any animal that does not discriminate*: (Zj, Mṣb, Ḳ:) pl. بَهَائِمُ. (Ṣ, Mṣb, Ḳ.)

[بَهِيمِىٌّ *Of, or relating to, beasts, or brutes.*]

[بَهِيمِيَّةٌ The *nature of beasts*, or *brutes.*]

أَبْهَمُ: see مُبْهَمٌ, in two places. — Also *i. q.* أَعْجَمُ [app. as meaning *Destitute of the faculty of speech* or *articulation, like the beasts*]. (Ḳ.)

إِبْهَامٌ The *thumb*, and the *great toe*; (M, Ḳ;) the *greatest* إِصْبَع, (JK, T, Ṣ,) *that is next to the forefinger, having two joints*, so called because it closes upon [the palm of] the hand, as a cover; (T, TA;) the *greatest of the* أَصَابِع *in the hand* and *in the foot*: (M, Ḳ:) of the fem. gender, (Ṣ, Mṣb,) accord. to common repute; (Mṣb;) and sometimes masc.: (Lḥ, M, Ḳ:) and ↓ بَهِيمٌ signifies the same; mentioned by Az in the T, and by others; but Az adds that one should not say بِهَامٌ: (TA:) the pl. of ابهام is أَبَاهِيمُ (JK, Ṣ, M, Mṣb, Ḳ) and أَبَاهِمُ, (M, Ḳ,) which latter is used by poetic license for the former, (M,) and إِبْهَامَاتٌ. (Mṣb.) أَقْصَرُ مِنْ إِبْهَامِ الضَّبِّ [*Shorter than the great toe of the* (*lizard called*) ضبّ], and من ابهام القَطَاة [*than the back toe of the* (*bird called*) قطاة], and من ابهام الحُبَارَى [*than the back toe of the* (*bird called*) حبارى], are proverbs of the Arabs. (Ḥar p. 335.)

مُبْهَمٌ, applied to a door, *Closed*, or *locked*, (JK, Ḳ,) *so that one cannot find the way to open it*: (JK, TA:) and *stopped up*: (TA:) or *having a lock upon it, with which it is fastened*. (Mgh.) — A wall *in which is no door*. (TA.) — A chest *having no lock* [*by means of which it may be opened*]. (IAmb, TA.) — *I. q.* مُصْمَتٌ [as meaning *Solid; not hollow*; in the CḲ أَصْمَتُ, which signifies the same]; as also ↓ أَبْهَمُ: (Ḳ:) *having no fissure in it*: and ↓ the latter, applied to a heart, is said to mean † *impenetrable by admonition*. (TA.) — † A thing, or an affair, *made to be dubious, confused*, or *vague*; (JK;) [*such that there is no way*, or *manner, of knowing it*; (see the verb;)] or *such that one knows not the way*, or *manner, in which it should be engaged in, done, executed*, or *performed*: (JK, Ṣ, Mgh, TA:) † speech, or language, [*that is dubious, confused*, or *vague*,] *such that there is no way*, or *manner, of knowing it*: (Mgh, TA:) applied to a road, † *unapparent*, or *hardly apparent*: (TA:) and, applied to the ordinance respecting the making up for the days in which one has broken a fast, [and to many other cases,] † *undefined*; in this instance meaning, as to whether the days may be interrupted, or whether they must be consecutive. (Mgh.) [Hence,] مُبْهَمَاتٌ † *Difficult things*, or *affairs, such that one cannot find the way to perform them*. (TA.) And الأَسْمَآءُ المُبْهَمَةُ, so termed by the grammarians, † *The nouns of indication*, (Ṣ, Ḳ,) *such as* هٰذَا *and* هٰؤُلَآءِ *and* ذَاكَ *and* أُولَآئِكَ: (Ṣ:) accord. to Az, الحُرُوفُ المُبْهَمَةُ signifies † *the particles which have no derivatives, and of which the roots are not known, as* الَّذِى *and* مَا *and* مَنْ *and* عَنْ *and the like*. (TA.) — Applied to a vow, and to [certain ordinances respecting] marriage and divorce and emancipation, † *From which there is no getting out*, or *extricating of oneself; as though they were closed doors with locks upon them*: (Mgh:) and, applied to prohibited things, † *not allowable in any manner*, (T, Ḳ, TA,) *nor for any cause*; (T, TA;) or *prohibited unconditionally*; (Mgh;) *as the prohibition of* [*the marriage with*] *the mother, and the sister*, (T, Mgh,* Ḳ, TA,) *and the like*: (T, TA:) such a woman is said to be مُبْهَمَةٌ عَلَى الرَّجُلِ † [*absolutely prohibited to the man; as though she were closed against him*, or *inaccessible to him*]. (Mṣb. [But in this last work it seems to be مُبْهِمَةٌ, which is not agreeable with common usage.]) In the copies of the Ḳ, بُهُمٌ and بُهْمٌ are given as pls. of this word: but it seems that there is an omission or a misplacement in the passage; for these are said to be pls. of بَهِيمٌ, as shown above. (TA.) — † *In a state of swooning* or *insensibility, speechless, and without discrimination*; in consequence of a blow [&c.]. (TA.) — See also بَهِيمٌ.

مُسْتَبْهِمٌ عَنِ الكَلَامِ † *Debarred from the faculty of speech*. (Nifṭaweyh, TA.)

بهو

1. بَهَا, (JK, Mṣb, Ḳ,) aor. يَبْهَا, (JK,) or يَبْهُو; (Mṣb, Ḳ;) and بَهُوَ, aor. يَبْهُو; and بَهِىَ, aor. يَبْهَى; (Ṣ,* Ḳ;) and بَهِىَ, [first pers. بَهِيتُ,] aor. يَبْهَى; (Ḳ;) inf. n. بَهَآءٌ and بَهَاءَةٌ; (JK, TA;) *He* (a man, Ṣ) or *it, was*, or *became, characterized by*, or *possessed of*, بَهَآء, meaning *beauty*, or *goodliness* [&c.]. (JK, Ṣ, Mṣb, Ḳ.) — بَهُوتُهُ and بَهِيتُهُ: see 3. — بَهِىَ, (Ṣ, Ḳ,) aor. -َ, (Ḳ,) inf. n. بَهًا, (TA,) *It* (a tent, Ṣ, Ḳ) *was*, or *became, empty*, or *vacant*: (Ḳ:) or *it was*, or *became, rent*, or *pierced with holes, and rendered vacant*. (Ṣ, TA.) — بَهِىَ بِهِ *i. q.* بَهَأَ بِهِ [q. v.]. (JK.) And بَهُوا بِهِ occurs in a trad., as they relate it, for بَهَؤُوا بِهِ. (A'Obeyd, TA in art. بهأ.)

2. بَهَّاهُ, inf. n. تَبْهِيَةٌ, *He made it wide*, or *ample*; or *widened it*; and *made it*; namely, a بَيْت [i. e. tent, or house]. (Ḳ.)

3. بَاهَاهُ, (TA,) [and بَاهَى بِهِ, as will be seen from what follows,] inf. n. مُبَاهَاةٌ, (Ṣ, TA,) *He vied*, or *competed, with him*, or *contended with him for superiority, in beauty*, or *goodliness*, or *in glorying*, or *boasting*, or *in glory*, or *excellence*; *he emulated*, or *rivalled, him therein*; or, simply, *he vied with him*; syn. بَارَاهُ; (TA in art. بهج;) and فَاخَرَهُ. (Ṣ,* TA.) Hence, in a trad. respecting 'Arafeh, تُبَاهِى بِهِمُ المَلَائِكَةُ [*The angels vie with them*]. (TA.) You say, ↓ بَاهَانِى فَبَهَوْتُهُ (Lḥ, JK, Ḳ*) and ↓ فَبَهِيتُهُ (Lḥ, JK) i. e. [*He vied*, or *competed, with me*, or *contended with me for superiority, in beauty*, or *goodliness*, &c.,] *and I became*, (Lḥ,) or *I was*, (JK,) *more beautiful*, or *goodly*, [&c.,] *than he*, (Lḥ, JK,) or *I surpassed him in beauty*, or *goodliness* [&c.]. (Ḳ.)

4. ابهى *He* (a man) *was*, or *became, beautiful*, or *handsome, in face*. (Ḳ.) — ابهاهُ [*He deprived*

it of beauty, or *goodliness;* the ا being a privative, as it often is, like the Greek *α*: this is probably the primary signification: (see Freytag's Arab. Prov. ii. 604:) and hence, —] *He made it empty*, or *vacant:* (Ḳ:) or *he rent it*, or *made holes in it:* (JK:) or *he rent it, or made holes in it, and rendered it vacant:* (Ṣ:) namely, a tent. (JK, Ṣ, Ḳ.) Hence the saying, المِعْزَى تُبْهِى وَلَا تُبْنِى [explained in art. بنى]: (JK, Ṣ:) applied to him who injures and does not profit. (JK.) — *He emptied it;* namely, a vessel. (A'Obeyd, JK, Ṣ, Ḳ.) — ابهى الخَيْلَ *He freed the horses from service* (JK, Ṣ, Ḳ) *in warfare;* (Ṣ, Ḳ;) i. e. *he did not go to war upon the horses:* (TA:) or *he divested the horses of their furniture, and did not ride them:* or *he supplied the horses amply with fodder, and gave them rest:* but the first is the approved explanation. (TA.)

6. تَبَاهَوْا *They vied*, or *competed*, or *contended for superiority, one with another*, [*in beauty*, or *goodliness*, or] *in glorying*, or *boasting*, or *in glory*, or *excellence; they emulated*, or *rivalled, one another therein;* or, simply, *they vied, one with another;* syn. تَفَاخَرُوا. (Ṣ, Ḳ.)

8. يَبْتَهِى occurs in a verse of El-Aạshà for يَبْتَهِئُ. (O, TṢ, L, on the authority of Aṣ, in art. بهأ, q. v.)

بَهْوٌ *Ampleness;* or *an ample state*, or *condition:* so in the saying, هُوَ فِى بَهْوٍ مِنَ العَيْشِ [*He is in an ample state*, or *condition, of life*]: and this is [said to be] the primary signification. (Aṣ, TA.) — Anything *ample, wide*, or *spacious*. (Ḳ.) [Hence,] نَاقَةٌ بَهْوَةُ الجَنْبَيْنِ *A she-camel wide in the two sides*. (TA.) — *A wide*, or *spacious, tract of land*, (Ḳ, TA,) *in which are no mountains, between two elevated tracts*. (TA.) — *A wide covert*, or *hiding-place, of a* [*wild*] *bull*, (JK, Ḳ, TA,) *which he makes for himself at the foot of the kind of tree called* أَرْطَى [q. v.]: (TA:) pl. [of pauc.] أَبْهَآءٌ and [of mult.] بُهُوٌّ and [quasi-pl.-n.] بُهِىٌّ. (Ḳ.) — Any *vacant*, or *intervening, space*. (TA.) — The *interior of the chest*, or *breast*, (Ḳ, TA,) of a man and of any beast: (TA:) or the *space that intervenes between the two breasts and the uppermost part of the chest* (Ḳ, TA) is called بَهْوُ الصَّدْرِ: (TA:) or the *part between* [or *within*] *the extremities of the ribs that project over the belly:* (TA:) and in her that is pregnant, (JK, Ḳ,) whatever she be, (JK,) the *resting-place of the fœtus, between the two haunches:* (JK, Ḳ:) pl. [of pauc.] أَبْهَآءٌ and أَبْهٍ and [of mult.] بُهِىٌّ and [quasi-pl. n.] بُهِىٌّ [in the TA بِهِىٌّ, which seems to be a mistake]. (Ḳ.) — *A tent that is placed in advance, before the other tents:* (JK, Ṣ, TA:) pl. أَبْهَآءٌ. (JK.) In a trad., Arabs are spoken of as removing with their أَبْهَآء. (TA.)

بَهٍ [originally بَهِوٌ]: see بَهِىٌّ, in two places.

بَهَآءٌ *Beauty*, or *goodliness:* (Ṣ, Mṣb, Ḳ:) *beauty of aspect, of mien*, or *of external state* or *condition:* (Mṣb:) *a beautiful aspect, that excites admiration, and satisfies the eye:* (TA:) and, as an attribute of God, (Mṣb,) *greatness*, or *majesty*. (Mṣb, Ḥar p. 271.) — ‡ The *froth of milk:* (JK:) or the *glistening of the froth of milk*. (Ḳ.) = As an epithet applied to a she-camel, it belongs to art. بهأ [in which it is explained]. (Ṣ.)

بَهِىٌّ *Possessing the quality*, or *attribute, of* بَهَآء [i. e. *beauty*, or *goodliness*, &c.]; (JK, Ṣ, Mṣb;) *the beauty of which*, (JK,) or *the pleasing appearance of which*, (TA,) *satisfies the eye;* (JK, TA;) as also ↓ بَهٍ and ↓ بَاهٍ: the fem. of بَهِىٌّ is بَهِيَّةٌ; of which the pl. is بَهِيَّاتٌ and بَهَايَا: and the fem. of ↓ بَهٍ is بَهِيَةٌ; and the pl. is أَبْهِيَآءُ. (TA.)

بَاهٍ: see بَهِىٌّ. = Also, applied to a بَيْت [or tent (see بَهِىَ)], *Empty*, or *vacant;* (JK, Ṣ, Ḳ;) *containing nothing:* (Ṣ:) or *containing little furniture*, or *few goods* or *utensils*. (TA.) — بِئْرٌ بَاهِيَةٌ *A wide-mouthed well*. (Ḳ.)

أَبْهَى [*More*, and *most, beautiful*, or *goodly;*] *surpassingly*, or *superlatively, beautiful*, or *goodly:* fem. بُهْيَا; which is applied to a woman, and, by Ḥoneyf El-Ḥanátim, to a she-camel. (Az, TA.) [Hence,] one says, إِنَّ هٰذَا لَبُهْيَاىَ [*This is my superlatively beautiful quality;* or] *this is of the things in which I vie with others*. (AA, ISk.)

بهى

1. بَهِىَ, as an intrans. v.: and بَهَيْتُهُ: see art. بهو.

بو

بَوٌّ *A skin of a young unweaned camel stuffed* (Lth, T, Ṣ, M, Ḳ) *with straw* (Lth, T, M, Ḳ) *or with* ثُمَام [i. e. *panic grass*] (M, Ḳ) *or with dry herbage*, (M,) *to which a she-camel is made to incline* (Lth, T, Ṣ) *when her young one has died:* (Ṣ:) *it is brought near to the mother of the young camel* [*that has died*], *in order that she may incline to it, and yield her milk* (M, Ḳ) *over it*. (M.) — Also *A she-camel's young one*. (M, Ḳ.) — And † *Stupid; foolish; having little sense*, or *intellect;* as also ↓ بَوِّىٌّ; (IAạr, T, Ḳ;) applied to a man: (IAạr, T:) fem. بَوَّةٌ. (Ḳ.) — And البَوُّ, (Ḳ,) or بَوُّ الأَثَافِى, (Lth, T, Ṣ, M,) ‡ *Ashes:* (Lth, T, Ṣ, M, Ḳ:) so called [as being lifeless,] by way of comparison [to the stuffed skin of a young camel]. (M.)

بَوِّىٌّ: see above.

بُوبَاةٌ, mentioned in this art. in the Ṣ, and also, as well as in art. بوب, in the Ḳ: see the latter art.

بوا

جُوزُ بُوَا, also written جُوزُ بُوَّى: see art. جوز. = خُبْزُ بُوَاءٍ: see art. خبز.

بوأ

1. بَآءَ إِلَيْهِ, (M, Mgh,* Mṣb,* Ḳ,) aor. يَبُوْءُ, (M, Mgh, Mṣb,) inf. n. بَوْءٌ, (M, Mgh,) *He returned, went back*, or *came back*, (M, Mgh, Mṣb, Ḳ,) *to it*, (M, Ḳ,*) namely, a thing: (M:) or *he withdrew* [from a person or persons, or a place,] *to it*, or *him;* or, perhaps, *he made himself solely and peculiarly a companion*, or *an associate, to him*, or *it;* syn. اِنْقَطَعَ [q. v.]: (Ḳ:) but in some copies of the Ḳ, the latter explanation is connected with the former by وَ [and] instead of أَوْ. (TA.) وَبَآؤُوا بِغَضَبٍ مِنَ ٱللّٰهِ [in the Ḳur ii. 58 and iii. 108] means *And they returned with anger from God;* (Akh, Ṣ, Bḍ in ii. 58, and Jel in the same and in iii. 108;) i. e. the anger of God came upon them: (Akh, Ṣ:) or *they returned deserving anger from God:* (Bḍ in iii. 108:) or *they became deserving of anger from God:* from بَآءَ فُلَانٌ بِفُلَانٍ *such a one was deserving of being*, or *fit to be, slain in retaliation for such a one*, (Ksh and Bḍ in ii. 58,) *because his equal:* (Ksh ibid.:) the primary signification of بَوْءٌ being [said to be] that of *equalling*, or *being equal with*. (Bḍ in ii. 58.) [See a similar phrase, also from the Ḳur, below.] — بُؤْتُ بِهِ إِلَيْهِ [*I returned with it to him:* and hence,] *I returned it, took it back*, or *brought it back, to him;* (M, Ḳ;) as also ↓ أَبَأْتُهُ, (Th, M, Ḳ,) and بُؤْتُهُ, (Ks, M, Ḳ,) but this last is rare. (M.) — بَآءَ بِإِثْمِهِ, aor. and inf. n. as above, (T, Ṣ,) signifies, accord. to Akh, *He returned* [laden] *with his sin:* (Ṣ:) or, accord. to Aṣ, *he acknowledged it*, or *confessed it:* (T:) or, accord. to others, (TA,) بَآءَ بِذَنْبِهِ, (T,* M, Mṣb, Ḳ,) aor. as above, inf. n. بَوْءٌ and بَوَآءٌ, (M, Ḳ,) *he bore*, or *took upon himself, the burden of his sin*, or *crime*, or *offence;* syn. اِحْتَمَلَهُ; (Aboo-Is-ḥáḳ, T, M, Ḳ, TA;) *and became* [*as though he were*] *the abiding-place thereof:* (TA:) or *he became burdened*, or *laden, with it:* (Mṣb:) or *he became*, or *made himself, answerable, responsible*, or *accountable, for it, by an inseparable obligation;* syn. اِلْتَزَمَهُ; for the primary signification of بَوَآءٌ is [asserted to be] لُزُومٌ [i. e. *adhesion*, &c.]; and it is afterwards used in every case [so as to imply a meaning of this kind] according to the exigency of that case; as is said in the Nh, and expressly stated by Z and Er-Rághib: (TA:) or *he acknowledged it*, or *confessed it*. (M, Ḳ.) إِنِّى أُرِيدُ أَنْ تَبُوْءَ بِإِثْمِى وَإِثْمِكَ, in the Ḳur v. 35, means *Verily I desire that thou return* [laden] *with the sin committed against me* in slaying me, *and thy sin* which thou hast committed previously: (Jel:) or *I desire that thou shouldst bear* (تَحْمِلَ) *my sin* if I were to extend my hand towards thee, *and thy sin* in extending thy hand towards me: or *the sin committed against me* in slaying me, *and thy sin* for which thine offering was not accepted: and each noun is in the place of a denotative of state; i. e., [it means] *that thou return involved in the two sins; bearing them:* and perhaps the speaker may have meant, if that must inevitably take place, I desire that it may be thine act, not mine; so that the real meaning is, that it should not be his, not that it should be his brother's: or by the إِثْم may be meant the *punishment* thereof; for the desire of the punishment of the disobedient is allowable: (Bḍ:) accord. to Th, the meaning is, if thou have determined upon slaying me, the sin will be in thee, not in me. (M.) فَبَآؤُوا بِغَضَبٍ عَلَى غَضَبٍ

[in the Ḳur ii. 84] is explained by Aboo-Is-ḥáḳ as meaning *So they bore the burden of anger upon anger*; syn. اِحْتَمَلُوا; this being said by him to be the proper signification of the verb: or, as some say, the meaning is, [*they bore the burden of*] *sin for which they deserved the fire* [*of Hell*] *following upon sin for which they deserved the same*: or *they returned* [laden *with anger upon anger*]: (T:) or *they became deserving of anger upon anger*. (Ksh.) [See a similar phrase, also from the Ḳur, above.] It is said in a form of prayer, أَبُوْءُ إِلَيْكَ بِنِعْمَتِكَ, meaning *I acknowledge*, or *confess, to Thee thy favour* [towards me, as imposing an obligation upon me]. (Mgh.) You say also, بَآءَ بِحَقِّهِ; (Ṣ;) and بِدَمِهِ; (M, Ḳ;) *He acknowledged*, or *confessed*, [*himself to be answerable, responsible*, or *accountable, for*] *his right, due*, or *just claim*; (Ṣ;) and so [*for*] *his blood*: (M, Ḳ:) the verb expresses acknowledgment, or confession, always of something for which its agent is, as it were, indebted, or answerable; not the contrary. (Ṣ.) — بَآءَ بِكَفِّى, in a poem of Ṣakhr-el-Ghei, means *It* [referring to a sword] *became in my hand; my hand became to it a* مَبَآءَة, i. e. مَأْوًى [or *place of abode*]; *it returned, and became in my hand*: or, accord. to Ibn-Ḥabeeb, *i. q.* اِسْتَقَلَّ [app. a mistranscription for اِسْتَقَرَّ *it rested*, or *remained*; the verb بَآءَ in this phrase being from بَوَآءٌ signifying لُزُومٌ, explained above]. (Skr p. 16.) = بَآءَ also signifies *It* (a thing, TA) *suited, matched, tallied, corresponded*, or *agreed*. (Ḳ.) [Hence,] بَآءَ فُلَانٌ بِفُلَانٍ (inf. n. بَوَآءٌ, TA) *Such a one was the like, or equal, of such a one, to be slain* [*in retaliation*] *for him*: (T:) or *became his like, or equal, so that he was slain* [*in retaliation*] *for him*: (Mgh:) and *was slain for him*, (AZ, T, Ṣ,) *and his blood became a compensation for the blood of the other*: (T:) or *was deserving of being, or fit to be, slain in retaliation for him*, (Ksh and Bḍ in ii. 58,) *because his equal*: (Ksh ibid.:) or *was slain for him, and so became equal with him*; (Ḳ,* TA;) as also ↓ أَبَآءَ, and ↓ بَاوَأَهُ. (M, Ḳ.) One says, بُؤْ بِهِ, i. e. *Be thou of such as are slain* [*in retaliation*] *for him*. (Ṣ.) And it is said in a prov., بَآءَتْ عَرَارِ بِكَحْلٍ *'Arári became slain for Kaḥl*: these were two cows, which smote each other with their horns, and both died: the proverb is applied to any two that become equal. (Ṣ in this art.; and the same and Ḳ in art. عر. [See also Freytag's Arab. Prov. i. 151.]) — بَآءَ دَمُهُ بِدَمِهِ, (T,* M, Ḳ,) inf. n. بَوْءٌ and بَوَآءٌ, (M,) *He made his blood equal with* [or *an equivalent for*] *his* [i. e. *another's*] *blood* [*by shedding the former in retaliation*]. (M, Ḳ.) And بَآءَهُ, [or بَآءَهُ بِهِ] (M,) or ↓ أَبَآءَهُ بِهِ, (T, Ṣ,) and ↓ اِسْتَبَآءَهُ بِهِ, (Ṣ,) *He slew him* [*in retaliation*] *for him*; (T, Ṣ, M;) i. e., the slayer for the slain. (Ṣ.) أَبَآءَ ↓ فُلَانًا بِفُلَانٍ [*He slew such a one in retaliation for such a one*] is said when the Sulṭán has retaliated for a man upon another man: and ↓ أَبَآءَهُ, inf. n. إِبَآءَةٌ, signifies *he* (the Sulṭán, or another,) *slew him in retaliation*. (T.) = بَآءَ signifies also *He exalted himself*, or *was proud*: app. formed by transposition [of the second and third radical letters, the ى being changed into ا,] from بَأَى. (Fr, T.)

2. بَوَّأَهُ مَنْزِلًا *He lodged him in an abode*; (Fr, T, M, Ḳ;) as also بَوَّأَهُ فِى مَنْزِلٍ, (M, Ḳ,) and بَوَّأَ لَهُ مَنْزِلًا: (T,* M, Ḳ:) or, as also ↓ أَبَآءَهُ مَنْزِلًا, (the latter mentioned by Fr, T,) *he prepared for him an abode*, (Ṣ, Mgh,) *and assigned*, or *gave, him a place therein*: (Ṣ:) and بَوَّأْتُهُ دَارًا and بَوَّأْتُ لَهُ دَارًا *I lodged him in a house*: (Mṣb:) and ↓ تَبَوَّأْتُكَ بَيْتًا *I took for thee a house*: and تَبَوَّآ لِقَوْمِكُمَا بِمِصْرَ بُيُوتًا [in the Ḳur x. 87] means *take ye two, for your people, in Egypt, houses*: (Akh, T:) or ↓ تَبَوُّؤٌ [or تَبَوُّؤُ مَكَانٍ] signifies a man's *putting a mark upon a place, when it pleases him, that he may abide there*: (El-'Itreefee, T:) or ↓ تَبَوَّأَهُ *he put it* [a place] *into a right*, or *proper, state*; and *prepared it*: (Sh,* T:) or ↓ تَبَوَّأَ بَيْتًا *he took a house as a place of abode*, or *as a dwelling*: (Mṣb:) or ↓ تَبَوَّأَ مَنْزِلًا *he looked for the best place that could be seen, and the most level, or even, and the best adapted by its firmness, for his passing the night there, and took it as a place of abode*; (Fr, T;) or *he took for himself a place of abode*; (T, Mgh;) or *he alighted and sojourned in a place of abode*: and ↓ اِسْتَبَآءَهُ *he took it as a* مَبَآءَة [or *place of abode*]: (Ṣ:) and بَوَّأَ المَكَانَ and ↓ أَبَآءَ بِهِ (Ḳ) and ↓ تَبَوَّأَ [i. e. تَبَوَّأَ بِهِ] (Sh, T, Ḳ) *he alighted in the place, and stayed, or dwelt, in it*: (Sh, T, Ḳ:) or ↓ أَبَآءَ بِهِ *he stayed, or dwelt, in it*, i. e., a place: (Akh, T:) and ↓ تَبَوَّأَ المَكَانَ *he alighted and abode in the place*: (M:) [whence, in the Ḳur lix. 9,] وَالَّذِينَ تَبَوَّؤُوا الدَّارَ وَالْإِيمَانَ [*and they who have made their abode in the City* of the Prophet *and in the faith*]; the faith being likened to a place of abode; or the meaning may be مَكَانَ الإِيمَانِ [*the place of the faith*]. (M.) ↓ أَبَآءَهُمْ منزلًا (AZ, M) and بَوَّأَهُمْ مَنْزِلًا (AZ, TA) also signify *He alighted and abode with them by the fo..., or front, of a mountain, where it rose from its base*, (AZ, M, TA,) or *next to a river, or brook*. (AZ, TA.) = [Hence, (see بَآءَة,)] بَوَّأَ (inf. n. تَبْوِئَةٌ, Ḳ) † *Inivit* [feminam]: and *he married* [a woman]; *took* [her] *in marriage*: syn. نَكَحَ: (M, Ḳ:) and also تَزَوَّجَ. (TA. [There mentioned as a distinct signification.]) The verb is trans. in these two senses. (TḲ.) = بَوَّأَ الرُّمْحَ نَحْوَهُ *He directed the spear towards him*; (T, Ṣ;) and (T) *confronted him with it*; (T, M, Ḳ;) and *prepared it*, or *made it ready* [*to thrust it towards him*]. (TA.)

3. بَاوَأَهُ: see بَآءَ فُلَانٌ بِفُلَانٍ.

4. أَبَآءَهُ: see بُؤْتُ بِهِ إِلَيْهِ, near the beginning of this art. — أَبَآءَ الإِبِلَ, (T, Ṣ, O, L, and so in some copies of the Ḳ, in other copies of which we find أَبَآءَ بِالإِبِلِ,) inf. n. إِبَآءَةٌ, (T,) *He brought back the camels to the* مَبَآءَة (T, Ṣ, O, L) or مَعْطِن, (Ḳ,) both of which signify the *place where they are made to lie down, at the watering-place*. (L.) And أَبَآءَ الإِبِلَ, (T, M,) inf. n. as above, (T,) *He made the camels to lie down* [*in the* مَبَآءَة], *one beside another*. (T, M.) And أَبَآءَ عَلَيْهِ مَالَهُ *He drove back*, or *brought back, to their nightly resting-place, for him, his cattle*, (Ṣ, M, TA,) i. e., *his camels*, or *his sheep* or *goats*. (Ṣ, TA.) And [hence,] أَبَآءَ اللّٰهُ عَلَيْهِمْ نَعَمًا لَا يَسَعُهَا المُرَاحُ [*God bestowed upon them cattle* (i. e. *camels &c.*) *which the nightly resting-place thereof would not contain*]. (TA.) — See also 2, in four places. — أَبَآءَ الأَدِيمَ *He put the skin, or hide, into the tanning liquid*. (Ḳ.) In the O, the action is ascribed to a woman. (TA.) = أَبَآءَ مِنْهُ *He fled from him*. (M, Ḳ.) — فَلَاةٌ تُبِىْءُ فِى فَلَاةٍ *A desert that extends* (lit. *goes away*) *into a desert*, (T, Ṣ, Ḳ,) *by reason of its amplitude*. (TA.) = أَبَآءَهُ *I made him to acknowledge*, or *confess*. (M.) [It seems to be indicated in the M that one says, أَبَأْتُهُ بِدَمِ فُلَانٍ, meaning *I made him to acknowledge, or confess, himself to be answerable, responsible, or accountable, for the blood of such a one*.] = See also 1, (towards the end of the paragraph,) in four places.

5: see 2, in eight places. — الرَّجُلُ يَتَبَوَّأُ مِنْ أَهْلِهِ كَمَا يَتَبَوَّأُ مِنْ دَارِهِ *The man possesses mastery, or authority, and power, over his wife, like as he possesses the same over his house*; syn. يَتَمَكَّنُ مِنْهَا. (Ṣ, Mgh, Mṣb.) — See also 10.

6. تَبَاوَآ *They two* (namely, two slain men, M) *became equal* [*by being slain, one in retaliation for the other*]. (M, Ḳ.) It is said in a trad., أَمَرَهُمْ أَنْ يَتَبَاوَؤُوا; incorrectly related as being يَتَبَاءَوُا; (Ṣ, Mgh;) meaning *He* (the Prophet) *ordered them that they should be equal in retaliation*, in their fighting: (Mgh:) the occasion of the order was this: there was a conflict between two tribes of the Arabs, and one of the two tribes had superior power over the other, so they said, "We will not be content unless we slay, for the slave of our party, the free of their party; and for the woman, the man:" A'Obeyd holds the former reading to be the right. (T.)

10. اِسْتَبَآءَهُ: see 2. — In the following verse of Zuheyr Ibn-Abee-Sulmà,

* فَلَمْ أَرَ مَعْشَرًا أَسَرُوا هَدِيًّا * وَلَمْ أَرَ جَارَ بَيْتٍ يُسْتَبَآءُ *

ISk says that the هَدِىّ is *one who is entitled to respect, or honour, or protection*; and that يُسْتَبَآءُ is syn. with ↓ يُتَبَوَّأُ, meaning *whose wife is taken as a wife* [by another man]: but Aboo-'Amr Esh-Sheybánee says that يُسْتَبَآءُ is from البَوَآءُ, meaning "retaliation:" [and accord. to this interpretation, which is the more probable, the verse may be rendered, *And I have not seen a company of men who have made captive one entitled to respect, or honour, or protection, nor have I seen one who has begged the protection of the people of a house, or of a tent, slain in retaliation*:] for, he says, he came to them desiring to beg their protection, and they took him, and slew him in retaliation for one of themselves. (T.) See 1, near the end of the paragraph. — اِسْتَبَأْتُ الحَكَمَ, and بِالحَكَمِ, *I asked the judge to retaliate upon a slayer; to slay the slayer for the slain*. (M.)

بَآءٌ : see بَآءَةٌ. — A *libidinous* man. (TA in باب الالف اللّيّنة.) — The *name of the letter* ب, q. v.; as also بَا : pl. of the former بَآءَاتٌ; and of the latter أَبْوَآءٌ. (TA ubi suprà.) The dim. is بُيَيَّةٌ, meaning *A little* ب : and *a* ب *faintly pronounced:* [and app. بُوَيَّةٌ also, as the medial radical is generally held to be و :] and in like manner is formed the dim. of every similar name of a letter. (Lth, on the letter حَآء, in TA, باب الالف اللّيّنة.)

بَآءَةٌ : see مَبَآءَةٌ, in three places. — Also, (T, Ṣ, M, Mgh, Mṣb, Ḳ,) and † بَآءٌ, (IAṣr, T, Ṣ, M, Ḳ,) and بَاهَةٌ, with the ء changed into ه, (TA,) and بَاهٌ, (IAṣr, T, Mṣb,) with ا and ه, but IḲt asserts this last to be a mistranscription, (Mṣb, TA,) [though it is of very frequent occurrence,] and IAmb says that بَآءَةٌ is sing., or n. un., of بَآءٌ, and بَآءٌ [or بَآءَةٌ] has for pl. بَآءَاتٌ, (TA,) ‡ *Coitus conjugalis:* and *marriage:* syn. جِمَاعٌ (T, Mṣb) and نِكَاحٌ (Aṣ, Fr, T, Ṣ, M, Mgh, Ḳ) and تَزْوِيجٌ : (T:) from بَآءَةٌ signifying *a place of abode;* [see مَبَآءَةٌ;] (T, Ṣ,* Mgh, Mṣb;) because it is generally in a place of abode; (Mgh, Mṣb;) or because the man possesses mastery, or authority, and power, over his wife, like as he possesses the same over his house: (Ṣ, Mgh, Mṣb: see 5:) بَآءَةٌ is applied [also] to the *marriage-contract;* because he who takes a woman in marriage lodges her in a place of abode. (T.) [See also بَاهٌ, in art. بوه.] It is said in a trad., مَنِ ٱسْتَطَاعَ مِنْكُمُ البَآءَةَ فَلْيَتَزَوَّجْ *He who is able, of you, to marry, let him marry:* (T:) or a prefixed noun is here suppressed; the meaning being, *he who finds* [or *is able to procure*] *the provisions* (مُؤَن) *of marriage, let him marry.* (Mṣb, TA.) And one says, فُلَانٌ حَرِيصٌ عَلَى البَآءَةِ *Such a one is vehemently desirous of marriage.* (Aṣ, T.)

بِيئَةٌ a subst. from بَوَّأَهُ مَنْزِلًا. (M, Ḳ.) [See 2; and] see also مَبَآءَةٌ. — *A mode,* or *manner, of taking for oneself a place of abode:* (M:) and [hence,] *a state,* or *condition.* (AZ, T, Ṣ, M, Ḳ.) You say, إِنَّهُ لَحَسَنُ البِيئَةِ *Verily he has a good mode, or manner, of taking for himself a place of abode:* (M:) or *verily he is of good state* or *condition.* (Ṣ.) And بَاتَ بِبِيئَةِ سَوْءٍ *He passed the night in an evil state* or *condition* (AZ, T, Ṣ,* M.)

بَوَآءٌ *Equal; equivalent; like; alike; a match;* (Akh, T, Ṣ, M, Mgh, Ḳ;) and particularly, *if slain in retaliation for another.* (M.) It is applied to one, and to two, and to more: so that you say, فُلَانٌ بَوَآءُ فُلَانٍ *Such a one is the equal,* &c., *of such a one if slain in retaliation for him:* (M:) and هُوَ بَوَآءٌ *He is an equal,* &c.; and so هِيَ *she:* and هُمْ بَوَآءٌ *They are equals,* &c.; and so هُنَّ *they,* referring to females: (Mgh:) and هُمْ بَوَآءٌ فِى هٰذَا الأَمْرِ *They are equals in this affair.* (T.) Hence, in a trad. of 'Alee, respecting witnesses, إِذَا كَانُوا بَوَآءً *When they are equals in number and rectitude.* (Mgh.) And مَا فُلَانٌ لِفُلَانٍ بِبَوَآءٍ *Such a one is not an equal,* &c., *to such a one.* (T.) And دَمُ فُلَانٍ بَوَآءٌ لِدَمِ فُلَانٍ *The blood of such a one is an equivalent for the blood of such a one.* (Ṣ.) And الجِرَاحَاتُ بَوَآءٌ *Wounds are to be retaliated equally:* a trad. (T, Mgh.) And القَوْمُ عَلَى بَوَآءٍ *The people,* or *company of men, are in a state of equality.* (T.) And قُسِمَ المَالُ بَيْنَهُمْ عَلَى بَوَآءٍ *The property was divided among them equally.* (T. [A similar ex. is given in the Mgh, and explained in the same manner; but there I find عَنْ بَوَآءٍ; perhaps a mistranscription.]) And كَلَّمْنَاهُمْ فَأَجَابُوا عَنْ بَوَآءٍ وَاحِدٍ [in a copy of the M عَلَى بواء واحد] *We spoke to them, and they replied with one reply:* (T, Ṣ, O, Ḳ:*) i. e., their reply was not discordant: عَنْ being here used in the sense of بِ. (TA.) — Also *Retaliation.* (T.) [See 1, near the end of the paragraph: as well as in other places.] It is related in a trad., that Jaafar Eṣ-Ṣádiḳ, being asked the reason of the rage of the scorpion against the sons of Adam, said, تُرِيدُ البَوَآءَ [*It desires retaliation*]; i. e., it hurts like as it is hurt. (TA.)

بَائِىٌّ and † بَاوِىٌّ rel. ns. of بَآءٌ and بَا the names of the letter ب; (TA in باب الالف اللّيّنة;) and † بَيَوِىٌّ is a rel. n. of the same. (M in art. ب.)

بَاوِىٌّ : } see بَائِىٌّ.
بَيَوِىٌّ : }

مَبَآءَةٌ The *nightly resting-place* of camels; (T;) the *resting-place* of camels, *where they are made to lie down, at the watering-place;* (T, Ṣ,* M,* L, Ḳ;*) and of sheep or goats likewise; also termed † مُتَبَوَّأٌ : (L, TA:) or the *place to which camels return;* (Mgh;) as also † بَآءَةٌ : (Mgh, Mṣb:) this is the primary signification. (Mgh.) — Hence, (Mgh,) *A place of abode* (T, Ṣ, M, Ḳ) of a people, *in any situation;* (T, Ṣ;) as also † مُبَوَّأٌ (Bḍ and Jel in x. 93) and † بِيئَةٌ (M, Ḳ) and † بَآءَةٌ; (Ṣ,* M, Mgh, Mṣb,* Ḳ;) which last is hence applied in another sense, explained before, voce بَآءَةٌ : (Mgh, Mṣb:) or *a place where people alight and abide next to a valley,* or *to the face,* or *front, of a mountain, where it rises from its base;* [see بَوَّأَهُمْ مَنْزِلًا;] as also † بَآءَةٌ. (T.) [Hence,] هُوَ رَحِيبُ المَبَآءَةِ † *He is largely bountiful.* (TA.) — Also The *covert* of the wild bull. (Ṣ, Ḳ.*) — *A nest of bees in a mountain:* (M, Ḳ:) or, accord. to the T, the *nightly resting-place* of bees; not there restricted by mention of the mountain. (TA.) — The *part* of the womb *where the child has its abode;* (M;) the *part* thereof *which is the child's* † مُتَبَوَّأٌ. (Ḳ.) — A well has what are termed مَبَآءَتَانِ, which are The *place where the water returns to* [*supply the place of*] *that which has* [*before*] *collected in the well* [*and been drawn*], (M,) or the *place where the water collects in the well;* (TA voce مَآبَةٌ;) and the *place where stands the driver of the* سَانِيَة [q. v.]. (M.) [See also مَثَابَةٌ; and مَثَابٌ.]

حَاجَةٌ مُبِيئَةٌ *A want that is vehement,* or *pressing,* (Ḳ, TA,) *and necessary.* (TA.)

مُبَوَّأٌ : } see مَبَآءَةٌ, in three places.
مُتَبَوَّأٌ : }

بوب

1. بَابَ لَهُ, aor. يَبُوبُ, (M, Ḳ,) quasi-inf. n., if there be such a verb, بِوَابَةٌ, with the و not changed into ى because it is not an inf. n. properly speaking, but a subst., (Lth, T,) *He was,* or *became, a door-keeper,* or *gate-keeper, to him;* (M, Ḳ;) namely, a Sulṭán (M) [or other person].

2. بوّب [app., †*He practised what are termed* أَبْوَابُ الحَرْبِ, meaning *the expedients, tricks,* or *stratagems, of war, battle,* or *fight.* — And hence,] †*He charged upon, attacked,* or *assaulted, the enemy.* (AA, T.) — بَوَّبْتُ الأَشْيَآءَ †*I made the things to be divided into distinct* أَبْوَاب [meaning *kinds,* or *sorts;* or *I disposed, arranged, distributed,* or *classified, the things under distinct heads*]. (Mṣb.) And بَوَّبَ الأَبْوَابَ † [*He disposed, arranged, distributed, classified,* or *set in order, the kinds, sorts, classes, chapters, heads,* or *the like*]. (TA voce أَصَّلَ, q. v.) And بَوَّبَ المُؤَلِّفُ كِتَابَهُ † [*The author disposed,* or *divided, his book in,* or *into, distinct chapters*]. (A.) [See بَابٌ.]

5. تبوّب, (A,) or تَبَوَّبَ بَوَّابًا, (Ṣ, M, Ḳ,) *He took for himself a door-keeper,* or *gate-keeper.* (Ṣ, M, A, Ḳ.)

بَابٌ, originally بَوَبٌ, (M, Mṣb,) *A door; a gate; a place of entrance:* and the *thing with which a place of entrance, such as a door or gate, is closed; of wood &c.:* (MF, TA:) pl. أَبْوَابٌ (Ṣ, M, Mṣb, Ḳ) and بِيبَانٌ (M, Ḳ) and أَبْوِبَةٌ, (Ṣ, M, Ḳ,) [a pl. of pauc., said to be] only used for conformity with another word mentioned therewith, as in the saying (of Ibn-Muḳbil, so in a copy of the Ṣ),

هَتَّاكُ أَخْبِيَةٍ وَلَّاجُ أَبْوِبَةٍ

[*A frequent render of tents, a frequent enterer of doors*], (Ṣ, M,) not being allowable when occurring alone; (Ṣ;) but IAṣr and Lḥ assert that it is a pl. of باب without its being used for conformity with another word; (M;) and this is extr.; (M, Ḳ;) for باب is of the measure فَعَلٌ, and a word of this measure has not a pl. of the measure أَفْعِلَةٌ [by rule]. (M.) You say, بَابُ البَيْتِ [*The door of the house*]; and بَابُ الدَّارِ [*the door of the house,* and *of the chamber,* and *of the tent*]; (Mṣb;) and بَابُ البَلَدِ [*the gate of the town* or *city*]. (The Lexicons &c. passim.) And Bishr Ibn-Abee-Ḥázim assigns a باب to a grave; calling the latter a بَيْت. (M.) It is also applied to *an opening,* or *a channel, made for water, to irrigate seed-produce:* pl. أَبْوَابٌ. (Mgh.) [And in Egypt, it is applied also to *A sepulchral chamber, grotto,* or *cave, hewn in a mountain;* from the Coptic βηβ: pl. بِيبَان only.] — Hence, i. e. in a secondary application, the primary signification being "a place of entrance," it is used as meaning ‡ *A means of access,* or *of attainment, to a thing:* (B, Kull, TḲ:) as in the saying, هٰذَا العِلْمُ بَابٌ إِلَى عِلْمِ كَذَا ‡ *This science is a means of attainment to such a science.* (B, TḲ.) — [And hence, †*An expedient, a trick, a stratagem,* or *a process, by which something is to be effected:* pl. أَبْوَابٌ : as in أَبْوَابُ الحَرْبِ *the expedients,* &c.,

of war, battle, or *fight;* and بَابٌ مِنَ النُّجُومِ *a process of the science of the stars,* meaning *astrology* or *astronomy;* and بَابٌ مِنَ السِّحْرِ *a process of enchantment;* see an ex. voce سِحْرٌ. Compare Matt. xvi. 18, πύλαι ᾅδου οὐ κατισχύσουσιν αὐτῆς, probably meaning "the stratagems of Hell shall not prevail against it."] — [Also †*A mode, kind, sort, class,* or *category.*] Suweyd Ibn-Kuráa uses metaphorically the pl. أَبْوَاب in relation to rhymes; saying,

أَتَيْتُ بِأَبْوَابِ القَوَافِى كَأَنَّمَا • أَذُودُ بِهَا سِرْبًا مِنَ الوَحْشِ نُزَّعَا

‡[*I gave utterance to the various kinds of rhymes as though I were driving with them a herd of wild animals desirous of the males,* or *of their wonted places of pasture*]. (M, L.) [You say also, هُوَ مِنْ هٰذَا البَابِ † *It is of this mode, kind, sort, class,* or *category:* a phrase of frequent occurrence in lexicons &c. See also بَابَةٌ.] — [Also †*A chapter;* and sometimes *a section,* or *subdivision, of a chapter;* of a book or writing;] conventionally, †*a piece consisting of words relating to matters of one kind;* and sometimes, *to matters of one species:* (Kull:) pl. أَبْوَابٌ. (A.) See also بَابَةٌ. — [Also † *A head,* or *class of items* or *articles,* in an account, or a reckoning; as in the saying,] بَيَّنْتُ لَهُ حِسَابَهُ بَابًا بَابًا †[*I explained,* or *made clear, to him his account,* or *reckoning, head by head,* or *each class of items* or *articles by itself*]; a phrase mentioned by Sb: (M:) [or, sometimes,] بَاب (M, Ḳ) and ▼بَابَةٌ (T, M, Ḳ) are used in relation to حُدُود [which here means the punishments so termed], and to an account, or a reckoning, (T, M, Ḳ,) and the like, (T, M,) as signifying the *extreme term* or *limit;* syn. غَايَةٌ; (M, Ḳ;) but IDrd hesitated respecting this, and therefore it is not mentioned in the Ṣ. (TA.)

بَابَةٌ † *A mode,* or *manner;* syn. وَجْهٌ: (ISk, Ḳ:) pl. بَابَاتٌ. (Ḳ.) [See also بَابٌ, which has a similar, and perhaps the same, signification.] Hence, هٰذَا مِنْ بَابَتِى means † *This is of the mode,* or *manner, that I desire;* (TA;) *this is suitable to me:* (IAmb, TA:) and هٰذَا شَىْءٌ مِنْ بَابَتِكَ, (Ṣ,) or هٰذَا بَابَتُكَ, (A,) †*this is a thing suitable to thee:* (Ṣ, A:) and هٰذَا بَابَتُهُ † *this is suitable to him.* (Ḳ.) Accord. to most of the critics, it is tropical. (TA.) You say also, فُلَانٌ أَهْوَنُ بَابَاتِهِ الكَذِبُ † *Such a one, the lightest of the kinds* (أَنْوَاع) *of his wickedness is lying.* (A.) — † *A habit: a property; a quality; nature; natural disposition:* or *a practice;* or *an action:* syn. خَصْلَةٌ. (Abu-l-'Omeythil, TA.) [Hence, perhaps, the last of the exs. cited above from the A.] — † *A condition;* syn. شَرْطٌ: as in the saying, هٰذَا بَابَةُ هٰذَا †[*This is the condition of this*]. (M, Ḳ.*) — بَابَاتُ الكِتَابِ † *The lines of the book* or *writing:* (M, A, Ḳ:) or it may mean *its* ▼أَبْوَاب [i. e. *chapters,* or *sections of chapters*]: (M:) this has no sing.: (A, Ḳ:) [ISd says,] I have not heard any sing. of it. (M.) — See also بَابٌ; last signification.

بُوبَاةٌ *A desert;* or *a desert in which is no water;* syn. فَلَاةٌ: (T, IJ, M, Ḳ:) as also مُومَاةٌ; (T, MF;) the ب being changed into م, as is often the case. (MF.) [It is mentioned in the Ṣ, and again in the Ḳ, in art. بو, as *syn. with* مَفَازَةٌ.]

بِوَابَةٌ The *office,* or *occupation, of a door-keeper,* or *gate-keeper.* (M, Ḳ.) [See 1.]

بَوَّابٌ *A door-keeper,* or *gate-keeper.* (Ṣ,* M, Mṣb, Ḳ, TA.)

أَبْوَابٌ مُبَوَّبَةٌ † [*Kinds, sorts, classes, chapters, heads,* or *the like, disposed, arranged, distributed, classified,* or *set in order,*] is a phrase similar to أَصْنَافٌ مُصَنَّفَةٌ. (Ṣ.) You say also كِتَابٌ مُبَوَّبٌ † [*A book disposed in,* or *divided into, distinct chapters*]. (A.)

Quasi بوج

بَاجٌ; pl. أَبْوَاجٌ: see art. بأج. AZ mentions it as without ء: ISk, as with ء. (ISd, TA.)

بوح

1. بَاحَ, (A, Mṣb, Ḳ,) aor. يَبُوحُ, (Mṣb,) inf. n. بَوْحٌ, (A, Mṣb,) *It* (a secret, A, or a thing, Mṣb) *became apparent,* or *manifest.* (A, Mṣb, Ḳ.) You say, بَاحَ مَا كَتَمْتُ [*What I concealed became apparent*]. (A.) And أَعُوذُ بِاللّٰهِ مِنْ بَوْحِ السِّرِّ وَكَشْفِ السِّتْرِ [*I seek protection by God from the appearing of the secret, and the removing of the veil,* or *covering*]. (A.) = بَاحَ بِهِ, (Ṣ, A, Mṣb, Ḳ,) [aor. as above,] inf. n. بَوْحٌ and بُؤُوحٌ and بُؤُوحَةٌ, (Ḳ, TA,) *He revealed,* or *disclosed, it;* (Ṣ, A, Mṣb, Ḳ;) namely, a secret, (Ṣ, A, Ḳ,) or a thing; (Mṣb;) as also ▼اباحهُ. (A, Mṣb, Ḳ.) It (the former) is said to be from ▼الإِبَاحَةُ [the inf. n. of the latter] signifying *The showing* a thing *to the beholder in order that he who will may take it.* (TA.) You say, أَبَاحَهُ ▼ سِرًّا فَبَاحَ بِهِ *He revealed to him a secret, and he* (the latter) [*revealed it, i. e.,*] *did not conceal it.* (TA.) And بُحْ بِٱسْمِكَ وَلَا تَكْنِ عَنْهُ [*Reveal thou thy name, and make not a mere allusion to it*]. (A.)

4. اباح, inf. n. إِبَاحَةٌ: see 1, in three places. — إِبَاحَةٌ and ▼ٱسْتِبَاحَةٌ are used as syn.: but it is said that the former signifies The *making* a thing *allowable,* or *free,* to him who desires it, or seeks it: and the latter, the *taking* a thing *as allowed, allowable, free,* or *lawful.* (MF.) You say, اباح الشَّىْءَ *He made the thing allowable,* or *free.* (L.) And اباح مَالَهُ *He gave permission either to take or let alone his property; made it allowable,* or *free, either way one might choose to take.* (Mṣb.) And أَبَحْتُكَ الشَّىْءَ *I made,* or *have made, the thing allowable, free,* or *lawful, to thee,* (Ṣ, L, Ḳ, TA,) *to take it,* [*or let it alone,*] *or do it,* [*or make use of it,*] *or possess it;* but not by the law of the religion, for to do this belongs to God and his apostle; except in the language of this law. (MF, TA.) [Hence it is said that] إِبَاحَةٌ bears a signification similar to that of نُهْبَى [i. e. *Spoliation; a taking of spoil;* or the *taking* a thing *as spoil;* a signification more properly belonging to the inf. n. of 10, q. v.]. (L.)

10. استباحهُ *He deemed it,* or *esteemed it, to be allowed, allowable, free,* or *lawful;* namely, the property of another: (A:) or *he took it as allowed, allowable,* &c. (A,* MF.) See 4. — *He took it as spoil,* or *plunder.* (TA.) — *He made an attack upon it;* namely, the property of another. (Mṣb.) — *He took him captive, making him as a lawful possession to him.* (TA.) — And ٱسْتَبَاحُوهُمْ, (Ḳ,) or ٱسْتَبَاحُوهُمْ, (Ṣ,) *He,* or *they, extirpated,* or *exterminated, them.* (Ṣ, Ḳ.)

بُوحٌ has the following various significations assigned to it in explanations of the saying, ٱبْنُكَ ٱبْنُ بُوحِكَ يَشْرَبُ مِنْ صَبُوحِكَ: (Ṣ, TA:) The *penis:* (Ṣ, Ḳ, Ḥar p. 336:) the فَرْج [or *pudendum,* app. meaning, of a woman]: (Ḳ, Ḥar p. 328 on the authority of AO:) the نَفْس [meaning one's *self*]: (IAạr, T, Ṣ, Meyd, L:) *coitus;* syn. وَطْءٌ (Ṣ) or جِمَاعٌ: (Ḳ:) and accord. to the last but one of these renderings, [and virtually accord. to the others also,] the saying means *Thy son is the son of thyself,* [*who drinks of thy morning-draught*]; (T, TA;) *he whom thou hast begotten,* not he whom thou hast adopted: (IAạr, and Mṭr in Ḥar p. 328:) or بوح, here, is pl. of بَاحَةٌ; (A, TA, Ḥar p. 336;) and the meaning is, *he who has been born within the courts of thy house;* (A;) or, *in the court of thy house,* (TA, Ḥar,) not in the house of another: (TA:) or بوح is here a subst. from بَاحَ بِالشَّىْءِ; and the meaning is, *thy son is he whom thou hast openly acknowledged* (بُحْتَ بِهِ), and whom his mother hath also, agreeably with thee: (Ḥar p. 328:) [accord. to some,] it signifies also *i. q.* أَصْلٌ [i. e. *origin;* or *race,* or *stock,* which it may mean in the saying above: or *original,* or *primary, state,* or *condition*]; (Ḳ, Ḥar p. 328;) [for] one says, رَجَعَ إِلَى بُوحِهِ [*He returned,* or *reverted, to his original,* or *primary, state,* or *condition*]. (Ḥar p. 328.)

بَاحَةٌ The *court;* or *a spacious vacant part,* or *portion, in which is no building;* syn. سَاحَةٌ, (Ṣ, A, Ḳ,) and عَرْصَةٌ; (A, TA;) of a house or dwelling: (Ṣ, TA:) pl. بُوحٌ [q. v.]. (A, TA.) Hence [is said to be derived] بُحْبُوحَةُ الدَّارِ [mentioned in art. بح]. (TA.) One says also, نَحْنُ فِى بَاحَةِ الدَّارِ, meaning *We are in the middle,* or *midst,* or *best part, of the abode,* or *district,* or *country;* i. e. أَوْسَطِهَا. (TA.) And hence, accord. to Fr, تَبَحْبَحَ [explained in art. بح]. (Az, TA.) It is said in a trad., لَيْسَ لِلنِّسَآءِ مِنْ بَاحَةِ الطَّرِيقِ شَىْءٌ, meaning [*Women have no right*] *in the middle of the road.* (TA.) — Also The *main part* or *body of water:* (Ḳ:) applied by most of the lexicologists to the *sea.* (TA.) [In the present day applied to *A deep part of the sea, distant from land;* the *deep;* the *main,* or *main sea.*] — And *Many palm-trees.* (Aboo-Ṣárim El-Bahdalee, IAạr, Ḳ.)

أَمَرَهُ بِمَعْصِيَةٍ بَوَاحًا *He ordered him to disobey,* or *rebel, openly.* (Ḳ.) The last word occurs in this sense in two trads.; but in one of them, accord. to one recital, it is بَرَاحًا. (TA.)

هُوَ بُؤُوحٌ بِمَا فِى صَدْرِهِ *He is one who reveals, or discloses, what is in his bosom;* as also بَيْحَانٌ and بَيَّحَانٌ; (Ḳ;) the ى being originally و. (TA.)

مُبَاحٌ *Allowed* or *allowable* [*to be taken, or let alone, or done, or made use of, or possessed;* see 4]; *made allowable, free,* or *lawful; contr. of* مَحْظُورٌ. (Ṣ, A.)

المُبِيحُ *The lion.* (Ḳ.)

بوخ

1. بَاخَتِ النَّارُ, (Ṣ, A, L, Ḳ,) aor. تَبُوخُ, inf. n. بَوْخٌ and بُؤُوخٌ and بَوَخَانٌ, (L,) *The fire abated;* or *became allayed:* (Ṣ, L, Ḳ:*) or *became extinguished,* or *quenched.* (A.) And بَاخَ الحَرُّ *The heat abated,* or *became allayed.* (Ṣ, A, TA.) — [Hence,] بَاخَتِ الحُمَّى † *The fever abated,* or *became allayed.* (Ṣ.) And بَاخَ عَنْهُ الوِرْدُ ‡ *His fever abated,* or *remitted.* (A, TA.) And بَاخَ غَضَبُهُ ‡ *His anger abated,* or *became assuaged.* (Ṣ,* A, Ḳ.*) And بَيْنَهُمْ حَرْبٌ مَا يَبُوخُ سَعِيرُهَا ‡ *Between them is war of which the fire does not become extinguished,* or *quenched.* (A.) — [Hence also,] بَاخَ likewise signifies ‡ *He became fatigued,* (Ṣ, L, Ḳ,) *and out of breath.* (L.) You say, عَدَا حَتَّى بَاخَ (Ṣ, A, L) ‡ *He ran until he became fatigued* (Ṣ, L) *and out of breath.* (L.) — † *He* (a man) *flagged;* or *became remiss,* or *languid.* (TA.) — Also, inf. n. بُؤُوخٌ, † *It* (flesh-meat) *became altered,* or *changed in odour or otherwise for the worse,* (Ḳ, TA,) *and corrupted,* or *tainted.* (TA.)

4. اباخ *He extinguished,* or *quenched,* fire. (A, Ḳ.) And *He* (God) *abated,* or *allayed,* the heat. (A.) — [Hence,] اباخ النَّائِرَةَ بَيْنَهُمْ ‡ [*He extinguished,* or *assuaged, the discord,* or *rancour,* or *enmity, that was between them*]. (A, TA.) — And أَبِخْ عَنْكَ مِنَ الظَّهِيرَةِ † *Stay thou until the midday-heat shall have become allayed, and the air be cool.* (IAạr, TA in art. فيح and in the present art.)

بُوخٌ *A state of confusion,* or *perplexedness.* (Ṣ, Ḳ.) You say, هُمْ فِى بُوخٍ مِنْ أَمْرِهِمْ *They are in a state of confusion,* or *perplexedness, with respect to their affair,* or *case.* (Ṣ, Ḳ.*) And it is said in a prov., وَقَعُوا فِى دُوكَةٍ وَبُوخٍ, meaning *They fell into evil,* or *mischief, and altercation.* (Meyd, TA.)

بود

1. بَادَ, inf. n. بَوْدٌ and بَوَادٌ: see art. بيد.

بور

1. بَارَ, (Ṣ, M, Mṣb,) aor. يَبُورُ, (Mṣb,) inf. n. بُورٌ (Lth, T, Ṣ, M, Ḳ) and بَوْرٌ, (M, Ḳ,) or بَوَارٌ, (Mṣb,) *He,* (Ṣ,) or *it,* (Mṣb,) *perished.* (Lth, T, Ṣ, M, Mṣb, Ḳ.) You say, بَادُوا وَبَارُوا [*They became extinct, and perished*]. (A.) — [Hence,] بَارَتِ الأَرْضُ ‡ *The land was,* or *became, in a bad,* or *corrupt, state, and uncultivated;* (Ḳ,* TA;) *was unsown.* (A.) — And بَارَ عَمَلُهُ † *His work was,* or *proved, vain,* or *ineffectual:* such is the signification of the verb in the Ḳur xxxv. 11. (Ṣ, Ḳ.) — And بَارَ, (T, Ṣ, &c.,) aor. as above, inf. n. بَوَارٌ, (Mṣb,) ‡ *It* (a thing, Mṣb, or commodity, T, Ṣ, A, Mgh) *was,* or *became, unsaleable,* or *difficult of sale,* or *in little demand:* (T, Ṣ, A, Mgh, Mṣb:) because a thing, when neglected, becomes of no use, and thus resembles that which perishes. (Mṣb.) — And بَارَتِ السُّوقُ, (T, M,) inf. n. بَوْرٌ and بَوَارٌ, (Ḳ,) ‡ *The market was,* or *became, stagnant,* or *dull, with respect to traffic.* (T, M, Ḳ.) — And بَارَتِ الأَيِّمُ, (A,) inf. n. بَوَارٌ, (T, Ṣ, Ḳ,) ‡ *The woman without a husband was not desired,* or *sought for:* (A:) or *remained in her house long without being demanded in marriage.* (T, Ḳ.) — [بَارَ] is also used as an imitative sequent of حَارَ; like as بَائِرٌ is of حَائِرٌ: see exs. in art. حور. — بَارَ النَّاقَةَ, (T, Ṣ, A, Ḳ,) aor. as above, (T, Ṣ, A,) inf. n. بَوْرٌ, (Ṣ,) *He brought the she-camel to the stallion to see if she were pregnant or not:* (T, Ṣ, A, Ḳ:) for if she is pregnant, she voids her urine in his face (Ṣ, Ḳ) when he smells her. (Ṣ.) — Also *He* (the stallion) *smelt the she-camel to know if she were pregnant or not;* (T, Ṣ, M, Ḳ;) and so ▼ ابتارها. (Ṣ, M.) — Hence the saying, بُرْ لِى مَا عِنْدَ فُلَانٍ ‡ *Try thou,* or *examine, and learn, for me, what is in the mind* (نَفْس Ṣ) *of such a one.* (Ṣ, A.*) You say, بَارَهُ, (T, Ṣ, M, Ḳ,) aor. as above, (T, Ṣ,) inf. n. بَوْرٌ; (T, M, Ḳ;) and ▼ ابتارهُ, (M,) inf. n. اِبْتِيَارٌ; (Ṣ, Ḳ;) meaning ‡ *He tried him; assayed him; proved him by experiment* or *experience; examined him.* (T, Ṣ, M, Ḳ.) El-Kumeyt says,

* قَبِيحٌ بِمِثْلِى نَعْتُ الفَتَا * ةِ إِمَّا ٱبْتِهَارًا وَإِمَّا ٱبْتِيَارَا ▼ *

(T, Ṣ) ‡ *It were foul in the like of me to characterize the damsel either by false accusation or by trying, with speaking truth, to elicit what is in her mind* (مَا عِنْدَهَا [i. e. مَا فِى نَفْسِهَا, agreeably with an explanation given above]): (Ṣ, TA:) or ▼ ابتيارا, which is without ء, here signifies *by asserting with truth my having had sexual intercourse with her:* (TA:) [for] ابتارها signifies *he asserted with truth that he had had sexual intercourse with her;* and ابتهرها "he asserted the same falsely:" (A'Obeyd, T:) and the former signifies also *he had sexual intercourse with her* (Ḳ, TA) *by force; he ravished her:* (TA:) or ابتار signifies *he charged,* or *upbraided,* a person *with that which was not in him;* and ابتهر "he charged, or upbraided, with that which was in him." (TA in art. بهر.)

4. اباره *He* (God) *destroyed him; caused him to perish.* (Ṣ, M, A, Ḳ.)

8: see 1, in four places.

أَرْضٌ بَوْرٌ, (A'Obeyd, T, &c.,) in which the latter word is an inf. n. [of 1] used as an epithet, (IAth,) ‡ *Land not sown;* (A'Obeyd, T, Ṣ, IAth;) as also ▼ بَوَارٌ, [likewise an inf. n. used as an epithet,] of which the pl. is بُورٌ: (A, IAth:) or *land before it is prepared for sowing* (AḤn, M, Ḳ) *or planting:* (AḤn, M:) or *land that is left to lie fallow one year, that it may be sown the next year:* (Ḳ:) and أَرْضٌ بَائِرٌ ▼, (Zj, M, Ḳ,) and بَائِرَةٌ ▼, (Zj, Ḳ,) and بُورٌ ▼, [which is originally an inf. n.,] (Ḳ,) or بُورُ ▼ الأَرْضِ, [in which the former word may be pl. of بَوَارٌ, mentioned above,] (M,) ‡ *land that is in a bad state, and uncultivated,* (Ḳ,* TA,) *unsown,* (M, TA,) *and not planted:* (TA:) or *left unsown.* (Zj, M.) You say also, أَصْبَحَتْ مَنَازِلُهُمْ بُورًا ▼ †*Their abodes became void, having nothing in them.* (Fr, T.) — See also بُورٌ.

بُورٌ *A bad,* or *corrupt,* man; (Ṣ, A, Ḳ;) and one (M, Ḳ) *in a state of perdition;* (Ṣ, M, A, Ḳ;) *in whom is no good;* (Ṣ, Ḳ;) originally an inf. n., (Fr, T,) and [therefore, as an epithet,] applied also to a female, (AO, T, Ṣ, M, Ḳ,) and to two persons, and more: (AO, T, M, Ḳ:) [but see what here follows:] بَائِرٌ ▼, also, signifies *bad,* or *corrupt; destitute of good;* (Zj, M;) a man *in a state of perdition;* (AO, T, Ṣ;) and its pl., (Ḳ,) or rather quasi-pl., (M, TA,) is بَوْرٌ ▼, (M, Ḳ,) like as نَوْمٌ is of نَائِمٌ, and صَوْمٌ of صَائِمٌ; (M, TA;) and another pl. of the same is بُورٌ, (AO, T, Ṣ, M,) like as حُولٌ is of حَائِلٌ, or, accord. to some, as Akh states, this is a dial. var., not a pl., of بَائِرٌ. (Ṣ.) — See also بَوْرٌ, in three places. — إِنَّهُمْ لَفِى حُورٍ وَبُورٍ (A, TA [but in the latter, حور is put for جور]) *Verily they are in a state of deficiency,* or *detriment.* (TA.) See also بَائِرٌ. [And see حُورٌ.] You say also, ذَهَبَ فُلَانٌ فِى الحَوَارِ وَالبَوَارِ ▼ *Such a one went away in a defective and bad state.* (L, TA in art. حور.)

بَارِىٌّ and بُورِىٌّ ▼ and بَارِيَّةٌ ▼ (Aṣ, Ṣ, M, Ḳ) and بُورِيَّةٌ ▼ (M, Ḳ) and بَارِيَآءُ ▼ and بُورِيَآءُ ▼, (Ṣ, M, Ḳ,) all arabicized words, from the Persian, (M,) *A woven mat,* (M, Ḳ,) *made of reeds;* (Ṣ;) *what is called in Persian* بُورِيَا: (Aṣ, Ḳ:) or *a rough* حَصِير [or *mat*]. (Mṣb in art. برى [to which the words belong accord. to Fei, and the same is asserted to be the case by some others].) [The pl. is بَوَارِىُّ.] It is said in a trad., كَانَ لَا يَرَى بَأْسًا بِالصَّلَاةِ عَلَى البُورِىِّ ▼ explained as meaning *He did not see any harm in praying upon a mat made of reeds.* (TA.) — Accord. to some, (M,) *A road;* syn. طَرِيقٌ: (Ḳ, M:) [so, perhaps, in the trad. cited above:] arabicized. (Ḳ.)

بُورِىٌّ: see بَارِىٌّ, in two places. — Also *A kind of fish;* [*a species of mullet, the mugil cephalus* of Linnæus, of the roe and milt of which is made what the Italians call botargo, and the Arabs بَطَارِخ, and, accord. to Golius, بوترغا;] so called from a town in Egypt, named بُورَةُ, (Ḳ,) between Tinnees and Dimyáṭ, of which there are now no remains. (TA.)

بَارِيَّةٌ: }
بُورِيَّةٌ: } see بَارِىٌّ.
بَارِيَآءُ: }
بُورِيَآءُ: }

بَوَارٌ, an inf. n. of 1: see بُورٌ, last sentence. — [Hence,] بَوَارِ, like قَطَامِ, [an indecl. noun,] *Perdition*: (El-Aḥmar, Ṣ, M, Ḳ:) as in the saying, نَزَلَتْ بَوَارِ عَلَى الكُفَّارِ *Perdition fell upon the unbelievers.* (El-Aḥmar, Ṣ, TA.) = See also بُورٌ.

بَوَّارِىٌّ *A seller of mats of the kind called* بَارِىٌّ &c. (Ḳ.)

بَائِرٌ: see بُورٌ. — You say also, رَجُلٌ حَائِرٌ بَائِرٌ (T, Ṣ, M, A, Ḳ,) and ▼فِى حُورٍ وَبُورٍ, (A,) meaning *A man who does not apply himself rightly,* (T, Ṣ, TA,) or *has not applied himself rightly,* (Ḳ,) *to anything;* (T, Ṣ, Ḳ;) *erring; losing his way;* (T;) *who will not do right of his own accord, nor obey one directing him aright:* (Ḳ:) it may be from the signification of laziness, or sluggishness, and it may be from that of perdition: (M:) [or] بائر is here an imitative sequent of حائر. (Ṣ.) [Respecting the latter phrase, see also art. حور.] — See also بُورٌ, in two places.

فَحْلٌ مُبُورٌ *A stallion-camel that knows the state of the female, whether she be pregnant or not.* (M, A, Ḳ.)

مُبِيرٌ A *destructive* man, *acting exorbitantly in destroying others.* (TA, from a trad.)

بوز

بَازٌ *i. q.* بَازٍ; [see art. بزو;] (Ṣ, Ḳ;) a dial. var. of the latter; (Ṣ;) as also بَأْزٌ: (IJ, TA:) dual. بَازَانِ: (Ḳ:) pl. [of pauc.] أَبْوَازٌ and [of mult.] بِيزَانٌ: (Ṣ, Ḳ:) the dual of بَازٍ is بَازِيَانِ; (Ḳ;) and the pl. is بُزَاةٌ (Ṣ, Ḳ) and بَوَازٍ. (Ḳ.)

بوس

1. بَاسَهُ, aor. يَبُوسُهُ, (Ṣ,) inf. n. بَوْسٌ, a Persian word, arabicized, (Ṣ, A, Ḳ,) *He kissed him.* (Ṣ, A, Ḳ.) You say also, بَاسَ لَهُ الأَرْضَ *He kissed the ground to him.* (A, TA.)

مَبُوسٌ *Kissed:* you say, اليَوْمَ بِسَاطُكَ مَبُوسٌ وَغَدًا أَنْتَ مَحْبُوسٌ [*To-day thy carpet is kissed, and to-morrow thou art imprisoned*]. (A.)

بوش

1. بَاشَ, aor. يَبُوشُ, inf. n. بَوْشٌ, *He mixed,* or *confounded.* (Fr.) See also شَابَ, in art. شوب. — *He associated with* بَوْش, meaning, *people of the lowest* or *basest* or *meanest sort.* (IAạr.) — بَاشُوا, (Ḳ,) inf. n. as above, (A, Ḳ,) *They* (mixed people, A, Ḳ, of the lowest or basest or meanest sort, TA) *cried out,* or *vociferated;* or *did so calling for aid or succour;* or *in distress and impatience;* or *in fear.* (A, Ḳ.)

2. بَوَّشُوا, inf. n. تَبْوِيشٌ, *They became mixed,* or *confused:* (Ḳ:) or *numerous, and mixed* or *confused:* (TA:) and ▼تبوّشوا signifies the same. (Ḳ.)

5. see 2.

بَوْشٌ *A mixed* or *confused assembly* or *company:* (A, Ḳ:) or *an assembly,* or *a company, of mixed* or *confused people:* (Ṣ:) or only *of different tribes:* or *a multitude of men:* as also ▼بُوشٌ, in these several senses: (Ḳ:) and, accord. to the women of Temeem, *of beasts* also: (Aboo-'Adnán, TA in art. هوش:) or *people of the lowest* or *basest* or *meanest sort:* (IAạr:) or *a family,* or *household:* (ISd:) and [it is said by F that] it also signifies *sons of the same father, when assembled together:* (Ḳ:) resembling a contr. signification to that mentioned above, which restricts the application to such as are of different tribes: but it is said in the O, that بَنُو الاباء, [app. a mistake for بَنُو الأَبِ, meaning sons of the same father,] when assembled together, are not called by this name: (TA:) أَوْبَاشٌ is a pl. of this word, formed by transposition. (Ṣ.) You say, جَاؤُوا فِى هَوْشٍ وَبَوْشٍ *They came in assemblage and multitude.* (A.) And جَآءَ مِنَ النَّاسِ الهَوْشُ وَالبَوْشُ *The multitude of the people came:* (AZ:) or *the assembly and family* or *household.* (ISd.) And تَرَكْتُهُمْ هَوْشًا بَوْشًا *I left them* [*in great numbers* and] *in confusion.* (Ḳ.) And ▼بَوْشٌ بَائِشٌ, (Ṣ, Ḳ,) or ▼بُوشٌ ▼بَائِشٌ, (CḲ,) [app. *A numerous,* or *large, assembly of mixed or confused people.*] And ▼جَآءَ بِالبَوْشِ البَائِشِ, *He came with multitude,* or *the multitude.* (TA.)

بُوشٌ: see بَوْشٌ, in three places.

بَوْشِىٌّ A *poor* man *having a numerous family* or *household:* (Ṣ, Ḳ:) or *having a family* or *household:* (Aboo-Sa'eed:) and one *of the baser and common sort of men:* as also ▼بُوشِىٌّ. (Ḳ.)

بُوشِىٌّ: see what next precedes.

بَائِشٌ: see بَوْشٌ, in three places.

بوع

1. بَاعَ, (Ṣ, TA,) aor. يَبُوعُ, (TA,) inf. n. بَوْعٌ, (Ṣ, Ḳ, TA,) *He extended his arms to their full reach;* expl. by بَسَطَ بَاعَهُ; (TA;) and the inf. n. by مَدُّ البَاعِ; with a thing; as also ▼تبوّع. (Ḳ.) — *He* (a camel) *stretched forth his fore legs to the full* (مَدَّ أَبْوَاعَهُ); as also ▼تبوّع; and in like manner a gazelle: (TA:) and *he* (a horse) *stepped far,* or *took long steps,* in his running; (Ṣ, Ḳ;) and in like manner one says [بَاعَت] of a she-camel. (Ṣ.) You say, مَرَّ يَبُوعُ, and ▼يَتَبَوَّعُ, *He went along stretching forth his fore-legs to the full extent of his step.* (L.) — بَاعَ بِالمَالِ, aor. يَبُوعُ, (TA,) inf. n. بَوْعٌ, (Lth, Ḳ,) *He extended his arm,* or *hand,* [*liberally,* or *bountifully,*] *with the property.* (Lth, Ḳ, TA.) You say also, بُعْ بُعْ, meaning † *Stretch forth thine arms,* or *hands,* (بَاعَيْكَ,) *in acts of obedience to God.* (IAạr.) And ▼تَبَوَّعَ لِلْمَسَاعِى ‡ *He stretched forth his arms* (مَدَّ بَاعَهُ) [*to attain means of honour and elevation*]. (TA.) And ▼مَا يُدْرَكُ تَبَوُّعُهُ †*The point to which he has reached is not to be attained:* (Ḳ, TA:) and, as Lḥ says, ▼لَا تَبْلُغُونَ تَبَوُّعَهُ †*Ye will not,* or *shall not, reach the point to which he has attained:* originally, his length of step. (TA.) — ▼إِذَا بَاعَ ٱنْبَاعَ *When he accomplishes his want, he goes away.* (Ḥar p. 592.) = بَاعَ الحَبْلَ, (Mṣb, TA,) first pers. بُعْتُهُ, (Ṣ,) aor. and inf. n. as above, (Ṣ, Mṣb, TA,) *He measured the rope by the* باع [or *fathom*]; (Mṣb;) *he extended his* باع [or *arms stretched to the full reach*] *with the rope;* (Ṣ;) or *he extended the rope with his* باع; or, which is nearly the same in meaning, *he extended his arms with the rope until it became a* باع [or *fathom in measure*]; (TA;) like as you say, شَبَرْتُهُ from الشِّبْرُ. (Ṣ, TA.) — [And hence,] يَبُوعُ الأَرْضَ *He traverses the ground with wide step and quick motion.* (Ḥam p. 720.)

5: see 1, in six places: — and see 7.

7. انباع and ▼تبوّع, said of a rope, signify the same [app. *It was measured by the* باع, or *fathom*]. (Ḳ, TA.) — انباعت الحَيَّةُ *The serpent extended itself, after gathering itself together and coiling itself, in order to spring.* (Lḥ, Ḳ.) — Also انباع, said of a man, *He leaped,* or *sprang, after being still:* or *he made an assault;* or *leaped,* or *sprang, and made a violent seizure.* (TA.) [Hence,] مُخْرَنْبِقٌ لِيَنْبَاعَ *Silent in order to leap,* or *spring,* (Ḳ, and Ṣ in art. خربق,) *when he finds an opportunity;* (Ṣ in that art.;) *on account of a misfortune which he desires* [*to effect*]; (Ṣ, Ḳ, in that art.;) or *in order to make an assault:* (TA:) or *looking,* or *waiting, for an opportunity to leap,* or *spring, upon his enemy,* or *the object of his want, when able to do so;* and in like manner, مُخْرَنْطِمٌ لِيَنْبَاعَ: (TA in art. خربق:) a prov., (Ḳ,) applied to a man who is silent respecting a misfortune [which he desires to effect]; (TA;) or applied to a man who is long silent until he thinks his object inadvertent, and who is possessed of cunning: (Aṣ, TA in art. خربق:) accord. to one relation, لِيَنْبَاقَ, i. e. to bring about, or effect, a بَائِقَة, meaning a calamity, or misfortune: (Ḳ:) or لينباع may be for لِيَنْبَعَ, from نَبَعَ المَآءُ. (Ḥar p. 62.) [Hence also,] انباع الشُّجَاعُ مِنَ الصَّفِّ *The courageous man went,* or *came, out,* or *forth, from the rank.* (AAF.) — انباع لِى فِى سِلْعَتِهِ *He treated me in an easy manner in the sale of his commodity,* or *article of merchandise, and strained himself* (امْتَدَّ) *to give his consent to it.* (Ḳ, TA.) And hence, ▼اِنْبِيَاعٌ, as used by Ṣakhr-el-Ghei in describing the conduct of a man towards a beautiful woman, or, accord. to one relation, ▼اِبْتِيَاعٌ, The *acting,* or *behaving,* towards another, *boldly, in a free and easy manner,* or *without shyness;* syn. اِنْبِسَاطٌ; as also نَبْعٌ. (TA.) — انباع also signifies *He ran in a gentle manner, with a bending and a twisting of himself;* from بَاعَ, aor. يَبُوعُ. (Aḥmad Ibn-'Obeyd.) — *And he went away.* (Ḥar p. 592: see 1.) — And *It* (sweat) *flowed:* (Mṣb, Ḳ:) or, as El-Fárábee says, *extended.* (Mṣb.) 'Antarah says, describing the sweat of a she-camel,

* يَنْبَاعُ مِنْ ذِفْرَى غَضُوبٍ جَسْرَةٍ *

[*Flowing,* or *extending, from the part behind the ear of a she-camel quickly angered, spirited,* or *tall,* or *tall and bulky,* or *strong, and bold to endure travel*]: ينباع being originally يَنْبَوِعُ; or, as most of the lexicologists say, originally يَنْبَعُ, the ا being inserted after the fet-ḥah of the ب to render its sound full. (TA.)

8. اِبْتَاعَ: see 7, in the latter half of the paragraph.

بَاعٌ *A fathom; the space that is between* [*the extremities of*] *the two hands when they are extended to the right and left;* (Mṣb;) the *measure of the extension of the two arms* (Ṣ, Ḳ, TA) *with what is between them of the body;* (TA;) as also ↑ بَوْعٌ and ↑ بُوعٌ; (Ḳ;) the last of the dial. of Hudheyl: (TA:) said by AḤát to be of the masc. gender: (Mṣb:) pl. أَبْوَاعٌ (Mṣb, Ḳ) and بِيعَانٌ. (Ḥam p. 475.) — [And hence,] †The *body, including the limbs;* [because a fathom in height;] as in the phrase رَجُلٌ طَوِيلُ البَاعِ † *A man tall in the body;* which has also another meaning, to be seen below: but you do not say, قَصِيرُ البَاعِ as meaning short in the body. (TA.) — [Also The *arms;* and particularly *when extended to their full reach;* as also the pl.: and in like manner, the *fore legs* of a beast: see several examples in the first paragraph of this art.] — [And hence, ‡ *Reach; power;* or *ability.*] You say, هُوَ قَصِيرُ البَاعِ ‡ *He is lacking in power,* or *ability:* a phrase which has also another meaning, to be seen below. (TA.) And قَصُرَ بَاعُهُ عَنْ ذٰلِكَ ‡ *He was unable to attain,* or *to do,* or *effect, that:* in this case, ↑ بوع is not used. (TA.) — And ‡ *Reach, power,* or *ability, in the means,* or *causes, of attaining honour;* or *in generous,* or *honourable, qualities* or *actions:* (TA:) ‡ *eminence; nobility; honour; generosity:* (Lth, Ṣ, Ḳ:) in which senses, ↑ بوع is not used. (Lth.) A poet says,

* لَهُ فِى المَجْدِ سَابِقَةٌ وَبَاعُ *

[*He has precedence and eminence in glory, honour, dignity,* or *nobility*]. (Lth.) And رَجُلٌ طَوِيلُ البَاعِ ‡ *A man of large generosity.* (TA.) And قَصِيرُ البَاعِ ‡ *Niggardly:* a phrase which has also another meaning, mentioned above. (TA.)

بَوْعٌ and بُوعٌ: see بَاعٌ, in four places. — The former also signifies *A place that is broken,* or *crushed,* (مَكَانٌ مُنْهَضِمٌ,) *in a small ravine* (لِصْب) *of a mountain.* (Ibn-'Abbád, Ḳ.)

بَاعَةٌ The *court* (سَاحَة) of a house: (Ibn-'Abbád, Ḳ:) a dial. var. of بَاحَة. (TA.)

بَوَّاعٌ † A *large-bodied* camel. (TA.)

بَائِعٌ *A young gazelle that stretches forth its fore legs to the full* (يَبُوعُ) *in going along:* (Ḳ, TA:) an epithet in which the quality of a subst. is predominant: (TA:) pl. بُوعٌ (Ḳ) and بَوَائِعُ. (TA.) And ↑ أَبْوَاعُ, a determinate noun, is applied to *The ewe,* because she does so in going along: and she is called to be milked thereby; (Ibn-'Abbád, Ḳ;) by saying, أَبْوَاعُ أَبْوَاعُ. (Ibn-'Abbád.) You say also نَاقَةٌ بَائِعَةٌ *A she-camel that steps far,* or *takes long steps:* pl. بَوَائِعُ. (TA.) And ↑ فَرَسٌ بَيِّعٌ, (Ḳ,) originally بَيْوِعٌ, (TA,) *A horse that steps far,* or *takes long steps.* (Z, Ḳ.)

بَيِّعٌ: } see بَائِعٌ.
أَبْوَاعُ: }

مُنْبَاعٌ Anything *that flows;* or *extends:* (Mṣb:) anything *sweating,* or *exuding sweat.* (TA.)

بوق

1. بَاقَ, (Ḳ,) aor. يَبُوقُ, inf. n. بَوْقٌ, (TA,) *He came with,* or *brought,* or *effected, evil,* or *mischief, and altercations.* (Ḳ.) — بَاقَتِ الدَّاهِيَةُ *The calamity, misfortune,* or *disaster, befell, betided,* or *happened.* (Mṣb.) And بَاقَتْهُمُ الدَّاهِيَةُ, (Ṣ,) or البَائِقَةُ, (JK, Ḳ,) aor. and inf. n. as above, (Ṣ,) *The calamity, misfortune,* or *disaster, befell them,* or *smote them;* (Ṣ, Ḳ;) as also ↑ انباقت عَلَيْهِمْ: (JK, *Ḳ:) and ↑ انباقت عَلَيْهِمْ بَائِقَةُ شَرٍّ *A calamity,* &c., *burst upon them;* syn. اِنْفَتَقَتْ; (Ṣ, Ḳ;*) like انباجت, (Ṣ,) from which IF thinks it to be changed: (TA:) and ↑ انباق عَلَيْهِمُ الدَّهْرُ *Fortune assaulted them,* or *assailed them, with calamity, like as the sound issues from the trumpet* (البُوق): (Ṣ:) and بُقْتُهُمْ [*I assaulted them,* or *assailed them, with a calamity,* &c.]. (JK.) And in like manner, one says, بَاقَتْهُمْ بُؤُوقٌ, (Ṣ, TA,) inf. n. بُؤُوقٌ and بَوْقٌ, *A vehement calamity* or *misfortune* or *disaster befell them,* or *smote them.* (TA.) — Also بَاقَ, (Ḳ,) aor. as above, inf. n. بَوْقٌ, (TA,) *He wronged a man; treated him wrongfully,* or *unjustly:* or *he came upon a people,* or *company of men, suddenly,* or *unawares, without their permission;* as also ↑ انباق: (Ḳ:) [or,] as some say, بَاقُوا عَلَيْهِ *they slew him:* (TA:) and ↑ انباق به *he wronged him.* (Ḳ.) And بَاقَ بِكَ *He* (a man, JK) *came up,* or *forth, upon thee, from a low,* or *depressed, place.* (JK, Ḳ.) And بَاقَ بِهِ *He encompassed,* or *surrounded, him.* (JK, Ḳ.) And بَاقَ القَوْمُ عَلَيْهِ, (Ḳ,) inf. n. بَوْقٌ, (TA,) *The people,* or *company of men, gathered themselves together against him, and slew him wrongfully:* (Ḳ,* TA:) but some say that it means, as explained before, *they slew him.* (TA.) And بَاقَهُمْ, (Ibn-'Abbád, JK, Ḳ,) aor. as above, (JK,) inf. n. بَوْقٌ, (Ibn-'Abbád, TA,) *He stole from them; robbed them.* (Ibn-'Abbád, JK, Ḳ.)

7: see 1, in five places. مُخْرَنْبِقٌ لِيَنْبَاقَ, a prov., thus related by some, instead of لِيَنْبَاعَ, means *Silent in order to bring about,* or *effect, a* بَائِقَة, i. e., a *calamity,* or *misfortune:* (Ḳ in art. بوع, q. v.:) or, *to launch forth, and manifest what is in his mind.* (TA.) You say also, انباق عَلَيْنَا بِالكَلَامِ *He broke forth upon us with evil speech.* (JK.) And انباق بالضَّحِك *He broke forth with laughter.* (JK.) And انباقت المَطْرَةُ *The shower of rain poured forth with vehemence.* (TA.) And انباق المَآءُ *The water became copious,* or *much in quantity.* (JK.)

بَوْقٌ *Abundance of rain;* as also ↑ بُوقٌ. (TA.) — See also the next paragraph.

بُوقٌ [*A trumpet;*] *a certain thing in which one blows;* (IDrd, Ṣ, Mgh, Ḳ;) *in which one blows as in a musical pipe:* (Kr, Ḳ:) [mostly used in war, but] mentioned by a poet, cited by Aṣ, as used by the Christians: (Ṣ:) IDrd says, The Arabs used this word, but I know not its origin: Esh-Shiháb says, in the 'Ináyeh, that it is arabicized, from [the Persian] بُورِى: (TA: [but this is obviously improbable:]) pl. بُوقَاتٌ (Mgh, Mṣb) and بِيقَانٌ (Mṣb [in my copy of the Mgh, erroneously, بِيقَاتٌ]) [and أَبْوَاقٌ, a pl. of pauc., commonly used in the present day]. نَفَخَ فِى البُوقِ [*He blew the trumpet,* lit., *in the trumpet,*] means [also] ‡ *he spoke that in which was no profit.* (TA.) — [Hence,] † *One who does not conceal a secret;* (Lth, JK, Ḳ;) as also ↑ بَوْقٌ. (Ḳ.) — Also *A certain thing in which the miller blows;* (JK, Ḳ;) accord. to the copies of the Ḳ, *resembling a* مِنْقَاب; but this is a mistake: (TA:) it is *a thing resembling a* [*shell of the kind called*] مِنْقَاف, *the hole of which is twisted; and sometimes the miller blows in it, raising his voice; and what he means thereby is known.* (Lth, TA.) — See also بَوْقٌ.

بَاقَةٌ *A bundle of herbs,* or *leguminous plants.* (Ṣ, Ḳ.) [And in modern Arabic, *A bunch of flowers.*]

بُوقَةٌ *A shower, fall,* or *storm, of rain,* (JK, Ṣ,) *that has burst forth with a dash:* (Ṣ, TA:) or *such as is vehement;* or *disapproved, disliked,* or *deemed evil:* (Ḳ:) pl. بُوَقٌ. (JK, Ḳ.)

دَاهِيَةٌ بَؤُوقٌ, or بُؤُوقٌ, *A vehement calamity* or *misfortune* or *disaster.* (TA.) — And the former, applied to a man, *Thievish; a great thief.* (JK.)

بَائِقَةٌ *A calamity, misfortune,* or *disaster;* (JK, Ṣ, Mṣb, Ḳ;) *a vehement evil* or *mischief;* (Mṣb;) *a trial that befalls a people:* (TA:) pl. بَوَائِقُ. (Ṣ, Mṣb, Ḳ.) It is said in a trad., لَا يَدْخُلُ الجَنَّةَ مَنْ لَا يَأْمَنُ جَارُهُ بَوَائِقَهُ, meaning, accord. to Ḳatádeh, [*He will not enter Paradise whose neighbour is not secure from*] *his wrongful,* or *injurious, conduct:* or, accord. to Ks, *his malevolent,* or *mischievous, dispositions, and his evil conduct.* (Ṣ.)

IF says, in the "Maḳáyees," that بوق is not an accredited root, and that there is not, in his opinion, any correct word belonging to it. (TA.) [But this is a strange assertion.]

بول

1. بَالَ, (T, Ṣ, &c.,) aor. يَبُولُ, (Ṣ, M, Mṣb,) inf. n. بَوْلٌ (M, Mṣb) and مَبَالٌ, (Mṣb,) [*He urined, discharged his urine, made water,* or *staled;*] said of a man, (M, Mṣb,) and of a beast, (Mṣb,) &c. (M.) — [Hence,] بَالَ بَوْلًا شَرِيفًا فَاخِرًا ‡ *He* (a man) *begat offspring resembling him* (El-Mufaddal, T, TA) *in form and natural dispositions.* (El-Mufaddal, TA.) — A poet, using the verb metaphorically, says,

* بَالَ سُهَيْلٌ فِى الفَضِيخِ فَفَسَدْ *

‡ [*Canopus made water in the beverage prepared from unripe dates, and it became spoiled,* or *marred*]: (M:) meaning, that when Canopus

rises [aurorally, which it does, in central Arabia, early in August, the making of that beverage is stopped, for] the season of unripe dates has passed, and they have become ripe. (L in art. فضخ.) بَالَ سُهَيْلٌ is also a prov., said when winter has come. (MF in art. حرت.) [See سُهَيْلٌ.] —— بَوْلٌ also signifies † The *having vent, so as to flow forth*: (Ḳ:) whence بَوَّالٌ as an epithet applied to a wine-skin: see this word below. (TA.) —— And بَالَ † *It melted*, or *dissolved*: (Ḳ:) said of fat. (TA.)

2. بَوَّلَ أَصْلَ الشَّجَرَةِ (Ḳ in art. فرخ) [*He made water upon the root*, or *stem, of the tree*: or] *he put urine at the root of the tree to render its fruit abundant*. (TḲ in that art.)

3. لَا أُبَاوِلُهُ, from البَالُ, *I will not*, or *I do not, cause him*, or *it, to move*, or *occur to, my mind*. (Z, TA in art. بلو. See لَا أُبَالِيهِ in that art.)

4. ابال الخَيْلَ, and ♦ استبالها, [*He*, or *it, made*, or *caused, the horses to stale*: or] *he stopped the horses for the purpose of* [*their*] *staling*. (TA.) One says, (in threatening, PṢ,) لَنُبِيلَنَّ الخَيْلَ فِى عَرَصَاتِكُمْ [*We will assuredly make the horses to stale in your courts*]. (Ṣ.) And it is said in a prov., بَالَ حِمَارٌ فَٱسْتَبَالَ ♦ أَحْمِرَةً *An ass staled, and caused some (other) asses to stale*: applied to a case in which people help one another to do what is disagreeable. (Meyd.)

10. استبال *He desired*, or *required, to make water*. (KL.) —— See also 4, in two places. —— El-Farezdaḳ says,

* وَإِنَّ الَّذِى يَسْعَى لِيُفْسِدَ زَوْجَتِى *
* كَسَاعٍ إِلَى أُسْدِ الشَّرَى يَسْتَبِيلُهَا *

meaning [*And verily he who strives to corrupt my wife is like one betaking himself to the lions of Esh-Sharà* (a certain road abounding with those animals)] *to receive their urine in his hand*. (Ṣ.)

بَالٌ *A state, condition*, or *case*; syn. حَالٌ (T, Ṣ, M, Mṣb, Ḳ) and شَأْنٌ: (T:) or *a state, condition*, or *case, for which one cares*; wherefore one says, مَا بَالَيْتُ بِكَذَا, inf. n. بَالَةٌ, meaning "I cared not for such a thing:" (TA:) or *a thing* [or *things*] *for which one cares*: (Ḥar p. 94:) and البَالُ signifies also بَالُ النَّفْسِ, i. e. *care*, or *concern*; and hence is [said to be] derived بَالَيْتُ, having for its inf. n. بَالَةٌ. (T.) One says, مَا بَالُكَ *What is thy state*, or *condition*, or *case?* (Ṣ.) [See the Ḳur xii. 50 and xx. 53: and see an ex. in a verse cited in this Lex. voce إِيه.] When it was said to a man, in former times, "How hast thou entered upon the morning?" he used to reply, بِخَيْرٍ أَصْلَحَ ٱللّٰهُ بَالَكُمْ [*With good fortune: may God make good your state*, or *condition*]. (Ḥam p. 77.) وَيُصْلِحُ بَالَهُمْ, in the Ḳur [xlvii. 6], means *And He will make good their state*, or *condition, in the present world*: (I 'Ab, T:) or *their means of subsistence in the present world, together with their recompense in the world to come*. (M.) One says also, هُوَ رَخِىُّ البَالِ *He is in ample and easy circumstances* (T, Mṣb) *of life*; (T;) *he is not straitened in circumstances, nor troubled*: (T:) or *he is in an easy*, or *a pleasant, state* or *condition*: (TA in art. رخو:) or *he is easy*, or *unstraitened, in mind*: (Ṣ:) [for] البَالُ, (T, M, Ḳ,) or رَخَآءُ البَالِ, (TA,) signifies *ampleness and easiness of life*: (T, M, Ḳ, TA:) or البال signifies *an easy*, or *unstraitened, state of the mind*. (Ṣ.) And هُوَ كَاسِفُ البَالِ *He is in an evil state* or *condition*: (TA:) or *he is straitened in his hope*, or *expectation*: for البال is said to signify *hope*, or *expectation*: (T:) so says El-Hawázinee. (TA.) And لَيْسَ هٰذَا مِنْ بَالِى *This is not of the things for which I care*. (Ṣ.) And it is said in a trad., كُلُّ أَمْرٍ ذِى بَالٍ لَمْ يُبْدَأْ فِيهِ بِحَمْدِ ٱللّٰهِ فَهُوَ أَبْتَرُ, i. e., *Every honourable affair, for which one cares, and by which one is rendered solicitous*, [*in which a beginning is not made by praising God, is cut off from good*, or *prosperity*:] or *every affair of importance*, or *moment*. (TA in two places in this art.) —— Also The *heart*, or *mind*; syn. قَلْبٌ, (T, Ṣ, Mṣb, Ḳ,) and خَلَدٌ, (Ḥam pp. 76 and 77,) and نَفْسٌ, (AZ, T,) and خَاطِرٌ. (M, Ḳ, Kull p. 179.) You say, خَطَرَ بِبَالِى, (Mṣb, Kull ubi suprà,) and عَلَى بَالِى, (Kull ibid.,) i. e., [*It* (an affair, or a thing, Kull) *occurred to*, or *bestirred itself in*, or *moved*,] *my heart*, or *mind*. (Mṣb, Kull.) And لَمْ يَخْطُرْ بِبَالِى ذٰلِكَ الأَمْرُ, i. e., [*That affair did not occur to*, or *bestir itself in*, or *move, my heart*, or *mind*; or] *did not move me*, or *distress me*. (T.) And مَا يَخْطُرُ فُلَانٌ بِبَالِى, i. e. [*Such a one does not occur to*, or *move*,] *my heart*, or *mind*. (Ṣ.) —— [And hence, *Mind*, or *attention*. You say, أَعْطِنِى بَالَكَ *Give me thy mind*, or *attention*. And] لَا أُلْقِى إِلَيْهِ بَالًا [*I will not*, or *I do not, give*, or *pay, any attention to him*, or *it*]. (Z, TA in art. بلو.) ══ [The *whale*;] *a great fish*, (Ṣ, Ḳ,) *of the fish of the* بَحْر [here meaning *sea*]; (Ṣ;) *a certain bulky fish, called* جَمَلُ البَحْرِ; (M;) it is *a fish fifty cubits long*: (MF:) [Ḳzw describes it as being *from four hundred to five hundred cubits in length*, and says that *it sometimes shows the extremity of its fin, like a great sail, and its head also, and blows forth water rising into the air higher than an arrow can be shot*: these and other exaggerated particulars he mentions in his account of the Sea of the Zenj: and in a later place he says, that *it eats ambergris, and dies in consequence; and a great quantity of oil is procured from its brain, and used for lamps*:] the word [in this sense] is not Arabic: (Ṣ:) in the O it is said to be arabicized, from [the Persian] وَالْ. (TA.) ══ The *spade* (مَرٌّ [in the CḲ erroneously written مُرٌّ]) *with which one works in land of seed-produce*. (M, Ḳ.) ══ See also بَالَةٌ, in three places.

بَوْلٌ, originally an inf. n., (Mṣb,) [*Urine*; *stale*:] pl. أَبْوَالٌ. (Ṣ, Mṣb, Ḳ.) —— أَبْوَالُ البِغَالِ *The seminal fluid of mules*. (Aṣ, TA.) And hence, as being likened thereto, because it is fruitless, (Aṣ, TA,) † *The* سَرَاب [or *mirage*: in the CḲ الشَّرابُ]. (Aṣ, Ḳ, TA.) It is also applied to the road of El-Yemen, which is not travelled but by mules: see also art. بغل. (TA.) —— بَوْلُ العَجُوزِ † *Cow's milk*. (TA.) —— بَوْلٌ signifies also ‡ *Offspring*. (M, Ḳ, TA.) —— And ‡ *A large number*. (Ḳ, TA.) —— See also أَبْوَلُ.

بَالَةٌ *A* [*flask*, or *bottle, such as is called*] قَارُورَة: (M, Ḳ:) pl. [or rather coll. gen. n.] ♦ بَالٌ. (TA.) —— *A* [*bag such as is called*] جِرَاب, (T, M, Ḳ,) *small* and *large, in which musk is put*: (T:) or (M [in the Ḳ "and"]) the *receptacle of perfume*: (Ṣ, M, Ḳ:) a Persian word, (Ṣ, M,) arabicized; (Ṣ;) in Persian بِيلَه, (T, Ṣ, M,) or بَالَه: (M:) pl. [or coll. gen. n.] ♦ بَالٌ. (T.) —— It is said to signify also *An odour*; *a smell*; (T;) on the authority of Aboo-Sa'eed Eḍ-Ḍareer; (TA;) from بَلَوْتُهُ meaning "I smelled it, and tried, proved, or tested, it;" originally بَلْوَةٌ; the و being transposed, and changed into ا. (T.) —— And *A staff with a pointed iron at the end, used by the hunters of El-Baṣrah, who throw it at the game*: pl. [or coll. gen. n.] ♦ بَالٌ. (T, TA.) —— And hence it is applied by the vulgar to *A small elongated sword*. (TA.) ══ It is also an inf. n. of بَالَى, which see in its proper art. (TḲ.)

بُولَةٌ The *origin* (مَنْبِت [so in copies of the Ḳ accord. to the TA)] or *daughter* (بِنْت [so in some copies of the Ḳ]) of a man; (Ḳ;) on the authority of El-Mufaḍḍal. (TA.)

بِيلَةٌ a subst. from بَالَ, (Ṣ, M, Ḳ,) [meaning *A discharging of urine, making water*, or *staling*: or *a mode*, or *manner, thereof*; as appears probable from its form, and from J's adding that it is] like جِلْسَةٌ and رِكْبَةٌ; (Ṣ;) [and also from the following phrase:] إِنَّهُ لَحَسَنُ البِيلَةِ [*Verily he is one who has a good mode of discharging his urine*]; from البَوْلُ. (M.)

بُوَلَةٌ *That discharges much urine*; syn. كَثِيرُ البَوْلِ; (M, Ḳ;) applied to a man; (M;) and so ♦ بَوَّالٌ applied to a camel. (TA.)

بُوَالٌ *A disease occasioning much*, or *frequent*, بَوْل [or *discharging of urine*]: (M, Ḳ:) *a disease that attacks sheep*, or *goats, such that they discharge urine until they die*. (Ḥam p. 77.) You say, أَخَذَهُ بُوَالٌ *He was taken with much, or frequent*, بَوْل [or *discharging of urine*]. (Ṣ.)

بَوَّالٌ: see بُوَلَةٌ. —— [Hence,] † A wine-skin *from which the wine runs out*. (TA.) —— And شَحْمَةٌ بَوَّالَةٌ † *A piece of fat that quickly melts* or *dissolves*. (IAạr, TA.)

أَبْوَلُ مِنْ كَلْبٍ *More frequent in making water than a dog*: or it may mean *more abundant in offspring*. (Meyd. [Freytag adds, in his Arab. Prov. i. 199, on the authority of Sharaf-ed-Deen, that ♦ بول (i. e. بَوْلٌ) may signify *urine* or *coitus* or *offspring*.])

مَبَالٌ [The *place of urine*, or *of the urinary discharge*; meaning] the فَرْج [or *pudendum* of a man and of a woman]: whence the phrase, مَبَالٌ فِى مَبَالٍ occurring in a trad. (TA.)

مُبْوِلَةٌ [*A diuretic; a provocative of urine*]. You say, كَثْرَةُ الشَّرَابِ مَبْوَلَةٌ (Ṣ, Ḳ,*) i. e., *Much beverage occasions a discharging of urine.* (TA.)

مِبْوَلَةٌ [*A urinal;*] a vessel (كُوز) *in which one makes water.* (Ṣ, Ḳ.*)

بوم

بُومٌ and بُومَةٌ *A certain bird;* [namely, the *owl;*] each word applying to the *male* and the *female:* (Ṣ, Ḳ:) or the former signifies the *male,* or *males,* (so in different copies of the M,) *of the* هَام [or *owl-kind*]; and the latter is its n. un.: (M, TA:) said by Az to be genuine Arabic: (TA:) pl. of the former أَبْوَامٌ. (IB, TA.)

بُومٌ بَوَّامٌ [*An owl,* or *male owls,*] *that cries,* or *that cry, much.* (TA.)

بون

1. بَانَهُ, aor. يَبُونُ, (Ṣ in art. بين, Mṣb, Ḳ,) inf. n. بَوْنٌ, (Mṣb, TA,) *i. q.* بَانَهُ, aor. يَبِينُ, (Ṣ ubi suprà, Ḳ,) inf. n. بَيْنٌ, (TA,) meaning *He excelled him;* (Ṣ* ubi suprà, Mṣb;) *he surpassed him in excellence and in manly virtue:* so in the Iḳtiṭáf. (TA.)

بَانٌ [a coll. gen. n., The *ben-tree; a species of moringa;* so in the present day;] *a kind of tree,* (Ṣ, Mgh, Mṣb, Ḳ,) *well known:* (Mṣb:) n. un. with ة: (Ṣ, Mgh, Mṣb:) *its seed,* or *grain,* [*called* حَبُّ البَانِ *and* فُسْتُقُ البَانِ *and* جَوْزُ البَانِ, *the glans unguentaria,* or *nux unguentaria,* or *ben-nut,*] *has a good,* or *pleasant,* [*fragrant*] *oil,* (Ḳ,) *called* دُهْنُ البَانِ [*oil of ben*], (Ṣ, Mgh, Mṣb,) *and simply* بَانٌ, the prefixed noun being suppressed: (Mgh:) [Az says,] it is the pl. of بَانَةٌ, which is *a certain tree having a fruit,* or *produce, which is perfumed with aromatics, after which its oil is expressed, of a good* [or *fragrant*] *quality:* (T in art. بنى:) *its seed,* or *grain, is good for* [*removing*] *the* [*affections of the skin termed*] نَمَش *and* بَرَش *and* كَلَف *and* حَصَف *and* بَهَق *and* سَعْفَة *and the mange,* or *scab, and for the peeling of the skin, applied in the form of a liniment with vinegar; and for hardness of the liver and the spleen, made into a beverage with vinegar; and a* مِثْقَال *thereof, drunk, is an emetic, which loosens crude phlegm:* (Ḳ:) AḤn says, (TA,) *it is a kind of tree that grows tall, in a straight,* or *an erect, manner, like as grows the* [*species of tamarisk called*] أَثْل, *and its leaves are* [*of the kind termed*] هَدَب, *like those of the* اثل, *but its wood has no hardness:* the n. un. is with ة: Aboo-Ziyád says, *it is of the* [*trees called*] عِضَاه, *and has long* هدب, *intensely green; it grows upon* [*hills,* or *what are termed*] هَضْب; *and its fruit resembles the pods of the* [*species of kidney-bean called*] لُوبِيَآء, *except that its greenness is intense; and in it is a seed,* or *grain, from which is extracted the oil of the* بَان: *on account of the straightness of its growth and of the growth of its branches, and their length and tenderness, the poets liken thereto the tender girl of tall and beautiful,* or *just, stature; saying* كَأَنَّهَا بَانَةٌ [*As though she were a ben-tree*], and كَأَنَّهَا غُصْنُ بَانٍ [*As though she were a branch of the ben-tree*], &c.: thus does Ḳeys Ibn-El-Khaṭeem: (M in art. بين:) and so does Imra-el-Ḳeys. (TA.) [See an ex. voce بَرَهْرَهَةٌ.] — [It is also applied in the present day to *A species of willow,* the *salix Aegyptia* of Linnæus, properly called in Arabic خِلَاف: and this is said to be meant by modern Arab poets when they liken an elegant girl to a twig of the بان; but probably from their erroneously supposing this tree to be meant in the same case by the older poets.]

بَوْنٌ *Excellence: an excellent quality;* (Ṣ in art. بين, Mṣb;) as also ↓ بُونَةٌ: (IAạr, T:) or the *distance, space,* or *interval, between two things;* as also ↓ بُونٌ. (M, Ḳ.) You say, بَيْنَهُمَا بَوْنٌ بَعِيدٌ (T, Ṣ, Mṣb*) and بَيْنٌ بَعِيدٌ (T, Ṣ) [*Between them two* (meaning two men) *is a wide distance*]; i. e. *between their two degrees of rank* or *dignity,* or *between the estimations in which they are commonly held:* (Mṣb:) the former phrase is the more chaste: (Ṣ:) when corporeal distance is meant, one says, بَيْنَهُمَا بَيْنٌ, with ى; (Mṣb;) or in the case of [literal] distance, one says, إِنَّ بَيْنَهُمَا لَبَيْنًا; not otherwise. (Ṣ.)

بُونٌ: see بَوْنٌ.

بُونَةٌ: see بَوْنٌ. — Also *Mutual separation.* (IAạr, T.)

بوه

1. بَاهَهَا, (JK, Ḳ,) [aor. يَبُوهُ,] inf. n. بَوْهٌ, (TA,) *He lay with her;* syn. جَامَعَهَا; (Ḳ;) like بَاكَهَا. (JK.) — بَاهَ لَهُ, aor. يَبُوهُ, (JK, Ḳ,) inf. n. بَوْهٌ; (Ḳ;) as also بَاهَ لَهُ, aor. يَبَاهُ, (JK,* Ḳ,) inf. n. بَيْهٌ; (Ḳ;) *His attention became roused to it;* (Ḳ;) *he knew it,* or *understood it;* or *knew,* or *had knowledge, of it; was cognizant of it:* (JK, TA:) like بَاهَ, and أَبِهَ or أَبَهَ. (TA.) And مَا بُهْتُ لَهُ; as also مَا بِهْتُ لَهُ; *I did not know it,* or *understand it;* or *did not know,* or *had not knowledge, of it; was not cognizant of it:* (JK, Ṣ, Ḳ:) the inf. n. of the former is بَوْهٌ; and that of the latter, بَيْهٌ. (TA.)

بَاهٌ a dial. var. of بَآءَةٌ (IAạr, Ṣ) and of بَآءٌ, (IAạr, TA,) signifying *Coitus:* (Ṣ, Ḳ:*) and *marriage:* (Ḳ,* TA:) as also ↓ بَاهَةٌ: (TA:) or *a share of coitus;* (JK, TA;) occurring in this sense in a trad., in which a woman is mentioned as having adorned herself for it: (TA:) also *venereal passion:* (TA in art. خفش:) [or the *venereal faculty;* as when one says of a drug or some other thing, يَزِيدُ فِي البَاهِ *It increases the venereal faculty:*] IḲt says, of this word, بَاهٌ, [though it is of very frequent occurrence,] that it is a mistranscription [app. meaning for بَآءٌ]. (Mṣb and TA in art. بوأ.) [See also بَآءَةٌ.]

بَاهَةٌ: see بَاهٌ. — Also The *court* of a house; or *a spacious part,* or *portion,* of a house, *in which is no building;* (JK, Ḳ, TA;) *where people alight;* or *lodge:* (JK:) a dial. var. of بَاحَةٌ. (TA.)

بَاهِىٌّ *That strengthens the venereal* [*faculty* or] *appetite.* (TA in art. جزر, &c.)

بى

2. بَيَّيْتُ الشَّىْءَ, (T, Ḳ,) inf. n. تَبْيِىٌ, (Ḳ,) *I made the thing apparent, manifest, evident, clear, plain,* or *perspicuous.* (Aṣ, T, Ḳ.*) — Also, (Ḳ, as in the TA,) or ↓ تَبَيَّيْتُ الشَّىْءَ, (M, and so in several copies of the Ḳ,) [both confirmed by what follows,] *i. q.* تَعَمَّدْتُهُ [meaning *I directed myself,* or *my course,* or *aim, to,* or *towards, the thing; made for it,* or *towards it; made it my object;* &c.]. (M, Ḳ.) — In the saying, حَيَّاكَ اللّٰهُ وَبَيَّاكَ, the phrase حيّاك الله means *May God make thee to have dominion:* (Ṣ, M:) or *may God prolong thy life:* (M:) and بيّاك means أَعْتَمَدَكَ بِالتَّحِيَّةِ [*may He bring thee prolongation of life;* lit. *may He direct himself to thee,* or the like, *with* the gift of *prolongation of life*]; (Aṣ, Ṣ;) or قَصَدَكَ بِالتَّحِيَّةِ [which is the same]: (IAạr, T:) or اعْتَمَدَكَ بِالْمُلْكِ [*may He bring thee dominion*]; (M;) so too says IAạr: (TA:) or *may He make thy state,* or *condition, to be good:* (TA:) or *may He make thee to laugh:* (T, Ṣ, M, Ḳ:) so some say, accord. to Aṣ: (T:) and it is related that these words were addressed to Adam, in consequence of his having remained a hundred years without laughing after his son had been slain: (T, Ṣ:) so says A'Obeyd, on the authority of Sa'eed Ibn-Jubeyr: (T:) or it means *may He bring thee near* [*unto Himself*]: (Aboo-Málik, Aṣ, T, M, Ḳ:) or *may He bring thee:* (IAạr, Ṣ, M:) or *may He prepare for thee an abode; i. q.* بَوَّأَكَ مَنْزِلًا, (Ḳ,) or بَوَّأَكَ; the verb being here altered in order to assimilate it to the preceding verb, حَيَّا: (El-Aḥmar, T, Ṣ:) this explanation was approved by Aṣ: (Ṣ:) the meaning intended thereby is, *may He lodge thee in an abode in Paradise:* (TA:) or, as some say, the verb in this case is an imitative sequent to that preceding it: (A'Obeyd, Ṣ, Ḳ:*) but this is naught: (Ḳ:) A'Obeyd says that in his opinion it is not an imitative sequent, because an imitative sequent is scarcely ever coupled with what precedes it by و. (Ṣ.) As an ex. of بَيَّا in the sense of قَرَّبَ, Aboo-Málik cites this verse:

* بَيَّا لَهُمْ إِذْ نَزَلُوا الطَّعَامَا * أَلْكِبْدَ وَالْمَلْحَآءَ وَالسَّنَامَا *

[*He brought near to them,* i. e., *placed before them, when they alighted, the food,* namely, *the liver, and the flesh of the back extending from the withers to the rump, and the hump*]. (T.) And IAạr, explaining بيّاك as meaning قصدك بالتحيّة, cites the following verse:

* لَمَّا تَبَيَّيْنَا ↓ أَبَا تَمِيمِ * أَعْطَى عَطَآءَ اللَّحِزِ اللَّئِيمِ *

(T.) Accord. to J, the meaning in this instance may be agreeable with the explanation of بيّاك by اعتمدك بالتحيّة [so that the verse may be rendered *When we betook ourselves with salutation to the father of Temeem,* or, as the verse is cited in the Ṣ, *to the brother of Temeem* (أَخَا تميم), *he gave the gift of the niggardly, the mean*]: or it may mean *we brought:* and the verb admits of the same double rendering in other instances. (TA.) — بَيَّيْتُ بَآءً حَسَنَةً and حَسَنًا [*I made,* or *wrote, a beautiful* ب]. (TA in باب الالف اللّيّنة.)

5. تبيًّا *It was, or became, apparent, manifest, evident, clear, plain, or perspicuous, being near;* syn. تَبَيَّنَ مِنْ قُرْبٍ. (Aṣ, T.) ═ See also 1, in two places.

البَىُّ *The low, ignoble, mean, or contemptible, man;* as also ↓ ابْنُ بَيَّانَ, (IAạr, T, Ḳ,) and ابن هَىّ بْنِ بَىّ, (IAạr, T,) and ابن بَىّ, (Ḳ,) or هَيَّانَ, and ↓ هَيَّانُ بْنُ بَيَّانَ: (Lth, T:) or the last two signify *he whose stock and branch are unknown:* (M:) or the same two, *he who is unknown, and whose father also is unknown:* (Ḳ in art. هى; and so the latter of them is explained in the Ṣ, both there and in the present art.:) and one says, مَا أَدْرِى أَىُّ هَىّ بْنِ بَىّ هُوَ, meaning *I know not what man he is.* (Ṣ.) Accord. to some, (Lth, T,) هَىُّ بْنُ بَىّ was one of the sons of Adam, that went away in the earth when the rest of his children dispersed themselves, and no trace of him was afterwards perceived. (Lth, T, Ḳ.)

ابْنُ بَيَّانَ: see البَىُّ, in two places.

بَيَوِىٌّ rel. n. of بَآءٌ or بَا: whence قَصِيدَةٌ بَيَوِيَّةٌ [as also بَائِيَّةٌ and بَاوِيَّةٌ] *A* قصيدة *of which the* رَوِىّ *is* ب. (M in art. ب.)

بيب

البَيَبُ: see أَبٌ, in art. ابو.

بيت

1. بَاتَ, (T, Ṣ, M, &c.,) aor. يَبِيتُ and يَبَاتُ, (Ṣ, Mṣb, Ḳ,) inf. n. بَيْتُوتَةٌ (Lth, T, Ṣ, A, Mṣb, Ḳ) and مَبِيتٌ (Mṣb, Ḳ) and مَبَاتٌ (Mṣb) and بَيْتٌ and بَيَاتٌ, (Ḳ,) has two meanings: in that which more commonly obtains, the action is restricted to the night: (Mṣb:) it is by night, or in night; not in sleep: (M:) you say, بَاتَ يَفْعَلُ كَذَا, meaning *He did such a thing by night, or at night:* (Ṣ, Mṣb, Ḳ:) [or *he was in the night, or at night, or during the night, doing such a thing:* and *he passed, or spent, the night, or a night, or a part thereof,* or, as will be seen below, *he entered upon the night, doing such a thing:*] like as one says, ظَلَّ يَفْعَلُ كَذَا as meaning "he did such a thing by day," or "at day-time:" (Ṣ, Mṣb:*) IḲooṭ and Es-Saraḳusṭee and IḲṭṭ say that it has this meaning, and not "he slept:" (Mṣb:) [F adds,] وَلَيْسَ مِنَ النَّوْمِ, (Ḳ,) which is said to mean, "and the action is not one of sleep;" so that when one sleeps by night, or at night, it is not correct to say, بَاتَ يَنَامُ: or, accord. to some, "its meaning is not that of sleeping;" so that one may say, بَاتَ زَيْدٌ نَائِمًا [*Zeyd was in the night,* &c., or *passed, or spent, the night,* &c., *sleeping*]: (MF:) [Fei says,] it is only when one remains awake in the night: and hence the saying in the Ḳur [xxv. 65] وَٱلَّذِينَ يَبِيتُونَ لِرَبِّهِمْ سُجَّدًا وَقِيَامًا [*And those who pass the night prostrating themselves to their Lord and standing up* in prayer]: (Mṣb:) Fr says that بَاتَ الرَّجُلُ means *The man remained awake all the night,* engaged in acts of obedience or of disobedience: (T, Mṣb:) [or it means *the man entered upon the night; or he was in the night, or at night, or during the night,* in any state, or engaged in any action; for] Zj says, (M,) بَاتَ is said of any one whom the night has overtaken, (M, Ḳ,*) whether he have slept or not slept: (M:) and Lth says, البَيْتُوتَةُ signifies *the entering upon the night:* one says, بِتُّ أَصْنَعُ كَذَا وَكَذَا [*I entered upon the night doing such and such things*]: and he adds, (T,) he who says بَاتَ as meaning *he slept* commits an error; for you say, بِتُّ أُرَاعِى النُّجُومَ [*I entered upon, or passed, the night*] *looking at the stars:* and how can he be sleeping who is looking at them? (T, Mṣb:) but Mullà 'Abd-El-Ḥakeem, in his Commentaries on the Muṭowwal, says that بَاتَ sometimes means *he remained, continued, stayed, or dwelt,* and *he alighted and abode, by night, or at night,* whether he slept or not: (MF:) and Ibn-Keysán says that it may be used in the same manner as نَامَ [*he slept*]; and also, [as will be explained below,] in the same manner as كَانَ. (TA.) You say, بَاتَ بَيْتُوتَةً صَالِحَةً (T) or طَيِّبَةً (A) [*He passed, or entered upon, the night, or a night, in a good manner*]. And بِتُّ القَوْمَ and بِتُّ بِهِمْ and بِتُّ عِنْدَهُمْ [*I passed, or entered upon, the night, or a night, with, or at the abode of, the people, or company of men:* the last of these phrases is the most common]. (A'Obeyd, M, Ḳ.) — Secondly, it is used in the sense of صَارَ [*He became*]; (Mṣb;) or in the same manner as كَانَ [*he was*]. (Ibn-Keysán, TA.) One says, بَاتَ بِمَوْضِعِ كَذَا *He became* [or *was*] *in such a place;* whether in night-time or in day-time. (Mṣb.) And hence the saying of the lawyers, بَاتَ عِنْدَ ٱمْرَأَتِهِ لَيْلَةً *He became* [or *was*] *with his wife one night;* [which is the same as *he passed a night* &c.; though this, it will be observed, is not in this instance the signification of the verb alone;] whether sleeping or not. (Mṣb.) — [Thus it is used both as a "complete," i. e. an attributive, verb, and also as an "incomplete," i. e. a non-attributive, verb.] — بَاتَ, aor. يَبِيتُ, inf. n. بَيْتٌ, (T, M, Ḳ,) also signifies ‡ *He married, or took a wife:* (T, A:) [see بَيْتٌ below:] or † *he gave in marriage;* syn. of the inf. n. تَزْوِيجٌ. (Kr, M, Ḳ.)

2. بَيَّتَ البَيْتَ *He constructed, or built, the* بيت [i. e. *tent, or house,* &c.]. (M.) ═ بَيَّتَ الأَمْرَ, [inf. n. as below,] *He did, or performed, the thing, or affair, by night, or at night:* (M:) and *he thought, or meditated, upon it, considering its end, or issue, or result,* (Zj, T, Ṣ, M, A, Mṣb, Ḳ,) or *entered into it,* (Zj, T,) *by night, or at night.* (Zj, T, Ṣ, M, &c.) And one says, بُيِّتَ بِلَيْلٍ, (T, A,) meaning the same as دُبِّرَ بِلَيْلٍ [*It was thought, or meditated, upon,* &c., *by night, or at night*]: (T:) [for] بَيَّتَ الشَّىْءُ also signifies [simply] *the thing was thought upon, and considered as to its end, issue, or result;* syn. قُدِّرَ. (Ṣ.) Accord. to El-Marzooḳee, they say of a thing that is not done deliberately, and with good consideration of its issue or result, هٰذَا أَمْرٌ قُدِّرَ بِلَيْلٍ; [in the text from which this is taken, without the syll. signs;] and hence the saying in the Ḳur [iv. 83], بَيَّتَ طَائِفَةٌ مِنْهُمْ غَيْرَ ٱلَّذِى تَقُولُ [*A part of them meditateth by night upon doing otherwise than that which thou sayest;* as is indicated in the M, where this is cited; and in like manner, يُبَيِّتُونَ, in the continuation of the same passage of the Ḳur, is explained in the T as meaning يُدَبِّرُونَ, and يُقَدِّرُونَ, (i. e. مِنَ السُّوْءِ,) لَيْلًا]: but Aboo-Hilál says that a thing is meditated upon in the night in order that one may apply himself to it with strong purpose, and not be diverted by other things, so that it may be done with more firmness; and he cites the same passage of the Ḳur. (Ḥam p. 130.) And hence, in the Ḳur [iv. 108], إِذْ يُبَيِّتُونَ مَا لَا يَرْضَى مِنَ القَوْلِ *When they meditate,* &c., (Ṣ, M, Bḍ, Jel,) *by night,* (Ṣ, M,) [*what He will not approve, of speech,*] *and prepare it* [*in their minds*] (يُزَوِّرُونَهُ [see art. زور]). (Bḍ.) It is said in a trad., لَا صِيَامَ لِمَنْ لَمْ يُبَيِّتِ الصِّيَامَ *There is no fasting to him* [meaning *his fasting is null*] *who does not purpose it from the night.* (TA. [See another reading, voce بَتَّ.]) And you say, بَيَّتَ النِّيَّةَ *He decided upon the purpose, or intention, by night, or in night-time.* (Mṣb.) And بَيَّتَ رَأْيَهُ *He thought upon his opinion, and concealed it, or conceived it, in his mind.* (TA.) — بَيَّتَهُمْ, (inf. n. تَبْيِيتٌ, (Mṣb, TA,) *He came upon them,* (Mgh, but the verb is there pl.,) or *made a sudden attack upon them, and engaged with them in conflict,* (Mṣb,) or *made a great slaughter among them, or engaged with them in vehement conflict,* (Ṣ, M, Ḳ,) namely, the enemy, (Ṣ, Mgh, Ḳ,) or a people, (M,) *by night:* (Ṣ, M, Mgh, Mṣb, Ḳ:) *he came upon them* (the sons of such a one) *in the night, and made a sudden attack upon them, while they were heedless:* (T:) *he attacked them* (the people of a house or place of abode) *by night: he went to them* (the enemy) *in the night, without their knowledge, and took them by surprise.* (TA.) — كَانَ لَا يُبَيِّتُ مَالًا وَلَا يُقَيِّلُهُ *He used not to retain property until night, nor to retain it until noon,* when it came to him; but used to hasten the dividing of it. (TA, from a trad.) — See also 4. ═ بَيَّتَ النَّخْلَ *He trimmed, or pruned, the palm-trees, by cutting off the stumps of the branches, or by cutting off the straggling branches, not in the best part thereof.* (Ḳ.) ═ See also 5.

4. اباتهُ, inf. n. إِبَاتَةٌ, *He* (God) *made him, or caused him, to pass, or spend, the night,* [or *a part thereof,*] or *to enter upon the night.* (T, M, Ḳ.) You say, أَبَاتَكَ ٱللّٰهُ بِخَيْرٍ [*May God make thee to pass, or enter upon, the night with happiness*], (Ṣ,) and أَبَاتَهُ حَسَنَةً [*in a good manner of doing so*]. (T, A.) And [in like manner,] ↓ بَيَّتَكَ ٱللّٰهُ فِى عَافِيَةٍ [*May God make thee to pass, or enter upon, the night in health and safety*]. (A.) And أَبَاتَهُ ٱللّٰهُ أَحْسَنَ بِيتَةٍ *God made him to pass, or enter upon, the night in the best manner of doing so.* (M, Ḳ.*)

5. تبيّتهُ عَنْ حَاجَتِهِ [so in the TA and in a MS. copy of the Ḳ: in the CḲ ↓ بَيَّتَهُ:] *He withheld,* or *debarred, him from the thing that he wanted.* (Ḳ.)

10. [استبات seems to signify *He asked for,* or *required,* بيت, or بِيتَةٌ, i. e. *food:* (see مُسْتَبِيتٌ:) and also to have the contr. signification; i. e. — *He possessed food:* for you say,] لَا يَسْتَبِيتُ لَيْلَةً *He possesses not a night's food.* (T, Ḳ.) And لَا يَسْتَبِيتُ *He has not food.* (A.)

بَيْتٌ [signifies *A tent; properly, having more than one pole;* but often applied without this restriction: and also *a house; a chamber; an apartment; a closet;* and *the like*]: a بَيْت is [*a tent*] *of* [*goats'*] *hair* (شَعَر), (M, A, Mgh, Mṣb, Ḳ,) or *of wool:* (Mgh:) *a* بيت *of hair* [i. e. *hair-cloth*] *is that kind* [*of tent*] *which has more than one pole:* the word is masc.: and applies to *small* and *large:* (M:) tents of goats' hair are peculiar to people of cold countries and of fertile regions, where the goats have abundant hair; for the goats of the Arabs of the desert have short hair, not long enough to be spun: (T in art. بنى:) a خِبَآء is a small بيت of wool or of hair: a بيت is *what is larger than a* خباء: next is the مظلّة, which is larger than the بيت; but the term بيت is also applied to *a* مظلّة *when it is large and* مُرَوَّق [i. e. *furnished with a* رِوَاق, q. v.]: (T:) Ibn-El-Kelbee says that the Arabs have six kinds of بيت; namely, a قُبَّة, which is of skins, or tanned hides; a مِظَلَّة, of hair; a خِبَآء, of wool; a بِجَاد, of soft hair (وَبَر); a خَيْمَة, of trees; an أُقْنَة, of stone; and a سُوط, of hair; or this is the smallest of them: El-Baghdádee says that the خباء is a بيت made of soft hair (وَبَر), or of wool, or of hair [commonly so called] (شَعَر), upon two poles, or three; and that a بيت is [*a tent*] *upon six poles, or more, to the number of nine:* in the Towsheeḥ it is said that the term خباء is applied to a بيت of any kind: (TA:) a بيت is also [*a structure*] *of clay,* or *tough or cohesive clay or earth;* (A, Ḳ;) [and *of baked bricks;* and *of stone;*] the name being likewise applied to *a structure of a kind other than the structures which are called* أَخْبِيَة [or *tents*]; (M;) signifying *a habitation* [*of any kind; an abode; a dwelling*]: (Mṣb:) a man's *house;* syn. دَارٌ: (T:) [and particularly *a chamber;* i. e.] *a single roofed structure* (Mgh, Kull) *having a place of entrance;* مَنْزِلٌ being applied to what comprises more than one [such] بيت, and a roofed صَحْن [or vacant part, and a kitchen, inhabited by a man with his family]; and دَار, to that which comprises more than one [such] بيت and more than one [such] مَنْزِل and a [court, or] صَحْن without a roof: (Kull:) the pl. is بُيُوتٌ, (Ṣ, M, Ḳ, &c.,) also pronounced بِيُوتٌ, (TA,) and أَبْيَاتٌ, (Ṣ, M, Ḳ,) the latter a pl. of pauc.; (TA;) and pl. pl. بُيُوتَاتٌ (M, Mgh, Ḳ) and أَبَايِيتُ (Sb, Ṣ, M, Ḳ) and أَبْيَاوَاتٌ, (Fr, M, Ḳ,) which last is extr.: (M:) the dim. is ▼ بُيَيْتٌ, also pronounced ▼ بِيَيْتٌ; (Ṣ, Ḳ;) and the vulgar say, بُوَيْتٌ, (Ṣ,) which is not allowable. (Ḳ.) You say, هُوَ جَارِى بَيْتَ بَيْتَ, (T, Ṣ, M,) *He is my neighbour* [*tent to tent, or house to house,* i. e.,] *by contiguity* [*of our habitations*]: بَيْتَ بَيْتَ being made indecl. with fet-ḥ for the termination because they are two nouns made one: (Ṣ:) Sb says that some of the Arabs make them [thus] indecl., like خَمْسَةَ عَشَرَ, and some make the former a prefixed noun governing the latter in the gen. case, [saying بَيْتَ بَيْتٍ,] except when used as a denotative of state: (M:) one says also, بَيْتًا لِبَيْتٍ, and بَيْتٌ لِبَيْتٍ; (Fr, T;) which last, or بَيْتٌ إِلَى بَيْتٍ, is the original form. (Ḥar p. 353.) بَنَى فُلَانٌ عَلَى ٱمْرَأَتِهِ بَيْتًا [lit. *Such a one constructed a tent over his wife,*] means *such a one had his wife conducted to him on the occasion of his marriage, and brought her, or had her brought, into a pitched tent, having conveyed thither the utensils and furniture and other things that they required.* (T.) And أَهْلُ بَيْتِ النَّبِىِّ [*The people of the house of the Prophet,*] means *the Prophet's wives and his daughter and 'Alee:* and so أَهْلَ ٱلْبَيْتِ [i. e. يَخُصُّ أَهْلَ البَيْتِ *He means particularly,* or *peculiarly, the people of the house*], in the Ḳur xxxiii. 33: بَنُو and مَعْشَر and أَهْل and آل, as prefixed nouns, being, as Sb says, the nouns most frequently occurring in the accus. case [for the reason indicated above, or, as the Arabian grammarians express it,] عَلَى الاِخْتِصَاص. (M.) — It also signifies *A* [*pavilion, palace,* or *mansion, such as is called*] قَصْر: (T, Ḳ:) whence the saying of Gabriel, بَشِّرْ خَدِيجَةَ بِبَيْتٍ مِنْ قَصَبٍ, i. e. [*Rejoice thou Khadeejeh by the announcement of*] *a pavilion* (قصر) *of hollow pearls,* (T, TA,) or *of emerald.* (TA. [See also art. قصب.]) بُيُوتًا غَيْرَ مَسْكُونَةٍ [*Uninhabited houses*], in the Ḳur xxiv. 29, means *buildings for the reception of travellers, or for merchants and their goods, and the shops of the merchants, and places in which things are sold, the entering of which is allowed by their owners:* or *ruins which a man enters for the purpose of easing nature.* (M.) And the بُيُوت which God has permitted to be raised, mentioned in the same chapter, verse 36, are *Mosques,* or *places of worship:* or, accord. to El-Ḥasan, *Jerusalem* (بَيْتُ المَقْدِس); the pl. being applied to it as a mark of honour. (Zj, M.) البَيْتُ [*The House*] applies particularly to ‡*the Kaạbeh* [*of Mekkeh*]; (Ḳ;) as also بَيْتُ ٱللّٰهِ [*the House of God*]; (AAF, M;) and البَيْتُ الحَرَامُ [*the Sacred House*]; (T;) and البَيْتُ العَتِيقُ [*the Ancient House*]; (Ṣ and Ḳ &c. in art. عتق;) and accord. to some, البَيْتُ المَعْمُورُ, q. v. (Bḍ in lii. 4.) [بَيْتُ المَالِ signifies *The treasury of the state.* And بَيْتُ المَآءِ is a euphemism for *The privy;* because water is put there for the purpose of ablution: also called بَيْتُ الفَرَاغِ, &c.] — Also † The *ark* of Noah: so in the Ḳur lxxi. last verse. (T.) — ‡ *A grave;* (M, IAth, Ḳ;) app. by way of comparison. (M.) So in a trad. of Aboo-Dharr: كَيْفَ تَصْنَعُ إِذَا مَاتَ النَّاسُ حَتَّى يَكُونَ البَيْتُ بِالوَصِيفِ, meaning *How wilt thou do when men shall die so that the grave shall be sold for the* [*servant-*] *boy?* (IAth.) — † The *habitation* of the سُرْفَة, which it constructs in a beautiful manner, (A'Obeyd, M,) of fragments of sticks; (Yaạḳoob, M;) and of the صَيْدَنَانِىّ, which it makes in the interior of the earth, and covers over: (A'Obeyd, M:) and † the *burrow,* or *hole,* of the ضَبّ &c.: and † the *web* of the spider: all, app., as being likened to the بَيْت of a man. (M.) — ‡ A man's *household.* (Ṣ, Ḳ, TA.) — ‡ The *wife* (Aṣ, IAạr, T, M, A) of a man. (M, A.) So in the saying,

• أَكِبَرٌ غَيَّرَنِى أَمْ بَيْتُ •

[*Hath old age altered me, or a wife?*]: (Aṣ, T:) or here it means *a household.* (Ṣ.) — The *nobility* of the Arabs; (T, Mṣb, Ḳ;*) as when one says, بَيْتُ تَمِيمٍ فِى بَنِى حَنْظَلَةَ [*The nobility of Temeem is in the sons of Ḥandhaleh*]: (T, Mṣb:*) or the *family that comprises the nobility of a tribe;* as آلُ حِصْنٍ of the فَزَارِيُّون, and آلُ الجَدَّيْنِ of the شَيْبَانِيُّون, and آلُ عَبْدِ المَدَانِ of the حَارِثِيُّون; which three were asserted by Ibn-El-Kelbee to be the highest of the families thus called of the Arabs: (M:) [see a verse of El-Lahabee cited voce أَخْضَرُ:] pl. بُيُوتٌ and بُيُوتَاتٌ, (T, M,) the latter being pl. of the former. (T.) You say, هُوَ مِنْ أَهْلِ البُيُوتَاتِ *He is of the people of nobility:* and مِنْ بَيْتٍ كَرِيمٍ [*of a generous,* or *noble, house,* or *family*]. (A.) [See also بَنَى.] — *A noble person:* (M, Mgh, Ḳ:) pl. بُيُوتٌ and بُيُوتَاتٌ. (Mgh.) You say, فُلَانٌ بَيْتُ قَوْمِهِ *Such a one is the noble person of his people.* (Abu-l-'Omeythil El-Aạrabee, M.) — ‡ The [*furniture termed*] فَرْش, (A, Mgh, Ḳ,) or مَتَاع, (TA,) *of a tent* or *house,* (Mgh, Ḳ,) or *that is sufficient for a tent* or *house.* (A.) You say, تَزَوَّجْتُ فُلَانَةَ عَلَى بَيْتٍ ‡ *I married,* or *took as a wife, such a woman for* [*my giving*] *furniture sufficient for a tent* or *house,* (A,) or *furniture of a house* or *tent.* (Mgh.) [See 1, last sentence.] — A بَيْت of poetry, (T, Ṣ, M, Mṣb,) or of the poet, (Ḳ,) is ‡ [*A verse;* i. e.] *what consists of certain known divisions* [or *feet*] *called* أَجْزَآءُ التَّفْعِيلِ; being termed بيت metaphorically, because of the conjoining of its component parts, one to another, in a particular manner, like as those of a tent are conjoined in its construction; (Mṣb;) because it consists of words collected together in a regular manner, and so resembles a tent, which is composed of a سَقْف and كِفَآء and رِوَاق and عُمُد: (T:) it is derived from the same word signifying a خِبَآء [or tent], and applies to the small and the great, as the رَجَز and the طَوِيل; and is [said to be] thus called because it comprises words like as the tent comprises its inhabitants; wherefore its component parts are termed أَسْبَاب and أَوْتَاد, as being likened to the اسباب and اوتاد of tents: (M:) pl. أَبْيَاتٌ and بُيُوتٌ, (M, A, Mṣb,) the latter mentioned by Sb and IJ, (M,) [but rare,] and [pl. pl.] أَبَايِيتُ: (A:) Abu-l-Ḥasan says that if the بيت of poetry be likened to the بيت which is a tent or other kind of structure, there is no reason why it should not have the same pl. forms as the latter has. (L.) By the following words of a poet,

• وَبَيْتٍ عَلَى ظَهْرِ المَطِىِّ بَنَيْتُهُ •
• بِأَسْمَرَ مَشْقُوقِ الخَيَاشِيمِ يَرْعُفُ •

[*Many a* بيت *upon the back of the camel have I*

constructed with a tawny thing slit in the nose and bleeding], is meant, many a بَيْت of poetry have I written with the reed-pen. (Ṣ.) [البَيْتَ, written after a quotation of a part of a verse of poetry, means اِقْرَإِ البَيْتَ *Read thou the verse.*] بَيْتُ القَصِيدَةِ [*The* chief *verse of the poem*] is a phrase employed when a person composes a poem in praise of any one from whom he would obtain some object of desire and want, being applied to *that verse of the poem in which the author's want is mentioned:* and is a proverbial expression relating to that which is extraordinary and strange, and used in denoting the superiority of a part of a thing over the whole of it [regarded as a whole]: [hence,] one says, فُلَانٌ أَوَّلُ الجَرِيدَةِ وَبَيْتُ القَصِيدَةِ † [*Such a one is the first of the detachment of horsemen, and the* chief *verse of the poem*]. (Ḥar p. 441.)

بَيْتٌ: see بِيتَةٌ, in two places.

بِيتَةٌ a subst. from بَاتَ: and signifying *A manner or mode, and state,* or *condition, of passing,* or *entering upon, the night.* (M.) [See 4; last sentence.] — *Food,* or *victuals;* and so ↓بَيْتٌ: (A, Ḳ:) [or particularly, of a night: for] you say, مَا لَهُ بَيْتُ ↓ لَيْلَةٍ, (Ṣ, M, A, Ḳ,) and بِيتَةُ لَيْلَةٍ, (T, Ṣ, M, A,) مِنَ القُوتِ, (T,) *He has not a night's food,* or *victuals.* (T, Ṣ, M, A, Ḳ.)

بَيَاتٌ *A coming upon the enemy by night;* (Mgh;) *a sudden attack upon, and conflict with, the enemy by night;* (Mṣb;) *a great slaughter* (Ṣ, M) *among the enemy,* (Ṣ,) or *a people,* (M,) *and vehement conflict with them;* (Ṣ, M;) *a coming upon people in the night, and making a sudden attack upon them, while they are heedless;* (T;) *an attack upon a people by night; a going to the enemy in the night, without their knowledge, and taking them by surprise:* (TA:) a subst. from 2; (Ṣ, M, Mgh, Mṣb;) like سَلَامٌ from سَلَّمَ. (Mgh.) — أَتَاهُمُ الأَمْرُ بَيَاتًا *The thing,* or *event, happened,* or *came, to them in the latter part of the night.* (T.)

بُيَيْتٌ, also pronounced بِيَيْتٌ, dim. of بَيْتٌ, q. v. (Ṣ, Ḳ.)

بَيُوتٌ *That has remained throughout a night* [*and so become stale; stale from being a night old*]; as also ↓بَائِتٌ: both, in this sense, [but the latter more usually,] applied to bread. (Ṣ, Ḳ.) — *Cold,* or *cool,* water, (M, Ḳ,) *that has become so from its having remained throughout a night:* (M:) or water *that remains during the night beneath the sky:* (Ḥam p. 553:) or water *that has been cooled in the leathern bag by night;* and in like manner, milk; for [Az says,] I heard an Arab of the desert say, اِسْقِنِى مِنْ بَيُوتِ السِّقَآءِ, meaning *Give thou me to drink of the milk that has been milked at night and left in the skin so that it has become cold,* or *cool, by night.* (T.) In the saying,

• فَصَبَّحَتْ حَوْضَ قَرًى بَيُوتَا •

the meaning seems to be, قَرَى حَوْضٍ بَيُوتًا, i. e., [*And they* (app. camels) *came in the morning to*] *the collected water of a trough, which water had remained throughout the night and so become cold,* or *cool;* the phrase being inverted. (M.) — أَمْرٌ بَيُوتٌ †*An affair,* or *event, for which,* or *on account of which, one passes the night in anxiety* or *grief.* (Ṣ, Ḳ.) — هَمٌّ بَيُوتٌ †*Anxiety,* or *grief, that has remained during the night in the bosom.* (M.) — سِنٌّ بَيُوتَةٌ *A tooth that does not fall out,* or *become shed.* (Ḳ.)

بَائِتٌ [*Passing,* or *spending, the night,* or *a night,* or *a part thereof;* or *entering upon the night;* &c.;] act. part. n. of 1. (Mṣb.) — See also بَيُوتٌ.

مَبِيتٌ *A place in which one passes,* or *enters upon, the night.* (M, A.)

مُتَبَيِّتَةٌ A woman *who has obtained a* بَيْت [i. e. *tent* or *house,* or *the furniture thereof,*] *and a husband.* (M, Ḳ.)

مُسْتَبِيتٌ *Poor,* or *needy;* [as though meaning *asking for,* or *requiring,* بَيْت or بِيتَة, i. e. *food;* or *possessing food, and nothing beside;*] syn. فَقِيرٌ [q. v.]. (IAạr, T, Ḳ.)

Quasi بيح

بَيْحَانٌ and بِيَحَانٌ: see بُوحٌ, in art. بوح.

بيد

1. بَادَ, aor. يَبِيدُ, inf. n. بَيْدٌ (T, Ṣ, M, &c.) and بُيُودٌ (Ṣ, M, L, Mṣb, Ḳ) and بَيَادٌ (M, L, Mṣb, Ḳ) and بَيْدُودَةٌ (Lḥ, M, L, Ḳ) and بَوَادٌ (L, Ḳ) and بُيُودٌ, (CḲ,) the last but one disapproved by MF, (TA,) [and the last equally doubtful,] *He,* or *it, perished;* (T, Ṣ, A, Mgh, L, Mṣb;) *went away; passed away; became cut off,* or *extinct; came to an end.* (M, L, Ḳ.) — بَادَتِ الشَّمْسُ, inf. n. بُيُودٌ, *The sun set.* (Sb, M, Ḳ.)

4. أَبَادَهُمْ *He* (God) *destroyed them;* (T, Ṣ, A, Mgh,* Mṣb;) *caused them to go away, pass away, become cut off* or *extinct,* or *come to an end.* (M.*)

بَيْدَ, (T, Ṣ, M, L, Mughnee, Ḳ,) as also ↓بَايْدَ, (L, Ḳ,) or بَائِدَ, (so in the Mughnee and in a MS. copy of the Ḳ and in the CḲ, and in a MS. copy of the Ḳ omitted,) a noun inseparably prefixed to أَنَّ with its complement, (Mughnee,) used as *syn. with* غَيْرَ, (Ks, T, Ṣ, M, &c.,) but never otherwise than in the accus. case, nor as an epithet, nor otherwise than as an exceptive in a case in which the thing excepted is disunited in kind from that from which the exception is made. (Mughnee.) You say, هُوَ كَثِيرُ المَالِ بَيْدَ أَنَّهُ بَخِيلٌ *He is possessed of abundant,* or *much, wealth, but he is niggardly.* (ISk, Ṣ, M, A, Mṣb, Mughnee.) — Also as *syn. with* عَلَى, (M, Ḳ,) as some say; (A'Obeyd, M;) but to render it in the former manner is preferable. (M.) Accord. to some, (L,) it is syn. with عَلَى in the following trad.: نَحْنُ الآخِرُونَ السَّابِقُونَ يَوْمَ القِيَامَةِ بَيْدَ أَنَّهُمْ أُوتُوا الكِتَابَ مِنْ قَبْلِنَا وَأُوتِينَاهُ مِنْ بَعْدِهِمْ [*We, the* latter people, *shall be those who will precede on the day of resurrection, although they were given the Scripture before us, and we were given it after them*]: (T, L:) El-Umawee holds it to be so: (T:) but Ks says that it here signifies غَيْرَ [as in the former ex.]: (T, L: [and so says IHsh in the Mughnee:]) accord. to one recital, it is بَايْدَ; (L;) or بَائِدَ; so in the Musnad of the Imám Esh-Sháfi'ee: (Mughnee:) IAth says, I have not found this in the classical language in the sense of عَلَى: some say that it is بِأَيْدٍ, i. e. *by means of strength,* or *power;* and that the meaning is, *we shall be those who will precede* to Paradise *on the day of resurrection by means of strength,* or *power,* given us by God. (L.) — Also, [accord. to some,] as *meaning* مِنْ أَجْلِ: (L, Mughnee, Ḳ:) as in the saying of Moḥammad, أَنَا أَفْصَحُ العَرَبِ بَيْدَ أَنِّى مِنْ قُرَيْشٍ وَنَشَأْتُ فِى بَنِى سَعْدٍ [*I am the most chaste in speech of the Arabs because I am of the tribe of Ḳureysh and I grew up among the children of Saad*]: (T, L: [in the Mughnee given somewhat differently:]) but Ibn-Málik and others say that it here, also, means غَيْرَ, after the manner in which the latter is used in the saying [of a poet],

• وَلَا عَيْبَ فِيهِمْ غَيْرَ أَنَّ سُيُوفَهُمْ •
• بِهِنَّ فُلُولٌ مِنْ قِرَاعِ الكَتَائِبِ •

[And there is no blemish in them, save that their swords have in them notches from the conflicting of the troops]. (Mughnee.) This manner of praising is termed by Abu-l-'Abbás Moḥammad Ibn-Yezeed اِسْتِثْبَاتٌ. (Ḥam p. 474.) — مَيْدَ is also a dial. var. of the same. (A'Obeyd, T, Mughnee.)

بَيْدَآءُ *A desert;* or *a waterless desert:* (Ṣ, M, A, Mgh, Mṣb, Ḳ:) or *one that is plain,* or *level, in which horses are made to run:* (M:) or *one wherein is nothing:* (TA:) so called, accord. to IJ, because it [often] destroys him who alights, or sojourns, in it: (M, Mṣb:*) or *a plain tract, slightly elevated, with few trees, and without herbage, extending to the distance of a day's journey,* or *half a day's journey,* or *less, rugged and hard, and only in a country of mould,* or *clay:* (ISh:) pl. بِيدٌ: (Ṣ, M, Mṣb, Ḳ:) it has a pl. of a form proper to epithets because it is originally an epithet: (M:) by rule it should be بَيْدَاوَاتٌ. (M, Ḳ.)

بَيْدَانَةٌ *A she-ass;* a subst. applied to that animal: (Ṣ:) or *a wild she-ass:* (M, Ḳ:) or one *that inhabits a desert* (بَيْدَآء); (T, Ḳ;) [an epithet;] not a subst. applied to the animal; J being in error in asserting it to be such: (Ḳ:) the [wild] she-ass is thus called, accord. to most of the lexicologists, because it inhabits the بيداء; and if so, the ن is an augmentative letter: or, accord. to some, because it is *large in the body* (البَدَن); and if so, the ن is a radical letter: (L:) the pl. is بَيْدَانَاتٌ. (L, Ḳ.)

بَايْدَ, or بَائِدَ: see بَيْدَ.

Quasi بير

بِيرٌ; pl. of pauc. أَبْيَارٌ: see بِئْرٌ, in art. بأر.

بيص

حَيْصَ بَيْصَ, وَقَعَ فِى حَاصِ بَاصِ, &c.: see art. حيص.

بَيْصٌ *Difficulty; straitness;* (IAạr, Ḳ;) as also ↓ بِيصٌ. (Ḳ.) See above.

بِيصٌ: see above.

بيض

1. بَاضَهُ, (Ṣ, Ḳ,) first pers. بِضْتُ, (M,) aor. يَبِيضُ, for which one should not say يَبُوضُ, [though it would be agreeable with a general rule respecting verbs denoting surpassingness,] (Ṣ, O,) *He surpassed him in whiteness.* (Ṣ, M, O, Ḳ.) = بَاضَتْ, (Ṣ, M, Mṣb, Ḳ, except that in the M and Mṣb we find the masc. form, بَاضَ, followed by الطَّائِرُ,) aor. تَبِيضُ, (Mṣb,) inf. n. بَيْضٌ, (M, Mṣb,) said of an ostrich, (M,) or a hen, (Ḳ,) or any bird, (Ṣ, M, Mṣb,) and the like, (Mṣb,) *She laid her eggs,* (M, Mṣb, TA,) or *egg.* (Mṣb.) — بَاضَ السَّحَابُ ‡ *The clouds rained.* (IAạr, O, Ḳ.) A poet says, [using a phrase from which this application of the verb probably originated,]

* بَاضَ النَّعَامُ بِهِ فَنَفَّرَ أَهْلَهُ *
* إِلَّا المُقِيمَ عَلَى الدَّوَى المُتَأَفِّنِ *

(IAạr,) i. e. ‡ *The* نعام, meaning the نَعَائِم, [or Twentieth Mansion of the Moon,] *sent down rain upon it, and so put to flight its occupants, except him who remained incurring the risk of* dying from *disease, wasting away:* [the last word being in the gen. case, by poetic license, because the next before it is in that case; like خَرِبٍ in the phrase هٰذَا جُحْرُ ضَبٍّ خَرِبٍ:] the poet is describing a valley rained upon and in consequence producing herbage; for the rain of the asterism called النعائم is in the hot season, [when that asterism sets aurorally, (see مَنَازِلُ القَمَرِ, in art. نزل,)] whereupon there grows, at the roots of the حَلِىّ, a plant called نَشْر, which is poisonous, killing beasts that eat of it: the verse is explained as above by El-Mohellebee: (IB:) or, as IAạr says, the poet means rain that falls at the نَوْء [by which we are here to understand the setting aurorally] of النعائم; and that when this rain falls, the wise flees and the stupid remains. (O.) — بَاضَ بِالمَكَانِ ‡ *He remained, stayed,* or *abode, in the place* [like as a bird does in the place where she lays her eggs]. (O, Ḳ.) — بَاضَتِ الأَرْضُ † *The earth produced* كَمْأَة [or *truffles,* which are thus likened to eggs]: (A, TA:) or † *the earth produced the plants that it contained:* or † *it became changed in its greenness to yellowness, and scattered the fruit,* or *produce, and dried up.* (M, TA.) — بَاضَ الحَرُّ ‡ *The heat became vehement,* or *intense.* (Ṣ, A, Ḳ.) = بَاضَ القَوْمَ; &c.: see 8, in three places.

2. بَيَّضَ, (Ṣ, M, Ḳ,) inf. n. تَبْيِيضٌ, (Ṣ,) *He whitened* a thing; *made* it *white;* (Ṣ, M;) *contr. of* سَوَّدَ. (Ḳ.) *He bleached* clothes. (M.) [*He whitewashed* a wall &c. *He tinned* a copper vessel or the like.] You say, بَيَّضَ اللّٰهُ وَجْهَهُ [lit., *God whitened his face:* or *may God whiten his face:* meaning ‡ *God rendered his face expressive of joy,* or *cheerfulness;* or *rejoiced,* or *cheered, him:* or *may God* &c.: and also *God cleared his character;* or *manifested his honesty,* or *the like:* or *may God* &c.: see the contr. سَوَّدَ]. (TA.) And بَيَّضَ لَهُ [*He left a blank space for it;* namely, a word or sentence or the like: probably post-classical]. (TA in art. شمس; &c.) — [*He wrote out fairly,* after having made a first rough draught: in this sense, also, opposed to سَوَّدَ: probably post-classical.] — ‡ *He filled* a vessel: (M, A, Ḳ:*) or *he filled* a vessel, and a skin, *with water* and *milk.* (Ṣ, O.) — And ‡ *He emptied* (A, Ḳ) a vessel: (A:) thus it bears two contr. significations. (Ḳ.)

3. بَايَضَهُ, (Ṣ, M,) inf. n. مُبَايَضَةٌ, (TA,) *He contended with him for superiority in whiteness.* (Ṣ, M.) — بَايَضَنِى فُلَانٌ ‡ *Such a one acted openly with me;* syn. جَاهَرَنِى: from ↓ بَيَاضُ النَّهَارِ [the whiteness of day, or daylight]. (A, TA.)

4. أَبْيَضَتْ and أَبَاضَتْ *She* (a woman) *brought forth white children:* and in like manner one says of a man [أَبْيَضَ and أَبَاضَ, meaning *He begat white children*]. (M, TA.) — See also 9, in two places.

8. ابتاض *He* (a man, Ṣ) *put upon himself a* بَيْضَة [or *helmet*] (Ṣ, Ḳ, TA) *of iron.* (TA.) = ابتاضهم *He entered into their* بَيْضَة [or *territory,* &c.]: (A, TA:) and ابتاضوا القَوْمَ *They exterminated the people,* or *company of men; they extirpated them;* (M, Ḳ;*) as also ↓ بَاضُوهُمْ: (M:) and ابْتِيضُوا [originally ابْتُيِضُوا; in the CḲ, incorrectly, ابْتَيَضُوا;] *They were exterminated,* or *extirpated,* (Ḳ, TA,) *and their* بَيْضَة [or *quarter,* &c.,] *was given up to be plundered:* (TA:) and ابْتَضْنَاهُمْ *We smote their* بيضة [or *collective body,* &c.,] *and took all that belonged to them by force;* as also ↓ بِضْنَاهُمْ: and ↓ بِيضَ الحَىُّ *The tribe was so smitten* &c. (TA.)

9. ابيضّ, (Ṣ, M, Mṣb, Ḳ,) and, by poetic license, ابْيَضَضَ, [of which see an ex. voce خَفَضَ, and see also 9 in art. حو,] (M, TA,) inf. n. ابْيِضَاضٌ, (Ṣ, Mṣb,) *It was,* or *became, white;* (Ṣ, M, Mṣb;) *contr. of* اِسْوَدَّ; (Ḳ;) as also ↓ ابياضّ, inf. n. ابْيِيضَاضٌ; (Ṣ;) *contr. of* اِسْوَادَّ; (Ḳ;) and ↓ أَبَاضَ: which ↓ last also signifies *it* (herbage or pasture) *became white, and dried up.* (M, TA.) [You say also, ابيضّ وَجْهُهُ, lit., *His face became white:* meaning ‡ *his face became expressive of joy,* or *cheerfulness;* or *he became joyful,* or *cheerful:* and also *his character became cleared;* or *his honesty,* or *the like, became manifested:* see 2.]

11: see 9.

بَيْضٌ: see بَيْضَةٌ, in three places.

بَيْضَةٌ *An egg* (Mṣb) of an ostrich, (Mgh,) and of any bird, (Ṣ, Mgh, Mṣb, Ḳ,) and the like, i. e. of anything that is termed صَمُوخ [or having merely an ear-hole] as distinguished from such as is termed أَذُون [or having an ear that is called أُذُن]: so called because of its whiteness: (TA:) n. un. of ↓ بَيْضٌ: (Ṣ, M,* Mṣb, Ḳ:) pl. [of the former] بَيْضَاتٌ (M, Ṣgh, Ḳ) and بَيَضَاتٌ, which latter is irreg., (M, Ṣgh,) and only used by poetic license; (Ṣgh;) and (of بَيْضٌ, M) بُيُوضٌ. (M, Ḳ.) You say, أَفْرَخَتِ البَيْضَةُ *The egg had in it a young bird.* (ISh.) And أَفْرَخَ بَيْضَةُ القَوْمِ † *What was hidden, of the affair,* or *case, of the people,* or *company of men, became apparent.* (ISh.) [See also art. فرخ.] بَيْضَةُ البَلَدِ signifies *The egg which the ostrich abandons.* (Ṣ, M, Ḳ.) And hence the saying, هُوَ أَذَلُّ مِنْ بَيْضَةِ البَلَدِ ‡ *He is more abject,* or *vile, than the egg of the ostrich which it abandons* (Ṣ, A,* Ḳ) *in the desert.* (TA.) You say also, هُوَ بَيْضَةُ البَلَدِ in dispraise and in praise. (IAạr, Aboo-Bekr, M.) When said in dispraise, it means ‡ *He is like the egg of the ostrich from which the young bird has come forth, and which the male ostrich has cast away, so that men and camels tread upon it:* (IAạr, M:) or *he is alone, without any to aid him; like the egg from which the male ostrich has arisen, and which he has abandoned as useless:* (TA:) or *he is an obscure man,* or *one of no reputation, whose lineage is unknown.* (Ḥam p. 250.) And when said in praise, it means ‡ *He is like the ostrich's egg in which is the young bird;* because the male ostrich in that case protects it: (IAạr, M:) or *he is unequalled in nobility;* like the egg that is left alone: (M:) or *he is a lord,* or *chief:* (IAạr, M:) or *he is the unequalled of the* بَلَد [or *country* or *the like*], *to whom others resort, and whose words they accept:* (Ḳ:) or *he is a celebrated,* or *well-known, person.* (Ḥam p. 250.) [See also art. بلد. And for another meaning of بَيْضَةُ البَلَدِ see below.] — ‡ *A helmet of iron,* (AO, Ṣ,* M,* Mgh,* Ḳ,*) *which is composed of plates like the bones of the skull, the edges whereof are joined together by nails; and sometimes of one piece:* (AO:) so called because resembling in shape the egg of an ostrich: (AO, M, Mgh:*) in this sense, also, n. un. of ↓ بَيْضٌ. (Ṣ, Ḳ: [in the CḲ, for والحَدِيدُ we should read والحديد.]) This may be meant in a trad. in which it is said that a man's hand is to be cut off for his stealing a بَيْضَة. (Mgh.) — † *A testicle:* (Ṣ, Ḳ:) pl. بَيْضَانٌ. (TA.) — ‡ The *bulb* of the saffron-plant [&c.]: as resembling an egg in shape. (Mgh.) — † [*A tuber:* for the same reason.] — † *A kind of grape of Eṭ-Ṭáïf, white and large.* (M.) — ‡ The *core* of a boil: as resembling an egg. (M.) — ‡ The *fat* of a camel's hump: for the same reason. (M.) — بَيْضَةُ البَلَدِ, in addition to its meanings mentioned above, also signifies †*The white truffle:* (O, Ḳ:) or simply *truffles;* syn. الكَمْأَةُ; (TA;) or these are called ↓ بَيْضُ الأَرْضِ. (A.) — بَيْضَةٌ also signifies ‡ The *continent,* or *container,* or *receptacle,* (حَوْزَة,) of anything. (Ṣ, Ḳ, TA.) And [hence] بَيْضَةُ الإِسْلَامِ ‡ *The place* [or *territory*] *which comprises El-Islám* [meaning *the Muslims*]; like as the egg comprises the young bird: (Mgh:) or this signifies *the congregation,* or *collective body, of the Muslims.* (AZ, M.) And بَيْضَةُ القَوْمِ

‡ *The quarter, tract, region,* or *district, of the people,* or *company of men:* (Ṣ, Ḳ:) *the heart;* or *midst,* or *main part, of the abode thereof:* (Ṣ, TA:) *the principal place of abode* (أَصْل) *thereof;* (M, TA;) *the place that comprises them; the place of their government,* or *regal dominion;* and *the seat of their* دعوة [i. e. دَعْوَة or *kindred and brotherhood*]: (TA:) *the midst of them:* (M:) or, as some say, *their* [*kinsfolk such as are termed*] عَشِيرَة: (TA:) but when you say, أَتَاهُمُ العَدُوُّ فِى بَيْضَتِهِمْ, the meaning is [*the enemy came to them in*] *their principal place of abode* (أَصْل), and *the place where they were congregated.* (TA.) And بَيْضَةُ الدَّارِ ‡ *The midst of the country* or *place of abode* or *the like:* (AZ, M, TA:) *the main part thereof.* (TA.) And بَيْضَةُ المُلْكِ *i. q.* حَوْزَتُهُ † [*The seat of regal power: or the heart,* or *principal part, of the kingdom*]. (Ṣ and Ḳ in art. حوز.) — بَيْضَةُ الخِدْرِ (M, A, Ḳ) ‡ *The damsel* (M, Ḳ) *of the* خدر [or *curtain* &c.]: (Ḳ: [in the CḲ, جَارِيَتُهَا is erroneously put for جَارِيَتُهُ:]) because she is kept concealed within it. (TA.) You say also, هِىَ مِنْ بَيْضَاتِ الحِجَالِ ‡ [*She is of the damsels of the curtained bridal canopies*]. (A, TA.) بَيْضَةٌ is used by a metonymy to signify ‡ *A woman,* by way of likening her thereto [i. e. to an egg] in colour, and in respect of her being protected as beneath the wing. (B.) [See Ḳur xxxvii. 47.] — بَيْضَةٌ also signifies † *White land, in which is no herbage;* opposed to سَوْدَةٌ: (TA:) and ▼ بِيضَةٌ, with kesr, *white, smooth land;* (Ḳ;) thus accord. to IAạr, with kesr to the ب: (Sh:) and أَرْضٌ ▼ بَيْضَآءُ signifies *smooth land, in which is no herbage;* as though herbage blackened land: or *untrodden land:* as also بَيْضَةٌ. (M.) — بَيْضَةُ النَّهَارِ *The whiteness of day;* [*daylight;*] *i. q.* ▼ بَيَاضُهُ; (Ḳ;) i. e. *its light.* (Ḥar p. 222.) You say, أَتَيْتُهُ فِى بَيْضَةِ النَّهَارِ *I came to him in the whiteness of day.* (TA.) — بَيْضَةُ الحَرِّ † *The vehemence,* or *intenseness, of heat.* (M.) And بَيْضَةُ القَيْظِ ‡ *The most vehement,* or *intense, heat of summer,* or *of the hottest period of summer, from the* [*auroral*] *rising of* الدَّبَرَان *to that of* سُهَيْل; [i. e., reckoning for the commencement of the era of the Flight, in central Arabia, *from about the 20th of May to about the 4th of August, O. S.;*] (A,* TA;) as also ▼ بَيْضَآءُ القَيْظِ. (A, TA.) And بَيْضَةُ الصَّيْفِ † *The main part of the* صيف [or *summer*]: (M, TA:) or *the vehement,* or *intense, heat thereof.* (Ḥam p. 250.)

بِيضَةٌ: see بَيْضَةٌ, in the latter part of the paragraph.

بَيَاضٌ *Whiteness;* contr. of سَوَادٌ; in an animal, and in a plant, and in other things; and, accord. to IAạr, in water also; (M;) the colour of that which is termed أَبْيَضُ: (Ṣ, Mṣb,* Ḳ:) they said بَيَاضٌ and ▼ بَيَاضَةٌ, (Ṣ, M, Ḳ,) like as they said مَنْزِلٌ and مَنْزِلَةٌ: (Ṣ:) بَيَاضَةٌ being applied to *a whiteness* in the eye. (M.) You say, هٰذَا أَشَدُّ بَيَاضًا مِنْ كَذَا [*This is whiter than such a thing*]: (Ṣ, Ḳ:*) but not ▼ أَبْيَضُ مِنْهُ: (Ṣ:) the latter is anomalous; (Ḳ;) [like أَسْوَدُ مِنْهُ; q. v.;] but it was said by the people of El-Koofeh, (Ṣ, Ḳ,) who adduced as authority the saying of the rájiz,

* جَارِيَةٌ فِى دِرْعِهَا الفَضْفَاضِ *
* أَبْيَضُ مِنْ أُخْتِ بَنِى إِبَاضِ *

[*A damsel in her ample shift, whiter than the sister of* the tribe of *Benoo-Ibád*]: Mbr, however, says that an anomalous verse is no evidence against a rule commonly approved: and as to the saying of another,

* إِذَا الرِّجَالُ شَتَوْا وَٱشْتَدَّ أَكْلُهُمْ *
* فَأَنْتَ أَبْيَضُهُمْ سِرْبَالَ طَبَّاخِ *

[*When men experience dearth in winter, and their eating becomes vehement, thou art the whitest of them,* or rather *the white of them, in respect of cook's clothing,* having little or nothing to do with entertaining them], the word in question may be considered as an epithet of the measure أَفْعَلُ that is followed by مِنْ to denote excess: but it is only like the instances in the sayings هُوَ أَحْسَنُهُمْ وَجْهًا and أَكْرَمُهُمْ أَبًا, meaning حَسَنُهُمْ وَجْهًا and كَرِيمُهُمْ; so it is as though he said فَأَنْتَ مُبْيَضُّهُمْ سِرْبَالًا; and as he has prefixed it to a complement which it governs in the gen. case, what follows is in the accus. case as a specificative. (Ṣ.) This latter verse is by Ṭarafeh, who satirizes therein 'Amr Ibn-Hind; and is also differently related in respect of the first hemistich, and the first word of the second. (L, TA.) — بَيَاضُ النَّهَارِ: see 3; and see بَيْضَةٌ, near the end of the paragraph. — بَيَاضٌ is also used elliptically for ذُو بَيَاضٍ; and thus means † *White clothing;* as in the saying, فُلَانٌ يَلْبَسُ السَّوَادَ وَالبَيَاضَ *Such a one wears black and white clothing.* (Mgh.) [Hence, also, it has other significations, here following.] — † *Milk.* (Ḳ.) See an ex., voce سَوَادٌ. — [† The *white* of an egg.] — بَيَاضُ الأَرْضِ † *That part of land wherein is no cultivation nor population and the like.* (M.) — بَيَاضُ الجِلْدِ † *That part of the skin upon which is no hair.* (M.) — بَيَاضٌ ‡ also signifies ‡ *A man's person;* like سَوَادٌ; syn. شَخْصٌ; as in the saying, لَا يُزَايِلُ سَوَادِى بَيَاضَكَ ‡ *My person will not separate itself from thy person.* (Aṣ, A, TA.)

بَيُوضٌ A hen *that lays many eggs;* (Ṣ, M, A,* Ḳ;*) as also ▼ بَيَّاضَةٌ: (M:) [but in the Mṣb it is evidently used as signifying simply *oviparous:*] pl. (of the former, Ṣ, M*) بُيُضٌ (Ṣ, M, A, Ḳ) and بِيضٌ, (Ṣ, M, Ḳ,) the latter in the dial. of those who say رُسْلٌ for رُسُلٌ, the ب being with kesr in order that the ى may remain unchanged; (Ṣ, M;) but sometimes they said بُوضٌ. (M.)

بَيَاضَةٌ: see بَيَاضٌ.

بَائِضٌ A hen, (Az, Ḳ,) or bird, (Ṣ, Mṣb,) and the like, (Mṣb,) *laying an egg* or *eggs:* (Az, Ṣ,* Mṣb, Ḳ:*) without ة because the cock does not lay eggs: (Az, TA:) or it is applied also to a cock, (M, TA,) and to a crow, (M, A, TA,) [as meaning *begetting an egg* or *eggs,*] in like manner as one uses the word وَالِدٌ. (M, TA.)

بَيَّاضٌ *A bleacher of clothes;* as a kind of rel. n.; not as a verbal epithet; for were it this, it would be مُبَيِّضٌ. (M.) — *A seller of eggs.* (M.) — بَيَّاضَةٌ: see بَيُوضٌ.

أَبْيَضُ *White;* contr. of أَسْوَدُ; (A, Ḳ;) *having whiteness:* (Mṣb:) fem. بَيْضَآءُ: (Mṣb:) pl. بِيضٌ, originally بُيْضٌ, (Ṣ, Mṣb, Ḳ,) the ḍamm being converted into kesr in order that the ى may remain unchanged, (Ṣ, Ḳ,) [i. e.] to suit the ى. (Mṣb.) In the phrase أَعْطِنِى أَبْيَضَّهْ, mentioned by Sb, as used by some of the Arabs, meaning أَبْيَضَ, [i. e. *Give thou to me a white one,*] ه is subjoined as it is in هُنَّهْ for هُنَّ, and the ض is doubled because the letter of declinability cannot have ه subjoined to it; wherefore the letter of declinability is the first ض, and the second is the augmentative, and for this reason it has subjoined to it the ه whereof the purpose is to render plainly perceivable the vowel [which is necessarily added after the doubled ض]: Aboo-'Alee says, [app. of the ه,] that it should properly have neither fet-ḥ nor any vowel. (M.) — Applied to a man &c., it was sometimes used to signify *White in complexion:* but in this sense they generally used the epithet أَحْمَرُ. (IAth, TA in art. حمر.) They also said, فُلَانَةٌ بَيْضَآءُ الوَجْهِ and فُلَانٌ أَبْيَضُ الوَجْهِ, meaning *Such a man,* and *such a woman, is clear, in face, from freckles or the like, and unseemly blackness.* (Az, TA.) And they used بِيضَانٌ, (Ṣ, Ḳ,) a pl. of أَبْيَضُ, (TA,) in the contr. of the sense of سُودَانٌ, (Ṣ, Ḳ,) [i. e. as signifying *Whites,*] applied to men: (Ṣ:) though they applied the appellation أَبُو البَيْضَآءِ to *the Abyssinian:* (TA in art. عور:) or to *the negro:* and أَبُو الجَوْنِ to the white man. (ISk.) But accord. to Th, أَبْيَضُ applied to a man signifies only ‡ *Pure; free from faults:* (IAth, TA in art. حمر:) or, so applied, *unsullied in honour, nobility,* or *estimation;* (Az, Ḳ;) *free from faults;* and *generous:* and so بَيْضَآءُ applied to a woman. (Az.) [In the lexicons, however, (see, for ex., among countless other instances, an explanation of بَضَّةٌ in the Ṣ,) and in other post-classical works, it is generally used, when thus applied, in its proper sense, of *White;* or *fair in complexion.*] — كَتِيبَةٌ بَيْضَآءُ *An army,* or *a portion thereof, upon which the whiteness of the* [*arms or armour of*] *iron is apparent.* (M.) — And بَيْضَآءُ alone, [as a subst.,] *A piece of paper* [*without writing*]. (Ḥar p. 311.) — الأَبْيَضُ *The sword:* (Ṣ, A, Ḳ:) because of its whiteness: (TA:) pl. بِيضٌ. (Ṣ.) — *Silver:* (A, Ḳ:) because of its whiteness: like as gold is called الأَحْمَرُ [because of its redness]. (TA.) — *The saliva* (رضاب) *of the mouth.* (Ḥam p. 348.) — *A certain star in the margin of the milky way.* (A, Ḳ.) — البَيْضَآءُ *The sun:* because of its whiteness. (M.) — *Waste,* or *uncultivated,* or *uninhabited, land:* (Ḳ,* TA: [in the CḲ الجِرَابُ is erroneously put for الخَرَابُ:]) opposed to السَّوْدَآءُ: because dead lands are white; and when planted, become black and green. (TA.) See also بَيْضَةٌ, near the end. — *Wheat:* (Ḳ:) as also السَّمْرَآءُ. (TA.) — *Fresh* [*grain of the kind called*] سُلْت. (El-

Khaṭṭábee, Ḳ.) —— *A certain kind of wood; that which is called* الحَوَرُ: (Ḳ in art. حور:) because of its whiteness. (TA in that art.) [See حَوَرٌ.] —— *The cooking-pot;* as also أُمُّ بَيْضَآءَ. (AA, Ḳ.) —— *The snare with which one catches game.* (IAạr, Ḳ.) —— الأَبْيَضَانِ *Milk and water.* (ISk, Ṣ, M, A, Ḳ.) A poet says,

وَمَا لِىَ إِلَّا الأَبْيَضَيْنِ شَرَابُ

[*And I have not any beverage except milk and water*]. (ISk, Ṣ, M.) —— *Bread and water:* (Aṣ, M, Ḳ:) or *wheat and water:* (Fr, Ḳ:) or *fat and milk.* (AO, Ḳ.) —— *Fat and youthfulness* (AZ, IAạr, M, A, Ḳ.) You say, ذَهَبَ أَبْيَضَاهُ *His fat and youthfulness departed.* (TA.) —— مَا رَأَيْتُهُ مُذْ أَبْيَضَانِ *I have not seen him for,* or *during, two days:* (Ks, M, A, Ḳ:) or *two months.* (Ks, M, Ḳ.) —— أَيَّامُ البِيضِ, (Mṣb, Ḳ,) or simply البِيضُ, (Mgh,) for أَيَّامُ اللَّيَالِى البِيضِ; [*The days of the white nights;*] i. e. *the days of the thirteenth and fourteenth and fifteenth nights of the month;* (Mgh, Mṣb, Ḳ;) so called because they are lighted by the moon throughout: (Mṣb:) or *of the twelfth and thirteenth and fourteenth nights:* (Ḳ:) but this is of weak authority, and extr.: the former is the correct explanation: (MF, TA:) you should not say الأَيَّامُ البِيضُ: (Ibn-El-Jawáleekee, IB, Ḳ:) yet thus it is in most relations of a trad. in which it occurs; and some argue for it; and the author of the Ḳ has himself explained الأَوَاضِحُ by الأَيَّامُ البِيضُ. (TA.) —— سَنَةٌ بَيْضَآءُ † *A year* [*of scarcity of herbage,*] *such as is a mean between that which is termed* شَهْبَآءُ *and that which is termed* حَمْرَآءُ. (TA in art. شهب.) —— كَلَامٌ أَبْيَضُ ‡ *Language expounded* or *explained.* (M.) —— كَلَّمْتُهُ فَمَا رَدَّ عَلَىَّ سَوْدَآءَ وَلَا بَيْضَآءَ ‡ *I spoke to him, and he did not return to me a bad word nor a good one.* (M.) —— يَدٌ بَيْضَآءُ † *A demonstrating,* or *demonstrated, argument, plea, allegation,* or *evidence.* (M.) —— And † *A favour,* or *benefit, for which one is not reproached;* and *which is conferred without its being asked.* (M.) [See also يَدٌ.] —— المَوْتُ الأَبْيَضُ † *Sudden death;* (Ḳ, TA;) *such as is not preceded by disease which alters the complexion:* or, as some say, *death without the repentance, and the prayer for forgiveness, and the accomplishment of necessary duties, usual with him who is not taken unawares;* from بَيَّضَ signifying "he emptied" a vessel: so says Ṣgh: opposed to المَوْتُ الأَحْمَرُ, which is slaughter. (TA.) —— بَيْضَآءُ also signifies † *A calamity,* or *misfortune:* (Ṣgh, Ḳ:) app. as a term of good omen; like سَلِيمٌ applied to one who is stung by a scorpion or bitten by a serpent. (TA.) —— بَيْضَآءُ القَيْظِ: see بَيْضَةٌ, last sentence but one. —— هٰذَا أَبْيَضُ مِنْ كَذَا; &c.: see بَيَاضٌ.

مَبِيضٌ *A place for laying eggs.* (ISd, TA in art. فحص.)

مُبِيضَةٌ A woman *who brings forth white children:* the contr. is termed مُسْوِدَةٌ: (Fr, Ḳ:) but مُوضِحَةٌ is more commonly used in the former sense. (O.)

[مُبَيَّضَةٌ The *fair copy,* or *transcript, made from a first rough draught;* which latter is called مُسَوَّدَةٌ: probably post-classical.]

مُبَيِّضٌ A man *wearing white clothing.* (TA.) —— Hence, المُبَيِّضَةُ *A sect of* [*the class called*] *the* ثَنَوِيَّة, (Ṣ, Ḳ,) the companions of المُقَنَّع; (Ṣ;) *so called because they made their clothes white, in contradistinction to the* مُسَوِّدَة, *the partisans of the dynasty of the 'Abbásees;* (Ṣ, Ḳ;*) *for the distinction of these was black: they dwelt in Ḳaṣr 'Omeyr.* (TA.) [See also الحَرُورِيَّةُ.]

بيع

1. بَاعَهُ, (Ṣ, Mgh, &c.,) aor. يَبِيعُ, (Ṣ, Mṣb, Ḳ,) inf. n. بَيْعٌ (Ṣ, Mgh, Mṣb, Ḳ) and مَبِيعٌ, (Ṣ, Mṣb, Ḳ,) which latter is anomalous, (Ṣ,) the regular form being مَبَاعٌ, (Ṣ, Ḳ,) has two contr. significations: *He sold it:* and *he bought it:* (Ṣ, Mgh, Mṣb, Ḳ:) and ↓ ابَاعَهُ is a dial. var. of the same: (IḲṭṭ, Mṣb:) [but app. only in the former sense:] or this last signifies *he offered it for sale;* or *exposed it to sale:* (Ṣ, Ḳ:) and ↓ ابتاعهُ, as well as بَاعَهُ, signifies *he bought it.* (Ṣ,* Mgh,* Mṣb, Ḳ.) The primary signification of بَيْعٌ is The *exchanging,* or *exchange, of property;* or the *making an exchange with property;* as in the phrases بَيْعٌ رَابِحٌ [*an exchange of property bringing gain*], and بَيْعٌ خَاسِرٌ [*an exchange of property occasioning loss*]: and this is a proper signification when it relates to real substances: but it is tropically used to signify the *making the contract* [*of sale and purchase*]; because this is the means of giving [and obtaining] possession: [though this signification is what is termed حَقِيقَةٌ عُرْفِيَّةٌ, i. e., a sense so common as to be conventionally regarded as proper:] the phrase صَحَّ البَيْعُ, or بَطَلَ, and the like, mean صَفْقَةُ البَيْعِ; [i. e. *The contract of sale,* or *purchase, was valid,* or *was null;*] but the prefixed n. being suppressed, and its complement [alone] used for it, and this being masc., the verb is made masc. (Mṣb.) بَاعَ [mostly signifies *He sold:* and] is doubly trans., both by itself and by means of مِنْ prefixed to the second object; (Mgh, Mṣb;) this prep. being thus used as a corroborative: (Mṣb:) you say, بَاعَهُ الشَّىْءَ and بَاعَهُ مِنْهُ [*He sold to him the thing* and *He sold it to him*]: (Mgh:) and بِعْتُ زَيْدًا الدَّارَ and بِعْتُ مِنْ زَيْدٍ الدَّارَ [*I sold to Zeyd the house:* (see also an explanation of the phrase اِسْتَبَعْتُهُ الشَّىْءَ: and see بَاعَهُ مِنَ السُّلْطَانِ: to which might be added countless similar instances; for when باع signifies *he sold,* مِنْ is generally prefixed to the noun or pronoun denoting the person to whom the thing is sold:)] and sometimes لِ is put in the place of مِنْ; so that you say, بِعْتُكَ الشَّىْءَ and بِعْتُهُ لَكَ [*I sold to thee the thing* and *I sold it to thee*]; the لِ being redundant [when the verb has this meaning, though not when it has the contr. meaning, as will be seen below]. (Mṣb.) Of the contr. signification we have an ex. in the saying of El-Farezdaḳ,

إِنَّ الشَّبَابَ لَرَابِحٌ مَنْ بَاعَهَا
وَالشَّيْبُ لَيْسَ لِبَائِعِيهِ تِجَارُ

[*Verily youthfulness, he who buys it is a gainer; but hoariness, there are no traffickers for its sellers;* the part. n. being here from the verb in the former sense]: (Ṣ, TA:) and [often in a case in which the verb is followed by لِ; as] in بَاعَ لَهُ الشَّىْءَ *He bought for him the thing;* (Mgh;) [the لِ not being redundant when the verb is used in this sense;] and as in the saying of Ṭarafeh,

وَيَأْتِيكَ بِالأَخْبَارِ مَنْ لَمْ تَبِعْ لَهُ
بَتَاتًا وَلَمْ تَضْرِبْ لَهُ وَقْتَ مَوْعِدِ

[*And he will bring thee tidings for whom thou hast not bought travelling-provisions, and for whom thou hast not assigned an appointed time* for his bringing them]: (TA:) and in the saying, بَاعَ دُنْيَاهُ بِآخِرَتِهِ ‡ [*He purchased his enjoyments of the present world at the expense of his enjoyments of the world to come*]: (Z, TA:) and [in like manner] you say, ↓ ابتاع زَيْدٌ الدَّارَ, meaning *Zeyd bought the house:* and ↓ ابتاعها لِغَيْرِهِ *He bought it for another person.* (Mṣb.) The verb has this signification, also, in the trad., لَا يَبِعْ بَعْضُكُمْ عَلَى بَيْعِ أَخِيهِ [*One of you shall not buy in opposition to the buying of his brother when an agreement has been manifested but the contract has not been concluded*]; (Ṣ, IAth, Mgh, Mṣb; [but in the Ṣ and Mṣb and by IAth, the trad. is related thus; لَا يَخْطُبِ الرَّجُلُ عَلَى خِطْبَةِ أَخِيهِ وَلَا يَبِعْ عَلَى بَيْعِ أَخِيهِ; (see art. خطب:)]) as is shown by the relation of Bkh, لَا يَبْتَاعُ ↓ الرَّجُلُ عَلَى بَيْعِ أَخِيهِ: (Mgh, Mṣb:) or it may here have the contr. meaning: (IAth:) Az says that the seller and buyer are equal in offence when either of them does thus to another. (TA.) [Similar to this is the saying, لَا يَسُومُ الرَّجُلُ عَلَى سَوْمِ أَخِيهِ: see art. سوم. See also بَاعَ عَلَى بَيْعِهِ below, used in a tropical sense.] You say also, بَاعَ عَلَيْهِ القَاضِى, meaning *The judge sold against his will;* (Mgh;) *sold without his consent.* (Mṣb.) —— The pass. form is بِيعَ [*It was sold:* and *it was bought*]: (Ṣ, Ḳ:) optionally either [thus] with kesr to the ب, or [بُيعَ] with ḍamm to the ب, (Ṣ,) [or rather with a sound between that of ḍamm and that of kesr, which pronunciation is termed إِشْمَامٌ;] and some say بُوعَ; (Ṣ, Ḳ;) changing the ى into و: and thus in the cases of كِيلَ and قِيلَ and the like: (Ṣ:) [but Ibn-Málik requires ḍamm or اشمام in the passive of a verb of which the medial radical is ى, and kesr or اشمام in the passive of a verb of which the medial radical is و, to prevent the mistaking of an active verb for a passive in such cases as بِعْتُ and سُمْتُ: others, however, only prefer what Ibn-Málik absolutely requires in these cases. (See I'Aḳ p. 131.)] —— You say also, بَاعَهُ مِنَ السُّلْطَانِ, [lit. *He sold him to the Sultán,*] meaning ‡ *he slandered him,* or *calumniated him,* to the Sulṭán. (Ḳ, TA.) —— And بَاعَ فُلَانٌ عَلَى بَيْعِهِ, [of which the lit. meaning has been shown above,] meaning ‡ *Such a one superseded him, or occupied his place, in respect of honourable and elevated station or rank, and gained the mastery over him;* (Ḳ,* TA;) and so حَلَّ بِوَادِيهِ: (TA:) or بَاعَ فُلَانٌ عَلَى بَيْعِ فُلَانٍ means ‡ *such a one gained the mastery over such a one, and wrested from him that which he sought to obtain from him;* and is an old proverb, applied by the Arabs to a man who contends with another, and seeks to obtain a thing from him by superior power or force, when he has succeeded in doing as above explained; and similar to it is the saying شَقَّ فُلَانٌ غُبَارَ فُلَانٍ. (El-Mufaḍḍal Eḍ-Ḍabbee, TA.) One also says, مَا بَاعَ عَلَى بَيْعِكَ أَحَدٌ, meaning † *Not any one has equalled thee.* (TA.) ═ بَيْعٌ is also used in the sense of اِنْبِسَاطٌ. (TA in art. بوع. [See اِنْبَاعَ in that art.])

3. بَايَعَهُ, (Ṣ, Mgh, TA,) inf. n. مُبَايَعَةٌ and بِيَاعٌ, (TA,) is from البَيْعُ; and so is ▼ التَّبَايُعُ; (Ṣ, TA;) this being syn. with المُبَايَعَةُ. (Ḳ, TA.) You say, بَايَعَا and ▼ تَبَايَعَا, meaning *They two sold and bought, each with the other:* (TḲ:) and ▼ تَبَايَعْنَا [*We sold and bought, one with another*]: (Mgh:) and بايعهُ also signifies *He bartered,* or *exchanged commodities, with him.* (TA.) [See 1; where a citation from the Mṣb indicates that this latter is the primary signification accord. to the author of that work.] —— It is also from البَيْعَةُ; and so is ▼ التَّبَايُعُ: (Ṣ, TA:*) المُبَايَعَةُ and ▼ التَّبَايُعُ from البَيْعَةُ signifying The *making a covenant, a compact, an engagement,* or *the like; as though each of the two parties sold what he had to the other, and gave him his own special property, and his obedience, and all that pertained to his case.* (TA.) [Hence,] بايع الأَمِيرَ *He promised,* or *swore, allegiance to the prince; making a covenant with him to submit to him the judgment of his own case and of the cases of the Muslims* [in general], *not to dispute with him in respect of anything thereof, but to obey him in whatever command he might impose upon him, pleasing and displeasing:* in doing which, it was usual for the person making this covenant to place his hand in the hand of the prince, in confirmation of the covenant, like as is done by the seller and buyer; wherefore the act was termed بَيْعَةٌ, an inf. n. [of un.] of بَاعَ. (Ibn-Khaldoon, in De Sacy's Chrest. Ar., 2nd ed., ii. 256—7.) [And hence the phrases, بُويِعَ لَهُ and بُويِعَ بِالخِلَافَةِ *He had the promise,* or *oath, of allegiance made to him as being Khaleefeh.*] You say also, بايعهُ عَلَيْهِ, inf. n. مُبَايَعَةٌ, *He made a covenant, a compact, an engagement,* or *the like, with him, respecting it,* or *to do it:* and ▼ تبايعوا عَلَى الأَمْرِ [*they made a covenant, &c., respecting,* or *to do, the thing,* or *affair*]; like as you say أَصْفَقُوا عَلَيْهِ. (TA.)

4: see 1, first sentence.

6: see 3, throughout.

7. انباع *It was,* or *became, saleable,* or *easy of sale; it had an easy,* or *a ready, sale:* (Ibn-'Abbád, Ḳ:) as though quasi-pass. of بَاعَهُ [and therefore primarily signifying *it was,* or *became, sold,* or *bought*]. (TA.)

8: see 1, in four places.

10. اِسْتَبَعْتُهُ الشَّىْءَ *I asked him to sell the thing to me;* expl. by سَأَلْتُهُ أَنْ يَبِيعَهُ مِنِّى; (Ṣ, Ḳ;*) for instance, عَبْدَهُ [*his slave.*] (Mgh.)

بَيْعٌ inf. n. of 1 [q. v.]. —— It also signifies The *hire,* or *hiring,* of land. (TA.) ═ Also *A thing sold,* or *bought:* (Mgh, Mṣb, TA:) a subst. in this sense: (Mgh, TA:) pl. بُيُوعٌ: (Mgh, Mṣb, TA:) which is also used as a pl. of the inf. n., to signify *Kinds of selling and buying.* (Mgh.) See also بِيَاعَةٌ.

بَيْعَةٌ [inf. n. of un. of بَاعَ. —— Hence,] *A striking together of the hands of two contracting parties in token of the ratification of a sale.* (Mṣb, TA.) —— And [hence,] The *act of* مُبَايَعَة [or *promising,* or *swearing, allegiance and obedience,* as explained above, (see 3,)] *and submission,* or *obedience.* (Mṣb, TA.) Whence, أَيْمَانُ البَيْعَةِ [*The oaths of allegiance and obedience*]; (Ibn-Khaldoon, in De Sacy's Chrest. Ar., 2nd ed., ii. 257; and Mṣb;) which the Khaleefehs exacted; (Ibn-Khaldoon;) and which El-Ḥajjáj appointed, including hard, or difficult, matters, relating to divorce and emancipation and fasting and the like. (Mṣb.)

بِيعَةٌ *A mode,* or *manner, of selling* or *buying.* (Ṣ, Mgh, Ḳ.) Hence, صَاحِبُ بِيعَةٍ [*A person occupying himself in any kind of selling* or *buying*]: occurring in a trad. of Ibn-'Omar. (Mgh, TA.) And إِنَّهُ لَحَسَنُ البِيعَةِ [*Verily he is good in the manner of selling* or *buying*]. (Ṣ, Mgh, TA.) ═ [*A Christian church;*] *a place of worship* (Ḳ) *pertaining to the Christians:* (Ṣ, Mgh, Mṣb, Ḳ:) or, as some say, *a synagogue of the Jews:* (TA:) pl. بِيَعٌ, (Ḳ, TA,) or بِيعٌ. (Mṣb: [but this I think a mistake: if correct, it is a coll. gen. n.])

بَيُوعٌ: see بَيِّعٌ.

بِيَاعَةٌ *An article of merchandise;* (Lth, Ṣ, Ḳ;) as also ▼ بَيْعٌ [q. v. suprà]: (Mgh:) pl. of the former بِيَاعَاتٌ. (Ḳ.)

بَيِّعٌ: see بَائِعٌ, in five places. —— Also A man *who sells,* or *buys, well;* and so ▼ بَيُوعٌ: fem. of the former with ة: pl. masc. بَيِّعُونَ, and pl. fem. بَيِّعَاتٌ; neither the masc. nor the fem. having a broken pl. (TA.)

بَيَّاعٌ A man *who sells,* or *buys, much.* (TA.)

بَائِعٌ *Selling,* or *a seller:* and *buying,* or *a buyer:* (Mṣb, Ḳ,* TA:) as also ▼ بَيِّعٌ: (Ḳ:) the former signification is the more obvious when بائع is used without restriction: (Mṣb:) and ▼ بَيِّعٌ also signifies [accord. to some] *a bargainer,* or *chafferer;* (Ḳ, TA;) not a seller nor a buyer; but Esh-Sháfi'ee and Az deny that this epithet is applied to a man before he has concluded the contract: (L, TA:) the pl. of بائع is بَاعَةٌ: (ISd, Ḳ:) and the pl. of ▼ بَيِّعٌ is بَيَعَةٌ [or rather this is a quasi-pl. n.] and أَبْيِعَاءُ: (Ḳ:) and Kr holds that بَاعَةٌ is pl. of بَيِّعٌ. (TA.) ▼ البَيِّعَانِ signifies *The seller and the buyer;* (Ṣ, Mgh;) and so ▼ المُتَبَايِعَانِ. (TA.) It is said in a trad., ▼ البَيِّعَانِ بِالخِيَارِ مَا لَمْ يَتَفَرَّقَا, and in another, ▼ المُتَبَايِعَانِ, [*The seller and the buyer have the option of cancelling the contract as long as they have not separated.*] (TA.) —— اِمْرَأَةٌ بَائِعٌ ‡ *A woman who easily obtains a suitor;* or *who is much in demand; by reason of her beauty:* (Ḳ, TA:) as though she sold herself: like نَاقَةٌ تَاجِرَةٌ. (Z, TA.)

مَبِيعٌ *Sold:* and *bought:* as also ▼ مَبْيُوعٌ: (Ṣ, Ḳ:) in the latter sense syn. with ▼ مُبْتَاعٌ. (Mṣb.) Kh says that the letter suppressed in مَبِيعٌ is the و of the measure مَفْعُولٌ, because it is augmentative: but Akh says that the letter suppressed is the medial radical; for when they made the ى quiescent, they transferred its vowel to the letter before it, so that it became maḍmoomeh, [the word thus being altered to مُبْيُوعٌ,] then they changed the ḍammeh into kesreh because of the ى after it, then the ى was suppressed, and the و was changed into ى, like the و of مِيزَانٌ, because of the kesreh: accord. to El-Mázinee, each of these sayings is good; but that of Akh is the more agreeable with analogy. (Ṣ.)

مَبْيُوعٌ: } see مَبِيعٌ.
مُبْتَاعٌ: }

مُتَبَايِعٌ: see بَائِعٌ, in two places.

بيلون

بَيْلُونٌ [*Fullers' earth, which is used for scouring cloths, and is sometimes used in the bath, instead of soap;*] the *yellow* [or rather *yellowish,* or *yellowish gray,* and sometimes *white,* or *whitish,*] *earth known by the name of* طَفْل. (TA, from Esh-Shiháb El-'Ajamee.)

بين

1. بَانَ, (M, Mgh, Mṣb, Ḳ,) [aor. يَبِينُ,] inf. n. بَيْنُونَةٌ and بُيُونٌ (M, Mgh, Ḳ) and بَيْنٌ, (M, Ḳ,) *It* (a thing) *became separated, severed, disunited,* or *cut off,* (M, Mgh, Mṣb, Ḳ,) عَنِ الشَّىْءِ *from the thing.* (Mgh.) And بَانَتْ, (M, Ḳ,) or بَانَتْ بِالطَّلَاقِ, (Mṣb,) *She* (a wife) *became separated by divorce,* (M, Mṣb, Ḳ,) عَنِ الرَّجُلِ *from the man.* (M, Ḳ.) And بَانَتْ said of a girl, [*She became separated from her parents by marriage;*] *she married:* (ISh, T:) as though she became at a distance from the house of her father. (ISh, TA.) And بَانَ, (M,) or بَانَ بِمَالٍ, aor. يَبِينُ, (T,) inf. n. بُيُونٌ (T, M) and بَيْنٌ, (M,) *He became separated from his father,* or *mother,* or *both, by property* [*which he received from him,* or *her,* or *them,*] (AZ, T, M,) *to be his alone:* (AZ, T:) and El-Fárisee states, on the authority of AZ, that one

says also, بَانَهُ and بَانَ عَنْهُ [the former app. meaning *he became separated thus from him*, i. e., from his father; and the latter being syn. with أَبَانَهُ, q. v.]. (M.) And بَانَ الخَلِيطُ, inf. n. بَيْنٌ and بَيْنُونَةٌ, [*The partner*, or *copartner*, or *sharer*, &c., *became separated from the person*, or *persons, with whom he had been associated*.] (T.) And بَانَتْ يَدُ النَّاقَةِ عَنْ جَنْبِهَا, inf. n. بُيُونٌ, [*The fore leg of the she-camel became withdrawn*, or *apart, from her side*.] (T.) And بَانَ, (Ṣ, M, Mṣb,) and بَانُوا, (Ḳ,) aor. يَبِينُ, (Ṣ,) inf. n. بَيْنٌ and بَيْنُونَةٌ, (Ṣ, M, Mṣb, Ḳ,) *He separated himself*, or *it separated itself*; (Ṣ; [in one copy of which it is said of a thing;]) and *they separated themselves*: (Ḳ:) or *it* (a tribe, M, Mṣb) *went, journeyed, went away*, or *departed*; and *went, removed, retired*, or *withdrew itself, to a distance*, or *far away*, or *far off*. (Mṣb.) — بَانَ, (T, Ṣ, M, &c.,) aor. يَبِينُ, (T, Mṣb,) inf. n. بَيَانٌ; (T, Ṣ, Mgh, Ḳ;) and ▼ابان, (T, Ṣ, M, &c.,) inf. n. إِبَانَةٌ; (T, Mṣb;) and ▼بيّن, (T, Ṣ, M, &c.,) inf. n. تَبْيِينٌ; (Ṣ;) and ▼تبيّن; and ▼استبان; (T, Ṣ, M, &c.,) all signify the same; (T, M, Mṣb;) i. e. *It* (a thing, T, Ṣ, M, Mgh, or an affair, or a case, Mṣb) *was*, or *became*, [*distinct, as though separate from others*; and thus,] *apparent, manifest, evident, clear, plain*, or *perspicuous*: (Ṣ, Mgh, Mṣb, Ḳ:) and *it was*, or *became, known*. (Ḳ.) You say, بَانَ الحَقُّ [*The truth became apparent*, &c.; or *known*]; as also ▼ابان. (T.) And

قَدْ بَيَّنَ ▼ الصُّبْحُ لِذِى عَيْنَيْنِ

The dawn has become apparent to him who has two eyes: a prov.: (Ṣ, M:) applied to a thing that becomes altogether apparent, or manifest. (Ḥar p. 542.) And it is said in the Ḳur [ii. 257], قَدْ تَبَيَّنَ ▼ الرُّشْدُ مِنَ الغَيِّ [*The right belief hath become distinguished from error*]. (TA.) And the lawyers, correctly, use the phrase, كَصَوْتٍ لَا يَسْتَبِينُ ▼ مِنْهُ حُرُوفٌ [*Like a sound whereof letters are not distinguishable*]. (Mgh.) — [It seems to be indicated in the TA that بَانَ, aor. يَبِينُ, inf. n. بَيْنٌ and بَيْنُونَةٌ, also signifies *It was*, or *became, united*, or *connected*; thus having two contr. meanings; but I have not found the verb used in this sense, though بَيْنٌ signifies both disunion and union.] — بَانَهُ, aor. يَبِينُ, inf. n. بَيْنٌ: see بَانَهُ, aor. يَبُونُ, inf. n. بَوْنٌ, in art. بون. — See also 2, in two places.

2. بيّن, intrans., inf. n. تَبْيِينٌ: see 1, in two places. — You say also, بَيَّنَ الشَّجَرُ ‡ *The trees*, (Ḳ,) or *the leaves of the trees*, (TA,) *appeared, when beginning to grow forth*. (Ḳ, TA.) And بَيَّنَ القَرْنُ ‡ *The horn came forth*. (Ḳ, TA.) — بيّن بِنْتَهُ: see 4. — بيّنهُ, (T, Mṣb, Ḳ,) inf. n. تَبْيِينٌ (T, Ṣ) and ▼تِبْيَانٌ (T, Ṣ,* Ḳ*) and تَبْيَانٌ; (Ḳ;) the second of which three is an anomalous inf. n., (T, Ṣ, Ḳ,) for by rule it should be of the measure تَفْعَال; (T, Ṣ;) but تَبْيَانٌ is not known except accord. to the opinion of those who allow the authority of analogy, which opinion is outweighed by the contrary; (TA;) and تِبْيَانٌ is the only inf. n. of its measure except تِلْقَآءٌ, (T, Ṣ,) accord. to the generality of the leading authorities; but some add تِمْثَالٌ, as inf. n. of مَثَّلَ; and El-Ḥareeree adds to these two, in the Durrah, تِنْضَالٌ, as inf. n. of نَاضَلَهُ; and Esh-Shiháb adds, in the Expos. of the Durrah, تِشْرَابٌ, as inf. n. of شَرِبَ الخَمْرَ; asserting تِشْرَابٌ also to have been heard, agreeably with analogy; [and to these may be added تِبْكَآءٌ and تِمْشَآءٌ, and perhaps some other instances of the same kind;] but some disallow تِفْعَالٌ altogether as the measure of an inf. n., saying that the words transmitted as instances thereof are simple substs. used as inf. ns., like طَعَامٌ in the place of إِطْعَامٌ; (MF, TA;) and Sb says that تِبْيَانٌ is not an inf. n.; for, where it so, it would be تَبْيَانٌ; but it is, from بَيَّنْتُ, like غَارَةٌ from أَغْرْتُ; (M, TA;) [*He made it distinct, as though separate from others*; and thus,] *he made it* (namely, a thing, T, Ṣ, Mgh, or an affair, or a case, Mṣb) *apparent, manifest, evident, clear, plain*, or *perspicuous*; (Ṣ, Mṣb, Ḳ;) as also ▼ابانهُ, (Ṣ, Mgh, Mṣb, Ḳ,) inf. n. إِبَانَةٌ; (Mṣb;) and ▼تبيّنهُ; (Ṣ,* Mṣb, Ḳ;) and ▼استبانهُ: (Mgh, Mṣb, Ḳ:) [بيّنهُ is the most common in this sense: and often signifies *he explained it*: and *he proved it*:] and ▼all these verbs signify also *he made it known*; *he notified it*: (Ḳ:) or ▼اِسْتَبَنْتُهُ signifies, (Ṣ,) or signifies also, (Mgh,) *I knew it*, or *became acquainted with it*, [or *distinguished it*,] (Ṣ, Mgh,) *clearly*, or *plainly*; (Mgh;) and so ▼تَبَيَّنْتُهُ; (Ṣ,* Mgh;) [and بَيَّنْتُهُ, as appears from an ex. in what follows, from a verse of En-Nábighah:] ▼بِنْتُهُ and ▼أَبَنْتُهُ and ▼اِسْتَبَنْتُهُ and بَيَّنْتُهُ all signify the same as ▼تَبَيَّنْتُهُ [app. in all the senses of this verb]: (M:) or, of all these verbs, ▼بَانَ is only intrans.: (Mṣb:) and ▼اِسْتَبَنْتُهُ signifies *I looked at it*, or *into it*, (namely, a thing,) *considered it, examined it*, or *studied it, repeatedly, in order that it might become apparent, manifest, evident, clear*, or *plain, to me*: (T, TA:) and ▼تبيّنهُ *he looked at it*, or *into it*, (namely, an affair, or a case,) *considered it, examined it*, or *studied it, repeatedly*, or *deliberately, in order to know its real state by the external signs thereof*. (T.) A poet says,

وَمَا خِفْتُ حَتَّى بَيَّنَ الشُّرْبُ وَالأَذَى
بِقَانِئَةٍ أَنِّى مِنَ الحَىِّ أَبْيَنُ ▼

[*And I feared not until the drinking*, or *the time of drinking, and molestation, made manifest*, or *plainly showed, by a deep-red* (*sun*), *that I was separated from the tribe*: see قَانِئٌ]. (M.) And it is said in the Ḳur [xvi. 91], وَأَنْزَلْنَا عَلَيْكَ الكِتَابَ تِبْيَانًا لِكُلِّ شَىْءٍ [*And we have sent down to thee the Scripture to make manifest everything*]; meaning, we make manifest to thee in the Scripture everything that thou and thy people require [to know] respecting matters of religion. (T.) See also بَيَانٌ, in the latter half of the paragraph. En-Nábighah says,

إِلَّا الأَوَارِىَّ لَأْيًا مَا أُبَيِّنُهَا

[*Except the places of the confinement of the beasts: with difficulty did I distinguish them*]; meaning ▼أَتَبَيَّنُهَا. (Ṣ.) You say also, ▼تبيّن مَا يَأْتِيهِ, meaning *He sought*, or *endeavoured, to see*, or *discover, what would happen to him*, of good and evil. (M in art. بصر.) [See also 5, below.] وَلِتَسْتَبِينَ ▼ سَبِيلَ المُجْرِمِينَ, in the Ḳur [vi. 55], means *And that thou mayest* the more *consider*, or *examine, repeatedly, in order that it may become manifest to thee, the way of the sinners*, O Mohammad: (T:) or *that thou mayest seek*, or *endeavour, to see plainly*, or *clearly*, &c.; syn. وَلِتَسْتَوْضِحَ سَبِيلَهُمْ: (Bḍ:) but most read, وَلِيَسْتَبِينَ سبيلُ المجرمين; the verb in this case being intrans. (T.)

3. بَايَنَهُ, (Ḳ,) inf. n. مُبَايَنَةٌ, (Ṣ,) *He separated himself from him*; or *left, forsook*, or *abandoned, him*: (Ṣ, TA:) or *he forsook*, or *abandoned, him, being forsaken*, or *abandoned, by him*; or *cut him off from friendly or loving communion or intercourse, being so cut off by him*; or *cut him*, or *ceased to speak to him, being in like manner cut by him*. (Ḳ.) [And *It became separated from it*.]

4. ابان, intrans., inf. n. إِبَانَةٌ: see 1, in two places. — ابانهُ, (inf. n. as above, TA,) *He separated it, severed it, disunited it*, or *cut it off*. (M, Mṣb, Ḳ, TA.) You say, ضَرَبَهُ فَأَبَانَ رَأْسَهُ مِنْ جَسَدِهِ (Ṣ, Ḳ) *He smote him and severed his head, from his body*. (Ṣ, TA.) And ابان المَرْأَةَ *He* (the husband) *separated the woman*, or *wife*, by divorce. (Mṣb.) And ابان بِنْتَهُ, and ▼بيّنها, (T, Ḳ,) inf. n. of the former as above, and of the latter تَبْيِينٌ, (TA,) *He married*, or *gave in marriage, his daughter*, (T, Ḳ,) *and she went to her husband*: (T:) from بَيْنٌ signifying "distance:" as though he removed her to a distance from the house, or tent, of her mother. (TA.) And ابان ٱبْنَهُ بِمَالٍ, (M,) or ابانهُ أَبَوَاهُ, (T,) *He separated from himself his son*, (M,) or *his two parents separated him from themselves*, (T,) *by* [*giving him*] *property*, (T, M,) *to be his alone*: (T:) mentioned on the authority of AZ. (T, M.) And ابان الدَّلْوَ عَنْ طَىِّ البِئْرِ *He drew away the bucket from the casing of the well, lest the latter should lacerate the former*. (M.) — See also 2, in three places. — [Hence, ابان signifies also *He spoke*, or *wrote, perspicuously, clearly, plainly*, or *distinctly, as to meaning*; or, *with eloquence*: from بَيَانٌ, q. v.] And ابان عَلَيْهِ *He spoke perspicuously, clearly, plainly*, or *distinctly, and gave his testimony*, or *evidence*, or *gave decisive information, against him*, or *respecting it*. (TA.) [The verb thus used is for ابان كَلَامَهُ, and شَهَادَتَهُ.] One says of a drunken man, مَا يُبِينُ كَلَامًا *He does not speak plainly*, or *distinctly*; lit., *does not make speech plain*, or *distinct*. (Ks, T in art. بت.) — مَا أَبْيَنَهُ [*How distinct, apparent, manifest, evident, clear*, or *plain, is it!* See an ex. voce بَسَلَ. — And *How perspicuous*, or *chaste*, or *eloquent, is he in speech*, or *writing! how good is his* بَيَان!]

5. تبيّن, intrans.: see 1, in two places. — As a trans. verb: see 2, in seven places. — [Hence,

الأَمْرَ being understood,] *He sought, or sought leisurely or repeatedly, to obtain knowledge [of the thing], until he knew [it]; he examined, scrutinized, or investigated:* (Bḍ in xlix. 6:) *he sought, or endeavoured, to make the affair, or case, manifest, and to settle it, or establish it, and was not hasty therein:* (Idem in iv. 96:) or *he acted, or proceeded, deliberately, or leisurely, in the affair, or case; not hastily:* (Ks, TA:) or it has a signification like this: in the Ḳur ch. iv. v. 96 and ch. xlix. v. 6, some read فَتَبَيَّنُوا, and others فَتَثَبَّتُوا; and the meanings are nearly the same: التَّبَيُّنُ was said by Moḥammad to be from God, and العَجَلَةُ [i. e. "haste"] from the devil. (T.)

6. تباينا *They two* (namely, two men, and two copartners,) *became separated, each from the other:* (M, TA:) or *they forsook, or abandoned, each other; or cut each other off from friendly or loving communion or intercourse; or cut, or ceased to speak to, each other.* (Ḳ.) And تباينوا *They, having been together, became separated:* (Mṣb:) or *they forsook, or abandoned, one another; or cut one another off from friendly or loving communion or intercourse; or cut, or ceased to speak to, one another.* (Ṣ.) — [Hence, *They two were dissimilar:* and *they two* (namely, words,) *were disparate;* whether contraries or not: and *they two* (namely, numbers,) *were incommensurable.*]

10. استبان, intrans.: see 1. ═ As a trans. verb: see 2, in six places.

بَانٌ a coll. gen. n.: n. un. with ة: see art. بون.

بَيْنٌ has two contr. significations; (T, Ṣ, Mṣb;) one of which is *Separation,* or *disunion* [of companions or friends or lovers]. (T, Ṣ, M, Mṣb, Ḳ.) Hence, ذَاتُ البَيْنِ as meaning *Enmity,* and *vehement hatred:* and the saying لِإِصْلَاحِ ذَاتِ البَيْنِ, i. e. *For the reforming,* or *amending, of the bad,* or *corrupt, state subsisting between the people,* or *company of men;* meaning *for the allaying of the discord, enmity, rancour,* or *vehement hatred:* (Mṣb:) [but this has also the contr. meaning, as will be seen below: and it is explained as having a vague import; for it is said that] فِى إِصْلَاحِ ذَاتِ البَيْنِ means *In the reforming,* or *amending, of the circumstances subsisting between the persons to whom it relates, by frequent attention thereto.* (Mgh.) [Hence also,] غُرَابُ البَيْنِ [*The raven of separation* or *disunion;* i. e., whose appearance, or croak, is ominous of separation: said by some to be] *the* غراب *termed* أَبْقَع [i. e. *in which is blackness and whiteness;* or *having whiteness in the breast*]; (Ṣ, Ḳ;) so described by the poet 'Antarah: (Ṣ:) or *that which is red in the beak and legs;* but the black is called الحَاتِمُ, because it makes [or shows] separation to be absolutely unavoidable, (Abu-l-Ghowth, Ṣ, Ḳ,) according to the assertion of the Arabs, i. e., by its croak: (Mṣb in art. حتم:) [or it is *any species of the corvus:*] Ḥamzeh says, in his Proverbs, that this name attaches to the غراب because, when the people of an abode go away to seek after herbage, it alights in the place of their tents, searching the sweepings: (Ḥar p. 308:) but accord. to the Ḳáḍee of Granada, Aboo-'Abd-Allah Esh-Shereef, this appellation, so often occurring in poetry, properly signifies *camels that transport people from one district, or country, to another;* and he cites the following verses:

غَلِطَ الَّذِينَ رَأَيْتُهُمْ بِجَهَالَةٍ
يَلْحَوْنَ كُلُّهُمُ غُرَابًا يَنْعَقُ
مَا الذَّنْبُ إِلَّا لِلْأَبَاعِرِ إِنَّهَا
مِمَّا يُشَتِّتُ جَمْعَهُمْ وَيُفَرِّقُ
إِنَّ الغُرَابَ بِيُمْنِهِ تُدْنُو النَّوَى
وَتُشَتِّتُ الشَّمْلَ الجَمِيعَ الأَيْنُقُ

[*Those have erred whom I have seen, with ignorance, all of them blaming a raven croaking: the fault is not imputable save to the camels; for they are of the things that scatter and disperse their congregation: verily the place that is the object of a journey is brought near by the raven's lucky omen; but the she-camels discompose the united state*]: and Ibn-'Abd-Rabbih says,

زَعَقَ الغُرَابُ فَقُلْتُ أَكْذَبُ طَائِرٍ
إِنْ لَمْ يُصَدِّقْهُ رُغَآءُ بَعِيرِ

[*The raven cried; and I said, A most lying bird, if the grumbling cry of a camel on the occasion of his being laden do not verify it*]. (TA in art. غرب.) — Also *Distance,* (Ṣ, M, Mṣb, Ḳ,) *by the space,* or *interval, between two things.* (Mṣb.) You say, بَيْنَ البَلَدَيْنِ بَيْنٌ *Between the two countries,* or *towns,* &c., *is a distance, of space,* or *interval:* (Mṣb:) and بَيْنَهُمَا بَيْنٌ *Between them two is a distance,* with ى, when corporeal distance is meant: (Idem in art. بون:) or إِنَّ بَيْنَهُمَا لَبَيْنًا [*Verily between them two is a distance*], not otherwise, in the case of [literal] distance. (Ṣ.) And you say also, بَيْنَهُمَا بَيْنٌ بَعِيدٌ (T in art. بون, Ṣ, M*) and بَوْنٌ بَعِيدٌ (T in art. بون, Ṣ, M,* Mṣb* in art. بون) *Between them two* [meaning two men] *is a* [*wide*] *distance;* (M;) i. e. *between their two degrees of rank* or *dignity,* or *between the estimations in which they are commonly held:* (Mṣb in art. بون:) in this case, the latter is the more chaste. (Ṣ.) You also say, [using بين to denote *An interval of time,*] لَقِيتُهُ بُعَيْدَاتِ بَيْنٍ [*I met him after,* or *a little after, an interval,* or *intervals,*] when you have met him after a while, and then withheld yourself from him, and then come to him. (Ṣ, M, Ḳ. [See also بَعْدُ.]) ═ Also *Union* [of companions or friends or lovers]; (T, Ṣ, M, Mṣb, Ḳ;) the contr. of the first of the significations mentioned above in this paragraph. (T, Ṣ, Mṣb.) [Hence ذَاتُ البَيْنِ as meaning *The state of union* or *concord* or *friendship* or *love subsisting between a people* or *between two parties;* this being likewise the contr. of a signification assigned to the same expression above: whence the phrase, إِفْسَادُ ذَاتِ البَيْنِ (occurring in the Ṣ and Ḳ in art. ابر, and often elsewhere,) *The marring,* or *disturbance, of the state of union* or *concord* &c.: and] hence the saying, سَعَى فُلَانٌ لِإِصْلَاحِ ذَاتِ البَيْنِ مِنْ عَشِيرَتِهِ [*Such a one laboured for the improving of the state of union* or *concord* &c. *of his kinsfolk;* but in this instance, the meaning given in the second sentence of this paragraph seems to be more appropriate]. (Ḥam p. 560.) — ذَاتُ بَيْنِهِمْ may also be used as meaning *The vacant space* (سَاحَة) *that is between their houses,* or *tents.* (Ḥam p. 195.) ═ بَيْنَ is also an adverbial noun, [as such written بَيْنَ,] (Ṣ, M, Mgh, Mṣb, Ḳ,) capable of being used as a noun absolutely: (M, Ḳ:) it relates only to that which has space, as a country; or to that which has some number, either two or more, as two men, and a company of men; and denotes [intervention in] the interval between two things, or the middle, or midst, of two things, (Er-Rághib, TA,) or the middle of a collective number: (Ṣ:) [thus it signifies *Between,* and *amidst,* and *among:*] its meaning is [therefore] vague, not apparent unless it is prefixed to two or more [words, or to a word signifying two or more], or to what supplies the place of such a complement: (Mṣb:) it must necessarily be prefixed, and may not be otherwise than in the manners just explained: (Mgh:) [i. e.] it may not be prefixed to any noun but such as denotes more than one, or to a noun that has another conjoined to it by و, (M,) not by any other conjunction, (M, Mṣb,) accord. to the usage commonly obtaining. (Mṣb.) You say بَيْنَ الرَّجُلَيْنِ [*Between the two men*]: (Er-Rághib, TA:) and المَالُ بَيْنَ القَوْمِ [*The property is between the company of men*]: (M, Mṣb, Er-Rághib:*) and المَالُ بَيْنَ زَيْدٍ وَعَمْرٍو [*The property is between Zeyd and 'Amr*]: and هُوَ بَيْنِى وَبَيْنَهُ [*He,* or *it, is between me and him*]: (M:) and جَلَسْتُ بَيْنَ القَوْمِ *I sat in the middle of* [or *amidst* or *among*] *the company of men:* (Ṣ, Ḳ:) and بَيْنَكُمَا البَعِيرَ فَخُذَاهُ, with البعير in the accus. case, [*See between you two the camel, therefore take him*], a saying heard by Ks: (L in art. عند:) and فَسَدَ مَا بَيْنَهُمْ [*The state subsisting among them became bad,* or *marred,* or *disturbed*]: (Ṣ and Ḳ in art. ميط:) and بَيْنَ الأَيَّامِ (M and Ḳ in art. ندر) and فِيمَا بَيْنَ الأَيَّامِ (Ṣ and Mṣb in that art.) [*In,* or *during, the space of* (*several*) *days*]: and عَوَانٌ بَيْنَ ذٰلِكَ, in the Ḳur [ii. 63], is an ex. of its being prefixed to a single word supplying the place of more than one; (Mgh, Mṣb;) the meaning being, *Of middle age, between that which has been mentioned;* namely, the فَارِض and the بِكْر. (Bḍ.) Some allow that two words to the former of which بَيْنَ is prefixed may be connected by فَ, citing as an evidence the phrase used by Imra-el-Ḳeys, بَيْنَ الدَّخُولِ فَحَوْمَلِ [as though meaning *Between Ed-Dakhool and Ḥowmal*]: but to this it has been replied that الدخول is a name applying to several places; so that the phrase [means *amidst Ed-Dakhool* &c., and] is similar to the saying, المَالُ بَيْنَ القَوْمِ [mentioned above, or جَلَسْتُ بَيْنَ القَوْمِ, also mentioned above]. (Mṣb.) [You say also, بَيْنَ ظَهْرَيْهِمْ, بَيْنَ أَظْهُرِهِمْ and, &c., meaning *In the midst of them.* (See art. ظهر.) And بَيْنَ يَدَيْهِ, and بَيْنَ يَدَيْهِمْ, meaning *Before him,* and *before them.*] بَيْنَ is also often used absolutely as a noun: thus it is in the Ḳur lxxxvi. 7, يَخْرُجُ مِنْ بَيْنِ الصُّلْبِ وَالتَّرَائِبِ *Coming* *forth from between*, or *amidst*, *the spine and the breast-bones*: and in xxxvi. 8 of the same, وَجَعَلْنَا مِنْ بَيْنِ أَيْدِيهِمْ سَدًّا *And we have placed before them* (lit. *between their hands*) *a barrier*.] It is said in the Ḳur [vi. 94], لَقَدْ تَقَطَّعَ بَيْنَكُمْ, as some read; or بَيْنُكُمْ, as others: (T, Ṣ, M:) the former means *Verily your union hath become dissevered*: (AA, T, Ṣ, M:) the latter, *that which was between you*; (مَا بَيْنَكُمْ, Ibn-Mes'ood, T, Ṣ, or ٱلَّذِى كَانَ بَيْنَكُمْ, IAar, T;) or *the state wherein ye were, in respect of partnership among you*: (Zj, T:) or *the state of circumstances*, or *the bond*, or *the love*, or *affection*, [*formerly subsisting*] *among you*, or *between you*; or, accord. to Akh, بَيْنَكُمْ, though in the accus. case as to the letter, is in the nom. case as to the place, by reason of the verb, and the adverbial termination is retained only because the word is commonly used as an adv. n.: (M:) AḤát disapproved of the latter reading; but wrongly, because what is suppressed accord. to this reading is implied by what precedes in the same verse. (T.) — [It is often used as a partitive, or distributive; as also مَا بَيْنَ: for ex.,] you say, هُمْ بَيْنَ حَاذِفٍ وَقَاذِفٍ, (Ṣ and TA in art. قذف,) or هم مَا بَيْنَ حاذفٍ وقاذفٍ, (TA in art. حذف,) i. e. [*They are partly*, or *in part*,] *beating with the staff*, or *stick*, *and* [*partly*, or *in part*,] *pelting with stones*; [or *some beating* &c., *and the others pelting* &c.] (Ṣ and TA, both in art. قذف, and the latter in art. حذف.) [See also an ex. in a verse cited voce خَيْطَةٌ.] — هٰذَا بَيْنَ بَيْنَ means *This* (namely, a thing, Ṣ, or a commodity, Mṣb) *is between good and bad*: (Ṣ, Mṣb, Ḳ:) or *of a middling*, or *middle*, *sort*: (M:) these two words being two nouns made one, and indecl., with fet-ḥ for their terminations, (Ṣ, Mṣb, Ḳ,) like خَمْسَةَ عَشَرَ. (Mṣb.) الهَمْزَةُ المُخَفَّفَةُ [i. e. the hemzeh uttered lightly] is called هَمْزَةُ بَيْنَ بَيْنَ, (Ṣ, M, Ḳ,*) i. e. *A hemzeh that is between the hemzeh and the soft letter whence is its vowel*; (Ṣ, M;) or هَمْزَةُ بَيْنٍ بَيْنٍ, the first بين with kesreh but without tenween, and the second with tenween, (Sharḥ Shudhoor edh-Dhahab,) [i. e. *the hemzeh* &c.:] if it is with fet-ḥ, it is between the hemzeh and the alif, as in سَالَ, (Ṣ, M,) for سَأَلَ; (M;) if with kesr, it is between the hemzeh and the yé, as in سَئِمَ, (Ṣ, M,) for سَئِمَ; (M;) and if with ḍamm, it is between the hemzeh and the wáw, as in لَوُمَ, (Ṣ, M,) for لَؤُمَ: (M:) it is never at the beginning of a word, because of its nearness, by reason of feebleness, to the letter that is quiescent, (Ṣ, M,) though, notwithstanding this, it is really movent: (Ṣ:) it is thus called because it is weak, (Sb, Ṣ, M,) not having the power of the hemzeh uttered with its proper sound, nor the clearness of the letter whence is its vowel. (M.) 'Obeyd Ibn-El-Abraṣ says,

* تَحْمِى حَقِيقَتَنَا وَبَعْـ * ـضُ القَوْمِ يَسْقُطُ بَيْنَ بَيْنَا *

i. e. [*Thou defendest what we ought to defend*, or *our banner*, or *standard*, *while some of the people*, or *company of men*,] *fall, one after another, in a state of weakness, not regarded as of any account*: (Ṣ:) or it is as though he said, *between these and these*; like a man who enters between two parties in some affair, and falls, or slips, or commits a mistake, and is not honourably mentioned in relation to it: so says Seer: (IB, TA:) or *between entering into fight and holding back from it*; as when one says, Such a one puts forward a foot, and puts back another. (TA.) — بَيْنَا ↓ and بَيْنَمَا ↓ are of the number of inceptive حُرُوف: (M, Ḳ:) this is clear if by حروف is meant "words:" that they have become particles, no one says: they are still adv. ns.: (MF, TA:) the former is بَيْنَ with its [final] fet-ḥah rendered full in sound; and hence the ا; (Mughnee in the section next after that of وا, and Ḳ;) [i. e.,] it is of the measure فَعْلَى [or فَعْلَا] from البَيْنُ, the [final] fet-ḥah being rendered full in sound, and so becoming ا; and the latter is بَيْنَ with مَا [restrictive of its government] added to it; and both have the same meaning [of *While*, or *whilst*]: (Ṣ:) or the ا in the former is the restrictive ا; or, as some say, it is a portion of the restrictive ما [in the latter]: (Mughnee ubi suprà:) and these do not exclude بَيْنَ from the category of nouns, but only cut it off from being prefixed to another noun: (MF, TA:) they are substitutes for that to which بَيْنَ would otherwise be prefixed: (Mgh:) some say that these two words are adv. ns. of time, denoting a thing's happening suddenly, or unexpectedly; and they are prefixed to a proposition consisting of a verb and an agent, or an inchoative and enunciative; so that they require a complement to complete the meaning. (TA.) One says, بَيْنَا نَحْنُ كَذٰلِكَ إِذْ حَدَثَ كَذَا [*While we were in such a state as that, lo*, or *there*, or *then, such a thing happened*, or *came to pass*]: (M, Mgh,* Ḳ:*) and بَيْنَمَا نَحْنُ كَذَا [*While we were thus*]: (Mgh:) and

* بَيْنَا نَحْنُ نَرْقُبُهُ أَتَانَا *

[*While we were looking*, or *waiting*, *for him, he came to us*]; (Ṣ, M;) a saying of a poet, cited by Sb; (M;) the phrase being elliptical; (Ṣ, M;) meaning بَيْنَ أَوْقَاتِ نَحْنُ نَرْقُبُهُ, (M,) i. e., بَيْنَ أَوْقَاتِ رِقْبَتِنَا إِيَّاهُ [*between the times of our looking*, or *waiting*, *for him*]. (Ṣ, M.) Aṣ used to put nouns following بَيْنَا in the gen. case when بَيْنَ might properly supply its place; as in the saying (of Aboo-Dhu-eyb, which he thus recited, with kesr, Ṣ),

* بَيْنَا تَعَنُّقِهِ الكُمَاةَ وَرَوْغِهِ *
* يَوْمًا أُتِيحَ لَهُ جَرِىءٌ سَلْفَعُ *

[*Amid his embracing the courageous armed men, and his guileful eluding, one day a bold, daring man was appointed for him*, to slay him]: (Ṣ, Ḳ:) in [some copies of] the Ḳ, تَعَنُّقُهُ; but in the Deewán [of the Hudhalees], تَعَنُّقِهِ: [in the Mughnee, ubi suprà, تَعَانُقِهِ:] the meaning is بَيْنَ تَعَانُقِهِ; the ا being added to give fulness to the sound of the [final] vowel: (TA:) Aṣ used to say that the ا is here redundant: (Skr, TA:) others put the nouns following both بَيْنَا and بَيْنَمَا in the nom. case, as the inchoative and enunciative. (Skr, Ṣ, Ḳ.) Mbr says that when the noun following بينا is a real subst., it is put in the nom. case as an inchoative; but when it is an inf. n., or a noun of the inf. kind, it is put in the gen., and بينا in this instance has the meaning of بَيْنَ: and Aḥmad Ibn-Yaḥyà says the like, but some persons of chaste speech treat the latter kind of noun like the former: after بينما, however, each kind of noun must be in the nom. case. (AA, T.) [See an ex. in a verse cited towards the end of art. اذ.]

بَيْنَا: } see بَيْنَ.
بَيْنَمَا: }

بَيْنٌ *A separation*, or *division*, (T, M, Ḳ,) *between two things*, (T,) or *between two lands*; (M, Ḳ;) *as when there is a rugged place, with sands near it, and between the two is a tract neither rugged nor plain*: (T:) *an elevation in rugged ground*: (M, Ḳ:) *the extent to which the eye reaches*, (T, M, Ḳ,) *of a road*, (T,) or *of land*: (M:) *a piece of land extending as far as the eye reaches*: (T, Ṣ:) and *a region, tract*, or *quarter*: (AA, T, M, Ḳ:) pl. بُيُونٌ. (Ṣ, TA.)

بَيَانٌ is originally the inf. n. of بَانَ as syn. with تَبَيَّنَ, and so signifies The *being* [*distinct* or] *apparent* &c.; (Kull;) or it is a subst. in this sense: (Mṣb:) or a subst. from بَيَّنَ, [and so signifies the *making distinct* or *apparent* &c.,] being like سَلَامٌ and كَلَامٌ from سَلَّمَ and كَلَّمَ. (Kull.) — Hence, conventionally, (Kull,) The *means by which one makes a thing* [*distinct*,] *apparent, manifest, evident, clear, plain*, or *perspicuous*: (Ṣ, Er-Rághib, TA, Kull:) this is of two kinds: one is [*a circumstantial indication* or *evidence*; or] *a thing indicating*, or *giving evidence of, a circumstance*, or *state, that is a result*, or *an effect, of a quality* or *an attribute*: the other is *a verbal indication* or *evidence, either spoken or written*: [see also بَيِّنَةٌ:] it is also applied to *language that discovers and shows the meaning that is intended*: and *an explanation of confused and vague language*: (Er-Rághib, TA:) or the *eduction of a thing from a state of dubiousness to a state of clearness*: or *making the meaning apparent to the mind so that it becomes distinct from other meanings and from what might be confounded with it*. (TA.) — Also *Perspicuity, clearness, distinctness, chasteness*, or *eloquence, of speech* or *language*: (T, Ṣ:) or simply *perspicuity thereof*: (Ḥar p. 2:) or *perspicuity of speech with quickness*, or *sharpness, of intellect*: (M, Ḳ:) or *perspicuous*, or *chaste*, or *eloquent, speech, declaring*, or *telling plainly, what is in the mind*: (Ksh, TA:) or the *showing of the intent*, or *meaning, with the most eloquent expression*: it is an effect of understanding, and of sharpness, or quickness, of mind, with perspicuity, or chasteness, or eloquence, of speech: (Nh, TA:) or *a faculty*, or *principles*, [or *a science*,] *whereby one knows how to express* [*with perspicuity of diction*] *one meaning in various forms*: (Kull:) [some of the Arabs restrict the science of البيان to *what concerns comparisons and tropes and metonymies*; which last the Arabian rhetoricians distinguish from tropes: and some make it to include *rhetoric* altogether:] Esh-Shereeshee says, in his Expos. of the Maḳámát [of El-Ḥareeree] that the difference between بَيَانٌ and تِبْيَانٌ ↓ is this: that the former denotes *perspicuity of meaning*; and the latter, the *making the meaning to be understood*; and the former is to another person, and the latter to oneself; but sometimes the latter is used in the sense of the former: (TA:) or the former is the act of the tongue, and the latter is the act of the mind: (Ḥar p. 2:) or the former concerns the verbal expression, and the latter concerns the meaning. (Kull.) It is said in a trad., إِنَّ مِنَ البَيَانِ سِحْرًا (Ṣ) or لَسِحْرًا (TA) [*Verily there is a kind of eloquence that is enchantment*: see this explained in art. سحر]. The saying in the Ḳur [lv. 2 and 3], خَلَقَ ٱلْإِنْسَانَ عَلَّمَهُ ٱلْبَيَانَ means *He hath created the Prophet: He hath taught him the Ḳur-án wherein is the manifestation of everything* [*needful to be known*]: or *He hath created Adam*, or *man* as meaning all mankind: *He hath* [*taught him speech, and so*] *made him to discriminate, and thus to be distinguished from all* [*other*] *animals*: (Zj, T:) or *He hath taught him that whereby he is distinguished from other animals*, namely, *the declaration of what is in the mind, and the making others to understand what he has perceived*, for the reception of inspiration, and the becoming acquainted with the truth, and the learning of the law. (Bḍ.) — It is also applied to *Verbosity, and the going deep*, or *being extravagant, in speech, and affecting to be perspicuous*, or *chaste, therein*, or *eloquent, and pretending to excel others therein*; or some بيان is thus termed; and is blamed in a trad., as a kind of hypocrisy; as though it were a sort of self-conceit and pride. (TA.)

بِئْرٌ بَيُونٌ *A well of which the rope does not strike against the sides, because its interior is straight*: or *that is wide in the upper part, and narrow in the lower*: or *in which the drawer of water makes the rope to be aloof from its sides, because of its crookedness*: (T:) or *deep and wide*; (Ṣ, Ḳ;) *because the ropes are wide apart from its sides*; (Ṣ;) as also ▼ بَائِنَةٌ: (Ṣ, TA:) or *that is wide between the two* [*opposite*] *sides*: (M:) pl. [regularly of the latter epithet] بَوَائِنُ. (T, Ṣ.)

بَيِّنٌ [*Distinct, as though separate from others*; and thus,] *apparent, manifest, evident, clear, plain*, or *perspicuous*; (T, Ṣ, Mṣb, Ḳ;) as also ▼ بَائِنٌ (T) and ▼ مُبِينٌ: (T, Ṣ:) pl. [of mult.] أَبْيِنَآءُ (Ṣ, Ḳ) and [of pauc.] بِيِنَةٌ. (Ḳ.) Hence, الكِتَابُ ▼ المُبِينُ [as applied to the Ḳur, q. v. in xii. 1, &c.,] *The clear, plain, or perspicuous, book* or *writing* or *scripture*: or, as some say, this means *the book &c. that makes manifest all that is required* [*to be known*]: (T:) or, *of which the goodness and the blessing are made manifest*: or, *that makes manifest the truth as distinguished from falsity, and what is lawful as distinguished from what is unlawful, and that the prophetic office of Moḥammad is true, and so are the narratives relating to the prophets*: (Zj, T:) or, *that makes manifest the right paths as distinguished from the wrong*. (M, TA.) And كَلَامٌ بَيِّنٌ *Perspicuous, clear, distinct, chaste*, or *eloquent, language*. (T.) — A man, or thing, *bearing evidence* of a quality &c. that he, or it, possesses. (Ṣ and Ḳ and other Lexicons passim.) — A man (M) *perspicuous*, or *clear*, or *distinct, in speech* or *language*; or *chaste therein*; or *eloquent*; (ISh, T, M, Ḳ;) *fluent, elegant, and elevated, in speech, and having little hesitation therein*: (ISh, T:) pl. أَبْيِنَآءُ (T, M, Ḳ) and بَيِّنَآءُ and [of pauc.] أَبْيَانٌ: (Lḥ, M, Ḳ:) the second of these pls. is anomalous: the last is formed by likening فَعِيلٌ to فَاعِلٌ: [for بَيِّنٌ is a contraction of بَيِيِنٌ:] but the pl. most agreeable with analogy is بَيِّنُونَ: so says Sb. (M.)

بَيِّنَةٌ *An evidence, an indication, a demonstration, a proof, a voucher*, or *an argument*, (Mgh, TA,) *such as is manifest*, or *clear, whether intellectual or perceived by sense*; (TA;) [originally بَيِيِنَةٌ,] of the measure فَيْعِلَةٌ, from بَيْنُونَةٌ, [see 1, first sentence,] and بَيَانٌ [q. v.]: (Mgh:) and the *testimony of a witness*: pl. بَيِّنَاتٌ. (TA.)

بَائِنٌ *In a state of separation* or *disunion*; or *separated, severed, disunited*, or *cut off*; (M,* Mṣb;) as also ▼ أَبْيَنُ, occurring in a verse cited above, voce بَيْنَ. [Hence,] اِمْرَأَةٌ بَائِنٌ *A woman separated from her husband by divorce*; (M, Mṣb, Ḳ;) as also ▼ مُبَانَةٌ: the former without ة: (Mṣb:) like طَالِقٌ and حَائِضٌ: you say [to a wife] أَنْتِ بَائِنٌ [*Thou art separated* from me *by divorce*.] (Mgh.) — طَلَاقٌ بَائِنٌ is a tropical phrase; and so is طَلْقَةٌ بَائِنَةٌ; (Mgh;) [signifying the same as] تَطْلِيقَةٌ بَائِنَةٌ (Ṣ, M, Mṣb, Ḳ) † *A divorce that is* [*as it were*] *cut off*; *i. q.* ▼ مُبَانَةٌ [in the second and third of these phrases, and ▼ مُبَانٌ in the first]: (ISk, Mṣb:) بائنة being here used in the sense of a pass. part. n.: (Ṣ, Ṣgh, Mṣb:) or it [is a possessive epithet, and thus] means *having separation*: this kind of divorce is *one in the case of which the man cannot take back the woman unless by a new contract*; (TA;) *nor without her consent*. (MF in art. بت.) — قَوْسٌ بَائِنَةٌ, (Ṣ, M, Ḳ,) and بَائِنٌ, (M, Ḳ,) *A bow that is widely separate from its string*: (Ṣ, M, Ḳ:) *contr. of* بَانِيَةٌ; (Ṣ, M;) this signifying one that is so near to its string as almost to stick to it: (Ṣ:) each of these denotes what is a fault. (Ṣ, M.) — بِئْرٌ بَائِنَةٌ: see بَيُونٌ. — نَخْلَةٌ بَائِنَةٌ *A palm-tree of which the racemes have come forth from the spathes, and of which the fruit-stalks have grown long*. (AḤn, M.) — البَائِنُ also signifies *He who comes to the milch beast* [meaning *the she-camel, when she is to be milked*,] *from her left side*; (Ṣ, Ḳ;) and المُعَلِّى, he who comes to her from her right side: (Ṣ:) or the former, *he who stands on the right of the she-camel when she is milked, and holds the milking-vessel, and raises it to the milker, who stands on her left, and is called* المُسْتَعْلِى: (T:) two persons are engaged in milking the she-camel; one of them holds the milking-vessel on the right side, and the other milks on the left side; and the milker is called المُسْتَعْلِى and المُعَلِّى; and the holder, البائن: (M:) pl. بُيُنٌ. (T.) It is said in a prov., اِسْتُ البَائِنِ أَعْرَفُ, or, as some say, أَعْلَمُ; meaning †*He who has superintended an affair, and exercised himself diligently in the management thereof, is better acquainted with it than he who has not done this*. (T. [See Freytag's Arab. Prov. i. 606.]) — طَوِيلٌ بَائِنٌ *Excessively tall, far above the stature of tall men*. (TA.) ═ See also بَيِّنٌ.

طَلَبَ إِلَى أَبَوَيْهِ البَائِنَةَ *He asked*, or *begged, of his two parents, the separation of himself from them, by* [*their giving him*] *property*, (AZ, T, M,) *to be his alone*. (T.)

فُلَانٌ أَبْيَنُ مِنْ فُلَانٍ :أَبْيَنُ see بَائِنٌ. ═ *Such a one is more perspicuous, clear, distinct, chaste*, or *eloquent, in speech* or *language, than such a one*. (Ṣ, TA.)

تِبْيَانٌ an anomalous inf. n. (T, Ṣ, Ḳ) of 2, q. v.: (T:) or a subst. used as an inf. n.; (MF, TA;) i. e., a subst. from 2. (Sb, M, TA.) See بَيَانٌ.

مُبَانٌ; and its fem., with ة: see بَائِنٌ, in three places.

مُبِينٌ *Separating, severing, disuniting*, or *cutting off*; (Ṣ, Ḳ;) as also مُبْيِنٌ, like مُحْسِنٌ: (Ḳ:) but [the right reading in the Ḳ may be وَمُبِينٌ كَمُحْسِنٍ, meaning "and مُبِينٌ is like مُحْسِنٌ:" if not,] مُبْيِنٌ is a mistake. (TA.) ═ See also بَيِّنٌ, in two places.

مَبَايِنُ الحَقِّ [in which the former word is app. pl. of مُبِينَةٌ] signifies *The things that make the truth to be apparent, manifest, evident, clear*, or *plain*; or *the means of making it so*; syn. مُوَاضِحُهُ. (TA.)

بيه

1. بَاهَ لَهُ, aor. يَبِيهُ, inf. n. بَيْهٌ; and مَا بِهْتُ لَهُ: see 1 in art. بوه.

ت

The third letter of the alphabet: called تَآءٌ and تَا [respecting which latter see the letter ب]: the pl. [of the former is تَآءَاتٌ; and of the latter,] أَتْوَآءٌ. (TA in باب الالف الليّنة.) It is one of the letters termed مَهْمُوسَة [or non-vocal, i. e. pronounced with the breath only, without the voice], and of those termed نِطْعِيَّة [and نَطْعِيَّة and نَطَعِيَّة and نَطَعِيَّة pronounced by pressing the tip of the tongue against the upper gums and suddenly withdrawing it with an emission of the breath]: these latter are ط and د and ت, three letters that are among those which are changed into other letters. (TA at the commencement of باب التآء.) ═ It is one of the augmentative letters: (Ṣ:) and is movent when added at the beginning of a noun, and at the end of a noun, [and at the beginning of a verb,] and at the end of a verb, and is also quiescent at the end of a verb. (Mughnee, Ḳ.) ═ Added at the beginning of a noun, it is a preposition, or particle governing the gen. case, significant of swearing, (Ṣ,* Mughnee, Ḳ,) and denoting wonder; (Mughnee, Ḳ;) and [accord. to general usage] it is peculiarly prefixed to the name الله; (Ṣ, Mughnee, Ḳ;) as in تَاللّٰهِ لَقَدْ كَانَ كَذَا [*By God, verily it was thus*, or *verily such a thing was*]; (Ṣ;) and تَاللّٰهِ لَأَفْعَلَنَّ كَذَا [*By God, I will assuredly do such a thing*]: (TA:) but sometimes they said, تَرَبِّى [*By my Lord*], and تَرَبِّ الكَعْبَةِ [*By the Lord of the Kaabeh*], and تَالرَّحْمٰنِ [*By the Compassionate*], (Mughnee, Ḳ,) as is related on the authority of Akh; deviating from common usage. (TA.) Thus used, it is a substitute for و, (Ṣ, Mughnee,) as it is also in تَتْرَى and تُرَاثٌ and تُجَاهَ and تُخَمَةٌ [&c.]; (Ṣ;) and the و is a substitute for ب; (Ṣ, Mughnee;) but the ت has the additional meaning of denoting wonder: so says Z. (Mughnee.) ═ Added at the end of a noun, it is a particle of allocution: (Mughnee, Ḳ:) it is thus added in أَنْتَ [*Thou*], (Ṣ, Mughnee, Ḳ,) addressed to a male, (TA,) and أَنْتِ [*Thou*], (Mughnee, Ḳ,) addressed to a female; (TA;) uniting with the noun, as though the two became one; not being an affixed noun governed in the gen. case. (Ṣ. [See أَنْ.]) ═ It is added in [the beginning of] the second person of the future, (Ṣ,) [i. e.,] in the beginning of the aor., (TA,) [as a particle of allocution,] as in أَنْتَ تَفْعَلُ [*Thou dost*, or *wilt do*]. (Ṣ, TA.) — It is also added, as a sign of the fem. gender, in the beginning of the future, [or aor.,] as in هِىَ تَفْعَلُ [*She does*, or *will do*]. (Ṣ, TA.) — It is also added in the beginning of the third person [fem.] of the [aor. used as an] imperative, [as a sign of the fem. gender,] as in لِتَقُمْ هِنْدُ [*Let Hind stand*]. (TA.) — And sometimes it is added in the beginning of the second person of the [aor. used as an] imperative, [as a particle of allocution,] as in the phrase in the Ḳur [x. 59, accord. to one reading], فَبِذٰلِكَ فَلْتَفْرَحُوا [*Therefore therein rejoice ye*]: and in the saying of the rájiz,

* قُلْتُ لِبَوَّابٍ لَدَيْهِ دَارُهَا * تِئْذَنْ فَإِنِّى حَمْؤُهَا وَجَارُهَا *

[explained in art. اذن]: and [thus] it is added in the beginning of [the second person of] the [aor. used as an] imperative of a verb of which the agent is not named, as in لِتُزْهَ يَا رَجُلُ [*Be thou proud, vain, boastful*, or *self-conceited, O man*], from زُهِىَ: but Akh says that the adding of the ل in the beginning of the second person of the [aor. used as an] imperative [except in the case of a pass. verb or a verb of which the agent is not named] is a bad idiom, because the ل is not needed. (Ṣ, TA.) ═ The movent ت added at the end of a verb is a pronoun, as in قُمْتُ [*I stood*], (Mughnee, Ḳ,) and قُمْتَ [*Thou stoodest*, addressed to a male], and قُمْتِ [*Thou stoodest*, addressed to a female]: (Mughnee:) thus added in the first and second persons of the pret., it is a pronoun denoting the agent. (Ṣ.) — The quiescent ت added at the end of a verb is a sign of the fem. gender, (Mughnee, Ḳ,) i. e., a particle applied to denote the fem. gender, (Mughnee,) as in قَامَتْ [*She stood*]. (Mughnee, Ḳ.) J says [in the Ṣ] that, when thus added at the end of the pret., it is a pronoun: but IB says [correctly] that it is a particle. (TA.) ═ It is also, sometimes, affixed to رُبَّ and ثُمَّ; and in these cases it is most commonly movent with fet-ḥ, (Mughnee, Ḳ,) so that one says رُبَّتَ and ثُمَّتَ. (TA.) [See arts. رب and ثم.] ═ ت is an imperative of أَتَى. (M in art. اتى.) ═ [As a numeral, ت denotes *Four hundred*.]

تا

تَا fem. of ذَا; (M;) *i. q.* ذِهْ [*This* and *that*]; (T;) a noun of indication, denoting that which is female or feminine; like ذَا (Ṣ, Ḳ) applied to that which is male or masculine; (Ṣ;) and you say also تِهْ, like ذِهْ: (Ṣ, Ḳ:) the dual is تَانِ: and the pl., أُولَآءِ. (Ṣ, Ḳ.) En-Nábighah [Edh-Dhubyánee] says, (T, Ṣ,) excusing himself to En-Noamán [Aboo-Ḳáboos], whom he had satirized, (TA,)

* هَا إِنَّ تَا عِذْرَةٌ إِنْ لَمْ تَكُنْ نَفَعَتْ *

* فَإِنَّ صَاحِبَهَا قَدْ تَاهَ فِى البَلَدِ *

[*Now verily this is an excuse: if it profit not, then verily its author has lost his way in the desert*, or *in the waterless desert*]: (T, Ṣ: but in the latter, لا is put in the place of لم:) تا here points to the قَصِيدَة [or ode]; and عذرة is a subst. from اِعْتِذَارٌ; and تاه means تَحَيَّرَ; and البلد means المَفَازَة. (TA.) The dim. of تَا is تَيَّا, (T, Ṣ, M, Ḳ,) which is anomalous, like ذَيَّا the dim. of ذَا, &c. (I'Aḳ p. 343. [Much has been written respecting the formation of this dim. to reduce it to something like rule, but I pass it over as, in my opinion, unprofitable and unsatisfactory; and only refer to what is said respecting the duals أَلَيَّا and أُلَيَّآءِ in art. الى. See an ex. voce مَرَّةٌ.]) — هَا is prefixed to it (T, Ṣ, Ḳ) [as an inceptive particle] to give notice of what is about to be said, (Ṣ,) so that one says هَاتَا [meaning *This*], (T, Ṣ, Ḳ,) as in هَاتَا فُلَانَةُ [*This is such a woman*]; (T;) and [in the dual] هَاتَانِ; and [in the pl.] هٰؤُلَآءِ: and the dim. is هَاتَيَّا. (Ṣ.) — When you use it in addressing another person, you add to it ك [as a particle of allocution], and say تَاكَ (Ṣ, Ḳ) and تِيكَ and تِلْكَ (T, Ṣ, Ḳ) and تَلْكَ, which is a bad dial. var., (Ṣ, Ḳ,) and تَالِكَ, (T, Ṣ,) which is the worst of these: (T:) [all meaning *That*:] the dual is تَانِكَ and تَانِّكَ, the latter with teshdeed, (Ṣ, Ḳ, [but in some copies of the Ṣ, only the latter is mentioned,]) and تَالِكَ [which, like تَانِّكَ, is dual of تِلْكَ or تَلْكَ, which are contractions of تَالِكَ; these two duals being for تَانِلِكَ, the original, but unused, form]: (Ḳ:) the pl. is أُولٰئِكَ and أُولَاكَ and أُولَآلِكَ [or أُولَآئِكَ] [respecting all of which see أُلَى, in art. الى]: (Ṣ, Ḳ:) and the dim. is تَيَّاكَ and تَيَّالِكَ: (Ḳ: [in the TA, the latter is erroneously written تَيَّانِكَ:]) the ك relates to the person or persons whom you address, masc. and fem. and dual and pl.: [but in addressing a female, you may say تَاكِ &c.; in addressing two persons, تَاكُمَا &c.; in addressing more than two males, تَاكُمْ &c.; and in addressing more than two females, تَاكُنَّ &c.:] what precedes the ك relates to the person [or thing] indicated, masc. and fem. and dual and pl. (Ṣ.) — هَا is also prefixed to تِيكَ and تَاكَ, so that one says, هَاتِيكَ and هَاتَاكَ هِنْدُ [*This*, or *that, is Hind*]. (Ṣ, Ḳ.*) Abu-n-Nejm says,

* جِئْنَا نُحَيِّيكَ وَنَسْتَجْدِيكَا *

* فَافْعَلْ بِنَا هَاتَاكَ أَوْ هَاتِيكَا *

meaning [*We have come saluting thee and seeking of thee a gift: then do thou to us*] *this or that*: [give us] a salutation or a gift. (Ṣ.) The هَا that is used to give notice of what is about to be said is not prefixed to تلك because the ل is made a substitute for that هَا: (Ṣ, TA:) or, as IB says, they do not prefix that هَا to ذٰلِكَ and تِلْكَ because the ل denotes the remoteness of that which is indicated and the هَا denotes its nearness, so that the two are incompatible. (TA.) —— تَا and تَأْ *Names of the letter* ت: see that letter, and see arts. توا and تى. —— تَاسَ and تًا or تَأْ for تَبًّا: see (near its end) art. ا.

تأ

R. Q. 1. تَأْتَأَ, inf. n. تَأْتَأَةٌ, *He reiterated the letter* ت *in speaking.* (S, K.) —— تَأْتَأَ بِالتَّيْسِ, (T, M,) inf. n. as above (T, M, K) and تِئْتَاءٌ, (M,) or تَأْتَأَ, (K,) *He called the he-goat to copulate,* (T, M, K,) or *to approach,* (M,) *saying* ↑ تَأْ تَأْ. (M.)

تَأْ تَأْ : see what next precedes.

تَأْتَأَةٌ *An onomatopœia* [*imitative of the sound made in reiterating the letter* ت *in speaking:* or, *in calling a he-goat to copulate,* or *to approach:* see the verb, above]. (T, K.)

تَأْتَاءٌ A man *who reiterates the letter* ت *in speaking.* (S, K.*)

تأر

4. أَتْأَرْتُ إِلَيْهِ النَّظَرَ *I continued to look at him time after time* (تَارَةً بَعْدَ تَارَةٍ): (T, TA:) or *I looked at him sharply,* or *intently.* (Fr, T, M, K.) And أَتْأَرْتُهُ بَصَرِى, (T, S, M, K,) and أَتْأَرْتُ إِلَيْهِ البَصَرَ, (K,) *I followed him with my eye; made my eye to follow him.* (S, M, K.) [See also art. تور.]

تَارَةٌ, without ء on account of frequent usage, (IAar, T, Msb in art. تور, and K,) *A time; one time;* [in the sense of the French *fois;*] syn. مَرَّةٌ: (Msb, K:) or *a time, whether long or short;* syn. حِينٌ: (IAar:) sometimes, however, it is pronounced تَأْرَةٌ: (Msb:) pl. تِئَرٌ (T, Msb, K) and تِئَارٌ: (Msb:) these are pls. of تَأْرَةٌ; but the pl. of تَارَةٌ without ء is تَارَاتٌ (Msb) and تِيَرٌ (S in art. تير, and K in art. تور,) and تِيَارٌ. (S in art. تير.) [See also art. تور.]

مُتْأَرٌ in the saying

فَصِرْتُ كَأَنِّى فَرَأٌ مُتَارُ

is [said by ISd to be] for مُتْأَرٌ [pass. part. n. of أَتْأَرَ; so that the meaning is, *And I became as though I were a wild ass looked at sharply* or *intently,* or *followed by the eye,* in order to be captured or shot]. (M, TA. [But see art. تور.])

تأم

3. تَاءَمَ أَخَاهُ, (K, TA, [in the TT, as from the M, written تَأَمَ, and so by Golius,]) inf. n. مُتَاءَمَةٌ, (TA,) *He was twinborn with his brother.* (M, K, TA.) —— تَاءَمَ, (S,) or تَاءَمَ ثَوْبًا, (M, K, TA, [in the TT, again, written تَأَمَ,]) inf. n. as above, (S, TA,) † *He wove a piece of cloth of threads two and two together* (S, M, K) *in its warp and its woof.* (K.) [See مِتْآمٌ, and see also نِيرٌ.] —— تَاءَمَ الفَرَسُ, (K, [written by Golius تَأَمَ,]) inf. n. as above, (TA,) † *The horse fetched run after run.* (K.)

4. أَتْأَمَتْ *She* (a mother, K, or a woman, S, M, Msb, and any pregnant animal, M) *twinned,* or *brought forth two at one birth.* (T, S, M, Msb, K.) —— أَتْأَمَهَا i. q. أَفْضَاهَا [like أَتْمَهَا, q. v. in art. اتم]. (S, K.) [Golius and Freytag have rendered it as though it meant أَفْضَى إِلَيْهَا.]

هُوَ تِتْئِمُهُ, whence تِتْئِمٌ, }
هُوَ تَتْئِيمُهُ, whence تَتْئِمٌ, } see تَوْأَمٌ.

تُؤَامِيَّةٌ *A pearl;* (M, K;) so called in relation to تُؤَامٌ, (TA,) which is a town twenty leagues from the metropolis of 'Omán, (K, TA,) in the tract next the sea, (TA,) a city of 'Omán whence pearls are purchased, (M,) erroneously called by J تَوْأَمٌ, [but in one copy of the S I find it written تُوَام,] and said by him to be the metropolis of 'Omán; (K;) as also ↑ تَوْأَمِيَّةٌ, (TA, [and thus it is written in copies of the S, but in one copy I find it written تُوَامِيَّةٌ,]) thought by En-Nejeeremee to be thus called in relation to the oyster-shell, because this is always what is termed تَوْأَمٌ, q. v. (TA.)

تَوْأَمٌ *A twin; one of two young,* (S, M, Mgh, Msb, K,) *and of more,* (M, K,) *brought forth at one birth,* (S, M, Mgh, Msb, K,) *of any animals; whether a male or a female, or a male* [*brought forth*] *with a female;* (M, K;) and تَوْأَمَةٌ is [also] applied to *a female:* (S, M, Mgh, Msb, K:) it occurs in poetry contracted into تَوْمٌ: (M:) the pl. is تَوَائِمُ and تُؤَامٌ, (S, M, Msb, K,) the latter of which is of a rare form, not without parallels, (M,) said by some to be a quasi-pl. n., and by some to be originally [تِئَامٌ,] with kesr, but the assertion of these last is condemned by AHei; (MF;) and تَوْأَمُونَ is allowable as applied to human beings: (S, TA:) you say, هُوَ تَوْأَمُهُ [in the TA, erroneously, تُؤْمُهُ, with damm,] and ↑ تِتْئِمُهُ and ↑ تَتْئِيمُهُ [in the CK تَتْيِمُهُ] (AZ, M, K) [meaning *He is his twin-brother*]: and هُمَا تَوْأَمَانِ (S,* M, Mgh, Msb,* K) and تَوْأَمٌ (M, K) [*They two are twin-brothers*]: or تَوْأَمٌ applies only to one of the two; (Msb;) it is a mistake to say هُمَا تَوْأَمٌ and هُمَا زَوْجٌ: (Mgh:) [but see زَوْجٌ:] Lth says that تَوْأَمٌ applies to *two sons,* or *young ones,* [*born*] *together;* and that one should not say هُمَا تَوْأَمَانِ, but هُمَا تَوْأَمٌ: this, however, is a mistake: correctly, as ISk and Fr say, تَوْأَمٌ applies to one, and تَوْأَمَانِ to two. (T, TA.) It is of the measure فَوْعَلٌ, (Kh, S, IB, Msb,) in the opinion of some, (IB,) and originally وَوْأَمٌ, (Kh, T, S, IB,) like as تَوْلَجٌ is originally وَوْلَجٌ; (Kh, T, S;) from الوِئَامُ, (T, IB,) "the being mutually near," (T,) "mutually agreeing," (T, IB,) "being mutually conformable;" (IB;) so that it means *one that agrees with,* or *matches, another,* (IB.) —— It is metaphorically used in relation to all things resembling one another [so that it means ‡ *One of a pair*]. (M.) A poet says,

قَالَتْ لَنَا وَدَمْعُهَا تُؤَامُ
كَالدُّرِّ إِذْ أَسْلَمَهُ النِّظَامُ
عَلَى الَّذِينَ ٱرْتَحَلُوا السَّلَامُ

† [*She said to us, while her tears fell in pairs,* or *in close succession, like large pearls when the string lets them drop off, Upon those who have departed be peace*]. (S.) [This citation, and what immediately follows it in the S, mentioning the pl. تَوْأَمُونَ, not تُؤَامُونَ, have been misunderstood by Golius; and Freytag has followed him in this case.] —— التَّوْأَمُ is also [a name of] † *A certain Mansion* [*of the Moon;* namely, *the Sixth; more commonly called* الهَنْعَةُ;] *pertaining to* الجَوْزَاء [here meaning *Gemini*]; (M, K;) *one of two* [*asterisms*] *called* التَّوْأَمَانِ: (M:) التَّوْأَمَانِ is †*The Sign of Gemini.* (Kzw.) —— [The pl.] تَوَائِمُ also signifies † *Clusters,* or *what are clustered together,* (مَا تَشَابَكَ,) of stars, and of pearls. (M, K.) —— And تَوْأَمَانِ, † *A pair of pearls,* or *large pearls, for the ear:* each of them is termed a تَوْأَمَةٌ to the other. (TA.) —— And التَّوْأَمَانِ, [in the CK التُّوأمانُ,] † *A certain small herb,* (AHn, M, K,) *having a fruit like cumin-seed,* (AHn, M, and K in art. وأم,) *and many leaves, growing in the plains, spreading long and wide, and having a yellow flower.* (AHn, TA.) —— التَّوْأَمُ also signifies †*The arrow of the kind used in the game called* المَيْسِر: (M:) or *a certain arrow of those used in that game:* (K:) or *the second of those arrows;* (S, M, K;) said by Lth *to have two notches, and to entitle to two portions* [*of the slaughtered camel*] *if successful, and to subject to the payment for two portions if unsuccessful.* (M.) —— And تَوْأَمَاتٌ, †*A kind of women's vehicles* [*borne by camels*], (T, K,) *like the* مَشَاجِر, (T, TA,) erroneously said in the copies of the K to be like the مَشَاجِب, (TA,) *having no coverings,* or *canopies:* the sing. is تَوْأَمَةٌ. (T, K.)

تَوْأَمِيَّةٌ: see تُؤَامِيَّةٌ.

مُتْئِمٌ *Twinning,* or *bringing forth two at one birth;* (S, M, Msb, K;) applied to a mother, (K,) or a woman, (S, M, Msb,) and to any pregnant animal; (M;) without ة. (Msb.)

مِتْآمٌ *Accustomed to twin,* or *bring forth two at one birth;* (S, M, K;) applied to a mother, (K,) or a woman, (S, M,) and to any pregnant animal: (M:) pl. مَتَائِيمُ. (Har p. 613.) —— Hence, (Har ubi suprà,) ثَوْبٌ مِتْآمٌ, (S, Har,) or ↑ مُتَاءَمٌ, (TA, PS,) [both app. correct,] †*A piece of cloth woven of threads two and two together in its warp and its woof.* (S, Har, TA.) —— Hence, also, أَبْيَاتٌ مَتَائِيمُ ‡ *Verses consisting of words in pairs whereof each member resembles the other in writing.* (Har ubi suprà.) [See also مُتَوْأَمٌ.]

مُتَاءَمٌ: see مِتْآمٌ.

فَرَسٌ مُتَائِمٌ † *A horse fetching,* or *that fetches, run after run.* (S, M.)

تَجْنِيسٌ مُتَوْأَمٌ † *The using two words resembling each other in writing but not in expression;* as in the saying, غَرَّكَ عِزُّكَ فَصَارَ قُصَارُ ذٰلِكَ ذُلَّكَ فَاخْشَ فَاحِشَ فِعْلِكَ فَعَلَّكَ تُهْدَا بِهٰذَا [*Thy might, or elevated rank, hath deceived thee, and the end of that has become thine ignominy: fear then thine exorbitant deed, and may-be thou wilt be made to follow a right course by this*]. (Ḥar p. 269.)

تب

1. [تَبَّ, aor. ـِ, inf. n. تَبٌّ, and perhaps ▼تَبَبٌ and ▼تَبَابٌ and ▼تَبِيبٌ, *He, or it, suffered loss,* or *diminution;* or *became lost:* and *perished,* or *died:* as also ▼تبّب, inf. n. تَتْبِيبٌ: and app. تُبَّ also.] تَبٌّ (M, A, Ḳ) and ▼تَتْبِيبٌ (M, Ḳ) [as inf. ns.] signify The *suffering loss,* or *diminution;* or *being lost:* and *perishing,* or *dying:* or [used as substs.] *loss,* or *diminution;* or the *state of being lost:* and *perdition,* or *death:* (M,* A, Ḳ:*) and so ▼تَبَابٌ, (T, Ṣ, A, Mṣb, Ḳ,) [said to be] a subst. from تَبَّهُ, with teshdeed, (Mṣb,) and ▼تَبَبٌ and ▼تَبِيبٌ: (Ḳ:) or the last three signify [simply] *perdition,* or *death:* (M:) and ▼تَتْبِيبٌ is explained as signifying *loss,* or *diminution, that brings,* or *leads, to perdition* or *death;* (IAth, TA;) and so ▼تَبَابٌ; (Bḍ in cxi. 1;) and the *causing to perish.* (T, TA.) Hence you say, ▼تَبًّا تَبَابًا [meaning, in an emphatic manner, *May he suffer loss,* or *be lost,* or *perish*]. (Ṣ.) And تَبًّا لَهُ May God decree *to him loss,* or *perdition;* or cause *loss,* or *perdition,* to cleave *to him:* (Ṣ, M,* Mṣb,* Ḳ:*) تَبًّا being in the accus. case as an inf. n. governed by a verb understood. (Ṣ.) And ▼تَبًّا تَبِيبًا, [in the CḲ تَتْبِيبًا,] meaning the same in an intensive, or emphatic, manner: (M, Ḳ:) and ▼تَبًّا تَبَابًا. (TA.) And تَبَّتْ يَدَاهُ, (T, Ṣ, M, Ḳ,) and تَبَّتْ يَدُهُ, aor. ـِ, (Mṣb,) inf. n. تَبٌّ and ▼تَبَابٌ, but IDrd says that the former of these seems to be the inf. n., and the latter the simple subst., (M,) *May his arms,* or *hands,* and *his arm,* or *hand, suffer loss,* or *be lost,* or *perish:* (T, M, Mṣb, Ḳ, and Bḍ in cxi. 1:) or ‡*may he himself suffer loss,* &c., (Mṣb,* and Bḍ ubi suprà,) i. e., ‡*his whole person:* (Jel in cxi. 1:) or ‡*his good in the present life and that in the life to come.* (Bḍ ubi suprà.) — [Hence,] تَبَّ (A, TA) and ▼تَتَبَّبَ (T, Ḳ) ‡ *He became an old man:* (T, A, Ḳ:) the loss of youth being likened to تَبَاب. (TA.) = تَبَّ, [aor., accord. to rule, ـُ,] *He cut,* or *cut off,* a thing. (Ḳ.) And تُبَّ *It was cut,* or *cut off.* (TA.)

2. تبّب, inf. n. تَتْبِيبٌ: see 1, in three places. = تبّبهُ, (inf. n. as above, Ṣ,) [*He caused him to suffer loss,* or *to become lost:* or] *he destroyed him,* or *killed him.* (Ṣ, Ḳ.) — *He said to him* تَبًّا: (M, Ḳ:*) [i. e.] *he imprecated loss,* or *perdition,* or *death, upon him.* (A.)

4. اتبّ ٱللّٰهُ قُوَّتَهُ ‡ *God weakened,* or *impaired,* or *may God weaken,* or *impair, his strength.* (Ḳ, TA.)

10. استتبّ ‡ *It* (a road) *became beaten,* or *trodden, and rendered even, or easy to walk or ride upon, or easy and direct.* (A.) — ‡ *It* (an affair) *was,* or *became, rightly disposed* or *arranged; in a right state:* (Ṣ, M, A, Mṣb:) or *it followed a regular,* or *right, course; was in a right state; and clear,* or *plain:* from مُسْتَتِبٌّ applied to a road, explained below: (T, TA:) or *it became complete, and in a right state:* lit. *it demanded loss,* or *diminution,* or *destruction;* because these sometimes follow completeness: (Ḥar p. 35:) or the ب may be a substitute for م; the meaning being استتمّ. (TA.)

R. Q. 1. تَتَبَّبَ: see 1.

تَبَّةٌ *A difficult,* or *distressing, state* or *condition.* (Ḳ.)

تَبَبٌ: } see 1, in several places.
تَبَابٌ: }
تَبِيبٌ: }

تَبُوبٌ i. q. مَهْلَكَةٌ [*A place of perdition,* or *destruction;* or *a desert;* or *a desert such as is termed* مَفَازَة]. (Ḳ.) = [It is also said in the Ḳ to signify *What the ribs infold:* but I think it probable that this meaning has been assigned to it from its having been found erroneously written for تَبُوتٌ, a dial. var. of تَابُوتٌ.]

تَابٌّ ‡ An *old* man; (AZ, T, M, A, Ḳ;) fem. with ة: (AZ, T, M, A:) and † *weak:* pl. أَتْبَابٌ: of the dial. of Hudheyl; and extr. [with respect to analogy]. (M.) You say, كُنْتُ شَابًّا فَصِرْتُ تَابًّا [*I was a young man, and I have become an old man*]. (A.) And أَشَابَّةٌ أَنْتِ أَمْ تَابَّةٌ [*Art thou a young woman or an old woman?*] (A.) — Also, (T, Ḳ,) or تَابُّ الظَّهْرِ, (T,) † An ass, and a camel, *having galls,* or *sores, on his back:* (T, Ḳ:) pl. as above. (Ḳ.) — [See also بَاتٌّ.]

مُسْتَتِبٌّ, applied to a road, ‡ *Furrowed by passengers, so that it is manifest to him who travels along it:* and to this is likened an affair that is clear, or plain, and in a right state. (T.) [See the verb, 10.]

تبت

تَبُوتٌ i. q. تَابُوتٌ; (Ḳ;) a dial. var. of the latter. (TA.) See both in art. توب.

تبر

1. تَبَرَ, aor. ـِ, (Lth, T, M, Mṣb, Ḳ,) inf. n. تَبَارٌ; (Lth, T, M;) and تَبِرَ, aor. ـَ; (Mṣb;) *He,* or *it,* (a thing, Lth, T, M,) *perished.* (Lth, T, M, Mṣb, Ḳ.) = See also 2.

2. تبّرهُ, inf. n. تَتْبِيرٌ; (Zj, T, Ṣ, M, Mṣb,* Ḳ;) and ▼تَبَرَهُ, aor. ـِ, inf. n. تَبْرٌ; (Ḳ;) *He broke it:* (Ḳ:) or *he broke it in pieces;* (Ṣ, M;) *and did away with it:* (M:) or *he crumbled it,* or *broke it into small pieces, with his fingers:* (Zj, T:) and *he destroyed it:* (Zj, T, Ṣ, Mṣb, Ḳ:) *He* (God) *destroyed him.* (A.)

تِبْرٌ [a coll. gen. n., of which the n. un. is with ة: *Native gold, in the form of dust* or *of nuggets:* this is the sense in which the word is generally used in the present day:] *broken gold:* (M:) it is not so called unless *in the dust of its mine,* or *broken:* (IJ, M:) or *gold,* and *silver, before it is wrought:* (Lth, T, IF, Mṣb:) or *broken,* or *crumbled, particles of gold,* and *of silver, before they are wrought:* when they are wrought, they are called ذَهَبٌ and فِضَّةٌ: (IAṭr, T, Ḳ:) or *uncoined gold* (Ṣ, Mgh, Mṣb) and *silver:* (Mgh:) when coined, it is called عَيْنٌ: (Ṣ, Mṣb:) [properly,] the term تبر should not be employed save as applied to gold; but some apply it to silver also: (Ṣ:) the تبر of silver, as well as of gold, is mentioned in a trad.: (TA:) or *gold* (M, Ḳ) universally: (M:) and *silver:* (Ḳ:) or *what is extracted from the mine,* (M, Ḳ,) *of gold* and *silver* and *all* جَوَاهِر [here meaning *native ores*] *of the earth,* (M,) *before it is wrought* (M, Ḳ) *and used:* (M:) or *any* جَوْهَر [or *native ore*] *before it is used, of copper* (Zj, T, Mgh, Mṣb) and *brass* (Zj, T, Mgh) or *iron* (Mṣb) *&c.:* (Zj, Mgh, Mṣb:) and *any* جوهر [or *native ore*] *that is used, of copper and brass:* (Ḳ:) the word is sometimes applied to other minerals than gold and silver, as *copper* and *iron* and *lead,* but generally to *gold;* and some say that its primary application is to gold, and that the other applications are later, or tropical: (TA:) also *broken pieces of glass.* (Zj, T, M, Ḳ.)

تِبْرِيَةٌ a dial. var. of هِبْرِيَةٌ, (AO, Ṣ,) i. e. [*Scurf on the head;*] *what is formed at the roots of the hair, like bran.* (AO, Ṣ, Ḳ.)

تَبَارٌ *Destruction,* or *perdition:* (Zj, T, Ṣ, M, &c.:) inf. n. of تَبَرَ. (Lth, T, M.)

مُتَبَّرٌ *Broken up* [*and*] *destroyed:* so in [the saying in the Ḳur vii. 135,] هٰؤُلَآءِ مُتَبَّرٌ مَا هُمْ فِيهِ [*As to these people, that wherein they are* shall be *broken up and destroyed*]. (Ṣ.) — رَأْىٌ مُتَبَّرٌ *Counsel destroyed,* or *brought to nought.* (TA, from a trad.)

مَتْبُورٌ [*Destroyed;*] *in a state of destruction:* (IAṭr, T, Ḳ:) and *defective,* or *deficient.* (IAṭr, T.)

تبع

1. تَبِعَهُ, (Ṣ, Mgh, Mṣb, Ḳ, &c.,) aor. ـَ, inf. n. تَبَعٌ (Ṣ, Mṣb, Ḳ) and تَبَاعَةٌ, (Ṣ, Ḳ,) *He followed;* or *went,* or *walked, behind,* or *after;* (Ṣ, Mgh, Mṣb, Ḳ;) *him,* (Mgh, Mṣb, Ḳ,) or *it;* namely, a people, or company of men: (Ṣ:) or [in the CḲ "and"] *he went with him,* or *it, when the latter had passed by him:* (Ṣ, Mgh, Mṣb, Ḳ:) and ▼اِتَّبَعَهُ signifies the same; (Lth, Ṣ, Ḳ;*) and so does ▼أَتْبَعَهُ: (Lth, Mgh, Ḳ:) or ▼أَتْبَعْتُهُمْ signifies *I overtook them, they having gone before me;* (Fr,* A'Obeyd, Ṣ, Mṣb,* Ḳ;) as also تَبِعْتُهُمْ: (Fr, Ḳ:) Akh says that تَبِعْتُهُ and ▼أَتْبَعْتُهُ signify the same: and hence the saying in the Ḳur [xxxvii. 10], ▼فَأَتْبَعَهُ شِهَابٌ ثَاقِبٌ [*and a shooting star piercing the darkness by its light overtaketh him*]: (Ṣ:) and the saying in the same [vii. 174], ▼فَأَتْبَعَهُ ٱلشَّيْطَانُ *and the devil overtook him:* (TA:) and

the saying in the same [xx. 81], فَأَتْبَعَهُمْ ▾ فِرْعَوْنُ بِجُنُودِهِ *and Pharaoh overtook them with his troops: or almost did so:* (Ibn-'Arafeh, Ḳ:) or this signifies *made his troops to follow them;* (TA;) the ب, accord. to some, being redundant: (Bd:) or ▾ أَتْبَعَهُ signifies *he followed his footsteps;* and *sought him, following him:* (TA:) but اتّبعهم signifies *he went* [*after them,* or *followed them,*] *when they had passed by him;* as also تَبِعَهُمْ, inf. n. تَبَعٌ: you say, مَا زِلْتُ أَتَّبِعُهُمْ ▾ حَتَّى أَتْبَعْتُهُمْ, i. e. [*I ceased not to follow them*] *until I overtook them:* (A'Obeyd:) Fr says that ▾ أَتْبَعَ is better than ▾ اِتَّبَعَ; for the latter signifies *he went behind,* or *after, him, when the latter person was going along;* but when you say, ▾ أَتْبَعَهُ, it is as though [you meant that] you followed his footsteps: (TA:) and ▾ اِتَّبَعَ ▾ فُلَانٌ فُلَانًا [as in the L and TA, but perhaps a mistake for ▾ أَتْبَعَ,] signifies also *he followed him, desiring to do evil to him;* like as Pharaoh followed Moses: (L, TA:) some say, تَبِعْتُ الشَّىْءَ, inf. n. تُبُوعٌ, meaning *I went after the thing:* and تَبِعَ الشَّىْءَ, inf. n. تَبَعٌ and تَبَاعٌ, †[*he followed the thing*] *in respect of actions:* (L, TA:) you say, تَبِعَ الإِمَامَ †*he followed the Imám* [*by doing as he did*]: (Mṣb:) [but in this last sense, more commonly,] one says, ▾ اِتَّبَعَهُ, meaning †*he did like as he* [another] *did:* (TA:) and ▾ اِتَّبَعَ القُرْآنَ †*he followed the Ḳur-án as his guide; did according to what is in it:* (TA:) and you say also, ▾ تَابَعَهُ عَلَى الأَمْرِ; (Mṣb;) or على كَذَا, inf. n. مُتَابَعَةٌ and تِبَاعٌ; (Ṣ;) †[*he followed him,* or *imitated him, in the affair;*] (Mṣb;) *he followed him,* or *imitated him, in doing such a thing:* (PṢ:) [but this last phrase has another meaning: see 3.] In the saying, لَا يُتْبَعُ بِنَارٍ إِلَى القَبْرِ, [in which the verb may be pass. of تَبِعَ or of ▾ أَتْبَعَ,] or, accord. to one relation, ▾ لا يُتَّبَعُ, each in the pass. form, [*Fire shall not be made to follow to the grave,* though it may be rendered *one shall not follow with fire to the grave,* it is said that] the ب is to render the verb transitive. (Mgh.) — تَبِعْتُ الرَّجُلَ بِحَقِّى; and ▾ تَابَعْتُهُ بِهِ, inf. n. مُتَابَعَةٌ [and probably تِبَاعٌ also]; and ▾ اِتَّبَعْتُهُ بِهِ; *I prosecuted,* or *sued, the man for my right,* or *due.* (TA.) The saying in the Ḳur [ii. 173], فَاتِّبَاعٌ ▾ بِالْمَعْرُوفِ means [*Then*] *prosecution* for the bloodwit [shall be made *with lenity*]. (TA.) — تَبِعَ, of which the aor., يَتْبَعُ, occurs in a trad., [see 4,] (Mgh, TA,) pronounced by the relaters of trads. with teshdeed, [▾ يَتَّبِعُ,] (TA,) also signifies †*He accepted a reference from his debtor to another for the payment of what was owed to him.* (Mgh, TA.*)

2. تَبَّعَ ٱللّٰهُ لِفُلَانٍ, inf. n. تَتْبِيعٌ, *May God make a thing to be followed by another thing to such a one,* is said in relation to good and to evil; like سَبَّعَ لَهُ. (TA in art. سبع.) ═ See also 5.

3. تِبَاعٌ [and مُتَابَعَةٌ, the inf. ns. of تَابَعَ,] *i. q.* وِلَاءٌ [The *making a consecution,* or *succession, of one to the other,* بَيْنَ أَمْرَيْنِ *between two things,* or *affairs:* and the *making consecutive, successive,* or *uninterrupted, in its progressions,* or *gradations,* or *the like:* see 6]. (Ṣ, Ḳ.) It is said in a trad., تَابِعُوا بَيْنَ الحَجِّ وَالعُمْرَةِ [*Make ye a consecution between the* حج *and the* عمرة; meaning *make ye the performance of the* حج *and that of the* عمرة *to be consecutive*]; (TA;) i. e. *when ye perform the* حج, *then perform ye the* عمرة; *and when ye perform the* عمرة, *then perform ye the* حج: or *when ye perform either of these, then perform ye after it the other, without any length of time* [*intervening*]: but the former [meaning] is the more obvious. (Marginal note in a copy of the Jámi'-eṣ-Ṣagheer of Es-Suyooṭee.) And you say, تَابِعْ بَيْنَنَا وَبَيْنَهُمْ عَلَى الخَيْرَاتِ †*Make thou us to be followers,* or *imitators, of them in excellencies.* (TA.) And تابع الأَغَانِىَّ ‡[*He sang songs consecutively, successively,* or *uninterruptedly*]. (Ṣ and Ḳ in art. جور.) And تابع إِسْقَاطَهُ [*He made it to fall, fall down, drop, drop down,* or *tumble down, in consecutive portions* or *quantities*]. (M and Ḳ in art. سقط: in the CḲ اَسْقَاطَهُ.) And تابع الفَرَسُ الجَرْىَ † [*The horse prosecuted,* or *continued, the course,* or *running, uninterruptedly*]. (Ḳ voce هَلَبَ; &c.) And هُوَ يُتَابِعُ الحَدِيثَ ‡*He carries on the narrative,* or *discourse, by consecutive progressions,* or *uninterruptedly:* or, as Z says, *pursues it,* or *carries it on, well.* (TA.) [See also a similar phrase in what here follows.] — تابع القَوْسَ †*He pared,* or *trimmed, the bow well, giving to each part thereof what was its due.* (Ḳ, TA.) Skr says that the phrase تُوبِعَ بَرْيُهَا, used by Aboo-Kebeer El-Hudhalee in describing a bow, means *The paring,* or *trimming, of which has been executed with uniformity, part after part.* (TA.) — Hence, (TA,) the saying of Abu-l-Wáḳid El-Leythee, (Ṣ, TA,) in a trad., (Ṣ,) تَابَعْنَا الأَعْمَالَ فَلَمْ نَجِدْ شَيْئًا أَبْلَغَ فِى طَلَبِ الآخِرَةِ مِنَ الزُّهْدِ فِى الدُّنْيَا (Ṣ, TA) †*We have practised works with diligence, and acquired a sound knowledge of them,* [*and we have not found anything more efficacious in the pursuit of the blessings of the world to come than abstinence in respect of the enjoyments of the present world.*] (Ṣ,* TA.) You say also, تابع عَمَلَهُ, meaning †*He made his work sound,* or *free from defect:* (Kr, Ṣ:) and in like manner, كَلَامَهُ *his language,* or *speech.* (Kr.) — [Hence also,] تابع المَرْعَى الإِبِلَ ‡*The pasture fattened the camels well and thoroughly.* (Ḳ, TA.) — تابعهُ عَلَى الأَمْرِ †*He aided, assisted,* or *helped, him to do the thing,* or *affair.* (TA.) — See also 1, where another meaning of the same phrase is mentioned, in the latter half of the paragraph. — تَابَعْتُهُ بِحَقِّى: see 1, near the end of the paragraph.

4. اتبعهُ: see 1, from the beginning nearly to the end. ═ Also *He made him to follow;* or *to overtake:* (Ṣ, Ḳ:) *he made him to be a follower:* (Mgh, Mṣb:) or *he urged him,* or *induced him, to be a follower.* (Mgh.) You say, [making the verb doubly trans.,] أَتْبَعْتُهُمْ غَيْرِى [*I made them to follow,* or *overtake, another, not myself*]. (Ḳ.) And أَتْبَعْتُهُ الشَّىْءَ فَتَبِعَهُ [*I made him to follow,* or *overtake, the thing, and he followed it,* or *overtook it*]. (Ṣ.) And أَتْبَعْتُ زَيْدًا عَمْرًا *I made Zeyd to be a follower of 'Amr:* (Mgh, Mṣb:) or *I urged,* or *induced, Zeyd to be a follower of 'Amr.* (Mgh.) And أَتْبَعَهُ نَفْسَهُ مُتَحَسِّرًا عَلَى مَا فَاتَ ‡[*He made his mind,* or *desire, to follow after it, regretting what had passed away*]. (TA in art. عجز.) [See also 10.] It is said in a prov., (TA,) أَتْبِعِ الفَرَسَ لِجَامَهَا [*Make thou its bit and bridle to follow the horse*]: or النَّاقَةَ زِمَامَهَا [*her nose-rein, the she-camel*]: or الدَّلْوَ رِشَاءَهَا [*its rope, the bucket*]: used in bidding to complete a favour, or benefaction: (Ḳ, TA:) A'Obeyd says, I think the meaning of the first prov. to be, Thou hast liberally given the horse, and the bit and bridle are a smaller matter; therefore satisfy thou completely the want, seeing that the horse is not without need of the bit and bridle. (TA.) — Hence the trad., مَنْ أُتْبِعَ عَلَى مَلِىٍّ فَلْيَتْبَعْ ‡*Whoso is referred, for the payment of what is owed to him, to a solvent man, let him accept the reference:* (Mgh, TA:*) [see also 1, last meaning:] the verb being made trans. by means of على because it conveys the meaning of إِحَالَةٌ. (Mgh.) You say [also], أُتْبِعَ فُلَانٌ بِفُلَانٍ ‡*Such a one was referred, for the payment of what was owed to him, to such a one.* (Ṣ, TA.) And أَتْبَعَهُ عَلَيْهِ ‡*He referred him, for the payment of what was owed to him, to him.* (TA.) — [See also إِتْبَاعٌ, below.]

5. تتبّعهُ, inf. n. تَتَبُّعٌ, (Lth, Ṣ, Mṣb,* Ḳ,) for which ▾ اِتِّبَاعٌ is used by El-Ḳuṭámee, tropically, (Ṣ,) or, accord. to Sb, because the same in meaning; (TA;) and ▾ تبّعهُ, inf. n. تَتْبِيعٌ; (Ṣ, Ḳ;*) *He pursued it; investigated it; examined it; hunted after it; prosecuted a search after it; made successive,* or *repeated, endeavours to attain it, to reach it,* or *to obtain it;* or *sought it, sought for it,* or *sought after it, successively, time after time,* or *repeatedly,* or *in a leisurely manner,* or *by degrees, gradually, step by step, bit by bit,* or *one thing after another,* (Lth, Ṣ,* Mṣb, Ḳ,* TA,) *following after it.* (Ṣ.) Hence the saying of Zeyd Ibn-Thábit, respecting the collecting of the Ḳur-án, فَعَلِقْتُ أَتَتَبَّعُهُ مِنَ اللِّخَافِ وَالعُسُبِ [*And I set myself to seeking to collect it successively,* &c., *from the thin white stones and the leafless palm-branches* upon which it was written]. (TA.) And تتبّع البِلَادَ يَخْرُجُ مِنْ أَرْضٍ إِلَى أَرْضٍ [*He investigated the countries, going forth from land to land*]. (Ṣ and Ḳ in art. قرى.) And فُلَانٌ يَتَتَبَّعُ أَثَرَ فُلَانٍ [*Such a one pursues,* &c., *the track of such a one*]. (TA.) And يَتَتَبَّعُ مَسَاوِىَ فُلَانٍ [*He seeks successively,* &c., *to discover the vices, faults,* or *evil qualities* or *actions, of such a one*]. (TA.) And يَتَتَبَّعُ مَدَاقَّ الأُمُورِ وَنَحْوَ ذٰلِكَ [*He pursues small,* or *little, affairs; and the like thereof:* or *he seeks successively,* &c., *to obtain a knowledge of the subtilties, niceties, abstrusities,* or *obscuri-*

ties, of things, or affairs; and the like thereof]. (TA.) And تَتَبَّعَ الحَبْلَ [He took successive holds of the rope]: said of a man descending from a part of a mountain such as is termed شِيق, by means of a rope tied to that part, to a place in which honey was deposited. (TA in art. شيق.)

6. تتابع *It was, or became, consecutive, successive,* or *uninterrupted, in its progressions,* or *gradations,* or *the like;* syn. تَوَالَى. (K.) You say, تتابع سُقُوطُهُ [*Its falling, falling down, dropping, dropping down,* or *tumbling down, was,* or *became, consecutive,* &c.; i. e. *it fell, fell down,* &c., *in consecutive portions or quantities*]. (M and K in art. سقط.) And تتابع القَوْمُ *The people,* or *company of men, followed one another.* (Msb.) And تَتَابَعَتِ الأَشْيَآءُ, and الأَمْطَارُ, and الأُمُورُ, *The things,* and *the rains,* and *the events, came one after another, each following near upon another.* (Lth.) And it is said in a trad., تَتَابَعَتْ عَلَى قُرَيْشٍ سِنُو جَدْبٍ [*Years of dearth, drought,* or *sterility, came consecutively upon Kureysh*]. (TA.) — تتابع الفَرَسُ ‡ *The horse ran evenly, not raising one of his limbs* [*above its fellow*]. (TA.) — تتابعتِ الإِبِلُ ‡ *The camels became fat and goodly.* (TA.)

8: see 1, throughout: and see also 5.

10. استتبعهُ *He desired,* or *demanded, of him that he should follow him:* (TA:) or *he made him to follow him.* (L.) [See also 4.]

تِبْعٌ *A follower* of women: (Lh,* Az:) or *a passionate lover, and follower,* of a woman, (K,) whithersoever she goes: (TA:) and with ة, of a man. (Lh:) and ↓ تُبَّعٌ *a sedulous seeker* of women. (K.) [See تَابِعٌ.] You say also, هُوَ تِبْعُ ضِلَّةٍ, meaning *He is a follower of women:* and تِبْعُ ضِلَّةٍ *one in whom is no good, and with whom is no good:* or, accord. to Th, you only say تِبْعُ ضِلَّةٍ. (TA.) — هٰذَا تِبْعُ هٰذَا *This is what follows this.* (M in art. تلو.) — See also تَبِيعٌ, in two places.

تَبَعٌ: see تَابِعٌ, in six places.

رَجُلٌ تُبَعٌ لِلْكَلَامِ *A man who makes his speech consecutive, one part to another.* (Yoo, K.*)

بَقَرَةٌ تَبْعَى *A cow desiring* [and therefore *following*] *the bull.* (Ibn-'Abbád, K.)

تَبِعَةٌ and ↓ تَبَاعَةٌ signify the same; (T, S, O, L, K;) [*The consequence* of an action: and] *a claim which one seeks to obtain for an injury,* or *injurious treatment,* and *the like:* (T, O, L, K; and so the Msb in explanation of the former word:) the former is also explained as signifying *a right,* or *due, annexed to property, claimed from the possessor of the property:* (L:) pl. [of the former] تَبِعَاتٌ and [of the latter] تَبَاعَاتٌ. (TA.) A poet says,

أَكَلَتْ حَنِيفَةُ رَبَّهَا ۞ زَمَنَ التَّقَحُّمِ وَالمَجَاعَهْ

لَمْ يَحْذَرُوا مِنْ رَبِّهِمْ ۞ سُوْءَ العَوَاقِبِ وَالتَّبَاعَهْ

[*Haneefeh ate their lord, in the time of experiencing dearth,* or *drought,* or *sterility, and hunger: they did not fear, from their lord, the evil of the results, and the consequence* of their action]: for they had taken to themselves a god consisting of حَيْس, [i. e. dates mixed with clarified butter and the preparation of milk called أَقِط, kneaded together,] and worshipped it for some time; then famine befell them, and they ate it. (S.) And one says, مَا عَلَيْهِ مِنَ ٱللّٰهِ فِى هٰذَا تَبِعَةٌ, and ↓ تَبَاعَةٌ, *There is not, against him, on the part of God, in this, any claim on account of wrong doing.* (TA.)

تَبِيعٌ [One who is *prosecuted,* or *sued,* for a right, or due; of the measure فَعِيلٌ in the sense of the measure مَفْعُولٌ, from تَبِعْتُهُ بِحَقِّى;] one *who owes property to another,* (S, K, TA,) *and whom the latter prosecutes,* or *sues, for it.* (TA.) ═ The *young one of a cow in the first year;* (S, Msb, K;) so says Aboo-Fak'as El-Asadee: (TA:) or *that is a year old;* (Az, Mgh, TA;) not so called until he has completed the year; erroneously said by Lth to signify *a calf ripening to his perfect state:* (Az, TA:) thus called because he yet follows his mother; (Mgh, Msb;) the word in this sense being of the measure فَعِيلٌ in the sense of the measure فَاعِلٌ: (Msb:) and ↓ تِبْعٌ signifies the same: (TA:) fem. of the former with ة: (S, Msb, K:) pl. تِبَاعٌ and تَبَائِعُ; (AA, S, O, K;) both pls. of تَبِيعٌ; (AA, S, O;) or the former is pl. of تَبِيعَةٌ; (Msb;) and the pl. of تَبِيعٌ is أَتْبِعَةٌ [a pl. of pauc.]; (L, Msb;) and أَتَابِعُ and أَتَابِيعُ, the latter of which is extr., are pls. of أَتْبِعَةٌ: (L:) the pl. of ↓ تِبْعٌ in the above-mentioned sense is أَتْبَاعٌ. (TA.) Accord. to Esh-Shaabee, (IF,) One *whose horns and ears are equal* [*in length*]: (IF, K:) but this is a judicial explanation; not deduced from the rules of lexicology. (IF.) — *I. q.* ↓ تَابِعٌ [as signifying One *who prosecutes,* or *sues,* for a right, or due; and particularly for blood-revenge]. (S, K.) Hence the saying in the Kur [xvii. 71], ثُمَّ لَا تَجِدُوا لَكُمْ عَلَيْنَا بِهِ تَبِيعًا *Then ye shall not find for you any to prosecute for blood-revenge, nor any to sue, against us therein:* (Fr, S, K:) or *ye shall not find for you any to sue us for the disallowing of what hath befallen you, nor for our averting it from you:* (Zj:) [or *any aider against us;* for] تَبِيعٌ also signifies *an aider;* and especially *against an enemy.* (Lth, K.) — See also تَابِعٌ, latter half.

تَبَاعَةٌ: see تَبِعَةٌ, in three places.

تُبَّعٌ *An appellation of each of the Kings of El-Yemen* (S, K) *who possessed Himyer and Hadramowt,* (K, TA,) *and,* as some add, *Seba;* (TA;) but not otherwise; (K, TA;) and the like of this is said in the 'Eyn: (TA:) so called because they followed one another; whenever one died, another took his place, following him in his course of acting: (TA:) pl. تَبَابِعَةٌ, (S, K,) with ة added as having the meaning of a rel. n.; [as though it were pl. of تُبَّعِىٌّ, like as حَنَابِلَةٌ is pl. of حَنْبَلِىٌّ;] erroneously written in some of the copies of the K تتابعة: (TA:) the تبابعة of Himyer were like the أَكَاسِرَة of the Persians and the قَيَاصِرَة of the Romans. (Lth.) In the Kur xliv. 36, it is said in a trad. to mean a particular king, who was a believer, and whose people were unbelievers. (Zj.) — And hence, (TA,) *A species of the* يَعَاسِيب [or *kings of the bees*], (K,) *the greatest and most beautiful thereof, whom the other bees follow:* (TA:) pl. تَبَابِيعُ; (K;) in the L, تَتَابِعُ [which is probably a mistranscription for تَبَابِعُ]. (TA.) — *A species of* طَيْر [which means any *flying things,* as well as *birds;* and may therefore, perhaps, be meant to indicate what next precedes]. (S.) — The *shade,* or *shadow;* (S, K;) because it follows the sun; as also ↓ تُبْعٌ. (K.) A poet says, (S,) namely, Soadà El-Juhaneeyeh, (TA,) or Selmà El-Juhaneeyeh, (marginal note in a copy of the S,) bewailing her brother, As'ad,

۞ يَرِدُ المِيَاهَ حَضِيرَةً وَنَفِيضَةً ۞

۞ وِرْدَ القَطَاةِ إِذَا ٱسْمَأَلَّ التُّبَّعُ ۞

(S) [*He comes to the waters when people are dwelling,* or *staying, there,* (but see حَضِيرَةٌ,) *and when no one is there, as the bird called katáh comes to water*] *when the shade has become contracted at mid-day:* or, accord. to Aboo-Leylà, the meaning is, *the shade of night;* i. e., this man comes to the waters in the last part of the night, before any one: though it means also the shade of day-time: (TA:) or, accord. to Aboo-Sa'eed Ed-Dareer, the meaning here is [*the star,* or *asterism, called*] الدَّبَرَان; and this is very probably correct; for the bird above mentioned comes to the waters by night, and seldom by day; and hence the saying, أَدَلُّ مِنْ قَطَاةٍ. (Az, TA.) See تَابِعٌ. — See also تِبْعٌ. — مَا أَدْرِى أَىُّ تُبَّعٍ هُوَ *I know not who of men he is.* (Ibn-'Abbád, K.) — تُبَّعٌ is also a pl. of تَابِعٌ [q. v.]. (TA.)

تُبْعٌ: see تُبَّعٌ.

تُبُوعُ الشَّمْسِ *A certain wind,* (K, TA,) *also called* التُّكَيْبَاءُ, (TA,) *which blows* (K, TA) *in the early morning,* (TA,) *with the rising of the sun,* (K, TA,) *from the direction of the wind called* الصَّبَا, *unaccompanied by rising clouds,* (TA,) *and veers round through the various places whence winds blow until it returns to the place from which blows the wind called* الصبا, (K, TA,) *whence it commenced in the early morning:* (TA:) the Arabs dislike it. (Z, TA.)

تَابِعٌ *Following; a follower:* (TA:) and ↓ تَبَعٌ also signifies the same as تَابِعٌ; (K;) *a thing that follows in the track* of a thing; (Lth, Az;) or *that is at the hinder,* or *latter, part* of anything; (TA;) but is used alike as sing. and pl.: (S, Msb, K:) the pl. of تَابِعٌ is تُبَّعٌ and تُبَّاعٌ (TA) [and, applied to rational beings, تَابِعُونَ]: and the pl. of ↓ تَبَعٌ is أَتْبَاعٌ; (S, K;) or this may be used as a pl. of تَبَعٌ; (Msb;) or it is pl. of تَابِعٌ, like as خَدَمٌ is pl. of خَادِمٌ, (Kr, Mgh,) and طَلَبٌ of طَالِبٌ, &c.; (Ḳ;) or, correctly speaking, it is a quasi-pl. n. (Sb, TA.) You say, ▼ المُصَلِّى تَبَعٌ لِإِمَامِهِ [*The person praying is a follower of his Imám*]: and النَّاسُ تَبَعٌ لَهُ [*The people are followers of him*]. (Mṣb.) And it is said in the Ḳur [xiv. 24, and xl. 50], ▼ إِنَّا كُنَّا لَكُمْ تَبَعًا [*Verily we were followers of you*]: (Ṣ, TA:) in which the last word may be a quasi-pl. n. of تَابِعٌ; or it may be an inf. n., meaning ذَوِى تَبَعٍ. (TA.) ▼ تُبَعٌ is applied as an epithet to the legs of a beast: (Lth, T:) and is also used as [an epithet in which the quality of a subst. is predominant,] signifying The *legs of a beast*. (Ḳ.) — *A jinnee, or genie, that accompanies a woman and follows her whithersoever she goes,* (Ḳ, TA,) *loving her:* (TA:) and تَابِعَةٌ *a jinneeyeh, or female genie, that does the same to a man:* (Ṣ,* Ḳ, TA:) or the ة is added in the latter to give intensiveness to the signification, or to denote evilness of nature, or to convey the meaning of دَاهِيَةٌ, q. v.: the pl. is تَوَابِعُ: and this means *female associates*. (TA.) — *A servant;* as also ▼ تَبِيعٌ. (TA.) أَوِ ٱلتَّابِعِينَ غَيْرِ أُولِى الإِرْبَةِ, in the Ḳur [xxiv. 31], accord. to Th, means *Or the servants* of the husband, *such as the old man who is perishing by reason of age, and the aged woman.* (TA.) — See also تَبِيعٌ. — [Also *One next in the order of time after the* صَحَابَة; like ▼ تَابِعِىٌّ. — And in grammar, *An appositive.*] — تَابِعُ النَّجْمِ [*The follower of the asterism;* i. e., *of the Pleiades;*] *a name of* الدَّبَرَان [*the Hyades;* or *the five chief stars thereof;* or *the brightest star among them, α of Taurus*]: this name being given to it as ominous of good; (Ḳ;) or as ominous of evil: (O:) or so called because it follows the Pleiades: (T:) also called التَّابِعُ, (T in art. دبر, Sb, IB, and others,) and تُوَيْبِعٌ, (Ḳ,) which is the dim., (TA,) or التُّوَيْبِعُ, (T in art. دبر,) and ▼ تُبَعٌ, (Ḳ,) or التُّبَّعُ [q. v.], (Aboo-Sa'eed Eḍ-Ḍareer, T,) and ▼ التَّبَعُ, (IB, Z,) and التَّالِى, and الحَادِى, (IB,) or حَادِى النُّجُومِ, (Ṣ in art. جدح,) or حَادِى النَّجْمِ. (Ḳzw and others.) [See also المِجْدَحُ.]

تَابِعِىٌّ: see تَابِعٌ.

تُوَيْبِعٌ: see تَابِعٌ, last sentence.

إِتْبَاعٌ in language is when one says the like of حَسَنٌ بَسَنٌ (Ṣ, Ḳ) and قَبِيحٌ شَقِيحٌ: (Ṣ:) The *putting, after a word, an imitative sequent,* i. e. *another word similar to the former in measure or in its* رَوِىّ, *by way of pleonasm, or for fulness of expression, and for corroboration;* (Mz 28th نوع, and Kull p. 11;) *the latter word being one not used alone, and having no meaning by itself, as in* حَسَنٌ بَسَنٌ; *or being one which has a meaning of its own, as in* هَنِيْئًا مَرِيْئًا. (Kull ubi suprà.) — [Also The *latter of such two words;* i. e. *an imitative sequent.* — And used in the former sense, as an inf. n., it denotes various other kinds of assimilation, i. e., of one word to another preceding or following it, and of one vowel to another preceding or following it in the same word.]

مُتْبِعٌ She *who has with her children,* or *young ones:* (Lḥ:) or a ewe, or she-goat, and a cow, and a girl, *having her offspring following her:* (Ḳ:) or a cow *having a* تَبِيع, q. v.: and IB mentions also مُتْبِعَةٌ as signifying the same: and a female servant *followed by her offspring whither she comes and goes.* (TA.)

مَتْبُوعٌ [pass. part. n. of 1. — In grammar, The *antecedent of a* تَابِع, i. e., *of an appositive.*]

مُتَابَعٌ †Anything *made,* or *executed, soundly, thoroughly, well,* or *so as to be free from defect.* (Ḳ,* TA.)

مُتَتَابِعٌ *Consecutive, successive,* or *uninterrupted, in its progressions,* or *gradations,* or *the like.* (TA.) You say لُؤْلُؤٌ مُتَتَابِعٌ *Pearls following one another,* or *doing so in uninterrupted order.* (TA.) And صِيَامُ شَهْرَيْنِ مُتَتَابِعَيْنِ *The fasting of two consecutive months.* (TA.) — غُصْنٌ مُتَتَابِعٌ ‡ *An even,* or *a uniform, branch, in which are no knots.* (Ḳ,* TA.) And فَرَسٌ مُتَتَابِعُ الخَلْقِ ‡ *A horse symmetrical in make,* (A, Ḳ,) *justly proportioned in his limbs* or *parts.* (A, TA.) And رَجُلٌ مُتَتَابِعُ العِلْمِ ‡ *A man whose knowledge is uniform, consistent, without incongruity.* (K,* TA.)

تبل

1. تَبَلَهُ, (Lth, T, M,) aor. ـِ, (M,) inf. n. تَبْلٌ, (Lth, T, M,) *He pursued him with enmity,* or *hostility:* (Lth, T:) or *he bore enmity,* or *was hostile, to him.* (M.) — تَبَلَهُمُ الدَّهْرُ, (Ṣ, M, Ḳ,) inf. n. تَبْلٌ, (M,) ‡ *Time,* or *fortune, smote them with its vicissitudes,* (M, Ḳ,) and (Ḳ) *destroyed them;* (Ṣ, Ḳ;) as also ▼ أَتْبَلَهُمْ. (Ṣ, TA.) — تَبَلَهُ الحُبُّ, (Ṣ, M,) or الهَوَى, (T,) aor. ـِ, (M,) inf. n. تَبْلٌ; (T, Ḳ;) and ▼ اتبلهُ, (Ṣ, M,) inf. n. إِتْبَالٌ; (Ḳ, TA;) *Love made him sick,* or *ill;* (T, Ṣ, M, Ḳ; [in the CḲ, والاَسْقامُ كالاَتْبالِ is erroneously put for والإِسْقَامُ كالإِتْبَالِ;]) and *caused him to be in a bad,* or *unsound, state:* (Ṣ:) or, as some say, تَبَلَهُ signifies, (M,) or signifies also, (Ḳ,) *it took away his reason,* (M, Ḳ,) and *bewildered him.* (TA.) — You say also, of a woman, تَبَلَتْ فُؤَادَ الرَّجُلِ, (M, Ḳ,) inf. n. as above, as though meaning, (M,) *She smote the man's heart with* ▼ تَبْل [app. meaning *love-sickness*]. (M, Ḳ.) — See also Q. Q. 1.

2 and 3: see Q. Q. 1.

4. اتبلهُ, inf. n. إِتْبَالٌ, *He made him a victim of blood-revenge,* or *retaliation of murder or homicide.* (Ṣ: the meaning is indicated there, but not expressed.) — See also 1, in two places.

Q. Q. 1. تَوْبَلَ القِدْرَ, (A'Obeyd, T, Ṣ, M, Mṣb, Ḳ,) and تَأْبَلَهَا, with hemz, (IJ, M,) or ▼ تَابَلَهَا, [without ء,] (Ḳ,) mentioned by Ibn-Abbád in the Moḥeeṭ, (TA,) and ▼ تَبَّلَهَا, (T, M, Ḳ,) said by Lth to be allowable, (T,) and ▼ تَبَلَهَا, (Ḳ,) *He seasoned* [*the contents of*] *the cooking-pot with* تَابَل; (Mṣb;) *he put* تَابَل *into the cooking-pot;* (Ḳ;) *i. q.* قَزَّحَهَا and فَحَّاهَا: (A'Obeyd, T:) from تَابَل. (Ṣ, M.*) — [Hence,] تَوْبَلَ كَلَامَهُ ‡ *He seasoned* [meaning *he embellished*] *his speech,* or *language;* syn. قَزَّحَهُ (TA) and بَزَّرَهُ. (A in art. بزر.)

تَبْلٌ [originally inf. n. of 1, q. v. —] *Enmity,* or *hostility,* (Lth, T, M, Ḳ, TA,) *in the heart,* (TA,) *with which one is pursued:* (Lth, T:) pl. تُبُولٌ (Lth, T, M, Ḳ) and ▼ تَبَابِيلُ, which latter is extr. (Ḳ.) You say, لِى عِنْدَهُ تَبْلٌ [*He has enmity,* or *hostility, towards me, with which he pursues me*]. (T.) — *I. q.* تِرَةٌ (Ṣ) and ذَحْلٌ (Ṣ, M, Ḳ) [by the former of which may be intended the meaning explained above, or, as appears to be meant by the latter, *blood-revenge;* or *retaliation of murder or homicide;* or *prosecution for blood;* or *a desire of,* or *seeking for, retaliation of a crime or of enmity*]: pl. تُبُولٌ. (Ṣ.) التَّبْلُ as meaning الذَّحْلُ is likened by Yezeed Ibn-El-Ḥakam Eth-Thakafee to a debt which one should be paid. (Ḥam p. 530.) And one says, أُصِيبَ بِتَبْلٍ [*He was made a victim of blood-revenge,* or *retaliation of murder or homicide:* or, perhaps, *of enmity,* or *hostility*]. (Ṣ.) And بَيْنَهُمْ تُبُولٌ [*Between them are blood-revenges,* &c.]. (TA.) — *Love-sickness.* (Kull p. 167. [See حُبٌّ.]) See 1.

دَهْرٌ تَبِلٌ, (M,) or ▼ تَابِلٌ, (TA,) ‡ *Time,* or *fortune, that smites people with its vicissitudes,* (M, TA,) *and destroys them.* (TA.) And ▼ دَهْرٌ مُتْبِلٌ خَبِلٌ, occurring in a poem of El-Aạshà, †*Time,* or *fortune, that destroys,* or *carries off, family and children.* (Ṣ.)

مَتْبُولٌ: see تَبِيلٌ.

تَبَابِيلُ: see تَبْلٌ.

تَبَّالٌ *A possessor* [or *seller*] *of* تَوَابِل pl. of تَابَل. (Ḳ.)

تَابَلٌ, (A'Obeyd, T, Ṣ, M, Mṣb, Ḳ,) also pronounced تَأْبَلٌ, with ء, (IJ, M,) and ▼ تَابِلٌ, (Ṣ, Mṣb, Ḳ,) and ▼ تَوْبَلٌ, (IAạr, T, Ḳ,) *Seeds* (أَبْزَار, Mṣb and Ḳ) *that are used in cooking, for seasoning food;* (T, Ṣ,* M, Mṣb, Ḳ;) *i. q.* فِحًا; (T, M;) *such as cumin-seeds and coriander-seeds:* (TA voce قزح:) said to be arabicized: Ibn-El-Jawáleeḳee says that the vulgar distinguish between تابل and ابزار, [in the manner explained voce بزر,] but the [classical] Arabs do not: (Mṣb:) pl. تَوَابِلُ. (T, Ṣ, Mṣb, Ḳ.)

تَابِلٌ: see تَبِلٌ: — and see تَابَلٌ.

تَوْبَلٌ: see تَابَلٌ.

تُوبَالٌ [from the Persian تُوبَال or تُوپَال?] *What falls in consecutive portions,* or *particles, on the occasion of the hammering* of copper and of iron: *a* مِثْقَال *thereof, with hydromel, drunk, powerfully alleviates the* [*ejection of*] *phlegm.* (Ḳ.)

مُتْبِلٌ : see تَبْلٌ.

مَتْبُولٌ A man *rendered love-sick;* (T;) as also ▾تَبِيلٌ: (M:) and the former, *a lover who is not granted that which he wants.* (TA.)

تبن

1. تَبَنَ, aor. ـِ, (Ṣ, M, Ḳ,) inf. n. تَبْنٌ, (Ṣ,) *He fed* a beast *with* تِبْن [q. v.]. (Ṣ, M, Ḳ.) — Also *He sold* [تِبْن, i. e.] *straw.* (KL.) = تَبِنَ, (T, Ṣ, M, Ḳ,) aor. ـَ, (Ṣ, Ḳ,) inf. n. تَبَنٌ, (T, Ṣ,) or تَبْنٌ, (M, Ḳ,) and تَبَانَةٌ (T, Ṣ,* M, Ḳ) and تَبَانِيَةٌ, (M,) *He was,* or *became, intelligent, sagacious, skilful,* or *knowing;* syn. فَطِنَ, (Ḳ,) or صَارَ فَطِنًا; (Ṣ;) *and nice,* or *minute, in inspection* (Ṣ, Ḳ) *into affairs:* (Ṣ:) or تَبَانَةٌ signifies the *being very intelligent* or *sagacious* or *skilful* or *knowing, and nice,* or *minute, in inspection;* as also طَبَانَةٌ; accord. to AO and AA: (T:) these two words signify the same (T, Ṣ, M*) accord. to [most of] the leading authorities: (T:) and Yaḳoob asserts that the ت is a substitute for ط: (M:) [or the reverse seems to be the case in the opinion of Az, who here remarks that there are many instances of the change of ت into ط:] or the former is *in evil;* and the latter, in good: (M:) or, accord. to Lth, طَبِنَ means in evil; and تَبِنَ, *in good;* so that he makes طبانة to be in deceiving, or beguiling, and suddenly, or unexpectedly, attacking or destroying: but En-Naḍr says the contr.; and accord. to him, طَبْنٌ signifies the having knowledge of affairs, and intelligence, or sagacity, and science: (T:) and ▾تَبَّنَ, inf. n. تَتْبِينٌ signifies the same as تَبِنَ: (Ḳ:) or *he inspected nicely,* or *minutely:* as in a trad. in which it is said, respecting a woman whose husband has died leaving her pregnant, يُنْفَقُ عَلَيْهَا مِنْ جَمِيعِ المَالِ حَتَّى تُبَيِّنُوا, or مَا تَبَنْتُمْ, meaning [*She shall be expended upon from the whole of the property*] *until ye make a nice,* or *minute, inspection* [into the circumstances of the case], and say otherwise, (T, Ṣ,) i. e., that she shall be expended upon from her own share: (T:) and so in another trad., in which it is said, إِنَّ الرَّجُلَ لَيَتَكَلَّمُ بِالكَلِمَةِ يُتَبِّنُ فِيهَا يَهْوِى بِهَا فِى النَّارِ (A'Obeyd, T, M,) i. e. [*Verily a man will say a saying*] *in which he will be nice,* or *minute* [in expression], *whereby he will fall into the fire of* Hell]: (TA:) here A'Obeyd thinks the meaning to be the making language obscure, or abstruse, and disputing in a matter of religion. (T.) You say also, تَبِنَ لَهُ (T, M, TA) *He understood it;* or *knew it;* or *had knowledge,* or *was cognizant, of it;* (TA;) *i. q.* طَبِنَ. (M.)

2. تَبَّنَ, inf. n. تَتْبِينٌ: see 1. = تَبَّنَهُ, inf. n. as before, *He clad him with a* تُبَّان. (TA.)

8. اِتَّبَنَ *He clad himself with a* تُبَّان. (Ḳ.)

تِبْنٌ: see what next follows.

تِبْنٌ (Ṣ, M, Mṣb, Ḳ, &c.) and ▾تِبِنٌ (M, Ḳ) *Straw;* i. e. the *stalks,* or *stems,* (عَصِيفٌ, M, Ḳ,) or the *stalk,* or *stem,* (سَاق, Mṣb,) *of seed-produce,* (M, Mṣb, Ḳ,) *such as wheat and the like,* (M, Ḳ,) [generally] *after it has been trodden or thrashed* [*and cut*]; (Mṣb;) *wheat when it has been trodden or thrashed* [*and cut*] *by the feet of beasts or by repeatedly drawing over it the* [*machine called*] مِدْوَس [q. v.]: (Mgh in art. دوس:) [a coll. gen. n.:] n. un. with ة [signifying *a straw,* or *piece of straw*]. (Ṣ, M.) You say أَقَلُّ مِنْ تِبْنَةٍ [*Less than a straw,* or *piece of straw*]. (TA.) = Also, the former, *A great bowl:* (Ṣ:) or *a bowl that satisfies the thirst of twenty:* (Ḳ:) or the *greatest of bowls, that almost satisfies the thirst of twenty:* (Ks, Ṣ, M:) next is the صَحْن, which is nearly equal thereto: then, the عُسّ, that satisfies the thirst of three and of four: then, the قَدَح, that satisfies the thirst of two men: then, the قَعْب, that satisfies the thirst of one man: then, the غُمَر: (Ks, Ṣ:) or *a bowl of rude,* or *rough, make; not made neatly,* or *skilfully.* (M.) — [Hence, probably,] †*A liberal,* or *bountiful, and noble, chief.* (Ḳ.) — And *A wolf.* (Ḳ.)

تِبْنٌ *Intelligent, sagacious, skilful,* or *knowing; and nice,* or *minute, in inspection* (Ṣ, M, Ḳ) *into affairs;* (Ṣ;) as also طِبْنٌ: (M:) [or *very intelligent, &c.:* and accord. to some, *in evil:* or *in good:* see تَبِنَ.] — And One *who plays with his hand with everything.* (Ḳ.)

تَبَّانٌ *A seller of* تِبْن: (Ṣ, M, Ḳ:) thus, perfectly decl., if of the measure فَعَّال, from التِّبْنُ: but if of the measure فَعْلَان, from التَّبُّ [the act of cutting (for تِبْن is generally cut by the thrashing-machine)], it is [تَبَّانُ,] imperfectly decl. (Ṣ.)

تُبَّانٌ *Small* سَرَاوِيل [or *breeches*], (Ṣ, Mgh, Ḳ,) *without legs,* [i. e. *having only two holes through which to put the legs,*] (TA in art. ثفر,) [*made of linen,* and *of leather,*] *of the measure of a span,* (Ṣ, Mgh,) *such as to conceal the anterior and posterior pudenda* (Ṣ, Mgh, Ḳ, TA) *only;* (TA;) *worn by sailors* (Ṣ, Mgh) [*and by wrestlers*]: or *a thing like* سراويل: (M, Mṣb:) or *a thing like small* سراويل: (T:) [it is an arabicized word, from the Persian تُنْبَان:] the Arabs make it masc. (T, M, Mṣb) and fem.: (Mṣb:) pl. تَبَابِينُ. (T, Mṣb.)

تِبَانَةٌ (TA) and ▾مَتْبَنَةٌ (Mgh, Mṣb, TA) and ▾مَتْبَنٌ (Mgh, Mṣb) The *place,* (TA,) or *house,* or *the like,* (Mgh, Mṣb,) *of* [or *for*] تِبْن. (Mgh, Mṣb, TA.)

مَتْبَنٌ :
مَتْبَنَةٌ : } see تِبَانَةٌ.

مَتْبُونٌ, applied to a horse such as is termed بِرْذَوْن, *Of the colour of* تِبْن [or *straw*]. (TA.)

تبه

تَابُوهٌ a dial. var. of تَابُوتٌ, of the dial. of the Anṣár. (Ṣ and Ḳ in art. توب, q. v.)

تبو

تَابُوتٌ: see art. توب. Accord. to some, it belongs to the present art., and was originally تَابُوَةٌ.

تتر

التَّتَرُ [and التَّاتَارُ and التَّتَارُ] *A certain people,* or *nation,* (Ḳ,) [called by us *the Tartars,*] *in the furthest countries of the East, in the mountains of* طغماج*, on the confines of China,* (TA,) *bordering upon the Turks,* (Ḳ,) *more than six months' journey from Má-waráä-n-nahr:* so in the Murooj edh-Dhahab. (TA.)

تَتْرَى and تَتْرًى: see art. وتر.

تجر

1. تَجَرَ, (Ṣ, A, Mṣb, Ḳ,) aor. ـُ, (Ṣ, Mṣb,) inf. n. تَجْرٌ (Ṣ, Mṣb, Ḳ) and تِجَارَةٌ, (Ṣ, A, Ḳ,) or the latter is a simple subst., (Mṣb,) or quasi-inf. n., (Mgh,) and مَتْجَرٌ; (A;) and ▾اِتَّجَرَ, (Ṣ, A, Mṣb, Ḳ,) of the measure اِفْتَعَلَ; (Ṣ;) *He practised traffic, merchandise,* or *commerce; trafficked; traded; dealt; sold and bought;* (Ḳ;) *employed property for the purpose of gain.* (A.) You say, تَجَرَ تِجَارَةً رَابِحَةً [*He practised a profitable,* or *lucrative, traffic*]. (A.) And فُلَانٌ يَتَّجِرُ▾ فِى البَرِّ وَالبَحْرِ [*Such a one traffics on land and sea*]. (A.) There can hardly, if at all, be found any other instance of ت immediately followed by ج, except رتج and نتج: the ت in تُجَاهَ is originally و. (Mṣb.)

3. تَاجَرَهُ, (A,) inf. n. مُتَاجَرَةٌ, (A, KL,) *He practised with him* [and (as is implied in the A) *he vied with him in practising*] *traffic,* or *selling and buying.* (KL.)

8. اِتَّجَرَ: see 1, in two places. = See also 8 in art. وجر.

تَجْرٌ :
التَّجْرُ : } see تَاجِرٌ.

تِجَارَةٌ a subst. from 1; (Mṣb;) or quasi-inf. n.; (Mgh;) [The *practice of traffic, merchandise,* or *commerce; traffic; trade; selling and buying;*] the *trade of the* تَاجِر, i. e., *of him who sells and buys for gain;* (Ksh in ii. 15;) the *seeking of gain by selling and buying.* (Bḍ ibid.) [See also 1.] — Also *Merchandise,* meaning *what is sold and bought, of goods,* or *commodities,* or *household-furniture,* and *the like;* a quasi-inf. n. used in the sense of a pass. part. n. (Mgh.) [Hence the saying,] عَلَيْكُمْ بِتِجَارَةِ الآخِرَةِ ‡ [*Keep ye to the merchandise of the life to come*]. (A.)

تَاجِرٌ *A merchant; one who practises traffic, merchandise,* or *commerce; a trafficker; a trader,* or *tradesman; a dealer; one who sells and buys;* (Ḳ;) *one who sells and buys for gain:* (Ksh in ii. 15:) and *a vintner,* or *seller of wine,* (Ṣ, Ḳ,) was also called thus by the Arabs: (Ṣ:) accord. to IAth, this latter is said to be the primary signification: and hence the saying in a trad., إِنَّ التَّاجِرَ فَاجِرٌ [*Verily the vintner is a transgressor*]: (TA:) pl. تِجَارٌ and تُجَّارٌ and ▾تَجْرٌ, (Ṣ, Mṣb, Ḳ,) [or rather this last is a quasi-pl. n.,] like as صَحْبٌ is of صَاحِبٌ, (Ṣ, Mṣb,) and تُجُرٌ, (Ḳ,) or this may be a pl. of تِجَارٌ. (ISd, TA.) ▾التَّجْرُ,

occurring in a verse of El-Akhtal, [for التَّاجِرُ,] is thought by ISd to be like طُهْرٌ [for طَاهِرٌ]. (TA.) — [Hence,] ‡ A man *skilful in an affair*. (Ḳ, TA.) The Arabs say, إِنَّهُ لَتَاجِرٌ بِذٰلِكَ الأَمْرِ ‡ *Verily he is skilful in that affair.* (IAạr, TA.) — And ‡ A she-camel *that is saleable*, or *easy of sale*, or *in much demand, in traffic*, and *in the market*; (A'Obeyd, Ṣ, Ḳ;) as also تَاجِرَةٌ: (Ḳ:) or the latter, a she-camel *that is goodly, and saleable*, or *in much demand*: (A:) or *that is easy of sale when offered, by reason of her excellence*: (T:) or simply, *that is easy of sale*, or *in much demand*: (Ṣ:) as though, by reason of her beauty, or goodliness, and fatness, she sold herself: (Ksh in ii. 15:) *contr. of* كَاسِدَةٌ: (Ṣ,* TA:) the pl. of تاجرة is تَوَاجِرُ. (T, A.) You say also, عَلَيْكَ بِالسِّلَعِ التَّوَاجِرِ ‡ [*Keep thou to the commodities*] *that are saleable*, or *in much demand*. (A.) And هُوَ عَلَى أَكْرَمِ تَاجِرَةٍ † *He is upon a most noble horse.* (Ḳ.)

أَرْضٌ مَتْجَرَةٌ [in the TA, مُتْجِرَةٌ, but this is wrong,] *A land in which traffic, merchandise, or commerce, is practised*; (Ṣ, L, Ḳ;) and *to which people go for the purpose of practising the same*: (Ḳ:) pl. مَتَاجِرُ. (TA.)

Quasi تجه

1. تَجَهَ, aor. ـَ, (AZ, Ḳ, art. وجه,) inf. n. تَجْهٌ; (AZ, TA, in that art.;) or, as Aṣ says, تَجُهَ, with ḍamm; (TA in that art.;) *i. q.* وَجَهَ and تَوَجَّهَ (Ḳ in that art.) and اِتَّجَهَ. (Ḳ in art. تجه.) See art. وجه.

تُجَاهَ (Ṣ, Mṣb, Ḳ, in art. وجه) and تِجَاهَ (Ṣ, Ḳ, in that art.) and تَجَاهَ (Ḳ in that art.) *i. q.* وُجَاهَ, (Ṣ, Mṣb, Ḳ, in that art.,) which is seldom used; the و being generally changed into ت. (Mṣb, ibid.)

تحت

تَحْتَ is the *contr. of* فَوْقَ: (Mṣb, Ḳ:) and التَّحْتُ [signifying *The location that is beneath, below*, or *under*,] is opposed to الفَوْقُ, and is used in relation to that which is separate from another thing; الأَسْفَلُ being used in relation to that which is united with [or a part of] another thing. (Kull.) Sometimes, (Ḳ,) تَحْتَ is an adv. n., (Mṣb, Ḳ,) having a vague signification, its meaning not being clear unless it is prefixed to another word, as in the phrase هٰذَا تَحْتَ هٰذَا [*This is beneath, below*, or *under, this*]. (Mṣb.) And sometimes, it is a simple noun; (Ḳ;) in which case, [not having the article ال,] it is indecl., with ḍammeh for its termination, (Ḳ, and I'Aḳ p. 204,) provided that the noun to which it should be prefixed is suppressed, and the meaning of this is intended to be understood, but not the word itself; (I'Aḳ ubi suprà;) as in مِنْ تَحْتُ [*Beneath, below*, or *under*]; (Ḳ;) and in the saying,

أَقَبُّ مِنْ تَحْتُ عَرِيضٌ مِنْ عَلُ

[*Lean beneath; broad above*]: otherwise, it is decl.; (I'Aḳ ibid.;) as in تَجْرِى مِنْ تَحْتِهَا الأَنْهَارُ [*Rivers running beneath them*]; (Ḳur ii. 23, &c.;) i. e., beneath their trees, (Bḍ, Jel,) and their pavilions. (Jel.) [You say also, فُلَانٌ تَحْتَ أَمْرِ فُلَانٍ † *Such a one is under the command, rule*, or *authority, of such a one*. And فُلَانٌ تَحْتَهُ فُلَانَةُ † *Such a one has as his wife such a woman*: see an ex. in a verse cited voce إِذَا.] The dim. is تُحَيْتَ: you say, هٰذَا تُحَيْتَ هٰذَا, and مِنْ تُحَيْتِ هٰذَا, *This is a little beneath, below*, or *under, this*.] — التَّحْتُ is also the sing. of التُّحُوتُ, (IAth, TA,) which latter [in the CḲ erroneously written التُّحُتُ] signifies *The low, base, vile*, or *ignoble, persons*. (A, IAth, Ḳ.) It is said in a trad., لَا تَقُومُ السَّاعَةُ حَتَّى تَظْهَرَ التُّحُوتُ وَتَهْلِكَ الوُعُولُ, i. e. [*The hour of resurrection will not come until*] *the low*, or *ignoble, persons* [*shall prevail*], *and the noble persons* [*shall perish*]: (A, IAth, TA:) or, as some say, *until the treasures that are beneath the earth appear*. (TA.) And in another trad. it is said that among the signs of the resurrection shall be this: أَنْ يَعْلُوَ التُّحُوتُ الوُعُولَ *That the weak of mankind shall have ascendency over the strong*. (TA.)

تَحْتَانِىٌّ [*Of*, or *relating to, the location that is beneath, below*, or *under*; *inferior*; *lower*;] rel. n. of تَحْت, like as فَوْقَانِىٌّ is of فَوْق: ا and ن being very often added in the rel. n. (TA.)

[تُحَيْتَ dim. of تَحْتَ, q. v.]

تحف

4. اتحفهُ بِهِ [*He presented him with it*; or *gave it to him as a* تُحْفَة, q. v.]: (Ṣ, Mṣb:) and اتحفهُ تُحْفَةً [*He made a present to him*; or *gave him a* تُحْفَة; and so اتحفهُ alone, as in an ex. cited voce أَنْفَخ]: (Ḳ, TA:) *i. q.* أَطْرَفَهُ بِتُحْفَةٍ [which properly means *He presented him with a novel*, or *rare, and pleasing present*; or *a gift not given to any one before*; or *a gift of which he* (the recipient) *did not possess the like, and which pleased him*]: and اِتَّحَفَهُ signifies the same as أَتْحَفَهُ. (TA.)

8. اِتَّحَفَهُ: see above. [Perhaps originally اِوْتَحَفَهُ: see what follows.]

تُحْفَةٌ and تُحَفَةٌ (Ṣ, Mṣb, Ḳ, &c.) *i. q.* بِرٌّ [as meaning *A gratuitous gift*, or *favour*; or *a bounty*, or *benefit*]; and لُطْفٌ [meaning *a present*; i. e. *a thing sent to another in token of courtesy* or *honour*]; (Ḳ;) in some copies of the Ḳ, لُطَف; (TA;) [i. e.] التحفة signifies مَا أَتْحَفْتَ بِهِ الرَّجُلَ (Ṣ;) or [simply] مَا أَتْحَفْتَ بِهِ مِنَ البِرِّ وَاللُّطْفِ غَيْرَكَ: (Mṣb:) and *a* طُرْفَة [which properly signifies *a gift not given to any one before*; or *of which the recipient did not possess the like, and which pleases him*;] (Ḳ, TA:) *of fruit*, and *of sweet-smelling flowers*: (TA:) [it generally means simply *a present*; or *a rare*, or *pleasing*, or *rare and pleasing, present*:] pl. تُحَفٌ. (Ṣ, Ḳ.) Accord. to some, it is originally وُحْفَةٌ: (Ḳ, TA:) Az says that its ت is originally و: (Mṣb:) and تَوَحَّفَ is quasi-pass. of أَتْحَفَهُ: (Lth, TA:) so that it should be mentioned in art. وحف: (Ḳ, TA:) being like تُهَمَة and تُخَمَة &c. (TA.) It is said in a trad., تُحْفَةُ الصَّائِمِ الدُّهْنُ وَالمِجْمَرُ [*The pleasing present for the faster is oil, and aloes-wood* or *the like*]; i. e., these dispel from him the grievousness and distress occasioned by the fasting. (TA.) And in another, respecting dates, تُحْفَةُ الكَبِيرِ وَصُمْتَةُ الصَّغِيرِ [i. e. The date is *the pleasing gift for the big*, or *full-grown*, or *old, and the quieter of the little one*, or *child*]. (TA.) And in another, تُحْفَةُ المُؤْمِنِ المَوْتُ [*The boon for the believer is death*]. (TA.)

تحين

تَحِينَ: see arts. حين and ليت.

تخ

1. تَخَّ, (JK, Ṣ, L, Ḳ,) aor. ـِ, (JK, L,) inf. n. تُخُوخٌ, (JK, L, and so in a copy of the Ṣ,) or تُخُوخَةٌ, (Ḳ, and so in a copy of the Ṣ,) or both, (TA,) *It* (dough) *became sour*: (JK, Ṣ, L, Ḳ:) *it became soft by reason of too much water*: and in like manner, clay, or mud, *so that one could not plaster with it*. (L.) Also, said of dough, *It became leavened*; or *mature*. (JK.)

4. اتخّهُ *He made it sour*; namely, dough: (JK, Ṣ, L, Ḳ:) *he made it soft by putting into it too much water*; namely, dough: and in like manner, clay, or mud, *so that he could not plaster with it*. (L.)

تَخٌّ *Sour dough*: (JK, Ṣ, A, L, Ḳ:) *such as is soft by reason of too much water*. (L.) — Also *Dregs of sesame-grain from which the oil has been expressed*; (JK, L, Ḳ;) *also called* كُسْبٌ. (TA.)

تَاخٌّ *Having no desire for food* [app. *by reason of acidity in the stomach*]. (JK, Ḳ.)

تخت

تَخْتٌ *A repository in which clothes are kept*; (Ḳ;) [*a chest for clothes*; *a wardrobe*: pl. تُخُوتٌ:] a Persian word sometimes used by the Arabs. (IDrd.) — [The following significations of the word seem to be post-classical. — *A throne*: *a seat*: *a seat of government*: *a moveable wooden bench*, or *sofa*: all which are Persian. Hence, تَخْتَرَوَانٌ, from the Persian, *A kind of covered litter, like a palanquin, borne by two camels or horses, one before and the other behind, or by two or four mules*. — So too تَخْتَةٌ *A board*, or *plank*: likewise of Persian origin. Hence the verb تَخَّتَ *He boarded*, or *planked*.]

تخذ

1. تَخِذَ, aor. ـَ, inf. n. تَخْذٌ and تَخَذٌ: see 8 in art. اخذ.

8. اتّخذ: see 8 in art. اخذ.

اِسْتَخَذَ, an irregularly formed verb: see 8 in art. اخذ.

تخرص

تِخْرِيصٌ and تِخْرِيصَةٌ (Lth, Ḳ) dial. vars. of دِخْرِيصٌ and دِخْرِيصَةٌ, (Lth,) *A* بَنِيقَة [or *gore*] of a garment: arabicized words, from تِيرِيزْ, (Lth, Ḳ, which is Persian. (Lth.)

تخم and quasi تخم

1. تَخِمَ, [originally وَخِمَ,] aor. َ, (Mṣb, and Ḳ in art. وخم,) inf. n. تَخَمٌ; (Mṣb;) and تَخُمَ, aor. ُ; (Ḳ ubi suprà;) and ↑اِتَّخَمَ; (Mṣb, and Ṣ and Ḳ &c. in art. وخم;) *He suffered from indigestion, or heaviness of the stomach arising from food which it was too weak to digest;* (Mṣb in art. وخم;) *he suffered from a disease produced by unsuitable* [or *unwholesome*] *food,* (Ḳ and TA in art. وخم,) or *by fulness of the stomach:* (TA in that art.:) followed by مِنَ الطَّعَامِ and عَنِ الطَّعَامِ. (Ṣ and TA in that art.)

3. تاخم, [inf. n. مُتَاخَمَةٌ,] *It* (a land or country) *bordered upon,* or *was conterminous with* or *to,* another land or country. (AHeyth, Mgh, Ḳ.)

4. اتخمهُ, (Ṣ and Ḳ in art. وخم,) originally أَوْخَمَهُ; (Ṣ in that art.,) or formed from تُخَمَةٌ, in consequence of imagining the ت in this word to be radical; (MF;) said of food, *It caused him to suffer from* تُخَمَة [or *indigestion*]. (Ṣ and Ḳ in art. وخم.)

8: see 1.

تَخْمٌ The *limit,* or *boundary,* (Ṣ, Mṣb,) of any town (Ṣ) or land: (Ṣ, Mṣb:) pl. تُخُومٌ: (Ṣ, Mṣb:) a poet (Aboo-Ḳeys Ibn-El-Aslat, TA) says,

يَا بَنِىَّ التُّخُومُ لَا تَظْلِمُوهَا

(Fr, Ṣ,) or, as some relate it, ↑التَّخُومُ: (TA:) accord. to the former reading, Fr says, the meaning is, [*O my sons,*] *the limits,* or *boundaries,* [*misplace ye not them*], for he does not say تَظْلِمُوهُ: but ISk says, I heard AA say, it is ↑تَخُومٌ, and the pl. is تُخُمٌ; like صَبُورٌ and صُبُرٌ: (Ṣ:) both IAạr and ISk say that the sing. and pl. are like رَسُولٌ and رُسُلٌ: (Mṣb:) but the latter mentions also تُخُومٌ, with ḍamm, as a pl. form, having no sing.: (TA:) or ↑تَخُومٌ signifies *a sign,* or *mark* [*of a boundary* or *of a way*]: and *limits,* or *boundaries:* and is sometimes with ḍamm [to the ت]: (Mgh:) Lth says that تخوم [written without any vowel-sign] signifies *a division,* or *place of division, between two districts* and *two towns* or *villages;* and the *limit,* or *boundary, of the land of any district* and *town* or *village* is its تخوم: and AHeyth says that this word signifies *limits,* or *boundaries:* (TA:) or تُخُومٌ, with ḍamm, signifies *a sign,* or *mark,* and *a limit,* or *boundary, that is a division between two lands;* and is of the fem. gender: and the pl. is تُخُومٌ also, and تُخُمٌ: (Ḳ:) this app. means that these are pls. of تُخُومٌ; but the former is a word that is used as a sing. and as a pl.; and the latter is pl. of تَخُومٌ, like as صُبُرٌ is of صَبُورٌ, and غُفُرٌ of غَفُورٌ: (TA:) or (as ISk says, TA) the sing. is ↑تَخُومٌ and تَخْمٌ (Ḳ) and ↑تَخُومَةٌ: (AHn, Ṣ,* Ḳ:) accord. to A'Obeyd, the Arabic lingnists say ↑تَخُومٌ, like صَبُورٌ, making it fem. and sing.; but the people of Syria say تُخُومٌ, with ḍamm to the ت, making it pl., and the sing. is تَخْمٌ: accord. to IB, one says ↑تَخُومٌ and تُخُومٌ, and عَذُوبٌ and عُذُوبٌ; and no fourth instance of the kind is known; [but see عَذُوبٌ;] and the Baṣrees pronounce it with ḍamm [to the ت], and the Koofees with fet-ḥ. (TA.) It is said in a trad., مَلْعُونٌ مَنْ غَيَّرَ تُخُومَ الأَرْضِ, meaning, accord. to A'Obeyd, [*Cursed is he who alters*] *the limits,* or *boundaries, of land;* and *the signs,* or *marks, of the way:* or, as some say, *the limits,* or *boundaries, of the sacred territory.* (TA.) And اجعل همّك تخوما, [or rather اِجْعَلْ لِهَمِّكَ ↑تَخُومًا,] means ‡[*Set thou to thy purpose*] *a limit,* to which go thou, and pass not beyond it. (TA.) And هُوَ طَيِّبُ التُّخُومِ †*He is good in respect of ancestry,* or *origin:* (JK:) or *in respect of natural dispositions;* or, as some relate the saying, ↑التَّخُومِ. (TA.) تُخُومٌ also signifies †*A state,* or *condition, that one desires* [app. as the limit of his wish]. (IAạr, Sh, Ḳ.)

تُخْمٌ: see تَخْمٌ.

تُخَمَةٌ, (Mṣb in the present art., and Ṣ and Ḳ in art. وخم,) originally وُخَمَةٌ, (Mṣb, and Ṣ in art. وخم,) and تُخْمَةٌ, (Mṣb, and Ṣ and Ḳ in art. وخم,) the latter vulgar, (Ṣ in art. وخم,) but occurring in poetry, (Ṣ and Ḳ in that art.,) *Indigestion, or heaviness of the stomach arising from food which it is too weak to digest;* (Mṣb in art. وخم;) *a disease produced by unsuitable* [or *unwholesome*] *food,* (Ḳ and TA in that art.,) or *by fulness of the stomach:* (TA ibid.:) pl. تُخَمَاتٌ (Ṣ and Ḳ ibid.) and تُخَمٌ. (Mṣb, and Ṣ and Ḳ in art. وخم.)

تَخُومٌ: see تَخْمٌ, in seven places.

تُخُومٌ pl. of تَخْمٌ, which see throughout: and also used as a sing.

تَخُومَةٌ: see تَخْمٌ.

طَعَامٌ مُتْخِمَةٌ, (JK, and Ṣ and Ḳ in art. وخم,) originally مَوْخَمَةٌ, (Ṣ in art. وخم,) *Food that causes one to suffer from* تُخَمَة [or *indigestion*]. (JK, and Ḳ in art. وخم.)

مُتَاخِمٌ *Conterminous* to a land (لِلْأَرْضِ). (Mgh.) You say also, هُوَ مُتَاخِمِى *He is my neighbour, his house,* or *tent, adjoining mine.* (TA in art. جمد.)

تر

1. تَرَّ, (T, M, A, Ḳ,) aor. ِ and ُ, (M, Ḳ,) the latter irregular, (TA,) inf. n. تَرٌّ and تُرُورٌ, (M, Ḳ,) *It* (a bone, M, Ḳ, or anything, M,) *became severed, separated,* or *cut off,* (T, M, Ḳ,) by a blow, or stroke [of a sword &c.]. (M, A.) And تَرَّتْ يَدُهُ, inf. n. تُرُورٌ, *His arm,* or *hand, became cut off;* (M;) and in like manner, any member: (TA:) or *fell off;* as also طَرَّتْ. (Ṣ in art. طر.) — تَرَّتِ النَّوَاةُ, (Ṣ, M, A,) aor. ِ, (Ṣ, M,) and ُ, (Ṣ,) inf. n. تُرُورٌ, (T, M,) *The date-stone leaped,* (T, M,) or *went forth,* (Ṣ, A,) from the [mess called] حَيْس [in the process of kneading], (T,) or from the stone with which it was to be broken. (Ṣ, A.) — تَرَّ عَنْ قَوْمِهِ *He was,* or *became, apart,* or *separated, from his people.* (Aṣ, T.) — تَرَّ عَنْ بَلَدِهِ *He was,* or *became,* or *went, far from his country,* or *town.* (Ṣ, M, Ḳ.) = تَرَّ, (M,) aor. ِ, (TA,) inf. n. تَرٌّ, (Ḳ,) *He* (an ostrich) *ejected what was in his belly.* (M, Ḳ.) — تَرَّ بِسَلْحِهِ, aor. ُ and ِ, *He ejected his excrement.* (AA, T.) — See also 4, in two places. = تَرَّ, (T, M, Ḳ,) sec. pers. تَرِرْتَ, (Ṣ,) aor. َ, (T, M,) and [sec. pers. تَرَرْتَ, aor.] ِ, (M,) [and app. sec. pers. تَرُرْتَ, aor. ُ,] inf. n. [of تَرِرْتَ or تَرَرْتَ] تُرُورٌ (M, Ḳ) and [of تَرُرْتَ] تَرَارَةٌ, [which last is the most common,] (Lth, T, Ṣ, M, Ḳ,) *He was,* or *became, plump:* (T in explanation of the first verb:) or *his body became plump, and his bones full of moisture:* (Lth, T, M, Ḳ:) or *he became fat, soft, thin-skinned, and plump.* (Ṣ.) — And تَرَّ, aor. ِ, *He was,* or *became, relaxed,* or *flaccid, from impatience or some other cause.* (T. [See تَارَّ.])

4. اترّ; (T, Ṣ, M, A, Ḳ;) and ↑تَرَّ, (IDrd, M, Ḳ,) inf. n. تَرٌّ; (IDrd, M;) or the former only; (M;) *He cut off* (T, Ṣ, M, Ḳ) a man's arm, or hand, by a blow, or stroke, (T, Ṣ, M, A,) of a sword; (T, Ṣ, A;) *made it to fall off:* (Ṣ:) and in like manner, any member: (M:) as also اطرّ and اطنّ. (T.) — And the former, (Ṣ, A, TA,) or ↑the latter, (M, as in the TT,) *He* (a boy) *made the piece of wood called* قُلَة *to fly away* [by striking it] *with the* مِقْلَاء. (T, Ṣ,* M,* A,* TA.) — اترّهُ قَوْمُهُ *His people separated him from themselves.* (Aṣ, T.) — اترّهُ القَضَآءُ *Fate drove him far away from his country, or town.* (Ṣ, M, Ḳ.)

R. Q. 1. تَرْتَرَهُ, inf. n. تَرْتَرَةٌ, *He moved, put in motion, put into a state of commotion, agitated,* or *shook, him,* or *it:* (Ṣ, M, Ḳ:) *he shook him vehemently:* (M:) *he seized his* (a man's) *arms,* or *hands, and shook him:* (Lth, T:) *he shook him* (a drunken man) *violently, and ordered him to breath in his face, that he might know what he had drunk;* (AA, T, Ḳ;) as also تَلْتَلَهُ, and مَزْمَزَهُ: (TA:) or تَرْتَرَةٌ and تَلْتَلَةٌ and مَزْمَزَةٌ all signify the act of *shaking, agitating,* or *putting in motion, vehemently.* (Mgh.)

R. Q. 2. تَتَرْتَرَ *He became moved, put in motion, put into a state of commotion, agitated,* or *shaken.* (Ṣ, Ḳ.)

تُرٌّ: see تَارٌّ: = and تُرٌّ.

تُرٌّ The *string,* or *line, which is extended upon,* or *against, a building,* (Aṣ, Ṣ, M,) *and according to which one builds, called in Arabic the* إِمَام; (Aṣ, M;) the *string,* or *line, by which a building is proportioned:* (Aṣ, T, M, Ḳ:) a Persian word, (T, M,) arabicized; (M;) not Arabic: (IAạr:) *it is called in Arabic the* مِطْمَر. (Aṣ, T.) A man, when angry, says to another, لَأُقِيمَنَّكَ عَلَى التُّرِّ ‡[*I will assuredly make thee to conform to the rule of right behaviour*]. (Lth, T, Ṣ, A.) = *I. q.*

أَصْلٌ: (IAạr, T, Ḳ:) so in the saying, لَأَضْطَرَّنَّكَ إِلَى تُرِّكَ وَقُحَاحِكَ [*I will assuredly impel thee, or drive thee, against thy will, to the utmost point to which thou canst go, or be brought or reduced: or constrain thee to do thine utmost*]: (IAạr, T, and L in art. قح: see قُحَاحٌ:) [accord. to ISd,] لَأَضْطَرَّنَّكَ إِلَى تُرِّكَ means إِلَى مَجْهُودِكَ [i. e. *I will assuredly make thee to have recourse to thine utmost effort, or endeavour*]. (M. [In the Ḳ, the signification of المَجْهُودُ is erroneously assigned to ▼التُّرُّ. See also the saying لَأُلْجِئَنَّكَ إِلَى قُرِّ قَرَارِكَ explained voce قَرَارٌ.])

تَرِىٌّ An arm, or a hand, *cut off*. (Ḳ.)

تَرَاتِرُ [a pl. of which the sing. is not mentioned] *Great*, or *formidable*, or *terrible*, *things* or *events* or *affairs*: (Ṣ:) *distresses*, *afflictions*, or *calamities*; (M, A, Ḳ;) *such as are in war*. (A.)

تَارٌّ A man *apart*, or *separate*, *from his people*. (Aṣ, T.) ― *Plump* (Lth, T, Ṣ, A) *in body*, (Lth, T,) *and having the bones full of moisture*; (Lth, T, A;) *fat*, *soft*, *thin-skinned*, *and plump*: (Ṣ, TA:) applied to a youth: fem. with ة, applied to a girl; (A, TA;) meaning [*plump* &c.: or] *beautiful and foolish and soft* or *weak*. (T.) You say, غُلَامٌ تَارٌّ طَارٌّ [*A boy that is plump, and with bones full of moisture, whose mustache is growing forth*]. (A.) And قَصَبَةٌ تَارَّةٌ [*A bone of the kind called* قصبة *full of moisture*]. (A.) ― *Relaxed*, or *flaccid*, *by reason of impatience* (جَزَعٍ T) or *hunger* (جُوعٍ Ḳ) [or the contrary (see أَتَرُّ شَىْءٍ, below,)] *or some other cause*: (T, Ḳ:) so says Abu-l-'Abbás. (T.) ― A *tall* man; as also ▼تُرٌّ, which is app. [a contraction of تُرُرٌ,] of the measure فُعُلٌ. (M.)

أَتَرُّ شَىْءٍ A man *in the most relaxed state by reason of fullness of the belly*: (TA:) or, accord. to Abu-l-'Abbás, *by reason of fatigue*. (T, TA.)

ترب

1. تَرِبَ, (Ṣ, M, Ḳ,) aor. ـَ, (Ḳ,) inf. n. تَرَبٌ, (M,) *It* (a thing) *became dusted*, or *dusty*; *dust lighted upon it*: (Ṣ, TA:) *it* (a place, M,) *had much dust*, or *earth*; *abounded with dust*, or *earth*. (M, Ḳ, TA.) ― *He* (a man, M) *had dust*, or *earth*, *in his hand*. (M, Ḳ.) ― Also, (T, Ṣ, M, &c.,) inf. n. as above, (M,) *He clave to the dust*, or *earth*: (M, Ḳ:) or *he clave to the dust*, or *earth*, *by reason of poverty*; (M;) *he became so poor that he clave to the dust*, or *earth*: (A'Obeyd, T:) or *he became poor*, (T, Ṣ, Mṣb,) *as though he clave to the dust*, or *earth*: (Ṣ, Mṣb:) and *he suffered loss, and became poor*, (M, Ḳ,) *so that he clave to the dust*, or *earth*; (M;) inf. n. as above, (M, Ḳ,) and مَتْرَبَةٌ, (M,) or مَتْرَبٌ, (Ḳ,) or both of these: (TA:) *his wealth became little*; (A;) as also ▼اترب, (M, A, Ḳ,) and ▼تَرَّبَ: (Ḳ:) or ▼اترب signifies, (T, Ṣ, M,) or signifies also, (A, Ḳ,) and so تَرِبَ, (A,) and ▼تَرَّبَ, (Ḳ,) *his wealth became much*, or *abundant*, (T, M, A, Ḳ,) *so that it was like the dust*, or *earth*; which is the more known meaning of the verb; (M;) or *he became rich*; (Ṣ, Mṣb;) *as though he became possessed of wealth equal in quantity to the dust*, or *earth*: (Ṣ, A:) accord. to Abu-l-'Abbás, ▼تَتْرِيبٌ signifies [the *having*] *much wealth*; and also [the *having*] *little wealth*. (T.) You say, تَرِبَ بَعْدَ مَا ▼أَتْرَبَ, meaning *He became poor after he had been rich*. (A.) ― تَرِبَتْ يَدَاكَ, (T, Ṣ, A, Mṣb, in the M and Ḳ يَدَاهُ,) a form of imprecation, (Ṣ, Mṣb,) meaning [*May thine arms*, or *thy hands*, *cleave to the dust*, or *earth*, *by reason of poverty*; as is implied in the T: or] *may thy hands have in them dust*, or *earth*: (Ḥam p. 275:) or *mayest thou not obtain*, or *attain*, *good*: (Ṣ, Ḳ:*) or *mayest thou be unsuccessful*, or *fail of attaining thy desire, and suffer loss*: (A:) occurring in a trad., and as some relate, (A 'Obeyd, T,) not meant as an imprecation; (A 'Obeyd, T, Mṣb;) being a phrase current with the Arabs, who use it without desiring its fulfilment; (A'Obeyd, T;) but meant to incite, or instigate: (Mṣb:) some say that it means *may thy hands become rich*; but this is a mistake: (A'Obeyd, T:) and it is said to mean لِلّٰهِ دَرُّكَ [which see in art. در]: and some say that it is literally an imprecation: but the first assertion is the most worthy of respect, (that it is not meant as an imprecation,) and is corroborated by the saying, in a trad., انْعَمْ صَبَاحًا تَرِبَتْ يَدَاكَ [*Mayest thou have a pleasant morning: may thine arms*, or *thy hands*, &c.]. (TA.) تَرِبَ جَبِينُهُ [*May his forehead* (for so جبين here means, as it does in some other instances,) *cleave to the dust*, or *earth*,] was said by Mohammad in reproving a man, and is said to mean a prayer that the man might be frequent in prostrating himself in prayer. (TA from a trad.) And he said to one of his companions, تَرِبَتْ نَحْرُكَ [*May the uppermost part of thy breast cleave to the dust*, or *earth*], and the man was [afterwards] slain a martyr: therefore this is to be understood in its obvious sense. (TA.) ― See also 4, in four places.

2. تَرَّبَ, inf. n. تَتْرِيبٌ: see 1, in three places: ― and see also 4, in four places.

3. تَارَبَتْهَا *She became her* تِرْب; (M, Ḳ;) [i. e.] *she* (a girl) *matched her*, namely, another girl; *she was*, or *became*, *her match*, *fellow*, or *equal*; syn. حَاذَتْهَا. (A, TA.) ― [The inf. n.] مُتَارَبَةٌ also signifies The *associating*, or *consorting*, *of* أَتْرَاب [pl. of تِرْبٌ, q. v.]. (Ḳ.)

4. اترب: see 1, in three places. ― اتربهُ *He put dust*, or *earth*, *upon it*, (Ṣ, M, A, Ḳ,) namely, a thing; (Ṣ, M;) as also ▼تَرَّبَهُ: (A, Ḳ:) or the latter, inf. n. تَتْرِيبٌ, signifies *he defiled it*, or *soiled it*, (namely, a thing,) *with dust*, or *earth*: (Ṣ:) or you say, ▼تَرَّبَهُ, (TA,) or تَرَّبَهُ بِالتُّرَابِ, (Mṣb,) aor. ـِ, (Mṣb, TA,) inf. n. (TA,) [meaning *he sprinkled it with dust*,] namely, a writing [for the purpose of drying up the ink], (Mṣb,) or a paper; (TA;) and ▼تَرَّبَهُ, (T, Mṣb, TA,) with teshdeed, (Mṣb,) [meaning *he sprinkled much dust upon it*; or *sprinkled it much with dust*;] namely, a writing; (T, Mṣb, TA;) the latter having an intensive signification: (Mṣb:) or ▼the former of the last two verbs is used in speaking of anything that is improved, or put into a right or proper state [by means of dust or earth]; and ▼the latter of them, in speaking of anything that is injured or marred or spoiled [thereby]: you say, ▼تَرِّبِ الإِهَابَ [*She sprinkled*, or *put*, *dust*, or *earth*, *upon the hide*], to prepare it properly for use; and so of a skin for water or milk. (TA.) It is said in a trad., [accord. to one reading,] اتْرِبُوا الكِتَابَ [*Sprinkle ye the writing with dust*]. (Ṣ. [So in three copies of that work: probably أَتْرِبُوا; but perhaps ▼اتْرِبُوا: the reading commonly known is ▼تَرِّبُوا.]) ― اترب also signifies *He possessed a slave who had been possessed three times*. (T, Ḳ.)

5. تترّب *He*, (T,) or *it*, (Ṣ,) *became defiled*, or *soiled*, (T, Ṣ,) *in the dust*, or *earth*, (T,) or *with dust*, or *earth*: (Ṣ:) *it had dust*, or *earth*, *sticking to it*. (M.)

تَرْبٌ: see تُرَابٌ.

تُرْبٌ: see تُرَابٌ, in three places.

تِرْبٌ *One born at the same time with thee*; (M, Ḳ;) *a coëtanean*; *a contemporary in birth*; *an equal in age*: *an equal*; *a match*; *a fellow*; *a peer*, or *compeer*: syn. لِدَةٌ: (T, Ṣ, M, A, Ḳ:) and سِنٌّ: (M, A, Ḳ:) applied to a male and to a female; (TA;) but mostly to a female; (M;) or, accord. to an opinion confirmed by [most of] the leading lexicologists, only to a female; and سِنٌّ is applied, as also قِرْنٌ, to a male; and لِدَةٌ, to a male and a female: (TA:) pl. أَتْرَابٌ. (Ṣ, M, A.) [The following exs. are given.] You say, [applying it to a female,] هٰذِهِ تِرْبُ هٰذِهِ, (T, Ṣ,) and هِىَ تِرْبُهَا, (M,) and هِىَ تِرْبِى; (Ḳ;) and [applying it to females and males,] هُمَا تِرْبَانِ, (T, A,) and هُنَّ أَتْرَابٌ, (Ṣ, A,) and هُمْ أَتْرَابٌ. (A.) Accord. to Th, عُرُبًا أَتْرَابًا, in the Ḳur [lvi. 36], means [*Showing love to their husbands*;] *like*, or *equal*, *unto them*, or *resembling them*: which is a good rendering, as there is no begetting or bearing of children, [or rather as the latter word does not apply to females born or generated,] in that case. (TA.)

تَرِبٌ, applied to a place, (M, TA,) and to soil, (TA,) *Abounding with dust*; *dusty*: (T, M, TA:) and to food, (T,) or flesh-meat, (A,) *defiled*, or *soiled*, (T, A,) *in the dust*, (T,) or *with dust*. (A.) You say also ▼أَرْضٌ تَرِبَةٌ meaning *Land in which are dust and moist earth*. (M.) And رِيحٌ تَرِبَةٌ, (T, Ṣ, M,) and تَرِبٌ, (T,) *A wind that carries with it dust*: (T:) or *that brings dust*: (Ṣ:) or *that drives along the dust*: [or *having dust*: for] thus used it is a possessive epithet. (M.) ― Also *Cleaving to the dust by reason of want*; *having nothing between him and the earth*: (IAạr, T:) [*cleaving to the dust by reason of poverty*; see 1:] *poor*, *as though cleaving to the dust*: (Mṣb:) and [simply,] *poor*: (IAạr, T, TA:) or *needy*, or *in want*. (M.) [See also مُتْرِبٌ.]

تُرْبَةٌ: see تُرَابٌ, in seven places. ― Also A man's رَمْس [i. e. his *grave*: so in the present day: pl. تُرَبٌ: or the *earth*, or *dust, thereof*]: (M:) or *a cemetery, burial-place*, or *place of graves* or *of a grave:* [so, too, in the present day:] pl. تُرَبٌ. (Mṣb.)

تَرِبَةٌ: see the word next following.

تُرْبَةٌ The *end of a finger;* i. e. the *joint in which is the nail;* syn. أُنْمُلَةٌ: (Ṣ, Ḳ:) pl. تُرُبَاتٌ. (Ṣ.) — Also, (Ṣ, M, Ḳ,) and ▼ تَرِبَةٌ, and ▼ تُرَبَآءُ, (M, Ḳ,) *A certain plant,* (Ṣ, M, Ḳ,) *growing in the plains*, or *in soft land, having serrated leaves:* or, as some say, *a certain thorny tree, of which the fruit is like a suspended unripe date, growing in the plains*, or *in soft land, and in rugged ground, and in Tihámeh:* accord. to AḤn, the تُرْبَة is *a green herb*, or *leguminous plant, that has a purging effect upon camels:* (M:) [accord. to Meyd, as stated by Golius, *what is called in Persian* خنفج; i. e. the plant *thlaspi;* and to this it is applied in the present day.]

تُرَبَآءُ: see تُرَابٌ, in five places: — and see تَرِبٌ: — and تُرْبَةٌ.

تُرَبَآءُ: see تُرَابٌ.

تَرَبُوتٌ A *submissive*, or *tractable*, camel; applied to the male (T, Ṣ, M, Ḳ) and to the female: (T, Ṣ, Ḳ:) from تُرَابٌ, (Ṣ, M,) because of the abasement thereof; or, as Sb holds it to be, for دَرَبُوتٌ, by the change of د into ت: accord. to Lḥ, a [camel such as is termed] بَكْرٌ that is *trained*, or *rendered submissive* or *tractable;* and in like manner a she-camel, one *that will follow a person if he takes hold of her lip or her eyelash:* and Aṣ, who derives it from تُرَابٌ, says that this epithet is applied to land, or ground, and any other thing, that is ذَلُولٌ [i. e. *easy to walk or ride upon*, &c.]. (M.)

تُرَابٌ and ▼ تُرْبٌ (Lth, T, Ṣ, M, A, Mṣb, Ḳ) and ▼ تُرُبٌ (CK [but this I do not find elsewhere]) and ▼ تُرْبَةٌ (Ṣ, A,* Ḳ) and ▼ تُرْبَآءُ (Lth, T, Ṣ, A,* Ḳ) and ▼ تُرَبَآءُ (Ṣ, M, Ḳ) and ▼ تَوْرَابٌ and ▼ تَوْرَبٌ and ▼ تَيْرَابٌ and ▼ تَيْرَبٌ [and ▼ تِيرَبٌ as will be seen below] and ▼ تَرِيبٌ (Ṣ, M, Ḳ) and ▼ تِرْيَبٌ, (M, Ḳ) accord. to MF ▼ تَرْيَبٌ, which is perhaps a dial. var., and accord. to some ▼ تِرْيِبٌ, and ▼ تُرْيَابٌ, (TA,) signify the same, (Lth, T, Ṣ, M, A, Ḳ,) and are words of which the meaning is well known: (A, Ḳ:) [i. e. *Dust:* and *earth:* generally the former; i. e. *fine, dry, particles of earth;* as when we say, اَلرِّيحُ تَسُوقُ التُّرَابَ *The wind drives along the dust:* but we also use the expression تُرَابٌ نَدٍ, meaning *moist earth*, the explanation, in Lexicons, of the word ثَرًى: ثَرًى is تُرَابٌ; and when it ceases to be moist, it is still تراب, but is not then called ثرى: (Mṣb voce ثرى:) accord. to Fr, تُرَابٌ is a gen. n., from which is formed neither dual nor pl.: and its rel. n. is ▼ تُرَابِىٌّ: (TA:) [but when it means *a kind of dust* or *earth*, as ▼ تُرْبَةٌ also does sometimes, it has a pl.: in this case,] accord. to Lḥ, (M,) its pl. is أَتْرِبَةٌ [a pl. of pauc.] and تِرْبَانٌ [a pl. of mult.]; (Ṣ, M, Ḳ;) and some add تُرْبَانٌ: (TA:) [and when ▼ تُرْبَةٌ has this, or a similar, meaning, it has for its pl. تُرَبٌ; as in the phrase أَطْيَبُ التُّرَبِ *the best of the kinds of earth*, occurring in this art. in the A:] but no pl. of any of the other syn. words mentioned above has been heard: (M, Ḳ:) AAF says that تراب is the pl. of ترب; [app. meaning that تُرَابٌ is a quasi-pl. n. (which is often called in lexicons a pl.) of تُرْبٌ;] but MF observes that this requires consideration: (TA:) Lth says that ▼ تُرْبٌ and تُرَابٌ are syn.; but when the fem. forms of these words are used, they say, ▼ أَرْضٌ طَيِّبَةُ التُّرْبَةِ meaning *Land that is good in respect of the natural constitution of its dust* or *earth;* and ▼ تُرَابَةٌ when meaning *A layer*, or *lamina, of dust* or *earth, such as is not perceived by the sight, but only by the imagination:* (T:) or this last word and ▼ تُرْبَةٌ signify *a portion of dust* or *earth:* and ▼ تُرْبَةُ الأَرْضِ signifies *the exterior*, or *external part, of the earth:* (M:) and ▼ التَّرْبَآءُ, *the earth* (Ṣ, Ḳ) *itself.* (Ṣ.) The Arabs said, التُّرَابُ لَكَ [*Dust*, or *earth, be thy lot*]; using the nom. case, although meaning an imprecation, because the word is a simple subst., not an inf. n.: but Lḥ mentions the phrase التُّرَابَ لِلْأَبْعَدِ [*Dust*, or *earth, be the lot of the remote from good*]; saying that the accus. case is used, as though the phrase were an imprecation [of the ordinary kind, in which an inf. n. is used in the accus. case as the absolute complement of its own verb understood]. (M.) And لَهُ التُّرَابُ is a phrase used as meaning † [*He has*, or *shall have*, or *may he have*,] *disappointment*, (Mṣb in art. عهر,) or, *nothing.* (A'Obeyd, Mgh in art. فرش.) تُرْبًا ▼ لَهُ وَجَنْدَلًا is also a form of imprecation, in which substs. in the proper sense of the term are used in the manner of inf. ns., put in the accus. case by reason of a verb unexpressed; as though it were for تَرِبَتْ يَدَاهُ وَجُنْدِلَتْ [*May his arms*, or *his hands, cleave to the dust*, or *earth, and the stones*, by reason of poverty]: and some of the Arabs put the nouns in the nom. case, still using the phrase in the same sense, as though they were in the accus. (M.) One says also, ▼ بِفِيهِ التَّيْرَبُ and ▼ التِّيرَبُ and ▼ التَّوْرَبُ and ▼ التَّوْرَابُ and ▼ التُّرْبَآءُ [*In his mouth is dust*, or *earth:* or *may dust*, or *earth, be in his mouth;* i. e. may he die, or be in his grave]. (T.) It is said in a trad. that God created the ▼ تُرْبَة [meaning the *dust*, or *soil*, or, accord. to the TA the *earth* (أَرْض),] on the seventh day of the week; and created upon it the mountains on the first day; and the trees, on the second day. (T.) And one says, ▼ لَأَضْرِبَنَّهُ حَتَّى يَعَضَّ بِالتُّرْبَآءِ, (Lth, T, A,) meaning [*I will assuredly beat him so that he shall bite*] *the dust*, or *earth.* (Lth, T.) And ▼ بَيْنَهُمَا مَا بَيْنَ الجَرْبَآءِ وَالتَّرْبَآءِ, meaning [*Between them two is the space that is between*] *the heaven and the earth.* (A.)

تَرِيبٌ: see تُرَابٌ: — and see also تَرِيبَةٌ, in two places.

تِرْيَبٌ:
تَرْيَبٌ:
تِرْيِبٌ:
تُرَابَةٌ:
} see تُرَابٌ.

تَرِيبَةٌ, (Ṣ, M, TA,) or ▼ تَرِيبٌ, (TA,) sing. of تَرَائِبُ, (Ṣ, M, TA,) which signifies The *part of the breast which is the place of the collar*, or *necklace:* (T, M, Ḳ:) so by the common consent of the lexicologists: (T:) or the *bones of the breast:* (M, A, Ḳ:) or the *bones of the breast that are between the collar-bone and the pap:* (Ṣ:) or the *part of the breast*, or *chest, that is next to the two collar-bones:* or the *part that is between the two breasts and the collar-bones:* or *four ribs of the right side of the chest and four of the left thereof:* (M, Ḳ:) or the *two arms and two legs and two eyes:* (T, M, Ḳ:) it is also said that the تَرِيبَتَانِ are the *two ribs that are next to the two collar-bones:* IAth says that the تَرِيبَة is the *uppermost part of the human breast, beneath the chin;* and its pl. is as above: accord. to IF, in the Mj, the ▼ تريب is the *breast*, or *chest:* MF says that ترائب relates to males and females in common; but most of the authors on strange words affirm decidedly that it is peculiar to women: (TA:) the تَرِيبَة of the camel is the *part in which it is stabbed*, or *stuck;* syn. مَنْحَر. (M.)

تُرَابِىٌّ rel. n. of تُرَابٌ, q. v. (Fr, TA.)

تُرْيَابٌ: see تُرَابٌ.

تَوْرَبٌ:
تَيْرَبٌ:
تِيرَبٌ:
تَوْرَابٌ:
} see تُرَابٌ, first sentence, and near the end of the paragraph.

تَيْرَابٌ: see تُرَابٌ.

أَتْرَبُ: see what next follows.

مُتْرِبٌ *Possessing much wealth;* (T, Ḳ;) *rich; without want;* or *having wealth like the dust*, or *earth:* (Lḥ and M: [in the TA, اترب is mentioned as having this meaning; perhaps by a mistranscription: if not, it must be ▼ أَتْرَبُ:]) and *having little wealth:* thus it bears two contr. significations: (Ḳ:) but the former is the more known. (TA.)

مَتْرَبَةٌ The *suffering loss, and becoming poor, so as to cleave to the dust*, or *earth;* an inf. n. of تَرِبَ: (M:) or *poverty*, or *neediness:* (Ṣ, TA:) [or (as a word of the same class as مَجْبَنَةٌ and مَبْخَلَةٌ) *a cause of cleaving to the dust*, or *earth:* and hence,] ذُو مَتْرَبَةٍ *Poor, so as to be cleaving to the dust*, or *earth:* (T:) or [simply] *cleaving to the dust*, or *earth.* (Ṣ.)

Quasi ترث

تُرَاثٌ: see وِرْثٌ and وَرِثَ.

ترج

تُرُنْجٌ and تُرُنْجَةٌ: see what follows.

أُتْرُجٌّ, (Ṣ, Mṣb, Ḳ, &c.,) the most chaste of the forms here mentioned, (Az, Mṣb, MF, TA,) a pl., (AḤát, MF, TA,) [or rather a coll. gen. n.,] and ▼ تُرُنْجٌ, (AZ, Ṣ, Mṣb, Ḳ, &c.,) [which is Persian,] a dial. var. of weak authority, (Mṣb,) by some disallowed, (MF, TA,) used by the vulgar, (TA,) the ن in which is by common consent held to be augmentative, (MF, TA,) likewise a pl., (TA,) [or coll. gen. n.,] and ▼ أُتْرُنْج, mentioned by Ibn-Hishám El-Lakhmee, in his Faseeḥ, and also used by the vulgar, (TA,) and by some of the people of Ḥims, (Lth cited in the L voce حُمَّ, q. v.,) [and this is likewise a coll. gen. n.,] and أُتْرُجَّةٌ, (Ṣ, Mṣb, Ḳ, &c.,) which is the sing. of the first, (AḤát, MF, TA,) or its n. un., (L, Mṣb,) also pronounced أُتْرُجَةٌ, without teshdeed, (TA,) and ▼ تُرُنْجَةٌ, (AZ, Ṣ, L, &c.,) likewise a n. un., (L,) *A certain fruit,* (Mṣb,) *well known,* (L, Mṣb, Ḳ,) *plentiful in the land of the Arabs, but not growing wild,* (L, TA,) [*of the species citrus medica,* or *citron; of which there are two varieties in Egypt; one, of the form of the lemon, but larger, there called* تُرُنْج بَلَدِىّ; *the other, ribbed, and called* تُرُنْج مُضَبَّع: accord. to Golius, *citrons of a large size, which have a sweeter peel than others, and are of a size nearly equal to that of a melon:*] *the sour sort allays the lust of women, clears the complexion, and removes the* [*discoloration of the face termed*] كَلَف, (Ḳ, TA,) *that arises from phlegm;* (TA;) *the peel thereof, put among clothes, preserves them from the moth-worm:* (Ḳ, TA:) *it is also beneficial as an antidote against the various kinds of poison; the smelling it in times of plague,* or *pestilence, is beneficial in the highest degree; and jinn,* or *genii, do not enter the house in which it is;* wherefore a reciter of the Ḳur-án is appropriately likened to it: (TA:) the pl. of أُتْرُجَّةٌ is أُتْرُجّ as well as أُتْرُجَّات: [or rather the latter is a coll. gen. n., as stated above:] but one should not say تُرُنْجَاتٌ [app. because it is vulgar; for it is agreeable with analogy as pl. of تُرُنْجَةٌ; as is also أُتْرُنْجَات as pl. of ▼ أُتْرُنْجَةٌ]. (AḤát, MF, TA.)

أُتْرُنْج and أُتْرُنْجَة: see above.

ترجم

Q. 1. تَرْجَمَهُ, (Ṣ in art. رجم, and Mṣb and Ḳ in the present art.,) and تَرْجَمَ عَنْهُ, (Ḳ,) inf. n. تَرْجَمَةٌ, (KL,) *He interpreted it,* (Ṣ, Mṣb, KL, Ḳ,) or *explained it in another language;* (Ṣ, Mṣb, KL;) namely, the speech, or language, (Ṣ, Mṣb, Ḳ,) of another person: (Mṣb:) or, as some say, *translated it from one language into another:* (TA:) and *he explained it;* namely, his own speech. (Mṣb.) [This verb is essentially the same in Arabic, Chaldee, and Ethiopic.] — تَرْجَمَهُ, inf. n. as above, also signifies *He wrote his life; wrote a biography,* or *biographical notice, of him.* (TA, passim; and other works of post-classical times.) — Accord. to the Ḳ, the ت in this verb is a radical: but see تُرْجُمَانٌ, below. (TA.)

تَرْجَمَةٌ [inf. n. of the verb above: used as a simple subst., *An interpretation: a translation:* pl. تَرَاجِمُ. — Also] *A life,* or *biography,* or *biographical notice,* of any person: pl. as above. (TA, passim; and other works of post-classical times.) — And *An article, a head, chapter, section,* or *paragraph,* of a book. (TA, passim; and other works of post-classical times.)

تَرْجَمَانٌ and تُرْجُمَانٌ and تَرْجُمَانٌ, (Ṣ in art. رجم, and Mṣb and Ḳ in the present art.,) of which three dial. vars. the first is the best, (Mṣb,) and is that which commonly obtains, (TA,) *An interpreter;* (Ṣ, Mṣb, Ḳ;) *an explainer of speech in another language:* (Ṣ, Mṣb:) [*a translator:* (see the verb, above:)] pl. تَرَاجِمُ and تَرَاجِمَةٌ; which latter favours the opinion of those who hold the word to be of foreign origin. (Ṣ, Mṣb.) The ت and م are [said to be] radicals; but J makes the ت to be augmentative, and ترجمان is mentioned in the T [as well as in the Ṣ] in art. رجم, though the author of the T has mentioned the verb among quadriliteral-radical words; and there is a reason [for deriving it from رَجَمَ], for one says لِسَانٌ مِرْجَمٌ meaning "a tongue that is chaste, or perspicuous, and copious, in speech:" most, however, hold the ت to be a radical. (Mṣb.) It is said in the Ḳ that the verb shows the ت to be radical; whereas J and AḤei and IḲt hold it to be augmentative; but there is a difference of opinion whether it be from الرَّجْمُ بِالحِجَارَةِ [the throwing stones], or from الرَّجْمُ بِالغَيْبِ [the conjecturing, or speaking conjecturally]; and also whether it be Arabic, or arabicized from ترغمان [a word which I do not know in Persian nor in any other language]: (MF, TA:) if arabicized, the present is its proper place. (TA.)

مُتَرْجَمٌ [*Interpreted:* or *translated.* — And also The *subject of a biography,* or *biographical notice.* — And] † *Confused,* or *dubious.* (Ḥar p. 537.)

ترح

1. تَرِحَ, aor. ـَ, inf. n. تَرَحٌ, *He grieved; he was,* or *became, sorrowful, unhappy,* or *anxious;* (Mṣb, Ḳ;) syn. حَزِنَ; (Mṣb;) [*contr. of* فَرِحَ; (see تَرَحٌ, below;)] as also ▼ تترّح. (Ḳ.) — [Also *He perished,* or *died: became cut off; was put an end to;* or *came to an end:* so accord. to explanations of تَرَحٌ given below on the authority of IAth.]

2. ترّحهُ, (Ṣ, A, Ḳ,) inf. n. تَتْرِيحٌ; (Ṣ, Ḳ;) and ▼ اترحهُ; (A, Mṣb;) *It* (an affair, or an event, &c., TA,) *grieved him; it made him sorrowful, unhappy,* or *anxious.* (Ṣ, A, Mṣb, Ḳ.) A poet cited by IAạr says,

قَدْ طَالَ مَا تَرَّحَهَا المُتَرِّحُ

[*Long did that which made unhappy make her,* or *them, unhappy*]; meaning that the pasturage rendered troublesome her, or their, state. (Th, AZ, TA.)

4: see 2.

5: see 1.

تَرْحٌ *Poverty; need; indigence.* (Ḳ.)

تَرَحٌ *Grief, sorrow, unhappiness,* or *anxiety;* syn. حُزْنٌ, (Mṣb,) or هَمٌّ, (Ḳ,) or غَمٌّ; (Ḥar p. 141;) *contr. of* فَرَحٌ. (Ṣ, A.) [It is the inf. n. of 1; but used as a subst., it has a pl., namely, أَتْرَاحٌ, like أَفْرَاحٌ. Hence the saying,] مَا الدُّنْيَا إِلَّا فَرَحٌ وَتَرَحٌ [*The present world,* or *life, is nothing but* a scene, or state, of *joy and grief*]. (A.) — *A perishing,* or *dying: becoming cut off; being put an end to;* or *coming to an end.* (IAth, TA.) — *A descending, going down,* or *going down a declivity;* syn. هُبُوطٌ. (Ibn-Munádhir, Ḳ.) One says, مَا زِلْنَا مُذُ اللَّيْلَةِ فِى تَرَحٍ i. e. [*We have not ceased from the beginning of this night to be*] *in a state of descending,* &c. (Ibn-Munádhir.)

تَرِحٌ *Grieving; sorrowing; unhappy.* (Mṣb.) — A man (A) *who possesses,* or *does, little,* or *no, good,* (A, Ḳ,) *so that he who asks of him grieves.* (A.)

تَرْحَةٌ *A grief; a sorrow; an unhappiness.* (L.) [Hence the saying,] مَا مِنْ فَرْحَةٍ إِلَّا وَبَعْدَهَا تَرْحَةٌ [*There is no joy but there is after it a grief*]. (A.)

مُتْرَحٌ, or مُتَرَّحٌ, accord. to different copies of the Ḳ, (TA,) One *who ceases not to hear and see that which does not please him.* (Ḳ.)

[مَتْرَحَةٌ *A cause of grief, sorrow, unhappiness,* or *anxiety:* pl. مَتَارِحُ. Hence the saying,] تَرَّحَتْهُ المَتَارِحُ [*Misfortunes* (lit. *the causes of grief,* &c.,) *grieved him,* or *made him sorrowful,* &c.]. (A.)

مُتَرَّحٌ *Strait, difficult,* or *distressful,* life. (A, Ḳ.) — *A scanty* torrent, or flow of water, *in which is a stopping,* or *an interruption.* (Ḳ.) — A garment, or piece of cloth, *dyed so as to be saturated with the dye.* (Az, Ḳ.)

مِتْرَاحٌ A she-camel *whose milk soon comes to an end,* or *stops:* (Ṣ, L:) pl. مَتَارِيحُ. (L.)

ترس

1. تَرَسَ البَابَ, aor. ـُ, inf. n. تَرْسٌ, *He fastened,* or *closed, the door* [with a bar or] *in any manner.* (TA.)

2. ترّس, inf. n. تَتْرِيسٌ, *He made* a person *to arm himself with a shield.* (KL.) — See also 5.

5. تترّس, (Ṣ, A, Ḳ,) or تترّس بِتُرْسٍ, (M,) *He defended himself with a* تُرْس [or *shield*]; (Ṣ, M, A,* Ḳ;) as also ▼ ترّس, inf. n. تَتْرِيسٌ; (Ṣ, Ḳ;) and ▼ اِتَّرَسَ, (Sb, M, A, TA,) inf. n. اِتِّرَاسٌ, of the measure اِفْتِعَالٌ: (TA:) and تترّس بِشَىْءٍ *he made a thing to be as a* تُرْس; *he defended,* or *protected, himself with it.* (Mṣb.) You say also, تَتَرَّسْتُ بِكَ مِنَ الحَدَثَانِ فَتَتَرَّسْتُ مِنْ نِبَالِ الزَّمَانِ ‡ [*I protected myself by thee from calamities, and so shielded myself from the arrows of fortune*]. (A.) And أَخَذَتْ إِبِلِى سِلَاحَهَا وَتَتَرَّسَتْ بِتُرْسِهَا, meaning ‡ *My camels became fat and goodly, and prevented their owner from slaughtering them.* (A, TA.) [See سِلَاحٌ.]

8. see 5.

تُرْسٌ [*A shield;*] *a certain piece of defensive*

armour; (M, TA;) a thing well known: (A, Mṣb, Ḳ:) pl. تِرَسَةٌ and تِرَاسٌ (Ṣ, M, Mṣb, Ḳ) and تِرَاسَةٌ (Ṣ) and تُرُوسٌ, [all pls. of mult.,] and أَتْرَاسٌ, [a pl. of pauc.,] (Ṣ, M, Mṣb, Ḳ,) but not أَتْرِسَةٌ. (ISk, Ṣ, Mṣb.) A تُرْس that is made of skins, without wood and without sinews in it, is called حَجَفَةٌ and دَرَقَةٌ. (Mṣb.) — Also ‡ The *disk* of the sun. (A,* TA.) — And ‡ *A smooth, round, level piece* of ground: (A, TA:) or *a rugged piece* of hard, or hard and level, ground. (Ibn-'Abbád, Ḳ.) — See also مَتْرَس.

تِرَاسَةٌ The *art of making shields.* (Ḳ.)

تَرَّاسٌ A man *having a shield;* (Ṣ, M, A, Ḳ;) as also ▾ تَارِسٌ. (Ṣ, A.) — And *A maker of shields.* (Ḳ.)

تَارِسٌ : see تَرَّاسٌ.

مَتْرَسٌ; so accord. to El-Ḥáfidh Ibn-Ḥajar, and this is the correct form; written in the T and the Towsheeḥ مِتْرَسٌ; and by some, مَتْرِسٌ [as in the CḲ]; and by some, مُتْرِسٌ [as I find it in two copies of the Ṣ and in a copy of the Ḳ]; (TA;) [*A wooden door-bar;*] *a piece of wood that is put behind the door;* (Ṣ, Ḳ;) the شِجَار [or *wooden bar*] *that is put against the door as a stay:* (T, L, TA:) [مَتْرَسٌ is] a Persian word, [having the above-mentioned signification, but originally a contraction of مَهْ تَرْسْ, and] meaning "fear not thou," with it [being here understood]: (T, Ḳ, TA:) or the name of this piece of wood in Arabic is ▾ تُرْسٌ: (M, TA:) which also signifies *a piece of wood with which a couch-frame* (سَرِير) *is repaired, by its being affixed as a* ضَبَّة: (M:) [and the Arabic word شِجَار has this latter signification also:] the Persian word is مَتَرْسْ. (M, TA.) — Their saying مَتَرْسْ, with fet-ḥ to the م and ت, and sukoon to the ر, means [also] *Security* [*is given*] *to thee, therefore fear thou not:* it is said to be Persian. (Mṣb.)

مِتْرَسَةٌ, (M, A,) or مَتْرَسَةٌ, (Ḳ, accord. to the TA, [and so I find in a MS. copy of that work, and in the CḲ, but the former is probably the correct form, being agreeable with analogy, like مِشْمَلَةٌ and مِجْنَبَةٌ &c.,]) *Anything by which one is defended,* or *protected.* (M, Mṣb, Ḳ.) You say also هُوَ مِتْرَسَةٌ لَكَ ‡ [*He is a cause of defence,* or *protection, to thee*]. (A.)

بَابٌ مَتْرُوسٌ *A door fastened,* or *closed,* [*with a bar,* or] *in any manner.* (TA.)

ترع

1. تَرِعَ, aor. ـَ , inf. n. تَرَعٌ, *It* (a vessel, Ṣ, or a thing, TA) *was,* or *became, full,* or *filled;* (Ṣ, Z, Ḳ;) as also ▾ اِتَّرَعَ: (Ṣgh, Ḳ:) or *it was,* or *became, very full,* or *much filled.* (Lth, in TA. [But it is said in the TA, in one place, that Lth ignored the verb in this sense; and in another place, that he said, I have not heard them say, تَرِعَ الإِنَآءُ.]) == *He hastened to do evil,* or *mischief;* (Ks, Ḳ;) and *to do a thing:* (TA:) and تَتَرَّعَ بِهِ إِلَى الشَّرِّ, accord. to the Ḳ; but accord. to the Ṣ and O and L, ▾ تَتَرَّعَ إِلَيْهِ بِالشَّرِّ; (TA;) *he hastened to him to do evil,* or *mischief.* (Ṣ, O, L, Ḳ.) — *He rushed headlong into affairs by reason of excessive briskness, liveliness,* or *sprightliness.* (Lth, Ḳ.) == تَرَعَهُ, inf. n. تَرْعٌ, [app. a mistake for تَرَعٌ,] *He hastened to him, forbidding* [*him to do a thing*]. (L.) — تَرَعَهُ عَنْ وَجْهِهِ *He averted him,* or *turned him back, from his course,* or *manner of acting* or *proceeding.* (Ibn-'Abbád, Ṣgh, L, Ḳ.)

2. تَرَّعَ البَابَ, inf. n. تَتْرِيعٌ, *He locked,* or *closed, the door;* syn. أَغْلَقَهُ [which has both these significations]. (Ḳ.) In the Ḳur [xii. 23], some read, وَتَرَّعَتِ الأَبْوَابَ *And she locked,* or *closed, the doors,* instead of غَلَّقَتْ. (O, TA.)

4. اترعهُ *He filled it;* (Ṣ, Ḳ;) namely, a vessel. (Ṣ.)

5: see 1, in two places.

8: see 1.

تَرْعٌ *Full;* applied to a watering-trough or tank for beasts &c.; (Ṣ, Ḳ;) and to a mug: (Ṣ:) an inf. n. used as an epithet: (TA:) the regular form is ▾ تَرِعٌ, which signifies the same. (Ḳ.)

تَرِعٌ : see تَرْعٌ. — Also A cloud *containing much rain.* (TA.) — عُشْبٌ تَرِعٌ *Fresh, juicy,* or *sappy, herbs* or *herbage.* (Sgh in art. درع, and L.) == A man *quick to do evil,* or *mischief,* (Ks, Ṣ,) *and to become angry:* (Ṣ:) *ready and quick to become angry:* and ▾ مُتْتَرِعٌ *evil,* or *mischievous, hastening to do what is not fit,* or *proper, for him.* (TA.) — One *who rushes headlong into affairs by reason of excessive briskness, liveliness,* or *sprightliness:* (O, L, TA:) thus correctly written; but in the copies of the Ḳ, ▾ تَرِيعٌ. (TA.) — *Light-witted; weak and stupid; deficient in intellect;* or *light and hasty in disposition* or *deportment.* (TA.) — And, with ة, A woman *who transgresses the proper bounds* or *limits,* and *is light* [*in conduct*]. (TA.)

تُرْعَةٌ The *mouth of a streamlet* or *rivulet;* (IB, Mṣb, Ḳ;) i. e. *a place hollowed out by the water in the side of a river, whence it flows forth:* (Mṣb:) pl. تُرَعٌ (IB, Mṣb) and تُرُعَاتٌ and تُرَعَاتٌ and تُرْعَاتٌ: (Mṣb:) in the Ṣ it is said to signify the *mouths of streamlets* or *rivulets;* but correctly the sentence should be, تُرَعٌ is pl. of تُرْعَةٌ, and has this signification. (IB.) — *A canal,* or *channel of water, to a meadow* or *garden* or *the like:* (L, TA:) this is the meaning commonly known [in the present day: the general name in Egypt for a canal cut for the purpose of irrigation, conveying the water of the Nile through the adjacent fields]. (TA.) — The *opening,* or *gap,* of a watering-trough or tank, *by which the water enters, and where the people draw it:* (Az, Mgh,* Ḳ,* TA:) and, (Ḳ,) accord. to AA, (TA,) the *station of the drinkers at the watering-trough* or *tank;* as in the O and Ḳ; or, as in the L, the *part* of the watering-trough or tank *which is the station of the drinkers.* (TA.) — *A meadow,* or *garden,* or *the like,* (Ṣ, Ḳ,) *in an elevated place:* (Ḳ:) if in low land, it is called رَوْضَةٌ. (TA.) — *A stair;* or *a flight of steps by which one ascends;* syn. دَرَجَةٌ: (Ṣ, Ḳ:) so accord. to some in a trad., which see in what follows: (Ṣ,* TA:) and particularly the *flight of steps of a pulpit.* (AA, Ṣgh, Ḳ.) — ‡ *A door,* or *gate:* (Ṣ, Ṣgh, Mṣb, Ḳ:) pl. تُرَعٌ. (Ḳ.) You say, فَتَحَ تُرْعَةَ الدَّارِ ‡ *He opened the door of the house.* (TA.) And it is said in a trad., إِنَّ مِنْبَرِى هٰذَا عَلَى تُرْعَةٍ مِنْ تُرَعِ الجَنَّةِ, (Ṣ, TA,) as though meaning, ‡ *Verily this my pulpit is at a gate of the gates of Paradise:* thus explained by Sahl Ibn-Saad Es-Sá'idee, the relater of the trad.; and A'Obeyd says, وَهُوَ الوَجْهُ ["and it is the proper," or "the valid and obvious, way," of explaining it], meaning that it is the preferable explanation: but the author of the Ḳ, mistaking his meaning, makes وَجْهٌ to be another signification of تُرْعَةٌ: or the meaning of this trad. is, he who acts according to the exhortations recited upon the steps of my pulpit will enter Paradise: or, accord. to Ḳt, prayer and praise in this place are means of attaining to Paradise; so that it is as though it were a portion of Paradise. (TA.) In the same manner Sahl explained his other trad., إِنَّ قَدَمِى عَلَى تُرْعَةٍ مِنْ تُرَعِ الحَوْضِ ‡ [*Verily my foot is at a gate of the gates of the pool* of Paradise]. (TA.)

تَرِيعٌ : see تَرِعٌ.

تَرَّاعٌ A torrent *filling the valley;* as also ▾ أَتْرَعُ: (Ḳ:) or a torrent *which fills the valley:* (Ṣ:) and ▾ the latter, a *vehement* torrent. (TA.) J says, in the Ṣ, that ▾ سَيْرٌ أَتْرَعُ signifies شَدِيدٌ; and he cites the words of a poet thus:

* فَافْتَرَشَ الأَرْضَ بِسَيْرٍ أَتْرَعَا *

ascribed by some to El-'Ajjáj, but correctly, accord. to IB, the words of Ru-beh; making two mistakes, in saying افترش, in the sing., and بسير: moreover, the last word in the citation is a pret. verb: [the right reading is]

* فَافْتَرَشُوا الأَرْضَ بِسَيْلٍ أَتْرَعَا *

[*And they travelled the land with* a multitude like *a torrent that filled* the valleys]: the poet describes the Benoo-Temeem, and their travelling the land like the torrent by reason of multitude. (Ṣgh, TA.) == †*A door-keeper.* (Th, Ṣ, Ḳ.)

أَتْرَعُ : see تَرَّاعٌ, in three places.

حَوْضٌ مُتْرَعٌ *A filled watering-trough* or *tank:* (TA:) and جَفْنَةٌ مُتْرَعَةٌ *a filled bowl.* (Ṣ.)

مُتْتَرِعٌ : see تَرِعٌ.

ترف

1. تَرِفَ, aor. ـَ, (Ṣgh, Ḳ,) inf. n. تَرَفٌ, (M, TA,) *He enjoyed,* or *led, a plentiful, and a pleasant* or *an easy, and a soft* or *delicate, life;* or *a life of ease and plenty;* (M, Ṣgh, Ḳ;) as also ▾ تترّف. (Ḳ.) — And the former verb, †*It* (a plant, or herbage,) *was,* or *became, luxuriant, flourishing, succulent,* or *sappy;* or *bright and fresh, by reason of plentiful irrigation.* (M, TA.)

2: see 4, in two places. — تَتْرِيفٌ [app. as the inf. n. of the pass. verb, تُرِّفَ, also signifies] *Good feeding.* (M.) — And تَرَّفَ الرَّجُلَ, and ↓ اترفهُ, *He rendered the man submissive;* or *made him to submit:* and *he made the man king,* or *prince:* [in both senses] like رَفَّلَهُ. (M.)

4. أَتْرَفَتْهُ النِّعْمَةُ [*Wealth,* or *what God bestowed upon him,*] *made him to behave exorbitantly; to be excessively disobedient* or *rebellious; to exalt himself, and be inordinate in infidelity;* or *to be extravagant in acts of disobedience and in wrongdoing:* (Ṣ, Ḳ:) and so سَعَةُ العَيْشِ [*plentifulness and easiness of life*]: and in like manner, ↓ تَرَّفَتْهُ *it caused him to exult,* or *to exult greatly,* or *excessively, and to behave insolently and unthankfully,* or *ungratefully.* (TA.) And [*Wealth,* or *what God bestowed upon him,*] *made him to enjoy,* or *lead, a plentiful, and a pleasant* or *an easy, and a soft* or *delicate, life;* or *a life of ease and plenty;* as also ↓ تَرَّفَتْهُ. (Ḳ.) — اترف الرَّجُلَ *He gave the man the object of his eager desire;* or *of his yearning,* or *longing,* or *appetency.* (Lḥ, M.) — See also 2. — اترف also signifies *He persevered in,* or *persisted in,* or *resolved upon, transgression,* *wrongdoing,* or *deviation from the right way.* (El-'Ozeyzee, Ḳ.)

5: see 1.

10. استترف *He magnified himself;* or *behaved proudly, haughtily,* or *insolently: he behaved exorbitantly; was excessively disobedient* or *rebellious; exalted himself, and was inordinate in infidelity;* or *was extravagant in acts of disobedience and in wrongdoing.* (Z, Ṣgh, Ḳ.)

تُرْفَةٌ *Plentifulness, and pleasantness* or *easiness, and softness* or *delicacy, of life; a life of softness* or *delicacy, and ease, comfort,* or *affluence;* or *ease and plenty;* syn. نَعْمَةٌ, (T, Ḳ, TA,) and سَعَةُ العَيْشِ: (TA:) or i. q. نِعْمَةٌ [i. e. *wealth;* or *what God bestows upon one;* &c.]. (Mgh, and so in the CḲ. [But this I think a mistranscription, for نَعْمَة.]) — *Good, sweet,* or *pleasant, food.* (IDrd, M, Ḳ.) — *A new,* or *strange, thing,* (شَىْءٌ طَرِيفٌ, [in some copies of the Ḳ, ظَرِيف is put in the place of طَرِيف,]) *that one appropriates,* or *peculiarly assigns,* [*as a gift*] *to a friend;* or *by* [*the gift of*] *which one distinguishes a friend:* (Ḳ:) *any* طُرْفَة [i. e. *gift not given to any one before;* or *of which the recipient did not possess the like, and which pleases him;* or *novel,* or *rare, and pleasing, present*]. (M, TA.) — *A thing protuberant in the middle of the upper lip, by nature.* (Lth,* T,* Ṣ, M, Ḳ.) — *A* مِسْقَاة [q. v.] *with which one drinks.* (M, TA.)

أَتْرَفُ *Having a natural protuberance in the middle of his upper lip, called* تُرْفَة. (Lth,* T,* M, Ḳ.)

مُتْرَفٌ [pass. part. n. of 4, q. v.] One *left to do what he will; not prevented from doing so.* (Ibn-'Arafeh, Ḳ.) — And hence, (Ibn-'Arafeh, TA,) One *enjoying,* or *leading, a plentiful, and a pleasant* or *an easy, and a soft* or *delicate, life;* or *a life of ease and plenty:* (Ibn-'Arafeh, M, Ḳ, TA:) *luxurious,* or *indulging himself largely in the pleasures,* or *delights, of the present life, and in its appetites,* or *eager desires:* (Ibn-'Arafeh, TA:) one *who is not prevented from enjoying himself:* (Ḳ, TA:) and one *whose means of subsistence are made ample,* or *plentiful;* as also ↓ مُتَرَّفٌ: (M:) one *whom plentifulness, and pleasantness* or *easiness, and softness* or *delicacy, of life,* or *whom a life of ease and plenty,* (T,) or *whom wealth,* or *what God has bestowed upon him, and plentifulness and easiness of life,* (Mgh,) *causes to exult,* or *to exult greatly,* or *excessively, and to behave insolently and unthankfully,* or *ungratefully:* (T, Mgh:) and i. q. جَبَّارٌ [i. e. one *who magnifies himself;* or *behaves proudly, haughtily,* or *insolently;* &c.]: (Ḳ:) so says Ḳatádeh, in explaining the phrase أَمَرْنَا مُتْرَفِيهَا, in the Ḳur [xvii. 17: see أَمَرَ]: or, accord. to some, مترفيها here means *the worst of its chiefs; and the leaders in evil.* (TA.) — Also, (TA,) or ↓ مُتَرَّفٌ, (T,) *A boy made soft,* or *delicate, in body, and rendered submissive.* (T, TA.)

مُتَرَّفٌ: see مُتْرَفٌ, in two places.

ترق

Q. Q. 1. تَرْقَيْتُهُ, (ISk, JK, Ṣ, Ḳ,) inf. n. تَرْقَاةٌ, (ISk, Ṣ, Ḳ,) *I hit,* or *hurt, his* (a man's, ISk, JK, Ṣ) تَرْقُوَة [or *collar-bone*]. (ISk, JK, Ṣ, Ḳ.)

تَرْقُوَةٌ The *collar-bone; the bone between the pit at the uppermost part of the chest and the shoulder,* (JK, Ṣ, Mgh, Ḳ,) *on either side, connecting those two parts,* (JK, Mgh,) of a man &c.; (TA;) *each of the two prominent bones in the uppermost part of the chest, from the head of each shoulder to the edge of the pit above mentioned:* (TA in art. ترب:) [and sometimes, as in a phrase which see below,] the *fore part of the* حَلْق [here app. meaning the *throat*], *at the uppermost part of the chest, the place into which the soul* [for النَّفْس, in copies of the Ḳ, I read النَّفَس] *rises* [*when one is at the point of death*]: (Ḳ in art. رقو:) pl. تَرَاقٍ (JK, Mgh, Ḳ) and تَرَائِقُ; (JK, Ḳ;) the latter formed by transposition: (JK:) Fr says that the latter pl. is used by some for the former: (TA:) the sing. is of the measure فَعْلُوَةٌ, (JK, Ṣ, Ḳ,) as is shown by the verb mentioned above, (Ḳ,) though it is repeated in the Ḳ in art. رقو: (TA:) one should not say تُرْقُوَة, with ḍamm to the ت. (Ṣ, Ḳ.) إِذَا بَلَغَتِ التَّرَاقِىَ, in the Ḳur lxxv. 26, means *When it* (the soul) *reaches the uppermost parts of the chest;* [or, *the parts of the throat next the chest;*] for النَّفْس is understood: (Bḍ:) said when one is at the point of death. (TA.)

تِرْيَاقٌ, an arabicized word, (Ṣ, Mṣb, Ḳ,) from the Greek, (Mṣb, Ḳ,) [i. e. from θηριακὰ,] or originally Persian, (Ṣ, O,) also written and pronounced دِرْيَاقٌ, (JK, Mṣb,) and طِرْيَاقٌ; (Mṣb;) or, as some say, from الرِّيقُ, because containing the spittle of serpents, and, if so, it is Arabic [in origin]: (Mṣb:) [*Theriac;* also called *treacle;*] *an antidote for poisons;* (Ṣ, O;) *a certain compound medicine,* (Ḳ,) *comprising many ingredients, at most ninety or ninety-six, and at least sixty-four,* (TA,) *sometimes including the flesh of vipers,* (Ḳ, TA,) *and that of asses, which cause it to be prohibited and impure, or, as some say, it is prohibited without restriction:* (TA:) *it is a remedy against the bite or sting of rapacious venomous reptiles and the like, and poisonous potions:* (Ḳ: [I omit some unprofitable and absurd particulars respecting the compounds thus termed, in the Ḳ and other lexicons &c.:]) pl. تَرَايِيقُ. (Ḳ in art. فرق.) The best kind is called التِّرْيَاقُ الفَارُوقُ, (Ḳ in art. فرق,) vulgarly تِرْيَاقٌ فَارُوقِىٌّ. (TA in that art.) [A principal ingredient of this kind is the best sort of Jews-pitch, i. e. asphaltum, also called mumia, and in Arabic مُومِيَا: (see De Sacy's "Rel. de l'Égypte par Abd-allatif," p. 274:) and this mumia, by itself, is called التِّرْيَاقُ التُّرْكِىُّ.] — [It is sometimes applied to *Treacle,* as meaning the *sirop that drains from sugar.*] It is also said to be applied to the فَادْزَهْر [or *Bezoar-stone*], likewise termed مَسُوس. (TA in art. مس.) — Also, and ↓ تِرْيَاقَةٌ, † *Wine;* (Ṣ, O, Ḳ;) because it dispels anxiety; (Ṣ;) or because it is a remedy for anxieties; (O;) wherefore it is also termed صَابُونُ الهُمُومِ. (TA.)

تِرْيَاقَةٌ: see the last sentence above.

[بَاذَنْجَانٌ تِرْيَاقِىٌّ *Zanthium.*]

ترك

1. تَرَكَهُ, (Ṣ, M, Mṣb, Ḳ, &c.,) aor. ـُ, (Ṣ, M,) inf. n. تَرْكٌ (Ṣ, M, Mṣb, Ḳ, &c.) and تِرْكَانٌ, with kesr, (Fr, Ḳ,) *He left it, forsook it, relinquished it, abandoned it, deserted it,* or *quitted it;* either *intentionally, and by choice,* or *by constraint, and of necessity:* (Er-Rághib, TA:) *he left it, forsook it,* &c., as above; namely, a thing that he desired, or wished for, and also a thing that he did not desire, or did not wish for: (Ibn-'Arafeh, TA:) *he left it, quitted it, went away from it,* or *departed from it;* namely, a place: and *he left him, forsook him, relinquished him, abandoned him, deserted him, quitted him,* or *separated himself from him:* (Mṣb:) *he cast it,* or *threw it, away, as a thing of no account; rejected it; discarded it; cast it off; left it off:* (MF, TA:) *he left it, left it alone, let it alone; ceased, desisted, forbore,* or *abstained, from it; neglected it, omitted it,* or *left it undone;* syn. خَلَّاهُ; (Ṣ, A, O;) or وَدَعَهُ; (M, Ḳ;) as also ↓ اتّركهُ. (Ḳ. [But respecting this latter verb, see what follows.]) وَاتْرُكِ البَحْرَ رَهْوًا, in the Ḳur xliv. 23, *And leave thou the sea opened with a wide interval;* or *motionless,* in the same state as before thy passing through it, and strike it not with thy rod, nor alter anything thereof; (Bḍ;) or *motionless, parted asunder;* (Jel;) so that the Egyptians may enter it; (Bḍ, Jel;) is an instance of the verb meaning leaving intentionally, and by choice: (Er-Rághib, TA:) and كَمْ تَرَكُوا مِنْ جَنَّاتٍ وَعُيُونٍ, in the next verse, *How many gardens and springs did they leave!* (Jel,) is an instance of the verb meaning leaving by constraint, and of necessity. (Er-Rághib, TA.) In a phrase such as تَرَكَ حَقَّهُ, meaning *He made his right,* or *due,* or *claim, to be null,* or *he rejected it,* and such as تَرَكَ رَكْعَةً مِنَ الصَّلَاةِ, meaning *He neglected, omitted,* or *left unperformed, a*

ركعة *of the prayer*, [it is said (but I think it doubtful) that] the verb, having an ideal substantive for its objective complement, is used metaphorically. (Mṣb.) مَا قَالَ فِيهِ فَمَا أَتْرَكَ ♦ means تَرَكَ شَيْئًا [i. e. *He strove, laboured,* or *exerted himself,* (اِجْتَهَدَ,) *in it, and neglected not,* or *omitted not, anything* in his power]: the verb is of the measure اِفْتَعَلَ. (Ṣ.) مَنْ أَوْصَى بِالثُّلُثِ وَلَمْ ♦ يَتَّرِكْ شَيْئًا is a mistake for وَلَمْ يَتْرُكْ شَيْئًا, or ولم يَتَّرِكْ ♦ without شَيْئًا, or فَمَا أَتْرَكَ; for this verb is not trans., except, sometimes, in poetry; and the meaning is, وَلَمْ يَتْرُكْ فِيمَا أُذِنَ لَهُ فِيهِ شَيْئًا [i. e. *He who bequeaths the third* of his property, *and does not omit anything* of what he is allowed (to leave, or anything of the third part, for this is all that he is allowed to bequeath)]: it is from the saying فَعَلَ فَمَا أَتَّرَكَ ♦ [*He did* such a thing, *and neglected not,* or *omitted not, anything*]. (Mgh.) You say also, تَرَكَ المَيِّتُ مَالًا, i. e. *The deceased left property.* (Mṣb.) — وَتَرَكْنَا عَلَيْهِ فِى الآخِرِينَ, (Ḳ,) in the Ḳur [xxxvii. 76 &c.], (TA,) means *And we have perpetuated* (Ḳ, Jel, TA) *to him* a eulogy *among the later generations* (Jel, TA) of the prophets and peoples to the day of resurrection, [namely,] Salutation &c. (Jel.) — التَّرْكُ is also *syn. with* الجَعْلُ, (Lth, Ḳ, TA,) in some instances; (Lth, TA;) as though it had two contr. significations: (Ḳ:) [i. e.,] when تَرَكَ is doubly trans., it has the meaning of صَيَّرَ, (MF, TA,) or جَعَلَ. (TA.) So in the saying, تَرَكْتُ الحَبْلَ شَدِيدًا *I made,* or *rendered, the rope strong;* or *made it,* or *caused it, to be,* or *become, strong.* (TA.) So too in the Ḳur ii. 16, وَتَرَكَهُمْ فِى ظُلُمَاتٍ *And maketh,* or *causeth, them to be in darknesses.* (Ksh, Bḍ, MF.) And sometimes one says of any action that has come at last to a certain state, مَا تَرَكْتُهُ هٰكَذَا [*I did not make it,* or *cause it, to be thus*]. (TA.) = تَرِكَ, aor. ـَ, (IAạr, Ḳ,) inf. n. تَرَكٌ, (TḲ,) *He* (a man, IAạr) *married,* i. e. *took to wife, a* تَرِيكَة, (IAạr, Ḳ,) meaning *a woman that had remained a virgin, unmarried, until she had become of middle age,* or *long after she had attained to puberty, in the house,* or *tent, of her parents.* (TA.)

3. تاركه [inf. n. مُتَارَكَةٌ] is *syn. with* خَالَاهُ (Ṣ in art. خلو) [which is explained in the Ḳ, in art. خلو, as *syn. with* تَرَكَهُ, *He left, forsook, relinquished, abandoned,* &c., *him or it;* and thus it may often be well rendered: but it properly signifies *he left him, forsook him,* &c., *being left,* &c., *by him;* whence it is said in the Mgh, in art. ودع, that مُوَادَعَةٌ is syn. with مُصَالَحَةٌ because it is مُتَارَكَةٌ: Golius, as on the authority of Ibn-Maạroof, explains تاركه as signifying *he dismissed him, and did not molest him: he left him unmolested* is one of its meanings, but is not the primary signification: accord. to the TḲ, متاركة signifies the *leaving,* &c., *anything in the state in which it is:* and the *leaving,* &c., *one another*]. One says also, تَارَكْتُهُ البَيْعَ, (Ṣ, Mgh, but in the latter تَارَكَهُ, and in the TA وَفِى البَيْعِ,) وَغَيْرَهُ, (Mgh,) inf. n. مُتَارَكَةٌ, (Ṣ,) [app. meaning *I relinquished with him,* i. e. *concurrently with him, the sale,* &c.: see 6, by which this rendering is confirmed: Golius, as on the authority of J, who has not explained it, says that it means *I relinquished to him the merchandise,* or *commodity;* and Freytag follows him.] — [Hence,] مُتَارَكَةٌ is metonymically used as meaning The *making peace* [or *a truce*], or *reconciling oneself, with another* or *others.* (Mgh.) — In the saying, لَا بَارَكَ اللّٰهُ فِيهِ وَلَا تَارَكَ وَلَا دَارَكَ, it is an imitative sequent, (Ḳ,) all of these verbs having the same meaning [so that the saying may be rendered *May God not bless him nor felicitate him nor make him happy*]: (TA:) [or the meaning may be, *nor preserve him,* or *prolong his life;* for] IAạr says that تَارَكَ means أَبْقَى. (TA.)

6. تَتَارَكُوا الأَمْرَ بَيْنَهُمْ, (Ḳ,) or الأَمْرَ فِيمَا بَيْنَهُمْ, (Mgh,) *They relinquished* [*concurrently*], *one with another, the affair that was between them.* (TḲ.)

8. اِتَّرَكَ: see 1, in five places.

تَرْكٌ: see تَرِيكَةٌ. = Also *A* [*drinking-cup* or *bowl such as is called*] قَدَح *which a man lifts,* or *carries, with his two hands.* (Ibn-'Abbád, TA.)

التُّرْكُ *A certain nation;* (Ṣ, Mṣb, Ḳ;) [namely, *the Turks:*] تُرْكِىٌّ is its n. un.: (Mṣb, TA:) [and signifies also *Turkish:*] pl. أَتْرَاكٌ. (Mṣb, Ḳ.) It is said in a trad., اُتْرُكُوا التُّرْكَ مَا تَرَكُوكُمْ [*Leave ye alone the Turks as long as they leave you alone*]. (TA.) [تُرْكِىُّ الوَجْهِ often occurs in post-classical works as meaning *Having a Turkish face;* i. e. *round-faced,* or *broad-faced;* opposed to عَرَبِىُّ الوَجْهِ.]

تَرْكَةٌ: see تَرِيكَةٌ, in two places. — Also † *A woman such as is termed* رَبْعَة [i. e. *of middling stature*]: (Ibn-'Abbád, Ḳ:) pl. تَرَكَاتٌ. (TA.) — It is said in a trad., جَآءَ الخَلِيلُ إِلَى مَكَّةَ يُطَالِعُ تَرْكَتَهُ † [*El-Khaleel* (i. e. Abraham) *came to Mekkeh to get knowledge of his* تركة], meaning Hagar, and her son Ishmael: (Ḳ:) the word originally means an ostrich's egg, and is here used metaphorically; for the ostrich lays but one egg in the year, and then leaves it and goes away: (TA:) Z says, in the Fáïḳ, that it is thus related, with the ر quiescent; (Nh, O, TA;) but it would be a proper way if it were with kesr to the ر, [تَرِكَتَهُ ♦,] as meaning *the thing that he had left,* or *forsaken,* &c. (Nh, O, Ḳ.)

تَرِكَةٌ: see what next follows.

تَرِكَةٌ *A thing that is left, forsaken, relinquished, abandoned, deserted,* or *quitted;* like طَلِبَةٌ meaning "a thing desired, or sought;" (TA;) see also تَرِكَةٌ: particularly, the *inheritance,* or *property that is left,* of a person deceased; (Ṣ, Mṣb, Ḳ;*) also pronounced ♦ تِرْكَةٌ: pl. تَرِكَاتٌ. (Mṣb.)

تَرَاكِ an imperative verbal noun, meaning اُتْرُكْ [*Leave thou,* &c.]. (Ṣ, TA.) Hence the saying, تَرَاكِ تَرَاكِ صُحْبَةَ الأَتْرَاكِ [*Leave thou, leave thou, the companionship of the Turks*]. (TA.) Yoo says that تَرَاكَ is a dial. var. of the same; but this is only when it is used as a prefixed noun, as in تَرَاكَهَا for تَرَاكِهَا. (TA.)

تَرِيكٌ: see the next paragraph, in two places.

تَرِيكَةٌ *A woman that is left unmarried;* (Ṣ, Ḳ;) *that has remained a virgin, unmarried, until she has become of middle age,* or *long after she has attained to puberty, in the house,* or *tent, of her parents:* (TA:) it is not applied to a male: (Lḥ, TA:) pl. تَرَائِكُ. (Ṣ.) — *A meadow the depasturing of which has been neglected:* (Ṣ, Ḳ:) or *a pasture-land where people have pastured their beasts, either in a desert or upon a mountain, and of which the beasts have eaten until there remain* [*only*] *some relics of wood.* (TA.) — *Water left by a torrent:* (IB, Ḳ:) used in this sense by El-Farezdaḳ. (IB.) — *An egg after the young bird has gone forth from it:* (Ḳ:) or *an ostrich's egg* (Ṣ, Ḳ) *which she forsakes* (Ṣ, TA) *in the desert after it has become empty:* (TA:) or, as some say, *an ostrich's eggs left solitary:* (TA:) and ♦ تَرْكَةٌ signifies the same. (Ḳ.) [For the pl., see the next sentence.] — † *An iron helmet;* (Ḳ;) in the opinion of ISd, as being likened to the egg thus termed; (TA;) and so ♦ تَرْكَةٌ: (Ṣ, Ḳ:) the pl. [of the former] is تَرَائِكُ [mentioned in the Ṣ as pl. of the former applied to an ostrich's egg] and ♦ تَرِيكٌ and ♦ تَرْكٌ [the latter of which is termed in the Ṣ pl. of تَرْكَةٌ] are coll. gen. ns. of which تَرِيكَةٌ and تَرْكَةٌ are the ns. un.]. (Ḳ.) — *A raceme of dates* (كِبَاسَة [in the CḲ, erroneously, كُنَاسَة]) *after it has had what was upon it shaken off,* (AḤn, Ḳ, TA,) *and is left:* pl. تَرَائِكُ: (AḤn, TA:) and ♦ تَرِيكٌ signifies *a raceme* (عُنْقُود) *when what was upon it has been eaten;* (AḤn, Ḳ, TA;) and *a raceme of dates* (عِذْق) *that has had what was upon it shaken off,* (Ḳ, TA,) *so that nothing remains upon it:* so AḤn says in one place. (TA.) — It is said in a trad., إِنَّ لِلّٰهِ تَرَائِكَ فِى خَلْقِهِ, meaning [*Verily to God are referrible*] *conditions which He hath perpetuated in mankind,* of hope and heedlessness, so that they apply themselves thereby with boldness, forwardness, presumptuousness, or arrogance, to the things of the present world. (TA.)

مَتْرُوكٌ [pass. part. n. of تَرَكَ, *Left, forsaken,* &c. —] In lexicology, *Obsolete.* (Mz 10th نوع.)

تركمان

التُّرْكُمَانُ [*The Turkumán;*] *a certain people,* or *race, of the Turks;* [absurdly said to be] so called because two hundred thousand of them became believers in one month; wherefore they said تُرْكُ إِيمَانٍ [the Turks of belief]; which was afterwards contracted into تُرْكُمَانُ: (Ḳ, TA:) [a coll. gen. n.: n. un., and rel. n., تُرْكُمَانِىٌّ:] pl. تَرَاكِمَةٌ. (TA.)

ترما

لَا تَرْمَا i. q. لَا سِيَّمَا [which see in art. سوى]. (Ḳ.)

ترمس

تُرْمُسٌ [vulgarly pronounced in the present day تِرْمِس; from the Greek θέρμος, or Coptic θαρμος; *Lupines; or the lupine;*] *a certain grain, well known, of the description termed* قُطْنِيَّة; (Mṣb;) the *produce of a tree* [or *plant*] *which has a grain ribbed and notched:* (Lth, M,* Ḳ:) or *i. q.* بَاقِلَّى مِصْرِىّ: (the Minháj and Ḳ:) [but if this be the same as the بَاقِلَّى قِبْطِىّ, it is a mistake, accord. to Ibn-Beyṭár, to identify it with the ترمس:] AḤn says that it is the جِرْجِير مِصْرِىّ, and is *of the description termed* قُطْنِيَّة; and under the head of the letter ج, he says that the جرجير is the بَاقِلَّى: accord. to the Minháj, it is *a grain of an expanded shape, of bitter taste, hollowed in the middle; and the wild kind is smaller than the other, and stronger: and the* ترمس *approaches more to medicine than to food: the best is the white, large, and heavy:* (TA:) some say that the ت is augmentative, and that the word is from رَمَسَ, signifying "he concealed" a thing: (MF, TA:) the n. un. is with ة. (Mṣb.)

ترن

تُرْنَى an appellation applied to *A female slave;* (T, Ḳ;) and to *a fornicatress, an adulteress,* or *a prostitute;* (M, Ḳ;) as also فُرْتَنَى: (T, Ḳ:) and اِبْنُ تُرْنَى means *the son of a fornicatress* or *an adulteress* or *a prostitute;* (T, Ḳ;) as also ابن فُرْتَنَى: (T:) or *one that is base-born:* (Ṣ in art. رنو:) but it is said that تُرْنَى is of the measure تُفْعَل, from الرُّنُوّ: (M:) it may be from رُنِيَتْ, meaning "she was looked at continuously." (T, Ḳ.)

ترنج

تُرُنْجَةٌ and تُرُنْجٌ: } see art. ترج.
أُتْرُنْجَةٌ and أُتْرُنْجٌ: }

ترنجبين

تُرُنْجَبِينٌ and تَرَنْجَبِينٌ and تَرَنْجُبِينٌ [thus variously written, in the last manner in the TA, and there said to be "with ḍamm;" from the Persian تَرَنْگَبِين; *A kind of manna;* the *manna of the thorny plant called by the Arabs the* حَاجّ, *and hence by European botanists "alhagi:"* accord. to Dr. Royle (art. "Man" in Kitto's Cycl. of Bibl. Lit.), it is *a sweetish juice which exudes from the alhagi maurorum, concretes into small granular masses, and is usually distinguished by the name of Persian manna:* he also states that the alhagi maurorum and another species, alhagi desertorum, are 'called in Mesopotamia "agool," according to some authorities, while by others this is thought to be the name of another plant:' by "agool" is meant عَاقُول, q. v.:] *a kind of dew* (طَلّ), *that falls mostly in Khurásán and in Ma-wará-n-nahr, and, in our country, mostly upon the* حاج: *the best thereof is that which is fresh,* or *moist, and white:* (Ibn-Seenà, or "Avicenna," vol. i. of the Arabic ed., p. 262:) the مَنّ [or *manna*] *mentioned in the Ḳur-án* [ii. 54]. (Ksh, Bḍ, Jel, TA.) [See also "Ibn Baithar" (Ibn-Beyṭár), vol. i. p. 207.]

تره

1. تَرِهَ, aor. ـَ, *He fell into what are termed* تُرَّهَات, said to signify, originally, [*deserts, such as are termed*] قِفَار, and to be metaphorically applied to ‡*false,* or *vain, sayings* or *actions* or *affairs; unprofitable sayings:* (Ḳ,* TA:) or †*the uttered false and confused and vain speech, with somewhat of embellishment,* (Lth, TA,) or *without foundation,* or *order,* or *method.* (Akh, TA.)

تُرَّهٌ: see what next follows, in two places.

تُرَّهَةٌ *A small road branching off from a main road:* (Aṣ, Ṣ, Ḳ:) a Persian word, arabicized: (Aṣ, Ṣ:) pl. تُرَّهَاتٌ (Aṣ, Ṣ, Ḳ) and تُرُهَاتٌ. (TA.) — *A* [*desert, such as is termed*] قَفْر, (see 1,) or] صَحْرَاءُ, *and* مَفَازَة. (JK.) — The first in this paragraph is the primary signification: (TA:) and hence, metaphorically, (Aṣ, Ṣ,) ‡ *A false,* or *vain, saying* or *action* or *affair;* (Aṣ, JK, Ṣ, Ḳ;) as also ↓ تُرَّهٌ: (Ṣ, Ḳ:) pl. of the former, تُرَّهَاتٌ (JK, Ṣ, Ḳ*) [and تُرُهَاتٌ, as above]; and of the latter, تَرَارِيهُ: (Ṣ, Ḳ:*) or the primary signification of تُرَّهَاتٌ is قِفَار: [see 1:] and it is metaphorically applied to ‡*false,* or *vain, sayings* or *actions* or *affairs;* (Ḳ;) and *unprofitable sayings:* (Z, Ḳ, TA:) or, accord. to Az, *false,* or *vain, affairs:* and the sing. is ↓ تُرَّهٌ: or, accord. to IB, this last is pl. of تُرَّهَةٌ: [or rather a coll. gen. n.:] or, as some say, it is a sing.: (TA:) and accord. to Lth it signifies the act of *lying,* and *confusing* [*truth and falsehood*]. (Ḥar p. 165.) [Sometimes it is followed by a syn., to give greater force to the signification:] one says التُّرَّهَاتُ البَسَابِسُ and التُّرَّهَاتُ الصَّحَاصِحُ: and sometimes the former word is used as a prefixed noun governing the gen. case [so that one says تُرَّهَاتُ البَسَابِسِ and الصَّحْصَحُ: تُرَّهَاتُ الصَّحَاصِحِ is mentioned in the Ḳ, in this art., as a syn. of التُّرَّهَةُ]. (S.) — Also *A calamity; a misfortune; an evil accident:* (JK,* Ḳ:) pl. [تُرَّهَاتٌ and] تَرَارِيهُ. (JK.) — *Wind.* (JK, Ḳ.) — *Clouds,* or *a collection of clouds.* (JK,* Ḳ.) ═ *A certain small creeping thing* (دُوَيْبَّة) [*found*] *in the sand.* (JK, Ḳ.)

تسع

1. تَسَعَهُمْ, aor. ـَ (Ṣ, Mṣb, Ḳ) and ـُ (Yoo, Mṣb, Ḳ) and ـِ, (Mṣb,) inf. n. تَسْعٌ, (TḲ,) *He took the ninth part of their possessions:* or *he became the ninth of them:* (Ṣ, Mṣb, Ḳ:) or *he made them to be nine with himself;* (Ḳ;) they having before been eight. (TA.) [See also 2.]

2. تَسَّعَهُ *He made it nine.* (Esh-Sheybánee, and Ḳ voce وَحَّدَ.) [See also 1.] — تَسَّعَ لِاْمَرَأَتِهِ, or عِنْدَهَا, *He remained nine nights with his wife:* and in like manner the verb is used in relation to any saying or action. (TA voce سَبَّعَ.)

4. اتسعوا *They became nine:* (Ṣ, Ḳ:) and *they became ninety.* (M and L in art. ثلث.) — *They were,* or *became, persons whose camels came to water* [*on the ninth day, counting the day of the next preceding watering as the first;* i. e.,] *after an interval of nine days,* [*of which the first or last, or each of these, was not complete,*] *and eight nights.* (Ṣ,* Ḳ,* TA.)

تَسَعٌ: see تِسْعَةٌ.

تُسْعٌ *A ninth part; one of nine parts;* (Ṣ, Mṣb, Ḳ;) as also ↓ تُسُعٌ; (Mṣb;) and ↓ تَسِيعٌ, (Ṣ, Mṣb, Ḳ,) agreeably with a rule which some hold to be applicable in the case of every similar fractional number; but Sh says, I have not heard تَسِيع on any authority but that of AZ. (TA.)

تِسْعٌ fem. of تِسْعَةٌ, q. v. — Also *A certain* ظِمْء *of the* أَظْمَآء *of camels;* (Ṣ, Ḳ, TA;) i. e., *their coming to water* [*on the ninth day, counting the day of the next preceding watering as the first;* or, in other words,] *after an interval of nine days,* [*of which the first or last, or each of these, is not complete,*] *and eight nights.* (TA.) — Also *The ninth young one,* or *offspring.* (A in art. ثلث.)

تُسَعٌ The *seventh and eighth and ninth nights of the* [*lunar*] *month;* (Ḳ;) the *three nights of the month which are after the* نُفَل, *because the last night of these is the ninth;* (Ṣ;) among the nights of the month are three called غُرَر, [pl. of غُرَّة,] and after these are three called نُفَل, and after these are three called تُسَع because the last of them is the ninth night: (Az, TA:) or the *three nights of the commencement of the month,* as some say; but the first of these explanations is more agreeable with analogy. (TA.)

تُسُعٌ: see تُسْعٌ.

تِسْعَةٌ, applied to denote a number, [namely *Nine,*] is masc.; and ↓ تِسْعٌ, so applied, is fem.: (Ṣ:) the latter is also written ↓ تِسَعٌ, with fet-ḥ to the ت; and is thus pronounced in the Ḳur xxxviii. 22, (Bḍ, MF,) accord. to one reading. (Bḍ.) You say تِسْعَةُ رِجَالٍ [*Nine men*], and تِسْعُ نِسْوَةٍ [*Nine women*]. (Ḳ.) When it means the things numbered, not the amount of the number, تسعة is imperf. decl., being regarded as a proper name: thus you say, تِسْعَةُ أَكْثَرُ مِنْ ثَمَانِيَةَ [*Nine things are more than eight things*]. (TA.) It is said in the Ḳur [xvii. 103], وَلَقَدْ آتَيْنَا مُوسَى تِسْعَ آيَاتٍ بَيِّنَاتٍ [*And we formerly gave unto Moses nine evident signs;* generally understood to mean the principal miracles which he was empowered to perform, and which are differently enumerated in the Ḳ and other works; but by some supposed to mean statutes]. (Ḳ,* TA.) — In تِسْعَةَ عَشَرَ, which is masc., and تِسْعَ عَشْرَةَ, which is fem., [each signifying *Nineteen,*] each of the two words ends with fet-ḥ in every case, because they are two nouns which are regarded as one noun. (TA.) The former is pronounced by some of the Arabs تِسْعَةْ عَشَرَ: and the latter, thus in the dial. of El-Ḥijáz [and of most of the Arabs], is pronounced تِسْعَ عَشِرَةَ in the dial. of Nejd. (Ṣ in art. عشر.) In the Ḳur lxxiv. 30, some read, تِسْعَةَ عْشَرَ, making the ع in عشر quiescent, instead of تِسْعَةَ عَشَرَ, from a dislike of this consecution of vowels in what is like one word. (Bḍ, TA.*)

[تِسْعُونَ *Ninety:* and *ninetieth.*]

[تُسَاعَ, as meaning *Nine and nine,* or *nine and nine together,* or *nine at a time and nine at a time,* seems not to have been in use.] A'Obeyd says that more than أُحَادَ and ثُنَاءَ and ثُلَاثَ and رُبَاعَ has not been heard, except عُشَارَ occurring in a verse of El-Kumeyt. (TA in art. عشر.)

تُسْعٌ: see تَسِيعٌ.

تَاسِعٌ [*Making to be nine with himself,* or *itself:* and hence, *ninth*]. You say, هُوَ تَاسِعُ تِسْعَةٍ [*He is the ninth of nine*]: and تَاسِعُ ثَمَانِيَةٍ [He is *making eight to be nine with himself*]: but it is not allowable to say, تَاسِعُ تِسْعَةً. (TA.)—[تَاسِعَ عَشَرَ and تَاسِعَةَ عَشْرَةَ, the former masc. and the latter fem., meaning *Nineteenth,* are subject to the same rules as ثَالِثَ عَشَرَ and its fem., explained in art. ثلث, q. v.]

تَاسُوعَآءُ, (Mṣb, TA, &c.,) or التَّاسُوعَآءُ, (Ṣ, Ḳ,) *The tenth day of* [*the month*] *El-Moharram;* (Mṣb, TA;) [*the day*] *before the day of* العَاشُورَآء, (Ṣ,) or *before the day of* عَاشُورَآء: (Ḳ:) or, accord. to some, *the same as the day of* العاشوراء: (TA:) [see عاشوراء, where this is explained:] it is a post-classical word: (Ṣgh, Ḳ:) J says, in the Ṣ, I think it post-classical: (Mṣb, TA:) but [SM says,] this requires consideration; for it was used by the Prophet: (TA:) one ought to say, that, with عاشوراء, it has this form for the sake of resemblance; but as used alone, it must be conceded that it has not been heard [from the Arabs of the classical times]. (Mṣb.)

[مُتَسَّعٌ pass. part. n. of 2, q. v. See also مُثَلَّثٌ.]

مَتْسُوعٌ A rope *consisting of nine strands.* (TA.)

تشرين

تِشْرِينٌ [in Chaldee תִּשְׁרִי] *A Greek name of each of two months,* (Ḳ,) *of the months of Autumn, called* تِشْرِينُ الأَوَّلُ *and* تِشْرِينُ الثَّانِى, [*and both together* تِشْرِينَانِ, *the two Syrian months corresponding, respectively, to October and November O. S.,*] *before the two months whereof each is called* كَانُونٌ. (TA.)

تع

R. Q. 1. تَعْتَعَ فِى الكَلَامِ, (Mgh, Ḳ,) inf. n. تَعْتَعَةٌ, (Ṣ, Mgh,) *He reiterated in speech, by reason of an impediment,* or *inability to say what he would;* (Ṣ, Mgh, Ḳ;) as also ↓ تَتَعْتَعَ: (Ḳ:) and *he was unable to say what he would,* or *to find words to express what he would say:* (El-Ghooree, Mgh:) تَعْتَعَةٌ is the *speech of him who is termed* أَلْثَغ. (TA.) And تعتع فِى القُرْآنِ *He reiterated in reciting the Ḳur-án, and his tongue stuck fast in his doing so.* (TA.)—تَعْتَعَتِ الدَّابَّةُ, (Ḳ,) inf. n. as above, (Ṣ,) *The beast stuck fast* in the sand, (Ṣ, Ḳ,) or soft soil, (Ṣ,) or mire: (TA:) sometimes the verb is thus used. (Ṣ.) And تعتع said of a camel &c. signifies *His feet sank* into the soft soil, or soft sands. (TA.)=تَعْتَعَهُ *He dragged him* (namely another man) *roughly,* or *vehemently, and agitated him:* (Ṣ:) or *he shook him,* or *shook him vehemently,* (AA, Ḳ,) *backwards and forwards, and treated him roughly:* (AA:) *he shook him roughly:* (IDrd, Ḳ:) or *he compelled him against his will, in an affair, so that he became disquieted,* or *agitated.* (IF, Ḳ.)—تُعْتِعَ فُلَانٌ *Such a one had his saying rebutted, rejected,* or *repudiated, as wrong,* or *erroneous.* (TA.)

R. Q. 2. تَتَعْتَعَ: see R. Q. 1, first signification.

تُعْتُعٌ *i. q.* فَأْفَأٌ or فَأْفَاءٌ [accord. to different MSS., as meaning One *who reiterates his words much in speaking*]. (AA, Ḳ.)

وَقَعُوا فِى تَعَاتِعَ, [app. pl. of the inf. n. تَعْتَعَةٌ,] *They fell into convulsing perplexities, arising from evil and discordant and false rumours or the like,* (فى أَرَاجِيف, q. v.,) *and confusion.* (AA, Ṣ, Ḳ.)

مُتَعْتَعٌ *Afflicted by an injury which disquiets* or *agitates.* (TA, from a trad.)

تعب

1. تَعِبَ, (Ṣ, A, Mṣb, Ḳ,) aor. ـَ, (A, Ḳ,) inf. n. تَعَبٌ, (Ṣ, Mṣb,) *He* [a man and a beast] *was,* or *became, fatigued, tired, wearied* [*by labour* or *journeying* &c.], or *jaded;* (Ṣ, A, Mṣb;) *contr. of* اِسْتَرَاحَ. (Ḳ.) [تَعَبٌ, which, used as a simple subst., may be rendered *Fatigue, tiredness, weariness,* or the *state of being jaded,* is here said in the TA to be *contr. of* رَاحَةٌ; and to signify شِدَّةُ العَنَآءِ, which may be rendered *much fatigue* &c.; but accord. to an explanation of the verb of عَنَآءٌ in the Ṣ and TA in art. عنى, this word and تَعَبٌ signify the same. See also مَتْعَبٌ.]

4. اتعب *He fatigued, tired, wearied,* or *jaded,* another; (Ṣ, Mṣb, Ḳ;) and himself, in a work that he imposed upon himself, or in which he laboured; and his travelling-camels, by urging them quickly, or by hard journeying. (TA.)—‡ *He broke* a bone *again after it had been set,* or *consolidated:* or *he caused* a bone *to have a defect in it, after it had been set, so that there remained in it a constant swelling,* or *resulted a lameness:* اتعب العَظْمَ signifying أَعْنَتَهُ بَعْدَ الجَبْرِ: (so in the CḲ:) or أَعْتَبَهُ بعد الجبر. (So in MS. copies of the Ḳ and in the TA. [In the latter, in art. عتب, this reading is confirmed; but a remark below, voce مُتْعَبٌ, rather favours the former reading, that of the CḲ.])—‡ *He filled* a vessel; (A, Ḳ;) as, for instance, a drinking-cup, or bowl. (A.)=اتعب القَوْمُ *The people's cattle became fatigued, tired, wearied, or jaded.* (Ḳ.)

تَعِبٌ *Fatigued, tired, wearied,* or *jaded;* as also ↓ مُتْعَبٌ; (Ṣ, Mṣb, Ḳ;) but not مَتْعُوبٌ. (Ṣ, Ḳ.) [↓ تَعْبَانُ, for تَعِبٌ, fem. with ة, is used in this sense in the present day.]

تَعْبَانُ: see what next precedes.

مَتْعَبٌ *A place of* تَعَب [or *fatigue,* &c.]:—and tropically, *syn. with* تَعَبٌ: pl. مَتَاعِبُ. (Ḥar p. 431.)

مُتْعَبٌ: see تَعِبٌ.—Also ‡ A camel *that has had a bone of one of his fore legs or hind legs broken and set, and has been fatigued beyond his power of endurance before the bone has consolidated, so that the fracture has become complete:* whence the phrase عَظْمٌ مُتْعَبٌ [app. meaning ‡ *a bone broken again after its having been set,* or *consolidated:* see 4]. (TA.)—A vessel, as, for instance, a drinking-cup, or bowl, ‡ *filled.* (TA.)—Water ‡ *squeezed forth,* or *expressed, from the earth,* to be drunk. (A, TA.)

مَتْعَبَةٌ [*A cause of fatigue* or *weariness:* a word of the same class as مَجْبَنَةٌ and مَبْخَلَةٌ: loosely explained in Ḥar p. 475 as meaning *a place of fatigue*]. One says, اِسْتِخْرَاجُ المُعَمَّى مَتْعَبَةٌ لِلْخَوَاطِرِ [*The eliciting of the meaning of that which is made enigmatical is a cause of fatigue to minds*]. (A.)

تعس

1. تَعَسَ, aor. ـَ, inf. n. تَعْسٌ; (Ṣ, A, Mṣb, Ḳ, &c.;) and تَعِسَ, aor. ـَ; (Sh, AHeyth, A, IAth, Ḳ;) but the latter is not chaste; (A, TA;) or the former is used in addressing a person, saying تَعَسْتَ; and the latter, in narration; (Ḳ;) accord. to Sh; but ISd says that this is strange; (TA;) *He fell, having stumbled; contr. of* اِنْتَعَشَ: this is the primary signification: (Ṣ:) or *he stumbled and fell* (AHeyth, A, IAth, Ḳ) *upon his hands and mouth,* (AHeyth, TA,) or *upon his face:* (IAth, TA:) or *he fell upon his face:* (Er-Rustamee, Mṣb, TA:) [and this may also be meant by one of the explanations of the inf. n. in the TA, which is نُكْسٌ فِى سَفَالٍ:] or *he fell in any manner.* (TA.) You say, by way of imprecation, تَعَسَ وَٱنْتَكَسَ, meaning *May he fall upon his face, and not rise after his fall until he fall a second time.* (Mṣb.) And تَعَسَ فَمَا ٱنْتَعَشَ وَشِيكَ فَلَا ٱنْتَقَشَ [*May he fall, having stumbled,* or *stumble and fall, &c., and not rise again; and may he be pricked with a thorn, and not extract the thorn*]. (TA.) And accord. to certain of the Kilábees, تَعَسَ signifies *He missed his proof in litigation,* and *the object of his search in seeking.* (TA.)—*He perished.* (Aboo-'Amr Ibn-El-'Alà, Ṣ, Ḳ.) You say, تَعَسْتَ, as though meaning *Mayest thou perish.* (ISh, TA.)—*He became far removed.* (A, Ḳ.)—*He became lowered,* or *degraded.* (A, Ḳ.) You say also, تَعَسَ جَدُّهُ [*His fortune,* or *good fortune, fell:* or *may his fortune,* or *good fortune, fall*]. (Ḳ in art. عثر.)=تَعَسَهُ ٱللّٰهُ, [aor. ـَ, inf. n. تَعْسٌ;] (A'Obeyd, A, Mṣb, Ḳ;) and ↓ اتعسهُ; (AHeyth, Ṣ, A, Mṣb, Ḳ;) the former unknown to Sh; (Az, TA;) *God made him to fall, having stumbled:* (Ṣ:) or *to stumble and fall* (AHeyth, A, Ḳ) *upon his hands and mouth,* (AHeyth, TA,) or *upon his*

face: (TA:) or *to fall upon his face:* (Mṣb:) or *to fall in any manner.* (TA.) — *God destroyed him;* or *made him to perish.* (A'Obeyd, Ṣ, Ḳ.) — *God made him to become far removed.* (A, Ḳ.) — *God lowered,* or *degraded, him.* (A, Ḳ.) — You say, by way of imprecation, تَعْسًا لَهُ *May he* [*fall, having stumbled:* or, *stumble and fall:* or, *stumble and fall upon his hands and mouth:* or, *upon his face:* or] *fall upon his face:* (Mṣb:) or *may God make destruction to cleave to him:* (Ṣ, TA:) [or *may God destroy him.*] Aboo-Is-ḥáḳ says, in explanation of the phrase فَتَعْسًا لَهُمْ, in the Ḳur xlvii. 9, that it may be in the accus. case as meaning أَتْعَسَهُمْ ↑ ٱللّٰهُ. (TA.) A man also says, by way of imprecation, to his swift and excellent camel, when it stumbles, تَعْسًا, meaning *May God throw thee down upon thy nostrils:* expressing his disapproval of the stumbling of a beast of such age and strength: but if it be not a swift and excellent beast, and stumble, he says to it لَعًا. (TA.) You say also, أَتْعَسَ ↑ ٱللّٰهُ جَدَّهُ [*May God make his fortune,* or *good fortune, to sink!*] (A.)

4: see تَعَسَهُ, in three places.

تَعْسٌ inf. n. of 1 [which see, throughout]. — Also *Evil; mischief.* (Ḳ.)

تَعِسٌ: see what next follows.

تَاعِسٌ (A, Ḳ) and ↑ تَعِسٌ (Mṣb, Ḳ) act. part. ns. of 1, [i. e., respectively, of تَعَسَ and تَعِسَ, accord. to rule, used intransitively,] (A, Mṣb, Ḳ,) both applied to a man: (Ḳ:) and the former, to fortune, or good fortune. (A.)

مَتْعَسَةٌ [*A cause of falling after stumbling:* or *of stumbling and falling* &c. (See 1.)] You say, هٰذَا ٱلْأَمْرُ مَنْحَسَةٌ مَتْعَسَةٌ [*This affair is a cause of ill luck; a cause of falling* &c.]. (A, TA.)

تفث

1. تَفِثَ, aor. ـَ, inf. n. تَفَثٌ, *He left off,* or *abstained from, anointing himself, and shaving his pubes, and in consequence became dirty:* (Mṣb:) or تَفَثٌ signifies the *state of being dirty;* (Mgh;) the *state of having matted and dusty hair, or a dusty head, long left unanointed:* (T, Mgh, Ḳ:) so in relation to the rites and ceremonies of the pilgrimage: (T, Ḳ:) thus explained by ISh; but not by any [other] of the lexicologists: he says that it is *one of the rites and ceremonies of the pilgrimage;* (T;) which is a conventional term of the professors, or lecturers, of the colleges: (Mgh:) accord. to I'Ab, it signifies the *shaving, and shortening,* or *clipping, of the beard and mustache and* [*the hair of*] *the armpit, and slaughtering* [*of the victims*], *and casting* [*of the pebbles*]: accord. to Fr, the *slaughtering of the* [*victims termed*] بُدْن, *and other victims, namely, kine, and sheep or goats, and shaving the head, and paring the nails, and the like:* (T:) AO says that no poem is adduced as presenting an ex. of it: (Mṣb, TA:) and Zj says that it is not known by the lexicologists except from the expositors of the Ḳur-án; (T, M;) who say that it is the *clipping the mustache, and paring the nails, and plucking out the hair of the armpit, and shaving the pubes, and clipping the hair* [*of the head*]: (T:) or the *plucking out the hair, and paring of the nails, and deviating from all that is prohibited to the* مُحْرِم: (M:) as though it were a passing from the state of إِحْرَام to the state of إِحْلَال: (T, M:) or, in the rites and ceremonies of the pilgrimage, the *doing such things as paring the nails, and clipping the mustache, and shaving the pubes* (Ṣ, Ḳ) *and the head, and casting the pebbles, and slaughtering the* بُدْن, (Ṣ,) *&c.:* (Ṣ, Ḳ: [but in two copies of the Ṣ, this art. is omitted:]) or the *doing away with the matted and dusty state of the hair, and pollution and dirt, absolutely.* (TA.) Accord. to ISh, قَضَآءُ ٱلتَّفَثِ means *The doing away with the matted and dusty state of the hair by shaving, and paring the nails, and the like:* (T:) or it means *the doing away with the state of* تَفَث, *by clipping the mustache, and paring the nails, and plucking out the hair of the armpit, and shaving the pubes.* (Mgh.) Accord. to IAạr, ثُمَّ لْيَقْضُوا تَفَثَهُمْ [in the Ḳur xxii. 30] means *Then let them accomplish their needful acts of shaving and cleansing:* (T:) or it means *then let them do away with their dirtiness, by clipping the mustache, and paring the nails, and plucking out the hair of the armpit, and shaving the pubes, on the occasion of* إِحْلَال: (Bḍ:) it is an allowance, after entering the state of إِحْلَال, of that which was forbidden them in the state of إِحْرَام. (Mṣb.) — فَتَفِثَتِ ٱلدِّمَآءُ مَكَانَهُ occurs in a trad., meaning *And the blood* (lit. *bloods*) *contaminated the place thereof.* (TA.)

تَفِثٌ, (T, Mgh, Ḳ,) accord. to ISh, applied to a man, (T, Mgh,) *Altered* [*in odour or the like*], (مُتَغَيِّرٌ, T,) or *dusty,* (مُغْبَرٌّ, Mgh, Ḳ, or مُتَغَبِّرٌ, TA,) *having matted and dusty hair, not having anointed himself,* (T, Mgh, Ḳ,*) *nor shaven his pubes.* (T, Mgh. [In the former it is implied that this explanation is doubtful.])

تفح

4. اتفحهُ [*He gave him an apple*]. You say, أَتْحَفَكَ مَنْ أَتْفَحَكَ [*He makes a present to thee who gives thee an apple*]. (A: there immediately following the saying, فُلَانٌ تُحْفَتُهُ تُفَّاحَةٌ.)

تَفْحَةٌ *A sweet odour.* (Abu-l-Khaṭṭáb, L.)

تُفَّاحٌ, of the measure فُعَّالٌ; an Arabic word; [not arabicized;] (Mṣb;) [The *apple,* or *apples;*] *a certain fruit,* (L, Mṣb,) *well known,* (Ṣ, L, Mṣb, Ḳ,) *plentiful in* [*the cooler parts of*] *the land of the Arabs:* (AḤn, TA:) the word is said by Abu-l-Khaṭṭáb to be derived from تَفْحَةٌ "a sweet odour:" (L:) the n. un. is with ة: (Ṣ, L, Mṣb:) the pl. is تَفَافِيحُ: (T:) and the dim. of the n. un. is ↑ تُفَيْفِيحَةٌ. (L.) You say, فُلَانٌ تُحْفَتُهُ تُفَّاحَةٌ [*Such a one, his present is an apple*]. (A.) — تُفَّاحٌ ذَهَبِىٌّ and تُفَّاحُ ٱلْجِنِّ: see بَاذَنْجَانٌ. — تُفَّاحُ ٱلْبِرِّ: see يَبْرُوحٌ, in art. برح. — ٱلتُّفَّاحَةُ also signifies ‡ *The head of the thigh-bone, which is in the haunch-bone.* (Kr, A, Ḳ.) — لَطَمْنَ بِٱلْعُنَّابِ ٱلتُّفَّاحَ [lit. *They* (women) *slapped, with the jujubes, the apples*] means, ‡ *with the fingers,* or *the ends of the fingers, the cheeks.* (A.)

تُفَيْفِيحَةٌ: see تُفَّاحٌ.

مَتْفَحَةٌ *A place where apples grow* (L, Ḳ) *in abundance.* (L.)

تفرق

تُفْرُوقٌ The قِمَع [or *base*] *of a date;* (Ibn-'Abbád, Ḳ;) a dial. var. of ثُفْرُوقٌ [q. v.]: pl. تَفَارِيقُ. (TA.)

تفل

1. تَفَلَ, [in the CḲ, erroneously, تَفِلَ,] aor. ـِ, (Ṣ, M, Mṣb, Ḳ) and ـُ, (Ṣ, Mṣb, Ḳ,) inf. n. تَفْلٌ, (T, Ṣ, M, Mṣb,) *He spat;* syn. بَصَقَ: (M, Ḳ:) [or rather, *he spat, emitting a small quantity of saliva,* generally *in scattered portions, as when one spits forth some minute thing:*] ٱلتَّفْلُ is *similar to* ٱلْبَزْقُ, *but less in degree:* (Ṣ, Mṣb:*) the first degree is ٱلْبَزْقُ; then, ٱلتَّفْلُ; then, ٱلنَّفْثُ; and then, ٱلنَّفْخُ: (Ṣ:) ٱلتَّفْلُ with the mouth is [*an action*] *never without somewhat of spittle:* a blowing without spittle is [said to be] termed نَفْثٌ. (T.) Hence, تَفْلُ ٱلرَّاقِى [*The spitting of the charmer, in which he emits a small quantity of saliva at a time, in scattered portions:* see also نَفَثَ]. (Ṣ.) One says also, ذَاقَ مَآءَ ٱلْبَحْرِ فَتَفَلَهُ, i. e. [*He tasted the water of the sea, and*] *spirted it forth,* by reason of dislike thereof. (TA.) ═ تَفِلَ, (M, Ḳ,) aor. ـَ, (Ḳ,) inf. n. تَفَلٌ, (Ṣ, M, Mgh, Ḳ,) *He,* or *it,* (a thing, M,) *became altered for the worse in odour, ill-smelling,* or *frouzy:* (M, Ḳ:) *he neglected,* or *left off the use of, perfume:* (M:) *he was unperfumed:* (Ṣ:) *he neglected,* or *left off the use of, perfume, and so became altered for the worse in odour, ill-smelling,* or *frouzy:* (Mgh, TA:) and تَفِلَتْ, aor. and inf. n. as above, *she* (a woman) *stank, by reason of having neglected,* or *left off the use of, perfume and ointments:* and also *she perfumed herself:* thus bearing two contr. significations. (Mṣb.)

4. اتفلهُ *He,* or *it, made him,* or *it, to be altered for the worse in odour, ill-smelling,* or *frouzy,* (Ḳ,) or *unperfumed.* (Ṣ.) The rájiz says,

• وَتُتْفِلُ ٱلْعَنْبَرَ وَٱلصُّوَارَا •

[*And she makes ambergris and musk,* or *the vesicle of musk, to have a bad odour,* or *to lose their fragrance*]. (Ṣ.) And it is said of the sun, تُتْفِلُ ٱلرِّيحَ [*It makes the odour* of the person *to be bad*]. (TA, from a trad.)

تَفْلٌ: see what next follows.

تُفَلٌ, (Ḳ,) or ↑ تُفْلٌ, (M, accord. to the TT,) and ↑ تُفَالٌ, (M, Ḳ,) vulgarly ↑ تِفْلٌ and ↑ تِفَالٌ, (TA,) *Spittle,* or *saliva, ejected from the mouth;* syn. بُصَاقٌ; (M, Ḳ;) as also ↑ تَفْلٌ: (Ibn-Abi-l-Ḥadeed, TA:) or it is *similar to* بُصَاق. (TA.) [See 1.] — And *Froth,* or *foam,* (M, Ḳ,) of the sea; (TA;) and *the like thereof.* (M.)

تفل: see تَفَلَ. — مَا أَصَابَ فُلَانٌ مِنْ فُلَانٍ إِلَّا تَفْلًا طَفِيفًا *Such a one obtained not from such a one save a little.* (T.)

تَفَلٌ: see تُفْلٌ.

تَفِلٌ, applied to a man; (Ṣ, M, Ḳ;) and تَفِلَةٌ, applied to a woman, (T, M, Mgh, Mṣb, Ḳ,) as also ▼مِتْفَالٌ, (T, Ṣ, M, Mṣb, Ḳ,) which is a possessive epithet, (M,) or an intensive epithet, (Mṣb,) *Altered for the worse in odour, ill-smelling,* or *frouzy:* (M, Ḳ:) *who has neglected,* or *left off the use of, perfume:* (M:) *unperfumed:* (T, Ṣ:) *who has neglected,* or *left off the use of, perfume, and so become altered for the worse in odour, ill-smelling,* or *frouzy:* (Mgh, TA:) *stinking,* (T, Mṣb,) *by reason of having neglected,* or *left off the use of, perfume and ointments:* (Mṣb:) the pl. of تَفِلَةٌ is تَفِلَاتٌ; (T, Mgh, Mṣb;) applied to such women as are not to be prevented from going to the mosque, and in this case meaning *unperfumed.* (T,* Mgh,* TA.) — قَوْمٌ سَفِلَةٌ تَفِلَةٌ [*A company of men of the lowest and vilest sort*]. (TA.)

تُفَالٌ and تِفَالٌ: see تُفْلٌ.

الشَّمْسُ مَتْفَلَةٌ [*The sun makes the odour of the person to be bad*]. (TA.)

مِتْفَلَةٌ *A spittoon,* or *vessel in which to spit;* syn. مِبْزَقَةٌ. (TA.)

مِتْفَالٌ: see تَفِلٌ.

تفه

1. تَفِهَ, aor. ـَ, (Ṣ, Mgh, Mṣb, Ḳ,) inf. n. تَفَهٌ, (JK, Mṣb, Ḳ, TA,) or تَفْهٌ, (Mgh, CḲ,) and تُفُوهٌ (Ḳ) and تَفَاهَةٌ, (Mṣb, TA,) or this last is a mistake; (Mgh;) and تَفَهَ, aor. ـُ, inf. n. تُفُوهٌ; (JK;) *It* (a thing, JK, Mgh, Mṣb) *was,* or *became, paltry, sorry, mean, contemptible,* or *inconsiderable;* (JK, Ṣ, Mgh, Mṣb;) and *little,* or *small, in quantity* or *number.* (JK, Ṣ, Ḳ.) — تَفِهَ, aor. ـَ, inf. n. تُفُوهٌ, *He* (a man) *was,* or *became, stupid,* or *foolish.* (JK, Ḳ.) And تَفِهَتْ نَفْسُهُ *His mind became weak.* (JK.) — تَفِهَ, aor. ـَ; and تَفَهَ, aor. ـُ; *He,* or *it, was,* or *became, lean,* or *meagre;* syn. غَثَّ. (Ḳ.) It is said in a trad. (Ṣ, Ḳ) of Ibn-Mes'ood, (Ḳ,) القُرْآنُ لَا يَتْفَهُ وَلَا يَتَشَانُّ, (Ṣ, Ḳ, [in the CḲ, erroneously, يُتْفَهُ and يُتَشانُّ, and in some copies of the Ḳ, for the latter is put يتنان,]) i. e. † لَا يَغِثُّ وَلَا يَخْلَقُ [*The Ḳur-án will not become meagre, nor will it become worn out*]: (Ḳ: [in the CḲ, erroneously, لا يُغَثُّ ولا يُخْلَقُ:]) it is implied by the context in the Ṣ, that لا يتفه means *will not become paltry,* or *mean:* لا يتشانّ means *will not become worn out* by reason of much repetition; from شَنٌّ signifying "a worn-out water-skin." (TA.)

4. اتفه فى عطائه [*He was paltry, sorry, mean,* or *niggardly, in his gift;*] *he made his gift little,* or *small.* (TA.)

تَفِهٌ: see تَافِهٌ. — Also *Insipid; tasteless;* and so ▼تَافِهٌ. (KL.) You say أَطْعِمَةٌ تَفِهَةٌ *Kinds of food having no taste of sweetness,* or *of sourness,* or *of bitterness;* and some include bread and flesh-meat among these. (Ḳ.)

تَافِهٌ (Ṣ, Mgh, Mṣb, KL, TA) and ▼تَفِهٌ (Mgh, KL, TA) applied to a thing, (JK, Mgh, Mṣb,) and the former to a man also, (TA,) *Paltry, sorry, mean, contemptible,* or *inconsiderable:* (JK, Ṣ, Mgh, Mṣb, KL, TA:) and *little,* or *small, in quantity* or *number.* (JK, Ṣ, TA, and KL in explanation of the former.) — تَافِهُ العَقْلِ A man *having little sense,* or *intellect;* (TA;) *stupid,* or *foolish.* (JK.) — See also تَفِهٌ. — تَافِهٌ also signifies *Afflicted,* or *distressed, by reason of disease and fatigue.* (JK.)

مُتَفَّهَةٌ; (JK, TA;) so in the handwriting of Ṣgh; in the Ḳ, مُتْفَهَةٌ; (TA;) *Easy, submissive,* or *tractable;* applied to a she-camel. (JK, Ḳ.)

تقد

تِقْدَةٌ (JK, Ṣ, L, Ḳ) and تَقْدَةٌ (Hr, L, Ḳ) and تَقِدَةٌ (JK, L) *Coriander-seed;* syn. كُزْبَرَةٌ. (IAạr, JK, Ṣ, L, Ḳ.) — And *Caraway-seed;* syn. كَرَوْيَاءُ. (IAạr, Th, L, Ḳ.)

تقن

2. تَقَّنُوا أَرْضَهُمْ, (JK, Ḳ,) inf. n. تَتْقِينٌ, (Ḳ,) *They watered their land with thick,* or *muddy, water,* [or *water containing* تِقْن,] (JK,* Ḳ,) *in order that it might become good.* (Ḳ.)

4. اتقنهُ, (Ḳ,) inf. n. إِتْقَانٌ, (JK, Ṣ,) *i. q.* أَحْكَمَهُ, [*He made it,* or *rendered it,* (namely, a thing, JK, or an affair, Ṣ and Ḳ,) *firm, stable, strong, solid, compact, sound,* or *free from defect* or *imperfection, by the exercise of skill; he made it firmly, strongly, solidly, compactly, so that it was firmly and closely joined* or *knit together, soundly, thoroughly, skilfully, judiciously,* or *well; he so constructed, constituted, established, settled, arranged, did, performed,* or *executed, it; he put it into a firm, solid, sound,* or *good, state,* or *on a firm, solid, sound,* or *good, footing*]. (JK, Ṣ, Ḳ.) [And اتقن لهُ signifies the same as اتقنهُ: or *he exercised,* or *possessed, the skill requisite for it;* namely, an affair.] الَّذِى أَتْقَنَ كُلَّ شَىْءٍ, in the Ḳur xxvii. 90, means *Who hath created everything firmly, strongly, solidly,* &c., (أَحْكَمَ خَلْقَهُ,) *and made it, fashioned it,* or *disposed it, in the fit, proper,* or *right, manner.* (Bḍ.) [You say also, اتقن عِلْمَهُ, meaning *He made his knowledge sound;* or *made himself thoroughly learned.*] And اتقنهُ عَنْهُ *He knew it,* or *learned it,* (namely, a tradition [&c.],) *soundly, thoroughly,* or *well, from him.* (TA in art. دبر.)

تِقْنٌ The رُسَابَة *of water,* (JK, Mgh, Ḳ,) *in a rivulet or in the channel of a torrent,* (Ḳ,) *in the* [*season called*] رَبِيع; (Lth, JK, Mgh;) i. e., (Mgh,) [*its sediment,* or] the *thick matter that is borne by it* [*and that sinks to the bottom; used for improving land*]: (Lth, JK, Mgh:) and (Ḳ) the تُرْنُوق *of a well* (Mgh, Ḳ) and *of the channel of a torrent;* i. e., the *slime, mixed with black,* or *black and fetid, mud;* accord. to the Jámi' of El-Ghooree. (Mgh.) — *A thing by means of which one subsists, and makes good,* or *improves, the performance,* or *execution,* or *management, of an affair; as iron, and other things, of the* جَوَاهِر [i. e. *precious stones,* or *native ores,*] *of the earth:* and *anything by means of which a thing is made good,* or *improved,* is called its تِقْن. (TA.) — *A skilful* man: (JK, Ṣ, Ḳ:) pl. أَتْقَانٌ. (TA.) — [Hence, probably,] تِقْنٌ [or ابْنُ تِقْنٍ] is also the name [or surname] of a certain man proverbial for his excellence in shooting. (Ṣ, Ḳ. [In the latter it is implied that this name or surname is التِّقْنُ.]) The rájiz says,

يَرْمِى بِهَا أَرْمَى مِنِ ابْنِ تِقْنِ

[*One more skilled in shooting than Ibn-Tiḳn shoots it*]. (Ṣ.) — *Nature,* or *natural disposition.* (JK, Ṣ, Ḳ.) You say, الفَصَاحَةُ مِنْ تِقْنِهِ *Chasteness of speech,* or *eloquence, is* [a quality] *of his nature.* (Ṣ.)

Quasi تقى: or, accord. to some, تقو

1. تَقَى, aor. ـِ, (T, Ṣ, Ḳ, in art. وقى) and ـَ, (T, TA,) or تَقِىَ, aor. ـَ, (Mṣb, [but the correctness of this I greatly doubt, unless, as appears to be the case, it is meant to be understood as an intrans. verb,]) inf. n. تَقْىٌ, (Ṣ and TA in art. تقى, [which art. I find in only one copy of the Ṣ,]) or تُقًى, (Ḳ,) or تُقَاةٌ, (Mṣb, and also mentioned in the TA,) of which تُقًى is pl., or coll. n., (Ḳzz, IB, Mṣb,) and تَقِيَّةٌ (Ḳ) and تِقَاءٌ; (Lḥ, Ḳ;) and ▼اِتَّقَى, (T, Ṣ, Mṣb, Ḳ,) inf. n. اِتِّقَاءٌ (Mṣb) and [quasi-inf. n.] تَقِيَّةٌ and تُقَاةٌ; (Ṣ, art. وقى;) *He feared* God: (Ṣ and TA in art. تقى: all else that follows is from art. وقى except where reference is made to another art.:) or *he was cautious of* a thing; *guarded,* or *was on his guard, against* it; *prepared, prepared himself,* or *was in a state of preparation, against* it; or *feared* it: (Ḳ:) or *he looked forward to* a thing, *and guarded against* it, *sought to avoid* it, or *was cautious of* it. (T, TA.) [For other explanations of the latter verb, which apply also to the former, see art. وقى.] ▼اِتَّقَى is originally اِوْتَقَى; (T, Ṣ;) then اِيتَقَى; then اِتَّقَى; and when this came to be much in use, they imagined the ت to be a radical part of the word, and made the word اِتَّقَى, aor. يَتَقِى, with fet-ḥ to the ت in each case, and without teshdeed; and not finding any analogue to it in their language, they said تَقَى, aor. يَتْقِى, like قَضَى, aor. يَقْضِى: (Ṣ:) or, as is said in the T, they suppressed the ا, and the و changed into ت, in اِتَّقَى, and said تَقَى, aor. يَتْقِى. (TA.) A poet says, (namely, Khufáf Ibn-Nudbeh, TA,)

جَلَاهَا الصَّيْقَلُونَ فَأَخْلَصُوهَا
خِفَافًا كُلُّهَا يَتْقِى بِأَثْرِ

or, as some read it, يَتَقِى, with the ت movent, but without teshdeed; (Ṣ;) and this latter, accord.

to IB, is the right reading. (TA.) [See this verse explained in art. اثر.] IB adds that Aboo-Sa'eed [app. meaning Aṣ] disallowed تَقَى, aor. يَتْقِى, inf. n. تُقًى; saying that it would require the imperative to be اِتْقِ, which is not said; and this, he states, is right: [for] J says that the imperative used is تَقِ [*Fear thou*, or *beware thou*, &c.], as in تَقِ ٱللّٰهَ [*Fear thou God*]; and to a woman, تَقِى; formed from the verb اِتَّقَى, without teshdeed, by the suppression of the ا. (TA.)

4. مَا أَتْقَاهُ لِلّٰهِ (Ṣ, TA) *How great is his reverential, or pious, fear of God!* (TA.) — ما اتقاه is also said of a saddle, as meaning *How good is it for not galling the back!* (TA.)

8: see 1, in two places; and see also art. وقى.

تَقْوَى: see تُقًى.

تُقَاةٌ: see تَقْوَى, in two places. — In the phrase in the Ḳur [iii. 27], إِلَّا أَنْ تَتَّقُوا مِنْهُمْ تُقَاةً, it may be an inf. n. [so that the meaning may be *Unless ye fear from them with* a great *fearing* (see 1)]: or it may be a pl. [app. of تَقِىٌّ, like as كُمَاةٌ is pl. of كَمِىٌّ, so that the meaning may be *unless ye fear from them, being fearful*]: but it is better to regard it as an inf. n. because another reading is تَقِيَّةً. (M, TA.)

تَقِىٌّ, applied to a man, (Mṣb, Ḳ, TA,) i. q. وَقِىٌّ (TA) and مُتَّقٍ (Ṣ) [*Fearing; cautious;* &c.: (see 1:) and particularly *having a reverential*, or *pious, fear of God:* or simply *pious:* or *one who preserves*, or *guards, himself*, accord. to some, *exceedingly*, or *extraordinarily, from sin, either of commission or of omission:* (see 8 in art. وقى:)] accord. to IDrd, one *who preserves*, or *guards, himself from punishment* [*in the world to come*], *and from acts of disobedience, by righteous conduct:* from وَقَيْتُ نَفْسِى: said by the grammarians to be originally وَقُوىٌ; then, تَقُوىٌ: or, accord. to Aboo-Bekr, [originally] of the measure فَعِيلٌ, as is indicated by the first of its pls. mentioned below: but he who says that it is [originally] of the measure فَعُولٌ says that it has that pl. because it has become like a word [originally] of the measure فَعِيلٌ: (TA:) or *righteous, virtuous, just*, or *honest;* (Mṣb in art. تقى;) contr. of فَاجِرٌ: (idem in art. بر:) pl. أَتْقِيَاءُ (Mṣb in art. تقى, and Ḳ) and تُقَوَاءُ, (Ḳ,) which is extr., and of a class disallowed by Sb, (TA,) [and app. also تُقَاةٌ, q. v. suprà.]

تَقِيَّةٌ: see what next follows.

تَقْوَى, or تَقْوًى, accord. to different readings in the Ḳur ix. 110, (Bḍ,) [of which readings the former is the more common,] is originally تَقْيَا, (Ḳ,) [or تَقْيًا,] or [rather وَقْيَا, or وَقْيًا, and then] وَقْوَى, of the measure فَعْلَى, from وَقَيْتُ, (ISd, TA,) or, accord. to MF, the right opinion is that it is [وَقْوَى,] of the measure فَعْوَلٌ, (TA,) and is thus transformed in order to make a distinction between the subst. and the epithet such as خَزْيَا and صَدْيَا: (Ḳ:) it is a subst. from اِتَّقَى or وَقَى; (Mṣb, Ḳ;) [and signifies *Fear; caution;* &c.: (see 1:) and particularly *reverential*, or *pious, fear of God:* or simply *piety:* or the *preservation*, or *guarding, of oneself*, accord. to some, *exceedingly*, or *extraordinarily, from sin, either of commission or of omission:* or the *preservation*, or *guarding, of oneself from punishment in the world to come, and from acts of disobedience, by righteous conduct:* or *righteousness, virtue, justice*, or *honesty:* (see تَقِىٌّ:) its explanations in relation to religion are many and various, but are all resolvable into *fear of God*, or *of sin;* or the *preservation*, or *guarding, of oneself from sin:*] and تَقِيَّةٌ ▼ and تُقَاةٌ ▼ are syn. with each other (Ṣ) and with تَقْوَى, (Mṣb,) and are used as inf. ns. of اِتَّقَى: (Ṣ:) and تُقًى ▼ [also] is syn. with تَقْوَى (Ṣ;) or it is pl. of تُقَاةٌ ▼, or a coll. n., (Ḳzz, IB, Mṣb,) like as طُلًى is of طُلَاةٌ, (Ḳzz, IB,) and as رُطَبٌ is of رُطَبَةٌ. (Mṣb.) وَآتَاهُمْ تَقْوَاهُمْ, in the Ḳur xlvii. 19, means *And hath explained to them*, (Bḍ,) or *suggested to them*, (Jel, TA,) *what they should fear*, or *that from which they should preserve themselves:* (Bḍ, Jel, TA:) or *hath aided them to practise their* تَقْوَى: (Bḍ:) or *hath given them the recompense of their* تقوى. (Bḍ, TA.) And هُوَ أَهْلُ ٱلتَّقْوَى, in the Ḳur lxxiv. last verse, means *He is entitled*, or *worthy, to be feared;* or *to be reverentially*, or *piously, feared.* (Bḍ, Jel, Ḳ.)

هُوَ أَتْقَى مِنْ فُلَانٍ [*He is more fearing*, or *cautious*, &c., *than such a one; more reverentially*, or *piously, fearful of God;* or *more pious;* &c.;] *he has more* تَقْوَى *than such a one.* (TA.)

تك

10. اِسْتَكَّ ٱلتِّكَّةَ, (IDrd, Ḳ,) or بِٱلتِّكَّةِ, (Mṣb,) *He inserted the* تِكَّة *in* [*the double upper border of*] *the drawers*, or *trousers.* (IDrd, Mṣb, Ḳ.) You say also, هُوَ يَسْتَتِكُّ بِٱلْحَرِيرِ *He makes use of a* تِكَّة *of silk.* (A.)

تِكَّةٌ The *band* [*that is inserted in the double upper border*] *of the drawers*, or *trousers;* (IDrd, Ḳ;) [*generally, a strip of cotton, which is often embroidered at each end; sometimes, of net-work; and*] *sometimes, of silk:* (A:) IDrd thinks it to be an adventitious word, though used in ancient times; (TA;) and IAmb says, I think it to be arabicized: (Mṣb:) pl. تِكَكٌ. (Ṣ, Mṣb, Ḳ.)

مِتَكٌّ The *thing by means of which the* تِكَّة *is inserted in* [*the double upper border of*] *the drawers*, or *trousers.* (TA.) [*It is generally a slender piece of wood, having at one end a loop through which a portion of the* تِكَّة *is passed.*]

Quasi تكأ

تَكِئٌ &c.: see art. وكأ.

Quasi تكل

1. تَكَلَ عَلَيْهِ, aor. ـُ, a dial. var. of اِتَّكَلَ. (Ibn-'Abbád, Ḳ.) See art. وكل; where, also, see تُكَلَةٌ, &c.

تل

1. تَلَّهُ, (T, Ṣ,* M, Mṣb, Ḳ,) aor. ـُ, inf. n. تَلٌّ, (M, Mṣb,) *He prostrated him*, or *threw him down;* (T, Ṣ, M, Mṣb, Ḳ;) [as some say,] *upon the* تَلّ: (TA:) or *he threw him down* (M, Ḳ, TA) *upon his* تَلِيل, i. e., (TA,) *upon his neck*, and *his cheek:* (M, Ḳ, TA:) but the former is the more approved; and thus it is explained as used in the phrase وَتَلَّهُ لِلْجَبِينِ [in the Ḳur xxxvii. 103], (M,) *and he prostrated him*, or *threw him down*, (Aboo-Is-ḥák, T, Ṣ, Bḍ,) *upon his side, so that the side of his forehead fell upon the ground;* (Bḍ;) or *upon his mouth;* (Ḳatádeh, T;) or *upon his face.* (Bḍ.) And تَلَّ ٱلنَّاقَةَ *He made the she-camel to lie down upon her breast.* (TA.) — *He threw it upon the ground:* said of any corporeal thing. (M.) — تَلَّ, aor. ـُ (IAạr, T, Ḳ) and ـِ, (Ḳ,) [the latter anomalous in this case, and doubtful,] also signifies *He poured* (IAạr, T, Ḳ, TA) into the hand of another. (TA.) And تَلَّ ٱلشَّىْءَ فِى يَدِهِ *He gave*, or *delivered, the thing to him:* (M, Ḳ*:) or *he threw*, or *put, the thing into his hand.* (Ḳ.) The Prophet says, بَيْنَا أَنَا نَائِمٌ أُتِيتُ بِمَفَاتِيحِ خَزَائِنِ ٱلْأَرْضِ فَتُلَّتْ فِى يَدِى, i. e. [*While I was sleeping, I had the keys of the treasures of the earth brought to me*,] *and they were poured into my hand:* (IAạr, T, M:) or *were thrown*, or *put, into my hand.* (IAmb, M.) — Also, (Ḳ,) inf. n. تَلٌّ, (M,) *He lowered*, or *let down, the rope into the well*, (M, Ḳ,) *with the hand, on the occasion of drawing water.* (M.) — تَلَّهُ بِتَلَّةِ ▼ سَوْءٍ, [aor. ـُ, accord. to rule,] *He charged him*, or *upbraided him, with an evil*, or *a foul, thing.* (Th, M, Ḳ.) = تَلَّ, aor. ـِ (IAạr, T, M, Ḳ) and ـُ, (Ḳ,) [the latter anomalous in this case, and doubtful,] *He was*, or *became, prostrated*, or *thrown down;* (M, Ḳ;) *he fell*, or *fell down.* (IAạr, T, M, Ḳ.) = تَلَّ جَبِينُهُ, (M, Ḳ,) aor. ـِ (T, M, Ḳ) and ـُ, (Ḳ,) [the latter anomalous in this case also, and doubtful,] inf. n. تَلٌّ, (T, M,) *The side of his forehead sweated*, or *exuded sweat.* (M, Ḳ.) And in like manner the verb is used in relation to a watering-trough. (Lḥ, M.) = تَلِلْتُ is an imitative sequent to ضَلِلْتُ. (M.)

4. اتلّ المائعَ *He made the fluid*, or *liquid, to drop*, or *fall in drops.* (Ḳ.)

R. Q. 1. تَلْتَلَهُ, (Ṣ,) inf. n. تَلْتَلَةٌ, (M, Ḳ,) *He moved him, agitated him, shook him, put him into a state of motion* or *commotion;* (Ṣ, M, Ḳ;) or *did so vehemently:* (Ṣ, Ḳ, and Mgh in art. تر:) *he shook him*, or *shook him violently*, (namely, a drinker,) *and ordered him to breathe in his face, that he might know whether he had drunk* [*wine or the like*], *or not;* (TA in this art. and art. تر;) as also تَرْتَرَهُ, and مَزْمَزَهُ. (TA in the latter art.) — تَلْتَلَةٌ also signifies *Hard journeying:* and *rough*, or *severe*, or *vehement, driving.* (Ḳ.) You say, تَلْتَلَ ٱلرَّجُلُ *The man was rough*, or *severe*, or *vehement, in his driving.* (M.) = تَلْتَلَةُ بَهْرَآءَ is [The tribe of] *Bahrá's pronouncing the* ت *of*

تَفْعَلُونَ *with kesr;* (M, Ḳ;) *saying* تِفْعَلُونَ, *and* تِشْهَدُونَ, *and the like.* (M.)

تَلٌّ, accord. to Lth, [and accord. to general present usage,] *A mound,* or *hill, of dust,* or *earth,* [or *rubbish,*] *pressed together, not natural:* but this is a mistake [if meant as an explanation of the proper application], for with the Arabs it signifies *a natural hill:* En-Naḍr says that *it is of the smaller sort of* إِكَام [pl. of أَكَمَةٌ]; *it is of the height of a house,* or *tent, and the breadth of its back is about ten cubits; it is smaller than the* أَكَمَة, *has fewer stones, gives growth to nothing good, and its stones are compacted together exactly like those of the* أَكَمَة: (T:) [the mound, or artificial hill, above mentioned, is what is meant by its being said,] the تَلّ of dust, or earth, is well known: and the word signifies also *a heap of sand:* (M, Ḳ:*) in both of these senses from التَّلّ signifying "the throwing upon the ground" anything of a corporeal kind: (M:) also *a hill* (M, Ḳ, TA) *overtopping what is adjacent to it:* (TA:) pl. [of pauc.] أَتْلَالٌ (M, TA) and أَتُلٌّ (TA) and [of mult.] تِلَالٌ (T, Ṣ, Mṣb, Ḳ) and تُلُولٌ. (TA.) ═ Also *A pillow:* pl. أَتْلَالٌ, which is extr.: or the pl. signifies *certain sorts of cloths,* or *of garments:* (Ḳ, TA:) or, as some say, *of pillows.* (TA.)

تَلَّةٌ [inf. n. un. of 1, by Golius erroneously written تُلَّةٌ, and wrongly explained by him,] *A single act of pouring* [&c.]. (T, Ḳ.) — *A single act of lying upon the side.* (Ḳ.) ═ See also تَلْتَلَةٌ.

تِلَّةٌ *A mode,* or *manner, of lying upon the side.* (Fr, Ḳ.) — *Sluggishness, laziness,* or *indolence.* (Fr, T, Ḳ.) — *A state,* or *condition.* (Ṣ, M, Ḳ.) You say, هُوَ بِتِلَّةِ سَوْءٍ *He is in an evil state* or *condition;* like as you say بِبِيئَةِ سوء: (Ṣ:) and بَاتَ بِتِلَّةِ سَوْءٍ *He passed the night in an evil state* or *condition.* (M.) — *A thing;* as in the saying, تِلَّهُ بِتِلَّةِ سَوْءٍ [explained above]: see 1. (Th, M, Ḳ.) ═ *I. q.* بِلَّةٌ, (T, M,) or بَلَلٌ, as also ↓ تَلَلٌ: (Ḳ:) Abu-s-Semeydaʼ says that تَلَلٌ and بَلَلٌ and تِلَّةٌ and بِلَّةٌ are all one [i. e. *Moisture*]. (T.) One says, [app. to a person suspected of having drunk wine or the like,] مَا هٰذِهِ التِّلَّةُ بِفِيكَ i. e. البِلَّةُ [*What is this moisture in thy mouth?*]. (T, M.)

تَلَلٌ: see تِلَّةٌ.

التَّلَالِ in the phrase هُوَ الضَّلَالُ بْنُ التَّلَالِ is an imitative sequent. (Ṣ, Ḳ.)

تَلِيلٌ *Prostrated,* or *thrown down;* as also ↓ مَتْلُولٌ: (IAạr, T, M, Ḳ:) [pl. of the former تَلَّى, like as صَرْعَى is pl. of صَرِيعٌ, and قَتْلَى of قَتِيلٌ, &c.; as in the phrase] قَوْمٌ تَلَّى *A company of men prostrated,* or *thrown down.* (M, Ḳ.) ═ The *neck:* (T, M, Ḳ:) and the *cheek:* (TA:) pl. [of pauc.] أَتِلَّةٌ and [of mult.] تُلُلٌ and تَلَائِلُ. (M, Ḳ.) You say, لَهُ تَلِيلٌ كَجِذْعِ السَّحُوقِ [*He has a neck like the trunk of the tall palm-tree*]. (TA.)

التَّلَالَةُ is an imitative sequent to الضَّلَالَةُ. (T,* Ṣ, M,* Ḳ.)

تَلْتَلَةٌ inf. n. of R. Q. 1 [q. v.]. — Also *Hardship, difficulty, distress,* or *adversity:* (M, Ḳ:) pl. تَلَاتِلُ, (TA,) signifying *hardships, difficulties,* &c. (Aboo-Turáb, T, Ṣ, M.) ═ *A drinking-vessel that is made of the envelope* (قِيقَاءَةٌ, Ṣ, or قِيقَاءٌ, M and Ḳ) *of the spadix of a palm-tree;* (Ṣ, M, Ḳ;) so called because what it contains is poured into the throat; (T;) as also ↓ تَلَّةٌ: (M, Ḳ:) it is said that نَبِيذ is drunk with it. (TA.)

تَالٌّ is an imitative sequent to ضَالٌّ. (T,* Ṣ, M,* Ḳ.)

مَتَلٌّ *A place of prostrating.* (TA.)

مِتَلٌّ [as a subst.] *A thing with which one prostrates:* (M, Ḳ:) and hence *a spear:* (Mṣb:) and [as an epithet], applied to a spear, *with which one prostrates:* (T,* Ṣ, M:) or, applied to a spear, *erect;* or *even and erect.* (Ḳ.) — *Strong;* (Ṣ, M, Ḳ;) applied to a man and to a camel (M, Ḳ, TA) &c. (TA.) — A man *erect in prayer:* (T, M, Ḳ:) so accord. to Lth, who cites the saying,

* رِجَالٌ يُتِلُّونَ الصَّلَاةَ قِيَامُ *

but this is a mistake; for يَتْلُونَ is from تَلَى, and means, who make prayer to follow prayer. (T.)

مُتَلْتِلٌ One *who prostrates much,* or *often; who does so by twisting his leg with the leg of another.* (T.)

مَتْلُولٌ: see تَلِيلٌ.

تلأب

Q. 4. اِتْلَأَبَّ: &c.: see art. تلب.

تلان

تَلَانَ *i. q.* أَلْآنَ [*At the present time; now*]: (Aṣ, Ḳ:) the ت is added, as in تَحِينَ. (AʼObeyd &c.) See art. اين.

تلب

Q. Q. 4. اِتْلَأَبَّ, (T, Ṣ, M, &c.,) inf. n. اِتْلِئْبَابٌ, (Ṣ, Ḳ,) *It* (a thing, M, or an affair, or a case, Ṣ, Ḳ, or a road, A) *was,* or *became, uniform* or *undeviating,* (A,) *right,* or *rightly directed* or *ordered:* (Ṣ, M, A, Ḳ:) or (M) *it* (a thing, M, or a road, Ṣ, Ḳ) *was,* or *became, extended,* (Fr, T, Ṣ, M, A, Ḳ,) and *right, direct, even,* or *uniform:* (Ṣ, M, Ḳ:*) or (M) *it* (a thing, M) *was,* or *became, set up,* or *erect.* (M, A, Ḳ.) You say, مَرُّوا فَاتْلَأَبَّ بِهِمُ الطَّرِيقُ [*They went along, and the road was, or became, uniform, &c., with them;* i. e., *their road was, or became, uniform,* &c.]. (A.) And اتلأبّ أَمْرُهُمْ [*Their affair,* or *case, was,* or *became, right,* or *rightly directed* or *ordered*]. (A.) — *He* (an ass) *raised his breast and head.* (Ṣ, Ḳ.) — This verb and its derivatives are mentioned in the [T and] Ṣ and Ḳ in the present art.; but they are held by [ISd and] IB to be radically quadriliteral. (TA.)

تَلْبٌ *Loss;* or the *state of being lost;* or *perdition.* (A, Ḳ.) One says, تَبًّا لَهُ تَلْبًا, (Lth, T,) or تَبًّا لَهُ وَتَلْبًا [which may be rendered May God decree *loss and perdition to him*]. (Ḳ.)

تُلَأْبِيبَةٌ a subst. (Ṣ, M, Ḳ) from اِتْلَأَبَّ; (Fr, T, Ṣ, M, Ḳ;) [signifying The *state of being uniform* or *undeviating, right,* &c.;] like طُمَأْنِينَةٌ [from اِطْمَأَنَّ]. (TA.)

تَوْلَبٌ, perfectly decl. [when used as a proper name as well as when used as an appellative], because it is of the measure فَوْعَلٌ; (Sb, Ṣ;) for we judge its ت to be a radical, and its و to be augmentative, because فَوْعَل is more common [as the measure of a noun] than تَفْعَل; (M;) but accord. to Suh, the ت is a substitute for و, and, if so, it should be mentioned in art. ولب; (TA;) *A young ass;* syn. جَحْشٌ: (Ṣ, Ḳ:) or the *foal of a wild ass, when he has completed a year.* (M.) And أُمُّ تَوْلَبٍ is an appellation given to *The she-ass.* (Ṣ.) — The former is sometimes metaphorically applied to ‡ *A* [*young*] *man:* (M:) or *a boy.* (Ṣ.)

مُتْلَئِبٌّ [*Uniform* or *undeviating,*] *right,* or *rightly directed* or *ordered* [&c.: see the verb]; as also مُسْلَحِبٌّ. (Aṣ, T.) Also applied to a rule, (A, TA,) as meaning *Uniform, undeviating,* or *of general application; uniformly,* or *constantly, obtaining.* (TA.)

مَتَالِبُ [app. pl. of مَتْلَبٌ or مَتْلِبٌ] The *places where a wound causes* death; syn. مَقَاتِلُ. (IAạr, T.)

Quasi تلج

أَتْلَجَ: and تَوْلَجٌ: see art. ولج.

تلد

1. تَلَدَ, aor. ـِ (T, Ṣ, M, Mṣb, Ḳ) and ـُ, (T, Ṣ, M, Ḳ,) inf. n. تُلُودٌ; (Ṣ, M, Mṣb, Ḳ;) [and ↓ اِتَّلَدَ; (see Ḥam p. 609;)] *It* (property, consisting of camels or the like, syn. مَالٌ, T, Ṣ, M, &c.) *was,* or *became, old,* or *long-possessed;* (Mṣb;) *such as is termed* تِلَاد. (T, Ṣ, M, Mṣb, Ḳ.) — تَلَدَ فُلَانٌ عِنْدَنَا *Such a one was born of parents at our abode,* or *home.* (L.) — And تَلَدَ, (T, Ṣ, M, Ḳ,) aor. ـُ, (M, Ḳ,) inf. n. as above; (T, L;) and تَلِدَ, aor. ـَ; (Ḳ;) *He remained, stayed, abode,* or *dwelt,* (Aṣ, T, Ṣ, M, Ḳ,) فِى بَنِى فُلَانٍ *among the sons of such a one,* (Ṣ,) and بَيْنَهُمْ *among them,* (M,) and بِمَكَانٍ *in a place.* (Aṣ, T, L.) ═ See also 2.

2. تلّد, (IAạr, T, Ḳ,) inf. n. تَتْلِيدٌ; (Ḳ;) or ↓ تَلَدَ; (so in the L as on the authority of IAạr, and accord. to Lḥ as is said in the TA;) *i. q.* جَمَعَ *and* مَنَعَ [app. as meaning *He collected and defended property*]; (IAạr, T, L, K;) said of a man. (IAạr, T, L.)

4. اتلد, (T, Ṣ, L,) and اتلد مَالًا, (T, M, Mṣb, Ḳ,) *He got, obtained,* or *acquired,* (اِتَّخَذَ,) *property* [*such as is termed* تِلَاد, as is implied in the T and M and Ḳ]: (T, Ṣ, L, Mṣb:) or *he possessed*

property such as is termed تِلَادٌ. (So accord. to the explanation of the act. part. n., q. v., in the Mgh.)

8: see 1.

تَلْدٌ: see تِلَادٌ, in two places.

تُلْدٌ: see تِلَادٌ, in two places. —— Also The *young one of an eagle.* (M, Ḳ.)

تَلَدٌ: see تِلَادٌ: —— and تَلِيدٌ.

تِلَادٌ, applied to مَالٌ [i. e. property, consisting of camels or the like], (T, Ṣ, M, &c.,) *Old*, or *long-possessed;* as also ↓ تَالِدٌ and ↓ تَلِيدٌ, (Mgh, Mṣb,) both of these meaning *old, original,* property, (A,) and ↓ مُتْلَدٌ: (L:) or *original, old,* or *long-possessed, born at one's own abode,* or *home;* as also ↓ تَالِدٌ and ↓ إِتْلَادٌ: (Ṣ:) *contr. of* طَارِفٌ (Ṣ, A, Mgh, Mṣb) *and* طَرِيفٌ: (Mgh, Mṣb:) or *born at the owner's abode,* or *house; or that brings forth there;* (M, Ḳ;) as also ↓ تَالِدٌ (Ḳ) and ↓ تَلِيدٌ and ↓ تَلْدٌ (M, Ḳ) and ↓ تَلَدٌ (Ḳ) and ↓ تُلْدٌ and ↓ إِتْلَادٌ, (M, Ḳ,) like إِسْنَامٌ, (M, [in the CḲ written أَتْلَاد, and so accord. to the MṢ,]) and ↓ مُتْلَدٌ; (M, Ḳ; [written in a copy of the M مُتَلَّد;]) wherefore, [i. e. because of the meaning,] Yaḳḳoob judges that the ت is a substitute for و; [as is said to be the case in the Ṣ;] but this is not a valid decision; for, were it so, the word in some of its variations would be reduced to its original: (M:) or any *old,* or *long-possessed,* property, (T, M, L,) consisting of animals &c., (M, L,) *inherited from parents;* (T, M, L;) as also ↓ تَالِدٌ (T, L) and ↓ تَلِيدٌ and ↓ مُتْلَدٌ (T, M, L [the last written in a copy of the T مُتْلِدٌ, and in a copy of the M مُتَلَّد,]) and ↓ تَلْدٌ and ↓ تُلْدٌ and ↓ إِتْلَادٌ, as above: (M:) or slaves, or pasturing beasts, *that breed at one's own abode,* or *home, and become old,* or *long possessed:* (ISh, as related by Sh:) or that *which you yourself breed,* or *rear.* (Aṣ, T.) [See also تَلِيدٌ, below. —— Hence,] هُنَّ مِنْ تِلَادِى, said by a man, (namely, Ibn-Mes'ood, M,) in reference to certain chapters (سُوَر) of the Ḳur-án, meaning ‡ *They are of those which I acquired* (or *learned,* L) *long ago* from the Ḳur-án: (Ṣ, M, L:) thus saying, he likened them to the property, or camels &c., called تِلَاد. (M, L.) —— [Az says,] I heard a man of Mekkeh say, تِلَادِى بِمَكَّةَ, i. e. مِيلَادِى [app. meaning *My birth was in Mekkeh*]. (T.)

تَلِيدٌ: see تِلَادٌ, in three places. —— Also That *which is born at the abode,* or *home, of another than thyself, and which, while young, thou afterwards purchasest, and which remains with thee:* (Aṣ, T:) or one *who is born in a foreign country, and is carried away while young to the territory of the Arabs:* (Mgh:) or one *who is born in a foreign country, and then brought away while young, and who grows up in the territory of the Muslims;* (Ṣ, Ḳ;) as also ↓ تَلَدٌ: (Ḳ:) or i. q. مُوَلَّدٌ and مُوَلَّدَةٌ, [masc. and fem.,] meaning one *that is born at thine own abode,* or *home:* (ISh, T: [see also تِلَادٌ:]) or one *who has parents at thine own abode,* or *home;* whereas مُوَلَّد signifies one who has only one parent there: (Mgh, from the Tekmileh [of the 'Eyn]:) the fem. is with ة; (Ṣ;) signifying a female slave *who is born in a foreign country, and is carried away, and grows up in the territory of the Arabs:* (Ḳt, T:) or a female slave *whose father and family and all her relations are in one country and who is herself in another:* (ISh, L in art. ولد:) or a female slave *born the property of a people with whom are her parents:* (L in art. ولد:) or a female slave *inherited by her owner;* if born at his own abode, or home, [of a mother already belonging to him,] she is called وَلِيدَةٌ: (T, L:) you say رَجُلٌ تَلِيدٌ; pl. تُلَدَآءُ: and اِمْرَأَةٌ تَلِيدٌ [and تَلِيدَةٌ]; pl. تَلَائِدُ (Lḥ, M, L) and تُلُدٌ. (Lḥ, L.) It is related in a trad. of Shureyḥ, that a man purchased a female slave, and the two parties made it a condition that she should be a مُوَلَّدَة; but the purchaser found her to be a تَلِيدَة, and therefore returned her: (Ṣ, Mgh:) a مُوَلَّدَة is like a تِلَاد, i. e. born at thine own abode, or home; (Ṣ;) or born in the territory of the Muslims. (Mgh.) —— Also, metaphorically, ‡ *A child,* absolutely. (Ḥar p. 317.)

تَالِدٌ: see تِلَادٌ, in four places. —— تَالِدٌ بَالِدٌ: see art. بلد.

إِتْلَادٌ, by some written أَتْلَادٌ: see تِلَادٌ, in three places.

مُتْلَدٌ, applied to مَالٌ, (Ṣ, Mṣb,) pass. part. n. of 4: (Mṣb:) see تِلَادٌ, in three places. —— [Hence,] خُلُقٌ مُتْلَدٌ, (M, L, TA,) in the Ḳ, مُتَلَّدٌ, said to be like مُعَظَّمٌ, but this is a mistake, (TA,) [and in the CḲ, خَلْقٌ is erroneously put for خُلُقٌ,] † *An old,* or *a long-possessed, natural disposition,* or *quality.* (M, L, Ḳ.) IAạr cites as an ex. this verse:

مَا ذَا وُزِينَا مِنْكِ أُمَّ مَعْبَدِ
مِنْ سَعَةِ الحِلْمِ وَخُلْقٍ مُتْلَدِ

[app. meaning *What has been experienced from us, on thy part, Umm-Maạbad, of largeness of forbearance, and of long-possessed good natural dispositions,* or *qualities?* وُزِينَا seems to be here used for رُزِئْنَا; or the latter may be the correct reading]. (M, L.)

مُتْلِدٌ [act. part. n. of 4:] *A possessor of property such as is termed* تِلَاد: and hence, —— *A first owner* or *proprietor;* as the weaver of a piece of cloth, and the man who delivers his she-camel [and is owner of her young one]. (Mgh.)

تلع

تَلْعَةٌ *High,* or *elevated, land* or *ground:* (AO, Ṣ, Ḳ:) and *low,* or *depressed, land* or *ground:* (AO, Ṣ, Mṣb, Ḳ:) thus bearing two contr. significations, (Ṣ, Ḳ,) accord. to AO: (Ṣ:) or it has not these significations, but means *a water-course from the upper part of a valley to its lower part;* therefore sometimes *its upper part* is described [by this name], and sometimes *its lower part:* (IAạr, IB, TA:) or it has the second of the significations above, (Mṣb, Ḳ,) and the first, (Ḳ,) and signifies also *a water-course* (Mṣb, Ḳ) *from the upper part of a valley:* (Mṣb:) and also, (Ḳ,) or, accord. to IDrd, (TA,) the *wide part of the mouth of a valley:* and *a high,* or *an elevated, piece of land* or *ground:* (IDrd, Ḳ:) sometimes, says IDrd, it has this last application; but the former is the original signification: (TA:) it is also said to signify *high,* or *elevated, and rugged, land* or *ground, in which the torrent goes to and fro, and from which it then pours to another* تلعة, *lower than it; and which is fertile in plants,* or *herbage:* (L, TA:) or *a water-course from the higher part of the ground to the bottom of a valley:* (AA, Ṣ:) pl. تِلَاعٌ (AA, Ṣ, Mṣb, Ḳ) and تَلَعَاتٌ: (Ḳ:) and, (Ḳ,) or, accord. to Sh, (TA,) تِلَاعٌ signifies *water-courses flowing from acclivities and the* [*eminences termed*] نِجَاف *and the mountains, until they pour into the valley:* (Sh, Ḳ:) to which Sh adds, *the* تلعة *of the mountain being formed by the water's coming and furrowing and excavating it until it escapes from it:* (TA:) *but* تلاع *are nowhere except* [the word إِلَّا has been dropped in the CḲ] *in the* صَحَارَى [or *deserts*]; (Sh, Ḳ;) *and sometimes a* تلعة *comes from a distance of five leagues* (فَرَاسِخ) *to the valley; and when it flows from the mountains, and falls into the* صحارى [or *deserts*], *it excavates in them what resembles a moat: when it becomes so large as to be like the half, or two thirds, of the valley, it is termed* مَيْثَآءُ: (Sh, TA:) تَلْعَةٌ is also said to be like رحبة [i. e. رَحْبَةٌ or رُحْبَةٌ, app. as meaning the *part* of a valley *in which its water flows into it from its two sides*]; and the pl. [or rather coll. gen. n.] is said to be تَلْعٌ. (TA.) It is said in a trad., فَيَجِىْءُ مَطَرٌ لَا يَمْتَنِعُ مِنْهُ ذَنَبُ تَلْعَةٍ [*And a rain will come, in consequence of which the end of a water-course will not be impeded*]: meaning to denote its abundance, and that no place will be exempt from it. (TA.) And in a prov., فُلَانٌ لَا يَمْنَعُ ذَنَبَ تَلْعَةٍ [*Such a one will not impede the end of a water-course*]: (Ḳ,* TA:) applied to the abject and contemptible. (Ḳ.) And in another, (ISh,) لَا أَثِقُ بِسَيْلِ تَلْعَتِكَ [*I do not, or will not, trust in the flow of thy water-course*]: applied to him in whom one does not trust: (ISh, Ḳ:) i. e. I do not, or will not, trust in what thou sayest, and what thou adducest: characterizing the person as a liar. (ISh.) And in another, (IAạr,) مَا أَخَافُ إِلَّا مِنْ سَيْلِ تَلْعَتِى [*I fear not save from the flow of my water-course*]: i. e., from the sons of my uncle, and my relations: (IAạr, Ḳ:) for he who descends the water-course is in danger: if the torrent come, it sweeps him away. (IAạr.)

تلف

1. تَلِفَ, (Ṣ, M, Mṣb, Ḳ,) aor. ـَ, (Ḳ,) inf. n. تَلَفٌ, (Lth, T, Ṣ, M, &c.,) *He,* or *it,* (a thing, Lth, T, Ṣ, Mṣb, of any kind, Lth, T,) *perished, passed away, was not, was no more, became non-existent* or *annihilated;* or *went away, no one knew whither;* or *became in a bad,* or *corrupt, state; became corrupted, vitiated, marred,* or *spoiled;* [in this sense the verb is often used in the present day;] or *he died*: syn. هَلَكَ; (M, Ḳ;) and of the inf. n., عَطَبٌ (Lth, T,) and هَلَاكٌ. (Lth, T, Ṣ.) [See also تَلَفٌ, below.]

4. اتلفهُ *He caused him*, or *it*, (a thing, Ṣ, Mṣb, or property, M,) *to perish, pass away*, or *be no more; or to go away, no one knew whither; or to become corrupted, vitiated, marred*, or *spoiled*: (Ṣ, M:) or *he made it* (his property, T) *to pass away, come to an end, come to nought*, or *be exhausted; destroyed, wasted, consumed*, or *exhausted, it*; (T, Ḳ;) *by prodigality*. (T.) [See an ex. in a verse of Ibn-Muḳbil cited voce أَخْلَفَ.] — El-Farezdaḳ says,

* وَقَوْمٍ كِرَامٍ قَدْ نَقَلْنَا إِلَيْهِمِ *
* قِرَاهُمْ فَأَتْلَفْنَا المَنَايَا وَأَتْلَفُوا *

(so in the T and L,) or

* وَأَضْيَافِ لَيْلٍ قَدْ نَقَلْنَا قِرَاهُمُ *
* إِلَيْهِمْ وَأَتْلَفْنَا المَنَايَا وَأَتْلَفُوا *

(so in some copies of the Ḳ,) or قَدْ بَلَغْنَا قِرَاهُمُ, (so in other copies of the Ḳ and in the TA,) or قد فَعَلْنَا قراهم, (so in the O,) i. e., [accord. to the different readings, *How many a generous company of men* has there been, or *how many guests of the night* have there been, *to whom we have brought their entertainment, and*] *we have found the fates to be destructive*, (T, Ḳ,*) *and they have found them to be so*: (T:) it is like the phrase أَتَيْنَا فُلَانًا فَأَبْخَلْنَاهُ and أَجْبَنَّاهُ: (TA:) or *we found the fates to destroy us, and they found them to destroy them*: or *we made the fates to be destruction to them, and they made them to be destruction to us*: (ISk, Ḳ:) he means, we engaged with them in vehement fight, and slew them. (TA.)

تَلَفٌ *A perishing, passing away*, &c. [See 1.] (Lth, T, Ṣ, &c.) It is said in a trad., (TA,) إِنَّ مِنَ القَرَفِ التَّلَفَ (T, TA) *Verily, from the being near to pestilence*, or *epidemic disease, there results death*, or *perdition*. (T.) And in a prov., السَّلَفُ تَلَفٌ [*The paying for a thing beforehand is a* cause of *perishing* to one's property]. (TA.) And one says, ذَهَبَتْ نَفْسُهُ تَلَفًا and طَلَفًا, (Ṣ, Ḳ,) both meaning the same, (Ṣ,) *His blood went for nothing, or as a thing of no account, unretaliated, and uncompensated by a mulct*. (Ṣ, Ḳ.)

تَلِفٌ, (M,) or ▼تَالِفٌ, (Mṣb, TA,) part. n. of 1, *Perishing*, &c.; (M, Mṣb,* TA;) as also ▼تَلْفَانُ, which is post-classical. (TA.)

تَلَفَةٌ *A* [*hill, mountain*, or *mass of rock, such as is termed*] هَضْبَة, *difficult of access, so that he who attempts it fears perdition*, or *death*. (El-Hejeree, M.)

تَلْفَانُ: } see تَلِفٌ.
تَالِفٌ: }

مَتْلَفٌ *A place of perishing* or *perdition*: (Ḳ:) *a* [*desert such as is termed*] مَفَازَة; (Ṣ, Ḳ;) because most of those who traverse it perish; and so ▼مَتْلَفَةٌ; (TA;) or the latter signifies *a* [*desert such as is termed*] قَفْر: (M:) the pl. of the former [or of both] is مَتَالِفُ. (TA.)

رَجُلٌ مِتْلَفٌ لِمَالِهِ, (Mṣb,) or ▼مِتْلَفٌ, and ▼مِتْلَافٌ, (M,) *A man who destroys*, or *wastes, his property*: (M:) or the last has an intensive signification, (Mṣb,) meaning *who destroys*, or *wastes, his property much*. (Ṣ.) You say also, رَجُلٌ مُخْلِفٌ مُتْلِفٌ, (Ḳ, and Ḥar p. 312,) or مِخْلَفٌ مِتْلَفٌ▼, (TA in art. خلف,) and مِخْلَافٌ ▼مِتْلَافٌ, (Ḳ, and Ḥar ubi suprà,) meaning *A man of courage and liberality, who makes what he takes as spoil, of the property of his enemies, to supply the place of that which he consumes by expenditure to satisfy the claims of his friends*. (Ḥar ubi suprà.)

مِتْلَفٌ: see the next preceding paragraph, in two places.

مَتْلَفَةٌ: see مَتْلَفٌ. — Also *A deep hollow, cavity*, or *pit, where one looks down upon destruction*. (M.)

مِتْلَافٌ: see مُتْلِفٌ, in two places.

مَتْلُوفٌ [*i. q.* مُنْكَرٌ, q. v.; i. e.] *contr. of* مَعْرُوفٌ: but this is post-classical. (TA.)

تلك

تِلْكَ and تَلْكَ and تَالِكَ: see art. تا.

تلمذ

Q. 1. تَلْمَذَ *He was*, or *became, a* تِلْمِيذ [or *disciple*, &c.], لِفُلَانٍ *to such a one*. (TA, passim.)

تِلْمِيذٌ *A disciple; a pupil; a learner*: or *a special servant of a teacher*: so says 'Abd-El-Ḳádir El-Baghdádee, who composed a treatise solely on this word: (MF, TA:) or simply *a servant; a follower; a dependant*: pl. تَلَامِيذُ (L, TA) [and تَلَامِذَةٌ].

تلو

1. تَلَا *He followed*; or *went*, or *walked, behind*, or *after*. (IAạr, T.) You say, تَلَوْتُهُ, (Ṣ, M, Mṣb, Ḳ,) aor. ـُ, (Ṣ, Mṣb, Ḳ,) inf. n. تُلُوٌّ (Ṣ, M, Mṣb, Ḳ) and تُلْوٌ, (Er-Rághib, MF,) *I followed him or it; or went*, or *walked, behind*, or *after, him or it*; (Ṣ, M, Mṣb, Ḳ;) namely, a man [&c.]; (Ṣ, Mṣb;) *immediately*, or *without intervention*; and sometimes it means *bodily* [or *in reality*]; and sometimes, *virtually*, or *in effect*: (Er-Rághib:) and so تَلَيْتُهُ; (Ḳ;) and ▼تَتَلَّيْتُهُ, (Aṣ,* T,* Ḳ,) inf. n. تَتَلِّيَةٌ. (Ḳ.) The phrase, in the Ḳur xci. 2, وَالقَمَرِ إِذَا تَلَاهَا means *By the moon when its rising follows the rising thereof*; i. e., the rising of the sun; at the beginning of the lunar month: (Bḍ:) or, *when it follows in rising the setting thereof*, (Bḍ, Jel,) on the night of the full moon: (Bḍ:) or, *when it follows it in becoming round, and in fullness of light*; (M,* Bḍ;) i. e., *when it follows it in the way of imitation, and in respect of rank*; for the moon borrows its light of the sun, and is to it in the place of a successor. (Er-Rághib.) Here, Ks pronounced تلاها with imáleh, [either because تَلَيْتُ is a dial. var. of تَلَوْتُ, or] because, although it has و for its last radical letter, it occurs with words that may be so pronounced, namely, يَغْشَاهَا and بَنَاهَا. (M.) — تَلَوْتُ الإِبِلَ ‡ *I drove*, or *brought*, or *gathered, the camels together, from their several quarters*: because the driver follows the driven. (A, TA.) — هُوَ يَتْلُو فُلَانًا *He imitates such a one, and follows what he does; he follows him in action*. (T.) — تَلَا, (T,) first pers. تَلَوْتُ, (Ṣ, M, Mṣb, Ḳ,) aor. ـُ, (T,) inf. n. تِلَاوَةٌ, (T, Ṣ, M, Mṣb, Ḳ,) *He read*, or *perused*, or *he recited*, (T, M, Ḳ,) the Ḳur-án, (Ṣ, M, Mṣb, Ḳ,) or any discourse, or piece of language: (M, Ḳ:) or *he followed* it, (I 'Ab, T, Ṣ,* M,) *and did according to it*; (I 'Ab, Mujáhid, T;) namely, the Scripture: (I 'Ab, Mujáhid, T, M:) or the inf. n. specially signifies the *following* God's revealed Scriptures, sometimes *by reading*, or *perusing*, or *by reciting*, and sometimes *by conforming therewith* [as well as by reading, &c., but not otherwise, for] every تِلَاوَة is قِرَآءَة, but the reverse is not the case. (Er-Rághib, TA.) [You say also, تَلَا عَلَيْهِ *He recited*, or *related, to him* a narrative &c.: see Ḳur v. 30, &c.] And فُلَانٌ يَتْلُو عَلَى فُلَانٍ, and يَقُولُ عَلَيْهِ, *Such a one lies*, or *says what is false, against such a one*. (TA.) وَاتَّبَعُوا مَا تَتْلُو الشَّيَاطِينُ, in the Ḳur ii. 96, means [*And they followed*] *what the devils related*, or *rehearsed*, ('Aṭà, T,) or *spoke*; (A 'Obeyd, T;) or, *what the devils* of the Jinn, or of mankind, or of both, *read*, or *recited*, or what they *followed*, of the writings of enchantment: (Bḍ:) some here read ▼تَتَلَّى. (T.) Hence the saying, لَا دَرَيْتَ وَلَا تَلَيْتَ: (T:) or, accord. to Yoo, it is ▼وَلَا أَتْلَيْتَ: (T, Ṣ:) and others say that it is وَلَا ٱتْتَلَيْتَ, from أَلَوْتُ. (T. [See these three readings explained in the latter part of the first paragraph of art. الو.]) — *He remained behind*, or *held back*. (IAạr, ISk, T.) You say, تَلَا بَعْدَ قَوْمِهِ *He held back*, or *lagged behind, after his people*, or *company, and remained*. (TA.) And تَلَوْتُهُ, (AZ, A 'Obeyd, T, Ṣ, M, Ḳ,) and تَلَوْتُ عَنْهُ, (AZ, T, M, Ḳ,) aor. ـُ, (AZ, T,) inf. n. تُلُوٌّ, (AZ, T, M,) *I left him, and held back from going with him*: (AZ, T:) *I held back from him*, or *from aiding him, and left him*: (AZ, A 'Obeyd, T, Ṣ, M, Ḳ:) thus the verb bears two contr. significations. (Ḳ.) — *He bought a* تِلْو, meaning *the young one of a mule*. (IAạr, T, Ḳ.) — تَلِيَتْ لِي مِنْ حَقِّي تَلِيَّةٌ, and تَلَاوَةٌ, aor. ـَ, (ISk, Ṣ,) inf. n. تَلًا, (TA,) *There remained to me, of my right*, or *due, a remainder*. (ISk, Ṣ.) And تَلِيَتْ لِي عِنْدَهُ تَلِيَّةٌ *There remained to me, with him*, or *there remained owing to me by him, a remainder*. (Aṣ, T.) And تَلِيَ مِنَ الشَّهْرِ كَذَا, (M, Ḳ,) inf. n. تَلًا, (M,) *There remained, of the month, such a portion*. (M, Ḳ.)

2: see 1, in two places. — هُوَ يُتَلِّي بَقِيَّةَ حَاجَتِهِ *He demands, and seeks to obtain, the remainder of that which he wants*. (T.) — تَلَّى صَلَاتَهُ, (T, M, Ḳ,) inf. n. تَتْلِيَةٌ, (Ḳ,) *He made his prayer to be followed by other prayer*: (T:) or *he made his prescribed prayer to be followed by supererogatory prayer*. (Sh, M, Ḳ.) — تَلَّى, inf. n. as above, [is also said to signify] *He stood erect for prayer.* (TA. [But see مُتَلٍّ, in art. تل.] — Also *He accomplished*, or *fulfilled, his vow.* (IAạr, M, Ḳ.) — And *He was at the last gasp.* (AZ, Ṣ, M, Ḳ.) ═ See also 4.

3. تالاهُ, inf. n. مُتَالَاةٌ, i. q. رَاسَلَهُ [meaning, فِى الغِنَآءِ, i. e. *He relieved him,* or *aided him, in singing, by taking up the strain when the latter was unable to prolong his voice sufficiently for the accomplishing of the cadence; or he did so with a high voice:* see مُتَالٍ, below]. (TA.)

4. أَتْلَيْتُهُ إِيَّاهُ *I made him to follow him;* or, *it to follow it.* (M, Ḳ.) Hence, (TA,) اتلاهُ اللّٰهُ أَطْفَالًا *God made him,* or *may God make him, to have little children following him.* (Ṣ, TA.) And أَتْلَتْ *She* (a camel) *had her young one following her:* (Ṣ, Ḳ:) whence the saying, لَا دَرَيْتَ وَلَا أَتْلَيْتَ; accord. to Yoo: (Ṣ:) but see 1, where two other readings are mentioned, with a reference to the explanations. — [Hence also,] أَتْلَيْتُهُ *I preceded him, outwent him, outstripped him,* or *got before him.* (Ṣ.) And مَا زِلْتُ أَتْلُوهُ حَتَّى أَتْلَيْتُهُ *I ceased not to follow him until I became before him.* (Ṣ.) — أَتْلَيْتُ حَقِّى عِنْدَهُ *I left a remainder of my due with him.* (Ṣ, Ḳ.) And أَتْلَيْتُ عِنْدَهُ تَلِيَّةً *I left with him a remainder* (T, M) *of a thing,* or *of a debt,* or *of a needful thing.* (M.) أَتْلَيْتُهُ عَلَى فُلَانٍ — *I referred him,* or *turned him over, for the payment of what was owing to him, to such a one, transferring the responsibility for the debt to the latter.* (T, Ṣ,* Ḳ.*) — اتلاهُ ذِمَّةً *He gave him a bond,* or *an obligation, whereby he became responsible for his safety:* (Ṣ, Ḳ:) and اتلاهُ alone (T, M, Ḳ) signifies the same; (T;) *he gave him what is termed* تَلَآء, (M, Ḳ,) i. e. ذِمَّةٌ, (Ḳ,) or جِوَارًا, (M, Ḳ,) and meaning also *an arrow on which was written his* (*the giver's*) *name,* (Ḳ,* TA,) *in order that, when he went to a tribe, he might show it to them, and they would not harm him:* (TA:) and اتلاهُ سَهْمًا † *he gave him an arrow whereby to demand protection,* (M, Ḳ, TA,) *in order that he might not be harmed:* and اتلاهُ نَعْلًا *he gave him a sandal for that purpose:* (TA:) and it means ‡ *he made him his* تِلْو [or *follower*], *and his companion.* (TA.) ▼ تَلَّى, also, signifies, like أَتْلَى, *He gave him his bond,* or *obligation, by which he became responsible for his safety.* (TA.)

5. تتلّى *He sought repeatedly,* or *in a leisurely manner,* or *by degrees,* (T, Ṣ, M, Ḳ,) *to obtain* his right, or due, *until he received it fully,* or *wholly,* (T, Ṣ,) or *to obtain* a thing. (M, Ḳ.) — *He collected much wealth.* (IAạr, T.) — تَتَلَّيْتُ حَقِّى عِنْدَهُ *I left with him,* or *in his possession, somewhat remaining of my right,* or *due.* (IAạr, T.) ═ *Somewhat remained of his debt.* (IAạr, T.)

6. تَتَالَتِ الأُمُورُ *The things,* or *events, were consecutive; they followed one another.* (M, Ḳ.) And جَآءَتِ الخَيْلُ تَتَالِيًا *The horses,* or *horsemen, came consecutively.* (Ṣ.)

10. استلاهُ الشَّىْءُ *He,* or *it, invited him to follow the thing.* (M, Ḳ.) — اسْتَتْلَيْتُ فُلَانًا *I made such a one to follow me.* (IAạr, T.) — And *I looked for, expected, awaited,* or *waited for, such a one.* (IAạr, T.) ═ استلى فُلَانًا also signifies ‡ *He sought,* or *demanded, of such a one, the arrow of protection* [called تَلَآء, q. v.]. (TA.)

تَلًا : see تَلِيَّةٌ.

تِلْوٌ *A thing that follows another thing:* (Ḳ:) and *a follower* of another man. (TA.) See also تَالٍ. تِلْوُ الشَّىْءِ means *That which follows the thing:* (Ṣ:) and هٰذَا تِلْوُ هٰذَا *This is what follows this.* (M.) [Hence,] تِلْوُ النَّاقَةِ *The she-camel's young one that follows her:* (Ṣ:) and تِلْوٌ [alone] *a ewe's,* or *she-goat's,* (M,) or *she-camel's,* (Ḳ,) *young one when weaned, and following the mother;* pl. أَتْلَآءٌ; and fem. with ة: (M, Ḳ:) and the *young one of the ass;* (M, Ḳ;) because he follows his mother: (M:) and the *young one of a mule:* (IAạr, T, Ḳ:) and, accord. to En-Naḍr, *a kid,* and *a lamb, that has become large in the stomach* or *belly* (استكرش) *and in no need of his mother;* fem. with ة: (T:) or the fem. signifies *a she-kid that has passed beyond the limit of those that are termed* أَجْفَار [pl. of جَفْرٌ, q. v.], (M, Ḳ,) *until she has completed a year* [*from her birth*] *and so become a* جَذَع. (M.) And a تِلْوَة of sheep or goats is *One that is brought forth,* or *that brings forth,* [the verb is تُنْتَجُ, which has both of these meanings,] *before the* صَفَرِيَّة [q. v.]. (Ṣ, Ḳ.) ═ Also *High,* or *lofty.* (Ḳ.) One says, إِنَّهُ لَتِلْوُ المِقْدَارِ, *Verily he,* or *it, is high,* or *lofty, in measure.* (TA.)

تَلَآءٌ *A bond,* or *an obligation, by which one becomes responsible for the safety of another:* (Ṣ, M, Ḳ:) and *an arrow upon which the giver writes his name,* (M, Ḳ, [in the CḲ, المُتْلِىّ is erroneously put for المُتْلِى,]) *and which he gives to a man, who, when he goes to a tribe, and shows it to them, passes unmolested:* (M:) and, accord. to IAmb, *responsibility,* or *suretiship.* (TA.) — Also The *transfer of a debt,* or *of a claim, by shifting the responsibility from one person to another.* (Z, TA.)

تُلُوٌّ A man *incessantly following:* (IAạr, M, Ḳ:) not mentioned by Yaạḳoob among the instances of this measure which he has limited; as حُسُوٌّ and فُسُوٌّ. (M.)

تَلِىٌّ [accord. to the CḲ, erroneously, تِلْىٌ,] *Using many oaths* (كَثِيرُ الأَيْمَانِ): and *Having much wealth.* (IAạr, T, Ḳ.)

تَلِيَّةٌ [accord. to the CḲ, erroneously, تَلْيَة,] and ▼ تُلَاوَةٌ (ISk, T, Ṣ, M, Ḳ) and ▼ تَلًا (M, TA) *A remainder* (ISk, T, Ṣ, M, Ḳ) of a thing, (M,) or of a right or due, (ISk, Ṣ,) or of a debt, (Ṣ, M, Ḳ,) and of a thing wanted, (ISk and T in explanation of the second word, and M,) &c. (Ḳ.) One says also, ذَهَبَتْ تَلِيَّةُ الشَّبَابِ ‡ *The remainder of youthfulness,* or *youthful vigour, departed.* (TA.) And فُلَانٌ تَلِيَّةُ الأَحْرَارِ ‡ [*Such a one is the last remaining of the ingenuous*]. (TA.) — وَقَعَ كَذَا تَلِيَّةَ كَذَا *Such a thing happened after such a thing.* (M.)

تُلَاوَةٌ : see تَلِيَّةٌ.

تَلَوِّى *A kind of boat:* (M, Ḳ:) of the measure فَعَوَّلٌ, (M, TA,) or فَعَلْوَلٌ: (TA:) so called because it follows the larger vessel: mentioned by Aboo-'Alee in the Tedhkireh. (M.)

تَلَّآءٌ لِلْقُرْآنِ One *who reads, peruses,* or *recites, the Ḳur-án,* or *who follows it,* or *acts according to it, much,* or *often.* (Mgh.)

تَالٍ act. part. n. of تَلَا; *Following; going,* or *walking, behind,* or *after;* [*immediately,* or *without intervention;* either *in reality,* or only *in effect;* (see 1;)] (T, Mṣb;) as also ▼ تِلْوٌ. (Mṣb.) — التَّالِى *The fourth of the ten horses that are started together in a race.* (TA voce سُكَيْت &c., and Ḥam p. 46.) — Also, (Sh, TA voce مُجْدَح,) and تَالِى النَّجْمِ [meaning *The follower of the Pleiades*], (Ḳzw,) *the star called* الدَّبَرَان. (Sh, Ḳzw.) — And تَالِيَاتُ النُّجُومِ *The last of the stars;* [app. *the last that are seen in the morning-twilight;*] (TA;) as also التَّوَالِى. (M, TA.) [تَالِيَاتٌ and تَوَالٍ are both pls. of تَالِيَةٌ, fem. of تَالٍ.] — التَّوَالِى also signifies *The last* of women journeying in vehicles upon camels; (M, Ḳ;) and in like manner, of camels. (M.) — Also *Hinder parts, posteriors,* or *rumps:* and *the hinder parts* of horses: or (of a horse, M) *the tail and hind legs.* (M, Ḳ.) One says, إِنَّهُ لَخَبِيثُ التَّوَالِى and سَرِيعُ التَّوَالِى [app. meaning *Verily he is quick in the hind legs*]. (M.) And the Arabs say, لَيْسَ هَوَادِى الخَيْلِ كَالتَّوَالِى, i. e., *The necks of horses are not like their hinder parts.* (TA.) — فَالتَّالِيَاتِ ذِكْرًا [in the Ḳur xxxvii. 3] means *And those* angels, or angels and others, *that recite* the *praise* of God. (M.)

مُتْلٍ and مُتْلِيَةٌ (T, M) A mother, (T,) or a she-camel, and a female wild animal, (M,) *having her young one following her:* pl. مَتَالٍ. (T, M.) — Also, both sings., A she-camel *that brings forth in the last portion of the breeding-time:* or the latter sing. signifies one *that is late in bringing forth;* and the former sing. has the first of the meanings explained in this paragraph: (M:) or, as some say, the latter sing. signifies one *that has become heavy by pregnancy, so that the head of her fœtus has turned towards the tail and the vulva;* a meaning not agreeing with the derivation: (IJ, M:) or, as some say, this word signifies [simply] *pregnant:* (Ḥam p. 688:) accord. to El-Báhilee, the pl. signifies she-camels *of which some have brought forth, and others have not.* (TA.) You say, إِبِلُهُمْ مَتَالٍ, meaning *Their camels have not brought forth until the season called the* صَيْف, (Ḳ, TA,) which is the last part of the breeding-time. (TA.)

مُتَالٍ One *who relieves,* or *aids, another,* in *singing,* and *in work, by taking up the strain,* or *the work, when the latter is unable to continue it:* (IAạr, T:) or one *who so relieves,* or *aids, the singer, with a high voice:* (Ṣ, TA:) and one *who sings to camels to urge them on, or excite them.* (TA.)

مُسْتَتْلٍ [act. part. n. of 10, q. v. It is said in the T to have a signification derived from تَلَآءٌ in the last of the senses assigned to the latter word above; so that it seems to mean *Seeking, or demanding, the transfer of a debt, or claim, or the like, by shifting the responsibility from one person to another*].

تلى

1. تَلِيَتْهُ: see تَلَوْتُهُ.

تَلِىٌّ &c.: see art. تلو.

تم

1. تَمَّ الشَّىْءُ, (T, Ṣ, M, Ḳ, &c.,) aor. ـِ, (T, M, Ḳ,) inf. n. تَمَامٌ, (T, Ṣ,) or تِمَامٌ, (M,) or both, and تُمَامٌ, (Ḳ,) and تَمَامَةٌ (M, Ḳ) and تِمَامَةٌ, (Ḳ,) and تَمٌّ and تُمٌّ and تِمٌّ, (M, Ḳ,) of which last three forms the first is said to be the most chaste, (TA,) [*The thing was, or became, complete, entire, whole, or full;* i. e., *without, or free from, deficiency:* and sometimes, *the thing was, or became, consummate, or perfect;* which latter signification is more properly expressed by كَمَلَ:] accord. to the author of the Ḳ, as is shown in art. كمل, and accord. to some others, تَمَامٌ and كَمَالٌ are syn.; but several authors make a distinction between them: the former is said to signify a thing's *being,* or *becoming, without,* or *free from, deficiency;* and the latter, to signify تمام and something more, as, for instance, goodliness, and excellence, essential or accidental; though each is sometimes used in the sense of the other: or, as some say, the former necessarily implies previous deficiency; but the latter does not: (MF, TA:) or, accord. to El-Ḥarállee, the latter signifies the attaining to the utmost point, or degree, in every respect: or, as Ibn-El-Kemál says, when one says of a thing كَمَلَ, he means that what was desired of it became realized. (TA.) [See also تَمَامٌ, below.] You say, تَمَّ خَلْقُهُ [*His make, or formation, was, or became, complete, or perfect; he* (a child or the like, and a man,) *was, or became, fully formed or developed, or complete in his members;* and *he* (a man) *was, or became, full-grown*]: (TA:) [whence, probably,] تَمَّ الشَّىْءُ [as meaning] *The thing became strong and hard.* (Mṣb.) And تَمَّ القَمَرُ, (T, Ṣ, Mṣb,) or ↓اتمّ, (M, Ḳ,) *The moon became full, so that it shone brightly.* (M, Ḳ.) And, of her who is pregnant, تَمَّتْ أَيَّامُ حَمْلِهَا [*The days of her gestation became complete*]. (Ṣ.) — تَمَّ إِلَى كَذَا *He reached, attained, arrived at, or came to, such a thing;* as, for instance, eminence or nobility, or the means of acquiring eminence or nobility. (TA.) — تَمَّ إِلَى مَوْضِعِ كَذَا, and ↓اتمّ إِلَيْهِ, *He repaired,* or *betook himself, to, or towards, such a place; he went to it.* (Ḥar p. 508.) Aboo-Dhu-eyb says,

فَبَاتَ بِجَمْعٍ ثُمَّ تَمَّ إِلَى مِنًى

[which may be rendered *And he passed the night in Jema* (a name of El-Muzdelifeh): *then he repaired,* or *went, to Minè;* there completing the ceremonies of the pilgrimage; wherefore ISd says,] I think that, by تَمَّ, [or rather تمّ الى منى,] he means *he completed his pilgrimage.* (M.) — تَمَّ بِهِ, and تَمَّ عَلَيْهِ: see their syn. اتمّهُ (4). — [Hence,] تَمَّ عَلَيْهِ *He performed it,* or *executed it; he accomplished it;* namely, an affair; a fast; a purpose, or an intention. (Mgh.) — And *He persevered in it;* (Mgh, TA;) as also تَمَمَ عَلَيْهِ, without teshdeed, as in the phrase إِنْ تَمَمْتُ عَلَى مَا أُرِيدُ [*If she persevere in what I desire*], occurring in a trad.; but IAth says that the verb here means ↓تَمَّمَتْ. (TA.) You say, تَمَّ عَلَى الإِبَآءِ *He persevered in refusal,* or *dislike,* or *disapproval.* (Mgh.) ═ تُمَّ *It was broken.* (T.) — And i. q. بلغ [app. بُلِغَ, i. e. *He was jaded, harassed, distressed, fatigued,* or *wearied*]. (T.)

2. تَمَّمَهُ: see its syn. اتمّهُ; and see also 1, near the end of the paragraph. — *He,* or *it, destroyed it; made it to reach its appointed term of duration.* (Sh, T, Ḳ.) — تَمَّمَهُمْ *He gave them the share of their arrow in the game called* المَيْسِر; (IAạr, M, Ḳ;) i. e. *he gave them to eat the flesh which was their share.* (M.) Accord. to Lth, التَّتْمِيمُ in the game called الميسر signifies A man's *taking what has remained, so as to complete the shares, or make up their full number, when the players have diminished from the slaughtered camel* [*by taking their shares*]. (T.) — تَمَّمَ عَلَى الجَرِيحِ ‡ *He hastened and completed the slaughter of the wounded man;* or *made his slaughter sure,* or *certain.* (M, Ḳ, TA.) ═ تَمَّمَ الكَسْرُ, (M, Ḳ,) and ↓تتمّم, (M, TA,) in the copies of the Ḳ, erroneously, تَمَّ, (TA,) [in the CḲ, تمم again,] i. e. [*The fracture,* or *the broken bone,* or simply *the bone,*] *cracked, without separating* (وَلَمْ يَبِنْ): or *cracked, and then separated.* (M, Ḳ.) You say, تَمَّمَ الكَسْرُ فَتَمَّمَ and ↓تَتَمَّمَ [*He,* or *it, completed the fracture,* or *cracked the broken bone,* or *the bone, and it cracked,* &c.]. (M.) And ↓ظَلَعَ فُلَانٌ ثُمَّ تَتَمَّمَ, i. e. [*Such a one limped,* or *halted,* or *was slightly lame: then*] *his lameness became complete by fracture:* from تُمَّ signifying "it was broken:" (T:) [or تَتَمَّمَ signifies *his lameness became complete by an increased fracture, after he had had a fracture with which he was able to walk:* this is what is meant by the following loose explanation:] التَّتَمُّمُ مَنْ كَانَ بِهِ كَسْرٌ يَمْشِى بِهِ ثُمَّ أَبَتَّ فَتَتَمَّمَ. (Ḳ. [In the CḲ, تمّم; and أَبَتَّ is here erroneously put for أَبَتْ.]) ═ تَمَّمَ المَوْلُودَ *He hung* تَمَائِم, (Th, M,) or *a* تَمِيمَة, (Ḳ,) *upon the new-born child,* or *young infant.* (Th, M, Ḳ.) — تَمَّمْتُ عَنْهُ العَيْنَ *I repelled from him the evil eye by hanging* [*upon him*] *the* تَمِيمَة. (A, TA.) ═ تمّم also signifies *He became, in the inclination of his mind,* (Lth, T, M, Ḳ,) *and in his opinion, and his place of abode or settlement,* (Lth, T, Ḳ,) *as one of the tribe of Temeem;* (Lth, T, M, Ḳ;) as also ↓تتمّم; (Ḳ, TA; [in the CḲ, تمّم again;]) or accord. to analogy it would be تتمّم, like تمضّر and تنزّر. (T.) And *He asserted himself to be related to the tribe of Temeem.* (M.)

3. مُتَامَّةٌ [inf. n. of تَامَّ] The *vying,* or *contending, with another in completeness,* or *perfection.* (KL.) [You say, تامّهُ *He vied,* or *contended, with him* &c.]

4. اتمّ, said of the moon: see 1. — Said of a plant, *It became tall and full-grown;* or *became of its full height, and blossomed.* (M, Ḳ.) — أَتَمَّتْ, said of one that is pregnant, *She completed the days of her gestation:* (Ṣ:) or, said of a woman and of a she-camel, (M,) *she became near to bringing forth.* (M, Ḳ.) — اتمّ إِلَى مَوْضِعِ كَذَا: see 1. ═ اتمّ الشَّىْءَ, (Ṣ, M, Ḳ,) or الأَمْرَ, (Mgh,) and اتمّ بِهِ, (M,) inf. n. إِتْمَامٌ; (TA;) and ↓تمّمهُ, (T, Ṣ, M, Ḳ,) inf. n. تَتْمِيمٌ and تَتِمَّةٌ; (T, TA;) and ↓استتمّهُ; (Ṣ, Mgh, Ḳ;) and ↓تَمَّ بِهِ, and ↓تَمَّ عَلَيْهِ; (M, Ḳ;) signify the same; (Ṣ, Mgh;) i. e. جَعَلَهُ تَامًّا (M in explanation of all but the last, and Ḳ in explanation of all that are mentioned therein,) and أَكْمَلَهُ (M in explanation of the last) [*He made the thing,* or *the affair, complete, entire, whole,* or *full;* i. e., *without,* or *free from, deficiency; he completed it:* and sometimes, *he consummated,* or *perfected, it*]. وَأَتِمُّوا الحَجَّ وَالعُمْرَةَ, in the Ḳur [ii. 192], means *And perform ye,* or *accomplish ye, completely, the rites and ceremonies* [*of the pilgrimage and the minor pilgrimage*]; (M,* Bḍ;) accord. to some: or, as some say, إِتْمَامُ الحَجِّ means that the money, or the like, that one expends in performing the pilgrimage should be lawfully obtained, and that one should refrain from doing what God has forbidden. (M.) And فَأَتَمَّهُنَّ, in the Ḳur [ii. 118], means *And he performed them,* or *accomplished them, completely,* (Bḍ, Jel,) *and rightly:* (Bḍ:) or *he did according to them.* (Fr, TA.) ═ اتمّهُ *He gave him what are termed* تِمَم, pl. of تِمَّةٌ, and meaning جِزَز [explained below, voce تِمَّةٌ], (M, TA,) *in order that he might complete therewith his web.* (TA.) [In consequence of its being misplaced in the Ḳ, this is there made to signify *He gave him a* تِمّ, meaning a فَأْس or a مِسْحَاة.]

5: see 2, in four places.

6. تَتَامُّوا *They came,* [and also, accord. to Golius, app. on the authority of a gloss in a copy of the KL, *they drank,*] *all of them, and were complete.* (Ṣ, Ḳ.) One says, اِجْتَمَعُوا فَتَتَامُّوا عَشَرَةً [*They collected themselves together, and came, all of them, making altogether ten*]. (TA.) And it is said in a trad., تَتَامَّتْ إِلَيْهِ قُرَيْشٌ, i. e. *Kureysh obeyed his call, and came to him, all of them, following one another.* (TA.)

10. استتمّهُ: see 4. — استتمّ النِّعْمَةَ *He asked for the completion of the benefit,* or *boon,* or *favour.* (M, Ḳ.) ═ *He sought, demanded,* or *requested, of him what are termed* تِمَم, pl. of تِمَّةٌ, and meaning جِزَز [explained below, voce تِمَّةٌ], (M, TA,) *in order that he might complete therewith his web.* (TA.) [In consequence of its being misplaced in the Ḳ, this is there made to signify *He sought, demanded,* or *requested, of him a* تِمّ, meaning a فَأْس or a مِسْحَاة.]

R. Q. 1. تَمْتَمَةٌ is the inf. n. of تَمْتَمَ, (Mṣb,) and signifies The *reiterating in uttering the letter* ت: (Mbr, Zj in his "Khalḳ el-Insán," T, Ṣ, Mṣb:) [if so, *syn. with* تَأْتَأَةٌ:] or the *tongue's pronouncing indistinctly, missing the place of the letter,* [i. e. *the place of its pronunciation in the organs of speech,*] *and recurring to an utterance like* ت *and* م, *though this be not distinct:* (Lth, T:) or the *making the speech* [or *tongue*] *to revert* [*repeatedly*] *to* ت *and* م: (M, Ḳ:) or the *jabbering, or hurrying in one's speech, so as hardly, or not at all, to make a person understand:* (M:) or the *uttering in such a manner that one's speech proceeds rapidly to the roof of his mouth.* (M, Ḳ.)

تَمٌّ an inf. n. of 1, in the first of the senses explained above. (M, Ḳ.) See تَمَامٌ, in two places. — See also تُمَّةٌ.

تِمٌّ an inf. n. of 1, in the first of the senses explained above. (M, Ḳ.) See تَمَامٌ, in two places.

تُمٌّ an inf. n. of 1, in the first of the senses explained above. (M, Ḳ.) See تَمَامٌ, in five places: — and تَامٌّ, in three places. — Also *i. q.* فَأْسٌ [app. here meaning *A kind of hoe*]: (IAạr, T, Ḳ:) or *i. q.* مِسْحَاةٌ [*a spade,* or *a shovel*]: (Ḳ:) pl. تِمَمَةٌ (IAạr, T,) or تِمَمٌ. (So in the TA.)

تُمَّةٌ: see what next follows, in two places.

تِمَّةٌ (M, Ḳ) and ↓ تُمَّةٌ (TA) [the former written in the CḲ تُمَّةٌ] sings. of تِمَمٌ (M, Ḳ, TA) and تُمَمٌ, (Ḳ, TA,) or ↓ تِمَمٌ, which [ISd says] I think to be a quasi-pl. n., (M,) or ↓ تُمٌّ is the quasi-pl. n.: (Ḳ:) these, i. e. the pls. and quasi-pl. n., signify *Shorn crops* (جِزَز [in the CḲ جِزَر, for which Golius appears to have found حِرز, for he has rendered it by "amuletum," and Freytag has done the same,]) *of* شَعَر [meaning *goats' hair*], *and of camels' hair, and of wool,* (M, Ḳ, TA,) *of that wherewith a woman* [*or a man*] *completes her* [*or his*] *web:* (TA:) and ↓ تُمَّةٌ signifies *what is given, of wool, or camel's hair,* [*or goats' hair,*] (Ṣ, TA, [and mentioned also in the Ḳ, but there, by misplacement, made to relate to تُمٌّ instead of تُمَّةٌ,]) *for a man to complete therewith the weaving of his* كِسَآء; (Ṣ;) as also ↓ تُمَّى. (Ḳ,* TA.)

تُمَّى: see تُمَّةٌ.

تَمَمٌ: see تَامٌّ, in four places: — and see also تِمَّةٌ.

تَمَامٌ (T, Ṣ, Ḳ) and ↓ تِمَامٌ (M, Ḳ) and ↓ تُمَامٌ (Ḳ) inf. ns. of 1, in the first of the senses explained above; (T, Ṣ, M, Ḳ;) as also ↓ تَمٌّ and ↓ تُمٌّ and ↓ تِمٌّ. (M, Ḳ.) [Hence,] وَلَدَتْهُ لِتِمٍّ ↓ and ↓ لِتَمَامٍ and لِتِمَامٍ *She brought him forth at the completion of formation;* (Ḳ, TA;) i. e., *when his formation was complete:* (TA:) [or, *at the completion of gestation:*] and, accord. to Aṣ, وَلَدَتْهُ التَّمَامِ, with the art. ال; not indeterminate, except in poetry. (IB, TA.) And وَلَدَتْ لِتَمَامٍ and ↓ لِتِمَامٍ [*She brought forth at the completion of formation; or, of gestation*]. (Ṣ.) And أَلْقَتِ الوَلَدَ لِغَيْرِ تَمَامٍ and ↓ تِمَامٍ [*She cast the child at a period not that of the completion of formation; or, of gestation; i. e., prematurely*]. (Mṣb.) And وُلِدَ المَوْلُودُ لِتَمَامٍ and ↓ لِتِمَامٍ [*The infant was born at the completion of formation; or, of gestation*]. (T,* Ṣ.) And وُلِدَ الوَلَدُ لِتَمَامِ الحَمْلِ and ↓ لِتِمَامِ الحَمْلِ [*The child was born at the completion of gestation*]. (Mṣb.) [These exs., and others following, show that an assertion of IDrd, mentioned in the M, namely, that one says, وُلِدَ الغُلَامُ لِتِمٍّ ↓ and ↓ لِتِمَامٍ, and ↓ بَدْرُ تِمَامٍ, and that in every other case it is تَمَامٌ, with fet-ḥ, requires consideration.] You say also, بَدْرُ تَمَامٍ and ↓ تِمَامٍ [lit. *The full moon of completion*]: and ↓ بَدْرٌ تَمَامٌ [lit. *A complete full moon*]: all meaning *the moon, or a moon, when it is full, so that it shines brightly:* (M, Ḳ:) and قَمَرٌ تَمَامٌ and ↓ تِمَامٌ *A complete,* or *full, moon.* (Ṣ.) And لَيْلَةُ التَّمَامِ and لَيْلَةُ تَمَامِ القَمَرِ, with fet-ḥ to the ت, (ISh, T,) or ↓ لَيْلَةُ التِّمَامِ, with kesr, [which seems to be at variance with general usage,] and sometimes with fet-ḥ, (Mṣb,) [*The night of the completion of the moon;* i. e.] *the night of the full moon;* (ISh, T, Mṣb;) which is *the thirteenth night;* (ISh, T;) or *the fourteenth.* (T.) And ↓ لَيْلُ التِّمَامِ, with kesr only, (T, Ṣ, M, Ḳ, &c.,) thus distinguished from what next precedes, (ISh, T,) as also ↓ لَيْلٌ تِمَامٌ, and in like manner, لَيْلٌ ↓ تِمَامٌ (T) and ↓ لَيْلٌ تِمَامِيٌّ, (T, Ḳ,) *The longest night of the year;* (Lth, T, Ṣ;) *the longest night of winter;* (Aṣ, ISh, T, M, Ḳ;) *that in which our Lord Jesus was born:* (Aṣ, T:) or *each of three nights of which no deficiency is apparent:* (Lth, T, M, Ḳ:) or *the night that is from thirteen to fifteen hours in length:* (Aboo-'Amr Esh-Sheybánee, T:) or *the night that is twelve hours or more in length:* (AA, T, M, Ḳ:) and *any night that is long, or tedious, to one, and in which one does not sleep,* is called ↓ لَيْلَةُ التِّمَامِ, or said to be like the night thus called. (IAạr, T.) And رُئِيَ الهِلَالُ لِتِمِّ الشَّهْرِ [*The new moon was seen at the completion of the month;* showing that another month was commencing]. (T.) And أَبَى قَائِلُهَا إِلَّا تِمًّا and ↓ تَمًّا and ↓ تُمًّا, (Ṣ, M,) three dial. vars., of which the first is the most chaste, i. e., تَمَامًا [meaning *The sayer thereof refused,* or *did not consent to,* aught *save completion*]; *he executed,* or *accomplished,* or *kept to, his saying; he did not go back from it.* (Ṣ, TA.) — تَمَامٌ (with fet-ḥ only, AZ, AAF, M) also signifies The *complement* of a thing; the *supplement* thereof; the *thing by the addition of which is effected the completion* or *perfection* of a thing; (AZ, T, AAF, M, Ḳ;) and so ↓ تَمَامَةٌ (M, Ḳ) and ↓ تَتِمَّةٌ. (T, M, Ḳ.) You say, هٰذِهِ الدَّرَاهِمُ تَمَامُ هٰذِهِ المِائَةِ, and ↓ تَتِمَّةُ هٰذِهِ المِائَةِ, *These dirhems are the complement of this hundred;* or, *what complete this hundred.* (T.) [And ↓ تَتِمَّةُ كِتَابٍ *The supplement of,* or *to, a book.*] — See also تَامٌّ, in two places.

تُمَامٌ: see تَمَامٌ, first sentence.

تِمَامٌ: see تَمَامٌ, throughout the greater part of the paragraph: — and see also تَامٌّ.

تَمِيمٌ *Strong; firm; hard:* (A'Obeyd, T, Ṣ, M, Mṣb, Ḳ:) or *strong in make,* or *formation:* (TA:) or *complete,* or *perfect, in make,* or *formation, and strong:* (M:) applied to a man and to a horse: (M, TA:) fem. with ة. (TA.) See also تَامٌّ. — Also *Tall;* (T;) applied to a man. (TA.) — See also تَمِيمَةٌ.

تَمَامَةٌ: see تَمَامٌ, near the end of the paragraph.

تُمَامَةٌ *A remainder,* or *remaining portion,* (Ḳ,) of anything. (TA.)

تَمِيمَةٌ *A kind of amulet* (عُوذَةٌ, T, Ṣ) *which is hung upon a human being;* forbidden to be worn: (Ṣ:) or *a kind of bead:* (Ṣ, Mgh:) erroneously imagined by some to be the same as مُعَاذَةٌ: (El-Ḳutabee, Mgh:) but as to the مُعَاذَات that are inscribed with something from the Ḳur-án, or with the names of God, in these there is no harm: (Ṣ, Mgh:) *a speckled bead, black speckled with white, or the reverse, which is strung upon a thong, and tied to the neck:* (M, Ḳ:) sing. of تَمَائِمُ and [n. un. of] ↓ تَمِيمٌ: (T, M, Ḳ:) تَمَائِمُ signifies *certain beads which the Arabs of the desert used to hang upon their children, to repel, as they asserted, the evil eye:* (T, Mgh:) or the تَمِيمَة is, accord. to some, *a necklace* (قِلَادَة) *upon which are put thongs and amulets* (عُوَذ): (M:) or *a necklace* (قِلَادَة) *of thongs:* and is sometimes applied to the *amulet* (عُوذَة) *that is hung upon the necks of children:* (T:) but he who makes تمائم to signify *thongs* is in error: El-Farezdaḳ uses the phrase سُيُورُ التَّمَائِمِ because they are *beads which are perforated, and into which are inserted thongs or strings whereby they are suspended:* (T, Mgh:) Az says, I have not found among the Arabs of the desert any difference of opinion respecting the تميمة, as to its being the bead itself: (TA:) but accord. to En-Nakha'ee, the Prophet disapproved of everything hung upon a child or grown person, and said that all such things were تمائم: (Mgh:) the تميمة is [said to be] thus called because by it the condition of the child is rendered complete. (Ḥar p. 22.)

تِمَامِيٌّ: see تَمَامٌ.

تَمْتَامٌ One *whose utterance is such as is termed* تَمْتَمَةٌ: (Ṣ, M, Mgh, Mṣb, Ḳ:) [see R. Q. 1: accord. to most authorities,] one *who reiterates in uttering the letter* ت: (Ṣ, Mgh, Mṣb:) or, accord. to AZ, one *who jabbers, or hurries in his speech, so as not to make another understand:* (Mgh, Mṣb:) fem. with ة. (M, Ḳ.)

تَامٌّ [part. n. of 1 in the first of the senses explained above]: (T, M, Ḳ, &c.:) *Complete, entire, whole,* or *full; without,* or *free from, deficiency:* and *consummate,* or *perfect:* (MF, TA:) as also ↓ تَمَامٌ, [which see above,] (M,* KL,) [and ↓ تِمَامٌ,

of which see three exs. voce تَمَامٌ,] and ▼تِمٌّ, (Kh, T, Ḥar p. 82,) and ▼تَتِمٌّ. (TA.) Thus تَامُّ الخَلْقِ signifies *Complete*, or *perfect, in make*, or *formation; without any deficiency in his members*; applied to a man; (MF, TA;) [and, thus applied, signifying also *full-grown*, as does, sometimes, تَامٌّ alone: and likewise applied to a new-born child, meaning *fully formed* or *developed*:] and ▼تِمِّيمٌ signifies the same, (M, Ḳ,) applied to a man and to a horse, (M,) and ▼تَمِرٌّ also; and in like manner is used the phrase ▼خَلْقٌ تَمِرٌّ [*a complete*, or *perfect, make* or *formation*]. (TA.) جَذَعٌ تَامٌّ [applied to a goat] signifies *That has completed the time in which he is termed* جَذَع, *and attained to that in which he is termed* تَيْس. (TA.) And ▼تَمِرٌّ is applied to a bull, or an ox, *That is in the stage of growth next before that in which all his teeth are grown*; in which latter stage he is termed عَمَمٌ. (L voce غَضَبٌ, on the authority of Eṭ-Ṭáifee.) You say also كَلِمَةٌ تَامَّةٌ, and دَعْوَةٌ تَامَّةٌ; [meaning *A perfect*, or *faultless, sentence*, and *oath*;] using the epithet تامّة in these instances because of the mention of God therein; for which reason there may not be in aught of either of them any deficiency or defect. (TA.) And ▼جَعَلَهُ تِمًّا i. e. ▼تَمَامًا [*He made it complete*, or *perfect*]. (M.) And ▼جَعَلْتُهُ لَكَ تِمًّا *I made it*, or *have made it, to be thine*, or *I assigned it*, or *have assigned it, to thee, completely*, or *wholly*. (T.) — [Hence, فِعْلٌ تَامٌّ meaning *A complete*, i. e. *an attributive, verb*: opposed to فِعْلٌ نَاقِصٌ.]

تَتِمَّةٌ: see تَمَامٌ, in three places, at the close of the paragraph.

مُتَمٌّ The *place of cutting*, or *termination*, (مُنْقَطَع, in the CḲ مُنْقَطِع,) *of the vein* (عِرْق [app. meaning *chord*]) *of the navel*. (Ḳ.)

مُتِمٌّ, applied to one that is pregnant, (Ṣ,) or to a woman, (M, TA,) and a she-camel, (M,) *That has completed the days of her gestation*: (Ṣ:) or *that is near to bringing forth*: (M:) or *that is at the point of bringing forth*. (TA.)

مُتَمِّمٌ One *whose arrow wins time after time* [*in the game called* المَيْسِر], *and who feeds the poor with the flesh* [*of the camel which constitutes the shares*] *thereof*: (M, Ḳ:) or *who, when players in the game called* الميسر *have diminished the slaughtered camel* [*by taking their shares*], *takes what has remained, so as to complete the shares*, or *make up their full number*. (Ḳ. [See 2. In the CḲ, نَقَصَ أَيْسَارَ جَزُورِ المَيْسِرِ is erroneously put for نَقَّصَ أَيْسَارُ جَزُورَ المَيْسِرِ.])

الجَهَالَةُ المُسْتَتِمَّةُ *Consummate ignorance*: improperly written المُسْتَتِمَّة, though this latter is explainable [as meaning *that completes* the extent to which it can go, or the like]. (Mgh.)

مُسْتَتِمٌّ One *who seeks, demands*, or *requests, wool*, or *camels' hair, to complete therewith the weaving of his* كِسَاء: so in a poem of Aboo-Duwád, (Ṣ,) where he says,

* فَهْىَ كَالبَيْضِ فِى الأَدَاحِىِّ لَا يُو *
* هَبُ مِنْهَا لِمُسْتَتِمٍّ عِصَامُ *

i. e., *And they* (referring to certain camels) *are*, in respect of the care that is taken of them, and in smoothness, *like the eggs* [*in the places where the ostrich has deposited them in the sand*]; *there may not be* found upon them to be *given from them, to one who demands a* تِمَّة, [even so much as] *a tie for a water-skin*; for they have become fat, and cast their hair. (TA.)

تمر

1. تَمَرَ, (Ṣ, M, Ḳ, &c.,) aor. ِ, (M, TA,) or ُ, (Mṣb,) inf. n. تَمْرٌ; (Ṣ, Mṣb, Ḳ;) and ▼تمّر, (M, Ḳ,) inf. n. تَتْمِيرٌ; (TA;) and ▼اتمر; (M, Ḳ;) *He fed* people *with*, or *gave* them *to eat*, تَمْر [or *dried dates*]. (Ṣ, M, Mṣb, Ḳ.)

2. تمّر, inf. n. تَتْمِيرٌ, *He dried* (Ṣ, M, Ḳ) dates. (Ṣ.) — ‡ *He dried* flesh-meat: (T, Ṣ:) or *he cut* flesh-meat *into small pieces*, (M, A,* IAth, Ḳ,) *like dates*, (IAth,) *and dried it*. (M, A, IAth, Ḳ.) It is said in a trad., كَانَ لَا يَرَى بِالتَّتْمِيرِ بَأْسًا ‡*He used not to see any harm in cutting flesh-meat into small pieces, like dates, and drying it*: meaning, in a Moḥrim's thus preparing flesh-meat for travelling-provision; or in one's drying the flesh of wild animals before the state of iḥrám. (IAth.) — See also 1: — and 4, in two places.

4. اتمر *He possessed many*, or *a large quantity of*, تَمْر [or *dried dates*]. (Ṣ, M, Ḳ.) — اتمرت النَّخْلَةُ, (T, M, A, Ḳ,) and ▼تمّرت, (M, Ḳ,) *The palm-tree bore* تَمْر [or *dry dates*]: (M, Ḳ:) or *had ripe dates upon it*. (Ḳ.) — اتمر الرُّطَبُ; (T, Ḳ;) and ▼تمّر, inf. n. تَتْمِيرٌ; (Ḳ;) *The ripe dates became in the state in which they are termed* تَمْر. (Ḳ.) — See also 1.

5. تتمّر *It* (flesh-meat) *was cut into strips*, or *small pieces, and dried*. (A.)

تَمْرٌ, a coll. gen. n.; (Ṣ, A;) masc. in one dial. and fem. in another [like other nouns of the same class]; (Mṣb;) *Dates*, or the *fruit of the palm-tree*: (M:) or *dried dates*, like زَبِيبٌ as applied to grapes, by general consent of the lexicologists: (Mgh, Mṣb:) the dates are left upon the palm-tree, after they have become ripe, until they are dry, or nearly so, when they are cut, and left in the sun to dry thoroughly; and sometimes, as AḤát says, the fruit of the palm-tree is cut when full-grown but unripe, to lighten the tree, or from fear of theft, and left until it becomes تَمْر: (Mṣb:) the n. un. is with ة: and the pl. of تَمْر is تُمُورٌ and تُمْرَانٌ, (T, Ṣ, M, Mṣb, Ḳ,) meaning *sorts* or *varieties* [*of* تَمْر]; for a coll. gen. n. has not a pl. in the proper sense: (Ṣ:) and in like manner the dual تَمْرَانِ means *two sorts* [*of* تَمْر]: (Sb cited in the M in art. بسر:) the pl. of تَمْرَةٌ is تَمَرَاتٌ. (Ṣ, Ḳ.) [See also بُسْرٌ.] Hence the prov., أَعْطِ أَخَاكَ تَمْرَةً فَإِنْ أَبَى فَجَمْرَةً [*Give thou thy brother a dried date; and if he refuse it, a live coal*]. (A, TA.) And التَّمْرُ بِالسَّوِيقِ [*Dried dates with meal of parched barley* or *wheat*] is another prov., used in allusion to requital. (Lḥ.) And one says, وَجَدَ عِنْدَهُ تَمْرَةَ الغُرَابِ, meaning ‡ *He found with him*, or *at his abode, what he approved*. (A.) And نَفْسُهُ تَمِرَةٌ بِكَذَا ‡ *His mind is pleased*, or *agreeably affected, with*, or *by, such a thing*; or *consents to such a thing*. (A, Ḳ.* [Accord. to the TA, it is here like فَرِحَة; but this seems to be true as to the meaning; not as to the form of the word. See also art. ثمر, voce ثَمِرٌ.]) And دَعْنِى إِنَّ نَفْسِى غَيْرُ تَمِرَةٍ ‡ [*Leave thou me*, or *let me alone: verily my mind is not pleased*, or *happy*]. (A.) — تَمْرٌ هِنْدِىٌّ [The *fruit of the tamarind-tree*; thus called in the present day;] *i. q.* حُمَر and حُومَر. (Ḳ in art. حمر.)

تَمْرِىٌّ One *who loves* تَمْر [or *dried dates*]. (Ṣ, A, Ḳ.)

تَمَّارٌ *A seller of* تَمْر [or *dried dates*]. (Ṣ, A, Ḳ.)

تَامِرٌ *Possessing* تَمْر [or *dried dates*]; (Ṣ, M, A, Mṣb;) like لَابِنٌ "possessing milk:" (Ṣ, Mṣb:) or تَامِرٌ, (Lḥ, M, Ḳ,) or ▼مُتْمِرٌ, (Ṣ, A,) signifies *possessing many*, or *a large quantity of*, تَمْر: (Lḥ, Ṣ, M, A, Ḳ:) the former of these two words is held by ISd to be a possessive epithet: (TA:) and sometimes it may signify *feeding* people *with*, or *giving* them *to eat*, تَمْر. (Ṣ, TA.)

تَامُورٌ and تَامُورَةٌ and تُومُورٌ and تُومُرِىٌّ &c.: see art. امر.

مُتْمِرٌ: see تَامِرٌ.

مُتَمَّرٌ *Furnished with* تَمْر [or *dried dates*] *for travelling-provision*. (Ṣ, Ḳ.)

تمك

1. تَمَكَ, aor. ُ (Ṣ, Ḳ) and ِ, (Ḳ,) inf. n. تَمْكٌ (Ṣ, Ḳ) and تُمُوكٌ, (Ḳ,) *It* (a camel's hump) *was*, or *became, tall*, or *long and high*: (Ṣ, Ḳ:) *it was*, or *became, juicy, and compact*, (O, Ḳ,) *and plump*. (M, TA.) — [Hence,] تَمَكَ فِيهِ الحُسْنُ [app. †*Beauty became fully developed*, or *consummate, in him*]. (TA.)

4. اتمك سَنَامَهُ [*It made his* (a camel's) *hump to become tall*, or *long and high*, or *juicy and compact, and plump*]; said of the [herbage called] رَبِيع. (A, TA.) And اتمك النَّاقَةَ *It* (herbage) *made the she-camel fat*. (IDrd, Ḳ.)

تَامِكٌ, applied to a camel's hump, *Tall*, or *long and high*: (Ṣ, TA:) or *high*: or *juicy, and compact, and plump*: (TA:) or *a camel's hump, in whatever state it be*. (M, Ḳ.) — A she-camel *having a large hump*: (ISd, Ḳ:) pl. تَوَامِكُ. (TA.) — A *high*, or *lofty*, building. (TA.) — You say also, إِنَّهُ لَتَامِكُ الجَمَالِ [app. meaning † *Verily he is a person of fully-developed*, or *consummate, beauty*]. (TA.) — And شَرَفُكَ تَامِكٌ وَإِقْبَالُكَ سَامِكٌ ‡ [*Thy nobility is lofty, and thy good fortune is high*]. (A, TA.)

تموز

تَمُّوزُ [sometimes written تَمُوزُ, without teshdeed,] *The* [*Syrian*] *month* [*sacred*, in ancient times, *to the god of that name*, (mentioned in Ezek. viii. 14,) *corresponding to July, O. S.*,] *after* حَزِيرَانُ. (Ṣ in art. حزر.)

تن

1. تَنَّ بِالمَكَانِ, [aor., accord. to rule, ـِ, i. q. [تَنَأَ] *He remained, stayed, dwelt,* or *abode, in the place.* (M.)

3. تَانَّ بَيْنَهُمَا, (Ḳ,) inf. n. مُتَانَّةٌ, (TA,) *He measured,* or *compared, them two together.* (Ḳ.)

4. اتنّ, (Ḳ,) inf. n. إِتْنَانٌ, (TA,) *He,* or *it, was,* or *became, distant,* or *remote.* (Ḳ.) ═ اتنّهُ *It* (a disease) *stunted him,* (AZ, IAạr, T, Ṣ, M, Ḳ,) namely, a child, or boy, (IAạr, T, Ṣ, M, Ḳ,) *so that he did not attain to the stature of his equals in age,* (AZ, T,) or *so that he did not attain to full growth.* (IAạr, T, Ṣ, M, Ḳ.)

R. Q. 1. تَنْتَنَ [in the CḲ تَنْتَنَ] *He* (a man, IAạr, T) *left,* or *deserted, his friends, and associated with others.* (IAạr, T, Ḳ.)

تَنٌّ: see تِنٌّ. ═ See also a poetical citation voce تَوٌّ.

تُنٌّ and تُنَّةٌ The *tunny-fish.* (Golius on the authority of Ibn-Beyṭár; and so in the present day; but the former is a coll. gen. n., and the latter is a n. un.)

تِنٌّ *A like; an equal, a match,* or *a fellow;* (Ṣ, M, Ḳ;) as also ↓ تَنِينٌ; (Ḳ, TA [in the CḲ [تِنِّين];) *an equal in age;* (T, M;) *an equal in intellect,* or *in weakness,* or *in strength,* or *in manliness,* or *manly virtue:* (ISk, Ṣ:) or *a companion:* (M:) pl. أَتْنَانٌ. (T, M.) You say, فُلَانٌ تِنُّ فُلَانٍ [*Such a one is the like,* or *equal,* &c., *of such a one*]. (Ṣ.) And هُوَ سِنُّهُ and تِنُّهُ and حِتْنُهُ [*He is his like,* or *equal,* &c.]. (T.) And هُمَا تِنَّانِ *They two are equals in intellect,* or *in weakness,* or *in strength,* or *in manliness,* or *manly virtue.* (ISk, Ṣ.) And صِبْوَةٌ أَتْنَانٌ [*Boys that are like each other,* or *equals,* &c.]. (T.) And هُمْ أَسْنَانٌ أَتْنَانٌ *They are equals in age.* (IAạr, T.) — *A boy stunted by disease,* (Lth, T, M,) *so that he does not attain to full growth;* (Lth, T;) as also ↓ تَنٌّ. (M.) — Also i. q. شَخْصٌ [The *body,* or *corporeal form, of a man or other thing, which one sees from a distance;* or *a person; an individual*]. (T.) — And i. q. مِثَالٌ [*A model; a pattern;* &c.]: (T:) and ↓ تِنَانٌ [likewise] signifies the مثال of a thing. (Ḳ.)

تِنٌّ: see تِنٌّ.

تِنِّينٌ [in Hebr. תַּנִּין] *A great serpent;* (Ḳ;) *a kind of serpent,* (Lth, T, Ṣ, M,) *one of the greatest of serpents,* (Lth, T,) or *like the greatest thereof:* (M:) it is related that a company of soldiers, on the shore of the Sea of Syria, saw a cloud divide upon the sea, and then rise, and they saw the tail of the تنّين in a state of commotion in the fringe of the cloud: it is also related that a cloud carries the تنّين to the country of Yájooj and Májooj [or Gog and Magog], and casts it down there, and they assemble thereupon, and eat its flesh: (T:) [these stories are fanciful accounts of the natural phenomenon called *a water-spout*, to which this name is applied by the Arabs in the present day: but the word is generally understood to mean *a dragon:* and *a great sea-monster;*] *an aquatic animal, great in make, terrible in appearance, long and broad in the body, large in the head, having very glistening eyes, wide mouth and inside, and many teeth: it swallows many animals; the animals of the land and of the sea fear it; and when it moves, the sea becomes agitated with waves by reason of its great strength: in its first state, it is a malignant serpent, that eats what it sees of the beasts of the land; and when its mischief becomes great, God sends an angel that carries it away, and throws it to Yájooj and Májooj: it is related of one that was seen to fall, that it was found to be about two leagues in length, of a colour like that of the leopard, with scales like those of a fish, two great fins in form like those of a fish, a head like a great hill, resembling the head of a man, two long and great ears, and two round eyes; and from its neck branched forth six other necks, every one of them nearly twenty cubits long, and every one of them having a head like that of the serpent.* (Ḳzw.) [Golius thinks it to mean The *shark* ("*carcharias*").] — Hence, التِّنِّينُ is †*A certain* نَجْم [or *constellation; the constellation of the Dragon*]; thus named as being likened to the serpent so called; (M;) *a constellation containing thirty-one stars within the figure; among which are those called* العَوَائِذُ *and* الرَّاقِصُ *and* الرُّبَعُ *and* الذِّئْبَانِ &c. (Ḳzw, TA.*) — [Also, app., †*A certain imaginary figure in the heavens, extending along the line of the nodes of a planet, which are called the dragon's head and the dragon's tail, in Arabic* الجَوْزَهَرُ (from the Persian گُوزِهْر), or الجَوْزَهَرَانِ, and also نَعْقَدَتَانِ, and, to distinguish each from the other, الرَّأْسُ وَالذَّنَبُ: this line is supposed by Golius to be meant by the following description; but I incline to regard it as the result of a confusion of a description of this line with a description of the zodiacal light, a phenomenon supposed to have been unnoticed by the Arabs:] *a slight whiteness in the sky,* (Lth, T, Ḳ,) *not an asterism,* (Lth, T,) *the body of which is in six signs of the zodiac, and the tail, which is slender, black, and twisted, in the seventh sign: it changes place like the planets; is called in Persian* هُشْتَنْبُرْ, (Lth, T, Ḳ,) [app. a mistranscription of هُشْتَبُرْ,] *in astrological computation; and is inauspicious:* (Lth, T:) accord. to J, *a certain place in the sky;* which is a correct explanation, though said in the Ḳ to be a mistake. (TA.)

تِنَانٌ: see تِنٌّ. ═ Also *A wolf:* (Ḳ, in this art. and in art. تين:) but used only by El-Akhṭal. (TA.)

تنأ

1. تَنَأَ, aor. ـَ, inf. n. تُنُوءٌ, *He remained, stayed, dwelt,* or *abode,* (T, Ṣ, M, Mṣb, Ḳ,) بِهِ *in it,* namely, a country, or town, (Ṣ, Mṣb,) or a place; (M;) *he settled* therein: (Mṣb:) as also تَنَا, (M, Mṣb,) not a dial. var., but formed by substitution [of ا for أ], (M,) [i. e.] by suppression of the ء. (Mṣb.) — تَنَأَ عَلَى كَذَا *He kept,* or *adhered, to such a thing, inseparably.* (TA.) ═ Also, inf. n. as above, *He was,* or *became, rich, wealthy, possessed of much property.* (Mṣb.)

تَنَاءَةٌ a subst. from تَنَأَ, (Ṣ, Ḳ,) meaning *A remaining, staying, dwelling,* or *abiding* [in a country, or town, or place]. (TḲ.)

تَانِئٌ *Remaining, staying, dwelling,* or *abiding,* (T, Mṣb,) in a country, or town [&c.]; *settling* therein: also pronounced تَانٍ, by suppression of the ء: (Mṣb:) *one who remains, stays,* or *abides, in his country,* or *town;* (Th, TA;) i. q. دِهْقَانٌ [app. as meaning *a man having a fixed abode in a district of cultivated land, or in a village or town of such a district:* but see below]: (Th, Ḳ, TA:) pl. تُنَّاءٌ. (T, Ṣ, Mṣb, Ḳ.) It is said in a trad., لَيْسَ لِلتَّانِئَةِ شَىْءٌ, meaning *For those who remain in their abodes, and go not forth with the soldiers on expeditions against the enemy, there shall be nothing;* i. e., no share of the spoil. (TA.) — *Rich; wealthy; possessing much property.* (Mṣb.) [Or *A man possessing much land or other immoveable property:* for this is a signification assigned to دِهْقَانٌ.]

تنر

تَنَّارٌ [and ↓ تَنُّورِىٌّ] *A maker of ovens of the kind called* تَنُّور. (M, Ḳ.)

تَنُّورٌ *A sort of* كَانُون [or *fire-place*]; (M;) the *thing,* (Ṣ, Mṣb,) or كانون, (Ḳ,) *in which bread is baked;* (Ṣ, Mṣb, Ḳ;) *but different from the* فُرْن: (Ṣ in art. فرن:) [it is *a kind of oven, open at the top, in the bottom of which a fire is lighted, and in which the bread, in the form of flat cakes, is generally stuck against the sides; either portable, and made of baked clay, wide at the bottom, and narrow at the top, where it is open; and if so, the bread is sometimes stuck upon the outside, to bake; or fixed, and in this case made of baked clay likewise, or constructed of bricks; or it is a hole made in the ground, and lined with bricks or tiles or the like, against which the bread is stuck, to bake; and sometimes flesh-meat, cut into small pieces, is roasted in it, or upon it, on skewers:*] such, accord. to some, is the meaning in the Ḳur xi. 42 and xxiii. 27; (T;) and the word is said to have the same meaning in every language; (Lth, T, M;) but this is not correct: (Ḥam p. 793:) it is an arabicized word; (T, M;) not genuine Arabic; (AḤát, Mṣb;) originally Persian: (M:) [in Hebrew תַּנּוּר:] Aḥmad Ibn-Yaḥyà [i. e. Th, as is stated in Ḥam, ubi suprà,] says that it is of the measure تَفْعُولٌ from النَّارُ, (M, and Ḥam ubi suprà,) or from النُّورُ; originally تَنْوُورٌ; (Ḥam;) but this is wrong: (M:) the pl. is تَنَانِيرُ. (M, Mṣb.) Moḥammad is related to have said to a man wearing a garment dyed with bastard-saffron, "If thy garment were in the تنّور of thy family, or beneath their cooking-pot, it were better:" whereupon he went away, and burned it: but he meant, "Wert thou to spend its price for flour to make bread, or for fire-wood with which to cook, it were better for thee:" as though he disliked a garment so dyed. (IAth.) —— The *surface of the ground:* (T, Ṣ, M, Ḳ:) so in the Ḳur ubi suprà, (T, Ṣ,) accord. to 'Alee (Ṣ) and I'Ab. (TA.) —— The *highest part of the earth* or *ground:* so in the same passages of the Ḳur accord. to Ḳatádeh. (TA.) —— *Any place from which water pours forth.* (M, Ḳ.) —— *A place where the water of a valley collects.* (M, Ḳ.) —— The *shining of the dawn:* so accord. to some in the Ḳur ubi suprà: (T:) and 'Alee is related to have said that وَفَارَ التَّنُّورُ means *and daybreak rose* or *rises:* (TA:) or it relates to the welling forth of water from the place of the mosque of El-Koofeh: (T:) or التنّور here signifies a well-known spring of water: (Hr, TA:) or a certain mountain near El-Maṣeeṣah; (I'Ab, Ḳ, TA;) i.e., (TA,) 'Eyn-el-Ward, in El-Jezeereh; (I'Ab, T, TA;) or 'Eyn-Wardeh. (Bḍ in xi. 42.)

تَنُّورِىٌّ: see تَنَّارٌ.

تنف

تُنُفٌ, [a pl. of which the sing. is not mentioned,] applied to [deserts such as are termed] تَنَائِفُ, [pl. of تَنُوفَةٌ,] meaning *Of which the extremities are far apart;* (Ibn-'Abbád, Ḳ;) *wide,* or *spacious.* (Ibn-'Abbád.)

تَنُوفَةٌ (T, Ṣ, M, Ḳ, &c.) and ↓ تَنُوفِيَّةٌ, (Ṣ, Ḳ,) like دَوٌّ and دَوِّيَّةٌ, the latter a rel. n. from the former, (Ṣ,) *A* [*desert such as is termed*] مَفَازَة: (T, Ṣ, Ḳ:) or *a land such as is termed* قَفْر [i. e. *vacant,* or *void,* or *desert, destitute of vegetable produce and of water;* or *destitute of human beings, but sometimes containing a little herbage* or *pasturage*]: (M:) or *a wide,* or *spacious, land, of which the extremities are far apart:* (El-Muärrij, Ḳ:) or *a desert* (فَلَاة) *in which is no water nor any person to cheer one by his company, though it may have,* or *produce, herbage;* (El-Muärrij, T;) so says ISh: (TA:) or *a far-extending desert, in which is a collection of herbage, but such as cannot be depastured because of its remoteness:* (Aboo-Kheyreh, T:) pl. تَنَائِفُ. (T, M.)

تَنُوفِيَّةٌ: see تَنُوفَةٌ: and see an ex. voce نَذْرٌ.

تنم

1. تَنَمَ, (M, Ḳ, [in the CḲ, erroneously, تَنَوَّمَ,]) without teshdeed to the ن, (M, TA,) *He* (a camel) *ate the* تَنُّوم. (M, Ḳ.)

تَنُّومٌ *A kind of trees* (Ṣ, M, Ḳ) *having a small fruit,* (Ṣ, M,) *like that of the* خِرْوَع [or castor-oil plant], (M,) *which, bursting, discloses grains, that are eaten by the people of the desert:* (Ṣ, M:) *as the sun declines, it follows it with the* [upper] *sides of its leaves:* (M:) *its fruit, with* خَرْوع, (Ḳ,) i. e. حَبُّ الرَّشَادِ [q. v.], (TA,) *and water, drunk, expels worms; and the application of its leaves, with vinegar, in the manner of a poultice, draws forth warts:* (Ḳ:) n. un. with ة: (Ṣ, M, Ḳ:) AḤn says, it is *a kind of dust-coloured trees, of those termed* أَغْلَاث, *eaten by ostriches and gazelles, and of those among which gazelles are snared: its grain, when the coverings thereof open, becomes black; and it has a root* (عِرْق), *sometimes made into a* زَنْد [*for producing fire*]: *the places where it grows are mostly the sides of valleys:* IAạr says, the تنّومة is *a tree of the kind called* جَنْبَة, *of large size, in which grow grains like hemp-seed, used for ointment, and as a seasoning,* or *condiment: it dries up at the beginning of winter, and disappears:* all this is from AḤn: (M:) A'Obeyd says, it is *one of the plants of the earth, in which, and in the fruit whereof, is a blackness: it is eaten by the ostrich:* the pl. [or coll. gen. n.] is تَنُّومٌ: (T: the author of which then adds,) I say, *it is a tree which I have seen in the desert: the colour of its leaves inclines to blackness, and it has grains like hemp-seed, or a little larger: I have seen the women of the desert bruise its grains, and express from them a blue oil, in which is a viscosity; and they anoint their hair with it when they comb themselves:* AA says, *the* تنّوم *has a grain which is oily and dust-coloured:* En-Naḍr says, *the* تنّومة *is of an ill savour, and the beasts do not like it,* or *eat much of it:* (T:) [it is erroneously said in the Ḳ, voce طَلَّامٌ, to be *hemp-seed* (حَبُّ الشَّاهْدَانِج): and] some say that it is the *hemp-plant* (شجر الشهدانج). (Ḥam p. 135.) The sun, when eclipsed, is said in a trad. to have become black, and like a تنّومة. (T.) And a poet, who married a woman, and found her to be pretty, but with hoary hair, and who had a youthful wife at his abode, likens the hair of the former to the flower of the أُقْحُوَان, and black hair to تنّوم; saying

وَلَمَّا رَأَيْتُ الأُقْحُوَانَ مُنَوِّرًا •
وَلَمْ أَرَ تَنُّومًا تَذَكَّرْتُ مَنْزِلِى •

[*And when I saw the chamomile flowering, and saw not tennoom, I remembered my abode*]. (Ḥam ubi suprà.)

ته

R. Q. 1. تَتْهَتَةٌ, [inf. n. of تَهْتَهَ,] i. q. لُكْنَةٌ [The *having an impotence,* or *an impediment,* or *a difficulty,* or *barbarousness,* or *vitiousness, in speech*]: (Ḳ:) or [the *having*] *a distortion in the tongue,* (TA,) *like what is termed* لُكْنَة: (Ṣ, TA:) accord. to Az, تَهْتَهَةٌ and هَتْهَتَةٌ signify the *twisting,* or *distorting, of the tongue in speaking.* (TA in art. هت.) —— And تَهْتَهَ signifies رَدَّدَ فِى البَاطِلِ, (Ḳ, TA,) or فِى الأَبَاطِيلِ, (TA,) [app. meaning *He repeated,* or *used repetitions, in uttering false,* or *vain,* or *unprofitable, sayings:* but Golius and Freytag render it as meaning *he applied himself to vain things.*]

تَهْ, (JK,) or تَهْ تَهْ, (Ḳ,) *An expression imitative of the* ↓ مُتَتَهْتِه, [i. e., *of him who has the faulty utterance termed* تَهْتَهَة,] (JK, Ḳ, TA, [in the CḲ, المُتَتَهْتِه is put for المُتَهْتِه,]) *consisting in a distortion of the tongue.* (JK.) —— تَهْ تَهْ is also *A cry by which one chides the camel,* (Ḳ, TA,) *and which makes him to run away.* (TA.) —— And *A call to a dog.* (Ḳ.)

تَهْ: see art. تَا.

تَهَاتِهُ *False,* or *vain, sayings* or *actions* or *affairs;* or *unprofitable sayings.* (JK, Ṣ, Ḳ.)

مُتَتَهْتِهٌ: see تَهْ.

تهر

تَاهُورٌ [probably, in its primary acceptation, a dial. var. of تَيْهُورٌ; for the signification here following is said in the TA to be tropical:——] ‡*Clouds;* or *a collection of clouds:* (JK, Ḳ, TA:) pl. تَوَاهِيرُ. (JK.)

تَيْهُورٌ, said by Az to be of the measure فَيْعُول, from الوَهْرُ; originally وَيْهُورٌ, like as تَيْقُورٌ is [said to be] originally وَيْقُورٌ; but the ت is held by ISd [and J and F and others] to be a radical: (TA:) *Low,* or *depressed,* sand: (T, TA:) or sand *that falls apart, and does not hold together:* (A, TA:) or *elevated* sand: (TA:) or sand *having a* جُوف [or *part carried and eaten away by torrents*]: (Aṣ, Ṣ, Ḳ:) pl. تَيَاهِيرُ and تَيَاهِرُ. (Ṣ, Ḳ.) —— *Low,* or *depressed,* land, or ground. (Ḳ.) —— The *part between the top and bottom of the side of a valley,* and *of a mountain:* (JK, Ḳ,* TA:) of the dial. of Nejd, and of that of Hudheyl. (TA.) —— *High waves of the sea* or *of a great river.* (Ḳ.) —— Applied to a man, [like تَيَّار, q. v.,] †*Vain,* or *having a fond opinion of himself,* (Ṣ, Ḳ,) and *proud.* (Ḳ.) [For ذَاهِبًا in one copy of the Ṣ, and ذَاهِبًا in another and in the L, in the phrase إِذَا كَانَ ذَاهِبًا بِنَفْسِهِ بِهِ تِيهٌ, or ذَاهِبًا, I read زَاهِيًا.]

تهم

1. تَهِمَ, (JK, Mṣb, Ḳ,) aor. ـَ, (Mṣb, Ḳ,) inf. n. تَهَمٌ, (Mṣb,) or تَهَامَةٌ, (JK,) *It* (flesh-meat, JK, Mṣb, Ḳ, and milk, Mṣb, and oil, Ḳ) *became altered for the worse, and stank:* (JK,* Mṣb, Ḳ:*) *it* (flesh-meat, TḲ) *had a foul odour; it stank.* (Ḳ.) —— *It* (the heat) *was,* or *became, vehement,* or *intense, with stillness of the wind.* (Mṣb.) —— Also, inf. n. تَهَمٌ, *He* (a camel) *was penetrated by the heat:* (JK:) or *was smitten by the hot wind, and in consequence became lean,* or *emaciated.* (TA.) —— And, (JK, Ḳ,) inf. n. تَهَمٌ, (TA,) *He* (a camel) *ate much of the pasture* (اِسْتَكْثَرَ مِنَ المَرْعَى), *and it was not wholesome:* (JK:) or *disapproved the pasture* (اِسْتَنْكَرَ المَرْعَى), *and did not find it wholesome,* (Ḳ, TA,) *and his condition became bad.* (TA.) —— And, said of a man, *His impotence,* or *inability, became apparent, and he became confounded,* or *perplexed, and unable to see his right course.* (Ḳ.)

3: see 4.

4. اتهم *He* (a man, Ṣ) *went,* (Ṣ,) or *came,* (Ḳ,) *to Tihámeh:* (Ṣ, Ḳ:) Er-Riyáshee says, I have heard the Arabs of the desert say thus of him who has descended from the mountain-roads of Dhát 'Irḳ: (TA:) or *he alighted,* or *abode, therein:* (Ḳ:) as also ↓ تَاهَمَ, (JK, Ḳ, TA, [in the CḲ, erroneously, تَاهَرَ,]) in the latter sense,

(JK,) and ▼ تَتَهَّمَ; (Ḳ;) or these mean *he came to Tihámeh.* (TA.) — [Accord. to Golius, on the authority of a gloss. in the KL, it signifies also, *He went into a region of hot air:* and this, if correct, may be the primary meaning.] ═ اتهم البَلَدَ *He found the country,* or *town, to be insalubrious,* (Ḳ, TA,) *and to have a bad,* or *foul, odour.* (TA.) ═ اتهم, inf. n. إِتْهَامٌ; in measure like أَكْرَمَ, inf. n. إِكْرَامٌ; (Mṣb;) [originally اوهم; or] formed from تُهْمَةٌ, in consequence of imagining the ت in this word to be radical; (MF in art. وهم;) [like as is said of اتَّخَذَ;] *He did a thing that made him an object of suspicion:* (JK and Mṣb and TA in the present art.:) or *he was an object of suspicion:* (Ḳ in art. وهم: [in the CḲ and TḲ, erroneously, اتّهم:]) or *there was in him that which induced suspicion:* you say of a man, when you suspect him, أَتْهَمْتُ, inf. n. إِتْهَامٌ; like أَدْوَأَتْ, inf. n. إِدْوَآءٌ. (Ṣ in art. وهم.) ═ اتهمه *He suspected him; thought evil of him;* as also ▼ اتَّهَمَهُ [which is the more common]. (Mṣb in this art.) You say, اتهمهُ بِكَذَا, (Ḳ, and so in some copies of the Ṣ, both in art. وهم,) inf. n. إِتْهَامٌ; (Ḳ in that art.;) or ▼ اتَّهَمَهُ بِهِ, (Mṣb and Ḳ, and so in some copies of the Ṣ, all in that art.;) and أَوْهَمَهُ; (Ḳ in that art.;) *He suspected him of such a thing; imputed it to him;* (Mṣb and Ḳ* and TA, all in that art.;) [and *he accused him of such a thing;*] i. e., a thing attributed to him. (TA.) And ▼ اتَّهَمْتُهُ فِى قَوْلِهِ [*I suspected him in respect of his saying;*] *I doubted of the correctness,* or *truth, of his saying.* (Mṣb in art. وهم.)

5: see 4.

8: see 4, in three places.

تَهَمٌ [in the CḲ, erroneously, تَهْم] *Land descending* (أَرْضٌ مُتَصَوِّبَةٌ [in the CḲ, here and afterwards, erroneously, مُتَصَوِيَة]) *to the sea;* as also ▼ تَهْمَةٌ; (Ḳ, TA;) mentioned by IḲṭ, from Ez-Ziyádee, from Aṣ: (TA:) these two words seem to be [originally] inf. ns. from تَهَامَةُ: (Ḳ:) [and accord. to F,] ▼ التَّهَمَةُ is a dial. var. of ▼ تِهَامَةُ: (Ḳ:) [but J says,] ▼ التَّهَمَةُ is used in the place of ▼ تِهَامَةُ, as though it were [originally] the inf. n. un., accord. to the saying of Aṣ that التَّهَمُ, with fet-ḥ to the medial radical, is an inf. n. from ▼ تِهَامَةُ: (Ṣ:) for the ▼ تَهَائِمُ [pl. of تِهَامَةُ, and thus meaning the *parts of Tihámeh,* or, accord. to the JK, meaning *lands descending to the sea,*] do descend to the sea: (Ḳ, TA:) so says Aṣ: (TA:) and [hence] the rájiz says, (namely, Sheyṭán Ibn-Mudlij, TA,)

• نَظَرْتُ وَالعَيْنُ مُبِينَةُ التَّهَمْ •

[*I looked, the eye distinguishing Et-Taham*], (Ṣ, and Ḥam p. 659,) meaning *Et-Tihámeh.* (Ḥam ibid.) — [As inf. n. of تَهِمَ, q. v.,] التَّهَمُ also signifies *Vehemence of heat, and* [or *with*] *stillness of the wind.* (Ḳ.) And hence Tihámeh is said to be thus called. (TA.)

تَهِمٌ, applied to flesh-meat, *Altered for the worse;* (JK;) *having a foul odour; stinking.* (JK,* Ḳ.) — أَرْضٌ تَهِمَةٌ *A land vehemently,* or *intensely, hot.* (Er-Riyáshee, TA.) ═ *Sleeping;* (JK;) *i. q.* تَهِنٌ. (TA in art. لعث.)

التَّهَمَةُ: see تَهَمٌ. — It, (Ḳ,) or ▼ التَّهْمَةُ, (JK,) signifies also البَلْدَةُ [app. as meaning *Mekkeh,* like ▼ تِهَامَةُ; as though *the city of cities*]: (JK, Ḳ:) so in the phrase ▼ أَهْلُ التَّهَمَةِ [which may mean *The people of Mekkeh;* and also, *of Tihámeh,* in the more extended sense of the latter appellation]. (JK.)

تَهْمَةٌ: see تُهَمَةٌ.

فِيهِ تَهَمَةٌ *In it is a foul odour; a stink.* (Ḳ.) — See also التَّهَمَةُ — تَهَمٌ: see تَهَمٌ, and التَّهَمَةُ; the latter in two places.

تُهْمَةٌ, (Ṣ, M, Ḳ, &c., in art. وهم, and Mṣb in that art. and in the present also,) of which ▼ تُهَمَةٌ is a dial. var. mentioned by El-Fárábee (Mṣb, and TA in art. وهم) and by several other authors, or, accord. to Ibn-Kemál, the latter is an inf. n. and the former is a simple subst., but Esh-Shiháb doubts of this; (TA;) originally وُهْمَةٌ, (Ṣ, ISd, Mṣb, &c.,) like as تُخَمَةٌ is originally وُخَمَةٌ; (ISd, TA;) a subst. from اتَّهَمَهُ; (Ṣ, Mṣb, both in art. وهم;) *Doubt:* and [more commonly] *suspicion,* or *evil opinion;* or *doubt combined with suspicion or evil opinion:* syn. شَكٌّ: and رِيبَةٌ: (Mṣb in the present art.:) or *i. q.* ظَنٌّ [which is *a preponderating wavering between the two extremes of indecisive belief;* and often means *suspicion*]: (ISd and TA in art. وهم:) or *a thing for which one is suspected:* (Ḳ in that art.: [and this is often meant by رِيبَةٌ, one of the syns. mentioned above:]) the pl. of تُهَمَةٌ is تُهَمٌ, mentioned by Sb, who argues that it is a pl. [and not a coll. gen. n.] from their saying هِىَ التُّهَمُ [*They are suspicions,* &c.], and not saying هُوَ التُّهَمُ like as they say هُوَ الرُّطَبُ. (TA in art. وهم.)

تِهَامِىٌّ: see تَهَامٍ.

تَهِيمٌ *Suspected; thought evil of;* (JK in this art., and Mṣb in this and in art. وهم;) [as also ▼ مُتَّهَمٌ and ▼ مُتْهَمٌ:] or *being an object of suspicion;* as also ▼ مُتْهِمٌ. (Ḳ in art. وهم. [In the CḲ, the latter is erroneously written مُتَّهِمٌ.])

تِهَامَةُ a name of *Mekkeh:* (JK, Ḳ:) and [more commonly] *a certain land,* (Mṣb, Ḳ,) *well known,* (Ḳ,) *commencing from Dhát 'Irḳ,* (Mṣb, TA,) *towards Nejd,* (Mṣb,) *and extending to Mekkeh and beyond it to the distance of two days' journeys* (Mṣb, TA) *and more, then uniting with the Ghowr, and extending to the sea: some say that it adjoins the land of El-Yemen; and that Mekkeh is of* تِهَامَةُ اليَمَنِ: (Mṣb:) [F says that] J has erred in terming it a بَلَد: (Ḳ:) [but by بلد, J may mean both a city and a country or province:] some say that its name is from تَهِمَ in the first of the senses assigned to this verb above, because it is low in relation to Nejd, so that its odour is bad; and some, that it is from the same verb in the sense explained in the second sentence, because of its vehement heat: (Mṣb:) [it seems to have تَهَائِمُ for a pl.:] see تَهَمٌ, in four places; and التَّهَمَةُ.

تَهَامِىٌّ *Of,* or *belonging to, Tihámeh;* as also ▼ تَهَامٍ, (T, Ṣ, M, Mṣb, Ḳ, [in the CḲ, erroneously, تَهامٌ,]) with fet-ḥ, (Mṣb, Ḳ,) irregularly formed; (M, Mṣb;) fem. تَهَامِيَةٌ; like رَبَاعٍ and رَبَاعِيَةٌ: (T, Mṣb:) when it is pronounced with fet-ḥ to the ت, it is without teshdeed [to the ى when you say رَجُلٌ تَهَامٍ and تَهَامِيَةٌ التَّهَامِى]; as in the instances of شَآمٍ and يَمَانٍ, except that the ا in تَهَامٍ is of the original word, and that in شَآمٍ and يَمَانٍ is a substitute for the two ىs of the [regular] rel. n., (Ṣ,) or rather, for one of those two ىs: (Aboo-Zekereeyà, TA:) and you say قَوْمٌ تَهَامُونَ [*A people,* or *company of men, of Tihámeh*], like يَمَانُونَ: (Ṣ, Ḳ:) and accord. to Sb, some say تَهَامِىٌّ and يَمَانِىٌّ and شَآمِىٌّ, with fet-ḥ, and with teshdeed [to the ى]. (Ṣ.)

مُتْهَمٌ: see تَهِيمٌ.

مُتْهِمٌ [*Going,* or *coming, to Tihámeh:* or *alighting,* or *abiding, therein:* and] *alighting,* or *abiding, in Mekkeh.* (TA.) — وَادٍ مُتْهِمٌ *A valley of which the water pours to Tihámeh.* (TA.) ═ See also تَهِيمٌ.

مِتْهَامٌ *Often coming to Tihámeh:* (Ṣ, Ḳ:) pl. مَتَاهِيمُ (Ṣ, TA) and مَتَاهِمُ, (TA,) applied to men (Ṣ, TA) and to camels. (TA.)

مُتَّهَمٌ: see تَهِيمٌ.

تو

4. اتوى, said of a man, signifies جَآءَ تَوًّا, i. e. *He came alone; by himself:* opposed to أَزْوَى meaning "he came with another." (T.) ═ See also art. توى.

تَوٌّ [app. from the Persian تُوْ, meaning "a fold," or "a single fold,"] *One, and no more; single; sole.* (T, Ṣ, M, Ḳ.) You say, كَانَ تَوًّا فَصَارَ زَوًّا *He,* or *it, was one only, and became a pair.* (TA.) And it is said in a trad., الطَّوَافُ تَوٌّ وَالِاسْتِجْمَارُ تَوٌّ, (Ṣ, TA,) i. e., *The circuiting* [of the Kaabeh] *is one action, and the casting of the pebbles* [in the valley of Minè] *is one action.* (TA.) You say also, جَآءَ تَوًّا, meaning *He came alone; by himself:* (T, Ṣ, M:) or *he came by a direct course, nothing making him to deviate, and not stopping anywhere in the road;* for if he stop anywhere in the road, he is not said to be تَوٌّ. (AZ, A'Obeyd, M, Ḳ.) And عَقَدْتُهُ بِتَوٍّ وَاحِدٍ *I tied it with a single knot; by turning the cord, or the like, once:* so says AZ; and he cites the following ex.:

• جَارِيَةٌ لَيْسَتْ مِنَ الوَخْشَنِّ •

• لَا تَعْقِدُ المِنْطَقَ بِالمَتْنِّ •

• إِلَّا بِتَوٍّ وَاحِدٍ أَوْ تَنِّ •

i. e., [*A girl that is not of the wild,* or *shy, sort: she does not tie the zone with the fist, but with a* *single knot, or] half a knot:* the ن in تَنّ [and in مُشْتَنّ and وَخْشَنّ] is redundant: تَنّ being originally تَ, which is a contraction [or rather the half, both as to the letter and the meaning,] of تَوٌّ. (T.) — *A rope that is twisted of a single strand:* pl. أَتْوَآءٌ. (T, M, Ḳ.) — [It is said that] it signifies also *A thousand horses,* or *horsemen.* (AZ, T, Ḳ.) [But this requires consideration: for] one says, وَجَّهَ فُلَانٌ مِنْ خَيْلِهِ بِأَلْفٍ تَوٍّ, (AZ, T, Ṣ,) meaning [*Such a one sent a troop of his horses*] *with a thousand men;* i. e., *with one thousand:* (Ṣ, TA:) or, as some say, *with one complete thousand.* (TA.) ═ Also One who is *unoccupied by the business of the present world and of the world to come.* (AA, T, Ḳ.*) ═ Also A structure *elevated, reared,* or *erected.* (T, Ḳ.)

تَوْءَةٌ *A period,* or *a short period,* (سَاعَةٌ, AA, T, Ḳ,) *of time.* (AA, T.) You say, مَضَتْ تَوْءَةٌ مِنَ اللَّيْلِ, and النَّهَارِ, *A period,* or *a short period,* (ساعة,) *of the night passed,* and *of the day.* (TA.) And مَا مَضَى إِلَّا تَوْءَةٌ حَتَّى كَانَ كَذَا *There passed not save a short period* (ساعة) *to the time that such a thing happened.* (IAạr, T.) Hence the saying of the vulgar, تَوْءَةٌ قَامَ [commonly pronounced تَوَّه] *Just now* (السَّاعَةَ) *he rose,* or *stood.* (TA.)

توأ

تَآءٌ *The name of the letter* ت, q. v.; as also تَا: pl. [of the former تَآءَاتٌ; and of the latter] أَتْوَآءٌ. (TA in باب الالف الليّنة.)

تَاوِىٌّ and تَائِىٌّ rel. ns. of تَآءٌ and تَا the names of the letter ت; as also تَيَوِىٌّ: (TA ubi suprà:) whence قَصِيدَةٌ تَائِيَّةٌ and تَاوِيَّةٌ and تَيَوِيَّةٌ (T, Ḳ, TA, ubi suprà, [the last written in the CḲ تَيْوِيَّةٌ,] and the second is also mentioned in the Ṣ) *A* قصيدة *of which the* رَوِىّ *is* ت. (TA ibid.)

توب

1. تَابَ, (T, A,) or تاب إِلَى ٱللّٰهِ, (Ṣ, M, Ḳ,) aor. يَتُوبُ, (Mṣb,) inf. n. تَوْبَةٌ and تَوْبٌ, (T, Ṣ, M, Mṣb, Ḳ,) both of these signifying the same, (T, Ṣ, M, Mṣb,) the ة in the former being added to denote the fem. gender, or, as some say, the former is a n. un. like ضَرْبَةٌ, (Mṣb,) or, as Akh says, تَوْبٌ is pl. [or a quasi-pl. n.] of تَوْبَةٌ, like as عَوْمٌ is of عَوْمَةٌ, (Ṣ,) or like as لَوْزٌ is of لَوْزَةٌ, and this is the opinion of Mbr, (M,) and تَابَةٌ, (M, Ḳ,) which is for تَوْبَةٌ, (M,) and مَتَابٌ (Ṣ, M, A, Ḳ) and تَتْوِبَةٌ, (Ṣ,* M,* Ḳ,) of the measure تَفْعِلَةٌ, (Ṣ, M,) an anomalous form, (TA,) syn. with تَوْبَةٌ, mentioned in the Book of Sb; (Ṣ;) [*He repented;* or *repented toward God;* as will be shown by what follows:] originally, *he returned unto God,* (T, TA,) عَنْ كَذَا and مِنْ كَذَا [*from such a thing*]: (TA:) or *he returned,* [or *returned unto God,*] (Ṣ, M, A, Ḳ,) *from sin,* (Ṣ,) or *from his sin,* (A,) or *from disobedience* (M, Ḳ) *to obedience:* (M:) or تَابَ مِنْ ذَنْبِهِ signifies *he desisted from his sin:* (Mṣb:) تَوْبَةٌ signifies the *repenting of sin;* i. e. the *grieving for it,* or *regretting it, with the confession of having no excuse for the commission thereof.* (Kull.) It is said in a trad., النَّدَمُ تَوْبَةٌ [*Repentance is*] *a returning from sin.* (Ṣ.) The time of El-Islám is termed زَمَنُ التَّوْبَةِ as being *The time of returning from* [or *repenting of*] *the belief in a plurality of gods.* (A.) A poet says,

* تُبْتُ إِلَيْكَ فَتَقَبَّلْ تَابَتِى *
* وَصُمْتُ رَبِّى فَتَقَبَّلْ صَامَتِى *

[*I have repented toward Thee, and accept Thou my repentance; and I have fasted, O my Lord, and accept Thou my fast*]; meaning تَوْبَتِى and صَوْمَتِى. (M.) — تَابَ ٱللّٰهُ عَلَيْهِ *God returned to forgiveness towards him; became again forgiving to him:* (T:) or *disposed,* or *adapted, him to repentance,* or *returning from sin* or *disobedience:* (Ṣ, Ḳ:) or *reverted from severity to mildness towards him:* or *returned to him with his favour,* or *grace, and his acceptance,* or *approbation; became again propitious to him:* (A, Ḳ:) all these meanings are correct: (TA:) or *God forgave him, and saved him from acts of disobedience:* (Mṣb:) or *accepted his repentance:* (Jel in ii. 35 &c.:) or *returned towards him with mercy, and acceptance of repentance.* (Bḍ ibid.)

10. استتابهُ *He proposed to him that he should return* [*to obedience unto God*], (T, A,) *and repent of that which he had committed:* (T:) *he asked him to return from sin,* or *disobedience:* (Ṣ, Ḳ:) or *he asked him to desist from his sin.* (Mṣb.)

تَابُوتٌ, originally تَوْبُوتٌ, the ت not being the characteristic of the fem. gender, (Z, MF, TA,) of the measure فَعْلُوتٌ, and meaning *A chest,* or *box,* from التَّوْبُ, because what is taken out from it continually returns to it: (AAF, IJ, Z, MF, TA:) or originally تَابُوَةٌ; (Ṣ, Ḳ; [in the CḲ تَأْبُوَةٌ;]) the و being made quiescent, and the ة changed into ت: (Ṣ, Ḳ:) [in Chald. תֵּיבוּתָא: in Hebr. תֵּבָה:] it signifies also the *ribs, with what they contain, as the heart and the liver &c.;* as being likened to a chest, or box; (IAth, TA in art. تبت;) the *chest, breast,* or *bosom:* (A in that art.:) or [primarily] the *ribs, with what they contain, as the heart &c.:* and [hence] applied to *a chest,* or *box:* (Towsheeh, MF, TA:) also written تَبُوتٌ. (Ḳ in art. تبت.) [It is generally applied in the present day to *a bier: a coffin:* and *an oblong case that is placed over a grave:* the pl. is تَوَابِيتُ.] El-Ḳásim Ibn-Maạn says that it is the only word in the Ḳur-án in respect of which the dialects of Ḳureysh and the Anṣár differ; the former pronouncing it تَابُوتٌ; (Ṣ;) and the latter, تَابُوهٌ. (Ṣ, Ḳ.) But IB denies that its last letter is originally ة, the fem. termination; asserting the final ت to be a radical letter, the measure of the word to be فَاعُولٌ, and its proper place in art. تبت: he says that the final ت is changed in a case of pause, but not generally, into ه, as is that of الفُرَاتُ [the Euphrates], in which the ت is not the fem. termination. (L, TA.) You say, مَا أَوْدَعْتُ تَابُوتِى شَيْئًا فَفَقَدْتُهُ, meaning *I have not deposited in my bosom anything* of knowledge, or science, *that I have lost.* (A in art. تبت.)

تَوَّابٌ, applied to a man, [One *who repents much* or *often;*] *returning from disobedience to obedience* [*to God*] (M, Ḳ, TA) *much* or *often.* (TA.) — And applied to God, *One who returns* [*much* or *often*] *to forgiveness towards his servant who returns unto Him:* (T:) or *who* [*often*] *disposes,* or *adapts, to repentance,* or *returning from sin* or *disobedience;* or *reverts from severity to mildness;* or *returns with his favour* or *grace, &c.:* (A, Ḳ: [see 1, last sentence:]) or *who forgives much, and saves from acts of disobedience.* (Mṣb.)

تَائِبٌ [*Repenting of sin:* (see 1:) originally,] *returning from disobedience* (M, Ḳ) *to obedience* to God. (M.)

توت

تُوتٌ (ISk, T, Ṣ, M, Mgh, Mṣb, Ḳ) and تُوثٌ; (Mgh, and L and Ḳ in art. توث, q. v.;) the latter sometimes used; (Mṣb;) or this is not allowable; (ISk, T, Ṣ, Mṣb;) for the word, which is app. Persian, is pronounced by the Arabs with ت for the final as well as for the initial letter; (T, Mṣb;) [The *mulberry;* and especially the *white mulberry;*] *i. q.* فِرْصَادٌ: (ISk, T, Ṣ, M, Mgh, Mṣb, Ḳ:) or, accord. to the people of El-Baṣrah, (Mṣb,) or some of the people of El-Baṣrah, (Mgh,) توت is the name of the *fruit,* and فرصاد is that of the *tree;* (Mgh, Mṣb;) and this is what is commonly held: (Mṣb:) or, accord. to IDrd and others, توت is an arabicized word, and فرصاد is the Arabic name: (TA:) [توت is a coll. gen. n.:] the n. un. is with ة. (M.) [Golius says, in his Lex., on the authority of Zeyn El-'Aṭṭár, that there are three kinds: "توت حلو," i. e. حُلْو, "the *sweet and white mulberry,* peculiarly called فرصاد; and "توت حامض," i. e. حَامِض, "the *sour and black mulberry;* and "توت وحشى," i. e. وَحْشِىّ, "and "توت العليق," i. e. العُلَّيْق, "the *wild mulberry,* i. e., *with red fruit.*" In Egypt, توت is applied to the *sweet mulberry, white* and *black,* and especially to the *former,* as also توت بَلَدِىّ; and توت شَامِىّ to the *latter.* In the present day, توت العُلَّيْق is applied to the *raspberry;* as also توت وَحْشِىّ: and توت شَوْكِىّ, I believe, to the *blackberry.* توت أَرْضِىّ and توت إِفْرَنْجِىّ are applied to the *strawberry.*]

تُوتِيَآءُ, [of the masc. gender, as is shown by the phrase توتياء مَعْدِنِىٌّ, and therefore perfectly decl.,] an arabicized word, (Ṣ, Mṣb,) [*Tutia,* or *tutty; an impure protoxide of zinc;*] *a certain stone* [or *mineral*], (Ṣ, Ḳ,) *well known,* (M, Ḳ,) *employed as a collyrium.* (Ṣ, Mṣb.) [It is also applied in the present day to several kinds of *vitriol;* the *sulphates of zinc* and *of copper* and *of iron.* De Sacy says, on the authority of Ibn-Beyṭár, that there are two species thereof; one which is found in mines; the other, in the furnaces in which copper is melted, like *cadmia;* and this latter species is what the Greeks call *pompholyx:* of the fossil tutia there are three varieties; one is white; another, greenish; the third, yellow, with a strong tinge of red: the white is the finest variety; the green, the coarsest. (Chrest. Arabe, 2nd ed., iii. 453; where see more.) Golius, on this word, in his Lex., says, "Optima est quæ vel naturalis, sc. Indica, cærulea, et pellucida; vel artificialis, sc. Carmanica, alba cum partis viridioris strictura. Zein." i. e. Zeyn El-'Aṭṭár. "Ex plumbi præstantissimi, quod dicitur قلعى, fuligine concrescere præstantissimum genus, commune vero ex fuligine æris, tradit Jacutus ex Abulfed."]

توتيا

تُوتِيَآءُ : see the art. next preceding.

توث

تُوثٌ *i. q.* فِرْصَادٌ ; a dial. var. of تُوتٌ, [q. v.,] mentioned by IF, (L, Ḳ,) and by AḤn, who cites a verse in which it occurs, and says that he had not heard any one pronounce it with ت, but only with ث, though توث is Persian and توت is Arabic; (IB, TA;) but it is disallowed by El-Ḥareeree and others: (TA:) in the Expos. of the work entitled Adab el-Kátib, it is said that توت is an arabicized word, originally توث and توذ : (Mz, MF:) the n. un. is with ة. (L, Ḳ.)

توج

2. تَوَّجَهُ ***He crowned him; invested him with the crown.*** (Ṣ, A, Mṣb,* Ḳ.) — *He made him a prince, lord, or chief.* (Mṣb,* TA.) — † *He turbaned him; invested him with the turban.* (TA.)

5. تتوّج ***He was,*** or ***became, crowned,*** or ***invested with the crown.*** (Ṣ, A, Ḳ.) [For the verb تَاجَ, in this or a similar sense, mentioned in the Lexicons of Golius and Freytag, in the former as from the Ḳ, I find no authority: on the contrary, it is said in the TA that no verb answering to تَائِجٌ has been heard.] — *He was made,* or *became, a prince, lord,* or *chief.* (TA.) — † *He was,* or *became, turbaned,* or *invested with the turban.* (TA.)

تَاجٌ *A crown;* (Ṣ, A, Ḳ, TA;) i. e. *a thing that is made for kings, of gold and jewels;* (TA;) *peculiar to the* عَجَم [or *Persians and other foreigners*]: (Mṣb:) [a Persian word:] pl. [of mult.] تِيجَانٌ (Ṣ, A, Mgh, Mṣb, Ḳ) and [of pauc.] أَتْوَاجٌ. (TA.) — † *A turban;* as being likened to a crown. (TA.) It is said in a trad., (TA,) العَمَائِمُ تِيجَانُ العَرَبِ [*Turbans are the crowns of the Arabs*]; (Ṣ, TA;) i. e. turbans are to the Arabs as crowns to the kings; for the Arabs in the deserts are [or were] mostly bare-headed or wearing قَلَانِس [pl. of قَلَنْسُوَةٌ, q. v.]; turbans among them being few. (TA.) — Also *Silver.* (TA.) [See what next follows.]

تَاجَةٌ *An ingot of purified silver:* originally تَازَهْ, a Persian word, applied to a dirhem recently coined. (TA.)

تَائِجٌ *Having a* تَاج [i. e. *crown,* or † *turban*]; an epithet applied to an إِمَام : (Ḳ:) it is a possessive epithet, like دَارِعٌ, for we have not heard any verb answering to it. (TA.)

مُتَوَّجٌ *Crowned;* applied to a king: (A, TA:) †*made a prince, lord,* or *chief:* †*turbaned.* (TA.)

مَتَاوِجُ [a pl. of which the sing. is not mentioned,] occurring in the saying of Jendel Er-Rá'ee,

وَهُنَّ يَعْمِينَ مِنَ المَلَامِجِ
بِقَرِدٍ مُخْرَنْطِمِ المَتَاوِجِ

signifies [properly The *parts of the head*] *where one is crowned* (حَيْثُ يُتَتَوَّجُ) *with the turban:* (Ḳ,* TA:) [but it is evidently here used in a tropical manner: the poet is speaking of she-camels:] the ملامج are the mouths; [or the parts around the mouths;] and the قَرِد, a word like كَتِف, is the accumulated foam which the camel casts forth from his mouth. (TA.) [It seems that the poet means, *And they cast forth, from the parts around the mouth, accumulated foam, elongated in the extremities:* مُخْرَنْطِم being app. syn. with مُخَرْطَم, as meaning "elongated like a خُرْطُوم," or "snout."]

توح

1. تَاحَ, aor. يَتُوحُ, inf. n. تَوْحٌ : see تَاحَ in art. تيح.

تور

1. تَارَ, aor. يَتُورُ, (TA in art. تير,) inf. n. تَوْرٌ, (Ḳ,) *It* (water, TA) *ran,* or *flowed:* (Ḳ, TA:) but this verb is obsolete. (TA in art. تير.) — تِيرَ الرَّجُلُ [app. for أُثْئِرَ] *Blood-revenge was had of the man.* (M. [See also تَارَةٌ.])

3. تاوره *He returned to him,* or *it, time after time;* syn. عَاوَدَهُ. (A. [See also 4.])

4. اتاره *He repeated it,* or *did it again, time after time.* (Ṣ in art. تير, M, Ḳ.) — *He continued to look at him,* or *it, time after time.* (TA.) And أَتَرْتُ إِلَيْهِ النَّظَرَ, (T, Ḳ,*) and الرَّمْىَ, inf. n. إِتَارَةٌ, (T,) *i. q.* اتارته, (Ḳ,) i. e. *I looked at him sharply,* or *intently:* (TA:) [or *time after time:*] and *I cast,* or *shot, at him time after time.* (T.) — فُلَانٌ يُتَارُ عَلَى أَنْ يُؤْخَذَ is said by AA to mean *Such a one is encompassed,* or *gone round,* (يُدَارُ,) *in order that he may be taken:* and he cites, from a poem of 'Ámir Ibn-Ketheer El-Moḥáribee,

لَقَدْ غَضِبُوا عَلَىَّ وَأَشْقَذُونِى
فَصِرْتُ كَأَنَّنِى فَرَأٌ يُتَارُ

[as though meaning *They have been angry with me, and driven me away, and I have become as though I were a wild ass encompassed* in order to be taken]: or, accord. as some relate it, ▼مُتَارُ: (Ṣ:) [and it is said that] this signifies *cast at,* or *shot at, time after time.* (T, L. [See also art. تأر.])

تَارٌ : see تَارَةٌ.

تَوْرٌ *A messenger* (Ṣ, M, A, Mṣb, Ḳ) *between people,* (Ṣ, M, Ḳ,) or *that goes about between lovers:* (A:) accord. to IDrd, (Ṣ,) a genuine Arabic word: (Ṣ, M:) pl. أَتْوَارٌ. (Mṣb.) And تَوْرَةٌ *A girl who is sent on messages between lovers.* (IAạr, T, Ḳ.) — *A vessel,* (Ṣ,) *a certain well-known vessel,* (T, Mṣb,) *a small vessel,* (A, Mgh, Ḳ,) *from which one drinks:* (Ṣ, Mgh, Ḳ:) *a vessel of brass,* or *of stone, like the* إِجَّانَة : (TA:) *sometimes also used for the ablution termed* وُضُوء : (A, Mgh, TA:) so called from the same word as signifying the act of "running" or "flowing" [of water], (TA,) because it is mutually borrowed and returned; or from the same word as signifying "a messenger:" (A, TA:) of the masc. gender: (T, A, Ḳ:) [or fem., for Z says,] I passed, at the Gate of El-'Omrah, [of the Temple of Mekkeh,] by a woman who was saying to her female neighbour, أَعِيرِينِى تُوَيْرَتَكِ [*Lend thou to me thy little* تَوْر]: for had she considered تور as masc., she would have said تُوَيْرَكِ. (A.) — تَوْرُ نُحَاسٍ *A cooking-pot of copper.* (Mgh.) — تَوْرُ المَآءِ *i. q.* طُحْلُبٌ, i. e. *A green substance that overspreads stagnant water.* (Mṣb.)

تَارَةٌ, originally with ء, which is suppressed on account of frequent usage, (IAạr, Mṣb,) and sometimes pronounced with ء; (Mṣb;) or its ا is [originally] و [and therefore it is mentioned in most of the lexicons in the present art.]; (Lth, T;) [or ى, for it is mentioned in the Ṣ in art. تير;] *A time; one time;* [in the sense of the French *fois;*] syn. مَرَّةٌ : (Ṣ, M, A, Mṣb, Ḳ:) and *a time, whether long or short;* syn. حِينٌ : (M, Ḳ:) sometimes [pronounced ▼تَارٌ,] without ة : (Ṣ:) pl. تَارَاتٌ (Lth, T, Ṣ, M, Mṣb, Ḳ) and تِيَرٌ ; (Lth, T, Ṣ, M, Ḳ;) the latter a contraction of تِيَارٌ ; like as they said قَامَاتٌ and قِيَمٌ, because of the unsound letter. (Ṣ. [See also art. تار.]) You say, فَعَلَ ذٰلِكَ تَارَةً بَعْدَ تَارَةٍ *He did that time after time.* (Ṣ.) And هٰذِهِ شَرُّ تَارَاتِكَ *This is the worst of thy times.* (A.) — يَا تَارَاتِ فُلَانٍ [app. meaning *O the blood-revenge of such a one!*] (M, Ḳ) is mentioned by Lḥ, (M,) or AA, (TA,) but not explained by him: and he cites the saying of Ḥassán,

لَتَسْمَعَنَّ وَشِيكًا فِى دِيَارِهِمُ
اللهُ أَكْبَرُ يَا تَارَاتِ عُثْمَانَ

[which probably means *Thou wilt assuredly hear speedily, in their abodes, "God is most great! O the blood-revenge of 'Othmán!"* for ISd says,] in my opinion, (M,) تارات is formed by transposition from وِتْرٌ signifying *blood* [or rather *blood-revenge*], (M, Ḳ,*) though not agreeing with it in measure: (M:) and وشيكا here means سَرِيعًا : so says IB. (TA in art. وشك.) [See also تَارٌ.]

تَائِرٌ *Applying himself constantly,* or *perseveringly, to work, after remitting,* or *remissness.* (Ḳ.)

تِيَارٌ : see art. تير.

مُتَارٌ : see 4.

توق

1. تَاقَ إِلَيْهِ, (Ḳ,) aor. يَتُوقُ, (TA,) inf. n. تَوْقٌ and تُؤُوقٌ and تِيَاقَةٌ and تَوَقَانٌ, *He yearned towards, longed for,* or *desired, him* or *it*; (Ḳ, TA;) *his soul yearned towards, longed for,* or *desired, him* or *it.* (TA.) And تَاقَتْ نَفْسِى إِلَى الشَّىْءِ, (JK, Ṣ, Mgh, Mṣb, but in the latter two نَفْسُهُ,) inf. n. تَوْقٌ (JK, Ṣ, Mṣb) and تُؤُوقٌ (JK, Mṣb) and تَوَقَانٌ, (Ṣ, Mgh, Mṣb,) *My soul yearned towards, longed for,* or *desired, the thing*; (JK, Ṣ, Mgh, Mṣb;) *and hastened to it*: (Mṣb:) and so تاقت الشَّىْءَ. (TA.) —— تَاقَ إِلَى الشَّىْءِ also signifies ‡ *He desired,* or *purposed, to do the thing*: and *he was brisk,* or *prompt, to do it*: (JK, Ḳ, TA:) so in the Moḥeeṭ. (TA.) You say, تاق إِلَى الغَايَةِ ‡ *He hastened, with briskness,* or *promptness, to the goal.* (TA.) And تُقْ إِلَىَّ يَا فُلَانُ ‡ *Hasten thou to me, O such a one.* (TA.) —— تَاقَ القِدْحُ *The gaming-arrow came forth on the occasion of the shuffling* in the game of المَيْسِر: (JK,* Ḳ, TA:) so says Ibn-'Abbád. (TA.) —— تَاقَتِ الدُّمُوعُ ‡ *The tears issued from their channels.* (JK, Ḳ, TA.) —— تَاقَ بِنَفْسِهِ, inf. n. تَوَقَانٌ (JK, Ḳ) and تَوْقٌ, (Ḳ, TA,) or تَوَقٌ, (CḲ,) *i. q.* جَادَ بِنَفْسِهِ [*He gave up his spirit*: or *he was near to die*]: (JK, Ḳ:) said of a man: (JK:) AA says that التُّؤُوقُ signifies *the being in the very agony of death*; like السُّوقُ. (TA.) —— تَاقَ is also *syn. with* أَشْفَقَ, (JK, Ḳ,) accord. to Ibn-'Abbád. (TA.) You say, تَاقَ مِنْهُ, meaning *He was cautious,* or *in fear, of him* or *it.* (TḲ.)

5. تتوّق إِلَى الشَّىْءِ *He was,* or *became, excited by a yearning towards, a longing for,* or *a desire for, the thing*; or *he affected and showed a yearning towards it, a longing for it,* or *a desire for it*; syn. تَشَوَّقَ. (TA.)

تَوَقَةٌ Persons *convalescent*; or *in a state of recovery from disease, but not yet completely restored to health and strength*: (IAạr, Ḳ:) app. pl. of ▼تَائِقٌ. (TA.)

تَوَّاقٌ *i. q.* شَوَّاقٌ [app. *Yearning, longing,* or *desiring, much,* or *vehemently*; or *very desirous*: but some regard it as a simple epithet, syn. with ▼تَائِقٌ; for it is said that] نَفْسٌ تَوَّاقَةٌ signifies the same as ▼تَائِقَةٌ [*A yearning, longing, desiring,* or *desirous, soul*]. (JK, Mṣb.) It is said in a prov., (TA,)

• المَرْءُ تَوَّاقٌ إِلَى مَا لَمْ يَنَلْ •

[*Man is desirous,* or *very desirous, of that which he has not attained*]. (Ṣ, TA.) —— One *whose soul yearns towards, longs for,* or *desires, every low,* or *base, action.* (TA.)

تَائِقٌ, fem. with ة: see تَوَّاقٌ, in two places; and see تَوَقَةٌ.

تَيِّقَانٌ, originally تَيْوِقَانٌ, A man *who leaps, springs,* or *bounds, vehemently.* (Ibn-'Abbád, Ḳ.)

مُتَوَّقٌ *Yearned towards, longed for, desired,* or *desired eagerly.* (IAạr, Ḳ.)

تولب

تَوْلَبٌ: see art. تلب.

توم

تُومٌ: see تُومَةٌ, below, in two places.

تَوْمٌ: see تَوْأَمٌ, in art. تأم.

تُومَةٌ sing. of تُومٌ [in the CḲ, erroneously, تُوَمٌ] and [n. un.] of ▼تُومٌ; (M, Ḳ;) *One of the things called* تُوم; (Ṣ, Mṣb;) i. e. *a* قُرْط [as meaning *a silver bead fashioned like a pearl*]: (Lth, T:) or *a* قُرْط [as meaning *an earring*] *in which is a large* حَبَّة [or *bead*]: (M, Ḳ:) or *a thing,* (T,) or حَبَّة [i. e. *bead*], (Ṣ, Mṣb,) *made of silver,* (T, Ṣ, Mṣb,) *like a pearl,* (T, Ṣ,) or *like a large pearl,* (Ṣ,) *of a round form, which a girl puts in her ear.* (T.) —— And hence, as being likened to this, (T,) †*A large pearl*: (AA, T:) or *a pearl.* (M, Ḳ.) And أُمُّ تُومَةَ ‡ *The pearl-shell*: (Ḳ, TA:) a proper name, and therefore imperfectly decl. (TA.) —— And ‡ *An ostrich's egg*: (M, Ḳ, TA:) pl. as above: (M:) ostriches' eggs are called ▼تُومٌ (A'Obeyd, T, Ṣ) as being likened to pearls, which are thus called: (T:) they are so called by Dhu-r-Rummeh, where he says,

• وَحَتَّى أَتَى يَوْمٌ يَكَادُ مِنَ اللَّظَى •
• بِهِ التُّومُ فِى أُفْحُوصِهِ يَتَصَيَّحُ •

[*And until there came a day in which, by reason of the flaming heat, the ostriches' eggs, in the place where they were deposited in the sand, almost dried up.*] (A'Obeyd, Ṣ, M.) —— التُّومَتَانِ is an appellation applied to two ḳaṣeedehs of Jereer, in praise of 'Abd-El-'Azeez Ibn-Marwán. (T.)

مُتَوَّمٌ *Having a* قِلَادَة [or *necklace*] *put upon his neck*; syn. مُقَلَّدٌ. (Ḳ. [In the CḲ, erroneously, مُقَلِّد.])

توه

1. تَاهَ, aor. يَتُوهُ, inf. n. تَوْهٌ (Mṣb, Ḳ) and تُوهٌ, (AZ, Ḳ,) is *syn. with* تَاهَ *having for its aor.* يَتِيهُ; (Mṣb, and TA in the present art. and in art. تيه;) [and with طَاحَ, aor. يَطُوحُ and يَطِيحُ;] signifying *He deviated from,* or *lost,* or *missed, the right way*; *he lost his way*; (Mṣb, TA;) in the desert: (Mṣb:) or *he was,* or *became, confounded,* or *perplexed, and unable to see his right course*: (TA in the present art.:) or *he went away* (Ḳ, TA) in the land, *confounded,* or *perplexed, and unable to see his right course*: (TA in art. تيه:) or, as some say, (TA,) *his mind,* or *intellect, was,* or *became, disordered, confused,* or *unsound*: (Ḳ, TA:) and *he perished*: (Ḳ, TA:) accord. to ISd, the ى in يَتِيهُ is shown to be originally و by their saying, مَا أَتْوَهَهُ, as syn. with مَا أَتْيَهَهُ. (TA.) AZ says, A man of the Benoo-Kiláb said to me, أَلْقَيْتَنِى فِى التُّوهِ, with ḍamm, meaning [*Thou hast thrown me into*] *destruction.* (TA.) —— Also, [like تَاهَ aor. يَتِيهُ, q. v.,] *He magnified himself*; or *behaved proudly, haughtily,* or *insolently.* (Ḳ.)

2. تَوَّهَهُ, (Mṣb, Ḳ,) inf. n. تَتْوِيهٌ, (TA,) *i. q.* تَيَّهَهُ, [and طَوَّحَهُ and طَيَّحَهُ,] i. e. *He made him to deviate from,* or *lose,* or *miss, the right way*; *made him to lose his way*: (Mṣb:) [or *he made him to be,* or *become, confounded,* or *perplexed, and unable to see his right course*: &c.: see 1; and see تَيَّهَهُ, in art. تيه:] or *he destroyed him.* (Ḳ.)

4. مَا أَتْوَهَهُ *i. q.* مَا أَتْيَهَهُ [*How extraordinary is he in deviating from,* or *losing,* or *missing, the right way! in losing his way!* or *in confusion,* or *perplexity, and inability to see his right course!* &c.: see 1]: (Ḳ in the present art., and Ṣ and Ḳ in art. تيه:) as also مَا أَطْوَحَهُ (TA in art. تيه) and مَا أَطْيَحَهُ. (Ṣ and TA in that art.)

10. استتاهه [*He,* or *it, invited him to deviate from,* or *lose,* or *miss, the right way*; *to lose his way*]; from تَاهَ, aor. [يَتُوهُ and] يَتِيهُ, signifying ضَلَّ. (Ḥam p. 685.)

فَلَاةٌ تُوهٌ (with ḍamm) [*A desert,* or *waterless desert, in which one loses his way*; or *in which one is confounded,* or *perplexed, and unable to see his right course*: or *in which one perishes*]: in the Ḳ, فُلَانٌ is erroneously put for فَلَاةٌ; (TA;) [and in the CḲ, تَوْهٌ for تُوهٌ; which last, in the CḲ, is made a pl.:] the pl. is أَتْوَاهٌ and أَتَاوِيهُ: (Ḳ, TA:) the latter is a pl. of the former pl. (TA.)

تَائِهٌ part. n. of 1; *Deviating from,* or *losing,* or *missing, the right way*; *losing his way*: &c.: see 1; and see also art. تيه. (TA.)

هُوَ أَتْوَهُ النَّاسِ *He is the most extraordinary of men* [*in deviating from,* or *losing,* or *missing, the right way*; *in losing his way*: or] *in confusion,* or *perplexity, and inability to see his right course*: as also أَتْيَهُ النَّاسِ: but the former is more common. (TA.) —— [It may also mean *He is the proudest,* or *vainest, of men.*]

يَا مُتَوَّهُ [*O misled! O misguided!* or *O thou who art made to deviate from,* or *lose,* or *miss, the right way!*] is said in reviling: and one says also, مَا بَالُ ذَاكَ المُتَوَّهِ يَفْعَلُ كَذَا [*What is the case of that misled,* or *misguided,* man, *that he does thus?*] (TA.)

توى

1. تَوِىَ, (T, Ṣ, M, Mgh, Ḳ,) in the dial. of Ṭeiyi تَوَى, (AAF, M,) aor. ـَ, (Ṣ, Ḳ,) inf. n. تَوًى, (T, Ṣ, M, Mgh, Ḳ,) *It perished*; *came to an end*; (Ṣ, Mgh, Ḳ;) *it passed away* (T, M, Mgh) *unhoped for*: (T, M:) said of property. (T, Ṣ, M, Mgh.) Hence the saying, in a trad., لَا تَوَى عَلَى مَالِ امْرِئٍ مُسْلِمٍ [*There shall be no perishing of the property of a man that is a Muslim*]: applied to the case of a man to whom is transferred the responsibility for a debt, and who dies insolvent; meaning that the responsibility shall return to him who transferred it. (Mgh.)

4. اتواهُ *He* (God, M, Ḳ, or another, Ṣ) *destroyed it, made an end of it,* or *caused it to perish* or *come to an end*; (Ṣ, Ḳ;) *he made it away*; (T, M;) namely, property, (Ṣ, M,) or his property. (T.) —— See also art. تو.

تَوٍ (Ṣ, M, Mgh, Ḳ) and ↓ تَاوٍ (Mgh) *Perishing; coming to an end;* (Ṣ, Mgh, Ḳ;) *passing away* (M, Mgh) *unhoped for:* (M:) applied to property. (Ṣ, M, Mgh.)

تَوَآءٌ *A perishing* of property; its *coming to an end;* or *becoming lost.* (TA.)

تُوِىٌّ *Remaining, staying, dwelling,* or *abiding:* (IAạr, M, Ḳ:) but ثُوِىٌّ, with ث, is better known in this sense. (M.)

تَاوٍ : see تَوٍ.

الشُّحُّ مَتْوَاةٌ [*Niggardliness,* or *avarice, is a cause of perishing* to property]: a saying of the Arabs, meaning, if thou withhold property from its right disposal, God will make it to pass away in that which is not its right disposal. (M.)

تى

2. تَيَّيْتُ تَآءً حَسَنَةً [and حَسَنًا *I made,* or *wrote, a beautiful* ت]. (Lth, T.)

تَيْوِىٌّ ; and قَصِيدَةٌ تَيْوِيَّةٌ : see تَائِىٌّ, in art. توأ.

تيا

تَيًّا, and تَيَّاكَ, and تَيَّالِكَ : see art. تا.

تيتل

تَيْتَلٌ a dial. var., or a mispronunciation, of تَيْتَلٌ. (TA.)

تيح

1. تَاحَ, aor. يَتِيحُ, inf. n. تَيْحٌ, *It* (a thing) *was,* or *became, easy,* and *facilitated,* or *prepared.* (Mṣb.) And تَاحَ لَهُ, (Ṣ, L, Ḳ,) aor. as above, (Ḳ,) and so the inf. n.; (TA;) and ↓ أَتْيَحَ; (Ṣ, Ḳ;) *It* (a thing) *was appointed,* or *ordained, to him,* or *for him:* (Ṣ:) or *was prepared for him;* as also تَاحَ لَهُ, aor. يَتُوحُ, (Ḳ,) inf. n. تَوْحٌ: (TA:) and *it* (an event) *was appointed, ordained,* or *decreed, to betide him.* (L.) One says, وَقَعَ فِى مَهْلَكَةٍ فَتَاحَ لَهُ رَجُلٌ فَأَنْقَذَهُ [*He fell into a place of destruction, and a man was appointed,* or *ordained,* or *prepared, for him, and he saved him*]: (Lth, TA:) or فَأُتِيحَ ↓ لَهُ مَنْ أَنْقَذَهُ and تَاحَ لَهُ مَنْ خَلَّصَهُ [*and there was appointed,* &c., *for him he who saved him*]. (A.) — تَاحَ فِى مِشْيَتِهِ *He affected an inclining of his body from side to side in his gait,* or *manner of walking.* (Ṣ, Ḳ.)

4. اتاحهُ, (Ṣ, A, Mṣb, Ḳ,) inf. n. إِتَاحَةٌ, (Mṣb,) *He* (God, Ṣ, A, Mṣb, Ḳ) *made it* (a thing) *easy; facilitated it;* (Mṣb;) or *prepared it:* (Mṣb, Ḳ:) or *appointed it,* or *ordained it;* (Ṣ, A;) whether good or evil; (TA;) لَهُ *to him,* or *for him.* (Ṣ, A.) One says, وَقَعَ فِى مَهْلَكَةٍ فَأَتَاحَ ٱللّٰهُ لَهُ مَنْ أَنْقَذَهُ [*He fell into a place of destruction, and God appointed,* or *prepared, for him, him who saved him*]. (Lth, TA.) And it is said in a trad., لَأُتِيحَنَّهُمْ فِتْنَةً [*I will assuredly appoint,* or *ordain,* or *prepare, for them trial,* or *punishment,* or *conflict and faction,* or *the like*]. (TA.) See also 1, in two places.

تَيِّحَانٌ, (T, Ṣ, A,) or تَيَّحَانٌ, (so in one copy of the Ṣ,) or both, (L, Ḳ,) like شَيِّحَانٌ and شَيَّحَانٌ applied to a horse, and هَيِّبَانٌ and هَيَّبَانٌ applied to a man, the only other instances of the kind, (L,) or the former is not allowable, (Ḥam p. 58,) so says Sb, as is stated in a marginal note in a copy of the Ṣ, (TA,) applied to a horse, meaning *That goes obliquely,* (Ṣ, A, Ḳ,) *by reason of briskness, liveliness,* or *sprightliness,* (Ṣ, Ḳ,) *and bends over on each side;* (Ṣ, A;) as also ↓ تَيَّاحٌ and ↓ مِتْيَحٌ: (Ṣ, A, Ḳ:) or *that runs vehemently:* and all signify, applied to a horse, *fleet, swift,* or *excellent in running.* (T, TA.) AlLeyth explains the first and second as meaning *Tall,* or *long.* (TA.) — It is also applied to a man, meaning *Who addresses himself to every generous action, and difficult affair:* (T, TA:) or *forward, officious, meddling,* or *a busybody,* (A, and Ḥam pp. 58 and 505,) *who says that which does not concern him:* (Ḥam p. 505:) or *who obtrudes himself,* or *interferes, in affairs:* (Abu-l-'Alà El-Ma'arree in a marginal note in a copy of the Ṣ, and Ḥam p. 58:) or, as also ↓ مِتْيَحٌ, (Ṣ, Ḳ,) and ↓ تَيَّاحٌ, (Ḳ,) *who obtrudes himself,* or *interferes, in that which does not concern him:* (Ṣ, Ḳ:) or *who falls into trials,* or *afflictions:* (Ḳ:) or ↓ مِتْيَحٌ, (TA,) which is also applied as an epithet to a heart, (Ṣ, A, TA,) signifies *who obtrudes himself,* or *interferes, in everything, and falls into that which does not concern him;* or *who incessantly falls into trials,* or *afflictions;* and its fem. is with ة; (TA;) or *who intrudes among a people whose affair,* or *business, is not his:* (IAạr, T, TA:) and ↓ مِتْيَاحٌ, (Ḳ,) applied to a man, (TA,) signifies *much in motion; forward, officious, meddling,* or *a busybody.* (Ḳ,* TA. [In the CḲ, العَرِيضُ is erroneously put for العِرِّيضُ.])

تَيَّاحٌ : see تَيِّحَانٌ, in two places.

مُتَاحٌ A thing *appointed, ordained,* or *decreed;* as also ↓ مِتْيَاحٌ. (Ḳ.)

مِتْيَحٌ : see تَيِّحَانٌ, in three places.

مِتْيَاحٌ : see تَيِّحَانٌ : — and مُتَاحٌ.

تير

تَارٌ and تَارَةٌ (mentioned in this art. in the Ṣ): see the latter in art. تور.

تِيرٌ *A beam between two walls:* (Ḳ: [in which this word, with the art. ال, is explained by الجَائِزُ الحَاجِزُ بين الحائطين, : in the M, بَيْنَ الحَائِطَيْنِ, i. e. *a partition between two gardens,* or *walled gardens of palm-trees:* the former I regard as the right reading (though SM thinks the contrary); for it expresses a well-known meaning of تير in Persian; and it is said that تِير is] a Persian word, arabicized. (M.) — † *Vanity,* or *a fond opinion of oneself,* (Ḳ,) and *pride.* (TA.)

تَيَّارٌ *Waves:* (Ṣ, M, A, Mṣb:) or *waves of the sea,* or *of a great river,* (M, IAth, Ḳ,) *having a current;* (Ḳ,* TA;) and *its main body,* or *deep:* (IAth, TA:) [in the present day, the *current,* or *main current, of a sea* or *great river:*] or *vehemence of flow* or *current:* (Mṣb:) accord. to some, of the measure فَعَّالٌ, from تير; (Mṣb;) i. e., from تِير signifying "vanity" and "pride:" (TA:) accord. to others, of the measure فَيْعَالٌ, (Mṣb, TA,) from تَارَ, aor. يَتُورُ, though this verb is obsolete, (TA,) originally تَيْوَارٌ, the و being changed into ى and then incorporated into the preceding ى. (Mṣb.) — Applied to a man, ‡ *Vain,* or *having a fond opinion of himself,* (A, Ḳ,) and *proud;* (Ḳ;) *who swells up like waves, in his vanity.* (A.) — ‡ A horse *that rises like waves in his running.* (A.) — ‡ A vein *that runs,* or *flows, quickly,* when cut. (Ṣ, A, Ḳ.)

تيس

1. تَاسَ, [aor. يَتِيسُ,] *He* (a kid) *became a* تَيْس. (M, TA.) — [Also, app., ‡ *He became like a he-goat in stupidity:* for what immediately follows appears to be the fem. of the imp. of this verb.] ↓ تِيسِى is a word used in declaring a thing to be vain, and false: (M, Ḳ:) or it is an exceration; [for لُعْبَةٌ, an evident mistake, which I find in copies of the Ḳ, and in the TA, I read لَعْنَةٌ;] and a reproach: (Ḳ:) the vulgar say تِيزِى, changing the س into ز. (TA.) One says to a she-hyena, تِيسِى جَعَارِ, (A,* Ḳ,) meaning ‡ *Be thou like the he-goat* (تَيْس) *in stupidity, O she-hyena:* and these words are a proverb applied to a stupid man. (A, TA.) The same words were directed, by Aboo-Eiyoob, as is related in a trad., to be said to a غُول, (M, TA,) as though one said to her, *Thou liest,* or *hast lied, O girl.* (TA.) And one says to a man, تِيسِى, and احْمَقِى, [as though he were a she-hyena, or a woman,] when he speaks foolishly, or stupidly, or says what is not like anything. (AZ, TA.)

3. تَايَسَ قِرْنَهُ, (A,) inf. n. مُتَايَسَةٌ and تِيَاسٌ, (A, Ḳ,) ‡ *He strove, struggled, contended,* or *conflicted, with his adversary;* syn. مَارَسَهُ: (A:) [*he strove with his adversary to repel him,* like as a he-goat strives with another:] the inf. n. signifies the same as مُمَارَسَةٌ, and مُكَابَسَةٌ, and مُدَافَعَةٌ. (Ḳ.)

6. تَتَايَسَ المَآءُ ‡ *The waves of the water conflicted,* or *dashed together.* (A, TA.)

10. اسْتَتْيَسَتِ العَنْزُ ‡ *The she-goat became like the* تَيْس [or *he-goat*]: (M, [but in a copy of that work, for العَنْزُ I find الشَّاةُ,] A, Ḳ:) like اسْتَنْوَقَ الجَمَلُ: (Ṣ:) a prov. applied to a vile man who becomes mighty, (A,) or who magnifies himself: (Ḳ:) one should not say استاست. (Th, M, TA.)

تَيْسٌ *A he-goat;* the *male of the* مَعْز: (Ṣ,* M, A, Ḳ:) and the *male of the mountain-goat:* (A, Ḳ:) and *of the gazelle:* (Ṣ, M, A, Ḳ:) the female of the last [as well as of the first and second] is called عَنْزٌ: (Ṣ, M:) or *that has completed a year:* (A, Ḳ:) or *a yearling he-goat:* before the year it is called جَدْىٌ: (AZ,* Mṣb, TA:) pl. (of pauc.,

M) أَتْيَاسٌ (Ṣ, M, Ḳ) and أُتْيُسٌ, (M, TA,) and (of mult., M) تُيُوسٌ (Ṣ, M, Mṣb, Ḳ) and تِيَسَةٌ and ✝ مَتْيُوسَآءُ [like مَشْيُوخَآءُ, q. v.]: (Ḳ:) the last [which is properly a quasi-pl. n.] signifies the same as تُيُوسٌ, (Ṣ,) or *a herd of* تُيُوس. (M.) You say of the نَكَّاح, [i. e. of him who marries often, or the like,] هُوَ مِنْ مَتْيُوسَآءِ✝ بَنِى فُلَانٍ ‡ [lit. *He is of the he-goats of the sons of such a one*]. (A, TA.)

تَيَسٌ The *quality*, in a she-goat, *of having horns like those of the mountain-goat*, (Ḳ, TA,) *in length*. (TA.)

تَيْسِىٌّ: see 1.

عَنْزٌ تَيْسَآءُ *A she-goat having long horns*, (M, A,) *like the* تَيْس: (A:) or *having horns like those of the mountain-goat*, (Ḳ, TA,) *in length*. (TA.)

فِيهِ تَيْسِيَّةٌ [*In him is goatishness*]: some say ✝تَيْسُوسِيَّةٌ, [in the TA تُيُوسِيَّةٌ, but the former, which is found in the L as well as in the Ṣ and Ḳ, seems, from what here follows, to be the right,] (Ṣ, L, Ḳ,) and [in like manner, for كَيْفِيَّةٌ they say] كَيْفُوفِيَّةٌ, but [J says] I know not what is the truth thereof: (Ṣ:) the former word is preferable. (O, TA.)

تَيْسِيَّةٌ : see تَيْسُوسِيَّةٌ.

تَيَّاسٌ *A possessor of* تُيُوس [or *he-goats*]: (M:) or *one who holds the* تَيْس. (Ṣ, Ḳ: explained in the former by اَلَّذِى يُمْسِكُ التَّيْسَ: and in like manner in the latter, by مُمْسِكُهُ.)

مَتْيُوسَآءُ: see تَيْسٌ, in two places.

تيك

تِيكَ: see art. تا.

تيل

تِيلٌ [*Hemp, of which ropes and cloths are manufactured*; thus called by the Arabs in the present day; perhaps from the Persian تيلا "a rope;"] *a certain thing resembling flax, that comes forth from the sea*; [possibly meaning that it is imported into Arabia;] *and of which cloths are woven*. (TA.)

تيم

1. تَامَ, [aor. يَتِيمُ, inf. n. تَيْمٌ,] *He loved excessively*: (T:) [or *he became enslaved*, or *brought into subjection, by love*; (see 2;) and so ✝تتيّم, as explained in Kull p. 165: (see حُبٌّ:) or *his reason departed*, and *became disordered, in consequence of love and desire*; for] تَيْمٌ signifies the *departing of reason*, and *its becoming disordered*, (T, TA,) *in consequence of love and desire*. (TA.) — *He became alone, apart from others*. (T, TA.) — تَامَتْهُ, (T, Ṣ, M, Ḳ,) aor. تَتِيمُهُ, (T,) inf. n. تَيْمٌ; (T, M, Ḳ;) and ✝تَيَّمَتْهُ, (T, M, Ḳ,) [which is the more common,] inf. n. تَتْيِيمٌ; (Ḳ;) *She* (a woman) *enslaved him* (Ṣ, M, Ḳ) *by love of her*, (M,) and *brought him into subjection*: (Ṣ, Ḳ:) and *she enslaved it, and brought it into subjection*; namely, his heart: (Ṣ:) or *she deprived him of his reason; disordered his reason*. (T.) And تَامَهُ, (Ḳ,) inf. n. as above; (M, Ḳ;) and ✝تَيَّمَهُ; (Ṣ, Ḳ;) *It* (love, Ṣ, Ḳ, or love and desire, M, and excessive love, Ḳ) *enslaved him*, (Ṣ, M, Ḳ,) and *brought him into subjection*. (Ṣ, Ḳ.)

2: see 1, in two places.

5: see 1.

8. اِتَّامَ, (T, Ṣ,) inf. n. اِتِّيَامٌ, (T, Ṣ, M,) *He* (a man) *slaughtered his* تِيمَة [q. v.]: (T, Ṣ, M:) and in like manner, اِتَّامَتْ, said of a woman: (T:) or اتّيام signifies the *slaughtering camels, and sheep or goats, for no cause*. (IAạr, T.)

تَيْمٌ *i. q.* عَبْدٌ [as meaning *A slave*, and *a servant* or *worshipper* of God or of a false god]: whence the names تَيْمُ ٱللّٰهِ [*The servant of God*] and تَيْمُ اللَّاتِ [*The servant of El-Lát*]: (Ṣ, M, Ḳ:) pl. تُيُومٌ: it is originally an inf. n., from تَامَهُ: or an epithet like its syn. عَبْدٌ: J says that it is from تَيَّمَهُ الحُبُّ. (TA.)

تِيمَةٌ (as also تِئْمَةٌ, with hemz, Ḳ) *A ewe*, or *she-goat, which her owner milks for himself*, (A'Obeyd, T, Ṣ, M, Ḳ,) *in his abode*, (Ṣ, M, Ḳ,) *of those which he has reared*, (A'Obeyd, T,) *not left to pasture where she pleases*; (A'Obeyd, T, Ṣ, M, Ḳ;) *but sometimes slaughtered, when her owner is in want of flesh-meat*: (A'Obeyd, T:) or *one that is slaughtered in a time of famine*: (AZ, T, M, Ḳ:) or *one beyond forty, until the number attains to the next amount that requires one to be given for the poor rate*: (M, Ḳ:) or *one that is slaughtered gratuitously, not for a compensation, when persons desire flesh-meat*. (AHeyth, T.) = Also *A* [*kind of amulet, such as is called*] تَمِيمَة, *that is hung upon a child*: (Ḳ:) app. a contraction of تميمة. (TA.)

أَرْضٌ تَيْمَآءُ *A* [*desert*] *land such as is termed* قَفْرَة, *that causes one to lose his way and to perish*: or *a wide tract of land*: (M, Ḳ:) or *a land in which is no water*: (T:) and تَيْمَآءُ alone *a* [*desert such as is termed*] فَلَاة; (T, Ṣ, Ḳ;) because one loses his way therein: (T:) and *a wide* فَلَاة. (T.) = التَّيْمَآءُ *The stars of* الجَوْزَآء [app. meaning *Gemini*, also called التَّوْءَمَانِ]. (Ḳ.)

أَتْيَمُ [*More, and most, enslaved by love*]. Hence أَتْيَمُ مِنَ المُرَقِّشِ [*More enslaved by love than El-Murakkish*: a prov.: see Freytag's Arab. Prov. i. 255]. (TA.)

مُتَيَّمٌ: see what follows.

مَتْيُومٌ *Enslaved*, and *brought into subjection, by love*: (Ṣ:) *having the heart enslaved*, and *brought into subjection, and affected with vehement love so as to be deprived of his reason*: (Abu-l-'Abbás El-Ahwal, TA:) or *deprived of his reason; disordered therein; by women*; as also ✝مُتَيَّمٌ: and *led astray*. (T.)

تين

تِينٌ The *tree of the* بَلَس [or *common fig*; *ficus carica*]: or the بلس *itself*: (M:) [or *both*; i. e.] *a certain well-known kind of tree*; and the *fruit thereof*: (TA:) [or the latter only;] *a certain thing that is eaten*, (Ṣ, Mṣb,) *well known*: (Mṣb, Ḳ:) *fresh and ripe, it is the most approved of fruits, and the most nutritious, and the least flatulent; drawing, dissolvent, having the property of opening obstructions of the liver and spleen, and laxative; and the eating much thereof engenders lice*: (Ḳ: [the last word in this explanation in the Ḳ is مُقَمِّل, which I render agreeably with the TḲ, having found no authoritative explanation of it: but in my own opinion, the meaning of this word is *fattening*, for قَمِلَ signifies "he became fat after being lean;" and my opinion is confirmed by what here follows:]) it is *a pleasant fruit, having nothing redundant, and a nice food, quick of digestion, and a very useful medicine, for it has a laxative property, dissolves phlegm, purifies the kidneys, removes sand of the bladder, opens obstructions of the liver and spleen, and fattens the body*: it is also said, in a trad., that *it stops hemorrhoids, and is good for the gout*: (Bḍ xcv. 1:) AḤn says, *there are many kinds thereof; that of the desert, that of the cultivated land, that of the plains, and that of the mountains; and it is abundant in the land of the Arabs*: and he adds, on the authority of an Arab of the desert, of the Saráh, that *it is, in the Saráh, very abundant, and allowed to be commonly taken; and is eaten by the people there in its fresh state, and also dried and stored*: (M:) the word is Arabic: (Mṣb:) [a coll. gen. n.:] n. un. with ة. (Ṣ, M, Mṣb.) This is what is meant in the Ḳur [xcv. 1], where it is said, وَالتِّينِ وَالزَّيْتُونِ, (T, Ṣ, M, Mṣb,) accord. to I'Ab, (T, Ṣ, Bḍ, Jel,) and the generality of the interpreters: (Mṣb:) or these two words mean two mountains (Ṣ, M, Bḍ, Jel) of Syria, (Ṣ, Jel,) or of the Holy Land, (Bḍ,) that produce the two fruits thus named: (Jel:) or, accord. to a Syrian interpreter, certain mountains extending from Ḥulwán to Hemdán, and the mountains of Syria: (Fr, T:) or Damascus and Jerusalem: (M, Bḍ:) or the mosque of Damascus and that of Jerusalem: (Bḍ:) or two mosques in Syria: accord. to AḤn, the former is the name of a mountain in the country of Ghaṭafán; but there is no mountain thus called in Syria. (M.) — Among the kinds of تين is that called تِينُ الجُمَّيْزِ [*The sycamore-fig; ficus sycomorus*; also called *the Egyptian fig*]; described voce جُمَّيْزٌ, q. v. (AḤn.) — التِّينُ الشَّوْكِىُّ and التِّينُ الإِفْرَنْجِىُّ [are appellations applied in the present day to *The Indian fig*, or *prickly pear; cactus opuntia*: Forskål (Flora Aegypt. Arab. p. lxvii) applies the former name to *the cochineal Indian fig; cactus cochinillifer*.] — التِّينَةُ also signifies †*The anus*: (AḤn, M, Ḳ:) [opposed to الجُمَّيْزَةُ as meaning "the pudendum muliebre."]

تِينَانٌ: see art. تن.

تَيَّانٌ *A seller of* تين [or *figs*]. (TA.)

مَتَانَةٌ [originally مَتْيَنَةٌ] *A fig-garden*. (KL.) And أَرْضٌ مَتَانَةٌ *A land abounding with* تين [or *figs*]. (TA.)

تيه

1. تَاهَ, (Ṣ, Mgh, Mṣb, Ḳ,) aor. يَتِيهُ, (Ṣ, Mṣb,) inf. n. تَيْهٌ (Ṣ, Mgh, Mṣb, Ḳ) and تِيْهٌ (Ḳ) and تَيَهَانٌ, (Ṣ, Ḳ,) is *syn. with* تَاهَ *having for its aor.* يَتُوهُ; (Mṣb, TA;) [and with طَاحَ, aor. يَطِيحُ and يَطُوحُ;] signifying *He deviated from,* or *lost,* or *missed, the right way; he lost his way;* (Mgh, Mṣb, Ḳ, TA;) in the desert: (Mgh, Mṣb:) *he was,* or *became, confounded,* or *perplexed, and unable to see his right course:* (Mgh:) *he went away* in the land, *confounded,* or *perplexed, and unable to see his right course:* (Ṣ, TA:) [or *his mind,* or *intellect, was,* or *became, disordered, confused,* or *unsound:* (see تَاهَ in art. توه:)] and *he perished.* (TA in art. توه.) You say also, تَاهَتْ بِهِ سَفِينَتُهُ *His ship deviated from the right course with him.* (TA.) And تَاهَ عَنِّى بَصَرُكَ *Thine eye,* or *thy sight, passed me over;* syn. تَخَطَّى. (Aboo-Turáb, TA.) تَاهَ بَصَرُهُ [in the CḲ, erroneously, قَصْرُهُ] signifies also تَاقَ, (Ḳ, TA, [in the CḲ تَافَ,] i. e., accord. to 'Arrám, *He looked at a thing continually,* or *continuously* (فِى دَوَامٍ) [app. *as one confounded,* or *perplexed, and unable to see aright*]). (Aboo-Turáb, TA.) — Also, تَاهَ, (Ṣ, Ḳ,) aor. يَتِيهُ, (Ṣ,) inf. n. تِيهٌ, (Ṣ, Ḳ,) and تَيْهٌ is said to be a dial. var. of this, but is doubtful; (MF;) [like تَاهَ having for its aor. يَتُوهُ;] *He magnified himself;* or *behaved proudly, haughtily,* or *insolently:* (Ṣ, Ḳ:) and *he affected to be commended for,* or *praised for,* or *he gloried in, that which he did not possess;* [i. e. *he was,* or *became, conceited,* or *vain-glorious;* or *he behaved conceitedly,* or *vain-gloriously;*] or *he overpassed the due bounds in elegance of mind* or *manners* or *address* or *speech* or *person* or *attire* and *the like, and arrogated to himself superiority therein, through pride:* (Ḳ:) [or rather, *he was,* or *became, vain;* or *he behaved vainly:* for] Er-Rághib makes a distinction between مُعْجَبٌ and تَائِهٌ; saying that the معجب believes himself with respect to the opinion or judgment that he forms of himself indecisively, from evidence outweighed in probability; whereas the تائه believes himself decisively. (MF and TA in art. عجب.) One says, هُوَ يَتِيهُ عَلَى قَوْمِهِ [*He behaves proudly,* or *conceitedly,* or *vainly, towards his people*]. (TA.)

2. تَيَّهَهُ i. q. تَوَّهَهُ [and طَيَّحَهُ and طَوَّحَهُ], i. e., *He made him to deviate from,* or *lose,* or *miss, the right way; made him to lose his way:* (Mṣb:) [or *he made him to be,* or *become, confounded,* or *perplexed, and unable to see his right course:* &c.: see 1:] *he destroyed,* or *lost,* or *left* or *neglected, him* or *it.* (Ḳ.) And تَيَّهَ نَفْسَهُ *He made himself to be,* or *become, confounded,* or *perplexed, and unable to see his right course;* (Ṣ, TA;) as also تَوَّهَهَا and طَوَّحَهَا: (Ṣ:) or *he destroyed himself.* (TA.)

4. مَا أَتْيَهَهُ: see مَا أَتْوَهَهُ, in art. توه.

10. اِسْتَتَاهَهُ: see art. توه.

تَيْهٌ: see تِيهٌ.

تِيهٌ [originally an inf. n.: see 1, throughout:] *A* مَفَازَة [i. e. *desert,* or *waterless desert,* &c.,] (Ṣ, Mṣb, Ḳ) *in which one loses his way,* (Ṣ,) *wherein is no sign,* or *mark, whereby one may be guided therein;* as also ▾ تَيْهَآءُ: (Mṣb:) pl. أَتْيَاهٌ and أَتَاوِيهُ, (Ṣ, Ḳ,) the latter of which is a pl. of the former pl., (TA,) and أَتَاوِهَةٌ. (Meyd, in Freytag's Lex.) [Hence,] التِّيهُ, [also called تِيهُ بَنِى إِسْرَائِيلَ,] *The place* [or *desert*] *in which the Children of Israel lost their way, between Egypt and the 'Aḳabeh* [*at the head of the eastern gulf of the Red Sea*], *unable to find the way of egress from it.* (TA.) — أَرْضٌ تِيهٌ and ▾ تَيْهٌ and ▾ تَيْهَآءُ (Ḳ) and ▾ مَتْيَهَةٌ, (Ṣ, Ḳ,) originally [مَتْيَهَةٌ,] of the measure مَفْعَلَةٌ, (Ṣ,) and ▾ مَتِيهَةٌ and ▾ مُتَيِّهَةٌ and ▾ مَتْيَهٌ (Ḳ) and ▾ مُتَيَّهَةٌ (TA) *A land wherein one loses his way,* (Ṣ, Ḳ, TA,) *wide, and having in it no signs,* or *marks, of the way, nor mountains nor hills.* (TA.) And ▾ بَلَدٌ أَتْيَهُ *A country to which,* and *in which, one cannot find his way.* (TA.)

تَيْهَآءُ: see تِيهٌ, in two places.

تَيْهَانٌ: see تَائِهٌ, in two places. — Also, and ▾ تَيَّهَانٌ and ▾ تَيْهَانٌ, *Daring,* or *bold; who pursues a random,* or *heedless, course, without any certain aim* or *object, in affairs:* applied to a man: and in like manner to a camel: and, with ة, to a she-camel. (TA.)

تَيَّهَانٌ and تَيْهَانٌ: see تَيْهَانٌ: and see also تَائِهٌ.

تَيَّاهٌ: see تَائِهٌ, in two places.

تَائِهٌ *Deviating from,* or *losing,* or *missing, the right way; losing his way;* (Mgh; see also art. توه;) and so ▾ تَيْهَانٌ and [in an intensive sense, like مِتْيَهٌ,] ▾ تَيَّاهٌ: (Ḳ:) *deviating from the right way and magnifying himself* or *behaving proudly* or *haughtily* or *insolently:* or *deviating from the right way and being confounded* or *perplexed, unable to see his right course.* (TA.) — ‡ *Deviating from the right way in opinion:* (Mgh:) *desiring a thing and unable to find the right way.* (Mṣb.) — *Magnifying himself;* or *behaving proudly, haughtily,* or *insolently: affecting to be commended for* or *praised for,* or *glorying in, that which he does not possess;* or *overpassing the due bounds in elegance of mind* or *manners* &c.: [see 1, last sentence but one: it is best rendered *behaving proudly,* or *conceitedly,* or *vainly:*] and in like manner ▾ تَيَّاهٌ; (Ḳ;) but this has an intensive signification; [meaning, like مِتْيَهٌ, *very proud* or *conceited* or *vain;*] (TA;) and ▾ تَيْهَانٌ and ▾ تَيَّهَانٌ and ▾ تَيْهَانٌ: (Ḳ:) or only تَائِهٌ and تَيَّاهٌ, accord. to IDrd. (TA.)

هُوَ أَتْيَهُ النَّاسِ: see أَتْوَهُ in art. توه, where it is explained on the authority of the TA. [In the Ṣ it seems to be indicated by the context that the meaning is *He is the proudest of men.*] — See also تِيهٌ, last sentence.

مَتْيَهٌ: see تِيهٌ.

مِتْيَهٌ A man *having much* تِيه [meaning *pride,* or *conceit,* or *vanity*]: or *who deviates from,* or *loses,* or *misses, the right way,* or *who loses his way, much,* or *often.* (TA.)

مَتْيَهَةٌ and مَتِيهَةٌ and مُتَيِّهَةٌ and مُتَيَّهَةٌ: see تِيهٌ.

ث

The fourth letter of the alphabet: called ثَآءٌ and ثَا [respecting which latter see the letter ب]: the pl. [of the former] is ثَاآتٌ; and [of the latter,] أَثْوَآءٌ and أَثْيَآءٌ. (TA in باب الالف اللّيّنة.) It is one of the letters termed مَهْمُوسَة [or non-vocal, i. e. pronounced with the breath only, without the voice], and of those termed لِثَوِيَّة [or gingival], which are ث and ذ and ظ. (TA at the commencement of باب الثآء.) — It is sometimes substituted for ف, as in the instance of حُثَالَةٌ and حُفَالَةٌ; and for س, as in the instance of جُثْمَانٌ and جُسْمَانٌ; and for other letters. (TA in the latter place.) ═ [As a numeral, it denotes *Five hundred.*]

ثا

ثا and ثَآءٌ: see the letter ث, and arts. ثوأ and ثى.

ثأ

R. Q. 1. ثَأْثَأَ *He watered* camels *to their satisfaction:* (Ṣ, M, Ḳ; but in some copies of the Ṣ, the verb is made trans. by means of ب:) or *he watered* them (T, M) *so as to quench their thirst,* (T,) *but not so as to satisfy them.* (T, M.) — Also, contr., *He kept* camels *thirsty;* i. e. *he did not water* them *at all;* or *he watered* them *little, so that they were not satisfied.* (Ḳ,* TA.) — *He extinguished* fire. (Ṣgh, Ḳ.) — *He stilled* another's anger. (TA.) And ثَأْثَأَ عَنْهُ غَضَبَهُ *He quenched his anger.* (M.) [Or this may be rendered *He dispelled from him his anger:* agreeably with what follows.] — *He removed* (IDrd, M, Ḳ) a thing (M) *from its place.* (IDrd, M, Ḳ.) — ثَأْثَأَ عَنِ القَوْمِ *He repelled from,* or *defended, the people,* or *company of men,* (Aṣ, Ṣ, Ḳ,) *and rendered them reciprocal aid.* (Aṣ, TA.) — ثَأْثَأَ, (T, M, Ḳ,) inf. n. ثَأْثَأَةٌ, (T,) also signifies *He restrained,* or *withheld,* (T, M, Ḳ,) a man (T, M,) from (عَنْ) another man, (T,) or from (عَنْ) a thing, or an affair. (M.) ═ ثَأْثَأَتِ الإِبِلُ *The camels drank to their satisfaction:* (M, Ḳ:) or *drank, but not so as to satisfy themselves.* (M.) — And, contr., *The camels thirsted.* (Ḳ.) — And ثَأْثَأَ *It became stilled;* (Ḳ;) said of anger. (TA.) — See also R. Q. 2. ═ ثَأْثَأَ بِالتَّيْسِ, (AA, AZ, M, Ḳ,) inf. n. ثَأْثَأَةٌ, (Ḳ,) like تَأْتَأَ, (TA,) *He called the he-goat* (AA, AZ, M, Ḳ) *to copulate.* (AA, Ḳ.)

R. Q. 2. تَثَأْثَأَ *He deemed it right that he should abide,* or *remain, where he was,* (AZ, T, Ḳ,) *and abstain,* (AZ, TA,) *after he had desired to make a journey* (AZ, T, Ḳ) *to a country,* or *land.* (AZ, TA.) And ثَأْثَأَ ▼ عَنِ تَثَأْثَأَ عَنِ الأَمْرِ, (M,) or الشَّىْءِ, (TA,) *He deemed it right that he should abstain from the affair,* or *thing,* (M, TA,) or *that he should pause at it,* (M,) *after he had desired it.* (M, TA.) — لَقِيتُ فُلَانًا فَتَثَأْثَأْتُ مِنْهُ *I met such a one, and feared him.* (Aṣ, Ṣ, Ḳ.*)

ثأب

1. ثُئِبَ, ('Eyn, T, M, Ḳ,) like عُنِىَ, (Ḳ,) and ثَئِبَ, (IḲoot, L, and so in a copy of the A,) inf. n. ثَأْبٌ, (Ḳ,) or ثَأَبٌ, (M,) *He became relaxed and sluggish;* said of a man: (A:) or *he became affected with sluggishness and languor;* (M;) as also ▼ تَثَاءَبَ: (M, A:) or *he became affected with sluggishness and languor like the languor of drowsiness;* as also ▼ تَثَأَّبَ and ▼ تَثَاءَبَ; (Ḳ;) which last is approved by IDrd and Thábit Es-Saraḳustee, who disallow ▼ تَثَأَّبَ, though this is the form commonly known and approved, and is the most chaste form: (TA:) or *he became affected with languor like the heaviness of drowsiness, in consequence of something that he had eaten or drunk, without becoming insensible;* (T;) as also ▼ تَثَاءَبَ: (L:) or ▼ this last signifies *he yawned,* or *opened his mouth,* (Mgh, Mṣb,) *by reason,* (Mgh,) or *on the occasion,* (Mṣb,) *of languor* (Mgh, Mṣb,) *like the heaviness of drowsiness;* (Mgh;) or *he yawned,* or *opened his mouth, and stretched himself, on being affected by sluggishness or drowsiness or anxiety;* (MF, TA, on the authority of IDrst;) or *he yawned,* or *opened his mouth, and emitted wind from his stomach, by reason of some affection thereof:* (TA on the authority of Et-Tedmuree:) التَّثَاؤُبُ is from الثُّؤَبَآءُ; (AZ, T, Ṣ, Mgh;) and is on the occasion of one's stretching himself, and being languid: (Lth, T:) one should not say تَثَاوَبَ; (AZ, T, Ṣ, O, Mgh;) [for] this is vulgar. (Mṣb.) Hence, إِذَا تَثَاءَبَ ▼ أَحَدُكُمْ فَلْيُغَطِّ فَاهُ [*When any one of you yawns, he should cover his mouth* with the back of his left hand; for it is believed that the devil leaps into the uncovered yawning mouth]. (Mgh.)

5: see 1.

6: see 1, in six places.

ثُؤَبَآءُ, (T, Ṣ, M, Ḳ, &c.,) as also ثُؤْبَآءُ, accord. to Ibn-Mis-hal, but this is strange, (TA,) is a subst. derived from التَّثَاؤُبُ, like التَّمَطِّى from مُطَوَآءُ; (T;) or from ثُئِبَ; and means *A state of relaxation and sluggishness:* (A:) or *sluggishness and languor* (M, Ḳ) *like the languor of drowsiness:* (Ḳ:) or *languor like the heaviness of drowsiness, in consequence of something that one has eaten or drunk, not attended by insensibility:* (T, L:) or *a yawning,* or *opening the mouth, by reason of languor like the heaviness of drowsiness:* (Mgh:) or *a yawning,* or *opening the mouth, and stretching oneself, on being affected by sluggishness or drowsiness or anxiety:* (IDrst, MF, TA:) or *a yawning,* or *opening the mouth, and emitting wind from the stomach, by reason of some affection thereof.* (Et-Tedmuree, TA.) Hence the prov., أَعْدَى مِنَ الثُّؤَبَآءِ, (Ṣ, A, TA,) and [الثُّوَبَآءُ,] without ء, as some say; (MF;) or the pronunciation without ء is vulgar, (IDrst, TA,) or erroneous; (TA;) [*More catching than yawning;*] for when a man yawns (اذا تثاءب) in the presence of others, they become affected as he is. (TA.)

مَثْؤُوبٌ *Affected with sluggishness and languor like the languor of drowsiness:* from ثُئِبَ, q. v. (Ḳ.)

ثأر

1. ثَأَرَهُ, (T, Ṣ, Mṣb,) and ثَأَرَ بِهِ, (T, Ṣ, M, Mṣb, Ḳ,) aor. ـَ, (Mṣb, Ḳ,) inf. n. ثَأْرٌ and ثُؤُورَةٌ, (Ṣ,) or the latter is a simple subst., as is also ثُؤْرَةٌ, (Lh, M, Ḳ,) *He revenged,* or *avenged, his blood, by retaliating his slaughter; he slew his slayer.* (T, Ṣ, M, Mṣb, Ḳ.) [Hence, ثُئِرَ مَقْتُولُهُ and بِمَقْتُولِهِ *The blood of his slain* relation *was revenged,* or *avenged, by retaliation of his slaughter:* see 10.] — [Hence also,] لَا ثَأَرَتْ فُلَانًا يَدَاهُ, (Ḳ,) or عَلَى فُلَانٍ, (A,) ‡ *May his arms,* or *hands, not profit such a one.* (A, Ḳ.) — Also ثَأَرَهُ, and ثَأَرَ بِهِ, (M, Ḳ,) and ثَأَرَ القَوْمَ, inf. n. ثَأْرٌ, (T,) *He sought to revenge,* or *avenge,* or *retaliate,* (T, M, Ḳ,) *his blood,* (M, Ḳ,) and *the blood of the people,* or *party.* (T.) It is said in a prov., لَا يَنَامُ مَنْ ثَأَرَ [*He will not sleep who seeks to revenge,* or *avenge,* or *retaliate, blood*]: in the Kámil of Mbr, [and in some copies of Meyd,] ▼ مَنِ اثَّأَرَ [which seems to signify the same]. (TA.) — [And ثَأَرَهُ and ثَأَرَ بِهِ signify also *He slew him in blood-revenge,* or *in retaliation of the blood of a relation:* see مَثْؤُورٌ.] — ثَأَرْتُكَ بِكَذَا *I have obtained my blood-revenge,* or *retaliation, of thee by such* [a deed, or *person*]. (Ṣ, Ḳ.)

4: see 8.

8. اِثْتَأَرَ, originally اِثْتَأَرَ, *He obtained his blood-revenge,* or *retaliation;* syn. أَدْرَكَ ثَأْرَهُ; (T, Ṣ, M, Ḳ;) *from him;* مِنْهُ (T, Ṣ;) as also ▼ أَثْأَرَ: (M, Ḳ:) and اِثَّأَرَ مِنْهُ *he slew the slayer of his relation.* (T.) Lebeed says,

وَالنِّيبُ إِنْ تَعْرُ مِنِّى رِمَّةً خَلَقًا
بَعْدَ المَمَاتِ فَإِنِّى كُنْتُ أَثَّئِرُ

[*And the old she-camels, if they seek to obtain benefit from a worn rotten bone of me after death, I used to retaliate* upon them by anticipation]: (T, Ṣ:) i. e., I used to slaughter [some of] them for guests, and so I have retaliated upon them during my life for their nibbling my rotten bones after my death: for when camels do not find herbage of the kind called حَمْض, they eat the bones of dead men and of camels instead thereof. (T.) — See also 1.

10. استثار *He* (a relation of a slain man, A) *sought*, or *asked, aid, in order that the blood of his slain* [relation] *might be revenged*, or *avenged, by retaliation of his slaughter* (لِيُثْأَرَ بِمَقْتُولِهِ), (AZ, Ṣ, Ḳ,) or *in order that he might take*, or *seek, revenge*, or *vengeance, for his slain* [relation]. (A.)

ثَأْرٌ, (Ṣ, M, A, Mgh, Mṣb, Ḳ,) which may be also pronounced ثَارٌ, i. e., with the ء suppressed, (Mṣb,) and ▼ثَأْرَةٌ, (A,) and ▼ثُؤْرَةٌ, (Ṣ,) which last is a subst. [from ثَأَرَ], as also ▼ثُؤُورَةٌ, (Lḥ, M, Ḳ,) *Blood-revenge*; or *retaliation of murder* or *homicide*: or *a seeking to revenge*, or *avenge*, or *retaliate, blood*: [see 1, of which ثَأْرٌ is an inf. n.:] or *a desire*, or *seeking, for retaliation of a crime* or *of enmity*: or *retention of enmity in the heart, with watchfulness for an opportunity to indulge it*: syn. ذَحْلٌ: (Ṣ, A, Mṣb:) or طَلَبٌ بِالدَّمِ: (M, Ḳ:) or حِقْدٌ: (Mgh:) or (so accord. to the M; but accord. to the Ḳ, "and") *blood* (M, Ḳ) *itself*: (M:) pl. أَثْآرٌ and آثَارٌ; the latter formed by transposition. (Yaạḳoob, M.) You say, أَدْرَكَ ثَأْرَهُ (Ṣ, Mgh, Ḳ) and ▼ثُؤْرَتَهُ (Aṣ, T, Ṣ) [*He obtained*, or *attained*, or *took, his blood-revenge*, or *retaliation*: or] *he attained the object of his pursuit* [*for blood-revenge*, or *retaliation*]; from ثَأْرَهُ: (Aṣ, T:) or *he slew the slayer of his relation*. (Mgh.) And طَلَبَ بِثَأْرِهِ *He sought to obtain his blood-revenge*, or *retaliation*; syn. طَلَبَ بِذَحْلِهِ. (Ṣ and Mṣb in art. ذحل.) And أَنَا أَطْلُبُ ثَأْرِى عِنْدَهُ *I seek my blood-revenge of him*; syn. ذَحْلِى. (A.) And ثَأْرِى عِنْدَ فُلَانٍ *My blood-revenge is a debt owed to me by such a one*; syn. ذَحْلِى: meaning *such a one is the slayer of my relation*. (A.) — ثَأْرٌ also signifies, (A,) or ▼ثَائِرٌ, (T,) *One who seeks blood-revenge*, or *retaliation of the slaughter of his relation*: and *one of whom is sought blood-revenge*, or *retaliation of the slaughter of a relation*: (T, A:) the latter primarily signifies *a slayer*; and hence, *a slayer of a person's relation in vengeance*, or *retribution*: (Ḥam p. 637:) and the former, *one who is sought*, or *pursued, for blood-revenge*; an inf. n. used as a subst.: (Ḥam p. 87:) the *slayer of a person's relation*; (Ṣ, M, A, Ḳ;) as also ▼ثَائِرٌ: (A:) pl. of the former أَثْآرٌ and آثَارٌ [as above] (Ḳ) and ثَأْرَاتٌ: (Ṣ, A, Ḳ:) the first of which three is [also] pl. of ثَائِرٌ. (T.) You say, هُوَ ثَأْرُهُ *He is the slayer of his relation*. (Ṣ.) And يَا ثَأْرَاتِ فُلَانٍ *O slayers of such a one*. (T, Ṣ, Ḳ.) يَا ثَارَاتِ عُثْمَانَ, occurring in a trad., which is also related with the substitution of ثَارَات for ثَأْرَات, may be explained in the same manner; or it may mean *O ye seekers of the blood-revenge of 'Othmán*, aid me to obtain it; the prefixed noun طَالِبِى, or أَهْل, being understood. (Nh, TA. [See also ثَارَةٌ in art. ثور.]) ثَأْرٌ مُنِيمٌ [*A slayer of one's relation who causes* his slayer *to sleep*,] means *one with whom the seeker* [*of blood-revenge* or *retaliation*] *is contented, if he find him* [*and slay him*], *so that he sleeps after*; (Ṣ, Ḳ;) *one who, if slain, causes the pursuer of blood-revenge to cease from the pursuit*: (Ḥam p. 87:) or *a person who is an equivalent for the blood of one's relation* [*and who therefore, by his being slain in retaliation, makes the avenger to sleep*]: (T:) or *a person of rank*, or *note, in whom* [i. e. *by the slaughter of whom*] *one has his full desire accomplished*. (A.) In a trad. of Mohammad Ibn-Selemeh, relating to the day of Kheyber, occur the words, أَنَا لَهُ يَا رَسُولَ ٱللّٰهِ ٱلْمَوْتُورُ ▼لِلثَّائِرِ, meaning [*I am for him*, i. e. I am he who should slay him, *O Apostle of God*:] *the seeker of blood-revenge* [*is for him of whom blood-revenge is sought*]. (L. [The explanation there given is clearly shown to relate to الموتور.]) — ثَأْرٌ signifies also *An enemy*: pl. أَثْآرٌ: so explained as occurring in the following words of a trad.; لَا تُغْمِدُوا سُيُوفَكُمْ عَنْ أَعْدَائِكُمْ فَتُوتِرُوا أَثْآرَكُمْ *Do not sheathe your swords from your young ones*, [neglecting to teach them the use thereof,] *and so make your enemies to attain their desire of blood-revenge*. (TA.)

ثَأْرَةٌ: see ثَأْرٌ.

ثُؤْرَةٌ; said in the Ṣ to be an inf. n. of 1: see ثَأْرٌ, in two places.

ثُؤُورَةٌ: see ثَأْرٌ.

ثَائِرٌ: see ثَأْرٌ, in three places. — Also One *who does not pity anything* (لَا يُبْقِى عَلَى شَيْءٍ) *so that he may obtain his blood-revenge*, or *retaliation*. (Ṣ, Ḳ.)

مَثْؤُورٌ and مَثْؤُورٌ بِهِ [*Revenged*, or *avenged, by the retaliation of his slaughter*; *by the slaughter of his slayer*: and also *slain in blood-revenge*, or *in retaliation for the blood of a relation of the slayer*]: these two expressions [thus] apply to one's enemy as well as to one's relation. (A.) — Also, the latter, [simply,] *Slain*. (T, and Ḥam p. 87. [But retaliation is generally meant to be understood.])

ثال

Q. Q. 1. ثُؤْلِلَ *He* (a man, M, Mgh) *had* ثَآلِيل [i. e. *warts*] *come forth upon him*. (M, Mgh, Ḳ.)

Q. Q. 2. تَثَأْلَلَ جَسَدُهُ (T, M, Ḳ) بِالثَّآلِيلِ (T, TA) *His person had* ثَآلِيل [or *warts*] *come forth upon it*. (T, M, Ḳ.)

ثُؤْلُولٌ, (T, Ṣ, M, &c.,) which may also be pronounced with the ء suppressed, [ثُولُولٌ,] (Mṣb,) [*A wart*; thus called in the present day;] *a certain excrescence* (M, Mgh, Ḳ) *on the person of a man*, (Mgh,) *small*, (Ḳ,) *hard, and round*, (Mgh, Ḳ,) *and of various forms*; *one description being inverted*; *another, cracked and scabrous*; *another, pendent*; *another, nail-shaped, large in the head and slender at the root*; *another, long, and bent backward*; *another, opened*; *all arising from a thick, tough humour, phlegmatic*, or *bilious*, or *a compound of both these kinds*: (Ḳ, TA:) pl. ثَآلِيلُ. (T, Ṣ, Mgh, Mṣb, Ḳ.) — Also, (as being likened to the excrescence above mentioned, TA,) The *nipple of the breast*. (Kr, M, Ḳ.)

ثبت

1. ثَبَتَ, (Ṣ, M, A, &c.,) aor. ـُ, (M, Mṣb,) inf. n. ثُبُوتٌ (Ṣ, M, A, Mgh, Mṣb, Ḳ) and ثَبَاتٌ, (Ṣ, M, Mgh, Ḳ,) or this latter is a simple subst., (Mṣb,) [unexplained in the Ṣ and M and A and Ḳ, as being well known,] *It* (a thing, Ṣ, M, Mṣb) *continued, subsisted, lasted, endured, remained, remained fixed* or *stationary, stood*, or *rested*; *it was*, or *became, permanent, constant, firm, steady, steadfast, stable, fixed, fast, settled*, or *established*: *it obtained*, or *held*: syn. دَامَ: (Mgh, Mṣb:) and اِسْتَقَرَّ: (Mṣb:) [*it stood, as a fact* or *truth*; *it stood*, or *held, good*; *it was*, or *became, a fact* or *truth*, or *a settled*, or *an established, fact* or *truth*:] *it was*, or *became*, or *proved, sound, valid, substantial, real, sure, certain, true, right, correct, just*, or *proper*; syn. صَحَّ. (Mṣb.) — ثَبَتَ بِالْمَكَانِ, inf. n. ثُبُوتٌ, *He continued, remained, dwelt*, or *abode, in the place*. (T.) — ثَبَتَ الجَرَادُ, and ▼ثبّت, and ▼اثبت, *The locusts stuck their tails into the ground to lay their eggs*. (T.) — ثَبَتُّ عَلَى الأَمْرِ [*I kept constantly, firmly, steadily, steadfastly*, or *fixedly, to the affair*]. (Ḳ in art. زمع.) — ثَبَتَ لِبْدُكَ ‡ *May thy case*, or *state*, or *condition, be permanent*. (A, TA.) — [ثَبَتَ عِنْدَهُ كَذَا *Such a thing was*, or *became, a settled*, or *an established, fact*, or *truth, with him*, or *in his opinion*; *it became established, substantiated, made good*, or *verified, in his opinion* or *estimation*: like صَحَّ. And ثَبَتَ عَلَيْهِ *It was*, or *became, established against him*. Hence, ثَبَتَ لَهُ عَلَيْهِ كَذَا *Such a thing became established*, or *verified, as due to him from him*: like صَحَّ. And hence,] ثَبَتَ is also *syn. with* وَجَبَ [as meaning *It was*, or *became*, or *proved to be, binding, obligatory, incumbent*, or *due*: and *it was*, or *became, necessitated, necessary*, or *requisite*: so that ثَبَتَ عَلَيْهِ means also *it was*, or *became*, or *proved to be, binding, obligatory*, or *incumbent, on him*; or *it rested*, or *lay, on him*; *as a debt*, or *a duty*: and *it* (a sentence &c.) *became necessitated to take effect upon him*: and ثَبَتَ لَهُ *it was*, or *became*, or *proved to be, due to him*, or *owing to him*]. (Telweeḥ, TA in art. وجب.) — [ثَبَتَ لَهُ also signifies *It belonged*, or *appertained, as an attribute*, or *a quality*, or *a property, to him*, or *it*; *it was affirmable*, or *predicable, of him*, or *it*.] — ثَبُتَ, (Ṣ, M, A, Mṣb, Ḳ,) aor. ـُ, (Mṣb, Ḳ,) inf. n. ثَبَاتَةٌ (M, A, Ḳ) and ثُبُوتَةٌ, (M, Ḳ,) *He was*, or *became, firm in intellect, understanding*, or *mind*: (Ṣ:) or *firm*, or *steady, in fight*, or *in speech*, or *discourse*: (M:) or *intelligent, and possessing self-restraint*: or *seldom erring* or *making a mistake* or *committing a fault*: (A:) or *firm of heart* in war: (Mṣb:) or *courageous as a horseman*, (Ḳ, TA,) *earnest in the charge*. (TA.)

2. ثَبَّتَ الجَرَادُ: see 1. — ثَبَّتَهُ: see 4, in two

places. — ثَبَّتَهُ عَنِ الأَمْرِ i. q. ثَبَّطَهُ [*He hindered him, withheld him,* or *prevented him,* &c., *from doing the affair,* or *thing*]. (M.)

3. مُثَابَتَةٌ i. q. مُمَاوَتَةٌ [meaning The *vying with another in firmness,* or *steadiness,* or *the like*]. (TA in art. موت.) — See also 4.

4. اثبت الجَرَادُ : see 1. = اثبتهُ trans. of ثَبَتَ, as also ▼ ثبّتهُ, (Ṣ, M, Mṣb, Ḳ,) signifying *He made it to continue, subsist, last, endure, remain, remain fixed* or *stationary, stand,* or *rest; to be,* or *become, permanent, constant, firm, steady, steadfast, stable, fixed, fast, settled,* or *established: he made it to obtain,* or *hold:* [*he made it to stand, as a fact* or *truth; to stand,* or *hold, good; to be,* or *become, a settled,* or *an established, fact* or *truth:*] *he made it,* or *rendered it, sound, valid, substantial, real, sure, certain, true, right, correct, just,* or *proper.* (Mṣb.) — طَعَنَهُ فَأَثْبَتَ فِيهِ الرُّمْحَ *He thrust him, and made the spear to penetrate into him so that the extremity protruded while part remained within him;* syn. أَنْفَذَهُ. (M.) — اثبتهُ بِوِثَاقٍ [*He made him fast with a bond,* or *ligature*]. (TA.) — لِيُثْبِتُوكَ, (Ṣ, Mgh, Ḳ,) or ▼ لِيُثَبِّتُوكَ, (CḲ,) in the Ḳur [viii. 30], means ‡*That they might inflict upon thee a wound by reason of which thou shouldst not be able to rise:* (Ṣ, Mgh, Ḳ, TA:) or *that they might confine thee* [*to thy place*]. (Ḳ, TA.) You say, طَعَنْتُهُ فَأَثْبَتُّهُ ‡ *I thrust him,* or *pierced him, and confined him to his place, so that he could not quit it.* (TA from a trad.) And ضَرَبُوهُ حَتَّى أَثْبَتُوهُ ‡ *They smote him,* or *beat him, so that they enervated him* [*and rendered him motionless*]. (A, TA.) And أَثْبَتَ الجَرِيحَ † *He weakened the wounded man so that he was unable to move.* (Mgh.) And أَثْبَتَتْهُ جِرَاحَةٌ ‡ *A wound rendered him unable to move:* (T,* A:) and in like manner one says of a malady. (A.) And أُثْبِتَ ‡ *His malady became violent,* or *a wound affected him, so that he did not* [or *could not*] *move.* (T, TA.) — اثبت حُجَّتَهُ *He established his evidence,* or *proof, and made it clear, plain,* or *manifest.* (M.) — اثبتهُ, (M, Ḳ,) inf. n. إِثْبَاتٌ, (TA,) also signifies ‡ *He knew him,* or *it, certainly,* or *assuredly;* and so ▼ ثابتهُ, (M, Ḳ, TA,) inf. n. مُثَابَتَةٌ. (TA.) And you say, نَظَرْتُ إِلَيْهِ فَمَا أُثْبِتُهُ بِبَصَرِى ‡ [*I looked at him,* or *it, but I did not know him,* or *it, surely with my eye*]. (A, TA.) And اثبت الشَّىْءَ مَعْرِفَةً ‡ [*He knew the thing certainly, completely,* or *thoroughly*]. (A. [Explained in a copy of that work, followed in the TA, by قَبِلَهُ; but this is undoubtedly a mistranscription for قَتَلَهُ, q. v.]) — Also, (i. e. اثبتهُ alone,) *He verified it.* (Ḥar p. 175.) — And ‡ *He wrote it,* [*set it down, registered it,* or *recorded it,*] i. e., a man's name, (A, Mṣb, TA,) فِى الدِّيوَانِ [*in the register of soldiers* or *pensioners* or *accounts*]. (A, TA.) — [And i. q. أَوْجَبَهُ as meaning *He made it,* or *declared it to be, binding, obligatory,* or *incumbent,* (عَلَيْهِ *on him,*) or *due* (لَهُ *to him*): and, said of a sentence &c., as meaning *he necessitated it to take effect,* or *necessitated its taking effect,* عَلَيْهِ *upon him:* see حَقَّهُ. — And *He affirmed it; he averred it;* i. q. أَوْجَبَهُ as *contr. of* نَفَاهُ. And hence, اثبتهُ لَهُ signifies also *He made it,* or *declared it,* or *asserted it, to belong,* or *appertain, as an attribute,* or *a quality,* or *a property, to him,* or *it; he affirmed it,* or *predicated it, of him,* or *it.* — And *He authorized it;* namely a word, a signification, &c.] — اثبت فُلَانًا *He kept, clave,* or *held fast, to such a one; scarcely,* or *never, quitting him.* (Mṣb.) And اثبتهُ السَّقَمُ, i. e. [*The malady clave to him;*] *did not quit him.* (Ṣ.)

5. تثبّت فِى الأَمْرِ, (T, Ṣ, M, A, TA,) and الرَّأْيِ; (T, TA;) and ▼ استثبت; (Ṣ, M, A, Ḳ, TA;) *He acted,* or *proceeded,* [*firmly, steadily,*] *deliberately,* or *leisurely,* (T, M, A, Ḳ, TA,) *in the affair,* (T, M, A, TA,) and *the opinion, judgment,* or *counsel;* (T, TA;) *not hastily:* (T, M, TA:) both signify the same: (Ṣ:) [or] ▼ استثبت فِى أَمْرِهِ *he consulted respecting his affair, and sought for information respecting it,* or *investigated it.* (T, TA.) [In the KL, تَثَبُّتٌ is explained by the words درنگ كردن وبجاى آوردن, perhaps meaning The *delaying* in an affair *and* (*then*) *executing* or *performing.*]

10. استثبت : see 5, in two places. — [Also *He sought,* or *desired,* or *demanded, confirmation, evidence, proof, demonstration, verification, assurance,* or *positive* or *certain information,* عَنْهُ *respecting him,* or *it.* — And *He desired,* or *meant, an affirmation:* see a remark on a verse cited voce بَيْدَ.] = استثبتهُ *He found it to be sound, valid, substantial, real, sure, certain, true, right, correct, just,* or *proper:* (Ḥar p. 175:) and *he assured,* or *certified, himself of the true state of his case.* (Idem, p. 420.) You say, صَغَّرَ عَيْنَهُ لِيَسْتَثْبِتَ النَّظَرَ † [*He contracted his eye in order to assure himself of the correctness of the view;* i. e., *to obtain a sure view*]. (M in art. وص.) — It is also said to mean *He made him,* or *asserted him to be, firm of heart:* but Er-Rázee says, I have not met with this verb used as one that is immediately transitive. (Ḥar p. 426.)

ثَبْتٌ : see ثَابِتٌ. — Also A man *firm,* or *steady, of heart;* (Ṣ;) and so ثَبْتُ الجَنَانِ; (A, Mṣb, TA;) pl. ثُبُتٌ: (TA:) or a man *who acts,* or *proceeds,* [*firmly, steadily,*] *deliberately,* or *leisurely,* (A, Mṣb,) *in his affairs:* (Mṣb:) and *a courageous horseman,* (M, Ḳ, TA,) *earnest in the charge;* (TA;) as also ▼ ثَبِيتٌ: (M, Ḳ, TA:) both of which signify also *intelligent, and possessing self-restraint;* or *seldom erring* or *making a mistake* or *committing a fault.* (A, TA.) And ثَبْتُ المُقَامِ A man *who does not quit his station,* or *abode.* (M.) And ثَبْتُ القَدَمِ [*Firm-footed;*] one *who makes no slip in contention,* or *in fight.* (A, TA.) And ثَبْتُ الغَدَرِ A man *firm,* or *steady, in fight,* or *in speech,* or *discourse:* (M, L, TA:) or *whose tongue makes no slip in contentions.* (Ṣ, TA.) — See also ثَبَتٌ: — and ثَبِيتٌ.

ثَبَتٌ *Firmness of heart* in war. (Mṣb, TA.) You say, لَهُ ثَبَتٌ عِنْدَ الحَمْلَةِ *He has firmness,* or *steadiness, on the occasion of the charge,* or *assault.* (Ṣ, A.) And لَهُ ثَبَتٌ عِنْدَ الحِمَامِ *He has firmness on the occasion of death.* (L.) [See also ثَبَاتٌ.] — Hence, (Mṣb,) *A proof, an evidence,* or *a voucher.* (Ṣ, Mgh, Mṣb, TA.) You say, لَا أَحْكُمُ بِكَذَا إِلَّا بِثَبَتٍ *I will not decide so unless on the ground of proof,* or *evidence.* (Ṣ.) And it is said in a trad. respecting the day of doubt, [i. e. the day of which one doubts whether it be the last of Shaabán or the first of Ramaḍán,] ثُمَّ جَآءَ الثَّبَتُ أَنَّهُ مِنْ رَمَضَانَ *Then came the proof,* or *evidence,* or *voucher, that it was of Ramaḍán.* (TA.) — And hence, (Mgh,) applied to a man, (A, Mgh, [in which latter it is said to be tropical when thus applied, but not so in the A,]) and sometimes written ▼ ثَبْتٌ, (TA,) † *One who is an authoritative evidence,* or *voucher, by reason of his trustworthiness in that which he relates:* (A, TA:) or ‡ *one who is trustworthy* (Mgh, Ḳ*) *in that which he relates:* (Mgh: [in the Ḳ, only the pl. is mentioned:]) or † *one who is just,* or *equitable,* [*in that which he relates,*] *and exact,* or *honest:* (Mṣb:) pl. أَثْبَاتٌ. (A, Mgh, Mṣb, Ḳ.) — Also †*An index,* or *a table of contents, in which a relater of traditions collects a list of what he has related from others, and of his sheykhs* [*who are his authorities*]: said by some to be a conventional term of the relaters of traditions: perhaps tropical. (TA.)

ثَبَاتٌ, a subst. from ثَبَتَ, [or an inf. n., like ▼ ثُبُوتٌ, used as a simple subst.,] *Continuance, subsistency, lastingness, permanence, endurance, remanence, remanence in a fixed* or *stationary state, a state of standing* or *resting, constancy, firmness, steadiness, steadfastness, stableness* or *stability, fixedness, fastness, settledness, establishment* or *a state of being established:* &c.: and *soundness, validness* or *validity, substantiality* or *substantialness, reality, sureness, certainty, trueness* or *truth,* &c. (Mṣb.) [See also ثَبَتٌ.]

ثُبَاتٌ, (A,) or دَآءٌ ثُبَاتٌ, (Ḳ, TA,) ‡ *A disease that renders one unable to move.* (A,* Ḳ, TA.)

ثِبَاتٌ The *two threads* or *strings,* or *each of the two threads* or *strings, of* [*the kind of face-veil called*] a بُرْقُع, *by which the woman* [*draws and*] *binds* [*the two upper corners of*] *it to the back of her head.* (Ḳ.) — And *A strap,* or *thong, with which a camel's saddle* (رَحْل) *is bound:* (M, Ḳ:) pl. أَثْبِتَةٌ. (M.)

ثُبُوتٌ : see ثَبَاتٌ.

ثَبِيتٌ : see ثَابِتٌ. — Also *Firm in intellect, understanding,* or *mind:* (Ṣ, Ḳ, TA:) and *firm in strength and intellect:* (TA:) or *firm of heart* in war: (Mṣb:) see also ثَبْتٌ. — And, applied to a horse, *Sharp, and light,* or *active, in his running;* (M, Ḳ;) as also ▼ ثَبْتٌ. (TA.)

ثَابِتٌ part. n. of ثَبَتَ; (M, A, Mṣb, Ḳ;) as also ▼ ثَبْتٌ (M, A, Ḳ) and ▼ ثَبِيتٌ; (Ḳ;) *Continuing, subsisting, lasting, enduring, remaining, remaining fixed* or *stationary, standing,* or *resting, permanent, constant, firm, steady, steadfast, stable, fixed, fast, settled,* or *established: obtaining,* or *holding:* [*standing, as a fact* or *truth; standing,* or *holding, good; having the quality of a fact or truth, or a settled, or an established, fact or truth*:] *sound, valid, substantial, real, sure, certain, true, right, correct, just,* or *proper*: (Mṣb: see 1:) dim., when it is used as an epithet, ثُوَيْبِتٌ; but when it is a proper name, its dim. is ثُبَيْتٌ. (T.) — ثَابِتٌ بِمَكَانٍ *Continuing, remaining, dwelling,* or *abiding, in a place.* (TA.) — الكَوَاكِبُ الثَّابِتَةُ [and الثَّوَابِتُ] *The fixed stars.* (Ḳzw &c.) — سُنُونَ ثَابِتَةٌ *Years lasting long.* (TA in art. فعس.) — قَوْلٌ ثَابِتٌ *A sound, valid, true, right, correct, just,* or *proper, saying.* (M.) بِالْقَوْلِ الثَّابِتِ in the Ḳur xiv. 32 means *By the assertion of the unity of God.* (Jel.)

مُثْبَتٌ *Bound with the strap,* or *thong, called* ثِبَات; applied to a camel's saddle (رَحْل). (M, Ḳ.) — ‡ *Motionless by reason of disease* (T, Ḳ, TA) *that has become violent,* or *by reason of a wound*: (T, TA:) or the same, (M,) or in this sense ▼ مُثْبِتٌ, (Ḳ, TA,) ‡ *heavy* (M, Ḳ, TA) *by reason of old age or some other cause,* (TA,) *and not quitting the bed.* (M, Ḳ, TA.) — [كَلَامٌ مُثْبَتٌ lit. *An affirmed sentence*; i. q. مُوجَبٌ as contr. of مَنْفِيٌّ; virtually *the same as* ▼ كَلَامٌ مُثْبِتٌ *an affirming,* or *affirmative, sentence.*]

مُثْبِتٌ: see مُثْبَتٌ, in two places.

ثبج

1. ثَبَجَ, (Ṣ, Ḳ,) aor. ـِ, (Ḳ,) inf. n. ثُبُوجٌ, (Ṣ,) *He sat with his buttocks against his heels, resting upon the extremities of his feet,* (Ṣ, Ḳ,) *as one does in performing the act termed* اِسْتِنْجَآء. (TA.) ═ [ثَبِجَ: see the next paragraph.]

2. ثَبَّجَ بِالعَصَا, (Ṣ,) inf. n. تَثْبِيجٌ; (Ṣ, Ḳ;) and تَثَبَّجَ بِهَا; (A, Ḳ;) *He* (a pastor, Ṣ, A) *put the staff,* or *stick, upon,* or *against, his back, and put his arms,* or *hands, behind it*: (Ṣ, A, Ḳ:) thus he does when he is fatigued. (TA.) ═ ثَبَّجَهُ, (Ṣ, A, TA,) inf. n. as above, (Ṣ, Ḳ,) *He made it obscure*; (Ḳ;) *he did not make it distinct,* or *plain*; (Ṣ, A, Ḳ;) namely, writing, (Ṣ,) [i. e.] handwriting; (A, Ḳ;) and speech, or language: (Ṣ:) *he did not express it in the proper mode,* or *manner,* namely, speech, or language. (A.) And ثُبِّجَ, inf. n. as above; [and app. ▼ ثَبِجَ, aor. ـَ, inf. n. ثَبَجٌ, q. v. infrà;] said of writing; [and of speech, or language;] *It was,* or *was made, confused* [&c.]. (Lth, TA.)

5: see 2.

ثَبَجٌ The *part between the* كَاهِل [app. here signifying the *base of the neck*] *and the back*: (Ṣ, A, Mṣb, Ḳ:) or the *circuit of the upper part of the* كاهل, *extending to the breast*; as is shown by the phrase أَثْبَاجُ القَطَا: [see what follows:] (Aboo-Málik, TA:) or the *part between the shoulder-blades and the* كاهل: and the *main part* of the back, and the *part in which are the places of curvature of the ribs*: or the *part between the buttocks and the base of the neck*: accord. to AO, the *part from the rump-bone,* or *root of the tail, to the hair of the withers* [of a horse]: (TA:) also the *breast* of the bird called القَطَا: (Ḳ:) or the *middle part* of that bird: pl. أَثْبَاجٌ. (A, TA.) — † The *middle* (Ṣ, Ḳ) of a thing, (Ḳ,) of anything: (Ṣ:) and the *main part* thereof; (Ḳ;) so of a heap, or tract, of sand: (A'Obeyd, Ṣ:) and the *higher,* or *highest, part* of a thing: pl. [of pauc.] أَثْبَاجٌ and [of mult.] ثُبُوجٌ. (TA.) ‡ The *middle* of the sea: the *main part* thereof; and of the night: (A,* TA:) the *height of the middle* of the sea, *where the waves meet one another*: the *higher,* or *highest, parts of the waves.* (TA.) مِنْ ثَبَجِ المُسْلِمِينَ † *Of the middle class of the Muslims*: or *of the higher,* or *highest,* or *chief, class of them.* (TA from a trad.) ═ The *quality denoted by the epithet* أَثْبَجُ, q. v.; as also ▼ ثُبْجَةٌ. (L.) — *Incongruity and confusion of speech,* or *language*: and *obscurity,* or *indistinctness, of handwriting.* (Ḳ. [App. an inf. n.: see 2, last sentence.])

ثُبْجَةٌ A thing *of the middling sort, between good and bad*: (Ḳ, TA:) the fem. ة is affixed because the word is changed from a subst. to an epithet: it occurs in this sense applied to the contribution termed صَدَقَة. (TA.) ═ See also ثَبَجٌ.)

أَثْبَجُ *Broad,* or *wide, in the part called the* ثَبَج; (Ṣ, Ḳ, Mṣb, TA;) and *large in the* جَوْف [i. e. *chest,* or *belly*]: (TA:) or *protuberant,* or *prominent, in the* ثَبَج: (Ṣ, A, Mgh, Mṣb, Ḳ:) or *humpbacked*: (TA in this art., and in art. عجر on the authority of Fr:) and *having a projecting,* or *prominent, breast,* or *chest*: (L:) dim. ▼ أُثَيْبِجُ, occurring in a trad. (Ṣ, Mgh, Mṣb,* Ḳ.)

أُثَيْبِجُ: see what next precedes.

ثبر

1. ثَبَرَهُ, (M, TA,) aor. ـِ, (M,) or ـُ, (TA,) inf. n. ثَبْرٌ, (M, Ḳ,) *He confined him*; or *restrained, withheld, hindered,* or *prevented, him*; (M, Ḳ;) as also ▼ ثَبَّرَهُ, (M,) inf. n. تَثْبِيرٌ. (Ḳ.) You say, ثَبَرَهُ بِالشَّىْءِ, aor. ـُ, inf. n. as above, *He confined, restricted,* or *limited, him* (a man) *to the thing.* (Mṣb.) And ثَبَرَهُ عَنْهُ, (T, Ṣ, M,) aor. ـِ, (T,) or ـُ, (Ṣ, M,) inf. n. as above; (Ṣ, Ḳ;) and ▼ ثَبَّرَهُ; (IAạr, TA;) *He,* or *it, restrained, withheld, hindered,* or *prevented, him from it*; (IAạr, T, Ṣ, Ḳ;) *turned him away,* or *back, from it.* (AZ, IAạr, T, M, Ḳ.) And مَا ثَبَرَكَ عَنْ حَاجَتِكَ *What restrained, withheld, hindered,* or *prevented, thee,* (T,* Ṣ, A,) or *retarded thee,* (A,) or *diverted thee,* (T, A,) *from* [*accomplishing,* or *attaining,*] *thy want?* (Ṣ, A.) And مَا ثَبَّرَ ▼ النَّاسَ *What hath turned the people away, or back, and withheld, or prevented, them,* from obeying God? or *what hath retarded them* therefrom? (TA from a trad.) — Also, (TḲ,) inf. n. as above, (Ḳ,) *He denied him,* or *refused him,* or *prohibited him from attaining,* or *debarred him from, what he desired* or *sought*; *he disappointed him,* or *caused him to fail of attaining his desire*; *rendered him unsuccessful*; *disappointed,* or *frustrated, his desire,* or *hope.* (Ḳ.) — *He drove him away, expelled him,* or *banished him.* (Ḳ.) — *He cursed him.* (Ḳ.) — Also, (M, A, Mṣb,) aor. ـُ, (Mṣb,) inf. n. ثُبُورٌ, (Mṣb, Ḳ,) *He* (God, M, A, Mṣb) *destroyed him* (M, A, Mṣb, Ḳ*) *with a destruction from which he should not rise again.* (M, A.) ═ ثَبَرَ, aor. ـُ, (Mṣb,) inf. n. ثُبُورٌ, (Ṣ, Mṣb, Ḳ,) *He perished*: (Ṣ, Mṣb, Ḳ:) *he suffered loss*; *erred,* or *went astray*; or *became lost.* (Ṣ.) [See also ثُبُورٌ below.] — Also, (M,) inf. n. ثَبْرٌ, (Ḳ,) *It* (the sea) *ebbed.* (M, Ḳ.)

2: see 1, in three places.

3. ثَابَرَ عَلَيْهِ, (T, M, A, Ḳ,*) inf. n. مُثَابَرَةٌ, (T, Ṣ, A, Mgh, Mṣb,) *He kept, attended,* or *applied himself, constantly, perseveringly,* or *assiduously, to it,* (T, Ṣ, M, A, Mgh, Mṣb, Ḳ,*) namely, a thing, (Ṣ, M, Mṣb,) or an affair, (TA,) as, for instance, learning: (A:) *he was eager to say it, or to do it, and kept to it constantly, perseveringly,* or *assiduously.* (IAth.)

6. تَثَابَرَا, (Ḳ,) or تَثَابَرَتِ الرِّجَالُ, (M,) *They two,* (Ḳ,) or *the men,* (M,) *leaped,* or *sprang,* (M, Ḳ,) *each upon,* or *at, the other,* (Ḳ,) or *one upon,* or *at, another,* in war, or fight. (M.)

11. اِثْبَارَرْتُ عَنْهُ *I was heavy,* or *sluggish, and held back from it.* (Ḳ.)

ثُبُورٌ *Perdition*: (Ḳatádeh, T, Ṣ, M, Ḳ:) *loss*; *a going astray*; or *becoming lost*: (Ṣ:) *woe*: (Ḳatádeh, T, M, Ḳ:) *destruction* (M, A, Ḳ) *from which there is no rising again.* (M, A.) Hence it is said that the people of Hell will call out, وَا ثُبُورَاهْ *Alas for destruction from which there is no rising again!* (M, A.) In the Ḳur xxv. 14 and 15, ثُبُورًا is in the accus. case as an inf. n., as though they said, ثَبَرْنَا ثُبُورًا; and, being an inf. n., it is used as a sing. and pl. (Fr, Zj, T.)

ثَابِرٌ *Suffering loss; erring,* or *going astray*; or *becoming lost,* or *perishing*; syn. خَاسِرٌ: so in the saying of El-Kumeyt,

* وَرَأَتْ قُضَاعَةُ فِى الأَيَا * مِنِ رَأْىَ مَثْبُورٍ وَثَابِرْ *

And Ḳuḍá'ah, in asserting their relationship to El-Yemen, formed the opinion of one who is made to suffer loss, or to err, &c., and one who is suffering loss, or *erring,* &c.; مثبور here meaning مَخْسُور. (Ṣ.)

مَثْبُورٌ, as used in the Ḳur xvii. 104, *Overcome*; *withheld,* or *prevented, from attaining what is good*: (Fr, T:) *driven away; expelled; banished; outcast*: *punished; chastised*: (IAạr, T:) *cursed; accursed*: (Fr, IAạr, T:) *made to lose,* or *suffer loss*; *to err,* or *go astray*; or *to become lost,* or *to perish*: so in the saying of El-Kumeyt cited above, voce ثَابِرٌ: (Ṣ:) *in a state of destruction.* (Mujáhid, T.)

ثبط

1. ثَبِطَ, aor. ـَ, [inf. n., accord. to rule, ثَبَطٌ,] (Ḳ,) or, as Ṣgh says, [judging from the part. n. ثَبِطٌ,] thus analogy requires that it should be, (TA,) *He was,* or *became, stupid in his work,* or *action*; *and weak*: and he (a man, and a horse, Ḳ and TA, said of a horse with respect to covering,

TA) *was*, or *became, heavy, sluggish*, or *slow*. (Ḳ,* TA.) ═ See also 2, in two places.

2. ثَبَّطَهُ عَنِ الأَمْرِ, (Lth, IDrd, Ṣ, Mṣb, Ḳ,) or الشَّىْءِ, (TA,) inf. n. تَثْبِيطٌ, (Ṣ, Mṣb,) *He hindered him, withheld him*, or *prevented him*, (IDrd, Mṣb, Ḳ, TA,) *and retarded him*, (IDrd, Ḳ, TA,) *from doing the affair*, or *thing*; (IDrd, Mṣb, Ḳ, TA;) as also ↓ ثَبَطَهُ: (IDrd, Ḳ:) *he diverted him from it, by occupying him otherwise*: (Lth, Ṣ, Mṣb:) or *he prevented him from doing it by inducing him to be cowardly and weak-hearted*: (Mṣb:) or تثبيط signifies one's *turning* a man *back*, or *away, from a thing that he would do*: (Aboo-Is-ḥáḳ:) or one's *intervening as an obstacle between a man and a thing that he desires*. (TA.) The verb occurs in the Ḳur ix. 46. (TA.) — ثَبَّطَهُ عَلَى الأَمْرِ, inf. n. as above, *He made him to pause*, or *wait, at the thing*, or *affair*; (TA;) as also ↓ ثَبَطَهُ عَلَيْهِ, (Ḳ,* TA,) inf. n. ثَبْطٌ; (TA;) syn. وَقَّفَهُ عَلَيْهِ [which here has the meaning assigned to it above, as is shown by the explanation of the quasi-pass. تَثَبَّطَ immediately following in the Ḳ: in the CḲ, we find, erroneously, وَقَفَ عليه]. (Ḳ, TA.)

4. اثبطهُ المَرَضُ *The disease scarcely*, or *never, quitted him*. (Ṣ, Ḳ.)

5. تثبّط [quasi-pass. of 2, *He became hindered, withheld*, or *prevented*, &c.; عَنِ الأَمْرِ *from the affair*, or *thing*. This signification and that next following are well known.—] *He paused*, or *waited*; [عَلَى الأَمْرِ at the thing, or affair; as is implied in the Ḳ and TA;] syn. تَوَقَّفَ. (Ḳ, TA.)

Q. Q. 3. اِثْبَأْطَطْتُ عَنِ الأَمْرِ *I held back*, or *hung back, from the affair*, or *thing, relinquishing it*. (TA.)

ثَبِطٌ *Stupid in his work*, or *action; and weak: heavy, sluggish*, or *slow*; applied to a man, and to a horse; (Ḳ;) to the latter, *with respect to covering*: (TA:) and a man *who will not move from his place*: (TA:) fem. with ة: (Ḳ:) and pl. [of pauc.] أَثْبَاطٌ and [of mult.] ثِبَاطٌ, (Ḳ,) and, applied to men, ثَبِطُونَ also. (TA.)

ثبن

1. ثَبَنَ الثَّوْبَ, aor. ـِ, inf. n. ثَبْنٌ and ثِبَانٌ, *He folded the extremity of the garment, and sewed it*; (Ṣ, Ḳ;) [*he made a tuck in the garment, to shorten it*;] like خَبَنَهُ: (Ṣ:) or, (Ḳ,) i. e. ثَبَنَ, (TA,) *he put a thing into the receptacle* [*thereof*] *and carried it before him*; as also ↓ تثبّن: and in like manner, *he folded and sewed over a thing the doubled upper border of his trousers in front*: (Ḳ,* TA:) or ↓ تثبّن شَيْئًا has this last meaning; and signifies also *he put a thing into a* ثِبَان [q. v.] *and carried it before him*: (Ṣ:) and ثَبَنَ فِى ثَوْبِهِ, aor. and inf. ns. as above; (M;) and ↓ اثبن فيه, (M, Ḳ, as in the CḲ,) accord. to [some of] the copies of the Ḳ اِثَّبَنَ, but the former is the right reading; (TA;) and ↓ ثبّن; (M;) *he put a thing into the receptacle* [*thereof*] *and carried it before him* [*in his garment*]: (M, Ḳ:*) [see also أَخْبَنَ:] or you say, ↓ ثَبَّنَهُ فِى ثَوْبِهِ *he made it a* ثِبَان (or *thing carried* [*before him*]) *in his garment*: (T:) and ↓ تثبّن ثِبَانًا *he made a receptacle in which he* [*so*] *carried a thing before him*. (T.)

2: see 1, in two places.

4: see 1.

5: see 1, in three places.

ثُبْنَةٌ: see what next follows, in four places.

ثِبَانٌ *A receptacle, such as when one folds the skirt of his shirt and puts in it a thing and carries it before him*: (Ṣ:) or the *part, of the garment, which is the place wherein one carries, when he wraps it around his body, or puts a portion thereof under his right shoulder and another portion over his left shoulder, then folds before him a part of it, and puts a thing in it*; as also ↓ ثُبْنَةٌ: (M:) or the *part, of one's garment, which is the place wherein he carries; folding its extremity, and sewing it, before him, and then putting in it some dates or other things*: as also ↓ ثَبِينٌ and ↓ ثُبْنَةٌ: (Ḳ:) and the *extremity of the* [*garment called*] رِدَآء, *when one folds it before him and sews it* [*and puts a thing in it to carry*]: (M:) or *a receptacle in which one carries a thing before him*; (T:) and ↓ ثُبْنَةٌ, of which the pl. is ثُبَانٌ, (T,) or its pl. is ثُبَنٌ, like as the pl of خُبْنَةٌ [which has a similar meaning] is خُبَنٌ, (Ḥar p. 427,) the *doubled upper border of the trousers or waist-wrapper, in which one carries* [*before him*] *fruit and other things*: [see also خُبْنَةٌ:] or, as some say, ثِبَانٌ does not signify a receptacle, but *dates that are put and carried in a receptacle or some other thing*: and sometimes *what a man carries in his sleeve*; and ↓ ثُبْنَةٌ signifies only *what one carries before him, that is little in quantity*: and what is great is not called ثِبَانٌ. (T.) It is said in a trad. of 'Omar, إِذَا مَرَّ أَحَدُكُمْ بِحَائِطٍ فَلْيَأْكُلْ مِنْهُ وَلَا يَتَّخِذْ ثِبَانًا [*When any one of you passes by a garden of palm-trees, let him eat thereof, but not take for himself*, or *make, a* ثبان]: i. e., when a necessitous hungry person passes by a man's garden of palm-trees, he may eat of their dates what will repel his hunger. (T. [See also another reading voce خُبْنَةٌ.]) And one says, قَدِمَ فُلَانٌ بِثِبَانٍ فِى ثَوْبِهِ مَا أَدْرِى مَا هُوَ [*Such a one came with a* ثبان *in his garment: I know not what it was*]. (T.)

ثَبِينٌ: see ثِبَانٌ.

مِثْبَنَةٌ *A bag in which a woman puts her mirror and apparatus*: (M, Ḳ:) of the dial. of El-Yemen. (M.)

ثبو or ثبى

1. ثَبَوْتُ لَهُ خَيْرًا بَعْدَ خَيْرٍ, or شَرًّا, *I sent him good after good*, or *evil* [after evil]. (TA.) [See also 2.]

2. تَثْبِيَةٌ, [inf. n. of ثَبَّى, mentioned in the T and Ḳ, in all its senses, in art. ثبى, and so in the M, except in the first of the following senses, which is there mentioned in art. ثبى and also in art. ثبو,] The act of *collecting* (Ḳ, TA) *in successive assemblages* (↓ ثُبَةً ثُبَةً). (TA.) You say, ثَبَّاهُ *He collected it*, namely, a thing, (M,) and water: (M* and TA in art. ثبو:) and *he added to it, and collected it*. (M, TA.) — The *collecting what is good*: and also, *what is bad*, or *evil*: thus bearing two contr. significations. (Ḳ.) — [And hence,] The *praising* a man *in his life-time*: (AA, Ṣ, Ḳ:) or *praising* him *time after time in his life-time*: (TA:) or *praising* him *much*; as though relating to him collections (↓ ثُبَات) of praise: (Z, TA;) or the *mentioning of the sundry good qualities or actions*: (Er-Rághib, TA:) and the *magnifying* [a person]; or *honouring* [him]. (T,* Ḳ.) You say, ثَبَّى الرَّجُلَ, (M,) or ثَبَّى عَلَى الرَّجُلِ, (T,) *He praised the man in his life-time*: (T, M:) because the doing so implies the collecting his good qualities or actions. (T,* M.) — [Hence also the contr. signification,] The *blaming*, or *censuring, much; collecting blame*, or *censure, from this and that source*. (TA. [The act. part. n. is rendered in the M agreeably with this explanation.]) — The act of *completing* [*and augmenting* a thing]. (Ḳ.) You say, ثَبِّ مَعْرُوفَكَ *Complete and augment* [*thy beneficence*, or *bounty*, or *favour*]. (T.) And ثَبَّى ٱللّٰهُ لَكَ النِّعَمَ [*May God complete and augment to thee benefits*, or *blessings*: or] *may God send to thee benefits*, or *blessings*. (TA.) [See also 1.] — The *putting* a thing *into a good, right*, or *sound, state, and augmenting it*. (T, Ḳ.*) — ثَبَّى المَالَ *He kept, preserved, guarded*, or *took care of, the property*. (Kr, M.) ═ ثَبَّيْتُ عَلَى الشَّىْءِ, (Aṣ, Ṣ,) inf. n. تَثْبِيَةٌ, (Aṣ, T, Ṣ, M, Ḳ,) *I kept constantly*, or *perseveringly, to the thing*. (Aṣ, T, Ṣ, M, Ḳ.) — The inf. n. signifies also The *keeping*, (T,) or *pursuing*, (Ḳ,) *the way, course, mode of acting, or the like, of one's father*: (T, Ḳ:) or the *doing*, or *acting, like one's father*. (M.) — Also The *complaining of one's state*, or *case, and of one's want; and asking aid*, or *assistance, and vengeance*, or *avengement*. (Ḳ.) [One of the meanings assigned to the verb by Golius, as on the authority of the Ḳ, and by Freytag after him, is "Disposuit paravitque se:" app. from the former's having found الإِسْتِعْدَاد written in a copy of the Ḳ for الإِسْتِعْدَآء.] ═ أَنَا أُعَرِّفُهُ تَثْبِيَةً *I know him*, or *it, with a seeming, not a certain, knowledge*. (T, TA.)

ثُبَةٌ *A company* (T, Ṣ, M, Ḳ) *of men*; (T, M;) as also ↓ أُثْبِيَّةٌ; (M, Ḳ; [in the CḲ erroneously written أَثْبِيَة;]) and ↓ أُثْبِيَّةٌ: (TA:) *a company in a state of separation or dispersion*; or *a distinct body*, or *company, of men*: (T:) and *a troop of horsemen; such as is termed* عُصْبَةٌ: (M, Ḳ: [in the CḲ, العَصَبَةُ is erroneously put for العُصْبَةُ:]) the pl. is ثُبَاتٌ and ثُبُونَ (T, Ṣ, M, Ḳ) and ثِبُونَ (Ṣ, M) and (the pl. of أُثْبِيَّةٌ, TA) أَثَابِىُّ and أَثَابِيَةٌ, in which last the ة is a substitute for the last ى [of أَثَابِىُّ]: (M, TA:) or [accord. to some,] أَثَابِىُّ, which signifies *companies*, has no sing.; but, as some say, its sing. is ↓ أُثْبِيَّةٌ, of the measure أُفْعُولَةٌ, [originally أُثْبُويَةٌ,] which means *a numerous company*: (Ḥam p. 796:) [it is also said that] ثُبَى is a pl. of ثُبَةٌ as meaning *a company*; (L in art. ثوب, and Ḥam p. 271;) and hence the phrase الثُّبِى العَالِى, for الثُّبِى العَالِيَةُ, [*the high*, or *exalted, companies*,] the former word being made masc. because it is like زُلَمٌ [which is sing. and masc.]; but some say that this word here means *the assemblies of the nobles*: (Ḥam ubi suprà:) IAạr says, الثُّبِى العَالِى مِنْ مَجَالِسِ الأَشْرَافِ; but [ISd observes,] this is extraordinary, and I have not heard it except in the poetry of El-Find Ez-Zimmánee. (M.) Accord. to some, it is from ثَابَ, being originally ثُوَيْبَةٌ; and its dim. is ثُوَيْبَةٌ: (T:) or it is originally ثُبَىٌ: (Ṣ:) accord. to Er-Rághib, the letter elided from ثُبَةٌ as meaning "a company," but not as relating to a watering-trough or tank, is ى; and ISd holds it to be ى: and [if so,] its dim. is ↓ ثُبَيَّةٌ: (TA:) [but ISd adds,] IJ says that the elided letter is و, because it is this in most cases, as in أَبٌ and أَخٌ and سَنَةٌ and عِضَةٌ &c. (M in arts. ثبو and ثبى.) [See also art. ثوب. It seems to signify also *An assemblage*, or *a collection*, of things of any kind:] see 2, in two places. — Also The *middle* of a watering-trough or tank, (T, Ṣ, M, Ḳ,) *to which the water returns* [*when it has been emptied*], (Ṣ,) or *to which what remains of the water returns*: (T:) and the *place where the water collects in a valley or low ground*: (Aboo-Kheyreh, T:) but this is from ثَابَ; (T, Ṣ;*) the ة is a substitute for the و, the medial radical, which is suppressed; for it is originally ثُوَبٌ: (Ṣ:) or it is originally ثُوبَةٌ: (T:) or it may be from ثَبَّيْتُ "I collected:" but Aboo-Is-ḥáḳ makes it to be from ثَابَ المَآءُ, aor. يَثُوبُ; and this he infers to be the case from their saying that the dim. is ثُوَيْبَةٌ. (M.) [See also art. ثوب.]

ثُبِىّ One *who praises men much* [*while they are living*: see 2]. (TA.)

ثُبَيَّةٌ: see ثُبَةٌ, of which it is said to be the dim.

أُثْبِيَّةٌ: see ثُبَةٌ, in two places.

مُثَبًّى Property *collected together*. (TA.)

ثتل

Q. Q. 1. ثَيْتَلَ, (Ḳ and TA, in the CḲ تَثَيْتَلَ,) *He feigned himself stupid after feigning himself intelligent*: (Ḳ, TA:) accord. to some copies, *after feigning himself negligent*, or *inadvertent*: (تَغَافُل being put in the place of تَعَاقُل:) [app. from the subst. below:] but the word as mentioned by IAạr is تنتل [app. a mistranscription for تَتْتَلَ]. (TA.)

ثَيْتَلٌ The وَعِل [or *mountain-goat*], (M, Ḳ,) as a general term: (M:) [in the present day, but vulgarly pronounced تَيْتَل, applied to the *wild goat of the Arabian and Egyptian deserts and mountains*; the *capra jaela* of Hamilton Smith; called by some an *ibex*; as is also بَدَن:] or *an old* وَعِل: (Ṣ, M, Mgh, Ḳ:) or the *male of the* أَرْوَى: (Sh, T, M, Ḳ: [this is the same as the first explanation:]) En-Naḍr says that *it has small horns*: (T:) Aboo-Kheyreh, that *it is of the* وُعُول, *does not quit the mountain, and its horns have branches*: (T, Mgh:*) he says that the وعول are dusky, or dingy, or of a hue inclining to black and dust-colour, with whiteness in their lower parts; and the ثَيَاتِل [pl. of ثَيْتَل] are like them in their colours, and only distinguished from them by the horns; the وَعِل having long horns, which extend backwards until they meet over his tail: (T:) also *a species of* [*the bovine antelope called*] بَقَرُ الوَحْشِ, (M, Ḳ,) *that abides in the mountains*. (M.) — A man *who sits with women*. (TA.) — *Incapable of going in to women*; or *not desirous of women*. (Ḳ.) — A bully, or *corpulent*, man, *in whom one thinks there is good* (AA, Ḳ, TA) *when there is no good in him*: (AA, TA:) but, as mentioned by Aṣ, it is تيتل. (TA.)

ثج

1. ثَجَّ, (A, L, Mṣb, Ḳ,) aor. ـِ, (A, Mṣb, TA,) inf. n. ثَجٌّ, (L, Mṣb, TA,) or ثَجِيجٌ, (A, TA,) or ثُجُوجٌ, (TA,) *It* (water) *flowed*: (Ḳ:) or *poured forth vehemently*, (A, Mṣb, TA,) or *much*: or, as some say, *it* (much water) *poured forth*: (L, TA:) and ↓ انثجّ and ↓ تَثَجْثَجَ signify the same. (Ḳ.) ثَجٌّ also signifies The *flowing* of the blood of a victim brought for sacrifice to the sacred territory of Mekkeh. (Ṣ, Ḳ, TA.) == ثَجَّهُ, (Ṣ, A, Mgh, Mṣb, Ḳ,) aor. ـُ, (Ṣ, A, Mgh, Mṣb,) inf. n. ثَجٌّ, (Ṣ, Mgh, Mṣb,) *He made it to flow*; (Ṣ, A, Mgh, Mṣb, Ḳ;) *poured it forth*; (Mṣb;) namely, water, (Ṣ, A, Mgh, Mṣb, Ḳ,) and blood (Ṣ, A, Mgh, Mṣb) of a victim for sacrifice; (Mgh, Mṣb;) as also ↓ ثَجْثَجَهُ; and ↓ اثجّهُ may also be used in the same sense. (TA.) Hence, (Mgh, Mṣb,) أَفْضَلُ الحَجِّ العَجُّ والثَّجُّ, (Ṣ, Mgh, Mṣb,) a saying of Mohammad, (TA,) meaning *The most excellent of the actions of the pilgrimage are* (Mgh) *the raising of the voice in the* تَلْبِيَة [see 2 in art. لبى] *and the shedding of the blood of the victims brought for sacrifice to the sacred territory*. (Mgh, Mṣb.)

4: } see 1.
7: }
R. Q. 1: }
R. Q. 2: }

حَلَبَ فِيهِ ثَجًّا *He milked into it milk abundantly flowing*. (TA from a trad.)

ثَجُوجٌ A source *yielding abundance of water*. (TA.) — See also ثَجَّاجٌ.

ثَجِيجٌ [originally an inf. n. (see 1)] *A torrent*, or *flow*. (Ṣ, Ḳ.) So in the saying, أَتَانَا الوَادِى بِثَجِيجِهِ [*The valley brought us its torrent*, or *flow*]. (Ṣ.) — The *sound of the pouring forth* of water. (TA.) — See also ثَجَّاجٌ.

ثَجَّاجٌ Water *pouring forth vehemently*: (Mṣb:) or *poured forth*; as also ↓ ثَجُوجٌ: (TA:) or *flowing*: (Ḥar p. 138:) or *flowing much*: (Id. p. 393:) and rain *pouring forth vehemently*; (Ṣ, TA;) as also ↓ ثَجِيجٌ and ↓ مِثَجٌّ: (TA:) and blood *poured forth*: (TA:) and a cloud *pouring forth*. (A.) Applied to water [or rain, and to blood,] it may have the meaning of a pass. part. n., or, which is preferable, that of an act. part. n. (IDrd, M.) — [Hence,] فُلَانٌ غَيْثُهُ ثَجَّاجٌ وَبَحْرُهُ عَجَّاجٌ ‡ [lit. *Such a one, his rain is such as pours forth vehemently, and his sea is noisy*, or *copious*: meaning *such a one is abundant in bounty* or *munificence*]. (A.)

مِثَجٌّ: see ثَجَّاجٌ. — Also, (Ḳ,) or خَطِيبٌ مِثَجٌّ, (A,) ‡ *An eloquent*, or *able*, *speaker* or *orator*; (Ḳ, TA;) *who pours forth a copious flow of words*. (TA.)

ثجر

1. ثَجَرَ, aor. ـُ, *He mixed the* ثَجِير *of dates* [i. e. *the dregs of pressed dates*] *with other* [*dates*] *in the beverage called* نَبِيذ: (Ṣ:) or *he mixed the dregs of pressed unripe dates with dried dates in making* نبيذ: (Mgh:) or ثَجَرَ التَّمْرَ *he mixed the dried dates with the dregs of pressed unripe dates*. (Ḳ.) The doing so is forbidden in a trad. (Ṣ, Mgh.)

ثَجِيرٌ, an arabicized word, (Mṣb,) pronounced by the vulgar with ت, (Ṣ, Mṣb,) The *dregs of anything that is pressed*; (Ṣ, A, Mgh, Mṣb;) as of pressed unripe dates: (Ḳ:) or the *dregs of pressed unripe dates, which are mixed with dried dates in making the beverage called* نَبِيذ: (TA:) or the *expressed juice of dates*; or the *dregs of pressed dates*: (Aṣ, Mṣb:) or *pressed grapes from which the juice has run, and of which the dregs remain*. (Lth, TA.)

ثخن

1. ثَخُنَ, (T, Ṣ, M, Mṣb, Ḳ,) aor. ـُ; (Ḳ;) and ثَخَنَ, (El-Aḥmar, ISd, Mṣb, TA,) aor. ـُ; (TA;) inf. n. ثَخَانَةٌ (T, Ṣ, Mṣb, Ḳ, &c.) and ثُخُونَةٌ (ISd, Mṣb, Ḳ) and ثِخَنٌ (Z, Mṣb, Ḳ) and ثُخْنٌ; (TA;) *It* (a thing, Ṣ, Mṣb) *was*, or *became, thick, big, gross*, or *coarse*; and *hard, firm, stiff, tough*, or *strong*: (Ṣ, Ḳ:) *it was*, or *became, thick, dense*, or *compact*: (M, TA:) [*it* (a garment, or piece of cloth,) *was thick*, or *close, in texture*: (see ثَخِينٌ:)] *it* [a semiliquid of any kind] *was*, or *became, thick, so that it did not flow, nor continue in its passing away*. (Er-Rághib, TA.)

4. اثخنهُ [in its primary sense, *He*, or *it, rendered it* ثَخِين, i. e. *thick*, &c. — And hence,] ‡ *He*, or *it*, (a man, JK, T, Mgh, Mṣb, and a wound, Ṣ, Mgh, and disease, Bḍ in viii. 68,) *rendered him heavy*: (JK, T, Bḍ ubi suprà, TA:) or *weakened him, rendered him languid*, or *enervated him*. (Ṣ, Mgh, Mṣb, Ḳ, TA.) You say, اثخنهُ ضَرْبًا † *He rendered him heavy by beating*: (JK:) or *he beat him much*, or *vehemently*, or *excessively*. (TA.) And أَثْخَنْتُهُ بِالجِرَاحَةِ † *I weakened him, rendered him languid*, or *enervated him, by the wound*, or *wounds*. (Mṣb.) — إِذَا أَثْخَنْتُمُوهُمْ, in the Ḳur xlvii. 4, means † *When ye have made much slaughter among them*: (Jel:) or *when ye have made a great and vehement slaughter of them*: (Bḍ:) or *when ye have overcome them, and wounded them much*, or *inflicted*

many wounds upon them, (Abu-l-'Abbás, Ḳ, TA,) *so that they give with their hands.* (Abu-l-'Abbás, TA.) —— اثخن فى العدوّ ‡ *He made a great,* or *vehement, slaughter,* (A,) or *a great,* or *vehement, wounding,* (Ḳ,) *among the enemy.* (A, Ḳ.) —— اثخن فى الأرض † *He made much slaughter in the earth,* or *land:* (Bḍ in viii. 68, Mgh, TA: in the Ṣ, اثخن فى الأرض قتلًا, which means the same: TA:) or *he went against the enemy, and made a wide,* or *large, slaughter of them* [*in the land*]: (Mṣb:) or *he fought vehemently in the earth,* or *land.* (Jel in viii. 68.) —— اثخن فى الأمر † *He exceeded the usual,* or *the just, bounds,* or *degree, in the affair; strove,* or *exerted himself, vigorously,* or *strenuously, therein;* or *did his utmost therein.* (TA.) —— اثخنهُ قولُهُ † *His saying took,* or *had, an effect upon him;* or *distressed,* or *afflicted, him.* (TA.) —— أَثْخَنْتُ فُلَانًا مَعْرِفَةً ‡ *I knew such a one,* or *was acquainted with him, thoroughly,* or *very well.* (TA.)

8. اِثَّخَنَ, in the saying of El-Aạshà,

تَمَهَّلَ فِى الحَرْبِ حَتَّى ٱثَّخَنْ

[*He acted deliberately in war until he became heavy,* or *weakened,* or *languid,* or *enervated, by wounds*], is contracted by idghám from اِثْتَخَنَ. (Ṣ, TA.)

10. استثخن منهُ النّومُ ‡ *Sleep overcame him.* (JK, Ḳ, TA.) استثخن بَيْنَ المَرَضِ وَالإِعْيَآءِ ‡ *He became overcome by* [lit. between] *disease and fatigue.* (A, TA.)

ثُخْنٌ an inf. n. of ثَخُنَ: [commonly used as a simple subst., meaning *Thickness,* &c.:] one says ثَوْبٌ لَهُ ثُخْنٌ [*A garment,* or *piece of cloth, having thickness,* or *closeness, of texture*]. (TA.)

ثَخَنٌ *i. q.* نقلة [app. a mistranscription for ثَقَلَةٌ or ثِقْلَةٌ, meaning † *A heaviness in the chest* or *body,* or *a heaviness and langour,* or *a heaviness on the heart*]; as also ↓ ثَخَنَةٌ: El-'Ajjáj says,

حَتَّى يَعِجَّ ثَخَنًا مَنْ عَجْعَجَا

[app. meaning *So that he who cries out cries out by reason of heaviness,* &c.]: (TA: [this saying is also cited in the Ṣ, in art. عج; but there, in one copy, I find ثَخَنًا; and in another, ثِخَنًا; and in both, مِنْ instead of مَنْ:]) and hence he received the surname of العَجَّاج: (Ṣ and TA in art. عج:) so says IDrd. (TA in that art.) [Golius explains ثَخَنٌ as meaning "crassities, spissitudo;" on the anthority of Ibn-Maạroof and Ibn-Beyṭár; but I suspect that he found ثَخَنٌ in their works written for ثُخْنٌ or ثِخَنٌ, both inf. ns. of ثَخُنَ.]

ثَخَنَةٌ: see ثَخَنٌ.

ثَخِينٌ part. n. of ثَخُنَ; (Ṣ, Mṣb;) *Thick, big, coarse,* or *gross;* and *hard, firm, stiff, tough,* or *strong:* (Ṣ:) [*thick, dense,* or *compact:* &c.: see 1: pl. ثِخَانٌ.] You say ثَوْبٌ ثَخِينٌ *A garment,* or *piece of cloth, thick,* or *close,* or *full, in texture,* and, as Az adds, *in warp.* (TA.) —— Applied to a man, *Completely armed:* (KL:) or ثَخِينُ السِّلَاحِ has this meaning. (Ṣ.) —— Also (JK, TA) ‡ *Forbearing, clement, grave, sedate,* or *calm:* (JK, Ḳ,* TA: [in some copies of the Ḳ, الحَكِيمُ is erroneously put for الحَلِيمُ:]) in the M, *heavy in his sitting-place.* (TA.)

مُثْخَنٌ [pass. part. n. of 4, q. v.]. You say, تَرَكْتُهُ مُثْخَنًا وَقِيذًا [*I left him weakened, languid, enervated,* or *much wounded; beaten until he was at the point of death*]. (TA.) —— † *Forbearing, clement, grave, sedate,* or *calm, in mind,* or *intellect.* (TA.) [See also ثَخِينٌ.] —— Metonymically applied by the people of Syria to ‡ *One who causes laughter; who is quick, brisk,* or *lively, in his motions.* (TA.)

مُثْخِنٌ † *One who exceeds the usual,* or *the just, bounds,* or *who does his utmost, in narration, and in the rehearsal of sayings.* (TA.) —— And, with ة, ‡ *A large, corpulent, fleshy,* woman. (JK, A, Ḳ.)

ثدأ

ثُنْدُؤَةٌ and ثُنْدُوَةٌ, (M,) or ثَنْدُوَةٌ, (Lth, T,) or ثُنْدُوَّةٌ, of the measure فُنْعُلَةٌ, with damm to the ف and ع, or, accord. to some, the ن is radical and the و augmentative, the measure being فُعْلُوَةٌ, (Mṣb in art. ثدى,) or ثُنْدُؤَةٌ and ثَنْدُوَةٌ, (ISk, T, Ṣ, Mgh, Mṣb, Ḳ,) with damm to the ث if with ء, (ISk, T, Ṣ, Mgh, Mṣb,) and of the measure فُعْلُلَةٌ, (ISk, Ṣ,) and with fet-ḥ to the ث if with و, without ء, (ISk, T, Ṣ, Mgh, Mṣb, Ḳ,) and in this case of the measure فَعْلُوَةٌ, (ISk, Ṣ, Ḳ,) like قَرْنُوَةٌ and عَرْقُوَةٌ, (ISk, Ṣ,) [the ن in both cases, accord. to ISk, being radical,] so in the Bári', (Mṣb,) and so says Ḳṭr, (TA,) but A'Obeyd says that the Arabs in general pronounced the word without ء, (Mṣb,) The ثُنْدُوَة [which generally signifies the *breast,* or *mamma,* but sometimes the *pap,* or *mamilla,*] *of a man:* (Mgh:) or the *part, of a man, that corresponds to the* ثَدْى *of a woman:* (T, Ṣ, Mṣb, Ḳ:) or the *flesh of the* ثَدْى: (Lth, T, M, Mgh:) or the *flesh that is around the* ثَدْى: (ISk, T, Ṣ, Ḳ:) or the *base of the* ثَدْى: (Aṣ, Zj in his "Khalḳ el-Insán," Ṣ, Mṣb, Ḳ, KL*:) or the *portion of flesh that is at the base thereof:* (Mṣb:) or *i. q.* ثَدْى: (TA:) and the *pap,* or *mamilla, of a woman* and *of a man:* (KL:) accord. to the author of the Wá'ee, the pl. [of ثندؤة] is ثَنَادِءُ, [with ء substituted for ى, unless the former be a mistranscription for the latter,] (TA,) and [that of ثندوة is] ثَنَادٍ. (Mṣb, TA.) The word ثدى is used in relation to men in the Ṣaḥeeḥ of Muslim, and ثندوة in relation to women in the Sunan of Aboo-Dáwood; and many of the lexicologists incline to the opinion that ثدى is common to men and women. (MF in art. ثند.) —— ثُنْدُوَةُ الأَنْفِ, occurring in a trad., *The tip,* or *fore part, of the nose.* (IAth, TA.)

ثدو

1. ثَدَاهُ, aor. ـُ: see art. ثدى.

ثدى

1. ثَدِىَ, aor. ـَ, *It became moist* or *moistened.* (T, Ḳ.) ثَدِيَتِ الأَرْضُ *i. q.* سَدِيَت [*The land became moistened by much dew*]: mentioned by Yaạḳoob, who asserts that the ث in the former is a substitute for the س in the latter; but is not known. (M.) —— ثَدَاهُ, aor. ـُ (T, Ḳ) and ـِ, (T,) *He moistened it.* (T, Ḳ.) —— And ثداهُ [so in the TT, as from the T, without teshdeed,] *He fed him,* or *nourished him:* (T, TT:) [or the verb in this sense is ↓ ثَدَّاهُ, for its inf. n.] تَثْدِيَةٌ signifies the act of *feeding,* or *nourishing.* (Ḳ.)

2: see 1.

ثَدْىٌ (T, Ṣ, M, Mgh, Mṣb, Ḳ, &c.) and ثُدْىٌ and ثَدًى: (Ḳ:) the first of these is the form most commonly obtaining: (TA:) [The *breast,* or *mamma;*] the *part of the chest whereof the* حَلَمَة *is the head; each of the two parts whereof the* حَلَمَتَانِ *are the two heads:* (Zj in his "Khalḳ el-Insán:") [and sometimes, but not properly, the حَلَمَة alone; i. e, the *pap, nipple,* or *mamilla:*] you say ثَدْىٌ مُقْعَدٌ *a breast that is swelling, prominent,* or *protuberant,* (Ṣ, A, L, Ḳ, in art. قعد,) *that fills the hand,* (A in that art.,) *and has not yet become folding:* (Ṣ, L, Ḳ, in that art.:) and رَضَعَ ثَدْىَ أُمِّهِ [*he sucked the breast,* meaning *the pap,* or *nipple, of his mother*]. (IḲṭṭ in TA, art. رضع:) it is *peculiar to woman;* (T, Ḳ:) or *common to woman and man;* (Ṣ, Mṣb, Ḳ;) being sometimes used in relation to a man; (Mṣb;) accord. to the opinion held to be most chaste and best known by the lexicologists [in general]: (TA:) and is masc.; (T, M, Mgh;) or masc. and fem.; (Ṣ, Mṣb, Ḳ;) but most chastely masc.: (TA:) the pl. [of pauc.] is أَثْدٍ, (Ṣ, M, Mṣb, Ḳ,) [originally أَثْدُىٌ,] of the measure أَفْعُلٌ, (Mṣb,) and [of mult.] ثُدِىٌّ, (Ṣ, M, Mṣb, Ḳ,) [originally ثُدُوىٌ,] of the measure فُعُولٌ, (Ṣ, Mṣb,) and ثِدِىٌّ, with kesr to the ث because of the kesr to the letter following, (Ṣ,) and sometimes ثِدَآءٌ, [originally ثِدَاىٌ,] like سِهَامٌ; (Mṣb;) and a poet says,

وَأَصْبَحَتِ النِّسَآءُ مُسَلِّبَاتٍ
لَهُنَّ الوَيْلُ يَمْدُدْنَ الثُّدِينَا

[*And the women became widowed,* or *bereft of relations, and without their ornaments,* or *in mourning, having woe, pulling the breasts*]; but this is something like a mistake; and it may be that he meant الثُّدِيَّا, and changed the [latter] ى into ن for the sake of the rhyme. (M.) It is said in a prov., تَجُوعُ الحُرَّةُ وَلَا تَأْكُلُ ثَدْيَيْهَا, meaning, أُجْرَةَ ثَدْيَيْهَا, [i. e. *The ingenuous woman will be made to hunger and will not eat the hire of her breasts,*] the prefixed noun being suppressed; or, as some relate it, بِثَدْيَيْهَا, which is plain [as meaning, *by means of her breasts*]: it is applied in relation to a man's preserving himself from ignoble means of acquiring wealth. (Mgh.) And جُدَّ ثَدْىُ أُمِّهِ, *May his mother's breast be cut off,* is a form of imprecation against a man, and used to imply a wish for his separation. (Aṣ, L in art. جد.) The saying of 'Alee, on the day of his slaughter of the Khawárij, أُنْظُرُوا فَإِنَّ فِيهِمْ

رَجُلًا إِحْدَى يَدَيْهِ مِثْلُ ثَدْيِ الْمَرْأَةِ [*Look ye, for among them is a man one of whose arms is like the breast of the woman*], not احدى ثُدَيَّيْهِ as some relate it, was applied to a man who had, in the place of one arm, a lump of flesh upon his shoulder-joint, which lump, when it was stretched, became equal in length to his other arm, and when it was left, returned [to its original form]. (Mgh.) Respecting ▾ ثُدَيَّةٌ, the dim., whence the surname ذُو الثُّدَيَّةِ, he who holds ثَدْىٌ to be masc. [only] says that the ة is added because the word [virtually] means اليَد, [which is fem.,] for the man thus surnamed had a short arm, of the size of the ثَدْى, as is indicated by the fact that they also called him ذُو اليُدَيَّةِ: (Ṣ:) or, accord. to Fr, (A 'Obeyd, T,) ة is added, in this instance, in the dim., though ثَدْىٌ is masc., because it applies to what resembled the remains (بَقِيَّة) of a ثَدْى, the greater part of it having gone, so that it is like لُحَيْمَةٌ and شُحَيْمَةٌ [dims. of لَحْمَةٌ and شَحْمَةٌ]: (T, M:) or the ة is added because the word is regarded in this case as meaning البَضْعَةُ [the piece, or lump, of flesh]: (Mgh:) some say that it is the dim. of ثَنْدُوَةٌ; (Mgh, TA;) but this requires consideration. (Mgh.)

ثُدَيَّةٌ: see ثَدْىٌ. — Also *A repository,* or *receptacle,* (AA, Ḳ,) *of the size of the fist,* (AA,) *in which the horseman carries the* [*sinews called*] عَقَب [*of which the bow-string is made, and which are bound round a bow, and round an arrow, to repair a fracture in it,* (see عَقْبٌ and عَقَبٌ,)] *and the feathers* [*which he may require to attach to any of his arrows*]. (AA, Ḳ.)

ثُدَّاءُ *A certain plant* [*growing*] *in the desert.* (Ṣ.)

ثَدْيَاءُ A woman *large in the* ثَدْيَانِ [or *breasts*]: أَثْدَى, the masc. form, is not used. (Ṣ, M.)

ثُنْدُوَةٌ, [written by some ثُنْدُؤَةٌ, as well as ثَنْدُوَةٌ and ثُنْدُوَةٌ,] mentioned here in the Ṣ, and in art. ثدأ: see the latter art.

ثرب

1. ثَرَبَهُ, aor. ـِ, (Ḳ,) inf. n. ثَرْبٌ, (TḲ,) [probably, in its primary sense, *He stripped it of its* ثَرْب: see 2: — and hence,] †*He stripped him of his garment;* namely, a sick man. (Ḳ.) — See also 2, in three places.

2. تَثْرِيبٌ, in its primary sense, is The *removing of the* ثَرْب, i. e., the *fat that forms the integument of the stomach of a ruminant:* so says Z. (Ḥar p. 187.) — And hence, ‡The act of *blaming; reproving;* and *punishing,* or *chastising, for an offence,* or *a crime:* (Ḥar ubi suprà:) or ‡ *severe blaming* or *reproving, that rends reputations, and takes away the brightness of countenances:* (Z in Ḥar ubi suprà:) which last meaning it has in the Ḳur xii. 92: (Bḍ:) or لَا تَثْرِيبَ عَلَيْكُمْ there means †*No evil,* or *mischief, shall come upon you:* (Zj, T:) or †*your offences,* or *crimes, shall not be mentioned:* (Th, M:) تثريب signifies †the act of *blaming,* or *reproving;* (Ṣ, Mgh;) or *doing so severely,* or *angrily;* or, *with the utmost severity* or *harshness:* the act of *upbraiding,* or *reproaching:* and the *going to the utmost length in blaming* or *reproving:* one says, لَا تَثْرِيبَ عَلَيْكَ †[*No blame,* &c., *shall be laid on thee*]: and it is from الثَّرْبُ [as explained above]. (Ṣ.) You say, ثَرَّبَ and ▾ ثَرَبَ and ▾ اثرب, meaning †*He blamed,* or *reproved;* or *did so severely,* or *with the utmost severity;* or *reproached,* or *upbraided:* (T:) and ثَرَّبَ عَلَيْهِ, (Ṣ, M, Ḳ,) and ثَرَّبَهُ; (A, Ḳ;) and ▾ ثَرَبَهُ, [and ثَرَبَ عليه,] aor. ـِ, (Ḳ,) inf. n. ثَرْبٌ; (TḲ;) and ▾ اثربهُ; (A, Ḳ;) †*he blamed him,* or *reproved him; upbraided him,* or *reproached him,* (M, A, Ḳ,) *with,* or *for, his offence,* or *crime;* (M, Ḳ;) and *reminded him thereof;* (M;) *he showed him his deed to be foul, abominable,* or *bad:* (Aṣ, Ṣ:) or ▾ ثَرَبَ عليه, aor. ـِ, signifies †*he blamed him,* or *reproved him;* and, as Suh says, ثَرَّبَ عليه, †*he blamed him,* or *reproved him, much.* (Mṣb.) — Also †The *acting ill,* or *corruptly; doing evil,* or *mischief; creating confusion,* or *disorder.* (TA.) = It is also said in the Ḳ to be *syn. with* طَىٌّ, which means The *building* [or *casing* a well] *with stones:* but [SM says,] I fear that this is a mistranscription for تَثْوِيب, with و. (TA.)

4. *He* (a ram) *increased in his fatness:* (Ḳ:) or *acquired a* ثَرْب, *having increased in fatness.* (TA.) = See also 2, in two places.

ثَرْبٌ *A thin integument of fat that covers the stomach of a ruminant and the bowels* or *intestines;* (Lth, T, Ṣ, M, Mṣb, Ḳ;) the *fat that is spread over the bowels,* or *intestines:* (T:) pl. (of mult., TA) ثُرُوبٌ (M, Ḳ) and (of pauc., TA) أَثْرُبٌ, and pl. pl. أَثَارِبُ. (Ḳ.) Hence, صَارَتِ الشَّمْسُ كَالأَثَارِبِ *The sun* [upon the ground] *became like the integuments above-mentioned:* i. e., scattered; being upon one place and not upon another, towards sunset: a phrase occurring in a trad., in which it is said that when this is the case, it is forbidden to perform the afternoon-prayer: and in another trad. occurs the phrase, صَارَتِ الشَّمْسُ كَثَرْبِ النَّاقَةِ [*The sun* upon the ground *became like the* ثرب *of the she-camel*]. (TA.) — And [hence,] †*A land of which the stones are such as those of the* حَرَّة [q. v.], *save that they are white.* (L.)

ثَرَبَاتٌ, (Ḳ,) or ثَرِبَاتٌ [like تَرِبَاتٌ, with which it is nearly, or perhaps exactly, syn.], (M,) The *fingers.* (M, Ḳ.)

أَثْرَبُ, (TA,) fem. ثَرْبَآءُ, (T, Ḳ,) A sheep *having a large* ثَرْب; (T, TA;) i. e. (TA) a *fat* sheep. (Ḳ, TA.)

مُثْرِبٌ †One *who gives little,* (Ḳ, TA,) *reproaching for that which he has given.* (TA.)

مُثَرِّبٌ *Upbraiding* [&c.: see the verb, 2]: (M:) or *acting ill,* or *corruptly; doing evil,* or *mischief; creating confusion,* or *disorder.* (M, Ḳ.)

ثرد

1. ثَرَدَ, aor. ـُ, (M, L,) or ـِ, (so in one place in the TT,) inf. n. ثَرْدٌ, (T, M, Mgh, L,) *He broke* a dry or hollow thing: (T, Mgh, L:) *he crumbled* a thing, or *broke* it *into small pieces, with his fingers.* (M, L.) [Hence,] ثَرَدَ خُبْزًا, (Ṣ, M, A, Mṣb, Ḳ,) aor. ـُ, (Mṣb,) inf. n. as above, (Ṣ, Mṣb,) *He crumbled bread,* or *broke it into small pieces, with his fingers,* (M, A, Mṣb, Ḳ,) *then moistened it with broth,* (A, Mṣb,) *and then piled it up in the middle of a bowl:* (A:) or *he broke bread:* (Ṣ:) and in like manner ▾ اِثَّرَدَهُ, originally اِثْتَرَدَهُ; and ▾ اِتَّرَدَهُ: (Ṣ, Ḳ:) and ▾ اثّرد ثَرِيدًا, and ▾ اِثَّرَدَهُ, *he made,* or *prepared,* ثريد [i. e. *bread crumbled &c. as above described*]. (M.) — *He rubbed and pressed* a testicle *with the hand, in lieu of castrating;* (Ḳ;) inf. n. as above. (Mgh.) — See also 2. — *He dipped* a garment, or piece of cloth, *in dye:* (Ḳ:) *he dyed* it with saffron [&c.]. (TA from a trad.) — ثُرِدَ مِنَ المَعْرَكَةِ, (so in a copy of the T, and in some copies of the Ḳ, and in the CḲ,) or ▾ ثُرِّدَ, (so in some copies of the Ḳ, and in the TA,) *He* (a man, IAạr, T) *was carried away from the place of fight wounded much but having life remaining in him.* (IAạr, T, Ḳ.)

2. ثَرَّدَ, (T, M, Ḳ,) inf. n. تَثْرِيدٌ; (T, Ṣ, Mgh;) and ▾ ثَرَدَ; (Ḳ;) [ISd says,] I think that the latter is a dial. var. of the former; (M;) *He killed* an animal that should be slaughtered *without cutting the* أَوْدَاج [or *external jugular veins*] *so as to make the blood flow;* (M, Ḳ;) i. e., (TA,) *he killed* it *with a blunt knife, so that he broke,* [*or tore, the flesh &c.,*] *and did not cut so as to make the blood flow:* (A, TA:) or *he killed* it *by squeezing and pressing the* اوداج, *without cutting, and making the blood to flow:* (Mgh:) or *he killed* it *with a thing that did not make the blood to flow freely:* or *he killed it without practising the method prescribed by the law:* (T:) or تثريد in slaughtering is the *breaking* [*the bones* or *joints &c. of the animal*] *before it is cold;* and this is forbidden. (Ṣ.) [See also مُثَرَّد.] — See also 1, last sentence. — And see ثَرِد, below.

4. [It seems that Golius found أَثْرَدَ erroneously written in a copy of the Ṣ and in a copy of the Ḳ for اِثَّرَدَ.]

8. اِثَّرَدَ and اِتَّرَدَ: see 1, in four places.

ثَرْدٌ *Weak rain.* (IAạr, M, Ḳ.)

ثَرَدٌ (Ṣ, Ḳ) and ▾ تَثْرِيدٌ (A) ‡ *A chapping* in the lips. (Ṣ, A, Ḳ.)

ثُرْدَةٌ: see what next follows.

ثَرِيدٌ and ▾ مَثْرُودٌ Bread *crumbled,* or *broken into small pieces, with the fingers, and then moistened with broth:* (Mṣb:) or [simply] *broken* bread. (Ṣ.) — Also, the former, (T, A,) and ▾ ثَرِيدَةٌ (T, M, A, Ḳ) and ▾ ثُرْدَةٌ (Ṣ, M, A, Mṣb) and ▾ ثُرُودَةٌ (M, Ḳ) and ▾ مَثْرُودَةٌ (Ḳ accord. to the TA) and ▾ أُثْرُدَانٌ, (Fr, M,* Ḳ,) *Bread,* itself, *crumbled,* or *broken into small pieces, with the fingers,* (T,* Ṣ,* M, A, Mṣb, Ḳ,*) *then moistened with broth* (T, A, Mṣb) *&c.,* (T,) *and then piled up in the middle of a bowl;* (A;) *generally having some flesh-meat with it:* (L:) or ▾ ثَرِيدَةٌ signifies *a mess,* or portion, of ثَرِيد [or bread crumbled or broken &c.]; (T;) [and so ▾ثَرُودَةٌ, and ▾ مَثْرُودَةٌ:] that of Ghassán is said by common consent to have been *prepared with marrow*, and *with eggs*, or *the yolks of eggs*; and there was no kind more delicious than these two kinds. (TA.) The pl. of ثَرِيدَةٌ is ثَرَائِدُ and ثُرُدٌ and ثُرْدٌ; (A, and Ḥam p. 524;) the last of which is a contraction of that next preceding it. (Ḥam ubi suprà.) A poet, as cited by IAạr, says,

أَلَا يَا خُبْزُ يَا ٱبْنَةَ يَثْرُدَانِ▾
أَبَى ٱلْحُلْقُومُ بَعْدَكَ لَا يَنَامُ

[*Now surely, O bread, O daughter of two preparers of* ثَرِيد, *the throat refuses, after* swallowing *thee, to rest*, by reason of desire for more]: he says that the poet calls the bread after two young men, or slaves, who were preparing ثريد, and gives tenween to يثردان by a poetic license, instead of saying يَثْرُدَانِ, which, as it is [originally] a verbal phrase, he should have said by rule: but the word, as Fr relates it, is ▾أُثْرُدَانِ; and [ISd says,] I think that this is a determinate subst., for الثَّرِيد or المَثْرُود, and therefore properly imperfectly decl., but here made perfectly decl. by a poetic license. (M.) It is said in a trad. that the excellence of 'Áïsheh above other women is as the excellence of ثريد above other kinds of food; but it is said that what is here meant is food prepared with flesh-meat, together with ثريد, because this is generally prepared with flesh-meat, and it is said to be one of the two things called لَحْم. (TA.)

ثَرُودَةٌ : ثَرِيدَةٌ : أُثْرُدَانٌ : see ثَرِيدٌ; for each, in two places.

مِثْرَدَةٌ *A* [*bowl such as is called*] قَصْعَة [app. *for* ثَرِيد]. (TA.)

مُثْرِدٌ One who *slaughters* (an animal intended to be slaughtered, M) *with a stone or a bone*, (M, Ḳ,) or *the like thereof*; to do which is forbidden: (M:) or one *whose iron instrument is not sharp*, (IAạr, M, Ḳ,) *so that he mangles the flesh*. (IAạr, M.)

مِثْرَادٌ *A stone*, or *bone*, or *blunt iron instrument*, *with which an animal is slaughtered* [*in a bungling manner:* see مُثْرِدٌ]. (M, Ḳ.)

مَثْرُودٌ : see ثَرِيدٌ. — Also A garment, or piece of cloth, *dipped in dye*. (ISh, T.)

مَثْرُودَةٌ : see ثَرِيدٌ, in two places.

يَثْرُدَان : see ثَرِيدٌ.

ثرم

1. ثَرِمَ, (T, Ṣ, M, Mṣb, Ḳ,) aor. ـَ, (Mṣb, Ḳ,) inf. n. ثَرَمٌ, (T, Ṣ, M, Mṣb,) *He* (a man, T, Ṣ, Mṣb) *had one of his central incisors broken:* (AZ, T, Mṣb:) or *he had a central incisor fallen out:* (Ṣ:) or *he had a tooth broken out entirely;* (M, Ḳ;) or *one of his fore teeth, such as the central incisors and the teeth between the central incisors and the canine teeth;* (M, Ḳ;*) or, peculiarly, *a central incisor:* as also ▾ انثرم. (M, Ḳ.) — ثَرَمَهُ, (T, Ṣ, M, Mṣb, Ḳ,) aor. ـِ, (M, Ḳ,) or ـُ, (Mṣb,) inf. n. ثَرْمٌ; (Ṣ, M, Mṣb;) and ▾ اثرمهُ; (T, M, Ḳ;) *He* (a man, T, Ṣ, Mṣb) *broke one of his central incisors:* (T, Mṣb:) or *rendered him* أَثْرَم: (M, Ḳ:) or the former, *he struck him on his mouth, so that one of his central incisors fell out:* and ▾ the latter, *He* (God) *rendered him* أَثْرَم. (Ṣ.) And ثَرَمْتُ ثَنِيَّتَهُ *I broke his central incisor*. (T, Ṣ.)

4: see 1, in two places.

7: see 1. — Also انثرمت ثَنِيَّتُهُ *His central incisor became broken*. (T, Ṣ, Mṣb.)

أَثْرَمُ, applied to a man, *Having one of his central incisors broken:* (T, Mṣb:) or *having a central incisor fallen out*, (Ṣ, and Ḥam p. 613,) *so as to have a gap between two of his teeth:* (Ḥam ib.:) or *having a tooth broken out entirely;* (M, Ḳ;) or *one of his fore teeth, such as the central incisors and the teeth between the central incisors and the canine teeth;* (M, Ḳ;*) or, peculiarly, *a central incisor:* (M, Ḳ:) fem. ثَرْمَآءُ: (M, Mṣb, Ḳ:) pl. ثُرْمٌ. (Mṣb.) — الأَثْرَمَانِ † *Night and day:* (M, Ḳ:) and † *time*, or *fortune, and death*. (TA.)

ثرو

1. ثَرَا القَوْمُ, (Aṣ, Ṣ, M, Ḳ,) aor. ـُ; (Aṣ, Ṣ;) and ثَرِىَ; (T, TT;) inf. n. ثَرًا; (M;) *The people*, or *company of men, became many, much*, or *great in number* or *quantity; and increased:* (Aṣ, T, Ṣ, M, Ḳ:) and in like manner, المَالُ, (Aṣ, Ṣ, M, Ḳ,) i. e., *the cattle*, or *other property, became many, much*, or *great in number* or *quantity*. (Aṣ, Ṣ, M.) — ثَرِىَ, (T, M, Ḳ,) aor. ـَ, inf. n. ثَرًى [or ثَرًا ?] and ثَرَآءٌ, (T, TA,) *He* (a man, T, Ḳ) *was*, or *became, abundant in cattle*, or *other property;* (T, M, Ḳ;) as also ▾ اثرى, (T, Ṣ, M, Mgh, Ḳ,) and أَثْرَى: (M:) or ▾ اثرى signifies *he was*, or *became, in a state of competence* or *sufficiency, in no need*, or *rich;* syn. استغنى: (Mṣb:) or it signifies *more than* استغنى: (T:) and ثَرِيتُ بِكَ, *I became*, or *have become, abundant* [*in property*] *by means of thee:* (T, Ṣ:) and ثَرِيتُ بِفُلَانٍ *I became in no need of other men by means of such a one*. (T, Ṣ, M.) A poet says, (Ṣ,) namely, El-Kumeyt, praising the Benoo-Umeiyeh,

لَكُمْ مَسْجِدَا ٱللّٰهِ المَزُورَانِ وَالحَصَى
لَكُمْ قِبْصُهُ مِنْ بَيْنِ أَثْرَى▾ وَأَقْتَرَا

[*Ye have the two visited mosques* of Mekkeh and El-Medeeneh, *and ye have the number of the pebbles of such as are between* him who *is wealthy and* him who *is poor*]: he means, مِنْ بَيْنِ مَنْ أَثْرَى وَمَنْ أَقْتَرَ; i. e., مِنْ بَيْنِ مُثْرٍ وَمُقْتِرٍ. (Ṣ.) — ثَرِيتُ بِكَ, (T,) or بِهِ, inf. n. ثَرًا, (M,) also signifies *I rejoiced* (T, M) *in thee*, (T,) or *in him*, or *it:* (M:) and ثَرِىَ بِذٰلِكَ, aor. ـَ, *He rejoiced in*, or *by reason of, that*. (ISk, Ṣ.) — ثَرَوْنَاهُمْ *We were*, or *became, more than they:* (AA, Ṣ, M:) or *more in cattle*, or *other property*. (K.) — ثَرَا القَوْمَ *He* (God) *made the people*, or *company of men, to be many*, or *numerous; multiplied them*. (AA, T, Ṣ.)

4: see 1, in three places. — لَا يُثْرِينَا العَدُوُّ *The enemy will not say much respecting us*. (M, TA.)

ثَرًا; dual ثَرَوَانِ: see ثَرًى, in art. ثرى.

ثَرٍ : see ثَرِىٌّ. — أَنَا ثَرٍ بِهِ *I am in no need of other men by means of him;* (T, Ṣ, M;) as also ▾ ثَرِىٌّ. (M.) — See also art. ثرى.

ثَرْوَةٌ *Many*, or *a great number*, (Ṣ, M, Ḳ,) of men; and of cattle, or other property: (M, Ḳ:) or *much*, or *a great quantity*, of property; (Mgh, Mṣb;) as also ▾ ثَرَآءٌ: (Ṣ, M,* Mgh:) and فَرْوَةٌ signifies the same as ثَرْوَةٌ; the ف being a substitute for the ث. (M.) One says, إِنَّهُ لَذُو ثَرْوَةٍ وَذُو ثَرَآءٍ▾, (ISk, Ṣ,) or إِنَّهُ لَذُو ثَرَآءٍ▾ وَثَرْوَةٍ, (T,) *Verily he possesses a number* [of men] *and much property*. (ISk, T, Ṣ.) Accord. to IAạr, one says ثَرْوَةٌ مِنْ رِجَالٍ and ثَرْوَةٌ, meaning *A great number of men:* but only ثَرْوَةٌ مِنْ مَالٍ. (TA.) — Also The *night of the conjunction of the moon and* الثُّرَيَّا [or *the Pleiades*]. (M, Ḳ.)

ثَرْوَانُ, fem. ثَرْوَى : see ثَرِىٌّ.

ثَرَآءٌ : see ثَرْوَةٌ, in three places. — Also *A state of competence* or *sufficiency;* or *richness*. (Mṣb.)

ثَرِىٌّ *Many*, or *numerous;* [applied to a company of men;] and so ثَرِيَّةٌ applied to spears (رِمَاحٌ): (TA:) also *many*, or *much*, cattle, or other property; (Ṣ, M, Ḳ, TA;) and so ▾ ثَرٍ. (T, TA.) — Also A man *possessing many*, or *much*, *cattle*, or *other property;* and so ▾ أَثْرَى; (M, Ḳ;) and ▾ مُثْرٍ: (T:) so too ▾ ثَرْوَانُ; (T, Ṣ, Mgh;) or *abounding* (M, Ḳ, TA) *in cattle*, or *other property:* (TA:) and [its fem.] ▾ ثَرْوَى, applied to a woman, (T, Ṣ, M, Ḳ,) likewise signifies *possessing many*, or *much*, *cattle*, or *other property:* (T, Ṣ, Ḳ:) the dim. of this last is ثُرَيَّا. (T, Ṣ, M, Ḳ.) — See also ثَرٍ. — And see art. ثرى.

ثُرَيَّا : see ثَرِىٌّ. — الثُّرَيَّا [*The Pleiades; the Third Mansion of the Moon:* it is believed to be the most beneficial, in its influences on the weather, of all the Mansions of the Moon, on account of the period of its auroral setting, which, in central Arabia, about the commencement of the era of the Flight, began on the 12th of Nov., O. S.: (see مَنَازِلُ القَمَرِ, in art. نزل; and see also نَوْءٌ:) hence what is said of it in Job xxxviii. 31; and hence, as being the most excellent of all asterisms, it is called by the Arabs] النَّجْمُ [*the Asterism*]: (Ṣ, Ḳ:) the former appellation is given to it because it comprises, in appearance, many stars in a small space; (M, Ḳ;*) for it is said that amid its conspicuous stars are many obscure stars; (IAth, TA;) the number altogether being said to be four and twenty, agreeably with an assertion of the Prophet: some say that it is so called because of the abundance [of the rain] of its نَوْء [here meaning auroral setting]: (TA:) the word is thus applied only in the dim. form, which is used in this instance to denote magnification. (M, TA.) —— ثُرَيَّا also signifies † *A cluster of lamps, generally resting in holes in the bottom of a lantern:* see an engraving in my "Modern Egyptians," ch. vi.] The ثُرَيَّا of lamps is so called as being likened to the asterism above mentioned. (M.)

أَثْرَى : } see ثَرًى : ═ and see also art. ثرى.
مُثْرٍ :

مَثْرَاةٌ *A cause of multiplying,* or *rendering abundant;* syn. مَكْثَرَةٌ : so in the saying, هٰذَا مَثْرَاةٌ لِلْمَالِ [*This is a cause of multiplying,* or *rendering abundant, cattle, or other property*]. (Ṣ, Ḳ.)

أَنَا مَثْرِيٌّ بِهِ *I am rejoiced in him.* (ISk, TA in art. ثرى.) ═ See also art. ثرى.

ثرى

1. ثَرِيَتِ الأَرْضُ, aor. ـَ, inf. n. ثَرًى, *The earth,* or *land, became moist and soft, after drought and dryness:* (M, Ḳ:) or *became watered by rain that penetrated to its moisture.* (Mṣb.) ═ See also the same form of the verb in the first paragraph of art. ثرو, in six places.

2. ثَرَّى, (T, Ṣ, M, Ḳ,) inf. n. تَثْرِيَةٌ, (Ṣ, Ḳ,) *He moistened* (T, Ṣ, M, Ḳ) a place, (T,) or earth, or the ground, or dust, (M, Ḳ,) and سَوِيق [or meal of parched barley or wheat], (Ṣ, TA,) and any other thing: (TA:) *he sprinkled* a place: (Ṣ, Ḳ:) *he poured water upon, and then stirred about, and mixed up,* [the preparation of milk termed] أَقِط, (M, Ḳ,) and سَوِيق. (M.) ═ *He made his hands to cleave to the ground* (T, Ḳ) *between the two prostrations in prayer, not separating them therefrom until he performed the second prostration.* (T.)

4. اثرى *It* (rain) *moistened the earth.* (Ṣ.) —— أَثْرَتِ الأَرْضُ *The land,* or *earth, had much moisture; became abundant in moisture:* (Ṣ, M, Mṣb, Ḳ:) or *it became compact with moisture.* (AḤn, M.) [See also مُثْرٍ.]

ثَرًى *Moisture; humidity;* (Ṣ, M, Ḳ;) of the earth: (Ṣ, Mṣb:) and *moist earth;* (Ṣ, M, Mṣb, Ḳ;) that is not moist is not called ثَرًى ; تُرَاب (Mṣb;) or *such as, when moistened, does not become cohesive mud or clay;* (M, Ḳ;) as also ▼ ثَرْيَآءُ [an epithet used as a subst.]: (AO, T,* Ḳ, TA: [in the CḲ, erroneously, ثَرِيَاء:]) and the *earth;* (M, Ḳ;) مَا تَحْتَ الثَّرَى, in the Ḳur [xx. 5], being explained as meaning *what is beneath the earth:* (M:) الثَّرَى and ▼ أَثْرَى both signify *the earth;* and the latter, being thus used as a proper name, is imperfectly decl.: (Ḥam p. 351:) dual ثَرَيَانِ (Ṣ, M, Ḳ) and ثَرَوَانِ: (Lḥ, M, Ḳ: [but the sing. of the latter should be written ثَرًا:]) pl. أَثْرَآءٌ. (M, Ḳ.) اِلْتَقَى الثَّرَيَانِ [*The two moistures met,* or *have met,*] is said when the rain has sunk into the ground so that it has met the moisture of the earth. (Ṣ, M, Ḳ.) Accord. to IAạr, it was also said by a man, (M,) or by an Arab of the desert, (Ḳ,) who, (M, Ḳ,) being naked, (Ḳ,) clad himself with a fur-garment, (M, Ḳ,) without a shirt; (M;) meaning *the hair of the pubes and the soft hair of the fur-garment.* (M, Ḳ.) And the Arabs say, شَهْرُ ثَرَى وَشَهْرُ تَرَى وَشَهْرُ مَرْعَى وَشَهْرُ ٱسْتَوَى, meaning *A month* [*of moisture*] *in which the rain begins, and sinks into the ground, and moistens and softens the earth;* for شَهْرٌ ذُو ثَرًى : *and a month in which thou seest the heads of the herbage grown forth;* for شَهْرٌ تَرَى فِيهِ رُؤُوسَ النَّبَاتِ : *and a month in which the herbage is tall enough to be pastured upon by the cattle:* (Aṣ, Ṣ,* M:) *and a month in which it is full-grown and erect.* (Aṣ, M.) One says also, بَدَا ثَرَى المَآءِ مِنَ الفَرَسِ, meaning *The sweat of the horse appeared.* (Ṣ,* M.) And إِنِّى لَأَرَى ثَرَى الغَضَبِ فِى وَجْهِ فُلَانٍ, meaning † *Verily I see the effect of anger in the face of such a one.* (T.) And هُوَ ٱبْنُ ثَرَاهَا † *He is the knowing with respect to it.* (T in art. بنى.) —— [Hence, as being likened to moist earth,] i. q. خَيْر †[*Good; anything good;* &c.]. (M, Ḳ. [For خَيْر, Golius appears to have found, in a copy of the Ḳ, حَيِّز; and this, which he has rendered "Terræ tractus," he has given as a signification, not of ثَرًى, but of ثَرَاةٌ, which, like ثَرًى, he also explains as meaning "terra."]) So in the saying, فُلَانٌ قَرِيبُ الثَّرَى [app. meaning † *Such a one is a person from whom good is easy of attainment:* or it may mean, *a person from whom good seems to be easy of attainment:* in either case likened to land of which the moist earth is near the surface: that the phrase may have the latter meaning appears from what here follows]. (M.) You say, إِنَّ فُلَانًا لَقَرِيبُ الثَّرَى بَعِيدُ النَّبَطِ, meaning † *Verily such a one is a person who promises but who does not fulfil.* (IAạr, T.) —— [Hence also, † *Fresh and vigorous friendship.*] You say, لَمْ يَيْبَسِ الثَّرَى بَيْنِى وَبَيْنَهُ † [*The fresh and vigorous friendship between me and him has not withered*]: whence the phrase, مَا بَيْنِى وَبَيْنَ فُلَانٍ ▼ مُثْرٍ † [*That* friendship *which is between me and such a one is fresh and vigorous*]; i. e., it has not ceased, or become severed. (Ṣ,* M.) Jereer says,

فَلَا تُوبِسُوا بَيْنِى وَبَيْنَكُمُ الثَّرَى •
فَإِنَّ الَّذِى بَيْنِى وَبَيْنَكُمُ مُثْرِى ▼ •

[*And wither not the fresh and vigorous friendship between me and you; for that which is between me and you is fresh and vigorous*]. (Ṣ, M.)

ثَرٍ, [fem. ثَرِيَةٌ, *Moist; humid.*] You say أَرْضٌ ثَرِيَةٌ, (M, Mṣb,) like عَمِيَةٌ, (Mṣb,) or ▼ ثَرِيَّةٌ, like غَنِيَّةٌ, (Ḳ, [but this is anomalous, as part. n. of ثَرِيَتْ,]) and ▼ ثَرْيَآءُ, (Mṣb, Ḳ,) *Earth,* or *land, that has become moist and soft, after drought and dryness:* (M, Ḳ:) or *watered by rain that has penetrated to its moisture:* (Mṣb:) or the last, *land of just,* or *moderate, moisture:* (AḤn, M:) or *moist land;* (T, Ṣ, M;) and so the first. (M.) And ▼ مَكَانٌ ثَرْيَانُ *A place of which the earth has in it moisture.* (TA.) And ▼ يَوْمٌ ثَرِىٌّ *A humid day.* (TA.) ═ See also art. ثرو.

ثَرِىٌّ, fem. ثَرِيَّةٌ : see ثَرٍ, in two places: ═ and see also art. ثرو.

ثَرْيَآءُ : see ثَرٍ : —— and see also ثَرًى.

ثَرْيَانُ : see ثَرٍ.

ثُرَيَّا : see art. ثرو.

أَثْرَى : see ثَرًى : ═ and see also art. ثرو.

أَرْضٌ مُثْرِيَةٌ [مُثْرٍ, fem. مُثْرِيَةٌ, part. n. of 4, q. v.] [is explained as meaning] *Land of which the earth has not become dry.* (T, TA.) —— See also ثَرًى, last two sentences. ═ And see art. ثرو.

مُثْرِىٌّ a pass. part. n. having no verb; used as an intensive epithet in the phrase ثَرًى مُثْرِىٌّ [*Very moist earth*]. (M.) ═ See also art. ثرو.

ثط

1. ثَطَّ, aor. ـِ; (Lth, TA;) [app. accord. to him who says رَجُلٌ أَثَطُّ; for Lth adds,] and, accord. to him who says رَجُلٌ ثَطٌّ, (Lth, TA,) ثَطَّ, aor. ـَ and ـُ; (Lth, Ḳ;) inf. n. [of ثَطَّ of which the aor. is ـِ,] ثَطَطٌ, (Lth, IDrd, Ṣ, Ḳ,) and [of the verb of which the aor. is ـَ,] ثَطٌّ, and [of that of which the aor. is ـُ, the second pers. of the pret. being app. ثَطُطْتَ,] ثَطَاطَةٌ and ثُطُوطَةٌ; (Lth, Ḳ;) or the last two, accord. to IDrd, are simple substs., and ISd approves of this distinction; (TA;) *He* (a man, Lth, Ṣ) *was,* or *became, such as is termed* ثَطٌّ and أَثَطُّ [explained below]. (Lth, IDrd, Ṣ, Ḳ.)

ثَطٌّ and ▼ أَثَطُّ, (Lth, Ṣ, Ḳ,) but the former is the more correct and the more common, (Lth,) or the former only, (IDrd, and IB on the authority of Ibn-El-Jawáleekee, and Ḳ,) the latter being vulgar, (IDrd, Ḳ,) but AZ asserted his having heard the latter, (AḤát, cited in the Jm,) [and the latter only is mentioned in the Mgh,] A man (Ṣ, Mgh) *having no hair upon the sides of his face, but only upon his chin;* syn. كَوْسَج : (Ṣ, Mgh, Ḳ:) or *having a scanty beard:* (IDrd:) or the former signifies *having little hair in the beard,* and *in the eyebrows:* (Ḳ:) or [when you mean the latter] you say رَجُلٌ ثَطُّ الحَاجِبَيْنِ, (Ḳ,) *a man having thin,* or *scanty, eyebrows;* as also ▼ أَثَطُّ الحَاجِبَيْنِ; (TA;) the mention of the eyebrows being indispensable; (IAạr, Ḳ;) and اِمْرَأَةٌ ثَطَّةُ الحَاجِبَيْنِ [*a woman having thin,* or *scanty, eyebrows*]: (Ṣ, TA:) pl. (of pauc., TA) أَثْطَاطٌ (Kr, Ḳ) and (of mult., TA) ثُطَّانٌ and ثِطَطَةٌ (AZ, Ḳ) and ثُطُطٌ, (IAạr,) [all of which may be of either sing.,] and ثِطَاطٌ, (AZ, Ṣ, Ḳ,) which is of the former sing., (Ṣ,) and ثُطٌّ, (AZ, Ṣ, Ḳ,) which is of the latter. (Ṣ.) You say also اِمْرَأَةٌ ▼ ثَطَّآءُ *A woman having no* إِسْب, (Lth, TA,) i. e. *hair on the pubes;* in the copies of the Ḳ incorrectly written اِسْت. (TA.) And ▼ عَارِضٌ أَثَطُّ *A side of the cheek,* or *of the face, having the hair falling off.* (Mgh.) —— Also, the former, *Heavy in the belly;* (Ḳ, TA;) *slow;* applied to a man. (TA.) ═ The former also signifies *Human excrement* or *ordure;* or *thin human excrement* or *ordure;* syn. سَلْح. (Ṣgh, Ḳ.) [See also ثَلْط.]

أَثَطُّ, and its fem. ثَطَّآءُ : see ثَطٌّ, in four places. —— الثَّطَّآءُ also signifies *The spider:* or *another creeping thing, that stings, or bites, vehemently:* (Ḳ:) this is from Lth, as in the O and L: but in the Tekmileh we find الثُّطَآءُ, like شَقَّآءُ, [app. a mistake for الثَّطَآءُ, like شِقَآءُ,] *a certain small creeping thing:* or, as some say, it is الثُّطَا, of the measure of قَفًا. (TA.)

ثعب

1. ثَعَبَهُ, (Ṣ, A, Ḳ,) aor. ـَ, (Ḳ,) inf. n. ثَعْبٌ, (Ṣ,) *He gave vent to it;* or *made it to flow forth, run,* or *stream;* namely, water, (Ṣ, A, Ḳ,) and blood, and the like. (Ḳ.) ثعب دَمًا, [thought by MF to be ثَعَبَ, but I see no reason why it should not be ثَعِبَ,] said of a wound, means *It flowed,* or *ran, with blood.* (TA.)

7. انثعب *It* (water) *had vent;* or *it flowed forth, ran,* or *streamed;* (Ṣ, A, Ḳ;) in, or through, a مَثْعَب: (Ṣ, TA:) and in like manner, rain: (TA:) and blood from the nose. (Ṣ, TA.) — [Hence,] صَاحَ بِهِ فَٱنْثَعَبَ إِلَيْهِ ‡ *He called out to him and he sprang up and ran to him.* (A, TA.)

ثَعْبٌ, applied to water, (Ḳ,) and to blood, (TA,) *Flowing, running,* or *streaming;* as also ▼ثَعِبٌ and ▼أُثْعُوبٌ and ▼أُثْعُبَانٌ. (Ḳ, TA.) You say ▼سَيْلٌ أُثْعُوبٌ [*A flowing torrent*]. (A.) — And [hence,] ▼شَرٌّ أُثْعُوبٌ ‡ [*Evil that takes its course like a stream*]. (A.) — See also what next follows.

ثَعَبٌ, (so in the Ṣ, expressly said to be بِالتَّحْرِيكِ,) or ▼ثَعْبٌ, (so in the Ḳ,) in some copies of the Ḳ, erroneously, مَثْعَب, (TA,) *A water-course of a valley; a channel in which water flows in a valley:* (Ṣ, Ḳ:) accord. to Lth, the *rubbish and scum that collect in the channel in which the rain-water flows;* but Az disapproves of this explanation of the word, and says that it signifies, in his opinion, the channel itself: (TA:) the pl. is ثُعْبَانٌ. (Ṣ, Ḳ.) One says, سَالَتِ الثُّعْبَانُ كَمَا سَالَ الثُّعْبَانُ, i. e. *The torrent* [or rather *the torrents*] *ran like the serpent called* ثعبان]. (A, TA.) — See also ثَعْبٌ.

ثُعْبَانٌ *A kind of long serpent:* (Ṣ:) *a great serpent;* applied to the *male* and the *female:* (Mṣb:) *a bulky and long serpent,* (Sh, Ḳ, TA,) *that hunts the rat or mouse, to which latter animal the name is sometimes metaphorically applied, and that is more useful in the house than are cats:* (Sh, TA:) or particularly the *male* [*serpent*], (Ḳtr, Ḳ,) *that is yellow,* and *ruddy:* (Ḳtr:) or the *serpent in general,* (ISh, Ḳ,) *male* and *female, great* and *small:* (ISh:) [also applied to *an enormous fabulous serpent;* described by Ḳzw and others:] pl. ثَعَابِينُ. (Ṣ, Mṣb.) — [رَئِيسُ الثَّعَابِينِ *The basilisk.* (Golius, from a Glossary.)] — دَمُ الثُّعْبَانِ: see دَمٌ.

فُوهُ يَجْرِي ثَعَابِيبَ, (Aṣ, Ṣ, Ḳ,) or فَمُهُ, (TA,) and سَعَابِيبَ, (Ṣ,) *His mouth runs with clear water, having an extended* [or *a ropy*] *flow.* (Aṣ, Ṣ, Ḳ.)

أُثْعُبَانٌ: see ثَعْبٌ.

أُثْعُوبٌ: see ثَعْبٌ, in three places.

مَثْعَبٌ [The *outlet,* or *place of outpouring, of the water* of a watering-trough &c.;] the *place of passage for the water, in the side of a watering-trough* or *tank:* and *a channel,* or *conduit, for water:* (KL:) pl. مَثَاعِبُ. (Ṣ, A.) You say مَثْعَبُ الحَوْضِ [*The outlet for the water of the watering-trough* or *tank*]: (Ṣ, A:) and مَثْعَبُ السَّطْحِ [*the outlet for the water of the house-top*]: (A:) and مَثْعَبُ المَطَرِ [*the outlet,* or *channel, for the rain-water*]: (TA:) from ثَعَبَ المَآءَ "he gave vent to the water," or, "made it to flow forth," &c. (A, TA.) And مَثَاعِبُ المَدِينَةِ, meaning *The channels,* or *places of flowing, of the water of the city:* (Ḳ, TA:) whence it appears that MF has erred in saying that مَثْعَبٌ signifies [only] *a* مِزْرَاب [or *spout for conveying away water from a house-top* &c.]: not a channel, or place of flowing. (TA.) [See also صُنْبُورٌ, and تَوْلَبٌ.]

ثعد

ثَعْدٌ, as an epithet applied to a leguminous plant, or to an herb, *Fresh, juicy,* or *sappy;* (Ṣ, A, Ḳ;) *soft,* or *tender.* (Ṣ, A.) You say ثَعْدٌ مَعْدٌ in this sense; (Ṣ, A;) the latter word being an imitative sequent, not [generally] used alone; but some use it alone: (Ṣ:) and it is said to be syn. with the former. (TA.) You say also رُطَبَةٌ ثَعْدَةٌ مَعْدَةٌ, meaning *A fresh, juicy, ripe date.* (IAạr, TA.) And ثَرًى ثَعْدٌ *Soft, moist earth;* (Ṣ, Ḳ;) as also جَعْدٌ. (Ṣ.) — [As a coll. gen. n.,] *Fresh ripe dates:* or *dates for the most part in a state of ripeness:* (Ḳ:) or *ripening dates when they have become soft:* n. un. with ة: (Aṣ, Ṣ:) that which is ripening, but as yet hard and indigestible, is termed جُمْسَةٌ. (Aṣ, TA.) [See بُسْرٌ.] — *Fresh butter:* so accord. to Is-ḥáḳ Ibn-Ibráheem El-Ḳurashee, in a trad. related by him. (IAth, TA.) — مَا لَهُ ثَعْدٌ وَلَا مَعْدٌ *He possesses not little nor much.* (Ḳ.) [Here, again,] the last word is an imitative sequent. (TA.)

ثعل

1. ثَعِلَ, aor. ـَ, inf. n. ثَعَلٌ, *His teeth were irregular in their places of growth, and overlying one another:* (Mṣb:) [or *he had a tooth,* or *teeth, in excess,* or *exceeding the usual number, and growing behind the others:* see what follows.] And ثَعِلَتِ السِّنُّ *The tooth exceeded the usual number,* (Mṣb, Ḳ,) *being behind the other teeth:* or *entered beneath another, being irregular in the place of growth.* (Ḳ.) [See also ثُعْلٌ.]

4. اثعلوا, said of guests, *They were,* or *became, numerous,* or *many,* (Ḳ, TA,) *and straitened,* or *crowded, one another:* (TA:) so, too, said of men coming to water. (Ḳ, TA.) — اثعلوا عَلَيْنَا *They acted contrarily,* or *adversely, to us; they opposed us.* (Lth, Ṣ, Ḳ.) — اثعل said of a recompense, or reward, *It was,* or *became, great.* (Ḳ.) — And said of an affair, *It was so great that one knew not how to apply himself to it:* (Ḳ:) it implies incongruity. (TA.)

ثَعْلٌ: see ثُعْلٌ.

ثُعْلٌ (Ḳ, and Ḥam p. 647) and ▼ثَعْلٌ and ▼ثُعْلُولٌ, (Ḳ,) the last from Ibn-'Abbád, (TA,) *A tooth in excess,* or *exceeding the usual number,* (Ḳ, and Ḥam ubi suprà,) *behind the other teeth:* (Ḳ:) or the *entering of a tooth beneath another, with irregularity in the place of its growth:* (Ḳ:) or ▼ثَعَلٌ signifies *superfluities in the teeth, and irregularity in their places of growth, so that they overlie one another:* (Ṣ:) or the *teeth's overlying one another, and the excess of a tooth among them* [*beyond the usual number*]. (Ḥar p. 243.) — And ثُعْلٌ (Ṣ, Ḳ, and Ḥam ubi suprà) and ▼ثَعْلٌ and ▼ثُعَلٌ (Ḳ) *An excess,* or *a redundance,* (Ḳ and Ḥam,) [i. e.] *a small teat in excess,* [*in addition to the usual number,*] (Ṣ,) *in,* or *among, the teats of a sheep* or *goat,* (Ṣ, Ḳ, Ḥam,) and *of a she-camel,* (Ṣ, Ḳ,) and *of a cow:* (Ḳ:) *it does not yield milk, though hyperbolically described as doing so.* (Ṣ. [But see ثَعُولٌ.]) — Also ثُعْلٌ, [not ثُعَالٌ as in Freytag's Lex.,] *A certain animalcule that appears in a skin used for holding water or milk when its odour has become bad.* (Ibn-'Abbad, Ḳ.*)

ثَعَلٌ: see ثُعْلٌ, in three places.

ثُعَلٌ: see ثُعَالَةُ. — One says in reviling a man, هٰذَا الثُّعَلُ وَالكُعَلُ, meaning *This ignoble fellow, that is naught.* (Ibn-'Abbád, TA.)

ثُعْلُولٌ: see ثُعْلٌ. — Also A ewe, or she-goat, *that may be milked from three places, or four,* (Ibn-'Abbád, Ḳ,) *by reason of an excess in the* [*number of*] *teats.* (Ibn-'Abbád, TA. [See also ثَعُولٌ.]) = *Angry.* (Lth, Ḳ.)

ثَعَالٍ: pl. of ثَعْلَبٌ [q. v.]. (Ḳ in art. ثعلب.)

ثُعَالٌ: see ثُعَالَةُ.

ثَعُولٌ, applied to a she-camel, a cow, and a sheep or goat, *Having an excess,* or *a redundance, in the* [*number of*] *teats:* or *having, above her teat, a small teat:* or *having a nipple in excess:* (Ḳ:) or a ewe, or she-goat, *having a* ثُعْل [q. v.]: or, accord. to some of the lexicologists, a ewe, or she goat, *that may be milked from her* ثُعْل. (Ḥam p. 647. [See also ثُعْلُولٌ.]) — طَعْنَةٌ ثَعُولٌ *A wound made with a spear or the like from which the blood is scattered,* or *sprinkled.* (TA.) — جَيْشٌ ثَعُولٌ *A numerous army.* (TA.) And كَتِيبَةٌ ثَعُولٌ *An army,* or *a collected portion thereof, having with it much rabble and many followers:* (Ḳ:) regard is had in it to multitude and crowding. (TA.)

ثُعَالَةُ, a determinate noun, *The* ثَعْلَب [or *fox*]; (Ṣ, O;) as also ▼ثُعَلٌ: (IDrd, TA:) or *the female* ثعلب; as also ▼ثُعَالٌ. (Ḳ.) = ثُعَالَةُ الكَلَإِ *Dry herbage:* or ثُعَالَةُ is [*the plant commonly called*] عِنَبُ الثَّعْلَبِ [see art. ثعلب]: (Ḳ:) this is from AḤn. (TA.)

أَثْعَلُ A man *whose teeth are irregular in their places of growth, and overlying one another:* (Mṣb:) or *having superfluities in his teeth, and irregularity in their places of growth, so that they overlie one another:* (Ṣ:) or *having a tooth in excess,* (Mgh, Ḳ,) *behind the other teeth:* (Ḳ:) or *having a tooth entering beneath another, being irregular in the place of growth:* (Ḳ:) fem. ثَعْلَآءُ, applied to a woman; (Ṣ, Mgh, Mṣb, Ḳ;) and also to a gum (لِثَةٌ): (Ḳ:) pl. ثُعْلٌ. (Mṣb, TA.) — *A portly,* or *corpulent, personage,* or *chief, characterized by superabundances of benificence,* or *bounty.* (Lth, Ḳ.)

مُثْعَلٌ *Spread, scattered,* or *sprinkled.* (TA.) — وِرْدٌ مُثْعِلٌ [*A company of men coming to water*] *straitening,* or *crowding, one another.* (Ḳ.) — جَآءَ القَوْمُ مُثْعِلِينَ *The people,* or *company of men, came in a connected,* or *continuous, body.* (TA.)

أَرْضٌ مُثْعَلَةٌ *A land in which are many* ثَعَالِب [or *foxes*]; (Ṣ, Ḳ;) like مَعْقَرَةٌ meaning "a land in which are many عَقَارِب [or scorpions];" (Ṣ;) as also مُثْعَلِبَةٌ. (Ḳ in art. ثعلب. [But see this last word.])

ثعلب

Q. 1. ثَعْلَبَ *He* (a man) *was cowardly, and eluded,* or *turned away,* or *went this way and that,* or *to the right and left, quickly, and deceitfully,* or *guilefully;* as also ▾ تَثَعْلَبَ: his doing so being thus likened to the running of the ثَعْلَب. (TA.) And ثعلب مِنْهُ فَرَقًا [*He was cowardly, and eluded him,* or *turned away from him,* &c., *through fear*]; i. e., from another man. (TA.)

Q. 2. تَثَعْلَبَ: see above.

ثَعْلَبٌ [The *fox; canis vulpes* of Linn.: but in the dial. of Egypt, the *jackal; canis aureus* of Linn.: the former animal being there called أَبُو الحُصَيْن, as it often is by the Arabs of other countries:] *a certain beast of prey;* (TA;) *well known:* (Ṣ, Ḳ:) applied to the *male* and the *female;* so that one says ثَعْلَبٌ ذَكَرٌ and ثَعْلَبٌ أُنْثَى; but if one would designate the male by a single word applying to it only, he says ▾ ثُعْلُبَانٌ, with ḍamm to the ث and ل: (IAmb, Mṣb:) or the former applies to the *female:* (Ḳ:) or the *female* is called ▾ ثَعْلَبَةٌ; (Ks, Ṣ, Mṣb, Ḳ;) and the *male,* ▾ ثُعْلُبَانٌ (Ks, Ṣ, Ḳ) and ثَعْلَبٌ, (Ḳ,) [accord. to some,] like as one says عَقْرَبَةٌ [and عُقْرُبَانٌ] and عَقْرَبٌ: (Mṣb:) or ثَعْلَبٌ is the *male;* and the *female* is called ▾ ثُعَالَةُ: (Az, TA: [but see this word in art. ثعل:]) the pl. of ثعلب is ثَعَالِبُ and ثَعَالٍ, (Ḳ,) accord. to Lḥ: but ISd disapproves of this [latter pl.]; and Sb does not allow it except in poetry. (TA.) F charges J with error in citing, as a proof that ▾ ثُعْلُبَانٌ signifies the *male,* the following verse:

أَرَبٌّ يَبُولُ الثُّعْلُبَانُ بِرَأْسِهِ ❊
لَقَدْ ذَلَّ مَنْ بَالَتْ عَلَيْهِ الثَّعَالِبُ ❊

[*Is he a Lord, upon whose head the he-fox makes water?* (the ب in برأسه being syn. with عَلَى: so in the Mughnee, in art. ب:) *Vile indeed is he upon whom the foxes make water!*] said by a man who was keeper of an idol, on seeing a he-fox make water upon it: but in this, F opposes also Ks and others; and it is asserted by several authorities that the correct reading of the word ثعلبان in a trad. whereby F attempts to establish his charge against J is not ثَعْلَبَانِ, dual. of ثَعْلَبٌ, as he pronounces it to be, but ثُعْلُبَانٌ, which is said to be the masc. of ثَعْلَبٌ, like as أُفْعُوَانٌ and عُقْرُبَانٌ are mascs. of أَفْعَى and عَقْرَبٌ. (TA.) — دَآءُ الثَّعْلَبِ [for which Golius seems to have found in a copy of the Ḳ دَوَاءُ الثَّعْلَبِ] *A well-known disease,* [namely, *alopecia,*] (Ṣ, Ḳ,) *in consequence of which the hair falls off.* (Ṣ.) — عِنَبُ الثَّعْلَبِ [*Fox-grape:* rendered by Golius "*uvæ vulpinæ,* i. e. *solanum:*" but now applied by some to the *gooseberry:* and the solanum nigrum, or garden-nightshade, is now commonly called عِنَبُ الذِّئْبِ:] *a certain astringent, cooling plant: seven* (or, as in one copy of the Ḳ, *nine*) حَبَّات [which here seems to mean *berries*] *thereof, swallowed, are a cure for the jaundice* (اليَرَقَان), *and stop pregnancy,* (Ḳ, TA,) *like the berries of the* خِرْوَع [or *castor-oil-plant*], *for the year,* or, *as some say, absolutely.* (TA.) = *A hole,* or *aperture,* (جُحْر,) *whence rain-water flows.* (TA.) [And particularly,] The *outlet, hole,* or *aperture,* (مَخْرَج, Ṣ and Mṣb, or جُحْر, Ḳ, or ثَقْب, TA,) *whence the rain-water flows from the place where dates are dried.* (Ṣ, Mṣb, Ḳ, TA.) And The *place whence the water flows forth* (L, Ḳ) *from,* (L, TA,) or *to,* (Ḳ, [probably a mistake,]) *a watering-trough* or *tank.* (L, Ḳ.) = The *upper extremity of a spear-shaft that enters into the head thereof.* (Ṣ, Ḳ.) — The *lowest part of a palm-shoot when it is cut from* [*the root of*] *the mother-tree:* or the *lowest part of a* [*shoot such as is termed*] رَاكُوب, *on the trunk of a palm-tree.* (AA, Ḳ.)

ثَعْلَبَةٌ: see ثَعْلَبٌ. = Also The *os coccygis,* or *tail-bone;* syn. عُصْعُص. (Ḳ.) — And The *podex,* or the *anus;* syn. اِسْتٌ. (Ḳ.)

ثُعْلُبَانٌ: see ثَعْلَبٌ, in three places.

ثَعْلَبِيَّةٌ *A running of the horse like the running of the dog.* (Ḳ.)

ثُعَالَةُ: see ثَعْلَبٌ, and see art. ثعل.

أَرْضٌ مُثَعْلِبَةٌ *A land having* ثَعَالِب [or *foxes*]: (Ṣ:) or, *having many thereof;* as also أَرْضٌ مَثْعَلَةٌ; (Ḳ;) which is from ثُعَالَةُ; or it may be from ثَعْلَبٌ, like مَعْقَرَةٌ applied to "a land having many عَقَارِب [or scorpions]." (Ṣ, L.)

ثغر

1. ثَغَرَهُ, (T, A, Ḳ,) aor. ـُ, (Ḳ,) inf. n. ثَغْرٌ, (T,) *He broke it;* (T, A;) namely, a part of a wall; (A;) *he demolished it:* this is [said to be] the primary signification: *he demolished it,* or *pulled it down;* namely, a wall: (T:) and *he broke it* (namely, anything, [as a wall and a vessel, &c.,] A) *so as to make a gap in it,* or *a hollow in its edge.* (A, Ḳ.) — Also, (IAṭr, Ṣ, Mṣb, Ḳ,) aor. as above, (Mṣb, Ḳ,) *He broke his* ثَغْر [or *front teeth*], (Ṣ, Mṣb, Ḳ,) or *his teeth.* (IAṭr, and TA as from the Ḳ.) And ثُغِرَ, in the pass. form, inf. n. ثُغُورٌ, *He* (a boy) *had his* ثَغْر [or *front teeth*] *broken.* (Mṣb.) — ثَغَرْتُ سِنَّهُ *I pulled out his tooth.* (El-Hujeymee, TA.) And ثُغِرَ *He* (a man) *had a tooth,* or *teeth, pulled out.* (Aṣ, TA.) — Also ثُغِرَ, (AZ, Ṣ, Mgh, Mṣb, Ḳ,) inf. n. ثَغْرٌ, (AZ, Mṣb,) *He* (a boy) *shed his central milk-teeth,* (AZ, Ṣ, Mgh, Ḳ,) or *his* ثغر [or *front teeth*]: (AZ, Mṣb:) or ▾ أَثْغَرَ has this latter meaning, (A, Ḳ,) or ▾ اِثَّغَرَ; (Aṣ, TA;) and ثَغِرَ, (Ḳ,) or ▾ اِتَّغَرَ, (Sh, TA,) or ▾ اِثَّغَرَ, (Mṣb,) signifies *he shed his teeth:* (Sh, Mṣb, Ḳ:) ثُغِرَ is said to have this last signification in the Kifáyet el-Mutaḥaffiḍh; and ▾ اثّغر and ▾ اتّغر are there said to have the contr. signification, explained below [see 8]. (Mṣb.) — ثُغِرَ also signifies *He had his mouth bruised;* and so ▾ أُثْغِرَ. (Ḳ.) = ثَغَرَ الثُّلْمَةَ, aor. ـَ, *He stopped up,* or *obstructed, the gap,* or *breach:* thus the verb bears two contr. significations. (Ḳ.) And ثَغَرْنَاهُمْ *We stopped up,* or *obstructed, against them the gaps,* or *passes of the mountain;* (Ṣ, TA;) *we stopped up,* or *obstructed, against them the place of exit, so that they knew not what way to take.* (A.)

4: see 1, in two places: — and 8 also, in two places.

8. اِثَّغَرَ (AZ, Sh, Ṣ, Mgh, Mṣb, Ḳ) and اِتَّغَرَ (AZ, Mgh, Mṣb) and اِدَّغَرَ, (Ḳ,) originally اِثْتَغَرَ, (AZ, Ṣ, Ḳ,) *He* (a boy) *bred his central milk-teeth,* (Ṣ,) or *his* ثغر [or *front teeth*]; (Sh,* Mṣb, Ḳ;) as also ▾ أَثْغَرَ: (Ḳ:) or *he bred his teeth after the former ones had fallen out:* (AZ, Mgh:) and ▾ أَثْغَرَ, inf. n. إِثْغَارٌ, of the measure of أَكْرَمَ, inf. n. إِكْرَامٌ, *he grew his* ثغر [or *front teeth*] *after the former ones had fallen out:* by some, اثّغر and اتّغر are used specially in relation to a beast: the Benoo-Kiláb thus used the former; not in relation to a boy. (Mṣb.) — See also 1, in five places.

ثَغْرٌ The *front teeth;* (Ṣ, A, Ḳ;) syn. مَبْسِمٌ; (Mṣb;) described by a poet as *eight in number, four upper and four lower:* (TA:) afterwards applied to the *central incisors:* (Mṣb:) or *all the teeth* (TA) *while they remain in their places of growth,* (Ḳ, TA,) *before they fall out:* (TA:) or the *teeth,* (Ḳ, TA,) *all of them, whether in their places of growth or not:* (TA:) or the *mouth:* (Ḳ:) pl. ثُغُورٌ. (TA.) [Hence, ضَحِكَ ثُغْرُهُ *He laughed so as to show his front teeth,* or *his teeth.*] — *Any gap, opening, interstice,* or *open intervening space,* (M, Ḳ,) in a mountain, or in the bottom of a valley, or in a road along which people pass; (TA;) as also ▾ ثُغْرَةٌ: (A,* TA:) or the latter signifies *a gap,* or *breach,* in a wall &c.; the *hollow* of the broken edge of a vessel &c.; and its pl. is ثُغَرٌ. (Ṣ.) You say, هٰذِهِ مَدِينَةٌ فِيهَا ثُغْرٌ ▾ *This is a city in which are gaps,* or *breaches.* (Ṣ.) — †*A frontier-way of access to a country,* [in the CḲ, فُرُوح is erroneously put for فُرُوج, the word occurring in its place in MSS. of the Ḳ and in the Ṣ,] *such as is a place of fear;* (Ṣ, Ḳ;) as also ▾ ثُغْرُورٌ: (Ḳ:) the *part of a country from which the invasion of the enemy is feared;* so that it is like a gap in a wall, from which one fears the invasion of the robber: (Mṣb:) *a place from*, or *through, which one fears the enemy's coming, in a mountain or fortress:* (T, TA:) the *frontier of a hostile country:* (Ḳ:) *a place that is a boundary between the countries of the Muslims and the unbelievers:* (IAth, TA:) pl. ثُغُورٌ. (Mṣb.) You say, فُلَانٌ يَسُدُّ الثَّغْرَ ‡ [*Such a one stops up*, or *obstructs, the frontier-access of the country* by his bravery]. (A.) — See also ثُغْرَةٌ, in two places. — أَمْسَوْا ثُغُورًا ‡ *They became dispersed*, or *scattered*, (JK, A, Ḳ,) *and lost*, or *in a state of perdition:* (A, Ḳ:) sing. ثَغْرٌ. (JK, Ḳ.)

ثُغْرَةٌ; pl. ثُغَرٌ: see ثَغْرٌ, in two places. — Also The *pit of the uppermost part of the breast*, or *chest, between the two collar-bones;* (Ṣ, M, Ḳ;) the *pit in the middle of the* نَحْر: pl. as above: (Mṣb:) in a camel, the *pit which is the stabbing-place:* and in a horse, [the *part*] *above the* جُؤْجُؤ, (Ḳ,) which is the *prominent portion of the* نَحْر, *between the upper parts of the* فَهْدَتَانِ [or *two portions of flesh on the right and left of the breast*]. (TA.) — *A tract*, or *quarter, of the earth*, or *of land;* (JK, Ḳ;) as also ↓ ثَغْرٌ. (TA.) You say, مَا بِتِلْكَ الثُّغْرَةِ مِثْلُهُ *There is not, in that tract*, or *quarter, of the earth, his*, or *its, like*. (TA.) — *A plain, level*, or *even, road;* (Ḳ;) as also ↓ ثَغْرٌ: (TA:) or *any road that people tread*, or *pass along, with ease;* because they furrow its surface: (T, TA:) pl. as above. (A.) [Hence,] ثُغَرُ المَسْجِدِ *The ways leading to the mosque:* or ثُغْرَةُ المَسْجِدِ means *the upper part of the mosque* [app. *next to the ḳibleh*]. (TA.) And هُوَ يَخْتَرِقُ ثُغَرَ المَجْدِ ‡ [*He travels*] *the ways of glory*. (A.)

ثُغْرُورٌ: see ثَغْرٌ.

ثَاغِرَةٌ The *root*, or *lower part, of a tooth:* pl. ثَوَاغِرُ. (JK.)

مَثْغَرٌ The *place through which a tooth passes*, in the head [or gum]. (TA.)

مُثْغَرٌ: see what follows.

مَثْغُورٌ *Having his* ثَغْر [or *front teeth*], (A,) or *his teeth*, (IAạr, TA,) *broken*. (IAạr, A, TA.) — *Having his mouth bruised;* as also ↓ مُثْغَرٌ. (TA.) — A boy (AZ, Ṣ) *shedding his central milk-teeth*, (AZ, Ṣ, Ḳ,) or *his* ثَغْر [or *front teeth*]. (AZ, A, Mṣb.)

ثغم

4. اثغم *It* (a valley) *produced the kind of plant called* ثَغَام: (Ḳ:) or *abounded therewith*. (A, TA.) — And ‡ *It* (the head) *became like the* ثَغَامَة *in whiteness*. (Ḳ, TA.)

ثَغَامٌ *A kind of plant*, (Ṣ, Mṣb, Ḳ, TA,) *generally* (Mṣb) *found in the mountains*, (Ṣ, Mṣb,) *having a green stem*, (TA,) *which becomes white when it dries*, (Ṣ, Mṣb, TA,) *and to which hoariness is likened;* (Ṣ, Mṣb; [Golius, app. misled by a false reading in a copy of the Ṣ, says "simile anetho;"]) *it has a thick* [*head*, or *blossom, such as is called*] سَنَمَة, *and* [*it is said that*] *it does not grow save upon a black mountain-top, and is found in Nejd and Tihámeh:* (TA:) A'Obeyd says that it is *a kind of plant*, (TA,) IF, that it is *a tree*, (Mṣb,) *with a white blossom and fruit*, (Mṣb, TA,) *to which hoariness is likened:* (TA:) it is *called in Persian* درمنه; (Ḳ; [written in different copies of that work دِرْمَنْه and دَرْمَنْه and دَرْمَنَه; the last of which is said in the TA to be the right reading; a word said to mean *wormwood*, and *hyssop;* or, accord. to Meninski, as mentioned by Freytag, *zedoary;* but this last is called in Persian زُرُنْبَا, with which word درمنه may have been confounded;]) or درمنه اسپيد, (Ṣ,) or دَرْمَنَه إِسْپِيد, in which [SM thinks] the former word is a contraction of دَرْ مِيَانَه; the two together meaning "in the middle white:" (TA:) the n. un. is with ة: (Ṣ, Ḳ:) and ↓ أَثْغِمَآءُ is a quasi-pl. n.; (Ḳ;) as though the ء were a substitute for the ة of أَثْغِمَة. (TA.)

ثَاغِمٌ A colour *white like the* ثَغَام: (Ḳ:) in the L, a head *wholly white*. (TA.)

أَثْغِمَآءُ: see ثَغَامٌ.

ثغو

1. ثَغَتْ, aor. ـُ, (Ṣ, Mgh, Ḳ,) inf. n. ثُغَآءٌ, (Ṣ, [in a copy of the Mgh, ثُغَاةٌ,]) *She*, or *it, bleated*, or *cried*, (Ṣ, Mgh, Ḳ,) [*on the occasion of bringing forth*, and *on other occasions;*] said of a sheep or goat [&c.]. (Ṣ, Mgh, Ḳ, TA.)

4. اثغى *He made* a sheep or goat [&c.] *to utter the cry termed* ثُغَآء. (Ḳ.) = أَتَيْتُهُ فَمَا أَثْغَى *I came to him and he gave not anything:* (Ḳ:) or فَمَا أَثْغَى وَمَا أَرْغَى *and he gave not a sheep or goat, &c., that uttered the cry termed* ثُغَآء, *nor a camel that uttered the cry termed* رُغَآء. (TA.)

ثَغْوَةٌ *A single cry of the kind termed* ثُغَآء. (TA.)

ثُغَآءٌ The *bleating*, or *crying*, or *cry*, (Ṣ, Ḳ,) of the sheep and goat and the like, (Ṣ,) or of the sheep or goat, and gazelle, &c., *on the occasion of bringing forth*, (M, Ḳ,) and *on other occasions;* (M;) as also ↓ ثَاغِيَةٌ, like رَاغِيَةٌ in relation to camels, and صَاهِلَةٌ in relation to horses. (TA.) = Also, (Ḳ,) thus we find in the copies of the Ḳ, but correctly ↓ ثُغَايَةٌ, as in the Tekmileh [and in the JK], (TA,) The *fissure in the lip of the sheep* or *goat*. (Ḳ.)

ثُغَايَةٌ: see what next precedes.

ثَاغٍ [part. n. of ثَغَى: and hence, —] *A sheep* or *goat* [&c.]; (TA;) as also [its fem.] ثَاغِيَةٌ. (Ṣ, Ḳ, TA.) You say, مَا لَهُ ثَاغٍ وَلَا رَاغٍ (TA) and مَا لَهُ ثَاغِيَةٌ وَلَا رَاغِيَةٌ (Ṣ, TA) *He has not a sheep or goat, nor a camel:* (Ṣ, TA:) or مَا لَهُ رَاغِيَةٌ وَلَا ثَاغِيَةٌ *he has not a she-camel nor a sheep or goat*. (Ḥar p. 333.) And مَا بِالدَّارِ ثَاغٍ وَلَا رَاغٍ †*There is not in the house any one*. (Ṣ, TA.)

ثَاغِيَةٌ fem. of ثَاغٍ [q. v.]. — See also ثُغَآءٌ.

ثفأ

ثُفَّآءٌ, (T, Jm, Ṣ, M, Ḳ,) of the measure فُعَّالٌ, (Ṣ,) or ثُفَآءٌ, (Mgh, Mṣb,) of the measure of غُرَابٌ, (Mṣb,) [a coll. gen. n.,] *i. q.* خَرْدَلٌ [i. e. *Mustard*]; (Ṣ, M, Ḳ;) in the dial. of the people of El-Ghowr: (M:) or خَرْدَلٌ *worked together*, or *mixed up*, or *compounded*, (مُعَالَج,) *with* صِبَاغ [i. e. *sauce*, or *fluid seasoning*]: (M, Mgh:) or *what is called* حُرْفٌ (Ṣ, M, Ḳ, TA) *in the dial. of the people of El-Ghowr*, (TA,) or, (M,) which is the same thing, (TA,) *what is called* حَبُّ الرَّشَادِ (M, Mgh, Mṣb, TA) *in the dial of the people of El-'Irák*, (TA,) *which is eaten in case of necessity:* (Mṣb: [see art. رشد:]) n. un. with ة: (Ṣ, M, Ḳ:) the ء may be original, or it may be substituted for و or ى: (M:) Ṣgh says, in the O, that he thinks the latter to be the case. (TA.) It is said in a trad., مَا ذَا فِى الأَمَرَّيْنِ مِنَ الشِّفَآءِ الصَّبِرِ وَالثُّفَّآءِ [*What remedy is there in the two most bitter things, aloes and the* ثُفَّآء?]. (T, Mgh: but in the latter, the last word is without teshdeed to the ف.)

ثفر

1: and 2: see 4.

4. اثفرهُ *He bound, tied*, or *fastened, upon him a* ثَفَر [or *crupper*]; (Ṣ, M, A, Mṣb, Ḳ;) namely, a beast, a horse, an ass, or a camel: (Ṣ,* M,* TA, &c.:) or *he made for him* (namely, a camel or an ass &c., TA) *a* ثَفَر [or *crupper*]. (M, Ḳ.) [Hence,] أَثْفَرْتُهُ بَيْعَةَ سُوْءٍ ‡ [app. *I imposed upon him a bad sale so that he could not rid himself of it;* lit.] *I stuck a bad sale to his backside*. (A, Ḳ.) — ‡ *He drove him*, or *urged him on, from behind;* (A, Ḳ;) as also ↓ ثفّرهُ, inf. n. تَثْفِيرٌ; (Ḳ;) in some copies of the Ḳ, ↓ ثَفَرَهُ, aor. ـِ. (TA.) — اثفرت *She* (a goat) *showed*, or *gave evidence of, pregnancy*, or *bringing forth*. (Ḳ: in the CḲ, بَيَّنَتِ الوِلَادَ: in MS. copies of the Ḳ, and in the TA, الوِلَادَةَ.)

10. استثفر ‡ *He* (a man, M) *put* [*a part of*] *his* إِزَار [or *waist-wrapper*] *between his thighs, twisted together;* (M, Ḳ;) *he* (a wrestler) *turned back the extremity of his garment* [*between his thighs*] *and stuck it in the part where it was bound round his waist:* (A:) or استثفر بِثَوْبِهِ, (Ṣ, Mṣb,) or بِإِزَارِهِ, (T, Mgh,) or استثفر إِزَارَهُ, (Mgh,) *he* (a man) *turned back the extremity of his garment between his legs to the part where it was bound round his waist;* (Ṣ;) or *he* (a wrestler, T, Mgh) *bound his garment*, (IF, Mṣb,) or *his* ازار, (T, Mgh,) *round the lower part of his body*, (IF, Mgh, Mṣb,) or *round his thighs*, (T,) *and then turned back its extremity between his legs, and stuck it in the part where it was bound round his waist, behind*. (T, IF, Mgh, Mṣb.) — استثفرت, said of a menstruous woman, signifies the like; (Mṣb;) ‡ *i. q.* تَلَجَّمَتْ; (A, Mṣb;) *She closed her vulva with a broad piece of rag*, or *stuffed it with some cotton, and fastened the* [or *each*] *extremity of the bandage to a thing tied round her waist*. (T, L.) — And استثفر, (M,) or استثفر بِذَنَبِهِ, (Ṣ, A, Mṣb, Ḳ,) said of a dog, ‡ *He put his tail between his thighs*, (Ṣ, M, A,* Mṣb, Ḳ,) *making it to cleave to his belly*. (M, Ḳ.)

ثَفْرٌ (Ṣ, M, Mṣb, Ḳ) and ↓ ثُفْرٌ (M, Ḳ) The *vulva*

of an animal of prey, (Aṣ, T, Ṣ, M, Mṣb, Ḳ,) and of any creature that has claws, or talons: (Ṣ, Mṣb, Ḳ:) or the *vagina* thereof: (M, Ḳ:) and metaphorically used in relation to other animals: (Mṣb:) thus applied to that of a cow, (Ṣ, M, TA,) and of a mare, and of a ewe, and of a woman: or applied to that of a cow it is proper, not tropical. (M, TA.) — Also, accord. to AA and others, The *anus*. (Mz 44th نوع.) — See also ثَفَرٌ.

ثُفْرٌ: see ثَفَرٌ.

ثَفَرٌ, (Ṣ, M, A, Mṣb, Ḳ,) and sometimes ↓ ثَفْرٌ, (Ḳ,) The [*crupper*, or] *strap*, or *thong, at the hinder part of the saddle;* (M, Ḳ;) the *appendage of the saddle that is put beneath the tail* (Mgh) of a beast, (Ṣ, A, Mgh, Mṣb,) of a horse, an ass, or a camel: (T, TA:) *its two ends are bound to the* دَفَّتَانِ: (IDrd in his book on the Saddle and Bridle, p. 4:) pl. أَثْفَارٌ. (Mṣb.)

مِثْفَرٌ: see what follows.

مِثْفَارٌ A beast *that throws its saddle backwards.* (Ṣ, M, A, Ḳ.) — ‡ *A catamite;* syn. مَأْبُونٌ; (Ḳ;) الَّذِى يُؤْتَى; (M;) as also ↓ مِثْفَرٌ. (M, Ḳ.)

ثفرق

ثُفْرُوقٌ The قِمَع [or *base*] of a date: (Ṣ, Ḳ:) or the قمع of a full-grown unripe date; i. e., the *round portion of its covering, surrounding the stalk, and adhering to the upper part* of the date: (Mgh:) or the *part* (El-'Adebbes, A 'Obeyd, Ṣ, Ḳ) of the date (El-'Adebbes, A 'Obeyd, Ṣ) *to which the* قمع *adheres:* (El-'Adebbes, A 'Obeyd, Ṣ, Ḳ:) or, accord. to Lth, the *connecting medium* (علاقة) *between the stone* of the date *and the* قمع; and AZ says the like: (TA: [see فَرْضٌ as signifying a sort of dates of 'Omán:]) or *a raceme of which the dates have been eaten*, or *of which all the dates have been stripped off except one or two or three:* (ISh, TA:) pl. ثَفَارِيقُ; (Ṣ, Ḳ;) explained by Ks as meaning the أَقْمَاع of full-grown unripe dates. (Ṣ.) تُفْرُوقٌ is a dial. var. thereof. (TA in art. تفرق.) The pl. also signifies The *bases* (أَقْمَاع) of grapes: (JK:) or the ثُفْرُوق of a grape is *what adheres to the raceme;* and *a closed perforation therein.* (Mgh.) — [Hence,] مَا لَهُ ثُفْرُوقٌ † *He possesses not anything.* (JK, Ibn-'Abbád, Ḳ.)

ثفل

1. [ثَفَلَ, accord. to Golius, as on the authority of J, quasi سَفَلَ, *i. q.* رَسَبَ, i. e. *It subsided;* said of any sediment: but I do not find this in the Ṣ, nor in any other lexicon.] — ثَفَلَ الرَّحَى, (Ḳ,) aor. ِ, inf. n. ثَفْلٌ; (TA;) or ↓ ثَفَّلَهَا; (so in a copy of the M;) *He placed a* ثفال [q. v.] *beneath the hand-mill.* (M, Ḳ.) — ثَفَلَهُ, (Lth, T, Ḳ,) aor. ِ, (TA,) inf. n. ثَفْلٌ, (T, M,) *He left it, or cast it away as a thing of no account,* or *neglected it,* (تَرَكَهُ, Lth, T, M,) or *he scattered it, strewed it,* or *dispersed it,* (نَثَرَهُ, Ḳ,) *all of it,* (Lth, T, TA,) *at once.* (Lth, T, M, Ḳ.)

2. ثَفَّلَ عَنِ اللَّبَنِ بِالطَّعَامِ, inf. n. تَثْفِيلٌ, *He ate wheat,* or *other food, with the milk.* (Ibn-'Abbád, Ḳ.) — See also 1.

3. [ثافل probably signifies † *He ate* ثُفْل, i. e. *grain,* &c.; as Golius has assumed from the explanation, in the Ṣ and Ḳ, of the act. part. n., which see below: or ثافلهُ *he ate* ثُفْل *with him.*] — Accord. to Ibn-'Abbád, (TA,) ثافلهُ is syn. with ثَافَنَهُ, q. v. (Ḳ, TA.)

4. اثفل *It* (wine, or beverage,) *had in it* ثُفْل [meaning *a sediment,* or *dregs*]. (Zj, Ḳ.)

5. تثفّلهُ ‡ *It* (a radical, or hereditary, evil quality) *withheld him from generous actions.* (Ibn-'Abbád, Ḳ, TA.) — ‡ *He overcame him,* or *subdued him,* [as though] *putting him beneath him like the* ثِفَال. (TA.)

ثُفْلٌ The *sediment,* or *settlings,* of anything; (Ṣ;) the *dregs; lees;* or *thick,* or *turbid, portion that sinks to the bottom* of a thing, (T, M, Mṣb, Ḳ,) *beneath the clear portion;* (T, Mṣb;) as, for instance, of water, and of broth, (TA,) and of medicine, (T, TA,) and the like, and of a cooking-pot, [i. e. of its contents,] (T,) &c.; (TA;) as also ↓ ثَافِلٌ. (IDrd, M, Ḳ.) — ‡ *Grain,* (T, Ṣ, M, Ḳ, TA,) and *whatever is eaten of flesh-meat* or *bread* or *dates;* and particularly *when people are in want of milk:* (T:) or *flour;* and *what is not drunk,* as *bread,* and *the like:* (TA:) or the *refuse,* or *worse sort, of* طَعَام [i. e. *wheat,* or *other food*]. (Ḥam p. 768.) You say, شَرِبَ المَآءَ عَلَى غَيْرِ ثُفْلٍ ‡ [*He drank water,* or *the water, not upon,* i. e. *not having eaten, grain,* or *flesh-meat,* &c.]. (A in art. بحت.) — See also ثِفَالٌ.

ثَفْلٌ: see ثِفَالٌ.

ثَفِلٌ ‡ One *who eats* ثُفْل. (Ḳ. [It seems to be there indicated that the latter word is to be understood in this case in the former of the senses assigned to it above; but it is not so.]) One says, لَيْسَ الثَّفِلُ كَالْمَحْضِ, i. e. ‡ *He who eats* ثُفْل [or *grain,* &c.,] *is not like him who drinks pure milk.* (TA.) And ↓ هُمْ مُثَافِلُونَ ‡ *They are eating* ثُفْل, i. e. *grain,* (T, Ṣ, M, Ḳ, TA,) or *flesh-meat,* or *bread,* or *dates,* (T,) [&c.,] being in want of milk; (T, Ṣ;) the hardest of the means of subsistence (T, Ṣ, M) to the Bedawee. (T, Ṣ.)

ثُفْلَةٌ, (T,) or ثُفَلَةٌ, (TA,) † *Somewhat remaining* (T) of dates, in a sack: on the authority of a person of the tribe of Suleym. (T, TA.)

ثَفَالٌ *Slow;* (Ṣ, M, Mgh, Ḳ;) applied to a camel (T, Ṣ, M, Mgh, Ḳ) &c.; as also ↓ ثَفِلٌ; (Ḳ;) and ثُفَالٌ: (Ḳ in art. ثقل:) one *that will not rise and go save with reluctance:* (T:) the first thus written with fet-ḥ [to the ث] in the generality of books; but in the Tekmileh [of the 'Eyn] ↓ ثِفَالٌ, and there said to be applied to a beast and to a man. (Mgh.)

ثُفَالٌ: see the paragraph next following.

ثِفَالٌ The *thing by which the mill is preserved from the ground;* as also ↓ ثُفْلٌ: (M, Ḳ:) it is *a skin that is spread beneath the hand-mill to preserve the flour from the dust;* (T;) *a skin,* (Ṣ, Mṣb,) or *the like, that is put beneath the mill,* (Mṣb,) [i. e.,] *which is spread, and whereon is placed the mill, which is turned with the hand,* (Ṣ,) *in order that the flour may fall upon it.* (Ṣ, Mṣb.) When the ثفال has another thing to preserve it from the ground, this latter is called the وِقَاض. (M.) Zuheyr says, (T, Ṣ, Ḳ,) describing war, (T,)

فَتَعْرُكُكُمْ عَرْكَ الرَّحَى بِثِفَالِهَا

(T, Ṣ, Ḳ,*) meaning [*And it frets you as frets the mill*] *when it is with its* ثفال: for they do not place a ثفال beneath the mill except when grinding. (Ḳ.) — Also, (sometimes, Ṣ,) The *nether,* or *lower, mill-stone;* (Ṣ, Ḳ;) and so ↓ ثُفَالٌ. (Ḳ.) — And *A ewer;* syn. إِبْرِيقٌ: (IAạr, T, M, Ḳ:) occurring in a trad. in which mention is made of washing the hand therewith. (T, M.) — See also ثَفَالٌ.

ثَافِلٌ: see ثُفْلٌ. — Hence, as some say, metonymically, (M,) *Dung; ordure;* syn. رَجِيعٌ. (M, Ḳ.)

ثَفِلٌ: see مُثَافِلٌ.

ثفن

1. ثَفِنَتْ يَدُهُ, (Ṣ, M, A, Ḳ,) aor. َ, (Ṣ, Ḳ,) inf. n. ثَفَنٌ, (Ṣ, M,) ‡ *His hand was,* or *became, rough,* or *callous,* [as though resembling a ثَفِنَة of a camel,] (Ṣ, M, A, Ḳ,) *and blistered,* (A,) *from work.* (M.) — ثَفَنَتْهُ, (Ṣ, Ḳ,*) aor. ِ, inf. n. ثَفْنٌ, (Ṣ,) *She* (a camel) *struck him with her* ثَفِنَات [pl. of ثَفِنَة, q. v.]. (Ṣ, Ḳ.*) — And ثَفَنَهُ, (T, M, Ḳ,) aor. as above, (Ḳ,) and so the inf. n., (T, M,) *He impelled, pushed, thrust,* or *drove, him;* or *pushed, thrust,* or *drove, him away,* or *back:* (T, M, Ḳ:) and *struck,* or *beat, him.* (M.) — Also, (T, M, Ḳ,) aor. ِ (M, Ḳ) and ُ, (M,) inf. n. ثُفُونٌ, (T, M,) *He followed him:* (M, Ḳ:) or *he came to him from behind him:* (T, Ḳ:) or you say, جَآءَ يَثْفِنُ as meaning *he came closely pursuing a thing, having almost overtaken,* or *reached, it:* and يَثْفِنُهُمْ, and مَرَّ يَثْفِنُهُمْ, *he went along,* or *away, following them.* (M.) — And ثَفِنَ الشَّىْءَ, aor. َ, inf. n. ثَفَنٌ, *He kept, clave, clung,* or *held fast, to the thing.* (M.) — And ثَفَنَ الرَّجُلَ *He associated with the man in such a manner that nothing of his case was hidden from him.* (T.) [See also 3.]

3. ثافنهُ, (T, Ṣ, Ḳ,) inf. n. مُثَافَنَةٌ, (T,) *He sat with him:* (Ṣ, Ḳ:) said to be derived from ثَفِنَة: as though meaning *he made the* ثَفِنَة [or *lower portion of the fore part*] *of his knee to cleave to the* ثَفِنَة *of the knee of the other:* (Ṣ:) or *he sat with him, knee to knee,* or *each sitting upon his knees, fighting with him.* (T.) — *He kept, clave,* or *clung, to him,* (T, Ḳ,) *speaking to him.* (T.) [See also 1.] — *He consulted with him in order to know what was in his mind;* and *kept, clave,* or *clung, to him, that he might know his inward state or case,* or *his opinion,* or *his mind.* (M.) [See 1, last signification.] — ثافنهُ عَلَى الشَّىْءِ *He aided,* or *assisted, him to do the thing.* (Ṣ, M.)

4. اثفن يَدَهُ *It* (work) *rendered his hand rough,* or *callous.* (Ṣ, Ḳ.) [See 1, first signification.]

ثَفْنٌ *Weight:* or *a weight:* syn. ثِقْلٌ. (T.)

ثَفَنٌ *A disease in the* ثَفِنَة [q. v.]. (Ḳ.)

ثُفْنُ مَزَادَةٍ *The sewed sides of a leathern water-bag.* (Ṣ.)

ثَفِنَةٌ [The *callosity,* or *callous protuberance, upon*] *the knee; and what touches the ground,* [*in the act of lying down,*] *of* [*the callosity upon the breast called*] *the* كِرْكِرَة *and the* سَعْدَانَة, [two words having the same meaning, for the latter of which the Ḳ erroneously substitutes the pl. form,] *and of* [*each of the stifle-joints,* i. e.,] *the roots,* or *lower parts, of the thighs;* of the camel: (M, Ḳ:*) pl. ثَفِنٌ and ثِفَانٌ (M, Ḳ) and ثَفِنَاتٌ: (T, Ṣ, M:) the ثَفِنَات of the camel are the *parts that fall upon the ground when the animal lies down, and that become rough,* or *callous, such as the two knees, &c.;* (Ṣ;) the *parts that are next the ground when the camel lies down, one of them being the* كِرْكِرَة, *with which they are five in number* [as explained above]: or, as some say, the ثَفِنَة is [only *the stifle-joint,* i. e.,] the *joint between the thigh and the* سَاق [or *leg* properly so called], *internally,* [meaning *anteriorly,*] and [the *knee,* i. e.,] the *joint between the shank and the arm:* (T:) or, accord. to some, *any part that is next the ground, of any quadruped, when he lies down like the camel and like the sheep.* (M.) — Hence, (TA,) [The *stifle-joint,* i. e.,] the *joint between each thigh and leg, internally,* [meaning *anteriorly,*] of a horse. (M, Ḳ.) — Hence also, (TA,) The *knee of a man:* or [so accord. to the M, but in the Ḳ "and,"] the *place of union of the shank and thigh:* (M, Ḳ:) [or the *lower portion of the fore part of the knee, which becomes callous in consequence of much kneeling:* see 3, first sentence. Hence,] 'Abd-Allah Ibn-Wahb Er-Rásibee was surnamed ذُو الثَّفِنَاتِ (Ṣ, M, Ḳ*) from his much praying, (M,) because long prostration produced an [indurating] effect upon his ثفنات: (Ṣ, Ḳ:) and 'Alee Ibn-El-Ḥoseyn Ibn-'Alee, (Ḳ, TA,) known by the appellation of Zeyn-el-'Ábideen, (TA,) was [likewise] so surnamed, (Ḳ, TA,) because those parts of him upon which he prostrated himself were like the ثفنة of the camel in consequence of his much praying: (TA:) so too was 'Alee Ibn-Abd-Allah Ibn-El-'Abbás. (A, Ḳ.) — الثَّفِنَةُ مِنَ الجُلَّةِ, (Ḳ, [in some of the copies of the Ḳ الحُلَّة, which, as is said in the TA, is a mistake,]) or ثَفِنَتَا الجُلَّةِ, (AḤn, M,) *The two edges of the lower part of the* جُلَّة, (AḤn, M, Ḳ,) [meaning,] *of the dates* [*contained in the receptacle thus called;* app. because the dates in the edges become more dry and hard than the main portion]. (AḤn, M.) ═ Also *A number,* and *a company, of men.* (M, Ḳ.) ═ And [as fem. of ثَفِنٌ, which is perhaps unused,] *A she-camel that strikes with her* ثَفِنَات [here meaning her *stifle-joints*] *on the occasion of her being milked.* (M, Ḳ.) Her case is easier than that of the ضَجُور. (M.)

مُثْفَنٌ, (M,) or ▼مُثَفَّنٌ, (TA,) may mean *Large in the* ثَفِنَات. (M, TA.)

مُثْفِنٌ: see مُثْفَنٌ: ═ and see also مُثَافِنٌ.

مُثْفِنٌ لِخَصْمِهِ A man *who keeps, cleaves, clings,* or *holds fast, to his adversary,* or *antagonist.* (M.) [See also مُثَافِنٌ.]

مُثَفَّنٌ: see مُثَافِنٌ.

مُثْفَانٌ A camel *whose* ثَفِنَة [here meaning his *stifle-joint*] *has hit,* or *hurt, his side and his belly,* (Ḳ, TA,) *usually.* (TA.)

مُثَافِنٌ *Keeping to a person,* or *thing, constantly, perseveringly,* or *assiduously:* (T, M:) or *keeping, cleaving,* or *clinging, to another:* as also ▼مُثْفِنٌ or ▼مُثَفِّنٌ (Ḳ, accord. to different copies,) [or, probably, مُثْفِنٌ, q. v.].

ثفو

1. ثَفَاهُ, aor. ـُ: see art. ثفى.

ثفى

1. ثَفَاهُ, aor. ـِ (M, Ḳ) and ـُ, (Ḳ,) *He followed him;* (M, Ḳ;) as also أَثْفَهُ: or *he was with him, near after him,* or *at his heels, as though treading in his footsteps:* (TA:) or ثَفَوْتُ الرَّجُلَ signifies *I was with the man, near after him,* &c.: and جَآءَ يَثْفُوهُ, *he came following him.* (M.) — ثَفَيْتُ القَوْمَ *I drove away,* or *drove away and pursued closely,* or *hunted, the people,* or *company of men;* syn. طَرَدْتُ: (Ḳ:) perhaps from أَثْفَهُ, which also signifies طَرَدَهُ. (TA.)

2. ثَفَّى القِدْرَ, (Ṣ, M, Ḳ, [in the CḲ, the verb is erroneously without teshdeed,]) *He put the cooking-pot upon the* أَثَافِى [pl. of أُثْفِيَّةٌ, q. v.]; (Ṣ, M, Ḳ;*) as also ▼أَثْفَاهَا; (M, Ḳ;) and اثّفها, (Ḳ,) inf. n. تَأْثِيفٌ; (TA;) and أَثْفَهَا; (so in some copies of the Ḳ;) or آثَفَهَا, (so in other copies of the Ḳ, and in the TA,) inf. n. إِيثَافٌ: (TA:) or ▼اثفاها signifies *he put,* or *made, for it* أَثَافِى. (Ṣ.) — [Hence,] ثُفِّيَتِ المَرْأَةُ ‡ *The woman was a wife of a man who had two wives beside herself; she being the third of them;* they being likened to the أَثَافِى of the cooking-pot. (M.) And ▼أَثْفَى † *He took three women as his wives.* (Ḳ.)

4. اثفى القِدْرَ: see 2, in two places. See also Q. Q. 1 in art. اثف. — And اثفى said of a man: see 2.

5. تَثَفَّى فُلَانًا عِرْقُ سَوْءٍ. [*Evil origin,* or *a bad hereditary disposition,*] *withheld such a one* (قَصَّرَ بِهِ) [in the CḲ, erroneously, قَصُرَ بِهِ]) *from generous actions.* (Ḳ.)

ثُفَاءٌ, or ثُفَّآءٌ; n. un. with ة: see art. ثفأ.

أُثْفِيَّةٌ (Ṣ, M, Ḳ, &c.) and إِثْفِيَّةٌ (Fr, A 'Obeyd, Ḳ) The *stone* [*which is one of the three*] *whereon the cooking-pot is placed:* (M,* Ḳ:) it is *a stone like the head of a man:* (T, TA:) pl. أَثَافِىُّ and أَثَافٍ. (Ṣ, Ḳ, &c.) [See more in art. اثف.]

مُثَفًّى, and its fem. مُثَفَّاةٌ: see what next follows, in three places.

مُثَفًّى, (M,) or ▼مُثْفًى, (Ḳ, [but this is probably a mistranscription,]) † A man *of whom many wives die:* (M, Ḳ:) or *of whom three wives have died:* (M, Ḳ:*) and مُثَفَّاةٌ, (T, M,) or ▼مُثْفَاةٌ, (Ḳ, [but this, again, is probably a mistranscription,]) † a woman *of whom many husbands die:* (M, Ḳ:) or *of whom three husbands have died:* (M:) or it signifies also (Ḳ) a woman *who has buried three husbands:* (IAạr, T, Ḳ:) or مُثَفَّاةٌ signifies [like مُؤَثَّفَةٌ] † a woman *whose husband has two wives beside her; she being the third of them;* they being likened to the أَثَافِى of the cooking-pot: and ▼مُثْفِيَةٌ, † a woman *of whom three husbands have died:* and ▼مُثْفٍ, † a man *of whom three wives have died.* (Ṣ.) — مُثَفَّاةٌ, (Ṣ,) or ▼مُثْفَاةٌ, (Ḳ,) also signifies † *A brand,* or *mark made with a hot iron, upon an animal, resembling the* أَثَافِى [*of the cooking pot*]. (Ṣ, Ḳ.)

مُثْفٍ, and its fem. مُثْفِيَةٌ: see what next precedes.

قِدْرٌ مُؤَثْفَاةٌ *A cooking-pot put upon the* أَثَافِى. (Ḳ* and TA, and M in art. اثف, q. v. [In the CḲ, erroneously, مُؤَثْفَاةٌ.])

ثقب

1. ثَقَبَ, (Ṣ, A, Ḳ, &c.,) aor. ـُ, (JK, Mṣb,) inf. n. ثَقْبٌ, (JK, Ṣ, Mṣb,) *He made a hole in* a thing (JK,* Ṣ,* A, Mgh, Mṣb, Ḳ) with a مِثْقَب; (A, Mṣb;) meaning, *a hole of small size;* (Mgh;) *such as passed through; he perforated, bored,* or *pierced,* it: (A, Mgh, Ḳ:) and in like manner, ▼ثَقَّبَ, (Ḳ,) but this signifies he did so *much,* or to several, or many, things; (Ṣ, TA;) and ▼تثقّب. (Ḳ, TA.) You say, ثَقَبَ الدُّرَّ [*He bored,* or *perforated,* or *pierced, the pearls*]; (A, TA;) and الأُذُنَ [*the ear*]. (Mgh.) And ثَقَبَ القَرْحَ *He pierced,* or *punctured, the purulent pustule, in order that the fluid,* or *water, in process of excretion, might issue.* (A, TA.) And ثَقَبَ الحَلَمُ الجِلْدَ *The* [*ticks called*] حَلَم *pierced holes in the skin.* (A, TA.) And ▼ثَقَّبْنَ البَرَاقِعَ (A, Mgh) *They made holes in the face-veils,* (Mgh,) لِعُيُونِهِنَّ [*for their eyes*]: (A:) said of women. (Mgh.) — [Hence,] ثَقَبَ الكَوْكَبُ, (Ḳ, and Ḥam p. 701,) [aor. ـُ,] inf. n. ثُقُوبٌ, (JK, Ḥam,) ‡ *The star shone brightly* [*as though it pierced through the darkness:* see ثَاقِبٌ]: (Ḳ:) or *shone and glistened intensely.* (Ḥam ubi suprà.) And ثَقَبَتِ النَّارُ, (Ṣ, L, Ḳ,) aor. ـُ, (Ṣ, L,) inf. n. ثُقُوبٌ (Ṣ, L, Ḳ) and ثَقَابَةٌ, (Ṣ, L,) ‡ *The fire burned brightly; burned, blazed,* or *flamed, up.* (Ṣ, L, Ḳ.) And ثَقَبَ الزَّنْدُ, (JK, TA,) aor. ـُ, inf. n. ثُقُوبٌ, (TA,) † [*The* زند *emitted fire*]: said when the spark falls (JK, TA) upon [or from] the زند [or wooden instrument for producing fire]. (JK.) — ثَقَبَتِ الرَّائِحَةُ ‡ *The odour diffused itself, and rose.* (Ḳ, TA.) — ثَقَبَ رَأْيُهُ, (Ḳ,) inf. n. ثُقُوبٌ, (TA,) ‡ *His judgment was penetrating;* syn. نَفَذَ. (Ḳ.) — ثَقَبَتِ النَّاقَةُ, (JK, Ṣ, Ḳ,) aor. ـُ, inf. n. ثُقُوبٌ, (JK, TA,) ‡ *The she-camel had*

much milk; abounded with milk. (JK, Ṣ, Ḳ.) — ثَقُبَ, aor. ـُ, (Ḳ,) inf. n. ثَقَابَةٌ, (JK, A, Ḳ,) ‡ He (a man, JK, A) was, or became, very red; (JK, A, Ḳ;) so as to be likened to the flame of fire. (A, TA.)

2. ثقّب: see 1, in two places. — [Hence,] ‡ *He* (a bird) *soared high, piercing the region of the air next to the clouds:* (A, TA:) or *reached, or ascended to, the midst of the sky.* (TA.) — ثَقَّبَهُ الشَّيْبُ, (JK, A, Ḳ,) inf. n. تَثْقِيبٌ; (JK, Ḳ;) and ثَقَّبَ فِيهِ; (IAạr, Ḳ;) ‡ *Hoariness appeared upon him:* (Ḳ:) or *began to appear upon him:* (A, TA:) or *became intermixed in his hair;* or *appeared and spread upon him;* or *his blackness and whiteness of hair became equal.* (A, TA.) And ثَقَّبَ الشَّيْبُ بِاللِّحْيَةِ ‡ *Hoariness commenced in the sides of the beard.* (A.) — ثقّب عُودُ العَرْفَجِ ‡ *The stalk of the* عرفج [q. v.], *the plant being rained upon, became soft:* (Ṣ:) or *the sap ran in it, and it put forth leaves.* (JK, A.) When it has become blackish, one says of it, قَمِلَ: when it has increased a little, أَدْبَى; in which state it is fit to be eaten: and when its خُوص are perfect, أَخْوَصَ. (Ṣ.) — ثقّب, (A, Ḳ,) inf. n. تَثْقِيبٌ, (Ṣ, Ḳ,) also signifies ‡ *He made* a lamp, and a fire, *to burn, shine, glisten,* or *gleam, very brightly, as though piercing through the darkness, and dispelling it;* and so ↓ اثقب; (A, TA;) and the latter, *he kindled* a fire (TA) with tinder, (A, TA,) or camel's dung, or the like: (A:) or both signify *he made* a fire *to burn brightly; to burn, blaze,* or *flame, up;* (Ṣ, Ḳ;) and so ↓ تثقّب: (Ḳ:) or, accord. to AZ, ↓ اثقب النَّارَ, inf. n. إِثْقَابٌ, signifies *he scraped a hole for the fire, in the ground, then put upon it,* [i. e. the fire] *dung, such as is called* بَعْر, *and small pieces of fire-wood* or *similar fuel, and then buried it in the dust;* and so ↓ تثقّب النَّارَ, and ↓ تثقّب بِهَا; as also مَسَّدَ بِالنَّارِ, inf. n. تَمْسِيدٌ: and ↓ تثقّب النَّارَ signifies also *he struck fire:* and ↓ اثقب, inf. n. as above, *he made* a spark *to fall* from a زَنْد, q. v. (TA.)

4: see 2, in three places.

5: see 1, first sentence: — and see also 2, in four places: — and 7, in two places.

7. انثقب *It was,* or *became, perforated, bored,* or *pierced;* and in like manner, [but properly, as quasi-pass. of 2, signifying *it was,* or *became, perforated,* &c., *much* or *in many places,*] ↓ تثقّب. (Ḳ.) You say, ↓ تثقّب الجِلْدُ *The skin was,* or *became, pierced with holes* by the [ticks called] حَلَم. (Ṣ, A.)

ثَقْبٌ (Ṣ, A, Mgh, Mṣb, Ḳ) and ↓ ثُقْبٌ (Mṣb) and ↓ ثُقْبَةٌ (Ṣ, A, Mgh, Mṣb) *A hole, perforation,* or *bore, that penetrates,* or *passes through, a thing;* (A, Mgh, Ḳ;) accord. to Mṭr, (Mṣb,) only *such as is small;* (Mgh, Mṣb;) such as is large being termed نَقْبٌ, with ن: (Mgh:) or *a hole that is not deep:* or, as some say, *a hole descending into the earth:* (Mṣb: [but this last explanation is not of general application:]) said to be opposed to شَقٌّ: (TA:) pl. [of mult.] (of the first word, Ṣ, Mṣb, Ḳ) ثُقُوبٌ (Ṣ, A, Mṣb, Ḳ) and [of pauc.] أَثْقُبٌ (Ḳ) and (of ثُقْبَةٌ, Ṣ, Mṣb) ثُقَبٌ (Ṣ, A, Mṣb) and ثُقْبٌ. (Ṣ [in which this last is said to be with damm, meaning, to the ق, not (as some have supposed) to the ث only,] and A.)

ثُقْبٌ: / ثُقْبَةٌ: } see ثَقْبٌ.

ثِقَابٌ: see what next follows.

ثَقُوبٌ ‡ *Fuel;* or *a thing with which fire is kindled, or made to burn brightly, or to burn, blaze, or flame, up;* (JK, Ṣ, A;) as also ↓ ثِقَابٌ; (Ḳ;) *consisting of small sticks,* (Ṣ, TA,) or *dung, such as is called* بَعْر; (A, TA;) and *tinder.* (JK, A, TA.)

ثَقِيبٌ ‡ A man *very red;* (JK, A, Ḳ;) *so as to be likened to the flame of fire:* (A:) fem. with ة. (JK, A.) — See also ثَاقِبٌ, in three places.

ثَاقِبٌ ‡ A star, and a lamp, and fire, (A,) or a flame of fire, or a shooting star, (Ṣ,) *shining brightly:* (Ṣ:) or *shining, glistening,* or *gleaming, very brightly, as though piercing through the darkness, and dispelling it.* (A, TA.) النَّجْمُ الثَّاقِبُ [in the Ḳur lxxxvi. 3] means ‡ *The star,* or *asterism, brightly shining;* (Fr, Bḍ, L;) as though it pierced through the darkness, or the celestial spheres, by its light: (Bḍ:) or *the star,* or *asterism, that is high, above the others:* or *the planet Saturn:* (L, Ḳ:) or *the Pleiades,* or *any star* or *asterism, brightly shining;* because it pierces through the darkness by its light. (Jel.) — † A زَنْد (q. v.) *that emits fire, when struck.* (TA.) — ‡ Applied to حَسَب [i. e. nobility, or grounds of pretension to respect or honour], it means *Famous and exalted:* (Lth, JK, A,* TA:) or *bright; brilliant.* (Aṣ, TA.) — And hence, ‡ applied to knowledge [as meaning *Penetrating,* or *brilliant*]. (Aṣ, TA.) You say also ثَاقِبُ العِلْمِ, for ثَاقِبٌ فِي العِلْمِ, meaning ‡ *Brilliant* [or *penetrating*] *in knowledge;* as also ↓ مِثْقَبٌ: (TA:) which latter signifies also ‡ *learned, and sagacious,* or *intelligent;* (TA;) *penetrating in judgment:* (Ḳ:) and ثَاقِبُ الرَّأْيِ ‡ a man *of sound and penetrating judgment, sagacity,* or *intelligence.* (A, TA.) — أَتَتْنِى عَنْهُمْ عَيْنٌ ثَاقِبَةٌ, (JK,) or عَنْكَ, (A, TA,) ‡ *There came to me, from them,* or *from thee, certain,* or *sure, news* or *information.* (JK, A, TA.) — نَاقَةٌ ثَاقِبٌ ‡ *A she-camel having much milk; abounding with milk;* (AZ, JK, Ṣ, A, Ḳ;) as also ↓ ثَقِيبٌ; (AZ, JK, Ḳ;) and ↓ ثَقِيبَةٌ: (TA, voce نَقِيبَةٌ:) pl. (of the former, A) نُوقٌ ثُقَّبٌ, (so in a copy of the A,) or ثُقُبٌ. (TA.) One says also, إِنَّهَا لَثَقِيبٌ مِنَ الإِبِلِ, meaning *Verily she is one that vies with the other camels abounding with milk, and surpasses them in abundance thereof.* (TA.)

أَثْقَبُ [*More, and most, piercing,* or *penetrating:* &c.] — [Hence,] † أَثْقَبُ حَطَبٍ نَارًا [*The most excellent of fire-wood in yielding fire*]. (TA in art. مرخ.)

أُثْقُوبٌ † A man (TA) *who enters,* or *penetrates, much into affairs.* (Ḳ, TA.)

مَثْقَبٌ † *A great road,* (Ḳ, TA,) *which people* [*as it were*] *pierce,* or *perforate, by their tread.* (TA.) [See also what next follows.]

مِثْقَبٌ *An instrument with which one perforates, bores,* or *pierces; a drill,* or *the like:* (Ṣ, A, Mṣb, Ḳ:) pl. مَثَاقِبُ. (A.) — And hence, ‡ *A road passing through a mountain;* as though perforating it: (A, TA:) or *a road passing through a stony and rugged tract:* (L, TA:) and, with the article ال, particularly applied to the road of El-'Irák, (A, Ḳ,) from El-Koofeh (Ḳ) to Mekkeh: (A, Ḳ:) or a road between El-Yemámeh and El-Koofeh: (L, TA:) and a road between Syria and El-Koofeh: (Ḳ:) or, accord. to El-Bekree and the Maráṣid, a road called after a man named مثقب. (MF, TA.) Hence the saying, هُوَ طَلَّاعُ الثَّنَايَا, i. q. طَلَّاعُ المَثَاقِبِ [q. v. voce ثَنِيَّةٌ]. (A, TA.) — See also ثَاقِبٌ.

دُرٌّ مُثَقَّبٌ (Ṣ, A) i. q. ↓ مَثْقُوبٌ [i. e. *Bored, perforated,* or *pierced, pearls*]: (Ṣ, TA:) the pl. of the latter is مَثَاقِيبُ. (TA.) — إِهَابٌ مُثَقَّبٌ *A hide pierced with holes* by [the ticks called] حَلَم. (A, TA.) — حَنَّ كَمَا حَنَّ اليَرَاعُ المُثَقَّبُ [*He,* or *it, uttered plaintive sounds like the reed pierced with holes;* i. e., the musical reed]. (A, TA.)

مَثْقُوبٌ: see مُثَقَّبٌ.

ثقف

1. ثَقُفَ, aor. ـُ, inf. n. ثَقَافَةٌ; and ثَقِفَ, aor. ـَ, inf. n. ثَقَفٌ (Ṣ, Ḳ) and ثِقْفٌ; (Ḳ;) *He* (a man, Ṣ) *became skilled,* or *skilful; and light, active, quick,* or *sharp; and intelligent,* or *sagacious.* (Ṣ, Ḳ, TA.) — ثَقُفَ, aor. ـُ, inf. n. ثَقَافَةٌ, is also said of vinegar (خَلٌّ), meaning *It was,* or *became, very acid;* and so ثَقِفَ. (TA. [But I suspect that this may have been taken from a MṢ. in which خَلٌّ has been erroneously put for رَجُلٌ. In the JK, I find رَجُلٌ ثَقِيفٌ وَقَدْ ثَقُفَ ثَقَافَةً].) — ثَقِفْتُ الشَّىْءَ, aor. of the latter ـُ: see 3. — ثَقِفَهُ, aor. ـَ, inf. n. ثَقَافَةٌ and ثُقُوفَةٌ, *I was,* or *became, skilled in the thing.* (Ḥam p. 772.) — And ثَقْفٌ signifies The *learning* a thing *quickly:* [its verb is ثَقِفَ or ثَقُفَ:] you say, ثَقِفْتُ العِلْمَ فِي أَوْحَى مُدَّةٍ, and الصِّنَاعَةَ, *I acquired knowledge,* or *the science,* and *the art,* or *handicraft, quickly* [*in the shortest period*]: (TA:) and ثَقِفْتُ الحَدِيثَ *I understood the narration,* or *tradition,* &c., *quickly.* (Mṣb.) — ثَقِفَهُ, aor. ـَ, (Ṣ, Mṣb, Ḳ,) inf. n. ثَقْفٌ, (Ṣ, Ḳ,*) or ثَقَفٌ, (Mṣb,) [but the former is better known,] primarily signifies, *He perceived it,* or *attained it, by knowledge,* or *by deed:* (Bḍ ii. 187:) or *he perceived it,* or *attained it, by his sight, by expertness in vision:* and hence, (Er-Rághib, TA,) ‡ *he reached him,* or *overtook him,* (IF, Mṣb, Ḳ, and Er-Rághib,) in war, or fight: (Mṣb:) or (Ḳ) † *he found him:* (Ṣ, Ḳ, and Bḍ in ii. 187 &c.:) or † *he found him in the way of taking and overcoming:* (Ksh in ii. 187:) or (Ḳ) † *he took him,* or it, (Lth, Mṣb, Ḳ,) namely, a thing: (Mṣb:) or (Ḳ) by implication, (Bḍ in ii. 187,) † *he gained the victory*, or *mastery, over him; overcame him;* (IDrd, Mṣb, Ḳ, and Bḍ ubi suprà;) or *got possession of him.* (IDrd, Mṣb, Ḳ.) It is said in the Ḳur [ii. 187 and iv. 93], وَٱقْتُلُوهُمْ حَيْثُ ثَقِفْتُمُوهُمْ *And slay ye them wherever ye find them:* (Ksh, Bḍ, Jel, TA:) or *wherever ye take them,* or *overcome them,* or *overtake them.* (TA.) And exs. occur also in the Ḳur [iii. 108 and] viii. 59 and xxxiii. 61 [and lx. 2]. (TA.) For another ex., see 4, below. — ثَقِفَهُ also signifies *He thrust him,* or *pierced him,* [with a spear or the like,] namely, a man. (Ḥam p. 772.) — See also 2.

2. ثقّفهُ, (Ṣ, Mṣb, Ḳ,) inf. n. تَثْقِيفٌ, (Ṣ, Mgh, Ḳ, KL,) *He straightened it,* or *made it even,* (Ṣ, Mgh, Ḳ, KL,) or *straightened what was crooked thereof;* (Mṣb;) namely, a spear, (Ṣ, KL,) [and a bow, (see ثِقَافٌ,)] or a crooked thing; *with the* ثِقَاف: (Mgh:) [and so ✝ ثَقَفَهُ, accord. to an explanation of the inf. n. ثَقْفٌ in the KL.] تَثْقِيفُ السَّهْمِ عَلَى القَوْسِ, as meaning *The directing the arrow upon the bow straightly towards the object aimed at,* is not approved. (Mgh.) — Hence, (Mgh,) ‡ *He disciplined him,* or *educated him well, and amended him,* or *improved him.* (Mgh, TA.) You say, لَوْلَا تَثْقِيفُكَ وَتَوْقِيفُكَ مَا كُنْتُ شَيْئًا ‡ [*But for thy disciplining,* or *good educating, and amending,* or *improving, and thy teaching, I had not been anything*]. (TA.) — You say also, of vinegar, يُثَقِّفُ الطَّعَامَ, i. e. *It makes food acid.* (Ḥar p. 227.)

3. ثَاقَفَهُ ✝ فَثَقَفَهُ, (Ḳ,) inf. n. of the former مُثَاقَفَةٌ and ثِقَافٌ, (TA,) and aor. of the latter ـُ, (Ḳ,) *He vied with him,* or *strove to surpass him, in skill,* (Ḳ, TA,) *and intelligence,* or *sagacity, and the perceiving,* or *attaining, of a thing, and the doing thereof,* (TA,) *and he surpassed him therein.* (Ḳ, TA.) Er-Rághib says that this is metaphorical. (TA.) [Accord. to J,] المُثَاقَفَةُ is from ثَقُفَ in the first of the senses explained above. (Ṣ.) — ثِقَافٌ also signifies The *contending with another:* and particularly *in fight,* or *with the sword:* (Ḳ: [see also ثَقْفٌ, below:]) and the *using of,* or *performing with, the sword;* like ثِقَافَةٌ. (TA.) And ثاقفهُ, inf. n. مُثَاقَفَةٌ, *He played with him with the sword,* or *some other weapon.* (TA.)

4. أُثْقِفْتُهُ [*I was made to gain the mastery over him,* or *to overcome him:* or, which is virtually the same,] *he was appointed for me* [*that I might have the mastery over him*]. (Ṣgh, Ḳ.) 'Amr Dhu-l-Kelb says,

* فَإِنْ أُثْقِفْتُمُونِى فَٱقْتُلُونِى *
* وَإِنْ أَثْقَفْ ✝ فَسَوْفَ تَرَوْنَ بَالِى *

And if ye [*be made to*] *gain the mastery over me,* i. e. *if it be appointed for you to meet me* [*and overcome me*], *then slay me: but if I meet* [*you and overcome*], *then shall ye see my condition:* but some relate it thus: وَمَنْ أَثْقَفْ, meaning *but whom I meet,* of you, I will slay him: (Skr, Ṣgh, TA:) [and J gives it thus:] فَإِمَّا تَثْقَفُونِى الخ [meaning *And if ye meet me* &c.]. (Ṣ.)

5. تثقّف ‡ [*He was,* or *became, disciplined,* or *educated well, and amended,* or *improved;* quasi-pass. of 2, q. v.] You say, هَلْ تَثَقَّفْتُ إِلَّا عَلَى يَدِكَ ‡ [*Was I,* or *have I been, disciplined,* &c., *save by thy agency,* or *means?*]. (A, TA.)

6. تَثَاقَفُوا *They contended,* or *played, one with another, with swords,* or *other weapons.* (TA.)

ثَقْفٌ *Skilled,* or *skilful; and light, active, quick,* or *sharp; and intelligent,* or *sagacious;* as also ✝ ثَقِفٌ and ✝ ثَقُفٌ (Ṣ, Ḳ) and ✝ ثَقِيفٌ and ✝ ثِقِّيفٌ: (Ḳ:) or ✝ ثَقِيفٌ signifies *quick in understanding a narration:* (Mṣb:) and ✝ ثَقَافٌ, applied to a woman, *intelligent,* or *sagacious.* (Ḳ.) You say also ✝ رَجُلٌ ثَقْفٌ لَقْفٌ and ثَقِفٌ لَقِفٌ, meaning *A man who is a relater, a poet, an archer or a caster of the spear* &c.: (Lth, JK, TA:) or *light, active, quick,* or *sharp, and skilful:* (Ṣ and Ḳ in art. لقف:) or *quick in understanding what is said to him; and in taking what is thrown to him:* or *skilful in his art,* or *handicraft:* (TA in that art.:) or *a man who keeps, preserves,* or *guards, and manages,* or *orders, well, that which he possesses:* (ISk, TA:) and Lḥ adds ✝ ثَقِيفٌ لَقِيفٌ: and Ibn-'Abbád, ✝ ثِقِّيفٌ لِقِّيفٌ. (TA.) — A man *quick in taking,* or *seizing, his opponents,* or *adversaries.* (Ksh ii. 187.) ═ ثَقْفٌ, or (as it is written in one place in the TA) ✝ ثَقَفٌ, also signifies *Contention:* and particularly *in fight,* or *with the sword:* like ثِقَافٌ [inf. n. of 3, q. v.]. (TA.)

ثَقِفٌ : } see ثَقْفٌ.
ثَقُفٌ : }

ثَقَافٌ : see ثَقْفٌ, in two places.

ثُقَّافٌ : see ثَقْفٌ.

ثِقَافٌ *Skill,* and *intelligence,* or *sagacity;* as also ✝ ثُقُوفَةٌ. (TA.) ═ Also *An instrument with which spears are straightened,* (Ṣ, Ḳ, TA,) *and bows also,* (TA,) *and* [*other*] *crooked things;* (JK, Mgh, TA;) *made of iron:* (JK, TA:) or *a strong piece of wood, a cubit in length, having at its extremity a hole large enough to admit the bow,* [*or the spear*], *which is inserted into it, and pinched and pressed in the part that requires this to be done until it becomes in the state that is desired; but this is not done to bows nor to spears until they have been greased, and prepared with fire,* or *exposed thereto so as to have become altered in colour:* (AḤn, TA:) the pl. [of pauc.] is أَثْقِفَةٌ and [of mult.] ثُقُفٌ. (JK, TA.) — [Also The *handle* of a shield of the kind called حَجَفَةٌ: see إِخَادَةٌ.]

ثَقِيفٌ : see ثَقْفٌ, in three places. — Also *Very acid;* applied to vinegar; (Ḳ;) and so ✝ ثِقِّيفٌ, (Ṣ, Ḳ,) like حِرِّيفٌ applied to the onion. (Ṣ.) And أَبُو ثَقِيفٍ ‡ *Vinegar* [itself]; so named because it makes food acid. (Ḥar p. 227.) — Also, and ✝ مَثْقُوفٌ, A thing *skilled in.* (Ḥam p. 772.) — And both these words, A man *thrust* or *pierced* [with a spear or the like]. (Ḥam ibid.)

ثَقَافَةٌ The *use of,* or *performance with, the sword;* like ثِقَافٌ [inf. n. of 3, q. v.]. (TA.) You say, هُوَ حَسَنُ الثَّقَافَةِ بِالسَّيْفِ [*He is good in respect of performance with the sword*]. (TA.)

ثُقُوفَةٌ : see ثِقَافٌ.

ثِقِّيفٌ : see ثَقْفٌ, in two places: — and see ثَقِيفٌ.

أَثْقَفُ *More,* and *most, skilled,* or *skilful,* [in a general sense, and particularly] *in contending,* or *playing, with the sword,* or *other weapon.* (TA.)

مُثَقَّفٌ A spear *straightened,* or *made even.* (TA.) [Accord. to Freytag, it is poetically used as signifying *A spear* itself; and so with ة.]

مَثْقُوفٌ : see ثَقِيفٌ.

ثقل

1. ثَقُلَ, aor. ـُ, inf. n. ثِقَلٌ (Ṣ, Mṣb, Ḳ, &c.) and ثِقْلٌ, a contraction of the former, (Mṣb,) and ثَقَالَةٌ, (Ḳ, TA, in the CḲ ثِقالة, but) like كَرَامَةٌ, (TA,) *It* (a thing, Ṣ, Mṣb) *was,* or *became, heavy, weighty,* or *ponderous.* (Ṣ, Ḳ.) [See ثِقْلٌ, below.] — See also 4. — [† *It was,* or *became, heavy, weighty,* or *preponderant, ideally.*] فَأَمَّا مَنْ ثَقُلَتْ مَوَازِينُهُ, in the Ḳur ci. 5, means † *And as to him whose good deeds shall be preponderant.* (Bḍ, Jel.) [See also Ḳur vii. 7 and xxiii. 104.] — [† *It was,* or *became, heavy,* or *weighty,* as meaning *onerous, burdensome, oppressive, afflictive, grievous,* or *troublesome.*] You say, ثَقُلَ القَوْلُ ‡ *The saying was* [*heavy,* or *weighty,* &c.; or] *unpleasant to be heard.* (TA.) And it is said in the Ḳur vii. 186, ثَقُلَتْ فِى السَّمٰوَاتِ وَالأَرْضِ † *It* (the time of the resurrection) *will be momentous,* or *formidable,* [*in the heavens and on the earth,* or] *to the inhabitants of the heavens and the earth,* (Bḍ, Jel,) *to the angels and men and genii;* app. alluding to the wisdom shown in concealing it: (Bḍ:) or it means *the knowledge thereof* [*is difficult*]: (Ibn-'Arafeh, TA:) or *it is occult,* or *hidden.* (Kt, TA.) [ثَقُلَ is also said of a word, and of a sound, meaning † *It was heavy,* or *not easy, of utterance;* or *heavy to the ear:* see 2. And of an affair, or action, meaning † *It was afflictive, grievous, troublesome,* or *difficult.* In these and similar senses, it is trans. by means of عَلَى: you say, ثَقُلَ عَلَيْهِ † *It was,* or *became, heavy, weighty, onerous,* &c., *to him.* In like manner also it is said of food, meaning † *It was,* or *became, heavy to the stomach; difficult of digestion.*] You say also, ثَقُلَ سَمْعُهُ ‡ [*His hearing was,* or *became, heavy;* or] *his hearing partially went.* (Ḳ, TA.) — ‡ *He* (a man) *was,* or *became, heavy* in sickness, or disease: [and in like manner, in his sleep:] the verb is thus, with ḍamm to the ق; though said in the Ḳ to be ثَقِلَ, like فَرِحَ, as meaning *his disease became violent;* (Fet-ḥ el-Báree, TA;) not improbably through error or inadvertence. (MF.) — [† *He was,* or *became, heavy, slow, sluggish, indolent, lazy, dull, torpid,* or *drowsy; wanting in alacrity, activity, agility, animation, spirit,* or *intelligence; stupid.*] You say, يَثْقُلُ عَنْ قَبُولِ مَا يُلْقَى إِلَيْهِ † [*He is averse from receiving,* or *accepting,* or *admitting,* or *is*

slow to receive, &c., what is said to him]. (TA.) — Also, said of the عَرْفَج, and of the ثُمَام, ‡ Its shoots became luxuriant, or succulent, or sappy. (Ḳ, TA.) ═ ثَقَلَهُ, (JK, Ṣ, Ḳ,) بِيَدِهِ, (Ḳ,) aor. ُ, (TA,) inf. n. ثَقْلٌ, (Ḳ,) *He tried the weight of it,* (JK, Ṣ, Ḳ,) namely, a thing, (Ḳ,) or a sheep or goat, (Ṣ,) *by lifting it* [*with his hand*] *to see if it were heavy or light.* (Ṣ, TA.) — ثَقَلَ الشَّىْءُ الشَّىْءَ فِى الوَزْنِ, aor. and inf. n. as above, (Ṣ,) *The thing surpassed the thing in weight; outweighed it.* (PṢ.) — See also 2.

2. ثقّلهُ, inf. n. تَثْقِيلٌ, *He,* or *it, made it,* or *him,* ثَقِيل [i. e. *heavy,* properly and tropically]: (Ḳ:) تثقيل is the *contr. of* تَخْفِيفٌ; (Ṣ;) and signifies the *making heavy in weight* [&c.]; as also ثَقْلٌ [inf. n. of ▼ ثَقَلَهُ]. (KL.) — [Hence, † *He made it* (a word or a sound) *heavy,* or *not easy, of utterance;* or *heavy to the ear:* and particularly a word *by uttering hemzeh with its true,* or *proper, sound,* which is commonly termed تَحْقِيقُ الهَمْزَةِ, and opposed to تَخْفِيفُهَا; and *by making a single consonant double;* and *by making a quiescent consonant movent:* often occurring in these senses in lexicons and grammars: opposed to خَفَّفَهُ.]

4. اثقلهُ *He,* or *it,* (a load, Ṣ, or a thing, Mṣb,) [*burdened him:* or] *burdened him heavily:* (Ḳ:) or *beyond his power; overburdened him.* (JK, Mṣb, TA.*) — † In the latter sense, said also of a debt: and of sickness, or a disease: (JK:) or, said of sickness, or a disease, and of sleep, and of meanness, or sordidness, ‡*it* [*burdened him,*] *overcame him, and rendered him heavy.* (Ḳ,* TA,* TḲ.) ═ اثقلت, said of a woman, *She became gravid; her burden became heavy in her belly:* (Ṣ:) or *she had a burden,* (Akh, Ṣ, and Bḍ in vii. 189,) *by reason of the greatness of the child in her belly:* (Bḍ, Jel:) or *her pregnancy became apparent,* or *manifest;* as also ▼ ثَقُلَتْ. (Ḳ.)

6. [تثاقل عَلَى شَىْءٍ *He pressed heavily,* or *bore his weight, upon a thing:* see مُتَثَاقِلٌ.] — تثاقلوا † [*They were heavy, sluggish,* or *spiritless:*] *they did not rise and hasten to the fight when commanded to do so.* (IDrd, Ḳ.) And تثاقل إِلَى الأَرْضِ, (Ṣ and Ḳ in art. ارض, &c.,) and اِثَّاقَلَ الى الارض, the former being the original form of the verb, (Bḍ and Jel in ix. 38,) † *He was,* or *became, heavy, slow,* or *sluggish,* (Bḍ, Jel,) *averse from warring against the unbelievers,* (Jel,) *and inclining to the earth,* or *ground;* (Bḍ, Jel;) or *propending thereto.* (Bḍ.) And اِثَّاقَلَ إِلَى الدُّنْيَا † *He propended to the present world.* (TA.) And تثاقل عَنْهُ † *He was heavy,* or *sluggish, and held back from it.* (Ḳ.)

10. استثقلهُ *contr. of* اِسْتَخَفَّهُ; (Ṣ and Ḳ and TA in art. خف;) *He deemed it,* or *him,* ثَقِيل [i. e. *heavy,* properly and tropically]. (TA in that art.) — [Hence, † *He deemed it* (a word or a sound) *heavy,* or *not easy, of utterance;* or *heavy to the ear:* often occurring in this sense in lexicons and grammars.] — أُسْتُثْقِلَ نَوْمًا ‡ [*He was overcome, and rendered heavy, by sleep:* and in like manner, مَرَضًا, *by sickness* or *disease:* and لُؤْمًا, *by meanness* or *sordidness:* see its pass. part. n., below]. (JK.)

ثِقْلٌ *Weight:* or *a weight:* syn. وَزْنٌ: (Ṣ, Mṣb, KL:) pl. أَثْقَالٌ. (Ṣ.) So in the phrase أَعْطِهِ ثِقْلَهُ [*Give thou him his,* or *its, weight*]. (Ṣ, Mṣb.) See also مِثْقَالٌ. You say also, أَلْقَى عَلَيْهِ ثِقْلَهُ or ▼ ثَقَلَهُ [*He threw upon him his weight:* see مِثْقَالٌ, last sentence: and see جِرْمٌ]. (Ṣ in art. اوق &c., accord. to different copies.) — And *A load,* or *burden:* (KL:) or *a heavy load* or *burden:* pl. as above. (Ḳ.) وَتَحْمِلُ أَثْقَالَكُمْ, in the Ḳur xvi. 7, means *And they carry your loads,* or *burdens;* (Bḍ;) or *your heavy loads* or *burdens.* (TA.) — أَثْقَالٌ (as pl. of ثِقْلٌ, Ḳ, or of ▼ ثَقَلٌ, Bḍ) also signifies ‡ The *treasures,* or *buried treasures,* of the earth: and its *dead,* or *corpses.* (Ḳ, TA, and Bḍ and Jel in xcix. 2.) — Also (as pl. of ثِقْلٌ, Ḳ) ‡ *Sins.* (JK, Ḳ.) So in the saying in the Ḳur [xxix. 12], وَلَيَحْمِلُنَّ أَثْقَالَهُمْ وَأَثْقَالًا مَعَ أَثْقَالِهِمْ ‡ [*And they shall assuredly bear their sins, and sins* (of others whom they have seduced) *with their sins*]. (TA.)

ثَقَلٌ *A thing,* or *things, that a man has with him, of such things as burden him:* (Ḥam p. 295:) [and particularly] the *household-goods,* or *furniture and utensils,* (El-Fárábee, JK, Ṣ, Mgh, Mṣb, Ḳ, Ḥam ubi suprà, and Bḍ in xcix. 2,) and (accord. to El-Fárábee, Mṣb) the *household and kindred and party,* or *domestics,* or *servants,* (JK, Ṣ, Mgh, Mṣb, Ḳ, and Ḥam,) of a man, (Ḥam,) or of a traveller: (JK, Ṣ, Mgh, Mṣb, Ḳ:) [or the *travelling-apparatus and baggage and train,* of a man:] pl. أَثْقَالٌ; (JK, Ṣ, Mgh, Mṣb, Ḳ;*) with which ▼ ثَقَلَةٌ is syn., (JK, Ṣ, Ḳ,) as are also ▼ ثَقْلَةٌ and ▼ ثِقْلَةٌ and ▼ ثُقْلَةٌ and ▼ ثِقَلَةٌ; (Ḳ;) as meaning *all the household-goods* or *furniture and utensils* of persons going on a journey. (Ṣ, Ḳ.) — See also ثِقْلٌ. — † The *requisites* and *apparatus, instruments, tools,* or *the like,* of a man: (Ḥam ubi suprà:) as, for instance, ‡ the *books and writing-reeds* of the learned man: every craftsman has what is thus termed. (TA.) By the saying

• كِلَا ثَقَلَيْنَا طَامِعٌ بِغَنِيمَةٍ •

the author thereof, Iyás Eṭ-Ṭá-ee, means *Each of our two armies, the possessors of the* ثَقَلَانِ [or *apparatus,* or *weapons,* &c., *of war, is longing for spoil*]: or an army may be termed ثَقَلٌ because it is heavy in assault. (Ḥam ubi suprà.) — *Anything held in high estimation, in much request, and preserved with care.* (Ḳ, TA.) Hence the trad., إِنِّى تَارِكٌ فِيكُمُ الثَّقَلَيْنِ كِتَابَ ٱللّٰهِ وَعِتْرَتِى [*Verily I am leaving among you the two objects of high estimation and of care, the Book of God, and my kindred,* or *near kindred*]: (Ḳ:) or they are thus called because of the heaviness of acting in the manner required by them: (Th, TA:) or as being likened to the requisites and apparatus, instruments, tools, or the like, of a man. (Ḥam ubi suprà.) — Also *Eggs of the ostrich;* because he who takes them rejoices in them, and they are food. (TA.) — الثَّقَلَانِ *Mankind and the jinn* or *genii;* (Ṣ, Mṣb, Ḳ;) because, by the discrimination that they possess, they excel other animate beings. (TA.) It may also mean *The Arabs and the foreigners:* or *mankind and other animate beings.* (Ḥam ubi suprà.)

ثِقَلٌ *Heaviness; weight,* or *weightiness; ponderousness; gravity; contr. of* خِفَّةٌ: (Ṣ, Ḳ, and Er-Rághib:) and *preponderance:* in its primary acceptation, relating to corporeal objects: then, to ideal objects. (Er-Rághib, TA. [See ثَقُلَ, throughout.]) See also ثِقْلٌ. — فِى أُذُنِهِ ثِقَلٌ ‡ [*In his ear is a heaviness,* or *dulness,*] is said of him whose hearing is not good; as though he were averse from receiving, or accepting, or admitting, or slow to receive, &c., what is said to him. (TA.)

ثَقْلَةٌ: see ثَقَلٌ. — Also † *A fit of drowsiness,* or *of slumber, that overcomes one:* (JK, M, Ḳ:) and ‡ *a heaviness experienced in the chest,* (Ḳ, TA,) or *in the body,* (TA,) *from food:* as also ▼ ثَقَلَةٌ: (Ḳ, TA:) or the former, or ▼ the latter, (accord. to different copies of the Ṣ,) † *a heaviness and languor* in the body: (Ṣ:) and ▼ the latter, † *a heaviness that is experienced on the heart.* (JK.)

ثُقْلَةٌ: see ثَقَلٌ.

ثَقَلَةٌ: see ثَقَلٌ: — and see ثَقْلَةٌ, in three places.

ثِقَلَةٌ: } see ثَقَلٌ.
ثِقْلَةٌ: }

ثَقَالٌ: see ثَقِيلٌ, in two places. — Also, applied to a woman, (JK, Ṣ, Ḳ,) *Heavy;* (Ṣ;) *large in the hinder part,* or *posteriors:* (JK,* Ṣ,* Ḳ, TA:) or *heavy* (Ḳ, TA) *in an ideal sense.* (TA.)

ثُقَالٌ: see ثَقِيلٌ.

ثَقِيلٌ part. n. of ثَقُلَ; (Ṣ, Mṣb, Ḳ;) *Heavy, weighty,* or *ponderous:* (Ṣ, Ḳ, and Er-Rághib:) and *so in relation to another thing; preponderant:* primarily applied to a corporeal thing: (Er-Rághib, TA:) and ▼ ثَقَالٌ and ▼ ثُقَالٌ signify the same: (Ḳ:) pl. ثِقَالٌ and ثُقُلٌ and ثُقَلَآءُ [which last, however, seems to be applied only to rational beings, agreeably with analogy]. (Ḳ.) — [Like its verb,] it is also applied to an ideal thing. (Er-Rághib, TA.) [Thus it signifies † *Heavy,* or *weighty,* in the sense of *onerous, burdensome, oppressive, afflictive, grievous,* or *troublesome: momentous,* or *formidable: difficult: heavy,* or *not easy, of utterance;* or *heavy to the ear;* applied to a word and a sound; and particularly to a word *in which a single consonant is made double,* and to one *in which a quiescent consonant is made movent,* like ▼ مُثَقَّلٌ: *heavy to the stomach; difficult of digestion: heavy* applied to the hearing: see the verb.] قَوْلًا ثَقِيلًا, in the Ḳur [lxxiii. 5], means †*A heavy,* or *weighty, saying.* (TA.) النُّونُ الثَّقِيلَةُ means † [*The heavy-sounding* ن; as in يَفْعَلَنَّ &c.;] *the contr. of* الخَفِيفَةُ. (TA in art. خف.) — It is also applied to a man, (JK,) meaning ‡ [*Heavy in sickness,* or *disease;* or] *suffering a violent disease:* (Ḳ:) [and †*heavy, slow, sluggish, indolent, lazy, dull, torpid,* or *drowsy; wanting in alacrity, activity, agility, animation, spirit,* or *intelligence; stupid*:] and so is ▼ مُسْتَثْقَلٌ: (JK:) which also means, particularly, †*overcome, and rendered heavy*, by sleep (نَوْمًا), (JK,* Ḳ,* TḲ,) and by sickness or disease (مَرَضًا), and by meanness or sordidness (لُؤْمًا). (Ḳ.) ثِقَالُ النَّاسِ [expressly said in the TA to be with kesr, but in the CḲ, erroneously, ثُقَال,] and ثُقَلَآءُ النَّاسِ mean †*Those men whose company is disliked*; (Ḳ;) *whom others deem heavy*: each is pl. of ثَقِيلٌ. (TA.) One says, أَنْتَ ثَقِيلٌ عَلَى جُلَسَائِكَ †[*Thou art heavy, or dull, or unwelcome, to thy companions with whom thou sittest*]. (TA.) And (to him who is ثَقِيل, TA in art. نسم,) مَا أَنْتَ إِلَّا ثَقِيلُ الظِّلِّ بَارِدُ النَّسِيمِ †[*Thou art no other than one who casts a gloom upon others, and chills them*: lit., *heavy of shade, or shadow; cold of breeze*]. (TA.) ثَقِيلٌ, applied to a man, is mostly used in dispraise: but sometimes, in praise: (Er-Rághib, TA:) used in praise, it signifies †*Grave, staid, steady, sedate, or calm*. (Kull.) Applied to a horse, †*Slow*; (Kull;) and so ▼ ثَقَالٌ applied to a camel; (Ḳ;) a meaning also assigned to ثُقَال, with ف; (TA;) and ▼ مُثْقَلٌ, applied to a horse or the like. (JK.) اِنْفِرُوا خِفَافًا وَثِقَالًا, in the Ḳur [ix. 41], means †[*Go ye forth to fight*] *prompt and not prompt*: (Ḳatádeh, Bḍ, Jel, TA:) or *whether moving be easy to you or difficult*: (Bḍ,* TA:) or *riding and walking*: or *lightly armed and heavily armed*: or *healthy and sick*: (Bḍ:) or *strong and weak*: (Jel:) or *rich and poor*: (Jel, TA:) or *young and old*. (TA.)

ثَاقِلٌ A deenár *of full weight*; (Z;) *not deficient*: (Ṣ, Ḳ:) pl. ثَوَاقِلُ. (Ṣ, Z, Ḳ.) — أَصْبَحَ ثَاقِلًا †*He became*, or *became in the morning, heavy by reason of sickness*, or *disease*. (Aboo-Naṣr, Ḳ, TA.)

أَثْقَلُ *More* [and *most*] *heavy*. (TA.)

مُثْقَلٌ *Heavily burdened*: (TA:) or *burdened beyond his power; overburdened*. (JK, TA.) — †*Weighed down*, or *oppressed*, by sickness, or disease, (JK,) and by debt. (JK, Er-Rághib.) — See also ثَقِيلٌ.

مُثْقِلٌ, applied to a woman, *Gravid; whose burden has become heavy in her belly*: (Ṣ:) or *whose pregnancy has become apparent*, or *manifest*. (Ḳ.)

مُثَقَّلٌ: see ثَقِيلٌ. — Also †*Ill received; disapproved; not rendered an object of love to hearts*. (Ḥam p. 37.)

مُثَقَّلَةٌ *A stone of marble*; (JK;) *a piece of marble by which a carpet is made heavy*: (Ḳ:) by rule it should be with kesr to the ق. (TA.)

مِثْقَالٌ The *weight* (مِيزَان, JK, Ṣ, Ḳ, or وَزْن, Mṣb, TA, and Jel in iv. 44 and x. 62 and xxi. 48, or زِنَة, TA) of a thing, (JK, Ṣ, Mṣb, Ḳ,) *of the like* thereof (مِنْ مِثْلِهِ [but why this is added I do not see]); (Ṣ, Mṣb, Ḳ;) [i. e.] its *equal in weight*; (PṢ, and Bḍ in x. 62;) its *quantity* (مِقْدَار). (Bḍ in xxi. 48.) مَا يَعْزُبُ عَنْ رَبِّكَ مِنْ مِثْقَالِ ذَرَّةٍ, in the Ḳur x. 62, means *There is not hidden from thy Lord aught of the weight of the smallest ant*: (Jel:) or *a thing equal in weight to a small ant*; or *to the motes that are seen in a ray of the sun that enters through an aperture*. (Bḍ.) — *A thing with which one weighs*; as also ▼ ثِقْلٌ; i. e., *any of the weights of the balance*. (Er-Rághib, TA.) — *A certain weight, of which the quantity is well known*; (JK;) *a dirhem and three sevenths of a dirhem*; (Mṣb, and Ḳ in art. ملك;) i. e., the *seventh part of ten dirhems*: (Mṣb:) or [*a dirhem and a half*; so in the present day; i. e.,] *seventy-two sha'eerehs*: (El-Karmánee, TA:) or *twenty ḳeeráṭs*. (Hidáyeh, TA.) — [*A certain coin*;] i. q. دِينَارٌ, q. v.; (Mṣb in art. دنر;) *a* مِثْقَال *of gold*: pl. مَثَاقِيلُ. (Ṣ, Ḳ.) — أَلْقَى عَلَيْهِ مَثَاقِيلَهُ *He threw upon him his weight*, or *burden*; syn. مَؤُونَتَهُ [perhaps meaning *the burden of supporting him*]. (Aboo-Naṣr, Ṣ, Ḳ.) [See also ثِقْلٌ.]

مُتَثَاقِلٌ *Bearing one's weight upon a thing*: whence the saying, وَطِئَهُ وَطْأَةَ الْمُتَثَاقِلِ [*He trod upon him, or it, with the tread of him who bears his weight, or presses heavily*]. (TA.)

مُسْتَثْقَلٌ: see ثَقِيلٌ.

ثكل

1. ثَكِلَتْهُ, (Ṣ, Mgh, Mṣb,) aor. ـَ, (Mṣb,) inf. n. ثَكَلٌ, (Ṣ, Mṣb,) or ثُكْلٌ, (Mgh,) or this is a simple subst., (Mṣb,) and ثَكْلٌ, (Mgh,) [or this last is also a simple subst.,] *She* (a mother) *lost him*, or *became bereft of him*; namely, her child, (Ṣ, Mgh, Mṣb,) *by death*: (Mgh:) and ثَكِلَهُ, aor. ـَ, (Ḳ,) inf. n. ثَكَلٌ, (TA,) *he lost him*; namely, a friend, or person beloved, or a child. (Ḳ.) ثَكِلَتْكَ أُمُّكَ [lit. meaning *May thy mother be bereft of thee*] is an imprecation against him to whom it is addressed, not said with the desire of its having effect, but on an occasion of vehement love, like لَا أَبَا لَكَ, [and قَاتَلَكَ ٱللّٰهُ,] &c. (Ḥar p. 165.)

4. أَثْكَلَتْ *A state of bereavement clave to her*; (Ḳ;) namely, a woman: or *she became in a state of bereavement*. (TA.) — أَثْكَلَهَا ٱللّٰهُ وَلَدَهَا *God made her to be bereft of her child* [*by death*]. (Mṣb, Ḳ.) And أَثْكَلَهُ ٱللّٰهُ أُمَّهُ *God made him to be bereft of his mother* [*by death*]. (Ṣ.)

ثَكْلٌ: see what next follows.

ثُكْلٌ The *loss*, or the *state of being bereft, of a child* [*by death*], (Ṣ, Mṣb, Ḳ,) or *of a friend*, or *person beloved*; (Ḳ;) i. e., a *woman's loss of her child*; (Ṣ, Mṣb;) as also ▼ ثَكَلٌ [which is the inf. n. by general consent], (Ṣ, Ḳ,) and ▼ ثَكْلٌ. (TA.) It is said in a prov., الْعُقُوقُ ثُكْلُ مَنْ لَمْ يَثْكَلْ [*Undutiful treatment of a parent is* (like) *the bereavement of him who is not* (really) *bereft of his child*]. (TA.) — Also *Death*: and *a state of perdition* or *destruction*. (Ḳ.)

ثَكَلٌ: see ثُكْلٌ.

ثَكْلَانُ; fem. ثَكْلَى and ثَكْلَانَةٌ: see ثَاكِلٌ.

ثَكُولٌ: see ثَاكِلٌ. — فَلَاةٌ ثَكُولٌ ‡*A desert in which the traveller becomes lost*. (Ḳ, TA.)

ثَاكِلٌ, applied to a man, *Bereft of a child*, or *of a friend*, or *person beloved*; as also ▼ ثَكْلَانُ or ثَكْلَانٌ [with or without tenween, as is shown by the two forms of the fem. mentioned in what follows, but generally without]: (Ḳ:) and applied to a woman; (Ṣ, Mṣb, Ḳ;) and sometimes ثَاكِلَةٌ; (Mṣb;) as also ثَكْلَى (Ṣ, Mṣb, Ḳ) and ثَكْلَانَةٌ, (IAṭr, Ḳ,) which is rare, (Ḳ,) and ▼ ثَكُولٌ; (Ṣ, Ḳ;) meaning *bereft of her child* [*by death*]; (Ṣ, Mṣb;) pl. (of ثَاكِلٌ, TA, [and of ثَاكِلَةٌ,]) ثَوَاكِلُ, [and of ثَكْلَى also ثَاكِل, as is implied in the TA voce عُبْر,] and (of ثَكْلَى, TA) ثَكَالَى. (Mṣb, TA.)

إِثْكَالٌ and ▼ أُثْكُولٌ i. q. عِثْكَالٌ (Ṣ, Ḳ) and عُثْكُولٌ, i. e., The *fruit-stalk* (شِمْرَاخ) *upon which are the ripening dates*: pl. أَثَاكِلُ, [app. a contraction of أَثَاكِيلُ, like عَثَاكِيلُ,] occurring in poetry. (Ṣ.) These two words are mentioned here by J and Ṣgh, and F has followed them; but they should be mentioned among words whose first radical letter is hemzeh, for the ا is a radical, substituted for ع. (TA.)

أُثْكُولٌ: see what next precedes.

مُثْكِلٌ A woman *whose state of bereavement is constant*: (Ḳ:) or *who is in a state of bereavement*: (TA:) pl. مَثَاكِيلُ (Ḳ) [or this is pl. of مِثْكَالٌ]. Hence, نِسَآءُ الْغُزَاةِ مَثَاكِيلُ [*The wives of the warriors are constantly bereft*, or *often bereft, of their husbands*]. (TA.) — قَصِيدَةٌ مُثْكِلَةٌ ‡*An ode in which bereavement is mentioned*. (Ibn-'Abbád, Z, Ḳ.)

رُمْحُهُ لِلْوَالِدَاتِ مَثْكَلَةٌ [*His spear is a cause of bereavement to mothers*] (Ṣ, Ḳ) is a saying similar to الْوَلَدُ مَبْخَلَةٌ وَمَجْبَنَةٌ [explained in art. بخل]. (Ṣ.)

مِثْكَالٌ A woman *much*, or *often, bereft of her children*: (Mṣb, TA:) pl. مَثَاكِلُ (TA) [or مَثَاكِيلُ: see مُثْكِلٌ]. — And A she-camel *that is accustomed to lose her young by death or by slaughter or by gift*: pl. مَثَاكِيلُ. (Ḥam p. 746.)

ثل

1. ثَلَّ, (T, Ṣ, Ḳ,) aor. ـُ, inf. n. ثَلٌّ, (T,) *He put* [or *poured*] *back* the earth into a grave, and a well, after digging it: (T:) or *he poured* the earth into a well, (Ṣ, Ḳ,) &c. (Ṣ.) — Also, (Ṣ, M, Ḳ,) aor. as above, (M,) and so the inf. n., (Ṣ, M,) *He poured forth* pieces of money. (Ṣ, M, Ḳ.) — Also, (Ḳ,) aor. and inf. n. as above; (TA;) and ▼ ثَلْثَلَ; (M, Ḳ;) *He moved*, or *put in motion, with his hand*, or *he broke at one of its sides*, [app. *so as to make it pour down*, or *fall*,] a quantity of earth collected together, or a sand-heap, (M, Ḳ,) or a house: (O, TA:) or *he dug it*. (TA.) — And the former, (Ṣ, M, Ḳ,) aor. as above, (Ṣ, M,) and so the inf. n., (M, TA,) *He threw down*, or *demolished*, a house, (Ṣ, M, Ḳ,) *by digging beneath the wall, and then pushing, so that it fell in ruins*: (Ṣ, TA:) and *he demolished*, and *broke*, a thing. (M.) — [Hence,] ثَلَّ ٱللّٰهُ عَرْشَهُمْ ‡*God destroyed their dominion*:

and ثُلَّ عُرُوشُهُمْ ‡ *Their might,* or *power, departed:* (Ṣ:) or ثَلَّ ٱللّٰهُ عَرْشَهُ ‡ *God caused him to die;* or *caused his dominion,* or *his might,* or *power, to depart:* (Ḳ, TA:) and ثُلَّ عَرْشُهُ, inf. n. ثَلٌّ, ‡ *His means of support became destroyed, and ceased;* (M, A;*) or *he became abased,* or *in an abject condition;* (IDrd, M;) or, accord. to Er-Rághib, it means أُسْقِطَتْ ثُلَّةٌ مِنْهُ [perhaps *a company of men* (ثُلَّة) *was made to fall away from him*]: (TA:) El-'Otbee says that عرش here has two meanings; namely, *a throne,* and *a booth,* or *shed, constructed for shade.* (TA. See art. عرش.) You say also, ثُلَّ عَرْشُهُ and عُرْشُهُ, meaning † *He was slain:* and a poet says, of a sword, ثَلَّ عُرُوشَهُ, meaning † [*It severed*] *the base of his neck; the part where his neck was set on his back.* (IDrd, M.) — And ثَلَّ, (Aṣ, Ṣ, M, Ḳ,) aor. as above, (Aṣ, Ṣ, M,) inf. n. ثَلٌّ (Aṣ, Ṣ, M, Ḳ) and ثَلَلٌ, (Aṣ, Ṣ, Ḳ,) *He killed,* or *destroyed,* (Aṣ, Ṣ, M, Ḳ,) a man, (Aṣ, Ṣ,) or men. (M, Ḳ.) And ثَلَّ *He died,* or *perished.* (T.) — ثَلَّ البِئْرَ, (M, Ḳ,) aor. ـُ, inf. n. ثَلٌّ, (M,) *He took,* or *cast, forth the earth from the well;* (M, Ḳ;) and *the mud from the bottom of the well.* (M.) — ثَلَّ الوِعَآءَ, aor. and inf. n. as in the next preceding case, *He took what was in the receptacle;* as also ▼اِثْتَلَّهُ; the latter from Ibn-'Abbád. (TA.) == ثَلَّتِ الدَّابَّةُ, (Ṣ, Ḳ,) and ثَلَّ الحَافِرُ, (M, O,) aor. ـُ [irregularly], (Ṣ, TA,) inf. n. ثَلٌّ, (TA,) *The beast,* and *the solid-hoofed animal, dunged.* (Ṣ, M, O, Ḳ.) — And ثَلَّ *He became rich,* or *in a state of competence.* (T.)

4. اثلّ *He* (a man, Ṣ) *abounded in what is termed* ثَلَّة, (Ṣ, Ḳ,) which may mean either *wool* or *a flock of sheep* or *goats:* both these meanings are assigned to it in this case by Z. (TA.) == اثلّه *He ordered,* or *commanded, the repairing of it;* (M;) or *the repairing of what had been thrown down,* or *demolished, of it.* (IAạr, Ṣ, Ḳ.)

5. تثلّل *It* (a house) *became thrown down,* or *demolished;* (Ḳ;) as also ▼انثلّ: (TA:) or *it* (a house) *became thrown down,* or *demolished, and it fell by degrees, part after part.* (M.) And تَثَلَّلَتِ الرَّكِيَّةُ *The well became demolished.* (TA.)

7. انثلّ *It* (a thing) *poured forth,* or *became poured forth.* (TA.) — اِنْثَالُوا i. q. اِنْثَلُّوا [app. as meaning *They poured themselves forth*]. (Ḳ.) You say, انثلّوا عَلَيْهِ *They poured forth,* or *down, upon him,* or *against him.* (Z, TA in art. ثلم.) — See also 5.

8: see 1, near the end.

R. Q. 1. ثَلْثَلَ: see 1, near the beginning.

ثَلَّةٌ *The earth that is taken forth from a well:* (T, Ṣ, M, Ḳ:) and the *mud that is taken forth from the bottom of a well:* (M:) and the *space upon which is cast the earth taken forth from a well, around its mouth;* which space, when the well has been dug in a place that is not the property of any one, belongs exclusively to the owner of the well: (A 'Obeyd, T:) pl. ثُلَلٌ. (Ḳ.) — ▼ثَلَّةٌ مَثْلُولَةٌ *A grave* (تُرْبَةٌ) *filled up with earth, after it has been dug.* (T.) == *A thing that is made of clay,* or *mud,* (M,) *like a* مَنَارَة [q. v.], (Ḳ,) *in the desert, for the sake of its shade.* (M, Ḳ. [Erroneously written by Golius and Freytag مَثَلَّةٌ, and compared to مَظَلَّةٌ.]) == *Wool,* (T, Ṣ, M, Ḳ,) *alone:* (M, Ḳ:) or *a portion of wool collected together:* (Er-Rághib, TA:) and *wool and goats' hair* (شَعَر) *and camels' hair* (وَبَر) *together;* (Aboo-Yoosuf, T, Ṣ, Ḳ;) but not the second of these alone, nor the third alone: (Aboo-Yoosuf, T, Ṣ:) or it signifies *camels' hair* (وبر) also: (T:) or *wool and* شعر *and* وبر *together;* but none of these alone. (M.) كِسَآءٌ جَيِّدُ الثَّلَّةِ is said to mean *A* كساء *of good wool:* (Ṣ, M:) and حَبْلُ ثَلَّةٍ, *a rope of wool.* (Ṣ.) It is said in a prov., لَا تَعْدَمُ صَنَاعٌ ثَلَّةً [*A clever woman is not without wool* to spin or weave when she has nothing else to do]: applied to a skilful man. (TA.) And you say, عِنْدَ فُلَانٍ ثَلَّةٌ كَثِيرَةٌ, meaning *Such a one has much wool and goats' hair* (شعر) *and camels' hair* (وبر). (Aboo-Yoosuf, Ṣ.) [Hence,] فُلَانٌ كَثِيرُ الثَّلَّةِ [sometimes] means ‡ *Such a one has much hair on his body.* (TA.) — *A flock of sheep or goats,* (T, M, Ḳ,) *whether many or few:* (M:) or *many thereof:* (M, Ḳ:) or specially *a flock of sheep:* or *sheep, absolutely:* (M:) or *a numerous flock of sheep:* (ISk, T, Ṣ, Ḳ:) and *numerous sheep and goats together:* many goats are not thus called; but are called حَيْلَةٌ: (Aboo-Yoosuf, Ṣ, M:) pl. ثُلَلٌ, (Ṣ, M, Ḳ,) which is extr., (M,) and ثِلَالٌ. (M, Ḳ.) — *Many pieces of money;* or *much money;* (M, Ḳ;) as also ▼ثُلَّةٌ. (Ibn-'Abbád, Ḳ.) == In relation to the times of camels' coming to water, (فِى مَوَارِدِ الإِبِلِ, TA, [in the copies of the Ḳ, فى is omitted, and مَوَارِدُ is put for مَوَارِدِ,]) *The interval of two days,* or *keeping from water during two days, between two drinkings.* (Ḳ, TA. [The word to which this signification is assigned is erroneously written by Golius and Freytag مَثَلَّة; and explained as meaning "Locus ubi aquantur cameli postquam per biduum non biberint."])

ثُلَّةٌ *A party of men;* (T;) *a company of men:* (Ṣ, M, Ḳ:) or *a numerous company.* (Bḍ in lvii. 13.) You say, فُلَانٌ لَا يُفَرِّقُ بَيْنَ الثَّلَّةِ وَالثُّلَّةِ [*Such a one will not distinguish*] *between a flock of sheep or goats and a company of men.* (Z, TA.) — See also ثَلَّةٌ.

ثُلَّةٌ *Death;* or *a state of perdition* or *destruction;* (Ḳ;) and so ▼ثَلَلٌ; (Ṣ, M, Ḳ;) which latter is also an inf. n. of ثَلَّ signifying "he killed," or "destroyed:" (Aṣ, Ṣ, Ḳ:) pl. of the former ثُلَلٌ. (Ḳ.)

ثُلَّى ‡ *Might, power,* or *elevated condition, perishing,* or *passing away.* (Ḳ, TA.)

ثَلَلٌ: see ثُلَّةٌ.

مُثِلٌّ A man (Ṣ, M) *abounding in what is termed* ثَلَّة. (Ṣ, M, Ḳ. [See 4. أَثَلَّ, mentioned by Golius with this word, as syn. therewith, and as from the Ṣ and Ḳ, is not in either of those Lexicons.])

مُهْرٌ مِثَلٌّ [*A colt that dungs much*]. (M. [The meaning is there indicated, but not expressed.])

مُثَلِّلٌ *Collecting wealth,* (Ibn-'Abbád, Ḳ,) *and disposing it well,* or *putting it into a good state* or *condition.* (Ibn-'Abbád, TA.)

مَثْلُولٌ A house *thrown down,* or *demolished.* (TA. [See 1.]) — See also ثَلَّةٌ, second sentence.

ثلب

1. ثَلَبَهُ, (Ṣ, M, A, Mṣb, Ḳ,) aor. ـِ, (M, Mṣb, Ḳ,) inf. n. ثَلْبٌ (T, Ṣ, M, A, Mṣb) and مَثْلَبٌ, (T,) *He blamed him; reprehended him; found fault with him; imputed to him,* or *charged him with, a fault, vice,* or *the like:* (M, A, Mṣb, Ḳ:) or *he charged him plainly,* or *openly, with a fault, vice,* or *the like;* (Ṣ;) *spoke against him;* (TA;) *censured him, reproached him, detracted from his reputation,* or *impugned his character:* (Ṣ, Mṣb:) or *he blamed him severely;* and *assailed him with his tongue; as is done in punishings and the like.* (Lth, T.) — ثَلَبَهُ, (M, Ḳ,) inf. n. ثَلْبٌ, (M,) also signifies *He drove him* (a man, M) *away; expelled him;* or *put him at a distance, away,* or *far away.* (M, Mṣb, Ḳ.) — And *He turned it* (a thing, M) *upside down,* or *over,* or *inside out;* or *changed its manner of being,* or *state.* (M, Ḳ.) — And *I. q.* ثَلَمَهُ: (M, Ḳ:) formed from the latter by substitution of ب for م. (M.) == ثَلِبَ, (M,) inf. n. ثَلَبٌ, (M, Ḳ,) *It* (one's skin, M, or a garment, TḲ) *was,* or *became, dirty,* or *filthy:* (M, Ḳ:) and *it* (a thing, TḲ) *was,* or *became, contracted.* (Ḳ, TḲ.) — Also *It was,* or *became, broken in the edge* or *middle,* [like ثَلِمَ,] and *split,* or *cracked.* (KL.)

2. ثلّب, (Aṣ, Ṣ, M,) inf. n. تَثْلِيبٌ, (Ṣ,) *He* (a camel) *became such as is termed* ثِلْب. (Aṣ, Ṣ, M.)

ثِلْبٌ *Blamed; reprehended; found fault with; charged with a fault, vice,* or *the like;* as also ▼ثَلِبٌ; applied to a man. (M, Ḳ.) — Also A camel *extremely old,* or *old and weak,* (M, A,) *and having his teeth much broken:* (M:) or a camel *whose canine teeth are broken* (Ṣ, Ḳ) *much* (Ḳ) *by reason of extreme old age,* or *age and weakness, and the hair of whose tail has fallen off by degrees:* (Ṣ, Ḳ:) fem. with ة; (Ṣ, M, Ḳ;) but some disallow this, and say that the female is termed نَابٌ: (M:) pl. [of pauc.] أَثْلَابٌ (M, Ḳ) and [of mult.] ثِلَبَةٌ. (Ṣ, Ḳ.) — Hence, (A,) ‡ A man *extremely old,* or *old and weak,* (A, TA,) *whose teeth are much broken:* (TA:) or an *aged* man; a man *advanced in years:* (IAạr, M, Ḳ:) [said to be] of the dial. of Hudheyl; but IAạr mentions it without assigning it to the dial. of any particular tribe of the Arabs. (M.) — Also A camel *that does not impregnate.* (M, Ḳ.*) — See also what next follows.

ثَلِبٌ: see ثِلْبٌ. — Also, applied to a spear, (Ṣ, M, A, Ḳ, but in a copy of the A written ▼ثَلِبٌ,) *Much notched,* or *broken in the edges* [*of the head*]: (Ṣ, M, Ḳ:) or *weak*, or *weak and soft*. (A.) You say ثِلْبٌ عَلَى ثِلْبٍ وَبِيَدِهِ ثِلْبٌ [*An extremely old, or old and weak, man, whose teeth are much broken, upon a camel in the like condition, and having in his hand a spear that is much notched, or weak, or weak and soft*]. (A, TA.)

ثَالِبَةُ الشَّوَى A woman *having cracked*, or *chapped, feet*: (Ṣ, Ḳ:) from ثِلْبٌ as an epithet applied to a spear. (Ṣ.)

أَثْلَبٌ and إِثْلَبٌ, (Fr, T, Ṣ, M, Ḳ,) the former of which is the more common, (Fr, T,) *Dust*, or *earth*; and *stones*: (Fr, T, M, Ḳ:) or *small fragments*, or *particles, of stones*, (Ṣ, Ḳ,) and *of dust* or *earth*: (Ṣ:) or *stone* (A 'Obeyd, Sh, T) in the dial. of El-Ḥijáz: and *dust*, or *earth*, in the dial. of Temeem: (T:) and El-Hejeree says, الأَثْلَمُ is like الأَثْلَبُ; but [ISd says,] whether it be formed by substitution or be a dial. var., I know not. (M, TA.) One says, بِفِيهِ الأَثْلَبُ and الإِثْلَبُ *In his mouth are*, or *be, dust*, or *earth, and stones*; (Fr, T;) or, *particles of stones and of dust* or *earth*. (Ṣ.) Lḥ mentions the phrase الأَثْلَبَ لَكَ or الإِثْلَبَ [*Dust, or earth, and stones, be thy lot*]; and التُّرَابَ: and he says that the noun is thus put in the accus. case, as though the phrase were an imprecation [of the ordinary kind]: he means, as though the noun were an inf. n. used in an imprecation; though it is a simple subst. (M.) لِلْعَاهِرِ الإِثْلَبُ or الأَثْلَبُ, occurring in a trad., means *For the adulterer*, or *fornicator, stone* (الحَجَرُ) [but see this word, and see also art. عهر]: or *dust*, or *earth*: or *small stones*. (TA.)

مِثْلَبٌ *Accustomed to blame, reprehend*, or *find fault*. (A, TA.)

مَثْلَبَةٌ (Ṣ, M, Mṣb, Ḳ) and مَثْلُبَةٌ (M, Ḳ) *A fault, vice*, or *the like*: (Ṣ, M,* Ḳ:*) or [properly] *a cause of* [*blame* or] *reviling*: (Mṣb:) pl. مَثَالِبُ. (Ṣ, A, Mṣb.) You say, مَا عَرَفْتُ فِى فُلَانٍ مَثْلَبَةً [*I have not known in such a one a fault*, or *vice*, or *cause of blame*, &c.]. (A, TA.)

ثلث

1. ثَلَثَ القَوْمَ, aor. ُ, (Ṣ, M, Mṣb, Ḳ,) inf. n. ثَلْثٌ, (TA,) *He took the third of the goods*, or *property, of the people*, or *company of men*. (Ṣ, M, Mṣb, Ḳ.) And ثُلِثَتِ التَّرِكَةُ *The property left at death had a third of it taken*. (A.) And ثَلَثَ, aor. ِ, [but in this case it seems that it should be ُ, as above,] is also said to signify *He slew a third*. (L.) — ثَلَثَ القَوْمَ, (T, Ṣ, Ḳ,) or الاِثْنَيْنِ, (Fr, T, M,) or الرَّجُلَيْنِ, (Mṣb,) aor. ِ, (Ṣ, M, Mṣb, Ḳ,) [thus distinguished from the verb in the first sense explained above,] inf. n. ثَلْثٌ, (TA,) signifies *He was*, or *became, the third of the people*, (T, Ṣ, Ḳ,) or *a third to the two*, (Fr, T, M,) or *to the two men*: (Mṣb:) or *he made them, with himself, three*: (T, Ṣ, Ḳ:) and similar to this are the other verbs of number, to ten [inclusive], except that you say, أَرْبَعُهُمْ and أَسْبَعُهُمْ and أَتْسَعُهُمْ, with fet-ḥ, because of the ع. (Ṣ.) A poet says, (IAṣr, Ṣ,) namely, Abd-Allah Ibn-Ez-Zubeyr El-Asadee, satirizing the tribe of Ṭeiyi, (IB, TA,)

فَإِنْ تَثْلِثُوا نَرْبَعْ وَإِنْ يَكُ خَامِسٌ
يَكُنْ سَادِسٌ حَتَّى يُبِيرَكُمُ القَتْلُ

[*And if ye make up the number of three, we will make up the number of four; and if there be a fifth of you, there shall be a sixth of us; so that slaughter shall destroy you*]: (IAṣr, Ṣ, IB:) he means, if ye become three, we will become four: or *if ye slay three*. (IB, TA.) — Also; (Ṣ, M, TA;) in the Ḳ, "or," but this is wrong; (MF, TA;) ثَلَثَ القَوْمَ signifies *He made the people, with himself, thirty*; (A 'Obeyd, Ṣ, M, Ḳ;) they being twenty-nine: and in like manner one uses the other verbs of number, to a hundred [exclusive]. (A 'Obeyd, Ṣ.) And ثَلَثَ also signifies *He made* twelve *to be thirteen*. (T.) — ثَلَثَ الأَرْضَ *He turned over the ground three times for sowing*, or *cultivating*. (A, TA.) — See also 2. — ثَلَثَ, (T, M, L, TA,) [as though intrans., an objective complement being app. understood,] or ▼ ثَلَّثَ, (Ḳ, [but the former is app. the right reading, unless both be correct,]) said of a horse, *He came* [*third in the race*; i. e., *next*] *after that which is called* المُصَلِّى: (T, M, L, Ḳ: [in the CḲ, الذى, after الفَرَسُ, should be omitted:]) then you say رَبَعَ: then, خَمَسَ. (T, M, L.) And in like manner it is said of a man [as meaning *He came third*]. (T.) — لَا يَثْنِى وَلَا يَثْلِثُ, (so in a copy of the M in art. ثنى, but in the present art. in the same copy written لا يثنى ولا يثلث,) or ▼ لَا يُثَنِّى وَلَا يُثَلِّثُ, (so in a copy of the A, [in the CḲ in art. ثنى, and in Freytag's Arab. Prov. ii. 545, لَا يُثَنِّى وَلَا يُثَلِّثُ,]) or ▼ لَا يُثْنِى وَلَا يُثْلِثُ, (so in a copy of the Ḳ in art. ثنى, [in the TA, in the present art. and in art. ثنى, without any syll. signs,]) said of an old man, meaning *He cannot rise*, (M, A, TA,) when he desires to do so, a first time, nor can he (M, TA) *the second time, nor the third*. (M, A, TA.)

2. ثَلَّثَهُ *He made it three*; or *called it three*: (Esh-Sheybánee, and Ḳ in art. وحد:) تَثْلِيثٌ signifies the *making* [a thing] *three* [*by addition* or *multiplication* or *division*]; as also ▼ ثَلْثٌ [inf. n. of ثَلَثَ]: and the *calling* [it] *three*. (KL.) — [Hence, ثَلَّثَ, inf. n. تَثْلِيثٌ, *He asserted the doctrine of the Trinity*.] — [Hence also,] فُلَانٌ يُثَنِّى وَلَا يُثَلِّثُ *Such a one counts two Khaleefehs*, namely, the two Sheykhs [Aboo-Bekr and 'Omar], *and* [*does not count three*, i. e.,] rejects the other [that succeeded them]: and فُلَانٌ يُثَلِّثُ وَلَا يُرَبِّعُ *Such a one counts three Khaleefehs*, [namely, those mentioned above and 'Othmán,] *and* [*does not count a fourth*, i. e.,] rejects ['Alee,] the fourth. (A, TA.) — لَا يُثَنِّى وَلَا يُثَلِّثُ: see 1. — ثَلَّثَ لِامْرَأَتِهِ, or عِنْدَهَا, *He remained three nights with his wife*: and in like manner the verb is used in relation to any saying or action. (TA voce سَبَّعَ.) — ثَلَّثَ بِنَاقَتِهِ *He tied*, or *bound, three of the teats of his she-camel with the* صِرَار (Ṣ.) — ثَلَّثَتْ said of a she-camel, and of any female: see 4. — ثَلَّثَ said of a horse in a race: see 1. — ثَلَّثَ البُسْرُ, (M, Ḳ,) inf. n. as above, (Ḳ,) *The full-grown unripe dates became, to the extent of a third part of them, ripe*, or *in the state in which they are termed* رُطَب. (M, Ḳ.) — تَثْلِيثٌ also signifies The *watering seed-produce* بَعْدَ الثُّنْيَا [*on the third day*, i. e.,] *another time* [which app. means *after excepting*, or *omitting, one day*]. (M.) — And The *making* [a thing] *triangular* [or *trilateral*]. (KL.) — [The *making* a letter *three-pointed*; *making it to have three dots*.] — The *making* [a thing] *to be a third part*. (KL.) — The *making the electuary*, or *confection, of aromatics*, or *perfumes, that is called* مُثَلَّث. (KL.)

4. اثلث القَوْمُ *The party of men became three*: (Th, Ṣ, M, L, Ḳ:) and similar to this are the other verbs of number, to ten [inclusive]: (Ṣ:) also *The party of men became thirty*: and so in the cases of other numbers, to a hundred [exclusive]. (M, L.) — اثلثت *She* (a camel, and any female,) *brought forth her third young one*, or *offspring*; (Th, M;) and so ▼ ثَلَّثَت, or ▼ اثتلثت. (TA in art. بكر.) — لَا يُثْنِى وَلَا يُثْلِثُ: see 1. — اثلث said of a grape-vine, *It had one third of its fruit remaining, two thirds thereof having been eaten*. (M.)

8: see 4.

ثَلْثٌ: see ثُلُثٌ.

ثِلْثٌ The *third young one* or *offspring*, (M, A, Ḳ,) of a she-camel, (M, Ḳ,) and, accord. to Th, of any female: (M:) and in like manner others are termed, to ten [inclusive]. (A.) But one should not say نَاقَةٌ ثِلْثٌ [after the manner of ثِنْىٌ, q. v.]. (M.) — سَقَى نَخْلَهُ الثِّلْثَ *He watered his palm-trees once in three days*: (A:) or *he watered them* بَعْدَ الثُّنْيَا [which app. means *after excepting*, or *omitting, one day*]. (Ḳ.) ثِلْثٌ is not used [thus] except in this case: there is no ثِلْث in the watering of camels; for the shortest period of watering is the رِفْه, when the camels drink every day; then is the غِبّ, which is when they come to the water one day and not the next day; and next after this is the رِبْع; then, the خِمْس; and so on to the عِشْر: so says Aṣ: (Ṣ, TA:) and this is correct, though J's assertion that ثلث is not used except in this case is said by F to require consideration. (TA.) — حُمَّى الثِّلْثِ i. q. حُمَّى الغِبِّ, [*The tertian fever*;] *the fever that attaches one day and intermits one day and attacks again on the third day*; called by the vulgar ▼ المُثَلَّثَة. (Mṣb.)

ثَلَثٌ: see what next follows.

ثُلُثٌ (T, Ṣ, M, A, Mṣb, Ḳ) and ▼ ثُلْثٌ (Mṣb, Ḳ) and ▼ ثَلَثٌ, which last is either a dial. var. or is so pronounced to make the utterance more easy, (MF,) *A third*; *a third part* or *portion*; (Ṣ, A, Mṣb, Ḳ;) as also ▼ ثَلِيثٌ, (Aṣ, T, Ṣ, M, Mṣb, Ḳ,) like خَمِيسٌ and سَدِيسٌ and سَبِيعٌ and ثَمِينٌ and نَصِيفٌ, (Ṣ,) though AZ ignored ثَلِيثٌ (T, Ṣ) and

خَمِيس : (Ṣ:) [and ▼مِثْلَاثٌ, q. v., app. signifies the same:] the pl. of ثُلْث, (M, Mṣb,) and of ثليث also, (M,) is أَثْلَاثٌ. (M, Mṣb.) It is said in a trad., دِيَةُ شِبْهِ العَمْدِ أَثْلَاثًا [*The expiatory mulct for that* homicide *which resembles what is intentional* shall be *thirds*]; i. e., thirty-three she-camels each such as is termed حِقَّة, and thirty-three of which each is such as is termed جَذَعَة, and thirty-four of which each is what is termed ثَنِيَّة. (TA.)

إِنَآءٌ ثَلْثَانُ *A vessel in which the corn &c. that is measured therein reaches to one third of it*: and in like manner one uses this expression in relation to beverage, or wine, &c. (M, L.)

ثُلْثَانٌ, (so in a copy of the M,) or ثَلْثَانٌ, and ثِلْثَانٌ, (Ḳ,) *I. q.* عِنَبُ الثَّعْلَبِ; (Ḳ;) the *tree thus called.* (M, TA.)

ثُلَاثٌ, also written ثُلْثٌ: see ثَلَاثَةٌ, in six places: and ثُلَاثٌ, in two places.

ثُلَاثُ and ▼مَثْلَثُ (Ṣ, L, Ḳ) *Three and three; three and three together*; or *three at a time and three at a time*; (L;) imperfectly decl. [because] changed from the original form of ثَلَاثَةٌ ثَلَاثَةٌ; (Ḳ;) or because of their having the quality of epithets and deviating from the original form of ثَلَاثَةٌ: they are epithets; for you say, مَرَرْتُ بِقَوْمٍ مَثْنَى وَثُلَاثَ [*I passed by a party of men two and two, and three and three, together*]: (Sb, Ṣ:) or they are imperfectly decl. because they deviate from their original as to the letter and the meaning; the original word being changed as above stated, and the meaning being changed to ثَلَاثَةٌ: but the dim. is ▼ثُلَيْثٌ, perfectly decl., like أُحَيْدٌ &c., because it is like حُمَيْرٌ [dim. of حِمَارٌ], assuming the form of that which is perfectly decl., though it is not so in the cases of أُحَيْسِنُ and the like, as these words, in assuming the dim. form, do not deviate from the measure of a verb, for مَا أُحَيْسِنَهُ [How goodly is he!] is sometimes said. (Ṣ.) It is said in the Ḳur [iv. 3], فَٱنْكِحُوا مَا طَابَ لَكُمْ مِنَ ٱلنِّسَآءِ مَثْنَى وَثُلَاثَ وَرُبَاعَ, i. e. *Then marry ye such as please you, of women, two* [and] *two, and three* [and] *three, and four* [and] *four*: [meaning, *two at a time*, &c.:] here مثنى &c. are imperfectly decl. because deviating from the original form of اِثْنَيْنِ اِثْنَيْنِ, &c., and from the fem. form. (Zj, T, L.) And one says ▼مَثْلَثَ مَثْلَثَ, like ثُلَاثَ ثُلَاثَ. (T.) You say also, فَعَلْتُ الشَّىْءَ مَثْنَى وَثُلَاثَ وَرُبَاعَ, meaning *I did the thing twice and twice, and thrice and thrice, and four times and four times.* (L.) — [ثُلَاثٌ is app. fem. of ثُلَاثَةٌ, a dial. var. of ثَلَاثَةٌ, of which the fem. is ثَلَاثٌ: and hence,] ذُو ثُلَاثٍ, with ḍamm [to the initial ث], A camel's [*girth of the kind called*] وَضِين. (Ḳ.) You say, اِلْتَقَتْ عُرَا ذِى ثُلَاثِهَا ‡ [lit., *The loops of her girth met together*]; (A, TA; [but in a copy of the former, ▼ذِى ثَلَاثِهَا;]) meaning, *she was,* or *became, lean,* or *lank in the belly.* (A. [See a similar saying voce بِطَانٌ.]) And a poet says,

* وَقَدْ ضَمَرَتْ حَتَّى بَدَا ذُو ثَلَاثِهَا *

[*And she had become lean,* or *lank in the belly, so that her girth appeared*]: but some say that ذو ثلاثها [here] means *her belly, and the two skins,* [namely,] *the upper, and that which is pared,* or *scraped off, after the flaying*: (TA:) or, accord. to some, the phrase is حَتَّى أَرْتَقَى ذو ثلاثها, meaning, *so that her fœtus rose* to her back; the ثلاث [here again in a copy of the A written with fet-ḥ to the initial ث, and in like manner ثَلاثها,] being the سَابِيَآء and the سَلَا and the womb. (A, TA.) You say also, عَلَيْهِ ذُو ثَلَاثٍ▼, [so I find it written, but perhaps it should be ذُو ثُلَاثٍ,] meaning, ‡ *Upon him is a* [*garment of the kind called*] كِسَآء *made of the wool of three sheep.* (A, TA. [In the latter without any syll. sign to show that ثلاث here differs from the form in the exs. cited before.])

ثُلَاث : see ثَالِثٌ.

ثَلُوثٌ A she-camel *that fills three vessels* (Ṣ, M, A, L, Ḳ) *such as are called* أَقْدَاح, (M, L,) *when she is milked,* (Ṣ, Ḳ,) [i. e.,] *at one milking.* (A.) This is the utmost quantity that the camel yields at one milking. (IAạr, M.) — Also A she-camel *three of whose teats dry up*: (Ṣ, M, A, Ḳ: [accord. to the TA, it is said in the T that such is termed ▼مَثْلُوثٌ; but I think that this is a mistranscription:]) or *that has had one of her teats cut off* (IAạr, T, M, L, Ḳ) *by cauterization,* which becomes a mark to her, (IAạr, M,) *and* [in some copies of the Ḳ "or"] *is milked from three teats*: (T, M, L, Ḳ:) or *that has three teats*; (IAạr, TA;) [and] so ▼مُثَلَّثَةٌ: (T, TA:) or a she-camel *having one of her teats dried up in consequence of something that has happened to it.* (ISk.)

ثَلِيثٌ : see ثُلْثٌ.

ثَلَاثَةٌ, also written ثَلٰثَةٌ, a noun of number, [i. e. *Three,*] is masc., (Ṣ, M, Mṣb,) and is also written and pronounced ▼ثُلَاثَةٌ, with ḍamm: (IAạr, M, TA:) the fem. is ▼ثَلَاثٌ, also written ثَلٰثٌ; (Ṣ, M, Mṣb;) [and app. ثُلَاثٌ also, mentioned above, under the head of ثُلَاثُ, but only as occurring with ذُو prefixed to it.] You say ثَلَاثَةُ رِجَالٍ [*Three men*]: and ▼ثَلَاثُ نِسْوَةٍ [*three women*]. (Mṣb.) In the saying of Mohammad, رُفِعَ القَلَمُ عَنْ ثَلَاثٍ▼ [*The pen* of the recording angel *is withheld from three* persons] ثلاث is for ثَلَاثُ أَنْفُسٍ. (Mṣb. [See art. رفع.]) [In like manner, ▼ثَلَاثٌ occurs in several trads. for ثَلَاثُ خِصَالٍ; as, for instance, in the saying,] ثَلَاثٌ مَنْ كُنَّ فِيهِ حَاسَبَهُ ٱللّٰهُ حِسَابًا يَسِيرًا [There are *three* qualities: *in whomsoever they be, God will reckon with him with an easy reckoning*]: these are, thy giving to him who denies thee, and forgiving him who wrongs thee, and being kind to him who cuts thee off from him. (El-Jámi' eṣ-Ṣagheer.) The people of El-Ḥijáz say, أَتَوْنِى ثَلَاثَتُهُمْ [*The three of them came to me*], and أَرْبَعَتُهُمْ, and so on to ten [inclusive], with naṣb in every case; and in like manner in the fem., أَتَيْنَنِى ثَلَاثَتُهُنَّ▼, and أَرْبَعَتُهُنَّ: but others decline the word with the three vowels, making it like كُلُّهُمْ: after ten, however, only naṣb is used; so that you say, أَتَوْنِى أَحَدَ عَشَرَهُمْ [and ثَلَاثَةَ عَشَرَهُمْ], and إِحْدَى عَشْرَتَهُنَّ [and ثَلَاثَ عَشْرَتَهُنَّ]. (Ṣ.) The saying وَلَدُ الزِّنَا شَرُّ الثَّلَاثَةِ means [*The offspring of adultery,* or *fornication, is the worst of the three*] if he do the deeds of his parents. (Mgh.) [It is said that when ثلاثة means the things numbered, not the amount of the number, it is imperfectly decl., being regarded as a proper name; and so are other ns. of number. (See ثَمَانِيَةٌ.) See also سِتَّةٌ.—] ثَلَاثَةَ عَشَرَ [indecl. in every case, meaning *Thirteen,*] is pronounced by some of the Arabs ثَلَاثَةَ عْشَرَ: and [the fem.] ثَلَاثَ عَشْرَةَ, thus in the dial. of El-Ḥijáz [and of most of the Arabs], is pronounced ثَلَاثَ عَشِرَةَ in the dial. of Nejd. (Ṣ in art. عشر.)

ثُلَاثَةٌ : see ثَلَاثَةٌ.

الثَّلَاثَآءُ, also written الثَّلٰثَآءُ, (Lth, T, Ṣ, M,) or يَوْمُ الثَّلَاثَآءِ or الثَّلٰثَآءِ, (A, Mṣb, Ḳ,) and ▼الثُّلَاثَآءُ, with ḍamm, (A, Ḳ,) [meaning *The third day of the week, Tuesday,*] has this form for the sake of distinction; for properly it should be الثَّالِثُ: (Ṣ, M:) or it has meddeh in the place of the ة in the noun of number [ثَلَاثَةٌ] to distinguish it from the latter: (Lth, T:) [it is without tenween in every case; when indeterminate as well as when determinate; being fem.:] the pl. is ثَلَاثَاوَاتٌ (Ṣ, M, Mṣb) and أَثَالِثُ. (Th, M.) It has no dim. (Sb, Ṣ in art. امس.) Lḥ relates that Aboo-Ziyád used to say, مَضَى الثَّلَاثَآءُ بِمَا فِيهِ [*Tuesday passed with what* occurred *in it*]; making ثلاثاء sing. and masc.; [but this he did because he meant thereby يَوْمُ الثَّلَاثَآءِ ; يوم being masc.:] Th is related to have said, بِمَا فِيهَا; making it fem.: and Abu-l-Jarráḥ used to say, مَضَتِ الثَّلَاثَآءُ بِمَا فِيهِنَّ, treating the word as a numeral. (M.)

الثُّلَاثَآءُ : see الثَّلَاثَآءُ.

ثُلَاثِىٌّ a rel. n. from ثَلَاثَةٌ, anomalously formed, (M,) [or regularly formed from ثُلَاثَةٌ,] *Of,* or *relating to, three things.* (T, TA.) — *Three cubits in length,* or *height*; applied in this sense to a garment, or piece of cloth; (T, A;) and to a boy. (T.) — A word *comprising,* or *composed of, three letters* [*radical* only, or *of three radical letters with one or more augmentative*; i. e., *of three radical letters with,* or *without, an augment*]. (T, TA.)

ثَلَاثُونَ, [also written ثَلٰثُونَ,] the noun of number, [meaning *Thirty,* and also *thirtieth,*] is not considered as a multiple of ثَلَاثَةٌ, but as a multiple of عَشَرَةٌ; and therefore, if you name a man ثَلَاثُونَ, you do not make the dim. to be ثُلَيْثُونَ, but [you assimilate the noun from which it is formed to a pl. with و and ن from عَشَرَةٌ, or to عِشْرُونَ, and say] ▼ثُلَيْثُونَ. (Sb, M.)

ثُلْثُونَ : see what immediately precedes.

ثُلَاثَاوِىٌّ One *who fasts alone on the third day of the week.* (IAạr, Th, M.)

ثُلَيْثٌ : see ثُلَاثٌ.

ثَالِثٌ [*Third*]: fem. with ة. (T, &c.) The final ث in الثَّالِثُ is sometimes changed into ى. (M.) You say, هُوَ ثَالِثُ ثَلَاثَةٍ [*He, or it, is the third of three*]: thus you say when the two [terms] agree, each with the other; but not ثَالِثٌ ثَلَاثَةً; ثالث being regarded in the former case as though it were a subst.; for you do not mean to convey by it a verbal signification, but only mean that he, or it, is one of the three, or a portion of the three: (Fr, ISk, T, Ṣ:) and in like manner you say, هِىَ ثَالِثَةُ ثَلَاثٍ [*She is the third of three*]; but when there is among the females a male, you say, هِىَ ثَالِثَةُ ثَلَاثَةٍ, making the masc. to predominate over the fem. (T.) When the two [terms] are different, you may make the former to govern the gen. case or to govern as a verb; saying, هُوَ رَابِعُ ثَلَاثَةٍ or هُوَ رَابِعٌ ثَلَاثَةً, like as you say ضَارِبُ زَيْدٍ and ضَارِبٌ زَيْدًا; and thus you also say, هٰذَا ثَالِثُ اثْنَيْنِ and هٰذَا ثَالِثٌ اثْنَيْنِ, meaning *This makes two to be three, with himself*, or *itself*. (ISk, T,* Ṣ. [In most copies of the Ṣ, for ثَالِثُ اثْنَيْنِ is put ثَالِثُ اثْنَيْنِ; and, in the explanation of this phrase, ثَلَثَ اثْنَيْنِ for ثَلَّثَ اثْنَيْنِ: IB has remarked that these are mistakes.]) ثُلَاثٌ ▼ occurs in the sense of ثالث in a trad. cited voce ثَانٍ in art. ثنى. (Sh, T in art. ثنى.) — ثَالِثَةُ الأَثَافِى means *A projecting portion of a mountain, by which are placed two pieces of rock, upon all which is placed the cooking-pot.* (Ṣ, Ḳ.) Hence the saying, رَمَاهُ اللّٰهُ بِثَالِثَةِ الأَثَافِى [explained in art. اثف]. (TA.) — [ثَالِثَ عَشَرَ and ثَالِثَةَ عَشْرَةَ, the former masc. and the latter fem., meaning *Thirteenth*, are generally held to be indecl. in every case without the art.; but with the art., most say in the nom. الثَّالِثُ عَشَرَ, accus. الثَّالِثَ عَشَرَ, and gen. الثَّالِثِ عَشَرَ; and in like manner in the fem. Accord. to some,] you say, هُوَ ثَالِثُ عَشَرَ as well as هُوَ ثَالِثَ عَشَرَ [*He, or it, is a thirteenth*]: he who uses the former phrase says that he means هُوَ ثَالِثُ ثَلَاثَةَ عَشَرَ, (T, Ṣ,) i. e. *He, or it, is one of thirteen*, (T,) and that he suppresses ثلاثة, and leaves ثالث decl. as it was; and he who uses the latter phrase says that he likewise means this, but that, suppressing ثلاثة, he gives its final vowel to the word ثالث, (T, Ṣ,) to show that there is a suppression: (Ṣ:) but IB says that the former of these two phrases is wrong; that the Koofees allow it, but that the Basrees disallow it, and pronounce it a mistake. (L.) [And accord. to J, one says, هٰذَا الثَّالِثَ عَشَرَ and هٰذِهِ الثَّالِثَةَ عَشْرَةَ *This is the thirteenth, or this thirteenth*: for he adds,] and you say, هٰذَا الحَادِىَ عَشَرَ and الثَّانِىَ عَشَرَ and so on to twenty [exclusive]; all with fet-ḥ; for the reason which we have mentioned: and in like manner in the fem., in which each of the two nouns is with ة. (Ṣ.) You say also, ثَالِثَ عَشَرَ ثَلَاثَةَ عَشَرَ [*The thirteenth of thirteen*]; and so on to تَاسِعَ عَشَرَ تِسْعَةَ عَشَرَ: and in like manner in the fem. (I 'Aḳ p. 316.)

[الثَّالُوثُ *The Trinity.*]

مُثَلَّثٌ and مُثْلَثٌ: see ثُلَاثٌ. — مثلث [i. e. مُثَلَّثٌ] signifies *A chord* [*of a lute*] *composed of three twists*: that which is of two twists is called مثنى [i. e. مَثْنًى]: or, as some say, these two words signify [respectively] the *third chord* and the *second*: their pls. are مَثَالِثُ and مَثَانٍ. (Ḥar p. 244.)

مُثْلِثٌ A she-camel, and any female, *bringing forth her third young one, or offspring*: one should not say نَاقَةٌ ثَلِثٌ. (M.) — See also مُثَلِّثٌ.

مُثَلَّثٌ A thing *having three angles* or *corners*, *triangular* [or *trilateral*]; *a triangle*. (Ṣ, Ḳ.) You say مُثَلَّثٌ حَادٌّ [*An acute-angled triangle*]: and مُثَلَّثٌ قَائِمٌ [*A right-angled triangle*]. (TA.) And أَرْضٌ مُثَلَّثَةٌ *A three-sided piece of land*. (TA.) — A thing *composed of three layers* or *strata*, or *of three distinct fascicles* or *the like*; (M, TA;) [see also مَثْلُوثٌ;] and in like manner what are composed of four, and more, to ten [inclusive], are called by similar epithets: (TA:) or a thing *of three folds*. (Lth, T.) — [As a conventional term in lexicology, A word *having a letter which has any of the three vowels*: ex. gr., بَدْأَةٌ is مُثَلَّثَةُ البَآءِ; i. e., it is written بَدْأَةٌ and بُدْأَةٌ and بِدْأَةٌ. As such also, A verb *having its* عَيْن (or *middle radical letter*) *movent by any of the three vowels*: ex. gr., بَهَأَ بِهِ is مُثَلَّثٌ; i. e., it is written بَهَأَ and بَهُؤَ and بَهِئَ. And as such, مُثَلَّثَةٌ (not مُثَلِّثَةٌ) signifies *Three-pointed*; *having three diacritical points*: it is an epithet added to ثَآء, to prevent its being mistaken for بَآء or تَآء or يَآء.] — *Wine* (شَرَاب) *cooked until the quantity of two thirds of it has gone*; (Ṣ, Ḳ;) *the expressed juice of grapes so cooked*. (Mgh.) — And *A certain electuary*, or *confection*, *of aromatics*, or *perfumes*. (KL.)

مُثَلِّثٌ *A calumniator*, or *slanderer*, *of his brother* [or *fellow*] *to his prince*; because he destroys three; namely, himself and his brother and his prince: (Sh, T, M,* Ḳ:) as also ▼ مُثْلِثٌ; (Ḳ;) or thus accord. to Aboo-'Owáneh. (Sh, T.) — See also ثِلْثٌ, last sentence: — and see ثَلُوثٌ.

مِثْلَاثٌ from ثُلُثٌ is like مِرْبَاعٌ from رُبُعٌ. (M.) See ثُلُثٌ and مِرْبَاعٌ.

مَثْلُوثٌ Property *of which a third part has been taken*. (A.) — [Applied to a verse,] That *of which a third has been taken away*: (M, Ḳ:) whatever is مَثْلُوثٌ is مَنْهُوكٌ: (TA:) or the former word signifies as above, and the latter signifies that of which two thirds have been taken away: this is the opinion of the authors on versification with respect to the metres called رَجَز and مُنْسَرِح: (M, TA:) the مثلوث in poetry is that *whereof two feet out of six have gone*. (TA.) — A rope *composed of three strands* (Lth, T, Ṣ, M, A, Ḳ) *twisted together*, (Lth, T, A,) and in like manner *woven*, or *plaited*: (Lth, T:) and ropes composed of four, five, six, seven, and nine, strands, but not of eight nor of ten, are similarly called. (M.) — A garment of the kind called كِسَآء *woven of wool and camels' hair* (وَبَر) *and goats' hair* (شَعَر). (Fr, T.) — مَزَادَةٌ مَثْلُوثَةٌ *A* مزادة [or leathern water-bag] *made of three skins*. (T, Ṣ, A, Ḳ.) — أَرْضٌ مَثْلُوثَةٌ *Land turned over three times for sowing or cultivating*. (A.) — See also ثَلُوثٌ.

ثلج

1. ثَلَجَتِ السَّمَآءُ, aor. ـُ and ـِ, *The sky snowed; let fall snow*. (A, TA.) [Here, and in other cases, throughout this art., the meaning of ثَلْج is assumed to be well known.] — ثَلَجَتْنَا السَّمَآءُ, (Ṣ, Mṣb, Ḳ,) aor. ـُ; (Ṣ, Mṣb;) and ▼ أَثْلَجَتْنَا; (Mṣb,* Ḳ;) *The sky snowed upon us*; (Ṣ, Mṣb, Ḳ;) like as one says مَطَرَتْنَا. (Ṣ.) And ثُلِجُوا *They were snowed upon*. (TA.) You say, ثُلِجْنَا العَامَ ثَلْجًا كَثِيرًا [*We were snowed upon this year much*]. (A.) And ثُلِجَتِ الأَرْضُ, (A, Mṣb, TA,) and ▼ أُثْلِجَت, (TA,) *The land was snowed upon*. (A,* Mṣb, TA.*) — [ثُلِجَ, said of water &c., *It was cooled*, or *made cold, with snow*: see an ex. voce مَثْلُوجٌ. In the present day, ▼ ثَلَّجَهُ signifies *He cooled it*, or *made it cold, with snow* or *ice*; *iced it*; *froze it*.] — See also 4. — [Hence,] ثَلَجَ, (IAạr, Ḳ,) aor. ـَ, (Ḳ,) inf. n. ثَلْجٌ, (TA,) † *His heart became cool*, or *refreshed, and relieved of a thing*: (IAạr:) and *he rejoiced*; or *was*, or *became, joyful, glad*, or *happy*: (IAạr, Ḳ:) and *he was*, or *became, at ease, at rest, tranquil*, or *free from disquietude*. (TA.) And ثَلِجَتْ نَفْسُهُ بِكَذَا ‡ *His mind became refreshed and happy by means of such a thing*. (A.) And ثَلِجَتْ نَفْسِى, aor. ـَ, inf. n. ثُلُوجٌ; (AA, Ṣ, Ḳ;) and ثَلَجَتْ, aor. ـُ, inf. n. ثَلْجٌ; (Aṣ, Ṣ, Ḳ; [in the CḲ ثَلْج ثَلَج;]) and ▼ أَثْلَجَتْ; (Ḳ;) بِالشَّىْءِ; (TA;) † *My mind became at ease, at rest, tranquil, or free from disquietude*, (AA, Ṣ, Ḳ, TA,) *and became healed, by means of the thing*: (TA:) or *I knew it, and was rejoiced at it, or by it*: or *my mind became at ease, and I confided*, or *trusted, in the thing*: as also ثلجت إِلَيْهِ; and ثلج صَدْرِى: or this last, accord. to Sh, means *my bosom became dilated* [*with joy*], لِلْأَمْرِ, *at the event*. (TA.) And ثلجت بِمَا خَبَّرْتَنِى ‡ *I became healed, and my heart became at rest, or tranquil, by means of the information which thou gavest me*. (ISk, TA.) And ثَلَجَ قَلْبُهُ and ثَلِجَ, the latter mentioned by Lb, on the authority of 'Abd-El-Ḥaḳḳ, ‡ *His heart became certified*, or *assured*. (TA.) ثَلْجٌ is said to mean ‡ *Certitude*, or *assurance*, because it is taken from the delight that one has in water rendered cool, or cold, by means of snow and the like. (TA.) — ثُلِجَ فُؤَادُهُ ‡ *He was*, or *became, stupid, dull, wanting in*

intelligence: (IAạr, A, TA:) *his heart,* or *his mind,* or *intellect, quitted him.* (TA.) —— ثَلَجَهُ, (Sh, Ḳ,) aor. ـُ, inf. n. ثَلْج, (Sh, TA,) also signifies *He,* or *it, soaked it; moistened it.* (Sh, Ḳ, TA.)

2: see 1.

4. اثلج *It* (a day, Ṣ, Ḳ, or a year, A) *was,* or *became, snowy.* (Ṣ, A, Ḳ.) —— *He reached, came upon,* or *lighted on, snow;* (Ḳ;) as also ثلج [written without any syll. signs, app. ↓ ثَلَّجَ]. (TA.) *He entered upon* [*a tract,* or *time,* or *season, of*] *snow.* (TA.) —— أَثْلَجَتْنَا السَّمَآءُ: and أَثْلَجَتِ الأَرْضَ: see 1. —— [Thus the verb is intrans. and trans. And hence,] أَثْلَجَتْ نَفْسِى: see 1. —— And اثلجهُ † *He rejoiced him; made him joyful, glad,* or *happy.* (Ḳ.) And اثلج صَدْرِى ‡ *It* (news, or information,) *healed and tranquillized me.* (A,* TA.) And مَا أَثْلَجَنِى بِهٰذَا الأَمْرِ † *How joyful,* or *happy, am I made by this thing,* or *event!* (TA.) —— [Hence also,] حَفَرَ حَتَّى اثلج ‡ *He dug until he reached the clay,* or *mud,* (AA, Ṣ, Ḳ, TA,) or *the cold of the moist earth,* (A,) or *the moist earth and the water.* (TA.) —— اثلج مَآءُ البِئْرِ ‡ *The water of the well ceased,* or *stopped.* (A, Ḳ.) And hence, (TA,) اثلجت عَنْهُ الحُمَّى ‡ *The fever quitted him.* (A, TA.) —— إِثْلَاجٌ [the inf. n.] is also syn. with إِفْلَاجٌ [inf. n. of أَفْلَجَ, q. v.]. (Ḳ.)

ثَلْجٌ [*Snow;*] *a thing well known,* (Ṣ, A, Mṣb, Ḳ,) *that falls from the sky:* (TA:) pl. ثُلُوجٌ. (Mṣb.)

ثَلِجٌ *Cold:* (Ḳ:) applied to water. (TA.)

ثُلُجٌ †Men *joyful, glad,* or *happy, by reason of news.* (IAạr, TA.) —— † Men who are *stupid, dull,* or *wanting in intelligence.* (TA.) [See also مَثْلُوجٌ.]

ثَلْجِىٌّ: see ثَلَّاجٌ.

ثُلَاجِىٌّ ‡ *Very white:* applied to an iron head of an arrow or of a spear or of a sword or the like: (A, Ḳ:) fem. with ة. (A.)

ثَلَّاجٌ *A seller of snow;* (Ḳ;) as also ↓ ثَلْجِىٌّ. (TA.)

مَثْلَجَةٌ *A place in which is* [*kept*] *snow* [*for cooling water &c. in summer*]. (Ḳ.)

مَثْلُوجٌ: fem. with ة: the latter applied to land (أَرْض), meaning *Snowed upon.* (Ṣ, A, Mṣb.) —— Water *cooled,* or *made cold, with snow.* (TA.) A poet says, speaking of a woman's mouth,

يُخَالُ مَثْلُوجًا وَإِنْ لَمْ يُثْلَجِ •

[*It would be thought to be cooled with snow, though it was not cooled therewith*]. (TA.) —— مَثْلُوجُ الفُؤَادِ ‡ A man (Ṣ) *stupid, dull,* or *wanting in intelligence.* (Ṣ, A, Mṣb, Ḳ.) [See also ثُلُجٌ.]

ثلط

1. ثَلَطَ, aor. ـِ, (Az, Ṣ, Ḳ,) inf. n. ثَلْطٌ, (Az, Ṣ,) *He* (a camel, Ṣ, IAth, Ḳ, and a bull, IAth, Ḳ, and an elephant, mostly said of these three animals, IAth, and a man, Az, and a child, Ḳ) *voided his dung in a thin state.* (Az, Ṣ, Ḳ.) It is said in a trad., (Ṣ, TA,) of 'Alee, (TA,) كَانُوا يَبْعَرُونَ بَعْرًا وَأَنْتُمْ تَثْلِطُونَ ثَلْطًا, (Ṣ, TA,) meaning that the former ate little, and that the latter ate much and of various kinds. (TA.) ═ ثَلَطَ فُلَانًا *He threw* ثَلْط, (Ḳ, TA,) i. e. *thin dung,* (TA,) *at such a one:* (Ḳ, TA:) and *he befouled him,* or *smeared him, therewith.* (Ḳ, TA.)

ثَلْطٌ *Thin dung* of an elephant and the like, (Lth, Ḳ,) and of anything, when it is thin. (TA.)

مَثْلَطٌ, (Ḳ, TA, [but by rule it should be مَثْلِطٌ,]) or مَثْلَطَةٌ, (CḲ,) The *place of exit of* ثَلْط. (Ḳ.)

ثلم

1. ثَلَمَهُ, aor. ـِ, (T, Ṣ, M, Mṣb, Ḳ,) inf. n. ثَلْمٌ, (Ṣ, M, Mṣb,) *He broke its edge;* (Ṣ,* M, Mṣb, Ḳ;) namely, that of a vessel, (M, Mṣb, Ḳ,) and of a sword, and the like; (M, Ḳ;) as also ثَلِمَهُ, aor. ـَ; (Ḳ, TA; [but I suspect that this latter form of the verb has been taken from a copy of the Ṣ in which the intrans. verb ثَلِمَ has been erroneously made trans.;]) and ↓ ثَلَّمَهُ; (M, Ḳ;) or this last signifies he did so *much,* or *in many places:* (Ṣ:) and the first signifies also *he made a gap,* or *breach, in it;* namely, a wall. (T,* Ṣ.) —— [Hence,] ثُلِمَ فِى مَالِهِ, (TA,) or ثَلْمَةً, (M,) ‡ *He suffered the loss of somewhat of his property.* (M, TA.) And هٰذَا مِمَّا يَثْلِمُ الدِّينَ وَيَثْلِمُ اليَقِينَ † [*This of the things that wound religion and impair sure faith*]. (TA.) ═ ثَلِمَ, aor. ـَ, inf. n. ثَلَمٌ; (Ṣ;) and ↓ انثلم, and ↓ تثلّم; (Ṣ, M, Mṣb, Ḳ;) said of a thing, (Ṣ,) a vessel, (M, Mṣb, Ḳ,) a sword, and the like, (M, Ḳ,) *It was,* or *became, broken in its edge:* (Ṣ,* M, Mṣb, Ḳ:) [or ↓ the last, being quasi-pass. of **2**, *it was,* or *became, broken much,* or *in several places, in its edge:*] and ↓ انثلم and ↓ تثلّم are said of a wall [as signifying *it had a gap* or *breach,* or *gaps* or *breaches, made in it*]. (T.) ثَلَمٌ, [the inf. n. of ثَلِمَ,] when relating to a valley, signifies The *having its* حَرْف, (T, M, Ḳ, and so in a copy of the Ṣ, [meaning *brink,* or *edge,*]) or its جُرُف, (so in other copies of the Ṣ, [meaning its *abrupt, water-worn, bank,*]) *broken;* (T, Ṣ, M, Ḳ, TA;) i. e., *broken down:* (TA:) and in like manner, in relation to a trench dug round a tent to prevent the rain-water from entering it, and in relation to a watering-trough, or tank. (M, TA.) [Golius and Freytag have explained it as signifying the *part so broken;* but I do not think that this can be meant by the explanation given above.]

2: see 1.

5: see 1, in three places.

7: see 1, in two places. —— You say also, انثلموا عَلَيْهِ *They poured forth,* or *down, upon him,* or *against him;* as also انثلّوا. (Z, TA.)

ثَلْمٌ *A break of the edge* in a vessel (ISk, T, Ṣ) and in a sword. (T, Ṣ.) [See also what next follows.]

ثُلْمَةٌ *A gap,* or *breach,* (Ṣ, M, Mṣb, Ḳ,) in a wall &c., (Ṣ, Mṣb,) or *of a thing that is broken,* and *of a thing ruined,* (Ḳ,) or *of a broken edge:* (M:) or *a place that has been broken in an edge,* or *that has had a gap,* or *breach, made in it:* (T, TA:) *a broken place* of a vessel: (TA:) pl. ثُلَمٌ. (T, Mṣb.) [See also ثَلْمٌ.] —— [Hence,] مَوْتُ فُلَانٍ ثُلْمَةٌ فِى الإِسْلَامِ ثُلْمَةٌ لَا تُسَدُّ ‡ [*The death of such a one is* an occasion of *a gap in the body of the Muslims; a gap that will not be filled up*]. (TA.) [See also its syn. خَلَّةٌ.]

أَثْلَمُ A thing [such as a vessel and a sword and the like] *broken in its edge:* (Ṣ:) a watering-trough, or tank, *broken in its side.* (TA.) ═ أَثْلَمُ *Dust,* or *earth;* and *stones;* like أَثْلَبُ; accord. to El-Hejeree: but [ISd adds,] whether it be a dial. var. or formed by substitution, I know not. (M.)

ثم

1. ثَمَّهُ, (Ṣ, M,* Ḳ,) aor. ـُ, (Ṣ, M,) inf. n. ثَمٌّ, (T, Ṣ, M,) *He repaired it;* or *put it into a good, sound,* or *right, state;* (T, Ṣ, M, Ḳ;) [*by filling up its interstices, &c.,*] *with* ثُمَام [q. v.]. (Ṣ.) Hence the saying, ثَمَمْتُ أُمُورِى † *I put my affairs into a good, sound, right,* or *proper, state; restored them to such a state;* or *set them right,* or *in order.* (Ṣ.) And hence also the saying, كُنَّا أَهْلَ ثَمِّهِ وَرَمِّهِ † [*We were the fit persons to put it into a good, sound, right,* or *proper, state;* &c.]; (Ṣ;) occurring in a trad.; accord. to the relaters thereof, ↓ ثُمِّهِ وَرُمِّهِ; but A'Obeyd holds the former reading to be the right. (T.) —— *He spread* ثُمَام *for it,* namely, a skin of milk, *and put it* [ثمام] *above it, in order that the sun might not strike it, and its milk become consequently decomposed,* or *curdled.* (T.) —— [*He stuffed it,* either with ثُمَام or absolutely: for] ثُمَّ signifies *it was stuffed.* (T.) —— *He collected it together;* (Ṣ, M, Ḳ;) namely, a thing; (Ṣ, M;) mostly used in relation to dry herbage. (M, Ḳ.) You say, ثُمَّ لَهَا, i. e. *Collect thou* [*for them;* namely, the cattle &c.; like قُمَّ لَهَا, from قَمَّ]. (TA.) And هُوَ يَثُمُّهُ وَيَقُمُّهُ *He sweeps it, and collects the good and the bad.* (Ṣ.) —— ثَمَّ الطَّعَامَ, (M, Ḳ,) [aor. and] inf. n. as above, (M,) *He ate the good of the food and the bad thereof;* (M, Ḳ;) as also قَمَّهُ. (TA.) —— ثَمَّتْهُ, (T,* Ṣ, M, Ḳ,) aor. and inf. n. as above, (M,) *She* (a ewe or a goat, M, Ḳ, or, as some say, only the latter, M) *pulled it,* or *plucked it, up,* or *out, with her mouth;* (T, Ṣ, M, Ḳ;) namely, a thing, (T, M,) or a plant, (Ṣ, Ḳ,) and anything by which she passed. (TA.) —— ثَمَّ يَدَهُ بِالحَشِيشِ, (M, Ḳ,) or بِالأَرْضِ, (Ṣ, M,) [aor. and] inf. n. as above, (TA,) *He wiped his hand* (Ṣ, M, Ḳ) *with the dry herbage,* (M, Ḳ,) or *upon the ground.* (Ṣ, M.)

ثَمَّ *There;* syn. هُنَاكَ; (Zj, Ṣ, M, Ḳ;) a noun of indication, (Zj, T, M, Mṣb, Mughnee, Ḳ,) denoting a place that is remote (Zj, T, Ṣ, M, Mughnee, Ḳ) from the speaker, (Zj, T, M,) like as هُنَا denotes that which is near; (Zj, T, Ṣ;) or denoting a place other than that of the speaker: (Mṣb:) it is an adverbial noun, not to be used otherwise than as such; (Mughnee, K;) indecl. because of its vagueness, and with fet-ḥ for its termination to avoid the concurrence of two quiescent letters. (Zj, T, M.) Thus in the saying [in the Kur xxvi. 64], وَأَزْلَفْنَا ثَمَّ الآخَرِينَ [*And we brought near, there, the others*]. (Mughnee.) He who makes it decl. as an objective complement (Mughnee, K) in this ex., (Mughnee,) and in the saying in the Kur [lxxvi. 20], وَإِذَا رَأَيْتَ ثَمَّ رَأَيْتَ نَعِيمًا, is in error: (Mughnee, K:*) Zj says that the meaning is, *And when thou castest thine eyes*, or *thy sight, there, thou shalt behold* [scenes of] *enjoyment*: that Fr asserted the meaning to be, إِذَا رَأَيْتَ مَا ثَمَّ [*when thou seest what is there*]; but that this is an error; for ما, accord. to this interpretation, is a conjunct noun, and it is not allowable to suppress a conjunct noun and leave its complement. (T.) — [مِنْ ثَمَّ is used by post-classical writers as meaning *Therefore; for that reason; on that account.*]

ثُمَّ, (T, Ṣ, M, &c.,) for which one also says فُمَّ, (M, Mughnee,) substituting ف for the ث, (M,) and ثُمَّتَ (T, Ṣ, M) and ثُمَّتْ, (M, TA,) but ثُمَّ is the more common, (Mughnee and K on the letter ت,) and فُمَّتَ and فُمَّتْ, (M, TA,) [meaning *Then*, i. e., *afterward*, or *afterwards*,] a particle, (M, K,) or conjunction, (Zj, T, Ṣ, Mṣb, Mughnee,) denoting order (Zj, T, Ṣ, M, Mṣb, Mughnee) and a delay, (Ṣ, Mṣb,) or having three properties, namely, that of virtually associating in the same case [the latter of the two members which it conjoins with the former of them], and denoting order, and denoting a delay; but respecting all of these there is a difference of opinions. (Mughnee, K.*) As to the associating in the same case, Akh and the Koofees assert that it sometimes fails to have this property, by its occurring redundantly, so as not to be a conjunction at all; and they hold to accord with this assertion the saying in the Kur [ix. 119], حَتَّى إِذَا ضَاقَتْ عَلَيْهِمُ الأَرْضُ بِمَا رَحُبَتْ وَضَاقَتْ عَلَيْهِمْ أَنْفُسُهُمْ وَظَنُّوا أَنْ لَا مَلْجَأَ مِنَ اللّٰهِ إِلَّا إِلَيْهِ ثُمَّ تَابَ عَلَيْهِمْ [*Until, when the earth became strait to them, notwithstanding its amplitude, and their minds became straitened to them, and they knew that there was no repairing for refuge from God save unto Him, then He returned to forgiveness towards them*]: (Mughnee, K:*) but this has been resolved by the subaudition of the complement [of what precedes ثُمَّ, as though the meaning were, *then* (*they betook themselves unto Him, begging forgiveness, and*) *He returned* &c.]. (Mughnee.) And as to its denoting order, some hold that there are exs. of its not necessarily implying this; (Mughnee, K;*) one of which is the saying in the Kur [xxxix. 8], خَلَقَكُمْ مِنْ نَفْسٍ وَاحِدَةٍ ثُمَّ جَعَلَ مِنْهَا زَوْجَهَا: (Mughnee: [in which are added other similar exs., one of which is given in the K:]) but to this there are five replies: 1st, that this passage is elliptical; the meaning being, *He created you from one person* (*which He originated*); *then He made therefrom its mate*: 2nd, that the meaning is, *He created you from a person that was alone; then* &c.: 3rd, that the progeny of Adam were made to come forth from his back like little ants; then Eve was created from his [rib called the] قُصَيْرَى: 4th, that the creation of Eve from Adam being unusual, ثُمَّ is used to notify its order and posteriority in respect of wonderfulness and of the manifestation of power; not to denote order and posteriority of time: 5th, that ثُمَّ is here used to denote the order of enunciation; not the virtual order: the replies preceding this last are better than it, inasmuch as they verify the order and the delay; whereas the last verifies the order only, as there is no delay between the two enunciations; but the last reply is of more common application, applying to the ex. given above and to others: (Mughnee:) Fr says that the meaning of the ex. given above is, *He created you from a person* (*which He created*) *single; then* &c.; and in like manner says Zj. (T.) And as to its denoting a delay, Fr asserts that sometimes this is not the case, as is shown by the saying, أَعْجَبَنِي مَا صَنَعْتَ الْيَوْمَ ثُمَّ مَا صَنَعْتَ أَمْسِ أَعْجَبُ [*What thou didst to-day excited my wonder*, or *admiration*, or *pleasure*; *then* (*I tell thee*) *what thou didst yesterday was more wonderful*, or *admirable*, or *pleasing*]; for ثُمَّ is here used to denote the order of the enunciation; not a delay between the two enunciations. (Mughnee, K.*) — [It is said that] it denotes order and a delay when it conjoins single words: but Akh says that it has the meaning of وَ [*And*], because it is used in cases in which there is no order; as in وَاللّٰهِ ثُمَّ وَاللّٰهِ لَأَفْعَلَنَّ [*By God, and* (*I say again,*) *By God, I will assuredly do* such a thing]: and when it conjoins propositions, it does not necessarily denote order, but has the meaning of وَ: (Mṣb:) it has the meaning of وَ, (Ṣ, Mṣb,) the conjunction, (Ṣ,) in the saying in the Kur [x. 47], ثُمَّ اللّٰهُ شَهِيدٌ عَلَى مَا يَفْعَلُونَ [*And God is witness of what they do*]. (Ṣ, Mṣb.) — The Koofees allow its being used in the manner of فَ and وَ so as that the aor. immediately following it after a conditional verb may be manṣoob: and Ibn-Málik allows its being thus used so as that the aor. immediately following it after the expression of a desire that the thing shall not be done may be marfooa and mejzoom and manṣoob. (Mughnee.)

ثُمٌّ: see ثُمَامٌ. — In the saying مَا لَهُ ثُمٌّ وَلَا رُمٌّ [*He has not* ثُمّ *nor* رُمّ], the former of these two nouns signifies *water-skins*, or *milk-skins, and vessels*; (M;) or *what is bad*, or *the worst, of those things*, (Ṣ, K,) accord. to ISk; (Ṣ;) or *men's household-goods*, or *furniture and utensils, and their water-skins*, or *milk-skins, and vessels*; (T, TA;) which last is the right meaning: (TA:) and the latter noun signifies مَرَمَّةُ الْبَيْتِ [app. meaning, accord. to analogy, (for I find no suitable explanation of it in any of the lexicons,) *the means by which a house*, or *tent, is put into a good state*; and therefore, *good furniture and utensils*]. (ISk, Ṣ, M, K.) You say also, مَا يَمْلِكُ ثُمًّا وَلَا رُمًّا, meaning the same: (Ṣ, TA:) or *he possesses not little nor much*: it is not used save with a negation. (M, TA.) An Arab of the desert said, جَعْجَعَ بِي الدَّهْرُ عَنْ ثُمِّهِ وَرُمِّهِ, [thus in some copies of the Ṣ, and in the TA, in which latter the last two nouns are expressly said to be with ḍamm, but in two copies of the Ṣ, in this instance, erroneously written, ثَمِّهِ وَرَمِّهِ,] i. e. [*Fortune has debarred me*] *from its little and its much*. (Ṣ, TA.) And hence the saying of the vulgar, جَآءَ بِالثِّمِّ وَالرِّمِّ, except that they pronounce both these nouns with kesr, meaning *He brought little and much*. (TA.) — See also 1.

ثُمَّةٌ: see ثُمَامٌ.

ثُمَّةٌ *A handful of dry herbage*. (Ṣ, M, K.) — Also n. un. of ثُمٌّ, which is syn. with ثُمَامٌ: see the next paragraph in six places.

ثُمَامٌ [*Panicum*, or *panic grass*; applied to several species thereof; but restricted by Forskål (Flor. Aeg. Ar., descr. plant., p. 20, where its Arabic name is written "tummâm,") to *panicum dichotomum*; called by Delile (Flor. Aeg., no. 58, where its Arabic name is written "temâm,") *pennisetum dichotomum*; and described by him in the "explication des planches" accompanying his Flora, plate 8: *the Arabs use it for making thatch for their huts*:] *a kind of plant*, (T, Ṣ, Mṣb, K, [in the M termed شَجَر,]) *well known in the desert, not desired*, or *not much eaten, by the camels*, or *cattle, except in a case of scarcity*, or *drought*; (T;) *weak*, or *frail*; *having what are termed* خُوص [q. v.], *or what resemble* خوص, *sometimes used for stuffing*, (Ṣ, TA,) *and for stopping up the interstices of houses*; (Ṣ, Mṣb, TA;) *and sometimes used for removing whiteness from the eye*: (K:) accord. to Az, *it is of several species, one of which is the* ضَعَة, *and another is the* جَلِيلَة, *and another is the* غَرَف, *which resembles rushes* (أَسَل), *and brooms are made of it, and water-bags are covered with it to protect them from the sun, causing the water to become cool*: (TA:) [see also أُمْصُوخَةٌ:] it is also called ثُمَامَى, (K,) and ثُمَّةٌ, [but see what follows,] (T, M,) which is sometimes contracted into ثُمَةٌ; (T;) or it is also called ثُمٌّ, of which ثُمَّةٌ is the n. un.: (AḤn, TA:) the n. un. of ثُمَام is [likewise] with ة. (Ṣ, M, Mṣb, K.) You say of a thing that may be reached, or taken with the hand, without difficulty, هُوَ عَلَى طَرَفِ الثُّمَامِ, (T, Z, K,) (IAạr, T, M, Z, K,*) i. e. †*It is easy to thee*, or *within thy reach, no obstacle intervening between thee and it*: (IAạr, M:) because the ثمام is not tall, (T, K,) so that the reaching it should be difficult. (T.) And هُوَ لَكَ عَلَى رَأْسِ الثُّمَّةِ [meaning the same]. (M.) And لَكَ ذٰلِكَ عَلَى رَأْسِ الثُّمَّةِ, (TA,) or عَلَى رَأْسِ الثُّمَّةِ, †[*That is easy of attainment to thee*], (M,) is a prov. used in relation to the attainment of a thing that one wants. (M, TA.) The Arabs also say, هُوَ أَبُوهُ عَلَى طَرَفِ الثُّمَّةِ, meaning †*He is like his father*: and some of them say الثَّمَّة, with fet-ḥ. (TA.) And it is said in a trad. of 'Omar, اُغْزُوا وَالْغَزْوُ حُلْوٌ خَضِرٌ قَبْلَ أَنْ يَصِيرَ ثُمَامًا ثُمَّ رُمَامًا ثُمَّ حُطَامًا †[*Engage ye in predatory warfare while it is sweet and fresh*], meaning, while ye see, and make abundant, your spoils, *before it become feeble like the* ثمام;

[*then, decayed; then, broken up.*] (TA.) — It also signifies *What has become dry, or dried up, of the branches that are placed beneath the* نَضَد [q. v.]. (M.)

ثَمُومٌ A sheep (T, Ṣ, M, Ḳ) or goat (Ṣ, M, Ḳ) *that pulls, or plucks, up, or out, with her mouth,* (T, Ṣ, M, Ḳ,) *a thing,* (T, M,) or *a plant:* (Ṣ, Ḳ:) and *that eats* ثُمَام. (M, TA.)

ثَمُومٌ: see ثُمَامٌ.

مِثَمٌّ (like مِسَنٌّ, Ḳ [in the CḲ, erroneously, like مُسِنٌّ, مُثِمٌّ,]) One *who pastures for him who has no pastor,* (T, Ḳ,) or *no pasturage,* (TA,) *and lends a beast or camel for riding or carrying, to him who has no beast or camel for riding or carrying* (يُفْقِرُ مَنْ لَا ظَهْرَ لَهُ), [in the CḲ, erroneously, يُفْقِرُ,]) *and sets right* (يَثُمُّ [in the CḲ, erroneously, يُثِمُّ,]) *what the tribe are unable to manage, of their affair:* (T, Ḳ:) so explained by ISh. (T.) And A man *who is strong; who comes after, and aids, those who have recourse to him in need; and bears, or carries, what is redundant,* or *in excess; and repels the riders.* (T.) And رَجُلٌ مِعَمٌّ مِثَمٌّ مِلَمٌّ *A man who sets right an affair, and manages it,* or *acts vigorously in it.* (IAạr, T.) — رَجُلٌ مِثَمٌّ وَمِعَمٌّ and ▼ مِثَمَّةٌ وَمِعَمَّةٌ, (Ṣ, Ḳ,) in which latter phrase the ة is added to give intensiveness to the signification, (Ṣ,) *A man who sweeps and collects the good and the bad of a thing:* (Ṣ:) or *who eats the good of the food and the bad thereof.* (Ḳ.) [See also مِعَمَّةٌ, in art. عم.]

مِثَمَّةٌ: see what next precedes.

مَثْمُومٌ, applied to a house or chamber, (M, Ḳ,) and to a skin containing milk [&c.], (M,) *Covered with* ثُمَام. (M, Ḳ.)

ثمت

ثُمَّتَ and ثُمَّتْ: see ثُمَّ.

ثمد

1. ثَمَدَهُ, aor. ـُ, inf. n. ثَمْدٌ, *He took forth, or dug out, from it* (i. e. a ثَمَد q. v. infrà) *the earth, in order that the water might come forth;* (M, L;) as also ▼ اثمدهُ, (so in the TA, and in the TT from the M,) or ▼ اثّمدهُ, (accord. to the L,) and ▼ استثمدهُ. (M, L.) — Also, (Ḳ,) aor. and inf. n. as above, (TA,) *He took it* (اتّخذهُ) *as a* ثَمَد; and so ▼ اثمدهُ and ▼ استثمدهُ. (Ḳ, TA. [But see 8 below.]) — [Hence,] ‡ *He begged of him until he exhausted him of what he possessed.* (A meaning indicated, but not expressed, in the A.)] — And ثَمَدْتُ النَّاقَةَ بِالحَلْبِ ‡ *I exhausted the she-camel by milking.* (A.) — And ثَمَدَتْهُ النِّسَآءُ ‡ *Women exhausted him of his seminal fluid.* (T, Ṣ, M, A, Ḳ. In the CḲ ثَمَّدَتْهُ.) = ‡ *He gave him a gift.* (A.) = ثَمِدَ, (Ḳ,) inf. n. ثَمَدٌ, (TA,) *He* (a man, TA) *was, or became, fat;* as also ▼ اِثْمَادَّ (Ḳ) and ▼ اِثْمَأَدَّ. (ISh, TA.)

4: see 1, in two places. = اثمد عَيْنَهُ *He applied* إِثْمِد *as a collyrium to his eye.* (A, TA.)

8. اثّمد and اتّمد *He* (a man, Ṣ) *came to a* ثَمَد [q. v.] *to drink.* (Ṣ, Ḳ.) — اثّمد ثَمَدًا *He made,* or *prepared,* (اتّخذ,) *a* ثَمَد. (ISk, L.) See also 1.

10. استثمدهُ: see 1, in two places. — [Hence,] ‡ *He sought of him a gift,* (A,) or *a benefit, a favour,* or *an act of kindness.* (Ḳ.)

11. اِثْمَادَّ: see 1.

Q. Q. 4. اِثْمَأَدَّ: see 1.

ثَمْدٌ: see what next follows.

ثَمَدٌ (T, Ṣ, M, A, Ḳ) and ▼ ثَمْدٌ (Ṣ, M, Ḳ) and ▼ ثِمَادٌ, (M, Ḳ,) or the last is a pl. of one of the two preceding words, (MF,) *Water that is little in quantity,* (Lth, T, Ṣ, M, Ḳ,) *that has no continual increase:* (Ṣ, M, A, Ḳ:) or *a little water remaining in a tract of hard, or hard and level, ground:* or *what appears in winter and goes away in summer* (الصَّيْف): (M, Ḳ:) or *a small round hollow or cavity* (قَلْت) *in which the rain-water collects and from which men drink during two months of the spring-season* (الصَّيْف), *but which fails when the summer* (القَيْظ) *comes:* (IAạr, T:) and *rain-water that remains retained beneath the sand, and, when this is removed, is yielded by the ground:* (A:) pl. ثِمَادٌ (T, A) and أَثْمَادٌ [a pl. of pauc.]: (so in the L:) some say that ثِمَادٌ signifies *holes dug* or *excavated, in which is a little water;* and hence A'Obeyd says, سُجِرَتِ الثِّمَادُ, meaning that the holes &c. were filled by the rain; but he does not explain it: (M:) or ثِمَادٌ signifies *wells dug around a place which has been prepared to receive the water of the rain, where there is continually rain-water, this place having water-courses, and the said wells being filled therefrom:* men drink the water that lies open to view until it becomes dried up by the effect of the hot winds of summer; the wells remaining. (Aboo-Málik, T.)

ثِمَادٌ: see ثَمَدٌ.

ثَامِدٌ A lamb or kid or calf *that has begun to eat.* (Ṣ.)

إِثْمِدٌ [*An ore of antimony:* or *antimony itself; stibium;* or *stimmi:*] *collyrium-stone* (حَجَرُ الكُحْل), (Ḳ, TA,) *which is black inclining to red, the mines whereof are in Iṣpahán, whence the best is obtained, and in the West, whence the hardest is obtained:* (TA:) *a certain stone used as a collyrium:* (Ṣ:) *a certain stone from which collyrium* (كُحْل) *is prepared:* or *collyrium* (كُحْل) *itself:* (M:) or *a substance resembling it:* (Seer, M:) or *a species thereof:* (Lth, T:) or *black* كُحْل, *the mine whereof is in the East:* said by some of the lawyers to be *that of Iṣpahán:* and said to be an arabicized word. (Mṣb.) The women of the Arabs used also to sprinkle [or rub] it upon the lips and gums, in order that the teeth might glisten the more. (EM p. 62.) [And for the same purpose, many of them tattoo their lips, so as to make them of a uniform dull bluish hue.] — One says of a man who remains awake at night, journeying or working, فُلَانٌ يَجْعَلُ اللَّيْلَ إِثْمِدًا [*Such a one makes the night a collyrium*]; the blackness of the night being as though it were a collyrium to his eyes because he labours all the night in seeking the means of attaining to eminence. (AA, T, L.)

مَثْمُودٌ A water *exhausted by the crowding of men to it,* (Ṣ, M, Ḳ,) *except the smaller portion of it.* (Ṣ, Ḳ.) — And [hence,] ‡ A man *exhausted of what he possessed,* (T, Ṣ, M, A, Ḳ,) *by his giving when asked,* (M, Ḳ,) or *in consequence of much begging.* (T, Ṣ, M, A.) — And ‡ A man *exhausted of his seminal fluid by women.* (Ṣ, A, Ḳ.)

ثمر

1. ثَمَرَ: see 4, in three places. — Also *It* (fruit) *was,* or *became, ripe.* (T.) — ثَمَرَ لِلْغَنَمِ *He collected trees* (which are called ثُمَر, TA [or rather *shrubs*]) *for the sheep* or *goats.* (Ḳ.) = ثَمُرَ, aor. ـُ, ‡ *It* (a man's wealth) *became abundant.* (A, TA.) — فُلَانٌ مَجْدُودٌ مَا يَثْمُرُ ‡ [*Such a one is fortunate in the abundance of his wealth:* or] *such a one possesses wealth.* (A, TA.)

2. ثمّر, inf. n. تَثْمِيرٌ, *It* (a plant) *shook off its blossoms,* [or *shed them,*] *and organized and compacted* (in the M عَقَدَ, and in the Ḳ عَقَّدَ) *its fruit.* (AḤn, M, Ḳ.) — ثمّر السِّقَآءُ, inf. n. as above; and ▼ اثمر; ‡ *The skin* [*of milk*] *showed upon it the forming of the butter in little clots:* (Ṣ, M,* Ḳ:) and ثمّر اللَّبَنُ, and ▼ اثمر, (T,* A,) ‡ *the milk, being churned, showed upon it what resembled dry scabs on the skin,* (T, A,) *previously to their becoming large and collecting together and forming butter:* and you say of the skin [containing it], ثمّر and ▼ اثمر: (T:) and ▼ اثمر الزُّبْدُ † *the butter collected together.* (T.) = Also † *He* (God) *made* a man's wealth *abundant.* (Ṣ.) And ‡ *He* (a man) *increased, and made abundant,* his wealth. (M, Ḳ.)

4. اثمر, [inf. n. إِثْمَارٌ,] *It* (a tree) *put forth its fruit:* (T, Ṣ:) or *put forth its fruit yet unripe:* (IAạr:) or *began to put forth its fruit:* (T, Mṣb:) or *bore fruit;* as also ▼ ثَمَرَ, (M, Ḳ,) aor. ـُ: (TA:) or [اثمر signifies *it bore fruit;* and ▼ ثَمَرَ, *it attained the time of bearing fruit:* or the former, *it bore unripe fruit;* and the latter, *it bore ripe fruit:* or the former, *it attained the time for the plucking of its fruit;* and the latter, *it put forth its fruit:* for it is said that] ▼ مُثْمِرٌ signifies *bearing fruit;* and ▼ ثَامِرٌ, *that has attained the time of bearing fruit:* or the former, *unripe* fruit; (M;) and the latter *ripe* fruit: (T, M:) or the former, *that has attained the time for plucking;* (AḤn, M, Ḳ;) and the latter, *that has put forth its fruit:* (Ḳ:) or the latter of these epithets is applied to a tree, signifying *bearing ripe fruit;* and to fruit, signifying *ripe.* (IAạr, TA.) — *He* (a man) *had fruit that had come forth but that was not yet ripe.* (T.) — ‡ *He* (a man) *became abundant in wealth;* (T, Ṣ, M, A, Ḳ;) as also ▼ ثَمَرَ, (A, Ḳ,) aor. ـُ, (TA,) inf. n. ثُمُورٌ. (A, TA.) — مَا أَثْمَرَ ابْنُ ▼ ثَمِيرٍ ‡ [*As long as the*

moonlight-night renews itself, or *recurs;* i. e. *ever*]. (TA.) — See also 2, in four places. = This verb is mentioned by most of the lexicologists only as intrans.; but it is also trans., signifying *It* (a tree, or ‡ other thing,) *produced* fruit, ‡ &c. (Shifá el-Ghaleel, MF.) — Also *He fed* a person *with fruits.* (TA.)

ثُمُرٌ : see ثَمَرٌ, in two places.

ثَمَرٌ (T, Ṣ, M, A, Mṣb, Ḳ) and ▼ ثُمْرٌ (Sb, M, A) and ▼ ثِيمَارٌ, (M,) [coll. gen. ns.,] The *fruit of trees;* (M, Ḳ;) the *several kinds of fruits;* (T;) the *fruit which a tree produces, whether it is eaten or not eaten:* (Mṣb:) pl. of the first, ثِمَارٌ; and pl. pl. (i. e. pl. of ثِمَارٌ, Fr, Ṣ, M, Mṣb) ثُمُرٌ; and pl. pl. pl. (i. e. pl. of ثُمُرٌ, Ṣ, Mṣb) أَثْمَارٌ; (Ṣ, Mṣb, Ḳ;) and the pl. of أَثْمَارٌ is أَثَامِيرُ; (IHsh, TA:) or ثُمُرٌ is pl. of ثَمَرٌ; (AHeyth, TA;) or it may be pl. of ثَمَرَةٌ, because it is of a form more common as that of a pl. of a word of this form than of the form of ثِمَارٌ: (M:) ثَمَرَةٌ is the n. un. of ثَمَرٌ, (Ṣ, M, Ḳ,) and ثُمْرَةٌ is that of ثُمْرٌ: (Sb, M, Ḳ:*) the pl. of ثَمَرَةٌ is ثَمَرَاتٌ (Ṣ, Mṣb) and ▼ ثَمْرَآءُ: (Ḳ:) [or rather this last is a quasi-pl. n.:] ثُمْرَةٌ, which none but Sb mentions, has, accord. to him, no broken pl.: (M:) IHsh says that there is no word like ثُمُرٌ in its series of pls. except أُكُمٌ. (MF: see أَكَمَةٌ.) — Also ثَمَرٌ, (M, A, Ḳ,) or ▼ ثُمُرٌ, (T, Ṣ,) and ▼ ثُمْرٌ, (Ṣ,) and ▼ ثَمَارٌ, (Ḳ,) or ▼ ثِيمَارٌ, (M,) or ▼ ثَيْمَارٌ; (TA;) of which last three, the first (ثمار) is disapproved by several writers; and some say that it is for ثَمَرٌ, the second vowel being lengthened for the sake of metre; (MF;) ‡ *Property,* or *wealth,* (T, Ṣ,) *increased* and *multiplied:* (Ṣ:) or *various kinds of property* or *wealth,* (I 'Ab, M, Ḳ,) *increased* and *multiplied,* and *gained,* or *acquired, for oneself:* (I 'Ab, B:) or, accord. to Mujáhid, ثَمَرٌ, in the Ḳur, means *fruit;* and ▼ ثُمُرٌ, *property,* or *wealth;* but Yoo did not admit this, app. holding both to mean the same: (T:) in the Ḳur xviii. 32, AA read ▼ ثُمْرٌ, and explained it as signifying *kinds of property* or *wealth.* (Ṣ.) — ثَمَرٌ also signifies ‡ *Gold* and *silver:* (AAF, M, Ḳ:) so accord. to Mujáhid in the Ḳur xviii. 32; but this is not known in the proper language. (AAF, M.) — And *Trees* [or *shrubs*]: (TA:) and ثَمَرَةٌ *a tree* [or *shrub*]. (Th, M, Ḳ. [In the CḲ, erroneously, ثُمْرَةٌ.]) — And [the n. un.] ثَمَرَةٌ, [in the CḲ, erroneously, ثُمْرَةٌ,] ‡ *A child,* or *son;* (Ḳ, B, TA;) as also ثَمَرَةُ القَلْبِ, [of which other meanings will be found below,] and ثَمَرَةُ الفُؤَادِ [lit., like the next preceding expression, *fruit of the heart*]: accord. to some, in the Ḳur ii. 150, الثَّمَرَاتُ means الأَوْلَادُ [or *children*] and الأَحْفَادُ [or *grandchildren,* &c.]. (B, TA.) — † *Progeny;* or *offspring.* (Ḳ.) [Whence, app.,] قُطِعَتْ ثَمَرَتُهُ † *His* [*power of*] *procreating was cut off:* or *his appetite for sexual intercourse.* (TA from a trad.) [Another meaning of this phrase will be found below.] — † The *fruit,* as meaning the *profit,* of a thing: (Mṣb, TA:) as that of knowledge, namely, good works; and that of good works, namely, Paradise. (TA.) Hence, لَيْسَ لَهُ ثَمَرَةٌ † *There is no profit pertaining to it.* (Mṣb.) [Hence also,] ثَمَرَةُ مَالٍ ‡ *The increase of property.* (A.) — ‡ The *knot of the extremity,* (A,) or *of the extremities,* (Ḳ,) of a whip; (A, Ḳ;) because like a fruit in its form and in its manner of hanging: (B, TA:) and ثَمَرٌ, the *knots of the extremities* of whips: (Ṣ, Mj, Mgh:) or the former signifies the *end,* or *extremity,* of a whip: (T:) or, more correctly, the *tail, which is* [*the appendage that forms*] *the end,* or *extremity,* of a whip; its عَذَبَة. (Mgh.) — ‡ The *extremity,* (T, Ḳ,) or *tip,* (A,) of the tongue: (T, A, Ḳ:) or its *lower extremity.* (IAth, TA.) — ‡ A man's *prepuce:* pl. ثِمَارٌ: so in the phrases قُطِعَتْ ثَمَرَةُ فُلَانٍ, and قُطِعَتْ ثِمَارُهُمْ, meaning ‡ *Such a one was circumcised,* and *they were circumcised.* (A.) [Another meaning of the former of these phrases has been mentioned above.] — † The *skin* of the head. (ISh, T, Ḳ.) — ثَمَرَةُ القَلْبِ [of which one meaning has been given above] also signifies † *The heart's core;* or *the black,* or *inner, part of the heart;* syn. سُوَيْدَاؤُهُ, and حَبَّتُهُ. (Ṣ in art. حب.) [Hence,] خَصَّنِى بِثَمَرَةِ قَلْبِهِ ‡ [*He distinguished me peculiarly,* or *specially,*] *by his love,* or *affection.* (A, TA.) And أَعْطَاهُ صَفْقَةَ يَدِهِ وَثَمَرَةَ قَلْبِهِ ‡ [*He gave him his ratification of the bargain, and*] *his sincerest agreement.* (A, TA.) — فِى السَّمَآءِ ثَمَرَةٌ and ثَمَرٌ ‡ *In the sky is a small portion,* or *quantity, of cloud.* (A, TA.) — ثَمَرُ الحِنَّآءِ: see art. حنأ. — See also ثَمِيرٌ.

ثُمْرٌ : see ثَمَرٌ, in three places.

ثَمِرٌ ‡ Wealth *blessed with increase:* (A, TA:) or *much,* or *abundant,* wealth; as also ▼ مَثْمُورٌ. (Ḳ.) — ثَمْرَآءُ : see ثَمِرَةٌ. — مَا نَفْسِى لَكَ بِثَمِرَةٍ ‡ *My mind has no sweetness for thee:* (Ḳ, TA:) but accord. to Z, in the A, art. تمر, the last word in this phrase is with ت, and so it is written in the Ḳ in that art., and explained as meaning طَيِّبَة [or *agreeably affected*]. (TA.)

ثَمْرَآءُ : see ثَمَرٌ, first sentence. = شَجَرَةٌ ثَمْرَآءُ *A tree having fruit;* (Ṣ;) *of which the fruit has come forth:* (Ḳ:) or *abounding with fruit;* as also ▼ ثَمِيرَةٌ: or this latter signifies the *same as* ▼ مُثْمِرَةٌ; and its pl. is ثُمُرٌ. (AḤn, M.) And أَرْضٌ ثَمْرَآءُ *Land abounding with fruit;* as also ▼ ثَمِيرَةٌ, (AḤn, M, Ḳ,) or ▼ ثَمِرَةٌ. (So in some copies of the Ḳ, and in the TA.)

ثَمَارٌ : see ثَمَرٌ, second sentence.

ثَمِيرٌ; fem. with ة: hence شَجَرَةٌ ثَمِيرَةٌ, and أَرْضٌ ثَمِيرَةٌ : see ثَمْرَآءُ. — ثَمِيرٌ also signifies † *Milk of which the butter has not come forth;* (M, Ḳ;) and so ▼ ثَمِيرَةٌ: (Ḳ:) or both signify *milk of which the butter has appeared:* (M, Ḳ:) or لَبَنٌ ثَمِيرٌ, *milk of which the butter has not been taken forth:* (TA in art. جهر:) or *milk of which the butter has formed into little clots:* (IAth, TA:) and لَبَنٌ مُثْمِرٌ [in like manner], *milk fit for churning, and showing upon it the formation of little clots of butter:* (Aṣ, M:) and ▼ ثَمِيرَةٌ, (as some say, M,) ‡ *what appears, of butter, before it collects together* (Ṣ, M,* Ḳ) *and attains the time of its becoming in a good,* or *proper, state:* (Ṣ, M:) and ▼ ثَمَرٌ, *what is seen upon milk, when it has been churned, resembling dry scabs on the skin,* (T, A,) is also termed the ▼ ثَمِيرَة of milk. (T.) [See 2.] — ابْنُ ثَمِيرٍ ‡ *The moonlight-night,* (Ṣ, M, Ḳ,) *when the moon is full;* (TA;) [*contr. of* ابْنُ سَمِيرٍ.] See 4.

ثَمِيرَةٌ fem. of ثَمِيرٌ. — Also a subst.: see ثَمِيرٌ, in three places.

ثَامِرٌ : see 4. — ثَامِرُ الحِلْمِ ‡ *Perfect,* or *complete, in respect of forbearance,* or *clemency;* like ripe fruit. (IAṣr, M.) — الثَّامِرُ *The flower of the* حُمَّاض [or *rose-coloured sorrel*]; (AḤn, M, Ḳ;) *which is red.* (TA.) — *The* لُوبِيَآء [*dolichos lubia* of Forskål]. (AḤn, M, Ḳ.)

ثِيمَارٌ, or ثَيْمَارٌ : see ثَمَرٌ, in three places.

مُثْمِرٌ : see 4; and see also ثَمْرَآءُ. — عَقْلٌ مُثْمِرٌ † [*Fruitful intellect;*] the *intellect of the Muslim:* opposed to عَقْلٌ عَقِيمٌ [barren intellect;] the intellect of the unbeliever. (M, TA.)

مُثْمِرَةٌ : see ثَمِيرٌ.

مَثْمُورٌ : see ثَمِرٌ. — قَوْمٌ مَثْمُورُونَ ‡ *A people,* or *company of men, abounding in wealth.* (Ḳ,* TA.)

ثمل

1. ثَمَلَ, [aor., app., ـِ and ـُ,] inf. n. ثَمْلٌ, *It* (water) *remained* in a watering-trough or tank. (Mṣb.) — Also, (T, TA,) aor. ـِ and ـُ, (TḲ,) inf. n. ثَمْلٌ (T, M, Ḳ) and ثُمُولٌ, (M, Ḳ,) *He* (a man, T) *remained, stayed, resided, dwelt,* or *tarried.* (T, M, Ḳ.) You say, ثَمَلَ فُلَانٌ فَمَا يَبْرَحُ *Such a one remained,* &c., *and does not quit his place.* (T.) And ارْتَحَلَ بَنُو فُلَانٍ وَثَمَلَ فُلَانٌ فِى دَارِهِمْ, i. e., [*The sons of such a one removed,* or *departed, and such a one*] *remained* [*in their abode*]. (T, TA.) = ثَمَلَهُ *He steeped it,* or *macerated it, and left it,* or *kept it, long;* namely, poison. (Skr p. 194.) [See ثُمَالٌ.] — ثَمَلَتِ الصِّبْيَانَ, aor. ـُ, [inf. n., app., ثَمْلٌ,] *She* (a woman) *was a support to the children, remaining,* or *abiding, with them.* (M.) And ثَمَلَهُمْ, (T, M, Ḳ,) aor. ـُ (T, Ḳ) and ـِ, (Ḳ,) inf. n. ثَمْلٌ, (M,) *He aided them,* or *succoured them,* (T, Ḳ,) namely, his party, kinsfolk, or tribe, (Ḳ,) *and undertook,* or *managed, their affairs:* (Ibn-Buzurj, T, Ḳ:) *he fed them, and gave them drink,* (M, Ḳ,) namely, orphans, (M,) *and undertook,* or *managed, their affairs.* (M, Ḳ.) — مَا ثَمَلَ شَرَابَهُ بِشَىْءٍ (Yoo, T, Ṣ, M, Ḳ) مِنْ طَعَامٍ (Yoo, Ṣ) *He ate no food before drinking.* (Yoo, T, Ṣ, M, Ḳ.) — You say also, أَكَلَتِ المَاشِيَةُ مِنَ الكَلَإِ مَا يَثْمُلُ مَا فِى أَجْوَافِهَا مِنَ المَآءِ *The cattle ate of the herbage what was equal to the water that they had drunk.* (T.) — And ثَمَلَ, aor. ـُ, *He ate* (Ḳ) food. (TḲ.) = ثَمِلَ, (Ṣ, M, Ḳ,) aor. ـَ, (Ḳ,) inf. n. ثَمَلٌ, (Ṣ, M, Ḳ,*) *He* (a man, Ṣ) *became intoxicated.* (Ṣ, M, Ḳ.)

2. ثَمَّلَ as an intrans. v.: see 4. ═ ثَمَّلَهُ, inf. n. تَثْمِيلٌ, *He made it*, or *caused it, to remain; he left it*; or *reserved it*; (Ṣ, Ḳ; [in the former of which, for the explanation بَقَّاهُ, Golius found نَقَّاهُ;]) as also ▼ اثملهُ. (Ṣ, TA.) You say, أَحْقِنِ الصَّرِيحَ وَأَثْمِلِ ▼ الثُّمَالَةَ, i. e., [*Collect thou the clear* milk *in a skin, and*] *leave the* ثمالة [or *froth*] in the milking-vessel. (T.) — ثَمَّلْتُ الحُبَّ *I took forth the* ثُمَالَة [or *remaining water* or *the like*] *from the bottom of the jar*; as also ▼ أَثْمَلْتُهُ. (TA.)

4. اثمل *It* (a thing, Ṣ, or milk, TA) *had much* ثُمَالَة, i. e., *froth*; (Ṣ,* TA;) as also ▼ ثَمَّلَ. (TA.) — اثملت *She* (a camel) *gave much froth in her milk.* (TA in art. حلب.) ═ See also 2, in three places.

5. تثمّل *He supped*, or *sipped*, what was in a vessel. (Ibn-'Abbád, Ḳ.)

ثَمْلٌ: see ثَمَلٌ, in four places.

ثُمْلٌ: see ثُمْلَةٌ.

ثَمَلٌ *Remanence, stay, residence*, or *tarriance*; like ▼ ثَمْلٌ: (T, M, Ḳ:) [the latter is an inf. n.: see 1:] and both signify also *ease; repose; easiness of life, and ampleness of the circumstances thereof.* (T.) You say دَارُ ثَمَلٍ (T, M) and ▼ ثَمْلٍ (M) *An abode of* [*fixed*] *residence*, (T, M,) *and of ease*, or *repose*, &c. (T.) And ▼ مَكَانٌ ثَمْلٌ *A place peopled, inhabited, well stocked with people and the like.* (Th, AAF, M.) And دَارُ بَنِى فُلَانٍ ثَمَلٌ and ▼ ثَمْلٌ *The abode of the sons of such a one is an abode of* [*fixed*] *residence.* (IDrd, TA.) — *Shade*, or *shadow.* (M, Ḳ.) ═ *Intoxication*: (Ḳ:) inf. n. of ثَمِلَ. (Ṣ, M.) ═ See also ثُمْلَةٌ, in two places.

ثَمِلٌ *Intoxicated.* (Ṣ, M, Ḳ.) — أَنَا ثَمِلٌ إِلَى مَوْضِعِ كَذَا ‡ *I have a love for such a place.* (Ḳ,* TA.)

ثَمْلَةٌ, (T, M,) or ▼ ثُمْلَةٌ, (Ḳ,) *Mud taken forth from the bottom of a well.* (AZ, T, M, Ḳ.) — See also ثُمْلَةٌ, in two places.

ثُمْلَةٌ *Grain*, and *meal of parched barley or wheat* (سَوِيق), and *dates, of which half* and *less*, (AZ, T, M, Ḳ,) or *half* and *more*, (M, Ḳ,) *is* [*remaining*] *in the receptacle*, or *bag*; (AZ, T, M, Ḳ;) as also ▼ ثَمْلَةٌ (Ḳ) and ▼ ثَمِيلَةٌ: (M, Ḳ:) pl. (of the first, TA) ثُمَلٌ and (of the last, TA) ثَمَائِلُ. (Ḳ.) — And in like manner, *A* [*heap such as is termed*] صُبْرَة *of wheat.* (TA.) — Also, and ▼ ثَمْلَةٌ, (AA, Ṣ, M, Ḳ,) and ▼ ثَمَلَةٌ, (Ḳ,) and ▼ ثُمَالَةٌ, (Ṣ, M, Mṣb,) and ▼ ثَمِيلَةٌ, (Ḳ,) *A remainder*, (AA, Ṣ,) or *water remaining*, (Mṣb,) or *a little water remaining*, (M, Ḳ,) *in a watering-trough*, (Mṣb,) or *in the bottom of a watering-trough*, (Ṣ, M, Ḳ,) or *of a skin*, (M, Ḳ,) or *of a vessel* (AA, Ṣ, M) *of any kind*, (M,) &c.; (AA, Ṣ;) and the same, (TA,) or ▼ ثَمِيلَةٌ, of which ثَمِيلٌ is the pl. [or rather coll. gen. n.], (Ṣ,) *water*, (Ṣ,) or *a little water*, (TA,) *remaining in a rock*, or *in a valley*: (Ṣ, TA:) or these two words signify *water remaining in pools left by torrents, and in hollows that have been dug.* (T.) [See an ex. of ▼ ثُمَالَة in a verse cited voce قَصْرٌ.] — بِهِ ثُمْلَةٌ and ▼ ثُمَلٌ †*In him is somewhat* [*remaining*] *of intelligence, and prudence*, (Ḳ, TA,) *and judgment, to which regard*, or *recourse, may be had.* (TA.) — See also ثُمْلَةٌ. — And see ثُمْلَةٌ.

ثَمَلَةٌ: see ثُمْلَةٌ. — Also, (IF, TA,) or ▼ ثَمَلٌ, (M,) *Some tar remaining in a vessel.* (IF, M, TA.) — And (hence, IF, TA) the former, *A piece of rag*, (IF, M,) *dipped in tar*, (M,) or *a tuft of wool*, (Ṣ, Ḳ,) *with which a camel is tarred*, (IF, Ṣ, M, Ḳ,) [to cure him of, or preserve him from, the mange, or scab,] *and with which a skin for water or milk is anointed*; (M, Ḳ;) as also ▼ ثُمْلَةٌ (M, Ḳ) and ▼ مِثْمَلَةٌ. (Ṣ, Ḳ.) — And (hence, as being likened thereto, TA) The *rag of the menses*: pl. [or rather coll. gen. n.] ▼ ثَمَلٌ. (M, Ḳ.)

ثُمَالٌ *Steeped*, or *macerated, poison*; as also ▼ مُثَمَّلٌ: (T, Ṣ, Ḳ: [in the CḲ, المُنْتَقِعُ is put for المُنْقَعُ:]) or ▼the latter signifies poison *that has been long steeped, and has remained*: (Ṣ,* M:) or *that has been steeped in a vessel, and remained steeped for some days, until it has fermented*: (Ibn-'Abbád, Z:) or poison *with which has been mixed something that strengthens it and excites its energy, that it may be more penetrating*, or *more effective*: (Ḥam p. 215:) and simply *poison.* (T.) [The *poison of a serpent or other thing.* (Golius, from Meyd.)] — [Hence,] رَنَّحَهُ مُثَمَّلُ ▼ الكَرَى ‡ [*The infection of drowsiness made him to incline from side to side*]. (TA.) — See also ثُمَالَةٌ.

ثِمَالٌ *An aider*, or *a succourer, who undertakes*, or *manages, the affairs*, of his party, kinsfolk, or tribe: (T, Ṣ, Ḳ:) their *stay*, or *support*: (M:) the *aider*, or *succourer*, of orphans: (Lḥ, M:) *a refuge*, or *protector.* (Mgh. [See also مَثْمِلٌ.]) Hence, (Mgh,)

ثِمَالُ اليَتَامَى عِصْمَةٌ لِلْأَرَامِلِ

[*The aider*, &c., or *the stay*, or *support*, or *the refuge, of the orphans; a defence to the widows*]; (Mgh, TA;) said by Aboo-Ṭálib, in praising Mohammad. (TA.) [See also another ex. in a verse cited voce أَنْ.]

ثَمِيلٌ: see ثُمْلَةٌ.

ثُمَالَةٌ: see ثُمْلَةٌ, in two places: — and see ثَمِيلَةٌ. — Also, (Ṣ, M, Mgh, Mṣb, Ḳ,) and ▼ ثُمَالٌ, (M, Mgh,) accord. to Th, (M,) or the latter is pl. of the former, (Ṣ, M, Mṣb, Ḳ,) [or rather coll. gen. n.,] *Froth*, (Ṣ, M, Mgh, Mṣb, Ḳ,) *of any kind*: (M:) or *froth of milk* (Th, M) *when it is drawn.* (M.)

ثَمِيلَةٌ: see ثُمْلَةٌ, in three places. — Also *Remains of food*, (M, Ḳ,) or *of herbage*, or *fodder*, (Ṣ,) or *of fresh pasture and of fodder*, (T,) *and of drink*, (Ṣ, Ḳ,) *in the belly*, (Ṣ, M, Ḳ,) or *in the intestines and other parts*, (T,) *of a camel*, or *other animal*; (Ṣ;) as also ▼ ثُمَالَةٌ: (Ḳ:) and *food that has been eaten before drinking*: (T, Ṣ:) and *any remains*, or *anything remaining*: (Ṣ:) pl. ثَمَائِلُ. (TA.) — Also The *part* (Lḥ, M, Ḳ) *of the belly* (Ḳ) *of a man* (Lḥ, M) *in which are the food and drink*: (Lḥ, M, Ḳ:) and the *part in which is the drink in the belly of the ass.* (Lḥ, M.)

مَثْمِلٌ, (Ṣ, Ṣgh, Ḳ,) like مَنْزِلٌ, (Ḳ, TA, but in one copy of the Ṣ مِثْمَلٌ, and in another مُثْمَلٌ, and in the CḲ like مِنْبَرٌ,) *A refuge; an asylum.* (Ṣ, Ṣgh, Ḳ. [See also ثِمَالٌ.])

مُثْمِلٌ Milk *having froth*; [or, app., *having much froth*; see 4;] as also ▼ مُثَمِّلٌ. (M, Ḳ.)

مِثْمَلَةٌ: see ثَمَلَةٌ.

مُثَمَّلٌ: see ثُمَالٌ, in three places.

مُثَمِّلٌ: see مُثْمِلٌ.

ثمن

1. ثَمَنَهُمْ, aor. ـُ, (Ṣ, M, Mgh, &c.,) inf. n. ثَمْنٌ, (M,) *He took the eighth of their goods*, or *property.* (Ṣ, M, Mgh, Mṣb, Ḳ.) — And, aor. ـِ, *He was*, or *became, the eighth of them*: (Ṣ, Mgh, Mṣb, Ḳ:) or *he made them, with himself, eight.* (Ṣ in art. ثلث.) And *He made them*, they being seventy-nine, *to be eighty.* (A'Obeyd, Ṣ in art. ثلث.) ═ ثَمُنَ, [aor. ـُ,] inf. n. ثَمَانَةٌ, *It* (a commodity) *was*, or *became, precious, costly, of high price*; and ▼ اثمن [signifies the same; or] *it had a price*, or *value.* (TA. [See ثَمِينٌ.])

2. ثمّنهُ *He made it eight*: or *called it eight.* (Esh-Sheybánee, and Ḳ in art. وحد.) — [*He made it octangular.*] — ثمّن لِامْرَأَتِهِ, or عِنْدَهَا, *He remained eight nights with his wife*: and in like manner the verb is used in relation to any saying or action. (TA in art. سبع.) ═ Also, (T, TA,) inf. n. تَثْمِينٌ, (TA,) *He collected it together.* (T, TA.) ═ Also, inf. n. as above, (Mṣb, TA,) *He made known*, or *notified*, [or *he set*, or *assigned it*,] *its price*; i. e., the price of a commodity; like قَوَّمَهُ: (TA:) or *he assigned it a price by conjecture*: (Mṣb:) and ▼ اثمنهُ *he named a price for it.* (TA.)

4. اثمن القَوْمُ *The party of men became eight*: (Ṣ, Ḳ:) and also *the party of men became eighty.* (M and L in art. ثلث.) — أَثْمَنَتْ *She brought forth her eighth offspring.* (TA in art. بكر.) — اثمن said of a man, *He was*, or *became, one whose camels came to water* ▼ ثِمْنًا, (Ṣ, Ḳ,) i. e., *on the eighth night* [*after the next preceding watering*]. (Ḳ.) ═ اثمن said of a commodity: see 1. ═ اثمنهُ *He sold it for a price.* (Mṣb.) — See also 2. — اثمن الرَّجُلَ مَتَاعَهُ, (T, Ṣ,) or بِسِلْعَتِهِ, (Ḳ,) and اثمن لَهُ, (T, Ṣ, Ḳ,) [i. e. اثمن له متاعه, or سلعته,] signify the same, (T, Ṣ,*) *He gave the man the price of his commodity*: (Ḳ:) or اثمن الرَّجُلَ بِمَتَاعِهِ, and اثمن لَهُ مَتَاعَهُ, *he named to the man a price for his commodity, and assigned it to it, or to him.* (Mgh.)

ثُمْنٌ: see ثُمُنٌ.

ثِمْنٌ The *eighth young one or offspring.* (A in art. ثليث.) ═ *One of the periods between two drinkings*, or *waterings, of camels*: (Ṣ:) [or the *end of one of those periods*; namely, the *night of coming to water which is*] *the eighth night of a period between two drinkings*, or *waterings, of camels*, (Ḳ,) [*counting the night of the next preceding drinking*, or *watering, as the first*: see رِبْع and خِمْس &c.] See also 4.

ثَمَنٌ The *price* of a thing; i. e. the *thing that the seller receives in return for the thing sold, whether money* or *a commodity*; (Er-Rághib, TA;) the ثَمَن of a thing sold: (Ṣ:) and also (Er-Rághib, TA) *a compensation*, or *substitute*, (Mgh, Mṣb, Er-Rághib, TA,) *whatever it be, for a thing*, (Er-Rághib, TA,) i. e., *for a thing that is sold*; but in the sense commonly known, *such as it is incumbent upon one to pay, of pieces of silver, and of gold* [or *other money*]; *not commodities and the like*: (Mgh:) or the *value*, or *worth*, of a thing; (Ḳ;) its قِيمَة: (T:) or the *estimated value*, or *worth*, of a thing, *by mutual consent, even though it be really excessive or deficient*; whereas the قيمة is its real value or worth, its equivalent: (MF:) pl. أَثْمَانٌ (T, Mgh, Mṣb, Ḳ) and أَثْمُنٌ, (Ṣ, Mṣb, Ḳ,) the latter used only as a pl. of pauc., (Mṣb,) and [so] أَثْمِنَةٌ. (CḲ: not in the TA.) The saying in the Ḳur [ii. 38 and v. 48], وَلَا تَشْتَرُوا بِآيَاتِى ثَمَنًا قَلِيلًا is metaphorical, meaning ‡ *And take ye not in exchange for my signs a small substitute*: [i. e. purchase not in exchange for belief in my word the happiness, or enjoyments, of the present life.] (Mgh.) With respect to this saying, Fr remarks, when ثَمَنًا occurs in the Ḳur, with ب prefixed to the name of the thing sold or bought, in most cases it relates to two things whereof neither is a ثمن in the sense commonly known, i. e., such as pieces of gold and of silver: and such is the case when you say, اِشْتَرَيْتُ ثَوْبًا بِكِسَآءٍ [*I purchased a garment with a* كساء, q. v.]: either of these may be termed a ثمن for the other: but in speaking of pieces of silver and of gold, you prefix the ب to the ثمن [only]; as is done in [the chapter of] Yoosuf, [i. e. ch. xii., v. 20, where it is said,] وَشَرَوْهُ بِثَمَنٍ بَخْسٍ دَرَاهِمَ مَعْدُودَةٍ [*And they sold him for a deficient*, or *an insufficient, price: for pieces of silver* not many, so as to require their being weighed, but few, and therefore *counted*]: for pieces of silver are always a ثمن: and when you purchase pieces of silver and of gold with the like, you prefix the ب to whichever of the two you will, because each of them in this case is a purchase and a price. (T.)

ثُمْنٌ (Ṣ, M, Mgh, Mṣb, Ḳ) and ▼ ثُمُنٌ (M, Mṣb, Ḳ) *An eighth; an eighth part* or *portion*; as also ▼ ثَمِينٌ; (Ṣ, M,* Mgh, Mṣb, Ḳ;) agreeably with a general rule applying to fractions, accord. to some; (M, Ḳ;) but ثَلِيث was ignored by AZ (T and Ṣ in art. ثلث) and by others, (TA,) and so was خَمِيس: (Ṣ in art. ثلث:) pl. أَثْمَانٌ. (M, Ḳ.)

ثَمَانٌ and ثَمَانٍ: see ثَمَانِيَةٌ.

ثَمِينٌ: see ثُمْنٌ. — Also *High-priced*; or *of high value*; (Ṣ, TA;) and ▼ مُثْمِنٌ [signifies the same; or] *having a price*, or *value*: (TA:) but accord. to the Durrat el-Ghowwáṣ, the assertion that the former has the meaning here assigned to it is a mistake; for it means [only] the same as ثُمْنٌ; and a thing that has a price, or value, is termed مثمن [app. مُثْمِنٌ, as above; but perhaps مُثْمَنٌ, q. v.]. (Ḥar p. 42.)

ثَمَانِيَةٌ a noun of number, well known; [meaning *Eight*;] as also ▼ ثَمَانٍ, (M, TA,) which is like يَمَانٍ, (M, Ḳ,) in form: (M:) the former is the masc. form: the latter, the fem.: (Mṣb:) this is not a rel. n. [though likened above to يَمَانٍ]: (M, Ḳ:) or it is originally a rel. n. from الثُّمْنُ, because it is the part, or portion, that makes seven to be eight, so that it is its eighth: they make the first letter to be pronounced with fet-ḥ, because they make changes [in some other cases] in the rel. n., (Ṣ, Ḳ,) as when they say سُهْلِىٌّ and دُهْرِىٌّ, [which are rel. ns. of سَهْل and دَهْر,] (Ṣ,) and they suppress one of the two ى which are characteristic of the rel. n., and compensate it by the insertion of ا, as they do in the rel. n. of اليَمَنُ [when they say يَمَانٍ, originally يَمَنِىٌّ], for يَمَانِىٌّ: (Ṣ, Ḳ: [and the like is said in the Mgh:]) El-Fárisee says that the ا of ثَمَانٍ is the characteristic of the rel. n., because this word is not a broken pl. like صَحَارٍ; and IF assents to this, and says that were it not so, the ة would be inseparable, as it is in عَبَاقِيَة &c. (M.) You say ثَمَانِيَةُ رِجَالٍ [*Eight men*], (T, Ṣ, Mgh,) and ثَمَانِيَةُ أَيَّامٍ [*eight days*]. (Mṣb.) And when ثمان is prefixed to another noun, its ى is retained, like the ى in القَاضِى: (Ṣ, Mṣb, Ḳ:) and it is decl. in the same manner as words of the class to which this last belongs: (Mṣb:) you say ثَمَانِى نِسْوَةٍ [*Eight women*], (T, Ṣ, Mgh, Mṣb, Ḳ,) and ثَمَانِى مِائَةٍ [*eight hundred*], (Ṣ, Mṣb, Ḳ,) [in the nom. and gen. cases;] and رَأَيْتُ ثَمَانِىَ نِسْوَةٍ [*I saw eight women*], pronouncing the fet-ḥah [at the end, in this case]. (Mṣb.) When it is with tenween, the ى is dropped in the nom. and gen. cases, but it is retained in the accus. case: (Ṣ, Ḳ:) [i. e.,] when the fem. form is not prefixed to another noun, you say, عِنْدِى مِنَ النِّسَآءِ ثَمَانٍ [*I have with me, of women, eight*], and مَرَرْتُ مِنْهُنَّ بِثَمَانٍ [*I passed by, of them, eight*], and رَأَيْتُ ثَمَانِيًا [*I saw eight*]. (Mṣb.) It sometimes occurs, in poetry, indecl.: (Ṣ, M:) this is because it is fancied to be a pl.; (Ṣ;) or because it is likened, as to the letter, but not as to the meaning, to جَوَارِىَ. (M.) The people of El-Ḥijáz pronounce the masc. and the fem. with naṣb in every case, in phrases like أَتَوْنِى ثَلَاثَتَهُمْ and أَتَيْنَنِى ثَلَاثَهُنَّ; and so on to ten [inclusive]. (Ṣ voce ثَلَاثَةٌ, q. v.) Th mentions ▼ ثَمَانٌ; (TA;) and some instances of its occurrence are cited; but Aṣ disallows it. (T, Mgh, TA.) كِسَآءٌ ذُو ثَمَانٍ means *A* [*garment of the kind called*] كساء *made of eight fleeces*. (T.) تُقْبِلُ بِأَرْبَعٍ وَتُدْبِرُ بِثَمَانٍ [*She advances with four and goes back with eight*] is a saying of one of the مُخَنَّثُون of El-Medeeneh; meaning, with four creases (عُكَن) of the belly, and with eight extremities thereof; each crease having two extremities, towards the two sides of the woman spoken of. (Mgh in art. هيت.) The saying الثَّوْبُ سَبْعٌ فِى ثَمَانٍ should properly be فِى ثَمَانِيَةٍ, (Ṣ,) which means, *The garment*, or *piece of cloth, is seven* cubits in length *by eight* spans in breadth; (Mṣb;) because the length is measured by the ذِرَاع, which is fem., and the breadth by the شِبْر, which is masc.; but they use the fem. when they do not mention things; as when they say, صُمْنَا مِنَ الشَّهْرِ خَمْسًا [We fasted, of the month, five], though meaning days: (Ṣ:) or because ذراع is fem. in most instances, and شبر is masc. (Mṣb.) [But it is said that when ثمانية means the things numbered, not the amount of the number, it is imperfectly decl., being regarded as a proper name: thus] you say, تِسْعَةُ أَكْثَرُ مِنْ ثَمَانِيَةَ [*Nine things are more than eight things*]. (TA voce تِسْعَةٌ, q. v.) [See also سِتَّةٌ.] — When you make it a compound [with the number ten], you say, عِنْدِى ثَمَانِيَةَ عَشَرَ رَجُلًا [*I have with me eighteen men*]: and in the case of the fem., you may either make the ى to be with fet-ḥ or make it quiescent, saying, عِنْدِى مِنَ النِّسَآءِ ثَمَانِىَ عَشْرَةَ امْرَأَةً or ثَمَانِىْ عَشْرَةَ [*I have with me, of women, eighteen women*]; but the former is the more chaste; and in one dial., the ى is elided, on the condition of [saying ثَمَانَ عَشْرَةَ,] making the ن to be with fet-ḥ; (Mṣb;) or in this case you say ثَمَانِ عَشْرَةَ, with kesr. (T.) A poet says, (T, Ṣ,) namely, El-Aạshà, (Ḳ,)

• فَلَأَشْرَبَنَّ ثَمَانِيًا وَثَمَانِيًا •
• وَثَمَانِ عَشْرَةَ وَٱثْنَتَيْنِ وَأَرْبَعَا •

[*And I will assuredly drink eight* cups of wine, (a pl. of كَأْس, which is fem., being understood,) *and eight more, and eighteen, and two, and four*]: (T, Ṣ, Ḳ: but in the Ṣ and Ḳ, وَلَقَدْ شَرِبْتُ; and in the Ḳ, and in one copy of the Ṣ, وَثَمَانِ:) he should properly have said ثَمَانِىَ عَشْرَةَ or ثَمَانِىْ عَشْرَةَ, (accord. to different copies of the T and Ṣ and Ḳ,) but he elides the ى after the dial. of him who says طِوَالُ الأَيْدِ [for الأَيْدِى], (Ṣ, Ḳ,) and he makes the ن to be with kesr in order to indicate the ى. (T.) — The dim. of ثَمَانِيَةٌ may be formed either by suppressing the ا, which is the preferable way, so that you say ▼ ثُمَيْنِيَةٌ, or by suppressing the ى, saying ▼ ثُمَيِّنَةٌ, changing the ا into ى and incorporating into it the ى that is the characteristic of the dim.; and you may compensate for both [of these suppressed letters by saying ▼ ثُمَيِّنَةٌ and ▼ ثُمَيْنِيَةٌ]. (Ṣ.) — الثَّمَانِى is also the name of *A certain plant*. (Aṣ, T, Ḳ.)

ثَمَانُونَ a well-known noun of number; [meaning *Eighty*;] sometimes used as an epithet: El-Aạshà says,

• لَئِنْ كُنْتَ فِى جُبٍّ ثَمَانِينَ قَامَةً •
• وَرُقِّيتَ أَسْبَابَ السَّمَآءِ بِسُلَّمِ •

[*Assuredly if thou wert in a well eighty fathoms deep, and wert made to ascend the tracts of heaven by a ladder*]: he uses it thus as meaning deep. (TA. [But in this verse, as cited in the present art. in the TA, أَبْوَابَ is put in the place of اسباب, which is the reading commonly known, and given in the Ṣ and TA in art. سب, and in the TA in art. رقى.]) أَحْمَقُ مِنْ صَاحِبِ ضَأْنٍ ثَمَانِينَ [*More stupid than an owner of eighty sheep*], (Ṣ, Ḳ,) or مِنْ رَاعِى ضَأْنٍ ثَمَانِينَ [*than a pastor of eighty sheep*], as in some of the copies of the Ṣ, or, as in the Proverbs of Aboo-'Obeyd, مِنْ طَالِبِ ضَأْنٍ ثَمَانِينَ [*than a demander of eighty sheep*], (TA,) is a saying that originated from the fact that an Arab of the desert announced to Kisrà an event that rejoiced him, whereupon he said, "Ask of me what thou wilt;" and he asked of him eighty sheep. (Ṣ, Ḳ.) — [It also signifies *Eightieth*.]

ثَمَانِيَةٌ and ثُمَيِّنَةٌ and ثُمْنِيَةٌ and ثُمْنِيَّةٌ : see ثُمْنٌ, last sentence but one.

ثَامِنٌ [*Eighth*: fem. with ة]. (Ṣ, Ḳ, &c.) — [ثَامِنَ عَشَرَ and ثَامِنَةَ عَشْرَةَ, the former masc. and the latter fem., meaning *Eighteenth*, are subject to the same rules as ثَالِثَ عَشَرَ and its fem., explained in art. ثلث, q. v.] — إِبِلٌ ثَوَامِنُ, [the latter word pl. of ثَامِنَةٌ,] *Camels that come to water on the eighth night* [*after the next preceding watering*]: from ثِمْنٌ. (TA.)

أَثْمَنُ *Of more* [and *of most*] *price or value*. (Ṣ.)

مُثْمَنٌ *Sold for a price*: (Mṣb:) or *having a price named for it, and assigned to it*. (Mgh.) [See also ثَمِينٌ.]

ثَمِينٌ : see مُثْمَنٌ.

مُثْمَنَةٌ *A* مِخْلَاة [or *nose-bag*]: (IAạr, T:) or the *like thereof*. (Ṣ.)

مُثَمَّنٌ *Octangular*. (Ṣ, Ḳ.) — *A verse composed of eight feet*. (TA.) — *Collected together*. (T, TA.) — *Poisoned*; syn. مَسْمُومٌ. (Ḳ.) — *Fevered*; syn. مَحْمُومٌ. (Ḳ.)

ثن

2. ثَنَّنَ *He* (a horse) *lifted his* ثُنَّة [or *fetlock*] *so that it did not touch the ground in his running, by reason of his briskness, or lightness*: (M:) [or] *his* ثُنَّة *touched the ground in consequence of his being ridden by a heavy person*. (T.)

4. اثَنَّ *He* (a weak old man) *became wasted and worn out*. (Ḳ.)

5. تَثَنَّنَ *He pastured*, or *fed, upon* ثِنّ [q. v.]. (T.)

ثِنٌّ *Dry herbage*: (Ṣ:) or *dry herbage when it lies heaped together, one part upon another*: (T:) or *dry herbage*, (Ḳ,) or *what has become dried up of* حَلِىّ *and* بُهْمَى *and* حَمْض, (M,) *when it is much in quantity, and lies heaped together, one part upon another*: or *what has become black of any branches*, or *twigs; not consisting of* بَقْل *nor of* عُشْب: (M, Ḳ:) or *dry herbage broken in pieces*: (IDrd, M:) or [simply] *herbage*, or *pasture*: (Th, M:) or *herbage that is weak, and soft*, or *easily broken*. (IJ.)

ثُنَّةٌ, of a human being, (Lth, T,) *The part below the navel*, (Lth, T, M,) *above*, (Lth, T,) or *extending to*, (M,) *the hair of the pubes*, (Lth, T, M,) *in the lower part of the belly*; (Lth, T;) the *part between the navel and the hair of the pubes*: (Ṣ:) or the *thin skin* (مُرَيْطَآء) *between the navel and the hair of the pubes*: (M, Ḳ:) or the *hair of the pubes*, (T, M, Ḳ,) *itself*. (M.) — And, of a horse (T, Ṣ, M, Ḳ) and the like, (T, Ṣ, Ḳ,) The *fetlock*; i. e. the *hairs on the hinder part of the pastern-joint*, (T, Ṣ, M, Ḳ,) *hanging down* (Ṣ, M) *over the part called* أُمُّ القِرْدَانِ *so as nearly to reach the ground*: (Ṣ:) pl. ثُنَنٌ. (Ṣ, M.) — كُنَّا فِى ثُنَّةٍ مِنَ الكَلَامِ وَغُثَّةٍ ‡ [app. meaning *We were engaged in light and confused talk*] is a metaphorical saying, borrowed from the ثُنَّة of the horse and the singing [or humming or buzzing of the flies and other insects] of the meadow or garden. (A, TA.)

ثُنَانٌ *Numerous*, or *abundant, and tangled*, or *luxuriant, plants or herbage*. (T, Ḳ.)

ثنتان

ثِنْتَانِ fem. of اِثْنَانِ, which see in art. ثنى.

ثندأ and ثند

ثُنْدُؤَةٌ and ثَنْدُوَةٌ and ثُنْدُوَةٌ and ثَنْدُؤَةٌ : see art. ثدأ.

Quasi ثنو

اَلثَّنَوِىُّ : ثَنَوِيَّةٌ and ثَنَوِىٌّ : ثُنًى and ثَنْوَى and مَثْنَوِيَّةٌ : مَثْنَوِىٌّ : see art. ثنى.

ثنى

1. ثَنَاهُ, (T, Ṣ, M, Mgh, Mṣb, Ḳ,) said in the Ḳ to be like سَعَى, implying that the aor. is َ, but this is a mistake, (MF, TA,) [for it is well known that] the aor. is ِ, (Mṣb,) inf. n. ثَنْىٌ, (Ṣ, M, Mṣb, &c.,) *He doubled it*, or *folded it*; (T;) *he turned one part of it upon another*; (M, Ḳ;) *he bent it*; (T, Ṣ, Mgh, Mṣb, TA;) *he drew*, or *contracted, one of its two extremities to* [or *towards*] *the other*; or *joined*, or *adjoined, one of them to the other; thus bending it*; (Mgh;) namely, a stick, or branch, or twig, (Mgh,) or a thing, (T, Ṣ, M, Mṣb, Ḳ,) of any kind. (T.) One says of a man with the mention of whom one begins, in relation to an honourable or a praiseworthy quality, or in relation to science or knowledge, بِهِ تُثْنَى الخَنَاصِرُ, (T,) meaning *With* [the mention of] *him*, (T, and Mṣb in art. خصر,) among others of his class, (Mṣb ib.,) *the little fingers are bent*. (T, and Mṣb ubi suprà. [For the Arabs, in counting with the fingers, first bend the tip of the little finger down to the palm of the hand; then, the tip of the next; and so on; bending the thumb down upon the other fingers for five; and then continue by extending the fingers, one after another, again commencing with the little finger.]) And a poet says,

فَإِنْ عُدَّ مَجْدٌ أَوْ قَدِيمٌ لِمَعْشَرٍ
فَقَوْمِى بِهِمْ تُثْنَى هُنَاكَ الأَصَابِعُ

[*And if glory, or any old ground of pretension to honour, be reckoned as belonging to a body of men, it is my people, with the mention of them, in that case, the fingers are bent*]; meaning that they are reckoned as the best; (IAạr, M;) for the best are not many. (M.) One says also, ثَنَى وَرِكَهُ فَنَزَلَ [lit. *He bent his hip, and alighted*], meaning he alighted from his beast. (T.) And ثَنَى رِجْلَهُ عَنْ دَابَّتِهِ, meaning *He drew up his leg to his thigh*, and alighted. (M.) But قَبْلَ أَنْ يَثْنِىَ رِجْلَهُ, occurring in a trad., means *Before he turned his leg from the position in which it was* in the pronouncing of the testimony of the faith. (IAth.) ثَنَى صَدْرَهُ, aor. and inf. n. as above, [lit. *He folded his breast*, or *bosom*,] means † *he concealed enmity in his breast*, or *bosom*: or *he folded up what was in it, in concealment*. (TA.) It is said in the Ḳur [xi. 5], أَلَا إِنَّهُمْ يَثْنُونَ صُدُورَهُمْ, meaning [*Now surely*] *they infold and conceal* [*in their bosoms*] *enmity and hatred*: (Fr, T:) or *they bend their breasts*, or *bosoms, and fold up, and conceal, what is therein*: (Zj, T:) I 'Ab read, تَثْنَوْنِى ↓ صُدُورُهُمْ: you say, اِثْنَوْنَى صَدْرُهُ عَلَى البَغْضَآءِ, meaning *his breast*, or *bosom, infolded*, or *concealed, vehement hatred*: (T:) or the phrase in the Ḳur, accord. to the former reading, means *they bend*, or *turn, their breasts*, or *bosoms, from the truth; they turn themselves away therefrom*: or *they incline their breasts*, or *bosoms, to unbelief, and enmity to the Prophet*: or *they turn their backs*: (Bḍ:) [for] — ثَنَاهُ, (T, Ṣ, Mṣb, TA,) aor. as above, (Mṣb,) and so the inf. n., (T, Mṣb, TA,) also signifies *He turned him*, or *it, away* or *back*. (T, Ṣ, Mṣb, TA.) Also *He turned him*, or *turned him away* or *back*, (Lth, T, Ṣ,) *from the course that he desired to pursue*, (Lth, T,) or *from the object of his want*: (Ṣ:) or you say, ثَنَاهُ عَنْ وَجْهِهِ, (Mgh,) and عَنْ حَاجَتِهِ, (TA,) and عَنْ مُرَادِهِ, (Mṣb,) *he turned him*, or *turned him away* or *back*, (Mgh, Mṣb, TA,) *from his course*, (Mgh,) and *from the object of his want*, (TA,) and *from the object of his desire*. (Mṣb.) One says also, فُلَانٌ لَا يُثْنَى عَنْ قِرْنِهِ وَلَا عَنْ وَجْهِهِ [*Such a one will not be turned*, or *turned away* or *back, from his antagonist, nor from his course*]. (T.) — Also *He tied it*; or *tied it in a knot* or *knots*; or *tied it firmly, fast*, or *strongly*. (TA.) You say, ثَنَيْتُ البَعِيرَ بِثِنَايَيْنِ, meaning, accord. to Aṣ, as related by A 'Obeyd, *I bound both the fore legs of the camel with two bonds*: but correctly, *I bound the two fore legs of the camel with the two ends of a rope*; the last word meaning a single rope: (T:) عَقَلْتُهُ بِثِنْيَيْنِ means *I bound one of his fore shanks to the arm with two ties*, or *tyings*. (T, M.) — ثَنْىٌ [as inf. n. of ثَنَى] also signifies The act of *drawing*, or *joining*, or *adjoining, one* [*thing*] *to another*; (Lth, T, Mgh;) and so ↓ تَثْنِيَةٌ [inf. n. of ثَنَّى]. (Mgh.) — [As ثَلَثَهُمْ signifies "he took the third of their property," and "he made them, with himself, three," and other verbs of number are used in similar senses, so] ثَنَاهُمْ signifies *He took the half of their property*: or *he drew*, or *adjoined, to him what became with him two*: (TA:) or ثَنَيْتُهُ, (Ṣ, Mṣb,) aor. and inf. n. as above, (Mṣb,) signifies *I became* (Ṣ, Mṣb) *to him*, (Ṣ,) or *with him,* (Mṣb,) *a second;* (Ṣ, Mṣb;) or *I was a second to him,* or *it:* (Er-Rághib:) or one should not say thus, but that AZ says, (M,) هُوَ وَاحِدٌ فَاثْنِهِ (M, Ḳ [but in the latter, هٰذَا in the place of هُوَ, and in the CḲ, ▼فَاثْنه,]) *he is one, and be thou a second to him.* (M, Ḳ.) — ثَنَى, aor. as above, also signifies *He made* eleven *to be twelve.* (T in art. ثلث.) — ثَنَى الأَرْضَ, inf. n. as above, *He turned over the land,* or *ground, twice for sowing,* or *cultivating:* (Mgh, and A* and TA* in art. ثلث:) and ▼ثَنَّيَة [inf. n. of ثَنَّى] and ثُنْيَانٌ [app. another inf. n. of ثَنَى, and app. correctly written ثُنْيَانٌ] are often used by [the Imám] Mohammad in the sense of ▼ثَنْيٌ: he who explains ثَنْيَةٌ as signifying the *turning over* [the land, or ground,] *for sowing,* or *cultivating, after the harvest,* or as signifying the *restoring land to its owner turned over for sowing,* or *cultivating,* commits an inadvertence. (Mgh.) — فَاثْنِنِى, occurring in a poem of Kutheiyir 'Azzeh, is explained as meaning *Then give thou to me a second time:* (M, TA:) but this is strange: (TA:) [ISd says,] I have not seen it in any other instance. (M.) — لَا يَثْنِى وَلَا يَثْلِثُ, (a phrase mentioned by IAạr, M,) or لَا يُثَنِّى ▼ وَلَا يُثَلِّثُ, or لَا يُثْنِى ▼ وَلَا يُثْلِثُ: see 1 in art. ثلث.

2. ثَنَّاهُ, (Ṣ, M, Mṣb, Ḳ,) inf. n. تَثْنِيَةٌ, (Ṣ, Ḳ,) *He made it two;* or *called it two.* (Ṣ, M, Mṣb, Ḳ.) [Hence,] ثَنَّى means also *He counted two;* whence the saying, فُلَانٌ يُثَنِّى وَلَا يُثَلِّثُ; see art. ثلث: (A and TA in art. ثلث:) [and so, app., ▼اِثَّنَى; for] a poet says,

• بَدَا بِأَبِى ثُمَّ اثَّنَى بِأَبِى أَبِى •

[which seems plainly to mean *He began with my father; then counted two with the father of my father*]. (M.) — [*He dualized it,* namely, a word; *made it to have a dual.* — *He marked it with two points,* namely, a ت or a ى.] — *He repeated it; iterated it.* (Mgh.) See 1, in three places. — ثَنَّى لِامْرَأَتِهِ, or عِنْدَهَا, *He remained two nights with his wife:* and in like manner the verb is used in relation to any saying or action. (TA voce سَبَّعَ.) — ثَنَّى بِالأَمْرِ *He did the thing immediately after another thing.* (T.) — تَثْنِيَةٌ also signifies A man's *requesting others* [*who are playing with him at the game called* المَيْسِر] *to return, for* [*a chance of*] *the stakes, his arrow, when it has been successful, and he has been secure, and has won.* (Lḥ, M.) — See also 4.

4. أَثْنَتْ, or ▼اِسْتَثْنَتْ, *She brought forth her second offspring.* (TA in art. بكر.) — See also 1, in two places. — اثنى, (inf. n. إِثْنَآءٌ, TA,) *He shed his tooth called the* ثَنِيَّة; (Ṣ, Mgh, Mṣb;) *he became what is termed* ثَنِىّ; said of a camel [&c.]: (M, Ḳ:) *he shed his* رَوَاضِع [pl. of رَاضِعَة which is the same, in this case, as ثَنِيَّة]; said of a horse [&c.]. (IAạr, T.) — اثنى عَلَيْهِ, (T, Ṣ, M, Mṣb, Ḳ, &c.,) inf. n. إِثْنَآءٌ; (T;) and ▼ثَنَّى, inf. n. تَثْنِيَةٌ, accord. to the Ḳ, but this is a mistake for ▼ثَنَّى, inf. n. تَثْنِيَةٌ; (TA;) *He praised, eulogized, commended,* or *spoke well of, him:* and *he dispraised, censured, discommended,* or *spoke ill of, him:* (T,* M, Mṣb, Ḳ:) the object is either God or a man: (T:) or it has the former meaning only: (M, Ḳ;) or the former meaning is the more common: (Mṣb:) accord. to IAạr, اثنى signifies *he spoke,* or *said, well,* or *good;* and *ill,* or *evil;* and اثنى, "he defamed," or "did so in the absence of the object;" and "he disdained, scorned, shunned, disliked, or hated," a thing: (T:) and you say, اثنى عَلَيْهِ خَيْرًا [*He spoke,* or *said, well,* or *good, of him*]; (Ṣ, and TA from a trad.;) and شَرًّا [*ill,* or *evil*], also. أَثْنَيْتُ (TA from the same trad.) One says also, عَلَى فِعْلِهِ فِعْلَهُ [*I praised his deed*]; meaning; or because أَثْنَى means مَدَحَ. (Ḥam p. 696.)

5. تثنّى: see 7. — Also *He affected an inclining of his body, or a bending,* or *he inclined his body,* or *bent, from side to side;* syn. تَمَايَلَ: (Ḥar pp. 269 and 271:) and *he walked with an elegant and a proud and self-conceited gait, with an affected inclining of the body from side to side;* or *with a twisting of the back, and with extended steps;* syn. تَبَخْتَرَ. (Idem p. 271.) You say, تَثَنَّى فِى مِشْيَتِهِ (Ṣ, and Ḥar p. 269) *He affected an inclining of his body, or a bending,* or *he inclined his body,* or *bent, from side to side, in his gait.* (Ḥar ib.) [And in like manner, and more commonly, one says of a woman.]

7. انثنى, (T, Ṣ, M, Ḳ,) and ▼تثنّى, and ▼اِثَّنَى, of the measure اِفْتَعَلَ, (M, Ḳ,) originally اِثْتَنَى, (M,) and ▼اِثْنَوْنَى, (T, Ṣ, Ḳ,) of the measure اِفْعَوْعَلَ, (T, Ṣ,) *It was,* or *became, doubled,* or *folded;* (T;) *it had one part turned upon another;* (M, Ḳ;) *it was,* or *became, bent.* (T, Ṣ.) — [Hence,] انثنى signifies also *He turned,* or *turned away* or *back,* (Ḥar pp. 44 and 120,) عَنْ أَمْرٍ *from an affair,* after having determined to do it. (Lth in TA art. زمع.)

8: see 7, and 4: — and see also 2.

10. استثناهُ *He set it aside as excluded;* or *he excluded it,* or *excepted it;* مِنْ شَىْءٍ *from a thing;* syn. حَاشَاهُ: (M:) or *he set it aside,* or *apart, for himself:* and in the conventional language of the grammarians, [*he excepted it;* i. e.] *he excluded it from the predicament in which another thing was included, or in which other things were included:* (Mgh:) الاِسْتِثْنَآءُ [in grammar] is *the turning away the agent from reaching the object of the* اِسْتِثْنَآء: (Mṣb:) in the case of an oath [and the like], it means *the saying* إِنْ شَآءَ ٱللّٰهُ [*If God will*]. (Mgh.) [See ثُنْيَا.]

12. اثنونى: see 7; and see also 1.

ثِنْىٌ *A duplication,* or *doubling,* of a thing: (T,* Ṣ, Mṣb:) pl. أَثْنَآءٌ; (Ṣ, Mṣb;) or the sing. may be ▼ثِنًى. (Mṣb.) — *A folding:* so in the saying, أَنْفَذْتُ كَذَا ثِنْىَ كِتَابِى, (Ṣ, TA,) or فِى ثِنْىِ كِتَابِى, (so in a copy of the Ṣ,) i. e., فِى طَيِّهِ [lit. *I sent,* or *transmitted, such a thing within the folding of my writing,* or *letter;* meaning *infolded,* or *enclosed, in it;* and *included in it*]. (Ṣ, TA.) — *A duplicature,* or *fold,* of a garment, or piece of cloth: (TA:) or *what is turned back* of the extremities thereof: (T:) pl. as above: whence, in a trad. of Aboo-Hureyreh, كَانَ يَثْنِيهِ عَلَيْهِ أَثْنَآءً مِنْ سَعَتِهِ [*He used to fold it upon him in folds by reason of its width*]; meaning the garment. (TA.) [Hence the saying,] وَكَانَ ذٰلِكَ فِى أَثْنَآءِ كَذَا, i. e., فِى غُضُونِهِ [lit. *And that was in the folds,* meaning, *in the midst, of such a thing,* or *such an affair,* or *event*]. (TA.) And جَآؤُوا فِى أَثْنَآءِ الأَمْرِ *They came in the midst of the affair,* or *event.* (Mṣb.) [And hence, app.,] مَضَى ثِنْىٌ مِنَ اللَّيْلِ *An hour,* or *a period,* or *a short portion, of the night passed;* (M, Ḳ;*) syn. سَاعَةٌ, (Th, M, Ḳ,) or وَقْتٌ. (Lḥ, M, Ḳ.) [See also what is said below respecting its pl. in relation to a night.] — Also sing. of أَثْنَآءٌ meaning The *parts of a thing that are laid together like the strands of a rope, or that are laid one upon another as layers* or *strata,* or *side by side as the things that compose a bundle;* (M;) and طَاقَاتُهُ; [rendered by Freytag "virtutes, facultates rei;"]) and ▼مَثَانٍ, of which the sing. is ▼مَثْنَاةٌ and ▼مِثْنَاةٌ, signifies the same. (M, Ḳ.) — Also *A bending of the neck* of a sheep, or goat, *not in consequence of disease:* (Ḳ: but in the M, ثَنْىٌ [inf. n. of 1]:) and a serpent's *bending,* or *folding, of itself:* (M, Ḳ:) and also (thus in the M, but in the Ḳ "or") *a curved part* of a serpent that has folded itself; (M, Ḳ;) pl. أَثْنَآءٌ, (M,) i. e. the *folds* of a coiled serpent. (T.) The pl. is used metaphorically [as though meaning ‡ The *turns*] of a night. (M. [But see explanations of the sing. as used in relation to a night in what precedes.] — *A part that is bent,* or *folded,* or *doubled,* of a وِشَاح [q. v.]; (TA;) pl. as above: (T, TA:) and so of a rope: (Ṣ:) or *a portion of the extremity* of a rope *folded,* or *doubled,* [*so as to form a loop,*] *for binding therewith the pastern of the fore leg of a beast, to serve as a tether.* (T.) Ṭarafeh says,

• لَعَمْرُكَ إِنَّ المَوْتَ مَا أَخْطَأَ الفَتَى •
• لَكَالطِّوَلِ المُرْخَى وَثِنْيَاهُ بِاليَدِ •

[*By thy life, death, while missing the strong young man, is like the tether that is slackened while the two folded extremities thereof are upon the fore leg,* or *in the hand:* see طِوَلٌ]: (T, Ṣ:) he means that the young man must inevitably die, though his term of life be protracted; like as the beast, though his tether be lengthened and slackened, cannot escape, being withheld by its two extremities: (so in a copy of the T:) or by ثنياه he means *its extremity;* using the dual form because it is folded, or doubled, upon the pastern, and tied with a double tie: (so in another copy of the T:) or he means, *while its two extremities are in the hand* of its owner: (EM p. 91:) by ما اخطا, he means فِى إِخْطَائِهِ, (Ṣ in art. طول,) or مُدَّةَ إِخْطَائِهِ: and the ل [prefixed to the ك of comparison] is for corroboration. (EM ubi suprà.) You say also, رَبَّقَ أَثْنَآءَ الحَبْلِ, meaning *He made loops in the middle of the rope to put upon the necks of the young lambs or kids.* (T.) — Also *A bend,* or *place of bending,* of a valley, (Ṣ, M,* Ḳ,) and of a mountain: (Ṣ:) pl. as above: (M,

Ḳ:) and ▼مَثَانٍ [likewise] signifies the *bends* of a valley. (T, Ḳ.) ═ A she-camel *that has brought forth twice,* (Ṣ,) or *two,* (M,) or *a second time:* (Ḳ:) or, as some say, *that has brought forth once:* but the former is more analogical: (M:) one does not say ثِلْثٌ [as meaning "that has brought forth thrice"], nor use any similar epithet above this: (Ṣ, TA:) pl. ثُنَآءٌ, like ظُؤَارٌ pl. of ظِئْرٌ, accord. to Sb, (M, TA,) and أَثْنَآءٌ accord. to others: (TA:) in like manner it is applied to a woman, (Ṣ, M,) metaphorically: (M:) and to the she-camel's *second young one:* (Ṣ, M:) accord. to Aṣ, as related by A'Obeyd, a she-camel that has brought forth once: also that has brought forth twice: [so says Az, but he adds,] but what I have heard from the Arabs is this; that they term a she-camel that has brought forth her first young one بِكْر; and her first young one, her بِكْر; and when she brought forth a second, she is termed ثِنْىٌ; and her young one, her ثِنْى: and this is what is correct. (T.) [Hence the saying,] مَا هٰذَا الأَمْرُ مِنْكَ بِكْرًا وَلَا ثِنْيًا ‡ *This thing, or affair, is not thy first nor thy second.* (A and TA in art. بكر.) — See also ثُنْيَانٌ.

ثَنًى: see ثِنْىٌ, first sentence.

ثُنًى: see ثِنًى: — and see also ثُنْيَانٌ: — and اِثْنَانِ.

ثِنًى The *repetition of a thing; doing it one time after another:* (Aboo-Sa'eed, TA:) or *a thing,* or *an affair, done twice:* (Ṣ, Mṣb, TA:) this is the primary signification: (TA:) and ▼ثُنًى signifies the same. (IB, TA.) It is said in a trad., لَا ثِنَى فِى الصَّدَقَةِ *There shall be no repetition in the taking of the poor-rate;* (IAth, TA;) [i. e.] *the poor-rate shall not be taken twice in one year:* (Aṣ, Ks, T, Ṣ, M, Mgh, Ḳ:) or *two she-camels shall not be taken in the place of one for the poor-rate:* (M, IAth, Ḳ:*) or *there shall be no retracting of an alms;* or *no revoking it:* (Mgh, Ḳ,* TA:) this last is the meaning accord. to Aboo-Sa'eed, (Mgh, TA,) i. e. Eḍ-Ḍareeree, (Mgh,) who, in explaining this trad., as relating to the giving an alms to a man and then desiring to take it back, says he does not deny that ثِنًى has the meaning first assigned to it above in this paragraph. (TA.) — See also ثُنْيَانٌ: — and اِثْنَانِ.

ثَنْوَى and ثُنْوَى: see ثُنْيَا, in four places.

ثَنْيَةٌ: see ثُنْيَا, in three places.

ثُنْيَةٌ The *lowest, most ignoble,* or *meanest,* of the people of his house; applied to a man. (Ṣ, TA.) — Also pl. of ثُنْيَانٌ, q. v. (Ṣ, Ḳ.)

ثُنْيَا a subst. from اِسْتِثْنَآءٌ; (Ṣ, Mgh, Mṣb;) as also ▼ثَنْوَى; the former with ḍamm, and the latter with fet-ḥ: (Ṣ, Mṣb:) both are syn. with اِسْتِثْنَآءٌ [used as a subst., meaning *An exception*]; (T;) as also ▼ثَنْيَةٌ, (T, Ḳ,) or ▼ثُنْيَةٌ, (accord. to one copy of the T,) and ▼مَثْنَوِيَّةٌ: (T:) so in the saying, حَلَفَ يَمِينًا لَيْسَ فِيهَا ثُنْيَا and ▼ثَنْوَى and ▼ثَنْيَةٌ or ▼ثُنْيَةٌ and ▼مَثْنَوِيَّةٌ [*he swore an oath in which there was not an exception*]; for when the swearer says, "By God I will not do such and such things unless God will otherwise," he reverses what he [first] says by God's willing otherwise: (T: [see 10:]) [and so in the saying,] ▼حَلْفَةٌ غَيْرُ ذَاتِ مَثْنَوِيَّةٍ *a swearing not made lawful* [*by an exception*]: (M:) [so too in the saying,] ▼بَيْعٌ مَا فِيهِ مَثْنَوِيَّةٌ [and ثُنْيَا &c.] (Ḳ in art. لحج) *a sale in which there is not an exception:* (TA in that art.:) or ثُنْيَا signifies *a thing excepted,* (M, Mgh, Ḳ,) *whatever it be;* (Ḳ;) as also ▼ثُنْوَى, (M, Ḳ,) with و substituted for ى, (M,) or ▼ثَنْوَى, (so in the TA, [but probably through inadvertence,]) and ▼ثُنْيَةٌ, (M, Ḳ,) or ▼ثَنْيَةٌ. (TA.) In a sale, it is unlawful when it is the exception of a thing unknown; and when one sells a slaughtered camel for a certain price and excepts the head and extremities: (T, TA:) or when an exception is made from things sold without measuring or weighing or numbering: and in a contract with another for labour upon land on the condition of sharing the produce, it is when one excepts a certain measure after the half or the third. (IAth, TA.) The saying of Moḥammad, مَنِ ٱسْتَثْنَى فَلَهُ ثُنْيَاهُ means *Whoso maketh an exception, his shall be what he excepteth:* (M, TA:*) as, for instance, when one says, "I divorce her thrice, save once:" or "I emancipate them, except such a one." (TA.) — It also means particularly The *head and legs* of a slaughtered camel; (T, M,* Ḳ;) because the seller of the camel used, in the Time of Ignorance, to except them; (T;) and IF adds, but incorrectly, the *back-bone:* (Ṣgh, TA:) whence, applied to a she-camel, مُذَكَّرَةُ الثُّنْيَا, (T, M,) meaning *Resembling the make of the male in* [*the largeness of*] *her head and legs;* (Th, M;) or جُمَالِيَّةُ الثُّنْيَا, *having thick legs, like those of the male camel in thickness.* (T.) [Also, app., The *exception,* or *omission, of a day, in irrigation:* see 3 in art. ثلث, and ثِلْثٌ in the same art.] And ▼ثَنِيَّةٌ signifies also *A palm-tree that is excepted from a bargain.* (M, Ḳ.) And The *martyrs whom God has excepted from those who shall fall down dead* or *swooning:* (M, Ḳ:) these, accord. to Kaab, are ▼ثَنِيَّةُ ٱللّٰهِ فِى الأَرْضِ [*those whom God has excepted on the earth*]; (T, M;) alluded to in the Ḳur [xxxix. 68], where it is said, "And the horn shall be blown, and those who are in the heavens and those on the earth shall fall down dead, or swooning, except those whom God shall please [to except]." (T.)

ثُنْيَانٌ The *second chief;* the *person who comes second as a chief;* (A'Obeyd, T;) the *person who is* [*next*] *below the* سَيِّد, (Ṣ, M, Ḳ, [in some copies of the Ḳ, erroneously, سيل,]) *in rank;* (Ṣ;) as also ▼ثُنًى (A'Obeyd, T, Ṣ, M, Ḳ) and ▼ثِنًى (A'Obeyd, T, Ṣ, Ḳ) and ▼ثِنْىٌ: (Ḳ:) pl. (of the first, Ṣ) ثُنْيَةٌ [which is also a sing., mentioned above]. (Ṣ, Ḳ.) [See an ex. in a verse cited voce بَدْءٌ.] — A man *having no judgment nor intelligence,* or *understanding.* (M, Ḳ.) — Applied to judgment, or an opinion, (M, Ḳ,) ‡ *Wrong,* or *having a wrong tendency;* (M;) *bad, corrupt, unsound,* or *wrong.* (Ḳ, TA.) ═ Also a pl. of ثَنِىٌّ [q. v.]. (Ṣ, M, &c.)

ثَنَوِىٌّ rel. n. of اِثْنَانِ, and of اِثْنَا عَشَرَ, when either or these is used as the proper name of a man; as also ▼اِثْنِىٌّ [with ا when connected with a preceding word]; like بَنَوِىٌّ and اِبْنِىٌّ as rel. ns. of اِبْنٌ. (Ṣ.) — And الثَّنَوِيَّةُ [*The Dualists;*] *the sect who assert the doctrine of Dualism* [الاِثْنَيْنِيَّة]. (TA.)

ثَنَآءٌ, [and accord. to the CḲ, ثَنِيَّةٌ, but this is a mistranscription for تَثْنِيَةٌ, inf. n. of ثَنَّى, and تَثْنِيَةٌ is a mistake for تَثْبِيَةٌ, inf. n. of ثَبَّى, (see 4,)] *Praise, eulogy,* or *commendation,* (T, Ṣ, M, Mṣb, Ḳ,) of a man, (T, M,) and of God: (T:) and *dispraise, censure,* or *discommendation,* (T, M, Mṣb, Ḳ,) of a man: (T, M:) or the former only: (M, Ḳ:) or more frequently the former: (Mṣb:) so termed because it is repeated: (Ḥam p. 696:) that it relates to good speech and evil is asserted by many. (TA.)

ثُنَآءٌ and ثِنَآءٌ: see مَثْنًى.

ثِنَآءٌ The *cord,* or *rope, with which a camel's fore shank and his arm are bound together;* (Ṣ, Ḳ;) and *the like; consisting of a folded,* or *doubled, cord,* or *rope: each of the folds,* or *duplicatures, thereof* would be thus termed if the word were used in the sing. form: (Ṣ:) Ibn-Es-Seed [in the CḲ, erroneously, Ibn-Es-Seedeh] allows it; and therefore it is given as on his authority in the Ḳ: (TA:) and Lth allows it; but in this instance he allows what the Arabs do not allow: (T:) you say, عَقَلْتُ البَعِيرَ بِثِنَايَيْنِ, meaning *I bound together the fore shanks and the arms of the camel with a rope,* (Ṣ,) or *with two ropes,* (M, [but this is probably a mistake of a copyist,]) or *with the two ends of a rope;* (AZ, T, Ṣ, M;) without ء because the word has no sing.: (Kh, Sb, T, Ṣ:) Lth allows one's saying بِثِنَاءَيْنِ also; but the Baṣrees and Koofees [in general] agree that it is without ء: (T:) IB says that it has no sing. because it is a *single rope, with one end of which one fore leg is bound, and with the other end the other leg;* and IAth says the like: (TA:) this rope is also called ▼ثِنَايَةٌ; but a single rope for binding one fore shank and arm is not thus called. (T.) See also ثِنَايَةٌ. — And see ثَانٍ. ═ The فِنَآء [or *court,* or *open* or *wide space, in front,* or *extending from the sides,*] (M, Ḳ,) of a house: (M:) [in the CḲ, الغناء is erroneously put for الفناء:] accord. to IJ, from ثَنَى, aor. يَثْنِى, because there one is turned back, by its limits, from expatiating; but A'Obeyd holds the ث to be a substitute for ف. (M.)

ثَنِىٌّ *Shedding his tooth called the* ثَنِيَّة [q. v.]: (Ṣ, M, Mṣb:) or *that has shed the tooth so called:* (T, Mgh:) applied to a camel &c., as follows: (T, Ṣ, M, &c.:) or, as some say, to any animal that has shed that tooth, except man: (M:) fem. with ة: (T, Ṣ, M, Mṣb, Ḳ:) a camel *in the sixth year;* (T, Ṣ, M, IAth, Mgh, Mṣb, Ḳ;) the least age at which he may be sacrificed: (T:) and a horse *in the fourth year;* (IAạr, T, Mgh, Ḳ;) or *in the third year:* (Ṣ, Mṣb:) and a cloven-hoofed animal, (Ṣ, Mgh, Mṣb,) or a sheep or goat and an animal of the bovine kind, [respecting which last see عَضْبٌ,] (T, IAth, Ḳ,) *in the third year:* (T, Ṣ, IAth, Mgh, Mṣb, Ḳ:) or a sheep and a goat, (M,) the latter accord. to the persuasion of Aḥmad [Ibn-Ḥambal], (TA,) *in the second year:* (M:) and a gazelle *after the age at which he is termed* جَذَعٌ: (M: [see شَصَرٌ:]) in all cases, *after what is termed* جَذَعٌ *and before what is termed* رَبَاعٌ: (Mgh:) pl. (masc., Ṣ, TA) ثُنْيَانٌ and ثِنَآءٌ (Ṣ, M, Mgh, Mṣb) and ثُنَآءٌ, and, accord. to Sb, ثُنٍ; (M;) and pl. fem. ثَنِيَّاتٌ. (Ṣ.)

الثَّنَى, or الثُّنِىُّ: see اِثْنَانِ.

ثَنِيَّةٌ *I. q.* عَقَبَةٌ: (AA, M, Mgh, Ḳ:) or the latter means *a long mountain that lies across the road, and which the road traverses;* and the former, *any such mountain that is traversed:* (T:) so called because it lies before the road, and crosses it; or because it turns away him who traverses it: (Mgh:) or the *road of what is termed* عَقَبَةٌ: (Ṣ; and so in copies of the Ḳ:) or *a high road of what is thus termed:* (Ḳ accord. to the TA:) or *a road in,* or *upon, a mountain,* (M, Ḳ,) *like that which is termed* نَقْبٌ [q. v.]: (M:) or *a road to a mountain:* (M, Ḳ:) or *a mountain* (M, Ḳ) *itself:* (M:) or *a part of a mountain that requires one, in traversing it, to ascend and descend;* as though it turned the course of journeying: (Er-Rághib, TA:) pl. ثَنَايَا: (T, Ṣ:) which signifies also [*such roads as are termed*] مَدَارِج. (T.) Hence the phrase, فُلَانٌ طَلَّاعُ الثَّنَايَا *Such a one rises to eminences,* or *to lofty things* or *circumstances,* or *to the means of attaining such things;* like the phrase طَلَّاعُ أَنْجُدٍ [q. v.]: (Ṣ:) or, like the latter phrase, *is accustomed to embark in,* or *undertake,* or *to surmount,* or *master, lofty and difficult things:* (Mgh:) or *is hardy, strong,* or *sturdy; one who embarks in,* or *undertakes, great affairs.* (TA. [See an ex. under the heading of اِبْنُ جَلَا, in art. جلو: and see also art. طلع.]) — Also, (T, Ṣ, M, &c.,) pl. ثَنَايَا (T, Ṣ, Mgh, Mṣb) and ثَنِيَّاتٌ, (Mṣb,) *One of certain teeth,* (T, Ṣ, M, Mgh, Mṣb, Ḳ,) *the foremost in the mouth,* (M,) [namely, *the central incisors,*] *four in number,* (T, M, Mgh, Mṣb,) to man, and to the camel, (T, M, &c.,) and to the wild beast, (M,) *in the fore part of the mouth,* (T, Mgh, Ḳ,) *two above and two below:* (T, M, Mgh, Ḳ:) so called as being likened to the ثَنِيَّة of a mountain, in form and hardness; (TA;) or because each of them is placed next to its fellow. (Mgh.) — Also fem. of ثَنِىٌّ [q. v.]. (T, Ṣ, M, &c.) — See also ثِنْيًا, in five places.

ثِنَايَةٌ *A cord,* or *rope, of goats' hair* (شَعَر), or *of wool,* (Ṣ, Ḳ,) or *of other material;* (Ḳ;) as also ▼ ثِنَآءٌ (Ḳ) and ▼ مِثْنَاةٌ and ▼ مَثْنَاةٌ; (M, Ḳ;) which last is explained by IAạr as signifying [simply] *a cord,* or *rope:* (M:) [or] the first has the meaning assigned to it above, voce ثِنَآءٌ; syn. with ثِنَايَانِ: and signifies also *a long rope;* whence the saying of Zuheyr, describing the [she-camel termed] سَانِيَة,

تَمْطُو الرِّشَآءَ وَتُجْرِى فِى ثِنَايَتِهَا
مِنَ المَحَالَةِ ثَقْبًا رَائِدًا قَلِقًا

(T,) meaning [*She draws the well-rope, and causes to run,*] *with her* ثناية *upon her,* (ISk, T,) [*a wabbling, unsteady, sheave* (?) *of the large pulley;*] the ثناية here being *a rope of which the two ends are tied to the saddle* (قَتَب) *of the* سانية; *the* [*upper*] *end of the well-rope being tied to its* ▼ مِثْنَاة [which here means the *folded middle part*]: (T:) but Aboo-Sa'eed says that it [here] means *a piece of wood by which are connected the two extremities of the cheeks,* or *side-pieces,* (طرفا الميلين, [the latter of which words I here render conjecturally, supposing it to be similar in meaning to القَعْوِ or القَعْوَيْنِ,]) *above the* محالة, and *a similar piece below; the* محالة *and* [qu. or] *the sheave turning between the two pieces thus called.* (T, in a later portion of the art.)

ثُنَائِىٌّ [a rel. n. from اِثْنَانِ, anomalously formed, but analogous with other rel. ns. from ns. of number, as رُبَاعِىٌّ, ثُلَاثِىٌّ, &c., *Of,* or *relating to, two things*]. — كَلِمَةٌ ثُنَائِيَّةٌ *A word comprising,* or *composed of, two letters;* as يَدٌ and دَمٌ [or دَمْ?]. (TA.)

ثِنْتَانِ a fem of اِثْنَانِ, q. v.

ثَانٍ [act. part. n. of 1; *Doubling,* or *folding;* &c.]. Hence, وَهُوَ ثَانٍ رِجْلَهُ *While he was bending his leg* before rising, or standing up. (TA from a trad.) [And جَآءَ ثَانِىَ عِطْفِهِ: see art. عطف.] One says of a horseman who has bent the neck of his beast on the occasion of his vehement running, جَآءَ ثَانِىَ العِنَانِ [*He came bending the* rein by pulling it with both hands a little apart]: (T:) or جَآءَ ثَانِيًا مِنْ عِنَانِهِ [*he came bending* a part *of his* rein]. (Ṣ.) And of the horse himself, one says, جَآءَ سَابِقًا ثَانِيًا, i. e. *He came outstripping, with bent neck,* by reason of briskness; because when he is fatigued, he stretches out his neck; and when he is not fatigued nor jaded by running, but comes in his first run, he bends his neck: and hence the saying of the poet,

وَمَنْ يَفْخَرْ بِمِثْلِ أَبِى وَجَدِّى
يَجِئْ قَبْلَ السَّوَابِقِ وَهْوَ ثَانِى

i. e. [*And he who glories in the like of my father and my grandfather, let him come before the mares that outstrip,*] *he being* like the horse that outstrips [all others], *with bent neck;* or it may mean, *he bending* the neck of his horse which has outstripped the others. (T.) [Hence also,] شَاةٌ ثَانِيَةٌ *A sheep,* or *goat, bending the neck, not in consequence of disease.* (M, Ḳ.) — [Also *Second;* the ordinal of two: fem. with ة.] You say, هٰذَا ثَانِى هٰذَا [*This is the second of this*]; i. e. *this is what has made this a pair,* or *couple:* (M:) and فُلَانٌ (T) or هٰذَا (Ṣ) ثَانِى اثْنَيْنِ, (T, Ṣ,) i. e. *Such a one,* or *this, is* [*the second of two,* or] *one of the two;* (T, Ṣ;) like as you say ثَالِثُ ثَلَاثَةٍ; and so on to عَشَرَةٍ: but not with tenween: (Ṣ:) [i. e.,] you may not say ثَانٍ اثْنَيْنِ: (T: [see ثَالِثٌ:]) but if the two [terms] disagree, you may use either mode; (Ṣ;) you may say, هٰذَا (Ṣ) or هُوَ (Mgh) ثَانِى وَاحِدٍ and ثَانٍ وَاحِدًا, (Ṣ, Mgh,) i. e. *This has become a second to one,* (Ṣ,) [or rather, *becomes* &c. (i. e. يُثَنِّى rather than ثَنَّى),] or *he,* or *it, makes one, with himself,* or *itself, to be two.* (Mgh.) ▼ ثِنَآءٌ also signifies the same in a trad. respecting the office of commander, or governor, or prince; where it is said, أَوَّلُهَا مَلَامَةٌ وَثِنَاؤُهَا نَدَامَةٌ وَثِلَاثُهَا عَذَابُ يَوْمِ القِيَامَةِ إِلَّا مَنْ عَدَلَ, i. e. [*The first result thereof is blame, and*] *the second* [*is regret, and*] *the third* [*is the punishment of the day of resurrection, except* in the case of *him who acts equitably*]: so says Sh. (T.) — And الثَّوَانِى [pl. of الثَّانِيَةُ] signifies [*The second horns;*] *the horns that are* [*next*] *after the* أَوَائِل. (M.) — [ثَانِىَ عَشَرَ and ثَانِيَةَ عَشْرَةَ, the former masc. and the latter fem., meaning *Twelfth,* are subject to the same rules as ثَالِثَ عَشَرَ and its fem., explained in art. ثلث.]

أَثْنَآءٌ pl. of ثِنْىٌ and of اِثْنَانِ: and also syn. with this latter, q. v.

ثَنَوِىٌّ: see اِثْنِىٌّ.

اِثْنَانِ a noun of number; (Ṣ, Mṣb;) applied to the dual number; (Mṣb;) meaning [*Two;*] the *double of* وَاحِدٌ; (M, Ḳ;) with a conjunctive ا [when not immediately preceded by a quiescence, written اَثْنَانِ]; (T, Ṣ, Mṣb;) but this is sometimes made disjunctive when connected with a preceding word by poetic license: (T, Ṣ:) of the masc. gender: (Ṣ:) fem. اِثْنَتَانِ, (T, Ṣ, Mṣb,) in which, also, the ا is conjunctive; (T, Mṣb;) and ▼ ثِنْتَانِ; (T, Ṣ, M, Mṣb, Ḳ;) the latter sometimes used, (T,) [much less frequently than the former, though the only fem. form mentioned in the M and Ḳ,] and of the dial. of Temeem; (Mṣb;) like as one says, هِىَ بِنْتُهُ and هِىَ ٱبْنَةُ فُلَانٍ: (T:) the ت in the dual is a substitute for the final radical, ى, (M, TA,) as it is in أَسْنَتُوا, the only other instance of this substitution except in words of the measure اِفْتَعَلَ: (Sb, M, TA:) in اِثْنَانِ, the final radical, ى, is suppressed: (Mṣb:) it has no sing.: (Lth, T:) if it were allowable to assign to it a sing., it would be اِثْنٌ [for the masc.] and اِثْنَةٌ [for the fem.], like اِبْنٌ and اِبْنَةٌ: (Ṣ:) accord. to some, (Mṣb,) it is originally ثِنْىٌ; (T, Mṣb, CḲ;) and hence the dual ثِنْتَانِ: (Mṣb:) or it is originally ثَنَىٌ, (M, Mṣb, and so in a copy of the Ḳ,) the conjunctive ا being then substituted for the ى, whence the dual اَثْنَانِ, like اَبْنَانِ: (Mṣb:) this is shown by the form of its pl., which is أَثْنَآءٌ, (M, Ḳ,) like أَبْنَآءٌ [pl. of اِبْنٌ, which is originally بَنَوٌ or بَنَىٌ,] and آخَآءٌ [pl. of أَخٌ, which is originally أَخَوٌ]. (M.) In the saying in the Ḳur [xvi. 53], لَا تَتَّخِذُوا إِلٰهَيْنِ اثْنَيْنِ [*Take not to yourselves two gods*], the last word is added as a corroborative. (M.) The phrase ثِنْتَا حَنْظَلٍ occurs, by poetic license, for حَنْظَلَتَانِ, اِثْنَتَانِ مِنْ حَنْظَلٍ, meaning [*Two colo-*

cynths]. (Ṣ.) You say also, شَرِبْتُ أُثْنَاةَ ↓ القَدَحِ, and شَرِبْتُ ٱثْنَىْ هٰذَا القَدَحِ, meaning [*I drank*] *twice as much as the bowl*, and *as this bowl*: and in like manner, ٱثْنَيْنِ and شَرِبْتُ ٱثْنَىْ مُدِّ البَصْرَةِ بِمُدِّ البَصْرَةِ [*I drank twice the quantity of the* مُدّ *of El-Baṣrah*]. (M.) And a poet says,

• فَمَا حُلِبَتْ إِلَّا الثَّلَاثَةَ وَالثُّنَى ↓ •
• وَلَا قُيِّلَتْ إِلَّا قَرِيبًا مَقَالُهَا •

meaning [*And she was not milked save*] *three vessels and two*, [*nor was she given her midday-drink save when her midday-resting was near.*] (IAạr, M.) —— Hence, (Mṣb,) يَوْمُ الاِثْنَيْنِ, (Ṣ, Mṣb,) or الاِثْنَانِ alone, (M, Ḳ,) *One of the days of the week*; [*the second*; namely, *Monday*;] because the first, with the Arabs, is الأَحَدُ; (M;) as also ↓ الثِّنَى, like إِلَى; (Ḳ;) so in the copies of the Ḳ; [or,] accord. to some, ↓ الثُّنِىُّ, [originally الثُّنُوىُ,] of the measure فُعُول, like ثُدِىّ [pl. of ثَدْىٌ], is used in this sense; (TA;) or ↓ اليَوْمُ الثُّنِىُّ, [so in the M, accord. to the TT,] mentioned by Sb, on the authority of certain of the Arabs: (M:) the pl. is أَثْنَآءٌ and أَثَانِينُ, (M, Ḳ,) the latter mentioned on the authority of Th: but it has no dual: and those who say أَثْنَآءٌ form this pl. from الاِثْنُ, although this has not been in use: (M:) or it has neither dual nor pl., (Ṣ, Mṣb,) being itself a dual; (Ṣ;) but if you would form a pl. from it, you would regard it as itself a sing., and make its pl. أَثَانِينُ: (Ṣ, Mṣb:) IB says that أَثَانِينُ has not been heard [from the Arabs], and is only mentioned by Fr, on the ground of analogy; that it is far-fetched in respect of analogy; and that the pl. heard is أَثْنَآءٌ: Seer and others mention, as heard from the Arabs, إِنَّهُ لَيَصُومُ الأَثْنَآءَ [*Verily he fasts on the Mondays*]. (TA.) الاثنين in يوم الاثنين has no dim. (Sb, Ṣ in art. امس.) IJ says that the article ال in الاثنين is not redundant, though the word is not an epithet: Abu-l-'Abbás says that the prefixing of the article in this case is allowable because the virtual meaning is اليَوْمُ الثَّانِى [*the second day*]. (M.) The saying اليَوْمُ الاِثْنَانِ means The name of *to-day* [*is* الاثنان]; and is like the saying اليَوْمُ يَوْمَانِ [to-day is two days] and اليَوْمُ خَمْسَةَ عَشَرَ مِنَ الشَّهْرِ [to-day is fifteen of the month]. (Sb, M.) Sometimes, يَوْمُ ٱثْنَيْنِ, without the article ال, occurs in poetry. (M, Ḳ.) When a pronoun refers to الاثنان [as meaning Monday], this word may be treated in two ways, [as a sing. and as a dual,] but the more chaste way is to treat it as a sing., as meaning the day: (Mṣb:) [thus,] Aboo-Ziyád used to say, مَضَى الاِثْنَانِ بِمَا فِيهِ [*Monday passed with what occurred in it*]; making it sing. and masc.; and thus he did in the case of every day of the week, except that he made الجُمُعَة fem.: Abu-l-Jarráḥ used to say, مَضَى الاِثْنَانِ بِمَا فِيهِمَا, treating the word as a numeral; and thus he treated the third and fourth and fifth days, saying in each of these cases بِمَا فِيهِنَّ. (M.) —— [اِثْنَا عَشَرَ, fem. اِثْنَتَا عَشْرَةَ; respectively, in a case of naṣb and khafḍ, اِثْنَىْ عَشَرَ and اِثْنَتَىْ عَشْرَةَ; and with ا when not immediately preceded by a quiescence; mean *Twelve*: see عَشَرَة.]

اِثْنَوِىٌّ, [with ا when not immediately preceded by a quiescence, in the CḲ erroneously written اَثْنَوِى,] One *who fasts alone on the second day of the week.* (IAạr, Th, M, Ḳ.)

الاِثْنَيْنِيَّةُ [*The doctrine of dualism*: see ثَنَوِىٌّ]. (TA.)

مَثْنَى (Ṣ, Mgh) and ↓ ثُنَاءَ (T, Ṣ) [*Two and two*; *two and two together*; or *two at a time and two at a time*]: they are imperfectly decl., in like manner as [مَثْلَثُ and] ثُلَاثُ, as explained in art. ثلث; (Ṣ, TA;) [because] changed from the original form of ٱثْنَانِ ٱثْنَانِ; (T, Mgh, TA;) or because of their having the quality of epithets and deviating from the original form of ٱثْنَانِ; (Sb, Ṣ in art. ثلث, q. v.;) or because they deviate from their original as to the letter and the meaning; the original word being changed as above stated, and the meaning being changed to ٱثْنَانِ ٱثْنَانِ. (Ṣ ibid.) You say, جَاؤُوا مَثْنَى and ↓ ثُنَاءَ (M, Ḳ) or مَثْنَى مَثْنَى, (Ṣ,) but this is a repetition of the word only, not of the meaning, (Mgh,) and in like manner one says of women, (M, Ḳ,*) i. e. *They came two* [*and*] *two.* (Ṣ, M, Ḳ.) And it is said in a trad., صَلَاةُ اللَّيْلِ مَثْنَى مَثْنَى, i. e. *The prayer of night is two rek'ahs* [*and*] *two rek'ahs* (رَكْعَتَانِ رَكْعَتَانِ). (TA.) [See also other exs. voce ثُلَاثُ.] —— مَثْنَى الأَيَادِى *The repeating a benefit*, or *benefaction*; or *reiterating it*; *conferring it twice*, or *thrice*; (Aṣ, T, Ḳ;) or *twice*, or *more than twice*: (Ḳ:) or *the shares remaining of the slaughtered camel* (A'Obeyd, T, Ṣ, M, Ḳ) *in the game called* المَيْسِر, (A'Obeyd, T, Ṣ, Ḳ,) *which shares a bountiful man used to purchase, and give for food to the* أَبْرَام, (A'Obeyd, T, Ṣ, M, Ḳ,) i. e., *those who took no part in the game, not contributing*: (M:) or *the taking a portion time after time.* (AA, T, Ṣ, M.) —— مَثَانٍ [is pl. of مَثْنًى as signifying *A place of doubling*, or *folding* &c.: and hence means —] The *knees* and *elbows* of a horse or similar beast. (T, Ḳ.) —— And The *bends* of a valley. (T, Ḳ. See ثِنْىٌ.) —— And, as pl. of مَثْنًى, The *chords of the lute that are after the first*: (M, Ḳ:) or مثنى signifies *a chord* [*of a lute*] *composed of two twists*: or, as some say, the *second chord.* (Ḥar p. 244. See مَثْلَث.) —— مَثْنًى also signifies The زِمَام [or *nose-rein*] of a she-camel: and Er-Rághib says that the مثناة [i. e. ↓ مَثْنَاة or ↓ مِثْنَاة] is the *doubled*, or *folded, part of the extremity of the* زِمَام. (TA.) —— المَثَانِى as relating to the Ḳur-án is pl. of مَثْنًى, (Mgh,) or of ↓ مَثْنَاةٌ: (AHeyth, T, Mgh:) it has three applications, accord. to A'Obeyd: (T, Mgh:) it signifies *The Ḳur-án altogether*; (A'Obeyd, T, Ṣ, M, Mgh, Ḳ;) so in the Ḳur xxxix 24; (A'Obeyd, T, Mgh;) meaning that the mention of reward and punishment is repeated, or reiterated, in it; (Fr, T;) or so called because the verse of mercy is conjoined with that of punishment; (Ṣ;) or because narratives and promises and threats are repeated in it; or because one peruses it repeatedly without being wearied: (Mgh:) or it signifies, (M, Ḳ,) or signifies also, (A'Obeyd, T, Ṣ, Mgh,) [*the first chapter*, called] *the* فَاتِحَة, (A'Obeyd, T, Ṣ, M, Mgh,) or الحَمْد, (Ḳ,) which means the same; (TA;) so in the Ḳur xv. 87; (A'Obeyd, T, Mgh;) because it is repeated, or recited twice, in every [act of prayer termed a] رَكْعَة, (Fr, Zj, AHeyth, T, Ṣ,) or with every chapter, (Th, M,) or in every prayer; (Mgh;) or because containing praise of God: (Zj, T, Mgh:) [but see سَبْعَة voce السَّبْعُ المَثَانِى:] or it signifies, (M, Ḳ,) or signifies also, (A'Obeyd, T, Ṣ, Mgh,) *the chapters that are less than those containing a hundred verses*, (Ṣ, M, Mgh,) or *that are less than the long ones* (الطُّوَل, q. v.), *and less than those containing a hundred verses*, (A'Obeyd, T, Ḳ, but in [most of] the copies of the Ḳ دُونَ المِائَتَيْنِ is put in the place of دُونَ المِئِينَ, which is the right reading, TA,) *and more than* [*those of the portion called*] *the* مُفَصَّل, (A'Obeyd, T, Mgh, Ḳ,) as is related on the authority of the Prophet by Ibn-Mes'ood and 'Othmán and Ibn-'Abbás; (AHeyth, T;) because, (Mgh,) or as though, (T,) occupying the second place after those containing a hundred verses: (T, Mgh:) or *the chapters*, (T, Ḳ,) *six and twenty in number*, (T,) *entitled* الحَجّ *and* القَصَص *and* النَّمْل *and* النُّور *and* الأَنْفَال *and* مَرْيَم *and* العَنْكَبُوت *and* الرُّوم *and* يٰس *and* الفُرْقَان *and* الحِجْر *and* الرَّعْد *and* سَبَأ *and* المَلَائِكَة *and* إِبْرَاهِيم *and* صٓ *and* مُحَمَّد *and* لُقْمَٰن *and* الغُرَف *and* المُؤْمِن *and* الزُّخْرُف *and* السَّجْدَة *and* الأَحْقَاف *and* الجَاثِيَة *and* الدُّخَان (T, Ḳ) *and* الأَحْزَاب, (Ḳ,) which last has been omitted by the copyists of the T: (TA:) or *the chapters of which the first is the* بَقَرَة, *and the last is* بَرَآءَة: or *what is repeated, of the Ḳur-án, time after time.* (M, Ḳ.)

مَثْنَاةٌ; pl. مَثَانٍ: see ثِنْىٌ: and ثِنَايَةٌ: and مَثْنًى; the last in two places. —— It is said in a trad. that one of the signs of the resurrection will be the public reading, or reciting, of the مَثْنَاة, (T, Ṣ,) which means *That which has been desired to be transcribed from a source other than the Book of God*: (T:) or *a certain book*, (T, Ḳ,) [*the Mishna*,] *which the learned men, and the recluses, of the Children of Israel, after Moses, composed after their own desire, from a source other than the Book of God*, as A'Obeyd says on the authority of a man learned in the books of the earlier times, (T,) *containing the histories of the Children of Israel after Moses, in which they allowed and disallowed what they pleased*: (Ḳ:) or *what is sung*: (Ḳ:) or *what is called in Persian* دُو بَيْتِى, (Ṣ, Ḳ,) *which means two verses, each composed of a pair of hemistichs*; (TA;) i. e. *what is sung*; but A'Obeyd explains it otherwise than thus: (Ṣ:) it is *what is known among the 'Ajam by the term* ↓ مَثْنَوِىّ, as though this were a rel. n. from مَثْنَاة: the vulgar say [erroneously] ذُو بَيْت, with the pointed ذ. (TA.)

مُثْنَاةٌ ; pl. مَثَانٍ : see ثِنْىٌ : and ثِنَايَةٌ ; the latter in two places : and see also مَثْنًى.

مُثَنًّى [pass. part. n. of 2. — *Dualized* : a *dual.* — مُثَنَّاةٌ فَوْقِيَّةٌ *Marked with two points above* : an epithet added to تَآء to prevent its being mistaken for بَآء or ثَآء or يَآء. And مُثَنَّاةٌ تَحْتِيَّةٌ *Marked with two points below* : an epithet added to يَآء to prevent its being mistaken for بَآء or تَآء or ثَآء.] — الطَّوِيلُ المُثَنَّى † *That which passes away* [*out of sight*, or *disappears*,] *by length* ; mostly used of a thing that is long without breadth. (TA.)

مُثَنًّى [pass. part. n. of 1; *Doubled* or *folded* &c.] — أَرْضٌ مُثْنِيَةٌ *Land*, or *ground, turned over twice for sowing*, or *cultivating.* (Mgh, and A and TA in art. ثلث.)

مَثْنَوِىٌّ : see مُثْنَاةٌ.

مَثْنَوِيَّةٌ : see ثُنْيَا, in four places.

ثو

ثُوَّةٌ [mentioned in the M under the head of ثو, as the radical letters, but in the T and K in art. ثوى,] sing. of ثُوًى, (IAar, T, K,) which latter, (IAar, T,) or the former, (K,) signifies The *goods*, or *utensils and furniture, of a house* or *tent* : (IAar, T, K :) or the former, *pieces of rag made in the form of a ball of thread* or *string, upon a peg*, or *stake, upon which the skin of milk is agitated to make butter, lest it should become lacerated* ; as also ▼ ثُوِىٌّ ; (M, K ;) which latter we hold to be from ثوو because syn. with ثُوَّةٌ, like قُوَّةٌ : (ISd in the M :) or *a piece of rag, which is moistened, and put upon the skin of milk when it is agitated to make butter, lest it should become lacerated* : (T :) or it signifies, (K,) or signifies also, (M,) *a piece of rag*, (M, K,) or *some wool wound upon the head of a peg*, or *stake*, (IB, TA,) *put beneath the skin of milk when it is agitated to make butter, in order to preserve it from being injured by the ground* ; (M, IB, K ;) pl. ثُوًى : (IB, TA :) or it signifies, (K,) or signifies also, (M,) *an elevated and a rugged spot, upon which, sometimes, stones are set up in order that one may be directed thereby to the right way* ; (M, K ;) like صُوَّةٌ. (M. See also ثَايَةٌ, in art. ثوى.)

ثُوِىٌّ : see above.

ثوأ

4. أَثْأَتُهُ بِسَهْمٍ, (S in art. ثأ, [incorrectly there mentioned, as is said by IB and others and in the K,] and K in the present art. and in art. ثأا,) inf. n. إِثَآءَةٌ, (S,) *I shot him*, or *shot at him, with an arrow* ; (S, K ;) so says AA, and Ks says the like ; (S ;) as also أَثْوَتُهُ, and, accord. to As, أَثْأَيْتُهُ, (TA in art. ثأ,) which is a strange word. (TA in the present art.) It is mentioned in the present art. by Sgh ; (K in art. ثأا ;) and this is its proper place ; (TA in the present art. ;) the verb, accord. to him, being like أَقَامَ : (TA in art. ثأا :) A'Obeyd has mentioned it in art. ثأا, (K in that art.,) as also Az ; holding the verb to be like صَنَعَ ; and so IKtt and IKoot assert it to be. (TA.)

ثَآءٌ *The name of the letter* ث, q. v. ; as also ثَا : pl. [of the former,] ثَآءَاتٌ ; and [of the latter,] أَثْوَآءٌ and أَثْيَآءٌ. (TA in باب الالف الليّنة.) ═ It also stands for ثَنَآءٌ, and ثَوَابٌ, and the like. (Idem ubi suprà.) ═ Also The *best* of anything ; as, for instance, of wheat, and of flesh-meat, and of sugar. (Kh, TA ubi suprà.)

ثَائِىٌّ and ثَاوِىٌّ rel. ns. of ثَآءٌ and ثَا, the names of the letter ث ; as also ثَيَوِىٌّ. (TA ubi suprà.)

ثوب

1. ثَابَ, (T, S, M, &c.,) aor. يَثُوبُ, (S, Mgh, &c.,) inf. n. ثَوْبٌ (S, M, Msb, K) and ثَوَبَانٌ (S) and ثُؤُوبٌ, (M, K,) *He*, or *it*, (a thing, M,) *returned* ; (M, Mgh, Msb, K ;) as also ▼ ثَوَّبَ, inf. n. تَثْوِيبٌ : (M, K :) *he returned to a place to which he had come before* ; or *it returned* &c. : (T :) *he* (a man) *returned, after he had gone away.* (S.) You say, تَفَرَّقُوا ثُمَّ ثَابُوا i. e. [*They became separated*, or *dispersed : then*] *they returned.* (A.) — ثَابَ إِلَى ٱللّٰهِ, like تَابَ, † *He returned* [*from disobedience*] *to obedience to God* ; *he repented* ; as also أَثَابَ. (T.) — ثاب also signifies † *He returned to a state of advertency*, or *vigilance* ; or *he had his attention roused.* (Th, T.) — Also † *He returned to a state of health*, or *soundness* : (TA, from a trad. :) *he became convalescent, and fat, after leanness.* (Mgh.) And ثَابَ جِسْمُهُ, (M, A, K,) inf. n. ثَوَبَانٌ ; (M, K ;) and ▼ أَثَابَ جِسْمُهُ ; (IKt, M ;) and ثَابَ إِلَيْهِ جِسْمُهُ ; (T, M, A ;) and ▼ أَثَابَ, alone ; (S, M, A ;) ‡ *He became fat, after leanness* ; (A ;) *his good state of body returned to him* ; (S, M, K ;*) *his condition of body became good, after extenuation* ; *and health*, or *soundness, thereof returned to him.* (T.) — ثَابَ إِلَيْهِ عَقْلُهُ ‡ [*His reason*, or *intellect, returned to him*] : and حِلْمُهُ [*his forbearance*, or *clemency*]. (A.) — ثَابَ ٱلْمَآءُ † *The water of a well returned*, or *collected again* : (T :) *the water attained again its former state after some had been drawn* : (M :) *the water collected* [*again*] *in a watering-trough, or tank.* (S.) — ثَابَ ٱلنَّاسُ † *The people collected themselves together, and came.* (S.) And ثَابَ ٱلْقَوْمُ † *The company of men came following one another* : the verb is not used in this sense in speaking of one person. (M.) — ثاب said of a man's property, ‡ *It became abundant, and collected.* (A.) — Said of dust, ‡ *It rose*, or *spread*, or *diffused itself, and became abundant.* (A.) — Said of a watering-trough, or tank, (T, M, A, K,) inf. n. ثَوْبٌ (AZ, T, M, K) and ثَوَبَانٌ (AZ, T) and ثُؤُوبٌ, (M, K,) ‡ *It became full* : (AZ, T, M, A, K :) or *nearly full.* (AZ, T, M, K.)

2. ثَوَّبَ, inf. n. تَثْوِيبٌ : see 1, first sentence. — ثَوَّبَ بَعْدَ خَصَاصَةٍ ‡ [*He returned to a state of richness*, or *competence, after poverty*, or *straitness*, or *being in an evil condition*]. (A, TA.) — تَثْوِيبٌ meaning The *calling*, or *summoning*, (M, Mgh, K,) *to prayer*, (M, K,) and *to other things*, (M,) is said to be from ثَوْبٌ "a garment," (Mgh,) because a man, when he comes crying out for aid, makes a sign with his garment, (M, Mgh,) moving it about, raising his hand with it, in order that he to whom he calls may see it, (Mgh,) and this action is like a calling, or summoning, (M, Mgh,) and an announcing, to him ; so the calling, or summoning, by reason of frequent usage of this word [as meaning the *making a sign with a garment*], came to be thus called ; and one said of the caller, or summoner, ثَوَّبَ : (Mgh :) or it means the *calling*, or *summoning, twice* ; (M, K ;) or the *repeating a call* or *summons* ; from ثاب "he returned :" (Mgh :) you say, ثَوَّبَ, inf. n. as above, (T, Msb,) meaning *he called*, or *summoned, one time after another* ; (T ;) *he repeated his call*, or *cry* : (Msb :) and hence تثويب in the أَذَان ; (T, Msb ;) i. e., the *saying* of the مُؤَذِّن, *after having, by the* اذان, *called the people to prayer*, ٱلصَّلَاةَ رَحِمَكُمُ ٱللّٰهُ ٱلصَّلَاةَ [*Prayer : may God have mercy on you ! Prayer !*] ; thus calling to it a second time : (T :) or his *saying*, (S, TA,) *in the morning call to prayer*, (S,) ٱلصَّلَاةُ خَيْرٌ مِنَ ٱلنَّوْمِ [*Prayer is better than sleep*] ; (S, TA ;) for he resumes his call by saying this after he has said, حَىَّ عَلَى ٱلصَّلَاةِ [and حَىَّ عَلَى ٱلْفَلَاحِ] ; desiring the people to hasten to prayer : (TA :) or his *saying, in the morning call to prayer*, الصلاة خير من النوم *twice*, (T, K,) *after having said*, حىّ على الصلاه حىّ على الفلاح : (T :) or the old تثويب was the *saying* of the مُؤَذِّن, *in the morning call to prayer*, الصلاة خير من النوم : and the modern, ٱلصَّلَاةَ ٱلصَّلَاةَ or قَامَتْ قَامَتْ. (Mgh.) It also signifies The إِقَامَة ; (Mgh, K, TA ;) [meaning, the *chanting*, by the مُبَلِّغُون, in a mosque, not by the مُؤَذِّن, *the common words of the* أَذَان, *with the addition of* قَدْ قَامَتِ ٱلصَّلَاةُ (*The time of prayer has come*), *pronounced twice after* حىّ على الفلاح ;] i. e. the اقامة *of prayer* : (IAth, TA :) and this is what is meant by the phrase, in a trad., إِذَا ثُوِّبَ بِٱلصَّلَاةِ [*When the words of the* اقامة *are chanted*]. (IAth, Mgh, TA.) And The *praying after the prayer divinely ordained.* (Yoo, T, K.) You say, ثَوَّبَ, meaning *He performed a supererogatory prayer after the prescribed* ; تثويب being only after the prescribed ; being the *praying after praying* : (T :) and ▼ تَثَوَّبَ signifies the same. (K.) And ثَوَّبَ بِرَكْعَتَيْنِ *He performed two rek'ahs as a supererogatory act.* (A.) But this and the similar significations are said to be post-classical. (MF.) — See also 4, in four places. ═ ثَيَّبَتْ, (T, S, Mgh,) inf. n. تَثْيِيبٌ ; (T, Mgh ;) formed from ثَيِّبٌ, upon supposition [that the medial radical letter of this word is ى, whereas many hold that letter to be و] ; (Mgh ;) or ▼ تَثَيَّبَتْ ; (K in art. ثيب ; [the author of which seems to have supposed that, for ثَيَّبَتْ, one should read ثَيِّبَتْ ; and therefore he gives مُثَيِّب as syn. with ثَيِّب ;]) *She* (a woman) *became what*

is termed ثَيِّب. (T, Mgh, Ḳ.) — [Accord. to my copy of the Mgh, it also signifies *She* (a camel) *became what is termed* ثَابَ: but I think that, in this instance, it is a mistranscription, for نَيَّبَتْ.] ═ [See also the last sentence of the second paragraph of art. ثوب; and compare, with what is there said by SM, meanings assigned below to مَثَابٌ and مَثَابَةٌ.]

3. الخُطَّابُ يُثَاوِبُونَهَا *The suitors return to her* (namely, a woman such as is termed ثَيِّب,) *time after time.* (A, Mgh.)

4. اثاب: see 1, in two places. — It may also mean †*It* (a valley, or a well,) *had a return of water after a stoppage thereof.* (Ḥam p. 598.) ═ اثاب ٱللّٰهُ جِسْمَهُ ‡ *God restored him to fatness, after leanness;* (A;) *restored his body to a good state,* or *condition.* (TA.) — إِنَّ عَمُودَ الدِّينِ لَا يُثَابُ بِالنِّسَآءِ إِنْ مَالَ † *Verily the column of the religion cannot be set upright again by women, if it incline:* said by Umm-Selemeh to 'Áisheh, when the latter desired to go forth to El-Baṣrah. (T, L.) — اثابهُ ٱللّٰهُ, (T, Ṣ,* M, A, Mṣb, Ḳ,) inf. n. إِثَابَةٌ; (Mgh;) and أَثْوَبَهُ [dev. from rule]; (M, Ḳ;) and ▼ثَوَّبَهُ, (T, A,) inf. n. تَثْوِيبٌ; (T, Mgh;) *God recompensed, compensated, requited,* or *rewarded, him:* (T, Ṣ,* M, A, Mgh,* Mṣb, Ḳ:) said in relation to good and to evil. (T.) And اثابهُ, (Lḥ, M,) and أَثْوَبَهُ, (T,) مَثُوبَةً حَسَنَةً, (Lḥ, T, M,) and مَثْوَبَةً, (Lḥ, M,) *He* (God) *gave him a good recompense, compensation,* &c. (M.) And ▼ثَوَّبَهُ مَثُوبَتَهُ *He gave him his recompense,* &c. (M, Ḳ.) It is said in a trad., أَثِيبُوا أَخَاكُمْ, i. e. *Recompense ye your brother for his good deed.* (TA.) And in the Ḳur [lxxxiii. last verse], هَلْ ▼ثُوِّبَ الكُفَّارُ مَا كَانُوا يَفْعَلُونَ *Have the unbelievers been recompensed for what they did?* (T, Ṣ, M.) And one says also, اثابهُ مِنْ هِبَتِهِ, meaning *He gave him a substitute, something instead* or *in exchange,* or *a compensation, for his gift.* (Mgh,* and TA in art. جنب.) And ▼ثَوَّبَهُ مِنْ كَذَا, (M,) inf. n. تَثْوِيبٌ, (Ḳ,) *He gave him a substitute,* &c., *for such a thing.* (M, Ḳ.*) — اثاب الثَّوْبَ, inf. n. إِثَابَةٌ, *He sewed the garment,* or *piece of cloth, the second time:* when one sews it the first time, [in a slight manner,] you say of him مَلَّهُ [and شَلَّهُ, i. e. "he sewed it in the manner termed 'running'"]. (T.) — اثاب الحَوْضَ ‡ *He filled the watering-trough,* or *tank:* (Ḳ, TA:) or *nearly filled it.* (Ḳ.)

5. تَثَوَّبَ — and تَثَيَّبَتْ: see 2, in the latter part of the paragraph. — The former also signifies *He gained,* or *earned, a* ثَوَاب [or *recompense,* &c.]. (Ḳ.) But this is said to be post-classical. (MF.)

6. تثاوب: see تَثَأَّبَ, in art. ثأب.

10. استثاب مَالًا *He restored to himself,* or *repossessed himself of, property;* syn. اِسْتَرْجَعَهُ; (T, A, Ḳ;) his property having gone away. (T, A.) And اِسْتَثَبْتُ بِمَالِكَ *I restored to myself,* or *repossessed myself of, property, by means of that which thou gavest me;* my property having gone away. (A.) El-Kumeyt says,

• إِنَّ العَشِيرَةَ تَسْتَثِيبُ بِمَالِهِ •
• فَيُغِيرُ وَهْوَ مُوَفِّرٌ أَمْوَالَهَا •

[*Verily the tribe restore to themselves wealth by means of his property; and he makes incursions into hostile territories* at his own expense, *making their property abundant* by the spoil that they gain with him]. (T, TA.) — اسْتَثَابَهُ *He asked him to recompense, compensate, requite,* or *reward, him.* (Ṣ, Ḳ.)

ثَوْبٌ *A garment,* (M, Mgh, Mṣb, Ḳ,) [or *piece of cloth* or *stuff,*] *that is worn by men, composed of linen, cotton, wool, fur,* خَزّ [q. v.], (Mgh, Mṣb,) *silk,* or *the like;* (Mṣb;) but [properly] *not what is cut out of several pieces, such as the shirt, and trousers, or drawers, &c.;* (Mgh;) [though often applied to a shirt or shift (قَمِيص) or درع) and to a جُبَّة &c.:] it seems to be so called because the wearer returns to it, or it to the wearer, time after time: (Mgh:) [also *a garment worn by women and girls over the shift;* (see أُصْدَةٌ;) app., as in the present day, *a long gown, reaching to the feet, with very wide sleeves:*] pl. ثِيَابٌ [the pl. of mult.] (T, Ṣ, M, A, Mgh, Mṣb, Ḳ) and أَثْوَابٌ [a pl. of pauc.] (Ṣ, M, Mṣb, Ḳ) and أَثْوُبٌ and أَثْؤُبٌ, (Ṣ, M, Ḳ,) the last two being pls. of pauc., and the latter of them being thus pronounced with ء by some of the Arabs because the ḍammeh immediately after و is deemed difficult of utterance; for which reason they substitute ء for و in all instances like this. (Ṣ.) — *Curtains,* and *the like,* are not [properly] called ثِيَاب; but أَمْتِعَةُ البَيْتِ: (Mgh, Mṣb:) though Es-Sarakhsee uses the phrase ثِيَابُ البَيْتِ. (Mgh.) تَعَلَّقَ بِثِيَابِ ٱللّٰهِ ‡ [*He clung to the curtains* of the House *of God*], i. e., *to the curtains of the Kaabeh,* is a tropical expression.* (A.) — Sometimes, ثَوْبٌ is used metonymically to signify ‡ *A thing* [*of any kind*] *that veils, covers,* or *protects:* as in the saying of a poet,

• كَثَوْبِ ٱبْنِ بِيضٍ وَقَاهُمْ بِهِ •
• فَسَدَّ عَلَى السَّالِكِينَ السَّبِيلَا •

[*Like the means of protection adopted by Ibn-Beed: he protected them by it, and closed the way against the passengers*]. (TA.) Ibn-Beed was a wealthy merchant of the tribe of 'Ád, who hamstrung his she-camel upon a mountain-road, and stopped the way [to his abode] with it. (Ḳ in art. بيض.) — In the same manner, also, ثِيَابٌ is used to signify ‡ *Weapons.* (Ḥam p. 63.) — And أَثْوَابٌ is sometimes employed to signify †The *wearers of garments;* the wearers' *bodies.* (R, TA.) Esh-Shemmákh says, (T,) or Leylà, describing camels, (TA,)

• رَمَوْهَا بِأَثْوَابٍ خِفَافٍ فَلَا تَرَى •
• لَهَا شَبَهًا إِلَّا النَّعَامَ المُنَفَّرَا •

i. e. *They mounted them,* namely, the travelling-camels, (T,) *with* their [*light,* or *agile,*] *bodies:* [*and thou seest not anything like them, except ostriches scared away.*] (T, TA.) And in like manner, also, the dual is employed to signify †The wearer's *body,* or *self;* or *what the garments infold:* and ثِيَاب is employed in the same manner. (TA.) You say, لِلّٰهِ ثَوْبَاهُ, i. e. ‡ *To God be he* [meaning *his excellence*] *attributed!* [for nothing but what is excellent is to be attributed to God:] (A:) or it means لِلّٰهِ دَرُّهُ [*To God be attributed the good that hath proceeded from him!* or *his good deed!* &c.: see arts. اله and در]. (Ḳ.) And فِى ثَوْبَىَّ أَبِى أَنْ أَفِيَهُ meaning ‡ [*On me and on my father it rests,* or *lies,* or *be it, that I pay it:* or] فِى ذِمَّتِى وَذِمَّةِ أَبِى [*on my responsibility and the responsibility of my father*]. (Ḳ, TA.) And أُسْلُلْ ثِيَابَكَ مِنْ ثِيَابِى ‡ *Withdraw,* or *separate, thyself from me.* (A.) — [The following exs. are mostly, or all, tropical.] — إِنَّ المَيِّتَ لَيُبْعَثُ فِى ثِيَابِهِ الَّتِى يَمُوتُ فِيهَا, (Ḳ,* TA,) a saying of Moḥammad, repeated by Aboo-Sa'eed El-Khudree, when, being about to die, he had called for new garments, and put them on: (TA:) it means *Verily the dead will be raised in his garments in which he dies;* accord. to some; and was used in this sense by Aboo-Sa'eed: (El-Khaṭṭábee, MF, TA:) or † [*agreeably with*] *his works* (Ḳ, TA) *with which his life is closed:* (TA:) or † *in the state in which he dies,* according as it is good or evil. (TA.) — وَثِيَابَكَ فَطَهِّرْ, in the Ḳur [lxxiv. 4], means *And purify thy garments:* (Abu-l-'Abbás, T:) or *shorten thy garments;* for the shortening them is a means of purity: (T:) or †*put not on thy garments in a state of disobedience or unrighteousness:* (I'Ab, T:) or † *be not perfidious;* for [figuratively speaking,] he who is so pollutes his garments: (Fr, T:) or, as some say, †*purify thy heart:* (Abu-l-'Abbás, T, Ḳ:) or † *purify thyself* (IḲt, T, TA) *from sins,* or *offences:* (IḲt, TA:) or †*rectify thine actions,* or *thy conduct.* (TA.) — You say, فُلَانٌ نَقِىُّ الثَّوْبِ, meaning ‡ *Such a one is free from vice,* or *fault:* (A:) and طَاهِرُ الثَّوْبِ ‡ [*the same;* or *pure in heart,* or *conduct,* or *reputation*]. (TA in art. نصح.) And دَنِسُ الثِّيَابِ ‡ *Vicious,* or *faulty:* (A:) or *perfidious:* (Fr, T:) or *foul,* or *evil, in reputation,* (T, TA,) *in conduct,* or *actions,* and *in the way that he follows* [*with respect to religion and morality*]. (TA.) أَعْرَضُ ثَوْبِ المُتَشَبِّعِ: see كَلَابِسِ ثَوْبَىْ زُورٍ — ثَوْبُ المَآءِ: see عَرَضٌ and المِلْبَسِ and المُلْبَسِ &c. — † [*The membrane called*] *and* الغِرْسُ السَّلَى. (Ḳ. See these two words.)

ثِيبٌ: see ثَائِبٌ, in two places.

ثُبَةٌ The *place where the water collects in a valley or low ground;* so called because the water returns to it: (Aboo-Kheyreh, T:) and the *middle of a watering-trough or tank,* (T, Ṣ, M,) *to which the water returns when it has been emptied,* (Ṣ,) or *to which what remains of the water returns;* (T;) as also ▼مَثَابٌ: (Ṣ:) the ة is a substitute for the و, the medial radical, which is suppressed; (Ṣ, L;) the word being from ثَابَ, aor. يَثُوبُ: (L:) Aboo-Is-ḥáḳ infers that this is the case from its having for its dim. ▼ثُوَيْبَةٌ: but it may be from ثَبَّيْتُ "I collected together:" (M:) it is mentioned in the Ḳ in art. ثبى or ثبو, and not here. (TA.) See also art. ثبو or ثبى. — Also *A company of men;* (T, M, L;) and so أُثْبِيَّةٌ: (M:) or *a company of men in a state of separation* or *dispersion;* (T;) *a distinct body,* or *company, of people:* (Yoo, T:) and *a troop of horsemen:* (M:) pl. ثُبَاتٌ and ثُبُونَ (T, M) and ثِبُونَ: (Ṣ and M in art. ثبى, and M in art. ثبو also:) accord. to some, from ثَابَ, being originally ثُوبَةٌ; and its dim. is ▾ ثُوَيْبَةٌ: accord. to others, it is originally ثُبَيَةٌ; (T, L;) and its pl. is ثُبًى. (L.) Hence, in the Ḳur [iv. 73], فَانْفِرُوا ثُبَاتٍ, i. e. [*And go ye forth* to war against the unbelievers] *in troops,* (Fr, T,) or *in distinct bodies.* (Yoo, T.) See, again, art. ثبو or ثبى.

ثُوَبَاءُ: see ثُؤَبَاءُ, in art. ثأب.

ثَوَابٌ (T, Ṣ, M, Mgh, Mṣb, Ḳ) and ▾ مَثَابَةٌ (T, Mṣb) and ▾ مَثُوبَةٌ (T, Ṣ, M, Ḳ) and ▾ مَثْوَبَةٌ, (Et-Temeemee, T, M, Ḳ,) the last anomalous, (M,) and unknown to the Kilábees, who knew the second of these words, (T,) *A recompense, compensation, requital,* or *reward,* (T, Ṣ, M, Mgh, Mṣb, Ḳ,) *of obedience* [*to God*]: (Ṣ:) or *absolutely; for good* and *for evil;* as appears from the words of the Ḳur, هَلْ ثُوِّبَ الكُفَّارُ [cited above, see 4]; but *more especially and frequently, for good.* (IAth, L, MF, TA.) — ثَوَابٌ is also used as a quasi-inf. n., in the sense of إِثَابَةٌ; and in this case, accord to the Koofees and Baghdádees, it may govern as a verb, [like the inf. n.,] as in the saying,

• لِأَنَّ ثَوَابَ ٱللّٰهِ كُلَّ مُوَحِّدٍ •
• جِنَانٌ مِنَ الفِرْدَوْسِ فِيهَا يُخَلَّدُ •

[*For God's rewarding every believer in his unity* will be the giving *gardens of Paradise, wherein he will be made to abide for ever*]. (Expos. of the Shudhoor edh-Dhahab.) — It signifies also ‡ *Honey;* (Ḳ, TA;) i. e. (TA) *the good that proceeds from bees.* (A, TA.) — And in like manner, ‡ [*Rain;* i. e.] the *good that results from the winds.* (A, TA. [See ثَائِبٌ.]) — And † *Bees;* (M, Ḳ;) because they return [to their hives]. (M.)

ثَيِّبٌ, [like سَيِّدٌ; originally ثَيْوِبٌ, or ثَوْيِبٌ; i. e.] of the measure فَيْعِلٌ, (Mgh,) or فَيْعَلٌ; (Mṣb;) *A woman who has become separated from her husband* (Lth, T, M, Mgh, Ḳ) *in any manner:* (Lth, T, M, Mgh:) or *a woman whose husband has died,* or *who has been divorced, and has then returned to the marriage-state:* (A Heyth, TA:) or *one that is not a virgin:* (IAth, TA:) or *a woman to whom a man has gone in;* and *a man who has gone in to a woman:* (Ks, ISk, Ṣ, Mgh, Ḳ:) or *a person who has married:* (Mṣb:) applied to *a man* and to *a woman;* (Aṣ, Ṣ, M, Mṣb;) like بِكْرٌ and أَيِّمٌ: (Mgh, Mṣb:) from ثَابَ; (IAth, Mgh, Mṣb;) because they generally return time after time to the marriage-state: (Mgh:) but mostly applied to *a woman;* because she returns to her family in a manner different from the first [state]; (Mṣb;) or because the suitors return to her time after time: (Mgh:) or it is not applied to a man (Lth, El-'Eyn, T, M, Mgh, Ḳ) except in the dual form, as when one says وَلَدُ الثَّيِّبَيْنِ: (Lth, El-'Eyn, T, M, Ḳ:) and a woman is also termed ▾ مُثَيِّبٌ; (M;) or ▾ مُثَيَّبٌ, like مُعَظَّمٌ: (Ḳ: [but see 2, last sentence but two:]) the pl. of ثَيِّبٌ applied to a woman is ثَيِّبَاتٌ, (T, Mgh, Mṣb,) and the post-classical writers say ثُيَّبٌ, which has not been heard as genuine Arabic: (Mgh,* Mṣb:) its pl. if applied to a man is ثَيِّبُونَ. (Mṣb.) It is said in a trad., الثَّيِّبَانِ يُرْجَمَانِ وَالبِكْرَانِ يُجْلَدَانِ وَيُغَرَّبَانِ [*The two persons of whom each has previously had carnal intercourse in marriage with one of the other sex shall be stoned* if they commit adultery together; *and the two who have previously had no connubial intercourse with others shall be flogged and banished* if they commit fornication together]. (T.) — It is also applied to † *A woman who has attained the age of puberty, though a a virgin;* tropically, and by extension of its proper signification. (IAth, TA.) — This word is mentioned in the Ḳ [and M] in art. ثيب; and its mention in art. ثوب is said by the author of the Ḳ to be wrong: but IAth and many others decisively assert that it is from ثَابَ, aor. يَثُوبُ, "he returned." (MF, TA.)

ثُوَيْبَةٌ: see ثُبَةٌ, in two places.

ثِيَابَةٌ and ثُيُوبَةٌ, as meaning The *state of being a* ثَيِّب, are not of the genuine language of the Arabs. (Mgh.)

ثِيَابِىٌّ *One who takes care of the clothes in the bath.* (Ḳ.) [A post-classical word.]

ثَوَّابٌ i. q. تَوَّابٌ [One *who repents,* or *returns from disobedience to obedience to God, much* or *often*]. (T.) — *A seller of garments,* or *pieces of cloth:* (AZ, T, L, Ḳ:) and *a possessor thereof.* (Sb, Ṣ, L, Ḳ.)

بِئْرٌ لَهَا ثَائِبٌ ‡ *A well into which water returns after one has drawn from it;* (A, TA;) see مَثَابٌ; and in like manner, [but in an intensive sense in the second of the following phrases,] ذَاتُ ثَيِّبٍ ▾ and بِئْرٌ لَهَا ثَيِّبٌ ▾ وَعَيِبٌ [in which وعيب is an epithet]: (T, L, TA:) or the first of these three phrases means *a well of which the water stops sometimes, and then returns.* (Ḥam p. 598.) You say of a well (بئر), مَا أَسْرَعَ ثَائِبَهَا † *How quick is its returning supply of water!* (T.) — ثَائِبُ البَحْرِ † *The water of the sea when it flows after ebbing.* (Ḳ.) Hence, كَلَأٌ مِثْلُ ثَائِبِ البَحْرِ † *Fresh, sappy,* [*green,*] *herbage.* (T, L.) — قَوْمٌ لَهُمْ ثَائِبٌ ‡ *A people,* or *number of men, who come company after company.* (A, TA.) — ثَائِبٌ also signifies ‡ *A violent wind that blows at the beginning of rain.* (Ṣ, Ḳ, TA.)

مَثَابٌ: see مَثَابَةٌ, in four places: — and see ثُبَةٌ. — Also † The *place from which the water returns* [*to supply the place of that which has been drawn, in a well*]: whence بِئْرٌ لَهَا ثَائِبٌ ▾ [see ثَائِبٌ]. (TA.) — And † The *station of the water-drawer,* (A 'Obeyd, T, Ṣ, M, Ḳ,) *above the* عُرُوش [which means the *pieces of wood upon which he stands*], (A 'Obeyd, T,) or *at the brink, where is the* عَرْش [sing. of عُرُوش], (Ṣ,) or *which forms part of the* عُرُوش, (M,) *of a well:* (A 'Obeyd, T, Ṣ, M, Ḳ:) or the *middle* of a well: (Ḳ:) or it has this meaning also: (M:) pl. مَثَابَاتٌ. (T, M.) [See also مَثَابَةٌ.] — And † The *construction,* or *casing, of stones* (طَىُّ الحِجَارَةِ) *that succeed one another from top to bottom* [*round the interior of a well*]. (IAạr.) [See again مَثَابَةٌ.]

مَثَابَةٌ (accord. to Aboo-Is-ḥáḳ originally ▾ مَثْوَبَةٌ, T) *A place to which people return,* (ISh, Aboo-Is-ḥáḳ, T, Ṣ, Mṣb,) or *to which one returns,* (ISh, Ṣ, Mṣb,) *time after time;* (Ṣ;) and ▾ مَثَابٌ signifies the same: (Aboo-Is-ḥáḳ, T:) and the former, *a place of assembly* or *congregation:* (ISh:) or *a place where people assemble,* or *congregate, after they have separated,* or *dispersed;* as also ▾ the latter word: (M, Ḳ:) and *a place of alighting* or *abode; an abode;* or *a house;* because the inhabitants thereof return to it (ISh, Ṣ) after having gone to their affairs: (Ṣ:) the pl. is مَثَابَاتٌ; [also mentioned above as pl. of مَثَابٌ;] (ISh;) or it is مَثَابٌ ▾; (Ṣ;) [or this is a coll. gen. n.;] or, accord. to Fr and others, مَثَابَةٌ and ▾ مَثَابٌ are the same: Th says that *a house,* or *tent,* (بَيْت,) is called مَثَابَةٌ; and some say ▾ مَثُوبَةٌ; but no one reads thus [in the Ḳur]. (TA.) It has the first of all these meanings in the Ḳur ii. 119: (T, Ṣ, Bḍ, Jel, TA:) or it there means *a place of recompense* or *reward* for the pilgrimage to the Kaạbeh and the visitation thereof. (Bḍ.) — And, sometimes, The *place where the hunter,* or *fowler, puts his snare.* (Ṣ.) — مَثَابَةُ البِئْرِ ‡ *The place where the water of the well collects:* (A, TA:) or *the place reached by the water of the well when it returns and collects after one has drawn from it.* (M, Ḳ.) [Hence,] جَمَّتْ مَثَابَةُ جَهْلِهِ ‡ *His ignorance became confirmed.* (A, TA.) And كَانَ يَسْتَجِمُّ مَثَابَةَ سَفَهِهِ ‡ [*He used to wait for his lightwittedness,* or *silliness, to attain its full degree*]: a metaphorical phrase, occurring in a trad. (Ḥar p. 68.) — Also † *The stones that project, or overhang, around the well,* (M, Ḳ,) *upon which the man sometimes stands in order that the bucket* (دلو or غرب) *may not strike against the side of the well:* (M:) or *the place where it is walled round within* (مَوْضِعُ طَيِّهَا): (Ḳ:) or, accord. to IAạr, it means طَىُّ البِئْرِ; but [ISd says,] I know not whether he mean thereby مَوْضِعُ طَيِّهَا, or *the building it* [or *walling it round within*] *with stones;* though it is rarely that a word of the measure مَفْعَلَةٌ [like مثابة] is an inf. n. (M.) [See مَثَابٌ: and see what is said of تَثْوِيبٌ in the last sentence of the second paragraph of art. ثرب.] — مَثَابَاتٌ [the pl.] also signifies † The *foundations of a house.* (IAạr, T.) — See also ثَوَابٌ.

مُثُوبَةٌ: see ثَوَابٌ.

مَثْوَبَةٌ: see مَثَابَةٌ, in two places: — and see also ثَوَابٌ.

مُثَيَّبٌ and مُثَيِّبٌ: see ثَيِّبٌ.

because

مُسْتَثَابَاتُ الرِّيَاحِ ‡ *Winds that are attended by prosperity and blessing; from which one hopes for a good result* [i. e. *rain*]. (A, TA.)

ثوخ

1. ثَاخَ and سَاخَ both signify *He*, or *it, sank* into the ground; and Yaakoob asserts that the ث in the former is a substitute for the س in the latter. (L, TA.) You say, ثَاخَتْ قَدَمُهُ بِالوَحْلِ, (Ṣ,) or فِى الوَحْلِ, (L,) aor. تَثِيخُ and تَثُوخُ, *His foot sank*, or *entered, into the mire.* (Ṣ, L.) And ثَاخَتِ الإِصْبَعُ, aor. as above, (L, Ḳ,) inf. n. ثَوْخٌ, (L,) *The finger entered*, or *sank*, into a swollen, or tumid, or a soft, or yielding, substance; (L, Ḳ;) as also سَاخَتْ, (L,) and تَاخَتْ: (Lth:) but this last is disapproved by IDrd, and J and others do not mention it. (TA in art. توخ.)

ثور

1. ثَارَ, aor. يَثُورُ, (M,) inf. n. ثَوْرٌ and ثُؤُورٌ and ثَوَرَانٌ, (M, Ḳ,) *It* (a thing, M) *became raised, roused, excited, stirred up*, or *provoked*; syn. هَاجَ; (M;) syn. of the inf. n. هَيَجَانٌ: (Ḳ:) as also ↓ تثوّر. (M, Ḳ.) — Said of dust, (Ṣ, M, A, Mgh, Mṣb,) and of smoke, (M, A,) and of other things, (M, TA,) inf. n. ثَوْرٌ and ثُؤُورٌ (Ṣ, M, Mṣb, Ḳ) and ثَوَرَانٌ, (Ḳ,) ‡ *It became raised*, or *stirred up*; (Mgh, Mṣb;) *and spread*: (Mgh:) or *rose*, (Ṣ, M, A, Ḳ,) *and appeared*; (M;) as also ↓ تثوّر: (Ḳ:) also said of the redness in the sky after sunset, inf. n. ثَوْرٌ and ثَوَرَانٌ, ‡ *it spread upon the horizon, and rose*: (TA: [see ثَوْرٌ:]) and ثار, said of anything, means † *it appeared and spread.* (Mgh.) — Said of a camel lying upon his breast, *He became roused*, or *put in motion* or *action*; as also ↓ تثوّر. (TA.) — Said of the bird called القَطَا, (M, A,) inf. ns. as first mentioned above, (Ḳ,) or ثَوْرٌ and ثَوَرَانٌ, (M,) *It rose* (M, A, Ḳ) from the place where it lay; (M, A;) as also ↓ تثوّر: (Ḳ:) and of a swarm of locusts, *it rose*; (M, Ḳ;) as also ↓ تثوّر: (Ḳ:) or *appeared*; as also ↓ انثار. (TA.) — Also, (Ṣ, M,) inf. ns. as first mentioned above, (M, Ḳ,) *He leaped*, or *sprang*; (M, Ḳ;) as also ↓ تثوّر. (Ḳ.) You say, ثار إِلَيْهِ *He leaped*, or *sprang, to*, or *towards, him*, or *it.* (M.) And ثار بِهِ النَّاسُ *The people leaped*, or *sprang, upon him.* (Ṣ.) And ثار إِلَى الشَّرِّ *He rose*, or *hastened, to do evil*, or *mischief.* (Mṣb.) — ثار المَآءُ *The water flowed forth with force; gushed forth.* (TA.) — ثار بِهِ الدَّمُ, (TA,) inf. ns. as first mentioned above, (Ḳ,) ‡ *The blood appeared in him*; as also ↓ تثوّر. (Ḳ,* TA.) And ثار الدَّمُ فِى وَجْهِهِ ‡ *The blood appeared in* [or *mantled in* or *mounted into*] *his face*; as also ↓ انثار. (M.) — ثارت به الحَصْبَةُ, (Ṣ, M, A,) inf. n. ثَوْرٌ and ثُؤُورٌ and ثُوَارٌ [or ثُؤَارٌ?] and ثَوَرَانٌ, (M,) ‡ *The measles spread* [or *broke out*] *in him*: (M:) and in like manner one says of anything that appears: (M:) one says, ثار, inf. n. ثَوْرٌ and ثَوَرَانٌ, meaning † *it appeared.* (T.) And accord. to Lḥ, one says, ثار الرَّجُلُ, inf. n. ثَوَرَانٌ, meaning ‡ *The man had the measles appearing in him.* (M.) — ثار بِالمَحْمُومِ الثُّوْرُ ‡ *Pimples*, or *small pustules, breaking out in the mouth, appeared in the fevered man.* (A.) — ثارت الحُمَّى † [*The fever rose*, or *became excited*]. (TA from a trad.) — ثارت نَفْسُهُ ‡ *His soul* [or *stomach*] *heaved*; or *became agitated by a tendency to vomit*; syn. جَشَأَتْ, (T, Ṣ,) i. e. اِرْتَفَعَتْ; (T;) or جَاشَتْ, (TA,) i. e. فَارَتْ. (T.) — ثار الغَضَبُ, (Mṣb,) inf. n. ثَوْرٌ, (M,) † [*Anger became roused*, or *excited*, or *inflamed*: or *became roused*, or *excited in the utmost degree*: or *boiled*: or *spread*: (see ثَائِرٌ, below:) or] *became sharp.* (M, Mṣb.) — ثارت بَيْنَهُمْ فِتْنَةٌ وَشَرٌّ (A, Mṣb*) ‡ *Discord*, or *dissension*, or *the like, and evil*, or *mischief, became excited among them*, or *between them.* (Mṣb.)

2: see 4, in three places. — You say also, ثَوَّرَ الأَمْرَ, inf. n. تَثْوِيرٌ, † *He searched*, or *sought, for*, or *after, the thing*, or *affair*; *inquired*, or *sought information, respecting it*; *searched*, or *inquired, into it*; *investigated, scrutinized*, or *examined, it.* (M.) And ثوّر القُرْآنَ † *He searched after a knowledge of the Kur-án*, (Ṣ, Ḳ,) or *its meanings*: (M:) or *he read it, and inquired of*, or *examined, diligently, those skilled in it, respecting its interpretation and meanings*: (Sh:) or *he scrutinized it, and meditated upon its meanings, and its interpretation, and the reading of it.* (TA.)

3. ثاورهُ, (T, M, A, Ḳ,) inf. n. مُثَاوَرَةٌ (Ṣ, M, Ḳ) and ثِوَارٌ, (Lḥ, M, Ḳ,) *He leaped*, or *sprang, upon him*, or *at him*; *he assaulted*, or *assailed, him*; syn. وَاثَبَهُ, (T, Ṣ, M, A, Ḳ,) and سَاوَرَهُ. (T, A.)

4. اثارهُ, (T, Ṣ, M, A, Mgh, Ḳ,) and أَثْرَهُ, and هَثَرْتُهُ, (Ḳ,) [but in the M, I find أَثَرْتُهُ and هَثَرْتُهُ, (in the latter of which the ه is substituted for the أ of the former, as in هَرَاقَ for أَرَاقَ,) and it is evident that the author of the Ḳ erroneously supposed them to be from أَثَرَ and هَثَرَ, whereas they are from أَثَارَ and هَثَارَ, and are originally أَثْوَرْتُهُ and هَثْوَرْتُهُ, but, for أَثْرَهُ, SM appears to have read أَثَّرَهُ, for he says that it is formed by transposition,] inf. n. إِثَارَةٌ and إِثَارٌ; (Lḥ, M;) and ↓ ثوّرهُ; (M, Ḳ;) and ↓ استثارهُ; (T, M, A, Ḳ;) *He raised, roused, excited, stirred up*, or *provoked, him* or *it*; (Ṣ, M, A, Mgh, Ḳ;) [as, for instance,] an object of the chase or the like, (T, M, A,) a beast of prey, (T,) a lion, (M, A,) † dust, (M, Mgh,) † smoke, and any other thing: (M:) or *he drew it forth*: (M:) ↓ استثارهُ is [often used in this last sense, or as meaning *he disinterred it, exhumed it*, or *dug it up* or *out*,] said of a thing buried. (Ḳ in art. سوع.) You say, اثار فُلَانًا *He roused such a one for an affair.* (T.) And اثار البَعِيرَ *He roused the camel lying upon his breast*, or *put him in motion* or *action.* (T.) And ↓ ثوّر البَرْكَ, and ↓ استثارها, *He roused the camels lying upon their breasts, and made them to rise.* (Ṣ.) — اثار التُّرَابَ بِقَوَائِمِهِ *He* [a beast] *scraped up the earth*, or *dust, with his legs.* (T, M.) — اثار الأَرْضَ, (M, Mgh, Mṣb,) and أَثْوَرَهَا, (M,) *He tilled the ground*, or *land*; *cultivated it by ploughing and sowing*: (Mgh, Mṣb:) *he turned the ground over upon the grain after it had been once opened*: (M, TA:) *he ploughed and sowed the land, and educed its increase, and the increase of its seed.* (TA.) And أَثَارَتِ الأَرْضَ [*She* (a cow) *tilled the ground*]. (TA.) — اثار الفِتْنَةَ ‡ *He* (an enemy) *excited discord*, or *dissension*, or *the like.* (Mṣb.) And ↓ ثوّر عَلَيْهِمُ الشَّرَّ (inf. n. تَثْوِيرٌ, Mṣb) ‡ *He excited evil*, or *mischief, against them*, (T, Ṣ, A,* Mṣb,*) *and manifested it.* (Ṣ.)

5: see 1, in seven places.

7: see 1, in two places.

10: see 4, in three places.

ثَارٌ: see ثَأْرٌ.

ثَوْرٌ *A bull*: (Ṣ, M, Mṣb, Ḳ:) and ↓ ثَوْرَةٌ *a cow*: (Ṣ, M, Mṣb:) pl. [of pauc.] أَثْوَارٌ (M, Mṣb, Ḳ) and ثِيَرَةٌ (Ṣ, M, Ḳ) and [of mult.] ثِيرَانٌ and ثِيَارٌ (T, Ṣ, M, Mṣb, Ḳ) and ثِوَرَةٌ (Ṣ, M, Ḳ) and ثِيَارَةٌ (M, Ḳ) and ثِيَارَةٌ; (M, TA:) Sb says of the pl. ثِيَرَةٌ that و in it is changed into ى because of the kesreh before it, though this is not accordant to general rule: (Ṣ:) accord. to Mbr, they said ثِيَرَةٌ to distinguish it from the ثِوَرَةٌ of أَقِطٌ, and that it was originally of the measure فِعَلَةٌ: (Ṣ, M:*) accord. to Aboo-'Alee, it is a contraction of ثِيَارَةٌ. (M.) [Hence,] الثَّوْرُ ‡ [*The constellation Taurus*;] *one of the signs of the Zodiac.* (Ṣ, M, Ḳ.) — † *A lord, master*, or *chief*, (M, A, Ḳ,) of a people. (A.) 'Othmán is called, in a trad., الثَّوْرُ الأَبْيَضُ; the epithet الابيض being added because he was hoary; or it may denote celebrity. (M.) — † *Stupid; foolish; of little sense*: (T, Ḳ:) *a stupid, dull man, of little understanding.* (T.) — † *Possessed by a devil*, or *insane*, or *mad*; syn. مَجْنُونٌ; so in copies of the Ḳ; but in some copies, [and in the CḲ,] جُنُونٌ [*diabolical possession*, or *insanity*, or *madness*]. (TA; and thus in Ḥar p. 415.) = *A piece*, (T, Ṣ, Mgh, Mṣb,) or *large piece*, (M, Ḳ,) *of* أَقِطٌ, (T, Ṣ, M, Mgh, Mṣb, Ḳ,) i. e. *milk which* [*has been churned and cooked and then left until it*] *has become congealed and hard like stone*: (TA:) pl. [of mult.] ثِوَرَةٌ (T, Ṣ, M, Ḳ) and أَثْوَارٌ. (M, Ḳ.) = The *green substance that overspreads stale water*; (T, M, Ḳ;) this is called ثَوْرُ المَآءِ; (Ṣ, Mṣb;) syn. طُحْلُبٌ, (AZ, T, Ṣ, M, Mṣb, Ḳ,) and عَرْمَضٌ, and غَلْفَقٌ; (M;) and the *like thereof*: (T, M:) and *small rubbish*, or *broken particles of things*, (Mṣb, TA,) or *anything*, (Ḳ,) *upon the surface of water*, (Mṣb, Ḳ, TA,) *which the pastor beats to make the water clear for the bulls or cows.* (Mṣb.) Accord. to some, it has the first of these meanings in the following verse of Anas Ibn-Mudrik El-Khath'amee:

* إِنِّى وَقَتْلِى سُلَيْكًا ثُمَّ أَعْقِلَهُ *

* كَالثَّوْرِ يُضْرَبُ لَمَّا عَافَتِ البَقَرُ *

[*Verily I, with respect to my slaying Suleyk and then paying the price of his blood, am like the green substance upon the surface of stale water, that is beaten when the cows loathe the water*]: but accord. to others, by الثور the poet means *the bull*; for the cows follow him: (M, TA:) the cows are not beaten, because they have milk; but the bull is beaten that they may be frightened and therefore drink. (Ṣ.) [See a slightly-different reading, and remarks thereon, in Ḥam p. 416: and see Freytag's Arab. Prov. ii. 330. The latter hemistich is used as a prov., applied to him who is punished for the offence of another.] —— † *Pimples, or small pustules, breaking out in the mouth*, in a person who is fevered. (A.) —— ‡ The *redness shining*, (نَائِرَةٌ, Ḳ,) or *spreading and rising*, (ثَائِرَةٌ, M,) *in the faint light that is seen above the horizon between sunset and nightfall*: (M, Ḳ:) or ثَوْرُ الشَّفَقِ *the spreading appearance of the redness above the horizon after sunset*. (Ṣ, A, Mgh.) You say, سَقَطَ ثَوْرُ الشَّفَقِ [*The spreading appearance of the redness above the horizon after sunset sank down*, or *set*]. (Ṣ, A.) With its سُقُوط commences the time of the prayer of nightfall. (TA.) —— † The *whiteness in the lower part of the nail* (M, Ḳ) *of a man*. (M, TA.)

ثِيرٌ *A covering of* [or *film over*] *the eye*. (Ḳ.) One says, عَلَى عَيْنِهِ ثِيرٌ *Upon his eye is a covering* [or *film*]. (TḲ.)

ثَوْرَةٌ: see ثَوْرٌ. —— † *An excitement*: so in the saying, اِنْتَظِرْ حَتَّى تَسْكُنَ هٰذِهِ الثَّوْرَةُ [*Wait thou until this excitement become stilled*]. (Ṣ.) —— † *Many*; *a great number*; *much*; or *a large quantity*; of men; (T, M, Ḳ;) and of wealth, or of camels or the like; (T, Ḳ;) like ثَرْوَةٌ: (T, M:) or not of wealth; for of this one says ثروة only. (M.)

ثُوَارَةٌ The [*part of the body called the*] خُوْرَان [q. v.]. (Ḳ.)

دَبًى ثَائِرٌ [*Locusts before they have wings*] *just coming forth from the dust, or earth*. (T, Ṣ.) —— ثَائِرُ الرَّأْسِ ‡ *Having the hair of his head spreading out in disorder, and standing up*: (Aṣ, T,* Ṣ,* TA:) or *shaggy*, or *dishevelled*. (T, A.) —— رَأَيْتُهُ ثَائِرًا فَرِيصُ رَقَبَتِهِ ‡ [*I saw him with his external jugular veins, or with the sinews and veins of his neck, swelling* by reason of anger]. (A.) —— ثَائِرٌ also signifies † *Angry*. (T.) —— And ‡ *Anger*: (Ṣ, A, Ḳ:) [or *an ebullition of anger, rage*, or *passion*: whence the phrase,] فَارَ ثَائِرُهُ, (T, Ṣ, M, A,) like فَارَ فَائِرُهُ, (T, A,) ‡ *He was angry*: (T:) or *his anger became roused*, or *excited*, (Ṣ, M,) or *inflamed*: (A:) or *became roused, or excited, in the utmost degree*: (TA:) or *boiled*: (Ṣ in art. فور:) or *spread*. (TA in that art.)

أَرْضٌ مُثَارَةٌ *Land ploughed up*. (T.)

أَرْضٌ مَثْوَرَةٌ *A land abounding with bulls* [and *cows*]. (Th, M, Ḳ.)

مُثِيرَةٌ A cow *that tills the ground*; (Mgh, Ḳ;) and in like manner applied to bulls (مُثِيرَةٌ). (T.)

ثول

1. ثَالَ, (T, Ṣgh, Ḳ,) aor. يَثُولُ, inf. n. ثَوْلٌ, (T,) *He* (a man, T) *was, or became, stupid, foolish*, or *disordered in his intellect*: (Ḳ:) or *he was, or became, affected with incipient madness* or *demoniacal possession, not such as had become confirmed*. (T, Ṣgh, Ḳ.) You say to a man, when you order him to be stupid and ignorant, ثُلْ ثُلْ. (IAạr, Th, T.) —— And ثَوِلَ, (T, M, Mṣb, Ḳ,) aor. يَثْوَلُ, (T,) inf. n. ثَوَلٌ, (T, M,) *He* (a man, and any animal,) *was, or became, affected with confirmed madness* or *demoniacal possession*: (T:) *he* (a sheep or goat) *was, or became, affected with what is termed* ثَوَلٌ, explained below; (M, Mṣb, Ḳ;) as also, accord. to Sb, ↓اثول; (so in the TT, as from the M;) or ↓اثْوَلَّ, inf. n. اِثْوِلَالٌ. (Ḳ.) ═ ثَالَ الوِعَآءَ, (Ṣgh, Ḳ,) aor. يَثُولُ, inf. n. ثَوْلٌ, (TA,) *He poured forth what was in the receptacle*. (Ṣgh, Ḳ.)

4: see 1.

5. تَثَوَّلَتِ النَّحْلُ *The bees collected themselves together, and became dense*. (M, Ḳ.) See also 7. —— تَثَوَّلَ عَلَيْهِ *He*, (a man, TA,) or *they*, (a company of men, Ṣ, M,) *assailed him*, or *overcame him, with reviling* (Ṣ, M, Ḳ) *and beating* (Ṣ, M) *and oppressive conduct*; (M, Ḳ;) as also ↓انثال. (M.)

7. انثال *It poured forth*: (Ḳ:) or *it poured forth at once*. (Mṣb.) انثال عَلَيْهِ التُّرَابُ *The dust, or earth, poured forth upon him*. (Ṣ.) —— [Hence,] انثال عَلَيْهِ النَّاسُ مِنْ كُلِّ وَجْهٍ *The people poured forth upon him*, or *against him, from every quarter*: (Ṣ, TA:) or *collected themselves together against him*: (Mṣb:) [for] انثالوا also signifies *they collected themselves together*; and so ↓تثوّلوا. (TA. [See also 7 in art. ثل.]) —— See also 5. —— انثال عَلَيْهِ القَوْلُ † *Speech suggested itself to him uninterruptedly and abundantly, so that he knew not with what to begin*. (M, Ḳ.)

9: see 1.

ثَوْلٌ *A number*, or *collection*, or *swarm, of bees*: (Aṣ, T, Ṣ, M, Ḳ:) or simply *bees*: (IAạr, Th, T:) a word having no proper sing.; (Aṣ, T, Ṣ, M, Ḳ;) and of the fem. gender: (M:) or the *male bee*; (M, Ḳ;) thus Lth explains it; but the right explanation is the first, that of Aṣ. (T.) —— And *A company of men*. (Ibn-'Abbád, TA.) —— Also The *kind of trees called* خَمْخَم. (M, Ḳ.)

ثُولٌ a dial. var. of ثِيلٌ, meaning The *sheath of the penis* of the camel. (Nh, TA.)

ثَوَلٌ *Madness*, or *demoniacal possession*: (IAạr, Th, T:) or *madness*, (Ṣ,) or *an affection like madness*, (Lth, T, M, Ḳ,) [i. e.] *a certain disease resembling madness*, (Mṣb,) *that befalls a sheep or goat*, (Lth, T, Ṣ, M, Mṣb,* Ḳ,) *in consequence of which the animal will not follow the other sheep or goats, but turns, or goes, round in his place of pasturage*: (Ṣ, M, Ḳ:) or *a laxness in the limbs of a sheep or goat*; (M, Ḳ;) *a certain disease that attacks a sheep or goat, occasioning a laxness in the limbs*. (IF, Mṣb.)

ثُوْلُولٌ: see ثُؤْلُولٌ, in art. ثأل.

ثُوَيْلَةٌ *A company*, or *an assemblage*, of men *come from detached*, or *scattered, houses* or *tents*; (Ṣ, Ḳ;* [in Ḥar p. 261, written ثُوَيْلَة; but in the TA, said to be like سَفِينَة, as written in the Ṣ and Ḳ;]) and of boys, or children; and of camels or the like (مال): mentioned by Yaạḳoob, on the authority of Aboo-Ṣá'id. (Ṣ.) —— Also *A place in which fresh herbage is*, or *becomes, collected together*. (Th, M, Ḳ.)

ثُوَالَةٌ *A swarm*, or *large number, of locusts*; (Aṣ, T, M, Ḳ;) a subst., like جُبَانَةٌ (M, Ḳ) and جُثَالَةٌ: (M:) or *an assemblage of locusts*, and *of men*. (IAạr, Th, T.)

أَثْوَلُ *Mad*, or *possessed*: and *stupid, foolish*, or *disordered in intellect*: (M, Ḳ:) and, applied to a ram (M, Mṣb) or he-goat, (Ṣ, Mṣb,) *affected by what is termed* ثَوَلٌ, explained above; fem. ثَوْلَآءُ, applied to a ewe (Ṣ, M, Mṣb) or she-goat; (Ṣ, Mṣb;) or this, applied to a ewe or she-goat &c., signifies *mad*: (Mgh:) pl. ثُولٌ. (Mṣb.) —— Also *Slow in aiding*, or *in aiding against an enemy*: and *slow in doing good, and in acting*: and *slow in running*: pl. as above. (Ḳ.) And ↓أُثَاوِلَةٌ, applied to old men, *Slow* (Ḳ, TA) *in doing good*, or *in acting*, or *in running*. (TA.)

أُثَاوِلَةٌ: see what next precedes.

ثوم

ثُومٌ [*Garlic*; the *allium sativum* of Linn.;] *a kind of* بَقْل, (AḤn, M,) *well known*, (Ṣ,) *abundant in the country of the Arabs*; (AḤn, M;) *of two sorts*; *wild*, (AḤn, M, Ḳ,) and *growing in the cultivated tracts*, (AḤn, M,) or *in gardens*: (Ḳ:) *the former sort is called* ثُومُ الحَيَّةِ, *and is the stronger*, (Ḳ,) *and is brought from Syria*: (TA:) *each of them is heating, expels flatulence and worms, and is strongly diuretic*; *and this is the most excellent* [*property*] *that is therein*: *it is good for obliviousness, and asthma, and chronic cough, and* [*pain in*] *the spleen and the flank, and colic, and sciatica*, &c.: (Ḳ: [in which are added many other supposed uses:]) n. un. with ة. (AḤn, M, Ḳ.) —— Hence, as being likened thereto, (M,) ثُومَةٌ signifies also ‡ The *pommel of a sword*. (Ṣ, M, Ḳ.) Whence, أُمُّ ثُومَةَ, said to be the name of a certain woman, may mean ‡ *A sword*. (M.) —— [Hence, also,] ثُومَةُ ذَكَرِ رَجُلٍ † [*The glans of a man's penis*]. (Az, in TA voce طُرْثُوثٌ.) —— الثُّومَةُ also signifies *The channel* [or *oblong depression*] *between the two mustaches, against the partition between the two nostrils*; (IAạr, TA;) *i. q.* الخُنْعُبَةُ, &c. (TA in art. خنعب.) ═ ثُومٌ is also a dial. var. of فُومٌ, meaning *Wheat*. (Lḥ, T, M.) And the latter is used in the [ordinary] sense of the former. (T.)

ثوى

1. ثَوَى (T, Ṣ, M, Mgh, Mṣb, Ḳ) بِالمَكَانِ, (Ṣ, M, Mgh, Mṣb, Ḳ,) and فِيهِ, (Mṣb,) and ثَوَى المَكَانَ, (Ṣ,* M, Mṣb, Ḳ,) aor. ـِ, (T, Ṣ, Mṣb,

K,) inf. n. ثَوَآءٌ (T, Ṣ, M, Mgh, Mṣb, K) and ثُوِىٌّ (Ṣ, M, Mgh, K) and مَثْوًى; (T, M;) and ▼اثوى (T, Ṣ, M, Mṣb, K) بالمكان, (Ṣ, M, K,) or فيه; (so in the CK;) *He remained, stayed, dwelt,* or *abode,* (T, Ṣ, Mgh, Mṣb,) *in the place:* (Ṣ, Mgh, Mṣb:) or *he remained, stayed, dwelt,* or *abode, long* (Lth, T, M, K) *therein:* (M, K:) or *he alighted,* or *alighted and abode, in the place:* (K:) or ثَوَى signifies also *he alighted,* or *alighted and abode,* (M,) or *he settled,* (TA,) بالمكان *in the place.* (M.) Hence, إِنَّا نُطِيلُ الثَّوَى فِى دَارِ الحَرْبِ [*Verily we prolong the stay in the seat of war*]. (Mgh.) [You say also, ثَوَى إِلَى المَرْأَةِ *He betook himself to the woman to remain, stay, dwell,* or *abide, with her:* see ثَوِيَّةٌ.] — [Hence,] ثَوَى, (T, M, IB, TA,) aor. ـِ; in the K, incorrectly, ▼ثوّى, inf. n. تَثْوِيَةٌ; (TA;) signifies also *He was slain,* (T, M,) *and remained where he was:* (M:) or *he remained in his grave:* (IB, TA:) or, as the latter verb is explained in the K, *he died.* (TA.) [See a verse cited in art. حسب, conj. 2.] ═ ثُوِىَ *He was buried:* (M, K:) because there is no longer dwelling than that of him who is buried. (M.)

2: see 4: ═ and see also 1.

4. اثوى: see 1. ═ اثواهُ *He made him to remain, stay, dwell,* or *abide;* (Ṣ, Mṣb, K;) or *to remain,* &c., *long;* (M, K;) in a place; (M, K;) and ▼ثوّاه, (Kr, Ṣ, M, K,) inf. n. تَثْوِيَةٌ, (Ṣ,) signifies the same. (Kr, Ṣ, M, K.) [In the CK, ثَوَّيْتُهُ is erroneously put for ثَوِيْتُهُ.] — And *He lodged him; made him his guest;* or *entertained him as a guest.* (M, K.) You say, أَنْزَلَنِى فَأَثْوَانِى ثَوَآءً حَسَنًا [*He lodged me, and entertained me well as a guest*]. (T.)

5. تثوّاه *He became his guest.* (TA.)

ثَا [mentioned in this art. in the K, as "*A certain letter of the alphabet,*" namely, ث]: see art. ثوا: ISd holds its ا to be originally و. (TA.)

ثَاىٌ:
ثَاوَةٌ: } see what next follows.

ثَايَةٌ, (Ṣ, M, K,) without ء, (Ṣ,) formed by permutation from ثَوِيَةٌ, though the author of the Kitáb [i. e. Sb] holds the ا to be originally ى, (M,) *The lodging-place,* or *nightly resting-place, of camels,* (ISk, Ṣ, M, K,) and *of sheep* or *goats,* (ISk, Ṣ,) *when they have gone away to a distance in the pasture,* or *around the tents* or *houses;* (ISk, Ṣ, M, K;) as also ▼ثَوِيَّةٌ and ▼ثَاوَةٌ: (K:) or the first and second, (AZ, T, Ṣ, M,) and the third also, (M,) signify the *lodging-place,* or *nightly resting-place, of sheep* or *goats,* (AZ, T, Ṣ, M,) and *of oxen,* or *bulls and cows;* (M;) and the last is app. formed by permutation from the first. (M.) — Also *A combination of two or three trees, upon which is thrown a piece of cloth, used for shade,* or *shelter from the sun.* (IAạr, M. [And in like manner ثَايَةٌ is explained in the T, in art. ثأى.]) — Also, (AZ, T, Ṣ, M,) and ▼ثُوَيَّةٌ, (M,) *Stones elevated for a sign of the way to direct the pastor when he returns by night:* (AZ, T, Ṣ, M:) and the former, or latter, (M,) or both, and ▼ثُوَّةٌ, (K,) with damm, (TA, [in the CK ثَوَّةٌ,]) the *lowest sign of the way, of the height of a man in a sitting posture.* (M, K.) — Also The *part which is the place of stabbing* of a slaughtered camel. (TA.) — The pl. of ثَايَةٌ is ▼ثَاىٌ: (Lh, M:) [or rather the latter is a coll. gen. n., of which the former is the n. un.]

ثُوَّةٌ: see art. ثو: and see ثَايَةٌ in the present art., above.

ثَوِىٌّ *A guest:* (IAạr, T, Ṣ, M, K:) the vulgar erroneously pronounce it ثُوِىٌّ. (TA. [See also مَثْوًى.]) — *Remaining, staying, dwelling,* or *abiding;* as also ثَاوٍ; but the former is better known in this sense. (M in art. ثوى.) — *One who abides* (مُجَاوِرٌ) [generally meaning *for the purpose of study*]) *in either of the two sacred cities* or *territories* [*of Mekkeh and El-Medeeneh*]. (IAạr, T, K.) — *One who is very patient in military and predatory expeditions, who is detained in the territory of the enemy,* or *on the frontier of the enemies' country.* (IAạr, T.) — *A captive.* (Th, M, K.) ═ *A chamber,* or *house,* or *tent, prepared for a guest:* (T, M, K:) and, (M,) accord. to Lth, (T,) *a chamber within a chamber.* (T, M.)

ثُوِىٌّ: see art. ثو. ═ Also an inf. n. of 1. (Ṣ &c.)

ثَوِيَّةٌ: see ثَايَةٌ, above, in two places. ═ Also *A woman* (K, TA) *to whom one betakes himself to remain, stay, dwell,* or *abide, with her* (يُثْوَى إِلَيْهَا). (TA.)

ثَاوٍ part. n. of 1; (Mṣb;) [*Remaining,* &c.: or *remaining,* &c., *long:*] *a stranger remaining, staying, dwelling,* or *abiding, in a country,* or *town:* (T:) or ثَاوِى بَلْدَةٍ *a stranger who keeps to a country,* or *town.* (M.) — A man *remaining in his grave.* (IB, TA.)

ثَاوِىٌّ: see ثَائِىٌّ, in art. ثوا. You say قَافِيَةٌ ثَاوِيَّةٌ [in the CK, erroneously, ثاوِيَةٌ] *A rhyme of which the characteristic is* ث. (K,* TA.)

مَثْوًى *A place where one remains, stays, dwells,* or *abides;* (T;) *a place of alighting* or *abode, an abode,* or *a dwelling,* (T, M, Mgh, Mṣb,) of a man: (T:) pl. مَثَاوٍ (T, M, Mgh, Mṣb, K.) Hence, أَبُو المَثْوَى *The master* (M, K) *of the house* or *tent,* (M,) or *of the place where one alights* or *abides,* or *of the abode* or *dwelling.* (K.) And أُمُّ المَثْوَى *The mistress of the house* or *tent.* (M.) And أَبُو مَثْوَى الرَّجُلِ *The master of the place of alighting,* or *of the abode, of the man:* (Ṣ:) *the host who entertains the man; to whom he betakes himself for lodging, and at whose abode he stays:* (Ḥar p. 595:) and *the guest whom the man entertains.* (M, K.* [See also ثَوِىٌّ.]) And أُمُّ مَثْوَى الرَّجُلِ *The mistress of the place of alighting,* or *of the abode, of the man:* (Ṣ:) *the mistress of the man's place of alighting,* or *abode, in which he passes the night;* occurring in this sense in a trad., not meaning his wife. (TA.) — It is also an inf. n. of ثَوَى. (T, M.)

ثى

2. ثَيَّيْتُ ثَآءً حَسَنًا and حَسَنَةً [*I made,* or *wrote, a beautiful* ث]. (TA in باب الالف اللّيّنة.)

ثِيَةٌ* The *lodging-place,* or *nightly resting-place, of sheep* or *goats* [*when they have gone away to a distance in the pasture,* or *around the tents* or *houses*]; (IB, K;) a dial. var. of ثَايَةٌ [q. v. in art. ثوى]. (IB, TA.)

ثَاىٌ:
ثَايَةٌ: } see art. ثوى.

ثُيَوِىٌّ: see ثَائِىٌّ, in art. ثوا.

ثيب

For several words mentioned in the M and K as belonging to this art., see art. ثوب.

ثيتل

ثَيْتَلٌ:
ثَيْتَلٌ: } see art. ثتل.

ثيخ

1. ثَاخَ, aor. يَثِيخُ: see art. ثوخ.

ثيل

ثِيَلٌ: see what next follows.

ثِيلٌ The *sheath of the penis* of a camel (Lth,* AZ, T, Ṣ, M, K) &c.; (K;) [i. e.,] of a he-goat also, and of a bull: (M:) or the *penis* itself: (Lth, T, M, K:) sometimes also used in relation to a man: (M:) and ▼ثِيَلٌ signifies the same; (K;) mentioned by Ibn-'Abbád; and IAth adds ثُوَلٌ. (TA.) Hence the prov., أَخْلَفُ مِنْ ثِيلِ الجَمَلِ [*More contrary* to what is usual *than the sheath of the penis,* or *than the penis, of the camel*]: for the camel, like the lion, is a retromingent. (TA.) ═ *A kind of plant;* (Ṣ, K;) as also ▼ثِيَلٌ: (K:) *a certain plant having a root and stem; when short, called* نَجْمٌ: and *a certain herb,* or, as some say, *a plant, that is found on the banks,* or *sides, of rivers, in meadows:* and, some say, *a species of the* [*plants,* or *trees, called*] جَنْبَةٌ, *which grows in the territory of* [*the tribe of*] *Temeem, and becomes large, so that the sheep,* or *goats, lie in its shelter:* (M:) AHn says, (M,) in the "Book of Plants," (Mgh,) the ثيل, (M,) or ▼ثِيَلٌ, (Mgh,) [both appellations now applied to *triticum repens,* or *dog's grass,*] is the نَجْمَةٌ; *called in Persian* ريزوپادله[?]; (Mgh;) *its leaves are like those of wheat, but shorter, and it spreads upon the face of the ground, extending far, and becoming com-*

plicated, or *tangled, so as to be like felt* (M, Mgh) *upon the ground;* (M;) *it has many joints*, or *knots, and short internodal portions; and scarcely*, or *never, grows anywhere but over water, or in a place beneath which is water;* (M, Mgh;) *and it is one of the plants that are regarded as indicative of the existence of water:* n. un. with ة: (M:) Lth says that the ثيل is *a certain plant that tangles upon the ground:* Th, on the authority of IAạr, says that it is *a kind of plant said to be that called* لِحْيَةُ التَّيْسِ: and Sh says that the ثِيلَة is *a green small tree* [or *plant*] *resembling the first shoots that come forth from grain.* (T.)

ثَيَلٌ: see ثِيل, in two places.

أَثْيَلُ A camel *large in the* ثِيل; (T, Ṣ, M, Ḳ;) *wide therein:* (M:) pl. ثِيل. (Ḳ.)

مَثْيَلَةٌ *A place in which is the kind of plant called* ثِيل. (Mgh.)

END OF THE FIRST PART OF BOOK I.